LABOR RELATIONS

LAW, PRACTICE AND POLICY

SECOND EDITION

By

JULIUS G. GETMAN

Professor of Law, Yale Law School

and

JOHN D. BLACKBURN

Associate Professor of Business Law,
Ohio State University

Mineola, New York
THE FOUNDATION PRESS, INC.
1983

COPYRIGHT © 1978 THE FOUNDATION PRESS, INC.
COPYRIGHT © 1983 By THE FOUNDATION PRESS, INC.
Printed in the United States of America

Library of Congress Cataloging in Publication Data

Getman, Julius G.
   Labor relations.

   Includes bibliographies and index.
    1. Labor laws and legislation—United States.
I. Blackburn, John D.   II. Title.
KF3369.G47 1983   344.73'01   82–21042
                    347.3041

ISBN 0–88277–102–7

Professor Getman dedicates this book to the memory of his father, Samuel Getman, worker and scholar. Professor Blackburn dedicates this book to the memory of his grandfather, Orville W. Hubbard, Esq.

*

PREFACE TO SECOND EDITION

This book is a revision of the earlier text authored by Professor Getman. The revision has primarily been done by Professor Blackburn working with the advice and consultation of Professor Getman.

A revision is in order for a number of reasons. Changes and developments in the field since publication of the earlier edition require that the materials be brought up to date. Furthermore, experimentation with the first edition, together with the constructive criticism of some of its users, have pointed out ways in which the materials could be improved.

Virtually every chapter starts with a case study. The case studies have been derived from actual experiences confronting real companies, the identities of which have been changed. The case studies can be effectively used to explore some of the issues that are raised by the material which follows.

All of the chapters have been re-written to reflect changes and new concepts. New readings and cases have been added or substituted where appropriate. For example, the chapter on union organizing includes an expanded treatment of determination of the appropriate bargaining unit; and the Getman, Goldberg and Herman study, reproduced at great length in the first edition, has been textually summarized in the revision. The dynamic nature of labor law is illustrated by one recent change which occurred after this book was in production. The Board's decision in Midland National Life Insurance Company, which was released after this book was in page proof, is included in Appendix D herein. It should be read and considered in connection with the Board's decision in General Knit of California at page 129, which it overrules.

The chapter on employer-employee cooperation now includes a discussion of the legality of Scanlon plans. The chapter on collective bargaining contains a discussion of the social and economic functions of collective bargaining, and an expanded treatment of mandatory and permissive subjects of bargaining. The chapter on arbitration presently includes more readings regarding the practice and procedure of arbitration. The chapter on strikes includes a discussion of recent empirical research on strike activity. The chapter on public sector bargaining has been expanded to include the constitutional right to join a union, bargain, and to strike, and the due process protections applicable to the discharge of public employees. Finally, the chapter on equal employment opportunity has been replaced with a chapter on the emerging rights of individual employees, which includes a discussion of the duty of fair representation, changes in the employment-at-will doctrine, and OSHA, in addition to a textual treatment of equal employment opportunity law.

Professor Blackburn wishes to thank the many people who gave him useful criticism in preparing the second edition. In particular, many thanks to Mr. Thomas E. Murphy, Esquire, of Cincinnati, Ohio, formerly Associate Dean and Professor of Labor Law at the University of Cincinnati College of Law; and to Mr. Arthur B. Smith, Jr., Esquire, partner in the prestigious law firm of Vedder, Price, Kaufman & Kammholz in Chicago, Illinois; two distinguished labor attorneys who helped with their insights, expertise, and suggestions. Neither of these gentlemen is responsible for the views expressed or materials used. Any errors are attributable to the authors.

JULIUS G. GETMAN
JOHN D. BLACKBURN

November, 1982

PREFACE TO FIRST EDITION

This book was developed from a course on government regulation of labor relations, offered to Business School students at Stanford University. In trying to select a textbook for that course I realized that while traditional legal materials were too technical and focused too much on the role of law, labor relations texts for undergraduate courses were frequently inaccurate, outdated or both. That realization led me to explore the development of teaching materials which would accurately reflect the richness of the field. Labor relations is not a field which respects disciplinary boundaries and these materials therefore range over a wide area. They are intended to introduce students to relevant governmental decisions and policies and also to show how labor relations in fact operates.

I have tried to illustrate the powerful human emotions which are at work in the various situations dealt with. Passion, violence and anger are part of the picture and must be recognized to understand the nature of labor relations. The regulation of organizing campaigns for example is only understandable if one is attuned to the emotions, tactical considerations and basic arguments of the contending sides. Similarly the term collective bargaining often suggests a more rational process to the uninitiated than it does to one who has experienced it. I have included materials to illustrate why this is so. In addition, I have tried to either present or distill the best and most challenging scholarly work from various disciplines on the theory that exposure to sophistication is a good way to achieve it. Finally, the book is meant to be useful for those who will continue to learn about the subject and also to those whose exposure will end with one course.

I have had considerable help in the course of preparing these materials; I wish in particular to thank Dean Charles Myers and Associate Deans Keith Mann and Joseph Leininger of the Stanford Law School for their help, support and understanding. I also wish to acknowledge the contributuion of my colleague in the Stanford course, Professor Robert Flanagan and Mr. Lou Rodriguez, my research assistant at Yale. Numerous colleagues at Yale and Stanford read over parts of the manuscript and I am grateful to them all for their help. I would particularly like to thank my wife, Roberta Filzer Getman, who read the entire manuscript, making helpful and important changes with her usual perceptiveness.

Crucial financial support for this book came from the Project in Law for Undergraduates at Stanford University. That project has been financed by the National Endowment for the Humanities, the Claremore Fund of Los Angeles, the George H. Sandy Foundation of San Francisco, the Andrew Norman Foundation of Los Angeles and the

Swig Foundation of San Francisco. None of these worthy groups nor any of the other people mentioned are responsible for the views expressed or materials used.

JULIUS G. GETMAN

Stanford, Calif.
May, 1978

TABLE OF CONTENTS

Chapter I

HISTORICAL DEVELOPMENT AND OVERVIEW OF LABOR MANAGEMENT REGULATION

Chapter II

UNION ORGANIZING

Chapter III

EMPLOYER–EMPLOYEE COOPERATION AND THE CONCEPT OF COMPANY UNIONS: THE REACH OF § 8(a)(2)

Chapter IV

COLLECTIVE BARGAINING

Chapter VIII

INDIVIDUAL EMPLOYMENT RIGHTS

Appendices

TABLE OF CASES

LABOR RELATIONS

LAW, PRACTICE AND POLICY

*

Chapter I

HISTORICAL DEVELOPMENT AND OVERVIEW OF LABOR MANAGEMENT REGULATION

A. EARLY HISTORY

When unions first organized in the United States in the 16th and 17th century it was generally believed that concerted activity by workers violated the criminal law. Although there was no specific statute which made union activity a crime, the common law doctrine of criminal conspiracy was applied. Under this doctrine, a combination of workers might constitute an illegal conspiracy if the court thought that the goals sought or the means used were sufficiently improper. The essence of conspiracy was combination. The same action when undertaken by an individual might be perfectly lawful. The first American labor law case to apply the conspiracy doctrine was the Philadelphia Cordwainers case tried in 1806. A group of cordwainers (shoemakers) were charged with conspiracy because of a strike to increase their rate of pay. They were convicted. The charge to the jury by the trial judge stated:

> "A combination of workmen to raise their wages may be considered in a two-fold point of view: one is to benefit themselves, the other is to injure those who do not join their society. The rule of law condemns both. One man determines not to work under a certain price and it may be individually the opinion of all: in such case it would be lawful in each to refuse to do so, for if each stands alone, * * * fettered by no promises to the rest, many might have changed their opinion as to the price of wages and gone to work; but * * * they were bound down by their agreement and pledged by mutual engagements to persist in it however contrary to their own judgment. The continuance in improper conduct may therefore be attributed to the combination." [1]

The conspiracy doctrine helped to delay the emergence of a strong trade union movement. As labor became politically more potent, however, some prosecutors refused to prosecute, some judges refused to sustain indictments and some juries refused to convict. Finally, in the case of Commonwealth v. Hunt,[2] decided in 1842, the Supreme Judicial Court of Massachusetts, in a highly influential opinion by Chief Justice Shaw rejected the notion that unions as such

---

1. The Philadelphia Cordwainers Cases, *III Common Documents History of American Independent Society* (1958), p. 233.

2. 4 Metc. (45 Mass.) 111 (1842).

were conspiracies. The indictment charged that the formation of the union was a criminal conspiracy and that many actions undertaken on behalf of the union were also illegal. In his opinion, Justice Shaw responded to the conspiracy argument.

> The averment is that the defendants and others formed themselves into a society, and agreed not to work for any person, who should employ any journeyman or other person, not a member of such society, after notice given him to discharge such workman.

> The manifest intent of the association is, to induce all those engaged in the same occupation to become members of it. Such a purpose is not unlawful. *   *   *   But in order to charge all those, who become members of an association, with the guilt of a criminal conspiracy, it must be averred and proved that the actual, if not the avowed object of the association, was criminal.   *   *   *

> Nor can we perceive that the objects of this association, whatever they may have been, were to be attained by criminal means. The means which they proposed to employ, as averred in this court, and which, as we are now to presume, were established by the proof, were, that they would not work for a person, who, after due notice, should employ a journeyman not a member of their society. Supposing the object of the association to be laudable and lawful, or at least not unlawful, are these means criminal? The case supposes that these persons are not bound by contract, but free to work for whom they please, or not to work, if they so prefer. In this state of things, we cannot perceive, that it is criminal for men to agree together to exercise their own acknowledged rights, in such a manner as best to subserve their own interests.

This decision was formally binding only in Massachusetts, but it was uniformly accepted in other states as establishing the legality of unions and of traditional strikes for higher wages or improved working conditions. However, it did not establish the legitimacy of all possible union goals and it specifically acknowledged that the use of improper means by union members could make concerted activity illegal. Thus, even after Commonwealth v. Hunt, it was still not certain what union purposes would justify picketing or other concerted activity nor which tactics other than peaceful picketing could safely be employed. This uncertainty would probably not have provided a serious hindrance to the union movement if employers had to rely on the criminal law, since as mentioned earlier, prosecutors were generally not eager to bring cases against trade unionists. Starting around 1880, however, employers began to combat union activity by use of injunctions. Injunctions are orders by judges directed to individuals or groups requiring them to take or refrain from taking certain action. An injunction could be issued against conduct found to be illegal or against conduct of doubtful legality if such conduct threatened irreparable injury to property interests.[3] Individual judges had great discretion in deciding whether to issue an injunction. Failure to obey was contempt of court, which could be punished by fine or imprisonment without jury trial. The uncertainty of the law made it likely that in any particular jurisdiction, at least one judge could be persuaded that a strike threatened serious harm and was of sufficiently doubtful legality to justify the grant of an injunction. The potential for abuse, inherent in this system, was frequently realized, as the following anguished statement by a federal judge written in 1899 makes clear.

> The modern writ of injunction * * * has taken the place of the police powers of the State and nation. * * * With it the judge not only restrains and punishes the commission of crimes defined by statute, but he proceeds to frame a criminal code of his own, as extended as he sees proper, by which various acts, innocent in law and morals, are made criminal; such as standing, walking, or marching on the public highway, or talking, speaking, or preaching, and other like acts. In proceedings for contempt for an alleged violation of the injunction the judge is the lawmaker, the injured party, the prosecutor, the judge and the jury. It is not surprising that uniting in himself all these characters he is commonly able to obtain a conviction. * * * It is said the judge does not punish for a violation of the statutory offense but only for a violation of his order prohibiting the commission of the statutory offense. Such reasoning as this is what Carlyle calls "logical cobwebbery." The web is not strong enough to deprive the smallest insect of its liberty much less an American citizen.
>
> The extent and use of this powerful writ finds its only limitation in that unknown quantity called judicial discretion, touching which Lord Camden, one of England's greatest constitutional lawyers, said: "The discretion of a judge is the law of tyrants; it is always unknown; it is different in different men; it is casual and depends upon constitution, temper, and passion. In the best it is oftentimes caprice; in the worst it is every crime, folly, and passion to which human nature is liable." Mr. Burke pointed out the danger of investing "any sort of men" with jurisdiction limited only by their discretion. He said: "The spirit of any sort of men is not a fit *rule* for deciding on the bounds of their jurisdiction; first because it is different in different men and even different in the same at different times, and can never become the proper directing line of law; and next because it is not reason but feeling, and when it is irritated it is not apt to confine itself within its proper limits."
>
> A jurisdiction that is not required to stop somewhere will stop nowhere.

---

3. A form of injunction called a temporary restraining order might be issued to preserve the existing situation without even granting the party to be enjoined a hearing.

Prof. Baird says fish have no maturity but continue to grow until they die. This curious characteristic of fish is present in a very intensified form in the equitable octopus called injunction, for that has no maturity and *never dies*, and its jurisdiction grows and extends perpetually and unceasingly.[4]

The development of the injunction as an anti-labor weapon during the 1890's was dramatic. In strike after strike, workers were faced with court orders, phrased in broad and legalistic language. As the workers sarcastically put it, they forbade "whomsoever from doing whatsoever".

The employers' arsenal and their ability to obtain injunctions was strengthened unexpectedly in 1896 by passage of the Sherman Anti Trust Act, which made unlawful " * * * every * * * combination * * * or conspiracy in restraint of trade". The Act was aimed at business monopolies, but it was soon used against unions. The Act provided for injunctions to remedy violations and also specified that anyone injured by a violation could obtain damages up to three times the amount of the injury. The question of the Act's application to unions came before the U. S. Supreme Court in the Danbury Hatters case, Loewe v. Lawlor.[5] The complaint charged the defendants, members of the United Hatters of America, with attempting to restrain trade through strikes and boycotts in order to unionize all of the workers in the industry, regardless of the workers' desires. The lower court dismissed the complaint on the grounds that unions actually did not fall under the Act. The Supreme Court reversed, holding that a valid complaint was stated. It rejected the argument that there was an implicit exemption for unions, in the Sherman Act for it stated, "The Act made no distinction between classes. It provided that 'every' contract combination or conspiracy in restraint of trade was illegal".

The Supreme Court in Hitchman Coal v. Mitchell [6] also upheld the use of injunctions to prevent union organizers from interfering with existing contracts under which employees promised not to join a union during the course of their employment. These agreements, known as "yellow dog contracts" to labor and their supporters, became a powerful anti-union device after this opinion because their existence could be the basis of an injunction against union organizing which the court described as "an effort to subvert" existing contractual relations.

The widespread use of labor injunctions, the enforcement of yellow dog contracts, and the application of the Sherman Anti Trust Act to unions led the union movement to establish as one of its major priorities the enactment of legislation which would deal with legitimate union activity and eliminate the use of injunctions. As the

---

4. Henry Clay Caldwell, Trial by Judge and Jury, 33 American L.Rev., pp. 321, 327–329.

5. 208 U.S. 274, 28 S.Ct. 301, 52 L.Ed. 488 (1908).

6. 245 U.S. 229, 38 S.Ct. 65, 62 L.Ed. 260 (1918).

union movement grew in strength and political power during the period from 1890 to 1914, these aims came to be increasingly respectable. In 1914 Congress passed the Clayton Anti Trust Act. This act contained two provisions responsive to Labor's concerns, Section 6 purported to grant unions an exemption from the antitrust laws and Section 20 purported to eliminate the use of injunctions in labor disputes.[7]

Although Samuel Gompers, founder and president of the American Federation of Labor, hailed them as "the Magna Carta of Labor," their impact was significantly reduced by the U. S. Supreme Court in the famous Duplex Printing case. The majority and the minority opinions in that case, parts of which are reproduced below, reflect the contrasting points of view from which different judges evaluated the legality and desirability of union activity.

DUPLEX PRINTING PRESS CO. v. DEERING

Supreme Court of the United States, 1921.
254 U.S. 443, 41 S.Ct. 172, 65 L.Ed. 349.

* * *

The Clayton Act, in § 1, includes the Sherman Act in a definition of "anti-trust laws," and, in § 16 (38 Stat. 737), gives to private par-

---

7. Section 6.

" * * * nothing contained in the anti trust laws shall be construed to forbid the existence and operation of labor, agricultural, or horticultural organizations * * * or restrain individual members of such organizations from lawfully carrying out the legitimate objectives thereof: nor shall such organization or members thereof be held or constricted to be illegal combinations or conspiracies in restraint of trade under the anti trust laws."

See Section 20.

"That no restraining order or injunction shall be granted by any court of the United States, or a judge or the judges therof, in any case between an employer and employees, or between employers and employees, or between employees, or between persons employed and persons seeking employment, involving, or growing out of, a dispute concerning terms or conditions of employment, unless necessary to prevent irreparable injury to property, or to a property right, of the party making the application, for which injury there is no adequate remedy at law, and such property or property right must be described with particularity in the application, which must be in writ-

ing and sworn to by the applicant or by his agent or attorney.

"And no such restraining order or injunction shall prohibit any person or persons, whether singly or in concert, from terminating any relation of employment, or from ceasing to perform any work or labor, or from recommending, advising, or persuading others by peaceful means so to do; or from attending at any place where any such person or persons may lawfully be, for the purpose of peacefully obtaining or communicating information, or from peacefully persuading any person to work or to abstain from working; or from ceasing to patronize or to employ any party to such dispute, or from recommending, advising, or persuading others by peaceful and lawful means so to do; or from paying or giving to, or withholding from, any person engaged in such dispute, any strike benefits or other moneys or things of value; or from peaceably assembling in a lawful manner, and for lawful purposes; or from doing any act or thing which might lawfully be done in the absence of such dispute by any party thereto; nor shall any of the acts specified in this paragraph be considered or held to be violations of any law of the United States."

ties a right to relief by injunction in any court of the United States
*   *   *.

*   *   *

The substance of the matters here complained of is an interference with complainant's interstate trade, intended to have coercive effect upon complainant, and produced by what is commonly known as a "secondary boycott," that is, a combination not merely to refrain from dealing with complainant, or to advise or by peaceful means persuade complainant's customers to refrain ("primary boycott"), but to exercise coercive pressure upon such customers, actual or prospective, in order to cause them to withhold or withdraw patronage from complainant through fear of loss or damage to themselves should they deal with it.

*   *   *

Upon the question whether the provisions of the Clayton Act forbade the grant of an injunction under the circumstances of the present case, the Circuit Court of Appeals was divided; the majority holding that under § 20, "perhaps in conjunction with section 6," there could be no injunction.   *   *   *   As to § 6, it seems to us its principal importance in this discussion is for what it does *not* authorize, and for the limit it sets to the immunity conferred. The section assumes the normal objects of a labor organization to be legitimate, and declares that nothing in the anti-trust laws shall be construed to forbid the existence and operation of such organizations or to forbid their members from *lawfully* carrying out their *legitimate* objects; and that such an organization shall not be held in itself—merely because of its existence and operation—to be an illegal combination or conspiracy in restraint of trade. But there is nothing in the section to exempt such an organization or its members from accountability where it or they depart from its normal and legitimate objects and engage in an actual combination or conspiracy in restraint of trade. And by no fair or permissible construction can it be taken as authorizing any activity otherwise unlawful, or enabling a normally lawful organization to become a cloak for an illegal combination or conspiracy in restraint of trade as defined by the anti-trust laws.

The principal reliance is upon § 20. This regulates the granting of restraining orders and injunctions by the courts of the United States in a designated class of cases, with respect to (a) the terms and conditions of the relief and the practice to be pursued, and (b) the character of acts that are to be exempted from the restraint; and in the concluding words it declares (c) that none of the acts specified shall be held to be violations of any law of the United States. All its provisions are subject to a general qualification respecting the nature of the controversy and the parties affected. It is to be a "case between an employer and employees, or between employers and employees, or between employees, or between persons employed and persons seeking employment, involving, or growing out of, a dispute concerning terms or conditions of employment."

The first paragraph merely puts into statutory form familiar restrictions upon the granting of injunctions already established and of general application in the equity practice of the courts of the United States. It is but declaratory of the law as it stood before. The second paragraph declares that "no *such* restraining order or injunction" shall prohibit certain conduct specified—manifestly still referring to a "case between an employer and employees,   *   *   *   involving, or growing out of, a dispute concerning terms or conditions of employment," as designated in the first paragraph.   *   *   *

The majority of the Circuit Court of Appeals appear to have entertained the view that the words "employers and employees," as used in § 20, should be treated as referring to "the business class or clan to which the parties litigant respectively belong"; and that, as there had been a dispute at complainant's factory in Michigan concerning the conditions of employment there—a dispute created, it is said, if it did not exist before, by the act of the Machinists' Union in calling a strike at the factory—§ 20 operated to permit members of the Machinists' Union elsewhere—some 60,000 in number—although standing in no relation of employment under complainant, past, present, or prospective, to make that dispute their own and proceed to instigate sympathetic strikes, picketing, and boycotting against employers wholly unconnected with complainant's factory and having relations with complainant only in the way of purchasing its product in the ordinary course of interstate commerce—and this where there was no dispute between such employers and their employees respecting terms or conditions of employment.

We deem this construction altogether inadmissible. Section 20 must be given full effect according to its terms as an expression of the purpose of Congress; but it must be borne in mind that the section imposes an exceptional and extraordinary restriction upon the equity powers of the courts of the United States and upon the general operation of the anti-trust laws, a restriction in the nature of a special privilege or immunity to a particular class, with corresponding detriment to the general public; and it would violate rules of statutory construction having general application and far-reaching importance to enlarge that special privilege by resorting to a loose construction of the section, not to speak of ignoring or slighting the qualifying words that are found in it. Full and fair effect will be given to every word if the exceptional privilege be confined—as the natural meaning of the words confines it—to those who are proximately and substantially concerned as parties to an actual dispute respecting the terms or conditions of their own employment, past, present, or prospective. The extensive construction adopted by the majority of the court below virtually ignores the effect of the qualifying words. Congress had in mind particular industrial controversies, not a general class war. "Terms or conditions of employment" are the only grounds of dispute recognized as adequate to bring into play the exemptions; and it would do violence to the guarded language employed were the exemption extended beyond the parties affected in a proximate and substantial, not merely a sentimental or sympathetic, sense by the cause of dispute.

Nor can § 20 be regarded as bringing in all members of a labor organization as parties to a "dispute concerning terms or conditions of employment" which proximately affects only a few of them, with the result of conferring upon any and all members,—no matter how many thousands there may be, nor how remote from the actual conflict—those exemptions which Congress in terms conferred only upon parties to the dispute. That would enlarge by construction the provisions of § 20, which contain no mention of labor organizations, so as to produce an inconsistency with § 6, which deals specifically with the subject and must be deemed to express the measure and limit of the immunity intended by Congress to be incident to mere membership in such an organization. At the same time it would virtually repeal by implication the prohibition of the Sherman Act, so far as labor organizations are concerned, notwithstanding repeals by implication are not favored; and in effect, as was noted in Loewe v. Lawlor, 208 U.S. 274, 28 Sup.Ct. 301, 52 L.Ed. 488, would confer upon voluntary associations of individuals formed within the States a control over commerce among the States that is denied to the governments of the States themselves.

* * *

The extreme and harmful consequences of the construction adopted in the court below are not to be ignored. The present case furnishes an apt and convincing example. An ordinary controversy in a manufacturing establishment, said to concern the terms or conditions of employment there, has been held a sufficient occasion for imposing a general embargo upon the products of the establishment and a nation-wide blockade of the channels of interstate commerce against them, carried out by inciting sympathetic strikes and a secondary boycott against complainant's customers, to the great and incalculable damage of many innocent people far remote from any connection with or control over the original and actual dispute—people constituting, indeed, the general public upon whom the cost must ultimately fall, and whose vital interest in unobstructed commerce constituted the prime and paramount concern of Congress in enacting the antitrust laws, of which the section under consideration forms after all a part.

Reaching the conclusion, as we do, that complainant has a clear right to an injunction under the Sherman Act as amended by the Clayton Act, it becomes unnecessary to consider whether a like result would follow under the common law or local statutes; there being no suggestion that relief thereunder could be broader than that to which complainant is entitled under the acts of Congress.

There should be an injunction against defendants and the associations represented by them, and all members of those associations, restraining them, according to the prayer of the bill, from interfering or attempting to interfere with the sale, transportation, or delivery in interstate commerce of any printing press or presses manufactured

by complainant, or the transportation, carting, installation, use, operation, exhibition, display, or repairing of any such press or presses, or
the performance of any contract or contracts made by complainant
respecting the sale, transportation, delivery, or installation of any
such press or presses, by causing or threatening to cause loss, damage, trouble, or inconvenience to any person, firm, or corporation concerned in the purchase, transportation, carting, installation, use, operation, exhibition, display, or repairing of any such press or presses, or
the performance of any such contract or contracts; and also and especially from using any force, threats, command, direction, or even
persuasion with the object or having the effect of causing any person
or persons to decline employment, cease employment, or not seek employment, or to refrain from work or cease working under any person, firm, or corporation being a purchaser or prospective purchaser
of any printing press or presses from complainant, or engaged in
hauling, carting, delivering, installing, handling, using, operating, or
repairing any such press or presses for any customer of complainant.
Other threatened conduct by defendants or the associations they represent, or the members of such associations, in furtherance of the
secondary boycott should be included in the injunction according to
the proofs.

Complainant is entitled to its costs in this court and in both courts
below.

Decree reversed, and the cause remanded to the District Court for
further proceedings in conformity with this opinion.

MR. JUSTICE BRANDEIS, dissenting, with whom MR. JUSTICE
HOLMES and MR. JUSTICE CLARKE concur.

The Duplex Company, a manufacturer of newspaper printing
presses, seeks to enjoin officials of the machinists' and affiliated unions from interfering with its business by inducing their members not
to work for plaintiff or its customers in connection with the setting
up of presses made by it. *　*　* there is here no charge that defendants are inducing employees to break their contracts. Nor is it
now urged that defendants threaten acts of violence.

*　*　*

The defendants admit interference with plaintiff's business but
justify on the following ground: There are in the United States only
four manufacturers of such presses; and they are in active competition. Between 1909 and 1913 the machinists' union induced three of
them to recognize and deal with the union, to grant the eight-hour
day, to establish a minimum wage scale and to comply with other
union requirements. The fourth, the Duplex Company, refused to
recognize the union; insisted upon conducting its factory on the open
shop principle; refused to introduce the eight-hour day and operated
for the most part, ten hours a day; refused to establish a minimum
wage scale; and disregarded other union standards. Thereupon two
of the three manufacturers who had assented to union conditions, notified the union that they should be obliged to terminate their agree-

ments with it unless their competitor, the Duplex Company, also entered into the agreement with the union, which, in giving more favorable terms to labor, imposed correspondingly greater burdens upon the employer. Because the Duplex Company refused to enter into such an agreement and in order to induce it to do so, the machinists' union declared a strike at its factory, and in aid of that strike instructed its members and the members of affiliated unions not to work on the installation of presses which plaintiff had delivered in New York. Defendants insist that by the common law of New York, where the acts complained of were done, and where this suit was brought, and also by § 20 of the Clayton Act, 38 Stat. 730, 738, the facts constitute a justification for this interference with plaintiff's business.

First. As to the rights at common law: Defendants' justification is that of self-interest. They have supported the strike at the employer's factory by a strike elsewhere against its product. They have injured the plaintiff, not maliciously, but in self-defense. They contend that the Duplex Company's refusal to deal with the machinists' union and to observe its standards threatened the interest not only of such union members as were its factory employees, but even more of all members of the several affiliated unions employed by plaintiff's competitors and by others whose more advanced standards the plaintiff was, in reality, attacking; and that none of the defendants and no person whom they are endeavoring to induce to refrain from working in connection with the setting up of presses made by plaintiff is an outsider, an interloper. In other words, that the contest between the company and the machinists' union involves vitally the interest of every person whose cooperation is sought. May not all with a common interest join in refusing to expend their labor upon articles whose very production constitutes an attack upon their standard of living and the institution which they are convinced supports it? Applying common-law principles the answer should, in my opinion, be: Yes, if as matter of fact those who so cooperate have a common interest.

The change in the law by which strikes once illegal and even criminal are now recognized as lawful was effected in America largely without the intervention of legislation. This reversal of a common-law rule was not due to the rejection by the courts of one principle and the adoption in its stead of another, but to a better realization of the facts of industrial life. It is conceded that, although the strike of the workmen in plaintiff's factory injured its business, the strike was not an actionable wrong; because the obvious self-interest of the strikers constituted a justification. * * *

* * *

So, in the case at bar, deciding a question of fact upon the evidence introduced and matters of common knowledge, I should say, as the two lower courts apparently have said, that the defendants and those from whom they sought cooperation have a common interest which the plaintiff threatened. *   *   *

*   *   *

Second. As to the anti-trust laws of the United States: Section 20, of the Clayton Act, *   *   * [sets out certain acts which had previously been held unlawful, whenever courts had disapproved of the ends for which they were performed; it then declared that, when these acts were committed in the course of an industrial dispute, they should not be held to violate any law of the United States. In other words the Clayton Act substituted the opinion of Congress as to the propriety of the purpose for that of differing judges; and thereby it declared that the relations between employers of labor and workingmen were competitive relations, that organized competition was not harmful and that it justified injuries necessarily inflicted in its course.] *   *   *

This statute was the fruit of unceasing agitation, which extended over more than twenty years and was designed to equalize before the law the position of workingmen and employer as industrial combatants. Aside from the use of the injunction, the chief source of dissatisfaction with the existing law lay in the doctrine of malicious combination, and, in many parts of the country, in the judicial declarations of the illegality at common law of picketing and persuading others to leave work. *   *   * It was objected that, due largely to environment, the social and economic ideas of judges, which thus became translated into law, were prejudicial to a position of equality between workingman and employer; that due to this dependence upon the individual opinion of judges great confusion existed as to what purposes were lawful and what unlawful; and that in any event Congress, not the judges, was the body which should declare what public policy in regard to the industrial struggle demands.

By 1914 the ideas of the advocates of legislation had fairly crystallized upon the manner in which the inequality and uncertainty of the law should be removed. *   *   *

The Duplex Company contends that § 20 of the Clayton Act does not apply to the case at bar, because it is restricted to cases "between an employer and employees, or between employers and employees, or between employees, or between persons employed and persons seeking employment, involving, or growing out of, a dispute concerning terms or conditions of employment"; whereas the case at bar arises between an employer in Michigan and workingmen in New York not in its employ, and does not involve their conditions of employment. But Congress did not restrict the provision to employers and workingmen *in their employ.* By including "employers and employees" and "persons employed and persons seeking employment" it showed that it was not aiming merely at a legal relationship between a specific employer and his employees. Furthermore, the plaintiff's contention proves too much. If the words are to receive a strict technical construction, the statute will have no application to disputes between employers of labor and workingmen, since the very acts to which it applies sever the continuity of the legal relationship. The further contention that this case is not one arising out of a dispute concerning the conditions of work of one of the parties is, in my opinion, founded upon a misconception of the facts.

Because I have come to the conclusion that both the common law of a State and a statute of the United States declare the right of industrial combatants to push their struggle to the limits of the justification of self-interest, I do not wish to be understood as attaching any constitutional or moral sanction to that right. All rights are derived from the purposes of the society in which they exist; above all rights rises duty to the community. The conditions developed in industry may be such that those engaged in it cannot continue their struggle without danger to the community. But it is not for judges to determine whether such conditions exist, nor is it their function to set the limits of permissible contest and to declare the duties which the new situation demands. This is the function of the legislature which, while limiting individual and group rights of aggression and defense, may substitute processes of justice for the more primitive method of trial by combat.

QUESTIONS

1.   Is the majority or the dissent more persuasive?

2.   What assumptions does the majority make about the desirability of unionization? The dissent?

3.   What changes, if any, in the language of §§ 6 and 20 would have been adequate to achieve a different result?

––––––––

The decision in *Duplex Printing* outraged labor and its supporters. The role of the courts in labor relations in general, and the injunction in particular, were once again the subject of attack. A particularly influential scholarly statement detailing its history and abuses in labor relations came from Felix Frankfurter and Nathaniel Greene.[8]

––––––––

"The restraining order and the preliminary injunction invoked in labor disputes reveal the most crucial points of legal maladjustment. Temporary injunctive relief without notice, or, if upon notice, relying upon dubious affidavits, serves the important function of staying defendant's conduct regardless of the ultimate justification of such restraint. The preliminary proceedings, in other words, make the issue of final relief a practical nullity. Undoubtedly, the law is here confronted with a very perplexing situation. Where the plaintiff on the surface presents a meritorious case, he should not be exposed to the peril of irreparable damage before the court can make available to

8.   Frankfurter and Greene. *The Labor Injunction*, (1930) pp. 200–203.

him its slower, though much more scrutinizing, processes of fact-finding. This form of relief presents no difficulty when the temporary suspension of defendant's activities results in no very great damage to him, at least no damage that cannot be adequately compensated by money, security for which is provided by plaintiff's bond. In labor cases, however, complicating factors enter. The injunction cannot preserve the so-called *status quo*; the situation does not remain in equilibrium awaiting judgment upon full knowledge. The suspension of activities affects only the strikers; the employer resumes his efforts to defeat the strike, and resumes them free from the interdicted interferences. Moreover, the suspension of strike activities, even temporarily, may defeat the strike for practical purposes and foredoom its resumption, even if the injunction is later lifted. Choice is not between irreparable damage to one side and compensable damage to the other. The law's conundrum is which side should bear the risk of *unavoidable* irreparable damage. Improvident denial of the injunction may be irreparable to the complainant; improvident issue of the injunction may be irreparable to the defendant. For this situation the ordinary mechanics of the provisional injunction proceedings are plainly inadequate. Judicial error is too costly to either side of a labor dispute to permit perfunctory determination of the crucial issues; even in the first instance, it must be searching. The necessity of finding the facts quickly from sources vague, embittered and partisan, colored at the start by the passionate intensities of a labor controversy, calls at best for rare judicial qualities. It becomes an impossible assignment when judges rely solely upon the complaint and the affidavits of interested or professional witnesses, untested by the safeguards of common law trials—personal appearance of witnesses, confrontation and cross-examination.

"But the treacherous difficulties presented by an application for an injunction are not confined to the ascertainment of fact; the legal doctrines that must be applied are even more illusory and ambiguous. Even where the rules of law in a particular jurisdiction can be stated, as we have tried to state them, with a show of precision and a definiteness of contour, the unknowns and the variables in the equation—intent, motive, malice, justification—make its application in a given case a discipline in clarity and detachment requiring time and anxious thought. With such issues of fact and of law, demanding insight into human behavior and nicety of juristic reasoning, we now confront a single judge to whom they are usually unfamiliar, and we ask him to decide forthwith, allowing him less opportunity for consideration than would be available if the question were one concerning the negotiability of a new form of commercial paper. We ease his difficulty and his conscience by telling him that his decision is only tentative.

"Emphasis upon procedural safeguards in the use of the injunction must therefore rank first. Whatever differences there may be as to the particular stages of the procedure at which changes are to be made or as to the character of the changes, there should be no reasonable basis for opposing such correctives, once the unique elements that enter into labor litigation are fully recognized."

———

A more personal reaction, giving some sense of the outrage which unionists felt towards the courts as a result of the use of labor injunctions, is contained in the testimony of Edward Doyle, a mine worker and union official, before the Commission on Industrial Relations of 1915.[9]

* * *

Chairman Walsh. What is your age?

Mr. Doyle. Twenty-eight. * * *

Chairman Walsh. I wish you would sketch, as briefly as you can, what you have done in the way of work, labor, all your life, beginning at the first, but of course not confining it to the particular jobs, but the localities and the character of your employment?

Mr. Doyle. I commenced work at the age of 12 in the mines of Illinois, in Spring Valley, Ill.

Chairman Walsh. In what capacity?

Mr. Doyle. As trapper boy.

Chairman Walsh. And what does a trapper boy have to do?

Mr. Doyle. He tends to the trapdoors. The current of air in a mine is controlled by doors, and also by canvas curtains; where the current is too strong, they use a door, and the trapper boys attend to those doors and permit the teams of coal to go through and act really as flagmen for drivers, etc.

Chairman Walsh. Underground?

Mr. Doyle. Underground; yes sir.

Chairman Walsh. How long did you work at that?

Mr. Doyle. I should judge I worked at that—oh, about two years, when I was put on spragging.

* * *

Mr. Doyle. After trapping at this place I got to spragging. That is a position that boys of a little more experience than trappers are put to work on. I was put to spragging cars. That is what you call it; you might call it on a railroad, braking. I was spragging the wheels in order to keep them from running too fast, and to handle them, and so forth, from the places to the cage. After that I went to digging coal, mining coal with a brother of mine. First with another party and then with a brother of mine.

Chairman Walsh. How old were you when you began digging coal?

9. *Report of the Commission on Industrial Relations*, 38819 S.Doc. 415, 64–1, Vol. 7–31, pp. 66174 et seq.

Mr. Doyle. I should judge 17. I was only getting a dollar and a quarter a day for spragging. I was very large for my age and wanted to drive a mule—which was paying $1.75. Not getting it, I thought I could make more money. I believed by working perhaps—not hard—at mining coal on the tonnage basis than spragging, and secured a job of mining.

Chairman Walsh. At the age of 17?

Mr. Doyle. Yes, sir.

Chairman Walsh. What were your wages mining? What did you earn as a miner when you began?

Mr. Doyle. Well, I don't remember exactly. I know that the biggest pay as a trapper I got, I could not make in a half month over $9.75.

Chairman Walsh. And then as a spragger?

Mr. Doyle. As a spragger I made $1.25 a day.

Chairman Walsh. And as a miner?

Mr. Doyle. As a miner we were paid 76 cents a ton, I believe. It was later increased to 82½ cents, if I remember correctly.

*   *   *

Chairman Walsh. You are the present secretary-treasurer for the United Mine Workers?

Mr. Doyle. Yes sir; secretary-treasurer for the district organization; not for the national—

Chairman Walsh (interrupting). When were you in jail for contempt of court?

Mr. Doyle. The first time on December 23, 1910; and the second time July 14, 1911.

Chairman Walsh. How long were you in the first time?

Mr. Doyle. Two months.

Chairman Walsh. And the second time?

Mr. Doyle. Four months. Each time I was sentenced a year, and the second time it was a year and $500 fine.

Chairman Walsh. Briefly, in what did the contempt consist?

*   *   *

Mr. Doyle. There wasn't any contempt. It was all a put-up job on the part of the judge and one of the companies, and they railroaded us—

Chairman Walsh. Where did this occur?

Mr. Doyle. Occurred in Denver. We were on strike in Weld and Boulder Counties, and they secured an injunction from Judge Greeley Whitford in Denver County, an injunction that forbade us to do anything, in fact, but eat or sleep. We couldn't fly banners, post notices, hold meetings, talk to a neighbor or to strangers, and if you would say a word about it he could pronounce you guilty, or find you guilty for anything you did or didn't do and on the 17th of December, 1910, a fight was supposed to have taken place on the streets of Lafayette, which I believe did take place; and about the 20th 16 miners from Lafayette were arrested, charged with violating the injunction and brought to Denver for a farcical trial without a jury and were sentenced to jail after a two days' supposed hearing.   *   *   *

We didn't know what we were arrested for and couldn't find out until the day before the trial. We were released on bonds—$300 or $400—I think $300, I ain't sure—and when we returned to Lafayette there was a great crowd at the station when we got back to welcome us, and that was used as evidence against us for being congregated at the depot. That was evidence in our trial.

We were placed on trial—I forgot to state in the beginning that the miners' organization did not appear and oppose the issuance of the temporary injunction, knowing that the judge would not consider such a thing under the circumstances; that he had his mind made up to issue it regardless of what opposition was made. So we didn't waste any time or money by appearing. And when we were set for trial the 16 of us were denied a jury and we were compelled to sit in the jury box—12 of them and 4 in chairs in front of the jury box—and we were compelled to be seated always in the same places in order that the witnesses could identify us and could tell who we were by a certain place—

*   *   *

Mr. Doyle.   And after two days of a farcical trial—it was a joke, so far as a trial was concerned—we were sentenced to one year in the county jail in the city of Denver. During that trial witnesses appeared on the stand that could not pick out their men that they said was there in the fight, or anything else. When we would change a seat in the jury box purposely so they would not know, the judge would tell us to get back and take our seat. We could understand the conspiracy as to the whole thing. We were convinced to our own satisfaction—

Chairman Walsh.   That feeling, whether or not it was correct, did it cause a bitter feeling among the men involved in the strike and your friends?

Mr. Doyle.   It certainly did. And during the trial I might mention—I don't know whether any of the members of the commission are superstitious or not, but for the further information of any, if there are any such—during the trial—we were tried in the courthouse down here in Denver and the goddess of justice is standing up there on the dome holding the scales of justice in her hand; this is the way she did it, showing one balance stood up close to the statue of justice and the other part down, and when we were sentenced to jail—after we were sentenced she throwed the scales on top of the roof and they are there yet.

During that trial the record will show that the judge overruled practically everything; it was absolutely ridiculous the way the judge overruled the attorneys for the miners. I tallied—I don't know, for

about an hour and 10 minutes at one time; I think an hour and 10 minutes, or 2 hours and 10 minutes. I don't remember exactly, but I scored a while, being in there—on a piece of paper the number of matters overruled by the judge, on our side and the number on the other; and I had 111 matters on our side overruled and 11 on the company's side; and I mention that to show that there wasn't any chance during the trial at all. The facts were, as near as I could learn afterwards, that out of those 16 men 1 man was in the group that had the fight and 15 were not, and I later was, as I said before, put in for telling the men that I thought they ought not to obey the injunction, and advised them before any arrests were made. * * *
And while in jail, and after getting out, I wrote some letters to our official paper published at Indianapolis, Ind., called the United Mine Workers' Journal, and in those letters I told my honest opinion of the judge and what I thought about him. In July, 18 more miners were arrested. I was among the 18; again for alleged contempt of this so-called injunction.

Chairman Walsh. The same injunction?

Mr. Doyle. The same injunction.

* * *

Chairman Walsh (interrupting). Did the supreme court pass upon your case?

Mr. Doyle. No; they did not. They were to pass upon that later.

* * *

Chairman Walsh. What effect did the whole matter have upon the minds of the working people generally, if you observed?

Mr. Doyle. Well, if I am any judge, it only served to show them that the powers that be; that is, the corporations, as great as they are, that a judge will serve it; that the workmen as such need not expect any justice at the hands of courts that these people can get control of, and have control of, and you might as well not make any defense; and you may just as well, whether you violated the law or not, realize, if you are accused, you are guilty, and you have to prove yourself innocent instead of being innocent until you are proved guilty. And I believe the worst part of it was that way. Later this judge was charged with having been bribed to send the miners—a woman made the statement that she gave him $3,000—and he had the nerve to ask another district judge to get a jury to investigate his case, and yet he wouldn't give the miners a jury to hear their case.

Chairman Walsh. What is the feeling among the working people generally in Colorado with reference to the courts at this time?

Mr. Doyle. Well, as far as I know, as far as labor is concerned as such, I think there is not very much feeling in certain parts of the State, because things have not got to that stage. But in certain counties and with certain members of the supreme bench I think labor believes it cannot and will not get a fair deal.

B. THE DEMAND FOR A NATIONAL LABOR POLICY

Political agitation by labor and its supporters against the labor injunction was successful. In 1932 Congress passed the Norris La-Guardia Act, which severely restricts the availability of the injunction in labor disputes. Mindful of the fate of § 20 of the Clayton Act, particular care was taken in drafting the new law. Felix Frankfurter, then a law professor, later a member of the Supreme Court, played a major role in this effort.

The Act declares that "no court of the U. S. shall have jurisdiction to issue any restraining order or temporary or permanent injunction in a case involving or growing out of a labor dispute, except in strict conformity with this Act." The term labor dispute is broadly defined. Section 4 prohibits any injunction against strikes, peaceful union activity under any circumstances. Section 7 permits the grant of injunctions against unlawful acts, but only after a hearing in which a heavy burden of justification is placed upon the person seeking the injunction. At the time of its passage, there was considerable doubt about Congress' ability to enact such a law for the purpose of regulating labor relations: The law was thus framed as a limitation on the jurisdiction of the Federal courts, in order to insure its constitutionality. This technique limited the Act's effectiveness, however, because. it did not apply to state courts, which were, if anything, more willing than Federal courts to issue injunctions in labor disputes. Many state legislatures, however, adopted so-called "baby Norris LaGuardia" acts which applied the language or approach of Norris LaGuardia to their own courts.

While passage of the Norris LaGuardia Act was a notable victory for the union's movement, the Act's scope was limited. It did not establish a national labor relations policy, other than one of "hands off", and by the time of its passage in 1932, more was needed. Labor relations had, from its beginning, always been a turbulent—sometimes violent, area of human endeavor. By the 1900's however, passions had grown stronger. The numbers of people involved had swelled into the millions, and the techniques of battle on both sides had become violent. The following three excerpts give some of the flavor of labor disputes during the early years of the Twentieth Century.

1. THE McKEESPORT STRIKE OF 1909 AGAINST PRESSED STEEL CAR CO.

The immediate cause of the strike was the refusal of the company to restore pay cuts made during the panic of 1907—when wages went from $3 a day to 50 cents a day in 1909 for the least skilled worker.

In general, conditions at the factory were deplorable—a pool system of payment was used, so that payment depended on the whole group's performance. Rates of pay were not announced so that workers did not know how much they were earning, and safety conditions were so bad that investigators found that an average of one man a day was killed. Although they were basically unorganized on July 14, 1909, 5,000 men walked off the job.

Attempts to bring in strike breakers failed as did initial attempt to evict strikers and their families from company houses despite the use of 300 deputy sheriffs and 200 state constables. All attempts on the part of the union to meet with the company president were turned down.

The strike finally succeeded, but at the cost of 13 lives and 500 wounded. Public opinion was so aroused against company tactics that the sheriff prohibited the importation of strike breakers and money was raised for strikers in nearby Pittsburgh.

N. Y. TRIBUNE

July 16, 1909.

Pittsburg, July 15.—A day of rioting and bloodshed at the Mc-Kee's Rocks plant of the Pressed Steel Car Company was closed about 10 o'clock to-night after an hour's fighting between strikers and fifty mounted men of the state constabulary, in which at least fifty strikers were injured by the constables' bullets or by being run down by the horses. Hardly one of the fifty constables escaped the showers of rocks and missiles with which the strikers met them each time they tore through the crowd.

Elmer Jrtsen, a trooper, is in the hospital, as the result of being knocked from his horse and rolled on by the animal, but it is not thought he will die. Fred Frash, of the constabulary, is also in the hospital, suffering from wounds inflicted by thrown rocks in a riot at noon to-day. The hospital is filled with wounded from rioting which begun about noon to-day and continued until late to-night. It is conservatively estimated that 250 persons were injured to-day. About six of them will die.

With twenty-two alleged strike leaders under arrest, herded together in a box car, and the Pennsylvania State Constabulary over-awing the 3,500 strikers by the free use of riot maces and revolvers, comparative quiet reigned at midnight.

The officials of the company said to-night that they could not understand why the strikers were rioting, as the entire plant of the company was idle and no attempt was being made to work any department.

The most serious riot occurred at noon, when for an hour four thousand strikers fought the constabulary, the deputy sheriffs and the special officers. It was no concentrated battle, but a series of battles all over the town. The most serious rioting occurred when Frash and six others tried to disperse a crowd of seven hundred strikers. They were met with a volley of stones, and Frash was knocked from his horse.

He was dazed, but, climbing on his horse again, began shooting over the heads of the mob. His shots brought only another volley of rocks.

STRIKERS SEIZE BREWERY

Then Frash and his fellow officer began to shoot in earnest, and the mob stampeded. It is certain that eight injured men were carried ahead of the retreating mob, but they cannot be found. Frash and his fellows pursued the strikers, captured two alleged leaders, handcuffed them and chained them to a tree while Frash was taken to the hospital. About this time the McKee's Rocks Brewery was seized by five hundred strikers, who started to serve free beer in the town, where all saloons were closed. It took one hundred deputies an hour to throw them out and close the brewery.

Efforts to evict families of striking miners from the company's houses this evening produced an impressive scene. Hundreds of women, many of them with lighted torches, drove the special mounted constables back, threatening to set fire to that part of the town if any attempt was made to carry out the orders by the officers, who retired.

The situation was quiet this morning. Following a night of wild disorder, in which thirty persons were shot or beaten, a detachment of the Pennsylvania state constabulary arrived early to-day, and soon afterward the rioting stopped. The men were temporarily awed by the police.

CONSTABULARY ATTACKED

When the police reached the plant they stationed their horses inside the gates and then took up positions outside the fence. A moment later a brick struck one of the troopers. Instantly the mill gate was thrown open, several troopers vaulted into the saddle, and the next minute were dashing fiercely into a crowd of strikers and their sympathizers. As they galloped through the crowd the state police struck right and left with heavy riot clubs. The crowd became demoralized under the terrific assault and fled in all directions.

At 9 o'clock the strikers, with their wives, children and sympathizers, were gathered about the gates of the mill. There are seven gates, but only two of them are the main arteries of the plant. At these gates almost a solid wall of Winchester muzzles protected the openings.

Frank N. Hoffstet, president, and J. W. Friend, vice-president, of the Pressed Steel Car Company were out of the city yesterday, but are said to be on their way here.

An investigation of conditions in the Pressed Steel plant is urged by friends of the foreign workmen, who assert that a system of graft has been in operation for years. The workmen say they have been compelled to pay from $10 to $50 for a job at the plant, and that even after paying this their places were not secure, and in many cases they were discharged after a few weeks. Discharged workmen were not barred from reapplying for work again, according to the strikers, who say they could get their old jobs back just as often as they had the money to pay for them. It is alleged that when the plant was running full time and over time this graft from workmen wanting employment amounted to as much as $10,000 a month.

The pooling system, which has so outraged the workmen, is explained by them as a plan to make the workmen pay the wages of each foreman. Until 1907 the company paid the wages of the foremen, but since that time, * * * the 25 to 40 cents an hour for foremen has been taken out of the pool formed of the workmen's wages. The workmen aver also that they have been compelled to deal at the company store, being peremptorily discharged if they dealt elsewhere. The store is owned and operated by the Pressed Steel Car Company in a roundabout way, it is said, as there is a law in Pennsylvania against company stores.

Men said to be agents from the Hungarian and Italian consulates at Washington visited the strike district to-day and took statements concerning the grievances of the workmen. Complaint to the consulates has been made.

The Pressed Steel Car Company has been in existence only ten years, having been incorporated in 1899; nevertheless, it controls practically all the pressed steel car manufacturing plants in the United States.

At the outset its preferred and common stock amounted to only $25,000,000, ran equal amounts of each; there were no bonds offered. For several years the company operated on that capital; then further to extend its activities it issued a block of $5,000,000 notes in 1901, maturing in 1911. To date the company has paid off all but $500,000 of these.

Preferred dividends have been paid regularly since the company's organization at 7 per cent a year, but in 1905 the common dividend was suspended, after the troublesome year of 1904. Since then the common stockholders have had to get along without sharing the company's profits, the management deeming it wisest to accumulate a comfortable bank account before resuming dividends on their stock. In this way the company's total surplus, which was $2,588,000 at the close of 1905, was brought to $6,413,000 on December 31, 1907.

In several instances the men claim that their employers, taking advantage of their recent prolonged idleness, are offering them low wages for their work. The officials assert conditions do not warrant higher remuneration at this time.

Other grievances are the alleged violation of the eight-hour workday, non-recognition of organized labor, a controversy over the use of so-called "safety" powder for coal mine blasting and better conditions generally.

2.   THE COLORADO COAL STRIKE

The Colorado coal mining area was the scene of violent labor struggles from 1890 to 1915.   Violence was resorted to by both sides but state and county governments strongly supported the mine operators.   As a result, state militia were called out and martial law declared at the employers' request, and forceable deportations took place.   A statement by a former U. S. Senator who tried to settle the strike of 1904, made to the Commission on Industrial Relations of 1915 makes clear how strong was management's objection to granting union recognition.[10]

TESTIMONY OF HON. THOMAS M. PATTERSON

Chairman Walsh.   Please state your name, Senator.

Senator Patterson.   Thomas M. Patterson.

Chairman Walsh.   What is your profession, please?

Senator Patterson.   I am not following any now.   I have been a practicing lawyer.

Chairman Walsh.   You have been an attorney at law by profession?

Senator Patterson.   Yes, sir.

Chairman Walsh.   And the publisher of newspapers?

Senator Patterson.   Yes, sir—journalist.

Chairman Walsh.   And a member of the Senate of the United States?

Senator Patterson.   Yes, sir.

Chairman Walsh.   Have you had anything to do with the coal industry of Colorado?

Senator Patterson.   Yes.

Chairman Walsh.   In what way?

Senator Patterson.   I have been a part owner in one small mine for quite a number of years, and for the last 10 years, perhaps, a part owner in two small mines.   *   *   *

Resuming where I left off.   Gov. Ammons and I that morning held a consultation, and very early, perhaps on that visit, I found that Mr. White, Mr. Hayes of the national organization, Mr. Lawson the president of the State organization of the miners, and, perhaps, Mr. McLennan, although I am not certain about that, were in one of the governor's rooms, and the governor and I went into the room where they were.   They were told briefly what we were going to do to try to bring about a peaceable settlement of the strike.   They expressed a very great desire that it should be done, and that, so far as they were concerned, they would do everything in their power to have it settled, and that they would make every reasonable concession that

10.   Report pp. 6474 et seq.

could be asked of them to have it settled. And shortly afterwards the governor called up the mine operators and told them that he would like to see them. They told him they would come up immediately, and they came, as I recall it now, Mr. Osgood, Mr. Welborn, and Mr. Brown. The governor told them that he was very, very anxious to bring about a settlement and that he had requested me to help him in bringing it about and he wanted to know what could be done. Of course, it is impossible for me to give consecutively what was said by the one or the other. I can only give the general nature of the conversation with some of the details. We told the operators of the talk we had had with the representatives of the union, and that they were willing and very anxious to have the matter settled. The operators said they were also anxious to have it settled, but they soon gave us to understand that they would not meet with the miners—I mean with White, Hayes, and Lawson. They said, "We are willing to talk with the men themselves, any man whom the men will select from among the workers—the miners, we are willing to confer with them—but we will not have any conference with Mr. White, Mr. Hayes, or Mr. Lawson." We had several conferences, one, perhaps, again that afternoon, and then the next day—all to the same effect.

Between two of these interviews with the operators' committee, we understanding that Messrs. Osgood, Welborn, and Brown represented the body of the operators, we had a talk with Mr. White, Mr. Hayes, and Mr. Lawson, and possibly Mr. McLennan, in which, in substance we told them that there had to be some concrete proposition made; we told them of the attitude of the operators and that, unless they could give us an opening to proceed with the efforts, they would have to stop, and finally, Mr. White—I think it was Mr. White, it was either Mr. White or Mr. Lawson, I am quite certain it was Mr. White—made this statement, addressed to the governor and myself: He said, "We have this to say: That if the operators will but grant us a conference we know that this strike will be settled. All we want to do is to have a conference with these men so that we can understand each other, and if they will but grant us a conference we know that this strike will be settled." I said to them: "Gentlemen, do you understand the import of your language? You know that the operators will not recognize the union. It is generally understood that you will insist upon recognition of the union as a sine qua non of a settlement. Now, the fair inference from your language is that you are willing to reach a settlement upon some other basis than the recognition of the union." Mr. White replied: "Whatever the import of our language is, I reiterate that if the operators will confer with us we know there will be a settlement." Gov. Ammons and I felt that in view of that statement there was some hope, and we called up the operators very promptly and they shortly came. The same gentlemen met us and I put the matter before them. I said: "Gentlemen, I believe that a settlement can be reached. These men say that if you will but grant them a conference they know that the strike will be settled. Now, that must mean that they will surrender their demand for the recognition of the union, and, I think, you ought to grant them a conference. They are right out here in the adjoining room—there was but a brick wall separating the operators, the governor, myself, and the representatives of the miners." They said: "No; we will not hold any conference with them." And they indulged in some very, very bitter language in talking—referring to these men. They said they were merely interlopers, they were intermeddlers, they had no business here, they did not live in this State, and then some bitter names were applied to them that placed the responsibility for the violence that had occurred in the south upon their shoulders, and for that reason they would not meet them. I said: "Gentlemen I don't think that you have a right to regard them as interlopers or intermeddlers; they are the officers of the national union of which the local unions are a part; it is their duty and their right to visit the different unions of the national organization in the different States wherever they may be; it is their duty and their right to give advice and to ask for information, and if the striking miners wish them to help them it is their duty to help them. They can't be stigmatized under those circumstances as interlopers or intermeddlers, and I do not think that your objections are well taken." "Well," they said, "to confer with them would be recognition of the union—practical recognition." I said: "That is foolish, gentlemen. A conference with them simply gives you the opportunity of learning whether you can meet upon common ground or not. If you find you can't, that ends the matter, and you are just as far from the recognition of the union then as you are now. These men have a right to be represented in conference by men of their own selection, and it requires men of experience and knowledge to meet such gentlemen as you and properly represent the men." One of the gentlemen remarked: "If they were to come into this room now we would go out. We won't be in the same room with them."

I protested, and so did the governor, tried to reason the matter, but upon that one proposition they were absolutely fixed and unrelenting, they would not meet nor they would not confer with the men. I want to say right now that I believe, as I believe and know I am sitting here, that if they had but granted a conference that they would have reached a settlement of the strike, no matter to what extent the representatives of the unions had to withdraw their claims. And to my mind the violence and whatever else has followed the continuation of the strike rests right there.

3.   THE STEEL STRIKE OF 1919

From its creation in 1901, the U. S. Steel Corporation's policy had been one of firm opposition to unionization.

The Amalgamated Association of Iron, Steel and Tin Workers attempted to extend their toehold to new mills after the corporation was formed. They lost. With few exceptions the unions lost strike after strike against U. S. Steel. The union was expelled from the last of the union mills in 1909. In 1919, after 100,000 men had been signed up by the union, demands for recognition, collective bargaining, eight hour day, and reinstatement of men discharged for union activities, were made. A strike began on September 22, 1919 with 375,000 men going out. The strike was defeated—with the aid of strike breakers, the suppression of civil liberties and the help of the press, which created the impression that the strikers were well paid and that the strike was a Bolshevik plot.

Because of U. S. Steel's immense size and influence, its successful anti-union policy set the tone for much of the union policy of big industry.

The Interchurch Commission, a specially established committee from various Protestant churches, investigated the strike and issued a widely discussed report which spotlighted Company attitudes towards labor and unions.[11]

REPORT ON STEEL STRIKE

In normal times, the Steel Corporation had no adequate means of learning the conditions of life and work and the desires of its employees.

The President of the Carnegie Steel Company declared to the Commission that there was "no real way of getting hold of the foreigner." The head of the Corporation's Sanitation, Safety and Welfare Department, Mr. C. L. Close agreed with this statement. Neither seemed to think that this inability was due to a lack of machinery and it was apparent that steel officials generally relied on some other method for information than an openly organized system of studying the minds and needs of the workers. A suggestion that companies might foster and enlist the aid of organizations of the workers themselves for the purpose of insuring such information was commented on by company officers with surprise not to say suspicion. Mr. Gary gave the clearest testimony in confirmation of his subordinates, though that was not his immediate purpose. He told the Senate Committee that his men were "contented." He said he knew this to be the case and that he had adequate means for knowing it; that there was "no cause" for the strike and that "the men were not complaining; the workmen had found no fault; we are on the best of terms with our men and have always been, with some very slight exceptions, very inconsequential exceptions." Then he volunteered the following, (quoted from the Senate Testimony, Volume I, pages 161 and 162):

Senator Walsh. "How did you personally know that hundreds and thousands of your men were content and satisfied?"

Mr. Gary. "Senator, I know it because I make it my particular business all the time to know the frame of mind of our people. Not that I visit every man; I do not do that; of course, I could not do

11. Commission of Inquiry of Interchurch World Movement Report on Steel Strike of 1919.

that; not that there could be something done or something said in the mills that I would not know; but, in the first place, my instructions regarding the treatment of the men are absolutely positive, given to the presidents at the presidents' meetings regularly—plenty of my remarks to the presidents have been printed and can be exhibited if necessary—and because I am inquiring into that; and we have a man at the head of our welfare department, Mr. Close, who is here, who is around among the works frequently, and all the time, more or less, trying to ascertain conditions; because public writers, unbeknown to us, have been among our works making inquiry and reporting and writing articles on the subject; and because we come in contact with the foremen and often with the men, going through the mills, Mr. Farrell and myself, and others from time to time; because we have a standing rule, and have had, that if any of our men in any department are dissatisfied in any respect they may come singly or they may come in groups, as they may choose, to the foremen and ask for adjustments, make complaints, and if necessary they may come before the president of the company, or they may come to the chairman of the Corporation."

The Corporation relies upon other means of information than a system of open and cooperative machinery operating within the mills. Mr. Gary's testimony on this subject is brief: (Senate Testimony, Volume I, Page 177:)

Senator Walsh. "Have you a secret service organization among your employees at any of the subsidiary plants of the Steel Corporation?"

Mr. Gary. "Well, Senator, I cannot be very specific about that, but I am quite sure that at times some of our people have used secret service men to ascertain facts and conditions."

It was not the original intention of the Interchurch Commission to gather evidence on the widespread charges of "company spy systems," "industrial espionage," etc. Steel workers and their spokesmen asserted that such spy systems were the ever-present instruments resulting in an ever-present fear,—some workers called it "terrorization,"—evident among the rank and file of steel workers. For one thing, it would have seemed impossible to get such secret evidence. For another thing, the Commission doubted its importance. But it became apparent that some officials of some steel companies were so accustomed to look upon their secret service reports as the basis on which their, or any company's, labor policy would have to be formed that they showed no hesitancy in producing information about them from their secret files.

* * *

For the country at large, the source of information about conditions in the steel industry and the progress of the strike, was, of course, principally the press. The wide discrepancies between the facts now disclosed and most of the press reports at the time are the subject of exhaustive analysis elsewhere. The findings are that most newspapers, traditionally hesitant in reporting industrial matters, failed notably to acquaint the public with the facts, failed to take steps necessary to ascertain the facts, failed finally to publish adequately what was brought out by the brief investigation of the U. S. Senate committee.

Within the steel communities themselves the facts about the organization of the steel industry are not known. Even in the case of the American workers, the conditions of their jobs, their hours, rates of pay, methods of promotion and attitude to the companies are not common knowledge. Even in normal times it is difficult to get American skilled steel workers to discuss their jobs. These men say when pinned down, "How do I know who you are? Even in the mill I can't talk about conditions. If I talk, I may find myself transferred to a worse job or laid off. I can't afford to talk."

In the case of the "foreigner," the facts lie behind the further screen of physical and mental segregation.

The situation, then, during the strike, and existent now, is that the fundamental facts about the steel industry and especially about the masses of unskilled foreign workmen are not known and that this ignorance breeds a public fear akin to panic.

"Bolshevism":

The second preliminary phase of the report concerns the charge, widely current, that the strike was a product of Bolshevism. The evidence, from steel company officials, strike committee records, local and national governmental officers and from observations by the Commission and its investigators is completely adequate for forming a judgment.

A stranger in America reading the newspapers during the strike and talking with steel masters both in and out of steel communities must have concluded that the strike represented a serious outbreak of Bolshevism red hot from Russia. The chief memory that American citizens themselves may have a few years from now may well be that the strike was largely the work of Reds. " 'Reds' back of the Steel Strike" was a frequent headline in September. As late as January 4, 1920, an article in *The New York Times* contained the following:

> "Radical leaders planned to develop the recent steel and coal strike into a general strike and ultimately into a revolution to overthrow the government, according to information gathered by federal agents in Friday night's wholesale round-up of members of the Communist parties. These data, officials said, tended to prove that the nation-wide raids had blasted the most menacing revolutionary plot yet unearthed."

The history of the Steel Corporation's dealings with labor since 1901 shows a consistent and successful carrying out of the anti-union policy. Largely by shutting down mills "conceded" to be "union" and by discharging workmen for forming other unions this result has come about: whereas in 1901 one-third of the Corporation's mills dealt with unions, in 1919 these and all other unions had been ousted;

no unions were dealt with. Besides the stockholders' report of 1912 hitherto quoted, which "justifies" the Corporation's "repression of the workmen," Mr. Gary made plain to the Senate Investigating Committee that the same ideas and the same methods held all along.

He told the Senate Committee that "unionism is not a good thing for employer or employee." At the same time he declared that the Corporation did not carry this belief into practice by "opposing labor unions as such"; that no workman "was discriminated against because he was a union man"; that the Corporation did not attempt to crush unions.

The Commission's data show that the practice of the antiunionism alternative by the Corporation and by a large number of independents entailed in 1919—

1. Discharging workmen for unionism, just as the twelve men were discharged at Wellsville in 1901 "for forming a lodge"; also the eviction of workmen from company houses and similar coercions.

2. Blacklisting strikers.

3. Systematic espionage through "under-cover men."

4. Hiring strike-breaking spies from "labor detective agencies."

Attempts to thwart union organization and refusals to recognize unions were a major issue in most of the major strikes in the early part of this century. Indeed it was these issues rather than questions of wages or working conditions which gave rise to the intense passions which were aroused. Blue Ribbon and Congressional commissions of inquiry appointed to investigate strikes began to recommend that the government play a more positive role in setting the ground rules for labor relations. Specifically, it was urged that the right to form, join and participate in unions should be safeguarded; that orderly processes should be established for determining when employees wanted to be represented by a union and that management be required to recognize and bargain with unions selected by their employees.[12] The first major statute embodying these principles was the Railway Labor Act passed in 1926. This Act reflected the special Congressional concern with ensuring uninterrupted transportation service.

C. THE 1930s—THE DEVELOPMENT OF A NATIONAL LABOR POLICY

The Railway Labor Act provided for collective bargaining supported by an intricate system of Boards and Commissions to help resolve disputes.

---

12. Much of this history is spelled out in Magruder. "A Half Century of Legal Influence Upon the Development of Collective Bargaining," 50 Harv.L.Rev. 1071 (1937).

Grievances under existing agreements were settled through boards of adjustment. Efforts to negotiate new agreements were left to the parties assisted by mediation, arbitration and emergency boards. This Act was the culmination of a long history of heavy regulation of railroads, and it was not intended to, and did not set a pattern for industry generally.[13]

Despite considerable agitation, a statute establishing rights to union organization and collective bargaining for employees generally had to wait until after the Great Depression of 1929, which shook confidence in the effectiveness of the existing economic system. In 1933, the New Deal Administration of President Franklin Roosevelt came to power. Roosevelt pledged strong action to deal with economic problems and a greater voice for labor within the existing capitalist system.

Originally, the New Deal's labor policy was included in the National Industrial Recovery Act of 1933 (NIRA), which, in Section 7 sought to insure the rights of union organization and collective bargaining. When the NIRA was declared unconstitutional, it was replaced by the Wagner Act, officially the National Labor Relations Act, which still remains at the core of national labor policy. Section 7 of the Act, largely unchanged to this date, granted employees " * * * the rights to self organization to join or assist labor organizations to bargain collectively through representatives of their own choosing and to engage in concerted activities for the purpose of collective bargaining or other mutual aid or protection". These rights were protected through unfair labor practice provisions outlawing certain employer conduct. Section 8(1) outlawed employer interference with Section 7 rights. Section 8(2) made employer domination or support as a labor organization illegal. Section 8(3) prohibited employer retaliation either through discharge or other reprisal against those who engaged in union activity. Section 8(5) required an employer to bargain with the representatives chosen by his employees. To administer the Act, the National Labor Relations Board was established. The Board was instructed to hold elections to determine whether or not a majority of employees in an appropriate unit wished union representation. Several important features of the Act were shaped by historical developments.

1. The establishment of the National Labor Relations Board to administer the Act was a reflection of labor's distrust of the courts. Indeed, the Act was drafted to minimize the role of the courts as much as possible in its enforcement.[14]

2. The focus of the statute was on eliminating barriers to organization and collective bargaining. Unlike labor laws in other nations, the Wagner Act did not seek to regulate the relationship of the par-

13. Because of its special nature, this Act despite its importance will not be considered in any detail in this book.

14. For constitutional reasons, court enforcement of Board orders was required if a respondent did not obey. Courts were instructed to enforce whenever the Board's order was supported by substantial evidence, regardless of the court's view of the soundness of the Board's decision.

ties once recognition was achieved and good faith bargaining begun. This reflects the central role which attempts to combat union organization and refusals to recognize played in the major labor management conflicts of the preceding half century. It also reflects the relatively positive experience with collective bargaining once undertaken. Neither union nor management desired governmental involvement in setting wages and working conditions.

3. A unique and important feature of the Wagner Act was the crucial role assigned to elections to determine whether a majority of employees desired union representation. An employer was obliged to bargain in good faith only with a union selected by a majority. The union then represented all of the employees, not just its members. And it soon became clear that the employer could not recognize or deal with individuals or other unions. Thus, under the election system established by the Act, a union either represented everyone or no one. In part, this majoritarian emphasis in the labor statute is a reflection of its prevalence in our political system. It also reflects the historical dispute between unions and management concerning the wishes of employees. Management's public posture in rejecting unions almost always involved the claim that most employees were satisfied with existing conditions and did not want union representation. Many of the court opinions limiting strikes or picketing arose in a context in which this claim was most plausible. Unions on the other hand regularly claimed that management policies overrode the wishes of employees. Thus a system of elections was geared to resolving the competing factual claims which historically underlay pro and anti union positions.[15]

The avowed purposes of the National Labor Relations Act were to stimulate collective bargaining and to provide a forum for the peaceful resolution of disputes concerning union representation. Both of these goals were substantially advanced during the period following the Act's passage.[16] Union membership and the number of employees covered by collective bargaining agreements increased dramatically, from 4 to 15 million. Simultaneously, the right of employees to choose became more readily accepted. The Supreme Court, which upheld the constitutionality of the Act also affirmed the Board's central role in determining and protecting employee freedom of choice. Passage of the NLRA also served to nationalize labor relations policy. Previously each state was free to establish its own labor laws, but it was soon held that except for certain limited purposes such as the prevention of violence, states could not legislate with regard to matters which came within the Board's sphere of regulation, even if their laws were consistent with the national Act.

15. The election system also had the benefit of resolving claims between competing unions which was a growing problem at the time the Act was passed.

16. There is a lively, scholarly debate about how much of the change was attributable to the Act.

D. THE TAFT-HARTLEY ACT

During World War II, labor pledged not to strike and a system for resolving disputes through arbitration was established.[17] Issues not resolved through collective bargaining were submitted to a tripartite arbitration panel under the auspices of the War Labor Board. However, the War Labor Board could not deal effectively with disputes about wages or other major terms of employment. As a result, the period immediately following World War II was marked by a significant number of important strikes in major industries. This led to growing public concern about the power of labor, concern already mounting as a result of strikes in the mines called by John L. Lewis during World War II. The problem was exacerbated by a number of jurisdictional strikes in which services were shut down because of disputes between rival labor groups. After World War II, management groups directed their political activity not to repealing the Wagner Act but toward "limiting the power of big labor", an approach which turned out to have potent political appeal. The Congressional elections of 1946 resulted in a series of major victories for conservative Republicans; many pledged to support significant amendments to the Wagner Act. In 1947, Congress after prolonged, emotional debate, enacted the Taft-Hartley Act. As the following excerpts demonstrate, both proponents and opponents of the Act seemed to treat it as a referendum on the Wagner Act, the role of labor unions in our society and a major turning point in the development of U. S. labor relations.

93 CONG. RECORD

pp. 3443–4 (1947).

Mr. Gwinn of New York. One other reason why this bill must be amended is that men who violate the law have been exempted from the processes of the law under the Wagner Act. One of the most evil things that has been rolling up under this bill for the last 14 years is utter lawlessness and violence, because men who commit violence cannot be prosecuted successfully under the Wagner Act supported by the LaGuardia Act.

The interpretation of these acts by the Board and the courts has been that respectable robbery could be committed without liability. The new Hartley Act now before us for passage changes that and makes all men subject to the law and subject to damages for unlawful, concerted, monopolistic acts to destroy property and to injure persons.

This is one more step back to the restoration of freedom, one more rededication of Government to its primary function of protecting indi-

---

17. The War Labor Board experience with arbitration helped to establish labor arbitration as an acceptable means for resolving minor disputes, particularly disputes concerning the meaning of collective bargaining agreements.

vidual freedom in America. The sum total of many individual freemen is the fundamental source of a good society. The formation of groups to exercise compulsion and intimidation over individual men ends in strife and violence which has multiplied threefold since the Wagner Act.

The American workman who was once free has been cajoled, coerced, intimidated, and on many occasions beaten up for the alleged good of the group he was forced to join. His whole economic life has been subject to the complete domination and control of unregulated monopolists. To get a job he has had to pay them. He has been forced to join these groups against his will because he feared them. At other times when he has desired to join a group he trusted he has been forced to join one he has mistrusted. He has been compelled to pay assessments for causes and candidates for public office which he opposed. He has been shut up in meetings and fined or expelled for expressing his own mind about right and wrong on public issues. He has been denied the right to arrange the terms of his own employment. He has frequently, against his will, been called out on strikes and violence which have resulted in wage losses representing years of his savings. He has been ruled by Communists and other subversive influences because he has had no right to vote. In short his mind, his soul, and his very life have been subject to a tyranny more despotic than one could think possible in a free country.

The committee report finds the employer's plight has been equally bad and dangerous. He has played an unhappy enforced part in rising prices and reduced production and resulting scarcity under a new form of monopoly called laboristic monopoly. He has been required to employ or reinstate individuals who have assaulted him and his employees and want only to destroy his property. When he has tried to discharge Communists and trouble makers he has been prevented from doing so by a board which called this union bating (sic). He has had to stand by helpless while employees desiring to enter his plant legally to work have been obstructed by violence, mass picketing, and general rowdyism. He has been unable to speak against irresponsible slander, abuse, and vilification against him.

His business often has been brought to a standstill by jurisdictional fights and disputes for which he himself had no responsibility or possibility of settling. And finally, he has been compelled by the laws of the greatest democratic country in the world to be a part of a rising tide of industrial warfare three times greater than ever before witnessed, in this land of 165 years of liberty, because of the Wagner Act.

The public has suffered most of all.

By default in our legislative branch of Government, Americans have been separated into contending factions because they have ignored and set aside established constitutional law. The administative and judicial departments of our Government have with equal shame participated.

This is the sordid story unfolded before the committee in its hearings.

RESUMPTION OF AMERICAN PRINCIPLES

The bill is a restatement of the inalienable rights of the individual and a rededication of Government to its primary function of protecting those rights of individuals. It has been drafted on the principle that when individual rights are protected and free men are truly free in their life, work, and pursuit of happiness, as our Constitution provides, the whole of society achieves its greatest good.

The bill rejects the contention that organized groups may assert and force an individual to give up his basic rights for any alleged higher right of a group. The committee finds such so-called group rights lead to the exploitation of individuals as well as of the public generally.

93 CONG. RECORD

p. 3439 (1947).

<u>Mr. Kelley.</u> I believe the reader will find that the minority report clearly points out the danger of this drastic amendment to the National Labor Relations Act, of the host of unfair labor practices by employees, of the destruction of union security, of the amendments to the Clayton Act, the Norris-LaGuardia Act, the Corrupt Practices Act, and others, and shows beyond a doubt that the ultimate objective of the bill is to weaken labor unions in their collective-bargaining procedures.

It should be borne in mind here that all management is not interested in this kind of legislation. We have been hearing from a most articulate and vociferous group in management, but I am not convinced that this group speaks for management as a whole. I think management would find this legislation a nuisance. If the managers think they have trouble now, just let them try to operate under this proposed legislation. They will be coming down here to Congress and crying to high heaven for relief. If the legislators who are the proponents of this measure imagine for 1 minute that it is going to bring peace between labor and management, they are in for a sudden and serious awakening. The American workingman is a long-suffering individual, as past history will prove, but he will subject himself to chains only so long. The day will always come when he will rise up and smite his enemies. The supporters of H. R. 3020 must overlook the fact that anything that circumscribes the liberties of the workingman and his right to improve his working conditions and security is violently resented, because it is not only he but his family who is affected. It is the threatened impoverishment of his children, the deprivation of proper food and clothing and education, which creates bitterness in him. So we had better weigh well the consequences of any kind of legislation that affects the intimate life of our working people.

In any legislation we should attempt to raise the standard of living, not drive it down. All society is benefited by such a positive approach rather than a negative one. We should not forget that there are between 55 and 60 million working people in this country who have families. They are the great bulk of our population. The imposition of this kind of legislation by a few is contrary to the concepts of a free people. Again I say that what we need at this time are enlightened physicians, not medicine men.

———

Despite the emotional tone of the debate, the Taft-Hartley Act is noteworthy for what it did not do. It did not eliminate the basic protection of organizing rights established by the Wagner Act. All of the original unfair labor practices essentially remained intact, as did the Act's election procedures. Nor was the Board's role in labor relations reduced. By not amending the heart of the Wagner Act, the Taft-Hartley amendments in fact, established its permanency. Taft-Hartley did however, make significant additions to the NLRA for the purpose of correcting what were considered the abuses. In order to make the Board and the Act more neutral with respect to collective bargaining, the Taft-Hartley Act for the first time in Section 8(b) established union unfair labor practices. These included coercing or restraining employees in the exercise of Section 7 rights, refusing to bargain in good faith or engaging in or endorsing secondary boycotts or jurisdictional strikes. The Norris-LaGuardia Act was also amended to permit the Board to obtain injunctive relief against secondary activity under certain specified procedures. Injunctions at the request of employers were not resurrected. Section 7 was amended to recognize the employees' right to refrain from engaging in concerted activity. Taft-Hartley forbade closed shop agreements which required the employer to hire only union members, but it did permit agreements under which employers could be required to pay dues and fees as a condition of employment. Even this limited form of union security was made vulnerable, by Section 14b, to state right to work laws. The Taft-Hartley Act also provided for presidential power to limit strikes in National Emergency situations and for special techniques of mediation and fact finding in such strikes through the newly created Federal Mediation and Conciliation Service.

One of the most important provisions of the Taft-Hartley Act turned out to be Section 301, which simply provided for the enforcement of collective bargaining agreements by the Federal Courts. This provision was later held to establish an unwritten federal law of labor agreements, the major feature of which is the encouragement of arbitration to resolve disputes during the term of an agreement.

It is difficult to assess the impact of the Taft-Hartley Act on labor relations. With the exception of the secondary boycott provisions, the union unfair labor practices were not of major importance. Although they did serve to provide a federal remedy against violence or threats of violence, the secondary boycott provisions of the Act were the subject of considerable litigation. Their complexity made it difficult for the Board and Courts to enforce them in a consistent and understandable fashion. As a result, neither unions nor employees knew what was punishable. With sound legal advice, unions were largely able to avoid the application of the law, while applying economic pressure. However, a mistake concerning the law's application made a union vulnerable to injunction and damages.

In the decade after Taft-Hartley, the percentage of employees who were organized actually declined. It is unlikely that the law played a significant role in this development, since the basic organizational procedures and protections remained intact. It is arguable that by 1950 those segments of the work force most easily amenable to organization were already organized. Those who remained were (a) in the south or rural areas, where employee attitudes towards unions were less favorable (b) white collar or professional employees who often felt that union organization was inconsistent with their professional self image or (c) governmental and other employees not covered by the Act. Moreover, the economy developed in such a way as to increase the percentage of those groups least susceptible to unions. In some industries, employers anxious to avoid unions structured working conditions so as to make them seem unnecessary. That these factors, rather than the change in the law were responsible for the slackening of union organization is indicated by the fact that in recent years the unions have had their greatest organizing successes in the public sector, sometimes without any statutory protection and rarely with laws more favorable than Taft-Hartley.

E.   RECENT DEVELOPMENTS AND CURRENT TRENDS

In the 1950's and in 1960, union management relations matured in those industries already organized. Collective bargaining agreements adopted certain ways of structuring working conditions as a matter of course. The employer's right to discharge was limited by the concept of just cause. Seniority became the standard by which jobs and benefits were allocated and layoffs determined. Grievance procedures were established for the resolution of disputes concerning the meaning of the collective bargaining agreement. Under the typical grievance system, the union and employer seek to resolve disputes informally through meetings between various levels of company and union officials. if they are unable to agree, the matter is submitted to an arbitrator whose decision the parties agree to accept as final. The War Labor Board experience during World War II provided evidence of the usefulness of arbitration, and it also provided a core group of neutal experts acceptable to both sides as arbitrators.

In organized industry, the enforcement of negotiation and collective bargaining rights was controlled by the union. This made rank and file employees dependent upon official union action for protection of their interests and placed individuals or groups disfavored by union officials at a significant disadvantage. The law was slow in responding to this problem. For a long time, internal union relations were treated like membership disputes in private clubs; essentially outside the law's concern. This approach gradually changed. The courts determined that a union which acted as a bargaining agent was under a duty to represent all employees fairly. In 1959, Congress, after a highly publicized investigation of union corruption, enacted the Landrum-Griffen Act which was the first comprehensive Federal regulation of internal union affairs. The Act sought to require unions to function democratically. Members were given rights of free speech and protest and union officials required to be elected democratically. The Landrum-Griffen Act also amended the NLRA. It lightened restrictions on secondary boycott activity and it limited organizational picketing.

The Landrum-Griffen protections have turned out to be less successful than its drafters had hoped and the problem of developing adequate protection for individual interests continues to concern the labor department, Board and the Courts. The 1959 Act did not, except tangentially, deal with questions of racial, sexual or religious discrimination in employment. This problem was addressed in 1964, when Congress, through Title VII of the Civil Rights Act, outlawed acts of discrimination in employment, either by unions or employers. Title VII was a weakly drawn compromise bill not intended, nor expected, to have much impact. But under the leadership of the EEOC and the courts, the language was interpreted to reach employment practices neutral on their face but discriminatory in practice. Moreover, the use of the class action made Title VII litigation attractive to plaintiffs and to lawyers while the courts' willingness to consider statistical proof of violation made it easier to prove unlawful conduct. The Act was also amended in 1972 to make it stronger. The result was a statute, the enforcement of which came to play an increasingly significant role in labor relations.

The Sixties and Seventies have witnessed the re-emergence of state law once thought to have been rendered meaningless by the NLRA. Several factors account for this development. The 1959 amendments to the NLRA gave the states jurisdiction over matters outside the Board's jurisdictional standards. State law was held not to be preempted in important areas such as internal union affairs. Most significantly the growth of unions in areas outside the jurisdiction of the NLRA made state regulations applicable to a growing number of situations. The NLRA excluded both agricultural and governmental employees from its protection. In the Sixties both of these groups of employees became attracted to unions. In agriculture Cesar Chavez and the United Farm Workers through a series of strikes and consumer boycotts, forced many of the growers to grant them recognition. The lack of statutory machinery for conducting elections led to a protracted dispute between the Teamsters and the UFW, and to charges and counter charges between the growers and the unions. For the same reasons which led Congress to pass the

NLRA, California passed an Agricultural Labor Relations Act similar in language and administrative set up to the NLRA. The development of unionization among public employee groups forced the enactment of various state laws to regulate labor relations in the public sector. These laws are typically modeled after the NLRA and much of the language is similar or identical, but the scope of bargaining is generally limited. Instead of the right to strike a complex system of dispute resolution using arbitrators or fact finding is established.

F. THE AMERICAN LABOR MOVEMENT

In order to understand labor relations it is necessary to understand the diverse structure and goals of the labor movement. Unions vary in size, from the mammoth teamster organization with two million members to the Italian Actors Union with a total membership of 75 at last count and no locals. Unions vary similarly in terms of the occupations which they represent. There are special unions for laborers, clerks, physicians, sanitation workers, basketball referees, airline pilots and college professors. Some unions such as Shoemakers can trace their history back before the founding of the Republic. Many were organized in the last 15 years. Some unions are organized by industry, such as the steel workers (U.S.A.), auto workers (UAW) and mine workers (UMW). Others are organized by craft such as meat cutters or carpenters. The building trades and the dock unions frequently control the distribution of jobs through union referral or hiring halls; in most industries this is left to the employer. In some unions most policy decisions are made on the national level; in some the local unions have almost complete autonomy.[18] Some rely heavily on lawyers others may not use them at all. Unions vary in political and social ideology. While many unions have politically supported the claims of ethnic minorities, blacks and women, others have been guilty of open discrimination. In many unions the leadership has publically offered support while the members have privately resisted. The union movement played a leading role in the passage of the 1964 Civil Rights Act but since then unions have frequently been defendants under the Act.

Despite its diversity certain general characteristics distinguish the American labor movement and give it its special flavor.

1. LIMITED GOALS

The labor movement does not seek to fundamentally alter the society. It does not accept the concept of an increasing class struggle. It is not seeking to eliminate or substantially reduce capitalism. Essentially it seeks a greater share for its members of the wealth produced by the existing system.

---

18. Unions are generally composed of local units and regional federations or districts. The central union is often called the international because it oper- ates in Canada and in the U. S. Generally local unions are more important in craft unions and the international in industrial unions.

2.   THE CENTRALITY OF COLLECTIVE BARGAINING

American unions rely primarily on collective bargaining. To increase wages and employee benefits, the bargaining power of unions comes from their ability to strike. The power of a strike is determined in part by the extent to which the employees are organized. Therefore, unions are concerned with protecting and expanding their ability to strike and with organizing the unorganized. The legislative agenda for labor always gives these goals the highest priority. Conversely, most American unions, unlike many of their foreign counterparts, want to keep government involvement in the bargaining process to a minimum. They do not want the government to resolve bargaining disputes.

3.   WORKING THROUGH EXISTING PARTIES

Because its political goals are limited, labor is content to work through the existing party structure. It cultivates the good will of key members of both parties and in each session of Congress it seeks passage of a small number of bills. Its legislative goals often supplement its bargaining demands. For example, unions generally try to increase the minimum wage in order to provide a floor for bargaining.

4.   SUPPORT FOR INDUSTRY

A union's ability to achieve its goals through bargaining is greatest when the employer's economic position is strong. Unions politically support the economic well-being of their industry. Thus, the UAW has opposed energy programs thought harmful to the automobile industry and the machinists have supported defense construction to provide jobs for their members. The garment workers have run ads on behalf of American garment industries.

5.   LIMITED ROLE IN PLANT MANAGEMENT

The unions have rarely sought to become involved in decisions concerning production, except to the extent such decisions have direct impact on the continuation of existing jobs. Nor have they become involved in questions of management personnel. They have been content to leave such decisions to management.

6.   LOCAL AUTONOMY—LOOSE CONFEDERATION

The focus on collective bargaining and grievance arbitration, with individual employers, has tended to make the local union much more important and powerful in the United States than it is elsewhere. Historical factors have also tended to reinforce the significance of the local union. In addition, the AFL–CIO, which is the federation of international unions has very little control over its members. It does not play a significant role in bargaining or organizing, and its political positions are frequently rejected by members.

This diversity has prevented the development of a consistent ideology. The absence of a labor movement ideology has helped to foster diversity.

There are several reasons why American labor has relied so heavily on collective bargaining and has not acquired a coherent political philosophy. The American Federation of Labor grew out of the ashes of the Knights of Labor. The Knights which dominated the American union movement until 1884 had a broad legislative program through which they hoped to remake the society. The founders of the AFL concluded that this contributed to the collapse of the Knights and, specifically, sought to limit themselves to what could be achieved through Labor's own power. Moreover, the lack of ideology in the American labor movement is consistent with the lack of faith in ideology which is common to American society and which also shapes our political parties and educational institutions.

The American labor movement's faith in collective bargaining supported by the strike weapon is also understandable. The relatively short supply of labor, and technological sophistication, have combined to give organized labor considerable bargaining power by making its members crucial to the process of production and difficult to replace. Similarly, the willingness of labor to accept the existing system of production and distribution is attributable to material wealth which it has provided for its members.

————

There is disagreement about the effects of the labor movement upon the economy. Some view unions as having major positive effects on the economy; others stress the adverse effects unions have on productivity. The following article examines both views.

RICHARD B. FREEMAN & JAMES L. MEDOFF, THE TWO FACES OF UNIONISM *

* * * [S]ocieties have two basic mechanisms for dealing with divergences between desired social conditions and actual conditions. The first is the classic market mechanism of exit and entry, individual mobility: The dissatisfied consumer switches products; the diner whose soup is too salty seeks another restaurant; the unhappy couple divorces. In the labor market, exit is synonymous with quitting, while entry consists of new hires by the firm. By leaving less-desirable jobs for more-desirable jobs, or by refusing bad jobs, individuals penalize the bad employer and reward the good—leading to an overall improvement in the efficiency of the social system. The basic theo-

* Richard B. Freeman & James L. Medoff, "The Two Faces of Unionism," The Public Interest 69 (Fall, 1979).   Reprinted with permission of the authors and publisher; ©1979 by National Affairs, Inc.

rem of neoclassical economics is that, under well-specified conditions, the exit and entry of persons (the hallmark of free enterprise) produces a "Pareto-optimum" situation—one in which no individual can be made better off without making someone worse off. Economic analysis can be viewed as a detailed study of the implications of this kind of adjustment and of the extent to which it works out in real economies. As long as the exit-entry market mechanism is viewed as the only efficient adjustment mechanism, institutions such as unions must necessarily be viewed as impediments to the optimal operation of a capitalist economy.

There is, however, a second mode of adjustment. This is the political mechanism, which Albert Hirschman termed "voice"   *   *   *. "Voice" refers to the use of direct communication to bring actual and desired conditions closer together. It means talking about problems: complaining to the store about a poor product rather than taking business elsewhere; telling the chef that the soup had too much salt; discussing marital problems rather than going directly to the divorce court. In a political context, "voice" refers to participation in the democratic process, through voting, discussion, bargaining, and the like.

*   *   *

In the job market, voice consists of discussing with an employer conditions that ought to be changed, rather than quitting the job. In modern industrial economies, and particularly in large enterprises, a trade union is the vehicle for collective voice—that is, for providing workers as a group with a means of communicating with management.

Collective rather than individual bargaining with an employer is necessary for effective voice at the workplace for two reasons. First, many important aspects of an industrial setting are "public goods," which affect the well-being   *   *   *   of every employee. As a result, the incentive for any single person to express his preferences, and invest time and money to change conditions (for the good of all), is reduced. Safety conditions, lighting, heating, the speed of a production line, the firm's policies on layoffs, work-sharing, cyclical-wage adjustment, and promotion, its formal grievance procedure and pension plan—all obviously affect the entire workforce in the same way that defense, sanitation, and fire protection affect the entire citizenry. "Externalities" (things done by one individual or firm that also affect the well-being of another, but for which the individual or firm is not compensated or penalized) and "public goods" at the workplace require collective decision-making. Without a collective organization, the incentive for the individual to take into account the effects of his or her actions on others, or express his or her preferences, or invest time and money in changing conditions, is likely to be too small to spur action.   *   *   *

A second reason collective action is necessary is that workers who are not prepared to exit will be unlikely to reveal their true preferences to their bosses, for fear of some sort of punishment. The essence of the employment relationship under capitalism * * * is the exchange of money between employer and employee in return for the employer's control over a certain amount of the worker's time. The employer seeks to use his employee's time in a way that maximizes the value of the output the employee produces. Even in the case of piece rates, employers monitor employee activity to assure the quality of output. As a result, the way in which the time purchased is utilized must be determined by some interaction between workers and their boss. Since the employer can fire a protester, individual protest is dangerous; so a prerequisite for workers' having effective voice in the employment relationship is the protection of activists from being discharged. * * *

The collective nature of trade unionism fundamentally alters the operation of a labor market and, hence, the nature of the labor contract. In a nonunion setting, where exit and entry are the predominant forms of adjustment, the signals and incentives to firms depend on the preferences of the "marginal" worker, the one who will leave (or be attracted) by particular conditions or changes in conditions. The firm responds primarily to the needs of this marginal, generally younger and more mobile worker and can within some bounds ignore the preferences of "infra-marginal," typically older workers, who— for reasons of skill, knowledge, rights that cannot be readily transferred to other enterprises, as well as because of other costs associated with changing firms—are effectively immobile. In a unionized setting, by contrast, the union takes account of the preferences of *all* workers to form an average preference that typically determines its position at the bargaining table. Because unions are political institutions with elected leaders, they are likely to be responsive to a different set of preferences from those that dominate in a competitive labor market.

In a modern economy, where younger and older workers are likely to have different preferences * * *, the change from a marginal to an average calculus is likely to lead to a very different labor contract. When issues involve sizeable fixed costs or "public goods," a calculus based on the average preference can lead to a contract which, ignoring distributional effects, is socially more desirable than one based on the marginal preference—that is, it may even be economically more "efficient."

As a voice institution, unions also fundamentally alter the social relations of the workplace. Perhaps most importantly, a union constitutes a source of worker power in a firm, diluting managerial authority and offering members a measure of due process, in particular through the union innovation of a grievance and arbitration system. While 99 percent of major U.S. collective-bargaining contracts provide for the filing of grievances, and 95 percent provide for arbitration of disputes that are not settled between the parties, relatively few nonunion firms have comparable procedures for settling disagreements between workers and supervisors. More broadly, the entire industrial jurisprudence system—by which many workplace decisions are based on negotiated rules (such as seniority) instead of supervisory judgement (or whim), and are subject to challenge through the grievance/arbitration procedure—represents a major change in the power relations within firms. As a result, in unionized firms workers are more willing and able to express discontent and to object to managerial decisions.

Thus, as a collective alternative to individualistic actions in the market, unions are much more than simple monopolies that raise wages and restrict the competitive adjustment process. Given imperfect information and the existence of public goods in industrial settings, and conflicting interests in the workplace and in the political arena, unionism provides an alternative mechanism for bringing about change. This is not to deny that unions have monopolistic power to raise wages for a select part of the workforce. The point is that unionism has two "faces," each of which leads to a different view of the institution; One, which is at the fore in economic analysis, is that of a monopoly; the other is that of "a voice institution," i.e., a sociopolitical institution. * * *

Although the American labor movement may be characterized as not ideological, the following article proposes that there is nevertheless an ideology of industrial relations.

JACK BARBASH, THE AMERICAN IDEOLOGY OF INDUSTRIAL RELATIONS *

The idea that I want to get across here is that there is an American ideology of industrial relations. But it's an ideology that needs to change with changing circumstances. By ideology, I don't mean anything fancy except a more or less fixed or systematic way of looking at the world.

Ideology is not good or bad in itself. It's good if it provides a perspective, an outlook, or a scheme of values which helps one to understand or interpret complexities—*and* if the ideology is constantly tested against reality and plausibility. This is what I call an *open* ideology.

Ideology is bad if it interposes a screen between the true believer and reality, if it becomes a total secular faith. I call this kind of ideology a *closed* ideology.

The American ideology of industrial relations is not contained in a "great book" of some sort, but that doesn't make it less of an ideology. Even if there is no great book, the American ideology can, nonetheless, be read from how the participants perform in their industrial relations.

* Jack Barbash, "The American Ideology of Industrial Relations," 30 Labor Law Review 453 (1979).   Reprinted with the permission of the author; ©1979 by Jack Barbash.

By industrial relations, I mean the theory and management of the labor problem under industrial conditions. Industrial relations is not limited to collective bargaining, but collective bargaining undoubtedly sets the pace for dealing with labor problems outside of collective bargaining.

As I see it, two leading principles govern the American ideology of industrial relations: the adversary principle and the principle of voluntarism. I don't claim that these are universal principles. Rather, I stress that the principles grow out of the American experience.

The adversary principle means that the two parties limit their *mutual* interests to the preservation and enlargement of the common pot which finances their respective factor shares. The parties recognize that wages and profits both require a prosperous enterprise. Beyond that, the relationship is dominated by a running dispute over the distribution of the enterprise's net proceeds between wages and nonwages. Not only is this the way it is, but I think this is how the parties seem to want it.

Management prefers the adversary relationship, because it fears that union collaboration will dilute management authority and thereby impair efficiency. The union prefers it that way, because the adversary relationship is most consistent with the maintenance of the union as a bargaining organization, and bargaining is what the union is all about.

The adversary principle in the American ideology best serves the public or general interest, too. In the ideal form, the logic runs something like this: "adversaryism" via competition in the product market is what keeps costs and prices from getting out of hand. The union's adversary stance in the labor market prevents the employer's exploitative impulse from getting out of hand. For its part, the union cannot press its adversary claims too far without pricing its product, and therefore the jobs and membership that go with it, out of the market.

There emerges the precept that tension among the participants, far from being pathological or aberrant, is normal and, if kept in bounds, even desirable. The assumption is that the parties can only be kept "honest," so to speak, by these countervailing checks and balances.

This benign view of the effects of industrial relations tension is not altogether shared by other disciplines. If I am not mistaken, harmony is the ideal state for organizational behavior and what used to be called human relations.

The adversary principle is workable because it *is* kept within bounds. Give-and-take and live-and-let-live are the ruling maxims of industrial relations. What keeps adversaryism in bounds is this spirit of moderation which deters the parties from stretching tensions to the breaking point.

Tension, I think, is probably a better word than conflict to describe the essence of industrial relations. Conflict implies one side

vanquishing the other; tension, on the other hand, implies an equilibrium or balance of forces—which is what collective bargaining and
industrial relations are more nearly about.

Tensions are kept within bounds, I am suggesting, by a kind of
civilizing or rationalizing process that derives from: (1) the practical,
pragmatic, incremental, compromising bent of the parties; (2) the in-
stitutionalization of tension; and (3) the ability of the economy and
enterprise to pay out wages and profits in some equitable combination.

The parties demonstrate their pragmatism by their willingness to
settle for something less than their maximum position and, further,
by their willingness to move to their larger goals piece by piece rather than wholesale.

In accordance with the maxim of live-and-let-live, each party concedes the other's right to exist. The union accepts the management's
function, and management accepts the union's function, even as both
sides jockey to secure maximum advantage from each other—but
within the bounds of "mutual survival," as Wight Bakke put it a generation ago.

Paradoxically, it is the strike and other forms of withholding that
operate to civilize tensions. The strike is like a stabilizer or governor
which warns the parties off extreme positions by confronting them
with the costs of intransigence.

The parties make the adversary relationship tolerable by institutionalizing the bargaining game. Bargaining is played according to
rules and procedures which, to an increasing degree, are established
by the state.

Moreover, bargaining is a game increasingly played by professionals. On the union side, representation is more and more a function of
a full-time staff, replacing the union volunteer who mostly manned
the union in earlier times. Professionalization is even more marked
on the management side, where a corps of personnel specialists, consultants, lawyers, and associations are the movers and shakers of the
industrial relations community.

The professionals operate through bargaining *structures* which
establish the organizational channels for the adversary relationship
to travel. Multi-employer bargaining, human relations committees,
and health and welfare trusts are some of the forms that normalize
the adversary relationship.

Industrial relations has not been lacking in visions of more constructive, integrative, cooperative, problem-solving, and trusting relationships—to use the terms that have been variously applied to the
"higher" stage of industrial relations development. Nobody has ever
really thought that the adversary principle could be supplanted entirely, but many have hoped at the very least to abate action-reaction
and thrust-and-parry in favor of more direct collaboration. Indeed,
there are interesing experiments going on right now.

That the quest for a "better" way has not been successful—if I am not mistaken—is not due to the lack of trying and experimentation. That the parties to the experiments invariably revert to a "harder" line may be saying something about the seeming fitness of the adversary principle in the American environment.

Voluntarism

Voluntarism is the other great foundation stone of the American ideology of industrial relations. Voluntarism in the American context means that the bilateral parties are given maximum freedom in working out their relationship on their own power.

State intervention, the principle of voluntarism asserts, should be limited to the referee's role, that is, to the function of setting and monitoring the rules but not determining the results. The rules should be focused on the maintenance of a power balance among the parties. Underlying voluntarism is a kind of populist creed that self-determination by the people affected is superior to control from the outside.

For the unions, voluntarism extends historically to keeping the movement free of domination by intellectuals. The late Nat Goldfinger, the AFL–CIO's chief economist and IRRA president, "exposed" (his word) the "macroeconomist mandarins who dominate the economics departments of the leading universities *   *   * as bankrupt." The British TUC takes this tone, too. Their "mandarins" are the "administrative elite [who] because of their common educational background [can] be objectively described as the Establishment. Theirs is a very different perspective from that of the working people of Britain. *   *   * ”

Seventy years ago, John R. Commons distinguished between the "lower idealism" of the working class with its "demand for rights" and the "higher idealism" of the "transcendental philosophers" which "resurrected man but not the real man." For Commons, the intellectual served better as adviser than as the maker of policy in his own right.

Intervention in the System

By most standards, the adversary principle has worked well enough in the private sector. The question now is whether it hasn't lost something in the translation to the public sector. In the private sector, the costs of the adversary principle are borne mostly by the parties. The costs of strikes by firefighters, police, sanitation and hospital workers, and teachers are borne mostly by the public. Indeed, public hardship is deemed part of the game.

Another problem with the adversary principle is that not all of the interests have been fully represented in the formal bargaining. Typically excluded have been the interests of women and the disadvantaged ethnic groups. Nor has the general interest in curbing inflation been sufficiently represented. Also, the dominant money-wage orientation of collective bargaining has, until recently, under-emphasized the quality of worklife and occupational health.

To compensate for these defects in the operation of the adversary principle, voluntarism is being subjected to attrition by increased doses of state intervention. More and more, the state is displacing the bilateral parties in shaping the *results* of collective bargaining. Virtually every postwar administration, Democrat as well as Republican, has had a go at wage-price manipulation of some sort. Judicial and administrative interventions are remaking the seniority system. And, it is not unlikely that, when the full scenario is played out, the Occupational Safety and Health Act (OSHA) and the Employee Retirement Income Security Act (ERISA) may turn out to have the most radical impact of all the interventions.

Several facts stand out about state intervention. The state has become a third party in the bargaining process, critically modifying the two-party adversary relationship. It is not accurate any longer, if it ever was, to talk about state intervention which is limited to procedure. The state is now moving in to regulate the results as well as the procedure of bargaining. The point of all of this, it needs to be stressed, is not so much to pass judgment on the merits as to recognize how fundamentally we are moving away from voluntarism and the two-party adversary principle.

Industrial Relations Research

Research in industrial relations, it seems to me, must take some of its cues from these profound changes. It has been a source of great strength for industrial relations research that it has stayed pretty close to practice.

But practice-oriented research has the weaknesses of its strengths. One of the weaknesses frequently referred to is the absence of a Theory, that is, theory with a capital T, which means quantitative-type generalizations at a high plane of abstraction. This is Theory in which the rigor of the method becomes more important than the usefulness of the results.

But capital-T Theory does not come naturally to industrial relations, because its origins lie with problems. My fear is that a major preoccupation with upper-case Theory must come at the expense of a diminishing interest in the live problems that clamor for serious, responsible, and detached inquiry—indeed, for theory with a small t.

I am not, of course, arguing against lower-case theory. Theory is how we make sense out of complex situations. Industrial relations needs theory to understand, appraise, and generalize about the labor problems in its infinite diversity, but it has to be a theory that does not stray too far from the imperfect human beings who populate it.

Quantitative method is indeed one of the essential tools of any theory, but a quantitative mode of theorizing that excludes history and philosophy does so at the peril of its usefulness and insights. On this point, I want to recall some wise words by J. Douglas Brown who called attention in his 1952 IRRA presidential address, to the "inherent existence of value judgments in industrial relations research."

"Industrial relations, like all other subdivisions of what we call social science, is truly a branch of the humanities. Social science uses the proper sciences more as a *tool* than as a *determinant*. Industrial relations is the study of a humane art with the use, where relevant, of scientific methodology. Industrial relations is not a science. Rather, it is the study of the values arising in the minds, intuitions, and emotions of individuals as these values become embodied in group organization and action. The understanding and solution of problems of group organization and action can never be divorced from the more basic understanding of the values which determine individual behavior. No matter how useful scientific methodology may be along the way, the goal of industrial relations research and practice lies beyond the 'timberline' of science."

The research agenda has to give greater recognition to the large problems of the adversary principle and voluntarism. I think we can give greater substance to these concepts using the established methodologies of the social sciences. I think we need also to probe the values that underlie these concepts.

The adversary principle in industrial relations operates on the assumption that egoism and aggression are inherent in the human situation and that a system of checks and balances has to be maintained to protect the parties from themselves and from each other and to protect the general interest from joint aggression by both in collusion. This is Douglas McGregor's Theory X of the situation.

Is a Theory Y possible? Is it possible to draw on impulses of altruism and social responsibility? I know that all of this is utopian. But might not this be a time ripe for a dash of *utopian* research and reflection? Isn't this the time to be deeply concerned about (with Alan Fox) "the ever extending network of commercialized relations which pervade[s] every aspect of human existence: the offering of specific service in exchange for specific sums of money; the carefully calculated and jealously guarded reciprocation; the draining from the transaction of all expressive or other extraneous considerations; the quick suspicion of fraud or default; the ever increasing battery of State-initiated protections and penalties designed to control and punish the bad faith that otherwise increasingly accompanied the impersonal specific contract"?

G.   THE NATIONAL LABOR RELATIONS BOARD

Much of this book (chapters 2 through 5) considers the body of federal law regulating union organizing and collective bargaining, commonly referred to as the National Labor Relations Act (NLRA). The NLRA is administered by the National Labor Relations Board. The following discussion of the NLRB is taken from *A Guide to Basic Law and Procedures Under the NLRA*, a Board publication:

The rights of employees declared by Congress in the National Labor Relations Act are not self-enforcing. To ensure that employees may exercise these rights, and to protect them and the public from unfair labor practices, Congress established the NLRB to administer and enforce the Act.

The NLRB includes the Board, which is composed of five members with their respective staffs, the General Counsel and staff, and the Regional, Subregional, and Resident Offices. The General Counsel has final authority on behalf of the Board, in respect to the investigation of charges and issuance of complaints. Members of the Board are appointed by the president, with consent of the Senate, for 5-year terms. The General Counsel is also appointed by the President, with consent of the Senate, for a 4-year term. Offices of the Board and the General Counsel are in Washington, D.C. To assist in administering and enforcing the law, the NLRB has established 33 Regional and a number of other field offices. These offices, located in major cities in various States and Puerto Rico are under the general supervision of the General Counsel.

The Agency has two main functions: to conduct representation elections and certify the results, and to prevent employers and unions from engaging in unfair labor practices. In both kinds of cases the processes of the NLRB are begun only when requested. Requests for such action must be made in writing on forms provided by the NLRB and filed with the proper Regional office. The form used to request an election is called a "petition," and the form for unfair labor practices is called a "charge." The filing of a petition or a charge sets in motion the machinery of the NLRB under the Act. Before discussing the machinery established by the Act, it would be well to understand the nature and extent of the authority of the NLRB.

The NLRB gets its authority from Congress by way of the National Labor Relations Act. The power of Congress to regulate labor-management relations is limited by the commerce clause of the United States Constitution. Although it can declare generally what the rights of employees are or should be, Congress can make its declaration of rights effective only in respect to enterprises whose operations "affect commerce" and labor disputes that "affect commerce." The NLRB, therefore, can direct elections and certify the results only in the case of an employer whose operations affect commerce. Similarly, it can act to prevent unfair labor practices only in cases involving labor disputes that affect, or would affect, commerce.

"Commerce" includes trade, traffic, transportation, or communication within the District of Columbia or any Territory of the United States; or between any State or Territory and any other State, Territory, or the District of Columbia; or between two points in the same State, but through any other State, Territory, the District of Columbia, or a foreign country.   Examples of enterprises engaged in commerce are:

- A manufacturing company in California that sells and ships its product to buyers in Oregon.

- A company in Georgia that buys supplies in Louisiana.

- A trucking company that transports goods from one point in New York State through Pennsylvania to another point in New York State.

- A radio station in Minnesota that has listeners in Wisconsin.

Although a company may not have any direct dealings with enterprises in any other State, its operations may nevertheless affect commerce.   The operations of a Massachusetts manufacturing company that sells all of its goods to Massachusetts wholesalers affect commerce if the wholesalers ship to buyers in other States.   The effects of a labor dispute involving the Massachusetts manufacturing concern would be felt in other States and the labor dispute would, therefore, "affect" commerce.   Using this test, it can be seen that the operations of almost any employer can be said to affect commerce.   As a result, the authority of the NLRB could extend to all but purely local enterprises.

Although the National Labor Relations Board could exercise its powers to enforce the Act in all cases involving enterprises whose operations affect commerce, the Board does not act in all such cases. In its discretion it limits the exercise of its power to cases involving enterprises whose effect on commerce is substantial.   The Board's requirements for exercising its power or jurisdiction are called "jurisdictional standards."   These standards are based on the yearly amount of business done by the enterprise, or on the yearly amount of its sales or of its purchases.   They are stated in terms of total dollar volume of business and are different for different kinds of enterprises.

Ordinarily if an enterprise does the total annual volume of business listed in the standard, it will necessarily be engaged in activities that "affect" commerce.   The Board must find, however, based on evidence, that the enterprise does in fact "affect" commerce.

The Board has established the policy that where an employer whose operations "affect" commerce refuses to supply the Board with information concerning total annual business, etc., the Board may dispense with this requirement and exercise jurisdiction.

Finally, Section 14(c)(1) authorizes the Board, in its discretion, to decline to exercise jurisdiction over any class or category of employers where a labor dispute involving such employees is not sufficiently substantial to warrant the exercise of jurisdiction, provided that it cannot refuse to exercise jurisdiction over any labor dispute over which it would have asserted jurisdiction under the standards it had in effect on August 1, 1959.   In accordance with this provision the Board has determined that it will not exercise jurisdiction over racetracks, owners, breeders, and trainers of racehorses, and real estate brokers.

In addition to the foregoing limitations the Act states that the term "employee" shall include any employee *except* the following:

- Agricultural laborers.
- Domestic servants.
- Any individual employed by his parent or spouse.
- Independent contractors.
- Supervisors.
- Individuals employed by an employer subject to the Railway Labor Act.
- Government employees, including those employed by the U.S. Government, any Government corporation or Federal Reserve Bank, or any State or political subdivision such as a city, town, or school district.

Supervisors are excluded from the definition of "employee" and, therefore, not covered by the Act. Whether an individual is a supervisor for purposes of the Act depends on that individual's authority over employees and not merely a title. A supervisor is defined by the Act as any individual who has the authority, acting in the interest of an employer, to cause another employee to be hired, transferred, suspended, laid off, recalled, promoted, discharged, assigned, rewarded, or disciplined, either by taking such action or by recommending it to a superior; or who has the authority responsibly to direct other employees or adjust their grievances; provided, in all cases, that the exercise of authority is not of a merely routine or clerical nature, but requires the exercise of independent judgment. For example, a foreman who determined which employees would be laid off after being directed by the job superintendent to lay off four employees would be considered a supervisor and would, therefore, not be covered by the Act; a "strawboss" who, after someone else determined which employees would be laid off, merely informed the employees of the layoff and who neither directed other employees nor adjusted their grievances would not be considered a supervisor and would be covered by the Act.

All employees properly classified as "managerial," not just those in positions susceptible to conflicts of interest in labor relations, are excluded from the protection of the Act. This was the thrust of a decision of the Supreme Court in 1974.

The term "employer" includes any person who acts as an agent of an employer, but it does *not* include the following:

- The United States or any State Government, or any political subdivision of either, or any Government corporation or Federal Reserve Bank.
- Any employer subject to the Railway Labor Act.

The authority of the NLRB can be brought to bear in a representation proceeding only by the filing of a petition. Forms for petitions must be signed, sworn to or affirmed under oath, and filed with the Regional Office in the area where the unit of employees is located. If employees in the unit regularly work in more than one regional area, the petition may be filed with the Regional Office of any of such regions. Section 9(c)(1) provides that when a petition is filed, "the Board shall investigate such petition and if it has reasonable cause to believe that a question of representation affecting commerce exists shall provide for an appropriate hearing upon due notice." If the Board finds from the evidence presented at the hearing that "such a question of representation exists, it shall direct an election by secret ballot and shall certify the results therof." Where there are three or more choices on the ballot and none receives a majority, Section 9(c)(3) provides for a runoff between the choice that received the largest and the choice that received the second largest number of valid votes in the election. After the election, if a union receives a majority of the votes cast, it is certified; if no union gets a majority, that result is certified. A union that has been certified is entitled to be recognized by the employer as the exclusive bargaining agent for the employees in the unit. If the employer fails to bargain with the union, it commits an unfair labor practice.

The procedure in an unfair labor practice case is begun by the filing of a charge. A charge may be filed by an employee, an employer, a labor organization, or any other person. Like petitions, charge forms, which are also available at Regional Offices, must be signed, sworn to or affirmed under oath, and filed with the appropriate Regional Office—that is, the Regional Office in the area where the alleged unfair labor practice was committed. Section 10 provides for the issuance of a complaint stating the charges and notifying the charged party of a hearing to be held concerning the charges. Such a complaint will issue only after investigation of the charges through the Regional Office indicates that an unfair labor practice has in fact occurred.

In certain limited circumstances where an employer and union have an agreed-upon grievance arbitration procedure which will resolve the dispute, the Board will defer processing an unfair labor practice case and await resolution of the issues through that grievance arbitration procedure. If the grievance arbitration process meets the Board's standards, the Board may accept the final resolution and defer to that decision. If the procedure fails to meet all of the Board standards for deferral, the Board may then resume processing of the unfair labor practice issues.

An unfair labor practice hearing is conducted before an NLRB administrative law judge in accordance with the rules of evidence and procedure that apply in the U.S. District Courts. Based on the hearing record, the administrative law judge makes findings and recommendations to the Board. All parties to the hearing may appeal the administrative law judge's decision to the Board. If the Board considers that the party named in the complaint has engaged in or is engaging in the unfair labor practices charged, the Board is authorized to issue an order requiring such person to cease and desist from such practices and to take appropriate affirmative action.

Section 10(b) provides that "no complaint shall issue based upon any unfair labor practice occurring more than six months prior to the filing of the charge with the Board and the service of a copy thereof upon the person against whom such charge is made." An exception is made if the charging party "was prevented from filing such charge by reason of service in the armed forces, in which event the six-month period shall be computed from the day of his discharge." It should be noted that the charging party must, within 6 months after the unfair labor practice occurs, file the charge with the Regional Office *and* serve copies of the charge on each person against whom the charge is made. Normally service is made by sending the charge by registered mail, return receipt requested.

If the Regional Director refuses to issue a complaint in any case, the person who filed the charge may appeal the decision to the General Counsel in Washington. Section 3(d) places in the General Counsel "final authority, on behalf of the Board, in respect of the investigation of charges and issuance of complaints." If the General Counsel reverses the Regional Director's decision, a complaint will be issued. If the General Counsel approves the decision not to issue a complaint, there is no further appeal.

To enable the NLRB to perform its duties under the Act, Congress delegated to the Agency certain powers that can be used in all cases. These are principally powers having to do with investigations and hearings.

As previously indicated, all charges that are filed with the Regional Offices are investigated, as are petitions for representation elections. Section 11 establishes the powers of the Board and the Regional Offices in respect to hearings and investigations. The provisions of Section 11(1) authorize the Board or its agents to

- Examine and copy "any evidence of any person being investigated or proceeded against that relates to any matter under investigation or in question."

- Issue subpenas, on the application of any party to the proceeding, requiring the attendance and testimony of witnesses or the production of any evidence.

- Administer oaths and affirmations, examine witnesses, and receive evidence.

- Obtain a court order to compel the production of evidence or the giving of testimony.

The National Labor Relations Act is not a criminal statute. It is entirely remedial. It is intended to prevent and remedy unfair labor practices, not to punish the person responsible for them. The Board is authorized by Section 10(c) not only to issue a cease-and-desist order, but "to take such affirmative action including reinstatement of employees with or without back pay, as will effectuate the policies of this Act."

The object of the Board's order in any case is two fold: to eliminate the unfair labor practice and to undo the effects of the violation as much as possible. In determining what the remedy will be in any given case, the Board has considerable discretion. Ordinarily its order in regard to any particular unfair labor practice will follow a standard form that is designed to remedy that unfair labor practice, but the Board can, and often does, change the standard order to meet the needs of the case. Typical affirmative action of the Board may include orders to an employer who has engaged in unfair labor practices to:

- Disestablish an employer-dominated union.

- Offer certain named individuals immediate and full reinstatement to their former positions or, if those positions no longer exist, to substantially equivalent positions without prejudice to their seniority and other rights and privileges, and with backpay, including interest.

- Upon request, bargain collectively with a certain union as the exclusive representative of the employees in a certain described unit and sign a written agreement if an understanding is reached.

Examples of affirmative action that may be required of a union which has engaged in unfair labor practices include orders to:

- Notify the employer and the employee that it has no objection to reinstatement of certain employees, or employment of certain applicants, whose discriminatory discharge, or denial of employment, was caused by the union.

- Refund dues or fees illegally collected, plus interest.

- Upon request, bargain collectively with a certain employer and sign a written agreement if one is reached.

The Board's order usually includes a direction to the employer or the union or both requiring them to post notices in the employer's plant or the union's office notifying the employees that they will cease the unfair labor practices and informing them of any affirmative action being undertaken to remedy the violation. Special care is taken to be sure that these notices are readily understandable by the employees to whom they are addressed.

* * *

Section 10(j) allows the Board to petition for an injunction in connection with any unfair labor practice after a complaint has been issued. This section does not require that injunctive relief be sought, but only makes it possible for the Board to do so in cases where it is considered appropriate.

If an employer or a union fails to comply with a Board order, Section 10(e) empowers the Board to petition the U.S. Court of Appeals for a court decree enforcing the order of the Board. Section 10(f) provides that any person aggrieved by a final order of the Board granting or denying in whole or in part the relief sought may obtain a review of such order in any appropriate circuit court of appeals. When the court of appeals hears a petition concerning a Board order, it may enforce the order, remand it to the Board for reconsideration, change it, or set it aside entirely. If the court of appeals issues a judgment enforcing the Board order, failure to comply may be punishable by fine or imprisonment for contempt of court.

In some cases the U.S. Supreme Court may be asked to review the decision of a circuit court of appeals particularly where there is a conflict in the views of different courts on the same important problem.

H. RECOMMENDED READING

1. Commons and Associates, *History of Labour in the United States* (Macmillan, 1918).
2. S. Perlman, *A Theory of the Labor Movement* (1928).
3. Mills and Montgomery, *Organized Labour* (1945).
4. Ullman, *The Rise of the National Trade Union* (1955).
5. Foner, *History of the Labor Movement in the United States*, Vol. I (1947).
6. Taft, P., *Organized Labor in American History* (1964).
7. Pelling, *American Labor* (1960).
8. A. Blum, *A History of the American Labor Movement* (1972).
9. G. Bloom and H. Northrup, *Economics of Labor Relations* (8th Ed. 1977).

Chapter II

UNION ORGANIZING

As the materials in the first chapter show, prior to World War II, union organizing in major American industries was a turbulent, often violent, process. The passionate commitment of the organizer, who saw in unionism the potential for a just society and a more equal distribution of wealth, was likely to be matched by the fierce resistance of the employer, who saw it as a radical movement seriously threatening established institutions. Today, forty years after passage of the NLRA, much of the passion is gone from both sides. Organizing campaigns in the private sector are conducted by unemotional professionals. Sophisticated techniques of persuasion are used by employers and standardized rhetoric has largely replaced the earlier emotionalism of the union's campaign. Echoes of the bygone attitudes still regularly surface, but these are more likely to be used as a tactic than expressed as a matter of deep belief.

A. CASE STUDY: THE ALPHA COMPANY

Background

The Alpha Company, headquartered in Chicago, Illinois, operates a retail food chain. In 1976 Alpha operated 1,173 stores and had sales of 386 million dollars. By 1979 Alpha became the nation's second largest food retailer with 1,237 stores in 26 states, having sales of 6.1 billion dollars.

Alpha's Manufacturing Division consists of plants which manufacture and process products, such as bakery, candy and delicatessan products, for sale in Alpha's stores as well as to non-Alpha owned food establishments, In 1976 the Manufacturing Division had sales of 826 million dollars. By 1979 the Manufacturing Division's sales had reached 1.2 billion dollars. In 1976 the Manufacturing Division's market share was 14.8%; in 1979 it was 14.5%. During the same three year period, the Manufacturing Division opened 5 new production facilities.

On September 1, 1980 Alpha purchased the Beta Products Company from the Delta Corporation. Beta Products is located in Jasper, Indiana, a town with a population of 20,000. Beta manufactures and processes pet food products. It employs 53 nonsupervisory employees in its processing plant and warehouse. The employees are not unionized. While Beta was under Delta ownership, two card signing attempts made in 1976 and 1978 by the United Food and Commercial Workers resulted in less than 10 signed cards in each attempt.

The Plant Manager that came with the plant from Delta was John Jones. Jones was replaced by Dana Blass, the manager of an Alpha candy plant in St. Louis. Blass was transfered to Jasper pursuant to Alpha's policy of Alphatizing the Jasper operation.

All of the foremen at Beta are former Delta employees. Starting in January 1981 they and other members of the management team are scheduled to attend Alpha Management Supervisor services conducted in Jasper by Brian Brown, Alpha Manufacturing Division Training Supervisor. The foremen feel closer to the hourly employees than to Alpha or the Plant Manager.

The Wage and Benefit Package

Before the Alpha takeover of Beta, Jones' practice regarding wage and benefit determination was to make a salary review each September and to base the compensation package on whatever the parent company plant in Chillicothe, Ohio settled their union plant for. Following this practice, Jones sent the following letter to the Jasper employees on September 10, 1979:

TO: Jasper, Indiana Employees

FROM: J. A. Jones

SUBJECT: Wage Increase Effective October 1, 1979

Pursuant to the past, the company has granted wage and benefit increases effective October 1 of every year. It is the intention of the Delta Company to continue this program to keep our employees wages and benefits at a competitive level in our area.

With this in mind, the following wages and benefits will be changed effective October 1, 1979:

1. Wages

    A 55¢ per hour increase in general wages will be granted. There will be *no* cost of living adjustments made during the period of 10/1/79 thru 10/1/80.

2. Life Insurance

    Life insurance benefits will increase from $6,000 to $8,000.

3. Accidental Death & Dismemberment Insurance

    The accidental death and dismemberment insurance will increase from $2,500 to $8,000.

4. Vacations

    The vacation schedule will change where 4 weeks vacation will be granted after 15 years instead of 20 years as it was previously.

5. Sickness and Accident Benefits

    Weekly sickness and accident benefits will increase from $80 to $90 per week.

6. Shift Differential

The shift differential will change as follows:

2nd Shift: from 10¢ per hour to 20¢ per hour.

3rd Shift: from 20¢ per hour to 30¢ per hour.

Now I think it is time for us to do our part and show our appreciation. This can be done in numerous ways. For example, we can do a better job of housekeeping, be more productive, and take better care of the equipment that we do have even if it may be worn out.

I personally feel Delta has done their part, so now it is our turn. Let's show them we do care by being as productive as possible and keep our plant as clean as we can. The pet food business today is more competitive than ever so we must be as efficient as possible.

s/ _____

John Jones

As part of Alpha's assessment of whether to purchase Beta from Delta, Tom Adams, Alpha's Regional Personnel Manager reviewed the wage structure of the Jasper plant in May of 1980. In a report sent to George Baker, Alpha's Labor Relations Director in Chicago, Adams stated that as a result of determining the wage structure according to the Chillicothe settlement, the Jasper employees "are paid one of the top rates for the area and all seem to be very happy in the non-union environment. My recommendations are not to change their past practices and to review the plant in September following the same trend in wage proposal whatever Chillicothe settles for."

Adams also reviewed the Beta Benefit Plan and compared it with the Alpha Benefit Plan. He proposed the adoption of the Alpha Plan for the Beta Plant. Whereas the Beta Plan provided the same benefits to the salaried and hourly employees, the Alpha plan established separate plans for management, office and hourly employees. Adams' proposal included (1) providing coverage in all areas currently covered by the Beta Plan; (2) improving coverage for sick pay, major medical, some insurance options, dental and vision and prescription drug to offset less coverage in basic life, hospitalization, and surgical medical coverage; (3) standardizing coverage in each group to minimize problems in claim processing, certificates and plan information booklets.

Baker adopted Adams recommendations. In a report to Charles Webster, Alpha's Vice President for Industrial Relations, Baker included Adams' proposals, stating: "All of the proposals are developed by using existing plans and integrating them with Alpha plans. This will standardize the system and provide programs that are equal to or better than existing plans."

After the Alpha takeover of Beta, Blass sent the following letter to the Beta employees on September 18, 1980:

"It is with great pleasure that I can announce that effective on Oct. 1, 1980 all hourly employees will receive a $.60/hour increase.

In addition, the following benefits will be improved:

(1) Voluntary life insurance *added.*

(2) Salary continuation *increased* from $90 wk to $125 wk.

(3) Surgical and medical *increased* to $1500.

(4) Diagnostic X-Ray *increased* to $75/person.

(5) Supplemental insurance *added* at $100/accident.

(6) Maximum medical *increased* to $50,000.

(7) Dental program *added.*

(8) Pension program *increased* to Alpha/income plan.

(9) Vacation scheduled *improved* to get 3 wks after 8 years.

s/John Blass

_____

Plant Manager"

Included with Blass' letter was the following summary of the Benefit Plan:

BENEFITS FOR YOU AND YOUR FAMILY

ALPHA PAYS THE PREMIUMS FOR THE FOLLOWING COVERAGE:

A. Medical Benefits

(1) Blue Cross Hospitalization

120-day coverage for semi-private room—paid in full.

(2) Hospital Medical Benefits

$10.00 per day to cover doctor's calls during hospital confinement that is due to an injury or sickness and results in a room and board charge.

(3) Surgical Benefits

$1,500.00 maximum to pay your doctor's fee for a covered surgical procedure up to the limit for the procedure in the surgical schedule. Effective 3/15/81, $2,000.00 maximum.

(4) Diagnostic X-Ray and Laboratory Expense Insurance

$75.00 for diagnostic x-ray and laboratory examinations per calendar year. Effective 3/15/81, $100.00.

(5) Supplemental Accident Expense Insurance

Payments, up to $100.00, will be made towards the expenses which are not paid under other parts of the group plan.

(6) Major Medical Expense Benefit—$50,000

After you or a covered dependent has satisfied the deductible ($100.00 per person) during a calendar year, benefits will be paid at the rate of 80% for all eligible expenses incurred by that individual during the rest of the year. Effective 3/15/81, $100,000.

(7) Dental Expense Benefit

Covers basic and major services maximum $800.00.

B. Insurance

(1) Alpha Income Protection

Protects against loss of income due to an off-the-job accident or illness that prevents you from working.

Coverage maximum $125.00 per week.

(2) Term Life Insurance—$5,000.00

Your term life insurance will be paid to any beneficiary you name if you die from any cause. Effective 3/15/81, $10,000.

(3) Accidental Death and Dismemberment Insurance—$5,000.00

This insurance will be paid for any of the losses outlined in the insurance certificate as the result of an accident occurring on or off the job while you are injured. Effective 3/15/81, $10,000.

(4) Voluntary Life Insurance—Optional

If you wish, you may purchase additional term life insurance (employee paid) up to $22,000.00 according to your salary. Effective 3/15/81, $30,000.00.

SUMMARY OF BENEFIT CHANGES—EFFECTIVE 3/15/81:

(1) Major Medical Expense Benefit will increase from $50,000.00 to $100,000.00.

(2) Surgical Expense Benefit will increase from $1,500.00 to $2,000.00.

(3) Diagnostic X-ray and Laboratory Expense Benefit will increase from $75.00 to $100.00.

(4) Your Term Life Insurance will increase from $5,000.00 to $10,000.00.

(5) Your Accidental Death and Dismemberment Insurance will increase from $5,000.00 to $10,000.00.

(6) Your Term Life Insurance (Voluntary) will increase from $22,000.00 to $30,000.00.

Also included with Blass' letter were insurance claims forms and enrollment cards. Benefit plan booklets were not available to distribute to employees because the National Insurance Company was in the process of reprinting due to changes in the publication.

The next day, Arthur White, and Paul Lakin, two hourly employees at the Beta processing plant, were discussing Blass' letter in the employee lunch room with Morris Simpson, an hourly employee at the Beta warehouse. White said that he had heard many of the other employees grumbling that they had been short changed on benefits when Alpha took over. The prime reason, according to White, was the reduction in the term life insurance from $8,000 to $5,000. Both

Lakin and Simpson said that they had heard the same complaint from many of the other employees. They said that they had also heard several of the older employees complain about not knowing anything about their Alpha retirement coverage.

The Soft Drink Machine Fund

Under Delta ownership of Beta, a practice had developed with regard to two soft drink machines located in the employee lunch room. The machines had been purchased several years ago through a collection taken up by the employees. The company operated the machines and profits from the machines went into a fund. At the end of each year Jones and an employee committee selected by Jones determined how the fund would be distributed. In previous years the fund had been used to purchase a microwave oven and a refrigerator for the lunch room. On November 13, 1980 the soft drink machines were sold for $50 each, and the proceeds along with the remaining money in the fund ($727.40) were put into the Alpha account.

The Company Christmas Party

Each December, Jones and the employee committee traditionally had planned the annual company Christmas party. On December 10th Blass discussed the plans for the party with the committee. The employees told Blass that they did not want a party because it always turned into a "drunken brawl" and only a few employees went to it. Blass agreed that something else would be done, but the committee did not have any ideas. Blass told the employees that the cost of the party would be distributed to the employees in the form of a Christmas gift in lieu of the party. An investigation by Blass revealed that the 1979 Christmas party cost $1,000–$1,500 and 20 to 25 employees attended.

Blass decided to give each employee a cheese tray for Christmas and have a deli lunch in the plant on Christmas Eve. The deli lunch was brought in for all shifts; however, the first shift had lunch and took home what was left. The second and third shifts did not get lunch. Many of the employees thought the cheese trays were bought with the money in the soft drink fund. The cheese trays were uniformly detested by the employees, who would have preferred to have a $10 certificate or a ham or turkey.

The Organizing Effort

In late December, 1980 Tony Delmonico, an organizer for the Teamsters had a discussion with Arthur White. White told Delmonico that the plant was a good location for an organizing drive. He gave Delmonico the names of Paul Lakin and Morris Simpson whom he believed to be pro-union. Delmonico contacted them and found out that in fact they were interested in unionization. An inside organizing committee was formed among them, and they began signing up employees secretly.

On January 12, 1981 Damon Borden, President of Teamsters Local 028 in Evansville informed Blass of the organizing drive. He told

Blass that they had secured cards from all but 3 of the 53 hourly employees, and requested that Blass check the authenticity of the signatures. Blass did not agree to a card check and communicated the conversation to George Baker and Lee Bower, an attorney in the Alpha law department.

On January 16, 1981 Blass posted the following notice in the employee parking lot, at entrance drives and on the employee bulletin board:

NOTICE!!

"SOLICITATION" "TRESPASSING" or "DISTRIBUTION OF LITERATURE" on these premises is "PROHIBITED"

In addition, the following notice was posted on the employee bulletin board:

January 16, 1981

TO: Our Employees

SUBJECT: The Meaning of Non-Union Status

1. To The Alpha Co.

   Complete personnel administration, uninhibited employee communication, unimpeded research and development, growth for the company and our employees.

2. To the Employees

   Direct dealing with the company, no intermediate bossism by the union, no out-of-pocket payment to a union, freedom from duties prescribed by a union, undisturbed co-worker relations, good relationships with your supervisors, absence of strikes and other interferences.

3. To the Supervisors

   Unobstructed assignment of work, rights of promotion and transfer of employees, independent grievance resolution, absence of unneeded stewards and committees.

4. For the Customer

   Continuous flow of product, good quality assurance, absence of pressures of strikes, boycotts, and picketing.

5. For the Community

   No strikes, no violence, lessened unemployment, fewer on welfare roles, encouragement to new industry.

If anyone is caused trouble in the plant, or put under pressure to join the union, you should let your foreman know, and we will see to it that it is stopped.

On February 9, 1981 a petition for certification was filed by Teamsters Local 028 with the NLRB regional office Indianapolis, requesting certification as the bargaining agent for all 53 plant and warehouse employees at the Jasper plant. The Board hearing was set for February 23, 1981.

On February 17 and 18, 1981 Blass delivered the following speech to the assembled employees during work hours on all three shifts:

Text

A letter was mailed to you on Thursday, 2/12/81, telling you that the Teamsters, Local 028, filed a petition for election with the National Labor Relations Board. We received the petition from the Board on the same day—Thursday.

I want to tell you a little about what will now happen:

- The Labor Relations Board will conduct a hearing to determine the appropriate unit (the people in the plant who can vote).

- When that is decided, the Board will set a date for an election. The date will probably be March 19th from 7 a.m. to 4 p.m.

- A *secret* ballot vote will be held in the plant and everyone who is eligible will have a chance to vote.

- Everyone in the eligible unit can vote, even if you did not sign a card. *You don't have to vote for the union just because you signed a card*, but we do urge everyone to vote.

- The results of the vote will be certified by the Labor Board as soon as they are counted and all challenges are worked out. The Company and the union will have the right to challenge any votes they feel are illegal.

- If the Company wins the election, we will go on with business as usual.

So everything you now have can be put on the bargaining table and you could end up with the same or fewer or more wages and benefits that you now have. If we do not reach an agreement and if there is a deadlock, the union can try to force us to agree by pulling you out on strike. How many of you have been out of work on strike?

A campaign will be conducted between now and the election by both the Company and the union. We hope both sides will tell you the truth about the situation. We know we will.

You will have questions about the election. I will put up a box for questions.

There are a few facts I would like to pass on to you:

1. Our Plant has found itself in great financial difficulty in the eight (8) months since The Alpha Co. purchased the Plant. In that time, we have lost over two hundred thousand dollars ($200,000). While this has happened, we have made sure everyone has worked a full week and no one has been laid off (except one day at Christmas time).

2. Your future and ours rests on how well we are able to regain the customers we have lost and keep the ones we have.

3. If we can maintain a low price for our customers, then we will be able to meet competition and survive.

4. If we do not do better than our competitors, then job security will not exist for any of us.

5. The only way to keep our Plant operating is by getting new customers and keeping our prices reasonable. No union or union contract can provide work for this plant.

6. Some union plants have been forced out of business because they did not survive the competition by other companies who charged lower prices. A good example happened next door within the last few months—National Tidbit closed down on October 15, 1980, and 175 people lost their jobs. One of the major reasons they went out of business was a two (2) week strike over wages and working conditions.

7. A union does not necessarily mean automatic improvements for anyone. Job security comes only from the Company's ability to meet competition, not from any union contract.

We will continue to have meetings, pass information on to you and answer your questions. Thank you for your support.

After the speech to the first shift, several employees approached Blass privately in his office and commented that they personally did not support the union. One employee, Rufus King, asked Blass why the company did not get rid of the three employees who were pushing the union. Blass responded: "Rufus, if you are harassed, coerced or threatened in any way by the Teamsters or those three, either at work or at home, please let me or your foreman know immediately. You do not have to tolerate it and we will see to it that it is stopped."

Blass then asked "Rufus why do you think some of the employees want a union?" King replied, "There are always going to be trouble makers. However, several of the workers were really teed off when you sold those Coke machines. You should tell those Alpha people that those were our machines and we would like to have them back or the money you got for them spent on the lunchroom."

After King left Blass' office, Blass phoned the Ace Vending Company and ordered a soft drink machine and a sandwich machine to be installed in the employee lunch room. The next day the machines were installed. A week later the following notice was posted above the question box:

February 25, 1981

Dana Blass

Plant Manager

NOTICE TO ALL EMPLOYEES

1. Question: Has the Alpha Co. actually lost money operating this plant since they have purchased it, or is it as the union

people say: That they have just not made as much money as they expected to, and call this money lost??

Answer: What I said at our meeting still stands. No strings attached, nothing shady, no accounting deceptions.

To make this even clearer—let me say it this way—we have made *no* money, we have only *lost* money!! At the time I stated that we had lost over $200,000, it is now closer to $300,000 *loss* clean, clear, *LOSS*.

The union has absolutely no way of knowing our profit or loss figures. Any statement that they make in regards to our profit or losses, will only be an effort on their part to deceive you.

I hope you know me well enough by now to know that I will not lie to you.

2. I appreciate knowing that you like the sandwich and soft drink machines. Thanks for telling me.

On March 1st, the following letter was included in the employees' pay envelope:

Dear Beta Employee:

The fact that your present wages, hours, and benefits are equal to those of union represented employees is the result of Beta's long standing policy to provide wages and working conditions to all employees regardless of whether employees are union represented or not.

Thus, I believe you already receive in wages and benefits *all* that you can reasonably expect the union to obtain for you. And you receive *equal* wages and benefits without having to pay union dues or being subject to union bylaws or regulations.

Teamster Local 028 in Evansville currently collects *$18.00 each month* from all members. This means that the employees in our Plant could pay $11,016 each year, which will guarantee you—NOTHING. Look at your check and imagine this month's check with $18.00 less.

In 1979, Local 028 paid their officers and employees of the Local $149,614. They need your money to continue to pay these people.

But what are you going to get in return?—NOTHING.

Sincerely,

s/ _____

Dana Blass
Plant Manager

On March 10th the following letter was sent to the employees:

March 10, 1981

Dear Beta Employee,

When the Alpha Co. purchased the Delta Plant on 9/1/80, you were provided with a list of the benefits and the explanation of how the plan was coordinated with the Alpha/National Insurance benefit programs.

A review in 1980 indicated the need to make improvements in the benefit plans in all locations included in the Alpha benefit plan. The following changes were approved at that time for your location to be effective on 3/15/81:

Major Medical Expense Benefit increased to $100,000; Surgical Benefit Increase to $2,000; Diagnostic X-Ray and Laboratory Expense Benefit increased to $100 per person; Term Life Insurance, Company paid, increased to $10,000; Accidental Death and Dismemberment Insurance, Company paid, increased to $10,000; Voluntary Life Insurance, Employee paid, increased to $30,000.

New booklets will be printed showing the improved coverage and distributed in the near future.

Because a union has petitioned to represent our production and maintenance employees and an election is pending, we can be charged with unfair labor practice whenever we change an employee's wages or benefits. Because our hands are tied, we regret that the planned increase in benefits cannot go into effect. If we give increased wages or benefits, we can be charged with trying to buy votes.

Sincerely,

s/

_____

Dana Blass

Plant Manager

On March 15th, the following notice was included in each employee's pay envelope:

YOU HAVE SOMETHING TO LOSE BY VOTING FOR A UNION

YOU CAN LOSE JOB SECURITY

Which Comes Only From The Combined Efforts Of All Employees To Keep Your Business Successful Many Union Professionals Try To Mislead Employees Into Believing That Union Contracts Provide Job Security. They Do Not! Only A Successful And Progressive Business With All Of Us Working As A Team Can Give You Real Security

It Has Happened Elsewhere—Don't Let It Happen To Us!

Stay Ahead Of Our Competition!

If There Are Any Questions—See Me.

DANA BLASS
PLANT MANAGER

On March 17th and 18th, Blass delivered the following speech to the assembled employees on all three shifts:

BETA PRODUCTS
JASPER, INDIANA

March 17/18, 1981

Text: Dana Blass

You all know that an election is going to be held here Thursday to determine whether or not an outside third party will come between us. I have been here long enough to know most of *you* pretty well. Well enough to have confidence in your judgment and I think well enough to know that you will *not* bring an outside union into this plant. But just in case a few of you still have some doubts, let me tell you why I am personally against the union here. You can see that I have got the things I am going to say written down today. I've done that for legal reasons—because of the election. However, I don't need any of these things I want to say written down. Because these things involve me personally. They involve you personally. They involve this plant and are extremely important to all of us.

There has never been a union in this plant. This is a compliment to you and to prior mangement and I hope to me. This is what gives you the right to think and talk for yourself.

You all know about the Delta Plant in Chillicothe with a union. We were told that Chillicothe had a turnover of 48.8% in 1971. The year before you had a union attempt to get in here. If that sounds high to you, you're right. There were on the average 117 workers at Chillicothe and 57 of these employees left the Company during 1971 for one reason or another. Averaging that out over the year, that means that more than one employee every week was coming and going at Chillicothe.

Compare the kind of turmoil with the working conditions you have had here at Jasper. Since June, 1980, when Alpha purchased this Plant, there has been only one person leave and that was for not coming to work. We think this shows the real difference in working conditions that we have here at Beta as compared to a union pet food plant.

Let's take a closer look at Jasper, Indiana, for just a minute. There are 27 manufacturing plants here in town. There are only 4 plants in town which have unions: Acme, Carmet, Unarco and Vega Sporting Goods Company. The 23 plants in Jasper without a union have had *no* strikes. On the other hand, some of the plants in Jasper with unions have had strikes. National Tidbit had a strike last summer. They are now closed because of business and profit problems. Where there are unions, strikes generally take place. During this time, you have not had to walk a picket line or lost any money due to a strike for even one day because there is no union here at our plant.

Compare what we have here with what employees at these union plants have here in Jasper. And keep in mind that employees in

these union plants pay dues, fines and assessments to an outside
third party which you don't have to pay. In three (3) of the larger
plants in Jasper with unions, the top production wage rate is $5.44
per hour and the top maintenance rate is $6.05. Compare that with
our rates and tell me how much you had to pay to a union to get that
for you. Do you think it is worth up to $240 each year in union dues?

Actually, this comparison doesn't tell the whole story. Because
some of these employees had to suffer through a strike to receive an
increase. Here is an idea of how long it takes you to recover what
you would lose in wages for a 3 week strike. (Pass out "Your Personal Strike Computer," Appendix A and discuss). If you take home
$115 per week, you lose $345 in 3 weeks. If you get 10¢ per hour
more by going on strike, it takes 1 year and 34 weeks (86 weeks) to
recover the $345. If you take home $230 per week, you lose $690 and
it takes 172 weeks. Can you imagine being out on strike for 3 weeks
with only the $45 per week that I understand the Teamsters would
pay you? Who gets hurt during these strikes? The paid union organizers? Hardly. They keep getting their regular pay checks from
the union. The ones that get hurt are the employees who aren't getting a paycheck from the Company. The ones who get hurt are the
employees who aren't getting unemployment compensation because
you cannot collect unemployment when you are on strike. These are
the people who get hurt and their families. Strikes ordinarily take
place only where you have a union. Everybody knows that, and
everybody knows that strikes mean lost work, lost pay, and possibly
lost jobs.

Frankly, the strike record of the Teamsters union is pretty lousy.
Local 028 is out of Evansville and they took the employees at the
Alpha warehouse in Evansville on a 13 day strike in 1976. That cost
these employees a lot of lost wages and frankly it cost the Company
a lot in lost sales. Nobody wins in a strike. It could be possible that
the Teamsters union will tell you to go on strike to support a strike in
Evansville or somewhere else. This is called—support your union
and your union brother. Well, you will not get anything for this type
of strike—and could even lose your job.

There is one thing we shouldn't forget. Voting for this union will
not automatically bring any wage increases or any other benefits to
you. If this union were to be voted in, there would still be no way
that it could force your Company to do anything that we are not already willing or able to do. All wages and benefits would be negotiable. You could get more, you could stay the same, or you could get
less. The only thing that the union could do without our consent, is
call you out on strike. And we have no intention of yielding to any
sort of union strike pressure.

Now, let's look to the future. It is definitely our hope, and our
intention, to keep your wages and your benefits moving upward as
we have in the past. You can count on that without any union! I'll
repeat that. It is definitely our hope and our intention to keep your

wages and benefits moving upward as we have in the past. You can count on that without any union.

Union organizers will always try to turn you against the management—against us. But who do you believe is really more interested in your welfare. We, who are responsible for running this business and are trying to carry it on in the best possible manner? Or these organizers, who want to collect union dues, assessments and fines from you? Who do you think you will do better with? With us, whom you know, and with this Company, which keeps the operation going and meets our payroll. Or with paid union organizers, who are here today to organize you and gone from here tomorrow. The Teamsters do not represent any employee in Jasper. How much time do you think they will spend working with you? We have a Dairy in Ohio represented by the Teamsters. A lot of the employees recently signed a petition to kick them out because they (the Teamsters) do not spend enough time on the employees problems. This is a typical problem with unions. *We* will take enough time to listen to your problems and take care of them. We have proved this to you. And you do not have to pay us to do it.

Bear in mind that you now have the individual right and freedom to come in and settle with us personally any problem you may have. You now have the right to think and talk for yourself. With a union, we couldn't always work things out together. In many cases, there would be the union standing between us, pulling us apart.

We are all striving to maintain and build up this operation. As Plant Manager, I would like to guarantee the success of this plant. I want to assure jobs for you and security for you and your families. A successful future for this plant and security for you and your jobs here *cannot* be accomplished by any union! It can only be accomplished through your continued loyalty and cooperation—and by all of us working and pulling together—and *not* letting some outsider pull us apart.

When this election is held, it is important that all of you vote. Don't stand aside on the idea that the outcome won't affect you. It *will* affect you. Take a hand in the matter. Make sure it goes the way you want it to go. The way you know is best for you and your family. Otherwise, you might find yourself with a union you don't really want. By all means, *everyone* should vote in this election.

Remember, all of you have a right to vote against this union by voting *"NO"*—even though some time or other you may have signed a union card or gone to a union meeting. I know just as sure as I'm standing here today that *you* stand to gain by keeping this union *out* of this plant.

Here are some questions that I have heard asked and the answers to those questions. (Pass out questions and answer sheet, Appendix

B).   Let's read them together.   (Read questions and answers.   After each answer—Does anybody want to talk about this one?)

Remember—Vote, it is important.   Vote NO UNION.   That is also important.

APPENDIX A

YOUR PERSONAL STRIKE COST COMPUTER

TAKE HOME PAY	YOU LOSE	0¢	1¢	2¢	3¢	4¢	5¢	6¢	7¢	8¢	9¢	10¢
						You Strike For To Get It Back It Will Take You						
$ 80	$240	Never	11 yrs 28 wks	5 yrs 40 wks	3 yrs 44 wks	2 yrs 46 wks	2 yrs 16 wks	1 yr 48 wks	1 yr 34 wks	1 yr 23 wks	1 yr 14 wks	1 yr 8 wks
$ 85	$255	Never	12 yrs 12 wks	6 yrs 6 wks	4 yrs 5 wks	3 yrs 3 wks	2 yrs 23 wks	2 yrs 2 wks	1 yr 39 wks	1 yr 28 wks	1 yr 19 wks	1 yr 12 wks
$ 90	$270	Never	12 yrs 50 wks	6 yrs 25 wks	4 yrs 17 wks	3 yrs 12 wks	2 yrs 31 wks	2 yrs 8 wks	1 yr 44 wks	1 yr 32 wks	1 yr 23 wks	1 yr 15 wks
$ 95	$285	Never	13 yrs 36 wks	5 yrs 44 wks	4 yrs 29 wks	3 yrs 22 wks	2 yrs 38 wks	2 yrs 15 wks	1 yr 50 wks	1 yr 37 wks	1 yr 27 wks	1 yr 19 wks
$100	$300	Never	14 yrs 22 wks	7 yrs 11 wks	4 yrs 42 wks	3 yrs 32 wks	2 yrs 46 wks	2 yrs 21 wks	2 yrs 3 wks	1 yr 42 wks	1 yr 31 wks	1 yr 23 wks
$105	$315	Never	15 yrs 7 wks	7 yrs 29 wks	5 yrs 2 wks	3 yrs 40 wks	3 yrs 1 wk	2 yrs 27 wks	2 yrs 8 wks	1 yr 46 wks	1 yr 35 wks	1 yr 26 wks
$110	$330	Never	15 yrs 45 wks	7 yrs 48 wks	5 yrs 15 wks	3 yrs 50 wks	3 yrs 9 wks	2 yrs 33 wks	2 yrs 13 wks	1 yr 51 wks	1 yr 39 wks	1 yr 30 wks
$115	$345	Never	16 yrs 30 wks	8 yrs 15 wks	5 yrs 27 wks	4 yrs 7 wks	3 yrs 16 wks	2 yrs 29 wks	2 yrs 19 wks	2 yrs 3 wks	1 yr 43 wks	1 yr 34 wks

PERIOD WEEKS

APPENDIX B

BETA PRODUCTS COMPANY
JASPER, INDIANA

March 17, 1981

Here are some questions that some of you have asked and the answers to those questions and other common questions about a union and what they *can* and *cannot* do for you.

1. Do we have to pay the union if they win?

   Answer. You Bet! They haven't said much about their dues, assessments, initiation charges and other fees, but union members could pay as much as $20.00 a month just in dues. What's more, the union's constitution allows them to increase your dues.

2. If the union is voted in, when do we get a wage increase?

   Answer. You don't get an increase just because a union is voted in. The union has no way of forcing the Company to agree to anything it does not want to agree to. If we can't afford to pay an increase, we have the right to tell the union: "No, we won't pay what you demand". *THE COMPANY CONTROLS WAGES—NOT THE UNION—NOT THE CHAMBER OF COMMERCE OR THE MAYOR OF JASPER.*

3. What happens if the Company and the union don't agree on wages?

   Answer. Ask your co-employees who are in favor of the union what they think. If you get the answer, let us know.

4. If we vote to keep the union out, what will the Company do for us?

   Answer. We can't answer that one now, because under the law a Company can't make any promises to employees during a campaign. That's considered to be unfair and we would be in trouble with the Federal Government if we did so. However, we will always try to do the best we can and we hope business will improve.

5. How come the *union* can make us promises?

   Answer. They're allowed! Under the law, a union can make you all the promises in the world to get you to vote for them. BEWARE OF PHONY PROMISES. Ask the union people how they will make good on their fancy promises.

6. Who will answer questions that are in favor of the union? For instance, what good can they do for us?

   Answer. We honestly believe that the union will not do any good here. As a matter of fact, we believe that the union's reputation is so bad that all it will do here is cause trouble and bring regret to our employees.

7. Why is the Company so afraid of the union coming in?

    Answer. Our Company is opposed to any union coming between the Company and its employees. We feel that in the last year wages, benefits and working conditions have been greatly improved. The Company did not need a union to make these improvements. Our policy is to constantly review our wages, benefits and working conditions so as to make sure that our employees are receiving fair compensation. You don't need to pay dues to the union to insure this kind of fair treatment.

8. If the union called us out on strike over wages and other conditions of employment, would we get paid while the strike is going on?

    Answer. No. If you don't work, you won't get paid. The Company won't pay your wages, and neither will the union. Sometimes unions pay a few dollars to strikers who carry a picket sign in all kinds of weather. But the union continues to pay the big salaries of the professional union organizers from your union dues while YOU are out of work on strike!

9. Can we collect unemployment compensation while we are out on strike?

    Answer. No. Under our state laws you CANNOT collect unemployment compensation while you are out of work on strike.

10. If the union decided to call a strike over wages and other conditions of employment, could I lose my job?

    Answer. Yes. Under the federal law, if the union made you strike to try to force the Company to agree to the Union's wage and other economic demands, the Company is free to PERMANENTLY REPLACE ALL STRIKERS with new workers. This means that after the strike is over you may no longer have a job, and the law does NOT force the Company to rehire you if you are an economic striker and have been permanently replaced by someone willing to work in your job.

11. I'm not that interested in the union; do I have to vote?

    Answer: Yes, it is very important that everyone vote. If you don't the pro-union employees will vote for the union and we will have a union whether you like it or not. The Union does not have to get a majority of the employees eligible to vote but only a majority of those ACTUALLY VOTING. For example, if 40 employees vote then all the union needs is 21 votes to win. DON'T LET OTHERS DO THE VOTING FOR YOU. IT IS YOUR FUTURE—VOTE.

12. Can the Company give an increase to employees now?

    Answer. Under the law, the federal government has rules prohibiting a Company from making any promises or giving increases to certain employees or to everyone in general while a campaign is going on. (The union, however, is legally allowed

to make all the promises they want.) So we can't give an increase to anyone now as it would appear as a bribe and would
be an unfair labor practice.

If you have any additional questions, ask them! We will give you the
best answer we can—FAST.

John Jones

Plant Manager

B. THE WAY ORGANIZING BEGINS

Most organizing efforts begin when a group of employees contacts a union organizer. The impulse to organization is likely to
spring from a combination of deep-rooted dissatisfaction and some recent unsettling development on the job. Employees are usually
aware of the possibility of unionizing because of their own previous
membership or that of a close family member. After they decide to
seriously investigate unionizing, the employees must decide which
union to contact. The choice is often between a union whose jurisdiction and history seems particularly appropriate for the company being unionized and the teamsters, a union with catchall jurisdiction.
The teamsters are attractive to many employees because they are
powerful. They are perceived as capable of obtaining concessions
and of protecting the employees from reprisal. On the other hand,
the teamsters also suggest industrial strike, exploitation of the workers by the union and corruption. Despite these concerns, the teamsters are involved in about one-third of all NLRB elections, and it is
often the employees who contact them.

An initial meeting between the union organizer and a group of
workers generally begins the organizing drive. The success of this
meeting is highly important to the union campaign. The organizer
will discuss the history and role of unions, and he will attempt to
persuade the employees of the power of the union to redress their
grievances. An employee or "inside" organizing committee is
formed. As company employees, its members have greater access to
the other employees than the professional organizer does. The committee's formation demonstrates that local employees will control the
union, and its membership is thought to indicate the nature of the
union's leadership, should it be successful. Accordingly, it is very
important to the union that those on the committee have the respect
of their fellow employees. An experienced organizer typically uses
this meeting to anticipate company statements and actions. He will
inform the employees that they will soon be bombarded with company "love letters", and he will outline many of the arguments regularly contained in them.

Generally, efforts will be made to keep the organizing drive secret
to protect against employer reprisal. Some organizers, however, feel
that informing the employer of the local union's formation is a bold
stroke, dramatizing the security which the union can provide and si-

multaneously protecting the employees whose names are listed against employer reprisal.

Thus the Ladies Garment Workers Union will frequently send the employer a telegram stating, "Please be advised that the following employees are members of the committee in favor of unionization. * * * We will expect you to accord these members all the rights and guarantees to which they are entitled under the National Labor Relations Act". Garment worker organizers feel that the possibility of a secret campaign doesn't really exist where more than a handful of employees is involved.

During the period which follows the initial meeting, union supporters try to persuade other employees to sign cards, which authorize the union to act as their collective bargaining agent. Obtaining signed authorization cards is critically important to the union. Thirty percent of the employees in the unit must sign in order to obtain an election. Also, a card majority may be used to obtain bargaining rights without an election, or despite an election loss, if the employer commits unfair labor practices which the NLRB considers likely to have a substantial impact on the employees' vote.

Most unions do not collect dues from employees who sign up during this period. The prospect of paying dues to a union not currently capable of bargaining on their behalf might discourage some employees from joining up. Moreover, union dues are certain to be a focus of the employer's anti-union campaign, and most organizers feel that the impact of this tactic can be lessened by waiving all dues until a collective agreement is signed.

If the organizing effort is successful, the union organizer will write what is known as a "recognition letter" to the company president informing him that the union has signed up a majority of employees, offering to prove this to an impartial observer, and requesting that the employer bargain with the union.

An employer may respond to the request for recognition by entering into immediate collective bargaining relationship. Such action is legal if the union in fact represents a majority. However, immediate bargaining is rare. Most employers strongly desire to avoid dealing with a union, and they have a right to insist on an election under the law. At this point, if he hasn't already done so, the employer is likely to contact a labor lawyer, who will draft a letter challenging the union's claim to majority status and insisting that the union win an election before bargaining will take place.[1] The employer will be instructed by the lawyer not to question the employees about the union and not to discharge or discipline anyone because of union membership, at least not without checking with the lawyer.

---

1. In the past, certain unions such as the Ladies Garment Workers would strike in protest of the refusal of recognition. Such tactics are rarely used today. They are of doubtful legality, and quick resort to strikes will play into the employers' common argument that the unions necessarily mean strikes.

C. THE ORGANIZATIONAL CAMPAIGN

When its request for recognition is rejected, the union's response is to file a petition before the Labor Board, seeking an election, to determine its right to represent the employees.

The stakes in the election are high. If the union wins a valid election, even by a single vote, it becomes the exclusive bargaining representative for all employees in the unit. The employer may not then deal individually with his employees, and he may not unilaterally change their wages, hours, or working conditions without bargaining with the union. If the union loses a valid election, it ends up bargaining for no one, not even its members.

The union's petition will indicate generally which employees it claims to represent. A typical claim might include all production and maintenance workers, or it might be limited to warehouse workers or drivers. The employer may challenge the petition by raising the argument that the unit described is inappropriate under Board standards. This claim rarely succeeds, but it can cause delay. The parties may also disagree about which employees are eligible to vote in a given unit. Usually the terms of the election and the questions of eligibility are worked out by agreement of the parties. Frequently, it is the union which makes concessions in order to forestall a Labor Board hearing on these matters. It is generally thought that the delay caused by technical wrangling favors the employer, and the employer's ability to delay the election by raising these technical questions is one of the things unions would like changed by law.

Before the election takes place, a series of tactical decisions have to be made by each side, particularly by the employer. The employer must decide how intense and forceful a campaign to run, whether to stay within the NLRB's guidelines or not and which supervisors to use as spokespeople. The style of the company campaign will be in part a reflection of the style and approach of the company's lawyer. Because many labor lawyers handle such campaigns regularly, they are thought to be experts not only concerning the law, but also about what works in persuading people to vote against union representation.

Management lawyers today generally urge their clients to adopt a moderate approach to the campaign and to avoid bitter personal attacks on the union or its members. There are several reasons why this is so. Most company lawyers feel that too bitter a campaign is likely to backfire. Also they fear that if the union wins after a bitter campaign, it will be difficult to establish a good working relationship. Management lawyers often deal with the same union on behalf of other clients, and some are concerned that an emotional campaign will harm their existing bargaining relationship. Moreover, experience dealing with unions has made most management lawyers less fearful of the consequences of unionization than their clients generally are. Thus neither their emotions nor their tactical judgments are likely to urge them toward a vitriolic campaign.

Not all management lawyers urge moderation on their clients. There are still a goodly number who despise unions and who feel that frightening employees is an effective technique for getting them to vote against unionization. Lawyers vary similarly in their willingness to urge or participate in action deemed improper by the Labor Board. Some reject it on a combination of legal and ethical grounds. Some engage in or counsel unlawful behavior as a matter of course, concluding that legal problems following an election are better for their client than a union victory and are profitable for them. Almost all lawyers, however, seek to avoid too flagrant violations for fear of provoking the Board to issue a bargaining order which remedies unfair labor practices by instructing the employer to bargain with a union despite its having lost a previously held majority. As one lawyer who regularly uses illegal tactics stated, "but you don't want it to reach the point where a bargaining order issues because that's when you really hurt".

The employer must also decide how strenuous a campaign to run. While most employers are initially eager to mount a major campaign against the union, devoting considerable time and personnel to this effort, there are a variety of factors cutting against such a course. It is expensive. It means high lawyers' fees and loss of productivity. Management time will be taken up in working on the campaign, and employee time will be taken up in meetings and discussion. It increases the likelihood of inadvertant misconduct. In addition, some feel that a too openly vigorous company campaign will signal to the employees the power of the union and its ability to shape managerial behavior. Thus, it is common for the company's formal campaign to be relatively low-key, involving several letters and two or three meetings. Supervisors are often told not to foment discussion of unionization or even to take part in them, but to keep track of expressions of sentiments and report back. Intelligence on employee attitudes is customarily desired, not as a prelude to reprisal, but for the same reasons that political campaigners use polls: to know which voters need to be won over and the issues about which the employees are concerned.

The climax of the employer campaign is usually a meeting on company premises in which all the employees eligible to vote are gathered to hear an address delivered by the president or other high company official. The employees are paid for attending, and it is not uncommon for beer and refreshments to be served. Sometimes this meeting is set up by an intense but low-keyed effort to make the person giving it better acquainted or on a first-name basis with the employees. If the company official is thought to be knowledgeable about the law and capable of avoiding misstatements, he may be permitted to speak extemporaneously and to answer questions. Extemporaneous talks have the advantage of permitting the employer to speak without sounding contrived, but in the heat of discussion, the employer may forget to say certain things, and he may inadvertently say other things which violate the law. A question and answer format is even more risky. A question asking point-blank whether the employer plans to take certain action favored by the employees puts him in a difficult situation. If he says the action will be taken, he has made a promise of benefits which is an unfair labor practice that can be used to get the election set aside if the union loses. If the employer says the desired action will not be taken, the employees will be angered. If he refuses to answer, the employees may be disappointed and conclude he is using Board rules to avoid making a desirable commitment. A well versed union organizer might deliberately plant such a question. The following colloquy handled by a knowledgeable company spokesman is typical.

Question: "There is a little girl here that asks me every morning if by summer we can't have an ice cream machine."

Answer: "Well, I think it would be nice to have ice cream here in the summertime."

Question: "Well, are you going to tell her when you're going to have it? That is what she wants to know."

Answer: "The National Labor Relations Board has several rules which the company is under. We can't make any threats and we can't make any promises, but the unions can make all kinds of promises."

The employer cannot circumvent the problem by not recognizing well known union adherents in answering questions for he will be accused of being afraid of them. Thus it is common for the employer to carefully read a speech written for him by his lawyer, after an apology similar to the following: "I would much prefer to talk with you informally without any notes; however, because of the importance of this matter and so there won't be any question or misunderstanding about what I have to say, I have decided to read these remarks to you." The message which the employer delivers will vary, but certain basic arguments and approaches are virtually certain to be used.

Commonly, the employer will begin in a friendly non-partisan way. He will urge the employees to listen to both sides, to make up their own minds and to be sure to vote. He will usually promise to abide by the employees' decision and will remind them that the ballot is secret. He will stress the importance of the vote as a way designed to make employees apprehensive about the consequences of unionization, "You are on the brink of making a momentous decision".

Next, the employer will stress whatever is positive about existing wages and working conditions. He will argue that wages and benefits are as high as he could reasonably make them and that only increased profitability for the company, something which the union endangers, could lead to improved benefits. He will refer to any benefits recently granted, and suggest that such grants are part of a continuing plan or pattern which obviates the need for a union. "In the past, the company has given you all the wage increases and fringe benefits it could afford and still stay competitive. We have given you these things voluntarily and without your having to pay one cent to any outsider or having to strike. We have done this because we want this to be as good a place for you to work as this company's financial ability and business will permit us to do." The employer will discuss the friendly and informal atmosphere which has existed in the past, and mention special favors which he has done for employees. He will contend that this easy-going atmosphere will be threatened by a union victory, which will force both him and the employees to go through the union to resolve problems. The following excerpt from a speech of a professional management consultant is typical of this approach: "The thing that I resent most about a union coming into an organization of this size is the fact that it changes the culture of the environment that you live in for the better part of every day and every week. The culture that changes is that many people are met on a give-and-take basis in meeting their problems as they occur. With the rigidity of a union you lose that. Now this shop has a lot of women. Many of you girls are the sole support of your family; you've got children, you do the best you can to get a babysitter, but sometimes things go wrong. And I resent deeply to be bound by a union contract that says when somebody exceeds a limit of, say five days a year, I've got to let her go regardless of the reason she was out. That's no heart! When we lose sight of the fact that a company like ours exists to serve people we're in trouble!"

The theme of the union leadership as outsiders who will disrupt a successful relationship between the company and its employees is used repeatedly. As one company statement in an election involving the ILGWU put it, "If the union wins this election, your affairs will then be in the hands of union dictators in New York and Ohio. Unions cannot exist without trouble. If there isn't any trouble, the outside troublemaker of the Ladies Garment Workers Union will probably make some."

Employers stress that a union victory does not guarantee improvements. The union must bargain with the employer and win his approval before any benefits are granted. The employer will probably promise to bargain in good faith, but announce his intention to bargain hard, and if the union makes unreasonable demands, to resist. "The only way a union can attempt to force your company to meet unrealistic union demands would be to pull you out on strike. Now without intending to seem harsh or abrupt, I hope you will realize and understand—while there is yet time—that we have no intention of yielding to any such pressure as that ever."

To exploit apprehension concerning the consequences of strikes, a variant of the following argument appears in almost all employer campaigns. "Strikes are a brutal and unpleasant experience. You get no wages, no unemployment compensation, and new employees may be hired to permanently replace you. Strikes generate ill will. Violence is not uncommon. Most strikes last a long time, several weeks or even months. Consider the money you would lose. Suppose you work 40 hours per week and make $1.70 per hour. If you were on strike for a period of five weeks, you would lose $340.00. If you made 20 cents an hour gain because of the strike, you would have to work 3400 hours in order to make up the lost wages. This is approximately one and one-half years. Management loses during a strike too. In a strike, everyone loses, except the union organizer. He will draw his pay fifty-two weeks a year."

Exorbitant union salaries might be mentioned at this point as a lead-in to another focus of anti-union speeches, union dues. The employer will claim that the desire to collect union dues to pay his salary is the real reason for the union's interest. An employer letter states bluntly, "What the union organizers want is money. Your money! These union organizers are out here for the thousands and thousands of dollars that they hope to get out of you in the form of initiation fees, union dues, and union assessments. You must decide whether to let these outsiders get their hands in your pockets. But make no mistake, it is your money that this union is really after."

Employers today will frequently acknowledge the positive contributions of unions at other times and in other industries. This puts the employer in a reasonable stance and permits him to express an attitude widely shared in our society. But, the employer will argue that the union movement today has lost its crusading zeal and become a profitable business.

An employer speech which gives the flavor of this line of argument went as follows, "Now I'm not going to say that unions haven't done a fine job. They have done a great job in the country. We've needed it. In years gone by, I'm sure John L. Lewis did great things for the coal miners, but let's take a good look at unions today. They're big, they're rich, they've got investments in Florida, big night clubs down there. * * * They're spitting in the face of the President of the United States. There are union members not too far away from here that are paying themselves $150,000 bucks a year. Now do you want to help them do that? Do you want to give them more money to squander on these things?"

Many employer speeches will try to suggest that union representation could lead to layoffs or even plant closing. For legal and tactical reasons, this is rarely couched in terms of employer reprisal. As one management official stated, "I think it would have pretty well convinced them that they did need a union here, if they thought their job security was not based on job performance, but rather on whims of management, why I think they would want greater security than that." Instead, the employer argues that the union will increase costs, which will cause the employer to lose customers and the loss of customers may force the company to curtail or shut down its operation. It is a popular tactic to place the responsibility for potential adverse consequences on the reaction of customers to unionization. This is thought to create apprehension about unions among the employees, to indicate that the apprehension is a sensible one, shared by business people, without detracting from the employer's desired image of fairness. Generally, a variation of the following argument stated by a manufacturer of industrial seats is used. "Our company is the sole supplier that many of these customers have. What do you think these customers would do if we became unionized? They would buy half as many seats from us as they are now and obviously this would reduce our business and it would reduce our employment."

"The union has said we are interested in profits and that is the only true thing they have ever told you. We are not ashamed of being interested in profits. After all, if it wasn't for profits, there would be no reason for us to stay in business or to provide jobs for you." Reference might be made either obliquely or directly to plants in the surrounding area which were unionized and which have since been shut down or sold. "Fortunately, all of you have had a chance to see these bakers in action. They have represented Jones Bakery, the Onion Works and Colonial. Only one of these is still in business. I'm not saying the Bakers caused them to go out of business. You know as well as I what happened. * * * But the Bakers sure as hell didn't stop these plants from going out of business."

While employers' counsel are wary of suggesting reprisal because of their fear of a backlash, there is general feeling that the promise of benefits is more likely to be effective, particularly if the promise is to correct or improve the very condition which gave rise to the original organizing effort. Employer counsel would thus often try to imply a promise in a statement which points out that the employer is legally prevented from making promises.

"People say we need a pension program here at Quincy. I want you and the National Labor Relations Board to understand that I am not promising you anything, but one of the things we have been kicking around and talking about is what we call income protection insurance."

A typical company campaign letter concludes, "Why pay dues and why run the risk of a union forced strike * * * to get what you can get free to you." The statement is purposely ambiguous. For legal reasons the employer does not state whether he means that the union cannot get more than is currently being granted or that he will grant benefits equal to those customary under a union contract. He would be satisfied with either interpretation.

The union campaign is the frequent target of employer criticism. Organizing drives in the Southern textile industry often become particularly heated. "I have read the two handbills passed out recently by the ILGWU at our plant. If I had not seen these handbills with my own eyes, it would have been hard for me to believe that anyone, even this union, would be willing to win an election using misrepresentation, deceit, and just plain outright, barefaced lies. Last week, the outside union organizers tried to insult me because I stumbled over a word in my talk to you. * * * The union organizers are stooping pretty low if all they have to talk about is how I pronounce words."

Employers' campaign literature generally stress the same themes as their speech. An effort is made to make the tone friendly, using first names on salutation and closing. Frequently, the literature will take the tone of either correcting factual errors in the union's campaign or of conveying information about the election process. Often employer propaganda literature will be labeled "fact sheet" contrasting union claims on the one hand with what are euphemistically characterized as facts on the other. Often the letters will respond to fictitious employee questions.

"Dear Ed:

"I would like to share with you some of the typical questions we have heard from our employees in the past few weeks.

"Who would be the union leaders and officers, if the union wins? * * *

You all know the answer to this question by just looking around in the plant. Only a very few will profit in this regard from this union.

"If I have signed a union card, can I still vote against this union in the election? * * *

Yes, it doesn't make any difference whether you signed a union card or went to a union meeting. * * * "

One technique used by several company counsel to demonstrate the powerlessness of unions is the "guarantee letter".

"Dear [Employee]:

"To protect yourself against irresponsible promises by Union Officials which the Union does not have the ability to carry out, it is suggested you get some of the Union's promises GUARANTEED to you by having the Union Officials sign their promises in writing.

"Some promises that you may be interested in having the Union Officials sign and GUARANTEE in writing are as follows:

1. Have the Union Official GUARANTEE you that the Union will pay your wages in the event you are out of work because of labor trouble or a strike.

Signed: _____ Date: _____
                    Union Official

2. Have the Union Official GUARANTEE you that if you are called out on strike—that you will get your job back regardless of whether you have been permanently replaced or not.

Signed: _____ Date: _____
                    Union Official

    *   *   * "

The company may try to get a loyal employee to publically present the document to the organizer.

With respect to plant management during the campaign, there is a wide variation in approach. Some employers seek to use the period to show their good will, responding generously to requests for time off, making popular changes in supervision, etc. Others will tighten up to demonstrate that the company might or could turn nasty in response to unionization. One company counsel described his campaign strategy as "no more vacationland U.S.A." Most company counsel, however, feel that any changes suggest the power of the union and its ability to affect company decisions and urge the employer to adopt a business as usual approach.

The union, like the employer, must make various tactical decisions concerning the focus and nature of its campaign. The union cannot call a meeting on company premises during working time, and typically, the union organizer, as a non-employee, may be kept off the premises. The organizer must therefore decide whether to try and utilize meetings held during non-working hours off the premises, whether to make home visits or whether to focus on letters. Under existing Labor Board rules, the union is entitled to a list of the names and addresses of eligible employees. There are drawbacks to any of the methods named. After hours meetings may be poorly attended because of the inconvenience of attending, and the poor attendance may be thought to signal waning of interest. The inside organizers are inexperienced and giving them too much prominence may raise concern among other employees about whether the union will function democratically if it is successful. Home visits might be resented as an invasion of privacy. Therefore, although organizers recognize the impersonality of letters, it is common for union campaigns to rely on them substantially.

The union's basic argument in any medium is that the employees acting together have more power than any individual has acting alone. As a Teamster form letter states, "One individual has no power to change his economic condition, but when he combines with his fellow employees for this purpose, he can move mountains. The power is the collective strength of all. All for one and one for all is the method which organized American workers have used for the past two centuries to improve their wages and living conditions. You and your fellow employees can do it election day."

The union will refer to wages and benefits they have achieved for the employees of other companies and discuss the security and dignity which comes from having a contract which limits the employer's ability to discharge people arbitrarily or to play favorites in promotions. The importance of an enforceable agreement "get it in writing" is a common theme. The union will frequently point out that high company officials are protected by long term contracts.

The union has campaign tactics and arguments to counter each standard employer statement or action. Knowledgeable organizers will attempt to blunt the effect of the company campaign from the very first meeting by predicting in advance what the company will say. He will warn employees that threats or predictions of plant closing are frequent during a campaign, but rare in reality. The union will affirm its desire to be reasonable and permit the employer a fair profit. It will stress that in the vast majority of cases, contracts are negotiated without a strike. Moreover, the union will add, decisions concerning bargaining positions are made by the employees themselves. The union may try to demonstrate this by soliciting employee ideas concerning the collective bargaining agreement to be negotiated. A common UAW form states: "List below the benefits that you would like to have in your UAW contract. We are now in the process of writing up the benefits that L&R Gear Workers want and need. We will consolidate all worker suggestions and they will be used as a basis for your contract proposals when we begin negotiations after the Labor Board election." This tactic is also designed to suggest to the employees the union's power to make their wishes come true.

Experienced organizers will try to turn around the argument about their inability to guarantee improvements. One organizer presented with the guarantee letter responded, "Hell, I wouldn't guarantee that tomorrow will be Tuesday. What you get from the Company depends upon what you want and how strong you are. It's your local union and if you all support it, you'll be successful". Another response to the Company's guarantee letter is a union guarantee letter which makes specific assurances concerning dues and strikes.

"We the undersigned guarantee that:

1. No one currently working at Jones will pay an initiation fee.
2. No one will pay dues until a contract containing higher wages, improved benefits and job security is voted on and accepted by a majority of employees.
3. There will be no strike unless the employees so vote by a two-thirds vote."

All of these points are standard operating procedures for most unions and are almost certain to be used to rebut employer arguments.

The union will respond to claims of personal favors to employees by arguing that such favors would not have been necessary in a unionized shop. "Mathews claims to be proud that employees have come to him with family, personal, and financial problems. Most or all of these problems have been financial. The employees had a problem living on the wages paid by the company and needed more money. This is not the type of problem Mathews should be proud to have his employees discuss with him. The answer to your problems is not to go to the plant manager. The answer is your union!"

Most unions will stress that they are an accepted part of the American industrial system and they will seek to demonstrate this through endorsements from noted public figures. President Eisenhower's statement that "only a fool would try to deprive working men and women of the right to form a union of their choice" is often quoted as are similar statements by Presidents Roosevelt, Truman, Kennedy, and Ford. Statements from Pope Pius XII and Pope John

XXIII are used where Catholic workers are involved. If a sizeable
number of Black employees are eligible to vote, the comment made
by Martin Luther King that "The labor hater is always a two-headed
creature spewing anti-Negro talk from one mouth and anti-union
propaganda from the other" is frequently quoted.

If promises or improvements are made by the employer, the union
will claim credit for them. "It took Local 561 to make the company
discuss your needs, but have you been promised anything definite?
Is it in writing? Is it signed? Whose word do you have that conditions will improve? The word of the company? Up to now it hasn't
been worth much to you." The union will become indignant at some
aspect of the company's campaign. "I just finished reading the hate
and scare letters that have been mailed to you. I have never read
such distorted bunk. It's a shame that the tremendous fee that is
being paid Mr. Flynn is not used as pay raises for you, instead of its
being used for scare letters." [2]

The union will claim that the employer is trying to win the election
by unfairly frightening the employees or trying to buy off their union
sympathizers. The frequently circulated steelworker pamphlet,
"Bombs Away," describes the typical company campaign as follows:
"Love 'em and scare 'em is managements' miracle method of defeating unions. Sometimes it's 'love letters' to your home with tidbits
about one happy family—Then there's the fear program, rumors that
the company may move if unionized, scare talks about strikes and
violence inflated stories about union dues. * * * If the company's
really interested in your welfare, what's wrong with giving you a
voice in it?" Unions respond to arguments about being the outsider
by stressing local control. "You are the union" is a line which is
used in virtually every union campaign.

Typical is a leaflet used by the Laborers union entitled "Managements' Most Delicate Operation: Taking the You out of Union",
which states "The bosses scarewords about 'outsiders' and 'agitators'
may look like they are aimed at someone else. But its you who gets
hit. You *Are* the Union. What weakens the union weakens you.
What strengthens the union strengthens you." The union will also
stress the democratic nature of its organization. A form entitled
"What you should Know about the UAW", states, "All UAW members have their own local unions, elect their own officers, committeemen and stewards, and control their own treasury." It also points
out that "In the UAW before any settlement becomes final, it must
be presented to the full membership for their acceptance or rejection." These statements are true for most unions, and variations appear in their boiler-plate campaign propaganda.

---

2. On occasion, the union will criticize
the company's claim to have conveyed information. "Scattered throughout their
letters to you is the use of the word 'fact'
or 'facts'. Steve's letter of July 25
promises honest and complete answers to
your question. Yet not a single fact is
contained in it. Who is he referring to
where he talks about 'union forced
strike'? Where does he obtain his fact,
not one name, date or location is given?"

The theme of local control is stressed in a variety of ways. Union letters and campaign literature constantly refer to "your union" or "your organizing committee". The word "your" is as common in union material as the adjective "outsider" is in company propaganda. Sometimes the union letters will feature the names of employees favorable to the union with a short statement by each concerning his reasons for joining. The union may use a letter of support from other unionized employees in the area, urging the employees to reject the employer's arguments. A letter used by the ILGWU stated, "We are your neighbors and residents of Kentucky. Most of us have all been through the same unfounded rumors and distortions that our employers put out before we voted yes and got our unions." The union will also point out that the employer has utilized outside help in the form of a lawyer. It might question whether the official who signed the company's letters really wrote them. The union will argue that the employer's willingness to spend this money on lawyers is proof that he fears the power of the union once installed. "Remember, before you cast your ballot that the Teamsters must be good for you or management would not have fought so hard to keep us out of your plant."

Large unions will stress their power. "Local 743 has the full support of the Teamsters Union. The largest and strongest union in the world."

Union support generally decreases during the pre-election campaign. Not infrequently, a union which had a card majority loses an election. Unions are likely to attribute their defeats to the employers' campaign and the fear of reprisal which it was able to engender. Employers, on the other hand, feel that their campaign successes stem from the persuasiveness of their message. They feel that NLRB regulation is already much too pervasive, often holding as improper legitimate employer argument.

QUESTIONS

In reading the material which follows, consider whether any of the campaign excerpts quoted above might violate the Act or otherwise constitute grounds for setting aside an election. Consider also whether the Board's system of regulation is defensible.

D. BOARD REGULATION OF REPRESENTATIONAL ELECTIONS

1. AN OVERVIEW OF BOARD REGULATION

The following is taken from *A Guide To Basic Law and Procedure Under The NLRA*, a Labor Board publication:

Although the Act requires that an employer bargain with the representative selected by its employees, it does not require that the representative be selected by any particular procedure so long as the representative is clearly the choice of a majority of the employees. As one of the methods by which employees can select a bargaining representative the Act provides for the NLRB to conduct representation elections by secret ballot.

The NLRB can conduct such an election only when a petition has been filed requesting one. A petition for certification of representatives can be filed by an employee or a group of employees or any individual or labor organization acting on their behalf, or it can be filed by an employer. If filed by or on behalf of employees, the petition must be supported by a substantial number of employees who wish to be represented for collective bargaining and must state that their employer declines to recognize their representative. If filed by an employer, the petition must allege that one or more individuals or organizations have made a claim for recognition as the exclusive representative of the same group of employees.

The Act also contains a provision whereby employees or someone acting on their behalf can file a petition seeking an election to determine if the employees wish to retain the individual or labor organization currently acting as their bargaining representative, whether the representative has been certified or voluntarily recognized by the employer. This is called a decertification election.

Provision is also made for the Board to determine by secret ballot whether the employees covered by a union-shop agreement desire to withdraw the authority of their representative to continue the agreement. This is called a union-shop deauthorization election and can be brought about by the filing of a petition signed by 30 percent or more of the employees covered by the agreement.

* * *

The same petition form is used for any kind of Board election. When the petition is filed, the NLRB must investigate the petition, hold a hearing if necessary, and direct an election if it finds that a question of representation exists. The purpose of the investigation is to determine, among other things, the following:

1. Whether the Board has jurisdiction to conduct an election.

2. Whether there is a sufficient showing of employee interest to justify an election.

3. Whether a question of representation exists.

4. Whether the election is sought in an appropriate unit of employees.

5. Whether the representative named in the petition is qualified.

6. Whether there are any barriers to an election in the form of existing contracts or prior elections.

The jurisdiction of the NLRB to direct and conduct an election is limited to those enterprises that affect commerce.   *   *   *

Regarding the showing of interest, it is the policy to require that a petitioner requesting an election for either certification of representatives or decertification show that at least 30 percent of the employees favor an election. The Act also requires that a petition for a union-shop deauthorization election be filed by 30 percent or more of the employees in the unit covered by the agreement for the NLRB to conduct an election for that purpose. The showing of interest must be exclusively by employees who are in the appropriate bargaining unit in which an election is sought.

Section 9(c)(1) authorizes the NLRB to direct an election and certify the results thereof, provided the record shows that a question of representation exists. Petitions for certification of representatives present a question of representation if, among other things, they are based on a demand for recognition by the employee representative and a denial of recognition by the employer. The demand for recognition need not be made in any particular form; in fact, the filing of a petition by the representative itself is considered to be a demand for recognition. The NLRB has held that even a representative that is currently recognized by the employer can file a petition for certification and that such petition presents a question of representation provided the representative has not previously been certified.

A question of representation is also raised by a decertification petition which challenges the representative status of a bargaining agent previously certified or currently recognized by the employer. However, a decertification petition filed by a supervisor does not raise a valid question of representation and must be dismissed.

*   *   *

A unit of employees is a group of two or more employees who share common employment interests and conditions and may reasonably be grouped together for purposes of collective bargaining. The determination of what is an appropriate unit for such purposes is, under the Act, left to the discretion of the NLRB. Section 9(b) states that the Board shall decide in each representation case whether, "in order to assure to employees the fullest freedom in exercising the rights guaranteed by this Act, the unit appropriate for the purposes of collective bargaining shall be the employer unit, craft unit, plant unit, or subdivision thereof."

This broad discretion is, however, limited by several other provisions of the Act. Section 9(b)(1) provides that the Board shall not approve as appropriate a unit that includes both professional and non-professional employees, unless a majority of the professional employees involved vote to be included in the mixed unit.

Section 9(b)(2) provides that the Board shall not hold a proposed craft unit to be inappropriate simply because a different unit was previously approved by the Board, unless a majority of the employees in the proposed craft unit vote against being represented separately.

Section 9(b)(3) prohibits the Board from including plant guards in the same unit with other employees. It also prohibits the Board from certifying a labor organization as the representative of a plant guard unit if the labor organization has members who are nonguard employees or if it is "affiliated directly or indirectly" with an organization that has members who are nonguard employees.

Generally, the appropriateness of a bargaining unit is determined on the basis of the common employment interests of the employees involved. Those who have the same or substantially similar interests concerning wages, hours, and working conditions are grouped together in a bargaining unit. In determining whether a proposed unit is appropriate, the following factors are also considered:

1. Any history of collective bargaining.

2. The desires of the employees concerned.

3. The extent to which the employees are organized. Section 9(c) (5) forbids the Board from giving this factor controlling weight.

Section 2(4) of the Act provides that the employee representative for collective bargaining can be "any individual or labor organization." A supervisor or any other management representative may not be an employee representative. It is NLRB policy to direct an election and to issue a certification unless the proposed bargaining agent fails to qualify as a bona fide representative of the employees. In determining a union's qualifications as bargaining agent, it is the union's willingness to represent the employees rather than its constitution and bylaws that is the controlling factor. The NLRB's power to certify a labor organization as bargaining representative is limited by Section 9(b)(3) which prohibits certification of a union as the representative of a unit of plant guards if the union "admits to membership, or is affiliated directly or indirectly with an organization which admits to membership, employees other than guards."

The NLRB has established the policy of not directing an election among employees presently covered by a valid collective-bargaining agreement except in accordance with certain rules. These rules, followed in determining whether or not an existing collective-bargaining contract will bar an election, are called the NLRB contract-bar rules.

Not every contract will bar an election. Examples of contracts that would *not* bar an election are:

- The contract is not in writing, or is not signed.
- The contract has not been ratified by the members of the union, if such is expressly required.
- The contract does not contain substantial terms or conditions of employment sufficient to stabilize the bargaining relationship.
- The contract can be terminated by either party at any time for any reason.
- The contract contains a clearly illegal union-security clause.
- The bargaining unit is not appropriate.
- The union that entered the contract with the employer is no longer in existence or is unable or unwilling to represent the employees.
- The contract discriminates between employees on racial grounds.
- The contracting union is involved in a basic internal conflict with resulting unstabilizing confusion about the identity of the union.
- The employer's operations have changed substantially since the contract was executed.

Under the NLRB rules a valid contract for a fixed period of 3 years or less will bar an election for the period covered by the contract. A contract for a fixed period of more than 3 years will bar an election sought by a contracting party during the life of the contract, but will act as a bar to an election sought by an outside party for only 3 years following its effective date. A contract of no fixed period will not act as a bar at all.

If there is no existing contract, a petition can bring about an election if it is filed before the day a contract is signed. If the petition is filed on the same day the contract is signed, the contract bars an election, unless the contract is effective immediately or retroactively and the employee has not been informed at the time of execution that a petition has been filed. Once the contract becomes effective as a bar to an election, no petition will be accepted until near the end of the period during which the contract is effective as a bar. Petitions filed not more than 90 days but over 60 days before the end of the contract-bar period will be accepted and can bring about an election. These time periods for filing petitions involving health care institutions are 120 and 90 days, respectively. Of course, a petition can be filed after the contract expires. However, the last 60 days of the contract-bar period is called an "insulated" period. During this time the parties to the existing contract are free to negotiate a new contract or to agree to extend the old one. If they reach agreement in this period, petitions will not be accepted until 90 days before the end of the new contract-bar period.

In addition to the contract-bar rules, the NLRB has established a rule that when a representative has been certified by the Board, the certification will ordinarily be binding for at least 1 year and a petition filed before the end of the certification year will be dismissed. In cases where the certified representative and the employer enter a valid collective-bargaining contract during the year, the contract becomes controlling, and whether a petition for an election can be filed is determined by the Board's contract-bar rules.

Section 9(c)(3) prohibits the holding of an election in any collective-bargaining unit or subdivision thereof in which a valid election has been held during the preceding 12-month period. A new election may be held, however, in a larger unit, but not in the same unit or subdivision in which the previous election was held. For example, if all of the production and maintenance employees in Company A, including draftsmen in the company engineering office, are included in a collective-bargaining unit, an election among all the employees in the unit would bar another election among all the employees in the unit for 12 months. Similarly, an election among the draftsmen only would bar another election among the draftsmen for 12 months. However, an election among the draftsmen would not bar a later election during the 12-month period among all the production and maintenance employees including the draftsmen.

It is the Board's interpretation that Section 9(c)(3) prohibits only the holding of an election during the 12-month period, but does not prohibit the filing of a petition. Accordingly, the NLRB will accept a petition filed not more than 60 days before the end of the 12-month period. The election cannot be held, of course, until after the 12-month period. If an election is held and a representative certified, that certification is binding for 1 year and a petition for another election in the same unit will be dismissed if it is filed during the 1-year period after the certification. If an election is held and no representative is certified, the election bars another election for 12 months. A petition for another election in the same unit can be filed not more than 60 days before the end of the 12-month period and the election can be held after the 12-month period expires.

Section 9(c)(1) provides that if a question of representation exists, the NLRB must make its determination by means of a secret ballot election. In a representation election employees are given a choice of one or more bargaining representatives or no representative at all. To be certified as the bargaining representative, an individual or a labor organization must receive a majority of the valid votes cast.

An election may be held by agreement between the employer and the individual or labor organization claiming to represent the employees. In such an agreement the parties would state the time and place agreed on, the choices to be included on the ballot, and a method to determine who is eligible to vote. They would also authorize the NLRB Regional Director to conduct the election.

If the parties are unable to reach an agreement, the Act authorizes the NLRB to order an election after a hearing. The Act also authorizes the Board to delegate to its Regional Directors the determination on matters concerning elections. Under this delegation of authority the Regional Directors can determine the appropriateness of the unit, direct an election, and certify the outcome. Upon the request of an interested party, the Board may review the action of a Regional Director, but such review does not stop the election process unless the Board so orders. The election details are left to the Regional Director. Such matters as who may vote, when the election will be held, and what standards of conduct will be imposed on the parties are decided in accordance with the Board's rules and its decisions.

To be entitled to vote, an employee must have worked in the unit during the eligibility period set by the Board and must be employed in the unit on the date of the election. Generally, the eligibility period is the employer's payroll period just before the date on which the election was directed. This requirement does not apply, however, to employees who are ill, on vacation, or temporarily laid off, or to employees in military service who appear in person at the polls. The NLRB rules take into consideration the fact that employment is typically irregular in certain industries. In such industries eligibility to vote is determined according to formulas designed to permit all employees who have a substantial continuing interest in their employment conditions to vote.

* * *

Ordinarily, elections are held within 30 days after they are directed. Seasonal drops in employment or any change in operations which would prevent a normal work force from being present may cause a different election date to be set. Normally an election will not be conducted when unfair labor practice charges have been filed based upon conduct of a nature which would have a tendency to interfere with the free choice of the employees in an election, except that, in certain cases, the Board may proceed to the election if the charging party so requests.

NLRB elections are conducted in accordance with strict standards designed to give the employee-voters an opportunity to freely indicate whether they wish to be represented for purposes of collective bargaining. Election details, such as time, place, and notice of an election, are left largely to the Regional Director who usually obtains the agreement of the parties on these matters. Any party to an election who believes that the Board election standards were not met may, within 5 days after the tally of ballots has been furnished, file objections to the election with the Regional Director under whose supervision the election was held. The Regional Director's rulings on these objections may be appealed to the Board for decision except in the case of elections that are held by consent of the parties, in which case the Regional Director's rulings are final.

An election will be set aside if it was accompanied by conduct that the NLRB considers created an atmosphere of confusion or fear of reprisals and thus interfered with the employees' freedom of choice.

In any particular case the NLRB does not attempt to determine whether the conduct actually interfered with the employees' expression of free choice, but rather asks whether the conduct tended to do so. If it is reasonable to believe that the conduct would tend to interfere with the free expression of the employees' choice, the election may be set aside. Examples of conduct the Board considers to interfere with employee free choice are:

- Threats of loss of jobs or benefits by an employer or a union to influence the votes or union activities of employees.

- Misstatements of important facts in the election campaign by an employer or a union where the other party does not have a fair chance to reply.

- An employer firing employees to discourage or encourage their union activities or a union causing an employer to take such action.

- An employer or a union making campaign speeches to assembled groups of employees on company time within the 24-hour period before the election.

- The incitement of racial or religious prejudice by inflammatory campaign appeals made by either an employer or a union.

- Threats or the use of physical force or violence against employees by an employer or a union to influence their votes.

- The occurrence of extensive violence or trouble or widespread fear of job losses which prevents the holding of a fair election, whether or not caused by an employer or a union.

2. DETERMINATION OF THE APPROPRIATE BARGAINING UNIT

Employers and unions spend a great deal of time and money litigating over what constitutes an appropriate bargaining unit. They do so because the scope of the bargaining unit will often determine whether a union can organize employees and with what economic power the union can come to the collective bargaining negotiations. To understand how the bargaining unit can be so important consider the potential bargaining unit configurations at the hypothetical KLD Company.

KLD is a manufacturing concern which employs 35 skilled tool-and-die makers, 40 unskilled press machine operators, and 80 part-time students who perform a wide range of simple tasks. KLD is located in a rural area with a large supply of unskilled workers and students but with very few skilled tool-and-die makers other than those KLD already employs.

Assume that two unions would like to represent KLD's employees. Union A which primarily represents skilled craftsmen is favored by the tool-and-die makers. Union B which has a reputation for representing unskilled workers is favored by the press machine operators. The students do not want to be represented by a union because they fear that KLD will reduce their working hours if confronted with the need to pay union scale wages and benefits. Each group is unanimous in its preferences.

The way the bargaining unit is defined will determine which if either union will be able to muster the majority vote from employees necessary to compel the employer to bargain with it. If it is decided that all the employees together constitute one appropriate unit, there will be no union representation in the plant because the part-time students who are opposed to unionization will have an absolute majority. If it is decided that all full-time employees constitute the appropriate unit, union B will be victorious because there are more press operators than tool-and-die makers. If it is determined that each group alone constitutes an appropriate bargaining unit, then union A will be chosen to represent the pressmen.

Which of these alternative units is determined as appropriate is of great interest to KLD as well as to the employees. If the appropriate unit is deemed to be one including all employees, KLD will not be required to deal with any union, an outcome KLD would greatly prefer. If this is not possible, KLD will much prefer union B because it will have a majority composed of unskilled workers who may be afraid to strike because they can be so easily replaced.

KLD does not want to have to negotiate with union A because of the leverage the tool-and-die makers would have in negotiations. If the tool-and-die makers went on strike KLD would have to close down. Union A might thus demand much more for tool-and-die makers than union B, which is more concerned with the unskilled workers.

While greatly oversimplified, this hypothetical situation illustrates the important stake that various parties have in the determination of the appropriate bargaining unit. Realizing the significance of bargaining unit decisions, Congress delegated to the NLRB in the Taft-Hartley Act the duty to determine the appropriate bargaining unit in a manner consistent with the Act's purpose of " *   *   * protecting the exercise by workers of full freedom of association, self-organization, and designation of representatives of their own choosing. *   *   * "

Congress provided little in the way of guidelines to assist the NLRB in carrying out this responsibility. The U. S. Supreme Court interpreted Congress' action as giving the NLRB broad discretion in developing a policy for unit determinations. The Court has, however, cautioned the NLRB that "wide variations in the forms of employee self-organization and the complexities of modern industrial organization make difficult the use of inflexible rules as the test of an appropriate unit." [3]

Finding that it has indeed been faced with an infinite variety of situations in which it must determine the appropriate bargaining unit,

3. N.L.R.B. v. Hearst Publications, 322 U.S. 111, 134, 64 S.Ct. 851, 862, 88 L.Ed. 1170 (1944).

the NLRB has heeded the Supreme Court's advice and has refrained from establishing any hard and fast rules. The NLRB has instead delineated a number of factors which it will examine in every case as a means of insuring consistent decision-making. The Board will consider:

1. the similarity in skills, interests, duties and working conditions;

2. the nature of the employer's organization to:

   a. functional integration of tasks

   b. commonality of supervision

   c. interchange among employees

   d. physical proximity among the employees;

3. employees' desires;

4. bargaining history; and

5. the extent of union organization among employees.

The intent of this "factor analysis" is to insure that the bargaining unit deemed to be appropriate is one marked by "that community of interest among the employees which is likely to further harmonious organization and facilitate collective bargaining." [4]

The NLRB is called upon to perform this analysis in a number of different procedural settings:

1. initial organization—where there is no history of employee organization for the purpose of collective bargaining (the situation referred to in the KLD Company illustration above);

2. severance—where a group of employees wishes to split off from an existing bargaining unit to negotiate separately;

3. unit clarification—where uncertainty exists concerning the proper scope of an existing unit;

4. unit modification—where changed circumstances require a reconsideration of the boundaries of an existing unit; and

5. accretion—where distinct groups of employees wish to merge into a single large grouping for the purpose of collective bargaining.

The need to clarify, modify or accrete to existing bargaining units usually arises when a company reorganizes its workforce, adding or changing job classification; relocates certain of its production facilities; and merges with or acquires other enterprises. In these cases the Board will engage in its factor analysis to determine if "substantial changes" have occurred in the community of interests among employees.

The NLRB has decided to supplement its community of interest analysis with more concrete guidelines for cases in which skilled craftsmen wish to remove themselves from larger groupings in favor of their own unit. These guidelines constitute what is known as the

4.   3 N.L.R.B. Ann.Rep. 174 (1938).

NLRB's "Mallinckrodt doctrine".[5] Mallinckrodt delineates relevant "areas of inquiry" that the NLRB must examine before rendering its decision. These are:

> 1.   Whether or not the proposed unit consists of a distinct and homogeneous group of skilled journeymen craftsmen performing the functions of their craft on a nonrepetitive basis, or of employ-ces constituting a functionally distinct department, working in trades or occupations for which a tradition of separate representation exists.

> 2.   The history of collective bargaining of the employees sought at the plant involved, and at other plants of the employer, with emphasis on whether the existing patterns and bargaining are productive of stability in labor relations, and whether such sta-bility will be unduly disrupted by the destruction of the existing patterns of representation.

> 3.   The extent to which the employees in the proposed unit have established and maintained their separate identity during the period of inclusion in a broader unit, and the extent of their partic-ipation or lack of participation in the establishment and mainte-nance of the existing pattern of representation and the prior opportunities, if any, afforded them to obtain separate representa-tion.

> 4.   The history and pattern of collective bargaining in the in-dustry involved.

> 5.   The degree of integration of the employer's production processes, including the extent to which the continued normal op-eration of the production processes is dependent upon the per-formance of the assigned functions of the employees in the pro-posed unit.

> 6.   The qualifications of the union seeking to "carve out" a separate unit, including that union's experience in representing employees like those involved in the severance action.

The "community of interests" analysis does not apply to all em-ployee classifications. Congressional action and NLRB and Court de-cisions have established special analyses to be applied to certain em-ployee classifications.

In the Taft-Hartley Act, Congress developed special rules to deal with situations involving professional employees and guards, and ex-cluded supervisory employees from the Act's protections. Section 9(b) of the NLRA provides that "the Board shall not * * * decide that any unit is appropriate * * * if said unit includes both pro-fessional employees and employees who are not professional employ-ees unless a majority of such professional employees vote for inclu-sion in such a unit * * * "

The NLRB has interpreted section 9(b) as restricting its discretion only with respect to units containing professionals and nonprofession-

---

als, and has remained unrestricted in its determinations as to the appropriateness of units containing one or more professional groups. Section 2(12) of the Act defines "professional employee", and it is the NLRB's interpretation of this section of the Act which determines who is a professional employee for the purposes of this restriction.

In section 9(b)(3) of the NLRA, Congress imposed even greater restrictions upon the representation of guards. Guards are not to be included in a unit including other employees. Further, and more restrictive, a union may not be certified to represent guards if its membership is open to employees other than guards, or if it is affiliated with a labor organization that represents non-guards. This restriction precludes separate guard locals in large unions, thereby forcing guards to be represented by unaffiliated unions established solely for the purpose of representing guards. Section 9(b)(3) defines those to whom this restriction applies as "any individual employed as a guard to enforce against employees and other persons rules to protect property of the employer and protect the safety of persons on the employer's premises".

The NLRB's exclusion of supervisory employees from the Act's protection (the effect of which is to give supervisor unions no legal recourse to compel an employer to bargain with them) created for the NLRB the problem of determining who is a "supervisor". Congress addressed this problem by defining supervisor in section 2(11) of the Act. This definition outlines thirteen specific tasks that make an "employee" a "supervisor" and thus outside the purview of the Act. The statute states:

> The term "supervisor" means any individual having authority, in the interest of the employer, to hire, transfer, suspend, lay off, recall, promote, discharge, assign, reward, or discipline other employees, or responsibly to direct them, or to adjust their grievances, or effectively to recommend such action, if in connection with the foregoing the exercise of such authority is not of a merely routine or clerical nature, but requires the use of independent judgment.

Although helpful, this definition has not completely eradicated NLRB difficulties in labeling certain employees as supervisors. There may exist an infinite number of gradations of authority in any given industrial setting and the NLRB must be careful not to construe the term supervisor too broadly, because the employee who is deemed a supervisor is denied the protection of concerted activity that the Act was designed to administer. The Board has developed "secondary indicia" to aid in determining supervisory status. These include whether the individual attends management meetings, receives a higher salary than his co-workers, and is considered to be a supervisor by other employees.

The NLRB itself has developed special principles to be applied to confidential and clerical employees. The NLRB's longstanding policy has been that "confidential employees" should be excluded from bargaining units composed of rank-and-file employees so that management is not required to handle their labor relations matters through members of the unions with which the employer must deal. The NLRB has defined "confidential employees" to include those who, in the regular course of their duties, assist and act in a confidential capacity to persons who exercise managerial functions only in the field of labor relations.

The NLRB distinguishes between "office clerical" and "plant clerical" employees, finding the former to be white collar office workers who may not be included in a production and maintenance unit. The NLRB has developed certain relevant factors to distinguish between the two groups. For example, plant clericals are those whose work is closely related to production operation, are located in the plant, have common supervision and interchange with production employees, and work under the same conditions as production employees.

The Supreme Court has mandated that managerial employees be excluded from the Act's protection. As a result the NLRB has had to develop a standard for determining who is a managerial employee.

After much deliberation, the NLRB has established a policy whereby it will weigh the facts "to determine whether or not the persons at issue are involved in the formulation, determination, and effectuation of management policies by expressing and making operative the decisions of their employer, and whether they have discretion in the performance of their job duties independent of their employer's established policies." [6]

This standard has not always proven easy to apply. A controversy over who is a managerial employee currently exists over the status of faculty members at private colleges and universities. The NLRB has repeatedly found that professors may organize and are neither managerial nor supervisory employees excluded from the protection of the Act. The Circuit Courts have rejected the NLRB's position. In 1980 the Supreme Court found, in N.L.R.B. v. Yeshiva University,[7] that full-time faculty members who develop and enforce employer policy are managerial employees within the meaning of the Act. Depending upon how it is interpreted, the *Yeshiva* decision may have profound consequences on NLRB policy concerning who should be excluded from the Act's protection as a managerial employee.

Another area of conflict has arisen from the 1974 Amendments to the NLRA which have eliminated the section 2(2) exclusion of employees of non-profit hospitals from the protection offered by the Act. Congress accompanied this amendment with a committee statement that "[D]ue consideration should be given by the Board to preventing proliferation of bargaining units in the health care industry." The NLRB has struggled to reconcile this congressional concern with unit proliferation with its own traditional community of interests analysis. While claiming to adhere to its traditional analysis, the NLRB has taken the congressional admonition seriously and has attempted to

6. Simplex Industries, 243 N.L.R.B. No. 13 (sl.op. p. 3) (1974).

7. N.L.R.B. v. Yeshiva University, 444 U.S. 672, 100 S.Ct. 856, 63 L.Ed.2d 115 (1980).

mold bargaining units into one of six categories; these being: physicians, nurses, all other professional employees, technical employees including LPNs, office clerical employees, and service and maintenance employees.

As this discussion illustrates, determining an appropriate bargaining unit is not an easy task. "The absence of congressional guidance, the broad discretion granted the Board by the courts, and the conflicting interests of the parties combine to confront the NLRB with a most difficult and sensitive task." [8] The NLRB's decision to proceed on a flexible case-by-case basis and the resulting difficulties the parties have in predicting the outcome of an NLRB hearing on their dispute have helped cause unit determinations to be a heavily litigated and controversial area of NLRB jurisdiction.

The following regional level decision of the Board illustrates how the Board's approach to unit determination must be flexible to take into account novel forms of labor relations.

K. B. SPECIALTY FOODS CO., EMPLOYER, AND UNITED FOOD & COMMERCIAL WORKERS, LOCAL NO. 610, PETITIONER

Before the National Labor Relations Board, Region 25 (October 13, 1981).
Case No. 25–RC–7739.

WILLIAM T. LITTLE, Regional Director

The Employer,[3] contrary to the Petitioner, urges that a unit composed exclusively of maintenance employees is not appropriate for the purpose of collective bargaining. The plant involved herein began operations in January 1974 with approximately sixty employees. Since that time it has increased its workforce to include ninety-eight employees in the warehouse area, about forty-nine employees in the production area and three lab employees. Additionally, there are seven employees in the maintenance classification, whose function is to repair and maintain chopping, dicing, cooking and packaging equipment used in the Employer's food production processing. In this capacity, it is found their maintenance work is routine and repetitive and intimately related to production. There is no history of collective bargaining at the Greensburg, Indiana plant.

The record reveals that the Employer operates the plant under what it denominates as a "team concept." Beginning on or about August 1, 1981, the Employer assigned its maintenance employees to teams composed of either production or warehouse employees. Two maintenance employees were assigned to each of two production teams, while one maintenance employee was assigned to each of the three warehouse teams. Maintenance employees are accountable to

---

8. Abodeely, R. Hammer & A. Sandler, The NLRB and the Appropriate Bargaining Unit 8 (1981).

3. The Employer, a division of the Kroger Co., an Ohio Corporation, with principal offices in Cincinnati, Ohio and the facility herein located at Greensburg, Indiana is engaged in the production and distribution of food products to the various retail outlets of the Employer.

the coordinator (supervisor) over each team. Prior to this change, the maintenance employees reported directly to the maintenance coordinator (supervisor), who is responsible for the coordination of the repair schedules of all outside contractors, ordering repair and replacement parts, and the scheduling of the major maintenance work. Since on or about the August 1 change, he no longer supervises the maintenance employees, but does on occasion counsel the other team coordinators about their maintenance work problems. Major maintenance work on electrical and refrigeration systems, lift trucks and other equipment has been and is presently being performed by outside contractors.

There are no specific educational requirements for an individual to become or remain in the maintenance classification. The Employer does not have a maintenance apprenticeship program. Although some maintenance training has been provided to employees in the maintenance classification, such training has required as little as two hours in its plant, to as much as a single 40 hour course away from the plant. Of the seven employees presently in the maintenance classification all but two were transfers from other production jobs. Moreover, one employee was transferred from maintenance to production while she was in training to become a production coordinator (supervisor). Additionally, all employees receive the same fringe benefits and are subject to the same three step pay scale system which it labels as pay groups I, II and III (group III being the highest paid class). The Class "A" mechanics, which are the highest paid classification of maintenance employees, share the "group III" pay level with laboratory technicians and coordinator (supervisory) trainees. However, "class B mechanics" are in the group II pay rates, along with half of the various other production classifications.

The duties performed by the maintenance employees include changing, greasing and repairing the "dicing" mechanisms, repairing overhead doors and walkways and changing light bulbs. Additionally, maintenance employees have performed certain undefined work on "hydraulics", tuning up and "trouble shooting" such equipment as the "Bobcat" loader, cleaning of the boiler and scheduled lubrication of machinery. Sometime about August 1, 1981, the maintenance employees also installed a garbage disposal and a water softener. There is a maintenance room where maintenance employees store some of their tools and on unspecified occasions perform work. Although no exact percentages were given, the record reveals that the maintenance employees spend the greatest majority of their time performing their assignments in the production or warehouse area.

The Petitioner, contrary to the Employer, argues that the maintenance employees possess interests sufficiently separate from those of the production and warehouse employees because of the following alleged facts: (1) they were selected for their jobs because of their specialized knowledge and experience; (2) the Employer has equipped them with special skills and has encouraged them to take special courses; (3) they perform "major repair" work on machinery and install industrial equipment; (4) the maintenance coordinator continues to impart advice to them; and (5) there is no history of collective bargaining. Additionally, the Petitioner also asserts that the restructuring of maintenance employees' duties and supervision, effective about August 1, 1981 coincided with the Petitioner's organizational effort. However, it proffered insufficient proof as to the latter conclusion on items 1 through 4, supra. Additionally, anent Item (1) and (2) there was no showing that any maintenance employees, save one, had any formal training that would qualify him/her to perform complex maintenance work and the training which the Employer has provided to the maintenance employees was limited to preparing employees to handle the routine problems of maintaining machinery peculiar to the Employer. With regard to Item (3), there is insufficient evidence indicating that any major maintenance operations have been undertaken by maintenance employees since the restructuring of their duties on or about August 1, 1981. As to Item (4), there was no showing that the maintenance coordinator retained supervisory authority over the maintenance employees after the August 1 date.

Additionally, there is nothing in the record which demonstrates that the maintenance employees had attained the level of skill, or are performing the type of work, which the Board would find supportive of a true craft unit. Furthermore, it is clear that the absence of a collective bargaining history is not sufficient to justify the Petitioner carving out an inappropriate unit. Timber Products Co., 164 N.L.R.B. 1060 and see Mallinckrodt Chemical Works, 162 N.L.R.B. 387. The record further reveals that maintenance employees work on a daily basis with production employees, share common fringe benefits and supervision with them; spend a clear majority of their working time on the production floor and form an integral part of its production process. Although the Employer encourages maintenance employees to acquire skills on their own time, there is no obligation for them to do so. No apprentice system impedes attainment of a maintenance position. On occasion maintenance and production employees are called upon to perform some of the more routine maintenance chores and upon some occasions maintenance employees are called upon to perform production chores. Additionally, the majority of maintenance employees' work time is spent in the production-warehouse areas performing what can be fairly characterized as routine maintenance work on the Employer's production and warehouse equipment.

Accordingly, based upon the foregoing, it can be fairly said that maintenance employees do not possess a community of interest sufficiently separate from production and warehouse employees to justify their separation from them for the purpose of collective bargaining. Beecham, Inc., 251 N.L.R.B. 731; Peterson/Puritan, Inc., 240 N.L.R.B. 1051; F & M Schaefer Brewing Co., 198 N.L.R.B. 323; Timber Products Co., supra. Inasmuch as the Petitioner has not demonstrated a sufficient showing of interest in a unit composed of the Employer's production, maintenance and warehouse employees, the petition is hereby dismissed.

3. BOARD REGULATION OF CAMPAIGN CONDUCT

(a) THE CONCEPT OF "LABORATORY CONDITIONS"

NLRB REGULATION OF CAMPAIGN TACTICS: THE BEHAVIORAL ASSUMPTIONS ON WHICH THE BOARD REGULATES *

The Board has developed an elaborate system of rules to govern campaign tactics:

* * *

The Board has said that in election proceedings it seeks to provide a laboratory in which an experiment may be conducted, under conditions as nearly ideal as possible, to determine the uninhibited desires of the employees. [General Shoe Corp., 77 N.L.R.B. 124, 127.] Where for any reason the standard falls too low the Board will set aside the election and direct a new one. Unsatisfactory conditions for holding elections may be created by promises of benefits [International Shoe Co., 123 N.L.R.B. 682], threats of economic reprisals [L. C. Ferguson and E. F. Seggern, d/b/a Shovel Supply Co., 121 N.L.R.B. 1485], deliberate misrepresentations of facts by an employer [United States Gypsum Co., 130 N.L.R.B. 901] or a union [The Gummed Products Co., 112 N.L.R.B. 1092], deceptive campaign tactics by a union [Heintz Division, Kelsey-Hayes Co., 126 N.L.R.B. 151], or by a general atmosphere of fear and confusion caused by a participant or by members of the general public [P. D. Gwaltney & Co., 71 N.L.R.B. 371].

The Board enforces its rules relating to campaign conduct in two ways. The losing party may file objections to conduct allegedly affecting the outcome of the election; if the Board finds such objections valid, it will set aside the election and order a new one. Alternatively, the loser may file an unfair labor practice charge, alleging that the winning party has interfered with the right of employees to "bargain collectively through representatives of their own choosing." Interference with this right constitutes an unfair labor practice which the Board is empowered to remedy by ordering the offending party, employer or union, to cease the forbidden practice. The Board also possesses the power, if it deems the interference with employee choice sufficiently serious, to order an offending employer to recognize the union as the representative of his employees and bargain with it even though the union lost the election.

* Getman, Goldberg and Herman, "National Labor Relations Board Regulation of Campaign Tactics: The Behavioral Assumptions On Which The Board Regulates," 27 Stanford Law Review 1465 (1975); © 1975 by the Board of Trustees of the Leland Stanford, Jr. University. Reprinted by permission of the publisher and Fred B. Rothman & Co.

An unfair labor practice almost always will constitute grounds for setting aside the election. In addition, "[c]onduct that creates an atmosphere which renders improbable a free choice will sometimes warrant invalidating an election, even though that conduct may not constitute an unfair labor practice." Tactics which fall into this category include those which are thought to impede a reasoned choice, such as misrepresentations of fact or law or appeals to racial prejudice. The Board thus possesses the power, either through objections proceedings or unfair labor practice proceedings, to regulate a broad spectrum of pre-election conduct.

The Board has frequently stated that its objective in regulating the pre-election campaign is to protect employee freedom of choice. By "freedom of choice" the Board means the opportunity of exercising a "reasoned, untrammeled choice" for or against union representation. * * * [T]he Board * * *, seeks to encourage, a model of employee voting behavior similar to that once thought to prevail in political elections; in theory, the political voter attends to the issues and candidates and decides how to vote by weighing the campaign information in light of his own and the country's best interests.

While a campaign preceding a political election is generally free of restrictions on campaign tactics, the Board, explicitly rejecting this aspect of the political analogy, has opted for stringent regulation of campaign conduct. The decision to regulate closely was a natural outgrowth of the historical circumstances and economic philosophy which led to passage of the National Labor Relations Act. The decades preceding passage of the Act were marked by stormy efforts to organize employees in major industries. Employers often sought to defeat unionization by capitalizing on their economic power over employees. The techniques employed included mass discharges, yellow dog contracts, and company unions. In response to the use of such tactics, the framers of the Act, who sought to "encourage by developing the procedure of collective bargaining, * * * equality of bargaining power," established unfair labor practice procedures. They hoped thereby to overcome "the relative weakness of the isolated wage earner." In this context it was probably inevitable that the Board would reject the model of unregulated political elections and seek to prevent employers from relying upon the threat or use of economic power to influence employee voting decisions.

* * * The Board has used the metaphor of "laboratory conditions" to describe the atmosphere necessary for a fair union representation election. The comparison with a laboratory suggests that an atmosphere of pristine calm and purity is both attainable and necessary to determine the uninhibited desires of the employees. * * *

Thus, the Board has adopted a model of employee voting behavior adapted from the political ideal, while at the same time assuming that this model can be realized in union representation elections only with governmental protection.

(b) Access To Employees

The self-organizational rights of employees came into conflict with the property and managerial rights of an employer when union organizational activity is attempted on company property. The Board has sought to insure that the union has an adequate opportunity to reach employees with its campaign. It was settled quite early in the administration of the National Labor Relations Act that an adequate union opportunity requires that employees be free to solicit on behalf of the union during nonwork time on company premises. An employer violates § 8(a)(1) when it prohibits solicitation by employees during their free time in nonworking areas. The rationale for this rule is that solicitation of this sort does not interfere with production and discipline, and the employee is already on the employer's premises.

An employer's rule prohibiting employee solicitation in the work place during nonwork time is presumed invalid, unless the employer can show that special circumstances exist to warrant the rule. The Board has found special circumstances warranting an employer's no-solicitation rule in work areas during free time in cases involving retail establishments and restaurants, where the public is present and solicitation would thus interfere with the employer's business.

An employer's rule prohibiting employee solicitation in the work place during work time is presumed valid, unless the rule is enforced discriminatorily in violation of § 8(a)(3). An example of discriminatory enforcement would be where two unions attempt to organize an employer's workers, and the employer applies its rule to only one.

An employer is allowed to make a different rule with regard to distribution of union literature. Distribution differs from solicitation, which refers generally to oral communication, but also includes the handing out of authorization cards. Distribution of written material may be limited both to the employees nonworking time and to nonwork areas.

The thrust of the Board's approach to an employer's solicitation and distribution rules as applied to employees is to balance the employer's property and managerial interests against the § 7 organizational rights of employees. The burden is on the employer to justify its rule. In the following case, note the balancing of employer managerial rights and protected employee organizational solicitation and distribution.

BETH ISRAEL HOSPITAL v. N.L.R.B.

Supreme Court of the United States, 1978.
437 U.S. 483, 98 S.Ct. 2463, 57 L.Ed.2d 370.

Mr. Justice Brennan delivered the opinion of the Court.

[The petitioner is a nonprofit hospital covered under the 1974 amendments to the National Labor Relations Act. In 1970, before the advent of the Union, the Hospital announced a rule barring solicitation and distribution of literature in any area to which patients and visitors have access; these activities were to be permitted only in certain employee locker rooms and adjacent restrooms. In 1975, the Hospital's rule was formulated explicitly to ban employee solicitation or distribution in "patient-care and all other work areas, and areas open to the public such as lobbies, cafeteria and coffee shop, corridors, elevators, gift shop, etc." In October 1975, an employee distributed the Union newsletter in the Hospital cafeteria, approaching only persons she believed to be employees. The newsletter, among other things, disparaged the Hospital's ability to provide adequate patient care, primarily because of understaffing. The Hospital's general director observed her engaged in such distribution and ordered her to stop; she was also given a written notice warning her that further violation of the Hospital rule would result in her dismissal.

Upon unfair labor practice charges filed by the Union, the Board found the issuance and maintenance of the Hospital's rule to violate Section 8(a)(1), and the discipline of the employee to violate Section 8(a)(3). It ordered, among other things, that the Hospital rescind its rule barring union solicitation and distribution in its cafeteria and coffee shop. The court of appeals enforced.]

I

A

Although petitioner employs approximately 2,200 regular employees, only a fraction of them have access to many of the areas in which solicitation is permitted. Solicitation and distribution are not permitted in all locker areas. Rather, of the total number of locker areas only six separate and scattered locker areas containing 613 lockers are accessible to all employees for these purposes. Moreover, most of these rooms are divided and restricted on the basis of sex, and in any event are not generally used even by petitioner to communicate messages to employees. The cafeteria, on the other hand, is a common gathering room for employees. A 3-day survey conducted by petitioner revealed that 77% of the cafeteria's patrons were employees while only 9% were visitors and 1.56% patients. The cafeteria is also equipped with vending machines used by employees for snacks during coffee breaks and other nonworking time.

Petitioner has itself recognized that the cafeteria is a natural gathering place for employees on nonworking time, for it has used and permitted use of the cafeteria for solicitation and distribution to employees for purposes other than union activity. For example, petitioner maintains an official bulletin board in the cafeteria for communicating certain messages to employees. On occasion it has set up special tables in or near the cafeteria entrance to aid solicitation of contributions for the United Way or United Fund charities, the Jewish Philanthropies Organization Drive, the Israel Emergency Fund, and to recruit members for the credit union. * * *

"[T]here are relatively few places where employees can congregate or meet on hospital grounds or in the nearby vicinity for the purpose of discussing nonwork related matters other than in the cafeteria; secondly, the area in the neighborhood of the hospital is congested and provides no ready access to employees"; 223 N.L.R.B. 1198 (opinion of administrative law judge). Petitioner, moreover, has adopted the policy of refusing to make available to unions the names and addresses of employees unless ordered to do so by the Board. App. 33. Petitioner has also made antiunion statements in a newsletter distributed to employees with their paychecks at their work stations.   *   *   *

II

*   *   *   In a unanimous opinion, in St. John's Hospital & School of Nursing, Inc., 222 N.L.R.B. 1150 (1976), the Board concluded that the special characteristics of hospitals justify a rule different from that which the Board generally applies to other employers. On the basis of evidence and aided by the briefs *amici curiae* filed by the American Hospital Association and District 1199 of the National Union of Hospital and Health Care Employees, the Board found:

> That the primary function of a hospital is patient care and that a tranquil atmosphere is essential to the carrying out of that function. In order to provide this atmosphere, hospitals may be justified in imposing somewhat more stringent prohibitions than are generally permitted. *For example* a hospital may be warranted in prohibiting solicitation even on nonworking time in strictly patient care areas, such as the patients' rooms, operating rooms, and places where patients receive treatment, such as x-ray and therapy areas. Solicitation at any time in those areas might be unsettling to the patients—particularly those who are seriously ill and thus need quiet and peace of mind." Ibid. (emphasis added).

The Board concluded that prohibiting solicitation in such situations was justified and required striking the balance against employees' interests in organizational activity. The Board determined, however, that the balance should be struck against the prohibition in areas other than immediate patient care areas such as lounges and cafeterias absent a showing that disruption to patient care would necessarily result if solicitation and distribution were permitted in those areas. The Board concluded, on a record devoid of evidence which contradicted that assessment, that the possibility of disruption to patient care in those areas must be deemed remote.

*   *   *

D

Petitioner's argument that it is irrational to hold, as the Board has, on the one hand, that a rule prohibiting solicitation in the dining area of a public restaurant is lawful because solicitation has the tendency to upset patrons, while one prohibiting like activity in a hospital's cafeteria is unlawful absent evidence that nonemployee-patrons would be upset, on the other, has only superficial appeal. That argument wholly fails to consider that the Board concluded that these rules struck the appropriate *balance* between organizational and employer rights in the particular industry to which each is applicable. In the retail marketing and restaurant industries, the primary purpose of the operation is to serve customers, and this is done on the selling floor of a store or in the dining area of a restaurant. Employee solicitation in these areas, if disruptive, necessarily would directly and substantially interfere with the employer's business. On the other hand, it would be an unusual store or restaurant which did not have stockrooms, kitchens and other nonpublic areas, and in those areas employee solicitation of nonworking employees must be permitted. In that context, the Board concluded that, on balance, employees' organizational interests do not outweigh the employer's interests in prohibiting solicitation on the selling floor.

In the hospital context the situation is quite different. The main function of the hospital is patient care and therapy and those functions are largely performed in areas such as operating rooms, patients' rooms, and patients' lounges. The Board does not prohibit rules forbidding organizational activity in these areas. On the other hand, a hospital cafeteria, 77% of whose patrons are employees, and which is a natural gathering place for employees, functions more as an employee service area than a patient care area. While it is true that the fact of access by visitors and patients renders the analogy to areas such as stockrooms in retail operations less than complete, it cannot be said that when the primary function and use of the cafeteria, the availability of alternative areas of the facility in which § 7 rights effectively could be exercised, and the remoteness of interference with patient care are considered, it was irrational to strike the balance in favor of § 7 rights in the hospital cafeteria and against them in public restaurants. The Board's explanation of the consistent principle underlying the different results in each situation cannot fairly be challenged. St John's Hospital & School of Nursing, Inc., 222 N.L.R.B. 1150–1151, n. 3.

IV

* * * We therefore hold that the Board's general approach of requiring health-care facilities to permit employee solicitation and distribution during nonworking time in nonworking areas, where the facility has not justified the prohibitions as necessary to avoid disruption of health care operations or disturbance of patients, is consistent with the Act. We hold further that, with respect to the application of that principle to petitioner's cafeteria, the Board was appropriately sensitive to the importance of petitioner's interest in maintaining a tranquil environment for patients. * * *

PROBLEM

On March 30, 1982, employee E. A. Smith handed out union literature to two fellow employees in the patient lounge of the Charity Hospital. Mr. Smith, at the time, was on his morning break. The other two employees were also on their break time. The patient lounge is not open to the general public and is mainly used by patients who are convalescing. Occasionally, visitors of patients accompany them to this area. Employees are requested to only be in the patient lounge area when they are working.

On the afternoon of the 30th, forty-five minutes after Mr. Smith's shift was over, he entered an employee break room area in the hospital and handed out union authorization cards to two employees who were scheduled to be in the hospital, but were on break time.

The hospital has a no-solicitation and no-access policy that reads as follows:

I. *Solicitation*

  *   *   *

(ii) No employee shall solicit another employee at any time in any patient care area within the hospital as such "patient care areas" are hereinafter defined.

II. *Distributions*

  *   *   *

(b) Employees—(i) No employee shall distribute materials of any kind, including printed or other literature, if either or any party to such distribution is on working time for the hospital.

(ii) No employee shall distribute materials of any kind, including printed or other literature (unless such material is distributed pursuant to the employee's work duties and is related to the hospital's operations) in any patient care area or in any working area, as hereinafter defined, for any purpose at any time.

III. *Definitions and Exemptions*

(a) The foregoing rules regarding solicitation and distribution do not apply to authorized services to patients (such as newspaper delivery) to the hospital's purchasing and supply operations, or to hospital volunteer organizations (such as Auxiliary, Twigs, etc.).

(b) "Patient Care Areas" are areas in which patients receive treatment or care (including rest, recuperation and therapeutic recreation) and include, but are not limited to, patient rooms, treatment areas, and other areas in which patients customarily are present where the occurrence of solicitation or distribution would have an unsettling effect on such patients, the care of whom involves quiet and peace of mind.

(c) "Working Areas" include not only all patient care areas, but all other areas within the hospital where employees customarily work, such as nursing stations, workshops, laboratories, offices and the like, other than employee break areas, the main reception areas, and the like.

IV. *Access Policy*

Due to the limited physical facilities of the hospital, including limited parking areas, and due to the necessity of maintaining a peaceful and tranquil environment for our patients, the following policy shall be enforced:

Only authorized persons are allowed in the hospital.

Individuals on official business with the hospital and visitors of patients, are authorized persons.

For purposes of this rule, employees are considered unauthorized personnel except when on duty, on their lunch or coffee breaks, during a period of thirty minutes prior to coming to duty and during a period of fifteen minutes after going off duty.

All employees are to report any unauthorized persons in the hospital to their supervisor and/or security personnel immediately.

The above policy has been uniformly enforced, except that the hospital has permitted solicitations for United Way by hospital employees and has also permitted the hospital auxiliary groups to solicit in the hospital for money for hospital related projects.

Smith's supervisor on April 1, 1982, after learning that the Union was seeking to represent hospital employees, and after learning of Smith's activities, suspended Smith for three days for violating the hospital's no-solicitation and no-access policy.

After the election, the Union filed unfair labor practice charges against the hospital for such disciplinary action alleging that the hospital was restraining or coercing Smith in the exercise of his rights under the National Labor Relations Act.

The hospital states the charge is without merit. The union claims the hospital has violated the National Labor Relations Act.

It has been more difficult to resolve whether adequacy of union communication requires: (1) that nonemployee organizers be allowed to solicit on company premises and (2) that the union be allowed an opportunity to respond, on company time and premises, to anti-union speeches delivered by the employer on company time and premises (known as "captive audience" speeches). As to both, decisions of the Supreme Court indicate that the appropriate test is whether the employer's refusal to allow union communication on his premises "truly diminishe[s] the ability of the labor organizations involved to carry their messages to the employees" or creates an "imbalance in the opportunities for organizational communication."

While the stated tests appear to pose somewhat different issues—adequacy of union opportunity to communicate as compared to equality of opportunity—the Board's response has been the same. Except in unusual circumstances, such as when employees are isolated because they work on a ship, an inaccessible island, or a resort hotel, the Board has rejected union demands for access to company premises by nonemployee organizers, whether to solicit generally or to respond to an anti-union speech. The Board assumes that unions generally have adequate opportunity to present their views to employees by means of employee solicitation on company premises combined with traditional off premise channels of communication, such as letters, telephone calls, and union meetings.

In order to increase unions' ability to correspond with employees by mail, the Board requires employers to provide unions with the names and addresses of employees eligible to vote in pending elections.[9] One emperical study has concluded that employers still have a significant edge in communicating with employees because of their ability to call employees together during work time to deliver an anti-union speech. The authors recommend that unions be granted equal time to respond.[10]

(c) Campaign Propaganda

Communication is the very heart of an election campaign. The union and the employer vie for employee votes by communicating their respective positions to the employees via signs, literature, speeches, and informal conversations.

Section 8(c) provides:

"The expressing of any views, argument, or opinion, or the dissemination thereof, whether in written, printed, graphic, or visual form shall not constitute or be evidence of an unfair labor practice under any provision if this Act, if such expression contains no threat of reprisal or force or promise of benefit."

Section 8(c) was added to the Act in 1947 in order to take the muzzle off of management's right of free speech, however it provides freedom-of-speech protection to both employers and unions. Section 8(c) does not provide protection for threats of reprisal or force or promise of benefit. Such statements are considered coercive and are unfair labor practices under § 8(a)(1).

Section 8(c) pertains only to unfair labor practices. In General Shoe Corp.[11] the Board held that campaign conduct by the winning party that makes an untrammeled free choice by the employees improbable warrants setting aside an election under the Board's § 9 supervisory authority over representation elections, even if no unfair labor practices are committed. Although any conduct that constitutes an unfair labor practice will usually result in the setting aside of an election, under *General Shoe* campaign conduct that upsets the laboratory conditions constitutes an interference of an election although it may not constitute an unfair labor practice.

9. Excelsior Underwear, Inc., 156 N.L.R.B. 1236 (1960).

10. J. Getman, S. Goldberg, J. Herman, *Union Representation Elections:* *Law and Reality* (Russell Sage Foundation, 1976).

11. 77 N.L.R.B. 124 (1948).

The following article excerpt illustrates the NLRB's approach to analyzing whether employer campaign tactics are consistent with the Board's concept of laboratory conditions.

NLRB REGULATION OF CAMPAIGN TACTICS: THE BEHAVIORAL ASSUMPTIONS ON WHICH THE BOARD REGULATES *

Employers are free to inform employees of their opposition to unionism and frequently do so. However, when ambiguous statements about the effect of unionism are made by the employer, the Board generally assumes that employees will infer threats of reprisal or promises of benefit. For example, in *Singer Co.* the employer stated that one of his chief reasons for opening a plant in the particular community was to take advantage of lower labor costs. He further stated that costs had risen at other plants after unionization with the result that work had been transferred and nearly 1,000 people had lost their jobs. Although the employer's comment could have been interpreted as a legal prediction of the economic consequences of unionization, the Board found the remarks contained an implied threat of reprisal. In *Thomas Products Co.*, the employer's constant reference to strikes was found not to suggest that union intransigence might cause a strike, but that the employer would take an unyielding bargaining stance, forcing employees to strike to obtain benefits. This statement, too, was seen as a threat of reprisal. In *Rein Co.*, the employer said that he was not required to negotiate present benefits into a union contract, nor prohibited from telling employees that such benefits could be discontinued. Although these statements were legally accurate, they were found to threaten the loss of existing benefits in retaliation for unionization.

Questions as well as statements may contain implied threats of reprisal or promises of benefit. If the employer tries to find out which employees support the union, the Board assumes that, lacking specific safeguards, his questioning will be understood as a threat of reprisal against union supporters. If the employer asks employees why they want a union, or what their grievances are, the Board assumes the employees will infer a promise to correct the grievances that prompted the effort to organize. Surveillance of union activities is impermissible because it demonstrates the employer's anxiety regarding unionization, thus causing the employees to fear economic retaliation.

Many of the Board's decisions setting aside elections on the basis of employers' statements appear to rest on the assumption that employees know little about labor-management relations or the effect of unionization on such relations, and that nearly all their information on this subject will be a product of the campaign. In *Boaz Spinning*

* Getman, Goldberg and Herman, "National Labor Relations Board Regulation of Campaign Tactics: The Behavioral Assumptions on Which the Board Regulates," 27 Stanford Law Review 1465 (1975); © 1975 by the Board of Trustees of the Leland Stanford, Jr. University. Reprinted by permission of the publisher and Fred B. Rothman & Co.

Co. the employer set out in some detail the history of other plants (one of which he had operated) that had closed after prolonged strikes called by a union seeking representation rights. He discussed possible results of a strike, including loss of jobs, loss of income, violence, bloodshed, and disruption of family and community life. The Board set aside the election, lost by the union, on the ground that the employer had unfairly given the employees the impression that their only choice was between union and a strike:

> In arguing against unionism, an employer is free to discuss rationally the potency of strikes as a weapon and the effectiveness of the Union seeking to represent his employees. It is, however, a different matter when the employer leads the employees to believe that they *must* strike in order to get concessions. A major presupposition of the concept of collective bargaining is that minds can be changed by discussion, and that skilled, rational, cogent argument can produce change without the necessity for striking. * * * Policy considerations dictate that employees should not be led to believe, before voting, that their choice is simply between no union or striking. That narrow choice is essentially what this Employer gave them.

Implicit in the Board's decision is the assumption that the employees had not previously considered the possibility of a strike and were unaware of the possible negative consequences of striking. Also implied in the Board's discussion is the assumption that employees will see their choice solely as presented by the employer—no union or strike—and will be unaware that many employers who adamantly oppose unionization ultimately accept a union contract rather than risk a damaging strike.

The assumption that employees lack sophistication is also present in the Board doctrine that an employer may not bargain with one union when a rival union claim raises a question concerning representation under the Act. Bargaining with one union, the Board has said, bestows an "unwarranted prestige" on the recognized union and thereby prevents a free choice by the employees. The Board's theory must be that substantial prestige will accrue to the recognized union due to its position of authority in the plant. Union leaders will be dealing with management officials with respect to grievances and the negotiation of an agreement; from these dealings the union will acquire an aura of responsibility giving it a significant advantage over rivals in a forthcoming election. This theory presupposes that employees will be so impressed by the union's acting in a responsible role that they will be unable to consider the likelihood that another union could do likewise. Hence, they are deprived of freedom of choice.

The assumption of unsophistication, even if accurate, could not justify setting aside elections without still another assumption—that the impact of such tactics cannot be neutralized by the union. If the employer threatens to close the plant contingent on a union victory, presumably the union organizer will respond that the employer will not do so as long as the plant is profitable, and that the union has no intention of making it unprofitable. If the employer promises to raise wages contingent on a union loss, undoubtedly the organizer will reply that mere words are not equal to a union contract. If the employer recognizes one union, the other will counter that the favored union is an employer puppet and that the unrecognized union will negotiate a more favorable contract. The Board must assume either that employees will not attend to the union's counterassertions or that the impact of the employer's threatened use of his economic power vis-à-vis employees is so great that counterassertions will be ineffective. Hence, self-policing of the campaign by the parties is ruled out and governmental regulation is deemed necessary.

The Board assumes that an employee's decision to vote for or against union representation is tenuous and easily altered by the campaign. This assumption is so inherent in Board regulation that it is rarely articulated save when the Board discusses those tactics it considers particularly effective in unfairly influencing voting. Foremost among these impermissible tactics are threats and acts of reprisal, and promises and grants of benefits. The Board has concluded that such tactics impress employees with the employer's economic power over them and thus interfere with their free choice. This conclusion rests on two further assumptions: (1) unless reminded of the employer's economic power during the campaign, employees will not fully appreciate its meaning or consider the possibility of its exercise; (2) once reminded of that power, employees will be inclined to vote against the union. Implicit in the second assumption is the conclusion that employees otherwise contemplating a vote for union representation will vote against the union either to prevent the employer from exercising his economic power in ways harmful to them or to encourage him to exercise that power in ways favorable to them. Many Board decisions reflect these assumptions.

1. *Threats and acts of reprisal.*

Of all reminders of employer power, threatened or actual loss of employment is considered among the most coercive. In *Cornelius American, Inc.* the Board held that actual reprisals, even against a single worker, would invalidate an election. Threats, even when implicit, are also thought to have great impact if the speaker is in a position to effectuate them. Thus, in *Thomas Products Co.*, the president of the parent company of the employer involved in the election made a speech in which he stated that the operations of the employer had not been successful and that other plants that had not succeeded had been closed, including one which had endured one union turmoil after another. He also told the employees, "I *am* a businessman and I have to make business decisions." The Board found his comments likely to coerce employees into voting against the union in order to prevent retaliation. The Board's assumptions in setting aside the election were clearly stated:

> Power can persuade, and substantial power can persuade substantially. When an employer who controls a multiplant operation

stands before employees and verbally juggles the factories, blithely reminding them of his ability to close this, that, or the other one, it is a display of enormous economic power, calculated to put the fear of unemployment in the minds of employees. Such a demonstration is unnecessary to a reasoned discussion of the pros and cons of unionism and can only tend to make employees believe that, should they incur the employer's displeasure, he could easily find a formidable way to express his dissatisfaction.

In *General Stencils, Inc.* the Board went a step further and issued a bargaining order based upon a threat of discharge.

2. *Promises and grants of benefits.*

Promises or grants of benefits made to discourage union support are considered exceedingly potent, whether or not made contingent on the union's defeat. For example, the Board stated in *Hudson Hosiery Co.*:

> [T]he presentation of economic benefits to employees in order to have them forego collective bargaining is a form of pressure and compulsion no less telling in its effect on employees because benign. * * * We can perceive no logical distinction between threats to withdraw economic benefits, for the purpose of thwarting self-organization of employees, and promises of better things to come, for the same objective.
>
> What is unlawful under the Act is the employer's granting or announcing such benefits (although previously determined bona fide) *for the purpose* of causing the employees to accept or reject a representative for collective bargaining.

Frequently, the grant of benefits is held to exert so powerful an influence on employee free choice that the Board issues a bargaining order on the theory that setting the contaminated election aside and holding another would be futile.

The theory on which promises or grants of benefits are assumed to interfere with rational decisionmaking has never been fully articulated by the Board. In N.L.R.B. v. Exchange Parts Co. the Supreme Court found an implicit threat of reprisals in the bestowal of benefits:

> The danger inherent in well-timed increases in benefits is the suggestion of a fist inside the velvet glove. Employees are not likely to miss the inference that the source of benefits now conferred is also the source from which future benefits must flow and which may dry up if it is not obliged.

The Board has in some cases, by citing *Exchange Parts*, suggested a wholly different explanation for treating grants and promises of benefits as illegal. In *Texas Transport & Terminal Co.*, the employer threatened reprisals and granted wage increases to discourage union support. The Board commented: "The threats were the stick, the grant of wage increases the carrot." The Board's theory in this case would thus appear to be that by granting benefits, the employer is attempting to win favor among employees and to persuade them that they will receive satisfactory wages and working conditions without the assistance of the union.

The vice of a last-minute grant of benefits that attempts to demonstrate that employees do not need a union to assure favorable treatment is by no means clear. One theory on which such conduct might be held unlawful is suggested by the court's statement in *Exchange Parts* that "[t]he beneficence of an employer is likely to be ephemeral if prompted by a threat of unionization which is subsequently removed." In other words, a last-minute grant of benefits for the purpose of discouraging union activity may represent only the employer's response to the immediate prospect of unionization rather than a long-range policy of maintaining a high level of benefits. Because of their assumed lack of sophistication, the employees will be unaware of the ephemeral nature of the last-minute grant of benefits, and hence will be misled into believing that unionization is unnecessary to secure future benefits.

While only those grants of benefit that the employer intends to influence employee voting choice are unlawful, the employer's intent need not be communicated explicitly to the employees in order to have the desired influence. For example, in *Texas Transport & Terminal Co.*, the employer decided to give a wage increase during the campaign. The Board found that the timing of the increase was influenced by the campaign. Although the employer did not couple the announcement of the increase with the campaign in any way, the Board assumed that the employees would make the connection on their own.

Even when a change is decided upon for business reasons unrelated to unionization if it is announced during the campaign it is assumed that employees will regard it as a response to their efforts to organize.

3.   Other reminders of employer power.

The Board's view of the fragility of rational decisionmaking is further demonstrated by cases holding that certain forms of employer campaigning are so potent that they are inconsistent with freedom of choice regardless of the content of the statements made. In *General Shoe Corp.* the company's general manager and the personnel manager met in their offices with small groups of employees to urge them to vote against the union. Their statements were found to be moderate in tone but the Board still set aside the election because they were made in the "locus of final authority."

Home visits by the employer for the purpose of campaigning against the union are also prohibited. In *Peoria Plastics Co.* the Board equated such visits with calling employees into the employer's office individually and concluded that they interfered with free choice, regardless of whether the employer's remarks were coercive.

4.   Interference with free choice unrelated to employer power.

The freedom of employees to vote for or against union representation is thought to be vulnerable to a variety of campaign tactics that do not trade upon the employer's economic power over the employees, but that nonetheless prevent employees from acting in a rational and nonemotional fashion. All campaign speeches on working time to massed assemblies of employees within 24 hours of the election are prohibited because such speeches "have an unwholesome and unsettling effect and tend to interfere with * * * sober and thoughtful choice."

Appeals to racial prejudice, when regarded by the Board as inflammatory, are proscribed because "[t]hey create conditions which make impossible a sober, informed exercise of the franchise." Similarly, linking the trade union movement to communism may be a basis for setting aside an election. Even statements made by outside parties unrelated to the employer or the union may provide a basis for setting aside an election if the Board concludes that these statements created an atmosphere in which rational decisionmaking could not take place.

Some rules appear to be based on both the Board's desire to protect its processes and its assumption of the fragility of free choice. Thus, the distribution of a facsimile of an official ballot marked to suggest that the Board endorses a particular choice is grounds for setting aside an election, as is the addition of a partisan message to an official Board notice entitled "Rights of Employees." Sustained conversation with prospective voters waiting to cast their ballots is prohibited to maintain order in the polling area and to prevent last-minute distraction and pressures on employees so that they may "consult their own consciences without interference."

* * *

The *Dal-Tex* and *Turner Shoe* opinions which follows are typical of many Board decisions. Carefully evaluating employer speech, consider how employees are likely to perceive such comments and how it is likely to affect their vote.

DAL–TEX OPTICAL CO.

137 N.L.R.B. 1782, 1962.

The Employer's president delivered speeches to employees in the plant on September 18, 19, and 21, 1961. The September 18 speech included the following statements:

> Two years ago the I.U.E. Union tried to organize this plant. They went to every length to cause trouble. They misrepresented all of the facts. They conducted a vicious campaign. They did not then, nor do they now, represent any optical laboratory in Texas. Our employees were not fooled and voted against the Union by a large majority. The Union lost the election. This election was conducted by a secret ballot and was a fair election, but the Union could not stand being beaten and attempted to set aside the

election. They introduced evidence before the Board, which I considered then, and do now consider, to be false and perjured. A year and a half after the election the National Labor Relations Board, based upon such evidence, decided that the election should be set aside and a new one held. After another six months the Board then decided to hold another election next week. The Company does not agree with the Board, and has maintained and is going to maintain that the election held two years ago was a valid election. And the Courts are going to have to decide whether this first election was valid. In the meantime, the Company is permitting the holding of this new election on Company property on September 22nd, because it feels that your rights can be better protected. If the Union should win this election, which I don't think it can, the Courts are still going to have to determine whether the Board was right or wrong. If the Board was wrong, which I firmly believe, the election to be held on September 22nd will not mean a thing if the Union wins it. My guess is that it will be another couple of years before this matter is settled. In the meantime, we will go on just as we are without any Union. I am explaining all of this to you so you will understand that wild promises by this Union of what is going to happen here if the Union wins don't mean a thing. I believe in law and order. When the Courts decide the matter I will abide by the decisions of the Courts.

* * *

[After detailing some of the benefits employees were receiving.]

So, why should you want a Union to represent you? Is it because you believe they can get you more than you now have, or have you been told the Union will run this plant? I have made it a practice of giving back in increased wages all efficiency gains during the year. During the year 1959 there were 270 individual raises given. During the year 1960 there were 298 raises given, and during this year already there have been 349 raises given. These are merit raises. These are wages that you get in addition to your profit sharing and pension plans. I not only provide for your old age and your family in case of your death, but as the efficiency improves you get the benefit of it in increased wages. Do you want to gamble all of these things? If I am required by the Court to bargain with this Union, whenever that may be, I will bargain in good faith, but I will have to bargain on a cold-blooded business basis. You may come out with a lot less than you have now. Why gamble because agitators make wild promises to you? If I am required to bargain and I cannot agree there is no power on earth that can make me sign a contract with this Union, so what will probably happen is the Union will call a strike. I will go right along running this business and replace the strikers. There has been a lot of talk about your being skilled workers. You only do one operation and in a short period I can train anybody to do any of these operations, as we trained most of you. I am not afraid of a strike. It won't hurt the Company. I will replace the strikers. They will lose all of their benefits. Strikers will draw no wages, no unemployment compensation and be out of a job. The Union won't pay you wages. The Union has nothing to lose. You do all of the losing. No employee is so important that he or she cannot be replaced. I am not afraid of threats. Before the last election this Union tried everything. Before this election is over, you will see how dirty the Union will get. It has no responsibility. It is not reasonable to believe that you would give up your individual rights to outside agitators and not be able to come to me as you have in the past with your problems. I cannot believe you want to change to the cold blooded bargaining basis that must follow.

In the September 19 speech he stated, among other things:

Will the Union get you more wages? No, who pays the wages? I do. I built this plant. I invest the capital. I see to it that it runs 52 weeks a year. I see that the orders come in. I have consistently turned back to you in increased wages all efficiency gains made by the Company. I give hundreds of increases in wages that are merited. In 1960 I gave 349 raises. This year I have already given 442 raises. This is the right way to handle wages. The result is that you have the highest wages in the industry. This I can assure you, it is my position now, and it will be my position at all times, that you will get merit raises just as I have been giving them over the years. If you don't merit them, you will not get them. This is nothing new. It is the system I have operated on from the beginning. I do not have to, nor will I, change it. If you believe promises the Union makes you, you will find out the Union doesn't pay wages. I do. The Union doesn't give raises. I do. Now, please remember you have to compare your wages with those of other optical laboratories in Dallas, Texas. We are at the top. It does not make any difference what Collins Electric pays or any other industry. It is what is paid in our industry. No Union and no company in our industry in Texas can match our wages and benefits.

Even a cursory reading of these portions of the speeches of the Employer's president demonstrates that they were couched in language calculated to convey to the employees the danger and futility of their designating the Union. After listing some of the existing benefits, he queried whether they wanted "to gamble all of these things," stated that if required to bargain he would do so on "a cold-blooded business basis" so that the employees "may come out with a lot less than you have now," and emphasized his own control over wages. This was a clearcut, readily understandable threat that the Employer would bargain "from scratch" as though no economic benefits had been given, and the employees would suffer economic loss and reprisal if they selected the Union. Also, the reference to the probability of a strike accompanied by the threat to replace strikers with the emphasis upon their expendability and resultant loss of all their benefits was calculated to create a fear that there would necessarily be a loss of employment and financial security if the Union won. These latter statements had even greater meaning and weight occurring, as they did, after the Employer engaged in a series of unfair labor practices, including, most recently, the discharge of three employees for acting contrary to the Employer's wishes.

In addition to and intermingled with the above threats were statements by which the Employer clearly conveyed the idea that designation of the Union was futile and that the Employer would not sign a contract even if required to engage in bargaining. The Employer informed the employees that in the event the Union won it would not mean a thing because the "Courts are still going to have to determine" the issue and "my guess is that it will be another couple of years before this matter is settled;" that if required to bargain and unable to agree, no power on earth could make the Employer sign a contract " * * * so what will *probably* happen is the Union will call a strike" (emphasis supplied); and that the Employer did not have to and would not change its wage policy. While these comments may appear to be mere statements of the Employer's legal rights and his intention to adhere to them, in the present context they assume quite a different character. The statement that the Employer could not be compelled to sign a contract in the absence of agreement seems innocuous on the surface. But when the same sentence was completed by pointing out the probability of a strike, when the entire sentence followed immediately after the threat to abrogate existing benefits and, in effect, bargain "from scratch," and when it was succeeded by the graphic description of the results of their replacement during the predicted strike, the entire import and impact of the comment was changed to a clear message that the Employer would not sign a contract even if required to negotiate. This message was reinforced by the other statements noted above, particularly the Employer's position that it *would not* change its wage policy, undeniably it was thus announcing a predetermination not to bargain on the subject of wages.

Prior cases involving objections to elections, have held, although not uniformly, statements similar to those involved herein to the effect that the employer would not bargain, were merely an expression of the Employer's "legal position." On the other hand, it has long been well settled that the same type of statement is not within the "free speech" protection of Section 8(c) of the Act but, rather, constitutes interference, restraint, and coercion of employees within the meaning of Section 8(a)(1) of the Act. We find no logic or sound reason for this disparity of treatment depending on the nature of the proceeding in which the issue is raised before the Board. Conduct violative of Section 8(a)(1) is, *a fortiori*, conduct which interferes with the exercise of a free and untrammeled choice in an election. This is so because the test of conduct which may interfere with the "laboratory conditions" for an election is considerably more restrictive than the test of conduct which amounts to interference, restraint, or coercion, which violates Section 8(a)(1). Accordingly, to the extent they are inconsistent herewith, we hereby overrule *National Furniture Company, Inc.*, supra, and similar cases holding such statements to be privileged under Section 8(c).

To adhere to those decisions would be to sanction implied threats couched in the guise of statements of legal position. Such an approach is too mechanical, fails to consider all the surrounding circumstances, and is inconsistent with the duty of this Board to enforce and advance the statutory policy of encouraging the practice and procedure of collective bargaining by protecting the full freedom of employees to select representatives of their own choosing. Rather, we shall look to the economic realities of the employer-employee relationship and shall set aside an election where we find that the employer's conduct has resulted in substantial interference with the election, regardless of the form in which the statement was made.

Under all the circumstances, as analyzed in the above discussion, we find that the entire content of the Employer's speeches, taken as a whole, with the clear threats and the implied anticipatory refusal to bargain if the Union should win the election generated an atomosphere of fear of economic loss and complete hostility to the Union which destroyed the laboratory conditions in which the Board must hold its elections and prevented the employees' expression of a free choice in the election. We therefore sustain objections Nos. 2 and 4.

TURNER SHOE CO.

249 N.L.R.B. 144 (1980).

By Chairman Fanning and Members Jenkins and Truesdale.

Pursuant to a Stipulation for Certfification Upon Consent Election approved by the Regional Director for Region 24 on January 10, 1979, an election by secret ballot was conducted on February 15, 1979, under the direction and supervision of the Regional Director for Region 24, among the employees in the stipulated unit. At the conclusion of the election, the parties were furnished a tally of ballots which showed that, of approximately 724 valid ballots, 178 were cast in favor of the Petitioner, 514 were against the Petitioner, and there were 32 challenged ballots. The number of challenged ballots was not determinative of the results of the election. Thereafter, the Petitioner filed timely objections to the election.

* * *

Although the Hearing Officer found that none of the Employer's conduct was objectionable in and of itself, she further found that the overall impact of the Employer's campaign speeches and literature created a coercive atmosphere which interfered with the results of the election. We agree with the Hearing Officer's recommendation that the election be set aside but also find, contrary to the Hearing Officer, that specific conduct by the Employer constituted objectionable conduct. As set forth more fully below, we find that the Employer engaged in objectionable conduct by making threats of plant closure and loss of jobs, and that, within the context of such threats, the Employer's repeated statements about strikes, plant closure, and loss of jobs had a coercive impact on the employees which also interfered with the results of the election.

The Employer conducted a vigorous campaign against the Union consisting of speeches and distribution of campaign literature. Between January 28–29, 1979, the Employer delivered a speech in both Spanish and English to small groups of employees. In this speech the Employer made several statements associating the Petitioner with strikes, plant closings, and loss of jobs.

Shortly after this speech, the Employer distributed a campaign leaflet entitled "The Death of a Shoe Factory" and a leaflet which described plant closings where employees had been represented by The Amalgamated Meat Cutters Union. The leaflet was printed in the form of a prayer card distributed at Catholic funerals and stated in Spanish:

OBITUARY (DEATH NOTICE)

DEAD: Dorado Shoe Co., Augadilla, P.R.

BORN: 1965

UNIONIZED BY: Meat Cutters Union, 1970 Three Week Strike

DEAD: 1971

The Meat Cutters Union alleges that if it goes into a plant it guarantees your job.

The Company Dorado Shoes was a very successful company when it was organized by the Meat Cutters Union. In 1970, six months later, the Meat Cutters Union called the employees to a strike at the Company which lasted three weeks.

Six months thereafter, one year after the Meat Cutters Union came into the Company, the Meat Cutters Union negotiated a close out of the plant.

WHY DID THIS HAPPEN?

Because the plant could not successfully compete in the shoe industry and the plant closed. This was the death of a shoe factory.

LESSON:

Our job security depends on the working together as a team and of the mutual cooperation and ability to produce shoes of quality at competitive prices so that we can sell our shoes to our customers.

BUT NOT WITH UNION PROMISES. VOTE NO

The pamphlet on plant closings was also printed in Spanish and stated:

Job security is very important to you. What job security does the Meat Cutters give its members?

You be the judge.

CLOSING OF PLANTS, CLOSING OF PLANTS, CLOSING OF
PLANTS

The Meat Cutters Union was the representative of these plants
that closed recently.

CLOSED—Swift & Co., Scottsbluff, Nebraska; Swift & Co., Wil-
son, N. C.; Hygrade Packing Co., Richmond, Va.; Goetz Packing,
Baltimore, Md.; Clayman Packing, Philadelphia, Pa.; Swift & Co.,
Telleson, Arizona; Hygrade Packing, Indianapolis, Ind.; Swift &
Co., Nashville, Tenn.; Dukeland Packing, Baltimore, Md.; Swift &
Co., Kearney, N. D.; Dorado Shoe Co., Aguadilla P. R.; G. H.
Meyer Sons, Richmond, Virginia; Marhoeffer Co., Muncie, Indiana
(Pictures of plants with the words CLOSED across the picture it-
self.)

What job security did the employees of these plants receive from
the Meat Cutters Union?   Vote No.

The final aspect of the Employer's campaign was a speech delivered to groups of employees in Spanish and English on February 13,
1979, 2 days before the election.   After telling its employees that
unionization could mean strikes, plant closure, and loss of jobs, the
Employer stated near the end of the speech that "If we are not careful a disaster could hit and we could lose it all."

In evaluating the Employer's campaign conduct we must carefully
balance the Employer's right to express its views on the subject of
unionization with the right of its employees to make a reasoned decision regarding unionization in an atmosphere free of coercion and
threats.   In N.L.R.B. v. Gissel Packing Co., Inc., 395 U.S. 575, 618, 89
S.Ct. 1918, 1942, 23 L.Ed.2d 547 (1969), the Supreme Court pointed
out that:

> (A)n employer is free to communicate to his employees any of his
> general views about unionism or any of his specific views about a
> particular union, so long as the communications do not contain a
> "threat of reprisal or force or promise of benefit."   He may even
> make a prediction as to the precise effect he believes unionization
> will have on his company.   In such a case, however, the prediction
> must be carefully phrased on the basis of objective fact to convey
> an employer's belief as to demonstrably probable consequences
> beyond his control or to convey a management decision already
> arrived at to close the plant in case of unionization.   See Textile
> Workers v. Darlington Mfg. Co., 380 U.S. 263, 274, fn. 20 (1965).
> If there is an implication that an employer may or may not take
> action solely on his own initiative for reasons unrelated to econom-
> ic necessities and known only to him, the statement is no longer a
> reasonable prediction based on available facts but a threat of re-
> taliation based on misrepresentation and coercion, and as such
> without the protection of the First Amendment.

In *Gissel* the Court found the employer, in its election campaign,
had informed its employees that other area plants had closed because
of unionization, that the union was strike happy, and that the union

would probably engage in a strike which would result in plant closure and a loss of jobs. The Court further found, in agreement with the Board, that there was no record support for the employer's underlying assumptions that the union would have to strike or that other area plants had closed because of unionization. In the absence of an objective basis to support its message of probable strikes and plant closure, the Court found that the employer's statements were not permissible predictions of economic consequences but were implicit threats of job loss and constituted objectionable conduct sufficient to set aside the election.

Our evaluation of the campaign conduct of the Employer in the instant case reveals a striking similarity to the conduct of the employer in *Gissel*. The employer's campaign was geared to convey to its employees the message that unionization would lead to strikes, plant closure, and loss of jobs. Thus, the Employer distributed a pamphlet entitled "The Death of A Shoe Factory" which related the "death" of a nearby factory subsequent to unionization. Although the pamphlet did not directly attribute the closing of the factory to unionization, the graphic presentation of the plant closing in the form of an obituary notice was a clear attempt to communicate by form if not by words a clear message to employees-unionization caused a nearby plant to close and unionization would likewise cause the Employer to close its plant. Similarly, in its February 13 speech, 2 days before the election, the Employer told its employees that the union was strike happy, unionization could lead to a long and costly strike, striking employees could be permanently replaced, other area union plants had been forced to close, and if the employees were not careful "a disaster could hit" and everything could be lost. The Employer's reference to an impending disaster just 2 days before the election conveyed the not too subtle message that a vote for the Union would lead to a strike and permanent strike replacements or plant closure and a resulting loss of jobs. Thus, the Employer sought to take advantage of employee concerns about job security and informed its employees that the only way to protect their jobs was to vote against the Union.

The record in the instant case, like the record in *Gissel*, contains no demonstrable record evidence to support the Employer's message that unionization caused the closure of other area plants or that unionization would lead to strikes, plant closure, job loss, and other unidentified disasters. Therefore, the Employer failed to convey a permissible noncoercive prediction that unionization might lead to an economic dispute that could result in a loss of jobs. Instead, in the context of the employer-employee relationship, the Employer's leaflet in the form of an obituary notice and its February 13 speech constituted threats of plant closure and job loss since "employees who are particularly sensitive to rumors of plant closings, take such hints as coercive threats rather than honest forecasts."

We find no merit to the Employer's contentions that it did not threaten its employees with job loss because none of its campaign material or statements directly or explicitly attributed strikes, plant closings, or job loss to unionization. Communications which hover on the edge of the permissible and the unpermissible are objectionable as "(i)t is only simple justice that a person who seeks advantage from his elected use of the murky waters of double *entendre* should be held accountable therefor at the level of his audience rather than that of sophisticated tribunals, law professors, scholars of the nicetics of labor law, or 'grammarians.' " As the Supreme Court has noted, an employer "can easily make his views known without engaging in 'brinksmanship' when it becomes all too easy to 'overstep and tumble (over) the brink,' *Wausau Steel Corp. v. N.L.R.B.*, 377 F.2d 369, 372 (7th Cir. 1967). At the least he can avoid coercive speech simply by avoiding conscious overstatements he has reason to believe will mislead his employees." The Employer's use of a leaflet in the form of an obituary notice and its reference to an impending disaster are examples of "brinksmanship" which overstepped and tumbled over the brink.

We also find that in the context of these specific threats of plant closure the Employer's repeated statements in its speeches and campaign material associating the Petitioner with strikes, plant closures, and loss of jobs had a coercive impact on the employees. In its January 22–29 speech the Employer told the employees that "the Meat Cutters were involved in 1,235 strikes in the last four years," that "hundreds of plants that the Meat Cutters union was in have closed," and that "25,000 Meat Cutters union members lost their jobs." Two days before the election the Employer informed the employees in its February 13 speech that "with 40% unemployment in Aguadilla, the union still does not give one job to one single person," that "the Meat Cutters was one of the most strike-happy Unions," and that although two area plants were union plants, they closed "throwing hundreds of workers out of work." In addition, the Employer's campaign material emphasized the themes of a strike-happy union, plant closures, and the loss of jobs. Within the context of the threats of plant closure and loss of jobs, as found above, we find that the Employer's constant references to strikes, plant closure, and loss of jobs constituted additional objectionable conduct which prevented the employees from exercising their free choice in the election.

Moreover, even if we did not find that the Employer's distribution of the death notice or its threat of an impending disaster constituted specific threats of plant closure, we would find that the overall impact of the Employer's campaign created a coercive atmosphere sufficient to set aside the election. We have found such a coercive atmosphere, even in the absence of a specific finding of objectionable conduct, in cases where an employer has emphasized campaign themes such as the likelihood of strikes, plant closure, and loss of jobs if the union won the election. Thomas Products Co., Division of Thomas Industries, Inc., 167 N.L.R.B. 732 (1967); Amerace Corp., ES-NA Division, 217 N.L.R.B. 850 (1975). As indicated above, the Employer in the instant case constantly emphasized job security to its employees and attempted to link the Petitioner with strikes, plant closure, and loss of jobs. Therefore, we find that the Employer's over-all campaign created a coercive atmosphere and tended to create the impression that strikes, plant closure, job loss, and other adverse consequences would be a direct result of unionization. Accordingly, we find merit to the Petitioner's Objection 1, and find that a second election should be directed.

As the following excerpt shows, the Board is not limited to holding a rerun election to remedy improper campaign behavior.

NLRB v. GISSEL PACKING CO.*

Supreme Court of the United States, 1969.
395 U.S. 575, 89 S.Ct. 1918, 23 L.Ed.2d 542.

MR. CHIEF JUSTICE WARREN delivered the opinion of the Court.

These cases involve the extent of an employer's duty under the National Labor Relations Act to recognize a union that bases its claim to representative status solely on the possession of union authorization cards, and the steps an employer may take, particularly with regard to the scope and content of statements he may make, in legitimately resisting such card-based recognition. The specific questions facing us here are whether the duty to bargain can arise without a Board election under the Act; whether union authorization cards, if obtained from a majority of employees without misrepresentation or coercion, are reliable enough generally to provide a valid, alternate route to majority status; whether a bargaining order is an appropriate and authorized remedy where an employer rejects a card majority while at the same time committing unfair practices that tend to undermine the union's majority and make a fair election an unlikely possibility; and whether certain specific statements made by an employer to his employees constituted such an election-voiding unfair labor practice and thus fell outside the protection of the First Amendment and § 8(c) of the Act, 49 Stat. 452, as amended, 29 U.S.C.A. § 158(c). For reasons given below, we answer each of these questions in the affirmative.

* * *

NOS. 573 and 691.

* * * In each case, the union waged an organizational campaign, obtained authorization cards from a majority of employees in the appropriate bargaining unit, and then on the basis of the cards, demanded recognition by the employer. All three employers refused to bargain on the ground that authorization cards were inherently unreliable indicators of employee desires; and they either embarked on,

----

* [The Board found that each of the employees had committed serious unfair labor practices].

or continued, vigorous antiunion campaigns that gave rise to numerous unfair labor practice charges.   *   *   *

*   *   *

The first issue facing us is whether a union can establish a bargaining obligation by means other than a Board election and whether the validity of alternate routes to majority status, such as cards, was affected by the 1947 Taft-Hartley amendments. The most commonly traveled route for a union to obtain recognition as the exclusive bargaining representative of an unorganized group of employees is through the Board's election and certification procedures under § 9(c) of the Act (29 U.S.C.A. § 159(c)); it is also, from the Board's point of view, the preferred route. A union is not limited to a Board election, however, for, in addition to § 9, the present Act provides in § 8(a)(5) (29 U.S.C.A. § 158(a)(5)), as did the Wagner Act in § 8(5), that "it shall be an unfair labor practice for an employer   *   *   *   to refuse to bargain collectively with the representatives of his employees, subject to the provisions of section 9(a)." Since § 9(a), in both the Wagner Act and the present Act, refers to the representative as the one "designated or selected" by a majority of the employees without specifying precisely how that representative is to be chosen, it was early recognized that an employer had a duty to bargain whenever the union representative presented "convincing evidence of majority support." Almost from the inception of the Act, then, it was recognized that a union did not have to be certified as the winner of a Board election to invoke a bargaining obligation; it could establish majority status by other means under the unfair labor practice provision of § 8(a)(5)—by showing convincing support, for instance, by a union-called strike or strike vote, or, as here, by possession of cards signed by a majority of the employees authorizing the union to represent them for collective bargaining purposes.

We have consistently accepted this interpretation of the Wagner Act and the present Act, particularly as to the use of authorization cards. *   *   *

*   *   *   We agree with the Board's assertion here that there is no suggestion that Congress intended § 9(c)(1)(B) to relieve any employer of his § 8(a)(5) bargaining obligation where, without good faith, he engaged in unfair labor practices disruptive of the Board's election machinery. And we agree that the policies reflected in § 9(c) (1)(B) fully support the Board's present administration of the Act; for an employer can insist on a secret ballot election, unless, in the words of the Board, he engages "in contemporaneous unfair labor practices likely to destroy the union's majority and seriously impede the election."   *   *   *

*   *   *

Remaining before us is the propriety of a bargaining order as a remedy for a § 8(a)(5) refusal to bargain where an employer has committed independent unfair labor practices which have made the holding of a fair election unlikely or which have in fact undermined a union's majority and caused an election to be set aside. We have

long held that the Board is not limited to a cease-and-desist order in
such cases, but has the authority to issue a bargaining order without
first requiring the union to show that it has been able to maintain its
majority status. See NLRB v. Katz, 369 U.S. 736, 748, n. 16, 82 S.Ct.
1107, 1114, 8 L.Ed.2d 230 (1962); NLRB v. P. Lorillard Co., 314 U.S.
512, 62 S.Ct. 397, 86 L.Ed.2d 380 (1942). And we have held that the
Board has the same authority even where it is clear that the union,
which once had possession of cards from a majority of the employees,
represents only a minority when the bargaining order is entered.
Franks Bros. Co. v. NLRB, 321 U.S. 702, 64 S.Ct. 817, 88 L.Ed.2d
1020 (1944). We see no reason now to withdraw this authority from
the Board. If the Board could enter only a cease-and-desist order and
direct an election or a rerun, it would in effect be rewarding the employer and allowing him "to profit from [his] own wrongful refusal to
bargain," Franks Bros., supra, at 704, while at the same time severely curtailing the employees' right freely to determine whether they
desire a representative. The employer could continue to delay or disrupt the election processes and put off indefinitely his obligation to
bargain; and any election held under these circumstances would not
be likely to demonstrate the employees' true, undistorted desires.

     The employers argue that the Board has ample remedies, over and
above the cease-and-desist order, to control employer misconduct.
The Board, can, they assert, direct the companies to mail notices to
employees, to read notices to employees during plant time and to give
the union access to employees during working time at the plant, or it
can seek a court injunctive order under § 10(j) (29 U.S.C.A. § 160(j))
as a last resort. In view of the Board's power, they conclude, the
bargaining order is an unnecessarily harsh remedy that needlessly
prejudices employees' § 7 rights solely for the purpose of punishing
or restraining an employer. Such an argument ignores that a bargaining order is designed as much to remedy past election damage as
it is to deter future misconduct. If an employer has succeeded in
undermining a union's strength and destroying the laboratory conditions necessary for a fair election, he may see no need to violate a
cease-and-desist order by further unlawful activity. The damage will
have been done, and perhaps the only fair way to effectuate employee rights is to re-establish the conditions as they existed before the
employer's unlawful campaign. There is, after all, nothing permanent in a bargaining order, and if, after the effects of the employer's
acts have worn off, the employees clearly desire to disavow the
union, they can do so by filing a representation petition. * * * we
should reemphasize, where there is also a showing that at one point
the union had a majority; in such a case, of course, effectuating as-
certainable employee free choice becomes as important a goal as deterring employer misbehaviour. In fashioning a remedy in the exercise of its discretion, then, the Board can properly take into
consideration the extensiveness of an employer's unfair practices in
terms of their past effect on election conditions and the likelihood of
their recurrence in the future. If the Board finds that the possibility
of erasing the effects of past practices and of ensuring a fair election

(or a fair rerun) by the use of traditional remedies, though present, is slight and that employee sentiment once expressed through cards would, on balance, be better protected by a bargaining order, then such an order should issue.

We emphasize that under the Board's remedial power there is still a third category of minor or less extensive unfair labor practices, which, because of their minimal impact on the election machinery, will not sustain a bargaining order. There is, the Board says, no *per se* rule that the commission of any unfair practice will automatically result in a § 8(a)(5) violation and the issuance of an order to bargain.

———

The questionable nature of the behavioral assumptions underlying Board regulation has been pointed out by several commentators and has even been adverted to by members of the Board. A recent major field study [12] has concluded that many of the Board's assumptions are erroneous.

The study, conducted by Getman, Goldberg, and Herman examined how employees involved in organizing campaigns react to employer and union campaign tactics. The purpose of the study was to examine the validity of the behavioral assumptions underlying NLRB doctrines for regulating union representation elections. It focused on the validity of what the authors argue is the central assumption guiding Board policy: that employees are attentive to the union and management election campaigns and that their votes are significantly influenced by the campaigns.

The authors identified the following additional assumptions as being implicit in Board decisions: (1) employees will interpret ambiguous statements by employers as threats or promises; (2) employees are unsophisticated about labor relations; (3) free choice is jeopardized by tactics such as threats, promises of benefits and misuse of employer economic power; (4) equal opportunity to communicate to employees is critical; (5) signing of an authorization card is an indicator of union support or lack of support but does not imply that a carefully reasoned judgment was made in deciding whether to sign or not to sign.

To test the validity of these assumptions, the authors used a research design adapted from studies of voting behavior in political elections. They interviewed employees as soon as possible after the direction of the election and again after the election was held. The authors measured the potential confounding variables and controlled their efforts through statistical analysis. Thirty-one elections held in the lower Midwest were studied. The number of employees eligible to vote in these elections was 2,907.

Getman, Goldberg, and Herman found that the vast majority of votes cast in elections studied were influenced primarily by pre-

12. J. Getman, S. Goldberg, J. Herman, Union Representation Elections: Law and Reality (Russell Sage Foundation, 1976).

campaign attitudes of the employees and not by the campaign. Eighty-one percent of the voters had their minds made up prior to the campaign. This finding disputes the validity of the guiding premise that the campaign is central for the average voter. In examining factors related to a vote for the union, the authors found that positive attitudes toward unions in general and job dissatisfaction were highly productive.

Employees did not remember the many issues raised in the campaigns. During the campaigns, management raised about 30 issues, on the average, with employees remembering about 3. Unions campaigned on the average of 25 issues with employees remembering about 2. Meeting attendance, either at union or management sponsored gatherings, was significantly related to a familiarity with issues but had little effect on voting if the meeting was company sponsored. Persons who expressed familiarity with the issues were more likely to vote for the side expressing issues they remembered.

The study reported that generally, unions won elections only in units where authorization card majorities existed before the filing of the petition for an election. Between the filing of the petition and the election, average erosion of unions support was about 4 percent. Attendance at union meetings appeared to motivate undecided employees toward the union. The author provided no clear answers for why some undecided employees vote for the company, but concluded that exposure to company information may play a role.

The authors had an administrative law judge examine the campaign for violations of the Board's rules regarding campaign conduct. The administrative law judge found violations in 22 of the 31 elections. Nine had violations so serious that a bargaining order would have been imposed. The study found that union supporters were not more likely to switch their vote in a tainted campaign than in a clean campaign.

The major conclusions that the authors reached on the basis of their analysis were that the decision to vote for or against a union is largely a function of precampaign attitudes and that the campaign does not cause most employees to switch. Rather, the impact of the campaign is more likely to reinforce employee precampaign attitudes and intentions to vote since employees selectively perceive and distort information to which they are exposed in the campaigns. Finally, those individuals who do switch away from their predispositions do so for reasons that are independent of the campaign. On the basis of these conclusions the authors recommend that the Board eliminate rules governing campaign tactics, eliminate the need for the Board to make judgments regarding the impact of campaign tactics, provide employees equal access to employees in campaigns where the employer campaigns on company time or premises, and impose severe penalties on severe violations to the law.

The Board's policy regarding election campaign misrepresentations has oscillated in recent years. In 1962, in Hollywood Ceramics [13] the Board held that if substantial misstatements were made in a campaign and the opponent did not have time to respond, the Board would set aside the election results and order a new election. In 1977, the Board reversed the *Hollywood Ceramics* doctrine in the case of Shopping Kart Food Market, Inc., holding that elections would no longer be set aside solely because of misleading campaign statements.[14] However, it maintained this position for only one year. In General Knit of California the Board overruled *Shopping Kart* and readopted its prior standard of reviewing allegations of election campaign misrepresentations. The *General Knit* decision is reprinted below.

[The Board's oscillation continued even while this book was set in page proof. The Board decision in Midland National Life Insurance Co., 263 N.L.R.B. 24 (1982), wherein the Board repudiated *General Knit* and reinstituted the rule of *Shopping Kart* is included in Appendix D of this text. Read both decisions and consider which seems best reasoned and most sensible in result.—Ed.]

GENERAL KNIT OF CALIFORNIA

99 L.R.R.M. 1687 (1978).

[A certification election was conducted of the employees of General Knit of California, Inc. (employer). 134 ballots were cast in favor of representation by the United Steelworkers of America, AFL-CIO (petitioner), and 104 ballots were cast against the petitioner. The employer filed objections to the union's campaign conduct with the NLRB's regional director, charging that the union distributed leaflets which falsely listed the employer's net worth and its profits from the previous year. The figures in the leaflet made it appear that the employer had gathered considerable profits, when in fact it had sustained a $5 million loss. The regional director issued a report recommending that General Knit's objections be overruled and that the union be certified as the bargaining agent of the employer. General Knit filed exceptions with the Board to the regional director's report, and the union responded. The Board reversed.]

Opinion of the Board:

* * *

* * * After much deliberation, we have decided that the principle expressed in the majority and concurring opinions in Shopping Kart is inconsistent with our responsibility to insure fair elections. Accordingly, we hereby overrule Shopping Kart Food Market, Inc., and return to the standard of review for alleged misrepresentations most cogently articulated in Hollywood Ceramics Company, Inc. That standard indicates that:

"[A]n election should be set aside only where there has been a misrepresentation or other similar campaign trickery, which in-

---

13. Hollywood Ceramics Co., Inc., 140 N.L.R.B. 221 (1962).

14. Shopping Kart Food Market, Inc., 228 N.L.R.B. 1311 (1977).

volves substantial departure from the truth, at a time which prevents the other party or parties from making an effective reply so that the misrepresentation, whether deliberate or not, may reasonably be expected to have a significant impact on the election."

In Shopping Kart, which itself overruled Hollywood Ceramics, a Board majority determined that elections would no longer be set aside solely because of misleading campaign statements.

In disagreeing with the principles of Hollywood Ceramics, the Shopping Kart majority, in essence, disagreed with the general proposition that misrepresentations may, in fact, affect the way employees vote and thereby undermine the integrity of our electoral processes. As support for its view, the Shopping Kart majority relied on certain findings of one empirical study and what that study purported to prove. In that study, its authors attempted to verify empirically certain assumptions which they believed underlay the Board's regulation of election conduct—most importantly, the Board's assumption that electioneering by the employer and union affects the employee's decision as to how to cast his or her ballot. They concluded that this assumption was not supported by voter behavior in the 31 elections they studied. Rather, the authors found, on the basis of interviews with voters, both before and after the elections involved, that the parties' electioneering had not affected the decision of 81 percent of the voters. Thus, 81 percent voted in accordance with the intent they expressed to interviewers prior to the bulk of the union-management campaign. From this finding, the authors concluded that the voters' decisions seemed to be determined by their attitudes toward unions and toward their jobs, both of which had been established prior to the campaign, and which for 81 percent of the voters remained unchanged during the campaign. Of the remaining 19 percent, 6 percent were undecided at the first interview, while 13 percent voted contrary to the intent they had expressed to interviewers immediately after the filing of a petition for an election. Interestingly, in attempting to determine how voters in these two groups made their voting decisions, the authors found that the votes of the undecided 6 percent correlated with their "familiarity" with the unions' campaigns. Thus, those employees who voted for a union recalled significantly more issues raised by the union than did those who voted against the union. A similar pattern existed for the 13 percent who switched their votes. Finally, the authors found that the votes of the undecided and switchers were determinative in 9 of the 31 elections; that is, in 29 percent of the elections they studied.

In evaluating the findings summarized above, the authors speculated that the campaign itself had had little effect on voting decisions, but that the extent of familiarity with and reaction to each side's campaign was determined by a voter's initial attitude toward unions in general. However, the study was not designed to investigate the actual reasons for the reaction of voters to the campaigns, and theirs is by no means the only possible conclusion to be drawn from the data. The results of 43 years of conducting elections, investigating objections, and holding hearings at which employees testify concerning their recollection of campaign tactics convince us that employees are influenced by certain union and employer campaign statements. Even the authors acknowledged that, of the 19 percent, those who ultimately voted against the union may have been influenced by the employer's campaign, even though they did not recall specific issues.

The authors' final recommendations, including the suggested deregulation of misrepresentations, were based on their findings vis-à-vis the 81 percent of voters rather than the 19 percent. Such a narrow focus might have been warranted if the authors had concluded either that the votes of the 19 percent had not affected the results of a significant number of elections or that the 19 percent, in deciding how to vote, had not based that decision on information provided during the campaign. But where, as this study indicates, not only are a substantial minority of employees influenced by the campaign, but their votes also affected the outcome of over a quarter of the elections, we find this persuasive evidence for maintaining reasonable procedures to insure that the employees exercise their franchise in an atmosphere free from substantial and material misrepresentations.

Even if this particular study were clearly supportive of all of the authors' conclusions, however, we would still not find it an adequate ground for rejecting a rule which had been well established for 15 years. While we welcome research from the behavioral sciences, one study of only 31 elections in one area of the country—although it may provide food for thought—is simply not sufficient to disprove the assumptions upon which the Board has regulated election conduct, especially since, in our experience, statements made by either side can significantly affect voter preference.

*   *   *   In returning to the rule of Hollywood Ceramics, we are convinced that the rule better enhances employee free choice and the fairness of Board elections than did Shopping Kart. The Hollywood Ceramics rule further assures the public that the Board will not tolerate substantial and material misrepresentations made in the final hours of an election campaign and thereby gives stability to any bargaining relationship resulting from the election. The aims of insuring employee free choice, fairness of elections, and bargaining stability are high, but they are achievable under Hollywood Ceramics. It is for the foregoing reasons that we now return to the rule of that case.

(d) RETALIATION AGAINST UNION MEMBERS

Employers may sometimes respond to union organization by action as well as speech. It is unlawful, however, either to retaliate against union supporters or to make a selective or a general grant of benefits in order to defeat the union. Employers frequently consider discharging a marginal or unsatisfactory employee whom they know or consider to be a union supporter. The presence of legitimate grounds does not make the action lawful. As long as the employee's union activity or membership played a role in the decision, discipline violates the Act. The only question is one of proof of the employer's motive. A side issue which frequently arises is whether the Board may consider a lawful anti-union speech in determining the motive for a discharge. Although Section 8(c) provides that expressions of opinion are not to be considered evidence of an unfair labor practice, the Board does consider such statements as part of the background of the case. Where an unlawful discharge is found, the employee is ordered reinstated with backpay plus interest. Such action will frequently be a major factor in the issuance of a bargaining order.

The only situation in which avowed employee retaliation against employees for engaging is protracted actually does not violate the law is when the employer closes down his business entirely. The Supreme Court so held in Textile Workers v. Darlington Mfg. Co., 380 U.S. 263, 85 S.Ct. 994, 13 L.Ed.2d 827 (1965).

The case arose when the employees of Darlington Manufacturing Company voted for union representation. In response the stockholders voted to dissolve the corporation. Darlington discontinued operations in November and sold the plant. The Board found that Darlington thereby violated Section 8(a)(3).

The Board also found that Darlington "occupied a single employer status with [another respondent], Deering Milliken and its affiliated corporations." A separate order was directed to Deering Milliken making it liable for backpay to the same extent as Darlington and ordering it to offer the discharged employees positions at other locations to the extent they were available. The Fifth Circuit, sitting en banc, denied enforcement.

The Supreme Court remanded. It stated that if Darlington should be regarded as a single employer it was privileged to go out of business even if "the liquidation [was] motivated by vindictiveness towards the union * * * ." On the other hand the Court held that the closing down of the Darlington Plant might constitute an unfair labor practice because of its impact on other parts of Deering Milliken's enterprise. It announced a three-step test for determining whether a plant closing violates Section 8(a)(3):

> If the persons exercising control over a plant that is being closed for anti-union reasons (1) have an interest in another business, whether or not affiliated with or engaged in the same line of commercial activity as the closed plant, of sufficient substantiality to give promise of their reaping a benefit from the discouragement of unionization in that business; (2) act to close their plant with the purpose of producing such a result; and (3) occupy a relationship to the other business which makes it realistically foreseeable that its employees will fear that such business will also be closed down if they persist in organizational activities, we think that an unfair labor practice has been made out.[15]

The case was returned to the court of appeals to consider whether Darlington was a single employer under the newly-established test.

15. Textile Workers v. Darlington Mfg. Co., 380 U.S. 263, at 275, 276, 85 S.Ct. 994 at 1002, 13 L.Ed.2d 827 (1965).

QUESTION

What sort of evidence would be necessary to prove a violation under the second and third parts of the Darlington partial closing test?

E. RECOMMENDED READING

In addition to the books and articles excerpted in the chapter, among the best legal discussions are:

1. Williams, James and Huhn, National Labor Relations Board, *Regulation of Election Conduct* (1974).
2. Getman and Goldberg, "The Myth of Labor Board Expertise," 390 Univ. of Chi.L.Rev. 681 (1972).
3. Bok, "The Regulation of Campaign Tactics In Representation Elections Under the National Labor Relations Act," 78 Harv.L. Rev. 38 (1964).
4. Samoff, "NLRB Elections: Uncertainty and Certainty," 117 U. of Pa.L.Rev. 228, (1968).
5. Schlossberg, *Organizing and the Law* (1967).

For field research, see:

6. Karsh, *Diary of a Strike* (1958).
7. Brotslaw, "Attitude of Retail Workers Toward Union Organization," 81 Labor L.J. 149 (1967).

For practical management guides for responding to union organizing efforts, see:

8. Fulmer, "Step By Step Through A Union Campaign," Harv. Bus.Rev. 94 (July-August 1981).
9. Kilgour, *Preventive Labor Relations* (1981).
10. Swann, *NLRB Elections: A Guidebook for Employers* (1980).
11. DeMaria, *How Management Wins Union Organizing Campaigns* (1980).

*

Chapter III

EMPLOYER–EMPLOYEE COOPERATION AND THE CONCEPT OF COMPANY UNIONS: THE REACH OF § 8(a)(2)

A. CASE STUDY: THE ACACIA COMPANY

The Acacia Company is headquartered in Springfield, Ohio, which is 60 miles west of Columbus, Ohio. Its major facility consists of 187,000 square feet under one roof. At this facility there are 775 employees of which 500 are in Manufacturing. Since 1965, Acacia has been supplying electronic instrumentation to the agricultural industry. Typical electronic products are planter monitors, combine monitors, grain moisture testers and control systems for liquid sprayers and granular spreaders. In addition, Acacia produces sophisticated systems that are used in processing grain and measuring protein, oil, moisture and other constituents of grain.

Acacia's Springfield plant is a vertically integrated manufacturing facility, which means it does numerous primary operations such as machining, metalworking, painting, molding and making liquid crystal displays, as well as assembling the electronic components into consoles and systems. The facility operates under a traditional organizational structure with a philosophy of participative management whenever practical and possible.

Acacia started experiencing production quality problems in the late-1970's. In 1979, 40–50% of its control systems for liquid sprayers and granular spreaders were produced with missing or faulty parts, up from 10% in 1973. In addition, productivity during this period fell by 25%. Furthermore, employee dissatisfaction became apparent during this period. Employee turnover and absenteeism had greatly increased. The number of employee quits rose by 50% from 1977 to 1979. During this two-year period it was necessary for Acacia to recruit 25% of its workforce each year. Absenteeism rose from an average of two work days per year per worker in 1977 to an average of 9 work days per worker in 1979. Management attributed the high turnover and absenteeism rate to the shifting demographics of its workforce. Starting in the mid-1970's, Acacia employed more women who had never worked in a factory before. The women workers generally found factory routine and discipline difficult. Women workers also experienced difficulties in finding suitable child care facilities. Also starting in the mid-1970's Acacia employed a younger workforce than it had employed in the 1960's and early 1970's. The post W. W. II baby boom was being felt at Acacia. Acacia's younger workers were generally better educated workers who no longer want-

135

ed to confront the same job routine every day. Due to shifting housing patterns, many of Acacia's employees lived farther from work than in the past. Thus Acacia's workers were commuting longer distances.

In early 1979, Jim Bookmiller, Acacia's Vice-President of manufacturing started reading numerous articles in magazines and receiving promotion brochures in the mail on Quality Circles.

Quality Circles are small groups of employees doing similar or related work who meet regularly to identify, analyze and solve product-quality and production problems and to improve general operations. Such diverse matters as safety and absenteeism may be scrutinized. Workers are given training in a variety of statistical techniques designed to help them correctly evaluate information. Bookmiller brought up the subject of Quality Circles in a staff meeting in January, 1979, as something which seemed to make sense to Acacia's type of operation and which might be of value to Acacia. After one of the managers investigated it further and made a presentation to the staff, the staff decided to pursue its investigation by attending a one-day seminar in February, 1979 on the subject in Chicago and visiting a company which had an active Quality Circle program. Three people attended the seminar and plant visit.

The three staff members were impressed at what they found. They learned that Quality Circles sometimes solved problems that baffled professional engineers. In their trip report they stressed how effectively Quality Circles motivated workers by enriching their jobs and increasing their sense of participation. The report also noted the strong support top management gave to the program and the obvious involvement of the workers in their jobs. The three staff members came back enthused with the Quality Circle concept. At a staff meeting in March, 1979, they made the following presentation:

Quality Circle Presentation

 1. Concept

    The concept of Quality Circles originated in Japan after World War II as one means of upgrading their product quality. Many people feel it plays a major role in their attaining a world-wide position of supplying high quality products. It first appeared in the U. S. under this name in 1970. (It should be noted however that similar activities have been conducted by numerous other companies under different names for many years.)

 2. Definition

    A Quality Circle is defined as   *   *   *   "A small group of three to twelve people from the same work area who voluntarily get together on a regular basis, to identify, analyze and solve product quality and other problems in the work they are doing."

3. Philosophy

The Quality Circles philosophy is based on the simple concept that "nearly all people will take more pride and interest in their work if they are allowed to make meaningful contributions which influence decisions made about their work".

4. Objectives

The overall objective of Quality Circles is improved productivity but that is attained through the following more definite ways:

(a) Improved communications.

(b) Providing a better climate for motivation.

(c) Provide a means or opportunity for the people to analyze and solve problems, not just identify them thus improving quality and efficiency.

(d) Reduce conflicts and improve teamwork.

(e) Educate and generate awareness of costs, operations, and goals.

(f) Provide for personal and job growth opportunities.

5. How it Operates

The operation of Quality Circles consists of five elements:

(a) A Steering Committee

(b) Facilitators

(c) Circle Leaders

(d) Circle Members

(e) Management

The Steering Committee as the name implies, advises, sets policies, objectives and rules to give the program guidance and direction. Generally, it is composed of the facilitators and management representing the major functions of the company.

The facilitator is probably the key element of the program. The facilitator does the training, coordinating, communicating and is most responsible for the overall program.

The circle leader is normally the person responsible for one circle. The leader trains, participates, guides and reports on the circle activities. Generally, the leader is the regular supervisor of the work area the circle is from and a volunteer.

The circle members are strictly volunteers and for best results, do similar type of work. The members bring up and select the problems, analyze them and solve them.

Management fits into the program from the standpoint of providing support, assistance and, if appropriate, participates. They are also the recipients of the circles presentations and may frequently be asked to approve the problem solutions, particularly if they involve funding or operation changes.

The three staff members concluded their presentation with a recommendtion that Acacia adopt a Quality Circle program. The staff adopted the recommendation, concluding that it fit Acacia's management philosophy of participation. It was decided that the Quality Circles concept fit Acacia's type of operation and could help the company be more efficient and productive.

Organization of the Quality Circle Program

Selection of the Steering Committee and the Facilitator:

The first step the staff took in implementing the Quality Circle program was the formation of the Steering Committee. After discussing the concept and the role of the Steering Committee with several managers, the staff decided that the Steering Committee would consist of the Vice President of Manufacturing, the Quality Control Manager, and the production managers of the initial circles. These individuals were chosen because of their involvement and relationship to the expected circle activities. Although the Steering Committee was established with managers, the staff established the policy that the Steering Committee members need not necessarily be managers.

The staff next named a facilitator. The facilitator is the most critical element in the program. The facilitator conducts much of the initial training and also serves as a resource person for the Quality Circles. The facilitator's task is to help the Quality Circle concept take hold and make it grow. He or she coordinates the activities, trains the leaders, follows-up on projects, attends the Quality Circle meetings, and participates in the Steering Committee meetings. The staff reviewed the available personnel and went over the various qualifications, which were: experience in manufacturing and quality control, communication ability, interest in the program, and people oriented. The staff selected Dennis Yerkes, one of the staff members as the facilitator.

Philosophy, Goals and Scope of the Program

Before going into operation, the staff felt it important to put into writing the philosophy, goals, and scope of the program. These were generated by Yerkes with considerable discussion and review by the Steering Committee. In May the following statement of philosophy, goals and scope were issued:

Quality Circles Philosophy at Acacia

It is a philosophy of Acacia to continually seek ways and means through which to make the work of all Acacia people both interesting and rewarding.

In adopting the Quality Circles concept of having people from the same work area, voluntarily work together to identify and solve quality and other problems, we are dedicated to the following goals.

Quality Circles Goals

- Improve communications throughout the company.

- Make work more interesting and meaningful.

- Have circles learn more about the company and interface with other functions and operations.

- Keep both members and non-members informed of circle activities.

- Develop a greater trust and understanding throughout Acacia.

- Gradually expand circles throughout Acacia.

- Reduce scrap, workmanship errors and vendor problems.

- Develop problem prevention techniques.

- Maintain records of quality circle achievements.

Quality Circles Scope

The Quality Circles Program is to begin with five circles within the Manufacturing Department. Expansion of additional circles will be at a rate of two every two months.

Circle size may range from approximately eight to ten members each, with supervisors being leaders during the initial phase. All circles will be scheduled to meet for one hour each week, to have members voluntarily participate in the task of identifying, analyzing, and solving quality and other problems in their own work area.

The Steering Committee will be made up of officers, managers, and facilitators during the first six months of operation and will be responsible for overseeing circle activities and providing direction. After six months of successful operation, the committee may review its own make-up to allow both members and leaders to participate in meetings.

Facilitator responsibilities are to include handling of all daily operations of Quality Circles, such as scheduling meetings, training leaders and members, contacting support groups, publicity and regularly report circle activities to the Steering Committee.

Circles may elect to work on problems involving paperwork, workmanship, assembling methods, material handling, product flow and productivity. Matters that deal with electronic circuit designs, customer designs, or company policies such as wages, vacations and benefits will continue to be handled by supervision or the specific area of responsibility.

The scope of Quality Circles may be revised at anytime to allow for future growth and new challenges at the recommendation of the Steering Committee.

The Program's Implementation

Circle Area Selection:

Bookmiller's staff decided to start the program with five circles and add two circles every two months. The decision on what areas the five would come from involved several questions, such as: (1) Is the supervisor from that area interested in Quality Circles? (2) Are the activities of that group fairly similar? (3) Could that area benefit from the program quickly and easily?

Leader Training:

Having established the five circles, it was then that the supervisors of the areas, who would be the Quality Circle leaders, had to be trained. The leader training was conducted by the facilitator. The leaders were introduced to the Quality Circles concept in a seminar. They were instructed in the techniques of organizing, training, and maintaining the circles.

Selection of Members:

After successfully completing this course, the leaders presented the concept to their subordinates. After explaining the program and answering questions, the employees were asked to volunteer for membership. Each circle was formed with eight to ten members. Where more than ten workers in a circle area volunteered for membership, the leader selected ten workers who he or she thought to be most suited for membership.

Circle Start-Up and Training:

The circle member began meeting once a week, with the first few meetings spent familiarizing members with the basic Quality Circle techniques in which the leader had been trained. The objective of the training program was to teach leaders and members to apply simplified, basic techniques to the selection of actual problems in the area where they work. As part of the learning phase the members apply the techniques to real problems. The same basic techniques the members were trained in were:

(1) Data Gathering—Check Sheets. The objective is to analyze only after having accurate data which is organized. Training was conducted on establishing a foremat for check sheets.

(2) Pareto Analysis. The purpose of learning Pareto's Law was so the members would apply their efforts to accomplish the greatest return. Members were taught how to graphically depict on a Pareto chart a problem's frequency so that a decision could be made on which problems to work on. Pareto Analysis was thus used to select problems to solve and to establish their priority, not as a problem-solving tool.

(3) Data Gathering Theory. Members were trained in sampling, including the conditions of bias, depression and repeatability.

(4) Brainstorming. Brainstorming was to be used for listing possible courses of a problem. Members were told that an important aspect of brainstorming in Quality Circles is the suggest-

ed rule: No criticisms, do not evaluate or judge the ideas during brainstorming, participation should be subsequently and only one idea per turn.

(5) Decision Analysis. The members were taught the advantages and disadvantages of group decision-making, the encouragement of tactful dissent, and the means of obtaining good decisions.

(6) Presentation Techniques. Training in presentation techniques was undertaken to assure that the solution being recommended would get a fair hearing when approval was required.

(7) Cause and Effect Problem Solving. Members received training in cause and effect analysis to facilitate identification of the cause or causes of a problem so that corrective action could be undertaken.

The Program's Operation

By August 1979 the first circles were in operation. The Steering Committee decided that circles should meet for one hour per week in the plant cafeteria. The members set to work identifying and solving workshop problems using the techniques described above.

Each circle designated one member to record minutes which were circulated to the Steering Committee and to appropriate department managers. Department managers are the next higher level of Supervision over the line supervisors. Department managers have full responsibility over budgeting, efficiency, quality control, personnel in their departments. Although the department managers are not organizationally involved with the circles, a special effort was made to communicate to the department managers the circle objectives, activities, and results. This was done through circulation of minutes, and discussions between Yerkes and the department managers and supervisors.

Consultations with each circle member were conducted by Yerkes. In August problems had been listed and corrective action had begun. Routine conversation with circle members indicated a good deal of enthusiasm. However Yerkes noted the following questions raised by circle members:

— "I'm putting forth this extra effort for the company, what effect will it have on my performance review?

— "Will participation in the circle help my chances of promotion?

— "If we save the company money, shouldn't I get some amount of financial reward?"

Additional comments came from those employees not in circles, ranging from curiosity to complaints about circle members getting out of work.

In response to the question on financial reward, the Steering Committee explained its philosophy in the following statement sent to circle members:

"Whether we like to admit it or not, a company does not consist of just owners or management or production personnel. It requires all three groups working together to make it succeed. You might consider the company as a partnership of three groups pulling and working in unison for common goals. Therefore, as part of their future, their livelihood, their compensation and return, it is essential they contribute all of their skills, their knowledge and capability while at work. To this end, each of them has a responsibility, an obligation and all are being compensated to use their heads along with the rest of their bodies   *   *   * "

We could go on and cover the drawbacks of financial incentive systems and all the administrative problems, but the point is whatever job you are assigned or whatever position you hold, it is part of your job and pay, to think and submit ways of improvement.

Results

By the end of 1981 there were 20 circles in the Acacia Springfield plant. Employee turnover absenteesim had been reduced and production quality improved. In 1980, the average circle listed 35 separate problems, and solved 24.

In January 1982 Local 076 of the International Brotherhood of Electrical Workers succeeded in signing up the necessary 30% of the 500 hourly employees in the Manufacturing Division at Acacia's Springfield plant. A NLRB certification election was held in April 1982. Of the 435 employees who voted, 220 voted against having the IBEW as its bargaining representative and 215 voted in favor of the union. Local 076 has petitioned the Board's Regional Director to set aside the election, charging that Acacia committed an unfair labor practice by supporting a labor organization in violation of § 8(a)(2) when it implemented its Quality Circle Program.

B.   THE SCOPE AND OPERATION OF § 8(a)(2)

Section 8(a)(2) of the NLRA Act makes it unlawful for an employer to "dominate or interfere with the formation or administration of any labor organization or contribute financial or other support to it." This section was primarily intended to prevent the company union, an organization which claims to represent the employee but is in fact controlled by the employer, but as the materials below will show its application today goes well beyond that limited purpose.

Where employer control is proved, the Board will characterise the offending union as a "dominated labor organization". It will then order the union "disestablished" which means the employer is barred from ever recognizing it as the representative of his employees or bargaining with it again. The Board finds domination when managerial employees play a major role in the formation or in the operation of a union. The use of company unions to defeat organization has waned in recent years not only because they are outlawed but because such organizations have the potential for escaping from employer control and putting the employer in the situation of having created the type of union which he was seeking to forestall.

An employer may be guilty of illegal support short of domination in which case he will be ordered to withhold recognition until such time as the union becomes certified by the Board after a fair election.

Various types of employer conduct in support of a union might constitute unlawful support as where an employee contributes money or permits a supervisor to solicit for the union on company time. The mere expression of employee sentiment on behalf of a union is not unlawful however. It is protected by the free speech language of § 8(c). Employer recognition of a minority union constitutes illegal support even if done in the good faith belief that the union had a majority at the time and the Board will order recognition withdrawn even if the union has in the meantime acquired majority support.[1]

When two or more unions vie for employer support, the Board applying its so-called Midwest Piping doctrine holds that anytime an election is pending or would be appropriate the employer must withhold recognition even if he correctly estimates that one of the unions is supported by a majority. The employer may not even continue to recognize an incumbent union for the purpose of negotiating a new agreement. The courts have been very hostile to the doctrine in these circumstances and have frequently refused to enforce Board Midwest Piping decisions.

C. SECTION 8(a)(2) AND NEW FORMS OF LABOR–MANAGEMENT RELATIONS

One important question which has not yet been answered is whether § 8(a)(2) prevents experimentation with new forms of labor participation. Such programs may often be characterized as efforts to co-opt employees and make unions unnecessary in managerial decision making. The Act's sweeping language makes it possible to find a dominated labor organization whenever a group of employees has a role in determining labor policies.

LABOR BOARD v. CABOT CARBON CO.

Supreme Court of the United States, 1959.
360 U.S. 203, 79 S.Ct. 1015, 3 L.Ed.2d 1175.

MR. JUSTICE WHITTAKER delivered the opinion of the Court.

The question for decision in this case is whether "Employee Committees" established and supported by respondents at each of their several plants for the stated purposes of meeting regularly with man-

---

1. The Supreme Court dealt with these questions in ILGWU v. N.L.R.B. (The Bernhart-Altman case) 366 U.S. 731, 81 S.Ct. 1603, 6 L.Ed.2d 762 (1961).

agement to consider and discuss problems of mutual interest, including grievances, and of handling "grievances at nonunion plants and departments," are, in the light of their declared purposes and actual practices, "labor organizations" within the meaning of § 2(5) of the National Labor Relations Act.

Respondents are * * *, and for many years have been, engaged in operating a number of plants, principally in Texas and Louisiana, primarily for the purposes of manufacturing and selling carbon black and oil field equipment. Pursuant to a suggestion of the War Production Board in 1943, respondents decided to establish an Employee Committee at each of their plants. To that end, respondents prepared, in collaboration with employee representatives from their several plants, a set of bylaws, stating the purposes, duties and functions of the proposed Employee Committees, for transmittal to and adoption by the employees in establishing such Committees. The bylaws were adopted by a majority of employees at each plant and by respondents, and, thus, the Employee Committees were established. Those bylaws, and certain related company rules, were later published by respondents in a company manual called "The Guide," and are still in effect.

In essence, the bylaws state: that the purpose of the Committees is to provide a procedure for considering employees' ideas and problems of mutual interest to employees and management; that each plant Committee shall consist of a stated number of employees (ranging from 2 to 3) whose terms shall be one year, and that retiring members, with the help of plant clerks, will conduct the nomination and election of their successors; that each plant Committee shall meet with the plant management at regular monthly meetings and at all special meetings called by management, shall assist the plant management in solving problems of mutual interest, and that time so spent will be considered time worked; and that "It shall be the Committee's responsibility to: * * * Handle grievances at nonunion plants and departments according to procedure set up for these plants and departments."

In November 1954, International Chemical Workers Union, AFL-CIO, filed with the National Labor Relations Board, and later several times amended, an unfair labor practice charge against respondents, alleging, in part, that respondents were unlawfully dominating, interfering with and supporting labor organizations, called Employee Committees, at their several plants. Thereafter the Board, in April 1956, issued a complaint against respondents under § 10(b) of the Act (29 U.S.C.A. § 160(b)), alleging, *inter alia*, that the Employee Committees were labor organizations within the meaning of § 2(5) (see note 1), and that respondents, since May 1954, had dominated, interfered with, and supported the Committees in violation of § 8(a)(2) of the Act.

* * *

We turn first to the Court of Appeals' holding that an employee committee which does not "bargain with" employers in "the usual concept of collective bargaining" does not engage in "dealing with" employers, and is therefore not a "labor organization" within the meaning of § 2(5). Our study of the matter has convinced us that there is nothing in the plain words of § 2(5), in its legislative history, or in the decisions construing it, that supports that conclusion.

Section 2(5) includes in its definition of "labor organization" any "employee representation committee or plan * * * which exists for the purpose, in whole or in part, of *dealing with* employers concerning grievances, labor disputes, wages, rates of pay, hours of employment, or conditions of work." (Emphasis added). Certainly nothing in that section indicates that the broad term "dealing with" is to be read as synonymous with the more limited term "bargaining with." The legislative history of § 2(5) strongly confirms that Congress did not understand or intend those terms to be synonymous. * * *

* * *

We therefore conclude that there is nothing in the amendment of § 9(a), or in its legislative history, to indicate that Congress thereby eliminated or intended to eliminate such employee committees from the term "labor organization" as defined in § 2(5) and used in § 8(a) (2).

Respondents argue that to hold these employee committees to be labor organizations would prevent employers and employees from discussing matters of mutual interest concerning the employment relationship, and would thus abridge freedom of speech in violation of the First Amendment of the Constitution. But the Board's order does not impose any such bar; it merely precludes the employers from dominating, interfering with or supporting such employee committees which Congress has defined to be labor organizations.

The judgment of the Court of Appeals is reversed and the cause is remanded for further proceedings not inconsistent with this opinion.

Reversed and remanded.

———

The reach of the *Cabot Carbon* decision has become a matter of considerable importance in light of the growing interest in the concept of worker participation or co-determination. As the materials which follow show, schemes to give workers a greater voice in setting working conditions have been established with varying degrees of success in Europe. Similar programs have been developed or are under consideration in the United States. However, the *Cabot Carbon* decision and subsequent Board and Court rulings have raised doubt about the legality of such programs under § 8(a)(2) of the NLRA.

ROBERT BALL, THE HARD HATS IN
EUROPE'S BOARDROOMS *

In recent years, many American businessmen have become vaguely aware of a European phenomenon known by its tongue-twisting German name, *Mitbestimmung*. Some not so vaguely, if their companies have subsidiaries in the North European countries where *Mitbestimmung* is firmly established as an industrial way of life. But sometimes direct exposure only deepens the bafflement. Workers on the board? Worker councils with influence over management decisions to hire and fire? An obligation for management to consult employees about new capital-investment projects? It sounds like the end of capitalism.

Well, no, but the confusion is understandable. It begins with the word itself, for which there is no satisfactory English equivalent. Co-determination, co-management, participation—all of them miss the German term's associations of joint command, of two hands on the tiller. Co-determination and co-management have a blurred meaning; participation can cover anything from the employee suggestion box to all sorts of programs for job enrichment.

America did get a whiff of the idea in the late Sixties, when all sorts of protest movements took up the demand for "participation"— for the view that people should be able, in some way, to influence decisions affecting them. In the business world, this was reflected in the more widely accepted view that the corporation itself had a broader responsibility to society than that implied by accountability to stockholders and obedience to the law of the land. Businessmen who accepted the idea of "corporate social responsibility" were increasingly responsive to claims having to do with ecology, consumerism, and the rights of minorities and women.

Significantly, most American unions stood aside from the campaign for "participation." They have consistently taken the line that a sharing of management responsibilities would hamper the unions' freedom of action in collective bargaining. The A.F.L.-C.I.O. rejects the idea of workers on the board, and some officials have scoffed that European unions are simply trying by other means to get the degree of effective shop-floor control that American unions already have. The only significant exception in the U. S. labor movement is the United Automobile Workers, who have recently been asking Chrysler to put some unionists on its board.† But even some U.A.W. officials believe the emphasis should be on co-managing the job rather than the enterprise itself.

AN IDEA WITH MOMENTUM

Many European unions operate on the premise that worker interests are best served if employees have a say in management. Union pressure has provided the momentum for the remarkable recent

---

* Reprinted from the June '76 issue of Fortune Magazine by special permission; © 1976 Time, Inc.

† [At publication, Douglas Fraser, UAW president, is seated on the Chrysler board.—Ed.]

spread of co-determination institutions. In the last few years, laws requiring worker representation in the boardroom have gone on the books in the Netherlands, Luxembourg, Austria, Norway, Sweden, and Denmark. Similar "industrial democracy" legislation has been promised by the present governments of France and Britain. In West Germany, that citadel of the entrepreneurial spirit, the Bundestag last March, by an almost unanimous vote, raised employees to near-equality with stockholders on the boards of all companies with more than 2,000 persons on the payroll—some 650 enterprises.

This impressive forward march of the hard hats into European boardrooms does not mean that co-determination has become noncontroversial. Employers in France and Britain are strongly opposed to their governments' legislative plans, and Italian employers are also cool to any compulsory form of co-determination. The conservative Swiss last spring defeated by two-to-one margins a pair of referendum proposals on co-determination. And in the Latin countries the unions themselves remain skeptical.

Even where co-determination has been adopted, employers have fought a stubborn rearguard action to stop employee-union representation in the boardroom somewhere short of half and half. Employers feel, with some reason, that the interests of stockholders and employees are not identical when it comes to such decisions as the introduction of laborsaving machinery or building a plant abroad. They worry that the union could end up negotiating with itself.

Yet the evidence shows that, up to now, co-determination has worked. Indeed, some observers, looking at Germany's extraordinary record of good industrial relations, rapid economic growth, and export success, have jumped to the conclusion that *Mitbestimmung* is a universally applicable magic formula for industrial success. That it certainly is not.

The fairest reading of the evidence would seem to be that co-determination works when the stockholder side has a slight but decisive edge, and when, within the enterprise, awareness of the diverging interests of employers and employees is matched by a sense of common interest in the future of the company. Then the paradigm of employer-employee relations becomes not a rectangular bargaining table, but a round boardroom table.

IT'S A TWO–TIER SYSTEM

Worker representation is much easier to build into a German board (or into those of companies in the North European countries that follow the German pattern of company law) than into the board of a British or American corporation. This is because German corporations have what is usually referred to as a two-tier system.

The upper tier is the *Aufsichtsrat*, or supervisory board, and it is this board that worker representatives have been joining. However, the *Aufsichtsrat* does not get entangled in the actual running of the business. Its members normally include no executives of the company, and the board meets infrequently (about four times a year on average). Its principal power is that of hiring and firing the senior executives who make up the *Vorstand*—the lower tier—and monitoring their performance, though it may also review major investment plans.

The boardroom is not the only arena in which European workers can exert influence. Another is the *Betriebsrat* or works council. This body, elected by the employees of each large plant, has a key role in labor relations. It, rather than the union, is the focus of shop-floor grievance procedures and monitors the carrying out of labor agreements. It is the negotiating partner if management wants to change the organization of production, has certain veto rights over hiring and firing, and is the main channel through which management conveys information to employees. It is close to union thinking, but is no mere appendage of the union. In Germany, where workers have strong loyalties to their companies, works councils often show an independent spirit.

Mitbestimmung tends to be popular among many of Europe's socialists, but it is not really a socialist idea. It is, in fact, an alternative to socialism, if the latter means nationalization of the means of production. The name itself postulates a partnership between owners and employees, and in Western countries this implies survival of private ownership of enterprises. Co-determination differs clearly from the Yugoslav system of worker self-management and the various forms of co-op or worker ownership in Western countries in that workers are involved in management but do not own the company.

Nothing like co-determination exists in the countries of the so-called "socialist camp," where the rule is a hierarchical command structure beyond the dreams of any Western reactionary. Many Western Communist parties condemn co-determination as a fraud perpetrated by capitalists on the working class. It is no accident that co-determination has developed most strongly in those countries in which Communist parties are weak and leftist demands for nationalization are faint.

D. JENKINS, DEMOCRACY IN THE FACTORY *

Though discontent has obviously been fermenting for sometime, only very recently have the problems of work received much notice in the United States. The press has devoted a modicum of attention to the issue, and it is no longer a novelty to observe that most jobs are stupefyingly boring. (A U. S. Army recruiting poster, reflecting the increased awareness of the question, perceptively coaxed: "If your job puts you to sleep, try one of ours.") The new concern about work has only begun to lead to an intensive search for solutions.

It should be emphasized that the situation is very different in Europe, where there is—and has been for some years—a widespread resolution to deal with problems of work. Specifically, there is a well-established movement to modify or abolish authoritarianism in industry and to replace it by some form of democracy. Although the reforms being promoted vary from country to country, they have one point in common: the transfer of decision-making power to employees. This movement, whose first tremors are only now being felt in the United States, might best be called "industrial democracy." In almost every West European country, student groups, political factions, independent organizations, social thinkers, writers, and labor leaders are actively urging democratic reform of business enterprises, and anyone in these countries drawing up a list of social reforms would surely put near the top some version of industrial democracy.

In the United States, paradoxically, there is a vast reservoir of *knowledge* of organizations. During the past three or four decades, the study of organizations by behavioral scientists has made enormous strides, and since the 1950s the knowledge has been spreading into managerial ranks. Previously, psychologists in industry were usually restricted to technical chores such as testing, recruiting, and thinking up "human relations" gimmicks with which to create spurious feelings of "belongingness" among employees. And "organization specialists" were people who concentrated on reshaping organization charts to create clearer and more effective lines of authority. Recently this has been changing, as the behavioral scientists have begun to persuade managers to think of organizations in terms of their human components.

But there is still only limited interest in industrial democracy in America. Almost no groups here—neither student activists nor journalists (as in France), nor the state (as in Yugoslavia), nor labor unions (as in Germany), nor intellectual leaders (as in Sweden), nor radical leftists groups (as in Great Britain), nor the workers themselves (as in many European countries)—are agitating for the spread of democracy within enterprises.

This anomalous situation cannot be expected to endure for long, particularly in view of the deepening dissatisfaction with work and the pressure toward industrial democracy implicit in these organizational studies. It is difficult to see how a convergence of these two can be avoided, and when it takes place, the impact could be far-reaching.

Most advanced American approaches to industrial organization contain some "democratic" elements—that is, they alter power structures, they give increased power and freedom to lower-level employees, and they help diffuse decision-making throughout the organization. But they tend to be limited.

The handful of companies that have gone the furthest have adopted a philosophy, variously described as an "open sytems," "total systems," or "sociotechnical" approach. This approach actively encourages employees to influence their working environment, and it attempts to integrate technological systems with social systems, so that production methods serve human as well as corporate needs.

The two companies that have made the most progress along these lines are General Foods and Procter & Gamble.

The General Foods philosophy has been put into practice at a pet-food factory in Topeka, Kansas. Lyman Ketchum, an organizational specialist at General Foods headquarters in White Plains, New York, explained to me that the new approach grew to a great extent out of experience at a pet-food plant in Kankakee, Illinois, of which he had been manager. In the late 1960s, with the advent of an ever younger work force, an unfamiliar atmosphere was developing. "We discovered there was something different happening," Ketchum told me. "People were not aware of why they were behaving differently; they were just reacting in different ways." Ketchum mentioned poor quality production, vandalism, and graffiti on the walls as symptoms of the discontent. He told me: "Bad quality is inevitably a product of alienation."

To attack these problems, management took an entirely new stance at the Topeka plant. The planning group analyzed the plant's operation in terms of human needs: the employees' self-esteem, sense of accomplishment, autonomy, and increasing knowledge. The group also looked at data on employees' performance. As a consequence of the study, the company minimized the work force so as to make each job more challenging. * * * Along the same lines, the planners omitted as many specialized functions as possible. "We tried to put all the responsibilities and all the skills in the teams," Ketchum said. There are no foremen, there are "team leaders."

After about eighteen months of operation, the reorganization of the Topeka plant appeared to be working out very much as planned. Ed Dulworth, plant manager, told me that all the unusual features had been retained; indeed, employees were being given more freedom than planned: "People are free to come and go when they wish. In the plant, operators are free to arrange the tasks among themselves. The scheduling—who does what and when—is all handled by the people in the plant. Everybody is very involved in all aspects of the business. We have committees for safety, spare parts, welfare and benefits, recreation, and so on. Almost everyone has some part in the committee work."

There are two teams—an eight-man processing team and a sixteen-man packaging-warehousing team—operating on three shifts. There are about ninety employees, including office staff. Normally, there would be cleaners, helpers, process operators, mechanics, boiler operators, quality control technicians, fork truck drivers, grain unloaders, and others on each shift. But here everybody learns every job.

Everyone learns at his own pace—his progress being judged by his fellow team members—and moves up the pay scale according to his own progress (regardless of seniority or how many others are moving up at the same time). Starting pay in mid-1972 was $136 a week; by learning a full team's jobs, employees move up to $142; by learning more jobs "across the plant," they move gradually up to

$170; and by acquiring—in addition to all this—an unusual skill or expertise, they can go to $192 (a step nobody had reached at the time of my visit). Dulworth says: "We feel that the more jobs a person knows the better he can do any job, since lots of things that happen affect several jobs. We're paying for knowledge beyond what is required. For example, you can get people to do jobs like loading materials eight hours a day rather cheaply. But that's an undesirable job, and the people here share the undesirable jobs."

In addition to responsibilities specified in the reorganization plan, employees have taken on the job of hiring and firing. Potential new employees are screened by the teams and, occasionally, are expelled on the decision of their teammates.

Overall costs of the product are considerably lower than would customarily be expected in a conventional plant, and quality is higher because of greater worker involvement. The attitudes of workers are overwhelmingly positive.

Without doubt the most radical organizational changes made on a practical, day-to-day basis in the United States have taken place at Procter & Gamble, one of America's largest companies and well known for its hard-boiled, aggressive management practices. Primarily devoted to making good soap and fat profits, P&G has minimal interest in management methods of modish nomenclature. But Charles Krone, the head of organizational development at P&G's Cincinnati headquarters, in discussing his approach, says: "I call it industrial democracy."

The new P&G program was first put into operation in the late 1960s at a plant in Lima, Ohio, employing about 125 people in three shifts, producing two consumer products, one in a batch process and the other in a continuous process. Krone explained to me that the new ideas were designed into the plant, which uses rather advanced technology and is highly automated: "The plant was designed from the ground up to be democratic. The technology—the location of instruments, for example—was designed to stimulate relationships between people, to bring about autonomous group behavior, and to allow people to affect their own environment." Conference rooms, laboratories, and other service functions are located immediately adjacent to the production area, so that any needed action can be taken without delay.

Just as there are no physical barriers, so there are no barriers between jobs. Indeed, there are no jobs at all in the ordinary sense. In an orthodox plant of this type, there might be sixteen to twenty job classifications—at Lima there are none. Not everybody can do every job, but every member of "the community" (as Krone refers to the employees) is constantly adding to his own skills in some specialized field. Krone says, "Each individual defines the direction in which he wants to grow." The community decided, however, that every member must continue to share responsibility for day-to-day operations. "You might be a laboratory technician," Krone says, "but you also handle operating jobs. Everybody carries the same minimum responsibility. No matter where you go, you always have to go back to the operation—you cannot become exclusively a specialist. One guy became a very skilled machinist and wanted to concentrate on his skill—so the community fired him. They told him there was plenty of opportunity for that on the outside. This system grew up naturally at the wish of the members—it was not imposed."

The members of this unusual community, were judged to have, when they were hired, "high innate capacity," but they did not have any special training or skills. "However," Krone points out, "after the plant has been in operation for three years, they are by now probably among the most highly skilled people in the company. One man who was a farmer would now be called a very highly skilled instrument specialist. He designed the plant's whole instrument control system, and did it entirely on his own initiative, working with manufacturers."

The workers have virtually complete control of the plant. There are no time clocks or other symbols of petty "class" distinctions, and everybody is on straight salary. "The manager," says Krone, "has very little decision-making power. Usually, instead of being seen as a resource, he is seen as an invader, fulfilling a directive and controlling role—there is much less of that here." Among other things, the members of the community work out the pay scales themselves and all the salaries are known to everyone.

In speaking of the results of democratic management, it is possible to document a favorable impact, both on the morale of employees and on productivity and quality.

These advanced management methods have been introduced in U. S. companies primarily because they "work" in conventional terms. But they also lead toward a true democratization of companies—breaking up orthodox power patterns and diffusing influence throughout the organization.

There is, to repeat, little recognition of this fact in America. Most of the people who have been developing these methods dislike the use of the word. The issue extends far beyond mere terminology. In much of the recent discussion of work-related problems in America, there is the assumption that since a main curse is an abundance of tedious jobs created by shortsighted managements, the answer is the creation of fascinating jobs by farsighted managements. A great deal of attention is given to the rearrangement of tasks in "job enlargement" or "job enrichment" or "job design" projects.

But the basic problem is not a faulty arrangement of jobs, it is a question of faulty power patterns; the arrangements of jobs are only surface symptoms. To be sure, any job reshuffling that gives workers increased control is a step on the road to democracy. And the assembly-line worker who sees the time span of his job increased from, say, forty to seventy seconds, and his task widened from tightening one bolt to tightening two bolts will doubtless appreciate the change. But strictly speaking, only those organizational systems that regard employee influence as a healthy and desirable phenomenon, and that are planned from the ground up to nurture and encourage such influence, can be called democratic.

Surprisingly few of the companies I have visited have given much thought to where the changes they are promoting in their organizations might ultimately lead them, even though they often see a process developing that tends to have a life of its own. But it is apparent that the ultimate scope of the changes may be rather large. Job enrichment experts in America are increasingly recommending that the employees themselves participate in reforming their own jobs and that the change process, in order to work, has to be continuous.

RICHARD E. WALTON, HOW TO COUNTER ALIENATION IN THE PLANT *

The lesson we must learn in the area of work reform is similar to one we have learned in another area of national concern. It is now recognized that a health program, a welfare program, a housing program, or an employment program alone is unable to make a lasting impact on the urban-poor syndrome. Poor health, unemployment, and other interdependent aspects of poverty must be attacked in a coordinated or systemic way.

So it is with meaningful reform of the workplace: we must think "systemically" when approaching the problem. We must coordinate the redesign of the way tasks are packaged into jobs, the way workers are required to relate to each other, the way performance is measured and rewards are made available, the way positions of authority and status symbols are structured, and the way career paths are conceived. Moreover, because these types of changes in work organizations imply new employee skills and different organizational cultures, transitional programs must be established.

A PROTOTYPE OF CHANGE

A number of major organization design efforts meet the requirements of being systemic and comprehensive. One experience in which I have been deeply involved is particularly instructive. As a recent and radical effort, it generally encompasses and goes beyond what has been done elsewhere.

During 1968, a large pet-food manufacturer was planning an additional plant at a new location. The existing manufacturing facility was then experiencing many symptoms of alienation. There were frequent instances of employee indifference and inattention that, because of the continuous-process technology, led to plant shutdowns, product waste, and costly recycling. Employees effectively worked only a modest number of hours per day, and they resisted changes toward fuller utilization of manpower. A series of acts of sabotage and violence occurred.

* Richard E. Walton, "How to Counter Alienation in the Plant." Harvard Business Review November-December 1972. Copyright © 1972 by the President and Fellows of Harvard College all rights reserved.

Because of these pressures and the fact that it was not difficult to link substantial manufacturing costs to worker alienation, management was receptive to basic innovations in the new plant. It decided to design the plant to both accommodate changes in the expectations of employees and utilize knowledge developed by the behavioral sciences.

Key Design Features

The early development of the plant took more than two years. This involved planning, education, skill training, and building the nucleus of the new organization into a team.

During this early period, four newly selected managers and their superior met with behavioral science experts and visited other industrial plants that were experimenting with innovative organizational methods. Thus they were stimulated to think about departures from traditional work organizations and given reassurance that other organizational modes were not only possible but also more viable in the current social context. While the consultations and plant visits provided some raw material for designing the new organization, the theretofore latent knowledge of the five managers played the largest role. Their insights into the aspirations of people and basically optimistic assumptions about the capacities of human beings were particularly instrumental in the design of the innovative plant. In the remainder of this section, I shall present the nine key features of this design.

1. *Autonomous work groups*: Self-managed work teams are given collective responsibility for large segments of the production process. The total work force of approximately 70 employees is organized into six teams. A processing team and a packaging team operate during each shift. The processing team's jurisdiction includes unloading, storage of materials, drawing ingredients from storage, mixing, and then performing the series of steps that transform ingredients into a pet-food product. The packaging team's responsibilities include the finishing stages of product manufacturing—packaging operations, warehousing, and shipping.

A team is comprised of from 7 to 14 members (called "operators") and a team leader. Its size is large enough to include a natural set of highly interdependent tasks, yet small enough to allow effective face-to-face meetings for decision making and coordination. Assignments of individuals to sets of tasks are subject to team consensus. Although at any given time one operator has primary responsibility for a set of tasks within the team's jurisdiction, some tasks can be shared by several operators. Moreover, tasks can be redefined by the team in light of individual capabilities and interests. In contrast, individuals in the old plant were permanently assigned to specific jobs.

Other matters that fall within the scope of team deliberation, recommendation, or decision making include:

- Coping with manufacturing problems that occur within or between the teams' areas of responsibilities.

- Temporarily redistributing tasks to cover for absent employees.

- Selecting team operators to serve on plantwide committees or task forces.

- Screening and selecting employees to replace departing operators.

- Counseling those who do not meet team standards (e.g., regarding absence or giving assistance to others).

2. *Integrated support functions*: Staff units and job specialties are avoided. Activities typically performed by maintenance, quality control, custodial, industrial engineering, and personnel units are built into an operating team's responsibilities. For example, each team member maintains the equipment he operates (except for complicated electrical maintenance) and housekeeps the area in which he works. Each team has responsibility for performing quality tests and ensuring quality standards. In addition, team members perform what is normally a personnel function when they screen job applicants.

3. *Challenging job assignments*: While the designers understood that job assignments would undergo redefinition in light of experience and the varying interests and abilities on the work teams, the initial job assignments established an important design principle. Every set of tasks is designed to include functions requiring higher-order human abilities and responsibilities, such as planning, diagnosing mechanical or process problems, and liaison work.

The integrated support functions just discussed provide one important source of tasks to enrich jobs. In addition, the basic technology employed in the plant is designed to eliminate dull or routine jobs as much as possible. But some nonchallenging, yet basic, tasks still have to be compensated for. The forklift truck operation, for example, is not technically challenging. Therefore, the team member responsible for it is assigned other, more mentally demanding tasks (e.g., planning warehouse space utilization and shipping activities).

Housekeeping duties are also included in every assignment, despite the fact that they contribute nothing to enriching the work, in order to avoid having members of the plant community who do nothing but menial cleaning.

4. *Job mobility and rewards for learning*: Because all sets of tasks (jobs) are designed to be equally challenging (although each set comprises unique skill demands), it is possible to have a single job classification for all operators. Pay increases are geared to an employee mastering an increasing proportion of jobs first in the team and then in the total plant. In effect, team members are payed (sic) for learning more and more aspects of the total manufacturing system. Because there are no limits on the number of operators that can qualify for higher pay brackets, employees are also encouraged to teach each other. The old plant, in contrast, featured large num-

bers of differentiated jobs and numerous job classifications, with pay increases based on progress up the job hierarchy.

5. *Facilitative leadership*: Team leaders are chosen from foreman-level talent and are largely responsible for team development and group decision making. This contrasts with the old plant's use of supervisors to plan, direct, and control the work of subordinates. Management feels that in time the teams will be self-directed and so the formal team leader position might not be required.

6. *"Managerial" decision information for operators*: The design of the new plant provides operators with economic information and managerial decision rules. Thus production decisions ordinarily made by supervisors can now be made at the operator level.

7. *Self-government for the plant community*: The management group that developed the basic organization plan before the plant was manned refrained from specifying in advance any plant rules. Rather, it is committed to letting these rules evolve from collective experience.

8. *Congruent physical and social context*: The differential status symbols that characterize traditional work organizations are minimized in the new plant. There is an open parking lot, a single entrance for both the office and plant, and a common decor throughout the reception area, offices, locker rooms, and cafeteria.

The architecture facilitates the congregating of team members during working hours. For example, rather than following the plan that made the air conditioned control room in the process tower so small that employees could not congregate there, management decided to enlarge it so that process team operators could use it when not on duty elsewhere. The assumption here is that rooms which encourage ad hoc gatherings provide opportunities not only for enjoyable human exchanges but also for work coordination and learning about others' jobs.

9. *Learning and evolution*: The most basic feature of the new plant system is management's commitment to continually assess both the plant's productivity and its relevance to employee concerns in light of experience.

I believe pressures will mount in this system with two apparently opposite implications for automation:

- On the one hand, people will consider ways of automating the highly repetitive tasks. (There are still back-breaking routine tasks in this plant; for example, as 50-pound bags pile up at the end of the production line, someone must grab them and throw them on a pallet.)

- On the other hand, some processes may be slightly deautomated. The original design featured fully automated or "goof-proof" systems to monitor and adjust several segments of the manufacturing process; yet some employees have become confident that they can improve on the systems if they are allowed to intervene with their own judgments. These employees suggest that organizations may benefit more from operators who are alert and who care than from goof-proof systems.

Implementation Difficulties

Since the plant start-up in January 1971, a number of difficulties have created at least temporary, and in some cases enduring, gaps between ideal expectations and reality.

The matter of compensation, for example, has been an important source of tension within this work community. There are four basic pay rates: starting rate, single job rate (for mastering the first job assignment), team rate (for mastering all jobs within the team's jurisdiction), and plant rate. In addition, an employee can qualify for a "specialty" add-on if he has particular strengths—e.g., in electrical maintenance.

Employees who comprised the initial work force were all hired at the same time, a circumstance that enabled them to directly compare their experiences. With one or two exceptions on each team, operators all received their single job rates at the same time, about six weeks after the plant started. Five months later, however, about one third of the members of each team had been awarded the team rate.

The evaluative implications of awarding different rates of pay have stirred strong emotions in people who work so closely with each other. The individual pay decisions had been largely those of the team leaders who, however, were also aware of operators' assessments of each other. In fact, pay rates and member contributions were discussed openly between team leaders and their operators as well as among operators themselves. Questions naturally arose:

- Were the judgments about job mastery appropriate?
- Did everyone have an equal opportunity to learn other jobs?
- Did team leaders depart from job mastery criteria and include additional considerations in their promotions to team rate?

Thus the basic concepts of pay progression are not easy to treat operationally. Moreover, two underlying orientations compete with each other and create ambivalences for team leaders and operators alike:

- A desire for more equality, which tends to enhance cohesiveness.
- A desire for more differential rewards for individual merit, which may be more equitable but can be divisive.

* * *

Management, too, has been a source of difficulty. For example, acceptance and support from superiors and influential staff groups at corporate headquarters did not always come easily, thus creating anxiety and uncertainty within the new plant community.

QUESTIONS

Is there any legitimate basis for the lack of enthusiasm by most of the American labor movement for the concept of worker participation? Is there any reason why an employer should be legally inhibited from developing such a program? Consider in this regard the persuasiveness of the following articles.

DOES EMPLOYER IMPLEMENTATION OF EMPLOYEE PRODUCTION TEAMS VIOLATE SECTION 8(a)(2) OF THE NATIONAL LABOR RELATIONS ACT? *

Sections 2(5) and 8(a)(2) of the National Labor Relations Act (NLRA) establish the ambits of permissible employer involvement with a labor organization. These sections were designed to maintain the independence of employee organizations in order to ensure the fair operation of the collective bargaining process, and they presuppose the existence of employers and employees as separate entities with conflicting interests. In applying these sections, the National Labor Relations Board (NLRB) and the courts have traditionally focused upon the questions of what constitutes a labor organization, and what specific indicia of employer involvement amount to illegal support, domination and interference. Recent employer efforts to redesign the conventional workplace, by organizing employees into production teams and giving those teams the responsibility of making recommendations or decisions about certain aspects of production as well as certain terms and conditions of employment, have added a new dimension to analysis under these sections.

Although the efforts of Swedish manufacturers, particularly Volvo, to introduce team production have perhaps received the widest public attention, several American companies have also implemented the team form of production in recently built plants. A major difference between the Swedish and American organizational changes, however, is that the Swedish plans are the joint product of the employers and the unions, whereas in the United States the plans, for the most part, have been unilaterally implemented by the employer in a nonunion context.

*   *   *

THE TEAM CONCEPT

To combat the growing alienation among employees, manifested by industrial strife, high rates of personnel turnover, absenteeism, and low productivity, several employers have attempted to redesign the workplace in accordance with new theories of management. One such theory, participative decisionmaking, attempts to enhance the meaning of an employee's involvement in and sense of responsibility for his job. The fullest implementation of the theory of participative decisionmaking requires a major organizational redesign of traditional plant operations. The organizational model most widely discussed

---

* Note, "Does Employer Implementation Of Employee Production Teams Violate Section 8(a)(2) Of The National Labor Relations Act?" 49 Indiana Law Journal 19 (1974); © 1974 by the Trustees of Indiana University. Reprinted with the permission of the Indiana Law Journal and Fred B. Rothman & Co.

in the United States is that which assigns production employees into a number of teams which are delegated certain decisionmaking responsibility along with their productive tasks.

Plants utilizing the team concept commonly assign all production employees into a number of teams with responsibility for an entire segment of plant operations delegated to each. Each team usually has a team leader, either appointed by management or elected by the team members. In addition to its productive tasks, each team is given the responsibility for making recommendations or decisions about some or all of the following matters:

(1) individual job assignments;

(2) interviewing job applicants and hiring;

(3) establishing and changing work rules;

(4) evaluation of individual job performance;

(5) progression within the compensation system;

(6) coping with manufacturing problems that occur within or between the team's areas of responsibility;

(7) selecting team operators to serve on plant-wide committees or task forces.

Deliberation on problems falling within these areas occurs routinely in conjunction with the team members' performance of their productive tasks. The teams are purposely structured, both in terms of size and assigned functions, to facilitate a high degree of team member interaction which serves as the basis for recommendations or decisions.

With some decisional authority delegated by the company to the team, this form of organization is designed to change the structure of the traditional employee-employer relationship by minimizing distinctions between employees and employers as separate identifiable groups with independent and conflicting interests. Instead, this plan attempts to substitute for the more conventional structure a cooperative relationship based on mutuality of interest and involvement in a common enterprise.

Development of the employees' sense of identification with the company is crucial to the plan's success. At one plant, for example, the company, in addition to increasing the employees' participation in decisionmaking, has made a conscious effort to reduce the physical symbols of hierarchy, characteristic of conventional plants, on the premise that employee involvement with the company is promoted when an employee is treated as though his place within the organization is an important one.

The fundamental conflict between the theory of labor relations underlying the team and the basic policies of the NLRA is apparent. The Act presupposes conflicts of interest and provides the neutral process of collective bargaining to resolve those conflicts. The theory on which the team is based, however, assumes that the employer can establish a mutuality of interest through the implementation of the team model. The resolution of this basic conflict must be made by reference to the specific provisions of the NLRA dealing with the permissible scope of employer involvement in employee affairs.

Is the Team a "Labor Organization" Under § 2(5) of the NLRA?

One of the basic statutory prohibitions designed to assure the full effectiveness of the collective bargaining process is § 8(a)(2) of the NLRA which prohibits employer domination of, interference with, or support of a labor organization. This section is meant to ensure the independence of labor organizations, and it represents the most obvious legal obstacle to the implementation of the team concept.

Section 8(a)(2) is applicable only where the employer is allegedly dominating a "labor organization" as defined by § 2(5). Therefore, to determine whether § 8(a)(2) has any impact on the team concept, the question whether the team is a "labor organization" must first be explored.

The Structural Requirement of § 2(5)

For an organization to be a "labor organization" within the meaning of § 2(5), it must meet structural, subject matter, and functional requirements. The structural requirement is met by "any organization of any kind *   *   * in which employees participate. *   *   *" Courts have consistently refused to establish any extrastatutory formal requirements for a labor organization, thus indicating that the statutory provision be read as broadly as written. Organizations in which employees participate have been found to qualify as labor organizations where they lacked a formal structure, a constitution or bylaws, officers, the practice of collecting dues, or even continuity of existence. Accordingly, the team would seem to qualify.

*   *   *

The Subject Matter Requirements of § 2(5)

The second requirement that an organization must meet to fall within § 2(5) is that its relationship with management concern "grievances, labor disputes, wages, rates of pay, hours of employment, or conditions of work." In NLRB v. Cabot Carbon Co., a case in which the company was charged with dominating an assortment of employee committees, the Supreme Court of the United States established that an organization's concern with only one of these matters satisfies this subject matter requirement. At least two areas of responsibility often delegated to teams appear to meet the requirements of § 2(5). Teams delegated the responsibility for establishing and changing work rules are concerned with items falling under the § 2(5) category of "conditions of work." Similarly, teams making decisions about an individual's progression within the compensation system are concerned with subject matter within the headings of "wages" or "rates of pay." The purpose of participative decision-making which is to give employees a voice in decisions that shape the quality of life in the workplace, naturally involves team concern with "conditions of work." Since the subject matter requirement of § 2(5) is met by an organization dealing with any one of the enumerated subjects, most teams will meet this requirement.

The Functional Requirement of § 2(5)

The functional requirement of § 2(5) is met if a team exists "For the purpose, in whole or in part, of dealing with" the employer. If a company has purposely involved a team in the determination of § 2(5) matters, the team, if it does in fact "deal" with the employer, necessarily exists, at least in part, for that purpose.

The Court in *Cabot Carbon* unequivocally established that "dealing with" did not exclusively mean "bargaining with." Further, it specified that the term "dealing" encompassed employee recommendations to management. Although the facts of *Cabot Carbon* did not warrant further elaboration on the meaning of "dealing," other courts have found "dealing" between the employer and a labor organization where the parties merely discussed § 2(5) subjects and, also, where one of the parties merely asked questions, or provided information.

If the team makes recommendations to management relating to § 2(5) subjects, the conclusion is apparent. The team would fall squarely within the *Cabot Carbon* holding that an organization's act of making recommendations to the employer constitutes dealing within the meaning of the statute. If, however, the team makes actual decisions relating to § 2(5) matters, the question whether it is "dealing" with the employer becomes more difficult. For there to be "dealing," there must be contact between the two parties. Here, it might be argued, no contact occurs. When the team operates within its delegated domain of responsibility, management provides no input into the team's decision. Management does not suggest what the decision should be; it does not even discuss with the team the issues to be decided. Since the team unilaterally makes and implements its decision, it is not "dealing with" the employer.

The problem with this argument is that although the team makes a totally unilateral decision, that decision is not necessarily final. Implicit in the company's delegation of decisionmaking responsibility to the team is management's ultimate power to review or even overrule the team's decision. If a team's decision is final in practice, its finality is attributable not to the team's authority, but to management's ultimate authority to let the decision stand. Conceptually, it is at least arguable that team decisions subject to review by management amount only to recommendations which become final when management decides not to exercise its veto. If this view is accepted, *Cabot Carbon* would again necessitate a finding that the team is "dealing" with the employer.

Another basis for a finding that the team is dealing with management, that of discussion with the employer about issues of employment, is implicit in the employer's ultimate power of review. Practically, the employer's power to review seems to imply that the team, at least occasionally, would have the burden of justifying its decisions to management personnel. Any discussions between the team and management in which the team is required to justify its action would thus constitute "dealing" in the broad sense of that term which the courts have adopted.

Conceivably, an employer might avoid a finding that it was engaged in "dealing" with a team if it could persuade the NLRB and courts that it had not and would not exercise its formal power of review and that team decisions were thus final. In order to make this claim, however, the employer must have imposed carefully structured limits on the domain of team decisionmaking responsibility. Assuming that the employer requires a control mechanism of some type over team decisions, in order to protect itself against the possibility of decisions which undercut the company's economic position, the employer would have to argue that it had limited the domain of team decisionmaking so that management was indifferent to any decision which the team might make within that domain—Arguably the employer has not engaged in "dealing"—because it has delegated to the team the full power to make unilateral decisions about the wage levels of individual employees.

Conceptually, this argument is persuasive. An employer who has implemented such a plan, however, will face serious practical problems in realizing the positive features of team organization while maintaining this carefully structured division of decisionmaking responsibility. Such a careful division of authority undercuts a major purpose of implementing the team concept which is to improve employee morale by decreasing the hierarchal distance between employer and employees. In the situation described above, the employer, to avoid the deliberations which would constitute "dealing," would have to issue its unilateral decisions concerning § 2(5) subject in the form of directives not open to discussion. Thus communication between the employer and the team would be marked by an artificial formality inconsistent with the cooperative atmosphere which the team is designed to promote.

Moreover, confining all team decisions about § 2(5) subjects within employer imposed limits could prevent the employees from developing the sense of involvement with the company which is a prerequisite to improve productivity. It would seem that, to be truly effective, the team form of organization would permit employee involvement in more meaningful types of decisions.

The typical team, then, generally will meet the structural and functional requirements of a § 2(5) labor organization, since employees will be participants and the team will be involved in "dealing with" the employer regardless of whether a team leader participates in its affairs. In addition, the subject matter requirements of § 2(5) will be met, for team involvement in determining "conditions of work" is one of the primary goals of the concept itself. Thus, since virtually all teams will satisfy the structural, subject matter, and functional requirements of § 2(5), they will qualify as "labor organizations" and will therefore be subject to the § 8(a)(2) prohibition of employer domination.

A major purpose of the Act was to allow employees the freedom to exert economic pressure against the employer in order to force the employer to agree to terms it would not accept if not economically coerced. The structurally dominated or supported labor organization is incapable of launching this kind of economic attack. An employer can cripple its effectiveness by disordering its internal operations or withdrawing its support.

Moreover, the problem of the structurally dominated labor organization goes even deeper than its basic vulnerability to employer sabotage. Not only is such an organization weak, but it also preempts the creation by the employees, of an independent organization outside the employer's sphere of influence. Its very existence nurtures employee reliance on a dispute resolution system which clearly favors the employer because, unlike true collective bargaining, it does not permit the employees full exertion of economic pressure.

* * *

To implement the policy of protecting a labor organization's structural independence, the NLRB and the courts have strictly scrutinized the relationship between the employer and the labor organization. They have found illegal support, for example, where the employer has provided office facilities or clerical assistance, or where the employer has allowed the organization to meet on company time without deducting from the employees' pay for time spent at such meetings. Illegal domination or interference has also been found where the employer initiated or implemented the organization, participated in the drafting of its rules or procedures, participated in its meetings, or selected or controlled its membership.

Assessed in terms of these specific prohibitions and viewed against the basic policy underlying § 8(a)(2), the team is clearly a dominated and supported labor organization. Employers conceive and implement it as an organizational form; the employer has the power to destroy it as the basic productive unit and to substitute some other form of productive organization; the employer dictates the § 2(5) subject matter with which the team is allowed to concern itself; * * *.

Furthermore, the implementation of the team effectively inhibits the employees from attempting to construct their own labor organization. In fact, one of the intended effects of the team and related management theories is to prevent unionization. The team provides resolution machinery capable of accommodating minor disputes or grievances and thereby pre-empts the creation of an independent labor organization. The incompatibility of unionism and the team concept is reflected in the management practice of implementing the team form of organization through the opening of a new plant rather than in a plant already in operation. The rationale for this practice, as explained by one management official, is that "[n]o power groups will exist within the organization that create an anti-management posture."

* * *

Under the cases delineating the traditional meaning of employer domination, then, implementation of the team concept would be a clear violation of § 8(a)(2) whenever a team satisfied the § 2(5) definitional requirements of a "labor organization." In recent years, however, the United States Courts of Appeals, by employing a three-pronged analysis, have given a new policy emphasis to § 8(a)(2) which may undercut the conclusiveness of this determination. The Seventh Circuit departed from the policy underlying the *Newport News* approach in its decision in Chicago Rawhide Manufacturing Co. v. NLRB. Emphasizing, instead, the policy of cooperation, *Chicago Rawhide* and its progeny reflect a willingness of the courts to be influenced in § 8(a)(2) cases by the existence of a harmonious relationship between employees and employers. In accordance with the new policy emphasis on cooperation, these courts have developed an approach to § 8(a)(2) which permits employer involvement which is clearly illegal under the *Newport News* analysis. Since the team concept, if successfully implemented by the employer, promotes harmony and cooperation between employees and their employer, this harmony could be a major factor in the decision of a court assessing the team under § 8(a)(2). For this reason it is necessary to explore the limits of the circuit courts' approach to ascertain, first, whether the team would be permissible and, second, whether it should be.

As articulated in *Chicago Rawhide*, the new approach hinges on three elements: (1) a subjective standard for domination, from the point of view of the employees, (2) a distinction between illegal "support," and cooperation or aid which does not involve "control;" and (3) distinctions between actual domination or interference which is illegal, and potential domination or interference which the court stated was not a violation because it was always implicit in the employee-employer relationship. Operating together, these three elements seem to change the traditional § 8(a)(2) analysis in two ways. First, use of a subjective standard for domination shifts the focus from the institution of the labor organization to the individual employees. Second, distinctions (2) and (3) shift from scrutiny of the structural relationship between the employer and the labor organization to scrutiny of the specific impact of employer conduct on the employees.

* * *

A court strongly motivated by the concern for preserving a cooperative relationship between employers and employees might find the team permissible under § 8(a)(2). Under this interpretation, § 8(a)(2) might be deemed violated only upon a showing that the employer has actually influenced employees to change their position on issues which are traditionally the subject of collective bargaining. If a showing of actual employer domination of particular employees is required, a § 8(a)(2) violation in the team context would be extremely difficult to establish. The employer has specifically designed the team to accommodate greater employee participation and influence than is possible in the conventional workplace. Within the team each employee enjoys a greater freedom of involvement than his traditional counterpart.

Thus, if a court were to focus exclusively on the individual team members as opposed to the team as an entity, it could conceivably find that there is no illegal domination. However, to take this position, a court would be forced to abandon the literal meaning of § 8(a)(2) which is to protect and guarantee the independence of a labor organization, as well as to violate the policy behind that provision as framed by Congress and interpreted by the NLRB and the Supreme Court. As written, § 8(a)(2) does not directly protect the individual employee; it protects, instead, the independent labor organization which, as the vehicle for collective employee action, enables the employees to protect themselves.

KENT F. MURRMANN, THE SCANLON PLAN JOINT COMMITTEE AND SECTION 8(a)(2) *

The Scanlon Plan, originally developed during the 1930s by steelworker Joseph Scanlon, is a system of principles used to focus the joint efforts of employees and management on productivity improvement. Its philosophy emphasizes the common interest of employees and management in maintaining a viable firm as a reliable source of employment and return on investment. A key element of the Scanlon Plan is the use for formalized, joint employer-employee committees as vehicles for employee collaboration on productivity improvement. An equally important aspect of the system is the use of a jointly determined bonus system, intended to insure that any cost savings resulting from the joint productivity effort are shared equitably between employees, managers, and stockholders.

The Scanlon Plan has drawn increasing attention in recent years. It has been shown to be an effective approach to productivity improvement for numerous individual firms in a variety of settings. It is noteworthy that this has occurred during a period when productivity improvement becomes increasingly difficult to attain. However, it also has been identified by some unionists as part of a growing movement by employers to avoid unionization. Concern has been expressed that various "participative management" schemes are being used widely by employers to unlawfully supplant or alleviate the need for a union.

Despite its noted success in the area of productivity improvement, does such a system constitute a violation of the National Labor Relations Act? This paper will examine the typical Scanlon Plan joint committee and attempt to answer the question.

* * *

* Kent F. Murrmann, "The Scanlon Plan Joint Committee and Section 8(a) (2)," 31 Labor Law Journal 299 (1980).   Reprinted with special permission; © 1980 by Kent Murrmann.

THE JOINT COMMITTEE

The Scanlon Plan joint committee system varies little across organizations or time. Its basic structure consists of two committee layers. The bottom layer is composed of several production committees, and the top layer is comprised of a screening committee. Each serves to focus the joint attention of employees and management on productivity problems. A separate production committee usually is established for each department. The production committees consist of the departmental supervisor and one or more rank-and-file employees. The supervisor serves as management's representative on the committee. The employee committee members are elected through a secret ballot procedure by all department employees.

The employee committee members assist other employees in the formulation of written suggestions, collaborate with the supervisor in evaluating the merit of suggestions, inform employees of the status of their suggestions, and share with employees information learned from management. The committee meets monthly or more often if necessary to examine production problems and to evaluate suggestions.

The production committee typically has the authority to reject any suggestions that lack merit and to implement suggestions that do not involve other departments or expenditure in excess of a certain dollar amount. It may refer to the screening committee any suggestions on which production committee members fail to agree or that involve more than one department or excessive expenditures.

The membership of the screening committee typically is evenly divided between management and employee representation. Employee representation on the screening committee includes one employee elected by secret employee vote from each department. The management members are appointed by the chief executive officer and represent all staff and functional areas in the organization.

The screening committee meets monthly to evaluate and resolve suggestions referred to it by the production committees, to share and evaluate information about economic forces affecting the organization, and to share and evaluate information concerning specific production problems affecting bonus earnings. Employee members then share this information and any decisions reached by the committee with their fellow employees.

An important issue involved here concerns the role of employee committee members in the decisionmaking process. Much emphasis is given to the principle that neither the production committee nor the screening committee is a decisionmaking body. Rather, final decisions are reserved for management. However, the chief executive officer ordinarily makes decisions on the basis of all responsible recommendations furnished to him by the various management and employee members of the screening committee. Though in principle the making of final decisions is reserved to management, employee representatives share substantially in the process of formulating recommendations that more often than not become final decisions.

The prohibition of employer dominance provided in Section 8(a)(2) applies only to bona fide labor organizations as defined in Section 2(5). In order for any organization to qualify as a labor organization under Section 2(5) it must possess certain structural, functional, and subject matter attributes. Accordingly, we will determine the status of the Scanlon Plan joint committee in light of these criteria.

STRUCTURAL AND FUNCTIONAL REQUIREMENTS

Structurally, a labor organization may be "any organization of any kind, or any agency or any employee representation committee * * * in which employees participate * * *." The courts have refused to further specify the intent of this statutory language, and so the statutory language applies as broadly as it is written. Under this language, organizations in which employees participate that lack a formal structure, a constitution or bylaws, officers, dues requirements, or a continuing existence have been found to be labor organizations. The Scanlon Plan joint committee is a formal organization, with election and membership provisions, in which employees participate. It clearly meets the structural requirements of Section 2(5) in terms of the court-established criteria.

The functional requirement of Section 2(5) provides that an organization must exist "for the purpose, in whole or in part, of dealing with" the employer. Interpretation of this provision by the U. S. Supreme Court in *Cabot Carbon* established that "dealing with" is not limited to collective bargaining but may include employees making recommendations to management. Other courts have found "dealing with" to include mere discussion, or the asking of questions, or the providing of information.

In view of these criteria, it is conclusive that the Scanlon Plan joint committee falls within the Section 2(5) functional requirements. In the production committee, employees receive information, ask questions, make recommendations, and share in making decisions in their relationship with the management representative on the committee.

In the screening committee, employees have the same types of dealing directly with the organization's chief executive officer. Though the chief executive officer retains the right to make the final decision in all matters, his decisions generally affirm recommendations supported by a consensus of views in the screening committee.

SUBJECT MATTER REQUIREMENTS

The third requirement of Section 2(5) is that the subject matter dealt with concerns "grievances, labor disputes, wages, rates of pay, hours, or conditions of work." In *Cabot Carbon*, where the employer organized a committee to "provide a procedure for considering employees' ideas and problems of mutual interest to the employees and management," the court established that an organization need deal with the employer with respect to only one of the categories in order to fulfill the Section 2(5) subject matter requirement. The Scanlon Plan joint committee fulfills the subject matter requirement in three categories.

First, the typical joint committee deals with rates of pay through its involvement with the determination of the bonus formula. The bonus formula is periodically reviewed by the screening committee. When changes in the formula are required, the screening committee evaluates the formula and makes recommendations that materially influence the content of the formula. Also, the adoption of a formula must be supported by a consensus of the screening committee. In this way, the screening committee deals with the employer concerning rates of pay.

"Conditions of work" is another Section 2(5) subject matter area that the joint committee often becomes involved with. The NLRB has established that work standards and work rules, working hours, work schedules, and work loads constitute conditions of work. These factors directly affect productivity and are routinely dealt with in joint committee schemes to improve productivity.

Finally, grievances or complaints concerning working conditions are discussed and even resolved in many joint committees though in principle they should be excluded from their consideration. Grievances are a subject of importance to employees, and as a practical matter it is difficult at best for management to establish and rigorously apply a distinction between grievances and productivity related suggestions. This may be especially difficult if there are no regular alternate means for handling grievances acceptable to employees.

VIOLATION OF SECTION 8(a)(2)?

Section 8(a)(2) of the NLRA provides that it is unlawful for an employer to "dominate, contribute financial aid or other support to, or interfere with" the formation or administration of any labor organization. Under the original policy, the NLRB and the courts found labor organizations to be unlawfully dominated, supported, or influenced by the employer where the employer could veto decisions of the organization or provide office facilities or clerical assistance. Also, if the organization was allowed to meet on company time without employees' pay being deducted for the time spent in meetings, the organization was unlawfully dominated. A more recent policy emphasis, established in *Chicago Rawhide*, allowed some form of cooperation between employers and labor organizations so long as the labor organization retained its ability to act independently of the employer.

Under either policy, it can be concluded that the Scanlon Plan joint committee in its usual form is dominated, supported, and influenced in violation of Section 8(a)(2). The joint committee is established in large part through the initiative and leadership of the employer, is fully supported in terms of office and clerical needs by the employer, and is heavily influenced by employer representation in its membership. Finally, the joint committee's decisions are subject to review by the employer.

CONCLUSION

National labor policy embodied in Section 8(a)(2) requires that labor organizations be independent of employer control so that they may freely represent the special interests of employees. The Scanlon Plan joint committee, despite its value as a method of attacking productivity problems, is clearly a violation of Section 8(a)(2). Under the operation of the joint committee, the protection of employee interest depends on the good will of the employer rather than on the strength of an independent employee representative. By its very nature, the joint committee precludes the form of relationship between independent parties envisioned by the NLRA, while it undertakes to resolve matters that may be dealt with properly only between independent parties.

Two fundamentally opposite approaches to solution of this problem are conceivable. First, the subject matter dealt with by the joint committee could be limited so that the joint committee no longer fulfills the Section 2(5) definition of a labor organization. This would require that the joint committee be excluded from determination and administration of the bonus formula, as well as from consideration of any "conditions of employment" in its efforts to develop solutions to productivity problems. These limitations may significantly reduce the joint committee's potential impact on productivity by reducing the scope of solutions that it may consider. Yet, without these limitations, implementation of the joint committee inevitably will supplant the statutory prerogatives of a labor organization.

A more far-reaching solution would require new legislative enactment. Under this approach, Section 8(a)(2) would be revised to permit committee participation in the determination of bonus formulas and changes in working conditions that are strictly incidental to bona fide productivity suggestions. Current policy provides that employers and employees may lawfully deal with one another concerning Section 2(5) matters only in either a "one-on-one" relationship, i.e., an employer dealing with an individual employee, or through the collective form of relationship specified in Sections 2(5) and 8(a)(2). This revision would allow carefully limited exceptions in the case of legitimate productivity programs. However, before such a change could be undertaken, Congress would have to once again carefully examine the conflicting interests of employees and employers and determine if those interests, even within carefully defined boundaries, can be properly reconciled through representation procedures controlled by the employer.

THE WEST GERMAN MODEL OF CODETERMINATION UNDER SECTION 8(a)(2) OF THE NLRA *

Industries in the United States have been experimenting with innovative forms of labor relations in an effort to enhance peaceful industrial relations. Models have been designed to increase employee input into the decisionmaking process and to create more challenging and interesting jobs for workers. Due to the apparent success of West Germany's *Mitbestimmung*, or codetermination, such a system may become attractive to business enterprises in the United States.

Codetermination is a type of corporate structure in which those who provide their services to the corporate entity determine and execute corporate policies equally with those who represent the financial resources. Under this model, parity in the decisionmaking process is sought at the level of the board of directors.

THE WEST GERMAN MODEL OF CODETERMINATION, CORPORATE STRUCTURE

As opposed to the American corporation with its single board of directors, German corporations have two boards: the supervisory board, *Aufsichtrat*, and the managing board, *Vorstand*. At the top of the corporate hierarchy is the supervisory board which is designed to be an intermediary between management and stockholders. It does not conduct the business of the corporation, but has the limited functions of appointing and overseeing the managing board. The actual determination and execution of corporate policy is left to the managing board which consists of three directors, a sales director, a production director, and a labor director, who operate independently in their areas of specialty, and collectively on matters of overall policy.

Codetermination

The key to the German model of full codetermination is its provision for equal representation of stockholders and employees on the supervisory board. Thus, of a normal supervisory board of 11 directors, five would be labor representatives. The German Trade Union Federation (*Deutsche Gewerkschaftsbund*, or *DGB*) selects one director, and the industry *DGB*-affiliated union selects another. Another two directors are selected by the Works Council, which itself is directly elected by the employees. The fifth labor director is selected by the other four. He may not be an employee or union member, and usually is a labor expert or a public figure. Five more directors are elected by the stockholders, and the eleventh director, who is to represent the public interest, is chosen by the two factions. Although the purpose of this eleventh director is to provide a tie-breaking vote, in practice the eleventh director seldom casts the deciding vote, and

* Note, "The West German Model Of Codetermination Under Section 8(a)(2) Of The NLRA," 51 Indiana Law Journal, 795 (1976); © 1976 by the Trustees of Indiana University. Reprinted with the permission of the Indiana Law Journal and Fred B. Rothman & Co.

his function is more aptly described as mediation. In addition to equal representation on the supervisory board, the other key provision of the full codetermination model is that the labor director on the managing board must be approved by the majority of the labor faction on the supervisory board. Thus, in addition to gaining equal participation on the supervisory board, employees have gained the ability to influence the decisions of the labor director of the managing board—the corporate official most closely connected with the corporation's day-to-day labor policies.

The Implications of Codetermination

It is evident from Germany's use of the full codetermination model that the ideal of equal participation in management has not been achieved. There has, however, been established a degree of labor influence over corporate policy. Although the managing board conducts the business of the corporation and has discretion in promoting the corporate interest, the supervisory board can influence corporate policy indirectly by its authority to select the managing board. Since there is parity on the supervisory board, labor theoretically has equal influence over corporate policy.

Although the results of full codetermination in West Germany are not conclusive, it is generally conceded that it has had a beneficial impact. Peaceful industrial relations, less man hours lost through strikes, increased industrial morale, better working conditions, better job security, more fringe benefits, and higher wages have all been attributed to full codetermination.

*   *   *

Codetermination in the United States

The NLRA reflects two premises: the existence of an inherent conflict between employers and employees, and an inequality of bargaining power between a single employee and his employer. The Act attempts to alleviate this inequality by encouraging collective bargaining and protecting concerted activities directed at organizing workers. Employee independence in these activities has been ensured by prohibiting employer involvement, which has resulted in limiting industrial communications to collective bargaining with a recognized union. In such a setting, codetermination as a substitute for collective bargaining could enhance industrial communication and combat worker alienation from the interests of the enterprise.

However, implementation of codetermination in the United States would certainly be viewed with apprehension by American labor unions, since collective bargaining has evolved into the institution for solving labor relations problems in the United States. Implementing codetermination would diminish the role of collective bargaining, and therefore such proposals lack union support. Thus, legislative endorsement of codetermination seems speculative. Realistically, codetermination could only be attained by voluntary implementation by a non-union employer.

At first glance, it may appear unrealistic to expect a non-union employer to consider implementing codetermination. However, in a situation where unionization seems imminent, the employer could confer employee influence over corporate policy through codetermination as an alternative to unionization. Although unionization and codetermination involve similar concessions by the employer, the adversary stance of collective bargaining would be avoided. Employee influence would be achieved by a framework which would promote cooperation, enhance communications, and induce a better understanding between employers and employees.

*   *   *

CODETERMINATION AND THE NLRA

In examining whether the NLRA would pose barriers to the implementation of codetermination by an employer, the initial question is whether the codetermination framework would merit the same protection under the NLRA as other labor organizations. More specifically, the inquiry under the NLRA would be whether a codetermination board constitutes a labor organization under Section 2(5) of the Act. If this inquiry is answered in the affirmative, the next question would be whether employer implementation of codetermination constitutes an unfair labor practice under Section 8(a)(2) of the Act which prohibits employer interference with the activities of a labor organization.

*   *   *

3. Functional Requirement

An organization "which exists for the purpose, in whole or in part of dealing with employers" fulfills the functional requirement of the definition of a "labor organization."

*   *   *

Common usage of the term "dealing with" could lead one to conclude that under full codetermination the labor faction is dealing with the stockholder faction since they are equally represented. However, in delineating the scope of "dealing with," the courts premised the analysis on the fact that the final decision would always rest with the employer. On this basis the interaction between the labor faction and the stockholder faction can be distinguished. The labor faction does not recommend certain action and then await the decision of the stockholder faction; rather, it makes the decision together with the stockholder faction. With equal representation on the board, there will be no majority vote and therefore no decision, unless representatives of either faction are swayed to accept the other's point of view. Unless a decision is reached the status quo remains, and the stockholder faction cannot unilaterally implement its point of view. In the case of an additional board member elected by both factions, the situation in a deadlock would resemble arbitration. Neither faction can break the deadlock, and the decision is finally made by a person who has been mutually entrusted with the power to make an equitable decision.

Applying this distinction, it is arguable that the labor faction on a full codetermination board does not fulfill the functional requirement. The NLRA intended to bring within the parameters of the definition of a "labor organization" all organizations which have the purpose of promoting employee interests, so as to subject such organizations to the protection of Section 8(a)(2). The protection against employer interference was deemed necessary due to the inherently coercive nature of the employment relationship. In this light, it can be argued that a codetermination board has no need for special protection, since the employer no longer has unfettered discretion with respect to corporate policy, and more particularly subject matters contained in Section 2(5). Policies cannot be developed unless the labor faction acquiesces in the proposals. Therefore, the inherently coercive nature of the employment relationship no longer exists, and a full codetermination board could be deemed not to be a labor organization.

Section 8(a)(2)

Section 8(a)(2) provides that it is an unfair labor practice for an employer:

> To dominate or interfere with the formation or administration of any labor organization or contribute financial or other support to it.

The specific evil which this section is designed to eliminate is the "company union," a device used by the employer to thwart genuine collective bargaining by dominating the union.

Under this section the courts have strictly scrutinized employer involvement in activities of labor organizations on the basis of a subjective test from the perspective of the employee:

> [T]he question is whether the organization exists as the result of a choice freely made by the employees, in their own interests, and without regard to the desires of their employer, or whether the employees formed and supported the organization, rather than some other, because they knew their employer desired it and feared the consequences if they did not.

* * *

Pursuant to this test, which was designed to insure the development of truly independent unions, any employer support, no matter how meager and regardless of the employer's good faith, was prohibited. This test is based upon a belief in an irreconcilable conflict of interests between the employer and employee, which leads to the conclusion that the only reason an employer would interfere with his employees' representative organization would be to further his own interests and thus defeat the best interests of his employees.

However, this assumption of irreconcilable conflict is of questionable validity in the contemporary employment relationship. The working class—managerial class distinction has faded, and American workers perceive themselves as middle-class citizens with specialized occupational ideologies. Consequently, the idea that the NLRA must have contemplated a permissible range of industrial cooperation has emerged.

This change in attitude has resulted in a judicial approach which encourages cooperation between management and labor.

* * *

In summary, the use of these three criteria signal a shift in labor policy by the courts. Under the old policy, which stressed the importance of independent employee organizational acitivity, the courts closely scrutinized any employer involvement in the organizational activity. Focusing on the impact that the employer involvement had on the employees was an effective means to this end. With the current emphasis on encouraging industrial cooperation, this narrow outlook is inadequate, and a broader view in which all the interests are considered is necessary. By broadening the inquiry into the three factors discussed above, employee interests are not the only considerations which dictate unlawful interference. An approach wherein employer interests are also considered is better suited to effectuate the new policy and results in a range of permissible employer involvement.

One of the difficulties of implementing the West German model of codetermination in the United States lies in the difference in structure of West German and American corporations. American corporations do not have a two-tier board of directors; rather they have a single-tier board (although it should be pointed out that the propensity of American corporate boards to delegate much work to committees of the board constitutes a de facto two-tier board operation). To view how codetermination might be implemented with an American board, it is helpful to examine a recent British Parliamentary attempt to introduce codetermination to British corporations, since British boards have the same basic structure as their American counterparts.

JOHN D. BLACKBURN, WORKER PARTICIPATION ON CORPORATE DIRECTORATES: IS AMERICA READY FOR INDUSTRIAL DEMOCRACY? *

Although Great Britain presently does not have co-determination legislation, the idea has recently received serious consideration. A departmental commission, the Bullock Commission, studied the idea in 1976 and recommended a plan to implement it. In 1978, the Labour Party proposed a similar plan. The Bullock Commission's plan, after generating heated debate, probably will not be enacted into law due to a direct confrontation between management and labor. The

* John D. Blackburn, "Worker Participation On Corporate Directorates: Is America Ready For Industrial Democracy?" 18 Houston Law Review 349 (1981); © 1981 by the Houston Law Review. Reprinted with permission of the publisher.

Labour Party Plan, referred to as the "White Paper," lost much of its support with the ouster of the Labour government at the polls.

* * *

The Unitary Board Model

Despite adoption of the two-tier board model by the European Economic Community in its proposals for the harmonization of European company law, the British Bullock Report, published in 1977, proposed employee representation on a unitary board. The Bullock Report suggested a unitary rather than the two-tier model in order to adapt the co-determination concept to British company structure and British corporate law. British companies are not composed of supervisory and management boards as are German enterprises. British companies have unitary boards which have the powers and responsibilities of the two German boards combined. Although it was suggested during the Bullock Commission's investigations that development of a two-tier model would be more conducive to cooperation by reducing the likelihood of friction over day-to-day managerial matters, this suggestion was rejected because it would involve a major overhaul of British corporate law and would introduce complexity into the corporate structure that appeared both unwarranted and unwanted by the Commission. The composition of the unitary board by the Bullock Report was presented by the following formula: $2X + Y$, with shareholders and employees constituting one X each, and with the third group, Y, being elected to the board by the two groups for their managerial expertise.

To ensure that the effectiveness of worker participation would not be diluted by delegation of board powers to management in the articles of incorporation, the Bullock Report proposed a statutory definition of board powers. The Report recommended that five functions be nondelegable with the board possessing the exclusive right to submit resolutions to the shareholders concerning each of the following: winding up, changes in the capital structure, changes in the articles of incorporation, shareholder dividends, and the disposal of a substantive part of the undertaking. The Report suggested that two functions, the control and appointment of management and the disposition of resources not governed by capital structure and dividends, should be the "ultimate responsibility" of the board so that management could not take unilateral action on them. Although management would continue to run the company's day-to-day activities and would be charged with implementing board decisions, the board would retain the right of veto on matters falling within its exclusive control. Similarly, under the Bullock Report's recommendations, shareholders would retain a veto power. This latter power may defeat any notion of employee parity with shareholders.

After heated debate between Britain's Trades Union Congress and the Confederation of British Industry, the British Labour government was unable to muster sufficient support for the Bullock Commission's recommendations to pass legislation based on them, and the possibility of their being adopted now seems slim. Management's main objection to the plan was that the unitary board brought employees too close to the day-to-day management of the corporation, and management consequently supported the two-tier model proposed by the Bullock Commission's Minority Report. The fact that management groups supported some form of worker representation suggests that the concept may be enacted in some form in the future.

QUESTIONS

1. Are the two Indiana Law Journal articles inconsistent? If so, which one is more persuasive?

2. Are the cases which follow consistent with the Cabot Carbon decision?

HERTZKA AND KNOWLES v. NLRB

United States Court of Appeals, Ninth Circuit, 1974.
503 F.2d 625, cert. denied 423 U.S. 875, 96 S.Ct. 144, 46 L.Ed.2d 106 (1975).

CHOY, CIRCUIT JUDGE:

This case arises out of a labor dispute at Hertzka & Knowles, a medium-sized architectural firm located in San Francisco. In September of 1971 its professional employees voted to have the Organization of Architectural Employees (OAE) as their bargaining agent. After months of negotiations failed to produce an agreement with management, one of the then 25 employees in the bargaining unit petitioned the National Labor Relations Board to decertify OAE. The Board set an election for December 6, 1972.

Prior to the election, management representatives spoke to the employees on several occasions. What occurred at a December 1st meeting formed the basis for OAE charges, filed with the Board after the election, that Hertzka & Knowles violated § 8(a)(1) of the National Labor Relations Act by allegedly making certain threats of reprisal.

OAE lost the election by a vote of 14 against continuing representation and 11 for.

Immediately after the election, a meeting attended by both the employees and the partners of the firm produced a new plan for employee bargaining. It called for five in-house committees with each to be composed of five employees and one management representative. Each was to have a particular zone of competence—for example, employee remuneration. In its charges before the Board, OAE claimed that this committee system violated § 8(a)(2) of the Act which requires that an employer not "dominate or interfere with the formation or administration   *   *   *   or contribute financial or other support to" any labor organization.

The Board agreed, after a hearing before a trial examiner, that the employer had committed the unfair labor practices OAE charged. 206 N.L.R.B. No. 32 (1973). Its order requires Hertzka & Knowles to cease and desist from threatening its employees with reprisals and to withdraw recognition and support from and disestablish the employees' committees. Additionally, the Board set aside the decertification and called for a new election.

Hertzka & Knowles petitions here to set aside, and the Board cross-petitions to enforce, this order insofar as it pertains to the unfair labor practices. We enforce the order as to the alleged threats of reprisal, but refuse to enforce that part based on the § 8(a)(2) charges. [The court's discussion of the § 8(a)(1) charge is omitted— Ed.]

The § 8(a)(2) Charges—The Committee System

When the results of the decertification election became clear on December 6, Hanna, a partner in the firm, called a meeting of both partners and professional personnel for the next morning. The meeting was opened by Hanna who commented that the eleven pro-union votes indicated a degree of dissatisfaction which had to be taken into account. He then asked for suggestions from the floor on how to accomplish a management-employee dialogue.

Employee Smith suggested the committee system previously described. The source of the idea, he later testified, was a proposal put forth by OAE during their unsuccessful negotiations with Hertzka & Knowles prior to decertification. The idea of adding a management representative to the committees was Smith's; he felt it would lessen what he termed the "long, tedious process" of negotiating with management that had been experienced with OAE as the bargaining agent. Smith's motion to adopt this system was seconded by two other employees and was approved by the employees, in the examiner's words, "overwhelmingly." An employee then suggested that the partners vote on the proposal. The suggestion was enthusiastically embraced, and the proposal passed unanimously.

The committees, though at the time of the Board hearing still in a nascent state, operate in a not unusual fashion. Their purpose is to discuss and formulate proposals for changes in employment terms and conditions; in some cases, it was contemplated that proposals would have to be passed on to management. Meetings are sometimes held on company time without loss of pay. On some committees the management member votes but apparently not on others. The firm representative, like other committee members, is consulted on meeting times and participates fully in the proceedings.

The issue for our consideration is whether the employer's participation in the system's approval and operation represents an illicit degree of interference, under § 8(a)(2), with its information and administration.

Central to the National Labor Relations Act is the facilitation of employee free choice and employee self-organization. Indeed, § 8(a)(2) is, in part, a means to that end, for it seeks to permit employees to freely assert their demands for improvements in working conditions. Literally, however, almost any form of employer cooperation, however innocuous, could be deemed "support" or "interference." Yet such a myopic view of § 8(a)(2) would undermine its very purpose and the purpose of the Act as a whole—fostering free choice—because it might prevent the establishment of a system the employees desired. Thus the literal prohibition of § 8(a)(2) must be tempered by recognition of the objectives of the NLRA.

In saying this, we are merely repeating what Senator Wagner said of § 8(a)(2) when he introduced his bill to the Senate:

> The erroneous impression that the bill expresses a bias for some particular form of union organization probably arises because it outlaws the company-dominated union. Let me emphasize that nothing in the measure discourages employees from uniting on an independent—or company-union basis, if by these terms we mean simply an organization confined to the limits of one plant or one employer. Nothing in the bill prevents employers from maintaining free and direct relations with their workers. * * * The only prohibition is against the sham or dummy union which is dominated by the employer, which is supported by the employer, which cannot change its rules and regulations without his consent, and which cannot live except by the grace of the employer's whims.

Statutory History of the United States: Labor Organization 278–79 (R. Koretz, ed. 1970) (remarks of Feb. 21, 1935).

For this same reason courts have emphasized that there is a line between cooperation, which the Act encourages, and actual interference or domination considered from the standpoint of the employees, which the Act condemns. * * * In N.L.R.B. v. Wemyss, 212 F.2d 465 (9th Cir. 1954), we declined to approve a Board finding that an employer interfered with and dominated the administration of an in-house committee system. Judging the § 8(a)(2) issue from the subjective standpoint of the employees, we said:

> [T]he question is whether the organization exists as the result of a choice freely made by the employees, in their own interests, and without regard to the desires of their employer or whether the employees formed and supported the organization, rather than some other, because they knew their employer desired it and feared the consequences if they did not.

Id. at 471. We indicated that the employer must be shown to have interfered with the "freedom of choice" of the employees. Id. at 472. The sum of this is that a § 8(a)(2) finding must rest on a showing that the employees' free choice, either in type of organization or in the assertion of demands, is stifled by the degree of employer involvement at issue.

Judged by this standard, we do not think there is substantial evidence, in the totality of circumstances, that Hertzka & Knowles violated § 8(a)(2). Unlawful support is not shown by the fact the committees meet at the firm and on firm time. Nor is it a weighty circumstance that Hanna called and opened the meeting at which the committee system was adopted. The idea was still that of an employee, and it was approved by the employees. There was no evidence produced at the hearing, that the employees' preference was affected by this fact. Finally, that the partners voted on the proposal is relatively meaningless; it was the result of a suggestion made by an employee and its enthusiastic acceptance by the body of employees.

The question essentially comes down to the significance of having management partners on the committees. True, this may mean bargaining is "weaker" than if there were a formally organized union. Yet this feature too was chosen by the employees, and it is one with which, for all the record shows, they are not dissatisfied. This is perhaps not unreasonable given the close contact that must exist between partners and professional associates in an architectural firm. There is no evidence, furthermore, of actual interference with the assertion of employee demands through the committees. At most, there is the management vote on some committees, and even where the partner votes, the employees can easily outvote him.

For us to condemn this organization would mark approval of a purely adversarial model of labor relations. Where a cooperative arrangement reflects a choice freely arrived at and where the organization is capable of being a meaningful avenue for the expression of employee wishes, we find it unobjectionable under the Act.

GENERAL FOODS CORPORATION AND AMERICAN FEDERATION OF GRAIN MILLERS, AFL–CIO AND ITS LOCAL 70

Case No. 8-CA-2657, Affirmed 231 N.L.R.B. No. 122 (1977).
96 L.R.R. M. 1204.

WALTER H. MALONEY, JR., Administrative Law Judge.   *   *   *

B. THE UNFAIR LABOR PRACTICES ALLEGED

Respondent operates a large manufacturing plant at St. Anne, Illinois, near Kankakee, where it produces dog food and other varieties of pet food. Its production and maintenance unit is organized and is represented by the Charging Party to this proceeding. Ancillary to the production plant is a research and testing facility known as Gaines Nutrition Center where about 25–30 non-supervisory workers are employed. This research and testing facility houses about 500 dogs and 250 cats which are used for testing both the food produced by the Respondent and its competitors and for research related to the production of new and different kinds of pet foods.

The Charging Party attempted to organize the Gaines Nutrition Center, went to an election on August 15, 1974, and lost by a vote of 10 to 13 * * *.

In addition to its ATG compensation plan, General Foods has embarked upon what is called a job enrichment program for many groups and classifications of employees. The job enrichment program is based upon certain premises derived from behavioral psychology which hold that employees desire to have a larger and more meaningful role in their day-to-day work activities than is normally assigned to them in a mechanical production line operation. The program is based upon the further assumption that employees desire to make a recognized contribution to the business organization of which they are a part. Accordingly, the Respondent has, at the Gaines Nutrition Center, made an effort to enlarge the powers and responsibilities of all its rank-and-file employees and to give them certain powers or controls over their job situations which are normally not assigned to manual laborers. Employees are divided into four teams. In theory if not always in practice, each team, acting by a concensus of its members, makes job assignments to individual team members, assigns job rotations, and schedules overtime among team members. A team has no disciplinary power. However, from time to time individuals who are drawn from these teams have conducted job interviews with applicants for vacancies at the Nutrition Center.

The Respondent has retained Dr. Bruce Wheatley, a professor of communications at Eastern Illinois University, as a consultant to assist in its job enrichment program. Dr. Wheatley described his periodic meetings with the various teams as attempts to improve the internal communications among team members and to build "trust levels" among them by conducting "team building" exercises. These meetings have occurred over a period of two years and are declining in frequency, since the success of Dr. Wheatley's efforts necessarily means that his work with the teams should diminish and ultimately terminate. Some of these meetings have occurred away from the Company's premises while other meetings have occurred at the Nutrition Center. First line supervisors normally attend these meetings. Dr. Wheatley expressed the opinion that his efforts in building "trust levels" was bearing fruit as to three teams but, in the Acceptability Team supervised by William Doan, he felt that he was not making such progress. As a result, only two or three meetings of the Doan Team were held with Dr. Wheatley after August 4, 1975, the cut-off date for the period of limitations in this case.

Apparently Dr. Wheatley's efforts at stimulating communications had some effect, even on Doan's team. At a team meeting in the fall of 1975, Kennelman Richard Hurst took advantage of the occasion to outline to team members, to Dr. Wheatley, and to Dr. Merl Parlin, the Director of the Center who was in attendance, an idea for the more equitable rotation of overtime within a crew. Dr. Parlin asked the opinions of the other team members about Hurst's suggestion. As they did not all agree with him, Parlin did not put the suggestion into effect. At one of the team meetings, Hurst asked either Dr. Wheatley or Mairs whether the ATG compensation plan, relating to managing by objectives, would mean more money for employees, since he felt it was a waste of time to prepare detailed descriptions and related documents for persons who were essentially manual laborers. He was informed that it would mean more money.

Other employees besides Hurst voiced opinions at team meetings as to what they liked or disliked about their jobs. On one occasion,

Hurst registered a complaint to the management in attendance about a raise that had recently been given to a female employee. He complained that supervisors were catering to female employees and were not assisting the other employees enough in performance of their chores as they were supposed to do. Other and similar complaints about lack of promotions were aired. Hurst testified that supervisors discontinued these objectionable practices after the matters were brought to Dr. Parlin's attention. Employees also discussed the job expectations which were a part of the management "contract" each employee had to reach with his supervisor and reviewed copies of other employees' job descriptions which they had prepared. More recently, the practice of requiring employees to write up job descriptions was discontinued.

C. ANALYSIS AND CONCLUSIONS

All parties agree that the nub of the issue in this case is whether the four teams which, in their aggregate, constitute the entirety of the non-supervisory work force at the Gaines Nutrition Center are labor organizations within the meaning of Section 2(5) of the Act.

The Charging Party correctly points out in its brief that none of the conventional accoutrements of a labor organization—constitution, by-laws, officers, and the like—is a prerequisite for eligibility to be a labor organization as envisioned by the Act. If the contrary were true, these teams would surely fall outside the definition set forth above, since none of them have officers, constitution, by-laws, election of delegates, regular membership meetings, dues, property, charter, formal recognition by the Employer, or formal designation by team members as a spokesman of any kind. While these factors are not essential in determining the existence of a labor organization the absence of all such normal features of labor organizations, or of organizations of any kind provides an insight which should be considered in determining the status of the Respondent's teams within the framework of this law.

In their essence, the teams, and each of them, are nothing more or less than work crews established by the Respondent as administrative subdivisions of its entire employee complement at the Gaines Nutrition Center. It is virtually uncontested that the Respondent's original purpose in establishing these crews had nothing to do with labor relations, as that term is generally understood. The teams exist and were created for the purpose of performing the various jobs that must be done in operating the Nutrition Center. As new jobs and new functions arose at the Center, new teams came into existence. Unlike many of the cases cited by the Charging Party and the General Counsel, the teams herein were not established to head off incipient organizing drives by outside unions nor did they come into existence in response to any unrest in the bargaining unit which was sensed by the Respondent. Four teams now exist at the Nutrition Center because, in the judgment of the Respondent's management, this is the best way to organize the work force to get the work done.

Having been established for reasons quite apart from labor relations matters, the teams, or any of them, can only become "labor organizations" within the meaning of the Act by virtue of some *de facto* status they may have acquired by virtue of events which have taken place at the Respondent's kennels within the period of limitations which began on August 4, 1975.

In addressing the issue in this case, a second and serious structural question relating to the teams also exists. In every case cited by the General Counsel or the Charging Party in which the Board or the courts have accorded labor organization status to an informal or loosely-knit employee group, the group or committee so designated is at least an entity which is different and is set apart from the totality of the bargaining unit which it has been called upon to represent. To my knowledge an entire bargaining unit, viewed as a "committee of the whole," has never been accorded *de facto* labor organization status. The essence of a labor organization, as this term has been construed by the Board and the courts, is a group or a person which stands in an agency relationship to a larger body on whose behalf it is called upon to act. When this relationship does not exist, all that can come into being is a staff meeting or the factory equivalent thereof. The fact that, for convenience sake, these staff meetings take place in four different groupings which in their aggregate constitute the whole unit should not change the status of the groups. Viewed in a certain light, the teams have a "meeting" each time their members come to work. The meetings focused upon evidence in this case are simply occasions when the Respondent's management has elected to interrupt the normal daily routine of the teams to bring to the attention of its employees certain matters of managerial concern. At these formalized meetings, certain employees have on occasion elected to voice their complaints individually to the management representatives who were present, but there is no evidence that the team as such ever acted as an agent on behalf of any irate employee to assist him on pressing his case. Indeed, a team could not do so because it lacked sufficient internal functional cohesiveness to be regarded as a unit or an entity separate and apart from its membership. A team could not be a bargaining agent because it lacked the structure and capacity to be an organization or an agent of any kind. No team had a team spokesman. At every team meeting, those who spoke did so on their own behalf and in their own individual capacities. If such a set of circumstances should give rise to the existence of a labor organization, no employer could ever have a staff conference without bringing forth a labor organization in its midst. I cannot believe that the Act intended or provided for such a result.

Thus, Hurst complained at a team meeting about supervisory favoritism toward female employees and outlined to management on one occasion his ideas concerning rotation of overtime. This was Hurst speaking individually to the Respondent. Hurst did not call upon, did not receive, and in the nature of things could not receive the intercession of the team on his behalf in pressing these matters. The fact that these matters constitute grievances or involve conditions of employment does not mean that the team took up the cudgels on Hurst's behalf in dealing with the Respondent. Hurst was dealing directly with management, as the proviso to Section 8(a)(2) authorizes both the Respondent and its employees to do.

The closest evidence to team dealing with the employer on behalf of employees to be found in this record are hearsay statements by Mairs that Dr. Parlin, the Director of the Center, reported to him at Christmas time that the teams had come to him ("I guess," as Mairs put it) to talk about the work schedule over the Christmas-New Years holiday season and had made request about changing the schedule to provide a greater amount of free time. In accordance with the previous custom at the Center, the holiday schedule was changed in accordance with the "recommendations of the teams." Mairs' information as to what exactly transpired between Parlin and the teams was fuzzy and his characterization that the recommendations originated with teams rather than individual employees or the total unit were his own. The matter is, in my judgment, *de minimis* and isolated from an entire history and pattern of events in which teams existed as unstructured assemblies of employees, without spokesman or leadership and without any agency relationship to its components, while team meetings served as occasions for management to communicate directly with its employees and vice versa. The testimony of Mairs on these matters does not, in my opinion, serve to transform the teams into either *de facto* or *de jure* labor organizations.

Accordingly, the Complaint herein must be dismissed.

D. RECOMMENDED READING

In addition to the material excerpted or referred to in the text the following articles should be helpful in analyzing the legal problems presented.

1. *"Note:* New Standards for Domination and Support Under § 8(a)(2)," 82 Yale L.J. 510 (1973).

2. Getman, "The Midwest Piping Doctrine," 31 U. of Chi.L.Rev. 292 (1964). On the Issue of Worker Participation the non-legal literature is vast. In addition to the articles excerpted see Carson, "Preparing Workers for Participation," 28 Int'l Mgmt. Jan. 1973. Meyers, "Overcoming Union Opposition to Job Enrichment" 49 Harv.Bus.Rev. (May/June 1971.)

3. Hulin & Blood, "Job Enlargement, Individual Differences and Worker Responses," 69 Psychological Bull. 41 (1968).

4. Jackson, "An Alternative to Unionization and the Wholly Unorganized Shop: A Legal Basis For Sanctioning Joint Employer-Employee Committees and Increasing Employer Free Choice," 28 Syracuse L.Rev. 809 (1977).

5. Schurgin, "The Limits Of Organized Employer-Employee Relations In Non-Union Facilities: Some New Evidence of Flexibility," 57 Chi.Kent L.Rev. 615 (1981).

For a discussion of Quality Circles, See:

6. Cole, "Made in Japan—Quality Control Circles," 16 Conf.Bd. 72 (Nov. 1979).

Chapter IV

COLLECTIVE BARGAINING

A. CASE STUDY: OHIO STEEL *

I. Background: Ohio Steel

Shortly after its founding as a small malleable iron foundry in Columbus, Ohio, in 1883, management discovered a major void in the marketplace. The rapidly expanding American railroad system was in desperate need of a safe, efficient and reliable method of coupling cars.

Railroading was the growth industry in turn-of-the-century America. In less than fifty years, the iron horse had transformed the United States from a rural, largely pioneer society, into an urban, industrial giant. But, while the railroads were quickly steaming civilization into the heartland of America, in preparation for the sophistication of the 20th century, the old link-and-pin-style coupler system continued to haunt passengers, shippers and workers alike. It was inefficient, unreliable and extremely hazardous to railroad workers.

By the 1880's, management of the then struggling Ohio Malleable Iron Company made the conscious decision to create its own marketplace. Working with railroad pattern maker James A. Timms, the company devoted many years to expensive research and development, which paid off with the creation of a safe, efficient and reliable automatic coupler.

At the turn of the century, larger locomotives and longer trains demonstrated that malleable iron was not strong enough to haul the products of American industry. Once again, Ohio management anticipated a need and responded. In 1902 Ohio Malleable converted from malleable iron to steel castings in a modern plant in Columbus, launching another era of growth and change. A name change to Ohio Steel followed. The expansion permitted Ohio's research and development engineers to probe for new markets.

The company's industrial innovation and growth potential did not go unnoticed. By 1905, the company had attracted not just the attention, but the investment capital and personal interest of the Rockefeller family. Frank Rockefeller, brother of the legendary John D., served as president of Ohio until 1907.

* This case was prepared by Dr. Marcus Sandver, associate professor of labor and human resources, College of Administrative Science, The Ohio State University. Published with the permission of the author.

During the early part of the 20th century, Ohio diversified into the manufacture of virtually every case part required on a railroad freight car. Today, more than 90 years after its founding, the Steel Castings Division, the largest steel foundry at one location in the United States, supplies products to virtually every railroad in the country—products ranging from couplers, four and six wheel side frames, bolsters, car frames, and underbodies.

The railroad market, with its characteristic cyclical peaks and valleys was the sole business served by Ohio Steel Castings for more than half a century, except for those periods during World Wars I and II when armaments assumed an important share. By the 1960's, Ohio management recognized that the spread of the interstate highway system would have a profound effect upon the railroads. Industry would become increasingly dependent upon long-haul trucks for freight handling, and the public would become more dependent upon the auto for intercity transportation. Management embarked upon a cautious but determined search for new, untapped markets.

By the mid-1960's, management had made one of its most important decisions—to enter the growing plastic molding industry because the automotive and appliance industries were committed to the conversion of many metal, wood and leather parts to plastic and there did not appear to be dominant leaders in the custom plastic molding industry. Before the auto makers would commit to significant conversion to plastic parts from outside suppliers, they required assurance that there would be ample plant capacity for their growing needs, recognition of rigid quality and production requirements and sophisticated management skills. Ohio Steel filled the void, much as it did 75 years earlier for the railroad industry. With this change, Ohio Steel Castings became Ohio International, Inc.

Today, just a decade after this diversification decision, the company's plastic operations account for more than $50 million in sales or over three and one-half times the combined sales of the plastic companies at the time of their acquisition. Ohio Steel, meanwhile, likewise expanded its market to provide steel castings ranging in size from 200 pounds to 30 tons each. In the process the company diversified into mass transit, armaments and many industrial markets, making castings for mining, oil exploration and heavy construction. Extensive machining and welding operations were added. Nonrailroad volume now accounts for 40 percent of Ohio Steel's sales. A multi-million dollar expansion program that will increase Ohio Steel's production capacity by 65 percent is now underway.

Beginning in the spring of 1980 Ohio Steel began to feel the effects of the recession which had begun earlier in the year in the auto industry. By the summer of 1980 the company was forced to lay off 200 workers from its production force of 2,000 employees; in October Ohio Steel laid off 200 more production employees and 75 office and clerical workers from an office staff of about 450 employees. In January of 1981 the company laid off 350 more production employees.

In the wake of these massive layoffs the company and the union met for their first bargaining session on February 9, 1981.

II. Background—Steelworkers Local 2342

Since 1942, the employees at Ohio Steel have been represented by Local 2342 of the United Steelworkers of America. Prior to 1942, during the 1920's and 1930's, the employees at Ohio Steel were enrolled in a company union. A ruling by the NLRB in 1942 established the United Steelworkers of America as the exclusive representative for the employees at Ohio Steel.

Although labor relations at Ohio Steel during the 1940's and 1950's were sometimes tumultuous, the climate of labor-management relations during the 1970's was generally peaceful and mature. The company and the union did have a six-week strike over wages during the last contract negotiation in 1978, however. The local union at Ohio Steel has about 1,000 working members with 650 members on layoff subject to recall.

The leaders of Steelworkers 2342 pride themselves on their responsiveness to their members' wishes and on the firm and aggressive stance they take in dealing with management. The current president, secretary-treasurer and first vice-president of Steelworkers 2342 all have been in office over six years; all were on the bargaining committee which negotiated the contract in 1978 and all are on the current bargaining committee.

The membership of Steelworkers Local 2342 is predominately comprised of unskilled and semi-skilled production workers. Only 150 of the currently employed workforce occupy skilled labor positions and 35 of these persons are in a separate bargaining unit represented by the Patternmakers League of North America. The vast majority of the members of Local 2342 are male (90 percent) and a large proportion of the labor force is black (65 percent). The president and the secretary-treasurer of the local union and the International Representative of the Steelworkers union (the fourth member and spokesman for the union's bargaining team) are all black and all have at least 15 years of shop floor working experience at Ohio Steel.

III. Union's Initial Demands

When bargaining began on February 9, 1981, the union presented the company with the following list of initial demands:

1. An increase in the shift differential to 35¢ per hour for second shift and 40¢ per hour for the third shift.

2. Change in the cost of living formula to provide a 1¢ per hour wage increase for every .3 percentage change in the C.P.I.

3. A general across-the-board wage increase for all job grades listed in Appendix B of the labor agreement

   75¢ for the first year

   40¢ for the second year

   40¢ for the third year

   in addition to the cost of living allowances.

4. Bereavement pay of $200 upon the death of an immediate family member.

5. Increase vacation schedule by 1 week for each length of service category.

6. Add two new paid holidays:

   a. January 15th—Martin Luther King's Birthday

   b. November 11th—Veterans' Day

7. An increase in life insurance to:

   a. $11,500 the first year

   b. $13,500 the second year

   c. $15,000 the third year

8. An increase in sickness and accident benefits to:

   a. $200 per week the first year

   b. $225 per week the second year

   c. $235 per week the third year

9. An increase in the duration of sickness and accident benefits to 50 weeks.

10. Increase pension multiplier to $15.50 per year of service.

11. An addition of a new section of the contract with the following language:

SUBCONTRACTING

a. Production, service, maintenance, repair and installation work performed by members of the bargaining unit shall not be contracted out by the company unless agreed to in advance by a contracting-out committee.

b. Production, service, maintenance, repair and installation work shall never be contracted out when employees in occupations appropriate to perform such work are on layoff status.

c. A committee consisting of four persons, two designated by the union and two designated by the company shall attempt to resolve all questions in connection with the contracting out of work.

d. Should the committee be unable to resolve any questions arising out of a sub-contracting issue the matter may be submitted to the grievance procedure up to and including arbitration.

12. Any grievance arising out of company actions dealing with discharge and discipline may be submitted to an expedited arbitration procedure. Under the rules of this expedited procedure the arbitrator must render an award within 48 hours after the close of the hearing and the arbitrator's fee is limited to $250. The expedited arbitration procedure is to conform with the "Rules of Procedure for Expedited Arbitration" as established by the American Arbitration Association.

IV. Company Demands

In its initial demands the company is seeking three main goals:

1. Increased flexibility in utilizing the labor force currently employed.
2. Moderating across the board wage increases.
3. Limiting the amount of money going to pay for COLA increases (see attached memo).

In particular, the company will be asking the union to:

1. Cap the COLA escalator (see attached memo) to a maximum of 15¢ per year.
2. Surrender super seniority for union stewards.
3. Agree that ability to perform the work shall be the major determining criteria in promotions, filling job vacancies, layoff and recall.
4. Agree that employees can be worked up to ten hours per week by mandatory overtime.
5. Agree that limitations on Saturday and Sunday overtime be eliminated from the contract.
6. Agree to a 10¢ per hour per year across the board wage increase.
7. Agree to no change in present insurance and hospitalization.
8. Agree to no change in present pension benefits.

The company realizes that it will not be able to get everything it wants in the negotiations, but Ohio Steel feels increasing pressure from competition and realizes that it needs *changes* in the labor agreement if it is going to remain in business.

MEMORANDUM

DATE: February 9, 1981

TO: Steelworkers Local #2342 Negotiating Team

FROM: John Adams, President, Ohio Steel

Gentlemen:

As we begin our negotiations to effect a new Contract in mid-April 1981, I believe it is extremely important to both the Steelworkers of America and Ohio Steel to review and act upon a financial situation which has grown (over the years) and is now seriously threatening the competitiveness and, hence, employment within Ohio Steel.

I refer to the fact of Ohio Steel granting an *Uncapped* Cost-of-Living provision effective in 1973 vs. our competition holding to a *Capped* Cost of Living down through the years.

Rather than a lot of talk, I am detailing a comparison history (since the COLA was originally instituted at Ohio Steel) between ourselves and two of our major competitors for our mutual review. See Exhibit A attached.

Obviously, the Uncapped COLA in effect at Ohio Steel has resulted in a series of automatic wage increases far in excess of our competition.

I am not criticizing the fact our Ohio Steel people *have kept pace* with the staggering inflation going forth throughout our country nor am I bemoaning the fact Ohio Steel went along with an uncapped cost-of-living provision and our competition did not.

I am pointing out—Many, many people and unions must use the words today, "Catch up with inflation," and I can't readily disagree with this sentiment.

However—

In the case of Ohio Steel, we have kept pace with inflation *automatically* whenever the federal indices have moved and—

We now find ourselves hard pressed in a competitive war for any available work which means *jobs* within Ohio Steel.

No, I am not proposing our people take any "cuts in pay" similar to other hard-pressed industries which are faced with being wiped out by competition but—

I am calling for a very responsible negotiation between your Steelworkers and our Company which will enable Ohio Steel (and *all* its people) to "stay in the competition race" and not become unemployed victims.

Very Truly Yours,

J. T. Adams

J. T. Adams
President

EXHIBIT A

See J. T. Adams' letter dated February 9, 1981

Contract Year		Ohio Steel	ASF	National
1972	Gen. Increase	$ .35	$ .11	$ .10
	COLA Increase	—	.11	—
1973	Gen. Increase	.10	.11	.12
	COLA Increase	.11	.12	.12

Contract Year		Ohio Steel	ASF	National
1974	Gen. Increase	.10	.28	.38
	COLA Increase	.45	.25	.22
1975	Gen. Increase	.27	.16	.16
	COLA Increase	.29	.25	.22
1976	Gen. Increase	.14	.16	.16
	COLA Increase	.23	.23	.20
1977	Gen. Increase	.14	.40	.60
	COLA Increase	.28	.26	.25
1978	Gen. Increase	.40	.20	.20
	COLA Increase	.36	.35	.35
1979	Gen. Increase	.20	.20	.20
	COLA Increase	.61	.35	.35
1980	Gen. Increase	.20	.25	.60
	COLA Increase	.71	.35	.35
1981	COLA Increase (Effective 1/1/81)	$ .17		

AGREEMENT

This Agreement dated April 15, 1978 is entered into between Ohio Steel Castings Company, Columbus, Ohio, (hereinafter called the "Company") and the United Steelworkers of America (hereinafter called the "Union").

SECTION I—INTENT AND PURPOSE

1. It is the intent and purpose of the parties hereto that the Agreement will promote and improve industrial and economic relationships between those employees who are in the Bargaining Unit and the Company, and to set forth herein the basic Agreement covering rates of pay, hours of work, and other conditions of employment to be observed by the parties hereto.

2. The term "employee", as used in the Agreement shall include all production, maintenance, and hourly rated shop clerical employees of the Company, excluding foremen, plant guards, watchmen, pattern makers and pattern maker apprentices, and all office clerical and salaried employees.

3. The Company agrees not to negotiate working conditions, wages, rates, hours of employment, or grievances, except through a committee appointed or elected by the Union. This Section shall not be construed to deprive any employee of his rights under Federal or State Laws.

SECTION II—RECOGNITION

1. The Company recognizes the Union as the exclusive bargaining agency for all employees of the Company as defined in Section I.

2.   The Company recognizes and will not interfere with the rights of its employees to become members of the Union. The Union and the Company agree that neither it, nor any of its officers or members, will engage in any Union activity while such employees are on Company time, and the Company may discipline any employee who shall be proved guilty of violating this provision. Any dispute as to the facts shall be adjusted in accordance with the provisions of Section VII—Adjustment of Grievances.

3.   Any employee who is a member of the Union in good standing on the effective date of this Agreement shall, as a condition of employment, maintain his membership in the Union to the extent of paying membership dues and assessments uniformly levied against all Union members.

(a) Any employees hired on or after the effective date of this Agreement shall become a member of the Union after the completion of two (2) calendar months of employment. Such employee shall thereafter maintain his membership in the Union to the extent as provided in Paragraph 3(b).

(b) Initiation fees for membership in the Union shall not exceed the minimum prescribed by the Constitution of the International Union at the time the employee becomes a member.

4.   During the term of this agreement, the Company will deduct Union initiation fees, monthly membership dues and any assessments permitted by law as designated and directed by the International Treasurer of the Union and as authorized by individually signed checkoff authorization cards submitted to the Company.

SECTION III—WAGES

1.   Job classifications, labor grades, and occupational hourly wage rates for production, maintenance, and shop clerical employees in the bargaining unit effective April 15, 1978, April 15, 1979 and April 15, 1980 are set forth in Appendices A and B.

2.   The Company shall establish production standards for incentive work where applicable and shall use recognized time study principles and methods.

3.   The Company will pay a premium of 20¢ per hour for hours worked on second shift and 25¢ per hours worked on third shift, effective April 15, 1978.

4.   Effective each adjustment date, a Cost-of-Living Adjustment equal to 1¢ per hour for each full .4 of a point change in the Consumer Price Index shall become payable for all hours.

5.   Cost-of-Living Adjustments will be an add-on during the contract period April 15, 1978–April 14, 1981.

6.   There will be no cap on the Cost-of-Living during the life of the contract.

7. Increases in wages during the term of this agreement will be as follows for those jobs listed in Appendix A.

April 15, 1978—40¢

April 15, 1979—20¢

April 15, 1980—20¢

SECTION IV—HOURS OF WORK AND OVERTIME

1. This Section is intended to provide a basis of calculating overtime and shall not be construed as a guarantee of hours per workday or workweek.

2. Time and one-half shall be paid for all hours worked in excess of eight (8) hours in a workday and for all hours worked in excess of forty (40) hours in a workweek.

3. Time and one-half shall be paid for Saturday work and double time shall be paid for Sunday work and holidays worked. All time worked between 7:00 a. m. Sunday and 7:00 a. m. Monday is to be paid at double time rate.

4. There shall be no duplication or pyramiding of overtime payments. If more than eight (8) hours are worked on Saturday or Sunday shifts only the overtime rate provided for such shifts shall be paid for such excess hours.

5. Any employee called or scheduled back to work after finishing his regular turn and before sixteen (16) hours rest, is guaranteed four (4) hours at the overtime rate or until the start of employee's regular shift, whichever comes first.

6. The Company will distribute regularly scheduled overtime equitably among qualified experienced employees in the same job occupation. No employee shall be scheduled for such overtime for more than two (2) weeks as against other employees qualified and experienced in the work to be performed.

No employee will be required to work more than two (2) consecutive weekends, nor be required to work in excess of a total of eight (8) hours a day on Saturday or Sunday.

SECTIONS V—VACATIONS

1. Each employee with continuous service as defined in Section VIII of this Agreement as of July, 1975 and each subsequent July 1 thereafter, during the term of this Agreement shall be entitled to vacation and/or vacation allowance as follows:

Years of Continuous Service	Number Weeks Vacation
6 months but less than 1	0
1 year but less than 3	$1\frac{1}{2}$
3 years but less than 5	2
5 years but less than 10	3
10 years but less than 15	4
15 years but less than 20	$4\frac{1}{2}$

Years of Continuous Service	Number Weeks Vacation
20 years but less than 25 5	
25 years and over 6	

SECTION VI—SENIORITY

1. The parties recognize that promotional opportunity and job security in event of promotions, decreases of forces, and rehirings after layoffs, should increase in proportion to length of continuous service and that in the administration of this Section the intent will be that full consideration shall be given continuous service in such cases. Further, it is the intent in the administration of this Section there shall be no discrimination because of sex, race, creed, or national origin. In recognition, however, of the responsibility of the Company for the efficient operation of the plant, it is understood and agreed that in all cases of:

(a) Promotions (except promotions to positions excluded under the definition of "Employee" herein above): the following factors as listed below shall be considered; however, only when factors (2) and (3) are relatively equal, length of continuous service (factor 1) shall govern.

(1) Continuous service

(2) Ability to perform the work

(3) Physical fitness

2. All job vacancies will be posted plantwide. Promotions to job vacancies will follow the provisions set forth above.

3. Job vacancies will be posted for three (3) working days, and include the following information:

(1) shift/department, job title, and rate

(2) location of job

(3) incentive/non-incentive

(4) job description available in Personnel Department at time of bid

4. The parties recognize that job security, in the event of decrease in forces and recall after layoff, should be in relation to length of continuous service. The following factors shall be considered, however, only where factors (b) and (c) are relatively equal, length of service (a) shall govern.

(a) Continuous service

(b) Ability to perform the work

(c) Physical fitness

5. It is agreed that all elected officers and grievance committee personnel shall hold super seniority for layoff purposes only in the department in which each holds seniority.

SECTION VII—ADJUSTMENT OF GRIEVANCES

1. The Grievance Committee for the plant shall consist of not less than three (3) employees of the plant and not more than twelve (12) such employees designated by the Union, who will be afforded such time off without pay as may be required:

(a) to attend regular scheduled Committee meetings;

(b) to attend meetings pertaining to discharge or other matters which cannot reasonably be delayed until the time of the next scheduled meeting; and

(c) to visit departments other than their own at all reasonable times, only for the purpose of handling grievances, after notice to the head of the department to be visited and permission from their own departmental superintendent or the superintendent's designated representative.

(d) the Company will pay the committee for six (6) hours per month for grievance hearings.

2. Should difference arise between the Company and the Union which involves the interpretation of or application of or compliance with the provisions of the Agreement, there shall be no suspension of work on account of such differences, and an earnest effort shall be made to settle such difference promptly in the manner outlined:

Step 1. Any employee or group of employees having a complaint in connection with his or their work shall first see his immediate foreman, and at the option of the employee or group may be with or without a Union Representative. The foreman cannot refuse the request of the employee or group for Union Representation. Such meeting shall be held within a seventy-two (72) hour period from the time the incident occurred (two weeks involving pay/incentive problem) causing the complaint, or such complaint shall be considered void and not subject to the grievance procedure. The employee shall request the presence of his Union Representative at the meeting. The foreman shall verbally give his answer to the complaint promptly but not later than forty-eight (48) hours from the time of discussion.

Step 2. If the complaint is not settled in Step 1 above, it may be appealed to the next higher step of this procedure. It shall then be reduced to writing on the form provided and submitted not later than at the end of the third working day after the date of the disposition by the foreman and presented to the general foreman and/or superintendent of the department. If the general foreman and/or superintendent and the Union departmental representative feel the need for aid in arriving at a decision, they may, by agreement invite such additional Company and Union representatives as may be necessary or available to participate in the discussion and investigation, but such additional participants shall not relieve the general foreman and superintendent or the Union departmental representative from responsibility for resolving the problem. Such appeal will be heard not later than the end of the third working day following the date of the appeal, but not during the hours of the employee's shift.

Step 3.   If the grievance is not settled at Step 2 above, it may be appealed to the next higher step of this procedure. Such an appeal shall be so indicated on the forms provided, and not later than the end of the third working day after the date of the disposition stated in Step 2. The Company agrees to provide for a meeting at the Company offices between the members of the Grievance Committee, a representative of the International Union and representatives of the Company, if requested, within five (5) days from the date of the request for the purpose of discussing grievances not settled in the preceding steps. Not later than two (2) working days immediately preceding the date set for such meetings, the International Representative shall submit to the Industrial Relations Director of the Company a list of grievances to be discussed at the next scheduled meeting. It is agreed that only those grievances so listed will be discussed unless otherwise mutually ageed by the parties. If requested, two (2) copies of accurate minutes of such meetings will be prepared and submitted to the International Representative. The representative of the Company shall answer the grievance not later than the end of the fifth working day following such meeting unless mutually agreed to extend.

Step 4.   Grievances involving the interpretation, application or violation of specific terms of this Agreement shall upon the request of either party within fifteen (15) days from the date of the decision made in Step 3, be submitted to an impartial arbitrator, who shall be selected by the parties within ten (10) days from the date of the request to arbitrate.

Step 5.   The award of the arbitrator shall be final and binding upon the parties except as otherwise provided by law. The expense of any arbitration proceeding shall be shared equally by the Company and the Union. The arbitrator shall not have the authority to add to, detract from or in any way alter the terms of this Agreement. Grievances which are not appealed in the manner and within the time aforesaid shall be considered settled on the basis of the decision last made and shall not be eligible for further appeal.

SECTION VIII—MANAGEMENT

The Management of the plant and the direction of the working forces including the right to hire, promote, suspend, demote, discharge for cause, transfer, or change processes, and the right to relieve employees from duties because of lack of work or other reason which may arise, is vested exclusively in the Company. The Company will not, however, use the provisions of this Section for the purpose of discrimination against any member of the Union because of such membership or Union activity.

SECTION IX—HOLIDAYS

The following days shall be considered holidays:

New Year's Day	Labor Day
President's Day (effective 1980)	Thanksgiving Day
Good Friday	Day after Thanksgiving
Memorial Day	Day before Christmas
July Fourth	December 31

1. All employees, other than probationary employees, shall be paid for holidays not worked on the basis of employee's hourly straight time earnings from week preceding holiday times eight (8). The cost-of-living adjustment will be included in the computation of holiday pay.

SECTION X—INSURANCE AND HOSPITALIZATION

1. The following insurance, hospital and surgical benefits for employees will be provided effective April 15, 1978.

Effective April 15, 1978

$ 8,500.00	Group Life Insurance
$ 8,500.00	Accidental Death
$ 8,500.00	Accidental Dismemberment
125.00	Weekly Sick Benefit and Weekly Non-Occupational Accident Benefit (such benefits payable beginning eighth day of sickness and non-occupational accident and to continue for maximum of 26 weeks).

Effective April 15, 1979

$ 9,000.00	Group Life Insurance
$ 9,000.00	Accidental Death
$ 9,000.00	Accidental Dismemberment
130.00	Weekly Sick Benefit and Weekly Non-Occupational Accident Benefit

Effective April 15, 1980

$10,000.00	Group Life Insurance
$10,000.00	Accidental Death
$10,000.00	Accidental Dismemberment

Effective April 15, 1980

    135.00   Weekly Sick Benefit and Weekly Non-Occupational Accident Benefit

2.   Effective April 15, 1979 a Vision Care Plan, as negotiated by the parties will be instituted. The Hospitalization, Major Medical, Dental Program, and Drug Plan will continue in force for the duration of the Agreement.

SECTION XI—TERMINATION

This Agreement shall remain in effect until midnight April 14, 1981. Either party may on or before February 15, 1981, give notice to the other party by registered mail of the desire of the party giving such notice to negotiate with respect to all of the terms of this Agreement.

If such notice is given the parties shall meet within thirty (30) days after February 15, 1981, and if the parties fail to agree with respect to such terms, either party may resort to strike or lockout, as the case may be, in support of its position.

APPENDIXES & EXHIBITS

APPENDIX A

JOB OCCUPATIONS

MOLDING DEPARTMENTS

Job Title	Evaluated Job Class
Tool Room Attendant	6
Steel Pouring	15
Supervisor—Molding Gangs	15
Inspector—Pouring Floor	10
General Labor	2
Operating Forklift Truck	6
Core Carrier—West Molding	4
Machine Men—Moldmaster	5

CORE DEPARTMENTS

Making Class I Cores	11
Core Maker Helper	3
Labor—General	2
Oven Tender	10
Operator—Sand Coating Machine	5
Oven Tender—Industrial Cores	6

FINISHING DEPARTMENTS

Chainman (Coupler)	6
Craneman (Coupler)	8
Stationary Grinder	7
Welder	9
Operator—Cold Press	10
Tool Room Blacksmith	9

Job Title	Evaluated Job Class
PRODUCTION MACHINING	
Operator—Turret Lathe	12
Operator—Surface Grinder	8
Operator—Radial Drill Press	8
Machinist—All Around	19
Group Leader—Machinists	21
Tool Grinder/Utility Man	15
MECHANICAL DEPARTMENT	
Tool Room Attendant	14
Tool Room Helper	9
Electrician	19
Maintenance Man	11
Mechanic	16
YARD DEPARTMENT	
Locomotive Crane Helper	6
Locomotive Crane Operator	12
PATTERN DEPARTMENT	
Aluminum Molder	13
Maintenance of Molding Equipment and Patterns	10
POWER DEPARTMENT	
Stationary Engineer	17
QUALITY CONTROL DEPARTMENTS	
Inspector—Finishing Departments	10
Quality Control Inspector—Finishing Departments	14
Quality Control—Precision Layout Finishing Departments	17

APPENDIX B

CHANGES IN RATES OF PAY—NONINCENTIVE WORK

Class Number	Rate Effective April 15, 1978 *	Rate Effective April 15, 1979 *	Rate Effective April 15, 1980
1	5.73	5.93	6.13
2	5.73	5.93	6.13
3	5.79	5.99	6.19
4	5.85	6.05	6.25
5	5.91	6.11	6.31
6	5.97	6.17	6.37
7	6.03	6.23	6.43
8	6.09	6.29	6.49
9	6.15	6.35	6.55
10	6.21	6.41	6.61
11	6.27	6.47	6.67

* Plus Quarterly Cost of Living Adjustments beginning April 1, 1978 through April 1, 1981 or a minimum cost of living adjustment of ten cents (10¢) per year.

Class Number	Rate Effective April 15, 1978 *	Rate Effective April 15, 1979 *	Rate Effective April 15, 1980
12	6.33	6.53	6.73
13	6.39	6.59	6.79
14	6.45	6.65	6.85
15	6.51	6.71	6.91
16	6.57	6.77	6.97
17	6.63	6.83	7.03
18	6.69	6.89	7.09
19	6.75	6.95	7.15
20	6.81	7.01	7.21
21	6.87	7.07	7.27

* Plus Quarterly Cost of Living Adjustments beginning April 1, 1978 through April 1, 1981 or a minimum cost of living adjustment of ten cents (10¢) per year.

PENSION AGREEMENT

Exhibit 1

This Pension Agreement dated the Fifteenth day of April, 1978, is between Ohio Steel Castings (hereinafter referred to as the "Company") and the United Steelworkers of America, AFL–CIO, (hereinafter referred to as the "Union").

The parties hereto having reached an agreement on the subject of a revised Pension Plan to become effective April 15, 1978, it is, therefore, agreed between the parties as follows:

SECTION I—ELIGIBILITY

A. Eligibility for Employees Retiring on or after April 15, 1978

1. Any employee in the Bargaining Unit who retires from the service of the Company on or after April 15, 1978, and:

(a) has attained the age of sixty-two (62), and

(b) has had no less than ten (10) years of continuous service as defined in Section III herein shall be entitled to receive a pension benefit upon retirement in the amount specified in Section II, Paragraph A–1.

2. Any employee in the Bargaining Unit who completes thirty (30) years of continuous service as defined in Section III herein, shall be entitled to receive a benefit upon retirement in the amount specified in Section II, Paragraph A–1 regardless of his physical age.

3. Any employee in the Bargaining Unit who shall become permanently and totally disabled, and who shall have no less than ten (10) years of continuous service, as defined in Section III, herein, prior to becoming permanently and totally disabled shall be eligible to receive a pension on the conditions specified in this agreement and in the amount specified in Section II, Paragraph B–1.

SECTION II—AMOUNT OF PENSION

A. Normal Retirement

1. An employee who retires on or after April 15, 1978, and who meets the eligibility requirements of Section I, Paragraphs A–1 and 2 shall receive a monthly benefit based upon his years of continuous service in monthly installments equal to ten dollars ($10) multiplied by such years of continuous service, subject to all the deductions provided for in other provisions of the Agreement.

OHIO STEEL FINANCIAL DATA

(Dollars in thousands, except per share amounts)	1980	1979	1978
FINANCIAL RESULTS Year ended May 31			
Net Sales and Revenues	$71,604.25	$69,538.50	$47,875.25
Cost of Goods Sold	57,512.50	56,432.00	39,016.25
Gross Margin	14,091.75	13,106.50	8,859.00
Operating Expenses			
Selling, General and Administrative	5,441.00	4,497.00	2,880.25
Interest	1,082.50	763.75	500.00
Total	6,523.50	5,260.75	3,380.25
Earnings Before Taxes	8,052.00	7,845.75	5,478.75
Income Taxes	3,647.75	3,809.00	2,706.25
Net Earnings	4,404.25	4,036.75	2,772.50
Per Share	.40	.368	.255
Depreciation	866.50	673.25	482.25
Funds from Operations	5,532.25	5,102.00	3,495.75
Cash Dividends	1,359.50	989.00	607.00
Per Share	.120	.090	.056
Capital Expenditures—Net	2,902.25	940.50	922.00
Average Shares Outstanding	2,761.25	2,746.75	2,724.25
FINANCIAL POSITION at May 31			
Current Assets	$29,516.25	$20,649.50	$15,723.75
Current Liabilities	16,258.00	9,328.25	8,472.25
Working Capital	13,258.25	11,321.25	7,251.50
Fixed Assets	25,283.25	9,441.75	9,370.00
Total Assets	55,970.75	30,696.50	25,601.75
Long-Term Debt	16,402.00	7,640.75	6,622.00
Shareholders' Equity	21,203.00	12,827.75	9,791.50
Per Share	1.715	1.168	.890
Total Capitalization	37,605.00	20,468.50	16,413.50
Shares Outstanding	3,090.75	2,746.75	2,747.50

B. THE SOCIAL AND ECONOMIC FUNCTIONS
OF COLLECTIVE BARGAINING

D. BOK & J. DUNLOP, LABOR AND THE
AMERICAN COMMUNITY*

If society is to evaluate the institution of collective bargaining and compare it with alternative procedures, its social and economic functions must be clearly perceived. Five functions seem particularly important.

ESTABLISHING THE RULES OF THE WORKPLACE

Collective bargaining is a mechanism for enabling workers and their representatives to participate in establishing and administering the rules of the workplace. Bargaining has resulted in the development of arbitration and other safeguards to protect the employee against inequitable treatment and unfair disciplinary action. More important still, the sense of participation through bargaining serves to mitigate the fear of exploitation on the part of the workers. Whether or not wages would be lower in the absence of bargaining, many employees would doubtless feel that their interests would be compromised without the presence of a union or the power to elect a bargaining representative. In view of these sentiments, collective bargaining may well serve as a substitute for sweeping government controls over wages as a device for insuring adequate, visible safeguards to protect the interests of employees.

CHOOSING THE FORM OF COMPENSATION

Collective bargaining provides a procedure through which employees as a group may affect the distribution of compensation and the choices between money and hours of work. One of the most significant consequences of collective bargaining over the past two decades has been the growth of fringe benefits, such as pensions, paid holidays, health and welfare, and vacations with pay. If unions had not existed, it is unlikely that individual workers would have spent added income in exactly the same way; indeed, it is doubtful whether, in the absence of collective bargaining, health and pension plans at present prices would have grown widespread. Moreover, though speculations of this kind are treacherous, the history of social-insurance legislation in the United States suggests that, under a system where the government was responsible for setting wages and terms of employment, fringe benefits would not have grown to the extent they have.

These fringe benefits have had a significant impact upon the whole economy. There can be little question that collective bargaining played a major role in focusing priorities and attention upon medi-

* D. Bok & J. Dunlop, *Labor And The American Community* 222–227 (1970); © 1970 by the Rockefeller Brothers Fund, Inc. Reprinted by permission of SIMON & SCHUSTER, a Division of Gulf & Western Corporation.

cal care in the past decade. With the growth of health and welfare plans, information about medical care has been widely disseminated and developed; a body of experts in business and labor have arisen, and the pressures for public programs in the medical field have been accelerated. In much the same way, the extent of expansion in vacation-oriented industries—motels, resorts, transportation, boating, and leisure goods—must be partly attributed to the emphasis in collective bargaining on greater vacation benefits for employees.

STANDARDIZATION OF COMPENSATION

Collective bargaining tends to establish a standard rate and standard benefits for enterprises in the same product market, be it local or national. Labor contracts in the ladies' garment industry seek to establish uniform piece rates (and labor costs) for all companies that produce the same item within the same general price brackets; all the firms in the basic steel industry confront virtually the same hourly wage schedule for all production and maintenance occupations; and all construction firms bidding on contracts in a locality confront known and uniform wage schedules.

Such uniformity is naturally sought by unions. As political institutions, they desire "equal pay for equal work" in order to avoid the sense of grievance that results when one group of members discovers that another group is performing the same job in another plant at a higher wage. Thus, unless there are strong economic reasons for maintaining wage differentials, unions will normally push hard for standardization.

From the standpoint of employers, it should be observed that uniform wage rates do not necessarily imply uniform labor costs. Firms paying the same hourly rates may have varying wage costs as a result of differences in equipment and managerial efficiency. But competition tends to remove these differences and promote more uniform labor costs among close rivals. In highly competitive industries, employers often have a keen regard for such standardization; it protects the enterprises from uncertain wage rate competition, at least among firms subject to the collective agreement.

From the standpoint of the economy as a whole, the effects of standardization are mixed. In some instances, wage uniformity may be broadened artificially beyond a product market area, as when the wage rates in a tire company are extended to apply to its rubber-shoe work. The effect is to produce a less efficient use of economic resources. The resulting premium over the wages paid in other rubber-shoe plants eventually will compel the tire companies to give up doing business in the rubber-shoe field. In a more important sense, however, the effect of uniformity has been positive in that it has favored the expansion of more profitable, more efficient firms. In a country like France, on the other hand, bargaining establishes only minimum rates, so that backward companies can often survive by paying lower wages than their competitors if they can somehow manage to retain the necessary work force.

DETERMINING PRIORITIES ON EACH SIDE

A major function of collective bargaining is to induce the parties to determine priorities and resolve differences within their respective organizations. In the clash and controversy between the two sides, it is easy to assume a homogeneous union struggling with a homogeneous management or association of employers. This view is erroneous and mischievous. In an important sense, collective bargaining consists of no less than three separate bargains—the agreement by different groups within the union to abandon certain claims and assign priorities to others; an analogous process of assessing priorities and trade-offs within a single company or association; and the eventual agreement that is made across the bargaining table.

A labor organization is composed of members with a conglomeration of conflicting and common interests. The skilled and the unskilled, the long-service and the junior employees, the pieceworkers and the day-rated workers, and those in expanding and contracting jobs often do not have the same preferences. A gain to one of these groups often will involve a loss to another. Thus, in George W. Taylor's words, "To an increasing extent, the union function involves a mediation between the conflicting interests of its own membership."

Similarly, corporate officials may have differing views about the negotiations, even in a single company. The production department and the sales staff may assess differently the consequences of a strike. The financial officers may see an issue differently from the industrial-relations specialists. These divergences are compounded where an association of companies bargains with a union, for there are often vast differences among the member firms in their financial capacity, vulnerability to a strike, concern over specific issues, and philosophy toward the union.

One of the major reasons that initial demands of both parties often diverge so far from final settlements is that neither side may have yet established its own priorities or preferences, or assessed the priorities of the other side. In many cases, these relative priorities are established and articulated only during the actual bargaining process. (This view of the bargaining process helps to explain the sense of comradeship that labor and management negotiators often develop through the common task of dealing with their respective committees and constituents.)

This process of accommodation within labor and management is central to collective bargaining. It should not be disparaged as merely a matter of internal politics on either side. In working out these internal adjustments in a viable way, collective bargaining serves a social purpose of enormous significance. The effective resolution of these problems is essential to the strength of leadership and to the continued vitality of both the company and the union.

REDESIGNING THE MACHINERY OF BARGAINING

A most significant function of collective bargaining in this country is the continuing design and redesign of the institution itself. While it is true that the national labor policy—as reflected in legislation, administrative rulings, and court decisions—has a bearing on some features of collective bargaining, the nature of the institution is chiefly shaped by the parties themselves. As previously noted, the collective-bargaining process largely determines the respective roles of individual bargaining and union-management negotiations. It defines the subjects to be settled by collective bargaining. It determines the structure of bargaining relationships. It establishes the grievance procedures and prescribes the uses of arbitration and economic power in the administration of an agreement. It decides the degree of centralization and decentralization of decision making. It influences the ratification procedures of the parties. The results are seldom fixed. The bargaining parties must reshape their bargaining arrangements from time to time in response to experience and emerging new problems. Thus, the design of collective bargaining and its adaptation to new challenges and opportunities have much to do with its capacity to fulfill its social functions effectively and without undue cost to the public.

C. THE LEGAL FRAMEWORK FOR COLLECTIVE BARGAINING

When a union is certified or has otherwise established its right to represent the employers in an appropriate unit, § 8(a)(5) of the Act, requires the employer to "bargain collectively" with it. There are two separate concepts enforced through section 8(a)(5). The first exclusive representation is defined in § 9(a). The second is good faith bargaining, dealt with in § 8(d) of the Act.[1]

1. EXCLUSIVE REPRESENTATION

Section 9(a) provides that Representatives designated or selected for the purpose of collective bargaining by a majority of the employees in a unit shall be the exclusive representatives of all the employees in such unit for the purpose of collective bargaining in respect to wages, hours of employment, or other conditions of employment. The concept of exclusive representation means that an employer may not deal with individual employees or any other group for the purpose of setting wages or working conditions. In addition, he may not make changes in any of these areas without first bargaining with the union. Pre-existing individual contracts do not provide a basis for refusing, even temporarily, to negotiate with the exclusive represen-

---

1. The duty to bargain also arises if an employer accepts the union's claim to majority status or if a bargaining order is issued.

tative since they may be superseded by a subsequent Collective Agreement.[2]

2. GOOD FAITH BARGAINING

Section 8(d) of the Act defines the term "bargain collectively" as the mutual obligation to meet at reasonable times and confer in good faith with respect to wages, hours, and other terms and conditions of employment or the negotiation of an agreement. Section 8(d) requires the parties to put their agreement in writing if either side so wishes, but it states that "such obligation does not compel either party to agree to a proposal or require the making of a concession". The last provision reflects a strong national policy against allowing the Board to dictate terms of collective bargaining agreements. As a result of this policy § 8(a)(5) is not a major factor in the negotiation process and it provides only meager protection for a union against an employer who is determined not to come to an agreement. Two separate factors combine to make § 8(a)(5) essentially useless in achieving agreement when the employer doesn't desire one. First, as illustrated in the case below the employer may, without violating his obligation under the law, insist upon an agreement so favorable to himself that it is bound to be unacceptable to the union. Such a proposed agreement may contain harsh substantive terms or it may insist upon the employer's continued ability to set wages or working conditions by himself. Second, even if an unfair labor practice is found, the Board's remedial power is extremely limited. The process of determining illegality and obtaining court enforcement is so time-consuming that as a practical matter the remedy will probably be determined long after either an agreement has been reached or the union has been effectively destroyed. In addition the Board's remedial order will not be able to undo the effects of the unfair labor practice. The H. K. Porter case which follows makes clear the limits on the Board's remedial capabilities.

WHITE v. N.L.R.B.

United States Court of Appeals, Fifth Circuit, 1958.
255 F.2d 564.

[W]e find that we are at last required to determine whether, in an otherwise unassailable attitude of collective bargaining, the employer may nevertheless be found guilty of a failure to bargain in good faith solely upon a consideration of the content of the proposals and counter proposals of the parties. In other words may the charge of refusal to bargain in good faith be sustained solely by reference to the terms of the employment contract which management finally says

---

2. The leading cases defining the concept of exclusive representation are J. I. Case Co. v. National Labor Relations Board, 321 U.S. 332, 64 S.Ct. 576, 88 L.Ed.2d 762 (1944), dealing with the relationship between collective and individual bargaining, and N.L.R.B. v. Katz, 369 U.S. 736, 82 S.Ct. 1107, 8 L.Ed.2d 230 (1962), dealing with the limits on unilateral employer conduct.

it is willing to sign if such proposed contract could fairly be found to be one which would leave the employees in no better state than they were without it.   For the purpose of considering this question we may assume that the Board could find that the terms of the contract insisted on by the company requiring the surrender by the employees of their right to strike and their agreeing to leave to management the right to hire and fire and fix wages in return for agreements by the company respecting grievances and security that gave the union little, if any, real voice in these important aspects of employment relations would in fact have left the union in no better position than if it had no contract.   It is perfectly apparent that the company representatives approached the bargaining table with a full understanding of their obligations to meet with, and discuss with, representatives of the employees any terms and conditions of employment that either party put forward; that they must at least expose themselves to such argument and persuasion as could be put forward, and that they must try to seek an area of agreement at least as to some of the terms of employment; that if they were able to arrive at such agreement they must be willing to reduce it to writing and sign it.   It is of some significance that at the fourth of the six bargaining sessions, when challenged by the employees' bargaining agent [15] the company's managing partner signed the company's proposed complete contract and tendered it to the union, which declined to accept it.   The question is: Can the company's insistence on terms overall favorable to it in net result be taken as proof that it did not approach the bargaining table in good faith, but that it approached the bargaining table only to give the outward sign of compliance when it had already excluded the possibility of agreement?   *   *   *

We start with the statute which states specifically that the "obligation [to bargain collectively] does not compel either party to agree to a proposal or require the making of a concession."   The Board, in its brief, recognizes this but fails to give effect to it in stating its contention.   Thus the Board is saying that although the statute says no concession need by made and no item need be agreed upon, if a company fails to concede *anything* substantial, then this is too much, and such failure amounts to bad faith.

The language of the Courts is not, as it cannot be, in construing this difficult statute, entirely clear, but we find no case which precisely supports the proposition here asserted by the Board.   The principal basis of the Board's attack here is the broad management function clause and the failure to agree to a real arbitration clause in which the arbitrators have final powers.   The remaining provisions criticized by the Board could not conceivably be considered as proof of bad faith by the petitioners.   As to the inclusion of a broad management functions clause and thus a refusal to permit matters relating

---

15. Burton, the union representative, said: "I told him personally I didn't believe they would sign their own contract. He called my bluff and had John White sign it."

to hiring, discharging, hours and working conditions to be subject to grievance procedures and arbitration, the Supreme Court has said:

"Congress provided expressly that the Board should not pass upon the desirability of the substantial terms of labor agreements. Whether a contract should contain a clause fixing standards for such matters as work scheduling or should provide for more flexible treatment of such matters is an issue for determination across the bargaining table, not by the Board. If the latter approach is agreed upon, the extent of union and management participation in the administration of such matters is itself a condition of employment to be settled by bargaining.

"Accordingly, we reject the Board's holding that bargaining for the management functions clause proposed by respondent was, per se, an unfair labor practice." National Labor Relations Board v. American National Insurance Co., 343 U.S. 395,[20] 72 S.Ct. 824, 832, 96 L.Ed. 1027.

If such a clause is not per se proof of failure to bargain in good faith then *a fortiori* insistence on physical examination by the company's own doctor, refusal to include terms of a Christmas bonus, a refusal to grant specified wage increases, refusal to "freeze" rent and utility charges on company-owned houses and like issues could not either separately or collectively constitute such proof.

We do not hold that under no possible circumstances can the mere content of the various proposals and counter proposals of management and union be sufficient evidence of a want of good faith to justify a holding to that effect. We can conceive of one party to such bargaining procedure suggesting proposals of such a nature or type or couched in such objectionable language that they would be calculated to disrupt any serious negotiations. A careful study of the record before us, and viewed with all the adverse emphasis the Board has placed upon the challenged actions of the company in its brief, footnote [16] supra, leaves us with the clear impression that the Board erred in finding adequate proof of a failure to bargain in good faith.

RIVES, CIRCUIT JUDGE, dissenting. * * * Collective bargaining is at the very heart and core of the Labor Management Relations Act. If, in any particular case, effective collective bargaining is not had and cannot be required, then in that case the Act is nothing. It follows that there must be some protection against "merely going

20. The terms of the management functions clause there before the Court was:

"The right to select and hire, to promote to a better position, to discharge, demote or discipline for cause, and to maintain discipline and efficiency of employees and to determine the schedules of work is recognized by both union and company as the proper responsibility and prerogative of management to be held and exercised by the company, and while it is agreed that an employee feeling himself to have been aggrieved by any decision of the company in respect to such matters, or the union in his behalf, shall have the right to have such decision reviewed by top management officials of the company under the grievance machinery hereinafter set forth, it is further agreed that the final decision of the company made by such top management officials shall not be further reviewable by arbitration."

through the motions of negotiating," "a predetermined resolve not to budge from an initial position," "surface bargaining" accompanied by "a purpose to defeat it and wilful obstruction of it," "shadow boxing to a draw," "giving the Union a runaround while purporting to be meeting with the Union for the purpose of collective bargaining."
*   *   *

The Board sometimes finds the employer's entire course of conduct in negotiations indicated the desire not to reach agreement in violation of § 8(a)(5). Some such Board opinions have been enforced by the courts,[3] but the *White* opinion illustrates how much deference is given to the concept of "hard bargaining" in defining the reach of § 8(a)(5).

H. K. PORTER CO. v. N.L.R.B.

Supreme Court of the United States, 1970.
397 U.S. 99, 90 S.Ct. 821, 25 L.Ed.2d 146.

BLACK, J. After an election respondent United Steelworkers Union was, on October 5, 1961, certified by the National Labor Relations Board as the bargaining agent for certain employees at the Danville, Virginia, plant of the petitioner, H. K. Porter Co. Thereafter negotiations commenced for a collective-bargaining agreement. Since that time the controversy has seesawed between the Board, the Court of Appeals for the District of Columbia Circuit, and this Court. This delay of over eight years is not because the case is exceedingly complex, but appears to have occurred chiefly because of the skill of the company's negotiators in taking advantage of every opportunity for delay in an act more noticeable for its generality than for its precise prescriptions. The entire lengthy dispute mainly revolves around the union's desire to have the company agree to "check off" the dues owed to the union by its members, that is, to deduct those dues periodically from the company's wage payments to the employees. The record shows, as the Board found, that the company's objection to a checkoff was not due to any general principle or policy against making deductions from employees' wages. The company does deduct charges for things like insurance, taxes, and contributions to charities, and at some other plants it has a checkoff arrangement for union dues. The evidence shows, and the court below found that the company's objection was not because of inconvenience, but solely on the ground that the company was "not going to aid and comfort the union." Efforts by the union to obtain some kind of compromise on the checkoff request were all met with the same staccato response to the effect that the collection of union dues was the "union's business" and the company was not going to provide any assistance.

---

3. One of the few cases of the type is NLRB v. Reed & Prince Mfg. Co., 205 F.2d 131 (1st Cir. 1955). The opinion contains a painstaking analysis by the Judge and shows how strong the evidence must be before a subjective finding of bad faith will be found.

G. & B. Labor Rel. 2nd Ed. MCB—8

Based on this and other evidence the Board found, and the Court of Appeals approved the finding, that the refusal of the company to bargain about the ckeckoff was not made in good faith, but was done solely to frustrate the making of any collective-bargaining agreement. In May 1966, the Court of Appeals upheld the Board's order requiring the company to cease and desist from refusing to bargain in good faith and directing it to engage in further collective bargaining, if requested by the union to do so, over the checkoff. United Steelworkers of America v. NLRB, 124 U.S.App.D.C. 143, 363 F.2d 272, cert. denied, H. K. Porter, Inc., Disston Division—Danville Works v. N.L.R.B., 385 U.S. 851, 87 S.Ct. 90, 17 L.Ed.2d 80.

In the course of that opinion, the Court of Appeals intimated that the Board conceivably might have required petitioner to agree to a checkoff provision as a remedy for the prior bad-faith bargaining, although the order enforced at that time did not contain any such provision.

The object of [the Wagner] Act was not to allow governmental regulation of the terms and conditions of employment, but rather to ensure that employers and their employees could work together to establish mutually satisfactory conditions. The basic theme of the Act was that through collective bargaining the passions, arguments, and struggles of prior years would be channeled into constructive, open discussions leading, it was hoped, to mutual agreement. But it was recognized from the beginning that agreement might in some cases be impossible, and it was never intended that the Government would in such cases step in, become a party to the negotiations and impose its own views of a desirable settlement.

* * *

In reaching this conclusion the Court of Appeals held that § 8(d) did not forbid the Board from compelling agreement. That court felt that "[s]ection 8(d) defines collective bargaining and relates to a determination of whether a * * * violation has occurred and not to the scope of the remedy which may be necessary to cure violations which have already occurred." 389 F.2d, at 299. We may agree with the Court of Appeals that as a matter of strict, literal interpretation that section refers only to deciding when a violation has occurred, but we do not agree that that observation justifies the conclusion that the remedial powers of the Board are not also limited by the same considerations that led Congress to enact § 8(d). It is implicit in the entire structure of the Act that the Board acts to oversee and referee the process of collective bargaining, leaving the results of the contest to the bargaining strength of the parties. It would be anomalous indeed to hold that while § 8(d) prohibits the Board from relying on a refusal to agree as the sole evidence of bad-faith bargaining, the Act permits the Board to compel agreement in that same dispute. The Board's remedial powers under § 10 of the Act are broad, but they are limited to carrying out the policies of the Act itself. One of these fundamental policies is freedom of contract. While the parties' freedom of contract is not absolute under the Act, allowing the Board to compel agreement when the parties themselves are unable to agree would violate the fundamental premise on which the Act is based— private bargaining under governmental supervision of the procedure alone, without any official compulsion over the actual terms of the contract.

In reaching its decision the Court of Appeals relied extensively on the equally important policy of the Act that workers' rights to collective bargaining are to be secured. In this case the court apparently felt that the employer was trying effectively to destroy the union by refusing to agree to what the union may have considered its most important demand. Perhaps the court, fearing that the parties might resort to economic combat, was also trying to maintain the industrial peace that the Act is designed to further. But the Act as presently drawn does not contemplate that unions will always be secure and able to achieve agreement even when their economic position is weak, or that strikes and lockouts will never result from a bargaining impasse. It cannot be said that the Act forbids an employer or a union to rely ultimately on its economic strength to try to secure what it cannot obtain through bargaining. It may well be true, as the Court of Appeals felt, that the present remedial powers of the Board are insufficiently broad to cope with important labor problems. But it is the job of Congress, not the Board or the courts, to decide when and if it is necessary to allow governmental review of proposals for collective-bargaining agreements and compulsory submission to one side's demands. The present Act does not envision such a process.

The judgment is reversed.

QUESTION

In the *Gissel* case, the court held that the Board could remedy unfair labor practices which inhibited union organizing election by putting the parties in the position the Board concluded they would have been in had there been no illegality. In *H. K. Porter*, the Board denied similar power in the bargaining area. Can you explain the difference?

The Board has accepted a limited view of its function with respect to collective bargaining, as the following statement of a former Board member reveals.

PETER D. WALTHER, THE BOARD'S PLACE AT THE BARGAINING TABLE*

The declared purpose of the National Labor Relations Act is to promote and protect the "friendly adjustment of industrial disputes" through the practice of collective bargaining. This is the principal objective of the Act and it is upon the accomplishment of this objective that the Act's success rests. In order to accomplish this objec-

* Peter D. Walther, "The Board's Place At The Bargaining Table," 28 Labor Law Journal 181 (1976). © 1976 Peter D. Walther. Reprinted with the permission of the author. Mr. Walther was a member of the National Labor Relations Board.

tive, the Act does several things: (1) it gives employees the right to organize for the purposes of collective bargaining or refrain from engaging in collective bargaining if they so desire, and protects them in the exercise of these rights; (2) it establishes and administers the process under which employees may choose a collective bargaining representative; (3) it imposes upon employers the duty to engage in collective bargaining with the employees' duly authorized representative; and (4) it attempts to insure that the parties negotiate in good faith with a view toward reaching agreement if possible.

A cursory glance at the Act thus shows that it is concerned to a great extent with maneuvering the parties to the bargaining table. The Board, under the Act, is constituted as the midwife of the bargaining relationship. It oversees the birth of that bargaining relationship and attempts to prevent any miscarriages. But once the parties have passed the threshold into the bargaining arena, the Board has accomplished much of what it can do. After that threshold is passed, the Board's further involvement with the collective bargaining process is limited to defining the subjects about which the parties must bargain and to seeing that the bargaining is not simply a charade. Although these are not negligible tasks, they do not compare in importance to the Board's task of getting the parties safely to the table for meaningful bargaining.

No matter what happens at or on the way to the bargaining table, the Board cannot go so far as to compel the making of a concession or the agreement to any proposal. Even where, as sometimes happens, the employer engages in patently illegal activity which undermines the union's support and destroys its bargaining strength, the Board must limit itself (perhaps through imposition of a bargaining order) to bringing the parties to the bargaining table; anything beyond this is not permitted.

To those who argue that this is lamentable or unfair, it is sufficient to observe that collective bargaining, as envisioned by the Act, is at heart a consensual process. There are good reasons, practical and otherwise, why this should be so. The collective bargaining agreement is an excellent vehicle for the adjustment of disputes (and correlatively for promoting employees' welfare) primarily because it is a privately negotiated, consensual document. Its strengths lie in the fact that it is self-enforcing and flexible—strengths which themselves derive from the fact that the agreement is the product of the parties' consent.

Only an agreement consented to by both parties and negotiated without undue interference from an outside agency will be truly self-enforcing. Similarly, only an agreement negotiated in the absence of substantive restraints will be sufficiently flexible to effectively meet the difficult unforeseen problems that can and will arise in the collective bargaining relationship. The parties alone know what they want. Absence of control by the Board is thus warranted if the agreement is to best balance each party's expectations.

Additionally, only by making collective bargaining a free and cooperative action of the parties can the Act achieve what the Act intends the collective bargaining relationship to achieve. It is paradoxically the Act's insistence upon consent in collective bargaining that has made the Act such an effective regulatory device. Like every piece of comprehensive social legislation, the National Labor Relations Act has both a regulative and an educative function—two functions which, because they work in tandem, are inseparable. Each function complements and is dependent upon the other.

Unless the public had become, through time, educated in and acquiescent to the goals of the Act, the Board, as the agency empowered to enforce the Act, would have found itself mired in a hopeless regulative task. That this has not happened is a tribute to the Act's educative successes. The fact that the Act stops short of compelling consent to the terms of collective bargaining agreements has, I feel, been chiefly responsible for these educative successes and has brought about the widespread acceptance of unionization and collective bargaining that is vital to the realization of the Act's objectives.

Where, therefore, an employer—through the employment of illegal tactics—effectively undermines the union's bargaining power before being shepherded to the bargaining table, the Board can perhaps attempt to mitigate the effect of this unlawful conduct by devising a remedy which restores to the union some of its bargaining power. But forcing either party to make bargaining concessions and making the Board the final arbiter of what goes into a collective bargaining agreement would irreparably damage the collective bargaining process and would in the long run do more harm than good.

It follows from the above that, just as the Board cannot compel the making of a concession, so the Board should be very reluctant to disturb the terms of the collective bargaining agreement once negotiated. A collective bargaining agreement is a fragile latticework of trade-offs and compromise, which often represents the results of months of negotiation. If the Board voids a provision of the agreement, it upsets the delicate balance arranged by the parties and in the process makes it probable that one of the parties will be disproportionately prejudiced by the Board's action. Obviously, such a result should be avoided if possible.

This is not to say that the Board should stand idly by if a negotiated agreement clearly sacrifices employee rights or is written in blatant disregard for the provisions of the Act. However, where the parties' agreement represents a reasonable accommodation between competing employer and union interests and does not trample on the employees' rights guaranteed by the Act, the Board should not intrude. Although the Board cannot compel agreement, it has established rules policing the forms and procedures of bargaining. The Board's rules have practical significance because they help to determine the reinstatement rights of the striking employees.[4] Thus, em-

---

4. See pages 172–73 below.

ployers and unions, particularly those bargaining in good faith, are likely to try and abide by these rules, which include the following:

(a) The parties must be willing to meet at reasonable times and to put their agreement in writing;

(b) The employer must furnish the union with information in his possession relevant to positions taken at the bargaining table. If an employer asserts financial inability, he must permit the union to examine relevant corporate ledgers;

(c) Neither side may adopt a "take-it-or-leave-it" attitude;

(d) The employer must address his arguments initially to the union's bargaining committee. He may not seek to bypass the committee and try to persuade the employees generally of the reasonableness of his position;

(e) When negotiating a new contract, both sides must bargain over proposals directed to "wage, hours, and other terms and conditions of employment". Failure to do so is an unfair labor practice. However, if a proposal falls outside the statutory definition, the other party may refuse to discuss it and the proposing party commits an unfair labor practice if it insists, to the point of impasse, on any such proposal.

While the system of bargaining developed under the National Labor Relations Act does not contemplate a significant role for legal compulsion in achieving agreement, it also does not assume that agreement will be achieved solely through the persuasive power of reason. Rather, the emphasis is on economic pressure from both sides. The role of economic pressure in the bargaining process was stressed by the Supreme Court first in the *Insurance Agents* case which follows.

NATIONAL LABOR RELATIONS BOARD v. INSURANCE AGENTS' INTERNATIONAL UNION, AFL–CIO

Supreme Court of the United States, 1960.
361 U.S. 477, 80 S.Ct. 419, 4 L.Ed.2d 454.

MR. JUSTICE BRENNAN delivered the opinion of the Court.

This case presents an important issue of the scope of the National Labor Relations Board's authority under § 8(b)(3) of the National Labor Relations Act, which provides that "It shall be an unfair labor practice for a labor organization or its agents * * * to refuse to bargain collectively with an employer, provided it is the representative of his employees * * *." The precise question is whether the Board may find that a union, which confers with an employer with the desire of reaching agreement on contract terms, has nevertheless refused to bargain collectively, thus violating that provision, solely and simply because during the negotiations it seeks to put economic pressure on the employer to yield to its bargaining demands by sponsoring on-the-job conduct designed to interfere with the carrying on of the employer's business.

Since 1949 the respondent Insurance Agents' International Union and the Prudential Insurance Company of America have negotiated collective bargaining agreements covering district agents employed by Prudential in 35 States and the District of Columbia. The principal duties of a Prudential district agent are to collect premiums and to solicit new business in an assigned locality known in the trade as his "debit." He has no fixed or regular working hours except that he must report at his district office two mornings a week and remain for two or three hours to deposit his collections, prepare and submit reports, and attend meetings to receive sales and other instructions. He is paid commissions on collections made and on new policies written; his only fixed compensation is a weekly payment of $4.50 intended primarily to cover his expenses.

In January 1956 Prudential and the union began the negotiation of a new contract to replace an agreement expiring in the following March. Bargaining was carried on continuously for six months before the terms of the new contract were agreed upon on July 17, 1956. It is not questioned that, if it stood alone, the record of negotiations would establish that the union conferred in good faith for the purpose and with the desire of reaching agreement with Prudential on a contract.

However, in April 1956, Prudential filed a § 8(b)(3) charge of refusal to bargain collectively against the union. The charge was based upon actions of the union and its members outside the conference room, occurring after the old contract expired in March. The union had announced in February that if agreement on the terms of the new contract was not reached when the old contract expired, the union members would then participate in a "Work Without a Contract" program—which meant that they would engage in certain planned, concerted on-the-job activities designed to harass the company.

A complaint of violation of § 8(b)(3) issued on the charge and hearings began before the bargaining was concluded. It was developed in the evidence that the union's harassing tactics involved activities by the member agents such as these: refusal for a time to solicit new business, and refusal (after the writing of new business was resumed) to comply with the company's reporting procedures; refusal to participate in the company's "May Policyholders' Month Campaign"; reporting late at district offices the days the agents were scheduled to attend them, and refusing to perform customary duties at the offices, instead engaging there in "sit-in-mornings," "doing what comes naturally" and leaving at noon as a group; absenting themselves from special business conferences arranged by the company; picketing and distributing leaflets outside the various offices of the company on specified days and hours as directed by the union; distributing leaflets each day to policyholders and others and soliciting policyholders' signatures on petitions directed to the company;

and presenting the signed policyholders' petitions to the company at its home office while simultaneously engaging in mass demonstrations there.

* * *

The hearing examiner found that there was nothing in the record, apart from the mentioned activities of the union during the negotiations, that could be relied upon to support an inference that the union had not fulfilled its statutory duty; in fact nothing else was relied upon by the Board's General Counsel in prosecuting the complaint. The hearing examiner's analysis of the congressional design in enacting the statutory duty to bargain led him to conclude that the Board was not authorized to find that such economically harassing activities constituted a § 8(b)(3) violation. The Board's opinion answers flatly "We do not agree" and proceeds to say "* * * the Respondent's reliance upon harassing tactics during the course of negotiations for the avowed purpose of compelling the Company to capitulate to its terms is the antithesis of reasoned discussion it was duty-bound to follow. Indeed, it clearly revealed an unwillingness to submit its demands to the consideration of the bargaining table where argument, persuasion, and the free interchange of views could take place. In such circumstances, the fact that the Respondent continued to confer with the Company and was desirous of concluding an agreement does not *alone* establish that it fulfilled its obligation to bargain in good faith * * *."

However, the nature of the duty to bargain in good faith thus imposed upon employers by § 8(5) of the original Act was not sweepingly conceived. The Chairman of the Senate Committee declared: "When the employees have chosen their organization, when they have selected their representatives, all the bill proposes to do is to escort them to the door of their employer and say, 'Here they are, the legal representatives of your employees.' What happens behind those doors is not inquired into, and the bill does not seek to inquire into it."

We believe that the Board's approach in this case—unless it can be defended, in terms of § 8(b)(3), as resting on some unique character of the union tactics involved here—must be taken as proceeding from an erroneous view of collective bargaining. It must be realized that collective bargaining, under a system where the Government does not attempt to control the results of negotiations, cannot be equated with an academic collective search for truth—or even with what might be thought to be the ideal of one. The parties—even granting the modification of views that may come from a realization of economic interdependence—still proceed from contrary and to an extent antagonistic viewpoints and concepts of self-interest. The system has not reached the ideal of the philosophic notion that perfect understanding among people would lead to perfect agreement among them on values. The presence of economic weapons in reserve, and their actual exercise on occasion by the parties, is part and parcel of the system that the Wagner and Taft-Hartley Acts have recognized.

Abstract logical analysis might find inconsistency between the command of the statute to negotiate toward an agreement in good faith and the legitimacy of the use of economic weapons, frequently having the most serious effect upon individual workers and productive enterprises, to induce one party to come to the terms desired by the other. But the truth of the matter is that at the present statutory stage of our national labor relations policy, the two factors—necessity for good-faith bargaining between parties, and the availability of economic pressure devices to each to make the other party incline to agree on one's terms—exist side by side. One writer recognizes this by describing economic force as "a prime motive power for agreements in free collective bargaining." Doubtless one factor influences the other; there may be less need to apply economic pressure if the areas of controversy have been defined through discussion; and at the same time, negotiation positions are apt to be weak or strong in accordance with the degree of economic power the parties possess. A close student of our national labor relations laws writes: "Collective bargaining is curiously ambivalent even today. In one aspect collective bargaining is a brute contest of economic power somewhat masked by polite manners and voluminous statistics. As the relation matures, Lilliputian bonds control the opposing concentrations of economic power; they lack legal sanctions but are nonetheless effective to contain the use of power. Initially it may be only fear of the economic consequences of disagreement that turns the parties to facts, reason, a sense of responsibility, a responsiveness to government and public opinion, and moral principle; but in time these forces generate their own compulsions, and negotiating a contract approaches the ideal of informed persuasion." Cox, The Duty to Bargain in Good Faith, 71 Harv.L.Rev. 1401, 1409.

For similar reasons, we think the Board's approach involves an intrusion into the substantive aspects of the bargaining process * * *. Thus the Board in the guise of determining good or bad faith in negotiations could regulate what economic weapons a party might summon to its aid. And if the Board could regulate the choice of economic weapons that may be used as part of collective bargaining, it would be in a position to exercise considerable influence upon the substantive terms on which the parties contract. As the parties' own devices became more limited, the Government might have to enter even more directly into the negotiation of collective agreements. Our labor policy is not presently erected on a foundation of government control of the results of negotiations. See S.Rep.No.105, 80th Cong., 1st Sess., p. 2. Nor does it contain a charter for the National Labor Relations Board to act at large in equalizing disparities of bargaining power between employer and union.

As the Insurance Agents case makes clear, the use and threatened use of economic pressure is an important part of the process of bargaining. The role of the law has generally been in defining when pressure tactics are legitimate and what responses may be legally made to them.

3. BARGAINING PRESSURE UNDER THE NATIONAL LABOR RELATIONS ACT [5]

One of the central purposes of the Wagner Act was to counterbalance the power of employers by facilitating the use of strikes and other forms of economic pressure by employees. To this end section 7 of the act granted to employees the right to engage in concerted activity for mutual aid or protection, while section 8 limited the ability of employers to respond. Although there have been many changes made in the NLRA since 1935, the use of economic pressure by employees remains a highly significant factor in the scheme of labor relations contemplated by the act.

The right to prevent application of state conspiracy laws and also to prohibit employers from using participation in such activity is grounds for disciplinary action. It was not intended, however, that an employer be required to yield to his employees' demands. The scheme of the act contemplates that an employer may resist employee pressure and subject the union to a test of economic power. A natural tension exists between the policy forbidding an employer to discipline employees for using economic pressure and the policy permitting him to defend his own economic interests. The National Labor Relations Board and the courts are often required to characterize particular employer responses as unfair labor practices or as legitimate steps to resist union pressure. The line between these concepts is vague; accordingly, the extent to which sections 8(a)(1) and 8(a)(3) limit employer responses to economic pressure has been a source of continual difficulty in the enforcement of the act.

Another source of difficulty arises from the fact that the statutory scheme does not recognize economic pressure as a legitimate means of solving all disputes. The Taft-Hartley and Landrum-Griffin amendments have specifically prohibited the use of economic pressure to achieve certain purposes. The Board and the courts have refused to protect economic pressure in other circumstances on the grounds that the nature of the dispute was such as to make its use unjustified. In areas of traditional management concern, it sometimes has been held that the employer should be able to make decisions without running the risk of economic combat. Alternatively the employer's involvement in an issue which concerns his employees may be so slight that it is considered improper for the employees to cause him economic hardship in pursuing their own interests. In many such cases the policy of the statute, which is aimed at preventing the spread of industrial disputes, militates against holding the economic pressure protected.

5. This discussion is an updated and slightly amended version of J. Getman, *The Protection of Economic Pressure* by Section 7 of the National Labor Relations Act, 115 U. of Pa.L.Rev. 1195 (1967).

From time to time the courts have also indicated that certain forms of economic pressure go beyond the purpose of equalizing economic power and give employees an unfair advantage.

*   *   *

Where a bargaining relationship is established there is less need to permit the use of economic pressure by individual employees. The existence of a recognized representative serves to counterbalance the employer's economic power. Collective bargaining agreements generally provide peaceful alternatives which make the use of economic pressure unnecessary. Moreover, the use of independent economic pressure is often inconsistent with a recognized union's status as sole bargaining representative. As a result of these considerations, pressure brought by employees independently of their recognized bargaining representative is almost always held unprotected.

*   *   *

(a) THE MEANING OF "PROTECTED"

The extent to which conduct described in section 7 is protected by the act depends upon the construction of sections 8(a)(1) and 8(a)(3). Section 8(a)(1) makes it an unfair labor practice to "interfere with, restrain or coerce employees in the exercise of   *   *   *"   section 7 rights. Section 8(a)(3) prohibits "discrimination in regard to   *   *   * any term or condition of employment to encourage or discourage membership in any labor organization: *   *   * ."

*   *   *

If an employer punishes an employee for engaging in activity protected by section 7, he violates section 8(a)(1) and, if union activity is involved, section 8(a)(3) as well. This does not mean, however, that an employer is helpless in the face of protected activity. In many situations, an employer acting to protect his business can legitimately respond to protected activity in such a way as to make it costly for the employees to continue such activity. Although such cases involve "interference" with section 7 rights and generally involve "discouragement" of union membership, the literal language of the act is limited to minimize interference with the employer's ability to run his business as he wishes.

On the other hand, the mere fact that an employer's response to economic pressure is motivated by legitimate business considerations does not necessarily mean that his conduct is permitted by the act. A violation of section 8(a)(1) may be found regardless of the employer's motivation if the interference with the employee rights is considered sufficiently severe to outweigh the employer's economic interests. Violations of section 8(a)(3) have been found on the basis of a similar balancing of interests.

An employer may take a variety of steps in response to employee economic pressure without violating the act. He need not pay employees for the time they spend engaged in such economic pressure activity. Employee absence for union activity may be taken into account in computing bonuses, and in certain circumstances economic pressure by employees will justify a lockout or a unilateral subcontracting of work. Possibly the most significant permissible response is the employer's ability to hire permanent replacements for striking employees. This employer prerogative was recognized by the Supreme Court, in dictum, in NLRB v. MacKay Radio & Tel. Co., and since has been largely unquestioned.

* * *

Theoretically, an employer's ability to permanently replace striking employees is limited to cases in which such action is taken for economic motives. An employer may permanently replace strikers in order to continue his business, but not in order to punish employees for engaging in protected activities. The difficulty, once again, is in trying to categorize the employer's conduct. Is he replacing for economic motives or discharging for punitive motives?

* * *

The Board, in fact, does not seek to evaluate the employer's state of mind in order to determine the legality of his conduct. Instead, the Board has devised a fairly mechanical test to distinguish between replacement (legal) and discharge (illegal). Unless it can be demonstrated that the employer has singled out for replacement those whom he knows to be active union members, he is permitted to lay off permanently any striking employees, as long as they are not notified that they are replaced or treated as having been replaced before new employees are hired. Employees are improperly discharged if, before replacements are hired, official action is taken to indicate that they may not return to work after the strike. This test, which has been approved by the courts, is related partly to the employer's reasons for acting. It is more likely to indicate whether the employer had competent counsel than to indicate his motives for acting. As long as the basic assumptions of the *MacKay* doctrine are accepted, however, the current rule is probably as good as any which can be devised. The rule prohibits flagrant attempts to punish protected activity and spells out what may be done with sufficient clarity.

THE REPLACEMENT OF EMPLOYEES FOR HONORING PICKET LINES

The Board and the courts are in general agreement with respect to the employer's ability to hire permanent replacements for striking employees. There is less agreement about the related problem of an employer's ability to respond when his employees refuse to cross a picket line at the premises of another employer. The Board has held that such activity is protected, nevertheless [an employee can justify discharge for refusal to cross a picket line by proving]:

(a) that the refusal to cross the picket line constituted a substantial interference with respondent's business which could not be overcome by merely assigning another employee to do the work.

(b) that replacements were in fact hired.

(b) Limitations on the Reach of Section 7 Based on the Purpose for Which Economic Pressure Is Used

The purposes for which concerted activity may be undertaken are broadly stated. In particular, the statutory phrase, "mutual aid or protection" can be read to encompass almost any goal-oriented group action. However, the reach of section 7 has been reduced by finding limitations suggested not by its language but by other sections and policies of the act. Section 8(b) prohibits various types of concerted activity. Such specifically prohibited activity properly falls outside the protection of section 7. It would make little sense to hold that section 7 protects that which section 8(b) prohibits.[6]

One of the central unanswered questions about the scope of section 7 is the extent to which lawful economic pressure for a legitimate purpose may be held unprotected. In NLRB v. Washington Aluminum Co., the Supreme Court rejected the position that economic pressure could be held unprotected if its use was deemed unwise or unreasonable. In that case, the Court held that a walkout by employees to protest cold working conditions was protected. The company argued that the activity was unprotected since it was already taking steps to alleviate the trouble and the employees had not presented a specific demand to which the company could respond. The Court rejected this argument:

> The fact that the company was already making every effort to repair the furnace and bring heat into the shop that morning does not change the nature of the controversy that caused the walkout. At the very most, that fact might tend to indicate that the conduct of the men in leaving was unnecessary and unwise, and it has long been settled that the reasonableness of workers' decisions to engage in concerted activity is irrelevant * * *

In *Washington Aluminum*, economic pressure was used to protest working conditions—an area of traditional employee concern. In subsequent cases, the courts of appeals also have found the use of economic pressure for traditional purposes protected without regard to its reasonableness. But the courts have not necessarily held economic pressure protected in all cases where employees have acted for mutual aid or protection. They have indicated, without really addressing themselves to the problem, that on the outer boundaries of the concept of mutual aid or protection, there are subjects with respect to which the act will protect expressions of employee sentiment, but not the use of economic pressure.

---

6. The major limitation on bargaining pressure which arises from 8(b) is the restriction on secondary pressure enacted in § 8(b)(4). This issue is dealt with more fully below.

The conclusion that economic pressure for a legitimate purpose is unprotected has been adopted most often with respect to employee action to protest changes in supervision. The Board usually holds such activity protected by section 7 but the courts have generally held it unprotected. Some of the early opinions suggested that employees do not have a legitimate interest in the selection of supervision, so that no concerted activity for the purpose of protesting the employer's actions in this area would be protected. The leading case is NLRB v. Reynolds International Pen Co. in which employees staged a short walkout to protest a change in foremen. The court simply announced that the change of foremen was a "prerogative of management" and therefore held the activity unprotected.

* * *

Several cases raise the question of whether management's interest in a subject might be so remote and tangential that economic pressure about the subject ought to be unprotected. Two situations raise the question: those involving demands made of third parties and instances where employees of one employer seek to support employees of another.

* * *

It has long been recognized that employee efforts to influence parties other than their own employer may be for "mutual aid or protection." Honoring a picket line, assisting organizing efforts at another employer's business, agitating for new legislation, protesting to a government agency and expressing solidarity with striking milk producers, have all been held protected, although involving matters outside the control of the employer. In Bethlehem Ship Bldg. Corp. v. NLRB, an employer objected to employee activity "to give public endorsement to a bill pending in the Massachusetts legislature increasing weekly benefits under the Workmen's Compensation Act."

Judge Magruder, speaking for the First Circuit, concluded that such employee activity was protected:

> But the right of employees to self-organization and to engage in concerted activities, now guaranteed by Section 7 of the National Labor Relations Act, is not limited to direct collective bargaining with the employer, but extends to other activities for "mutual aid or protection" including appearance of employee representatives before legislative committees.

* * *

(c) Making Common Cause with Other Employees: Refusals to Cross Picket Lines

It is generally accepted that employee activity in support of employees of another employer who are involved in a labor dispute is activity for "mutual aid or protection." The reasons for this were expressed by Judge Learned Hand in a characteristically compelling passage in N.L.R.B. v. Peter Cailler Kohler Swiss Chocolates Co.

The case arose when the chocolate company fired an employee who called a meeting of the local union to encourage employees of the company to express support for a union of milk suppliers. The Board held that the activity was protected. The Second Circuit affirmed. Judge Hand rejected the argument that the activity was unprotected because the members of the milk union were not members of the bargaining unit and were not "employees" under the act.

> Certainly nothing elsewhere in the act limits the scope of the language to "activities" designed to benefit other "employees"; and its rationale forbids such a limitation. When all the other workmen in a shop make common cause with a fellow workman over his separate grievance, and go out on strike in his support, they engage in a "concerted activity" for "mutual aid or protection," although the aggrieved workman is the only one of them who has any immediate stake in the outcome. The rest know that by their action each one of them assures himself, in case his turn ever comes, of the support of the one whom they are all then helping; and the solidarity so established is "mutual aid" in the most literal sense, as nobody doubts. So too of those engaging in a "sympathetic strike," or secondary boycott; the immediate quarrel does not itself concern them, but by extending the number of those who will make the enemy of one the enemy of all, the power of each is vastly increased. It is one thing how far a community should allow such power to grow; but, whatever may be the proper place to check it, each separate extension is certainly a step in "mutual aid or protection." * * * It is true that in the past courts often failed to recognize the interest which each might have in a solidarity so obtained * * *, but it seems to us that the act has put an end to this.

As indicated, the Wagner Act embraced the philosophy that employees should be free to support each other. The Taft-Hartley and Landrum-Griffin amendments, however, severely limited the extent to which economic pressures can be used to make common cause with employees of other companies. The policy that employees should be free to engage in secondary pressure was largely replaced by a policy against the spread of industrial disputes. Most traditional forms of secondary pressure were declared unfair labor practices by the additions of sections 8(b)(4) and 8(c) and hence are unprotected.

The refusal of employees to cross a primary picket line at another employer's premises in the course of their work is not prohibited by section 8(b)(4). The Board has held that this is protected activity because it comes within the literal meaning of section 7. It is activity for mutual aid or protection of another union and is concerted activity, even when undertaken by an individual employee on his own. By definition, the employee who honors a picket line does not act alone. He is in concert of action with the pickets. * * *

(d) Limitations Based on the Nature of the Economic Pressure

If read literally, the term "concerted activity" would encompass almost all economic pressure applied by two or more employees. However, as is true with respect to practically all of the broad language of the act, its meaning has been limited by other recognized policies. Thus, violence, threats of violence, efforts to seize or destroy company property and conduct which violates the policy of other federal statutes are all unprotected activities. As to these there is little or no theoretical dispute. The only important questions concern the degree of misconduct necessary to make conduct unprotected. It is only slightly less apparent that strikes in breach of a no-strike clause should be unprotected since such strikes conflict with the federal policy favoring the establishment of orderly procedures for resolving disputes in an established bargaining relationship.

Confusion exists, however, concerning the extent to which unorthodox pressure tactics—neither violent nor unlawful—may be held unprotected in circumstances in which traditional forms of economic pressure would be held protected. In some of its early decisions defining the reach of section 7, the Supreme Court held unorthodox activity unprotected. In its more recent decisions, however, the Court has apparently rejected the concept of picking and choosing among lawful economic weapons. It has also indicated a willingness to read section 7 more broadly. As a result, the continued vitality of the older cases is subject to question. A brief review of the cases indicates the nature of the conflict between the older and more recent decisions.

The first case in which the Court held the use of otherwise lawful but unorthodox economic pressure unprotected was UAW v. Wisconsin Employment Relations Bd. (Briggs & Stratton). In support of its bargaining demands, the union called a series of intermittent work stoppages in the guise of union meetings to disrupt the employer's production and delivery schedule. The Court held that such activity was unprotected by section 7. Distinguishing this conduct from a total strike, the Court held that it constituted an improper bargaining weapon. The conclusion of impropriety was supported by three considerations: (1) it is unfair to draw pay from a man while applying pressure against him; (2) such conduct is much more effective than a total strike, since the employer is helpless to protect himself against it; and (3) the employer was not given adequate notice of how he could respond to prevent or to stop the activity.

The reasons supporting the conclusion that partial strikes are unprotected has largely been eroded. It is clear that employers are not helpless, but many lock out employees who engage in partial strikes, thus treating the situation as though there had been a total strike which would have been protected. Moreover, the Supreme Court, in several opinions during the 1960s, made clear that only obviously improper or dangerous conduct should be treated as unprotected.

In Local Lodge 76 v. Wisconsin Employment Relations, another recent court decision concerning the status of partial strikers, the Supreme Court declined to follow *Briggs & Stratton* and invited the Board to reconsider on a "case-by-case" basis the status of partial strikes.

(e) THE IMPACT OF UNION RECOGNITION ON THE PROTECTED STATUS OF ECONOMIC PRESSURE

ECONOMIC PRESSURE BY A LABOR ORGANIZATION

When no collective agreement is in force, the use of economic pressure by an incumbent union in support of its bargaining demands is protected if the subject matter of the demand constitutes a mandatory subject of bargaining. However, once the agreement is negotiated, the use of economic pressure is normally unprotected. Most collective bargaining agreements contain no-strike clauses in which the union agrees not to use economic pressure for any purpose during the term of the agreement. If such a pledge is not explicit, it will be implied to cover matters which are subject to grievance machinery. Moreover, it is an unfair labor practice to strike in order to "terminate or modify" the agreement during its term.

*   *   *

ECONOMIC PRESSURE BY EMPLOYEES ACTING INDEPENDENTLY OF THE UNION

The use of economic pressure by employees acting independently of the union is usually held to be unprotected. During bargaining negotiations, any attempt by employees to bargain independently violates the scheme of exclusive representation set forth in section 9(a) of the act. As the Supreme Court stated in Medo Photo Supply Corp. v. N. L. R. B.:

> That it is a violation of the essential principle of collective bargaining and an infringement of the Act for the employer to disregard the bargaining representative by negotiating with individual employees, whether a majority or a minority, with respect to wages, hours, and working conditions was recognized by this Court * * *. The statute guarantees to all employees the right to bargain collectively through their chosen representatives. Bargaining carried on by the employer directly with the employees, whether a minority or majority, who have not revoked their designation of a bargaining agent, would be subversive of the mode of collective bargaining which the statute has ordained, as the Board, the expert body in this field, has found.

The *Medo* case held that an employer who bargained with individual employees violated section 8(a)(5). In order to prevent the employer from being faced with economic pressure to which he cannot lawfully yield, it follows that economic pressure in support of separate bargaining demands should be unprotected. Moreover, since the process of collective bargaining is so intimately connected with the use of economic pressure, independent employee pressure contrary to the wishes of the union—even in support of the union's bargaining position—should be treated as a form of independent bargaining and, hence, unprotected.

The importance of the policy of limiting bargaining pressure to the incumbent union was underlined recently when the Supreme Court held in Emporium Capwell Co. v. Western Addition Community Organization, that it superceded even the right to protest racial discrimination. The Court stated that an employer could legitimately discharge two employees who picketed to support their demands for a new policy to combat discrimination. The Court, in an opinion by Justice Marshall, stated,

> The policy of industrial self determination as expressed in § 7 does not require fragmentation of the bargaining unit along racial or other lines [to consist with] the national labor policy against discrimination.

A union is an institution in which employee sentiment can be crystallized and expressed. If the union adopts a position, the employer knows that he may legally yield to the pressure and he may assume that a majority of his employees would want to see him do so. Where concerted activity is undertaken without support of the union, the employer has no way of knowing whether the position advanced has substantial support among the employees. He probably has cause to suspect that it does not, and that granting the request would raise more problems for him than it would solve. One of the significant functions which a union performs is providing a forum in which employee sentiment may be expressed and consensus reached. Consequently, it is reasonable to require an employee who seeks to bring about a change to first direct his attention to winning the support of his fellow employees and the union.

(f) Employer Economic Pressure

In American Ship Building Co. v. N. L. R. B., the Supreme Court held that an employer was justified, under the Act, in locking out his employees in order to put pressure on them after an impasse in bargaining was reached. The Board had held that such conduct violated § 8(a)(1) and 8(a)(3). Quoting at length from its opinion in the *Insurance Agents* case, the Court reversed. In its opinion the Court stated, "Having protected employee organization in counterbalance to the employers bargaining power, and having established a system of collective bargaining whereby the newly co-equal adversaries might resolve their dispute, the act also contemplated resort to economic weapons should more peaceful measures not avail. Sections 8(a)(1) and 8(a)(3) do not give the Board general authority to assess the relative economic power by the adversaries in the bargaining process and to deny weapons to one party or the other because of the assessment of that party's bargaining power."

QUESTIONS

1. Is the court's reasoning in the *American Shipbuilding* case convincing? Can you argue that it is inaccurate as applied to employer action under economic pressure? Under the court's reasoning:

   (a) Would the employee need to wait for an impasse?

   (b) Could he permanently replace the employees laid off by the lock out?

2. Should partial strikes be held protected activity under § 7 of the NLRA?

3. Why should the NLRA discourage employees from independently protesting racial discrimination?

The government can play a role in settling strikes through the process of mediation which is provided for under § 8(d) of the Act. However, a federal mediator only helps to facilitate private agreement. The mediator has no power to enforce, or even formally recommend, the terms of settlement. Where public health and safety are threatened, a more active role may be played. Section 8(g) provides for a mediator in disputes arising in private health care facilities. The Act also provides for the appointment of a Board of inquiry which might recommend the terms of a settlement in the health care industry. Sections 206–210 provide special procedures including a "cooling-off" period enforced by injunction and a presidential board of inquiry where a dispute endangers the national "health or safety."

4.   THE SUBJECTS OF BARGAINING

There are three categories of bargaining subjects: mandatory subjects, permissive subjects, and prohibited subjects. The classification of a subject into one of these categories determines whether the parties must discuss it or be held to having committed an unfair labor practice, whether they may decide to discuss it voluntarily, or whether they should not waste time discussing it because any agreement on the subject would not be binding.

If either party makes a proposal on a mandatory subject during negotiations, the other party cannot refuse to bargain on the proposal. Section 8(d) requires bargaining on "wages, hours, and other terms and conditions of employment," but the NLRA does not define what subjects can be classified as falling under these headings. However, by its decisions the board has developed what may be described as an exhaustive list of mandatory subjects. These include retirement benefits, vacations, rest periods, and work assignments.

Permissive subjects are those that either party may refuse to bargain on without committing an unfair labor practice. Among permissive subjects are corporate organization, the size of the supervisory force, and the location of plants.

Neither the board nor the courts will enforce agreements on prohibited subjects. Illustrations of prohibited subjects are: provisions for a closed shop (requiring that the employer hire only union members) and hot cargo clauses (stating that workers will not be required to handle goods of a nonunion employer).

The following cases reveal the complexity of these classifications.

FIBREBOARD PAPER PRODUCTS CORP. v. N. L. R. B.

Supreme Court of the United States, 1964.
379 U.S. 203, 85 S.Ct. 398, 13 L.Ed.2d 233.

Mr. Chief Justice Warren:

* * *

* * * We are concerned here only with whether the subject upon which the employer allegedly refused to bargain—contracting out of plant maintenance work previously performed by employees in the bargaining unit, which the employees were capable of continuing to perform—is covered by the phrase "terms and conditions of employment." * * *

The subject matter of the present dispute is well within the literal meaning of the phrase "terms and conditions of employment." A stipulation with respect to the contracting out of work performed by members of the bargaining unit might appropriately be called a "condition of employment." The words even more plainly cover termination of employment which, as the facts of this case indicate, necessarily results from the contracting out of work performed by members of the established bargaining unit.

The inclusion of "contracting out" within the statutory scope of collective bargaining also seems well designed to effectuate the purposes of the National Labor Relations Act. One of the primary purposes of the Act is to promote the peaceful settlement of industrial disputes by subjecting labor management controversies to the mediatory influence of negotiation. The Act was framed with an awareness that refusals to confer and negotiate had been one of the most prolific causes of industrial strife. To hold, as the Board has done, that contracting out is a mandatory subject of collective bargaining would promote the fundamental purpose of the Act by bringing a problem of vital concern to labor and management within the framework established by Congress as most conducive to industrial peace.

The conclusion that "contracting out" is a statutory subject of collective bargaining is further reinforced by industrial practices in this country. * * * Experience illustrates that contracting out in one form or another has been brought, widely and successfully, within the collective bargaining framework. Provisions relating to contracting out exist in numerous collective bargaining agreements, and "(C)ontracting out work is the basis of many grievances. * * *

* * *

The facts of the present case illustrate the propriety of submitting the dispute to collective negotiation. The Company's decision to contract out the maintenance work did not alter the Company's basic operation. The maintenance work still had to be performed in the plant. No capital investment was contemplated; the Company merely replaced existing employment with those of an independent contractor to do the same work under similar conditions of employment. Therefore, to require the employer to bargain about the matter would not significantly abridge his freedom to manage the business.

The Company was concerned with the high cost of its maintenance operation. It was induced to contract out the work by assurances from independent contractors that economies could be derived by reducing the work force, decreasing fringe benefits, and eliminating overtime payments. These have long been regarded as matters peculiarly suitable for resolution within the collective bargaining framework, and industrial experience demonstrates that collective negotiation has been highly successful in achieving peaceful accommodation of the conflicting interest   *   *   *   although it is not possible to say whether a satisfactory solution could be reached, national labor policy is founded upon the congressional determination that the chances are good enough to warrant subjecting such issues to the process of collective negotiation.   *   *   *

FIRST NATIONAL MAINTENANCE CORP. v. N. L. R. B.

Supreme Court of the United States, 1981.
452 U.S. 666, 101 S.Ct. 2573, 69 L.Ed.2d 318.

JUSTICE BLACKMUN delivered the opinion of the Court.

Must an employer, under its duty to bargain in good faith "with respect to wages, hours, and other terms and conditions of employment," §§ 8(d) and 8(a)(5) of the National Labor Relations Act, as amended (the Act), 29 U.S.C. §§ 158(d) and 158(a)(5), negotiate with the certified representative of its employees over its decision to close a part of its business? In this case, the National Labor Relations Board (the Board) imposed such a duty on petitioner with respect to its decision to terminate a contract with a customer, and the United States Court of Appeals, although differing over the appropriate rationale, enforced its order.

I

Petitioner, First National Maintenance Corporation (FNM), is a New York corporation engaged in the business of providing housekeeping, cleaning, maintenance, and related services for commercial customers in the New York City area. It supplies each of its customers, at the customer's premises, contracted-for labor force and supervision in return for reimbursement of its labor costs (gross salaries, FICA and FUTA taxes, and insurance) and payment of a set fee. It contracts for and hires personnel separately for each customer, and it does not transfer employees between locations.

During the Spring of 1977, petitioner was performing maintenance work for the Greenpark Care Center, a nursing home in Brooklyn. Its written agreement dated April 28, 1976, with Greenpark specified that Greenpark "shall furnish all tools, equiptment [*sic*], materials, and supplies," and would pay petitioner weekly "the sum of five hundred dollars plus the gross weekly payroll and fringe benefits." Its weekly fee, however, had been reduced to $250 effective November 1, 1976. The contract prohibited Greenpark from hiring any of petitioner's employees during the term of the contract and for 90 days thereafter. Petitioner employed approximately 35 workers in its Greenpark operation.

Petitioner's business relationship with Greenpark, seemingly, was not very remunerative or smooth. In March 1977, Greenpark gave petitioner the 30 days' written notice of cancellation specified by the contract, because of "lack of efficiency." This cancellation did not become effective, for FNM's work continued after the expiration of that 30-day period. Petitioner, however, became aware that it was losing money at Greenpark. On June 30, by telephone, it asked that its weekly fee be restored at the $500 figure and, on July 6, it informed Greenpark in writing that it would discontinue its operations there on August 1 unless the increase were granted. By telegram on July 25, petitioner gave final notice of termination.

While FNM was experiencing these difficulties, District 1199, National Union of Hospital and Health Care Employees, Retail, Wholesale and Department Store Union, AFL–CIO (the union), was conducting an organization campaign among petitioner's Greenpark employees. On March 31, 1977, at a Board-conducted election, a majority of the employees selected the union as their bargaining agent. On July 12, the union's vice president, Edward Wecker, wrote petitioner, notifying it of the certification and of the union's right to bargain, and stating: "We look forward to meeting with you or your representative for that purpose. Please advise when it will be convenient." Petitioner neither responded nor sought to consult with the union.

On July 28, petitioner notified its Greenpark employees that they would be discharged 3 days later. Wecker immediately telephoned petitioner's secretary-treasurer, Leonard Marsh, to request a delay for the purpose of bargaining. Marsh refused the offer to bargain and told Wecker that the termination of the Greenpark operation was purely a matter of money, and final, and that the 30-days' notice provision of the Greenpark contract made staying on beyond August 1 prohibitively expensive. Wecker discussed the matter with Greenpark's management that same day, but was unable to obtain a waiver of the notice provision. Greenpark also was unwilling itself to hire the FNM employees because of the contract's 90-day limitation on hiring. With nothing but perfunctory further discussion, petitioner on July 31 discontinued its Greenpark operation and discharged the employees.

The union filed an unfair labor practice charge against petitioner, alleging violations of the Act's §§ 8(a)(1) and (5). After a hearing held upon the Regional Director's complaint, the administrative law judge made findings in the union's favor.   *   *   *

*   *   *

The National Labor Relations Board adopted the administrative law judge's findings without further analysis   *   *   *

The United States Court of Appeals for the Second Circuit, with one judge dissenting in part, enforced the Board's order.   *   *   *

*   *   *

II

*   *   *

Although parties are free to bargain about any legal subject, Congress has limited the mandate or duty to bargain to matters of "wages, hours, and other terms and conditions of employment." A unilateral change as to a subject within this category violates the statutory duty to bargain and is subject to the Board's remedial order. NLRB v. Katz, 369 U.S. 736, 82 S.Ct. 1107, 8 L.Ed.2d 230 (1962). Conversely, both employer and union may bargain to impasse over these matters and use the economic weapons at their disposal to attempt to secure their respective aims. NLRB v. American National Ins. Co., 343 U.S. 395, 72 S.Ct. 824, 96 L.Ed. 1027 (1952).[13] Congress deliberately left the words "wages, hours, and other terms and conditions of employment" without further definition, for it did not intend to deprive the Board of the power further to define those terms in light of specific industrial practices.

Nonetheless, in establishing what issues must be submitted to the process of bargaining, Congress had no expectation that the elected union representative would become an equal partner in the running of the business enterprise in which the union's members are employed. Despite the deliberate open-endedness of the statutory language, there is an undeniable limit to the subjects about which bargaining must take place:

> "Section 8(a) of the Act, of course, does not immutably fix a list of subjects for mandatory bargaining   *   *   *. But it does establish a limitation against which proposed topics must be measured. In general terms, the limitation includes only issues that settle an aspect of the relationship between the employer and the employees." Chemical & Alkali Workers v. Pittsburgh Plate Glass Co., 404 U.S. 157, 178, 92 S.Ct. 383, 397, 30 L.Ed.2d 341 (1971).

---

13. A matter that is not a mandatory subject of bargaining, unless it is illegal, may be raised at the bargaining table to be discussed in good faith, and the parties may incorporate it into an enforcea-ble collective-bargaining agreement. Labor and management may not, however, insist on it to the point of impasse. NLRB v. Borg-Warner Corp., 356 U.S. 342, 78 S.Ct. 718, 2 L.Ed.2d 823 (1958).

Some management decisions, such as choice of advertising and promotion, product type and design, and financing arrangements, have only an indirect and attenuated impact on the employment relationship. See *Fibreboard*, 379 U.S., at 223, 85 S.Ct., at 409 (Stewart, J., concurring). Other management decisions, such as the order of succession of layoffs and recalls, production quotas, and work rules, are almost exclusively "an aspect of the relationship" between employer and employee. *Chemical Workers*, 404 U.S., at 178, 92 S.Ct., at 397. The present case concerns a third type of management decision, one that had a direct impact on employment, since jobs were inexorably eliminated by the termination, but had as its focus only the economic profitability of the contract with Greenpark, a concern under these facts wholly apart from the employment relationship. This decision, involving a change in the scope and direction of the enterprise, is akin to the decision whether to be in business at all, "not in [itself] primarily about conditions of employment, though the effect of the decision may be necessarily to terminate employment." *Fibreboard*, 379 U.S., at 223, 85 S.Ct., at 409 (Stewart, J., concurring). Cf. Textile Workers v. Darlington Co., 380 U.S. 263, 268, 85 S.Ct. 994, 998, 13 L.Ed.2d 827 (1965) ("an employer has the absolute right to terminate his entire business for any reason he pleases"). At the same time, this decision touches on a matter of central and pressing concern to the union and its member employees: the possibility of continued employment and the retention of the employees' very jobs.

Petitioner contends it had no duty to bargain about its decision to terminate its operations at Greenpark. This contention requires that we determine whether the decision itself should be considered part of petitioner's retained freedom to manage its affairs unrelated to employment.[15] The aim of labeling a matter a mandatory subject of bargaining, rather than simply permitting, but not requiring, bargaining, is to "promote the fundamental purpose of the Act by bringing a problem of vital concern to labor and management within the framework established by Congress as most conducive to industrial peace," *Fibreboard*, 379 U.S., at 211, 85 S.Ct., at 403. The concept of mandatory bargaining is premised on the belief that collective discussions backed by the parties' economic weapons will result in decisions that are better for both management and labor and for society as a whole.[16] This will be true, however, only if the subject proposed for

---

15. There is no doubt that petitioner was under a duty to bargain about the results or effects of its decision to stop the work at Greenpark, or that it violated that duty. Petitioner consented to enforcement of the Board's order concerning bargaining over the effects of the closing and has reached agreement with the union on severance pay. App. to No. 79–4167 (CA2), at 21–22.

16. "The Act does not compel agreements between employers and employees. It does not compel any agreement whatever. It does not prevent the employer 'from refusing to make a collective contract and hiring individuals on whatever terms' the employer 'may by unilateral action determine.' * * * The theory of the Act is that free opportunity for negotiation with accredited representatives of employees is likely to promote industrial peace and may bring about the adjustments and agreements which the Act in itself does not attempt to compel." NLRB v. Jones & Laughlin Steel Corp., 301 U.S. 1, 45, 57 S.Ct. 615, 628, 81 L.Ed. 893 (1937). Cf. John Wiley & Sons, Inc. v. Livingston, 376 U.S. 543, 549, 84 S.Ct. 909, 914, 11 L.Ed.2d 898 (1964) ("The objectives of national labor

discussion is amenable to resolution through the bargaining process. Management must be free from the constraints of the bargainig process [17] to the extent essential for the running of a profitable business. It also must have some degree of certainty beforehand as to when it may proceed to reach decisions without fear of later evaluations labeling its conduct an unfair labor practice. Congress did not explicitly state what issues of mutual concern to union and management it intended to exclude from mandatory bargaining.[18] Nonetheless, in view of an employer's need for unencumbered decisionmaking, bargaining over management decisions that have a substantial impact on the continued availability of employment should be required only if the benefit, for labor-management relations and the collective bargaining process, outweighs the burden placed on the conduct of the business.

* * *

With this approach in mind, we turn to the specific issue at hand: an economically-motivated decision to shut down part of a business.

III

A

Both union and management regard control of the decision to shut down an operation with the utmost seriousness. As has been noted, however, the Act is not intended to serve either party's individual interest, but to foster in a neutral manner a system in which the conflict between these interests may be resolved. It seems particularly important, therefore, to consider whether requiring bargaining over this sort of decision will advance the neutral purposes of the Act.

A union's interest in participating in the decision to close a particular facility or part of an employer's operations springs from its legitimate concern over job security. The Court has observed: "The words of [§ 8(d)] * * * plainly cover termination of employment which * * * necessarily results" from closing an operation.

policy, reflected in established principles of federal law, require that the rightful prerogatives of owners independently to rearrange their businesses and even eliminate themselves as employers be balanced by some protection to the employees from a sudden change in the employment relationship.").

17. The employer has no obligation to abandon its intentions or to agree with union proposals. On proper subjects, it must meet with the union, provide information necessary to the union's understanding of the problem, and in good faith consider any proposals the union advances. In concluding to reject a union's position as to a mandatory subject, however, it must face the union's possible use of strike power. See generally Fleming, The Obligation to Bargain in Good Faith, 47 Va.L.Rev. 988 (1961).

18. The subjects over which mandatory bargaining has been required have changed over time. Employers and unions have been required to bargain over such diverse topics as profit-sharing plans, Winn-Dixie Stores, Inc. v. NLRB, 567 F.2d 1343 (CA5), cert. denied, 439 U.S. 985, 99 S.Ct. 576, 58 L.Ed.2d 656 (1978); layoffs and recalls, see Awrey Bakeries, Inc. v. NLRB, 548 F.2d 138 (CA6 1976); contractual clauses concerning race discrimination, see Wichita Eagle & Beacon Publishing Co., 222 N.L.R.B. 742 (1976); and "most favored nation" clauses, Dolly Madison Industries, Inc., 182 N.L.R.B. 1037 (1970). See also Borg-Warner, 356 U.S., at 353, 78 S.Ct., at 724 (Harlan, J., concurring in part and dissenting in part).

Fibreboard, 379 U.S., at 210, 85 S.Ct., at 402. The union's practical purpose in participating, however, will be largely uniform: it will seek to delay or halt the closing. No doubt it will be impelled, in seeking these ends, to offer concessions, information, and alternatives that might be helpful to management or forestall or prevent the termination of jobs. It is unlikely, however, that requiring bargaining over the decision itself, as well as its effects, will augment this flow of information and suggestions. There is no dispute that the union must be given a significant opportunity to bargain about these matters of job security as part of the "effects" bargaining mandated by § 8(a)(5). And, under § 8(a)(5), bargaining over the effects of a decision must be conducted in a meaningful manner and at a meaningful time, and the Board may impose sanctions to insure its adequacy. A union, by pursuing such bargaining rights, may achieve valuable concessions from an employer engaged in a partial closing. It also may secure in contract negotiations provisions implementing rights to notice, information, and fair bargaining.

Moreover, the union's legitimate interest in fair dealing is protected by § 8(a)(3), which prohibits partial closings motivated by anti-union animus, when done to gain an unfair advantage. Textile Workers v. Darlington Co., 380 U.S. 263, 85 S.Ct. 994, 13 L.Ed.2d 827 (1965). Under § 8(a)(3) the Board may inquire into the motivations behind a partial closing. An employer may not simply shut down part of its business and mask its desire to weaken and circumvent the union by labeling its decision "purely economic."

Thus, although the union has a natural concern that a partial closing decision not be hastily or unnecessarily entered into, it has some control over the effects of the decision and indirectly may ensure that the decision itself is deliberately considered. It also has direct protection against a partial closing decision that is motivated by an intent to harm a union.

Management's interest in whether it should discuss a decision of this kind is much more complex and varies with the particular circumstances. If labor costs are an important factor in a failing operation and the decision to close, management will have an incentive to confer voluntarily with the union to seek concessions that may make continuing the business profitable. Cf. U.S. News & World Report, Feb. 9, 1981, p. 74; BNA, Labor Relations Yearbook–1979, p. 5 (UAW agreement with Chrysler Corp. to make concessions on wages and fringe benefits). At other times, management may have great need for speed, flexibility, and secrecy in meeting business opportunities and exigencies. It may face significant tax or securities consequences that hinge on confidentiality, the timing of a plant closing, or a reorganization of the corporate structure. The publicity incident to the normal process of bargaining may injure the possibility of a successful transition or increase the economic damage to the business. The employer also may have no feasible alternative to the closing, and even good-faith bargaining over it may be both futile and cause the employer additional loss.

There is an important difference, also, between permitted bargaining and mandated bargaining. Labeling this type of decision mandatory could afford a union a powerful tool for achieving delay, a power that might be used to thwart management's intentions in a manner unrelated to any feasible solution the union might propose.

* * *

While evidence of current labor practice is only an indication of what is feasible through collective bargaining, and not a binding guide, see *Chemical Workers*, 404 U.S., at 176, 92 S.Ct., at 396, that evidence supports the apparent imbalance weighing against mandatory bargaining. We note that provisions giving unions a right to participate in the decisionmaking process concerning alteration of the scope of an enterprise appear to be relatively rare. Provisions concerning notice and "effects" bargaining are more prevalent. See II BNA, Collective Bargaining Negotiations and Contracts § 65:201–233 (1981); U.S. Dept. of Labor, Bureau of Labor Statistics, Bull. 2065, Characteristics of Major Collective Bargaining Agreements, January 1, 1978, pp. 96, 100, 101, 102–103 (charting provisions giving interplant transfer and relocation allowances; advance notice of layoffs, shutdowns, and technological changes; and wage-employment guarantees; no separate tables on decision-bargaining, presumably due to rarity). See also U.S. Dept. of Labor, Bull. No. 1425–10, Major Collective Bargaining Agreements, Plant Movement, Transfer, and Relocation Allowances (July 1969).

* * *

We conclude that the harm likely to be done to an employer's need to operate freely in deciding whether to shut down part of its business purely for economic reasons outweighs the incremental benefit that might be gained through the union's participation in making the decision, and we hold that the decision itself is *not* part of § 8(d)'s "terms and conditions," over which Congress has mandated bargaining.

D. THE PRACTICE OF COLLECTIVE BARGAINING

1. THE UNION'S POSITION

When a union has been selected as representative of the employees, it must quickly prepare itself for the collective bargaining process. A bargaining committee representing different groups within the union will be selected to meet with company representatives and a list of bargaining demands and priorities will be established. The union's proposals will be typically of three types:

(a) Those helpful to the union as an institution.

(b) Those seeking changes in working conditions.

(c) Those dealing with wages and wage-related fringe benefits.

(a) Institutional Proposals

Three types of institutional proposals are commonly presented

(a) A union security clause under which all employees in the unit must become members of the union within 30 days of employment.[7]

(b) A dues checkoff clause which provides that union dues are deducted before the employee's paycheck is prepared. Such a practice has the advantage of saving the union the cost and effort of collecting dues and it probably makes the reduction of income less noticeable.

(c) Clauses under which union officials are given time off, to conduct union business with pay and superseniority to protect them in case of layoffs.

The unions argue that all of these clauses are necessary to ensure the union's ability to function adequately on behalf of the employees it represents. Employees used to argue that such clauses were put in by labor bosses over the objections of the rank and file.

The Taft-Hartley Act as originally passed required a separate vote on union security clauses. However, employees voted overwhelmingly in favor of union security clauses in the vast majority of such special elections and the requirement was soon eliminated from the Act. The votes were attributable to the employee's desire to eliminate "free riders"—unit members who get the benefit of union representation without paying for it. Even where no union security clause exists, sentiment against free riding often runs high.

(b) Non–pecuniary Working Conditions

The union's non-pecuniary proposals generally focus on 4 areas:

(a) Seniority;

(b) Grievance machinery;

(c) Work protection;

(d) Work scheduling.

Seniority has been described as the "soul" of a collective bargaining agreement. Under a typical seniority system, benefits, raises, va-

---

7. Such clauses are permitted under a proviso to § 8(a) 3 but, in order to justify discharging an employee for failure to become a member: (a) membership must have been available, and (b) the employee must be terminated for failure to tender dues and initiation fees "uniformly required". Section 14b permits states to outlaw such clauses.

cations, and promotions are all allocated to favor those employees who have worked longest. Layoffs are determined inversely on the basis of seniority. Although there is generally broad support within the union for the concept of seniority, there is often considerable disagreement as to whether the appropriate unit for calculation of seniority should be "plant-wide," "departmental," or "job". Generally older less skilled workers desire a wider unit and more high skilled younger employees a narrower one.

Differences about the content of proposals and about priorities are bound to exist within the union. The process by which they are resolved is complex. Several factors significantly influence the union's proposals:

(a) The wishes of the majority of the membership;

(b) The desire to keep the allegiance of significant subgroups, particularly those such as skilled workers whose support would be crucial for a strike;

(c) Contractual provisions in force elsewhere in the industry. The international union which exerts considerable influence over bargaining posture will typically strive to achieve uniform standards within an industry. Existing contractual provisions also eliminate the problems involved in selecting new language adequate to achieve the union's purpose. The proper choice of language may be difficult to achieve for a local union without much technical expertise.

QUESTIONS

Why do unions so frequently propose the use of seniority? Are there circumstances under which seniority might not be stressed in a union's proposal?

Almost all unions seek a grievance system for resolving disputes arising during the term of the agreement. Typically, the union's proposal will give it or its members the right to file a "grievance" whenever it is claimed that employee rights under the agreement are being violated. The proposal will call for meetings between successive levels of union and management personnel to try and resolve the grievance. If the grievance is not settled by agreement, the union will have the option of submitting the issue to an arbitrator selected by the parties whose decision shall be final and binding.

The union will usually seek to protect work currently done by its members through a series of clauses. The following are typical union proposals:

(a) No work normally done by unit employees is to be done by supervisors;

(b) No unit work is to be done by non-unit personnel;

(c) No unit work is to be subcontracted.

(c) WAGE RELATED PROPOSALS

It is commonplace of industrial relations that with respect to wages and benefits unions seek "more". But unions must determine how much to ask for and how to divide their request between wages and other benefits. Where a union represents different categories of workers, it must decide how to allocate its requests among them. In order to maintain the support of the rank and file, industrial unions have traditionally favored the less highly paid workers. They have, for example, frequently sought "across-the-board" increases which would contribute a higher percentage for the lower paid and proportionally more than they could obtain if the wages were set by the market. In recent years, however, the more highly skilled members of industrial unions have protested this practice. They have threatened not to support a strike, or even to form their own union, and, as a result, unions as the UAW have had to make special efforts on behalf of the skilled craftsmen they represent. They have also given skilled workers special voice in deciding whether to ratify the agreement negotiated in the settlement.

Unions frequently seek fringe benefits rather than simple wage increases which each member can spend as he chooses. Fringe benefits are sought instead of straight wages for economic and institutional reasons.

Thus unions sometimes have access to group rates for life and medical insurance. These rates are cheaper than the rates available to individuals. While many union members would buy insurance on their own if the collective agreement did not provide for it, insuring through the agreement is more efficient than insuring individually. Similarly, group pension plans may generate more benefits than could be received by the same number of individuals saving separately. In addition there may be favorable tax consequences which follow from the negotiation of group benefits. When many employees work in a plant, however, it becomes quite expensive for the employer to negotiate with each of them respecting vacations. It is usually less expensive and inconvenient for the employer to negotiate with a single entity, the union, respecting provision for additional leisure time. Sometimes the psychological value of obtaining special benefits is greater than the monetary value would justify, as with pension or educational benefits. Negotiating such benefits indicates breadth of the union's concern with improving its members life style. Sometimes by demands for increased vacations or a shorter work week, the union is recognizing the preference of wealthier employees for leisure rather than income. It might be administratively difficult for employees to negotiate individually concerning leisure time because of the problems of scheduling which would arise. Unions seek increased leisure when their membership is relatively well-paid.

Do unions in fact always seek the largest possible wage increase they can obtain for their members? Such a policy might ultimately mean that since the cost of labor becomes more expensive, the employer will hire fewer workers or expand less rapidly, and the union will have fewer members. Therefore tension exists between the union's desire for increased wages and its interest in maintaining or increasing its membership. Studies have suggested that union wage policies take this tension into account, and that both the desire to improve wages and the desire to increase or maintain membership play a part in the union's wage demands. In addition, unions are restrained by the desire not to put the employer at too great a disadvantage competitively relative to other firms and therefore put him out of business. Thus, where an industry is generally organized, unions will seek similar increases from all employers even if some might be particularly vulnerable and willing to grant more. In order to avoid a strike where the industry is, for the most part unorganized, the union will not want to give non-union employees too great an advantage, and so might limit its demands. Sometimes, the financial situation of a particular employer is such that he cannot afford the general rate in a unionized industry. Most unions will take this into account in establishing their demands. However, some unions feel that the importance of maintaining general union standards is so great that they would prefer to force a particular employer to close down rather than have the union wage undercut.

With respect to work scheduling, the union will seek to define work shifts to limit the regular hours and to provide for rest, lunch, and clean-up breaks. Usually a premium will be sought for those working less desired shifts, although unions will try not to make the premium so high that the employer will want to eliminate extra shifts. There is sometimes a conflict of interest between the union and some of its members concerning how extra work should be handled. The union might prefer to see more employees added to increase its membership and to prevent current members from being overworked. Many individual employees would prefer to do the extra work so that they can earn more money. This conflict is usually resolved by seeking substantial premiums for overtime work. Premiums create incentive to add employees and reduce the amount of overtime desired by employees to meet their financial needs.

2. THE EMPLOYER'S BARGAINING POSITION

The employer wants to set wages sufficiently high enough to maintain his current work force and to permit him to recruit new workers. To keep most of the existing work force, it is not necessary to match what other employers are paying. This is so because, for most employees, there are economic and social costs involved in changing jobs which would have to be overcome. Even for non-unionized employees, a job change is likely to mean the loss of some benefits based on longevity. Costs also include the time and expense involved in finding another job, and the need to retrain to the new employer's methods. Some employees however are likely to be highly mobile, and these are likely to be the most highly skilled. In general, skilled employees can more readily find other employment and generally need less retraining. In addition to problems of retention, recruitment of new employees is difficult if the starting rate is too low.

Thus in an inflationary period the employer does not usually want to keep wages at the pre-contract level and his own proposals will probably call for an increase. Sometimes the employer will enter collective bargaining not only willing but eager to grant additional wages in the interest of staying competitive. However, proposals will be limited by the difficulty of reducing wage increases once given and by concern that all benefits granted to the union will set a standard for his non-union employees.

Employers are generally ambivalent concerning the use of seniority. As benefits accrue to senior employees their mobility decreases (except to the extent the benefits are transferrable), thus providing the employer with a stable experienced work force. On the other hand, the desire to employ personnel as efficiently as possible requires more flexibility than is possible under a rigid seniority system. Thus, the employer is likely to accept the use of seniority for many purposes, but to seek to temper its application in promotion and lay-off situations so that decisions based on qualifications might be made. Employers are not happy to give up their absolute power to discharge or discipline, but this power is the focus of much employee unhappiness and its limitation is almost always a major union goal. Just cause limitations are common; as a result, most employers accept the basic union proposal after bargaining.

Employer reaction to union security and dues checkoff proposals are likely to vary with the strength of their opposition to unions. There is little expense to the employer in accepting such provisions. However, some employers have a strong ideological resistance to forcing anti-union employees to join up. Also, denying these clauses to the union, will weaken it financially and, perhaps, cause dissension. Thus an employer who strongly opposes unions may resist and, perhaps, even take a strike on this issue. For most employers, however, it is a proposal which because of the strength of the union's desire can be used to obtain provisions which management feels strongly about, such as a broad "no-strike" clause. It should be noted that acceptance of clauses deemed essential by the union is a good way to acquire the good will of union officials. Ultimately, this is a strong plus for any employer whose business is unionized.

Employers are also often ambivalent about establishing a grievance system leading to binding arbitration. A grievance system replaces employer discretion, and it involves the union in the process of discipline from the beginning. The thought of having an outsider with final power, one who must be acceptable to the union and who will determine the legitimacy of a wide range of management decisions is often disturbing. On the other hand, establishing grievance machinery has important advantages for management. It provides recognized channels for dealing with and resolving complaints which might otherwise fester. Sometimes mistakes can be corrected and sometimes the process serves to legitimate controversial management action either because it is accepted by the union in the lower stages or upheld by the arbitrator in the final stage. Management lawyers generally support establishment of a grievance system and the use of arbitration. They prefer arbitration because it is a quick, peaceful, informal and relatively inexpensive method of resolving disputes. They have confidence in their ability to select knowledgeable arbitrators who will consider legitimate management concerns. The law also encourages management to utilize arbitration. An arbitration clause is the necessary prerequisite for an injunction against a strike in breach of contract. Thus management is likely to accept a grievance system and binding arbitration, although it may seek to put limits on what is grievable and who may file a grievance. Management will also seek to structure the contract so that the arbitrator will feel reluctant to sustain grievances too easily. Almost all the promises in a collective agreement are by management and the employer would prefer not to have them read expansively. In particular, employers do not want to be forced to do things on the basis of an arbitrator's understanding "shop custom." Management will propose that the arbitrator be limited to interpretation of the language of the agreement in dealing with grievances. Management will also seek a clause acknowledging its power to make decisions with regard to those matters not explicitly dealt with in the contract. Such clauses, called "reserved rights" or "management prerogative" clauses, appear in most agreements. A typical clause will state that such matters as scheduling production, directing work, hiring, firing (subject to good cause), arranging schedules, and promotions, shall be "vested solely in management". Unions generally accept the inclusion of such a clause but add language such as "except as otherwise provided in this agreement" to make clear that in case of conflict the management rights clause is subordinate to clauses dealing with seniority or work preservation.

QUESTION

1. How useful are management right clauses likely to be in interpreting the agreement?

As to most of the other non-pecuniary clauses proposed by the union, management will object, but not strongly, on the grounds that they limit management discretion. Usually management is willing to trade off a certain amount of discretion in return for an acceptable pecuniary settlement, particularly since the collective agreement does have the benefit of making clear to the employees what is expected of them.

The most important concession which management seeks is a promise not to strike during the terms of the agreement. Management wants an unqualified pledge by the union not to call a strike. It would also like an express obligation by the union to make efforts to stop a strike undertaken independently by the employees.

No-strike clauses are, to many militant union members, what union security clauses are to some management officials; a betrayal of basic ideological commitments. Although the union will argue strongly about breadth, it will generally accept some form of a no-strike clause, particularly because the courts will read one by implication into a contract with a grievance system, even though no such language appears.

3.　THE PROCESS OF BARGAINING

The positions which the parties take at the start of negotiations are likely to differ substantially. Some of the differences reflect bargaining technique. The parties are prepared to moderate their proposals. But important differences about such matters as wages, the scope of the grievance system, fringe benefits, the uses of seniority and the breadth of the no-strike clause, are customary. The ultimate goal of negotiation is to obtain an acceptable compromise on these issues of substantial disagreement. As we have already noted, the law does not play a significant role in this process. Bargaining power which stems from the relative ability of the parties to withstand the closing down of the company by a strike, and their psychological willingness to subject themselves to this test, largely defines the possible range of settlement. Negotiating skills help to determine where within the possible range the parties actually agree and in some circumstances, whether they will agree at all.

4.　THE ROLE OF ECONOMIC PRESSURE

If the union strikes, it inflicts damage on the employer and on itself and its members. The amount of damage to the employer will depend on several factors:

(1) The union's ability to close down or substantially reduce operations for a prolonged period. This in turn will be determined by:

(a) The percentage of employees who will support the strike;

(b) The extent to which the employer's operation is dependent on labor rather than on machinery;

(c) The extent to which the striking workers have skills not readily available in the market or possessed by supervisors;

(d) The extent to which the strikers can either physically bar entrance or frighten away replacements;

(e) The extent to which employees who make pick ups from or deliveries to the plant would refuse to cross a picket line.

Attempts to continue operations during a strike, particularly when replacements are hired, is a very dangerous step which the employer must carefully consider. It almost inevitably carries a risk of violence. Generally, if the replacements are permanent, it means lowering the quality of the work force and it often means a long period of hard feeling between management and unions after the strike. As a result, employers in well organized industries today rarely try to continue to operate during a strike. When employers do try to operate, it is often a calculated risk undertaken in hopes of destroying the union.

  (2) The potential cost to an individual employer is increased if his competitors continue to operate because of the possibility that customers will be lost to non-struck competitors.

  (3) The harm to the employer is greater when demand for his product is strong. He then usually has little inventory to cushion the impact and a greater likelihood of losing customers.

  (4) The cost to a struck employer is greater if he has relatively high fixed costs which continue during the strike.

  (5) The cost of a strike is greater if the employer cannot make up for lost work hours by compensating scheduling after the strike ends. This would be the case for example where the employer provides a service such as transportation.

  (6) The cost of a strike will be greater if the unit being struck is an integral part of the employer's overall operation.

The cost to the union and its members stems from lost wages and benefits. Neither the strikers nor the union get paid during a strike. Both have expenses. The burden of a strike on union members will be lessened if they have alternative employment opportunities available during the period of the strike and by union strike benefits. These come from the International Strike Fund. Strike benefits are likely to be greater if only a single employer is involved, because such a strike puts less of a strain on the fund. Since a strike, against a single employer also maximizes the likelihood of losing business to competitors, it is generally true that a union's bargaining power is greatest when it is in a position to strike many employers at one time. The union's position is strongest when a large international union is striking against a small company.

A strike is likely to become more painful the longer it goes on for employees also. As a strike continues savings dwindle, bills become overdue, enforced leisure starts to grate, and substitute jobs often grow increasingly unpleasant.

For the union as an institution, a strike means loss of dues and depletion of the strike fund. If the strike drags on, it might mean loss of support. Sometimes, the membership becomes so disgusted that it votes to oust the union after a long, unsuccessful strike. A long strike might also cost the union much in public good will, and each side permanently damages its relation with the other. Thus, in a prolonged strike, both sides suffer substantially. The victor, if any, is likely to be the side best able to absorb economic and psychological punishment. Because a strike can be so destructive, labor relations professionals on both sides caution their clients against precipitating one. This desire to avoid a strike generally assures that a good-faith effort will be made to reach agreement peacefully; and, in the vast majority of cases, agreements are reached during negotiations without the need for a strike.

Nevertheless, strikes do occur. They sometimes occur because the bargaining positions of the parties are irreconcilable from the start, sometimes because the negotiations exacerbate tension or because the parties have placed themselves inadvertently in a position where they must strike to retain credibility. Sometimes strikes occur because preexisting management/union relations were so bad that the parties were eager to do battle against each other. Sometimes one of the parties feels a strike is necessary to maintain its credibility for future negotiations.

Although lengthy strikes are almost always costly, it has been claimed that a short strike can have a useful effect for the union; releasing tensions, creating a feeling of employee solidarity and even providing an enjoyable departure from routine.

It should also be noted that as Albert Rees has pointed out:

> The ability of unions to win strikes does not necessarily govern the frequency with which they strike. If their power is great mere threat of a strike may be all that is necessary. The willingness of a union to strike also depends in part on the philosophy and attitudes of its leaders and members. A high propensity to strike by unions of miners, seamen, and longshoremen has been noted for several countries.[8]

5. THE PROCESS OF NEGOTIATION

The parties generally meet to negotiate an agreement with each side recognizing that failure to agree will result in a potentially harmful strike, but with each side determined not to yield in its position beyond a certain point. Each hopes to convince the other of the futility of resistance. The process is a delicate and complex one. The skills of the negotiators and the way the bargaining relationship is structured are both important factors in determining how successful the negotiations will be.

D. BOK & J. DUNLOP, LABOR AND THE AMERICAN COMMUNITY *

The process of negotiating a new agreement varies widely from one firm to another. In a number of industries, for example, the smaller firms will usually follow the pattern set by a larger competitor; bargaining for them will mean little more than seeking to make a few minor adjustments in the pattern-setting agreement to take account of special conditions. In larger firms—and particularly in the

---

8. Rees, The Economics of Trade Unions (U. of Chicago 1963) p. 37.

* D. Bok & J. Dunlop, *Labor And The American Community* 217–219 (1970);

pattern-setting companies—bargaining will be a much more elaborate and difficult process.

When bargaining involves more than simply accepting a standard agreement, there will normally be much preparation on both sides. The union will develop a series of demands through local meetings, consultation among officials, and sometimes the use of surveys and questionnaires. Management will likewise develop its position through meetings among its officers and staff. Both parties will normally arm themselves with research data; for example, they may study the nature of prior grievances, draw upon studies of market and employment trends, and analyze the financial and competitive position of the firm itself.

Once these preparations are complete, the process of bargaining often proceeds through a series of stages. At the outset, the union customarily presents a long and extravagant list of demands. In many instances, the company will respond by submitting its own proposals, which are typically far apart from those of the union. Although this exchange may seem as irrelevant and ritualistic as the mating dance of the great crested grebe, it can serve a variety of purposes. By putting forward many exaggerated demands, the parties create trading material for later stages of negotiations. They disguise their real position and thus give themselves room for maneuver as bargaining progresses. They explore a wide range of problems that may have been bothering each side, and they have the opportunity to explain concerns to each other. They manage to satisfy their constituents or principals by seeming to back numerous proposals, only to scale down many of the demands or abandon them altogether later on in the negotiations when it is more expedient to do so. A proposal may be advanced and explored, only to be put aside for more serious negotiation in subsequent years.

After the initial presentations, there normally is a period of exploration in which each side tries to clarify the proposals of the other and marshal arguments against them. At this stage of negotiation, little change can be expected in the positions of the parties. As bargaining progresses, each side will begin to formulate a combination of proposals, or "package," which it considers an appropriate basis for settlement. The package offered by each side gives the other party a clearer sense of the priorities attached to various items and the possible concessions to be gained. In this process, more than one package may be put forward by either side.

Eventually, before or after a stoppage, an agreement will be reached. The meeting of the minds will normally be arrived at first during informal talks between key negotiators, and the proposed settlement will then be discussed before the full negotiating committees on either side. Thereafter, the tentative agreement must be reduced to contract language, usually with the advice of lawyers and after much further discussion over details of wording.

After the agreement is reduced to writing, ordinarily it must be ratified or approved by the principals involved. On the union side, ratification may be required by the membership of the union, by a specified group of elected delegates, or by an elected wage policy committee, as in the case of the basic-steel agreement. Management negotiators in a single company will need the approval of the president or the board of directors. In association bargaining, the approval of the elected directors or the full membership of the association is typically required.

The ratification of settlements by union members serves a variety of purposes. By obtaining an explicit vote of approval for the settlement, subsequent enforcement of the agreement by management, by union officers, or by an arbitrator is made easier. Ratification also requires union negotiators to explain and "sell" the agreement to the membership. In doing so, ratification provides a check to insure that the negotiators keep in touch with the rank and file and reflect their interests in the bargaining process.

The quality of union leadership and its influence on the membership are subtly reflected in collective bargaining and ratification. In many bargaining relationships, ratification on the union side is a formality. The negotiators, by common consent, are in touch with the membership or wage policy committee with power to ratify; the negotiators are highly respected, and their views and recommendations carry great weight. In other instances, the union leaders occupy a more tenuous position; they lack the influence and prestige to guarantee acceptance even of a satisfactory contract.

As previously observed, there has been a marked increase in the proportion of settlements that have been rejected in the ratification process. According to federal mediators, the most common reasons for rejection are dissatisfaction with the size of wage and fringe benefits, lack of understanding by the leaders of the real desires of the members, internal political rivalries, and inadequate ratification procedures that give undue weight to the views of dissident members. At times, however, a rejection can be a deliberate tactic in the bargaining process. Union representatives may take a management offer to the members to demonstrate the unity and the sentiments of the rank and file. They may appear to accept a proposal and later oppose ratification in order to extract further concessions from management. Such stratagems normally are harmful to bargaining relationships. Management is unlikely to make its best offer at the bargaining table once it has been burnt by the use of a rejection as a tactical maneuver; it will save its best offer for a later date, thus causing the agreement-making process to become more difficult.

(a) STRUCTURING NEGOTIATIONS

SLICHTER, HEALY, LIVERNASH, THE IMPACT OF COLLECTIVE BARGAINING ON MANAGEMENT *

The representation of employees and management in collective bargaining takes an almost indefinite variety of forms. The simplest case of employee representation is that of a local union dealing with an employer. Even this is handled in various ways. Representation is usually by a business agent or a bargaining committee. Business agents who are in a strong position locally may handle the negotiations themselves and may not submit the result to ratification by the rank and file—indeed, some business agents would refuse to negotiate without the authority to make a binding settlement. Other business agents negotiate subject to the approval of the rank and file, which is expected as a matter of course. Some local unions negotiate through specially-elected bargaining committees that report to the membership. The men on the bargaining committee are likely to be the active leaders in the union.

Many unions use lawyers in several ways in their negotiations. Sometimes they are used as advisers to the regular union negotiators; sometimes the lawyers assume the principal burden of negotiating. Two general types of lawyers represent unions. One tries to dominate the local union and to make it dependent on him, frequently by persuading the union to take extreme positions so that it is in constant trouble with the employer. A second type of lawyer may be described as the constructive type. He is a true expert in industrial relations and interested in negotiating the kind of labor-management contract that will benefit both the union and the employer. There is an increasing number of this latter type who are devoted to the trade union movement and are of great assistance to many local unions that for one reason or another receive little guidance from their national unions.

Most national unions, especially the older ones, exercise some control over the freedom of local unions to involve themselves in the hazards and costs of strikes. In its milder form this control involves refusal of the national to support strikes financially unless its prior approval has been obtained. The stricter degree of control requires the national's approval for a strike. Before a national either agrees to share in the cost of the strike or to permit the local to conduct a strike, the national is likely to try to settle the dispute through the intervention of a national vice-president or international representative. Although national intervention sometimes undermines real bargaining by the local union representatives, more often than not the international representative provides constructive leadership and guidance that may be lacking or limited in perspective at the local level.[3]

3. The following is a vivid account of how an international representative

When a union negotiates a master contract covering several plants of a multiplant company, the union is usually represented by a negotiating committee of representatives from each plant, though actual negotiations may be conducted by a small part of the committee or by several subcommittees. Negotiations covering 15 or 20 plants usually mean a very large negotiating group. If the union committee has representatives from each plant, management is likely to want to have representatives from each plant. In negotiating the master contract in one large multiplant company, the United Steelworkers have about 45 representatives and management a few less. In negotiations with two other large companies, the steelworkers start off with 75 to 100 people on the committee. In the flat glass industry the

works with local union negotiators, as given by an international representative of one of the older AFL unions:

Suppose wage negotiations are to start on Monday. The international representative, if he is conscientious, and he usually is, comes to town early, maybe on Friday or Saturday and contacts the local activators to find out just what the local members want. The international man talks the situation over with the local activators, and later with the president and negotiating committee of the local union.

The local people tell the international representative, "we want 35¢." He mutters under his breath "it's a nickel this year," but instead of blowing his top, he asks, "Is that all! Where's the rest of your demands?" So they give him their list, which might run from the top of the table to the floor. He does not squelch them. The international representative has the instinct to feel the reactions of people before they are aware of them themselves. It is not facts that he deals with. He has to deal with the political situation. People like Boulware think collective bargaining is looking at the facts and deciding what is right. Hah! they miss the boat.

Maybe there is a stranger in the meeting that the international representative has never seen before. The international representative figures he is a new committee member or activator and keeps a watch on him to size him up. The stranger might say he wants all of the local union's demands. "Ah hah," says the international representative to himself, "a radical." But he has to find out if he is serious or a blowhard. If he is serious, and if he is competent as well, it is dangerous. The only thing to do is to have him made a foreman or put him on the international staff.

The international representative tries to bring in what other plants have got. For instance, it might be a nickel. He treats what the others have got as a

"good agreement" and builds it up, so by the time they enter negotiations, they all know what they want. But he does not chop down their demands. Let the employer do that. Why should we (the union) tell the people what *not* to ask for? It is dangerous and the employer will do it for us anyway. Let the employer do it.

The prime function of the international representative is to crystalize the local situation in his own mind, to anticipate and reveal the feelings of the local union almost before the union itself does. The international man must be sensitive and alert to the local political situation. He must recognize the radicals and determine whether they are competent and seriously militant. But seriously, the international representative must skillfully determine and reveal the local situation to the local union in the light of the situation in the rest of the industry.

If they all leave the negotiations with the feeling that it is not too hot a settlement but it is O.K., what else do you want. You made a settlement the men will work under for another year or two, and that is what you are after. The leadership of a union is interested in a wage settlement—the best wage settlement possible in the light of the local and industry-wide situation. Actually the union leaders are interested in a settlement and that is all. The personnel officer and the union spokesmen are the only ones with the same interests—the need for a settlement. In each group (union and management), there are major differences of opinion, but the union leaders and the personnel people have the same opinion, the need for a settlement. The union comes to the bargaining table committee to get a settlement at almost any cost. A settlement means members, keeping the old ones and getting new ones, dues and the flow of funds to the union, and, specifically, my job.

union sent a large committee to bargain with the two major companies. In one automobile negotiation in 1959 the union committee had 17 members, of whom 11 were hourly-paid employees and the others full-time representatives of the union.

If negotiations are to be conducted reasonably, there must be unified leadership among the negotiators who speak for the union and accept or reject company propositions. In an important negotiation in 1955 there was divided leadership in the union committee. The members of the committee could not agree to accept anything the company offered, and a strike resulted. Only with great difficulty and with the help of an outside conciliator was agreement finally reached.

Large committees have both advantages and disadvantages. The advantages involve the educational and democratic value of keeping reasonably large numbers of representatives closely informed on the content of negotiation and of securing some degree of participation by them. The major disadvantage is the difficulty of conducting negotiations with large groups. In many situations negotiations begin with large committees on each side, but bargaining teams are reduced after an initial exploration of issues. If teams are not reduced, settlement is likely to take place in informal meetings of key individuals outside of the formal meetings. In some cases small committees conduct the negotiations in the presence of larger groups in a sort of fish-bowl atmosphere. Also negotiations may take place in small committees that continuously report to larger groups. Unions with strong democratic traditions have difficulties in devising representative mechanisms that are not a stumbling block in achieving settlements. Some managements welcome large committees on the ground that representation from every plant gives the company a better chance to spread information about the company and about the management's viewpoint. If the union has a large committee, some managements want a large committee also. Managements say that they want someone present from each plant who has first-hand information of any local conditions that the union negotiators may bring up.

MANAGEMENT REPRESENTATION IN NEGOTIATIONS

Management may be represented in negotiations by operating officers, employers' associations, lawyers or industrial relations consultants, industrial relations staffs, or combinations thereof.

Representation by Operating Officers

This was the original method of representation, and it is still frequently used, especially in companies too small to have industrial relations departments. Negotiations by operating officers help keep the terms of labor-management agreements properly related to operating conditions and problems. This method has the great disadvantage that operating men can ill afford to take time from their jobs to engage in bargaining, and they are not necessarily capable bargainers. Nothing is more likely to produce bad bargains for employers than impatience on the part of management representatives to get back to their regular jobs. A labor relations staff is selected partly to obtain individuals skilled in the art of negotiation.

Representation through Associations of Employers

The association may be quite informal, consisting of little more than a bargaining committee (as when contractors in small communities negotiate with unions), or it may be a formal organization with dues and a professional staff. There are two general types of associations—specialized organizations confined to employers in a given industry, such as the associations in the construction industry, the printing trades, the tool and die industry, the coal industry, and general associations covering plants in various industries throughout a city or area. Especially in industries where there are numbers of small competing employers, the competitive equality made possible by bargains between associations of employers and unions is important alike to the employers and their employees. General associations covering a variety of industries, such as the Associated Industries of Cleveland, and the San Francisco Employers Council, can be invaluable to their members. The Cleveland association makes regular surveys of the provisions of union-management contracts in the city, so that it is prepared to inform its members on prevailing rates of pay, and what are customary contract provisions with respect to vacations, pensions, sick benefit plans, and the like. It also knows whether a union that is negotiating with Plant A is considering a strike against Plant B. The Cleveland association, in addition to giving information and advice, also helps conduct negotiations for members—an important service to many employers too small to maintain specialized industrial relations departments. In 1956, for example, it negotiated 25 contracts with the United Automobile Workers and helped in the negotiation of 10 or 12 more.

Representation through Lawyers and Industrial Relations Consultants

Some companies, finding themselves suddenly organized and without an industrial relations staff (or a staff experienced in labor law), turn to lawyers for representation. Some of the lawyers are tough and sharp, but they are employed to fight the union, not to develop good relations with it. As management and unions learn how to get along together, the demand for representation through anti-union lawyers seems to be diminishing. But many employers who are too small to have their own industrial relations departments and who do not have the services of an employers' association use labor consultant services or attorneys who do not specialize in fighting unions. There are today a considerable number of law firms and labor consultants well qualified either to advise employers during negotiations or to take on the responsibility of negotiating for them.

Representation through Industrial Relations Staffs

In the largest companies there is a strong tendency for the responsibility for conducting negotiations to be assigned to the director of industrial relations and his staff. In large companies it is recognized that handling industrial relations is sufficiently important to call for a man of stature who is well qualified to negotiate for the company. The practice of handling negotiations through the industrial relations staff is steadily spreading to companies of medium size. In a large company the negotiating team is likely to include such members of the industrial relations staff as are needed, plus some one from finance and the legal department, and some representation from operations. The addition of a representative from the legal department is important because with the growth of arbitration, management (as well as the union) wants to be sure that the language finally adopted means precisely what it is intended to mean.

Representation through Plant Managers and the Industrial Relations Staff

Some companies follow the policy of building up the importance of the plant managers by giving them the responsibility of conducting negotiations with unions. The managers are assisted by the industrial relations staff. The practice of concentrating responsibility for negotiations in plant managers is usually found in multiplant companies where the plants are numerous and small and where separate local agreements are made for each plant. In one large company with many small plants a representative from the national industrial relations staff of the company regularly sits with the manager during negotiations.

There is reason to believe that the efforts of some multiplant companies to transfer negotiations to plant managers are not entirely successful. Some managers enjoy negotiating, but many do not, and even those that like to negotiate find themselves handicapped by the fact that the union committee has far more time for negotiating than the manager can take from running the plant. Hence, if the plant is large enough to have an industrial relations department, this department is likely sooner or later to take over negotiations. Of course most important is not who represents the company, but whether a wise position is taken by the company representatives with respect to the several interests of the firm.

TECHNICAL AND SPECIAL ISSUES IN REPRESENTATION

With the extension of negotiations to such matters as pensions and health and welfare funds, both unions and employers have made greater use of technical advisers in negotiations. A company may bring its economist into negotiations for a day or two in order to answer the economists of the union. A few of the larger unions have established pension departments, health and welfare departments, or social security departments that can furnish technical aid; outside sources, such as insurance underwriters and consulting actuarial firms, are used by both unions and employers. On technical matters much of the real negotiating may be handled by the technicians.

Subcommittees may be created during negotiations to handle special problems. In the negotiations with one of the Big Three in the automobile industry in 1958 subcommittees were set up to work on seniority problems, problems of the skilled crafts, and the particular problems connected with one of the special operations of the company.

LIAISON BETWEEN NEGOTIATORS AND ADMINISTRATORS

Whether a union-management contract is practical and well thought-out is likely to depend in considerable measure on whether the men who negotiate it are in close touch with operating conditions. It is not essential that the negotiators be operating men, but it is important that there be good teamwork between the men who make the agreement and those who must operate under it. The problem of proper liaison arises when negotiations are conducted by a lawyer or by employers' associations, when national union representatives enter the negotiations, and even when responsibility for negotiations within a company is turned over to the industrial relations staff.

A large company complains that it must negotiate its agreement with the central staff of the steelworkers, who have nothing to do with the administration of the agreement. There are 16 district directors of the union who oversee the activities of the locals under the agreement, but they are not present at the negotiations. In addition, the district directors are responsible for the activity of many other locals in other industries. The company has no one to whom it can go in the administration of the contract who has participated in the negotiations and who understands what changes were made in the contract and why they were made. * * *

Few general rules can be laid down as to what determines the preference of employers or unions for different bargaining units. Sometimes different unions dealing with the same company have different preferences, for example, the United Steelworkers and the International Association of Machinists in dealing with the large can manufacturers. The steelworkers have obtained master agreements covering a number of plants; the machinists prefer to negotiate separate agreements for each plant. If the employers turn out a more or less standard product and if labor costs are important and competition is keen, the pressure is likely to be strong among both employers and employees for area-wide or industry-wide contracts. Roughly equal competitive conditions in terms of the labor contract are thus established. There are many such area-wide contracts in American industry but few industry-wide contracts. Furthermore, the tendency of a large part of industry to produce differentiated products and of each enterprise to develop its own methods of production plus the tendency for one large company to pay about what its principal competitors pay diminishes the pressure for industry-wide or area-wide contracts.

Multienterprise bargaining increases the problem of maintaining adequate liaison between those who negotiate the agreement and those who work under it. The task increases in difficulty as the number of plants or enterprises increases. When bargaining is for a number of plants or enterprises, the special problems of particular enterprises, plants, or local unions may receive little attention. A manufacturer of glass tableware withdrew from an industry-wide bargaining arrangement because other employers were not interested in its special problems. In this industry the national agreement failed to cover day-to-day problems and was described by the leading employer as an "umbrella for the inefficient." Industry-wide bargaining among the railroads has handicapped managements in bargaining for rules changes since rules that are burdensome to some roads are not burdensome to others. Some unions oppose industry-wide bargaining on the ground that it holds back the strongest locals of the union from pushing for better conditions. Also various unions prefer the tactical advantage of bargaining company by company and selecting different companies as pattern setters under different circumstances and at different times.

There are sharp differences within the ranks of employers and unions in their preferences for multiplant as opposed to individual-plant agreements. Some unions have a strong preference for multienterprise, or at least company-wide, agreements; others prefer individual plant agreements. The same differences exist among employers. In general, however, the proportion of unions preferring multiplant or multienterprise agreements is greater than the proportion of employers with this preference. From the union standpoint company-wide agreements have the advantage of enabling the union to get the same terms for its members in all plants, thus avoiding charges that the workers in some plants are being favored over those in other plants. From the standpoint of management, company-wide agreements have the advantage of simplicity (the same rules apply in all plants), and they prevent the union from whipsawing the company by using the settlement with one plant to get a still better settlement for the employees in other plants. Regardless of the position taken by a company with respect to individual-plant or company-wide agreements pertaining to operations, virtually all concerns prefer company-wide pension schemes. The negotiation of such pension schemes on a company-wide basis has tended to bring into common meetings representatives from all plants of the company and thus indirectly to lay the foundation for company-wide agreements pertaining to operations.

Company-wide agreements (as well as industry-wide agreements) have the disadvantage from the standpoint of labor of preventing the strongest local unions from moving ahead as rapidly as they might. This is the reason why the machinists' union has preferred plant-by-plant agreements in the metal container industry. Company-wide agreements have the danger from the standpoint of management that they lack flexibility and impose conditions uniformly throughout operations where variation of working rules is required. A manufacturer of flat glassware that is now committed to company-wide bargaining would prefer plant-by-plant bargaining because it fears that company-wide bargaining will lead to the spread of wasteful rules and wage payment systems from old plants of the company to new plants. Company-wide agreements make it easier for the union to tie up all of the company's operations by a strike. Company-wide agreements may be inappropriate and subject the company to important competitive disadvantages in case the different plants of the company make different products and sell under very different competitive conditions. In late 1958 and early 1959 an auto parts company went through a long strike to replace a company-wide agreement with the UAW with plant-by-plant agreements. The company makes a considerable variety of products, and its several plants compete with different rivals and under different conditions.

Setting up machinery for company-wide or area-wide bargaining may involve political problems for the union. An illustration is furnished by thirteen locals of the Amalgamated Association of Meat Cutters and Butcher Workmen that negotiates with a New England chain store. The locals have set up a Food Council of delegates, chiefly business agents and presidents, selected by the various local executive boards. The larger locals have more representation on the council than the smaller locals—the Boston local, the largest, has three representatives. The council selects a negotiating committee of thirteen—one from each local. Use of the thirteen-man committee was prompted by the fear of each local that its interests would not be protected if it did not have a man present at the negotiations. The thirteen-man committee proved cumbersome, and with the development of greater cooperation and unanimity among the locals, the actual work of negotiating was delegated to a smaller group of five or six of the thirteen. The smaller group may not consummate a settlement of its own but must report for approval to the full thirteen-man committee. Each of the contracting locals agrees to make no separate agreement with the company once the Food Council's negotiating committee has signed the contract.

It is difficult to summarize what is the trend with respect to the unit of negotiation. It is perhaps true that in the long run the tendency is for the unit to become larger. But in a few instances there has been movement away from company-wide bargaining units. A related and important question is what bargaining issues are appropriate for negotiation in the company-wide master contract and what issues should be left to local determination in local supplements. In practice there is clear variation in the way managements and unions have defined the scope of central and local bargaining.

PREPARATION FOR NEGOTIATIONS

Preparation for negotiations ordinarily involves consideration of two principal matters: (1) the general position that the union or the company will take in negotiations, and (2) the specific contract changes that the union or the company intends to make.

General Positions of the Parties

Unions and employers need to be making continuous studies of changes in wages, markets, technology, and of industrial trends generally in order to decide what changes are needed in the labor-management contract. As a basis for determining the approximate size of the package that would be appropriate, companies and unions participate in local, regional, or national surveys of changes in wages and employee benefits and draw on materials issued by the U.S. Bureau of Labor Statistics and various employer associations, such as the American Newspaper Publishers' Association, the Associated Industries of Cleveland, the San Francisco Employers' Council, the Glass Container Manufacturers' Association, the National Metal Trades Association, the wage settlement reports of the National Industrial Conference Board, the Bureau of National Affairs, and others. The data are fairly abundant but scattered and often quite incomplete, especially with respect to employee benefits. A good regular statistical picture of wages in the United States is lacking. A few large companies regularly exchange information on the earnings of their employees.   *   *   *

Specific Union Proposals for Change

In the 1948 General Motors negotiations the union proposed deletion or changes in 132 paragraphs, leaving only 32 minor paragraphs unchanged, and in 1950 the union asked changes in 40 percent of the 152 paragraphs. In the 1959 steel negotiations the union asked for over 250 changes. The large number of proposed changes do not mean that the union thought the contract was worthless. Someone in almost every local is likely to want to have certain language changed. It is easier for the union to pass on the proposals to the employer than to assume the onus of rejecting them.

Unions have different ways of selecting their demands. Local union bargaining committees may receive instructions from the local meeting. It is often easier to approve a proposal that some member or group wants to make than to alienate some members of the union by refusing to include their pet idea. Consequently there may be little connection between the nominal demands of the union and the proposals for which the negotiators seriously bargain. But the negotiators have a good idea of what the members really want. Rank and file influence is shown by the large number of wage settlements that have taken the form of straight cents-per-hour increases in contrast with percentage increases. It is shown also by the rapid spread of health and welfare funds, when a desire for this protection developed in the postwar years.

In the case of multiplant bargaining the various locals are given an opportunity to submit proposals. The result is likely to be the long lists of demands already referred to. The employees in each plant (or some groups of employees) are likely to want certain changes in the labor-management contract. But in multiplant bargaining, as well as local bargaining, the proposals on which the union negotiators really concentrate are determined largely by a few leaders of the union in the light of their knowledge of the desires of the rank and file. In the case of prominent national agreements, such as in steel and automobiles, the influence of the leaders is particularly outstanding. The rank and file may find themselves proposing something, such as supplemental unemployment compensation, that they had not thought of, or they may find themselves suddenly demanding the sharing of profits only a few years after their leaders had strongly denounced profit sharing.

National unions exercise varying degrees of control over the proposals made by local unions. For example, the Upholsterers' International Union has established minimum standards which it expects its local unions to obtain. Locals that do not negotiate the minimum standards are required to give an explanation to the national. Various degrees of such influence and control are to be found.

As a matter of historical curiosity, the rather formal arrangements for proposing changes in the contract that prevailed for many years in the national collective bargaining in the flint glass industry should be mentioned. The agreement was negotiated each year in August at Atlantic City. The national constitution of the American flint glass workers' union provided that proposals for changes in the agreement must be considered by the local unions in January. Any changes recommended by a local were sent to the national secretary in February. He sent the collected proposals to the trade in March, and the various locals voted approval or disapproval. The result of the vote was announced in May, and the secretary sent the proposed changes to the manufacturers' association that month. The union held a convention early in July, at which a final position was taken on proposed changes in the agreement. Negotiations began late in July or early in August, and propositions were taken up one by one—first a proposition from the union, next one from the employers.

A recession produces special demands of temporary significance, such as the one made on one of the Big Three automobile makers in 1958 that overtime be limited to two hours a day and eight hours on Saturday. This demand stayed on the table for several months. A recession also makes unions sensitive to the contracting out of work, and demands for restrictions on contracting out were numerous in 1958 and 1959. But in spite of the recession some companies succeeded in broadening their right to contract out work.

Specific Company Proposals for Change

Management must be prepared to answer the union demand for changes in the contract. In addition, the management is sure to find that some parts of the contract have been giving trouble and must be prepared to propose specific and carefully considered changes that would relieve the difficulties. One of the Big Three automobile manufacturers found that 60 per cent of the grievance case load was generated by five sections in the agreement—those dealing with (1) foreman working, (2) overtime, (3) rates and classifications, (4) discipline, and (5) promotion.   Another automobile company is not content to study only those parts of the contract that are causing problems. That company, among others, studies how *all* parts of the contract are working and says that it learns as much from studying the parts that are working well as from those that are causing trouble.

Various steps are taken by different managements to prepare company proposals for improvements in the contract. A manufacturer of electronic equipment prepares management's proposals (1) by reviewing all grievances that have reached the third step in the grievance procedure during the last year (such grievances are likely to indicate ambiguity in the language of the agreement) and (2) by conferences between division industrial relations staffs and operating staffs on changes or special features needed in the agreement. For example, the rule governing management's right to work short time before invoking seniority needs to be different in some divisions of the company from others. An increasing number of managements keep systematic watch on how each section of the labor-management contract is working so that management at all times has a quite definite idea what changes are needed. A large maker of flatglassware maintains a "bargaining book." Two pages are devoted to each clause in the labor-management contract. On the left-hand page is the clause as it now stands; on the right-hand page is the clause as management would like to see it written. The help of operating men, including foremen, is sought in working out changes that would improve the agreement. *   *   *

In general one may say that there is a close connection between the quality of the administration of the union-management contract and the quality of the preparation for negotiations. Good administration by a management (or a union) means that the management or union is well informed and is able to take an intelligent position in negotiation. Managements should bear in mind that the opportunity given by negotiations to answer questions raised by the union is an extremely valuable one. No information registers quite so strongly as that given in response to a specific question or objection raised by the other party.

Recession affects the choice of proposals by management as well as by unions. Thus, the competitive pressures accentuated by the recession of 1958 led a few companies to insist on breaking away from company-wide contracts and to take strikes in order to win separate plant contracts.

A large milk processor and distributor, which makes many local agreements negotiated by plant managers, does a large part of its preparation after the first session with the union. Management at the first session makes no proposals or suggestions and does not argue over issues.

Negotiations are becoming more orderly and businesslike, although they leave much to be desired. The union and management delegations are frequently headed by men who have served before as chairman and who have learned the need for order. There is general agreement that profanity is less frequently used, and some managements have made it clear that their representatives will promptly leave the meeting if abusive language is used.

Agreements that the two sides will refrain from publicity during negotiations are becoming increasingly common and appear to be closely observed. With large committees there may be some speaking to the gallery, at least during the early stages of negotiation, even though it does no good without publicity. Indeed, with a large committee of forty or more members, time may be allowed to permit the local representatives to present their views. But then serious negotiations must be undertaken by a small group of union and management people.

The teamsters in negotiating with one association wanted to hold closed sessions, with only one or two people on each side rather than with a full union committee as the association preferred. The teamsters wanted commitments for future years without making these commitments known to anyone but the negotiators. In the judgment of the employers, the union did not want active interest and participation by members.

This association has taken a firm stand against this kind of negotiation, and its members expect to know what is going on. Furthermore, they feel secret and unwritten agreements create a suspicion of dishonesty and sellouts. Finally, secret negotiations conflict with the policy of the association of encouraging interest and participation by its members in its affairs.

Particularly in the case of critical national negotiations involving issues that relate to public policy or that have pattern-setting consequences, the external pressures on the parties are likely to be very great. These pressures may come from other companies, unions, or the government. Under such circumstances, especially when an impasse develops in negotiations, the parties tend to feel strongly that public statements are necessary for support. An effective public relations program necessitates the oversimplification of issues and the use of slogans. The public statements make it harder to resolve the issues, and there is no easy answer to this dilemma. From the standpoint of the collective bargaining process, public commitments complicate enormously the problem of reaching a settlement.

Complete stenographic transcripts of negotiations have been made in a few cases (in the General Motors-UAW negotiations at one time, for example) but are now unusual. One union officer observed that it is bad enough to quarrel over the meaning of the contract without getting involved over arguments as to the meaning of the transcript. Stenographic records have other disadvantages. They discourage talking by some members of the committee, and they encourage formal speechmaking "for the record." Stenographic records retard the give-and-take of negotiations by forcing frequent recesses for "off the record" consultations and caucuses. But in one important negotiation both parties want a transcript and read agreed interpretations of the contract into the record. The contract is changed less frequently than the interpretations. Both parties approve the flexibility they have developed in modifying interpretations.

Negotiations are easier if the committee has definite proposals to work from. The usual procedure in negotiation is to put aside difficult issues and concentrate on items on which the parties are not far apart. All agreements on specific items, of course, are tentative—depending on acceptance of the agreement as a whole. By beginning with problems on which agreement can be obtained it is possible to establish a pattern of agreement. Success in disposing of a few of the easier issues puts the parties in the best possible mood for attacking the thorny problems.

Agreements gain in authority if they are ratified by some body considerably larger than the negotiating committee. When agreements are negotiated by a local union, submission to the membership for ratification is usual. In the case of a multiplant or multienterprise agreement, submission to the entire membership may be cumbersome and impracticable. Hence, it may be ratified by a representative body.

(b) THE TACTICS OF NEGOTIATIONS

The process of negotiation in labor relations is complex. Although directed to attorneys, the following article provides valuable insight into the tactics of negotiation for the labor relations specialist, who often is the principal negotiator representing management at the negotiation table.

JACOB P. HART, TECHNIQUES OF COLLECTIVE BARGAINING *

PREPARATION FOR BARGAINING

One of the most difficult tasks confronting the management negotiator is to become as knowledgeable about the company that he represents as the others at the bargaining table. The members of management are, of course, familiar with the intricacies of their company. The union's team, consisting of persons who work for the company and one or more union officials who probably spend most of their time representing employees of the company or in the same industry, will also understand the physical and economic characteristics of the company's business. The management negotiator, too, must develop a knowledge of the processes by which raw material is turned into finished product, the economics of the company's operation, and, most important of all, the conditions under which the members of the bargaining unit work.

* Jacob P. Hart, "Techniques Of Collective Bargaining," 26 The Practical Lawyer 9 (1980); © by The American Law Institute. Reprinted with the permission of *The Practical Lawyer*. Subscription rates $18 a year; $3.75 a single issue. This article appeared in the January 15, 1980 issue of *The Practical Lawyer*.

Without exception, a management negotiator should not bargain without undertaking a fairly intensive tour of the facilities of the plant, with special emphasis upon the different types of jobs performed by members of the bargaining unit. Inevitably, questions will arise at the bargaining table concerning particular jobs or locations within the plant believed by members of the bargaining unit to be exceptionally onerous and therefore deserving of higher rates or special working considerations. Unless the negotiator has been there, he has no idea of the legitimacy of the concerns expressed by the union. The views of his client often tend to be biased. On the other hand, it is extremely effective at the bargaining table to be able to speak of personally touring a particular area or watching a particular job being performed, thus having a personal basis upon which to disagree with the union representative.

Cost Union Proposals

If a written copy of the union's contract proposals can be secured in advance, the cost of each proposal should be established before the first bargaining session. If an advance copy cannot be obtained, the cost of the proposals should be determined before the second meeting. Although there are many ways to cost proposals, the union probably is used to thinking in terms of cents per hour, and since this serves as an effective shorthand, compute the company's costs on that basis.

Appendix A contains a list of seven hypothetical union demands and instructions showing how to determine their cost. In order to communicate with the union in the same language, certain ground rules for costing proposals should be established early in the negotiations. The method commonly utilized is a noncumulative, straight-time, hourly cost for each proposal. Under this procedure, the hypothetical demands total 79.2 cents per hour in increased labor costs in the first year of the contract, an additional 61 cents in the second year, and an additional 66 cents for the third year. The total cost of the contract is $2.062. Most of the literature on contract settlements will express costs in this way.

Obviously, to obtain a true picture of the increased labor costs over the entire contract, it will be necessary to cumulate the figures. For example, the first year increase of 79.2 cents is actually incurred three times. In fact, over the life of the contract the seven demands will cost an additional $4.256 cents per hour. The most effective means of referring to the cumulative calculation at the bargaining table is to translate the cents per hour into dollars. Thus, the union's hypothetical proposals will, over the life of the contract, increase labor costs by $1,655,413.

A common shortcut used in the costing of proposals, which unfortunately works to the detriment of the employer, is the computation of all nonwage proposals on the basis of existing hourly rates. To illustrate, in the hypothetical, the cost of three additional holidays was set at five cents per hour. In fact, however, were the union successful in increasing the average straight-time hourly rate from $4.57 to $5.07, as proposed, the cost of these holidays would be six cents per hour. While costing each item on the basis of the increase to be negotiated is the accurate method, since the ultimate wage settlement cannot be predicted, it is more practical to calculate all the elements of the wage package on the basis of existing straight-time hourly rates.

Similarly, the real cost of any wage increase is a function not only of the straight-time rate, but also of all overtime, holiday, and vacation pay. Here again, in calculating costs, this "roll up" is usually not taken into consideration. Moreover, it is practically impossible to get a union to credit the employer with these hidden costs. It may be true that a 50 cents per hour wage increase will actually cost the company 55 cents, but that fact will probably carry little weight at the bargaining table.

Study Past Negotiating History

In order to appreciate the importance of various union demands, a new management negotiator must delve into the past bargaining history. If a benefit now being sought—for example, plant-wide seniority for layoffs, as opposed to departmental seniority—was requested during previous negotiations but dropped relatively quickly, this proposal probably does not carry any special weight. If, on the other hand, the demand was hotly debated during the previous negotiations and only reluctantly abandoned by the union, the employees will, most likely, be anxious to press the demand.

A study of previous settlements will also enable the negotiator to point to some of the benefits that the union has achieved in recent years, for it is usually impossible to tell how old an existing benefit is simply by looking at the labor agreement itself. Of course, the management negotiator must read the agreement from cover to cover. The interrelationships between contract clauses may result in a proposal having an impact or a portion of the contract not immediately involved in the proposal itself. Furthermore, during the course of a collective bargaining negotiation, any clause in the contract may be discussed, even though it does not appear on the union's list of written demands.

Know the Union's Negotiators

The company's final contract offer will almost never be accepted by the rank and file unless it is recommended by the union negotiating team. Hence, it is extremely important that the individuals at the bargaining table support the proposed settlement. In the typical case, the union bargaining committee will consist of one or more union officers, together with a cross-section of bargaining-unit employees. Know in advance each committee member's department, his hourly rate, his seniority date, and any particular grievances that this employee has had or is likely to have in the near future.

No matter how attractive a wage offer might otherwise be, if one member of the union's negotiating team believes that his pet grievance has not been addressed, he may sabotage the entire agreement by opposing the proposed settlement at the membership meeting. On the other hand, if a particular management proposal tends to benefit one or more members of the negotiating team, human nature being what it is, those members will probably look favorably upon the entire management package. A thorough knowledge of the economic relationships of the union representatives with the company can be critical when illustrating the impact of proposals on members of the bargaining unit. If a particular offer will affect the actual paychecks of the people in the room, a firm basis for negotiations will exist, since the union side will be unable to dispute the accuracy of the data.

Even more important than the employee members of the committee is the chief union spokesman. It is advisable to get as much information about him as possible, particularly if he has recently negotiated agreements with similar companies. Thus, if the union negotiator has obtained a recent settlement with a company he perceives to be in a competing or similar industry, any offer that he will receive will be considered by him in light of the previous contract settlement. Obviously, copies of other agreements negotiated by the union in general, or by the negotiator in particular, are useful to have.

Pick the Management Team with Care

Unless the company is very small and the chief executive officer is in daily contact with members of the bargaining unit, it is not advisable to include him on the management team. Although the National Labor Relations Act ("Act") requires that the management representatives have authority to consummate an agreement, this provision really means that the parties must negotiate in good faith. There is no harm in stating occasionally that a particular union proposal is beyond the scope of the bargaining team's present authority, and that further discussions with upper management will be necessary before a response can be made. This assertion may be a convenient way to end a particular meeting.

It can be very embarrassing for a chief company officer to be "called on the carpet" by members of the rank and file during a volatile negotiating session. Pointed questions might be asked which, because top management is in the room, cannot be sidestepped until later. The company negotiator may lose control because someone of sufficiently high rank is sitting at the table and is expected to provide immediate answers. Furthermore, it is critical to establish early in a negotiation that only the principal spokesmen for each side should make proposals and counterproposals, and this is extremely difficult to secure if the top-ranking member of management is present.

Probably the best management team consists of three individuals. The first should be a personnel representative, who not only will be the member of management most conversant with the terms of the labor agreement, but will also be aware of all of the company benefits, including those not set forth in the agreement. The personnel officer usually has the most frequent contact with the union, since he is involved in the handling of grievances and other matters touching the employment relationship.

The second member should be a high-ranking operations official. No matter how attractive a particular proposal may appear from a personnel viewpoint, it is impossible in every case to understand the complete impact of a proposal on the company's operations without the input of someone who oversees them.

The third member should be a high-ranking executive with close ties to the chief officer of the company. Preferably, he should be someone with a sound financial background. Although the company controller need not be present, if this third individual is aware of the financial condition of the company, he will be able to assist in calculating the cost impact of union proposals. He should also be someone who has the trust and confidence of the company president or other chief operating officer and who could help to persuade the company to make or refrain from certain moves.

Prepare the Management Team

As soon as the management team has been selected, begin asking for the limits of your negotiating authority. This may prove to be a most difficult task. Management often comes to the bargaining table without a firm idea of how many cents per hour it is willing to spend in order to reach a contract without a strike. If the company has not yet fixed upon the amount, begin forcing the team from the very first meeting to think in this direction. Use the concepts of a "red line" and a "blue line" bargaining limit. The blue line represents the cost of a package that the company believes will make a desirable settlement. The red line should be that figure beyond which the company is prepared to take a strike.

Of course, both the red and blue line amounts can change during the course of negotiations. Nevertheless, it is extremely advantageous to focus on these two figures as soon as possible. In this way, both the negotiator and the team know, at the table and in caucus, whether they are moving too slowly or too fast, and, in general, whether strategies are having their desired effect.

AT THE BARGAINING TABLE

Since, particularly in the case of a renewal agreement, the company usually would be happy to continue the existing contract, it is the union that normally indicates a desire to commence negotiations. Consequently, management often has little to do with the date on which negotiations begin.

Generally, most unions prefer to do the bulk of their bargaining during the last month or two months of the collective bargaining agreement. Under the Act, should a rival union be interested in replacing the incumbent as the certified bargaining agent, the rival's petition must be filed with the National Labor Relations Board ("Board") no later than 60 days or earlier than 90 days before the end of the current agreement. Seldom, therefore, will an incumbent union wish to begin bargaining more than 60 days prior to the end of the present contract.

Furthermore, unless the employer anticipates extremely difficult or complex negotiations, it is usually advisable not to start bargaining too early. If the parties sit too long at the bargaining table, either the employer will make significant concessions or the bargaining atmosphere will become increasingly hostile. If possible, contract renewal negotiations are best left for the last month of the contract, and, at least in the beginning, marathon negotiating sessions or meetings on several successive days are generally unwise.

Management should not make a stenographic or taped record of the negotiations, for this conduct may suggest to the union that what occurs during bargaining will not be kept confidential or that management thinks that the labor team will distort what transpires. The Board takes a dim view of employers insisting on tape recording negotiating sessions. Architectural Fiberglass, 165 N.L.R.B. 238 (1967). So long as the parties are careful to reduce all agreements to writing as the negotiations progress, tapes or stenographic notes of negotiations are really unnecessary.

The Bargaining Location

As a general rule, negotiating at the union hall puts the employer at a disadvantage and may lead to more explosive conduct by the union. Negotiations on the premises of the employer are preferable, but there must be a suitable place that is sufficiently isolated from the work force, so that the presence of active bargaining does not interfere with production. When negotiating on company property, a conference room or some other meeting facility is to be preferred over the offices of any particular member of management.

The most desirable location is neutral territory. The lawyer's office represents an ideal setting, being away from the company's premises and requiring less travel time by the lawyer-negotiator. Of course, the parties can agree to negotiate on truly neutral ground, such as a hotel meeting room, with each party sharing the cost of the facility. Particularly when many people are expected, as in multiemployer or multiunion negotiations, the hotel room often provides the most businesslike and tranquil atmosphere.

Often overlooked, but of real importance, is the physical arrangement of the negotiating room. Since usually both sides will bring a lot of papers, a large conference table is needed. When sitting "across the table" from the other side, it is desirable for the chief negotiators to occupy positions on opposite sides, rather than opposite ends, of the table. There is no substitute for eye contact, and stationing two negotiators 15 to 20 feet apart is not very helpful.

A caucus room, to which either side may adjourn for private meetings, should be available nearby. This room should be sound proof, since even parties acting in the best of faith often cannot resist the temptation to pay close attention to the sounds of a caucus that are clearly audible.

.At some point during negotiations the parties may decide to move to the office of a federal or state mediator. One of the immediate advantages of using a mediator is that the government provides meeting rooms, with the sobering impact that such quarters can produce.

The Opening Meeting

Little actual bargaining usually takes place during the opening meeting. However, some essential ground rules should be laid by the parties at that time if the remaining sessions are to proceed in an orderly and businesslike manner.

First, there should only be one official spokesman for each side. Particularly when no written record is made of the proceedings, a meeting at which many people talk at once often leaves both sides confused as to what was proposed or decided. Most union negotiators are quite willing to accept this ground rule, if only to give them greater control over their own bargaining team.

Also tell the management team that you expect to be the spokesman during the actual negotiations. Of course, be very clear about the value of the team's input. In fact, in caucus, the members of the team are free to say anything, including "you're fired." However, for the lawyer-negotiator to be most effective, he must be the lightning rod drawing the union's fire, and to do this, he must control the management side of the table during all open meetings.

Obviously, there will be times during negotiations when the views of the management team will be solicited, particularly on questions involving technical aspects of the operation or the status of present benefits. But while all of the members of the team can expect to be involved in the proceedings, they will speak only when instructed to do so, and will not otherwise engage in dialogue with the union.

The substance of the initial meeting will often consist of an exchange of proposals. Particularly when the parties are bargaining over the terms of an initial contract, each side must understand the precise meaning of the other side's terms. In the case of a renegotiation of an expiring contract, no matter how clear the proposals may appear in writing, the union spokesman should be asked to review them one at a time and to make whatever comments he feels appropriate. The alert management negotiator should be able to learn much simply by listening to the manner in which the union spokesman states the initial demands.

If the number of proposals appears to be large, and especially if an initial contract is being negotiated, bring to the table duplicate looseleaf notebooks, each of which contains on the left and right sides of the looseleaf rings the proposals and counterproposals, subject by subject. Present one of these notebooks to the union negotiator for his use during the talks. The book facilitates the cataloging of differences between the parties and helps both sides to discuss the same clause at any given time. By drawing a red pencil through any proposals that have been dropped by the parties and circling in blue pencil items that have been agreed upon, together with their modifications, the notebook provides a visual picture of how far the parties are apart on any particular provision.

Conduct During Negotiations

Negotiate the noneconomic items first. The terms "economic" and "noneconomic" distinguish between collective bargaining proposals directly susceptible to monetary evaluation, such as wages, vacations, holidays, and pension and welfare contributions, and those that, while usually affecting an employer's operating costs, are more in the nature of labor or management restrictions, such as the no-strike, picket line, seniority, grievance and arbitration, and assignment of overtime clauses.

Most management representatives prefer to negotiate the noneconomic issues first. Since the union negotiating committee is usually concerned primarily with the money items on the table, particularly wages, it may be possible to obtain prompt and favorable agreements on the noneconomic matters in order to turn the bargaining to areas of more significant labor concern.

Occasionally, a union will object to negotiating initially the noneconomic items. Management should proceed with caution in the face of such an objection; at least one Board decision has held that the employer commits an unfair labor practice by insisting, against the union's will, on negotiating noneconomic items first. Federal-Mogul Corp., 212 N.L.R.B. 950 (1974), enforced, 524 F.2d 37 (6th Cir. 1975).

Prepare and initial acceptable language as items are settled. Often the parties are so relieved that a particular point has been tentatively agreed upon and are so anxious to move on to the next item that they are forced to rely on skimpy and often inconsistent notes when drafting the precise language of their agreement. Particularly in the case of a first contract, when the language of many basic clauses, whether dealing with union security, management rights, or a no-strike pledge, will be forged, to be left unchanged for years thereafter, the bargaining committees must concur, prior to completing negotiations, not only on the concepts, but on the full contract language. Although it is advisable to secure an understanding that all items agreed upon during the negotiations are subject to the successful completion of a total package, nevertheless, written and initialed memoranda of all accepted items of contract language should be prepared as the talks progress.

Present and discuss the economic items as a package. Both sides will gain increased flexibility if they can reach an accord concerning the manner in which economic proposals are made. Preferably, all the economic items should be presented together, with the understanding that the "package" is a single proposal. Thus, for example, if the union requests improvements in wages, vacations, holidays, and pension and welfare contributions, the management should respond to all four items at one time, even if, as to some, no concessions are made. If the economic issues are put on the table as a total package, then management retains the option of rearranging the dollars in subsequent offers, even if, as to a particular element such as vacations, the subsequent offer is less generous than a previous one.

If this arrangement is not made in advance, the employer could be accused of simply withdrawing items that had been previously offered. An employer who insists, against the union's will, on the right to reserve, modify, or withdraw proposals that were accepted, runs some risk of violating the Act. Cf. Holmes Tuttle Broadway Ford, Inc., 186 N.L.R.B. 73 (1970), enforced, 465 F.2d 717 (9th Cir. 1972).

Periodically summarize the status of the negotiations. Particularly if there are many items proposed by each side, occasionally provide the union with a written list showing which items have been agreed upon and which remain to be discussed. Omit any reference to items that either side has dropped from the table completely. This summary can help ascertain whether particular proposals have been withdrawn. Sometimes, the union's chief negotiator must be very careful when he abandons an item that is strongly favored by one or more of his committee members. As a result, management may not be completely certain whether the proposal has been dropped by the union or has simply been omitted from discussion on a temporary basis. The written summary permits the tacit abandonment of items not included in the open list.

Whenever possible, work from documents. The basic rule that a negotiator work from a document is particularly important in labor bargaining, where contract language often survives for a long time with little or no change.

Many unions have standard contract clauses they want management to adopt. Particularly in the case of a first collective bargaining agreement, the union contract proposed at the beginning of negotiations will usually be a collection of the very best clauses that the union has been able to secure from other employers over a period of years. If management simply accepts the union's language on critical matters, it may find itself with a basically unacceptable contract that will be very difficult to change in the future. By contrast, since a union negotiating an initial agreement is usually very desirous of securing a quick contract, thereby putting to rest what could be a volatile labor situation, it will often accept management's terms on these important clauses.

Learn how to be silent. The statement that "the first one who talks loses the point," while generally applicable to all negotiations, is particularly relevant in labor bargaining. In an atmosphere than can easily become emotionally charged, it is sometimes difficult, if not impossible, to refrain from elaborate explanations designed to cut the tension in the room. The negotiator who can make his point quickly and succinctly, then sit back and allow the other side to respond no matter how long it takes, will often find that the response contains some concession or movement. If the management team is well trained, so that the members will not feel compelled to break the silence by injecting a thought of their own, someone on the union negotiating committee may not be as well disciplined, and will volunteer information, or at least express a reaction to a proposal, that can be extremely helpful in the future.

Never say no without a reason. One of the most important things for a management negotiator to achieve is credibility with the other side. The union may approach a negotiation with a certain inbred hostility toward, and maybe even distrust of, management. The members of the shop committee may particularly resent being patronized by a company spokesman. Quite properly, these employees view collective bargaining as an opportunity to meet with management on even ground. They deserve respect.

An excellent way to show consideration is never to respond to a proposal with a simple "no." Although the union might not agree with the logic behind management's rejection, some reason should always be given, even if it is based on assumptions that only management believes. Whenever management makes a wage proposal, for instance, there should be some basis, be it cost of living, comparison with other plants, comparison with raises in the past, or productivity. On the other hand, a union proposal should only be rejected if there is a good and sufficient reason, which the union is entitled to know. Often the union is quite willing to listen to, and even accept, an explanation for management's rejection of a proposal.

Make only one "final" offer. A good way for a management negotiator to get into trouble is to style some intermediate position as the company's "final offer." All it takes is a second final offer to convince the union that this term is being used for bargaining purposes only and is not, in fact, an indication of the employer's ultimate position on a given subject. Inform the union in advance that no offer will be final unless it actually is. In this way, the significance of that offer will be enhanced, when and if it is actually made.

When the final offer is made, if at all possible, it should be conditioned on an agreement by the union negotiating team to recommend that offer to the rank and file for ratification. The management negotiator can say: "If you will agree to recommend, then we shall offer the following." This is not mere rhetoric. Rather, it is an attempt to preserve to management the option of not officially making an offer unless the union agrees to recommend it. In this way, management is able to withdraw the offer if the union rejects it. This technique avoids an accusation that the offer was made in bad faith. It also avoids a situation in which management makes its final offer, only to have it summarily rejected.

Under ideal circumstances, the union will propose a settlement that management can accept. Then there is immediate assurance that the union negotiating committee will recommend the settlement. To achieve this result, it may be necessary for the chief spokesmen to meet privately "off the record." These sessions are extremely desirable, since both negotiators are free to explore the other side's limits, without, however, making or extracting any binding commitments.

Once the parties have reached a tentative settlement, the final meeting should never adjourn until the terms have been reduced to writing and signed by every member of the negotiating team for each side. Not only does the signed writing memorialize what is going to be taken to the rank and file for ratification, but, even more important, there is a written commitment from each member of the union team to support that final offer. It is excellent insurance to prevent changes of heart when the rank and file assemble at the union hall to cast their ballots.

The management representative should draft the written final offer and preface it with a statement like: "As the final settlement of all outstanding issues between the parties, the company proposes, and the union negotiating committee agrees to recommend, the following total package." The written final offer should also contain a statement that all the terms and conditions of the present contract not affected by the final offer remain unchanged.

Do not bid against yourself. A successful labor negotiation must remain a give and take process. Whenever possible, therefore, the next offer should come from the recipient of the previous one. Often management falls into the trap of simply "upping the ante" following each union rejection of a proposal. This kind of bargaining results in an unsatisfactory agreement for management, since the union is never required to make a concession, simply saying "no" until management satisfies labor's demands.

Make clear from the very outset of negotiations that whenever management makes a proposal, it expects a rational response, not merely a statement that "your proposal is rejected; come up with another one." No matter how slight the movement, so long as both sides continue to whittle away at the differences between them a satisfactory settlement should result.

Also, by expecting the union to respond with a counterproposal that is more than a simple rejection, management is better able to flush out those items on the union's list of demands that are not essential to settlement. By bidding against itself, management will almost always include in the settlement items that the union would have eventually dropped or modified significantly had it been forced to make counterproposals.

Never offer benefits that the union has not requested. Employers often believe that they know much more about what their employees really want than does the union. Unless the management negotiator dispels this notion quickly, he can be offering benefits that the union does not expect.

Someone may suggest in caucus, for example, that the employees really do not want three more personal holidays, as requested by the union, but instead would prefer more vacation time for the senior men; therefore management should offer five weeks vacation after 25 years of service—a demand not made by the union—if the union drops its holiday proposal. Inevitably, the union will respond by accepting the extra vacation time while keeping their own proposal on the table. Now the management negotiator is faced with the task of retrieving from the table a benefit labor knows the company can afford, while still trying to deal with the three personal holidays. The tactic simply does not work.

Turning to Mediation

The role of the mediator is widely misunderstood; in fact, he is often confused with an arbitrator or a fact finder. The mediator is a government official, working either for the Federal Mediation and Conciliation Service or for a similar state or local agency. His function is to assist both sides to reach an amicable contract settlement.

Except in the health care industry, where the 1974 amendments to the Act added a fairly elaborate, mandatory mediation procedure, the use of a mediator is strictly voluntary. Furthermore, even when a mediator is employed, he is not empowered to bind either side. His role is simply to help bring the parties together.

By contrast, an arbitrator, whether he is asked to resolve a grievance or decide the terms of a collective bargaining agreement, does have the power to bind the parties. He is like a judge, hearing "cases" and determining a winner and loser. Occupying a middle ground between the mediator and the arbitrator is the "fact finder." Except in the health care industry, the fact finder is voluntarily selected by the parties to assist in the settlement of contract disputes. Like the arbitrator, the fact finder—or fact finders, since they often work in panels—sits as a judge, listening to testimony and receiving evidence. However, the fact finder's product, a recommended contract settlement, is not binding on either side. Moreover, the fact finder, unlike the mediator, does not actually participate in the talks themselves.

If a mediator is to be used, it is important to remember that he is not an advocate for either side; he is concerned only with reaching a settlement. The good mediator can make each side give or yield more than it was willing to do on its own.

Ironically, when either party approaches mediation unmindful of this role, often believing the mediator really is its advocate, it stands to lose. For example, if management mistakenly believes that the mediator is there to assist it, he may be told everything there is to know about management's ultimate position. If the union holds something back, the settlement that the mediator will produce probly will be at the maximum level of management's authority and likely more than the union needed to settle.

The physical facilities that are available to a mediator are one of the major advantages of using him. Therefore, unless the company is located in a city where there is no mediation office, utilize the mediator's location.

In the first place, the mediator may have a number of conference rooms available, so that each side has a large caucus room within which to conduct private discussions. Second, the psychological impact on both sides of moving the situs of the talks to a neutral place provided by the government is an aid towards desirable compromise. Finally, the mediator will be more accessible in his own office; from there, he can simultaneously work on more than one negotiation.

As a general proposition, the main purpose of the mediator is to convey exploratory offers. He will often shuttle from one caucus room to another, trying to extract in private from the parties commitments that they are as yet unwilling to make across the table. The mediator is well equipped to play the game of: "If the union agrees to X, will you agree to Y?" In addition, some mediators take an aggressive role in prolonging talks that appear otherwise stalled, in breaking off talks to await a better day, or in actually scheduling bargaining sessions when the parties have not done so on their own.

The mediator may not be subpoenaed to testify in arbitrations or other proceedings concerning his participation in negotiations. Over the years, the Federal Mediation and Conciliation Service has successfully defended the immunity of their mediators from testifying, in order to preserve their "confessor" role at the bargaining table. Therefore, everything the mediator does is truly "off the record."

* * *

CONCLUSION

The negotiation of a collective bargaining agreement on behalf of management requires knowledge of the company, psychological acumen, preparation, and stamina. It ranks among the most challenging aspects of labor law.

Appendix A

CALCULATING THE COST OF UNION DEMANDS

I. Background facts

    a.   There are 187 members in the bargaining unit.

    b.   Twenty-three are in "skilled trades."

    c.   Each year, 388,960 straight-time hours were worked or paid for (187 employees $\times$ 40 hours per week $\times$ 52 weeks per year).

    d.   The average straight-time hourly rate is $4.57.

    e.   The present vacation schedule allows two weeks after three years, and three weeks after ten years.

f. At the present time, 25 employees have more than two-years' seniority, but less than three; 37 employees have more than eight years but less than ten.

g. Overtime at time and a half is now paid only after 40 hours per week. Last year, 250 man-hours of daily overtime—more than eight hours worked in one day—were worked by employees who did not work over 40 hours in the week. The same number of man-hours were worked on Saturdays by employees who did not otherwise work 40 hours in the week.

II. **The new union proposal for a three-year contract**

a. Across-the-board hourly wage increases of 50, 45, and 50 cents.

b. A skilled trade bonus of 5, 5, and 5 cents.

c. Three additional holidays.

d. Increased hourly contributions to the Union Pension and Welfare Plan of 20, 15, and 15 cents.

e. Two-weeks' vacation after two years and three-weeks' vacation after eight years.

f. Time and a half for all hours worked in excess of eight in a day.

g. Time and a half for all hours worked on Saturday.

III. **Calculation of increased straight-time costs in cents per hour (non-cumulative)**

Benefit	1st YEAR	2nd YEAR	3rd YEAR
A	50.0	45.0	50.0
B	01.0 [1]	01.0	01.0
C	05.0 [2]		
D	20.0	15.0	15.0
E	03.0 [3]		
F	00.1 [4]		
G	00.1 [5]		
Totals	79.2	61	66

or $2.062 over the life of the contract.

[1] Assume 23 people get 5 cents for 2080 hours. The cost is $2346. Divided by 388,960 (assumption Ic), the cost is .6 cent, or one cent per hour.

[2] Based on the present hourly rate.

[3] See assumption If. 62 people will receive an extra week of vacation—62 × 40 hours × $4.57 ÷ 388,960.

[4] See assumption Ig.

[5] See assumption Ig.

* * *

A MANAGEMENT LAWYER LOOKS AT NEGOTIATIONS

Interview: August 5, 1977, between Julius G. Getman and Leland Cross, Esq., an experienced management attorney. Location: Indianapolis, Indiana.

Q: What role do you as a management lawyer usually play in negotiations?

A: Well, there is no typical role that I play. Usually I appear as the principal spokesman representing the employer along with other representatives of the employer. Hopefully no more than two or three. I ask that I be the only person who speaks in behalf of the employer—sometimes this fails. Normally, I have a caveat though, that is, other members of the employer and negotiating team may speak if I direct a question to them. We have a series of signals when they are authorized to speak.

Q: Do you have specific goals?

A: Yes. I have specific goals in mind, indeed, agreed upon with my client that we will seek to achieve and we evaluate our negotiations based upon the success we have had in reaching those goals.

Q: Do you also have in mind a specific point past which you will not compromise?

A: Yes, in fact very early in the negotiations we establish end points in our authority with regard to language and usually at midpoint or perhaps two-thirds through the negotiations, we establish end points with regard to economics. We have a firm understanding with the client that we are not to go beyond these designated end points. And we also have the understanding that if the client has any idea that it may amend those end points that they advise us very early. It has a very serious impact on our credibility as a negotiator if we say we will only go as far as X and later end up going to X plus 1 or X plus 2—both with respect to language and with respect to economics. So, it is crucial to establish the end point of the authority.

Q: You mentioned that your credibility with the union is very important.

A: It is probably more important than any expertise we bring to the table.

Q: OK. Yet you certainly do not want them to know what your end points are. Correct?

A: Ordinarily the adversary in the negotiating process does not know. Although in some cases where we have an established relationship with the other side, I find it to our advantage to advise them that this is as far as we will go. It is usually done by a side-bar technique. This means a meeting (and not in the presence of the client and not in the presence of the union negotiating committee) in which we have a very candid discussion—both the union representative and myself as to how far each will go and to what are *must* items on each party's agenda.

Q: But, now before you get to that point where you are leveling with the chief union negotiator—would it contribute to a successful negotiation for the union to think that you will give less than in fact you will give?

A: Yes. But we would not say we will only go as far as X when we intend to go as far as X plus 2. We may intimate this is as far as we will go, but we will not say that in specific terms.

Q: What might you say to try to convey this without risking your credibility?

A: We would say, for example, with respect to a wage offer that a 10% increase is consistent with what our competitors are doing, consistent with the industry pattern, and is what we think we should give to get a contract. At no point there do I say it is all we will give. Indeed, we may want to give more to be competitive in the employee market.

Q: There are two points I want to pursue. One is that you mentioned you may want to give more. Does that mean that you would not necessarily want to continue the old wage rates but would, in fact, want to arrive at a wage rate which permits you to compete with other employers for the best employees?

A: That's quite correct. I have had four or five cases in the last couple of years where because of ineptness on the part of the negotiator representing the union, he has accepted less than I in fact wanted to give and as a result, we found ourselves rather seriously disadvantaged in the local labor market with respect to our ability to obtain the kind of employees we wanted. In some of these cases, we literally had to ask the mediator to force the union to ask for more or if they had not accepted what we wanted them to take, to come back later and reopen the contract voluntarily in order to give more to the union. This is a very clumsy situation to be in. It damages the credibility of the union representative which disadvantages us as well as the union representative.

Q: That's fascinating. I knew this was theoretically possible but I never knew that it really arose.

A: It does happen. It has happened a number of times.

Q: Now on the other hand, if you are dealing with a skillful union negotiator who gets to know you, wouldn't he realize that he can push you up to that point where you say that this is as far as you go? That is, doesn't he realize that there will be more give until you tell him this is it?

A: Well, if he is a person with whom I have had an ongoing relationship and a candid relationship, he will realize what I am doing but the more he knows about my style, the more conservative my technique is in dealing with him.

Q: Have you ever been in negotiations where you have seen the union not wanting to push too much for fear of making the employer noncompetitive?

A: This is a rare case. We have had a couple of cases in which the union representative, knowing that we were in bad business circumstances, said "we don't want you out of business—we are not going to strike, but we do want everything you can give us consistent with your capacity to exist and compete and keep jobs available."

For example, the Teamsters, are extremely businesslike negotiators and we have had just those kinds of circumstances and we have been very candid with them saying: "Look, this is as far as we will go—if we go beyond this—we are going to be in *serious* trouble with regard to our capacity to compete. We will be in serious trouble regarding our capacity to provide jobs. X cents is going to be it." And sometimes they will even say: "That's great—that's all we want to know—don't give us X cents until about a minute before the contract expires. Come in about a dime or seven cents below that and hang on!"

Q: When you are bargaining with the union for the first time with respect to matters dealing with the union, for example, union security, or super-seniority or time-off for union, how do you decide whether to grant these clauses?

A: It is usually a very easy decision if you want to avoid a strike. We know those are strike issues accordingly, assuming that we want a contract—and we don't always want a contract—we will grant those usually as one of the final concessions. It is usually a trade-off with respect to a good management rights clause, a good arbitration clause and the like. Obviously, we don't have that kind of trade the next time around.

Q: Do you ever have an employer who decides that it is a matter of principle not to grant union security?

A: I would say that maybe 1 out of 25 or 30 will talk at some length about the principle involved in checkoff or the principle involved in union security, but that if that employer does have any basic intelligence and does want to avoid a strike, we are usually able to convince him that: (1) they are better off with it than without it. For example, we can tell them that if they want to avoid the highly competitive situation where unions are constantly trying to resell themselves to the employees by demonstrating their aggressive tactics, by demonstrating their willingness to represent any kind of claim the employees might have, that, the best trick is to institutionalize the union by giving them union security so they don't have to engage in continuing manhood contests to demonstrate to the employees that a union is good and a union will represent them. We can make a good case that it is in the employer's interest to have union security. Secondly, we can make a good case that the employer is better off checking off union dues than to have the union stewards running around throughout the plant collecting them every 30 days. This is disruptive.

Q: How about seniority? Would you advise an employer generally to accept the basic concept of seniority which unions almost always advocate?

A: Yes. With certain safeguards—namely that an employee must have the ability to do the job on a bump situation and a layoff and that an employee must have the ability to do or to learn reasonably quickly the job in a job bidding situation.

Q: So, you feel that seniority has advantages for management as well as for the union?

A: Certainly.

Q: How about grievance systems. Do you try to limit the scope of the grievance system? First of all, do you think that a well organized grievance system leading to arbitration is in management's interest?

A: Absolutely! We think anything that brings order to the handling of employee complaints and there will be employee complaints no matter what we do is directly related to the capacity of the company to be productive.

Q: Can you discuss the relative weight of economic power and negotiating skill in achieving an agreement?

A: I would say that economic power is number one and negotiating skill is number two. The use of power in negotiations is much more influential than the use of skill. The best way to negotiate is to accommodate the use of power with the maximum amount of skill.

Q: When you negotiate, are you concerned with future relations with the union?

A: Absolutely. Sometimes unions will make proposals they do not understand themselves. Sometimes their own proposals have features that could come back to haunt the union. These features could seriously disadvantage the union and sometimes the employer's proposals have fish hooks in them—sometimes deliberately and sometimes not deliberately.

Q: What do you mean by a fish hook?

A: Well that is a language item which has in it the capacity for the employer to take advantage of in the future which the union itself does not perceive at the time it negotiates it. Gimmicks like whether the day before and the day after a holiday is the day before or the day after on the employer's work schedule. I would much prefer to pull the fish out from under the table and say: "Look, this is what it means—this is how it works—and I want everyone to make sure that we understand each other on this." Sometimes the adversary does not comprehend drafting as well as he or she should and I really don't want to be the kind of person who has the reputation of having slipped one by the other side. Because the matter will probably end up an arbitration case. Perhaps we'll even win that arbitration case, nonetheless I am more concerned with my capacity to be forceful and effective based on my credibility the next time around. And this is the difference, perhaps the most significant difference, in style between different kinds of management representatives and their views of the long-term relationships with the parties. I realize that when I shake hands with the union and walk out of the negotiating room, my client is going to have to live for two or three years on that collective bargaining agreement and if I have tricked the union—if I have set land mines or fish hooks in the contract language which are going to come back to haunt the union—I know I'll pay for it the next time around! Not only because they are going to be mad at me, not only because that language will have to come out and be changed, but because what I tell them will be that much less believable and they will perceive me as someone who has tricked them.

Q: Would you ever accept a less favorable agreement than you could otherwise get in order to be sure to maintain the good will with the union?

A: I don't know if I would "buy good will" by accepting a less favorable contract. I don't believe I can do that in good conscience. I certainly couldn't do it unless the client expressly understood it. But I will tell you what I have done. I have proposed final packages which were more than I thought might fly rather than risk a non-ratification because I did not have confidence in the capacity of the union leadership to adequately sell a lesser package to the membership. I sweetened the pot—so to speak.

Q: When negotiations are completed, assuming the contract is signed, does one side usually feel dissatisfied like they have been beaten? Or is it typically that both sides feel they have triumphed?

A: My experience is that the employer ordinarily feels it gave more than it should. The union ordinarily feels that it took less than it should. This is particularly true when there is a substantial majority vote in favor of the ratification meeting. In fact, my favorite ratifications are where the contracts are ratified by about 5 or 10 per cent margin. Then I know I didn't give away too much. But I have the view that part of this is just a rationalization and my typical experience is that I end up settling for about what I anticipated I would have to and the union ends up holding out at a point about where I anticipated they would hold out. I am not really surprised and I think my most sophisticated clients are not really surprised at the settlements because if you do the proper job of conditioning your client in terms of what to expect, both with regard to what the union will be demanding and where it will settle, you will end up pretty close to the mark if you are doing your job and both sides will be preconditioned to a certain degree as to where the actual area of the meeting of minds will be.

Q: What if anything do you tell new clients concerning the risk of a strike?

A: Well, when we are costing out economic packages I also make them go through the exercise of giving me the cost of a strike. I feel this is a good way to condition the client—to having a realistic view of what a strike really is about. I've tried to get my client to say pretty honestly—"well a strike will cost me X dollars a week, my potential loss of clients could be perhaps Y, my cost of running the plant's overhead without the work force there is essentially a cost Z"—so that they have a realistic idea of what the expense items are. I also tell them the risk of a short strike because if a short strike occurs—1, 2, 3, 4, 5, days—the employees never really get hurt very bad. The company gets hurt immediately and in the long-term, employees learn that a short strike that doesn't hurt them much is what it takes to get what they want and you really educate the employees that a strike is the only way they will get what they want! So a short strike is a very uneconomic thing for the employer both with regard to the immediate time and in the future.

Q: When you do face a strike situation, do you use the legal right to hire replacements very frequently?

A: Most infrequently.

Q: Why is that?

A: Because realistically we know that we are not going to supplant the union, that we are not going to make the union go away. We realize that in 1977 a union is here to stay and that the union will come back. At the end, the strike will not settle unless we reinstate all the replaced employees. Typically the only time we engage in replacements is where it is a so-called fight to the death and we intend to really move the union out of the picture. It has serious consequences in terms of employee moral. There are friendly strikes and there are unfriendly strikes and the turning point of most strikes between the friendly strike and the unfriendly strike is when the replacements start rolling through the gates. We only do it when we think that it is the only thing we can do to keep in business and we need to keep in business unless our goal is to remove from the scene permanently.

Q: When you negotiate with the union, would you prefer the union negotiator to be a knowledgeable and able representative or would you prefer to have somebody who is, by your lights, incompetent?

A: I would much prefer a very strong leader and a very able person. First of all, these persons are more easy to anticipate than an incompetent. Secondly, you don't need to constantly be worried about overreaching such a person. You can assume they mean what they say in writing and orally and you can assume that they understand what you say orally and in writing. They're much easier to deal with. You don't have the problem of holding them up with one hand and bargaining with him with the other, and that is a tremendous advantage. The most difficult negotiations we have, indeed the negotiations most likely to end in strike, are negotiations where the other side is represented by someone who is weak or technically incompetent.

Q: Now, would this vary from union to union or is it just a matter of circumstance?

A: It may vary from union to union. Very infrequently do you run into an incompetent with the Teamsters, the U.A.W. or the Steelworkers. They hire strong people, they work in developing them, they have good leadership programs and as a result we'll have many less strikes with unions like that.

Q: When collective bargaining relationships mature, is the employer worse off than he was before the union came on the scene?

A: I guess it turns on where the employer started from. The employer that does not effectively administer a personnel program because it doesn't care or doesn't know how, is the employer most likely to be organized. The employer who can effectively administer a personnel program is least likely to be organized. In my judgment a union frequently forces upon an employer the responsibility of effectively administering its personnel program and that employer may then be better off. I have in mind a plant here in town of 40 employees that had no personnel system, no personnel function, no personnel records. It was organized by the Teamsters' Union about 6 years ago. That employer was forced to hire someone who knew something about personnel and labor relations, which was expensive of course. He was forced to establish policies, forced to establish procedures, and with the contract, was forced to provide equitable personnel treatment to his rank and file employees. That employer is measurably better off now than he was before he was organized. But I also believe that the employer, had he cared, could have come to someone like myself or to a good labor relations consultant and done all of those things voluntarily, and have been somewhat better off. But the point is, he wouldn't have. Necessity was the mother of that invention and happily that invention was probably much improved labor relations.

RUBIN AND BROWN, THE SOCIAL PSYCHOLOGY OF BARGAINING AND NEGOTIATION *

In developing a bargaining strategy * * * the parties must each resolve a rather complex dilemma. Consider, for example, the problem confronting the union leadership. By being tough, they stand to receive the necessary and desired support of their constituency ("Those guys are really in there fighting for us"). At the same time, however, they run the risk of driving the other side away from the bargaining table, in which case they may well lose the very membership support they initially had. On the other hand, in pushing for an agreement that has a good chance of being acceptable to the board, they run the risks of settling for less than necessary, as well as of losing the confidence and support of the union membership ("Those guys are a bunch of lily-livered sellouts"). Thus each party must, in effect, bargain not only with the other side but with his own constituency as well. * * * Regarding the pressure generated by the union constituency, McKersie, Perry, and Walton report:

> The rank and file can best be characterized by high aspirations backed by strong emotions. * * * Commensurate with the strength and level of rank-and-file aspirations are strong expectations about appropriate behavior for their elected representative.

Management negotiators faced similar pressures:

> Similarly, the Company negotiator was the target of conflicting expectations. Top management and other line managers expected settlements which did not increase labor costs excessively or reduce management flexibility. * * * At the same time they expected him to avoid a stoppage in production. The behavioral implications of such objectives were clear—hard defensive bargaining. * * * Failure to cope adequately * * * could lead either to a deterioration in interorganizational relations or to a weakening of his position within his organization.

In the case of the Union representatives, failure to comply with the accountability pressures had the following kinds of implications:

> The rank and file, through their delegate on the committee, expected the chief negotiator to accept their demands and to bargain aggressively for all of them. The negotiator was not expected to differentiate among issues or to be afraid to use power in an attempt to secure a favorable settlement. The fact that the Union had frequently resorted to strike action in support of its demands and that some locals had engaged in wildcat strikes during previous negotiations * * * acted as a reminder of the behavior which was considered appropriate.

As a result,

> A good number of delegates perceived high costs in failing to advocate their constituent's demands. Many of the delegates faced serious challenges to their leadership from organized factions within the membership and could be said to have chosen their orientation in response to implicit political sanctions.

The results of this investigation suggest that labor and management constituencies, and dependent audiences in general, often have the power to apply sanctions to their representatives when the latter fail to satisfy accountability requirements.

Another perspective on the results of this study may be gained by taking a closer look at the nature of commitment, particularly in terms of the limitations that it may impose on an individual's ability to creatively manipulate his environment. Roby has proposed that while commitment may have beneficial effects, it may also function to limit one's awareness of alternatives and one's latitude to make alternate choices. Roby implies that in a sense excessive commitment leads to "insulation" from information, a proposition similar to that advanced by Schelling who speaks of the "binding" qualities of commitment. It is thus possible to view the study by Blake and Mouton as one in which the structure of the situation—characterized as it was by exclusive ingroup activities prior to negotiation, a focus on issues that were zero sum in nature, and public exposure while bargaining—probably intensified the strength of the loyalty, commitment, and advocacy pressures and thereby limited the ability of group representatives to recognize and accept solutions that were more efficacious than their own.

THE AVAILABILITY OF THIRD PARTIES

A second, social structural component that may markedly affect bargaining behavior is reflected in the availability or presence of third parties. Such individuals may function in a variety of formal or informal conflict resolution roles. Whether formal or informal, however, the interventions made by third parties may be either apparent to the casual observer or nonapparent, and they may range from the structuring of physical space, to the establishment and reinforcement of norms, to the diagnosis and satisfaction of a bargainer's personal needs.

Examples of formal third party roles include those of conciliator, mediator, arbitrator, and fact finder; examples of the informal type include those of intermediary and special envoy. There are considerble differences between the formal and the informal. For instance, formal third party roles are often defined legally or on the basis of prior formal agreement between the participants. In many instances some form of licensure, such as certification by an appropriate outside agency attesting to the third party's competency and impartiality, may be required. Also, formal third parties, such as mediators, are normally equally accessible to each of the opposing parties. From the perspective of the participants in a dispute, when there is formal third party involvement the opposing sides are normally bound to recognize at least the legitimacy of such an individual's involvement, although they are not necessarily compelled to abide by his recommendations. While formal third parties may indeed have the authority to make interventions affecting both sides, this in itself is no guarantee that a given intervention will be heeded or seen as impartial. The effectiveness of formal third parties rests to a large extent on their personal characteristics, on their demonstrated and reputed impartiality and authoritativeness and on situational constraints.

Formal third parties, especially when they are seen as impartial and authoritative, generate pressures toward agreement through the reduction of differences. This is true not only in bargaining situations per se but seems to occur in a variety of other kinds of conflict situations as well. For example, the ombudsman whose function it is to resolve differences between individuals and institutions, the judge who resolves differences between claimants and defendants, and the marital counselor concerned with resolving differences between husbands and wives are all instances in which pressures toward the reduction of differences may be generated by third parties having formally vested authority to serve in this capacity. It is also interesting to note that in bargaining—as perhaps in each of the instances mentioned above—these pressures can be seen to operate prior to, as well as following, third party intervention.

In other words, the mere availability of a third party may itself generate pressures toward agreement. The mere knowledge, for example, that a declaration of impasse will bring a mediator into a negotiation, may push bargainers toward creating an impasse so that they may then make concessions—ostensibly at the mediator's suggestion rather than on their own initiative.   *   *   *

The mediator's suggestion in this case permits a concession that, if proffered by the bargainer himself, could be seen as a sign of weakness by the opposing party or even by his own constituency. A concession made on the advice of a mediator may reduce a bargainer's accountability for having made that concession and may thereby ameliorate negative evaluations of him. On the other hand, third party interventions may also serve to illuminate alternatives that are not readily apparent to bargainers because of their commitment to their own or to their constituency's positions.

In general, then, *the pressures toward agreement generated by third parties may emanate from the mere knowledge of their presence and/or future involvement, from their specific attributes (such as personality and reputation), and most directly from the interventions which they initiate.* In large part these pressures push bargainers in two primary directions: toward deference to norms of fairness, social responsibility, reciprocity, and equity of exchange; and toward the search for alternatives to their preferred positions.

The Effectiveness of Third Parties

Perusal of any major daily newspaper informs us that formal third parties become involved in a surprising number of community disputes, labor-management negotiations, and international conflicts. Also widely publicized are numerous accounts of smaller scale conflicts (e.g., divorce and child possession proceedings, grievances by individuals against institutions, etc.) in which neutral third parties are introduced in order to ease conflict resolution between the protagonists. The overall impression gained from these accounts is that third parties, although they may fall far short of optimal effectiveness, are generally useful in helping to bring about more rapid and effective conflict resolution.

The Functions Served by Third Parties

The evidence we have examined so far seems to suggest that, when neither impartiality nor authoritativeness are in question, formal third parties are likely to generate pressures that drive bargainers toward agreement. However, having reached an affirmative answer to the question of whether or not third parties are effective, we must now confront the broader problem of determining the reasons for their effectiveness. To gain a toehold on this question, it may be useful to examine the range of functions which third parties provide in bargaining. Since we know of no empirical investigations of the effects of differing third party roles, we shall borrow heavily from conceptual analyses in this area.

In a discussion of the resolution of industrial conflict (Ken 1954), points out that a mediator may provide any of the following forms of assistance:

   1. *Reducing irrationality*, by providing the parties with " * * * an opportunity to vent their feelings to him, by keeping personal recriminations out of joint discussions, and by drawing the attention of the parties to the objective issues in dispute and to the consequences of aggressive conflict [pp. 236–237]."

   2. *Reducing nonrationality*, by making interventions that enable the parties to clarify their intentions and their expected gains and costs;

   3. *Exploring alternative solutions*, by recasting issues on which positions may be solidified in terms that evoke less rigidity;

   4. *Providing opportunities for graceful retreat or face saving*, in the eyes of one's adversary, one's constituency, the public, etc., (a) by removing concession making from face-to-face or public exposure, (b) by controlling the pace of retreat, and (c) by taking responsibility for concessions made;

   5. *Facilitating (constructive) communication between opposing parties*, by acting as a go-between or providing opportunities for informal communication;

   6. *Regulating the costs of conflict*, " * * * by bringing or threatening to bring public wrath down on [the bargainers] heads, by persuading their allies to withdraw their support, by threatening retribution (or reward) from government or customers or some other source * * * ;

   7. *Regulating public intervention or interference;*

   8. *Identifying and promoting the use of additional resources not initially apparent to the parties; and*

   9. *Establishing and reinforcing norms and rules of procedure.*

In a slightly more general vein, Walton has examined the kinds of interventions that third parties may make to bring about "constructive confrontation." Walton's formulation is intended to be applicable to a broad range of conflicts, ranging from those that are primarily interpersonal to more structured bargaining situations. He thus argues that:

The third party can facilitate a productive confrontation by assessing and managing the following ingredients in the interaction setting: motivation, situational power, timing, pacing, tension level, communicative signs, and the group norms, process skills, and support relevant to openness.

Specifically, Walton points out that third parties may exert influence over: *the structure of the confrontation*, including the neutrality of the site, the formality of the setting, the time constraints, and the composition of the meeting with respect to others who are present; and over *the dialogue process*, including refereeing the interaction, initiating agenda, restating issues and views, eliciting reactions, offering observations, and diagnosing aspects of the conflict.

Psychological Mechanisms Determining the Effectiveness of Third-Party Interventions

Although it is clear that formal third parties such as mediators may perform a variety of functions (and may even perform several of these simultaneously), it is equally clear that to do so effectively there must be sufficient trust in their integrity and confidence in their ability for them to execute this role. * * *

As reported by Kressel's respondents, the trust factor seems to embody at least two different dimensions: the safeguarding of privileged information and the commitment to being "a servant of the parties and of nobody else * * *". It was also reported that trust in a mediator generally required a demonstrable concern on his part with the particular dispute, and an empathic, nonjudgmental understanding of each side's position. With respect to the ability factor, the interviewees indicated that among the main criteria often employed in assessing a mediator's competency are manifest signs that he understands the intricacies of the bargaining process, the real issues at stake, and the relationship between the parties.

We view "trust in integrity" and "confidence in ability" as major factors that mediate responsiveness to third party interventions. We therefore hypothesize that *other things being equal, the greater the trust and confidence in a third party, the more effective his interventions are likely to be.* Stated somewhat differently, the strength of the pressures toward agreement generated by third parties will be a function of the amount of trust and confidence placed in them by bargainers.

A factor pointing to the necessity of trust and confidence may be extracted from the often stated view that the task of a mediator consists largely of "trying to persuade each party to accept the largest concession which the other is willing to make * * *." If, as implied by use of the word "persuade," we view third parties as influence agents, then it becomes possible—and interesting—to think of such individuals as themselves functioning in a bargaining role. Viewed in these terms, a mediator is merely another party to a bargaining relationship—one whose primary interests lie in the area of promoting agreement between the principal opponents rather than in competing for the specific outcomes which they seek.

Toward this end the mediator has a variety of devices at his disposal for promoting agreement. He may: attempt to heighten the salience of norms having to do with reciprocity, fairness, equity, social responsibility, etc.; act to protect the parties against excessive position and image loss; exercise power over the participants, as this may be derived from his legitimacy, expertise, or reputation as well as his ability to reward or punish them; and reveal alternatives that the opposing parties may have been unable to perceive by themselves.

However, in order to do any of these effectively, he must have the trust and confidence of the disputants.

To summarize briefly: Effective third party interventions generally create pressures toward agreement. These pressures drive bargainers to make concessions and narrow the differences between them, or at least to demonstrate that they have given serious consideration to alternatives to their initially preferred positions. Authoritativeness and impartiality, as these affect confidence and trust in a third party, seem to be the foundations of effective intervention. Pressures toward agreement may be strengthened by structuring the situation (physically or normatively or both) to protect against excessive position or image loss to the conceding party. This may involve the subtle provision of rewards by the third party when a desirable concession is made (such as the obtaining of a reciprocal concession from the opposing party or the giving of public praise to the conceder), or subtle threats of increased position or image loss for failure to make an appropriate concession. A third party's reward-punishment potential may be grounded in his personal prestige (e.g., his prior reputation for promoting equitable agreements), his institutional role (e.g., his status as a representative of "the people," national interests, etc.), and the opportunity he provides for bargainers to attribute their concessions to him.

QUESTIONS

1. a. There has been considerable discussion concerning the type of people who should act as principal negotiators for either side. On the basis of the materials just considered, would management do better with (1) A member of its industrial relations staff, (2) lawyer, (3) an economist or (4) a social psychologist?

   b. What accounts for the prominent role played by lawyers in the process?

   c. What background and personality traits should a good management negotiator have?

   d. Are there any special qualifications needed by a good union negotiator?

   e. What kind of person should unions seek to handle negotiations for them?

2. The XYZ Manufacturing Company has a small canteen area where employees go for lunch. It contains a machine which dispenses bottled soda pop, a cigarette machine, and a coffee machine. Traditionally, there have been no formal limits on the use of these machines. Foremen have been complaining that employees are taking too much time off to use the machines, disrupting work and causing litter. A sign stating "The machine is to be used only during

lunch time and after finishing work" has been widely ignored. Several management people want to seek a clause in the contract stating:

> Use of the machines in the canteen area is not permitted during working time, and failure to abide by this rule shall make an employee subject to discipline.

Is this a wise provision to include?

How else might you deal with this problem as a management negotiator?

ANDREW L. SANDLER, A CASE HISTORY IN NEGOTIATION STRATEGY: COLLECTIVE BARGAINING AT GENERAL ELECTRIC—BOULARISM AND THE BIRTH OF COORDINATED BARGAINING *

The struggle between unions and employees to gain the upper hand at the bargaining table has been the source of many different bargaining strategies. One of the classic management/union struggles has been the one between the unions and companies comprising the electrical products industry.

The General Electric Company has traditionally been the industry leader in collective bargaining negotiations. General Electric has put more time, effort, and money into industrial relations than almost any other company. As a result, some of the most well-known bargaining strategies have emanated from General Electric and the unions with which it bargains. Other companies in the industry typically use General Electric's collective bargaining agreements as models for their own.

General Electric first experienced unionization in 1906, when the Pattern-Makers League of North America established a local at General Electric's Schenectady, New York, plant. The informal bargaining relationship established between the Company and the Pattern-Makers ultimately spread to other General Electric facilities. General Electric prided itself on being a good employer and worked hard to preserve that image in future years.

During the depression years, General Electric employees increasingly turned to unionism for job security. The newly formed Electrical Workers Union (UE), a CIO affiliate, signed up most of those looking for a union affiliation. By 1946, the UE had over 400,000 members and represented 96% of unionized General Electric employees, fully 60% of the Company's workforce.

The year 1946 was a militant one for all unions. War-time wage and price controls were relaxed, the economy was booming and prices were rising.

It was a year when fully 10% of the country's workforce were rising. It was a year when fully 10% of the country's workforce struck their employers. Not surprisingly the UE picked this opportu-

---

* Reprinted with the permission of the author.

nity to test its strength. General Electric was unprepared for the UE's militant bargaining posture, negotiations quickly broke down and a nine week nationwide strike ensued.

The strike had a profound effect on General Electric management. The Company had always prided itself on being a fair and considerate employer. It was inconceivable to top management that it was a victim of the 1946 strike wave.

The company's reaction was articulated by one high official as follows:

> At the time   *   *   *   we looked back not only on having had the highest wage scales that were feasible and proper by all product and labor market standards, but also to our having voluntarily pioneered our employees suggestions systems in 1906, safety and health programs in 1907, pensions in 1912, savings plans in 1917, insurance in 1920, relief and labor plans in the 1930's, ambitious experiments in work and pay guarantees—including the guaranteed annual wage—in the 1930's and profit-sharing plans in the 1930's and 1940's.[1]

The Company's response was rapid. As soon as a contract was signed with the striking UE, GE President Charles Wilson, embarked on a search for someone to examine and redefine General Electric's labor relations policies. The job ultimately went to Lemuel Boulware, a General Electric Vice-President, who had managed seven affiliated companies that were uneffected by the strike. Boulware immediately set out "to correct the ridiculous situation where—despite the best of intentions and the best practices known—the company was distrusted and disapproved of by employees and neighbors in some very important matters."[2]

Boulware found that the Company's problem was in its failure to disseminate information to its workers and the community concerning the Company's contributions to the general good, and the realistic limitations on company and government largesse. He developed a comprehensive new employee and community relations program to address these shortcomings.

The keystone of the program was a new approach towards contract negotiations. Under the slogan "do good voluntarily in the balanced best interest of all," Boulware embarked on a "job marketing" program. The Company set out to identify what was most important to the employees and to incorporate these perceived employee "needs" into the contract GE would offer. The goal, according to Boulware, was to come "as close as we could possibly come to an exact copy of the principles and practices we had long used with comparative good success in meeting our customers' requirements for (1) the basic material rewards and (2) the extra human satisfactions."[3]

1. L. Boulware, *The Truth About Boulwarism* 18 (1969).

2. Id at 3.

3. Id at 24.

The most controversial part of this new approach to employee relations was its effect on collective bargaining. In preparation for the first set of negotiations under Boulware in the spring of 1948, the Company went directly to the workers for their input, offered the union representatives opportunities for discussion, and considered GE's economic position and expectations. As Boulware tells it:

> [W]hen it finally seemed evident that all the individual items of current interest, together with all the available related information of real significance, had been fully considered and discussed to the point of exhausting all the possibilities, we made a comprehensive and complete offer. This offer was made up of that combination of gives and takes—that combination of eliminations, continuances, and additions—which would constitute the appropriate "new model" job at what the market indicated was the right market price in pay and benefits.[4]

Having arrived at this "comprehensive and complete offer," Boulware presented it to the union as *the* GE offer. At the same time, GE launched a direct appeal to its employees, extolling the virtues of the benefits package being offered.

While General Electric concentrated its energy and resources on preparing for collective bargaining negotiations, the union became engaged in a fight for its survival. The wave of strikes in 1946 had caused a great furor. A congressional investigation of the causes of the 1946 strike quickly came to focus on communist domination of the union movement.

Due to heavy government pressure, the CIO attempted to purge communists from leadership positions in affiliated unions. UE resistance to these efforts led to its expulsion from the CIO in 1949. At that time, the CIO established a rival union, the International Union of Electrical, Radio and Machine Workers (IUE).

As a result of the expulsion, open season was declared on UE membership and the IUE, IBEW and UAW began raiding the outlaw union of its members. It was a terrible time for the union movement as the widespread interunion fighting and agitation drained union coffers, brought new organizing to a standstill, and prevented effective preparation for the key collective bargaining negotiations ahead.

At the time the 1948 negotiations began, the UE was already caught up in the series of events which would lead to its expulsion from the CIO. When GE presented the union with its "take it or leave it" offer, the Union accepted, thankful that the Company did not take greater advantage of its weakened position.

Over the course of the next few years the union raiding wars continued to take their toll. The Company used this time of almost complete domination of collective bargaining negotiations to further improve and refine "Boulwarism", as its industrial relations policy came to be called.

4. Id at 87.

The 1956 negotiations were as amicable as such a process could be. The economy was booming and General Electric's sales were envied throughout the industry. The Company offered its employees a generous five year contract with provisions to reopen the contract and deal with certain job security issues in 1958. The IUE, which had by this time supplanted the UE as GE's dominant union was still preoccupied with solidifying its position, and happily accepted.

The negotiations proved to be the last that Lemuel Boulware actively participated in. In 1957, Boulware turned over his negotiating responsibilities to others, remaining a GE Vice-President and special consultant until 1960, when in compliance with General Electric's mandatory retirement policy, he left the Company.

Although Boulware absented himself from future negotiations, Boulwarism remained General Electric's bargaining strategy. It was destined to itself become a prime issue in future negotiations. The new leadership of the IUE, led by James Carey, believed that Boulwarism itself was preventing them from reaching satisfactory agreements with GE. They believed that they could only achieve equality at the bargaining table by forcing GE to abandon Boulwarism. This remained their main goal for the next twelve years.

The IUE's President, James Carey, first came to national attention in 1933 when he led the employees of the Philco Radio-Philadelphia Battery Works out on a strike that resulted in recognition for his local and a strong collective bargaining agreement for the workers. Shortly thereafter, Carey became President of the newly formed UE.

Carey was a very poor administrator and his failure to focus proper attention on the internal administration of the rapidly growing union created a leadership vacuum. While Carey was traveling around the country in an effort to enhance his personal stature as a national labor leader, others stepped in and took control of the day-to-day operation of the UE. In 1941, the UE's Secretary Treasurer Jules Emspak and Director of Organization James Matles rejected Carey's efforts to rid the organization of communists. In the bitter presidential election campaign that followed, they engineered Carey's defeat by Albert Fitzgerald, a local union leader.

CIO President Philip Murray placed Carey at the helm of the new IUE in 1949, and by 1958 the IUE had successfully raided 75% of the UE's membership. With Carey back at the table and Boulware no longer there, the 1958 negotiations marked the beginning of a new era in General Electric/Union relations.

The Company's commitment to Boulwarism and Carey's insistance that it be abandoned created an instant impasse in negotiations. Decreased demand for GE products caused heavy layoffs, creating enormous pressure on union leadership to negotiate better job security provisions. The IUE demanded many modifications including a very expensive new supplemental unemployment benefits package. General Electric balked at any such modifications, feeling that the 1956 contract was very generous and that the Union must be shown that Boulwarism was to remain in effect.

Carey quickly came to the conclusion that a strike was the only way to get the Company to modify its position. Carey could not muster the two-thirds "yes" vote that the IUE constitution required for a strike to be called and was thus forced to settle on the Company's terms. He immediately began planning for the 1960 negotiations. He left little doubt about his future plans, telling a "Steel Magazine" interviewer "I owe GE a strike".

As 1960 approached, GE and the unions prepared for difficult negotiations. For the first time since the UE was expelled from the CIO in 1949, the unions, led by the IUE, were in a position to negotiate with some leverage. The GE labor relations staff spent 18 months preparing for the negotiations. Carey attempted to consolidate his position and enlisted the Industrial Union Department (IUD) of the AFL–CIO in an attempt to form a coalition of GE unions. A tentative alliance was formed among the UAW, IBEW, AFTE and Carey's IUE.

Negotiations between GE and the IUE began on July 19, 1960, almost a full month prior to the contractually designated date. The early sessions were devoted to the problems of "employment security." Two things became quickly apparent. First, GE had no intention of abandoning "Boulwarism" and second, Carey was spoiling for a strike and was not going to accept any company offer—no matter what it included.

As the deadline approached each side used the media to convey to the public the impression that the other side was intransigent and that its own proposals were reasonable. Negotiations were interrupted for the IUE convention in September. When they resumed one week later, the IUE attempted to bring in various public officials to mediate. The Company rejected outside intervention, accepting only the services of the Federal Mediation Service. As the October strike date approached Carey suffered a major setback when, one by one, local units of the IAM and UAW accepted the GE offer.

Cracks in IUE unity also began to develop. Carey gambled that a strike would bring solidarity and the IUE walked out on October 2nd as Carey had promised they would. Carey's hopes for a unified front were immediately shattered when the large Schenectady local remained on the job. Schenectady did not join the strike until three days later and never exhibited much enthusiasm for the walk-out. AFL–CIO support of the strike was lukewarm. Other union leaders had been urging Carey to hold off until after the national elections, so that all efforts could be concentrated on electing John F. Kennedy and pro-labor Congress. The strike was a dismal failure and the final blow came on October 20th, when the IUE's Westinghouse locals announced an agreement with Westinghouse on terms very similar to those GE was offering. Without the support of the other unions and reinforcement from its own Westinghouse locals, the IUE could not maintain a credible strike. The Union was forced to call off the strike without receiving any increased benefits. A. H. Raskin of *The*

New York Times called the abortive strike "the worst setback any union has received in a nationwide strike since WWII." [5]

As a result of the 1960 strike fiasco the General Electric unions became embroiled in a new set of internal struggles.

Carey's stature suffered immeasurable harm in 1960 and his militant opposition to General Electric's 1963 offer was rejected by the IUE Board which promptly agreed to terms with the Company.

Sensing the weakness of the IUE, the UAW and IBEW began campaigns to swallow up the IUE by merger.

In a bitter 1964 election campaign, Paul Jennings, an IUE local president successfully challenged Carey. It took Labor Department intervention, however, to get him installed in office because the Carey forces had rigged the election.

Soon after Jennings' election, preparation began for the 1966 negotiations. The picture confronting the IUE and other industry unions was bleak. While industry employment was steadily rising, only one in four new production workers were union members; industry wage scales were lagging behind those in other durable goods industries; other employers were successfully using the General Electric agreements as models for their own union contracts; and the IUE's lawsuit charging that Boulwarism was a refusal to bargain in good faith and thus an unfair labor practice under the NLRA was meandering through the federal courts with no chance of being decided until after the 1966 negotiations were completed.

It was clear that the unions needed to develop a strategy to effectively combat Boulwarism at the bargaining table. At the urging of Jennings, AFL–CIO President George Meaney threw his support behind the formation of a "Committee on Collective Bargaining" (CCB) to explore cooperative efforts among AFL–CIO affiliated unions representing electrical manufacturing industry employees. The CCB was formed by seven unions: IUE, Machinists (IAM), UAW, Allied Industrial Workers of America (AIW), IBEW, Sheet Metal Workers (SMWIA) and American Federation of Technical Employees (AFTE).

Its initial function was to coordinate union preparation for the 1966 negotiations with the General Electric Company and the Westinghouse Electric Corporation.

Conspicuously missing from the CCB membership was the UE. Still an outcast independent union, the UE was not eligible for membership. Under Jennings' direction, however, the IUE informally shared information with the UE.

A steering committee was immediately formed under the chairmanship of David Lasser, an IUE executive. The Industrial Union Department (IUD) of the AFL–CIO, which under the leadership of Walter Reuther had long promoted coordinated bargaining, praised the formation of the CCB and offered its complete support. At its 1965 convention, the IUD signaled the importance the whole labor

    5. "G.E.'s Labor Formulation," The
New York Times, October 25, 1960, p. 8.

movement attached to the CCB efforts, adopting a resolution in support of the GE-Westinghouse coalition which stated in part:

> * * * nowhere are a joint program and a common front more necessary than in dealing with General Electric and Westinghouse. If either or both of these corporations are permitted to maintain substandard conditions, or to flout the legal obligation to bargain collectively, they will exert a drag upon the whole field of collective bargaining. Therefore, no negotiation in 1966 will be more important than those involving GE and Westinghouse.[6]

Coordination began in earnest and a unity theme was repeatedly stressed. In March of 1966 the original seven CCB members were joined by the American Flint Glass Workers (AFGW) at a meeting which became known as the "unity conference", and which concluded with a pledge of mutual cooperation, mutual understanding, and mutual support. A series of grass roots meetings were scheduled to spread the theme of cooperation. At GE this took the form of a "unity day" where cooperation was pledged and unity buttons were distributed.

While the unions prepared to present a unified front, General Electric set about preparing for the 1966 negotiations in its accustomed manner. The Company arrived at its offer and developed plans to explain the virtues of the offer to its employees and the general public. The Company also decided that it would not under any circumstances negotiate with more than one union at a time.

On several occasions in late 1965 and early 1966, the CCB Steering Committee offered to meet with GE negotiators. The CCB letters to GE pointed out that:

> since our eight unions have a jointly-developed approach on how to create the most successful type of meetings and since your management has a national policy on this matter, the simplest and most effective solution is a conference between us.[7]

GE repeatedly refused to engage in any such discussions. One letter addressed to the IUE explained that:

> As you know, we are very receptive to appropriate prenegotiation discussions with the IUE, but as we have already elaborated before in greater detail to you and your associates, we do not intend to participate in any eight-union coalition discussions or in any other steps in the direction of industry-wide bargaining.[8]

The IUE responded in a letter conveying its disappointment with the Company decision that it would not engage in a joint meeting with representatives of CCB member unions. The letter concluded by promising to drop the matter in the hope that negotiations could begin. GE promptly replied by offering to meet with the IUE on May 4, 1966. When GE negotiators entered this meeting, representa-

---

6. 1965 Proceedings, Industrial Union Department, AFL–CIO, 6th Constitutional Convention, Washington D.C., at 113–114.

7. See General Electric Co. v. NLRB, 71 L.R.R.M. 2418 (1969).

8. General Electric, "Employer Relations News," April 4, 1966.

tives of the seven other unions were present. Each was careful to state that he was there representing the IUE. The IUE insisted that it was merely exercising its right to select its own bargaining representatives. "In the face of this subterfuge" the GE negotiators recessed the meeting "until such time as the IUE is ready to deal with us in a sincere effort to form GE–IUE prenegotiation sub-committees." [9]

Shortly after adjournment of this meeting both sides filed unfair labor practice suits with the NLRB. The Board's general counsel granted the unions' petition and requested the District Court to issue an order enjoining GE from refusing to bargain with the committee chosen by the IUE. District Court Judge Marvin Frankel issued the order after four days of hearings. On Appeal, the Circuit Court dissolved the injunction, criticizing the use of such an extraordinary remedy.[10]

Supreme Court Associate Justice John Harlan subsequently stayed the Circuit Court decision, pending Supreme Court review.[11] Thus, GE was forced back to the bargaining table with the "travelling circus" that the IUE chose to represent it.

Bargaining proceeded slowly, the CCB members denounced the Company's offer as "completely unacceptable." A review committee was established, with George Meaney as chairman, to evaluate any new offer from GE. The parties fought a media war, extolling the virtues in their respective positions and villifying the other side for its intransigence. On October 2nd, just four hours before the strike deadline, President Johnson intervened and summoned the parties to Washington. A two week extension was agreed to and three Cabinet members were brought into the negotiations. A settlement was reached twelve days later, and the UE signed an almost identical contract with General Electric two days later.

The results of the 1966 negotiations were heartening to the unions. They had maintained a cohesive front and found in coordinated bargaining an effective method to combat Boulwarism. Further, with the assistance of government intervention they had forced General Electric to modify its initial offer—thereby violating a fundamental element of the Boulware approach.

General Electric management viewed the 1966 negotiations differently. Government and court intervention had forced the Company to negotiate with the "union coalition" and pressured it into an earlier settlement than it would have preferred. In spite of this result, the Company felt Boulwarism had been preserved, the final agreement being little more than the shifting around of benefits that the Company had always engaged in.

---

9. BNA, Daily Labor Report, May 14, 1966 at p. A–2.

10. McLeod v. General Electric Co., 63 L.R.R.M. 2065 (2d Cir. 1966).

11. The Supreme Court later refused to review the NLRB decision, ruling that the decision was moot since a subsequent agreement had been reached by the litigants.

Both sides waited anxiously for NLRB and court deliberation of the various unfair labor practice charges to be completed. The unions hoped to make their perceived victory complete by having Boulwarism declared a violation of the NLRA and General Electric hoped for Supreme Court support of their position that they need not bargain with the CCB "travelling circus" each time a specific union's contract came up for renegotiation.

In 1969, the Supreme Court finally disposed of the coordinated bargaining issue. The Court ruled that the union could choose whatever representatives it wished and that General Electric had committed an unfair labor practice by refusing to bargain with the unions' designated representatives.[12]

While the fate of Boulwarism as a collective bargaining strategy was still winding its way through the courts, the unions, bolstered by judicial support of coordinated bargaining set out to defeat Boulwarism at the bargaining table. Meticulous planning for the 1969 negotiations began. The IUD developed a teletype system to insure rapid and accurate communications between the coordinated unions. The IUE's Jennings solidified his position as the CCB's leader and Meaney relaxed restrictions on coordination with non-affiliated unions, allowing the Teamsters, UAW and UE to join the coordinated effort. A large strike fund was amassed and plans were developed to pressure the government to support the employees in the event of a long strike.

General Electric also carefully planned for the eventuality of a strike. The Company elicited a public promise of non-intervention from the Nixon Administration and built up enough inventory to get through the Christmas shopping period in the event of a long strike. Just as negotiations were to begin the Company released its offer accompanied by an elaborate public relations campaign explaining to employees and the general public the attributes of the offer and the reasons why GE neither could nor would offer more.

The unions just as publicly rejected the offer as inadequate. It became readily apparent that a strike was unavoidable. As one commentator noted "The issue was far deeper * * * than the amount or timing of wage increases over the following three years. The showdown over Boulwarism was at hand." [13]

A last minute union request for arbitration was rejected by the Company and on October 26, 1969, the strike began. Both sides dug in for a long work stoppage. One month later the AFL–CIO announced the formation of a GE Strike Fund, contributions reached two million dollars and the UAW added another million. A consumer boycott against the General Electric Company was announced and great pressure was brought to bear on elected officials to encourage public welfare agencies to assist the workers and their families. GE

12. McLeod v. General Electric Co., 71 L.R.R.M. 2418 (1969).

13. J. Kuhn, *"Electrical Products,"* in *Collective Bargaining: Contempora-* *ry American Experience* 245 (G. Sommers, Ed. 1980).

countered with a huge advertising campaign explaining its position and hammering home the idea that a loss of business due to the boycott would translate into a loss of jobs. GE also used its influence to prevent the use of public funds to support the strikers.

By January, everybody was feeling the effects of the strike. General Electric's production fell to 10%, the IUE and other unions were coming to the end of their financial resources, and employees were finding it impossible to continue to support their families on the meager strike funds they were receiving. Also, the many communities in which General Electric was the primary employer were beginning to see their economic base crumble. On January 8, 1970, the Director of the Federal Mediation and Conciliation Service entered the negotiations and pressed the parties to settle. An agreement was soon reached.

The terms of the agreement ultimately reached could not be characterized as a great victory for either side. What the agreement did indicate was that Boulwarism was no longer a viable bargaining strategy [14] and that coordinated bargaining was not going to give unions the kind of power at the bargaining table that Boulwarism had once given the Company. Rather, the industry was entering an era which was to be characterized by a balance of power at the bargaining table.

The tone that future General Electric-Union negotiations were to take was clearly signalled by the statement of the Company's new chief negotiator, C. R. Greley, at the outset of the 1973 negotiations. He stated:

> General Electric will proceed according to a different kind of negotiations process this year, adopting a procedure that permits more give and take, more flexibility, and one that attempts to achieve solutions that strike a balance between the priorities of the company and the union. [15]

The 1973 negotiations proved to be difficult. The gloomy economic and industry forecasts convinced the Company of the need to tighten its belt. Actual and expected layoffs made job security the union's priority concern. An agreement to extend the deadline staved off a strike and led to a contract that none were happy with but all could live with under the dismal economic situation confronting the industry. The 1973 negotiations were most noticeable for what they lacked. No vituperative exchanges in the media accompanied these negotiations. They seemed to be characterized by grudging respect among the one-time virulent antagonists. After the contract was signed, IUE President Jennings commented, "GE has now entered the Twentieth Century." [16]

The 1976 negotiations at General Electric were low key and business-like. The issues were a 12.3% industry unemployment rate and

---

14. Boulwarism was later found to violate the NLRA's requirement of good faith bargaining at NLRB v. General Electric Co., 418 F.2d 736 (1970).

15. "G.E. takes a new Path" Unity III 2, (1973).

16. Business Week, June 16, 1973 at 92.

rising inflation. A mutually acceptable COLA formula was devised and some progress was made on job security provisions, the issue that continued to be the most difficult one for the parties to resolve.

The 1979 negotiations followed the pattern established in 1973 and 1976. Negotiations proceeded in a quiet and professional manner, with job security again proving to be a most difficult issue to resolve.

The 1979 negotiations may well have provided a sneak preview of what the pattern of negotiations in the 1980's will be. The unions' main concern was General Electric's construction of new production facilities in non-union areas and the effect the transfer of much of its existing production to these new facilities was having on the availability of jobs for union members.

It remains to be seen what union response this new Company tactic will provoke, but it is certain to shatter the relatively harmonious collective bargaining that has existed since 1972.

N.L.R.B. v. GENERAL ELECTRIC CO.

United States Court of Appeals, Second Circuit 1970.
418 F.2d 736.

IRVING R. KAUFMAN, CIRCUIT JUDGE.

Almost ten years after the events that gave rise to this controversy, we are called upon to determine whether an employer may be guilty of bad faith bargaining, though he reaches an agreement with the union, albeit on the company's terms. * * *

* * *

The Board * * * chose to find an overall failure of good faith bargaining in GE's conduct. Specifically, the Board found that GE's bargaining stance and conduct, considered as a whole, were designed to derogate the Union in the eyes of its members and the public at large. This plan had two major facets: first, a take-it-or-leave-it approach ("firm, fair offer") to negotiations in general which emphasized both the powerlessness and uselessness of the Union to its members, and second, a communications program that pictured the Company as the true defender of the employees' interests, further denigrating the Union, and sharply curbing the Company's ability to change its own position.

* * *

GE argues forcefully that it made so many concessions in the course of negotiations—concessions which, under section 8(d), it was not obliged to make—that its good faith and the absence of a take-it-or-leave-it attitude were conclusively proven, despite any contrary indicia on which the Trial Examiner and the Board rely. * * *

The Company's stand, however, would be utterly inexplicable without the background of its publicity program. Only when viewed in that context does it become meaningful. We have already indicated that one of the central tenets of "The Boulware approach" is that the "product" or "firm, fair offer" must be marketed vigorously to the "consumers" or employees, to convince them that the Company, and not the Union, is their true representative.   *   *   *

The Company's refusal to withhold publicizing its offer until the Union had had an opportunity to propose suggested modifications is indicative of this attitude.   Here two interests diverged.   The command of the Boulware approach was clear: employees and the general public must be barraged with communications that emphasized the generosity of the offer, and restated the firmness of GE's position. A genuine desire to reach a mutual accommodation might, on the other hand, have called for GE to await Union comments before taking a stand from which it would be difficult to retreat.   GE hardly hesitated.   It released the offer the next day, without waiting for Union comments on specific portions.

The most telling effect of GE's marketing compaign was not on the Union, but on GE itself.   Having told its employees that it had made a "firm, fair offer," that there was "nothing more to come," and that it would not change its position in the face of "threats" or a strike, GE had in effect rested all on the expectation that it could institute its offer without significant modification.   Properly viewed, then, its communications approach determined its take-it-or-leave-it bargaining strategy.   Each was the natural complement of the other; if either were substantially changed, the other would in all probability have to be modified as well.   It is only in this context that GE's incomprehensible insistence on a January 1 starting date for the pension benefits, and the "explanations" that followed it, can be understood.

All this was brought into the open during the September 28 meeting.   Virtually on the eve of the strike, Union negotiators were searching for a way to save face by reconstituting their SUB proposal within the outlines of the Company's costs.   Far from being frivolous as the dissent seems to suggest, such last minute attempts at compromise are the stuff of which lasting accommodations and productive labor-management relations are made.   The substance of the Company's response to this effort was well put by their chief negotiator, Philip Moore:

"After all our month of bargaining and after telling the employees before they went to vote that this is it, we would look ridiculous to change it at this late date; and secondly the answer is no."

The Company, having created a view of the bargaining process that admitted of no compromise, was trapped by its own creation.   It could no longer seek peace without total victory, for it had by its own words and actions branded any compromise a defeat.

*   *   *

While it is clear that the Board is not to control the substantive terms of a collective bargaining contract, nonetheless the parties must do more than meet.   *   *   *

*   *   *

In order to avoid any misunderstanding of our holding, some additional discussion is in order. We do not today hold that an employer may not communicate with his employees during negotiations. Nor are we deciding that the "best offer first" bargaining technique is forbidden. Moreover, we do not require an employer to engage in "auction bargaining," or, as the dissent seems to suggest, compel him to make concessions, "minor" or otherwise.   *   *   *

*   *   *   We hold that an employer may not so combine "take-it-or-leave-it" bargaining methods with a widely publicized stance of unbending firmness that he is himself unable to alter a position once taken. It is this specific conduct that GE must avoid in order to comply with the Board's order, and not a carbon copy of every underlying event relied upon by the Board to support its findings. Such conduct, we find, constitutes a refusal to bargain "in fact." It also constitutes, as the facts of this action demonstrate, an absence of subjective good faith, for it implies that the Company can deliberately bargain and communicate as though the Union did not exist, in clear derogation of the Union's status as exclusive representative of its members under section 9(a).

*   *   *

Enforcement granted.

GEORGE H. HILDEBRAND, COORDINATED BARGAINING— AN ECONOMIST'S POINT OF VIEW*

I view coordinated bargaining as an attempt by unions to alter certain existing bargaining systems primarily to increase their bargaining power, that is, their ability to extract more concessions from the employers with whom they deal. Coordination as such, of course, is nothing new. It began with the city building trades in the '80s and '90s; it was introduced to the railroad industry by the operating crafts starting in 1902; and found use in West Coast pulp and paper in 1934. More recently, it has been widely extended by the Industrial Union Department of the AFL–CIO to deal with a variety of special situations in manufacturing. Even here there was ample precedent in meat packing, farm implements and aerospace.

Cooperative bargaining efforts by unions can extend all the way from tacit collusion among separately negotiating organizations to a formal alliance involving common demands, common negotiations and a common settlement.

BARGAINING PROGRAM SYSTEMS

Taking the IUD program as it has evolved since April 1964, one can identify the following typical situations: (1) Several locals affiliated with one or more international unions and bargaining traditionally on a plant-by-plant basis join together in an effort to obtain joint com-

---

* George H. Hildebrand, "Coordinated Bargaining—An Economist's Point Of View," 19 Labor Law Journal 524 (1968);   ©1968 by George H. Hildebrand. Reprinted by permission.

pany-wide bargaining. Such attempts were made with a mixture of success and failure in American Home Products, Wilson Sporting Goods, and Union Carbide. (2) Two or more international unions, bargaining nationally with multi-plant concerns frame common demands, perhaps in alliance with locals of other unions, to strenthen their bargaining position by an effort to curtail the employer's ability to use divide-and-conquer tactics. An example here would be the coalition formed by IUE, IBEW, and many plant locals of other unions, to deal with General Electric and Westinghouse. (3) A key international industrial union bargaining separately at the successive stages of production in a vertically integrated company forms an alliance with a competing international and with a diverse group of craft unions in a program of common company wide demands with common expiration dates, to gain in strike effectiveness. This was done in copper under the leadership of the Steelworkers, in a coalition that started from a tradition of decentralized bargaining and that embraced the four major producers.

In all three variants, one finds bargaining systems that contain the following ingredients in varying degrees: multiple unionism, decentralized bargaining, incomplete organization of the relevant product market by any single union, and a company-wide unit of employer policymaking in bargaining and labor relations. Numerous other cases correspond generally to this pattern.

BARGAINING EFFECTIVENESS

I now venture the following hypothesis: as a general proposition, the effort to introduce coordinated bargaining is an admission of union weakness under the systems hitherto prevailing. The common employer view, that coordination is a bid for more union power is correct. But the source lies more in weakness than in existing strength.

To be an effective bargainer in behalf of its pecuniary and regulatory purposes, any union seeks to extend its organizational reach to embrace all sources of supply for a common product market. It must encompass all competing plants of a given employer, and all competing employers in the market. This is the meaning of the traditional slogan, "taking wages out of competition." Only when wages and benefits are made uniform for all competing sources of product supply can a given union adequately check the ability of buyers to substitute against the plants most favorable to the union.[2]

Consider now some of the types of bargaining weakness which coordination seeks to overcome. (1) Two or even three internationals having parallel jurisdictions may deal with different competing plants in a given industry, some of them belonging to the same employer. This is the situation in aluminum, meat packing, farm implements, and until very recently, domestic copper. Absent coordination, differential wage settlements are likely. This will widen differences be-

2. Internal union politics can be another reason for seeking wage uniformity. However, the main thrust derives from the discipline imposed by the product market.

tween high- and low-cost plants, with ensuing employment and bargaining disadvantages for certain locals. In this situation, coordination is a feasible remedy from the unions' point of view. Indeed, it becomes all the more attractive when compared to the alternative solution, the very difficult device of union merger.

(2) A given corporate giant with multiple plant operations may have some plants organized by one international, others by another, and perhaps others without any union, and these plants may be substitutes for one another as regards product lines. Collaterally, the company may also enjoy two other advantages: local plant contracts with divergent expiration dates. If there is no coordination between the unions, strikes by either one will be incomplete and largely ineffective. Even with coordination this weakness can be overcome only by seeking common expiration dates, which in turn will require a chain strike in the first instance. It should also be noted that divergent expiration dates can be a weakening agent in the parallel union case previously cited.

(3) The corporate conglomerate can be an independent source of union weakness, particularly when it is the product of recent mergers. Product diversity involves different technologies and different skill mixes. Thus there is a strong likelihood of multiple unionism, with different organizations involved according to particular plant and product line. In consequence, any long-established conglomerate is likely to have a plant-by-plant local bargaining system. Such fragmentation and decentralization make it extremely difficult to mount effective strikes. The reason is that just as product diversification is a method of hedging risks in the product market, the fractional bargaining system to which it gives rise enables the firm to reduce the overall risks deriving from strikes and from settlements with given unions.

Recent high levels of merger activity involving the formation or enlargement of conglomerate corporations exacerbates these sources of union weakness. Prior to its acquisition, a component smaller concern may have been effectively organized by a single major industrial union. After absorption, the locus of business decision-making power shifts upward to the central offices of the absorbing corporation. In this shift of managerial power, the union now finds itself a unit in a decentralized group of labor organizations, and thereby loses negotiating effectiveness. It must confront a unified management that is able to take a local strike because it has hedged its risks by assembling a product conglomerate, in the process establishing or extending a decentralized system of local unit bargaining.

In military parlance, the conglomerate corporation can fight on interior lines against a diverse set of weak opponents, each acting independently and hence vulnerable to divide-and-conquer strategies. Even without conglomerate status in production, the multiple plant concern that bargains on a local basis enjoys a similar strategic advantage, although this can be reduced if a single international has effective representation in all of the relevant plants.

A more general hypothesis to account for the recent upsurge of coordinated bargaining by industrial unions would run as follows. Large concerns typically now involve one or more of the following characteristics: multiple plants, vertical integration, horizontal integration and conglomerate production. Typically, local negotiations prevail in these contexts. The recent wave of corporate mergers has increased the incidence of these situations. Thus we have emergent here a special kind of environment for bargaining, while mergers are converting old environments to this same type. This, then, is the challenge to which coordinated bargaining is the response. To match business bargaining power, the unions are seeking increased power for themselves, by centralizing the ambient of negotiations. To do so, they must sacrifice the tradition of local negotiations and organizational autonomy, a price that they seem quite willing to pay.

I turn now to some other aspects of coordinated bargaining. Such groupings seem easiest to achieve and to maintain when the problem is simply one of getting two parallel industrial unions to concert their negotiating activities. The reason is that both organizations have strong interests in common and little to divide them. Both can gain by cooperating. The effective reach of strikes can be extended, while the attainment of common terms of settlement will reduce the problem of competition between low- and high-cost plants. By the same token, the employer loses the advantage of divide-and-conquer tactics, while his ability to take a strike and maintain partial operation is correspondingly reduced. By extending the coordination to all competing companies, the two unions can approach a kind of industry-wide bargaining, checking the adverse effects of cost-differentials created by divergent settlements caused by their acting independently. Coordination in meat packing, farm implements, and aerospace, already long established, are cases in point of durable coalitions of this type.

"Importance of Being Unimportant"

The difficulties become much greater when the attempt involves an industrial union together with a diverse collection of craft organizations. The fact that the employees jointly represented by the participating organizations are all wage workers does not mean that these employees share a set of economic interests in common—as completing rather than competing organizations, as it were. Alfred Marshall's principle that a well-situated small skilled craft can achieve a relative wage advantage if it exploits "the importance of being unimportant" can still hold—if it has the advantages of a low elasticity of technical substitution, a low ratio of its labor cost to total production cost, and, conceivably, a low elasticity of supply for cooperating factor inputs, at least where sunk capital bulks large in the production function. Why should such a craft, for example the brick masons or copper smelting, give up its independent advantage simply to join a coalition? And if it does, how long before it decides that it can do better by pulling out?

In answer, I suggest first that when a group of crafts join a coalition with an industrial union, the outcome for wage structure takes the same characteristics as if all the employees were represented by a single industrial union. The tendency will be strong to seek flat general increases; compression of the structure will begin; and at some point breakaway tendencies by the skilled groups will assert themselves. The role of the Machinists in the recent railroad shop crafts dispute is an interesting case of this very phenomenon. Years of parallel increases achieved by a craft coalition finally caused the Machinists to rebel, once they recognized how narrow their differential had become and had begun comparing the fruits of such bargaining with what Machinists were earning for comparable work in the air transport and motor bus industries.

Yet there are situations in which common collateral demands and standards of settlement do make sense and can keep this type of coalition viable. Fringe issues such as pensions and medical plans inherently lend themselves to company-wide uniformity even from the employer's point of view and even where negotiations are on a plant-by-plant basis. The problem here for the unions is to gain a greater voice in such matters. Coordination can provide this because it calls for the creation of a company-wide negotiating unit on the union side as well.

Furthermore, even wage rates conveniently can come under this logic when questions of changes in level take precedence over those of structure, as in times of inflation. In such cases, flat general increases make sense to employees of all different kinds. But here are contained the latent centrifugal forces that could ultimately disrupt the coalition. For if such increases are the continuing response to persistent inflation, the squeezing effects upon skill differentials will make it necessary for one or more crafts either to obtain special concessions or to break away and go it alone. By contrast, if the inflation is eventually halted, questions of wage structure will come back into prominence. At that point it will become extremely difficult to hold the coalition together, and centrifugal forces could well take over.[7]

Diverse coalitions with many participating organizations contain another threat to their stability, deriving from the complex pattern of separate interests involved. Coalition can be preserved only at the price of including these interests. If it is possible to compel a large employer to shift from fractional to central bargaining on a company-wide level, it seems inevitable that the agenda for such bargaining will be made lengthy and complex, and that a lower tier of complicated plant-by-plant bargaining also will become mandatory, simply to accommodate the interests of the diverse locals involved. Much of the malaise, including severe inflationary potential, of British collec-

---

7. In his very able account of coordinated bargaining in Westinghouse and General Electric, David Lasser shows that decision was made to center upon national goals such as general increases, fringes, a cost-of-living escalator, and reduction of excessive area differentials—all developed against a background of below-average gains since 1960. Questions of internal occupational wage structure apparently had no place in this situation.

tive bargaining seems to have emerged from a variant of this double-decker system, which may be a portent for this country as well.

Because one of the basic purposes of any form of coordination is to increase negotiating strength by enlarging strike effectiveness, a difficult question becomes posed: will it increase the potential for long and costly strikes?

The question permits an equivocal answer. Experience at Union Carbide and in copper suggests the affirmative, but obviously is not conclusive. Pointing in the contrary direction is the case of city newspaper, where uncoordinated fractional bargaining for years has produced the economic demands, leap-frogging the rival organizations, extremist strategical long strikes, and the demise of several dailies. Coalition brought about extreme demands and a long and very difficult strike in copper. Lack of coalition has had the same result in newspapers. If there is a moral in all this, I cannot say what it is.

The Conglomerate Enterprise

I have already suggested that mixed alliances containing a large number of participating organizations are inherently unstable. There is a big potential for dissolution, or alternatively, for converting the alliance for a more stable organizational form. By contrast, simpler coalitions or parallel industrial unions promote considerable staying power, particularly if the concerns with which they deal are predominantly in a particular industry, such as meat packing. Here however, continued success under coordination might well promote members of internationals as a simpler and more durable surrogate for cooperative activity.

On this reasoning, the conglomerate case would seem to be the most difficult from the standpoint of putting a coalition together and of keeping it intact. Such concerns usually are spread over several industries and therefore are in none. Because their product lines and technologies are diverse, they are likely to have a large and mixed collection of locals, affiliated with several different national unions, or in some cases with none. After coordination is achieved, to which international unions will these locals gravitate? No single product-oriented union may be able to pull them together, while continuing cooperation among internationals will be difficult. As Herbert Lahne has suggested, if coordination can be made to work, its focal point will have to be the conglomerate enterprise itself. The fascinating possibility then arises that this turning inwards of the interests of these diverse locals might ultimately lead them to combine in a new organizational form, an American version of Japanese "enterprise unionism." If so, we would witness a major deviation from the traditional trend toward national union affiliation, a displacement initially invoked in a shift in the environment within which a given bargaining structure functions, to which coordinated bargaining is the initial response, and a change in organizational forms as its ultimate consummation.

E. NEW APPROACHES TO BARGAINING

New approaches to bargaining are frequently suggested. Some of the more interesting new developments are discussed below. Consider the advantages and disadvantages of each system and the likelihood of its spreading.

MATTHEW KELLY, TECHNIQUES FOR MINIMIZING CRISIS *

CONTINUOUS BARGAINING ISSUE DIFFERENTIATION AND SUB COMMITTEES

Continuous bargaining, in a sense, is perhaps one of the oldest forms of labor-management efforts at minimizing bargaining crisis since it has its base in labor-management cooperative committees established under an existing agreement and these go back in one form or another to the earliest days of our collective bargaining relationship. But continuous bargaining goes beyond these joint committees and, despite its apparent connotation, does not mean round-the-clock bargaining, however desirable and useful this may prove at times. Rather, continuous bargaining is a recognition that collective bargaining is a continuous process and not like treaty-making where one meets, makes an agreement and walks away from it—not to meet again until there is another treaty to be made.

Continuous bargaining, where practiced successfully by labor and management, calls for systematic and periodic meetings of the negotiators, or their representatives, throughout the life of a contract. Operations under the contract are reviewed together and efforts at improving contract language, or removing ambiguities, or dealing with potential problems are done in these weekly or monthly sessions before they give rise to grievances and tensions.

There is, of course, nothing that is really great or new or fresh about this approach. But the will to make labor-management committees a positive force for problem-solving and minimizing the day-to-day crises which give rise to industrial conflict is, as yet, so far from general that it fits the category of being innovative.

Once continuous bargaining has been established as an on-going approach, its application is unlimited and the opportunities for creativity and imagination in the labor-management relationship are great. Some labor and managements have utilized the format to go beyond the day-to-day plant relationship and have discussed, and established among others, joint programs for furthering and improving the industry and its job opportunities; for joint public relations promoting the industry and its union-produced product; for studying the economics of the industry and the labor and product markets in particular; for joint programs with city, state and federal governments

---

* 14 Collective Bargaining, Negotiations & Contracts 451 et seq. (©BNA 1969). Reprinted by permission.

for the mutual well-being of labor and management in the industry; for the recruitment, hiring and training of the hard-core unemployed in the industry, and the like.

Continuous bargaining, where practiced, often leads to issue differentiation and a great reliance on labor-management subcommittees in contract negotiations. The negotiators, of course, need to determine and bargain the costs of the contract as a unit. But related issues like the eligibility or nature of a pension program within the negotiated cost limits; or the details of a welfare program; or the provisions of an apprentice program, and other such items, can be delegated to labor-management subcommittees. These can, and frequently do, serve as a special labor-management subcommittee endeavor which continues throughout the life of a contract.

In a sense, the parties do this frequently as joint trustees in a pension or welfare program, or as a joint apprenticeship committee, or in the educating, schooling and retraining of skilled craftsmen. More recently, however, many industries have relied on labor-management subcommittees and the continuous bargaining format to develop and administer special funds and programs for softening the impact of mechanization and automation and for the retraining of displaced employees.

It is clear that the continuous bargaining and subcommittee approach lend themselves to the consideration of many other issues which normally might be debated in cursory fashion at the bargaining table until the groundswell of resentment and the upsurge of crisis compel a more intelligent approach.

"PRE–CRISIS" MEDIATION

Some labor and managements have found it helpful in their effort to minimize crisis to turn to mediation before the crisis sets in. Here the mediator is present almost from the beginning of the negotiations and assists the parties whenever they feel he can be helpful. In a sense, then, this is a modified and ad hoc partial reliance on the mediation role in collective bargaining which gave rise to the Impartial Chairman.

The Federal Mediation and Conciliation Service is happy to be of assistance to the parties should they seek "pre-crisis" mediation and, in fact, has urged its greater use. But there are two schools of thought here and the approach is by no means widespread. Many feel strongly that the mediator should be used sparingly and that his greatest contribution is lending a fresh approach where there is truly a problem between the parties. And at this tension point in negotiations, it is preferred that the mediator be uninhibited and uncontaminated, if you will, by the prior arguments and positions of the parties which, in the final analysis, had all served to prevent rather than to arrive at an agreement.

Be that as it may, "pre-crisis" mediation, or mediation from the start of negotiations rather than at the point of deadlock, is a technique which some labor and managements have found most helpful in minimizing crisis and negotiators generally should be aware of its availability and potentials to them.

COORDINATED BARGAINING—A LABOR AND MANAGEMENT MEANS FOR CRISIS AVOIDANCE

Much has been written about coordinated bargaining as a union tool for improving its bargaining strength and we are all familiar with the now famous GE case, the recent copper negotiations and other dramatic examples of recent union efforts at coordinated bargaining. And, in some instances, as for example in the recent Washington D.C. newspaper negotiations and the subsequent commercial printing negotiations, management has found it possible to "take a leaf" out of this union experience and adopt an employer coordinated approach to give it greater bargaining strength.

But coordinated bargaining, in addition to being an innovative approach to aid either labor or management at the bargaining table, has been used as a joint undertaking of some labor and managements to lessen tensions and minimize potential for crisis. A case in point is the coordinated bargaining approach agreed to by the San Francisco newspapers and printing unions to end their recent strike.

In brief, both the San Francisco printing unions and the newspaper publishers have agreed to a coordinated bargaining approach to be followed in their next negotiations with the mutual conviction that it will lessen the possibility of strike and stoppage. The contract termination dates for each of the several printing trade union contracts with the newspaper publishers are identical. Each contract, however, remains separate and each union retains its autonomy over it with the full power of acceptance or rejection.

The publishers negotiate as an association with key bargaining representatives from each of the unions. Thus the negotiations with each of the unions are not only conducted at the same time, but all together and in the same room. All members of the bargaining team from each of the unions and the newspapers are on hand for all joint negotiating sessions. While only the "spokesman" for each of the unions and the newspapers are at the bargaining table, all bargaining team members are present in adjoining rooms for as long as the joint sessions go on both for availability for policy consultation as well as to share in the emotion, atmosphere and tension which normally surrounds a contract negotiation. Sam Kagel who served as the mediator in helping to settle the San Francisco newspaper strike has stressed that this physical presence and involvement of all bargaining team representatives is essential for the success of coordinated bargaining of this type.

Under the San Francisco newspaper coordinated bargaining approach, the joint bargaining sessions are held on economic and common industry related items only. All other bargaining issues are negotiated individually, and prior to the joint coordinated negotiations of economic items.

In order to expedite the individual negotiations on non-economic items and to prevent an undue delay or stalling on these matters, the San Francisco publishers and unions have agreed to an interesting and effective approach. If there is need for more time in the discussion of the non-economic items and the parties are falling behind the established time schedule for getting on to the joint coordinated bargaining on basic economic issues, there is the general understanding that these individual negotiations would be postponed until after agreement has been reached on the basic economic terms of a new agreement. It is further understood that if the individual parties fail to reach agreement on the unresolved non-economic items within a reasonable period of time, they would be submitted to arbitration.

Thus, in effect, there is voluntary terminal arbitration for all non-economic items which the parties are unable to resolve prior to the joint coordinated sessions or after a reasonable period. The publishers and unions, however, are free to strike or lockout if they fail to reach agreement on the economic issues being negotiated in the joint coordinated bargaining sessions.

Once an economic settlement has been arrived at in the joint coordinated bargaining sessions, it is ratified individually by each union. However, the settlement is not put into effect for any union until it has been ratified by all of the unions.

The San Francisco newspaper publishers and unions have discussed the application of a "no retroactivity" agreement in order to put the maximum pressure on all unions to ratify the jointly negotiated economic settlement promptly. Although there seems to be a willingness to adopt this approach, partial retroactivity is a possible alternative to a "no retroactivity" agreement. Under such an arrangement, retroactivity would be provided to the date of ratification of each union but in each instance would not be provided until all unions have ratified. Thus, there would be an automatic penalty for the union which ratified late but no penalty for the union which ratified promptly.

WAGE–REOPENER, IMPARTIAL CHAIRMAN AND THE "SWING" THIRD YEAR

Another interesting innovation in traditional collective bargaining adopted by labor and management to minimize the potential for crisis in negotiations takes place in the New York Hotel Industry. Here, association bargaining and joint union coordinated bargaining was first entered into in the early '30's and it has been largely successful in putting an end to the chaos and strife which marked that industry's labor-management relations in earlier years. In addition to the joint coordinated bargaining approach, the parties appointed an impartial chairman who is not only used in handling day-to-day grievances which arise during the life of a contract, but also at the time of new contract negotiations.

The parties write long-term contracts—usually three-year agreements, although four-year agreements have been agreed to on occasion—with a wage and hour reopener the last year of the contract. The parties then use the reopening period to negotiate a whole new contract, even though technically the reopening is for wages and hours for the last year of the contract only.

The Hotel employers association and the unions have been successful in this approach over the years. They are convinced that in negotiating a full year before the absolute contract termination date, they have been free of the tensions and crisis atmosphere of working against a time deadline and that this has permitted them to problem-solve and to work out their differences peacefully together. The "crutch" or "safety-valve" in this bargaining procedure, of course, is the Impartial Chairman who is empowered in the event the parties fail to reach agreement on a new contract to set the wage and hour terms for the third or fourth year of the existing contract, as the case may be. In their entire relationship, however, the Impartial Chairman in the New York Hotel Industry has never been called upon to do this and the parties have never failed to write a new agreement at the wage reopening time.

"PRE–ACTIVITY" OR EARLY SETTLEMENT EFFECTIVE UPON RATIFICATION

"Pre-Activity" is another form of innovation at the bargaining table which is directed at minimizing crisis and is really retroactivity in reverse. Early negotiations and early agreements, although far from frequent, are hardly new or unusual in collective bargaining. What is new, however, is the "pre-activating" of the terms of an early settlement upon early ratification.

Usually, where agreement is reached early by the parties, the terms of the new contract are traditionally not put into effect until the old one expires even though the ratification of the new agreement was prior to the old contract termination date. Under the "pre-activity" approach, however, the parties seek to encourage early agreement and early ratification with the additional understanding that the new contract terms will be put into effect immediately upon membership acceptance.

Although the advantages of this approach are somewhat clear, there are some limitations which need be borne in mind by negotiators and those who might consider its application in their own bargaining relationship.

In the first place, there need be some incentive on both sides of the table to put the new terms of a contract into effect early. Union members need be satisfied, of course, that the settlement is consistent with established patterns, that there isn't more to be had by waiting, and that there are some disadvantages, or risks at least, in failing to ratify early and in going beyond the contract termination date.

Employers, too, need some inducement to pay out the costs of a new contract early and before they would be required to do so legally or contractually under the old agreement. They need to feel that there are distinct advantages in encouraging ratification. This may well be in the possibilities for minimizing the potential of contract rejection and strike. Or, it might be because of the possibility of avoiding the instability and the nuisance of interferences with normal operations that often surround the extention of negotiations beyond a contract termination date. In addition, it would seem that there need be consideration of the possibility for some concessions being obtained at the bargaining table which might not have been available if early settlement had not been reached.

"PACKAGE BARGAINING" AND INDIVIDUAL EMPLOYEE INVOLVEMENT

One of the major problems in collective bargaining has been the loss of individual or member involvement through centralized bargaining structures and centralized agreements. The individual union member has been increasingly "turned off", not only because—in large industries like steel and automobiles—he doesn't feel his local plant problems are getting proper attention at the bargaining table, but also because he doesn't have much control over the "results" of the bargain.

A number of labor and managements have been mindful of this and have endeavored to minimize the crisis potential of grass-root revolt by bargaining techniques which have presented greater choice to the individual union member in determining how the "results" of the bargain are to be utilized. A classic example of a centrally negotiated contract not meeting local needs would be the provision of a new contract paid holiday, say, Lincoln's Birthday to employees in Southern plants in a wider than regional bargaining unit. Here, obviously the Southern employees would much prefer Jefferson Davis Day to a Lincoln's Birthday holiday since it is then that their children will be home from school and their friends working under locally negotiated contracts will be off.

Much friction, tension and even crisis could be avoided at the local level if there were some modification in the centralized structure of bargaining. "Package" bargaining presents just such an opportunity for the maximization of self-determination by employees of the results of the bargain. It affords a freedom of choice in determining how to "divide" the "package" that has been negotiated and this is of value whether the contract is negotiated individually, company-wide, regionally or industry-wide.

Where a contract is negotiated for, say, a $10 weekly package, management could, within limits, permit the employees to determine as a unit how much of the "package" is to go to wages and how much to welfare or pensions, additional holidays, vacations, and the like. Management, of course, is not likely to permit employees a wholly free and unlimited determination in this regard, however strong its basic desire for self-determination, even though it was within the basic cost limits of the "package". Management is concerned, properly, with the extent of employee choice since it would not normally agree to increases in non-productive time or employee benefits which might tend to encourage malingering. But within these limits, much free choice can—and should—be permitted employees through the "package" bargaining approach. The few labor and managements which have recognized this and have adopted the "packaging" approach at the bargaining table have found it to be a powerful means for minimizing the potential of bargaining crisis and maximizing individual worker involvement in, and satisfaction with, the "results" of the collective bargaining agreement.

There is much advantage in permitting the individual union member to make the decisions as to how the results of the bargaining agreement are to be apportioned directly rather than indirectly through their spokesmen and representatives at the bargaining table. There was a time, perhaps, when union officers and union negotiating representatives would have strongly questioned this procedure and resented any inference that they didn't know what their members really wanted. But many labor and managements today are jointly exploring ways by which they can put such bargaining innovations into effect and gain greater individual union member involvement and support in the collective bargaining process.

CONCLUSION

No doubt the increase of late in the number of member rejections of union negotiated agreements and the current increase in the amount of membership second-guessing of achievements by the union leadership at the bargaining table have encouraged the parties to take another look at their traditional bargaining approach and to endeavor to increase individual union member involvement—and satisfaction—to the fullest extent possible. And, despite the transitional turmoil and disruption this might occasion in the modification of established ways of bargaining, this is all to the good.

"Package" bargaining lends itself greatly to this approach, as do the other means of innovative bargaining which direct themselves to the minimization of crisis through the extension of greater individual involvement in the bargaining process and in the determination of the "results" of the bargain.

Whatever else might be said of the collective bargaining process, it is an essentially democratic process. And, whatever its failings, its improvement is dependent on finding ways to make the process more, and not less, democratic. This is why tidy legal answers to the contract rejection problem in the form of legislation to prohibit ratification and require union representatives to come to the bargaining table with the same final authority as management are essentially short-sighted and self-centered at best.

There is nothing basically wrong with the collective bargaining process and much that is wholesome and, in fact, essential to the freedoms which are the very foundation of our economic and social system. But we need continually remind ourselves of the basic purpose of the collective bargaining process and make every effort to encourage and improve it to fit the needs of the working man for whom it was basically established. Efforts of labor and management, voluntarily arrived at and mutually initiated, to minimize the potential of crisis by shifting the centralized base of decision-making wherever possible and to increase the direct involvement of the individual employee in the results of the bargain cannot help but strengthen the process and ensure its durability and value in the years ahead.

ELLIOT BREDHOFF, NEW METHODS OF BARGAINING AND DISPUTE SETTLEMENT *

Although there has not been a basic steel strike since 1959, the possibility of a strike has led to a "boom and bust" production cycle every negotiating year. Steel customers, fearful that a strike may develop and cut off their supply of steel, begin purchasing excessive quantities of steel, much of it from foreign producers, long in advance of a possible steel strike.

CONSEQUENCES OF A STRIKE

The unhappy consequences were four-fold:

(1) If no strike occurred, customers did not need steel for several months and massive numbers of employees would be laid off. For example, in 1971, 100,000 Steelworkers were laid off, some even before the deadline, and the rest right after the close of negotiations. Many remained laid off for seven or eight months.

(2) The American balance of payments was adversely affected because steel customers built at least part of their stockpiles through the purchase of foreign steel. In addition, the inroads made by the foreign steel producers during the stockpiling season tend to be permanent. In many cases foreign steel mills demand long term commitments before selling to American customers. Thus, in 1972, steel imports remained very close to their 1971 level of over 18 million tons, indicating that new customers won by the foreign steel producers during the 1971 negotiations continued to give them business.

(3) The industry incurred substantial extra expenses in connection with the inventory buildup from the starting-up of marginal facilities and the scheduling of considerable overtime. These sums could have been better used to benefit employees as well as the companies.

(4) The industry's incentive to reach a meaningful collective bargaining solution was reduced, and its willingness to incur a strike was increased, by knowledge that the demand for steel

* This article appeared in the *Proceedings* of New York University's 27th Annual Conference on Labor, published by Matthew Bender & Co., Copyright © 1975, New York University. Reprinted with the permission of the author and of the Institute of Labor Relations at New York University.

would inevitably be light in the months following such a solution, and striking employees (unlike those laid off following a settlement) were not entitled to supplemental unemployment benefits financed by the companies.

It was apparent that stronger measures were required to prevent the stockpiling phenomenon which reached records levels in the succeeding negotiating periods in 1963 (reopener) and 1965. In 1967, well in advance of the scheduled termination date, the parties seriously flirted with the only solution destined to work; an advance agreement that should negotiations fail to produce a settlement, the outcome would be arbitration rather than an industry strike. Unfortunately, the 1967 effort foundered, not over that basic principle, as both parties recognized its desirability, but over inability to agree upon means for translating that principle into reality. Thus, the steel companies were unwilling to accept certain preconditions which the Union regarded as essential if it were to surrender its right to strike.

The companies' proposal in 1967 was to negotiate without preconditions or guarantees. But, the union sensed considerable disquiet about an open surrender of the right to strike. Employees, after all, had come to recognize the strike weapon as their key vehicle for attaining substantial economic and contractual improvements. To surrender that weapon simply for an adjudicated solution in the event of impasse was believed to be contrary to the membership's wishes.

Of course, rational arguments could be made that the employees were likely to do as well through arbitration as through a more traditional round of negotiating with the strike weapon. However, certain psychological factors deter employee acceptance of these arguments. Many employees, rightly or wrongly, see a vast gulf between their interests and life-styles and those of arbitrators, whose education and economic levels differ from their own. To place one's economic future in those hands, without more, would be a traumatic step for the average worker.

In addition, employees derive an important sense of identity and pride from the knowing that they have an economic weapon, the strike, which their employer respects. After three years of working under a system whereby management directs and the employee obeys, the cyclical opportunity to deal with management as an equal, and even threaten to bring it to its knees, is important to the worker's self-respect. Thus, more than a rational demonstration that arbitration is "as good as" the strike weapon was needed to convince employees that such an innovation is in their interest.

It is valuable to analyze the pre-conditions which, because missing in 1967, led to the ultimate inability to reach agreement upon arbitration as a substitute for the right to strike. As will be seen, this year's success has resulted from the ENA's provision of pre-conditions lacking in 1967.

NEGOTIATION OF THE ENA AND DESCRIPTION
OF ITS PROVISIONS

The most recent agreements in the basic steel industry, covering approximately 385,000 employees, were to expire August 1, 1974. More than a year and one-half before that date, the union and the companies began serious discussions of possible solutions to their dilemma. These discussions culminated in the ENA, agreed to *voluntarily* in late March, 1973, a full 16 months prior to the contract expiration date. As will be seen, the essence of the agreement, procedurally, was to substitute binding arbitration, if necessary, as the final step of the negotiation process for the traditional weapons of the strike and lockout.

ENA and Collective Bargaining

Before proceeding to the provisions of the agreement, momentary reflection on the relationship between the Experimental Negotiating Agreement and the hallowed institution of *free* collective bargaining would be helpful. This institution cannot function properly or equitably without the right to invoke economic force. Compulsory arbitration and other government restrictions on the right to strike would sound the death-knell for free collective bargaining, and the industrial democracy it makes possible. Without a doubt, considerations such as these prompted President Eisenhower to proclaim that there are worse societal ills than strikes, for example, the loss of freedom itself inherent in prohibiting the right to strike.

Thus, a fundamental credo of the labor movement, and of progressive management as well, is that the right to strike (or lockout) must be preserved inviolate. The question then arises whether violence is done to this fundamental credo when parties agree to eschew economic force and substitute voluntary arbitration as the terminal point of contract negotiations. Does schizophrenia begin to set in at that juncture?

The author does not believe so. The right to use economic force carries with it the concomitant obligation to exercise it responsibly, sparingly, and only when no other means of arriving at settlements are feasible. Because of the inevitable losses and economic distortions entailed in many strikes and lockouts, parties to a collective bargaining relationship owe it to themselves and the public to delimit using these weapons to the greatest extent possible.

Utilization of *voluntary* arbitration as a terminal negotiating facility is one significant method of achieving this end without infringing on the overriding *right* to engage in economic battle, if this method does not satisfy both parties.

The key is in the word voluntary. So long as the parties preserve among themselves, without governmental interference, the freedom to revert to use of their economic power in a future negotiation, utilization of voluntary arbitration does not undercut the indispensable ingredient of free collective bargaining. The desirability of waiving the strike or lockout in favor of voluntary grievance arbitration during a contract term is recognized and accepted. In effect the parties to a voluntary interest arbitration arrangement are deferring, for a period longer than the term of a particular contract, the possible need to resort to strike or lockout in connection with future negotiations.

The Experimental Negotiating Agreement and Its Guarantees

The essential feature of the Experimental Negotiating Agreement is that there would not be a nationwide strike or lockout if the parties failed to agree on the terms of new collective bargaining contracts. Instead, nationwide disputes would be submitted to an Impartial Arbitration Panel for solution. However, there would be a right to strike at the plant level in support of local collective bargaining issues. Because customers knew that there could not be a nationwide steel strike, an absence of stockpiling in 1973 and 1974 was anticipated.

In consideration for this understanding, the companies agreed to important benefits for their employees. The minimum guarantees included in the ENA were:

(1) *Bonus.* Each member having employee status as of August 1, 1974, would receive a $150 bonus, "in consideration of the contribution made by employees to stability of steel operations * * * ."

The companies agree to this bonus in recognition of the production savings anticipated from the avoidance of stockpiling.

The union understandably felt that the employees, whose surrender of their ultimate economic weapon was the direct cause of this financial benefit to the companies, should share in that financial benefit, and the bonus reflects that sharing. Reluctance of the companies to commit themselves to such a sharing in 1967 was a significant reason for the union's decision to reject the arbitration approach at that time.

(2) *The "guaranteed" wage increase.* There was *no* limit to the amount of wage increase, or any other benefit, which the Union could seek in negotiations. The agreement *did*, however, provide a guaranteed "floor," which employees were assured of receiving regardless of what developed in negotiations.

(3) *Cost of living adjustment.* The Agreement provided that the cost of living adjustment would continue throughout the three-year agreement. There will be no "floor" or "ceiling" on cost of living adjustments which can become payable during the 1974 agreement.

(4) *Protection of certain important contractual provisions.* There are certain fundamental safeguards in the collective bargaining agreements which each side wanted to insulate and preserve. Accordingly, the ENA listed a series of issues which could not be submitted to the Impartial Arbitration Panel. These provisions, in addition to the wage, bonus and cost of living provisions

described above, included: (a) the local working conditions provisions; (b) the union shop and checkoff provisions; (c) the no strike and no lockout provisions; and (d) the management rights provisions.

Thus, the 1973 solution, by providing a guaranteed minimum economic settlement, a major pre-condition missing in 1967, was designed to overcome the natural employee reluctance described above.

Right to Strike Over Local Plant Issues Retained

Another crucial ingredient of the 1973 solution, lacking in 1967, was retention of the right to strike over local plant issues such as past practices, scheduling, parking lots, lunchrooms and coffee breaks, etc. While the parties were committed to arbitration of any company-wide issues which could not be resolved, they reserved the right to strike (or lockout) at individual plants over local issues related solely to that plant. This feature was especially attractive to the employees.

Local issues are, of course, considerably important to employees. Frequently, those at a particular plant view them with greater concern than industry-wide economic or contractual issues. During the past several negotiations, the parties have created elaborate procedures, and made enormous progress, toward resolving the vast majority of local issues. A small number, however, including some deemed important at specific locations, have remained problems at the conclusion of overall negotiations.

Despite continual improvement in resolving local issues, the feeling persisted among many employees that these issues received inadequate attention in the past. The industry-wide format for dealing with the main issues led some to believe that local issues were deemphasized. Additionally, the traditional view that any steel strike would be industry-wide, rather than plant-wide, heightened the employees' feeling that, when the crunch came, local issues would receive secondary attention.

The ENA elevated the status of local issues in the bargaining process. By establishing the possibility of single plant strikes, and making local issues the sole permissible ground for such strikes, it assured that both sides would work hard to solve their local problems. Moreover, by retaining a right to strike over at least some issues, the ENA provided psychological satisfactions, which employees derive from having a cyclical opportunity to deal with management on equal terms.

Both parties felt confident that the number of local issues strikes would be relatively few. The reasons were (i) the improved track record on settling local issues in the last few rounds of negotiations, (ii) the additional incentive for resolving local issues generated by the reservation of the right to strike or lockout, and (iii) the careful procedures provided for rank and file and International Union authorization before a local issues strike may occur. Thus, not only was there assurance against a nationwide strike, but also there was every prospect the number of individual plant shutdowns, if any, would be small.

Finally, the pre-conditions described served an important function beyond the specific substantive issues covered. For, in the eyes of the employees, they were a significant and tangible demonstration that management was not trying to weaken or undermine the union, or seeking a diversionary means to obtain a "cheap" settlement.

An Experiment In Voluntary Arbitration

One additional factor bearing on employee acceptance deserves mention. The parties have had limited prior experience with interest arbitration in the area of incentives. In the 1968 negotiations, the difficult issues of incentive coverage and yield seemed irreconcilable and threatened to prevent a peaceful settlement. At the zero hour, the parties agreed to submit these issues to arbitration, if a study committee failed to resolve them. In a sense the parties were experimenting with voluntary arbitration as a terminal facility on one subject, even though they had failed to agree in 1967 on a broader voluntary arbitration arrangement. Fortunately, the experiment was successful. The incentive issues went to arbitration in 1969 and the award was, generally, well received by the employees. No doubt, it was influential in building employee confidence in a voluntary arbitration experiment.

The Course of National Negotiations

The Agreement provided that on or before February 1, 1974, a full six months prior to expiration of the current agreements, the Union and the steel companies would begin negotiations at the national level, and try to reach agreement on the terms of a new contract by April 15, 1974. Particular issues not resolved by then could be submitted by either party to the Impartial Arbitration Panel, which had authority to render a "final and binding decision" on such issues. This Panel had one Union representative, one representative of the companies, and three impartial arbitrators selected by the parties, at least two of whom were to be thoroughly familiar with collective bargaining agreements in the steel industry.

The Impartial Arbitration Panel would begin to hear disputes in May 1974 and would have to decide by July 10. The Union and companies would then attempt to implement the panel's decision, but if unable to do so by July 20, the panel would take such action as required to implement its decision by July 31, 1974.

Thus, at the time the ENA was agreed to in March, 1973, a full 16 months prior to the contract expiration date, the parties and the world, particularly and most importantly steel consumers, knew that new three-year agreements in the basic steel industry would definitely be consummated without an industry-wide strike or lockout, guaranteeing freedom from such at least until August 1, 1977.

Reaction to ENA

As Steelworkers President I. W. Abel stated on March 29, 1973, the day the ENA was agreed to:

"We have today embarked on an unprecedented experiment that we think will prove there is a better way for labor and management to negotiate contracts.

*   *   *

"The new bargaining procedure will not only relieve both sides of the pressures of a potential shutdown but also offers us a genuine opportunity to achieve results equal to those obtainable when the threat of a strike exists.

"We have carefully preserved the nature and role of our collective bargaining relationship. We are, in this instance, extending and refining the tools of collective bargaining to solve the boombust cycle that occurs during our negotiations and after the resulting settlements. Fourteen years of uninterrupted industrial peace in the Steel Industry have gradually established the maturity and respect for each other that warrants this sort of an advanced bargaining experiment.

"We look forward to the coming negotiations with optimism and a fervent hope that we can conclude our differences fairly, promptly and—if possible—without resort to the voluntary arbitration machinery that has been established.

"We are confident this experiment can work. We believe it will vindicate our faith in the free process of collective bargaining. Both sides are determined to make this a successful endeavor so that those we represent can continue to enjoy substantial economic progress and the rest of America can be assured of continued stability in this most essential industry."

It should be emphasized, however, that both parties labelled this Negotiating Agreement as "Experimental," and that title was not inadvertent. It was indeed an experiment, which both parties hoped and expected to work. If it did not, both sides were free in the next and future rounds of bargaining to resort once again to their traditional methods of strike and lockout, or the threat thereof.

How, then, did the parties fare under the ENA?

ENA EXPERIENCE IN THE 1974 STEEL
INDUSTRY NEGOTIATIONS

On April 12, 1974, after six weeks of intense negotiations, the Steelworkers and the major steel companies agreed to new three-year national agreements. Thus, under the ENA negotiating procedures, the parties reached agreement, *without* resort to arbitration, a full 3½ months ahead of the August 1 expiration date of the prior contracts.

How did employees fare in this round of bargaining, after foregoing their right to strike? The consensus of virtually everyone is that the settlement was excellent. It was approved overwhelmingly by the Union's Basic Steel Industry Conference, consisting of the Presidents of all local unions in the industry.

* * * "(a)s a result of these fine bargaining achievements at the industry, company and plant level, it was the virtually unanimous judgment of the members of the Basic Steel Industry Conference * * * that the Settlement was outstanding and that the new negotiating procedure (ENA) had been a successful experiment. Accordingly, it was the conclusion of the parties, concurred in by the Basic Steel Industry Conference, that we should renew the ENA and negotiate in the same manner in 1977."

Thus, the ENA was so successful that it has been renewed, and therefore no industry-wide steel strike or lockout is assured at least until August, 1980.

An editorial by Steelworkers President Abel, which appeared in the Union's monthly newspaper, provides an excellent summary:

"Our union and the companies this year made labor-management history. For the first time, we concluded a complete, major settlement in a critical industry without the threat of an industry-wide strike or lockout. This is a new, revoluntionary event in the collective bargaining process because, until now, it was assumed no equitable settlement of this magnitude could possibly be concluded without the threat of brute force dominating the talks.

"This new bargaining procedure that we helped pioneer establishes the fact that it is possible, without brandishing the threat of national work stoppage, to negotiate agreements as effective as when the traditional weapons of labor and management are present at the bargaining table. The basic ingredient is a determination and a commitment by both sides to engage in good faith bargaining.

"The ENA provided a procedure under which each side had the same freedom and flexibility to negotiate as effectively as they did in the past when the threat of a strike or lockout existed. *The ENA did provide for standby arbitration machinery but neither side wanted to have contractual differences settled by an outsider. The mere knowledge that issues in dispute could go to an outside, third party for final and binding disposition, supplied enough pressure on both sides to keep the negotiations productive.* I can assure our members that rough, give-and-take bargaining dominated the negotiations. There was no change in that from past negotiations.

"The fact that we and the 10 companies had the good sense to resolve contractual terms without using the arbitration procedure will serve us well in the years to come. The terms of the 1974 settlement will work all the better for both sides because the terms are the product of mutual decision, not something arbitrarily imposed by an outsider without first-hand experience in the Basic Steel Industry.

"But most important of all, the ENA did what the parties intended it to do: Avoid the employment and production disruption that once plagued our negotiations in past years. With a healthy economy, we can look forward to a high level of employment and stabilized production for many years to come. And certainly, this time, there won't be any layoffs while inventory-laden steel customers use up their stockpiles.

"The ENA, which was the result of a determination by both sides to find a better way to negotiate, may well prove to be the most valuable new tool devised for resolving labor-management problems related to the collective bargaining process. It can add a fresh dimension to industries that are afflicted with 'boom-bust' problems associated with normal negotiations.

"If the ENA is adopted elsewhere, our union can take a great deal of pride in having helped fashion and participate in this new, effective approach to a 'better way.'" (Emphasis added.)

THE IMPROVEMENT OF THE PERFORMANCE OF COLLECTIVE BARGAINING *

* * * A number of alternatives are available. They may be divided into three broad groups: (1) measures to be taken by the parties themselves; (2) measures to be taken by the parties with the cooperation, assistance and even the prodding of government; and (3) further legislative action to improve the performance of collective bargaining.

WHAT CAN BE DONE BY PRIVATE PARTIES THEMSELVES

In the United States, collective bargaining is highly developed in prescribing detailed agreements to fix the terms of employment and elaborate mechanisms to resolve differences over the meaning and application of these terms. In contrast to many Western countries, however, the American industrial-relations system has been relatively underdeveloped and unimaginative in fashioning *procedures* to settle disputes over the terms of new or reopened agreements. The Taft-Hartley Act simply requires sixty days' notice to the other party of the proposed modification or termination prior to the expiration date of the agreement and thirty days' notice to the Federal Mediation and Conciliation Service. Rarely do the parties themselves agree on steps to improve upon the Taft-Hartley procedures. It is therefore worth inquiring whether private parties and government in this country can develop new ways to facilitate the resolution of conflict over the terms of agreements.

The cumulative experience of collective bargaining has developed a wide variety of measures to promote settlements without resort to stoppages. Some of these devices are as old as collective bargaining; others are new names for older developments, while some have come

* D. Bok & J. Dunlop, *Labor And The American Community* 241–252 (1970); © 1970 by the Rockefeller Brothers Fund, Inc. Reprinted by permission of Simon & Schuster, a division of Gulf & Western Corporation.

into prominence only recently. A common element of these techniques is that the parties do not wait until the eve of negotiations, when demands and tensions are accelerating, to shape the course of bargaining; they work at arrangements for peaceful negotiation during the term of the agreement. Among the more common procedures are the following:

Prenegotiation conferences to influence the proposals that are subsequently made by each side and to shape negotiation steps. The technique has been used historically particularly in the garment, clothing and hosiery industries.

Advanced joint selection of specialists—actuaries, accountants, engineers or economists—to secure agreed-upon cost estimates of possible proposals or to gather specified wage and earnings data in a form agreed to be relevant to negotiations.

Early negotiations carried out well in advance of the deadline. The Armour and Company negotiations with the Packinghouse Workers and Butcher Workmen completed in the spring of 1967, before the September 1 deadline, affords an apt illustration.

Private mediation, including possible fact finding and recommendations, by neutrals or a tripartite group selected by the parties. The Kaiser Steel-Steelworkers Long-Range Sharing Plan is illustrative.

National private joint machinery within an industry or sector to assist in mediation of terms of agreements between parties in a locality, or the commitment to settle nationally, disputes over such agreements not settled locally. The Industrial Relations Council in the electrical branch of the construction industry, established in 1919, is a notable case.

A continuing joint study committee, or human-relations committee, which provides a forum for periodic discussion of specific problems. These committees show wide variation in function and scope of issues considered. The basic steel industry has provided examples.

A formula-type arrangement under which the parties agree to resolve one or more issues by the adoption of a specified norm or formula, such as a measure of prevailing wages. Thus, occupational wage rates for the United Shoe Machinery corporation employees are determined periodically by a B.L.S. machinery wage survey in the Boston area, and elevator constructors' wages are set in relation to the wages paid other construction crafts in the same locality.

An advance commitment to voluntary arbitration. The collective-bargaining agreements of Schrafft's Restaurants and Bickford Company, two chain restaurants in New York, have included such a provision; the transit industry in many localities historically included such provisions; in the airline industry, Pan American Airways is signatory to such agreements with several crafts. The agreement between the Airline Pilots and United Air Lines con-

cerning cockpit-crew size for the Boeing 737 equipment provides
for extensive fact finding under two crew-size patterns, with review of the experience and arbitration if the dispute is not resolved in joint negotiations.

Voluntary arbitration over the terms of unresolved disputed
provisions of an agreement may be utilized without an advanced
commitment, as a deadline approaches.

Experienced mediators and neutrals have also sought to persuade
parties to use these procedures. The preventive mediation program
of the Federal Mediation and Conciliation Service and the American
Arbitration Association, particularly through its Labor Management
Institute, encourages private parties to adopt some of these steps, or
fashion their own variants, to achieve settlements without work stoppages. * * * Federal mediators, in cooperation with the parties,
seek to encourage prenegotiation conferences, training programs for
management supervisors and union stewards and continuing joint
study committees. The F.M.C.S. reports, "Substantial segments of
labor and management have fully embraced the concept of preventive
mediation as an extension of the free collective-bargaining procedures."

Taken as a group, these voluntary procedures are no doubt growing in American collective bargaining.

* * *

Work stoppages do not arise ordinarily as a result of a lack of
knowledge of techniques for settlement, but rather from the absence
of a mutual disposition to use the available procedures more extensively. There are, however, some sources of conflict that have been
growing in significance in recent years and for which parties to collective bargaining have been developing still other procedures to facilitate settlement.

In a significant number of negotiations, the ratification of the settlement agreed upon by the committees of the parties has been rejected by the union membership or, less frequently, by the top management or an association of employers leading to a strike or lockout.
William E. Simkin, former director of the Federal Mediation and Conciliation Service, reported that union members have rejected settlements in 10 to 15 percent of the cases in which the F.M.C.S. was actively involved. The ratification procedures are established by the
customs, practices and constitutional requirements of the parties, and
labor and management can often contribute to industrial peace by
jointly reviewing these procedures. In some cases, more authority
should be given to negotiators to make final settlements. In others,
it would be well to review the question of which members of a union,
or which members of a management association, should be allowed to
vote on particular settlements; union members have sometimes been
allowed to vote on contracts in which they have no direct interest and
hence no duty to strike if the agreement is rejected. In many cases,
ratification can more certainly be achieved if enough time is given
before the vote to allow the leaders to explain the settlement careful-

ly and advocate its approval effectively. Voting procedures, too, may need examination, since they influence the number and characteristics of the members who actually vote. The results of a ratification vote may be influenced by whether it takes place in open meeting, by secret ballot at a meeting, or by mail; a procedure that produces a light vote may prejudice the legions of satisfied, apathetic members in favor of the aroused and indignant minority. A vote against ratification of a settlement by union members also requires careful assessment, since a higher offer is not always the most appropriate response by management. Some rearrangement in the package settlement, or a new vote, may be all that is needed to settle the dispute. These procedural issues relating to ratification are vital to good-faith bargaining since the rejection of negotiated settlements tends to reduce the willingness of negotiators to put forward their best offer in future negotiations.

Careful and perceptive understanding of the problems of both bargaining-unit employees and supervisory personnel in advance of negotiation also can contribute substantially to the achievement of peaceful settlements. It is not enough for union officials to presume they know the problems of workers or for top management to assume that it has full knowledge of what is going on at the workplace. A long list of demands or proposals to amend the contract is also inadequate. It is important to know something of the intensity of views on various issues and the types of members or supervisors concerned with each. A workplace is not a monolith, and knowledge of the diversity of interests and views, and the way in which they change during the course of negotiations, is essential to agreement making. The use of surveys, questionnaires and small department meetings is growing and providing more precise knowledge for negotiators. In the course of negotiation as well, more care can be directed to the conscious choice of alternatives and formulation of priorities. Agreements might provide for more options, to permit individuals or groups to choose among alternative benefits. A savings plan, for instance, may be used for illness or specified emergencies or carried over to retirement.   *   *   *

WHAT CAN BE DONE BY PRIVATE PARTIES WITH THE INITIATIVE OF GOVERNMENT

In the past, too little imagination has been expended on the opportunities for government to influence the conduct of collective bargaining. Discussions of the role of government have oscillated from proposals for drastic regulation to critiques of conventional mediation in particular disputes. Yet there is a vast underdeveloped world between these two forms of governmental involvement in private collective bargaining. An active industrial-relations policy would use the government to suggest, to stimulate, to research and to advocate a variety of measures to reduce conflict.

From the 150,000 agreements in the United States, it should be possible to develop a short list of those that produce the greatest concern, both by the frequency of stoppages resulting from a breakdown of negotiations and by the economic impact of the eventual settlements. The maritime, East Coast longshore, construction, newspaper, railroad, airline, and copper industries undoubtedly would be included on the list. Detailed studies of bargaining problems and bargaining structure should be arranged by government officials in each of these industries, preferably with the cooperation of the parties. As a general rule, the studies should be made apart from pending negotiations and disputes. Some investigations might be made in the executive branch of government; others could be made by private bodies under government contract. Some might be undertaken under legislative auspices if Congress could develop a greater capacity for making dispassionate inquiries into labor-management problems than it has managed to display in recent decades.

Such studies would provide a careful review of recent experience, analyze the reasons for major difficulties, inform a wider audience of the problems, and formulate proposals for private and public discussion. The parties might, under the circumstances, be asked to react specifically to the analysis and the recommendations of a report. Through such procedures, an attempt could be made to create within the parties a sense of public accountability for their conduct and a resolve to improve their performance. These studies should also be designed to help labor and management leaders within a sector educate their constituents and members on the nature of the problems of the sector and the hard alternatives which confront the parties.

In some of these problem sectors, and preferably after a detailed preliminary study, the executive branch should formally appoint a group of outsiders to work with the parties to assist them to develop procedures, or in some instances, actually propose legislation to improve the performance of collective bargaining. The nature of the sector and its problems should determine the type of outsider to be chosen. At times, the group might include leaders of the AFL–CIO and representatives of managements from other sectors; at other times it might include Congressional and executive department representatives; and on still other occasions it might be composed of private neutrals. The group should be selected not only for its ability to work constructively with the parties, but also for its capacity to impress upon labor and management leaders, and their followers, the urgency of the public's concern.

Another approach to reducing excessive strikes and lockouts is to establish, at least for a limited period, an agency to resolve a range of collective-bargaining disputes in cases in which federal funds are substantially involved. The President's Missile Sites Labor Commission, which operated in the period 1961–67, and the Atomic Energy Labor Relations Panel are illustrative. Both these bodies were created under Presidential authority and have exercised varying degrees of pressure (in addition to mediation) in the resolution of disputes over the terms of collective-bargaining agreements. The tripartite Missile Sites Commission and the all-public Atomic Energy Panel provided specialized mediation and made recommendations which typically resolved disputes over the terms of agreements between the parties. These bodies also provided a basis for discussion between labor and management and the operating personnel of government procurement agencies. The Missile Sites Commission was concerned with more than labor-management disputes; it was also given authority to make findings regarding uneconomic work practices and unreasonable provisions of collective-bargaining agreements. The authority of the government to approve costs for purposes of reimbursement at these missile, space and atomic-energy installations enhanced the influence of these public bodies in collective bargaining. National leaders of labor and management recognized the need for more orderly dispute settlement at those vital installations, and saw in such agencies a means to strengthen their hand in dealing with isolated and often independent local groups. The threat of other forms of government intervention, particularly legislation, likewise helped to secure the cooperation of labor and management.

These precedents suggest that national leaders might agree for a period to substitute a public board for the strike or lockout in disputes over the terms of agreements in which governmental funds are heavily involved, as they are in the construction and maritime industries. In some instances, the board might actually fix the terms of the new contract. In others, it would be useful simply to provide for the postponement of a local stoppage until a tripartite body had the opportunity to review the dispute and recommend a settlement around which negotiations should proceed.

WHAT CAN BE DONE THROUGH ADDITIONAL LEGISLATION

Additional general legislation for the settlement of serious disputes does not seem appropriate, at least until measures of the type proposed above have been given a fair opportunity. But this does not imply that certain procedural and *ad hoc* legislation may not be appropriate on occasion for particular industries or disputes.

The seriousness of the defects of collective bargaining in certain problem sectors, noted at the outset of this section, might be brought home more forcibly to the parties if Congress, rather than the executive branch, were to require the studies proposed above. Such action might help to bring the bargaining parties together and give national leaders of labor and management a greater degree of influence over their respective organizations and members. Congress might further require labor and management in specified sectors to submit their proposals for bargaining reform by a certain date.

In the event that stoppages continue to be a major problem in a particular sector, Congress could even provide, for a specified period, that no strike or lockout over the terms of an agreement would be legal until local parties had submitted the dispute to a national body established by labor and management in the sector and until his body had the opportunity to resolve the controversy. The body would be empowered to recommend settlement terms if it should deem that this step would contribute to the resolution of the dispute. These procedures would not prohibit the resort to economic conflict, but they would postpone strikes or lockouts until the procedures had been exhausted. The body might be tripartite and include government or neutral members.

There is probably no great urgency for going beyond these limited proposals to revise the procedures contained in the emergency dispute provisions of the Taft-Hartley Act.* To be sure, these provisions contain many well-publicized defects. If taken literally, the definition of an "emergency" dispute is extremely narrow. Critics have also objected to the prohibition barring the statutory board of inquiry from making substantive recommendations for the settlement of the dispute. The statutory provisions seem particularly futile in requiring that the employees vote on the employer's last offer; this provision was enacted on the mistaken assumption that union leaders caused unnecessary strikes that would be prevented if the members could only express their views on the matter. In spite of these flaws, the procedures have worked out better than might have been expected. The ingenuity of public officials in designing mediation and special fact-finding procedures has often compensated for the formal deficiencies of the law. The possibility of legislative action if the procedures do not solve the dispute has been a factor helping to induce settlement. The courts have so defined "emergency dispute" that the law can be applied to some disputes in single plants. In all, the procedures in the Act have been invoked twenty-nine times in the past twenty years. Only in the longshore and maritime industries have strikes developed after the eighty-day period.

The record of the Railway Labor Act, which was developed for railroads in 1926, and applied to airlines in 1936, is less satisfactory. The emergency procedures * were invoked in a total of 171 cases up to 1967; in the twenty-year period 1947–67, they were used on 127

---

* The Taft-Hartley law provides that whenever, in the opinion of the President, a labor dispute affecting an entire industry, or a substantial part, imperils the national health or safety, he may appoint a board of inquiry to find the facts but make no recommendations. The President may then direct the Attorney General to seek an injunction restoring work operations, or precluding a stoppage, for a period of eighty days. If the dispute remains unresolved between the sixtieth and seventy-fifth day of the injunction, the N.L.R.B. shall take a secret ballot of the employees on the question whether they wish to accept the final offer of the employer. If the dispute still remains unresolved at the end of the eighty-day period, the injunction is dissolved and the President shall submit to the Congress a full report together with such recommendations as he may see fit to make for consideration and appropriate action. The law provides for no restraint on the strike or lockout after the eighty-day period.

* The Railway Labor Act provides that if a major dispute between a carrier and its employees, in the judgment of the National Mediation Board, threatens substantially to interrupt interstate commerce to a degree such as to deprive any section of the country of essential transportation service, after seeking to resolve the dispute by mediation and the proffer of voluntary arbitration, the Board shall notify the President, who may create an *ad hoc* emergency board to investigate and report respecting the particular dispute. By convention, the report almost invariably contains recommendations for the resolution of the dispute. The parties may not engage in strike or lockout, or change rules affecting rates of pay, rules, or working conditions for thirty days, during which the emergency board conducts its investigation and makes its report, and for thirty additional days.

occasions and strikes occurred in thirty-four cases after the procedures had been exhausted. In the period 1958–68, in the airline industry, the unions rejected recommendations of emergency boards in 60 percent of the disputes, and strikes occurred in all the principal cases. The procedures of the Railway Labor Act have led to a situation in which the parties do little, if any, genuine bargaining until after the report and recommendations of an emergency board. In the early stages of collective bargaining, when it should be most vigorous, collective bargaining has often become perfunctory. The procedures have been invoked so frequently on individual carriers that the notion of an emergency has been diluted. The managements have felt compelled by virtue of their extensive regulation by government to accept the recommendations of emergency boards, and they have argued, with some justice, that recommmendations have become a floor from which unions, backed by the threat of strike, demand higher settlements. The leading academic authority on the Railway Labor Act, Professor Benjamin Aaron, who is also a respected mediator and arbitrator, has proposed that the emergency procedures of the Railway Labor Act be repealed and railroads and airlines be included within the scope of Taft-Hartley. The railroad and airlines industries were earlier noted to be two of the economic sectors with the greatest problems in structure and procedures for the negotiation of agreements. Even if one does not now accept the solution proposed by Professor Aaron, these industries are high on the list for the type of governmental study and joint discussions proposed earlier in this chapter.

JAMES W. DRISCOLL, A BEHAVIORAL-SCIENCE VIEW OF THE FUTURE OF COLLECTIVE BARGAINING IN THE UNITED STATES *

Major new pressures confront labor and management representatives in collective bargaining in the United States. Rapid technological change, intense international competition, shifts in the location of manufacturing activities, and the rise of nonmanufacuring sectors threaten massive displacement of manufacturing jobs. The work force itself has changed as a better educated, more heterogeneous, and more cynical generation reaches maturity.

Perhaps the most significant change confronting bargainers is the expanding role assumed by government in shaping the terms and conditions of employment. Equal employment opportunity, occupational safety and health, pension reform, and wage guidelines create administrative problems for bargainers, while providing important new protections to disadvantaged groups.

These frequently laminated impositions on bargaining are usually discussed individually and in terms of the new bargaining items they raise. From a behavioral-science perspective, however, the greatest

The law contains no restraint on the strike or lockout after that period.

* James W. Driscoll, "A Behavioral-Science View Of The Future Of Collective

Bargaining In The United States," 30 Labor Law Journal 433 (1979); © by James W. Driscoll. Reprinted by permission.

impact of these challenges is cumulative and procedural. New bargaining relationships will probably be needed to cope with these challenges; in fact, signs of such a transformation are already evident. The purpose of this article is to describe the likely direction of these changes and to discuss their implications for the roles of negotiators and third parties who will be involved with these changes. But first, to better understand the challenges that face collective bargaining, it may be helpful to describe the new complex environment in more abstract terms.

CHALLENGES TO EXISTING BARGAINING PRACTICES

A wider range of issues confronts negotiators. Problems of women's and minority rights, actuarial projections of pension and health funds, and layoff protection complicate the economic tradeoffs of a simple era. Perhaps the strongest testimony to the increasing range of issues covered in bargaining is the sheer size of current agreements; contracts of several hundred pages are not uncommon in mature bargaining relationships.

Issues appear suddenly and change rapidly. The unexpected extension of age discrimination protection to age seventy shows how fast important new pressures can arise in the bargaining environment. New issues can stem from the legislative process, technical and electronic research, medical research, and competitive changes. All share two characteristics—unpredictability of result and immediate impact on current contract terms.   *   *   *

Cooperation between union and management is possible on many issues. For economic issues, the conflict between union and management is clear and largely inevitable—a dollar for wages is a cost to management and an income to a union member. But for many newly emerging issues, conflict is not so compelling. Both union and management face the threat of government sanction for discriminatory employment practices that arise under their agreement. Foreign competition affects both labor and capital. And most modern managers show concern for the health and safety of their work force, even beyond that stimulated by insurance premiums and workmen's compensation laws.

To summarize the termoil in the current bargaining environment, negotiators must cope with complicated, changing, and unpredictable issues and with the possibility that cooperation rather than conflict might resolve a particular issue more effectively. Not surprisingly, negotiators in many situations have acted positively to respond to this new environment. Some of these responses are discussed next.

CHARACTERISTICS OF THE NEW
BARGAINING RELATIONSHIPS

More issues are now routinely included in negotiations. It is a small, immature, or unprofessional negotiation that does not include some discussion of affirmative action, ERISA requirements, health hazards, technological forecasts, etc. Experts supplement negotiators on both sides of the table. More and more frequently, legal, economic, actuarial, medical, and industry specialists are included in negotiations or provide background material for union representatives and labor-relations managers.

Negotiators meet to consider issues outside of contract negotiations. Regular meetings during the life of the contract as part of the grievance procedure are common in U.S. bargaining. However, many negotiators or other representatives are meeting outside of the grievance procedure to discuss unexpected contract developments or to explore unresolved issues from past negotiations.

Joint problem-solving approaches are used. The number of joint union-management committees established to explore issues of common concern grows each day. Industry-level programs exist for specific purposes in retail food, over-the-road trucking, nuclear power plant constructions, and men's garments. Local communities have formed joint committees to deal with declining economies. In-plant committees tackle various problems—from productivity under the Scanlon Plan to the quality of work life—in major companies such as the Dana Corporation and General Motors.

These joint committees do not rely on the exchange of proposals and the threat of economic force that is characteristic of traditional negotiations. Rather, they share information in the careful identification of problems and attempt to generate creative solutions.

An intriguing example of a common concern overriding the conflict between union and management can be seen in the textile industry where representatives meet frequently to develop a coordinated industy position toward imports. Despite the acrimony that surrounds the national AFL–CIO boycott of J. P. Stevens, these discussions continue. It is even rumored that Stevens' representatives have occasionally participated. Some aspects of these new approaches can be best understood in the context of a specific example.

Since 1974, a group of top-level executives and union leaders in the retail food industry have met regularly to discuss common concerns. The issues range from rationalizing local contract negotiations to providing equal employment opportunity, occupational safety and health, pensions, health and welfare funds, and guidelines for equitable wage settlements.

The Joint Labor-Management Committee has two levels. The policy-level Executive Committee meets quarterly; the operational Steering Committee meets monthly. Both committees have relied on consulting firms and university-based research to supplement their own staff expertise in specific areas such as pensions and safety. While negotiators remain staunch adversaries in local contract negotiations (which occur continuously), the JLMC has adopted a problem-solving approach, especially in the Executive Committee and in specific subcommittees.

A BARGAINING BUREAUCRACY

The JLMC suggests some of the new collective bargaining procedures that will be needed to cope with increasing demands from the external environment. A paradigm for the current bargaining procedure might be stated as follows: When the (infrequent) expiration of the labor agreement approaches, bargaining committees meet occasionally to exchange demands. These meetings intensify and each side sends fewer representatives as the expiration looms. Proposals and counter-proposals are made until, under time pressure, the chief negotiators meet together, perhaps with the assistance of a mediator, to make final concessions needed to resolve their differences and avert a strike. For the life of the agreement, meetings between the two sides are confined (except at the lowest level) to discussions of specific grievances about the application or interpretation of the agreement.

The new form of collective bargaining that is evolving differs from this paradigm in many respects. (1) Meetings are frequent during the life of the contract and are independent of its expiration. (2) Discussions examine external events and potential problem areas rather than internal complaints about current practice. (3) Groups of experts play a major role in all stages of decisionmaking, including the final decision on some issues. (4) Representatives often adopt a problem-solving approach. A sociologist would describe this new form of collective bargaining as a *bureaucracy*, since it has a continuous life, specialized tasks are assigned to experts, and decisions are made on rational grounds rather than by resorting to tests of economic power.

Some of the characteristics popularly associated with bureaucracies can also be seen. Groups, rather than individuals, often make the final decisions; seemingly endless studies are undertaken on major issues; and subcommittees proliferate. However, these characteristics have been shown in research literature to be vital to work organizations faced with complicated and changing environments, such as those described for collective bargaining. They are not merely unpleasant side effects.

On balance, then, the bargaining bureaucracy is a logical evolutionary stage in a human decisionmaking system faced with an increasingly complex environment. We can expect the interests in collective bargaining—labor, capital, and the public—to be better served by this procedure than they can be by the episodic, personalistic rituals which served a simpler age.

Evolutionary processes, of course, are not completely predictable. and the external environment may not favor development of such a bargaining bureaucracy. American management, for example, may continue the assault on the labor movement that characterized the campaign against the labor law changes that were proposed in 1977. The mature relationship described here as a bargaining bureaucracy requires mutual acceptance by each party of the legitimate role of the other as a representative of interest groups in the society. Without that acceptance, collective bargaining may degenerate into a simple test of economic strength. Indeed, many observers of the American labor movement predict such a reaction to management's assault. The 1980s may see the emergence of a labor party to pursue labor's goals in the political arena and direct attacks on traditional managerial prerogatives, if an accommodation between labor and management is not reached.

Nonetheless, the accommodation assumed by the present analysis is also likely. An obvious question remains. What are the implications of a bargaining bureaucracy for negotiators and other third parties, most of whom learned their jobs under the traditional system?

THE NEGOTIATOR'S ROLE

The negotiator is no longer the "expert." It is no longer possible for the negotiator to understand all the ramifications of problems facing the employer or the union. The negotiator must depend on the advice of experts in various disciplines.

This transition will be very difficult. Negotiators may deny that it is needed and may try to maintain expertise in most or all problem areas. This allows the negotiator to avoid feelings of dependency or even helplessness that arise when the judgment of another must be substituted for his or her own. Unfortunately, such a denial is harmful for the new relationship. Decisions are made without all of the information that is available, and the negotiator wastes time and energy trying to keep up in a few areas, while neglecting the new duties he or she now has.

Negotiators must learn to manage groups of experts. If a negotiator has several experts working on a problem, such as the legal implications of an affirmative action plan, the negotiator must be able to facilitate group discussion and decisionmaking. The facilitator's role is complex, but some of its activities include insuring that the group has accurately defined the problem; that a reasonable range of alternatives has been examined; and that frank opinions from the entire group have been solicited. The negotiator must rely on the members of the groups as experts, so the negotiator's task becomes one of managing the decisionmaking process rather than directly making the final decision.

Negotiators must have behavioral flexibility. Joint problem solving and hard bargaining require quite different approaches. The former emphasizes the open exchange of information and rational analysis of alternatives, while the latter rewards secrecy and the forceful advocacy of firm positions.

The bargaining bureaucracy requires negotiators who can accurately assess which approach is appropriate for a given issue and who possess the ability to move easily from problem solving to bargaining and back again. The ability to take a hard line is not enough.

Negotiators must manage their side of the joint bureaucracy. The assignment of people to specific tasks in the bureaucracy raises important strategic decisions. What issues should be under discussion at the present time? Who should be assigned to participate in each discussion? At what level in the bargaining bureaucracy should the final decision be made? Are the various discussions making adequate progress? What remedial steps can be taken to get a discussion moving again? The successful negotiator in a bargaining bureaucracy will be the one who can most accurately diagnose his or her organization's performance and find ways to facilitate the work of the members of the bargaining team.

ROLE OF THE THIRD PARTY

Changes in the various third-party roles will reflect the evolution of the negotiators whom they serve. Neutral third parties will need a wider variety of strategies. Traditional collective bargaining has shaped two distinctive third-party roles in the United States: mediator and arbitrator. Mediating is discussed in some detail below.

The demand for grievance arbitration will remain, especially for cases of individual due process. In addition, arbitrators will be called to resolve factual disputes between the experts representing each party. Unlike interest arbitration, these decisions will often fall in very technical areas, such as the impact of specific chemicals on workers' health. Thus, the demand will grow for neutrals from disciplines that relate to the new bargaining issues. Expedited and "mini" arbitrations, should also become more common during the term of the contract.

Mediators will need many new skills. Mediators will probably bear the brunt of the changes in bargaining. They will have to help the parties manage their joint bureaucracies rather than simply help them resolve impasses during contract negotiations. The problem they are confronted with is how to get each side to work jointly on problems between negotiations. Mediators will encourage negotiators to diagnose their own collective bargaining system.

The Relationships by Objectives Program of the Federal Mediation Service is a tentative beginning in this major area. Whether the Mediation Service will provide that help directly, or train other consultants and experts, is still an open question.

Since negotiations will not be one-on-one interpersonal sessions, mediators must understand the problems facing negotiators who must manage groups of experts. Mediators will have to work with negotiators who do not personally have all the information they need for many tough issues.

Mediators will also have to help parties develop their own expertise in the complicated issues facing collective bargaining, or they will need to provide a source for experts who can assist the parties. It will be important to have a broad range of contracts across the spectrum of issues that will arise in bargaining.

Finally, mediators must be able to assess when a cooperative approach is appropriate and possible in a bargaining situation and develop a range of skills to facilitate that process. The skills appropriate for a cooperative process are probably quite different from the existing skills in mediation. This suggests that mediators will need to devote some time to acquiring new skills to serve the new bargaining bureaucracy.

SUMMARY

From a behavioral-science perspective, the cumulative impact of the various pressures on collective bargaining may transform contract negotiation and administration into a bargaining bureaucracy. The bargaining bureaucracy implies different skills, functions, and objectives for negotiators and third parties that are involved in collective bargaining situations. This evolution in American labor-management relations is by no means assured. Nonetheless, professionals should evaluate the possibility and implications of such fundamental change in their discipline and remain alert for signs of its development.

F.   RECOMMENDED READING

Legal. For good commentaries on the legal rules governing bargaining, see:

1. Cox, "The Duty to Bargain in Good Faith," 71 Harv.L.Rev. 1401 (1958).

2. Smith, "Evolution of the Duty to Bargain Concept," in American Law, 39 Mich.L.Rev. 1065 (1941).

3. Schatzki, "The Employers Unilateral Act or Per Se Violation," 44 Texas L.Rev. 470 (1966).

4. Cross, Cullen & Hanslowe, "Good Faith in Labor Negotiations: Tests & Remedies," 53 Cornell L.Rev. 1009 (1968).

5. J. O'Reilly & G. Simon, *Unions' Rights To Company Information* (1980).

On the Economics of Bargaining, see:

6. Rees, *The Economics of Work and Pay* (1972).

7. Stevens, *Strategy and Collective Bargaining Negotiations* (1963).

8. N. Chamberlain and Kuhn, *Collective Bargaining* (2nd ed. 1965).

Chapter V

THE ENFORCEMENT OF COLLECTIVE BARGAINING
AGREEMENTS: GRIEVANCE ARBITRATION

A. CASE STUDY: DISCHARGE FOR JUST CAUSE OR DOUBLE JEOPARDY?

Below is the transcript of an actual arbitration hearing, slightly amended followed by excerpts from the union's brief and the company's brief. Decide which side you favor and write a short opinion justifying your conclusions. If you uphold the grievance, what remedy would you apply?

Which side, the union or the company, is better represented? Does this seem to make a difference?

(a) TRANSCRIPT

In the Matter of the Arbitration between
LAIDLAW CORPORATION
OF THE WEST,
Employer,

and

UNITED STEELWORKERS
OF AMERICA,
AFL–CIO, Local No. 6729
Union.

ARBITRATION PROCEEDINGS RE: EDWARD MARK, Grievant

OPENING STATEMENT

By Mr. DiMaggio: The Grievant, Edward Mark, was discharged on Friday, March 5, 1976 for falsifying a doctor's memo which stated that his grandmother had been admitted to the Dameron Hospital on February 27, 1976. The Union admits that Mr. Wells did in fact falsify the memo. The Grievant also admitted this to his immediate supervisor, Mr. Alfred Hawkins, on March 1, 1976.

As a penalty for falsifying the doctor's memo, the Grievant was given a three-day suspension without pay. He was told to return to work on March 5, 1976. Subsequent to the issuance of the three-day suspension, the Company's Vice-President from Peoria, Illinois, who was in Stockton for collective bargaining talks with the Union, decided that the three-day suspension was not severe enough and instructed the Plant Manager, Mr. Creekmore, to rescind the three-day suspension and to discharge the Grievant, and this was done on March 5, 1976, the very day the Grievant was scheduled to resume work.

It is the Union's opinion that the discharge action placed the Grievant in double jeopardy inasmuch as the original three-day disciplinary suspension had been levied against and served by the Grievant; therefore, the discharge in the Union's opinion was not for just cause and should not be upheld by the Arbitrator. That concludes the opening statement, sir.

The Arbitrator: All right, thank you very much. Now, this being a discharge case, it would be customary for the Company to go first. Do you have any witnesses to call, Mr. Eckerty?

Mr. Eckerty: Just the Foreman involved.

ALFRED R. HAWKINS,

called as a witness by and on behalf of the Company, being first duly and regularly sworn by the Arbitrator, testified as follows:

[*Whereupon a two-page memo re: absenteeism and tardy control procedure was marked Company Exhibit 1.*]

Mr. Eckerty: To go along with that, we also have a copy of his attendance record that we would like to enter into evidence.

Mr. DiMaggio: This will be Company Exhibit 2, sir?

The Arbitrator: Yes, Company Exhibit 2.

[*Whereupon photocopy of a sheet relating to Mark, dated 5–1–75, was marked Company Exhibit 2.*]

DIRECT EXAMINATION

By Mr. Eckerty: Al, I guess I will turn it over to you.

A. Okay. On the night that he got the emergency phone call, I told him to bring a note back in with him whenever he comes back. And so he did. And it didn't—it didn't look right, so I called the hospital and asked them about it. And they said, no, that his grandmother had not been admitted to the hospital or nothing, so then I called—

The Arbitrator: Wait a minute, now, you are starting with an emergency phone call, but I don't know anything about it. You may have to start a little further back. He was at work and then he got a phone call?

The Witness: Yes. Saying that his grandmother had been admitted to the hospital, and that he was needed there. And also I told him to bring the note from the hospital back saying for—you know, some information to us to let us know that he was there. So he did, and it didn't look right to me.

The Arbitrator: Now, he brought back a statement; do you have that?

Mr. Eckerty: Yes, we do.

The Arbitrator: Introduce that as Company Exhibit 3.

[*Whereupon photocopy of a note bearing the words "Dameron Hospital, Emergency Room" was marked Company Exhibit 3.*]

The Witness: Then he brought it in. So I called the hospital, and they said, no, he hadn't—she had not been admitted. So I went back to his department and brought him into the office and asked him about it. And he said, yes, that he did, he wrote it up himself and signed it.

So then I went and—I got the grievance person and a witness and we went into the lunch room. And I asked him about it, and he said, yes, it was false, he admitted to it right in front of the grievance person, which was Brigette Mederios, and the witness, Bruce Burdette.

So then I told him, well, you know, that he had done that, I am going to have to go ahead and suspend him for it, for falsification of the document.

So then the next day we went in and had a meeting with Earl Creekmore, the Plant Manager, and he said to go ahead, suspend him, and with his record and stuff like that for that.

So then I guess it was Thursday, the Vice-President of the Company came out and we reviewed it thoroughly on his past record of all his emergency phone calls and stuff like that. And he says to go ahead and terminate him for—for that.

The Arbitrator: Which is what you did?

The Witness: Right.

Mr. Eckerty: Mr. Arbitrator, here is a copy of the plant rules, too. I think that should be in there. That covers the posted notice which has been on the board dealing with this.

Mr. DiMaggio: Excuse me, they are the plant rules that were in effect at the time the Grievant was discharged, is that right?

Mr. Eckerty: That has got the date. These are the ones that were on the board.

Mr. DiMaggio: Thank you.

Mr. Eckerty: Okay. Did you ever discuss his attendance record with Edward Mark?

A. No, but I'm sure he was aware of—

Mr. DiMaggio: Objection, sir, calls for a conclusion.

The Arbitrator: How would you know what was in his mind?

The Witness: Well, it must—he must have knew what was in his mind whenever he falsified that document.

The Arbitrator: All you can do is just testify as to where the—where the rules were posted and if employees were normally made aware of it, or something of that kind.

Mr. Eckerty: Now, were plant rules and everything posted to where the employees could see them?

A. Oh, yes.

Q. Would you state where, please?

A. By the—as you walk in the hall, the side door, that is, as they come through in the plant, it is on the right side and they pass it every day.

Q. Is this not called the Company—this is the Company bulletin board you are referring to?

A. Right.

The Arbitrator: Are new employees given a copy of these rules?

The Witness: Yes, they are.

The Arbitrator: As part of their—when they first come on, are they given a packet of materials or something including the rules?

The Witness: Umm, I don't—I don't think so. Are they?

Mr. Eckerty: Mr. Hawkins is not involved in the hiring, but to answer—I don't know if I can answer it or not, but they are, I know this is—

The Arbitrator: A little irregular but—any other questions you wanted to ask?

Mr. Eckerty: I can't think of any, Mr. Getman.

CROSS–EXAMINATION

By Mr. DiMaggio: Mr. Hawkins, I believe you testified that on a particular shift the Grievant, Mr. Mark, received a telephone call, and he informed you that he had to leave work to go to the Dameron Hospital?

A. Right.

Q. Is it your testimony that you contacted the hospital and found that the Grievant's grandmother had not been admitted to the hospital?

A. Right.

Q. So about that time then you called the Grievant into the office, is that correct?

A. Yes, it is.

Q. And you informed him that you determined that his grandmother had not been admitted to the hospital?

A. Right.

Q. Did the Grievant admit at that time that his grandmother had not been admitted to the hospital?

A. Yes, he did.

Q. Did the Grievant admit that he had falsified the doctor's note?

A. Yes, he did.

Q. Did he offer any reason for having done so?

A. Yes.

Q. What was the reason that the Grievant gave you?

A. He said that he was tired, and he was sleepy, and he wanted to take the night off.

Q. Did he tell you that he had suffered a lack of sleep the night before?

A. Yes.

Q. Did he tell you that he felt that in his condition that he didn't believe that he could work safely?

A. Yes, but—

Q. Now, correct me if I am wrong, but at that time I believe you told the Grievant that he would probably receive a disciplinary suspension for his action, but that you would have to first contact the Plant Manager, Mr. Creekmore, is that right?

A. Right.

Q. And didn't you tell the Grievant at that time that as far as you were concerned you did not want to see him discharged?

A. Yes.

Q. And you allowed the Grievant to go back to work at that time, did you not, while you checked with Mr. Creekmore?

A. Yes.

Q. Now, following your conversation—did you telephone Mr. Creekmore?

A. Yes, I did.

Q. Did you explain the situation to Mr. Creekmore?

A. Yes.

Q. What did Mr. Creekmore have to say about this?

A. He said to right now just go ahead and put him on suspension.

Q. Did Mr. Creekmore specify the duration of the suspension?

A. No.

Q. Did he tell you how much time on suspension to give Mr. Mark?

A. Well, he said to go ahead, put him on the three-day suspension for right now.

Q. Put him on the three-day suspension?

A. For right now, yes.

Q. After talking to Mr. Creekmore, did you then get back to the Grievant?

A. Yes, I did.

Q. And did you inform the Grievant that at that time he was being put on suspension?

A.   Yes, I did.

Q.   And did the Grievant leave the plant at that time?

A.   Yes, he did.

Q.   Prior to his leaving the plant, did you inform the Grievant that you would be in touch with him by telephone the following day?

A.   Yes.

Q.   And this was for the purpose of letting the Grievant know what the final determination had been?

A.   Right.

Q.   Was going to be, is that correct?

A.   Right.

Q.   Did you telephone the Grievant the following day?

A.   Yes, I did.

Q.   And that would have been Tuesday, March 2, 1976, is that correct?

A.   Right.

Q.   About what time did you telephone the Grievant?

A.   Umm—

Q.   Wasn't it some time in the morning, about 9:00 a. m.?

A.   I think it was, yeah, after we had the meeting, yeah.

Q.   Now, you testified that the swing shift ran from 3:00 p. m. to 11:00 p. m.; how was it that—were you—did you make the call from the plant, by the way?

A.   Yes, I did.

Q.   How is it that you were in the plant at that time of the morning?

A.   Because I came back and was talking to Earl, the Plant Manager, Mr. Creekmore, about it.

Q.   About Mr. Mark's situation, the suspension?

A.   Yes.

Q.   And in your conversations with Mr. Creekmore, the Plant Manager, that morning prior to telephoning the Grievant, wasn't it determined that the Grievant should be placed on a three-day suspension?

A.   Yes.

Q.   Did you tell the Grievant then—I believe you testified you telephoned him about 9:00 a. m. that morning?

A.   Yes, I think it was.

Q.   Did you inform the Grievant that it had been decided that he would be placed on a three-day suspension?

A.   Yes.

Q.   Did you tell the Grievant that he should return to work on the swing shift on Friday, March 5, 1976?

A. (Affirmative nod)

Q. Your answer is yes?

A. Yes.

Q. You didn't see or speak to the Grievant on the following day, Wednesday, March 3?

A. No.

A. Did you? Now, let me call your attention to Thursday, March 4, 1976. Did you see the—did the Grievant come into the plant to pick up his paycheck?

A. Yes, he did.

Q. Okay, fine. And the Grievant came in to pick up his paycheck; do you recall approximately what time the Grievant came in to the plant to pick up his check that Thursday?

A. I believe it was around 6:00.

Q. 6:00 in the evening?

A. Yes. Wasn't it?

Q. And at that time the intentions were that the Grievant would return to work the following day, Friday the 5th, is that right?

A. Yes.

Q. So you didn't tell the Grievant anything to the contrary when he picked up his paycheck, did you?

A. No.

Q. Now, when was it that—when was it that Mr. Edwards, the Vice-President—when was it that he came into the picture?

A. Thursday evening.

Q. Thursday evening. Was this following your—was this following the Grievant's coming into the plant to pick up his check?

A. (Affirmative nod)

Q. Were you present with Mr. Edwards?

A. Yes, I was.

Q. Would you describe what took—who else was present at that time?

A. Let's see, it was Mr. Creekmore, Larry, and myself.

Q. And at—during that meeting isn't it true that Mr. Edwards then reversed the decision that had been made locally and instructed local management to discharge the Grievant?

A. Right.

Q. Do you know when the Grievant was notified of this change?

A. Friday.

Q. Following day, Friday, March 5?

A. Right.

Q. Did you notify him?

A. No, I didn't.

Q. Do you know who did notify him?

A. Larry.

Q. Mr. Eckerty?

A. Yes.

Mr. DiMaggio: No further questions, sir.

The Arbitrator: Mr. Eckerty?

Mr. Eckerty: Yes, I have a question.

REDIRECT EXAMINATION

By Mr. Eckerty: On the night in question when Ed Mark received that phone call, did he at that time instruct you that he was tired and sleepy from lack of sleep the night before; was there any indication on his part at all that he couldn't perform his duties or anything at all that was brought to your attention concerning this?

A. No.

Q. So you were under the delusion that he was prepared for work as normally expected of an employee?

A. Right.

Mr. Eckerty: Okay.

Mr. DiMaggio: Nothing further.

The Arbitrator: May I ask you one thing, when Mr. Edwards decided that he should be discharged, did local management disagree with him?

The Witness: No.

The Arbitrator: Okay, thank you very much. I take it that is the Company's case?

Mr. Eckerty: The only thing I have here, is the—I don't know if this has any bearing on it or not, but it was a ruling from the Unemployment Office that went against Edward Mark. Can I offer that as evidence?

Mr. DiMaggio: I would object to its introduction, sir. I don't think it is relevant to these proceedings.

The Arbitrator: Well, this is actually a question that arises fairly frequently. Normally you can introduce it but—but I won't give it very much weight. I will make my own decision. This happens from time to time, but the situation is quite different than the unemployment.

The Arbitrator: Okay. Do you have any witnesses?

Mr. DiMaggio: Yes. Call the Grievant, Edward Mark.

EDWARD MARK,

the Grievant herein, being first duly and regularly sworn by the Arbitrator, testified as follows:

DIRECT EXAMINATION

By Mr. DiMaggio: Would you state your name for the record, please?

A. Edward Mark.

Q. Prior to your being discharged, how long had you been employed by the Laidlaw Corporation?

A. Approximately a year-and-a-half.

Q. And what was your job with the company?

A. Bar man.

Q. Calling your attention to Monday, March 1, 1976, did your supervisor, Mr. Hawkins, call you to the office?

A. Yes, he did.

Q. And you were working the 3:00 to 11:00 shift?

A. Yes, I was.

Q. Did he tell you that he had telephoned the Dameron Hospital and determined that the doctor's note you had given him earlier was false?

A. Yes, he did.

Q. Did you admit that you had falsified the note?

A. I did.

Q. Did you offer a reason for having done so?

A. I did.

Q. And what was the reason you gave Mr. Hawkins?

A. I told him that I had been up for quite a long time and only had a few hours sleep, and I considered myself a safety hazard to myself and fellow employees.

Q. And what did Mr. Hawkins have to say at that time?

A. He—he told me that he would have to call the Plant Manager, Earl Creekmore, for further investigation to see what to do on this matter, and then he sent me back to work.

Q. Did Mr. Hawkins speculate as to what the penalty might be, if any?

A. He told me that most likely I would probably be placed on a suspension.

Q. Did Mr. Hawkins say anything to you with regard to what his personal recommendation would be?

A. He told—I asked him that—that he didn't think I would be fired or terminated, and he told me no, and that he would put nothing down on record that he would want me terminated in any way.

Q. I see. Were you then allowed to return to work?

A. Yes, I was.

Q. Did Mr. Hawkins again contact you a short time later?

A. Yes, he did.

Q. And what did he say to you at that time?

A. He asked me to join himself and Brigette Mederios and Bruce Burdette to the lunch room to tell me what the Plant Manager, Earl Creekmore, had told him over the telephone.

Q. You mentioned Brigette Mederios, who is Brigette Mederios?

A. At the time she was Grievance Officer, or on that particular shift.

Q. And who was Mr. Burdette, I believe you said?

A. Bruce Burdette, he is Maintenance-man on the shift.

Q. And is Mr. Burdette—or was Mr. Burdette at that time a Union officer or Committeeman?

A. No, he wasn't.

Q. Do you have any idea why Mr. Burdette was there?

A. No. I don't.

Q. What did Mr. Hawkins say to you when all of you were in the lunch room?

A. Well, he explained to—in front of Brigette Mederios and Bruce Burdette exactly what I had done and showed them the doctor's slip and told them that Earl Creekmore had told—had told him to put me on suspension until further investigation, pending further investigation, and that he would call me on Tuesday and let me know exactly what was going to happen.

Q. Did Mr. Hawkins mention the possibility of discharge at any time during that meeting?

A. No, he didn't.

Q. I believe you just testified that Mr. Hawkins told you that he would telephone you the following day on Tuesday?

A. Yes, he did.

Q. Calling your attention to the following day, Tuesday, March 2, 1976, did you receive a telephone call at home from Mr. Hawkins?

A. Yes, I did.

Q. And about what time did you receive this call?

A. About 9:00 o'clock in the morning.

Q. Would you describe to the best of your recollection what was said?

A. Mr. Hawkins told me that after discussing it further and after further investigation had been taken, that the Company was placing me on three-day suspension, and that I was to return to work on Friday the 5th, my normal shift, which is 3:00 to 11:00.

And then I asked him, "Now, I am not fired, I am just suspended for three days?"

He says, "That's right."

And that was the end of the conversation.

Q. Did you hear anything more from the Company that day?

A. No, I didn't.

Q. Did you hear anything from the Company the next day, Wednesday, March 3, 1976?

A. No, I didn't.

Q. On Thursday, March 4, 1976, did you have occasion to go to the plant?

A. I did.

Q. For what reason?

A. To pick up my payroll check.

Q. And was this the regular plant payday?

A. Yes, it was.

Q. At about what time did you arrive at the plant?

A. It was about 8:30 in the evening.

Q. Did you receive your paycheck?

A. I did.

Q. From whom?

A. Al Hawkins, Plant—the Foreman on that shift.

Q. Did you say anything to Mr. Hawkins before you left the plant?

A. I said to Mr. Hawkins, "Well, I'll see you tomorrow at 3:00." And he goes, "Okay."

Q. Were there any witnesses to this conversation?

A. Sarah Gallagher was with me.

Q. Did you hear from the Company at any time later that evening after leaving the plant?

A. No, I did not.

Q. Calling your attention to the following day, Friday, March 5, 1976, did you receive a telephone call at home from the plant?

A. Yes, I did.

Q. And at about what time did you receive this call?

A. About 9:15 in the morning.

Q. Who was calling you?

A. The secretary at the time was Laura, I don't know her last name. And she—she told me that Larry Eckerty wanted to speak to me.

Q. I see. And did you speak to Mr. Eckerty?

A. I did.

Q. Who is Mr. Eckerty?

A. He is the Foreman on the first shift at Laidlaw.

Q. Would you describe the conversation with Mr. Eckerty to the best of your recollection?

A. He told me that Ralph Edwards and Earl Creekmore had called him from negotiations and told him to tell me that I was terminated at that time.

Q. What did you have to say, if anything?

A. I really didn't know what to say, so I just said, "Okay, Larry," and I hung up the telephone.

Q. What, if anything, did you do then?

A. I got up out of bed and got my clothes on and headed straight for the plant.

Q. And what did you do when you arrived at the plant?

A. When I got there Larry was sitting behind—was in the Manager's office. And I knocked and Laura, the secretary, was in the office at that time. And I wanted to speak to Larry privately. So I asked Laura if she would please leave so I could speak to him, and she told me no. After she told me no, I told him, well, this time I really didn't have too much to say right now because she wouldn't leave, and that they were wrong. And Larry says, "Well, there is nothing I can do, this is what they have decided."

Q. Did he mention who decided?

A. Well, he mentioned that Ralph Edwards and Earl Creekmore decided this and there is nothing he could do.

Mr. DiMaggio: I don't have any further questions of the witness, Mr. Arbitrator.

The Arbitrator: Do you have any questions?

Mr. Eckerty: Yes, I do.

CROSS–EXAMINATION

By Mr. Eckerty: Mr. Mark, on the day in question you were tired and everything, did you offer any of this to the Foreman, that you hadn't had any sleep and that you felt you were a safety hazard to be working back there; was there anything offered at all to your supervisor?

A. Al did come up and he said, "You look pretty tired." And I go, "I am." And he didn't say any more, he didn't ask any reason whatsoever, why I was tired at all.

Q. Mr. Mark, weren't you given prior notices by other supervisors before Hawkins on your attendance record to let you know that you were to the point of disciplinary action?

A. Yes, and I knew for myself that I was.

Q. Had you not had a prior written warning notice from a supervisor telling you that your next unexcused absence would result in possible suspension?

A. Yes, I did.

Q. So then you were well aware of the fact then?

A. Uh-huh. (Yes)

Q. Okay. But you didn't offer any—anything to the Foreman that you thought you should go home, that you don't think you could perform your duties?

A. Not—not at the beginning of the shift when he asked me, no.

Q. Mr. Mark, isn't it each employee's responsibility, and aren't they aware of it to come to work prepared to perform their duties?

A. Yes, it is.

Q. You are well aware—you know where the Company does have a bulletin board?

A. Uh-huh. (Yes)

Q. You know where it is at?

A. Uh-huh. (Yes)

Q. Had you seen the rules and regulations posted on the board?

A. I read them.

Q. So you are well aware of what the plant rules were?

A. Uh-huh. (Yes).

Q. And the disciplinary action was?

A. Uh-huh, yes, I did.

THOMAS J. DiMAGGIO,

called as a witness by and on behalf of the Union, being first duly and regularly sworn by the Arbitrator, testified as follows:

Mr. DiMaggio: Mr. Arbitrator, on Friday, March 5, 1976, some time subsequent to 1:00 p. m., I was told by Mr. Ralph Edwards, the Vice-President of Laidlaw Corporation, that he had personally made a decision that the Grievant Mr. Mark should be discharged from his employment with the Company; and that he had instructed the Plant Manager, Mr. Earl Creekmore, to follow through with this action. Mr. Edwards explained that he believed that in the past the Company had been too lax in enforcing the plant rules, but that in the future they would be strictly enforced.

Mr. Edwards stated that in the case of the Grievant. Mr. Mark, the three-day suspension originally imposed by Mr. Creekmore was not in his opinion severe enough; and, therefore, he, Mr. Edwards, had instructed Mr. Creekmore to disregard the three-day suspension and to discharge the Grievant. Mr. Edwards was here from the company's head office in Peoria, Illinois, and his comments were made during collective bargaining negotiations in the presence of Mr. Creekmore and the three members of the Local Union Negotiating Committee: Danny Lindley, Alex Azevedo, and Steve Guthrie.

Prior to being notified of the Company's position with regard to the discharge of Mr. Mark, we had had considerable discussion regarding the plant rules and the fact that the Company had in the past not—had not been enforcing the plant rules with even-handedness, that some individuals had been disciplined for infractions of the plant rules while other individuals were not disciplined; that there was no uniformity, and that in general the Company had been very lax in the enforcement of those rules.

On or about March 17, 1976 I received a telephone call at my office from Mr. Creekmore, the Plant Manager, who informed me that due to lax enforcement and confusion regarding the plant rules he had decided to remove any and all infractions of the rules from all the employees records, and that everyone would be starting with a clean sheet. He also stated that he had posted new rules and would send me a copy of the new rules.

I received those rules on March 19, 1976, and on the same date I submitted a letter to Mr. Creekmore making clear that the Union was not a party to the rules and reserved the right to challenge the application of the rules on an individual basis.

And at this time, Mr. Arbitrator, I would like to introduce a copy of the plant rules that were sent to me by Mr. Creekmore. These are dated March 9, 1976. This would be Union's Exhibit 1, sir.

The Arbitrator: Yes, Union Exhibit 1.

[*Whereupon plant rules dated March 9, 1976, were marked Union Exhibit 1.*]

Mr. DiMaggio: And that concludes my testimony, Mr. Arbitrator.

The Arbitrator: Okay. Any questions, Mr. Eckerty?

Mr. Eckerty: No. I think Tom presented a fair statement. We are not here to color the facts, you know.

DANNY LINDLEY,

called as a witness by and on behalf of the Union, being first duly and regularly sworn by the Arbitrator, testified as follows:

DIRECT EXAMINATION

By Mr. DiMaggio: Would you state your name for the record, please?

A. Danny Lindley.

Q. Where are you employed?

A. Laidlaw Corporation of the West.

Q. How long have you been employed there?

A. Eleven years and eleven months.

Q. And what is your job at the plant?

A. Swing man.

Q. Do you hold any Union positions?

A. Yes, I am a Grievance Man on the first shift and Financial Secretary of the Local Union.

Q. Calling your attention to Friday, March 5, 1976, were you in attendance at collective bargaining sessions between the Union and the Company?

A. Yes, I was.

Q. And who was there present for the Company?

A. Vice-President Ralph Edwards of Laidlaw Corporation, and Earl Creekmore, Plant Manager of Laidlaw Stockton.

Q. And who was present for the Union?

A. Representative Tom DiMaggio, President Alex Azevedo, Vice-President Steve Guthrie, and myself.

Q. Now, some time after 1:00 p. m. that day, did Mr. Edwards comment with regard to Mr. Mark having been discharged?

A. Yes, he did.

Q. And to the best of your recollection what did Mr. Edwards have to say?

A. Well, he wanted to inform us that he had made a decision that they probably would find out when they got back to the plant, so he wanted to let us know right there, where he had looked over a case where a person, Edward Mark, had been suspended, and he decided that that wasn't a severe enough penalty that the Plant Manager had given him, and that he was letting us know that he had decided that that person should have been fired.

Q. And did Mr. Edwards inform you that in fact Mr. Mark had been fired?

A. Yes. He said he had just called the office and told the people at the office that they should call him up at his home and let him know.

Q. On or about March 9, 1976, did the Company take any action regarding infractions of the Company rules that were listed and shown as employee's personnel records?

A. Yes, they did.

Q. And what action was taken?

A. They called the Union officers that were present on that shift into the office, and they informed us that since there was a new contract as of March the 9th that they were—wanted to start off fresh, and that they were going to clear everybody's records, but from then on he was strictly enforcing it from that point on, go from a year-to-year basis, your record.

Q. Do you know a Rick Kohl, K–O–H–L?

A. Yes, I do.

Q. Had Mr. Kohl been terminated by the Company prior to clearing the records?

A. Yes, they had.

Q. What happened to Mr. Kohl when everybody's records were cleared?

A. He informed us at the same meeting when clearing everybody's records he would be reinstated with full seniority and pay for the days off he had been fired.

Q. Do you recall why Mr. Kohl had been discharged?

A. I think he had been late too many times in a year's period.

Q. Did the Company post new rules on or about March 9, 1976?

A. Yes, they did.

Q. And did you attend the second-step grievance meeting where Mr. Mark's grievance was heard?

A. Yes, I did.

Q. And did anyone from the Union ask if a Suspension Notice had been issued to the Grievant?

A. Not yet. I asked the Plant Manager, who was sitting across the desk from me, if he had some kind of written statement, you know, saying why this person had been suspended. And he handed me a document.

Q. I'm handing you a document at this time, Danny. Can you identify that as—can you identify that as being a copy of the document that Mr. Creekmore handed you during the step-two meeting?

A. Yes, this is a copy of that document.

Mr. DiMaggio: The Union introduces this as a Union Exhibit, Mr. Arbitrator.

[*Whereupon Employee Warning Notice dated 3–1–76 was marked Union Exhibit 3.*]

Mr. DiMaggio: I have no further questions from Mr. Lindley.

Mr. Eckerty: I have no questions.

The Arbitrator: I want to ask you one thing, you have been there eleven years?

The Witness: Yeah.

The Arbitrator: Do you know of any other case where an employee was guilty of either falsifying records or having a phoney absentee slip or anything of this type, anything similar to what happened with Mr. Mark?

The Witness: No, sir. When people miss, they—you know, they ask the people to bring in slips, and people bring in all kinds of slips. I don't know of anyone who has been discharged for it.

The Arbitrator: Not discharged, do you know of anybody who has ever been found with one that didn't—

The Witness: No sir, I don't know of any other one.

LARRY ECKERTY,

called as a witness by and on behalf of the Company, being first duly and regularly sworn by the Arbitrator, testified as follows:

Mr. Eckerty: We had a management change, as everybody is aware of at the time, and the previous Plant Manager, who was out of the plant so much that we—things did get a little loose, I don't deny that. We had a new Plant Manager, who was Earl Creekmore, and Alfred Hawkins was the new supervisor.

To go back to Edward Mark, we had previous suspensions for the attendance and the tardies. He was well aware, both verbally and in writing, notices that were given him by management to his attendance. And at the time the infraction occurred when he notified his supervisor that he had an emergency phone call and his grandmother ws being admitted to the hospital for a leg injury, he was well aware that an unexcused absence would have warranted a three-day suspension. He didn't offer any—you know, he didn't tell his supervisor that he was tired or he felt that he was a safety hazard to be performing his duties, or perhaps it might have been handled differently to begin with.

The note was presented to Al Hawkins when he returned to work to justify him being off so as not to be given a three-day suspension. At the time when he presented the note—I mean, it was obvious that we have had many notes from Dameron Hospital and from doctors, and we had never, you know, received one that looked like this. And this is the reason that we questioned it. In fact, Edward Mark admitted that it was a phoney and everything.

Now, the supervisor suspended him at that time because that is how supervisors work out here, we do not have the authority to terminate, we suspend and then we contact the Plant Manager at the earliest convenience to go over the case. And the Plant Manager actually is the one that performs the discharge, and it was presented by Al Hawkins that morning. It was decided that he would be given a three-day suspension, which happened. The local corporate management, Mr. Ralph Edwards, Vice-President, General Manager, reviewed the situation when he came out, and that is when the decision was made. The rules are clear cut. They are posted and the employees are well aware of it. And in fact he knew he was ready for a three-day suspension, and that was the reason for the falsification of the document, and, therefore, as local management we responded at that point. We feel as local management that corporate does have the right to review our decisions, and so we acted accordingly.

(b) EXCERPT FROM UNION BRIEF

ARGUMENT

A. The Discharge Action Placed the Grievant In Double Jeopardy

The principle prohibiting double jeopardy is well established and has been consistently observed by Arbitrators in the adjudication of Union Management disputes. This principle provides that "once discipline for a given offense has been imposed and accepted, it cannot thereafter be increased" (see p. 427, How Arbitration Works, Elkouri & Elkouri).

In the instant dispute, there can be no doubt that the Grievant suffered double jeopardy and that the original three day suspension levied against the Grievant was enlarged upon via the discharge action. The Company admits that at the time of suspension, the Grievant was told by Supervisor Hawkins that he would be contacted on the following day, March 2, 1976, and informed of the Company's *final* determination; that Supervisor Hawkins met with Plant Manager Creekmore on the morning of March 2, 1976; that it was decided by Mr. Creekmore that the appropriate penalty should be a three day suspension; and that this information was communicated to the Grievant following the March 2, 1976, meeting. Any enlargement of this penalty subsequent to this notification to the Grievant constitutes double jeopardy.

Thus, when the Grievant was notified of his discharge on Friday, March 5, 1976, three days after the imposition of the three day suspension, there can be no question that he was placed in double jeopardy. The three day suspension had in fact already been accepted and served and the Grievant was due to report back for work at 3:00 p. m. that afternoon.

In 59 LA 414, Stauffer Chemical Company, Arbitrator Pierce Davis found that maintenance employees who were orally reprimanded for not using full face masks were improperly suspended for one week, three weeks later, since this constituted double punishment for the same offense. It should be noted that the suspension was imposed after the Company's Corporate Board investigated the matter; a situation similar to that in the instant dispute.

At Page 416, Arbitrator Davis comments as follows:

"The only question in this case is whether a second and more severe disciplinary penalty should have been imposed, approximately three weeks subsequent to the first discipline, upon each grievant."

On this issue, the arbitrator concludes that there was not proper cause to impose additional and more severe penalties. This conclusion is warranted solely on the basis of the principle of prohibition of double jeopardy. This principle is so well known and so well established as not to require specific explanation.

Arbitrator Davis ordered that the Grievants' should be compensated retroactively for their lost earnings. The Plant Manager is signatory to the Agreement and has the authority to settle grievances at the Second and Third steps of the Grievance procedure as per Article XV of the Agreement. Council (sic) for the Company even testified that it is within the authority of the Plant Manager to decide whether employees are to be suspended or discharged and that corporate management has never before reversed such decisions. Mr. Edwards involvement in the Grievants' discharge was clearly contrary to proper procedure. The Union also cites the following arbitration awards as being supportive of the Union's position on double jeopardy:

37 LA 860

39 LA 1

40 LA 87

46 LA 699

The Union therefore submits that the grievance should be sustained on the basis that the discharge constituted double jeopardy.

B.   The Company Imposed Disparate Treatment to the Grievant

Testimony of Union witnesses is uncontroverted regarding the fact that the Company expunged all employees' personnel records of any and all infractions of the plant rules effective March 9, 1976.

Also standing uncontroverted is testimony that in expunging the employee records, the Company reinstated discharged employee Rick Kohl with full seniority and back pay.

The fact that the Grievant was not granted the same consideration constitutes disparate treatment and should, in itself, be sufficient grounds for setting aside Grievant's discharge.

C.   The Company Did Not Give Fair Notice of a Change In Standards Relative to the Application and Enforcement of the Plant Rules

There is no dispute as to the fact that the Company had been very lax in the enforcement of the Plant Rules prior to the Grievant's discharge.   Even Council (sic) for the Company admitted that "things did get a little loose, I don't deny that."

It was this lax attitude on the part of the Company that concerned Mr. Edwards, the Vice President of the Company, and caused him to enlarge upon the three day suspension by insisting that the Grievant be discharged.

Thus, the Grievant was used as *the example* in proclaiming the end of lax rule enforcement.   Not only was this grossly unfair to the Grievant, but it didn't work.   The Company later found it necessary to clear all employee records and to revise and re-post the Plant Rules "due to lax enforcement and confusion regarding the plant rules".

It is a well known arbitration principle that employees are entitled to prior notice of a Company's intention to strictly enforce plant rules that have formerly been loosely enforced.   The Grievant was not afforded such prior notice and on this basis alone, the discharge should be set aside.

D.   The Company Did Not Apply the Plant Rule as Written

Joint Exhibit 2 is the grievance file.   The second document in that file is the Plant Manager's first-step response to the instant grievance, which states in part as follows:

"Page (2) of the Plant Rules, state that falsification of personal, personnel, or Company records is grounds for *immediate* discharge."   (emphasis added)

Company Exhibit 4 is a copy of the Plant Rules in effect at the time of the Grievant's discharge. These rules state in pertinent part, as follows:

> "The following acts will normally result in *immediate* discharge.
>
> 8. Falsification of personal, personnel or Company records." (emphasis added)

It is called to the Arbitrator's attention that the Company did not apply Rule No. 8 as written inasmuch as the Grievant was not *immediately* discharged as required by the rule.

The Union submits that since the Company knew on March 1, 1976, that the Grievant had falsified the doctor's note but did not discharge the Grievant until March 5, 1976, it did not follow the rule of *immediate* discharge and therefore, the discharge is procedurally defective and must be set aside. The three day suspension originally imposed by the Company serves only to compound the procedural defect.

(c) EXCERPT FROM COMPANY BRIEF

ARGUMENT

A. The Double Jeopardy Concept is Inapplicable in the Present Matter

1. The Grievant Herein is Not Being Punished Twice for the Same Offense

Double jeopardy means double penalty for the same offense: "once discipline for a given offense has been imposed and accepted it cannot thereafter be increased." Elkouri & Elkouri, *How Arbitration Works* 636 (1973). The fallacy of the Union's contention is that it assumes that the Grievant has been punished twice for the same offense, whereas, in fact, two distinct offenses were committed and two separate penalties were imposed: first, pursuant to the Plant Rules, he was suspended for three days upon his accumulation of a fifth unexcused absence within the calendar year; and second, pursuant to the Plant Rules, he was discharged for falsifying a personal record.

That both offenses arose from the same action does not mean that the Company must select only one of them for purposes of discipline. In Wagner Castings Co. and Allied Industrial Workers of America, Local 728, 59 LA 862 (1972), the Union alleged double jeopardy since the Grievant's absentee record could result not only in disciplinary action but also in job disqualification. Arbitrator Martin rejected this contention, explaining that:

> * * * It is not an attempt to punish him twice for the same alleged offense if, in fact, his actions can be said to have constituted separate offenses. It is possible for one to damage property

without stealing it. It is also possible to steal property without damaging it. Proof of violation of one rule does not depend on proof of violation of the other. There is, then, no double jeopardy in Company's charging Grievant with violation of two rules."

The same reasoning disposes of the double jeopardy claim in the present matter. The Grievant herein committed two offenses—five unexcused absences within the calendar year and a falsified record— and may be punished separately for each without double jeopardy attaching, even though both arose from the same wrongful act.

2. Assuming Arguendo that the Grievant was Punished for the Same Offense, Double Jeopardy Does Not Attach Because the Preliminary Penalty Determination was not Made on the Basis of a Full Hearing

Even should the Arbitrator find that the Grievant's suspension and discharge were imposed for the same offense, double jeopardy cannot attach because a complete investigation and review of the Grievant's record had not been made at the time the preliminary penalty—the suspension—was imposed. In International Harvester Co. and United Farm Equipment, etc., Local 236 (CIO), 13 LA 610 (1949), in which employees were first suspended and then discharged upon further investigation, Arbitrator Wirtz concluded:

"The Union's cry of 'double-jeopardy' is only an attempt to construct a technicality on which to base its case. The technicalities of criminal law are a poor guide to labor relations, and the particular rule relied on here is obviously inapplicable. The double-jeopardy rule assumes that a full hearing has once been held, and that a penalty has been invoked on the basis of the disclosures at that hearing. Normal industrial plant disciplinary procedures do not contemplate the kind of hearing which is the basis of this rule, and there was no such hearing in this case."

Id. at 613–14.

In the present matter, a complete review of the Grievant's conduct was not made until Thursday, March 4, at which time Messrs. Hawkins, Creekmore, Eckerty and Edwards met to discuss the appropriate final penalty. As Mr. Eckerty testified, they

"reviewed the situation　*　*　*　and that is when the decision was made. The rules are clear cut. They are posted and the employees are well aware of it. And in fact [the Grievant] knew he was ready for a three-day suspension, and that was the reason for the falsification of the document, and, therefore, as local management we responded at that point. We feel as local management that corporate does have the right to review our decisions, and so we acted accordingly."

A suspension prior to discharge and a later discharge "not unduly delayed" do not violate double jeopardy where the intervening investigation is terminated within a reasonable time.

B. The Discharge is Warranted Under the Collective Bargaining Agreement

1. The Arbitrator Must Defer to the Company's Business Judgment Unless Its Decision was Arbitrary and Capricious

"ARTICLE III. MANAGEMENT

The management of the Employer's operations and direction of working forces, including but not limited to the right to * * * discharge for cause * * * and to make such reasonable rules and regulations in connection with the Employer's operations and the conduct, work performance and duties of its employees, as are deemed advisable, is vested exclusively in the Employer, subject only to such limitations as are specifically set forth in this Agreement."

This article of the Agreement authorizes the exercise of the Company's judgment in discharge matters. In the present matter, the Grievant's culpability is conceded. He admits that, at the time he falsified the doctor's note, he was aware of both the Plant Rule proscribing falsification of personal records and the consequent penalty of discharge.

Under the contract between the parties, the Arbitrator lacks authority to decide *de novo* the appropriateness of disciplinary penalties. This authority is "vested exclusively" in the management. Under such a contractual provision,

"The only circumstances under which a penalty imposed by management can be rightfully set aside by an Arbitrator are those where discrimination, unfairness, or capricious and arbitrary action are proved—in other words, where there has been abuse of discretion."

Stockham Pipe Fittings Co., 1 LA 160, 196 (1945). This is "a well recognized and frequently applied principle of arbitration 'law'."

One of the most basic management prerogatives is that of imposing discipline because of industrial misconduct. The Arbitrator has no authority to upset such judgments if the actions of management and the discipline imposed are not arbitrary or capricious. Otherwise, it would be the Arbitrators running the plant, rather than the Company. This case presents the first instance of an employee falsifying records; the Company intends to establish a firm, uniform, and strict disciplinary policy to deter future misconduct of this nature. Unless the Arbitrator considers this business judgment to be arbitrary and capricious, he has no authority to revoke the discharge.

Accordingly, the grievance should be denied.

B. THE COLLECTIVE CONTRACT

At the conclusion of negotiations, the parties normally sign a collective bargaining agreement which will govern their rights and responsibilities during its term. Set forth in Appendix C are the table of contents and some excerpts from a typical agreement. Note the breadth of the agreement and the careful drafting which was employed. The use of seniority and the extensive reach of the grievance system are typical as is the elaborate process described for choosing an arbitrator and for limiting the arbitrator's jurisdiction.

QUESTIONS

1. Can you identify any clauses which indicate the probable give and take of the bargaining process?

2. How could the "no strike" clause be written to make it more favorable to management?

3. How could the contract have been written to give greater weight to seniority?

4. How could the arbitration clause be rewritten to give the arbitrator less power? Would this be desirable from management's point of view? From the union's?

C.   GRIEVANCE PROCEDURES

Although many issues affecting employment may be resolved in the collective bargaining agreement, controversies will continue to arise after the parties have entered into the contract. The parties are obligated to bargain in good faith over its interpretation. Most such disputes are settled informally, but others require formal procedures. Where agreement cannot be obtained, the collective bargaining agreement usually provides a grievance/arbitration procedure to handle grievances.

Almost all collective bargaining agreements establish procedures to be followed in resolving grievances. Collective bargaining agreements vary in the number of steps they provide in the grievance system; however, most contracts contain four steps. Step One usually consists of the grievant registering a complaint to the immediate superior. This may be done directly but is usually done by the employee's union steward. If the grievance is denied at Step One, the steward may proceed to Step Two, where the grievance is presented to the plant labor relations representative. If the grievance is denied there, the grievance may be pursued to Step Three. At Step Three the grievant will be represented either by the plant bargaining committee or a representative from the international union. Management will be represented at this level either by the plant manager or a top labor relations manager, depending upon how complex is the company structure. If the grievance is unresolved at Step Three, the grievance may be pursued to Step Four, which is arbitration.

D. ARBITRATION

---

1. THE NATURE OF LABOR ARBITRATION: AN OVERVIEW

The agreement included in Appendix as does over 95% of all collective bargaining contracts provides for arbitration to settle disputes which arise during its existence. The widespread use of a voluntary arbitration is a unique feature of the American industrial relation process and is of fairly recent origin.

FLEMING, THE LABOR ARBITRATION PROCESS *

* * *

In retrospect it is clear that World War II did three things insofar as voluntary arbitration is concerned. First of all, it encouraged wide-spread adoption of arbitration techniques. Second, it sharpened the distinction between arbitration over "rights" and "interests." Henceforth, it would be clear that the commitment of the parties was to grievance arbitration, not to arbitration of the terms of a new agreement or to substantive issues not covered by the contract. Finally, the War Labor Board served as a training ground for the men who subsequently served as arbitrators. This cadre has ever since constituted the hard core of the arbitration profession. Without the understanding which they brought to the job it is possible that grievance arbitration would have been less readily accepted.

After 1945 grievance arbitration was firmly established. The debate was no longer *whether* an arbitration clause should be included in the contract, but was concerned solely with mechanics. Should pressure be put on the government to provide a free arbitration service? (There was precedent for this in the railroad industry.) Was it better to have a permanent umpire, *ad hoc* appointees, or a rotating panel? Should the arbitration board be tripartite, or should a single impartial individual be asked to make the decision? How formal should the proceedings be? Should the parties be represented by lawyers, or train their own people to present the cases? Were the parties willing to have the arbitrator attempt to settle the case, or did they want him to remain aloof and detached? To what extent should the courts be involved in deciding what kinds of cases the parties had in fact agreed to arbitrate? How great should the remedy power of the arbitrator be? Was he to be a policeman in the industry, or only a decision-maker in questions on which the parties differed, with the proper remedy being left to their further negotiation?

* Fleming, *The Labor Artibration Process* (© Univ. of Ill. 1965). Printed by permission.

Some of these questions were answered; others were not. After experimenting with free arbitration services for a brief period, the Federal Mediation and Conciliation Service abandoned the practice on the advice of labor and management. Thereafter it would maintain a panel of arbitrators from which names could be supplied to the parties, but arrangements would be made directly by the parties and they would pay the bill. As to the other questions, most of them remained items of preference without any fixed pattern emerging.

This was the formal structure of grievance arbitration as it emerged from the war. What remained was to breathe life into the structure so that the dynamics of the process became clear.

To the uninitiated, grievance arbitration looks like a simple and logical terminal point for deciding contractual disputes on which the parties cannot agree. There are, in fact, many reasons for going to arbitration which have little or nothing to do with the merits of the dispute. The grievance procedure is not, and cannot be, isolated from the bargaining relationship between the parties to the contract. A good example is the familiar phenomenon of multiple grievances being slated for arbitration during the period of contract negotiations, but being withdrawn as soon as a contract is agreed upon. Bargaining pressure is simply being exerted through the grievance channel.

There are many other institutional problems which must be taken into account. No impartial machinery which is always limited to the same two parties can survive if one side always wins. In bringing cases the parties take this into consideration. Being a political organization is an additional problem for the union. Too rigid screening of grievances can alienate needed local support. It may be better to blame an adverse decision on an arbitrator than to assert that the grievance is wholly without merit. Newly elected officers may take cases to arbitration to fulfill campaign promises, or just to gain experience for the future. In an otherwise peaceful and quiet plant an occasional arbitration may inject some color and excitement to whet the interest of committeemen. On the management side, the company may prefer to back rather than reverse an erring foreman. Or a clash in views may exist between the operating and industrial relations divisions, with the latter preferring to have the arbitrator push the company in the direction they deem desirable or inevitable.

In short, the years between 1941 and 1957 made clear that grievance arbitration was not only a device for settling differences of opinion over the meaning and interpretation of contracts. It was also related to bargaining strategy, to human relations within the plant, and to organizational imperatives within the management and union structures. It was not, however, much concerned with the law.

SELECTING THE ARBITRATOR *

Most collective bargaining agreements containing arbitration provisions specify that the parties are to select the arbitrator on a case-by-case basis rather than to impanel a single arbitrator to hear every case during the life of the agreement.

In some industries, such as basic steel and auto manufacturing, the contract provides for a permanent panel or pool of umpires, whose members are designated to adjudicate every case that reaches arbitration. Smaller employers, however, need not select a permanent umpire, unless both parties can agree upon a mutually acceptable individual to hear every case arising during the life of the contract. Some arbitrators are better suited or more experienced to hear particular matters (e.g., discipline and discharge cases), and agreements limiting the selection of arbitrators to a few individuals may deprive both parties of the opportunity to bring in another arbitrator who may have more expertise in the subject matter of the grievance.

Typically, representatives of both labor and management each receive an identified list of arbitrators from either the American Arbitration Association (AAA) or the Federal Mediation and Conciliation Service (FMCS). Each party then crosses off any names to which he objects, numbers the remaining names according to his order of preference, and returns the list to the AAA or FMCS. If no names are mutually satisfactory, the rules of the AAA and the FMCS arbitration service provide that a new list be issued.

If no names on that list are mutually acceptable, the appropriate agency may make an appointment from among the other members of its national panel of labor arbitrators. Of course, if the parties do not choose to accept this method of selection, they are entirely free to agree to other methods such as the receipt of even more lists from the AAA or FMCS.

The selection of the arbitrator to hear a particular case is especially important. Unlike our judicial system, where the parties have little if any control over the selection of the judge who will hear their case, arbitration gives the parties the unique opportunity to control selection. Selection of the arbitrator is perhaps the most important single step in the entire arbitral process.

Most contracts provide that arbitration awards shall be "final and binding" upon the parties. The courts have therefore been reluctant to set aside arbitration awards, except under very limited circumstances involving either gross impropriety and prejudice on the part of the arbitrator or where the award departs completely from the

* Reprinted from Earle K. Shawe, "Preparation For The Arbitration Hearing," 31 Labor Law Journal 46, 47–49 (1980). © Earle K. Shawe. Reprinted with the permission of the author. Mr. Shawe is Senior Partner of Shawe & Rosenthal, Baltimore, Maryland, a firm which specializes in labor law representing management and has represented a large number of corporate clients with respect to arbitrations throughout the country. Mr. Shawe is former Co-Chairman, Labor Law Section, Committee on Practice and Procedures of the American Bar Association.

contract language and intent. The losing party in a judicial proceeding has an automatic right of appeal to the appellate courts, but the parties can rarely obtain judicial review of an arbitration award. Thus, in a sense, the arbitrator exercises even more unreviewable authority over industrial relations than any trial court.

For these reasons, the selection of an arbitrator is extremely important. Arbitrators come from a variety of backgrounds, including professional arbitrators, lawyers, law professors, judges, public officials, clergymen, and economists. Short biographical sketches concerning the most frequently used arbitrators are contained in Commerce Clearing House's *Labor Arbitration Awards* and other reporting services. Also, the AAA and FMCS provide information concerning the arbitrators whose names are supplied to the parties for selection.

While these directories may provide some information about the arbitrator, there is no substitute for personal experience before the arbitrator in question. Perhaps the next most reliable indicator of an arbitrator's abilities is his written opinions and awards, which are found in *Labor Arbitration Awards* and other services.

Reputations quickly develop in the arbitration field, and unions and employers are urged to consult with the participants named in the proceedings reported in these services, to share their impressions about the subject arbitrator. For this purpose, *Labor Arbitration Awards* and other services provide the names of the parties' representatives who tried the reported cases. A good arbitrator is one whose reputation indicates his understanding of contracts and the arbitral process, a clear grasp of facts and issues, the ability to conduct a fair and orderly hearing, and the articulation of awards based upon sound reasoning and fair interpretations of the subject contract.

Since these sources of information are readily available, it is advisable to make use of them in the initial stages of preparing for the arbitration hearing. If there are no serious objections to the reasoning contained in a proposed arbitrator's past decisions, the parties' representatives should check his or her other qualifications (such as experience, intelligence, honesty, and courage) to decide each case on its own merits rather than "splitting" awards. Often, the broader the arbitrator's background and experience, the more likely he is to understand the facts and decide correctly.

ELKOURI & ELKOURI, HOW ARBITRATION WORKS *

TIME, PLACE, AND NOTICE OF HEARING

No fixed rule exists for setting the date and locale of arbitration hearings. Ordinarily the arbitrator will meet at any time and place agreed to by the parties, if he can be available. If the parties cannot agree upon these matters, the arbitrator or the administering agency

* Reprinted by permission from *How Arbitration Works*, (3rd Ed. 1973) by Frank Elkouri and Edna Asper Elkouri, copyright © 1973 by The Bureau of National Affairs, Inc., Washington, D.C. 20037.

must set them. In this regard, it is generally accepted that the "arbitrator [or agency] should consult the convenience of the parties in fixing the time and place for the hearing but should not allow one party to delay unduly the fixing of a date for the hearing. Written and timely notice of the date, time and place of the hearing should be given."

Under some arbitration statutes the time and place for the hearing are fixed by the arbitrator, who may also be responsible for giving timely notice thereof. In any case, the arbitrator should always take action to insure adequate notice to the parties.

The hearing room itself is ordinarily selected by the parties or by an administering agency. Frequently some "neutral ground" such as a hotel suite is used; this may minimize interruptions that sometimes occur when the hearing is held at the plant. However, some parties prefer to use a conference room at the company since this may reduce costs, will make records and witnesses more quickly available, and will require less time for any visit by the arbitrator to the site of the dispute.

A conference table arrangement (with the arbitrator at the head of the table) is most satisfactory if there are not too many participants. A "courtroom" arrangement tends to be more formal, but it may be best if there are numerous participants.

TRANSCRIPT OF HEARING

A formal written record of the hearing is not always necessary. Use of a reporter is the exception rather than the general practice.

In simple cases the arbitrator can take adequate notes. Likewise, in cases involving contract interpretation only, there being no disputed facts, the arbitrator's notes and the parties' exhibits and/or briefs ordinarily make a transcript unnecessary. However, in complicated or lengthy cases stenographic records may be very helpful, if not indispensable; the transcript will aid not only the arbitrator in studying the case, but also the parties in preparing briefs. The transcript may be invaluable in any court review of the arbitration proceedings. It is said that the palest ink is more accurate than the most retentive memory.

PARTICIPATION BY ARBITRATOR IN HEARING

Arbitrators should be informed as fully as possible about the disputes they are to resolve. Accordingly, the arbitrator must feel free to participate personally in the hearing by asking questions, seeking information and exploring all angles to the extent reasonably necessary to satisfy himself that he has in fact been informed as fully as possible. Arbitrator Harry Shulman emphasized, in this regard, that the arbitrator "should be satisfied that he knows enough to be able to decide the case" and that he "cannot simply sit back and judge a debate. He must seek to inform himself as fully as possible and encourage the parties to provide him with the information."

Similarly, it has been emphasized that while the arbitrator obviously should not take sides, he must be free to ask questions and to explore all angles which he deems necessary to a full understanding of the case "even if they have not occurred to either one or both of the parties."

It has been observed that:

"Where testimony is controverted, it is quite proper for the Arbitrator to take the initiative, if necessary, in reconciling apparent contradictions, or in seeking insight into the motives of those whose testimony is at odds. It is the parties' primary responsibility to present facts and to rebut contrary testimony, but the Arbitrator may also use his office to elicit information or to secure insights where, in his opinion, such procedure is made necessary by the critical nature of the controverted testimony."

Likewise, arbitrators are justified in making an independent study of the entire collective agreement to insure consideration of all provisions that might be relevant to the disposition of the case.

ORDER OF PRESENTING CASE

There is no rigid order in which the parties must present their case in arbitration. The party asserting a claim usually presents its case first, or at least a preliminary or introductory case, but this practice may not be followed where the nature of the issue makes a different procedure preferable. A somewhat typical approach in regard to the presentation of proof is that under American Arbitration Association Rule 26:

"The party initiating the arbitration, or his counsel, shall [first] present his claim and proofs, and his witnesses, who shall submit to questions or other examination. The answering party or his counsel shall then present his proofs, and his witnesses, who shall submit to questions or other examination. *The Arbitrator may, in his discretion, vary this procedure* but shall afford full and equal opportunity to all parties and witnesses for presentation of any material or relevant proofs."

NEED FOR HEARING

A hearing in the presence of the arbitrator is deemed imperative in virtually all cases. In giving each party full and fair opportunity to be heard, the arbitration hearing simultaneously serves to inform the arbitrator fully regarding all material aspects of the dispute. However, in some cases the parties believe that the arbitrator can be adequately informed without a hearing in his presence, so they submit the dispute for decision entirely on the basis of stipulated facts, written briefs, and sometimes affidavits.

REPRESENTATIVES IN ARBITRATION

It is generally agreed that each party has the right to be represented in arbitration proceedings by persons of its own choosing. As

Arbitrator Morton Singer has declared, neither side "may compel the other side to retain or consult with any person other than one of their own free will and choice."

Some parties prefer to be represented in arbitration by the person who served as their spokesman in the pre-arbitral stages of the grievance procedure, since he is thoroughly familiar with the dispute. That person, however, may lack the skill needed to present the case clearly to an outsider who has no background knowledge of the parties or their dispute. This recognized, other representatives such as higher union or company officials may be used to present the case at the arbitration stage. Then, too, attorneys often are used by one or both parties.

Regarding use of attorneys, Arbitrator Benjamin Aaron has aptly observed that an attorney, if he is well-trained and if he understands the nature of collective bargaining and the purposes of arbitration, will have the ability to outline the dispute clearly and simply, to come directly to the point at issue, to present his evidence in an orderly fashion, and to sum up his arguments and relate them to the record made at the hearing. Legal training may be especially important in still other respects if the case is governed by any detailed arbitration statute.

Of course, some laymen possess the ability and experience to present cases very skillfully and effectively. Indeed, as one union consultant has been quoted, "a good union representative" may be "more than an even match for a company attorney."

Some arbitration statutes expressly state that either party has a right to be represented by an attorney and that waivers of this right are subject to limitations stated in the statute.

Logically, "the determination of the order of presentation in an arbitration case should depend exclusively on how the facts can best be developed in an orderly way." If the arbitrator can see at the outset of a hearing that one of the parties possesses the basic facts of the case and that the case of the other party will consist primarily of a rebuttal, the arbitrator upon his own initiative or at the request of a party may suggest or require that the party in possession of the basic facts present its case first.

After both parties have presented their basic case, each party in turn will be given full opportunity to present its rebuttal case. Indeed, the hearing will not be adjourned until each party has nothing further to add.

OPENING STATEMENTS AND CLOSING ARGUMENTS

Opening statements are brief, generalized statements in clear language designed to acquaint the arbitrator with each party's view of what the dispute is about and what the party expects to prove by its evidence. Use of opening statements is ordinarily optional with the parties, but sometimes the arbitrator specifically requests that each party make one.

Sometimes both parties make opening statements at the outset of the hearing, before any evidence is introduced by either party. This is especially helpful to the arbitrator as it enables him to grasp more quickly what the dispute is about. Another possibility is that each party will make its opening statement immediately prior to presenting its initial evidence; thus one party will have made its opening statement and presented its evidence before the other party makes its opening statement. Ordinarily the arbitrator will follow whatever procedure the parties desire, unless he is convinced that some particular procedure is essential for proper presentation of the case.

By making closing arguments after all the evidence of both parties has been presented, the parties "can render a real service to the arbitrator as well as to themselves by carefully analyzing and synthesizing the important aspects of the case, emphasizing the facts they feel they have proved and placing them in proper relation to the ultimate fact sought to be established or to the ultimate conclusion at which they seek to persuade the arbitrator to arrive."

The arbitrator will always permit the parties to make closing arguments (though he may limit the amount of time), and he sometimes requests specifically that they do so. Closing arguments and posthearing briefs sometimes serve much the same purpose, and while the parties sometimes choose to use both they more frequently choose only to use either one or the other.

EARLE K. SHAWE, PREPARATION FOR THE ARBITRATION HEARING *

Obviously, the arbitrator's entire picture of the case comes from the parties' presentations of evidence and argument, so no material fact should be left unstated at the hearing. * * * [K]now and understand all facts surrounding the controversy and cull out all irrelevant and immaterial information.

In some types of cases, the facts may not be in dispute, and the presentation may therefore be directed to fashioning a persuasive * * * argument as to how particular contractual language should be interpreted. Following is a list of actions that should be undertaken when preparing a case for arbitration.

(1) Review the preliminary steps of the grievance proceeding and the positions taken by the parties.

(2) Obtain copies of and analyze prior grievances and arbitration awards between the parties on the same or related issues. Be prepared to rely upon or distinguish the disposition of these matters.

* Earle K. Shawe, "Preparation For The Arbitration Hearing," 31 Labor Law Journal 46 (1980); © by Earle K. Shawe. Reprinted with the permission of the author. Mr. Shawe is Senior Partner of Shawe & Rosenthal, Baltimore, Maryland, a firm which specializes in labor law representing management and has represented a large number of corporate clients with respect to arbitrations throughout the country. Mr. Shawe is former Co-Chairman, Labor Law Section, Committee on Practice and Procedure of the American Bar Association.

Similarly, research other decisions of the designated arbitrator, especially if he has decided cases with related issues.

(3) Ascertain the authority of the arbitrator, since the scope of his jurisdiction only extends as far as the voluntary agreement by both parties.

(4) Read and analyze the entire collective bargaining agreement, with particular attention to the provisions at issue in the case. Try to obtain copies of prior or succeeding contracts to the one at issue in order to compare changes in language which might have an important bearing on interpreting what the parties intended. Learn what the parties' past practice has been in administering the collective bargaining agreement because such history will bear upon the arbitrator's interpretation of contractual rights.

(5) Interview all witnesses to an event or persons who can inform you about the company's organization, machinery, equipment, plant layout, work force, or other matters significant to your case. Obtain not only the facts favorable to you, but also those that your opponent is likely to rely upon. After all, you are going to have to meet their arguments head on and demonstrate to the arbitrator how your opponent's position compares unfavorably with yours. If you get a complete picture of the facts and arguments your opponent is likely to rely upon as early as possible, you may decide to recommend that the case be settled. You should not develop a blind spot to the possible merits of your opponent's case. At the very least, you will not be caught by surprise at the hearing.

(6) Prepare testimony outlines for those witnesses whom you propose to call. Explain to each of them the points that they are expected to make. Prepare them for your opponent and test their statements by a searching cross-examination. Remember that the arbitrator's only information about the facts of the case will come from the evidence presented, so prepare these persons well. Coordinate all your witnesses so that each knows what the other will say, the order of appearance, and what principles he or she will be establishing. This will help make the hearing proceed more orderly and efficiently.

(7) Inspect and copy all documents and records that are relevant. Organize them into the exhibits you plan to use, order them in the chronological sequence in which they will be introduced, and make sufficient copies for the arbitrator and your opponent. This material can save much testimony and often present a clearer picture.

(8) If practical, visit and inspect the premises if the case is one where it is important to visualize the event that gave rise to the dispute. If so, obtain photographs, diagrams, or blueprints, of the site in question. In particularly unique or unusual cases, the parties may want to ask the arbitrator to also visit the plant or significant locations in the dispute.

(9) Prepare an outline of the case, including exhibits, witnesses, and legal argument ordered in a logical progression. Remember that, in presenting the case, you will have to sort and prune many of

the facts that you have gathered because much will be irrelevant, not sufficiently convincing, cumulative, etc.

(10) Attempt to secure from your opponent a written stipulation of facts not in dispute. This will narrow the issues and expedite the hearing. Often, background information helps to give the arbitrator a good frame of reference. Also, lists of names, places, and equipment involved, as well as terms peculiar to the industry, will often be helpful. Some arbitrators find that a chronological list of events is helpful.

(11) Some parties present preliminary or prehearing briefs to the arbitrator, but such documents must necessarily be somewhat sketchy before actual testimony and exhibits are admitted at the hearing. We do not recommend that prehearing briefs be presented, since arbitration proceedings do not generally provide for pretrial discovery. Thus, a prehearing memorandum may turn out to be based on assertions or assumptions which are rendered of dubious validity at the hearing.

STATEMENT OF THE ISSUE

Once the hearing opens, the first order of business should be to precisely stipulate the issue to be resolved by the arbitrator. In fact, some arbitrators request that the parties make such a submission in advance of the hearing date. This is more likely to occur in novel or complex cases.

Since the arbitration process does not entail the formal pleadings required in judicial proceedings, it is important that the issues to be decided be formulated in some other manner. Usually, the demand or notice of arbitration provided for by the collective bargaining agreement will only identify the facts and dispute in very general terms, and it is often inartfully drafted. Since the arbitrator has jurisdiction to decree a particular application of the agreement, the scope of his authority should be precisely pinpointed at the outset.

Sometimes, however, the parties are not able to agree upon a specific statement of the issue. A good arbitrator probably will not let this disagreement degenerate into an additional dispute by unduly pressing the parties to arrive at a mutually agreeable statement. Instead, he may allow some testimony or exhibits to be received, after which the issue may appear more clearly. At that point, the arbitrator may himself discuss clarification of the issue with the parties and prepare a stipulation agreeable to the parties.

Assuming that the issue or issues can be initially stipulated to, the hearing then opens and certain preliminary matters should be completed. The following information should first be made part of any record of the proceeding: (1) names of the parties: (2) date, hour, and place of the hearing; (3) name of the arbitrator(s); (4) name and title of representatives for the parties; and (5) stipulation of facts, including a copy of the collective bargaining agreement and any special matters that exist.

Some parties prepare a written summary of their contentions and submit it to the arbitrator and opposing counsel at this point. However, this is a matter of personal taste or style and is not necessary in most cases.

ARBITRABILITY

Many arbitration cases never result in a decision on the merits of the dispute. Before an arbitrator may consider the merits of a particular grievance, a threshold question must first be answered: whether the subject grievance is arbitrable under the contract.

The authority of an arbitrator is confined to the powers he derives from the collective bargaining agreement. An arbitrator can only render awards consistent with and limited to his authority as defined in the contract. Where an arbitrator is asked to exceed his authority and determine disputes which are not cognizable under the contract, either party may properly challenge his authority to rule in the case.

One of the most obvious methods of challenging the arbitrator's jurisdiction to decide a case is where there is a dispute over the timeliness of the filing of the grievance. Most contracts provide strict time limits within which either party may file a grievance, such as "within five working days from the time the alleged violation arose or was discovered."

If a grievance was untimely filed, either party may raise this at any step of the grievance procedure and should certainly raise it before the arbitrator. Where a grievance was untimely filed, and there are no extenuating circumstances warranting the delay in the filing of the grievance, arbitrators have not been reluctant to conclude that they were without authority to rule on the grievance.

Similarly, arbitrators frequently determine that they lack the authority to rule on a grievance which seeks a remedy which is beyond their contractual authority to award, or where the grievance is not cognizable under the contract. A classic example of this situation is a union grievance protesting the discharge of a probationary employee, although the contract provides that probationers have no contractual rights to protest such action. In a clear situation such as this, an arbitrator probably will conclude that he lacks the authority to rule on the grievance and will dismiss the grievance as inarbitrable.

In sum, before the parties present their case on the merits of the grievance, a thorough review of the preliminary question of arbitrability should be made. If any question over the arbitrator's jurisdiction is raised, it should be disposed of before the trial begins. Indeed, if this preliminary issue is one on which there is a genuine dispute over the facts, such as the precise time when the grievance was filed, it should be tried first, before proceeding to the merits of the case. Some arbitrators even bifurcate the proceedings, taking testimony only on the issue of arbitrability and ruling on that point first before proceeding to the case on the merits.

TRANSCRIPTS AND BRIEFS

Use of a reliable court reporter to transcribe a record of the proceedings should always be considered, especially in cases that are expected to establish important precedent. A transcript will help the arbitrator to analyze the case, as well as help the attorney prepare a posthearing brief. It will furnish the most reliable record of the actual words of witnesses, should questions of credibility arise. Moreover, this record will be most helpful if there is subsequent court review of the arbitration.

The cost of a transcript will involve a moderate expense but will likely be shared equally, because neither party typically wishes to risk not ordering a copy and thereby relying only upon the possible frailties of memory alone, when the opponent has a written transcript. As in any litigation, if there is a great disparity in ability to pay this expense, there is a risk that one side may curtail its testimony slightly to minimize its expense while the other side may lengthen its case in order to discourage numerous future arbitrations. However, the arbitrator or either party can request that immaterial, irrelevant, or cumulative material be disposed of "off the record."

Most practitioners utilize posthearing briefs as a means to organize and argue their view of the case as it developed at the hearing. If one has any doubt whatsoever about how the arbitrator is going to rule, a brief should be filed. This provides an opportunity to highlight the evidence and present an extended discussion of case precedents, bargaining history, and policy arguments in favor of the advocate's position. Even if the determination will depend solely upon the resolution of conflicting oral testimony, a brief should be filed to argue why your witnesses should be credited and the others discredited.

Sometimes an arbitrator may specifically request that briefs not be filed, but usually he will receive the brief of any party who desires to submit one. Briefs are usually scheduled to be submitted both to the arbitrator and the opposing party on the same day, but an alternative system may provide for staggered due dates. In either case, reply briefs may be allowed but typically are not requested. The arbitrator will usually grant a reasonable request for an extension of time within which to file the posthearing brief provided the other party does not object or, if briefs are due simultaneously, has not already filed his brief.

The brief is an important tool whose function is to persuade the arbitrator of the merits of one's side of the case. It should get to the point immediately, avoiding too much detail or background discussion. It must be limited to the facts elicited at the hearing. It is too late for new matter at this point. The customary sections included in the arbitration brief are: a preliminary statement of the case and issue; citations to or quotations from the pertinent provisions of the collective bargaining agreement; a statement of the facts; the legal argument, including a response to the testimony and argument of the other side; and a short summary or conclusion setting forth what one has shown.

Since the arbitrator may not be completely familiar with the industry's peculiar terms, procedures, or equipment in the case before him, and in no event will he know these matters as well as those familiar with the company and its operations, facts must be spelled out very clearly. If technical facts are involved, define them in laymen's terms and assume no prior familiarity with them. As to the argument section, if other precedents are cited, the facts of the case at hand should parallel these as closely as possible. One should read the entire decision(s) relied upon and not rely upon headnotes alone, which often give an incomplete, or worse, misleading picture.

CONDUCT AT HEARING

This discussion requires a final comment on conduct at the proceedings. Keep in mind that scheduling the hearing requires commitments to time and place for a multitude of busy people. A spirit of mutual cooperation is required from all in arranging a mutually agreeable hearing date and location, as well as a willingness to be flexible in planning other work around this matter.

At the hearing itself, be punctual and even early. Lateness not only wastes everyone's time but can create a bad impression upon the arbitrator (not to mention the client). Arbitrators have also commented that bad impressions are created by an advocate's excessive shouting, use of provocative words or questions, and reference to former incidents of misconduct which are irrelevant to the present issues. The oral summation should be clear and nonrepetitious; it should not mix facts with arguments, which can be confusing and damaging to one's case. One should not interrupt the arguments or the summation of an opponent. Thus, the advocate and his witnesses will be protected from interruption and will have a full opportunity to cross-examine his opponent's witnesses. The proceeding is a quasi-formal adversarial hearing, not an informal grievance or bargaining conference where points can be interjected at will.

Finally, do not make baseless and unnecessary objections to testimony proffered by opposing witnesses. Repeated interruptions of this type are time consuming and can irritate the arbitrator. Once a particular line of objections has been called to his attention, an experienced arbitrator will be aware of the matter thereafter without further express mention of it and will appropriately discount testimony weakened by hearsay and irrelevancy. One should be particularly careful if his opponent is not a lawyer but rather a union representative or company official. If one appears to be overly technical or to browbeat an opponent excessively for ignorance of rules of evidence or other legal principles, the arbitrator may unconsciously rush to his defense or sympathize with him.

If an arbitration case is thoroughly prepared and well-organized, the advocate should win the good cases and his share of close ones and even occasionally win cases that are not so good. In the long run, the stakes involved usually far exceed the single grievance to be decided, and the time invested in the case will be well spent.

As with any court appearance, no arbitration case can be over-prepared. The better one's preparation and presentation, the more likely his success. Well tried arbitration cases are important tools in maintaining stable labor relations under a collective bargaining agreement.

J. ALAN LIPS, POINTERS FOR WITNESSES IN ARBITRATION *

1.   TELL THE TRUTH In an arbitration case, as in all other matters, honesty is the best policy. Furthermore, if you try and shade the truth it could undermine your entire credibility. Telling the truth means more than not telling a deliberate falsehood; it requires testifying accurately about what you know.

2.   UNDERSTAND THE QUESTION before you try to answer. You cannot possibly give a truthful and accurate answer unless you understand the question. If you don't understand a question, ask for it to be repeated. The reporter may be asked to read the question to you.

3.   TAKE YOUR TIME and give the question the thought it requires to understand it. Formulate your answer before you give it. Do not give a snap answer without thinking.

4.   DON'T LOOK AT THE COMPANY LAWYER FOR HELP when you are on the stand. If you look at the lawyer for your side when a question is asked on cross-examination or for his approval after answering a question, the arbitrator is bound to notice it and get a bad impression.

5.   ANSWER THE QUESTION that is asked and then *stop*. Don't volunteer information not called for by the question.

6.   GIVE A POSITIVE AND FIRM ANSWER when you can. *Do not say*, "I don't recall that it was," when you mean, "I know that it was not." If you know what did or did not happen, don't be afraid to "swear" to it. When you take the stand, you will be "sworn" to tell the truth to the best of your ability. Avoid such phrases as "I think," "I believe," "in my opinion," and "probably."

7.   DON'T GUESS if you really don't know. Just say you don't know.

8.   GIVE AN AUDIBLE ANSWER so the reporter can hear it.

9.   TALK LOUDLY ENOUGH so everybody can hear you. Don't chew gum. Keep your hands away from your mouth. Dress conservatively and be neat. Sit straight and look alive.

10.   BEWARE OF QUESTIONS INVOLVING DATES OR TIME. Think clearly about dates and time. If you cannot recall exactly, give

---

* Reprinted with the permission of the author. Mr. Lips is a partner in the law firm of Taft, Stettinius & Hollister in Cincinnati, Ohio.

the approximate date or time, saying, "about 9:00 a.m." or "between January 15 and 20." Be sure your estimates are reasonable.

11. KNOW YOUR NAME, where you live, your position with the company during the critical period, how long you held your position, and what your job duties were.

12. BE COURTEOUS. Being courteous is one of the best ways to make a good impression on the arbitrator. Be sure to answer "Yes, sir" and "No, sir."

13. DON'T ARGUE WITH THE REPRESENTATIVE of the other side. He has a right to question you. If you appear to be antagonistic the arbitrator may discount your testimony as reflecting personal bias. Don't respond to a question by asking a question unless the original question is not clear to you.

14. DON'T LOSE YOUR TEMPER no matter how hard you are pressed. Lose your temper, and you may lose the case. When you lose your temper, you play right into the hands of the other side.

15. AVOID JOKING AND WISE CRACKS. An arbitration is a serious matter.

16. DON'T BE AFRAID to look the arbitrator in the eye while you are testifying. He wants to hear what you have to say. Speak directly to the arbitrator frankly and openly as if he were a friend or neighbor.

17. IF ASKED WHETHER you have talked to the lawyer on your side or are being paid while at the hearing, admit it freely. It is entirely proper to discuss your testimony before the hearing. You would not be paid for your testimony; you would be reimbursed for the time you lose and your expenses.

18. WHEN AN OBJECTION IS RAISED TO A QUESTION, say nothing until the arbitrator rules on the objection. If he says that you are not to answer a question, do not try to answer the question.

19. REREAD THESE POINTERS.

NOTE

The development of arbitration as a method of settling labor management disputes is remarkable in many ways. It has been accomplished almost entirely by private agreement. There is no legal compulsion upon the parties to utilize arbitration, and until 1960 there was not even judicial encouragement. Although they perform a significant task very similar to that of a judge, arbitrators are private citizens. There is no requirement that they be lawyers or that they have any specific educational or professional background. Many arbitrators principally pursue other occupations. Arbitration is a flexible process whose attributes vary from situation to situation. Some arbitrations are conducted as informal meetings. Others resemble carefully prepared formal adjudications involving lawyers, court reporters and subpoenas. The success and the unusual features of arbitration have made it a popular subject for academic analysis. Much of the writing on arbitration is by academics who have served as arbitrators. In the vast majority of cases the overall appraisal has been favorable. Below are excerpts from three particularly thoughtful and influential articles.

HARRY SHULMAN, REASON, CONTRACT AND LAW IN LABOR RELATIONS *

Collective bargaining is today, as Brandeis pointed out, the means of establishing industrial democracy as the essential condition of political democracy, the means of providing for the workers' lives in industry the sense of worth, of freedom, and of participation that democratic government promises them as citizens. The modern industrial worker is not engaged to produce a specific result and left to himself for the performance. He is hired to work under continuous and detailed direction and supervision, in close association with hundreds or thousands of fellow workers, each of whom performs a very minute portion of the work that ultimately results in a finished product. The enterprise requires the continuous co-ordination of the work of this multitude of employees; and this poses numerous daily problems whether or not the employees are organized. So elementary a matter as leaving the job for a few minutes "to service the body," as they say in the shop, poses a serious problem which must be carefully analyzed and provided for, otherwise one might find the work of a hundred men held up every time one of them had to leave. Every day a number of employees may be absent or report late. Daily or almost daily some employees have to be laid off for a short period or indefinitely; some employees must be hired; changes must be made in job assignments, either by way of promotion or demotion or otherwise. And daily there are thousands of occasions for friction between employee and supervisor which may erupt in disciplinary action against the employee or a stoppage of work.

These and a host of similar problems are inherent in the necessity of co-ordinating the work of thousands of persons into an efficient operation. Even where there is no union, the employer needs statements of policy to guide the hundreds of persons through whom he must act, though he may be ready to invest them with large powers of discretion. Addition of the union alters the situation in at least two ways: First, the employees, through the union, must participate in the determinations. Second, the acceptance of unions and collective bargaining has increased the employee's confidence and his sense of dignity and importance; where previously there may have been submission, albeit resentful, there is now self-assertion.

One might conceive of the parties engaging in bargaining and joint determination, without an agreement, by considering each case as it arises and disposing of it by *ad hoc* decision. But this is, of course, a wholly impractical method, particularly for a large enter-

* Harry Shulman, "Reason, Contract and the Law in Labor Relations", 68 Harvard Law Review 999 (1955); © by The Harvard Law Review Association. Reprinted by permission.

prise. So the parties seek to negotiate an agreement to provide the standards to govern their future action.

* * *

No matter how much time is allowed for the negotiation, there is never time enough to think every issue through in all its possible applications, and never ingenuity enough to anticipate all that does later show up. Since the parties earnestly strive to complete an agreement, there is almost irresistible pressure to find a verbal formula which is acceptable, even though its meaning to the two sides may in fact differ. The urge to make sure of real consensus or to clarify a felt ambiguity in the language tentatively accepted is at times repressed, lest the effort result in disagreement or in subsequent enforced consent to a clearer provision which is, however, less favorable to the party with the urge. With agreement reached as to known recurring situations, questions as to application to more difficult cases may be tiredly brushed aside on the theory that those cases will never—or hardly ever—arise.

Then there is never, of course, enough time to do an impeccable job of draftsmanship after substantive agreement is reached—apart from the hazard that such an effort might uncover troublesome disagreement. Though the subject matter is complex and the provisions intricate, the language must nevertheless be directed to laymen whose occupation is not interpretation—the workers in the plant, the foremen, the clerks in the payroll office. For it is they whose actions must be guided by the agreement; and indeed, in the case of the union, the membership is asked to ratify or reject what is prior to its action only a proposed agreement.

* * *

The method employed by almost all industry today for the resolution of stalemates in the adjustment of grievances under the private rule of law established by the collective agreement is private arbitration by a neutral person. The largest enterprises provide for a standing umpire or arbitrator to serve for a stated period of time or so long as he continues to be satisfactory to both sides. The great majority of agreements provide for separate appointment of an arbitrator in each case. And the appointments in any case are made by the parties or by a method agreed upon by them. The wide acceptance of arbitration as a terminal step in the grievance procedure—as contrasted with its relatively limited use in the making of the contract in the first place—is explained generally on the grounds, first, that grievances involve interests of lesser importance than those in contract negotiation and, second, that the discretion of the arbitrator is confined by the agreement under which the grievances arise. Both statements require qualification. As umpire under one collective agreement, I have arbitrated cases ranging all the way from the claim of a single employee for fifteen minutes' pay to that of more than sixty thousand employees for a paid lunch period the direct cost of which was between seven and eight million dollars a year. And the restraining bonds of the collective agreement are found on occasion to be elastic indeed.

The parties do not generally restrict their own joint powers in the grievance procedure. But it is customary for the collective agreement to limit the arbitrator's jurisdiction with apparent strictness. Apart from the specific exclusion of certain subjects, as, for example, rates for new jobs or production standards, he is commonly confined to the resolution of grievances or disputes as to "the interpretation or application of the agreement," or of claims of "violation of the agreement." And quite frequently he is further enjoined not to "add to, subtract from, or modify any of the terms of the agreement." In the agreement with which I am most familiar he is admonished also that he has "no power to substitute his discretion for the Company's discretion in cases where the Company is given discretion" by the agreement, and no power "to provide agreement for the parties in those cases where they have in their contract agreed that further negotiations shall or may provide for certain contingencies."

Doubtless these are wise, perhaps even necessary, safeguards—at least before the parties develop sufficient confidence in their private rule of law to enable them to relax the restriction. And an arbitrator worthy of appointment in the first place must conscientiously respect the limits imposed on his jurisdiction, for otherwise he would not only betray his trust, but also undermine his own future usefulness and endanger the very system of self-government in which he works. But these are hardly provisions which would be inserted in the agreement to control the courts in an action on the contract. The judge, too, must decide only "according to law." Unlike the case of the arbitrator, however, the judge's authority and the law which he must interpret and apply do not derive entirely from the agreement of the litigants before him.

* * *

The parties rarely start with an enterprise from scratch; generally they negotiate an agreement for a going enterprise which has been in operation for some time and which has developed practices or precedents of varying degrees of consistency and force. What is the significance of the claimed "prior practice"?

For example, in [a case concerning the employees' obligation to work overtime] suppose that evidence is tendered that the employer never sought to compel acceptance of overtime assignments, or that the employees never refused such assignments without good excuse. Or suppose that, though the agreement is silent on the matters, the employer had been giving the employees a rest period of ten minutes in each half of the shift, or a lunch period on the employer's time, or a five minute wash-up period before lunch or at the end of the shift, or a money bonus at Christmas. Or, to vary the nature of the example, suppose the claim is that it had been customary for the employer to assign a rigger to assist pipefitters when they were required to lift pipe of four inches or more in diameter, or to assign an employee to hold the pieces which a welder had to weld. Now suppose that, during the term of the agreement, the employer changes these claimed practices over the union's strenuous objections, which are then carried through the grievance procedure to the umpire. In these cases it is the union which relies on the prior practice. But frequently the position is reversed. For example, an employer directs a punch press operator to paint his press when he has no punching to do; or he asks a crib attendant to paint the walls of his crib. In either case, the employee refuses on the ground that painting is not work in his classification, but rather in that of a painter. And the employer points to a claimed prior practice in accord with his direction.

It is more than doubtful that there is any general understanding among employers and unions as to the viability of existing practices during the term of a collective agreement. There may be some agreements which are negotiated upon a real or tacit assumption of continuance of existing practices except as modified by the agreement. There are certainly some agreements which specifically provide for the continuance of existing practices with variant limitations. But I venture to guess that in many enterprises the execution of a collective agreement would be blocked if it were insisted that it contain a broad provision that "all existing practices, except as modified by this agreement, shall be continued for the life thereof unless changed by mutual consent." And I suppose that execution would also be blocked if the converse provision were demanded, namely, that "the employer shall be free to change any existing practice except as he is restricted by the terms of this agreement." The reasons for the block would be, of course, the great uncertainty as to the nature and extent of the commitment, and the relentless search for cost-saving changes. The larger the enterprise, the more varied its operations, the more dependent it is on technological change, and the keener the competition the greater this uncertainty and search. * * * How much weight is to be attached in each case to the employer's judgment, particularly in view of the fact that it is precisely that judgment which is sought to be curbed by the grievance procedure? What significance is to be attached to the personality of the individual employee, his age, his seniority, his prior record, his promise? What consideration, if any, is to be given to probable effects on plant "morale," the morale of supervisors as well as of the workers, and the effects at the time the decision is to be made as well as at the time the penalty is imposed? The frequent instances of stoppage of work in a department or a whole plant because of a disciplinary penalty imposed on a single employee indicates that what is involved is not merely the case of an individual but a group dispute. Factors of this kind should be and doubtless are considered by the parties in the other stages of the grievance procedure. Do they become irrelevant when the case is appealed to the arbitrator? * * *

A proper conception of the arbitrator's function is basic. He is not a public tribunal imposed upon the parties by superior authority which the parties are obliged to accept. He has no general charter to administer justice for a community which transcends the parties. He is rather part of a system of self-government created by and confined to the parties. He serves their pleasure only, to administer the rule of law established by their collective agreement. They are entitled to demand that, at least on balance, his performance be satisfactory to them, and they can readily dispense with him if it is not.

To the extent that the parties are satisfied that the arbitrator is properly performing his part in their system of self-government, their voluntary cooperation in the achievement of the purposes of the collective agreement is promoted. When I speak of the satisfaction of the parties, I do not mean only the advocates who may present the case to the arbitrator, or the top echelons of management or union representatives. I mean rather all the persons whose cooperation is required—all the employees in the bargaining unit and all the representatives of management who deal with them, from the job foreman up.

Ideally, the arbitrator should be informed as fully as possible about the dispute which he is asked to resolve. He should hear all the contentions with respect to it which either party desires to make. For a party can hardly be satisfied that his case has been fully considered if he is not permitted to advance reasons which to him seem relevant and important.

The more serious danger is not that the arbitrator will hear too much irrelevancy, but rather that he will not hear enough of the relevant.

The arbitrator may have to take a more active part in the investigation than does a trial court. This is not merely because, being charged with the responsibility for decision he should be satisfied that he knows enough to be able to decide. * * * A court's erroneous findings of fact in a particular litigation may work an injustice to the litigants but rarely disturb the future; similar error by an arbitrator may cause more harm by disturbing the parties' continuing relationship than by the injustice in the particular case. * * *

Finally, in this connection the arbitrator must be quite circumspect in explaining his decision on the ground of inadequate presentation, for his usefulness may depend in large part on the very people so designated for responsibility. And so, for several reasons, the arbitrator cannot simply sit back and judge a debate. He must seek to inform himself as fully as possible and encourage the parties to provide him with the information.

His choice from the more or less permissible interpretations of the language of the agreement, keeping the basic conceptions in mind, requires an appraisal of the consequences of each of the possibilities. Though all the parts of the agreement do not necessarily make a consistent pattern, the interpretation which is most compatible with the agreement as a whole is to be preferred over one which creates anomaly. The effects on efficiency, productivity, and cost are important factors to be considered. So are also the effects on the attitudes and interests of the employees. The two sets of factors are not always in opposition. An apparent increased cost may in some circumstances be more than repaid by the increased productivity resulting from the greater stimulus to voluntary cooperation. Practicality of the interpretation in its day-to-day applications is a related value. The interpretation, no matter how right in the abstract, is self-defeating and harmful to both sides if its day-to-day application provides further occasion for controversy and irritation.

Appraisal of probable consequences and practicality is no easy task and is not made on the basis of indisputable proof. The parties, too, make the appraisal. They differ with one another and they may differ with the arbitrator. But disagreement with the arbitrator by one or the other of the parties is normal and expectable and, of itself, not at all unhealthy. Indeed, the surprising thing is the extent of agreement that his award may meet within the ranks of both parties. For while a party may speak with one voice at the hearing, the fact is that there may be considerable difference of opinion among the many people who make up the artificial entity called the party.

The important question is not whether the parties agree with the award but rather whether they accept it, not resentfully, but cordially and willingly. Again, it is not to be expected that each decision will be accepted with the same degree of cordiality. But general acceptance and satisfaction is an attainable ideal. Its attainment depends upon the parties' seriousness of purpose to make their system of self-government work, and their confidence in the arbitrator. That confidence will ensue if the arbitrator's work inspires the feeling that he has integrity, independence, and courage so that he is not susceptible to pressure, blandishment, or threat of economic loss; that he is intelligent enough to comprehend the parties' contentions and empathetic enough to understand their significance to them; that he is not easily hoodwinked by bluff or histrionics; that he makes earnest effort to inform himself fully and does not go off half-cocked; and that his final judgment is the product of deliberation and reason so applied on the basis of the standards and the authority which they entrusted to him.

An important factor tending toward such general acceptance is the opinion accompanying the arbitrator's award. It has been urged by some that an arbitrator's award should be made without opinion or explanation in order to avoid the dangers of accumulating precedents and subjecting arbitration to the rigidities of stare decisis in the law. Perhaps this view has merit when the particular arbitration is regarded as solely a means of resolving the particular stalemate and nothing else. It is an erroneous view for the arbitration which is an integral part of the system of self-government and rule of law that the parties establish for their continuing relationship.

When the parties submit to arbitration in the system of which I speak, they seek not merely resolution of the particular stalemate, but guidance for the future, at least for similar cases. They could hardly have a high opinion of the arbitrator's mind if it were a constantly changing mind. Adherence to prior decisions, except when departure is adequately explained, is one sign that the determinations are based on reason and are not merely random judgments.

The arbitrator's opinion can help in rationalizing the agreement and the parties' contentions with respect to it and in fostering greater appreciation by them of each other's views and needs with respect to the problem at hand. Its greatest utility lies in its effect, not merely on the advocates who presented the case or the higher authorities in the enterprise, but on what might be called the rank and file—the workers in the shop and their supervisors. It is the rank and file that must be convinced. For the temptation to resort to job action is ever present and is easily erupted. The less their private rule of law is understood by the workers and the more remote from their participation are the decisions made on their grievances, the greater is the likelihood of wildcat stoppages or other restraints on productivity. The likelihood can be decreased by bringing the arbitration close to the shop, not only in the hearings and investigations, but also in the opinion which explains the award. * * * The arbitration may be resented by either party as an impairment of its authority or power. It is susceptible of use for buck-passing and face-saving. And it may sometimes encourage litigiousness. But when the system works fairly well, its value is great. To consider its feature of arbitration as a substitute for court litigation or as the consideration for a no-strike pledge is to take a foreshortened view of it. In a sense it is a substitute for both—but in the sense in which a transport airplane is a substitute for a stagecoach. The arbitration is an integral part of the system of self-government. And the system is designed to aid management in its quest for efficiency, to assist union leadership in its participation in the enterprise, and to secure justice for the employees. It is a means of making collective bargaining work and thus preserving private enterprise in a free government. When it works fairly well, it does not need the sanction of the law of contracts or the law of arbitration. It is only when the system breaks down completely that the courts' aid in these respects is invoked. But the courts cannot, by occasional sporadic decision, restore the parties' continuing relationship; and their intervention in such cases may seriously affect the going systems of self-government. When their autonomous system breaks down, might not the parties be left to the usual methods for adjustment of labor disputes rather than to court actions on the contract or on the arbitration award? I suggest that the law stay out—but, mind you, not the lawyers.

ARCHIBALD COX, REFLECTIONS UPON LABOR ARBITRATION *

* * *

In the beginning it seems useful to observe the characteristics of a collective-bargaining agreement which might affect the terms in

* Archibald Cox, "Reflections Upon Labor Arbitration," 72 Harvard Law Review 1482 (1959); © by 1959 by The Harvard Law Review Association. Reprinted by permission.

which it is written and, consequently, the process of interpretation. One unique characteristic is the number of people affected.

* * *

A collective agreement also covers a wide range of conduct and an enormous variety of problems. No state or federal statute, except possibly the tax laws, covers as wide a variety of subjects or impinges upon as many aspects of the ordinary company's business or a worker's life—wages, hours of employment, working conditions, health and accident insurance, retirement, pensions, promotions, layoffs, discipline, subcontracting, technological changes, workloads, and a host of minor items. Yet a collective-bargaining agreement must also be kept short and simple enough for the ordinary worker to read and understand.

* * *

A labor contract operates prospectively over substantial periods. Nearly all run for at least one year. Many run for two or three years.

One consequence of these   *   *   *   characteristics is that many provisions of the labor agreement must be expressed in general and flexible terms. The concept of "just cause" is an obvious illustration. Sometimes the negotiators can do no more than establish an appropriate set of procedures for resolving a class of problems; witness the provisions for fixing work loads and piece rates in many textile contracts. A collective agreement rarely expresses all the rights and duties falling within its scope. One cannot spell out every detail of life in an industrial establishment, or even that portion which both management and labor regard as matters of mutual concern.

* * *

The resulting contract is essentially an instrument of government, not merely an instrument of exchange. "The trade agreement thus becomes, as it were, the industrial constitution of the enterprise, setting forth the broad general principles upon which the relationship of employer and employee is to be conducted." This background not only gives meaning to the words of the instrument but is itself a source of contract rights.

The generalities, the deliberate ambiguities, the gaps, the unforeseen contingencies, and the need for a rule even though the agreement is silent all require a creativeness in contract administration which is quite unlike the attitude of one construing a deed, a promissory note, or a 300-page corporate trust indenture. The process of interpretation cannot be the same because the conditions which determine the character of the instruments are different.   *   *   *

Occasionally arbitrators and courts have come into conflict because of the courts' failure to perceive this need for an industrial jurisprudence within the area of labor-management relations brought under the regime of the collective agreement. A Remington Rand contract provided: "Seniority   *   *   *   is defined to mean length of service with the Company since the last date of hire at whatever loca-

tion and in whatever capacity employed." An employee who had resigned was rehired on September 25, 1950. As a result of a mistake,
however, the company record gave him the seniority date of May 21,
1945, which was the date of his original employment prior to the resignation. The erroneous date was carried forward for five years in
published seniority listings. It was the basis upon which two prior
grievances had been adjusted at the local level. Thereafter the company attempted to correct the seniority date in offering an opportunity for promotion. The arbitrator held that the seniority list had become frozen despite the mistake. "[T]here must come a time when
past errors which have not been challenged or corrected by either
party, or by individual employees, must be accepted as the agreed
understanding and no longer subject to change." The Supreme
Court of New York vacated the award upon the employer's motion.
The judge declared that the ruling "flies in the face of the words of
the contract" and expressed wonderment that "highly qualified and
sincere arbiters" could have reached such a result. The explanation
is both simple and revealing. The arbitrator recognized that every
contract must be interpreted and applied through an industrial jurisprudence. The judge felt bound to the written word, although courts
have exercised greater liberality for centuries in applying the Statute
of Frauds. In my opinion the judge made a serious error.

*   *   *

At this point we may draw two conclusions:

First, it is not unqualifiedly true that a collective-bargaining
agreement is simply a document by which the union and employees
have imposed upon management limited, express restrictions of its
otherwise absolute right to manage the enterprise, so that an employee's claim must fail unless he can point to a specific contract provision upon which the claim is founded. There are too many people,
too many problems, too many unforeseeable contingencies to make
the words of the contract the exclusive source of rights and duties.
One cannot reduce all the rules governing a community like an industrial plant to fifteen or even fifty pages. Within the sphere of collective bargaining, the institutional characteristics and governmental nature of the collective-bargaining process demand a common law of the
shop which implements and furnishes the context of the agreement.
We must assume that intelligent negotiators acknowledged so plain a
need unless they stated a contrary rule in plain words.

Second, the "interpretation and application" of a collective-bargaining agreement through grievance arbitration is not limited to
documentary construction of language.

*   *   *

The "interpretation and application" of a collective-bargaining
agreement embraces the same two functions. The arbitrator applies
a common law of contracts to actions upon industrial agreements.
He performs the function because it is inescapable, even though the
collective agreement confines him to "interpretation and application."
Yet the task is markedly different in two important respects. Collec-

tive agreements, because of the institutional characteristics already mentioned, are less complete and more loosely drawn than many other contracts; therefore, there is much more to be supplied from the context in which they were negotiated. The governing criteria are not judge-made principles of the common law but the practices, assumptions, understandings, and aspirations of the going industrial concern. The arbitrator is not bound by conventional law although he may follow it. If we are to develop a rationale of grievance arbitration, more work should be directed towards identifying the standards which shape arbitral opinions; if the process is rational, as I assert, a partial systematization should be achievable even though scope must be left for art and intuition. I can pause only to note some of the familiar sources: legal doctrines, a sense of fairness, the national labor policy, pass practice at the plant, and perhaps good industrial practice generally. Of these perhaps past practice is the most significant; witness the cases in which it is argued that a firmly established practice takes precedence even over the plain meaning of the words.

* * *

V

Thus far I have stated only half my thesis. Although the very nature of the collective agreement calls for arbitrators to create and apply an industrial jurisprudence unrestricted by the bare meaning of its words, it is even plainer that there are limits to the arbitrator's function. Even though an arbitration clause covering only "disputes concerning the interpretation and application" of the collective agreement cannot mean barely the translation of words, it must impose some limit. The phrasing of the arbitration clause is often an important issue in collective bargaining. Experienced negotiators are thoroughly aware of their ability to choose between the comparatively narrow clause noted above and a wide-open undertaking to arbitrate "any dispute, difference, disagreement or controversy of any nature or character" which may arise during the term of the agreement. When the former clause is selected, the company believes that a limit has been imposed upon the power of the arbitrator. The union would also acknowledge that his authority is narrower than if the union had been able to persuade the company to accept a wide-open clause. There are many arbitration decisions sustaining the defense of nonarbitrability. The arbitrator, in short, is not free, as are courts of general jurisdiction, to draw upon a complete legal system to adjudicate all the rights and duties of the parties.

Accordingly we are driven to ask where the boundary line lies between the area in which an arbitrator may apply the law of the shop and the forbidden territory from which he is excluded by the admonition that he is to confine himself to the "interpretation and application" of the agreement.

* * *

It is conventional to refer such questions to "intent," and the governmental nature of a collective-bargaining agreement suggests that it should be interpreted in the manner of a basic statute creating an administrative agency, a process in which the accepted formula refers us to the intent of the legislature. Yet it is misleading to speak of intent. No one supposes that the tens of senators and hundreds of representatives who vote for a bill have one common state of mind. I trust, also, that arbitrators who speak of "the intent of the parties" do not mean to imply that they are concerned with the secret, unexpressed intent of either party. Those who listen seriously to the testimony of negotiators concerning what they understood, supposed, or intended run the risk of imposing upon one side the unilateral suppositions of the other. The true standard of interpretation must be objective. To speak of intent as if the legislators or negotiators had reached a conclusion upon the specific issue is also misleading. The troublesome issues during the administration of a statute or contract are usually those which the authors either refused to face or failed to anticipate. Yet to speak of intent, when the word is properly understood, serves two useful functions. It reminds the interpreter that a statute or a contract is a purposive instrument. The metaphor also cautions the interpreter that it is his duty to effectuate the will of the Congress—or of the parties to the contract—even though he himself might reach an infinitely wiser decision. The interpreter must strive, therefore, to apply the instrument on a doubtful occasion in the way which is most consistent with the provisions whose meaning is clear.

*   *   *

The task of finding where the boundaries would have been drawn if the parties who signed the contract had drawn them explicitly is a problem of interpretation, for it is the agreement that draws the boundary line even though it does not draw it expressly. The interpreter must remember that the contract goes a distance but also that it stops, because it is a product of competing wills and its policy inheres as much in its limitations as in its affirmations. Nor is the interpreter left wholly without guidance. Even a vague management-functions clause suggests that the boundaries may be narrower than under a contract without one. An integrated-writing clause bespeaks narrow interpretation. Surely an open-end arbitration clause indicates a wider area of joint sovereignty than a clause limiting the arbitrator to the "interpretation and application" of the contract. In the discharge case it would not be implausible to conclude, if the words of the contract are otherwise blind, that review of discharges to determine whether there is "just cause" is more consistent with a contract granting other forms of job security and industrial justice than is the reservation of untrammeled power to discharge for any reason which the employer deems sufficient. The plausibility is less, if indeed there is any, in the case of subcontracting or shift schedules.

Whatever the indicia, however, they must be found in the relationship created by the particular contract, and no obligation which is outside the context of the contract may be imposed upon a company by an arbitrator. In this sense the management-rights theory seems sound. The imperative which requires a body of "industrial jurisprudence" within the general area marked off for joint government has no place in deciding what area has been marked off.

A single word may be added in conclusion. Try as he must to penetrate the spirit of the agreement, the judge or arbitrator who is confronted with a borderline case will be influenced by his own philosphy concerning the arbitrator's function. He may be an activist and impose his view upon the agreement when its words leave scope, bringing doubtful territory into the joint realm because he thinks that he knows that this is fair and good industrial relations. A wise and respected man may do much good through this conception of the arbitrator's function. Or the arbitrator may follow the quieter role which Learned Hand and Felix Frankfurter assign a judge in interpreting a statute the reach of which is sharply disputed.

> [T]he judge must always remember that he should go no further than he is sure the government would have gone, had it been faced with the case before him. If he is in doubt, he must stop, for he cannot tell that the conflicting interests in the society for which he speaks would have come to a just result, even though he is sure that he knows what the just result should be. He is not to substitute even his juster will for theirs; otherwise it would not be the common-will which prevails, and to that extent the people would not govern.

Even here the parties can make the choice, for they select their arbitrator. * * *

LON L. FULLER, COLLECTIVE BARGAINING AND THE ARBITRATOR *

The purpose of this paper is to discuss two controversies which have surrounded labor arbitration almost from its inception.

* * *

The first of these controversies relates to the proper role of the arbitrator—how he should conceive his function, how he should conduct the hearings, and what limits he should impose on himself. The second relates to the principles he should follow in interpreting the collective bargaining agreement and in applying its provisions to the controversy before him. As this statement of the second issue implies, my concern here is primarily with arbitration arising under an existing agreement, and not with arbitration conducted to set the terms of a new contract.

One conception of the role of the arbitrator is that he is essentially a judge. His job is to do justice according to the rules imposed by the parties' contract, leaving the chips to fall where they may. He decides the controversy entirely on the basis of arguments and proofs presented to him "in open court" with the parties confronting one another face to face. He does not attempt to mediate or conciliate, for to do so would be to compromise his role as an adjudicator. He will strictly forego any private communication with the parties after the hearing. The friends of this conception see it as casting the arbitrator in the role of a man of principle, a man who respects the institutional limits of his task, who conscientiously refuses to exploit his powers for ulterior purposes, however benign. The critics of this conception have a less flattering view of it. To them it is unrealistic, prudish, purist, legalistic, an abandonment of common sense, a chasing after false models motivated perhaps by a secret hankering for the glamour and security of judicial office.

The opposing conception expects of the arbitrator that he should adapt his procedures to the case at hand. Indeed, in its more extreme form it rejects the notion that his powers for good should be restrained at all by procedural limitations. By this view the arbitrator has a roving commission to straighten things out, the immediate controversy marking the occasion for, but not the limits of, his intervention. If the formal submission leaves fringes of dispute unsettled, he will gladly undertake to tidy them up. If the arguments at the hearing leave him in doubt as to the actual causes of the dispute, or as to what the parties really expect of him, he will not scruple to hold private consultations for his further enlightenment. If he senses the possibility of a settlement, he will not hesitate to step down from his role as arbitrator to assume that of mediator. If despite his conciliatory skill negotiations become sticky, he will follow Harry Shulman's advice and—with an admonitory glance toward the chair just vacated—"exert the gentle pressure of a threat of decision" to induce agreement.

The critics of this view are seldom charitable in describing it. They say that arbitrators who accept it think they can "play God," though the actual motive of their actions is usually a base instinct to meddle in other people's affairs. The conception that encourages this intermeddling rests essentially on hypocrisy, for it enables a man who pretends to be a judge to enjoy the powers of his office without accepting its restraints. It is a Messianic conception, a patent abuse of power, a substitution of one-man rule for the rule of law. So the castigations mount. There is need for a neutral term. As the nearest approach I suggest that we describe this view as one that sees the arbitrator, not as a judge, but as a labor-relations physician.

The other major controversy is, as I have said, that which relates to the interpretation of the collective bargaining agreement. By one view a labor contract is like any other legal document and ought to be subject to the same principles of interpretation. If, as it commonly does, it states that the arbitrator shall have no power to add to or to detract from its terms, he must accept this limitation. His object is not to do justice, but to apply the agreement. If the agreement imposes hardships, it is no business of the arbitrator to alleviate them.

His powers and his duties lie wholly within the four corners of the written document.

The opposing view stresses the unique quality of the collective bargaining agreement. It is not quite like any other document ever conceived by the mind of man. It is at once a constitution and the written record of an economic trade. It is a charter of the parties' rights and a set of resolutions never really expected to be fully realized in practice. From the curiously mixed nature of the collective bargaining agreement there is derived (by a logic that is certainly not obvious) the conclusion that it must be construed freely. Unlike judges, arbitrators must eschew anything like a "literal" interpretation. Their task is not to bend the dispute to the agreement, but to bend the agreement to the unfolding needs of industrial life.

In presenting these two controversies I have purposely thrown the contending sides into a sharper opposition than commonly exists in practice. In reality the matter is never so black and white as I have just painted it. Even those arbitrators who purport to adhere to a fairly extreme position at one end or the other of the scale seldom practice entirely what they preach. * * *

The two controversies I have outlined are to some extent two aspects of a single dispute. One can generally predict that the arbitrator with strong instincts toward mediation will also be likely to favor free principles of contract construction. This is not necessarily so, however. There is no compelling reason why the strict constructionist should not, on occasion at least, undertake the role of mediator. Indeed, he is in an especially favorable position to coax an agreement by "the gentle threat of a decision," for in his case this threat may be fortified by a reputation for stiff interpretations. But with this allowance it still remains true that where one will take his position on each of the two controversies is likely to be influenced by a single disposition.

* * *

A viable system of law requires that parties be willing to settle the great bulk of disputes out of court. It requires not only a willingness to settle cases that are reasonably certain to be decided against the conceding party, but also to settle at least some cases he could be quite certain of winning if they were taken to litigation. The decision of a dispute by law is not always the same thing as a wise disposition of it. People who are always demanding their "rights" can be a menace to any society. One of the responsibilities of the parties to a collective bargaining agreement is to ease the strains on arbitration by not litigating cases where there is an obvious tension between the result demanded by the terms of the contract and that which accords with practical wisdom in labor relations.

I have just been asserting that a large part of the responsibility for maintaining the integrity of arbitration rests with the parties. I do not wish to be understood as suggesting, however, that the arbitrator is entitled to thrust on the parties the whole responsibility for his role. I emphatically reject the contention made by Harry Shulman that in appraising such practices as "meeting with the parties separately" the "dangers envisaged with respect to judges and other governmental personnel are not equally applicable" to the arbitrator, for "the parties' control of the process and their individual power to continue or terminate the services of the arbitrator are adequate safeguards against these dangers."

The democratic principle does not require us, I submit, to indulge in the fiction that whatever institutions develop in a particular situation must be viewed as approved by those affected by them. There is generally no real sense, for example, in which it can be said that the workers in a particular factory have approved either a loose or a strict interpretation of the arbitrator's role. In such a matter only a few key figures, chiefly the arbitrator himself, have that sense of alternatives which is required for intelligent choice.

It may be answered that in speaking of the consent of the "parties" Shulman meant, not the workers or the whole management staff, but simply those few officials on either side directly concerned with arbitration. That this is hardly an adequate justification on which to rest the arbitrator's practices becomes apparent.

* * *

Successful arbitration obviously depends upon successful collective bargaining. It is from the collective bargaining agreement that arbitration derives its standards. If those standards are clearly and properly set, they will shape the award toward the needs of industrial self-government as seen by those most directly in contact with its problems. Reasonably clear standards contractually established are also essential for the integrity of arbitration. Without them the bond of participation that characterizes adjudication may be lost. Carelessly drawn agreements invite, may indeed demand, a departure by the arbitrator from his proper role. In this case the damage done becomes cumulative, since arbitration is almost certain to become overloaded if there are no standards to govern the settlement of grievances short of arbitration.

Conversely, the institution of collective bargaining can be undermined if the arbitrator casts off all restraints, assumes a variety of discordant roles, and presides generally over a process of decision from which may emerge, almost indifferently, a half-coerced agreement or a half-agreed award. In any such procedural chaos the guideline of the agreement is inevitably forfeited. When the agreement ceases to play a significant role in arbitration, the incentive to draft it carefully and fairly is lost.

The institution of voluntary arbitration soundly administered is an essential of industrial self-government. The danger of an extension of judicial control over arbitration lies, not only in the delays, costs, and formalities it would entail, but in the kinds of interpretation it would produce. The whole purpose of a collective bargaining agreement can be frustrated by unresponsive interpretations. A collective bargaining agreement may be viewed as a series of answers to a series of problems. The answers cannot be understood without understanding the problems. If an adjudicator (whether he be judge or arbitrator) attempts to read answers out of the agreement without understanding the problems to which those answers are addressed, all the processes of industrial self-government are upset and thrown out of balance.

The mediating form-free arbitrator and his opposite number, the stiffly literal judge, are equally threats to effective collective bargaining. The first may dissipate the benefits of careful negotiation and draftsmanship by disregarding the contract in the resolution of disputes. The second may dissipate those benefits by projecting into the agreement incongruent meanings, foreign to the thinking of those who created it.

The purpose of these rather scattered observations is to drive home the point that the procedures of industrial self-government, whether they be formal or informal, stand in a relation of interdependence. They are all parts, one of another. The right functioning of the system as a whole depends upon the right functioning of each of its components.

Taking the system as a whole and viewing it across considerable periods of time, I should say that it works remarkably well.

* * *

QUESTIONS

1. Is there any basic conflict in the approach to arbitration taken by the three commentators?

In what ways do the 3 papers espouse a similar approach to arbitration?

2. Is there any significant difference in approach between Cox and Shulman?

Between Fuller and Shulman?

3. If so, which approach seems better?

a. To resolve particular disputes?

b. To make the institution of arbitration most useful?

4. From time to time, it has been suggested that reliance on the strike is outmoded and that if the parties fail to agree, the issues should be submitted to binding arbitration.

Would you favor such a suggestion?

What effect might such a system of resolving disputes have on collective bargaining?

Suppose the arbitrator were limited to accepting the final offer of one side or the other, would that make arbitration more or less desirable?

2. THE SUBJECTS OF ARBITRATION

Below are some excerpts from arbitration awards dealing with traditional questions of discipline, seniority and the protection of work to be done by employees in the unit. Note the types of considerations addressed by the arbitrator, and the flexibility shown in fashioning remedies.

(a) DISCIPLINE

PEPSI COLA GENERAL BOTTLERS, INC. AND BREWERY & SOFT DRINK WORKERS, LOCAL 20

Decision of Arbitrator, 55 LA 663 (1970).

VOLZ, Arbitrator:

The parties agreed upon the following statement of the issue:

"Did the Company violate Article V, Section 1, of the parties agreement when it discharged employee B— on May 25, 1970?"

Employed in November, 1969, as a Route Salesman in the City Sales Department, B— was discharged on May 25, 1970, for violating the Company's grooming code. This code was read to all sales personnel in the later part of April, 1970. It was posted on the bulletin boards on May 7, 1970. The code reads in part:

"The public gains many of its impressions of our Company from its contacts with our employees. It is, therefore, important for our people not only to be courteous and efficient, but also to contribute to our public image through proper dress, personal appearance, and a reasonable degree of personal cleanliness and neatness.

*   *   *

"Hair styles, beards, mustaches, and sideburns continue to be matters of personal preference. The Company's interests are principally due to the sanitation standards of the food industry and in being well represented by those employees who have public and customer contact.

"It is not our intention to interfere with anyone's right to self-expression, personal freedom, and creativeness. We simply want our people to know the ground rules so they will have some basis to judge for themselves what represents reasonable dress, grooming, and personal appearance.

"We realize the maintenance of an image essential to the prosperity of our Company in serving the public poses many complications. Therefore, we feel it has become necessary to establish some clear, unambiguous standards of dress, grooming, and personal appearance reasonably related to the business needs of the Company. These are as follows:

"1.   Sideburns shall not extend beyond the bottom of the ear.

"2.   Sideburns shall be of uniform width throughout their length, shall be in a straight line perpendicular to the horizontal plane of the head, and be well-trimmed so as to avoid the appearance of being bushy.

"3.   Hair styles should be of such type as to avoid having any part of the ear covered.

"4.   Hair shall be kept neatly trimmed on the sides and in back, and shall extend downward on the back of the head no further than a line one-half inch above the collar.

"5.   Mustaches must not extend below the upper lip and must be neat and well-trimmed.

"6.   Beards must not extend further than a perpendicular line drawn from the corners of the mouth, nor shall they extend more than one inch below the chin. In all cases, beards must be neat and well-trimmed."

The Union stresses the following points:

1.   At the time B— was hired on November 13, 1969, his hair was actually longer than at the time of discharge.

2.   The Company's rule must be interpreted in the light of current hair styles; hair styles in vogue currently vary widely, and no intelligent guidelines can be formulated; B—'s hair style was in line with the NOW generation; long hair and beards for men have been traditional while short hair historically has been the exception.

3.   The Company caters in its advertising to the NOW generation; the grievant's appearance did not adversely affect the Company's business; his monthly sales increased.

4.   The Company has retained employees with more extreme hair styles and facial adornments than the grievant.

5.   The grievant was discharged in violation of his constitutional and civil rights of personal expression and preference.
* * *

DISCUSSION

In Section 1 of Article V, the parties agree that the Company may "require employees to observe reasonable Company rules and regulations that are not inconsistent with this Agreement." The Contract is silent on the question of grooming. Therefore, no inconsistent provisions exist. The primary question for decision concerns the reasonableness of the Company's rules and regulations pertaining to hair and facial grooming. Reasonableness, as has been frequently noted, is a fact question and depends upon an objective evaluation of all the relevant facts and circumstances existing at the time. If a Company rule is reasonable, it may take disciplinary action appropriate to the offense for a violation of it or to bring an employee into conformity with it. For the reasons set out below, the arbitrator finds that the grooming code announced by the Company in late April and posted on May 7, 1970, was a reasonable exercise of managerial authority as recognized in Section 1 of Article V, at least as the grooming code applied to Route Salesmen, who must deal with the public.

1. The grooming code represents a middle ground between the concern of the Company to protect and improve its image with the public and the preference of an employee for self-expression and individuality through hair styling. It grants him considerable latitude. It allows, within moderation, sideburns, mustaches, beards, and reasonably long hair. An employee's right to personal expression was not unreasonably curtailed.

2. The grooming code was not based upon arbitrary or unrealistic standards outmoded by current mores but was predicated upon a legitimate and justifiable interest to preserve and promote successful operations through the maintenance of a popular public image. The economic well-being of the Company is, of course, vital to the employees as well as to management. In United Parcel Service, 51 LA 292, 69–1 ARB, Par. 8057 (1968), Arbitrator Turkus wrote:

> "The Company had a right to require its employees who came in contact with the public to be clean-shaven. The arbitrator finds that this is a reasonable rule promulgated with a view toward preserving the Company's public image."

An employee who deals with the public or who solicits sales has an added responsibility for presenting a pleasing appearance. As Arbitrator Sembower noted in American Airlines, Inc., 46 LA 737 (1966):

> "There are types of employment where this might not make much difference, but grievant did not associate himself with such."

3. Nothing in the Labor Agreement prohibits the establishment of reasonable rules on the personal appearance of employees who deal with the public.

4. Employees are entitled to know with reasonable certainty the grooming standards to which they are expected to conform. The announced and posted grooming code provided such knowledge by replacing a general standard of "hair and face well trimmed and groomed" with specific and well-defined guidelines.

5. The grievant was given adequate notice of the grooming code and sufficient opportunity and time to comply.

* * *

7. The grievant maintains that the grooming code violates his constitutional and civil rights to self expression. As previously noted, the interest of employees in the individuality of their personal appearance is a factor which must be weighed and balanced in determining the reasonableness of the Company's rules and regulations relating thereto. However, where such rules and regulations, as here, are reasonable, an employee has no constitutional or other right

to defy or violate them except at his own risk. He may have a constitutional right to self-expression, but he has no constitutional right to continued employment in clear violation of reasonable Company rules.

8. Finally, it cannot be found that the grievant was singled out for discriminatory treatment. Other employees also were sent warning letters on May 7, and they brought themselves into compliance. That after the grievant's discharge one employee may have deviated from the policy does not taint the Company's earlier action with discrimination. Nor does the fact that the grievant's monthly sales were on the increase discredit the Company's assumption that Route Salesmen with excessively long hair and excessive facial hair lessen the esteem of the public for the Company. He had built up little equity in his job in his six months of employment.

AWARD

The grievance must be, and is, denied.

ROSENBLUM BROTHERS CO.

51 LA 323 (1968).

KATES, Arbitrator:

In February, 1968, at the end of an absence of four months due to a kidney ailment, the Company considered that this long absence, coupled with her past record of absences since May, 1965, constituted a violation of Rule 4, thereby rendering it an "Intolerable Offense." Thereupon the Company discharged the grievant on that stated ground.

In my opinion, the Company misinterpreted and misapplied Rule 4. The essence of that rule is what it expressly states—habitual absence without reasonable cause. The Company itself has conceded that each absence of the grievant after May, 1965, was for justifiable (reasonable) cause, a number of which absences were with the Company's express permission, notice of all of which to the Company was duly reported in advance.

The evidence does not establish that Rule 4 was violated by the grievant, and the reason for discharge stated by the Company in its separation notice has not been proved in this case.

II. Propriety of Discharge for Reasons Not Stated in Separation Notice.

Just as technicalities ought not to be strictly applied to the language of grievances so as to exclude evidence of relevant facts, so, also, in my opinion, discharge notices ought not to be so technically construed as to exclude evidence of clearly related facts. Excessive absenteeism was the essential factor involved in the grievant's discharge, and I believe that evidence pertaining to that factor should be given consideration even though only Rule 4 was mentioned in the separation notice. It seems clear that the grievant and Union were not taken by surprise by the Company's offer of this evidence, and no continuance was requested by the Union. However, the Company's single reliance upon Rule 4 in the separation notice is a factor adverse to it which should be taken into account in considering the propriety of the grievant's discharge.

It is significant that the applicable labor agreement expressly contemplates possible leaves of absence of as long as two years without necessarily causing termination of employment (Section D–2 of Article XIII—Seniority).

Nevertheless, despite this provision for lengthy leaves of absence and even though there be no specific shop rule on the point, and regardless of whether the employee's absenteeism has been due to long or short illnesses or other reasons, an employee may be discharged if there is reasonable cause to conclude that such employee's attendance at work in the future will in all likelihood be so irregular as to destroy his value as an employee.

I believe the foregoing is a fair statement of the essence of the arbitration decisions cited by the Company when applied to the instant case.

By reason of the repetition of respiratory tract illnesses as a reason for some of the grievant's long absences, a layman might infer that the grievant was so vulnerable to respiratory tract ailments that such vulnerability could reasonably be expected to render her future attendance so irregular as to destroy her value as an employee and warrant her discharge. Also, by reason of the relatively great frequency of the grievant's long absences due to a variety of ailments, a layman might infer that the grievant possesses a special vulnerability to confining illnesses. However, I do not believe that either of such inferences could properly be drawn in connection with the proposed discharge of the grievant in the instant case without supporting medical opinion.

The Company apparently never sought to have the grievant or her health history examined in relation to the probability or lack of probability of future confining illnesses.

Moreover, the grievant's discharge followed a four-month seige due to a kidney ailment—which was not shown to have been related to her previous illnesses. The evidence does not sufficiently show, in my judgment, that any lengthy future absences are likely as a result of the grievant's general or any special health condition.

Although the Company's assumption of future irregularity of attendance is understandable, and appears to have been made in good faith, I believe that it should have been supported by medical opinion.

With respect to the one, two and three-day absences of the grievant, which appear to have been frequent, there was insufficient evidence to contrast the grievant's pattern of attendance in that regard with that of the other employees. Mere comparison of percentage of aggregate absent time, as between the grievant and others, is not significant in my opinion, in view of the inclusion by the Company, in its figures, of absences represented by express leaves of absence resulting from accidental injury, and also the inclusion of Company-approved time off for lack of work on days when she had actually reported for work.

On the other hand, the grievant had received written warning and a disciplinary suspension for excessive absenteeism, and, in the light of her history, was obligated in my opinion to be more careful in her attendance habits than others without her history.

Under all the circumstances of this case, including the grievant's long service, it is my judgment that the grievant ought to be reinstated to her job, but without any back pay or other monetary relief with respect to the period from the time of her suspension in February, 1968 to the date of such reinstatement.

My decision in this case is intended to be without prejudice to the Company's right to suspend or discharge the grievant in the future whenever it can produce sufficient evidence to show a reasonable probability that the grievant will be so irregular or inadequate in future attendance as to destroy her value as an employee.

AWARD

The grievant is to be reinstated to employment at the beginning of the first week following the Company's receipt of a copy of this award. Such reinstatement is to be without any loss of seniority, but also without any back pay or other monetary benefits with respect to the period from February 3, 1968 to the date of such reinstatement. This decision may be taken into account by the Company in evaluating the disciplinary penalty appropriate to any future violation of duty by the grievant, should any occur, and shall be without prejudice to the Company if, following any future absence of the grievant, it can adequately prove that the grievant can not be expected to be reasonably regular in future attendance at work.

QUESTIONS

Do you agree that the company did not have good cause for discharge? Do you agree with the decision not to award back pay?

INTALCO ALUMINUM CORP.

68 LA 66 (1977).

* * *

LACUGNA, Arbitrator:—At the request of the parties, I have written only a Summary Opinion.

I—, the Grievant, was employed by Intalco Aluminum Corporation from 29 May 1967 until his discharge on 14 July 1976. On 12 July 1976 the Grievant pled guilty to one count of unlawful delivery of a controlled substance (marijuana) and received a five year suspended sentence. The Grievant served a term in the Whatcom County jail from 23 August 1976 to 25 November 1976.

II. QUESTIONS

(1) Whether the Grievant, I—, was terminated for just cause?

(2) If not, what is the remedy?

III. ARGUMENT

To answer these QUESTIONS I have interpreted and applied Rule 9 which reads

"(9) Immoral conduct affecting the employee-Company relationship; commission of a crime, dishonest act or other conduct which is harmful to the interests of the Company or other employees."

(a) Interpretation of Rule 9

The language of Rule 9 and the language which determines the appropriate disciplinary action is clear and unambiguous (Company Exhibit #3). The language simply interpreted is that a crime is a major and serious offense, and is a "just" cause for discharge when the offense "is harmful to the interests of the Company or other employees." The cause puts the burden of proof on the Company to show that the Grievant's violation of Rule 9 did, in fact, adversely affect the Company and/or its employees.

(b) Application of Contract Language

The only evidence of direct and actual injury to either the Company or employees was the statement of the Industrial Director who said that some employees "said they didn't want to work with him." But this evidence was rebutted by the Union on cross-examination when the Industrial Director admitted that "no employee had refused to work with him" (the Grievant).

All other arguments of the Company are either hypothetical or speculative, to wit: "the Employer is concerned that (the Grievant) could be a destructive influence on other employees;" that there is a "reasonable basis for the inference that (the Grievant) uses drugs;" reinstatement "may cause other problems such as absenteeism and tardiness;" "continued employment would be damaging to the Employer's reputation" especially in a small community; "the drug problem threatens to reach acute proportions" and "there is a drug problem at Intalco." (Company Brief *   *   *)

The conclusion is, and must be, that the Company failed to adduce hard, specific, and compelling evidence to show the Grievant's act did actually and adversely affect the Company, and/or its employees. Hence, on the basis of the contract which binds the arbitrator, the arbitrator has no choice but to reinstate the Grievant.

Absent conclusive and persuasive evidence, the clause protects the Grievant against discharge. But the clause also seeks to protect the

Company's abiding, legitimate, significant, and compelling interest to protect itself against criminal activity in the future, here, the possible trafficking in drugs. The clause also protects the Company's substantial interest to discharge undesirable employees and to retain efficient and reliable ones. Although the Grievant's work was acceptable, his employment record shows seven unexcused absences, seven unexcused tardies, and two neglects of duty. The accumulated record plus the crime is not good.

Hence, I have attempted to fashion a remedy in the *Award* that not only insures the legal right of the Grievant but also protects the Company's vested right to pursue its objectives with minimal interruption and disturbances.

IV. CONCLUSIONS

Question Number 1: Whether the Grievant, I—, was terminated for just cause?

Answer: No.

Question Number 2: If not, what is the remedy?

Answer: The proper remedy is specified in the *Award*.

V. AWARD

1.   The Company is ordered to reinstate the Grievant at its administrative convenience on or before but not later than 17 January 1977.

2.   The reinstatement is without back pay.

3.   The Grievant accumulates no seniority from the date of his discharge to the date of his reinstatement.

4.   The reinstatement is conditional, i.e.,

(a) if the Grievant is found to possess marijuana on Company property, the Company is free to discharge him at will.

(b) if the Grievant is again found guilty of selling or buying marijuana outside the Company premises by a court, the Company is free to discharge at will.

(c) for the three calendar years from 17 January 1977 to 17 January 1980 the Grievant's absenteeism and lateness are subject to the following rules. Each calendar year is defined as the period from 17 January of one year to 17 January of the next year. The first calendar year runs from 17 January 1977 to 17 January 1978. The Company may discipline the Grievant as follows:

(a) for a second lateness, a suspension of five work days; for a fourth lateness, an additional suspension of 10 work days; for a sixth lateness, discharge.

(b) after two unexcused absences, the Company is free to discharge at will.

(c) the Grievant hereby loses all further protection under the just clause provision of the contract in criminal matters, absenteeism, and tardiness.

ANCHOR HOCKING CORP.

66 LA 480 (1976).

PERTINENT FACTS

EMERSON, Arbitrator:—Without prior notice, discussion, or negotiation with the local union or any of the affected company employees, the company lined up about 75 of them, who were on their way out of the plant about 11:00 p.m., February 10, 1975, and searched their lunch boxes or buckets. A mason jar, lids, and rings were found inside the boxes or buckets of each of the four grievants, and in due course they were discharged for theft and destruction of company property. At no time was any of the employees advised of his right to counsel or that he could have a union representative present. Cartons of quart jars, lids, and rings, like those found in the grievants' lunch boxes or buckets, retailed at $1.28. There are eight jars to a carton, with matching lids and rings included. During their tenure with the company none of the grievants had ever been given either a written reprimand, a suspension, or a prior discharge.

Article 7

Management and Union Responsibility Section 1. Except as limited by the other provisions of this Contract   *   *   *   the right *   *   *   to discipline and discharge employees for proper cause are the responsibility of management.

Section 2. These responsibilities of the Company shall not be exercised in an arbitrary or unreasonable manner.

ISSUES

One issue is whether the company had "proper cause" to discharge the grievants pursuant to Article 7, Section 1. A significant closely related issue is whether the company discharged them in an "arbitrary" or "unreasonable" manner in violation of Article 7, Section 2.

ARBITRATOR'S VIEWS

It is well settled that where alleged stealing, necessarily involving criminal elements is urged, arbitrators commonly hold that the company must prove its case to the level of the criminal standards of guilt beyond a reasonable doubt. For the same reasons the Miranda requirements of right to counsel or union representation, advise as to the charge, warning regarding adverse use of oral or written statements, and the like, should be given, because of the criminal aspect inherent. See Miranda v. U. S., 384 U.S. 436, 86 S.Ct. 1602, 16 L.Ed. 2d 694 (1966).

Another important matter is the right of privacy which clearly includes protection against search, among other things, of lunch boxes or buckets. The hallowed right of privacy was developed chiefly by former United States Supreme Court Justice, Mr. Justice Brandeis, in a famous law review article. See Warren and Brandeis, The Right to Privacy, 4 Harv.L.Rev. 193 (1890). It has stood for 86 years.

Yet another matter is also worthy of note. The retail value of the mason jar, lids, and rings, in question here was substantially under $1.28. Few, if any, police or county prosecutors or district attorneys, would seek indictments or convictions in exercise of their discretion where property of such negligible value as far less than $1.28 is involved. Much more substantial matters would necessarily preempt their time from such a worthless pursuit, especially as to first offenders.

The discharges were not for proper cause, and the grievances are granted with full back pay. The action taken was arbitrary and unreasonable.

AWARD

The arbitrator finds that no advice or warning was given to the grievants in connection with the grievants' alleged thefts or their right of privacy. The grievants further were alleged to have stolen property of substantially less value than $1.28, and had no previous written reprimands, suspensions, or discharges.

The arbitrator concludes that the discharges were not for proper cause and the grievances are granted with full back pay. The action was arbitrary and unreasonable.

(b) SENIORITY

OMAHA BODY & EQUIPMENT CO.

68 LA 322 (1977).

JOB POSTING

YAROWSKY, Arbitrator:—Prior to June, 1976, Mr. Mass was employed by the company as a Utility Equipment Mechanic. His employment terminated because of a back condition that had made it difficult for him to continue working. He was reemployed as a new hire on January 30, 1976, in the same job classification that he had at the earlier date. But he was now brought in to fill a job opening without the benefit of the opening having been posted or announced for bidding. There is no question whatever, relating to his ability or qualification to do the work as he had performed most satisfactorily during his previous employment. This is not the issue.

However, because the contractual procedure expressed in Article XVIII of the previous agreement was disregarded in filling this vacancy, the union filed a grievance in early February which questioned the regularity of the manner of hiring of Mr. Mass. This was the subject of grievance No. 18.

During the course of joint union-management discussions that followed the filing of the grievance, the company acknowledged that it had erred in overlooking the job posting requirement. It then agreed to post a job opening for this vacancy and in response, three individuals expressed interest in the opening principally for the reason that it was at a higher wage classification. But because of certain personal considerations, only one of the three employees that indicated initial interest remained active in seeking the job. The reasons given by the other two for declining to go forward were somewhat vague and no doubt, in part, the result of a misunderstanding of certain work-connected requirements.

In any case, Mr. Lawrence Strong successfully bid the belated job opening and was awarded the classification together with back wages that he would have earned had the opening been posted properly in the first instance. As a result of this company's response, the union withdrew grievance No. 18 and it is not the subject of this arbitration. However, the settlement of this grievance did not end the matter for the reason that the company retained Mr. Mass in the job classification *in addition to* awarding the opening to Mr. Strong.

This turn of events has provoked this arbitration whereby the union is now contending that it is obvious that there were in reality two job vacancies and the company has now only permitted bidding for one (Mr. Strong's). Thus grievance No. 20 was filed in May, 1976, when the company declined to report the job opening and permitted the two employees to continue in the same job classification.

The union's position is that this action of the company is in the nature of a continuing violation of the contract because it has an adverse impact on seniority inasmuch as other more senior employees have not now been given the opportunity to bid on the second job to replace Mr. Mass—on the assumption that there were two openings, not merely one, and further assuming that several senior employees would be potentially interested in bidding for the second vacancy.

Discussion

Although the question raised is not wholly free of doubt, it is difficult to sustain the grievance because it is based on several assumptions or possibilities that have numerous uncertainties attached. The first assumption is that there are, or may be, senior employees willing and qualified to bid the Utility Equipment Mechanic classification, whereas, just several months previously there was only one (Mr. Strong). Then there is the further assumption that if there were others, these others could qualify to do hydraulic repair work in addition to welding as hydraulic work is definitely written into the description of the job.

Then there is the assumption that there were actually *two openings* instead of one because two men are still working in the classification.

The fact is that there was only one opening at the time Mr. Mass was employed; but when the company realized it had disregarded the posting requirement, it created an additional job for Mr. Strong in order to rectify the oversight of posting. The company has made other practical adjustments of this type in the past and many of these have been of mutual benefit to it and to the union. It cannot be faulted for making an additional accommodation under these circumstances especially in view of the fact that with the supply problem looking more favorable, it was reasonable to plan ahead for an additional work load requiring more personnel.

But there are more substantial reasons for concluding that the grievance must be denied beyond the uncertainties and contingencies of the assumptions referred to above. This is the matter of whether a continuing violation was occurring by the mere fact that Mr. Mass was not dismissed because of reposting or posting of a second vacancy would not answer this objection so long as Mr. Mass remained at work. Then additional reposting, (third, fourth, etc.) would be required as long as he stayed on the job.

The arbitrator has concluded that this is not a continuing violation—that only one job opening was available at the time. Although two men are now employed, they were employed for different reasons. One was brought in because of his admitted qualifications and the other one was awarded the job opening as a part of the remedy for the company's error. It has already been pointed out that a not altogether exceptional accommodation was worked out by the company so that the *two* men could continue on in the classification.

Of course it is desirable and productive of good employee morale to promote from within the plant—but here, Mr. Mass was not entirely a stranger from the outside. He had been previously employed and was well qualified to work in this classification and would have continued on but for his back condition.

The principle of seniority is extremely important to rank and file workers and, except for the wage scale, it is the most important attribute of the employment relationship. It must be fully implemented and fairly administered by management and bargaining agents are justified in their insistence that it be strictly construed. However, even in these instances, it must be subject to the rule of reason for the union is ultimately as much benefitted by having the most qualified workers in the more skilled job as is the company. Maximum and efficient productivity benefits both parites. Even the federal government has the practice of bringing in personnel from outside the agencies when it finds out that there is a very limited or no choice of "best qualified" applicants for a job. But in those instances, it is not resorted to until after notification of an opening and posting of a vacancy.

While posting and bidding for job vacancies are the rule, in the majority of collective bargaining agreements with few exceptions; the element of ability and qualification is the most decisive part in the selection process. Some agreements disregard seniority altogether and give management full discretion in making these decisions. Some are just based on length of service with the company plus qualification or ability as judged by management. But the fact is that here management admitted its contractual infraction and has itself supplied the remedy after the earlier grievance was filed. Because the arbitrator has held that the violation is not a continuing one, even though two employees are now performing the work of the classification of Utility Equipment Mechanic and that only one vacancy existed—the second one being improvised as part of an overall settlement of the grievance—the arbitrator has, on the basis of these findings, denied grievance No. 20.

There has been no showing that the disregard of the posting and bidding provision of the previous contract was deliberate or designed so as to undermine the standing of the union or to make an attack on the seniority principle.

AWARD

It is, therefore, the award of the arbitrator that on the basis of a full consideration of all of the evidence and the arguments of the parties and further, on the basis of the prior settlement of grievance No. 18, this grievance (No. 20) is denied.

CITY PRODUCTS CORP.

68 LA 489 (1977).

FACTS

KAUFMAN, Arbitrator:—Grievants R— and K— were hired August 8, 1966, and August 22, 1967, respectively, and were laid off on or about May 7, 1976. Both Grievants had been employed in the Warehousemen classification at the Company's warehouse in Los Angeles. It is stipulated that at the time of the layoffs, there were less senior employees still working in the Skilled Warehousemen classification, which pays five cents more per hour.

1. *Alleged Past Practice:* The Company's Manager of Employee Relations, who has negotiated contracts between these parties since 1964, testified that it has been "Company policy" to permit only downward or lateral bumping, but not upward bumping. In his testimony, as in his correspondence with the Union concerning these grievances, he cited the "general principle that an employee acting to avoid layoff should not gain promotion to a classification he never held before" (CX 3, p. 2). It was also noted that Grievants "have had ample opportunity in the past to bid into" the higher classification (CX 3, p. 2).

DISCUSSION AND CONCLUSIONS

1. *Upward Bumping:* The threshold question is whether the contract permits upward bumping. The Union contends that it does,

noting that Article IX, Section 2(2), contains "no language * * * which prohibits" it (UB 1). That is true, but neither does the provision permit upward bumping in so many words. In industry, for the most part, bumping rights apply downward and laterally; so it is arguable that unless upward bumping is expressly provided for, it was not intended.

The Company notes that under Article IX, Section 2(2), displacement by a senior employee is allowed only with respect to a "classification in which he is qualified," and that under Article III, Sections 1 and 2, the Company has "the right to * * * prescribe the duties of employees" and "shall be the judge of the * * * qualifications of its employees"; and the Company argues that it "has properly determined that employees in the warehousemen classification are not 'qualified' to displace employees in the skilled warehousemen classification" (CB 3)—that "the formal classifications themselves are actually descriptive of the level of qualification necessary to perform the job function" (CB 9). The Company also argues that "consistent past practice" and "bargaining history" support its position (CB 4).

While recognizing the Company's right to judge employees' qualifications, the Arbitrator must reject the Company's initial argument, which is, in effect, that a Warehouseman, because he is a Warehouseman, is not qualified to be a Skilled Warehouseman for purposes of bumping. It is unrealistic to assume that an employee's qualifications are no greater than his classification calls for. To use an employee's current classification as the exclusive criterion of his qualifications for another classification is to distort management's right to judge qualifications, for the criterion serves, in effect, as a substitute for the exercise of judgment.

As for the Company's reliance on past practice and bargaining history, certainly there has been no practice of upward bumping under the agreement; and as the Company argues, "Where the contract language is ambiguous, the non-exercise of claimed rights is a relevant consideration" (CB 23). At the same time, it does not appear that the Company ever had occasion to deny a request for upward bumping. The only specific instance of past practice introduced by the Company was one in which the Company denied a Warehouseman's request that he, rather than a less senior Skilled Warehouseman, be recalled from layoff to the latter classification. But, as the Union notes, Article IX, Section 2(6), provides that "laid-off employees shall be recalled to their regular classifications"; and the Company's answer to that grievance was based on the cited provision almost verbatim.

So far as appears, then, whatever the "Company policy" (apparently unwritten), the precise issue has not previously arisen between the parties. As the Union notes, "the Company has failed to prove that it has established a contrary practice which the Union has agreed to or acquiesced in" (UB 4).

Thus, the fact that the layoff provisions have remained unchanged over several negotiations becomes less significant than the Company maintains.　As for the silence of the parties concerning this issue in the most recent negotiations, conducted while these grievances were pending, it seems fair to conclude that the parties were content to take their chances in arbitration rather than risk any adverse implication arising from a proposal to change the agreement.

The Arbitrator is mindful of the varying arbitral views on this issue.　There is the view, espoused by this Company, that an employee should not be allowed to gain a promotion through a layoff.　As the Company's Manager of Employee Relations testified, the Company has an obligation to protect the Skilled Warehousemen, who may have bid for their jobs, against being deprived of them by Warehousemen seeking to avoid a layoff.　But the same rationale would apply to downward or lateral bumping, where admittedly no such protection is afforded.　With upward bumping, however, especially by Warehousemen who have declined to bid on the higher-rated job, the Company's argument becomes more persuasive on an emotional level;　and upward bumping, to repeat, is the exception, not the rule.

There is, however, another view—that bumping is not intrinsically inconsistent with promotion, but is entirely a contractual matter, like any other aspect of seniority;　thus, where the contract provides for bumping without prohibiting upward bumping, an employee should be able to exercise his seniority in any direction his qualifications permit, and so long as the right is available to all qualified employees, it may not be considered unfair.

In the present case, although Article IX, Section 2(2), provides for bumping without stating the direction it may take, the Arbitrator is not left to choose between doctrines or implications of silence, but may still resolve the issue by reference to the terms, of the contract. Thus, while Article IX, Section 2(2), does not provide for displacing less senior employees in higher classifications in so many words, the third paragraph of that subsection plainly provides that the right to bump "shall supersede the provisions of Section 1 of Article XV—Bid Procedure."　Since the latter Section provides for posting of vacancies in "classifications bearing a greater rate of pay than the Warehouseman classification," the Arbitrator can only conclude that the contract contemplates not only downward and lateral bumping, but upward bumping as well.　General principles and even past practice must yield, of course, to express contractual terms.

AWARD

1.　The Company violated the collective bargaining agreement by arbitrarily refusing to allow the Grievants, R— and K—, to displace less senior Skilled Warehousemen in order to avoid layoff.

2.　The Company shall recall said Grievants to displace less senior employees in the Skilled Warehousemen classification.

3.　If said Grievants are able to perform the required work competently without additional training, the Company shall make each Grievant whole for all earnings and other benefits under the collective bargaining agreement lost as a result of its failure to allow each of them to displace less senior Skilled Warehousemen on or about May 7, 1976, minus the amounts of any interim earnings and unemployment insurance benefits each may have received.

4. The Arbitrator retains jurisdiction in the event any dispute arises concerning the interpretation or application of the remedy awarded hereunder, including the computation of back pay.

(c) WORKING CONDITIONS

STAR MANUFACTURING CO.

68 LA 148 (1977).

HALL, Arbitrator:—Two grievances were filed (Jt. Exhibits 2 and 3) in behalf of numerous employees, and they are substantially the same, each alleging that the company violated the terms of the labor contract, first, by not discussing a change in working hours with the union, and second, by allowing a number of employees to leave early on the date of July 24, 1975 and/or not requiring many to work at all on the date of July 25, 1975. Thus, the grievants are those men who worked; and they seek time off with pay, inasmuch as those coworkers who were allowed to be absent from work were compensated while off, they having hustled to complete their week's workload prior to leaving their workposts.

DISCUSSION

Based upon the contract in existence between these parties, the facts stated above, and the case precedents, I conclude that this Plant Superintendent sought to serve both his employer well and yet to be as fair as possible to his employees. In his effort to increase production and to eliminate overtime, he gave his men an incentive, and they accepted the challenge by doing a week's work in less than a week's time. Once committed to give them some time off, he lived up to his word.

But in doing so, he did violate the basic understanding of all labor agreements, that being that the recognized representative is entitled to advance notice of any changes in working conditions. As was held in Indian Head, Inc., 65 LA 706 (Oct., 1975), some advance notification provides the union with an opportunity to convince the employer to reverse its decision. Doubtless here, the union would have agreed to the incentive, but it probably would never have agreed to any disparity of treatment of various departments as resulted from the Plant Superintendent's honor. While the employer's failure to give advance notification was an honest oversight, this fact does not excuse a failure to comply with the Recognition [Article I] provision of the labor agreement.

This still leaves for the arbitrator two difficult issues to consider. First, no one knows exactly how much time off each man had once the two departments completed their tasks. It appeared at the hearing that some had as little as two hours off with pay, while others may have had as much as ten hours off with pay. It is important to recognize here however, that those men who got time off with pay had completed a workload of five days in less than five days, and that fact was never brought out in their favors at the hearing. In summary then, we should see that *every man got five days' pay for five days' production, although some were not there at all on the fifth day.* As an ancillary question, the arbitrator has wondered why the employees had not worked so well prior to this incident, and why it was necessary to so goad them into such efficient productivity. As was seen in the case of Kaiser Foundation Hospitals, 61 LA 1008 (Nov. 1973), an employer should not be penalized or obligated to pay employees damages as a result of an improper act on one occasion, it appearing that the employer utilized its available and qualified bargaining unit employees to the fullest possible extent. This is the final question for me to consider—how much, if any, should those employees who did not get time off, be entitled to in the way of compensation? As indicated above, every one was paid for five days' work. I cannot therefore penalize this employer for the fact that it had an overly-honest Plant Superintendent, although he did err in not conferring with the union representative.

For the reasons stated above, it should be apparent to all parties that if they cannot ascertain how much time off each man had, then there is no way an arbitrator might determine this.

AWARD

Accordingly, my awards are as follows. The grievance is sustained in behalf of those employees who had no time off on either July 24 or July 25, 1975, the matter being clearly arbitrable. Each man who was at work that July 24th and July 25th, but who was not offered the incentive to speed up and get out his work earlier than usual, shall be given five hours off with pay on a Friday of the company's choice, provided each such employee will have completed a full week's workload of production just as if he had worked a full forty-hour week. In other words, those employees who are now offered five hours off must give the employer the equivalent of a full week's production just as did the auto-weld department employees in the week of July 21-25, 1975. It is my intention, by this award, to eliminate the disparity of treatment and to sustain the union's grievance on its representative status, but at the same time, to acknowledge the employer's honorable treatment to its employees and to its entitlement of a full week's production from each and every employee.

INLAND CONTAINER CORP.

68 LA 259 (1977).

I. THE ISSUES

EDES, Arbitrator:—The issues posed by the facts in this case are as follows:

Whether the Company violated Article XV, Section 2 of the applicable Collective Bargaining Agreement by training nonbargaining unit personnel in the use and operation of the C–47 corrugator machine and obtaining saleable production as a result thereof.   If so, what is the remedy?

II. APPLICABLE CONTRACT PROVISIONS

Article VI, Section 1 of the Agreement of May 1, 1975, provides:

"The management of the plant and direction of the employees, including the right to * * * train, * * * employees * * * , the layout of production, the methods of processing, the products to be manufactured, the production scheduling and the means of manufacturing are solely and exclusively the responsibility of the Employer, provided the Employer does not violate this Agreement."

Article XV, Section 2 provides:

"No person not a member of the Bargaining Unit shall perform work customarily performed by employees who are members of the Bargaining Unit, which will result in lost time or pay to such employees, except in the case of emergencies, to prevent losses to the Employer.   In the event it is found that a foreman has been performing PRODUCTION work in violation of the spirit of this Agreement, the employee who would be eligible for such work in accordance with the Plant Supplement overtime agreement shall receive four (4) hours pay at the applicable rate.

"*   *   *"

III. THE FACTS

The Inland Container Corporation is engaged in the manufacture of corrugated shipping containers.   It operates numerous paper mills and box plants throughout the United States.   The present matter is a consolidation of two grievances which were filed at the Company's Middletown, Ohio, box plant on November 17, 1975 and December 1, 1975.

In August, 1975, the Company began to install a new corrugator machine at the Middletown plant.   This machine, known as the C–47, was a prototype machine.   It had been designed and developed by the Company in conjunction with various other equipment manufacturers. It was a highly complex piece of equipment and at the time of its installation, was the only machine of its kind in the world.

By the first week of November, 1975, the C–47 had been fully installed and at that time was able to produce a saleable product. Due to the newness and experimental nature of this machine, representatives from the various manufacturers who had produced component parts of the machine came to Middletown to assist in the installation and adjustment of their respective parts and to train Inland personnel in the operation of the C–47. The Company also had management and supervisory personnel from its various offices and divisions (including Middletown) present to learn and be trained in the operation of the machine and to assist in its set-up and the training of personnel. Bargaining unit employees who had been properly selected through the bidding procedure to operate the machine were present for the training and were in attendance at all times when the machine was in operation.

The training included both classroom work and on-the-job training in all phases of C–47 operation. In the course of the on-the-job training, Company supervisors operated the C–47 in order to familiarize themselves with its total operation as well as to train others, including bargaining unit employees, in its operation. As a result of this on-the-job training, a small amount of saleable product was produced by this machine.

IV. ANALYSIS AND CONCLUSIONS

The questions put to me by the grievances in this case require me to determine whether, under the provisions of Article XV, Section 2, the work performed by the Company's supervisory or other non-unit personnel was such as was customarily performed by bargaining unit employees and which resulted in lost time or pay to such employees. It cannot be denied, nor does the Company dispute that saleable product resulted from the operation of the C–47 by non-unit personnel. The Union relies upon this fact to establish that a violation of the Agreement took place. I do not believe, however, that the case can be so easily disposed of.

The Company clearly has the express right to "train" personnel, as well as to determine the layout of production, the methods of manufacturing and the means of manufacturing. These rights are exclusively reserved to the Employer under Article VI, Section 1 of the Agreement, limited only by the caveat that the Employer not violate the Agreement. The testimony indicated that even though some saleable product was produced, it was de minimis and merely a by-product of the on-the-job training and I do not think that such product can be deemed to be production work as that term is used in the Agreement.

Training employees to do a job very frequently results in the actual production of a product which can then be sold. But to hold that such a result constituted "production" within the meaning of Article XV, Section 2, would, in my opinion, be violative of the "spirit" of the

Agreement. It would very substantially curtail the right of management to train the work force and I do not see anything in the contract which would countenance, such a managerial limitation. The contract here does not condemn all work by non-unit employees. Wholly apart from emergency situations the contract prohibits only such work as is "customarily performed" by unit employees and which, in addition, "will result in lost time or pay to the employees who customarily perform the work involved." Moreover, the situation must be such as violates "the spirit" of the Agreement which, as the heading of the contract section indicates, is to protect the work of bargaining unit personnel.

The assignments which the Union here contests were not made to deprive unit employees of work or pay. The assignments were made in order that management's express and exclusive rights to determine "methods of processing" and "layout" and the like could be facilitated and that, in addition, supervisory employees who would thereafter be required to train employees could themselves be trained on the machine in question which was a wholly unique piece of equipment. I can read nothing in the provisions of Article XV, Section 2, which prohibits such work or such assignments.

Nor could the Union in this case be able to demonstrate that the work being performed at the start-up of the C–47 operation was "customarily performed" by unit employees. This would be true only to the extent that the end product of the machine would be the same. But the manner of performing the work on this unique equipment was entirely novel for everyone concerned—unit and non-unit employees alike. So much was this so that the entire end product of the first several days of the start-up had to be scrapped.

The introduction of the C–47 prototype could not in fact be accomplished without the actual work participation of supervisors, engineers, and the host of other persons who were involved in the design and manufacture of the machine and its later use once it was fully debugged and made efficiently and functionally operative. It would not matter how many additional unit employees the Company added to the group who were initially assigned to the start-up. Such additions, without active participation of the non-unit employees, would add nothing to the need of the Company to the successful operation of the equipment. On the other hand there is no showing that any unit employee who should have been assigned to the start-up crew was not included or that any unit employee—assigned or not—lost time or pay as a result of work performed by any non-unit employee.

I cannot here find that either the letter or the spirit of the Agreement was violated.

AWARD

1. The Company did not violate Article XV, Section 2 of the applicable Collective Bargaining Agreement by training and otherwise utilizing nonbargaining unit personnel in the use and operation of the

C–47 corrugator machine, which training resulted in the production of some saleable product.

    2.   The grievances are denied.

HI–RAM, INC.

68 LA 55 (1977).

DANIEL, Arbitrator:—This case involves the sub-contracting of salvage of a circuit breaker housing. The Union grieved immediately and shortly thereafter a layoff occurred which the Union complained affected members of the salvage crew who would otherwise have been able to continue performance of work if the work had not been previously subcontracted.

The Management Rights clause in the contract specifies that the company has "the sole right to   *   *   *   determine the products to be manufactured, the place where they are to be manufactured, the schedules of production, methods, processes and means of manufacture, and to   *   *   *   change or discontinue job classifications *   *   *   subject only to such restrictions as are expressly provided in this Contract."

The contractual clause upon which the grievance is based is Article XXV, Section 93,

> "*Sub-Contracting.* Production and maintenance work within the plant shall not be sub-contracted where the work has customarily been performed by employees now in this bargaining unit and appropriate equipment and qualified employees are available to do such work."

POSITIONS OF THE PARTIES

COMPANY: The Company maintains that the Management Rights clause expressly reserves the right of sub-contracting and that there is a very narrow and specific exception contained in Section 93. All parts of 93 must be fulfilled specifically before any restriction can be imposed upon management. The Company maintains that the work was not customarily performed by employees in the unit; that there were no employees available at the time and that there was not appropriate equipment to perform the work. It maintains that the Company is not obligated to anticipate layoffs and that the past practice of subbing out work was fully known to the Union which had not objected in the past to similar action. The Company also maintains that the language of the contract is ambiguous and that reference to past practice is necessary.

UNION: The Union maintains that the language is clear and that the work and circumstances met the qualifications specified under the clause. It notes that there was no urgent or sudden circumstance justifying the contracting out and that if the work had not been subcontracted it would have been available for continued employment of members of the salvage crew past the layoff date in November.

ISSUES

1. Is the contract language ambiguous?

2. Has past practice or Union acquiescence changed the meaning of the contract language?

3. Were the specific qualifications of Section 93 met in the particular case?

4. Was there mitigating circumstances of sudden or urgent need justifying sub-contracting if such were otherwise proscribed by the contract?

DISCUSSION

While the Company and Union had engaged in collective bargaining for a number of years it was in August of 1975 that new owners took over the Company. There is reason to believe from the record and various documents that the new ownership was determined to improve the operation and to reduce costs. This is evident in several actions of the Company both by way of consolidating plants, selling of equipment and attempts to contract out other work not here concerned. When the parties came to the process of collective bargaining in October of 1975 there was then pending a grievance complaining of the sub-contracting of certain coil winding and claiming that such was restricted by Section 93 which is the contractual clause here involved. In the course of negotiations the Company tried with considerable effort to have this particular clause removed from the contract and the Union persisted with equal vigor in its efforts to retain it. The evidence shows that the Union was successful and that at the time the parties contested over the retention of that clause in the contract they were well aware of the dispute over the interpretation and application of Section 93. It would seem that if there were any ambiguity to the contract or any uncertainty it would behoove the party who would have the greatest concern with its application to seek clarifying language. It does not appear that the Company set out to clarify the language but rather to remove it entirely. It is difficult then, at this time, to accept the argument that the language is ambiguous. The Company certainly must have known what it was agreeing to at the time of negotiations and must have percieved the urgency with which the Union regarded the clause as a protection of jobs. Contract language is not ambiguous simply because it requires some interpretation and application. It would be inappropriate to permit a party in an arbitration to argue the ambiguity of a contractual clause where having had the opportunity to clarify, if it so perceived it to be ambiguous, it declined to do so. I find that it is not ambiguous.

Reviewing Section 93 I find that this is production and maintenance work since the reworking of the housings was simply an extension and supplement to the production process. Certainly the work has customarily been performed by unit employees and this is true even though some of the work may have been done previously by outside contractors also. There was appropriate equipment and qualified employees. In this regard I reject the Company's argument that the lack of space to store the parts should be considered as a lack of appropriate equipment. While such interpretation of the term "equipment" may be appropriate in certain cases particularly dealing with available floor space for certain machinery I do not find it applicable under the circumstances. There is no showing that the Company endeavored at all to utilize its storage space more efficiently or to find additional storage space within the building or in other buildings which it owned. The Company may not by its inaction cause a problem to arise, such as lack of space, and then claim that as the excuse or one of the excuses for not observing terms of the contract. The contract language as I read it means, appropriate equipment in the sense that would normally be taken and that means machinery and tools.

There then is left the interpretation and application of the words "available to do such work" as contained in Section 93. For if there were no available employees to perform this work at the time of sub-contracting then it would appear that the contract language permits such an undertaking by the Company.

The Company maintains that at the time it made its decision to sub-contract the work out the salvage crew was working full-time plus over-time and was nevertheless not able to produce an inventory of these parts sufficient for the Company's purposes. It is contended that there was an urgent need for these reworked housings because the vendor who was making the original parts was experiencing some trouble. The Company also maintains that it wished to build up a backlog of these parts for future production purposes and that this was urgent and an immediate necessity.

The grievance in this case is filed on October 23, 1975 and subsequent layoff of a general nature in the plant occurred on November 14, 1975 at which time members of the salvage crew were laid off. The Union contends that there were available people working salvage in October of 1975 so that the Company could have taken them off other work if it was so urgent that the housings be reworked. The Company maintains that it has the right to determine what people will do what work and as long as the work force is fully occupied with proper work it was unavailable to perform this work which the Company then felt free to sub-contract out. The Company maintains it was unable to foresee the substantial slackening of orders for its products which resulted in the layoff approximately three weeks later. Furthermore, the Company has pointed out that it has consistently in the past contracted similar work out; that the Union has known about it or should have known about it and has not objected.

This attempt to negate the terms of the collective bargaining agreement through past practice seems unreasonable to this arbitrator. The language of the contract is clear and unambiguous and there is not established in any way the traditional facts and circumstances necessary to allow past practice to override contractual terms. The notice which the Union has had in the past has not been formal, if at all, and there does not appear any evidence that the Union has acquiesced or permitted or agreed to a revision of the specific contract terms.

It is difficult to credit the defense that the Company was unable to foresee the impending layoff or that its orders would so dramatically fall within just weeks. Certainly, testimony by Company witnesses establishes that the need which it sought to fill by contracting out was the building up of an inventory of parts and yet that theory seems inconsistent with the almost simultaneous downslide of business. It cannot be ignored that the sub-contracting out of a non-union shop had an additional advantage to the Company of less cost than if they had used their own employees. The Union asserts that in effect all the Company was doing when it was sub-contracting was borrowing time from future work that could be done by the regular salvage crew and giving it to an outside contractor and that the Company was utilizing full employment circumstances as justificaiton and disguise. Was there really an urgency or sudden need for this work and unforeseeability of future events as to justify the Company's decision *at the time it was made?*

While the Company may make decisions regarding the use of its work force, it may not use situations and circumstances which it has created, permitted or caused to come into existence, for the purpose of justifying subcontracting which otherwise would be prohibited. There is no substantial evidence that there was an urgent or sudden need for these particular parts existing at the time of the sub-contracting. Clearly the only need was for building an inventory but as it turned out the inventory was not needed since the drop in orders brought about substantial layoffs. It is demonstrated by exhibits that the sub-contracted work was delivered back to the Company on November 5, 10, and 12 shortly before the layoffs took place. In this case I find that the Company either had or should have had the ability to judge the work flow several weeks in advance so as to avoid contracting out work which could have been done by subsequently laid-off employees. Here the facts all occurring within a relatively short period of time and viewed in the light of the recently concluded negotiations allow little room for defense by the Company on the point of availability since it had full control over availability and appears to have created or allowed the circumstances which it now seeks to rely upon for justification. A similar case might arise where, due to longer periods of time of projection and expectation of orders or backlogs, a reasonable and acceptable explanation could be successfully urged. In that case this arbitrator would be less inclined to question motivations based upon hindsight review.

The facts and circumstances in this case are sufficiently persuasive that I must find if the Company did not act intentionally it certainly acted with disregard for the rights and interests of the employees. The employees of the salvage department were entitled to perform the work which was sub-contracted out on October 23, 1975.

It may be complicated to determine exactly the employees who are to be recompensed for lost wages since some employees who were members of the crew chose voluntary layoff when faced with the general layoff. However, the size of the crew as of the date in question is established and the work would have been done by that number of people in the salvage crew. I therefore direct that the parties attempt to determine and agree upon which individuals would comprise that work crew and to divide up between them the amounts of money, at straight time rate, which would have been earned by doing the work which was contracted out. I retain jurisdiciton, if necessary, upon the request of either party to reopen this hearing for the purpose of specifically directing the remedial action outlined above.

AWARD

Grievance granted. The work which was sub-contracted out was prohibited under the terms of the contract and should properly have been performed by members of the salvage crew. Members of the salvage crew shall be reimbursed for wages lost as a result.

E. LEGAL ASPECTS OF LABOR ARBITRATION

---

1. THE FAVORED POSITION OF ARBITRATION

Prior to 1960, there was considerable doubt about the legal status of agreements to arbitrate. It was not clear whether the courts would enforce them, nor was it clear what the legal status was of an arbitration award after it was rendered. In 1960, the Supreme Court, in a series of 3 opinions undertook to answer these questions. These opinions (known as the "Steelworkers trilogy") announced new federal policy strongly favoring the use of arbitration in labor-management relations. Relying heavily on the Shulman and Cox articles, Justice Douglas, who wrote the majority opinion, stated that promises to arbitrate should be freely found and routinely enforced and that courts should also regularly enforce arbitration awards where the company refused to comply.

The following excerpts give the flavor of the fullsome praise lavished upon the process.

UNITED STEELWORKERS OF AMERICA v. AMERICAN MANUFACTURING CO.

Supreme Court of the United States, 1960.
363 U.S. 564, 80 S.Ct. 1343, 4 L.Ed.2d 1403.

* * * The function of the court is very limited when the parties have agreed to submit all questions of contract interpretation to the arbitrator. It is confined to ascertaining whether the party seeking arbitration is making a claim which on its face is governed by the contract. Whether the moving party is right or wrong is a question of contract interpretation for the arbitrator. In these circumstances the moving party should not be deprived of the arbitrator's judgment, when it was his judgment and all that it connotes that was bargained for.

The courts, therefore, have no business weighing the merits of the grievance, considering whether there is equity in a particular claim, or determining whether there is particular language in the written instrument which will support the claim. The agreement is to submit all grievances to arbitration, not merely those which the court will deem meritorious. The processing of even frivolous claims may have therapeutic values of which those who are not a part of the plant environment may be quite unaware.

The union claimed in this case that the company had violated a specific provision of the contract. The company took the position that it had not violated that clause. There was, therefore, a dispute between the parties as to "the meaning, interpretation and application" of the collective bargaining agreement. Arbitration should have been ordered.   *   *   *

UNITED STEELWORKERS OF AMERICA v. WARRIOR & GULF NAVIGATION CO.

Supreme Court of the United States, 1960.
363 U.S. 574, 80 S.Ct. 1347, 4 L.Ed.2d 1409.

MR. JUSTICE DOUGLAS   *   *   *   "respondent refused arbitration. This suit was then commenced by the Union to compel it   *   *   *."

The collective bargaining agreement states the rights and duties of the parties. It is more than a contract; it is a generalized code to govern a myriad of cases which the draftsmen cannot wholly anticipate. See Shulman, Reason, Contract, and Law in Labor Relations, 68 Harv.L.Rev. 999, 1004–1005. The collective agreement covers the whole employment relationship. It calls into being a new common law—the common law of a particular industry or of a particular plant. As one observer has put it:

"   *   *   *   [I]t is not unqualifiedly true that a collective bargaining agreement is simply a document by which the union and employees have imposed upon management limited, express restrictions of its otherwise absolute right to manage the enterprise, so that an employee's claim must fail unless he can point to a specific contract provision upon which the claim is founded. There are too many people, too many problems, too many unforeseeable contingencies to make the words of the contract the exclusive source of rights and duties.   *   *   *"

The collective bargaining agreement is an effort to erect a system of industrial self-government. When most parties enter into contractual relationship they do so voluntarily, in the sense that there is no real compulsion to deal with one another, as opposed to dealing with other parties. This is not true of the labor agreement. The choice is generally not between entering or refusing to enter into a relationship, for that in all probability preexists the negotiations. Rather it is between having that relationship governed by an agreed-upon rule of law or leaving each and every matter subject to a temporary resolution dependent solely upon the relative strength, at any given moment, of the contending forces. The mature labor agreement may attempt to regulate all aspects of the complicated relationship, from the most crucial to the most minute over an extended period of time. Because of the compulsion to reach agreement and the breadth of the matters covered, as well as the need for a fairly concise and readable instrument, the product of negotiations (the written document) is, in the words of the late Dean Shulman, "a compilation of diverse provisions: some provide objective criteria almost automatically applicable; some provide more or less specific standards which require reason and judgment in their application; and some do little more than leave problems to future consideration with an expression of hope and good faith." Shulman, supra, at 1005. Gaps may be left to be filled in by reference to the practices of the particular industry and of the various shops covered by the agreement. Many of the specific practices which underlie the agreement may be unknown, except in hazy form, even to the negotiators. Courts and arbitration in the context of most commercial contracts are resorted to because there has been a breakdown in the working relationship of the parties; such resort is the unwanted exception. But the grievance machinery under a collective bargaining agreement is at the very heart of the system of industrial self-government. Arbitration is the means of solving the unforeseeable by molding a system of private law for all the problems which may arise and to provide for their solution in a way which will generally accord with the variant needs and desires of the parties. The processing of disputes through the grievance machinery is actually a vehicle by which meaning and content are given to the collective bargaining agreement.

Apart from matters that the parties specifically exclude, all of the questions on which the parties disagree must therefore come within the scope of the grievance and arbitration provisions of the collective agreement. The grievance procedure is, in other words, a part of the continuous collective bargaining process. It, rather than a strike, is the terminal point of a disagreement.

The labor arbitrator performs functions which are not normal to the courts; the considerations which help him fashion judgments may indeed be foreign to the competence of courts.

"A proper conception of the arbitrator's function is basic. He is not a public tribunal imposed upon the parties by superior authority which the parties are obliged to accept. He has no general charter to administer justice for a community which transcends the parties. He is rather part of a system of self-government created by and confined to the parties.   *   *   * " *Shulman*, supra, at 1016.

The labor arbitrator's source of law is not confined to the express provisions of the contract, as the industrial common law—the practices of the industry and the shop—is equally a part of the collective bargaining agreement although not expressed in it.   The labor arbitrator is usually chosen because of the parties' confidence in his knowledge of the common law of the shop and their trust in his personal judgment to bring to bear considerations which are not expressed in the contract as criteria for judgment.   The parties expect that his judgment of a particular grievance will reflect not only what the contract says but, insofar as the collective bargaining agreement permits, such factors as the effect upon productivity of a particular result, its consequence to the morale of the shop, his judgment whether tensions will be heightened or diminished.   For the parties' objective in using the arbitration process is primarily to further their common goal of uninterrupted production under the agreement to make the agreement serve their specialized needs.   The ablest judge cannot be expected to bring the same experience and competence to bear upon the determination of a grievance, because he cannot be similarly informed.

*   *   *

QUESTION

Is the Court's reliance on Shulman's article for its conclusion and for its description of arbitration, sound?

UNITED STEELWORKERS OF AMERICA v. ENTERPRISE WHEEL & CAR CORP.

Supreme Court of the United States, 1960.
363 U.S. 593, 80 S.Ct. 1358, 4 L.Ed.2d 1424.

The refusal of courts to review the merits of an arbitration award is the proper approach to arbitration under collective bargaining agreements.   The federal policy of settling labor disputes by arbitration would be undermined if courts had the final say on the merits of the awards.   As we stated in United Steelworkers of America v. Warrior & Gulf Navigation Co., 363 U.S. 574, 80 S.Ct. 1347, decided this day, the arbitrators under these collective agreements are indispensable agencies in a continuous collective bargaining process.   They sit to settle disputes at the plant level—disputes that require for their solution knowledge of the custom and practices of a particular factory or of a particular industry as reflected in particular agreements.

When an arbitrator is commissioned to interpret and apply the collective bargaining agreement, he is to bring his informed judgment to bear in order to reach a fair solution of a problem.   This is especially true when it comes to formulating remedies.   There the need is for flexibility in meeting a wide variety of situations.   The draftsmen may never have thought of what specific remedy should be awarded to meet a particular contingency. Nevertheless, an arbitrator is confined to interpretation and application of the collective bargaining agreement; he does not sit to dispense his own brand of industrial justice. He may of course look for guidance from many sources, yet his award is legitimate only so long as it draws its essence from the collective bargaining agreement. When the arbitrator's words manifest an infidelity to this obligation, courts have no choice but to refuse enforcement of the award.

The opinion of the arbitrator in this case, as it bears upon the award of back pay beyond the date of the agreement's expiration and reinstatement, is ambiguous. It may be read as based solely upon the arbitrator's view of the requirements of enacted legislation, which would mean that he exceeded the scope of the submission. Or it may be read as embodying a construction of the agreement itself, perhaps with the arbitrator looking to "the law" for help in determining the sense of the agreement. A mere ambiguity in the opinion accompanying an award, which permits the inference that the arbitrator may have exceeded his authority, is not a reason for refusing to enforce the award. Arbitrators have no obligation to the court to give their reasons for an award. To require opinions free of ambiguity may lead arbitrators to play it safe by writing no supporting opinions. This would be undesirable for a well-reasoned opinion tends to engender confidence in the integrity of the process and aids in clarifying the underlying agreement. Moreover, we see no reason to assume that this arbitrator has abused the trust the parties confided in him and has not stayed within the areas marked out for his consideration. It is not apparent that he went beyond the submission. The Court of Appeals' opinion refusing to enforce the reinstatement and partial back pay portions of the award was not based upon any finding that the arbitrator did not premise his award on his construction of the contract. It merely disagreed with the arbitrator's construction of it.   *   *   *

2.   CRITIQUE OF THE TRILOGY

The trilogy led to a rash of scholarly reaction. Most observers believed that Justice Douglas overstated the competence of arbitrators and the parties' willingness to have them consider non-contractually related matters in arriving at their decision. However, there was considerable support for the courts' decision to favor the process of arbitration. A few commentators however, disagreed more fundamentally with the Court's approach. The sharpest attack came from Judge Paul Hays of the Second Circuit Court of Appeals. A former arbitrator and labor law professor, Judge Hays not only criticized the trilogy, but the entire process of arbitration.

HAYS, LABOR ARBITRATION: A DISSENTING VIEW *

THE PRACTICE OF LABOR ARBITRATION

The preferred position which, according to the *Steelworkers* cases, is to be accorded to arbitration is, it seems, largely based upon the superior skills of labor arbitrators.

* * *

No authority whatever is cited for any of these statements. I know of no authority that would lend them support.

There is a surprising lack of objective factual studies of the arbitration process. Yet if we are to understand what the system really is and how it actually works in practice such studies are vital. The literature of arbitration today, and it is among the dullest and dreariest, consists almost entirely of subjective discussions of arbitration written by arbitrators, who are likely to know very little about arbitration outside their own experience—and about their own experience are not inclined to frankness. Whatever an arbitrator writes is eagerly sought out by his clients and prospective clients. Many articles on arbitration, like some of the books by lawyers, could appropriately have the legend "Advt" appended to them.

For whatever reason, there are few studies of the arbitration process written by its clients. Our knowledge of the subject would be considerably enhanced by frank and thoughtful studies of this kind.

But the greatest need, as I have suggested, is for factual studies. It may be difficult to collect material, for reasons suggested in my reference above to articles by arbitrators. However, the project would surely be worth the effort.

In the only study that I know of on the selection of arbitrators, based on very limited factual material and now certainly quite old, there is still a ring of truth in the grounds of selection given by the clients who were questioned. "The only essential factor in selection is whether or not an arbitrator is likely to render a favorable decision in the particular case at issue." While this is said to be the reply given by only one client, the methods of selection described, which include a careful study of the proposed arbitrator's background, previous awards, public utterances, etc., indicate that the parties are much more influenced in their choice by their desire to win on the specific issue in question than they are by the factors mentioned by the Supreme Court.

It is a well-known fact that there are commercial organizations which make it their business to issue ratings on arbitrators and prospective arbitrators. The standards of judgment used by these organizations and, therefore, the standards of those who avail themselves of the services of such organizations, are primarily in terms of "pro" or "anti" union bias.

* * *

Addressing himself specifically to certain aspects of the Supreme Court's view of how arbitrators are chosen, Davey says:

> Arbitrators, being human, cannot fail to be impressed with the respect which the Court manifests for the superior knowledge, ability and wisdom of arbitrators. This deference to the specialized knowledge of arbitrators, which the Court feels apparently cannot be equaled by the "ablest judge," is certainly most gracious. At the risk of appearing ungrateful and traitorous to the arbitration profession, I shall venture the observation that such unstinted praise is in many cases probably not deserved.

* * *

The   *   *   * description of how parties choose arbitrators does not conform with my own experience of some 16 years in arbitration. In fact, most employers and unions in my acquaintance do not want arbitrators to function in the "philosopher king" manner suggested by the Court's statement.

On the contrary, most employers and unions choose arbitrators who will go strictly by the *statute law* of their relationship (i.e., the contract) and not by the so-called common law of the shop which might in fact turn out to be nothing more than the arbitrator's personal view as to what would be "good" for the parties. The writer has arbitrated many cases where he felt the subjective considerations referred to in the Court's dictum, such as heightening or reducing tensions in the shop, called for one decision and the contract itself for another. In such cases, most parties expect the arbitrator to follow the contract and to eschew the temptation to become a statesman.

I add my own witness based upon nearly twenty-five years of experience in deciding hundreds of arbitration cases. Far from being chosen because of any "trust in my personal judgment to bring to bear considerations not expressed in the contract," I feel certain that, to the extent that choice was influenced by any such rational consideration, I was chosen more because of my legal training, which was thought to equip me to interpret the contract, than for any other single reason. I am absolutely certain that the parties would have been astonished (and outraged) if I had based any of my decisions on "the effect upon productivity of a given result" or upon whether tensions would be "heightened or diminished."

The fact of the matter is that arbitration cases ought to be decided in much the same manner as any other controversy in which violation of a contract is alleged. The process of decision in arbitration demands of the arbitrator much the same skills that a judge uses when he is deciding a contracts case.

The position I am taking when I say this is contrary to orthodox arbitration doctrine. But that doctrine mistakes what a judge does when he has a question of contract violation. The picture of the judge which the arbitrators attempt to draw is one in which the judge looks at the pleading, says to himself, "contract" and then proceeds to decide the case according to "the law of contract." But there are nearly as many different kinds of contracts as there are contract cases, and to reach a decision in any of them the judge must understand the background out of which the contract arose. Frequently the background is much more complex and demanding than is the usually fairly simple background of labor relations cases.

* * *

One of the most experienced students of labor law has warned against the dangers of such an approach:

The case with which one can show that collective bargaining agreements have characteristics which preclude the application of some of the familiar principles of contracts and agency creates the danger that those who are knowledgeable about collective bargaining will demand that we discard all the precepts of contract law and create a new law of collective bargaining agreements. I have already expressed the view that the courts would ignore the plea but surely it is unwise even if they would sustain it. Many legal rules have hardened into conceptual doctrines which lawyers invoke with little thought for the underlying reasons, but the doctrines themselves represent an accumulation of tested wisdom, they are bottomed upon notions of fairness and sound public policy, and it would be a foolish waste to climb the ladder all over again just because the suggested principles were developed in other contexts and some of them are demonstrably inapposite. * * * Cox, The Legal Nature of Collective Bargaining Agreements, in Collective Bargaining and the Law (Univ. of Mich.Law School), pp. 121–22.

Judges will do well to heed this admonition. Their experience makes them much more sure-footed in applying principles pertinent to the enforcement of contracts than they are likely to be in discerning the needs of wise industrial relations.

We should realize what we mean when we speak of the special expertise of the arbitrator and his knowledge of the common law of the plant. Fuller states that it takes about a half hour at the outset of the case to fill in a brand new arbitrator on the background of a grievance. I found that it was usually better to proceed at once with the presentation of evidence, not wasting time on a preliminary background statement. The necessary background was almost certain to emerge in the course of the presentation. In the extremely unusual case where it proved to be necessary to do so, I could get the required clarification by a few questions at the end of the presentation. Fuller thinks it would take a judge longer than a half hour to get the required background, not because judges are not as quick to grasp such things as are arbitrators, but because of the method of presenting testimony in court (that is, through expert witnesses, etc.). Fuller shares with many arbitrators the fallacy that courts are operated today with the rigidities of eighteenth-century technicality. There is, of course, no reason at all why the judge should not be told the background of the case in exactly the same way that Fuller has his arbitrator getting that background, through the preliminary statements of counsel. As a matter of fact, that method of getting background would be more common in court procedure than my method of waiting to pick up the background in the course of the presentation of evidence. * * * an unsatisfactory formulation. And, I may add, it is unsatisfactory even in those situations which will never get to the courts. This is for two reasons: first, because we do not know at any given point in the procedure whether this is one of the cases in which an appeal to the courts will be made; and second, because the availability of the courts as enforcing agencies presumably leads to the acceptance of many arbitration awards which would not be accepted if the courts were *not* available. Another reason for requiring high standards in arbitration is the fact that arbitrators are granted judicial immunity. If arbitrators are to enjoy the extraordinary privilege of being free from the necessity of answering to their clients for their acts, then surely the public has the right to demand that they maintain a high level of conduct.

What Judge Van Voorhis said in his dissent in *Matter of Arbitration between East India Trading Co. and Harali*, a commercial arbitration case, is equally applicable to labor arbitration cases:

> It is not an answer that the arbitrators are probably reasonable men, and will probably do what is right between the parties. This question is one of power. Sometimes arbitrators are unreasonable men or abuse power.

The Supreme Court's view of arbitration, as far as appears from its citations of authority, is based upon the work of Harry Shulman and Archibald Cox. Shulman was, and Cox is, the equal of the "ablest judges." Arbitration in Shulman's hands had a special quality, and he had a view of it that differed somewhat from the general view since he believed that the procedure should be purely voluntary and that there should be no appeal to the courts. In Cox's hands, as my quotations from his work have indicated, arbitration must have closely resembled curial adjudication at its very best.

But surely arbitration cannot properly claim the right to be judged by the standards established by its best exemplars. What of the "many" arbitrators whose work is characterized by "incompetence, maneuvering, and even downright chicanery"? What of the "rascals in arbitration" who have "in some fashion * * * to be made to conform to some ethical standards or be thrown out"? What of the arbitrators who indulge in "ambulance chasing" and "fee padding"? What of the arbitrators whose "interest" is in "how to perpetuate themselves" or of the arbitrator who in deciding a case asks himself, "How secure [am I] in [my] position"? "What is the importance of the relevant arbitration duties to [my] career"?

* * *

The fact is that we have no idea at all of who the arbitrators are, let alone what views they entertain or what is the mettle of their character. Of the thousands who act as arbitrators, about 300 belong to the professional association, the National Academy of Arbitrators. Apart from this handful there are no statistics, no figures, no studies.

A tiny proportion of arbitration awards is published. (It has been estimated to constitute about 4 per cent of the total number of awards rendered.) One of the publications is the *Labor Arbitration* series, put out by the Bureau of National Affairs. In connection with this series the BNA publishes a list of the labor arbitrators whose awards appear in the series, together with brief biographical sketches of some of them. I have studied this list rather carefully. There are 945 arbitrators listed, and there are biographical sketches for 652. I take it that when we discuss arbitrators we are talking about several thousand persons since, as I have said, it is estimated that at least 20,000 cases are heard every year.

Since the material for the biographical sketches in the BNA volume is submitted by the arbitrators themselves and since the usefulness of the book is to those who are looking for an arbitrator to hire, the sketches are presumably as favorable to the authors as possible.

Not only are there only a dozen or so persons whose records reveal any substantial distinction, but there are astonishingly few whose past experience, other than legal training, includes anything of importance that is relevant to arbitration.

There are only 29 who appear to be full-time arbitrators; 22 of the others list themselves as judges and 21 as former judges; 205 are lawyers, and 78 are law professors, including deans, associate professors and the like (of these 7 have listed themselves as teaching labor law, and one as a retired teacher of labor law). Professors of economics, including chairmen of departments, associate professors, lecturers, and economists, number 63, of whom 3 are retired. There are 50 professors of industrial relations, personnel management, business, and so forth. There are 3 industrial engineers. Twenty are members or on the staff of state and federal labor relations and mediation boards. Fourteen are deans of schools and colleges, university presidents, or other university officials. Eighteen are miscellaneous professors, including professors of sociology, mathematics (retired), philosophy, federal taxation, political science (retired), physics, social ethics, anthropology, and geology. Fourteen are management-labor consultants. Thirteen are clergymen, of whom one is retired. Six are business executives and two are industrial relations managers. Only one is a union official. Finally, 23 miscellaneous occupations include a sales agent, two Certified Public Accountants, a referee in bankruptcy, two high school principals, an insurance agent, a probation officer, and a superintendent of schools. (Incidentally the job seems to be a healthy one. Thirty-six of the persons listed are 75 years of age or over, 18 are 80 or over and 3 are over 90).

The arbitrators are asked to list their past experience; 159 listed experience which had no relevant relation to arbitration. Of the 437 who listed some relevant material, there was in almost all cases some connection with the National War Labor Board or the National Wage Stabilization Board, ranging from the merest brush on the part of a great many to a few who were members of regional boards.

Many of the descriptions of past experience are interesting. I have space here for only a few of the shorter ones. One arbitrator says that he was "formerly Principal of Eldred High School 1904–1911, Superintendent, McKean County Schools 1911–1946." Another arbitrator was "Formerly United States district attorney; Chairman, State Boxing Commission 1931–1939; District Attorney, District of Colorado, 1933–1947." Another lists nothing whatsoever except "Formerly U.S. Navy 1942–1946." Another arbitrator was "Formerly trial lawyer for seven years in office of district attorney, Houston, Tex." A longer sketch says "Formerly, U.S. Naval Reserve, active duty, 1942–46, 1951–52; Lecturer, Estate Planning Institute, Ohio State Bar Association, Denison University 1958; Cleveland Regional Tax Institute, 1959; Tax Institutes, Ohio State University, 1960–61; Guest Lecturer, Univ. of Cincinnati, College of Law 1958–."

The arbitrators are also asked to list their affiliations. The listed affiliations of 185 are totally irrelevant to arbitration; 35 listed one or more relevant affiliations, in almost all cases either the National Academy of Arbitrators or the Industrial Relations Research Association. Among affiliations listed by arbitrators are the following (in each case the full list of affiliations is given for the individual arbitrator):

> Affiliated with Elks; Training Association of Southern California; American Legion; Veterans of Foreign Wars; Disabled American Veterans (past state commander); Legion of Valor; California State Employees Association; International Association of Public Employment Services.

> Affiliated with Phi Beta Kappa; Beta Theta Pi, Faculty Club (Berkeley).

*   *   *

A number of arbitrators have written books or articles, some of them on arbitration, others on such varied subjects as: *Cases on Negotiable Instruments; water law; Gaps, Ambiguities and Pitfalls in the Utah Corporation Code; The German Reichsbank and Economic Germany; Administration of Estates; five novels; Law of Sheriffs; Future Interests in Colorado; County History for Public Schools; Covenants Implied in Oil and Gas Leases; Non-Trade and Non-Business Expense Deductions; Albert Schweitzer, The Man and His Work; Cases and Other Select Materials on the Law of Bankruptcy; Murder, Inc.; Chancery Practice in New Jersey.*

The biographical directory, then, affords no support for the theory that arbitrators in general have some special expertise in the labor relations area that gives them an advantage over even the "ablest judges." In fact, if any special expertise is apparent it is with respect to the law. Well over half of those listed have had legal training. We may assume, I think, that the law-trained arbitrators (in-

cluding 43 judges, past and present) have a special feeling for the
resolution of controversies by orderly procedure and for the elements
of procedural due process. It is my conviction that in addition to procedural expertise, lawyers are chosen most often in arbitration because the decisions which are sought involve the interpretation of
contracts. The assistance of lawyers is today almost always invoked
in the drafting of collective agreements. That lawyers should be
called upon to interpret such agreements follows almost a fortiori.
Study of the published awards will reveal that in practically every
case the arbitrator claims, at least, to be interpreting a clause of the
written contract between the parties.

But even if there were evidence to establish the distinctive abilities of some arbitrators, this would hardly answer to the purpose.
The biographical directory and the published awards suggest, for example, that in scores of instances arbitrators' experience has been
confined to a single case, and in hundreds of others is limited to very
few cases over a considerable period of time and involving different
enterprises. Yet it appears that, for example, a clergyman sitting on
his one and only arbitration case is as much entitled to the Supreme
Court's preferred position as any other arbitrator. This is to say
nothing of the incompetent and the dishonest, "the rascals in arbitration," to whose presence the literature attests.

The fact of the matter is that the undiscriminating praise which
has been heaped on labor arbitration since World War II has its origin largely in the work published by arbitrators. In the absence of
factual studies, few besides arbitrators have made any attempt to
evaluate the process. Only a few arbitrators have been critical. The
American Arbitration Association, whose officials I know to be privy
to a great deal of unfavorable material on labor arbitration, has as its
purpose the promotion of the arbitration process, and the work of its
staff consists largely in such promotion. Much the same could be
said, I suspect, about the Federal Mediation and Conciliation Service.

There are, however, two types of awards, the compromise award
and the rigged award, which have come in for considerable criticism.
We may assume, I think, that the use of these devices is fairly widespread, although we cannot say how wide.

Of the arbitrator whose position leads to the compromise award
Raffaele says:

> The goal of organized arbitrators is to make arbitration a pro-
> fession. This is meant to be taken in a laudatory sense and not
> intended to allude to the nonprofessional practices of professional
> organizations. In order to achieve this objective, the rascals in
> arbitration in some fashion have to be made to conform to some
> ethical standards or be thrown out. This goal presents difficulties
> that are inherent in the nature of the beast. There exists no pre-
> sumption in industrial relations of the specialist inequality be-
> tween the arbitrator and those to whom he is dispensing his ser-
> vices. Arbitrators like mediators live by consent of the
> contending parties who want their just due in return for the prof-

fer of employment. They are the employees of the parties who can dispense with their services by reconciling differences direct-ly. * * * They live at the sufferance of unions and manage-ment and are inclined to accept a code of behavior prescribed by the parties that hire them. * * *

The fact that the arbitrator is an appointee of the parties subjects him to the political pressures of those who control his appointment. He is thereby confronted with a situation akin to a judge having to fear the power reaction against him from the party against whom he is inclined to make his decision. Some arbitrators inure themselves against such pressures. Others, especially those whose sole income is derived from arbitration, become quite sensitive to what the union or management can do to their position in consequence of their acts.

* * *

Raffaele points out two ways in which the arbitrator's preoccupa-tion with his own "acceptability" serves to distort the decision of arbi-tration cases. In the first place arbitrators in order "to maintain their acceptability * * * may have to lean a little in the direction of that party which is more likely not to elect them and, by so doing, add to its already disparate collective bargaining power." On the other hand, says Raffaele, arbitration which started out as a simple method of enforcement of the collective agreement became some-thing quite different when the arbitrators began to equate "power positions" in order to perpetuate themselves in office.

Raffaele's last remark has a great deal to do with the approach to arbitration in terms of the necessity of considering "the common law of the shop," the "gaps" in the collective agreement, "past practice," "increased productivity," and the "lessening of tensions." These con-cepts were introduced, says Raffaele, for the purpose of permitting the arbitrator to decide more grievances for the union and thus to keep his job. It has "forced on employers a kind of arbitration they had little intention of purchasing."

A rigged award is an award which is actually the product of an agreement between the employer and union representatives but which appears as the decision of the arbitrator. A case or two will illustrate the meaning and the role of the rigged award.

A number of years ago, when I was comparatively new at arbitra-tion, two lawyers, one representing the employer, the other repre-senting the employees' union, requested that I arbitrate a wage dis-pute for them. They offered me $5,000, which was in that day an excellent fee. I was pleased and quickly expressed my willingness to accept the arbitration. I was then informed that it would be unneces-sary for me to hold any hearings or even to prepare an award. The award, it appeared, had already been prepared, and all I was required to do was to sign my name to it. It was reasonably clear to me, even though it was my first experience of this kind, that I was not being paid $5,000 for the physical act of signing my name. I declined to sign. I heard afterward that two or three other arbitrators had de-clined. Then a fourth arbitrator signed. I have never particularly begrudged him his fee of $5,000, but I have always felt that it was going a bit too far to give him a dinner and a medal for making the most important contribution to arbitration for that year.

I presume that in this first case the union officials were bribed to accept the terms of the employer. I would give you therefore a second case of a type which some have found to be more difficult. Let us take a situation in which completely honest officials of the union are willing to agree to terms which have been negotiated with a marginal enterprise. The officials are genuinely convinced that the enterprise cannot afford to pay more and that it will have to suspend operations if it is forced to grant a higher scale of wages. The union officials sincerely believe that the settlement which has been negotiated is in the best interest of the workers. However, there is among the employees a rank and file committee controlled by Communists who have no real interest in the welfare of the workers and whose sole purpose is to get control of the union. If the officials agree to the negotiated wages, they will be handing the Communist group the most effective possible weapon. Moreover they know that, once the Communist group gets control of the union, it is likely to settle with the employer on the same terms or on terms which are even less favorable to the employees. The union and company officials take their case to a third party with the suggestion that he may be willing to "arbitrate" the wage issue. The "arbitrator" makes an independent investigation of the situation and comes to the conclusion that the union officials are (1) completely honest and (2) correct in their conclusions about the ability of the industry to pay higher wages. The question is whether the arbitrator should agree to take the case and to announce as an award what is in fact an agreed-upon settlement.

Fleming reports, with the reservation that the evidence must support the agreed finding (but, of course, without the particulars which I have included in my hypothetical case to make it more appealing), that "perhaps" a majority of the arbitrators whom he questioned "felt that it was entirely appropriate to take an agreed case in the wage category."

Bernstein gaily calls the rigged award a "masquerade." "A tripartite board is," he says, "the appropriate structural form for the rigged wage case. This is, in part, because wage changes in general are not well adapted to one-man arbitration. More important, however, is the usefulness of a tripartite arrangement in supporting the masquerade through the dissenting opinion. By his dissent a partisan board member can give the appearance of striving valiantly in the interests of his constituents against insuperable odds. These opinions make impressive reading in union newspapers and employers' association newsletters."

In the category of grievances, we may take as an example a situation in which the employer agrees, at the instance of the union, to discharge a leader of a faction within the union who has been "making trouble" for the union leaders, but whose discharge will be unpopular and, if effected with the consent of the union, might strengthen the faction. The employer discharges the man on a trumped-up charge, say incompetence. The union demands arbitration and presents its case to the arbitrator at a hearing, having in the meantime informed the arbitrator that it does not want to win the case. The arbitrator then upholds the discharge. As we have seen the National Labor Relations Board will ordinarily accept the result of the arbitration. For contrast we may take the case of an employee discharged by the employer for stealing. The union agrees with the employer that the evidence shows the employee is guilty, but it insists on going through the form of an arbitration hearing because of the employee's popularity. Again the arbitrator is told that the union does not desire to win.

To me the rigged award in any of these cases is a shocking distortion of the administration of justice. It displays the arbitrator as the creature of the parties, a marionette operated by them, a ventriloquist's dummy. This attitude toward arbitration, which is reflected by participation in the rigged award, is that the arbitrator is the obedient servant of those who hire him and owes nothing whatever to the public interest or to the ends of justice. Worse than that, the attitude reflects faithlessness toward those whose interest he is pretending to protect. For while the arbitrator is chosen and hired by the union leaders, he is paid out of the union treasury. He knows that he is looked upon by the membership of the union as the defender of their rights, not as the creature of the leadership, who will accept the orders of the officials even when those orders direct the sacrifice of the rights of the membership. The report of the McClellan Committee deals with a similar situation involving counsel for the unions. The report condemns counsel for acting as the representative of the officials of the union, rather than as representatives of the union as a whole.

The compromise award, when it is rendered so that the arbitrator may keep his job, and the rigged award are both totally unacceptable in any decent system of justice. As long as they continue to exist as a part of the arbitration process, the claim of arbitration for a preferred position under law must be a weak claim indeed.

If we put the loftier claims for labor arbitration to one side and turn to the considerably narrower claims of superiority to court procedure which were formerly asserted, we find that there is criticism of the process even on these narrower grounds. Manson says:

> The original attractions of arbitration were speed, simplicity and inexpensiveness.   *   *   *   Now sluggish, complicated and costly, the process has nurtured some peculiar techniques for dubious ends.

According to Raffaele:

> Some arbitrators, to be sure a minority, have indulged in ambulance chasing practices and fee padding. A simple discharge case, taking two hours of hearing, may require a week of deliberation,

each day of reflection costing the parties a hundred dollars and sometimes much more.

With arbitrators' fees running as high as $500 a day or even more, and with other expenses such as lawyers' fees, transcripts, etc. about the same as they would be for a court case, it seems to me very doubtful whether labor arbitration is in many cases less expensive than court procedures.

As to speed, Ross in an article called "The Well Aged Arbitration Case" wrote that in 1955–56 it took an average of 44 days from griev-ance to filing, 112 days from filing to hearing, 46 days from hearing to award, or a total of 202 days. This was up considerably from the figures of ten years before (133.1 days), and I think we may assume that the time consumed has tended to increase since Ross's study.

Aaron says that an "arbitrator may unduly prolong a hearing by failing to maintain decorum, by refusing to work more than a few hours a day or by intruding persistently in the presentation of the case by the respective parties," and that "some arbitrators take too much time or, what is worse, charge for more time than they have spent."

*　*　*

The claim of simplicity for the arbitration process is based in large part on the absence of "legal technicalities." Arbitrators, particular-ly those without legal training, are proud of eschewing legalisms. In *Hughes Tool Co.*, the arbitrator (not without legal training) refused to decide that an issue was arbitrable because a court would so de-cide. His reasoning was that the Supreme Court had held that arbi-trators were better able to decide grievance cases than judges, and that they were by the same token better able to decide arbitrability. In another case an issue was held arbitrable on the ground that "to limit the arbitrator to disputes expressly covered in the contract would fail to recognize the difference between labor-management contracts and commercial contracts, wills, deeds of trust and similar consensual agreements."

However, legal forms and legal principles are usually beneficial and frequently vital to the just resolution of the kind of controversy which is treated in arbitration. A few examples will suffice.

In the criticisms of legalism much scorn has been heaped on the doctrine of precedent. It is said that precedent has no place in labor arbitration, that each case must be decided on its own peculiar facts. This position betrays the ignorance of the critic since, of course, the doctrine of precedent provides in itself for distinguishing cases on the basis of their facts. By denying the applicability of precedent, the critics of "legalism" are denying to arbitration the beneficent effects of the doctrine. * * * In view of what has already been said about what the Industrial Union Department of the AFL has called our "Avaricious Arbitrators," it may not be invidious to suggest that one of the reasons for the arbitrators' opposition to the use of prece-dent is that it would lessen the need for arbitration. Of course the use of precedent would have other beneficial results. The same language in different collective agreements is frequently construed in different ways, with the result that similar conduct is treated differently under different contracts. Surely it would be desirable to have such language mean the same thing in all cases. This use of precedent would permit draftsmen, who could rely upon it, to be certain of the meaning which would be given to the words they used, and to include or avoid language with confidence in the effect that such inclusion or exclusion would have.

Another of the legalisms that arbitrators are urged to avoid is the adoption of any rule concerning the burden of proof. But surely it is impossible for any adversary system to operate without such a rule. What the arbitrators are doing is failing to announce the rule, though they must use it. The failure to announce the rule seems unfair to the parties. It also may lead arbitrators, particularly those without legal training, to render compromise awards, as in a discharge case to order reinstatement without back pay because the arbitrator is not quite sure on the evidence whether or not the employee was guilty of the offense with which he was charged.

Another legalism often criticized and apparently usually excluded from arbitration is the parol evidence rule. With respect to that exclusion I can do no better than to quote a comment by Cox:

> When legal principles are invoked in arbitration proceedings it is well not to brush them aside impatiently but to recall that behind them lies the weight of thought tested by experience. If the policy behind the legal rule holds true, the case should turn upon it. If the policy is unimportant, the legal rule may safely be disregarded.

Time prevents pursuing an inquiry into the applicability of some of the legal principles most often invoked in labor arbitration. If I have not already provoked controversy, I am sure that on these questions there would be sharp differences of opinion. Possibly it is only lawyers who feel misgivings on observing the tendency of some labor arbitrators to receive testimony from the parties as to what they thought and said during the negotiation of the contract which an arbitrator is seeking to interpret.

On the other hand Fuller believes that arbitrators are generally more conservative and less flexible than judges, and certainly there are some instances in which the rules adopted by arbitrators are extremely technical. It seems, for example, to be quite generally held that, where a particular offense has been charged as the basis for discipline, proof of another offense, even though sufficient to justify the discipline, will not support the charge. In other words there is no opportunity afforded, as there would be in a court, to amend to conform the pleading to the proof.

Another severely technical arbitration rule is that all employees guilty of the same offense must receive the same punishment. This thoughtless application of the maxim "equality is equity" flies in the face of the beneficial rule that the background and job history of an employee are relevant to the question of justification for discipline.

Arbitration pays for its simplicity by not having those important aids to the administration of justice and the ascertainment of truth which are available in the courts, such as provisional remedies, discovery procedures, and provision for joinder of parties.

* * *

By describing some of the actual practices of labor arbitration, I have endeavored to raise the question of how far the courts *should* accord to labor arbitration a preferred position.

NOTE

Judge Hays concluded that the Courts should "not lend themselves at all to the arbitration process" but should return it to its previous status as a voluntary system. At the very least, Judge Hays urged that courts should review carefully the merits before enforcing awards. Does Judge Hays make a convincing case?

Is there any way that Courts of Appeals, which are bound to follow the Supreme Court's directions, can follow the approach suggested by Hays of carefully reviewing arbitrator's decisions before enforcing awards?

Hays' description of arbitration has been responded to widely and rigorously attacked. Typical was the response of Saul Wallen, a noted arbitrator, who reviewed Hays' book for the Harvard Law Review.[1] With respect to trilogy, Wallen commented, "If the Court erred in its emphasis, it did not err in the essence of its holdings". With regard to Hays' criticism of arbitrators and the process, Wallen responded: "The documentation for these sweeping changes is nonexistent. Hays admits as much in his book when he deplores the lack of objective studies of the arbitration process—empirical observation does seem to bear out the special competence of the arbitrators.

Hays accuses arbitrators of writing awards in order that they may be chosen for future cases. How arbitrators accomplish this feat, he does not explain. Arbitrators are nearly always the mutual choice of the parties—the irate loser can veto him for the future. And if he writes a decision that has a little bit in it for each party but not enough for either to accomplish justice, his cowardice becomes immediately apparent to both. The pressures on arbitrators are not primarily from the parties, they are from within.

As yet, there are few studies which reveal how successful the process is; whether arbitrators perform as Douglas and Wallen claim or as Hays argues. An essentially unscientific study by Professors Jones and Smith undertook to study how well the parties feel the process is doing.[2] They sent out 715 letters of inquiry to management

1. Wallen, "Labor Arbitration: A Dissenter's View" 81 Harv.L.Rev. 507 (1967).

2. Dallas Jones and Russel Smith. "Management and Labor Appraisals and Criticisms of the Arbitration Process: A

representatives receiving 364 useful responses, and 290 letters to union representatives from which 77 useful responses were received.

They asked two questions:

"1. Are you generally satisfied with the arbitration process, or, given a chance, would you prefer leaving all issues of contract application to the courts or to collective bargaining (including strike action)?

2. What suggestions do you have for improving the arbitration process?"

They report:

"By an overwhelming majority (over 95%) our respondents indicate that they prefer the arbitration process to the available alternatives."

QUESTION

Does the method used permit any generalization to be drawn from these responses? Are there alternatives not referred to in question 1?

A wide range of suggestions was received. Most of them were concerned with limiting the arbitrator's power and with increasing the level of review, although it is not clear how representative these suggestions were.

Despite reservations expressed by Hays and others, the trilogy has set labor policy for over 15 years.

The Court has, on numerous occasions, reaffirmed its support for arbitration and the federal policy encouraging its use. Most notably in Boys Markets, Inc. v. Retail Clerks Local 770, 398 U.S. 235, 90 S.Ct. 1583, 26 L.Ed.2d 199 (1970), the Supreme Court held that despite the language of the Norris-La Guardia Act, an injunction might issue against a strike in breach of a no-strike clause when, and only when, "it is over a grievance which both partners are contractually bound to arbitrate".[3]

The growth of arbitration together with the increasing complexity of other areas of labor law has inevitably posed the question of how arbitrators should deal with legal issues presented in the grievances which they hear and what weight other tribunals should give to arbitration in exercising their own statutory jurisdiction.

Report with Comments" 62 Mich.L.Rev. 1115 (1964).

3. The Norris-La Guardia Act contains no exemption for strikes in breach of a no-strike clause.

3. THE ROLE OF ARBITRATORS IN
ENFORCING STATUTORY RIGHTS

There is no question in labor relations which has stirred more debate than that of the responsibility of arbitrators to apply statutory law when deciding grievances. The issue might arise in a number of ways. The union might claim that failure to promote a black employee violates the contract, and also the law against employment discrimination, or it might argue that discipline of a union steward is not for good cause and also constitutes retaliation for union activity in violation of § 8(a)(1) and (3) of the NLRA. Some argue that arbitrators are hired by the parties to interpret their contract and that arbitrators should limit themselves to this function, ignoring statutory law unless it is specifically incorporated into the agreement. Others argue that arbitrators have a responsiblity for insuring that the relationship between the parties is in accordance with the law.

The following excerpt summarizes the different positions taken by prominent arbitrators and scholars. Consider which of the positions described makes the most sense:

MICHAEL I. SOVERN, WHEN SHOULD ARBITRATORS FOLLOW FEDERAL LAW? *

I. THE PREVIOUS DISCUSSIONS

The question put by the title of my talk has been ably explored by distinguished members of the Academy at two of our last three meetings. To understate the matter, no consensus has emerged. Some would have us ignore federal law; others would have us apply it; still others would apply it in some cases but not in others. Given that range of opinion, I was surprised to discover that I disagreed in important ways with *all* of the positions advanced.

In a moment I shall briefly recapitulate the high points of this dialog. Then I shall try to add something to it. But first let me be as explicit as I can about what is and what is not at issue.

The debate focuses on cases in which an arbitrator is asked to base his decision on a statute or other source of law instead of or in addition to the contract. Among the many examples considered at previous meetings were: a claim for travel time not supported by the collective agreement but allegedly required by the Fair Labor Standards Act; a dismissal required by a collective agreement but apparently unlawful under Section 8(a)(3) of the National Labor Relations Act; and a unilateral change in working conditions claimed to violate Section 8(a)(5) of the NLRA rather than any particular provision of the parties' contract.

* Reprinted by permission from *Arbitration and the Expanding Role of* *Neutrals*, copyright 1970 by The Bureau of National Affairs, Inc., Washington, D.C.

We begin with Bernard Meltzer's paper of three years ago, in which he concluded that arbitrators should respect "the agreement that is the source of their authority and should leave to the courts or other official tribunals the determination of whether the agreement contravenes a higher law. Otherwise, arbitrators would be deciding issues that go beyond not only the submission agreement but also arbitral competence.

*   *   *

This brief passage epitomizes Meltzer's two main arguments. I think of them alliteratively—consent and competence. The parties have consented only to the arbitrator's construing their contract, not to his conforming it to applicable law. And arbitrators are not competent—in the sense of qualified—to rule on questions of federal law.

Robert Howlett, in a paper deliverd at the same meeting of the Academy, was equally categorical, but flatly contra to Meltzer. He said:

> "There is a responsibility of arbitrators, corollary to that of the General Counsel and the NLRB, to decide, where relevant, a statutory issue, in order that the NLRB, consistent with its announced policy, may avoid a decision on the merits, and the statutory policy of determining issues through arbitration may be fulfilled."

According to Howlett, "[E]ach contract includes all applicable laws." He infers that an arbitrator charged with construing a contract is also authorized to interpret the applicable law.

Howlett did concede, however, that on occasion the arbitrator does better to stay his hand. Thus,

> "When an arbitrator meets one of those cases which might better be determined by the NLRB or EEOC (or some other agency), he may determine the General Counsel or the Commission, with its power of investigation, is in a better position to secure evidence than is an under- or non-represented employee whose dispute has been submitted to arbitration. He should so advise the parties and withdraw."

In the workshops that followed Howlett's paper, labor and management attorneys chose up sides largely without regard to the identity of their clients. That is to say, some who represented labor and some who represented management preferred Howlett while others lined up with Meltzer. This nonpartisan division of opinion as to the role of the arbitrator casts some doubt on the proposition that the parties have bargained solely for contract interpretation. At least some sophisticated practitioners of our discipline conscientiously believe they have contracted for more when they settle on a standard arbitration clause. I shall return to this point.

A year went by and Richard Mittenthal, true to our craft, tried "to occupy the middle ground" between Meltzer and Howlett. He convincingly rebutted Howlett's sweeping assertion that all relevant law is incorporated in the collective agreement, then turned to face Meltzer. On the matter of competence, he pointed out that "[S]ome of our members—Smith, Aaron, Cox, Meltzer himself, to name but a few—surely possess the necessary expertise. Such men are well equipped to decide grievance disputes which raise both contractual and legal questions." Mittenthal went on to suggest that parties are free to pick such a man when their case involves a difficult question of law.

Mittenthal's contract arguments led him to that middle ground between Meltzer and Howlett:

"The arbitrator should 'look to see whether sustaining the grievance would require conduct the law forbids or would enforce an illegal contract; if so, the arbitrator should not sustain the grievance.' This principle, however, should be carefully limited. It does not suggest that "an arbitrator should pass upon all the parties' legal rights and obligations.' * * * Thus, although the arbitrator's award may *permit* conduct forbidden by law but sanctioned by contract, it should not *require* conduct forbidden by law even though sanctioned by contract."

Let me illustrate Mittenthal's distinction with a simple case. Suppose a collective agreement provides that departmental seniority shall govern layoff and recall. Suppose further that application of this provision would require laying off black workers with considerable plant seniority who have just been allowed to transfer into previously segregated departments. The black workers affected claim that compliance with the agreement's departmental seniority system would violate their rights under Title VII of the Civil Rights Act of 1964. According to Mittenthal's thesis, if the employer lays off the blacks and they grieve to arbitration, the arbitrator should reply that the contract has not been violated and the blacks should seek their remedy under Title VII. If, on the other hand, the employer lays off whites with greater departmental seniority than the blacks and the whites grieve, a different response is called for. The contract has indeed been violated and the arbitrator should say so, but if he believes the contract is illegal, he should say that too and refuse to issue an award upholding the grievance. To repeat the key passage from Mittenthal: "[A]lthough the arbitrator's award may *permit* conduct forbidden by law but sanctioned by contract, it should not *require* conduct forbidden by law even though sanctioned by contract."

Mittenthal met the fate so often meted out to men who try the middle ground. Meltzer and Howlett both criticized him. And Ted St. Antoine joined them. All agreed that Mittenthal's distinction between an arbitrator's permitting and requiring illegal conduct would not do. Meltzer put it this way:

"[Mittenthal's formula] is not supported by the authority conferred on the arbitrator by the parties; or by the expertise imputed to arbitrators and courts; or by the twin desires for finality of arbitration awards and the limitation of judicial intervention. Under Mr. Mittenthal's approach, the role accorded to law would depend on how an employer resolved a controversy and not on its essential character or the functions properly delegated to different adjudicative agencies. In my opinion, such an approach transforms an accidental consideration into a decisive one."

* * *

I have not done Meltzer, Howlett, or Mittenthal full justice in this brief summary, but I believe I have put their central ideas before you. I turn now to mine.

II. COMPETENCE AND CONSENT

Anyone who would urge, as I intend to, that arbitrators should sometimes pass on the legality of a contract provision must first meet Meltzer's arguments on competence and consent. Some arbitrators are as qualified as reviewing judges to rule on the law and some are not.

I have another difficulty with Professor Meltzer's view concerning the ability of arbitrators to apply federal law. He accepts, as everyone does, the complete propriety of an arbitrator's construing an ambiguous agreement to preserve its legality.

If the arbitrator's qualifications allow that, I do not see how they can be inadequate to answer the very same antitrust question when urged as a reason for not ordering compliance with a clear provision. There may be other reasons for distinguishing between the two cases, but the arbitrator's lack of qualifications cannot be one of them.

I turn now to Meltzer's other key argument—the parties have authorized the arbitrator to construe the contract, not the law. Though this might once have been irrefutable, two factors combine to rob it of at least some of its force. I have already suggested one of these: The very considerable division of authority as to the proper response of an arbitrator when faced with a question of law. As long as many arbitrators and practitioners—though a minority—believe that an arbitrator does have the power to resolve statutory questions under the standard arbitration clause, it cannot be said with complete assurance that parties intend to withhold such power when they are silent on the subject.

Far more important is the Supreme Court's rejection of conventional intent analysis as the definitive approach to arbitration provisions. The Court has indicated that arbitration clauses are part of a system of administration that the Court will itself define in part. And the needs of that system as perceived by the Court can overrule any but the most explicit limitations on the arbitrator's power.

* * * [W]e can conclude that when a statutory question is intertwined with a contract question, whether the arbitrator has authority to resolve both is not solely a matter of the parties' intent. It is also a matter of federal labor policy. Meltzer himself put it perfectly: "[T]he critical question [is] whether arbitral assumption of such jurisdiction is a desirable method of coordinating a private system of adjudication with a governmentally imposed legal and administrative framework." And the Supreme Court has indicated that we

are free to seek the best answer to that question, whatever the parties may have intended, unless they have been fully explicit.

* * *

Like the judge who has been bribed by both sides, we are now free to address the matter on the merits. I believe that an arbitrator may follow federal law rather than the contract when the following conditions are met:

1. The arbitrator is qualified.

2. The question of law is implicated in a dispute over the application or interpretation of a contract that is also before him.

3. The question of law is raised by a contention that, if the conduct complained of does violate the contract, the law nevertheless immunizes or even requires it.

4. The courts lack primary jurisdiction to adjudicate the question of law.

* * *

My second condition—that the question of law be implicated in a contract-interpretation dispute that is also before the arbitrator—is necessary because unless it is met, the parties belong in some other forum altogether.

My third condition is at the center of the battle, the point where Meltzer, Howlett, and Mittenthal clash most sharply.

Suppose a dispute between a union and an employer over the meaning and legality of a union-security clause. The union demanded the dismissal of an employee who failed to become a member. The employer responded that the union-security clause did not require dismissal in these circumstances and that if it did, the clause was to that extent unlawful under the NLRA. If the employer remains adamant and the union takes him to arbitration before a qualified arbitrator, my formula permits a decision on the statutory question. The arbitrator is qualified; the statutory question is implicated in a contract-interpretation dispute; the employer is claiming that if his refusal to dismiss does violate the contract, the NLRA nonetheless requires him to stand fast;

Where does all this complexity and confusion lead us? It leads me to my third condition. When an employer claims that his conduct, if a contract breach, is nonetheless required by law, the arbitrator should decide that question because the alternatives seem worse. They are either decision by a court or a parceling out of the case among three forums—arbitrator, court, and Board. Decision by a qualified arbitrator at least holds out the possibility of a quick, correct decision.

When my third condition is not met, the arbitrator should not decide the question of law. The reason, as we have just seen, is that the consequences of decision seem worse than those of abstention. Abstention has the virtue of clarity: The arbitrator decides the contract question and the Board decides the statutory question, and everyone concerned can know who is to do what. If the arbitrator decides, there is always the chance that his decision will conclude the matter, but if it does not, he may have succeeded only in dragging the courts into the case in addition to or in place of the NLRB.

To put the point another way, when an employer claims his conduct, if a breach of contract, is required by law, the case is tangled enough to warrant an arbitrator's gambling on improving matters. Deciding the statutory question might help greatly and can't hurt much. When that condition is lacking, the case, though complex, is not so badly snarled and there is a serious risk that a decision by the arbitrator will make things much worse.

You may have noticed that my third condition is not all that different from Mittenthal's distinction between an award that *permits* illegal conduct and one that *requires* it. And his distinction strikes me as sound for the most part. To repeat, an award that would require conduct proscribed by the NLRA either drags the courts into NLRA decisions or provokes a three-forum journey. An award that permits illegal conduct does not have the same consequences.

But Mittenthal's formulation fails to allow for cases in which a court is an appropriate tribunal to decide the issue of law. In those cases, there is little reason not to pass even a claim of illegality along.

*   *   *

IV. CONCLUSION

Though labor law is our specialty, our subject today is really the administration of justice. In answering the question before us, we seek to have the best possible forum or forums resolve any particular dispute with the minimum of litigation possible under our trifurcated system. That has led me to ask, first, whether the arbitrator is qualified to decide the noncontractual issue. If he is not, he is obviously not the best possible forum and he ought not to decide the question.

If he is qualified, I ask next: What is the alternative to his deciding the legal issue? Unless the case also involves a contract question, the alternative is simply a proceeding in whatever tribunal normally would have heard the legal issue.

In general, arbitrators appear reluctant to address themselves to statutory issues. A study commissioned by the American Arbitration Association indicated that 338 of 2300 grievances studied contained issues under the NLRA. In only 54 cases were Board policies in some way acknowledged.[4] A survey of the National Academy of Ar-

4. Waks, "Arbitrator, Labor Board, or Both," Monthly Labor Rev. Dec. 1968.

bitrators led Professor Harry Edwards to conclude that, with respect to the law of employment discrimination:

> The evidence as to whether and how many arbitrators are professionally competent to decide legal issues in cases involving claims of employment discrimination is at best mixed. Furthermore, even assuming, *arguendo*, that most arbitrators are professionally competent to decide such issues, the nature of the arbitration process often will not allow for full and adequate consideration of an employee's Title VII rights. Finally, the evidence from the survey suggests that even when arbitrators are professionally competent to decide legal issues and when the arbitration process is adequate to allow for full consideration of legal questions arising pursuant to Title VII, still many arbitrators believe that they have no business interpreting or applying a public statute in a contractual grievance dispute.[5]

4. THE DIFFERENCE OF THE NLRB TO ARBITRATION

The question of how the NLRB should respond when arbitrators exercise jurisdiction over cases raising statutory questions has evoked considerable controversy.

In 1955, the NLRB announced that it would accept an arbitrator's decision which dealt with a claim arising under the National Labor Relations Act where three standards were met: 1). The parties had agreed to be bound by the results, 2). The arbitration proceedings were fair and regular, and 3). The arbitrator's decision was not "clearly repugnant to the purposes and policies of the Act".[6] This decision, however, dealt with an already rendered award. It did not determine what the Board would do when a charge dealt with a matter either pending before or subject to arbitration. In 1971, the Board addressed this issue in the case of Collyer Insulated Wire Co.[7] It held that it would automatically defer to arbitration in any case in which the matter before it was subject to and likely to be resolved through arbitration.

The Board majority in the *Collyer* case based their decision on "the policy favoring voluntary settlement of labor disputes through arbitral processes" and on the expertise of arbitrators in dealing with questions of contract interpretation.

> "In our view disputes such as these can better be resolved by arbitrators with special skill and experience in deciding matters arising under established bargaining relationships than of the application of this Board of a particular provision in our statute".

This decision was criticised by some who argued that the special skill of arbitrators was exaggerated and that the decision would deprive

5. Edwards, "Arbitration of Employment Discrimination Cases: An Empirical Study," Proceedings 28th Annual Meeting, National Academy of Arbitrators, BNA 1975, p. 59.

6. Spielberg Manufacturing Co., 112 N.L.R.B. 1080. This policy is generally referred to as the Spielberg doctrine.

7. 192 N.L.R.B. 837 (1971).

some employees of the statutory forum created by Congress to vindi-cate their rights.[8] The *Collyer* doctrine was praised by many observ-ers who argued that the Board function was to protect the basic stat-utory rights to organize and bargain collectively. They argued that it was a waste of resources for the Board to become involved in day-to-day grievance settlement, particularly where an established system already existed.[9] Both critics and supporters of the *Collyer* doctrine have persuasive arguments.

QUESTIONS

1. Would unions or employers be most likely to favor the *Collyer* doctrine?

2. What difference would it make to an employee with a griev-ance whether or not his case would be heard by the Labor Board? If arbitration is available?

The closeness of the issue has led to a compromise approach, un-der which the Board defers in some cases but not in others. If a grievance involves a statutory question, because it is claimed the em-ployer discharged or disciplined an employee in retaliation for the ex-ercise of § 7 rights in violation of § 8(a)(3) of the Act, the Board will not defer. If the statutory question concerns the employer's failure to bargain with the union before taking action, the Board will defer. Each of these decisions were reached by a 3–2 vote of the Board. Two members favored deferral generally, two opposed it in all situa-tions. The swing vote was provided by then Chairwoman Murphy in both cases. Thus the existence and reach of the *Collyer* doctrine are both subject to amendment with changes in the membership of the Board. Consider which of the following opinions is most convincing.

CENTRAL AMERICAN TRANSPORTATION CORP.

94 L.R.R.M. 1483 (1977).

FANNING & JENKINS, Members.

Although we agree with the Administrative Law Judge that this case should not be deferred to arbitration, our rejection of deferral is predicated on our longstanding opposition to the policy establishcd by Collyer and its progeny, and is not based merely on the particular circumstances of the instant case. As we pointed out initially in our dissenting opinions in Collyer, and thereafter reiterated in dissenting from the extension of the Collyer policy to cases involving alleged violations of sections of the Act other than Section 8(a)(5), we believe that the Board has a statutory duty to hear and to dispose of unfair

---

8. Attleson, "Disciplinary Discharge Arbitration and NLRB Deference," 20B of L.Rev. 355 (1971) Getman, "Collyer In-sulated Wire, a Case of Misplaced Modes-ty," 49 Ind.L. Journal 57 (1973).

9. See Schatzki, "NLRB Resolution of Contract Disputes, § 8(a)(5)" 50 Texas L.Rev. 225 (1972).

labor practices and that the Board cannot abdicate or avoid its duty [in] seeking to cede its jurisdiction to private tribunals. As we have repeatedly pointed out,[2] Section 10(a) of the Act is explicit that the Board's power to prevent unfair labor practices "shall not be affected by any other means of adjustment or prevention that has been or may be established by agreement, law, or otherwise. * * * Such a lack of power in the Board to make the public interest in the vindication of statutory rights "a plaything of private treaty and interpretation" is further underlined by the decision of Congress, reflected in Section 14(c)(1), limiting the extent to which the Board may exercise its discretion to refuse jurisdiction over any "class or category of employers."

Aside from the Board's lack of power to subcontract to private tribunals the adjudication of rights that arise solely by virtue of our Act, we believe the facts of the instant case convincingly demonstrate why, on practical as well as policy grounds, the Collyer doctrine of deferral has failed.

In the first place, as we noted in dissenting from the result reached in National Radio Company, Inc., 198 N.L.R.B. 527, 80 L.R. R.M. 1718 (1972), the lead case in which the Collyer majority ordered deferral in the context of an alleged discriminatory discharge in violation of Section 8(a)(3), our Act explicitly protects employees from on-the-job discrimination because they have engaged in, or have refrained from engaging in, union activities. The protection thus afforded employees by the Act is clearly an individual, as contrasted with a union or group, right. In the instant case, instead of pursuing arbitration, a route which for a myriad of reasons he concluded would prove futile, Charging Party Soape chose to seek vindication of his statutory rights before the Board. Were we to order deferral in these circumstances, there would be nothing voluntary about the arbitration to which Charging Party Soape would be forced. Hence the voluntary nature of arbitration, long trumpeted by the Collyer enthusiasts as the main reason for deferral, is revealed as a sham in cases, like the instant case, where the charging party is an individual discriminatee seeking to enforce his individual rights.

This case is also instructive insofar as it illustrates the uncertainty, indeed the outright confusion, that has attended the efforts of the Collyer advocates to stretch their original justification for deferral to cover nearly every conceivable situation. Thus, as we have had frequent occasion to point out, even had we accepted the rationale for deferral as initially propounded in the Collyer decision, in subsequent cases the Collyer adherents repeatedly ignored record facts that

---

2. See our dissenting opinions in Collyer Insulated Wire, 192 N.L.R.B. 837, 77 L.R.R.M. 1931 (1971); Southwestern Bell Telephone company; Madison Square Offset Company, Inc., and Xerographic Reproduction Center, Inc., 212 N.L.R.B. 396, 86 L.R.R.M. 1655 (1974); Electronic Reproduction Service, 213 N.L.R.B. 758, 87 L.R.R.M. 1211 (1974), among others.

Our dissenting colleagues' assertion that the arguments which we have advanced against deferral have been "rejected repeatedly" by the courts is both mistaken and misleading. In this regard, see our dissenting opinion in Roy Robinson, Inc., d/b/a Roy Robinson Chevrolet, 228 N.L.R.B. No. 103, 94 L.R.R.M. 1474, (1977), and cases discussed therein.

clearly militated against deferral. In so doing, they so blurred the announced guidelines and criteria under which the Collyer policy was to be applied as to make almost any case in which they found a contract and an arbitration clause a likely candidate for deferral.[3]

As we noted in dissenting from the result reached in Joseph T. Ryerson & Sons, Inc., 199 N.L.R.B. 461, 81 L.R.R.M. 1261, (1972), and similar cases, the Collyer adherents, by indicating that they would defer in any case where the contract incorporates sections of the Act and contains an arbitration clause, in effect invited parties to seek to contract themselves out of the Act, thus stripping employees of the protection afforded by the Act.

*   *   *

Given this record, our dissenting colleagues' claim that cases have not been deferred to arbitration "in an indiscriminate manner" has a decidedly hollow ring. Nor can we join our colleagues in findings, and applauding, the Collyer adherents self-styled sensitivity "to the statutory rights of employees in deciding whether to defer and whether to give effect to an arbitration award." As we have taken pains to point out in numerous opinions, it is precisely the statutory rights of employees, and the obligation of this Board to vindicate those rights, which the Collyer advocates have sought to undermine and abrogate. See, in this regard, McLean Trucking Co., supra, and cases cited in the dissenting opinion at 714–715.

The Collyer adherents cite figures showing that from May 1973 through December 1975 a total of 1,632 cases had been deferred under Collyer. Of those, an arbitration award issued in 473, and 437 were settled short of arbitration. Of those 473 where an award was made, our Regional Offices on request examined 159 (about a third) for compliance with Spielberg standards, revoking deferral in 33 (over 20 percent) and securing violation-settlement agreements in 24 of those. The dissenters cite these figures to establish that their doctrine is a successful and effective means of reducing the Board's workload while preserving statutory rights and voluntary resolution of disputes. The message these figures convey to us is a quite different one: half these deferred cases disappeared from view, with no assurance of any kind that any statutory rights involved had received any consideration or protection; nearly half the remainder, i.e., about one quarter, were settled short of arbitration, and these probably would have been settled short of appeal to the Board even had they not been deferred; and of the one quarter which went to arbitration, it was necessary that the Board examine over a third, and over one out of five of the awards examined proved to have flouted the Act. During this same period of time, 80,152 "C" or violation cases were filed with the Board, so the total Collyer deferrals amounted to about 2 per cent of our workload. These figures make it plain to us that Collyer is not assuring protection of statutory rights and that it is costing us some effort in reviewing awards and in determining which

3. For a fairly representative Collyer decision demonstrating this tendency see   United Aircraft Corporation, 204 N.L.R.B. 879, 83 L.R.R.M.

cases to defer. The reduction in our workload is insignificant and the sacrifice of statutory protection is substantial. We do not regard this trade-off as compatible with our responsibility to administer and apply the Act.

For all of the foregoing reasons, we affirm the Administrative Law Judge's conclusion that deferral is not appropriate. Inasmuch as we agree also with the Administrative Law Judge's findings on the merits, we shall direct the Respondent to comply with her recommended Remedy and Order.

MURPHY, Chairman, concurring:

I agree with the Administrative Law Judge and with my colleagues, that the substantive issues joined by the pleadings herein— i.e., whether Respondent discharged employee Soape because of his union or other protected concerted activities in violation of Section 8(a)(3) and (1) of the Act—are not suitable for deferral to the parties' contractual grievance-arbitration machinery under the principles enunciated in Collyer and National Radio. I disagree, however, with that portion of their rationale which argues that the Board lacks statutory authority to defer any unfair labor practice allegation to the parties' agreed-upon means of resolution.

In my concurring opinion in Roy Robinson Chevrolet, issued this day, I expressed my agreement with the threshold holding in Collyer, supra, that the Board has the necessary discretionary authority under the Act to defer to the parties' contractual grievance-arbitration machinery certain unfair labor practice allegations growing out of differences between them as to the interpretation and/or application of their collective-bargaining agreement. I reached this conclusion substantially for the reasons articulated in Collyer. I also stated, however, that I would not exercise this discretionary authority in every instance where the alleged unfair labor practice might also be a contract violation and where the parties have an agreement calling for binding arbitration of all contract disputes. Rather, I indicated that the Board should stay its processes in favor of the parties' grievance arbitration machinery only in those situations where the dispute is essentially between the contracting parties and where there is no alleged interference with the individual employees' basic rights under Section 7 of the Act. Complaints alleging violations of Section 8(a)(5) and 8(b)(3) fall squarely into this category, while complaints alleging violations of Section 8(a)(3), 8(a)(1), 8(b)(1)(A), and 8(b)(2) clearly do not. As discussed more fully below, in the former category the dispute is principally between the contracting parties—the employer and the union—while in the latter the dispute is between the employee on the one hand and the employer and/or the union on the other. In cases alleging violations of Section 8(a)(5) and 8(b)(3), based upon conduct assertedly in derogation of the contract, the principal issue is whether the complained-of conduct is permitted by the parties' contract. Such issues are eminently suited to the arbitral process, and resolution of the contract issue by an arbitrator will, as a rule, dispose of the unfair labor practice issue. On the other hand, in cases alleging violations of Section 8(a)(1), 8(a)(3), 8(b)(1)(A), and 8(b)(2), although arguably also involving a contract violation, the determinative issue is not whether the conduct is permitted by the contract, but whether the conduct was unlawfully motivated or whether it otherwise interfered with, restrained, or coerced employees in the exercise of the rights guaranteed them by Section 7 of the Act. In these situations, an arbitrator's resolution of the contract issue will not dispose of the unfair labor practice allegation. Nor is the arbitration process suited for resolving employee complaints of discrimination under Section 7. Accordingly, for the reasons discussed below, I find that our decision in National Radio, supra, was an unwise extension of the Collyer deferral policy into an area in which the Board should retain its preeminence. That decision and its progeny must, therefore, be reversed.

The distinction which I draw between purely contractual issues which I would defer to arbitration under the Collyer rationale and those which I would not so defer are based upon statutory, as well as policy and practical, considerations.

The National Labor Relations Act, as amended, is predicated upon two national policy objectives which the Board is charged with effectuating. These dual statutory purposes are stated in the last paragraph of Section 1 of the Act as follows:

The right of employees to full freedom of association is, after all, the cornerstone of all Section 7 rights and the protection of those rights is the very reason for the Board's existence. Therefore, I believe it would not further the fundamental aims of the National Labor Relations Act to defer to arbitration disputes alleging interference with the employees' Section 7 rights, even though such dispute may also involve an underlying disagreement between the parties as to the meaning and/or application of their contract. Although the rights enumerated in, and guaranteed by, Section 7 of the Act are phrased in terms of individual rights of employees, they have long been recognized as public rights enforceable by governmental rather than private action. Interference with these rights, or employment discrimination intended to encourage or discourage the free exercise of these rights, is an unfair labor practice under Section 8(a)(1) and (3) if committed by an employer, and under Section 8(b)(1)(A) and (2) if committed by a labor organization. Statutory rights, unlike rights created by contract, cannot lawfully be reduced or eliminated either by the employer, the union, or by both. By the same token, an allegation that an employee's statutory rights have been invaded by the employer, the union, or by both ought not to be adjudicated by the very party or parties charged with the wrongdoing.

There are also compelling policy and practical considerations for declining to defer to the parties' contractual grievance-arbitration machinery any dispute which alleges interference with, or discrimination grounded on, an employee's exercise of Section 7 rights. These rights, as stated, are public rights which, in my judgment, must be protected by the Board in its public capacity of giving effect to the declared public policy of the Act. Rights under a collective-bargaining agreement, on the other hand, are private rights created by the contract and enforceable under procedures established by the contract for that purpose and by suits under Section 301 of the Labor-Management Relations Act. A dispute as to the meaning and/or applicability of the contract is essentially one between the contracting parties—the employer and the union—in which the employee has virtually no role to play. Thus, an employee who feels aggrieved by some action of the employer can file a grievance under the contract but has no standing to compel the union to process the grievance through arbitration if the grievance is resolved against the employee. Arbitration is a costly process and unions for the most part lack the resources necessary to fully investigate and prosecute to arbitration every grievance filed. Indeed, short of a failure to fairly represent, unions have wide discretion in determining which grievances to pursue to arbitration and which to abandon or to trade off in favor of some other advantage. Even where the union proceeds to arbitration on an employee's grievance, the aggrieved employee is but an outsider—a third party—to such proceeding, having no standing to participate as a party, to have counsel different from union counsel, to examine witnesses, or to submit evidence. Finally, the arbitrator is generally authorized only to determine the contract issue presented by the grievance, i.e., whether the employee engaged in the conduct for which he or she was assertedly disciplined and whether the contract permitted such discipline for that conduct. If the employee claimed that the discipline was in reprisal for having engaged in protected concerted activities under Section 7, the arbitrator either would not or could not reach that issue without exceeding the power given him by the contract.

In sum, I shall continue to defer to arbitration those cases involving only contract interpretation issues, as in Roy Robinson Chevrolet. But I shall not defer to arbitration in those cases which involve unfair labor practices allegations affecting individual rights under Section 7 of the Act. Since the instant case is of the latter type, being concerned with whether Respondent's motive in discharging employee Soape was his union or other protected concerted activities. I find that the matter should not be deferred to arbitration and I agree with my colleagues' finding that the Respondent violated Section 8(a)(3) and (1) by the said discharge.

PENELLO and WALTHER, Members, dissenting:

Inasmuch as we believe that this case should be deferred to arbitration under the Collyer doctrine, we find it unnecessary to determine whether the Administrative Law Judge correctly decided that the Charging Party, Perry Soape, Jr., was discriminatorily discharged.

Members Fanning and Jenkins would not defer for the reasons stated in their dissenting opinions in Collyer and repeatedly reiterated since; namely, "that the Board has a statutory duty to hear and to dispose of unfair labor practices and that the Board cannot abdicate or avoid its duty by seeking to cede its jurisdiction to private tribunals." Chairman Murphy does not agree with this lack-of-power theory. On the contrary, she agrees with us, essentially for the reasons set forth in the majority opinion of Collyer, that the Board has discretionary authority under the Act to defer disputes arising under the parties' collective-bargaining agreement to the grievance-arbitration machinery established by such agreement. However, she would exercise that discretionary authority only in cases involving alleged violations of Section 8(a)(5) and 8(b)(3). She would not defer cases alleging violations of Section 8(a)(1), 8(a)(3), 8(b)(1)(A), and 8(b)(2). Inasmuch as the present case involves an alleged violation of Section 8(a)(3), she would therefore not defer this case to arbitration.

"The question whether, in fact, the policies and purposes of the Act will be furthered by abstention here and in similar cases is more complex. The crucial determinant is, we believe, the reasonableness of the assumption that the arbitration procedure will resolve this dispute in a manner consistent with the standards of Spielberg. As we noted in Collyer, contract grievances and arbitration procedures have become an integral part of virtually all collective-bargaining contracts in this country. Though arbitration like all systems for the resolution of disputes has its imperfections, the demand for and resort to services of skilled arbitrators has increased at a steady and heartening rate. The issue most often resolved by arbitrators is that of just cause for the imposition of discipline. Indeed, it is largely the insistence of unions upon procedures to protect employees against arbitrary treatment that has led to the modern ubiquity of contractual grievance and arbitration procedures. Wholly aside from considerations arising from the increasing caseload before this five-man Board, we believe the purposes of the Act are well served by encouraging the parties to those contracts to resolve their disputes without government intervention. The reference in Carey to the 'therapy of arbitration' is not simply rhetorical. The relationship of contracting parties is strengthened by the experience of mutual reliance on contract procedures. The intervention of this Board, by contrast, can sometimes be an unsettling force." [Citations omitted.]

The Board noted two factors which justified its belief that abstention was proper: (1) the parties had had a long-established, stable, and productive bargaining relationship; and (2) although the 8(a)(3) allegation subsumed union animus, there was no pattern of action subversive of Section 7 rights. The facts in this case are identical.

Following National Radio, the Board has deferred to grievance-arbitration procedures numerous cases involving 8(a)(3) allegations. The court of appeals in the United Aircraft case specifically approved deferral of such cases under the Collyer doctrine. The court pointed out that there is a strong congressional policy encouraging arbitration of labor disputes. The court cited in support the numerous Supreme Court decisions beginning with Lincoln Mills recognizing this congressional policy. It approved deferral even though there was evidence of employer hostility to the union as exemplified in a number of Board decisions finding that the employer had engaged in unfair labor practices. Nevertheless, the court said that "anti-union" animus would be a controlling factor only if that animus might prevent successful arbitration of the dispute.

"Final adjustment by a method agreed upon by the parties is hereby declared to be the desirable method for settlement of grievance disputes arising over the application or interpretation of an existing collective-bargaining agreement."

In the United Aircraft case, which as pointed out, involved 8(a)(3) and (1) allegations, the court said (525 F.2d at 239):

"The validity of the Collyer doctrine is no longer seriously in doubt. * * * The Supreme Court has since added further authority to the policy by quoting favorably from the Board's reasoning in the Collyer decision in William E. Arnold Co. v. Carpenters, 417 U.S. 12, 16–17, 86 LRRM 2212 (1974)."

The Chairman has [not] substantially emasculated the court-approved Collyer doctrine for reasons which we do not regard as valid. The Chairman says that in cases involving 8(a)(1), 8(a)(3), 8(b)(1)(A), and 8(b)(2) violations an arbitrator's resolution of the contract issue will not dispose of the unfair labor practice allegations and that the arbitration process is not suited for resolving employee complaints of discrimination under Section 7. This is a strange doctrine in view of the Board's experience under Spielberg and volumes of arbitrators' decisions. In Spielberg, the Board said that it would accept an arbitrator's award made pursuant to a contract arbitration procedure as dispositive of related unfair labor practices if the awards met certain standards. Pursuant thereto, the Board has in fact dismissed 8(a)(1) and (3) allegations because of Spielberg arbitral awards. As to the allegation that the arbitration process is not suited for resolving complaints of discrimination under Section 7, this presumably means that arbitrators are not competent to decide such issues. With all due respect to the Chairman, we cannot subscribe to this notion. As the Board majority said in National Radio Company, 198 N.L.R.B. at 531–532, 80 L.R.R.M. 1718, the issue most often resolved by arbitrators is that of just cause for the imposition of discipline, which frequently also requires the arbitrator to decide whether the cause was in fact union or concerted activities.

Even before Collyer and National Radio, the Board and the courts, including the Supreme Court, approved the arbitral process as a means of resolving disputes which involved violations of sections of the Act other than 8(a)(5) and 8(b)(3). In the International Harvester case which involved alleged violations of Section 8(a)(3) and (1) and 8(b)(2) and (1)(A) the Board deferred to an arbitration award and overruled a Trial Examiner's (now Administrative Law Judge) decision finding violations. The Board stated (138 N.L.R.B. at 926–927):

"The Act, as has repeatedly been stated, is primarily designed to promote industrial peace and stability by encouraging the practice and procedure of collective bargaining. Experience has demonstrated that collective-bargaining agreements that provide

for final and binding arbitration of grievance and disputes arising thereunder, 'as a substitute for industrial strife,' contribute significantly to the attainment of this statutory objective. Approval of the arbitral technique, which has become an effective and expeditious means of resolving labor disputes, finds expression in Section 203(d) of the Labor Management Relations Act, 1947.
* * *

* * *

"If complete effectuation of the Federal policy is to be achieved, we firmly believe that the Board, which is entrusted with the administration of one of the many facets of national labor policy, should give hospitable acceptance to the arbitral process as 'part and parcel of the collective bargaining process itself,' and voluntarily withhold its undoubted authority to adjudicate alleged unfair labor practice charges involving the same subject matter, unless it clearly appears that the arbitration proceedings were tainted by fraud, collusion, unfairness, or serious procedural irregularities or that the award was clearly repugnant to the purposes and policies of the Act."

Not only was the Board's International Harvester decision affirmed by the court of appeals, it has also been cited and its language quoted with approval by the Supreme Court.

The Chairman also argues that Section 7 rights are public rather than private rights, that Section 10(a) entrusts the Board with exclusive authority to protect those rights, and that a collective-bargaining agreement cannot lawfully strip the employees of their statutory rights nor the Board of its obligation to protect those rights. This argument is pretty much the argument which has been repeatedly advanced by Members Fanning and Jenkins, and the conclusion drawn therefrom repeatedly rejected by the Board majority and the courts. To take up the argument piecemeal: no one disputes that Section 7 rights are public rather than private rights and that the Board is charged with protecting those rights in the public interest. But the Section 7 public rights of individuals includes the right "to bargain collectively through representatives of their own choosing," and this right is vindicated by Section 8(a)(5) and 8(b)(3), yet the Chairman is prepared to defer to arbitration cases involving alleged violations of those sections. The reference to Section 10(a) seems to be advanced to justify a conclusion that the Board lacks discretion to defer to arbitration at least some alleged unfair labor practice violations. This seems to be contradictory to the opening paragraphs of the Chairman's concurring opinion in this case and in her concurring opinion in Roy Robinson Chevrolet.

Nor is the Board stripping the employees of their statutory rights or repudiating its obligation to protect those rights by deferring suitable cases to arbitration. In National Radio the Board, in rejecting this argument of abdication, said (198 N.L.R.B. 531):

"We may not abdicate our statutory duty to prevent and remedy unfair labor practices. Yet, once an exclusive agent has been chosen by employees to represent them, we are charged with a duty fully to protect the structure of collective representation and the freedom of the parties to establish and maintain an effective and productive relationship.

"In this context, abstention simply cannot be equated with abdication. We are, instead, adjuring the parties to seek resolution of their dispute under the provisions of their own contract and thus fostering both the collective relationship and the Federal policy favoring voluntary arbitration and dispute settlement. And by reserving jurisdiction we preserve the right of the Charging Party to seek from us vindication of statutory rights should the arbitration reach a result not tolerable under the statute."

The Board has not deferred cases to arbitration in an indiscriminate manner, nor has it been insensitive to the statutory rights of employees in deciding whether to defer and whether to give effect to an arbitration award. The standard it has used is reasonable belief that arbitration procedures would resolve the dispute in a manner consistent with the criteria of Spielberg. Thus, it has refused to defer where the interests of the union which might be expected to represent the employee filing the unfair labor practice charge are adverse to those of the employee, or where the respondent's conduct constitutes a rejection of the principles of collective bargaining. And where, after deferral, the respondent has refused to proceed to arbitration, the Board has rescinded the deferral and decided the case on the merits. Finally, if for any reason the arbitrator's award fails to meet the Spielberg standards, as for example, that it is repugnant to the policies of the Act, the Board will not give it effect.

The Chairman refers to alleged "practical considerations" to justify a refusal to defer to arbitration. Thus, she says that "Arbitration is a costly process and unions for the most part lack the resources necessary to fully investigate and prosecute to arbitration every grievance filed." There are several answers to this argument. In the first place, if a union has agreed that disputes are to be handled by a specific grievance-arbitration procedure, it is not in a position to complain about costs when it is called upon to live up to its agreement. In the second place, not all unions are poor and unable to defray the costs of arbitration. In the third place, the union involved in this case is not pleading poverty and is not opposed to having Soape's dispute submitted to the contract grievance-arbitration procedure. On the contrary, it has told Soape in no uncertain terms that it should be so submitted. In the fourth place, if a grievance is submitted it may be resolved without ever reaching the arbitration stage.

The Chairman also complains about the right of a union to represent employees in grievance and arbitration procedures to the exclusion of the employees involved. This complaint is really directed at the nature of the collective-bargaining process itself. The Board, which has the responsibility of fostering collective bargaining, ought not itself undermine that process by permitting the employee to ignore the bargaining representative short of finding that the union is not fairly representing the employee. In this case, there is no evidence that the Union is prepared to sacrifice Soape's rights to the benefit of other employees or that it will not fairly represent him.

Finally, the Chairman says that an arbitrator is generally authorized to determine only the contract issue presented by the grievance, i.e., whether the employee engaged in the conduct for which he was disciplined and whether the contract permitted such discipline, but could not decide whether the discipline, if so claimed, was in reprisal for having engaged in protected concerted activities. Whatever the validity of this argument as a general proposition, it has no application to the present case, for the collective-bargaining contract in this case in listing the causes for "proper discharge" contains the following proviso:

> " * * * The Contractor will not use these rights for the purposes of discrimination against any employee."

Under the proviso the arbitrator in deciding the contract issue would necessarily have to decide the very issue before the Board, i.e., whether Soape was discriminated against for impermissible reasons.

In an unpublished Board study of the effect of Collyer over a 2½ year period, from May 1973 through December 31, 1975, a total of *1,632* cases had been deferred by the Board's Regional Offices under Collyer. Arbitrators' decisions issued in 473 of these cases. Of these 473 decisions, the Regions scrutinized 159 at the request of the charging parties in light of the Spielberg standards. On 33 occasions, the Regions revoked the Collyer deferrals either because the respondents refused to proceed to arbitration or the arbitration awards were deficient under the Spielberg standards. In 24 of these 33 instances, issuance of a complaint was made unnecessary by the respondent's signing of a settlement agreement. *Further, of the 1,632 deferred cases, 437 were settled through the contract grievance procedure without the need of proceeding to arbitration.* The study concludes:

> "As between processing a dispute as a grievance vis-a-vis an unfair labor practice, the evidence that 437 cases were subsequently adjusted by the parties, themselves, following deferral by the Regional Office suggests that Collyer has forced the parties to rely less on the NLRB and more on collective bargaining via the contractual grievance machinery to settle certain disputes. More over, this same evidence indicates that there is a 50/50 chance of resolving the dispute short of arbitration. When it is necessary to arbitrate, however, the data indicates that arbitration, much like Board litigation, is a victim of delay."

Relevant to the problem of deferral are the Board's own statistics as to elapsed time from the time of deferral to the time of the issuance of the arbitrator's decision. According to the study previously mentioned, the median time for the issuance of an arbitration decision following deferral by the Regional Office is *140* days. In comparison, the elapsed time from the issuance of a complaint by the Regional

Office to the issuance of a decision by the Board is approximately twice as long.

The statistics by this Agency indicate that Collyer works, that it has encouraged the use of contract grievance-arbitration procedures and thus encouraged collective bargaining itself, that it has speeded up the disposition of some disputes, that it has resulted in the settlement of many disputes at the early stages of grievance procedures making arbitration unnecessary, and that it has lightened the workload of the Board.[48]

The reasons advanced by the Chairman for cutting back the Collyer doctrine are no more persuasive than those advanced by Members Fanning and Jenkins, as we have shown. Accordingly, we dissent.

"The issue in this case is fundamental, yet simple. In order to effectuate the purposes of the labor statutes employees are empowered to organize. This, of course, has resulted in enormous benefits but entails certain burdens as well. One of these is that to some extent the interests of particular individuals are subordinated to the interests of the group both at the contract negotiation stage and thereafter. * * * This is necessary if a union is to function efficiently. As a result, a union may properly determine not to pursue a member's grievance to the arbitration stage at all." [404 F.2d at 171.]

———

Some commentators have questioned the Board's power under the NLRA to refuse to hear cases because of the existence of an arbitration clause. The Supreme Court has not ruled directly on this point but it has indicated, in a case involving a different issue,[10] its acceptance of the Collyer doctrine. The Courts of Appeals have uniformly upheld the Board's power to defer to arbitration under the *Collyer* doctrine. A different approach to the overlap between statutory rights and arbitration has been taken however in the area of employment discrimination.

48. In citing the deferral statistics to show, in their view, that Collyer has failed because it has not significantly reduced the Board's caseload, Members Fanning and Jenkins confuse an incidental benefit of deferral (caseload reduction) with the purpose of deferral (collective-bargaining encouragement). Deferral requires parties (including individuals who are bound by the acts of their bargaining agent) to abide by their agreement to settle their disputes themselves through the collective-bargaining process. The statistics show that of 1,632 cases deferral has been revoked in only 33 cases, or 2 percent of the time. Thus, deferral has had a 98-percent success rate in achieving its purpose. And these figures do not reflect those disputes which the parties, looking to Collyer, have settled themselves without resort to the Board. We think that deferral has had a significant and beneficial impact in furthering the major purpose of the Act, to encourage the practice and procedure of collective bargaining.

10. William E. Arnold Co. v. Carpenter, 417 U.S. 12, 94 S.Ct. 2069, 40 L.Ed.2d 620 (1974). Since the *Collyer* doctrine was not before the court its offhand reference to *Collyer* would not have any formal legal significance. The Court might decide differently after hearing argument and fully considering the issue.

ALEXANDER v. GARDNER–DENVER CO.

Supreme Court of the United States, 1974.
415 U.S. 36, 94 S.Ct. 1011, 39 L.Ed.2d 147.

POWELL, J.   This case concerns the proper relationship between federal courts and the grievance-arbitration machinery of collective-bargaining agreements in the resolution and enforcement of an individual's rights to equal employment opportunities under Title VII of the Civil Rights Act of 1964.   Specifically, we must decide under what circumstances, if any, an employee's statutory right to a trial de novo under Title VII may be foreclosed by prior submission of his claim to final arbitration under the nondiscrimination clause of a collective-bargaining agreement.

I.

In May 1966, petitioner Harrell Alexander, Sr., a black, was hired by respondent Gardner-Denver Co. (the company) to perform maintenance work at the company's plant in Denver, Colorado.   In June 1968, petitioner was awarded a trainee position as a drill operator. He remained at that job until his discharge from employment on September 29, 1969.   The company informed petitioner that he was being discharged for producing too many defective or unusable parts that had to be scrapped.

On October 1, 1969, petitioner filed a grievance under the collective-bargaining agreement in force between the company and petitioner's union, Local No. 3029 of the United Steelworkers of America (the union).   The grievance stated: "I feel I have been unjustly discharged and ask that I be reinstated with full seniority and pay."   No explicit claim of racial discrimination was made.

Under Art. 4 of the collective-bargaining agreement, the company retained "the right to hire, suspend or discharge [employees] for proper cause."   Article 5, § 2, provided, however, that "there shall be no discrimination against any employee on account of race, color, religion, sex, national origin, or ancestry," and Art. 23, § 6(a), stated that "[n]o employee will be discharged, suspended or given a written warning notice except for just cause."   The agreement also contained a broad arbitration clause covering "differences aris[ing] between the Company and the Union as to the meaning and application of the provisions of this Agreement" and "any trouble aris[ing] in the plant." Disputes were to be submitted to a multi-step grievance procedure, the first four steps of which involved negotiations between the company and the union.   If the dispute remained unresolved, it was to be remitted to compulsory arbitration   *   *   *.

On December 30, 1969, the arbitrator ruled that petitioner had been "discharged for just cause."   He made no reference to petitioner's claim of racial discrimination.   Petitioner then filed the present action in the United States District Court for the District of Colorado, alleging that his discharge resulted from a racially discriminatory employment practice in violation of § 703(a)(1) of the Act.

The District Court granted respondent's motion for summary judgment and dismissed the action. 346 F.Supp. 1012 (1971). The court found that the claim of racial discrimination had been submitted to the arbitrator and resolved adversely to petitioner. It then held that petitioner, having voluntarily elected to pursue his grievance to final arbitration under the nondiscrimination clause of the collective-bargaining agreement, was bound by the arbitral decision and thereby precluded from suing his employer under Title VII. The Court of Appeals for the Tenth Circuit affirmed per curiam on the basis of the District Court's opinion. 466 F.2d 1209 (1972).

We granted petitioner's application for certiorari. * * * We reverse to sue under Title VII. Both courts evidently thought that this result was dictated by notions of election of remedies and waiver and by the federal policy favoring arbitration of labor disputes, as enunciated by this Court in Textile Workers Union v. Lincoln Mills, 353 U.S. 448, 77 S.Ct. 912, 923, 1 L.Ed.2d 972 (1957), and the Steelworkers trilogy. * * *

III.

Title VII does not speak expressly to the relationship between federal courts and the grievance-arbitration machinery of collective-bargaining agreements. It does, however, vest federal courts with plenary powers to enforce the statutory requirements; and it specifies with precision the jurisdictional prerequisites that an individual must satisfy before he is entitled to institute a lawsuit. In the present case, these prerequisites were met when petitioner (1) filed timely a charge of employment discrimination with the Commission, and (2) received and acted upon the Commission's statutory notice of the right to sue. * * * There is no suggestion in the statutory scheme that a prior arbitral decision either forecloses an individual's right to sue or divests federal courts of jurisdiction.

In reaching the opposite conclusion, the District Court relied in part on the doctrine of election of remedies. That doctrine, which refers to situations where an individual pursues remedies that are legally or factually inconsistent, has no application in the present context. In submitting his grievance to arbitration, an employee seeks to vindicate his contractual right under a collective-bargaining agreement. By contrast, in filing a lawsuit under Title VII, an employee asserts independent statutory rights accorded by Congress. The distinctly separate nature of these contractual and statutory rights is not vitiated merely because both were violated as a result of the same factual occurrence. And certainly no inconsistency results from permitting both rights to be enforced in their respectively appropriate forums. The resulting scheme is somewhat analogous to the procedure under the National Labor Relations Act, as amended, where disputed transactions may implicate both contractual and statutory rights. Where the statutory right underlying a particular claim may not be abridged by contractual agreement, the Court has recognized that consideration of the claim by the arbitrator as a contractual dispute under the collective-bargaining agreement does not preclude subsequent consideration of the claim by the National Labor Relations Board as an unfair labor practice charge.   Cf. Smith v. Evening News Ass'n, 371 U.S. 195, 83 S.Ct. 267, 9 L.Ed.2d 246 (1962). There, as here, the relationship between the forums is complementary since consideration of the claim by both forums may promote the policies underlying each.   Thus, the rationale behind the election-of-remedies doctrine cannot support the decision below.[14]

Moreover, a contractual right to submit a claim to arbitration is not displaced simply because Congress also has provided a statutory right against discrimination.   Both rights have legally independent origins and are equally available to the aggrieved employee.   This point becomes apparent through consideration of the role of the arbitrator in the system of industrial self-government.[16]   As the proctor of the bargain, the arbitrator's task is to effectuate the intent of the parties.   His source of authority is the collective-bargaining agreement, and he must interpret and apply that agreement in accordance with the "industrial common law of the shop" and the various needs and desires of the parties.   The arbitrator, however, has no general authority to invoke public laws that conflict with the bargain between the parties:

> "[A]n arbitrator is confined to interpretation and application of the collective bargaining agreement; * * * . He may of course look for guidance from many sources, yet his award is legitimate only so long as it draws its essence from the collective bargaining agreement.   When the arbitrator's words manifest an infidelity to this obligation, courts have no choice but to refuse enforcement of the award."   United Steelworkers of America v. Enterprise Wheel & Car Corp., 363 U.S. 593, 597, 80 S.Ct. 1358, 1361, 4 L.Ed.2d 1424 (1960).   If an arbitral decision is based "solely upon the arbitrator's view of the requirements of enacted legislation," rather than on an interpretation of the collective-bargaining agreement, the

---

14. Nor can it be maintained that election of remedies is required by the possibility of unjust enrichment through duplicative recoveries.   Where, as here, the employer has prevailed at arbitration, there, of course, can be no duplicative recovery.   But even in cases where the employee has first prevailed, judicial relief can be structured to avoid such windfall gains. * * * Furthermore, if the relief obtained by the employee at arbitration were fully equivalent to that obtainable under Title VII, there would be no further relief for the court to grant and hence no need for the employee to institute suit.

16. See Meltzer, "Labor Arbitration and Overlapping and Conflicting Remedies for Employment Discrimination," 39 U.Chi.L.Rev. 30, 32–35 (1971); Meltzer,

"Ruminations About Ideology, Law, and Labor Arbitration," 34 U.Chi.L.Rev. 545 (1967).   As the late Dean Shulman stated:

> "A proper conception of the arbitrator's function is basic.   He is not a public tribunal imposed upon the parties by superior authority which the parties are obliged to accept.   He has no general charter to administer justice for a community which transcends the parties.   He is rather part of a system of self-government created by and confined to the parties.   He serves their pleasure only, to administer the rule of law established by their collective agreement."   Shulman, "Reason, Contract, and Law in Labor Relations," 68 Harv.L.Rev. 999, 1016 (1955).

arbitrator has "exceeded the scope of the submission," and the award will not be enforced. Ibid. Thus the arbitrator has authority to resolve only questions of contractual rights, and this authority remains regardless of whether certain contractual rights are similar to, or duplicative of, the substantive rights secured by Title VII.

* * *

The District Court and the Court of Appeals also thought that to permit a later resort to the judicial forum would undermine substantially the employer's incentive to arbitrate and would "sound the death knell for arbitration clauses in labor contracts." * * * Again, we disagree. The primary incentive for an employer to enter into an arbitration agreement is the union's reciprocal promise not to strike. * * * It is not unreasonable to assume that most employers will regard the benefits derived from a no-strike pledge as outweighing whatever costs may result from according employees an arbitral remedy against discrimination in addition to their judicial remedy under Title VII. Indeed, the severe consequences of a strike may make an arbitration clause almost essential from both the employees' and the employer's perspective. Moreover, the grievance-arbitration machinery of the collective-bargaining agreement remains a relatively inexpensive and expeditious means for resolving a wide range of disputes, including claims of discriminatory employment practices. Where the collective-bargaining agreement contains a nondiscrimination clause similar to Title VII, and where arbitral procedures are fair and regular, arbitration may well produce a settlement satisfactory to both employer and employee. An employer thus has an incentive to make available the conciliatory and therapeutic processes of arbitration which may satisfy an employee's perceived need to resort to the judicial forum, thus saving the employer the expense and aggravation associated with a lawsuit. For similar reasons, the employee also has a strong incentive to arbitrate grievances, and arbitration may often eliminate those misunderstandings or discriminatory practices that might otherwise precipitate resort to the judicial forum.

V.

Respondent contends that even if a preclusion rule is not adopted, federal courts should defer to arbitral decisions on discrimination claims where: (i) the claim was before the arbitrator; (ii) the collective-bargaining agreement prohibited the form of discrimination charged in the suit under Title VII; and (iii) the arbitrator has authority to rule on the claim and to fashion a remedy.[17] Under respondent's proposed rule, a court would grant summary judgment and dismiss the employee's action if the above conditions were met. The rule's obvious consequence in the present case would be to deprive

17. Respondent's proposed rule is analogous to the NLRB's policy of deferring to arbitral decisions on statutory issues in certain cases. See Spielberg Mfg. Co., 112 N.L.R.B. 1080, 1082 (1955).

the petitioner of his statutory right to attempt to establish his claim in a federal court.

At the outset, it is apparent that a deferral rule would be subject to many of the objections applicable to a preclusion rule. The purpose and procedures of Title VII indicate that Congress intended federal courts to exercise final responsibility for enforcement of Title VII; deferral to arbitral decisions would be inconsistent with that goal. Furthermore, we have long recognized that "the choice of forums inevitably affects the scope of the substantive right to be vindicated." U. S. Bulk Carriers v. Arguelles, 400 U.S. 351, 359–360, 91 S.Ct. 409, 413–414, 27 L.Ed.2d 456 (1971) (Harlan, J., concurring). Respondent's deferral rule is necessarily premised on the assumption that arbitral processes are comensurate with judicial processes and that Congress impliedly intended federal courts to defer to arbitral decisions on Title VII issues. We deem this supposition unlikely.

Arbitral procedures, while well suited to the resolution of contractual disputes, make arbitration a comparatively inappropriate forum for the final resolution of rights created by Title VII. This conclusion rests first on the special role of the arbitrator, whose task is to effectuate the intent of the parties rather than the requirements of enacted legislation. Where the collective-bargaining agreement conflicts with Title VII, the arbitration must follow the agreement. To be sure, the tension between contractual and statutory objectives may be mitigated where a collective-bargaining agreement contains provisions facially similar to those of Title VII. But other facts may still render arbitral processes comparatively inferior to judicial processes in the protection of Title VII rights. Among these is the fact that the specialized competence of arbitrators pertains primarily to the law of the shop, not the law of the land. United Steelworkers of America v. Warrior & Gulf Navigation Co., 363 U.S. 574, 581–583, 80 S.Ct. 1347, 1352–1353, 4 L.Ed.2d 1409 (1960). Parties usually choose an arbitrator because they trust his knowledge and judgment concerning the demands and norms of industrial relations. On the other hand, the resolution of statutory or constitutional issues is a primary responsibility of courts, and judicial construction has proved especially necessary with respect to Title VII, whose broad language frequently can be given meaning only by reference to public law concepts.

Moreover, the factfinding process in arbitration usually is not equivalent to judicial factfinding. The record of the arbitration proceedings is not as complete; the usual rules of evidence do not apply; and rights and procedures common to civil trials, such as discovery, compulsory process, cross-examination, and testimony under oath, are often severely limited or unavailable. * * * And as this Court has recognized, "[a]rbitrators have no obligation to the court to give their reasons for an award."

* * *

We think, therefore, that the federal policy favoring arbitration of labor disputes and the federal policy against discriminatory employment practices can best be accommodated by permitting an employee to pursue fully both his remedy under the grievance-arbitration clause of a collective-bargaining agreement and his cause of action under Title VII. The federal court should consider the employee's claim de novo. The arbitral decision may be admitted as evidence and accorded such weight as the court deems appropriate.[21]

The judgment of the Court of Appeals is Reversed.

H. EDWARDS, ARBITRATION OF EMPLOYMENT DISCRIMINATION CASES: AN EMPIRICAL STUDY*

Since Gardner-Denver leaves open the issue as to how much weight, if any, should be accorded an arbitral decision, it is important to get more empirical evidence about the capacity of the arbitration process and arbitrators to deal with legal issues arising under Title VII. In an effort to do just this, this writer conducted a survey of all of the U.S. members of the National Academy of Arbitrators in February 1975. The survey questionnaire was sent to 409 persons; 200 arbitrators responded to the questionnaire. (See Appendices A and B attached hereto.) The average age of the responding arbitrators was 49 years, and the range of ages was from 31 to 77 years. The average years of arbitration experience among the respondents was 21 years (with the range being from 4 to 40 years).

The percentage of survey questionnaires returned from each region in the United States was approximately the same. (The lowest percentage was in the southeast region where 40 percent of the arbitrators returned their survey questionnaire; the highest percentage of returns came from the State of Michigan where nearly 63 percent of the arbitrators answered the survey questionnaire.)

The Capacity of Arbitrators to Decide "Legal" Issues in Cases Involving Claims of Employment Discrimination

One of the things that the survey attempted to determine was the extent to which arbitrators are competent to handle "legal" issues in employment discrimination cases. The findings on this score were most interesting.

---

21. We adopt no standards as to the weight to be accorded an arbitral decision, since this must be determined in the court's discretion with regard to the facts and circumstances of each case. Relevant factors include the existence of provisions in the collective-bargaining agreement that conform substantially with Title VII, the degree of procedural fairness in the arbitral forum, adequacy of the record with respect to the issue of discrimination, and the special competence of particular arbitrators. Where an arbitral determination gives full consideration to an employee's Title VII rights, a court may properly accord it great weight. This is especially true where the issue is solely one of fact, spe-

cifically addressed by the parties and decided by the arbitrator on the basis of an adequate record. But courts should ever be mindful that Congress, in enacting Title VII, thought it necessary to provide a judicial forum for the ultimate resolution of discriminatory employment claims. It is the duty of courts to assure the full availability of this forum.

* H. Edwards, "Arbitration Of Employment Discrimination Cases: An Empirical Study," Proceedings Of The 28th Annual Meeting Of The National Academy Of Arbitrators 59, 70–89; © by BNA, Inc. 1976. Reprinted with the permission of the publisher.

One of the questions asked of the respondents was whether they had ever read any *judicial* opinions involving a claim of discrimination under Title VII. One respondent appeared to think that the question was incredulous, and he or she asked, "What kind of arbitrator does not" read judicial opinions? The survey results do not indicate what kind of an arbitrator does not read judicial opinions; however, it does indicate that 77 percent of the respondents had read judicial opinions involving claims of discrimination under Title VII at one time or another, 16 percent of the respondents indicated that they had never read any such judicial opinions, and 7 percent of the respondents declined to answer the question.

The arbitrators were also asked whether they regularly read labor advance sheets to keep abreast of current developments under Title VII. On this question only 52 percent of the respondents indicated that they did read labor advance sheets, nearly 40 percent of the respondents answered that they did not, and 8 percent of the respondents declined to answer the question.

Another question asked the arbitrators was whether they could define "bona fide occupational qualification," "reasonable accommodation/undue hardship," and "preferential treatment" and accurately explain the current status of the law under Title VII with respect to each of these legal terms. It is significant that very few of the respondents felt that they could define these terms without first doing some legal research. Only 14 percent of the respondents indicated that they felt confident that they could accurately define each of the terms and explain the relevant law, 30 percent of the respondents stated that they could make a good "educated guess" but would not certify their answers as being accurate, and nearly 50 percent of the respondents indicated that they would prefer to research the question before answering.

Finally, the arbitrators were asked whether they felt that they were professionally competent to decide "legal" issues in cases involving claims of race, sex, national origin, or religious discrimination. It is extremely noteworthy that, in answer to this question, only about 72 percent of the respondents indicated that they felt professionally competent to decide legal issues in cases involving claims of employment discrimination. Sixteen percent of the respondents answered that they did not feel professionally competent to handle such cases, and 12 percent of the respondents declined to answer the question.

While these statistics raise some troublesome questions about the capacity of arbitrators to decide legal issues in cases involving claims of employment discrimination, they surely do not, without more, prove that arbitrators are incapable of handling such legal matters. There are some additional data from the survey, however, that raise more serious questions with respect to the capacity of arbitrators to decide legal issues in cases involving claims of employment discrimination.

Most of the respondents (83 percent) who indicated that they had never read a judicial opinion involving a claim of employment discrimination also indicated that they did not regularly read labor advance sheets to keep abreast of current developments under Title VII. Yet, 50 percent of this group of respondents nevertheless answered that they felt professionally competent to decide "legal" issues in cases involving claims of race, sex, national origin, or religious discrimination. Similarly, 70 percent of the group of respondents who indicated that they did not regularly read labor advance sheets to keep abreast of current developments under Title VII nevertheless indicated that they felt professionally competent to decide legal questions in cases involving claims of employment discrimination. From these facts, it is obvious that many arbitrators do not believe that these factors are relevant measures of the professional competence of arbitrators to decide legal issues in cases involving claims of employment discrimination.

However, it is interesting to note that 83 percent of the group of respondents who had never read a judicial opinion indicated that they could not define the three legal terms mentioned on the questionnaire without first doing some legal research. Only 13 percent of this group felt that they could make a good "educated guess" about the definition of the three legal terms, and only 3 percent of the group felt that they could do more than give an educated guess.

On this same score, 63 percent of the group of respondents who answered that they did not regularly read labor advance sheets also answered that they could not define the three legal terms without doing some research on the subject. Only 5 percent of this group indicated that they could do more than give an educated guess about the meaning of the legal terms in question.

Only 14 percent of the total group of respondents indicated that they felt that they were both (1) professionally competent to decide legal issues in cases involving claims of employment discrimination, and (2) able to define "bona fide occupational qualification," "reasonable accommodation/undue hardship," and "preferential treatment" without doing any research, and accurately explain the current status of the law with respect to each of these concepts. Of equal significance is the fact that only 18 percent of the group of respondents who felt that they were professionally competent to decide legal issues in employment discrimination cases stated that they could define the three legal terms with something more than a good "educated guess" and without doing any research on the subject. Finally, it is surprising to note that nearly 20 percent of the respondents who indicated that they *could* accurately define each of the three legal terms or make a good "educated guess" on the subject nevertheless indicated that they did *not* feel professionally competent to decide "legal" issues in cases involving claims of employment discrimination.

The question of professional competence would be of little interest if only qualified persons were being selected to hear and decide arbitration cases involving legal issues in connection with claims of employment discrimination. However, the survey data indicate that one half of the respondents who answered that they did not feel professionally competent to decide legal issues in cases involving claims of employment discrimination also answered that they had heard and decided such cases during the past year. Thus, there is no reason to believe that the arbitration-selection processes, as they presently exist, are designed to screen out persons who are not professionally qualified to decide legal issues in cases involving claims of employment discrimination.

It is obvious from the above data that many arbitrators feel that they are competent to handle employment discrimination cases (and to decide related legal issues) even though they are not otherwise knowledgeable about current developments in the law under Title VII. This is shown by the fact that there is no strong statistical relationship between arbitrators' ability to define three oft-cited legal terms (pertaining to the law under Title VII) and arbitrators' personal perceptions about their professional competence to decide "legal" issues in cases involving claims of employment discrimination. In fairness, however, it must be conceded that a great many of the persons who are members of the National Academy of Arbitrators clearly possess the intellectual wherewithall, general expertise in the field of labor and industrial relations, and sufficient "judicial" experience to make them potentially well qualified and highly able to decide most employment discrimination cases (and most "legal" issues associated with such cases). Indeed, many arbitrators are well able to research a "legal" issue, discover the relevant law, and issue a sound decision on the matter. However, it must be recognized that the judgment as to "qualifications" may be viewed as an abstract possibility or as a current reality. The data from the survey would suggest that many arbitrators are potentially, but not actually, well qualified to decide *legal* issues in cases involving claims of employment discrimination at the present time.

The Capacity of the Arbitration Process to Handle Employment Discrimination Cases Involving Legal Issues Cognizable Under Title VII

The problem here is compounded by some additional considerations having to do with the nature of the arbitration process and with the arbitrators' perceptions about their roles in cases involving legal issues. Even if it may be assumed, *arguendo*, that many arbitrators are professionally competent to decide *legal* issues in cases involving claims of employment discrimination, the nature of the arbitration process will often make it impossible, or at best difficult, for such arbitrators to render opinions that effectively resolve legal issues in cases involving claims of employment discrimination. The following facts, based on the evidence from the survey, appear to support this conclusion.

In many cases, lawyers do not appear as advocates for the parties in arbitration proceedings involving claims of employment discrimination. This is not to say that only lawyers are qualified to serve as advocates in arbitration proceedings; quite the contrary, because it is clear that there are many outstanding arbitration advocates on both sides of the table who have never had any legal training. However, it must be assumed that lawyers, because of their professional training, should be better able than nonlawyers to identify and argue about "legal" issues that might be relevant in employment discrimination cases.

The survey results indicate that lawyers represented both the union and the company in only 173 out of 328 employment discrimination cases heard during the period from February 1974 until February 1975 (i.e., 53 percent of all of the cases). Companies were represented by legal counsel in 76 percent of the cases; unions were represented by legal counsel in only 53 percent of the cases. On the basis of these data, and if it can be assumed that legal representation may be an advantage in an arbitration case involving claims of employment discrimination, then it may be concluded that employee-grievants are at least somewhat disadvantaged in approximately 25 percent of these cases where the company has legal representation and the union does not.

One way to overcome this problem might be to allow grievants to appear with their own legal counsel in arbitration cases involving claims of employment discrimination. However, the survey results indicate that this approach was followed in only 9 percent (30 out of 328) of the cases involving claims of employment discrimination heard in arbitration.

It also might be argued that, since employee-grievants are not foreclosed by arbitration from pursuing their legal remedies under Title VII, it should not matter whether they are given legal representation in arbitration. However, the survey results suggest that many of the employment discrimination cases that are decided in arbitration do not subsequently get reheard by the EEOC or by the courts. The evidence received from the arbitrators who responded to the survey reveals that employment discrimination charges had been filed with the EEOC or the courts in only 25 percent (84 out of 328) of all of the employment discrimination cases that were heard in arbitration. This figure may be deceptively low, either because some of the arbitrator respondents were unaware of all of the cases in which grievants filed charges under Title VII or because such charges were filed subsequent to the conclusion of the arbitration proceeding. However, it is nevertheless noteworthy that the number of duplicate charges (involving complaints of employment discrimination which are heard in arbitration and in the courts) does not appear to be nearly as high as some persons have suggested. If these figures are accurate, then they certainly negate the argument advanced by those who oppose the decision in *Gardner-Denver* on the ground that an employee should not get "two bites at the same apple."

Several other important problems were raised in connection with the capacity of the arbitration process to deal with legal issues in employment discrimination cases. One such problem has to do with the nature of the substantive issue that is actually decided by an arbitrator in a case involving a claim of employment discrimination. On this score, it must be recognized that an arbitrator cannot resolve a legal issue, or give due consideration to the relevant law, if the matter is not raised as an issue in arbitration. On this point, the survey results indicate that the relevance of Title VII was raised in only 31 percent (103) of the employment discrimination cases heard in arbitration. Furthermore, company officials argued that the legal precedents under Title VII were relevant and should be considered by the arbitrator in only 12 percent of the cases, and union officials argued in favor of relevance in only 22 percent of all of the employment discrimination cases heard in arbitration.

Another like problem arises because arbitrators only infrequently rely on Title VII and other relevant legal precedents when deciding employment discrimination cases. The evidence from the survey reveals the following: The responding arbitrators indicated that they had actually relied on Title VII legal precedents in only 12.5 percent of all of the employment discrimination cases heard in arbitration; and legal precedents were actually cited in these arbitrators' decisions in only 11 percent of all of the employment discrimination cases heard in arbitration.

Although the survey data indicate that the responding arbitrators ruled in favor of employee-grievants in 34 percent of the cases involving claims of employment discrimination, the arbitrators in these cases usually avoided "legal" issues. In instances in which the grievants won, the arbitrator found that the company or union ws guilty of discrimination *under the contract* in only 48 percent of the cases and guilty of discrimination *under the law* in only 21 percent of the cases; no information was furnished with respect to the remaining 31 percent of the cases.

In Footnote 21 in the *Gardner-Denver* decision, the Supreme Court stated that "where an arbitral determination gives full consideration to an employee's Title VII rights, a court may properly accord it great weight." Two of the measures of "full consideration" identified by the Court were "degree of procedural fairness" and "adequacy of the record with respect to the issue of discrimination." Some of the data gleaned from the survey speak to these two considerations.

The evidence from the survey indicates that official transcripts were made in only 43 percent (140) of all of the employment discrimination cases heard in arbitration. Furthermore, the evidence reveals that prehearing and/or posthearing briefs were submitted by both parties in only 52 percent (172) of all of the employment discrimination cases heard in arbitration.

It is also noteworthy that most of the employment discrimination cases decided in arbitration were resolved on the merits. This is clear from the facts that show that in only 11 cases (3.3 percent) did the company or the union argue that the claim of discrimination was not arbitrable under the collective bargaining agreement and in only 16 (4.8 percent) of the cases did the parties' collective bargaining agreement explicitly exclude discrimination claims from arbitration. However, only 25 percent of the responding arbitrators who heard and decided employment discrimination cases last year indicated that they had advised grievants of their statutory rights pursuant to Title VII. While there is no legal requirement that such advice be given by the arbitrator, it would be clear that many grievants who are not so advised, and who are otherwise not represented by counsel, may not realize that arbitration is not the forum of last resort for the resolution of employment discrimination cases.

Finally, and most significantly, it is somewhat amazing to note that many of the responding arbitators suggested that the quality of the evidence given in employment discrimination cases heard in arbitration was deficient. On this point, the survey questionnaire asked the arbitrators: "In how many of these [employment discrimination] cases did you feel that the record was complete enough so that all of the legal issues under Title VII could have been resolved in a court of law?" In response to this question, the responding arbitrators indicated that the record was complete in only about 55 percent of all the employment discrimination cases heard in arbitration. This fact alone would surely suggest that the courts ought to be very careful before they begin to accord great weight to arbitration opinions involving claims of employment discrimination. This is especially so in light of the evidence here, which indicates that (1) no transcript of the proceedings is made in more than half of the arbitration cases involving claims of employment discrimination, and (2) most of the arbitrators who have heard and decided these cases have admittedly declined to consider and resolve "legal" issues.

Arbitrators' Views Concerning the Role of the Arbitrator in Deciding Employment Discrimination Cases

Whether or not arbitrators are professionally competent to decide legal issues in cases involving claims of employment discrimination, it still must be realized that many arbitrators are loath to decide such issues. For many years, various members of the National Academy of Arbitrators have debated the question dealing with the proper role of the arbitrator in handling "legal" issues in arbitration cases. Several theories have been advanced, most notably by Bernard Meltzer, Robert Howlett, Richard Mittenthal, Theodore St. Antoine, and Michael Sovern. All of these theories were ably summarized by Dean Sovern in a paper entitled "When Should Arbitrators Follow Federal Law?" that was delivered during the 1970 meeting of the National Academy of Arbitrators. While these debates have been healthy academic exercises, they really have not told us much about what arbitrators are actually doing as a group (or what they feel that they ought to be doing) when presented with legal issues in connection with claims of employment discrimination in arbitration. One of the reasons for the current survey was to get better and more accurate empirical data on this subject. The results of the survey on this point are interesting but not surprising.

Nearly two thirds of the responding arbitrators stated that they believed that an arbitrator has no business interpreting or applying a public statute in a contractual grievance dispute. (However, nearly one half of the responding arbitrators did indicate that an arbitrator should be free to *comment* on the relevant law if it appears to conflict with the collective bargaining agreement.) Only one third of all of the responding arbitrators indicated that they believed a collective bargaining agreement must be read to include by reference all public law applicable thereto. In other words, most of the arbitrators rejected the view that an arbitrator should always apply constitutional, statutory, or common law principles to aid in the resolution of contractual grievance disputes.

Nearly all of the responding arbitrators who believed that an arbitrator has no business interpreting or applying a public statute in a contractual grievance dispute conceded that there were certain exceptions to this rule. Of these respondents, 85 percent agreed that an arbitrator may consider and interpret public law in order to avoid compelling a union or a company to do something that is *clearly* unlawful. Ninety-five percent of them agreed that an arbitrator may properly refer to the applicable law if it can be found that the parties have intentionally adopted a contract clause pursuant to an existing statute with the object of incorporating the body of public law into the contract. Finally, 97 percent of these respondents agreed that an arbitrator should consider public law when the parties have, by submission, conferred jurisdiction upon him or her to decide the contract issue in light of the applicable federal or state law.

Although most of the responding arbitrators appear to accept the view that an arbitrator generally has no business interpreting or applying a public statute in a contractual grievance dispute, except in limited and exceptional circumstances, the survey results on this point are nevertheless anomalous in certain respects. More than one third of all of the respondents disagreed with the result in the *Gardner-Denver* decision. This figure by itself is not surprising. However, nearly 30 percent of all of the respondents who stated that an arbitrator has no business interpreting or applying public law in a contractual grievance dispute also stated that they disagreed with the opinion in *Gardner-Denver*. This result would appear to be inherently illogical.

Most of the respondents (90 percent) who disagreed with the result in *Gardner Denver* felt that they were professionally qualified to resolve legal issues in employment discrimination cases. This surely is not surprising, nor is it surprising that these persons would prefer some kind of deferral rule as opposed to the principles stated in the *Gardner-Denver* decision. However, it is curious that nearly 20 percent of the responding arbitrators who stated that they were *not* professionally competent to handle legal issues in employment discrimination cases also stated that they disagreed with the decision in *Gardner-Denver*. This position is surely inherently illogical.

Not only did a substantial majority of the responding arbitrators who disagreed with the decision in *Gardner-Denver* indicate that they felt professionally competent to decide legal issues, but 86 percent of this group also stated that they had read judicial opinions involving claims of employment discrimination and 60 percent of the group stated that they regularly read labor advance sheets to keep abreast of current developments under Title VII. Taken together, these statistics not surprisingly suggest that those persons who are most familiar with the law under Title VII are more inclined to disagree with the result in *Gardner-Denver*.

However, these findings do not negate the data that reveal that only 71 percent of the responding arbitrators felt that they were professionally competent to decide legal issues in cases involving claims of employment discrimination; only 52 percent of the responding arbitrators indicated that they regularly read labor advance sheets to keep abreast of current developments under Title VII; and only 14 percent of the responding arbitrators felt confident that they could accurately define "bona fide occupational qualification," "reasonable accommodation/undue hardship," and "preferential treatment" and explain the relevant law under Title VII with respect to each of these legal concepts.

Regional Differences

The evidence from the survey reveals some minor, but no significant, distinctions in the attitudes expressed among the arbitrators from different geographic regions in the United States. For example, more than 50 percent of the responding arbitrators from every region in the country felt that they were professionally competent to decide legal issues in employment discrimination cases: The figures ranged from 94 percent in Michigan, 91 percent in the Midwest, 86 percent in the Southeast, 74 percent in the Southwest (including California and Hawaii), 67 percent in the Northeast, and 50 percent in the Northwest (including only Idaho, Washington, and Oregon).

Likewise, the proportional number of employment discrimination cases heard in arbitration appeared to be evenly divided throughout the various regions in the country. Of the respondents from the northeast region, 54 percent indicated that they had heard employment discrimination cases in arbitration during the past year; 50 percent of the respondents from the Southeast and the Northwest had heard such cases; 44 percent of the respondents from the Midwest and the Southwest had heard discrimination cases; and 67 percent of the respondents from Michigan had decided employment discrimination cases.

It is interesting that nearly 53 percent of the respondents from the midwest region indicated that they did not agree with the Supreme Court decision in *Gardner-Denver*. This percentge was nearly 20 points higher than the next highest region. The figure is not surprising, however, when it is coupled with the fact that 91 percent of all of the respondents in the Midwest felt that they were professionally competent to decide issues in cases involving claims of employment discrimination.

Conclusion

There is nothing wrong with arbitrators' deciding cases involving claims of race, sex, national origin, or religious discrimination. For, as the Supreme Court noted in *Gardner-Denver*, "where the collective-bargaining agreement contains a nondiscrimination clause similar to Title VII, and where arbitral procedures are fair and regular, arbitration may well produce a settlement satisfactory to both employer and employee." But it should not be assumed that merely because an arbitrator has heard a case involving a claim of employment discrimination that he has also resolved the underlying "legal" issues that may be posed. The data recovered from the survey strongly militate against any such conclusion.

The evidence as to whether and how many arbitrators are professionally competent to decide legal issues in cases involving claims of employment discrimination is at best mixed. Furthermore, even assuming, *arguendo*, that most arbitrators are professionally competent to decide such issues, the nature of the arbitration process often will not allow for full and adequate consideration of an employee's Title VII rights. Finally, the evidence from the survey suggests that even when arbitrators are professionally competent to decide legal issues and when the arbitration process is adequate to allow for full consideration of legal questions arising pursuant to Title VII, still many arbitrators believe that they have no business interpreting or applying a public statute in a contractual grievance dispute.

Given all of these considerations, the courts should be very wary about reading *Gardner-Denver* too expansively in a manner that might well result in the development of de facto schemes of deferral that effectively foreclose full and complete judicial resolution of employment discrimination claims.

Some of the arbitrators who responded to the survey, and who indicated that they were opposed to the decision in *Gardner-Denver*, argued that they were as competent as many judges to decide legal issues arising pursuant to Title VII. Whether or not this is true is really beside the point. One responding arbitrator put the problem in proper perspective with the following comment: "Subjectively and privately I feel as well qualified as many of the judges writing the decisions; but I would not publicly make this claim, nor would I be eager to assume that responsibility unless the parties explicitly so requested."

Another responding arbitrator commented that the *Gardner-Denver* decision

"permits the arbitrator to confine himself to interpreting the collective bargaining agreement with less strain on his conscience, particularly where the agreement and the law are not congruent, because the grievant now clearly has an alternative tribunal which is not confined to the terms of the collective bargaining agreement. I think this will tend to make many cases much less elaborate since there is no longer any question of meeting all the standards which would be relevant if deferral to arbitration by the courts or EEOC was a possibility."

Arbitrators, unlike judges, are accountable only to the parties and their decisions are rarely subject to close judicial review. The simple fact is that arbitrators are not responsible for developing principles of public law. As the Court in *Gardner-Denver* noted, "the specialized competence of arbitrators pertains primarily to the law of the shop, not the law of the land." Therefore, even if some arbitrators are better qualified than some judges to decide certain legal issues, this still would not militate in favor of a deferral rule in cases involving claims of employment discrimination.

The proper role of the arbitrator, as distinguished from arbitral competence, is the real reason why the Supreme Court should not dilute the *Gardner-Denver* decision in favor of any deferral rule. This point was best stated by Dean Shulman, in his oft-quoted article, "Reason, Contract and Law in Labor Relations," as follows:

> "A proper conception of the arbitrator's function is basic. He is not a public tribunal imposed upon the parties by superior authority which the parties are obliged to accept. He has no general charter to administer justice for a community which transcends the parties. He is rather part of a system of industrial self-government created by and confined to the parties. He serves their pleasure only, to administer the rule of law established by their collective agreement."

A modern-day version of this same idea was stated by one of the arbitrators who responded to the survey and made the following comments:

> "A national public policy on discrimination should and must be developed, under statutes, by public administrative quasi-judicial agencies and courts; not by private persons like me, selected by private parties to decide particular disputes which *they* have. A consistent and uniform body of 'law,' binding on the nation should not be the creation of private decision-makers but of public instrumentalities. Arbitration of labor-management disputes has been successful because of its restricted role. Freight it with the responsibility of law enforcement and the interpretation of statutes and great harm will be done to the institution as it presently exists. "[The *Gardner-Denver* decision] hasn't changed my thinking at all. I was always confident that when the question reached the Supreme Court, an arbitrator's decision on the application of a statute would not (and should not) be binding and final as his decision on the private disputes of parties under their contract. Those whose bowels are in an uproar over *Gardner-Denver* are acting in accordance with Maxim #244 of Publilius Syrus: 'The end justifies the means.' Occasionally this may be so; but there is no in-

sufficient justification in this case. The Court has decided wisely.''

QUESTIONS

1.   How likely are the courts to give great weight to arbitration
awards under footnote 21?

2.   Does the Court's reasoning in *Gardner-Denver* undercut the
Collyer doctrine?

3.   Can the two approaches be harmonized?

4.   Does the *Collyer* doctrine have any bearing on the Meltzer-
Howlett-Sovern debate?

F.   NOTE: THE ENFORCEMENT OF CONTRACTUAL RIGHTS IN THE ABSENCE OF ARBITRATION

About 4% of collective bargaining agreements do not provide for
arbitration.   When disputes arise about the meanings or application
of such contracts they may be finally resolved in one of three ways.
(a) Unless otherwise stated in the agreement, a law suit may be
brought either in Federal or State Court and the judge will interpret
the agreement.   Q. Why might parties prefer a law suit to arbitration?   Would such a system more likely favor management or the
union?   (b) Some agreements give to management the final authority
to accept or reject grievances.   Where such agreements exist, the
courts will permit management great leeway and will only intervene
where the grossest form of violation occurs.   (c) Some agreements
provide that if management rejects a grievance the union may strike
about it.   The UE and some Auto Worker locals prefer such clauses
to arbitration.   It has recently been decided that such clauses do not
prevent the union from suing in court.   Q. Would an employer ever
favor such a provision instead of arbitration?

G.   RECOMMENDED READING

The literature dealing with arbitration is vast.   There is no real
difference between the legal and non-legal writings.   The materials
excerpted include many of the best and most thoughtful commentaries.   The Annual Proceedings of the National Academy of Arbitrators is a rich source of useful commentary.   In addition the following
general texts are recommended:

1.   Fleming, *The Labor Arbitration Process* (1965).

2.   Elkouri and Elkouri, *How Arbitration Works* (3rd ed. 1973).

3.   Fairweather, *Practice and Procedure in Labor Arbitration*
(1974).

4.   Updegraff, *Arbitration of Labor Disputes* (1946).

*

Chapter VI

ILLEGAL STRIKES, PICKETING AND OTHER CONCERTED ACTIVITY IN THE PRIVATE SECTOR

―――――

A. CASE STUDY: HUBBARD FOOD

You have been hired as a labor relations specialist for the Hubbard Food Stores, a retail grocery chain headquartered in Louisville, Kentucky. You report to Mr. Hank West, the Director of Labor Relations at Hubbard. West reports to Howard Nickloy, Executive Vice President for Labor Relations.

In your first week at Hubbard, you receive the following memorandum from West:

MEMORANDUM

Attached is a report of the current strike and impasse activity confronting the Company. Howard Nickloy has requested that we provide him with a strategy for dealing with the current situation. Please read through the reports and draft a memo to me advising me of your views on what is the appropriate response.

s/
_____

Hank West

The Covington Store Strike

Beginning 4 days ago and continuing to today, members of the United Paperworkers International Union Local 001 has been picketing the premises of our Covington, Kentucky store. Local 001 is the exclusive bargaining representative for the employees of the Standard Paper Bag Manufacturing Company at its plants located in Ludlow and Lexington, Kentucky, but excluding truck drivers, salesmen, executives, and supervisors.

For four months Local 001 has been engaged in a lawful economic strike against Standard. Although local 001 has had a labor dispute with Standard, at no time has Local 001 had a labor dispute with Hubbard.

The picketers (at certain times one individual and at other times two) have picketed throughout most of the normal operating hours at Hubbard's Covington store. The picketers have carried picket signs which read as follows:

"Consumer Boycott
of
Standard Paper Bag
Manufacturing Co. Products

'B.Y.O.B.'
(Bring Your Own Bag)
Standard Paper Bag Mfg. Co.

UNFAIR

Local 001 United Paperworkers International Union, AFL–CIO"

In addition to carrying these signs, the picketers distributed to the customers of Hubbard's Covington store handbills, which read as follows:

"BOYCOTT LEAFLET
CONSUMER BOYCOTT

Please bring your own bag when you shop at this store, or ask for a box. Please do not use bags manufactured or supplied by THE STANDARD PAPER BAG MANUFACTURING CO.

THE STANDARD PAPER BAG MANUFACTURING CO. is unfair to members of Local 001, United Paperworkers International Union, AFL–CIO, who have been on strike for fair benefits for four months. We have no dispute with any other Employer.

— This handbill is directed at CONSUMERS ONLY.

— It is not an appeal to cease performing work for, or to cease deliveries to, any other employer.

— This organization has no dispute with any other employer.

BRING YOUR OWN BAG!

Local 001, United Paperworkers International Union, AFL–CIO"

Standard is our sole supplier of grocery bags to our Covington store.

Our Covington store, in the normal course of business, furnishes its customers with grocery bags for the transport from the store groceries purchased by its customers. In the normal course of business, the store furnishes boxes in lieu of grocery bags to an average of twelve customers per week. The store normally compresses and sells for scrap most of the cardboard boxes in which it receives goods.

During the picketing of our Covington store, a few customers, including some officers and members of Local 001, utilized their own containers, such as pillow cases, plastic bags, paper bags or cardboard boxes, to transport from the store the groceries they had purchased. During this same period, approximately seventy customers requested and received from our Covington personnel boxes in lieu of grocery bags to transport from the store the groceries they had purchased. During this same period, approximately fifteen other customers requested Hubbard personnel to furnish them with boxes in lieu of grocery bags. However, our personnel were unable to comply with these customers' requests because, having complied with prior customers' requests for boxes, they had run out of boxes.

During the picketing at our Covington store, we had approximately 2800 customers. Yesterday, one customer brought groceries to a checkout counter. The cashier rang up the total price and began to place the groceries in grocery bags. This customer then said that she did not want "any scab bags" and left the store without paying for or taking her groceries.

The Ludlow Store Wildcat Walkout

We received a phone call from the manager of our Ludlow store at 9:00 a. m. today informing us of a walkout at the store. The Meat Department and Delicatessen employees had reported for work that morning, milled around for approximately ten to fifteen minutes and left the plant with no explanation. The manager indicated that it was rumored that the cause of the walkout was dissatisfaction with the manager's decision to suspend a fellow worker for insubordination. The suspension was for three days.

The manager recommends that we discharge all the employees who participated in the walkout. He wants to know what he should do if the employees return to work tomorrow. As an alternative to discharging all the employees who participated in the strike, the manager proposes to hold a meeting with the stewards and the president of the union for the purpose of interrogating the stewards concerning their involvement in the strike. Depending on the explanations offered by the stewards, a likely result would be to impose a disciplinary lay off on the stewards who were involved in the strike.

The Candy Plant Impasse

Hubbard owns a candy plant in Ferdinand, Indiana. The plant provides candy products to the Hubbard chain and also sells candy to other food chains under a different brand name. An independent union represents the candy plant workers. The collective bargaining contract between the company and the union ran out last week, and the parties have not reached an agreement on a new contract. Several issues remain unresolved, with no movement being made in the last two weeks. The union is demanding a wage increase of 25 cents an hour, while the Company's proposal calls for a wage increase of 10 cents an hour and the elimination of the cost-of-living adjustment (COLA) provided for in the existing contract.

This is the first contract in 21 years in which a new contract has not been ratified before the expiration of the existing contract. The union membership voted to authorize the leadership to declare a strike when bargaining began two months ago. However, the union leadership has not indicated whether it will call a strike. Local management is divided on whether to lockout the employees. Production managers argue that a lockout would avoid material losses if the ovens must be shut down rapidly. The marketing executives want production maintained to satisfy existing purchase orders.

Hubbard's financial officers report that the candy plant can accept a flat wage increase of 15 cents an hour over the three year contract period. Unfortunately the union has remained adamant with regard to keeping the COLA provision in the contract.

We must recommend strategy to the candy plant.

B. EMPIRICAL RESEARCH ON STRIKES

To the public, a strike is an inconvenience if not a counterproductive activity. It appears that neither party "wins" a strike. Workers lose wages and companies lose profits. However, striking by a union or taking a strike by management may carry long term benefits. The union may feel that a strike is necessary to maintain the credibility of its threats. Management may feel that taking a strike is a necessary means to reducing union expectations.

A number of studies have been done to identify the variables associated with the incidence and duration of strikes. The following article examines the ability of the existing strike literature to explain the pattern of strike activity in the United States in the period 1967 to 1977. After demonstrating the limited ability of these models to explain the strike activity during this period, the authors propose an alternative model which is related to the "pure bargaining theories" that stress the role of economic forces in terms of their effect on uncertainty in the bargaining process.

**WILLIAM J. MOORE AND DOUGLAS K. PEARCE,
A COMPARATIVE ANALYSIS OF STRIKE
MODELS DURING PERIODS OF
RAPID INFLATION: 1967–1977 ***

I. INTRODUCTION

Economists have used three conceptual models in the analysis of strike frequency.[1] For lack of better terms, we refer to these three

* William J. Moore and Douglas K. Pearce, "A Comparative Analysis of Strike Models During Periods of Rapid Inflation: 1967–1977," 3 Journal of Labor Research 39 (1982); © 1982 by the Journal of Labor Research. All rights reserved.

1. Strike frequency refers to the number of work stoppages in a given unit of analysis over a specified time period.

approaches as: (1) The Pure Bargaining Theory Model; (2) The Tactical Advantage Model; and (3) The Political-Economic Model. In recent years the latter two approaches have come to dominate the empirical studies of strike frequency in the post World War II period. Yet, as demonstrated below, these approaches have some noticeable weaknesses in explaining the pattern of strike frequencies in the United States since the outbreak of rapid inflation in the later 1960s. An alternative model is proposed which is related to the Pure Bargaining Theories that stress the role of economic forces in terms of their effect on uncertainty in the bargaining process.

II. THE PURE BARGAINING THEORY MODEL

The classic reference in the bargaining theory literature on strike activity is Hicks' (1932) "Theory of Industrial Disputes". Under the key assumption that skilled bargainers will learn the precise shape of the other parties wage-strike length concession functions through the bargaining process, Hicks' obtained a determinate wage solution and a rationale for the absence of work stoppages. He argued there is a general presumption that it will be possible for the union to obtain more favorable terms by negotiating than by striking because an employer is willing to pay higher wages to avoid the costs associated with a strike. But once a strike has begun, all the employer can buy off is the remainder of the strike; the loss already incurred is sunk cost. Since in most cases the power of the union to hold out for some specified period of time in the future decreases as the actual strike progresses, the union can obtain its highest possible wage by negotiating a pre-strike settlement. Therefore, under conditions of perfect information, rational unions have no reason to strike. For this reason, he concluded the major cause of actual strikes is faulty negotiation. The majority of strikes arise "from the divergence of estimates, and from no other causes * * * adequate knowledge will always make a settlement possible." [2]

While Hicks explained that the actual positions of the two parties' concession schedules and hence the level of the negotiated wage are influenced by business conditions, he failed to draw any inferences regarding the business cycle and the divergence of expectations between the bargaining parties or the degree of imperfect information. Thus, Hicks never discussed the cyclical nature of strike activity. But as Shalev (1980) has noted, Hicks' analysis suggested that students of economic influences on strike propensity should focus their attention on how economic conditions affect the parties' cost of agreement and disagreement and the likelihood of divergent expectations between them.

For a discussion of this and other types of strike analysis, see Stern (1978).

2. Hicks also noted two lesser causes of industrial disputes. First, unions may have to strike periodically just to keep the strike threat credible. Second, differences of opinion between union leaders and the rank and file may result in unnecessary strikes. As we shall see below, Ashenfelter and Johnson (1969) have stressed this factor in their "political-economic model" of strike activity.

This is certainly not an easy task and few empirical studies have used the pure bargaining theory model as the basis for analyzing strike activity.[3] As Ashenfelter and Johnson (1969, p. 36) explained, "it is not apparent how the propensity of either or both of the parties to (a) miscalculate the intentions of the other or (b) to act irrationally would be systematically related to any of the conceptually observable variables in the system."

III. THE TACTICAL ADVANTAGE MODEL

Rees (1952) was the first to explain the cyclical nature of strike activity in terms of changes in the relative bargaining power of the union and firm over the business cycle. He argued (p. 381) that

> Rising employment and improving business conditions offer the unions a variety of strategic advantages: (1) the employer's reluctance to lose his share of the expanding market; (2) his observation of rising wages elsewhere lowers his resistance to union demands; (3) his ability to replace strikers with nonstrikers diminishes as employment rises; (4) the strikers have an increased chance of obtaining employment elsewhere if the employer succeeds in replacing them; (5) if the expansion produces a rising cost of living, workers in firms where wages lag behind this rise will protest; (6) in periods of falling employment there is a sharp drop in organizational strikes * * * because the bargaining power of the employers rise relative to their [unions]; and (7) workers who keep their full-time jobs during the early stages of depression usually get real wage increases without striking [because wages are sticky downward and prices fall first].

Rees stressed the fact that "most industrial disputes are caused by social and psychological forces or by encomic forces which are noncyclical in nature", and that the business cycle only influences the timing of strikes. He believed that union leaders store up labor grievances like durable goods and then utilize them as strike issues when business conditions promise that the strikes may be successful. Furthermore, Rees explicitly recognized that noneconomic variables such as government policy, political events (war), and public opinion may alter the basic relationship between strike activity and the business cycle.

The major criticism of the "tactical advantage" hypothesis is that it appears to be one sided.[4] If unions become more militant because they have greater relative bargaining power in upturns of the business cycle, why do employers not push their advantage in downturns. This hypothesis seems to assume that unions are the active parties in strike decisions while employers passively accept whatever decision the union reaches. Rees provided a partial explanation for this be-

---

3. One exception to this is the study by Vanderkamp (1970) which used Walton and McKersie's (1965) bargaining model to justify the inclusion of business cycle variables in the analysis of Canadian strike activity.

4. See also in this regard the studies by Weintraub (1965), O'Brien (1965), and Scully (1971).

havior. He argued "the strike peak probably represents a maximum in the divergence of expectations between employers and union." Unions pay close attention to employment which generally does not lead at the peak of the business cycle while employers are likely to focus on such things as business failures, investment, security issues, contracts, and orders which do lead at the peak of the business cycle. Hence, at this time employers will resist demands for which the unions are still willing to fight. On the other hand, the strike cycle lags behind the business cycle at the troughs because union leaders adopt a "wait and see" attitude, and they want assurance that the revival is genuine before risking the jobs of their members.

Rees provided empirical support for his hypothesis by showing that for the period 1915–1939 the peak of the strike cycle leads the peak of the business cycle and that the strike cycle lagged the business cycle as it went through the trough. In a recent study, Shalev (1980) has included three variables to capture the influence of tactical advantages in his analysis of aggregate strike frequency in the U. S. in the post World War II period. First, the employer's interest in the timing of disputes is represented by a relative profit variable measured by the ratio of profits to the wage bill, π_{t-1}^*. Although he recognized that the workers' wage demands might be positively related to relative profit increases and hence strikes as well, Shalev contended that this variable is of greater importance to the firm. For this reason, he hypothesized that increases in relative profits will alter the employers' ability and willingness to pay more than workers' wage demand so the variable will have a negative influence on strike frequency. Second, Shalev argued that periods of low unemployment offer workers favorable conditions for pressing their demands for reasons similar to those suggested by Rees. Even though he recognized the fact that the situation is reversed in periods of high unemployment he believed the unemployment affects the workers bargaining power more than that of the employer, so the aggregate unemployment rate should be negatively correlated with strike frequency. Lastly, he argued that unions are more sensitive than employers to fluctuations in the relative size of inventories. Therefore, an inverse relationship is expected to exist between the inventory/sales ratio and the frequency of strikes.

To capture the pressures on workers to seek higher wages, he included a second set of variables under the heading of "workers" economic grievances. This includes a variable measuring recent changes in nominal wages. He hypothesized that, holding prices constant, larger recent wage increases are likely to lessen workers' current wage demand and hence the likelihood of a strike. Also, he predicted that recent price increases will have a positive influence on union wage demands and hence strike frequency after "controlling" for past wage increases. Finally, like Ross (1948), Shalev believed that wage concessions won by other union members in recent periods will have a positive influence on current union wage demands and the probability of a strike. He hypothesized that a variable measuring the size of the first-year wage adjustments negotiated by other unions in the previous time period would be positively correlated with strike frequency.

The final set of strike determinants in the Shalev model are associated with opportunities to strike. Since most strikes in the U. S. occur in the process of negotiating new contracts, he hypothesized that the number of contracts expiring for large bargaining units of 1,000 or more workers in manufacturing would be positively associated with the number of strikes. For similar reasons, Shalev also included three seasonal dummy variables because contract expiration dates have seasonal components and workers have seasonal income preferences which influence their propensity to strike. He hypothesized that strikes will be relatively more frequent in the warmer months. Finally, Shalev argued that government wage restraint policies place ceilings on wage demands and hence reduce the number of strikes. To test this hypothesis, he included a dummy variable for periods of government wage controls and a second dummy variable for each year following the lifting of such controls. If wage controls do limit union wage growth, then worker grievances are stockpiled and will erupt once the controls are lifted.

Shalev used regression analysis to estimate his model on quarterly fluctuations in U. S. strike activity for the period 1954–1975 and obtained the regression equation reported in Column 2 of Table 1. In general, Shalev's model is quite successful in explaining the fluctuations in aggregate strike activity over the postwar period from 1954 through 1975. The model explains more than 90 percent of the variance in strike activity and all of the individual coefficients are statistically significant at the .05 level and have the predicted sign.

Table 1

Shalev's Regression Results on Strike Frequency in Postwar America

Independent Variables (1)	Entire Period 1954-1975 (2)	Early Postwar Period 1954-1965 (3)	Recent Postwar Period 1966-1975 (4)
Unemployment Rate,	− 114.1	− 6.3	− 84.7
	(− 9.3)	(0.2)	(2.2)
Profit/Compensation $_{t-1}$	− 792.2	81.0	− 803.0
	(− 6.6)	(0.3)	(− 3.1)
Seasonal 1	208.5	28.1	225.3
	(6.8)	(0.5)	(4.0)
Seasonal 2	666.3	490.4	753.6
	(22.5)	(12.2)	(15.3)
Seasonal 3	505.9	416.6	528.2
	(17.0)	(10.8)	(9.3)
Inventory/Sales $_{t-1}$	− 2028.9	− 1503.0	− 2139.1
	(− 6.8)	(− 4.5)	(− 3.6)
Wage Controls	− 89.2	− 53.9	− 162.8
	(− 3.3)	(− 1.7)	(− 2.2)
Post-Wage Controls	129.9	262.6	110.8
	(3.3)	(2.3)	(2.2)
Contract Expirations	0.49	0.64	0.49
	(2.2)	(2.7)	(0.8)
Inter-Contract Wage Changes	(− 14.8)	− 2.9	− 5.4
	(− 1.7)	(− 0.2)	(− 0.3)
Inter-Contract Price Changes	46.8	24.4	32.6
	(5.4)	(1.7)	(1.4)
Contract (Other) Wage	27.6	15.7	26.3
	(3.7)	(0.7)	(1.5)
Constant	4985.8	2857.8	5058.1
	(9.2)	(4.2)	(4.5)
R^2	.929	.928	.906
DW	1.78	1.89	1.85
SEE	91.8	65.2	101.6

[C5340]

(*t*-statistics in parentheses)

However, there is some question as to whether the relationships on which the model is based are stable over the entire postwar period. When Shalev reestimated the model for two sub-periods (1954–1965 and 1966–1975) some significant differences appeared for the individual coefficients in the two equations as indicated in Columns 3 and 4 of Table 1. The unemployment and profit variables are not significant in the early postwar period, but are highly significant and negative in the later postwar period. More important with respect to this paper is the fact that the three variables used by Shalev to capture the economic grievances of workers perform poorly in the sub-period equations, in sharp contrast to the results reported for the entire postwar sample period. The lagged variables on wage changes, price changes, and changes in other wages are not statistically significant in the most recent sub-period. This suggests that these variables may have been unable to adequately adjust to the influence that the rapid growth in inflation has had on strike decisions. We shall return to this point below.

IV. ASHENFELTER AND JOHNSON'S POLITICAL MODEL OF STRIKE ACTIVITY

Ashenfelter and Johnson (1969), hereinafter referred to as A&J, proposed a strike model derived from Ross (1948) in which there are three parties involved in the collective bargaining process: management, union leadership, and the rank and file union members. Unique to this model is the argument that union leaders have personal political goals as well as an interest in developing the union as an institution and in protecting the economic welfare of union members. Strikes occur in this model when the rank and files' expected wage increase is much greater than the management will accept. In such cases, union leaders will attempt to convince the membership to accept a smaller increase. If they are unable to do so, the leadership may very well call for a strike it knows the union cannot win rather than run the risk of signing a contract which the membership might fail to ratify. If members rejected the contract the leaders' position in the union might be severely weakened, whereas even in a losing strike they may strengthen their position in the union by rallying forces against management.

Although A&J developed their model in a collective bargaining framework, it is certainly not a bargaining model in the traditional sense. Bargaining is not permitted in their model.[5] They assumed that management has no concession schedule in the Hicksian sense, but the union has a "resistance schedule" that is known by management. That is, management knows the rate at which the union members will lower their wage demands to avoid a strike of a certain length. With this information, the strike simply becomes a profit instrument of the firm. Management decides to take a strike or meet the unions wage demands depending on which option is the most profitable.

In this framework, the likelihood of a strike depends upon the size of the members' demands and upon management's assessment of the union's concession schedule. By assuming the latter to be invariant in the short-run, A&J argued that the probability of a strike is directly related to the members' minimum wage demands which, in turn, are related to three major variables: (1) the unemployment rate, (2) the recent change in real wages; and (3) the recent level of relative profits. They argued when unemployment is low workers will have better alternative employment opportunities, higher strike funds, and lower employment effects if large wage increases are obtained. According to A&J, larger recent changes in real wages, which they esti-

---

5. This point has been made by Vanderkamp (1970), Edwards (1978), and Shalev (1980) as well.

mated using Almon lags, will satisfy workers' expectations of long term increases in standard of living and hence lessen current wage demands. Finally, they argued high recent profits, measured by the ration of profits to the wage bill, are likely to increase workers' wage demands. With respect to the profit variable, A&J admitted that management might be more likely to accede to union demands when profits are high so that the effect of this variable on strike activity is indeterminate.[6]

A&J included two additional types of variables in their model. For the same reasons as Shalev, they used three quarterly seasonal variables. They added a trend variable since they believed that increasingly effective methods for resolving recognition disputes and handling grievances have reduced the level of strike activity over time.

A&J provided empirical support for their model by estimating several regression equations on U.S. quarterly strike data for the period 1952I–1967II. We have reestimated their basic model for the entire postwar period from 1954 through 1977 and our results are shown in Column 2 of Table 2.[7] The model performs very well for the entire postwar period. All of the individual coefficients except the lagged real wage variables are highly significant and have the predicted sign.[8] Overall, the model explains about 86 percent of the variance in strike activity over the period.[9]

In order to test the stability of the A&J model we divided the postwar period into two sub-periods, 1954I–1967II and 1967II–1977IV, and estimated separate equations for each period.[10] The results, presented in Columns (3) and (4) of Table 2, indicate some significant

6. Edwards (1978) and Shalev (1980) have argued that the rational employer would evaluate the union demand relative to the state of labor and product markets and the performance of the firm. If so, the unemployment rate as well as the profit level should influence the employer wage offers and as an effect of both these variables a strike activity would become theoretically indeterminate.

7. We chose to reestimate the A&J model for the postwar period beginning with 1954 rather than 1952 to make our results more comparable with the Shalev study. We did, however, first estimate the A&J model for the 1952–1967 period to assure us that we were, in fact, replicating the A&J model correctly.

8. It is a bit odd that the simple deletion of the years 1952 and 1953 from the original sample period would cause the lagged real wage variable to decline from a high level of statistical significance as reported by A&J (and observed in our replications for the 1952–1967 period) to one being insignificant for the 1954–1967 period. Since the profits/compensation

variables also moved from being insignificant in the 1952–1967 period to significant for the 1954–1967 period, it would appear that the estimated values of the parameters are highly sensitive to the observation period chosen. Even more dramatic in this regard is the fact that the time dummy variable has a significant negative coefficient in the 1952–1967 regression equation and a significant positive coefficient in the 1954–1967 equation.

9. Two recent studies by Pencavel (1970) and Hibbs (1976) provide added empirical support for the A&J model.

10. We added a zero-one dummy variable to the A&J model for the periods in which the Nixon wage and price controls were in effect from 1971 to 1974. Separate work by the authors suggests that while the guidelines of the 1960's did not significantly effect strike activity, the Nixon controls lowered strikes by almost twenty per cent per month. See Douglas K. Pearce, "The Impact of Incomes Policy on Strike Activity: An Application of Intervention Analysis," mimeo, University of Missouri, June 1980.

differences between the two sub-sample estimates. A standard Chow (1960) test indicates that the hypothesis that there is no difference in the set of parameter estimates in these two equations should be strongly rejected.[11] We find that in the 1954–1967 equation (Column 3) the profit/compensation, seasonal 1, time, and wage control coefficients are not statistically significant, whereas these coefficients are significant in the entire regression equation (Column 2) and in the recent equation (Column 4). In contrast, the lagged real wage variable is significant in the 1954–1967 equation, but not in the other two period equations.

This last result, apparently, is associated with the recent increase in the rate of inflation. When the real wage variable is decomposed into nominal wage changes and price changes, as A&J reported in their study, some strange results appear. In the regression equation for the entire period both the lagged change in nominal wages ΣW_{t-1} and the lagged change in nominal prices ΣP_{t-1} have positive but statistically insignificant coefficients. In the two sub-period equations, the ΣP_{t-1} coefficients are positive and highly significant and the ΣW_{t-1} coefficients are negative and highly significant. These last results, of course, are the one hypothesized by A&J.

In general, A&J's model does not explain strike activity for the recent period as well as it did for the early postwar period. The explanatory power of their model declines from $R^2 = .91$ for the 1954–1967II period to $R^2 = .86$ for the 1967III–1978 period. Moreover, there is substantial reason to believe that the predictive power of the A&J model has declined over time.

To test the predictive power of the A&J model for each of the postwar periods, we utilized the estimated model for each period, to forecast the level of strike activity in the post-sample period. One step ahead forecasts were made for the next four quarters, using the realized value of the independent variables. To measure the relative forecasting accuracy of the model, we then calculated Theil's inequality coefficient.[12] This statistic compares the root-mean-square prediction error of the proposed model with that of a naive forecasting model which predicts that the level of strike activity next year is the same as this year, i.e., a no-change extrapolative model. For the A&J model to be a better forecaster than this naive alternative, the calculated Theil inequality coefficient should be less than unity.

The last two rows in Table 2 show the relevant statistics for evaluating the predictive power of the A&J model. Using the 1954–1977 equation estimates to predict strike activity in each of the four quarters in 1978, we find the Theil coefficient to be 1.002, which indicates virtually no difference between the predictive power of the A&J model and the no-change extrapolative model for this period. The

---

11. Since the DW statistic for the 1954–1977 equation indicates autocorrelated residuals, the Chow test should only be viewed as suggestive. For the Chow test we obtained an F = 8.35 with 10, 84 degrees of freedom, respectively.

12. Henri Theil, *Applied Economic Forecasting* (Amsterdam: North-Holland Press, 1966), pp. 27–29.

early period A&J regression performed significantly better than the no-change extrapolative model in predicting the level of strike activity for each of the four quarters from 1967III–1968II. The Theil coefficient for this case is .416, indicating that A&J's model had a root-mean-square prediction error which was approximately 42 percent of that for the naive model. Finally, A&J's model for the recent period is a particularly poor forecaster of recent strike activity. Using the values of the 1967III–1977IV period model equation to estimate the strike activity in 1968, we obtained a Theil coefficient of 1.356. This means that the root-mean-square prediction error of the A&J model was 35.6 percent larger than that for the naive model. Researchers interested in predicting future levels of strike activity can hardly be excited by these results.

V. AN ALTERNATIVE SPECIFICATION OF A&J'S MODEL

In an effort to improve the ability of strike models to explain recent strike frequency we constructed some new economic variables that emphasize expectations of employers and workers. Since the most dramatic change in economic conditions in recent years appears to be the growth in inflation rates, attention was focused on that variable. It is assumed that workers base their expectations with respect to price changes on the Consumer Price Index (CPI) and that firms worry about producer price changes as approximated by the Wholesale Price Index (WPI). By time series analysis of rates of change in manufacturing wage rates, the CPI, and the WPI we constructed forecasting models which give the best forecasts of the series under the assumption that information is restricted to the past observations on the series.[13] In other words, it was assumed that workers and firms form their price and wage predictions on the basis of narrow rational expectations. From this analysis, the following variables may be constructed:

13. In order to generate expectations we used the following procedures. First, we estimated time series models for 1949II–1965IV for rates of change in the manufacturing wage, the CPI and the WPI. Using these models we forecasted the rate of change over 4 and 8 quarter horizons for 1966I–1966IV. Next we updated the data by adding 4 or 8 quarters of data, re-estimated the time series models, and made a set of forecasts for 1967I–1967IV and 1967I–1968IV. Finally, this process was repeated through 1978IV.

Table 2

Ashenfelter & Johnson and Moore & Pearce Regression Results on Strike Frequency

Independent Variables (1)	Ashenfelter & Johnson			Moore & Pearce		
	Entire Period 1954-1977IV (2)	Early Period 1954I-1967III (3)	Recent Period 1967III-1977IV (4)	Entire Period 1954-1977IV (5)	Early Period 1954-1967II (6)	Recent Period 1967III-1977IV (7)
Unemployment Rate,	−63.09 (−5.10)	−124.69 (−4.19)	−167.13 (−2.2)	−52.74 (−3.64)	−38.85 (−1.26)	−66.31 (−2.34)
Profit/Compensation$_{t-1}$	−21.87 (−1.77)	−20.10 (−.88)	−60.87 (−2.46)	−10.51 (−.67)	27.72 (1.11)	−73.03 (−2.64)
Seasonal 1	85.93 (2.27)	9.84 (.32)	142.52 (2.5)	96.24 (2.54)	34.29 (.99)	160.01 (3.16)
Seasonal 2	608.34 (16.05)	481.93 (16.00)	719.34 (12.26)	623.56 (15.98)	562.85 (15.81)	735.86 (14.48)
Seasonal 3	447.16 (12.02)	417.84 (14.00)	467.87 (9.12)	458.14 (11.31)	525.24 (12.17)	460.29 (9.32)
Time	7.08 (11.1)	−2.21 (−1.38)	19.87 (2.6)	6.61 (6.49)	−.93 (−.58)	9.19 (2.31)
Wage Controls	−181.93 (−5.87)	−40.34 (−1.27)	−145.73 (−2.42)	−165.75 (−5.14)	−14.53 (−.34)	−121.40 (−2.16)
$\Sigma_{i=0}^{4}$ Real Wage$_{t-1}$	−4.40 (−.33)	−69.51 (−3.31)	−55.00 (−1.54)			
Expected Real Wage Change				−2.12 (−.06)	81.04 (1.27)	−92.89 (−1.85)
Expected Real Labor Cost Change				7.91 (.33)	22.25 (.40)	−19.08 (−.86)
Unexpected Change Real Wages $_{t-i}$				−7.47 (−.56)	−33.16 (−1.62)	21.71 (.89)
Unexpected Change Labor Cost $_{t-i}$				−7.64 (−.72)	−6.09 (−.29)	23.19 (1.94)
Constant	1022.76 (6.04)	1799.05 (4.29)	864.41 (4.0)	876.37 (4.51)	646.44 (1.57)	1411.1 (4.01)
R^2	.86	.91	.86	.86	.90	.88
DW	1.13	1.43	1.77	1.16	1.50	2.06
SEE	128.81	75.73	120.31	130.53	82.38	114.35
RMSE	412.07	136.84	146.78	424.39	557.55	459.37
Theil U	1.002	.416	1.356	1.032	.446	1.117

[C5339]

(*t*-statistics in parentheses)

(1) The expected annual rate of change in real wage rates over the next 4 or 8 quarters, which is the expected change in nominal wages deflated by the expected change in the CPI. This variable should have a negative influence on strike frequency. If workers expect larger real wage increases they are less likely to strike since their long-run expectations are being satisfied and the opportunity cost of a strike is higher.

(2) The exepected change in real labor costs over the next 4 or 8 quarters as viewed by employers since the expected change in the WPI is used to deflate the expected change in wages. This variable is posited to have a positive coefficient. That is, if firms expect greater increases in wages than in product prices, they are likely to oppose strongly union wage demands.

(3) The unexpected change in real wages over the past 4 or 8 quarters is measured as the difference between what workers expected for that period and the actual change in the CPI over the period. The sign of this variable is ambiguous. According to A&J and Shalev, larger recent changes in real wages will satisfy workers' expectations of long term increases in standard of living and hence lessen current wage demands and the likelihood of a strike.[14] But as Edwards (1978), Skeels (1971), and Welch (1975) have noted, it is possible that large increases in real wages in the past could lead workers to demand current increases which are at least as large and hence this variable could be positively related to strike activity.

(4) The unexpected change in real labor costs over the past 4 or 8 quarters as viewed by employers is measured by the actual nominal wage change minus the actual WPI change minus the expected change in wage/WPI. Larger than expected increases in past real labor costs are expected to increase employers' resistance to union wage demands and thus tend to increase the likelihood of a strike.

To test the significance of these four expectation variables we substituted them in the A&J model in place of the Almon lag variables on real wage changes and reestimated the model using quarterly data for the period 1967–1977. Both the 4 quarter and the 8 quarter horizons were tried; the latter fit the data better. Our results are shown in Column 7 of Table 2. It appears that our variable specification is only slightly superior to A&J for the recent period. The R^2 rises from .86 (Column 3) to .88 (Column 7) and the Durbin-Watson statistic clearly indicates that serial correlation in the residuals is less of a problem under our specification. Furthermore, the Theil inequality coefficient obtained when we use our 1967–1977 regression equation to predict strike activity in each of the four quarters in 1978 is 1.117 compared to 1.356 for A&J's 1967–1977 equation, as shown in the last row of Table 2. Although our model predicts 1978 strike activity more accurately than A&J's model, we are not satisfied with our model's performance since the root-mean-square prediction error for our model is 11.7 percent larger than that for the naive, no-change extrapolative model.

Comparing the individual coefficients for the regression equations for the recent time period we observe very little difference in the A&J model (Column 4) and in our model (Column 7). The non-wage and non-labor cost variables (unemployment rate, profit/compensation, seasonal dummy variables, Time, and wage control) have approximately the same size coefficients and all of the coefficients have the anticipated sign and are statistically significant. The

---

14. Shalev (p. 158) is careful to point out "that higher real wage gains by *other* workers will *inflate* real wage expectations," and thus have a positive effect on strikes. Only by controlling for this "inflation" effect by including his other worker wage variable, measured by the size of the first-year wage adjustment negotiated in the previous quarter, did Shalev feel confident in predicting "that higher real wage increases in the past would moderate present wage militancy."

increase in the explanatory power of the model (higher R^2) under our specification is due to the fact that A&J's real wage variable ($\Sigma^8_{i=0}$ Real Wage) is not significant, whereas several of our expectation variables have statistically significant coefficients. First, our expected real wage change variable has a significant negative coefficient as hypothesized. Apparently, if workers expect larger real wage increases they are less likely to strike since their long-run wage expectations are being satisfied and the opportunity cost of a strike is higher. Second, the lagged unexpected change in labor cost variable has a singificant positive coefficient. We interpret this to mean that employers faced with higher than expected past real labor costs attempt to hold the line with respect to union current wage demands and this action tends to increase the likelihood of a strike. Our other two expectation variables (expected real labor cost changes and unexpected changes in real wages) failed to obtain statistical significance in the recent period equation.

In general, our approach of separating A&J's measure of past real wage changes into variables measuring expected future changes in wages and labor costs and variables measuring past unexpected changes in wages and labor costs is successful in explaining strike activity during the recent period, characterized by rapid inflation. The same cannot be said for periods of moderate inflation. When our model is estimated for data covering the entire postwar period (1954–1977), none of the expectation variables have statistically significant coefficients, as indicated in Column 5 of Table 2. The reason for this is probably due to the fact that the expectation variables have small variances during periods of moderate inflation. In this regard, it should be noted that A&J's lagged real wage variable also failed to reach significance during the period as shown in Column 2. In fact, there is no significant difference in performance between A&J's model and our model for this period. The R^2's are identical and the predictive power of the two models, as measured by the Theil U-statistic are almost equal. In the early postwar period (1954–1967II) the A&J model specification is slightly superior to ours. As shown in Columns 2 and 5 in Table 2, the R^2 is slightly higher (.91 vs. .90) and the Theil U-statistic is slightly smaller (.416 vs. .446) in the A&J regression equation for this period.

In conclusion, we find that it is only during periods of rapid inflation that our wage and labor cost expectation variables become important, but this is precisely the period when the traditional economic variables fail to maintain their significance in models of strike frequency. A&J's lagged real wage variable and Shalev's three economic variables (inter-contract wage changes, inter-contract price changes, and other contract wage changes) all failed to achieve statistical significance in explaining strike activity in the late 1960s and 1970s. In this paper, attention was limited to expectation variables associated with the growth in inflation rates, i.e., expected changes in wages and labor costs and lagged unexpected changes in wages and labor costs. Having established the validity of this approach to a certain extent, in the future we plan to examine the influence of other expectational variables dealing with unemployment rates and relative profits on the level of strike activity.

REFERENCES

Ashenfelter, Orley and George Johnson, "Bargaining Theory, Trade Unions, and Industrial Strike Activity," American Economic Review 59 (March 1969), 35–49.

Chow, G. C., "Tests of Equality Between Subsets of Coefficients in Two Linear Regressions," Econometrica 28 (1960), 591–605.

Edwards, P. K., "Time Series Regression Models of Strike Activity: A Reconsideration of American Data," British Journal of Industrial Relations Vol. 16 (November 1978).

Hibbs Jr., D. A., "Industrial Conflict in Advanced Industrial Societies," American Political Science Review 70 (December 1976), 1033–1058.

Hicks, John R., Theory of Wages, London, MacMillan (1932).

O'Brien, "Industrial Conflict and Business Fluctuations: A Comment," Journal of Political Economy 73 (December 1965), 650–54.

Pencavel, J. H., "An Investigation into Industrial Strike Activity in Britain," Economica 35 (August 1970), 239–56.

Rees, Albert, "Industrial Conflict and Business Fluctuations," Journal of Political Economy 60 (October 1952), 371–82.

Ross, Arthur M., Trade Union Wage Policy, University of California Press, 1948.

Scully, G., "Business Cycles and Industrial Strike Activity," Journal of Business 44 (October 1971), 359–74.

Shalev, M., "Trade Unionism and Economic Analysis—The Case of Industrial Conflict," Journal of Labor Research 1 (Spring 1980), 133–174.

Stern, R. M., "Methodological Issues in Quantitative Strike Analysis," Industrial Relations 17 (February 1978), 32–42.

Vanderkamp, J., "Economic Activity and Strikes in Canada," Industrial Relations Vol. 9 (February 1970), 215–230.

Walton, R. E. and R. B. McKereie, A Behavioral Theory of Labor Negotiations, New York, McGraw-Hill, 1965.

Weintraub, A., "Prosperity Versus Strikes: An Empirical Approach," Industrial and Labor Relations Review 19 (January 1966), 231–38.

C. THE ROLE OF THE CONSTITUTION

HUDGENS v. N.L.R.B.

Supreme Court of the United States, 1976.
424 U.S. 507, 96 S.Ct. 1029, 47 L.Ed.2d 196.

MR. JUSTICE STEWART delivered the opinion of the Court.

A group of labor union members who engaged in peaceful primary picketing within the confines of a privately owned shopping center were threatened by an agent of the owner with arrest for criminal trespass if they did not depart. The question presented is whether this threat violated the National Labor Relations Act. The National Labor Relations Board concluded that it did, and the Court of Appeals for the Fifth Circuit agreed. We granted certiorari because of the seemingly important questions of federal law presented.

I

The petitioner, Scott Hudgens, is the owner of the North DeKalb Shopping Center, located in suburban Atlanta, Ga. The center consists of a single large building with an enclosed mall. Surrounding the building is a parking area which can accommodate 2,640 automobiles. The shopping center houses 60 retail stores leased to various businesses. One of the lessees is the Butler Shoe Co. Most of the stores, including Butler's, can be entered only from the interior mall.

In January 1971, warehouse employees of the Butler Shoe Co. went on strike to protest the company's failure to agree to demands made by their union in contract negotiations. The strikers decided to picket not only Butler's warehouse but its nine retail stores in the Atlanta area as well, including the store in the North DeKalb Shopping Center. On January 22, 1971, four of the striking warehouse employees entered the center's enclosed mall carrying placards which read: "Butler Shoe Warehouse on Strike, AFL-CIO, Local 315." The general manager of the shopping center informed the employees that they could not picket within the mall or on the parking lot and threatened them with arrest if they did not leave. The employees departed but returned a short time later and began picketing in an area of the mall immediately adjacent to the entrances of the Butler store. After the picketing had continued for approximately 30 minutes, the shopping center manager again informed the pickets that if they did not leave they would be arrested for trespassing. The pickets departed.

* * *

[The court of appeals enforced the Board's decisions that Hudgens had violated Section 8(a)(1). However, it was unclear whether the decision rested solely on Section 7 of the NLRA or more broadly on a constitutional right, recognized in earlier Court decisions, of access to private property (including shopping centers) classified as quasi "public" property.]

II

* * * In the present posture of the case the most basic question is whether the respective rights and liabilities of the parties are to be decided under the criteria of the National Labor Relations Act alone, under a First Amendment standard, or under some combination of the two. It is to that question, accordingly, that we now turn.

It is, of course, a commonplace that the constitutional guarantee of free speech is a guarantee only against abridgment by government, federal or state. Thus, while statutory or common law may in some situations extend protection or provide redress against a private corporation or person who seeks to abridge the free expression of others, no such protection or redress is provided by the Constitution itself.

* * *

We conclude, in short, that under the present state of the law the constitutional guarantee of free expression has no part to play in a case such as this.

III

From what has been said it follows that the rights and liabilities of the parties in this case are dependent exclusively upon the National Labor Relations Act. Under the Act the task of the Board, subject to review by the courts, is to resolve conflicts between § 7 rights and private property rights, "and to seek a proper accommodation between the two." Central Hardware Co. v. NLRB, 407 U.S., at 543, 92 S.Ct., at 2241. What is "a proper accommodation" in any situation may largely depend upon the content and the context of the § 7 rights being asserted. The task of the Board and the reviewing courts under the Act, therefore, stands in conspicuous contrast to the duty of a court in applying the standards of the First Amendment, which requires "above all else" that expression must not be restricted by government "because of its message, its ideas, its subject matter, or its content."

In the Central Hardware case, and earlier in the case of NLRB v. Babcock & Wilcox Co., 351 U.S. 105, 76 S.Ct. 679, 100 L.Ed. 975, the Court considered the nature of the Board's task in this area under the Act. Accommodation between employees' § 7 rights and employers' property rights, the Court said in Babcock & Wilcox, "must be obtained with as little destruction of one as is consistent with the maintenance of the other." 351 U.S., at 112, 76 S.Ct. at 684.

Both Central Hardware and Babcock & Wilcox involved organizational activity carried on by nonemployees on the employers' property. The context of the § 7 activity in the present case was different in several respects which may or may not be relevant in striking the proper balance. First, it involved lawful economic strike activity rather than organizational activity. Second, the § 7 activity here was carried on by Butler's employees (albeit not employees of its shopping center store), not by outsiders. See NLRB v. Babcock & Wilcox Co., supra, 351 U.S., at 111–113, 76 S.Ct. at 683–685. Third, the property interests impinged upon in this case were not those of the employer against whom the § 7 activity was directed, but of another.

The Babcock & Wilcox opinion established the basic objective under the Act: accommodation of § 7 rights and private property rights "with as little destruction of one as is consistent with the maintenance of the other." The locus of that accommodation, however, may fall at differing points along the spectrum depending on the nature and strength of the respective § 7 rights and private property rights asserted in any given context. In each generic situation, the primary responsibility for making this accommodation must rest with the Board in the first instance. See NLRB v. Babcock & Wilcox, supra, 351 U.S. at 112, 76 S.Ct. at 684; cf. NLRB v. Erie Resistor Corp., supra, 373 U.S. at 235–236, 83 S.Ct. 1149–1150; NLRB v. Truckdrivers Union, 353 U.S. 87, 97, 77 S.Ct. 643, 648, 1 L.Ed.2d 676. "The responsibility to adapt the Act to changing patterns of industrial life is entrusted to the Board." NLRB v. Weingarten, Inc., 420 U.S. 251, 266, 95 S.Ct. 959, 968, 43 L.Ed.2d 171.

For the reasons stated in this opinion, the judgment is vacated and the case is remanded to the Court of Appeals with directions to remand to the National Labor Relations Board, so that the case may be there considered under the statutory criteria of the National Labor Relations Act alone.

It is so ordered.

D. UNLAWFUL STRIKES AND PICKETING

Strikes and picketing may constitute unlawful activity under the NLRA, the Sherman Anti-Trust Act or state law. If picketing involves violence and the union as an institution is responsible for the violence or the threat of violence, the union violates Section 8(b)(1)(a) of the NLRA. In addition, such conduct may be dealt with under state law through criminal penalties, money damages or injunction. It is often difficult to tell whether or not the union as an institution is responsible for the violence. The mere fact of picket line violence by union members is not enough. It must be demonstrated that the violence is pursuant to union policy or was encouraged or engaged in by high ranking union officials.

States may rarely assert jurisdiction over picketing which does not involve substantial violence. Attempts by State Courts to issue injunctions in situations outside of state jurisdiction may legally be ignored by the union.

A union may also be guilty of an unfair labor practice if it strikes for an unlawful object such as an illegal union security clause. Sometimes a strike will be in violation of one of the Board's bargaining rules. A strike over a non-mandatory bargaining topic violates the union's duty to bargain collectively. Employers rarely bring charges under Section 8(b)(3), however, because of the Board's inability to provide an adequate remedy, see discussion, infra.

E. THE PROHIBITION OF SECONDARY ACTIVITY

The most important limit on the use of strikes and economic pressure under the NLRA is the effort to outlaw secondary boycotts. Sections 8(b)(4) and 8(e), which cover secondary activity, are among the most confused and technical provisions in the legal system. It is extremely difficult to know what is prohibited and what is permitted under the law. The article which is partially reprinted below gives some idea of the reach of the statute and of the different interests which the Board and courts have recognized in interpreting it.

RAYMOND GOETZ, SECONDARY BOYCOTT AND THE LMRA: A PATH THROUGH THE SWAMP *

Few pieces of federal legislation have received the scathing criticism that has been heaped upon the secondary boycott provisions of the Labor Management Relations Act. Ever since section 8(b)(4) was first enacted, its substance has been bitterly condemned by organized labor, its draftsmanship has been caustically appraised by partisans and scholars alike, and its interpretation by the National Labor Relations Board and the courts has been disputed on all sides—including Congress. The queasy feeling of many who have been compelled to work with this statute is expressed by one plain-spoken observer who called it a "dreadful mess."

This subject has not lacked for scholarly analysis. Yet the statute and the decisions weave such an "intricate tapestry" and the commentary is so erudite that there still seems to be a need for a complete explanation of the law of secondary boycotts that can be grasped by students and practitioners approaching this baffling subject for the first time or returning to it after prolonged absence. The purpose of this article is to try to fill that need.

I. BACKGROUND AND STRUCTURE OF THE STATUTE

Prior to 1947, secondary boycotts were a widely-used economic pressure tactic of organized labor for combatting nonunion employers and influencing other employers against whom a strike was impractical or ineffective. As a result of Supreme Court interpretations of the Norris-LaGuardia and Clayton Acts, such tactics were permissible under federal law. In 1947, the Taft-Hartley Act amended the National Labor Relations Act (Wagner Act) by making certain union ac-

* Raymond Goetz, "Secondary Boycott And The LMRA: A Path Through The Swamp," 19 Kansas Law Review 698 (1971); © 1971 by the Kansas Law Review, Inc. Reprinted by permission of the Kansas Law Review and Fred B. Rothman & Co.

tivities unfair labor practices. Section 8(b)(4) was enacted to outlaw secondary boycotts. As Senator Taft put it:

> [U]nder the provisions of the Norris-LaGuardia Act, it became impossible to stop a secondary boycott or any other kind of strike, no matter how unlawful it may have been at common law. All this provision of the bill does is to reverse the effect of the law as to secondary boycotts. It has been set forth that there are good secondary boycotts and bad secondary boycotts. Our committee heard evidence for weeks and never succeeded in having anyone tell us any difference between different kinds of secondary boycotts. So we have broadened the provision dealing with secondary boycotts as to make them an unfair labor practice.

The intended operation of this statute was explained as follows:

> [S]trikes or boycotts, or attempts to induce or encourage such action, were made unfair labor practices if the purpose was to force an employer or other person to cease using, selling, handling, transporting, or otherwise dealing in the products of another, or to cease doing business with any other person. Thus it was made an unfair labor practice for a union to engage in a strike against employer A for the purpose of forcing that employer to cease doing business with employer B. Similarly it would not be lawful for a union to boycott employer A because employer A uses or otherwise deals in the goods of, or does business with, employer B.

It can be seen that the basic purpose of the statute was to prohibit the exertion of pressure by a union against one employer in order to force him to cease dealing with another employer. It was felt that this kind of pressure should be outlawed because it is directed at neutral employers who are themselves powerless to resolve the union's dispute. As will be explained more fully below, the boycott is considered secondary because it is an indirect means of exerting pressure on the party whose conduct the union really wants to influence, the employer with whom it has a labor dispute.

The statute, however, does not use the term "secondary boycott," probably because no one can be quite certain exactly what it means. Instead, section 8(b)(4) is phrased in terms of making it an unfair labor practice for a union to engage in certain extremely specific activities directed at attaining certain prohibited objectives.

Two categories of union activity are prohibited. The first, set forth in clause (i), is either engaging in a strike or refusal to handle goods or perform services, or inducing or encouraging an employed individual to engage in a strike or refusal to handle goods or perform services. This inducement may take the form of picketing or simply directions or requests to union members to cease work. The second type of prohibited union activity, set forth in clause (ii), is threatening, coercing, or restraining any person engaged in commerce—generally an employer or managerial employee. This clause was added in 1959 because it had been held that the section did not prohibit threats of labor trouble made directly to the neutral employer but applied only to pressure exerted on the employer through his employees.

Union activity falling in either or both of the prohibited categories amounts to an unfair labor practice only if it has "an object" specified in clauses (A), (B), (C), or (D) of section 8(b)(4). Clauses (C) and (D) do not pertain to secondary boycotts. Clause (A), which was inserted in 1959, refers to the objective of obtaining an agreement of the type prohibited in section 8(e) and is discussed in the portion of this article dealing with hot cargo clauses. Thus our basic concern is with the objective specified in clause (B). It is controlling in determining whether a union's activities covered by (i) or (ii) constitute the type of *secondary* boycott the statute was intended to proscribe. The object made unlawful by the portion of the clause that we are concerned with here is forcing or requiring any person to cease handling products of any other producer or to cease doing business with any other person.

II.   THE PRIMARY–SECONDARY DICHOTOMY

Absolutely essential to an understanding of section 8(b)(4) is the distinction between primary and secondary union activity. So fundamental, yet elusive, is this distinction that the literature has accorded it the status of a dichotomy. It has become a basic part of the test of legality of union conduct under this section.

Although the statute itself does not use the adjective "secondary," section 8(b)(4)(B) has since 1959 included a proviso stating that "nothing contained in this clause shall be construed to make unlawful, where not otherwise unlawful, any primary strike or primary picketing." This much is now clear: primary strikes and primary picketing are beyond the reach of the prohibition.

Without this proviso, the convoluted phrasing of section 8(b)(4) could have been interpreted literally to restrict primary activity. This possibility was illustrated in NLRB v. International Rice Milling Co., one of the first Supreme Court encounters with this masterpiece of draftsmanship. There the Teamsters Union picketed a mill to obtain recognition as bargaining agent for mill employees. The employees themselves did not strike or participate in the picketing. In the course of this picketing, union representatives succeeded in stopping a customer's truck arriving at the mill to pick up some grain. The pickets told the two men in the truck that there was a strike in progress and that they should turn back, which they did.

The Court of Appeals for the Fifth Circuit held that the union pickets in this case were doing exactly what the wording of the statute prohibited. Their activity certainly encouraged the customer's employees in the truck to refuse, in the course of their employment, to transport goods or perform services. An object of this activity was to force the customer to cease handling, transporting, or otherwise dealing in products of the mill, or to cease doing business with it. This activity had the additional object of forcing the mill to recognize the union as the representative of mill employees. Thus, both the prohibited activity and the forbidden object appeared to be present.

But such a view of the case would have the effect of outlawing one of the major objectives of any picket line around the premises of an employer with whom a union has a dispute. Traditionally, these objectives are not only to induce employees of that employer to remain away from work, but also to induce employees of customers and suppliers to refrain from crossing the picket line to carry on their employer's trade with the offending employer.

Even though the primary proviso was not in the statute at the time, the Supreme Court in *Rice Milling* recognized that to prohibit activity of the type involved there would be to "interfere with, impede or diminish the union's traditional right to strike",   *   *   *   The Court also noted that Congress did not seek by section 8(b)(4) to interfere with the ordinary strike. Although the opinion made no attempt to distinguish between primary and secondary activity, it did make it clear that section 8(b)(4) does not prohibit union efforts, in conjunction with a picket line at the premises of an employer with whom it has a dispute, to induce employees of another employer individually to refrain from crossing the picket line to deal with the picketed employer. This is true whether the picketing is carried on by employees of that employer or—as in *Rice Milling*—by nonemployees or "strangers."

*   *   *

Thus, the overriding test of legality of union conduct seemingly within the express wording of the prohibition is whether that conduct is primary or secondary. This is based on Congressional intention in section 8(b)(4) to outlaw secondary boycotts and prevent union attempts to widen the area of conflict by "coercion of neutral employers, themselves not concerned with a primary labor dispute, through the inducement of their employees to engage in strikes or concerted refusals to handle goods."

The vexing question running through this entire subject is how can a given type of union activity be identified as primary or secondary? An oft-quoted statement by Judge Learned Hand provides some guidance:

> The gravamen of a secondary boycott is that its sanctions bear, not upon the employer who alone is a party to the dispute, but upon some third party who has no concern in it. Its aim is to compel him to stop business with the employer in the hope that this will induce the employer to give in to his employees' demands.

Thus, the starting point is to identify the employer with whom the union has its basic dispute. An employer with whom a union has a dispute about his labor relations with his employees is a primary employer. As such, he is a fair target for direct application of economic pressure tactics, such as strikes and picketing. Such activity is primary and protected under the proviso to section 8(b)(4)(B). The mill in *Rice Milling* was an example of such a primary employer, since the union had a dispute with it about representation of its employees. The fact that pressure may be applied by nonemployees does not make it secondary, so long as it is applied directly against the employer with whom the union has such a dispute.

On the other hand, a secondary employer is one with whom the union has no dispute about his labor relations with his employees. These are the neutrals the statute was designed to protect because they do not have it within their own power to resolve the underlying dispute. Usually they are customers or suppliers of the primary employer or have some other business relationship with the primary employer. The union's only dispute with them—if it can be called a dispute—concerns their dealings with another employer against whom the union wants to exert indirect pressure in order to change the latter's labor relations policies. Pressure applied directly on such an employer is generally secondary because it is at least one step removed from its real target. The customer employing the men in the truck in *Rice Milling* of course was such a secondary employer. Activity directed at employees of such a customer is in a broad sense secondary, but when it is only a traditional concomitant of permissible primary activity at the premises of the primary employer, this sort of secondary effect is considered incidental to appeals to primary employees and therefore lawful.

It can be seen that the primary-secondary dichotomy requires the drawing of lines "more nice than obvious." The difficulty of this task will become more apparent in the discussions of the "ally doctrine," common situs picketing, and hot cargo clauses, which follow.

III. THE ALLY DOCTRINE

An early problem with section 8(b)(4) concerned its application to apparently secondary employers having some business relationship with the primary employer that might give them an interest in a dispute between primary and his employees. To deal with one aspect of this problem, the "ally doctrine" was promulgated in 1948 by Federal District Court Judge Rifkind in Douds v. Metropolitan Federation of Architects, Engineers, Chemists & Technicians (Ebasco).

A. Performance of Farmed-Out Struck Work

Employees of Ebasco Services, Inc., had gone on strike over the terms of a new collective bargaining agreement—clearly a primary economic strike. For about a year prior to the strike, Ebasco (which was engaged in the business of providing engineering services for industrial and public utility installations) had subcontracted some of its work to Project Engineering Company, a completely separate business entity. After the strike started, Ebasco subcontracted additional work to Project, including some that had been started by striking Ebasco employees. Ebasco supervisors made regular visits to Project to oversee this work, and Ebasco paid Project on the basis of time spent by Project employees on the subcontracts, plus a factor for overhead and profit.

Unquestionably, Project employees were doing work that Ebasco employees themselves would have been doing if they had not been on strike. The union representing the Ebasco strikers asked Project to stop doing this work. When this request went unheeded, the union picketed Project and induced some of its employees to cease work.

This activity on the part of the union seemed to come squarely within the statutory prohibition. By picketing Project, the union was obviously inducing or encouraging employees of Project to engage in a strike or concerted refusal to perform services on Ebasco subcontracts; the avowed purpose was to compel Project to cease doing this business with Ebasco.

Judge Rifkind, relying on the legislative purpose, refused to apply the statute literally. In particular, he cited Senator Taft's statement that the section "makes it unlawful to resort to a secondary boycott to injure the business of a third person who is wholly unconcerned in the disagreement between an employer and his employees." Judge Rifkind reasoned that Project was not an innocent bystander or neutral with no interest in the dispute between Ebasco and its employees, but instead "had made itself a party to the contest" and "was firmly allied to Ebasco." He pointed out that the economic effect on Ebasco's employees "was precisely that which would flow from Ebasco's hiring strikebreakers to work on its own premises." Therefore, he viewed the conduct of the union in inducing Project's employees to strike no differently from inducing Ebasco's employees to strike. In other words, the union's activity was in effect primary rather than secondary, and there was no secondary boycott.

Thus, *Ebasco* stands for the broad general proposition that picketing an independent contractor, to whom the primary employer has subcontracted work that would have been done by his own employees but for the strike, will be viewed as tantamount to picketing the primary employer and therefore not a violation of section 8(b)(4). The ally doctrine as originated in this case is still the law. It has been adopted by the Board, approved by the Second Circuit, and endorsed by Congress, Senator Taft, and former President Eisenhower.

Once it has been determined that an employer has become an ally, picketing may lawfully induce a total work stoppage by his employees and need not be limited to inducing a refusal to perform the struck work. The ally is considered to be standing "in the shoes" of the primary employer, with the result that the union may lawfully exert against the ally the same type of pressure it could against the primary employer. The subcontractor has given up his status as a neutral by taking on the farmed-out struck work. Another factor seems to be concern that if employees of the ally engaged in a partial work stoppage involving only struck work, this might be "unprotected" activity for which they could be disciplined.

* * *

Whether such an arrangement must be originated by the struck employer in order to create an ally relationship of this type is not entirely clear.

*   *   *

Not every subcontracting arrangement between a primary employer and a secondary employer makes the secondary employer an ally. In the construction industry, for example, subcontractors frequently do work that might have been done by employees of the general contractor or other subcontractor. As long as the subcontract is not for the completion of work left unfinished by a strike, the ally doctrine does not apply. While construction unions might argue that employees of the subcontractor are no different from employees of the prime contractor on a construction site, this argument was lost in NLRB v. Denver Building & Construction Trades Council. Nor does the ally doctrine apply where the subcontractor is merely attempting to continue its normal business dealings with the contractor.

Another variation of the problem arises where employees are striking in protest over the contracting out by their employer of work they had formerly been doing. In these circumstances, the subcontractor is not an ally since it is the contracting out that has caused the strike, not vice versa. Consequently, this is not considered farmed-out struck work. But if the subcontract is entered into when a strike is imminent, in an effort to mitigate its effect, the subcontractor becomes an ally even though the subcontract may extend beyond the duration of the strike.

Where a single corporate entity does business at more than one location, employees on strike at one location sometimes picket other plants or facilities of the employer to enlist the aid of employees there. Where the work being done at the second location is unrelated to work of the strikers, the employees there could not realistically be viewed as "strikebreakers." Yet, the difference in work and location does not make the premises "neutral." A union may lawfully exert pressure against a struck employer at any place where he happens to be carrying on his business. The same employer is involved throughout, and the picketing does not have an object of forcing one employer to cease doing business with any *other* employer. Since no third person is involved, it is unnecessary to resort to the ally doctrine to find the picketing primary.

*   *   *

IV.   COMMON SITUS PICKETING AND RESERVED GATES

Unlawful secondary picketing can often be distinguished from lawful primary picketing by its location. As a general rule, picketing at the premises of an employer with whom the union has its real dispute is primary, while picketing at the premises of a neutral employer is secondary.

A. The Common Situs Problem

Location of the picketing, however, is not necessarily conclusive of legality. It is especially unreliable when the workplace of employees of the primary employer coincides with the workplace of neutral employees, at what the Board calls a "common situs." Such shared work sites are typical of the construction industry where employees of a general contractor and independent subcontractors work on different portions of a building project, as well as other industries where employees do not spend all their time at the premises of their own employer.

Picketing at such a common situs comes within the literal wording of the statute. For example, the desired effect of picketing a construction project is to cause all union tradesmen to lay down their tools and walk off the job. This is the type of activity described in section 8(b)(4)(i). It does "induce or encourage   *   *   *   individual[s] employed by a person engaged in an industry affecting commerce to engage in a strike or a refusal in the course of [their] employment   *   *   *   to perform   *   *   *   services." This activity also has "an object," prohibited under clause (B), of forcing or requiring some employers at the site "to cease doing business with [an]other person."

Yet, as we have seen, the same analysis can be made of nearly all picketing at premises of a primary employer. Consequently, the courts have recognized that the statute cannot be literally construed because to do so would ban most lawful primary activity. This is now reinforced by the proviso, discussed earlier, which prevents the statute from being construed to make unlawful any primary strike or primary picketing.

Since picketing at the premises of a primary employer that induces secondary employees to respect the picket line generally is primary and lawful, a question arises whether the same sort of activity with the same objectives should not be equally lawful when it occurs at a common situs. It can be argued that a union in these circumstances is only exerting pressure directly on the employer with whom it has a dispute at a place where the dispute exists, and that the refusal of employees of others to cross the picket line is merely an incidental and lawful secondary effect. Moreover, if all common situs picketing were banned, unions would be precluded from any effective picketing of a primary employer whose business does not have a fixed location of its own where work is performed by his employees. On the other hand, it is difficult to justify indiscriminate picketing at a common situs, simply because a struck employer may be working there, when it may have an objective of forcing a neutral employer to cease dealing with the struck employer.

B. The Moore Dry Dock Standards

The problem is one of "balancing the right of a union to picket at the site of its dispute against the right of a secondary employer to be free from picketing in a controversy in which it is not directly involved." Neither right is absolute. To strike a balance, the Board has developed the *Moore Dry Dock* standards, under which picketing at a common situs is deemed primary and lawful if:

    a. the picketing is strictly limited to times when the situs of dispute is located on the secondary employer's premises;

    b. at the time of the picketing, the primary employer is engaged in its normal business at the situs;

    c. the picketing is limited to places reasonably close to the location of the situs; and

    d. the picketing discloses clearly that the dispute is with the primary employer.

These four requisites, which have been generally accepted by the courts, are designed to confine the effect of the picketing as closely as possible to the primary employer without outlawing it altogether. Although picketing in compliance with these guidelines is bound to be somewhat less effective than designating an entire job unfair, they still leave open to unions the possibility of exerting some economic pressure at a common situs by properly structured picketing. In fact, picketing that scrupulously meets all four requirements may still reach employees of neutral employers who occupy the site, as it did in the *Moore Dry Dock* case itself, where the union was picketing a ship in a dry dock that was neither owned nor operated by the ship owners. The standards, however, attempt to limit this possibility to the incidental effect of primary picketing.

In keeping with the delicate balancing effort required by the *Moore Dry Dock* guidelines, the Board and some courts at one time felt there was no necessity to allow any picketing at a common situs when the union had an opportunity to picket at a separately maintained place of business of the primary employer. Currently, however, the existence of such a place of business is not controlling, but is merely one of the circumstances to be considered in determining the object of picketing at a common situs.

A major problem in applying the *Moore Dry Dock* standards is identifying the "situs" of the primary dispute. Generally speaking, this situs is located wherever any employees of the primary employer may be working. Therefore, the dispute may have what in Board jargon is called a "roving situs," as where the dispute is with a truck operator. In such cases, the union may picket at delivery and pickup locations by timing and stationing the pickets properly and wording the signs carefully. This is often done by pickets following the trucks or waiting for them on a standby basis at a predetermined stop.

Generally, the first and second *Moore Dry Dock* requirements cannot be met if picketing is carried on at a location where employees of the primary employer sometimes work, but when they are not physically present. At such times, it is presumed that the picketing must be aimed solely at the neutrals who are working. While the third and fourth requirements concerning location of the picketing and disclosure of the party to the dispute may seem rather technical, their basic purpose is to compel a picketing union to make clear the kind of pressure it is seeking to exert. If the picketing is conducted at a place where the primary employees cannot observe them, or if the signs label the entire job "unfair," there is a direct appeal to neutrals working at the site which unnecessarily draws them and their employer into the dispute.

* * *

C. Common Situs Picketing at Construction Projects

Common situs picketing probably has generated the most controversy in the construction industry, where employees of a general contractor and various subcontractors traditionally work side by side toward completion of the same construction project. A common source of dispute is employment of nonunion labor by one of the contractors. Clearly, if all the tradesmen were employed by the general contractor, a union protest of his employment of nonunion workers would be a primary dispute with the general contractor. The question is whether the presence of a subcontractor alters the situation. The Supreme Court answered in the affirmative in NLRB v. Denver Building & Construction Trades Council, holding that common situs picketing at a construction project to protest employment of nonunion labor by an electrical subcontractor violated section 8(b)(4). The Court stated:

> We agree with the Board also in its conclusion that the fact that the contractor and subcontractor were engaged on the same construction project, and that the contractor had some supervision over the subcontractor's work, did not eliminate the status of each as an independent contractor or make the employees of one the employees of the other. The business relationship between independent contractors is too well established in the law to be overridden without clear language doing so. The Board found that the relationship between Doose & Lintner and Gould & Preisner was one of "doing business" and we find no adequate reason for upsetting that conclusion.

Although the union argued it was merely picketing to force the general contractor to make the project an all-union job and therefore had a primary dispute with the general contractor, the Court noted that the union actually had a longstanding dispute with the nonunion subcontractor, and the only way the union could achieve its purpose would be to force the subcontractor off the job. Therefore "an object"—if not the only object—of the picketing was to force or require the general contractor to cease "doing business" with the subcontractor. In support of its denial of any special treatment for the construction industry, the Court stated:

> In the views of the Board as applied to this case we find conformity with the dual congressional objectives of preserving the right of labor organizations to bring pressure to bear on offending employers in primary labor disputes and of shielding unoffending

employers and others from pressures in controversies not their own.

The Court refrained from any mention of the *Moore Dry Dock* standards promulgated by the Board a year earlier, but it was clear from the nature of the picketing that those standards could not have been met. The picket signs stated "This Job Unfair to Denver Building and Construction Trades Council," and the avowed purpose was to notify union members that nonunion men were working on the job.

Nevertheless, by refusing to make the construction industry an exception to common situs picketing problems, the Court paved the way for application of the *Moore Dry Dock* standards to that industry. They are now generally applied there, but without strict adherence to the portion of the first guideline requiring that the dispute be on the secondary employer's premises. Usually, neither the general contractor nor any of the subcontractors who might be considered the secondary employers at whom the picketing in question is directed are the owners of the construction site.

* * *

The picketing of the construction site in *Denver Building Trades* could have been conformed to the *Moore Dry Dock* standards by limiting it to times when the electrical subcontractor's employees were on the job, by stationing the pickets near the entrance used by them, and by rewording the signs to indicate that the dispute was with the offending subcontractor instead of designating the entire job unfair. Nonetheless, such picketing might still have been unlawful because the union representative in that case had made it plain to the general contractor in advance that union men would not work on the job with nonunion men and that if the nonunion contractor remained on the job, it would be picketed. These are the kinds of actions and statements that would seem to reveal that the union's paramount purpose is to drive the subcontractor off the job by unlawfully pressuring the general contractor to cease doing business with him. Such a prohibited *object*, however, cannot be inferred simply from the *effect* of the picketing; otherwise, all common situs picketing would be effectively outlawed since union employees of neutral employers traditionally respect picket lines.

V.   HOT CARGO AGREEMENTS

Until 1959, the statutory restrictions on secondary boycotts left a loophole for "hot cargo" clauses—so-called because of their prevalence in collective bargaining agreements in the trucking industry. These clauses usually provide either that employees will not be required to handle goods of a nonunion or "unfair" employer or that the signatory employer will not do business with such an employer. Clauses of this type produce essentially the same result as prohibited secondary boycotts: neutral employers and their employees become involved in disputes not their own, and this involvement compels the neutral secondary employers to cease doing business with primary employers with whom the union has its real dispute. In effect, such clauses establish secondary boycotts by advance commitment.

[Before 1959 the Act] appeared to leave unions free to compel employers, by strike or threat of strike, to agree to hot cargo clauses and then enforce them either in the courts or by exerting on the employer subtle pressures not amounting to the kind of strike or inducement of employees prohibited by the act. By such devices, employers could lawfully be coerced into "pseudo-voluntary" boycotts. As a result of concern about this possibility and of investigation into use of hot cargo clauses by the Teamsters Union, Congress, as part of the Landrum-Griffin amendments in 1959, enacted section 8(e).

* * *

In sweeping language, this section makes it an unfair labor practice for a union and an employer "to enter into any contract or agreement, express or implied, whereby [the] employer ceases or refrains or agrees to cease or refrain from handling, using, selling, transporting or otherwise dealing in any of the products of any other employer, or to cease doing business with any other persons * * * ." Any such agreement was declared unenforceable and void. Limited exceptions were made for agreements concerning jobsite construction work and for agreements involving certain integrated operations in the garment industry. At the same time, a new clause (A) was inserted in section 8(b)(4) to add to the prohibited objectives that of forcing or requiring an employer to enter into an agreement prohibited by section 8(e). Thus, section 8(e) was an attempt by Congress to close the hot cargo agreement loophole in section 8(b)(4).

A work preservation objective, or possibly some other objective with respect to labor relations between the signatory employer and his employees, will make a clause primary and lawful; on the other hand, a clause aimed at some union objective elsewhere will be secondary and unlawful under section 8(e). In this way, the primary-secondary dichotomy under section 8(b)(4) has been carried over as the test of legality under section 8(e).

* * *

E. Union Signatory and Union Standards Clauses

The *National Woodwork* [decision by the Supreme Court] supports Board and courts of appeals decisions holding that agreements permitting employees to refuse to handle goods not bearing a union label or produced by nonunion employers, as well as agreements prohibiting contracting out to firms that do not employ union members, violate section 8(e). Such clauses are not addressed to labor relations of the contracting employer *vis-a-vis* his own employees, but rather are "tactically calculated to satisfy union objectives elsewhere;" a currently existing dispute with the boycotted (nonunion) employer is not necessary to make the clause unlawful. Accordingly, in *National Woodwork*, a clause prohibiting employees from working on millwork unless it was union made and bore the Carpenters Union label was held by the Board to violate section 8(e), and the Union did not seek judicial review of that determination.

*   *   *

A union cannot, however, accomplish unlawful secondary objectives through the guise of a union standards clause. If a clause does not serve to protect the integrity of the unit wage scale, but instead seeks to affect wages of other employer's employees, it loses its primary character and becomes unlawfully secondary.

*   *   *

VI.   FREE SPEECH, PUBLICITY, AND CONSUMER PICKETING

Restrictions on secondary activity by unions have raised fundamental questions concerning possible abridgement of constitutionally protected free speech. To illustrate, a newspaper advertisement publicizing the fact that a union has a labor dispute with a particular employer, designated as "unfair," presumably would represent a form of speech protected by the First Amendment, though the effect might be to induce some persons to cease doing business with the unfair employer. It has been argued that union appeals to the public by handbilling or picketing near the premises of a neutral employer, which may have a similar effect, should be treated as similarly protected forms of publicity.

A.   Thornhill and the Unlawful Purpose Qualification

Support for this argument comes from the landmark case of Thornhill v. Alabama, in which the Supreme Court stated: "[T]he dissemination of information concerning the facts of a labor dispute must be regarded as within that area of free discussion that is guaranteed by the Constitution." Consequently, a broad statutory prohibition on all forms of picketing was unconstitutional. Publicizing the facts of a labor dispute could not be prohibited simply because it might persuade some persons "to refrain from entering into advantageous relations with the business establishment which is the scene of the dispute," since "[e]very expression of opinion on matters that are important has the potentiality of inducing action."

Despite these generalizations (which happened to relate to primary rather than secondary picketing), it was later recognized that picketing, even where peaceful, may amount to something more than just free speech and is therefore not completely beyond legislative control. It is now clear that peaceful picketing may constitutionally be restrained where it has an unlawful purpose.

Picketing aimed at employees of neutrals, generally speaking, is deemed to have an unlawful objective that removes it from protection of the First Amendment (as well as from the free speech provisions of section 8(c) of the Act). Thus, proscription of peaceful secondary picketing by a solitary union representative carrying a placard stating "This job unfair" is not an unconstitutional abridgement of free speech because the placard is considered tantamount to a direction to strike. Since picketing of this sort is a common form of secondary activity, any other conclusion would have narrowly limited the effect of section 8(b)(4).

B. The Publicity Proviso

The free speech problem is much more acute, however, where picketing takes place at a retail outlet for the struck employer's product and is ostensibly designed to enlist support of consumers. Questions about this type of secondary activity grew out of the 1959 amendments to this section.

* * *

C. [There is a special provision which permits "publicity other than picketing" aimed at consumers]

To properly apply the proviso, picketing must be distinguished from other types of publicity, since it exempts only publicity *other than picketing*. The term "picketing" has rather "vague contours" and is not defined in the act. Traditionally, it involves patrolling by one or more persons bearing a placard or banner inscribed with a relatively brief union message concerning a dispute with some employer. Regardless of the precise wording, the signal conveyed to loyal union supporters, and other informed observers, is simply "Do not enter!" The effect has been decribed as a "psychological embargo" around the picketed premises. It is this tacit proscriptive effect, apart from the merits of any message explicitly communicated, that has caused picketing to be considered something more than the mere expression of ideas. Thus, a general test of whether activity constitutes publicity other than picketing might be whether, in the light of all the circumstances, it can realistically be viewed as purely dissemination of information, or whether the conduct of union representatives at the secondary site has somehow created the type of psychological barrier to entry associated with the traditional picket line. In other words, the test of picketing for purposes of the publicity proviso to section 8(b)(4) should focus on the same factors that have been invoked to distinguish protected free speech from activity that may constitutionally be proscribed.

On the basis of this test, advertisements by means of newspapers, radio, television, or skywriting obviously would be publicity other than picketing. A sound truck probably would fall in the same category. Generally, handbilling, or distribution of leaflets, which Senator Kennedy used to illustate the proviso and which was involved in *Servette*, would also come within the proviso (assuming it is truthful and does not cause a work stoppage). Although union representatives may be physically present, the coercive signal is lacking; people are accustomed to ignore or discard handbills with impunity; any response depends almost entirely on intellectual persuasion. But handbilling involving patrolling by numerous persons in close formation near an entrance may contain an element of physical restraint sufficient to take it out of the proviso. In such circumstances, the effect is indistinguishable from picketing. On the other hand, patrolling with placards was not considered picketing for purposes of the proviso where it did not involve "confrontation in some form" between union members and employees, customers or suppliers trying to enter the secondary employer's premises. A union sign standing unattended near a secondary site could hardly be considered picketing, but decisions under section 8(b)(7) indicate that if a sign is under surveillance by union representatives visible in nearby cars, the combination amounts to picketing.

*   *   *

The variety of available communication media and the ingenuity of union representatives preclude any mechanical test of publicity other than picketing. But even where a union's secondary activity plainly does constitute publicity *by means of picketing* and is therefore unprotected by the proviso, it is not necessarily within the prohibition of Section 8(b)(4)(B).

D. Consumer Picketing and the Tree Fruits Doctrine

In N.L.R.B. v. Fruit & Vegetable Packers & Warehousemen Local 760 (Tree Fruits), the Supreme Court distinguished two types of peaceful consumer picketing at secondary sites: (1) picketing to persuade customers of the secondary employer *not to trade with him at all* in order to force him to cease dealing with, or put pressure on, the primary employer, and (2) picketing to persuade customers of the secondary employer *not to buy the product* of the primary employer.

The picketing in *Tree Fruits* was of the second type, which the Court held was not proscribed by the 1959 amendments to Section 8(b)(4). The picketing there was directed only at customers of Safeway supermarkets in Seattle, as evidenced by the pickets' arrival only after the stores opened for business and departure before they closed, their location in front of customer entrances, and the wording of the picket signs. These placards only asked consumers not to buy Washington State apples, explaining that the 1960 crop was packed by 26 firms with which the union had a labor dispute. The placards expressly stated this was not a strike against any store or market, and pickets were forbidden to request customers not to patronize the store. No employees stopped work.

In these circumstances, the Court concluded that the union did not "threaten, coerce, or restrain" the employer within the meaning of clause (ii), stating:

> When consumer picketing is employed only to persuade customers not to buy the struck product, the union's appeal is closely confined to the primary dispute. The site of the appeal is expanded to include the premises of the secondary employer, but if the appeal succeeds, the secondary employer's purchases from the struck firms are decreased only because the public has diminished its purchases of the struck product. On the other hand, when consumer picketing is employed to persuade customers not to trade at all with the secondary employer, the latter stops buying the

struck product, not because of a falling demand, but in response to pressure designed to inflict injury on his business generally. In such case, the union does more than merely follow the struck product; it creates a separate dispute with the secondary employer.

* * *

Tree Fruits has established the general rule that picketing at a secondary site, which only asks customers to refrain from buying the product of a primary employer, does not violate section 8(b)(4)(ii)(B). Retailers—no matter how neutral—have no immunity against involvement to this extent.

VII. REMEDIES

Because of the strong public policy of protecting neutrals against involvement in labor disputes not their own, the Act provides two unusual remedies for violations of section 8(b)(4)(A) and (B), only one of which is available for violations of section 8(e).

A. Injunctions

Under section 10(*l*), preliminary investigation by the Board of an unfair labor practice charge under any of these sections must be made "forthwith" and given priority over all other cases, except cases of like character in the office handling the charge. Then, if the regional attorney finds reasonable cause to believe that the charge is true and that a complaint should issue, he *must* petition the federal district court for appropriate injunctive relief pending final adjudication by the Board. Such relief is not sought if it appears that the union has voluntarily ceased engaging in the conduct and a resumption is not threatened.

The district court has jurisdiction to grant such injunctive relief or temporary restraining order as it deems just and proper. The court's role is not to determine whether or not there has in fact been a statutory violation, but only whether the Board has reasonable cause to believe that a violation is being committed.

* * *

Disobedience of a Board order for which enforcement has been granted by a United States Court of Appeals, of course, exposes the union to citation for civil contempt.

B. Damages

Enforcement of a Board cease and desist order for the future does not remedy any harm already caused by a union's secondary activity. Therefore, section 303 of the Act permits anyone injured in his business or property by reason of any violation of section 8(b)(4)—but not section 8(e)—to sue the union to recover damages sustained by him and the cost of suit. The action may be brought in any federal district court, or in any other court having jurisdiction of the parties, but federal law will apply in all cases.

One purpose of this damage remedy was to provide an additional deterrent to secondary boycotts. Although secondary boycotts still flourish, the potential liability for damage claims under section 303 is undoubtedly more effective in this regard than the mere threat of an order to cease activity after it may have had the desired effect. In practice, however, damage actions are probably filed most often to induce a union to settle immediately a concurrently filed charge and bring a halt to the boycott activity, after which the lawsuit may be dismissed.

Violation of section 8(b)(4) is a prerequisite to the recovery of damages under section 303, and the same tests of illegality apply in both contexts. It is not necessary, however, that there be an advance determination by the Board that such an unfair labor practice has been committed, nor even that any charge be filed. The two remedies are completely independent of each other.

N.L.R.B. v. RETAIL STORE EMPLOYEES

Supreme Court of the United States, 1979.
447 U.S. 607, 100 S.Ct. 2372, 65 L.Ed.2d 377.

MR. JUSTICE POWELL delivered the opinion of the Court.

The question is whether § 8(b)(4)(ii)(B) of the National Labor Relations Act, 29 U.S.C. § 158(b)(4)(ii)(B), forbids secondary picketing against a struck product when such picketing predictably encourages consumers to boycott a neutral party's business.

I

Safeco Title Insurance Co. underwrites real estate title insurance in the State of Washington. It maintains close business relationships with five local title companies. The companies search land titles, perform escrow services, and sell title insurance. Over 90% of their gross incomes derives from the sale of Safeco insurance. Safeco has substantial stockholdings in each title company, and at least one Safeco officer serves on each company's board of directors. Safeco, however, has no control over the companies' daily operations. It does not direct their personnel policies, and it never exchanges employees with them.

Local 1001 of the Retail Store Employees Union became the certified bargaining representative for certain Safeco employees in 1974. When contract negotiations between Safeco and the Union reached an impasse, the employees went on strike. The Union did not confine picketing to Safeco's office in Seattle. The Union also picketed each of the five local title companies. The pickets carried signs declaring that Safeco had no contract with the Union,[2] and they distributed

---

2. The picket signs read:

"SAFECO NONUNION

DOES NOT EMPLOY MEMBERS OF OR HAVE CONTRACT WITH RETAIL STORE EMPLOYEES LOCAL 1001."

handbills asking consumers to support the strike by canceling their Safeco policies.[3]

Safeco and one of the title companies filed complaints with the National Labor Relations Board. They charged that the Union had engaged in an unfair labor practice by picketing in order to promote a secondary boycott against the title companies. The Board agreed. It found the title companies to be neutral in the dispute between Safeco and the Union. The Board then concluded that the Union's picketing violated § 8(b)(4)(ii)(B) of the National Labor Relations Act. The Union had directed its appeal against Safeco insurance policies. But since the sale of those policies accounted for substantially all of the title companies' business, the Board found that the Union's action was "reasonably calculated to induce customers not to patronize the neutral parties at all." The Board therefore rejected the Union's reliance upon NLRB v. Fruit Packers, 377 U.S. 58, 84 S.Ct. 1063, 12 L.Ed.2d 129 (1964) (*Tree Fruits*), which held that § 8(b)(4)(ii)(B) allows secondary picketing against a struck product. It ordered the Union to cease picketing and to take limited corrective action.

The United States Court of Appeals for the District of Columbia Circuit set aside the Board's order. The court agreed that the title companies were neutral parties entitled to the benefit of § 8(b)(4)(ii) (B). It held, however, that *Tree Fruits* leaves neutrals susceptible to whatever consequences may flow from secondary picketing against the consumption of products produced by an employer involved in a labor dispute. Even when product picketing predictably encourages consumers to boycott a neutral altogether, the court concluded, § 8(b) (4)(ii)(B) provides no protection.

We granted a writ of certiorari to consider whether the Court of Appeals correctly understood § 8(b)(4)(ii)(B) as interpreted in *Tree Fruits*. Having concluded that the Court of Appeals misapplied the statute, we now reverse and remand for enforcement of the Board's order.

II

Section 8(b)(4)(ii)(B) of the National Labor Relations Act makes it "an unfair labor practice for a labor organization   *   *   *   to threaten, coerce, or restrain" a person not party to a labor dispute "where   *   *   *   an object thereof is   *   *   *   forcing or requiring [him] to cease using, selling, handling, transporting, or otherwise dealing in the products of any other producer   *   *   *   or to cease doing business with any other person.   *   *   *"

In *Tree Fruits*, the Court held that § 8(b)(4)(ii)(B) does not prohibit all peaceful picketing at secondary sites. There, a union striking

---

3. The distribution of handbills has not been an issue in this case. Section 8(b)(4) of the National Labor Relations Act does not prohibit "publicity, other than picketing, for the purpose of truthfully advising the public   *   *   *   that a product or products are produced by an employer with whom the labor organization has a primary dispute and are distributed by another employer.   *   *   *" 61 Stat. 141, as amended, 73 Stat. 543, 29 U.S.C. § 158(b)(4).

certain Washington fruit packers picketed large supermarkets in order to persuade consumers not to buy Washington apples.   Concerned that a broad ban against such picketing might run afoul of the First Amendment, the Court found the statute directed to an " 'isolated evil.' "   The evil was use of secondary picketing "to persuade the customers of the secondary employer to cease trading with him in order to force him to cease dealing with, or to put pressure upon, the primary employer."   Congress intended to protect secondary parties from pressures that might embroil them in the labor disputes of others, but not to shield them from business losses caused by a campaign that successfully persuades consumers "to boycott the primary employer's goods."   Thus, the Court drew a distinction between picketing "to shut off all trade with the secondary employer unless he aids the union in its dispute with the primary employer" and picketing that "only persuades his customers not to buy the struck product."   The picketing in that case, which "merely follow[ed] the struck product," did not " 'threaten, coerce, or restrain' " the secondary party within the meaning of § 8(b)(4)(ii)(B).

Although *Tree Fruits* suggested that secondary picketing against a struck product and secondary picketing against a neutral party were "poles apart," id., at 70, the courts soon discovered that product picketing could have the same effect as an illegal secondary boycott. In Hoffman ex rel. NLRB v. Cement Masons Local 337, for example, a union embroiled with a general contractor picketed the housing subdivision that he had constructed for a real estate developer.   Pickets sought to persuade prospective purchasers not to buy the contractor's houses.   The picketing was held illegal because purchasers "could reasonably expect that they were being asked not to transact any business whatsoever" with the neutral developer.   468 F.2d, at 1192.   "[W]hen a union's interest in picketing a primary employer at a 'one product' site [directly conflicts] with the need to protect * * * neutral employers from the labor disputes of others," Congress has determined that the neutrals' interests should prevail.   Id., at 1191.[7]

Cement Masons highlights the critical difference between the picketing in this case and the picketing at issue in *Tree Fruits*.   The product picketed in *Tree Fruits* was but one item among the many that made up the retailer's trade.   If the appeal against such a product succeeds, the Court observed, it simply induces the neutral retailer to reduce his orders for the product or "to drop the item as a poor seller."   The decline in sales attributable to consumer rejection of the struck product puts pressure upon the primary employer, and the marginal injury to the neutral retailer is purely incidental to the product boycott.   The neutral therefore has little reason to become in-

---

7.   The so-called merged product cases also involve situations where an attempt to follow the struck product inevitably encourages an illegal boycott of the neutral party.   See K & K Construction Co. v. NLRB, 592 F.2d 1228, 1231–1234 (CA3 1979); American Bread Co. v. NLRB, 411 F.2d 147, 154–155 (CA6 1969); Honolulu Typographical Union No. 37 v. NLRB, 131 U.S.App.D.C. 1, 4–5, 401 F.2d 952, 954–955 (1968); Note, Consumer Picketing and the Single-Product Secondary Employer, 47 U.Chi.L.Rev. 112, 132–136 (1979).

volved in the labor dispute. In this case, on the other hand, the title companies sell only the primary employer's product and perform the services associated with it. Secondary picketing against consumption of the primary product leaves responsive consumers no realistic option other than to boycott the title companies altogether. If the appeal succeeds, each company "stops buying the struck product, not because of a falling demand, but in response to pressure designed to inflict injury on [its] business generally." Thus, "the union does more than merely follow the struck product; it creates a separate dispute with the secondary employer." Such an expansion of labor discord was one of the evils that Congress intended § 8(b)(4)(ii)(B) to prevent.

As long as secondary picketing only discourages consumption of a struck product, incidental injury to the neutral is a natural consequence of an effective primary boycott. But the Union's secondary appeal against the central product sold by the title companies in this case is "reasonably calculated to induce customers not to patronize the neutral parties at all." The resulting injury to their businesses is distinctly different from the injury that the Court considered in *Tree Fruits*. Product picketing that reasonably can be expected to threaten neutral parties with ruin or substantial loss simply does not square with the language or the purpose of § 8(b)(4)(ii)(B).[10] Since successful secondary picketing would put the title companies to a choice between their survival and the severance of their ties with Safeco, the picketing plainly violates the statutory ban on the coercion of neutrals with the object of "forcing or requiring [them] to cease   *   *   *   dealing in the [primary] produc[t]   *   *   *   or to cease doing business with" the primary employer. § 8(b)(4)(ii)(B); see *Tree Fruits*, 377 U.S., at 68, 84 S.Ct., at 1069.[11]

---

10. Representative Griffin, a sponsor of the Landrum-Griffin amendments that brought § 8(b)(4)(ii)(B) into law, emphasized to the Congress that the statute would outlaw secondary picketing likely to coerce the neutral party. "If the purpose of the picketing," he said, "is to coerce or to restrain the employer of that second establishment, to get him not to do business with the manufacturer—then such a boycott could be stopped." 105 Cong.Rec. 15673 (1959), reprinted in 2 National Labor Relations Board, Legislative History of the Labor-Management Reporting and Disclosure Act of 1959, p. 1615 (1959).

Senator McClellan, who offered a bill quite similar to the statute actually adopted, noted that secondary picketing is particularly likely to coerce neutrals who have based their businesses upon one manufacturer's products. He pointed out:

"[W]e have cases of merchants who for 20 years, 10 years, or for a long period of time, may have been handling a particular brand of product. A merchant may have built his business around the product, such as the John Deere plows or some kind of machinery from some other company. The merchant may have built up his trade entirely on that product." 105 Cong.Rec. 6667 (1959), reprinted in 2 Legislative History, supra, at 1194.

11. The picketing in *Tree Fruits* and the picketing in this case are relatively extreme examples of the spectrum of conduct that the Board and the courts will encounter in complaints charging violations of § 8(b)(4)(ii)(B). If secondary picketing were directed against a product representing a major portion of a neutral's business, but significantly less than that represented by a single dominant product, neither *Tree Fruits* nor today's decision necessarily would control. The critical question would be whether, by encouraging customers to reject the struck product, the secondary appeal is reasonably likely to threaten the neutral party with ruin or substantial loss. Resolution

III

The Court of Appeals suggested that application of § 8(b)(4)(ii)(B) to the picketing in this case might violate the First Amendment. We think not. Although the Court recognized in *Tree Fruits* that the Constitution might not permit "a broad ban against peaceful picketing," the Court left no doubt that Congress may prohibit secondary picketing calculated "to persuade the customers of the secondary employer to cease trading with him in order to force him to cease dealing with, or to put pressure upon, the primary employer." Such picketing spreads labor discord by coercing a neutral party to join the fray. In Electrical Workers v. NLRB, 341 U.S. 694, 705, 71 S.Ct. 954, 960, 95 L.Ed.2d 1299 (1951), this Court expressly held that a prohibition on "picketing in furtherance of [such] unlawful objectives" did not offend the First Amendment. We perceive no reason to depart from that well-established understanding. As applied to picketing that predictably encourages consumers to boycott a secondary business, § 8(b)(4)(ii)(B) imposes no impermissible restrictions upon constitutionally protected speech.

Accordingly, the judgment of the Court of Appeals is reversed, and the case is remanded with directions to enforce the National Labor Relations Board's order.

So ordered.

HOWARD LESNICK, THE GRAVAMEN OF THE SECONDARY BOYCOTT *

The rationale I have proposed tests the primary or secondary character of an appeal to secondary employees by asking whether the appeal seeks to subject the secondary employer to loss of the services of his employees broader than that which would flow from the unavailability of the services of primary employees were the strike to succeed in inducing them to quit work. In addition, because of considerations similar to those underlying the "struck work" doctrine, it must be asked whether the employment of the secondary employer enables the primary to avoid the impact of the loss of services of his own employees. Under this approach:

(1) Picketing at a primary site is primary and lawful, regardless of its appeal to secondary employees not to cross the picket line, unless:

(a) the work done by the secondary employees at the site is unrelated to the operations of the primary, in the sense that disruption of those operations by a successful strike against the primary would not cause it to suspend business with the secondary;

of the question in each case will be entrusted to the Board's expertise.

* Howard Lesnick, "The Gravamen of the Secondary Boycott," 62 Columbia Law Review 1363 (1962); © 1962 by the Directors of the Columbia Law Review Association, Inc. Reprinted by permission of the Columbia Law Review and Fred B. Rothman & Co.

(b) the work done by the secondary employees can be carried on without necessitating curtailment of the primary's operations; and

(c) (if the Supreme Court insists) the secondary employees enter the premises through a separate gate.

(2) Picketing at a secondary site is secondary and unlawful if it appeals to secondary employees not to cross the picket line or to perform services, unless they are performing work that can not be carried on:

(a) without the presence of primary employees at the secondary site; or

(b) without necessitating curtailment of the primary's operations.

(3) Picketing at a secondary site contains an appeal to secondary employees unless:

(a) the picketing takes place only at times when primary employees are present;

(b) the picketing is carried on as close to those employees as is reasonably possible;

(c) the pickets, by their signs and conduct, make clear that the primary employer is the offending employer, and the secondary is not;

(d) there are no overt attempts to deter secondary employees from entering the premises or performing services; and

(e) no secondary employees actually refuse to enter the premises or perform services.

QUESTIONS

1. A primary strike in a major industry will frequently have significant secondary effect, possibly shutting down both suppliers and customers. These effects add to the pressures for settlement, which may be part of the union design for achieving settlement. In light of this, does it make any sense to prohibit a union which has a dispute with one sub-contractor from attempting to shut down the entire job?

2. Can you imagine any reason for which a union might realistically want to apply pressure against an employer other than its own, where it would not have a legal way of doing so?

F. WILDCAT STRIKES: ENFORCING
THE NO–STRIKE CLAUSE

Wildcat strikes are basically defined as work stoppages not authorized by the union. They can occur when the collective bargaining contract has expired. However, in the common parlance of labor relations, a wildcat strike means a strike during the term of a contract that contains a no-strike clause. A wildcat strike, as such, violates the contract and is the appropriate subject for a lawsuit under § 301

of the LMRA for damages, discipline, in some cases unfair labor practice changes, and most importantly, injunctive relief. As the following case points out, with respect to injunctive relief, the employer
must prove that the work stoppage is related to a grievable issue and
would ordinarily be the subject of grievance/arbitration.

BOYS MARKETS, INC. v. RETAIL CLERKS
UNION, LOCAL 770

Supreme Court of the United States, 1970.
398 U.S. 235, 90 S.Ct. 1583, 26 L.Ed.2d 199.

MR. JUSTICE BRENNAN delivered the opinion of the Court.

In this case we re-examine the holding of Sinclair Refining Co. v.
Atkinson, 370 U.S. 195, 82 S.Ct. 1328, 8 L.Ed.2d 440 (1962), that the
anti-injunction provisions of the Norris-LaGuardia Act preclude a federal district court from enjoining a strike in breach of a no-strike obligation under a collective-bargaining agreement, even though that
agreement contains provisions, enforceable under § 301(a) of the Labor Management Relations Act, 1947, for binding arbitration of the
grievance dispute concerning which the strike was called. The Court
of Appeals for the Ninth Circuit, considering itself bound by *Sinclair*, reversed the grant by the District Court for the Central District of California of petitioner's prayer for injunctive relief. We
granted certiorari. Having concluded that *Sinclair* was erroneously
decided and that subsequent events have undermined its continuing
validity, we overrule that decision and reverse the judgment of the
Court of Appeals.

I

In February 1969, at the time of the incidents that produced this
litigation, petitioner and respondent were parties to a collective-bargaining agreement which provided, inter alia, that all controversies
concerning its interpretation or application should be resolved by adjustment and arbitration procedures set forth therein and that, during the life of the contract, there should be "no cessation or stoppage
of work, lock-out, picketing or boycotts * * * ." The dispute
arose when petitioner's frozen foods supervisor and certain members
of his crew who were not members of the bargaining unit began to
rearrange merchandise in the frozen food cases of one of petitioner's
supermarkets. A union representative insisted that the food cases be
stripped of all merchandise and be restocked by union personnel.
When petitioner did not accede to the union's demand, a strike was
called and the union began to picket petitioner's establishment.
Thereupon petitioner demanded that the union cease the work stoppage and picketing and sought to invoke the grievance and arbitration procedures specified in the contract.

The following day, since the strike had not been terminated, petitioner filed a complaint in California Superior Court seeking a temporary restraining order, a preliminary and permanent injunction, and

specific performance of the contractual arbitration provision. The state court issued a temporary restraining order forbidding continuation of the strike and also an order to show cause why a preliminary injunction should not be granted. Shortly thereafter, the union removed the case to the Federal District Court and there made a motion to quash the state court's temporary restraining order. In opposition, petitioner moved for an order compelling arbitration and enjoining continuation of the strike. Concluding that the dispute was subject to arbitration under the collective-bargaining agreement and that the strike was in violation of the contract, the District Court ordered the parties to arbitrate the underlying dispute and simultaneously enjoined the strike, all picketing in the vicinity of petitioner's supermarket, and any attempts by the union to induce the employees to strike or to refuse to perform their services.

* * *

As we have previously indicated, a no-strike obligation, express or implied, is the *quid pro quo* for an undertaking by the employer to submit grievance disputes to the process of arbitration. Any incentive for employers to enter into such an arrangement is necessarily dissipated if the principal and most expeditious method by which the no-strike obligation can be enforced is eliminated. While it is of course true, as respondent contends, that other avenues of redress, such as an action for damages, would remain open to an aggrieved employer, an award of damages after a dispute has been settled is no substitute for an immediate halt to an illegal strike. Furthermore, an action for damages prosecuted during or after a labor dispute would only tend to aggravate industrial strife and delay an early resolution of the difficulties between employer and union.

* * *

Even if management is not encouraged by the unavailability of the injunction remedy to resist arbitration agreements, the fact remains that the effectiveness of such agreements would be greatly reduced if injunctive relief were withheld. Indeed, the very purpose of arbitration procedures is to provide a mechanism for the expeditious settlement of industrial disputes without resort to strikes, lockouts, or other self-help measures. This basic purpose is obviously largely undercut if there is no immediate, effective remedy for those very tactics that arbitration is designed to obviate.

* * *

The literal terms of § 4 of the Norris-LaGuardia Act must be accommodated to the subsequently enacted provisions of § 301(a) of the Labor Management Relations Act and the purposes of arbitration. Statutory interpretation requires more than concentration upon isolated words; rather, consideration must be given to the total corpus of pertinent law and the policies that inspired ostensibly inconsistent provisions.

The Norris-LaGuardia Act was responsive to a situation totally different from that which exists today. In the early part of this century, the federal courts generally were regarded as allies of management in its attempt to prevent the organization and strengthening of labor unions; and in this industrial struggle the injunction became a potent weapon that was wielded against the activities of labor groups. The result was a large number of sweeping decrees, often issued *ex parte*, drawn on an *ad hoc* basis without regard to any systematic elaboration of national labor policy.

In 1932 Congress attempted to bring some order out of the industrial chaos that had developed and to correct the abuses that had resulted from the interjection of the federal judiciary into union-management disputes on the behalf of management. Congress, therefore, determined initially to limit severely the power of the federal courts to issue injunctions "in any case involving or growing out of any labor dispute * * *." § 4. Even as initially enacted, however, the prohibition against federal injunctions was by no means absolute. Shortly thereafter Congress passed the Wagner Act, designed to curb various management activities that tended to discourage employee participation in collective action.

As labor organizations grew in strength and developed toward maturity, congressional emphasis shifted from protection of the nascent labor movement to the encouragement of collective bargaining and to administrative techniques for the peaceful resolution of industrial disputes. This shift in emphasis was accomplished, however, without extensive revision of many of the older enactments, including the anti-injunction section of the Norris-LaGuardia Act. Thus it became the task of the courts to accommodate, to reconcile the older statutes with the more recent ones.

A leading example of this accommodation process is Brotherhood of Railroad Trainmen v. Chicago River & Ind. R. Co., 353 U.S. 30, 77 S.Ct. 635, 1 L.Ed.2d 622 (1957). There we were confronted with a peaceful strike which violated the statutory duty to arbitrate imposed by the Railway Labor Act. The Court concluded that a strike in violation of a statutory arbitration duty was not the type of situation to which the Norris-LaGuardia Act was responsive, that an important federal policy was involved in the peaceful settlement of disputes through the statutorily mandated arbitration procedure, that this important policy was imperiled if equitable remedies were not available to implement it, and hence that Norris-LaGuardia's policy of nonintervention by the federal courts should yield to the overriding interest in the successful implementation of the arbitration process.

The principles elaborated in *Chicago River* are equally applicable to the present case. To be sure, *Chicago River* involved arbitration procedures established by statute. However, we have frequently noted, in such cases as *Lincoln Mills*, the *Steelworkers Trilogy*, and *Lucas Flour*, the importance that Congress has attached generally to the voluntary settlement of labor disputes without resort to self-help and more particularly to arbitration as a means to this end. Indeed, it has been stated that *Lincoln Mills*, in its exposition of § 301(a), "went a long way towards making arbitration the central institution in the administration of collective bargaining contracts."

The *Sinclair* decision, however, seriously undermined the effectiveness of the arbitration technique as a method peacefully to resolve industrial disputes without resort to strikes, lockouts, and similar devices. Clearly employers will be wary of assuming obligations to arbitrate specifically enforceable against them when no similarly efficacious remedy is available to enforce the concomitant undertaking of the union to refrain from striking. On the other hand, the central purpose of the Norris-LaGuardia Act to foster the growth and viability of labor organizations is hardly retarded—if anything, this goal is advanced—by a remedial device that merely enforces the obligation that the union freely undertook under a specifically enforceable agreement to submit disputes to arbitration. We conclude, therefore, that the unavailability of equitable relief in the arbitration context presents a serious impediment to the congressional policy favoring the voluntary establishment of a mechanism for the peaceful resolution of labor disputes, that the core purpose of the Norris-LaGuardia Act is not sacrificed by the limited use of equitable remedies to further this important policy, and consequently that the Norris-LaGuardia Act does not bar the granting of injunctive relief in the circumstances of the instant case.

V

Our holding in the present case is a narrow one. We do not undermine the vitality of the Norris-LaGuardia Act. We deal only with the situation in which a collective-bargaining contract contains a mandatory grievance adjustment or arbitration procedure. Nor does it follow from what we have said that injunctive relief is appropriate as a matter of course in every case of a strike over an arbitrable grievance. The dissenting opinion in *Sinclair* suggested the following principles for the guidance of the district courts in determining whether to grant injunctive relief—principles that we now adopt:

"A District Court entertaining an action under § 301 may not grant injunctive relief against concerted activity unless and until it decides that the case is one in which an injunction would be appropriate despite the Norris-LaGuardia Act. When a strike is sought to be enjoined because it is over a grievance which both parties are contractually bound to arbitrate, the District Court may issue no injunctive order until it first holds that the contract *does* have that effect; and the employer should be ordered to arbitrate, as a condition of his obtaining an injunction against the strike. Beyond this, the District Court must, of course, consider whether issuance of an injunction would be warranted under ordinary principles of equity—whether breaches are occurring and will continue, or have been threatened and will be committed; whether they have caused or will cause irreparable injury to the employer; and whether the employer will suffer more from the denial of an injunction than will the union from its issuance." 370 U.S., at 228. (Emphasis in original.)

In the present case there is no dispute that the grievance in question was subject to adjustment and arbitration under the collective-bargaining agreement and that the petitioner was ready to proceed with arbitration at the time an injunction against the strike was sought and obtained. The District Court also concluded that, by reason of respondent's violations of its no-strike obligation, petitioner "has suffered irreparable injury and will continue to suffer irreparable injury." Since we now overrule *Sinclair*, the holding of the Court of Appeals in reliance on *Sinclair* must be reversed. Accordingly, we reverse the judgment of the Court of Appeals and remand the case with directions to enter a judgment affirming the order of the District Court.

It is so ordered.

G. STRIKES AND PICKETING AS ORGANIZATIONAL TECHNIQUES

The 1959 amendments to the NLRA limited the use of picketing for organizational purposes. Testimony before the senate indicated that some unions, particularly the teamsters, engaged in "top down" organizing. Without winning the allegiance of employees the union would attempt to get the employer to sign a collective bargaining agreement by picketing or threatening to picket his premise. An employer in a precarious economic position, or one dependent upon pick up and deliveries is particularly vulnerable to such a threat. He might either sign a contract without checking with his employees or else attempt to convince them to sign up for the good of the enterprise. In a series of cases decided before 1959, the Supreme Court had made clear that whatever constitutional protection picketing enjoyed as a form of free speech did not pertain to top down picketing. But the process of framing statutory language to prevent top down organizing proved to be extremely delicate. For one thing, it was difficult to frame a provision which was limited to such picketing. Picketing by employees to enlist the support of fellow workers was considered a legitimate organizational device. Before passage of the Wagner Act strikes were frequently called during organizing campaigns to protest refusals to recognize the unions or other unfair employer tactics. Given this historical use of the strike weapon during organizational drives it was inevitable that the union movement would strongly resist efforts to prohibit organizational strikes. A bitter debate ensued, and the resulting provision, 8(b)(7), reflected the fact that both sides had to compromise repeatedly. Section 8(b)(7)(c), in particular, is riddled with provisos and exceptions to provisos, which have made it extremely difficult to interpret.

Section 8(b)(7) outlaws picketing, or threats of picketing, where "an object thereof is" forcing an employer to recognize or bargain—or forcing or requiring the employees of an employer to—select such labor organization. If another union is lawfully recognized, or if a valid election was held during the previous year the prohibition against picketing for the stated objective is absolute. Difficult questions may arise as to whether the union is in fact picketing, and if so, whether it is doing so to force recognition. Although these problems can be troublesome, the Board has been able to cope with them in the relatively few cases which have arisen. Today unions rarely picket for recognition when another union is recognized or after losing an election.

However, enforcement of the statute becomes far more complex if no union is recognized or if an election has not recently been held. Under § 8(b)(7)(c), which applies in such circumstances, unions are permitted to engage in recognitional picketing for up to 30 days. If a petition for election is filed the union may continue to picket although an expedited representative election may then be held if the employer seeks one. The union may block the expedited election, however, by filing unfair labor practice charges. Until the charges are disposed of, the Board will not hold an election and the union can continue to picket. If the charges are found meritorious this might take a year or more. Under subsection C, even if the union is picketing for the proscribed objective, its picketing is lawful if its picket signs truthfully advise the public that the employer does not "employ members of, or have a contract with," the union. This exception, however, does not apply if the picketing has a substantial impact on pickups and deliveries. This brief outline should indicate that a carefully counseled union has many ways to avoid the reach of § 8(b)(7)(c). The intricacies of Section 8(b)(7)(c) could force a substantial hardship to enforcement of the statute if recognitional picketing was more common. However, the use of picketing for these purposes is rare. Most unions feel that picketing before obtaining recognition is likely to backfire, costing them good will and giving credence to the employer's arguments that unions inevitably cause strikes, and that they are unconcerned about the wishes of employees. Most unions do not engage in top-down organizing.

QUESTION

Is there any reason why unions should not be able to use the strike as an organizational technique?

H. UNIONS AND ANTI–TRUST

There is no more complicated question in labor law than the relation between unions and anti-trust. The following materials contain only the barest outline of the issues presented. The key question which the courts have not yet answered is the extent to which union activity should be exempt from the normal rules of anti-trust law.

MILTON HANDLER, LABOR AND ANTITRUST:
A BIT OF HISTORY *

The application—or, perhaps, I should say misapplication—of the restraint of trade concept to labor union activities falls roughly into five chronological periods.

First is the antecedent common law. As late as 1835 the courts in my state held that an agreement among workers to raise their wages constituted a criminal conspiracy. The court, in People v. Fisher, proceeding upon the premise that wages comprised a material portion of the value of manufactured articles, held that the demands of journeymen shoemakers which enhanced the price of boots was an act injurious to trade. The court was of the view that it is in the best interests of society that the price of labor be determined by the unfettered force of competition. It thus put concerted action to fix wage rates on the same footing as price fixing. Accordingly, strikes and the other traditional methods of implementing labor's demands were held *per se* unlawful.

From the purely conceptual point of view, it is not too difficult to understand why unionization, collective bargaining and strikes should have been deemed common law restraints. Analytically, a union is a common sales agency marketing the services of its members at a uniform price. Instinct in the very formation of a labor union is the elimination of price competition by workingmen in the sale of their labor to their employer. A strike, after all, is a species of boycott. It is a concerted refusal to deal. Picketing, no matter how peaceful, involves the inducement of third parties not to do business with the employer. And the boycott itself, whether it consists of a direct refusal of the strikers to patronize their employer or the persuasion of other unions or the public at large to withhold patronage, is no different in principle from the concerted refusals to deal which in a business context have been unqualifiedly interdicted.

In the initial enforcement of the Sherman Act—which brings us to the second period—it is noteworthy that more actions were instituted against labor than against capital combinations. Antitrust was employed to prevent organizational as well as economic strikes, picketing and boycotts—typically when these weapons were accompanied by violence, but under a rationale condemning even peaceful concerted acts whose effect was to interfere with the flow of interstate commerce. It was in this era that the evil of the labor injunction came into being and, significantly, it was the government, and not private parties, who invoked the injunction to frustrate the normal processes of unionization and collective bargaining.

A judicial retreat from an unqualified application of antitrust to labor was inevitable. This occurred when it became apparent that if every non-peaceful strike which interfered with interstate commerce

* Milton Handler, "Labor And Antitrust: A Bit Of History," 40 Antitrust Journal 233 (1971); © 1971 by the Antitrust Journal. Reprinted by permission.

were to be regarded as a Sherman Act infraction, that law would be converted into a police measure saddling the federal government and the federal judiciary with the ultimate responsibility of protecting life and property from acts of violence in the course of labor disputes.

Hence, in the third period, the Court developed a new rubric. Proceeding on what is now an antiquated and rejected concept of interstate commerce, in which manufacture was distinguished from the movement of goods across state lines, the Court limited the jurisdiction of antitrust over non-peaceful labor activities to cases where the purpose of the strike was to restrain and directly burden interstate commerce, as distinguished from interfering with the process of manufacture. Absent such intent, there was no liability no matter how pervasive might be the interference with commerce or how egregious and indefensible might be the conduct of the strikers. Nothing, of course, is more slippery than the element of intent, particularly since men's motives are invariably mixed. Accordingly, the courts under this approach had an accordion-like instrument with which to include or exclude labor union activities from antitrust's strictures, dependent upon the philosophic outlook of the individual judge.

The fourth period endowed unions with the equivalent of a statutory exemption where their activities did not affect market prices or restrain business competition or where they did not participate with management in arrangements violative of antitrust's commands. [It] did provide labor with a reasonably effective shelter against the promiscuous invocation of antitrust against the acts and practices of unions—whether peaceful or non-peaceful—thus placing beyond antitrust's effective reach the normal and usual aims of collective bargaining.

* * *

This is where we stood when *Pennington* and *Jewel Tea* were decided in 1965. * * *

* * *

A union is exempt from the operation of antitrust only if its conduct satisfies two standards:

First, it must act "unilaterally" in the pursuit of its own interest rather than "at the behest of or in combination with non-labor groups."

Second, even if the union's activities are unilateral, to be protected they must concern a subject "intimately" related to matters of "immediate and direct" union concern—wages, hours and working conditions—rather than to matters such as prices, which are of only indirect concern to the union.[19]

---

19. Justice Goldberg, on behalf of himself and Justices Harlan and Stewart, took a sharply different approach. To him all agreements resulting from collective bargaining based on mandatory subjects are within the exemption. Since the agreement in *Pennington* derived from bargaining about wages, even though it affected the wages to be demanded of other employers, Justice Goldberg regarded it as being exempt. And since the hours of Jewel's operation as well as the hours of work required of its employees were mandatory subjects of bargain-

It may be that all that Justice White intended was that in determining whether a matter is a mandatory subject of bargaining, the Court must find that it is intimately related to traditional trade union objectives and is of direct and immediate concern to the union.

Justice Goldberg's reservations in dissent may stem from a more expansive view of what constitutes a mandatory subject of bargaining. If this be so, one could conclude that whatever ultimately is held to fall within the ambit of mandatory bargaining—a matter on which the Justices, like others, may reasonably disagree—would necessarily be exempt from antitrust attack. But whether this is so is far from clear in the various opinions in these cases and, indeed, the intimations are to the contrary.

To me the test should be this: Whatever is required or expressly authorized under existing labor legislation should be exempt from the antitrust laws. And what is mandatory should be determined in the light of our national labor policy, which should override any countervailing antitrust considerations.

In short, I would treat as minimally exempt whatever is held under the National Labor Relations Act to be the subject of obligatory bargaining. Only in this way can we achieve any degree of security in the collective bargaining process, which the Labor Relations Act encourages and sanctions.[20]

What I find most disturbing in these two cases is the suggestion that agreements reached in good faith, in free and open negotiations between management and labor within the boundaries set for collective bargaining by the National Labor Relations Act should pose a risk of possible antitrust liability. To hold that the benefits to workers must be balanced against the detriments to the competitive system would be to subject the entire bargaining process to a degree of judicial and administrative regulation which is antithetical to the basic postulates of our national labor policy. If union agreements are to be subject to an *ex post facto* antitrust audit, is it not apparent that this will have a chilling effect on the entire process of collective bargaining?

All this, however, is a far cry from permitting labor to join with industry in a deliberate scheme to extinguish the business life of the competitors of the employers with whom it is bargaining. *Pennington* is quite understandable when it is read in these terms, although, to be sure, in practice it is always difficult to determine whether or not a union is acting unilaterally. It is equally difficult to distinguish between industry-wide bargaining on the one hand, which conceivably could harm the smaller competitors, and the arrangement

---

ing, Justice Goldberg concurred in Justice White's ruling that the union's conduct in that case was protected.

20. I do not foreclose the possibility, starting with this principle, of expanding the exemption to cover appropriate non-mandatory items in the common law tradition of reasoning by analogy on a case

by case basis as we learn more about this matter through experience. Antitrust should have no application to what the Labor Act specifically prohibits; otherwise the forbidden conduct would be subject to dual proceedings and double punishment.

in *Pennington,* where the union committed itself to demand the same standards from the smaller companies that it obtained from the larger ones under its collective agreements.

This brings us to the question of antitrust liability when union activity is held to be non-exempt. The principal danger of these recent rulings is that a finding of antitrust liability will automatically be made whenever the challenged conduct is held to be non-exempt. This would be a *per se* approach with a vengeance. Arrangements may fall outside the scope of mandatory bargaining and yet have no adverse effect on competition. We still must find whether the agreement restrains trade and whether the restraint is unreasonable. A fair reading of *Jewel Tea* satisfies me that the Court intended that there be a full-scale rule of reason inquiry in every instance in which a non-exempt activity is claimed to be in violation of antitrust. Indeed the restriction on the hours of operation in *Jewel Tea* presumably would have been sustained under antitrust even if that agreement had been held to be nonexempt under our labor policies.

Now *Pennington* could rest on two theories: Either the predatory intent to drive the smaller mine operators out of business, or the second theory, which the Court emphasizes, where illegality seemingly accrues from the fact that the union relinquished its freedom of action in respect of its bargaining with competing employers. Under this view, predatory intent would be immaterial.

It is the latter approach which I find ominous. The rationale suggests that the surrender by a union of its freedom of action with respect to its bargaining policies runs counter to antitrust policy—a concept which to me runs counter to the law of contracts, as well as prior antitrust law. After all, every agreement, whatever its nature, involves a surrender of the contracting parties' freedom of action; that is what the law of contracts is all about.

The Attorney General's Committee, in 1954, gave consideration to whether the Sherman Act should be reestablished as the principal legal instrument for curbing the misuse of economic power by labor unions. I strongly opposed using antitrust for this purpose. It wasn't clear to me then, and it isn't clear to me now, what specific abuses the proponents had in mind. Whatever they may have been, it seems to me that antitrust is ill-suited for this difficult task.

I believe that you will agree with me on the basis of this historical review—albeit a rather sketchy one—that labor-antitrust is not one of the most inspiring chapters in our jurisprudence. It hardly exhibits the judicial process at its very best.

We in antitrust have had to cope in the past two decades with a series of strange and sometimes revolutionary doctrines that have put under a cloud business arrangements whose lawfulness had hitherto been unquestioned. It would not be a happy prospect to have doctrines enunciated in the context of internecine labor-management disputes applied willy-nilly to relations among competitors or between sellers and buyers.

More fundamental, however, would be the effect upon this country's labor relations were antitrust to be applied across the board to collective bargaining agreements. Maybe these labor relations policies are not the best that man could devise. But I earnestly urge that before we employ antitrust as a method of repression we have a concrete bill of particulars as to what it is that we are seeking to eradicate. Then as lawyers we can determine what is the appropriate legal instrument to remedy such abuses and evils as may exist in labor-management relationships. In short, if there is to be legislative correction, our enactments should be exactly tailored to our specific needs.

I am far from suggesting that there are no problems and that the ugly facts should be swept under the rug. It is my conclusion that a proper solution of the serious problems which this nation faces in its national labor policies will not only be found in antitrust, but any attempt to harmonize the conflicting goals of labor and antitrust law by an expansion of antitrust's role will only compound a confusion which is already intolerable.

The one thing that antitrust does not need is new worlds to conquer.

* * *

THE LABOR–ANTITRUST CONFLICT *

Connell Construction Company v. Plumbers and Steamfitters Local Union No. 100 is the Supreme Court's latest attempt to reconcile the national policy favoring competitive markets with the frequently conflicting national policy favoring union organization and collective bargaining. The conflict has been concisely described as follows:

A central aim of the antitrust laws is the promotion of competition. A central aim of collective bargaining is the elimination of competition according to classical trade union theory, the elimination of wage competition among all employees doing the same job in the same industry.

The resolution of this disagreement is a problem the Court has been wrestling with since the enactment of the Sherman Act in 1890. Although *Connell* represents the latest round in this enduring struggle, it is not likely to be the last.

In *Connell*, the union attempted to force the general contractor to subcontract mechanical work to only those subcontractors who were parties to the union's collective bargaining agreement. The Court applied a balancing test in determining whether this union activity is violative of antitrust. It balanced the subcontracting agreement's effect upon the market against the interests of the union members. In a five to four decision, the Court struck the balance in favor of the unrestrained market. Writing for the majority, Justice Powell stated: "[The subcontracting agreement] could result in significant ad-

* Note, "The Labor-Antitrust Conflict," 1975 by the Baylor Law Review. 27 Baylor Law Review 812 (1975); © Reprinted by permission.

verse effect on the market and on consumers, effects unrelated to the union's legitimate goals of organizing workers and standardizing working conditions." The majority concluded that the agreement "contravenes antitrust policies to a degree not justified by congressional labor policy.   *   *   *"

To understand *Connell's* rationale it is necessary to first trace the prior Supreme Court decisions which provide its historical foundation. The modern legal history of the struggle to resolve the conflicting national policies of collective bargaining and unrestrained markets begins with United States v. Hutcheson. The Court in *Hutcheson* held that union activity was exempt from the Sherman Act if such activity was in the union's self-interest and not undertaken in "combination with non-labor groups." This is probably the origin of the "combination with non-labor" exception to labor's general antitrust exemption. In Allen Bradley Co. v. Local 3, I.B.E.W., the Court applied the "combination with non-labor rule" to hold that the union violated the Sherman Act when it combined with contractors and manufacturers to exclude competing electrical products and to fix prices. In *Allen Bradley,* the Court recognized at the first that it was required to reconcile two conflicting policies: "The one seeks to preserve a competitive business economy; the other to preserve the rights of labor to organize to better its condition through the agency of collective bargaining." The Court held the policies of the Norris-LaGuardia Act and the NLRA were to be subordinated to the policy of the Sherman Act when a union participated in a business monopoly to dominate markets and prices. The Court explained that this conclusion meant "the same labor union activities may or may not be in violation of the Sherman Act dependent upon whether the union acts alone or in combination with business groups." For practical purposes, it would seem that the "combination with non-labor" rule is illusory. Bargaining with employers demands that labor combines with "non-labor groups." The courts are left to draw the arbitrary lines of which "combinations with non-labor" are, and which are not, antitrust violations. The deceptive nature of this test raised a storm of critical law review comment.

The Supreme Court's decisions in United Mine Workers of America v. Pennington and Local Union No. 189, Amalgamated Meat Cutters v. Jewel Tea Co. represented a new approach to reconciling the policies of competitive markets and collective bargaining. The rationale offered by Justice White in *Jewel Tea* is especially instructive in understanding *Connell's* majority decision. In *Jewel Tea*, the union forced a marketing hour restriction upon the employer. With these facts, *Hutcheson's* "combination with non-labor test" was not applicable. Rather, Justice White stated that the issue was "whether the marketing hours restriction, like wages, and unlike prices, is so intimately related to wages, and working conditions   *   *   *" that the union's imposition of the restriction fell, "within the protection of the national labor policy and therefore exempt from the Sherman Act." This became known as the "intimately related test." It is a divergence from *Hutcheson's* "combination with non-labor test" in that a labor antitrust violation no longer depends upon a "combination with non-labor." A union can lose its antitrust exemption by its own unilateral act. In determining which unilateral acts are antitrust violations Justice White explained the test lay not in the agreement's form, "but its relative impact on the product market and the interests of union members." In American Federation of Musicians v. Carroll, the Court applied this test and, in the process, clarified which unilateral activities are antitrust violations. *Carroll* involved the protest of four band leaders with the price floor requirements imposed upon them by the union were violative of antitrust. Writing for the majority, Justice Brennan quoted the "intimately related" test formulated by Justice White in *Jewel Tea*. Applying this test, the majority concluded that the price floors offered sufficient protection to the union member's wages to justify their restraint on trade. *Carroll* indicates clearly that the Court interprets Justice White's test in *Jewel Tea* to be a test which balances the interests of the union members against the resulting market restraint. Justice White's dissent in *Carroll* indicates this balancing test is exactly what he intended in *Jewel Tea*. His dissent is only against the particular balance the majority strikes.

In this historical progression, *Connell* is a further delineation of those labor objectives which fall within and those which fall without labor's antitrust exemption. The objective of *Connell's* subcontracting agreement was the legitimate labor goal of monopolizing the labor force. The Court's majority holding is that this objective's benefits to labor are outweighed by its restraints upon the market. Consequently it falls without the labor's general antitrust exemption.

In *Connell*, the Court continues to pay respect to *Hutcheson's* "combination with non-labor" test. The Court explains that labor's "nonstatutory exemption offers no similar protection when a union and a non-labor party agree to restrain competition. * * *" Obviously, the Court has not abandoned the "combination with non-labor" test. At the same time, it makes clear that it will not be limited to only the "combination with non-labor" test in determining labor's antitrust violations. It warns that labor's exemption only "allows unions to accomplish *some* restraints by acting unilaterally. * * *" (emphasis added). Those unilateral restraints which will not be allowed are to be judged, as they are in *Connell*, by the balancing test.

Connell thus represents the Court's increasing commitment to this balancing test, and herein lies its primary importance. In *Connell*, Justice White joined with Blackmun, Burger, Powell, and Rehnquist, to form the five member majority which applied the balancing test. Of the dissent, only Justice Douglas raised the issue that the "combination with non-labor" test should be exclusively controlling. None of the other dissenters joined in this line of reasoning. Instead, they concurred with Justice Stewart, as did Justice Douglas, that Congress had provided the exclusive remedy for unlawful secondary activity, such as *Connell's* subcontracting agreement. Consequently, these dissenters did not need to determine whether the balancing test or some other test should be applied to *Connell's* facts. In *Carroll*, both Stewart and Brennan had concurred in the application of the balancing test. So, seven of the Court's nine members have now, either in *Connell* or *Carroll*, supported the balancing test.

CONCLUSION

The Court's recent balancing test raises some unanswered questions. Both *Carroll* and *Connell* demonstrate that in applying the balancing test the more important the Court deems the labor objective, the heavier the scale is weighted in labor's favor. But, no explicit criteria has been provided to the lower courts for determining the labor objective's importance. The Court's language in *Connell* may have also been unnecessarily broad. The Court voices disfavor with restraints on competitive advantages derived from greater efficiency. Previously, the Court held "make work provisions" valid. These provisions prohibit more efficient methods of production in favor of securing more jobs. The Court's language in *Connell* clashes head-on with this prior holding. The Court's increasing reliance upon antitrust laws as a means of policing collective bargaining also promises disruptive consequences for the bargaining process. Employers may temporarily give ground in collective bargaining which they hope to later recoup through antitrust litigation. In bargaining, the unions will attempt to artifically incorporate market restraining objectives into labor goals that previously have been held to justify such restraints.

In summary, it seems clear that the complete exemption of labor from antitrust scrutiny would severely interfere with our national policy of competitive markets. It also seems clear that the broad application of the antitrust laws to collective bargaining agreements would seriously hinder our national labor policy. In *Jewel Tea*, *Carroll*, and *Connell*, the Court has adopted a balancing test to mediate a middle ground between these two equally unacceptable results. Legislative guidance is needed in helping the courts to navigate this difficult middle ground. Without such guidance, a solution must temporarily come from the ad hoc determinations of judges and juries. It is yet to be seen whether such judges and juries can provide a solution to the labor-antitrust problem which does not unduly subordinate one to the other but rather achieves a desirable accommodation.

I. RECOMMENDED READING

On Secondary Boycotts:

1. See Lesnick, "Job Security on Secondary Boycotts: The Reach of NLRA Sections 8(b)(4) and 8e" 113 U. of Pa.L.Rev. 1000 (1965).

2. St. Antoine, "What makes Secondary Boycotts Secondary?" Southwestern Legal Foundation 11th Annual Institute on Labor Law 5 (1965).

3. With respect to organizational picketing see Dunau, "Some Aspects of the Current Interpretation of Section (b)(7)," 52 Geo. L.J. 220 (1964).

4. Meltzer, "Organizational Picketing and the NLRB Five on a Seesaw," 30 U. of Chi.L.Rev. 78 (1962).

5. Among the most interesting articles dealing with labor and antitrust are Winter, "Collective Bargaining and Competition," 73 Yale L.J. 14 (1963).

6. Meltzer, "Labor Unions Collective Bargaining," 32 U. of Chi.L. Rev. 659 (1965).

*

Chapter VII

UNIONS IN THE PUBLIC SECTOR

A. CASE STUDY: COLLECTIVE BARGAINING IN THE STATE OF CONFUSION

The State of Confusion is located in northeastern United States. Its population of 3.1 million people makes it the 24th most populous state in the nation. Its land area of 4,862 square miles ranks 48th in the nation. It has five cities with over 100,000 people.

In spite of its small size, Confusion is an important industrial state and a favorite vacationland. Manufacturing accounts for 97 percent of the value of goods produced in Confusion. Manufacturing industries employ about 395,000 workers, or a third of Confusion's labor force. Confusion's leading manufacturing activity is transportation equipment, nonelectrical machinery, fabricated metal products, and electrical machinery. Confusion's factories produce weapons, sewing machines, jet engines, helicopters, motors, hardware and tools, cutlery, clocks, locks, ball bearings, silverware, and submarines. Confusion is also a popular resort area with its 250 mile shoreline and many inland lakes.

In the mid-1970's, Confusion experienced a strong economy. Unemployment, 6.7% in 1977, dipped to 4.3% in 1978. The 1977 per capita income climbed to $8,061, second highest in the country.

Although Confusion ranks second among the states in per capita income, rapid industrial and population growth has brought many problems in the 1970s. Cities and highways are crowded. Costs for education and housing are soaring.

Protecting Confusion against pollution has become a major challenge. In the late 1960's and early 1970's the state legislature passed laws to reduce air and water pollution.

Efforts are being made to attack metropolitan problems on a regional basis. For example, the towns in the Capital City area are attempting to stop the sale of illegal drugs and to provide treatment for drug users.

Confusion's governmental structure consists of the Executive, a General Assembly consisting of a 36-member Senate and a 151-member House of Representatives, and the Judiciary. The current governor is Lester Adams, a Republican. The General Assembly is comprised of 26 Republicans and 10 Democrats in the Senate, and 103 Democrats and 48 Republicans in the House.

Confusion's 1978 budget totaled $2,396,896 in general expenditures. Its 1979 budget will require even more money. Confusion's 1978 expenditures are summarized in Table 1.

Table 1

Confusion Expenditures by Function
(in thousands of dollars)

Function:	Amount:
Education	$ 678,099
Public Welfare	492,821
Hospitals	71,779
Natural Resources	20,550
Highways	193,072
Health	40,524
Corrections	52,396
Financial Administration	31,113
General Control	47,647
Employment Security Administration	32,135
State Police	29,443
Total General Expenditures	2,396,896

A 7% retail sales tax is the state government's largest single source of revenue. This tax provides over half of the state's total income. Other state taxes include those on cigarettes (21¢ per pack), gasoline (11¢ per gal.), inheritances, personal and corporate incomes, property, and highway use by trucks. Federal grants and other U.S. programs provide about a fourth of the state's income. The remainder comes from such sources as state-owned liquor stores, the state lottery, and various state institutions such as hospitals. Table 2 summaries Confusion's revenues.

Table 2

Confusion Revenue by Sources
(in thousands of dollars)

Source:	Amount:
Taxes:	
Total	$1,550,424
General Sales	645,274
Motor Fuels Sales	161,058
Licenses:	
Total	105,073
Motor Vehicle	64,348
Individual Income Tax	75,616
Corporate Income Tax	199,569
Intergovernmental Revenue (federal funds)	647,283
Charges and Misc. General Revenue	348,817
Total General Revenue	2,546,524

By its constitution, the Confusion government's budget must balance expenditures with revenue. Governor Adams has taken a popular stand against any increase in state taxes. In the last campaign, Governor Adams campaigned on two themes represented by the slogans "Jobs for Confusion" and "No New Taxes."

The State of Confusion employs 45,341 full-time employees. Of these 40,000 fall under the state's civil service system. School employees, fire fighters and police are excluded from the civil service system. There are 1,259 state law enforcement personnel, of which 840 are sworn officers and 419 are civilians in a variety of jobs.

Of Confusion's full-time employees, 20,285 are represented by unions. The number of unions representing Confusion's employees is nine. There are 24 bargaining units in the state government. The Confusion State Police are represented by Local 005 of the Association of State Police Officers.

The breakdown of Confusion's employment and payroll is summarized in Table 3.

Table 3

Confusion Employment and Payroll, October 1978

Employee Category	Number of Employees	Monthly Payroll (in thousands of dollars)
Higher Education	10,310	$13,895
Other Education	2,297	2,822
Highway	2,910	3,243
Public Welfare	2,493	2,377
Hospitals	10,148	9,191
State Police	1,259	1,538
Corrections	3,023	3,638
Natural Resources	850	985
Financial Administration	1,457	1,650
General Control	2,728	3,310
Total	45,341	50,439

State of Negotiations

Negotiations between Local 005 and the State have been going on for four months. During that time, there have been considerable improvements from the standpoint of the union, the best of which has been a new grievance system and the development of the "just cause" standard for discharges. The issues which are still on the table are wages, where the State has offered seven percent. The union is willing to accept a basic seven percent increase but wants an additional four percent which could be indirectly obtained through the Cost of Living Allowance (COLA) or through upping the meal allowance from $5.00 to $8.50. Also, on the table are the seniority, pension issues, management rights, off-duty use of State vehicles, and lieutenants overtime. The current contract and the union proposals on these issues are provided below. Also included are certain sections of the Confusion General Statutes, which are referred to in the current contract and the union proposal. A description of the State and union negotiating team members is also included. Final decisions by the State must be cleared through the Governor's chief financial assistant.

The Current Contract

Article V
Management Rights

Section One. Except as otherwise limited by an express provision of this agreement, the State reserves and retains, whether exercised or not, all the lawful and customary rights, powers and prerogatives of public management. Such rights include but are not limited to establishing standards of productivity and performance of its employees; determining the mission of an agency and the methods and means necessary to fulfill that mission, including the contracting out of or the discontinuation of services, positions, or programs in whole or in part; the determination of the content of job classifications; the appointment, promotion, assignment, direction and transfer of personnel; the suspension, demotion, discharge or any other appropriate action against its employees; the relief from duty of its employees because of lack of work or for other legitimate reasons; the establishment of reasonable work rules; and the taking of all necessary actions to carry out its mission in emergencies.

Section Two. Those inherent management rights not restricted by a specific provision of this Agreement are not in any way, directly or indirectly subject to the grievance procedure.

Article XII
Seniority

Section One. Seniority shall be defined as length of State service, including war service, for the following purposes: a. longevity; b. length of vacation leave.

Section Two. Seniority shall not be computed until after completion of the working test period.

Section Three. State service while working in a trainee class shall not accrue until permanent appointment after successful completion of the training whereupon it shall be retroactively applied to include such service.

Section Four. Seniority shall be deemed broken by: a. termination of employment caused by resignation, dismissal, or retirement; b. failure to report for five working days without authorization. Seniority shall not be deemed broken by a resignation from another branch of state service in order to join the State Police Department.

In the State employer's discretion, credit for seniority up to a break in service may be restored to an employee who returns to service within one year of a service break.

Section Five. Seniority Lists. Seniority lists shall be maintained annually.

Article XVI
Hours of Work:
Work Schedules and Overtime

Section One. Basic Workweek. The regular workweek of all employees shall be in conformance with C.G.S. Section 5–246. Field personnel shall continue to work the so-called 5–3 schedule. Certain groups of employees not traditionally subject to a rotating work schedule, including but not limited to administrative employees, fire marshals, criminal investigators, resident troopers, and other personnel on specialized assignments, shall continue to receive no fewer days off in each eight week cycle than field employees. The existing one-half hour unpaid lunch period shall not be counted as time worked.

Section Two. Starting and Quitting Times.

(a) The parties recognize that stability of working hours and shift assignments is in the best interest of all concerned. It is further understood that management requires a degree of flexibility as to the starting time of shifts in order to meet the needs of the public and to utilize available manpower in the most efficient manner.

(b) Existing and future shift schedules are established for the purposes of allowing management to meet these needs based upon analysis of all relevant factors as they exist in any troop or division area. Management will not change starting times without first considering all workload and "associated time consumed" data as it relates to the affected troop(s) or division(s). In such cases the Department shall give the Union adequate notice to prepare documentation and be heard prior to any adjustment.

Section Three. Except in unusual circumstances the starting and quitting times for each shift shall remain constant during each five-day consecutive period of work.

Section Four. The shift schedule covering each cycle of rotation shall be posted at least three (3) weeks in advance.

Section Five. For platoon or assignment changes of a long-term nature, ten (10) days notice shall be given to the employee.

*   *   *

Section Eight. Employees to be transferred shall be notified no less than two (2) weeks prior to the transfer date.

Section Nine. Ordinarily short-term schedule changes shall not be made solely for the purpose of avoiding overtime, e.g. rescheduling an employee required to appear in court from the evening shift to the day shift. With respect to administrative and investigative employees, the above provision shall be applied in conformance with past practice.

Section Ten.   In emergency situations, the Employer may establish shifts of longer duration than those normally scheduled.

Section Eleven.   In decisions concerning lateral transfers and patrol assignments: If in the supervisor's discretion all factors—efficiency, training needs, operational needs, etc. are considered equal, the supervisor shall take into account departmental seniority.   The supervisor's decision concerning such factors is final; however, employees or the Union may grieve to the Commissioner of State Police, concerning a pattern of failure to give proper consideration to seniority as a factor, not justified by operational needs.

Section Twelve.   Meal Periods.   Meal periods shall be scheduled close to the middle of a shift consistent with the operating needs of the agency.

Section Thirteen.   Overtime.   (a) The provisions of this section shall be interpreted consistent with Section 5–245 except when specifically provided otherwise.   (b) The State will continue to pay overtime to eligible employees at time-and-one-half for hours worked over 40, except as provided otherwise by Section 5–245 for employees on rotating shifts and unscheduled positions and classes, and except for averaging schedules approved by the Personnel Commissioner.   (c) Exempt Employees.   During the life of this Agreement, Section 5–245(b)(1) shall be deemed to exempt from overtime pay employees above the rank of Sergeant, Grade SP–3.   Lieutenants (SP–4) shall continue to receive compensatory time off, consistent with existing practice.   (d) Overtime pay shall not be pyramided.   (e) When practicable, overtime checks shall be paid no later than the second payroll period following the overtime worked.

Article XVIII
Compensation

Section One.   Effective July 1, 1977, a new pay classification structure shall be adopted, as follows:

SP–1—all employees currently in Grade 17

SP–2—all employees currently in Grade 19

SP–3—all employees currently in Grade 21

SP–4—all employees currently in Grade 24

Section Two.   Effective October 1, 1977, all employees shall receive a $1,000 across-the-board salary increase.   Effect July 1, 1978, employees shall receive 5% across-the-board.   Across the board increases hereunder shall be reflected in the salary grade and employees shall continue to receive annual increments in accordance with pre-existing regulations.   The salary schedules effective October 1, 1977 and July 1, 1978 shall be appended hereto.

Section Three.   Widow's Allowance.   (a) For employees who die on or after July 1, 1977 before retirement the monthly allowance to the surviving spouse under C.G.S. Section 5–146 shall be increased from $175.00 to $275.00.

(b) In any fiscal year in which the amount of employee contribution exceeds the amount of payments under C.G.S. Sections 5–146 through 5–151 the excess shall be rebated on a pro-rata basis to those employees who made contributions for the entire year.

(c) Effective July 1, 1977, the maximum employee contribution under C.G.S. Section 5–148 shall be reduced from $84 to $50 per year. The amount of said reduction shall be applied to reduce by $34 the premiums of those employees who, on June 30, 1977, have elected family dependent coverage.

(d) The state shall enter concurrent legislation to conform all present and future recipients with the contractual limits negotiated herein in subsection (a) above.

* * *

Section Five.　In each year of this agreement the lump sum of $100 per unit employee shall be allocated to a fund for the purpose of reducing the premiums on a pro-rata basis, of those employees who are on the payroll June 30, 1977, have elected family dependent coverage, and who continue such coverage for the life of this Agreement.

Section Six.　Effective July 1, 1977, mileage will be increased plus three cents, where applicable.

Section Seven.　Night Shift Differential.　Effective January 1, 1978, the existing night shift differential shall be increased $.07/hour; effective January 1, 1979, it shall be further increased $.07/hour.

Section Eight.　Tuition Reimbursement.　The State will allocate $30,000 each year for the existing tuition reimbursement program.

Section Nine.　Accidental Death or Dismemberment.　The State will provide the same accidental death and dismemberment policy ($7,500 per employee) as was negotiated under the Protective Services Agreement.

Article XXVI
Off-Duty Use Of State Vehicles

During the life of this Agreement the Employer shall continue to permit the use of assigned vehicles while off-duty subject to those rules, regulations, and orders promulgated by the Commissioner of State Police and existing prior to the signature date of this agreement.

Union Proposal

Article XVIII
Compensation

Section One.　General Negotiated Increases.　All general negotiated increases provided in this section shall be added to and become part of the base salaries or wages of members of the bargaining unit and shall be additional to the annual salaries or wages to which unit members are entitled.   Each step of each salary group shall therefore be increased accordingly.

Section Two.   (a) Effective July 1, 1979, all employees shall receive a 12.5% across-the-board salary increase or $2000 whichever is greater.   Across-the-board increases hereunder shall be reflected in the salary grade and employees shall continue to receive annual increments in accordance with preexisting regulations.

(b) Cost of Living Allowance (COLA).   A cost of living allowance shall be paid to each employee based upon changes in the cost of living which shall be determined in accordance with increases in the Consumer Price Index for Urban Wage Earners and Clericals revised U.S. Cities Average (CPI).

Cost of living allowances shall be determined quarterly during this Agreement as follows:

Base CPI Period:	Payment Begins:
May, 1979–August, 1979	October 1, 1979
August, 1979–November, 1979	January 1, 1979
November, 1979–February, 1980	April 1, 1980
February, 1980–May, 1980	July 1, 1980

The cost of living allowance to be paid shall be $6.50 bi-weekly for each one (1) percent increase in the CPI for the base period and shall be added to the current wages and salary of each employee.

Article XVI

Hours of Work; Work Schedules And Overtime

Section Eight.   Short-term schedule changes shall not be made for the purpose of avoiding overtime, e.g. rescheduling any employees required to appear in court from the evening shift to the day shift.   With respect to administrative and investigative employees, the above provision shall be applied in conformance with past practice.

Section Nine.   In emergency situations, the Employer may establish shifts of longer duration than those normally scheduled.

Section Ten.   Meal Periods.   Meal periods shall be scheduled close to the middle of a shift consistent with the operating needs of the agency.

Section Eleven.   Overtime.   (a) The provisions of this section shall be interpreted consistent with Section 5–245 except when specifically provided otherwise.   (b) The State will continue to pay overtime to eligible employees at time-and-one-half for hours worked over 35 except as provided otherwise in Section 5–245 for employees on rotating shifts and unscheduled positions and classes, and except for averaging schedules approved by the Personnel Commissioner.   There shall be no exceptions or exemptions or exemptions from the overtime rules stated herein on the basis of pay grade or rank.   Overtime shall not be pyramided.   (c) Over-time checks shall be paid no later than the second payroll period following the overtime worked. Payroll checks shall indicate all sources of income and deductions with specificity, including amount earned as over-time above base pay. (d) "Construction" overtime shall be offered to all troopers so that the amount worked shall be equal so far as is possible. Other overtime assignments shall be rotated among full-time employees on the basis of departmental and rank seniority, with the most senior employee being given the opportunity to accept the assignment, and so on, until the assignment is accepted. If no one will accept the assignment, it may be assigned by the Commanding Officer who shall apply reasonable standards of fairness.

Section Twelve. A Minimum Patrol for each command shall be established by negotiations between the employer and the Union. Such minimums cannot be deviated from except in case of state-wide emergency.

Section Thirteen. No person not a member of the bargaining unit shall be employed or otherwise used to do work usually done by members of the bargaining unit. The provisions of this Article are subject to the Miscellaneous Article, Section Two, and no such provision shall be deemed to have been vitiated by reason of this Article.

Article XXV
Vacations

Section One. The vacation schedule in effect on June 30, 1977, shall remain in force, except that employees who have completed 20 years of service shall earn paid vacation credits at the rate of 2 work days for each completed calendar month of service. For all other employees, the following vacation leave shall apply:

0–15 years, $1\frac{1}{4}$ days per month

over 15 and under 20, $1\frac{2}{3}$ days per month

over 20, 2 days per month

An employee may accumulate unused vacation days up to a maximum accumulation of 120 days.

Section Two. Vacation Selection. Vacation leave shall be selected within each troop or division. Conflicting leave requests, not to exceed the annual accrual, will be resolved in favor of the employees with greater departmental seniority as defined in Article XII, Sections One, Five, and Six, by such scheduling adjustments as the Commanding Officer deems necessary.

Employees who receive Military Leave during the prime vacation period (May 1–September 30) shall be considered to have exercised their seniority rights under this section consistent with existing practice; except that employees who receive no more than 15 days annual Military Training during the Prime Vacation period shall ordinarily be permitted to select 5 consecutive days of vacation according to seniority.

Article XXVI
Off-Duty Use Of State Vehicles

During the life of this Agreement the Employer shall continue to permit the use of unmarked assigned vehicles while off-duty.

Article XII
Seniority

Section One.   Except as otherwise provided below, seniority shall be defined as length of State Police Department service, including war service.

Section Two.   Seniority shall not be computed until after completion of the training whereupon it shall be retroactively applied to include such service.

Section Three.   Seniority shall be deemed broken by: termination of employment caused by resignation, dismissal, or retirement;

(b) failure to report for five working days without authorization.

Credit for seniority up to a break in service shall be restored to an employee who returns to service within one year of a service break.

Section Four.   Except as otherwise provided in Section Five, seniority, within the State Police Department, and in rank shall be determinative in matters involving, but not limited to, promotions, patrols and assignments, vacations, overtime, holidays, and night shifts.

Section Five.   Length of service in State agencies other than the State Police Department shall be considered for longevity and length of vacation leave and when police seniority is equal, to resolve direct conflicts in other matters.

New Clause
Retirement

Section One.   Any employee who has completed twenty (20) years of service as a State Police Officer shall be retired on his own application.

Section Two.   Any increases in any pension payments or retirement benefits for any other state employees or former state employees shall be extended to members of these bargaining units and former members, including specifically, but not limited to any cost of living increase for retired employees and including specifically, but not limited to the five (5%) increase provided by Public Act No. 78–228.

Said plans shall also vest after five (5) years of service and guarantee the right to join at any time and the right at any time to purchase-in for any appropriate past service (including specifically part-time service).   Members of the unit shall retain the right to retire early in accordance with provisions of said plans in effect prior to the passage of P.A. 75–531.

Section Three. Any person who retires from the State Police Department for any reason and is employed by any other employer, shall be able to collect any additional income and accrue any additional retirement benefits by reason of his service in the other employment without diminishing the amounts of his retirement or disability payments from the State.

New Clause

Disability Retirement And Benefits

Section One. Members of the Union shall have and be protected in their rights to Disability Retirement as they existed prior to the passage of P.A. 75–628 including specifically the right of a disabled employee to work without penalty or reduction in benefits.

Statutes Referred to in the Current Contract and Union Proposal

Section 5–146. Allowances for survivors of state police officers. Effect of collective bargaining agreements. Valuation of fund by retirement commission.

(a) If any state police officer in employment on June 21, 1961, who has elected survivors' benefits, or any state police officer who commenced employment subsequent to June 21, 1961, dies before retirement from state service from any cause, leaving a surviving spouse or dependent unmarried children under the age of eighteen years, there shall be paid survivors' allowances, from the state employees retirement fund on the following basis:

(1) To the surviving spouse, a monthly allowance of two hundred seventy-five dollars commencing immediately upon the death of such state police officer payable for his or her lifetime or until his or her subsequent remarriage.

(b) Notwithstanding the provisions of subsection (a) of this section, survivors' allowances may be paid from the state employees retirement fund in such amounts and commencing on such dates as may conform to the terms of any prevailing collective bargaining agreement effective on or after July 1, 1979, between the state and the employees' representative for state police officers.

Section 5–151. Benefits for survivors of previously deceased police.

Any widow other than one who has received benefits under the provisions of section 5–146, and a dependent child or children of any state policeman or of a retired state policeman who would have been eligible for benefits under sections 5–146 to 5–151, inclusive, had said sections been in effect on July 1, 1945, or at any time subsequent thereto shall be entitled to such benefits provided such eligibility still exists. The survivors' benefits paid in accordance with this section shall be certified by the retirement commission to the comptroller, who shall draw his order on the treasurer for payment of such allowances.

Section 5–162 (Public Act 75–531).   Retirement date and retirement income.

(1) Each member who has completed twenty-five or more years of state service shall be retired on his own application on the first day of the month named in the application, and on or after the member's fifty-fifth birthday.

(2) Each member who has completed twenty-five or more years of state service and has reached his seventieth birthday and who is in an appointive position shall continue in service and shall be retired on the first day of the month on or after his seventieth birthday, upon notice from the retirement commission to the member, to the executive head of his agency and the comptroller.

Section 5–162b (Public Act 78–228)   Cost of living adjustment for employees retired on or before June 30, 1975.

On July 1, 1978, and on July first of each subsequent year, each employee and the spouse of each deceased employee who had elected the husband and wife retirement income option, retired under the state employees' retirement act on or before June 30, 1975, shall be entitled in addition to his original monthly retirement salary plus cost of living allowances from date of original retirement, to an additional five percent of living monthly allowance computed on the basis of his combined monthly retirement salary and cost of living allowances, if any, to which he was entitled as of the June thirtieth immediately preceding.   If on any July first, the retirement commission determines that the national consumer price index for urban wage earners and clerical workers for the previous twelve-month period has increased less than the cost of living allowance provided by this section, the cost of living allowance provided by this section shall be adjusted to reflect the change in such index provided such cost of living allowance shall not be less than three percent.

Section 5–245.   Standard workweek.   Overtime pay.

(a) The standard workweek of all state employees is thirty-five hours in five days.   Any state employee who performs work authorized by his appointing authority for a period in addition to the hours of the employee's regular, established workweek, or the standard workweek, whichever may contain fewer hours, shall receive compensation as follows:

(1) For that portion of such additional time worked which when added to the employee's regular, established workweek, or the standard workweek, whichever may contain fewer hours, does not exceed forty hours, the employee shall be compensated at an hourly rate based on his annual salary;

(2) for that portion of such additional time worked which when added to the employee's regular, established workweek, or the standard workweek, whichever may contain fewer hours, exceeds forty hours, the employee shall be compensated at a rate equal to one and one-half times an hourly rate based on his annual salary.

(b) The provisions of this section shall not be applied with respect to any employee employed in

(1) an executive, administrative or professional capacity as such terms may be defined and delimited from time to time by the commissioner of administrative services or

(2) a position or class which has been designated as unscheduled by the commissioner or administrative services, or

(3) a position, the regular work schedule of which requires rotating shifts as approved by the commissioner of administrative services and recorded in his office, which schedule shall not average more than five work days and thirty-five hours per week over a period of not more than eight weeks.

(c) Any person serving in a position referred to in subdivision (2) or (3) of this section who performs work authorized by his appointing authority for a period in addition to a weekly average of thirty-five hours per workweek shall receive compensation as follows:

(1) For those hours worked in any one workweek which are additional to his regularly scheduled hours for such week and which, when added to the employee's average workweek, do not exceed forty hours, the employee shall be compensated at an hourly rate based on his annual salary;

(2) for those hours worked in any one workweek which are additional to his regularly scheduled hours for such week and which, when added to the employee's average workweek, exceed forty hours, the employee shall be compensated at a rate equal to one and one-half times an hourly rate based on his annual salary, provided nothing in this section in conflict with section 5–246 shall be construed to apply to any member of the state police.

Section 5–246.   State police workweek.   Work for highway contractors.

(a)(1) Notwithstanding the provisions of any regulation issued under this chapter, no state policeman shall be required to be on active duty as such more than five days in any consecutive seven-day period except in case of emergency as determined by the commissioner of public safety. Subject to the provisions of subsection (b) of section 5–245, compensation at a rate equal to one and one-half times an hourly rate based on his annual salary shall be made in the case of any member or officer of the state police force who performs work authorized by the commissioner of public safety in addition to the hours of his regular workweek as established by said commissioner, provided the commissioner of public safety shall establish no workweek which, including home-to-duty station and duty station-to-home time, exceeds an eight-week average of forty hours per week.

(2) The commissioner of public safety may authorize any member or officer of the state police force to provide police services for private contractors at highway construction sites. Time spent in the performance of such police services shall be in addition to the as-

signed hours of the regular workweek and shall not be included in the total hours in an eight-week average of forty hours established under this subsection.   Each such state policeman shall be compensated by the state for the performance of such services at a rate equal to one and one-half times an hourly rate based on his annual salary.   Such private contractors shall reimburse the division of state police within the department of public safety for (A) the compensation of such policemen and (B) the costs related to the performance of such services at a rate to be determined by the commissioner of public safety, with the approval of the secretary of the office of policy and management.   Performance of such services under the provisions of this subsection shall not constitute state service for retirement purposes under the provisions of chapter 66.

(b) A state policeman employed in an executive, administrative or professional capacity as defined under the provisions of subsection (b) of section 5–245 who performs work authorized by the commissioner of public safety in addition to the hours of his regular workweek as established by said commissioner shall be granted equivalent time off with pay.

The Negotiating Teams

The following are members of the union negotiating team:

1.   Tony Jones is the union president. Tony may be characterized as tough, impatient, and very concerned not to "sell out" any part of the union local membership. Jones is personally opposed to having lieutenants in the bargaining unit. He would like to reduce management discretion. He is most concerned with economic issues. He is a road cop which he basically enjoys, and he mainly feels an affinity with the interests of the road cops. He is interested in improving disability pensions, to permit double-dipping and making it possible for people to retire after twenty years. Jones would be opposed to a strike but might be willing to support some form of job action if he became angry enough. He favors departmental seniority with respect to vacation. He is strong on economics.

2.   Sergeant Rich D'Aniello wants an agreement. He does not want to strike. He tends to be more willing to compromise than most other people on the committee. He is generally well respected as a police officer. His primary interest is in economic issues. He feels very strongly that vacation should be decided by seniority. He speaks for the sergeants and generally is in favor of improving disability benefits, and feels it should be made possible to retire after twenty years of service.

3.   June Heider is young, aggressive, and very interested in economics. She has ambitions for union leadership. She does not care very much about seniority or overtime for lieutenants. She would prefer departmental seniority in all matters. She is most concerned with economic issues. She would be opposed to a strike but might be willing to support some form of job action if she

became angry enough. She is eager to continue her existing excellent relations with the male troopers who, despite their normal male chauvinist pig attitudes, consider her "a regular guy". She is neutral about keeping lieutenants in the unit.

4. Sal Manola is a road cop who has been on the force for twenty years. He is dissatisfied with his current position. He has been passed over for special assignments and feels very strongly that the department is riddled with favortism. He is interested in economics but is unwilling to support any contract that does not have a strong seniority clause. He has a small but vocal following. He would like to improve disability pensions. If the question of a strike should arise, he would support one. He opposes having lieutenants in the bargaining unit. He is also interested in disabilities and favors a strong stand on economics. He strongly favors departmental seniority on vacations.

5. Lieutenant Bill Pace is a good officer, well liked by the troops. He is immune from the widespread feeling that lieutenants are more aligned with management than with the union. He is very interested in seeing to it that lieutenants are eligible for overtime pay at time-and-a-half. He is not particularly sympathetic to seniority for assignments because he feels that it hampers him in getting the right people to do jobs. He is opposed to a strike but might consider a job action if he became angry enough. He feels strongly about retirement.

6. The principal negotiator is Gary Becher. Becher wants a deal on the best terms possible. He feels 10% or anything like it would be a triumph. He is more favorable to pushing seniority than lieutenant overtime, but he feels priority of issues should come from the union.

The following are members of the state negotiating team:

1. The principal negotiator is Stan Macey. Macey wants an agreement with the police which will provide a precedent for keeping other unions in line at or under seven percent. He has no strong feelings against unions or seniority. He is under pressure from state officials as not being militant enough. On the other hand, the governor wants him to come to an agreement with the police and avoid a strike. He is under orders not to give on pension or retirement or manpower levels and not to give a COLA.

2. Commissioner Russell Lane wants an agreement. He does not want to be known as an enemy by the troops. He is beginning to form a good relationship with the union president. He is most concerned with preserving managerial discretion in running the department. He is also anxious to stay on good terms with the Governor and to demonstrate that he can cope effectively with the union. He is opposed to improving retirement because he feels it would create turnover problems.

3. Ms. Sandra Diamond is the state personnel representative. she is concerned with keeping costs down, with preventing eco-

nomic provisions which might be a precedent for other unions, and for avoiding any commitment on retirement or any yielding on management rights.

B. THE RISE OF COLLECTIVE BARGAINING

As late as 1950, unions and collective bargaining were extremely rare in the public sector. Today union strikes and collective bargaining are common. A variety of factors help to explain this development.

During the 60's the number of public employees, particularly at the state and local levels, grew dramatically and at a pace much faster than that of employees in private industry. This dramatic growth, together with the fact that the labor movement had organized or tried to organize most significant employee groups in private industry, made public employees an inviting target for union organization.

Because salaries for public employees are generally decided by legislative bodies whose procedures are cumbersome and slow, salaries for government workers did not in that inflationary period keep pace with those in private industry. Job dissatisfaction rose, and public employees became more responsive to the arguments of union organizers. As a result, during the 60's and early 70's, while the percentage of union membership in private industry stayed about the same or declined slightly, the percentage of union membership among public employees increased rapidly.

The growth in union organization was accompanied by a change in public and professional attitudes toward the concept of collective bargaining in public service. It was once considered too obvious for discussion that unionization was inappropriate for public employees. As a result, public employees were excluded from the coverage of the National Labor Relations Act (NLRA) and from most state labor acts as well. However, during the 60's the assumption that collective bargaining was inappropriate was subjected to increasingly critical analysis. Since it was based partly on what was considered to be the peculiar nature of government service, this assumption became more difficult to defend as government service expanded and the nature of the work done by government employees became more like that of employees in private industry. Moreover, conceptions of collective bargaining also changed. At one time it was thought to be concerned almost entirely with wages and hours which were generally established by law in the public service. It was thought that there was nothing about which public employees and management could bargain. But as people became aware that the establishment of grievance systems and orderly procedures was a key function of collective bargaining its suitability for the public sector became more readily apparent.

Union leaders, workers and impartial observers began increasingly to dispute the notion that collective bargaining was inappropriate in the public service at the same time that union organization and employee dissatisfaction were growing.

The initial reaction of the courts was to condemn collective bargaining and the possibility of strikes in the public sector. Two main arguments were used. It was often claimed that unions represented an infringement on the government's sovereignty. Since the concept of sovereignty is an elusive one, referring vaguely to the government's ability to exercise dominion within its jurisdiction, it was never clear what the argument meant. Generally it stood for nothing more than strongly held feelings that unions "had no proper place in the public sector." The other frequently used argument was that strikes of essential services could not be tolerated. Although this argument had force when applied to police or fire workers, critics were quick to point out that it could not justify a blanket prohibition of strikes of government workers many of whom provided less crucial services than private sector employees covered by the NLRA. The simplistic nature of the arguments against public sector unions led some commentators to reject the idea of a fundamental difference and to argue that public employees were entitled to the same rights as private sector employees. A rash of public sector bargaining legislation modeled in the Wagner Act was passed. In a few states a limited right to strike was granted. But experience with public sector unions has suggested that neither total acceptance nor total rejection of the private sector model would be sensible. Attempts to define more precisely how the two areas differed were made. In most states a hybrid system was developed involving limited application of private law processes.

C. THE DEBATE ABOUT THE APPROPRIATENESS OF PUBLIC SECTOR BARGAINING

The material below gives examples of both the law, the early reactions and the more current debate over the applicability of private sector models to the government. Because of the central role of the strike weapon in private sector labor relations much of the debate has focused on the question of whether such a right should be granted to public employees and also whether it is possible to structure a system of collective bargaining without such a right.

————

The Applicability of the Private Sector Model

ANDERSON FEDERATION OF TEACHERS v.
SCHOOL CITY OF ANDERSON

Supreme Court of Indiana, 1969.
252 Ind. 558, 251 N.E.2d 15.

*   *   *

The appellant is an organization of public school teachers employed by the appellee.

The appellee is a municipal corporation organized under the statutes of this state for the purpose of operating the public schools within the boundaries of the School City of Anderson, Indiana.

In the spring of 1968 the appellant and the appellees entered into negotiations concerning salary schedules for the following year. These negotiations apparently were not satisfactory to the appellant for on May 1, 1968, the appellant instituted a strike against the school corporation and established picket lines at the various schools operated by appellee. Evidence discloses that school children were unloaded in the public streets because of the presence of the picket lines. It was this action of picketing by the appellant which precipitated the temporary restraining order issued on May 2, 1968, and it was the continuation of this activity without regard for the restraining order upon which the trial court based its judgment after a hearing on May 6, 1968, that the appellant was in contempt of court for violating the restraining order.

The trial court was in all things correct in its finding and judgment of contempt of court.

It is the contention of the appellant that Indiana's "Little Norris-LaGuardia Act," also known as the anti-injunction statute, *   *   * is applicable in this case. This act prohibits the issuance of restraining orders and injunctions in matters involving labor disputes between unions and private employers. We do not agree with the appellant that this act is applicable to disputes concerning public employees. The overwhelming weight of authority in the United States is that government employees may not engage in a strike for any purpose.

The Supreme Court of the United States clearly enunciated the proposition that public employees did not have a right to strike and that the injunctive processes might properly be used to prevent or halt such strikes in the case of United States v. United Mine Workers (1947), 330 U.S. 258, 67 S.Ct. 677, 91 L.Ed. 884. This case has never been overruled or modified.

     " *   *   * The purpose of the Act is said to be to contribute to the worker's 'full freedom of association, self-organization, and designation of representatives of his own choosing, to negotiate the terms and conditions of his employment, and that he shall be free from the interference, restraint, or coercion of employers of labor, or their agents, in the designation of such representatives

* * * for the purpose of collective bargaining * * *.' These considerations, on their face, obviously do not apply to the Government as an employer or to relations between the Government and its employees."

We are in total accord with the above language and hold that it is equally applicable to the Indiana statute.

This same proposition has been followed generally in most of the other state jurisdictions where it has been repeatedly held that strikes by public employees are or should be prohibited and that injunctions should be granted to halt or prevent them. For reference see the following cases:

School Committee of City of Pawtucket v. Pawtucket Teachers Alliance (1966), 101 R.I. 243, 221 A.2d 806;

Minneapolis Federation of Teachers Local 59, AFL–CIO v. Obermeyer et al. (1966), 275 Minn. 347, 147 N.W.2d 358;

City of Minot v. General Drivers and Helpers Union (1966), N.D., 142 N.W.2d 612;

Board of Education of Community Unit School District No. 2 v. Redding (1965), 32 Ill.2d 567, 207 N.E.2d 427;

New Jersey Turnpike Authority v. American Federation et al. (1964), 83 N.J.Super. 389, 200 A.2d 134;

Donevero v. Jersey City Incinerator Authority (1962), 75 N.J. Super. 217, 182 A.2d 596;

South Atlantic & Gulf Coast District of International Longshoremen's Association, Independent v. Harris County (1962), Tex. Civ.App., 358 S.W.2d 658;

Hansen v. Commonwealth (1962), 344 Mass. 214, 181 N.E.2d 843;

Port of Seattle v. Int'l Longshoremen's and Warehousemen's Union (1958), 52 Wash.2d 317, 324 P.2d 1099;

City of Pawtucket v. Pawtucket Teachers Alliance (1958), 87 R.I. 364, 141 A.2d 624;

City of Manchester v. Manchester Teachers Guild (1957), 100 N.H. 507, 131 A.2d 59;

City of Alcoa v. Int'l Brotherhood of Electrical Workers (1957), 203 Tenn. 12, 308 S.W.2d 476;

International Brotherhood of Electrical Workers v. Grand River Dam Authority (1956), Okl., 292 P.2d 1018;

City of Detroit v. Division 26 et al. (1952), 332 Mich. 237, 51 N.W. 2d 228;

Norwalk Teachers Association v. Board of Education (1951), 138 Conn. 269, 83 A.2d 482, 31 A.L.R.2d 1133;

City of Los Angeles v. Los Angeles Building & Construction Trades Council (1949), 94 Cal.App.2d 36, 210 P.2d 305;

Miami Waterworks Local No. 654 v. City of Miami (1946), 157 Fla. 445, 26 So.2d 194, 165 A.L.R. 967.

We find only one case where an injunction to prevent a pending strike of public employees was denied. That case was Board of Education of City of Minneapolis v. Public School Employees Union (1951), 233 Minn. 141, 45 N.W.2d 797, 29 A.L.R.2d 424. That case, however was overruled in 1966 by the Supreme Court of Minnesota in Minneapolis Federation of Teachers Local 59, AFL–CIO v. Obermeyer, supra.

The Indiana Continuing Legal Education Forum in 1968 circulated a publication entitled MUNICIPAL EMPLOYEE NEGOTIATIONS AND STRIKES in which they point out that almost without exception the state and federal courts hold that strikes by public employees are illegal.

The publication also quotes from a letter written by President Franklin D. Roosevelt to the President of the National Federation of Federal Employees on August 16, 1937, in which he said:

> "Particularly, I want to emphasize my conviction that militant tactics have no place in the functions of any organization of Government employees * * * A strike of public employees manifests nothing less than intent on their part to prevent or obstruct the operations of Government until their demands are satisfied. Such action, looking toward the paralysis of Government by those who have sworn to support it, is unthinkable and intolerable."

In a New York Supreme Court case Justice Emilio Nunez in granting an injunction against striking teachers made the following observation:

> "Upon the signing of the Condon-Wadlin Act, Governor Dewey stated, in part, that 'Every liberty enjoyed in this nation exists because it is protected by a government which functions uninterruptedly. The paralysis of any portion of government could quickly lead to the paralysis of all society. Paralysis of government is anarchy and in anarchy liberties become useless.' " Board of Education of the City of New York v. Shanker and United Federation of Teachers, Local 2, Supreme Court (1967), 54 Misc.2d 941, 283 N.Y.S.2d 548, 552.

We thus see that both the federal and state jurisdictions and men both liberal and conservative in their political philosophies have uniformly recognized that to allow a strike by public employees is not merely a matter of choice of political philosophies, but is a thing which cannot and must not be permitted if the orderly function of our society is to be preserved. This is not a matter for debate in the political arena for it appears fundamental, as stated by Governor Dewey, public strikes would lead to anarchy, and, as stated by President Roosevelt, the public strike "is unthinkable and intolerable."

The Madison Superior Court, is, therefore, in all things affirmed.

ARTERBURN, J., concurs.

HUNTER, J., concurs with statement.

DeBruler, C. J., dissents with opinion in which Jackson, J., concurs.

Hunter, Judge (concurring).

Heretofore I announced my determination not to participate in this case by reason of the fact that the issues presented involved litigation in the City of Anderson, Indiana, my place of residence. However, my sense of judicial responsibility and duty now impels me to do so, because of the gravity of the legal issues of public policy in the area of public education.

Therefore I wholeheartedly concur in the opinion of Judge Givan in this case.

DeBruler, Chief Judge (dissenting).

I dissent from the opinion of the majority for two reasons:

I. The majority opinion offers absolutely no justification for its holding that every strike by any public employees, including teachers, is illegal and, therefore, enjoinable regardless of how peaceful and nondisruptive the strike is.

II. Indiana has an anti-injunction statute which is applicable to this case. Since the trial court did not follow the procedures required by that statute, it had no jurisdiction to issue a temporary restraining order or injunction without notice or hearing, or to find the teachers' union guilty of contempt without a jury trial.

I.

This teachers' strike was completely peaceful and minimally disruptive of the public service rendered by the schools. Only a small percentage of the public school teachers participated in the strike, the schools were never closed by the strike, and there was sufficient staff to insure that the classes were quiet, seated and at work. The picketing which accompanied this strike was at all times peaceful, nonthreatening, and at no time endangered the health or safety of the school or the community. The non-striking teachers and students entered and left the building freely.

In spite of this the majority labels this strike "illegal" and states that, therefore, the injunctive process may be used to halt it. The strike is called illegal because it is in violation of an alleged public policy of this State against all strikes by public employees. However, there has never been such a public policy in this State and there was none in May, 1968, when the teachers in this case went on strike. Our General Assembly has never declared such a public policy, on the contrary, the only legislation that can be interpreted to cover this subject is the anti-injunction statute discussed under Part II of this dissenting opinion, which runs directly counter to the majority opinion.

In the absence of any legislative guidelines, formulated after thorough public discussion and debate, the majority suddenly declares that there is an absolute prohibition against any strike by any group of public employees, no matter how peaceful or non-disruptive the strike may be.

The majority offers no *argument* to show why this Court should make such a declaration of policy. They merely set out a list of cases from other jurisdictions and quotes from two well-known politicians to the effect that *they* believed strikes by public employees were unthinkable and led to anarchy. Nowhere does the Court descend from these useless generalities and deal with the facts in the case before us.

The court decisions cited by the majority from other jurisdictions are not authority in Indiana except to the extent the reasoning therein is persuasive to this Court. The pertinent cases are those where, in the absence of any legislation, the appellate courts have declared the right to enjoin strikes by public employees, even though the strike is peaceful and minimally disruptive to the general community. I have read all the cases cited by the majority, and on this point I have found none whose reasoning supports a *per se* rule against strikes by public employees. All of the cases rely on the same arguments, and I will examine the main ones to show their weaknesses.

(1) "The terms of employment are not subject to bargaining and strike pressure because they are set by the legislative body and are not within the discretion of the agency which is the employer."

This assumes an old-fashioned, out-dated view of the purpose and value of collective bargaining. In Indiana the governing boards of the school corporations have a wide discretion in the allocation of the resources which are budgeted to them. In the case now before us, the appellee has bargained with appellant over salary schedules at least since 1952. Besides, there are many issues about which employees are anxious to bargain other than wages, which are within the discretion of the agency employer. This is shown by a policy statement by appellee, in effect prior to and during the strike which reads in part as follows:

> "Be it resolved, that the Board of School Trustees of the School City of Anderson will professionally negotiate with the Anderson Federation of Teachers with regards to employment salary schedules, grievance procedures, working conditions and administration policies."

All employees have a legitimate interest in establishing fair grievance procedures to control arbitrary and discriminatory dismissal or discipline. Teachers especially, as professionals, have a wide range of concerns other than purely monetary. They do and ought to have a strong interest in the establishment of the priorities in the allocation of the total school budget; they are interested in the details of the teacher transfer programs designed to promote integrated faculties; they are interested in the emphasis and techniques to be used in furnishing special services to underprivileged and ghetto children; they have an interest in controlling how much of their time must be given up to patrolling rest rooms searching out smokers, or collecting tickets at basketball games; they have an interest in the quality of texts and audio-visual materials to be used; they have an interest in the whole question of the substitute teacher system. The local governing boards do have discretion in these areas in addition to wide discretion with reference to salaries, job classification, job requirements, etc. The existence of this discretion means that there is something for teachers and local school boards to bargain about. It also means that there is a wide scope for arbitrary and unfair actions by those boards which can be avoided only if the teachers have the effective means to pressure the boards into good faith bargaining on the issue. If this argument against the right of all public employees to strike ever held water, it certainly does not any longer.

(2) "To say that public employees can strike is to say that they can deny the authority of government."

It must be kept in mind that the local governing boards of school corporations have a great deal of *discretion* over the terms and conditions of employment of teachers. Any decision within this discretionary area is authorized by the government and, therefore, obviously does not deny the authority of government. The teachers seek to compel choices within that discretionary area. They do *not* seek to destroy the body politic or pressure employers into violating their statutory duties.

In addition, I think the entire community benefits when the government recognizes the right in its employees and citizens to compel the human agents of that government to behave reasonably and fairly towards all those with whom they deal.

(3) "A strike by public employees is a strike against government itself, a situation so anomalous as to be unthinkable."

This is not a rational argument at all but a technique for avoiding dealing with the merits of the issue. This argument indicates a limitation in the thinker not attributable to the subject matter. In the case of a peaceful strike and no major disruption of the community, I find it very easy to think of a strike against the sovereign *and* to justify it. In fact, I find it unthinkable that any sovereign worthy of the name would strive to remain insulated from all pressures to act fairly and decently, without arbitrariness, towards its employees. The conflict of real social forces cannot be solved by the invocation of magical phrases like "sovereignty".

(4) "Public employees occupy a status entirely different from private employees because they are agents of the government serving a public purpose and a strike by them contravenes the public welfare and results in paralysis of the society."

First, I think we should note the basic similarities between the two categories of employees. They both involve people working for wages and seeking some control over their employment conditions. The potential for arbitrary and discriminatory practices against employees are the same. In both cases there is pressure on the employer to pay as little as possible and still retain the personnel. In both cases the employer has some areas of discretion which allow for bargaining with the employees.

Second, I believe that to avoid being in violation of the equal protection clause of the Fourteenth Amendment to the United States Constitution the dichotomy between public and private employees must have a rational basis in light of the purpose of the no-strike prohibition. Rinaldi v. Yeager (1966), 384 U.S. 305, 86 S.Ct. 1497, 16 L.Ed.2d 577. If some strikes by workers within the category of public employees would not appreciably disrupt the community or create anarchy, then there is no justification for treating those public employees differently than private employees, and, therefore, no justification for a *per se* rule against strikes by public employees. To justify such a prohibition against every strike by any public employees the results of a strike by such employees must be different from and more disruptive than a strike by private employees. That such is not the case can be easily demonstrated.

(a) There is no difference in impact on the community between a strike by employees of a public utility and employees of a private utility; nor between employees of a municipal bus company and a privately owned bus company; nor between public school teachers and parochial school teachers. The form of ownership and management of the enterprise does not determine the amount of disruption caused by a strike of the employees of that enterprise. In addition, the form of ownership that is actually employed is often a political and historical accident, subject to future change by political forces. Services that were once rendered by public enterprise may be contracted out to private enterprise, and then by another administration returned to the public sector.

(b) It seems obvious to me that a strike by some private employees would be far more disruptive of the society than the peaceful teachers' strike involved in this case, e.g., the truck drivers who deliver milk to the cities, the factory workers who work in defense plants, construction workers on missile and space launching sites, agricultural workers, etc.

(c) The state and municipal governments perform their many functions through a large number of different agencies of varying importance. The temporary cessation of work in one of those agencies will not *necessarily* interfere with the rest of the service. It is naive to think that *every* strike by *any* public employees will upset the whole operation of government.

Does the majority seriously believe that a strike by employees of municipal golf courses would result in anarchy? What of city parking lot attendants? What about janitors? What about referees at the high school basketball games? In this case there was absolutely no finding that the strike was unduly disrupting the community or causing social chaos.

It is clear then that the mere existence of some difference between public and private employees cannot justify an absolute strike prohibition.

It is true that a strike by public employees may result in some amount of disruption of the agency for which they work. In the absence of legislation dealing with this subject we believe that it is a judicial function to determine whether the amount of the disruption of the service is so great that it warrants overriding the legitimate interests of the employees in having effective means to insure good faith bargaining by the employer. This is a minimum requirement before a court can declare a strike by public employees illegal.

*   *   *

In our case there was not even that much harm shown.

I think it is a very unwise policy to allow a trial court to enjoin a peaceful strike, in the absence of any way to insure that the underlying dispute will be discussed and settled amicably. To prohibit a strike in a context where this amounts to ending any pressure on the employer to bargain in good faith with representatives of the employees is to invite arbitrary action by the employer, illegal strikes, violence, and bitter feelings which may do longlasting damage to the community.

Indiana needs a comprehensive labor relations act which would provide a mechanism to help settle labor disputes involving both public and private employees, without recourse to a strike. It is obvious the courts cannot create this machinery. It is equally obvious that the Court should not create an apparent substitute in the form of a *per se* rule against peaceful strikes by public employees regardless of the impact of the strike, when this substitute is wholly inadequate and seriously misleading as to its effects.

QUESTION

Is the majority or the dissent more persuasive?

THE TAX FOUNDATION, UNIONS AND GOVERNMENT EMPLOYMENT *

Although unionism among civil servants has not generally been an important factor in management-employee relationships until rather recently, private industry has had dealings with labor organizations for a number of decades. The question naturally arises: to what decree can the principles developed in the private sector be applied in the public case?

Some observers, particularly those representing labor interests, insist there is no meaningful difference between the two situations. They contend that the lessons so painfully learned can simply be transferred more or less intact to the state and local bargaining tables, thereby eliminating a repetition of the wasteful struggles which characterized many industries at the outset of the spread of unionization. Others maintain that some extremely important differences set the public and private labor problems apart, and render many ap-

---

* Unions and Government Employment
23–25; © by the Tax Foundation, Inc.

proaches which are valid in the private sector inappropriate and even harmful in the case of public employment.

In evaluating these two positions, a number of facets of the public sector need to be taken into account. These include the essential nature of some public services, the absence of many of the market constraints which normally permit valid tests of management-labor offers and demands, views of the sovereignty of the State, and the political intermesh often associated with public sector labor problems.

Lack of Market Factors

Many of the market factors which bring pressures of various sorts on employers and employees do not exist at all or are very weak in the public sector. Several characteristics of the public sector make for a bargaining situation which differs from that in private industry: (1) the absence of a profit constraint, (2) sharply limited, all but nonexistent possibilities for capital substitution, (3) weak constraints on wage ceilings, (4) less visible accountability for management commitments in settlements, and (5) more than the usual difficulties in determining employees' productivity, particularly when a social product is involved.

The very significant absence of a profit constraint inevitably weakens the motivation with which a government employer, compared with a private employer, will seek to keep costs of a settlement down. The situation bears no resemblance to the private market, where an increase in the price of the product means the loss of customers and probable reduction both in profits and number of jobs offered by the firm. Generally speaking, the government's "customers" cannot turn elsewhere if the cost of the "product" goes up, and, even if they do, they nonetheless will continue to pay, through taxes, for most government services whether they use them or not.

Another difficulty government shares with some industries in the private sector: the possibilities for capital substitution when wages go up are all but nil in many government jobs. In private industry, the possibility of mechanization of processes often serves as a tacit constraint on wage demands and an escape route for employers. It is true, of course, that opportunities are rampant for automating clerical and similar operations in government. But how to automate the job of a policeman or a fireman or a garbageman? Mechanization can be utilized, but largely to make the civil servant's chore less arduous or even more pleasant, possibly to make it more efficient, but rarely to eliminate it.

The weakness of constraints on wage ceilings also sets the public bargaining situation apart from the private negotiation. When a private employer claims that the cost of employee demands could drive him out of business, he may be mistaken or bluffing. But experienced labor negotiators know that sometimes, in fact, high labor costs do make it impossible for a firm to continue operations, and this knowledge to some degree tempers the bargaining. For government, this simply cannot happen; the public employee will never find he has bargained his boss out of business and himself out of a job. He may, indeed, discover his action has forced individual supervisors or politicians out—but the institution, and hence his job, will inevitably continue, or, at least, historically always has.

One other difference acts in the union's favor. A government manager-negotiator can sometimes hope to hide part of the financial consequences of his bargaining if it is in his political interest to do so, whereas an owner-manager would have no motive for doing so. For one thing, the cost impact of a settlement—particularly one that includes such fringe benefits as pension adjustments—may not be manifest for some time; for another, municipal and state budgets can be such complex instruments, a tacit agreement between labor and management to conceal evidence of full costs, i.e., by understated estimates, would not be overwhelmingly difficult to implement.

Yet another problem arises from the virtual impossibility of measuring the productivity of most service-oriented work such as characterizes public services. When there is a social product (such as guarding public safety) involved, the difficulties become insurmountable. That is to say, no one can really determine with certainty what the output of a particular employee is worth, when he is not making some tangible item or service which in turn will be sold on a freely competitive market. So there may exist a question as to what is a fair wage, in the mind of both employee and manager. Such indefiniteness would tend to act more in favor of the employee, who rightfully will push for the highest possible wage, than of the employer, who may hesitate to be unjust.

Crucial Services

The disruption of the supply of certain types of government goods or services makes virtually no difference to the general public, while deprivation of others can create severe problems. Whether a strike in a given area will generate a public crisis appears to depend on such matters as (1) how frequently the good or service involved must be renewed, (2) whether its use is related to health and/or safety, and (3) whether substitutes or alternative sources of supply are available.

The third point has special significance in the case of many government goods and services; the government generally fulfills functions precisely because they are best performed by a "monopolist," although of course this consideration is not always the primary reason for government involvement. The necessity for monopoly elements can be illustrated in the matter of, say, police protection. The fact that supplementary police-type protection can be bought privately through the use of guard service, alarm systems, etc., does not weaken the basic point. In the absence of an effective police force, individual investment in such supplements would have to be increased to points which would require very high expenditures, and very wasteful diseconomies of scale. Moreover, private police cannot be as effective as a government force, since the ultimate power of government could not underlie their efforts.

Certain government services must be available practically continuously. In this category would fall many services, such as transportation, police, fire, and military protection, and various public health functions including sanitation. Moreover, some of these services play an important part in protecting public health and safety.

Thus in considering government labor relations, the relatively high importance of the product should be held foremost in mind. When the public is deprived of the output of most industries in the private sector, only inconvenience and annoyance result, whereas, in contrast, when the community is deprived of the output from many segments of government, social harm can result.

Some writers have suggested a classification of government services on the basis of how essential they might be, prohibiting strikes and mandating arbitration and other procedures in the case of the more critical employees, such as police and firemen. For instance, the Boston and Montreal police strikes demonstrated that public safety breaks down very quickly when police protection is removed. Such a situation can in no way be compared to a strike which, say, halts auto production for a time.

CLYDE SUMMERS, PUBLIC SECTOR BARGAINING: PROBLEMS OF GOVERNMENTAL DECISION–MAKING *

I. THE UNIQUENESS OF PUBLIC SECTOR BARGAINING

It is a threadbare truism that bargaining in the public sector is different from bargaining in the private sector, but the differences are often described in unhelpful detail, too much like the four blind men describing an elephant. Such descriptions will not help us either to make it work or to keep it under control. We ought, therefore, to describe the differences in more general and fundamental terms. To do that, we must start with the basic question: What, exactly, is unique about public sector bargaining?

There is nothing unique about public employees; they are no different from employees in the private sector. They have the same capacities, the same needs, and the same values; they seek the same advantages and the same gains. Many public sector employees previously have been, and with present trends perhaps even more will again become, private sector employees.

There is nothing unique about the work which public employees perform. The private sector has school teachers, nurses and social workers, as well as secretaries, bookkeepers, janitors, maintenance employees, construction workers, and rubbish collectors. There are private police, private detectives, private armed guards, and even private firefighters. Nor is the work necessarily any more critical because it is performed by public employees. Strikes by parochial

* Clyde Summers, "Public Sector Bargaining: Problems Of Governmental Decision–Making," 44 University of Cincinnati Law Review 660, 668, 675 (1976); © by the University of Cincinnati Law Review Association. Reprinted with permission.

school teachers create substantially the same inconvenience as strikes by public school teachers. A strike by janitors in public buildings may create fewer problems than a strike by janitors in private apartment buildings. A disruption in garbage collection may be less serious than a disruption in electric power or telephone service.

The uniqueness of public employment is not in the employees nor in the work performed; the uniqueness is in the special character of the employer. The employer is government; the ones who act on behalf of the employer are public officials; and the ones to whom those officials are answerable are citizens and voters. We have developed a whole structure of constitutional and statutory principles, and a whole culture of political practices and attitudes as to how government is to be conducted, what powers public officials are to exercise, and how they are to be made answerable for their actions. Collective bargaining by public employers must fit within the governmental structure and must function consistently with our governmental processes; the problems of the public employer accommodating its collective bargaining function to government structures and processes is what makes public sector bargaining unique.

To state the difference another way, in private sector bargaining we have never been concerned with how the employer decided on the policy to be brought to the bargaining table. We have been concerned with the union's decisionmaking process, requiring the union to observe minimal democratic standards, but we have not been concerned with the corporation's decisionmaking process. All that the law has required is that the employer send someone to the bargaining table who has authority to speak for and to bind the employer. Who instructs the negotiator, how his instructions are determined, and what his instructions may be is for the corporation to decide. The corporation's decisionmaking process is of no concern in collective bargaining; it is of little concern to the law.

When the employer is government, however, the employer's decisionmaking process becomes of central concern in both legal and political terms. The policies brought to the bargaining table are governmental policies. State constitutions and statutes, city charters and ordinances may prescribe procedures as to how these policies are to be decided, specify what bodies or officials shall make those decisions, and impose limitations on the decisions which can be made.

More specifically, in the private sector, the employer must send someone to the bargaining table with authority to make a binding agreement. In the public sector this may not be legally possible or politically sensible. Wages and other benefits directly affect the budget and the tax rates; but adopting budgets and levying taxes are considered, within our governmental system, fundamental legislative policies to be decided by the legislative body, not by a negotiator at the bargaining table. Dismissal procedures may be subject to constitutional requirements which limit the procedures which can be negotiated. Promotion policies may be governed by civil service principles which are written into the city charter and cannot be eliminated by bargaining. Modifications in state pension plans cannot, in most states, be made binding by negotiators, but must be ratified by the legislature. In the public sector, agreement at the bargaining table may be only an intermediate, not a final, step in the decisionmaking process.

Collective bargaining by a governmental employer is different because governmental decisionmaking is different. The unique problems, and the ones of central concern, focus on how government makes its decision. The unique and interesting legal problems are created by legal limitations on governmental decisionmaking. Beyond the legal problems, however, are the far more important ones of how the governmental decisions in collective bargaining ought to be made. The problems are more in the realm of political science than of labor relations. Our central concern is not, as in the private sector, with what will facilitate bargaining and reaching agreement, but with what are appropriate processes for governmental decisionmaking.

Two cases illustrate this crucial difference between the central questions in public sector and private sector bargaining. In Madison School District v. Wisconsin Employment Relations Board, a school teacher at a public meeting of the school board presented a petition urging the board not to agree to a "fair shares" provision in the agreement then being negotiated with the union. The board was charged with a prohibited labor practice for allowing the teacher to speak and for accepting the petition. In the private sector such conduct is barred because it may weaken the union's position as exclusive representative and may interfere with the bargaining process. In the public sector, we must confront the question whether citizens, teachers or otherwise, shall be allowed to make their views known to public officials on public issues. Beyond the constitutional issues of free speech and the right to petition is the judgmental question whether those making governmental decisions should be barred from hearing all views and opinions of all citizens before making decisions. The central concern is not the collective bargaining process but the governmental process.

In Detroit Police Officers v. City of Detroit, the voters of the city wrote into the city charter the benefits payable under the police and firemen's pension plan. As a result, those benefits could be changed only by referendum. This, of course, impeded the bargaining process; but that does not end the inquiry in the public sector. The legal question is whether the collective agreement can override the results of a referendum, but the crucial political question is who should have the final voice in determining the city's pension obligations. When we realize that the pension plan may create a larger long term obligation than any bond issue, creating a lien of undefined size for an indeterminate period, there are strong arguments for requiring voter approval, even though that impedes bargaining. Again the question is not what will facilitate bargaining, but what is the appropriate way of making the governmental decision. If certain acts may, in some measures, impede bargaining as we have known it in the private sector, that cannot end our inquiry. Our ultimate concern is not to make collective bargaining work, but to make government work. My first and basic proposition, then, is that in public employee bargaining, the fundamental issue to which we should be addressing ourselves is how the decisions of government should be made.

My second and subordinate proposition is that the major decisions made in bargaining with public employees are inescapably political decisions. They are political decisions in at least three senses. First, they involve critical policy choices. The matters debated at the bargaining table and decided by the contract are not simply questions of wages, hours, vacations and pensions. Directly at issue are political questions of the size and allocation of the budget, the tax rates, the level of public services, and the long term obligations of the government. These decisions as to budgets, taxes, services, and debts are political in the second sense that, within our system of government, they are to be made by the political branches of government—by elected officials who are politically responsible to the voters. Indeed, these decisions generally are considered uniquely legislative and not subject to delegation. Finally, these decisions are political in the ultimate sense that those making the decisions will do in the political market what business men do in the economic market—maximize their gains and minimize their losses. Politically elected officials in bargaining seek to maximize votes rather than profits.

The major decisions made in public employee bargaining not only are political, but in my view must be, and ought to be, political. The size of the budget, the taxes to be levied, the purposes for which tax money is to be used, the kinds and levels of governmental services to be enjoyed, and the level of indebtedness are issues that should be decided by officials who are politically responsible to those who pay the taxes and seek the services. The notion that we can or should insulate public employee bargaining from the political process either by arbitration or with some magic formula is a delusion of reality and a denigration of democratic government.

These two propositions—that our central concerns should be the processes of governmental decisionmaking, and that the governmental decisions made in collective bargaining are political decisions—focus our inquiry on the working of our political processes when decisions concerning terms and conditions of employment for public employees are made. Within this framework, which has a multitude of facets and difficult questions, I want to deal briefly, and in grossly oversimplified fashion, with three questions, more to focus on problem areas than to provide solutions. First, what is the alignment of political interest groups when decisions concerning terms and conditions of employment are made? Second, how does collective bargaining change the political effectiveness of the competing interest groups? Third, what are some of the special conditions which may impair the political process or significantly affect the balance of political forces?

A. The Political Alignment in Public Employment Issues

In most general terms, the demands of public employees are at the expense of the taxpayers and the users of public services. This is true whether or not there is collective bargaining. If a city's employees demand a wage increase, this can be granted only by increasing taxes or by reducing the number of employees and, in turn, the level of services. If the police demand two men in a patrol car, this can be met only by hiring more police or by reducing the number of patrol cars. The political alignment in decisions concerning terms and conditions of employment for public employees, therefore, finds on one side the public employees, who want higher wages, and benefits with lesser work loads, and on the other side the taxpayers, who want lower taxes, and the users of public service, who want more and better services.

This clash of interests can be extremely sharp. Because wages normally make up 65 to 70 percent of a city's current budget, a general wage increase will increase significantly the tax burden. Where the city's primary revenue source is the property tax, any increase is plainly visible in the mill rate and keenly felt in the annual tax bill. Reductions in services may be less visible and may affect only selected groups, but they still generate significant opposition.

In the political contest, the public employees are greatly outnumbered by taxpayers and users of public services. Public employees may compensate for this by the intensity of their interest and political activity, their greater cohesiveness, and their easier access to the machinery of government. Even at best, however, they may be no match for organized taxpayers, parents, or community groups and others demanding public services. Whatever may be the balance of political power, and there may be sharp disagreement both as to what it is and what it should be, the basic alignment is the public employees on one side and the taxpayers and users of public service on the other side. Therefore, our inquiries ought to be directed not only to the question of the proper balance, but also to how various factors may affect that balance. Only after such inquiries can we decide sensibly how to construct and manage a public employee bargaining system.

B. The Effect of Collective Bargaining on the Political Balance

Collective bargaining creates a special process for making decisions concerning terms and conditions of employment. That process significantly increases the effectiveness of the public employees' voice in those decisions in several ways. First, the principle of exclusive representation gives public employees a unified and authoritative voice. The majority union becomes the sole spokesman for the employees, and an agreement with it settles the terms and conditions for all employees in the unit. The ability to speak with a single voice and to provide a binding settlement gives added force and political weight to that voice in the public forum.

Second, the bargaining process gives public employees special access to the political process. They are not limited to speeches at public meetings, petitions, circulars or personal presentations, as other interest groups are. The union, representing all employees in bargaining, can compel responsible officials to sit down at the bargaining table, confront them face to face, engage in discussion, respond to arguments, state positions, provide reasons and supply information. The process of interchange continues through countless meetings of interminable hours until either agreement is reached or all possibilities are exhausted. This direct and intensive access to responsible officials, with its structured process of persuasion, gives the union an especially effective voice in the decisionmaking.

Third, because bargaining normally comes before the budget is adopted, public employees may obtain prior consideration of their interests, with collective agreements worked out before other sets of decisions are made. Once the agreement is made, the ability to consider other interests becomes limited. Even tentative agreements made at the bargaining table by negotiators who do not have the power to bind cannot be rejected without political costs. The agreement carries a political force of its own, giving it a measure of priority over competing claims.

Fourth, if bargaining is conducted behind closed doors, as is customary in the private sector, the union's voice gains added effectiveness. The public official is confronted with the union's demands and arguments without direct exposure to the competing demands and arguments. The pressures of hard bargaining through extended sessions push toward acceptance of the union's demands at the expense of other interests which are unable to make their weight felt because they do not know what is being decided at the bargaining table. Once an agreement, even a merely tentative one, is reached at the bargaining table, the opposing interests are placed at a substantial political disadvantage. The issue becomes whether the agreement should be repudiated, rather than what agreement should be made in the first place.

Fifth, the union by obtaining bargaining rights can build an organizational structure and develop resources to be used in political forums other than bargaining. Practically, though not legally, it becomes the voice of the employees on all political issues. More importantly, it may provide the organizational base, if not the financial means, for electing those who support their bargaining demands and defeating those who oppose them.

I would emphasize that the political effectiveness of public employees and their organizations does not necessarily depend upon collective bargaining. Organizations of policemen and firemen were politically powerful in many cities long before they obtained bargaining rights. Teachers' organizations were able to obtain salary increases, reduced classes, and many other benefits even when they shunned the words "bargaining" and "negotiations." These organizations were able to bring effective pressure to bear through the ordinary political channels available to other interest groups.

Collective bargaining, however, does provide a special process available only to public employees, and equally available to all classes of public employees. It significantly increases the political effectiveness of public employees in determining their terms and conditions of employment, particularly relative to other competing political interest groups. This does not mean that collective bargaining gives public employees dominant political power or enables them to obtain more than their fair share. Arrayed against public employees are the massive interest groups of taxpayers and the users of public services. Nearly every voter is threatened in one or even both capacities by union demands which must increase either the size of the budget or the share allocated to labor costs or both. Those interest groups are not only massive, but are capable of effective political organization, as anyone who has confronted taxpayers' leagues, parents' organizations, property owners' associations, or chambers of commerce well knows. In my view, one of the principal justifications for public employee bargaining is that most public employees need this special process to give them an ability to counteract the overriding political strength of other voters who constantly press for lower taxes and increased services.

Even collective bargaining without the availability of the strike often leaves public employees in a vulnerable political position. I have seen too many cases of taxpayers who, having received wage and salary increases themselves, and daily paying more for every good and service they buy, adamantly insist that their public employees continue to render the same service at the same wage. The repeated refrain at bargaining tables by those representing the public employer, particularly during the last three years, has been: "We must hold the line. The taxpayers will not stand for an increase." Nor have these been empty claims, as the wreckage of defeated tax and bond referenda testify. Anyone who still believes that public employee unions can ride roughshod over opposing interest groups should examine the results of the recent voting, on both candidates and referenda, in San Francisco.

My central point here, however, is not that collective bargaining gives public employees too much or too little political effectiveness. That is a debate for another day. My purpose here is only to map out in the boldest relief the competing political forces which operate when decisions are made as to the terms and conditions of public employment, and to point out how collective bargaining affects the relative effectiveness of those competing political groups.

C. Some Special Problems of Political Process

Collective bargaining by public employees creates unfamiliar problems of political process which at times place unusual stress on that process. Our ability to construct and manage a system of public employee bargaining depends largely on our identifying and understanding those problems, five of which are briefly sketched below.

First is the problem of the smoke-filled room—the problem created by the parties' insistence that bargaining be carried on behind closed doors. It may be that in the private sector secret bargaining facilitates reaching agreement. However, the bargaining is often less secret in fact than in form. Moreover, though secrecy may facilitate agreement at the bargaining table, it may frustrate ratification by the members. But in the public sector, agreements made in smoke-filled rooms are necessarily suspect. In principle, it is inappropriate to have public decisions affecting taxes, budgets and public services made by unions and public officials behind closed doors, so that the public has no knowledge of what is going on until presented with an agreement.

Such secrecy, by precluding any political reaction by other interest groups while the agreement is being worked out at the bargaining table, creates debilitating consequences. When the tentative agreement is presented, the public does not know what the issues were at the bargaining table, what facts were presented, or what considerations entered into what compromises. One consequence is public apathy and a sense of hopelessness in making any critical judgment of the agreement, with the result of blind acceptance of questionable agreements. At the same time there is generated public distrust, with a willingness to blame the financial ills of the city on its collective agreements. The distrust, in turn, leads later to repudiation by the taxpayers of even the most modest agreements; ultimately it creates resistance at the bargaining table to reasonable union demands. The smoke-filled room manifestly frustrates the democratic process and ultimately impedes the bargaining process. I am suggesting not that public employee bargaining be conducted in a goldfish bowl, but only that the smoke-filled room be opened occasionally to let in a little light and fresh air, and to let out public knowledge of the issues, the positions of the parties, and the progress toward agreement.

The second problem I would like to sketch is the problem of the handwringing politician—the public official who claims he is unable to withstand the pressures generated by the union for unreasonable demands. If he believes the union's demands are unreasonable, he should be marshalling the opposing political forces—the taxpayers and the users of public services who have massive political potential—instead of wringing his hands. The voters often do not realize the ultimate consequences of a union demand and so do not react. If the police demand a 12 percent increase, the cost may not seem substantial, but granting this demand may require equivalent increases for all other public employees. By making taxpayers aware that what might seem like a minor cost increase will set off a chain reaction resulting in a 3 mill tax increase, a political leader can build a more than adequate political counterforce to offset the union's pressure. Similarly, demands for increases by employees in public works can be translated into terms understandable to voters, such as less snow removal, more potholes in the streets, unkempt parks, and un-lighted streets. A political leader who is unable to make that transla-tion and who informs the voters that he feels compelled to surrender to excessive union demands should be allowed to wring his hands a final time on election night.

The third problem is what I call the political buck-passer—the po-litical official who buys a settlement with the union by passing the financial burden on to future budgets and future taxes. The para-digm example is the increase in pension benefits which is not fully funded out of the current budget, so that taxpayers are not aware of the costs of settlement which they must bear in future years. A more visible, and therefore less effective, form of buck-passing is the two- or three-year contract with the rear-end load, or even the one-year contract made before election which requires no increased taxes until after election. In these cases, the employees appreciate fully the value of the benefits, but the taxpayers do not feel the cost until it is too late to respond politically, for those who made the settlement may have promoted themselves to higher office or retired to private life.

Eliminating political buck-passing entirely is impossible, but legal restrictions could be put on pension plans to require that current fi-nancing reflect current costs, and that future costs be realistically estimated and be approved in the same manner as that required for long term bonded indebtedness. Perhaps we also should put legal limits on contract duration, so that the political officials responsible for negotiations can be held politically responsible for their agree-ments.

The fourth problem is the problem of strange political bedfellows, a problem that is probably less prevalent in collective bargaining than in other political decisions, but which in many respects is more troub-ling. The normal political alignment, as I have pointed out, joins the taxpayers and the users of public services in opposition to the de-mands of public employees. But this is not always the case. If teachers demand a reduction in class size to lighten their teaching load, their demand may be supported by the parents who see smaller classes as providing better schools. Parents also may see higher teacher salaries, tuition payment benefits, and many other teacher de-mands as improving the quality of education for their children. Al-though the parents are taxpayers, they do not pay the full cost, for non-parents, parents with children no longer in school, businesses and industries must pay a share of the increased taxes. The result is that the parents, as users of the service and as taxpayers, become political bedfellows with the teachers' bargaining representative, leaving the remaining taxpayers vulnerable to their combined pressure.

This problem of political misalignment may take an even more troublesome form. When union demands impose increased costs, the political response may be not to increase taxes or to reduce services generally, but to obtain the necessary funds by selectively cutting services of politically impotent groups. Thus, wage increases may be granted by cutting welfare benefits, letting playgrounds deteriorate, closing public hospitals, or reducing garbage pick-ups in ghetto areas. The union is kept happy, the opposition of taxpayers is neutralized, and most users of public services are unaffected. The opposition is limited largely to groups whose political voice at the polls is less effective than the union's voice at the bargaining table.

Finally, I want to call attention to what may be the most difficult problem of all, the problem of anesthetized taxpayers—that is, taxpayers who are unaware of the pain of paying taxes. In local political units where most voters are homeowners and where the primary source of revenue is the property tax, every increase in taxes is felt keenly and generates strong political reaction. But in cities where many voters rent housing rather than own homes, tax increases will not generate as much reaction, for most renters are quite unaware of property tax increases, which are buried in rent increases. Even the best efforts of the landlord to persuade renters that their higher rent is due to higher taxes will seldom succeed. Although renters are in fact taxpayers, they do not react as taxpayers. As a consequence, they do not provide a reservoir of political resistance to union demands. In large cities where renters may constitute a majority of the voters, the dominant pressure may be for increased services and increased wages, regardless of the increased taxes. To the extent that reliance is placed on sales taxes or payroll taxes, the taxpayer may be roused from his slumber, but taxpayers are probably less sensitive to these than to property taxes.

I have no adequate answers for the last two problems—the problem of strange political bedfellows and the problem of anesthetized taxpayers. These exist quite apart from collective bargaining. The politics of budgetmaking is customarily one of promiscuous bedfellowship, and anesthetized taxpayers demand services with indifference as to costs, regardless of unions. The added pressures of collective bargaining have simply aggravated these problems and called them again to our attention.

These shifts in political alignments and the failure of taxpayers to react to increased labor costs create disparities in bargaining power and may lead, in some situations, to high labor costs. A partial, though admittedly unsatisfying, answer is that we accept comparable conditions in the private sector with scarcely a quibble. Although in some industries, such as the textile industry in the South, unions cannot bargain effectively and can barely survive, in other industries, such as local haulage, employers may be unable to resist union demands. In the private sector we have employers and unions purportedly bargaining against each other but actually combining to pass off high labor costs to the consuming public. There is one single difference: in the private sector the consumers who pay have no possibility of voting out of office those who negotiated the agreements. If we examined private sector bargaining as critically as we do public sector bargaining, we might conclude that it has as many, or more, troublesome problems than public sector bargaining.

III. CONCLUSION

My purpose here is not to judge whether public sector bargaining is a bane or a boon. Nor is it to argue that collective bargaining gives public employees too little or too much political effectiveness. My primary concern at the moment is that we ask the right questions, for that must precede finding the proper answers. The significant questions in public employee bargaining are questions of governmental decisionmaking: By what process shall these important policy decisions be made, and by whom? The answers will not be found by comparing bargaining in the public sector with bargaining in the private sector, nor by asking simply what will facilitate bargaining. They will be found only by examining critically the impact of bargaining on the political process and asking what will improve that process within the premises of democratic government. The five problems I have sketched are intended only as samples of the difficulties which we must recognize and try to meet as problems of political process. There are others of the same order, which we must confront if we are to construct and manage a system of collective bargaining appropriate to governmental decisionmaking.

HARRY H. WELLINGTON AND RALPH K. WINTER, JR., THE LIMITS OF COLLECTIVE BARGAINING IN PUBLIC EMPLOYMENT *

Good lawyers are good critics. The nature of their discipline makes this skill necessary, and the content of their work brings it inevitably to bear upon doctrines and concepts laboriously constructed by their predecessors. In approaching questions involving collective bargaining and public employment, union lawyers and academic commentators have for some years been criticizing the concept of the sovereignty of the public employer, and its offspring, the doctrine of the illegal delegation of power. These two lawyer-made constructs once had imposed formidable obstacles to collective bargaining in the public sector of our economy. But this criticism, vastly strengthened by the changing nature of government employment and the ever visible example of collective bargaining in the private sector, has led to a liberalized common law and a growing body of enacted law and has reduced to a whisper the counsel of restraint voiced by these constructs.

Consider sovereignty, that concept so elusive as an analytical tool, yet so fundamental to all notions of government. A law dictionary advises that it is the "supreme, absolute, and uncontrollable power by which any independent state is governed * * *." Since collective bargaining in the private sector is believed by many to be a system of countervailing power—a means, that is, by which the power of employees is increased to offset that of employers—one might easily see

* Harry H. Wellington and Ralph K. Winter, Jr., "The Limits Of Collective Bargaining In Public Employment," 78 Yale Law Journal 1107 (1970); © 1970 by the Yale Law Journal Company. Reprinted by permission of the Yale Law Journal Company and Fred B. Rothman & Company.

its establishment in the public sector as an infringement on governmental power and the sovereignty of the state itself. Viewing the
"supreme, absolute, and uncontrollable" sovereign in its role as an
employer, therefore, Franklin Roosevelt understandably said, "A
strike of public employees manifests nothing less than an intent on
their part to obstruct the operations of government until their demands are satisfied. Such action looking toward the paralysis of
government by those who have sworn to support it is unthinkable and
intolerable." [10]

But, to the lawyer-critics, sovereignty seems a weak reed when
the private analogy is pressed. It was 1836 when a judge observed
that if collective bargaining in the private sector were "tolerated, the
constitutional control over our affairs would pass away from the people at large, and become vested in the hands of conspirators. We
should have a new system of government, and our rights [would] be
placed at the disposal of a voluntary and self-constituted association."
Such sovereignty-related assertions are no longer thought to have applicability to the private sector, for private collective bargaining has
served as the nation's labor policy for more than a generation—not
without criticism, but surely without any sign of the apocalypse.
And so, conclude the critics, the notion of sovereignty as a bar to
collective bargaining is not a concept peculiar to the public employer,
but is merely an anti-union make-weight left over from an earlier day
when the law was hostile to all collective bargaining.

Sovereignty must also seem to the critics too elusive and too remote a concept to be of practical significance in the fashioning of labor policy. The issue is not, they say, whether government's power
is "supreme," but how government as an employer ought to exercise
that power. And the concept of sovereignty, while it locates the
source of ultimate authority, does not seem to speak to that issue.

* * *

II. THE CLAIMS FOR COLLECTIVE BARGAINING
IN THE PUBLIC SECTOR

In the area of public employment the claims upon public policy
made by the need for industrial peace, industrial democracy and ef-

---

10. Consider the following statement
of Charles E. Wilson made in 1948 when
he was President of General Motors:

If we consider the ultimate result of
this tendency to stretch collective bargaining to comprehend any subject
that a union leader may desire to bargain on, we come out with the union
leaders really running the economy of
the country; but with no legal or public responsibility and with no private
employment except as they may permit.

Under these conditions, the freedom of
management to function properly with-

out interference in making its everyday decisions will be gradually restricted. The union leaders—particularly
where they have industry-wide power—will have the deciding vote in all
managerial decisions, or at least, will
exercise a veto power that will stop
progress.

Only by defining and restricting collective bargaining to its proper sphere can
we hope to save what we have come to
know as our American system and
keep it from evolving into an alien
form, imported from East of the Rhine
* * *.

fective political representation point toward collective bargaining. This is to say that three of the four arguments that support bargaining in the private sector—to some extent, at least—press for similar arrangements in the public sector.

Government is a growth industry, particularly state and municipal government. While federal employment between 1963 and 1968 has increased from 2.36 million to 2.73 million, state and local employment has risen from 6.87 to 9.42 million, and the increase continues apace. With size comes bureaucracy, and with bureaucracy comes the isolation and alienation of the individual worker. His manhood, like that of his industrial counterpart, is threatened. Lengthening chains of command necessarily depersonalize the employment relationship and contribute to a sense of powerlessness on the part of the worker. If he is to share in the governance of his employment relationship as he does in the private sector, it must be through the device of representation, which means unionization. Accordingly, just as the increase in the size of economic units in private industry fostered unionism so the enlarging of governmental bureaucracy has encouraged public employees to look to collective action for a sense of control over their employment destiny. The number of government employees, moreover, makes it plain that those employees are members of an interest group which can organize for political representation as well as for job participation.

The pressures thus generated by size and bureaucracy lead inescapably to disruption—to labor unrest—unless these pressures are recognized and unless existing decision-making procedures are accommodated to them. Peace in government employment too, the argument runs, can best be established by making union recognition and collective bargaining accepted public policy.

Much less clearly analogous to the private model, however, is the unequal bargaining power argument. In the private sector that argument really has two aspects. The first * * * is affirmative in nature. Monopsony is believed sometimes to result in unfair individual contracts of employment. The unfairness may be reflected in wages, which are less than they would be if the market were more nearly perfect, or in working arrangements which may lodge arbitrary power in a foreman, i.e., power to hire, fire, promote, assign or discipline without respect to substantive or procedural rules. A persistent assertion, generating much heat, relates to the arbitrary exercise of managerial power in individual cases. This assertion goes far to explain the insistence of unions on the establishment in the labor contract of rules, with an accompanying adjudicatory procedure, to govern industrial life.

Judgments about the fairness of the financial terms of the public employee's individual contract of employment are even harder to make than for private sector workers. The case for the existence of private employer monopsony, disputed as it is, asserts only that some private sector employers in some circumstances have too much bargaining power. In the public sector, the case to be proven is that the governmental employer ever has such power. But even if this case could be proven, market norms are at best attenuated guides to questions of fairness. In employment as in all other areas, governmental decisions are properly political decisions, and economic considerations are but one criterion among many. Questions of fairness do not centrally relate to how much imperfection one sees in the market, but more to how much imperfection one sees in the political process. "Low" pay for teachers may be merely a decision—right or wrong, resulting from the pressure of special interests or from a desire to promote the general welfare—to exchange a reduction in the quality or quantity of teachers for higher welfare payments, a domed stadium, etc. And we are limited in our ability to make informed judgments about such political decisions because of the understandable but unfortunate fact that the science of politics has failed to supply us with either as elegant or as reliable a theoretical model as has its sister discipline.

Nevertheless, employment benefits in the public sector may have improved relatively more slowly than in the private sector during the last three decades. An economy with a persistent inflationary bias probably works to the disadvantage of those who must rely on legislation for wage adjustments. Moreover, while public employment was once attractive for the greater job security and retirement benefits it provided, quite similar protection is now available in many areas of the private sector. On the other hand, to the extent that civil service, or merit, systems exist in public employment and these laws are obeyed, the arbitrary exercise of managerial power is substantially reduced. Where it is reduced, a labor policy that relies on the individual employment contract must seem less unacceptable.

The second, or negative aspect of the unequal bargaining power argument, relates to the social costs of collective bargaining. As we have seen the social costs of collective bargaining in the private sector are principally economic, and seem inherently limited by market forces. In the public sector, however, the costs seem to us economic only in a very narrow sense and are on the whole political. It further seems to us that, to the extent union power is delimited by market or other forces in the public sector, these constraints do not come into play nearly as quickly as in the private.

* * *

In the public sector too, the market operates. In the long run, the supply of labor is a function of the price paid for labor by the public employer relative to what workers earn elsewhere. This is some assurance that public employees in the aggregate—with or without collective bargaining—are not paid too little. The case for employer monopsony, moreover, may be much weaker in the public sector than it is in the private. First, to the extent that most public employees work in urban areas, as they probably do, there may often be a number of substitutable and competing private and public employers in the labor market. When that is the case, there can be little monopsony power. Second, even if public employers occasionally have monopsony power, governmental policy is determined only in part by economic criteria, and there is no assurance, as there is in the private sector where the profit motive prevails, that the power will be exploited.

* * * market-imposed unemployment is an important restraint on unions in the private sector. In the public sector, the trade-off between benefits and employment seems much less important. Government does not generally sell a product the demand for which is closely related to price. There usually are not close substitutes for the products and services provided by government and the demand for them is inelastic. Such market conditions are, as we have seen, favorable to unions in the private sector because they permit the acquisition of benefits without the penalty of unemployment, subject to the restraint of non-union competitors, actual or potential. But no such restraint limits the demands of public employee unions. Because much government activity is, and must be, a monopoly, product competition, non-union or otherwise, does not exert a downward pressure on prices and wages. Nor will the existence of a pool of labor ready to work for a wage below union scale attract new capital and create a new, and competitively less expensive, governmental enterprise.

Even if we are right that a close relationship between increased economic benefits and unemployment does not exist as a significant deterrent to unions in the public sector, might not the argument be made that in some sense the taxpayer is the public sector's functional equivalent of the consumer? If taxes become too high, the taxpayer can move to another community. While it is generally much easier for a consumer to substitute products than for a taxpayer to substitute communities, is it not fair to say that, at the point at which a tax increase will cause so many taxpayers to move that it will produce less total revenue, the market disciplines or restrains union and public employer in the same way and for the same reasons that the market disciplines parties in the private sector? Moreover, does not the analogy to the private sector suggest that it is legitimate in an economic sense for unions to push government to the point of substitutability?

Several factors suggest that the answer to this latter question is at best indeterminate, and that the question of legitimacy must be judged not by economic, but by political criteria.

In the first place, there is no theoretical reason—economic or political—to suppose that it is desirable for a governmental entity to liquidate its taxing power, to tax up to the point where another tax increase will produce less revenue because of the number of people it drives to different communities. In the private area, profit maximization is a complex concept, but its approximation generally is both a legal requirement and socially useful as a means of allocating resources. The liquidation of taxing power seems neither imperative nor useful.

Second, consider the complexity of the tax structure and the way in which different kinds of taxes (property, sales, income) fall differently upon a given population. Consider, moreover, that the taxing authority of a particular governmental entity may be limited (a municipality may not have the power to impose an income tax). What is necessarily involved, then, is principally the redistribution of income by government rather than resource allocation, and questions of income redistribution surely are essentially political questions.

For his part, the mayor in our * * * case will be disciplined not by a desire to maximize profits, but by a desire—in some cases at least—to do a good job (to effectuate his programs), and in virtually all cases either to be reelected or to move to a better elective office. What he gives to the union must be taken from some other interest group or from taxpayers. His is the job of coordinating these competing claims while remaining politically viable. And that coordination will be governed by the relative power of the competing interest groups. Our inquiry, therefore, must turn to the question of how much power public employee unions will exercise if the full private model of collective bargaining is adopted in the public sector.

V.   PUBLIC EMPLOYEES STRIKES AND THE POLITICAL PROCESS

Although the market does not discipline the union in the public sector to the extent that it does in the private, the paradigm case, nevertheless, would seem to be consistent with what Robert A. Dahl has called the " 'normal' American political process," which is "one in which there is a high probability that an active and legitimate group in the population can make itself heard effectively at some crucial stage in the process of decision," for the union may be seen as little more than an "active and legitimate group in the population." With elections in the background to perform, as Mr. Dahl tells us, "the critical role * * * in maximizing political equality and popular sovereignty," all seems well, at least theoretically, with collective bargaining and public employment.

But there is trouble even in the house of theory if collective bargaining in the public sector means what it does in the private. The trouble is that if unions are able to withhold labor—to strike—as well as to employ the usual methods of political pressure, they may possess a disproportionate share of effective power in the process of decision. Collective bargaining would then be so effective a pressure as to skew the results of the " 'normal' American political process."

One should straightway make plain that the strike issue is not *simply* the essentiality of public services as contrasted with services or products produced in the private sector. This is only half of the issue, and in the past the half truth has beclouded analysis. The services performed by a private transit authority are neither less nor more essential to the public than those that would be performed if the transit authority were owned by a municipality. A railroad or a dock strike may be much more damaging to a community than "job action" by teachers. This is not to say that governmental services are not essential. They are, both because the demand for them is inelastic and because their disruption may seriously injure a city's economy and occasionally the physical welfare of its citizens. Nevertheless, essentiality of governmental services is only a necessary part of, rather than a complete answer to, the question: What is wrong with strikes in public employment?

What is wrong with strikes in public employment is that because they disrupt essential services, a large part of a mayor's political constituency will press for a quick end to the strike with little concern for the cost of settlement. The problem is that because market restraints are attenuated and because public employee strikes cause inconvenience to voters, such strikes too often succeed. Since other interest groups with conflicting claims on municipal government do not, as a general proposition, have anything approaching the effectiveness of this union technique—or at least cannot maintain this relative degree of power over the long run—they are put at a significant competitive disadvantage in the political process. Where this is the case, it must be said that the political process has been radically altered. And because of the deceptive simplicity of the analogy to collective bargaining in the private sector, the alteration may take place without anyone realizing what has happened.

Therefore, while the purpose and effect of strikes by public employees may seem in the beginning merely designed to establish collective bargaining or to "catch up" with wages and fringe benefits in the private sector, in the long run strikes must be seen as a means to redistribute income, or, put another way, to gain a subsidy for union members,[57] not through the employment of the usual types of political pressure, but through the employment of what might appropriately be called political force.

* * *

VI.　SOVEREIGNTY AND DELEGATION REVISITED

As applied to public employment, there is a concept of sovereignty entitled to count as a reason for making strikes by public employees illegal. For what sovereignty should mean in this field is not the location of ultimate authority—on that the critics are dead right—but the right of government, through its laws, to ensure the survival of the " 'normal' American political process." As hard as it may be for some to accept, strikes by public employees may, as a long run proposition, threaten that process.

Moreover, it is our view—although this would seem to be much less clear—that the public stake in some issues makes it appropriate

---

57.　Strikes in some areas of the private sector may have this effect, too. The difference in the impact of collective bargaining in the two sectors should be seen as a continuum. Thus, for example, it may be that market restraints do not sufficiently discipline strike settlements in some regulated industries, or in industries that rely mainly on government contracts. If this is so—and we do not know that it is—perhaps there should be tighter restraints on the use of the strike in those areas.

for government either not to have to bargain with its employees on these issues at all or to follow bargaining procedures radically different from those of the private sector. It is in this respect that the judicial doctrine of illegal delegation of power should have relevance.

J. F. BURTON & C. KRIDERER, THE ROLE AND CONSEQUENCES OF STRIKES BY PUBLIC EMPLOYEES *

A. BENEFITS OF COLLECTIVE BARGAINING

Wellington and Winter believe the benefits of collective action, including strikes, are less in the public sector than in the private sector since (1) the problem of employer monopsony is less serious, and (2) any use of monopsony power in the public sector which results in certain groups, such as teachers, receiving low pay may reflect, not a misallocation of resources, but rather a political determination of the desired use of resources.

*   *   *

Wellington and Winter assert that employer monopsony is less likely to exist or be used in the public than in the private sector. But as they concede, referring to Bunting, monopsony is not widespread in the private sector and, except in a few instances, cannot be used as a rationale for trade unions. They provide no evidence that monopsony is less prevalent in the public than in the private sector. Moreover, other labor market inefficiencies, common to the public and private sectors, are probably more important than monopsony in providing an economic justification for unions. For example, the deficiencies of labor market information are to some extent overcome by union activities, and there is no reason to assume that this benefit differs between the public and private sectors.

Assuming there is monopsony power, Wellington and Winter believe that collective bargaining in the private sector can eliminate unfair wages "which are less than they would be if the market were more nearly perfect." They assert, however, that low pay for an occupation in the public sector may reflect a political judgment which ought not to be countered by pressures resulting from a strike. To say, however, that the pay for an occupation would be higher if the employees had the right to strike than if they did not is not independent proof that strikes are inappropriate. The same criticism could be made of any activity by a public employee group which affects its pay. An independent rationale must be provided to explain why some means which are effective in raising wages (strikes) are inappropriate while other means which are also effective (lobbying) are appropriate. Whether the Wellington and Winter discussion of the politically based

* J. F. Burton & C. Kriderer, "The Role And Consequences Of Strikes By Public Employees," 79 Yale Law Journal 418 (1970); © 1970 by the Yale Law Journal Company. Reprinted with the permission of the Yale Law Journal Company and Fred B. Rothman & Co.

decision-making model for the public sector provides this rationale will be discussed in more detail subsequently.

B.   Costs of Collective Bargaining

Wellington and Winter's discussion of the cost of substituting collective for individual bargaining in the public sector includes a chain of causation which runs from (1) an allegation that market restraints are weak in the public sector, largely because the services are essential; to (2) an assertion that the public puts pressure on civic officials to arrive at a quick settlement; to (3) a statement that other pressure groups have no weapons comparable to a strike; to (4) a conclusion that the strike thus imposes a high cost since the political process is distorted.

Let us discuss these steps in order:

(1) *Market Restraints:* A key argument in the case for the inappropriateness of public sector strikes is that economic constraints are not present to any meaningful degree in the public sector. This argument is not entirely convincing. First, wages lost due to strikes are as important to public employees as they are to employees in the private sector. Second, the public's concern over increasing tax rates may prevent the decision-making process from being dominated by political instead of economic considerations. The development of multilateral bargaining in the public sector is an example of how the concern over taxes may result in a close substitute for market constraints. In San Francisco, for example, the Chamber of Commerce has participated in negotiations between the city and public employee unions and has had some success in limiting the economic gains of the unions. A third and related economic constraint arises for such services as water, sewage and, in some instances, sanitation, where explicit prices are charged. Even if representatives of groups other than employees and the employer do not enter the bargaining process, both union and local government are aware of the economic implications of bargaining which leads to higher prices which are clearly visible to the public. A fourth economic constraint on employees exists in those services where subcontracting to the private sector is a realistic alternative. Warren, Michigan, resolved a bargaining impasse with an American Federation of State, County and Municipal Employees (AFSCME) local by subcontracting its entire sanitation service; Santa Monica, California, ended a strike of city employees by threatening to subcontract its sanitation operations. If the subcontracting option is preserved, wages in the public sector need not exceed the rate at which subcontracting becomes a realistic alternative.

An aspect of the lack-of-market-restraints argument is that public services are essential. Even at the analytical level, Wellington and Winter's case for essentiality is not convincing. They argue:

> The Services performed by a private transit authority are neither less nor more essential to the public than those that would be performed if the transit authority were owned by a municipality. A railroad or a dock strike may be much more damaging to a com-

munity than "job action" by teachers. This is not to say that government services are not essential. They are both because they may seriously injure a city's economy and occasionally the physical welfare of its citizens.

This is a troublesome passage. It ends with the implicit conclusion that all government services are essential. This conclusion is important in Wellington and Winter's analysis because it is a step in their demonstration that strikes are inappropriate in all governmental services. But the beginning of the passage, with its example of "job action" by teachers, suggests that essentiality is not an *inherent* characteristic of government services but depends on the specific service being evaluated. Furthermore the transit authority example suggests that many services are interchangeable between the public and private sectors. The view that various government services are not of equal essentiality and that there is considerable overlap between the kinds of services provided in the public and private sectors is reinforced by our field work and strike data from the Bureau of Labor Statistics. Examples include:

1. Where sanitation services are provided by a municipality, such as Cleveland, sanitationmen are prohibited from striking. Yet, sanitationmen in Philadelphia, Portland, and San Francisco are presumably free to strike since they are employed by private contractors rather than by the cities.

2. There were 25 local government strikes by the Teamsters in 1965–68, most involving truck drivers and all presumably illegal. Yet the Teamsters' strike involving fuel oil truck drivers in New York City last winter was legal even though the interruption of fuel oil service was believed to have caused the death of several people.

(2) *Public Pressure:* The second argument in the Wellington and Winter analysis is that public pressure on city officials forces them to make quick settlements. The validity of this argument depends on whether the service is essential. Using as a criterion whether the service is essential in the short run, we believe a priori that services can be divided into three categories: (1) essential services—police and fire—where strikes immediately endanger public health and safety; (2) intermediate services—sanitation, hospitals, transit, water, and sewage—where strikes of a few days might be tolerated; (3) nonessential services—streets, parks, education, housing, welfare and general administration—where strikes of indefinite duration could be tolerated. These categories are not exact since essentiality depends on the size of the city. Sanitation strikes will be critical in large cities such as New York but will not cause much inconvenience in smaller cities where there are meaningful alternatives to governmental operation of sanitation services.

Statistics on the duration of strikes which occurred in the public sector between 1965 and 1968 provide evidence not only that public services are unequal essentially, but also that the a priori categories which we have used have some validity. Strikes in the essential services (police and fire) had an average duration of 4.7 days, while both the intermediate and the nonessential services had an average duration of approximately 10.5 days. It is true that the duration of strikes in the intermediate and nonessential services is only half the average duration of strikes in the private sector during these years. However, this comparison is somewhat misleading since all of the public sector strikes were illegal, and many were ended by injunction, while presumably a vast majority of the private sector strikes did not suffer from these constraints. It would appear that with the exception of police and fire protection, public officials are, to some degree, able to accept long strikes. The ability of governments to so choose indicates that political pressures generated by strikes are not so strong as to undesirably distort the entire decision-making process of government. City officials in Kalamazoo, Michigan, were able to accept a forty-eight day strike by sanitationmen and laborers; Sacramento County, California, survived an eighty-seven day strike by welfare workers. A three month strike of hospital workers has occurred in Cuyahoga County (Cleveland), Ohio.

(3) *The Strike as a Unique Weapon:* The third objection to the strike is that it provides workers with a weapon unavailable to the employing agency or to other pressure groups. Thus, unions have a superior arsenal. The Taylor Committee Report opposes strikes for this reason, among others, arguing that "there can scarcely be a countervailing lockout." Conceptually, we see no reason why lockouts are less feasible in the public than in the private sector. Legally, public sector lockouts are now forbidden, but so are strikes; presumably both could be legalized. Actually, public sector lockouts have occurred. The Social Service Employees Union (SSEU) of New York City sponsored a "work-in" in 1967 during which all of the caseworkers went to their office but refused to work. Instead, union-sponsored lectures were given by representatives of organizations such as CORE, and symposia were held on the problems of welfare workers and clients. The work-in lasted for one week, after which the City locked out the caseworkers.

A similar assertion is made by Wellington and Winter, who claim that no pressure group other than unions has a weapon comparable to the strike. But this argument raises a number of questions. Is the distinctive characteristic of an inappropriate method of influencing decisions by public officials that it is economic as opposed to political? If this is so, then presumably the threat of the New York Stock Exchange to move to New Jersey unless New York City taxes on stock transfers were lowered and similar devices should be outlawed along with the strike.

(4) *Distortion of the Political Process:* The ultimate concern of both the Taylor Committee and Wellington and Winter is that "a strike of government employees   *   *   *   introduces an alien force

in the legislative process." It is "alien" because, in the words of the Taylor Committee Report:

> Careful thought about the matter shows conclusively, we believe, that while the right to strike normally performs a useful function in the private enterprise sector (where relative economic power is the final determinant in the making of private agreements), it is not compatible with the orderly functioning of our democratic form of representative government (in which relative political power is the final determinant).

The essence of this analysis appears to be that certain means used to influence the decision-making process in the public sector—those which are political—are legitimate, while other—those which are economic—are not. For several reasons, we believe that such distinctions among means are tenuous.

First, any scheme which differentiates economic power from political power faces a perplexing definitional task. The *International Encyclopedia of the Social Sciences* defines the political process as "the activities of people in various groups as they struggle for—and use—power to achieve personal and group purposes." And what is power?

> Power in use invariably involves a mixture of many different forms—sometimes mutually reinforcing—of persuasion and pressure * * *.

> Persuasion takes place when A influences B to adopt a course of action without A's promising or threatening any reward or punishment. It may take the form of example, expectation, proposals, information, education, or propaganda * * *.

> Pressure is applied by A upon B whenever A tries to make a course of action more desirable by promising or threatening contingent rewards or punishments. It may take the form of force, commands, manipulation, or bargaining * * *.

> Physical force is a blunt instrument * * *. Besides, more flexible and reliable modes of pressure are available. Rewards, in the form of monetary payments, new positions, higher status, support, favorable votes, cooperation, approval, or the withdrawal of any anticipated punishment, may be bestowed or promised. Punishment, in the form of fines, firing, reduction in status, unfavorable votes, noncooperation, rejection, disapproval, or withdrawal of any anticipated reward, may be given or threatened * * *.

> Bargaining is a still more fluid—and far more persuasive—form of using pressure. In bargaining, all sides exercise power upon each other through reciprocal promises or threats * * *. Indeed, force, command, and manipulation tend to become enveloped in the broader and more subtle processes of bargaining.

We have quoted at length from this discussion of the political process because we believe it illustrates the futility of attempting to distinguish between economic and political power. The former concept would seem to be encompassed by the latter. The degree of overlap is problematical since there can be economic aspects to many forms of persuasion and pressure. It may be possible to provide an operational distinction between economic power and political power, but we do not believe that those who would rely on this distinction have fulfilled their task.

Second, even assuming it is possible to operationally distinguish economic power and political power, a rationale for utilizing the distinction must be provided. Such a rationale would have to distinguish between the categories either on the basis of characteristics inherent in them as a means of action or on the basis of the ends to which the means are directed. Surely an analysis of ends does not provide a meaningful distinction. The objectives of groups using economic pressure are of the same character as those of groups using political pressure—both seek to influence executive and legislative determinations such as the allocation of funds and the tax rate. If it is impossible effectively to distinguish economic from political pressure groups in terms of their ends, and it is desirable to free the political process from the influence of all pressure groups, then effective lobbying and petitioning should be as illegal as strikes.

If the normative distinction between economic and political power is based, not on the ends desired, but on the nature of the means, our skepticism remains undiminished. Are all forms of political pressure legitimate? Then consider the range of political activity observed in the public sector. Is lobbying by public sector unions to be approved? Presumably it is. What then of participation in partisan political activity? On city time? Should we question the use of campaign contributions or kickbacks from public employees to public officials as a means of influencing public sector decisions? These questions suggest that political pressures, as opposed to economic pressures, cannot *as a class* be considered more desirable.

Our antagonism toward a distinction based on means does not rest solely on a condemnation of political pressures which violate statutory provisions. We believe that perfectly legal forms of political pressure have no automatic superiority over economic pressure. In this regard, the evidence from our field work is particularly enlightening. First, we have found that the availability of political power varies among groups of employees within a given city. Most public administrators have respect for groups which can deliver votes at strategic times. Because of their links to private sector unions, craft unions are invariably in a better position to play this political role than a union confined to the public sector, such as AFSCME. In Chicago, Cleveland and San Francisco, the public sector craft unions are closely allied with the building trades council and play a key role in labor relations with the city. Prior to the passage of state collective bargaining laws such unions also played the key role in Detroit and New York City. In the No-Strike Model, craft unions clearly have the comparative advantage because of their superior political power.

Second, the range of issues pursued by unions relying on political power tends to be narrow. The unions which prosper by eschewing economic power and exercising political power are often found in cities, such as Chicago, with a flourishing patronage system. These unions gain much of their political power by cooperating with the political administration. This source of political power would vanish if the unions were assiduously to pursue a goal of providing job security for their members since this goal would undermine the patronage system. In Rochester, for example, a union made no effort to protect one of its members who was fired for political reasons. For the union to have opposed the city administration at that time on an issue of job security would substantially have reduced the union's influence on other issues. In Chicago, where public sector strikes are rare (except for education) but political considerations are not, the unions have made little effort to establish a grievance procedure to protect their members from arbitrary treatment.

Third, a labor relations system built on political power tends to be unstable since some groups of employees, often a substantial number, are invariably left out of the system. They receive no representation either through patronage or through the union. In Memphis, the craft unions had for many years enjoyed a "working relationship" with the city which assured the payment of the rates that prevailed in the private sector and some control over jobs. The sanitation laborers, however, were not part of the system and were able to obtain effective representation only after a violent confrontation with the city in 1968. Having been denied representation through the political process, they had no choice but to accept a subordinate position in the city or to initiate a strike to change the system. Racial barriers were an important factor in the isolation of the Memphis sanitation laborers. Similar distinctions in racial balance among functions and occupations appear in most of the cities we visited.

C. Conclusions in Regard to Strikes and the Political Process

Wellington and Winter and the Taylor Committee reject the use of the Strike Model in the public sector. They have endorsed the No-Strike Model in order "to ensure the survival of the 'normal' American political process." Our field work suggests that unions which have actually helped their members either have made the strike threat a viable weapon despite its illegality or have intertwined themselves closely with their nominal employer through patronage-political support arrangements. If this assessment is correct, choice of the No-Strike Model is likely to lead to patterns of decision making which will subvert, if not the "normal" American political process, at least the political process which the Taylor Committee and Wellington and Winter meant to embrace. We would not argue that the misuse of political power will be eliminated by legalizing the strike; on balance, however, we believe that, in regard to most governmental functions, the Strike Model has more virtues than the No-Strike Model.

IV. DIFFERENTIATION AMONG PUBLIC
SECTOR FUNCTIONS

The most important union for local government employees, The American Federation of State, County, and Municipal Employees (AFSCME), issued a policy statement in 1966 claiming the right of public employees to strike:

> AFSCME insists upon the right of public employees * * * to strike. To forestall this right is to handicap free collective bargaining process [sic]. Wherever legal barriers to the exercise of this right exists it shall be our policy to seek the removal of such barriers. Where one party at the bargaining table possesses all the power and authority, the bargaining becomes no more than formalized petitioning.

> In general, we believe that strikes in the public sector should be legalized for the same reasons they are legal in the private sector. For some public sector services, however—namely, police and fire protection—the probability that a strike will result in immediate danger to public health and safety is so substantial that strikes are almost invariably inappropriate. In these essential functions, the strike should be presumed illegal; the state should not be burdened with the requirement of seeking an injunction. We would, however, permit employees in a service considered essential to strike if they could demonstrate to a court that a disruption of service would not endanger the public. Likewise, we would permit the government to obtain an injunction against a strike in a service presumed nonessential if a nontrivial danger to the public could be shown.

D. PUBLIC SECTOR BARGAINING LEGISLATION

As the previous material suggest the debate over the applicability of the private sector model has been inconclusive. The scholarly debate excepted above has had its less sophisticated counterpart in political exchange between those favoring the grant of collective bargaining right to public employees and those offering it. The resolution of the political struggle has also been inconclusive and has varied from state to state. In no state has the private sector model been fully adopted whole for public employees, but in many states a special statute granting rights to organize and bargain have been passed. In some states these acts apply to all public employees, in some only to selected groups such as teachers or municipal workers. Generally parts of these statutes have been copied verbatim from the National Labor Relations Act but there are two main differences. In place of a right to strike special impasse procedures are established and the scope of collective bargaining is made narrower than it is under the NLRA.

HARRY T. EDWARDS, THE EMERGING DUTY TO BARGAIN IN THE PUBLIC SECTOR *

* * *

B. The Muddle of Bargaining Models in the Public Sector: "Meet and Confer" or "Collective Negotiations"

Statutes concerned with public sector bargaining may be divided into two categories: those providing for "collective negotiations" and the so-called "meet and confer" statutes. In states, such as Michigan, which have adopted the collective-negotiations approach, the statutory definition of the duty to bargain is often identical or very similar to that found in the NLRA. It is probably safe to assume that these statutes were intentionally designed to incorporate by reference private sector precedents. On this score, it is interesting to note that the Michigan Employment Relations Commission (MERC) frequently cites NLRB precedents in deciding cases under that state's Public Employment Relations Act.

Before attempting an appraisal of legislation based on the meet-and-confer model, it may be helpful to contrast it with the collective-negotiations approach presently recognized in the private sector. "Meet-and-confer negotiations" can be defined as the

> process of negotiating terms and conditions of employment intended to emphasize the differences between public and private employment conditions. Negotiations under "meet and confer" laws usually imply discussions leading to unilateral adoption of policy by legislative body rather than written contract, and take place with multiple employee representatives rather than an exclusive bargaining agent.

This definition fairly describes what was originally intended by the meet-and-confer standard of bargaining. Implicit in the *pure* meet-and-confer approach is the assumption that the private sector bargaining model would be overly permissive if applied without qualification to the public sector. In other words, it is argued that public employers should retain broad managerial discretion in the operation of a governmental agency, subject only to the recall of the electorate. Thus, under the pure meet-and-confer bargaining model, the outcome of any public employer-employee discussions will depend more on management's determinations than on bilateral decisions by "equals" at the bargaining table. In contrast, the parties in the private sector meet as equals and are free to negotiate to a point of impasse all "mandatory" subjects of bargaining—matters concerning wages, hours, and conditions of employment.

* * *

It is generally assumed that most states which have passed statutes dealing with public sector labor relations have opted for the col-

---

* Harry T. Edwards, "The Emerging Duty To Bargain In The Public Sector," 71 Michigan Law Review 885 (1973): © 1973 by the Michigan Law Review Association. Reprinted by permission.

lective-negotiations model over the meet-and-confer approach. Close study of the legislation, however, reveals that this conclusion appears to be somewhat overdrawn and, at best, misleading. Actually, most states have rejected the pure meet-and-confer bargaining model, but, by the same token, most have also rejected the collective-negotiations approach. In practice, most states have adopted either a *modified* meet-and-confer statute, which gives unions more bargaining power than the pure model, or a *modified* collective-negotiations statute, which is more restrictive from the union's viewpoint than its private sector counterpart. For this reason alone, it is often difficult to distinguish between meet-and-confer and collective-negotiations as viable working concepts in the public sector.

Most critics of meet-and-confer have argued that any bargaining structure which relegates the employees' representative to the status of a "conferee" or "discussant," rather than a negotiator, is patently deficient. But this criticism rests on the assumption that the bargaining process is in fact different under a meet-and-confer, as opposed to a collective-negotiations, model. However, the recent history of collective bargaining in the public sector suggests that there is relatively little difference in bargaining tactics or techniques under these two models. Unions in the public sector have pressed for the same type of demands and with the same vigor under both models. Moreover, many of the states which have passed meet-and-confer statutes have so distorted the pure meet-and-confer bargaining model that it is no longer accurate to say that the parties governed by these statutes do not meet as "equals."

While it is plain that in some states, the parties do not meet as equals at the bargaining table, there are other meet-and-confer jurisdictions in which the matter has not been so neatly resolved. In Kansas, for example, the duty to meet and confer encompasses more than a mere exhortation to the public employer to "consider" employees' proposals; it is a mutual obligation to "meet and confer in order * * * * *to endeavor to reach agreement* on conditions of employment." Other meet-and-confer statutes state even more explicitly that the employer's duty goes beyond listening to its employees' suggestions. For example, the Montana statute makes it an unfair labor practice for a government employer to refuse to "meet, confer, or negotiate *in good faith.*"

The concept of meeting and conferring *in good faith* has been supported by the Advisory Commission on Intergovernmental Relations (ACIR). In a lengthy report, the Commission opted for a modified meet-and-confer approach.

It is noteworthy that the ACIR recommendations, which have been followed by some states, include the suggestion that the parties may be required to bargain in "good faith" to a point of impasse. Surely, if this is a part of the definition of meet and confer, then the *bargaining process* is not much different from the collective-negotiations approach.

* * *

B.   The Impact of Pre-Existing Legislation and Civil Service Laws

Other statutory provisions restrict the scope of bargaining by giving precedence to pre-existing state law or municipal ordinance over a subsequent collective bargaining agreement.   For example, the Massachusetts municipal employee bargaining statute provides: "In the event that any part or provision of any such agreement is in conflict with any law, ordinance, or by-law, such law, ordinance, or by-law shall prevail so long as such conflict remains   *   *   * ."   Particularly important among pre-existing laws which may conflict with collective bargaining agreements are civil service statutes and regulations. Nine statutes in eight states apparently give precedence to civil service systems over collective bargaining agreements.   In two states the collective bargaining agreement is given precedence.   In Michigan, where the public employee bargaining statute makes no mention of precedence, the state supreme court has ruled that those provisions of local civil service laws covering mandatory subjects of bargaining are superseded *pro tanto* by the Michigan Public Employees Relations Act.   Whether this ruling will influence other states where the statutes do not contain a rule of precedence remains to be seen.

Arguably, of course, a rule of precedence deals with the enforcement of the completed agreement and not with the scope of bargaining per se.   But such a rule certainly has an impact on the scope of bargaining.   It may seriously impair the bargaining process if the public employer believes that certain subjects in issue are not "mandatory" items covered by the duty to bargain.   In other words, a public employer presumably will seek to avoid bargaining over matters covered by civil service laws, especially if inundated with a host of other union demands, on the plausible ground that any agreements reached in these areas would be unenforceable because of conflicting civil service rules.

Problems associated with the duty to bargain in the public sector are already too numerous to be compounded by overly broad and inconsistent civil service regulations.   While the civil service system was originally designed to favor workers by eliminating patronage and rewarding merit, it has gradually expanded to a point where many systems now cover other aspects of employee relations not essentially related to the merit principle.   In other words, the civil service system for many years filled the gap caused by the lack of public sector bargaining.   Now that this gap has been filled, a conflict has arisen between the civil service system and the duty to bargain in the public sector.   It is fairly clear that if the collective bargaining process is going to have any value at all, the civil service system in its broad expanded form must yield to bargaining.   Thus, it may well be that civil service should control, at the utmost, only hiring, promotions, and demotions.

Civil service laws are not the only source of conflict with collective bargaining legislation.   Of the other statutes which limit the scope of bargaining, the most interesting, in view of recent developments in Michigan, are the municipal "home rule" statutes.   A tug-of-war has recently developed between the Michigan courts and the Michigan Employment Relations Commission over the extent to which munici-pal residency requirements, passed pursuant to the state's Home Rule Cities Act, can restrict the scope of mandatory bargaining. A number of Michigan cities, including Detroit and Pontiac, have passed ordinances requiring certain city employees to reside within the city limits. The principal opposition to these ordinances has come from police officers, and local police officers' associations have placed the ordinances high on their priority lists for negotiations with city offi-cials. The issue has thus been joined: the right of municipalities to require a commitment to the city on the part of certain employees is pitted against the right of those employees to attempt to negotiate a relaxation of that commitment.

C.   Judicial Limitations on the Scope of Bargaining

Another source of restrictions on the scope of bargaining is nar-row judicial interpretation of statutory language. Just as courts have been hesitant to impose a duty to bargain on the public employ-er, so have they been reluctant to give expansive interpretations to the language governing the scope of bargaining. The desire to avoid illegal delegations of power, as well as the reluctance to permit em-ployee groups to encroach upon areas entrusted to the discretion of a political agency are unquestionably valid, if often overstated, con-cerns of the court. These concerns are reinforced by legislative poli-cy statements which virtually mandate a conservative approach to statutory interpretation.

Unfortunately, many public sector statutory provisions which are at variance with the private sector model do not make clear the legis-lative purpose behind the language modification. Indeed, some provi-sions merely appear to reflect the differences in the employment situ-ation seen in the public sectors, but do not otherwise indicate a legislative intention to narrow the scope of bargaining. For example, the Delaware statute covering teachers provides that the public em-ployer has a duty to negotiate in good faith with respect to "salaries, employee benefits, and working conditions." In other state statutes, however, the language employed is sufficiently ambiguous to make it unclear whether the scope of bargaining was intentionally defined to be more narrow than the definition in the NLRA. In Oklahoma, for instance, teachers and boards of education are required only to bar-gain with respect to "items affecting the performance of professional services," and the South Dakota public employee relations act re-quires bargaining only on "grievance procedures and conditions of employment."

In all these cases, the problem is essentially the same: state courts and/or public employee relations boards are forced to develop case law to accommodate the statutory variations. Given the exis-tence of the familiar NLRA model, which I would argue is sufficient-ly flexible to accommodate public service, the continued enactment of these oddball statutory provisions appears unnecessary. More impor-tantly, these ambiguous provisions may actually deter peaceful and effective bargaining. Faced with unfamiliar terms, which purport to define the subjects of mandatory bargaining, the employer is encouraged to test the parameters of the language by refusing to bargain on borderline issues. The prosecution of these court challenges is no less time-consuming, expensive, or irritating than traditional collective bargaining. Furthermore, even if the employer prevails in a single case, as in *West Hartford*, public employees are not likely to cease pressing their demands at the bargaining table and before the legislature in areas which they believe affect their employment situation.

D. Statutory Management-Rights Clauses

Delineating the scope of bargaining is even more difficult where statutory management-rights clauses and other statutory exclusions are involved. While the whole thrust of private sector case law is to define what is bargainable by constant refinement of the term "wages, hours and conditions of employment," statutory exclusions are attempts to define bargainability in terms of what is *not* bargainable. Furthermore, while deviations from NLRA language leave the scope of bargaining unclear, statutory exclusions create even more confusion. Some state statutes, for instance, provide that the public employer has the unfettered right to "maintain the efficiency of government operations." Others declare that the employer has no duty to bargain with respect to the mission of the agency or matters of inherent managerial policy. It surely is not clear what these terms mean. A public employer, for example, may claim that *anything* done by the agency before the advent of collective bargaining gives evidence of the "mission of the agency" or was done to "maintain the efficiency of government operations." Operationalizing such language in the context of the objectives of a collective bargaining statute is not only difficult, it is unnecessary.

*   *   *

The FLRC [Federal Labor Relations Council] may have discovered a method of dealing with statutory management-rights clauses that state public employee relations boards would do well to adapt. In effect, the FLRC ruled that management is free to invoke reserved-rights provisions at any time, but a relatively stiff burden will be placed on the employer to show that such an invocation is not capricious and that negotiations over the item in question would seriously deter the smooth functioning of the employer's operations.

*   *   *

E. The Expanding Scope of the Duty To Bargain

Actually, the tendency of both meet-and-confer and collective-negotiations states to limit the scope of bargaining rests on a fear that institutionalizing private sector practices in the public sector may ultimately pervert the political process. As the decision regarding allocation of resources in the public sector is a political rather than merely an economic choice, it has been argued that full collective bargaining in the public sector may give labor the means to enforce its will to the detriment of other, less highly organized suitors for government funds.

It cannot, of course, be controverted that, in theory, decisions on governmental priorities are properly political and should be responsive to the desires of the constituency as a whole rather than the values of a labor union. Yet, in reality, the process of resource allocation in government is the outcome of a tug-of-war between many organized interest groups.

Current developments in public sector labor laws indicate that we may expect to see a widening of the scope of bargaining in all states. The experience in Michigan furnishes ample evidence that public sector bargaining can be satisfactorily regulated under the private sector concept of the duty to bargain. A state public employment relations board is usually quite capable of deciding, on the basis of private sector precedents and public sector bargaining experiences, which subjects should be deemed "mandatory" for bargaining purposes. The case-by-case decision-making approach on mandatory subjects is vastly superior to a rigid legislative limitation on the scope of bargaining, because if experience proves the initial judgment to be erroneous, it is easier for a state board to reverse itself than it is to get a modification of a state statute in the legislature.

In this regard, one may ask whether it is ever sensible to attempt to limit the scope of bargaining by statute. The collective bargaining process is in part a therapeutic process, and it should permit the parties to address fully all problems which affect the bargaining relationship. If the employer is opposed to a given union demand, he can discuss the problem raised, and then, if appropriate, he can persist in rejecting it. This is a more satisfactory approach, in terms of achieving stable and harmonious labor relations, than to have the employer refuse to discuss an issue in the first instance because it is legally nonnegotiable. It may be worthwhile to recall the dissent of Justice Harlan in NLRB v. Wooster Division of Borg-Warner, where he argued:

> The bargaining process should be left fluid, free from intervention * * * leading to premature crystallization of labor agreements into any one pattern of contract provisions, so that these agreements can be adapted through collective bargaining to the changing needs of our society and to the changing concepts of the responsibilities of labor and management.

At the present time, the predicted trend toward a more liberal approach to the scope of bargaining in the public sector already appears to be developing. At the federal level, for example, a "Scope of Bargaining Project," currently underway at the Civil Service Commission, is preparing proposals for streamlining the *Federal Personnel Manual,* which is now the source of extensive restrictions on bargaining in the federal service. Civil Service Commission Chairman Robert Hampton recently outlined both the nature of these restrictions and the goals of the "Scope of Bargaining Project" in a speech before the Personnel Directors' Conference of the Federal Executive Institute, as follows:

* * *

The Objective of the Scope of Bargaining Project is to remove barriers in the [*Federal Personnel Manual*] to negotiations, not to determine what is negotiable or to come up with a laundry list of negotiable items. Instead, the project is designed to (1) pinpoint [Civil Service Commission] policies and regulations that might be undesirably restrictive, and (2) suggest how they might be changed to broaden or remove uncertainty about the scope of bargaining in the Federal Service.

* * *

At the state level, the public employment relations boards and courts in several states, notably Michigan, New York, Wisconsin, and Pennsylvania, have been in the forefront of the movement toward expanded public sector bargaining.

Notwithstanding the importance of the New York court's decision, most of the progress in defining the scope of bargaining in the public sector is an accomplishment of state labor boards. By far, the class of public employees who have most actively sought to test the scope of mandatory bargaining before state boards has been the public school teachers, and it is in this area that the boards have made the greatest expansion of the scope of bargaining. One of the first cases which suggested that the scope of management discretion over educational policy is not as broad as had been previously thought was a Michigan trial examiner's decision in *North Dearborn Heights School District*. Before the case was ultimately settled, the examiner caused a bit of a furor in Michigan education circles by holding all fourteen of the submitted issues to be bargainable, including curriculum, classroom schedules and class sizes, selection of textbook materials, and a number of other subjects formerly thought to be within the exclusive discretion of the board of education. While no labor board decision has gone as far since, the fear that collective bargaining over some of these matters may lead to abdication of the school board's responsibility and a loss of local control over schools has apparently lessened. Increasingly, formerly permissive or forbidden subjects have become mandatory. The Pennsylvania Labor Relations Board recently reversed an earlier decision by holding that five of twenty-one formerly nonbargainable subjects were negotiable and that the other sixteen "may be bargainable."

Public education provides an excellent environment for the development of the case-by-case method of defining the scope of bargaining. Such matters as the length of the school day, the academic calendar, classroom size, and extra-curricular assignments clearly relate to wages, hours, and other terms and conditions of employment. Yet, they also are matters closely connected with educational policy, usually considered to be within the authority of the school board. This potential overlap of management functions with bargainable subjects leads to some rather fine line-drawing by labor boards as

they attempt to strike a proper balance "between the duty of elected
officials to make decisions for the entire electorate and the statutory
right of employees to negotiate items directly affecting terms and
conditions of employment."

The difficulty of striking this kind of balance is illustrated by the
New York PERB decision in *West Irondequoit Board of Education*,
where the principal issue was class size. The hearing officer determined that class size was a mandatory subject, since it was an "integral component of the working environment." The Board, however,
modified the order, holding that class size was a policy decision. In
so doing, it drew a distinction between teaching load, a mandatory
subject of bargaining, and class size—a result which provoked the
dissenting member to observe that "the impact of numerical limitations of class size upon teaching load is so direct as to make a line of
demarcation impossible."

The New York PERB has reasoned similarly with respect to other
contract provisions. In *Triborough Bridge & Tunnel Authority*,
PERB upheld a hearing officer's decision that the authority could not
refuse longevity increases to employees whose anniversaries arose
after the expiration of a collective bargaining agreement and before a
new one could be negotiated, noting:

> [T]he statutory prohibition against an employee organization
> resorting to self help by striking imposes a correlative duty upon
> a public employer to refrain from altering terms and conditions of
> employment unilaterally during the course of negotiations. *This
> duty of an employer in the public sector to refrain from self
> help is greater than is the similar duty of private sector em-
> ployers.*

* * *

VIII. ENFORCEMENT OF THE DUTY TO BARGAIN

The need to appropriate public money to pay for negotiated increases in wages and benefits is another characteristic unique to the
public sector which creates enforcement problems. It may be conceded that, without its consent, a state legislature may not be compelled
to make apropriations; however, a public employer should not be able
to use a failure to appropriate as an excuse for either a refusal to
bargain or the total repudiation of an existing agreement. Rather,
both parties should be expected to make whatever adjustments are
necessary to accommodate the financial limitations of the employer.
In other words, the requirement of good faith bargaining should not
terminate in the face of fiscal obstacles.

Where public employers have attempted to use financial considerations as excuses for refusing to bargain or for repudiating an agreement, courts and labor boards have recently exhibited a willingness
to intervene. In a recent Michigan case, *City of Flint*, the city refused to bargain with the general employees of the municipality pending arbitration of a dispute involving the city firemen and possible

arbitration with police. The city claimed that it could not make a wage offer since it would not know how much money was available until after the arbitration. The Michigan Employment Relations Commission, however, determined that the city could not refuse to bargain with one group of employees because of the financial uncertainty resulting from a dispute with another group. The New York PERB reached an analogous result in *City of Albany.*

The lesson of the Michigan and New York cases is clear: financial uncertainty is no justification for a total refusal to bargain. It is just as clear, however, that such uncertainty can be a basis for a hard-line position in negotiations. Hard bargaining is not in itself an unfair labor practice, even in the private sector. The public employer can take appropriations cutbacks into consideration in bargaining, just as a private employer can take a sales decrease or a decline in profits into account. Similarly, the public employer can take into consideration the impact of bargaining on other units, as in cases where pattern settlements are the rule or wage-parity agreements are in effect. But there is a line between hard bargaining and no bargaining, and vigorous enforcement of the duty to bargain can help to clarify the contours of that line.

Administrations change, but the management problems linger. The Management Advisory Board report said, "The City has failed to develop a strong identity for its managers." This conclusion was also very much on the mind of Edward Hamilton, a deputy mayor under Lindsay, when he was interviewed by the State Charter Revision Commission a few years ago. Hamilton spoke of the need to develop a "management ethos," and went on to say, "The problem in most governments is that the challenge to middle management is greater than other places, because they have to deal with employees over whom they don't have the usual levers—they can't fire them, they can't lower their salaries, they can't usually do much about their promotion, they can't do any of the things that a middle manager expects to use as his stock in trade. * * * Public managers on the whole have to be superb people to really motivate people in a situation like that. Despite this, middle managers in the city have virtually nothing on the other side. * * * They had no training, they had no sense of being part of a management cadre which was somehow looking over the shoulder of people who did what they did for a long time, and so forth. There is no equivalent to the key to the executive washroom; there is no recognition, no feeling of peer-group identification, none of the things that help turn a person into a manager."

One reason the "management ethos" is missing is that many managers identify not with the city but with the union they belong to. They see the union as the source of their protection, of the push for higher salaries, of their health and welfare benefits. In the Fire Department, deputy chiefs, each of whom supervises from three to five battalions comprising from five to twelve companies and earns about forty thousand dollars a year, belong to a union. Last year, according to the Temporary Commission on City Finances, only fourteen out of more than eleven thousand Fire Department employees were outside the collective-bargaining system.   In the Police Department, the deputy chiefs, who also earn about forty thousand dollars a year, belong to a union.   In the Sanitation Department, everyone below the level of borough superintendent belongs to a union.   In the Housing Authority, housing-project managers belong to the same union as most of the people they are supposed to manage.   In the office of Code Enforcement of the Housing and Development Administration, according to the Productivity Council report, only four out of approximately fourteen hundred employees are not members of a union.   In the city comptroller's office, the auditors of District Council 37's Health and Security Plan are members of District Council 37.

Commissioner Russo sounds like a general who has lost his troops. "In the Parks Department, the only men we have who aren't union members are the borough park managers," he says. "The assistant park manager in each borough—the person responsible for discipline—belongs to Victor Gotbaum's union, District Council 37. In case of a strike, who opens the door to let in workers who want to work?

DAVID B. ARMBRUST, IMPASSE RESOLUTION PROCEDURES IN PUBLIC EMPLOYMENT NEGOTIATIONS *

* * *

MEDIATION

During the collective bargaining process, the public employer and the union meet, discuss and eventually agree upon the terms and conditions of the employment.   Often, however, the parties will fail to achieve a "meeting of the minds" and the conciliatory influence of a neutral third party will have a beneficial effect on the negotiations. A mediator is such a neutral third party.   He is neither a judge nor a referee, "but rather a conciliator who improves the negotiation atmosphere by emphasizing the common ground between the parties and helping to tear down obstacles to communication."   The mediator is not primarily responsible for the resolution of the impasse; his primary responsibility is to the parties in an attempt to have *them* resolve the impasse.

Of the various approaches to impasse resolution, mediation is said to be the most tried and reliable, largely because skilled mediators are able to use their neutral positions to offer suggestions and compromise proposals that are both *practical* and *face saving* for the parties.   Mediation is also said to be the most effective means toward the development of a practical and viable system of public employee

* David   B.   Armbrust,   "Impasse Resolution   Procedures   In   Public Employment Negotiations," 8 The Urban Lawyer 449 (1976); © 1976 by The Urban Lawyer. Reprinted by permission of The Urban Lawyer, the national quarterly journal of the American Bar Association, Section of Local Government Law.

labor relations. Presently, at least twenty-five states provide in some way for mediation of negotiation disputes. The use of mediation as a resolution mechanism follows a variety of patterns, and its effectiveness varies accordingly. In some states the form of mediation to be used varies with the class of employees who are involved. Mediation can also either be compulsory or voluntary.

Although the key to successful mediation depends to a large extent on the skills and impartiality of the mediator himself, mediation as a tool in the dispute settlement process has been demonstrated to be highly successful and probably the most desirable means of dispute settlement. In addition, its effectiveness increases when it is part of a "comprehensive program" in the public negotiating process. In other words, it appears to operate best as a link "in a chain of progressive measures * * * intended to decrease public employee strikes while treating their causes."

FACT–FINDING

If mediation fails in the private sector, the parties generally resort to self-help and the use of power tactics such as the strike; in the public sector, disputing parties frequently utilize a technique known as fact-finding, which is something more than mediation but falls short of compulsory arbitration. Although the findings generally are not legally binding on the parties, fact-finding carries more finality than does mediation.

The term fact-finding is somewhat misleading in that "it connotes objective, infallible precision and an ability of the fact-finder or need on the part of the disputants to arrive at the facts." In reality, the fact-finder's responsibility does not merely end with his determination of the facts, as he also has a duty to make recommendations to the parties in order to resolve the impasse. Since the recommendations are of a non-binding nature, the parties are free to comply or not, as they wish. At least twenty-three states use fact-finding as a technique in the dispute settlement procedure. While both sides in a dispute find it attractive because the recommendations are not binding, some authorities object to the fact that such a procedure does not assure a final settlement.

As with mediation, the process of fact-finding varies from state to state and no singular pattern emerges. While fact-finding involves some aspects of both mediation and arbitration it is really a separate procedure. While in some states, such as Montana, fact-finding is the only available impasse resolution procedure, at least twelve other states include it as merely a step in the process or an alternative which may be used in lieu of others. As in mediation, state statutes provide a variety of methods to invoke the fact-finding procedure. Maine provides voluntary fact-finding at the request of the parties, while the Hawaii act provides for its use when the parties cannot reach an agreement within a set number of days after the impasse.

The state of Massachusetts has a typical provision for fact-finding in the public sector, which since its enactment in the mid-1960s has proven to be a workable and effective tool in impasse resolution.   Application for fact-finding is a voluntary process which may be used by either party to the dispute.   Within a day after receiving an application for fact-finding, the Massachusetts Board of Conciliation and Arbitration appoints one of its agents to certify that an impasse exists and that reasonable attempts have been made to resolve it.   The state conciliator may work with the parties as long as six months before actually certifying the existence of an impasse, so that the parties may voluntarily agree to a settlement.   The fact-finder, who is given a great deal of freedom, may even decide to mediate the case if he deems mediation the best procedure under the circumstances. The Massachusetts act is designed to encourage voluntary settlements and indeed, formal fact-finding reports have been issued in only about one half of the cases.   The only significant change in the act since its enactment was designed to "add teeth" to the Board's findings should the process reach that stage.   The new amendment requires public notice of any impasse remaining unresolved ten days after the transmittal of such findings.   In the public sector negotiating process, this can potentially be a powerful pressure tactic.

While the flexibility of fact-finding has been praised as its greatest advantage, the fact-finding process also has been criticized as being too *rigid* by critics who are concerned with the effect of the findings of the parties.   The basis of the criticism is that once the fact-finding report is issued the positions of each side must harden and the lines of battle become more intense, while neither side, then, may be required to retreat from its position.   Since public pressure is a very formidable weapon in the public sector, the new Massachusetts publicity provision may prove a workable solution.

While both mediation and fact-finding are effective impasse resolution procedures, neither process assures a final settlement.   Because of dissatisfaction with these mechanisms or as a supplement to these procedures, some states employ the process of arbitration. Like both mediation and fact-finding, arbitration also involves the presence of a neutral third party.   The distinguishing factor, however, is the binding nature of the third party's findings or conclusions.

The American experience with arbitration has for the most part been limited to the settlements involving the interpretation of the terms of a collective bargaining agreement.   Interest arbitration has been used less frequently.   Under this mechanism, the neutral third party is introduced into the negotiation stage at a time when the parties have reached an impasse in their bargaining, and the dispute is settled without resort to a strike.   In essence, this form of arbitration is a speedy form of justice.

Currently, at least twenty-three states employ arbitration as a means of resolving public sector disputes and like mediation and fact-finding, there are numerous variations of the basic procedure.   Although it may be compulsory, it usually is voluntary, and the decision may be binding or merely advisory.   It may also assume exotic configurations such as "final offer" arbitration.   Some states utilize both voluntary and compulsory methods. Rhode Island, for example, allows either party in a municipal employee or teacher impasse to voluntarily request binding arbitration when the expenditure of money is not involved, while in police and fire impasses, compulsory binding arbitration is imposed upon the parties.

Voluntary arbitration has one obvious drawback: it may never be invoked unless the parties so desire. Experience shows this to be a major problem, since voluntary binding arbitration in public employment disputes has been used very infrequently. The questionable legality of arbitration in jurisdictions which have not specifically approved it by statute explains the reluctance of parties to agree to submit unresolved issues to a third party for a binding decision. Public employers also have been reluctant to voluntarily agree to third party arbitration on the grounds that without legislative approval, their delegation might be beyond the scope of their authority. Consequently, voluntary arbitration has not met with great success, in the words of one author: "It is certainly questionable whether a system that leaves so much to the good will of the parties * * * [in] * * * a highly-charged, often delicate, situation is worthwhile."

Compulsory arbitration, which has been adopted by a number of states, is most often designed to be a substitute for the strike as the final step in the collective bargaining process. Compulsory arbitration is a formidable mechanism because it effectively takes the collective bargaining process out of the hands of both parties. In fact, the major argument against compulsory arbitration focuses on whether or not it will destroy the collective bargaining process. Nevertheless, this means of impasse resolution is becoming more and more highly regarded. The American Bar Association's Section on Labor Relations recently reported that some evidence exists that fear of an arbitration award, like fear of a strike, induces compromise.

Several designs have been suggested to modify the harshness of compulsory binding arbitration and encourage voluntary settlements. For example, some authorities have proposed "mediation-arbitration" as a hybrid form of dispute resolution designed as another alternative. This plan envisions a mediator with powers of arbitration to be used only as a last resort. The plan's most obvious disadvantage is the dual role of the third party who is involved in the bargaining process and, in the event of a totally irreconcilable impasse, is then expected to function as a detached third party and thus made vulnerable to a charge of collusion with either of the disputants. Mediation arbitration is used rarely and its experimentation has been relatively restricted to the private sector.

Another attempt to improve compulsory binding arbitration has involved the introduction of a technique called "final offer" selection. In this procedure the employer and the union submit their best and final offers to the arbitrator after all other attempts at a voluntary settlement have failed. The arbitrator selects the more reasonable offer. Proponents of "final offer arbitration" argue that this method is extremely effective because it forces the parties to adopt reasonable positions, since failure to do so may result in the arbitrator enforcing the final offer of the other side.

In May of 1973, the University of Cincinnati College of Law sponsored a collective bargaining experiment comparing arbitration and final offer selection; the results of this experiment, in which experienced labor specialists negotiated two simulated contracts, are quite interesting. The early stages of bargaining revealed apparently little difference in the effect of the two procedures, but as the deadline for agreement approached, "final offer selection" began to emerge as the most favorable procedure. "Final offer selection," with its demand for reasonableness, forced most of the participants into a more moderate bargaining position. The reasonableness requirement also tended to narrow the issues. A majority of the negotiators concluded that the bargaining strategy did vary with the mode of impasse resolution and it is significant to note that five out of seven participants said they would prefer "final offer selection" to arbitration. Final offer selection actually seemed to affect the negotiations as it was designed to do. While the Unviersity of Cincinnati experiment indicates that "final offer selection" might become the wave of the future, its true success can only be measured through experience. To date, the states of Massachusetts, Michigan, Minnesota and Wisconsin have adopted some form of this technique, but its relative infancy prohibits generalizations concerning its success.

The final offer procedure itself can be easily modified. The arbitrator may be restricted to choosing one side's entire proposal or he may be able to select a proposal for each issue in dispute. Another alternative, untried anywhere, would allow the arbitrator to select from three proposals—"that of the employer, that of the union or that of the fact-finder." This last alternative merits close study because it provides a third solution where the parties both have unreasonable offers.

Most authorities seem to agree that arbitration has a "bright future" in the area of public-sector labor relations; however, the particular form to be used must be carefully structured in light of the particular circumstances and other available procedures.

THE STRIKE

The strike, which has been characterized as labor's ultimate weapon, has been used for years as labor's economic blockbuster. It has been said that "a free enterprise system without the right to strike is a contradiction in terms." In the public sector, however, the right to strike is viewed quite differently. In the words of Franklin Delano Roosevelt:

A strike by public employees manifests nothing less than an intent on their part to obstruct the operations of government until their demands are satisfied. Such action looking toward the paralysis of government by those who have sworn to support it is unthinkable.

Public employee strikes are generally regarded as the ultimate impasse resolution mechanism and when authorized at all, they are intended for use after all else fails. Legislative approaches to this "ultimate weapon" have basically taken one of two approaches: the no-strike model or the strike model.

Most states have adopted the no-strike approach, banning public employee strikes by statute, attorney general opinion or court decision. The fact that public employee strikes, slowdowns and sick-outs have increased at an astronomical rate, throughout the past decade, even in jurisdictions where strict penalties are imposed, illustrates that the deterrent effect is not great enough to overbalance the gains to be expected from strikes. "Experience has shown that the mere prohibition of strikes does not prevent them," and it is true that an economic strike could easily be converted into a strike for amnesty, with the result that the law is totally abandoned and the strike period lengthened. Several of the states which prohibit strikes also either totally or partially ban collective bargaining for public employees or attempt to substitute other impasse resolution mechanisms for the strike. The frequency of strikes in some form or another certainly indicates a flaw in the present system.

Although still a distinct minority, several states, which may be classified as falling within the no-strike model, are establishing a trend by liberalizing their no-strike provisions. About five years ago, Montana, Vermont, Hawaii and Pennsylvania began to liberalize their no-strike laws, and study commissions in Colorado, Maine and Maryland have recommended legislation granting a right to strike. In 1973, Oregon and Minnesota adopted a limited right to strike, and Vermont liberalized its laws even further. Vermont removed its "negative" statutory language and the statute now provides that strikes will not be prohibited *unless* they endanger the health, safety or welfare of the public. The Hawaii Act, which in 1970 was the first law to extend the right to strike to public employees, is a somewhat typical structure. The strike is used only after the failure of other impasse procedures such as fact-finding and even then the strike is not permitted to endanger the public health or safety. This act and others patterned after it have proved to be workable methods of regulating the public employee strike.

All strike laws in the public sector must contain some reference to essential services to be performed in spite of a strike or they will be totally unmanageable. Most laws use words such as "danger to health, safety or welfare" while some adopt other measures of protecting the public. In Canada, for example, the parties or the Conciliation Board *must* actually agree *before the strike* which classes of employees must remain on the job for the safety and security of the public. One noted authority in this area has proposed legislation authorizing the governor of a state to seek an injunction for a specified period through procedures similar to those for emergency disputes under the Taft-Hartley Act. He suggests that this would be a method of preventing strikes from endangering the public health or safety. This essential-services-distinction is criticized by at least one author. Arvid Anderson, who has said that by only allowing non-disruptive employees to strike, the state is only allowing those employees with the least leverage to speak for the union. This author concludes that sophisticated legislation is needed in this area providing for administrative supervision of the process. Indeed, the states which have experimented with the right to strike have found it necessary to create some form of administrative machinery to insure its success as Mr. Anderson has suggested. It is generally accepted that the development of an institution to administer and insure compliance with the law is essential to the stability and the success of the legislation. The explosive nature of the strike as an impasse resolution mechanism magnifies the importance of properly drafted legislation. Whatever the statutory scheme, it must take many aspects into account. As authorities call for legalized strikes in the public sector, it is logically expected that more and more states will adopt this approach. As they do, they should be watched for possible suggestions as well as latent defects.

One state has recently emerged with a rather novel proposal which may be classified as a quasi-strike. In 1973, a Connecticut public employee study commission proposed a new alternative. The committee proposed arbitration supplemented with economic constraints that would approximate those of a strike without actually engaging in a strike per se. The proposal provided that if either party rejected the arbitration award, a series of economic sanctions would be involved as follows:

> For a specified period of time, the employees would then receive 90% of their wages during which time the employer would also forfeit a specified amount of its funds. If no settlement were reached during that time, the sanctions would be increased, with wages reduced further and the forfeiture of government funds to be increased.

Since the obvious effect of this proposal applies economic pressures to the parties while still providing service to the public, it is difficult to classify it as a strike procedure or an arbitration mechanism in lieu of a strike. It certainly merits further attention by those states which are reluctant to extend the right to strike to their public employees.

SCHOOL COMMITTEE OF BOSTON v. BOSTON TEACHERS UNION

Supreme Judicial Court of Massachusetts 1977.
372 Mass. 605, 363 N.E.2d 485.

KAPLAN, J. After extended efforts, the School Committee of Boston and the Boston Teachers Union found themselves unable to resolve their differences in negotiating collective bargaining agreements for the school year 1974–1975. Accordingly, they agreed to submit the outstanding items to "interest" arbitration under G.L. c.

150E, Section 9 fifth paragraph. Following lengthy hearings, the arbitrator made his award on these items. Thereupon the School Committee (and the city of Boston and its mayor) commenced an action against the Teachers Union to vacate the award as to certain items, the contention being that these were beyond the arbitrator's authority even though within the scope of the agreed submission. The Teachers Union brought a cross-action to confirm the award. A judge of the Superior Court held in favor of the Teachers Union. We granted direct appellate review of these matters. * * *

As to the statutory framework: G.L. c. 150E grants public employees organizational and bargaining rights (Section 2) with provision for determining exclusive bargaining representatives (Sections 3–4). Section 6 obligates the employer and the bargaining representative to meet at reasonable times (including meetings in advance of the employer's budget-making process) and to "negotiate in good faith with respect to wages, hours, standards of productivity and performance, and any other terms and conditions of employment but such obligation shall not compel either party to agree to a proposal or make a concession." If agreement is reached, the employer submits to the relevant legislative body a request for any appropriation needed to make it effective (Section 7).

Section 9 describes what is to happen if agreement is not reached within a reasonable time. Either party may petition the State Board of Conciliation and Arbitration (see G.L. c. 23, Section 7) "for a determination of the existence of an impasse," and if that is found, the board appoints (or the parties agree upon) a mediator to assist the parties in resolving the impasse. After a reasonable period, the mediator reports to the board. If the impasse continues, then, upon either party's petition, or on the petition of the parties acting jointly, the board appoints or the parties select a fact finder. He transmits his findings and recommendations to the board and the parties; if the impasse continues thereafter, the issues are returned to the parties for further bargaining.

There is, however, a separate route, the one followed in the present case—"interest" arbitration. This depends on agreement of the parties and ends in a final and binding award. Section 9, fifth paragraph, provides:

> Any arbitration award in a proceeding voluntarily agreed to by the parties to resolve an impasse shall be binding on the parties and on the appropriate legislative body and made effective and enforceable pursuant to the provisions of * * * (G.L. c. 150C), provided that said arbitration proceeding has been authorized by the appropriate legislative body or in the case of school employees, by the appropriate school committee.

And under c. 150C (which by its own terms governs grievance arbitration under the provisions of a private-sector collective bargaining agreement) we find provision for enforcement by the court of the awards made in the arbitral proceedings (Sections 10–13). The grounds for vacating an award are set forth in Section 11, and the one of interest to us is: "(3) the arbitrators exceeded their powers or rendered an award requiring a person to commit an act or engage in conduct prohibited by state or federal law."

The School Committee's principal contention on this appeal is that the award was beyond the arbitrator's authority because the whole arbitral process under G.L. c. 150E, Section 9, fifth paragraph (quoted above), must be restricted to matters as to which the parties are obligated to negotiate in good faith under Section 6 (also above quoted) and the items involved were not of that kind. Of course Section 9, fifth paragraph, does not say this in terms. It is suggested, however, that the thought is conveyed by the work "impasse."

The courts have held under the National Labor Relations Act that a party violates his duty to bargain in good faith if he insists to the point of impasse on a matter as to which the statute does not impose a duty to bargain—a so called "nonmandatory" or "permissive" matter. This is the doctrine of NLRB v. Wooster Div. of Borg-Warner Corp., 356 U.S. 342, 78 S.Ct. 718, 2 L.Ed.2d 823 (1958), which has been endlessly elaborated in private-sector litigation.

We shall assume that the subjects of the three items in the present case fall outside the scope of mandatory bargaining described in G.L. c. 150E, Section 6. Suppose *Borg-Warner* is read into Section 9, fifth paragraph, so that an impasse under that provision must have arisen in connection with matters for mandatory bargaining. That was the situation at bar, for the list of outstanding items included many as to wages and so forth that were indubitably of the mandatory type. Such an impasse having arisen, the parties could voluntarily submit to arbitration not only those items but additional and different items in deadlock, and the arbitrator's authority extended to them. Analogically, when parties in fact include nonmandatory items in a collective bargaining agreement which contains an arbitration clause, disputes as to those items are subject to grievance arbitration with the rest, and awards regarding them are enforced without distinction from awards as to matters initially for mandatory bargaining. See United Steelworkers v. Enterprise Wheel & Car Corp., 363 U.S. 593, 599, 80 S.Ct. 1358, 4 L.Ed.2d 1409 (1960);   *   *   *   That is surely true, as well, of arbitration under our c. 150C, as Section 1 indeed indicates expressly. Of course there has never been any thought that interest arbitration by agreement between private parties must be limited to the mandatory subjects. See Chattanooga Mailers Local 92 v. Chattanooga News-Free Press Co., 524 F.2d 1305, 1314–1315 (6th Cir. 1975). The scope of voluntary interest arbitration in the public sector has its limits   *   *   *   but those cannot in reason be coterminous with the scope of mandatory bargaining.

As indicated, the draftsmen of Section 9, fifth paragraph, omitted any words confining voluntary interest arbitration to the field of mandatory bargaining. That the arbitration should extend more broadly is the result to which the draftsmen would have been led by their practical good sense. Many labor contracts reached in the usual course include, quite naturally, a miscellany of provisions thrown up by experience which are not at the core of bargaining over wages, hours, and the like. As the record proves, such has been conspicuously the case in contracts over the years between the present parties. Being at a standstill on a variety of subjects, the parties would have thought it odd indeed if they had been told that their Memorandum of Agreement under Section 9, fifth paragraph, which reflected the actual dimensions of irreconcilable dispute, was in part nugatory. On that view, it is extremely doubtful that they would have taken the step of submitting their quarrels to binding arbitration.

In a larger sense, it seems evident that if voluntary interest arbitration is to make an appeal to the parties and carry out its purpose of avoiding protracted strife, it must, optimally, imitate the range of the negotiation which it supersedes. The interplay and "tradeoff" of mandatory and other items which are described as "the very fabric of effective collective bargaining," Oil Workers Int'l Local 3–89 v. NLRB, 132 U.S.App.D.C. 43, 405 F.2d 1111, 1117 (1968), have their place in voluntary arbitration of the terms of a labor contract and will tend to improve and make more livable the arbitral result. Of course, if for any reason the parties prefer a more limited arbitration, they can provide for it by agreement. Here the parties agreed in the contrary sense.

We add that there is a general policy favoring voluntary arbitration in the labor field which speaks against imposing a narrowing interpretation on Section 9, fifth paragraph. On the other hand, there is an understandable attitude of wariness about arbitration forced on a party. Massachusetts Nurses Ass'n v. Lynn Hosp., 364 Mass. 502, 306 N.E.2d 264 (1974), was a case of forced arbitration under c. 150A, Section 9A (nurses in health care facilities), where we were, in addition, aided by express statutory language in finding that the arbitration was intended to be limited to the subjects of mandatory bargaining. The same theme appears in Section 4 of the statute (St. 1973, c. 1078) that enacted c. 150E, Section 9. Section 4 provided for forced interest arbitration in the event of impasse in bargaining between representatives of police officers or fire fighters and municipal authorities. It stated, in effect, that the arbitration in police matters was to be limited to the subjects of mandatory bargaining. By contrast, Section 9, fifth parargraph, which invokes voluntary arbitration, is to be understood as it reads, without artificial constriction. * * * (Judgment Affirmed).

E. PUBLIC SECTOR LABOR RELATIONS AND THE CONSTITUTION

In many instances there is little or no legislative context for dealing with labor relations in the public sector. Where this is the case, the U.S. Constitution is a source of authority for individual and collective bargaining rights. The following materials focus on the right to join a union, bargain, and strike; and conversely the right to not participate in union activity. Also considered is the public employee's right to job tenure, the employee's due process rights upon removal, and what constitutes cause for discipline or removal. The materials further consider the constitutional limits to federal legislation of state and local labor relations.

1. THE CONSTITUTIONAL RIGHT TO JOIN A UNION, BARGAIN, AND TO STRIKE

The NLRA protects the right to strike and the right to join or refrain from joining a union. Furthermore, sections 8(a)(5), 8(d), and 9 create an employer responsibility to recognize and bargain with the employees' union representative. However, in many states what legislation exists merely prohibits strikes by public employees and in no way fashions any collective bargaining rights and responsibilities, of public employer and employee. In such states, can public employees rely on the Constitution in asserting their right to join a union, to bargain, and to strike? If they do successfully bargain, can their contract rights be enforced? Consider the following cases.

ALABAMA LABOR COUNCIL v. FRAZIER

Alabama Circuit Court, Madison County, 1972.
81 L.R.R.M. 2155.

MAYHALL, JUDGE: * * *

This proceeding was for a declaratory judgment decreeing that certain Alabama statutes, commonly called and hereinafter referred to as the Solomon Act, more specifically described as Title 55, Sections 317(1), 317(2), 317(3) and 317(4), Code of Alabama, Recompiled 1958 as amended to be held to violate Amendment One and the Due Process and Equal Protection Clauses of Amendment Fourteen of the United States Constitution.

* * *

The only issue presented to the court by the pleadings was whether or not the Solomon Act is void as violative of the U.S. Constitution. The pleadings, factual evidence, and legal argument presented to the court clearly shows the Solomon Act to be unconstitutional and therefore void.

The Complainants proved that they had been stymied in their organization of state employees and that their goal in such organization was the betterment of wages and working conditions for state and local public employees.

Mr. Barney Weeks, President of the Alabama Labor Council, AFL–CIO, testified that since the enactment of the Solomon Act in 1953, public employee union membership has dropped from 3,787 members to 655 in June of 1972. This drop in membership cost his labor organization over the twenty-year period in excess of $100,000 in dues. During the twenty-year period when state and local public employment in Alabama increased by 106.7%, public employee union membership fell by 79.1%.   Additional evidence by union officials with Complainants' Locals 1279 and 660 showed loss in local union membership and dues because of the Solomon Act prohibition of public employee membership in labor unions.   The evidence of loss of membership and dues income was not disputed by the Respondents.

As of March 1972, approximately 162,200 Alabamians are employed with state and local government.   The U.S. Supreme Court has long since ruled in U.S. v. Robel (1967), 389 U.S. 258, that these public employees could belong to the Communist Party.   This court certainly thinks that they also have the right to join a labor union.

Section 317(2) of the Act clearly states that "any public employee" who joins or participates in a labor union loses all right, "afforded him under the state merit system, employment rights, re-employment rights, and other rights, benefits, or privileges which he enjoys as a result of his public employment."   Such sweeping language, without any further showing of a valid, specific need for governmental protection is fatally overbroad.   This court must conclude as have two recent federal courts that public employees have the same constitutional rights under the First Amendment as any other American citizen.   See: Atkins v. City of Charlotte (D.C.N.C.) 296 F.Supp. 1068, 70 LRRM 2732 (1969) and Melton v. City of Atlanta (D.C.Ga.) 324 F.Supp. 315, 76 LRRM 2511 (1971).

The Solomon Act effectively prohibits public employee membership in union by sweeping and harsh penalties.   And there has been no showing of a legitimate public interest to be protected by such law.   The courts in Atkins, supra and Melton, supra, also encountered state statutes very similar to our Solomon Act and both held that their statutes were void as violative of the U.S. Constitution.

The Court noted the wish of complainant-employees to join a union but for their fear of termination.   The presence of the Solomon Act hanging over the heads of public employees in Alabama deprives those employees of rights guaranteed in our constitution to assemble, to petition their government and to associate with whom they choose.

Finally this court would like to point to the exemptions from the Act for teachers, employees of municipalities, employees of the State Docks terminal railway, and employees of Bryce and Searcy Hospitals and Partlow State School.   There exists no rational basis or explanation for this discrimination which clearly violates the 14th Amendment.   This court cannot find any reasonable way to interpret the Act in a constitutional manner, nor can it find a constitutional field of operation for the Solomon Act.

IT IS, THEREFORE, ORDERED, ADJUDGED, AND DECREED BY THE COURT, AS FOLLOWS:

1.   That the declaratory judgment of the Complainants be and the same hereby is granted and that the Solomon Act or Title 55, Sections 317(1) through 317(4), Code of Alabama, Recompiled 1958, as amended, is declared void as repugnant to the 1st and 14th Amendments to the U.S. Constitution.

QUESTION

There seems to be little doubt that the Constitution supports the right of public employees to join a union. Is there a corollary to this right? Consider, Richmond Education Association v. Crockford.

RICHMOND v. CROCKFORD

United States District Court, Eastern District of Virginia, 1972.
80 L.R.R.M. 3116.

MERHIGE, DISTRICT JUDGE:—This is a class action brought pursuant to 28 U.S.C. §§ 1343(3) and (4) and 42 U.S.C. § 1983, seeking declaratory and injunctive relief against the School Board of the City of Richmond and its individual members in their representative capacities. Defendants have filed various motions and a memorandum in support thereof as follows:

> 1. Motion to Dismiss for Lack of Jurisdiction and/or failure to state a claim upon which relief can be granted.

* * *

Plaintiffs have filed their responses, and the legal issue raised are now ready for disposition.

The complaint and exhibits filed therewith reflect that plaintiff, Richmond Education Association ("REA"), is an unincorporated association organized under the laws of the Commonwealth of Virginia, whose sole purpose is to represent certified professional employees of the defendant school board, in their employment relationships. REA membership currently lists 2,085 members of an eligible 3,350. This action is based upon an alleged refusal of the defendants to meet and discuss with the REA concerning conditions of employment, to recognize REA as a representative of the aforementioned employees for purposes of discussion, and to recognize REA as the exclusive representative of the class which it purports to represent. The defendants have allegedly refused all recognition of and discussions with REA.

* * *

The plaintiffs herein premise their complaint in the First and Fourteenth Amendments to the Constitution of the United States. The Court is satisfied that jurisdiction exists pursuant to 42 U.S.C. § 1983 and 28 U.S.C. §§ 1343(3) and (4).

The complaint herein clearly and succinctly alleges that the plaintiffs have a constitutional right as public sector employees to organize and associate for the purpose of collectively representing their employment interests. It is contended that by their actions, the defendants have effectively blunted the exercise of these rights. The plaintiffs allege, in essence, that:

> Nothing could have a greater chilling effect upon plaintiffs' fundamental rights to associate and bargain collectively, than the stoppage of all communication and dealings between the School

Board and REA as a representative association. See, Plaintiffs' Memorandum in Opposition, at page 11.

The grant of approval to organize and associate without the corresponding grant of recognition may well be an empty and meaningless gesture on the part of the defendant School Board. See, Williams v. Rhodes, 393 U.S. 23, 41, 89 S.Ct. 5, 21 L.Ed.2d 24 (1968); NAACP v. Burton, 371 U.S. 415, 83 S.Ct. 328, 9 L.Ed.2d 405 (1963); Lamont v. Postmaster General, 381 U.S. 301, 85 S.Ct. 1493, 14 L.Ed.2d 398 (1965).

Without embarking into a discussion of a remedy herein, the Court finds that plaintiffs' allegation that the defendants' wrongful actions have a chilling effect upon the exercise of plaintiffs' First Amendment rights does indeed state a claim upon which relief, if due, can be granted. The plaintiffs have stated a constitutional claim, which on the present status of the pleadings is sufficient under the Constitution and laws of the United States.

NOTES

1. It is doubtful that the *Richmond* theory will prevail. See, Indianapolis Education Association v. Lewallen, 72 L.R.R.M. 2071 at 2072 (1969). In a Florida case, the state constitution was successfully used as a base to establish the employer's duty to bargain. See, Dade County Classroom Teachers' Association v. Legislature of the State of Florida, 269 So.2d 684 (Fla.1972).

2. For an excellent review of state legislation affecting labor relations in the public sector, see Blair, "State & Legislative Control over the Condition of Public Employment," 26 Vand.L.Rev. 1 (1973).

3. Is there a corollary to the right to bargain? What about strike?

POSTAL CLERKS v. BLOUNT

United State District Court, District of Columbia, 1971.
325 F.Supp. 879.

Per Curiam. This action was brought by the United Federation of Postal Clerks (hereafter sometimes referred to as "Clerks"), an unincorporated public employee labor organization which consists primarily of employees of the Post Office Department, and which is the exclusive bargaining representative of approximately 305,000 members of the clerk craft employed by defendant. Defendant Blount is the Postmaster General of the United States. The Clerks seek declaratory and injunctive relef invalidating portions of 5 U.S.C. Section 7311, 18 U.S.C. Section 1918, an affidavit required by 5 U.S.C. Section 3333 to implement the above statutes, and Executive Order 11491, C.F.R., Chap. II, p. 191. The Government, in response, filed a motion to dismiss or in the alternative for summary judgment, and plaintiff filed its opposition thereto and cross motion for summary judgment. A three-judge court was convened pursuant to 28 U.S.C. Section 2282 and Section 2284 to consider this issue.

5 U.S.C. Section 7311(3) prohibits an individual from accepting or holding a position in the federal government or in the District of Columbia if he

> (3) participates in a strike   *   *   *   against the Government of the United States or the government of the District of Columbia. *   *   *

Paragraph C of the appointment affidavit required by 5 U.S.C. Section 3333, which all federal employees are required to execute under oath, states (POD Form 61):

> I am not participating in any strike against the Government of the United States or any agency thereof, and I will not so participate while an employee of the Government of the United States or any agency thereof.

18 U.S.C. Section 1918, in making a violation of 5 U.S.C. Section 7311 a crime, provides:

> Whoever violates the provision of Section 7311 of Title 5 that an individual may not accept or hold a position in the Government of the United States or the government of the District of Columbia if he   *   *   *.

> (3) participates in a strike, or asserts the right to strike, against the Government of the United States or the District of Columbia   *   *   *   shall be fined not more than $1,000 or imprisoned not more than one year and a day, or both.

Section 2(e)(2) of Executive Order 11491 exempts from the definition of a labor organization any group which:

> asserts the right to strike against the Government of the United States or any agency thereof, or to assist or participate in such strike, or imposes a duty or obligation to conduct, assist or participate in such a strike   *   *   *.

Section 19(b)(4) of the same Executive Order makes it an unfair labor practice for a labor organization to:

> call or engage in a strike, work stoppage, or slowdown; picket any agency in a labor-management dispute; or condone any such activity by failing to take affirmative action to prevent or stop it; *   *   *.

Plaintiff contends that the right to strike is a fundamental right protected by the Constitution, and that the absolute prohibition of such activity by 5 U.S.C. Section 7311(3), and the other provisions set out above thus constitutes an infringement of the employees' First Amendment rights of association and free speech and operates to deny them equal protection of the law. Plaintiff also argues that the language to "strike" and "participate in a strike" is vague and overbroad and therefore violative of both the First Amendment and the Due Process Clause of the Fifth Amendment. For the purposes of this opinion, we will direct our attention to the attack on the constitutionality of 5 U.S.C. Section 7311(3), the key provision being challenged * * *.

At common law no employee, whether public or private, had a constitutional right to strike in concert with his fellow workers. Indeed, such collective action on the part of employees was often held to be a conspiracy. When the right of private employees to strike finally received full protection, it was by statute, Section 7 of the National Labor Relations Act, which "took this conspiracy weapon away from the employer in employment relations which affect interstate commerce" and guaranteed to employees in the private sector the right to engage in concerted activities for the purpose of collective bargaining. See discussion in Local 232 v. Wisconsin Employment Relations Board, 336 U.S. 245, 257–259, 69 S.Ct. 516, 93 L.Ed.2d 651 (1948). It seems clear that public employees stand on no stronger footing in this regard than private employees and that in the absence of a statute, they too do not possess the right to strike. The Supreme Court has spoken approvingly of such a restriction, see Amell v. United States, 384 U.S. 158, 161, 86 S.Ct. 1384, 16 L.Ed.2d 445, (1965), and at least one federal district court has invoked the provisions of a predecessor statute, 5 U.S.C. Section 118p-r, to enjoin a strike by government employees. Tennessee Valley Authority v. Local Union No. 110 of Sheet Metal Workers, 233 F.Supp. 997 (D.C.W.D.Ky.1962). Likewise, scores of state cases have held that state employees do not have a right to engage in concerted work stoppages, in the absence of legislative authorization. See, e.g., Los Angeles Metropolitan Transit Authority v. Brotherhood of R. R. Trainmen, 54 Cal. 684, 8 Cal.Rptr. 1, 355 P.2d 905 (1960); Board of Education, etc. v. Redding, 32 Ill.2d 567, 207 N.E.2d 427 (1965). It is fair to conclude that, irrespective of the reasons given, there is a unanimity of opinion on the part of courts and legislatures that government employees do not have the right to strike. See Moberly, "The Strike and Its Alternative in Public Employment," University of Wisconsin Law Review (1966) pp. 549–550, 554.

Congress has consistently treated public employees as being in a different category than private employees. The National Labor Relations Act of 1937 and the Labor-Management Relations Act of 1947, (Taft-Hartley) both defined "employer" as not including any governmental or political subdivisions, and thereby indirectly withheld the protections of Section 7 from governmental employees. Congress orginally enacted the no-strike provision separately from other restrictions on employee activity, i.e., such as those struck down in Stewart v. Washington, 301 F.Supp. 610 (D.C.D.C.1969) and NALC v. Blount, 305 F.Supp. 546, (D.C.D.C.1969), by attaching riders to appropriations bills which prohibited strikes by government employees. See for example the Third Urgent Deficiency Appropriation Act of 1946, which provided that no part of the appropriation could be used to pay the salary of anyone who engaged in a strike against the Government. Section 305 of the Taft-Hartley Act made it unlawful for a federal employee to participate in a strike, providing immediate discharge and forfeiture of civil service status for infractions. Section

305 was repealed in 1955 by Public Law 330, and reenacted in 5 U.S.C. Section 118p-r, the predecessor to the present statute.

Given the fact that there is no constitutional right to strike, it is not irrational or arbitrary for the Government to condition employment on a promise not to withhold labor collectively, and to prohibit strikes by those in public employment, whether because of the prerogatives of the sovereign, some sense of higher obligation associated with public service, to assure the continuing functioning of the Government without interruption, to protect public health and safety or for other reasons. Although plaintiff argues that the provisions in question are unconstitutionally broad in covering all Government employees regardless of the type or importance of the work they do, we hold that it makes no difference whether the jobs performed by certain public employees are regarded as "essential" or "nonessential," or whether similar jobs are performed by workers in private industry who do have the right to strike protected by statute. Nor is it relevant that some positions in private industry are arguably more affected with a public interest than are some positions in the Government service. While the Fifth Amendment contains no Equal Protection Clause similar to the one found in the Fourteenth Amendment, concepts of Equal Protection do inhere in Fifth Amendment Principles of Due Process. Bolling v. Sharpe, 347 U.S. 497, 74 S.Ct. 693, 98 L.Ed. 884 (1954). The Equal Protection Clause, however, does not forbid all discrimination. Where fundamental rights are not involved, a particular classification does not violate the Equal Protection Clause if it is not "arbitrary" or "irrational," i.e., "if any state of facts reasonably may be conceived to justify it." McGowan v. Maryland, 366 U.S. 420, 426, 81 S.Ct. 1101, 1105, 6 L.Ed.2d 393 (1961). Compare Kramer v. Union Free School District, 395 U.S. 621, 627–628, 89 S.Ct. 1886, 1889–1890, 23 L.Ed.2d 583 (1969). Since the right to strike cannot be considered a "fundamental" right, it is the test enunciated in *McGowan* which must be employed in this case. Thus, there is latitude for distinctions rooted in reason and practice, especially where the difficulty of drafting a no-strike statute which distinguishes among types and classes of employees is obvious.

Furthermore, it should be pointed out that the fact that public employees may not strike does not interfere with their rights which are fundamental and constitutionally protected. The right to organize collectively and to select representatives for the purposes of engaging in collective bargaining is such a fundamental right. Thomas v. Collins, 323 U.S. 516, 65 S.Ct. 315, 89 L.Ed.2d 430 (1945); NLRB v. Jones & Laughlin, 301 U.S. 1, 33, 57 S.Ct. 615, 622, 81 L.Ed. 893 (1937). But, as the Supreme Court noted in Local 232 v. Wisconsin Employment Relations Board, supra, "The right to strike, because of its more serious impact upon the public interest, is more vulnerable to regulation than the right to organize and select representatives for lawful purposes of collective bargaining which this Court has characterized as a 'fundamental right' and which, as the Court has pointed out, was recognized as such in its decisions long before it was given protection by the National Labor Relations Act." 336 U.S. at 259, 69 S.Ct. at 524.

Executive Order 11491 recognizes the right of federal employees to join labor organizations for the purpose of dealing with grievances, but that Order clearly and expressly defines strikes, work stoppages and slowdowns as unfair labor practices. As discussed above, that Order is the culmination of a longstanding policy. There certainly is no compelling reason to imply the existence of the right to strike from the right to associate and bargain collectively. In the private sphere, the strike is used to equalize bargaining power, but this has universally been held not to be appropriate when its object and purpose can only be to influence the essentially political decisions of Government in the allocation of its resources. Congress has an obligation to ensure that the machinery of the Federal Government continues to function at all times without interference. Prohibition of strikes by its employees is a reasonable implementation of that obligation * * *.

Accordingly, we hold that the provisions of the statute, the appointment affidavit and the Executive Order, as construed above, do not violate any constitutional rights of those employees who are members of plaintiff's union. The Government's motion to dismiss the complaint is granted. Order to be presented.

WRIGHT, C. J., concurring * * *. My following comments are addressed to the main issue raised in Part I of the opinion—the validity of that flat ban on federal employees' strikes under the Fifth Amendment of the Constitution. This question is, in my view, a very difficult one, and I cannot concur fully in the majority's handling of it.

It is by no means clear to me that the right to strike is not fundamental. The right to strike seems intimately related to the right to form labor organizations, right which the majority recognizes as fundamental and which, more importantly, is generally thought to be constitutionally protected under the First Amendment—even for public employees. See Melton v. City of Atlanta, 324 F.Supp. 315 (N.D. Ga.1971); Atkins v. City of Charlotte, 296 F.Supp. 1068 (W.D.N.C. 1969). If the inherent purpose of a labor organization is to bring the workers' interests to bear on management, the right to strike is, historically and practically, an important means of effectuating that purpose. A union that never strikes, or which can make no credible threat to strike, may wither away in ineffectiveness. That fact is not irrelevant to the constitutional calculations. Indeed, in several decisions, the Supreme Court has held that the First Amendment right of association is at least concerned with essential organizational activities which give the particular association life and promote its fundamental purposes. See Williams v. Rhodes, 393 U.S. 23, 89 S.Ct. 5, 21 L.Ed.2d 24 (1968); United Mine Workers v. Illinois State Bar Association, 389 U.S. 217, 88 S.Ct. 353, 19 L.Ed.2d 426 (1967). I do not suggest that the right to strike is coequal with the right to form labor organizations. Nor do I equate striking with the organizational activities protected in *Williams* (access to the ballot) or *United Mine Workers* (group legal representation). But I do believe that the right to strike is, at least, within constitutional concern and should not be discriminatorily abridged without substantial or "compelling" justification.

Hence the real question here, as I see it, is to determine whether there is such justification for denying federal employees a right which is granted to other employees of private business. Plaintiff's arguments that not all federal services are "essential" and that some privately provided services are no less "essential" casts doubt on the validity of the flat ban on federal employees' strikes. In our mixed economic system of governmental and private enterprise, the line separating governmental from private functions may depend more on the accidents of history than on substantial differences in kind.

Nevertheless, I feel that I must concur in the result reached by the majority in Part I of its opinion. As the majority indicates, the asserted right of public employees to strike has often been litigated and, so far as I know, never recognized as a matter of law. The present state of the relevant jurisprudence offers almost no support for the proposition that the government lacks a "compelling" interest in prohibiting such strikes. No doubt, the line between "essential" and "nonessential" functions is very, very difficult to draw. For that reason, it may well be best to accept the demarcations resulting from the development of our political economy. If the right of public employees to strike—with all its political and social ramifications—is to be recognized and protected by the judiciary, it should be done by the Supreme Court which has the power to reject established jurisprudence and the authority to enforce such a sweeping rule.

QUESTIONS

Should a union be able to insist upon a security clause, such as a union shop or agency shop clause? Under the NLRA, such agreements are valid and union insistence upon their inclusion will be protected. Should union security be considered differently in the public sector? Does a public employee have a constitutional right to refuse to join a union or to refuse to pay the equivalent of union dues to the union on the ground that to do so inhibits freedom of association? Consider the following case.

ABOOD v. DETROIT BOARD OF EDUCATION

Supreme Court of the United States, 1977.
431 U.S. 209, 97 S.Ct. 1782, 52 L.Ed.2d 261.

[In 1973 the Michigan legislature amended that state's Public Employment Relations Act to permit the negotiation of agency shop clauses. Public employers and unions representing their employees could require as a condition of continued employment the payment of a service fee equivalent to union dues. D. Louis Abood and other teachers in Detroit brought suit, alleging that the Detroit Federation of Teachers, to which they had become obligated to pay fees, engaged not simply in collective bargaining and contract enforcement but also in various unspecified political, economic, and social activities to which they objected. These programs and activities were asserted to be unrelated to the federation's duties as bargaining agent for the Detroit teachers. The Michigan Court of Appeals ruled that the agency shop amendment, as applied through the federation's use of compulsory service fees to further "political purposes" unrelated to collective bargaining "could violate plaintiffs' First and Fourteenth Amendment rights." The court determined that relief should be denied, however, because the plaintiffs had failed to specify the causes and candidates to which they objected. After the Supreme Court of Michigan denied review, the United States Supreme Court granted certiorari.]

* * *

Our decisions establish with unmistakable clarity that the freedom of an individual to associate for the purpose of advancing beliefs and ideas is protected by the First and Fourteenth Amendments. Equally clear is the proposition that a government may not require an individual to relinquish rights guaranteed him by the First Amendment as a condition of public employment. The appellants argue that they fall within the protection of these cases because they have been prohibited, not from actively associating, but rather from refusing to associate. They specifically argue that they may constitutionally prevent the Union's spending a part of their required service fees to contribute to political candidates and to express political views unrelated to its duties as exclusive bargaining representative. We have concluded that this argument is a meritorious one.

One of the principles underlying the Court's decision in Buckley v. Valeo, 424 U.S. 1, 96 S.Ct. 612, 46 L.Ed.2d 659, was that contributing to an organization for the purpose of spreading a political message is protected by the First Amendment. Because "[m]aking a contribution * * * enables like-minded persons to pool their resources in furtherance of common political goals," id., at 22, the Court reasoned that limitations upon the freedom to contribute "implicate fundamental First Amendment interests," id., at 23.

The fact that the appellants are compelled to make, rather than prohibited from making, contributions for political purposes works no less an infringement of their constitutional rights. For at the heart of the First Amendment is the notion that an individual should be free to believe as he will, and that in a free society one's beliefs should be shaped by his mind and his conscience rather than coerced by the State. * * *

We do not hold that a union cannot constitutionally spend funds for the expression of political views, on behalf of political candidates, or toward the advancement of other ideological causes not germane to its duties as collective-bargaining representative. Rather, the Constitution requires only that such expenditures be financed from charges, dues, or assessments paid by employees who do not object to advancing those ideas and who are not coerced into doing so against their will by the threat of loss of governmental employment.

There will, of course, be difficult problems in drawing lines between collective-bargaining activities, for which contributions may be compelled, and ideological activities unrelated to collective bargaining, for which such compulsion is prohibited. * * * The process of establishing a written collective-bargaining agreement prescribing the terms and conditions of public employment may require not merely concord at the bargaining table, but subsequent approval by other public authorities; related budgetary and appropriations decisions might be seen as an integral part of the bargaining process. We have no occasion in this case, however, to try to define such a dividing line. * * *

In determining what remedy will be appropriate if the appellants prove their allegations, the objective must be to devise a way of preventing compulsory subsidization of ideological activity by employees who object thereto without restricting the Union's ability to require every employee to contribute to the cost of collective-bargaining activities. This task is simplified by the guidance to be had from prior decisions. * * *

The Court * * * considered the remedial question in Railway Clerks v. Allen, 373 U.S. 113, 83 S.Ct. 1158, 10 L.Ed.2d 235. In that case employees who had refused to pay union-shop dues obtained injunctive relief in state court against enforcement of the union-shop agreement. The employees had not notified the union prior to bringing the lawsuit of their opposition to political expenditures, and at trial, their testimony was principally that they opposed such expenditures, as a general matter. Id., at 118–119, n.5. The Court held that the employees had adequately established their cause of action by manifesting "opposition to *any* political expenditures by the union," id., at 118 (emphasis in original), and that the requirement * * * that dissent be affirmatively indicated was satisfied by the allegations in the complaint that was filed, id., at 118–119, and n.6. * * *

The Court in *Allen* described a "practical decree" that could properly be entered, providing for (1) the refund of a portion of the exacted funds in the proportion that union political expenditures bear to total union expenditures, and (2) the reduction of future exactions by the same proportion. 373 U.S., at 122. Recognizing the difficulties posed by judicial administration of such a remedy, the Court also suggested that it would be highly desirable for unions to adopt a "voluntary plan by which dissenters would be afforded an internal union remedy." Ibid. This last suggestion is particularly relevant to the case at bar, for the Union has adopted such a plan since the commencement of this litigation.

*   *   *

The Court of Appeals thus erred in holding that the plaintiffs are entitled to no relief if they can prove the allegations contained in their complaints, and in depriving them of an opportunity to establish their right to appropriate relief * * *. In view of the newly adopted Union internal remedy, it may be appropriate under Michigan law, * * * to defer further judicial proceedings pending the voluntary utilization by the parties of that internal remedy as a possible means of settling the dispute.

The judgment is vacated, and the case is remanded for further proceedings not inconsistent with this opinion.

It is so ordered.

*   *   *

MR. JUSTICE POWELL, with whom THE CHIEF JUSTICE and MR. JUSTICE BLACKMUN join, concurring in the judgment.

The Court today holds that a State cannot constitutionally compel public employees to contribute to union political activities which they oppose. On this basis the Court concludes that "the general allegations in the complaints, if proved, establish a cause of action under the First and Fourteenth Amendments." Ante, at 237. With this much of the Court's opinion I agree, and I therefore join the Court's judgment remanding this case for further proceedings.

But the Court's holding and judgment are but a small part of today's decision. * * * [T]he Court apparently rules that public employees can be compelled by the State to pay full union dues to a union with which they disagree, subject only to a possible rebate or deduction if they are willing to step forward, declare their opposition to the union, and initiate a proceeding to establish that some portion of their dues has been spent on "ideological activities unrelated to collective bargaining." Ante, at 236. Such a sweeping limitation of First Amendment rights by the Court is not only unnecessary on this record; it is in my view unsupported by either precedent or reason.

*   *   *

* * * it is now clear, first, that *any* withholding of financial support for a public-sector union is within the protection of the First Amendment; and second, that the State should bear the burden of proving that any union dues or fees that it requires of nonunion employees are needed to serve paramount governmental interests.

* * * I agree with the Court as far as it goes, but I would make it more explicit that compelling a government employee to give financial support to a union in the public sector—regardless of the uses to which the union puts the contribution—impinges seriously upon interests in free speech and association protected by the First Amendment.

*   *   *

The ultimate objective of a union in the public sector, like that of a political party, is to influence public decisionmaking in accordance with the views and perceived interests of its membership. Whether a teachers' union is concerned with salaries and fringe benefits, teacher qualifications and in-service training, pupil-teacher ratios, length of the school day, student discipline, or the content of the high school curriculum, its objective is to bring school board policy and decisions into harmony with its own views. Similarly, to the extent that school board expenditures and policy are guided by decisions made by the municipal, State, and Federal Governments, the union's objective is to obtain favorable decisions—and to place persons in positions of power who will be receptive to the union's viewpoint. In these respects, the public-sector union is indistinguishable from the traditional political party in this country.

What distinguishes the public-sector union from the political party—and the distinction is a limited one—is that most of its members are employees who share similar economic interests and who may have a common professional perspective on some issues of public policy. Public school teachers, for example, have a common interest in fair teachers' salaries and reasonable pupil-teacher ratios. This suggests the possibility of a limited range of probable agreement among the class of individuals that a public-sector union is organized to represent. But I am unable to see why the likelihood of an area of consensus in the group should remove the protection of the First Amendment for the disagreements that inevitably will occur. Certainly, if individual teachers are ideologically opposed to public-sector unionism itself, as are the appellants in this case, ante, at 212–213, one would think that compelling them to affiliate with the union by contributing to it infringes their First Amendment rights to the same degree as compelling them to contribute to a political party.　*　*　*

Nor is there any basis here for distinguishing "collective-bargaining activities" from "political activities" so far as the interests protected by the First Amendment are concerned. Collective bargaining in the public sector is "political" in any meaningful sense of the word. This is most obvious when public-sector bargaining extends—as it may in Michigan—to such matters of public policy as the educational philosophy that will inform the high school curriculum. But it is also true when public-sector bargaining focuses on such "bread and butter" issues as wages, hours, vacations, and pensions. Decisions on such issues will have a direct impact on the level of public services, priorities within state and municipal budgets, creation of bonded indebtedness, and tax rates. The cost of public education is normally the largest element of a county or municipal budget. Decisions reached through collective bargaining in the schools will affect not only the teachers and the quality of education, but also the taxpayers and the beneficiaries of other important public services. Under our democratic system of government, decisions on these critical issues of public policy have been entrusted to elected officials who ultimately are responsible to the voters.

2. JOB TENURE: DUE PROCESS PROTECTION UPON REMOVAL

When government assumes the role of employer, it is not afforded unfettered discretion in dealing with its employees. The Due Process Clause of the U.S. Constitution provides a unique restriction not apparent in the private sector. Thus, even without a state or federal statute, public employees have some special constitutional protections which the following cases and materials illustrate.

BOARD OF REGENTS v. ROTH

Supreme Court of the United States, 1972.
408 U.S. 564, 92 S.Ct. 2701, 33 L.Ed.2d 548.

[Respondent was hired in 1968 for his first teaching job as an assistant professor at a state university for a fixed term of one academic year. The notice of his faculty appointment was so specified. He completed the academic year, but was informed that he would not be rehired for the next academic year. Under university rules the respondent was given no reason for the decision not to rehire him, nor was he given any opportunity to challenge the decision at any sort of hearing; because (1) he had acquired no tenure rights to continued employment under state statutory law, such rights inuring to the benefit of state university teachers only after 4 years of continuous employment, and (2) absent tenure rights, he was entitled to nothing under state law beyond his one-year appointment. Respondent brought suit in federal district court alleging violations of free speech and procedural due process protections provided by the First and Fourteenth Amendments of the U.S. Constitution. The district court granted summary judgment for respondent. The court of appeals affirmed. The U.S. Supreme Court reversed.]

I

The requirements of procedural due process apply only to the deprivation of interests encompassed by the Fourteenth Amendment's protection of liberty and property. When protected interests are implicated, the right to some kind of prior hearing is paramount. But the range of interests protected by procedural due process is not infinite.

* * * [T]o determine whether due process requirements apply * * * we must look * * * to the *nature* of the interest at stake. We must look to see if the interest is within the Fourteenth Amendment's protection of liberty and property.

"Liberty" and "property" are broad and majestic terms. They are among the "[g]reat [constitutional] concepts * * * purposely left to gather meaning from experience. * * * [T]hey relate to the whole domain of social and economic fact, and the statesmen who founded this Nation knew too well that only a stagnant society remains unchanged." National Mutual Ins. Co. v. Tidewater Transfer Co., 337 U.S. 582, 646, 69 S.Ct. 1173, 1195, 93 L.Ed. 1556 (Frankfurter, J., dissenting). * * * The Court has * * * made clear that the property interests protected by procedural due process extend well beyond actual ownership of real estate, chattels, or money. By the same token, the Court has required due process protection for deprivations of liberty beyond the sort of formal constraints imposed by the criminal process.

Yet, while the Court has eschewed rigid or formalistic limitations on the protection of procedural due process, it has at the same time observed certain boundaries. For the words "liberty" and "property" in the Due Process Clause of the Fourteenth Amendment must be given some meaning.

II

"While this Court has not attempted to define with exactness the liberty   *   *   *   guaranteed [by the Fourteenth Amendment], the term has received much consideration and some of the included things have been definitely stated. Without doubt, it denotes not merely freedom from bodily restraint but also the right of the individual to contract, to engage in any of the common occupations of life, to acquire useful knowledge, to marry, establish a home and bring up children, to worship God according to the dictates of his own conscience, and generally to enjoy those privileges long recognized   *   *   *   as essential to the orderly pursuit of happiness by free men." Meyer v. Nebraska, 262 U.S. 390, 399, 43 S.Ct. 625, 626, 67 L.Ed. 1042. In a Constitution for a free people, there can be no doubt that the meaning of "liberty" must be broad indeed. See, e.g., Bolling v. Sharpe, 347 U.S. 497, 499–500, 74 S.Ct. 693, 694, 98 L.Ed. 884; Stanley v. Illinois, 405 U.S. 645, 92 S.Ct. 1208, 31 L.Ed.2d 551.

There might be cases in which a State refused to re-employ a person under such circumstances that interests in liberty would be implicated. But this is not such a case.

The State, in declining to rehire the respondent, did not make any charge against him that might seriously damage his standing and associations in his community.   *   *   *

Similarly, there is no suggestion that the State, in declining to re-employ the respondent, imposed on him a stigma or other disability that foreclosed his freedom to take advantage of other employment opportunities.   *   *   *

To be sure, the respondent has alleged that the nonrenewal of his contract was based on his exercise of his right to freedom of speech. But this allegation is not now before us. The District Court stayed proceedings on this issue, and the respondent has yet to prove that the decision not to rehire him was, in fact, based on his free speech activities.

Hence, on the record before us, all that clearly appears is that the respondent was not rehired for one year at one university. It stretches the concept too far to suggest that a person is deprived of "liberty" when he simply is not rehired in one job but remains as free as before to seek another. Cafeteria Workers v. McElroy, supra, 367 U.S. at 895–896, 81 S.Ct. at 1748–1749, 6 L.Ed.2d 1230.

III

The Fourteenth Amendment's procedural protection of property is a safeguard of the security of interests that a person has already acquired in specific benefits.   *   *   *

*   *   *

*   *   * To have a property interest in a benefit, a person clearly must have more than an abstract need or desire for it. He must have more than a unilateral expectation of it. He must, instead, have a legitimate claim of entitlement to it. It is a purpose of the ancient institution of property to protect those claims upon which people rely in their daily lives, reliance that must not be arbitrarily undermined. It is a purpose of the constitutional right to a hearing to provide an opportunity for a person to vindicate those claims.

Property interests, of course, are not created by the Constitution. Rather, they are created and their dimensions are defined by existing rules or understandings that stem from an independent source such as state law—rules or understandings that secure certain benefits and that support claims of entitlement to those benefits.   *   *   *

*   *   * [T]he respondent's "property" interest in employment at Wisconsin State University-Oshkosh was created and defined by the terms of his appointment. Those terms secured his interest in employment up to June 30, 1969. But the important fact in this case is that they specifically provided that the respondent's employment was to terminate on June 30. They did not provide for contract renewal absent "sufficient cause." Indeed, they made no provision for renewal whatsoever.

Thus, the terms of the respondent's appointment secured absolutely no interest in re-employment for the next year. They supported absolutely no possible claim of entitlement to re-employment. Nor, significantly, was there any state statute or University rule or policy that secured his interest in re-employment or that created any legitimate claim to it. In these circumstances, the respondent surely had an abstract concern in being rehired, but he did not have a *property* interest sufficient to require the University authorities to give him a hearing when they declined to renew his contract of employment.

*   *   *

QUESTIONS

1. What did Mr. Roth want, and what do you think should be provided?

2. If Mr. Roth had had tenure, would the case have been decided differently? Why?

3. *Roth* establishes a test for determining the existence of property or liberty interests for purposes of determining whether procedural due process applies. What is it?

4. Suppose the dean of State College hires a secretary. Two months later she is discharged because the office finds out something of her past. She asks why she is being fired and the dean responds "Sex and drugs." What are the secretary's constitutional rights with regard to her removal? Suppose the dean had said nothing in response to her question? Is she entitled to an explanation?

3. FEDERAL POWER TO CONTROL STATE LABOR RELATIONS

Should the labor relations problems of state and local public employees be left to the multitude of state legislatures and city governments? Are there aspects of labor relations in the public sector which are so unique that they are not amenable to federal control? There are about 30 states which have laws which in some way govern labor relations in the public sector. For the most part, they differ in their approaches. With all the recent work stoppages and strife in the public sector, does the extensive impact of such problems warrant a national legislative response? Should there be a federal law? If so, what should it provide? Before these questions can be answered, a more fundamental question must be addressed: Would a federal law governing state and local public employment relations be constitutional? Consider the following case:

NATIONAL LEAGUE OF CITIES v. USERY

Supreme Court of the United States, 1976.
426 U.S. 833, 96 S.Ct. 2465, 49 L.Ed.2d 245.

REHNQUIST, J. * * *. In a series of amendments beginning in 1961 Congress began to extend the provisions of the Fair Labor Standards Act to some types of public employees. The 1961 amendment to the Act extended its coverage to persons who were employed in "enterprises" engaged in commerce or in the production of goods for commerce. And in 1966, with the amendment of the definition of employers under the Act, the exemption heretofore extended to the States and their political subdivisions was removed with respect to employees of state hospitals, institutions, and schools. We nevertheless sustained the validity of the combined effect of these two amendments in Maryland v. Wirtz, 392 U.S. 183, 88 S.Ct. 2017, 20 L.Ed.2d 1020 (1968).

In 1974, Congress again broadened the coverage of the Act. The definition of "employer" in the Act now specifically "includes a public agency," 29 U.S.C. Section 203(d). In addition, the critical definition of "enterprises engaged in commerce or in the production of goods for commerce" was expanded to encompass "an activity of a public agency," and goes on to specify that

The employees of an enterprise which is a public agency shall for purposes of this subsection be deemed to be employees engaged in commerce, or in the production of goods for commerce, or employees handling, selling, or otherwise working on goods or materials that have been moved in or produced for commerce. 29 U.S.C. Section 203(s)(5).

Under the Amendments "public agency" is in turn defined as including

the Government of the United States; the government of a State or political subdivision thereof; any agency of the United States (including the United States Postal Service and Postal Rate Commission), a State, or a political subdivision of a State; or any interstate governmental agency. 29 U.S.C. Section 203(x) * * *.

The Act thus imposes upon almost all public employment the minimum wage and maximum hour requirements previously restricted to employees engaged in interstate commerce. These requirements are essentially identical to those imposed upon private employers, although the Act does attempt to make some provision for public employment relationships which are without counterpart in the private sector, such as those presented by fire protection and law enforcement personnel. * * *.

This Court has never doubted that there are limits upon the power of Congress to override state sovereignty, even when exercising its otherwise plenary powers to tax or to regulate commerce which are conferred by Art. I of the Constitution. In *Wirtz*, for example, the Court took care to assure the appellants that it had "ample power to prevent * * * 'the utter destruction of the State as a sovereign political entity,'" which they feared. 392 U.S., at 196, 88 S.Ct. at 2024. Appellee Secretary in this case, both in his brief and upon oral argument, has agreed that our federal system of government imposes definite limits upon the authority of Congress to regulate the activities of the States as States by means of the commerce power. In *Fry*, supra, the Court recognized that an express declaration of this limitation is found in the Tenth Amendment:

While the Tenth Amendment has been characterized as a "truism," stating merely that "all is retained which has not been surrendered," United States v. Darby, 312 U.S. 100, 124 (1941), it is not without significance. The Amendment expressly declares the constitutional policy that Congress may not exercise power in a fashion that impairs the States' integrity or their ability to function effectively in a federal system * * * 421 U.S., at 547 * * *.

Appellee Secretary argues that the cases in which this court has upheld sweeping exercises of authority by Congress, even though those exercises preempted state regulation of the private sector, have already curtailed the sovereignty of the States quite as much as the 1974 amendments to the Fair Labor Standards Act. We do not agree. It is one thing to recognize the authority of Congress to enact laws regulating individual businesses necessarily subject to the dual sovereignty of the government of the Nation and of the State in which they reside. It is quite another to uphold a similar exercise of congressional authority directed not to private citizens, but to the

States as States. We have repeatedly recognized that there are attributes of sovereignty attaching to every state government which may not be impaired by Congress, not because Congress may lack an affirmative grant of legislative authority to reach the matter, but because the Constitution prohibits it from exercising the authority in that manner   *   *   *.

One undoubted attribute of state sovereignty is the States' power to determine the wages which shall be paid to those whom they employ in order to carry out their governmental functions, what hours those persons will work, and what compensation will be provided where these employees may be called upon to work overtime. The question we must resolve in this case, then, is whether these determinations are "functions essential to separate and independent existence," so that Congress may not abrogate the States' otherwise plenary authority to make them   *   *   *.

Judged solely in terms of increased costs in dollars, these allegations show a significant impact on the functioning of the governmental bodies involved. The Metropolitan Government of Nashville and Davidson County, Tenn., for example, asserted that the Act will increase its costs of providing essential policy and fire protection, without any increase in service or in current salary levels, by $938,000 per year. Cape Girardeau, Mo., estimated that its annual budget for fire protection may have to be increased by anywhere from $250,000 to $400,000 over the current figure of $350,000. The State of Arizona alleged that the annual additional expenditures which will be required if it is to continue to provide essential state services may total $2½ million dollars. The State of California, which must devote significant portions of its budget to fire suppression endeavors, estimated that application of the Act to its employment practices will necessitate an increase in its budget of between $8 million and $16 million.

Increased costs are not, of course, the only adverse effects which compliance with the Act will visit upon state and local governments, and in turn upon the citizens who depend upon those governments. In its complaint in intervention, for example, California asserted that it could not comply with the overtime costs (approximately $750,000 per year) which the Act required to be paid to California Highway Patrol cadets during their academy training program. California reported that it had thus been forced to reduce its academy training program from 2,080 hours to only 960 hours, a compromise undoubtedly of substantial importance to those whose safety and welfare may depend upon the preparedness of the California Highway Patrol   *   *   *.

Quite apart from the substantial costs imposed upon the States and their political subdivisions, the Act displaces state policies regarding the manner in which they will structure delivery of those governmental services which their citizens require. The Act, speaking directly to the States *qua* States, requires that they shall pay all but an extremely limited minority of their employees the minimum wage rates currently chosen by Congress. It may well be that as a matter of economic policy it would be desirable that States, just as private employers, comply with these minimum wage requirements. But it cannot be gainsaid that the federal requirement directly supplants the considered policy choices of the States' elected officials and administrators as to how they wish to structure pay scales in training, or those who wish to work on a casual basis, or those who for some other reason do not possess minimum employment requirements, and pay them less than the federally prescribed minimum wage. It may wish to offer parttime or summer employment to teenagers at a figure less than the minimum wage, and if unable to do so may decline to offer such employment at all. But the Act would forbid such choices by the States. The only "discretion" left to them under the Act is either to attempt to increase their revenue to meet the additional financial burden imposed upon them by paying congressionally prescribed wages to their existing complement of employees, or to reduce that complement to a number which can be paid the federal minimum wage without increasing revenue.

This dilemma presented by the minimum wage restrictions may seem not immediately different from that faced by private employers, who have long been covered by the Act and who must find ways to increase their gross income if they are to pay higher wages while maintaining current earnings. The difference, however, is that a State is not merely a factor in the "shifting economic arrangements" of the private sector of the economy, Kovacs v. Cooper, 336 U.S. 77, 95, 69 S.Ct. 448, 458, 93 L.Ed. 513 (1949) (Frankfurter, J., concurring), but is itself a coordinate element in the system established by the framers for governing our federal union.

The degree to which the FLSA amendments would interfere with traditional aspects of state sovereignty can be seen even more clearly upon examining the overtime requirements of the Act. The general effect of these provisions is to require the States to pay their employees at premium rates whenever their work exceeds a specified number of hours in a given period. The asserted reason for these provisions is to provide a financial disincentive upon using employees beyond the work period deemed appropriate by Congress. According to appellee,

> [t]his premium rate can be avoided if the [State] uses other employees to do overtime work. This, in effect, tends to discourage overtime work and to spread employment, which is the result Congress intended.

We do not doubt that this may be a salutary result, and that it has a sufficiently rational relationship to commerce to validate the application of the overtime provisions to private employers. But like the minimum wage provisions, the vice of the Act as sought to be applied here is that it directly penalizes the States for choosing to hire governmental employees on terms different from those which Congress has sought to impose   *   *   *.

Our examination of the effect of the 1974 amendments, as sought to be extended to the States and their political subdivisions, satisfies us that both the minimum wage and the maximum hour provisions will impermissibly interfere with integral governmental functions of these bodies. We earlier noted some disagreement between the parties regarding the precise effect the amendments will have in application. We do not believe particularized assessments of actual impact are crucial to resolution of the issue presented, however. For even if we accept appellee's assessments concerning the impact of the amendments, their application will nonetheless significantly alter or displace the States' abilities to police protection, sanitation, public health, and parks and recreation. These activities are typical of those performed by state and local governments in discharging their dual functions of administering the public law and furnishing public services. Indeed, it is functions such as these which governments are created to provide, services such as these which the States have traditionally afforded their citizens. If Congress may withdraw from the States the authority to make those fundamental employment decisions upon which their systems for performance of these functions must rest, we think there would be little left of the States' "separate and independent existence." Thus, even if appellants may have overestimated the effect which the Act will have upon their current levels and patterns of governmental activity, the dispositive factor is that Congress has attempted to exercise its Commerce Clause authority to prescribe minimum wages and maximum hours to be paid by the States in their capacities as sovereign governments. In doing so, Congress has sought to wield its power in a fashion that would impair the States' "ability to function effectively (with)in a federal system," Fry, supra, 421 U.S., at 547, 95 S.Ct. at 1796 n. 7. This exercise of congressional authority does not comport with the federal system of government embodied in the Constitution. We hold that insofar as the challenged amendments operate to directly displace the States' freedom to structure integral operations in areas of traditional governmental function, they are not within the authority granted Congress by Art. I, Section 8, cl. 3   *   *   *.

So ordered.

BRENNAN, WHITE, and MARSHALL, J. J., dissenting. The Court concedes, as of course it must, that Congress enacted the 1974 amendments pursuant to its exclusive power under Art. I, Section 8, cl. 3, of the Constitution "To regulate Commerce   *   *   *   among the several States." It must therefore be surprising that my Brethren should choose this Bicentennial year of our independence to repudiate principles governing judicial interpretation of our Constitution settled since the time of Chief Justice John Marshall, discarding his postulate that the Constitution comtemplates that restraints upon exercise by Congress of its plenary commerce power lie in the political process and not in the judicial process. For 152 years ago Chief Justice Marshall enunciated that principle to which, until today, his successors on this court have been faithful.

[T]he power over commerce   *   *   *   is vested in Congress as absolutely as it would be in a single government, having in its constitution the same restrictions on the exercise of the power as are found in the constitution of the United States. *The wisdom and the discretion of Congress, their identity with the people, and the influence which their constituents possess at elections, are * * * the sole restraints on which they have relied, to secure them from its abuse. They are the restraints on which the people must often rely solely, in all representative governments.* Gibbons v. Ogden, 9 Wheat. 1, 197 (1824) (emphasis added).

We said in United States v. California, 297 U.S. 175, 184, 56 S.Ct. 421, 424, 80 L.Ed. 391 (1936), for example, that "[t]he sovereign power of the states is necessarily diminished to the extent of the grants of power to the federal government in the Constitution * * *. [T]he power of the state is subordinate to the constitutional exercise of the granted federal power." This but echoed another principle emphasized by Chief Justice Marshall:

> If any proposition could command the universal assent of mankind, we might expect it would be this—that the government of the Union, though limited in its powers, is supreme within its sphere of action. This would seem to result necessarily from its nature. It is the government of all; its powers are delegated by all; it represents all, and acts for all * * *.

> The government of the United States, then, though limited in its powers, is supreme; and its laws when made in pursuance of the Constitution, form the supreme law of the land, "any thing in the constitution or laws of any State to the contrary notwithstanding." McCulloch v. Maryland, 4 Wheat. 316, 405–406 (1819).

"[It] is not a controversy between equals" when the federal government" is asserting its sovereign power to regulate commerce * * *. [T]he interests of the nation are more important than those of any state." Sanitary District v. United States, 266 U.S. 405, 425, 45 S.Ct. 176, 178, 69 L.Ed. 352 (1925) * * *.

We are left then with a catastrophic judicial body blow at Congress' power under the Commerce Clause. Even if Congress may nevertheless accomplish its objectives—for example by conditioning grants of federal funds upon compliance with federal minimum wage and overtime standards, cf. Oklahoma v. United States Civil Service Commission, 330 U.S. 127, 144, 67 S.Ct. 544, 554, 91 L.Ed. 794 (1947)—there is an ominous portent of disruption of our constitutional structure implicit in today's mischievous decision. I dissent.

F.　RECOMMENDED READING

1. Symposium, "Public Sector Impasses," 16 Industrial Relations, pp. 264 et seq. (1977).

2. Hamermesh (ed.), *Labor in the Public and Nonprofit Sectors* (1975)

3. Zagoria (ed.), *Public Workers and Public Unions* (1972)

4. Wellington & Winter, *The Unions and the Cities* (Brookings, 1971)

5. Summers, "Public Employee Bargaining: A Political Perspective," 83 Yale L.J. 1156 (1974)

Chapter VIII

INDIVIDUAL EMPLOYMENT RIGHTS

A. CASE STUDY: THE ALPHA COMPANY AND ZELMA MAZUKA

Zelma Mazuka was hired by the Alpha Company * as a cashier on November 13, 1977. On June 6, 1978, she was suspended for allegedly discounting to a customer. At that time, the Company had no evidence that Mazuka knew the customer.

Zelma notified her union steward, Elliot Klayman, who talked with the store manager, Gary Herbert. Following this, a grievance was filed by the Clerks Union on behalf of Mazuka. The grievance proceeded to a step two grievance procedure meeting. This meeting was attended by the grievant, Mazuka, Ron Racster and Frank Gibson, business agents for Local 001 of the Clerks Union; and by Herbert and Galen Hite, the divisional personnel director, for the Company.

Since the Company could not prove that Mazuka knew the customer involved, the grievance was resolved at this level by the Company agreeing that Mazuka could return to work on June 16th. It was further understood by the Union and the Company that if the Company got more evidence, such as a relationship between Mazuka and the customer, the Company could reopen the case. The Union further agreed that the Company could watch Mazuka more closely than normal because of its suspicion that she was deliberately discounting to friends.

On June 22nd, Mazuka filed a charge with the Equal Employment Opportunity Commission (EEOC), alleging that Alpha had engaged in unlawful employment discrimination. In her charge, she made the following statement:

On June 6, 1978, I was suspended from my job as a cashier by the Alpha Company. I was re-instated on June 16, 1978. Mr. Herbert, the store manager, suspended me until further investigation (the alleged reason—improper check out procedures). I believe that I am being discriminated against because of my race (black) due to the fact that since I have been re-instated, Mr. Herbert (white) has been constantly harassing me by threatening to pull mystery shopping on me, constantly watching me, and cutting my hours and giving my hours to the white part time bag boy cashiers.

---

* For background information regarding the Alpha Company, see the description of the Company contained in the case study to Chapter Two.

On June 20th, Luther King, one of the stock clerks, came forward and informed Herbert that he had seen the customer before at Mazuka's house and had seen Mazuka at the customer's house. He said that he was present on both occasions since he was dating Mazuka at the time.

Herbert informed Hite of this development. In turn, Hite phoned the Clerks Union and notified Adam Buddy, one of its business agents, of the development. Hite informed Buddy that he, Hite, was going to confront Mazuka when he was at the store the following week. Hite told Buddy to treat the information as extremely confidential; however, Buddy contacted Mazuka, told her that the Company had evidence that she and the customer were friends, and suggested that she quit. Later that day, Mazuka arrived at work as scheduled and handed Herbert the following letter:

> Zelma Mazuka
> 2929 Magnolia Avenue
> Connersville, Indiana 47331

The Alpha Company
2525 Washington Rd.
Connersville, Indiana 47331

Dear Mr. Herbert:

I (Zelma Mazuka), as of June 30th, 1978, resign from this store as cashier. The present store conditions, along with harassment, stemming from the *office personnel* and *yourself,* no longer make it possible for me to perform my job efficiently.

> Sincerely yours,
>
> s/ _____
> Zelma Mazuka

On February 1, 1979, the EEOC notified the Company of its determination as follows:

> EQUAL EMPLOYMEMT OPPORTUNITY
> COMMISSION
> Citizens Trust Building, Thirteenth Floor
> 77 Hoosier Avenue, S.E.
> Indianapolis, Indiana 47551

Zelma Mazuka
2929 Magnolia Avenue   Charging Party
Connersville, Indiana 47331

Alpha Store # 111
2525 Washington Rd.   Respondent
Connersville, Indiana

Determination

Under the authority vested in me by 29 CFR Section 1601.21(d) of the Commission's Procedural Rules 42 Fed.Reg. 47828 et seq. (September 23, 1977), I issue on behalf of the Commission the following determination as to the merits of the subject charge.

All the jurisdictional requirements have been met. Charging Party alleges Respondent discriminated against her on the account of her race (black) after reinstatement by constantly harassing her and cutting her hours which subsequently led to her resignation.

Examination of the evidence indicates there is reason to believe the allegations are true. The records reflect that Charging Party was previously suspended on one occasion for improper checkout procedures and later reinstated. Evidence obtained during the course of investigation is indicative of Charging Party's allegations that her hours were indeed cut. Further evidence reflected that four other white employees received far greater working hours than the Charging Party even though she possessed more seniority. Respondent's witness contends that Charging Party was scheduled less hours because she failed to contact the Charging Party due to threatening phone calls received from Charging Party's relatives. Such contention was unfounded. Accordingly, based upon the evidence obtained, there is reason to believe a violation of Title VII did occur.

Having determined that there is reasonable cause to believe the charge is true, the Commission now invites the parties to join with it in a collective effort toward a just resolution of the matter. A "Notice of Conciliation Process" is attached for your information; a representative of the Commission will contact each party in the near future to begin the conciliation process.

On Behalf of the Commission

2-1-'79	s/ Breslove Barrett
Date	District Director

The Company has conducted its own internal investigation of the case. The investigation was undertaken by the Assistant Director of Human Resources, Barney Ross, of the home office. The following information is taken from the investigation file. Included are Ross's notes regarding general background information; Zelma Mazuka's wage history; copies of her discipline records in the form of 3 "constructive advice records" and a "significant incident reminder"; statements and affidavits taken from the front end manager, who supervises the cashiers, and the clerk who came forward; copies of the results of Mazuka's "mystery shops"; and a summary of comparable discipline and discharge circumstances.

General Background Information

Zelma Mazuka:

— Hired 11-13-77.

— Suspended 6-6-78.

— Brought Back 6-16-78.

— Resigned 6-30-78.

Gary Herbert:
- — Store Manager (14 years with Alpha).
- — White male 39 years old.
- — Entered management training in 1967. Store manager for 10 years.
- — Co-manager for 2 years. Clerk and Department Head for 2 years.

Customer involved in incident:

Marcia Tompson

10i5 West Wineland Dr.

Apt. C Sans Souci Apts.

Connersville, Indiana (ph. 555–5235)

Joan Blankenship (front end manager):
- — With Alpha since 1971.

Interview with Gary Herbert (manager):
- — Agrees with incident as described in affidavit of Joan Blankenship.
- — Suspends Zelma shortly after incident. Zelma makes no comments or excuses for her actions.
- — Attended 2nd step grievance meeting on 6/14/78.

  —Present:

Company	**Union**
Herbert	Ron Racster, B.A.
Hite	Frank Gibson, B.A.
	Zelma Mazuka, grievant.

- — Zelma was asked if she knew the customer, to which she replied no.
- — Union theory: mistake. If Company could establish that she knew customer, it would reconsider grievance.
- — Decision to put Zelma back to work made by Personnel Dept.
- — Since the schedule was already posted, we had to squeeze her in. She did not get all the hours she was entitled to by seniority. She filed no grievance regarding the hours.

Zelma Mazuka's Wage History

Date:	Job Title:	Wage:
11/13/77	Checker	3.87
1/8/78	Checker	4.23
2/11/78	Checker	4.58
3/6/78	Checker	4.90
4/9/78	Checker	5.13
5/14/78	Checker	5.28

Zelma Mazuka's Discipline Records

CONSTRUCTIVE ADVICE RECORD #1

Discussion Date 11/14/77

Name: Zelma Mazuka Classification: Checker Store/Dept.#111

Nature of incident: Carelessness

"Spot checked a grocery order; $2.93 error in ringing up a $8.89 order."

Antiacid tablets $1.83

Tape .97

Corrective Effort:

Has the employee been placed on probation? "Yes" Until what date? 12–14–77.

The shop steward or union representative, David Bruno, has been fully informed of the details concerning this incident on 11/14/77.

s/ _____

Gary Herbert, Store Manager

Employee's Statement:

"Customer was talking. I thought I rang up $1.83, but it must have skipped by."

s/ Zelma Mazuka _____

CONSTRUCTIVE ADVICE RECORD #2

Discussion Date 12–8–77

Name: Zelma Mazuka Classification: Checker Store? Dept. #111

Nature of incident:

"Register came up $13.60 short on December 3, 1977."

Corrective Effort:

"Employe's drawer usually checks up good. She will be careful in the future."

Has the employee been placed on probation? "No" Until what date?

_____

The shop steward or union representative, David Bruno, has been fully informed of the details concerning this incident on 12/3/77.

s/ _____

Gary Herbert, Store Manager

Employee's Statement:

s/ _____

Zelma Mazuka

CONSTRUCTIVE ADVICE RECORD #3

Discussion Date <u>6–6–77</u>

Name: <u>Zelma Mazuka</u> Classification: <u>Checker</u> Store/Dept. <u>#111</u>

Nature of incident:

"Failed to ring disposal diapers $2.45; tissue, .86; lemons .59 for a total of $3.90.

Corrective Effort:

"Suspended until 6–16–78. Return under the following conditions (covered with Ron Racster) (1) If we get any new evidence, case will be reopened; (2) any shortages, overages, violations of check-out procedure will be just cause for discharge; (3) we will monitor her closely; (4) no back pay."

Has the employee been placed on probation? _____ Until what date? _____

The shop steward or union representative, _____, has been fully informed of the details concerning this incident on _____.

s/ _____

Gary Herbert, Store Manager

Employee's Statement:

s/ _____

SIGNIFICANT INCIDENT REMINDER

Date: <u>6/24/78</u>

Name: <u>Zelma Mazuka</u>

Briefly describe the incident:

"Cashier was not calling her prices."

Have you done something about it?

____ Commended the employee if the incident was favorable.

____ Discussed ways to prevent recurrence if the incident was unfavorable.

s/ _____	s/ Gary Herbert____
Employee	Employee's Supervisor

Statements and Affidavits

AFFIDAVIT OF JOAN BLANKENSHIP

City of Connersville
County of Fayette
State of Indiana

I, Joan Blankenship make this statement on the tenth day of May 1979 of my own free will. I currently reside at 3633 Bermuda Circle, Connersville, Indiana and am employed by the Alpha Company at store #111 located at 2525 Washington Rd., Connersville, Indiana. My current job title is front end manager and have been employed in this capacity since July 2, 1978. Prior to being front end manager I was a head checker for approximately eleven (11) months. I have been employed with the Alpha Company since 1971.

On June 6, 1978 I arrived for work at approximately 7:00 a. m. Zelma Mazuka was my morning cashier and started working at approximately 9:30 a. m. On this morning I assigned her to register #3, which is one of the registers used to ring out large orders. The store is equipped with one express register located next to the office. This express register is operated by various cashiers during the business day. All of the cashiers assigned to the registers other than the express are on "total accountability." By total accountability I mean that the cashiers are required to count their register cash till drawer and verify that there is eighty dollars ($80.00) in the cash drawer. The cashier is then assigned to a register which she operates throughout the day. No other cashier is permitted to ring the register of another cashier. At the conclusion of the work day the cashier counts her register down and verifies any overage or shortage.

On June 6, 1978 Zelma Mazuka did count her register cash drawer prior to beginning work at register #3. At approximately 10:15 a. m. Zelma was waiting on a white male customer. The transaction was not complete and the customer left the check lane to get another item from the sale floor to be purchased. While the customer was away from the check lane, a black female customer approached her lane. I recognized the customer as being a fairly regular customer who lived near the store. Zelma was familiar with the customer and always greeted her and spoke with her little boy. As the customer walked past the office and approached the check lanes, Zelma left register #3 and directed the customer to the express lane. At this point I was in the store office and heard the customer say "Where were you last night; I tried to call you?" The customer began unloading her bascart. There was more conversation, but I am not sure of the content of that conversation. Zelma proceeded to ring out the customer's order. Zelma completed the order and had the order bagged. She had placed one bag to her right on check lane #2. The second bag was placed on the express bagging area. There was one box of disposal diapers sitting on the check stand area. I knew she had finished the order because it was bagged and the customer was writing a check for the total, $9.27, which was displayed on the register indicator located in the window portion at the top of the register.

At this point, Mr. Herbert was walking past the office and brought to my attention that the male customer from register #3 had returned to the lane. I left the office and told Zelma that I would collect for the order and for her to return to register #3. She appeared to be nervous and somewhat apprehensive. I told her a second time to return to her register; that I would collect the check for the express order. At this point, Zelma totaled out the register. The register drawer opened and the customer receipt discharged from the register. Zelma closed the drawer and placed the receipt next to the customer on the check stand where she was entering the total on her check. Zelma then left the register and returned to register #3. I was somewhat surprised at the way that Zelma acted as she completed the transaction.

I looked down at the receipt and noticed that there were no items for more than two dollars ($2.00). I knew that the disposal diapers were more than two dollars and realized that they had not been rung up. At this point, Mr. Herbert was walking past and I made him aware that the disposal diapers were not rung up. He told me to re-ring the entire order. Up to this time nothing was said to the customer involved. Mr. Herbert and I re-rang the order, and we found that there were two other items in addition to the disposal diapers that had not been rung. These items were a package of toilet tissue and a half dozen lemons. When we rang the correct total, it came to $13.34. The customer wrote another check for the exact total.

Around this time, Zelma approached the register and inquired as to what the problem was. Mr. Herbert advised her that the order was not rung properly. She was shown what items were rung properly, and she made no comment. The customer paid for the groceries and then left the store. Mr. Herbert took the first customer receipt and went to his upstairs office. He returned a short time later and told me to get a girl to operate the express register and to call in someone to operate one of the large order check lanes.

Mr. Herbert called Zelma upstairs and sent her home. I counted Zelma's register down and it checked out o.k. Mr. Herbert advised me that Zelma had been suspended. I removed the detail tape and gave it to Mr. Herbert.

On June 14th I was asked to tell Ron Racster, a union business agent what had happened on June 6, 1978. I advised him the same things I have outlined in this statement.

On Friday, June 16, 1978, while Zelma was still on suspension, she came into the store to pick up her pay for the previous week worked. At the office window she stated, "One of these days you are going to get the shit out of you." I didn't know what to say, so I ignored her.

The schedule for the week ending June 24th had already been posted and Mr. Herbert was called by personnel and told to put Zelma back on the schedule. Since the schedule was already made out, Mr.

Herbert took hours scheduled to others and scheduled Zelma hours for Tuesday, Thursday, and Saturday for the week ending 6–24–78.

I made up the schedule for the week ending July 1, 1978, and Zelma was scheduled according to seniority. There was no one with less seniority with more hours. Zelma worked Sunday, June 25, 1978 and called in sick for the remainder of the week.

On Sunday, June 25, 1978, there were two till audits done on Zelma's register. The till audits consisted of counting the register drawers and verifying their contents. These audits were done at the direction of the Division Office. The head cashiers and front end managers were advised to periodically run two audits in one day on a particular cashier. These audits were done to improve cash control and security. There were numerous cashiers who were audited on a periodic and random basis. It is not uncommon to audit or mystery shop a cashier more than once in a day.

During the first week of Zelma's work after the suspension, I received a customer complaint that Zelma was rude, unfriendly, failed to call merchandise prices, and handled her merchandise improperly. The customer complained that Zelma had thrown her groceries around and had caused a gallon of milk to split. I advised Mr. Herbert of the complaint, and he talked to the customer.

Also, during Zelma's first week back, I received a phone call approximately forty five minutes after Zelma had left for the day. The caller asked for Zelma, and I advised her that she had left. The caller then said, "What are you doing to my daughter? I guess I'm going to have to come and beat the hell out of you." I hung up the phone and advised Mr. Biff, the co-manager, what happened. While I was telling Mr. Biff what happened, the phone rang again. We both picked up different extensions, and the same caller said "What do you think you're doing hanging up on me? I guess I'm going to come down there and beat the hell out of you." I replied that I didn't have to take that, and I hung up.

I should also point out that on June 25, 1978, Zelma's father was standing in the front of the store and staring at the office personnel. As Zelma left for home, she said in a loud voice to her father, "You better do something about this, they're still picking on me."

I, Joan Blankenship state that the above statement is true and complete to the best of my recollection.

s/ _____

Joan Blankenship

Gerald C. Brown
Notary Public, Indiana State at Large
My Commission expires February 13, 1983

AFFIDAVIT OF LUTHER KING

City of Connersville
County of Fayette
State of Indiana

I, Luther King, make this statement on the 10th day of May, 1979 on my own free will. I currently reside at 2618 Nanette Rd., Connersville, Indiana. I may be reached at my home telephone number of 317–555–4531. At the present time I am employed by the Midwestern Railway and may be reached by phone there at 317–555–4637.

I was employed by Alpha on a part-time basis as a stock clerk for the period encompassing January 1978 through January 1979. Prior to being employed by the Alpha Company, I was dating a Ms. Zelma Mazuka, who was employed at Alpha Store #111 on Washington Rd. in Connersville, Indiana. I continued dating Zelma into the month of July, which was shortly after her resignation with the Alpha Company.

On June 6, 1978 I was arriving for work at Alpha at approximately 10:50 p. m. Zelma approached me in the parking lot and told me that she had been suspended from work earlier that day. She told me that she was accused of passing some items through the register to a customer, which had not been rung up. I asked her if it was true, and she replied that there was some confusion due to her changing registers, and that some items had slipped by her without being rung up. She gave me the impression at the time that she did not do this deliberately.

I told her that if she was not guilty of anything, then not to worry about it. I told her that I would talk to her the following day.

On Wednesday, June 7, 1978 I went to Zelma's house. Her parents were upset and kept saying that Alpha was picking on her, and that the Company was trying to get rid of blacks. I thought that this was ridiculous, because the store manager, Mr. Herbert, was always fair and treated the employees impartially. Zelma also made comments about the store being unfair to blacks. This same day, Zelma told me that the customer involved in the incident was Marcia Tompson. I knew Marcia Tompson, because she was a friend of Zelma's. We had visited Marcia at her apartment in the Sans Souci Apartments, which are near the store. I have also been with Zelma at her house when Marcia came to visit.

On Saturday, June 17th, Zelma told me that on Friday, June 16th, she had told the head checker, Joan Blankenship that she was going to beat her ass.

Shortly after this day, while I was working, Mr. Herbert asked me if I knew Marcia Tompson. I told him that she was a friend of Zelma's and mine. He then told me that Marcia was the customer involved. I told Zelma that I had mentioned to Mr. Herbert that we knew Marcia, and she got all upset and told me that she had told **Mr.** Herbert that she did not know the customer.

On June 30, 1978, Zelma resigned from Alpha, and shortly after that, Zelma and I quit dating.

I have read the statement of the above and swear that it is true and complete to the best of my recollection.

s/ _____

Luther King

Gerald C. Brown
Notary Public, Indiana State at Large
My Commission expires February 13, 1983

MYSTERY SHOPS FOR ZELMA MAZUKA

The following memo to store managers explains the Alpha mystery shop:

Memo:

Zone K Store Managers
Subject: Mystery Shops

Mystery Customer Shops are a very valuable tool to check cashier accuracy and assist in shrink control.

I am listing below the procedure that will be followed in each store effective as 1/10/78

1.   Store manager, co-manager, or head cashier are the only ones to make mystery shops.

2.   Shops must be a surprise to the cashier and done at different times and days with no set pattern.

3.   Shops are to be made after the customer has been checked out.

4.   Shops should be recorded in a notebook and kept in the store office, listing the cashier's name, date of the shop, and comment on the shop. This is the responsibility of each store's head cashier to keep the records current and accurate.

5.   The shop's form should be forwarded to the zone manager each Saturday night with form 40 for medium eggs.

s/ R. K. Kelso

The following table shows the mystery shops conducted on the cashiers at Alpha Store #111 during the thirteen pay periods of 1977.

Mystery Shops: Store # 111

Name	1	2	3	4	5	6	7	8	9	10	11	12	13
J. Walker			3/11 (3/25x3)	4/15						9/29		4/30	
A. Cole				4/1			6/26	7/12 8/6	8/27 9/3 8/20	9/16			12/8
B. Ricter			Prod.	4/1 4/4 4/18	4/22 5/5	6/16			9/3	10/12	10/14 10/23		12/3 12/7 12/9
K. Merriman	Prod.	Prod.	Prod.	4/13	4/22 5/13	6/15	6/25	7/15	8/18	9/29	(10/11x2) 10/20		12/10
K. Jackob	2/11	2/24	3/3	3/30 4/20	4/23 5/6	6/10	7/12	8/3			10/14	11/17 11/28	11/30
M. Messer				4/15	4/22 4/21	5/29		7/21	9/6 9/8			11/26	
H. Lord		2/16	3/21	4/21	4/26 5/1		7/22	9/9	9/12				
S. Coombs	1/27	(2/24x2)	(3/14x2)	4/21	4/28			(7/13x3) 7/20	8/13 8/21			11/15	(11/30x2)
M. Boyle		2/23		4/15	4/22 5/6	5/28		8/2				11/27	12/9 12/10
Q. Andrews		2/17	(3/14x2)	3/29	5/5	5/21	STOCK CREW						
B. Miller	1/29	2/24	3/24	4/20	4/29		7/19		8/15	9/16		11/28	
M. Hew		N.C.	3/4	N.C.	4/22 4/27	N.C.		7/18					
L. Irvin	N.C.	N.C.		N.C.	N.C.	N.C.	N.C. STOCK CREW	N.C.	8/15	9/16	10/11	10/14	12/1 12/7
M. Gramza			3/23	4/15	STOCK CREW								
Z. Mazuka		2/10	3/15	4/13	(4/26x2)								
B. Johnson	1/14	2/23	8/7 8/15	4/18				8/2		9/20		11/10	12/9
T. Mark				4/12									
E. Lard					5/15	5/20		7/24	9/22			11/28	12/1 12/3
B. Sox											11/10		
S. Garden										9/12 9/23			
M. Hoffman								7/31	8/15	9/12	10/19	11/20	12/8 12/10
Y. Shafer													12/9

The following table summarizes the results of the mystery shops conducted on Zelma Mazuka.

Zelma Mazuka Mystery Shops

Date	Time	Amount Charged	Correct Amount	Comments
2–10–78	3:30 p.m.	$21.28	$21.28	
3–15–78	——	$16.18	$16.18	
4–13–78	3:00 p.m.	$29.47	$29.46	One item marked 2/99¢; rang both 50¢
4–26–78	10:30 a.m.	$30.22	$30.22	
4–26–78	3:00 p.m.	$13.02	$13.02	

SUMMARY OF COMPARABLE DISCIPLINE AND DISCHARGE CIRCUMSTANCES

A.   Discipline

1. Amy Cole—white, checker, female.

    a. C.A.R. 12/19/77—checker failed to collect for order totalling $24.11. Also rang multiple price items wrong in the next order.

    b. C.A.R. 6/26/78—register balanced $10.00 short for day of 6/25/78—placed on probation until 9/26/78.

2. Bonnie Johnson—white, checker, female.

    a. C.A.R. 2/25/78—register balanced $20.00 short for the day of 2/23/78. Checker was given one week disciplinary layoff without pay and placed on probation until 5/1/78.

3. Dan McKenny—white, clerk, male.

    a. C.A.R. 11/23/78—register balanced short $15.00 for day of 11/23/78. Clerk placed on probation until 1/11/79.

4. Mark Hoffman—white, clerk, male.

    a. C.A.R. 11/25/78—register balanced $20.70 short on 11/25/78. Placed on probation until 1/25/79.

5. Bertha Ricter—white, checker, female.

    a. C.A.R. 11/25/78—register balanced $5.40 short on 11/25/78. Placed on probation until 1/25/79.

B.   Discipline and/or Discharge

1. Deborah B. Tory—black, checker, female. Separated 5/31/77. Discharged—proven dishonesty—took $1.09 worth of merchandise from Deli without paying for it.

2. Rubenstein Green—black, checker, female. Separated effective 12/12/77.

    a. C.A.R. 12/12/77—charged only $23.67 for an order totalling $100.51—net loss of $76.84. Checker was suspended pending investigation.

    b. Discharged on 12/14/77 effective last day worked 12/12/77. Violation of Alpha policy on ringing merchandise.

3. Lisa Richman—white, checker, female. Separated effective 3/9/78.

Discharged for dishonesty—failure to ring up merchandise. On two consecutive mystery shops, shopper gave checker correct amount for merchandise and left store without receipt. Checker was observed pocketing money instead of ringing up merchandise.

4. Debbie Sanders—black, checker, female. Separated effective 3/31/79.

    a. Verbal (?) No C.A.R. in file. Register balanced short $20.16 on 3/14/79.

    b. C.A.R. 3/16/79. Spot till audit at 3:00 P.M. on 3/12/79, register balanced over $6.00. Register balanced short $11.00 at end of day.

    c. Bascart check on 3/31/79. Overcharged customer 53¢ through numerous errors on multiple priced merchandise.

    d. Manager observation. While assisting in bagging, store manager observed checker underring an item 20¢.

    e. Discharged 3/31/79. Unsatisfactory quality of work. The above incidents were summarized as the basis for discharge.

B. INTRODUCTION

Chapters 1 through 7 considered labor relations from the perspective of the relationship between the union and management. Labor relations, as such, was union-management relations. The policy embodied in the law regulating union-management relations is the fostering of free collective bargaining between the union, as representative of the employees, and the company management. The thrust of the law regulating the collective bargaining relationship is essentially indirect. The law seeks to impose a setting in which the parties are free to negotiate a contract which will govern their relationship. The national labor policy is not to impose a contract upon the parties, but to impose the conditions in which the parties may create their own contract.

In the collective bargaining model of labor relations, employee interests are promoted through the union in its role as the collective bargaining agent of the employees. Individual employee rights are subordinate to the interests of collective representation.

Beginning in the 1960s and 1970s, questions began to surface regarding the rights of individual employees. The emerging issue of individual employment rights has led one commentator to conclude that "many observers both inside and outside the corporation believe these demands for new individual rights, and the struggle over whether and how to provide them, will reach their mature status in the 1980s." [1]

The recognition of individual rights has been accomplished through direct governmental intervention in the employment relationship. The following discussion focuses on the issues involved in the recognition of the following rights of the individual employee: the right to fair representation, the right to equal opportunity in employment, the right to a just discharge, and the right to a safe workplace.

C. THE RIGHT TO FAIR REPRESENTATION

The doctrine of fair representation imposes upon labor organizations a duty to represent fairly all members of a bargaining unit. The NLRA does not explicitly require that a bargaining representative fairly represent all employees in its bargaining unit. Rather, the duty of fair representation has evolved judicially to protect individual employees stripped of traditional forms of redress from unfair treatment at the hands of their collective bargaining representative. The following article traces this judicial evolution and identifies the emerging principles of fair representation.

CLYDE W. SUMMERS, THE INDIVIDUAL EMPLOYEE'S RIGHTS UNDER THE COLLECTIVE AGREEMENT: WHAT CONSTITUTES FAIR REPRESENTATION? *

The only guides provided by the Supreme Court for measuring the union's duty of fair representation in contract administration are those articulated or applied in Humphrey v. Moore,[23] Vaca v. Sipes,[24] and Hines v. Anchor Motor Freight, Inc.[25] Although amorphous and incomplete, those guides provide a sense of direction and suggest some inchoate standards to be applied in concrete areas.

In Humphrey v. Moore, one trucking company absorbed the operations of a second company. The local union, which represented employees of both companies, recommended that the two seniority lists be dovetailed and this recommendation was adopted by the Joint Conference Committee. When employees of the first company who were laid off as a result of this dovetailing charged that they had not been fairly represented, the Court, in rejecting this claim, focused on four points. First, the section of the collective agreement relied upon by the Joint Committee in making its decision "reasonably meant what

---

1. *Individual Rights in the Corporation* xi (A. Weston & S. Salisbury, Ed. 1980).

* Clyde W. Summers, "The Individual Employee's Rights Under The Collective Agreement: What Constitutes Fair Representation," 126 University of Pennsylvania Law Review 251 (1977); © 1977 by the Trustees of the University of Pennsylvania. Reprinted by permission.

23. 375 U.S. 335, 84 S.Ct. 363, 11 L.Ed.2d 370 (1964).

24. 386 U.S. 171, 87 S.Ct. 903, 17 L.Ed.2d 842 (1967).

25. 424 U.S. 554, 96 S.Ct. 1048, 47 L.Ed.2d 231 (1976).

the Joint Committee said or assumed it meant." Second, the decision to dovetail "was neither unique nor arbitrary," but was a "familiar and frequently equitable solution" in such cases. Third, the local union was free to take a "good faith position * * * supporting the position of one group of employees against that of another," for it should not "be neutralized when the issue is chiefly between two sets of employees." Finally, the disfavored employees were not deprived of a fair hearing, for they had notice of the hearing, and three stewards representing them were present at the hearing and were given every opportunity to state their position. With these four elements present, the union fulfilled its duty of fair representation. Whether something less would have met the minimum standard, we cannot know, but these four elements are considered by the Court as relevant in determining the standard.

In Vaca v. Sipes, an employee, Owens, who had been on sick leave, was denied reinstatement because of his heart condition. The Court emphasized that the union had pressed the grievance through the grievance procedure, attempted to obtain evidence to support Owen's case, attempted to secure less strenuous work for him, and tried to help him be rehabilitated. Only after all these efforts did the union conclude that arbitration would be fruitless and dismissed the grievance. Beyond holding that this diligence in processing Owen's grievance met the standard of fair representation, the Court, by its choice of language and its analysis, provided additional guides as to the measure of that duty.

The Court in *Vaca* carefully and deliberately selected the terms for describing the duty, and in doing so distinguished between the standards to be used in contract negotiation and contract administration. Counsel for the union urged that the union's duty should be limited to acting in "complete good faith and honesty," the words used in Ford Motor Co. v. Huffman to describe the union's duty in negotiating an agreement. The Court, however, rejected these words as an inadequate description of the duty, in effect saying that in the settlement of grievances, "complete good faith and honesty" was not enough.

In contrast, the Court defined the duty in broader terms of "wrongfulness;" the individual could sue on the basis of the union's "*wrongful* refusal to process the grievance." Wrongfulness was elaborated by three principle adjectives, used in the alternative—"arbitrary, discriminatory, or in bad faith." Repeated emphasis was given to the word "arbitrary," which union counsel had urged the Court not to add to the standard stated in Ford Motor Co. v. Huffman. Wrongfulness was further elaborated by the Court to include ignoring a meritorious grievance or processing it in a perfunctory manner. Thus, the Court declared: "[A] union must, in good faith and in a nonarbitrary manner, make decisions as to the merits of particular grievances. * * * [T]he Union might well have breached its duty had it ignored Owens' complaint or had it processed the grievance in a perfunctory manner."

These carefully selected terms for describing the duty were more than elusive adjectives to create a mood; they were used to narrow the polar positions presented by arguments to the Court and to bring the standard of fair representation into clearer focus. Rejecting the polar extremes, the Court emphasized on the one hand that the individual employee has no "absolute right to have his grievance taken to arbitration regardless of the provisions of the applicable collective bargaining agreement," for if he could, "the settlement machinery provided by the contract would be substantially undermined." On the other hand, the Court emphasized that the union's exclusive control over grievance procedures did not carry with it "unlimited discretion to deprive injured employees of all remedies for breach of contract."

In narrowing the polar positions of the parties, the Court stated that the union did not breach its duty "merely because it settled the grievance short of arbitration." The Court approved the union's desire to assure that "frivolous grievances are ended prior to the most costly and time-consuming step in the grievance procedures." The union does not fulfill its duty, however, merely by refraining from "patently wrongful conduct such as racial discrimination or personal hostility." "[A] union must, in good faith and in a nonarbitrary manner, make decisions as to the merits of particular grievances."

Proof of violation of the duty of fair representation requires more than a showing that the evidence supports the individual's claim that he has been wrongfully discharged; the union's decision that a particular grievance "lacks sufficient merit to justify arbitration" does not become a breach of duty simply "because a judge or jury later found the grievance meritorious." But, said the Court, "a union may not arbitrarily ignore a meritorious grievance or process it in perfunctory fashion."

In *Hines v. Anchor Motor Freight, Inc.* a truckdriver was discharged for allegedly falsifying a motel receipt, and this discharge was upheld by a Joint Conference Committee. He claimed that had the union adequately investigated it would have discovered that the falsification was made by the motel clerk, and with this evidence obtained his reinstatement. Although the only issue before the Court was whether the employer could be sued for wrongful discharge when the union had failed to produce evidence at the Joint Conference Committee hearing, the Court restated and extended the standards articulated in *Vaca*. The "duty of fair representation has served as a 'bulwark to prevent arbitrary union conduct against individuals stripped of traditional forms of redress by the provisions of federal labor law.'" Although the duty does not require "pressing the employee's case to the last step of the grievance process," it does require that a union not "'arbitrarily ignore a meritorious grievance or process it in a perfunctory fashion.'" Congress, in putting its blessing on private dispute settlement anticipated that "the contractual machinery would operate within some minimum levels of integrity." If the union fails in its duty in presenting the case at arbitration, the individual employee is not bound by the award. Otherwise, "[w]rongfully discharged employees would be left without jobs and without a fair opportunity to secure an adequate remedy."

Although the Court's opinions in these three cases do not define the standard of the union's duty of fair representation, they do reject the polar extremes and mark some outer boundaries, thereby providing some guides as to the inner and outer limits of the duty. Those limits are further narrowed, and the standard is given substantive content by four interlacing policies or values which run through all of the Court's opinions from *Humphrey* to *Hines.*

First, the legally enforceable contractual rights that individual employees acquire under collective agreements are valuable personal rights and the union's ability to prevent employees from enforcing those rights should be limited. In the words of the Court in *Vaca,* "We cannot believe that Congress, in conferring upon employers and unions the power to establish exclusive grievance procedures, intended to confer upon unions such unlimited discretion to deprive injured employees of all remedies for breach of contract."

Second, arbitration should not be overburdened with frivolous grievances by allowing an individual employee unilaterally to invoke arbitration or to compel the union to take grievances to arbitration regardless of their merit. The union must be free to sift out wholly frivolous grievances that would only clog the grievance process and must have the power to settle the majority of grievances short of the costlier and more time consuming steps of arbitration.

Third, the union, as "statutory agent and as coauthor of the bargaining agreement" should be able to isolate the "major problem areas in the interpretation of the collective bargaining contract" and resolve those problems. Where bargaining has left ambiguities or gaps in the agreement, the union must be able to resolve those ambiguities or fill those gaps by settlement of grievances with the employer.

Fourth, there should be assurance that in settling disputes under collective agreements, "similar complaints will be treated consistently." A problem of interpretation, once settled by the parties in one case should settle the problem in all other cases. Individual grievants should not be subject to "the vagaries of independent and unsystematic negotiation."

* * *

V. EMERGING PRINCIPLES OF FAIR REPRESENTATION

These seven sample cases do not purport to cover the full spectrum of problem situations nor suggest the multitude of fact variations which arise. They are intended only to provide points of focus for applying the general guides and principles articulated by the Supreme Court to concrete fact situations. Reflection * * * however, does lead us to some more explicit standards for measuring the individual employee's rights under the collective agreement and the union's duty to represent the employee in enforcing the agreement. Six standards emerge quite clearly.

1. The individual employee has a right to have clear and unquestioned terms of the collective agreement that have been made for his benefit, followed and enforced until the agreement is properly amended. For the union to refuse to follow and enforce the rules and standards it has established on behalf of those it represents is arbitrary and constitutes a violation of its fiduciary obligation.

2. The individual employee has no right to insist on any particular interpretation of an ambiguous provision in a collective agreement, for the union must be free to settle a grievance in accordance with any reasonable interpretation of the ambiguous provision. However, the individual has a right that ambiguous provisions be applied consistently and that the provision mean the same when applied to him as when applied to other employees. Settlement of similar grievances on different terms is discriminatory and violates the union's duty to represent all employees equally.

3. The union has no duty to carry every grievance to arbitration; the union can sift out grievances that are trivial or lacking in merit. However, the individual's right to equal treatment includes equal access to the grievance procedure and arbitration for similar grievances of equal merit.

4. The individual employee has a right to have his grievance decided on its own merits. The union violates its duty to represent fairly when it trades an individual's meritorious grievance for the benefit of another individual or of the group. Majority vote does not necessarily validate grievance settlements, but may instead, make the settlement suspect as based on political power and not the merits of the grievance.

5. Settlement of grievances for improper motives such as personal hostility, political opposition, or racial prejudice constitutes bad faith regardless of the merit of the grievance. The union thereby violates its duty to represent fairly by refusing to process the grievance even though the employer may not have violated the agreement.

6. This union can make good faith judgments in determining the merits of a grievance, but it owes the employees it represents the duty to use reasonable care and diligence both in investigating grievances in order to make that judgment, and in processing and presenting grievances on their behalf.

These standards are obviously not exhaustive, and they lack definitive precision. They do, however, carry us a substantial step beyond the general guides and principles as stated in Humphrey v. Moore, Vaca v. Sipes and Hines v. Anchor Motor Freight. They give us a more meaningful understanding of the nature and content of the duty of fair representation and provide more workable guides for deciding concrete cases. Together, they protect the individual's right to representation in grievance handling, and, at the same time, allow the union sufficient freedom to fulfill its function in administering the agreement.

HINES v. ANCHOR MOTOR FREIGHT, INC.

Supreme Court of the United States, 1976.
424 U.S. 554, 96 S.Ct. 1048, 47 L.Ed.2d 231.

Mr. JUSTICE WHITE delivered the opinion of the Court.

The issue here is whether a suit against an employer by employees asserting breach of a collective-bargaining contract was properly dismissed where the accompanying complaint against the union for breach of duty of fair representation has withstood the union's motion for summary judgment and remains to be tried.

I

Petitioners, who were formerly employed as truck drivers by respondent Anchor Motor Freight, Inc. (Anchor), were discharged on June 5, 1967. The applicable collective-bargaining contract forbade discharges without just cause. The company charged dishonesty. The practice at Anchor was to reimburse drivers for money spent for lodging while the drivers were on the road overnight. Anchor's assertion was that petitioners had sought reimbursement for motel expenses in excess of the actual charges sustained by them. At a meeting between the company and the union, Local 377, International Brotherhood of Teamsters (Union), which was also attended by petitioners, Anchor presented motel receipts previously submitted by petitioners which were in excess of the charges shown on the motel's registration cards; a notarized statement of the motel clerk asserting the accuracy of the registration cards; and an affidavit of the motel owner affirming that the registration cards were accurate and that inflated receipts had been furnished petitioners. The Union claimed petitioners were innocent and opposed the discharges. It was then agreed that the matter would be presented to the joint arbitration committee for the area, to which the collective-bargaining contract permitted either party to submit an unresolved grievance. Pending this hearing, petitioners were reinstated. Their suggestion that the motel be investigated was answered by the Union representatives' assurances that "there was nothing to worry about" and that they need not hire their own attorney.

A hearing before the joint area committee was held on July 26, 1967. Anchor presented its case. Both the Union and petitioners were afforded an opportunity to present their case and to be heard. Petitioners denied their dishonesty, but neither they nor the Union presented any other evidence contradicting the documents presented by the company. The committee sustained the discharges. Petitioners then retained an attorney and sought rehearing based on a statement by the motel owner that he had no personal knowledge of the events, but that the discrepancy between the receipts and the registration cards could have been attributable to the motel clerk's recording on the cards less than was actually paid and retaining for himself the difference between the amount receipted and the amount recorded. The committee, after hearing, unanimously denied rehearing "because there was no new evidence presented which would justify a reopening of this case."

There were later indications that the motel clerk was in fact the culprit; and the present suit was filed in June 1969, against Anchor, the Union and its International. The complaint alleged that the charges of dishonesty made against petitioners by Anchor were false, that there was no just cause for discharge, and that the discharges had been in breach of contract. It was also asserted that the falsity of the charges could have been discovered with a minimum of investigation, that the Union had made no effort to ascertain the truth of the charges, and that the Union had violated its duty of fair representation by arbitrarily and in bad faith depriving petitioners of their employment and permitting their discharge without sufficient proof.

The Union denied the charges and relied on the decision of the joint area committee. Anchor asserted that petitioners had been properly discharged for just cause. It also defended on the ground that petitioners, diligently and in good faith represented by the Union, had unsuccessfully resorted to the grievance and arbitration machinery provided by the contract and that the adverse decision of the joint arbitration committee was binding upon the Union and petitioners under the contractual provision declaring that "[a] decision by a majority of a Panel of any of the Committees shall be final and binding on all parties, including the employee and/or employees affected." Discovery followed, including a deposition of the motel clerk revealing that he had falsified the records and that it was he who had pocketed the difference between the sums shown on the receipts and the registration cards. Motions for summary judgment filed by Anchor and the Unions were granted by the District Court on the ground that the decision of the arbitration committee was final and binding on the employees and "for failure to show facts comprising bad faith, arbitrariness or perfunctoriness on the part of the Unions." Although indicating that the acts of the Union "may not meet professional standards of competency, and while it might have been advisable for the Union to further investigate the charges * * *," the District Court concluded that the facts demonstrated at most bad judgment on the part of the Union, which was insufficient to prove a breach of duty or make out a prima facie case against it.

After reviewing the allegations and the record before it, the Court of Appeals concluded that there were sufficient facts from which bad faith or arbitrary conduct on the part of the local Union could be inferred by the trier of fact and that petitioners should have been afforded an opportunity to prove their charges. To this extent the judgment of the District Court was reversed. The Court of Appeals affirmed the judgment in favor of Anchor and the International. Saying that petitioners wanted to relitigate their discharges because of the recantation of the motel clerk, the Court of Appeals, quoting from its prior opinion in Balowski v. International Union, 372 F.2d 829 (CA6 1967), concluded that the finality provision of collective-bargaining contracts must be observed because there was "[n]o evidence of any misconduct on the part of the employer * * *" and wholly insufficient evidence of any conspiracy between the Union and Anchor.

It is this judgment of the Court of Appeals with respect to Anchor that is now before us on our limited grant of the employees' petition for writ of certiorari. We reverse that judgment.

II

Section 301 of the Labor Management Relations Act, 1947, provides for suits in the district courts for violation of collective-bargaining contracts between labor organizations and employers without regard to the amount in controversy. * * * Section 301 contemplates suits by and against individual employees as well as between unions and employers; and contrary to earlier indications § 301 suits encompass those seeking to vindicate "uniquely personal" rights of employees such as wages, hours, overtime pay, and wrongful discharge. Petitioners' present suit against the employer was for wrongful discharge and is the kind of case Congress provided for in § 301.

Collective-bargaining contracts, however, generally contain procedures for the settlement of disputes through mutual discussion and arbitration. These provisions are among those which are to be enforced under § 301. Furthermore, Congress has specified in § 203(d), that "[f]inal adjustment by a method agreed upon by the parties is declared to be the desirable method for settlement of grievance disputes * * *." * * *

Pursuant to this policy, we [have] held that an employee could not sidestep the grievance machinery provided in the contract and that unless he attempted to utilize the contractual procedures for settling his dispute with his employer, his independent suit against the employer in the District Court would be dismissed. *Maddox* nevertheless distinguished the situation where "the union refuses to press or only perfunctorily presses the individual's claim * * *. * * *

Humphrey v. Moore, supra, involved a seniority dispute between the employees of two transportation companies whose operating authorities had been combined. The employees accorded lesser seniority were being laid off. Their grievances were presented to the company and taken by the union to the joint arbitration committee pursuant to contractual provisions very similar to those now before us. The decision was adverse. The employees then brought suit in the state court against the company, the union, and the favored employees, asserting breach of contract by the company and breach of its duty of fair representation by the union. They sought damages and an injunction to prevent implementation of the decision of the joint arbitration committee. The union was charged with dishonest and bad-faith representation of the employees before the joint committee. The unions and the defendant employees asserted the finality of the joint committee's decision, if not as a final resolution of a dispute in the administration of a contract, as a bargained-for accommodation between the two parties. The state courts issued the injunction. Respondents argued here that "the decision of the Committee was obtained by dishonest union conduct in breach of its duty of fair representation and that a decision so obtained cannot be relied upon as a valid excuse for [their] discharge under the contract." We reversed the judgment of the state court but only after independently determining that the union's conduct was not a breach of its statutory duties and that the joint committee's decision was not infirm for that reason. Our conclusion was that the disfavored employees had not proved their case: "Neither the parties nor the Joint Committee exceeded their power under the contract and there was no fraud or breach of duty by the exclusive bargaining agent. The decision of the committee, reached after proceedings adequate under the agreement, is final and binding upon the parties, just as the contract says it is."

* * *

III

Even though under *Vaca* the employer may not insist on exhaustion of grievance procedures when the union has breached its representation duty, it is urged that when the procedures have been followed and a decision favorable to the employer announced, the employer must be protected from relitigation by the express contractual provision declaring a decision to be final and binding. We disagree. The union's breach of duty relieves the employee of an express or implied requirement that disputes be settled through contractual grievance procedures; if it seriously undermines the integrity of the arbitral process the union's breach also removes the bar of the finality provisions of the contract.

It is true that *Vaca* dealt with a refusal by the union to process a grievance. It is also true that where the union actually utilizes the grievance and arbitration procedures on behalf of the employee, the focus is no longer on the reasons for the union's failure to act but on whether, contrary to the arbitrator's decision, the employer breached the contract and whether there is substantial reason to believe that a union breach of duty contributed to the erroneous outcome of the contractual proceedings. But the judicial remedy in Humphrey v. Moore was sought after the adverse decision of the joint arbitration committee. Our conclusion in that case was not that the committee's decision was unreviewable. On the contrary, we proceeded on the basis that it was reviewable and vulnerable if tainted by breach of duty on the part of the union, even though the employer had not conspired with the union. The joint committee's decision was held binding on the complaining employees only after we determined that the union had not been guilty of malfeasance and that its conduct was within the range of acceptable performance by a collective-bargaining agent, a wholly unnecessary determination if the union's conduct was irrelevant to the finality of the arbitral process.

* * *

Anchor would have it that petitioners are foreclosed from judicial relief unless some blameworthy conduct on its part disentitles it to rely on the finality rule. But it was Anchor that originated the discharges for dishonesty. If those charges were in error, Anchor has surely played its part in precipitating this dispute. Of course, both courts below held there were no facts suggesting that Anchor either knowingly or negligently relied on false evidence. As far as the record reveals it also prevailed before the joint committee after presenting its case in accordance with what were ostensibly wholly fair procedures. Nevertheless there remains the question whether the contractual protection against relitigating an arbitral decision binds employees who assert that the process has fundamentally malfunctioned by reason of the bad-faith performance of the union, their statutorily imposed collective-bargaining agent.

Under the rule announced by the Court of Appeals, unless the employer is implicated in the Union's malfeasance or has otherwise caused the arbitral process to err, petitioners would have no remedy against Anchor even though they are successful in proving the Union's bad faith, the falsity of the charges against them, and the breach of contract by Anchor by discharging without cause. This rule would apparently govern even in circumstances where it is shown that a union has manufactured the evidence and knows from the start that it is false; or even if, unbeknownst to the employer, the union has corrupted the arbitrator to the detriment of disfavored union members. As is the case where there has been a failure to exhaust, however, we cannot believe that Congress intended to foreclose the employee from his § 301 remedy otherwise available against the employer if the contractual processes have been seriously flawed by the union's breach of its duty to represent employees honestly and in good faith and without invidious discrimination or arbitrary conduct.

* * *

Petitioners are not entitled to relitigate their discharge merely because they offer newly discovered evidence that the charges against them were false and that in fact they were fired without cause. The grievance processes cannot be expected to be error-free. The finality provision has sufficient force to surmount occasional instances of mistake. But it is quite another matter to suggest that erroneous arbitration decisions must stand even though the employee's representation by the union has been dishonest, in bad faith, or discriminatory; for in that event error and injustice of the grossest sort would multiply. The contractual system would then cease to qualify as an adequate mechanism to secure individual redress for damaging failure of the employer to abide by the contract. Congress has put its blessing on private dispute settlement arrangements provided in collective agreements, but it was anticipated, we are sure, that the contractual machinery would operate within some minimum levels of integrity. In our view, enforcement of the finality provision where the arbitrator has erred is conditioned upon the union's having satisfied its statutory duty fairly to represent the employee in connection with the arbitration proceedings. Wrongfully discharged employees would be left without jobs and without a fair opportunity to secure an adequate remedy.

Except for this case the Courts of Appeals have arrived at similar conclusions. As the Court of Appeals for the Ninth Circuit put it in Margetta v. Pam Pam Corp., 501 F.2d 179, 180 (1974): "To us, it makes little difference whether the union subverts the arbitration process by refusing to proceed as in *Vaca* or follows the arbitration trail to the end, but in so doing subverts the arbitration process by failing to fairly represent the employee. In neither case, does the employee receive fair representation."

Petitioners, if they prove an erroneous discharge and the Union's breach of duty tainting the decision of the joint committee, are entitled to an appropriate remedy against the employer as well as the Union. It was error to affirm the District Court's final dismissal of petitioners' action against Anchor. To this extent the judgment of the Court of Appeals is reversed.

So ordered.

D. THE RIGHT TO EQUAL OPPORTUNITY IN EMPLOYMENT

The right to equal opportunity in employment has been recognized by several federal statutes. Although a body of case law is developing, the cases have been generally concerned with interpreting statutes that provide the framework for preventing discrimination in employment. In brief, the statutes that will be discussed below are:

Title VII of the 1964 Civil Rights Act.

Basic to an understanding of fair employment practices law is Title VII of the 1964 Civil Rights Act, which was strengthened by the Equal Employment Opportunity Act of 1972. Title VII was enacted as part of a broad civil rights program dealing with discrimination in restaurants and hotels (public accommodations), educational institutions, and recipients of federal financial assistance as well as employment. This act was one congressional response to the civil rights movement and resulting strife of the 1950s and 1960s.

Title VII provides that it is unlawful for employers, unions, or employment agencies to make any decision concerning the employment or work status of an individual on the basis of race, sex, religion, or national origin. This prohibition covers private and public employers who have at least fifteen employees. One of the few defenses available under Title VII is the bona fide occupational qualification (bfoq). This provision allows an employer to hire and employ (or a union and employment agency to classify) on the basis of sex, religion, or national origin in limited circumstances where the sex, religion, or national origin of the individual is reasonably necessary to the operation of a business. This defense or exception has been narrowly construed by the courts and is discussed more fully later. Note that the bfoq provision does not mention race and, therefore, discrimination on the basis of race, if proven, cannot be justified by this exception.

The Equal Pay Act.

The Equal Pay Act of 1963 is an amendment to the Fair Labor Standards Act of 1938 (FLSA) which is the federal minimum wage and maximum hour law. Amendments to the Equal Pay Act in 1972 and 1974 broadened its coverage so that it mandates equal pay for equal work regardless of sex at professional and managerial levels, in state and local government, as well as in most private industries. The most difficult questions raised under the Equal Pay Act are determining whether male and female workers are actually doing substantially the same work, and if so, whether the pay differential is based on a factor other than sex. The nature of this inquiry demands in most instances a case-by-case analysis.

The Age Discrimination In Employment Act.

The Age Discrimination In Employment Act (ADEA) represents the congressional response to ameliorate the condition of the older worker. With the express purpose of promoting the employment of older workers on the basis of their ability rather than age, the ADEA prohibits discrimination against older workers by employers, employment agencies and labor organizations. The Secretary of Labor originally was charged with the Act's enforcement and administration. In 1979, jurisdiction over the ADEA and the Equal Pay Act was shifted to the EEOC.

The ADEA applies to employers, employment agencies and labor organizations, and it prohibits age discrimination in hiring and all other aspects of employment, referral for employment and membership in unions. Originally, only persons between the ages of 40 and 65 were protected by the Act. However in 1978, Congress raised the upper limit to age 70 for all non-federal employees covered by the Act.

1. THEORIES OF DISCRIMINATION

Before examining the statutes mentioned above, the principal theories of discrimination must be first considered.

The Supreme Court has established the essential elements of a prima facie case of employment discrimination in several cases involving Title VII. Under Title VII, the requirements of a plaintiff's prima facie case depend upon whether the individual alleges that he has been subjected to "disparate treatment" because of his race, religion, national origin or sex; or that he has been the victim of a facially neutral practice having a "disparate impact" upon his racial or religious group, or on others of his national origin or sex; or that he was denied an employment opportunity because the employer engaged in a "pattern or practice" of unlawful discrimination.

The Supreme Court established the elements of a prima facie case of employment discrimination through disparate treatment in McDonnell Douglas Corp. v. Green,[2] a Title VII case involving a refusal to rehire because of alleged unlawful racial discrimination. In *McDonnell Douglas*, the Court affirmed what has been the general understanding that the plaintiff bears the initial burden of establishing a prima facie case of employment discrimination. The Court held that the plaintiff had established such a case where he proved that he belonged to a racial minority; that he applied and was qualified for a job for which the employer was seeking applicants; that despite his qualifications, he was rejected; and that, after his rejection, the position remained open and the employer continued seeking applicants with the plaintiff's qualifications. The thrust of this approach is to require complainants to establish on a comparative basis that they have been denied an employment opportunity which they are qualified to perform. After the plaintiff establishes a prima facie case, the burden shifts to the defendant to state a legitimate, nondiscriminatory reason for its action. The Court further added a third stage to this process by holding that the plaintiff is to be accorded a final opportunity to establish that the reason offered by the defendant is a mere pretext.

Where the claim is that a facially neutral employment practice has a disparate impact on a group protected by Title VII, the Court has articulated a different method of establishing the claim. The Court defined the prima facie case on a disparate impact claim in Griggs v. Duke Power Co.,[3] a Title VII case involving the legality of an employer's use of a high school diploma requirement and standardized intelligence tests for employee selection. The Court in *Griggs* held that a prima facie case on a disparate impact claim is made by proof that the particular practice operates to exclude a disproportionate number of members of the protected group from an employment opportunity. Once the plaintiff has established the disparate impact of the practice, the burden shifts to the employer to show that the practice is justified by business necessity. Thus an employer is not liable under Title VII for employment practices that have a disparate impact if it can establish that those practices sufficiently serve a business purpose. This is known as the business necessity doctrine. The test is whether there exists an overriding legitimate business purpose such that the practice is necessary for the safe and efficient operation of the business. The dimensions of the business necessity doctrine are presently unclear. It appears to be a test of specificity in that the practice must be job-related. At least one court [4] has held that an employment criterion having a disparate impact can be justified only

---

2. 411 U.S. 792, 93 S.Ct. 1817, 36 L.Ed.2d 668 (1973).

3. 401 U.S. 424, 91 S.Ct. 849, 28 L.Ed.2d 158 (1971).

4. Johnson v. Pike Corporation of America, 332 F.Supp. 490 (C.D.Cal.1971).

by a showing that the criterion relates to job performance and not by a broader notion of business necessity. Other courts have said similar criteria may be justified with reference to such business related factors as employee morale and efficiency or the integrity and security of the business.

The inquiry does not necessarily end when the employer proves job-relatedness or business necessity. The court must still determine whether there exist other practices or selection criteria that would serve the employer's interest but without the undesirable impact.

In a pattern or practice case the plaintiff attempts to demonstrate that the defendant's policy has been to treat minorities less favorably than other employees. The pattern or practice case attempts to establish a general policy of discrimination.

2. THE ISSUE OF STATISTICAL PROOF

ARTHUR B. SMITH, JR. & THOMAS G. ABRAM, QUANTITATIVE ANALYSIS AND PROOF OF EMPLOYMENT DISCRIMINATION *

Quantitative analysis has become an important tool in the resolution of employment discrimination controversies. * * *

[I]n employment discrimination law, statistics on the employment of protected groups, such as women, minorities, or older workers, are introduced as circumstantial evidence. Quantitative analysis then determines whether the statistical evidence supports an inference that employment discrimination has occurred as a matter of law in a particular case.

* * *

Statistical evidence of hiring discrimination exists where the percentage of job offers made to minorities and women is less than their percentage representation in the qualified labor pool for that job. Similarly, statistical evidence of wage discrimination exists where individuals with the same productivity characteristics receive different wages, and the differences are systematically correlated with the race or sex of an individual.

A hypothetical demonstrates the application of these concepts. In support of a claim of discriminatory hiring practices against minorities, plaintiffs introduce evidence showing that in 1980, minority group members comprised forty percent of all qualified applicants for the employer's jobs, but of the applicants offered jobs, only thirty percent were minorities. Even assuming that the pool of qualified applicants is properly measured, the difficult task of establishing the probative value of the statistical evidence, to determine whether em-

* Arthur B. Smith, Jr. & Thomas G. Abram, "Quantitative Analysis And Proof Of Employment Discrimination," 1981 Illinois Law Review 33; © 1981 by the Trustees of the University of Illinois. Reprinted by permission.

ployment discrimination caused the disparity between minority availability and job offers, still remains.

Differentials in representation percentages in the availability and hiring of minorities or females, such as those found in the hypothetical, may support an inference that an employer's practices are infected by unlawful discrimination. In assessing whether the inference may be properly drawn, one must determine what the hire rates of the favored and unfavored group would be in the absence of discrimination. Labor economists * * * would not expect even a nondiscriminatory employer to at all times hire minorities and nonminorities at a rate exactly equal to their representation in the labor market. Thus, a minority hire rate lower than minority representation in the labor market may be attributable to the relative lack of qualified minority applicants or to chance fluctuations from parity rather than unlawful discrimination. Formal statistical tests, not *ad hoc* personal judgments, therefore, are needed to assess whether differentials between minority representation in the labor market and minority representation in new hirings are meaningful.

In drawing a statistical inference about an employer's behavior, one must determine whether the observed minority hire rate is consistent with the hypothesis that hiring decisions were nondiscriminatory. Tests for statistical significance are designed to choose between this assumption, termed the "null hypothesis," and an "alternative hypothesis." In this example, the alternative hypothesis is that hiring is race conscious.

To test the null hypothesis in the hypothetical, it is assumed that the nondiscriminatory employer will conduct its hiring by randomly drawing the names from a pool of qualified persons. Assume further that the pool precisely reflects the minority representation in the qualified labor force from which the employer recruits. This process of selection is repeated until 1,000 random draws have been made and the minority or non-minority status of each draw is recorded. The results of individual draws will be different, but a tabulation of results of all draws will produce a frequency distribution of selection rates. This distribution reflects the likelihood of any minority hire rate occurring if the selection process were conducted in accordance with a completely random drawing process.

Next, the null hypothesis is either accepted or rejected by comparing the actual minority hiring rate, thirty percent in the hypothetical, with the distribution of hire rate generated by random draws, and calculating the number of times in the 1,000 random draws the minority selection rate would be equal to or less than thirty percent. Standard statistical tests are employed in performing these calculations and making the appropriate comparisons. Selection of the proper test in each instance depends, inter alia, on the type of comparison being made, the possibility of measurement errors in the estimation of the qualified labor pool, and the size of the hire data sample.

The hypothesis of nondiscrimination (the null hypothesis) will be rejected if the probability that the observed minority rate (thirty percent) would have occurred is less than an agreed upon "significance" level. The significance level chosen depends on how confident the analyst wishes to be that the observed hiring rate would not be the outcome of a random nondiscriminatory hiring process. For instance, if a minority hiring rate of thirty percent or less would occur only twenty-five times out of 1,000 draws, the random model of hiring is an improbable description of the actual hiring process and at the .05 significance level, it can be said that the hiring process was not truly random. A truly random selection process, however, would still produce a thirty percent hire figure 2.5 percent of the time, so that even at this level of significance it cannot be concluded with absolute confidence that the hiring process is discriminatory.

Several observations flow from the preceding description of the principles of statistical inference in the context of labor market concepts of unlawful discrimination. First, applying tests of statistical inference to hiring data is appropriate only if certain prerequisites are met. The selection of each applicant must be independent of the selection of any other applicant, so that the selection of one applicant does not affect the probability of selecting another. The requirement of independence is satisfied if the applicants selected are a random sample of the relevant population.

Actual hiring practices, however, rarely approximate a random process. For instance, an employer may vary its recruitment practices over time. The employer might recruit in the suburbs one month and the inner city the next, or advertise job openings in a Spanish-language newspaper one week and a newspaper with a predominantly black readership the next. Thus, the selection of applicants resulting from these recruitment efforts may not, for any given time period, be truly random because the applicants may not be representative of the population in terms of ethnicity or socio-economic background. Because an employer's selection process cannot, by definition, be a random procedure, statistical inference cannot play as decisive a role in employment discrimination cases as it has in jury selection decisions. That an employer's selection process may not be random for any particular time period underscores the fact that economic concepts of labor supply and demand apply to employment patterns developed over the long term. Reliance on evidence from a narrow time period may be misleading, precluding reliable inferences about the nature of an employer's behavior.

Second, valid conclusions concerning the relationship of observed hiring patterns to employer behavior require application of an appropriate statistical test of significance. Notwithstanding the view of some commentators to the contrary, statistical significance tests are required even where the statistical comparison is based on complete count of the applicant or work force population for a given time period.

Statistical significance tests are also needed because the inferences to be drawn implicate the complete hiring process followed by an employer. Thus, data on hiring rates for a given period are properly viewed as only a part of the hiring process and as such are a sample for the purpose of applying traditional tests of statistical significance.

Minority and nonminority representation in the qualified labor pool, against which work force or hire rates are measured, moreover, are imperfectly estimated from census or applicant data, and data used in employment discrimination litigation typically does not represent the true availability or supply of qualified and interested persons for the jobs in question. Even if the estimates were conceptually accurate, errors in coding and transcription will produce random variation from correct values. Tests of statistical significance are also necessary to distinguish variations in representation attributable to errors of measurement from the true relationships in the data.

Third, despite the emphasis placed on the need for statistical tests of significance, a finding that disparities between minority and nonminority hire rates, employment figures, or earnings are statistically significant is neither a necessary nor a sufficient condition for establishing impermissible discrimination, at least from the standpoint of a labor market economist. A disparity in minority and nonminority hiring rates that is statistically significant at some level merely attests to the relative likelihood that the disparity resulted from a nonrandom selection process. A finding that a disparity in minority availability and hire percentages is statistically significant, however, does not establish by itself that a discriminatory hiring practice caused the disparity in hiring rates.

The adoption of a particular level or test of statistical significance, moreover, is arbitrary and depends upon the relative confidence one wishes to have in rejecting or accepting the null hypothesis. Thus, if the .05 significance level is adopted, the analyst is willing to infer that discrimination may have contributed to the appearance of the disparity, notwithstanding the fact that the disparity may have occurred by chance up to five percent of the time. The .05 significance level has been adopted by convention in a wide variety of uses in the social and natural sciences, but there is no *a priori* superiority advocating its use in employment discrimination cases. Accordingly, a finding of a statistically significant hiring disparity between minorities and nonminorities is useful only in informing an analyst of the likelihood that the disparity would have occurred in the absence of discrimination.

Similarly, the absence of statistically significant hiring disparities at the .05 level does not in all circumstances convince a labor market economist that nondiscriminatory hiring practices exist. For example, even if the disparities are statistically insignificant, a conclusion that an employer pursued discriminatory hiring policies may be inferred from evidence that, for ten years and in ten different occupational groups, minorities were hired at a rate less than the rate their appropriately defined ability should have produced.

Finally, inferences of unlawful discrimination from statistical data should be accepted only if the likelihood is small that nondiscriminatory practices contributed to the observed disparities and other non-statistical evidence establishes the existence of an employment practice which may have caused the statistical result. Because individuals exhibit characteristics other than minority group or sex attributes, differences in individual qualifications and preferences which affect the supply of labor must be controlled before drawing an inference about the causes of observed hiring or earnings disparities. In many, if not all, actual uses of statistical evidence in employment discrimination litigation, it may be impossible to gather data on many of these differences in qualifications and preferences. Consequently, there will likely be alternative explanations, not captured by the statistical analysis, for observed disparities in the employment of minorities or females. These alternative explanations must be taken into consideration in assessing the strength of the inference to be drawn from the statistical evidence.

B. THE LEGAL DEFINITION OF UNLAWFUL EMPLOYMENT DISCRIMINATION

* * *

A 1977 Supreme Court opinion, Hazelwood School District v. United States,[77] served as a primer on the proper marshalling of statistical proof in an employment discrimination action. In this pattern and practice Title VII case, the plaintiffs claimed that the low representation of minorities among the school district's faculty violated Title VII. The Supreme Court ordered a new trial because both the trial court and the court of appeals relied on erroneous comparisons of employment data. The Court declared that the trier of fact must compare the current percentage of minority faculty members with the racial composition of qualified public school teachers in a relevant labor market. A comparison of the minority composition of the teacher work force with the percentage of minority pupils in the school district was improper.

The Court also rejected the lower court's definition of the relevant labor market for comparison purposes, articulating five criteria for evaluation by the trial court on remand. In addition, the Court cautioned that simple comparisons between school district work force and qualified labor force data in a relevant geographic area must be analyzed in conjunction with the racial composition of hiring patterns after the effective date of an employer's coverage by employment discrimination law. The Court declared that an employer who, from the effective date of coverage, "made all its employment decisions in a wholly nondiscriminatory way would not violate Title VII even if it had formerly maintained an all-white work force by purposefully excluding Negroes."

Last, and perhaps most important, *Hazelwood* introduced the concept of statistical significance into the evaluation of employment statistics. Borrowing from Castaneda v. Partida,[82] a jury discrimination

---

77. 433 U.S. 299, 97 S.Ct. 2736, 53 L.Ed.2d 768 (1977).

82. 430 U.S. 482, 97 S.Ct. 1272, 51 L.Ed.2d 498 (1977).

case, the Court suggested that where the disparity between the actual percentage of minorities observed in a work force and the "expected percentage" in the work force is greater than what would occur if the employer hired randomly, then the hypothesis that hiring was accomplished without regard to race or some other prohibited characteristic would be suspect. To evaluate the significance of statistical disparities, the Court first suggested a calculation of the standard deviation of the number of minorities expected in the surrounding labor force. The Court observed that when large numbers of employees make up the data base, a difference of more than two or three standard deviations between the actual and expected minority representation percentages would occur less than five percent of the time if completely random hiring procedures were employed. If a disparity were observed which would occur less than five percent of the time using completely random procedures, the Court determined that the hypothesis that hiring is done without regard to race or other prohibited characteristics would be suspect.

The *Hazelwood* Court's observations about the legal importance of statistically significant disparities are apparently not intended as inflexible guidelines, or the final word on the issue. The cautious and tentative nature of these observations are noteworthy, for the discussion of statistical significance in *Hazelwood* contains two fundamental flaws. First, the Court's analysis of statistically significant disparities is premised on the questionable assumption that a nondiscriminating employer's work force will mirror the percentage of minorities or females in a surrounding labor force. As previously discussed, labor market economics recognizes that an employer does not engage in truly random hiring practices.

Second, the procedure described by *Hazelwood* for evaluating the statistical significance of a disparity does not, as the Court apparently suggests, lead to the inference that a statistically significant disparity is caused by prohibited employment practices. A statistically significant disparity requires the rejection of the hypothesis that the defendant employed completely random hiring procedures.

A statistically significant disparity does not identify which factor caused the deviation from the results expected of random procedures. Thus, the use of sophisticated mathematical tests for evaluating disparities presented by raw numbers in employment discrimination cases should not obscure the fact that numbers and mathematical tools alone do not contain a causal link between the observed and expected result.

Aside from these considerations, *Hazelwood's* emphasis on the concept of statistical significance should not detract from the importance of "practical significance" to the evaluation of data in employment discrimination cases. Whereas a measure of statistical significance provides a basis for inferring whether a disparity in results for minority and nonminority groups could be expected if random employment practices were used, practical significance refers to the magnitude of the disparity. It is quite conceivable that a statistically significant disparity—one which, for example, would be expected less than five percent of the time if random procedures were employed— may be quite small in practical terms. The Court's emphasis in * * * *Hazelwood* on evidence of "long-lasting and gross dispari- ties" suggests that more is required in the evaluation of statistical proof of disparate impact than statistically significant disparities.

In the Supreme Court, therefore, statistical evidence of dispari- ties, properly presented, may be probative evidence and sufficient to establish a prima facie case of discrimination. The prima facie case thereupon shifts the burden of going forward to the defendant, who must produce evidence in justification of the challenged employment practice. Statistical evidence standing alone, however, is not suffi- cient to establish guilt as a matter of law. Nor is it sufficient alone to establish innocence.

Another important directive can be derived from Supreme Court decisions on statistical inference. No single data format is sufficient in building or rebutting a case based on statistics. In a hiring dis- crimination case, for example, work force to labor force comparisons are useful. Statistics, however, on the number of minority applicants and the number of workers hired since the effective date of an enter- prise's coverage by employment discrimination law also seem neces- sary to establish a record sufficiently complete to support an infer- ence of discrimination. Some analytical methods are more probative than others, depending on the type of discrimination at issue. The weight the trier of fact accords the statistical evidence, moreover, de- pends on the inferences that may fairly be drawn from the record compiled for the particular case.

3.   TITLE VII

Probably the most significant piece of legislation dealing with equal employment opportunity is Title VII of the Civil Rights Act of 1964.[5] The Civil Rights Act of 1964 represents the most comprehen- sive step in civil rights since the days following the Civil War. It also represents a concerted attack upon discrimination in several forms. This discussion is concerned only with Title VII. Its objective is to prevent discriminatory practices in employment based on race, color, religion, national origin or sex and is administered by the EEOC.

(a) COVERAGE AND SCOPE

Title VII applies to employers, employment agencies and labor or- ganizations and prohibits them from discriminating on the basis of race, color, religion, national origin and sex in virtually all types of employment activity.

The coverage of Title VII extends to employers and labor organi- zations engaged in an industry affecting commerce and to employ-

5.   42 U.S.C.A. § 2000e, et seq. (1964).

ment agencies that serve such employers. The term "industry affecting commerce" leaves little doubt that Title VII's reach extends to any activity which Congress may properly regulate under the U. S. Constitution's Commerce Clause.

Besides being engaged in an industry affecting commerce, to be covered employers and unions must have 15 or more employees. Also, any union maintaining a hiring hall is covered regardless of the size of its membership.

Any person regularly undertaking with or without compensation to find employees for an employer is considered to be an employment agency under the Act. Is a college placement office an employment agency? Under one district court decision it is if it is the primary source employers use to hire the school's graduates and most students obtain employment through the placement office.[6] What about a newspaper which publishes sex-segregated help wanted advertising? The Supreme Court refused to review a decision which held that a newspaper is not an employment agency under Title VII. It let stand a lower court determination that newspapers do not engage in the business of finding employees, that their involvement in printing ads is negligible, and that their concern for aiding persons in obtaining employment is minimal.[7]

Under Title VII an employer cannot discriminate with regard to hiring, firing, compensation, terms, conditions, or privileges of employment on the basis of race, color, religion, national origin or sex. Neither can an employer limit, segregate, or classify employees in any way that tends to deprive any individual of employment opportunities or adversely affects his employment status because of any of these five bases. Labor organizations are prohibited from discriminating on any of these five bases with regard to membership. Employment agencies are forbidden to discriminate on these five bases in their referral activity. Furthermore, every entity covered by Title VII is forbidden to discriminate on the basis of race, color, religion, national origin or sex in apprenticeship and training programs. It is also illegal for any covered entity to indicate a preference or a discrimination on any of these five bases in employment advertisements.

(b) Exceptions

All of the above described prohibitions are subject to some important exceptions, namely the seniority exception, the exception accorded to bona fide occupational qualifications, and the allowance made for professionally developed ability tests.

---

6. Kaplowitz v. University of Chicago, 387 F.Supp. 42 (Ill.N.D.1974).

7. Brush v. San Francisco Newspaper Printing Co., 315 F.Supp. 577 (N.D.Cal. 1979).

(1) Seniority Systems

Section 703(j) permits an employer to apply different standards of employment pursuant to a "bona fide seniority or merit system" provided that it is not the result of an *intention* to discriminate. Seniority is the cornerstone to many union efforts. From organized labor's perspective, seniority provides a system of employment security to workers. Seniority systems eliminate favoritism. Senior workers are provided a preference in any promotion or layoff activity. From the employer's perspective, the rationale of seniority is that it adds to the safety and efficiency of the employer's place of business. The theory is that a more experienced worker will be safer and more efficient than a lesser experienced worker.

Seniority systems, especially those created before Title VII's effective date (1965), have resulted in a great deal of litigation. Seniority systems can be discriminatory. One example of a discriminatory seniority system would be where a plant maintains segregated seniority lines with minority workers or women assigned to a seniority line with less pay than seniority lines staffed by only white workers. In Franks v. Bowman Transportation Co.,[8] such a seniority system was held unlawful.

Seniority systems that were established before 1965 can also be discriminatory. For example, suppose that a plant has four departments, which in the order of pay from bottom to top are: maintenance, production, repair, and packing. Suppose further that each department has five grades within it. Now suppose that a worker must be the highest senior worker in one department (e.g. production) to move into the next highest department (e.g. repair). Within each department, the worker moves up to higher grade only on the basis of departmental seniority, not plant seniority. Now, suppose that before 1965, women in this plant could only work in the maintenance department. Under *Bowman Transportation*, this is now a violation of Title VII. However, even if the other departments are opened to women workers employed after 1965, for those women hired under the old seniority system, two problems are presented: (1) there is no incentive for a woman to move out of the maintenance department and into the production department because women would start out at the bottom grade of the production department—thus there will be a pay cut, and (2) a woman worker transferring from maintenance into production will lose her seniority from the maintenance department, thus making her vulnerable to layoffs since the first one to be laid off will be the worker at the bottom of the lowest grade. Thus, although the seniority system does not discriminate for new hirees, it serves as a neutral force which freezes or locks-in the discrimination practiced before 1965.

---

8.   424 U.S. 747, 96 S.Ct. 1251, 47 L.Ed.2d 444 (1976).

Before 1977, such seniority systems had been struck down by several lower federal courts. Their reasoning was that any seniority system that perpetuated past discrimination was not a "bona fide" seniority system. As the Fifth Circuit Court of Appeals stated in United Papermakers and Crown Zellerbach Corp. v. United States:

> Title VII expressly states the seniority system must be *bona fide*. The purpose of the act is to eliminate racial discrimination in covered employment. Obviously one characteristic of a bona fide seniority system must be lack of discrimination. Nothing in Title VII, or in its legislative history suggests that a racially discriminatory seniority system established before the act is a bona fide seniority system under the act.[9]

However, most of these lower courts permitted the seniority system to continue if the employer could establish the "business necessity" of the system. The *Papermakers* court stated that "When an employer or union has discriminated in the past and when its present policies renew or exaggerate discriminatory effects, those policies must yield, unless there is an overriding legitimate non-racial business purpose." Thus the appellate court developed a rule requiring an employer to prove that the departmental seniority system actually added to the safety and efficiency of workers. Other circuits refused even to recognize this business necessity justification for pre-Act seniority systems.

In a recent decision on the legal status under Title VII of a seniority system that perpetuated the effects of past discrimination, the Supreme Court breathed new life into the seniority system exception and reversed the *Papermakers* approach in a case which marks a retreat from the Court of Appeals "business necessity" justification standard. In International Brotherhood of Teamsters v. United States [10] the Court ruled that a seniority system which affords no constructive seniority to victims discriminated against before Title VII's effective date is bona fide and thus not unlawful under the Act. The Court expressly rejected the Government's argument, which had extensive support among the courts of appeal, that a seniority system which perpetuates the effects of past discrimination never could be "bona fide" under Title VII. The Court said that "Both the literal terms and the legislative history of Title VII demonstrate that Congress considered this very effect of many seniority systems and extended a measure of immunity to them * * * . Although a seniority system inevitably tends to perpetuate the effects of pre-Act discrimination * * * , the congressional judgment was that Title VII should not outlaw the use of existing seniority lists and thereby destroy or water down the vested seniority rights of employees simply because their employer had engaged in discrimination prior to the passage of the act." Justices Brennan and Marshall's dissenting opinion maintained that " * * * the different privileges of employ-

9. Local 189, United Papermakers and Paperworkers, AFL–CIO, et al. and Crown Zellerbach Corp. v. United States, 416 F.2d 980 (5th Cir. 1969).

10. 431 U.S. 324, 97 S.Ct. 1843, 52 L.Ed.2d 396 (1977).

ment   *   *   *   produced by petitioners' seniority system are precisely the result of prior intentional discrimination   *   *   *" and thus would have treated such seniority systems as falling within the exception's proviso that such seniority systems not be the product of an intention to discriminate.

(2) Bona Fide Occupational Qualifications and Ability Tests

The bona fide occupational qualification, or bfoq, is a statutory exception to those employment practices which might otherwise violate Title VII. This exception allows an employer to discriminate in its hiring where religion, national origin or sex is a "bona fide occupational qualification reasonably necessary to the normal operation of that particular business or operation." More will be said about this exception later in this chapter. However, two important items should be noted here: (1) the effect of this exception is to excuse sexual, religious and national origin discrimination in some hiring situations, and (2) no such justification is given to racial discrimination; the exception extends only to sexual, religious, and national origin discrimination. An employer also can utilize and act upon the results of any "professionally developed ability test" if it is not designed or used to discriminate.

(c) EEOC Administration And Enforcement

The Equal Employment Opportunity Commission (EEOC) administers Title VII. The principal method of enforcement is through the voluntary compliance efforts of conciliation and mediation; however, if these efforts fail, the Commission is authorized to initiate litigation in federal district court on behalf of aggrieved persons.

The EEOC normally becomes involved when an aggrieved person, called the "charging party," files a written charge in one of the Commission's regional offices, claiming that an unlawful discriminatory act has been directed toward him or her. Normally, the written charge must be filed within 180 days of the alleged discriminatory act. Although the written charge need not be in any specified form, it must be submitted under oath.

To allow state and local fair employment practices agencies the first chance to resolve the dispute, the EEOC is required to defer its activity until 60 days after state or local proceedings are commenced. If a charging party goes to the EEOC first, the EEOC will normally have him complete an EEOC charge form and a state or local charge form, then after sending the state or local form to the proper agency, wait 60 days before initiating any investigation. This process of deferring to any state or local fair employment practices agency is known as the "EEOC 60-day state deferral."

After the 60-day deferral period, the EEOC will initiate an investigation. A notice that a charge has been filed against him will be delivered to the employer, who is referred to as the respondent. The notice identifies the charging party. Title VII's anti-retaliation provision prohibits the employer from retaliating against an employee through punishment, discrimination or any other means for initiating or participating in any proceeding brought under Title VII. Thus, although an employer may be innocent of the charges filed with the EEOC, if the employer undertakes any activity that could be construed as retaliation against the charging party, the employer may find itself ultimately rendered liable to the charging party for violating Title VII's anti-retaliation provision.

The investigation conducted by the EEOC may take a variety of forms. Interrogatories may be sent to the respondent or a visit may be conducted of the respondent's plant. If interrogatories are propounded, they are normally sent along with the copy of the notice of charge. Any plant visit will normally occur only after the employer has been sent a copy of the notice of charge. The EEOC is given the power to subpoena any relevant documents.

The EEOC's investigation culminates in a determination that there is either no reasonable cause to believe that a Title VII violation occurred, or that there is reasonable cause that a violation exists, the charge is dismissed. If a finding of reasonable cause results, then the EEOC issues a "determination letter" to the respondent, notifying the respondent of the Commission's role of endeavoring to eliminate the alleged unlawful practice by the informal method of conciliation.

Section 706(b) of the Title VII states:

If the Commission determines after such investigation that there is reasonable cause to believe that the charge is true, the Commission shall endeavor to eliminate any such unlawful employment practice by informal methods of conference, conciliation and persuasion.

The section goes on to recite the confidentiality of anything said or done during the conciliation process.

The conciliation process will be undertaken between the charging party and the respondent, with the EEOC representing the charging party. The result of the conciliation process will be either a conciliation agreement or an impasse in the negotiations between the parties. The effect of a conciliation agreement is the same as a settlement agreement between the parties of a pending lawsuit.

At a conciliation conference the agency will be represented by one or more representatives of the EEOC and perhaps with counsel for the agency, such as an attorney who could eventually pursue the matter in court. The respondent is entitled to be represented by counsel at all stages of the proceeding. It is very unusual to find the charging party present at a conciliation conference. If present, the charging party is not generally allowed private counsel as the agency is his representative.

If the conciliation conference concludes with an agreement arrived at between the parties, a conciliation agreement will be executed. Final approval of the conciliation agreement must be obtained from the regional director in the region in which the charge is filed and will be kept on file in the regional office. The effect of a conciliation agreement on other legal actions is that most civil action which could be brought by the charging party against the respondent will be barred by the execution of a final and binding conciliation agreement which has been approved by the charging party.

If conciliation fails, two things may happen: (1) The regional office of the EEOC may send the case to one of its litigation centers scattered about the country for a determination by the litigation center whether the Commission will bring a direct action against the respondent. (2) The Commission will send the charging party a notice that conciliation has been fruitless and that the charging party has a right to sue in federal court within 90 days. Should the charging party elect to pursue this route, he or she would obtain private counsel and file suit in the appropriate federal court on behalf of the charging party or perhaps on behalf of an entire class of persons similarly situated.

No discussion of Title VII enforcement would be complete without some mention of the remedies which can be assessed those who are found to be in violation of the law. Title VII provides for broad and effective remedies for violations of its provisions. In addition to prohibiting the unlawful employment practice, a court may award such affirmative action or any other equitable relief as the court deems appropriate. A court may also assess up to two years of back pay, reinstatement to the job, and payment for attorney fees.

(d) RELIGIOUS DISCRIMINATION

Title VII prohibits discrimination in employment based upon religion. Section 701(j) states:

> The term 'religion' includes all aspects of religious observance and practice, as well as belief, unless an employer demonstrates that he is unable to reasonably accommodate to an employee's or prospective employee's religious observance or practice without undue hardship in the conduct of the employer's business.

This definition places the burden squarely on the employer to demonstrate that he is unable to "reasonably accommodate" to an employee's or prospective employee's religious observance, practice or belief without undue hardship to his business.

One issue initially encountered under this section is "What is a religion?" In determining what is a religion within the meaning of Title VII, the EEOC has been guided by the broad interpretation of religion used by the Supreme Court in construing the Universal Military Training and Service Act in several conscientious objector cases. In these cases the Court has defined broadly, stating that any belief in a supreme being, or even atheism constitutes a religion. Thus, the term "religion" means not only organized sects whose beliefs are common to a number of people, but may include intensely personal convictions which some may find incomprehensible or incorrect. Such groups as Black Muslims, the Salvation Army, and the World Wide Church of God have been held to be religion under Title VII. However, one federal district court upheld an employer's discharge of an employee because of his membership in the United Klans of America over the objection by the employee that the racially exclusive and anti-semitic nature of the organization transformed it into a racial or religious group.[11]

Another issue presented by Title VII's ban on religious discrimination in employment is its constitutionality under the U. S. Constitution's prohibition against the establishment of any religion. An argument can be made that Title VII's prohibition of intentional religious discrimination constitutes a congressional mandate requiring employers to accommodate an individual employee's religious belief, which arguably is a preference on account of religion. No federal court has held the provision unconstitutional. Those that have discussed the issue have held that the benefits to religion are incidental to the purpose of fulfilling nondiscrimination mandate. Although the Supreme Court has remained silent on the subject, two justices, Justice Brennan and Justice Marshall registered their conclusions supporting the section's constitutionality in a dissenting opinion.[12]

An exception to Title VII's provision has, however, been declared in dictum to be of "very doubtful constitutionality" by the D. C. Court of Appeals. Section 702 provides: This title * * * shall not apply * * * to a religious corporation, association, educational institution, or society with respect to perform work converted with the carrying on . . . of its activities." By going beyond religious activities and including even secular activities of a religious organization, the D. C. Court of Appeals noted in King's Garden, Inc. v. F. C. C.,[13] that the section's scope could violate the U. S. Constitution's establishment clause.

Religious discrimination is a far less frequent topic of litigation than other forms of forbidden discrimination, therefore the law regarding what is "reasonable accommodation" and what constitutes an "undue hardship" to the employer's business is not well developed. The most frequent charges of religious discrimination dealt with by the courts and the EEOC have not involved raw prejudice against an employee's religion, but have involved instances where a work rule of the employer, innocent in intent, results in a conflict with one of the religious beliefs of an employee. Two areas that have raised problems under Title VII involve work rules relating to (1) work schedules and (2) dress and attire. Work scheduling can create a conflict when an employer insists that his employees work on weekends during periods of time considered by some employees to be their Sabbath. For example, a work rule requiring all employees to work Saturdays con-

---

11. Bellamy v. Mason Stores, Inc., 368 F.Supp. 1025 (E.D.Va.1973).

12. Trans World Airlines v. Hardison, 432 U.S. 63, 97 S.Ct. 2264, 53 L.Ed.2d 113 (1977) (Brennan and Marshall dissenting).

13. 498 F.2d 51 (D.C.Cir. 1974).

tradicts with the religious beliefs of Jews and Seventh Day Adventists. Employer dress codes also can conflict with an individual employee's religious dress code, such as an employer's dress code requiring that Black Muslim women refrain from wearing ankle-length dresses.

Whether the religious practice can be "reasonably accommodated" or whether such accommodation would amount to an "undue hardship" to the employer's business requires a balancing of employer hardship against employee burdens, with the employer required to bear the burden of proving that the balance should be struck in its favor. The factors courts use in determining whether accommodation must be made include the following: (1) The nature of the job—if specialized or unique, the employer is given greater latitude, (2) The size of the employer's establishment—for example, larger employers will be required to show why other employees cannot be transferred to replace a Sabbath observing worker, (3) The effects of accommodation on employee morale. Undue hardships may be established by showing that scheduling problems, overtime pay requirements, and violations of a collective bargaining agreement would be presented by accommodating the employee's beliefs. Although these factors may be present, the duty to accommodate requires that employers make some effort toward accommodation. Thus, employers, should make some effort to transfer a Sabbath-observing employee to a position which does not require working on the prohibited days.

In 1977 the Supreme Court rendered a decision which limited an employer's duty to accommodate. In Trans World Airlines v. Hardison,[14] the Court held that the seniority rights of other employees need not be violated to protect the religious beliefs of an employee, nor must the employer incur more than minimal expenses for such things as overtime pay and loss of efficiency. In *Trans World Airlines*, the plaintiff, a member of the WorldWide Church of God, named three unions and his employer as defendants, claiming that enforcement of the collective bargaining agreement discriminated against him because the seniority system prevented the transfer of other employees to accommodate his Sabbath observance. The Court held that Congress did not intend that employers or unions be required to take action that would impinge seniority systems. In establishing a guideline for determining what is employer undue hardship, the Court stated: "To require TWA to bear more than a *de minimis* cost in order to give Hardison Saturdays off is an undue hardship."

The *de minimis* rule regarding proof of employer undue hardship makes it easier for employers to show that accommodating an employee's religious requirements is not necessary. The Court's decision also reversed the position taken by the EEOC and several circuit courts of appeal that, as the Sixth Circuit stated: "Undue hardship is something greater than hardship * * * to call * * * inconve-

---

14.   432 U.S. 63, 97 S.Ct. 2264, 53
L.Ed.2d 113 (1977).

nience * * * 'undue hardship' would be to venture into 'an Alice-in-Wonderland' world where words have no meaning." [15]

In the area of dress codes, the courts have held that an employer must reasonably accommodate an employee's religious dress requirements, unless the employer can establish the business necessity of the dress code.

Under Title VII, an employer may also assert the bfoq defense to justify religious discrimination in hiring. Thus, if a church-owned school wanted to hire only church members to teach religious classes, its policy would be justified because membership in that particular religion would be a bona fide occupational qualification.

(e) DISCRIMINATION BASED ON NATIONAL ORIGIN

Although discrimination on the basis of national origin is forbidden by Title VII, the Act does not define the term. An initial issue thus presented by the term "national origin" is the relationship between it and the concepts of alienage and ancestry. That is to say, are aliens, or non-citizens, included within the meaning of the term, or is the term's meaning restricted to citizens who are discriminated on the basis of their ancestry? For example, is the Irish woman fresh off the boat from Belfast, dressed in her tweeds and shawl, and not yet a U. S. citizen, protected from employment discrimination by Title VII just as much as her future American-born daughter? The Supreme Court considered this issue in Espinoza v. Farah Manufacturing, Inc.[16] In that case, plaintiffs, resident-Mexicans, sought a declaratory judgment and damages under Title VII because they were denied employment with a private employer because they were aliens. The Court declared that the employer did not violate Title VII because the term "national origin" did not encompass "citizenship;" ancestry, not alienage was the scope of Title VII's prohibition. The Court held that the term "national origin" on its face refers to the country where the person was born, or more broadly, the country from which one's ancestors come. The Court refused to recognize discrimination on the basis of citizenship as forbidden by Title VII, stating that while a citizenship requirement in some cases might be a part of a wider scheme of national origin discrimination, there was no evidence on the record that the employer's policy against employing aliens discriminated against persons of Mexican national origin.

Justice Douglas dissented in *Espinoza*, pointing out that under *Griggs*, practices or procedures that are neutral on their face violate Title VII if they create artificial, arbitrary, and unnecessary barriers to employment. Farah Manufacturing had explicitly conceded that the citizenship requirement was imposed without regard to an alien's job qualifications. Thus, Douglas would have applied the *Griggs* test and would have held Farah in violation of Title VII.

---

15. Cummins v. Parker Seal Co., 516 F.2d 544 (6th Cir. 1975).

16. 414 U.S. 86, 94 S.Ct. 334, 38 L.Ed. 2d 287 (1973).

Thus, the Supreme Court decision in *Espinoza* held that discrimination on the basis of citizenship is not per se national origin discrimination. Title VII does not protect aliens from employment discrimination. However, other laws and the U. S. Constitution may provide protection.

Title VII's non-applicability to aliens notwithstanding, the EEOC has issued guidelines regarding national origin discrimination directed against U. S. citizens. According to the Commission's guidelines, (29 C.F.R. 1606) employment differentials applied against employees or applicants based on the following factors will constitute unlawful national origin discrimination:

(1) Language requirements, i.e., the use of tests in the English language where English is not the individual's first language or mother tongue *and* where English language skill is not a requirement of the work to be performed.

(2) Marriage or association with members of a particular national origin.

(3) Membership in a lawful organization identified with or seeking to promote the interests of a given nationality or ethnic group.

(4) Attendance at a school or church commonly utilized by members of a particular national origin.

(5) Having a surname indicative of a certain national origin.

(6) Height and weight requirements.

Although Title VII provides a bfoq exception for national origin discrimination, the EEOC's guidelines point out that the exception shall be strictly construed. For example, suppose that an employer opens a French gourmet restaurant. Could the owner hire only waiters and waitresses who are of French ancestry and who speak flawless, unaccented French? An argument could be made that in this situation being of French national origin is a bona fide occupational qualification reasonably necessary for the normal operation of a French gourmet restaurant. However, suppose another enterprising restaurant owner opens Joe's White Anglo-Saxon Grill. Could he hire only white Americans of Anglo-Saxon ancestry? In Mejia v. New York Sheraton Hotel,[17] a federal district court held that a hotel's requirement of English language proficiency was justified by business necessity.

(f) Sex Discrimination

It is interesting to note that sex became a protected category under Title VII almost by accident. Efforts by opponents to block passage of the Civil Rights Act included the addition of sex to the bases upon which employment discrimination could be alleged. It was not until the last day of the House Rules Committee's consideration of

---

17.   459 F.Supp. 375 (S.D.N.Y.1978).

Title VII that a motion was submitted to include sex discrimination with the other types of employment discrimination the bill was designed to end. Two weeks of floor debate in the House of Representatives resulted in a formal amendment to include sex discrimination in Title VII. While this particular turn of events may not have seemed of great importance at the time, it has since changed the legal status of working women significantly.

Application of Title VII requires that it first be determined that a discrimination on the basis of sex has occurred. Obviously, if there is no sex discrimination the inquiry ends. Suppose an employer maintains separate grooming standards for men and women (i.e., forbidding male employees from maintaining hair below the earlobe but only requiring that female employees secure long hair so that it does not fall freely)—is this sex discrimination? The EEOC takes the position that such grooming standards are discriminatory and violate Title VII.[18] However, the numerous district and circuit courts which have considered the issue have generally reached the opposite conclusion. In Dodge v. Giant Food, Inc.,[19] the D. C. Circuit noted that "it is * * * clear that the regulations treat long-haired males differently than long-haired females. Thus, the regulations embody a distinction among employees based upon their sex." However, the court held that the distinction did not constitute unlawful discrimination within the meaning of Title VII. Analogizing hair-length regulations to an employer's requirement that men and women use separate toilet facilities or a rule that men not wear dresses, the court stated:

> The issue in these cases is one of degree. Few would disagree that an employer's blanket exclusion of women from certain positions constitutes "discrimination" within the meaning of Title VII. At the same time, few would argue that separate toilet facilities for men and women constitute Title VII "discrimination." The line must be drawn somewhere between these two extremes, and we draw the line to exclude Giant's hair-length regulations from the ambit of Title VII. We do not believe that Title VII was intended to invalidate grooming regulations which have no significant effect upon the employment opportunities afforded one sex in favor of the other.

Title VII prohibits not only overt sexual discrimination but subtle and unintended forms of sex discrimination as well. Thus, the use of facially neutral standards which disproportionately impact adversely the employment opportunities of women are forbidden in the same way such facially neutral devices directed against blacks and ethnic groups are prohibited. Height and weight requirements that adversely affect females more than males may not survive Title VII scrutiny unless they can be justified by business necessity.

Remember, where facially neutral standards are at issue, a prima facie case of illegal discrimination under Title VII requires a showing

18. Decision No. 72–0979, CCH EEOC Decisions ¶ 6343.

19. 488 F.2d 1333 (D.C.Cir. 1973).

of the device's "disproportionate impact" before the burden shifts to the employer to establish the "business necessity" of the practice. This two-step process is best illustrated in a sex discrimination context in the area of employer anti-nepotism rules. Anti-nepotism rules prohibit spouses from working in the same department or plant or prohibit totally the hiring of spouses by the employer. In Harper v. Trans World Airlines, Inc.,[20] the Eighth Circuit affirmed a judgment against a plaintiff who claimed that TWA's rule proscribing the employment of spouses in the same department. In upholding the anti-nepotism policy, the court stated: "we conclude that plaintiff is not entitled to avail herself of the protective shield of *Griggs* because she has failed to prove, by statistics or other probative evidence, that defendant's rule adversely affected women * * * Since plaintiff failed to prove a 'disparate effect' upon women due to the implementation of defendant's rule, the requisite threshold issue has not been met and there is no need for defendant to show any business necessity for the rule." In Yuhas v. Libbey-Owens-Ford Co.,[21] the Seventh Circuit upheld a similar challenge to a company policy against hiring spouses of its hourly employees, notwithstanding a factual showing that the rule had a substantially discriminatory impact upon women. The court concluded that the employer had demonstrated the job-relatedness of the rule by plausibly arguing that it is generally a bad idea to have both marriage partners working together.

Another form of indirect sex discrimination is referred to as "sex plus" discrimination. Sex-plus discrimination denotes that discrimination that exists when a constraint or requirement is imposed on some members of one sex but not on any member of the opposite sex. Thus, where only some members of a particular sex are discriminated against while no members of the opposite sex are so treated, "sex-plus" discrimination exists. For example, if an employer were to hire men regardless of educational background but hired only women with high school diplomas, this would be sex-plus discrimination. Although the employer hires both men and women, the employer requires a plus factor for women.

Another example of sex-plus discrimination is the requirement that female employees be single while males may be married. This policy was once prevalent in the airline industry, which generally required that female flight attendants (stewardesses) be single while males in the same category (stewards) could be married. The EEOC Guidelines (29 C.F.R. 1604) prohibit this practice in the following language: "The Commission has determined that an employer's rule which forbids or restricts the employment of married women and which is not applicable to married men is a discrimination based on sex prohibited by Title VII of the Civil Rights Act. It does not seem to us relevant that the rule is not directed against all females, but only against married females, for so long as sex is a factor in the application of the rule, such application involves discrimination based

20.   525 F.2d 409 (8th Cir. 1975).

21.   562 F.2d 496 (7th Cir. 1977).

on sex." This guideline was upheld by the Seventh Circuit in Sprogis v. United Air Lines, Inc.[22] It should be noted that a "no marriage" rule will be legal if the requirement is that all employees, male and female, be unmarried.

A third type of sex-plus discrimination that has been addressed by the courts concerns the condition of motherhood. An employer's policy of discriminating against females with pre-school age children, but not discriminating against males who are similarly situated may constitute illegal sex-plus discrimination in the absence of any evidence that females so situated have higher absentee rates than males. In Phillips v. Martin Marietta Corp.,[23] the Supreme Court addressed an employer's refusal to hire women with pre-school age children, although the employer did not discriminate against men with pre-school age children. The hiring practice of the employer did not appear to discriminate against women because: "at the time Mrs. Phillips applied, 70–75% of the applicants for the position she sought were women; 75–80% of those hired for the position assembly trainee, were women, hence no question of bias against women as such was presented." However, the Court ruled that since men with pre-school age children were hired where women were not the practice violated Title VII. Thus, sex discrimination existed because a certain class of females were discriminated against while their male counterparts were not.

As seen by the above discussion, the initial inquiry in determining whether an employer has violated Title VII's anti-sex discrimination provision is to ascertain that discrimination on the basis of sex has occurred. Such sex discrimination may be overt, indirect or take the form of sex-plus discrimination. However, if a court concludes that an employer has discriminated on the basis of sex then it is the employer's burden to establish that a "bona fide occupational qualification" (bfoq) reasonably necessary to the employer's business justifies the discriminatory practice. Title VII declares sex discrimination in employment to be unlawful in all employment situations except those hiring decisions that can be justified as involving sex as a bona fide occupational qualification (bfoq). The statute itself states in section 703(e) that there may be discrimination on the basis of sex if sex "is a bona fide occupational qualification reasonably necessary to the normal operation of that particular business or enterprise." This means that employers may discriminate on the basis of sex if the job by its nature requires that it be performed by a member of a certain sex. If an employer can prove that a particular job requires a job incumbent to be of a specific sex, it is allowable to employ only members of that sex in that job. Exactly what would be considered a bfoq has been the thrust of the judicial inquiry in cases involving sex discrimination to date.

22.   444 F.2d 1194 (7th Cir. 1977).

23.   400 U.S. 542, 91 S.Ct. 496, 27 L.Ed.2d 613 (1971).

The administrative Guidelines (29 C.F.R. 1604.2) developed by the EEOC take an extremely narrow stand on the applicability of the bfoq exception. The Commission's Guidelines on Discrimination Because of Sex were implemented in 1972. While these Guidelines are not substantive law, courts often defer to administrative expertise and place great weight upon the EEOC's interpretation of the statute because the agency has taken a consistent position on this subject. These guidelines state in pertinent part:

(a) The Commission believes that the bona fide occupational qualification exception as to sex should be interpreted narrowly. Labels—"Men's jobs" and "Women's jobs"—tend to deny employment opportunities unnecessarily to one sex or the other.

(1) The Commission will find that the following situations do not warrant the application of the bona fide occupational qualification exception:

(i) The refusal to hire a woman because of her sex based on assumptions of the comparative employment characteristics of women in general. For example, the assumption that the turnover rate among women is higher than among men.

(ii) The refusal to hire an individual based on stereotyped characteristics of the sexes. Such stereotypes include, for example, that men are less capable of assembling intricate equipment; that women are less capable of aggressive salesmanship. The principle of non-discrimination requires that individuals be considered on the basis of individual capacities and not on the basis of any characteristics generally attributed to the group.

(iii) The refusal to hire an individual because of the preferences of coworkers, the employer, clients or customers
    * * *.

What is a bfoq under the Guidelines? The EEOC provides only the example of an actor or actress in which a certain sex is necessary for authenticity purposes. It follows therefore that where sex is a function or an essential element of the job the Guidelines approach would recognize that a bfoq would lie: i.e., jobs calling for a wet nurse or a sperm donor. In deciding whether a bfoq lies, the Guidelines approach requires that one ask whether it is absolutely necessary that members of one sex perform the job. Thus only if the answer to the question "Can any member of the opposite sex perform this job?" is "no" will the Guidelines recognize the existence of a bfoq.

More important than the Guidelines is the manner in which the courts have applied the exception in real life situations. Two Fifth Circuit cases, Weeks v. Southern Bell Telephone and Telegraph Co.,[24] and Diaz v. Pan American World Airways, Inc.[25] are the principal cases defining a bfoq.

---

24. 408 F.2d 228 (5th Cir. 1969).   25. 442 F.2d 385 (5th Cir. 1971).

In *Weeks*, the plaintiff was denied a switchman position even though her seniority would have entitled her to the job. The company maintained that the position's arduous responsibilities, which including lifting over 30 pounds, did not reveal that the job could not be performed by women in general, and the plaintiff maintained that she was capable of performing the job. Deferring to the Commission's guidelines requiring that individuals be considered on the basis of individual capacities and not on characteristics generally attributed to groups as a whole, the court held that Southern Bell did not meet its burden of proof merely by showing conclusions based on stereotypes; that the bfoq exception requires a factual showing that the employer had reasonable cause to believe that all or substantially all women would be unable to perform safely and efficiently the duties of the job. Absent this showing, the employer must individually assess the abilities of each worker. The court in *dictum* noted that unverified yet reasonable generalizations based on sex may be permitted where it would be impossible or highly impracticable to make individual determinations.

The *Weeks* bfoq formula was elaborated upon in *Diaz* where a male was denied a job as an airline stewardess. The company argued that the exception should apply because of passenger preference indicating that women were superior to men in the nonmechanical functions of the job, such as attending to the psychological needs of passengers by providing a pleasurable environment. The court, however, held that the bfoq exception requires the application of a business necessity, not a business convenience test; meaning that sex can constitute a bfoq only where the essence of the business operation would be undermined by not hiring members of one sex exclusively. The court found that the nonmechanical aspects of a stewardess position were not enough to qualify the job for the exception, since they were not "reasonably necessary to the normal operation of the particular business." The court noted that Pan Am had not suggested that having male stewards would so seriously affect the operation of the business as to jeopardize or minimize the airline's ability to provide safe transportation.

Taken together, *Weeks* and *Diaz* establish that before sex can constitute a bfoq, it must be shown that (1) it is impracticable to find members of one sex who possess the abilities which members of the other sex possess, and (2) that those abilities are necessary to the performance of the job. Referred to as the *Weeks-Diaz* formula, in application it is the *Diaz* element which is considered first in the analysis. The initial thrust of the judicial inquiry is to ascertain the business necessity of the qualifications invoked by the employer to justify its discrimination; the *Diaz* element. Once it is established that the qualifications are necessary for job performance, the *Weeks* element must be met to establish that it is impracticable to find members of the excluded class who meet these qualifications; i.e., there may be a factual basis for believing that substantially all persons of a specified sex would be unable to perform safely and efficiently the duties of the job, or it may be impossible or impracticable to determine through medical examinations, periodic reviews of job performance, and other objective tests the capacities or abilities of these people to perform the job safely and efficiently.

Determination of the scope of the bfoq exception has focused the judicial attention upon two additional areas: (1) the area of state female protective legislation and (2) the area of privacy and public morality.

State female protective laws were enacted to "protect" women from certain perceived dangers or immoralities of the workplace. They generally require employers to limit women employee's overtime opportunities, restrict the weight-lifting requirements of women and provide special working conditions for women under the theory that to do otherwise will jeopardize the health of child-bearing women. Other laws forbid women from working between certain evening hours or serving as bartenders under the theory that these environments are dangerous to the safety and morals of women. In lawsuits alleging sex-bias in employment employers have claimed that they discriminated against women workers in an effort to comply with these state protective labor laws. For example, in *Weeks* the company attempted to assert that this reliance upon the Georgia protective law prohibiting women from lifting more than 30 pounds on the job constituted a bfoq. The Fifth Circuit held that the employer's burden of proving a bfoq was not met by merely showing reliance upon a state protective law. The conflict between Title VII's provisions and state protective labor laws is resolved by the United States Constitution's supremacy clause, which provides that federal law prevails over state laws that are in conflict. Further, 708 of Title VII specifically prohibits an employer's reliance upon any law conflicting with Title VII.

In the privacy-public morality area, the issue raised is whether a bfoq exists to permit sex discrimination out of respect for another's privacy or generally accepted notions of public morality. For example, should an employer be permitted to prohibit the hiring of female attendants in male rest rooms? May a men's clothing store require that fitters be male because of the sensitive nature of measuring a man's inseam? Although no federal cases exist on the subject, two state cases are noteworthy. The Massachusetts Commission Against Discrimination ruled that the city of Boston could not restrict the job of women's bath house attendant to women, that the first qualified applicant must be hired. The city responded and hired a man as attendant.[26] In another case the Wisconsin Department of Industry, Labor and Human Relations found a trucking company guilty of sex discrimination for refusing to permit a woman truck driver to operate a dual-team rig with a male driver other than her husband.[27]

Another particular concern that working women face is that of pregnancy and the manner in which employers deal with pregnancy.

26. Fair Employment Report, March 10, 1975, p. 50.

27. Lyon v. Pirkle Refrigerated Freight Lines, Inc., Fair Employment Report, January 29, 1973, p. 30.

The fact that women are biologically different from men in their ability to bear children caused several serious questions concerning discrimination to be raised in the courts. Most of the litigation concerned maternity leave policies and pregnancy benefit provisions in employee disability plans.

The exclusion of pregnancy from disability plans was a hotly contested issue which has been recently resolved. Employers took a cost-based position, maintaining that so long as the employer's cost for benefits provided to males equaled the cost of providing female benefits, no discrimination exists. Females argued that the exclusion of pregnancy benefits constituted sex discrimination. They maintained that because only women can become pregnant only women suffer from the exclusion of pregnancy from a disability plan. Therefore, women are discriminated against because of their biological role in the procreation of the species. In General Electric Co. v. Gilbert,[28] the Supreme Court addressed the issue, holding that the General Electric Company's exclusion of pregnancy benefits was not illegal discrimination. The Court concluded that the exclusion of pregnancy from the disability program was not discriminatory because both men and women were excluded, and monetarily both sexes received the same amount of disability protection. In fact, the Court considered that it would be conceivable that if normal pregnancies were insured men would suffer discrimination because they by no means could suffer a normal pregnancy—thus women would receive a benefit that men would be incapable of receiving.

In 1978, Congress responded to the *Gilbert* decision by enacting the Pregnancy Discrimination Act, which is an amendment to the definitional section of Title VII. It makes clear that the terms "because of sex" or "on the basis of sex," as used in Title VII includes "because of or on the basis of pregnancy, childbirth or related medical conditions." The Act further provides:

> women affected by pregnancy, childbirth, or related medical conditions shall be treated the same for all employment-related purposes, including the receipt of benefits under fringe benefit programs, as other persons not so affected but similar in their ability or inability to work * * * .

Therefore, Title VII forbids discrimination in employment against women affected by pregnancy or related conditions.

4. THE EQUAL PAY ACT

Sex discrimination in wages is specifically forbidden by the Equal Pay Act of 1963. Essentially, the Equal Pay Act, a short amendment to the Fair Labor Standards Act of 1938 (the Wage-Hour Law, which provides for the federal minimum wage and the payment of overtime pay), provides for the payment of equal wages for equal work between the sexes. Until 1979 it was enforced by the Wage-Hour Divi-

28.   429 U.S. 125, 97 S.Ct. 401, 50 L.Ed.2d 343 (1976).

sion of the Labor Department in the same manner as the rest of the Wage-Hour Law. After 1979, enforcement responsibility was transferred to the EEOC under the Carter Administration's reorganization of the federal civil rights program.

The Equal Pay Act provides that no difference in pay between the two sexes can exist when the employees are performing work that requires "equal skill, effort and responsibility," and is "performed under similar working conditions." The term "equal" in the phrase "equal skill, effort and responsibility" could be construed as an obstacle for a plaintiff in proving a violation of the Act. However, in Shultz v. Wheaton Glass Co.,[29] which was the first equal pay case to reach an appellate court, the Third Circuit Court of Appeals decided in 1970 that the "equal work" standard requires that the compared jobs need only be "substantially equal," not identical. Small differences in job content will not make jobs unequal so long as the men and women who perform those jobs do essentially the same work. In *Wheaton Glass*, male glass packers performed extra menial tasks for which the employer claimed they were receiving higher pay. The court however rejected this argument and held that the work of men and women workers need not be exactly identical, but only substantially equal.

The law defines work equality in terms of equality of "skill," "effort," "responsibility," under "similar working conditions." Congress chose these factors to serve as the Act's standard primarily because they were the criteria used in standard job classification systems to evaluate jobs for classification and pay purposes. Born out of the early time and motion studies, these methods essentially quantify work content. For example, the Kress method, which is used to identify the relative worth of each job to the company, and to provide a ranking or grading of jobs (and which was used by the Labor Department in investigating charges), utilizes a professional job evaluator, usually an engineer, to observe the disputed jobs in action, taking detailed notes of what the females and males do in their respective assignments. Each of the elements are then subcategorized in the following manner and graded weights are given each element:

1. Skill (50%)

    (a) scholastic content

    (b) learning period

2. Effort (15%)

    (a) mental application

    (b) physical resistance overcome by operator

3. Responsibility (20%)

    (a) seriousness of errors

    (b) originality of problems

    (c) degree to which work is supervised

29.   421 F.2d 259 (3rd Cir. 1970).

      (d) teamwork and public contacts required

      (e) supervision exercised by operator

  4. Working Conditions (15%)

      (a) hazards and disagreeable conditions

      (b) expense to operator

Using this analysis, each element of skill, effort and the like is awarded a total number of points which are within a given pre-determined weighted range. The job with the most points is eligible for a higher rate of pay.

Thus, in determining what constitutes equal skill, effort, etc., courts and administrators will most likely define those terms according to their industrial usage. For example, in Corning Glass Works v. Brennan,[30] the Supreme Court confronted the issue of whether day-night shift differentials were to be considered in determining whether female day-shift workers were working under similar working conditions as male evening-shift workers. The Court rejected the employer's argument that different shifts constituted different working conditions which justify a higher pay rate for male night-shift workers. The Court pointed out that as understood in industrial parlance, "working conditions" did not refer to the time of day during which work is performed.

There are several exceptions to the equal work-equal pay standard. These include situations where pay differentials arise due to a seniority system, a merit system, a system where earnings are measured by the quantity or quality of work, or where the differential is based upon a factor other than sex. The first three exceptions, fully explained by an Interpretative Bulletin (available from the EEOC) which is to be given great weight by the courts and which serves as guidance for employers, are relatively simple in their application. Thus, for example, where employees of both sexes doing identical work on an assembly line are paid an individual production piece rate, and thus receive different wages, there is no equal pay violation.

The burden of establishing these exceptions falls upon the employer. The most problems occur when the employer tries to show that a wage disparity is based on a "factor other than sex." Although wage differentials based on day-night shifts are not "working conditions," nevertheless higher pay to a male can be legitimately based upon a "factor other than sex" when the male's extra rate is paid because of the night shift differential. The "factor other than sex" exception exists also with a temporary or occasional reassignment of higher paid males into lower paid female work duties with a continuation of the premium rate for the male.

A current issue is whether economic factors may constitute a "factor other than sex." In the *Wheaton Glass* case, the employer claimed that male glass packers were paid an additional 10% because of the savings the company realized from the flexibility gained by

   30. 417 U.S. 188, 94 S.Ct. 2223, 41 L.Ed.2d 1 (1974).

having male workers perform certain additional tasks normally performed by those occupying the job of "snap-up boy." The circuit court held that the company had failed to establish the exception because it had failed to prove that the savings from this flexibility amounted to 10%. Thus under *Wheaton Glass*, if an employer claims an economic basis for wage differentials the employer must be able to prove a correlation between the savings to the company and the increased earnings of the employee. This has been criticized by one commentator who wrote:

> The requirement * * * that the employer show an economic benefit from the extra duties or from having male personnel available for extra duties "commensurate with the pay differential"—appears to place an unreasonable burden on the employer and one which is not warranted by the Act. An employer should be permitted to pay additional wages for extra duties or flexibility if he, in good faith, believes the benefits are worth the additional money, without having to show an actual financial benefit in the full amount of the wage differentials. He should be allowed to exercise business judgment in such cases, to the extent that it is not a subterfuge for discrimination on the basis of sex.[31]

No sex based wage discrimination exists where the wage disparity arises out of a bona fide training program, when males in training for management jobs are required to get exposure to all facets of the establishment and thus work temporarily with females while receiving a higher rate. However the Interpretative Bulletin cautions that "Training programs which are to be available only to employees of one sex, will, however, be carefully examined to determine whether such programs are in fact, bona fide."

In complying with the Act, an employer must raise the lower wage of the aggrieved sex to the higher wage of the opposite sex, who is found to be doing equal work. Thus, an employer cannot reduce all the pay of higher paid males in order to comply, but must raise the female's wage to equal that of the highest paid male found to be doing equal work. The presence of one member of one sex being paid a higher rate than members of another sex, who are all doing equal work, is sufficient to constitute a violation of the Act.

The employer found to be in violation is also required to pay the computed back pay, which may be calculated up to two years for regular violations, and three years for willful violations. The Act also allows "liquidated damages," amounting to a total of twice the underpaid wages. These are discretionary with the courts, and unavailable in cases brought by the government.

31. G. Ginsburg, *Cases And Materials On Equal Employment* 466 (3rd Ed. 1976).

5. THE AGE DISCRIMINATION IN EMPLOYMENT ACT *

ADEA's prohibitions generally parallel those contained in Title VII. Employers are prohibited from discriminating in the hiring, compensation or other conditions of employment against persons between the ages of 40 and 70. Any segregation or classification of the employees is unlawful when it is based on age. When there has been discrimination in the payment of wages, a reduction in the higher wage rate will not cure the violation. Employment agencies are not permitted to refer prospective employees to employers on the basis of age. Unions are prohibited from excluding from membership any individual because of age. As with employers, they cannot segregate or classify their membership; and like employment agencies they are not allowed to discriminate in their referral activity. This latter prohibition primarily is directed to union hiring hall practices prevalent in the construction and shipping industries. It is additionally unlawful for a union to cause an employer to discriminate on the basis of age.

In addition to the specific prohibitions provided for each covered entity in particular, the ADEA contains certain prohibitions which are common to all. Thus it is a violation of the ADEA for employers, employment agencies and unions to indicate any preference or age discrimination in a published notice or advertisement. Furthermore, retaliatory action against individuals having participated in proceedings or pursued rights granted under the ADEA is not permitted by any covered employer.

Certain affirmative requirements also are imposed on all those covered by the Act. Employers, employment agencies and unions are required to maintain a conspicuously posted notice explaining the Act's provisions. Recordkeeping requirements also have been imposed on all covered entities in order to effectuate the administration of the Act.

Notwithstanding the ADEA's prohibitions, the Act provides certain exceptions which if established will exonerate an employer's actions. Thus it is permissible for an employer to discriminate on the basis of age "where age is a bona fide occupational qualification reasonably necessary to the normal operations of a particular business." Practices based on reasonable factors other than age, and discharges or other discipline of individuals for cause also are allowed. Further allowance is made for discriminatory practices which are pursuant to a bona fide seniority system or an employee benefit plan. In addition to these exceptions, the EEOC is authorized to establish any additional exceptions which are necessary to the public interest.

The exception provided to age-based personnel practices where age is a bona fide occupational qualification (bfoq) is a recognition

* This discussion is a slightly amended version of J. Blackburn, "Charting Compliance Under The Age Discrimination In Employment Act," 57 Chicago-Kent Law Review 559 (1981).

that the purpose of the ADEA is to prohibit arbitrary age discrimination against those who are qualified to do a job notwithstanding their age; that the Act is not intended to require the employment of those who are not qualified for a particular position. Administrative guidelines narrowly construe the exception, giving as examples occupations involving the portrayal by actors of young or elderly characters and the hiring of persons to promote products directed toward young or elderly consumers (such as the Gerber baby). The thrust of these guidelines is similar to the approach of the guidelines for determining a bfoq under Title VII, which is to focus on the authenticity of the age requirement as an essential element of the job.

In Usery v. Tamiami Trail Tours, Inc.,[32] the Fifth Circuit Court of Appeals (the same folks who brought you the *Weeks* and *Diaz* decisions) had occasion to apply its bfoq formula in an age discrimination case involving an intercity bus carrier's policy of refusing to hire applicants over age 40 for the position of bus driver. Applying the *Weeks-Diaz* formula, the circuit court upheld the lower court's decision that Tamiami had justified its policy under the exception by (1) showing that it had a factual basis for believing that its business operations (safe transportation) would be undermined by hiring over-40 drivers, and (2) by demonstrating that the individual testing of applicants was impracticable. The circuit court observed that the *Diaz* requirement that an employer show its employment criteria to be necessary to the essence of its business operations varies with the business involved. Since the carrier's business was the safe transportation of people from one place to another, the company could invoke the criteria of safe driving ability as the necessary job qualification. Having established safe driving to be related to the essence of Tamiami's business operations, the court required the company to establish either that substantially all persons over 40 were unable to perform safely and efficiently the duties of intercity bus drivers, or that it was impracticable to ascertain the safe driving abilities of over-40 drivers on an individual basis. The circuit court examined the evidence and upheld the trial court's decision that individual testing was incapable of revealing the physiological and psychological changes with sufficient reliability to meet the carrier's special safety obligations.

Two related exceptions exist where an employment determination is based on "reasonable factors other than age," or where the discharge or discipline of an employee can be shown to be for cause. Both exceptions represent two sides of the same coin, since every good cause discharge or discipline of an employee will constitute an employment practice based on a reasonable factor other than age. These exceptions reflect a recognition that discriminatory personnel practices must be distinguished from legitimate exercise of employer judgment and control.

Judicial construction of the exceptions suggests that their application is governed by a recognition of both the dictates of compelling

32. 531 F.2d 224 (5th Cir. 1976).

business conditions and the spirit of the statute. The courts have fashioned a standard that balances an employer's business judgment against the ADEA's remedial purposes. Bishop v. Jelleff Associates [33] is illustrative of this judicial posture.

In *Bishop*, a women's specialty store catering to a clientele of mature women embarked on a program designed to reduce its personnel. This was necessitated by poor business conditions and excessive payroll expenses. By discharging its older employees and expanding its product line, the company additionally hoped to appeal to a younger market. In terminating one employee, the company gave as its reason the fact that "business was falling off;" another was terminated after being advised that "business was slow." Recognizing that the company's decision to change its image and clientele represented a business decision, the D.C. District Court nevertheless held that the employment decision resulted in age discrimination, which was outweighed by the ADEA's remedial spirit.

The court's holding represents a delicate balancing of an employer's business judgment and the ADEA's legislative objectives. The court held "that the statute is not violated in the case of terminations or other employer decisions which are premised upon a rational business judgment not activated by age bias." This good faith business judgment rule represents an appreciation of what constitutes an appropriate judicial function, and reflects the long-standing tradition of judicial self-restraint. "To conclude otherwise," wrote Judge Green, "would make the federal courts a super board of directors reviewing bona fide management decisions, a procedure Congress did not intend by passage of this Act." Thus questions of "whether employee layoffs were *actually* required by business conditions, whether reductions in personnel contribute to rather than alleviate poor sales, and whether an executive in conflict with management is an able businessman are not the kind of judgments the courts are permitted to make." However, the court tempered its recognition of an employer's business judgment by cautioning that "where business judgment exceeds those instances set forth above, and reductions are predominantly of older workers for no apparent, rational reason other than age,   *   *   *   the spirit of the statute is violated."

The precise issue presented in *Bishop* was whether economic reasons may fall under the reasonable factors other than age exception. In practical terms, the issue is whether an employer may respond to economic reversals by firing older workers because of the increased labor and benefit expenses of employing them, and whether an employer may hire only young workers to attract a younger clientele. Although both *Bishop* and the administrative guidelines prohibit economic reasons from serving as reasonable factors other than age, as has been seen, courts construing a similar exception to the Equal Pay Act have held otherwise.

In deciding whether an individual personnel determination is based on a reasonable factor other than age, courts rely heavily upon

33. 398 F.Supp. 579 (D.D.C.1974).

whether the employer used ordinary, objective and valid criteria. In Stringfellow v. Monsanto Co.[34] the discharge of older workers was held to be based on reasonable factors other than age where the discharge decisions were pursuant to an employee evaluation plan which utilized eighteen criteria (one of which was productivity, and none of which was age) derived from publications of the American Management Association and other similar recognized sources. Similarly, the discharge of a fifty-year-old chemist was upheld in Gill v. Union Carbide Corp.[35] because "management, in a careful and intelligent manner, undertook to establish a system to evaluate the qualifications of each employee * * *." Interestingly enough, Union Carbide's evaluation standards included age and length of service as employment factors; however, neither was used adversely in evaluating employees, but only operated to their benefit. Even if age is unlawfully used in making a preliminary decision to discharge an employee (i.e., by a foreman), such a discharge has been declared valid where the final employee evaluation was made by someone without knowledge of the employee's age (i.e., a supervisor).

Although relying upon employer use of employee evaluations, courts permit the employee to prove such criteria to be mere pretext for discriminating on the basis of age. Thus in Hodgson v. Ideal Corrugated Box Co.,[36] an ADEA violation was found where, among other things, the employer had asked three foremen to satisfy impossible production goals and used their failure as a pretext for dismissing them.

E. PROTECTION AGAINST UNJUST DISCHARGE

JACK STIEBER, THE CASE FOR PROTECTION OF UNORGANIZED EMPLOYEES AGAINST UNJUST DISCHARGE *

Unions in the United States, though collective bargaining, have provided workers with a guarantee of due process, including the right of appeal to arbitration, in situations involving discipline or discharge for on-the-job behavior. Government employees are usually afforded similar protection under civil service and teacher tenure laws. The restriction of this protection to organized workers and government employees has rarely been questioned. This might be somewhat understandable if unions were as pervasive in the United States as in some other industrialized nations where a substantial majority of all employees belong to labor organizations. However, since only about 25 percent of U. S. workers are covered by collective bargaining

---

34.   320 F.Supp. 1175 (W.D.Ark.1970).

35.   368 F.Supp. 364 (E.D.Tenn.1973).

36.   10 F.E.P. Cases 744 (N.D.W.Va. 1974).

* Jack Stieber, "The Case for Protection of Unorganized Employees

Against Unjust Discharge," Industrial Relations Research Association 32nd Annual Proceedings 155 (1979); © 1979 by the Industrial Relations Research Association. Reprinted by permission.

agreements, it is indeed strange that relatively little attention has been paid to the fact that a majority of all private-sector employees—numbering over 50 million people—may, in the language of a recent court decision, be discharged "for any or no reason."

In recent years, a number of industrial relations scholars have called attention to the need for judicial or legislative action to protect all employees against unjust discharge. However, thus far the courts have not heeded their advice and legislators, at both the federal and state levels, have not seen fit to deal with this problem.

*   *   *

A Comparative View

The United States stands almost alone among industrialized nations in not providing statutory protection against unjust discharge or "unfair dismissal" as it is commonly called in most countries. Protection against unfair dismissal has been the subject of an International Labour Organization Recommendation, a Proposal for Legislation in the European Common Market, and statutes in individual countries in Western Europe.

Recommendation 119 on "Termination of Employment at the Initiative of the Employer" was adopted by the International Labour Organization on June 26, 1963, by a vote of 196 to 74 with 10 abstentions. It provides: "Termination of employment should not take place unless there is a valid reason for such termination connected with the capacity or conduct of the worker or based on the operational requirements of the undertaking, establishment or service."

The Recommendation states that a worker who feels that his employment has been unjustly terminated should be able to appeal the termination to "a body established under a collective agreement or to a neutral body such as a court, an arbitrator, an arbitration committee or a similar body." If the termination is found to be unjustified, the tribunal should be entitled to order that the worker be reinstated or be paid "adequate compensation" or other appropriate relief. Except for cases of "serious misconduct," a terminated worker should be given "a reasonable period of notice or compensation in lieu thereof." Dismissal for serious misconduct should be limited to cases "where the employer cannot in good faith be expected to take any other course." A worker accused of serious misconduct should be given an opportunity to state his case promptly, with the assistance of a representative where appropriate.

A 1976 Report of the European Commission drew attention to the variation in conditions, procedures, and legal consequences of dismissal provisions in Member States, and put forward proposals to serve as a basis for an EC directive on individual dismissals. The Commission Report proposes that Member State laws and minimum standards be harmonized along the following lines:

1. Dismissal is justified only when "serious grounds" exist. "Serious grounds" is defined in terms of "urgent requirements of the firm," i.e., " *   *   * when it is impossible or unreasonable,

for economic or technical reasons or for reasons connected with the person or behavior of the worker, for the employer to continue the employment relationship."

(a) Personal grounds shall be deemed to exist only when a worker has, over a long period of time, shown himself to be incapable of carrying out his duties.

(b) Behavorial grounds for dismissal presuppose a serious breach of a worker's obligations under the individual contract of employment.

(c) Even when grounds exist, dismissal should be a last resort. When dismissal is unavoidable, employers should take account of a worker's age, length of service, future job prospects, and family circumstances.

2. A worker is entitled to written notice and, on request, a written statement of the grounds for dismissal. He should also be advised of his legal remedies.

3. Except in cases of "summary dismissal," minimum notice of 30 days should be given.

4. Summary dismissal should be resorted to only if the worker is guilty of such a severe breach of his obligations under the contract of employment that the employer cannot reasonably be expected to observe a notice period.

5. The legality of every dismissal must, at the request of the worker, be examined by an independent body.

6. Protection against dismissal should be provided only to employees with at least six months service in the undertaking.

Protection against unfair dismissal is provided by statute in all Common Market countries and in Sweden and Norway.

Most countries limit protection against unfair dismissal to employees who have completed a probationary period, usually six months. However, Sweden covers all workers except "supervisory and managerial" employees who are fairly high in the hierarchy, and Norway provides protection to all employees. Ireland excludes employees with less than one year of service. In Great Britain, the Conservative Government has raised the qualifying period from six to twelve months. Statutes in a few countries do not apply to employers with less than a minimum number of employees (5 in West Germany; 15 in Italy).

"Unfair dismissal" is defined in various ways: "socially unwarranted" in West Germany; not for "real and serious reasons" in France; not for "objectively valid grounds" in Sweden. In most countries, the burden of proving that a dismissal is "fair" rests on the employer. However, in France there is no clear onus of proof established by statute and in Britain, the Conservative Government has proposed "that the onus of proof as to reasonableness of a dismissal should be made neutral as between employer and employee."

An employee is entitled to be given reasons for dismissal, upon request, in all countries.

Advance notice, ranging from 40 hours to six months, is required for ordinary dismissal in all countries. However, advance notice is not required in cases of summary dismissal. In France, summary dismissal may only be for "flagrant" or "gross" misconduct. In Germany, dismissal without notice is permitted only when it is not reasonable to expect an employer to continue the employment relationship. Belgium limits summary dismissal to situations in which the employment is adjudged to be "immediately and definitely impossible." In the Netherlands, there must be "urgent cause" to justify summary dismissal. And in Norway, there must have been "a serious and fundamental breach of contract."

Reinstatement is rarely permitted and, where permitted, is rarely employed as a remedy by the courts which have jurisdiction over dismissal cases in most countries. Compensation is the most common remedy available to a worker who has been unfairly dismissed. The amount of compensation varies from one country to another. Six months' compensation in addition to notice payments is the maximum in several countries. Ireland, however, permits up to 104 weeks' compensation, Sweden up to 48 months' damages, and Norway provides for "reasonable" compensation with no upper limit.

Some Relevant Considerations

Robert Howlett will present "A Practical Proposal" for legislation in this session. There are, however, a few questions to be answered before considering ways of dealing with the problem.

How Significant Is the Problem?

There are no hard data which would permit us to determine accurately how many unorganized employees are dismissed without just cause in the United States during any given period. Indeed, we do not know how many discharge grievances are appealed to arbitration under collective bargaining agreements or what proportion are sustained. However, we do know that discipline and discharge questions are more frequently arbitrated than any other issue.

Apart from the logic and morality of affording protection against unjust discharge to all employees, there is evidence that the problem is one of considerable magnitude.

Of the 67 million private industry employees in 1977, some 17 million were covered by collective bargaining agreements, almost all of which include negotiated grievance and arbitration procedures. This leaves about 50 million unprotected employees.

Unpublished data from the Bureau of Labor Statistics indicate that the annual discharge rate in manufacturing industries is about 4.6 percent. There are no data available for other industries. Assuming that the nonmanufacturing discharge rate is approximately the same as in manufacturing and that there is no difference in the tendency to invoke discharge as between union and nonunion employers, there would have been about 2.3 million employees discharged for cause in 1977 by private-sector employers who were not unionized.

One could reasonably argue that employers should have complete freedom to dismiss employees who are still undergoing a probationary period without having to show just cause. In fact, most union agreements do not protect probationary workers against dismissal. Assuming a six-month probationary period, which is longer than is provided under most agreements, about 20 percent of all employees would not be entitled to protection. Since probationary employees are much more likely to be discharged than longer service employees, I have also assumed that the discharge rate for these employees is five times that for nonprobationary employees. Given these conservative assumptions, I estimate that about one million private industry employees with more than six months' service were discharged in 1977 without the right to a fair hearing and a decision by an impartial tribunal as to the justness of their termination.

What Proportion of These Discharges Are Likely to Have Been Unjustified?

Nobody knows for sure. However, it would appear from published arbitration decisions that as many as half of all discharges appealed to arbitration are found to have been made without "just cause." In such cases, arbitrators usually reinstate the grievant to his or her job with full, partial, or no back pay depending upon the circumstances of the case. It would be surprising if nonunion employers, who know that their decisions are not appealable to arbitration, would fare better at the hands of an impartial tribunal than union employers who know that there is a strong likelihood that they will have to persuade an arbitrator of the fairness of their discharge decisions. Unfortunately, there are no statistics on the proportion of all discharges that are appealed to arbitration under collective bargaining agreements. Assuming that one-third of all discharges are appealed to arbitration, which may be an underestimate in view of increasing union concern over unfair-representation complaints brought by members; and assuming further that nonunionized discharged employees would appeal and win their cases in the same proportion as unionized workers, some 150,000 to 200,000 of them would have been reinstated to their former jobs in 1977, if they had had recourse to an impartial tribunal. There is no reason to believe that 1977 was an atypical year.

Why Should Protection Against Unjust Discharge Be Treated Differently Than Other Contractual Advantages of Union over Nonunion Employees?

In principle, employees should be protected against all unjust discipline. However, I favor limiting initial statutory protection to discharge because it is the most severe penalty that an employer can assess against an employee. Not only does a discharged employee lose a job and the income and benefits that go with it; but, in addition, being fired may stigmatize an employee both as a worker and as a person. Typical reasons for discharge include: excessive absenteeism and/or tardiness, loafing or sleeping on the job, leaving work without permission, fighting, insubordination, use of profanity or abusive language to supervision, falsifying records, theft, dishonesty, disloyalty to the employer, incompetence, negligence or carelessness in work performance, gambling, possession or use of drugs or alcoholic beverages, chronic alcoholism, etc.

It is not surprising that employers may be reluctant to hire workers who have been discharged from previous jobs for one or more of the above reasons. As a result, discharged employees have difficulty finding new jobs and may have to accept less attractive employment than their education, training, and skill would otherwise warrant. Furthermore, in a work-oriented society such as we live in, being fired from a job can affect a person's relationships with spouse, family, friends, and the community, not to speak of the effect on one's own feelings of self-worth. In short, the consequences go far beyond the economic and other work-related disadvantages that may flow from working for a nonunion as opposed to a union employer.

Why Can't Employers Establish Procedures to Protect Against Unfair Dismissal on Their Own?

Many nonunion employers have recognized the need for procedures whereby employees can complain against unjust treatment by supervisors. The Bureau of National Affairs (BNA) recently published the results of a survey among nonunion companies regarding recourse provided their employees who feel that they have been disciplined unfairly. The BNA found that most of the 128 responding companies have a mechanism for employees to appeal disciplinary actions. But less than half have a formal complaint procedure, and often the procedures are not used. The major problems reported with procedures by the companies were delay in getting complaints resolved and employees' fear of reprisal from supervisors. Only two of the companies provided for outside arbitration as a final step in the complaint procedure, but neither company reported any experience with arbitration.

While these efforts by nonunion employers are meritorious, almost all lack the essential element of credibility among employees because they have been unilaterally instituted and, more important, the final decision on all complaints is made by management. No matter how well-intentioned, sincere, and honest their efforts, management decisions cannot have the acceptability of judgments made by an outsider with no ties to the company.

Conclusion

In discussing this subject before various groups, I have yet to find any one who takes issue with the principle that employees should be entitled to protection against unjust discharge. The questions most frequently raised are: (1) What evidence is there that employees need such protection? (2) How much will it cost?

I have tried to respond to the first question by showing, on the basis of available data and relatively conservative assumptions, that more than a million employees with at least six months' seniority are being deprived of their jobs each year without due process.   Even if—contrary to my assumptions—the discharge rate in nonmanufacturing is lower than in manufacturing, nonunion employers are less prone than union employers to discharge employees without just cause, the discharge rate for probationary employees is greater than five times that of employees with more than six months of service, and the proportion of discharges appealed to arbitration is less than one-third of the total, there would still be thousands of employees fired each year without just cause.

Consider the attention given by the media and Congress to employees who lose their jobs because they engage in political activities which are objectionable to their employers, or who "blow the whistle" on corporations knowingly producing and selling defective products or violating environmental protection laws, or who otherwise exercise their constitutional right of free speech and assembly.   Certainly these employees deserve to be protected, and there is already a move afoot to legislate in this area.   I would point out, however, that by providing due process for *all* discharged employees, we would be protecting not only the small number of activists mentioned above, but also thousands of others who are just as deserving of protection.

The cost of providing due process for discharged employees will depend on the specific provisions of the legislation and how many employees avail themselves of the protection.   A few years of experimentation, possibly with different state statutes, will be necessary before accurate cost estimates can be made.   We have long since determined that administration of laws dealing with wages and hours, equal employment opportunity, environmental protection, consumer protection, and private- and public-sector labor-management relations are proper government functions.   Protection against unjust discharge, which is already available to one-third of U. S. employees and is provided in other industrialized nations, is equally justifiable on moral, social, and economic grounds.

ROBERT G. HOWLETT, DUE PROCESS FOR NONUNIONIZED EMPLOYEES: A PRACTICAL PROPOSAL *

* * *

What should be included in legislation to protect employees from unjust discharge and discipline?   As in all legislation, the supporters must assess the political climate and strive for the "possible."

* Robert G. Howlett, "Due Process for Nonunionized Employees: A Practical Proposal," Industrial Relations Research Association 32nd Annual Proceedings 164 (1979); © 1979 by the Industrial Relations Research Association. Reprinted by permission.

Categories of Employees to Be Included

Length of Service

Probationary periods are common under collective bargaining agreements. Coverage under the act should be limited to employees who have developed some seniority with an employer. I suggest one year. By that time, an employee who has not performed at least reasonably well will have been terminated.

Supervisors

Anyone experienced in employer-employee relations knows that some of the most arbitrary and capricious discharges are those visited on supervisors. However, if legislation is to be enacted, it is advisable to exclude supervisors as defined in NLRA. Opposition of business representatives may be softened if supervisors are excluded.

Public Employees

There are two reasons (neither conceptual) to exclude public employees. First, public employees have protections, unavailable to private-sector employees, through court-enforced constitutional rights, civil service, and in the case of public school teachers, tenure acts. Second, political opposition to the statute will be intensified if an attempt is made to include public employees.

Administration of the Process

Nearly 40 states have agencies which administer public-sector employer-employee relations statutes and a few states have private-sector statutes. The act could be administered by the existing labor relations agency. I think there is merit, however, in placing jurisdiction under a Department of Labor or Department of Labor and Industry. There may be less political opposition to enactment if administration is separated from the employer-union relationship procedure. In addition, mediators and administrative law judges who deal with representation and unfair labor practice issues are experienced in and used to organizational, as distinguished from individual, procedures.

The statute should provide for a written request addressed to the administering agency. No filing fee should be required.

Coverage

Acts covered should include: (1) discharge and other involuntary termination, including termination alleged to be voluntary; (2) disciplinary suspension; and (3) promotion and demotion.

If disciplinary suspensions are not included, an employer could impose a lengthy suspension which would, in fact, be a discharge. The inclusion of promotions and demotions may excite political opposition. However, employees can be—and are—"punished" by demotion and refusal to promote.

With one caveat, I would exclude discrimination cases covered by statute, unless employer and employee agree to use of the process. However, complete exclusion is not possible as there are cases where a reason advanced for discipline or discharge is a cover-up for discriminatory action. In such cases, the process should be applicable, recognizing that under Alexander v. Gardner-Denver, 415 U.S. 36, 94 S.Ct. 1011, 39 L.Ed.2d 147, 7 FEP Cases 81 (1974), an employee has a right to institute court action following arbitration.

Mediation

The primary procedure for unresolved grievances should be mediation. As discussed above, I think it advisable not to use mediators from the agency which performs this service in collective bargaining relationships.

In a number of states, including Michigan, staff mediators perform a significant amount of grievance mediation.

Mediators serving in the nonorganized area can be expected to take affirmative positions more often than mediators in collective bargaining relationships. They will, more than in the organized sector, serve as "informal" arbitrators in grievance administration.

Impasse Resolution after Mediation

What if mediation does not resolve the disagreement? There are three possibilities: (1) end the procedure with mediation; (2) submit the dispute to fact-finding; or (3) submit the dispute to arbitration, either directly or following fact-finding.

Mediation, without more, is better than nothing. However, there cannot be a true determination of "just cause" for discipline or discharge without a quasi-judicial or judicial procedure.

Patently, arbitration is the better terminal process. But political realities may dictate only fact-finding.

The unions perform a screening process by deciding whether a complaint not resolved during the grievance procedure shall be submitted to arbitration. Under collective bargaining, an employee does not have power to submit his case to arbitration.

The administering agency should provide for a screening process before fact-finding or arbitration through an official who, like an examining magistrate or regional director of the National Labor Relations Board (NLRB), decides whether there is cause to believe that the grievance has merit. An affirmative decision will result in the case proceeding to fact-finding or arbitration.

Selection of the Arbitrator

Some state agencies maintain panels of arbitrators. Or, a state could employ the services of the AAA; or the Federal Mediation and Conciliation Service might be willing to perform this function for a state.

An alternative is to have the state employ a full-time hearing officer, or a hearing officer performing another quasi-judicial function until it is determined how heavy the case load will be. Another alternative is a full- or part-time hearing officer, and ad hoc arbitrators for overloads.

Payment for the Arbitration

This is a key political consideration. There will be opposition on the ground that the cost of arbitration is unknown, and could be great, although excessive cost seems unlikely if there is adequate screening. However, if a state is interested in "justice," cost considerations should be weighed against expected fair and equitable results.

Court systems are expensive, but justice for a state's citizens requires that the taxpayers pay this cost.

If the reviewing officer decides that the grievance is sufficiently meritorious to proceed to fact-finding or arbitration, the employee should be required to pay a small fee ($50 to $100).

Presentation of Cases to Fact-finding or Arbitration

An experienced official of the administering agency should be assigned to present the grievances to fact-finding or arbitration. In a number of states, including Michigan and Wisconsin, unfair labor practice cases are presented by charging parties, generally through a union represented by a lawyer or staff official. Individual employees seldom have the competence necessary to marshall evidence and present it effectively. The statute should authorize the arbitrator to direct reinstatement or award damages, and additional remedies as under the Canadian Labour Code.

Conclusion

A bill to provide the basic right of fair treatment to employees in nonorganized enterprises does not have much political attraction for legislators. Unorganized employees have no formal groups; hence, they have little impact on elections. However, there may be legislators who believe in individual human rights and who have the "guts" and ability to take such a bill and develop a "common man" lobby. Such a legislator might become a hero and, if not, his effort would help him to continue his legislative career with a clear conscience and with the knowledge that he is promoting justice and equity for a group for which it does not exist and which has no "special interest" political influence.

F. THE RIGHT TO A SAFE WORKPLACE

MORRIS E. DAVIS, WORKPLACE HEALTH & SAFETY— COLLECTIVE BARGAINING TRENDS *

Most American working men and women spend at least one-half of their waking hours in the workplace. Many are exposed at some time to health and/or safety hazards. Each year thousands are maimed, disabled, or killed from job-related injuries or diseases. Na-

* Morris E. Davis, "Workplace Health & Safety—Collective Bargaining Trends," 8 San Fernando Valley Law Review 59 (1980); © 1980 by the San Fernando Valley Law Review. Reprinted by permission.

tional Safety Council surveys have consistently estimated approximately 14,000 deaths due to accidents on the job and 2.2 million disabling injuries annually. In reference to the incidence of disease, the U. S. Department of Health, Education, and Welfare estimates 390,000 new cases of occupational disease each year, and in excess of 100,000 deaths caused by hazardous workplace exposures. Most recently, the National Cancer Institute and the National Institute of Environmental Health Sciences released a report associating increased incidence of nationwide cancer with occupational exposure to toxic substances. Workplace exposure to such substances as asbestos, arsenic, benzene, coal tar pitch volatiles, and chromium were estimated to cause 20–38 percent of all cancer incidence in forthcoming decades.

During the late 1960's such statistics provided the background for organized labor's role and the government response to this occupational safety and health epidemic. In 1969 the federal Coal Mine Health and Safety Act was passed on the heels of a mine explosion which killed 78 miners in Farmington, West Virginia. The enactment of this law coupled with increased pressure from industrial unions for equal coverage were the two major factors contributing to the eventual passage of the 1970 federal Occupational Safety and Health Act.

Prior to enactment of the 1970 Act, organized labor exhibited little evidence of a comprehensive bargaining strategy for workplace safety and health. Narrowly tailored federal legislation reflected this weakness and, hence, focused on special interest areas. For example, the Federal Bureau of Mines was established as early as 1910 to monitor mine safety. However, it did not receive authority to promulgate and enforce safety and health standards until 1952. In 1916 the Federal Employees Compensation Act was passed, providing compensation for job-related injuries incurred by federal employees. Protective legislation aimed at workers other than federal employees was enacted in 1936 with passage of the Walsh-Healey Public Contracts Act. The objective was to require employers with government contracts exceeding $10,000 to comply with specific safety and health standards.

Almost 30 years after enactment of the Walsh-Healey Act, Congress passed the McNamara-O'Hara Public Service Contract Act of 1965, which extended the same limited health and safety protections to suppliers of government services. It was, therefore, not until passage of the 1969 Coal Mine Health and Safety Act, that a major industrial union, the United Mine Workers of America, sought comprehensive federal legislation to address the increasing injury, disease, and death rates among its membership.

The provisions of the Coal Mine Health and Safety Act reflected significant issues which the UMW had unsuccessfully attempted to resolve through the bargaining process. Periodic site investigations and monitoring, general safety standards, respirable dusts exposure limits, adequate training, and jointly conducted inspections were all issues which the bargaining process had been unable to consistently resolve. In addition, the UMW sought to break new ground by attempting to obtain federal recognition of and compensation for an occupational disease: pneumoconiosis.

The subsequent Coal Mine Act, therefore, set mandatory health and safety standards for underground mines, appropriated aid to states for the implementation or improvement of state protection and compensation programs, and provided for federal funding of research into coal miners' pneumoconiosis, better known as "black lung" disease. The act also guaranteed compensation for disabled mine workers or their widows.

RELATIONSHIP OF THE OSHACT TO COLLECTIVE BARGAINING

The history of health and safety collective bargaining has been substantially affected by socio-economic and political conditions. The 1930's and 1940's showed a general lack of emphasis on workplace safety. The depression, coupled with World War II, required that organized labor concern itself with wages and the establishment of union rights. However, by the 1960's a new factor entered the picture: environmental control

"As the country became conscious of air and water pollution, a parallel concern about the polluted working environment developed. This coincided with several other elements: sharp increases in industrial accidents starting in 1958, research into the danger of new chemicals and other physical agents, and general prosperity which enabled unions to work for non-wage demands and management to pay for needed controls."

In addition, the 1967 decision of NLRB v. Gulf Power Co.[10] rejected the argument that workplace health and safety was a management function, and therefore not subject to negotiation. In this case, two International Brotherhood of Electrical Workers (IBEW) locals demanded negotiations on the company's safety rules for the following year's contract. The company contended that because it was required by statute to exercise a high degree of care in its utility operations, all safety matters were the prerogative of management and outside its duty to bargain collectively. In rejecting this argument, the 5th Circuit likened safety laws to minimum wage and other governmental regulations which establish minimum requirements on various subjects, but which do not preclude negotiations about the same issues. Finally, the court reasoned that Section 8(d) of the Taft-Hartley Act required employers to bargain in good faith on wages and other terms and conditions of employment. The phrase "other terms and conditions of employment" was sufficiently broad to include safety rules and practices.

This decision, coupled with the aforementioned environmental focus and increasing rates of job-related accidents, diseases, and deaths in the private sector, provided the forum from which the pending

10.   384 F.2d 822 (5th Cir. 1967).

1970 OSHAct would emerge. After considerable compromise, the
Federal Occupational Safety and Health Act of 1970 was enacted,
with its objectives being to "assure so far as possible every working
man and woman in the nation safe and healthful working conditions
and to preserve our human resources. * * * "

Generally the OSHAct encourages employers to reduce hazards in
the workplace and initiate new or improve existing safety and health
programs. The Act also: (1) authorizes the Occupational Safety and
Health Administration (OSHA) to establish mandatory safety and
health standards; (2) provides for compliance, enforcement, administrative appeal and research functions; and (3) encourages states to
administer and enforce their own safety and health programs "at
least as effective" as the federal program. The law therefore had
the potential of impacting on labor-management relations because it
required negotiators for both sides to increase their own knowledge
of the terminology and issues of concern related to securing safe and
healthful working conditions.

More specifically, the Act prescribed a general duty of the employer to provide a safe working environment. In order to insure active
involvement, the law grants workers the right to file a complaint with
OSHA when it is believed that a violation of a safety or health standard exists. Employers are also required under the Act to monitor
exposure to regulated harmful substances and permit the workers an
opportunity to observe the monitoring and to have access to the monitoring reports.

Worker and union access to management health and safety data
was one of the most critical issues raised during the pre-legislation
stage. In response, the Act requires warning signs and labels when
workers are exposed to regulated hazardous materials. In the event
of excessive exposure, the Act requires the employer to both inform
workers of each instance of exposure, and of corrective measures being taken to reduce or eliminate such exposures. To further insure
participation and utilization of the above provisions, the Act prohibits
any employer retaliation or discrimination against workers for filing
a complaint, testifying in a matter instituted under the Act, or exercising any other right afforded under the law.

Finally, the OSHAct establishes specific procedural processes
which complement the substantive obligations of the employer and
define the parameters for union involvement. For example, union
representatives may: (1) be present as witnesses during federal investigations; (2) accompany an inspector during the walk-around investigation; (3) directly file a federal complaint in behalf of affected
workers; (4) request an informal hearing if the inspector determines
that no violations exist; (5) elect "party" status or appear as witnesses in an employer contested enforcement matter before the Occupational Safety and Health Review Commission; (6) petition OSHA for
new or improved standards; and (7) challenge the validity of any
OSHA promulgated standard in the appropriate U. S. Circuit Court.

BRIDGING THE GAP BETWEEN OSHA AND COLLECTIVE BARGAINING

Notwithstanding the specific dictates of the OSHAct, many areas still require clearer guidelines if work-site safety programs are to be effective. Therefore, expanding on OSHA requirements, or establishing procedures and payment mechanisms to facilitate workplace programs, has been the focus of recent union attention. The following issues serve to illustrate the scope of bargaining activity since passage of the Act in 1970.

I. *General Duty Clause*

Securing the employers' commitment to provide a safe and healthful workplace, and to comply with all applicable state and federal health and safety laws.

II. *Specific Employer Obligations*

(a) To furnish, maintain and replace all required protective clothing and related mechanical devices.

(b) To furnish adequate heating, ventilation, lighting and noise control systems.

(c) To guarantee that all equipment and machine processes comply with state and federal standards.

(d) To furnish medical aid for job-related injuries; first aid training for supervisors; and immediate transportation for medical treatment in case of emergency.

(e) To furnish specific protections against working with hazardous and toxic materials.

(f) To furnish medical surveillance services for workers exposed to hazardous substances such as lead, arsenic, asbestos, benzene, or radiation exposure.

(g) To provide health and safety training for current, new and transferred workers.

III. *Specific Employee Rights*

(a) The right to refuse to work when confronted with hazards posing imminent danger.

(b) The right to rate retention if a worker is temporarily removed from a job due to occupational hazards.

(c) The right to return to work after an industrial injury or illness.

(d) The right to special seniority considerations in cases of industrial injury or illness.

(e) The right to be protected against discriminatory actions when engaging in health and safety activities.

(f) The right to supplemental pay in addition to compensation benefits in cases of industrial injury or illness.

(g) The right of fertile workers to be protected against substances which may cause damage to the reproductive system and for pregnant workers to have transfer rights during their pregnancy.

(h) The right to information on the types of chemicals being used and the generic description of substances for adequate identification.

(i) The right to work in accordance with adequate crew or staffing pattern requirements, with related prohibitions against speed-up.

(j) The right to strike in concert with other employees over health and safety issues.

(k) The right to jointly select physicians providing medical surveillance services, with direct access to written medical reports, reports, and files.

(l) The right to be paid while participating in discussions, meetings, and other activities relative to health and safety.

IV. *Specific Union Rights*

(a) The right of authorized representatives of the union to enter the workplace to investigate any health and safety problem.

(b) The right to investigate any accident, with unrestricted access to accident sites, samples, and related information.

(c) The right to commission its own consultants, engineers, and industrial hygienists to conduct independent surveys of the workplace.

(d) The right to tag a job or shut down an unsafe operation.

(e) The right to call for selective work stoppages or strikes over health and safety issues.

(f) The right to full information on chemical hazards encountered by its members.

(g) The right to send health and safety committee members to training programs, with expenses paid by the employer.

(h) The right to designate workers who shall be paid lost-time wages for health and safety related activities, or where appropriate, designate full and part-time health and safety representatives, paid by the employer.

(i) The right of access to employer information on the health conditions of members and to results of special health studies.

(j) The right to commission independent organizations to conduct occupational research on the health status of its members; with such studies to be financed through jointly administered trust funds.

(k) The right to be notified of any new machinery, work processes, or changes in plant design, prior to installation or operation.

(*l*) The right of full access to all workers' compensation records retained by the employer.

V. *Specific Union Procedural Rights*

(a) Clear recognition of union health and safety representatives.

(b) An orderly procedure for joint resolution of health and safety issues.

(c) The right to grieve and arbitrate any issue related to workplace health and safety.

(d) Provisions for regular meetings, record keeping, selection of agenda items, and rotation of officers in regards to joint health and safety committee functions.

(e) Accelerated procedures for effectively handling refusal to work situations.

DEVELOPING TRENDS IN WORKPLACE HEALTH AND SAFETY

The aforementioned areas of bargaining are by no means totally reflective of the most recent trends in this area. If one were to speculate about the future of occupational safety and health, several developments are instructional.

In 1976, a health and safety professional staff survey was conducted among the 15 international unions most active in this field. At that time 37 individuals were identified as having full or part-time responsibilities. In less than three years, that number has increased to more than 78 professionals working for 26 internationals and locals. In addition, a new occupational safety and health department, within the National AFL–CIO, was established in 1978. Furthermore, 42 new health and safety training programs have been established within the past eighteen months at universities throughout the country.

Another trend has been the promulgation of standards and the adoption of regulations by OSHA *after* the same issues have been negotiated through the bargaining process. For example, OSHA regulations were adopted for all of the following items after labor-management contractual provisions had been negotiated:

1. Lost-time pay for worker involvement in any OSHA-related investigation or other activity;

2. Individual and union receipt of all OSHA injury and illness reports, rather than simply being able to review such;

3. Rate retention provisions for workers removed from jobs involving hazardous exposures to toxic materials;

4. Direct worker and union access to and receipt of company financed medical opinions related to hazardous exposures;

5. Refusal to work provisions where unsafe conditions pose imminent danger; and

6. Specific training and educational programs for workers exposed to regulated substances or work processes.

In the area of research, international unions have conducted or commissioned significant mortality and morbidity studies for their members, using results to negotiate improved working conditions. For example, the United Rubber Workers have concentrated on such carcinogens as vinyl chloride, solvents, acrylonitrile, benzene, and toluene. The International Asbestos Workers Union is considered a pioneer in the field of asbestos-related cancer research and for providing compensation, diagnosis, and treatment services. The United Steelworkers of America negotiated an early retirement agreement for its foundry members after studies showed increased death rates from job-related lung cancer and other respiratory diseases.

In addition, we are beginning to see more and more coalition groups between labor unions and public interest groups around the issue of health and safety. Examples of this include the coalitions between the Oil, Chemical and Atomic Workers union, and the Washington D.C.-based Public Citizens Health Research Group. That effort in 1972 resulted in the promulgation of the first governmental regulations for work place exposure to 14 cancer causing agents. There have also been coalitions between the Amalgamated Clothing and Textile Workers Union and local chapters of the Brown Lung Association, specifically around the issue of improving working conditions for workers exposed to cotton dust, and also around the issue of pain and compensation for those workers who have incurred the respiratory illness referred to as byssinosis—so called "brown lung" disease.

There have also been a growing number of collaborative efforts around the country to create Committees on Occupational Safety and Health (COSH). These groups, composed of union, medical and legal representatives, have focused on efforts to improve worker compensation programs, represent the interests of minority workers, and monitor compliance and enforcement aspects of state and federal OSHA programs. These COSH groups have also been actively promoting a worker "right-to-know" campaign, with the objective being to require all employers to disclose the generic name of toxic substances to which workers are exposed. The campaign is also aimed at assuring worker access to employer-conducted medical examination and industrial hygiene monitoring data.

One other trend which should be mentioned is that in the past five years we have begun to see an increasing number of negligence suits brought by individual union members against their respective locals and internationals. These suits have focused primarily upon the union's inability to police the contract, especially where there is specific language imposing upon them a duty to do so; the lack of such policing resulting in death, injury, or disease to specific workers. Negligence suits have been successfully brought in the past five years throughout the country. The latest development in this area occurred in December 1978, when the United States Supreme Court refused to review a decision by the Missouri Court of Appeals whereby the court had awarded damages to an individual worker against the local, the international, and the individual shop steward who was present at the time this particular worker was electrocuted.

Finally, in the last five years organized labor has increased its involvement in the OSHA standard-setting process. It has successully petitioned for new or improved standards for 13 specific carcinogens, in addition to asbestos, inorganic arsenic, coke-oven emissions, and lead. It has also increased its court challenges of OSHA promulgated standards.

Therefore, it is safe to state that new ground has been broken in the field of labor relations and workplace health and safety. Labor, management, and government should be supported and encouraged for their collective efforts to "preserve our human resources."

Although the OSHAct represents a significant step in regulating workplace safety and health conditions, the act provides workers with limited redress. Several problems arise with an employee's use of the OSHAct to enforce his or her rights. An employee can report violations and be protected from discharge for doing so, but no private cause of action exists to enforce the act. Only the Department of Labor has such enforcement power. Further, problems with bureaucratic machinery and OSHA staff size cut into the act's practical uses. For private redress the worker must resort to an action at common law.

In most jurisdictions employers have a common law duty to provide employees with a reasonably safe place to work. Employee redress for breach of this duty is in the form of a civil action for negligence. The following case shows a state court applying common law to protect a nonsmoking employee from the dangers of "sidestream smoke," smoke that comes from the lighted end of a cigarette or is exhaled by smokers.

SHIMP v. NEW JERSEY BELL TELEPHONE COMPANY

New Jersey Superior Court, 1976.
145 N.J.Super. 516, 368 A.2d 408.

GRUCCIO, J. S. C.

This case involves a matter of first impression in this State: whether a nonsmoking employee is denied a safe working environment and entitled to injunctive relief when forced by proximity to smoking employees to involuntarily inhale "second hand" cigarette smoke.

Plaintiff seeks to have cigarette smoking enjoined in the area where she works. She alleges that her employer, defendant N. J. Bell Telephone Co., is causing her to work in an unsafe environment by refusing to enact a ban against smoking in the office where she works. The company allows other employees to smoke while on the job at desks situated in the same work area as that of plaintiff. Plaintiff contends that the passive inhalation of smoke and the gaseous by-products of burning tobacco is deleterious to her health. Therefore her employer, by permitting employees to smoke in the work area, is allowing an unsafe condition to exist. The present action is a suit to enjoin these allegedly unsafe conditions, thereby restoring to plaintiff a healthy environment in which to work.

The attorneys have submitted affidavits in lieu of oral testimony and it has been agreed that I will decide the issue upon submission of briefs by counsel. Plaintiff's affidavit clearly outlines a legitimate grievance based upon a genuine health problem. She is allergic to cigarette smoke. Mere passive inhalation causes a severe allergic reaction which has forced her to leave work physically ill on numerous occasions.

Plaintiff's representations are substantiated by the affidavits of attending physicians who confirm her sensitivity to cigarette smoke and the negative effect it is having upon her physical well-being. Plaintiff's symptoms evoked by the presence of cigarette smoke include severe throat irritation, nasal irritation sometimes taking the form of nosebleeds, irritation to the eyes which has resulted in corneal abrasion and corneal erosion, headaches, nausea and vomiting. It is important to note that a remission of these symptoms occurs whenever plaintiff remains in a smoke-free environment. Further, it appears that a severe allergic reaction can be triggered by the presence of as little as one smoker adjacent to plaintiff.

Plaintiff sought to alleviate her intolerable working situation through the use of grievance mechanisms established by collective bargaining between defendant employer and her union. That action, together with other efforts of plaintiff and her physician, resulted in the installation of an exhaust fan in the vicinity of her work area. This attempted solution has proven unsuccessful because of the fan was not kept in continuous operation. The other employees complained of cold drafts due to the fan's operation, and compromises involving operation at set intervals have proven ineffective to prevent the onset of plaintiff's symptoms in the presence of smoking co-employees. The pleadings indicate plaintiff has tried every avenue open to her to get relief prior to instituting this action for injunctive relief.

It is clearly the law in this State that an employee has a right to work in a safe environment. An employer is under an affirmative duty to provide a work area that is free from unsafe conditions. This right to safe and healthful working conditions is protected not only by the duty imposed by common law upon employers, but has also been the subject of federal legislation. In 1970 Congress enacted the Occupational Safety and Health Act (OSHA) which expresses a policy of prevention of occupational hazards. The act authorizes the Secretary of Labor to set mandatory occupational safety and health standards in order to assure safe and healthful working conditions. Under the general duty clause Congress imposed upon the employer a duty to eliminate all foreseeable and preventable hazards. OSHA in no way preempted the field of occupational safety. Specifically, 29 U.S.C.A. § 653(b)(4) recognizes concurrent state power to act either legislatively or judicially under the common law with regard to occupational safety.

* * *

Where an employer is under a common law duty to act, a court of equity may enforce an employee's rights by ordering the employer to eliminate any preventable hazardous condition which the court finds to exist. The courts of New Jersey have long been open to protect basic employees' rights by injunction. * * *

Since plaintiff has a common law right to a safe working environment, the issue remains whether the work area here is unsafe due to a preventable hazard which I may enjoin. There can be no doubt that the by-products of burning tobacco are toxic and dangerous to the health of smokers and nonsmokers generally and this plaintiff in particular.

In 1965 Congress officially recognized the dangerous nature of cigarette smoke and declared a national policy to warn the public of the danger and to discourage cigarette smoking. In 1970 the Public Health Cigarette Smoking Act, 15 U.S.C.A. § 1331 *et seq.*, strengthened the warning language which all cigarette packages were required by the 1965 statute to bear. 15 U.S.C.A. § 1331 declares:

> It is the policy of the Congress, and the purpose of this chapter, to establish a comprehensive Federal program to deal with cigarette labeling and advertising with respect to any relationship between smoking and health, whereby—

> (1) the public may be adequately informed that cigarette smoking may be hazardous to health by inclusion of a warning to that effect on each package of cigarettes * * *

In furtherance of this policy 15 U.S.C.A. § 1333 makes it unlawful to sell cigarettes in the United States unless they bear the statement, "Warning: The Surgeon General Has Determined That Cigarette Smoking Is Dangerous To Your Health," conspicuously imprinted on the side of every package.

Additionally, the Congress in 1970 determined that the hazardous nature of cigarettes is significant enough to warrant affirmative action to counteract the persuasive effect of cigarette advertising. 15 U.S.C.A. § 1335 bans the advertising of cigarettes from radio and television. The advertisements totally ignored the health hazards and promoted the idea that cigarette smoking is both pleasurable and harmless. Despite the presentation of anti-smoking commercials, such advertising on the popular media of radio and television tended to offset the effectiveness of the warnings. Consequently, Congress took remedial action in the public interest and banned cigarette promotion on the airwaves.

Where a matter is generally accepted by mankind as true and is capable of ready demonstration by means commonly recognized as authoritative, the court may use that matter as an aid in its consideration. The national policy to recognize and warn the public of the dangerous nature of cigarette smoke has made that fact generally accepted. Therefore, I take judicial notice of the toxic nature of cigarette smoke and its well known association with emphysema, lung cancer and heart disease.

The HEW report for 1975, *The Health Consequences of Smoking*, and the Surgeon General's report by the same title for 1972 reveal distressing new evidence in the continuing investigation of the toxic nature of cigarette smoke. The reports indicate that the mere presence of cigarette smoke in the air pollutes it, changing carbon monoxide levels and effectively making involuntary smokers of all who breathe the air. Prior to these reports it was generally accepted that smoking is a hazard voluntarily undertaken. To smoke or not to smoke was considered the choice of the individual, and a smoker once informed of the risk imperiled no one's health but his or her own when he or she chose to ignore the warnings.

The 1972 report of the Surgeon General has shown that such is not the case. The report indicates that a burning cigarette contaminates the air with "sidestream" smoke which comes from the burning cone and mouthpiece of the cigarette between puffs as well as with the smoke exhaled by the smoker. The presence of this smoke in the air not only contributes to the discomfort of nonsmokers, but also increases the carbon monoxide level and adds tar, nicotine and the oxides of nitrogen to the available air supply. These substances are harmful to the health of an exposed person particularly those who have chronic coronary heart or broncho pulmonary disease.

The Surgeon General's findings are supported strongly by the evidence which has been presented to me. The affidavit of Dr. Luthor Terry, who served as Surgeon General of the United States from 1961 to 1965 and is an expert in cardiovascular disease, divides the effects of tobacco smoke on nonsmokers into three categories. The first category includes that small percentage of the population who are genuinely sensitive to tobacco smoke and experience allergic manifestations. Dr. Terry notes that while he has not personally examined plaintiff, she appears to fall into this class of nonsmokers. The next category includes persons with chronic disease, especially cardiovascular disease and lung disease. These people are particularly vulnerable to the effects of involuntary smoking which may significantly exacerbate their medical conditions. Finally, a large proportion of the nonsmoking population finds it unpleasant and uncomfortable to be exposed to significant amounts of tobacco smoke. Having reviewed the scientific data and medical evidence available, Dr. Terry concludes that passive smoking in the workplace can be injurious to the health of a significant percentage of the working population.

This evidence is reiterated in the other affidavits before me. The affidavit of Dr. Jesse Steinfeld, Professor of Medicine at the University of California and a member of the American Association for Cancer Research, repeats the carcinogenic and otherwise toxic nature of the chemicals in tobacco smoke. Dr. Steinfeld states "While the primary toxic effects of tobacco smoking occur in the individual who inhales the mainstream smoke, it is quite clear that sidestream smoke contains a considerable amount of material which is toxic to the passive smoker who is near others who smoke."

Dr. Wilbert S. Aronow, a Cardiologist who is Chief of Cardiovascular Research at the University of California at Irvine, has submitted with his affidavit the results of extensive research and testimony collected in a paper entitled "The Effect of Passive Smoking on the Cardiovascular and Respiratory Systems." In that paper Dr. Aronow concludes that passive smoking not only aggravates the condition of persons with cardiovascular or pulmonary disease, but also may lead to increased respiratory tract infections and precipitate respiratory and other symptoms in *nonallergic* patients sensitive to tobacco.

In dealing with the question of allergy to tobacco smoke, several of the physicians submitting affidavits recognized such an allergy as a serious health problem which could produce severe symptoms and may lead to a deterioration of the patients overall condition. Dr. Michael Diamond, a specialist in allergy and immunology, estimates that 10% of the United States population has an allergy to tobacco smoke, producing symptoms such as coughing, wheezing, eye itching and headaches upon *minimal exposure* to smoke. Dr. Frank Rosen has submitted his study of a case in which a one-year-old child developed bronchial asthma due to allergy to tobacco smoke. A report of similar adverse effects upon children with smoking parents has been made by Drs. Hall and Hyde, Pediatricians associated with the University of Rochester Medical Center. Dr. Richard Brams, an allergy specialist who has personally treated plaintiff for her symptoms, has diagnosed her condition as respiratory allergy aggravated by the combination of tobacco smoke and poor ventilation at her work environment. Dr. Brams included with his affidavit scientific data and reports of allergy and respiratory specialists in support of his professional opinion that toxic cigarette smoke is the cause of plaintiff's on-the-job health problems and that she and others like herself should be protected from this hazard.

The opinion that tobacco smoke should be eliminated from the work environment is shared by specialists in the field of industrial medicine. Dr. Susan Daum is an internist who has done extensive work in the field of occupational safety in affiliation with the Environmental Science Laboratory at Mount Sinai School of Medicine and the Rutgers University Labor Education Center. Based on her experience she states:

Longterm health hazards causing or contributing to chronic disease are rarely recognized as work related and impede the collection of data necessary to promulgate a safe limit of low level expo-

sure. In the absence of such data or longterm scientific studies
dealing with a known noxious agent, it is a sound and accepted
procedure in the practice of preventive medicine to eliminate the
hazardous substance whenever possible until firm scientific guidelines can be established.

Dr. Donald Bews, a specialist in occupational medicine certified by
the American Board of Preventive Medicine, shares Dr. Daum's view
that tobacco smoke should be eliminated from the work area.   He
states that based on 28 years of experience in the field as medical
director to Bell Telephone of Canada, and having observed the deleterious effects of smoking on the health of the active and passive smoker, it is his professional judgment that the work environment should
be free of tobacco smoke, one of the major sources of air pollution.

The evidence is clear and overwhelming.   Cigarette smoke contaminates and pollutes the air, creating a health hazard not merely to
the smoker but to all those around her who must rely upon the same
air supply.   The right of an individual to risk his or her own health
does not include the right to jeopardize the health of those who must
remain around him or her in order to properly perform the duties of
their jobs.   The portion of the population which is especially sensitive
to cigarette smoke is so significant that it is reasonable to expect an
employer to foresee health consequences and to impose upon him a
duty to abate the hazard which causes the discomfort.   I order New
Jersey Bell Telephone Company to do so.

In determining the extent to which smoking must be restricted the
rights and interests of smoking and nonsmoking employees alike
must be considered.   The employees' right to a safe working environment makes it clear that smoking must be forbidden in the work
area.   The employee who desires to smoke on his own time, during
coffee breaks and lunch hours should have a reasonable accessible
area in which to smoke.   In the present case the employees' lunchroom and lounge could serve this function.   Such a rule imposes no
hardship upon defendant New Jersey Bell Telephone Company.   The
company already has in effect a rule that cigarettes may not be
smoked around the telephone equipment.   The rationale behind the
rule is that the machines are extremely sensitive and can be damaged
by the smoke.   Human beings are also very sensitive and can be damaged by cigarette smoke.   Unlike a piece of machinery, the damage
to a human is all to often irreparable.   If a circuit or wiring goes bad,
the company can install a replacement part.   It is not so simple in the
case of a human lung, eye or heart.   The parts are hard to come by,
if indeed they can be found at all.

A company which has demonstrated such concern for its mechanical components should have at least as much concern for its human
beings.   Plaintiff asks nothing more than to be able to breathe the air
in its clear and natural state.

Accordingly, I order defendant New Jersey Bell Telephone Company to provide safe working conditions for plaintiff by restricting
the smoking of employees to the nonwork area presently used as a

lunchroom.   No smoking shall be permitted in the offices or adjacent customer service area.

It is so ordered.

G.   RECOMMENDED READING

The articles excerpted are particularly good for describing the law in this area.   There have been many important articles and books on the subject.   Some of the more prominent include:

1. *Individual Rights in the Corporation: A Reader on Employee Rights* (A. Westin & S. Salisbury, Ed., 1980).

2. K. Loptka, "A 1977 Primer On The Federal Regulation Of Employment Discrimination," 1977 U. of Ill.L.F. 69.

3. Blackburn, "Restricted Employer Discharge Rights: A Changing Concept of Employment at Will," 17 Am.Bus.L.J. 467 (1980).

4. Summers, "Individual Protection Against Unjust Dismissal: Time For A Statute," 62 Va.L.Rev. 481 (1976).

5. Blackburn, "Charting Compliance Under The Age Discrimination In Employment Act," 57 Chi.-Kent L.Rev. (1981).

6. M. Sovern, *Legal Restraints on Racial Discrimination in Employment* (1966).

7. Fanning, "The Duty of Fair Representation," 19 Boston College L.Rev. 813 (1978).

8. Edwards & Zaretsky, "Preferential Remedies for Employment Discrimination," 74 Mich.L.Rev. 1 (1975).

9. F. Marshall, *The Negro and Organized Labor* (1965).

10. "Note, Employment Discrimination and Title VII of the Civil Rights Act of 1964," 84 Harv.L.Rev. 1109 (1971).

11. Foner, *Organized Labor and the Black Worker* (1974).

12. H. Hill, *Black Labor and the American Legal System* (1977).

13. Blackburn, "Legal Aspects of Smoking in the Workplace," 31 Labor Law Journal 564 (1980).

*

Appendix A

SELECTED PORTIONS NLRA

SHORT TITLE AND DECLARATION OF POLICY

Section 1. (a) This Act may be cited as the "Labor Management Relations Act, 1947."

(b) Industrial strife which interferes with the normal flow of commerce and with the full production of articles and commodities for commerce, can be avoided or substantially minimized if employers, employees, and labor organizations each recognize under law one another's legitimate rights in their relations with each other, and above all recognize under law that neither party has any right in its relations with any other to engage in acts or practices which jeopardize the public health, safety, or interest.

It is the purpose and policy of this Act, in order to promote the full flow of commerce, to prescribe the legitimate rights of both employees and employers in their relations affecting commerce, to provide orderly and peaceful procedures for preventing the interference by either with the legitimate rights of the other, to protect the rights of individual employees in their relations with labor organizations whose activities affect commerce, to define and proscribe practices on the part of labor and management which affect commerce and are inimical to the general welfare, and to protect the rights of the public in connection with labor disputes affecting commerce.

TITLE I—AMENDMENT OF NATIONAL LABOR RELATIONS ACT

Sec. 101. The National Labor Relations Act is hereby amended to read as follows:

FINDINGS AND POLICIES

Section 1. The denial by some employers of the right of employees to organize and the refusal by some employers to accept the procedure of collective bargaining lead to strikes and other forms of industrial strife or unrest, which have the intent or the necessary effect of burdening or obstructing commerce by (a) impairing the efficiency, safety, or operation of the instrumentalities of commerce; (b) occurring in the current of commerce; (c) materially affecting, restraining, or controlling the flow of raw materials or manufactured or processed goods from or into the channels of commerce, or the prices of such materials or goods in commerce; or (d) causing diminution of employment and wages in such volume as substantially to impair or

701

disrupt the market for goods flowing from or into the channels of commerce.

The inequality of bargaining power between employees who do not possess full freedom of association or actual liberty of contract, and employers who are organized in the corporate or other forms of ownership association substantially burdens and affects the flow of commerce, and tends to aggravate recurrent business depressions by depressing wage rates and the purchasing power of wage earners in industry and by preventing the stabilization of competitive wage rates and working conditions within and between industries.

Experience has proved that protection by law of the right of employees to organize and bargain collectively safeguards commerce from injury, impairment, or interruption, and promotes the flow of commerce by removing certain recognized sources of industrial strife and unrest, by encouraging practices fundamental to the friendly adjustment of industrial disputes arising out of differences as to wages, hours, or other working conditions, and by restoring equality of bargaining power between employers and employees.

Experience has further demonstrated that certain practices by some labor organizations, their officers, and members have the intent or the necessary effect of burdening or obstructing commerce by preventing the free flow of goods in such commerce through strikes and other forms of industrial unrest or through concerted activities which impair the interest of the public in the free flow of such commerce. The elimination of such practices is a necessary condition to the assurance of the rights herein guaranteed.

It is hereby declared to be the policy of the United States to eliminate the causes of certain substantial obstructions to the free flow of commerce and to mitigate and eliminate these obstructions when they have occurred by encouraging the practice and procedure of collective bargaining and by protecting the exercise by workers of full freedom of association, self-organization, and designation of representatives of their own choosing, for the purpose of negotiating the terms and conditions of their employment or other mutual aid or protection.

DEFINITIONS

Sec. 2.   When used in this Act—

(1) The term "person" includes one or more individuals, labor organizations, partnerships, associations, corporations, legal representatives, trustees, trustees in bankruptcy, or receivers.

(2) The term "employer" includes any person acting as an agent of an employer, directly or indirectly, but shall not include the United States or any wholly owned Government corporation, or any Federal Reserve Bank, or any State or political subdivision thereof, or any person subject to the Railway Labor Act, as amended from time to time, or any labor organization (other than when acting as an employer), or anyone acting in the capacity of officer or agent of such labor organization.

(3) The term "employee" shall include any employee, and shall not be limited to the employees of a particular employer, unless the Act explicitly states otherwise, and shall include any individual whose work has ceased as a consequence of, or in connection with, any current labor dispute or because of any unfair labor practice, and who has not obtained any other regular and substantially equivalent employment, but shall not include any individual employed as an agricultural laborer, or in the domestic service of any family or person at his home, or any individual employed by his parent or spouse, or any individual having the status of an independent contractor, or any individual employed as a supervisor, or any individual employed by an employer subject to the Railway Labor Act, as amended from time to time, or by any other person who is not an employer as herein defined.

(4) The term "representatives" includes any individual or labor organization.

(5) The term "labor organization" means any organization of any kind, or any agency or employee representation committee or plan, in which employees participate and which exists for the purpose, in whole or in part, of dealing with employers concerning grievances, labor disputes, wages, rates of pay, hours of employment, or conditions of work.

(6) The term "commerce" means trade, traffic, commerce, transportation, or communication among the several States, or between the District of Columbia or any Territory of the United States and any State or other Territory, or between any foreign country and any State, Territory, or the District of Columbia, or within the District of Columbia or any Territory, or between points in the same State but through any other State or any Territory or the District of Columbia or any foreign country.

(7) The term "affecting commerce" means in commerce, or burdening or obstructing commerce or the free flow of commerce, or having led or tending to lead to a labor dispute burdening or obstructing commerce or the free flow of commerce.

(8) The term "unfair labor practice" means any unfair labor practice listed in section 8.

(9) The term "labor dispute" includes any controversy concerning terms, tenure or conditions of employment, or concerning the association or representation of persons in negotiating, fixing, maintaining, changing, or seeking to arrange terms or conditions of employment, regardless of whether the disputants stand in the proximate relation of employer and employee.

(10) The term "National Labor Relations Board" means the National Labor Relations Board provided for in section 3 of this Act.

(11) The term "supervisor" means any individual having authority, in the interest of the employer, to hire, transfer, suspend, lay off, recall, promote, discharge, assign, reward, or discipline other employees, or responsibly to direct them, or to adjust their grievances, or

effectively to recommend such action, if in connection with the foregoing the exercise of such authority is not of a merely routine or clerical nature, but requires the use of independent judgment.

* * *

NATIONAL LABOR RELATIONS BOARD

Sec. 3. (a) The National Labor Relations Board (hereinafter called the "Board") created by this Act prior to its amendment by the Labor Management Relations Act, 1947, is hereby continued as an agency of the United States, except that the Board shall consist of five instead of three members, appointed by the President by and with the advice and consent of the Senate. Of the two additional members so provided for, one shall be appointed for a term of five years and the other for a term of two years. Their successors, and the successors of the other members, shall be appointed for terms of five years each, excepting that any individual chosen to fill a vacancy shall be appointed only for the unexpired term of the member whom he shall succeed. The President shall designate one member to serve as Chairman of the Board. Any member of the Board may be removed by the President, upon notice and hearing, for neglect of duty or malfeasance in office, but for no other cause.

* * *

RIGHTS OF EMPLOYEES

Sec. 7. Employees shall have the right to self-organization, to form, join, or assist labor organizations, to bargain collectively through representatives of their own choosing, and to engage in other concerted activities for the purpose of collective bargaining or other mutual aid or protection, and shall also have the right to refrain from any or all such activities except to the extent that such right may be affected by an agreement requiring membership in a labor organization as a condition of employment as authorized in section 8(a)(3).

UNFAIR LABOR PRACTICES

Sec. 8. (a) It shall be an unfair labor practice for an employer—

(1) to interfere with, restrain, or coerce employees in the exercise of the rights guaranteed in section 7;

(2) to dominate or interfere with the formation or administration of any labor organization or contribute financial or other support to it: *Provided,* That subject to rules and regulations made and published by the Board pursuant to section 6, an employer shall not be prohibited from permitting employees to confer with him during working hours without loss of time or pay;

(3) by discrimination in regard to hire or tenure of employment or any term or condition of employment to encourage or discourage membership in any labor organization: *Provided,* That nothing in this Act, or in any other statute of the United States, shall preclude an

employer from making an agreement with a labor organization (not established, maintained, or assisted by any action defined in section 8(a) of this Act as an unfair labor practice) to require as a condition of employment membership therein on or after the thirtieth day following the beginning of such employment or the effective date of such agreement, whichever is the later, (i) if such labor organization is the representative of the employees as provided in section 9(a), in the appropriate collective-bargaining unit covered by such agreement when made, and (ii) unless following an election held as provided in section 9(e) within one year preceding the effective date of such agreement, the Board shall have certified that at least a majority of the employees eligible to vote in such election have voted to rescind the authority of such labor organization to make such an agreement: *Provided further*, That no employer shall justify any discrimination against an employee for nonmembership in a labor organization (A) if he has reasonable grounds for believing that such membership was not available to the employee on the same terms and conditions generally applicable to other members, or (B) if he has reasonable grounds for believing that membership was denied or terminated for reasons other than the failure of the employee to tender the periodic dues and the initiation fees uniformly required as a condition of acquiring or retaining membership;

(4) to discharge or otherwise discriminate against an employee because he has filed charges or given testimony under this Act;

(5) to refuse to bargain collectively with the representatives of his employees, subject to the provisions of section 9(a).

(b) It shall be an unfair labor practice for a labor organization or its agents—

(1) to restrain or coerce (A) employees in the exercise of the rights guaranteed in section 7: *Provided*, That this paragraph shall not impair the right of a labor organization to prescribe its own rules with respect to the acquisition or retention of membership therein; or (B) an employer in the selection of his representatives for the purposes of collective bargaining or the adjustment of grievances;

(2) to cause or attempt to cause an employer to discriminate against an employee in violation of subsection (a)(3) or to discriminate against an employee with respect to whom membership in such organization has been denied or terminated on some ground other than his failure to tender the periodic dues and the initiation fees uniformly required as a condition of acquiring or retaining membership;

(3) to refuse to bargain collectively with an employer, provided it is the representative of his employees subject to the provisions of section 9(a);

(4)(i) to engage in, or to induce or encourage any individual employed by any person engaged in commerce or in an industry affecting commerce to engage in, a strike or a refusal in the course of his employment to use, manufacture, process, transport, or otherwise handle or work on any goods, articles, materials, or commodities or to perform any services; or (ii) to threaten, coerce, or restrain any person engaged in commerce or in an industry affecting commerce, where in either case an object thereof is:

(A) forcing or requiring any employer or self-employed person to join any labor or employer organization or to enter into any agreement which is prohibited by section 8(e);

(B) forcing or requiring any person to cease using, selling, handling, transporting, or otherwise dealing in the products of any other producer, processor, or manufacturer, or to cease doing business with any other person, or forcing or requiring any other employer to recognize or bargain with a labor organization as the representative of his employees unless such labor organization has been certified as the representative of such employees under the provisions of section 9: *Provided,* That nothing contained in this clause (B) shall be construed to make unlawful, where not otherwise unlawful, any primary strike or primary picketing;

(C) forcing or requiring any employer to recognize or bargain with a particular labor organization as the representative of his employees if another labor organization has been certified as the representative of such employees under the provisions of section 9;

(D) forcing or requiring any employer to assign particular work to employees in a particular labor organization or in a particular trade, craft, or class rather than to employees in another labor organization or in another trade, craft, or class, unless such employer is failing to conform to an order or certification of the Board determining the bargaining representative for employees performing such work;

Provided, That nothing contained in this subsection (b) shall be construed to make unlawful a refusal by any person to enter upon the premises of any employer (other than his own employer), if the employees of such employer are engaged in a strike ratified or approved by a representative of such employees whom such employer is required to recognize under this Act: *Provided further,* That for the purposes of this paragraph (4) only, nothing contained in such paragraph shall be construed to prohibit publicity, other than picketing, for the purpose of truthfully advising the public, including consumers and members of a labor organization, that a product or products are produced by an employer with whom the labor organization has a primary dispute and are distributed by another employer, as long as such publicity does not have an effect of inducing any individual employed by any person other than the primary employer in the course of his employment to refuse to pick up, deliver, or transport any goods, or not to perform any services, at the establishment of the employer engaged in such distribution;

(5) to require of employees covered by an agreement authorized under subsection (a)(3) the payment, as a condition precedent to becoming a member of such organization, of a fee in an amount which the Board finds excessive or discriminatory under all the circum-

stances. In making such a finding, the Board shall consider, among other relevant factors, the practices and customs of labor organizations in the particular industry, and the wages currently paid to the employees affected;

(6) to cause or attempt to cause an employer to pay or deliver or agree to pay or deliver any money or other thing of value, in the nature of an exaction for services which are not performed or not to be performed; and

(7) to picket or cause to be picketed, or threaten to picket or cause to be picketed, any employer where an object thereof is forcing or requiring an employer to recognize or bargain with a labor organization as the representative of his employees, or forcing or requiring the employees of an employer to accept or select such labor organization as their collective bargaining representative, unless such labor organization is currently certified as the representative of such employees:

(A) where the employer has lawfully recognized in accordance with this Act any other labor organization and a question concerning representation may not appropriately be raised under section 9(c) of this Act,

(B) where within the preceding twelve months a valid election under section 9(c) of this Act has been conducted, or

(C) where such picketing has been conducted without a petition under section 9(c) being filed within a reasonable period of time not to exceed thirty days from the commencement of such picketing: *Provided,* That when such a petition has been filed the Board shall forthwith, without regard to the provisions of section 9(c)(1) or the absence of a showing of a substantial interest on the part of the labor organization, direct an election in such unit as the Board finds to be appropriate and shall certify the results thereof: *Provided further,* That nothing in this subparagraph (C) shall be construed to prohibit any picketing or other publicity for the purpose of truthfully advising the public (including consumers) that an employer does not employ members of, or have a contract with, a labor organization, unless an effect of such picketing is to induce any individual employed by any other person in the course of his employment, not to pick up, deliver or transport any goods or not to perform any services.

Nothing in this paragraph (7) shall be construed to permit any act which would otherwise be an unfair labor practice under this section 8(b).

(c) The expressing of any views, argument, or opinion, or the dissemination thereof, whether in written, printed, graphic, or visual form, shall not constitute or be evidence of an unfair labor practice under any of the provisions of this Act, if such expression contains no threat of reprisal or force or promise of benefit.

(d) For the purposes of this section, to bargain collectively is the performance of the mutual obligation of the employer and the representative of the employees to meet at reasonable times and confer in good faith with respect to wages, hours, and other terms and conditions of employment, or the negotiation of an agreement or any question arising thereunder, and the execution of a written contract incorporating any agreement reached if requested by either party, but such obligation does not compel either party to agree to a proposal or require the making of a concession: *Provided,* That where there is in effect a collective-bargaining contract covering employees in an industry affecting commerce, the duty to bargain collectively shall also mean that no party to such contract shall terminate or modify such contract, unless the party desiring such termination or modification—

(1) serves a written notice upon the other party to the contract of the proposed termination or modification sixty days prior to the expiration date thereof, or in the event such contract contains no expiration date, sixty days prior to the time it is proposed to make such termination or modification;

(2) offers to meet and confer with the other party for the purpose of negotiating a new contract or a contract containing the proposed modifications;

(3) notifies the Federal Mediation and Conciliation Service within thirty days after such notice of the existence of a dispute, and simultaneously therewith notifies any State or Territorial agency established to mediate and conciliate disputes within the State or Territory where the dispute occurred, provided no agreement has been reached by that time; and

(4) continues in full force and effect, without resorting to strike or lockout, all the terms and conditions of the existing contract for a period of sixty days after such notice is given or until the expiration date of such contract, whichever occurs later:

The duties imposed upon employers, employees, and labor organizations by paragraphs (2), (3), and (4) shall become inapplicable upon an intervening certification of the Board, under which the labor organization or individual, which is a party to the contract, has been superseded as or ceased to be the representative of the employees subject to the provisions of section 9(a), and the duties so imposed shall not be construed as requiring either party to discuss or agree to any modification of the terms and conditions contained in a contract for a fixed period, if such modification is to become effective before such terms and conditions can be reopened under the provisions of the contract. Any employee who engages in a strike within any notice* period specified in this subsection, or who engages in any strike within the appropriate period specified in subsection (g) of this section,* shall lose his status as an employee of the employer engaged in the particular labor dispute, for the purposes of sections 8, 9, and 10 of this Act, as amended, but such loss of status for such employee shall terminate if and when he is reemployed by such employer. Whenever the collective bargaining involves employees of a health care institution, the provisions of this section 8(d) shall be modified as follows:

(A) The notice of section 8(d)(1) shall be ninety days; the notice of section 8(d)(3) shall be sixty days; and the contract period of section 8(d)(4) shall be ninety days.

(B) Where the bargaining is for an initial agreement following certification or recognition, at least thirty days' notice of the existence of a dispute shall be given by the labor organization to the agencies set forth in section 8(d)(3).

(C) After notice is given to the Federal Mediation and Conciliation Service under either clause (A) or (B) of this sentence, the Service shall promptly communicate with the parties and use its best efforts, by mediation and conciliation, to bring them to agreement. The parties shall participate fully and promptly in such meetings as may be undertaken by the Service for the purpose of aiding in a settlement of the dispute.

(e) It shall be an unfair labor practice for any labor organization and any employer to enter into any contract or agreement, express or implied, whereby such employer ceases or refrains or agrees to cease or refrain from handling, using, selling, transporting or otherwise dealing in any of the products of any other employer, or to cease doing business with any other person, and any contract or agreement entered into heretofore or hereafter containing such an agreement shall be to such extent unenforceable and void: *Provided,* That nothing in this subsection (e) shall apply to an agreement between a labor organization and an employer in the construction industry relating to the contracting or subcontracting of work to be done at the site of the construction, alteration, painting, or repair of a building, structure, or other work: *Provided further,* That for the purposes of this subsection (e) and section 8(b)(4)(B) the terms "any employer", "any person engaged in commerce or in industry affecting commerce", and "any person" when used in relation to the terms "any other producer, processor, or manufacturer", "any other employer", or "any other person" shall not include persons in the relation of a jobber, manufacturer, contractor, or subcontractor working on the goods or premises of the jobber or manufacturer or performing parts of an integrated process of production in the apparel and clothing industry: *Provided further,* That nothing in this Act shall prohibit the enforcement of any agreement which is within the foregoing exception.

(f) It shall not be an unfair labor practice under subsections (a) and (b) of this section for an employer engaged primarily in the building and construction industry to make an agreement covering employees engaged (or who, upon their employment, will be engaged) in the building and construction industry with a labor organization of which building and construction employees are members (not established, maintained, or assisted by any action defined in section 8(a) of this Act as an unfair labor practice) because (1) the majority status of such labor organization has not been established under the provisions of section 9 of this Act prior to the making of such agreement, or (2) such agreement requires as a condition of employment, membership in such labor organization after the seventh day following the beginning of such employment or the effective date of the agreement, whichever is later, or (3) such agreement requires the employer to notify such labor organization of opportunities for employment with such employer, or gives such labor organization an opportunity to refer qualified applicants for such employment, or (4) such agreement specifies minimum training or experience qualifications for employment or provides for priority in opportunities for employment based upon length of service with such employer, in the industry or in the particular geographical area: *Provided,* That nothing in this subsection shall set aside the final proviso to section 8(a)(3) of this Act: *Provided further,* That any agreement which would be invalid, but for clause (1) of this subsection, shall not be a bar to a petition filed pursuant to section 9(c) or 9(e).

(g) A labor organization before engaging in any strike, picketing, or other concerted refusal to work at any health care institution shall, not less than ten days prior to such action, notify the institution in writing and the Federal Mediation and Conciliation Service of that intention, except that in the case of bargaining for an initial agreement following certification or recognition the notice required by this subsection shall not be given until the expiration of the period specified in clause (B) of the last sentence of section 8(d) of this Act. The notice shall state the date and time that such action will commence. The notice, once given, may be extended by the written agreement of both parties.

REPRESENTATIVES AND ELECTIONS

Sec. 9. (a) Representatives designated or selected for the purposes of collective bargaining by the majority of the employees in a unit appropriate for such purposes, shall be the exclusive representatives of all the employees in such unit for the purposes of collective bargaining in respect to rates of pay, wages, hours of employment, or other conditions of employment: *Provided,* That any individual employee or a group of employees shall have the right at any time to present grievances to their employer and to have such grievances adjusted, without the intervention of the bargaining representative, as long as the adjustment is not inconsistent with the terms of a collective-bargaining contract or agreement then in effect: *Provided further,* That the bargaining representative has been given opportunity to be present at such adjustment.

(b) The Board shall decide in each case whether, in order to assure to employees the fullest freedom in exercising the rights guaranteed by this Act, the unit appropriate for the purposes of collective bargaining shall be the employer unit, craft unit, plant unit, or subdivision thereof: *Provided,* That the Board shall not (1) decide that any unit is appropriate for such purposes if such unit includes both professional employees and employees who are not professionl employees unless a majority of such professional employees vote for inclusion in such unit; or (2) decide that any craft unit is inappropriate for such purposes on the ground that a different unit has been established by a prior Board determination, unless a majority of the employees in the proposed craft unit votes against separate representation or (3) decide that any unit is appropriate for such purposes if it includes, together with other employees, any individual employed as a guard to enforce against employees and other persons rules to protect property of the employer or to protect the safety of persons on the employer's premises; but no labor organization shall be certified as the representative of employees in a bargaining unit of guards if such organization admits to membership, or is affiliated directly or indirectly with an organization which admits to membership, employees other than guards.

(c)(1) Wherever a petition shall have been filed, in accordance with such regulations as may be prescribed by the Board—

(A) by an employee or group of employees or any individual or labor organization acting in their behalf alleging that a substantial number of employees (i) wish to be represented for collective bargaining and that their employer declines to recognize their representative as the representative defined in section 9(a), or (ii) assert that the individual or labor organization, which has been certified or is being recognized by their employer as the bargaining representative, is no longer a representative as defined in section 9(a); or

(B) by an employer, alleging that one or more individuals or labor organizations have presented to him a claim to be recognized as the representative defined in section 9(a);

the Board shall investigate such petition and if it has reasonable cause to believe that a question of representation affecting commerce exists shall provide for an appropriate hearing upon due notice. Such hearing may be conducted by an officer or employee of the regional office, who shall not make any recommendations with respect thereto. If the Board finds upon the record of such hearing that such a question of representation exists, it shall direct an election by secret ballot and shall certify the results thereof.

(2) In determining whether or not a question of representation affecting commerce exists, the same regulations and rules of decision shall apply irrespective of the identity of the person filing the petition or the kind of relief sought and in no case shall the Board deny a labor organization a place on the ballot by reason of an order with respect to such labor organization or its predecessor not issued in conformity with section 10(c).

(3) No election shall be directed in any bargaining unit or any subdivision within which, in the preceding twelve-month period, a valid election shall have been held. Employees engaged in an economic strike who are not entitled to reinstatement shall be eligible to vote under such regulations as the Board shall find are consistent with the purposes and provisions of this Act in any election conducted within twelve months after the commencement of the strike. In any elec-

tion where none of the choices on the ballot receives a majority, a run-off shall be conducted, the ballot providing for a selection between the two choices receiving the largest and second largest number of valid votes cast in the election.

(4) Nothing in this section shall be construed to prohibit the waiving of hearings by stipulation for the purpose of a consent election in conformity with regulations and rules of decision of the Board.

(5) In determining whether a unit is appropriate for the purposes specified in subsection (b) the extent to which the employees have organized shall not be controlling.

* * *

(e)(1) Upon the filing with the Board, by 30 per centum or more of the employees in a bargaining unit covered by an agreement between their employer and a labor organization made pursuant to section 8(a)(3), of a petition alleging they desire that such authority be rescinded, the Board shall take a secret ballot of the employees in such unit and certify the results thereof to such labor organization and to the employer.

(2) No election shall be conducted pursuant to this subsection in any bargaining unit or any subdivision within which, in the preceding twelve-month period, a valid election shall have been held.

PREVENTION OF UNFAIR LABOR PRACTICES

Sec. 10. (a) The Board is empowered, as hereinafter provided, to prevent any person from engaging in any unfair labor practice (listed in section 8) affecting commerce. This power shall not be affected by any other means of adjustment or prevention that has been or may be established by agreement, law, or otherwise: *Provided,* That the Board is empowered by agreement with any agency of any State or Territory to cede to such agency jurisdiction over any cases in any industry (other than mining, manufacturing, communications, and transportation except where predominantly local in character) even though such cases may involve labor disputes affecting commerce, unless the provision of the State or Territorial statute applicable to the determination of such cases by such agency is inconsistent with the corresponding provision of this Act or has received a construction inconsistent therewith.

* * *

(c) The testimony taken by such member, agent, or agency or the Board shall be reduced to writing and filed with the Board. Thereafter, in its discretion, the Board upon notice may take further testimony or hear argument. If upon the preponderance of the testimony taken the Board shall be of the opinion that any person named in the complaint has engaged in or is engaging in any such unfair labor practice, then the Board shall state its findings of fact and shall issue and cause to be served on such person an order requiring such person to cease and desist from such unfair labor practice, and to take such affirmative action including reinstatement of employees with or without back pay, as will effectuate the policies of this Act: *Provided,* That where an order directs reinstatement of an employee, back pay may be required of the employer or labor organization, as the case may be, responsible for the discrimination suffered by him: *And provided further,* That in determining whether a complaint shall issue alleging a violation of section 8(a)(1) or section 8(a)(2), and in deciding such cases, the same regulations and rules of decision shall apply irrespective of whether or not the labor organization affected is affiliated with a labor organization national or international in scope. Such order may further require such person to make reports from time to time showing the extent to which it has complied with the order. If upon the preponderance of the testimony taken the Board shall not be of the opinion that the person named in the complaint has engaged in or is engaging in any such unfair labor practice, then the Board shall state its findings of fact and shall issue an order dismissing the said complaint. No order of the Board shall require the reinstatement of any individual as an employee who has been suspended or discharged, or the payment to him of any back pay, if such individual was suspended or discharged for cause. In case the evidence is presented before a member of the Board, or before an examiner or examiners thereof, such member, or such examiner or examiners, as the case may be, shall issue and cause to be served on the parties to the proceeding a proposed report, together with a recommended order, which shall be filed with the Board, and if no exceptions are filed within twenty days after service thereof upon such parties, or within such further period as the Board may authorize, such recommended order shall become the order of the Board and become effective as therein prescribed.

* * *

*

NORRIS–LAGUARDIA ACT

---

47 Stat. 70 (1932), 29 U.S.C.A. §§ 101–15

AN ACT

To amend the Judicial Code and to define and limit the jurisdiction of courts sitting in equity, and for other purposes.

Sec. 1. Issuance of restraining orders and injunctions; limitation; public policy.

No court of the United States, as herein defined, shall have jurisdiction to issue any restraining order or temporary or permanent injunction in a case involving or growing out of a labor dispute, except in a strict conformity with the provisions of this Act; nor shall any such restraining order or temporary or permanent injunction be issued contrary to the public policy declared in this Act.

Sec. 2. Public policy in labor matters declared.

In the interpretation of this Act and in determining the jurisdiction and authority of the courts of the United States, as such jurisdiction and authority are herein defined and limited, the public policy of the United States is hereby declared as follows:

Whereas under prevailing economic conditions, developed with the aid of governmental authority for owners of property to organize in the corporate and other forms of ownership association, the individual unorganized worker is commonly helpless to exercise actual liberty of contract and to protect his freedom of labor, and thereby to obtain acceptable terms and conditions of employment, wherefore, though he should be free to decline to associate with his fellows, it is necessary that he have full freedom of association, self-organization, and designation of representatives of his own choosing, to negotiate the terms and conditions of his employment, and that he shall be free from the interference, restraint, or coercion of employers of labor, or their agents, in the designation of such representatives or in self-organization or in other concerted activities for the purpose of collective bargaining or other mutual aid or protection; therefore, the following definitions of and limitations upon the jurisdiction and authority of the courts of the United States are enacted.

Sec. 3.   Nonenforceability of undertakings in conflict with public policy: "yellow dog" contracts.

Any undertaking or promise, such as is described in this section, or any other undertaking or promise in conflict with the public policy declared in section 2 of this Act is hereby declared to be contrary to the public policy of the United States, shall not be enforceable in any court of the United States and shall not afford any basis for the granting of legal or equitable relief by any such court, including specifically the following:

Every undertaking or promise hereafter made, whether written or oral express or implied, constituting or contained in any contract or agreement of hiring or employment between any individual, firm, company, association, or corporation, and any employee or prospective employee of the same, whereby

(a) Either party to such contract or agreement undertakes or promises not to join, become, or remain a member of any labor organization or of any employer organization; or

(b) Either party to such contract or agreement undertakes or promises that he will withdraw from an employment relation in the event that he joins, becomes, or remains a member of any labor organization or of any employer organization.

Sec. 4.   Enumeration of specific acts not subject to restraining orders or injunctions.

No court of the United States shall have jurisdiction to issue any restraining order or temporary or permanent injunction in any case involving or growing out of any labor dispute to prohibit any person or persons participating or interested in such dispute (as these terms are herein defined) from doing, whether singly or in concert, any of the following acts:

(a) Ceasing or refusing to perform any work or to remain in any relation of employment;

(b) Becoming or remaining a member of any labor organization or of any employer organization, regardless of any such undertaking or promise as is described in section 3 of this Act;

(c) Paying or giving to, or withholding from, any person participating or interested in such labor dispute, any strike or unemployment benefits or insurance, or other moneys or things of value;

(d) By all lawful means aiding any person participating or interested in any labor dispute who is being proceeded against in, or is prosecuting, any action or suit in any court of the United States or of any State;

(e) Giving publicity to the existence of, or the facts involved in, any labor dispute, whether by advertising, speaking, patrolling, or by any other method not involving fraud or violence;

(f) Assembling peaceably to act or to organize to act in promotion of their interests in a labor dispute;

(g) Advising or notifying any person of an intention to do any of the acts heretofore specified;

(h) Agreeing with other persons to do or not to do any of the acts heretofore specified; and

(i) Advising, urging, or otherwise causing or inducing without fraud or violence the acts heretofore specified, regardless of any such undertaking or promise as is described in section 3 of this Act.

Sec. 5. Doing in concert of certain acts as constituting unlawful combination or conspiracy subjecting person to injunctive remedies.

No court of the United States shall have jurisdiction to issue a restraining order or temporary or permanent injunction upon the ground that any of the persons participating or interested in a labor dispute constitute or are engaged in an unlawful combination or conspiracy because of the doing in concert of the acts enumerated in section 4 of this Act.

Sec. 6. Responsibility of officers and members of associations or their organizations for unlawful acts of individual officers, members, and agents.

No officer or member of any association or organization, and no association or organization participating or interested in a labor dispute, shall be held responsible or liable in any court of the United States for the unlawful acts of individual officers, members, or agents, except upon clear proof of actual participation in, or actual authorization of, such acts, or of ratification of such acts after actual knowledge thereof.

Sec. 7. Issuance of injunctions in labor disputes; hearings; findings of court; notice to affected persons; temporary restraining order; undertakings.

No court of the United States shall have jurisdiction to issue a temporary or permanent injunction in any case involving or growing out of a labor dispute, as herein defined, except after hearing the testimony of witnesses in open court (with opportunity for cross-examination) in support of the allegations of a complaint made under oath, and testimony in opposition thereto, if offered, and except after findings of fact by the court, to the effect—

(a) That unlawful acts have been threatened and will be committed unless restrained or have been committed and will be continued unless restrained, but no injunction or temporary restraining order shall be issued on account of any threat or unlawful act excepting against the person or persons, association, or organization making the threat or committing the unlawful act or actually authorizing or ratifying the same after actual knowledge thereof;

(b) That substantial and irreparable injury to complainant's property will follow;

(c) That as to each item of relief granted greater injury will be inflicted upon complainant by the denial of relief than will be inflicted upon defendants by the granting of relief;

(d) That complainant has no adequate remedy at law; and

(e) That the public officers charged with the duty to protect complainant's property are unable or unwilling to furnish adequate protection.

Such hearing shall be held after due and personal notice thereof has been given, in such manner as the court shall direct, to all known persons against whom relief is sought, and also to the chief of those public officials of the county and city within which the unlawful acts have been threatened or committed charged with the duty to protect complainant's property: *Provided, however,* That if a complainant shall also allege that, unless a temporary restraining order shall be issued without notice, a substantial and irreparable injury to complainant's property will be unavoidable, such a temporary restraining order may be issued upon testimony under oath, sufficient, if sustained, to justify the court in issuing a temporary injunction upon a hearing after notice. Such a temporary restraining order shall be effective for no longer than five days and shall become void at the expiration of said five days. No temporary restraining order or temporary injunction shall be issued except on condition that complainant shall first file an undertaking with adequate security in an amount to be fixed by the court sufficient to recompense those enjoined for any loss, expense, or damage caused by the improvident or erroneous issuance of such order or injunction, including all reasonable costs (together with a reasonable attorney's fee) and expense of defense against the order or against the granting of any injunctive relief sought in the same proceeding and subsequently denied by the court.

The undertaking herein mentioned shall be understood to signify an agreement entered into by the complainant and the surety upon which a decree may be rendered in the same suit or proceeding against said complainant and surety, upon a hearing to assess damages of which hearing complainant and surety shall have reasonable notice, the said complainant and surety submitting themselves to the jurisdiction of the court for that purpose. But nothing herein contained shall deprive any party having a claim or cause of action under or upon such undertaking from electing to pursue his ordinary remedy by suit at law or in equity.

Sec. 8. Noncompliance with obligations involved in labor disputes or failure to settle by negotiation or arbitration as preventing injunctive relief.

No restraining order or injunctive relief shall be granted to any complainant who has failed to comply with any obligation imposed by law which is involved in the labor dispute in question, or who has failed to make every reasonable effort to settle such dispute either by negotiation or with the aid of any available governmental machinery of mediation or voluntary arbitration.

Sec. 9. Granting of restraining order or injunction as dependent on previous findings of fact; limitation on prohibitions included in restraining orders and injunctions.

No restraining order or temporary or permanent injunction shall be granted in a case involving or growing out of a labor dispute, except on the basis of findings of fact made and filed by the court in the record of the case prior to the issuance of such restraining order or injunction; and every restraining order or injunction granted in a case involving or growing out of a labor dispute shall include only a prohibition of such specific act or acts as may be expressly complained of in the bill of complaint or petition filed in such case and as shall be expressly included in said findings of fact made and filed by the court as provided herein.

Sec. 10. Review by Court of Appeals of issuance or denial of temporary injunctions; record; precedence.

Whenever any court of the United States shall issue or deny any temporary injunction in a case involving or growing out of a labor dispute, the court shall, upon the request of any party to the proceedings and on his filing the usual bond for costs, forthwith certify as in ordinary cases the record of the case to the court of appeals for its review. Upon the filing of such record in the court of appeals, the appeal shall be heard and the temporary injunctive order affirmed, modified, or set aside with the greatest possible expedition, giving the proceedings precedence over all other matters except older matters of the same character.

Sec. 11. Contempts; speedy and public trial; jury.

In all cases arising under this Act in which a person shall be charged with contempt in a court of the United States (as herein defined), the accused shall enjoy the right to a speedy and public trial by an impartial jury of the State and district wherein the contempt shall have been committed: *Provided*, That this right shall not apply to contempts committed in the presence of the court or so near thereto as to interfere directly with the administration of justice or to apply to the misbehavior, misconduct, or disobedience of any officer of the court in respect to the writs, orders, or process of the court.*

---

* Sections 11 and 12 were repealed by Act of June 25, 1948 (62 Stat. 862), a codification of the provisions of Title 18 of the United States Code. The substance of Section 11 was reenacted in the same Act (62 Stat. 844, 18 U.S.C.A. § 3692); the substance of Section 12 is now found in Rules 42(a) and (b) of the Federal Rules of Criminal Procedure.

Sec. 12.* Contempts; demand for retirement of judge sitting in proceeding.

The defendant in any proceeding for contempt of court may file with the court a demand for the retirement of the judge sitting in the proceeding, if the contempt arises from an attack upon the character or conduct of such judge and if the attack occurred elsewhere than in the presence of the court or so near thereto as to interfere directly with the administration of justice. Upon the filing of any such demand the judge shall thereupon proceed no further, but another judge shall be designated in the same manner as is provided by law. The demand shall be filed prior to the hearing in the contempt proceeding.

Sec. 13. Definitions of terms and words used in chapter.

When used in this Act, and for the purposes of this Act—

(a) A case shall be held to involve or to grow out of a labor dispute when the case involves persons who are engaged in the same industry, trade, craft, or occupation; or have direct or indirect interests therein; or who are employees of the same employer; or who are members of the same or an affiliated organization of employers or employees; whether such dispute is (1) between one or more employers or associations of employers and one or more employees or associations of employees; (2) between one or more employers or associations of employers and one or more employers or associations of employers; or (3) between one or more employees or associations of employees and one or more employees or associations of employees; or when the case involves any conflicting or competing interests in a "labor dispute" (as hereinafter defined) of "persons participating or interested" therein (as hereinafter defined).

(b) A person or association shall be held to be a person participating or interested in a labor dispute if relief is sought against him or it, and if he or it is engaged in the same industry, trade, craft, or occupation in which such dispute occurs, or has a direct or indirect interest therein, or is a member, officer, or agent of any association composed in whole or in part of employers or employees engaged in such industry, trade, craft, or occupation.

(c) The term "labor dispute" includes any controversy concerning terms or conditions of employment, or concerning the association or representation of persons in negotiating, fixing, maintaining, changing, or seeking to arrange terms or conditions of employment, regardless of whether or not the disputants stand in the proximate relation of employer and employee.

(d) The term "court of the United States" means any court of the United States whose jurisdiction has been or may be conferred or defined or limited by Act of Congress, including the courts of the District of Columbia.

Sec. 14. Separability of provisions.

If any provision of this Act or the application thereof to any person or circumstance is held unconstitutional or otherwise invalid, the remaining provisions of this Act and the application of such provisions to other persons or circumstances shall not be affected thereby.

Sec. 15. Repeal of conflicting acts.

All acts and parts of acts in conflict with the provisions of this Act are repealed.

*

Appendix C

COLLECTIVE BARGAINING AGREEMENT

INDEX

PREAMBLE

This agreement is made and entered into this 10th day of March, 1975, by and between the Sacramento Plants of the AEROJET LIQUID ROCKET COMPANY and AEROJET NUCLEAR SYSTEMS COMPANY OF AEROJET-GENERAL CORPORATION, hereinafter referred to as the "Company," and the GRAND LODGE OF THE INTERNATIONAL ASSOCIATION OF MACHINISTS AND AEROSPACE WORKERS, A.F. of L.-C.I.O., and its Local Lodge No. 946, hereinafter referred to as the "Union."

ARTICLE I
RECOGNITION

101. The Aerojet Liquid Rocket Company and the Aerojet Nuclear Systems Company recognize the Union, party to this agreement, as the sole and exclusive agent for all its production and maintenance employees at their Sacramento Facilities and any other group of employees presently or hereafter recognized or certified, whose conditions may be negotiated at such time at the request of either party; excluding supervisory personnel as defined in the National Labor Relations Act, as amended, and also excluding any other employees presently certified to another Union.

102.   The Company acknowledges the requirement for security inherent in the nature of the Union's operations and the need for a feeling of job security on the part of its maintenance and production employees which places a responsibility upon the Company to avoid the assignment of presently established bargaining unit work to nonbargaining unit employees, which would have the direct result of undermining the bargaining agent, diluting the bargaining unit, or checking its natural growth.   The foregoing shall not cause the Company or the Union to violate any State or Federal laws.

103.   In light of the above, supervisors or any other nonbargaining unit personnel shall not perform any bargaining unit work or operations performed by employees covered by this agreement.

ARTICLE II
RIGHTS OF MANAGEMENT

201.   The Union and its members recognize that the management of the facility and the direction of the working force remain vested exclusively in the Company, and this shall include but shall not be limited to the right to: hire, properly classify, promote, or transfer; suspend, discipline, or discharge for just cause; or lay off employees for lack of work only; provided that the exercise of the foregoing shall not conflict with the provisions of this agreement.

ARTICLE III
STRIKES AND LOCKOUTS

301.   For the duration of this agreement, the Union and its members agree that it shall not call, sanction, or engage in any strike, slow-down or stoppage of work; and the Company agrees that it shall not cause or engage in any lockout.

ARTICLE IV
UNION SECURITY AND CHECK-OFF

401.   All employees covered by this agreement shall, as a condition of continued employment, become and remain members of the Union in good standing during the term of this agreement.

402.   All new employees covered by this agreement shall, as a condition of employment, become members of the Union immediately after thirty (30) calendar days of employment, and remain members in good standing during the term of this agreement.

403.   The Union will make membership in the Union available to all employees covered by this agreement on the same terms and conditions as are generally applicable to other members of the Union, and further, demands for termination of employment will not be made for reasons other than failure of an employee to tender the periodic dues and fees uniformly required as a condition of acquiring or retaining membership in the Union.

404. Upon receipt of authorization signed by the employee, the Company shall deduct from the employee's pay the initiation or reinstatement fee and monthly dues payable by him to the Union, in an amount as directed by the Union for the period specified, so long as he remains in the bargaining unit.

405. The Union shall indemnify and save the Company harmless against any and all claims, demands, lawsuits or other forms of liability that may arise out of or by reason of action taken by the Company at the direction of the Union in making payroll deductions of Union membership dues, reinstatement, initiation fees, or discharge of an employee at the Union's request in accordance with Section 403 of this article.

* * *

ARTICLE VI
STANDARD WORKDAY AND WORKWEEK

601. Standard Workweek

602. Five (5) standard workdays, Monday through Friday, shall constitute the standard workweek.

603. For the purpose of computing overtime pay of each employee, the workweek of an employee shall consist of seven (7) consecutive 24-hour days beginning at the regular starting time of his first assigned shift.

604. Standard Workday

605. An employee's standard workday shall begin at the regular starting time of his shift.

ARTICLE VII
OVERTIME

701. Payable time before and after an employee's regularly scheduled shift hours shall be paid for at the overtime rate that applies.

702. One and one-half (1½) times the employee's regular rate shall be paid an employee in the following instances.

703. a. For all payable time outside his regularly scheduled shift hours up to and including four (4) hours in his standard workweek workday.

704. b. For his regularly scheduled shift hours on Saturday.

705. Two (2) times the employee's regular rate shall be paid an employee in each of the following instances.

706. a. For all payable time outside the employee's regularly scheduled shift hours in the employee's Saturday workday.

707. b. For all payable time exceeding four (4) hours put in outside the employee's regularly scheduled shift hours during the employee's standard workweek workday.

708. c. All payable time on the employee's Sunday workday.

709. d. All payable time on holidays as outlined in Article X.

710. An employee who works twenty (20) hours or more in any workday shall be paid two (2) times his regular rate for all payable hours worked on the next day unless and until he is given time off for a four (4) hour continuous period.

ARTICLE VIII
VACATION

801. Eligibility

802. All employees covered by this agreement who have completed four (4) months of employment (seniority) shall be entitled to vacation benefits as outlined herein.

813. Vacation Benefits and Pay

814. An employee with less than ten (10) years of employment (seniority), and who is on the payroll on the computation date, shall be entitled to a maximum of two (2) weeks' vacation time off, and shall receive vacation pay in an amount equivalent to four percent (4%) of his gross earnings from the last computation date.

815. An employee with ten (10) years of employment (seniority) with the Company between June 1st and December 31st of the vacation year and who is on the payroll on the computation date shall be entitled to a maximum of three (3) weeks' vacation time off, and shall receive vacation pay in an amount equivalent to six percent (6%) of his gross earnings from the last computation date.

816. An employee with fifteen (15) years of employment (seniority) with the Company between June 1st and December 31st of the vacation year and who is on the payroll on the computation date, shall be entitled to a maximum of four (4) weeks' vacation time off and shall receive vacation pay in an amount equivalent to eight percent (8%) of his gross earnings from the last computation date.

ARTICLE IX
SICK AND ACCIDENT LEAVE

909. Sick and Accident Leave Pay

910. Pay for each full day of sick leave for an employee means pay for one (1) standard workday at an employee's regular rate of pay. Such pay shall be at the employee's regular rate of pay in effect at the time sick and accident leave days or units are used, or in the case of pay under Sections 912 and 913, at the employee's regular rate of pay in effect on the next computation date.

* * *

ARTICLE XII
REST PERIODS

1201. It is the policy of the Company to standardize established rest periods throughout the plant. The running break will be recognized as dictated by efficient work force and operational requirements. In the event it is deemed necessary by the Company to change an established rest period within a work organization, seven (7) calendar days' notification will be given to the Union prior to implementing such change.

1202. The length of rest periods will be ten (10) minutes during the first half of an employee's shift and ten (10) minutes during the last half of an employee's shift. In remote areas, i.e., test and processing, where transit time is deemed necessary by supervision for the employee to reach a rest period station, such transit time will be allowed in addition to the ten (10) minutes.

1203. The Company agrees not to change its present practices on washup time without prior negotiations with the Union.

ARTICLE XIII
WAGE RATES

1301. The bargaining unit job classifications and wage rates which shall be effective during the term of this agreement are set forth in Appendix "A" and made a part thereof.

ARTICLE XIV
PAYROLL DEDUCTIONS

1401. Payroll deductions will be made only when:

1402. Required by law.

ARTICLE XV
NEW OR REVISED JOB CLASSIFICATION

1501. It is recognized that the establishment of new or revised job classifications within the collective bargaining unit heretofore defined may be warranted because of changes in job content growing out of the introduction of new products, changes in equipment, tooling, or in methods of processing or in materials processed, etc. Under each circumstance, the Company shall prepare and submit to the Union for negotiation the descriptions and appropriate rate ranges and promotional group for such job classifications as will have been determined to be within the collective bargaining unit. If agreement has not been reached after ten (10) working days, the Company may place the job classification into effect. The Union shall have the right within thirty (30) days thereafter to file a grievance over any alleged improper job description and/or rate range and/or promotional group for such classification. If the Union does not file a grievance within the time limit specified above, the job classification, rate range, and promotional group established by the Company shall be considered to be fair and equitable and shall remain in effect.

ARTICLE XVI
SENIORITY AND PROMOTIONS

1601. General

1602. The purpose of this article is to provide a declared policy of work security for employees measured by length of service with the Company and to provide means by which job movements of employees will be regulated.

1603. Definitions

1604. **Hire date seniority** shall be defined as the employee's length of service with the Company since his date of hire or rehire, whichever occurs later.

1613. Layoffs and Downgrades

1614. General

1615. In administering layoffs and downgrades, seniority shall be applied as follows:

1616. The person having the least bargaining unit seniority within the affected job classification in the Company shall be the first displaced and the last recalled.

1617. An employee(s) who is unable to retain his present job classification due to a reduction in force shall apply his bargaining unit seniority to bump a less senior employee(s), if any, within his promotional ladder.

1618. In the application of Paragraph 1617, the employee will apply his bargaining unit seniority to displace less senior employees, if any, within his promotional ladder and his previously held jobs in descending labor grade order in an effort to retain the highest rated job classification possible. An employee's promotional ladder will be determined by the earliest date of entry into his highest rated job classification. All previously held job classifications will be integrated into into the employee's promotional ladder in descending labor grade order. In cases where an employee can bump to more than one job classification in the same labor grade, he will displace the least senior employee of those job classifications.

1619. An employee affected by reduction in the work force may bump to a higher rated classification only under the following conditions:

    a. That such classification was formerly held on a permanent basis and subsequently upgraded or converted from a classification that was formerly held on a permanent basis and subsequently upgraded.

    b. That the employee does not have recall rights to such classification, or that the employee has not refused recall to such classification.

c. That the employee must be affected by a reduction in force (lateral transfer, downgrade, or layoff) at the time he wishes to exercise his seniority to a higher classification.

1620. The application of this procedure is not intended to extend job assignment or work organization preference to the affected employee, but does provide maximum employment based on length of service with the Company. It is the intent of this article that an employee exercising any priority of placement must be the more senior in bargaining unit seniority to displace another employee within his promotional ladder in the event of a reduction in force.

1621. If two or more employees subject to a layoff or downgrade have an equal amount of bargaining unit seniority with the Company, the most senior employee will be determined on the basis of:

1622. a. Earliest date of hire at the Company.

1623. b. Lowest badge number.

1624. Employees may accept a layoff in lieu of downgrade. However, if the employee has been notified of his downgrade and requests layoff in lieu of downgrade, he must submit a confirmemo to his supervisor requesting layoff in lieu of downgrade to a particular job classification(s) prior to the end of his shift on the Tuesday following his notification. The supervisor will sign and date the confirmemo and be responsible for forwarding it to Labor Relations immediately. An employee may rescind a confirmemo providing he submits written notification to his supervisor in advance of publishing a layoff list on which the employee is affected. An employee who elects to accept a layoff in lieu of downgrade(s) shall forfeit recall rights to refused job classification(s) within his promotional ladder.

1625. In case of a layoff, the Company shall notify the affected employees at least five (5) regularly scheduled working days in advance unless advance planning is not possible due to unavoidable circumstances (mutually agreed upon as unavoidable, and if mutual agreement is not reached, such may be subject to the grievance procedure), or in cases where the employee is absent. In such instances the Company shall notify the affected employees as far in advance as possible.

1626. Emergency Layoff Procedure

1627. In the event the Company finds it necessary to make an emergency general layoff (in excess of 100 employees) or an entire operation (if less than 100 employees) due to cancellation of contracts without prior notice, or disaster requiring shutdowns, or other unavoidable circumstances (mutually agreed upon as unavoidable and if mutual agreement is not reached, such may be subject to the grievance procedure), the Company may lay off without regard to seniority all employees involved subject to the following:

1628. a. All employees with one (1) or more years of seniority shall be returned within five (5) working days to positions to which their seniority and qualifications would entitle them.

1626. b. All employees with less than one (1) year of seniority shall be returned within ten (10) working days to positions to which their seniority would entitle them.

1630. c. In the event the Company finds it necessary to have work performed during the above periods, the senior classified employee(s) of the classification utilized will be given the opportunity to perform the available work.

1631. Recall from Layoff or Downgrade

1632. Any employee who accepts a lower paid job classification in lieu of a layoff (downgrade) shall have recall rights within his promotional ladder.

1633. Laid-off, downgraded, or employees laterally transferred due to a reduction in the work force shall be recalled in the event of job openings in accordance with their bargaining unit seniority before the Company declares such openings available for promotion or lateral transfer.

1634. In the event an employee subject to recall accepts a job classification in the bargaining unit at a rate range equal or lower than jobs where he has recall rights as determined by the promotional ladder, he shall not lose recall rights to such job classification(s).

1639. General

1640. Loss of Seniority

1641. a. Resignation.

1642. b. Discharge for just cause.

1643. c. Failure to comply, report, or refusal of recall in accordance with the provisions of Section 1638.

1644. d. Layoff in excess of twenty-four (24) consecutive months out of the Company.

1645. e. Failure to return to the bargaining unit in accordance with the provisions of Sections 1649 and 1650.

1646. f. Failure to return from, or comply with, the provisions of Article XXVI—Leaves of Absence.

1647. g. Early retirement.

1648. No employee who has active seniority rights under this agreement shall be required to serve more than one probationary period within the bargaining unit unless he is discharged for just cause or quits.

1649. Retention of Seniority

1650. An employee who has voluntarily accepted a job classification with the Company outside of the bargaining unit may return to the bargaining unit provided that the employee returns within a total accumulative period of three (3) months. Such three-month period shall constitute all time spent outside of the bargaining unit during the course of employment with the Company.

1651. Super Seniority

1652. Union stewards, president, vice president, recording secretary, conductor, sentinel, three (3) trustees, secretary-treasurer, negotiating committee, permanent grievance committeeman, and Union safety committee chairman shall possess super seniority within his classification and area of representation for the purpose of layoff, transfer, downgrade and shift change during their period of service in such capacity. Super seniority for the above mentioned positions will be advanced for these representatives when in an "elect" status not to exceed thirty-one (31) days. It is the responsibility of the business representative and/or chief steward to provide Labor Relations with a current list of all employees entitled to such super seniority. This list shall continue in full force and effect until there is a signed notice of change furnished by the business representative and/or chief steward. In the event the business representative and/or chief steward fails to promptly provide Labor Relations with a change in the list, the Company shall not be responsible for any liability resulting from the lack of proper notification. If an employee maintains his classification solely as a result of super seniority, and subsequently loses that super seniority, the employee will continue in that classification for thirty-one (31) calendar days, at which time he will be placed in accordance with the normal seniority as outlined in this agreement.

ARTICLE XVII
UNION STEWARDS

1701. The union will designate one (1) chief steward for the Aerojet Liquid Rocket Company and Aerojet Nuclear Systems Company. One (1) permanent grievance committeeman will also be recognized and he shall perform duties similar to those of the chief steward. The permanent grievance committeeman may be designated to act as the chief steward when he is absent or at the request of the chief steward. The chief steward's duties shall be as follows:

1702. Act as chairman of the Union grievance committee.

1703. To investigate a grievance to determine the advisability of appealing it to the third step of the grievance procedure.

1704. To participate in the hearing of grievances that have been appealed to the third step of the grievance procedure.

1705. To investigate matters pertaining to safety and unsanitary working conditions within the Aerojet Liquid Rocket Company and Aerojet Nuclear Systems Company.

1706. To participate in arbitrations, negotiations, and other scheduled meetings with the Company pertaining to the bargaining unit within the Aerojet Liquid Rocket Company and Aerojet Nuclear Systems Company.

1707. To order, direct, and be responsible for all actions and activities of the permanent grievance committeeman, all zone and senior stewards, Union safety committee chairman, and all other employees within the Aerojet Liquid Rocket Company and Aerojet

Nuclear Systems Company who are on downtime for the purpose of conducting Company-Union business, including the policing of any unauthorized and excessive time spent on Union activity. Union representatives shall not be allowed to leave their area of representation or the plant premises to conduct Union business without prior approval of the chief steward and/or business representative. When employees are to be absent from their work station for the purpose of conducting Company-Union business, the chief steward and/or the business representative will notify the Labor Relations office no later than twenty-four (24) hours, if possible, prior to the day such employee will be absent in order to arrange for the necessary changes.

1708. To schedule weekly grievance meetings with Labor Relations on grievances which have been appealed from the second step.

1709. Senior Stewards

1710. In addition to the zone stewards as provided for in Section 1714, the Union may designate senior stewards not to exceed three' (3), except where by mutual agreement this number may be changed. Such senior stewards shall be appointed in accordance with mutually agreed upon location, work organization and shift. The senior stewards' duties shall be as follows:

1711. To order, direct and be responsible for the actions of the zone stewards under his jurisdiction, including the policing of any unauthorized or excessive time spent on Union activity.

1712. To investigate a verbal or written grievance within his area of jurisdiction that has not been satisfactorily adjusted at the first step of the grievance procedure.

1713. To consult with the chief steward to determine the advisability of appealing a grievance to the third step of the grievance procedure.

1714. Zone Stewards

1715. Zone stewards may be designated in accordance with areas mutually agreed upon by the Union and the Company. The Union will not exceed a ratio of one (1) zone steward to every fifty (50) bargaining unit employees.

1716. The zone stewards' duties shall be as follows:

1717. To investigate and discuss a grievance with an employee within his area of representation. If, after a discussion, there is a valid reason for the grievance, the zone steward may present an employee's grievance to the immediate supervisor in an effort to resolve the matter.

1718. To present to supervision an employee's written grievance.

1719. To consult with the senior steward when a written grievance has been answered at the first step of the grievance procedure to determine the advisability of appealing the grievance to the second step of the grievance procedure.

1720. General

1721. It is agreed that zone and senior stewards shall keep at a minimum the time spent in the performance of their duties as outlined in this article and at all other times continue to perform their assigned jobs.

1722. A steward before leaving his work station to perform any of his functions shall request permission from his immediate supervisor to conduct on Company time Union business falling within the provisions of this article and contract, state the nature of his activity, the approximate amount of time he will be gone, and such permission shall be immediately granted. A steward will not ask for immediate permission if operations will be adversely affected. He shall report to his supervisor upon completing such mission. Every effort shall be made by the zone steward to conduct Union business at the end of his regularly assigned shift.

1723. The chief steward and/or business representative shall give the Labor Relations Manager or his representative as much advance notification as possible in writing of any changes of stewards, designating the agreed-upon area, work organization, and shift in which they are certified to function. Such notification shall also be given upon removal of a steward. Stewards shall be recognized only upon receipt of an official Union letter of certification. Such written certification shall be addressed to Labor Relations.

1724. When mutually agreed-upon areas of representation are changed, the Union will notify the Company promptly of the employee to be recognized thereafter as the zone or senior steward since there can be no more than one (1) steward to each zone per shift.

1725. All ratios in this article shall be reapportioned on the basis of total bargaining unit employees on the payroll as of the last Sunday of each calendar month, and proper apportionment action shall be taken no later than three (3) weeks from that time.

1726. No Union steward will be transferred to another area or shift unless such transfer is mutually agreed to by the Company and the Union. Should an employee be temporarily assigned to a zone other than his regular zone, he will be represented by the steward of that zone to which he is temporarily assigned.

1727. All Union representatives will report to the cognizant supervisor, if available, or any available supervisor when entering an area supervised by a supervisor other than his own. He will inform the supervisor he is there to discuss Company-Union matters and the approximate length of his stay.

1728. Zone and senior stewards' super seniority will be on the basis of area of jurisdiction (zone area and shift) and classification. Senior stewards must have completed one (1) year of continuous employment within the bargaining unit. Zone stewards must have completed six (6) months of continuous service within the bargaining unit.

1729. The senior steward or the regular zone steward may designate an acting steward to act in his place when the regular steward is absent from the facility. Such acting stewards shall not have super seniority.

1730. The Company shall provide an office for use by the chief steward providing that the use of such office is not abused.

1731. The supplementary agreement regarding the total hours permitted by the Company to conduct all Union activity and representative(s) downtime is a part of this article.

ARTICLE XVIII
GRIEVANCE PROCEDURE

1801. For the purpose of this agreement, the term "grievance" means a dispute between the Company and the Union, or between the Company and any employee concerning the interpretation, application, claim of breach or violation of this agreement or any matters involving wages, hours, working conditions or other conditions of employment. Any group or general grievance involving more than one individual shall be taken up by a designated Union representative.

1802. Step 1

1803. An employee who believes he has cause for grievance shall contact his immediate supervisor alone, with, or through his zone steward. Prior to discussing the grievance the supervisor shall notify the zone steward, who shall be present at such discussion. If after discussions with the immediate supervisor, the employee and/or the zone steward do not feel that the grievance has been properly adjusted, the grievance may be reduced to writing by the zone steward. The zone steward is responsible for the written grievance at the first step. The grievance statement shall include the following:

1804. a. A statement of the grievance clearly indicating the question raised by the grievance and the article(s) and section(s) of the labor contract that is violated.

1805. b. The remedy or correction requested of the Company.

1806. The grievance form will be filled out with an original and six (6) copies, and shall be signed by the grieving employee and the zone steward, the date and time of presentation affixed thereto, and signed as received by the employee's immediate supervisor.

1807. The grieving employee's immediate supervisor shall give his answer to the grievance in writing within one (1) standard workday from the time he receives the grievance in writing. The supervisor's answer shall include the following:

1808. a. A complete statement of the Company's position and the facts upon which it is based.

1809. b. The remedy or correction which has been offered, if any.

1810. If the grievance is withdrawn, settled or denied, at the first or second step, the supervisor shall retain one copy for his file, forward the original to Labor Relations, and return the remaining copies to the zone steward.

1811. All available facts must be brought out at all steps of the grievance procedure.

1812. Step II

1813. The zone steward will deliver the grievance and answer to the senior steward, who will make the decision whether or not to appeal to the second step. The senior steward is responsible for the grievance at the second step.

1814. The appeal to the second step will be made within one (1) standard workday. The hearing of the grievance will be held within two (2) standard workdays from the date of appeal to second step, if possible, or in any event within three (3) standard working days of the second step appeal. The senior steward and designated representative of the department manager will meet in an effort to settle the matter. The Company's answer will be made two (2) standard workdays after the hearing is held. The Union has five (5) standard workdays to determine whether or not to appeal the grievance to the third step. The chief steward has the responsibility to determine if the grievance is appealed to the third step. By mutual agreement of the parties, the grieving employee, zone steward, and the supervisor who gave the first step answer may attend the second step hearing.

1815. Step III

1816. The chief steward and/or his designated representative and others by mutual agreement and the designated representative of Labor Relations will meet at regularly scheduled weekly meetings to hear grievances appealed to the third step. Grievances appealed to the third step of the grievance procedure shall be heard within ten (10) standard working days after the appeal to the third step of the grievance procedure. Labor Relations will be notified of the order of grievances to be heard at least forty-eight (48) hours prior to the mutually agreed scheduled meeting.

1817. The chief steward and/or his designated representative and Labor Relations Representative will meet in an effort to dispose of the matter. A written answer will be made within ten (10) standard workdays after the hearing.

1818. Arbitration

1819. If the third step answer is not satisfactory to the Union, the Union may appeal the grievance to arbitration. The request for arbitration must be given in writing to the Manager of Labor Relations by the designated representative of the Union within ten (10) standard workdays from the date of the third step answer.

1820. It is understood the Company's maximum liability in a continuing liability grievance shall not exceed three (3) calendar months from the date of the third step answer. Any grievance for which an arbitrator is not selected and a hearing date set within three (3) calendar months from the date of the Company's third step answer will be considered withdrawn without prejudice.

1821. An arbitrator may be selected by mutual agreement between the Manager of Labor Relations and the Directing Business Representative or their designated representatives.

1822. Should the parties fail to mutually agree on an arbitrator in the selection meeting referenced in Section 1821 above, within forty-eight (48) hours of such meeting, they shall immediately make a joint request to the Federal Mediation and Conciliation Service for a list of five (5) qualified arbitrators. The parties shall each strike two (2) names from the list and the remaining person shall be accepted as the arbitrator.

1823. In the event there is a violation of Article III, in addition to any other remedy either party may proceed immediately to arbitration, and the arbitrator will issue a final award within one (1) standard workday, which will be fully enforceable.

1824. Prior to the arbitration hearing the parties will endeavor to enter into a stipulation of facts concerning the matter to be arbitrated and further will attempt to define the issue to be arbitrated.

1825. If an employee witness is called by the Company, the Company will reimburse him for time lost. If a swing or graveyard shift employee is called in for an arbitration during the day shift, such employee may only work enough hours during his regular shift that would, in addition to the hours paid by the Company as an arbitration witness, total a standard eight (8) hour work shift. If an employee witness is called by the Union, except the chief steward or his designated representative, the Union will reimburse him for lost time.

1826. It is understood that the arbitrator will only interpret this contract and will in no instance add to, delete from, or amend any part thereof. The arbitrator's decision shall be final and binding on both parties to this agreement, and such decision shall be rendered within thirty (30) days after receipt of briefs, if filed, and/or transcripts, whichever is later.

1827. The fees of the arbitrator and the court reporter will be borne equally by the Union and the Company, except in those cases where either party proceeds to arbitration under Section 1823 of the labor agreement.

1828. Medical Arbitration

1829. If a grievance arises which is not settled between the parties as a result of an employee's medical condition, the following procedure will be followed:

1830. a. The Company physician and the employee's physician will select a third doctor who will make a medical evaluation of the employee's condition.

1831. b. The neutral physician's medical opinion on the extent of the disability and/or the reasonableness of the medical restriction shall be final.

1832. General

1833. In those instances where an employee believes he has cause for a grievance based on events occurring in a work organization other than his own, or based upon the act(s) of an employee assigned in a work organization other than his own, arrangements will be made for a responsible supervisor to attend the second step grievance hearing.

1834. A Union policy grievance, as distinguished from a grievance filed by an individual employee, may be filed at Step III of the grievance procedure by the chief steward.

1835. A written grievance involving more than one (1) employee will be filed by the zone steward for and on behalf of the employees.

1836. Settlements at Step I and Step II of the grievance procedure are not precedent setting and these dispositions will not be used in establishing a grievance precedent.

1837. No matter shall be considered as a grievance under this article unless it is presented in writing within thirty (30) calendar days after occurrence of the events on which the grievance was based, unless the aggrieved party did not know that grounds existed for such a claim prior to the expiration of such thirty (30) calendar day period, in which case such grievance must be filed within ten (10) calendar days after the discovery of the circumstances resulting in the grievance. However, under no circumstances will the grievance be processed if the events in the grievance are based on happenings two (2) months or more old as of the written submission. It is the intent of this provision that a grievance shall be filed as soon as practicable.

1838. No grievance decision covering any type of grievance shall provide for retroactive compensation for more than thirty (30) working days prior to the date such grievance was filed, except by mutual agreement between the parties, except that a bona fide pay discrepancy, with proper documentation, will be reviewed.

1839. Either party to this agreement shall, upon receipt of a written grievance, have the right to refuse to handle such grievance if the aggrieved party has not followed the steps outlined in this article for processing a grievance except that grievances of a general nature pertaining to matters not normally decided by shop supervisory personnel may be presented in Step III.

1840. If the Company does not meet time limits, the Union may process the grievance to the next highest step of the grievance procedure, and a hearing will be held the following workday. However, by mutual agreement the applicable representatives of the parties may extend the time limit for a grievance by a signed specified time extension. If no answer to a third step grievance is forthcoming within the appropriate time limits and no mutual agreement to extend the time limits in writing has been made, then the grievance will be granted in favor of the Union at the third step.

1841. The business representative, the chief steward, or his designated representative, the senior steward, and the zone steward shall have the authority to settle grievances for the Union or employees at their respective steps of the grievance procedure.

1842. An employee who is to be discharged shall be granted a hearing upon his request with a Labor Relations representative and such hearing will include the chief steward and/or business representative. The discharged employee will be given the reason for discharge in writing. In those cases where employees are suspended, the business representative and/or chief steward will be notified by Labor Relations.

1843. An unsettled grievance arising as a result of the discharge of an employee will be processed to arbitration immediately. If the parties are unable to agree upon the selection of an arbitrator within forty-eight (48) hours after the Company's third step answer, the Federal Mediation and Conciliation Service will be contacted by telegram or telephone for a list of five (5) qualified arbitrators and the selection of an arbitrator will be made within twenty-four (24) hours of receipt of such lists, in accordance with the provisions of Section 1822 of this article.

1844. An Employee Action Record shall be void and without effect twenty-four (24) months after the date of its issuance and the Company will remove such void Employee Action Record from the employee's personnel file and copies returned to the employee. However, the status of the Employee Action Record will be reviewed six (6) months subsequent to its issuance, and each six (6) months thereafter, by a designated member of management and the appropriate Union Steward.

1845. It is agreed that a copy of any documentation regarding an employee's conduct which is the basis of or is an Employee Action Record shall be given to the employee no later than sixty (60) days after the occurrence of the events on which the documentation is based. This will not apply to actions regarding unauthorized absences, excessive absenteeism and tardiness.

ARTICLE XIX
ACCESS TO COMPANY FACILITY

1901. Accredited representatives of the Union shall have the maximum access permissible under applicable security regulations to appropriate areas of the Company's facility during working hours for the purpose of conducting Union business pertaining to the provisions of this agreement. It is understood that all arrangements for visits of the accredited representatives of the Union to the Company's facility shall be made through Industrial Relations.

ARTICLE XX
NONDISCRIMINATION

2001. The Company and the Union agree not to discriminate in any way against any employee because of race, color, creed, religion, national origin, sex, age, or handicap.

2002. The Company agrees not to discriminate against any employee for Union activity.

ARTICLE XXI

BULLETIN BOARDS

2101. Space shall be provided on Company property at locations mutually agreed upon for Union bulletin boards for the posting of the following types of notices:

2102. a. Union recreational and social activities.

2103. b. Union elections.

2104. c. Union appointments and results of Union elections.

2105. d. Union meetings.

2106. e. Such other notices as may be mutually agreed upon by the Union and Manager of Labor Relations.

2107. Notices as referenced in (e) above and posted without prior mutual agreement by the Labor Relations Manager or his designated representative will result in the removal of such unauthorized notices by the Union upon request by Labor Relations.

2108. Glass-enclosed Union bulletin boards shall continue to be furnished by the Company. They are for the sole purpose of posting such notices as listed above. The size shall be 3 feet by 4 feet. The locks and keys shall be furnished and retained by the Union.

* * *

ARTICLE XXIV

AGE AND HEALTH OF EMPLOYEES

2401. It is mutually agreed that advanced age by itself will not be a deterrent to employment with the Company. This article is not to be used in any way to hinder or conflict with the pension plan covered by Article XXIX.

2402. The Company may require physical examinations of prospective employees to determine if they are physically qualified for employment.

2403. Periodic physical examinations will be provided for occupations where deemed advisable. This list of occupations selected for periodic physical examinations shall be subject to the grievance procedure. Such time spent by employees for such examinations shall be paid for by the Company.

* * *

ARTICLE XXVI
LEAVES OF ABSENCE

2601. For periods of short duration, not to exceed six (6) consecutive months, leaves of absence without pay shall be granted for the following reasons:

2602. a. Employee illness, accident or maternity. (The Company may require satisfactory proof of such illness, accident, or maternity.)

2603. b. Medically restricted employees incapable of performing the duties of their present classification.

2604. c. Appointment or election to a Union position.

2605. The Company may grant leaves of absence without pay for other reasons that the Company considers valid.

2606. Union Business

2607. Any officer of the Union, delegate, or committeeman, shall be granted a leave of absence without pay for the purpose of attending Union conventions or meetings or to accept full-time employment by the Union, with the following terms and conditions:

2608. a. In case of full-time employment by the Union, if conditions permit, at least ten (10) days' written notice of the necessity of such leave shall be given to the Company by the Union. Upon application in writing, leaves of absence with seniority unimpaired shall be granted to full-time officers and employees of the Union for the duration of their employment or term of office, provided such employees have completed their probationary period; provided such leave shall be subject to automatic renewal after three (3) years from date of commencement; and provided further that employees on such leave shall not accrue holiday, vacation, or sick leave. Union representatives on leaves of absence shall be allowed to return with the same privileges that are given employees on military service leave provided they do not take other employment before returning to the Company. They shall acquire active pension credits while off the Company's payroll. The Company will make available to full-time Union representatives the dental plan, group insurance, and life insurance provided that the actual cost will be reimbursed by the Union.

2609. b. Other notification for leaves of absence for Union business shall be made in writing by the Union with as much advance notification to the Company as possible.

MIDLAND NATIONAL LIFE INSURANCE COMPANY

263 NLRB 24 (1982).

The facts are not complex. On the afternoon of October 15, 1980, the day before the election, the Employer distributed campaign literature to its employees with their paychecks. One of the distributions was a six-page document which included photographs and text depicting three local employers and their involvements with the Petitioner. The document also contained a reproduction of a portion of the Petitioner's 1979 financial report (hereinafter LMRDA report) submitted to the Department of Labor pursuant to the provisions of the Labor Management Reporting and Disclosure Act of 1959. The Petitioner learned of the document the next morning, $3^{1}/_{2}$ hours before the polls were to open.

The first subject of the document, Meilman Food, Inc., was portrayed in "recent" pictures as a deserted facility, and was described in accompanying text as follows: "They too employed between 200 and 300 employees. This Local 304A struck this plant—violence ensued. *Now all of the workers are gone!* What did the Local 304A do for them? Where is the 304A union job security?" (Emphasis in original.) Jack Smith, the Petitioner's business representative, testified that Local 304A, the Petitioner, had been the representative of Meilman's employees, but that neither the Petitioner nor Meilman's employees had been on strike when the plant closed. He added that the employees had been working for at least $1^{1}/_{2}$ years following the strike and prior to the closure of the facility.

The second and third employers pictured and discussed in the document were Luther Manor Nursing Home and Blue Cross/Blue Shield. The text accompanying the pictures of Luther Manor explained that:

> [a]lmost a year ago this same union that tells you they will "make job security" (we believe you are the only ones who can do that) and will get you more pay, told the employees of LUTHER MANOR (again, here in Sioux Falls) * * * the union would get them a contract with job security and more money. Unfortunately Local 304A did not tell the Luther Manor employees what year or century they were talking about. Today the employees have no contract. Most of the union leaders left to work elsewhere. Their job security is the same (depends upon the individual as it always has). There has been no change or increase in wages or hours. The union has sent in three different sets of negotiators. Again, promises and performance are two different things. All wages, fringes, working conditions are remaining the same while negotiations continue.

The text accompanying the pictures of Blue Cross stated that "this same Local union won an election at Blue Cross/Blue Shield after promising less restrictive policies, better pay and more job security. Since the election a good percentage of its former employees are no longer working there. Ask them! The employees have been offered a wage increase—*next year* of 5% * * *." (Emphasis in original.)

Smith testified that the Petitioner took over negotiations at Luther Manor and at Blue Cross on or about July 1, 1980, after the Petitioner had merged with Retail Clerks, Local 1665, and that Retail Clerks, Local 1665, not the Petitioner, had conducted the prior negotiations and won the election at Blue Cross.

Assessing the statements concerning these local employers, the Hearing Officer concluded that, in its description of Meilman Food, the Employer intended to instill in the minds of its employees the false impression that the Petitioner had conducted a strike at Meilman, that violence had ensued, and that, as a direct result of the strike, all of the employees at Meilman were terminated. Evaluating the statements about Luther Manor and Blue Cross, the Hearing Officer found that the Employer had misrepresented the labor organization involved, and had implied that the Petitioner was an ineffectual and inefficient bargaining representative who would cause employees to suffer.

The Employer's distribution also included a portion of the Petitioner's 1979 LMRDA report which listed information concerning the Petitioner's assets, liabilities, and cash receipts and disbursements for the reporting period. Three entries on the reproduced page were underlined: total receipts, reported at $508,946; disbursements "On Behalf of Individual Members," reported at zero; and total disbursements, reported at $492,701. Other entries on the reproduced page showed disbursements of $93,185 to officers, and $22,662 to employees. The accompanying text stated that $141,000 of the Petitioner's funds went to "union officers and officials and those who worked for them," and the "NOTHING—according to the report they filed with the U.S. Government was spent 'on behalf of the individual members.' [sic]"

The Hearing Officer found that the report actually showed that the Petitioner disbursed only $115,847 to its officers and employees, a difference of $25,000, and that the Employer's statement attributed 19 percent more in income to the officials and employees than was actually received. He further found that, while the report showed that no sums had been spent "on behalf of the individual members," the instructions for the LMRDA report require that entry to reflect disbursements for "other than normal operating purposes," and that the Employer failed to include this fact in its distribution.

In accordance with his findings outlined above, the Hearing Officer concluded that the document distributed by the Employer contained numerous misrepresentations of fact of a substantial nature designed to portray the Petitioner as an organization staffed by highly paid officials and employees who were ineffectual as bargaining representatives, and that as a consequence employees would suffer with respect to job security and compensation. The Hearing Officer also determined that the document was distributed on the afternoon before the election, that the Petitioner did not become aware of it until approximately 10 a.m. election day, 2½ hours before the preelection conference and 3½ hours before the polls were to open, and that, owing to the nature of the misrepresentations, the Petitioner did not have sufficient time to respond effectively. Applying the standard found in *General Knit of California, Inc.*, and *Hollywood Ceramics Company, Inc.*, the Hearing Officer accordingly recommended that the objection be sustained and that a third election be directed.

We have decided to reject the Hearing Officer's recommendations and to certify the results of the election. We do so because, after painstaking evaluation and careful consideration, we have resolved to return to the sound rule announced in *Shopping Kart Food Market, Inc.*, and to overrule *General Knit* and *Hollywood Ceramics*.

* * *

We begin with the recognition that Congress has entrusted a wide degree of discretion to the Board to establish the procedures necessary to insure the fair and free choice of bargaining representatives by employees. N. L. R. B. v. A. J. Tower Co., 329 U.S. 324, 330 (1946). In carrying out this task, "the Board must act so as to give effect to the principle of majority rule set forth in § 9(a)" of the Act. Id. at 331.

Although the Board's exercise of discretion must be consistent with the principle of majority rule, the Supreme Court has held that the Board is not precluded from making "practical adjustments designed to protect the election machinery from the ever-present dangers of abuse and fraud." Id. In making these rules, the Board must weigh and accommodate not only the principle of majority rule, but several other conflicting factors, such as preserving the secrecy of the ballot, insuring the certainty and finality of election results, and minimizing unwarranted and dilatory claims by those opposed to the election results. Id.

Accordingly, a Board rule governing a representation proceeding need not be an "absolute guarantee" that the election will, without exception, reflect the choice of a majority of the voting employees. Rather, the rule simply must be "consistent with" and constitute a "justifiable and reasonable adjustment of the democratic process." Id. at 332, 333.

For numerous reasons, we find that the rule we announce today constitutes just such a "justifiable and reasonable adjustment" of our democratic electoral processes. By returning to the sound principles espoused in *Shopping Kart*, not only do we alleviate the many difficulties attending the *Hollywood Ceramics* rule, but we also insure the certainty and finality of election results, and minimize unwarranted and dilatory claims attacking those results.

As was discussed earlier, an election would be set aside under *Hollywood Ceramics*

> * * * only there has been a misrepresentation or other similar campaign trickery, which involves a substantial departure from the truth, at a time which prevents the other party * * * from making an effective reply, so that the misrepresentation, whether deliberate or not, may reasonably be expected to have a significant impact on the election.

An an initial matter, it is apparent that reasonable, informed individuals can differ on the multitude of subjective issues encompassed in this rule. When does a particular statement involve a "substantial" departure from the "truth"? Under what conditions has there been time for an "effective reply"? May the misrepresentation "reasonably be expected" to have a "significant impact" upon the election? As Professor Derek C. Bok concluded in his classic work on the Board's election procedures, restrictions on the content of campaign propaganda requiring truthful and accurate statements "resist every effort at a clear formulation and tend inexorably to give rise to vague and inconsistent rulings which baffle the parties and provoke litigation."

The Board's experience under the *Hollywood Ceramics* rule bears this out. As was found in *Shopping Kart*, although the adoption of the *Hollywood Ceramics* rule "was premised on assuring employee free choice its administration has in fact tended to impede the attainment of that goal. The ill effects of the rule include extensive analysis of campaign propaganda, restriction of free speech, variance in application as between the Board and the courts, increasing litigation, and a resulting decrease in the finality of election results."

In sharp contrast to the *Hollywood Ceramics* standard, *Shopping Kart* "draws a clear line between what is and what is not objectionable." Thus, "elections will be set aside 'not on the basis of the *substance* of the representation, but the deceptive *manner* in which it was made.' * * * As long as the campaign material is what it purports to be, i.e., mere propaganda of a particular party, the Board would leave the task of evaluating its contents solely to the employees." Where, due to forgery, no voter could recognize the propaganda "for what it is," Board intervention is warranted. Further, unlike *Hollywood Ceramics*, the rule in *Shopping Kart* lends itself to definite results which are both predictable and speedy. The incentive for protracted litigation is greatly reduced, as is the possibility of disagreement between the Board and the courts. Because objections alleging false or inaccurate statements can be summarily rejected at the first stage of Board proceedings, the opportunity for delay is almost nonexistent. Finally, the rule in *Shopping Kart* "furthers the goal of consistent and equitable adjudications" by applying uniformly to the objections of both unions and employers.

In addition to finding the *Hollywood Ceramics* rule to be unwieldly and counterproductive, we also consider it to have an unrealistic view of the ability of voters to assess misleading campaign propaganda. As is clear from an examination of our treatment of misrepresentations under the Wagner Act, the Board had long viewed employees as aware that parties to a campaign are seeking to achieve certain results and to promote their own goals. Employees, knowing these interests, could not help but greet the various claims made during a campaign with natural skepticism. The "protectionism" propounded by the *Hollywood Ceramics* rule is simply not warranted. On the contrary, as we found in *Shopping Kart,* "we believe that Board rules in this area must be based on a view of employees as mature individuals who are capable of recognizing campaign propaganda for what it is and discounting it."

This fact is apparently recognized to a certain extent even under *Hollywood Ceramics.* Thus, although the Board determined that a substantial misrepresentation had been made, the election would not be set aside if it also appeared that there had been ample time to respond. This result would obtain no matter how egregious the error or falsity, and regardless of whether in fact a response had been made.

We appreciate that today's decision is likely to cause concern, just as did *General Knit's* quick retreat from *Shopping Kart* in 1978. Accordingly, we do not take this step lightly. We take it because of our emphatic belief that the rule in *Shopping Kart* is the most appropriate accommodation of all the interests here involved, and should be given a fair chance to succeed. Unlike its predecessor, it is a clear, realistic rule of easy application which lends itself to definite, predictable, and speedy results. It removes impediments to free speech by permitting parties to speak without fear that inadvertent errors will provide the basis for endless delay or overturned elections, and promotes uniformity in national labor law by minimizing the basis for disagreement between the Board and the courts of appeals. Weighing the benefits flowing from reinstatement of the *Shopping Kart* rule against the possibility that some voters may be misled by erroneous campaign propaganda, a result that even *Hollywood Ceramics* permits, we find that the balance unquestionably falls in favor of implementing the standard set forth in *Shopping Kart.*

In reaching this decision, we note that "[a]dministrative flexibility is * * * one of the principal reasons for the establishment of the regulatory agencies [because it] permits valuable experimentation and allows administrative policies to reflect changing policy views." Boyd Leedom, et al. v. International Brotherhood of Electrical Workers, Local Union No. 108, AFL–CIO, 278 F.2d 237, 243 (D.C.Cir. 1960). As is obvious from today's decision, the policy views of the Board have changed. We cannot permit earlier decisions to endure forever if, in our view, their effects are deleterious and hinder the goals of the Act. The nature of administrative decisionmaking relies heavily upon the benefits of the cumulative experience of the decisionmakers. Such experience, in the words of the Supreme Court, "begets understanding and insight by which judgments * * * are validated or qualified or invalidated. The constant process of trial and error, on a wider and fuller scale than a single adversary litigation permits, differentiates perhaps more than anything else the administrative from the judicial process." N.L.R.B. v. J. Weingarten, Inc., 420 U.S. 251, 265–266 (1975).

Cumulative experience need not produce the same understanding and insight. Reasonable minds can and indeed have differed over the most appropriate resolution of this issue. That no one can dispute. However, we again express our emphatic belief that on balance the rule in *Shopping Kart* best accommodates and serves the interests of all.

In sum, we rule today that we will no longer probe into the truth or falsity of the parties' campaign statements, and that we will not set elections aside on the basis of misleading campaign statements. We will, however, intervene in cases where a party has used forged documents which render the voters unable to recognize propaganda for what it is. Thus, we will set an election aside not because of the substance of the representation, but because of the deceptive manner in which it was made, a manner which renders employees unable to evaluate the forgery for what it is. As was the case in *Shopping Kart*, we will continue to protect against other campaign conduct, such as threats, promises, or the like, which interferes with employee free choice.

Accordingly, inasmuch as the Petitioner's objection alleges nothing more than misrepresentations, it is hereby overruled. Because the tally of ballots shows that the Petitioner failed to receive a majority of the valid ballots cast, we shall certify the results.

MEMBERS FANNING and JENKINS, dissenting:

For the second time in 5 years, a bare majority of the Board has abandoned the flexible and balanced *Hollywood Ceramics* standard for determining when election campaign misrepresentations have overstepped the bounds of tolerability and substituted an ultra-permissive standard that places a premium on the well-timed use of deception, trickery, and fraud. In reestablishing the *Shopping Kart* rule, the present majority adds nothing to the debate that has accompanied the seesawing of Board doctrine in this area. Instead, the majority reiterates the familiar theme of the "unrealistic view of the ability of voters to assess misleading campaign propaganda" (which it attributes to *Hollywood Ceramics*) and the promise of elimination of delays caused by the processing of misrepresentation objections.

* * *

What the majority does now is to give up, in the interest of possibly reducing litigation, a speculative thing at best, any attempt to balance the rights of the employees and the campaigners. However, their goal, which, as the Board noted in *General Knit*, must never take precedence over preservation of the integrity of the electoral process, seems to have eluded the Board's prior attempt under *Shopping Kart*. For, according to an internal audit conducted for the General Counsel, the number of elections in which allegations of misleading statements were ruled on increased from 327 in 1976, the year before *Shopping Kart* was decided, to 357 in 1978, the first full year after *Shopping Kart* was in effect, this despite a decrease (from 8,899 to 8,464) in the total number of elections conducted in those respective years.

In return for the illusory benefits of speed and a speculative lightening of its workload, the majority today errs in relinquishing the Board's obligation to put some limits on fraud and deceit as campaign tools. It is apparent that the system contemplated by Section 9 of the Act for representation elections has survived reasonably well during the decades in which the Board has taken a role in insuring the integrity of its elections. Indeed, the majority does not suggest deregulating the election process other than with respect to misrepresentations. In this connection, we are especially puzzled by the distinction the majority draws between forgery, which it will regulate, and other kinds of fraud, which it will not. The majority states that forgeries "render the voters unable to recognize the propaganda for what it is." Yet it is precisely the Board's traditional perception that there are some misrepresentations which employees can recognize "for what they are" and others which, in the Board's considered judgment, they cannot, that has made the *Hollywood Ceramics* doctrine so effective. In place of this approach, under which judgments take into account the facts of each case, the majority creates an irrebuttable presumption that employees can recognize all misrepresentations, however opaque and deceptive, except forgeries. Employees' free choice in elections, the only reason we run elections, must necessarily be inhibited, distorted, and frustrated by this new rule. To the majority, this is less important than the freedom to engage in lies, trickery, and fraud. Under the new rule, important election issues will be ignored in favor of irresponsible charges and deceit. Under *Hollywood Ceramics*, the Board did not attempt to sanitize elections completely but only to keep the campaign propaganda within reasonable bounds. Those bounds have now disappeared. Why?

Albeit today's American employees may be better educated, in the formal sense, than those of previous generations, and may be in certain respects more sophisticated, we do not honor them by abandoning them utterly to the mercies of unscrupulous campaigners, including the expert cadre of professional opinion molders who devise campaigns for many of our representation elections. In political campaigns, which are conducted over a much longer period of time and are subject to extensive media scrutiny, the voters have ready access to independent sources of information concerning the issues. In representation campaigns, they do not. Thus, it has been observed that: "Promises are often written on the wind, but statements of fact are the stuff upon which men and women make serious value judgments * * * [and] rank and file employees must largely depend upon the company and union to provide the data * * *." As we said in our dissent in *Shopping Kart*, the very high level of participation in Board elections as compared with political elections speaks well for the Board's role in insuring a measure of responsibility in campaigning.   On the other hand, absent some external restraint, the campaigners will have little incentive to refrain from any last-minute deceptions that might work to their short-term advantage.

In sum, we are able to agree with the majority on very little. But one point of agreement is the majority's statement that, "The sole question facing us here is how [the fair and free choice of a bargaining representative] is best assured." For the reasons set forth above, and also for the reasons set forth in *General Knit* and our dissent in *Shopping Kart*, we find it impossible to answer that question by abandoning one of the most effective means the Board has yet devised for assuring that desired result.

Turning to the facts of the instant case, the Employer misrepresented to the employees that a strike called by the Union led directly to the closing of a large local employer and that the Union had bargained extensively with two other local employers without success. These were substantial misrepresentations concerning the central issue in the choice of a bargaining representative—its effectiveness. But the Employer did not limit itself to simple misrepresentations. It stepped beyond that and engaged in an elaborately conceived fraud when it presented and commented upon an excerpt from the Form LM–2 financial report the Union was required to file with the U.S. Department of Labor. Line 71 of the form, showing union disbursements "on behalf of individual members," appears to show that the Union made no such disbursements during the reporting year. The Employer both underlined that item and emphasized it in a separate notation. The Employer contrasted this negative disbursement figure with a figure which overstated by 19 percent the moneys paid to union officers and "those that worked for them." This contrast was designed, of course, to show that the hard-earned money collected from the Union's members benefited only union officials. What the excerpt and the Employer's notations concealed, however, was that the Labor Department's instructions for completing line 71 specifically exclude from disbursements "on behalf of individual members," all normal operating expenses. Thus, while a reader in possession of the instructions might realize that the Union's operating expenses, including salaries for the Union's staff, are incurred with the objective of benefiting all the members, the Employer carefully disguised this fact, egregiously distorted what the Union does with its members' money, and ingeniously made the Union itself appear to be the source of this misinformation. In addition, how many employees are going to read and understand this complicated form?

The Employer's fraudulent misstatement of the contents of this Government document is analogous to the mischaracterization of this Board's documents, and is at least equally objectionable. See *Formco, Inc.*, 233 NLRB 61 (1977). Here, in sum, we have a fraudulent misrepresentation of a most serious and extreme nature, forming part of a series of material misrepresentations. Such conduct can hardly have failed to affect the election, especially since, with a tally of 107 to 107, the change of a single vote may have changed the outcome.

The majority through this decision is giving our election processes, possibly the most important part of installing a viable collective-bargaining relationship, over to the possible excesses of the participants and eliminating the Board from its statutory oversight responsibilities. Why? Accordingly, we must dissent.

*

INDEX

References are to Pages

751

Nineteenth-Century Literature Criticism

Guide to Gale Literary Criticism Series

When you need to review criticism of literary works, these are the Gale series to use:

If the author's death date is: **You should turn to:**

After Dec. 31, 1959
(or author is still living)
CONTEMPORARY LITERARY CRITICISM

for example: Jorge Luis Borges, Anthony Burgess,
William Faulkner, Mary Gordon,
Ernest Hemingway, Iris Murdoch

1900 through 1959
TWENTIETH-CENTURY LITERARY CRITICISM

for example: Willa Cather, F. Scott Fitzgerald,
Henry James, Mark Twain, Virginia Woolf

1800 through 1899
NINETEENTH-CENTURY LITERATURE CRITICISM

for example: Fedor Dostoevski, Nathaniel Hawthorne,
George Sand, William Wordsworth

1400 through 1799
LITERATURE CRITICISM FROM 1400 TO 1800
(excluding Shakespeare)

for example: Anne Bradstreet, Daniel Defoe,
Alexander Pope, François Rabelais,
Jonathan Swift, Phillis Wheatley

SHAKESPEAREAN CRITICISM

Shakespeare's plays and poetry

Antiquity through 1399
CLASSICAL AND MEDIEVAL LITERATURE CRITICISM

for example: Dante, Homer, Plato, Sophocles, Vergil,
the Beowulf poet

(Volume 1 forthcoming)

Gale also publishes related criticism series:

CHILDREN'S LITERATURE REVIEW

This ongoing series covers authors of all eras. Presents criticism on
authors and author/illustrators who write for the preschool
through high school audience.

CONTEMPORARY ISSUES CRITICISM

This two volume set presents criticism on contemporary authors
writing on current issues. Topics covered include the social sciences,
philosophy, economics, natural science, law, and related areas.

ISSN 0732-1864

Volume 14

Nineteenth-Century Literature Criticism

Excerpts from Criticism of the
Works of Novelists, Poets, Playwrights,
Short Story Writers, Philosophers, and Other
Creative Writers Who Died between 1800
and 1900, from the First Published Critical
Appraisals to Current Evaluations

Cherie D. Abbey
Editor

Jelena Obradovic Kronick
Janet Mullane
Associate Editors

Gale Research Company
Book Tower
Detroit, Michigan 48226

STAFF

Cherie D. Abbey, *Editor*

Jelena Obradovic Kronick, Janet Mullane, *Associate Editors*

Gail Ann Schulte, Robert Thomas Wilson, *Senior Assistant Editors*

Rachel Carlson, Vivian L. Metcalf, Mary Nelson-Pulice, *Assistant Editors*

Sheila Fitzgerald, Phyllis Carmel Mendelson, Emily B. Tennyson,
Anna C. Wallbillich, *Contributing Editors*
Melissa Reiff Hug, *Contributing Assistant Editor*

Jeanne A. Gough, *Permissions & Production Manager*
Lizbeth A. Purdy, *Production Supervisor*
Denise Michlewicz Broderick, *Production Coordinator*
Eric Berger, *Assistant Production Coordinator*
Kathleen M. Cook, Maureen Duffy, Sheila J. Nasea, *Editorial Assistants*

Victoria B. Cariappa, *Research Coordinator*
Maureen R. Richards, *Assistant Research Coordinator*
Daniel Kurt Gilbert, Kent Graham, Michele R. O'Connell,
Keith E. Schooley, Filomena Sgambati, Vincenza G. Tranchida,
Mary D. Wise, *Research Assistants*

Linda Marcella Pugliese, *Manuscript Coordinator*
Donna Craft, *Assistant Manuscript Coordinator*
Maureen A. Puhl, Rosetta Irene Simms, *Manuscript Assistants*

Janice M. Mach, *Permissions Coordinator, Text*
Patricia A. Seefelt, *Permissions Coordinator, Illustrations*
Susan D. Battista, Margaret A. Chamberlain, Sandra C. Davis, Kathy Grell, *Assistant Permissions Coordinators*
Mabel C. Gurney, Josephine M. Keene, Mary M. Matuz, *Senior Permissions Assistants*
Margaret A. Carson, H. Diane Cooper, Colleen M. Crane, *Permissions Assistants*
Eileen H. Baehr, Anita L. Ransom, Kimberly F. Smilay, *Permissions Clerks*

Frederick G. Ruffner, *Publisher*
Dedria Bryfonski, *Editorial Director*
Ellen Crowley, *Associate Editorial Director*
Laurie Lanzen Harris, *Director, Literary Criticism Division*
Dennis Poupard, *Senior Editor, Literary Criticism Series*

Copyright © 1987 by Gale Research Company

Library of Congress Catalog Card Number 81-6943
ISBN 0-8103-5814-X
ISSN 0732-1864

Computerized photocomposition by
Typographics, Incorporated
Kansas City, Missouri

Printed in the United States

Contents

Preface

The nineteenth century was a time of tremendous growth in human endeavor: in science, in social history, and particularly in literature. The era saw the development of the novel, witnessed radical changes from classicism to romanticism to realism, and contained intellectual and artistic ideas that continue to inspire authors of our own century. The importance of the writers of the nineteenth century is twofold, for they provide insight into their own time as well as into the universal nature of human experience.

The literary criticism of an era can also give us insight into the moral and intellectual atmosphere of the past, because the criteria by which a work of art is judged reflect current philosophical and social attitudes. Literary criticism takes many forms: the traditional essay, the book or play review, even the parodic poem. Criticism can also be of several types: normative, descriptive, interpretive, textual, appreciative, generic. Collectively, the range of critical response helps us to understand a work of art, an author, an era.

The Scope of the Work

The success of two of Gale's current literary series, *Contemporary Literary Criticism (CLC)* and *Twentieth-Century Literary Criticism (TCLC)*, which excerpt criticism of creative writing from the twentieth century, suggested an equivalent need among students and teachers of literature of the nineteenth century. Moreover, since the analysis of this literature spans almost two hundred years, a vast amount of critical material confronts the student.

Nineteenth-Century Literature Criticism (NCLC) presents significant passages from published criticism on authors who died between 1800 and 1900. The author list for each volume of *NCLC* is carefully compiled to represent a variety of genres and nationalities and to cover authors who are currently regarded as the most important writers of their era as well as those whose contribution to literature and literary history is significant. The truly great writers are rare, and in the intervals between them lesser but genuine artists, as well as writers who enjoyed immense popularity in their own time and in their own countries, are important to the study of nineteenth-century literature. The length of each author entry is intended to reflect the amount of attention the author has received from critics writing in English and from foreign critics in translation. Articles and books that have not been translated into English are excluded. However, since many of the major foreign studies have been translated into English and are excerpted in *NCLC*, author entries reflect the viewpoints of many nationalities. Each author entry represents a historical overview of critical reaction to the author's work: early criticism is presented to indicate initial responses and later selections represent any rise or decline in the author's literary reputation. We have also attempted to identify and include excerpts from the seminal essays on each author as well as modern perspectives. Thus, *NCLC* is designed to serve as an introduction for the student of nineteenth-century literature to the authors of that period and to the most significant commentators on these authors.

NCLC entries are intended to be definitive overviews. In order to devote more attention to each writer, approximately fifteen authors are included in each 600 page volume compared with about fifty authors in a *CLC* volume of similar size. Because of the great quantity of critical material available on many authors, and because of the resurgence of criticism generated by such events as an author's centennial or anniversary celebration, the republication of an author's works, or publication of a newly translated work or volume of letters, an author may appear more than once. Usually, a few author entries in each volume of *NCLC* are devoted to single works by major authors who have appeared previously in the series. Only those individual works that have been the subject of extensive criticism and are widely studied in literature courses are selected for this in-depth treatment. Robert Louis Stevenson's *Strange Case of Dr. Jekyll and Mr. Hyde* and William Makepeace Thackeray's *Vanity Fair* are the subjects of such entries in *NCLC*, Volume 14.

The Organization of the Book

An author section consists of the following elements: author heading, biographical and critical introduction, principal works, excerpts of criticism (each preceded by explanatory notes and followed by a bibliographical citation), and an additional bibliography.

- The *author heading* consists of the author's full name, followed by birth and death dates. The unbracketed portion of the name denotes the form under which the author most commonly wrote. If an author wrote consistently under a pseudonym, the pseudonym will be listed in the author heading and the real name given in parentheses on the first line of the biographical and critical introduction. Also located at the beginning of the introduction are any name variations under which an author wrote, including transliterated forms for authors whose languages use nonroman alphabets. Uncertainty as to a birth or death date is indicated by a question mark.

- A *portrait* of the author is included when available. Many entries also feature illustrations of materials pertinent to an author's career, including manuscript pages, letters, book illustrations, and representations of important people, places, and events in an author's life.

- The *biographical and critical introduction* contains background information that elucidates the author's creative output. When applicable, biographical and critical introductions are followed by references to additional entries on the author in past volumes of *NCLC* and in other literary reference series published by Gale Research Company. These include *Dictionary of Literary Biography, Children's Literature Review,* and *Something about the Author.*

- The list of *principal works* is chronological by date of first book publication and identifies genres. In those instances where the first publication was in other than the English language, the title and date of the first English-language edition are given in brackets. Unless otherwise indicated, dramas are dated by the first performance, rather than first publication.

- *Criticism* is arranged chronologically in each author section to provide a perspective on any changes in critical evaluation over the years. In the text of each author entry, titles by the author are printed in boldface type. This allows the reader to ascertain without difficulty the works being discussed. For purposes of easier identification, the critic's name and the publication date of the essay are given at the beginning of each piece of criticism. Unsigned criticism is preceded by the title of the journal in which it appeared. For an anonymous essay later attributed to a critic, the critic's name appears in brackets at the beginning of the excerpt and in the bibliographical citation.

- Essays are prefaced with *explanatory notes* as an additional aid to students using *NCLC*. The explanatory notes provide several types of useful information, including the reputation of the critic, the importance of a work of criticism, a synopsis of the essay, the specific approach of the critic (biographical, psychoanalytic, structuralist, etc.), and the growth of critical controversy or changes in critical trends regarding an author's work. In some cases, these notes include cross-references to related criticism in the author's entry or in the additional bibliography. Dates in parentheses within the explanatory notes refer to other essays in the author entry.

- A complete *bibliographical citation* designed to facilitate the location of the original essay or book follows each piece of criticism.

- The *additional bibliography* appearing at the end of each author entry suggests further reading on the author. In some cases it includes essays for which the editors could not obtain reprint rights.

An appendix lists the sources from which material in the volume is reprinted. It does not, however, list every book or periodical consulted for the volume.

Cumulative Indexes

Each volume of *NCLC* includes a cumulative index listing all the authors who have appeared in *Contemporary Literary Criticism, Twentieth-Century Literary Criticism, Nineteenth-Century Literature Criticism,* and *Literature Criticism from 1400 to 1800,* along with cross-references to the Gale series *Children's Literature Review, Authors in the News, Contemporary Authors, Contemporary Authors Autobiography Series, Dictionary of Literary Biography, Something about the Author,* and *Yesterday's Authors of Books for Children.* Users will welcome this cumulated author index as a useful tool for locating an author within the various series. The index, which lists birth and death dates when available, will be particularly valuable for those authors who are identified with a certain period but whose death date causes them to be placed in another, or for those authors whose careers span two periods. For example, Fedor Dostoevski is found in *NCLC*, yet Leo Tolstoy, another major nineteenth-century Russian novelist, is found in *TCLC*.

NCLC also includes a cumulative nationality index to authors. Authors are listed alphabetically by nationality, followed by the volume numbers in which they appear.

A cumulative index to critics is another useful feature of *NCLC*. Under each critic's name are listed the authors on whom the critic has written and the volume and page where the criticism appears.

Acknowledgments

No work of this scope can be accomplished without the cooperation of many people. The editors especially wish to thank the copyright holders of the excerpts included in this volume, the permissions managers of the book and magazine publishing companies for assisting us in securing reprint rights, and the staffs of the Detroit Public Library, University of Michigan Library, and Wayne State University Library for making their resources available to us. We are also grateful to Anthony J. Bogucki for his assistance with copyright research. The editors also wish to acknowledge The Bettmann Archive, Inc., for the endpaper illustration of Robert Louis Stevenson.

Suggestions Are Welcome

The editors welcome the comments and suggestions of readers to expand the coverage and enhance the usefulness of the series.

Authors to Appear in Future Volumes

About, Edmond Francois 1828-1885
Aguilo I. Fuster, Maria 1825-1897
Aksakov, Konstantin 1817-1860
Aleardi, Aleadro 1812-1878
Alecsandri, Vasile 1821-1890
Alencar, Jose 1829-1877
Alfieri, Vittorio 1749-1803
Allingham, William 1824-1889
Almquist, Carl Jonas Love 1793-1866
Alorne, Leonor de Almeida 1750-1839
Alsop, Richard 1761-1815
Altimirano, Ignacio Manuel 1834-1893
Alvarenga, Manuel Inacio da Silva
  1749-1814
Alvares de Azevedo, Manuel Antonio
  1831-1852
Anzengruber, Ludwig 1839-1889
Arany, Janos 1817-1882
Arene, Paul 1843-1893
Aribau, Bonaventura Carlos 1798-1862
Arjona de Cubas, Manuel Maria de
  1771-1820
Arnault, Antoine Vincent 1766-1834
Arneth, Alfred von 1819-1897
Arnim, Bettina von 1785-1859
Arnold, Thomas 1795-1842
Arriaza y Superviela, Juan Bautista
  1770-1837
Asbjornsen, Peter Christian 1812-1885
Ascasubi, Hilario 1807-1875
Atterbom, Per Daniel Amadeus
  1790-1855
Aubanel, Theodore 1829-1886
Auerbach, Berthold 1812-1882
Augier, Guillaume V.E. 1820-1889
Azeglio, Massimo D' 1798-1866
Azevedo, Guilherme de 1839-1882
Bakin (pseud. of Takizawa Okikani)
  1767-1848
Bakunin, Mikhail Aleksandrovich
  1814-1876
Baratynski, Jewgenij Abramovich
  1800-1844
Barnes, William 1801-1886
Batyushkov, Konstantin 1778-1855
Beattie, James 1735-1803
Beckford, William 1760-1844
Becquer, Gustavo Adolfo 1836-1870
Bentham, Jeremy 1748-1832
Beranger, Jean-Pierre de 1780-1857
Berchet, Giovanni 1783-1851
Berzsenyi, Daniel 1776-1836
Black, William 1841-1898
Blair, Hugh 1718-1800
Blicher, Steen Steensen 1782-1848
Bocage, Manuel Maria Barbosa du
  1765-1805

Boratynsky, Yevgeny 1800-1844
Borel, Petrus 1809-1859
Boreman, Yokutiel 1825-1890
Borne, Ludwig 1786-1837
Botev, Hristo 1778-1842
Brinckman, John 1814-1870
Bronte, Emily 1812-1848
Brown, Charles Brockden 1777-1810
Browning, Robert 1812-1889
Buchner, Georg 1813-1837
Campbell, James Edwin 1867-1895
Campbell, Thomas 1777-1844
Carlyle, Thomas 1795-1881
Castelo Branco, Camilo 1825-1890
Castro Alves, Antonio de 1847-1871
Channing, William Ellery 1780-1842
Chatterje, Bankin Chanda 1838-1894
Chivers, Thomas Holly 1807?-1858
Claudius, Matthais 1740-1815
Clough, Arthur Hugh 1819-1861
Cobbett, William 1762-1835
Colenso, John William 1814-1883
Coleridge, Hartley 1796-1849
Collett, Camilla 1813-1895
Comte, Auguste 1798-1857
Conrad, Robert T. 1810-1858
Conscience, Hendrik 1812-1883
Cooke, Philip Pendleton 1816-1850
Corbiere, Edouard 1845-1875
Crabbe, George 1754-1832
Cruz E Sousa, Joao da 1861-1898
Desbordes-Valmore, Marceline
  1786-1859
Deschamps, Emile 1791-1871
Deus, Joao de 1830-1896
Dickinson, Emily 1830-1886
Dinis, Julio 1839-1871
Dinsmoor, Robert 1757-1836
Du Maurier, George 1834-1896
Echeverria, Esteban 1805-1851
Eminescy, Mihai 1850-1889
Engels, Friedrich 1820-1895
Espronceda, Jose 1808-1842
Ettinger, Solomon 1799-1855
Euchel, Issac 1756-1804
Ferguson, Samuel 1810-1886
Fernandez de Lizardi, Jose Joaquin
  1776-1827
Fernandez de Moratin, Leandro
  1760-1828
Fet, Afanasy 1820-1892
Feuillet, Octave 1821-1890
Fontane, Theodor 1819-1898
Freiligrath, Hermann Ferdinand
  1810-1876
Freytag, Gustav 1816-1895
Ganivet, Angel 1865-1898

Garrett, Almeida 1799-1854
Garshin, Vsevolod Mikhaylovich
  1855-1888
Gezelle, Guido 1830-1899
Ghalib, Asadullah Khan 1797-1869
Goldschmidt, Meir Aron 1819-1887
Goncalves Dias, Antonio 1823-1864
Griboyedov, Aleksander Sergeyevich
  1795-1829
Grigor'yev, Appolon Aleksandrovich
  1822-1864
Groth, Klaus 1819-1899
Grun, Anastasius (pseud. of Anton
  Alexander Graf von Auersperg)
  1806-1876
Guerrazzi, Francesco Domenico
  1804-1873
Gutierrez Najera, Manuel 1859-1895
Gutzkow, Karl Ferdinand 1811-1878
Ha-Kohen, Shalom 1772-1845
Halleck, Fitz-Greene 1790-1867
Harris, George Washington 1814-1869
Hayne, Paul Hamilton 1830-1886
Hazlitt, William 1778-1830
Hebbel, Christian Friedrich 1813-1863
Hebel, Johann Peter 1760-1826
Hegel, Georg Wilhelm Friedrich
  1770-1831
Heiberg, Johann Ludvig 1813-1863
Herculano, Alexandre 1810-1866
Hernandez, Jose 1834-1886
Hertz, Henrik 1798-1870
Herwegh, Georg 1817-1875
Hoffman, Charles Fenno 1806-1884
Holderlin, Friedrich 1770-1843
Hood, Thomas 1799-1845
Hooper, Johnson Jones 1815-1863
Hopkins, Gerard Manley 1844-1889
Horton, George Moses 1798-1880
Howitt, William 1792-1879
Hughes, Thomas 1822-1896
Imlay, Gilbert 1754?-1828?
Irwin, Thomas Caulfield 1823-1892
Issacs, Jorge 1837-1895
Jacobsen, Jens Peter 1847-1885
Jippensha, Ikku 1765-1831
Kant, Immanuel 1724-1804
Karr, Jean Baptiste Alphonse 1808-1890
Keble, John 1792-1866
Khomyakov, Alexey S. 1804-1860
Kierkegaard, Soren 1813-1855
Kinglake, Alexander W. 1809-1891
Kingsley, Charles 1819-1875
Kivi, Alexis 1834-1872
Koltsov, Alexey Vasilyevich 1809-1842
Kotzebue, August von 1761-1819
Kraszewski, Josef Ignacy 1812-1887

Kreutzwald, Friedrich Reinhold 1803-1882

Krochmal, Nahman 1785-1840

Krudener, Valeria Barbara Julia de Wietinghoff 1766-1824

Lampman, Archibald 1861-1899

Landon, Letitia Elizabeth 1802-1838

Larra y Sanchez de Castro, Mariano 1809-1837

Lebensohn, Micah Joseph 1828-1852

Leconte de Lisle, Charles-Marie-Rene 1818-1894

Lenau, Nikolaus 1802-1850

Leontyev, Konstantin 1831-1891

Leopardi, Giacoma 1798-1837

Leskov, Nikolai 1831-1895

Lever, Charles James 1806-1872

Levisohn, Solomon 1789-1822

Lewes, George Henry 1817-1878

Leyden, John 1775-1811

Lobensohn, Micah Gregory 1775-1810

Longstreet, Augustus Baldwin 1790-1870

Lopez de Ayola y Herrera, Adelardo 1819-1871

Lover, Samuel 1797-1868

Luzzato, Samuel David 1800-1865

Macedo, Joaquim Manuel de 1820-1882

Macha, Karel Hynek 1810-1836

Mackenzie, Henry 1745-1831

Malmon, Solomon 1754-1800

Mangan, James Clarence 1803-1849

Manzoni, Alessandro 1785-1873

Mapu, Abraham 1808-1868

Marii, Jose 1853-1895

Markovic, Svetozar 1846-1875

Martinez de La Rosa, Francisco 1787-1862

Mathews, Cornelius 1817-1889

McCulloch, Thomas 1776-1843

Merriman, Brian 1747-1805

Meyer, Conrad Ferdinand 1825-1898

Montgomery, James 1771-1854

Morton, Sarah Wentworth 1759-1846

Muller, Friedrich 1749-1825

Murger, Henri 1822-1861

Neruda, Jan 1834-1891

Nestroy, Johann 1801-1862

Newman, John Henry 1801-1890

Niccolini, Giambattista 1782-1861

Nievo, Ippolito 1831-1861

Nodier, Charles 1780-1844

Obradovic, Dositej 1742-1811

Oehlenschlager, Adam 1779-1850

O'Neddy, Philothee (pseud. of Theophile Dondey) 1811-1875

O'Shaughnessy, Arthur William Edgar 1844-1881

Ostrovsky, Alexander 1823-1886

Paine, Thomas 1737-1809

Peacock, Thomas Love 1785-1866

Perk, Jacques 1859-1881

Pisemsky, Alexey F. 1820-1881

Pompeia, Raul D'Avila 1863-1895

Popovic, Jovan Sterija 1806-1856

Praed, Winthrop Mackworth 1802-1839

Prati, Giovanni 1814-1884

Preseren, France 1800-1849

Pringle, Thomas 1789-1834

Procter, Adelaide Ann 1825-1864

Procter, Bryan Waller 1787-1874

Pye, Henry James 1745-1813

Quental, Antero Tarquinio de 1842-1891

Quinet, Edgar 1803-1875

Quintana, Manuel Jose 1772-1857

Radishchev, Aleksandr 1749-1802

Raftery, Anthony 1784-1835

Raimund, Ferdinand 1790-1836

Reid, Mayne 1818-1883

Renan, Ernest 1823-1892

Reuter, Fritz 1810-1874

Rogers, Samuel 1763-1855

Ruckert, Friedrich 1788-1866

Runeberg, Johan 1804-1877

Rydberg, Viktor 1828-1895

Saavedra y Ramirez de Boquedano, Angel de 1791-1865

Sacher-Mosoch, Leopold von 1836-1895

Saltykov-Shchedrin, Mikhail 1826-1892

Satanov, Isaac 1732-1805

Schiller, Johann Friedrich 1759-1805

Schlegel, August 1767-1845

Schlegel, Karl 1772-1829

Scott, Sir Walter 1771-1832

Scribe, Augustin Eugene 1791-1861

Sedgwick, Catherine Maria 1789-1867

Senoa, August 1838-1881

Shelley, Percy Bysshe 1792-1822

Shulman, Kalman 1819-1899

Sigourney, Lydia Howard Huntley 1791-1856

Silva, Jose Asuncion 1865-1896

Slaveykov, Petko 1828-1895

Slowacki, Juliusz 1809-1848

Smith, Richard Penn 1799-1854

Smolenskin, Peretz 1842-1885

Stagnelius, Erik Johan 1793-1823

Staring, Antonie Christiaan Wynand 1767-1840

Stendhal (pseud. of Henri Beyle) 1783-1842

Stifter, Adalbert 1805-1868

Stone, John Augustus 1801-1834

Taine, Hippolyte 1828-1893

Taunay, Alfredo d'Ecragnole 1843-1899

Taylor, Bayard 1825-1878

Tennyson, Alfred, Lord 1809-1892

Terry, Lucy (Lucy Terry Prince) 1730-1821

Thompson, Daniel Pierce 1795-1868

Thompson, Samuel 1766-1816

Thomson, James 1834-1882

Tiedge, Christoph August 1752-1841

Timrod, Henry 1828-1867

Tommaseo, Nicolo 1802-1874

Tompa, Mihaly 1817-1888

Topelius, Zachris 1818-1898

Turgenev, Ivan 1818-1883

Tyutchev, Fedor I. 1803-1873

Uhland, Ludvig 1787-1862

Valaoritis, Aristotelis 1824-1879

Valles, Jules 1832-1885

Verde, Cesario 1855-1886

Villaverde, Cirilio 1812-1894

Vinje, Aasmund Olavsson 1818-1870

Vorosmarty, Mihaly 1800-1855

Weisse, Christian Felix 1726-1804

Welhaven, Johan S. 1807-1873

Werner, Zacharius 1768-1823

Wescott, Edward Noyes 1846-1898

Wessely, Nattali Herz 1725-1805

Whitman, Sarah Helen 1803-1878

Wieland, Christoph Martin 1733-1813

Woolson, Constance Fenimore 1840-1894

Zhukovsky, Vasily 1783-1852

Émile Gaboriau

1832-1873

French novelist and journalist.

Often credited with the creation of the first detective novel, Gaboriau introduced in his popular and sensational crime novels many now-familiar narrative methods and detective techniques. Furthermore, scholars cite the series of five books featuring the investigators Lecoq and Père Tabaret as a significant link between Edgar Allan Poe's short stories of detection and Sir Arthur Conan Doyle's Sherlock Holmes tales. Though Gaboriau's work remains largely unread today, he continues to be recognized as a key figure in the development of the detective fiction genre.

Gaboriau was born in Saujon, France, to a bourgeois family. Though his father encouraged him to pursue a career in law, Gaboriau evaded legal studies by joining the cavalry in 1851. During his seven-year term of military service he reached the rank of sergeant major, but left the army when he saw no further opportunity for advancement. After moving to Paris, he took a variety of jobs to support himself: he worked as a shipping clerk, manager of a livery stable, editor of a minor periodical, ballad-writer for street singers, and composer of poetic mottoes for cakes, wrapping paper, and shopping bags. In 1859, he began to publish anecdotes of military life and sketches of famous Parisian actresses and royal mistresses in newspapers and magazines. This writing experience led to a position as secretary to Paul Féval, a popular author of lurid sensational romances that appeared as serial supplements to daily newspapers. Known as "feuilletons," the supplements were the French equivalent of the English "penny dreadfuls" or the American "dime novels." Gaboriau's duties as Féval's secretary probably included researching city morgues, prisons, and police stations for background information as well as ghost-writing some of the daily episodes of the feuilletons.

The knowledge of the French judicial system and Parisian criminal life that Gaboriau acquired as Féval's assistant served him well when he became a feuilletonist in his own right in 1861. During the next five years, Gaboriau produced seven serialized works, but these melodramatic accounts of society and manners attracted little attention until the appearance of *L'affaire Lerouge* (*The Widow Lerouge*). This serial, based on a contemporary crime, won Gaboriau both popular and financial success. Gaboriau's feuilleton included the customary elements of intrigue, crime, and confused identity, but the work was unique in its primary emphasis on the criminal investigation process and the detectives Lecoq and Père Tabaret. Because of this innovative focus many scholars recognize *The Widow Lerouge* as the first true detective novel. Between 1867 and 1869, Gaboriau produced four more novels that featured the idiosyncratic amateur investigator, Tabaret, and the dedicated, egotistical police detective, Lecoq. *Le crime d'Orcival (The Mystery of Orcival), Le dossier no. 113 (File No. 113), Les esclaves de Paris (The Slaves of Paris),* and *Monsieur Lecoq* follow the pattern established in *The Widow Lerouge*. Each work is composed of two volumes: the first opens with a mysterious crime and then describes the detective's efforts to solve it, while the second includes a lengthy digressive history of the characters and their motivations. Though the second vol-

umes were less popular than the action-oriented detective portions, Gaboriau's novels were avidly read, both as serials in periodicals and in book form. His popularity soon spread to England and America, where numerous translations and plagiarized versions were released. Gaboriau profited handsomely from the sale of his novels in France, but he continued writing at a frantic pace, producing five more novels that focused exclusively on society as well as a collection of shorter detective pieces. At the time of his death in 1873, he was at work on two new novels in which he hoped to escape the commercialism of the feuilleton. Some scholars conclude that these fragmentary manuscripts would have proved Gaboriau's best work, had he finished them. While his later writings are generally regarded as inferior to his detective novels, some critics consider *Le petit vieux des Batignolles (The Little Old Man of the Batignolles)*, a novella published posthumously with a collection of short stories, equal to his best work.

Criticism of Gaboriau's work focuses almost exclusively on his detective tales. Some early critics argued that these novels were marred by inconsistencies as well as by the discursive style that Gaboriau adopted as a feuilletonist. Generally, however, contemporary reviewers assessed his works very favorably; though sensational and crime-ridden, Gaboriau's novels never glorify the criminal elements and thus could not be faulted on moral grounds. Commentators also admired Gaboriau's use of scrupulously accurate legal detail, his effective settings, and his careful plot construction. Yet following the first glow of popularity, his books were generally forgotten, and Gaboriau was cited only as an important precursor to Doyle. In the 1920s and 1930s, his reputation enjoyed a brief revival, and his reissued works drew positive commentary from such critics as Valentine Williams and Dorothy L. Sayers, who praised Gaboriau's originality, style, and characterizations. Their critiques established his historical importance to the evolution of the detective genre, a position defended by E. F. Bleiler and R. F. Stewart in the latter part of the twentieth century.

Gaboriau's original detection techniques, which dazzled nineteenth-century readers and are still widely copied, have today earned his novels the status of classics in their genre. Though Gaboriau is of interest primarily to students of the history of mystery literature, many scholars have accorded him the title "the father of the detective novel."

*PRINCIPAL WORKS

Le 13e hussards (sketches) 1861
  [*The Thirteenth Hussars*, 1888]
Les gens de bureau (novel) 1862
  [*The Men of the Bureau*, 1880]
Les mariages d'aventure (sketches) 1862
  [Published in two volumes: *A Chance Marriage*, 1878;
    Promises of Marriage, 1883]
L'affaire Lerouge (novel) 1866
  [*The Widow Lerouge*, 1873]
Le crime d'Orcival (novel) 1867
  [*The Mystery of Orcival*, 1871]
Le dossier no. 113 (novel) 1867
  [*File No. 113*, 1875]
Les esclaves de Paris (novel) 1868
  [*The Slaves of Paris*, 1882]
Monsieur Lecoq (novel) 1869
  [*Monsieur Lecoq*, 1880]
La vie infernale (novel) 1870
  [*The Count's Secret*, 1881]
La clique dorée (novel) 1871
  [*The Clique of Gold*, 1891]
La dégringolade (novel) 1872
  [*The Downward Path*, 1883]
La corde au cou (novel) 1873
  [*Within an Inch of His Life*, 1873]
L'argent des autres (novel) 1874
  [*Other People's Money*, 1874]
Le petit vieux des Batignolles (novella and short stories)
  1876
  [*The Little Old Man of the Batignolles; or, A Chapter
    from a Detective's Memoirs*, 1880]

*Most of Gaboriau's works were first published in serial form in daily newspapers.

THE SATURDAY REVIEW, LONDON (essay date 1866)

[*The following excerpt is drawn from an early review of* The Widow Lerouge.]

The story [of *L'affaire Lerouge*] is well told, and is full of those fine and delicate touches, those epigrammatic sentences and incisive phrases, so peculiarly French; the ingenuity of the evidence is very clever, and the analysis of character and motive subtle and true. It is not ghastly and immoral like Germinie Lacerteux, and some others of late production, but it is neat, careful, well sustained, and interesting; and, if criminal, is also decent. (p. 738)

> A review of "L'affaire Lerouge," in The Saturday Review, London, Vol. 22, No. 581, December 15, 1866, pp. 737-38.

THE SATURDAY REVIEW, LONDON (essay date 1867)

[*The author of the following review of* File No. 113 *finds the novel lacking in ingenuity and claims that Gaboriau's concern with minute plot details led him to commit absurdities and gross oversights.*]

It will be easy for our readers to imagine for themselves the general nature of M. Gaboriau's plot [in *Le Dossier No. 113*]. We cannot say that we perfectly understand all the dark ramifications of plots and counterplots in which his persons lead a mysterious existence. There are two or three of the crimes which are generally most interesting. There is a villain who poisons his brother, and thereby possesses himself of a fortune. There is a theft which we can only compare to the Road murder; two persons, of apparently unimpeachable honour, have keys to a banker's safe, to which no one else has any apparent means of access; and one morning it appears to have been opened, and 350,000 francs subtracted from it. There is, further, an elaborate and diabolical system of *chantage*—the French name for extorting money by threats of exposure—which tortures two amiable women to the verge of insanity. The police authorities and their spies, the villains, the honest people, and above all the wonderful amateur detective [Père Tabaret] . . . are always plunged in a series of more or less unintelligible intrigues, which the reader can scarcely follow without giddiness. There are thrilling meetings in dark corners of Paris, where terrific threats are being exchanged; and it is not without a serious effort of thought that we can realize the position in which any one of the actors stands to the others, and remember what will be the effect of any given remark at a given moment. The writer of such a story has of course no very exalted ambition. He does not seek to give us any profound analysis of character, for it is evidently quite sufficient labour to drive such a perplexing team of personages, and to keep the reins tolerably distinct. The one aim that he can propose to himself is to amuse us by the ingenuity of the story; and the great difficulty is to keep the reader just at the right pitch of attention. If he thinks too little about what he is reading, he soon gets hopelessly muddled as to the various combinations of the plot; and if he thinks too much, he sees that they are all made of moonshine. The principle upon which all such stories depend is a very simple one, and was used with remarkable skill by Poe in his ghastly fiction of the *Murders in the Rue Morgue*. The artifice is something of this kind. When a man has constructed a riddle, he has of course little trouble in finding the answer to it; and if the reader followed the writer's mental process, he would not wonder at its ingenuity. Poe started by imagining a murder by a chimpanzee, and made the beast leave just enough hints of his performance to afford grounds for a guess at his agency. But he of course began by giving the reader the riddle without the explanation, and asked him to guess it. Here, he said, are the hints; what can you make of them? When the reader gave it up, he supplied the key, which of course fitted admirably. And most people forgot to remark how easy it was, when the crime was given, to invent the necessary evidence for its discovery, and also forgot to remark that a sensible man might with equal propriety have made a different guess; for it does not follow in such cases that, because one solution explains the facts, another will not do equally well. M. Gaboriau constantly makes use of this simple artifice. Thus the only trace left upon the safe which has been opened is a certain mysterious scratch. The super-excellent detective thinks about this for three days, and at last hits upon an explanation which solves the mystery and leads ultimately to the discomfiture of the villains. This is, that whilst one person was trying to press the key into the lock, another must have suddenly drawn back his arm by a jerk. When M. Gaboriau had settled the details of the crime, it was of course easy to invent this indication, and it is equally easy to call upon us to admire the marvellous sagacity of his detective in explaining it. And yet in practice such a scratch would admit of fifty other explanations, and a detective who stuck to this one theory would be making a foolish assumption, though it might accidentally turn out that he was right. In the meantime, whilst this astonishing inference is being made, no one else has thought of the most obvious expedient of all—that of getting the numbers of the stolen notes. The detective aforesaid mentions after a time that he has hit upon this plan, and quite confounds his hearer by the wisdom which he has thereby shown; but of course M. Gaboriau is bound to find some profounder device for discomfiting the rogues, and nothing more is heard of tracing the notes. Indeed, if people took the shortest way to their ends, no one could get a sufficiently complicated plot; and, in seeking to get matters into a duly ravelled condition, M. Gaboriau inevitably commits greater oversights than this. He is so careful to raise little entanglements that he forgets some of the most obvious difficulties; if his readers look at matters from a different point of view from his own, the absurdity of some of his assumptions becomes evident. Thus, at one part of his story, it is essential that a villain should be of most attractive appearance, and act the character of a young Frenchman of fortune and birth, whilst moving in good society. At another, the same villain, in obedience to other necessities, has to be the son of an English jockey, who has been better educated than usual, but has made his living by card-sharping in London. That such a youth should enter the house of a rich banker as a native Frenchman of high social position, is, we hope, slightly improbable. Or again, a certain Marquis de Clameran has killed two men, and been sentenced to several years' imprisonment. He escapes, but calmly comes back to France—after twenty years, it is true—but under the same name, and in great wealth and comfort; and it never occurs to any one but his brother that he is the old Marquis de Clameran come back.

In short, without exposing the absurdity of a tissue of absurdities, we may say that the absurdities are really not plausible enough even for a novel. We see the strings too plainly to care about the puppets. Moreover, the complication is mainly produced by a device which is rather tiresome—that of beginning the story in the middle and turning back half way through to tell what had happened before the book began; *à propos* to which we may remark that the amateur detective is supposed to relate these pre-introductory matters, and that in the course of a week he has discovered the particulars of conversations which took place twenty years before. The method by which he obtains this surprising result is by getting copies of letters written by another person about the time of his investigation, which certainly implies that his penetration must have been

An illustration of the murder scene from The Widow Lerouge.

enormous. We have, however, said enough to prove that *Le Dossier No. 113* is, in our opinion, wanting in the merit to which it aspires, that of being amusingly ingenious. (p. 546)

> *A review of "Le dossier no. 113," in* The Saturday Review, *London, Vol. 24, No. 626, October 26, 1867, pp. 545-46.*

THE SATURDAY REVIEW, LONDON   (essay date 1869)

[*In a survey of current French literature, this reviewer commends Gaboriau's* The Slaves of Paris *as entertaining reading.*]

If we must have sensational stories full of horrors and improbabilities, we should prefer applying to writers who, like M. Gaboriau, aim at nothing else but excitement pure and simple. *Les Esclaves de Paris* has no pretensions to teach philosophy or to recommend Red Republicanism; it does not form part of a triology destined to illustrate a grand social thought. M. Gaboriau's sole purpose is to amuse, and he does so thoroughly. It is hard to believe that what he calls *le chantage*— that is to say, the art of worming out people's secrets and trading with them—is as extensively practised in Paris as our novelist suggests; but *chantage* has afforded the groundwork for two interesting volumes.

A review of "Les esclaves de Paris," in The Saturday
Review, *London, Vol. 27, No. 710, June 5, 1869,
p. 758.*

THE SATURDAY REVIEW, LONDON (essay date 1878)

[In the following excerpt, the anonymous critic attributes Gaboriau's success to his careful attention to and consistency in plot details. The critic also dismisses moral objections to Gaboriau's novels, noting that the author demonstrated no sympathy with crime and "never failed to make his criminals utterly odious."]

The most successful author of novels of mystery was, beyond all doubt, the late Emile Gaboriau, some of whose curious and rather ghastly stories seem to be now as widely read as when they were first produced. *L'Affaire Lerouge* and *Le Crime d'Orcival* have gone through twelve editions, and *Le Dossier No. 113* through ten. A greater success could hardly be desired for any novelist; but it might perhaps be urged that nevertheless it is not one to be envied, inasmuch as Gaboriau's works are of a demoralizing nature. The criticism would, however, be unfounded, for, though he usually dealt with crime, he was totally free from any morbid sympathy with it, and never failed to make his criminals utterly odious. The success of his books, then, was certainly not due to any degrading characteristics, and, if it was not of a very lofty kind, it can hardly be denied that it was considerable, and that some of his works are found highly interesting by a great many people.

The point to which we now desire to draw attention is that the great effect which these romances produce on the reader is due not so much to the inventive genius of the writer as to the extraordinary care given by him to the arrangement of his story, and to the thought bestowed by him on every incident down to the most minute. He had considerable inventive power, no doubt; but in this respect other novelists, both English and French, have been quite equal to him. What gave such singular force to some of his fictions was the immense trouble he took to think out every detail of his plot; and that not during the progress of the work, but apparently before he put pen to paper. (p. 619)

[*L'Affaire Lerouge*], no doubt, is an ingenious story, but at the same time it does not show any very extraordinary originality or inventive power. Some parts of it, such as the silence of a man for fear of compromising a woman, and the reappearance of a person supposed to be dead, are old enough, and must be familiar to most readers; and yet *L'Affaire Lerouge* is perhaps the most successful novel of its kind ever written, and probably few of those who have read it can say with truth that it failed to interest them. Its force is due in part, no doubt, to its well-contrived story; but in still greater degree to the careful manner in which the writer, before beginning the work as it appeared, evidently thought out, not only his main plot, but everything connected with it, the sequence of all the facts, the exits and entrances, it may almost be said, of the leading characters. The author, therefore, when writing, developed his story according to a plan considered down to its minutest detail, and, having all the threads in his hand, was able to produce exactly the effect he desired. There is nothing at first apparently to connect the advocate with the murder of Claudine Lerouge; but when the mystery is at last made clear, the fact of his being the assassin is seen to be a necessary inference from the preceding parts of the work, and all the carefully considered incidents are seen to point to the same conclusion, except in one or two cases where the writer makes slight mistakes; but it is

probably almost impossible altogether to avoid these in a novel of this kind. On the whole, the work is wonderfully consistent. The reader who desires to verify what has been said as to Gaboriau's method can easily do so by turning back to the opening chapters after finishing the work. He will then see how completely everything connected with the story must have been present to the author's mind when those were written. If it be said that the opening chapters may have been composed last, the answer is that this cannot have been the case, as the small errors which have been mentioned are in these chapters, and would certainly have been avoided if they had been written after the rest of the book was completed. Probably *L'Affaire Lerouge,* like most of Gaboriau's works, appeared in *feuilletons,* so that the opening chapters must of necessity have been written first, and, once written, could not be altered. It certainly is not to be desired that English writers should imitate Gaboriau in his fondness for describing crimes and horrors; but perhaps some of those who wish to achieve success in what may now be considered as the business of novel-writing might do well to study the method which he followed in producing the most successful of his works. (pp. 619-20)

A review of "L'affaire Lerouge," in The Saturday
Review, *London, Vol. 45, No. 1177, May 18, 1878,
pp. 619-20.*

[A. INNES SHAND] (essay date 1879)

[Calling Gaboriau a pioneer in his genre, Shand points to Gaboriau's emphasis on individualized characters and ingenious plots as his main contribution to the crime fiction model established by Poe. For another discussion by Shand, see the excerpt dated 1890.]

It is nearly six years since the death of Emile Gaboriau, and no one has succeeded as yet in imitating him even tolerably, though he had struck into a line that was as profitable as it was popular. We are not inclined to overrate Gaboriau's genius, for genius he had of a certain sort. . . . [His] system was less difficult than it seems, since he must have worked his puzzles out *en revers,*—putting them together with an eye to pulling them to pieces. But his originality in his own *genre* is unquestionable, though in the main conception of his romances he took Edgar Poe for his model. But Gaboriau embellished and improved on the workmanship of the morbid American. The murders of the Rue Morgue and the other stories of the sort are hard and dry *procès-verbals,* where the crime is everything, and the people go for little, except in so far as their antecedents enlighten the detection. With Gaboriau, on the other hand, we have individuality in each character, and animation as well as coarser excitement in the story. The dialogue is lively, and always illustrative. Perhaps Gaboriau has had but indifferent justice done to him, because he betook himself to a style of romance which was supposed to be the speciality of police-reporters and penny-a-liners. His readers were inclined to take it for granted that his criminals were mere stage villains, and that his police-agents, apart from their infallible *flair,* were such puppets as one sets in motion in a melodrama. The fact . . . [is] that they are nothing of the kind. Extreme pains have been bestowed on the more subtle traits of the personages by which, while being tracked, examined or tried, they are compromised, condemned, or acquitted. Read Gaboriau carefully as you will, it is rarely indeed that you find a flaw in the meshes of the intricate nets he has been weaving. Or, to change the metaphor, the springs of the complicated action, packed away as they are, the one within the other, are always working in marvellous harmony towards the appointed end. The ingenuity of some of his combinations and suggestions is extraordinary; and we believe his works might be very profitable reading to public prosecutors as well as intelligent detectives. His *Maître Lecoq* and his *Père Tabaret* have ideas which would certainly not necessarily occur to the most *rusé* practitioner of the Rue Jerusalem; and they do not prove their astuteness by a single happy thought. On the contrary, the stuff of their nature is that of the heaven-born detective, who is an observer from temperament rather than from habit, and who draws his mathematical deductions from a comparison of the most trivial signs. The proof that Gaboriau's books are something more than the vulgar *feuilleton* of the 'Police News,' is that most of them will bear reading again, though the sensations of the dénouement have been anticipated. In reading for the second time, we read with a different but a higher interest. Thus in the *L'affaire Lerouge,* for example, there is an admirable mystification. The respectable and admirably conducted Noel Gerdy, who has coolly committed a brutal murder, plays the hypocrite systematically to such perfection that we can understand the famous amateur detective being his familiar intimate without entertaining a suspicion as to his nature and habits. The disclosure having been made, and Noel fatally compromised, the circumstances strike you as carrying improbability on the face of them; so you read again and are severely critical in the expectation of catching M. Gaboriau tripping. And we believe, by the way, that in that very novel we have come upon the only oversight with which we can reproach him, although it is not in the history of Noel's intimacy with Père Tabaret. It is a missing fragment of a foil, which is one of the most deadly *pièces de conviction* against the innocent Viscount de Commarin; and the fragment, so far as we can remember, is never either traced or accounted for. But exceptions of this kind only prove the rule; and when we think how the author has varied and multiplied the startling details in his criminal plots, we must admit that his fertility of invention is marvellous. The story of the *Petit Vieux des Batignolles,* the last work he wrote, though short and slight, was by no means the least clever. One unfortunate habit he had, which may perhaps be attributed to considerations of money. He almost invariably lengthened and weakened his novels by some long-winded digression, which was at least as much episodical as explanatory. When the interest was being driven along at high-pressure pace, he would blow off the steam all of a sudden, and shunt his criminals and detectives on to a siding, while, going back among his personages for perhaps a generation, he tells us how all the circumstances had come about. (pp. 698-99)

> [A. Innes Shand], "*Contemporary Literature, VI: French Novels,*" in Blackwood's Edinburgh Magazine, *Vol. CXXV, No. DCCLXIV, June, 1879, pp. 678-703.*

ALFRED E. GATHORNE HARDY   (essay date 1884)

[*Characterizing Gaboriau's novels as entertaining, well constructed, and intellectually challenging, Gathorne Hardy maintains that they are superior to those of Poe and Wilkie Collins and recommends them to students of French legal practice.*]

To those who are desirous of becoming acquainted with the French criminal procedure, and have not the leisure or inclination to study abstruse legal text-books, I pass on the advice given me many years ago by the late Mr. Justice Willes, when I was marshal on the Northern Circuit. "Young man," he said, "you mean to practice at the Bar, and will find it useful to

know the French criminal practice; you had better read Gaboriau's novels, and they will give you a thorough insight into it." Those who have shared with me the privilege of the friendship of that most learned judge and excellent man, will agree that his two distinguishing characteristics as a lawyer were accuracy and profundity, and that he himself would never have given such advice without having compared with the parent sources of code and commentary the streams which, in the form of light literature, he so recommended to others. I followed his advice at once, and have since devoured Gaboriau's works over and over again with infinite pleasure, and if it is necessary to cite more exalted critics in their favour, I believe that two men among the greatest of their generation—Prince Bismarck and Lord Beaconsfield—were great readers and admirers of these fictions. The ingenuity with which the plots are constructed, and the care and industry with which they are elaborated, even to their minutest details, in my opinion far outshine the greatest successes of Poe and Wilkie Collins in similar fields of literature, and I doubt whether anyone who is really fond of the what I may call puzzle class of novels could tear himself away from *Monsieur Lecoq* or *L'Affaire Le Rouge* until the answer to the riddle had been revealed, or the candle burnt down to the socket.

As a general rule the plan of Gaboriau's various works is uniform. A crime is committed under mysterious circumstances, and one portion of the book is devoted to detecting its author and proving the innocence of those who are wrongly suspected, while a second portion details the circumstances, often commencing at a remote date, which led to its commission. The general interest of the latter part is usually far inferior to that of the former. The reader must be prepared for murders, thefts, bigamy, and other crimes, and "moving accidents in flood and field"; but if Gaboriau wishes, like the fat boy in *Pickwick*, "to make your flesh creep," judging from my own experience he does not in the least degree succeed. My feelings are never at all harrowed by the woes of bereaved relations, plundered bankers, and betrayed damsels; who all seem to me as lay-figures constructed to set off to advantage the life-like personalities of the real heroes, the marvellous detectives whose instinctive perception of the true facts of a crime, and the motives of its perpetrators, far excel the wonders of modern thought-reading. . . . (pp. 593-94)

> *Alfred E. Gathorne Hardy, "The Examination of Prisoners: Emile Gaboriau," in* The National Review, *London, Vol. III, July, 1884, pp. 591-604.*

SIR ARTHUR CONAN DOYLE   (essay date 1887)

[*Doyle was a late nineteenth- and early twentieth-century English novelist and short story writer who is best remembered as the creator of Sherlock Holmes. The following excerpt from Dr. Watson's recounting of a dialogue with Sherlock Holmes is taken from Doyle's* A Study in Scarlet, *which was first published in* Beeton's Christmas Annual *in November, 1887. Although Holmes here claims superiority to Lecoq, later critics often link Gaboriau's and Doyle's creations in discussions of detective fiction.*]

'Have you read Gaboriau's works?' I asked. 'Does Lecoq come up to your idea of a detective?'

Sherlock Holmes sniffed sardonically. 'Lecoq was a miserable bungler,' he said, in an angry voice; 'he had only one thing to recommend him, and that was his energy. That book made me positively ill. The question was how to identify an unknown prisoner. I could have done it in twenty-four hours. Lecoq took six months or so. It might be made a text-book for detectives to teach them what to avoid.' (pp. 31-2)

Sir Arthur Conan Doyle, "The Science of Deduction," in his A Study in Scarlet, *Doubleday & Company, Inc., 1974, pp. 23-33.*

[A. INNES SHAND]   (essay date 1890)

[*In the following excerpt, Shand praises Gaboriau's consistently accurate, detailed plots and unique "systems" of detection, but faults the novelist's characterizations and digressive explanatory passages. For further commentary by Shand, see the excerpt dated 1879.*]

[Gaboriau] elaborated, if he did not invent, the romance which turns entirely on the detection of a crime. He glorifies and idealises the exploits of the *élite* of the handful of men who control the dangerous masses of Paris. If he is not incapable of the delineation of character—like Boisgobey, his most promising pupil—he is quite indifferent to it. The natures and temperaments of his heroes, as originally indicated, are continually contradicting themselves. He has his heroines; he is fond of arranging unequal marriages; he introduces love-affairs, but they only lead up to striking situations, and the sentimentalism and the pathos are alike fictitious. On the other hand, there are no inconsistencies in the careful construction of the plot. From the first to the final chapter it works smoothly and without a hitch. *En passant,* or incidentally, he lays himself out to explain away whatever seems improbable and incredible. He is inspired by the veritable genius of the detective business, and his superiority in his special department is undeniable. At the same time, he has his invariable "system," like his heroes of the Rue Jerusalem; and when we come to understand it, his successful ingenuity is less astonishing than it appears at first sight. He always works backwards: he argues backwards from prearranged and established facts; and his infallible sneers, with their instinctive *flair,* interpret to the ignorant the signs that are clear to them. Consequently his Père Tabaret and his Monsieur Lecoq are pure creations of the fancy, parading an intelligence they do not really possess. None the less do they serve his purpose and ours, inasmuch as we credit them with gifts approaching the miraculous. We are brought to share the blind confidence of the Père Absinthe, who, dazzled by the *clairvoyance* of his clever young colleague Lecoq, asks, with the best faith in the world, what the people they had been tracking said to each other.

The personages of Gaboriau's *mises-en-scène* are generally much the same. There is the "suspect" entangled in advance in the meshes of circumstantial evidence; there is a sulking somebody else whom sooner or later we begin to fancy may have had much to say to the atrocity; there is the *juge d'instruction,* always of rare sagacity, though he changes nature and methods in the different books; and there is the shrewd but kindly old surgeon, of rough or forbidding manners, who is told off for the autopsy of the corpse, and whose experience draws invaluable deductions. Above all, there is the brilliant detective, who, by the light of intuitive perception, follows out his profession as a science. He is an enthusiast, of course, whether he has taken to the pursuit in his ripe maturity like Tabaret, or in his boiling and ambitious *jeunesse* like Lecoq, who builds his hopes of fortune on the favour of the Prefecture. They are enthusiasts to the point that old Tabaret compromises his reputation without regret, keeping the most irregular hours; while young Lecoq is ready to sell a *masure* belonging to him,

that he may take his revenge on the subtle and mysterious Mai who has befooled him on several occasions at their game of blind-man's-buff. Those enthusiasts always go in terror of their lives—for sundry convicts have sworn to slay them on their return from Cayenne, or their dismissal from forced works at Melun or Fontrevault. No wonder the criminals they have hunted down owe them a bitter grudge, for the concentrated zeal they bring to the chase seems beyond the limits of fair professional business. . . . Nothing shows more the extreme care of Gaboriau's workmanship than his development of the "systems" he attributes to the Tabarets and Lecoqs. In the reflection in the fiction of the imaginary facts, the whole fabric is based on logical deduction; the minutest details must be mutually self-supporting; and the demonstration of some insignificant flaw involves the collapse of the entire structure. The demonstration of one of these mathematical problems is worked out indirectly when Tabaret throws up his hands in remorseful horror at the Vicomte de Caumarin, who is charged with an atrocious murder, but is not provided with an irrefutable *alibi*. Otherwise the circumstantial evidence is complete; but that fundamental omission is sufficient to invalidate it, and Tabaret is in despair because the prosecutors, clinging to the ideas he has been labouring assiduously to drive into their heads, are bent upon sending an innocent man to the guillotine. For of course the favourite trick of the criminal novelist is to send suspicion running on a false trail, as in the case of de Caumarin, or in that of Prosper Bertomy in the *Dossier, No. 113.* Then some detective of transcendental intelligence comes to the rescue, and the mining and countermining go briskly forward. (pp. 178-79)

Darkening the colours and accentuating details, Gaboriau has turned *chantage* to excellent purpose. The most thrilling sensations of *Le Dossier No. 113* depend upon it; and still more exciting is *La Corde au Cou,* of which *chantage* is the theme, as it supplies the title. We follow with sympathy and indignation each new pressure of the cord, as a turn of the operator's wrist intensifies the torture. We know that the victim must live on and endure; he can never find a refuge in suicide and repose in the Morgue, since his miseries are to end in a blissful *dénouement*. But those novels on *chantage* remind us of Gaboriau's worst fault as a story-teller. Explaining the source of the secrets—and it is the same, though in a lesser degree, with his mysterious murders—he wearies us with interminable and explanatory digressions. As a clever artist he must have known it was a mistake: we can only suppose that the method paid him. An innocent suspect is under lock and key: the real offender begins to have good cause to tremble, and our interest is being wrought up to the highest pitch, when, with the "crak-crak" of some chorus in a *vaudeville,* a dramatic chapter closes, and in commencing the next we are stagnating in the backwaters of some episode of family history which came off in the provinces forty years before. On the whole, we prefer the plan of *Monsieur Lecoq,* which devotes an entire volume to the crime, and the second and succeeding volume to its causes. Perhaps for that reason we rank the short and unpretentious *Petit Vieux des Batignolles* among the very best of Gaboriau's books. It goes straight to the point, and is all to the purpose. (p. 180)

[*A. Innes Shand*], *"Crime in Fiction," in* Blackwood's Edinburgh Magazine, *Vol. CXLVIII, No. DCCCXCVIII, August, 1890, pp. 172-89.*

THE BOOKMAN, LONDON   (essay date 1900)

[*The author of the following excerpt asserts that Gaboriau has been unjustly ignored by critics. Though the novelist had no pre-*

A climactic scene from The Widow Lerouge.

tensions to great literary style, this writer believes that he is to be commended for his creation of Lecoq and for his accurate descriptions of Parisian criminal life.]

Gaboriau is one of those writers who, while appealing strongly to thousands upon thousands of readers, are by the critics absolutely ignored as literary forces. He is, as a rule, passed by as a mere spinner of detective stories, a light and rather frivolous entertainer. Now, in his case, this seems to be particularly unjust. He made no pretension to literary style or effect. His love passages, as love passages pure and simple, are of the most conventional and threadbare. It is quite true that he was only making stories; but he wrote of a certain side of life as he knew it, and for his background he drew upon the store of experience acquired by years of watching the ebb and flow of Paris. It is said that the plots of his books were taken almost bodily from the secret archives of the Rue Jerusalem, and one may readily believe it. There is a little touch of the *Comédie Humaine* to be found in his works. He knew his Balzac and his Molière, and he made use of this knowledge. That dark under side of the criminal life of Paris with which Gaboriau deals furnished Balzac with some of his most powerful themes.

Justly or unjustly, Emile Gaboriau is regarded, first of all, as the creator of one powerful character. And yet we do not think that he himself ever wished to give such pre-eminence to Monsieur Lecoq or that he even realised the dramatic qualities of the great detective. Had he aimed to show Lecoq infallible, omniscient, would there have been a Père Tabaret? The real

Lecoq is a factor in only three books—*The Mystery of Orcival, Monsieur Lecoq* and *File No. 113.* In *Other People's Money* and *The Lerouge Case* he is a mere subordinate. Sherlock Holmes fleered at him as a bungler, a mere practical investigator, whose only merit was his patience and his capacity for hard work [see excerpt by Doyle dated 1887]. True, he was not a builder of fancy hypotheses; he did not show so well in the lime-light. But we defy any reader to take up Lecoq's arguments and evidence and be unconvinced. And his evolving a complete theory from the chance words, "It is the Prussians who are coming," let drop by the pretended May, in the first chapter of *Monsieur Lecoq,* shows an imagination of a very high order. (pp. 106-07)

A review of "L'affaire Lerouge" and other novels, in The Bookman, *London, Vol. XII, No. 2, October, 1900, pp. 106-07.*

THE LIVING AGE   (essay date 1901)

[*Though* Monsieur Lecoq *has many characteristics in common with sensational fiction, this critic claims that Gaboriau's craftsmanship and ingenuity raise the novel above the level of the English penny dreadful.*]

The re-issue, in a genteel *format,* of the enslaving works of Emile Gaboriau should be an event of special interest to a generation whose appetite for sensational serials surpasses that of any previous generation. For Gaboriau, besides being the chosen novelist of Bismarck, was the greatest mere sensation-monger, save one, that ever lived. His superior, of course, was Eugène Sue, author of the incomparable *Wandering Jew* and *The Mysteries of Paris.* (p. 129)

Gaboriau was a lesser figure [than Sue], but a figure not to be despised. He was more than a mechanical concoctor. In craftsmanship, though not in the amplitude of his inspiration, he excelled Sue, and he certainly had what is called "a pretty gift" of writing. The perusal of *Monsieur Lecoq,* and its sequel, "The Honor of the Name," has, we confess, impressed us with a sense of Gaboriau's sterling ability. The first book in which the afterwards famous Lecoq commences his career by a brilliant failure, begins with a murder, and is nothing more than a detective story; but it is a detective story conceived in the true romantic manner, and depending for effect more on its general atmosphere of a terrible mystery than on circumstantial ingenuities. Sherlock Holmes might have taught Lecoq many little dodges, but Lecoq was by far the greater intellect— an intellect that moved in larger curves on a higher plane. Character rather than event controls the progress of the tale, and this is clearly perceived in the sequel—an immense novel which distinctly recalls Balzac's *Les Paysans,* and is, moreover a very tolerable imitation of that sinister drama. From "The Honor of the Name" you perceive that Gaboriau, thereby proving himself an ambitious and intrepid artist, had drawn together in the murder the threads of a vast and complicated politico-social intrigue rooted in the national life of France. "The Honor of the Name," despite its sensational aspects, is quite a serious study of history; it shows the fatal war of class against class, and it is the record, not of a few individuals, but of a society. One cannot but observe that the French novelist has, as regards material, a two-fold advantage over the English: first, in the political vicissitudes of France during the nineteenth century, and, second, in the peculiar functions of the *Juge d' Instruction* under French criminal law. France seems to have made her history for the behoof of her novelists. As for the *Juge d'Instruction,* he is simply invaluable. Take, for an instance, the long examination of May by M. Segmuller in **Monsieur Lecoq;** it is almost the best thing in the book and serves a thousand ends. But Gaboriau could have succeeded without either French history or the *Juge d' Instruction.* The entrance of Blanche into the cottage and her poisoning of Marie Anne, in "The Honor of the Name," is an excellent sample of his rich inventive faculty. And his skill in *synthetizing* the significance of multitudinous facts in one item of evidence is finely exemplified in his use of the phrase uttered by the captured murderer—"It is the Prussians who are coming" (in **Lecoq**). Before reaching the conclusion of the sequel you are made to see that the whole tragedy is wrapped up in that phrase. In fine, it was not by chance that Gaboriau acquired his reputation. We in England have rather condescended towards him, as the artificer of a gloried penny-dreadful; that is a mistake. (pp. 129-30)

> *"The Sensational Serial: An Enquiry,"* in The Living Age, *Vol. CCXXX, No. 2974, July 6, 1901, pp. 129-32.*

ARTHUR BARTLETT MAURICE   (essay date 1902)

[*In this excerpt from his essay on the development of character types, Maurice briefly traces the influence of Gaboriau's Tabaret on Doyle's Sherlock Holmes.*]

If in one line we can trace the ancestry of Sherlock Holmes to Edgar Allan Poe's Dupin, in another we can work back to Gaboriau, not, however, to the great Lecoq, but to old Tabaret, better known to the official police who are introduced into the tales as Père Tirauclair. From Dupin, Holmes derived his intellectual acumen, his faculty of mentally placing himself in the position of another, and thereby divining that other's motives and plans, his raising of the observation of minute outward details to the dignity of an exact science. Père Tirauclair inspired him to that wide knowledge of criminal and contemporary history which enabled him to throw a light on the most puzzling problem and to find some analogy to the most *outré* case. With Lecoq, Holmes has absolutely nothing in common.

The deductions of Dupin and of Sherlock Holmes we are ready to accept, because we feel that it is romance, and in romance we care to refute only what seriously jars our sense of what is logical; we take those of Lecoq, because they convince beyond all question, because when one has been forced upon us, we are ready defiantly to maintain that no other is possible. (p. 235)

> *Arthur Bartlett Maurice, "The Detective in Fiction,"* in The Bookman, *New York, Vol. XV, May, 1902, pp. 231-36.*

FRANK WADLEIGH CHANDLER   (essay date 1907)

[*In this excerpt from his study of the connection between picaresque and detective literature, Chandler suggests that Gaboriau's novels display characteristics of both genres.*]

[Gaboriau perfected] the literature of crime-detection in France. In a succession of novels, from **L'Affaire Lerouge** . . . to **La Corde au Cou,** . . . as well as in two posthumous tales [**L'Argent des Autres** and **La Dégringolade**], . . . this prolific author developed his famous detectives, Lecoq the professional, and Père Tabaret the amateur. Both agree in the infinite zest and patience with which they track down criminals. They are not so much analysts as blood-hounds, keen on the scent from the first rumor of crime, and untiring in the chase. Action with them is everything. They cannot rest until their prey be found. Unlike Poe's Dupin, they indulge in no calm diagnosis of the case at home, and prepare no carefully constructed theory to be wrought out by others. And because they mix immediately with the world of crime, the account of their exploits is invariably melodramatic.

Gaboriau drew his inspiration from Vidocq, Balzac, and the Archives of the Rue de Jérusalem,—that arsenal of criminal records capable of furnishing forth a whole army of novelists. . . . Frequently Gaboriau dwells overmuch upon the intercalated history of his criminal, developing the motives that produced the crime in so great detail as to obscure the interest in crime-detection. Such passages, however, show the influence of the picaresque rather than of the detective formula, and they tacitly acknowledge the close relationship between the two. (pp. 529-30)

> *Frank Wadleigh Chandler, "The Literature of Crime-Detection," in his* The Literature of Roguery, *Vol. II, Houghton, Mifflin and Company, 1907, pp. 524-50.*

HARRY THURSTON PECK   (essay date 1909)

[*Gaboriau is the artistic link between Poe and Doyle, Peck asserts in the excerpt below. While Gaboriau's characterization of M. Lecoq is superior to Poe's detective characterizations, the French novelist lacked the human interest of Doyle's hero, Holmes.*]

[The defect in Poe's] tales lies in the fact that their author could not create a living, breathing character. His personages are nothing but abstractions. He moves them about like chessmen on a board, and we are interested, not in them, but in the problem with which they have to do.

In order that the detective story should be something more than mathematics applied to fiction—or, perhaps, fiction applied to mathematics—it was necessary that what Poe did should be combined with a sympathetic understanding of human nature. This combination was effected—imperfectly, to be sure, but still with great ability—by Émile Gaboriau in the best of his detective stories, **M. Lecoq.** (p. 262)

Gaboriau became fascinated by the thoroughness and precision of [the marvelously elaborate system of espionage established by Napoleon III in contemporary France]. He studied it in all its phases, and with the greatest care. As a result of this study, he wrote the novels which, with all their blemishes, are still read eagerly in many countries and in many languages.

Of these novels, the one best constructed and most deserving of fame is that entitled **M. Lecoq.** . . . In it is seen an ingenuity equal to that of Poe, while there is also shown a fair success in sketching character. Moreover, the author has introduced a new type of deductive reasoner which suggested to Conan Doyle the interesting Mycroft Holmes, brother of Sherlock Holmes, and that great detective's superior in the subtlety of his intellectual processes. (pp. 263-64.)

The scene of the prisoner's examination by [the] magistrate [in **M. Lecoq**] is one of thrilling interest, and it gives to us Anglo-Saxons a vivid picture of the workings of French law in its assumption that a prisoner is guilty unless he proves his innocence. The long, searching inquiry in which the judge alternately pleads with the accused and browbeats, threatens, and tortures him, hoping at last to break him down and wring from him a full confession, is wonderfully written. (pp. 265-66)

[In Gaboriau's characterization of Père Tirauclair] we find a conception more attractive even than that of [Poe's C. Auguste Dupin]; and the literary touches of Gaboriau and Doyle give us a genuine personality that far surpasses the interest of a mere calculating machine.

It is true that Gaboriau mars his story by injecting into it a long secondary narrative. Conan Doyle made precisely the same mistake in his first successful detective tale, *A Study in Scarlet;* but it was a mistake which he never repeated. Gaboriau, therefore, is a link between Edgar Allan Poe and Conan Doyle, just as Poe himself is a link between Voltaire and Gaboriau. (p. 268)

Gaboriau is superior to Poe [in characterization]. Had there been no Gaboriau, we might never have had that fascinating cycle of stories which Conan Doyle has written around the great detective who lived in Baker Street, and whose name is as well known all over the world to-day as that of Shylock, Falstaff, or any other creation of Shakespeare himself, with, perhaps, Hamlet as the one exception. (p. 270)

Gaboriau is an excellent literary artisan. His mysteries are very neatly constructed. The parts all dovetail perfectly. But they have little artistic value, and the unravelling of their complicated plots is like the dissection of a Chinese puzzle which interests by its ingenuity, but appeals neither to the intellect nor to the imagination. (p. 273)

> *Harry Thurston Peck, "The Detective Story," in his* Studies in Several Literatures, *Dodd, Mead and* Company, 1909, pp. 257-78.

BURTON EGBERT STEVENSON (essay date 1913)

[Including Lecoq and Tabaret in his list of the classic characters of detective fiction, Stevenson recounts two of Tabaret's greatest scenes. He faults Gaboriau only for his overuse of coincidence and inclusion of digressive romantic subplots.]

[Among] all the detectives, amateur and professional, who have appeared before the public and performed their little tricks, there are only four who are classic—C. Auguste Dupin, Tabaret, M. Lecoq, and Sherlock Holmes. These abide. Beside them, the others are mere shadows. And these four are memorable not because they never bungled, not because occasionally they struck home with a cleverness and certainty which makes us forgive their mistakes. Their supreme moments are moments to be remembered with delight. (p. 49)

Twenty years after Poe's death, Emile Gaboriau began [a] series of detective stories which still remain, on the whole, the best of their class. There is probably no scene more satisfying than that in which Tabaret arrives at the place of the murder in *The Lerouge Case,* and, after a short investigation, proceeds to reconstruct the crime. Here, plainly, is the genesis of Sherlock Holmes, and yet Holmes never quite rose to this height. And it is in this story that Tabaret reaches his supreme moment—the moment when, after having bound his chain about his victim, assured that there is not a single weak link in it, he sees it shiver to pieces. The accused man has been arrested, has been taken before a magistrate, and, although stunned and incoherent, has doggedly asserted his innocence, but has as doggedly refused to say where he was on the night of the crime. Finally he is led away and Tabaret enters.

"I have come," he says, "to know if any investigations are necessary to demolish the alibi pleaded by the prisoner."

"He pleaded no alibi," the magistrate replies.

"What? No alibi!" cries the detective. "He has, of course, then, confessed everything."

"No, he has confessed nothing. He acknowledges that the proofs are decisive: he cannot give an account of how he spent his time, but he protests his innocence."

Tabaret is thunderstruck—and reaches his supreme moment.

"Not an alibi!" he murmurs. "No explanations! It is inconceivable! We must then be mistaken: he cannot be the criminal. That is certain!"

The magistrate laughs at him, and Tabaret explains that the man who committed this crime, so carefully planned, so cleverly carried out, so audacious and yet so prudent, would, under no circumstances, have failed to provide himself with a convincing alibi, and that a man who has no alibi cannot possibly be the criminal. Still the magistrate laughs, and Tabaret proceeds to lay down a principle which all writers of detective fiction would do well to learn by heart:

> "Given a crime, with all the circumstances and details, I construct, bit by bit, a plan of accusation, which I do not guarantee until it is entire and perfect. If a man is found to whom this plan applies exactly in every particular, the author of the crime is found; otherwise one has laid hands upon an innocent person. It is not sufficient that such and such particulars seem to point to him; it must be all or nothing."

Those six words sum up the whole science of detection: it must be all or nothing. . . . [Writers dream] of some day writing a story in which the edifice of conviction is slowly and carefully built, four-square, like the frame of a sky-scraper, with every beam tested and every bolt rivetted, formidable and apparently impregnable, yet with a tiny hidden defect which, just as the last bolt is being placed, brings the whole structure smashing to the ground. That would be worth doing!

In the Lerouge case, Tabaret built such an edifice; but Gaboriau carries coincidence too far. It is admissible that both the real murderer and the man suspected of the crime should, on that particular evening, have been carrying an umbrella and wearing a high hat; perhaps it is admissible, since they are the same age and about the same build, that their shoes should be of the same size and shape; but when the author equips them both with lavender kid gloves he adds one coincidence too many. In his desire to strengthen the chain of evidence, he overleaps himself and loses the confidence of the reader. (pp. 51-2)

Tabaret has a worthy pupil in M. Lecoq, although it should not be forgotten that he remains a pupil, with many things unlearned, to the end of the chapter. Sherlock Holmes's gibe at him [see excerpt by Doyle dated 1887] seems to be the result of an unworthy envy. For Lecoq, though inferior to Tabaret, is far greater than Holmes—more picturesque, more subtle, more resourceful—and with a sense of humour. Probably his greatest moment occurs in *The Mystery of Orcival.* A murder has been committed and a house ransacked, the furniture upset, the clock thrown from the mantel. It has stopped at twenty minutes past three, and to every one it seems evident that it was at that hour the crime occurred. Lecoq replaces the clock on the mantel, and slowly pushes forward the minute-hand to half-past three. The clock strikes eleven.

That was a great idea—so great that no one will ever dare use it again without acknowledging its source. Sherlock Holmes came perilously near it, once, when he solved a mystery by re-winding a watch. But the honours belong to Gaboriau. And for another thing the Frenchman deserves all praise. He recognised the fact that, to hold the interest, it is not enough that a crime should be committed and the criminal in the end discovered. There must be something more than that. There must be a war of intellect, a clash of theories. There must be confronting investigators, one seeking to establish a man's guilt, the other to establish his innocence. For the reader, the real pleasure is in following, step by step, this contest.

In so far as detective work goes, Gaboriau's stories are far better than Conan Doyle's; but Gaboriau tried to do too much. He sought to add a love interest, and in that respect he failed. Every one of his tales is built upon the threadbare formula, "cherchez la femme"; every one turns back for its motive to an illicit love affair.... [I have] no patience with a plot which, for its explanation, must go back two or three generations; so these portions of Gaboriau's stories are to be skimmed rapidly, until Tabaret or Lecoq appears again upon the scene. Then not a word is to be missed. Amat Tabaret! (pp. 52-3)

> Burton Egbert Stevenson, "Supreme Moments in Detective Fiction," in The Bookman, New York, Vol. XXXVII, No. 7, March, 1913, pp. 49-54.

VALENTINE WILLIAMS (essay date 1923)

[In the following excerpt from his article commemorating the fiftieth anniversary of Gaboriau's death, Williams discusses the early critical reception and the circumstances surrounding the publication of Gaboriau's detective fiction. He also states that Gaboriau expanded the model for detective fiction established by Poe, introducing lively characterization and dramatic plots to the genre.]

The present year will mark the fiftieth anniversary of the death of Emile Gaboriau. He has an indisputable claim to be regarded as the father of the detective novel. Poe, it is true, was his precursor and his direct inspiration: but Gaboriau was far from being a feeble imitator. [A French writer justly observes:]

> He derived from this class of story . . . a new type, and impressed his own particular quality upon it so well that, instead of being a servile and insignificant plagiarist, he stands out as an original and fertile creator. . . .

Poe was the scientist who produced the text-book; Gaboriau seized upon his exposition and dramatized it. There is no "love interest" in Poe's [Dupin] trilogy; the dialogue is stilted, and the characters are merely chessmen set out to present a problem.

In each of his five great detective novels Gaboriau also has an intricate problem, but it is the centre of a highly dramatic plot with living figures (interspersed, it is true, with many dummies of the French feuilleton), a brisk dialogue and a keen perception of "situations." He is, first and last, a journalist, drawing, as one may clearly see, upon a well-filled notebook; but a journalist equipped with a brilliant analytical brain which, as his life story shows, circumstances never permitted to find its fullest and highest expression. (p. 612)

When fame, who so often limps far behind material prosperity, reached the feuilletonist's desk, she found an empty chair. To-day, fifty years after Gaboriau was laid to rest in the family vault at Jonzac, running through the coarse woof of plot and counter-plot which the concierges demanded from his stories for their daily sou, we may discern the scarlet thread of a brilliant mind. Here, through the jostling throng of desperately wicked dukes, of incredibly noble maids, of *banquiers véreux*, Monsieur Lecoq, simple agent of the Sûreté, comes stepping, fresh as a bridegroom, *un beau gars, à l'oeil clair, à l'air résolu*, or, as casual visitors saw him in his careful disguise, a sober personage of distinguished appearance, with his gold spectacles, his white tie, and his *mince redingote*.

Against a canvas of tiresome puppets he stands out a living figure, notwithstanding the curious metamorphoses to which, in the course of the stories, the exigencies of the feuilleton subjected him. He is as French as the crowing cock, which, with its proud motto, "Semper Vigilans," he chose as his device. His limpid mind, his crystal-clear reasoning, his dazzling deductions, his fluttering *panache*, his ups and downs, his hopes and fears, all these are wholly French.

When Gaboriau died, *Le Siècle* called him "the inventor of the *roman judiciaire*." The unknown writer, who thus shrewdly gave his dead *confrère* his due, would open his eyes to-day could he survey the large and lusty progeny of which Monsieur Lecoq is the father. But there is a hint of cold condescension in the way in which some of the contemporary newspapers dispose, in a brief *fait divers*, of "M. Emile Gaboriau, author of *romans judiciaires*, which have had the greatest success." (pp. 613-14)

[Marius Topin wrote in his *Romanciers contemporains* in 1876:]

> Gaboriau . . . has long been ranged among the facile scribes of the cheap newspapers, the hurried improvisers, the novelists who share with the police reports and the *faits divers* the breathless curiosity of the fishwives and porters. Gaboriau is classified, ticketed, numbered. There is nothing more to be said. That he is loved by so many common readers does not please the cultured. In the highly aristocratic republic of letters the innumerable suffrages of the plebs must not be confounded with the select opinions of a few delicate-minded censors.

And he proceeds to pay a warmly sincere tribute to the "scientific art" of Gaboriau's five great crime stories. (p. 614)

Monsieur Lecoq is said to be the faithful portrait of one of the highest officials in the Prefecture of Gaboriau's day; but Gévrol, nicknamed "The General," who flits in and out of the stories, the type of old-fashioned detective and a sore thorn in the side of Monsieur Lecoq; and Fanferlot (a detective in *Dossier 113*) with his "turned-up nose, thin lips, and small, round eyes of irritating mobility," are also clearly sketched from life. (p. 616)

[After] *Le Crime d'Orcival* only *La Corde au Cou*, not one of his happiest efforts, and a short tale *Le Petit Vieux des Batignolles*, which I hold to be in some respects the best detective story ever written, were in his especial vein. The rest were terrific romances of modern life with double-dyed villains and blameless heroines and mysterious love affairs. Their digressions, and digressions from digressions, are endless; the colours are laid on very thick; and to-day they possess little interest. (p. 618)

[Gaboriau] was a facile, but immensely conscientious, worker. He never sat down to write until his plot was clear in his mind, and it is recorded of him that he would fill from two to three thousand sheets of his specially prepared paper without correction or erasure. On the other hand, he devoted immense care to the revision of the proofs of his stories in book form and the galleys, as he returned them to the publisher, were almost unrecognizable.

A notebook was his constant companion. In it he would jot down such ideas as occurred to him, usually with a brief scenario. He has always on the lookout for types, and when he came across a character that seemed suitable to figure in a story he would sometimes even make a rough sketch so as to impress the salient features on his mind.

Like Charles Dickens, he took infinite trouble with the names of his personages, which, we are informed—an eloquent commentary on the sublime nonchalance of French feuilleton writing!—he frequently changed in the course of publication. One of his great amusements, Alfred d'Aunay records, was to study a passer-by in the street and try to glean, by processes of reasoning and observation, his mode of life and social standing, and then to shadow his victim to see if his deductions were correct.

It is suggested that Gaboriau's five great criminal romances (*L' Affaire Lerouge, Le Crime d'Orcival, Dossier 113, Monsieur Lecoq,* and *La Corde au Cou*) were the fruition of that early impulse of his to write *Les Récits Etranges* after the manner of Poe. However that may be, what is certain is that he wished to publish the five books under the general title, *Processes of Reasoning in Judicial Affairs.* (p. 619)

[The] fetters of the feuilleton galled the genius of Gaboriau. He wrote . . . in haste, twisting his plot and modifying his characters, often, no doubt, in deference to the wishes of his editor. The result is patchwork, and, in the case of his greatest creation, Monsieur Lecoq, this immortal character, as he passes through the stories, is cluttered up with a mass of incongruities which Gaboriau, had he lived, would surely have planed away. (p. 620)

[The] first volume of *Monsieur Lecoq* is incontestably Gaboriau's masterpiece. I say advisedly "the first volume," for the second, narrating at inordinate length the life history of a wicked duke from 1815 on, is one long yawn compared to the four hundred pages of vivid, pulsating prose of its companion.

Gaboriau's scheme in this splendid story is clear. He set himself to construct a ladder between the lowest and the highest levels of society. To Lecoq he allotted the task of following up the trail of a crime that led from a squalid cabaret outside the Paris fortifications to a ducal mansion in the Faubourg St. Germain. (pp. 621-22)

It is difficult for anybody with imagination to lay down the first volume of *Monsieur Lecoq* before he has read it through to the last page. With uncanny skill Gaboriau interests his readers, not only in his central figure, the detective, and his desperate fight against the stubborn incredulity of his chiefs, but also in the mysterious prisoner whose determination to mislead the police as to his identity is reinforced by secret associates outside the prison. It culminates in that thrilling chase through Paris when Lecoq, in despair of ever identifying

the accused, having deliberately let the prisoner escape, shadows him through the streets—and loses him. (p. 622)

Valentine Williams, "Gaboriau: Father of the Detective Novel," in The National Review, *London, Vol. LXXXII, No. 490, December, 1923, pp. 611-22.*

[T. S. ELIOT]   (essay date 1929)

[*Eliot, an American-born English poet, essayist, and critic, is regarded as one of the most influential literary figures of the first half of the twentieth century. In the following excerpt from his brief note on the reissue of* The Mystery of Orcival, *Eliot praises the novel, pointing out the importance of considering it in historical perspective.*]

[The] revival of Gaboriau is fully justified by a perusal of [*The Mystery of Orcival*]. . . . [We] protest that the publishers have not provided a short note about the author . . . , for the serious critic of such fiction knows how much the *date* at which a book was written matters. The elaborate and protean disguises of the detective ended with Sherlock Holmes, but in Gaboriau's time they were not only permissible but commendable. Lecoq, when one knows the dates, does wear extremely well. One of the merits of this story is that we know the criminal very early: the only difficulty is to prove the crime and to catch the culprit. (p. 760)

[T. S. Eliot], in a review of "The Mystery of Orcival," in The Criterion, *Vol. VIII, No. XXXIII, July, 1929, pp. 760-61.*

H. DOUGLAS THOMSON   (essay date 1931)

[*Announcing that "'The Great Gaboriau Revival' is under way," Thomson commends Gaboriau's psychologically and emotionally appealing detectives and cases, but finds that his novels are unsatisfying to modern readers because the mystery is not sustained long enough.*]

Until recently Gaboriau had fallen on evil days. He was once regarded as second only to Sir Arthur Conan Doyle, and his detective, Lecoq, was as famous as Sherlock Holmes. After a time the Victorians seemed to forget him, and the younger generation knew him only as a name. (p. 94)

[Today], "The Great Gaboriau Revival" is under way. . . . There is a growing habit amongst publishers of reprinting earlier examples of the genre—an act of grace which confers on the detective story a definite literary status. (p. 95)

Gaboriau, experimentalist that he was, had quite a definite opinion of what the detective story ought to be. "The inquest of a crime," he makes Lecoq say, in *Le Crime d'Orcival,* "is nothing more nor less than the solution of a problem. Given the crime, proved, patent, you commence by seeking out all the circumstances, whether serious or superficial; the details and the particulars. When these have been carefully gathered, you classify them, and put them in their order and date. You thus know the victim, the crime and the circumstances; it remains to find the third term of the problem, that is X, the unknown quantity—the guilty party. The task is a difficult one, but not so difficult as is first imagined."

Gaboriau's novels do not, however, quite satisfy our own notions. They are not so much detective stories, as stories in which a detective has helped, but only helped, to unravel a tangled skein of events. A prolonged course of reading may have prejudiced us against Gaboriau, in much the same way as reading a sequel before the original is apt to spoil the latter. . . . [Gaboriau's novels have] no grand dénouement. The reader having read only half the book can name the guilty person. The problem is not protracted enough; and even from a grossly material point of view the detection occupies only a fraction of the whole.

Nevertheless, Gaboriau does not seem to have made up his mind as to what constituted the *ideal* construction. Experience, in a way, handicapped him; for, knowing that court proceedings bulk largely in the history of any criminal case, he felt obliged to retain the proportion. Gaboriau's court scenes are delicious entertainment. In a few bold strokes he paints the examining magistrate, the prisoner, the detective all agog with excitement. He packs his novels with axioms of criminal procedure, and that type of psychology which betokens the witty precisian.

Gaboriau leant towards realism in another particular, chiefly in his later novels. He seems to have formed a preference for a more concrete type of investigation. What is said of Lecoq in *Monsieur Lecoq* is equally true of Gaboriau himself:—

> He next had recourse to a mode of investigation which is generally the last resort of the police, but which is generally successful, because it is so sensible and simple.
>
> He determined to examine all the books in which the law compels the proprietors of hotels and lodging houses to keep a record of their guests.
>
> Rising long before daybreak and going to bed late at night, he spent all his time in visiting the hotels, furnished houses and lodgings in Paris.
>
> (pp. 96-8)

This is one instance which shows that Gaboriau latterly tended to make his stories *romans policiers* pure and simple—chronicles of the police methods adopted to catch a known criminal.

Historically, Gaboriau is one of the pioneers. He was the father of the detective novel as opposed to the detective story. He made the way straight for Sir Arthur Conan Doyle. He was a master in the art of story telling. . . . Where Gaboriau improved on Poe was in his heightening of the interest and in the intensification of the human appeal. Gaboriau took no half measures. He decided in the first place to make the problem such that it would give rein to the emotions. Secondly, he gave the detective a personality. (pp. 98-9)

All Gaboriau's problems arise from family scandals and intrigues. A blot on the escutcheon and there was no saying to what crime it might not lead. Gaboriau saw that there is no secret so well kept as a family secret. Complication of the plot would be easier when the origin of the mystery might take one years back. (p. 99)

[Gaboriau] gave us two detectives, Père Tabaret and Lecoq. As far as reputation goes the pupil has quite eclipsed his master. Lecoq was certainly Gaboriau's favourite. His appearance is more frequent, and we are allowed to witness the development of his powers. Père Tabaret is a type of detective very much in the contemporary fashion. He took up detection, as we saw, to dispel his boredom. (There is a no more discontented class of people than the dilettante detectives, even at the present moment when unemployment and an aristocratic scorn for the dole would constitute a more cogent reason for adopting the pursuit.) Tabaret is an amateur at the game, the magnet from

time to time of the professionals' ridicule. He is also an amateur in the less flattering sense. Always liable to make mistakes, he was once actually responsible for the execution of an innocent man. He is as eccentric as Dupin, and his garrulous landlady has not got a dog's chance. His eccentricity gives comic relief, ''but unlike Holmes's does not give an impression of latent genius.'' . . . In his use of paradox he is almost as doctrinaire as Father Brown.

Lecoq is often mentioned in the same breath as Dupin and Sherlock Holmes. He is an amusing character; *that* needs no stressing. But it must occur to one that perhaps after all his name is just a shade greater than his deserts. His is borrowed plumage. (pp. 99-100)

Gaboriau's murders and robberies are not the meticulously planned affairs with which we are now familiar. Smith Minor would turn up his nose at them. Père Tabaret himself complained that criminals were not what they used to be. ''Blunderers as well as cowards,'' he styled them. And if they did not leave behind them their visiting-cards, they left quite enough evidence to be going on with.

Gaboriau's legacy is for all that a rich one. Many of his tricks and ruses have now become clichés. (p. 102)

Many of Gaboriau's stratagems are now hackneyed. Time stops whenever a murder is committed. The clock never escapes, and the deceitful hands play the deuce with one's calculations. . . . [Furniture] has a ''physiognomy.'' An escritoire and overturned chairs are never absent from the scene of the crime. We note too the never failing presence of a confusing number of wine glasses or coffee cups—seldom of plates, forks or spoons. Tobacco in some form or another of disintegration is another necessary stage property. Gaboriau makes one of his careless criminals leave behind him the end of a Trabucos cigar. Then there is the undergraduate's trick of rumpling the bed clothes to make the bed appear to have been slept in. But one rumples in vain if only the bolster is removed. ''A bed is one of those terrible witnesses which never misguide.'' Footprints are always being discovered; but at this stage they are used to trace movements, rather than for identification purposes. Lecoq once has recourse to a regular Austin Freeman expedient when he preserves the footprints in the melting snow by means of his plaster casts. Whether it is a piece of symbolism or realism, a murder is inevitably accompanied by a heavy fall of rain. Generally speaking the detection is of the familiar Sherlock Holmes variety—keen observation coupled with rapid inference. A leap of more than two yards to avoid a flower bed is assumed to prove that the man ''was active and, therefore, young.''

It was Gaboriau's idea to present the reader with a sketch plan of the scene of the crime. The idea is in itself a sound one; a picture may brighten a narrative as a graph may give life to tables of figures. But an excessive use of it has converted it into a mixed blessing. It is apt . . . to get on one's nerves. Gaboriau uses it properly and does not force the conscientious reader to turn back to it nor annoy the unconscientious by continual and unnecessary reference. (pp. 103-05)

L'Affaire Lerouge and *Le Crime d'Orcival* are undoubtedly Gaboriau's best novels. Of the rest the best that can be said of *Le Dossier No. 113* is that it would make an excellent film; of *Monsieur Lecoq* that the first part, ''L'Enquête,'' falls under the less attractive category of a pure *roman policier,* while the second, ''L'Honneur du Nom,'' as rather tedious family his-

Mascarin questions Paul in this illustration from Caught in the Net.

tory. The majority are nothing more or less than emotional blood and thunder novels. (p. 105)

> *H. Douglas Thomson, "The French Detective Novel,"
> in his* Masters of Mystery: A Study of the Detective
> Story, *1931. Reprint by Folcroft Library Editions,
> 1973, pp. 92-121.*

[DOROTHY L. SAYERS]   (essay date 1935)

*[Sayers is acknowledged as one of the great mystery writers of
the twentieth century. As a detective novelist, she is best remembered for her creation of the aristocratic amateur sleuth Lord
Peter Wimsey, who figures prominently in many of her mysteries.
Sayers's contribution to the genre lies in her attempt to transform
the detective novel into "a novel of manners, instead of a mere
crossword puzzle." In the following excerpt, Sayers praises Gaboriau's thematic breadth and his attempt to synthesize intellectual puzzles with human drama. She observes that although later
detective novelists have perfected the techniques Gaboriau introduced, few have balanced suspense and human psychology with
Gaboriau's success.]*

Emile Gaboriau, like some other literary pioneers, is to-day
probably more venerated than read. Everybody knows that he
was a master of detective fiction and that he created Monsieur
Lecoq; but when it comes to celebrating the centenary of his

birth the younger generation of readers is apt to feel like Miss
Codger on being presented to a Pogram by a Hominy:—

> A thrilling moment is it in its impressiveness
> on what we call our feelings. But why we call
> them so, or why impressed they are, or if im-
> pressed they are at all, or if at all we are, or if
> there really is, oh gasping one! a Lecoq or a
> Gaboriau, or any active principle to which we
> give those titles, is a topic, Spirit searching,
> light abandoned, much too vast to enter on, at
> this unlooked-for crisis.

Yet the present is a very good moment at which to ask ourselves
whether impressed we are at all and whether there is, in fact,
any active principle behind the lip-homage we offer to Gaboriau. . . .

The present-day reader may well be excused [from a study of
Gaboriau] if he feels that the topic is "much too vast to enter
on." The mere reading of the books presents a formidable
difficulty, for most of them are out of print and all of them
are fat. Faced with **Monsieur Lecoq** or with **La Corde au Cou**—
each containing, in the French edition, between four and five
hundred pages of ugly and sight-destroying letterpress—one
wonders whether the palm is worth the dust. "I suppose,"
says the reader, plaintively, "I shall find him very old-fashioned." He is old-fashioned; yet perhaps he was more so yesterday than he is to-day, while to-morrow may find him back
in the fashion. Mr. H. Douglas Thomson, writing in 1931 in
Masters of Mystery [see excerpt above], said of him:—

> Gaboriau's novels do not, however, quite sat-
> isfy our own notions. They are not so much
> detective stories as stories in which a detective
> has helped, but only helped, to unravel an en-
> tangled skein of events. . . . The mystery is
> gradually cleared up. The reader having read
> half the book can name the guilty person. The
> problem is not protracted enough; and even from
> a grossly material point of view the detection
> occupies only a fraction of the whole.

There is the modern case against Gaboriau, succinctly stated;
and it resolves itself into two counts: a division of interest, and
the lack of the "surprise" element to which we have become
accustomed. To these objections we may add two more: the
enormous length of the narrative and the slow amplitude of its
development. It is easy enough to account for all these characteristics historically; but in doing so we may find also an
artistic justification for them, as valid to-day as it was seventy
years ago. . . .

[For] the police and their methods . . . Gaboriau felt . . . glamorous enthusiasm; and therefore, though Tabaret the amateur
is his earliest detective hero, though Lecoq is Tabaret's pupil
and Tabaret the final court of appeal invoked when Lecoq by
himself has failed, it is Lecoq and not Tabaret, the professional
and not the amateur, who is the better known and the more
beloved of Gaboriau's heroes. Tabaret has the benevolent eccentricities, but Lecoq the great heroic moments; and it is
significant that *Le Crime d'Orcival,* in which Lecoq acts alone,
is Gaboriau's best book. It is as though the writer, dominated
at first by Poe's notion of contrasting amateur methods favourably with those of the police, had found his admiration
for the *Sûreté* too much for him, and had conceived the idea
of developing the contrast within the framework of the police
organization itself. Tabaret and Lecoq make common cause;

they triumph, not over routine police methods but over the jealousy of Lecoq's official rivals or over the personal prejudices of some provincial *juge d'instruction*. Thus, though Gaboriau is in a very real sense the model and precursor of Conan Doyle, he is also the precursor of Freeman Wills Crofts and of that whole school of modern detective writers whose true hero is Scotland Yard.

The moment was favourable to the development of the *roman policier* on both sides of the Channel. . . . Both in England and in France the mystery fiction of the sixties had its roots in real police work; Collins and Gaboriau—both enthusiastic students of Fenimore Cooper—undoubtedly read and influenced one another (the works of Collins were all translated into French, and the works of Gaboriau stood on Collins's bookshelves); and it is probable that behind both was the American influence, not only of Fenimore Cooper but of Edgar Allan Poe.

Yet neither Collins nor Poe succeeded, at that time, in founding a school of what we should now call pure detective fiction. The works of both contained large elements both of "sensation" and of *comédie de moeurs,* and it was these elements that were taken up and elaborated by their immediate successors. Not till we come to Conan Doyle do we again get stories in which the detection forms the whole interest as in those tales of Poe which were so precociously in advance of their time. The truth is that neither Collins nor Gaboriau aimed at writing what we should call detective stories. What we look upon as their defects were due to no failure of method but rather to a difference of purpose. With all their passion for secrets and puzzles, they were novelists, and they aimed at writing novels. They can certainly never have dreamed that the detective problem could come to stand as a book by itself, cut off from the great stream of human and literary tradition. For them, the character interest was as necessary as the plot interest.

That is why, to the modern fancier of the "chessboard" type of detective fiction, their books seem to be fumbling and uncertain in construction and stuffed with extraneous material; whereas to them, the work of a Doyle, a Connington, a Crofts or a Rhode would doubtless have appeared thin, dry and lacking in emotional power. Both parties would be, to some extent, right. It is significant that, when Conan Doyle did at length set detective fiction on the road which it was to follow for four decades he took it by way of the short story. (p. 677)

[With the great technical gain of modern detective literature] there went, however, a loss: the characterization, the human story, began to disappear from detective fiction. This happened, not only because the mere physical bulk of the novel was decreasing . . . but also because the "surprise ending" by its nature imposed restrictions upon the humanity of the narrative. If the be-all and end-all of the detective story is to conceal the identity of the criminal, then the most important and moving part of the human interest has to be omitted— namely, the character and motives of the criminal himself. He is the mainspring of the whole action, yet we may never see into the works; and this, even from the intellectual point of view, is unfortunate. Moreover, this restriction in its turn restricts the handling of all the other characters; for, if all but one are intimately analysed, then that remaining one must of necessity be the criminal; so that the author, to keep his secret, must leave the majority of his characters unanalysed. . . .

Of this integral artistic difficulty the early masters of the detective novel were quite aware. . . . Gaboriau, in *L'Affaire Lerouge,* tackled it along straight-forward lines of character-draw-

ing, but at the cost of taking the reader into his confidence behind the detective's back. While Tabaret still believes Noël Gerdy to be a model of youthful sobriety, we know that he is keeping an expensive mistress and is desperate for money. We understand and sympathize with Noël, but are all the readier to believe that, if money can be got by doing murder, then Noël is the man to do it. Consequently, we solve the mystery before the detective. This defect may have been less obvious in 1866 than it is to-day; the contrast between the false nobility of the claimant Noël and the true nobility of the real vicomte, Albert de Commarin, is delicately enough done to deceive the unsophisticated. Clearly, however, the author himself was dissatisfied. No doubt he felt that he had fallen between two stools. By trying to keep his secret he had prevented himself from extracting the full juice of emotion from Noël's agonizing situation; yet, in trying to make that situation clear he had more than jeopardized the secret. In his three succeeding books, [*Le Dossier No. 113, Le Crime d'Orcival*, and *Monsieur Lecoq*] . . . , he abandoned all attempt at compromise and used an expedient which to us appears clumsy and inartistic, but which offered perhaps the best scope for his peculiar talent.

These stories are built on the scheme used subsequently by Conan Doyle in *A Study in Scarlet* and *The Valley of Fear*. A crime is committed; the police investigations are put in hand; the inquiry is brought up to the point at which the detective is able to name the murderer and discover the motive for the crime. Then, instead of jumbling the necessary data into a brief summary by the detective or confession by the criminal, the author breaks off and retells the story in detail from the beginning, showing the whole emotional and dramatic interplay of circumstance and character. Finally, in a kind of coda, the detective action is taken up again, to show us the end of the inquiry and the fate of the criminal.

It is obvious that the great drawback to this kind of construction is the sudden and violent break in continuity. At the moment when we are most excited about Monsieur Lecoq we have to forget him and interest ourselves in an entirely different set of people. But if we make the effort we are to some extent rewarded by the greatly increased richness and significance of the book as an interpretation of life. We see the passions and interests which led to a sordid murder, not foreshortened into a paragraph but spread out over a prospect as wide as life itself, and moving ineluctably through a real time and space to a predestined end behind the grisly glass cases of the Morgue and under the chill light of a police investigation. Here is the case as Lecoq sees it; there were the passions as the people felt them. We may not care to see the thing done in this way; but it is as well to bear in mind, when we read Gaboriau, that the way was deliberately chosen for a definite artistic end. It is not that he is unable to write a detective story but that he prefers to write a human drama.

His drama, it is true, is melodrama; there was probably never a writer more ingenious in wringing the last ounce of agitation from an intrigue. "Intrigue" is the right word: his plots all turn upon illicit love and the humiliations sustained by noble families at the hands of their illegitimate scions. Compared with the work of his English contemporaries, Gaboriau's novels suffer from monotony of theme; but in dealing with that theme his nationality gives him an enormous advantage. His stage is narrow, but it is intensely lit; his plot makes contact with life at one or two points only, but the contact is ringingly made. He is a ferocious moralist, pursuing the sins of youth with savage retribution, but at least he is allowed to persuade us that the sins have been committed. . . . It is true that Gaboriau's noble young men and pure maidens are puppets as dreary as the virtuous young couples in Dickens or anybody else; and here he must yield the palm to Collins, who had an unexpected talent for making decent young people interesting. It is also a pity that Gaboriau, the son of a provincial notary, should have been so romantically intoxicated by the splendours of the ancient French nobility. The lustre of a great name and great riches dazzles his eyes; in their honour as in their dishonour, his dukes and counts and viscounts tower up always a little more than lifesize, rigid with caste, insolent with ineffable *morgue,* interminable rhetoricians upon the point of honour. Yet, though he sees them magnified, he can see them justly: and in **Le Crime d'Orcival** he can ruthlessly chastise his own weakness in Mme. Sauvresy and strip off the false glitter from de Trémorel to show the cheap and ugly clay beneath. In so doing, and particularly in the scene where this pinchbeck villain sets out to commit a spectacular suicide and fails absurdly through lack of courage to pull the trigger, he lifts his melodrama, for the first and only time, to the level of genuine high comedy.

But for us, the importance of Gaboriau lies, of course, in his police work. Here his eyes are not blinded with excess of light, and all his pictures are drawn with an exact and witty realism. He knows inside out the life of the *petit fonctionnaire,* the professional jealousies of the local magistracy, the cacklings of small-town gossip, the frictions between the *procureur* and the *maire,* the pomposities of the country doctor, the rivalry between the village policeman and the man sent down from the *Sûreté,* the difficulties in which a *juge d'instruction* may find himself when trying to steer a safe course between his political allegiance and the integrity of his professional conscience. He can show us the behaviour of every kind of suspect under the brutal onslaught of the French system of interrogation, from the cringing and plausible old offender to the despairing innocent caught in a hopeless trap of circumstance; his court scenes are ruthlessly authentic in minute detail; and his acquaintance with the topography of the Paris underworld and all its unpleasing fauna is "extensive and peculiar." If Lecoq himself sometimes appears to us rather as a superman than as an ordinary being, it is not because of any miracles of intuitive inspiration (for all his deductions are careful and logical) but merely because of his nerve-shattering facility in disguise and his inability to resist what Sherlock Holmes calls "a touch of the dramatic." . . .

It is easy for us to-day to dismiss the detective exploits of Tabaret and Lecoq as interesting specimens of a primitive art. We may feel ourselves greater than Gaboriau because we stand on his shoulders. But in that central problem of effecting a synthesis of intellectual and emotional interest have we come any nearer to a solution than he did? . . .

What Gaboriau, with all his faults of construction, with all his pedestrian dryness of style, with all his artificiality and absurdity of rhetoric has, which his successors have not, is breadth of treatment and, in a large sense, seriousness of aim. Crudely and melodramatically, but with enormous energy and gusto, he is writing novels and not anecdotes, attempting a criticism of life and not filling in time with cross-word puzzles related to nothing in particular. He never quite succeeded in synthesizing intellect and emotion, but at least he made the attempt. Now that books are once more growing longer there is an opportunity for the modern detective writer to make the attempt again and, with his perfected technique, to do it better. Ga-

boriau, who died suddenly in 1873 at the early age of thirty-eight, had only seven years of full literary life, and of his thirteen or fourteen books not all are detective stories. But in those seven years he left his mark upon detective history; and one fortress at least which bears the scars of his cannon has been left by those that came after, not only unachieved but unassaulted. (p. 678)

[*Dorothy L. Sayers*], *"Emile Gaboriau, 1835-1873: The Detective Novelist's Dilemma," in* The Times Literary Supplement, *No. 1761, November 2, 1935, pp. 677-78.*

HOWARD HAYCRAFT   (essay date 1941)

[*Haycraft argues that Gaboriau never realized his potential as a writer. His novels fail as detective fiction because the main characters' logical deductions are artistically incompatible with the melodramatic backgrounds and secondary characters Gaboriau uses.*]

Seven typically artificial and not very successful novels of military and fashionable life had come from Gaboriau's too facile pen before **L'Affaire Lerouge** began its serial career in a dying newspaper called *Le Pays* in 1866. In the sense that it was the first story of novel length to employ detection as an important theme, it is perhaps entitled to the appellation "the first detective novel"—though it bears little resemblance to what we mean by the term to-day. (p. 32)

When [Gaboriau] sticks to detection, it is excellent detection indeed; but . . . [rarely] did he succeed in so limiting himself. In **Monsieur Lecoq,** which many critics consider his masterpiece, he put all the detection into the first volume, devoting the entire second half to the narration of a tedious family chronicle. The family, it may be noted in passing, is the basis of most of Gaboriau's novels, as it was of most French fiction of his time. Family scandal is at the bottom of virtually all the problems investigated by his detectives, and the feuilletonist who knew his concierge and shop-girl audience missed few opportunities such a subject presented for melodramatic digression. The proportion of detection is no greater in the other novels. Furthermore, the solution by the detective is seldom the apex of the story. There is no single rise of action to a grand dénouement. We know the guilty party before the book is half through, and from that point forward we read (if we are able!) another story, or several sub-stories, about the same characters. (pp. 32-3)

[The] stories come to life when Lecoq is on the stage. The difficulty is that he is too often in the wings or hiding behind false faces.

In the conflict, described by Williams [see excerpt dated 1923], between Lecoq and his background, we find the key to Gaboriau's chief failure according to the standards of modern detective fiction. In his attempt to mix incompatible elements—the lurid unreality of the yellow-back and the cool logic of detection—he violates one of the prime requirements of the form: the semblance, at least, of plausibility. ("A sense of verisimilitude is essential to the detective novel."—Willard Huntington Wright.) The mésalliance he thus unwittingly and unfortunately began has persisted in the French detective story virtually to this day, to its undeniable detriment.

Nevertheless, Gaboriau's logic—when he does give it rein—is definitely of the better sort; it is only the backgrounds that are at fault. Many of Lecoq's devices are still in use to-day, although of course in altered and generally amplified form. His test to tell whether a bed has been slept in, the example of the striking clock to show that the hands have been set back— to mention but two—have been employed in principle at least by more fictional sleuths of a later day than one would care to estimate. There is nothing really new in Lecoq's reasoning; it stems directly from Dupin. But Gaboriau, drawing on his well-filled police-court notebooks and on Vidocq's *Mémoires,* elaborated Poe's abstractions with fresh illustrations and variations. (Sherlock Holmes, it is true, scorned Lecoq as "a miserable bungler" [see excerpt by Doyle dated 1887]. But in the same breath he dismissed Dupin as "a very inferior fellow." For all his exemplary qualities, it is to be feared that the Baker Street seer was not immune to professional jealousy!)

Because of the diverse elements in Gaboriau, it is difficult to classify the ultimate result with any degree of exactitude. He presented plot and detection virtually as separate entities. On the former side, his work was purely *physical;* on the latter, almost as elaborately *mental* as "Marie Rogêt." The issue of this mismating was a *divided* rather than a *balanced* detective story. Any final evaluation of his contribution must therefore distinguish carefully between promise and achievement. By a paradox that would have appealed to his French mind, his reputation to-day rests largely on the fact that he is so seldom read! For Gaboriau is one of those authors whom everybody talks about but whose works (if the truth be told) are virtually unknown. Few modern readers would have the patience to abide the tawdry puppetry, the fustian, the cheap sensationalism, the dull and irrelevant digressions, the dreary and artificial verbiage that are the feuilletonist at his too-frequent worst, in order to get at the few grains of highly competent detection. This is perhaps as well, for (to continue the metaphor) the greatest value of the grain was its germinal quality. (pp. 34-6)

It is for this implied rather than fulfilled promise that the world honors Gaboriau; for this, and for the impetus he gave the detective story in his own time. Had he lived to write the works that he planned, his honors on both scores would almost certainly have been greater. Even as it is, generations of later detective story writers are in his debt. He blazed no really new trails, but he tilled in honest peasant fashion a great deal of virgin soil. (p. 36)

> Howard Haycraft, "The In-Between Years (Development)," in his Murder for Pleasure: The Life and Times of the Detective Story, D. Appleton-Century Company Incorporated, 1941, pp. 28-44.

A. E. MURCH   (essay date 1958)

[*Murch recognizes Gaboriau as the originator of the French roman policier, or "police novel," a genre that he enriched with his creation of the likeable detective, Lecoq, and his introduction of the "red herring," or false lead. Further, Murch describes Gaboriau's struggle to combine episodic narrative structure with in-depth character study.*]

[Gaboriau's detective novels] are sensational and melodramatic, as such fiction had to be to please its public, but they differ from *romans-feuilletons* in that the reader's attention is focussed on the detection, not the commission, of crime. In them Gaboriau originated the '*roman-policier*' which was to form a major part of French popular fiction for the next quarter of a century. (p. 121)

In *L'Affaire Lerouge,* the opening chapters direct the limelight upon two official detectives of established reputation, M. Daburon, *le juge d'instruction,* and the celebrated Gévrol, *chef de la police de sûreté,* and it seems as though Gaboriau's original intention was to make them the central figures in his new novel of detection. But they are quickly eclipsed by two much more interesting characters, Père Tabaret and Monsieur Lecoq. (p. 122)

On his original appearance Lecoq is introduced with scant ceremony as a comparatively unimportant figure, merely Gévrol's junior assistant for the day, and Gaboriau describes him as 'an old offender now reconciled with the law,' a particularly interesting phrase because it places Lecoq, as an ex-convict turned policeman, in the same category as Vidocq, or Balzac's Gondureau, or the typical *agent de police* of any time in the previous hundred years. The term may have been used unthinkingly, simply as a conventional description—it has that air in the text—but Gaboriau seems to have regretted the phrase later, for as Lecoq became the central figure in the novels which followed, he went to some trouble to explain away this alleged stain on his hero's good name. (p. 123)

To enable Lecoq to fill his new rôle of French police-detective hero with brilliant efficiency. Gaboriau endowed him with powers derived from all his predecessors in detection. Lecoq can follow a trail as cleverly as the Princes of Serendip or Cooper's Indian braves, and he has all Vidocq's courage and intuition, his mastery of disguise, his familiarity with criminal ways. In view of Gaboriau's admiration for Edgar Allan Poe it is not surprising to find many points of similarity between Lecoq and Dupin, and they both regard a mysterious puzzle as a challenge to their powers of perception; they reason with mathematical precision and enjoy giving little lectures on 'algebraic analysis' to their associates. But whereas Dupin was an abstract logician, an arm-chair amateur detective, Lecoq threw himself with intense energy into the physical, as well as the mental, activities of practical police work, and over and above his inherited qualities he brought fresh skills of his own to the scientific detection of crime.... No-one, before him, used plaster to preserve a record of footprints, or drew a careful sketch of the scene of the crime, to be incorporated in the text. Lecoq and Père Tabaret are the first detectives to astonish the police (and the reader) by giving a detailed description of their suspect after making a brief examination of the scene of the crime. Père Tabaret, in *L'Affaire Lerouge,* takes a quick glance around, and remarks:—

> "He is a young man, below average height, elegantly dressed and wearing a top hat. He carried an umbrella, and was smoking a Havana cigar in a holder."

Lecoq, in "L'Enquête" (the first volume of *Monsieur Lecoq)* looks at the snow-covered ground outside an inn, and at once describes the man who walked across it half-an-hour ago:—

> "He is middle-aged and very tall, wearing a soft cap and a chestnut-coloured overcoat with a fleecy surface. He is very probably married."

In precisely the same way, twenty years or so later, Sherlock Holmes staggered his associates with such comments, . . . and Tabaret, Lecoq and Holmes are all alike in not revealing until some time later the simple indications that enabled them to make their dramatic pronouncements.

Lecoq is drawn as a man to be liked as a human being, not merely admired as a detective, and, clever though he is, he is not infallible. In "L'Enquête," he allowed himself to be baulked of almost certain success after a long, exhausting quest, simply because he could not credit that his missing suspect was really a Duke. A chat with old Tabaret gave him fresh heart and a new line of enquiry, and at the end of the second volume he brought his case to a triumphant conclusion.

Gaboriau further enriched detective fiction by his perception of the suspense value of the 'red herring,' and often sent suspicion running on a false trail laid by circumstantial evidence. Prosper Bertomy, in *Le Dossier No. 113* and *le vicomte de Caumarin* in *L'Affaire Lerouge,* seem almost certainly guilty until, at last, new information shows them to be wrongly suspected. The case against Caumarin is so strong that he is actually on trial for murder when Père Tabaret, learning that the prisoner has no alibi for the material time, deduces that he must therefore be innocent, and begins to reconsider the evidence against him. In *Le Crime d'Orcival* Lecoq is faced with a similar need to revise his conclusions in view of conflicting indications, and in this respect Gaboriau pointed the way to that subtle and delicately balanced see-saw of detective argument which was later brought to such perfection in the novels of Freeman Wills Crofts and Father Ronald Knox.

In view of the antipathy so long felt in France towards the police, it was a remarkable achievement to win popularity for a police-hero. Indeed, Gaboriau first followed Poe's example, and in the opening instalments of *L'Affaire Lerouge* it is the amateur detective, Père Tabaret, who shines most brightly. But as the tale developed, Gaboriau invested police affairs with a glamour that caught his readers' attention, and focussed their interest upon Monsieur Lecoq. He was so typically French, and the device of a crowing cock, which he chose for his personal symbol, so aptly expressed his high-stepping self assurance, his quick eye for trifles, his bedraggled dejection when success eluded him and his exultant bravado when he was lucky! The logical force of his soundly reasoned arguments appealed to French habits of thought, and readers could also enjoy his revelations of interdepartmental rivalries within the *Préfecture;* the jealousy of a village policeman for the man sent down by the *Sûreté;* the dilemma of a *juge d'instruction,* divided between professional duty and loyalty to personal ties; the routine of prison management; and the behaviour of various types of suspect when subjected to the gruelling French system of interrogation.

In developing his novels of Monsieur Lecoq, Gaboriau found himself faced with the artistic difficulty inherent in fiction of this type. In essence, a detective story concerns itself with an analytical enquiry into a given set of circumstances, and for that reason, though the enquiry may be protracted, the tale is really episodic. The most satisfying, the most technically perfect, examples of detective fiction—the tales of Dupin and of Sherlock Holmes, for instance—are short stories. It is difficult for a longer work to concern itself with a detective theme to the virtual exclusion of that intimate study of character which is the province of the true novelist. In writing a detective novel the author generally finds himself involved in two conflicting subjects, on one hand a complicated puzzle calling for the exercise of the reasoning powers, and on the other a human drama which appeals to the emotions.

Gaboriau attempted to overcome this difficulty in *L'Affaire Lerouge* by breaking off the thread of detection at a dramatic moment (in a manner very frustrating to a modern reader) and

A depiction of Parisian rogues from Caught in the Net.

interpolating the life-stories of the people concerned, even to the extent of taking the reader into his confidence behind the detective's back. In *Monsieur Lecoq* he went to the length of writing two separate volumes, the first setting forth the problem as Lecoq saw it, and the second relating, from the beginning, the human drama that culminated in the crime, with Lecoq completing his case in the final pages. *Le Crime d'Orcival* is much shorter, the interpolation less tedious, and Lecoq's investigations are not seriously interrupted. This book, in which Gaboriau more nearly approaches the technique of the twentieth century detective novel, is his best work by modern standards, with the possible exception of *Le Petit Vieux des Batignolles* . . . , which shows a further advance towards the 'pure' detective story, and foreshadows the device of the 'trick' ending. The murderer laid a false trail with meticulous care, and was caught only because the police, in ignorance of a material fact which he assumed they would know, blundered on the truth almost by accident. (pp. 124-27)

> *A. E. Murch, "The Rise of the 'Roman-Policier',"
> in his* The Development of the Detective Novel, *Philosophical Library, 1958, pp. 115-32.*

E. F. BLEILER   (essay date 1975)

[*Bleiler affirms Gaboriau's historical importance and the status of* Monsieur Lecoq *as a "perennial classic," but concludes that*

Gaboriau was "an author with a fine lesser imagination and an excellent skill at research, hampered by a lack of large-scale insight."]

Did Gaboriau really invent the modern detective novel? The answer is a qualified "Yes," if each of the three words "modern," "detective" and "novel" is taken with precision. Generally speaking, in both English and French, there had been a considerable body of crime fiction before Gaboriau's day, and some of this contained the germs of later developments, including primitive detectives and detection. But most of this material, like Victor's *The Dead Letter,* could not be considered modern, being only curious ancestral effigies for future generations to look upon. (p. x)

Gaboriau should not be seen as a collection of influences, but as a man who crystallized and solidified what may have been in the air around him. He unified a certain grouping of characteristics and created a form. Féval may have talked about ratiocinative deduction two or three years before Gaboriau, but he apparently did not care or was unable to develop the idea. Vidocq wandered about Paris in disguise, seeking criminals, and Balzac and Sue may have written long novels that combined comedy of manners with crime motives, but Gaboriau still has the distinction, in *L'Affaire Lerouge,* of having created the first modern novel that was clearly and unmistakably and consciously and primarily a detective story. (p. xii)

Gaboriau in a vague sort of way seems to have thought of the later novels, from *L'Affaire Lerouge* on, as segments of a consistent universe, a small *comédie humaine.* As a result there is a certain carry-over of names and personalities from one novel to another. The reader often finds a familiar face among the newcomers. This situation, unfortunately, is complicated by the fact that Gaboriau was careless in his chronology and cross-references, and is inconsistent almost as often as consistent. A further complication is that Gaboriau simply liked certain names and used them over.

A common frame of mind, similarly, permeates all the novels of Gaboriau, both detective and social. The ultimate spring of all his major work is scandal of the sexual sort. Forbidden amours, illegitimacy, golddigging, adultery—all provide final motivation for action. This is in striking contrast to the British novels that are roughly contemporary.... Wilkie Collins, in the two great novels, *The Woman in White* and *The Moonstone,* uses financial greed to motivate the stories. The ultimate in *The Woman in White* is Fosco's wish to obtain an inheritance, and the ultimate in *The Moonstone* is the monetary value of the gem. In Doyle's work, the ultimate is usually greed, with revenge a second consideration. For the other British Victorians—LeFanu, Miss Braddon, Mrs. Wood—the motivation is sometimes economic, sometimes the passion of anger, sometimes erotic, but never scandalous.

One could say simply and flippantly, that this simply means that Gaboriau was a Frenchman, and that his novels reflect the folkways of the time. But I do not know whether this is true. The psychologies of the characters—their violent passions and hatreds, their filial devotion, their raffishness, their strange innocences and pruderies—do they represent an aspect of life in the middle classes of Gaboriau's milieu, perhaps the ideals of his own pecksniffian family, or are they a literary convention, or perhaps both?

The motivations in Gaboriau are consistent and the personalities are consistent. A high problem of the generation before Ga-

boriau, one that entered very frequently in the fiction of the 1860's, was the haughty old revanchist nobility, returning in the post-Napoleonic restoration. There was the boom and bust of the Emperor Louis Napoleon; the extravagances of inverse machismo, when a chance act or word might ruin a girl's life, even though nothing significant had happened. Did this configuration of folkways really dominate mid-Victorian bourgeois France? I do not know, any more than if British lords in the comparable English literature perpetually tried to swindle their relatives. (pp. xvi-xviii)

For reasons now forgotten, Gaboriau's work was appreciated in America before England. (p. xix)

Before the appearance of Gaboriau's novels in America, the American detective story had been on the trivial side numerically. There were prehistoric detective stories before 1840 by Charles Brockden Brown and William Leggett; there was Poe's crystallization of the form and invention of ratiocinative deduction; but only a few minor successors to Poe. Then suddenly, shortly after the appearance of Gaboriau, the country was flooded with series after series of detective novels in dime-novel format. They were not modern detective stories, it is true; but they were novels that involved a crime, a detective (usually official), and some detection. I am inclined to think that this explosion of interest is the result of two foreign influences: to a lesser extent British detective casebooks (like "Waters"), as published by Dick and Fitzgerald, and to a larger extent, the long novels of Gaboriau.

In England Gaboriau's works began to appear in *Vizetelly's Sensational Novels* from 1883 on. Some of the translations may have been taken from American piracies; others may have been British in origin. This date 1883, it will be observed, is not far removed from 1887, the date of A. C. Doyle's *Study in Scarlet.* Doyle's diary notes reveal that he read certain of Gaboriau's novels, and in later years he recalled *The Widow Lerouge,* though somewhat dimly. Yet enough of the schema and details of Gaboriau's work remained in Doyle's mind that Doyle without Gaboriau would have been quite different. If Poe's Dupin was the father of Tabaret and Lecoq, Tabaret and Lecoq are the father and godfather of Sherlock Holmes. This is not to say, of course, that there were no other elements, or to deny Doyle's own ingenious contributions. (pp. xix-xx)

Gaboriau is obviously a historical link of the utmost importance [between Poe and Doyle] Is he more than this? Is he an author worth reading in his own right? My answer is a limited "Yes." While he has great weaknesses, he also has certain strengths that are almost unique.

Let us omit the question of Gaboriau's French style, which has been called alternately brilliant and whimsical, ironic and lyric. These qualities do not emerge in the translations, but the translations are admittedly bad. They are hastily, carelessly, insensitively prepared hackwork, which at times are neither French nor English.

Gaboriau is certainly one of the most accomplished plotters in the genre. He is capable of working out a complex group of life situations and interweaving them without boring the reader or confusing him.

Complex plots, of course, were a standby of Victorian popular literature, and in England G. W. M. Reynolds and Wilkie Collins specialized in comparable material. Yet it is safe to say that Gaboriau at his best excelled them both in ornateness.

Such erector-set stories, however, may not be the highest achievement in literature (especially since the twentieth century is likely to seek other values), but they are still achievements that demand respect.

The detective novel is a notoriously difficult form to plot, since, to express it in the lowest terms, the author must devise something to fill in the space between the crime and the revealment or detection. It is greatly to Gaboriau's credit that in what is the first modern detective novel he solved the problem as well [as] any one has done since. Where *The Widow Lerouge* has flaws, they are in other areas.

Gaboriau's second strength lies in his detailed factual backgrounds and in his criminological and legal accuracy. Strictly speaking, this is not purely a matter of literature, but the reader of one hundred years later can appreciate the care that went into the descriptions of judicial processes, quirks of law, detectional insights, and the whole philosophy of French criminal investigation. British jurists have been known to recommend Gaboriau's novels to juniors who wanted a rapid picture of French criminal procedure. Gaboriau's old chief, Féval, faked in such matters and relied on imagination to carry him through. Gaboriau was correct. If Gaboriau describes the powers of the examining magistrate, if he explains a point in the law of inheritance, if he describes a suicide by carbon monoxide from unventilated charcoal braziers, one can be sure that he has checked the point. For Gaboriau there are no giant sea anemones, no devil's foot. If a young man is sent to the war in French Indo-China, and a crime is committed there, as in *The Gilded Clique,* one can be sure that extradition and venue are correctly handled. All this mirrors a world strange to the American reader, a world where the prisoner is officially guilty unless he can prove his innocence, where police entrapment (as in the Epilogue to *Monsieur Lecoq*) is permissible.

Where does Gaboriau fail? His portrayal of people. His characters have been called cardboard, and the accusation is, for the most part, true. They do resemble the moving dummies in a shooting gallery. Yet this criticism is a little over-simple. While the various counts and barons, fake and real, that people the novels, the adulterous ladies and virtuous ingenues, the sincere young lovers with mistresses on the side—are statues or lay-figures that sustain a drapery of plot, Gaboriau did succeed in animating two major characters, Lecoq and Tabaret, the voices of realism, rather than of romance.

A little more consciousness of technique might have worked wonders for Gaboriau in this respect. When Gaboriau works through the mind of a single character, which he does to some extent with Lecoq and Tabaret, his skill at recognizing motivation and his ability to create small detail can work an animation. When Gaboriau, on the other hand, attempts to make his characters interact romantically, when he speaks remotely as a recording witness, he loses his honesty of emotion and de-sparks what might have been human. This is where melodrama comes in, and this is where disaster strikes.

Perhaps the safest judgment of Gaboriau as a whole is to call him an author with a fine lesser imagination and an excellent skill at research, hampered by a lack of large-scale insight. Too often he sets up trumpery effects that do not succeed, and too often he is false. This may seem to be a harsh judgment, but the reader can look at the works of Balzac to see what happens when a first-rate writer, even though he may lack smoothness, works on material somewhat similar to Gaboriau's.

Criticism should stay at criticism, and reading pleasure should remain reading pleasure. Despite a modern reader's occasional annoyance at Gaboriau's weaknesses, *Monsieur Lecoq,* Part One, is still very much worth reading; it is easily the most animated of Gaboriau's works. The ingenuity of the author's deductions; the piquant personality of the young man who is determined to make his way in his profession, despite obstacles of official stupidity and criminal cunning; the thrill of the psychological duel between the helpless prisoner in his cell and the imaginative detective—these are the factors that make *Monsieur Lecoq* a perennial classic. (pp. xxi-xxiii)

E. F. Bleiler, in an introduction to Monsieur Lecoq *by Émile Gaboriau, edited by E. F. Bleiler, Dover Publications, Inc., 1975, pp. v-xxviii.*

R. F. STEWART (essay date 1980)

[*Stewart emphasizes Gaboriau's significance in the development of detective fiction. Noting that Gaboriau was surprisingly acceptable to critics who generally considered sensationalistic crime fiction immoral, Stewart identifies several influences on Gaboriau's writings and concludes with the suggestion that the author has not received full credit for his impact on Doyle and succeeding detective novelists.*]

What kind of book was Gaboriau writing that it was accepted by both readers and critics and that it succeeded where English sensation novelists, treating the same topics of crime, mystery and detectives, were left far behind? In what did he differ so greatly from Miss Braddon and Collins that he overcame the critical hostility to this kind of novel and won readers in a country already well-catered for in the field of sensation?

That Gaboriau had achieved something both different and more acceptable is clear from the critics' broadly favourable reaction to him, though of course they had no reason at first to suspect that he was instituting a sub-division of sensation fiction which was to become so extensive and in some respects so apparently different as to be able in time to deny its parent. To begin with, Gaboriau's superiority and the grounds for his critical acclaim were indicated more by favourable comparisons than by positive appreciations. He was good because the rest were bad—and bad often in a moral sense. This is seen in the *Saturday's* comment . . . that *L'Affaire Lerouge* 'is not ghastly and immoral, like . . . some others of recent production', followed in haste and surprise at commending a book dealing with crime by, 'if criminal, [it] is also decent' [see excerpt dated 1866]. (pp. 237-38)

[The] tendency of sensationalists to exalt or exonerate evil was a sticking point for many critics, who saw themselves as the guardians of moral as well as of literary taste. In Gaboriau they seemed to find an author of whom they could approve even though he dealt in the hitherto reprehensible subject of crime. Black, in Gaboriau, was black, and white was white: the bad were punished and the good lived happily ever after; there were no complications except in the plot, no lessons except in detection, and analysis was confined to clues. So was born the ideology of the detective story. (p. 239)

[Gaboriau] was the first novelist deliberately, consistently and completely to swing the criminal romance away from the crime and the criminal and to focus on the detective. . . . Before Gaboriau there were novels with detectives, not novels about detectives or novels about detection. There are odd examples of works which approach Gaboriau's concentration on these themes—*The Notting Hill Mystery, Lady Audley's Secret, The Moonstone*—but even these lack that vital intention of exalting these elements. Again, none of these books was followed by others in quite the same vein or using the same characters, and their popularity was due at least as much to other factors as to their detectives and detection—the thrill of a beautiful murderess in *Lady Audley's Secret,* the interplay of character in *The Moonstone,* and even though *The Notting Hill Mystery* is presented from the investigator's point of view, the interest is centred on Baron R. But Gaboriau sets the detective in the centre of the stage, turns the limelight on him and puts him through his paces. And both author and character come through with flying colours.

In one direction Poe is Gaboriau's obvious inspiration. It may safely be assumed that he had read Poe in Baudelaire's translation which enjoyed immense success in France. (p. 240)

In another direction Gaboriau's stories have their roots firmly planted in a French tradition. Just as novels with detectives were being written in England for many years before Doyle, so too in France Gaboriau could draw on a wealth of fiction replete with mysteries and detectives, and just as Doyle fits into the English sensational tradition, so Gaboriau is part of the French. Balzac and Dumas are obvious influences, but the undergrowth was no less thick than England's—Zevaco, Decourcelle, Ponson du Terrail and Gaboriau's employer, Féval, to name but a few. (pp. 241-42)

Without the efforts of these predecessors Gaboriau might never have conceived and executed his detective stories. There is probably more of Balzac than of Poe in Gaboriau, [seen in] his habit of using the same characters over a series of novels and of modelling his aristocrats along Balzac's lines. . . .

Gaboriau's achievement was to produce something new from the old formulas, the old characters and the old plots of sensation fiction, This he did by arranging his people and events round the detective—the detective who had always been there but in the background. Nothing changed except the emphasis. (p. 242)

It is probably to his judicious intermingling of the new with the old that Gaboriau owes some of his success. In *Monsieur Lecoq,* for example, the man known as Mai, whose identity Lecoq spends most of the first part of the book trying to establish, is not the villain of the piece but the object of a plot. It is vital to Lecoq's pride that he find his answer; it is equally vital to Mai and his friends that his true identity is not established or the honour of his name will be compromised. The reader, however, is free to adopt either the interesting new angle of following with the hound—*in detail,* which had not happened before, or the edifying variation on the well-proven old angle—running with the *innocent* hare. Whichever the reader chooses, Gaboriau wins; of course the reader chooses to do both and Gaboriau doubles his winnings. (p. 245)

• • • • •

Doyle made two well-known comments about Gaboriau. The first is in *A Study in Scarlet* [see excerpt dated 1887]. . . . The second is in his autobiography, *Memories and Adventures* . . . : 'Gaboriau had rather attracted me by the neat dove-tailing of his plots'. There is a whiff of contradiction here, but since the first was written by Doyle in his capacity as a literary agent and the second by Doyle *qua* Doyle, I think we are justified in taking the autobiographical comment as nearer his true opinion.

Doyle does not elaborate on what he means by 'neat dove-tailing', but the structure of his own long stories leaves little doubt. Thus in both *A Study in Scarlet* and *The Valley of Fear* . . . Doyle faithfully follows Gaboriau's system of a first part concerned with a crime, its investigation and virtual solution, then a second part in which time is turned back and a new story started which from remote beginnings brings the reader to the commission of the crime discovered at the opening of the book. (p. 256)

This similarity of construction is a very obvious common factor in Gaboriau and Doyle, and is generally condemned in both. (p. 257)

Doyle owed rather more to Gaboriau than the histories tell us, a suspicion borne out by another, less well-known, reference to Gaboriau in Doyle's diary. John Dickson Carr mentions it in his biography of Doyle:

> 'I have read Gaboriau's *Lecoq the Detective*', he wrote; the first reference to Gaboriau in all his papers, '*The Gilded Clique,* and a story concerning the murder of an old woman, the name of which I forget.' Looking this up, he inserted *The Lerouge Case.* 'All very good. Wilkie Collins, but more so.'
>
> (p. 259)

No absolute disparagement of Doyle is intended here; only a suggestion that the distribution of recognition within detective fiction could bear some reorganisation. Doyle freely admitted his debt to Poe. Gaboriau, I am sure, would have admitted a similar debt. Nor can we doubt Doyle's sincerity when he wrote: 'As to work which is unconsciously imitative, it is not to be expected that a man's style and mode of treatment should spring fully formed from his own brain', but it was Poe alone that he seemed to have in mind here. Given the foregoing, one feels that he owes, for his start in life, a more immediate debt to Gaboriau, not for showing him that stories about detectives and detection could be written—Poe did that—but for showing him that they could become alive. That was the achievement of both Gaboriau and Doyle, and if in the long run Doyle did it better, could he have done it at all without Gaboriau's lead? (p. 260)

In a positive and deliberate sense, Gaboriau set out to write about detectives, their successes, their failures, to have them as his centrepieces, to propose them as superior alternatives to rogues and criminals. No, he was not writing 'detective fiction', but to say this is now to quibble. What he did write was, twenty years later, considered so distinctive and influential as to be worth the invention of the term. This is where Gaboriau differs from Collins and all the other writers of the time who employed detectives. To them—and to many later writers—the detective was useful. To Gaboriau he was vital.

So fascinated was Gaboriau by detectives that he set himself to render the unacceptable attractive. Beside Gaboriau's interest, Dickens' and Collins' appears negligible. (pp. 276-77)

Up to Gaboriau, no novelist—and Poe only in the short story—had taken a detective and thrust greatness upon him. Gaboriau differs radically from all [early detective novelists] in that he starts with a detective and finishes with a detective. Even Poe ends with a dissertation, and Robert Audley is a detective in spite of himself. With his long, historical flashbacks Gaboriau gives us rather more than we have come to expect. . . . [As] twentieth-century detective stories *Monsieur Lecoq* and *Le Dos-*

sier No. 113 are too long, but the detective parts are complete in themselves. Indeed, the first part of the former, **"L'enquête"**, is so self-contained that it has been published on its own on several occasions with no mention of its second part, **"L'honneur du nom"**. The 'digressions' in *L'Affaire Lerouge* and *Le Crime d'Orcival* are much more closely linked with the detective plot; they may seem long-winded, but they are Gaboriau's way of doing something that had never been done before. Moreover, the romances which make up the second parts of the other two books, especially that in *Le Dossier No. 113,* are entertaining in themselves if the reader can disabuse himself of the notion that the problem of who did it is necessarily central to the detective story.

Of course Gaboriau did not obey the rules. He was making them, or at least one, and that a much more basic one than anything to follow and on which all that followed depended; the rule, simply, that detective stories could be written and enjoyed. We can accept or reject, as we please, any or all of the explanations of his faults. . . . But whatever we do, we cannot deny that the intention to write novels about detectives and the achievement of that intention are Gaboriau's lasting contributions to literature. (pp. 278-79)

> *R. F. Stewart, "The Reader Learns Much That He Has Guessed" and "In Which an Important Act of Restitution Is Made," in his . . .* And Always a Detective: Chapters on the History of Detective Fiction, *David & Charles, 1980, pp. 231-52, 253-79.*

ADDITIONAL BIBLIOGRAPHY

Cambiaire, Célestin Pierre. "Poe and Émile Gaboriau." In his *The Influence of Edgar Allan Poe in France*, pp. 264-80. 1927. Reprint. St. Clair Shores, Mich.: Scholarly Press, 1971.
> Compares Poe's detective stories with Gaboriau's novels. While Cambiaire maintains that Poe was the superior artist, he grants that Gaboriau was not slavish in his imitations of Poe's technique.

Symons, Julian. "Dickens, Collins, Gaboriau: The Pattern Forms." In his *Mortal Consequences: A History—From the Detective Story to the Crime Novel*, pp. 36-53. New York: Harper & Row, Publishers, 1972.
> Claims that Gaboriau has been underrated. Symons finds that although Gaboriau's novels lack humor and skilled characterization, they display the author's analytical intelligence and thorough knowledge of French police procedures.

Wells, Carolyn. *The Technique of the Mystery Story*. Springfield, Mass.: Home Correspondence School, 1913, 336 p.
> Surveys the history and characteristics of detective fiction and credits Gaboriau, along with Poe and Doyle, with the invention of the genre.

Wright, Willard Huntington. "The Great Detective Stories." In *The Art of the Mystery Story: A Collection of Critical Essays*, edited by Howard Haycraft, pp. 33-70. New York: Simon and Schuster, 1946.
> Assesses Gaboriau's place in the history of detective fiction. Wright calls Gaboriau's *The Widow Lerouge* "the first great stride in the detective novel."

William Godwin

1756-1836

English philosopher, novelist, essayist, historian, dramatist, and biographer.

Godwin is recognized as a philosopher and author whose writings strongly influenced the English Romantic writers. His anarchistic and rationalistic beliefs are delineated in his philosophical masterpiece, *An Enquiry Concerning Political Justice and Its Influence on General Virtue and Happiness*. In this work, Godwin stated that humankind is innately good and capable of living harmoniously without laws or institutions. These tenets are dramatized in his best-known novel, *Things As They Are; or, The Adventures of Caleb Williams*, a didactic tale about the evils of government. Though Godwin wrote other novels as well as biographies and essays, critics point out that these works lack the emotional power and intellectual appeal of *Caleb Williams* and *Political Justice*. Despite his prolific career, Godwin's reputation has declined, and he is primarily known today as a figure of historical importance.

The seventh of thirteen children, Godwin was born in Wisbeach, England, to a Presbyterian minister and his wife. Raised in a strict, puritanical environment, Godwin trained for the ministry at an early age and became a Sandemanian clergyman in 1777. However, after studying the French revolutionary philosophers, he grew disenchanted with religion and eventually became an atheist. Leaving the church in 1783, Godwin moved to London, intending to make his living as an author. There he contributed to the *London Review* and wrote factual pamphlets and biographies; these writings, though intellectually rigorous, lack the philosophical content that distinguishes his subsequent work.

In 1793, Godwin published *Political Justice*, which contains the theoretical essence of all his later writings. In this work, Godwin denounced contemporary goverhments as corrupt and ineffective, hypothesizing that reason rather than law should provide the ruling force of society. Through the development of reason, he declared, humanity could become perfect. He also contended that property should not be accumulated by individuals, but should instead be held in trust for those in need. In discussing penal servitude, Godwin maintained that criminals should be reformed, not merely punished. Of all the arguments advanced in *Political Justice*, perhaps the best known is Godwin's disdain for the institution of marriage: he advocated that men and women should be united solely by a bond of mutual respect rather than a social and legal contract. Godwin was nearly prosecuted for these unconventional beliefs. However, among those who sympathized with its unorthodox tenets, *Political Justice* met with immediate acclaim, and its author was widely hailed as an influential philosopher.

Following the success of *Political Justice*, Godwin produced *Caleb Williams*, a novel inspired by his desire to disseminate the ideas of *Political Justice* through a more popular form. A tale of good triumphing over evil and an individual conquering a corrupt system, the novel tells the story of Caleb Williams, a man persecuted by his employer, Ferdinando Falkland, and jailed for a crime he did not commit. Godwin's plot combines historical events with psychological realism and Gothic and

detective elements. The original preface, in which the author defined the novel as "a study and delineation of things passing in the moral world," was considered politically subversive and was consequently suppressed for many years. *Caleb Williams* endures, however, as a record of the revolutionary spirit and as one of the first novels to successfully combine fiction and philosophy. Though undeniably propagandistic, the novel won critical praise for its synthesis of content and style. In particular, critics noted that Godwin's use of first-person narration lends an element of immediacy to *Caleb Williams*. With *Political Justice*, *Caleb Williams* provided Godwin with his only financial success.

Godwin was already an established and influential writer in 1796 when he met Mary Wollstonecraft, the author of *A Vindication of the Rights of Woman*, an attack on society's treatment of women. Their rapport was immediate, and soon the two began living together. When Wollstonecraft became pregnant a few months later, the two wed despite their mutual distaste for the institution of marriage because they wanted to ensure the legal rights of their child. By all accounts, both found great joy in wedlock, but their happiness was short-lived. Several days after the birth of their daughter in 1797, Wollstonecraft died of complications from the delivery. A desolate Godwin recorded his memories of their brief life together in *Memoirs of the Author of "A Vindication of the Rights of*

Woman,'' in which he wrote of his wife, ''I honoured her intellectual powers and the nobleness and generosity of her propensities; mere tenderness would not have been adequate to produce the happiness we experienced.'' Left with his infant daughter as well as a stepdaughter to care for, Godwin set out to find a mother for his children. He was turned down by one woman after another before marrying Mary Jane Clairmont, a harsh, cruel woman who treated his children poorly.

Despite the sorrows of his personal life, Godwin continued to write. In 1799, shortly before his marriage to Clairmont, Godwin had published St. Leon, a historical novel that reflects his interest in heroic drama and his desire to modify some of his earlier radical beliefs, which were considered harsh and insensitive. A sentimental depiction of the joys of domesticity, St. Leon is also a tribute to his late wife. Response to the novel was mixed, and critics termed St. Leon more ambitious in design than Godwin's range would permit. His next novel, Fleetwood, which appeared six years later, is considered both a synthesis of Romantic ideals and a reconstruction of Godwin's earlier philosophy. Though some critics praised Fleetwood's philosophical framework, most considered it poorly organized and overly didactic. Like St. Leon, Fleetwood sold poorly.

After the publication of Fleetwood, Godwin and his wife began publishing children's books, histories, and biographies in a desperate attempt to support their growing family. Godwin also relied heavily on the financial assistance of the young followers who sought his philosophical guidance; most notable among these was the Romantic poet Percy Bysshe Shelley. In 1814, Shelley, who was already married, eloped with Godwin's sixteen-year-old daughter, Mary. Though a furious Godwin disowned them both, he continued to demand Shelley's monetary support. Godwin's wrath diminished when the two married several years later, and he became once again extremely close to his daughter. Shelley remained a devoted disciple of his father-in-law and aided the initial reception of Godwin's Mandeville by writing a strongly favorable review. Inspired by the fiction of Sir Walter Scott, Mandeville is considered indicative of the general decline in Godwin's fiction following Caleb Williams. Godwin's last novels, Cloudesly and Deloraine, generated little positive response upon their publication and are today considered dull.

In addition to his fiction, Godwin published several book-length essays, including Thoughts on Man: His Nature, Productions, and Discoveries and Of Population: An Enquiry Concerning the Power of Increase in the Numbers of Mankind, Being an Answer to Mr. Malthus' Essay on That Subject. The latter work contests the political theories of Thomas Malthus as delineated in his Essay on the Principle of Population. While Malthus argued for a check on population growth, Godwin opposed any type of law or governing institution that would inhibit human nature. Despite his steady literary output, Godwin struggled financially until 1833, when he was appointed yeoman usher of the exchequer and was granted a government pension. Though no longer compelled by financial necessity, Godwin steadfastly continued to write until his death three years later.

At the time of his death, Godwin's contemporaries considered him a figure of historical and literary importance whose beliefs had briefly inspired such individuals as Samuel Taylor Coleridge and Robert Southey, who together created a pantisocracy, or egalitarian agricultural society, based on Godwin's theories. His revolutionary writings also influenced Shelley and

William Wordsworth, who both based their Romantic philosophies on his ideas on personal freedom. However, Godwin's works soon fell into relative obscurity, receiving attention only from such literary figures as Thomas De Quincey and Leslie Stephen, who both censured his verbosity and excessive didacticism. It was not until the turn of the century that critics began to demonstrate a renewed interest in Godwin as a philosopher and author. Early twentieth-century studies stressed the literary merits of Political Justice and its value as a philosophical and historical document. Caleb Williams, too, has enjoyed a revival. Since the 1940s, critics have analyzed various aspects of the work, including its elements of tragedy and mystery, the two endings for the novel, and the prose style. Critics differ on whether Godwin best articulated his philosophy in the essay or novel form. Nonetheless, they point out his ideological consistency: despite the variety of genres in which Godwin composed, the philosophical thread that he developed in Political Justice dominates every work.

Today, Caleb Williams continues to be read and studied widely; the profusion of articles written on the novel each year attests to its enduring popularity. Critics also regard the work as a seminal contribution to the evolution of the English novel. Political Justice endures as a testament to Godwin's talent at the peak of his powers and as one of the main documents of English Romantic philosophy. In addition, Godwin's importance derives from his influence on the Romantics, especially on the verse of Wordsworth and Shelley. Godwin's reputation today rests on three areas: Caleb Williams, his theories as expressed in Political Justice, and his imprint on contemporary and modern literature.

PRINCIPAL WORKS

An Account of the Seminary That Will Be Opened at Epsom (prospectus)   1783
The History of the Life of William Pitt   (biography)   1783
An Enquiry Concerning Political Justice and Its Influence on General Virtue and Happiness   (essay)   1793; also published in revised form as Enquiry Concerning Political Justice and Its Influence on Morals and Happiness, 1796
Things As They Are; or, The Adventures of Caleb Williams (novel)   1794; also published as The Adventures of Caleb Williams; or, Things As They Are, 1839
The Enquirer: Reflections on Education, Manners, and Literature   (essays)   1797
Memoirs of the Author of "A Vindication of the Rights of Woman"   (memoirs)   1798
St. Leon: A Tale of the Sixteenth Century   (novel)   1799
Life of Geoffrey Chaucer   (biography)   1803
Fleetwood; or, The New Man of Feeling   (novel)   1805
Faulkener [first publication]   (drama)   1807
Mandeville: A Tale of the Seventeenth Century in England (novel)   1817
Of Population: An Enquiry Concerning the Power of Increase in the Numbers of Mankind, Being an Answer to Mr. Malthus' Essay on That Subject   (essay)   1820
Cloudesly   (novel)   1830
Thoughts on Man: His Nature, Productions, and Discoveries (essay)   1831
Deloraine   (novel)   1833
Lives of the Necromancers; or, An Account of the Most Eminent Persons Who Have Claimed or to Whom Has

Been Imputed the Exercise of Magical Power
(biographical sketches)   1834
Essays Never Before Published   (essays)   1873

SAMUEL TAYLOR COLERIDGE   (poem date 1793)

[*An English poet and critic, Coleridge was central to the English Romantic movement and is considered one of the greatest literary critics in the English language. His sonnet, "To William Godwin," originally appeared in the* Morning Chronicle *on January 10, 1793.*]

O form'd t'illumine a sunless world forlorn,
As o'er the chill and dusky brow of Night,
In Finland's wintry skies the Mimic Morn
    Electric pours a stream of rosy light,

Pleas'd I have mark'd OPPRESSION, terror-pale,
    Since, through the windings of her dark machine,
    Thy steady eye has shot its glances keen—
And bade th'All-lovely 'scenes at distance hail.'

Nor will I not thy holy guidance bless,
    And hymn thee, GODWIN! with an ardent lay;
    For that thy voice, in Passion's stormy day,
When wild I roam'd the bleak heath of Distress,

Bade the bright form of Justice meet my way
And told me that her name was HAPPINESS.

> *Samuel Taylor Coleridge, " 'To William Godwin',"*
> *in* Godwin and the Age of Transition, *edited by A. E.*
> *Rodway, Barnes & Noble, Inc., 1952, p. 206.*

WILLIAM GODWIN   (essay date 1794)

[*Written in 1794, Godwin's preface to the first edition of* Caleb Williams *was suppressed and not published until much later. Because of the conservative political atmosphere at the time, booksellers feared that the preface might be considered traitorous.*]

The following narrative is intended to answer a purpose more general and important than immediately appears upon the face of it. The question now afloat in the world respecting THINGS AS THEY ARE is the most interesting that can be presented to the human mind. While one party pleads for reformation and change, the other extols in the warmest terms the existing constitution of society. It seemed as if something would be gained for the decision of this question, if that constitution were faithfully developed in its practical effects. What is now presented to the public is no refined and abstract speculation; it is a study and delineation of things passing in the moral world. It is but of late that the inestimable importance of political principles has been adequately apprehended. It is now known to philosophers, that the spirit and character of the government intrudes itself into every rank of society. But this is a truth highly worthy to be communicated to persons whom books of philosophy and science are never likely to reach. Accordingly it was proposed, in the invention of the following work, to comprehend, as far as the progressive nature of a single story would allow, a general review of the modes of domestic and unrecorded despotism by which man becomes the destroyer of man. If the author shall have taught a valuable lesson, without subtracting from the interest and passion by

which a performance of this sort ought to be characterised, he will have reason to congratulate himself upon the vehicle he has chosen. (pp. xix-xx)

> *William Godwin, in a preface to his* The Adventures
> of Caleb Williams; or, Things as They Are, *revised*
> *edition, Richard Bentley, 1849, pp. xix-xx.*

THE BRITISH CRITIC   (essay date 1794)

[*In the following excerpt, the critic harshly condemns* Caleb Williams, *stating that the novel represents "the evil use" of Godwin's talents.*]

[*Things as They Are; or, The Adventures of Caleb Williams*] is a striking example of the evil use which may be made of considerable talents, connected with such a degree of intrepidity as can inspire the author with resolution to attack religion, virtue, government, laws, and above all, the desire (hitherto accounted laudable) of leaving a good name to posterity.

In this extraordinary performance, every gentleman is a hard hearted assassin, or a prejudiced tyrant; every Judge is unjust, every Justice corrupt and blind. Sentiments of respect to Christianity are given only to the vilest wretch in the book; while the most respectable person in the drama abhors the idea of "shackling his expiring friend with the fetters of superstition."

In order to render the laws of his country odious, the author places an innocent prisoner, whose story he (avowedly) takes from the Newgate Calendar of the first George's reign, in a dungeon; the wretched, unhealthy state of which he steals (as avowedly) from one of the benevolent Howard's painful descriptions of a worse gaol than common. We will only add, that the character, on which the author seems to dwell with most pleasure, is that of a leader of robbers, one who dwells in a ruinous retreat, and dispatches felons and murderers, in parties, around the country.

When a work is so directly pointed at every band which connects society, and at every principle which renders it amiable, its very merits become noxious as they tend to cause its being known in a wider circle. (pp. 70-1)

> *A review of "Things as They Are; or, The Adventures*
> *of Caleb Williams," in* The British Critic, *Vol. IV,*
> *July, 1794, pp. 70-1.*

THE MONTHLY REVIEW, LONDON   (essay date 1794)

[*In the following excerpt from a review of* Caleb Williams, *the critic terms the plot "a whining love tale," but praises the novel as an outstanding example of philosophical fiction.*]

Between fiction and philosophy there seems to be no natural alliance:—yet philosophers, in order to obtain for their dogmata a more ready reception, have often judged it expedient to introduce them to the world in the captivating dress of fable. It was not to be supposed that the energetic mind of Mr. Godwin, long inured as it must have been to abstract speculation and sublime inquiry, would condescend to employ itself in framing a whining love tale. . . . In writing *The Adventures of Caleb Williams*, this philosopher had doubtless some higher object in view; and it is not difficult to perceive that this object has been to give an easy passport, and general circulation, to some of his favourite opinions. Having laid it down as a first principle that virtue consists in justice, or the wise and equal pursuit of general good, he thinks it necessary, in order to carry his system into effect, to investigate many sentiments which, though hitherto considered as the legitimate offspring of nature, and even as possessing some degree of moral value, are in his judgment only the creatures of error and prejudice. In this class he appears to rank that sense of honour which seeks its ultimate reward in the good opinion of mankind. Accordingly, this fictitious narrative seems to have been written chiefly for the purpose of representing, in strong colours, the fatal consequence of suffering the love of fame to become predominant.

Mr. Falkland, who ought, perhaps, rather than Caleb Williams, to be considered as the principal actor in this drama, exhibits a character wholly formed on the visionary principles of honour. Early tinctured with extravagant notions on this subject, by the heroic poets of Italy, he cherishes a romantic pride; which, notwithstanding his natural propensity toward benevolence, displayed in occasional acts of generosity, soon forms his ruling passion, and at length overwhelms him with accumulated wretchedness. He is the fool of honour; a man whom, in the pursuit of reputation, nothing could divert; who would purchase the character of a true, gallant, and undaunted hero, at the expence of worlds; and who thinks every calamity nominal except a stain on his honour. His virtue, his life, his everlasting peace of mind, are cheap sacrifices to be made at the shrine of fame; and there is no crime too horrible for him to commit in pursuit of this object. (pp. 145-46)

This visionary character is drawn with uncommon strength of conception and energy of language. The reader, while he respects and adores the virtues of Falkland, feels infinite regret that his mad passion for reputation should suppress every feeling of humanity, and become the source of unspeakable misery to himself, and of the most tragical calamity to others. The character, though original, will perhaps be admitted to be consistent; unless it should be thought difficult to reconcile the benevolence every where ascribed to Falkland, with the *deliberate* injustice and cruelty which were shewn in suffering the innocent Hawkins and his son to be executed, in preference to confessing his own guilt.—It will perhaps be said that the ruling passion of Falkland was not benevolence, but the love of fame; yet it may be questioned whether such benevolence, as is ascribed to Falkland, be not utterly incompatible with the tyrannical sway which is given in his character to the *selfish* passion of the love of fame. . . .

A farther object in this story appears to have been to exhibit an example of the danger of indulging an idle curiosity, merely for its own gratification; and the fatal consequences of this folly were perhaps never so impressively exemplified as in the story of Caleb Williams, the confidential servant of Falkland. (p. 147)

With due allowance for systematical eccentricity, (the reader will pardon the paradoxical expression,) this performance, interesting but not gratifying to the feelings and the passions, and written in a style of laboured dignity rather than of easy familiarity, is singularly entitled to be characterized as a work in which the powers of genius and philosophy are strongly united. (p. 149)

> E., "Godwin's 'Things as They Are'," in The Monthly Review, *London, Vol. XV, October, 1794, pp. 145-49.*

WILLIAM GODWIN (essay date 1799)

[*In the following excerpt from his 1799 preface to* St. Leon, *Godwin explains his desire to depict the joys of domestic life.*]

It has been said of Shakespeare, that he

> Exhausted worlds, and then imagined new:

but the burthen sustained by Shakespeare was too heavy for the shoulders of any other individual. I leave the first part of the task above mentioned to be divided among those celebrated novelists, living and dead, who have attempted to delineate the scenes of real life. In [*St. Leon*] I have endeavoured to gain footing in one neglected track of the latter province. The hearts and the curiosity of readers have been assailed in so many ways, that we, writers who bring up the rear of our illustrious predecessors, must be contented to arrive at novelty in whatever mode we are able. The foundation of the following tale is such as, it is not to be supposed, ever existed. But, if I have mixed human feelings and passions with incredible situations, and thus rendered them impressive and interesting, I shall entertain some hope to be pardoned the boldness and irregularity of my design.

Some readers of my graver productions will perhaps, in perusing these little volumes, accuse me of inconsistency; the affections and charities of private life being every where in this publication a topic of the warmest eulogium, while in the *Enquiry Concerning Political Justice* they seemed to be treated with no great degree of indulgence and favour. In answer to this objection, all I think it necessary to say on the present occasion is, that, for more than four years, I have been anxious for opportunity and leisure to modify some of the earlier chapters of that work in conformity to the sentiments inculcated in this. Not that I see cause to make any change respecting the principle of justice, or any thing else fundamental to the system there delivered; but that I apprehend domestic and private affections inseparable from the nature of man, and from what may be styled the culture of the heart, and am fully persuaded that they are not incompatible with a profound and active sense of justice in the mind of him that cherishes them. True wisdom will recommend to us individual attachments; for with them our minds are more thoroughly maintained in activity and life than they can be under the privation of them; and it is better that man should be a living being, than a stock or a stone. True virtue will sanction this recommendation; since it is the object of virtue to produce happiness, and since the man who lives in the midst of domestic relations will have many opportunities of conferring pleasure, minute in the detail, yet not trivial in the amount, without interfering with the purposes of general benevolence. Nay, by kindling his sensibility, and harmonising his soul, they may be expected, if he is endowed with a liberal and manly spirit, to render him more prompt in the service of strangers and the public. (pp. ix-x)

> *William Godwin, in a preface to his* St. Leon: A Tale of the Sixteenth Century, *Colburn and Bentley, 1831, pp. vii-x.*

ROBERT SOUTHEY (letter date 1800)

[*An English poet, historian, biographer, essayist, short story writer, and editor, Southey was a prominent literary figure of the late eighteenth and early nineteenth centuries and a key member of the Lake School of poetry. In the following extract from a letter to his friend Coleridge, Southey offers a mixed assessment of* St. Leon.]

How like you Godwin's novel [*St. Leon*]? It is at times powerfully written—but it is dilated or diluted. St. Leon always acts so like a fool that his conduct is the most unbelievable part of the volume, and Godwin is always exposing himself in a posture which says "come kick me!" The passage in the first volume about voluptuousness, which recommends a course of brothel studies, is very exceptionable, and Godwin ought to have recollected what allusion his enemies would immediately make. I was quite pained and irritated at the man's folly. (p. 213)

Robert Southey, in a letter to Samuel Taylor Coleridge in January, 1800, in his New Letters of Robert Southey: 1792-1810, Vol. 1, *edited by Kenneth Curry, Columbia University Press, 1965, pp. 212-14.*

T. R. MALTHUS (essay date 1806)

[*A nineteenth-century English political and economic theorist, Malthus is best known for his* Essay on the Principle of Population. *There, Malthus proposed his controversial thesis that population growth should be controlled. In the following excerpt from that work, he outlines his objections to Godwin's theories in* Political Justice. *Focusing on his ideas regarding marriage and his proposed system of providing for children "by general benevolence," Malthus argues that Godwin's social model would prove economically disastrous. Godwin later rebutted Malthus's statements in his* Of Population.]

In reading Mr. Godwin's ingenious [*An Enquiry Concerning Political Justice*], it is impossible not to be struck with the spirit and energy of his style, the force and precision of some of his reasonings, the ardent tone of his thoughts, and particularly with that impressive earnestness of manner which gives an air of truth to the whole. At the same time it must be confessed that he has not proceeded in his inquiries with the caution that sound philosophy requires. His conclusions are often unwarranted by his premises. He fails sometimes in removing objections which he himself brings forward. He relies too much on general and abstract propositions which will not admit of application. And his conjectures certainly far outstrip the modesty of nature.

The system of equality which Mr. Godwin proposes is, on a first view, the most beautiful and engaging of any that has yet appeared. A melioration of society to be produced merely by reason and conviction gives more promise of permanence than any change effected and maintained by force. The unlimited exercise of private judgment is a doctrine grand and captivating, and has a vast superiority over those systems, where every individual is in a manner the slave of the public. The substitution of benevolence, as the masterspring and moving principle of society, instead of self-love, appears at first sight to be a consummation devoutly to be wished. In short, it is impossible to contemplate the whole of this fair picture without emotions of delight and admiration, accompanied with an ardent longing for the period of its accomplishment. But alas! that moment can never arrive. The whole is little better than a dream—a phantom of the imagination. (pp. 98-9)

The great errour under which Mr. Godwin labours throughout his whole work is, the attributing of almost all the vices and misery that prevail in civil society to human institutions. Political regulations, and the established administration of property, are, with him, the fruitful sources of all evil, the hotbeds of all the crimes that degrade mankind. Were this really a true state of the case, it would not seem an absolutely hopeless task to remove evil completely from the world; and reason seems to be the proper and adequate instrument for effecting so great a purpose. But the truth is, that though human institutions appear to be the obvious and obtrusive causes of much mischief to mankind, they are, in reality, light and superficial, in comparison with those deeper-feated causes of evil which result from the laws of nature. (pp. 100-01)

Man cannot live in the midst of plenty. All cannot share alike the bounties of nature. Were there no established administration of property every man would be obliged to guard with force his little store. Selfishness would be triumphant. The subjects of contention would be perpetual. Every individual would be under a constant anxiety about corporal support, and not a single intellect would be left free to expatiate in the field of thought.

How little Mr. Godwin has turned his attention to the real state of human society will sufficiently appear, from the manner in which he endeavours to remove the difficulty of an overcharged population. He says,

> The obvious answer to this objection is, that to reason thus is to foresee difficulties at a great distance. Three fourths of the habitable globe are now uncultivated. The parts already cultivated are capable of immeasurable improvement. Myriads of centuries of still increasing population may pass away, and the earth be still found sufficient for the subsistence of its inhabitants.
>
> (pp. 102-03)

[Let] us imagine for a moment Mr. Godwin's system of equality realized in its utmost extent, and see how soon this difficulty might be expected to press, under so perfect a form of society. A theory that will not admit of application cannot possibly be just.

Let us suppose all the causes of vice and misery in this island removed. War and contention cease. Unwholesome trades and manufactories do not exist. Crowds no longer collect together in great and pestilent cities for purposes of court intrigue, of commerce, and vicious gratification. Simple, healthy, and rational amusements take place of drinking, gaming, and debauchery. There are no towns sufficiently large to have any prejudicial effects on the human constitution. The greater part of the happy inhabitants of this terrestrial Paradise live in hamlets and farm houses scattered over the face of the country. All men are equal. (pp. 103-04)

Mr. Godwin considers marriage as a fraud and a monopoly. Let us suppose the commerce of the sexes established upon principles of the most perfect freedom. Mr. Godwin does not think himself that this freedom would lead to a promiscuous intercourse; and in this I perfectly agree with him. The love of variety is a vicious, corrupt, and unnatural taste, and could not prevail in any great degree in a simple and virtuous state of society. Each man would probably select for himself a partner to whom he would adhere, as long as that adherence continued to be the choice of both parties. It would be of little consequence, according to Mr. Godwin, how many children a woman had, or to whom they belonged. Provisions and assistance would spontaneously flow from the quarter in which they abounded to the quarter in which they were deficient. And every man according to his capacity would be ready to furnish instruction to the rising generation.

I cannot conceive a form of society so favourable upon the whole to population. The irremediableness of marriage, as it is at present constituted, undoubtedly deters many from entering into this state. An unshackled intercourse on the contrary would be a most powerful incitement to early attachments; and as we are supposing no anxiety about the future support of children to exist, I do not conceive that there would be one woman in a hundred, of twenty-three years of age, without a family. (pp. 104-05)

There can be little doubt that the equalization of property which we have supposed, added to the circumstance of the labour of the whole community being directed chiefly to agriculture, would tend greatly to augment the produce of the country. But to answer the demands of a population increasing so rapidly, Mr. Godwin's calculation of half an hour a day would certainly not be sufficient. It is probable that the half of every man's time must be employed for this purpose. Yet with such or much greater exertions, a person who is acquainted with the nature of the soil in this country, and who reflects on the fertility of the lands already in cultivation, and the barrenness of those that are not cultivated, will be very much disposed to doubt whether the whole average produce could possibly be doubled in twenty-five years from the present period. (pp. 106-07)

During the next period where will the food be found to satisfy the importunate demands of the increasing numbers? Where is the fresh land to turn up? Where is the dressing necessary to improve that which is already in cultivation? There is no person with the smallest knowledge of land but would say, that it was impossible that the average produce of the country could be increased during the second twenty-five years, by a quantity equal to what it at present yields. Yet we will suppose this increase, however improbable, to take place. The exuberant strength of the argument allows of almost any concession. Even with this concession however, there would be eleven millions at the expiration of the second term unprovided for. (pp. 107-08)

Alas! what becomes of the picture, where men lived in the midst of plenty, where no man was obliged to provide with anxiety and pain for his restless wants; where the narrow principle of selfishness did not exist; where the mind was delivered from her perpetual anxiety about corporal support, and free to expatiate in the field of thought which is congenial to her. This beautiful fabric of the imagination vanishes at the severe touch of truth. (p. 108)

No human institutions here existed, to the perverseness of which Mr. Godwin ascribes the original sin of the worst men. No opposition had been produced by them between public and private good. No monopoly had been created of those advantages which reason directs to be left in common. No man had been goaded to the breach of order by unjust laws. Benevolence had established her reign in all hearts. And yet in so short a period as fifty years, violence, oppression, falsehood, misery, every hateful vice, and every form of distress which degrade and sadden the present state of society, seem to have been generated by the most imperious circumstances, by laws inherent in the nature of man, and absolutely independent of all human regulations.

If we be not yet too well convinced of the reality of this melancholy picture, let us but look for a moment into the next period of twenty-five years, and we shall see 44 millions of human beings without the means of support; and at the conclusion of the first century the population would be 176 millions, and the food only sufficient for 55 millions, leaving 121 millions unprovided for. In these ages want indeed would be triumphant, and rapine and murder must reign at large: and yet all this time we are supposing the produce of the earth absolutely unlimited, and the yearly increase greater than the boldest speculator can imagine.

This is undoubtedly a very different view of the difficulty arising from the principle of population, from that which Mr. Godwin gives, when he says, "Myriads of centuries of still increasing population may pass away, and the earth be still found sufficient for the subsistence of its inhabitants." (pp. 109-10)

It may be curious to observe in the case that we have been supposing, how some of the principal laws, which at present govern civilized society, would be successively dictated by the most imperious necessity. As man, according to Mr. Godwin, is the creature of the impressions to which he is subject, the goadings of want could not continue long before some violations of public or private stock would necessarily take place. As these violations increased in number and extent, the more active and comprehensive intellects of the society would soon perceive, that while population was fast increasing the yearly produce of the country would shortly begin to diminish. The urgency of the case would suggest the necessity of some immediate measures being taken for the general safety. Some kind of convention would then be called, and the dangerous situation of the country stated in the strongest terms. It would be observed, that while they lived in the midst of plenty it was of little consequence who laboured the least, or who possessed the least, as every man was perfectly willing and ready to supply the wants of his neighbour. But that the question was no longer whether one man should give to another that which he did not use himself; but whether he should give to his neighbour the food which was absolutely necessary to his own existence. It would be represented, that the number of those who were in want very greatly exceeded the number and means of those who should supply them; that these pressing wants, which, from the state of the produce of the country, could not all be gratified, had occasioned some flagrant violations of justice; that these violations had already checked the increase of food, and would, if they were not by some means or other prevented, throw the whole community into confusion; that imperious necessity seemed to dictate, that a yearly increase of produce should, if possible, be obtained at all events; that in order to effect this first great and indispensable purpose it would be advisable to make a more complete division of land, and to secure every man's property against violation by the most powerful sanctions. (pp. 111-13)

The next subject which would come under discussion, intimately connected with the preceding, is the commerce of the sexes. It would be urged by those who had turned their attention to the true cause of the difficulties under which the community laboured, that while every man felt secure that all his children would be well provided for by general benevolence, the powers of the earth would be absolutely inadequate to produce food for the population which would inevitably ensue; that even if the whole attention and labour of the society were directed to this sole point, and if by the most perfect security of property, and every other encouragement that could be thought of, the greatest possible increase of produce were yearly obtained; yet still the increase of food would by no means keep pace with the much more rapid increase of population; that some check to population therefore was imperiously called for; that the most natural and obvious check seemed to be to make every man provide for his own children; that this would operate in some respect as a measure and a guide in the increase of population, as it might be expected that no man would bring beings into the world for whom he could not find the means of support; that where this notwithstanding was the case, it seemed necessary for the example of others, that the disgrace and inconvenience attending such a conduct should fall upon that individual who had thus inconsiderately plunged himself and his innocent children into want and misery.

The institution of marriage, or at least of some express or implied obligation on every man to support his own children, seems to be the natural result of these reasonings in a community under the difficulties that we have supposed. (pp. 114-15)

> *T. R. Malthus, "Of Systems of Equality: Godwin," in his* An Essay on the Principle of Population; or, A View of Its Past and Present Effects on Human Happiness, Vol. II, *third edition, J. Johnson, 1806, pp. 98-133.*

PERCY BYSSHE SHELLEY   (letter date 1817)

[*Regarded as a major English poet, Shelley was a leading figure in the English Romantic movement. He was also married to Godwin's daughter Mary. Influenced and inspired by Godwin's philosophy all throughout his writing career, Shelley expresses his admiration for* Mandeville *in the following extract from a letter to Godwin. For additional commentary by Shelley, see excerpt below dated 1817.*]

I have read *Mandeville,* but I must read it again soon. For the interest is of that irresistible & overwhelming kind, that the mind in its influence is like a cloud borne on by an impetuous wind, like one breathlessly carried forward who has no time to pause, or observe the causes of his career. I think the *power* of *Mandeville* is inferior to nothing that you have done, & were it not for the character of Falkland, no instance in which you have exerted that power of *creation* which you possess beyond all contemporary writers might compare with it. Falkland is still alone: power is in Falkland not as in Mandeville. Tumult hurried onward by the tempest, but Tranquillity standing unshaken amid its fiercest rage! But *Caleb Williams* never shakes the deepest soul like *Mandeville.* It must be said that in the latter you rule with a rod of iron. The picture is never bright, & we wonder whence you drew the darkness with which its shades are deepened until the epithet of tenfold night almost ceases to be metaphor. The NOUN *smorfia* touches some cord within us with such a cold & jarring power, that I started, & for some time could scarce believe but that I was Mandeville, & that this hideous grin was stamped upon my own face.

In style & strength of expression *Mandeville* is wonderfully great, & the energy & the sweetness of the sentiments [are] scarcely to be equalled. Clifford's character as mere beauty is a divine & soothing contrast, & I do not think, if perhaps I except (& I know not if I ought to do so) the speech of Agathon in the *Symposium* of Plato that there ever was produced a moral discourse more characteristic of all that is admirable & lovely in human Nature more lovely & admirable in itself than that of Henrietta to Mandeville as he is recovering from madness—Shall I say that when I discovered that she was pleading all this time secretly for her lover, & when at last she abandoned—weakly abandoned poor Mandeville I felt an involuntary & perhaps an unreasonable pang? (pp. 573-74)

> *Percy Bysshe Shelley, in a letter to William Godwin on December 7, 1817, in his* The Letters of Percy Bysshe Shelley: Shelley in England, Vol. I, *edited by Frederick L. Jones, Oxford at the Clarendon Press, Oxford, 1964, pp. 572-74.*

ELFIN KNIGHT [PSEUDONYM OF PERCY BYSSHE SHELLEY] (letter date 1817)

[*Here, Shelley elaborates on the comments on* Mandeville *in his letter to Godwin (see excerpt above dated 1817) and additionally praises Godwin's literary, intellectual, and philosophical talents.*]

[The] author of *Mandeville* is one of the most illustrious examples of intellectual power of the present age. He has exhibited that variety and universality of talent which distinguishes him who is destined to inherit lasting renown from the possessors of temporary celebrity. If his claims were to be measured solely by the comprehension and accuracy of his researches into ethical and political science, still it would be difficult to name a contemporary competitor. Let us make a deduction of all those parts of his moral system which are liable to any possible controversy and consider simply those which only to allege is to establish, and which belong to that most important class of truths which he that announces to mankind seems less to teach than to recall.

[Godwin's] *Political Justice* is the first moral system explicitly founded upon the doctrine of the negativeness of rights and the positiveness of duties, an obscure feeling of which has been the basis of all the political liberty and private virtue in the world. But he is also the author of *Caleb Williams;* and if we had no other record of a mind but simply some fragment containing the conception of the character of Falkland, doubtless we should say, "This is an extraordinary mind, and undoubtedly was capable of the very sublimest enterprises of thought."

St. Leon and *Fleetwood* are molded, with somewhat inferior distinctness, in the same character of a union of delicacy and power. The *Essay on Sepulchres* has all the solemnity and depth of passion which belong to a mind that sympathizes, as one man with his friend, in the interests of future ages, and in the concerns of the vanished generations of mankind.

It may be said with truth that Godwin has been treated unjustly by those of his countrymen upon whose favor temporary distinction depends. If he had devoted his high accomplishments to flatter the selfishness of the rich or enforced those doctrines on which the powerful depend for power, they would no doubt have rewarded him with their countenance, and he might have been more fortunate in that sunshine than Mr. Malthus or Dr. Paley. But the difference would still have been as wide as that which must forever divide notoriety from fame. Godwin has been to the present age in moral philosophy what Wordsworth is in poetry. (pp. 308-09)

Mandeville is Godwin's last production. The interest of this novel is undoubtedly equal, in some respects superior, to that of *Caleb Williams.* Yet there is no character like Falkland, whom the author, with that sublime casuistry which is the parent of toleration and forbearance, persuades us personally to love, while his actions must forever remain the theme of our astonishment and abhorrence. Mandeville challenges our compassion, and no more. His errors arise from an immutable necessity of internal nature, and from much of a constitutional antipathy and suspicion, which soon sprang up into a hatred and contempt and barren misanthropy, which, as it had no roots in genius or virtue, produces no fruit uncongenial with the soil wherein it grew. Those of Falkland arose from a high, though perverted conception of the majesty of human nature, from a powerful sympathy with his species, and from a temper which led him to believe that the very reputation of excellence should walk among mankind, unquestioned and undefiled. So far as it was a defect to link the interest of the tale with anything inferior to Falkland, so is *Mandeville* defective. But if the varieties of human character, the depth and complexity of human motive, those sources of the union of strength and weakness, those useful occasions for pleading in favor of universal kindness and toleration are just subjects for illustration and development in a work of fiction. *Mandeville* yields in interest and importance to none of the productions of the author.

The language is more rich and various, and the expressions more eloquently sweet, without losing that energy and distinctness which characterizes *Political Justice* and *Caleb Williams*. The moral speculations have a strength and consistency and boldness which have been less clearly aimed at in his other works of fiction. The pleadings of Henrietta to Mandeville, after his recovery from madness, in favor of virtue and benevolent energy, compose in every respect the most perfect and beautiful piece of writing of modern times. It is the genuine doctrine of *Political Justice* presented in one perspicuous and impressive view, and clothed in such enchanting melody of language as seems scarcely less than the writings of Plato to realize those lines of Milton:

> How charming is divine Philosophy!
> Not harsh and crabbed, as dull fools suppose,
> But musical as is Apollo's lute.

Clifford's talk, too, about wealth has a beautiful and readily to be disentangled intermixture of truth and error. Clifford is a person who, without those characteristics which usually constitute the sublime, is sublime from the mere excess of loveliness and innocence. Henrietta's first appearance to Mandeville at Mandeville House is an occurrence resplendent with the sunrise of life; it recalls to the memory many a vision, or perhaps but one, which the delusive exhalations of unbaffled hope has invested with a rose-like luster as of morning, yet unlike morning a light which, once extinguished, never can return. Henrietta seems at first to be all that a susceptible heart imagines in the object of its earliest passion. We scarcely can see her, she is so beautiful. There is a mist of dazzling loveliness which encircles her and shuts out from the sight all that is mortal in her transcendent charms. But the veil is gradually withdrawn, and she "fades into the light of common day." Her actions and even her sentiments do not correspond with the elevation of her speculative opinions and the fearless purity which should be and is the accompaniment of truth and virtue. But she has a divided affection, and she is faithful there only where infidelity would have been self-sacrifice. Could the spotless Henrietta have subjected her love for Clifford to the vain and insulting accidents of wealth and reputation and the babbling of a miserable old woman and have proceeded unshrinkingly to her nuptial feast from the expostulations of Mandeville's impassioned and pathetic madness? It might be well in the author to show the foundations of human hope thus overturned, for his picture would otherwise have been illumined with one gleam of light; it was his skill to enforce the moral "that all things are vanity" and that "the house of mourning is better than the house of feasting"; and we are indebted to those who make us feel the instability of our nature that we may lay the knowledge which is its foundation deep and make the affections which are its cement strong. But one regrets that Henrietta, who soared far beyond her contemporaries in her opinions, who was so beautiful that she seemed a spirit among mankind should act and feel no otherwise than the least exalted of her sex; and still more that the author capable of conceiving something so admirable and lovely should have been withheld by the tenor of the fiction which he chose from executing it

to its full extent. It almost seems in the original conception of the character of Henrietta that something was imagined too vast and too uncommon to be realized; and the feeling weighs like disappointment on the mind.

But these considered with reference to the core of the story are extrinsical. The events of the tale flow on like the stream of fate, regular and irresistible, and growing at once darker and swifter in their progress; there is no surprise; there is no shock; we are prepared for the worst from the very opening scene, though we wonder whence the author drew the shadows which render the moral darkness every instant more profound and at last so appalling and complete. The interest is awfully deep and rapid. To struggle with it would be gossamer attempting to bear up against the tempest. In this respect it is more powerful than *Caleb Williams*—the interest of *Caleb Williams* being as rapid but not so profound as that of *Mandeville*. It is a wind which tears up the deepest waters of the ocean of mind. The reader's mind is hurried on, as he approaches the end, with breathless and accelerated impulse. (pp. 309-11)

> *Elfin Knight [pseudonym of Percy Bysshe Shelley], in a letter to the editor of "The Examiner," on December 28, 1817, in* Shelley's Prose; or, The Trumpet of a Prophecy *by Percy Bysshe Shelley, edited by David Lee Clark, The University of New Mexico Press, 1954, pp. 308-11.*

THE NORTH AMERICAN REVIEW   (essay date 1818)

[*In the following excerpt from a review of* Mandeville, *the critic faults the lugubrious tone and "forbidding air" of Godwin's writings, but acknowledges his insight into human nature.*]

Godwin is a writer of a severe and sombre cast, who seems to take a gloomy satisfaction in dwelling upon whatever is deplorable in the constitution of society, or execrable and loathsome in human nature. In many parts of each of his works, and more especially in *Caleb Williams* and *Political Justice,* he writes with the spirit of a conspirator against the moral government of the world; and seems to look upon all the order, and beauty, and harmony of the social system, as Satan contemplated the delights of Eden, when he first alighted on the Tree of Life,—as something to be blasted and spoiled.

But he has nothing of malignity in [*Mandeville*];—he every where speaks like one of benevolent dispositions; but his benevolence is ill directed; he does not, like Satan, regard mankind, as those 'whom he could pity' for the evils, his own labours are intended to bring upon them. He compassionates them for what constitutes the beauty, and dignity, and security of existence. Though he sometimes speaks in tones of condolence, he more frequently utters the language of indignation and reproach. 'Of what use,' says he, 'are talents and sentiments in the corrupt wilderness of human society? It is a rank and rotten soil, from which every finer shrub draws poison as it grows. All, that, in a happier field and purer air, would expand into virtue and germinate into usefulness, is thus converted into henbane and deadly nightshade.'

This, and a thousand other passages of a similar import, scattered through his writings, are not the occasional burstings out of a wronged and burthened mind, striving to pour off its bitterness in momentary exclamations. (p. 92)

It has been, and continues, in a degree, to be a favourite doctrine with him, that all the restraints of decorum, propriety, and law, are infringements of the inalienable liberties of man, and constitute a tyranny, that subdues and enslaves the noblest principles of our nature. One infers, from the general tenor of his speculations, that nations are only great prisons, differing, principally, in the number of prisoners and prison-keepers. (pp. 92-3)

Godwin's imagination peoples the world with an over proportion of the unfortunate good on the one hand, and, on the other, of foul and monstrous beings, bent upon mean pursuits, and in love with errour and folly—creatures, that contaminate the atmosphere they breathe, and communicate a moral pestilence by their touch. It becomes a noble mind to loathe such wretches, and show the purity and elevation of its nature by acting in opposition to the maxims of the world. Whenever domestick or social duties interfere with this high way of thinking and acting, they may be violated and spurned—the citizen may defy the government that protects him; the husband may desert his wife, and the son may brave and insult his father.

These sentiments are not always directly inculcated; they are sometimes denied; but whatever may be the letter, this is commonly the spirit of his lessons. Though they often present sound maxims of conduct to the understanding, they generally shed a pestiferous influence upon the heart. One reads, without any transports, without any of the free and expanding emotions, which the thoughts of more generous minds inspire; but not without sensations;—he presses forward eagerly, not more out of interest and curiosity, than from a desire to be relieved from an indescribable aching of the soul and suffocation of the feelings, with which the stories of Godwin invariably oppress the reader.

At the conclusion, he finds himself sickened and disgusted with the world, as a scene of misery and guilt; he is ready to exclaim against Providence, and reprobate the constitution of nature, by which it seems to be ordained, that virtue and vice, wisdom and folly, honour and meanness, shall be idle and futile qualities, and that men shall be endowed with sensibilities, only to feel more poignantly the ills to which they are born. If he adopts Godwin's notions,—that all the miseries of the world spring from the artificial system of civil society, and the influence of false prejudices,—he becomes affected with a scornful pity of his fellow beings; he has an enthusiastick desire that they should come to have new, though he hardly knows what, views of happiness, and dignity, and honour, and begin to act upon certain new and sublime principles, which, however, he can but imperfectly define; he only knows, that they are altogether opposite to what the world has been accustomed to, and something much better. (pp. 93-4)

Such are some of the leading characteristics and tendencies of Godwin's philosophy;—under which name may be comprehended the greater part of his works, for his fictions are philosophical treatises, no less than his *Political Justice*. His views of life, and his moral and political principles, are prominent parts of his thinking, and are always obtruding themselves. But notwithstanding all the absurdities, and distortions and misconceptions, with which his writings abound, they probably have not done much absolute mischief to mankind. (pp. 94-5)

Godwin is a writer of a forbidding air, arising partly from his affectation of stateliness and independence, and partly from his practice of mixing up too much of metaphysical and economical philosophy in his stories. He is violent and bold in the extreme, and sticks not to be coarse, if he can but be strong. His mind is well stored with knowledge, and he has reflected much and deeply, though not always justly, upon men and their

pursuits. He occasionally throws out great and striking thoughts upon the philosophy of the mind and the economy of society. Propriety and probability are counted for nothing with him, and he seems to pursue his eccentrick course with more energy, the further it carries him from nature. He rarely thinks in a generous, pathetick, or kindly strain, though there are not wanting touching passages in his works. The most remarkable of this sort, now in our recollection, is that, in which St. Leon is described as visiting his daughters, after he has renewed his life by drinking the elixir. But, whatever may be Godwin's faults, he has produced two masterpieces in their kind, in *St. Leon* and *Caleb Williams;* and this ought to satisfy his ambition. *Mandeville* is not likely to add to his reputation; it is indeed a falling off, and is so repulsive and hard featured a story, that not many readers, we believe, have resolution to go through it. (p. 97)

Godwin's other novels are very thin of events; this contains still fewer than those. His work has no resemblance to a dramatic representation of characters and actions, so constructed, that, in the perusal, a thousand associated images, recollections and sentiments, spontaneously spring up in the reader's mind, which are not directly expressed. It is rather the exhibition of his philosophical opinions in the form of dissertations,—a detail of the thoughts and feelings of his personages, and a consideration of the influences, which the incidents may be supposed to have, in determining their dispositions and characters. He is occupied with what passes within his persons, instead of what is taking place about them. His real actors seem to be certain principles and opinions and passions,—which are not qualities and ingredients, that go to the composition of his personages, and form a part of them, but rather make use of them as mere instruments. All this gives an abstract, metaphysical turn to his narratives, whence to readers, who flutter from novel to novel, in quest of vacant amusement, they have a rugged and forbidding aspect.

This effect is aggravated by his set, stately, inverted style of writing, and by his abundance of distant allusions, strained conceptions, and obsolete words and phrases, and forced expressions. Add to these, that his figurative expressions are violent, sometimes to absurdity. Take a few examples—his hate of Clifford hung, 'with insurmountable weight, *upon the neck of Henrietta's mind.'* . . .—'*Inhuman laughter flayed and mangled my ears, like a hundred lancets.'* . . .—'*Doors leaped from their hinges, to give Clifford entrance.'* . . .—'*Henrietta entered, with triumphant wheels, into the fortress of my heart.'* . . .—There were certain *muscles of my intellectual frame,* that had never been brought into play.' . . .—'These trials produced tremendous explosions and *earthquakes* in my bosom.' . . . He sometimes repeats the same thoughts in the same language, even when they are of little importance; and gives the characters of his persons again and again; and is not content with stating how things are, but must reckon up all the possibilities of their having been otherwise, and pursue these suppositions into all their consequences. It thus happens that the action is often at a stand, and the reader seems to himself as if he were on a voyage, in a vessel, which should lie by half the time, while the master might take observations and work up his reckoning.

If one is not repelled by these discouragements, he will open to himself in *Mandeville* a rich vein of sentiment and reflection. He will find in it the elevated strain of thinking, nervous eloquence and keen penetration, which are characteristic of its author. Like his other novels, it contains an important lesson, forcibly inculcated—it shows the forlornness and misery of a jealous, sullen, aspiring mind, that makes great claims on the world, without proper efforts to justify or enforce them. The author in this, as in his previous works, displays, with appalling truth, the despotic sovereignty and all searching observation of publick opinion, in so much, that one trembles with the consciousness of being subject to this tremendous power, which he cannot fly from or resist. No writer has perhaps more adequately expressed,—what every body feels,—how much of the good and ill of life is involved in reputation. The sentiments we excite in others become, in some sort, a part of ourselves; we either bear a good or an ill fame, that, like a charm, makes us invulnerable to 'the slings and arrows of fortune,' or exposes us, defenceless and sorely alive, to the shaft. The opinion of men pursues and hangs upon us like destiny, and our reputation encompasses us like a luminous atmosphere, that exhibits us, either blemished or fair, to the eyes of the world. (pp. 104-05)

"Godwin's 'Mandeville'," in The North American
Review, *Vol. VII, No. 1, May, 1818, pp. 92-105.*

WILLIAM HAZLITT (essay date 1825)

[*One of the most important commentators of the Romantic age, Hazlitt was an English critic and journalist. He is best known for his descriptive criticism in which he stressed that no abilities beyond judgment and analysis are necessary on the part of the critic. In the following excerpt, Hazlitt surveys Godwin's literary career, philosophy, and decline in popularity. For additional commentary by Hazlitt, see excerpt dated 1830.*]

The Spirit of the Age was never more fully shown than in its treatment of [William Godwin]—its love of paradox and change, its dastard submission to prejudice and to the fashion of the day. Five-and-twenty years ago he was in the very zenith of a sultry and unwholesome popularity; he blazed as a sun in the firmament of reputation; no one was more talked of, more looked up to, more sought after, and wherever liberty, truth, justice was the theme, his name was not far off. Now he has sunk below the horizon, and enjoys the serene twilight of a doubtful immortality. (p. 17)

[The] author of *Political Justice* and of *Caleb Williams* can never die; his name is an abstraction in letters; his works are standard in the history of intellect. . . .

No work in our time gave such a blow to the philosophical mind of the country as the celebrated *Enquiry Concerning Political Justice.* Tom Paine was considered for the time as a Tom Fool to him, Paley an old woman, Edmund Burke a flashy sophist. Truth, moral truth, it was supposed, had here taken up its abode; and these were the oracles of thought. . . .

Mr. Godwin indulged in extreme opinions, and carried with him all the most sanguine and fearless understandings of the time. What then? Because those opinions were overcharged, were they therefore altogether groundless? Is the very God of our idolatry all of a sudden to become an abomination and an anathema? Could so many young men of talent, of education, and of principle have been hurried away by what had neither truth nor nature, not one particle of honest feeling nor the least show of reason in it? (p. 18)

The fault . . . of Mr. Godwin's philosophy, in one word, was too much ambition—'by that sin fell the angels!' He conceived too nobly of his fellows (the most unpardonable crime against them, for there is nothing that annoys our self-love so much as being complimented on imaginary achievements, to which we are wholly unequal)—he raised the standard of morality

above the reach of humanity, and by directing virtue to the most airy and romantic heights, made her path dangerous, solitary, and impracticable. The author of the *Political Justice* took abstract reason for the rule of conduct and abstract good for its end. He places the human mind on an elevation, from which it commands a view of the whole line of moral consequences; and requires it to conform its acts to the larger and more enlightened conscience which it has thus acquired. He absolves man from the gross and narrow ties of sense, custom, authority, private and local attachment, in order that he may devote himself to the boundless pursuit of universal benevolence.

Mr. Godwin gives no quarter to the amiable weaknesses of our nature, nor does he stoop to avail himself of the supplementary aids of an imperfect virtue. Gratitude, promises, friendship, family affection give way, not that they may be merged in the opposite vices or in want of principle, but that the void may be filled up by the disinterested love of good and the dictates of inflexible justice, which is 'the law of laws, and sovereign of sovereigns.' All minor considerations yield, in his system, to the stern sense of duty, as they do, in the ordinary and established ones, to the voice of necessity. Mr. Godwin's theory, and that of more approved reasoners, differ only in this, that what are with them the exceptions, the extreme cases, he makes the every-day rule. No one denies that on great occasions, in moments of fearful excitement, or when a mighty object is at stake, the lesser and merely instrumental points of duty are to be sacrificed without remorse at the shrine of patriotism, of honour, and of conscience. (pp. 20-1)

The *Enquiry Concerning Political Justice* (it was urged by its favourers and defenders at the time, and may still be so, without either profaneness or levity) is a metaphysical and logical commentary on some of the most beautiful and striking texts of Scripture. Mr. Godwin is a mixture of the Stoic and of the Christian philosopher. To break the force of the vulgar objections and outcry that have been raised against the Modern Philosophy, as if it were a new and monstrous birth in morals, it may be worth noticing, that volumes of sermons have been written to excuse the founder of Christianity for not including friendship and private affection among its golden rules, but rather excluding them. Moreover, the answer to the question, 'Who is thy neighbour?' added to the divine precept, 'Thou shalt love thy neighbour as thyself,' is the same as in the exploded pages of our author—'he to whom we can do most good.' In determining this point, we were not to be influenced by any extrinsic or collateral considerations, by our own predilections, or the expectations of others, by our obligations to them or any services they might be able to render us, by the climate they were born in, by the house they lived in, by rank, or religion, or party, or personal ties, but by the abstract merits, the pure and unbiassed justice of the case.

The artificial helps and checks to moral conduct were set aside as spurious and unnecessary, and we came at once to the grand and simple question—'In what manner we could best contribute to the greatest possible good?' This was the paramount obligation in all cases whatever, from which we had no right to free ourselves upon any idle or formal pretext, and of which each person was to judge for himself, under the infallible authority of his own opinion and the inviolable sanction of his self-approbation. 'There was the rub that made *philosophy* of so short life!' Mr. Godwin's definition of morals was the same as the admired one of law, *reason without passion;* but with the unlimited scope of private opinion, and in a boundless field of speculation (for nothing less would satisfy the pretensions of the New School), there was danger that the unseasoned novice might substitute some pragmatical conceit of his own for the rule of right reason, and mistake a heartless indifference for a superiority to more natural and generous feelings. Our ardent and dauntless reformer followed out the moral of the parable of the Good Samaritan into its most rigid and repulsive consequences with a pen of steel, and let fall his 'trenchant blade' on every vulnerable point of human infirmity; but there is a want in his system of the mild and persuasive tone of the Gospel, where 'all is conscience and tender heart.' (pp. 21-3)

[If] it is admitted that Reason alone is not the sole and self-sufficient ground of morals, it is to Mr. Godwin that we are indebted for having settled the point. No one denied or distrusted this principle (before his time) as the absolute judge and interpreter in all questions of difficulty; and if this is no longer the case, it is because he has taken this principle, and followed it into its remotest consequences with more keenness of eye and steadiness of hand than any other expounder of ethics. His grand work is (at least) an *experimentum crucis* to show the weak sides and imperfections of human reason as the sole law of human action. (pp. 26-7)

Captain Parry would be thought to have rendered a service to navigation and his country, no less by proving that there is no North-West Passage, than if he had ascertained that there is one: so Mr. Godwin has rendered an essential service to moral science, by attempting (in vain) to pass the Arctic Circle and Frozen Regions, where the understanding is no longer warmed by the affections, nor fanned by the breeze of fancy! This is the effect of all bold, original, and powerful thinking, that it either discovers the truth or detects where error lies; and the only crime with which Mr. Godwin can be charged as a political and moral reasoner is, that he has displayed a more ardent spirit and a more independent activity of thought than others, in establishing the fallacy (if fallacy it be) of an old popular prejudice that *the Just and True were one,* by 'championing it to the Outrance,' and in the final result placing the Gothic structure of human virtue on an humbler, but a wider and safer, foundation than it had hitherto occupied in the volumes and systems of the learned.

Mr. Godwin is an inventor in the regions of romance, as well as a skilful and hardy explorer of those of moral truth. *Caleb Williams* and *St. Leon* are two of the most splendid and impressive works of the imagination that have appeared in our times. It is not merely that these novels are very well for a philosopher to have produced—they are admirable and complete in themselves, and would not lead you to suppose that the author, who is so entirely at home in human character and dramatic situation, had ever dabbled in logic or metaphysics. The first of these, particularly, is a masterpiece, both as to invention and execution. The romantic and chivalrous principle of the love of personal fame is embodied in the finest possible manner in the character of Falkland; as in Caleb Williams (who is not the first, but the second character in the piece) we see the very demon of curiosity personified. Perhaps the art, with which these two characters are contrived to relieve and set off each other, has never been surpassed in any work of fiction, with the exception of the immortal satire of Cervantes. The restless and inquisitive spirit of Caleb Williams, in search and in possession of his patron's fatal secret, haunts the latter like a second conscience, plants stings in his tortured mind, fans the flame of his jealous ambition, struggling with agonized remorse; and the hapless but noble-minded Falkland at length

falls a martyr to the persecution of that morbid and overpowering interest, of which his mingled virtues and vices have rendered him the object.

We conceive no one ever began *Caleb Williams* that did not read it through: no one that ever read it could possibly forget it, or speak of it after any length of time but with an impression as if the events and feelings had been personal to himself. This is the case also with the story of *St. Leon* which, with less dramatic interest and intensity of purpose, is set off by a more gorgeous and flowing eloquence and by a crown of preternatural imagery, that waves over it like a palm-tree! It is the beauty and the charm of Mr. Godwin's descriptions that the reader identifies himself with the author; and the secret of this is, that the author has identified himself with his personages. Indeed, he has created them. They are the proper issue of his brain, lawfully begot, not foundlings, nor the 'bastards of his art.' He is not an indifferent, callous spectator of the scenes which he himself pourtrays, but without seeming to feel them. There is no look of patch-work and plagiarism, the beggarly copiousness of borrowed wealth; no tracery-work from worm-eaten manuscripts, from forgotten chronicles, nor piecing out of vague traditions with fragments and snatches of old ballads, so that the result resembles a gaudy, staring transparency, in which you cannot distinguish the daubing of the painter from the light that shines through the flimsy colours, and gives them brilliancy.

Here all is clearly made out with strokes of the pencil, by fair, not by factitious means. Our author takes a given subject from nature or from books, and then fills it up with the ardent workings of his own mind, with the teeming and audible pulses of his own heart. The effect is entire and satisfactory in proportion. The work (so to speak) and the author are one. We are not puzzled to decide upon their respective pretensions. In reading Mr. Godwin's novels, we know what share of merit the author has in them. (pp. 27-9)

Mr. Godwin, in all his writings, dwells upon one idea or exclusive view of a subject, aggrandises a sentiment, exaggerates a character, or pushes an argument to extremes, and makes up by the force of style and continuity of feeling for what he wants in variety of incident or ease of manner. This necessary defect is observable in his best works, and is still more so in *Fleetwood* and *Mandeville;* the one of which, compared with his more admired performances, is mawkish, and the other morbid. Mr. Godwin is also an essayist, an historian—in short, what is he not, that belongs to the character of an indefatigable and accomplished author? (p. 30)

William Hazlitt, "William Godwin," in his The Spirit of the Age; or, Contemporary Portraits, *1825. Reprint by Oxford University Press, London, 1947, pp. 17-34.*

[WILLIAM HAZLITT]   (essay date 1830)

[In the following review of Cloudesly, *Hazlitt contends that Godwin's talents have declined markedly since the publication of* Caleb Williams. *Though he considers* Cloudesly *technically accomplished, Hazlitt deems it unoriginal and overly didactic. For additional commentary by Hazlitt, see excerpt dated 1825.]*

We find little of the author of *Caleb Williams* in [*Cloudesly*], except the name in the title-page. Either we are changed, or Mr Godwin is changed, since he wrote that masterly performance. We remember the first time of reading it well, though now long ago. In addition to the singularity and surprise occasioned by seeing a romance written by a philosopher and politician, what a quickening of the pulse,—what an interest in the progress of the story,—what an eager curiosity in divining the future,—what an individuality and contrast in the characters,—what an elevation and what a fall was that of Falkland;—how we felt for his blighted hopes, his remorse, and despair, and took part with Caleb Williams as his ordinary and unformed sentiments are brought out, and rendered more and more acute by the force of circumstances, till hurried on by an increasing and incontrollable impulse, he turns upon his proud benefactor and unrelenting persecutor, and in a mortal struggle, overthrows him on the vantage-ground of humanity and justice! There is not a moment's pause in the action or sentiments: the breath is suspended, the faculties wound up to the highest pitch, as we read. . . . Mr Godwin was thought a man of very powerful and versatile genius; and in him the understanding and the imagination reflected a mutual and dazzling light upon each other. His *St. Leon* did not lessen the wonder, nor the public admiration of him, or rather 'seemed like another morn risen on mid-noon.' But from that time he has done nothing of superlative merit. He has imitated himself, and not well. He has changed the glittering spear, which always detected truth or novelty, for a leaden foil. We cannot say of his last work (*Cloudesly*),—'Even in his ashes live his wonted fires.' The story is cast indeed something in the same moulds as *Caleb Williams;* but they are not filled and running over with molten passion, or with scalding tears. The situations and characters, though forced and extreme, are without effect from the want of juxtaposition and collision. Cloudesly (the elder) is like Caleb Williams, a person of low origin, and rebels against his patron and employer; but he remains a characterless, passive, inefficient agent to the last,—forming his plans and resolutions at a distance,—not whirled from expedient to expedient, nor driven from one sleepless hiding-place to another; and his lordly and conscience-stricken accomplice (Danvers) keeps his state in like manner, brooding over his guilt and remorse in solitude, with scarce an object or effort to vary the round of his reflections,—a lengthened paraphrase of grief. The only dramatic incidents in the coarse of the narrative are, the sudden metamorphosis of the Florentine Count Camaldoli into the robber St Elmo, and the unexpected and opportune arrival of Lord Danvers in person, carry the same prospect with you, like a map in your hand, the whole way. Mr Godwin has laid no ambuscade for the unwary reader—no picturesque group greets the eye as you pass on—no sudden turn at an angle places you on the giddy verge of a precipice. Nevertheless, our author's courage never flags. Mr Godwin is an eminent rhetorician; and he shows it in this, that he expatiates, discusses, amplifies, with equal fervour, and unabated ingenuity, on the merest accidents of the way-side, or common-places of human life. Thus, for instance, if a youth of eleven or twelve years of age is introduced upon the carpet, the author sets himself to show, with a laudable candour and communicativeness, what the peculiar features of that period of life are, and 'takes an inventory' of all the particulars,—such as sparkling eyes, roses in the cheeks, a smooth forehead, flaxen locks, elasticity of limb, lively animal spirits, and all the flush of hope,—as if he were describing a novelty, or some *terra incognita,* to the reader. . . . Every man's strength is his weakness, and turns in some way or other against himself. Mr Godwin has been so long accustomed to trust to his own powers, and to draw upon his own resources, that he comes at length to imagine that he can build a palace of words upon nothing. When he lavished the colours of style, and the exuberant strength of his fancy, on descriptions like those of the

character of Margaret, the wife of St Leon, or of his musings in the dungeon of Bethlem Gabor, or of his enthusiasm on discovering the philosopher's stone, and being restored to youth and the plenitude of joy by drinking the *Elixir Vitae;*—or when he recounts the long and lasting despair which succeeded that utter separation from his kind, and that deep solitude which followed him into crowds and cities,—deeper and more appalling than the dungeon of Bethlem Gabor,—we were never weary of being borne along by the golden tide of eloquence, supplied from the true sources of passion and feeling. But when he bestows the same elaboration of phrases, and artificial arrangement of sentences, to set off the most trite and obvious truisms, we confess it has to us a striking effect of the *bathos.* (pp. 147-49)

We have a graver charge yet to bring against Mr Godwin on the score of style, than that it leads him into useless amplification: from his desire to load and give effect to his descriptions, he runs different characters and feelings into one another. By not stopping short of excess and hyperbole, he loses the line of distinction, and 'o'ersteps the modesty of nature.' All his characters are patterns of vice or virtue. They are carried to extremes,—they are abstractions of woe, miracles of wit and gaiety,—gifted with every grace and accomplishment that can be enumerated in the same page; and they are not only prodigies in themselves, but destined to immortal renown, though we have never heard of their names before. This is not like a veteran in the art, but like the raptures of some boarding-school girl in love with every new face or dress she sees. It is difficult to say which is the most extraordinary genius,—the improvisatori Bernardino Perfetti, or his nephew, Francesco, or young Julian. Mr Godwin still sees with 'eyes of youth.' Irene is a Greek, the model of beauty and of conjugal faith. Eudocia, her maid, who marries the elder Cloudesly, is a Greek too, and nearly as handsome and as exemplary in her conduct. Again, on the same principle, the account of Irene's devotion to her father and her husband, is by no means clearly discriminated. The spiritual feeling is exaggerated till it is confounded with the passionate; and the passionate is spiritualized in the same incontinence of tropes and figures, till it loses its distinctive character. Each sentiment, by being over-done, is neutralized into a sort of platonics. It is obvious to remark, that the novel of *Cloudesly* has no hero, no principal figure. The attention is divided, and wavers between Meadows, who is a candidate for the reader's sympathy through the first half volume, and whose affairs and love adventures at St Petersburg are huddled up in haste, and broke off in the middle; Lord Danvers, who is the guilty sufferer; Cloudesly, his sullen, dilatory Mentor; and Julian, (the supposed offspring of Cloudesly, but real son of Lord Alton, and nephew of Lord Danvers,) who turns out the fortunate youth of the piece. The story is awkwardly told. Meadows begins it with an account of himself, and a topographical description of the Russian empire, which has nothing to do with the subject; and nearly through the remainder of the work, listens to a speech of Lord Danvers, recounting his own history and that of Julian, which lasts for six hundred pages without interruption or stop. It is the longest parenthesis in a narrative that ever was known. Meadows then emerges from his *incognito* once more, as if he had been hid behind a curtain, and gives the *coup-de-grace* to his own autobiography, and the lingering sufferings of his patron. The plot is borrowed from a real event that took place concerning a disputed succession in the middle of the last century, and which gave birth not long after to a novel with the title of *Annesley.* We should like to meet with a copy of this work, in order to see how a writer of less genius would get to the end of his task, and carry the reader along with him without the aid of those subtle researches and lofty declamations with which Mr Godwin has supplied the place of facts and circumstances. (pp. 150-51)

[The] fault of this and some other of the author's productions is, that the critical and didactic part overlays the narrative and dramatic part; as we see in some editions of the poets, where there are two lines of original text, and the rest of the page is heavy with the lumber and pedantry of the commentators. The writer does not call characters from the dead, or conjure them from the regions of fancy, to paint their peculiar physiognomy, or tell us their story, so much as (like the anatomist) to dissect and demonstrate on the insertion of the bones, the springs of the muscles, and those understood principles of life and motion which are common to the species. Now, in a novel, we want the individual, and not the *genus*. The tale of *Cloudesly* is a dissertation on remorse. Besides, this truth of science is often a different thing from the truth of nature, which is modified by a thousand accidents, 'subject to all the skyey influences;'—not a mechanical principle, brooding over and working every thing out of itself. (p. 152)

Mr Godwin's mind is, we conceive, essentially active, and therefore may naturally be expected to wear itself out sooner than those that are passive to external impressions, and receive continual new accessions to their stock of knowledge and acquirement:

> A fiery soul that working out its way,
> Fretted the pigmy body to decay,
> And o'er-inform'd its tenement of clay.

That some of this author's latter works are (in our judgment) comparatively feeble, is, therefore, no matter of surprise to us, and still less is it matter of reproach or triumph. We look upon it as a consequence incident to that constitution of mind and operation of the faculties. (pp. 152-53)

> [*William Hazlitt*], *"Mr. Godwin,"* in The Edinburgh Review, *Vol. LI, No. CI, April, 1830, pp. 144-59.*

[MARY SHELLEY] (essay date 1830)

[*An English novelist, Shelley achieved great fame as the author of* Frankenstein; or, The Modern Prometheus, *a classic tale of Gothic horror. She was also the daughter of Godwin and Wollstonecraft. In her review of* Cloudesly, *Shelley offers glowing praise for Godwin's characterization, narrative style, and didactic intent.*]

While other writers represent manners rather than passions, or passions at once vague and incomplete, [Mr. Godwin] conceives, in its entireness, the living picture of an event with all its adjuncts; he sets it down in its vivid reality: no part is dim, no part is tame. We have the clear and distinct representation of his conception, and are made to feel that his portraiture is endowed with the very essence and spirit of nature. (p. 711)

Of all modern writers, Mr. Godwin has arrived most sedulously, and most successfully, at the highest species of perfection his department of art affords. He sketches in his own mind, with a comprehensive and bold imagination, the plan of his work; he digs at the foundations, and learns all the due bearings of his position; he examines his materials, and sees exactly to what purpose each is best fitted; he makes an incident; he unerringly divines the results, both of the event and passion, which this incident will bring forth. By dint of the

mastery of thought, he transfuses himself into the very souls of his personages; he dives into their secret hearts, and lays bare, even to their anatomy, their workings; not a pulsation escapes him,—while yet all is blended into one whole, which forms the pervading impulse of the individual he brings before us. Who, remembering Falkland, but feels as if he had stood by that noble ruin, and watched its downfall! Who but writhes under the self-dejection of Mandeville, and feels the while his own heart whisper fearful oracles of the tameless and sad incongruities of our souls! Who but exulted madly with St. Leon, when he obtained his specious gifts! (p. 712)

Cloudesly is before us, a fresh example of what we have been saying. This tale contains a train of events, each naturally flowing one from the other, and each growing in importance and dignity as they proceed. We have no extraneous ornaments; no discursive flights. Comparing this book with others, we felt as if we had quitted gardens and parks, and tamer landscapes, for a scene on nature's grandest scale; that we wandered among giants' rocks, "the naked bones of the world waiting to be clothed." We use this quotation, because it suggested itself to our minds as we read these volumes, but we must guard our meaning from the idea of there being any turgidness in *Cloudesly*. Grace and dignity, joined to power, are its characteristics. The first volume is the least interesting. The author digs at the foundation, and then places the first stones; then we begin to feel the just proportions and promising beauty of the plan, till the tantalizing work of preparation finally yields to the full manifestation of the conception of the artist. If we may be permitted another metaphor, and this last is the most just, we will say that this work reminds us of the solemn strain of some cathedral organ. First, a few appropriate chords are fitfully and variously struck; a prelude succeeds to awaken our attention, and then rises the full peal, which swells upon the ear, till the air appears overcharged and overflowing with majestic harmonies. As far as an image can go, this exactly pourtrays our sensations on reading *Cloudesly*. The composer rapts us from ourselves, filling our bosoms with new and extraordinary emotions, while we sit soul-enchained by the wonders of his art. (pp. 712-13)

It is the peculiar excellence of Mr. Godwin's writing, that there is not a word too much, and curtailment of the narrative would be like displaying the unfilled-up outline of beauty; we might feel that it was there, and yet remain in ignorance of its peculiar features. The interest is imperative, but unconstrained; nature dwells paramount in every part. As it proceeds, it becomes high-wrought, without being harrowing. To the end, the tragedy is tempered by the softest spirit of humanity; it touches the verge of terror, only to bring us the more soothingly back to milder feelings. We close the book, not tantalized by a sense of the injustice of fate, nor tormented by a painful depicting of unrebuked guilt, but with a compassion for the criminal, and a love or admiration for the innocent, at once elevating and delightful. The few last pages are indeed a record of truths and sentiments, which, as coming from one who has lived so long, and, synonymous with this expression, suffered so much, inculcates a philosophy very opposite from the misanthropical one so prevalent a little while ago.

Mr. Godwin's style is at once simple and energetic; it is full, without being inflated. (p. 714)

Here is nothing harsh and crabbed, nothing morbid and disheartening: every page displays freshness and vigour, each one containing some lesson to teach us confidence, love, and hope. This philosophy, as emanating from experience, is a precious boon, such as, since the days of the philosophers of old, has seldom been bequeathed to us. Let the reader turn to the last page of the third volume, and learn thence, that a glory still remains to the earth, an attribute to our mortal natures, that must elevate and bless us while man remains; and let our hearts exult, when one of the wisest men of this or any age tells us, that "the true key of the universe is love." (p. 716)

> [*Mary Shelley*], in a review of "Cloudesly; A Tale," in Blackwood's Edinburgh Magazine, *Vol. XXVII, No. CLXVI, May, 1830, pp. 711-16.*

[J. A. HERAUD AND WILLIAM MAGINN] (essay date 1830)

[*Heraud was an English poet, dramatist, and critic. Maginn, one of the most prominent journalists in England during the first half of the nineteenth century, wrote prolifically for a number of English periodicals. Here they discuss the strengths and weaknesses of Godwin's novels, terming* Cloudesly *his best production to date.*]

Mr. Godwin is a veteran author—so much so, indeed, that he is looked upon by general readers rather as one of the by-gone, than as presently existing. This has been owing as much to the infrequency of his appearance, as to the transcending excellence of his productions, which is indeed such as to associate him at once in our minds with the mighty dead. This infrequency of appearance is the cause of the transcending excellence by which he has attained a living immortality. Mr. Godwin seems to have had no ambition of being esteemed a ready writer, capable of sending out his novel and a half a year. His ambition is of a higher mark—like Ben Jonson, while inferior authors thought only of making their works, plays—he has aimed at making his plays, works. Accordingly, we find in his novels no marks of haste or inattention, though, perhaps, more than enough of elaboration. (p. 381)

Mr. Godwin's sympathies in [*Cloudesley*] were all for the distant and future; the *endless* perfectibility of the human species engages more of his affection than the welfare of the present race of mankind, who, for the generations that may exist some centuries hence, are to suffer spoliation of property, and the destruction of established institutions. Not such is the moral code of the Gospel, in which all is practicable, all virtue is founded in mercy, kindness, benevolence, and comfort, alike to him that gives and him that takes. There we find no wild supposition of an interest which cannot be described, as it does not exist; no course of actions is proposed, without a motive direct and reflected. But ... Godwin's mind has been progressive—and he lived to outgrow much of what was erroneous in his opinions. (p. 384)

Mr. Godwin's mind is not poetical. ... By a poetical mind, we mean, in this instance, one that exercises, by turns or together, the faculties both of the fancy and the imagination. Mr. Godwin can only be said to exert one of these. In so far as imagination is poetry, Mr. Godwin's mind is poetical. Mr. Godwin images out an *idea* better than any other man living. But the idea is given too monotonously; it is aggrandized and exaggerated; but never realized. This was the case in his philosophical work [*Political Justice*]. ... It was the working out of one idea—pushing the argument founded on it to extremes; and sticking to an exclusive view of the subject in hand. Now, all this is very well for a trial of skill, but fails to discover truth, which is not confined in holes and corners in any such way, but is as free as the general air, as broad as the whole heavens. His novels, accordingly, want variety, because the

fancy is not exercised in aggregating poetical forms in order to the manifold exhibition of the ideal creation. The perfection of art is in the union of the ideal and the real—this is Shakspeare's excellence—it is also Sir Walter Scott's; but it is not Mr. Godwin's. Inasmuch as Mr. Godwin creates, (if he does create,) he is entitled to a high character even as a poet; but it is in the process of his work that he loses that character. He works like a mathematician, not like a poet; he demonstrates his conclusion, not suggests it. There is moreover, no surprise, in any of the incidents, no curiosity excited in the reader's mind. The reader is as much possessed, from the beginning, with the idea as the author himself; he anticipates the course of the work, he has no curiosity respecting the coming incidents, but only desires to discover how, and with what force of style they will be treated. Sometimes, also, as in the third volume of *Caleb Williams,* there is too much made of one section of the argument; but the reader feels, as well as the author, that the fault is committed to stuff the volume, and pities and forgives.

There is great want of material, such as picturesque scenery, local association, manners, and traditions, in *Caleb Williams*. The hint, as the author states, was suggested by the popular tale of *Blue Beard*. His idea was to exhibit the passion of curiosity. This he does in the person of Caleb Williams, a young man in the service of one Falkland, who feels, from some circumstances, a curiosity to know whether his master was not guilty of a murder for which other persons had been executed. The character of Falkland is constructed in the same way. The love of fame is his one principle of conduct. A brutal insult hurts his chivalrous feelings; in a moment of madness, he takes a fatal revenge, and, to preserve his character, he permits the vengeance of the law to fall upon the innocent. It is ascribing, after all, too much power to Williams's inveterate curiosity, that it should possess the fascination of extracting from such a man so important a secret. Supposing, however, that he should get possession of the secret, all the rest follows as a matter of course; that Falkland should endeavour to prevent Williams from divulging it. The means which he adopts for this purpose are so insufferable; his suspicion is so nice and extreme, that, in self-defence, his confidant is obliged to betray him. Falkland is a noble character; and, at the end, the magnificence of his nature breaks out afresh, and redeems him, through his last act of forgiveness, within the limits of human sympathy.

Throughout this work the novelist delights to shew the imperfections of our social institutions, and indulges in constant satire on the ordinary motives to conduct. All the common notions of society are set at nought, and his minor characters are made the objects of extreme contempt. Only the intellectual are represented as admirable. Now this is not true to nature, as, in the meanest specimens of humanity, some glimpses of the divinity are discernible, and moral worth frequently belongs to those who are most deficient in intellectual acquisitions.

But in the *Travels of St. Leon,* as the author has himself told us, he shews how good is individual conformity to the customs and usages of society, and how fatal to the possessor is an immunity from the common cares and anxieties of mortality. (pp. 385-86)

We have no doubt that Mr. Godwin thought that, in this novel, he was enforcing a fine moral, namely, that the possession of unlimited wealth, and the gift of immortality, were inconsistent with the present condition of the human race, and ineffectual for individual happiness.—This, however, will not be found to hold; the only moral that it inculcates is, that such a privilege bestowed on a single individual, would confer on him an invidious distinction, which would tend to his perpetual discomfort. It leaves the problem unsolved; what would be the effect of such powers, if possessed by every man?

We know not that it is necessary to allude to Mr. Godwin's novel of *Fleetwood,* as we do not recollect it ever having been brought into discussion, in any estimate of his merits, with which we are acquainted. There is in *Fleetwood,* as usual, an attempt at exhibiting the morally marvellous, which excites no illusion, and little sympathy; combined with frequent beauties of detail, striking eloquence of expression, great energy of intellect, and much to arouse and stimulate the better order of novel readers. The story acquires importance in its progress. The jealousy of the married Fleetwood is worked out with elaborate skill. This subject, however, was not sufficient to occupy the three volumes. (p. 386)

Original as his works are in construction and execution, the ideas which are the germs of each, were not the sole property of the author, but suggested by his course of reading, and determined by the degree of progression in which his mind found itself at the time of writing. His has not been the power of producing or creating ideas, but of conceiving them strongly, when presented by accident or study to his understanding. His mind is built up and edified by a certain process of self-instruction; and the force of his intellect drives on the acquired idea through all the forms of the understanding until the applicable categories are exhausted, and then ceases from its labour. This process is slow in its work of education, and its results are dependant upon the diligence of study. Besides this, Mr. Godwin has no facility in varying the form and costume of his intellectualizations. He cannot, like the Scots novelist, present a counterpart of previous characters and incidents in a new production—*"another, yet the same."* What he has once written, he has written; and another version would not only fail of interest, but be deficient in execution. Mr. Godwin dwells in an intellectual world; "a world of empty forms," as Kant would have said; not in the world of the senses. He can scarcely be said to embody, so much as to impersonate; but his persons, whatever their number, are the same in essence, and in unity of substance are but one; for they are not physical persons, but "beings of the mind." (pp. 386-87)

[It] is our opinion, that Godwin's last novel [*Cloudesley*] is his best. *Caleb Williams* has the advantage of old associations in its favour; it is the work on which the author's reputation has been established—with which his genius is identified. *Cloudesley,* also, has a strange defect. It is well-conceived—it is admirably executed—it is miserably constructed. But with all the claims of the first work on public regard, and this great drawback from the latter, we repeat, that we are of opinion, the judicious reader will decide in favour of its greater claims on permanent approbation. (p. 387)

The language of this novel is written in a less ambitious and inverted, and therefore better, style than most of Godwin's productions. In this respect, it is far superior to his *History of the Commonwealth,* which is composed in the worst species of what is called the historical style. The tone of composition in *Cloudesley* is quiet, calm, and graceful—the course of the narrative is gradual and even, not marked by any starts of passionate energy and expression, but patiently worked out to its conclusion—the doom of restitution and punition. The penitence of Lord Danvers is preferable to the unavailing remorse of Falkland—it is a more congenial representation of human

nature—shews more of the good in the evil—and is solemnly touched with the pencil of a master in his art. How fine is the idea of the retribution for his crime, in the loss, one by one, of his children, and, lastly, of his wife—so that he is left heirless, and without hope of progeny, and is, at length, fain to restore his brother's son to the heritage of his fathers. How exquisite is the description of the manner in which Cloudesley proceeded in the education of his ward, and the fatherly interest which became gradually generated in his mind towards the boy! Julian himself is a fine adumbration of a generous and ingenuous boyhood, too susceptible to temptation, with no more power of resistance than youths in general, without experience, are capable of exerting. This is much better than the subsidiary story of *Caleb Williams,* altogether descriptive as it is of the brutal parts of humanity, whether exhibited in stations of power or servility. There is "a relish of salvation in it," which is highly agreeable to a cultivated taste. To many of the readers of *Cloudesley,* perhaps, the interest of the main story and its adjuncts may be less intense—the passion less harrowing—the excitement less engrossing; but the judicious critic will perceive that the philosophy is more true, and the philanthropy more amiable, if not more profound, than in *Caleb Williams.* The intense energy characteristic of that work is a mark of inexperienced authorship—it is indicative of a state of mind in which the writer is possessed of, instead of being possessed with, an idea. We can see the enthusiast at work, watching and waiting for the inspiration, uncertain whither he shall be carried; but desirous of being rapt away, whatever the end may be. (p. 391)

Excellent, however, as this production is, and superior to every other novel published during the last season, it may, we think, be reasonably questioned, whether with novel readers it has had so much success as some of the more time-serving productions of the same kind. With this result, Mr. Godwin is no doubt well content. (p. 392)

The prime instrument employed by Mr. Godwin in his novels is analysis. In this he is . . . distinguishable from Sir Walter Scott, who proceeds synthetically; that is, by an accumulation of particulars, in which the character is presented at once in its integrity to the reader.

Mr. Godwin, however, in his preface to the present work, expresses his opinion, that

> Analysis is a science more commensurate to human faculties than synthesis.
>
> (p. 393)

We readily agree with Mr. Godwin, that to analyze is a far easier task than to synthesize. The novelist, however, would do the latter who consulted the oracle in his bosom, and *added* its responses in aid of those conclusions which he had otherwise obtained. We cannot, however, allow that this oracle is consulted by Mr. Godwin, if he intend by it what is usually meant by *the heart.* The only oracle he consults is his understanding; the process which he exercises constitutes a series of judgments.—The act of judging consists in an union of sensuous presentations in a consciousness; which union is either *analytical* by identity, or *synthetical* by the addition of such presentations to each other. But inasmuch as Mr. Godwin's personage is ideal, the origin of his judgments is not empirical, (as the Kantists would say,) but, *à priori,* as springing from the *pure* understanding and reason. And it is upon this account that, while we cannot bestow upon Mr. Godwin the highest philosophical degrees, we are willing to grant him, nevertheless, a very high diploma indeed, from the metaphysical college of which we profess ourselves to be unworthy members. Nevertheless, we cannot help regretting that Mr. Godwin's scheme of philosophy was not of the more elevated kind, because, what have we not reason to expect, in that case, might have been his success, with his philosophical tact, seeing what has already been that of Sir Walter Scott, without it, who, nevertheless, worked in the spirit of the higher philosophy, by force of that natural instinct, as it were, and that genius, which is also nature, and therefore, like nature, transcends all the results of art, with the most exquisite art, though without any appearance of it?

Would also, on another account, that his philosophy had been rather synthetical than analytical! His genius then would have attained a more elevated reach in his productions. It has been said, that Mr. Godwin is a metaphysician grafted on a dissenting preacher. Would that he had grafted again on the metaphysician the divine! The highest range of metaphysical inquiry, which the latter character implies, is only possible by means of synthesis. The understanding may overstep its limits into the mere field of intellectual beings; and Mr. Godwin has so far overstept its limits; but he has not exercised his mind in those high endeavours, in which it is no longer completely satisfied with an empirical use of the rules of understanding, this use being always conditional, but expels even the understanding itself from its sphere, to seek, entirely out of its limits, for those ideal beings, through which, by the aid of a strong imagination, it may, without any empirical conditions, complete its mighty labour. Then it rises, on the wings of the pure reason, to the contemplation of ideas, which are not only subjectively and necessarily real, but also objectively possible.

That Mr. Godwin's mind is capable of this elevated reach is, nevertheless, sufficiently evident. A passage of this kind occurs in *Mandeville.*

> Religion is the most important of all things, the great point of discrimination that divides the man from the brute. It is our special prerogative, that we can converse with that which we cannot see, and believe in that, the existence of which is reported to us by none of our senses. Such is the abstract and exalted nature of man. This it is that constitutes us intellectual, and truly entitles us to the denomination of reasonable beings. All that passes before the senses of the body, is a scenic exhibition: and he that is busied about these fantastic appearances, 'walketh in a vain shew, and disquieteth himself in vain.' Invisible things are the only realities; invisible things alone are the things that shall remain.

We say that this passage indicates power in Mr. Godwin to rise to the desired elevation so characteristic of a pure rationalist. But it is doubtful whether he speaks here in his own character or that of Mandeville. We are in doubt whether he did not intend it as a part of the attributes with which he has invested that fictitious personage, as belonging to that most repulsive form of Calvinism, which he describes as having so deleterious an effect upon his mind and character. At any rate, the principle which we are advocating exerts no practical influence upon Mr. Godwin's writings. This is a subject, with us, of great regret; not only as it has contracted the moral utility of his productions, but as it has confined the flight of his genius to a humbler quarry than that to which it was naturally destined.

The fact is, that all theological ideas are carefully excluded from this writer's compositions. He treats, ever and anon, of the subject of remorse—and he delineates it well. No man can better shew the writhings and contortions of his victims, who, in general, also, either expressly or by implication, are represented as repentant. But as this remorse is without religious consolation—so their repentance is without religious motive. It is the growth of circumstances—of dire necessity, or miserable expediency—never the result of any higher principles, than the beggarly elements of this world. (pp. 393-95)

We should be sorry, if any of our above remarks should be construed to amount to a charge either of practical or speculative atheism, whether in Mr. Godwin or in his writings; but, without scruple of any sort, we do accuse him of want of faith. We accuse Cromwell of want of faith. Such deficiency is inseparable from him who either does ill that good may come, or advocates the doing of it. Mr. Godwin has exercised all the lower faculties of his mind too long—let him rise to the exertion of that "which is the substance of things hoped for, the evidence of things not seen;" that, by which "the elders obtained a good report"—that, through which, "we understand that the worlds were framed by the word of God, so that things which are seen were not made of things which do appear."

It is not without propriety that we make this appeal to this illustrious writer, because it is not without hope. His mind, we have proved, has been progressive. From antipathy to social institutions, it has proceeded to sympathy with them; until, at length, as in his last work, his nature overflows with the spirit of charity. (p. 395)

> [*J. A. Heraud and William Maginn*], "Mr. Godwin's Novels," in Fraser's Magazine, Vol. II, No. X, November, 1830, pp. 381-96.

LEIGH HUNT (essay date 1831)

[*An English poet and essayist, Hunt is remembered as a literary critic who encouraged and influenced several Romantic poets, especially John Keats and Shelley. Here, Hunt praises* Caleb Williams *and notes that Godwin "succeeds far better in moving by pain than by pleasure." Hunt's comments were written in 1831.*]

Caleb Williams is a masterly work of absorbing interest. We do not think the character of *Falkland* a very natural one; that is to say, we do not think that any man, not under the influence of physical madness, could commit the crime that he does; and yet have been accustomed from childhood to those habits of self-restraint and the most amiable virtue. There would have been overt acts of impatience and resentfulness, many times, in such a man; or else his virtue would have set most uneasily upon him. *Falkland* is no fool of virtue, whatever the author may sometimes appear to have intended him; but he may be allowed to be a sort of *Sir Charles Grandison*, taking himself for what he was not. He is Richardson's hero in miniature, under the sad disadvantage of having committed a capital offence! The less varnished characters in this novel are admirably painted; *Tyrrel, Grimes* and all the rest, as far as we recollect them, for we have not seen the novel for many years . . .; [recently] we sat down incontinently, and read nearly seven chapters without being able to take our eyes from the book. This is the right thing. Criticism may or may not be all in an error. We think, however, it will be conceded that Mr. Godwin succeeds far better in moving by pain than by pleasure. His works are calculated to do more good to the unimaginative, than the reverse; or at least to those whose imaginations are not cultivated, and who are willing to have the rudiments of thought and feeling thrust upon them, at as much expense as the author pleases. We confess, for our own parts, we are among those who have had wounds enough, and are willing to have a little balm. We can dispense with being poked in the fifth rib, or taking our breakfast within hearing of the cries of a surgery. We think that the list of happy books might be increased without detriment to the salutary stock of dissatisfaction. But at the same time, we allow to the full the merit of such works as *Caleb Williams;* and having neutralized our criticism by saying what we read of it again without stopping, we shall proceed to redeem our character for a masculine endurance by saying that we shall infallibly read the whole volume through. Yes: we shall submit our scalp to Mr. Godwin, so tempting is his tomahawk. (pp. 373-74)

> Leigh Hunt, *"A Review of Cooper's 'The Pilot' and Godwin's 'Caleb Williams',"* in his Literary Criticism, *edited by Lawrence Huston Houtchens and Carolyn Washburn Houtchens, Columbia University Press, 1956, pp. 372-75.*

[WILLIAM MAGINN]   (essay date 1834)

[One of the most prominent journalists in England during the first half of the nineteenth century, Maginn wrote prolifically for a variety of English periodicals and was the founding editor of Fraser's Magazine for Town and Country, *from which the following excerpt is drawn. Here, Maginn surveys Godwin's career, focusing on his ideas and style.]*

Yonder walks William Godwin! The marks of age press heavily upon him; but there gleams out of that strange face and above that stranger figure the eye of fire which lighted up with the conceptions of *Caleb Williams* and *St. Leon.* Wonderful books! Once read, not only ever remembered, but ever graven on the mind of those who know how to read. We can enter into the feeling of Lord Byron's exclamation, when, after asking Godwin why he did not write a new novel, his lordship received from the old man the answer, that it would kill him. "And what matter," said Lord Byron; "we should have another *St. Leon.*"

But it was not to be. There is power, and stirring thought in *Fleetwood, Mandeville,* and *Cloudesly;* but they are not what Lord Byron called for. The promised *Seven Sleepers,* which was to be the conclusion of a new series of *St. Leon,* has never come; and of Godwin the novelist we suppose there is an end. Of Godwin the politician we have little good to say. He started in opposition to the received views of the world on all the most important affairs in which that world is concerned; and it is perfectly unnecessary to add, that the world beat in the end, as indeed in his case it deserved to beat. The principles of his *Political Justice,* derived as it was pretended from the Bible, would, if they could have been acted upon, have subverted all the honourable relations of society, and destroyed all the ennobling or redeeming feelings of the heart. Godwin himself, as he confesses in his preface to *St. Leon* [see excerpt dated 1799], was sorry for having insulted, in that cold-blooded and, we must say, absurd book, those charities and duties which are the links of life: we should be much surprised if he has not since repented of all the work. In his [*Of Population*], he shewed that true feelings were prevalent in his mind, though he failed in producing the fit refutation of the desperate quackery which he opposed, and which was destined to fall to destruction before the hand of Sadler. His *Thoughts on Man,* containing much

that is eloquent, contain but little that is profound; and we are sorry to find, that though his scepticism on the most vital points is not so recklessly urged as in former days, it is scarcely abated. His historical work on the Commonwealth is a failure. . . .

He has now taken his place in our world of authors; and we incline to think, that *Caleb Williams* and *St. Leon* are the only books of his which will be remembered. His mind is not productive,—therein singularly differing from that of Sir Walter Scott, with whom alone, as a novelist of power, he of all our contemporaries can be compared. There is a want of invention even in his best books; and we can believe the current story, that *Caleb Williams* was written to illustrate a system, or to prove that a novel might be composed without reference to the passion of love. Once fairly embarked in his book, he forgot his systems; but the idea of so originating them proves that there is a deficiency in the mind. The phrenologists inform us, that the organ of veneration is wholly and most singularly absent in his head;—we do not exactly believe in phrenology; but his works prove to us, that there is some want in his intellect which operates to control the impulses of his genius.

> [William Maginn], *"William Godwin, Esq.,"* in Fraser's Magazine, *Vol. LVIII, No. X, October, 1834, p. 463.*

[EDGAR ALLAN POE]   (essay date 1835)

[Considered one of America's most outstanding men of letters, Poe was a distinguished poet, novelist, essayist, journalist, short story writer, editor, and critic. Poe stressed an analytical rather than emotive approach to literature and emphasized the specifics of style and construction in a work instead of concentrating solely on the importance of ideological statement. Here, he favorably reviews Lives of the Necromancers *and praises Godwin's prose and philosophical insight.]*

The name of the author of *Caleb Williams,* and of *St. Leon,* is, with us, a word of weight, and one which we consider a guarantee for the excellence of any composition to which it may be affixed. There is about all the writings of Godwin, one peculiarity which we are not sure that we have ever seen pointed out for observation, but which, nevertheless, is his chief idiosyncrasy—setting him peculiarly apart from all other *literati* of the day. We allude to an air of mature thought—of deliberate premeditation pervading, in a remarkable degree, even his most common-place observations. He never uses a hurried expression, or hazards either an ambiguous phrase, or a premature opinion. His style therefore is highly artificial; but the extreme finish and proportion always observable about it, render this artificiality, which in less able hands would be wearisome, in him a grace inestimable. We are never tired of his terse, nervous, and sonorous periods—for their terseness, their energy, and even their melody, are made, in all cases, subservient to the sense with which they are invariably fraught. No English writer, with whom we have any acquaintance, with the single exception of Coleridge, has a fuller appreciation of the value of *words;* and none is more nicely discriminative between closely-approximating meanings.

The avowed purpose of [*Lives of the Necromancers*] is to exhibit a wide view of human credulity. "To know"—says Mr. Godwin—"the things that are not, and cannot be, but have been imagined and believed, is the most curious chapter in the annals of man.'' *In extenso* we differ with him.

> There are more things in Heaven and Earth, Horatio,
> Than are dreamt of in thy philosophy.

There are many things, too, in the great circle of human experience, more curious than even the records of human credulity—but that they form *one* of the most curious chapters, we were at all times ready to believe, and had we been in any degree skeptical, the **Lives of the Necromancers** would have convinced us. . . .

The design, if we understand it, is to display in their widest extent, the great range and wild extravagancy of the imagination of man. It is almost superfluous to say that in this he has fully succeeded. His compilation is an invaluable work, evincing much labor and research, and full of absorbing interest. The only drawback to the great pleasure which its perusal has afforded us, is found in the author's unwelcome announcement in the Preface, that for the present he winds up his literary labors with the production of this book. The pen which wrote **Caleb Williams,** should never for a moment be idle.

> [*Edgar Allan Poe*], ''*Godwin's Necromancy,*'' *in* The Southern Literary Messenger, *Vol. II, No. 1, December, 1835, p. 65.*

GEORGE GILFILLAN　(essay date 1845)

[*Gilfillan was a Scottish clergyman and poet as well as a prolific critic and biographer. In the following excerpt from his* Gallery of Literary Portraits, *Gilfillan praises the style and characterization of* Caleb Williams *and* St. Leon, *but considers Godwin's later works less successful. De Quincey disputes Gilfillan's assessment of* Caleb Williams *in the excerpt dated 1845-46.*]

While **Caleb Williams** is in every circulating library, and needs more frequently, we have heard, than almost any novel, to be replaced, the **Enquiry Concerning Political Justice,** is read only by a few hardy explorers, and reminds them, contrasting its past influence with its present neglect, of some cataract, once the terror and the glory of the wilderness, but which, by the fall of its cliff of vantage, has been robbed of its voice of thunder, shorn of its Samson-like locks of spray, dwarfed into comparative insipidity, deserted by its crowding admirers, and left to pine alone in the desert of which it was once the pride, and to sigh for the days of other years. And yet, while of **Caleb Williams** it was predicted by some sapient friend, that, if published, it would be the grave of his literary reputation, the other lifted him, as on dragon wings, into instant and dangerous popularity; the **Enquiry** was the balloon which bore him giddily up, the novel the parachute which broke his fall.

As a novelist, indeed, Godwin, apart from the accidents of opinion and popular caprice, occupies a higher place than as a philosopher. As a philosopher, he is neither altogether new nor altogether true; he is ingenious, but unsafe, and the width of the field he traverses, and the celerity with which he runs across it, and the calm dogmatism with which he announces the most extreme and startling opinions, excite suspicions as to the depth of his knowledge, and the comprehension of his views. They surround the figure of the sage with an air and edging of charlatanerie. As a novelist, on the contrary, he passes for no more than he is,—a real and robust original. He proceeds in this walk with the exulting freedom and confidence of one, who has hit on a vein entirely new. He imagines a character after his own heart; a quiet, curious, prying, philo-

sophical being, with a strong underdash of the morbid, if not of the mad; and he thickens around him circumstances, which, by making him altogether a misanthrope, and nearly a maniac, bring out all the powers and the passions of his nature. The main actor in each of his tales, at first recumbent, is, at length, ere you leave him, rampant with whatever may be the pervading principle of his being. And so with the author himself; he, too, catches fire by running. At first slow, embarrassed, uninteresting, commonplace, he becomes rapid, ardent, overpowering. The general tone of his writing, however, is calm. ''In the very whirlwind of his passion, he begets a temperance which gives it smoothness.'' His heat is never that of the sun with all his beams around him; but of the round rayless orb seen shining from the summit of Mont Blanc, still and stripped in the deep black ether. He has more passion than imagination. And even his passion he has learned more by sympathy than by personal feeling. And amid his most tempestuous scenes, you see the calm and stern eye of philosophic analysis looking on. His imagery is not copious, nor always original, but its sparseness is its strength; it startles you with unexpected and momentary brilliance; the flash comes sudden as the lightning; like it, too, it comes from the cloud, and like it, it bares the breast of heaven in an instant, and in an instant is gone. No preparatory flourish or preliminary sound,—no sheets of useless splendour;—each figure is a fork of fire which strikes, and needs no second blow. Nay, often his images are singularly commonplace, and you wonder how they move you so, till you resolve this into the power of the hand which jaculates its own energy in them. His style is not the least remarkable thing about his compositions. It is a smooth succession of short and simple sentences, each clear as crystal, and none ever distracting the attention from the subject to its own construction. It is a style in which you cannot explain how the total effect rises out of the individual parts, and which is forgotten as entirely during perusal as is the pane of glass through which you gaze at a comet or a star. The *form,* too, favours the general effect. Each narrative takes the shape of an autobiography, and the incessant recurrence of the pronoun *I* transports you to a confessional, where you hear told you, in subdued tones, a tale which might ''rouse the dead to hear.'' Systematically, he rejects the use of supernatural machinery, profuse descriptions, and mere mechanical horrors. Like Brockden Brown, he despises to summon up a ghost from the grave; he invokes the ''mightier might'' of the passions of living flesh; he excites terror often, but it is the terror which dilated man wields over his fellow, colossal and crushing, but distinct; not the vague and shadowy form of fear which springs from preternatural agency. His path is not, like that of Monk Lewis and Maturin, sulphureous and slippery, as through some swart mine; it is a *terribil via,* but clear, direct, above ground—a line of light passing through dark forests, over mountains, and by the brink of tremendous precipices. . . . His novels resemble the paintings of John Martin, being a gallery, nay, a world in themselves; and it is a gloomy gallery and a strange world. In both, monotony and mannerism are incessant; but the monotony is that of the sounding deep, the mannerism that of the thunderbolts of heaven. Martin might append to his one continual flash of lightning, which is present in all his pictures, now to reveal a deluge, now to garland the brow of a fiend—now to rend the veil of a temple, and now to guide the invaders through the breach of a city—the words, ''John Martin, his mark.'' Godwin's novels are not less terribly distinguished, to those who understand their cipher—the deep scar of misery, branded, whether literally, as in **Mandeville,** or figuratively, as in all his other tales, upon the brow of the ''Victim of Society.''

We well remember our first reading of *Caleb Williams.* We commenced it about nine o'clock at night, sitting by ourselves in a lonely room—read on and on, forgetful of time, place, and of the fact, especially, that our candle was going out, till, lo! at one of the most enchaining of its situations, it suddenly dropped down, and we were in darkness! It was a most provoking position. The family were "dead asleep," not a spark of light to be got, and there were we, sitting with the book we had been devouring in our hands, pressing it in our enthusiasm to our breast, and yet unable to see a syllable of its contents. It was, we remember, in our seventeenth year, and we did not bear the disappointment so philosophically as we would now. We went to bed intensely chagrined, were long of sleeping,—when we did sleep, dreamed stupid sulky dreams about Hawkins and Tyrrell, and by earliest dawn were up and tearing out its heart. There is about it a stronger suction and swell of interest than in any novel we know, with the exception of one or two of Sir Walter's. You are in it ere you are aware. You put your hand playfully into a child's, and are surprised to find it held in the grasp of a giant. It becomes a fascination. Struggle you may, and kick—but he holds you by his glittering eye. There is no convulsion in the narrative either, few starts or spasms, no string of asterisks, (that base modern device,) to quicken your flagging curiosity; no frightful chasms yawn in your face; the stream is at once still as a mill-lead, and strong as a rapid. But it has higher merits than that of mere interest—a very subordinate kind of excellence, after all; for does not a will interest more than a *Waverley?*—the letter of a friend, more than the most sublime production of the human mind? There is a uniqueness in the whole conception of the tale, the incidents are imagined with consummate art, and succeed each other with breathless rapidity; the moral, so far as it respects the then wretched state of prison discipline and legal forms, is strongly pointed; and the writing, though far from elegant or finished, has in parts the rude power of those sentences which criminals, martyrs, and maniacs, scrawl upon their walls or windows, in the eloquence of desperation. The characters are not Englishmen, (none of Godwin's characters, indeed, seem to belong to any country; they are all, like their creator, philosophers, and citizens of the world, be they thieves or jailors, highwaymen or hags, ruffians or gentlemen,) but they are generally men. We like Falkland least of all, though we tremble at him, as the terrible incarnation of the principle of honour. He is certainly a striking creation; but resembles rather one of the fictitious beings of heraldry, than a real man. No such noble nature was ever so soured into a fiend; no such large heart was ever contracted into a scorpion-circle of fire, narrowing around its victim. Godwin's Falkland is in truth a more monstrous improbability than his daughter's Frankenstein. He is described as a paragon of benevolence and virtue, and yet to preserve, not the consciousness of honour, but, as Fuseli remarked, its mere reputation; he sets himself deliberately, by every despicable art, by every enormous energy of injustice, to blast a being whom, all the while, he respects and admires. And you are expected, throughout the whole career of the injury, to blend admiration of the inflicter, with sympathy for the victim. It is an attempt to reconcile the most glaring moral contradictions, an attempt worthy of the author of the far-famed chapter on "Necessity," and an attempt in which, strange to say, he nearly succeeds. You never altogether lose your regard for Falkland; and this chiefly because Caleb Williams himself never does. . . . Williams himself is the creation of circumstances, and has all the prominent points in his character struck out by the rude collisions he encounters. Originally he is neither more nor less than a shrewd, inquisitive youth.

He is never much more, indeed, than a foil to the power and interest of his principal. Tyrrell is a brute, nor even an English brute; but a brute proper and positive. He is drawn sternly and *con amore.* The other characters, Miss Melville, Raymond, Collins, &c. are very insipid, with the exception of Gines, the bloodhound, who is painted with the force, gusto, and almost inhuman sympathy of a Landseer; and the hag who attempts the life of Caleb in the robber's den, a dire figure, pointed into powerful relief by her butcher's cleaver, a coarser Clytemnestra, if great things may be likened to small. Such is *Caleb Williams,* a work which made an era in the fictitious writing of the age, and which has not only created a school of imitators, but coloured insensibly many works, which profess and possess independent claims; such as the Paul Cliffords, Eugene Arams, Rookwoods, and Oliver Twists, of Bulwer, Ainsworth, and Boz, which, but for it, we verily believe, had never been. Written with the care and consciousness of one who felt himself writing for immortality, it still keeps its place amid the immense fry of ordinary tales, embalmed and insulated in the rough salt of its own essential and original power.

If *Caleb Williams* be the most interesting and popular, *St. Leon* is the most pathetic and imaginative of his tales. It does not, indeed, in our judgment, do full justice to the character of an alchymist;—a character which ought to attract more interest nowadays, when chemistry has approached the verge of transformations nearly as wonderful as that which he sought by self-denial, and abstinence, and unwearied perseverance, and solemn prayer. (pp. 18-25)

This is our ideal of an alchymist: and has Godwin satisfied this ideal? We must answer, No. St. Leon is not a seeker for the philosopher's stone, nor yet its finder. He gains it by no protracted and painful process; he stumbles upon it by chance. It is not a reward; it is not a result; it drops at his feet as from the clouds. He wears, therefore, its mystic crown awkwardly, and like a *parvenu.* He never, somehow, seems satisfied that he has a proper claim to it, nor are you. What right, you say, has this broken-down moody gambler and ex-count to a gift so rare, which so many prophets and righteous men have desired in vain? Unworthy of its possession, no wonder that it avenges itself by making him the most miserable of men. The evils, too, of the successful alchymist's position are, we think, somewhat overdrawn. Money, it is true, cannot unlock every dungeon, melt every refractory element, or quench the fury of devouring flames; but it is clearly not answerable for the calamities into which his own recklessness or extravagance, or the savage superstitions of his age, plunge the Count St. Leon. Because he neglects ordinary precautions, and indulges needless expense, must the power of gold, as an engine of vast benevolence and amelioration, be reduced to a negative quantity? Indeed, the book defeats its own apparent object. As a satire upon gold, it is dull and powerless. As a picture of its princely prerogatives, it is captivating in the extreme. More successfully still, though not more justly, does he depict the misery of immortality on earth. He impresses us with the deepest sense of the dreary position of a man, whose stupendous privileges have only rendered him "alone in the world." Who does not pity St. Leon burying his noble wife, bidding farewell to his charming daughters, and setting forward on his solitary journey, "friendless, friendless, alone, alone?" Who weeps not with him as he feels that his gift has insulated him for ever; that an immortal can form no abiding connexion with "the ephemeron of an hour?" This is the impression which the author wishes to give, and he does give it; and it is most melancholy. But, perhaps, he has not brought out with due force the other side of the medal;—the consolations of such a solitude; a solitude like that of the brideless sun, diffusing, unweariedly, his tide of power and splendour; of the solitary stars; of the "childless cherubs." . . . Still, St. Leon is a magnificent romance. We all remember the grand outburst of his feelings after he knows the secret; though it rises less from the fact that the mysteries of nature are open, than that they are open to *him*. Hence, in the celebrated exclamation, "For me the wheels of the universe are made to roll backwards," we must lay the emphasis on the second word. But, better than this is that melancholy figure of the stranger, whose name is not given; whose history you must guess from the disconnected expressions of his despair; whose mysterious entrance is announced in words so significant and thrilling, like a blast of trumpets, and whom you doubt, in your perplexity, to be an incarnation of the fiend; so disastrous is the influence he sheds on the cottage by the lake, and on the destiny of its inmates. He reminds us of Coleridge's "Ancient Marinere." Like him, he is nameless; like him, he passes "like Night from land to land;" like him, he has strange power of speech; like him, he carries a deep burden of secret upon his breast, which he must disclose; like him, he has a special message to an individual, which colours all the after history of his being. Like the wedding guest, St. Leon becomes a wiser and a sadder man.

And then there is the noble Marguerite de Damville, the ideal of a matron, a mother, a wife, a woman; whose very step moves to the music of lofty purpose, and before whom her husband, even while holding the keys of nature and of immortal life, dwindles into insignificance. Blessings on thee, William Godwin, for this fine creation! a creation realising all our fondest dreams of the majesty, purity, and wisdom which gracious Nature can build up, when she pleases, in one woman's form. (pp. 27-30)

And while she is the loveliest, Bethlem Gabor is the most terrific character in this or in almost any tale. He is a "bear bereaved of his whelps." His castle has been burned; his wife and babes, "all his pretty ones," murdered; and he steps up upon their corpses into a giant of misanthropy. His figure itself proclaims his character. His stature is Titanic; his hair, a dead black; his face, all scarred and scorched with sword and flame; one eye is gone, but the other has gathered up into its solitary orb the fury which fell from it, and glares with a double portion of demoniac meaning. His voice is thunder; and as he talks in a torrent of imprecation against man, and nature, and Eternal Providence, his stature dilates, his breast swells and heaves like an angry wave, and a "supernatural eloquence seems to inspire and enshroud him." His every thought is tinctured with gall. (p. 31)

Mandeville is, like Bethlem Gabor, a misanthrope, but wants the energy and grandeur of that extraordinary character. He is not maddened into the feeling by circumstances; he hates, because he has nothing else to do. It is but in him the escape of immeasurable ennui. Godwin was probably seduced into this miscreation by the success of Gabor, forgetting that to reproduce any character is dangerous, and that what will pass, nay, tell, in a sketch, may be intolerable in a full-length portraiture. The power of this tale,—and it has great power,—lies not in story, for story there is little; nor in variety, for variety there is none; nor in characters, for character of any prominence there is but one—Mandeville himself; but in the minute and pains-taking analysis of hatred, as it roots itself in the soil of one morbid spirit, and gradually, as it grows, covers all with the blackness of darkness; and in the eloquence of certain

insulated passages, collecting the pith of the fell passion, and reminding you of those dark, soundless wells in the wilderness, into which you tremble to look down at noonday. And what an exit the hero has at length, leaving the stage with that ghastly gash upon his face, which grins out the intelligence that Clifford has set his mark on him, and that he is his for ever. (p. 33)

Fleetwood and Cloudesly, with many beauties of thought and style, are but faint, moony reflexes of the others, and we may silently drop both from the catalogue of the works, begirt by which he shall yet stand "before the dread tribunal of To-come," to receive the verdict of immortality. . . .

[Godwin's] *Life of Chaucer* includes some ingenious dissertations, but is a total misnomer, inasmuch as it contains little or no biography. His *Essay on Sepulchres* is full of learning, and seems to have been a favourite with its author; but, crushed down under its ominous title, it is now safely deposited in the tomb of the Capulets. His *Lives of Milton's Nephews* were another still birth. He is better at writing the life of a fictitious, than a real personage. His Sermons,—called curiously *Sketches from History*,—which we glanced over, *à la* Charles Lamb, at a book-stall in Glasgow, a good many years ago, are desperately dry, and we do not wonder that he soon ceased to be a preacher. His tragedies were sins of youth, and—would it were so with all such!—are forgotten forever. His *Memoirs of the Author of "A Vindication of the Rights of Woman"* does not add to his reputation. (p. 34)

> *George Gilfillan, "William Godwin," in his* A Gallery of Literary Portraits, *William Tait, 1845, pp. 15-36.*

THOMAS DE QUINCEY (essay date 1845-46)

[*An English critic and essayist, De Quincey used his own life as the subject of his best-known work,* Confessions of an English Opium Eater, *in which he chronicled his addiction to opium. De Quincey also contributed reviews to a number of London journals and earned a reputation as an insightful if occasionally long-winded literary critic. Here, he responds to Gilfillan's essay (see excerpt dated 1845), disagreeing vehemently with his estimate of the popularity of* Caleb Williams. *De Quincey's remarks were first published in* Tait's Magazine *in November-December 1845 and January-April 1846.*]

[Men] of talent have raised *Caleb Williams* to a station in the first rank of novels; whilst many more, amongst whom I am compelled to class myself, can see in it no merit of any kind. A schism, which is really perplexing, exists in this particular case. . . . (pp. 328-29)

They who vote against it are in a large majority. The Germans, whose literature offers a free port to all the eccentricities of the earth, have never welcomed *Caleb Williams*. Chenier, the ruling *littérateur* of Paris in the days of Napoleon, when reviewing the literature of his own day, dismisses Caleb contemptuously as coarse and vulgar. It is not therefore to the German taste; it is not to the French. And, as to our own country, Mr. Gilfillan is undoubtedly wrong in supposing that it "is in every circulating library, and needs more frequently than almost any novel to be replaced." If this were so, in presence of the immortal novels which for one hundred and fifty years have been gathering into the garners of our English literature, I should look next to see the race of men returning from venison and wheat to their primitive diet of acorns. But I believe that the number of editions yet published would at once discredit this account of the book's popularity. Neither is it likely, *a priori*, that such a popularity could arise even for a moment. The interest from secret and vindictive murder, though coarse, is undoubtedly deep. What would make us thrill in real life,—the case, for instance, of a neighbour lying under the suspicion of such a murder,—would make us thrill in a novel. But then it must be managed with art, and covered with mystery. For a long time it must continue doubtful both as to the fact, and the circumstances, and the motive. Whereas, in the case of Mr. Falkland, there is little mystery of any kind: not much, and only for a short time, to Caleb; and none at all to the reader, who could have relieved the curiosity of Mr. Caleb from the first, if he were placed in communication with him. (pp. 332-33)

The possibility that any individual in the minority can have regarded Godwin . . . [in a positive light] seems to argue that we of the majority must be wrong. Deep impressions seem to justify themselves. *We* may have failed to perceive things which *are* in the object; but it is not so easy for others to perceive things which are *not*,—or, at least, hardly in a case like this, where (though a minority) these ''others'' still exist in number sufficient to check and to confirm each other. On the other hand, Godwin's name seems sinking out of remembrance; and he is remembered less by the novels that succeeded, or by the philosophy that he abjured, than as the man that had Mary Wollstonecraft for his wife, Mrs. Shelley for his daughter, and the immortal Shelley as his son-in-law. (p. 335)

Thomas De Quincey, ''Notes on Gilfillan's Literary Portraits: William Godwin,'' in his The Collected Writings of Thomas De Quincey, *edited by David Masson, A. & C. Black, 1897, pp. 326-35.*

LESLIE STEPHEN (essay date 1876)

[*Stephen is considered one of the most important English literary critics of the late Victorian and early Edwardian eras; he also wrote extensively on Godwin. In his criticism, which is often moralistic, Stephen argues that all literature is nothing more than an imaginative rendering, in concrete terms, of a writer's philosophy or beliefs. In the following excerpt, Stephen explicates Godwin's philosophy as outlined in* Political Justice *and offers a brief assessment of* St. Leon *and* Caleb Williams. *For additional commentary by Stephen, see excerpt dated 1902.*]

Godwin's [*Political Justice*] in its general design reminds us rather of French than of English models. He is what so few Englishmen are—a thorough-going ''ergotist.'' His treatise embodies what is called inexorable logic. In other words it represents the really illogical frame of mind which refuses to be shocked by a *reductio ad absurdum*. One principle is ridden to death. That principle is the supremacy and all-sufficiency of reason. As a true prophet of the era, Godwin makes a clean sweep of all tradition. He rejects all that implicit reason which has embodied the past experience of the race in dumb, instinctive prejudices, without becoming articulate in logical demonstrations. So far his affinities are distinctly French, and, like Tom Paine, he represents the English reaction of the French movement. But it is plain that he has sat at the feet of other teachers. He ranks Hume with ''the most illustrious and venerable of men'' for his logical profoundness; and it is chiefly from Hume that he borrows his philosophical armoury. The influence of the great sceptic is evident throughout the book. Following Hume, he rejects the social contract and the *à priori* doctrine of the rights of man, popular with the school of Rousseau. He borrows Hume's arguments against freewill, though perhaps not thoroughly understanding them, and accepts Hume's

utilitarianism and his admission of the unselfish impulses. Godwin's philosophy, in short, is derived from Berkeley and Hume; his sentiment from the revolutionary doctrines then triumphant in France; but he gives a turn of his own to the adopted materials. The main outlines of his curious system may be briefly indicated.

All the revolutionary theories, and Godwin's among them, start from the assumption of human equality. Man, in their dialects, means the colourless unit which remains when abstraction has been made of all the peculiarities of race, government, and religion that cause one man to differ from another. This metaphysical entity, admirably fitted to be the subject-matter of beautiful mathematical demonstrations, is then identified with the concrete animal; and it is assumed that because man, stripped of all specific qualities, must be everywhere the same, therefore men, as clothed with all those qualities, must be the same. Thus all appeals to history and experience may be summarily set aside as irrelevant, because referring to the accidents instead of the essence. But how are we to determine the qualities of human nature in the abstract? for some primitive quality must be left to afford a point of adhesion for our logic. Godwin's answer is again modelled upon Hume. Man is not only devoid of innate ideas, but almost, it would seem, of innate capacities. The mind, if there be a mind, is nothing but a series of thoughts and sensations, which may or may not inhere in some hypothetical substratum. Hence the person is entirely built up of the various ideas which have somehow cohered in what may or may not be a mind. We begin life without innate principles or instincts, and though some differences of animal structure must be admitted, they are comparatively trifling. ''It is the impression that makes the man, and compared with the empire of impression the mere differences of animal structure are inexpressibly unimportant and powerless.'' Large brains are made by many thoughts, not thoughts by the brain. It is needless to ask whether this doctrine be legitimately derived from Hume, or should not lead to a self-destructive scepticism. Godwin infers from it the indefinite modifiability of every human being. The embryo man is so nearly a zero that everything which makes the complete adult is due to the accumulation of ideas poured in since his birth. When the process takes place legitimately it is called reason. When illegitimately, we have the various forms of error which produce vice in morality, tyranny in politics, and inequality in society. We must naturally conquer error. The will is entirely determined by opinion, if the will be anything but opinion; and therefore truth is omnipotent. You have nothing to do but to exhibit to a man adequately the reasons for right conduct, and he will inevitably adopt it. The passions, even those which have been regarded as strongest, may be easily conquered, if only their nature is clearly exhibited. Man, therefore, is ''perfectible, or, in other words, susceptible of perpetual improvement.''

The morality founded upon this doctrine is utilitarian; but not in the ordinary sense. The weak side of the old utilitarianism was the necessary imperfection of its appeal to experience. In framing a calculus of human happiness it started from the individual, instead of the social, point of view. It tried, that is, to reckon the consequences of an action, without taking into account the history of the social organism which can alone explain its moral development. Godwin shares this weakness. But most utilitarians started also with the first principle that a man's own happiness could be the only end of his actions. Their doctrine was, therefore, identified with the doctrine of pure selfishness, whether backed or not by some reference to supernatural sanctions. The opposite school, which sought to discover the moral law in pure reason, endeavoured to dispense with any empirical test. Morality must have no reference to happiness, to save it from degenerating into mere prudence. Godwin borrows from both sides. He is an intellectual utilitarian. Morality, as he reiterates, is nothing but a calculation of consequences. It is a kind of moral arithmetic. That action is best which produces the greatest sum of happiness. Vice is a wrong calculation, and virtue a right calculation of consequences. (pp. 451-52)

Thus interpreted, utilitarianism seems to be fairly obnoxious to one of the alternative accusations generally levelled against it. It does not sanction selfishness, but it prescribes an impossible standard of heroism. I am to act as an angelic spectator, freed from all the ties and prejudices of my condition and animated only by an impartial desire for the happiness of all men, would wish me to act. Every man "is bound to consider himself a debtor in all his faculties, his opportunities, and his industry to the general welfare. This is a debt which must always be paying, never discharged." The least deviation from the path which leads to the greatest happiness of the species is a crime. Every man "should feel himself obliged to scruple" (qy. not to scruple?) "the laying out his entire strength and forfeiting his life upon any single instance of public exertion." This is in fact the creditor and debtor theory of Calvinism, translated into philosophy. When we have done all, we are unprofitable servants.

Man, then, is not merely a reasonable being, but is, so to speak, created by reason. He is hardly even the sheet of white paper, on which experience is to write its arguments. His very tissue is itself woven out of argument. Since good arguments naturally prevail over bad ones, man, could a hearing for the truth be secured, might be actually constructed of right reason. Reason should be the sole judge of truth; the sufficient sanction of morality; the sole agent in regenerating society. For somehow things have gone terribly wrong, and though man as he might be has indefinite capacities for wisdom and virtue, man as he is has been most accurately painted by Swift. He is a Yahoo, and is to be made into an angel. It has come to pass, as a matter of fact, that society is bound together by instincts, rather than by reasoned convictions. A modern utilitarian might appeal to experience as showing the paramount importance of those instincts. But with Godwin, who reasons from the nature of man considered as a colourless unit, provided only with a capacity for reason and for happiness, such an appeal is impossible. An instinct is not reason, and therefore must lead to superstition instead of science. . . . Reason, which starts from assuming the equality of mankind, must condemn monarchy and aristocracy, which imply some natural inequality. Therefore, as Godwin says, "it must be laid down as a first principle that monarchy is an imposture." But this is a trifle. "Government is nothing but regulated force;" but force is not argument, therefore all government is wrong. "That any man or body of men should impose their sense upon persons of a different opinion, is, absolutely speaking, wrong, and in all cases deeply to be regretted;" though in some cases the evil, essential to government, must be endured. The cases, however, on Godwin's showing, would be few. Association of any kind is bad, for even voluntary associations tend to suppress the free play of individual sentiment.

This simple logic makes a clean sweep of all political institutions. In an ideal country the constitution would consist of two articles; the first dividing it into equal electoral districts; the second prescribing means of electing a national assembly,

"not to say that the latter of these articles may very probably be dispensed with." Hence, he thinks, would speedily follow the breaking up of the empire into a confederacy of small republics, and another "sufficiently memorable" consequence—"the gradual extinction of law." Even criminal law, as he argues at length, is a blunder. The gallows is most illogical. It appeals to fear instead of reason. (pp. 453-54)

The good simple Godwin! After this it is a trifle to observe that he abolishes monarchy, aristocracy, churches, armies, laws, associations, inequality of property, and marriage. All promises are, in some degree, evil; for to promise is to limit in some degree the future exercise of my reason. The unalterable promise made in marriage is specially objectionable; and Godwin observes with his usual calmness that "the abolition of the present system of marriage appears to involve no evil." It is, he says, an important question whether in a reasonable state of society, the rule would be promiscuous intercourse, or an adherence of particular pairs, so long as they mutually agreed. He thinks the latter alternative the most probable, because "it is the nature of the human mind to persist for a certain length of time in its opinion or choice." Thus society is finally pulverized and reduced to a mere agglomeration of independent atoms combining and separating according to chance or the dictates of pure reason. This result itself is happily to be brought about, not by violence, but by the diffusion of sound reason. Modern worshippers of Individualism may seem to be feeble plagiarists from Godwin.

The result of applying Godwin's principles is of course to be the advent of the millennium. Everybody is to be good and happy. The labours of every man for half-an-hour a day will supply the wants of all men. The abolition of law will lead to the disappearance of crime. (p. 455)

It is one of his doctrines that a man should always be ready to revise his opinions, for how else can he be devoted to reason? and he availed himself liberally of the privilege. . . . Both volumes . . . [of *Political Justice*] contain much interesting writing. They have Godwin's characteristic merits. The style is rather too smooth, and Godwin is given to terribly trite classical illustrations after the old-fashioned model; but the style, if over smooth, is lucid, and the appropriate exponent of a mind always calm, candid, and in earnest. He argues fairly and thoughtfully; and even when he indulges in commonplaces, as, to say the truth, he indulges pretty freely, his evident conviction of their importance redeems them from contempt. The most pleasing part, to my taste at least, is that which deals with education. Godwin's sympathy with youth is always amiable, and in education we are still most in need of his favourite doctrine. The old brutal theories, which treat the infant mind as a mere receptacle into which ideas are to be crammed by main stress of birch and discipline, whether it be or be not capable of assimilating them, is not so rampant now as then; but it has left behind it some awkward legacies in various forms of scholastic pedantry. Godwin urges very forcibly that the teacher should aim at stimulating the desire for knowledge instead of injecting knowledge ready made; and should try to turn out youths of five-and-twenty with teachable minds, not with minds ready to teach the universe. A hint or two of this kind might be useful at our universities. It can hardly be said, however, that Godwin's essays have much permanent literary value. They have almost as little of Hazlitt's vigour as of Lamb's humour. (pp. 457-58)

Godwin's two successful novels, *Caleb Williams* and *St. Leon*, are of more interest than the *Essays*. They seem both to be connected with the speculations of the *Political Justice*. *Caleb Williams* was intended, as the original preface declared, to give a "general review of the modes of domestic and unrecorded despotism by which man becomes the destroyer of man" [see excerpt by Godwin dated 1794]. Godwin had himself explained sensibly enough, though with some queer illustrations, the obvious objection to the hybrid genus of pamphlet novels. Homer, he thinks, meant the *Iliad* as an "example of the fatal consequences of discord among political allies." In practice it has enhanced "the false lustre of military achievements." Whatever Homer meant, the efficient moral of a story is apt to differ from that intended by the author. In fact, the logical objection is as strong as the artistic. A novel can show at most what would happen if the novelist were in the place of Providence. From *Caleb Williams* it would be difficult to draw any decided inference. Falkland, the refined hero, is supposed to be a victim to the absurd superstitions of honour. This induces him, first, to murder a ruffian who has grossly insulted him; then to allow two innocent men to be hanged for the crime; and finally to carry out, for many years, a relentless persecution of poor Caleb Williams, who has divined his secret. The most obvious moral is that you ought not to have half a conscience. If Falkland had been thoroughly virtuous, he would not have committed murder; if thoroughly vicious, he would not have been tortured to death by remorse. But fortunately this childish design of enforcing a political theory did not spoil Godwin's story. The situation is impressive, and, in spite of many clumsy details, is impressively represented. The spectacle of a man of delicate sense of honour writhing under the dread of detection, and opposed by an incarnation of vulgar curiosity, moves us to forget the superfluous moral. (pp. 458-59)

Godwin has no ... mechanical skill, and little of what we should call poetical imagination. His characters do not live, and are not dexterously picked out. A love story which is intruded is commonplace and rather coarse. A rambling account of a den of thieves suggests recollections of *Gil Blas*. It is meant to be politically instructive, and is tiresome and irrelevant; and yet the story lays hold of us. The main reason is obvious. The author may not have mastered the story, but the story has mastered him. He is possessed and dominated by his characters. Though he is neither a Fielding nor a Scott, he interests us as he would have interested us by describing a real set of adventures of similar character. In the hands of a more powerful writer, Falkland and his victim might have been more alive; but few writers could have communicated to us more vividly the strong fascination by which Godwin watches the creatures of his fancy. His straightforward sincerity and the genuine interest of a moralist in the working out of an ethical problem are at the bottom of Godwin's success.

St. Leon is an inferior work. Here, too, indeed, there is a striking situation, possibly suggested by Godwin's speculations on human immortality. A ruined noble has retired to a quiet retreat to enjoy domestic happiness. He hospitably receives an old man, persecuted, broken down, and anxious to die, who slowly intimates that he is the possessor of the secret of immortality and of the philosopher's stone. St. Leon may only have it on condition of revealing it to no one. It has been a curse to its proprietor, who has learnt the folly of trying to "vary from the kindly ways of man." St. Leon's temptation, his unwillingness to possess a secret which will separate him from his family gradually yielding to the desire of boundless wealth and life, is strikingly set forth. Here Godwin has to deal with a problem to his taste; and he writes with a power reminding us of *Caleb Williams*. Enough is done to suggest

that the story might be impressive in other hands. . . . But Godwin makes the interest turn almost exclusively upon the difficulty felt by St. Leon in accounting for his sudden wealth. That is a difficulty which might surely have been surmounted by a man of talent with a possible eternity in front of him. The story becomes a rather commonplace romance, devoted in great part to an attack upon the Inquisition, and now barely readable. (pp. 459-61)

[Godwin's] creed deserves a word of notice, if only as greatly influencing and probably identical with the creed of Shelley. Godwin was called an Atheist, and, in a sense, may have deserved the name. We find his nephew, Charles Clairmont, lamenting pathetically that "the idea of God and a future state is so deeply rooted" in him that he fears that he will "never be able to get over it." Conscientious perseverance may do much in such matters. When, however, another disciple of Godwin boasts of having made a convert to Atheism, Godwin rebukes him, and calls his "zeal of proselytism" in such a cause unnatural. Godwin explains that he does not believe in an "intellectual God, a God made after the image of man," but that he thinks a man wrong who is without a sense of religion. From other passages it seems that Godwin was in a state of mind common enough, though not so commonly avowed. He distinctly disbelieves in the God of Christianity, and regards him as not only a fiction, but an immoral fiction. He does not "believe in God" as those words would be understood by a Deist, or even by a Pantheist. His belief, if it is to be called a belief, is too vague to be fixed in a formula. It vanishes when looked at directly. But he feels deeply the importance of those vague emotions of awful reverence which are prompted by a calm contemplation of the mysteries and infinities of the surrounding universe, and is anxious to preserve without attempting to explain or justify them. In later years he seems to have become more tolerant to the established order, and less anxious to upset existing beliefs. Yet the legacy of essays called by him *Christianity Unveiled*, after the familiar title of Holbach's essay, was meant as a destructive attack upon the popular creed, and it is significant of the change of feeling that a man so genuinely convinced of the supreme importance of a candid utterance of all opinions, did not think it a duty to fire the mine in his lifetime. (p. 461)

> Leslie Stephen, "William Godwin," in The Fortnightly Review, *Vol. XXVI, No. 118, October 1, 1876, pp. 444-61.*

LESLIE STEPHEN (essay date 1902)

[*Here, Stephen surveys Godwin's career and deems the author a "superlative bore" despite his numerous literary and philosophical accomplishments. This essay first appeared in the* National Review *in February 1902. For additional commentary by Stephen, see excerpt dated 1876.*]

Hazlitt has recorded a conversation in which he and his friends discussed an interesting problem: If you were able to summon from the dead any of the great men of old, whom would you select for an interview? . . . One thing, I fancy, is quite clear: Nobody would ask for an hour of William Godwin. His most obvious qualities, a remorseless "ergotism," squeezing the last drops out of an argument; a frigid dogmatism, not redeemed by the fervour which half excuses fanaticism; and a singular incapacity for even suspecting the humorous or fanciful aspects of life, are qualities which go far to make the superlative bore. They may be harmless or even advantageous in a man who wishes to compose a political Euclid, but that kind of author is not likely to be attractive at a supper-party, and certainly not likely to succeed in other branches of literary work. Yet it is odd that, without too much violence to language, we might describe Godwin as one of the most versatile authors of his time. Though a dealer in the most abstract speculations, he became an industrious Dryasdust, raking in the obscurest assortments of waste paper. In spite of his priggishness, he was a writer of popular books for children, and, without the smallest claims to poetic imagination, he was the author of one tragedy which escaped failure. A more remarkable fact, however, was his success as a novelist. He wrote in a comparatively barren period. The generation which had been impressed by the novels of Richardson, Fielding, Smollett, Sterne, and Goldsmith had passed away, and the novel of the nineteenth century had not yet come to life in Miss Austen and Scott. The novels which were produced in the interval, and can still be read by any one except conscientious professors of English literature, may be counted on the fingers—perhaps of one hand. Godwin's *Caleb Williams* is one of the few. It can be read without the pressure of a sense of duty. It has lived—though in comparative obscurity—for over a century, and high authorities tell us that vitality prolonged for that period raises a presumption that a book deserves the title of classic. Three generations must have accepted it, and as each naturally condemns the taste of the old fogies, its predecessors, the agreement implies some permanent attractiveness. There has been time for a reaction and a re-reaction. Living novelists, if one may judge from their practice, will say that *Caleb Williams* offends against all manner of sound canons of criticism. I am a little sceptical as to all such canons, and rather infer that a book which can survive in spite of such incompatibility must have had some of the seeds of life. Few writers, I fear, can be confident that their works will interest their great-great-grandchildren; and only such happy persons should be quite ready to throw the first stone. (pp. 111-13)

[Godwin] reminds us of a familiar difficulty which besets writers of fiction. When they introduce a bore for the sake of the comic effect of his tediousness, the tediousness is very apt to tire the reader. . . . [Godwin] was a bore by nature. Everybody, I hold, is a bore to some people, but Godwin was one of the unlucky persons capable of boring all round. He can never be amusing taken by himself, and we have to make the effort of seeing him among his fellow-actors before we catch any glimpse of the comedy in which he played a part. (p. 114)

Godwin, in any case, might well pass for a great philosopher. He dealt in what is called "inexorable logic." That is to say, that whenever he ran his head against a lamp-post, he calmly asserted that it did not exist. If the proper way of making a science of politics be to ignore all appeals to experience, his method was irreproachable. That happened to be precisely the opinion of a good many people at the time, and Godwin's Utopia [as presented in *Political Justice*], though liable to collapse at the first touch of common-sense, appeared to enthusiasts to be solid because self-consistent. Moreover, if we consider the merits of the exposition, apart from the validity of the theory expounded, it showed remarkable literary power. The style is simple and solid; the argument is well arranged; and, in short, the logical architecture leaves nothing to be desired if we will allow the architect to use for his material what is really mere moonshine. Nor can it be denied that he is appealing to the sense of justice and humanity of his readers; and that, if he is not impassioned, there is a general glow of benevolent sentiment which commended him to the more gen-

erous impulses of the revolutionary period. I have only to say, however, that it is easy to understand that Godwin would act the part of philosopher to perfection. . . . In Godwin's days, Newnham and Girton were not even conceivable; and a philosopher might hope to be taken seriously by a circle of feminine admirers. They could revere a man, not though, but because, he was a bore. Incapacity for lighter talk proved that his thoughts were absorbed in serious topics, and the absence of romance showed that in him the emotions were under the sway of reason. (pp. 121-22)

Posterity has long ceased to hanker after *Mandeville*. I, at least, have tried in vain to discover the slightest justification for Shelley's enthusiasm [see excerpts dated 1817]. Can we discover any grounds for such enthusiasm in Godwin's masterpiece? *Caleb Williams* was published when Godwin's fame was at its zenith—just before the trial of his friends. A preface, announcing its purpose, was suppressed for the time by the fears of his publisher [see excerpt dated 1794]. "It is now known to philosophers," says this document (philosophers had just been enlightened by *Political Justice*), "that the spirit and character of government intrude into every rank of life." The novel was to illustrate this truth, and to exhibit "the modes of domestic and unrecorded despotism by which man becomes the destroyer of man." That is to say, apparently, it is to show how the wicked aristocrat carries into private life the execrable principles of kings and ministers. *Caleb Williams* was, like *Uncle Tom's Cabin*, to rouse men to a sense of the evils of slavery. The reader, unassisted by the preface, would scarcely perceive this doctrine between the lines. Falkland, the hero, is a model country gentleman; not only a benevolent and public-spirited landlord, but a man of taste and a poet. Like his predecessor, Sir Charles Grandison, he shows his high qualities under the most delicate circumstances. (pp. 130-31)

[The book] suggests the question, What has become of the moral? How about the wickedness of government? The answer must be that it has passed out of sight. Something, indeed, is made of the social abuses of the time: there is a prison of the old pattern, and an innocent man who dies in it because he is too poor to pay for legal assistance; and an impossible band of robbers—imported apparently from the region described by Schiller—whose captain argues philosophically as to the rights of property with Williams. But such matters only supply accessories. Falkland, the centre of interest, is not the typical oppressor of the poor; and, whenever he is not murdering or concealing a murder, uses his influence for the best possible purposes. His mind has been poisoned, we are told, by the "idle and groundless romances of chivalry." He suffers from Don Quixote's complaint, but has managed to mislearn his lesson. The Don would certainly have felt bound to fight instead of meanly assassinating. Falkland is a perverse monomaniac, who will guard his reputation even by deserving infamy. That, no doubt, might suggest a very interesting motive. The psychology of hypocrisy—of the transition by which the sense of honour is replaced by a desire for being honoured—might be embodied in a lifelike hero, as it is common enough in real life. With Godwin, Falkland becomes a heap of contradictory qualities. Monomaniacs are rather in favour now, and a modern novelist would, perhaps, make Falkland into an illustration of heredity or the general corruption of society. But he is so obviously unreal, and all the incidents so frankly impossible, that we scarcely feel even the interest excited by a caricature of conceivable wickedness. Why, then, are we interested? In the first place, because mysterious crimes are always interesting. The interest may be wrong, but it is natural. But, in the next place, given the situation and shutting our eyes to impossibilities, Godwin shows the kind of power manifested by the *Political Justice*. The story is developed with admirable order and lucidity—if the machinery will not bear inspection we need not inspect—and the agony is slowly and steadily piled up till the catastrophe in which the victim suddenly changes places with the oppressor. . . . Godwin's hero does not pray—it would be against his principles—he invokes the force of reason; but the result is the same, and the gradual working up of the catastrophe, the slow and steady evolution of the diabolical agency, has a fascinating power. We catch something of the writer's own profound interest in the story, and admire at least the persistence and ingenuity (perverse as its means) with which variations are performed upon the theme which is always in view. Godwin, of course, had not a trace of the peculiar skill exemplified in *Pride and Prejudice,* where every incident is both perfectly natural and conducive to the effect. Yet his incidents are so well combined that the book has the same sort of unity and co-ordination, and even the formality of the style is congenial to his own ideals. (pp. 135-37)

Caleb Williams might be compared with Mrs. Clive's very striking Paul Ferroll. Ferroll combines the murderer and the polished gentleman far more intelligibly than Falkland, and refuses to let an innocent person suffer in his place. Godwin's book has, however, a certain advantage from the fervour due to his intended moral. The moral, it is true, eludes him. It reminds one of Lowell's description of an orator who tries in vain to get his subject properly laid down. He makes desperate attempts, wanders off in many directions, and in his last contortion "sees his subjick a-nosin' round arter him ag'in." Still, the pursuit of a subject gives a certain unction to oratory, and in the same kind of perverted and anomalous fashion, Godwin's moral gives a sort of momentum and diffused energy to his mass of incongruities.

Godwin's next novel, *St. Leon,* is, I suppose, the last—in spite of Shelley—which anybody has read in modern times, and marks a stage in his development. It appeared in 1799, and shows that he had learned something from his brief married life. He announces in the preface that he has now learned that there is really some good in the ''private affections'' [see excerpt dated 1799]. He adds calmly that this opinion is perfectly consistent with the rest of his doctrines—though to most readers the alteration required in them seems to be considerable. Anyhow, his new doctrine again provided him with a really striking situation. St. Leon is a French nobleman of the seventeenth century, though, it need hardly be said, Godwin takes very little trouble to give any genuine picture of the time. . . . The purpose is to show how miserable a man would become when his exemption from mortality made him incapable of sympathy with his ephemeral companions. That is the kind of text which might have been treated effectively in the old moral tale of the Candide variety. Godwin not only expands it into a long quasi-historical novel, with all manner of impossible adventures and coincidences, but contrives to miss the moral. The point of the situation in his version comes to be the difficulty which St. Leon finds in accounting for his sudden accession to boundless wealth. He has a perfect wife, supposed to be meant for a portrait of Mary Wollstonecraft, but the poor lady is tormented by a curiosity as keen as that of Caleb Williams. . . . Godwin had got further from realities than he was in *Caleb Williams,* and makes his characters indulge in a stilted declamation which he appears to have meant for passion. (pp. 139-42)

Godwin, by the time of *St. Leon,* was forcing his vein under pressure of embarrassment, and the usual result followed. In *Caleb Williams* it was by a kind of good luck that his philosophy provided him with an effective situation, and though it did not in the least prove his moral, and though characters and incidents are simply preposterous, gave a certain power to his elbow. . . . *Caleb Williams* is a kind of literary curiosity—a monstrous hybrid between different species—which gains its interest by a fortunate confusion. But if any one should be prompted to push his study into other novels, I fear that he is destined to disappointment. (p. 143)

> *Leslie Stephen, ''William Godwin's Novels,'' in his* Studies of a Biographer, Vol. III, *G. P. Putnam's Sons, 1907, pp. 111-43.*

GEORGE McLEAN HARPER (essay date 1912)

[*Harper discusses Godwin's philosophy as outlined in* Political Justice *and his reputation as a philosopher.*]

The share of Godwin's *Political Justice* in the intellectual movement of the nineteenth century was not at all considerable, if we set aside its influence on Wordsworth and Shelley and the Utilitarian school of philosophy. No other fact more strikingly illustrates the reactionary character of political theory in that century. (pp. 645-46)

Godwin has this . . . in common with Locke, that his philosophy is integral. It is rigorously deduced from a few chief principles. Thus its ethics cannot be held separately from its metaphysics, nor can its politics be detached from its psychology. The largest and the soundest parts of the *Enquiry Concerning Political Justice* are devoted to ethical and political considerations, which can, indeed, hardly be distinguished from one another, as it is his dearest purpose to show they should not be. Godwin insists that his conclusions in these departments of practical conduct depend on his doctrines of knowledge and will. He is a determinist, and the only weak element of his book is his insufficient argument for necessity. The many pleas in favor of free will which have suggested themselves to philosophers, as well as to humbler thinkers, he almost wholly fails to take into account.

Equally dogmatic, though not so audacious, because more widely shared, is his belief that experience is the source of all knowledge. 'Nothing can be more incontrovertible,' he asserts, 'than that we do not bring preëstablished ideas into the world with us.'

Justice, he contends, is the whole duty of man. And it seems that his criterion of justice is the greatest good of the greatest number; for he says, 'Utility, as it regards percipient beings, is the only basis of moral and political truth.' Reason is the only organ whereby men can discover what is just. 'To a rational being, there can,' he says, 'be but one rule of conduct, justice, and one mode of ascertaining that rule, the exercise of his understanding.' Intuition, and every form of mystical illumination, together with all authority, whether of numbers, antiquity, institutions, or 'inspired words,' are calmly set aside. Morality is a matter of knowledge: 'The most essential part of virtue consists in the incessantly seeking to inform ourselves more accurately upon the subject of utility and right.'

Godwin affirms these principles unhesitatingly, and as if they must of course be admitted by every thinking person to whom they are stated separately, each in its own strength. But he himself supplies, in his practical illustrations, difficulties which might not have occurred to a less acute mind. And it was upon these examples that his opponents seized. For instance, since man is a moral being and all his actions are either just or unjust, he has no rights, that is, no moral options, but only duties. And therefore there is no place for deeds of gratitude, for pardon, for partiality to friends or kindred, for charity, for vindictive punishment. Moreover, a promise has no sanctity, and an oath is an abomination; because 'an individual surrenders the best attribute of man the moment he resolves to adhere to certain fixed principles for reasons not now present to his mind, but which formerly were.' Marriage, accordingly, falls under his disapproval, in so far as it is a relation maintained solely in virtue of a promise. (pp. 646-47)

Some of these principles are to be found distinctly echoed— sometimes approved and sometimes painfully questioned, but certainly echoed—in Wordsworth's tragedy, *The Borderers;* and the slightly earlier poem, ''Guilt and Sorrow,'' indicates that he was imbued with Godwin's doctrine that 'under the system of necessity, the ideas of guilt, crime, desert, and accountableness have no place.' Godwin declares that since the will is not free, 'the assassin cannot help the murder he commits any more than the dagger.' Punishment, therefore, should be limited to restraining the criminal from repeating his act of injustice.

It is evident that a society holding such views must reject all but the barest essentials of government, must be reduced to the most extreme individualism. Accordingly we find Godwin insisting that 'government is an evil, an usurpation upon the private judgment and individual conscience of mankind.' . . . (p. 647)

To say that Godwin was lacking in historical feeling is putting the case too negatively. It is more correct to say that he chose not to be hampered by history. He regarded the present with keen perceptive powers and looked to the future. The absence of a background in his picture of human destiny is not due to shallowness of literary culture, but to a deliberate theory. He was one of the last of the philosophers of the Enlightenment in the eighteenth century. And his method, as regards the use of history, is precisely the method of that whole great movement.

A peculiarity of his own, however, is that he relies altogether upon his individual judgment, and not at all upon the collective judgment of his fellow men, which he mistrusts because it has been institutionally organized and thus clogged with the weight of selfish advantages. And even in his own case, he trusts, or professes to trust, only his perceptive and logical powers, and not at all his affections. He has, however, by no means succeeded in shutting out every emotional influence. To take him at his word in this respect is to do him an injustice. His principles are not cold-drawn. There is no fire more intense than the flame of pure intelligence. It is not conceivable that, without the tremor of inward burning, a man possessed, as Godwin was, with a sense of responsibility could write: 'The doctrine of the injustice of accumulated property has been the foundation of all religious morality.' The philosophy of the Enlightenment may well have been too difficult, too sheer, for minds accustomed to beaten tracks in the broad vales of thought, but it was not wanting in emotional splendor. Right or wrong, the man who could affirm that 'there must in the nature of things be one best form of government,' because 'the points in which human beings resemble are infinitely more considerable than those in which they differ,' was moved by a deep moral feeling, as well as by the perception of truths from which most men shrink. (pp. 648-49)

Godwinism soon fell into deep and undeserved disrepute. This was not due wholly to its peculiar features, some of which were beyond the comprehension of pragmatical minds, and others objectionable on the very grounds of general utility to which Godwin sought to refer his thinking. It was due chiefly to the inherent unattractiveness of the whole philosophy of the Enlightenment, and to the inauspicious character of the times. Pure rationalism can, perhaps, never be expected to win the favor of more than a small minority, even among reflective men. Its voice is in no age altogether silent, but the echoes nearly always come back mingled with alien notes, the note of classicism, the note of transcendentalism, the note of romanticism. (p. 649)

George McLean Harper, ''Rousseau, Godwin, and Wordsworth,'' in The Atlantic Monthly, *Vol. CIX, May, 1912, pp. 639-50.*

B. SPRAGUE ALLEN (essay date 1918)

[*Interpreting* St. Leon *and* Fleetwood *as sentimental works that indicate Godwin's belief in the joys of domesticity and love, Allen discusses the relationship in the two novels between the individual and society.*]

[In] his novels Godwin departed far from the rationalistic spirit of *Political Justice.* He has such an immoderate desire for emotion for its own sake, that, like many other sentimentalists, he makes no attempt to proportion the intensity of feeling to the importance of the object that excites it. The net result is extravagance, strained, ineffectual pathos, and frequently the defiance of common sense.

Two of Godwin's novels, *St. Leon* and *Fleetwood,* are deserving, I believe, of special treatment. . . . Godwin, after his marriage with Mary Wollstonecraft and in the interval between the publication of *Caleb Williams* and *St. Leon,* came to see the error of his inflexible statement that, under the guidance of his reason and without regard for the disquieting emotions of gratitude, patriotism, and love of kin, the individual is always under obligation to regulate his actions with a view to their ultimate utility to society, as it is thus only that he can achieve the ideal of justice and philanthropy. Godwin now admits the importance of feeling as a motive for conduct; instead of deprecating its influence, he grants its ethical justification, and in his Preface to *St. Leon* expresses the conviction that the cultivation of family affections is absolutely indispensable to the complete development of the individual, and, instead of checking, fosters wider social sympathy [see excerpt dated 1799]. Whether or not ''the culture of the heart'' invalidates the rationalistic theories of *Political Justice* is not the question here, and, at all events, it is a conclusion which Godwin himself denies. (pp. 16-17)

[Underneath] the forbidding exterior of *Political Justice* and more unmistakably in *Caleb Williams,* there flowed a current of sentimentalism, and Godwin's later attitude toward the tender emotions is probably not so much a complete change of front as a consistent outgrowth of existent tendencies. The upshot is that in *St. Leon* and in all his subsequent novels this new faith in domestic affection and his doctrine of love reinforce one another and gradually merge together into a sentimental gospel of love. (pp. 17-18)

In *St. Leon* Godwin shows the necessity of revising the ideals dominating the life of the individual. His method is to start his hero out in life under the guidance of false ideals, to subject him to a varied and painful experience in which his ideals, being tested, prove delusions, and, finally, to lead him by degrees to the perception of essential ethical values. St. Leon is an aristocrat, cherishing the typically false notions that wealth, display, and princely luxury, are the only means to happiness. Reduced in circumstances, he lives in retirement with his noble wife and four children what is really an idyllic existence, but he scarcely appreciates his blessings. When he learns from a stranger the secret of immortality and the philosopher's stone, all his sleeping ambitions burst into life. His imagination is inflamed by the hope of realizing splendid dreams of earthly glory and of restoring his wife and children to the position in society which was theirs by birth. With impressive, even if extravagant irony, Godwin exposes the fallacy of St. Leon's hope. His wealth increases his wants, and makes him dissatisfied with his peaceful life; and his inability to explain satisfactorily the source of his wealth estranges him from his son, breaks the heart of his wife, and entails unutterable misery upon himself.

In the terms of revolutionary philosophy what is the significance of *St. Leon*? In unmasking the hollowness of wealth, luxury, and worldly ambition Godwin meant to illuminate as truths the principle of human brotherhood and the joy and wisdom of a simple life. To these ideals St. Leon had, at first, been indifferent, but when it was too late, he realized their supreme value. The man who does not crave for the sympathy of his fellows, is abnormal, because, as Godwin insists, love is not an occasional or incidental need of man's nature, but a fundamental requirement of his soul. It quickens and, in fact, conditions the development of his whole spiritual being. Indeed, the possibilities of emotional life can be realized only in social communication; pleasurable feelings are intensified by the responsive joy of our fellows, and painful feelings are assuaged only by the sympathy of others. So the demands of his inmost being weave about the individual a network of a thousand ties which bind him inevitably and for his own good to the society in which he lives. Domestic affection is no longer selfish in its tendency and at variance with the principles of absolute morality, as Godwin had asserted in *Political Justice,* but it is a noble manifestation of a deeply rooted instinct. No wonder St. Leon, contemplating his family, cries, "What are gold and jewels and precious utensils? Mere dross and dirt. The human face and the human heart, reciprocations of kindness and love, and all the nameless sympathies of our nature, these are the only objects worth being attached to." Moreover, this affection does not blight the growth of social sympathy; rather, indeed, do the tender duties of the family circle awaken into activity a desire to help others not akin to us.

The love of wife and children does not, however, satisfy man's need for sympathy, Godwin assures us. The dependence of the individual upon society is portrayed with poignant force in St. Leon's awful realization that his superhuman powers have blasted a chasm between him and the whole human race. He perceives with anguish that, by reason of his exemption from earthly cares, his hopes and fears, joys and sorrows, all will be of another order, such as no mortal can comprehend. The very gift of immortality seems a curse, and he shrinks with loathing from the contemplation of the future to which he is doomed. It will be his cruel destiny to see the coming and going of successive generations of men, and love for him will be a futile passion because every mortal must inevitably be torn from him by death. "I can no longer cheat my fancy; I know that I am alone. The creature does not exist with whom I have any common language, or any genuine sympathy. Society is a bitter

and galling mockery to my heart; it only shows in more glaring colors my desolate condition." The philosophers of the "selfish theory" had claimed that man sought social intercourse not out of love of his kind, but merely for the sake of the personal material advantages which such an intercourse afforded. Godwin comes to the rescue of human nature, and shows that St. Leon, placed by his peculiar powers beyond all need of mortal assistance, craves, nevertheless, the society of men.

The sentimental literature of the day glorified charity. . . . But the philanthropic schemes of St. Leon outstrip them all. Filled with an ambition to achieve something commensurate with his superhuman powers, he journeys to Hungary, and, assuming the function of a god, undertakes to relieve the whole nation from the misery into which it has been plunged by the war. (pp. 18-21)

Over against St. Leon, the lover of his species, Godwin sets the Titanic misanthrope, Bethlem Gabor. Like Karl Moor of Schiller's *Robbers,* he is the embodiment of tremendous energy, his passions have superhuman violence, and in the blindness of egoism he would annihilate the whole human race for a personal wrong. But here a very definite distinction must be drawn between Godwin's attitude toward misanthropy and that of many other writers of the romantic period. The active misanthropy of Karl Moor as well as the contempt for mankind which is implied in the *Weltschmerz* of such characters as Saint-Preux and Werther, is portrayed as an expression of cynicism that is justified by the manners and insipidity of the average man; Rousseau, Goethe, and Schiller are, in reality, voicing their own discontent. Godwin, however, did not take misanthropy as his theme because he had lost faith in human nature. Far from it. To cherish bitter feelings toward mankind, he believes, is no assurance of superiority of soul, but a spiritual misfortune, cutting off the individual from all the ennobling advantages of social intercourse. The hatred of mankind is not sanctioned because evil may exist in human nature; in truth, misanthropy betokens a lamentable blindness to the excellence that is the possession of every man, woman, and child. In its origin Godwin regards misanthropy as a perversion of the inborn human craving for love. (pp. 21-2)

Had he possessed the lyrical power of Rousseau, Godwin's exaltation of [the] gospel of love would remind us more often of Jean-Jacques. At any rate, he floods his book with feeling. This excessive emotionalism has been justly struck at by the anonymous parodist of *St. Leon,* who, after burlesquing one of Godwin's domestic scenes, bursts out rapturously, "It was indeed a delicious sight, and I think I have well described it. I am but a bad hand at sublime description, but at the tender, pathetic, *homely scene,* I do not know my equal." From our point of view this ridicule seems well deserved, but the fact remains, to judge from the comments of Godwin's contemporaries, that *St. Leon* deeply impressed many of its readers. We may be assured it appealed to a host of Rousseauists who had been indifferent to the austere statement of the doctrine of benevolence in *Political Justice.* It is a book completely of its time, born of glowing optimism, and valuable as a revelation of what a revolutionary idealist thought of human nature. In its delineation of the tragedy of the individual cut off from opportunity to satisfy the longing of his being for companionship, it is in harmony with the spirit of the "Ancient Mariner" and *Frankenstein.* (pp. 22-3)

Fleetwood clarifies still further Godwin's judgment of the unhappy individual who is bound to society by no ties of sympathy, and reveals him in reaction against that particularly ignoble form of sentimentalism, the *Weltschmerz*. In so far as that is the case, the novel is interesting as Godwin's commentary on an emotional pose that many of his generation, and Byron in particular among Englishmen, regarded as distinctly "the correct thing" among fashionable swaggerers. Significantly enough, Godwin would cure this sentimental pessimism by a doctrine of optimism scarcely less sentimental in its own way.

Fleetwood is the spiritual brother of those languid epicures in feeling, Saint-Preux and Werther, Chateaubriand's René, Madame de Staël's Lord Nelvil, Sénancour's Obermann, and Lamartine's yet unborn Raphael. Nurtured among the wild Welsh mountains and in the pathetic solitude of a motherless childhood, Fleetwood has developed a most exquisite sensibility. After a period of dissipation on the continent, where he is deceived by two mistresses in turn, and after acquaintance with the insincerity of literary life and the corruption of politics, he realizes the chasm between the ideal and the actual and tastes all the bitterness of disillusionment. In his loneliness he travels for years to discover relief for his *ennui*, but all in vain. He finally arrives at the age of forty-five, hopeless of finding a true friend, contemptuous of all human interests, convinced of the insipidity of life and the spiritual emptiness of a world in which no one of his ideals comes to fruition. When we see Fleetwood in this mood, we expect that, like many another victim of impotent idealism, he will attempt to escape from hideous reality by suicide. Werther took the fatal step; Saint-Preux, René, Obermann, and Raphael contemplated it.

At this very point Godwin reacts, and reacts decisively, against the solution which most of his contemporaries would have given to Fleetwood's spiritual dilemma. He represents Fleetwood as becoming acquainted, at this crucial moment of his career, with Macneil, a disciple of Rousseau. This gentleman, who has a sublime faith in the essential goodness of humanity, quickly exposes the sophistry of Fleetwood's convictions. In protest against Fleetwood's contempt for man, Macneil assures him that almost every individual of the species is "endowed with angelic virtues," and that whenever he sees a man, he recognizes him as "something to love—not with a love of compassion, but with a love of approbation." Fleetwood's life is unnatural, because even a rapturous love of nature and of brute creation cannot satisfy man's inborn need for the society of his kind. (pp. 23-5)

What is the exact bearing of Godwin's reaction against the *Weltschmerz*? In the first place, convinced of the essential solidarity of the human race and the value of social intercourse, he rejects the notion that any individual can afford to hold himself aloof from his fellows in fancied superiority. To appreciate the importance of this protest one has only to read the literature of the romantic period to find, constantly recurring, the idea that genius is synonymous with martyrdom; to be harried by duties from which his talent should exempt him, and to be scorned by a dull, uncomprehending world is conceived as the unhappy lot of every finer spirit. In the second place, Godwin shows the utter futility of pursuing an unattainable ideal that alienates the individual from the world, and fallaciously enough, seems to relieve him of the necessity of doing what good lies in his power. The ideal is to be found in the actual; so Fleetwood discovers that in marriage he has realized the ideal of friendship for which he has sought so long. Furthermore, Godwin in this novel and elsewhere argues against sentimental passivity when he insists that it is nothing less than immoral for an individual to cherish unduly painful emotions

that will incapacitate him for useful benevolent activities. That delicacy of feeling which impairs a man's energy, is only another name for selfishness. To cure the *Weltschmerz* Godwin urges the hopeless sufferer to substitute altruistic motives for the egoistic impulses governing his life. Suicide is only a cowardly escape from every man's duty to do as much good as he can in the world. In a word, then, St. Leon wrecked his life, because he did not heed the gospel of love until it was too late; Fleetwood, after a bitter spiritual struggle, carries it into practice and enjoys the blessings which St. Leon had thrown away. Godwin should, indeed, have great credit for reacting against the peculiarly morbid form of sentimentalism that flourished more on the continent than in England, and of which the victims deserve pathological investigation no less than literary study. Without question his criticism of the pessimistic pose and his recognition of the power of social intercourse to discipline and develop character show the soundest thinking, but unfortunately his tendency to believe so well of human nature that he will not tolerate the attitude of the misanthropist, is tainted more than once by almost maudlin optimism. Curiously enough, Godwin's solution of the spiritual trouble of his age is akin to Goethe's ideal of self-renunciation; but whereas in its consummation Faust's philanthropy is purged completely of egotism, the altruism of St. Leon and Fleetwood is always associated with the delicious self-consciousness of the sentimentalist, seeking opportunities for indulging his feelings and enjoying the contemplation of his own benevolence. Godwin's doctrine of philanthropy is too deeply rooted in sentimentalism to attain to the noble dignity, the restraint, and self-forgetfulness of Goethe's ideal. (pp. 25-7)

> *B. Sprague Allen, "William Godwin as a Sentimentalist," in* PMLA, *33, n.s., Vol. XXXIII, No. XXVI, March, 1918, pp. 1-29.*

GEORGE SAINTSBURY (essay date 1920)

[*Saintsbury was an English literary historian and critic of the late nineteenth and early twentieth centuries. In the following excerpt, Saintsbury analyzes Godwin's doctrine in* Political Justice *and deems it a highly impractical form of government, created strictly on theory without any accounting for human nature. This essay was originally published in the* New World *in November 1920.*]

[*Political Justice*] is the most remarkable example extant in its own direction of what has been called the intellect left to itself, and working out consequences from certain assumed principles, without regard to experience, or expediency, or humour, or common sense. Appearing, as it did, just at the time when the practical excesses of the French Revolution had reached their highest, *Political Justice* arranged the Anarchist theory— the theory which regards all positive law, all regular institutions, all punishments, all interferences, in short, of any kind with the individual except in the way of kindness, as things utterly unjustifiable and radically bad. The antithesis between Justice and Law is at the very root of this book, and is not much less at the root of *Caleb Williams*.

Marriage, religion, monarchy, being all restraints, have to go; though Godwin is so preternaturally serious and thorough-going that he deprecates the use of force to overthrow institutions quite as strongly as the use of force to maintain them. (pp. 368-69)

[Though] very well and clearly written, . . . [*Political Justice* conducts] its demonstrations with a relentless and stolid contempt of all sense of the ridiculous on the one hand, and on the other of those appeals by rhetoric to passion, which are most formidable when addressed to popular audiences. Its effect on the unthinking was probably next to *nil;* its fallacies were seen at once by steady heads; but its influence on young and enthusiastic persons of more wits than experience was incalculable. (p. 370)

[Grave] and grotesque absurdity . . . [also] saturates Godwin's anarchism. Despite or through the varnish of amiability above-mentioned, there are germs of the worst results of Bolshevism itself. But we may find something equally amusing and suggestive in his serious proposition that "All attachments to individuals, *except in proportion to their merits,* are plainly unjust." One sees at once how extremely convenient this is, or would be, on one slight supposition—that human beings were not human beings. Attachment being a mere calculus of merits, envy, jealousy, hatred, malice and all uncharitableness would vanish at once. If my friend dropped me for another friend I should philosophically observe that the other friend's merits were no doubt superior to mine. If my wife left me in the same way, or if any young lady refused to be my wife, the same reflection would at once remove all soreness of feeling. If my father cut me off with a shilling—though indeed on Godwin's system there would be no shillings and no cutting off, with very dubious fatherhood—I should either acknowledge the paternal acuteness in perceiving my want of merit, or deplore the blindness in miscalculating my possession of it. Perhaps the following passage, which has to do with community of goods, is even funnier. Godwin was a student; and it seems to have occurred even to him that it would be rather a nuisance if another person came into his room and said: "Philosopher, I want this room to sit in and that table to work at." But his undoubting mind was never staggered long by any common-sense consideration. "Disputes," he says—and I am now quoting his very words—"would in reality be impossible. They are the offspring of a misshapen and disproportionate love of ourselves. Do you want my table? Make one for yourself; or, if I be more skilful in that respect than you, I will make one for you. Do you want it immediately? Let us compare the urgency of my wants and yours, and let justice decide." That an abstraction *can't* decide: that each disputant will be quite certain beforehand that she decides for him; and that the upshot of it will be either resort to brute force (which Godwin hated) or to that embodied Justice, to wit Law, which he perhaps hated less, but which his system compelled him to declare to be worse; that if you are perpetually to interrupt business and pleasure to discuss and compare respective claims to their implements life cannot go on for a day—these are the things which the plain man sees at once, but to which Godwin shut his eyes with that sublime, that inexpugnable, that utterly hopeless and desperately mischievous persistence which only implicit faith in theory can confer upon mankind. When a man decides, as Godwin does, that exactly half an hour's work per diem on the part of everybody will satisfy all the reasonable wants of the human race, he is beyond argument: you can only laugh at him or shut him up.

Caleb Williams—still a common enough book, not merely in libraries but in modern bookshops, ever willing to book orders—is a sort of fictitious illustration or object-lesson in the doctrines of the more abstract treatise. The hero by chance discovers the fact of a murder having been committed (under circumstances, it is true, of gross provocation) by a man of high reputation and otherwise unblemished character, and the whole story of the book, which is very ingeniously constructed, turns upon the efforts of the criminal to suppress the danger

of a revelation. Even here the indictment against society is of the most unpractical kind, and Godwin is apparently blind to the obvious retort that in his own ideal commonwealth private murder would probably be one of the most frequent of things, inasmuch as on the one hand there would be no other hope of redressing an injury, and on the other there would, on the strictest system of *Political Justice,* be no fear of punishment.

This point is of importance. It will be observed, and may be objected, that this "Bolshevism in its Cradle" lacks a good many things which are associated with the same creed, or no-creed, at the present day. There are no Soviets; there is no *special* anti-Capitalism; there is no *special* worship of the proletariat; and there *is* a special putting forward of sweet reasonableness and absence of violent methods. But then most of us in our cradles do differ considerably from our grown-up stages: even Lord Palmerston, who thought we were all "born good," certainly did not think that we all remained good. And while Godwinism was practically certain to develop all the corruptions of its maturity, that development would be as certain in some cases by reaction as in others by development proper. If Godwin did not say in so many words, *"La propriété c'est le vol,"* his own theory of temporary and readjustable property according to merit must (human nature being what human nature is) turn into Proudhon's; and it only wanted time and the Marxian miasma to spread the notion that capital is the worst form of property. (pp. 370-73)

That, as he grew older, Godwin grew in some respects wiser—not merely in the way of becoming, without the slightest regard to correlative merit, a sinecurist under Government, though he had previously held that everybody ought to work and that there ought to be no Government at all—is not surprising. The children (or indeed the parents) of Revolution generally grow wiser unless their offspring or parent devours them too soon. But he has also left very amusing letters to intending disciples who took *Political Justice* at the foot of its letter. And his last philosophical work, the *Thoughts on Man,* . . . would certainly not of itself suggest identity of authorship with his first. But this again is common, and, except to those who care only for the anecdotage of literature and history, adds nothing to the interest of *Political Justice* itself. That interest lies in the fact that the book is the first book in English, and one of the first books in any language, to advocate complete reversal, or at any rate removal, of all hitherto accepted principles of law in politics, religion, morals and everything that affects the *conduct* of men. The author's history and personality add a little to the interest of the book and supply comment, sometimes decidedly ironic, on its principles; nor is this addition, perhaps, quite accidental or uninstructive. But it is as an early gospeller of what in various modifications or developments has since been known as Anarchism, Nihilism, Communism (in the *Commune* sense), and finally Bolshevism, that Godwin most deserves attention and will best "repay perusal." (pp. 382-83)

> *George Saintsbury, "Bolshevism in Its Cradle," in his* The Collected Essays and Papers of George Saintsbury: 1875-1920, Vol. III, *E. P. Dutton & Co., 1923, pp. 365-83.*

C. H. DRIVER   (lecture date 1929-30)

[*Driver provides a detailed examination of* Political Justice, *focusing on the influences on Godwin's thought, his importance to future political movements, and the intent and consequences of his theories. Driver's comments were originally delivered as a lecture in 1929-30.*]

Political Justice is a work which holds a unique place in the history of English political theory; it is unique in doctrine and in scope. Before examining Godwin's teaching in detail it is necessary as a preliminary to stress two general features of his treatise which may help us the better to appreciate the nature of its teaching—namely, that it was written during a period of very rapid transition, wherein were mingled ideas and forces both new and old; and that its author intended it to be a comprehensive system embracing every aspect of society and essentially valid for all time. Godwin sought for the permanent beneath the flux, and found cause for unbounded hope as a result of his quest.

This book is essentially the product of the epoch which separates the old world from the new, the agricultural from the industrial. Much of the interest it has for us lies in the fact that it is thus symbolical, being both retrospective and prospective in its reference. Godwin confronts the problems of the future with intellectual preconceptions derived from the past. His work, on the one hand, is in a very real sense a synthesis of the speculation of the previous century, possessing all the general features of that speculation both as to attitude and as to method. On the other hand, it states for the future its major problems and provides the starting-point for much of its speculation.

Godwin was not an original thinker. His book is definitely the product of extensive reading (frequently acknowledged in footnotes), the results of which have been organised and integrated by a man of marked intellectual characteristics and of striking personal temperament. He sets out to build a Temple of Reason, and it is always easy to see whence he has quarried his materials; but he remains his own architect. It has been said that no single idea in *Political Justice* is original, and this is probably true. From Locke and the empiricists he borrowed his ideas of the nature and structure of mind; from Rousseau, Helvétius, and Holbach he learnt the effects which education and political institutions have on the formation of character; from Mably and others he accepted the idea of the uniformity of truth; Paine taught him the distinction between society and government; and from all these writers he took over the criticisms of monarchy and aristocracy. His criticism of private property is obviously inspired by Mably and by Wallace, and to a less extent by Plato and Sir Thomas More. Such a statement of his indebtedness could be extended to cover practically every page of his writing, but it would avail little. No catalogue of sources can explain a man. His originality is rather to be sought in the logical unity of his scheme and the intrepidity with which he pushed his system to its logical extreme, as no English philosopher had done before.

Being thus eclectic, *Political Justice* possesses all the main features associated with that line of Enlightenment speculation which derives chiefly from the Cartesian outlook. It is individualistic and atomistic in its attitude to society, regarding society as "nothing more than an aggregate of individuals." Moreover, it is uncompromisingly intellectualistic in tone, as examination of the doctrine reveals, and is completely lacking in that emotional driving power of romanticism which Rousseau introduced into political theory. If Rousseau stood for the idyllic imagination, . . . and Burke for the moral imagination, then Godwin above all stood for the rational imagination and its concomitants—the idea of progress and of human perfectibility—which resulted from the confluence of the Baconian and Cartesian influences. That rational imagination underlies all his writing, and is revealed at the beginning of *Political Justice.* (pp. 145-47)

Another characteristic of Godwin's work, which is derived from the preceding century, and which is an inevitable accompaniment of his rationalism, is its *a priori* method. Analysis will show how rigidly Godwin bases the whole of his political teaching on his doctrine of an immutable moral law from which particular deductions to meet particular exigencies can be made. (p. 148)

The importance of Godwin's work lies in the fact that he it was who first disclosed in England the essentially radical spirit inherent in the outlook of the Enlightenment. This was undoubtedly due to the influence of the French thinkers acting upon his own uncompromising Nonconformist dispositions. He turned these doctrines to account, not to make a plea for the enlightened despot who should remedy the abuses of organised society by purifying it and levelling it up through his wisdom, but to destroy social organisation entirely as something inevitably evil and opposed to reason.

But although Godwin's work is backward-looking so far as its intellectualism and its method are concerned, yet it has features which gave it marked significance for the future. For instance, his insistence on the doctrine of progress involved a *purposive* attitude to social phenomena, and that attitude—coming as it did at the beginning of the mightiest epoch of social change in our history—was destined to spread and to modify political life to an incalculable extent. . . . Godwin's entire work is a . . . vehement denunciation of the doctrine of indifference. The fact that he sought a remedy in exactly the opposite direction to that in which later generations have gone—in abolition of all restraint, instead of increasing social control—need not blind us to the essential significance of this protest. He had a keen sense of prevailing social misery and of the appalling waste of human life involved in the social system around him. . . . In the next century such an attitude of social purposiveness was to become general, instead of being the exception; and the dissemination of such an attitude was the prelude to democracy.

In a second respect, however, Godwin's work has a bearing on the future—in his realisation that the idea of property is the fundamental problem of human society. . . . Few other political philosophers in England had for a century considered it as the paramount *practical problem;* but such it was for Godwin. In this respect he shows greater detachment and more insight than most of the revolutionaries with whom he was associated. He says plainly that republicanism will not solve the social problems. Only a redistribution of property can do that. This issue had been raised during the Commonwealth period, but from the Restoration onward had fallen into the background of political speculation this side of the Channel. (pp. 148-50)

Apart from the attribute of social purposiveness and the question of property, there is another sense in which Godwin has significance for the century that followed, and that is in his emphasis on the necessity for leisure and education as the indispensable bases for the erection of democracy. This point of view—the complete antithesis of Burke's idea of the "swinish multitude"—follows from Godwin's conception of the perfectibility of man. He has a thoroughly evangelical regard for the intrinsic worth of every human being; his moral ideal involves the development of the reason latent in all men; and for him we fall short of this moral ideal so long as there remain any undeveloped potentialities in the soul of man. Adopting as he did the Socratic position that knowledge is virtue, Godwin sees in the extension of education the only medium of progress and reform. It was this fact which made him distrust violence and any form of collective endeavour such as leagues, societies, and unions; it was this fact which led him to break with Thelwall and the physical force men; and it was this fact also that led him to imply in many places in *Political Justice* that reform must come relatively slowly through the propaganda work of a small intellectual aristocracy.

Besides this double aspect of *Political Justice* as both retrospective and prospective there is another general feature of the work which needs emphasising, and that is its comprehensiveness. In one sense Godwin's book is misnamed; it is far more extensive in scope than its title at first glance would imply. But Godwin is careful to explain in what sense he is using his terms. For him politics does not mean merely the machinery of government and its construction; nor does justice mean merely a legal ideal. By politics he means rather the general science of human virtue and happiness. Politics is really a general ethical study. He tells us in the preface that he "conceived politics to be the proper vehicle of a liberal morality"; and in his first chapter he criticises the generally accepted meaning of the word "politics." He says that it has been used in too narrow a sense by writers hitherto, for they have not displayed "a consciousness of the intimate connection of the different parts of the social system, whether it relates to the intercourse of individuals or to the maxims and institutes of states and nations." . . . Godwin is accordingly at pains to show that "government is still more considerable in its incidental effects than in those intended to be produced." It is all-pervading in its influence; it "insinuates itself into our personal dispositions and insensibly communicates its own spirit to our private transactions"; it is the ever-present but invisible environment, controlling the life of every single member of the community by compelling the adaptation of the individual to itself, unconsciously, but none the less completely. No other English writer had conceived his subject in such a comprehensive way, although since Godwin's time the complexity of the issues involved in the problems of politics has been increasingly realised.

Since he adopted this viewpoint, it is not surprising that Godwin made his own work "perspicuous." It is not so much a treatise on politics as on sociology. Besides being what he himself calls a "political science," it is a treatise on ethics, on philosophy, and on individual and social psychology. It treats of education and religion; it roams from the problem of free will to the question of immortality. . . . Above all, he wrote with a practical intention. He clearly wanted to modify public opinion and to hasten the coming of the day of enlightenment. This was to be no mere academic treatise, but a work "from the perusal of which no man should rise without being strengthened in habits of sincerity, fortitude, and justice."

This last remark reveals another general trait of *Political Justice*. It was comprehensive not only in the sense that a large variety of subjects was dealt with, but also in the sense that its author was trying to look at the issues *sub specie eternitatis.* He writes on cosmic problems with a consummate self-confidence, and his political theory is in a direct sense the by-product of his cosmology. From beginning to end he is always asking what are the "general principles," not what are the facts; and he entertains no doubt in his own mind that once these general principles are found they can be applied to all concrete problems with ease. . . . He is completely convinced of the truth of his general principles; he is quite confident that they alone embody the entire truth; he is assured that his teaching is in perfect harmony with "the general scheme of things," so that even though the adventitious sin of man may postpone

the coming of the reign of reason, yet that reign must come sooner or later, and neither principalities nor powers will be able ultimately to prevent it. Godwin had dropped the specific tenets of the Calvinist creed; but his book is Calvinistic in spirit throughout, and a realisation of this fact helps us the better to appraise his teaching. For a discoverable God he substituted a discoverable universe. For grace working silently in the heart of man he substituted reason. Instead of righteousness as the principle of conduct he pleaded for enlightenment, since the mind—once awakened to the sublimity of eternal truth—must of necessity act in conformity with it. Lastly, and as a corollary of what has been said, for the need of conversion he substituted the need for education; man could attain his true status only by turning away from the intellectual errors into which he had fallen, and by contemplating the immutable laws of the universe. Godwin in more than one place seems to think that this awakening of the soul may happen suddenly, though he hopes the process may not be too sudden in the community as a whole. He prefers that the awakening should first occur among the spiritual *élite,* who should be, as it were, missionaries to their fellows. When the enlightenment has become general, then the whole political and social problem will be solved. The awakening to the truth means automatically that the calm period of reason will succeed, since "in reality the chains fall off themselves when the magic of opinion is dissolved." It is the old doctrine that the truth would make men free. (pp. 150-53)

[Godwin] reiterates his position to an almost wearisome degree, and recurs to his "first principles" with every specific problem. We will examine first, therefore, his theory of man; and next his conception of the universe, so far as he presents that as determining political theory.

His theory of man is fundamental. All men, whatever their colour and wherever they are born, are made in the same way. "All men are conscious that man is a being of one common nature, and feel the propriety of the treatment they receive from one another being measured by a common standard." The points in which human beings are alike "are infinitely more considerable than those in which they differ." This common nature has several marked features. First, all minds at birth are a *tabula rasa,* and we bring into the world with us no innate principles. Consequently at birth there is "no essential difference between the child of the lord and the porter." But in the second place man is born endowed with reason, or at least the potentiality of reason. "All men are partakers of the common faculty reason, and may be supposed to have some communication with the common preceptor truth." Godwin is always saying that man is an intellectual being; but he nowhere tells us clearly exactly what he means by reason. He appears to mean by that term the capacity, or the faculty, for discerning cause and effect in phenomena. But the strangest aspect of Godwin's doctrine is his contention that reason exerts a compulsive power over its possessor. Man always acts in accordance with such reason as he has, even though that may not be fully developed. No other faculty intervenes in action; indeed, given the perception of one or more causal relationships, action follows automatically in accordance with that perception. Hence it follows that "Man being, as we have now found him to be, a simple substance, governed by the apprehensions of his understanding, nothing further is requisite but the improvement of his reasoning faculty to make him virtuous and happy." So there can be no such thing as free will. Godwin devotes twenty pages to destroying the case for free will, and to showing that if there is to be a science of mind it must be based on the necessitarian hypothesis. The mind is itself built up of associated sequences of ideas derived from the perceptions of reason. Thus the inner world of mind, like the outer world of matter, is a causal system. Therefore "man is in reality a passive and not an active being"; "considered in himself he is merely a being capable of impression, a recipient of perceptions." This doctrine Godwin uses at almost every stage of his argument, and especially in connection with treatment of crime and punishment. Paradoxically enough, also, it is this doctrine which is going to give him his chief reason for optimism for the future.

Four important consequences follow from this conception of human beings as passive creatures without innate ideas, but endowed with a potential reasoning faculty. The first is that there is no distinction between will and intellect; action is automatic, for it is impossible to imagine, in the light of the above teaching,

> that, in the case of an intellectual faculty placed in an aptly organised body, preference can exist together with a consciousness (gained from experience) of our power to obtain the object preferred, without a certain motion of the animal frame being the necessary result. We need only attend to the obvious meaning of the terms in order to perceive that the will is merely, as it has been happily termed, the last act of the understanding.

The second consequence is the moral and intellectual equality of all human beings, at least potentially:

> From these simple principles we may deduce the moral equality of mankind. We are partakers of a common nature, and the same causes that contribute to the benefit of one contribute to the benefit of another. Our senses and faculties are of the same denomination. Our pleasures and pains will therefore be the same. We are all of us endowed with reason, able to compare, to judge, and to infer. The improvement therefore which is to be desired for the one, is to be desired for the other.

The third consequence, which again is utilised throughout *Political Justice,* is the doctrine that character is determined by environment, and by environment only:

> From these reasonings it sufficiently appears, that the moral qualities of men are the produce of the impressions made upon them, and that there is no instance of an original propensity to evil. Our virtues and vices may be traced to the incidents which make the history of our lives, and if these incidents could be divested of every improper tendency, vice would be extirpated from the world.

The fourth consequence which Godwin deduces from his view of the capacities of man is "the doctrine of benevolence." Man does not act from the impulse of self-love, for the understanding of virtue is itself a motive exciting to action; and by virtue he means conformity with the moral law, which commands the consideration of other people's needs as much as one's own. "Man is not originally vicious."

When we turn from Godwin's theories of the nature of man to his theories of the nature of the universe we find him no less explicit, and from the combination of the two doctrines

the whole of his political theory is derived. We may summarise his teaching under this head by the theorem that he conceived of the universe as a system of cause and effect, working by immutable laws, and implying a code of moral principles which are themselves rational and discernible by the human reason.

To begin with, it is a *system;* and the main purpose of ***Political Justice*** is to delineate that system. "I am myself part of a great whole," he says; and it is this whole that he means by the word "truth." . . . But it is a system which works by the immutable laws of cause and effect. He speaks of "the great chain of causes from which every event in the universe takes its rise." . . . These immutable laws involve a code of moral principles. Godwin is a utilitarian, and for him virtue and happiness are interchangeable terms. Virtue is thus organic to nature, in the sense that nature has ordained that all men shall pursue their own happiness; and in the attainment of that complete harmony which is real happiness they help to promote the happiness of others also. It is this harmony ordained by nature which constitutes the moral code, and which Godwin calls justice. "If truth be one," he says, "there must be one code of truths on the subject of our reciprocal duties," for "the course of nature and the course of perfect theory are the same." (pp. 154-58)

Such are Godwin's basic theories of man and the universe. Man is of one nature; the universe is one system; the moral law is one code; and necessity reigns everywhere. There follow certain consequences of great importance for politics, "leading to a bold and comprehensive view of man in society." Five such consequences have in particular to be noted.

In the first place, all doctrine of rights in the political sense completely disappears. The moral law prescribes what duty the individual owes to his neighbours and what duty they owe to him, and nothing more is necessary. The argument is simple. "By right . . . has always been understood discretion, that is, full and complete power of either doing a thing or omitting it, without the person's becoming liable to animadversion or censure from another." But

> the rights of one man cannot clash with, or be destructive of, the rights of another; for this, instead of rendering the subject an important branch of truth and morality (as the advocates of the rights of man certainly understand it to be), would be to reduce it to a heap of unintelligible jargon and inconsistency. If one man have a right to be free another man cannot have the right to make him a slave.

Nobody has a right to omit what his duty prescribes: "from hence it inevitably follows that men have no rights." Nothing is more surprising, says Godwin, than that two ideas so incompatible as man and rights should have been associated together, since either term "must be utterly exclusive and annihilatory of the other." Once posit that man is an intellectual being, it follows that he can learn from immutable justice what his duties are, and thereby all talk of rights becomes meaningless. . . . Society cannot change eternal truth. It can require of me everything that it is my duty to do, and no more (hence it cannot compel me to go to war on its behalf). Conversely, society is bound to do for its members everything that can contribute to their welfare (and on the strength of this Godwin later denies any absolute right to property).

A second consequence, no less important than the denial of inherent rights, follows from Godwin's views of man and his world, and this is the fact that there can be no such thing as legislation in any real sense. Law cannot be made, for it simply *is;* and the most venerable Senate "can only interpret and announce the law which derives its real validity from a higher and less mutable authority." And, again, legislation is

> a term not applicable to human society. Men cannot do more than declare and interpret law; nor can there be an authority so paramount as to have the prerogative of making that to be law which abstract and immutable justice had not made to be law previously to that inter-position—

though he admits that as a temporary expedient it might be found necessary to have an authority empowered to declare those general principles.

The third consequence is that no obedience is due to government as such. The object of government is the exertion of force; and the duty of man is the exercise of his reason. I am bound to submit to justice and truth, because they approve themselves to my judgment; but I submit to erroneous government only because there is no alternative.

> The compliance I yield to government independently of my approbation of its measures is of the same species as my compliance with a wild beast that forces me to run north when my judgment and inclination prompt me to go south.

So it follows that "no Government ought pertinaciously to resist the change of its own institutions," or to hinder the fullest possible discussion. The individual judgment is the only valid tribunal, and man is in all cases

> obliged to consult that judgement before he can determine whether the matter in question be of the sort provided for or no. So that from this reasoning it ultimately appears that no man is obliged to conform to any rule of conduct farther than the rule is consistent with justice.

The contrary doctrine has been the source of more calamities to mankind than all the other errors of the human understanding. "Depravity would have gained little ground in the world, if every man had been in the exercise of his independent judgement."

A fourth consequence of Godwin's general philosophical outlook is that there is one best form of government. Truth is one; and truth "cannot be so variable as to change its nature by crossing an arm of the sea"; it is at all times and in all places the same. Man's nature is everywhere the same in essentials also; therefore he always needs the same things. Hence "there must in the nature of things be one best form of government which all intellects sufficiently roused from the slumber of savage ignorance will be irresistibly incited to approve." Difference in climate need not modify political theory.

Such are the general premises of Godwin's political thinking, and such are the consequences which these premises involve for him. But if the living of a social life is part of the general problem of morality, and if on the other hand man is born morally neutral, but endowed with the potentialities of reason, the question then arises: What are the causes of moral improvement? The general nature of the answer to this question has already been implied, but Godwin examines it with considerable fullness.

There are three principal sources of moral improvement: literature, education, and political organisation. The first two are limited in their scope. Literature, although it has already "reconciled the whole thinking world respecting the great principles of the system of the universe," appeals only to a few. The bulk of the community has neither the time nor the capacity to devote to it, because of the inequitable distribution of wealth. Education, although in some respects a more powerful instrument, is also circumscribed in its influence; partly because of the difficulty of finding the sagacious and disinterested teacher, but mainly because its benefits will be neutralised by the evil environment when the youth passes into the world. The environment must first be altered before the other two instruments can be fully utilised. That is why political organisation is of such overwhelming importance. If that organisation be based on the true laws of morality, then man, being a creature passive to his environment, will himself grow moral. By creating the invisible but omnipresent social environment government has an incalculable power of suggestion, entering into every action and every thought of man. (pp. 158-62)

> *C. H. Driver, "William Godwin," in* The Social & Political Ideas of Some Representative Thinkers of the Revolutionary Era, *edited by F. J. C. Hearnshaw, George G. Harrap & Company Ltd., 1931, pp. 141-80.*

JOHN MIDDLETON MURRY (essay date 1938)

[*Murry was a noted English essayist, magazine editor, and literary critic who wrote during the first half of the twentieth century. In the following excerpt, he analyzes the philosophy of* Political Justice, *emphasizing that Godwin was one of the most humane and concrete political thinkers of his time.*]

It is impossible to understand Godwin, or his curious aloofness from the political movements of his day, except we appreciate that he was no more a mere democrat than Cromwell or Rousseau. He was concerned for the integrity of the individual man. Therefore, the political revolutionary or even the moderate political reformer did not know what to make of him. Without the faintest intention of paradox, he was always springing surprises. His denunciation in *Political Justice* of the fetish of majority worship, "that intolerable insult upon all reason and justice—the deciding of truth by the counting up of numbers," is of a piece with his spirited attack, forty years later, on the viciousness of vote by ballot in his final book of essays, *Thoughts on Man*. The ballot-box would, it is true, enable a man to vote as he pleased; but what was that compared to the fact that it will encourage him in duplicity and make dissimulation a necessity? That sounds almost fantastical: quite fantastical is his serious doubt at the end of *Political Justice* whether in a true society of real individuals its members would consent to play orchestral music or act in dramas, because of the attaint to their individuality. But what underlies his extraordinary generalization: "Everything understood by the term co-operation is in some sense an evil" is an impassioned conviction of the worth and potentialities of the individual, and an endeavour to implant in men's imaginations the conception of what human integrity might mean.

It was this strain in *Political Justice* which set young men's hearts on fire. The difference between Godwin and the enthusiasts who fell by the wayside, who (as Hazlitt sardonically put it) "lost their way in Utopia, and found it in Old Sarum," was that Godwin had the power to endure. He had come to his vision first through a long and peculiar religious tradition, and secondly through hard thinking on the basis of a religious struggle of his own. He was thirty-five, and a mature and well battered man when he conceived *Political Justice:* he had fought his way to his vision. Now he rationalized it. It was really all perfectly simple, as genuine religious vision always is.

Godwin saw, quite plainly, that men could be very much better than they are—so much better, indeed, as to be virtually quite different. The means of this regeneration of man was Reason. But reason in Godwin's argument was a peculiar thing; it was inherently compulsive. Godwin's Reason was, in fact, the same as the faculty of understanding the Truth in Blake's apothegm: "Truth cannot be uttered so as to be understood and not be believed." There is no difference between that and the Godwinian axiom that "Sound reasoning and truth, when adequately communicated, must always be victorious over error." (pp. 248-50)

"Universal benevolence" was, in Godwin's system, self-evident. The only problem is to understand why it is not in operation. The answer is, of course, simple. "Positive institutions"—Monarchy, Aristocracy, the Church, the property-system—have corrupted men, and made them opaque to its illumination. The problem shifts a plane. By what means can these diabolical "positive institutions" be changed? The answer is by the propagation of "universal benevolence," in idea and act, among those who are responsive to it. The problem shifts again. What are the desirable changes in positive institutions which the disciples of universal benevolence should pursue? This, more than any other, is the question which Godwin answers in *Political Justice*. And it is intelligible that he induced in his fellow political reformers a kind of uncomprehending despair. He seemed to be answering the same question as they; but, in fact, it was a quite different one. His real answer is that all positive institutions should be abolished. That is to say, his answer is on the same plane as his problem: not political at all, as we (like his associates) understand the word, but moral and religious. And once more Godwin's creed is better summed up by Blake than by himself: "Religion is Politics, and Politics is Brotherhood." The real solution, and ultimately the only solution, is the conversion, by "adequate communication" of the truth, of a number of men to self-evident "universal benevolence." Their example will be contagious, and the process of regeneration accelerated.

But in the meantime? Godwin was only partly interested in the meantime. He did not really believe in the efficacy of transitional measures; he could do no more than allow that they were better than nothing. In practical politics he was content to be a Whig of the radical kind; but though he was ready to intervene, as he did very effectively in the trial of the twelve reformers with his brilliant pamphlet, *Cursory Strictures on Chief Justice Eyre's Charge to the Grand Jury*, he was not to be implicated in revolutionary politics. He was willing to bear his witness to the evil of the existing order, and the good that might one day be; and he bore his witness bravely: but he profoundly mistrusted political organization toward the good. Let evolution begin at home, in the hearts and minds of men; it would last longer than the enthusiasms and extravagances of the London Corresponding Society. His attitude to the politics of reform was largely colored by his deep mistrust of State action, which proceeded less from his having imbibed the English political individualism of his century than from his having absorbed the religious individualism of Independency. He imagined that he was the antithesis of Rousseau in this matter; but in fact he did not understand Rousseau, who, it must be confessed, was a much more realistic and revolutionary *polit-*

ical thinker than Godwin. Rousseau's fundamental axioms that organized society, however calamitous its original advent might be deemed, was now necessary to human existence, and that now the specifically human problem was to moralize the organization of society, so that society might become the means to a new kind of human liberty—these positions were strictly incomprehensible to Godwin. The notion that men might need to be "forced to be free" was worse than a paradox to him; it was a blasphemy. Nevertheless, the conception is essential to any positive social thinking that is not to be stultified by atomism. That men may need to be "forced to be free" is merely an extreme assertion of the necessity of obedience to Law, without which a society cannot be imagined at all. The practical problem is to determine where the power that may "force men to be free" ought to reside, how it shall be placed there, and how men may be safeguarded from its perversion to quite other ends. These problems, into the consideration of which Rousseau entered as deeply as any man has done, can hardly be said to have been real to Godwin at all. His thought was, in essence, Protestant, millennial and anarchical.

So far as Godwin's conception can be reduced to practical terms, it meant the formation of a society within society—a little nucleus of the elect, practicing universal benevolence among themselves and seeking by their example to accelerate the normal process of political development, in which they participated without illusion and without repugnance. In this form, the kinship between his thought and that of the Independents is manifest; Godwinism is secular Sandemanianism. And the much-derided "perfectibility of man" is no more, and no less, than the reassertion in secular terms of the possibility of regeneration. That this regeneration ultimately involves the abolition of all coercive government is self-evident: in so far as the regeneration actually takes place what is good in such government becomes supererogatory, what is bad, a manifest evil.

But Godwin imagined that all government was coercive government. This is no more true than that all education is coercive, or indeed all experience whatsoever. Government is justified, in the eyes of imaginative reason, as the indispensable means for the formation of beneficent social habit—the habit of well-doing; to reject government, because it has been, and is always liable to be, diabolically abused, is to reject society itself. On the other hand, to accept the necessity of government does not involve rejecting the ideal of "universal benevolence." The assumption that these positions are destructive of one another, which Godwin appears always to be making, derives partly from the difficulty of expressing a religious intuition in secular terms, and partly from the evil condition of English government in his day. (pp. 250-52)

It was not so much against coercive government, as against coercion in general that Godwin protested. He was convinced that man could not enter the reign of love by compulsion, or even by organization. Hence the apparent paradox that political association for reform was almost as repugnant to him as governmental repression. Persuasion, working from individual to individual, was the only way to achieve a regeneration of society that was not superficial and specious. Godwin's seeming extravagance should not blind us to the element of truth in this. It is more apparent today than it was during the nineteenth century that political democracy will not yield more than you put into it in the way of social and moral regeneration. The difference between Godwin and Rousseau here is that Rousseau maintained (as I believe, rightly) that the very process of moral regeneration in the individual involved the recognition that organized society is necessary. The regenerated individual, in Rousseau's vision, works definitely to make society a fitting instrument of individual regeneration: to change secular society into a religious society.

This was beyond the range of Godwin's Independent and individualistic thought. But Godwin's faith in persuasion was not really excessive. There is no other process conceivable by which men can learn to love one another. What is odd is that Godwin appears to consider no other kind of persuasion than the least persuasive form of it, namely, logical argument. But that is only appearance. He means something different. (p. 253)

Posterity owes Godwin a rehabilitation which it will yet have to perform. For the moment he still lives on "in the serene twilight of a doubtful immortality," and in that deceitful medium he looms vaguely as a sort of fabulous monster of rationality. Yet when we come to regard him closely, he appears as one of the most human figures of his time. . . . The quality that is diffused through his whole work is rare and human and tender. In the eighteen-thirties, when even Charles Lamb was showing signs of panic at the doings of "Captain Swing," but no sign of comprehension of the appalling misery of the starved farm-laborer, Godwin was writing that "the merits and demerits of the public house were very unjustly rated by the fastidious among the more favored orders of society." The country ale-house was a place where discontent was fomented and sedition talked, said the frightened interests. Let them be shut! Godwin turns the tables with a vengeance. He calls the public house the laborer's university, where men are educated into citizenship. Such a degree of imaginative sympathy and tolerance toward the laborer was almost unparalleled among his most enlightened contemporaries. "Universal benevolence" was not a remote and ideal condition to Godwin: it was the way he felt. (pp. 256-57)

Such was Godwin's ideal: that men should be, instead of automata obedient to "positive institutions," "absolute human beings and genuine individuals." It is remarkable that he finds this ideal condition realized in the boy at play. That means simply that what he believed in, and strove to propagate as the goal of education, was human spontaneity and mutual tolerance. Somehow the spontaneity of the child was to be recreated in the grown and advised man.

From his noble conception of the individual, Godwin derived a criterion for a swift and searching criticism of the State. "The only legitimate object of political institutions," he wrote in one of the final chapters of *Political Justice*, "is the advantage of individuals. All that cannot be brought home to them— national wealth, prosperity and glory—can be advantageous only to the self-interested impostors." Godwin, who is generally reckoned one of the most abstract of political thinkers, was in fact one of the most concrete; but it is to be noted that even here his phrasing is deceptive. By "individuals" he means all individuals; and he takes it for granted that he will be so understood. The "wealth of nations" is humanly meaningless, and even a sinister equivocation, unless it involves the comfort and security of the individuals who compose the nation.

As often, the visionary is the true realist. He has the innocent eye which sees things as they are. But how was the condition to be achieved in which the welfare of individuals should become the sole object of political institutions? Ultimately, only by increasing the number of those to whom this *raison d'être* of government was self-evident. And Godwin could hardly help

being fascinated by the speculation that, if this became self-evident to many men, there would be no need of government. Undoubtedly he indulged this dream overmuch and rationalized it to excess; but that was partly because he lacked an idiom and philosophy of growth in which to express his thought. In fact, no man was more patient of the slowness of political and social improvement than Godwin. He was content to work a change in the hearts of a few by putting a vision before their imaginations. Thus a new motive would be introduced into that process of necessity which to the last Godwin believed governed the world of men. "The decisions of our will are always in obedience to the strongest motive." The acceptance of this psychological determinism Godwin, like Spinoza, held to be the highest spiritual achievement of man; it was for him the sole authentic fount of true tolerance. (pp. 258-59)

John Middleton Murry, "William Godwin," in his Heroes of Thought, *Julian Messner, Inc., 1938, pp. 245-59.*

ANGUS WILSON   (essay date 1951)

[*Wilson is one of the most important English novelists of the postwar years. In the following excerpt, he defends Godwin as an original and sensitive novelist.*]

[As] works of art [Godwin's novels] are all, in some degree, failures—three, at least, completely so. Excuses and explanations for Godwin's failure as a novelist can be offered: *Caleb Williams* is by far the most successful work, and it alone was written before external circumstances made writing a fight against time and debt and family warfare. Much of the failure of *St. Leon, Fleetwood,* and *Mandeville* may be accounted for by the pressure of miserable hackwork; the total collapse of *Cloudesly* and *Deloraine* may be charged to old age and spent forces. The fact remains, however, that Godwin's powers as a novelist were very limited; that, with every excuse made for difficult circumstances, he never developed them, and that this artistic limitation makes even the best, the most original of his novels, at times unendurable, and renders the weaker, the less original, worthless.

That any writer of such intellectual distinction, whose style and powers were so ill adapted to this medium, should have chosen to express himself in it, must seem curious. The choice is only partly, I think, explained by the growing popularity of the novel, and the large financial returns, which he always hoped for, but never succeeded in securing, to relieve his load of debts. The deeper reason lies in the nature of the material which he put into his novels. The guilt, the horror and the tragedy of the eighteenth century lay in the hinterland of the minds of its sensitive men. For many—politicians and men of affairs, even some artists—it was so well repressed, so covered over by hard work and harder play that it could only emerge in periodic madness which no formal social life, no tea with Mrs. Unwin or Mrs. Thrale, no midnight sessions in the House, or early morning gambling or debauch, could heal. Godwin found his relief in the symbolism of the novel. (pp. 38-9)

Had he lived half a century later, Godwin might well have given utterance to his emotions in a form that would have been adequate to its content, for by that time the creative genius of Dickens had transformed the old picaresque shape of *Pickwick Papers* into the great psychological social novels like *Bleak House* or *Our Mutual Friend*. The Victorian novelists were to carry the symbolisation of personal conflict in fictitious forms to the height of art. But Godwin was, in this respect, a pioneer without creative genius. He could imitate forms; he could not create them. The eighteenth-century forms which he had at hand were the least suited for the emotions he wished to express. The picaresque novels of Le Sage or Fielding or Smollett are no happy treasure-trove for the Freudian investigator, no deep reservoir of the subconscious. Yet it was the picaresque form with its central character moving from group to group that made the outline of Godwin's six novels. In *Caleb Williams* where 'things as they are'—the primary title of the novel—formed part of the subject matter, the old Fieldingesque method, so well adapted to simple social indignation, sufficed. Godwin, in the purely descriptive scenes of this novel—the gaol, the robbers' retreat, the lodgings of the odious Mr. Spurrel—showed a gift for caricature and dialogue that never appeared elsewhere in his work. But for the fall from grace of noble Falkland, his dark, resolute pursuit of Williams, the hero's nightmare flight from omnipotent anger, his final resolution and defiance, the forms of Fielding and Smollett gave no answer. So it was with the endless flight of St. Leon before the effects of his own magic powers, or of Mandeville's inescapable corruption from pride and suspicion.

Something Godwin may have found in the works of a greater novelist than Fielding or Smollett—Richardson, though mainly one suspects through his Continental imitators. Whether, however, by direct influence, or through the enervated medium of Rousseau or of Henry Mackenzie, there is an interesting parallel between Richardson's approach to his principal characters—his portrayal of the seeming omnipotence of the guilty Mr. B. and Lovelace, his emphasis upon the final victory of the innocent Pamela and Clarissa—and Godwin's greatest successes in his novels—the psychology of Falkland, Williams or Mandeville, and the moral order they symbolise. Richardson, of course, was an artist of a different class from Godwin, but there is also a similar parallel between their principal defects. The prolixity of *St. Leon, Caleb Williams,* and *Mandeville* springs, in some degree, from lack of formal sense, but it is also, in part, the logical outcome of that same itching obsession with human motive that produces the most tedious passages of *Clarissa* and *Grandison,* as it does the most brilliant.

Godwin, it must be noted, belongs on this side to the greatest stream of eighteenth-century fiction—that of Richardson, Prévost and Sade. Their analysis of power, guilt and pursuit were expressed in sexual symbols, his in the more trite language of social melodrama and historical romance.

In this choice of expression, of course, he followed the fashionable 'Gothic' trend of his day, the course of Mrs. Radcliffe and 'Monk' Lewis, the stage convention of his successful playwright friend, Holcroft, and his less successful playwright friend, Coleridge. . . . The stately, if somewhat stilted eighteenth-century style, so well suited for *Political Justice*, sits comically upon the narration of mystery and horror, and his reverence for the decencies of language forbade him the extravagances and vulgarities in which Lewis or Mrs. Radcliffe developed their Gothic tales. In this combination of formal language and romantic narrative he is more akin to Sir Walter Scott, whose work was still unwritten when *Caleb Williams* and *St. Leon* appeared. Indeed, some of his most successful passages—the description of the battle of Pavia and of the dungeons of Bethlem Gabor in *St. Leon,* the ill-fated Royalist rising in *Mandeville,* are a foretaste of Scott at his best.

But Gothic mysteries and historical romances were alike as inadequate as the picaresque to contain the subtle, psychological pessimism of Godwin's emotions. Like so many figures of the 'Romantic movement', he was drawn to the literature of an earlier age to satisfy his needs. (pp. 39-40)

There is a frightening chasm, a nightmare dissociation between the gloomy tortured lives of Godwin's heroes and the sweet reasonableness, the universal good sense of *Political Justice,* though the horror of the novels gives full answer to the facile criticism of Godwin's anarchism on the grounds of psychological naïveté and failure to consider the problem of evil. It is true that the dichotomy is there, damaging both political treatise and romance, but Godwin was fully aware of this schizophrenic tendency. After the publication of *Caleb Williams* in which he bade defiance to the morose tyranny of his Calvinist childhood—father, God and all the powers there are—he attempted in every successive novel to suggest an answer to man's solitude, fear and isolating pride. His answers were of two kinds, both, of course, embedded in the thought of his age. In *Fleetwood* we are offered the ennobling answer of man communing with nature in the person of the sage—almost Chinese in type—M. Ruffigny, who from the majestic heights of the Alps—the El Dorado of so much eighteenth-century aspiration—gives counsels of order, decency, the nobility of man and the sublimity of the rivers and hills. The excellent family of the Macneils, in the same novel, resident among the more picturesque but still ennobling scenes of the Lake District, suggest the second solution—the simple, cultivated, busy life of domestic bliss. But it is in the almost Swiss Family Robinson happiness of St. Leon's retreat on the Swiss lakeside that we get the crown of these two escapes from the awful choice between solitude and despair or the pursuit of power and degradation. It is in St. Leon's wife, Marguerite—the image of Mary Wollstonecraft—that the highest virtues are embodied. In the sublimity of nature, in the deep communings of a solitary mind is shown the path of Wordsworth. In the simple pleasures of amiable intercourse, in the domestic fireside, in the little polite group of compatible tempers, is offered the eighteenth-century answer. It was thus with his gardening schemes and his letter-writing that Shenstone fought melancholy; it was so with his hares and his tea with Mrs. Unwin that Cowper fought the inevitability of Hell; this was the solace of Streatham's garden and Dr. Burney's drawing-room for Johnson's agonised mind. The flames of the Manichaean dilemma leapt up and licked at the sensitive mind in the eighteenth century as in our own. For all those who cannot follow Mr. Huxley into his Yogic retreat from their ardour, or escape with Mr. Graham Greene into the solace of the Church, for all those who hate the forces of power—whether *laissez-faire* capitalism or State tyranny—and must yet find their solution in man's own natural goodness, the novels of Godwin, with all their absurdities, demand attention. (p. 40)

Angus Wilson, "The Novels of William Godwin," in World Review, *n.s. Vol. 28, June, 1951, pp. 37-40.*

P. N. FURBANK (essay date 1955)

[*Furbank surveys Godwin's novels and* Political Justice, *focusing on his "exact study and dramatization of morbid passion."*]

To read one's way through Godwin is to get more than one has bargained for. He is a richer study, there is more *to* him, than one is often given to believe; at least, this was the present writer's experience. One finds, it is true, an exploded thinker and a discredited character—a figure both comic and disreputable; but one finds also a serious artist and the absorbing history of a long intellectual development.

To understand Godwin it is necessary to take both his political writings and his novels into account, and to see the real links between them. For the novels are not reflections of the political writings; they are the complement of them, and in some ways a counterblast to them. The novels, apart from *Caleb Williams,* have a low reputation, I think certainly an unjustifiably low one. In part, this is because critics have as often as not been unwilling to accept the genre of his novels. It is one that we do not happen to have many examples of in English, though they are common in other languages: I mean the dramatized history of a state of mind, on the lines of *René, Werter, Hero of Our Own Times* etc. It is a form of confessional literature, and in France takes some of its inspiration from Rousseau's *Confessions.* (In England, so far as it exists, it derives in part from religious confessions: there is a fine example in Hogg's *Confessions of a Justified Sinner.*) It is a form which comes into being with the Romantic revival, and is, perhaps, the Romantic substitute for tragedy. Its most natural subject-matter is various forms of misanthropy. The greatest flowering of this genre is to be found in Dostoevsky: and the reader brought up on *Notes from Underground* and *The Insulted and Injured* should have no difficulty in recognizing the sort of thing Godwin is writing. It is important to point this out, however, because in the past Godwin has sometimes been linked with the 'roman philosophique' of Holcroft and Bage, which is quite a different genre—a species of picaresque novel with Voltairean dialogue, a form distinctly less important in the history of the novel.

There is a real affinity between Godwin and Dostoevsky, for all that the latter is so incomparably the greater writer. They are both truly first-hand historians of the conscience. Both are always fresh in their discoveries about the soul, because always true to their own inner experience. Godwin's later novels are almost intolerably bleak, the tract of experience that they deal with is excessively narrow and hideous in kind, but still burningly felt, and in its own way fresh—a contribution to our knowledge of psychology. The stir of life is there.—I speak of *St. Leon, Fleetwood* and *Mandeville.* It is less true of the last two novels, *Cloudesly* and *Deloraine.*

Common opinion is in the right, and *Caleb Williams* is certainly Godwin's best complete novel; and it has particular reasons for success which the later novels do not possess. All Godwin's novels are autobiographical or confessional, but *Caleb Williams* is so in a subtler and more adventurous way than the others. To put it briefly, the novel is a highly dramatized symbolical picture of Godwin himself in the act of writing *Political Justice.* I think it is important to point this out at once, for some of the brilliance and originality of the conception is missed if we fail to realize it. (pp. 214-15)

Caleb Williams is clearly Godwin himself, Falkland the *ancien régime,* and the opening of the trunk is the writing of *Political Justice.* The secret of the trunk is the secret which Godwin brings to the light of day in *Political Justice,* the guilty secret of government: and in describing Caleb's fierce glee and terror at making the discovery he is describing his own emotion at conceiving the theories of that work.

It is plain that Godwin was in a state of extreme excitement at the time of writing his famous political work. The cold-blooded rationalism of *Political Justice,* its apparently placid nihilism, was conceived in passion. It looks at first sight a paradox that the sedate anarchist and pedantic advocate of universal benevolence should also be the painter of the wild scenes of passion and mania that fill *Caleb Williams;* but the explanation is simple, it is that the emotions that fill the novel

are those which Godwin himself experienced in writing the celebrated treatise. 'Show me that you are afraid of my entertaining certain opinions or learning certain principles, and you will infallibly sooner or later awaken my curiosity': so says Godwin in *Political Justice;* and to satisfy this curiosity in whatever spirit of calm inquiry is in imagination most desperate, perhaps the most guilty, of acts.

The doctrine of *Political Justice* is that truth has only to be heard to prevail. . . . Tyrannical government holds its power not by force but by imposition. It hides its tyrannies behind the plausible fallacies of marriage and property-rights, and the sanctity of pledges, etc. To detect the fallacies is the whole of the battle. Touch the *secrets* of government, and, as with Falkland, you have touched the sore. In *Political Justice* Godwin talks as though the touching could be done with impunity, and seems to wish to represent the whole process of revolution as an innocent one. In *Caleb Williams* he does justice to the guilty side of the picture. The book, of course, was written under the shadow of the Terror.

What a powerful fable Godwin's plot is! And how brilliantly its implications are worked out. See for instance how much he makes of the complexity of Caleb's motives in prying into his noble master's secrets. Caleb's ruling passion is his curiosity, and it is both a good and an evil. It is this that has enabled him to improve his mind: and it is no vulgar curiosity. . . . On the other hand it has all the signs of an evil passion when it leads him to spy upon his master. . . . His most generous qualities (like Falkland's) help to precipitate him towards his fatal step. (pp. 215-17)

Falkland's tragedy is to be the victim of his own best impulses. In original character he is nobler than his servant; he has been brought up in the cult of honour and chivalry, and it is his passionate devotion to these which hurries him into the most despicable of crimes. It is a psychological law for Godwin that the best is in danger of turning into the worst. Falkland's tyrannical cruelty springs from hysteria, and not from original baseness. This is Godwin's way of doing justice to the *ancien régime.*

Godwin, in fact, has achieved something very difficult in this novel. He has found a human situation to parallel the impersonal issue of revolution: not a replica of it in miniature, but a psychological analogue. Something which, unlike the abstract issue, does not frustrate our sympathies at every turn. To do this, he depends very much on a favourite concept, the equivocalness of innocence and guilt: the book has a number of surprises, arising from this idea. (p. 218)

There is a further paradox, closely related to the guilty-innocence one, in Godwin's conception of necessity. The destiny which seems so cruel, destroying Falkland and turning Caleb into a trembling victim, turns out to have been beneficent after all. Caleb's vicious curiosity is revealed as the instrument of Providence—like the eye of God in the cautionary volume on which Godwin partly based his story, 'perpetually pursuing the guilty, and laying open their most hidden retreat to the light of day'. (pp. 218-19)

Caleb Williams . . . differs from the rest of Godwin in having symbolical applications. I have discussed the symbolical side of it, because it seems to me so interestingly conceived. It represents the writer's guilt-situation *vis-à-vis* revolution more satisfactorily than either Schiller's *Robbers* or Wordsworth's *Borderers.* (p. 219)

What *Caleb Williams* has in common with Godwin's other novels is the exact study and dramatization of morbid passion. Godwin is expert in describing the moment in which a passion first seizes upon the mind. He is the great master of *possession*. To read of Falkland's reaction to Tyrrel's insult is to know at once that something more than commonplace literary psychology is involved. . . . *St. Leon* gives us a whole series of these moments of possession. The book, indeed, is an analysis of a man's career in terms of such moments. Again, in *Fleetwood,* the newly married hero brings back his bride to his childhood home, and next morning shows her what had been his favourite room. He is about to rhapsodize about his love for it, when she innocently remarks that she thinks she will have it for her own. His 'animal spirits' are 'suddenly driven back upon his heart' by this; and a career of obsession begins for him.

Fleetwood and *Mandeville* are purely psychological studies, two case-histories of obsession. *St. Leon,* although also a case-history—in Gothic guise—has in addition some symbolical reference to contemporary political issues, and so stands nearer to *Caleb Williams.*

In his treatment of the passions, Godwin, in his own queer way, takes something from Elizabethan dramatists. The sudden madnesses of passion that attack Fleetwood and Falkland are those of Leontes and Lear: a mind hitherto immune to violent experience is suddenly swamped by it, and overset by the suddenness of the onrush. Fleetwood, in particular, is the Leontes *de nos jours. Fleetwood* is a duller work than its two predecessors, till we reach the third volume and Fleetwood's marriage: then it takes fire. (This part is probably Godwin's finest achievement outside *Caleb Williams.*) The novel is the natural history of, and also a satire on, a Man of Feeling. (pp. 219-20)

[*Fleetwood*] puts one in mind of . . . Jacobean tragedy; of Tourneur, for instance. Discovering the Elizabethan dramatists was the great intellectual event of [Godwin's] middle years. He speaks with joy of the immense new prospect of excitement it opened up to him. . . . The important likeness, of course, is in conception—in a view of the workings of passion—and not in language. When he is not vehement, Godwin is painfully prosy in language, and even his most vehement utterances often suffer in this way, though we forget the weakness in the fierceness and hurry of the sentiment. In dialogue he has a special aptitude for short, intense exchanges. . . . (p. 222)

Whilst Godwin obviously lacks certain qualities of the dramatist, he possesses some of the advantages of the novelist. He can handle relationships as well as individual psychology; and here too he has original discoveries to offer. Particularly is this true of *Fleetwood,* in which, as a change from the preceding novels, Godwin intended to deal with everyday life and manners. The story, according to Godwin, is to consist of 'such adventures, as for the most part have occurred to at least one-half of the Englishmen now existing'. . . . Many of his observations of behaviour and touches of feeling are truly original and good. He not only examines shades of feeling with great precision, he can make them play a part in the course of events. For instance, once Fleetwood has banished his wife from his house, she is inflexible to any suggestion of reconciliation. She considers that he would never have treated her so, if she had had a dowry. And on reflection, we realize she is right. Some time after Fleetwood has begun to woo her, she loses her dowry through a fraud. Fleetwood has no need of the money, and he loves her no less; but his relations with her change, notwithstanding. (pp. 223-24)

Godwin's character perhaps especially fitted him for his treatment of the passions. One seems to see him so clearly, the prosaic, argumentative prodigy of the dissenting academy, famous for his calm and unimpassioned discussion, a heart unusually unpractised in the emotions, devoted to a 'fearless tranquillity' as he calls it, suddenly infected by one great passionate excitement (I mean, at the time of writing *Political Justice*) and thereafter catching the passions, and observing himself catch them, one after one, like belated childhood diseases. . . . What often strikes one about Godwin is that he does not *want* to believe in the importance of the feelings; he is made to admit it rather against his will. Even then, he is always eager to explain their existence on mechanical lines. (p. 224)

[Few writers] have written more movingly of the pains of human existence; but fewer still at such a moment would have been so prosaically frank. He lets us down with a bump; and yet in so doing he in a way makes us admire him the more. I find this a great attraction in a character that is certainly no great shakes by ordinary standards. No doubt the cult of 'perfect sincerity' often enough turns Godwin into an object of fun, if not of contempt. He clings to the doctrine, pathetically, absurdly, often disreputably. (pp. 226-27)

> *P. N. Furbank, "Godwin's Novels," in* Essays in Criticism, *Vol. V, No. 3, July, 1955, pp. 214-28.*

JAMES T. BOULTON   (essay date 1963)

[*Boulton discusses the didacticism and psychological analysis in Godwin's writings, as well as the influence of William Shakespeare, Samuel Johnson, Coleridge, and Wordsworth on his use of language in the novels.*]

In his novels Godwin wished to possess his readers of 'all the circumstances' bearing on an individual in any given situation, the circumstances being both material and psychological. Psychological analysis was his *forté* as he realised:

> the thing in which my imagination revelled the most freely, was the analysis of the private and internal operations of the mind, employing my metaphysical dissecting knife in tracing and laying bare the involutions of motive, and recording the gradually accumulating impulses, which led the personages I had to describe primarily to adopt the particular way of proceeding in which they afterwards embarked.

The novelist's 'dissecting knife' is both a valuable and a dangerous tool: it can lay bare motive with great vividness and clarity, it can be used to demonstrate the connection between impulse and action, and so on, but if its use becomes an end in itself the patient is reduced to the level of an 'object' and ceases to be a living creature. . . . [It] is well to remember that Godwin was, as his prefaces make clear, a didactic novelist; at his best he surmounts the obstacles this title suggests, but at other times he was obstructed by them. 'We will enlighten you', he remarks in *Political Justice* and it is when this determination takes hold of the novelist—whether the enlightenment be moral or intellectual, through an exhaustive examination of motive and intention or through the giving of information— that he becomes tedious. And even if our final judgment emphasises his creative success in, say, *Caleb Williams* or the final volume of *Fleetwood,* the first two volumes of that novel and many wearying passages in *St. Leon* among others must not be left out of account.

The experience of writing *Political Justice* must not of course be held responsible only for Godwin's failures; it also contributed significantly to his success. As in that work, so in the novels, the essence of his manner is an inexorable deliberateness; 'the chain and combination of events, that proceeds *systematically* from link to link' is what fascinates him and gives a distinctive comprehensiveness to his novels. It is this which lends to the pursuit of Caleb by the seemingly omnipresent Falkland, or to the endless frustrations of St. Leon, or the gradual and inevitable oncoming jealousy in Fleetwood, an almost nightmarish dimension of relentless inevitability. All Godwin's chief characters suffer the agony described by St. Leon—'the snare, woven and drawing close round me on all sides for my destruction'—and if this experience is to be agonising it must be slow but not ponderous; there must be a high degree of inwardness in the presentation of characters and not mere psychological 'information' given about them; and general truths deriving from specific situations should seem to arise inevitably rather than being a principal objective.

To take an example: the following passage records Caleb's decision to watch Falkland in order to discover his apparently guilty secret:

> The instant I had chosen this employment for myself, I found a strange sort of pleasure in it. To do what is forbidden always has its charms, because we have an indistinct apprehension of something arbitrary and tyrannical in the prohibition. To be a spy upon Mr. Falkland! That there was danger in the employment, served to give an alluring pungency to the choice. I remembered the stern reprimand I had received, and his terrible looks; and the recollection gave a kind of tingling sensation, not altogether unallied to enjoyment. The further I advanced, the more the sensation was irresistible. I seemed to myself perpetually upon the brink of being countermined, and perpetually roused to guard my designs. The more impenetrable Mr. Falkland was determined to be, the more uncontrollable was my curiosity. Through the whole, my alarm and apprehension of personal danger had a large mixture of frankness and simplicity, conscious of meaning no ill, that made me continually ready to say every thing that was upon my mind, and would not suffer me to believe that, when things were brought to the test, any one could be seriously angry with me.

Here Godwin's slow, deliberate analysis is at its best. His concentration is on the movement of Caleb's mind, but his own fascination in the amalgam of a curious terror and pleasure, and in the attraction of 'brinkmanship' to a mentality which is at once alert and naïve, comes strongly through. In other words, though the record of this mental state is Caleb's, the zest with which it is communicated arises from the creative pleasure Godwin experienced while writing it. His tendency to generalise is kept subservient to the interest in Caleb's state of mind; the second sentence is a general statement, but it is valid, pertinent, and so placed that we cannot forget the specific situation that gives rise to it. And, finally, there is nothing static about the prose; the analysis is not an academic exercise, but is justified because it advances the plot and records, at a significant moment, the psychological condition of a central figure.

In such a passage—and the mental torment Fleetwood suffers after his marriage provides further examples—the psychological insights are first-rate and the deliberate slowness with which they are revealed largely accounts for Godwin's success: one feels that this *is* the way in which a man's mind motivated by both honesty and self-justification would work. But when urgency and creative excitement are absent the slowness develops into tedium, pleasurable discovery into laborious informativeness; habits of thinking and writing formed while composing *Political Justice* then become deleterious. (pp. 233-35)

Between these two qualitative extremes is a mid-way level of writing which might be described as analytic 'statement'; it lacks the dramatic immediacy and inwardness of the first passage and relies on first-person statements *about* a psychological condition. It is the equivalent in Godwin's novels of the descriptive method used in *Political Justice* to disprove the optimistic philosophers; in both analysis is present but the language keeps the felt experience at arm's length. (p. 236)

Godwin frequently fails to distinguish between conceptual truth arrived at through argument and logical exposition such as is appropriate in *Political Justice,* and the imaginative truth of a novel which is embodied in the facts of a created situation and validated by the intensity and completeness of our response to it. In this connection, Godwin's generalising mode, necessary in *Political Justice,* often proves deleterious in the novels. . . . *St. Leon* frequently suffers from this defect. Having modified his views about 'the culture of the heart' by 1799, Godwin takes every opportunity in this novel to speak of sexual attachment with 'the warmest eulogium', but he does so in general terms more appropriate to *Political Justice.* (p. 237)

A similarly uneven awareness of the difference between philosophical treatise and imaginative literature accounts for Godwin's variable success in handling dialogue. . . . [For] the most part Godwin's imagination is actively engaged in creating characters whose speech idiom is alive and appropriate. Particularly in [*St. Leon*] does he score with the many low-life characters; the very fact that they lack the philosophical sophistication that Godwin was accustomed to meet with in his personal life, the fact that they live intellectually in a recognisably different world compelled him to think creatively about their idiom. This was not invariably the case. In *St. Leon,* where a negro character appears, the narrator disdains 'the mimic toil of inventing a jargon . . . suitable to the lowness of his condition'. In *Caleb Williams,* however, Godwin does not sidestep the problem in this way, nor do we feel that he has invented a 'jargon'; consequently, characters like Tyrrel and Grimes live through their spoken language. Without a living idiom they would be nothing better than properties in a horror novel. . . . [For] the most part jailers and thieves, boors and labourers in *Caleb Williams* are made convincing by means of their idiom; they, too, form part of a society organised on one central principle of tyranny which affects the behaviour of all classes— and it was the recognition of this fact that stimulated Godwin's creative imagination.

When this compulsion is inoperative he lapses too easily into an undistinguished style which responds neither to the speaker nor to the occasion; it is solely a vehicle for the communication of ideas. To give proof of this claim would be tedious; suffice it to say that Godwin is capable merely of turning into direct speech the kind of meditation already quoted (on marriage) from *St. Leon.* At such times he notably lacks what can be called a common, workaday level of style which will crisply and effectively carry him over stretches of ordinary narrative;

instead he often has recourse to a clumsy version of the language he had been accustomed to using in *Political Justice*. (pp. 238-40)

Another test of Godwin's sensitivity to appropriate style is to examine the echoes of other writers—principally Shakespeare and Johnson—that one frequently comes across in the novels. Johnson's manner . . . provided some advantages (amplitude, comprehensiveness, attention to nuances and distinctions, and the like) as a model for the writing of *Political Justice;* it is a handicap as a *general* guide for writing a novel. . . . 'Learned without ostentation, refined without foppery, elegant without effeminacy'. This description of Falkland exactly reproduces the rhythm and balance of Johnson's remarks on Addison's prose style, and it is not out of place—but St. Leon's memory of his mother's affection is less appropriately cast in a Johnsonian mould:

> I was her darling and her pride, her waking
> study, and her nightly dream. Yet I was not
> pampered into corporeal imbecility, or suffered
> to rust in inactivity of mind.

Once Godwin drops into the Johnsonian triad of the first sentence he is, as it were, led into the pseudo-Johnsonian pomposity of the second. . . . And it is this accumulation of verbal weight that is one of Godwin's chief failings.

But it is Shakespeare on whom Godwin most often leans. In *Caleb Williams,* where Godwin's imagination works most effectively, the source-play for the majority of his allusions is *Macbeth,* the Shakespearean tragedy that is undoubtedly closest in mood and story to his own novel. Macbeth and Falkland are both pursued and pursuing, both are inexorably caught in the net of their own making, and both are the victims of ambition. To be reminded, therefore, of the play by 'curses, deep, not loud', 'misfortune comes so thick upon me', '"sleep no more"', or 'the milk of human kindness', might be regarded as valid and purposeful. But one's conviction is weakened by looking at the contexts of these allusions. The first relates to the social reaction to Tyrrel's brutal treatment of Emily, the second is spoken by the dispossessed tenant-farmer Hawkins, the third has reference to the suffering Caleb endured from the discovery of Falkland's secret, and the last is applied to the grotesque female who cooks for the band of thieves which befriends Caleb. There is indeed no thematic consistency about the use of these allusions; Godwin does not introduce them with a full understanding of their value, but indiscriminately as they occur to him by simple association. The extreme example of an allusion used as a cliché occurs in *St. Leon,* where the hero considers the advantages of wealth· 'I contemplated the honour, love, obedience, troops of friends, which are so apt to attend upon wealth.' The words are mere counters which happen to have been strung together and remain as a unit in Godwin's mind; the fact that Macbeth was lamenting the absence of these things and that the allusion inevitably evokes a sense of tragic decline and loss does not perturb Godwin in the least. (pp. 241-42)

In the final volume of *Fleetwood* Godwin blatantly exploits the Othello-Iago-Desdemona situation: Fleetwood is driven insane with jealousy because of his wife's supposed infidelity with his nephew, the soldier Kenrick, through the machinations of Gifford, also his nephew. The reliance on Shakespeare is in itself no disgrace, and it must be said that the device produces some of Godwin's most powerful writing. He relies on a detailed memory of *Othello:* Gifford's techniques were all learnt from Iago; Fleetwood is given a letter by Gifford which seems fully to incriminate Mary; he visits her bedroom, finds her asleep, disbelieves the affectionate words she speaks to him in a dream, and steals a kiss from her; and finally he denounces her. And yet, not only does Godwin allude, not to Iago but to Hamlet when describing Gifford—'thus did this damnable calumniator lead me on, with broken sentences, and "ambiguous givings-out"'—but when Fleetwood imagines Mary to be set on calming his misgivings he remarks:

> It was thus that Cleopatra inveigled Mark Antony to his ruin, when she had determined to
> play him false with his confident Dolabella. As
> my wife left the room, I saw her apply her
> handkerchief to her eyes. . . .

Such evidence of insensibility is scarcely credible.

Yet this kind of literary and verbal insensitivity is frequently found. In *Caleb Williams* even Falkland at times almost degenerates into the conventional figure of a horror novel, the man who gnashes his teeth and stamps in rage. . . . (p. 243)

On the other hand, it is vital to note occasions when Godwin's choice of language and metaphor is precise and effective. Three examples must suffice. The first is a brief one from *Caleb Williams;* it occurs when Caleb establishes his initially idyllic relationship with Laura Denison:

> While our familiarity gained in duration, it
> equally gained in that subtlety of communication by which it seemed to shoot forth its roots
> in every direction.

The metaphor is unobtrusive, almost casual, but it acts exactly as it should, stressing the living yet invisible growth of a developing acquaintance. The second comes from the point at which St. Leon experiences immortality as distinct from merely contemplating the idea of it. Godwin tries to capture the sensation vividly, and does so through an exploration of the difference between the Christian, who believes in 'eternal bliss' but has only a 'faint and indistinct picture' of it in his mind, and

> the feelings of the celebrated apostles, who had
> been taken up into the third heaven, and had
> beheld the new Jerusalem with all its jaspers,
> its chrysolites, its emeralds, and its sapphires.

The parallel is just, it is worked out with care, and one can feel the writer's determination to think concretely about the abstract issue: 'It is so different a thing to conceive a proposition theoretically, and to experience it in practice.' And the final example, from *Fleetwood,* involves a discrimination between the man of 'simple perception' (Sir Charles Gleed) and the man of 'imagination' (Fleetwood himself). The distinction is made by contrasting the responses to a landscape of a farmer and a poet, the former seeing the detail of soil, weather, and crops, the latter seeing 'a living scene, animated by a mysterious power, whose operations he contemplated with admiration and reverence'. 'The farmer's were perceptions; his were feelings'. That the distinction was a commonplace in the late eighteenth and early nineteenth centuries is immaterial; it is important that it should be made, and Godwin makes it with great care and vividness.

This is to take only one illustration from each of three novels, but the common factor in all is significant. Each example—and they were not initially chosen with this in mind—involves an attempt by Godwin to think precisely about a feature of human character, to assess and capture imaginatively some moral perception. Behind each lies an abstract issue which had stimulated the philosopher in him—the nature of human relationships, the difference between theory and practice, or the nature of perception; the intellectual stimulus excited clear, creative thought about the characters and situations which embodied these abstractions; and the result is fresh, lucid, and fluent prose.... On the other hand, where Godwin is not intellectually as well as emotionally involved the outcome is unconvincing. He is not so involved for most of the first two volumes of *Fleetwood*, for example, hence their tediousness for long stretches. The rakes and mistresses with whom Fleetwood associates do not come alive, they are merely verbal forms without body; consequently, when we learn that Fleetwood had 'passed the Rubicon of vice' and had become 'hardened and brutalised' we note them as statements that mean nothing on our pulses. Indeed, at one point Godwin implicitly confesses his lack of involvement. Fleetwood visits the court of Louis XV and Godwin remarks that it would be 'superfluous' for him to describe the depravity of a court which 'the reader may find in so many volumes amply and ambitiously detailed'. In thus avoiding his responsibility he may have had in mind those 'innocent and inexperienced readers' for whose safety he is scrupulous in *St. Leon*, but the truth is that he is writing as an observer and not as a man imaginatively involved in human actions. (pp. 244-45)

A major reason for the failure of *St. Leon* lies in Godwin's design: to '"mix human feelings and passions with incredible situations, and thus render them impressive and interesting"'; *St. Leon*, in other words, is Godwin's "Ancient Mariner." The story was to be of 'the miraculous class', necessitating the constant invention of novel and surprising situations; Godwin's ingenuity is kept at full stretch, but the reader becomes wearied by an incredible sequence of events, each of which increases the hero's misfortunes. There are incidental successes within the novel; even in the improbable happenings centring on the giant, Bethlem Gabor, Godwin's amazement at the resilience of the human mind brings St. Leon alive and momentarily saves him from being a puppet of circumstance; but as a whole the novel is insufficiently pervaded by intellectual vigour and, because of its design, Godwin is too intent on manipulating events. If, however, *St. Leon* is Coleridgean, *Caleb Williams* and *Fleetwood* are Wordsworthian. In them he is concerned with *'things as they are';* his purpose is to give the charm of novelty to things of every day. The first is a story of 'uncommon events' but 'entirely within the laws and established course of nature'; the second, even more Wordsworthian, is to give 'a certain kind of novelty' to 'common and ordinary adventures'. Thus, although inventive ingenuity was still called for, it was working on the material of ordinary life and—equally important—within a society in which operated the moral forces Godwin had examined in *Political Justice*. That *Fleetwood* does not make a forceful impact on the reader until the final volume is significant.... [The] novel comes to life with dramatic suddenness when a false estimate of rank and wealth distorts the moral perception of the central character, a man—as Godwin said of Burke—who was a strange mixture of 'dark and saturnine temper' with 'urbanity and a susceptibility of the kinder affections'.

This final volume of *Fleetwood* is the nearest approach both in mood and successful achievement to Godwin's best novel, *Caleb Williams*. And what most distinguishes these two among his other novels—besides a more intelligent choice of form,

A portrait of Mary Wollstonecraft shortly before her death.

the stimulus of intellectual excitement, and the concentration on 'things as they are'— is the presence in both of a powerful central figure driven to near insanity by a regard for rank and social eminence, a veneration for the values of aristocracy. He is a man in both cases whose moral vision is distorted by this obsessive veneration; he earns of the other characters and of the reader sympathy and admiration mixed with regret for misused talents; he excites a response, indeed, such as Burke aroused in Godwin.... [Here] was the most fearful evidence of the power of a traditional social morality to corrupt even the best human qualities, and the creative results, above all in *Caleb Williams*, are manifest. Instead of characters dissected as mere objects (as in *St. Leon* or the early volumes of *Fleetwood*), we are presented with an excited series of discoveries about the springs of human action; instead of the language of abstract speculation habitually used in *Political Justice*, we have an idiom that is generally alive and flexible; and instead of a writer who is a kind of bemused schoolmaster, we have Godwin imaginatively resolving the problem raised by a contemporary situation. (pp. 247-49)

James T. Boulton, "William Godwin, Philosopher and Novelist," in his The Language of Politics in the Age of Wilkes and Burke, *Routledge & Kegan Paul, 1963, pp. 207-49.*

WALLACE AUSTIN FLANDERS   (essay date 1967)

[*Flanders interprets* St. Leon *as an elaboration of the literary techniques Godwin used in* Caleb Williams *and of his philosophical theories in* Political Justice. *He argues, in addition, that in*

St. Leon *Godwin employed "the supernatural trappings of Gothic fiction for didactic purposes."*]

Godwin employed in *St. Leon* much more directly than he did in *Caleb Williams* the characteristic techniques of Gothic fiction, and used them to illustrate and elaborate on the ideas published earlier in *Political Justice*. Thus the novel is interesting partly as it extends the range of Gothic fiction, not so much in its introduction of "'criminal' and 'alchemical' elements," but in its combination of the two dominant schools of novel writing in the 1790's: the Gothic and the "philosophical." (p. 533)

Although there is in *Caleb Williams* an interest in subjective experience much like that of the Gothic novel, there is no attempt to introduce the supernatural, either directly, as in *The Monk*, or indirectly, as in Mrs. Radcliffe's pseudo horrors. *St. Leon*, on the other hand, uses the supernatural trappings of Gothic fiction for didactic purposes. In *Caleb Williams*, the institutions representing the evils which Godwin attacks are recognizably English and contemporary; in *St. Leon* Godwin turns to the strangeness and exoticism of the supernatural, to foreign countries and remote periods of history for a setting in which to play out the consequences of his ideas.

Godwin's reputation as a sternly rational thinker would not lead one to expect him to indulge in the sensational delights of Gothic fiction; yet, much like other writers of Gothic novels, in his fiction he was always interested in abnormal states of mind issuing from corruptions of human nature and reason. Like Swift, he seems to be more fascinated with aberrations than the norm he upholds. Then there were other reasons for exploring the Gothic style; *St. Leon* was perhaps the first of Godwin's mature works to be inspired by commercial reasons. Even though Godwin never ignores his serious purpose in the novel, he adopted its mode at least in part to attract readers, having the dual aims of the professional novelist and the moralist. (p. 534)

In spite of its Gothic framework, the central purpose of the novel is to inculcate moral truths. In the first edition of *Political Justice* Godwin classed literature as one of the "three principal causes of moral improvement." He said that "few engines can be more powerful, and at the same time more salutary in their tendency, than literature. Without enquiring for the present into the cause of this phenomenon, it is sufficiently evident in fact, that the human mind is strongly infected with prejudice and mistake. The various opinions prevailing in different countries and among different classes of men upon the same subject, are most innumerable; and yet of all these opinions only one can be true. Now the effectual way of extirpating these prejudices and mistakes seems to be literature." Godwin's speaking of literature as an "engine" is typical of his attitudes; he later spoke of the novel in the Preface to *Caleb Williams* as a "vehicle" for teaching "a valuable lesson" [see excerpt dated 1794]. Many of the moral concerns prominent in *Caleb Williams* recur in *St. Leon*, often in a similar guise, and this recurrence shows the constancy of his novelistic aims. (pp. 535-36)

The supernatural elements in *St. Leon* are closely involved with the central theme. The effects of St. Leon's possession of superhuman powers is the central subject of the novel, and their appeal to his ambition is his downfall. In St. Leon's career, as in Falkland's in *Caleb Williams*, Godwin shows that power which divides man from man is a curse. St. Leon's ambition and pride make him dissatisfied with a simple but

secure life in Switzerland. . . . Godwin has much to say in *Political Justice* about the effects of bad education on the moral state of both individuals and the society they form. In St. Leon's case vicious education has produced a temperament which leads him to turn away from the principles of justice and morality, based for Godwin perhaps most firmly in the dictate of absolute sincerity, to a systematic practice of deception for the purpose of furthering his ambition.

The secrecy which St. Leon is forced to maintain is the agent of his undoing, for in hiding his resources and his action he cuts himself off from all mankind. (pp. 536-37)

In the essay **"On Awakening the Mind"** in *The Enquirer* . . . Godwin stated that "Man is a social being. In society the interests of individuals are intertwisted with each other, and cannot be separated." This belief, whose operation in Godwin's mind is very close to that of sentimental benevolence, is fundamental to his ideas on political justice, and was important in determining the idea of *St. Leon*. The novel shows the calamity resulting when a man tries to alter his social relationships by untwisting the natural bonds tying man to man. In St. Leon's hyperbolic case these bonds are the basic conditions of human existence, such as the necessity of labor and the inevitability of death. When St. Leon suffers for the first time the fear and scorn of the ignorant, with whom he would never associate on a personal level but who now join in society's suspicious rejection of him, Godwin shows that even this apparently inconsequential breaking of the social bond is a "calamity." . . . Every step St. Leon takes toward freeing himself from the common hazards and necessities of human life takes away as well a portion of the potential happiness resulting from his common humanity and leaves him more unnatural and miserable. He refrains from taking the Elixir of Life until his preservation depends on it. Its baleful effect . . . is rather to heighten his sense of isolation than to reinvigorate him. . . . (pp. 537-38)

This misery adds up to a terrible indictment of what St. Leon has done. He learns that "it is indeed absurd, it may be termed profanation, to talk of solitary pleasure." . . . The word "profanation" indicates Godwin's meaning, for he condemns St. Leon's power as a profanation of human nature and the moral order of the world—parallels to God in Godwin's atheistic universe. The implications of this condemnation extend to any powers and privileges a man may claim which are not the common property of humanity. The source of the wrong here is the same as in *Caleb Williams*: like Falkland, St. Leon uses prerogatives to wrest from life what he desires and fails to gain respect for himself naturally and honestly. This divorce from natural justice makes both characters solitary and miserable. In *St. Leon* the supernatural becomes a metaphor for what is depicted in natural terms in *Caleb Williams*.

The novel's treatment of domestic affection as a morally cultivating exercise of benevolence is closely related to the main theme of the novel and therefore to the novel's Gothic elements. The natural blessings of domestic happiness are opposed to the objects of St. Leon's ambition. The corruption of his ideas brought about through his education and his life in Paris led him to accept unnatural and antisocial powers in the place of honest labor and affection. He never regains the flawed happiness of the sojourn in Switzerland after he abandons the confidence and hence the love of his family; no benevolence or philanthropy he attempts can succeed to the extent of the limited good he could have promoted by serving them. The miscarriage of his attempts at social benevolence in Hungary illustrates his failure in trying to transcend natural limitations. The loss of the respect of all mankind follows upon his rejection of natural affection and the social bonds of family life. This emphasis clearly reveals the middle-class sentimentalist leanings of Godwin's apparently revolutionary "rationalistic" ethics, which were strongly but perhaps less evidently present in his earlier *Political Justice.*

The didactic intentions of Godwin's development of these themes is well served by the wanderings of his outcast hero. St. Leon is morally condemned because his choice of evil destroys his bonds with humanity, but in his wanderings Godwin has many opportunities to display a variety of social injustices in society's reactions to the outcast himself. This device lends sympathy to St. Leon without changing Godwin's estimation of the worth of his motives. Showing kinship to the legend of the Wandering Jew but ultimately drawn from the example of the earlier uses of picaresque literature for social commentary, it reveals the moral corruption of both St. Leon and his persecutors. Godwin never condones persecution or torture, although they follow St. Leon because of his guilt. (pp. 538-39)

The idea that the issues with which he deals in the novel should grow out of the historical circumstances of its background does not seem to have occurred to Godwin; he rather grafted contemporary concerns onto his historical setting. . . . Godwin, as concerned as he was with the revolution and personally aware of its effects, in *St. Leon* still uses history in the classical manner; he writes a novel in which "not only the psychology of the characters, but the manners depicted are entirely those of the writer's own day" and in which there is no "derivation of the individuality of characters from the historical peculiarity of their age."

In his treatment of the Inquisition, Godwin uses his historical background characteristically as a pretense for introducing moral commentary on a contemporary theme. He openly connects the Inquisition with English attempts to suppress all liberal political ideas in the face of the French revolutionary threat. (pp. 539-40)

St. Leon's flight to Spain to escape persecution is the original device which enables Godwin to enlarge his didacticism. . . . Godwin counts on the British abhorrence of Catholicism and on the current literary associations of the black mysteries of the Roman Church to make his point. St. Leon refers to the prison of the Inquisition as a "scene of Horrors" and other details of the imprisonment lend it a Gothic cast; the prisoners are described as "mere shades of men, cold, inert, glaring bodies, which the heaven born soul has long since deserted and left to themselves." . . . In this case, unlike many similar treatments of the evil of the church, the Gothic horrors are intended to emphasize the evil of religious persecution rather than merely to produce a shiver of terror.

The other Gothic elements in the novel, whether actually supernatural or only atmospheric, also lead to the enforcement of ideas. Godwin, always interested in the psychological states of his characters, creates in St. Leon a variation on the theme of the haunted wanderer which lent much Gothic feeling to *Caleb Williams* and lends romantic feeling to his basically didactic intentions. St. Leon is remorseful over his past and regrets with anguish his loss of the means of giving his family those joys he covets for them. He wanders alone through conventionally wild landscapes in which he is tormented by his emotions. . . . This misery and self-condemnation amid the sublimity of nature prepare St. Leon for the acceptance of the stranger's gift, which proves his final ruin, and thereby provide an emotional tone suitable to the magnitude of his corruption. (p. 541)

Such tormenting guilt anticipates that of the Byronic villain-hero, but Godwin's interest in states of mind is generally more "scientific" than Byron's; he often introduces little discourses on the psychology of guilt. Even though he does not admire irrationality, he shows a constant awareness that there are depths of experience not revealed in the ideal rational man who is the ultimate product and agent of political justice. His despairing creatures fascinate him and at times seem to press him to a denial of his usual belief in the efficacy of reason as a control of human behavior. . . . St. Leon leaping from rock to rock in his frenzy and secret guilt reminds us of Manfred and the guilt-haunted heroes of Byron's Oriental Tales. Godwin's treatment of St. Leon is close in feeling to the romantic conception of the persecuted, sensitive misfit of Byron and Shelley although Godwin condemns the misfit instead of exalting him. (p. 542)

[St. Leon] remains a man to be pitied but a man whose anti-social emotions are never glorified. St. Leon is not a complete villain, however, for he reveals Godwin's ambiguity of feeling. Godwin's sensibilities are perhaps inevitably more stimulated by the aberration than the norm, and therefore he emphasizes the sufferings of the culpable St. Leon much as Evans notes. Intellectually, Godwin's moral commitment to the standards of *Political Justice* never wavers in *St. Leon* and finally gives a justification to its Gothicism. . . .

The Hungarian episode provides perhaps the most striking Gothic exercise in the novel and reveals as well the aesthetic problems with which Godwin was struggling in *St. Leon.* Here Godwin serves his didactic aims by pursuing the indictment of despotism as a variety of the unjust power which divides man from man. St. Leon is shocked to find the rulers of Hungary jealous of his attempts to aid the starving populace because any alleviation of their suffering lessens the government's despotic power. He is in great danger because he dares to lessen the misery on which tyranny feeds. He meets the wild and distorted misanthrope, Bethlem Gabor, who, because of the effects of injustice, is dedicated to hatred of mankind. As the prisoners of the Inquisition become mere shadows of men through the effects of despotism, Gabor becomes through the effect of despotic cruelty a sublimely magnified type of man's malignity. (p. 543)

The exaggerated psychology is in keeping with the incredibly exaggerated drawing of Gabor's whole character. It illustrates Godwin's theses about crime and harks back to the idea in *Political Justice* that evil is imposed on man by his institutions, chiefly political ones. Gabor turns against St. Leon, not only because he is suspicious and jealous of his magic powers but also because he has been taught to hate by men, who, like St. Leon, have tried to extend their power by unnatural and unjust means. St. Leon attempts benevolent actions in Hungary but fails because his power is founded not on natural justice but on unnatural wealth.

The sources of his misery combine against St. Leon in a Gothic nightmare of oppression. Gabor imprisons him in a dungeon— this indispensable asset of the Gothic novel is played upon with relish—and he escapes only by accident. Godwin portrays the kinship between the corruption of the two men at length; Gabor, a fully developed sublime villain, is a double for the outcast St. Leon. . . . (pp. 543-44)

The symbolic power inherent in the St. Leon-Gabor relationship is not fully realized because of Godwin's lack of literary skill. He tries for Gothic effects, as in his description of St. Leon's hunger pangs: "The gnawings I now felt in my stomach were intolerable. They were at one period so severe, that I can compare them to nothing but the sensation of having swallowed a glowing ember . . . the pain was diversified with intervals of a death-like and insupportable sickness—But no; I will not attempt to describe the horrors of hunger sublimed by despair, where the torture of the mind gives new pungency and uproar to the corporeal anguish." . . . No better and no worse than most such descriptions, this passage finds its relevance to Godwin's idea in its reference to the "tortures of the mind," which, although they are perhaps the essence of all Gothic terror, take on added significance in St. Leon's consciousness of his moral guilt.

Although Godwin employs in these ways the supernatural and Gothic effects as metaphor and illustration of the unjust and unnatural possession and exercise of power, they strain his somewhat limited literary powers—as the character of Gabor amply reveals. The problem of creating an aura of probability was for Godwin a vexing one. Although St. Leon is cut off from society because his magic removes for him some of the basic cares of mankind, Godwin must, in order to gain our sympathy, portray him as a vulnerable human being, subject to anxieties and concerns such as hunger and fear of death which should not touch him very deeply. (pp. 544-45)

Godwin was not successful in handling the Gothic elements, although he was able to endow them with meaning. His rationalistic temperament made it difficult for him to lose himself in an effect. The very intellectualism which led him to give didactic meaning to the supernatural kept him from making it fully effective. Yet in consistency of idea and intellectual interest *St. Leon* is superior to most contemporary didactic novels. As a work of Gothic fiction it is interesting for what it attempts to do; its serious metaphorical use of the supernatural was a rarity in the literature of the eighteenth century. In using Gothic subjects for his purposes, Godwin foreshadows later, more successful uses of such materials after Gothicism had faded. . . . Godwin was, in spite of his weaknesses, perhaps instrumental in extending the range of prose fiction through both *Caleb Williams* and *St. Leon*. (p. 545)

> *Wallace Austin Flanders, "Godwin and Gothicism: 'St. Leon'," in* Texas Studies in Literature and Language, *Vol. VIII, No. 4, Winter, 1967, pp. 533-45.*

ERIC ROTHSTEIN   (essay date 1967)

[*Rothstein contends that* Caleb Williams *is a unified moral tale whose narrative action moves from "the egoistic portrayal of external events to the objective . . . recognition of personal morality."*]

Largely because of Godwin's own insistence on ideology, the "message" of *Caleb Williams* seems curiously detachable from its literary artistry. Critics who have tried to reconcile the two have evoked such dubious genres as the Political Novel and the Psychological Novel, and have claimed that one is the vehicle or the complement of the other in satisfying Godwin's inner conflict between reform and romance. Some see a sadomasochistic Gothicism as setting and libretto for the victory of middle-class virtue over its feudal pursuers; some find a profound anatomy of obsession carried on, half intended, beneath the white sheets of Godwin's rationalism; or some discover both, in a muddled way, going on at once. I should like to propose a different approach. I contend that *Caleb Williams* is very much of a piece, that it is primarily moral, and that its social or psychological interests serve to exemplify or to express moral terms. Furthermore, I maintain that despite his stylistic limitations, Godwin succeeded in writing a skilfully planned and formally satisfying work of art. He did so by contriving an intricate *Bildungsroman*—or spiritual autobiography—in which Caleb learns about things as they are, within him and outside him, through a flow of actual events and of psychologically symbolic events connected by analogy.

This contention implies at least three postulates. The first is that *Caleb Williams* centres upon individual recognition, not social exposure; the second, that despite Godwin's sporadic determinism, the novel insists on moral action and choice; the third, that we must consider what happens in the novel as Caleb's renderings, not as objective fact. I believe that these postulates are not so precarious as they may seem. As to the first, we should observe that neither Caleb's curiosity nor Falkland's greed for reputation, the two characteristics that are the tinder of the plot, seems to be socially determined or even socially encouraged. . . . Falkland's fatal disposition comes from reading Italian romances, not from the society in which he actually moves. "Imagination" and "fancy," according to Caleb, encourage in Falkland a "temper perpetually alive to the sentiments of birth and honour," while philosophy, which was presumably what society brought to his education, "purged" his imagination. . . . Even the despotism of Barnabas Tyrrel, about which one hears in Chapter III, comes from his having been spoiled as a child, and must therefore have been latent within him. Given that these three men, portrayed in the opening three chapters, are the most important actors in the book, one may well be sceptical about Godwin's indicting society. It seems obvious that, ideologically, social malfeasances are extensions of personal evils. At most, the social stimulus makes individual corruption plausible or feasible in terms of verisimilitude; or it palliates the faults which it approves. But these are secondary refinements. Evil in *Caleb Williams* comes from individual human beings, whom society as a whole reflects. Men must change before society can.

To throw the moral burden upon individual action forces one to assume that people can make choices and follow them. Godwin at times undeniably claimed to believe that principles of necessity bind each man, and this claim appears to run counter to the moral freedom in *Caleb Williams*. In temper, it probably does. But *Caleb Williams* is no more obliged to work in terms of necessity than *Rasselas*, say, must work in moral terms because its author was a brilliant and insistent moralist. . . . [In *Caleb Williams*] Godwin limited himself formally by setting up as narrator a young man whose mind and conscience operate in terms of moral will. However we may judge Caleb's individual responses to his world, we cannot exclude those responses from our range of understanding. Moral praise, blame, and therefore choice, are intrinsic to the novel. Furthermore, our sense of Caleb's individuality, made quite marked by the first-person narration, works against our thinking of him deterministically.

By insisting on the importance of free will in the novel, one can see why Godwin threw aside his first conclusion, in which Caleb is finally rebuffed by Falkland and by the law, so that he ends his memoir broken, delirious, and impotent. The logic of the novel leads to a conclusion that throws the onus not on society and its squires, as Godwin must have perceived on re-reading, but on the freely chosen evil of the individual. The published conclusion, as a result, shows us Caleb's inner guilt after Falkland and society have cleared his name: ''it is now only,'' he tells us, ''that I am truly miserable.'' . . . One can also understand, following this line of argument, the short path between *Caleb Williams* and Godwin's next two novels, *St. Leon* and *Fleetwood*, in both of which the moral act is paramount.

Such an emphasis upon the individual and his moral choice leads directly to my third postulate, that one must consider the events in the novel as Caleb's renderings rather than as objective fact. Clearly, some of the events must represent Caleb's subjective re-creations, if not distortions, of a reality that hides from the reader in ambiguity. Information about Falkland's past involvement with Tyrrel and Emily Melville, transcriptions of private conversations and still more private feelings—these appear on Caleb's pages, although by any standard of literal accuracy he could not have discovered them. Unless one is to assume that Godwin pointlessly abrogated his narrative convention at the very beginning of the novel, when one would think that he might well be establishing it, one must agree that the first third of the novel, more or less, presents Caleb the narrator as an author rather than as an objective historian. . . . Godwin must have wanted Caleb to tell the flashback story in his own way. By so doing, Caleb could provide us with various moral patterns, later picked up by analogy, and with an index of his own mind and experience through the allusory structure of the story he tells. (pp. 18-20)

Godwin's obvious interest is not in neat causal plot, of the sort that a rational social reformer might fancy, but in the effect of events on Caleb and Caleb's moral development.

If we accept this sort of reading, we can understand Godwin's letting the plot turn on a series of malign accidents that appear more suitable to the professed purpose of Hardy's novels than to any fictional exposition of *Political Justice*. Caleb happens to wander to Mr. Forester's house just at the time that Mr. Falkland happens to arrive there, and so is suspected (with some reason) of chicanery. Falkland's spy Gines happens to be the same man whom Caleb had earlier served to humiliate, and Gines' brother happens to be the very printer to whom the disguised Caleb sends his pamphlets. If events are seen as shaped by the narrator, one does not balk at Godwin's balancing the humiliation of Falkland and the humiliation of Gines against one another. One accepts his playing off the capture of real criminals (Gines' task) with the capture of fictional ones (the printer's), thereby to embellish the theme of reality and imagination that pervades the novel. . . . [Examples] of different sorts all suggest a fatalism far removed from Godwin's ideas of necessity. The fatalism here is symbolic, and exists not in the structure of William Godwin's world but in that of Caleb's spiritual voyage.

To say that Caleb is in some way the creative poet of his own history, mingling world and self, is inevitably to remind oneself that Godwin was an almost exact contemporary of Blake and that *Caleb Williams* is only four years older than ''The Rime of the Ancient Mariner.'' . . . Godwin, the son of a dissenting minister, did not desert the tradition of Bunyan and Defoe, who brought the allegorical autobiography to its highest point at the turn of the eighteenth century. In the preface to *Caleb Williams*, Godwin mentions his reading John Reynolds' collection of providential tales, *God's Revenge Against Murder*, first published in 1635. He also was reading that most intricate of eighteenth-century spiritual journeys, *Clarissa*, while writ-

ing his own novel. Admittedly, Godwin has disembarrassed himself of the theology of these works. But he has adapted the form by keeping a kind of providential force, as the ''coincidences'' listed above should indicate. Caleb is driven toward truth, a recognition of his own blindness and his own egoism. That process is clarified for the reader through the systematic use of allusion and of analogous moral acts.

Caleb Williams itself begins with the flashback to the history of Falkland and Tyrrel, which presents a sort of moral lexicon for what is to happen later. When examining it closely, one finds that Caleb tells this history like a plagiarist, borrowing ideal schemes of action from several sources, most prominently from the novels of Richardson. Because Richardson was so extraordinarily popular in the late eighteenth century, close parallels with events in *Sir Charles Grandison* and *Clarissa* could not pass unnoticed: the allusions must be as intentional as they are thorough. Let me indicate how thorough they are. Falkland goes to Italy like Sir Charles Grandison, where he teaches English to a beautiful rich Italian girl, as does Sir Charles. The result in both novels is that the Englishmen must confront jealous Italian pretenders to the girl's hand—Count Belvedere in Richardson and Count Malvesi, which sounds like a negative inflected form of ''belvedere,'' in Godwin; in both novels, the Englishman subdues the Italian by his noble behaviour. . . . Surely these duplications of Richardson's plots, compressed into ten brief chapters, cannot be coincidental. They may demonstrate Godwin's poverty of imagination, or they may be intended to characterize Caleb, who tells us the history. The latter seems more likely. Caleb can only cast his story in terms that he knows, the terms of books rather than of men. His moral knowledge in this first part of the novel is confined by romance.

''Romance,'' for Godwin, would have included the Bible and perhaps also English history, from which other particulars of the flashback story are drawn by the naïve Caleb. After he gets past such allegorically conceived names as ''Clare'' for his famous poet, and ''Tyrrel'' for his rural tyrant, he moves to ''Barnabas,'' Tyrrel's Christian name, with ironic reference to the Apostle who, the Golden Legend says, ''was harmonious [*ordinatus*] in his three faculties, the rational, the concupiscible, and the irascible. . . . He was harmonious with God, deferring to the authority of God, to His majesty and His goodness. . . . He nourished his flock by word, good deeds, and example.'' The ironic joke appears in *Joseph Andrews*, and Caleb carries it to its logical end in all respects. ''Ferdinando Falkland'' conflates two English Civil War heroes, the parliamentary general Ferdinando Fairfax and the great royalist Lord Falkland, both of whom appear in Clarendon's *History of the Rebellion*. (pp. 21-3)

Within this double context of Bible and patriotism, Caleb's own name is expressive. Caleb in the book of Numbers . . . stills the rebellious people, and is thereby justified by the Lord and permitted to enter the Promised Land. Our hero wills himself to be this Caleb, blessed and powerful. Eventually, the name turns out to be ironic as ''Barnabas'' is ironic, and for the same reasons. Just as Tyrrel tries through the law and force to make the world an adjunct of his own ego, in a wild perversion of his apostolic name, so too Caleb tries. The methods differ: Caleb treats all men only as they relate to him, a conversion of reality into self-interest that parallels and anticipates his writing subjective memoirs like objective history. Reality twists into spiritual patterns when seen only from the standpoint of the self, as Caleb sees it and as the tradition of the allegorical autobiography sees it. But the autobiography has a social function. It transforms the self into a universal by explicating a general pilgrimage of the soul, by being written for social benefit, and by stressing the metaphysical reality that it can perceive from its own partial and humble point of view. Caleb writes only as a mental diversion and to clear his name with posterity . . . ; from these facts, we immediately learn the egocentrism of his proceedings. By itself, this egocentrism might be unimportant. It becomes important when seen as a shadow of the callousness, the selfishness, the spiritual despotism that Caleb practises toward Falkland during the early part of the novel, and that overwhelms him with remorse at the end.

Caleb's egoism is established for us by the end of the first chapter, in which Godwin establishes the nature of his sympathy: "My heart bleeds at the recollection of [Falkland's] misfortunes, as if they were my own. How can it fail to do so? To his story the whole fortune of my life was linked; because he was miserable, my happiness, my name, and my existence have been irretrievably blasted." All feeling for Caleb is self-centred; compassion is at best a literary delight. . . . To Falkland's forbearance and rational rebukes, Caleb remains insensible, like Tyrrel and unlike Malvesi. And these days of spying, of goading, of merciless persecution, Caleb calls "a more favourable period of my life." . . . (pp. 24-5)

Caleb's subsequent imprisonment as a thief corresponds, as he would see it, to the unjust imprisonments of young Hawkins and Emily Melville the social underlings whom Tyrrel had arrested respectively as thief and defaulter. Ignoring his own role in corrupting Falkland to a second Tyrrel, Caleb appears partially right. But his egoism and aggrievedness keep him from pressing his analogies further and from seeing that Falkland's dishonour at Tyrrel's hands (for embezzling Tyrrel's neighbourhood reputation) places Falkland too in the list of victims along with Emily and Hawkins. If one looks at the correspondences in these terms, Caleb, who has carried on the work of dishonouring his better, is the second Tyrrel. Again and again, he catches himself up in his simplifications.

A passage from Godwin's *Enquirer* . . . reveals still another twist: "one of the most sacred principles of social life, is honour, the forbearance that man is entitled to claim from man, that a man of worth would as soon steal my purse or forge a title-deed to my estate, as read the letter he sees lying on my table." The letter from Hawkins that Caleb reads . . . has slipped to the floor, but I do not think Godwin would admit such distinctions. Caleb's being accused as a thief, his having his box pried open and Falkland's valuables thrust into it, represents a symbolically accurate punishment. . . . Godwin is guiding us to understand Caleb's actions as the moral equivalents of crime, if not literally crime itself. Caleb is properly discredited and imprisoned, since the false accusation simply lends public arms to naked moral truth.

Prison is dehumanizing, and the keepers vain tyrants. In other words, prison duplicates, on a squalidly physical level, Caleb's own personality, which has made Falkland an object to watch and fetter close. Caleb, of course, claims that the prison is quite alien to his nature—amusingly enough, he insists that the turnkey need not exceed a set social function and threatens revenge for insolence . . . , not reflecting on his own relationship with his master. He tries twice to escape, and details for us his methods of doing so. His description, full of pride at his ingenuity and industry, goes on much longer than the mere narrative demands, and thus should be seen as part of his professed

rhetoric . . . , designed to impress us in his favour and to cheer himself. (pp. 25-6)

As Caleb has entered prison, the novel has moved from its earlier structure of patriotic romance to an anti-social romance or history, as Caleb senses his isolation and symbolically analogizes himself with a legendary criminal. These new terms reflect a fortunate loss of naïveté, but cannot stand up morally better than the old. Raymond's gang offers Caleb a close look at criminals, and permits him to discover for himself that they subsist on despair, self-deceit, and brutality . . . , epitomized by the old hag who attempts his life. Their violence discredits his narrow social condemnations. . . . (p. 27)

The last section of the novel proper, between Caleb's first accusation of Falkland and the "Postscript," picks up the moral, the literary, the spiritual, and the romance themes about which we have been talking. Images of divinity increase, compelling our attention to God and the Devil, those supreme imaginative creators of Truth and the Lie. The Biblical romance of the flashback story now produces a metaphysical echo. Falkland's agent Gines is "infernal" and "diabolic"; the "God-like Falkland" seems "burnt and parched by the eternal fire that burned within him," which can be compared to "the imaginary hell, which the great enemy of mankind is represented as carrying every where about with him." . . . Just as Falkland has earlier shaped a sort of objective truth from Caleb's inner condition, making him first a thief (in the eyes of society) and then a legendary villain, so now he makes Caleb's chosen disguises come true. Caleb finds himself a real beggar—"meagreness and poverty were the ordinary attendants of my course" . . .— and a real Wandering Jew. He has refused rest to Falkland, like the Jew who refused Christ rest on Calvary, and falls victim to the social lash of a retributive God. He thereby learns what reputation means; but he cannot infer from it the principle of utility, as he has not in the past, despite the warning of Collins that bare truth is no absolute . . . , despite the example of Falkland who has saved a village from total conflagration by destroying a few houses . . . , despite the implicit plea of Raymond that repentance should make past folly fade. Caleb once more resolves to create his own world of truth and to arraign the poet of his fate.

Caleb's pointless and malicious accusations against Falkland have no effect but to kill the man and tarnish his name; what is proved is Caleb's own blindness. The flashback story had warned him of this in the actions of Tyrrel—Emily and Falkland survive arrest from a sickbed three days each, in obvious parallelism—and his own story had warned him in the actions of a second Tyrrel, the corrupted Falkland. But Caleb cannot read experience morally, an exercise left for us, and through his act of will he falls unredeemable. In wresting the truth from Falkland and in revealing it, he has created his own hell about himself: now he must live within his sorry creation, newly rich with knowledge and newly powerless. . . . At this point the guilt that has been projected into symbolic action appears within the person who has exemplified its true source, Caleb himself; the narrative pattern has been completed by moving from the egoistic portrayal of external events to the objective (if not disinterested) recognition of personal morality. The memoirs that have been begun to cheer and vindicate the writer end with an unselfish zeal for expiation and a socially meaningful justice.

Caleb Williams is a novel of great polish and complexity, with obvious stylistic faults, with less obvious but far more significant imaginative virtues. It is a broader novel than its critics give it credit for. . . . I do not want to denigrate the seriousness of its social commentary—the prisons, the squirearchy, the magistracy are all as foul in Godwin's eyes as in Caleb's—but to place that social commentary in its proper moral terms. Nor would I deny . . . that *Caleb Williams* and *Political Justice* are closely related; the relation is reciprocal. From examining the two books as Godwin's thought evolves through them, one can see him moving toward the dictum that he enunciates in *Enquirer.* . . : "The first and most fundamental principle in the intercourse of man with man, is reverence." A better single motto for *Caleb Williams* would be hard to find. From its logic, Godwin moved to the overtly domestic fantasy of *St. Leon* and the overtly domestic psychometry of *Fleetwood,* both impressive but loose novels. *Caleb Williams* can by no means be called a loose novel: its matter is limited enough to be manageable and Godwin manages it brilliantly, brilliantly enough to make it one of the great artistic achievements of the late eighteenth century. (pp. 28-30)

> *Eric Rothstein, "Allusion and Analogy in the Romance of 'Caleb Williams',"* in University of Toronto Quarterly, *Vol. XXXVII, No. 1, October, 1967, pp. 18-30.*

JOHN PESTA   (essay date 1971)

[*Interpreting* Caleb Williams *as a tragic novel, Pesta discusses Caleb and Falkland's "wasted opportunity for love."*]

Caleb Williams is a tragic novel because the possibility for love between the hero Caleb and his enemy Falkland is wasted. At the end of the novel Caleb reflects: "I thought that if Falkland were dead, I should return once again to all that makes life worth possessing. I thought that if the guilt of Falkland were established, fortune and the world would smile upon my efforts. Both these events are accomplished; and it is now only that I am truly miserable." . . . Caleb comes to realize that his long sufferings—flight from Falkland, continuous fear of capture, years of anxiety and despair—have been trivial in comparison with the intense remorse he now feels after conquering his master. The novel ends on a note of tragic desolation. . . .

The standard interpretation of Godwin's novel depicts Caleb as a helpless individual within an unjust system and Falkland as a powerful aristocrat with the legal means to persecute his victim. But the relationship between Godwin's characters is more complicated than this statement suggests. Caleb and Falkland find much to admire and praise in each other. There is strong attraction as well as hostility between them, love as well as hate. To understand the novel properly, we must see how its tragic human dimension conforms to Godwin's social and political ideas. (p. 67)

Self-love hinders Caleb and Falkland from achieving a beneficial relationship based on selfless love. Their realization that through blind selfishness and misunderstanding they have caused each other's downfall accounts for the novel's moving conclusion. Tragic suffering results from a wasted opportunity for love. (p. 68)

Ultimately tragedy happens in *Caleb Williams* because two characters who could understand and benefit each other become not "father and son" but mortal enemies. Caleb flees, and Falkland takes advantage of his superior social position to persecute him. The novel becomes a tale of terror and pursuit in the Gothic mode. In the end Caleb triumphs by forcing Falkland to make a public confession. The destruction of Falkland's

pride and Caleb's deep remorse suggest the fierceness of struggle and the guilt and loneliness of triumph in an archetypal conflict between father and son.

Several lines of evidence support the theory that a father-son relationship exists between Godwin's central characters. First, Caleb and Falkland resemble and attract each other, for though they differ in social class and experience, they share essential personality traits. Second, throughout the novel Caleb displays a need to find a parent-figure to replace his own dead parents. Besides Falkland he tries to attach himself to Collins, Forester, Spurrel, and Laura, but all these attempts end in rebuffs. Third, there is an intriguing pattern of mythopoeic imagery, in which Falkland is represented as a supernatural being whom Caleb both fears and loves. (1) Although Caleb's curiosity instigates the fatal connection with Falkland, certain personal factors reveal their spiritual affinity. Both have literary pretensions. Both are intelligent and sensitive to each other's feelings. Most importantly, both are proud and egoistic, qualities that make it difficult for them to engage in a selfless relationship. Falkland's pride involves his obsession with honor and reputation. (p. 69)

Although a development toward friendship takes place early in the novel, Caleb's probing curiosity and Falkland's sense of guilt block this. In a discussion of Alexander the Great, Caleb inadvertently strikes at the root of his master's secret by condemning Alexander's deeds as the unjustifiable murders of a madman susceptible to momentary provocations. "The instant I had uttered these words," Caleb adds, "I felt what it was that I had done. There was a magnetical sympathy between me and my patron, so that their effect was not sooner produced upon him, than my own mind reproached me with the inhumanity of the allusion." . . . The feelings of Caleb and Falkland are so closely attuned that already Caleb can blame himself for distressing his master.

(2) At various times Caleb describes or speaks to several characters as parents. One of these is Collins, an old servant of Falkland's. "My father!" Caleb says to him, "I am your son! once your little Caleb, whom you a thousand times loaded with kindness." . . . Another is Laura—"my comforter, my friend, my mother!" . . .—the admirable woman Caleb meets after fleeing to Wales. Like Collins and Laura, another parent-figure, Falkland's brother Forester, rejects Caleb because of the crimes that Falkland falsely alleges against him, after Caleb attempts to expose his guilt. Falkland seems to interpose whenever Caleb comes near finding parental security. By doing so, Falkland at once persecutes Caleb as an enemy and retains control over him, as if in spirit he alone is Caleb's true parent. (p. 70)

(3) Certain mythic images intensify the love-hate relationship. No consistent pattern exists, for at different times Falkland appears to Caleb as godlike or infernal. A key passage early in the novel, when Caleb decides to spy on Falkland, brings out Caleb's feelings toward him as a divine being: "I determined to place myself as a watch upon my patron. The instant I had chosen this employment for myself, I found a strange sort of pleasure in it. To do what is forbidden always has its charms, because we have an indistinct apprehension of something arbitrary and tyrannical in the prohibition." . . . The editorializing here is related to Godwin's political theme, but more interesting is Caleb's state of mind, his "strange sort of pleasure." The wish for forbidden knowledge goes back to the Garden of Eden, and Caleb's transgression is a sort of Original

Sin from which all his sufferings flow. The arbitrary power is not only political but, perhaps, divine. (pp. 70-1)

A suprapersonal force of evil pervades the novel. Despite the apparent contradiction, however, the representation of Falkland as both godlike and demonic is in keeping with the novel's ambivalent emotional structure. In the supercharged world of *Caleb Williams* it is appropriate that Falkland's mixed qualities of good and evil, benevolence and egoism, should be presented in a heightened manner. The major effect of mythopoeic references is to elevate the personal involvement between Caleb and Falkland and to amplify, often to the point of melodrama, the tone of the novel. The God-man imagery lends strength to the claim that on the man-to-man level the relationship between Falkland and Caleb is that of father and son.

As the preceding outline shows, it is possible to infer a spiritual kinship between Caleb and Falkland and to find many direct statements of love and esteem on Caleb's part. But it remains necessary to determine whether the concrete action of the novel supports these hints and statements, and in particular whether Falkland gives any sign of sharing Caleb's affection. One point that readers generally overlook is that Falkland is not Caleb's constant enemy. In the last volume, after Caleb has been bound over for trial on the trumped-up charge of robbing Falkland, an event takes place that sheds light on Falkland's paternalistic attitude. On the day set for trial, Falkland does not appear, and Caleb is allowed to go free. Afterwards, at a meeting at an inn, Falkland denies that he has sought to injure Caleb. Instead it was Forester, Falkland's brother, who offered a reward for Caleb's capture because he regarded Caleb as an impertinent upstart seeking to slander Falkland. Falkland insists that his sole object has been the preservation of Caleb's life and that, in all his wanderings, Caleb has never been out of his sight. (pp. 71-2)

Within the time scheme of the novel, Falkland's pursuit of Caleb lasts several years, whereas Forester's pursuit covers only a few months. But in terms of space a far greater portion of the book is devoted to Forester's efforts. Godwin's handling of Forester represents a major weakness of the novel, for this character, who plays such a crucial role in the plot, is seldom onstage, and his comings and goings seem quite contrived. For instance, his absence from Caleb's trial, after he has taken great pains to apprehend Caleb, is altogether unsatisfactory. Nonetheless, readers who disregard Forester's role as initial pursuer and who reduce the relationship between Falkland and Caleb to a simple pursuer-pursued situation will fail to appreciate the complexity of their involvement. (pp. 72-3)

In depicting the development of Caleb's character, Godwin avoids a fallacy by having Caleb bring his story up to the present toward the end of the last volume. The opening of Chapter Fourteen makes clear that the last two chapters and especially the Postscript are written with a different attitude from that of the preceding chapters. Caleb's sense of guilt and sorrow develops only in this closing section. If the entire novel were written in long retrospect instead of reaching a present moment before the end, it would be fallacious in a first-person narrative not to represent the narrator's state of mind as the same at the start as at the end. Swift's narrator in *Gulliver's Travels* exemplifies such an omission.

My interpretation of *Caleb Williams* as a tragedy of wasted love lays much emphasis on events that occur near the end of the novel. (p. 74)

Do the tragic implications of *Caleb Williams* conflict with Godwin's political themes? If we accept the standard interpretation of *Caleb Williams,* which regards Caleb and Falkland simply as enemies, quasi-symbolic representations of innocence and oppression, then the reversal of roles that takes place at the end and Caleb's guilt and self-blame make no sense. But the standard conception of Godwin's doctrine is too narrow.... Not Falkland but Tyrrel represents the spirit of tyranny; Falkland stands for monarchy built on the ideal of honor. Godwin considered this ideal a total failure as a social code.... The failure of Falkland and Caleb to overcome egoism and to reach a profitable interchange of help and understanding suggests that society also will remain unsatisfactory so long as men fail to transcend selfishness and prejudice.... Godwin should not be held to a narrow polemical view that simply attacks tyranny. *Caleb Williams* offers a moral and emotional solution to human problems that is at once more moving and effective: love and understanding are needed for men to achieve peace, harmony, and justice, if man is not forever to be the destroyer of man.

To read *Caleb Williams* as a tragic novel is to extend its relevance beyond eighteenth-century historical circumstances into the timeless question of the human condition. A tragedy conceived in terms of personal relations is peculiarly modern, and the central situation of the novel, Caleb's search for a father, constitutes a dominant issue in modern literature. In an age when traditional religious beliefs have been shaken, strong emphasis has been placed on the beneficial, even salvific power of personal relationships. To this extent *Caleb Williams* anticipates the modern dilemma of an alienated individual searching for order and security in an uncertain world. (pp. 75-6)

> *John Pesta, "'Caleb Williams': A Tragedy of Wasted Love," in* Tennessee Studies in Literature, *Vol. 16, 1971, pp. 67-76.*

JOANN P. COBB   (essay date 1973)

[*Cobb contends that Godwin's novels are linked by the theme of human misery caused by both the perversion of human nature and such institutions as government and religion.*]

Caleb Williams and the five novels which succeeded it—*St. Leon* ..., *Fleetwood* ..., *Mandeville* ..., *Cloudesly* ..., and *Deloraine* ...—even though they contain a variety of character types, settings, and plots are very closely related thematically. The encompassing and pervasive theme which dominates the novels is human misery, the cause of which is two-fold: the institutions which dominate human life are a corrupting and limiting influence on human behavior, and individuals pervert human nature by actions which are contrary to reason and benevolence. Each novel involves a variation on this theme. The institution which is responsible for evil may be government, the law, aristocracy, or religion. The suffering protagonist may violate his conscience through passion, predisposition, or premeditation. The result is always the same—tragedy. It is significant that all six novels deal almost exclusively with disaster.

Caleb Williams demonstrates the iniquity which results from the perversion or denial of truth, and each succeeding novel continues the demonstration. Godwin used the novels to illustrate the validity of the basic conclusions of *Political Justice:* Political institutions coerce man, enforce prejudice, prevent enlightenment, subvert morality, and therefore produce unhappiness. "Truth is omnipotent"; if man is free to seek the truth, it will prevail and, in turn, promote rational progress and universal benevolence. To deny truth and submit to political coercion is to live in the misery depicted in Godwin's novels. He used the novels both as a proving ground for his philosophical conclusions and as a vehicle for disseminating his ideas. Because the novels were published during a forty-year period after the appearance of *Political Justice,* they also provided Godwin with the means of promulgating the emendation of his original thought. The fundamental conclusions of *Political Justice* are never denied in the fiction, but the study of each novel individually reveals a gradual modification of certain ideas. Each novel is related to *Political Justice* as the demonstration of the validity of its philosophical conclusions, as the modification or rejection of certain ideas, or both.

The 1798 edition of the *Enquiry Concerning Political Justice and Its Influence on Morals and Happiness* is considered the valid culmination of Godwin's thoughts on political justice. The title indicates that Godwin believed that the importance of politics lies in its relation to virtue and happiness, and his political philosophy is at the same time a moral philosophy. His doctrine of human perfectibility and rational progress depends upon the existence of absolute truth which becomes the standard for measuring progress. Man is capable of knowing these truths through reason which "collates" emotions and feelings, as well as ideas and apprehensions, and judges rightly the truth of a situation in relation to eternal truth.

Since man is capable of right judgment, lack of it indicates the subversion of human nature by false opinion inflicted upon man by outside force. Godwin emphasizes the importance of this conclusion in stating the corollaries of his fundamental position in regard to the power of truth: "Sound reasoning and truth, when adequately communicated, must always be victorious over error: Sound reasoning and truth are capable of being so communicated: Truth is omnipotent: The vices and moral weakness of man are not invincible: Man is perfectible, or in other words susceptible of perpetual improvement." Since truth is omnipotent, according to Godwin, he who knows the truth must act in accordance with it. Evil thus becomes only the absence of good or lack of knowledge. Vice will disappear when man gains enough knowledge, and this is the foundation for Godwin's belief in rational progress. (pp. 16-17)

The difficulty of full acceptance of Godwin's philosophy lies in his fundamental belief that man is basically good and primarily rational. The charge that Godwin ignores the problem of evil is, to a great extent, a valid criticism of *Political Justice.* A complete understanding of Godwin's thought requires an investigation of the novels which succeeded *Political Justice,* complemented it, and sometimes contradicted it. The problem of evil is fully investigated in the novels. Here it is depicted as a direct result of malevolence and error. The tortured lives of Godwin's heroes demonstrate the evil which prevails when men refuse to submit to truth or institutions enforce error. In Godwin's philosophy, pain and evil are synonymous and the aura of misery which pervades his novels gives evidence of his concern over the problem of evil.

The Preface to Godwin's first major novel, *Caleb Williams* . . . , points out the work's intention "to comprehend, as far as the progressive nature of a single story would allow, a general review of the modes of domestic and unrecorded despotism, by which man becomes the destroyer of man" [see excerpt dated 1794]. The major emphasis in this work is on law and the corruption which results from the imposition of it. Law represents institutional society in *Caleb Williams* as government represents all institutions in *Political Justice.* . . . (pp. 17-18)

Falkland and Tyrrel represent the decadent aristocracy which government and law encourage and sustain. Falkland, apparently a refined, sensitive, and benevolent man, is reduced by a momentary submission to passion to a life of suffering; Tyrrel, who is totally degenerate, ruins not only himself, but everything and everyone he touches. Falkland, a victim of Tyrrel's injustice, is in turn moved to inflict injustice on Caleb Williams, and it is the law which permits the machinations of the privileged to oppress and corrupt the rest of society. Falkland's compulsive dedication to his reputation results in the deaths of three men, the destruction of Caleb Williams, and the loss of his own physical and mental health. He is the first of Godwin's guilty, suffering, fictional characters who demonstrate the misery which results when human beings deny the omnipotence of truth and justice. Falkland's unjust and inhuman persecution of Caleb Williams, through the manipulation of the law, demonstrates its dehumanizing effects on both guilty and innocent, as well as the absurdity of "legal justice."

In *Political Justice* Godwin denies the efficacy of punishment, which may reasonably be inflicted only when it will produce an "overbalance of good." To punish a miscreant "for what is past and irrecoverable, and for the consideration of that only, must be ranked among the most pernicious exhibitions of an untutored barbarism." Punishment requires the use of force and "coercion first annihilates the understanding of the subject upon whom it is exercised, and then of him who employs it." Falkland coerces Caleb and destroys himself. Caleb's long flight from his oppressor takes him to prison, to the hideout of a band of robbers, to the London slums, and to a remote corner of Wales. The inhumanity of man is demonstrated in each of these places. Godwin, the revolutionary, speaks through Caleb Williams to demonstrate the depth of the ignominy and misery to which man may sink. (pp. 18-19)

Caleb Williams demonstrates the corruption of mankind as a result of the political institutions which inhibit the progress of truth. If the novel does not offer a solution to the misery of society, it offers an emphatic denunciation of "things as they are." The alternative may be found in *Political Justice.*

The Preface to the first edition of *St. Leon: A Tale of the Sixteenth Century* . . . offers further evidence that Godwin himself connected the opinions expressed in *Political Justice* with those of the novels. He realizes that the conclusions about marriage in this novel are a topic "of the warmest eulogium, while in the Enquiry concerning Political Justice they seemed to be treated with no great degree of indulgence and favour" [see excerpt dated 1799]. (p. 19)

St. Leon begins Godwin's long investigation of the institution of marriage which culminates in the ideal marriage depicted in *Deloraine.* It has been suggested that St. Leon's wife, Marguerite, is the image of Godwin's first wife, Mary Wollstonecraft, but if *St. Leon* is a criticism of man "as he is," it is evident in neither the representations of Godwin's personal life nor the setting of the novel. Though the events take place in the sixteenth century, the problems which assault the characters are timeless. St. Leon's gift of immortal life and the problems this gift entails represent man's search for power and immortality at the sacrifice of justice and benevolence in this life. St. Leon sacrifices both general and private benevolence to self-interest and, in the process, loses happiness for himself, his family, and everyone he encounters. (p. 20)

It is evident in *St. Leon* and the succeeding novels that man needs sympathy and understanding, and the private affections of a wife, family, and friends in addition to his rational benevolence toward mankind in general.

Godwin's third major novel, *Fleetwood: or The New Man of Feeling* . . . , is set in contemporary society and records incidents that "multitudes of readers have themselves passed through." The author forestalls criticism from those "certain persons who condescend to make my supposed inconsistencies the favourite object of their research," by asserting that *Political Justice* recommends not "a pitiful attempt by scattered examples to rennovate the face of society," but "a grand and comprehensive improvement of its members." Godwin has already admitted in *St. Leon* that he now approves of "private affections." (p. 21)

Godwin's next novel, *Mandeville: A Tale of the Seventeenth Century in England* . . . , assumes essentially the form of the memoirs of a madman. Like his predecessor, Fleetwood, Mandeville is a madman ultimately because he cannot perceive truth, goodness, and virtue; that is, he is out of contact with reality. His mature madness is a direct result of his abnormal childhood, and Godwin presents in this novel a case-study of the effects upon the human mind of bigotry and prejudice, horror and cruelty.

One of Godwin's fundamental theories in *Political Justice* is the primacy of environment over heredity in its influence on human lives: "The actions and dispositions of men are not the offspring of an original bias that they bring into the world in favor of one sentiment or character rather than another, but flow entirely from the operation of circumstances and events acting upon a faculty of receiving sensible impressions." Godwin rejects innate principles, instincts, and prenatal influences as critically important in directing the actions of human beings and concentrates on the effects of education: "It has appeared that the characters of men are determined in all their most essential circumstances by education. By education in this place I would be understood to convey the most comprehensive sense that can possibly be annexed to that word, including every incident that produces an idea in the mind, and can give birth to a train of reflections."

The education of the infant Mandeville plausibly produced a madman. At the age of three he witnessed the murder of his mother and father, and every other English Protestant in the company, during the religious wars in Ireland. The uncle who became his guardian was a neurotic recluse who had not put on his shoes to leave his room for twenty years and who could tolerate his nephew only once a month for two minutes. The memory of his uncle's gloomy, isolated estate and the teachings of his tutor, a Protestant Divine who hated the Roman church, formed the mature Mandeville. The detailed exposition of Bradford's opposition to the Catholic church permits Godwin to demonstrate his objection to the superintendence of opinion and the enforcement of prejudice which are a necessary complement to institutional religion.

In *Political Justice,* Godwin considers religious establishments under the section which deals with the political superintendence of opinion. Godwin asserts that "the system of religious conformity, is a system of blind submission"; "the tendency of a code of religious conformity is to make men hypocrites"; and, the clergy "are fettered in the outset by having a code of propositions put into their hands, in a conformity to which all their inquiries must terminate." But the primary objection of Godwin to institutional religion is that it impedes the progress of truth: "The direct tendency of science, is to increase from

age to age, and to proceed, from the slenderest beginnings, to the most admirable conclusions. But care is taken, in the present case [religion], to anticipate these conclusions, and to bind men, by promises and penalties, not to improve upon the science of their ancestors." Rational progress depends upon the assumption that "it is the characteristic of mind to be capable of improvement." To believe that the ultimate truth has been discovered is to become static rather than progressive. According to Godwin, religious institutions, like other political and social institutions, advocate permanence and stagnation and then, worst of all, use force to achieve these ends. (pp. 23-4)

Mandeville is unique among the Godwinian protagonists in his ultimate refusal to "see" truth. Each of the others submits at last to the irresistible power of reason. Circumstances have destroyed Mandeville's ability to perceive truth—he is mad. Modern psychological theory tends to support the conclusion that abnormal childhood conditions may provoke the onset of psychotic obsession in the adult. Though Godwin's pre-scientific psychology differs somewhat from post-Freudian theory, the ultimate conclusions are basically the same: human misery is learned and therefore is not inevitable. Godwin's case-study of the effect of two distinct kinds of "education" upon a brother and sister demonstrates his belief in the possibility of human progress. Mandeville's psychological maladjustment is a result of his early learning. In the words of Mandeville: "It is the express purpose of the narrative in which I am engaged, to show how the concurrence of a variety of causes operate to form a character." Reasonable causes, on the other hand, work to produce a well-adjusted and happy man.

Cloudesly: A Tale . . . , which was published a full thirteen years after its predecessor, bears certain resemblances to both *Mandeville* and *Caleb Williams* and adumbrates *Deloraine*. Earl Danvers, who is the real protagonist of the novel since Cloudesly plays only a minor role, is like Mandeville eclipsed by a rival and like Falkland and Deloraine is made to suffer terribly from remorse and guilt. Danvers' rival is his elder brother, who receives preferential treatment, but Danvers is saved from obsessive hatred by the benevolence of the elder brother himself. One mistake, the concealing of the true heir after his brother's death, leads to a lifetime of mental suffering and demonstrates the futility of sacrificing truth to material power. Danvers' life touches many people in many countries and allows Godwin to illustrate the difference between natural good and ambition, to investigate further the problems of education, and to remind his readers once more of the power of truth. (p. 24)

Though the "voice of truth" is not featured so blatantly in the other novels, its presence in each is too obvious to be denied. The disparity among the characters who are ultimately overcome by truth and reason in *Cloudesly* emphasizes Godwin's continuing belief in its power. In this novel, truth conquers an English nobleman and an English servant, an Italian nobleman, and a Turkish military leader. Godwin's attempt to demonstrate to man the need for truth and benevolence endures until the end of his career as a novelist. His failure to convince his readers of this necessity provokes the cry of Deloraine in the last novel.

Deloraine . . . , which was published when the author was seventy-seven years of age, reiterates the conclusion of his first novel: human guilt and remorse exact a heavier penalty upon the individual than any social or political institution could possibly impose. The debilitating effects of vengeance on both pursuer and pursued, the agony of guilt and remorse which follows crime and deception, and the inhumanity of political institutions are related again, with an important addition. In the person of Catherine Deloraine, Godwin concludes his career as a novelist with a last eloquent and very moving demonstration of the power of truth. (p. 26)

> *Joann P. Cobb, "Godwin's Novels and 'Political Justice'," in* Enlightenment Essays, *Vol. IV, No. 1, Spring, 1973, pp. 15-28.*

C. R. KROPF (essay date 1976)

[*Kropf interprets* Caleb Williams *as "a serious contribution to the ongoing controversy over the instructive purpose and method of fiction."*]

Caleb Williams contributes a statement to the continuing dispute over how fiction best fulfills its instructive intent and to the nearly related problem of the place which fiction should have in the whole educational process of the young.

Among the numerous ways in which the novel and education are related, two are of immediate relevance to *Caleb Williams*. Perhaps because of Richardson's and Fielding's examples, the novel of the eighteenth century took education as one of its major themes. Fielding uses education as an effective method of characterization, and Richardson's Pamela enters a lengthy debate over the best kind of education for her son and writes an extended commentary on Locke's *Thoughts Concerning Education*. (p. 81)

It seems fairly obvious that the phrase which acts as the title of Godwin's novel *Things as They Are* was popularly associated with the two closely related questions of how the reading audience best learns from fiction and how an author can most effectively furnish instruction, by providing vicarious experience in the manner of Fielding and the novel or by holding up models for imitation in the manner of Richardson and the romance. Readers of Godwin's works know that his interest in these and other questions concerning education is readily apparent. In *The Enquirer* he treats such standard questions as the place of the classics in education and the long disputed matter of public versus private (i.e., domestic) education, and his contemporary readers recognized that his novels were intended to instruct the public in the nature of education.... The title [*Things as They Are*] declares in very specific terms that the novel will present us with a fictional world more approximate to Fielding's than to Richardson's, a world of everyday realism and all its moral ambiguity, and that it will instruct by providing vicarious experience, not by holding up patterns of virtue and vice.

At the same time, the novel has something serious to say about the education of youth and about the educations of all three of the major characters at our first introduction to them. In each case the characters are recognizable stereotypes which had appeared repeatedly in earlier works to illustrate various facets of education. Williams is the young man who knows nothing of the world but is well acquainted with books. Falkland, with one unfortunate flaw, is a fine example of what an eighteenth-century gentleman's education should make of him, while Tyrrel is the typical boorish country squire, spoiled by his mother and fawned over by his tutor, a type which appears in *Joseph Andrews* in the person of the nameless country squire who "roasts" Parson Adams. It is reasonably accurate to say that the novel explores the consequences of the miseducation of Tyrrel and Williams. Falkland's polish contrasted to Tyrrel's

ill-mannered rusticity finally goads the latter into provoking Falkland fatally, and Williams's curiosity, undirected by worldly prudence, leads to his own tragedy.

Of more interest, however, is the related theme of how fiction instructs. Both Williams and Falkland are the victims of their reading in romance. Williams tells us that he has an "invincible attachment" to romances. "I panted for the unravelling of an adventure, with an anxiety, perhaps almost equal to that of the man whose future happiness or misery depended on the issue."... The statement, of course, is more true than Williams knows, for on the unravelling of Falkland's adventure his own happiness does indeed depend. Williams's own natural curiosity, misdirected by his reading about the world as it should be as depicted in romances and uninformed about the world as it is, is his destruction. Falkland's preoccupation with romance is no less destructive of his own happiness. (pp. 83-4)

The lives of both men are destroyed by their taking the exemplary world of the romance for a pattern to be imitated.... Falkland tries to live according to a set of values which has nothing to do with the world as it is. Somewhat less obviously Williams does the same thing. He pursues Falkland's secret with the same intensity with which he would watch a plot unwind.... Through at least the first half of the plot one gets the distinct impression that Williams is a character in the wrong novel, one used to living in the world as it should be and now floundering about in the world as it is. To survive, Williams must and does learn the devious ways of the world, but by then both he and Falkland have destroyed their own happiness because of the false ideals they have picked up from their youthful reading in romances.

To read *Caleb Williams* as an attack on romance is perhaps to discover the answer to one serious question about the novel: Why did Godwin rewrite the conclusion? In the original manuscript version the novel ends with Falkland's triumph in the final trial and Williams's subsequent defeat and madness. Apparently dissatisfied, Godwin rewrote the final few pages giving the victory to Williams and concluding with Falkland's death three days later. At first glance the new conclusion seems to be inconsistent with the internal logic of the novel, ... for in a world where injustice is presumably supreme, it gives the ultimate triumph to truth and justice. The new conclusion therefore seems to undermine the propagandistic thrust of the rest of the work. The problem is more apparent than real, however. That truth eventually triumphs does nothing to obviate the injustices which the characters have done to themselves and to each other. Indeed, the fact that truth does finally prevail gives one final and bitterly ironic twist to the novel, for all of the suffering which Falkland and Williams undergo is thereby robbed of what little meaning it may have had. Falkland dies lacking the one thing, a spotless reputation, which he had lived for, and Williams faces a future burdened with the knowledge that he is a murderer.... Godwin's point is not that truth will never prevail, but that the present state of society and its laws being what they are it will prevail only at an enormous and useless expense in human misery.

If anything it is the original conclusion which belies one major point the novel attempts to make. It will be recalled that in the dispute between the advocates of Fielding and the novel on one hand, and Richardson and romance on the other, one matter of contention is characterization. The romance is thought to perform its instructive intent by providing such exemplary characters as Sir Richard Grandison or such negative examples as Lovelace. In the novel, however, such moral oversimplification is not allowed, and the moral ambiguity of a character like Tom Jones is thought to provide useful instruction in the world as it is. The original ending of *Caleb Williams* places the work distinctly within the realm of romance according to this scheme of things. Falkland's character is thoroughly blackened, and Williams is depicted as the suffering innocent whose plight calls on our tears. But in a work which attacks the pernicious effects of romance it will not do to risk the charge of self-contradiction by employing the romance's favorite device of moral over-simplification. The revised version avoids this problem by placing the conflict in a morally ambiguous context. In the final paragraphs of his narrative Williams reflects on Falkland's death: "I have been his murderer. It was fit that he should praise my patience, who has fallen a victim, life and fame, to my precipitation! It would have been merciful in comparison, if I had planted a dagger in his heart." It is no longer very clear who has been persecuting whom. . . . (pp. 84-6)

Thanks to the miseducation inflicted on them by the authors of romances, Falkland and Williams are each victim and tyrant to the other. To read *Caleb Williams* in this manner is to see it as more than a fictional gloss on *Political Justice*. It presents its reader with a morally complex dilemma and makes a serious contribution to the ongoing controversy over the instructive purpose and method of fiction. (p. 86)

> C. R. Kropf, "'Caleb Williams' and the Attack on Romance," in Studies in the Novel, *Vol. VIII, No. 1, Spring, 1976, pp. 81-7.*

IAN OUSBY (essay date 1976)

[*Ousby discusses* Caleb Williams *as "a modernized version of the revenge tragedy" in which the detective and the criminal become symbiotically merged.*]

[Despite] Caleb's obvious courage, energy, and resourcefulness, the reader's view of his character is ultimately hostile. His detective activities involve, in a subtler and transmuted form, several of the themes associated with both Gines and his real-life counterparts. The characterization of Caleb thus shows how the sociologically determined suspicions of the detective manifest themselves in a complex fictional context.

In modern detective fiction the detective plays a role like that of the Duke in Shakespearean comedy: a moral hero and a figure of power, he establishes intellectual certainties and restores the order which has previously been threatened. Caleb Williams, on the contrary, is essentially a tragic figure, powerless in everything except his ability to catalyze discord. His discovery of Falkland's guilt does little good and a great deal of harm. (p. 21)

Even though Caleb is finally successful [at exposing Falkland], the import of the denouement is profoundly dissimilar from its equivalents in modern detective fiction. Superficially a moment of triumph for the detective, it is really a moment of psychological and moral defeat. It destroys even the detective's certainties about himself. . . .

[At the beginning of the novel Caleb] is clearly no simple hayseed, but his view of life and his knowledge of the world smack distinctly of the evening class and the midnight oil; they are bookish and theoretical rather than experiential. (p. 22)

His move from the village to Falkland's manor house involves him for the first time in a world of experience and complexity.

In contrast to the world of Caleb's youth, Falkland's world is one of social power and sophistication, of intellectual and cultural refinement. Through his acquaintance with Falkland and his detective investigations, Caleb is introduced to psychological and moral complexities for which neither village life nor his books had prepared him. (p. 23)

The hero of revenge tragedy undergoes a similar development. Like Caleb, Hamlet and Vindice are scholars thrust into a world of action, a world of decisions with direct human consequences rather than of abstract problems. Again like Caleb, Bussy D'Ambois is the blunt countryman forced to cope with the complexities of court life. In both literal and symbolic terms the court of Jacobean drama and Falkland's manor house function similarly: they epitomize the world of sophistication and complexity with which the hero must deal. Moreover, the complexities presented to Caleb by Falkland's life assume a form familiar in revenge tragedy: the hidden crime or sin which gives the lie to the avowed public standards of morality.

In these circumstances the reaction of the revenge hero is a delicate balance of attraction and repulsion. He becomes a railer at corruption, fascinated by what he attacks. Caleb's reaction to Falkland hinges on a similar paradox. Initially viewing his master as an unspotted emblem of innocence and purity, he then deliberately destroys this ideal image by embarking on his detective activities. Once Caleb has discovered the truth about Falkland's murder of Tyrrel, he oscillates between continued admiration and a hatred of both Falkland and the social system he represents. (pp. 23-4)

Caleb's curiosity, the motive that makes him turn detective, corresponds to the revenger's desire for revenge. In Jacobean drama revenge has an awkward habit of recoiling upon its actor's head, and the revenger commonly dies hoist with his own petard. Caleb's detection exposes him to the same fate. With his discovery of Falkland's crime Caleb's role—to use his own terminology—switches from the "offensive" to the "defensive." . . . Successful as a detective, he almost immediately finds himself in the dock rather than the witness box, and thereafter moves steadily toward social disgrace and psychological ruin. The stages of his destruction mirror his activities as a detective. (p. 24)

The revenger's fate as victim of his own machinations represents a judgment on his actions. As the dying Laertes sees, his death is an ironic stroke of justice. For revenge in Jacobean drama is a morally corrosive activity. Superficially it appears to make its actor the agent of justice; yet far from exemplifying his moral integrity, it calls into question and impairs that integrity. Corrupted by the pursuit of revenge, the revenger dies a victim of the disease he has begun by attempting to cure. Yet viewing a similar reversal in his own life, Caleb Williams can see only a grim irony of fate and an indictment of the social system. His resemblance to the revenger is completed by a nuance which eludes him: the element of punishment, of implicit judgment on the questionable morality of his own activities as a detective.

Caleb Williams, then, can be viewed as a modernized version of the revenge tragedy. The parallel serves to underline the book's essential movement and to suggest the terms by which its hero should be judged. Like the revenger, Caleb in his role as detective is subject to criticism for both his morals and his motives. The matter is complicated, however, by the fact that the entire story is told by Caleb himself: as an autobiographer, he is bent on self-vindication, not self-criticism. He distracts attention from his failings by describing his character in deceptively simple and laudatory terms. According to his own account, he is merely innocent and curious.

Caleb's protestations of innocence begin on the book's first page. "My own conscience," he declares, "witnesses in behalf of that innocence my pretensions to which are regarded in the world as incredible." . . . Indeed, he has undertaken the narrative to clear himself of the charge of theft which Falkland has used to blacken his character and render his adult life "a theatre of calamity." . . . As the narrative proceeds, however, it becomes apparent that Caleb aims at much more than a purely legal vindication.

To the word "innocence" are added other terms suggestive of broader qualities and often touching on key Godwinian concepts, terms such as "simplicity" and "sincerity." The insistence is not merely that Caleb is not a thief but also that he is innocent in more profound ways. He is, he implies, without guilt or sin. Exhibiting this purity in his youth and his early days at Falkland House, he has miraculously retained it through all the miseries and complexities of his relationship with Falkland.

In trying to seek out the precise nature of this vaunted innocence, the reader is likely to find himself in sympathy with Falkland, who at one point quotes with approval the dying words of Brutus: "O Virtue! I sought thee as a substance, but I find thee an empty name!" . . . For all the frequency with which Caleb invokes it, his innocence proves elusive and nebulous. Part of the reader's doubt arises from the very frequency with which Caleb resorts to the term to explain or justify his actions. Describing his first suspicion that Falkland is a murderer, and aware that "the reader will scarcely believe that the idea suggested itself to my mind," he immediately excuses himself on the grounds that: "It was but a passing thought; but it serves to mark the simplicity of my character." . . . The explanation is, in fact, open to objection on two counts. As the narrative makes clear, the suspicion is anything but passing. Moreover, the reader cannot lightly accept a definition of innocence or simplicity which includes such a readiness to believe evil of others; one imagines that innocence is distinguished by precisely the opposite tendency. (pp. 24-6)

[His] interviews with Falkland show not innocence but a convenient, false naiveté. Whether or not Caleb's actions are justifiable, it is clearly misleading to call them "innocent." Caleb himself admits as much when he refers to his own "air of innocence" and his "apparent want of design." . . . The effect of this admission, however, is somewhat decreased by his apparent lack of interest in drawing any distinction between the true and the false, between innocence and guile—a failing which he later insists to be one of the worst aspects of the world's opinion. (p. 26)

Caleb's use of the idea of innocence serves to draw attention to both his unreliability as narrator and his dubious moral status. Obviously he is innocent—as he claims to be—in the strictly legal sense. The substance behind his other claims seems merely to be an initial naiveté, an "ignorance of the world" . . . , which is distinguished primarily by the speed of its disappearance. (pp. 26-7)

Caleb's innocence is destroyed by his curiosity. He himself points to this quality as the mainspring of his character and the determinant of his fortunes. Listing its manifestations, he first mentions his "mechanical turn" . . . , shown later in his mastery of such diverse skills as lockpicking, carpentry, acting,

watchmaking, and writing. This vein of practical ingenuity, combined with a readiness to learn, aligns him with the tradition of sturdy Protestant heroes stemming from Robinson Crusoe. . . .

Fictional detectives are frequently characterized by pragmatism and by practical ingenuity. In Caleb's case, however, these qualities are strangely unrelated to that side of his curiosity which makes him turn detective. His resourcefulness and his willingness to learn are important primarily in helping him to resist and evade Falkland's tyranny, and are only marginally relevant to the events which provoke that tyranny. Caleb's ingenuity arises from a practical interest in the world around him and has an immediate, sometimes vital use. By contrast, his curiosity about Falkland is strictly nonutilitarian. (p. 27)

His eagerness is in response to an irrational obsession rather than a practical need. Caleb is the victim of "a kind of fatal impulse that seemed destined to hurry me to my destruction." . . . In imagery which suggests the similarity of his obsessive curiosity to Edgar Allan Poe's "imp of the perverse," Caleb speaks of the "demon" . . . which finally brings him to "the verge of the precipice." . . . (pp. 27-8)

A similar habit of self-aggrandizement characterizes the way in which Caleb describes that side of his curiosity which prompts him to become a detective. He is, he explains near the beginning of the narrative, "a sort of natural philosopher." . . . Reflecting ruefully on the causes of his misfortunes, he remarks, "My offence had merely been a mistaken thirst of knowledge." . . . Such remarks are vague in reference but have the unmistakable effect of suggesting that the reader should view Caleb as a noble Faustian overreacher or a daring speculator. (p. 28)

In fact, Caleb's curiosity is of precisely the sort that he himself had previously designated as "ignoble." . . . He develops an interest in Falkland unadorned by either moral concern or intellectual originality. Rather, his master affords him "an ample field for speculation and conjecture." . . . As if to emphasize the point that Caleb's speculation is that of the gossip rather than the moral philosopher, the reader is told that the other servants in the house regard Falkland in a strikingly similar manner. . . . Although Caleb's curiosity eventually leads him into realms of moral and intellectual complexity which a Faust or a St. Leon might well inhabit, this is essentially an accident—one that he hardly welcomes—and not the result of any intention on his part. Rather than being the overreacher which his narrative tone at times suggests, Caleb the detective is more the Peeping Tom and the gossip, a figure who invites criticism.

Caleb enters Falkland's service a young and inexperienced man, ignorant of the ways of the world. Under the pressure of curiosity about his master's life he outgrows his initial naiveté, replacing it with a feigned naiveté, an "air of innocence." Godwin's firm disapproval of the type of social manner and behavior adopted by Caleb is on record elsewhere. "Insincerity," he writes in *The Enquirer,* "corrupts and empoisons the soul of the actor, and is of pernicious example to every spectator." Indeed, sincerity—one of the terms that Caleb uses with so uncritical a liberality—is a vital concept in Godwin's vision of ideal social intercourse. However, the description of Caleb's activities as a detective does not reflect merely the social ethics of a philosopher who could on occasion take extreme positions. It also represents a specific response to contemporary issues.

In the novel Caleb is not called a "detective," for the term did not gain currency until the middle of the nineteenth century. He is called a "spy." . . . Then, as now, the term could refer simply to "one who spies upon or watches a person or persons secretly." In its more specialized sense it was applied to the professional snooper, in particular to the spy whose investigations served matters of foreign or military policy, or of internal security. (pp. 28-9)

[*Caleb Williams*] reflects not only the general hostility to spying but also the fear of the spy in its acutest form. That Caleb should be the servant of the man whose crime he uncovers is a fact of central importance to the narrative. Caleb's twin identity as servant and spy is implicit in his Christian name. . . .

Godwin, with his Calvinist upbringing and his youthful experience as a minister, would certainly have been aware of these references. Indeed, throughout the book Caleb's roles as servant and spy are continually brought into juxtaposition. The occasion on which the term "spy" is first used of Caleb also draws attention to his social status. Falkland threatens him: "You set yourself as a spy upon my actions. But bitterly shall you repent your insolence. Do you think you shall watch my privacies with impunity?" . . . Later Falkland reproves Caleb's attempts to draw him into conversation as "improper" . . . and warns him, "learn to be more respectful!" . . . In each case the criticism invokes not an abstract moral code but a code of conduct dictated by their positions as master and servant. (p. 34)

This deliberate juxtaposition is ironic. . . . A combination of faithful service and efficient surveillance is impossible, for spying requires of Caleb a violation of the duties involved in his assigned social role. The breach of fidelity takes on particular significance within the context of the master-servant relationship.

From the beginning of the narrative it is made clear that Falkland, despite the eccentricities caused by his private guilt, is in the salient respects a model employer. . . . "His manner was kind, attentive and humane" . . . , Caleb reports of their first meeting, adding: "My reception was as gracious and encouraging as I could possibly desire. Mr. Falkland questioned me respecting my learning, and my conceptions of men and things, and listened to my answers with condescension and approbation. This kindness soon restored to me a considerable part of my self-possession, though I still felt restrained by the graceful, but unaltered dignity of his carriage." . . . On the one hand, Falkland's behavior implicitly asserts the master's right to keep his servants at a respectful distance. On the other, his manner shows a kindness and sensitivity appropriate to the local squire who is offering to bring an orphaned youth under the protection of the "family." In view of this latter characteristic, Caleb's suspicions have about them an air of churlish ingratitude. They represent, as it were, a refusal to return kind attentions with kind thoughts. However, the burden of the criticism falls not so much on the suspicions themselves as on the course of conduct that they lead Caleb to pursue.

The air of frankness that he feigns in his conversations with Falkland in fact represents an exaggerated version of that "studied countenance" which Godwin noted in all servants. Inscrutability becomes supplemented by a calculated deceptiveness. From Falkland's point of view the effect is to increase the gap that separates him from his servant. From Caleb's viewpoint the gap is narrowed, for he renders himself deliberately unknowable in order to penetrate his master's privacies more successfully. On the psychological level, Caleb attempts to delve into the hidden recesses of his master's mind, to uncover the source of his private anguish. On the physical level, his activities involve a violation of his master's private possessions. (pp. 35-6)

Refusing to view his master's affairs from a respectful distance, Caleb is claiming an intimacy with Falkland to which even a social equal would have no right. By thus converting himself into Falkland's inquisitor rather than his servant, Caleb is not merely offending against the initial terms of the relationship, but threatening to reverse them. (p. 36)

Thus, although Caleb begins his detection with the interests of a gossip, he develops into a mischief-maker of a peculiarly potent sort. The magistrate's expostulation when Caleb finally presents evidence against Falkland reflects a very real fear in the contemporary audience: "There would be a speedy end to all order and good government, if fellows that trample upon ranks and distinctions in this atrocious sort, were upon any consideration suffered to get off." . . . The criticism is one that Caleb himself cannot entirely discount. Though it only serves to add spice to the adventure, he is on occasion uneasily aware of the "forbidden" . . . nature of his investigations. (pp. 36-7)

To this analysis of the judgments passed on Caleb it may be objected that they suggest a surprising degree of accord between Godwin the radical philosopher and the middle-class public of his day, as they imply an agreement between Godwin and Falkland, the epitome of the established system. The answer to the objection is that, on the issue of spying, such agreement exists. Caleb's detection involves a disregard for those basic qualities—sincerity and sensitivity—upon which Godwin's ideal social code was based. (p. 37)

Though Falkland's later treatment of Caleb is identified with that social tyranny which Godwin so hated, Caleb's actions also strongly resemble that rash revolutionism which the author criticized in his fellow radicals. Godwin's political writings look forward to the gradual evolution of a Utopian society while ruling out the desirability of revolution in the streets.

Eschewing revolution as a means of attaining his ideal goals, Godwin often adopts a stance of modified liberalism. It is perhaps unfortunate that his thought should be best known through *Political Justice*, a work which avowedly concentrates on abstract theory and favors expressions of absolute disapproval of various social institutions. As *The Enquirer* and the pamphlet writings show, Godwin had a flexible mind, and his practical response was usually to accept the fact that such institutions were here to stay for at least the foreseeable future and to suggest ways in which they might be made more liberal and humane.

To *Caleb Williams* this habit leads to a distribution of sympathy between Caleb, the assailant of the social order, and Falkland, the representative of "things as they are." Though Godwin later agrees with Caleb's fulminations against the system, he also sympathizes with Falkland's protests against the implications of Caleb's conduct as a spy. Falkland's angry dismissal of the detective as an "insolent domestic" . . . thus carries with it the endorsement of a writer who in practice often showed a cautious and pragmatic acquiescence to current institutions.

In *Caleb Williams* detection is not merely a transgression of social etiquette; it is also a complex psychological process that further renders Caleb's status as hero dubious. He achieves the intimacy with Falkland that he so passionately desires, but it proves a curse rather than a blessing. As his investigations progress, Caleb plunges deeper and deeper into moral uncertainties. Caleb and Falkland begin to resemble each other, and their fates become inextricably linked; by the end of the novel, detective and criminal appear more like symbiotic twins than antagonists.

Although Caleb's ultimate conduct toward his master smacks of churlish ingratitude, his initial response is a profound—indeed, an exaggerated—respect. In a book replete with purple rhetoric his declarations of feeling for Falkland loom especially hyperbolic. (pp. 37-8)

Caleb's assumption of the role of detective appears an act of involuntary iconoclasm against the idol he himself has created, a surrender to "the demon that possessed me." . . . Significantly, one of his first actions as a detective is to launch an oblique attack on Falkland by voicing doubts about the character of Alexander the Great, who attempted to "persuade mankind that he was the son of Jupiter Ammon." . . . Caleb cites the opinions of Fielding and Doctor Prideaux, which Falkland considers to be "Accursed blasphemy!" . . . But blasphemy is always an ambiguous activity, and disbelief does not supplant veneration in Caleb's mind. In fact, the story that originally sows the seed of suspicion also provides him with "a thousand fresh reasons to admire and love Mr. Falkland." . . .

Caleb's discovery of the truth about Falkland's past merely intensifies his emotional turbulence. He had earlier promised himself "an unknown gratification" . . . in the achievement of the secret, and he celebrated its pursuit as a means toward maturity and the expansion of his powers. It proves, however, to be an initiation into a world of frightening experience. . . . (p. 39)

In his "mistaken thirst of knowledge" . . . Caleb has encountered the problem of evil in a peculiarly complex and disturbing form. During his investigations he had been uneasily aware of their forbidden nature, if only in the most obvious sense that they went against Falkland's commands. He discovered that, despite his good intentions and his earnestness, he contained the seeds of evil within himself; he could, as he confesses to Falkland, yield to a "demon." . . . (pp. 39-40)

Expressed in abstract terms, the truth that Caleb has discovered is that good and evil, though apparently worlds apart, are in practice bedfellows. In his relationship with Falkland, Caleb enacts this truth for the rest of the novel. Rather than appearing as simple polar opposites, the detective and the criminal become inextricably connected. . . .

This close structural relationship is emphasized by the emotional bonds that develop between the detective and the criminal. Caleb eventually achieves an intimacy with Falkland, though of a type he neither expected nor welcomes. He has sympathy for Falkland. . . . (p. 40)

When apart, each is unable to rid himself of the mental presence of the other. After Caleb's departure from the manor and escape from prison, Falkland persists in remaining obsessed by his very existence. Even after his ex-master's death Caleb cannot forget him. . . . Brought together by their obsessive natures, they conclude by becoming obsessed with each other. The process involves something approaching a destruction of their separate identities. . . .

This destruction of their separate identities is aided by the manner in which Caleb progressively comes to resemble Falk-

land. The effect of detection upon Caleb is like the effect of the crime itself upon Falkland. The servant develops the master's desperate "sensibility to reputation" . . . ; this is actually his main motive for writing his memoirs. Energetic and youthful, he had initially appeared the antithesis of his decaying and neurotic master. Having become the sole sharer of Falkland's secret, unable to blot out the knowledge and reluctant to communicate it to others, Caleb ages as Falkland himself had aged after Tyrrel's death. (p. 41)

Their final confrontation, when Caleb at last publicly accuses his master of murder, brings to a climax the emotional bond and the similarity between the two men. The intimacy which Caleb's earlier detection had initiated is symbolically culminated and acknowledged. (pp. 41-2)

During one of his insinuating conversations with his master, Caleb had remarked that "innocence and guilt are too much confounded in human life." . . . He was referring to the fallibility of the world's opinion, but his remark might apply in another sense to the world to which his detective activities have introduced him. For the final effect of the relationship between the detective and the criminal is to introduce ambiguities on the psychological level similar to those on the social level. Detection begins as an activity apparently designed to establish moral and intellectual clarity. The detective, voluntarily or involuntarily, assumes the role of an agent of justice, seeking to distinguish good from evil and to identify the source of evil. Caleb's relationship with Falkland, however, progressively suggests that good and evil do not admit of so simple a polarization. Inextricably linked, the detective and the criminal are similar in their characters and in their fates. Rather than emerging as antithetical or antagonistic in their relations, they grow into symbiotic twins. (p. 42)

Ian Ousby, " 'Caleb Williams'," in his Bloodhounds of Heaven: The Detective in English Fiction from Godwin to Doyle, *Cambridge, Mass.: Harvard University Press, 1976, pp. 19-42.*

MITZI MYERS   (essay date 1981)

[*Myers argues that Godwin's biography of Wollstonecraft,* Memoirs of the Author of "A Vindication of the Rights of Woman," *reveals much about Godwin's own attitudes. According to Myers, the work can be read as "a part of Godwin's intellectual—and emotional—biography."*]

Though it has long been recognized that Wollstonecraft's effect on Godwin's later thought was complicated and profound, the **Memoirs** have received surprisingly little attention as an important document in Godwin's reformulation of **Political Justice**'s rationalistic doctrines. Yet their pervasive emphasis on feeling and their candid exploration of personal relationships epitomize philosophical issues, and Wollstonecraft is treated both as personality and as principle, at once individual woman and symbol of cultural values, even of an alternate cognitive mode. Generically, then, Godwin's memoir is an unusual hybrid, one which unites Wollstonecraft's notion of herself, Godwin's reading of her character, and his analysis of that character's impact on himself and his philosophy. Moreover, these variant species of life-writing mesh within a narrative framework structured both by Godwin's basic philosophical assumptions and his proclivities for romantic fiction.

It is not surprising that so complex a work should produce divergent responses. Its history tells much about changing conceptions of biography, as well as cultural attitudes toward women and feminism. The reception of the biography was remarkably stormy: both subject and author bore the stigmata of sans-culottic reform, and 1798 was clouded by political repression. Worse yet, Godwin's philosophical tenet of sincerity rendered him an opponent of biographical reticence and thus something of an innovator in life-writing. Indeed, his extreme frankness in publicizing his wife's sexual entanglements, suicide attempts, and unorthodox religious opinions so soon after her death still retains its power to surprise, if not to shock. The *Memoirs* spread far and wide facts which had not been generally known, juicy tidbits greedily seized by the conservative press for a brutal propaganda campaign. . . . Wollstonecraft became a horrible example of voracious female sexuality run wild, her life, her death, the *Memoirs* themselves warnings, intoned one pious clergyman, directly inspired by the hand of Providence. (pp. 300-01)

In their origin in crisis, in their interiorized presentation of subject and biographer alike, in their consequences for Godwin's later philosophy, the *Memoirs* are a congeries of romantic attitudes, their shaping of self and subject in terms of internal and private aspects a paradigm of romantic biography and, to some extent, of confessional autobiography as well.

The genesis and strategies of the *Memoirs* make them exemplary for the study of biography as the artistic construct resulting from the intersection of two personalities. The story of how the philosopher who pronounced marriage a pernicious institution and the feminist who had a child outside wedlock settled into satisfying if unconventional domesticity is best delineated in the almost daily notes of the lovers themselves. It is only necessary to notice here a basic pattern in their letters which clarifies Godwin's impetus in the *Memoirs:* the configuration of love as mutuality, as the reciprocal expansion of latent powers, as education in short. Godwin's confessional *disjecta membra* reiterate his "prominent vein of docility," that ductile teachability which is the constant companion of his scepticism, a willingness to learn from others that made him, thought Coleridge, almost "too persuadible a man." In this, his most stirring and deeply felt emotional relationship, Godwin, Wollstonecraft's "boy pupil," gladly learned as well as gladly taught. (pp. 303-04)

[His] portrayal of Wollstonecraft in the *Memoirs* [is] a portrayal which was further shaped by his reading and rereading of her most romantic works throughout their relationship, as his unpublished journal records; he was always a diligent student of what he wanted to understand.

Godwin's journal for their last month together suggests Wollstonecraft's tutelage and cryptically hints at self exploration. Stimulated by immersion in such romantic texts as *Werther, Julie,* the *Confessions,* and by her example, he worked on a "Life" in early August 1797, while concurrently studying Rousseau. Such reading nicely epitomizes his attitudes toward his wife and indicates the kind of confessional models he drew on for the *Memoirs.* . . . On 30 August, while Wollstonecraft was in labor, Godwin settled down to reread *Mary,* her first novel, an autobiographical fiction drenched in personal feeling. His entries from that day until the tenth of September when she died are succinctly painful. 10 September reads, "20 minutes before 8," followed by three blank heavily scored lines. He could not form the words, and he could not attend the funeral. The emotions suppressed in his journal poured out in letters to friends, "more like distracted lines than any thing rational," one recipient commented.

This grief-stricken correspondence enunciates the images and themes expanded in the *Memoirs,* sketches the just-discovered order of verities, the new mode of being, Godwin is trying to take in. He describes Wollstonecraft as without equal in the world, his guide to a kind of happiness he had previously been unable to imagine, indeed "scarcely admitted the possibility of it." She is a "light," whose memory will make him "wise and more human." His only pleasure is the cultivation of melancholy: he wants to weaken his stoicism and refine his sensibility. "I love," he writes, "to tread the edge of intellectual danger . . . and in this indulgence and this vigilance I place my present luxury." Godwin felt he had "half-destroyed" himself in writing such letters as these, but he soon found a more satisfactory employment. He abandoned the separate lodgings where he had always worked for his wife's study, enshrined her portrait as inspiriting muse, and steeped himself in her writings, as if he were trying to absorb her very essence. (pp. 305-06)

The *Memoirs,* then, were undertaken as a mode of self-therapy, in which the mourner seeks both to come to terms with his loss and, through empathically entering the beloved's personality, to assimilate and exemplify those emotional lessons he is conning. But the *Memoirs* are more than psychological self-help. They are also an imaginatively organized artistic construct drawing on Godwin's previous experience as thinker and novelist, a complex example of intergeneric, as well as interpersonal, reciprocity. Godwin was not a novice at biography: he had begun his literary career as a biographer, and he projected and published several lives besides the *Memoirs.* As a philosophical student of history, he had examined carefully the problems inherent in the writing of biography or individual history. In an unpublished essay from January 1797, parts of which later surfaced in the preface to his 1830 novel *Cloudesly,* Godwin considers the relationship "Of History and Romance." He finds the minute particularities and psychological details of individual history far more valuable than general historical abstractions, for the human mind naturally gravitates to "individualities." Biography leads to self-knowledge and imaginative moral enthusiasm; it instructs in motivation and the way passions operate. Significantly, Godwin pictures the student of individuals producing his collected materials to "engage in the solemn act of self-investigation . . . &, by a sort of magnetism, cause those particulars to start out to view in ourselves, which might otherwise have lain for ever undetected." Yet because of man's complexity—"the folds of the human heart, the endless intermixture of motive with motive"—Godwin concludes that biography is finally only a useful guess in the dark, an attempt to "hit on that thread" which will unravel the essence of the subject. It is, paradoxically, the author of fictitious narrative, of romance, who writes real history: the biographer is but a romantic writer without the "sublime license of imagination."

"True history" Godwin defines as "a delineation of consistent, human character, in a display of the manner in which such a character acts under successive circumstances, in showing how character increases & assimilates new substances to its own, & how it decays, together with the catastrophe into which by its own gravity it naturally declines," a relevant recipe for lives feigned or real. Whether the overt fable of romance or the covert fable of history, Godwin's "first enquiry is, Can I derive instruction from it? Is it a genuine praxis upon the nature of man?" Truth to human nature, grasped through sympathetic self-projection, is his criterion. The poet or novelist, he argues, is superior to the historian because he begins his task with "a preconception of the qualities'' that belong to his subject. Knowing ''the principle of [that subject's] actions,'' he need only educe from his premises and ''aid those conclusions by consulting the oracle in his bosom, the suggestions of his own heart,'' in order to unfold the ''seeds of character'' and the ''modes in which they expand themselves,'' the organic connection of plot and character. Such is the rationale for Godwin's romances, all psychological case histories of individuals, the same approach—analytic, autobiographical—also informs his history of his wife, in which he seeks to have the best of both worlds: the historian's factual accuracy, the novelist's psychological penetration and, always his desideratum, unity of effect. Godwin's wariness of scientific truth in life-writing . . . implies a rather sophisticated awareness that the story of a life, one's own or another's, is in important ways necessarily a fiction, the artistic recreation, even creation, of a character's essence. Godwin's developing romantic aesthetic offers one solution to that ''stiff'' artistic problem inherent in biography: how to infuse the ''granite-like solidity'' of factual truth with the ''rainbow-like intangibility'' of personality.

In the *Memoirs,* then, Godwin is exercising the imaginative freedom of the artist, demonstrating through his selection and shaping of fact, through his empathic narrator's thematic interposition, that sensitive affectivity he finds so exemplary in Wollstonecraft herself. Indeed, in his preface, Godwin presents his wife as a moral model, the detailing of whose gifts, especially those private ''virtues which discover themselves principally in personal intercourse,'' will promote public benefit, improvement contingent on his engaging readerly ''sympathy.'' . . . The outraged response to this edifying purpose might have been predicted even by Godwin himself, for he was still smarting from the slights Wollstonecraft suffered when they married . . . , thus forcing her acquaintances to recognize that she had never been Gilbert Imlay's wife and that her daughter Fanny was illegitimate. Yet he proceeds to elaborate not only this tragic liaison, but also Wollstonecraft's intense and unrequited passion for the married Henry Fuseli, the fact that she became Godwin's mistress shortly after her break with Imlay, and the information that the two married only because she was again pregnant. Godwin's extraordinary candor might be explained by his philosophic sincerity or Rousseau's example, but he did not in fact tell everything he knew. He omitted, for instance, what still remains one of the most problematic episodes in Wollstonecraft's career—her leading role in engineering her sister Eliza's separation from her husband. Godwin stresses that his practice is grounded in factual accuracy: he emphasizes his first-hand knowledge, the early notes he took as a student of human nature, the inquiries for further data he made. His facts are, so far as he could discover, true, but he is willing to make significant deletions when they do not serve his thematic purpose. That purpose, however, necessitates his including even the most intimate particulars which contribute to his interpretation of Wollstonecraft as an energetic and idealistic woman of genius whose trajectory was fueled by her attempts to realize those extraordinary emotional and imaginative capabilities she possessed. She is ''a lofty and undaunted spirit,'' a ''great soul''—a real life romantic heroine. . . . Every biographer of Wollstonecraft must decide how to resolve the complexities of her character and achievement, how to adjust her rationalism and her romanticism. Godwin's decision was clearly determined by his own needs. And it is Wollstonecraft as exemplar for him with which he is ultimately most concerned, her biography entailing his autobiography. (pp. 307-09)

Feeling, imagination, and sympathy constitute both his method and his theme. Disparaging private affections, the Godwin of *Political Justice* liked to talk of disinterestedness and universal benevolence, of judging human actions as an ''impartial spectator.'' Shifting from academic argument to palpable reality, Godwin the biographer tries hard to get inside his subject's skin, to understand how and why she developed as she did. He must feel his way into the subjective situation of a woman of ''ardent imagination'' who ''felt herself formed for domestic affection, and all those tender charities, which men of sensibility have constantly treated as the dearest band of human society,'' charities he, the man of rationality, had heretofore denigrated as impediments to perfectibility. . . . Comprehending this life requires that he reassess his former position step by step, a process not thoroughly accomplished until the reworked second edition of the *Memoirs* where he emerges as a full-fledged ''new man of feeling,'' to anticipate the subtitle of his 1805 novel *Fleetwood.* Beginning with an image to be quickened in his text, Godwin refines that image and himself in composition, as his pattern of analysis and defense, addition and revision, testifies. As his imaginative apperception of Wollstonecraft and the values she embodies matures, so his methodic efforts to become acquainted with himself mandate a change of heart, a tempering of system. Indicatively, with the draft of her biography ripening to fruition, ''Life (moi-même)''—Godwin habitually couches the emotionally charged in French—reappears in his journal by 29 November.

The biographer's subtle strategies foster the thinker's conversion; the writing of the life itself is for him a further lesson in his ongoing personal and philosophical quest for what nourishes human improvement. As he elsewhere remarks, one fully understands a subject because, not before, he has written about it. The second edition of the *Memoirs* was promptly followed by a crucially important autobiographical note in which he finds *Political Justice* ''essentially defective, in . . . not yielding a proper attention to the empire of feeling. The voluntary actions of men are under the direction of their feelings.'' Rather than the rational calculation of consequences, the spontaneity of virtue now kindles his interest. He had come to believe that man is inevitably spurred by motives peculiar to him as an individual, that domestic affections, ineradicable and infinitely powerful, are not only inseparable from the ''culture of the heart,'' but that they are premier instigators of morality. Godwin's succeeding works and personal memoranda bear continued witness to his new-found faith in feeling, domestic affections, and marriage; that institution once ''the worst of all laws,'' ''the worst of all properties,'' ''the worst of monopolies'' is transformed into ''the grand holiday of our human nature . . . the white spot, the little gleam of pure sunshine, which compensates for a thousand other hardships and calamities.'' Meticulously casting and recasting the audits of his mental experience, Godwin elaborated on the insights generated by Wollstonecraft and the writing of the *Memoirs* throughout his long life, his successive revisions calling to mind Nietzsche's equation of philosophy with ''confession . . . a species of involuntary and unconscious autobiography.''

Those biographical tactics which crystallized his conceptions Godwin blends from varied sources: his own memory and imaginative excursions into the mind of his subject, novels, essays, and autobiographies of sensibility, Wollstonecraft's fiction, the revelatory documents he was editing—a harmonious nexus resonant as the character he presents. For his is a less naive formulation than some critics allow. Like his successors (one reason Wollstonecraft lures biographers), he discovered in her transports and sorrows a ready-made tragic plot. He also found to hand in his literary models an organizing image, the paradigm of romantic genius within which Wollstonecraft's temperament and activities could be satisfyingly shaped. And it is an image consonant with his subject's view of herself, indeed explicitly sanctioned by her works.... Wollstonecraft is for Godwin "a female Werter," "endowed with the most exquisite and delicious sensibility," a spirit "almost of too fine a texture to encounter the vicissitudes of human affairs, to whom pleasure is transport, and disappointment is agony indescribable." ... (pp. 310-12)

But the tenderness Godwin treasures is not the whole of his account. The concomitant of Wollstonecraft's potent sensibility is resilient strength, the decisiveness and confidence, even the quick temper and imperious resentment whose existence he does not blink. Though his focus is the private individual rather than the public reformer—he finds her two *Vindications* harsh and rugged, not wholly typical of her "essential" nature—his integrating motif of romantic genius embraces affective range and social protest, stretches to accommodate both the independent champion of her sex and the "worshipper of domestic life." ... It also implies that remarkable intuitive gift he makes so much of in his autobiographical conclusion. Wollstonecraft filtered through such an alembic lets Godwin indulge his bent toward impressionism and psychological dissection, the latter perhaps most telling in his reconstruction of the Imlay debacle—that "ill-starred unhappy passion." ... His characteristic accent on motivation and determining matrix dovetails nicely with Wollstonecraft's own approach to her life. Unlike many early biographers, he furnishes an etiology of genius, a personality gradually assuming its own unique form, not just a finished and mature personage. He gives full weight to her childhood remembrance—the parental tyranny, the lack of love—and his rendering of her recollections, from brief phrases to whole portraits, is demonstrably colored by literary memory. He indicates how her life and temperament shaped her work and frequently notes the autobiographical strain in her writing; he was the first to stress the influence of her personal experience on her career, a fundamental point in modern explication. He cites with artistry, marrying his text to hers, appropriating her voice to express his own loss. (pp. 312-13)

Godwin's personal situation and mental history play an increasingly prominent role as the biography unfolds. Throughout, his interpretive assessments and philosophical asides operate self-referentially. He projects his experience as journalist or radical on Wollstonecraft's past (with occasional skewed results), considers such topics as religion, gratitude, cohabitation, and suicide in line with his peculiar tenets, and periodically calls attention to his privileged knowledge and his bereavement. His comments also, especially in connection with Wollstonecraft's traumatic loves, evince self-emendation, as in this concession to the emotive: "Moral reasoning is nothing but the awakening of certain feelings." ... But it is in the moving final chapters that he makes explicit the meaning for him of his interaction with Wollstonecraft, with, as he says, the same frank simplicity pervading the whole work. Turning from implicit to avowed autobiography, he traces minutely the growth of their affection, which he describes in terms of equality and mutual companionship: "friendship melting into love." Yet more revealingly, he delineates how one who "never loved till now" was initiated through that experience into fresh truths and new ways of knowing....

Godwin's central autobiographical theme is his thwarted access to enriched perception, developed through symbiotic spiritual profiles in which "the improvement I was in the act of re-

ceiving" is equated with "the leading traits of her intellectual character from which it flowed." ... His specialization in the fine psychological discrimination of complex and dynamic emotional states serves him well in appraising his own condition. With his customary exactitude, he sifts his nascent receptivity with analytical rigor. He and Wollstonecraft, he believes, cultivated their powers in divergent directions—logic and metaphysics versus a taste for the picturesque. But the difference between the two is not merely one of specialization.... Wollstonecraft ... incarnates for Godwin intuitive imagination, the alternate cognitive mode of romantic genius. Here too he could find warrant in her works, from the *Rights of Woman* to "On Poetry" to the "Hints." Enlarging on her unwavering intuition as established early in the *Memoirs* ..., Godwin relates how his "oscillation and skepticism were fixed by her boldness." He judges that this instantaneous insight, at once a feeling and a faculty of understanding, can be nurtured through "the daily recurrence of a striking example"; such attuned intelligence, then, is learnable through "responsive vibration" and reeducated habit.... Dissatisfied with this summation, however, Godwin recasts it, as well as other key passages, in the revised edition.

The second version of the *Memoirs* has received a bad press; it is usually dismissed without examination as a more discreet rendition of the first, its modifications intended merely to appease an irate public. But close collation invites a different view. Many of the variances are minor. As ever, Godwin corrected word by word; striving for precision, he rephrases, inserts new reflections. He was also clearly aware of widespread strictures. He excises some references to living people, occasional phrases which had struck a live nerve in reviewers ..., and a very few minor details which might be open to misinterpretation. But he leaves unaltered a much attacked section on Wollstonecraft's lack of deathbed religion, and he refuses to blur his central conception of his subject or to abridge his treatment of her unconventional acts. On the contrary, he copes with the criticism by probing those acts and their rationale yet more. He is alert to justify, but he does not apologize. His additions expand on the romantic motifs which unify the work. He repeats that his history is "personal," not solely a literary biography. He renews attention to Wollstonecraft's "two most cherished conceptions, the picturesque and the affectionate." ... His reworking of the by now notorious Imlay affair typifies his handling. Stressing that the narrow rules of vulgar morality cannot contain "the being who restlessly aspires to superior gratification," he locates Wollstonecraft's mistake not in the irregularity of the liaison, but in her misjudgment of the person. He insists that her desperate and prolonged attempts to hang on to her recalcitrant lover were the consequence of her idealism. The affectivity Godwin celebrates is not passive; he counters the reviewers' sneers at the "unresisting slave of feeling" with fresh emphasis on her native energy and elevation. Her very errors, he urges, "were connected and interwoven with the qualities most characteristic of her disposition and genius." ... (pp. 313-15)

Godwin's most extensive reconsiderations signify his own growing preoccupation with the inner life. In the interval between editions, he had worked out new views on marriage and solidified the philosophical underpinning of his solicitude for the affective. Selection of the beloved becomes the most important choice of private life, and he now terms prejudice his earlier support for individual nonconformity with marital custom, though he still believes that current laws demand reform.... Too, the wholly rewritten section on Wollstonecraft's relationship with Fuseli says even more about Godwin than his subject. The first edition dilates on Wollstonecraft's ideal of love as the principal solace of life; the second offers no timid toning down, but a position paper on domestic affections as vivifiers of sensibility and social sympathy which stands as Godwin's *locus classicus* on the topic, quoted and requoted in subsequent works. Such changes are not recantations, but expansions of his vision of human possibility. Nor does his remodeled conclusion betray the closet chauvinist, as some argue. His musing on the acculturated approaches of male and female discloses less sexism than self-exploration. In emblemizing himself and Wollstonecraft as representatives of the discursive and the intuitive, Godwin is trying both to grasp that quality in her cast of mind so superior to his own in valued ways and to ground more firmly his marital idyll of complementary reciprocity, mutual interdependence. Indeed, his marriage signifies for him the now desired fusion of reason and feeling, intellect wedding imagination. Intent on clarifying his new mental set and Wollstonecraft's role as catalyst, Godwin discards hazy wording for a sharper contrast between her imaginative strength and emotional spontaneity and his own diffident skepticism that anxiously examines and reexamines, a self-portrait he sketches again and again. Wollstonecraft as the guiding "light of my steps" suffuses both endings, but, revealingly, he adds to the second version a manifesto: "her sensibility determined me to a careful development of my feelings," a promise of personal evolution faithfully kept. . . . If Godwin's romantic heroine is not the whole of Wollstonecraft's complex nature, his portrayal is the generous artistic tribute of a diligent student to a gifted teacher, a light refracted through biographical involvement. (pp. 315-16)

Mitzi Myers, "Godwin's 'Memoirs' of Wollstonecraft: The Shaping of Self and Subject," in Studies in Romanticism, *Vol. 20, No. 3, Fall, 1981, pp. 299-316.*

DAVID MORSE (essay date 1982)

[*Morse suggests that Godwin's use of the Gothic form in* Caleb Williams *enabled him to combine psychological exploration with social criticism.*]

The correlation between a radical political vision and a Gothic mode of presentation characterises all the major novelists of the 1790s, but it was William Godwin . . . , in his *Caleb Williams* . . . , which bears the provocative alternative title 'Things as They Are'—a clear-enough indication that the domination that Godwin describes is not to be taken as mere fiction—who produced the most powerful articulation of the social nightmare of a class society. Indeed, in reading this novel we can scarcely avoid the connection between religious and political dissent, for Godwin was brought up in a Sandemanian environment and his novel is offered not as mere entertainment but as a discourse that is directly relevant to real life, a translation into more immediate terms of the principles of his *Political Justice*—though it is, of course, not simply to be regarded as a political-philosophical comic strip. In his Preface [see excerpt dated 1794] Godwin insisted that his purpose was both didactic and down-to-earth. . . . (p. 41)

Godwin's formulation is far from crude. It indicates a new type of fictional purpose: the delineation of a particular type of value system and a representation of the ways in which domination becomes institutionalised, legitimised and endlessly extended so that it reaches into the remotest corners of society, carrying its contagion everywhere with the relentless thoroughness of a plague. So provocative did this intention appear that Godwin was forced to withdraw it for the first edition of 1794. In *Caleb Williams* we find a more complex social vision and social critique than in any other Gothic novel, or in the other works of Godwin himself. For Godwin's criticism is not directed purely and simply at individuals, but is also directed at the social circumstances that determine the pattern of their actions. *Caleb Williams* is thus a determinist novel, but this term is not to be construed in any fatalist sense: for Godwin, determining circumstances can also generate a sense of freedom, as his description of the psychological processes of Caleb Williams testifies. But Godwin did believe that men were deeply influenced by their environment and the values and pressures by which they were surrounded. For this reason his thought, though characterised by great optimism about the possibility of human progress, to which he assigns no limit, is often unexpectedly pessimistic when it comes to a more immediate prognosis. In the section of *Political Justice* in which Godwin shows how men are influenced by their environment, and, in particular by the nature of political organisation, he writes,

> Political institution, by the consequences with which it is pregnant, strongly suggests to everyone who enters within its sphere, what is the path he should avoid, as well as what he should pursue. Under a government fundamentally erroneous he will see intrepid virtue proscribed, and a servile and corrupt spirit uniformly encouraged. But morality itself is nothing but the calculation of consequences. What strange confusion will the spectacle of that knavery which is universally practised through all the existing classes of society produce in the mind? The preceptor cannot go out of the world, or prevent the intercourse of his pupil with human beings of a character different from his own.

The connection between a social and political system where manipulation, intimidation and the brutal exercise of power are not the exception but the rule and the circumstances that affect the lives of every single individual is a constant if largely implicit thread running through the narrative of *Caleb Williams*. . . . The argument of the novel is . . . generalised through a series of parallels and analogies: Caleb's fate mirrors and is directly connected with that of Hawkins; while even the apparently kindly and well disposed Falkland comes to echo both the tyranny of Tyrrell and that of powerful rulers. Justice is therefore shown to be not an objective quality but a function of class position: 'justice' is used against *some* (the weak and poor) by *others* (the rich and powerful). For this reason also, Caleb Williams's period of imprisonment is far more than a transitory moment in the narrative. For Godwin and for his Romantic contemporaries the prison, though a place which few voluntarily visit and whose operations remain obscure to the majority, is nevertheless a crucial focus of moral indignation, because it simultaneously exemplifies both the torments to which one man can subject another and the heartless manner in which a man can be deprived of the use of the very faculties and abilities that make him what he is. (pp. 42-4)

[It] is patent that religious imperatives help to formulate and give edge to Godwin's social criticism. Man has been formed for freedom, and therefore to imprison him and to deprive him of his capacity for action is not simply gratuitous, immoral and cruel: it is a violation of the pattern of divine providence. The prison embodies the truth of modern culture and parodies all dreams of social justice and progress. . . . (p. 45)

But the prison also has a further significance for Godwin. Godwin belongs to the intellectual tradition of Shaftesbury, which laid great stress on man's social impulses, which are the source both of his moral capacity and of his disposition to expand and develop that capacity. But, when a prisoner is placed in solitary confinement in order to 'educate' and 're-form' him, the methods by which this is to be achieved are, in fact, calculated to achieve exactly the reverse:

> Shall we be most effectively formed to justice, benevolence and prudence in our intercourse with each other, in a state of solitude? Will not our selfish and unsocial dispositions be per-petually increased? What temptation has he to think of benevolence or justice, who has no opportunity to exercise it? The true soil in which atrocious crimes are found to germinate, is a gloomy and morose disposition. Will his heart become much either softened or expanded, who breathes the atmosphere of a dungeon?

This cascade of rhetorical questions from *Political Justice* makes it indisputably clear how great an evil imprisonment is for Godwin. But in *Caleb Williams* the notion of imprisonment is vastly expanded. For Godwin shows that in their different ways both Falkland and Caleb Williams become prisoners, because they are cut off from free communication of their thoughts and feelings to others. Falkland, because of the crime that he has committed and because of his failure to confess it, is locked up within himself in an agonising interior solitude that places him beyond the beneficent sphere of human communication. And, even when he is finally brought to the point where he has to reveal the whole story to Caleb Williams, his decision loses its virtue, because he insists on binding Caleb at one and the same moment to an oath never to disclose what his master has told him. From this action many evils flow. Falkland him-self continues to be tortured by guilt, remorse and, above all, anxiety that at some point or another Caleb will eventually reveal everything to persons who may be inclined to believe him. Consequently he employs the sinister and implacable Gines to pursue Caleb and to watch and observe his every action. Caleb's own existence becomes equally intolerable, since he is forced to adopt a variety of disguises and to flee from place to place; like Falkland before him, he cannot afford to open his heart to others, since any such action would only be one step towards his downfall. Disguise, for Godwin, heir to a puritan tradition, is a false mode of being, a dangerous step into inauthenticity and deceitful seeming. . . . (pp. 45-6)

But, in fairness, it must be added that Godwin has already shown the price that Caleb has paid for his various subterfuges and the torment of his continual loneliness and distrust. The point is that Caleb, like Falkland, forces himself to go *against nature* (to invoke the phrase that in French symbolism was later to acquire such resonance, though with more positive connotations), for at every moment when he yields to ordinary and normal human feelings he finds himself betrayed. . . . In-deed, perhaps the most interesting part of the novel is [the] depiction of Caleb Williams's frantic inner world in the closing stages of the narrative, which, while designed to show the agonies of internal isolation, has the paradoxical side-effect of showing the very processes of consciousness as a form of torture. This may well be Godwin's deepest and most enduring

fictional legacy. After Godwin it was scarcely possible to show men thinking calm, lucid and appropriate thoughts: the rep-resentation of consciousness from Poe to Dostoevsky and Kafka became rather a matter of frenzied leaps, switches and jumps, of thought doubling and redoubling upon itself, of ideas flood-ing recklessly and pell-mell into the mind, the revelation of a chaotic inner world. This is all of a piece with Godwin's views on the changeableness of human nature. (pp. 46-7)

In *Caleb Williams* there is no necessity that Falkland or Caleb Williams play the part of hypocrite or of false seemer; there is nothing inherent in the role or the position. It is rather society that creates it through the possibility it affords for one man to dominate and oppress another; because in the absence of a spirit of freedom and equality between all men there is also necessarily lacking an openness and sincerity in their mutual dealings. The doubling of Falkland and Caleb Williams has the effect of generalising the theme of the novel and of showing that the issue is not one of an unchangeable human nature that makes one man a hypocrite and another a miser, but rather of a particular form of social organisation which has the effect of isolating men from one another and of rendering their attempts to communicate with one another dubious and unstable, even destructive. But in this novel Godwin opened a fictional Pan-dora's box, which was to have repercussions spreading far beyond his own particular philosophy. For he initiated a whole series of novels in which men enter into mutual confidences and are oppressed by mysterious and enigmatic others, in which hypocrisy and an appearance of public righteousness are ex-posed by the mechanism of the double. The couple of the hypocrite and the double haunts Romantic and post-Romantic literature because of the very facility with which these fictional devices can speak the unspoken or unspeakable. These motifs are so popular because they lend themselves to a spirit of irreverence and bitter mockery: they expose the falsity and the hollowness of man in his public and social roles and point to deeper and more complex psychological realities which society cannot permit, and which even the individual may be reluctant to scrutinise too closely. At the same time the whole tradition of the examined self of the individual's scrutiny of his own motives becomes more and more problematic. The mind offers no certainties. As Godwin points out in *Political Justice,*

> Self-deception is of all things the most easy. Whoever ardently wishes to find a proposition true, may be expected insensibly to veer to-wards the opinion that suits his inclination. It cannot be wondered at, by him who considers the subtlety of the human mind, that belief should scarcely ever rest upon the mere basis of evi-dence, and that arguments are always viewed through a delusive medium, magnifying them into Alps, or diminishing them to nothing.

The Gothic becomes, *par excellence,* the genre of uncertainty: devoted not simply to an epistemological scepticism at a parade of fantastic and delusionary appearances, leaving the spectator baffled and bemused by puzzling and contradictory evidences; but, far more significantly, throwing into question the very reliability of the mind that scrutinises those appearances, and displaying the mind itself as fraught with division and contra-diction. Freudianism is simply the inheritor of this Gothic leg-acy—retaining, as did the nineteenth century, the fascination with unconscious and subconscious mental processes, but shed-ding the social critique to which the Gothic once emphatically gestured. (pp. 47-9)

David Morse, "The Social Novel and the Gothic," in his Romanticism: A Structural Analysis, *Barnes & Noble Books*, 1982, pp. 13-49.

ADDITIONAL BIBLIOGRAPHY

Allen, B. Sprague. "William Godwin and the Stage." *PMLA* XXXV, n.s. XXVIII, No. 3 (1920): 358-74.
Explores the relationship between several of Godwin's novels and various English, French, and American dramas. In addition, Allen discusses Godwin's friendship with the American playwright Thomas Cooper.

Baker, Ernest A. "The Novel of Doctrine." In his *The History of the English Novel: The Novel of Sentiment and the Gothic Romance*, pp. 228-55. London: H. F. & G. Witherby, 1934.
Contains an overview of Godwin's career. Baker describes Godwin's works as possessing "an express purpose; they all set forth his judgments on existing society in the light of his intellectualist philosophy, and in each case their particular object is defined at the outset."

Barker, Gerard A. "Justice to Caleb Williams." *Studies in the Novel* VI, No. 4 (Winter 1974): 377-88.
An analysis of the ending of *Caleb Williams*. Barker praises Godwin's conclusion, contending that "it turns Caleb's final confrontation into a moral triumph."

Brailsford, H. N. *Shelley, Godwin, and Their Circle*. London: Williams and Norgate, 1913, 256 p.
Describes the intellectual and political atmosphere in which Godwin lived.

Brown, Ford K. *The Life of William Godwin*. London: J. M. Dent & Sons, 1926, 387 p.
A biography of Godwin.

Clark, John P. *The Philosophical Anarchism of William Godwin*. Princeton: Princeton University Press, 1977, 343 p.
Examines Godwin's moral philosophy and his approach to social and political problems.

Dowden, Edward. "Theorists of Revolution." In his *The French Revolution and English Literature: Lectures Delivered in Connection with the Sesquicentennial Celebration of Princeton University*, pp. 47-89. 1897. Reprint. Port Washington, N.Y.: Kennikat Press, 1967.
A biographical study of Godwin and Wollstonecraft. Dowden also examines Godwin's presentation of his doctrine of revolution in *Political Justice*.

Dumas, D. Gilbert. "Things As They Were: The Original Ending of *Caleb Williams*." *Studies in English Literature 1500-1900* VI (1966): 575-97.
A discussion of the original, unpublished ending to *Caleb Williams*, discovered in the holograph manuscript of the novel. Dumas analyzes how the alternate ending—had it been published—would have affected the novel.

Fleisher, David. *William Godwin: A Study in Liberalism*. New York: Augustus Kelly, 1951, 155 p.
A detailed study of Godwin's ideas and themes, interspersed with biographical details. Fleisher considers Godwin primarily as a philosopher rather than as an author.

Gold, Alex, Jr. "It's Only Love: The Politics of Passion in Godwin's *Caleb Williams*." *Texas Studies in Literature and Language* 19, No. 2 (Summer 1977): 135-60.
Considers the influence of government upon Caleb's character.

Gross, Harvey. "The Pursuer and the Pursued: A Study of *Caleb Williams*." *Texas Studies in Literature and Language* I, No. 3 (Autumn 1959): 401-11.

An analysis of the historical and literary influences on *Caleb Williams*.

Grylls, Rosalie Glynn. *William Godwin and His World*. London: Odhams Press, 1953, 256 p.
A biography of Godwin that emphasizes the social and political environment of the late Enlightenment.

Harvey, A. D. "The Nightmare of *Caleb Williams*." *Essays in Criticism* XXVI, No. 3 (July 1976): 236-49.
Interprets *Caleb Williams* as an analysis of "the corrupting influence of society."

Hogle, Jerrold E. "The Texture of the Self in Godwin's *Things As They Are*." *Boundary 2* VII, No. 2 (Winter 1979): 261-81.
A semiotic study of *Caleb Williams*.

Locke, Don. *A Fantasy of Reason: The Life and Thought of William Godwin*. London: Routledge & Kegan Paul, 1980, 398 p.
A detailed study of Godwin's life and philosophical development.

Marshall, Peter H. *William Godwin*. New Haven: Yale University Press, 1984, 497 p.
A recent biographical study.

Monro, D. H. *Godwin's Moral Philosophy: An Interpretation of William Godwin*. London: Oxford University Press, 1953, 205 p.
Presents Godwin as a moralist rather than as a political reformer.

Murry, John Middleton. "William Godwin." In his *Countries of the Mind: Essays in Literary Criticism, second series*, pp. 181-87. London: Oxford University Press, 1931.
A discussion of Godwin's relationship with Wollstonecraft and his son-in-law, Shelley.

Paul, C. Kegan. *William Godwin: His Friends and Contemporaries*. 2 vols. London: Henry S. King and Co., 1876.
A biography based on Godwin's diaries, letters, and autobiographical fragments.

Pollin, Burton Ralph. *Education and Enlightenment in the Works of William Godwin*. New York: Las Americas Publishing Co., 1962, 293 p.
An analysis of the role of education in Godwin's literary and philosophical development.

———. *Godwin Criticism: A Synoptic Bibliography*. Toronto: University of Toronto Press, 1967, 659 p.
A bibliography of works by and about Godwin published between 1783 and 1966.

Priestley, F. E. L. "Platonism in William Godwin's *Political Justice*." *Modern Language Quarterly* 4, No. 1 (March 1943): 63-9.
Interprets *Political Justice* as a document influenced more by eighteenth-century Platonism than by the tradition of empirical philosophy.

Scheuermann, Mona. "Outside the Human Circle: Views from Hawthorne and Godwin." *The Nathaniel Hawthorne Journal* (1975): 182-91.
Studies the psychology of alienation as evidenced in the works of Godwin and Nathaniel Hawthorne.

Sherburn, George. "Godwin's Later Novels." *Studies in Romanticism* I, No. 2 (Winter 1962): 65-82.
An overview of Godwin's literary career following the publication of *Caleb Williams*.

Tysdahl, B. J. *William Godwin As Novelist*. London: Athlone, 1981, 205 p.
The first book-length study of Godwin's novels. Tysdahl assesses the novels in light of Godwin's philosophical writings and discusses the relationship between the two genres.

Uphaus, Robert W. "Moral and Tendency in *Caleb Williams*." In his *The Impossible Observer: Reason and the Reader in Eighteenth-Century Prose*, pp. 123-36. Lexington: University Press of Kentucky, 1979.
Considers *Caleb Williams* as a "psychological encounter with fears and desires."

Willey, Basil. "'Nature' in Revolution and Reaction." In his *The Eighteenth Century Background: Studies on the Idea of Nature in the Thought of the Period*, pp. 205-52. New York: Columbia University Press, 1941.

Assesses Godwin as a representative of eighteenth-century rationalism at its conclusion.

Woodcock, George. *William Godwin: A Biographical Study*. London: Porcupine Press, 1946, 266 p.

A study of Godwin's life and philosophy.

———. "The Man of Reason." In his *Anarchism: A History of Libertarian Ideas and Movements*, pp. 60-93. Cleveland: World Publishing Co., Meridian Books, 1967.

A discussion of Godwin's libertarian philosophy in the context of nineteenth-century anarchism.

Oliver Wendell Holmes

1809-1894

American essayist, poet, novelist, and biographer.

Holmes is considered one of the most versatile American authors of the nineteenth century. Though he wrote in a wide variety of genres, he is best known for his popular collection of essays *The Autocrat of the Breakfast-Table*. Critics believe that these fictional conversations provided Holmes with the ideal medium for expressing his views on humankind and its institutions and for acting, in his own words, as "his own Boswell." Holmes's novels, too, have attracted the interest of scholars. In these, most notably in *Elsie Venner*, he incorporated his pioneering theories of psychology and clarified his arguments against Calvinism and the concept of original sin. In addition to his literary works, Holmes was respected for his controversial scientific essays and for his brilliant skill as a conversationalist. Holmes's reputation has diminished considerably in recent years; perhaps the most famous and important figure in Boston intellectual circles during the second half of the nineteenth century, he is now remembered chiefly for the sparkling wit of *The Autocrat* and the spirit of free inquiry demonstrated by the wide range of his interests.

Holmes was born in Cambridge, Massachusetts, in 1809 to Sarah Wendell Holmes and the Reverend Abiel Holmes. A Calvinist minister, the Reverend Holmes was forced out of his parish in 1829 as a result of a conflict between the conservative and liberal factions within his congregation. For the younger Holmes, this event, as well as his early religious training, engendered a lifelong antagonism toward the Puritan strictures of Calvinism, which critics trace throughout his literary and scientific writings. Holmes attended Phillips Academy at Andover from 1824 to 1825 and then entered Harvard University. When he lost interest in his law studies, he transferred to medicine. After taking advanced courses in Paris in 1833, he returned to Harvard and completed the requirements for his medical degree in 1836. Holmes then practiced as a personal physician until 1839, when he was appointed to a professorship at Dartmouth College. The following year, he married Amelia Lee Jackson, with whom he had three children.

Holmes achieved distinction during the 1840s and 1850s as a teacher and scientific writer, and he later won great respect as Dean of the Harvard Medical School. He was also active on the lecture circuit, speaking on a wide variety of medical topics. In his 1842 essay, *Homeopathy and Its Kindred Delusions*, Holmes demonstrated the futility and danger of some existing medical treatments; in *The Contagiousness of Puerperal Fever*, written in 1843, he suggested that physicians themselves could be the carriers of disease. Despite the uproar of criticism that his essays elicited, he held his ground. Holmes retired from Harvard in 1882, yet remained active as a writer and public speaker. He once wrote that "life is a fatal complaint and an eminently contagious one," and having outlived most of his family and friends, he died at the age of eighty-five.

While his medical career was flourishing, Holmes was also gaining respect as a poet. His first public notice came in 1830 with the publication in a Boston newspaper of "Old Ironsides," a poem protesting the government's plans to dismantle the

frigate *U.S.S. Constitution*. The poem touched a patriotic nerve, and the ensuing public outcry saved the ship for its role as an historical relic. Buoyed by his early popular success, Holmes published *Poems* in 1836; expanded and revised editions of the collection followed in 1846, 1848, and 1849. Holmes wrote much serious poetry, but his output also included a large number of occasional verses composed in either heroic and octosyllabic couplets or in the meter of the folk ballad. Most of Holmes's poems express his views about the human condition and his hopes for its improvement. In "The Chambered Nautilus," for example, Holmes speculated on the growth of the soul; in "The Last Leaf," he depicted the problems of old age. Holmes is generally considered neither an innovator nor an influence on the development of American poetry, and many commentators point out that his style derives from the neoclassicism of the Augustan age of eighteenth-century England. Nevertheless, critics consistently note that he successfully used poetry as a forum for expressing his philosophy, particularly in such pieces as "The Deacon's Masterpiece; or, The Wonderful 'One-Hoss Shay'," his strongest poetic statement against Calvinism. Holmes's approach to writing also demonstrates his scientific bent of mind: he claimed that his meter was modeled on the pulse and respiration rate of a speaker reading poetry aloud. Scholars affirm that his many later collections, including *Songs in Many Keys*, *Soundings from the Atlantic*, *Songs of*

Many Seasons, and *The Last Leaf*, attest to the endurance of Holmes's poetic gift.

Already an established poet, Holmes began writing prose pieces in 1858 for the *Atlantic Monthly* at the invitation of its editor, James Russell Lowell. Holmes's first contributions, which were later collected as *The Autocrat*, present the breakfast-table conversations of a fictional group of boarding-house residents, narrated by a member nicknamed "the autocrat." Complete with well-developed characters and plot, this work is difficult to place within a genre, but is most often classified as a collection of essays. *The Autocrat* achieved enormous popular and critical success and helped to establish the *Atlantic Monthly*'s reputation. While some pieces were humorous, others contained Holmes's ideas for changing society, and still others satirized various aspects of Calvinism. Holmes especially delighted in debunking "any logical system . . . supposed by its authors to be perfect, uncorrectable, and therefore, everlasting." *The Autocrat* was followed by *The Professor at the Breakfast-Table* in 1860, *The Poet at the Breakfast-Table* in 1872, and *Over the Teacups* in 1891. These four collections comprise what is usually referred to as the Breakfast-Table series.

Just as he had used the Breakfast-Table books to present his views on society, Holmes utilized his so-called "medicated novels" to explore the causes and treatment of aberrant behavior. *Elsie Venner*, *The Guardian Angel*, and *A Mortal Antipathy* strongly attest to Holmes's scientific interest. Critics are divided in their views of these works: some consider these novels concerned with psychology, others regard them as scientific treatises presented in a fictional framework, while still others claim that Holmes's novels are not about science, but about morality. In the first, *Elsie Venner*, which originally appeared serially in the *Atlantic Monthly* as *The Professor's Story*, Holmes created a protagonist who is believed to be part human and part serpent as a result of a prenatal snakebite. In this novel, Holmes discourses on such topics as prejudice, the Calvinist concept of original sin, and human psychology and sexuality. Most critics contend that *Elsie Venner* lacks artistic merit, though they argue that Holmes's perceptive character studies anticipate the psychological theories of Sigmund Freud and Carl Jung. In *The Guardian Angel*, Holmes discussed the influences of heredity and environment on mental and physical health. The novel also warns against a Puritan upbringing for children. *A Mortal Antipathy*, which ran serially in the *Atlantic Monthly* as *The New Portfolio*, deals with the causes and cures of childhood trauma. Commentators stress that the issues in these "medicated novels" derive from their author's background as a scientist; indeed, in each the characters seek out doctors and professors for help—suggesting that Holmes looked to science, not theology, to provide the answers for humanity's complex problems.

Criticism of Holmes's literary efforts is as varied as his fields of expertise, and a consensus of opinion is difficult to obtain. Scholars have debated whether he is predominantly a literary figure or a scientist, focusing on the frequent incorporation of medical themes and terminology into his works. The critics S. I. Hayakawa and Howard Mumford Jones argued that those who view Holmes primarily as an artist overlook his most important quality: his scientific interest. They also point out that his essays on medical topics exhibit his best prose, free of Victorian constraints. Yet other commentators, both in the nineteenth and twentieth centuries, have chosen not to acknowledge as primary Holmes's scientific career, emphasizing instead his role as an author.

In assessments of Holmes as a writer, scholarly emphasis has shifted over time from his poetry to his fictional essays and then to his novels. While early critics of his verse stressed his humor, wit, and patriotism, some also stated that his poetry was shallow and dilettantish, and Holmes himself noted in a preface to an 1862 collection that his poetic promise remained unfulfilled. After he published *The Autocrat*, critics transferred their attention to his prose. Some reviewers praised his versatility and wit, yet others denounced the provincialism, elitism, and political conservatism of his sketches. Holmes's privileged financial and social position, in addition, led to charges of insularity: many critics faulted his failure to support the abolitionist and women's rights movements. Conversely, his sympathizers point out that despite his limited contact with persons and ideas outside of New England, Holmes was expansive in his interests and expertise, and the didactic tone of much of his writing can be read as his concern for the welfare of others. However, it is Holmes's novels that have proven most interesting to twentieth-century critics. Controversial when published because of their intimate look at human physiology and psychology, they remain so today. While *The Autocrat* is still considered his best work, Holmes's novels have attracted attention from modern critics, who praise them as important early psychological studies.

Though still valued for his contributions to literature, science, theology, and psychology, Holmes is no longer as popular with readers as he once was. Yet despite this diminution of his reputation, which many critics attribute to the decline of New England's influence on American culture, Holmes and his writings still attract considerable commentary. Today, *The Autocrat*, likened by Virginia Woolf to the taste of "champagne after breakfast cups of weak tea," continues to occupy an important place in American literature.

(See also *Dictionary of Literary Biography*, Vol. 1: *The American Renaissance in New England*.)

---

*PRINCIPAL WORKS

Poems (poetry) 1836; also published in revised form as
　　Poems, 1846, 1848, 1849
Homeopathy and Its Kindred Delusions (essay) 1842
The Contagiousness of Puerperal Fever (essay) 1843
Urania: A Rhymed Lesson (poetry) 1846
Astraea: The Balance of Illusions (poetry) 1850
The Autocrat of the Breakfast-Table (essays) 1858
The Professor at the Breakfast-Table (essays) 1860
Currents and Counter-Currents in Medical Science (essays)
　　1861
Elsie Venner: A Romance of Destiny (novel) 1861
Songs in Many Keys (poetry) 1862
Soundings from the Atlantic (poetry) 1864
The Guardian Angel (novel) 1867
Mechanism in Thought and Morals (essay) 1871
The Poet at the Breakfast-Table (essays) 1872
"Crime and Automatism" (essay) 1875; published in
　　periodical *Atlantic Monthly*
Songs of Many Seasons (poetry) 1875
John Lothrop Motley (memoir) 1879
The School-Boy (poetry) 1879
The Iron Gate, and Other Poems (poetry) 1880
Medical Essays, 1842-1882 (essays) 1883

*Many of Holmes's works were first published in the *Atlantic Monthly*.

THE NORTH AMERICAN REVIEW   (essay date 1837)

[*This critic praises Holmes's entertaining and humorous collection,* Poems.]

We have seldom had more genuine enjoyment in the course of our critical labors, than in examining [Mr. Holmes's *Poems*]. (p. 275)

Mr. Holmes does not write in [a] mezzotinto style; he reminds us more of the clear strong lines of the ancient engravers. His manner is entirely his own, manly and unaffected; generally easy and playful, and sinking at times into 'a most humorous sadness.' The latter is evidently his favorite style, and we think his best. . . . [All] poetry which has any relation to humanity, will deal in smiles as well as tears. The critic may demonstrate that it is undignified in the poet to entertain his readers; but, an appeal being open from criticism to nature, whoever makes us laugh in this care-worn world will always be sustained by the common gratitude of mankind.

The first of these poems, called ["**Poetry: A Metrical Essay**"] . . . , was recited at the last anniversary of the Phi Beta Kappa Society, at Cambridge. As it was pronounced, it seemed to us more like inspiration than most any thing which ever came our way. As readers, we find it finished with much care, and abounding in striking thoughts and illustrations; but we apprehend that it was not so great a favorite with the writer as some of the lyrical pieces, which were struck off with less labor, but more power. One or two fine specimens of the latter are inserted in the larger poem by way of illustration; and with most readers these will be regarded as the pearls, and the poem as the string. We would not, however, do it injustice; the chief defect is the want of clearness, in expressing the truths in relation to poetical materials and inspirations which it contains. Some passages in it require to be read twice, before the reader is sure of their meaning. This occasional obscurity is strongly contrasted with the easy and natural flow of the lyrical poems. Nothing need be more beautiful than the lines on the Cambridge Church-yard, a place to which many hearts are bound by strong associations; and ["**Old Ironsides,**"] the strain upon the plan proposed by the Navy Department for breaking up the Frigate Constitution, an unhappy suggestion of some one who was probably more familiar with national ship-yards than national feelings, will rank with the best martial songs of England.

We think that the comic pieces in this little collection are decidedly the best, or rather we should say those in which a quiet humor is blended with the pathetic so as to heighten the effect of the grotesque without destroying the plaintive character of the whole. An example of this is afforded in "**The Last Reader**"; it is evidently the kind of writing in which the author takes most pleasure; and if he should find room for poetical pursuits in the cares of his profession, we hope that this graceful style will be his choice. At the same time we must allow that his more comic pieces are exceedingly entertaining; particularly the lines upon the Comet, which is irresistible for its humor, and at the same time contains one or two passages of great power. The incident so well related in "**The Height of the Ridiculous**" might be fact, not fable.

We have not time to give an acount of the work in detail, nor is it necessary; a book so entertaining is by this time in the hands of a great proportion of our readers. They will agree with us in the opinion that the author is a man of genius, and in the hope that the favor with which his work has been received may induce him to come before the public again. (pp. 276-77)

> *"Holmes's 'Poems',"* in The North American Review, *Vol. XLIV, No. 94, January, 1837, pp. 275-77.*

THE YALE LITERARY MAGAZINE   (essay date 1837)

[*This anonymous critic praises Holmes's "humor and manly sentiment" in* Poems, *but censures the uneven quality of individual pieces.*]

The distinguishing characteristics of Mr. Holmes' [*Poems*] are manliness and humor. We say of his *book*, we shall give our notions on what we think are the true elements of his character (*id est* his poetic character) in the course of our article. The first thing that strikes is, that the writer has a way of saying a thing which is his own way, and that this is always manly. He casts his thoughts in a mould that shows his familiarity with the best writers; that he has been to the very fountain head for instruction, and come away benefitted by it. He knows how to be sentimental without silliness, and vigorous without violence; and in such situations as we would think him most likely to fail, he has contrived to acquit himself with credit. He does not for the sake of a thought let himself down to it, but if he must have it he brings it up to his own station. Neither does he seem to have yielded to that most besetting sin of all clever writers, a disposition to run as near to mawkishness as possible without falling into it, and by a delicacy and a mastery of good language produce something which we can't call bad, and yet for the life of us cannot give them credit for. We see nothing of this. On the contrary, there is too little sentimentality; and we could wish he had allowed himself more latitude where he shows himself so capable. He stops as if he were afraid of cloying us, and contents himself with saying a little less than just enough. Now though we honor the motive here we could wish it otherwise. We would have Mr. Holmes indulge himself in that delicate vein of simple melancholy which is so full of pathos, which is always found in every genuine poet, and which he himself possesses in an eminent degree; and though we know advice of this kind would let a host of evils on us if taken indiscriminately, yet we have no fears in giving it to a man like him whose good sense will surely never let him overstep the bounds of modesty.

The other characteristic of this book is, its playfulness. We don't recollect ever to have met before, in any one book and written by one person, so many pieces of sparkling humor.

Some of them are conceived in the happiest vein, and executed in the most felicitous manner. They have the advantage of being finished without the appearance of study—in fact seem to have dropped from the pen without effort. They open sly and soberly, about the middle you begin to suspect something, at last you lay aside the gentleman and literally roar. We notice also that there rarely or never recurs the same thought. . . . The thoughts in this book are rarely or never diluted; every line seems to have its business there, and the conclusion you come to after reading it is, that the thing is 'about done up.' Now this is saying a great deal. The art of writing a playful poem, easy yet vigorous, familiar yet original, and then to know just when to leave off, is the highest art of poetry. When we try to be natural, and select smooth and musical words to make the rhythm melodious, there is danger of letting the thought go *for* the word; and while we are chasing after this phrase or that, twisting it about and trying to knock the corners off that it may fit into the structure, the spirit is gone. Any one at all familiar with writing knows also, that the thoughts suggested in the heat of composition seem original often when they are not; and we take up many a manuscript after laying it by to cool, and find a work valueless which cost us a deal of labor. Mr. Holmes has steered clear of all this. Dean Swift's definition of a good style fits him exactly, 'proper words in proper places.' His words are well chosen, the rhythm is smooth, and in most cases the thought apparent at a glance. In his hands the language is made to twist itself many ways; yet the collocation is always natural and the spirit preserved. The conclusion we come to is, that Mr. Holmes is a poet of very fine powers, and that he deems his art of importance enough to be studied and studied well. His book has delighted us. . . . (pp. 116-18)

But we have not done with him. The reader will perceive we have all along carried the impression, of humor and manly sentiment being his chief characteristics. This is true of his book, in which, with one or two exceptions, these qualities are mostly prominent. But we said something back, of some different notions entertained by us about the true character of his genius—which we now return to. Nothing is more glaringly apparent in literary history, than the wonderful discrepancy we sometimes find, when we compare the *works* with the *ways* of literary men. An author before the public is like a belle in a drawing-room, in his very best; every thing offensive is put out of sight, out of compliment to the company. But this supposes the author's character bad—let us change the illustration. An author before the public is like a well educated lady, who out of favor to certain prejudices of the company avoids certain topics of conversation which are offensive to them. This suits our purpose better, and it is here we believe where our poet is. There is a delicate vein of the most melancholy witchery in him, which so far as we can judge he keeps aiming to suppress, and his reason is doubtless the fact, that the common mass of mankind speak coldly of or do not understand it. We believe we can understand him here; we believe that poetry with him is a sacred feeling; and if he ever brings it up and lets it gush forth in the full freshness of its own deep melody, he feels very much as the ancients did when strangers laid hands on their household gods, it seems to him like a kind of desecration. We believe this the secret of our poet's not indulging himself in this kind of writing, and yet in this vein we believe lies his power. We are strengthened in this by the fact, that the very finest specimens of real poetry in the book are of this character; and, also, that in the humorous pieces there is an under current of simple pathos, the more fascinating perhaps from the stinted quantities dealt out to us. (p. 118)

["**The Last Reader**"] is exquisite poetry. It melts into the heart like the melody of a dream when that heart is aching; and had our author written nothing else we should not soon forget him. The verse beginning:

> And when my name no more is heard,

is perfect; and what Coleridge says of Shakspeare, that you cannot add or diminish by a word to advantage, is true here. Would any one believe after reading [this] beautiful poem, that the same pen could trace the following, speaking of an old man—

> My grandmamma has said,—
> Poor old lady, she is dead,
>   Long ago,—
> That he had a Roman nose,
> And his cheek was like a rose
>   In the snow . . .

or this, of a girl's losing her lover:

> Down fell that pretty innocent as falls a snow white
>   lamb,
> *Her hair drooped round her pallid cheeks like sea-weed*
> *on a clam;*

or this, entitled ["**The Height of the Ridiculous**":] . . .

> He read the next; the grin grew broad,
>   And shot from ear to ear;
> He read the third; a chuckling noise
>   I now began to hear.
>
> The fourth; he broke into a roar;
>   The fifth; his waistband split;
> The sixth; he burst five buttons off,
>   And tumbled in a fit. . . .

Ye ghosts of Momus! look at it. The fellow holding his sides, frothing like a puppy got the hydrophobia, and the breeches flying. There's a scene for you to give tragedy the hysterics, or set the carved face on a brass door-knocker grinning. Well done, Mr. Holmes. (pp. 120-21)

We come now to the most disagreeable part of our work, viz. to censure; but, by the way, we think the 'why and wherefore' of our fault-finding will be that which reviews generally have passed over. We shall not stop to point out certain obscurities we have heard urged, though they may be urged perhaps with some propriety. There are a few passages which require to be re-read to be understood clearly; but when the reader will explain certain passages in Milton, and hundreds of them in Byron we can point him to, why then let him blame Mr. Holmes if he chooses. Nor shall we stop to mention an evident failure, in the winding up of one or two of the humorous pieces. A humorous composition, one that hits, one that gets hold of you, one that makes you laugh 'in resolution's spite;' such a poem must open ambiguously, begin to smoke in the middle, and go off with a flash. As a general thing he is very successful. As a specimen of genuine English humor we instance "**The Music Grinders**," and the "**Oysterman**," and for one evincing the true Elian spirit, we instance "**The Song of the Tread-mill**." In fact this little *morceau* gave us as much pleasure as some of Lamb's finest. We wish the last verse was better however— still, it is tart, pithy, and gloriously humorous. But the conclusion of the "**Mysterious Visitor**" is altogether unworthy of the body of that poem; and, as we understand it, the lines to the "**Portrait of a Lady**," are but little better. But for all this we are well compensated on the whole by the rest of the book, so we let it go. But what we *have* to blame our poet for is, a fault which himself has confessed, viz. the admission of certain confessedly *mediocre* poems, to fill out the volume. Our remarks shall be rather severe here, as the thing particularly offends us. In the preface he says, 'having written comparatively little, and nothing of late years until within a few months, I could ill afford to be over nice in my selection.' Now this is a most odious confession—odious because a man of his genius has no business to make it, and odious because the last part of the statement is false. He *can* afford to be nice in his selection: however, if he cannot, he has no business to select at all. The thought appendaged, also, that the publisher must be gratified, is abominable—just as if, in building up the cause of literature, the object is to well line the pockets of book-sellers. This is twisting things about with a vengeance. We always thought, that the supporting of publishers was a matter altogether incidental to the great work of advancing intelligence, and that the credit of *writing* a sound book took the precedence of the printing it. However it is one of the improvements of the age. We'll wager our poet any thing that we can pick out the very pieces inserted to swell the volume. What right have **"La Grisette," "A Souvenir," "My Companions," "The proud Pedestrian,"** and **"Evening, by a tailor"**—what right have these by the side of the splendid opening on the fourth page, **"The last Reader," "The last Leaf," "To a Katydid," "The dying Seneca,"** and twenty others we could mention? There never was such a coupling since the days of Job. It may be said, a man has a right to do what he likes with his own—we deny it totally and forever. A man who *can* write good poetry, has no more business to write bad, than a man whose character is up for truth telling, gets a charter thereby to lie when he chooses.... The truth of it is, we like Mr. Holmes; like his manner and method, and that too exceedingly, therefore we don't like to see him make himself unlikeable. (pp. 122-23)

Mr. Holmes has done well in this—his first volume we believe—and we hope soon to see him in another. His fresh and manly style of writing, we hesitate not in saying is very creditable to our literature, and will help refute the notion so vigorously cried up by a class of us, that this country is no place for poetry. (p. 123)

> *A review of "Poems," in* The Yale Literary Magazine, *Vol. II, No. 4, February, 1837, pp. 113-24.*

THE NORTH AMERICAN REVIEW   (essay date 1847)

[In the following excerpt from a largely favorable review of Urania, *the anonymous critic remarks on Holmes's mastery of style.]*

[*Urania*] is the modest and rather enigmatical title of a very lively and beautiful poem. (p. 208)

Though [Dr. Holmes] has published very little, he is one of the most popular of American poets, [and] . . . he deserves all his reputation. Some may object, that much of his popularity is to be ascribed to the exuberance of his wit, in which he easily surpasses all his contemporaries excepting Hood. To this we answer, that wit may justly be considered as one of the brightest ornaments of poetry; and in his case, as well as in that of his English predecessor to whom we have just alluded, it is by no means unattended by the higher and more characteristic excellences of his profession. His fancy teems with bright and appropriate images, and these are woven into his plan usually with exquisite finish and grace. His artistic merits are very great; his versification is never slovenly, nor his diction

meagre or coarse; and many of his shorter pieces are inwrought with so much fire and imagination as to rank among our best lyrics.

This is high praise, and in order to justify it, we should find it necessary to quote rather from the volume of his [*Poems*] . . . than from the brief "rhymed lesson," quite local and occasional in character, which is now before us. But we must not make citations from a work which is in the hands of nearly all our readers, while the choicer portions of it are as familiar to them as the songs of their childhood. *Urania*—a title which for some inexplicable reason he has chosen to annex to this later publication—has some striking faults; but it has also characteristic passages enough to support our high estimate of the writer's powers. It is a mere medley of bright thoughts and laughing satire, with here and there a momentary expression of deep feeling, which betrays a spirit that may be touched to nobler issues. The poet glances about like a butterfly from one topic to another, hardly resting on any one long enough to obtain more than a sip of its honey. The versification is uniformly flowing and harmonious, and the lines are never bolstered out with feeble or unmeaning expressions. (pp. 212-13)

[The description of a Sabbath morning in the city contains] vigorous and striking lines, which no living poet certainly need be ashamed to own. The deep and holy sentiment which pervades the latter portion of [those lines] may suffice to convince those of their error who have hitherto regarded Dr. Holmes only as a rhyming Momus. There are many felicities of expression in them which show great mastery of style, and perfect familiarity with the well of English undefiled. This, indeed, is one of the characteristic merits of our bard. His diction is uniformly terse, precise, and vigorous, never cheating the ear with sound that veils an ambiguity of meaning, nor violating by a hair's breadth the established usages of language. His words ring clear and shrill, like good coin tried on the counter. He has entire command of Anglo-Saxon phraseology, and the most familiar turns of speech, without ever sinking into baldness or vulgarity; and he often adapts colloquial expressions to his purpose with a felicity of setting which reminds one of Dean Swift. . . . There is much good sense, as well as pungent wit [in the poem]. . . . (p. 215)

[Dr. Holmes] has shown much versatility of power, and we hope, on greeting him again, to find that he has been wandering in some of the higher walks of poesy. Let him not seek excuse for keeping his wings folded, on the ground that his daily pursuits confine him to the prosaic side of life. He gives a laughing sketch, indeed, of the incongruity between the subjects of thought that are commended to him by his profession, and these furtive offerings to the Muse. But Aesculapius was the favorite son of Apollo, and the two deities were often worshipped at the same shrine. They will not quarrel with each other, if our author's homage is divided between them; nor can he be said to abandon the healing art who worships also the god of the silver bow, the slayer of the Python, and the author of the oracular responses given at Delphi. There are golden hours of leisure even in the practice of a successful physician, and these at least may be consecrated to more ambitious uses. (p. 216)

> *"Holmes's 'Urania'," in* The North American Review, *Vol. LXIV, No. 134, January, 1847, pp. 208-16.*

[JAMES RUSSELL LOWELL]   (poem date 1848)

[Lowell was a celebrated nineteenth-century American poet, critic, essayist, and editor of two leading journals, the Atlantic Monthly

and the North American Review. *He is noted today for his satirical and critical writings, including* A Fable for Critics, *a book-length poem featuring witty critical portraits of his contemporaries. In the following excerpt from that work, Lowell playfully describes Holmes's poetic style.*]

There's Holmes, who is matchless among you for wit;
A Leyden-jar always full-charged, from which flit
The electrical tingles of hit after hit;
In long poems 'tis painful sometimes and invites
A thought of the way the new Telegraph writes,
Which pricks down its little sharp sentences spitefully
As if you got more than you'd title to rightfully,
And if it were hoping its wild father Lightning
Would flame in for a second and give you a fright'ning.
He has perfect sway of what *I* call a sham metre,
But many admire it, the English hexameter,
And Campbell, I think, wrote most commonly worse,
With less nerve, swing, and fire in the same kind of
    verse,
Nor e'er achieved aught in't so worthy of praise
As the tribute of Holmes to the grand *Marseillaise.*
You went crazy last year over Bulwer's New Timon;—
Why, if B., to the day of his dying, should rhyme on,
Heaping verses on verses and tomes upon tomes,
He could ne'er reach the best point and vigor of
    Holmes.
His are just the fine hands, too, to weave you a lyric
Full of fancy, fun, feeling, or spiced with satyric
In so kindly a measure, that nobody knows
What to do but e'en join in the laugh, friends and foes.

(pp. 69-70)

[*James Russell Lowell*], *in his* A Fable for Critics; or, A Glance at a Few of Our Literary Progenies, *second edition, G. P. Putnam, 1848, 80 p.*

JOHN GREENLEAF WHITTIER   (essay date 1849)

[*Whittier was a noted American poet, abolitionist, journalist, and critic who encouraged the idea of American literary nationalism. In the following excerpt, he admires the wit and humor in* Poems, *but also values Holmes's ability to touch "the deeper chords of the heart."*]

If any of our readers (and at times we fear it is the case with all) need amusement, and the wholesome alterative of a hearty laugh, we commend them not to Dr. Holmes the physician, but to Dr. Holmes the scholar, the wit, and the humorist; not to the scientific medical professor's barbarous Latin, but to his poetical prescriptions, given in choice old Saxon. We have tried them, and are ready to give the doctor certificates of their efficacy. . . .

The volume [*Poems*] now before us gives, in addition to the poems and lyrics contained in the two previous editions, some hundred or more pages of the later productions of the author, in the sprightly vein, and marked by the brilliant fancy and felicitous diction for which the former were noteworthy. . . . "**Terpsichore,**" read at an annual dinner of the Phi Beta Kappa Society at Cambridge, sparkles throughout with keen wit, quaint conceits, and satire so good-natured that the subjects of it can enjoy it as heartily as their neighbors. (p. 516)

There are, as might be expected, some common-place pieces in the volume—a few failures in the line of humor. "**The Spectre Pig,**" the "**Dorchester Giant,**" "**The Height of the Ridiculous,**" and one or two others, might be omitted in the next edition without detriment. They would do well enough for an amateur humorist, but are scarcely worthy of one who stands at the head of the profession.

It was said of James Smith, of the "Rejected Addresses," that "if he had not been a witty man, he would have been a *great* man." Hood's humor and drollery kept in the back-ground the pathos and beauty of his soberer productions; and Dr. Holmes, we suspect, might have ranked higher, among a large class of readers, than he now does, had he never written his "**Ballad of the Oysterman,**" his "**Comet,**" and his "**September Gale.**" Such lyrics as "**La Grisette,**" "**The Puritan's Vision,**" and that unique compound of humor and pathos, "**The Last Leaf,**" show that he possesses the power of touching the deeper chords of the heart, and of calling forth tears as well as smiles. (p. 517)

Dr. Holmes has been likened to Thomas Hood; but there is little in common between them, save the power of combining fancy and sentiment with grotesque drollery and humor. . . . Holmes writes simply for the amusement of himself and his readers; he deals only with the vanity, the foibles, and the minor faults of mankind, good-naturedly and almost sympathizingly suggesting excuses for the folly which he tosses about on the horns of his ridicule. In this respect he differs widely from his fellow-townsman, Russell Lowell, whose keen wit and scathing sarcasm, in the famous *Biglow Papers,* and the notes of Parson Wilbur, strike at the great evils of society, and deal with the rank offences of church and state. Hosea Biglow, in his way, is as earnest a preacher as Habakkuk Mucklewrath, or Obadiah Bind-their-kings-in-chains-and-their-nobles-in-fetters-of-iron. His verse smacks of the old Puritan flavor. Holmes

A portrait of Holmes as a young man. The Granger Collection, New York.

has a gentler mission. His careless, genial humor reminds us of James Smith in his *Rejected Addresses* and "Horace in London." Long may he live to make broader the face of our care-ridden generation, and to realize for himself the truth of the wise man's declaration, that "a merry heart is a continual feast." (p. 518)

> John Greenleaf Whittier, "Mirth and Medicine," in Littell's Living Age, *Vol. XX, No. 251, March 10, 1849, pp. 516-18.*

MARY RUSSELL MITFORD (essay date 1852)

[*Mitford was an English sketch writer, dramatist, poet, novelist, and critic whose legacy to nineteenth-century literature includes some of the most endearing sketches of English country life. Here, Mitford praises Holmes's originality and his descriptions in* Astraea.]

Among the strange events of these strange days of ours, when revolutions and counter-revolutions, constitutions changed one week and rechanged the next, seem to crowd into a fortnight the work of a century, annihilating time, just as railways and electric telegraphs annihilate space,—in these days of curious novelty, nothing has taken me more pleasantly by surprise than the school of true and original poetry that has sprung up among our blood relations (I had well nigh called them our fellow-countrymen) across the Atlantic; they who speak the same tongue and inherit the same literature. And of all this flight of genuine poets, I hardly know any one so original as Dr. Holmes. For him we can find no living prototype; to track his footsteps, we must travel back as far as Pope or Dryden; and to my mind it would be well if some of our own bards would take the same journey—provided always, it produced the same result. Lofty, poignant, graceful, grand, high of thought, and clear of word, we could fancy ourselves reading some pungent page of "Absalom and Achitophel," or of the "Moral Epistles," if it were not for the pervading nationality, which, excepting Whittier, American poets have generally wanted, and for that true reflection of the manners and the follies of the age, without which satire would fail alike of its purpose and its name. (p. 399)

The grace and pathos of [Dr. Holmes's] introduction [to *Astraea*] must be felt by every one. It has all the sweetness of Goldsmith, with more force and less obviousness of thought.

The poem opens with a description of an American spring, equally true to general nature and to the locality where it is written. The truth is so evident in the one case, that we take it for granted in the other. The couplet on the crocus for instance, a couplet so far as I know unmatched in flower painting, gives us most exquisitely expressed an image that meets our eye every March. The "shy turtles ranging their platoons," we never have seen, and probably never shall see, and yet the accuracy of the picture is as clear to us as that of the most familiar flower of our border. (p. 402)

After this we are introduced to a winter room, delineated with equal taste and fidelity;—the very home of lettered comfort. . . . (p. 403)

Such is the opening of the *Astraea*. It speaks much for the man whose affluence of intellect could afford such an outpouring for a single occasion, the recitation of one solitary evening; and hardly less for the audience that prompted and welcomed such an effort. (p. 406)

> Mary Russell Mitford, "American Poets," in her Recollections of a Literary Life; or, Books, Places, and People, *1852. Reprint by Harper & Brothers, Publishers, 1855, pp. 399-410.*

[FRANK H. HILL] (essay date 1861)

[*In addition to criticizing Holmes's provincialism and lack of originality, Hill questions the propriety of his treatment of abnormality in* Elsie Venner, *commenting that the heroine's story "illustrates the fantastic extravagance, that lack of a controlling good taste, which mark American literature."*]

Dr. Holmes is indisputably and above all an entertaining writer. He thinks, and he can express his thought articulately. He flashes upon you an ingenious suggestion, or a whimsical paradox, clothed in fantastic guise, and without giving you time to pause upon the truth it contains, or to reflect even whether what seems so plausible is true, presents you with another and another in endless sequence. The general effect is somewhat kaleidoscopic. It suits, we suppose, the rapid hurry of the American mind, which cannot delay upon any thing, but which glances quickly over a thousand things; which is curious, but has its curiosity easily sated; which propounds countless questions, and is contented with the first plausible reply. Another source of Dr. Holmes's American popularity lies, no doubt, in the circumstance that he is a man of varied culture, accomplished in no ordinary degree; and that he addresses a people among whom a certain low average of education is universal, but among whom a high order of cultivation is rare. His writings abound in pleasant hints, stimulative to curiosity, of regions of thought and literature into which his readers have never penetrated; and they agreeably enlarge, though by fitful glimpses, which rapidly close in, the mental horizon of the great body of subscribers to the *Atlantic Monthly*. But though enriched with European culture, Dr. Holmes is essentially an American. Rub the varnish off the Russian, and the Tartar is seen beneath. There is the exaggerated provincialism of sentiment, the confusion of extent of territory with national greatness, of democratic equality with personal freedom, which characterise the typical American. (p. 363)

So far from admitting with [Dr. Holmes], however, that "America is the only place where man is full-grown," we contend that in America we have not the full-grown man, but only the over-grown boy. There is the boastful self-exaggeration, the inability of taking fair measure of its capacities and attainments as compared with those of its contemporaries and predecessors, which mark a people that has not yet cut its wisdom-teeth. The products of the American mind have no mellowness; there is a crude acidity about them. With all his intensely American feeling, however, Dr. Holmes is unable to make any advance towards the creation of a specifically American literature. He no sooner puts pen to paper than he becomes imitative. As in Washington Irving we have the revivication of the *Spectator* school of literature, as in Cooper we see only the pale and watery reflexion of Walter Scott, so in Dr. Holmes we have an American edition (expurgated) of Montaigne and Rabelais and Sterne. The modern work of English literature which the *Autocrat* and the *Professor* at the breakfast-table at once call to mind,—as much, perhaps, in the way of contrast as in the way of resemblance,—is the *Noctes Ambrosianæ*. The broad rollicking humour and strong sense of the Scotch professor, however, are in contrast as remarkable with the somewhat thin intellectual wit of the American, as the dry toast and tea of a Boston boarding-house are to the "strong waters" and meat-suppers of Ambrose's. The divinity student and school-dame and vexed female in bombazine are the proper hearers of the wisdom of the Autocrat, as the Shepherd and Tickler are the fitting interlocutors of North. The entire absence of dramatic powers in Holmes is, however, what chiefly differentiates him from Wilson. The boarders at his breakfast-table are only so many points to which the Autocrat attaches the threads of his conversation, so many mirrors in which he is variously reflected. They exist only as they are shone upon by him. We are sorry to speak in what appears disparagement of a writer for whom we entertain a very sincere admiration; from whom the reader is sure of entertainment and of a certain amount of mental stimulus; in whom we acknowledge wit, humour, fancy—real, if not of the highest order, shrewd observations of life, if not deep insight into character, ingenious if somewhat superficial criticism on art, literature, and philosophy. We are glad to add, without any qualification, that Dr. Holmes's sympathies are always large and humane; and that the most odious of tyrannies,—always associated in those who indulge it with a deep underlying scepticism, which suspects its own truth of being a cunningly disguised lie that may be found out, the tyranny which would suppress free thought on the most stupendous of all themes,—is thoroughly hated and despised by him. Seeing life by snatches rather than seeing it whole, apprehensive of the salient points of a character rather than grasping it in its living unity, endowed, in a word, with susceptible fancy rather than with a sterling imagination, Dr. Holmes's vocation would appear not to be towards fiction. It is in fragmentary "guesses at truth," rather than in completed delineations of life and character, that his strength hitherto has seemed to lie. Whether *Elsie Venner* confirms this pre-supposition, or rather the author's doctrine, that every man has at least one novel in him, and "that he (Dr. Holmes), as an individual of the human race, could write one novel, or story, at any rate, if he would;"—which of these alternatives is true remains to be seen. If he has succeeded, he has furnished the best refutation of Mr. Hawthorne's notion that American life and manners do not afford materials for a romance, by doing what was pronounced impossible. *Solvitur ambulando.*

The "destiny" which is referred to in the title-page is not, we may premise, the "manifest destiny" of which we used to hear so much in connexion with America,—romance though that appears now to have become. It refers to the doctrine, very prominent in all Dr. Holmes's writings, that character, mental and moral, is largely dependent on organization; that transmitted and congenital qualities form a determining force in life. This opinion is not peculiar to Dr. Holmes. Every man, not only of science, but of sense, holds it, with more or less limitation; and Dr. Holmes himself does not hold it altogether without limitation. In many cases, however, the limitation is held so strongly as practically to reduce the original truth to nothing; in others so slight a limitation is admitted as virtually to leave the doctrine unchecked, to drift into a materialistic fatalism. Apart from the nicely-balanced judgments of physiologists and psychologists, in the matter of truths admitted into any mind, there are some which, from a natural affinity, become operative in it, and are always present with it; they form the key by which it unlocks the secrets of character, the light in which it views nature and life, the interpretation of all mysteries. There are other truths, different of course in different persons, which, admitted in words, are practically ignored. To the former class, in the case of Dr. Holmes, belongs the doctrine of congenital qualities, coming to us by hereditary transmission. It is the clue by which he finds his way through the labyrinth. He deduces from it, as he well may, many lessons of practical wisdom, and of tender and enlarged charity. Not denying, occasionally in a sort of moral compulsion conceding,

that the mind has a self-determining power, operative under fixed conditions, he soon loses sight of the self-determining power, and remembers only the fixed conditions. Character, he allows, is destiny; but organisation is character, and organisation is an affair of race and parentage and external influences, moulding the individual as clay is moulded. This is the "destiny," the "romance" of which is told in *Elsie Venner.* It is there put in a very bold and startling, and what will be to some minds repulsive, shape. (pp. 365-67)

The conception of a literally brute nature in a human form is in itself by no means attractive. The idea of a reptile semi-parentage is still more repulsive. (p. 370)

We are quite incompetent to discuss the physiological basis of the story. We demur, however, to the propriety of illustrating a "grave scientific doctrine" by what may possibly be a wild and unscientific delusion; and still more to the artistic suitability of introducing into a story of prosaic modern life, abounding in Yankee vulgarisms, an incident so abnormal and unverified as that on which *Elsie Venner* hinges. Granting for the moment its possibility, granting its actuality, it still is out of place. The scenery and events, the tone and colouring of the tale, are not in keeping with it. The conception illustrates the fantastic extravagance, that lack of a controlling good taste, which mark American literature. It is "sensation writing;" the object is to startle. The best proof of this is that Dr. Holmes's serpent-woman does not excite awe, pity, or terror, but simply incredulity. *Elsie Venner,* so far as the heroine's character is concerned, has neither the verisimilitude of a story of real life, nor the instructiveness of avowed parable or allegory. Dr. Holmes is by no means the first to describe the gradual humanising of a character in which a nature lower than human predominates. Mr. Hawthorne has done so in his romance of *Transformation.* The stories of Undines and of Neckars are other instances. But these are avowedly only the mere play of a graceful or pathetic fancy, or the symbolical utterance of truths which we can detach from their exterior form. A case like that of Elsie Venner belongs to the morbid pathologist, and not to the novelist. To be treated with effect in fiction, it should be transferred to an age or country—to Egypt or Greece—where, in the strangeness of the surrounding scenery and costume, rites and beliefs, it would lose something of the monstrosity which attaches to it as actually presented.

The secondary characters in *Elsie Venner* are, to our mind, more happily conceived than that of the heroine. The work derives its chief value not from the "romance of destiny" which it contains, but from the glimpses which it affords us of ordinary American life in a provincial town of New England. The two ministers, Liberal and Calvinist, the Rev. Chauncy Fairweather and the Rev. Dr. Honeywood, each covertly leaning to the other's faith; Deacon Sloper and Colonel Sprowle and Mr. Silas Peckham, are, we dare say, faithful portraitures. The picture, if it be a correct one, is by no means flattering. It leaves an impression that over American society there is diffused an incurable vulgarity of speech, sentiment, and language, hard to define, but perceptible in every word and gesture. We do not pretend that in the middle classes of an English town we should find any remarkable degree of refinement. But here there is a pervading atmosphere of good breeding, which extends to those who do not themselves possess access to the immediate sources of cultivation. Even more conclusive, however, than the genuine vulgarity of the characters whom Dr. Holmes intends to paint as vulgar, is the real vulgarity of those whom he would represent to us as well-taught and highly-bred gentlemen, of whom Mr. Bernard Langdon is the type. His utter failure in this character would seem as if the model on which it was founded was not over common. His success in delineating the Slopers and Sprowles is in remarkable contrast. In the one, probably he draws from experience, in the other, from imagination. Be this as it may, the latter have an air of reality which is entirely wanting to the former. The inference which is suggested by this, as to the condition of American society outside of the great centres of intelligence, may be unjust, but it is not unnatural. (pp. 371-72)

[Frank H. Hill], in "Dr. Oliver Wendell Holmes and 'Elsie Venner'," in The National Review, *London, Vol. XIII, No. XXVI, October, 1861, pp. 359-72.*

OLIVER WENDELL HOLMES   (poem date 1862)

[In the following excerpt from his "To My Readers," written to introduce an 1862 edition of his collected poems, Holmes admits that his promise remains, as yet, unfulfilled.]

> Nay, blame me not; I might have spared
>   Your patience many a trivial verse,
> Yet these my earlier welcome shared,
>   So, let the better shield the worse.
>
> And some might say, "Those ruder songs
>   Had freshness which the new have lost;
> To spring the opening leaf belongs,
>   The chestnut-burs await the frost." . . .
>
> Deal gently with us, ye who read!
>   Our largest hope is unfulfilled,—
> The promise still outruns the deed,—
>   The tower, but not the spire, we build.
>
> Our whitest pearl we never find;
>   Our ripest fruit we never reach;
> The flowering moments of the mind
>   Drop half their petals in our speech.
>
> These are my blossoms; if they wear
>   One streak of morn or evening's glow,
> Accept them; but to me more fair
>   The buds of song that never blow.

(pp. 1-2)

Oliver Wendell Holmes, "To My Readers," in his The Complete Poetical Works of Oliver Wendell Holmes, *edited by Horace E. Scudder, Houghton Mifflin Company, 1895, pp. 1-2.*

[GERALD MASSEY]   (essay date 1867)

[Massey praises the manner in which Holmes uses humor to tell Americans "a few truths," thereby counteracting their provincialism.]

Oliver Wendell Holmes is . . . doing his best to tell his countrymen a few truths it was well they should learn, especially from their own writers. He can say the most unpalatable things in the pleasantest possible way. He does not appeal to the pride and pugnacity of his countrymen, or tell them that America is the only place in which a man can stand upright and draw free breath. He thinks there is 'no sufficient flavour of humanity in the soil' out of which they grow, and that it makes a man humane to 'live on the old humanized soil' of Europe. He will not deny the past for the sake of glorifying the present. 'They say a dead man's hand cures swellings if laid on them; nothing

like the dead cold hand of the past to take down our tumid egotism.' He is equally the enemy of 'high-falutin,' and spread-eagleism, and social slang. 'First-rate,' 'prime,' 'a prime article,' 'a superior piece of goods,' 'a gent in a flowered vest;' all such expressions are final. They blast the lineage of him or her who utters them, for generations up and down. He tells them that 'good breeding is surface Christianity.' He slyly consoles them with the thought that 'good Americans when they die go to Paris.' He is thoroughly national himself, and would have American patriotism large and liberal, not a narrow provincial conceit. The 'autocrat' is assuredly one of the pleasantest specimens of the American gentleman, and one of the most charming of all chatty companions; genial, witty, and wise; never wearisome. We fancy the *Autocrat of the Breakfast Table* is not so well known or widely read in this country as it deserves to be. A more delightful book has not come over the Atlantic. (pp. 233-34)

[Holmes] brings American humour to its finest point, and is, in fact, the first of American *Wits.* . . .

[A] speciality of Holmes's wit [is] the kind of *badinage* with which he quizzes common sense so successfully, by his happy paradox of serious straightforward statement, and quiet qualifying afterwards by which he tapers his point. (p. 234)

[Gerald Massey], "Yankee Humour," in The Quarterly Review, *Vol. CXXII, No. CCXLIII, January, 1867, pp. 212-37.*

THE NATION   (essay date 1867)

[This anonymous reviewer identifies several faults in The Guardian Angel, *contending that it contributed to the decline in Holmes's reputation as a novelist.]*

What "goes without saying," as the French put it, Dr. Holmes is very apt to say; that, we believe, is the thing which chiefly interferes with our enjoyment of his works. The third page of *The Guardian Angel* gives an example of what we mean. Is there any one who refuses to admit that his "local paper" is seldom to be called an admirable thing? No one, we are fully persuaded. So it is a little—or not a little—unpleasing when a ponderous, much-creaking piece of machinery is dragged out, and that somewhat aged truth—painfully true, we may call it—is violently driven into us, with every appearance of triumph on the part of the engineer. Surely it had several times before sunk through all our minds of its own weight. . . . [It] may have been a stroke of art in Dr. Holmes's work—his making his professor, when his lead-pencil is in hand, so stupid as he is. But it has not the appearance of being intended for stupidity. Thus Mr. Gridley goes on through his *Banner and Oracle*, advertisements and all; and with something of the same manner Dr. Holmes, as it appears to us, goes through his story—too often bearing on hard when only the lightest touch would have been pleasing, not to say sufferable; sternly breaking on his wheel the deadest of bugs and butterflies. For example, is a man "really *so* satirical" when he does this sort of thing? It is about Gifted Hopkins, the typical newspaper poet and village bard—a figure which has come to be, perhaps, the very least mirth-provoking of all with which satire deals. Satirists in kittenhood have played with it till the breath is long gone out of it. . . . (p. 390)

Of this fault of bearing on too hard, we repeat, the book itself, taken as a whole, is an example. When he had written the *Autocrat of the Breakfast Table,* Dr. Holmes would have done

Holmes's gambrel-roofed house in Cambridge.

well, as it has since appeared, had he ceased from satire. That series of papers gave him a brilliant reputation which from that time forward he has gone on damaging, diminishing it by each new book; diminishing the brilliance of it, at any rate, though it may well enough be that he has extended it among more people. He has never stopped hammering at the same nail which he hit on the head when he first struck. *The Professor* took away something from the estimation in which we had been holding the *Autocrat; Elsie Venner* took away a little more; and *The Guardian Angel* takes away a larger portion than was removed by either of the others.

We speak of the author as a satirist. That he is, mainly; he is hardly to be called a novelist. His characters are figures labelled and set up to be fired at, or are names about which a love story is told, or they embody some physiologico-psychological theory; but they are never to be called characters in any true sense of the word. Never is rather a large word, perhaps. We can remember "the young man called John"; and we remember him as almost entirely and always human. But this can be said of no other of the personages—boarding-house keepers, young lovers, artists, soldiers, ministers, boarding-school girls—with whose names Doctor Holmes's books are filled. The incidents of his stories and their arrangement into a plot are generally better invented than the characters, and answer well enough the main purpose of the book, which is always essentially an attack on some theological dogma, an attack made sometimes directly and sometimes by the setting forth of some such theory as this, for example—the one on which is built the novel before us: "It was the strife of her 'Vision,' only in another form— the contest of two lives her blood inherited, for the conquest of her soul." But the humorist and man of wit and satirist

leads the novelist astray. Most of his incidents, invented or borrowed, are of no special importance to his subject, and he is often compelled to come forward in his own person and tell us what he intends by them.

Of *The Guardian Angel* as a novel, then, it is hardly worth while to talk. The theory above quoted is well enough illustrated by the incidents which the author has used in *The Guardian Angel;* the narrative part of the novel is at any rate as good as the narrative part of *Elsie Venner* or *The Autocrat* or *The Professor,* and in all these novels the narrative part is good enough for the satirist's purpose. As to the doctrine which is put forward in all these works—the limitations of human moral responsibility, the effect on the soul of the bad company of the body—we profess ourselves believers in it as Dr. Holmes states it; as doctors generally state it, when they are not doctors of divinity, without humanity. He simply asks us to accept the facts of human nature instead of kicking against the pricks, in the fashion of the divines of a hundred years ago. If his persistence in preaching a doctrine now for a long time pretty generally accepted is going to be serviceable, we are not going to find fault with him in his capacity of preacher. Only, if it is permitted, we doubt whether his anxiety to preach is justified by the state of things around him; and very certainly we do not feel called on to say that his sermon is very new—in fact, we do feel called on to say that it is old, and old sermons have been said to be tiresome. It frequently happens to people to believe in a preacher's text, and even to accept the discourse of a preacher, without thinking the text the most valuable of texts, or the discourse extremely edifying to the hearer or creditable to the preacher.

Witty, Dr. Holmes is pretty sure to be; and the bright things in *The Guardian Angel* are numerous. (pp. 390-91)

On the whole, *The Guardian Angel* is far from being unreadable, unless one is too fastidious. Each reader of this notice can, we think, judge fairly for himself. For our own part, . . . we found in the volume [passages] worth reading, and we may say that we found enough of them and found them fresh enough to repay us tolerably for going through a good deal of triteness and dulness and flippancy. (p. 391)

A review of "The Guardian Angel," in The Nation, *Vol. V, No. 124, November 24, 1867, pp. 390-91.*

EDWIN P. WHIPPLE   (essay date 1876)

[*Whipple assesses Holmes as a vigorous, witty writer whose poetic talents can be seen in all of his writings.*]

Oliver Wendell Holmes—wit, satirist, humorist, novelist, scholar, scientist—is, above every thing, a poet, for the qualities of the poet pervade all the operations of his variously gifted mind. His sense of the ludicrous is not keener than his sense of the beautiful; his wit and humor are but the sportive exercise of a fancy and imagination which he has abundantly exercised on serious topics; and the extensive learning and acute logic of the man of science are none the less solid in substance because in expression they are accompanied by a throng of images and illustrations which endow erudition with life, and give a charm to the most closely linked chain of reasoning. The first thing which strikes a reader of Holmes is the vigor and elasticity of his nature. He is incapable of weakness. He is fresh and manly even when he securely treads the scarcely marked line which separates sentiment from sentimentality. This prevailing vigor proceeds from a strength of individuality which is often pushed to dogmatic self-assertion. It is felt as much in his airy, fleering mockeries of folly and pretension, as in his almost Juvenalian invectives against baseness and fraud—in the pleasant way in which he stretches a coxcomb on the rack of wit, as in the energy with which he grapples an opponent in the tussle of argumentation. He never seems to imagine that he can be inferior to the thinker whose position he assails, any more than to the noodle whose nonsense he jeers at. In argument he is sometimes the victor, in virtue of scornfully excluding what another reasoner would include, and thus seems to make his own intellect the measure of the whole subject in discussion. When in his *Autocrat,* or his *Professor,* or his *Poet, at the Breakfast Table,* he touches theological themes, he is peculiarly exasperating to theological opponents, not only for the effectiveness of his direct hits, but for the easy way in which he gayly overlooks considerations which their whole culture has induced them to deem of vital moment. The truth is that Holmes's dogmatism comes rather from the vividness and rapidity of his perceptions than from the arrogance of his personality. "This," he seems to say, "is not my opinion; it is a demonstrated law which you willfully ignore while pretending to be scholars." The indomitable courage of the man carries him through all the exciting controversies he scornfully invites. Holmes, for the last forty years, has been expressing this inexhaustible vitality of nature in various ways, and to-day he appears as vigorous as he was in his prime, more vigorous than he was in his youth. His early poems sparkled with thought and abounded in energy; but still they can not be compared in wit, in humor, in depth of sentiment, in beauty of diction, in thoughtfulness, in lyrical force, with the poems of the past twenty-five years of his life. It is needless to give

even the titles of the many pieces which are fixed in the memory of all cultivated readers among his countrymen. His novels, *Elsie Venner* and *The Guardian Angel,* rank high among original American contributions to the domain of romance. In prose, as in verse, his fecundity and vigor of thought have found adequate expression in a corresponding point and compactness of style. (p. 516)

Edwin P. Whipple, "The First Century of the Republic (Seventeenth Paper)," in Harper's New Monthly Magazine, *Vol. LII, No. CCCX, March, 1876, pp. 514-33.*

OLIVER WENDELL HOLMES   (essay date 1883)

[*In this excerpt from his preface to an 1883 edition of* Elsie Venner, *Holmes defends the premise of the novel, explaining that his aim "was to test the doctrine of 'original sin' and human responsibility."*]

[*Elsie Venner*] is the story which a dear old lady, my very good friend, spoke of as "a medicated novel," and quite properly refused to read. I was always pleased with her discriminating criticism. It *is* a medicated novel, and if she wished to read for mere amusement and helpful recreation there was no need of troubling herself with a story written with a different end in view.

This story has called forth so many curious inquiries that it seems worth while to answer the more important questions which have occurred to its readers.

In the first place, it is not based on any well-ascertained physiological fact. There are old fables about patients who have barked like dogs or crowed like cocks, after being bitten or wounded by those animals. There is nothing impossible in the idea that Romulus and Remus may have imbibed wolfish traits of character from the wet nurse the legend assigned them, but the legend is not sound history, and the supposition is nothing more than a speculative fancy. Still, there is a limbo of curious evidence bearing on the subject of pre-natal influences sufficient to form the starting-point of an imaginative composition.

The real aim of the story was to test the doctrine of "original sin" and human responsibility for the disordered volition coming under that technical denomination. Was Elsie Venner, poisoned by the venom of a crotalus before she was born, morally responsible for the "volitional" aberrations, which translated into acts become what is known as sin, and, it may be, what is punished as crime? If, on presentation of the evidence, she becomes by the verdict of the human conscience a proper object of divine pity and not of divine wrath, as a subject of moral poisoning, wherein lies the difference between her position at the bar of judgment, human or divine, and that of the unfortunate victim who received a moral poison from a remote ancestor before he drew his first breath?

It might be supposed that the character of Elsie Venner was suggested by some of the fabulous personages of classical or mediæval story. I remember that a French critic spoke of her as *cette pauvre Mélusine.* I ought to have been ashamed, perhaps, but I had not the slightest idea who Melusina was until I hunted up the story, and found that she was a fairy, who for some offence was changed every Saturday to a serpent from her waist downward. I was of course familiar with Keats's Lamia, another imaginary being, the subject of magical transformation into a serpent. My story was well advanced before Hawthorne's wonderful *Marble Faun,* which might be thought to have furnished me with the hint of a mixed nature,—human, with an alien element,—was published or known to me. So that my poor heroine found her origin, not in fable or romance, but in a physiological conception fertilized by a theological dogma. (pp. ix-x)

The story has won the attention and enjoyed the favor of a limited class of readers, and if it still continues to interest others of the same tastes and habits of thought I can ask nothing more of it. (p. xi)

> Oliver Wendell Holmes, "A Second Preface," in his *Elsie Venner: A Romance of Destiny*, Houghton, Mifflin and Company, 1892, pp. ix-xi.

THE NATION   (essay date 1885)

[*This reviewer of Holmes's biography of Ralph Waldo Emerson insists that it contains little new material and points out "conspicuous deficiencies" in Holmes's research, yet praises its wit and intrinsic interest.*]

[In Doctor Holmes's *Ralph Waldo Emerson*,] very little is . . . added to what we before knew of Emerson's career, while the greater part of what others have gathered is . . . omitted. Viewing the book merely as a memoir, the reader is disappointed; but taking it for what it is, a detailed review of the *opera omnia* of one man of genius by another, with running annotations, grave, gay, learned, and witty, it becomes both valuable and attractive. This is the form, evidently, in which Doctor Holmes has conceived his work—two-thirds of the pages (roughly estimating) being made of this sort of commentary. This is evidently done, to some extent, as task-work, though in a loyal spirit. There is a good deal that suggests the scissors and paste; and sometimes in the later pages, when the annotator comes back to the charge for the hundredth time, and says of an essay, "If I must select any of its wise words, I will choose," etc . . . , the reader is disposed to recall little Alice's answer when Humpty Dumpty says, "If it comes to that, I can repeat poetry as well as any one"; and he is tempted to reply hastily with Alice, "O, but it needn't come to that." And yet, when we think how many capital sayings, how many delicious *obiter dicta*, are scattered through these four hundred pages—how many single phrases here occur that we should recognize as the Autocrat's if we came upon them in the desert of Sahara or the Congressional Debates—we are ready to pardon everything to the inexhaustible lapidary who thus fills our hands with gems.

Such phrases occur, for instance, when he compares Thoreau to one who insists on "nibbling his asparagus at the wrong end" . . . , and Bowen reviewing Emerson to "a sagacious pointer making the acquaintance of a box-tortoise." . . .

It is among the most conspicuous deficiencies of this memoir that it leaves us almost wholly uninformed as to two of the most important aspects of Emerson's earlier life—his relations to the anti-slavery agitation and to the so-called transcendental movement. In both cases there is an obvious lack of personal knowledge, not filled by any assiduous inquiry. In the days when Emerson was in his prime, Holmes was but lately returned from Europe, full of zeal for his profession and his art—medicine and poetry; the latter then belonging almost wholly to the department of *vers de société*. It is pretty evident from some of his verses of that period—for instance, those on Jean Paul, whom he called "a German-silver spoon"—that transcendentalism simply bored him; while toward the anti-slavery agitation he probably had the usual prejudices of his social and professional circle, though not in any acrid form. On these two important and almost controlling aspects of Emerson's life, therefore, he was as unsympathetic as Ticknor or Everett; and though he makes some slight effort to describe that part of Emerson's environment, the sketch has neither amplitude nor life. He deals with Emerson as literature alone, and scarcely alludes to his surroundings. Where he does he is often in error: for instance, he utterly underrates Emerson's relations to the abolitionists, with whom he says that he "had never been identified." . . . It is impossible to say what Doctor Holmes means by being identified; Emerson no more merged himself in any anti-slavery society than in the "Saturday Club." But there is no doubt that from the day when his great address on West India Emancipation was delivered at Concord (August 1, 1844), the abolitionists, who were not at all given to claiming or even recognizing any half-converts, always accounted Emerson as their own. Doctor Holmes says of the Concord oration: "This discourse would not have satisfied the abolitionists" . . . , but he could easily have ascertained whether it actually did satisfy them or not by stepping into the Boston Public Library and looking at a file of the *Liberator* for 1844. He would then have perceived at once that the mere fact of Emerson's speaking at that time and place and on that subject was an act of self-identification with the unpopular party. . . .

Something of the same deficiency that mars Doctor Holmes's treatment of Emerson's anti-slavery attitude is likewise found when he comes to treat the "transcendental" movement. There is a disproportion almost absurd in giving six pages to the *Monthly Anthology*, because it was edited by Emerson's father, and only five pages to the *Dial*, into which Emerson put so much of his own intellectual life. Even of those five pages, nearly four are taken bodily from the Emerson-Carlyle correspondence, which is in everybody's hands. It is possible that the omission may be due to the fact that this period has already been well delineated in other volumes of the series. It is certainly a proof of the still living interest in that particular intellectual movement that four of the eight volumes of the "American Men of Letters" series have been devoted to its leaders; but, after all, each volume in the list should have a certain completeness in itself, even at the risk of some repetition. As a result of this want, we have Emerson isolated, whereas he can only be fitly viewed as the centre of a group.

As we go through the book, we find here and there some minor misapprehensions. Thus Doctor Holmes, like Matthew Arnold, makes the mistake of quoting in full . . . Emerson's characterization of the Whig and Democratic parties of forty years ago, and assuming it as still valid of the Democratic and Republican parties of today; the fact being not only that the lines are changed, but the positions almost reversed. (p. 99)

But all these deficiencies may be regarded as minor matters, since the main interest which will attract most readers to the book will lie in those literary estimates of which it chiefly consists. The very fact of the great difference in quality, if not in grade, of genius between the author and the subject will enhance this interest to the highest point. So remote, in truth, are the two men, that the book might almost be entitled 'Contributions to the Natural History of the Wood-Thrush, by a Canary Bird.' Sometimes, to our amazement, we find the two very dissimilar warblers singing the same note, as when Holmes endorses, with evident heartiness, Emerson's famous Divinity Hall address. Yet the divergence soon appears when the mystic bird of the woods sounds a note too high. Thus, Emerson's essay on "The Over-soul," in which so many have found, or thought they found, a jubilant delight, is to Holmes only a "rhapsody" . . . ; and he speaks with what can only be called contempt of the "Essay on Immortality." . . . But we must take a man, or a bird, for the notes that he can reach, not for those which do not properly belong to his genus or sub-order. On the whole, the criticisms on Emerson's prose, though they sometimes appear tame or perfunctory, are sympathetic as to the matter, and not unappreciative in respect to the manner; but it is when the critic comes to the poetry that we see how two fine minds may meet, despite all variations of temperament. Even here we find some criticism that is merely academical, as where Holmes complains of the redundant syllable in Emerson's line—

> By his own meek and incorruptible will—

and calls it a "span-worm line," lifting up its back in the middle. . . . One is led to suspect the critic of being rather led away and captured by his own stroke of wit, as will sometimes happen. . . .

It is a satisfaction to find, after this specimen, that when the same style of academical treatment is carried still further by Mr. Matthew Arnold, Doctor Holmes is all ready to protest against it, and declines, as it were, to allow any one else to prescribe for his venerated patient. . . .

[It] is the supreme merit of Holmes's criticism that he shows himself able to go beyond the limitations of his own school,

and do honor to a poet utterly dissimilar to himself. The reader can well forgive many a fault of omission and commission in a book that leaves to us the bequest of such generous praise for another. It is a fine act of self-abnegation when one who has so successfully cultivated his own well-defined field of genius expresses cordial admiration for a domain more vast. . . . (p. 100)

> *"Holmes's 'Emerson',"* in The Nation, *Vol. XL, No. 1022, January 29, 1885, pp. 99-100.*

EDMUND C. STEDMAN   (essay date 1885)

[*A major nineteenth-century American critic and anthologist, Stedman gained wide critical influence as the author of* Victorian Poets *and* Poets of America, *published in 1875 and 1895, respectively. In conjunction with his popular* American Anthology, *the latter work helped to establish a greater interest in and appreciation for American literature. Reviewing Holmes's long career as a poet, novelist, and essayist, Stedman notes the author's proficiency in several different genres, examines the reasons for his endurance as an artist, and suggests that Holmes's success owes much to his personality.*]

The distinction between [Holmes's] poetry and that of the new makers of society-verse is that his is a survival, theirs the attempted revival, of something that has gone before. He wears the seal of "that past Georgian day" by direct inheritance, not from the old time in England, but from that time in England's lettered colonies, whose inner sections still preserve the hereditary language and customs as they are scarcely to be found elsewhere. His work is as emblematic of the past as are the stairways and hand-carvings in various houses of Cambridge, Portsmouth, and Norwich. . . . Among living old-style poets, Dr. Holmes, the least complex and various, seems most nearly to the manner born; his work, as I say, being a survival, and not an experiment. It is freshened, however, by the animation which, haplessly for compilers of provincial literature, was wanting in the good Old Colony days. The maker wears the ancestral garb, and is a poet in spite of it. His verses have the courtesy and wit, without the pedagogy, of the knee-buckle time, and a flavor that is really their own. There are other eighteenth-century survivors, whose sponsors are formality and dullness; but Holmes has the modern vivacity, and adjusts without effort even the most hackneyed measures to a new occasion. Throughout the changes of fifty years he has practiced the method familiar to his youth, thinking it fit and natural, and one to which he would do well to cling. The conservative persistency of his muse is as notable in matter as in manner. On the whole, so far as we can classify him, he is at the head of his class, and in other respects a class by himself. (p. 503)

What one does easily is apt to be his forte, though years may pass before he finds this out. Holmes's early pieces, mostly college-verse, were better of their kind than those of a better kind written in youth by some of his contemporaries. The humbler the type, the sooner the development. The young poet had the aid of a suitable habitat; life at Harvard was the precise thing to bring out his talent. There was nothing of the hermit-thrush in him; his temper was not of the withdrawing and reflective kind, nor moodily introspective,—it throve on fellowship, and he looked to his mates for an audience as readily as they to him for a toast-master. He seems to have escaped the poetic measles altogether; if not, he hid his disorder with rare good sense, for his verse nowhere shows that he felt himself "among men, but not of them"; on the contrary, he fairly

Dr. Holmes in 1860.

might plume himself on reversing the Childe's boast, and declare ''I have loved the world, and the world me.'' (pp. 503-04)

As a versifier, he started with the advantage of hitting the public by buffo-pieces, and with the disadvantage of being expected to make his after-hits in the same manner,—to write for popular amusement in the major rather than the minor key. His verses, with the measured drum-beat of their natural rhythm, were easily understood; he bothered his audience with no accidental effects, no philandering after the finer lyrical distinctions. It is not hard to surmise what ''standard'' poets had been found on his father's book-shelves. Eloquence was a feature of his lyrics,—such as broke out in the line, ''Ay, tear her tattered ensign down!'' and the simple force of **''Old Iron-sides''** is indeed worth noting as it culminates in the last stanza. The making of verse that is seized upon by school-day spokesmen barely outlived the influence of Croly, of Drake and Halleck, of Pierpont with his ''Stand! the ground's your own, my braves!'' and Holmes himself would scarcely write in this way now. Yet one who sees, looming up by the Portsmouth docks, a fine old hulk to which these lines secured half a century of preservation will find them coming again to mind. **''The Meeting of the Dryads,''** another early poem, is marked by so much grace that it seems as if the youth who wrote its quatrains might in time have added a companion-piece to **''The Talking Oak.''** The things which he turned off with purely comic aim were neatly finished, and the merriment of a new writer, who dared not be ''as funny'' as he could, did quite as much for him as his poems of a higher class. The fashion of the latter, however, we see returning again. There is the pathetic silhouette of the old man, who so

> Shakes his feeble head,
> That it seems as if he said,
> 'They are gone.'

This equals the best recent knee-buckle verse, and excels most of it in simplicity. It taught a lesson to Locker and Saxe, and more than one among younger favorites look up to Holmes affectionately, conscious that the author of **''The Last Leaf,''** **''My Aunt,''** **''The Dilemma,''** and of later trifles still more refined, like **''Dorothy Q.,''** is the Nestor of their light-armed holiday encampment.

A poet so full of zest is wont to live his life, rather than to scorn delights in service of the thankless muse. Dr. Holmes's easy-going method, and a sensible estimate of his own powers, have defined the limits of his zeal. His poetry was and is, like his humor, the overflow of a nervous, original, decidedly intellectual nature; of a sparkling life, no less, in which he gathered the full worth of hey-day experiences. See that glimpse of Paris, a student's penciled sketch, with Clemence tripping down the Rue de Seine. It is but a bit, yet through its atmosphere we make out a poet who cared as much for the sweets of the poetic life as for the work that was its product. He had through it all a Puritan sense of duty, and the worldly wisdom that goes with a due perception of values, and he never lost sight of his practical career. His profession, after all, was what he took most seriously. Accepting, then, with hearty thanks, his care-dispelling rhyme and reason, pleased often by the fancies which he tendered in lieu of imagination and power,— we go through the collection of his verse, and see that it has amounted to a great deal in the course of a bustling fifty years. These numerous pieces divide themselves, as to form, into two classes,—lyrics and poetic essays in solid couplet-verse; as to purpose, into the lighter songs that may be sung, and the nobler

numbers, part lyrical, part the poems, both gay and sober, delivered at frequent intervals during his pleasant career. (p. 505)

His pieces light and wise—**''Contentment,''** the **''Epilogue to the Breakfast-table Series,''** **''At the Pantomime,''** **''A Familiar Letter,''** etc.—are always enjoyable. One or two are exquisite in treatment of the past. **''Dorothy Q.,''** that sprightly capture of a portrait's maiden soul, has given, like **''The Last Leaf,''** lessons to admiring pupils of our time. For sheer humor, **''The One-hoss Shay''** and **''Parson Turell's Legacy''** are memorable,—extravagances, but full of character, almost as purely Yankee as ''Tam O'Shanter'' is purely Scotch. In various whimsicalities, Holmes sets the key for Harte and others to follow. **''The First Fan,''** read at a bric-à-brac festival in 1877, proves him an adept in the latest mode. There is also a conceit of showing the youngsters a trick or two, in the story **''How the Old Horse Won the Bet,''** told to the class of '71 by the minstrel of the class of '29, and pointed with the moral that ''A horse *can* trot, for all he's old.''

Good and bright as these things are, some of his graver work excels them. Where most in earnest he is most imaginative; this, of course, is where he is most interested, and this again, in moods the results of his scientific bent and experience. Here he shows himself akin to those who have both lightness and strength. Thackeray's reverential mood, that was so beautiful, is matched by the feeling which Holmes, having the familiarity with Nature that breeds contempt in graver men, exhibits in his thoughts upon **''The Living Temple.''** The stanzas thus named, in measure and reverent effect, are not unworthy to be read with Addison's lofty paraphrase of the Nineteenth Psalm. Humility in presence of recognized law is the spirit of the flings at cant and half-truth in his rhymed essays. There are charity and tenderness in **''The Voiceless,''** **''Avis,''** **''Iris,''** and **''The Silent Melody.''** Another little poem, **''Under the Violets,''** reveals the lover of Collins. But **''The Living Temple''** and **''The Chambered Nautilus''** doubtless show us their writer's finest qualities, and are not soon to be forgotten. There is a group of his ''Vignettes,'' in recollection of Wordsworth, Moore, Keats, and Shelley, whose cadence is due to that gift of sympathetic vibration which poets seem to possess. These pieces are as good as any to furnish examples of the sudden fancies peculiar to Holmes's genius, whose glint, if not imagination, is like that of the sparks struck off from it. (pp. 506-07)

The things which, after all, sharply distinguish Holmes from other poets, and constitute the bulk of his work, are the lyrics and metrical essays composed for special audiences or occasions. Starting without much creative ambition, and as a bard of mirth and sentiment, it is plain that he was subject to faults which an easy standard entails. His aptitude for writing, with entire correctness, in familiar measures, has been such that nothing but an equal mental aptness could make up for the frequent padding, the inevitably thin passages, of his longer efforts, and for the conceits to which, like Moore and Hood, he has been tempted to sacrifice the spirit of many a graceful poem. To this day there is no telling whither a fancy, once caught and mounted, will bear this lively rider. Poetry at times has seemed his diversion, rather than a high endeavor; yet perhaps this very seeming is essential to the frolic and careless temper of society-verse. The charm that is instant, the triumph of the passing hour,—these are captured by song that often is transitory as the night which listens to it. In Holmes we have an attractive voice devoted to a secondary order of expression. Yet many of his notes survive, and are worthy of a rehearing. A true faculty is requisite to insure this result, and it is but just to say that with his own growth his brilliant occasional pieces strengthened in thought, wit, and feeling.

With respect to his style, there is no one more free from structural whims and vagaries. He has an ear for the "classical" forms of English verse, the academic measures which still bid fair to hold their own—those confirmed by Pope and Goldsmith, and here in vogue long after German dreams, Italian languors, and the French rataplan had their effect upon the poets of our motherland across the sea. His way of thought, like his style, is straightforward and sententious; both are the reverse of what is called transcendental. When he has sustained work to do, and braces himself for a great occasion, nothing will suit but the rhymed pentameter; his heaviest roadster, sixteen hands high, for a long journey. It has served him well, is his by use and possession, and he sturdily will trust it to the end. . . . (p. 507)

The mechanism of Holmes's briefer occasional poems is fully as trite and simple. Whether this may be from choice or limitation, he has accumulated a unique series of pieces, vivacious as those of Tom Moore, but with the brain of New England in them, and notions and instances without end. How sure their author's sense of the fitness of things, his gift of adaptability to the occasion,—to how many occasions, and what different things! . . . The half of his early collections is made up from efforts of this sort, and they constitute nine-tenths of his verse during the last thirty years. Now, what has carried Holmes so bravely through all this, if not a kind of special masterhood, an individuality, humor, touch, that we shall not see again? Thus we come, in fine, to be sensible of the distinctive gift of this poet. The achievement for which he must be noted is, that in a field the most arduous and least attractive he should bear himself with such zest and fitness as to be numbered among poets, and should do honor to an office which they chiefly dread or mistrust, and which is little calculated to excite their inspiration. (p. 508)

At forty-eight he began a new career, as if it were granted him to live life over, with the wisdom of middle-age in his favor at the start. Coming, in a sense, like an author's first book, *The Autocrat of the Breakfast-Table* naturally was twice as clever as any "first book" of the period. It appears that this work was planned in his youth; but we owe to his maturity the experience, drollery, proverbial humor, and suggestion that flow at ease through its pages. Little is too high or too low for the comment of this down-east philosopher. A kind of attenuated Franklin, he views things and folks with the less robustness, but with keener distinction and insight. His pertinent maxims are so frequent that it seems, as it was said of Emerson, as if he had jotted them down from time to time and here first brought them to application; they are apothegms of common life and action, often of mental experience, strung together by a device so original as to make the work quite a novelty in literature. The Autocrat holds an intellectual tourney at a boarding-house table; there jousts against humbug and stupidity, gives light touches of knowledge, sentiment, illustration, coins here and there a phrase destined to be long current, nor forgets the poetic duty of providing a little idyl of human love and interest. Here, also, we find his best lyrical pieces,—on the side of beauty, **"The Chambered Nautilus"** and **"The Living Temple"**; on that of mirth, **"The One-Hoss Shay."** . . . (pp. 508-09)

Two later books, completing the Autocrat series, follow in a similar vein, their scene the same boarding-house, their slight plots varied by new personages and by-play, the conductor of the Yankee symposia the same Autocrat, through the aid of a Professor and a Poet successively. The best comment on these works is made by their sagacious author, who likens them to the wine of grapes that are squeezed in the press after the first juice that runs of itself from the heart of the fruit has been drawn off. (p. 509)

The Professor is written somewhat in the manner of Sterne, yet without much artifice. The story of Iris is an interwoven thread of gold. The poems in this book are inferior to those of the *Autocrat,* but its author here and there shows a gift of drawing real characters; the episode of the Little Gentleman is itself a poem,—its close very touching, though imitated from the death-scene in Tristram Shandy. *The Poet at the Breakfast-Table,* written some years after, is of a more serious cast than its predecessors, chiefly devoted to Holmes's peculiar mental speculations and his fluent gossip on books and learning. He makes his rare old pundit a liberal thinker, clearly of the notion that a high scholarship leads to broader views. I do not think he would banish Greek from a college curriculum; but if he should, the Old Master would cry out upon him. Between the second and third works of this series, his [*Elsie Venner* and *The Guardian Angel*] had appeared,—curious examples of what a clever observer can do by way of fiction in the afternoon of life. As conceptions, these were definite and original, as much so as Hawthorne's; but that great romancer would have presented in a far more dramatic and imaginative fashion an Elsie Venner, tainted with the ophidian madness that so vexed her human soul,—a Myrtle Hazard, inheriting the trace of Indian savagery at war with her higher organization. The somewhat crude handling of these tales betrays the fact that the author was not trained by practice in the novelist's art. But they have the merit of coming down to fact with an exhibition of common, often vulgar, everyday life in the country towns of Massachusetts. This, and realistic drawings of sundry provincial types, Holmes produces in a manner directly on the way to the subsequent evolution of more finished works like Howells's *A Modern Instance* and *The Undiscovered Country.* Meanwhile he verifies his birthright by adapting these narratives to the debate on inherited tendency, limited responsibility, and freedom of the will. On the whole, the novels and the Autocrat volumes were indigenous works, in plot and style behind the deft creations of our day, but with their writer's acumen everywhere conspicuous. If their science and suggestion now seem trite, it must be owned that the case was opposite when they were written, and that ideas now familiar were set afloat in this way. Little of our recent literature is so fresh, relatively to our period, as these books were in consideration of their own. As Holmes's humor had relaxed the grimness of a Puritan constituency, so his prose satire did much to liberalize their clerical system. This was not without some wrath and objurgation on the part of the more rigid clergy and laity alike, and at times worked to the disadvantage of the satirist and his publishers. The situation now seems far away and amusing: equally so, the queer audacity of his off-hand pronunciamentos upon the gravest themes. He was responsible, I fear, for a very airy settlement of distracting social problems, to his own satisfaction and that of a generation of half-informed readers; for getting ready sanction to his postulate of a Brahmin caste, and leading many a Gifted Hopkins to set up for its representative. Yet his dialogues and stories are in every way the expression of a stimulating personage, their author,—a frank display of the Autocrat himself. If one would learn how to be his own Boswell, these five books are naïve examples of a successful American method.

Holmes's mental fiber, sturdier with use, shows to advantage in a few poems, speeches, and prose essays of his later years. These illustrate the benefits to an author of having, in Quaker diction, a concern upon him; each, like the speech **"On the Inevitable Crisis,"** is the outflow of personal conviction, or like **"Homeopathy vs. Allopathy," "The Physiology of Versification,"** etc., the discussion of a topic in which he takes a special interest. (pp. 509-10)

The notable prose essay on Edwards excites a wish that he oftener had found occasion to indulge his talent for analytic characterization. He has few superiors in discernment of a man's individuality, however distinct that individuality may be from his own. Emerson, for example, was a thinker and poet whose chartered disciples scarcely would have selected Holmes as likely to proffer a sympathetic or even objective transcript of him. Yet, when the time came, Holmes was equal to the effort. He presented with singular clearness, and with an epigrammatic genius at white heat, if not the esoteric view of the Concord Plotinus, at least what could enable an audience to get at the mold of that serene teacher and make some fortunate surmise of the spirit that ennobled it. I do not recall a more faithful and graphic *outside* portrait. (p. 510)

Holmes, among our poets, is . . . [an] original writer, but his prose is a setting for brilliants of a different kind; his shrewd sayings are bright with native metaphor; he is a proverb-maker, some of whose words are not without wings. When he ranges along the line of his tastes and studies, we find him honestly bred. Plato and the Stagirite, the Elzevir classics, the English essayists, the fathers of the healing art, must be in sight on his shelves. . . . (pp. 510-11)

But his proper study is man, the regard of people and movements close at hand. Somewhat distrustful of the "inner light," he stands squarely upon observation, experience, induction; yet at times is so volatile a theorist that one asks how much of his saying is conviction, and how much mirth or whim. His profession has put him on the alert for natural tendency, in the belief that fortune goes by inheritance. Crime and virtue are physically foreordained. He takes unkindly to sentimental attempts at reform. His temper and training so largely affect his writings that the latter scarcely can be criticised from the merely literary point of view. Holmes's conservatism, then, goes well enough with a poet of the old régime, and with the maker of light satires and well-bred verse. (p. 511)

If the question is asked, Would the verse of Doctor Holmes be held in so much favor if he had not confirmed his reputation by prose replete with poetic humor and analogy? the fairest answer may be in the negative. Together, his writings surely owe their main success to an approximate exhibition of the author himself. Where the man is even more lively than his work, the public takes kindly to the one and the other. The jester is privileged even in the court of art and letters; yet if one could apply to Holmes—the jester, homilist, and man of feeling—his own process, we should have analysis indeed. Were the theme assigned to himself, we should have an inimitably honest setting forth of his merits and foibles, from this keen anatomist of mind and body, this smile-begetter, this purveyor to so many feasts. As a New Englander he long ago was awarded the highest sectional praise,—that of being, among all his tribe, the cutest. His cleverness and versatility bewilder outside judges. Is he a genius? By all means. And in what degree? His prose, for the most part, is peculiarly original. His serious poetry scarcely has been the serious work of his life; but in his specialty, verse suited to the frolic or pathos of

occasions, he has given us much of the best-delivered in his own time, and has excelled all others in delivery. Both his strength and weakness lie in his genial temper and his brisk, speculative habit of mind. For, though almost the only modern poet who has infused enough spirit into table and rostrum verse to make it worth recording, his poetry has appealed to the present rather than the future; and, again, he has too curious and analytic a brain for purely artistic work. Of Holmes as a satirist, which it is not unusual to call him, I have said but little. His metrical satires are of the amiable sort that debars him from kinsmanship with the Juvenals of old, or the Popes and Churchills of more recent times. There is more real satire in one of Hosea Biglow's lyrics than in all our laughing philosopher's irony, rhymed and unrhymed. Yet he is a keen observer of the follies and chances which satire makes its food. Give him personages, reminiscences, manners, to touch upon, and he is quite at home. He may not reproduce these imaginatively, in their stronger combinations; but the Autocrat makes no unseemly boast when he says: "It was in teaching of Life that we came together. I thought I knew something about that, that I could speak or write about it to some purpose." Let us consider then, that if Holmes had died young, we should have missed a choice example of the New England fiber which strengthens while it lasts; that he has lived to round a personality that will be traditional for at least the time granted to one or two less characteristic worthies of revolutionary days; that— "'twas all he wished"—a few of his lyrics already belong to our select anthology, and one or two of his books must be counted as factors in what twentieth-century chroniclers will term (and here is matter for reflection) the development of "early" American literature. (p. 512)

> *Edmund C. Stedman, "Oliver Wendell Holmes," in* The Century, *Vol. XXIX, No. 4, February, 1885, pp. 502-12.*

EDWARD DELILLE   (essay date 1886)

[*Surveying Holmes's literary career, Delille argues that much of the author's work was superficial and finds in his writing "a certain general suggestion of great powers not exerted to the full."*]

With an aptitude for pure literature rarely if ever surpassed; with a technical training such as falls to the lot of very few men, and for the want of which many an aspiring spirit has sunk by the way; with, in a word, the finest gifts developed by the highest culture, what has Dr. Holmes accomplished? Has he written any pages which will remain as if graven in bronze? Has he struck out any such pregnant, irresistibly penetrating thoughts as those which render the names of Rochefoucauld and Chamfort immortal? Has he introduced any new formula of literary art, has he even achieved any searching general study of social life?

Dr. Holmes's sole work, in reality, has been to present in a graceful, able, and amusing way philosophy not transcending the bounds of the ordinarily intelligent mind, psychology which, however just and acute, is never especially profound, and objective observation wonderfully vivid and gay, but on the whole somewhat slight. His thought is not in the highest sense original, albeit originality is the quality of all others which his admirers claim for him. Precisely those views for which Dr. Holmes obtains the most credit have been condensed by other men into formulas more definite than his. His merit has consisted less in the conception of his ideas than in the concoction of the *sauce piquante* wherewith he serves them up.

Of course the maxim that nothing under the sun is new applies more completely to literature than to any other intellectual exercise. And it cannot fairly be contended, for the mere reason that every one of his clever little aphorisms and theories (that of the ''depolarization of ideas,'' for instance, or that of the ''triple mental strata'') may be met with in various French psychologists and moralists, from Montaigne downwards: it cannot on these grounds be contended that the author of *The Autocrat of the Breakfast-Table* lacks originality of thought. Most of these metaphysical subtleties and conceits, could they but be traced to their absolute source, would be found to belong to the very first philosopher that set sail on the sea of introspection; ideas must perforce be drawn from a common stock, and he is the best literary artist who can dress them in the most attractive garb. It is in Dr. Holmes's general attitude towards the weighty truths with which he loves lightly to deal that he reveals the want of that higher moral power which, in default of a better word, may be termed ''originality.'' (pp. 235-36)

[Judging] from the general tenor of his works, Dr. Holmes has always considered art and culture as being at least as essential to human welfare as universal suffrage. Indeed, in his own amiable way, he has occasionally laughed at his countrymen's ''new-wordly'' pretensions. The flapping of the American eagle's wings has never quite reconciled him to the harshness of the American peacock's scream, if a simile may be adapted from Emerson—himself a religious believer in all things American. But the spectacle of a great Government becoming an example when expected to remain a model might have inspired a *littérateur* so highly authorised as Dr. Holmes with comments somewhat more vigorous, were not his satiric pen dipped in *eau sucrée* instead of aquafortis. There was very little danger indeed of such a study as *Democracy* coming from the ''dean'' of American letters.

Dr. Holmes is too genial, it will be said, too tolerant, too kindly, to play the part of censor or polemical writer. He prefers agreeable pleasantry to denunciation. Very true; but then tolerance is a quality hardly compatible with high genius. Tolerance has never had much effect in redressing wrong. No reformer or moralist or satirist has ever been conspicuously ''tolerant.'' Can the deeper shades of feeling, in a word such as this, be supposed to exist without some admixture of passion? And have many of the world's great literary spirits succeeded in suppressing that strain of sensitive bitterness, generally called ''cynicism'' by the majority of the public who neither think nor feel? Perhaps, on the whole, it may be justly assumed that a writer so successful as is Dr. Holmes in escaping any similar charge owes this enviable result to a certain lack of profundity as well as to the ''sunniness'' of his humour. (p. 237)

It is rather in his poetry than his prose that Dr. Holmes's limitations stand revealed: and that a writer's faults and merits both appear the more plainly in his verse is probably a general rule, supposing, of course, he can handle verse quite freely, which is assuredly the case with Dr. Holmes. In the best of Dr. Holmes's poetry there is much delicacy of feeling, vivacity of observation, and literary elegance and ease; but his strain of song never rises so high or flows so strongly as that of poets born. There is always about his metrical achievements a hint of the somewhat paltry product called *vers de société*, to which true poets rarely condescend; nor would any true poet have fallen to the low level occupied so contentedly by much—by

perhaps the major part—of Dr. Holmes's verse. His would-be humorous pieces are often lamentably trivial. Witness the following stanza:

> Know old Cambridge? Hope you do.
> Born there! Don't say so! I was too;
> Born in a house with a gambrel roof—
> Standing still, if you must have proof—
> ('Gambrel? Gambrel?' Let me beg
> You'll look at a horse's hinder leg—
> First great angle above the hoof,
> That's the gambrel; hence gambrel roof.)

No, Dr. Holmes, not gambrel; doggerel.

To cite such rhymes as these in estimating, howsoever slightly, the poetical genius of a writer like Dr. Holmes, would scarcely be justifiable were they not a fair sample of a good many others by the same facile pen. To mistake wretched jingle for smartness; and to be merely ''chirpy'' when designing to be cheerful are tendencies in Dr. Holmes which all except his out-and-out-admirers will regret. (pp. 238-39)

The fact that Dr. Holmes is a versifier rather than a poet is emphasised by two particulars; one being his strong and perhaps personal consciousness of the tinkering mechanical side of rhyme-making (which has inspired him with several of his most entertaining prose passages), and the other his instinctive fondness for the graceful and highly-cultured but artificial and non-poetical manner of Pope. As an instance of Dr. Holmes's great proficiency in the latter style, and as a set-off against the nonsense-rhymes quoted above, some lines may now be given from the Prologue to *The Autocrat of the Breakfast-Table:*— . . .

> The victim knelt, still waiting for the blow.
> 'Why strikest not? perform thy murderous act,'
> The prisoner said (his voice was slightly cracked).
> 'Friend, I *have* struck,' the artist straight replied;
> 'Wait but one moment, and yourself decide,'
> He held his snuff-box—'now, then, if you please'—
> The prisoner sniffed, and with a crashing sneeze,
> Off his head tumbled—bowled along the floor—
> Bounced down the steps—the prisoner said no more.
>
> 'Woman! thy falchion is a glittering eye;
> If death lurks in it, oh how sweet to die!
> Thou takest hearts as Rudolph took the head;
> We die of love, and never dream we're dead.'

Words are not needed to point out the humour and literary grace of this delightful little *jeu d'esprit,* not unworthy in its elegance and spirit of the Augustan age. One could wish that throughout Dr. Holmes's poetic work there were more lines in the vein of the headsman Rudolph, with somewhat less of patter about ''gambrels'' and the like.

While there seems, on the whole, reason to conclude that Dr. Holmes is devoid of the higher poetical faculty, it must be recognised that many of his pieces gain a distinct value both from their clever execution, and from the tender affectionate sentiment, which . . . is the real keynote of the Bostonian humourist's nature.

There is in Dr. Holmes himself, as in most persons of keen sensibilities and quick intelligence, a certain suggestion of childhood, and his sympathy with, his love for, all that is childlike, is one of his finest traits. His tone in writing of children—whether in prose or in verse—is always delicately *ému,* to use an expressive French term without a parallel in

English. Thus, nothing could be more affecting than his description of the thrush-like thrill in the voice of a poor little girl, lying crushed by a cruel accident on a cot in a hospital in Paris. The feeling with which he speaks of this ''blessed angel's'' quietude in the arms of death is of the kind that wins on the instant the reader's affection to the writer. (pp. 239-40)

Dr. Holmes's three novels, *Elsie Venner, The Guardian Angel,* and *A Mortal Antipathy* (his latest production), are not only delightful reading, but afford palpable evidence of what their author might have, yet has not, done. It is indeed surprising that a writer capable of weaving tales thus brimful of human interest, and of portraying with such consummate skill the most idiosyncratic aspects of American life, should have been content, as it were, to sample the rich mine lying open at his feet, instead of exploring it fully—impossible, after reading *Elsie Venner,* to doubt that Dr. Holmes could have been (had he but wished it) *the* American novelist of the century. Hawthorne, unsurpassed as an artist and psychologist, was hardly the man to treat that every-day existence from which his dreamy soul recoiled. Mr. Howells, at the present day, is somewhat lacking in vigour and in breadth. But Dr. Oliver Wendell Holmes possesses in the highest degree the power of depicting characters; this is, among his various literary gifts, the most genuine and the foremost. (p. 241)

Dr. Holmes's works of fiction—taking *The Guardian Angel* and *Elsie Venner* for chief examples—are compounded of three principal elements namely, physiology, religion, and New England life. No praise could be too high for the manner in which Dr. Holmes treats the first and the last of these themes. Medical science has had few keener students than he, and who has ever discoursed on medical affairs so suggestively, so acutely, altogether so delightfully? His delineation of American provincial existence—indeed of American existence in general—is so excellently good, that the world ought to have had a dozen volumes full of it instead of only three. But in the matter of New England dogmatism Dr. Holmes has not done as much as was possible.

Having spent the almost entirety of a long life in New England, and being by training and taste a man of liberal ideas, Dr. Wendell Holmes has had every reason to know Puritanic orthodoxy for what it really is. (p. 242)

[He] has been enabled to perceive through his own daily experience to what extremes the spirit of creed may go in circles devoid of culture and art; and having had these things, as it were, within reach of hand, it would seem that he might have assailed them more effectually than by the means of witty innuedo and metaphysical discussion. Surely a little outspoken statement of opinion would have gone further—in the mouth of a great intellectual leader—than all the epigrammatic sayings about ''oaks being out of their place in flower-pots,'' and ''healthy people not needing to take the air in closed carriages,'' while the pages of brilliant hair-splitting were not needed to prove the dangerous and extraordinary facts that black is not blue nor the human heart a block of wood. One is convinced upon reading Dr. Holmes that his sentiments on the subject of dogmatism are far stronger than he ventures to express, which but renders one the more impatient at his constantly approaching, and never openly discussing, the theme of all others as to which frank speaking is most desirable. In short, one realises that this playing at fence with a question so vital as that of religious belief argues either a degree of indifference or else some lack of moral courage.

As matters now stand with Dr. Holmes, the three ''Breakfast-Table'' books constitute his greatest contribution to literature, and are those on which his fame chiefly depends. Few English or American readers are unacquainted with these admirable works. A very thesaurus might be drawn up from the pages of *The Autocrat, The Professor,* and *The Poet,* of wit and wisdom by Dr. Holmes. The Schoolmistress and Iris, Little Boston and the young man called John, the Model of all the Virtues, the Koh i-Noor, *et tutti quanti,* are familiar to most mouths as household words. The humour, the wit, the sentiment with which these characters are drawn no longer call for comment or for praise.

To seek the weakest link of a chain implies not weakness, but strength, in all the other links. Stress has been laid, above, on certain elements in Dr. Holmes's work which are conceived to be inferior to the rest. Perhaps this has mainly been because the rest is excellent beyond discussion. And yet not quite so either, for there seems to arise from these fascinating novels, delightful studies, sparkling essays and clever verses, a certain general suggestion of great powers not exerted to the full.

Dr. Oliver Wendell Holmes is a *bel esprit* of the finest water, a humourist of a high type, a ripe scholar, a brilliant stylist, an accomplished *gentilhomme de lettres.* But his possession of all these gifts rather enhances than diminishes the regret that they should be, to a certain extent, impaired by the spirit of a *dilettante.* (pp. 242-43)

Members of the Saturday Club, clockwise from top: Emerson, Hawthorne, Lowell, Longfellow, Whittier, Motley, and Holmes (center).

Edward Delille, "Oliver Wendell Holmes," in The Fortnightly Review, *n.s. Vol. XL, No. CCXXXVI, August, 1886, pp. 235-43.*

[A. INNES SHAND] (essay date 1892)

[*Shand asserts that while all Holmes's writings have the ability to surprise the reader and to combat dogmatism, the author is at his best in his novels, particularly* Elsie Venner.]

[Dr. Holmes] wrote—we were going to say at random—on anything and everything; he expressed his views and ideas with American frankness. . . . He was brimming over with the exuberance of animal spirits; instinctively he treated his subjects satirically, and he was overflowing with wit and fun and drollery. It was his nature to be logically or paradoxically aggressive, and when he had once fairly established his footing as the Autocrat, as he admits himself, he gave the rein to his aggressiveness in the *Professor,* and afterwards as *The Poet at the Breakfast-Table.* He expressed himself on the gravest questions of Time and Eternity, with a licence of speculation and a liberty of language which must often have shocked or scandalised New Englanders of the stricter sects. To much of his heterodoxy, whether outspoken or suggested, although it was based upon benevolence and broad philanthropy, we altogether take exception. We believe that, like some of the most respectable characters in his own novels, he was driven to extremes in the necessary reaction against the dogmatic Calvinism and the cruelly eclectic Predestinarianism, which revolted . . . his moral sense. On many minor matters, and especially on those concerning the orthodox practice of medicine, he had his prejudices, antipathies, and strong prepossessions. But we are persuaded that he always wrote according to his convictions; those convictions generally appear to have been abiding; and although he was intellectually emotional and impulsive, he was essentially a fair-minded man. So his essays, although desultory in the extreme, show, nevertheless, consistency in principles and thought. Their fascinations are infinite; but perhaps their principal attraction is that they are a self-revelation and a running commentary on the writer, whose personality is always conspicuous. They are full of the versatile individuality which gives them the changing colours of the chameleon—of instruction, of information, of entertainment. . . . [When] at his lightest he is essentially reflective and philosophic. A vein of introspective or subjective analysis runs under everything, even the drollery. As for his humour, it is dry and quaint, and has distinctly a piquant Transatlantic flavour, although it differs as widely from the humour of the Wild West as the sanctified and strait-laced capital of Massachusetts from the last-born mining township in Nebraska or Colorado. (pp. 194-96)

[Holmes's miscellaneous work has a distinct] American character. He lays the scenes of his monologues and colloquies in a society which is somewhat novel and unfamiliar to us. The characters and interlocutors he introduces to play their parts, as his puppets, are all of them genuinely Transatlantic types, and they were fresh when not distinctly original. His analogies, his illustrations, his metaphors, his inexhaustible and happily applicable reminiscences are drawn for the most part from the settled States in New England. There our English habits may have been modified by the soil, the climate, the circumstances, and republican institutions; but they still perpetuate the English traditions and memories which were affectionately cherished by the descendants of the patriotic Pilgrims. (p. 197)

He made his reputation in Europe by the *Autocrat of the Breakfast-Table,* and it is probably on the 'Autocrat' that his reputation may rest. But in our opinion he shows himself and his genius most characteristically in the novels, which have scarcely been sufficiently appreciated; and the most characteristic and the most striking is *Elsie Venner.* The conception is extremely original. We find a parallel, perhaps—although no plagiarism, for the two were conceived almost contemporaneously—in the *Transformation* of his countryman Hawthorne. In the prefaces to each of his novels he is apologetic, and that to *Elsie* is no exception. In the guise of fiction he has put forward some "grave scientific doctrine," but one of those doctrines born of a morbidly lively imagination, which more prosaically minded practitioners were disposed to ridicule. It underlies the delineation of the leading personalities, but it is evolved, insidiously, as it were, and with wonderful art, so as to give dramatic interest and power to the characters and situations. Nor is "insidious" an inappropriate term to employ, considering that this story turns on the venom of a serpent infused in the veins of a beautiful maiden, and tainting the fresh springs of her nature with the guile and cruelty of the rattlesnake. It is a wild fancy, given by the theorist for what it is worth, and mystery envelops the whole matter. From the beginning Holmes has made the most of the romantic materials to be found in New England. There is no lack in the back-settlements of striking and even of savage scenery, and the ancestral mansion of the house of Venner is environed by terrors and horrors. . . . [Elsie's] sad story is worked out with equal strength and pathos. That she is predestined to misery we know and feel: the question is, whether the magic of her magnetic attractions may not involve the life of some man doomed to love her more dearly than her father. The end is brought about and the spell is dissolved by natural and logical means, if we subscribe to the scientific theory. She sickens, she droops, and she dies at the period which nature has mercifully assigned to the venomous mortality of the rattlesnake. (pp. 198-99)

There is a great deal of the dramatic, too, in the career of the scapegrace who comes from the Wild West, claiming near kindred with the Venners. Cousin Richard has led a reckless life; with his callous conscience he is indifferent to crime, and only cares for its consequences. But the man of blood never went in for a more reckless venture than when he dreams of marrying his cousin, the snake-maiden, and that he soon realises. Nevertheless he still perseveres, and he sticks at nothing—not even, in defiance of Massachusetts law, at strangling the man he believes his rival. Like the frowning rattlesnake ledge, Cousin Richard is all the more effective that he comes into the peaceful society of Rockland like a raving wolf descending on the sheepfolds. But this fantastic and sensational novel has another side, and one which, as in Holmes's other pictures, makes it delightful reading to the humourist and the student of quaint manners in New England. Like Washington Irving, he seems to delight in lovingly satirising the simple characters and the odd fashions and customs which still linger in sequestered agricultural communities. It is literally a new world from our own into which we are introduced. The educational institutions, in particular, would appear to indicate primitive simplicity, if not primeval purity. . . . [The schoolmaster, Bernard] Langdon, with his susceptible heart, reminds us of Ulysses among the sirens. But he was assailed through the eyes rather than the ears, although he taught in a home of melodious voices. We should say that the strain was too severe upon mortal manhood, save that there was a certain security in the multiplicity of attractions. It was there he made the acquaintance of the passionate Elsie, but he might have been in the harem of an occidental voluptuary. The maidens of New England are always blooming and often beautiful. . . . (pp. 199-200)

The description of the great village or little township, like that of so many others in his novels, reminds us of an English Selborne. It still retains its rural character; it has never been approached by the speculative builder; its peaceful dulness warns away the enriched stock-jobber and the plutocrat of the petroleum springs. It reverences a local aristocracy like that of the Venners, who can trace their ancestry back for half-a-dozen of generations. But the select oligarchy of the place consists of the divines and the doctor, and one or two men who have made a comfortable independence in retail trade or any other respectable way. It boasts several of those venerable mansions which are the pride of Conservative New England—mansions like the old gambrel-house in which Holmes was born, and on which he dwells with loving minuteness of detail. . . . With their steep roofs and multifarious gables, and their old-fashioned gardens, with their bowers and carefully clipped hedges, they much resemble such English parsonages of Queen Anne's time as we see in the frontispiece to White's *Selborne*. And, like Selborne Rectory, they are surrounded by the secular elms which are always the pride of a New England village. One of these mansions was occupied by Colonel Sprowle, and it was in that mansion the Colonel gave his memorable party, which is admirably illustrative of the manners of the place, and an excellent specimen, moreover, of the dry and somewhat saturnine New England humour. It might have been a reminiscence by our old Nova Scotian friend Sam Slick [Thomas C. Haliburton]. (pp. 200-01)

In his monologues, in his essays, or in his novels, there are no characters whom Holmes analyses with greater enjoyment and subtlety—we may add, with more delicate humour—than that of the benevolent divine who has been bred a truculent Calvinist. The creed in which he has been educated, and which he feels bound to preach, is always clashing with his experiences, and still more often with his feelings. Waiving the doctrines of original sin and universal corruption, it is without conviction that he warns his tolerably decent-living flock that five-sixths of them are doomed to everlasting perdition. That was a matter on which Holmes felt very deeply, and in the reaction from the stern Calvinistic training of his youth he was driven latterly into the opposite extreme. (p. 202)

The Guardian Angel is also far-fetched and fantastic in its *motif*; but though there is a much more carefully constructed plot, it is also more conventional and commonplace in its treatment. There is the good old idea of the missing will, appropriately produced towards the *dénouement* to confound rascality and redress injustice. The story promulgates the moral notion of limited responsibility, founded on the scientific principle of heredity. We have the same sombre and romantic old houses as in *Elsie;* the same types of old characters who have been superannuated or shunted in a society which is progressing elsewhere at railway pace; the same austerity of dogmatic Calvinism, which casts gloomy clouds over sunny natures and repels the disciples it endeavours to enlist. But there is likewise the same agreeable relief in the undercurrent of quaint or sparkling humour, which is none the less pleasant that it is sometimes tinged with pathos. . . .

As for *A Mortal Antipathy,* the author may well avow in his preface that it was a very hazardous experiment. It is so ingeniously wrought out, with natural or possible details, that Holmes seems to have steered pretty wide of absurdity. But it is founded on a problematical case that might occur once in a

millennium, and the victim of a catastrophe is cured by a counter-shock which is less medical than melodramatic. (p. 203)

The Autocrat, and the kindred volumes which succeeded, demand intellectual congeniality or sympathy. We suspect that all who love them, love them almost to excess, and have fallen in love with them at first sight. Holmes is original, analytical, pathetical, satirical and sprightly, diffusive, desultory and discursive, without pretending to any great profundity. The range of his studies and reading has been extraordinarily wide; his tastes, or at least his interests, are endless; he is always striking unexpected attitudes or seeking for unfamiliar points of view. . . . [His] cynicism is assumed, and lies always on the surface; and his satire only stings when he is in solemn earnest, and rebelling against the gratuitous burdens which humanity imposes upon itself. (pp. 203-04)

The *Professor* and the *Poet* are in similar style, as is *Over the Teacups*, which closes the series. In the last there are still the old freshness and quaintness of thought, but they are tinged, like many of the later poems, with the melancholy of declining maturity. The old man speaks of accumulating years in the spirit of the philosopher; but with all its drawbacks he loves life well, and is very loath to leave it. He has known little or nothing of the sufferings of broken health; his strength has been more than sufficient for each day; he looks forward with vague hopes to a blissful futurity, but he shrinks from exchanging certainty for uncertainty. Holmes . . . is far from orthodox; and with less than Johnson's depth of well-reasoned and pious confidence, he really has Johnson's horror of death. He does not discourse "de Senectute," in the optimistic vein of the eloquent heathen sage. He is inclined to indulge in melancholy metaphor; sometimes he mocks his apprehensions, and seeks to console himself with grimly amusing satire. He is glad to remember that age is infinitely more cheerful in this nineteenth century than it used to be some two thousand years ago. . . . What he cannot away with is the modern writers who will make life out to be worse than it is, who paint the monstrosities of humanity as the normal state of mankind, or delight in dilating on actual horrors. Their realism, or rather their hyper-realism, is horribly unwholesome. . . . And as Holmes says indignantly, with great truth, the responsibility of immoral writers is terrible, for there are stains there is no possibility of effacing. "One who has had the mischance to soil his mind by reading certain poems of Swift, will never cleanse it to its original whiteness." As for the old 'Autocrat' himself, if his theology be somewhat broad, there is no question about the invariable purity of his morality; and his works, without exception, are absolutely free from the suggestion of vice or the suspicion of evil. (pp. 206-07)

[Holmes's] poetry is more diffuse and less emphatic than his prose. He shines most in such humorous satire and comical *vers de société Americaine* as "**The Deacon's Masterpiece,**" "**Parson Turell's Legacy,**" or "**How the old horse won the bet**"—which, by the way, although Holmes had a predilection for racing, is the record of a physically impossible feat, and flies in the face of all the canons of race-riding. His many songs of the War show that he was no Tyrtaeus, and among the most touching are those inspired by his innermost and abiding feelings, dealing with declining years and the inevitable decay of man. (p. 207)

[*A. Innes Shand*], *"Oliver Wendell Holmes," in* Blackwood's Edinburgh Magazine, *Vol. CLII, No. DCCCCXXII, August, 1892, pp. 194-207.*

Build thee more stately mansions, O my soul
 As the swift seasons roll!
 Leave thy low-vaulted past
Let each new temple, nobler than the last,
 Shut thee from heaven with a dome more vast
 Till thou at length art free,
Leaving thine outgrown shell by life's unresting sea!

1858

1892

Oliver Wendell Holmes

Boston, March 1st 1892.

Holmes's handwritten lines from "The Chambered Nautilus."

HENRY CABOT LODGE   (essay date 1894)

[Henry Cabot Lodge, a member of the U.S. House of Representatives (1887-93) and a U.S. senator from Massachusetts (1893-1924), is remembered for his biographies of George Cabot, Alexander Hamilton, Daniel Webster, and George Washington, as well as for his The Story of the Revolution *and* The Senate and the League of Nations. *In the following excerpt from an essay written several weeks after Holmes's death, Lodge discusses Holmes's literary career, deeming* The Autocrat *his best work and commending his patriotism.]*

Dr. Holmes is perhaps most often thought of as the poet of occasion, and certainly no one has ever surpassed him in this field. He was always apt, always happy, always had the essential lightness of touch, and the right mingling of wit and sentiment. But he was very much more than a writer of occasional poems, and his extraordinary success in this direction has tended to obscure his much higher successes, and to cause men to overlook the fact that he was a true poet in the best sense. The brilliant occasional poems were only the glitter on the surface, and behind them lay depths of feeling and beauties of imagery and thought to which full justice has not yet been, but surely will be, done. He felt this a little himself; and he never wrote a truer line than when he said:

> While my gay stanza pleased the banquet's lords,
> My soul within was tuned to deeper chords.

In his poetry and in his mastery of all the forms of verse, he showed the variety of talent which was perhaps his most characteristic quality. He had a strong bent toward the kind of poetry of which Pope is the best example, and possessed much in common with the author of the *Essay on Man.* He had the same easy flow in his verse, the same finish, wit of a kindlier sort, the same wisdom without any attempt at rhymed meta-physics, and the same power of saying, in smooth and perfect lines,

> What oft was thought,
> But ne'er so well expressed.

The metrical form which is so identified with Pope always seemed to appeal to Dr. Holmes, and, when he employed it, it lost nothing in his hands. But this was only one of many instruments which he used. He was admirable in narrative and ballad poetry, the poetry of energy and movement and incident, of which **"Bunker Hill Battle"** is as good an example as any. He ventured often into the dangerous domain of comic poetry, where so few have succeeded and so many failed, and he always came out successful, saved by the sanity and balance which one always feels in everything he wrote. Of a much higher order were the poems of dry humor, where a kindly satire and homely wisdom pointed the moral, as in the **"One Hoss Shay."** But he did work far finer and better than all this, excellent as this was in its kind. He was not one of

> The bards sublime,
> Whose distant footsteps echo through the corridors of
>   time.

Nor was he one of those who seem to have sounded all the depths and shoals of passion. I do not think he thought so himself or ever was under the least misapprehension as to the nature of his own work, and in this freedom from illusions lay one secret of his success and of the tact which never failed. . . . [The] aspiring note is often heard in his verse, and there are many poems by Dr. Holmes filled with the purest and tenderest sentiment. Such are the lines on the death of his classmate and friend, Professor Peirce; such is the **"Iron Gate,"** the tender and beautiful poem which he read at the breakfast given him on his seventieth birthday. Such, too, are his lyrics, which include much of his best work, and which have in a high degree the fervor and the concentration which the best lyric ought always to possess.

People generally link his name with a memory of wit and humor, for he had both in large measure, and the world is very grateful to any one who can make it laugh. But the sentiment and aspiration, which are of higher quality than wit and humor can ever be and which are felt oftenest in the poems that love of man or love of country inspired, as well as the perfection of the poet's workmanship, and the originality of his thought, are too often overlooked. This perfection of form and felicity of imagery never left him. In the poem on the death of Francis Parkman, written only a year before his own death, when he was well past eighty, there is neither weakness nor falling off. The sentiment is as true and simple as ever, the flow of the verse as easy, and when he puts England's conquest of France in Canada into the single line

> The Lilies withered where the Lion trod,

we need no critic to tell us that the old happiness of phrase and power of imagery remained undimmed to the last.

Yet when all is said of his poetry, of which he left so much fixed in our language to be prized and loved and remembered, I think it cannot be doubted that the work of Dr. Holmes, which will be most lasting is the *Autocrat of the Breakfast Table* and its successors.

The novel of *Elsie Venner* is a strong and interesting book. The story holds us fast, and the study of a strange and morbid state of mind has the fascination given to the snakes themselves. Such a book would have made the fame and fortune of a lesser man. But as lasting literature in the highest sense, it falls behind the *Autocrat*. There the whole man spoke. There he found full scope for his wit, and humor and mirth, his keen observation, his varied learning, his worldly wisdom, his indignation with wrong, and his tenderest sentiment. To attempt to analyze the *Autocrat* and its successors would be impossible. It is not the kind of work that lends itself to analysis or criticism. It is the study of many-sided humanity in the form of the essay rather than the novel, although the creation and development of character play in it a large part. Such books with life in them are few and rare, although many have attempted them, but when they have the great vital qualities they are not of the fashion of the day which passeth away but for all time, because they open to us the pages of the great book of human nature. Montaigne and Addison, Goldsmith and Sterne, and Charles Lamb are the best, perhaps the only ones really in this field, for the exact combination of wit and humor, of pathos and wisdom, of sense and sentiment, where the lesson of life runs close beneath the jest and the realities tread hard upon the fancies, is as essential as it is hard to find. To this small and chosen company Dr. Holmes belongs, and in it holds high place. All the qualities, all the diversities are there, and, most important of all, the perfect balance among them is there too. The style runs with the theme, always easy but never slovenly, always pure and good but never labored, like talk by the fireside, without either affection or carelessness, while over it all (and this is stronger in Dr. Holmes than in anyone else) hangs an atmosphere of friendliness which draws us nearer to the writer than any other quality. (pp. 673-76)

[Dr. Holmes] had one personal quality which ought not to be passed over without mention anywhere or at any time. He was a thorough American and always a patriot, always national and independent, and never colonial or subservient to foreign opinion. In the war of the rebellion no one was a stronger upholder of the national cause than he. In his earliest verse we catch constantly the flutter of the flag, and in his war poems we feel the rush and life of the great uprising which saved the nation. He was in the best sense a citizen of the world, of broad and catholic sympathies. But he was first and before that an American and a citizen of the United States, and this fact is at once proof and reason that he was able to do work which has carried delight to many people of many tongues, and which has won him a high and lasting place in the great literature of the English-speaking people. (p. 677)

> *Henry Cabot Lodge, "Dr. Holmes," in* The North American Review, *Vol. CLIV, No. 457, December, 1894, pp. 669-77.*

[ROWLAND E. PROTHERO]   (essay date 1895)

[Contending that Holmes was "above all, an American patriot," Prothero discusses the various influences on Holmes's style and sums up his contributions to American literature.]

The parentage, childhood, and early surroundings of a man of genius must always be matters of biographical interest. But in the case of Oliver Wendell Holmes they possess a special value for the literary critic. They imparted to his works a characteristic flavour; they shaped his views of literature and society; they dictated his choice of the audience to which he appealed; they directed his mind into the particular groove of thought that partially explains the welcome which his writings have always received in the Old World. Above all, they implanted and fostered those refined instincts, which led him to oppose the premature effort of his contemporaries to force originality, and to condemn as unreasonable the demand, made half a century ago, that Transatlantic literature should appear in a new shape, 'shaggy and unshorn, shaking the earth like a herd of buffaloes.' Nurtured in the best traditions of Old-World scholarship, he felt no sympathy with the young American movement for the assertion of literary independence. Bred upon English models, and living among cultivated men in an University town, he did not, like some of his contemporaries, revolt against the established canons of art, or push the principle of Republicanism into the world of letters. Careful in his choice of poetical subjects, and conservative in his adherence to accepted rules of rhyme or rhythm, he never echoed the impatience of Judge Story, who grew 'tired,' as he told his son, 'of the endless imitations of the forms and figures and topics of British poetry.'

To his ancestry and his early training Holmes owed, as we think, some of the most prominent features in the peculiar position that he occupied in the literary life of his country. From first to last he was a sturdy opponent of the lawless independence which at one time threatened to vulgarise the literature of the New World, and thence to extend its influence to England. Another reason for laying stress on the parentage of Holmes is supplied by two of his best-known novels. Though *Elsie Venner* and *The Guardian Angel* had the object of demonstrating the cruelty of the most extreme doctrine of original sin, they were also both written to illustrate the limits set to human responsibility by inherited tendencies. The theory was a favourite one with their author. It reappears, again and again, in his writings; it supplies the main argument to his essay on **"Crime and Automatism."** He would have said himself that in his mental equipments he was what his forefathers had made him. He compares the body in which we travel over the isthmus of life, not to a private carriage, but to an omnibus, filled inside and out with our ancestors. On his father's side he was descended from a Puritan family of importance which settled in Connecticut in the seventeenth century. Thus his paternal ancestors were those sturdy Roundheads who formed the aristocracy of New England, and he inherited blood

> Such as warmed the pilgrim sons of toil
> Who held from God the charter of the soil.
>
> (pp. 189-90)

From one point of view Holmes is a product of the leisured Augustan age, a cultured survival of the Georgian era of colonial history. From another he has all the alertness of the busy-brained enquiring man of science who adorns the present century. He is at once skilled in the conduct of the 'clouded cane,' and an adept in the use of the stethoscope. He excels in the patrician art of light *vers de société,* and delights in the 'straight-backed measure' which 'sheathed the steel-bright epigrams of Pope.' But he is also essentially a modern American in the nimbleness, vivacity, and concreteness of his mind, in the versatility that achieves success in widely different fields, and in the rapid intuition with which he links together incongruities by their hidden resemblances. It is the union of the two ages which gives a peculiar flavour to his writings. His manner and his general attitude towards men and things carry us back to the days when Pope was regarded as greater than Homer, when Bryant sate in Arctic isolation as the Dean of American poets, when Halleck was considered a rival to Byron, when Miss Sedgwick was the Miss Edgeworth of the New world, when Lydia Sigourney was a Transatlantic Felicia Hemans, and when Whittier seemed 'destined for the tar-pot, rather than the tripod.' His matter, on the other hand, transports us into an active bustling world of steam-engines and electricity, surrounds us with an atmosphere of polemics and controversies which was alien to the previous century, and keeps us abreast with, sometimes in advance of, the latest developments of modern thought. The shrewd observation and the strong practical sense of a nineteenth-century Franklin are tempered by the sympathies and expressed with the epigrammatic polish of an aristocratic age. He is at once master of the revels among the polished wits of the coffee-house, and the representative of the sagacious, alert, enterprising men of business who have made modern America.

Holmes's conservatism was strong. Republican though he was, he was essentially an aristocrat. . . . He ridiculed the appetite of his fellow-countrymen for high-sounding titles; he satirised the American love of superlatives; he laughed at the exaggeration of modesty which sometimes bordered perilously near to pruriency. (pp. 198-200)

The debt which the best American literature, and all who in the Old World and the New appreciate its mixture of freshness and refinement, owe to Holmes is very great. How great the debt was has not yet been fully recognized by his countrymen. When young America demanded that the political revolution which separated the Old and New Worlds should have its literary counterpart in a similar revolt, Holmes threw all his influence into the opposite scale. He urged, with keen satire as well as with the force of example, that even a Republic must recognize the laws of conventional decorum, and that those who enter the Temple of the Muses outrage propriety if they ostentatiously flaunt their working dress. To him, as much as to any other man, we owe it, that the Versailles of American

literature has not been invaded to a greater extent than it has by the vocabulary and manners of the 'Halles.' (p. 201)

Patrician in his tastes, aristocratic in his sympathies, Conservative in his opinions, anti-democratic but not anti-Republican, he was, above all, an American patriot. His war-songs ring true with loyalty to the nation; and his **"Hunt after my Captain"** is full of eager sympathy with the cause of the star-spangled banner.

As a poet Holmes is greater in equipment than in achievement. He is the master of a terse pointed style, at once clear and condensed: his versification is easy and simple; his choice of epithets is often felicitous; his works, whether grave or gay, have the clear-cut crispness and the brilliant sparkle of high polish. He blends comedy and seriousness, humour and pathos, wit and sentiment with the admirable dexterity that heightens their effect by harmonious contrast. His wildest freaks of humour are yet allied with manly feeling, shrewd observation, sound sense, and genial wisdom. (pp. 201-02)

But, *Figaro-ci, Figaro-lá,* in an evil hour for the full development of his gifts, Holmes has been called upon to write verses on every possible occasion. Stanzas to be read at banquets, addresses to distinguished visitors, panegyrics on dead friends, and songs in praise of good fellowship constitute the bulk of his work. In this department of literature he was unrivalled. His society-verse stands by itself in America. It is not merely that his work has the neat finish of a cultured leisured age, that despises the rough approximations of a century content with ready-made goods. Fastidious polish marks the product of all writers of his school. But Holmes was, as it were, born to the patrician industry which, since he began to write, others have cultivated assiduously. The art that they sought to revive was with him a survival, and, as a consequence, his lines ring true and genuine, while those of his successors necessarily bear the stamp of artificiality. Brilliant writers of occasional verses rarely reach the highest rank among poets; the careless ease which such poetry demands is generally incompatible with strength of feeling or massiveness of intellect. Holmes is no exception to the rule. His lively versatility, nimble wit, tender feeling, and eloquent rhetoric imposed upon his efforts limits that his extraordinary facility of composition and light-hearted gaiety only rendered more insurmountable. For power he substitutes refined taste. For imagination he offers us a fancy which, however light, sportive, and charming it may be, is rarely creative. Instead of ideality he gives us conceits that are often apt, often graceful, and often, it must be added, pushed too far. With him poetry seems to have been a diversion rather than a serious pursuit, a distraction but not a passion, and his compositions impress us as the work of a clever man of literary talent, not as the utterances of the man of genius. Holmes has, however, written many poems which suggest that, under other circumstances, his achievement might have been greater. Had he not been called upon to be the Scheherezade of American feasts, he might have given us more poems like **"The Chambered Nautilus"** and **"Dorothy Q.,"** or written ballads with the true ring of

> Come hither, God-be-Glorified,
>   And sit upon my knee;
> Behold the dream unfolding
>   Whereof I spake to thee,
> By the winter's hearth in Leyden,
>   And on the stormy sea.

Holmes has somewhere expressed the belief that 'every articulately speaking human being has in him stuff for *one* novel in three volumes.' 'All, after that,' he adds, 'are with some persons failures.' He has himself written three novels, none of which can, in our opinion, be called successful. They abound in homely wisdom and caustic humour; they contain shrewdly observed pictures of New England life; they are filled with thrilling incidents. But in constructive skill they are singularly deficient, and they show little dramatic power. The author is always on the stage directing the movements of his puppets, and bringing with him a 'medicated atmosphere.' The minor figures are coarsely drawn and harshly coloured; the chief actors are anatomical puzzles, concrete problems in heredity, examples of mental states, psychological instances scientifically, but not dramatically, constructed. No one can read *Elsie Venner* without feeling how differently the heroine would have fared in the hands of Hawthorne.

Wanting in the serious purpose of a poet, lacking the constructive and dramatic genius of the novelist, Holmes discovered in the *Autocrat* the form of expression which was most perfectly fitted for the display of his gifts. In 1857 the *Atlantic Monthly* was founded, and to its pages he contributed the rambling discursive series which established the reputation of the new review and his own best title to immortality. In table-talk we do not want the imaginative genius, the prophetic spirit, the reflective brooding of the poet. Its charm lies in the lightness and ease of its flow, the crispness and pungency of its reflections, the freshness and pertinence of its observations. Good conversation is, like occasional verse, a patrician art which Holmes inherited. In his hands it is the instrument by which he can teach without being didactic, preach without sermonising, and amuse without offending the most fastidious taste. Here the want of constructive power is not seriously felt, and the perpetual presence of the author's personality is a positive advantage. The figures on the stage of the boarding-house require no individuality, for they are only the puppets with which the Autocrat plays at his pleasure. Holmes did not wait till the age of forty-eight to discover the best means of displaying his brilliant gifts. More than a quarter of a century before, he had printed in the *New England Magazine* the first of two papers called **"The Autocrat of the Breakfast Table."** They attracted no attention; they were, as he himself says, 'the crude products of his uncombed literary boyhood.' But the idea of table-talk was not forgotten by their author. When he returned to his early experiment of 1831, he had gained the reflective maturity, the varied experience, the ripeness of judgment which are essential to the success of the essayist. The best work of a Lamb, a Sterne, or a Montaigne is the ripe fruit of middle life.

It is by the Autocrat that, in our opinion, the name of Holmes will live. The three volumes of table-talk which form the series are unequal in merit. They are neither narratives nor dramas; but collectively they form a treasure-house of practical philosophy. Incomparably the best is the first of the series, and it also contains two poems which, in very different styles, are two of the best representatives of his poetic gifts,—**"The Chambered Nautilus"** and **"The One-Hoss Shay."** The simple movement, the easy play, the frankness of the whole give it the appearance and the charm of a spoken soliloquy. We see the thought first as it appears in the rough clay, then pinched and patted here and there, till it is moulded into the shape of aphorism, or epigram, or apophthegm. Out of the medley of unexpected thoughts and quaint satire shine gleams of deeper feeling, sparks of brilliant fancy, penetrating rays of insight into men and things. It is full of earnest purpose; but the fight for the conditions of healthy national existence, the pursuit of

mental truth, the effort to enforce the laws of common sense and experience are conveyed by humorous suggestions, condensed into proverbs of homely wisdom, enforced by grotesque contrasts, drollery, and pathos. His nimbleness of wit and his keen appreciation of the resemblances which underlie apparent incongruities enable him to expound his subject by a variety of ingenius images, to decorate it with novel suggestions, and to illustrate it by a succession of fresh sidelights gathered from the maturity of his practical and reflective experience.

The whole of the series is replete with a homour which in America is rare, if not peculiar to Holmes. One set of circumstances checked, another fostered the growth of humour in the New World. Out of the shock of the opposing tides emerged the matter-of-fact, dry, sarcastic character of the national product. Puritan grimness restrained the flow of animal spirits, enforced the duty of concealing ridiculous ideas, and so determined its demure, covert character. At the same time the meeting of savagery and civilization sharpened to their keenest edge the sense of incongruities, the perception of concealed analogies, the appreciation of hidden resemblances. The native wit bears upon it the stamp of the influences of two contending forces. The broad buffoonery which often does duty for it is not a national product, though the attempt to obtain the sanction of Biblical phraseology undoubtedly represents one effect, and not always the most pleasing one, of this union of natural laughter and inherited sternness.

Holmes's humour was not the lean, joyless, silent laugh of the Puritan. It need scarcely be added that he is never a mere buffoon, and never attempts to eke out the poverty of his jest by flavouring it with the language of the Bible. His humour is not dry, sarcastic, rasping, cynical. It is the expression of a nature neither stoical nor ascetic, but cheerful, genial, and optimistic. It has the slyness of natural gaiety rathen than the demureness of conscious self-repression. It is sweet, wholesome, sympathetic, kindly, at once enjoying and enjoyable. It recognizes no moral evil in that happiness and delight of existence which Puritanism placed under so severe an interdict. It rests on a deeper basis than mere intellectual quickness or the keen perception of whimsical contrasts and absurd resemblances. It does not depend for its effect on the shock of surprise, on the raciness of exaggeration, or on the irony of understatement. There is in it something of the large humanity without the playful yet pathetic wistfulness of Thackeray. Both men approach their subject through the heart as well as through the head. There is neither cynical scorn nor ungenerous contempt in the humour of either. But the American is more confident in the progress of the world, more hopeful of society, more convinced of the natural goodness of his fellow-men. The one is, as it were, the product of the saddened experiences of an Old World, the other of the buoyant optimism that belongs to a society which is still in its youth. Holmes's humour bears re-reading, because it draws its inspiration from a deep but tender insight into human character and from the genial interest of life of a kindly-hearted, generous-natured man. No writer did more in his generation to soften the harshness of the Puritan temper, or to disperse with the cheerful warmth of innocent enjoyment the chilling gloom of its austere rule in New England. For this, even more than for his purely literary influences, he deserved, and gained, the affection of his fellow-countrymen. (pp. 202-06)

[Rowland E. Prothero], in a review of "The Writings of Oliver Wendell Holmes," in The Quarterly Review, *Vol. CLXXIX, No. CCCLIX, January, 1895, pp. 189-206.*

LESLIE STEPHEN (essay date 1896)

[Stephen is considered one of the most important English literary critics of the late Victorian and early Edwardian eras. In his criticism, which is often moralistic, Stephen argues that all literature is nothing more than an imaginative rendering, in concrete terms, of a writer's philosophy or beliefs. In the following excerpt, Stephen comments on The Autocrat, Elsie Venner, *and Holmes's later poetry, concluding with particular admiration for his freedom from the "mawkishness which sometimes makes good morality terribly insipid."]*

Few modern writers have roused a stronger feeling of personal affection than O. W. Holmes. (p. 626)

His works are not voluminous; and, though he had published some of his best verses before he was thirty, he was nearly fifty before he began the series of essays which really made him famous. Few popular authors have had a narrower escape from obscurity. He would, in any case, have been remembered in his own circle as a brilliant talker, and there would have been some curiosity as to the writer of the **"Last Leaf"** and two or three other poems. But had it not been for the judicious impulse given by his friend Lowell which induced him to make his appearance as the "autocrat," his reputation would have resembled that of Wolfe, of "not a drum was beat" celebrity. Who, it would have been asked, was the author of the few lines which we all know by heart? and we should have turned up the article devoted to him in a biographical dictionary. But he would not have revealed himself with that curious completeness upon which all his critics have remarked. He often heard, as he says in an interesting letter, that he "had unlocked the secret of some heart which others, infinitely more famous, infinitely more entitled to claim the freedom, have failed to find opening for them." He cannot help believing that "there is some human tone in his written voice which sometimes finds a chord not often set vibrating." The secret of this gift is not hard to penetrate. . . . He remarks in the same letter that his life was "rather solitary than social"; and the society which he did frequent was not in one of the greatest centres of intellectual movement. In certain ways, too, even Bostonians must admit that the social atmosphere was of a kind to nip some of the luxuriant growths congenial to older abodes of art and letters. Holmes' attachment to his surroundings was as keen as if the conditions had been of the most genial. . . . So Holmes cherished whatever could be called historically interesting in his own country, because the supply of the appropriate material was so limited. Men who live in the shadow of Westminster Abbey or go to universities which the great men of many centuries have filled with associations, are apt to become a little bored with the topic. . . . As he grew up his patriotism did not diminish in intensity. All that happened was that he became qualified to catch its comic aspects. When the "young fellow they call John" laid down the famous proposition that "Boston State House is the hub of the solar system," and adds that "you couldn't pry that out of a Boston man if you had the tire of all creation straightened out for a crowbar," the autocrat accepts the "satire of the remark," and admits that the "axis of the earth sticks out visibly through the centre of each and every town and city." But he does not pretend to conceal that the sentiment, outrageous if literally accepted, tickles his fancy agreeably. . . . Holmes as a man shares the young fellow's enthusiasm, though he wishes us to understand that he is aware in cold blood that it is not quite the whole truth. The little deformed gentleman in the *Professor* gives a still more vigorous mouthpiece of the same sentiment. "A new race, and a whole new world for the newborn human soul to work in! And Boston is the brain of it, and has been any time these hundred years! That's all I claim for Boston, that it is the thinking centre of the continent and therefore of the planet!"—in which respect its superiority to Philadelphia and New York is easily demonstrated. The little gentleman is one of Holmes' most spirited characters, and makes a very convenient organ for the utterance of opinions not to be turned into serious dogmas—but also not to be overlooked. Boston is an ideal as well as a real city; it represents "the American principle," whatever that may precisely be. It is the three-hilled city as opposed to the seven-hilled city or reason against Rome. Democratic America has a different humanity from feudal Europe "and so must have a new divinity." Religion has to be "Americanized," and Boston is in the van of the struggle.

This might suggest a good many remarks for which Holmes would, perhaps, leave his deformed gentleman to reply. He has not committed himself to an unreserved support of a personage who reflects only one of his moods. One point, however, has to be noticed. Holmes, like others, had revolted against Calvinism as represented by the Westminster Confession. Many pages in his essays are directed against the old-fashioned creed; and, as we are told, made him the object of warm denunciations by the orthodox. Young people . . . were forbidden to read the *Autocrat,* and *Elsie Venner* was regarded as a dangerous manifesto. This, it must be admitted, sounds strange at the present day. Were any books ever more obviously harmless? People who remember certain English controversies about [theologian Frederick Denison] Maurice, which happened a little before the appearance of the *Autocrat,* may succeed in understanding why, in the country of the Puritans, Holmes should have passed for a heresiarch. Yet it now requires an effort to put oneself in that position, and certainly Holmes' remarks would now hardly excite a shudder in the best regulated families. Still they represented what seems to have been the most important passage of his mental history. The old Puritanism, one may guess, appeared to him in a new light when he had sat at the feet of Parisian professors. The old Boston, at any rate, was not quite the "hub of the universe" in the physiologist's point of view; and he fancied, when the old and the new currents met, a good deal of the sediment of old-fashioned dogma would be precipitated. Still, the old problem which Calvinism had answered in its own way came up in a new form. The doctrine of hereditary sin might be abandoned, but the problems of scientific "heredity" took its place. Jonathan Edwards' discussions of moral responsibility have a serious meaning when they are dissociated from the ghastly visions of hell-fire. Holmes gave more place to these controversies than some of his readers liked; and I need say nothing as to the merit of his own conclusions. They interest us chiefly because they gave rise to that provoking book, *Elsie Venner*. I call it "provoking" merely because it will not square nicely with any orthodox canons of criticism. In the first place, it has an air of being didactic, or is a book with a tendency, or, in the old-fashioned phrase, is a novel with a purpose. I confess that I should have no objection to it upon that ground. I always found *Sandford and Merton* a delightful work in my childhood, and I partly preserve that degrading taste. I like books with a moral. Some authors, it is true, are cramped by their morals, and occasionally tripped up into flat absurdity. Still, a writer often gets a certain unction from the delusion that he is preaching as well as story-telling; and so long as anyone is working with a will, and defying the critics and all their ways, he has the root of the matter in him. Holmes, it must be remarked, did not suppose that he was proving anything in *Elsie Venner*; he recognized the truth of the axiom propounded in the *Rose and the Ring* that blank verse is not argument; and the imaginary behaviour of an impossible being cannot possibly lead to any conclusion. When we meet a being who is half woman and half a snake it will be time to settle the moral code for judging her. Holmes, in fact, says in his prefaces that he only took an imaginary case in order to call attention to the same difficulty in the common course of things. To that I can see no objection. Clearly, every great tragedy involves some interesting question of casuistry; and casuistry may repay the debt by suggesting a good plot for a novel. The only question is, whether the extravagant hypothesis, be it purely fantastic or contrived to illustrate a point in ethics, has really been turned to good account. Here I confess to a conflict of feeling which, I suspect, is shared by others. The book makes me read it just whenever I take it up, and yet I am never satisfied. Perhaps it is that I want more rattlesnake; I want to have the thrill which my ancestors felt when they told legends of werewolves; I wish the snake-woman to be as poetical as Coleridge's Geraldine, to tremble while I read, and to be encouraged in my belief by such an infusion of science as will reconcile me to the surroundings of the nineteenth century in New England. That is, no doubt, to wish at the lowest that Holmes could have been combined with Hawthorne—not to suggest the creator of Caliban—and that their qualities could have coalesced with as little interference as those of Elsie and the snake. So much is suggested that one wants a more complete achievement. The fact is simply, I suppose, that Holmes had not the essential quality of the inspired novelist. He did not get fairly absorbed in his story and feel as though he were watching, instead of contriving, the development of a situation. That, for example, is the way in which Richardson declares himself to have written, and which partly explains the fascination to our forefathers of his moralizing and long-winded narratives. Holmes is distinctly a spectator from outside, and his attention is too easily distracted. I do not, in the least object to a novelist discoursing or supplying comments if it be his natural vein; I am not simple-minded enough to care for the loss of the illusion. But the novelist should not give an analysis in place of a concrete picture, or wander into irrelevant remarks. Now, Holmes' intellect is so lively and unruly that the poor snake-lady gets too often squeezed into the background. He is struck by the peculiarities of New England villages, their houses, or their "collations," or their "hired men," and is immediately plunged into vivacious descriptions and disquisitions. We have to change moods too rapidly; to feel on one page a shudder at the uncanny being, with something not human looking out of her eyes; and, on the next, to be laughing at the queer social jumble of a village gathering. If, in spite of these artistic defects, the book somehow takes so firm a grasp of one's memory, it is the stronger proof of the excellence of the materials which form so curious a mosaic. After all, the writer never goes to sleep, and that is a merit which redeems a good many faults of design.

One condition of the excellence of the *Autocrat* and its successors is of course that in them this irrepressible vivacity and versatility finds in him a thoroughly appropriate field. They have, as we see at once, the merits of the best conversation. (pp. 629-33)

Talk, said Holmes, is "to me only spading up the ground for crops of thought." He was half the time "interviewing himself" and looking for his own thoughts, "as a school-boy turns his pockets inside out to find what is in them." The *Autocrat* is the outcome of this investigation. . . . The *Autocrat* might suggest a series of riddles or problems for some future examiner in English literature. Why is controversy like the Hydrostatic

Paradox? Why is a poem like a meerschaum? What is the "very obvious" resemblance between the pupil of the eye and the mind of the bigot? In what respects may truths be properly compared to dice and lies to marbles? Why should a trustworthy friend be like a cheap watch? How does the proper treatment for Guinea-worm illustrate the best mode of treating habitual drunkards? The answers to these and many equally ingenious parallels illustrate Holmes' power of perceiving analogies; and show, too, how his talent had been polished in the conversational arena. (pp. 634-35)

It is Holmes' special peculiarity that the childish buoyancy remains almost to the end, unbroken and irrepressible. He could hardly indeed have sympathized with the doctrine that heaven lies about us in our infancy, for we do not cherish that—illusion is it? or faith, till we are forced to admit that we can only see the light of common day. Holmes never seems to have lost the early buoyancy—only to have acquired new toys; even physiology which he studied seriously enough, and which is not generally regarded as amusing, supplies him with intellectual playthings, quaint fancies, and startling analogies to be tossed about like balls by a skilful juggler. The early poems, written in the pure extravagance of boyish fun, like the **"Spectre Pig"** and **"The Mysterious Visitor,"** show characteristics which may be overlaid but are never obliterated. I don't know that any of his poems are more thoroughly himself than the early lines on a portrait:—

> That thing thou fondly deem'st a nose,
>   Unsightly though it be,—
> In spite of all the world's cold scorn,
>   It may be much to thee.

The inimitable **"One-Horse Shay"** was written when he was near fifty, and the **"Broomstick Train,"** almost equally full of fun, when he was over eighty, and had sorrows enough to quench most men's last sparkles of vivacity. No human being ever fought more gallantly with the old enemy who defeats us all in the end. (pp. 639-40)

["**The Last Leaf**"], I humbly confess, does not quite touch me as it should, because it seems too ingenious. Like Blanco White's famous sonnet, it rather tempts me, at least, to think what reply I could make to the argument. But the **"Last Leaf"** might be made into the text of all that I wish to say. The exquisite pathos of the verse about the mossy marbles linked to the fun of the irresistible though sinful "grin" is the typical instance of Holmes' special combination of qualities. He is one of the writers who is destined to live long—longer, it may be, than some of greater intellectual force and higher imagination, because he succeeds so admirably in flavouring the milk of human kindness with an element which is not acid and yet gets rid of the mawkishness which sometimes makes good morality terribly insipid. (p. 641)

Leslie Stephen, "Oliver Wendell Holmes," in The National Review, *London, Vol. XXVII, No. 161, July, 1896, pp. 626-41.*

VIRGINIA WOOLF (essay date 1909)

[A British novelist, essayist, and short story writer, Woolf is one of the most prominent literary figures of the twentieth century. Like her contemporary James Joyce, with whom she is often compared, Woolf is remembered as one of the most innovative of the stream of consciousness novelists, and her critical writings, covering almost the entire range of literature, contain some of her finest prose. In her discussion of Holmes's work, Woolf praises

the gusto of The Autocrat *and observes that "it tastes like champagne after breakfast cups of weak tea." Woolf's essay, which was occasioned by the 1909 publication of Lewis W. Townsend's biography of Holmes, first appeared in the* Times Literary Supplement *on August 26 of that year.*]

Let us own at once that Dr. Holmes's works can hardly be said to survive in the sense that they still play any part in our lives; nor is he among the writers who live on without any message to deliver because of the sheer delight that we take in their art. The fact that there is someone who will write a centenary biography for a public that reads the *Autocrat* cannot be set down to either of these causes; and yet, if we seek it on a lower plane, we shall surely find reason enough. There is, to begin with, the reason that our own experience affords us. When we take it up at a tender age—for it is one of the first books that one reads for oneself—it tastes like champagne after breakfast cups of weak tea. The miraculous ease with which the talk flows on, the richness of simile and anecdote, the humour and the pathos, the astonishing maturity of the style, and, above all, some quality less easy to define, as though fruits just beyond our reach were being dropped plump into our hands and proving deliciously firm and bright—these sensations make it impossible to think of the *Autocrat* save as an elderly relative who has pressed half-sovereigns into one's palm and at the same time flattered one's self-esteem. Later, if some of the charm is gone, one is able to appraise these virtues more soberly. They have, curiously enough, far more of the useful than of the ornamental in their composition. We are more impressed, that is, by the honesty and the common sense of the *Autocrat*'s remarks, and by the fact that they are the fruit of wide observation, than by the devices with which they are decked out.

The pages of the book abound with passages like the following:

> Two men are walking by the polyphloesboean ocean, one of them having a small tin cup with which he can scoop up a gill of sea-water when he will, and the other nothing but his hands, which will hardly hold water at all—and you call the tin cup a miraculous possession! It is the ocean that is the miracle, my infant apostle! ... Nothing is clearer than that all things are in all things, and that just according to the intensity and extension of our mental being we shall see the many in the one and the one in the many. Did Sir Isaac think what he was saying when he made *his* speech about the ocean—the child and the pebbles, you know? Did he mean to speak slightingly of a pebble? Of a spherical solid which stood sentinel over its compartment of space before the stone that became the pyramids had grown solid, and has watched it until now! A body which knows all the currents of force that traverse the globe; which holds by invisible threads to the ring of Saturn and the belt of Orion! A body from the contemplation of which an archangel could infer the entire inorganic universe as the simplest of corollaries! A throne of the all-pervading Deity, who has guided its very atom since the rosary of heaven was strung with beaded stars!

This is sufficiently plausible and yet light in weight; the style shares what we are apt to think the typical American defect of over-ingenuity and an uneasy love of decoration; as though

they had not yet learnt the art of sitting still. The universe to [Dr. Holmes], as he says, 'swam in an ocean of similitudes and analogies'; but the imaginative power which is thus implied is often more simply and more happily displayed. The sight of old things inspires him, or memories of boyhood.

> Now, the sloop-of-war the Wasp, Captain Blakely, after gloriously capturing the Reindeer and the Avon, had disappeared from the face of the ocean, and was supposed to be lost. But there was no proof of it, and, of course, for a time, hopes were entertained that she might be heard from.... This was one of those dreams that I nursed and never told. Let me make a clean breast of it now, and say that, so late as to have outgrown childhood, perhaps to have got far on towards manhood, when the roar of the cannon has struck suddenly on my ear, I have started with a thrill of vague expectation and tremulous delight, and the long-unspoken words have articulated themselves in the mind's dumb whisper, *The Wasp has come!*

The useful virtues are there, nevertheless. The love of joy, in the first place, which raced in his blood from the cradle was even more of a virtue when the *Autocrat* was published than

The autocrat holding forth at the head of the breakfast-table.

it is now. There were strict parents who forbade their children to read the book because it made free with the gloomy morality of the time. His sincerity, too, which would show itself in an acrid humour as a young man, gives an air of pugnacity to the kindly pages of the *Autocrat.* He hated pomp, and stupidity, and disease. It may not be due to the presence of high virtues, and yet how briskly his writing moves along! We can almost hear him talk, 'taking the words out of one's mouth', in his eagerness to get them said. Much of this animation is due to the easy and almost incessant play of the *Autocrat*'s humour; and yet we doubt whether Dr. Holmes can be called a humourist in the true sense of the word. There is something that paralyses the will in humour, and Dr. Holmes was primarily a medical man who valued sanity above all things. Laughter is good, as fresh air is good, but he retracts instinctively if there is any fear that he has gone too deep:

> I know it is a sin
> For me to sit and grin—

that is the kindly spirit that gives his humour its lightness, and, it must be added, its shallowness. For, when the range is so scrupulously limited, only a superficial insight is possible; if the world is only moderately ridiculous it can never be very sublime. But it is easy enough to account for the fact that his characters have little hold upon our sympathies by reflecting that Dr. Holmes did not write in order to create men and women, but in order to state the opinions which a lifetime of observation had taught him. We feel this even in the book which has at least the form of a novel. In *Elsie Venner* he wished to answer the question which he had asked as a child; can we be justly punished for an hereditary sin? The result is that we watch a skilful experiment; all Dr. Holmes's humour and learning (he kept a live rattlesnake for months, and read 'all printed knowledge' about poison) play round the subject, and he makes us perceive how curious and interesting the case is. But—for this is the sum of our objections—we are not interested in the heroine; and the novel so far as it seeks to convince us emotionally is a failure. Even so, Dr. Holmes succeeds, as he nearly always does succeed, in making us think; he presents so many facts about rattlesnakes and provincial life, so many reflections upon human life in general, with such briskness and such a lively interest in his own ideas, that the portentous 'physiological conception, fertilized by a theological idea' [see excerpt dated 1883], is as fresh and almost as amusing as the *Autocrat* or *The Professor.* The likeness to these works, which no disguise of fiction will obscure, proves again that he could not, as he puts it, 'get out of his personality', but by that we only mean to define his powers in certain respects, for 'personality' limits Shakespeare himself. We mean that he is one of those writers who do not see much more than other people see, and yet they see it with some indescribable turn of vision, which reveals their own character and serves to form their views into a coherent creed. Thus it is that his readers always talk of their 'intimacy' with Dr. Holmes; they know what kind of person he was as well as what he taught. They know that he loved rowing and horses and great trees; that he was full of sentiment for his childhood; that he liked men to be strong and sanguine, and honoured the weakness of women; that he loathed all gloom and unhealthiness; that charity and tolerance were the virtues he loved, and if one could combine them with wit it was so much to the good. Above all, one must enjoy life and live to the utmost of one's powers. It reads something like a medical prescription, and one does not want health alone. Nevertheless, when the obvious objections are made, we need not doubt that it will benefit thousands in the future, and they will love the man who lived as he wrote. (pp. 235-40)

> Virginia Woolf, "Oliver Wendell Holmes," in her *Granite and Rainbow: Essays, Harcourt, Brace & World, Inc., 1958, pp. 232-40.*

JOHN MACY (essay date 1913)

[*Macy was an American literary critic and an editor of the* Boston Herald *and the* Nation. *His most important work is* The Spirit of American Literature, *which denounces the genteel tradition and calls for realism and the use of native materials in American literature. Macy argues that "Holmes is the single great discursive essayist that America has bound in its slender sheaf of literary harvest," but maintains that he viewed life from his comfortable place on "the sunny side of a clean street."*]

Holmes's views have been familiar for fifty years, and he now seems on the whole a witty, finely bred old gentleman, expressing over the teacups ideas that are mild and respectable, certainly not dynamical. It is to-day a little difficult to realize that he, too, was a revolter, that the first numbers of the *Atlantic Monthly,* made precious by *The Autocrat,* encountered opposition among some of the conventional religious barbarians who were a dull majority in our free and independent country. Holmes is the unsuperstitious man of the world, the rationalist, the spokesman of what in his time is radical science, protesting against the theological attitude toward life. His mind is inquisitive, discursive, fanciful, but very solidly sane. His manner is consciously well-bred, conciliatory, even elegant—a very innocent mask for some loaded guns that he fires while looking unconcernedly at something else. Having inspected the world and found it out, he does not attack it at full cry like a reformer; but in perfectly modulated tones, in a voice twinkling with laughter, though seldom yielding to the full chest tones of mirth, he discourses urbanely of men and their ways. Without quite knowing whence the shot came, the enemy has received a blow fairly amidships. Holmes touches profundities with an assumption of amateurish inquiry, which with him is a method of humour, and not, as with Matthew Arnold, a dodging, unconvincing modesty.

Because of Holmes's rationalism and urbanity, and also because his verse has a carven finish and intellectual glitter, he has been often referred to the eighteenth century which is preëminent for its town-bred essayists and witty versifiers. . . . Holmes is the single great discursive essayist that America has bound in its slender sheaf of literary harvest. It is easy, but not profoundly critical to say, "Holmes—essayist, and witty poet—eighteenth century, noted for essays and witty poems— ah, yes, Holmes had a belated eighteenth-century mind." The truth is he was a very modern man, wholly of his time and place. In form, in substance he is no closer to the eighteenth century than is Emerson or Thoreau. In the topics he discusses, in the nervous eclectic variety of his mind, he is characteristic of his day and generation. (pp. 155-57)

Holmes is a well-stored modern man. Moreover his is a foreward-looking, not a backward-looking mind. Despite all recent rapid changes of ideas and the silencing, if not the disappearance, of some prejudices that he attacked, he is closer to us than to any time before him. His old-fashioned garment is a dramatic costume, as was Lamb's. *The Autocrat* is a fresh, day-lit, life-lit book, tingling with present day issues, though we have lost the sense of stir which it made in the obdurate bosom of Calvinism. We do not recognize ourselves in the breakfast-eaters to whom Mr. Addison condescended so charmingly; indeed, it were better on some mornings to go back to bed if there were nothing more vital in the world than the *Spectator* brings. But the Autocrat is our neighbour. He can keep one up at night. Here is a champion of our kind of thought, a spirited, though half-disguised controversialist, a believer in intellectual courage, in which our world, Holmes's Boston especially, is, at this advanced date, deplorably lacking. "You never need think you can turn over any old falsehood without a terrible squirming and scattering of the horrid little population that dwells under it." So speaks Doctor Holmes of Beacon Street, our contemporary, though not the contemporary of the intellectual decadence of Beacon Street. "Do I think that the particular form of lying often seen in newspapers, under the title 'From Our Foreign Correspondent' does any harm? Why, no, I don't know that it does. I suppose it doesn't really deceive people any more than the *Arabian Nights* or *Gulliver's Travels* do." There speaks our contemporary, though not the contemporary of the men who edited the newspapers that the boy brought this morning.

The Autocrat came full-blooded and shapely of limb from the brow of humour, a new form, a new manner. There is nothing like it in the whole range of *causerie*. (pp. 158-59)

He belongs with the classic few . . . because the classic is a man who does something that other classics have not done. He joins them by writing a book in his own way without too much regard for established immortals. *The Autocrat* is a new mode of essay, "every man his own Boswell." It pretends to be a record of talk, and thereby gains the privileges of talk without sacrificing the advantages of literary phrasing when that is needed to put the thought in order. It is free from the rigours of the formal essay and secures a natural right to circle over the universe, alighting when it will and soaring when it will. (Holmes's grotesque delicious image is "putting his straw in the bung of the universe.") The table-talkers, Selden, Hazlitt, Coleridge have left fine fragments, epigrammatic, witty; sententious, poetical, of the conversational man or rather of the monologuizing man. Holmes, with an instinctive dramatic sense, favours a broader idea of human talk. He embodies himself in a variety of mouthpieces. The characters afford him opportunity to say things that he really means but which a Brahmin physician might not care to express *propria voce*. He enjoys in himself and others the habit of the human mind of jumping from topic to topic, and his table-talk form enables him to indulge the enjoyment. He drops with apparent casualness the conclusion of a life-long reflection on a pet idea, and then turns lightly to something else, so that the favourite thought does not betray how much the author thinks of it. Holmes was nearly fifty when he wrote *The Autocrat* and he had written little prose before; he drew on the untouched treasures of a mind at vigorous maturity, stocked full of experience.

It is from experience that he dips oftenest and deepest. He is a reader, an amateur of books, but not a bookish man. . . . Whenever he speaks of books, in *The Autocrat* or *The Professor,* he speaks with unerring perspicacity and individuality of judgment. . . . Holmes makes you close his book, with your finger between the pages, and let your fancy run on what he has been saying. He stands on his own feet thinking about life and does not sit on the shoulders of the literary giants of the ages.

Yet few of his more bookish contemporaries, devoted to purely literary questions, write so well as he does; only Hawthorne, of the New Englanders, equals him in unbroken perfection of style. Holmes is one of the masters of style in whose phrasing

there is no technical flaw, no expression blurred and but loosely approximate to the thought. His prose and his verse are free from false verbal notes. There is in his work not one of those sentences that somehow get neglected in the practical business of making manuscript, and which suffer for the healing touch of proofreader or editor. This is the more remarkable in view of the range of Holmes's thought. He expresses a great many kinds of idea. (The very index to *The Autocrat* is a work of humour.) He leaps from witty fooling and whimsicalities to some puzzling problem of psychology which he fetches into the light of his transparent logical style; then with an instinctive avoidance of tedium and long explanation, he leaves the problem and passes to a bit of sentiment, often on a high plane of feeling, where he is equally sure and in command of the resources of language. (pp. 161-62)

His thoughts on love in *The Professor* are beautiful, at once speculative and humane. He slips once or twice into the mists of poetical metaphysics (on the verge of the region where Emerson wanders in his essay on Love), but comes swiftly back to the persons at the table. He seldom quite lets go his moorings in life.

The Autocrat is the cream of a man's mind at fifty. Had he said the best that he had to say, and would the next book be a limping sequel unable to keep the pace of its predecessor? There are those who find *The Professor* even better than *The Autocrat.* Indeed it is a deepening and ripening of the Autocrat's method and quality of thought. The Professor argues a little more at length, moves more steadily in one subject, with less fantastic flitting, fewer wayward excursions in pursuit of lateral analogies. The old verve is there, with an admixture of a sharper satire. There is a reason why *The Autocrat* should have had a sequel. That gentle old fellow had, to his surprise, started some controversies by the fresh candour of his thoughts on life and religion. These controversies suggested new ideas, but they were not for the Autocrat to take up; they would have been out of character. (pp. 162-63)

The Poet and *Over the Teacups* are written in the Doctor's inimitable manner, or perhaps it would be fair to say in the manner that only Holmes could imitate. They suffer in comparison with himself alone. The sources of good talk are by no means run dry, though the stream is a little thinner. (p. 164)

His success in portraying characters and making them talk in the true idioms of life encouraged him to write a novel. *Elsie Venner* is an ingenious story, and it needs not to be said that it is well written; Holmes did not know how otherwise to write. But he had not the gifts of the genuine novelist. He might have discovered them in himself if he had begun to look for them at thirty instead of at fifty. The manager of *Elsie Venner* is the Professor; he shows through delightfully at times, in spite of the shivery tale. Perhaps we do not shiver now; for we have lived through Ibsen and other men of tragic genius, whose "problems" are more intense and harrowing than any idea of the Doctor's. *Elsie Venner* excites in us intellectual interest and gives the pleasure which a fine mind always offers even in some form of literature to which it is not best adapted. *The Guardian Angel,* another tale strung on a curious thesis, is more delightful than *Elsie Venner.* It is written in a lower key. If the Professor is stage manager of *Elsie Venner,* the director of *The Guardian Angel* is the Autocrat. The first half of the book, where the problems of the plot have not begun to close in and demand of the author a skill that he does not quite possess, is as full of wise fun as so many pages of the breakfast-table series.

From the time when Holmes, at twenty-one, struck the public fancy with his stirring, boyish verses, **"Old Ironsides,"** he was known as a writer of occasional poetry; he is perhaps the most uniformly skilful and delightful maker of rhymes in commemoration of local events to be found in English literature. He was ambitious to be known as a poet, as is every man of letters who has tasted at all of the divinest spring. His verses are among the most graceful pages of *The Autocrat,* and in their kind they are perfect. As he never wrote poor prose, so he never wrote bad poetry. And yet—he is not a poet of lofty rank. He is a neat versifier of humour, sentiment, and friendship, fundamentally sincere and dexterous in touching his modest lyre.... Holmes's most ambitious poem, the one which he was most eager to have remembered as poetry, is **"The Chambered Nautilus."** To me it seems an elaborated conceit, pretty but not moving. The best of his poems is **"The Last Leaf,"** which touches with a fine tenderness, through a playfully turned stanza, the true pathos of age. **"Wind-Clouds and Star Drifts,"** elevated in thought and well done in its way, is cold as prose. As the Poet at the Breakfast Table himself says of the verses: "They were evidently written honestly, and with feeling, and no doubt meant to be reverential." But the inexplicable inspiration never descended upon the Autocrat-Poet-Professor. The prose passage in *The Autocrat* about the sea and the mountains is essentially better poetry than any of Holmes's verse.... (pp. 164-66)

In the poetry of light sentiment, of humour and sparkling word-play Holmes is perfectly successful. He is the best possible maker of after-dinner verses. The spirit of college festivals and friendly reunions he caught and spun into cunning rhymes, not once but in fifty pieces. **"The Deacon's Masterpiece"** and **"The Broomstick Train"** possess that unquestionable merit which is settled once for all by the fact that no one else ever did anything like them. The Brahmin Doctor had only one peer in the versifying of Yankee humour and that was his neighbour across the river, Mr. Hosea Biglow.

Holmes belonged to the prosperous comfortable classes. He took very much to heart some of the problems of his time, the intellectual and religious problems. He was a very keen and advanced investigator of some questions of psychology, and no man ever phrased scientific knowledge more perspicuously for the layman. But life for him was easy, and he saw things from the sunny side of a clean street.... He writes for the few, not the many; he addresses those who can catch an idea as it flies. His odd combination of logic and fantasy makes his work a continuous delight; the process of his thought as he unfolds it is fascinating, and he himself watches it with a delighted sense of surprise. He is the most modest of egotists, and, except when he is attacking an enemy (always a generalized intellectual enemy, never a personal one), he suggests rather than asserts. His intellectual curiosity warily eludes closed final statements; to him the universe is going on all the time and was not concluded with the last remark that any of us happened to regard as ultimate. Every imagination that meets his is stimulated to go on thinking about a world that is so full of a number of things. (pp. 167-69)

> *John Macy, "Holmes," in his* The Spirit of American Literature, *Doubleday, Page & Company, 1913, pp. 155-70.*

HENRY JAMES   (essay date 1915)

[*James was an American-born English novelist, short story writer, critic, and essayist of the late nineteenth and early twentieth*

centuries. He is regarded as one of the greatest novelists of the English language and admired as a lucid and insightful critic. James was a frequent contributor to several prominent American journals, including the North American Review, *the* Nation, *and the* Atlantic Monthly. *James here praises* The Autocrat *as a classic and claims that Holmes was instrumental in the development of the American novel.*]

The *Atlantic* was for years practically the sole organ of that admirable writer and wit, that master of almost every form of observational, of meditational, and of humorous ingenuity, the author of *The Autocrat of the Breakfast Table* and of *Elsie Venner.... The Autocrat of the Breakfast Table,* the American contribution to literature, that I can recall, most nearly meeting the conditions and enjoying the fortune of a classic, quite sufficiently accounts, I think, for our sense not only at the time, but during a long stretch of the subsequent, that we had there the most precious of the metals in the very finest fusion. Such perhaps was not entirely the air in which we saw *Elsie Venner* bathed—since if this too was a case of the shining substance of the author's mind, so extraordinarily agile within its own circle of content, the application of the admirable engine was yet not perhaps so happy; in spite of all of which nothing would induce me now to lower our then claim for this fiction as the charmingest of the 'old' American group, the romances of Hawthorne of course always excepted.

The new American novel—for that was preparing—had at the season I refer to scarce glimmered into view; but its first seeds were to be sown very exactly in *Atlantic* soil.... (pp. 25-6)

> *Henry James, "Mr. and Mrs. James T. Fields," in* The Atlantic Monthly, *Vol. 116, No. 1, July, 1915, pp. 21-31.*

VERNON LOUIS PARRINGTON   (essay date 1927)

[*An American historian, biographer, and critic, Parrington is best known for his unfinished literary history of the United States,* Main Currents in American Thought, *written from the point of view of a Jeffersonian liberal. In the excerpt below, Parrington views Holmes as a spokesman for the Boston Brahmins.*]

Since the death of Holmes in 1894, his reputation has shrunk and dwindled with that of his group. With the rise of other literary schools, New England standards have been submitted to a somewhat rude overhauling, and Brahmin ideals are no longer reckoned so authoritative as they were once believed to be, nor the supremacy of Boston genius so indisputable. Concord has risen as Cambridge and Beacon Street have declined, and in the shadow of Emerson and Thoreau, the wit of Back Bay is in danger of being obscured. Unsupported by his physical presence, his writings seem far less vital than they did when the echoes of his clever talk were still sounding through them. Certain intellectual shortcomings are more obvious when his works are brought together in a library edition: in the mass his prose seems far more discursive and his verse thinner and more jingly than when the several bits appeared singly, personally sponsored by the author in whose cleverness everybody delighted. Read with sprightly vivacity to a group of sympathetic listeners at the mellowest hour of the dinner, his occasional verse must have sparkled brightly and have gone off with such a crackle of laughter as to convince the Back Bay that the asthmatic little gentleman with bubbling spirits was a veritable poet, on the same friendly footing with the muse that he was with Beacon Street. (p. 442)

[Though] a full-blown Victorian in manners and tastes, Holmes was something of a child of the eighteenth century at heart. The situation in which he found himself might have proved disconcerting if he had chosen to speculate upon it. By nature a thoroughgoing rationalist, he lived in a romantic age. A gentleman of "parts and learning," with a quick and lively fancy that blossomed in the pat phrase and neat couplet, he loved wit and hated dullness with true Augustan zeal. The great days of Queen Anne were a perennial inspiration to him. He clung to the heroic couplet through all the changes of romantic styles. He moralized in rime with the fluency if not the finish of Pope. He satirized Calvinism with an honest wrath that he might have learned of Swift. He commented in his table-talk on the manners of the times with the chatty discursiveness of Addison. Like the earlier wits, he discovered a deep sympathy for the maturity and ripe wisdom of the classics. (pp. 443-44)

Romantic garments fitted him ill, yet he persisted in trying them on. He even got to like them, and came finally to prefer **"The Chambered Nautilus"** above his other poems—a strange perversion of taste for a rationalist. **"The One-Hoss Shay"** is worth a volume of such pretty moralizing. **"Parson Turell's Legacy"** and **"The Moral Bully"** are in better vein—witty, lucid, critical—than any half-hearted ventures in romanticism. The eighteenth-century wit does not appear to advantage patched with Victorian sentiment, and he should have been rationalist enough to know it.

As a Beacon Street Victorian Holmes was as full of virtuous prejudices as an egg is full of meat; but as a rationalist, with a modest scientific equipment that came from his professional training, he kept the windows of his mind open to the winds of scientific inquiry that were blowing briskly to the concern of orthodox souls. Many a barnacled craft was foundering in those gales, and Holmes watched their going-down with visible satisfaction. He was perhaps the most militant Unitarian amongst Boston laymen. Hatred of Calvinistic dogma was an obsession with him; it dominated his thought and colored much of his work, *Elsie Venner* and his table-talk as frankly as **"The One-Hoss Shay."** The criticism to which he subjected the old-school dogmas was always vehement, often vindictive. Long after the battle had been won he kept annoying the retreating enemy. (p. 445)

On . . . [Calvinism] he was militantly radical, never shirking debate, but whetting the edge of his satire and impaling his victim neatly with his logic. He took sardonic delight in turning Calvinism against itself, in the clever *reductio ad absurdum* of the Edwardean argument. Perhaps this major intellectual interest appears most adequately in his picture of the Master, the autobiographical rationalist whom he introduces into *The Poet at the Breakfast Table*. A dabbler in the law, theology and medicine, a philosophic contemplator of the Order of Things, who refused to permit "the territory of a man's mind" to be "fenced in," who agreed with the Poet in thinking somewhat ill of the specialist who dedicated his life to the study of beetles, preferring to range widely through time and eternity, who followed Darwin and was deep in bacteriology, trying "curious experiments in spontaneous generation"—this was Holmes on the intellectual side, a genial disseminator of the latest scientific speculations, a tolerant amateur of the things of the mind, a friendly dabbler in absolute moralities, who hoped "to do some sound thinking in heaven" if he ever got there, but who was too pleasantly engaged with Beacon Street to settle things now. (p. 446)

In his literary work Holmes was always the talker rather than the writer. The charm of the vivid and racy colloquial marks every page. A clever aphorism or telling pun is the objective of every paragraph, and it explodes with a brilliant shower of sparks. But like every talker his discursiveness is inveterate; he wanders far in pursuit of his point and sometimes returns empty-handed. He was always an amateur; life was too agreeable for him to take the trouble to become an artist. The essay was his most congenial form—his novels are to be taken no more seriously than his occasional verse. *Elsie Venner* wraps up the familiar problem of moral determinism in pleasantly discursive chat of Yankee bumpkinism in contrast with Yankee Brahminism, and he returns his impeccable hero to Beacon Street, after his sojourn in the provinces, to reward him with the Brahmin rewards—a munificent practice, a charming wife, and an exalted social position. What richer reward could be desired by one who had tasted to the full the mellow flavor of that society? Staid, delightful, self-satisfied, righteous little Beacon Street! Last refuge and citadel of the old Brahmin respectability; basking in the afternoon sunshine of its culture, not realizing that its sun is already well past the meridian; in love with its own virtues and unaware that the morrow will see the invasion of the Huns and Vandals of plutocracy, to whose plethoric bank books Brahmin culture must eventually bow—who would not have liked it? It was something after all

A depiction of the professor and John from The Professor at the Breakfast-Table.

to have been its favorite wit, its ready oracle, its clever poet, who in praising his fellow Brahmins was well aware that he discreetly praised his own admirable qualities. Kindly, delightful, fortunate Dr. Holmes! chief citizen of the Hub of the Universe! He was born and lived with a silver spoon in his mouth, and if a grudging posterity inclines to rate him and his little world somewhat lower than he rated them, what difference can that make to him? Tolerant himself, we should perhaps emulate his example, and not insist too rudely that he is only a minor figure in American literature. (pp. 450-51)

> *Vernon Louis Parrington, "The Authentic Brahmin," in his* Main Currents in American Thought, an Interpretation of American Literature from the Beginnings to 1920: The Romantic Revolution in America, 1800-1860, *Vol. 2, 1927. Reprint by Harcourt Brace Jovanovich, Inc., 1954, pp. 442-63.*

GAY WILSON ALLEN (essay date 1935)

[*In the following excerpt, Allen provides a detailed analysis of Holmes's poetry and concludes that he had little influence on American versification.*]

There is almost every reason for us not to expect a prosodic system from Holmes, or even much prosodic thinking at all. He was first of all a physician and professor of anatomy, and most of his poetry is colored to some extent by the scientist, directly in subject-matter and idiom and indirectly in the scientific reserve that always held in check his poetic imagination.

In the second place, he was a "throw back," as most critics have pointed out (though they often over-emphasize it). He says in his note to [**"Poetry, A Metrical Essay"**] ... that, "This Academic Poem presents the simple and partial views of a young person trained after the schools of classical English verse as represented by Pope, Goldsmith, and Campbell, with whose lines his memory was early stocked." And in many respects, he remained an eighteenth-century neo-classicist all of his life. But even in this confession we must remember Holmes's statement that the poem, which would of course include the versification, represents only his "partial views." It is plain, however, that this young poet was not headed toward any sort of prosodic revolution.

In the third place, Holmes was always primarily an "occasional" poet, despite the fact that he did write some fine poetry for more serious purposes; and the occasional poet, like the journalistic versifier, may be counted upon to follow the conventions. For new forms divert attention to technique, whereas the "occasional" poet wants all attention focused on what he has to say. So long, therefore, as Holmes remained the writer of after-dinner verse (and such he did remain until the end of his days), he was practically compelled to continue using the familiar octosyllabic couplet, the heroic couplet, ballad meter, and other simple and accepted forms.

Nevertheless, we do find Holmes now and then speculating on prosodic questions. The most widely known instance, of course, is **"The Physiology of Versification,"** which is typical of Holmes the scientist, and which proclaims that there is a vital and necessary connection between the laws of versification and the respiration and the pulse, "the true time-keepers of the body." (pp. 193-94)

On the same grounds, Holmes argues that the "heroic line" is more difficult to read because only about fourteen verses are pronounced in a minute; so that, "If a breath is allowed to

each line the respiration will be longer and slower than natural, and a sense of effort and fatigue will soon be the consequence." Though the caesura is a "breathing-place," it "entirely breaks up the natural rhythm of breathing." The twelve- and the fourteen-syllable lines are also found difficult for the same reasons.

Now this argument is ingenious and interesting, but it is so "scientific" that it fails to take into account all the facts. Holmes admits that different persons have different respiratory rhythms, and hence his argument may not hold for all people. Moreover, he does not consider the fact that in enjambed octosyllabics, two, three, or several lines are read at one breath-sweep. And in blank verse, which is undoubtedly the most "natural" speaking verse (as Shakespeare's dramas are sufficient to prove), the irregular variation of short and long breath-sweeps gives us the most pleasing effects. But still more important is the fact that this theory is an attempt to explain conventional, classical, accepted prosody, in which end-stopped lines predominate. It is more physiological than prosodic. The attempt to explain prosody on physiological principles is commendable, yet the chief value of the essay for the student of prosody lies in the fact that it is the best proof we could ask that Holmes took conventional prosody for granted. (pp. 194-95)

And yet, strangely enough, there is in his 1836 preface [to *Poems*] a doctrine which sounds curiously "modern," even "modernistic" or "cubistic." In defending the "extravagant" in poetry, he says:

> A series of hyperbolical images is considered beneath criticism by the same judges who would write treatises upon the sculptured satyrs and painted arabesques of antiquity, which are only hyperbole in stone and colors. As material objects in different lights repeat themselves in shadows variously elongated, contracted, or exaggerated, so our solid and sober thoughts caricature themselves in fantastic shapes inseparable from their originals, and having a unity in their extravagance, which proves them to have retained their proportions in certain respects, however differing in outline from their prototypes.

But this preface is apparently a defence of the poems in the 1836 volume, all of which obey the conventional rules of versification. Apparently Holmes never thought of trying to convey his "hyperbolical images" and "caricature" by a "fantastic" or "exaggerated" technique.

Holmes did make valuable contributions to the practice of American versification, and exerted a powerful influence toward reinstating the French polish and perfection of eighteenth-century English ideals; yet we must study him as a versifier and not as a conscious prosodist.

Though Holmes early began to use practically all the verse forms that he ever used, the ballad measure seems to be most characteristic of his earlier period. He never surpassed **"The Spectre Pig,"** for instance, in his imitations of the genuine folk ballad, despite the fact that he insisted on placing it in the last section of his collected poems under the heading of "Verses from the Oldest Portfolio." It is difficult to find anywhere a more subtle, ironical, and satirical parody of the thought, diction, and rhythm of the ballad.

> It was the stalwart butcher man,
>   That knit his swarthy brow,
> And said the gentle Pig must die,
>   And sealed it with a vow.

And oh! it was the gentle Pig
Lay stretched upon the ground,
And ah! it was the cruel knife
His little heart that found.

These inversions and parataxes are not awkward, as we might expect, but produce a rhythm which is an unmistakable folk ballad tune. We also find the same "tune" in **"The Mysterious Visitor."**

"Old Ironsides" . . . is in the same ballad measure, yet is different in several details. The eight-line stanzas are fairly regular in meter and have a two-line thought-movement, as in **"The Spectre Pig"** and the genuine folk ballads; but only four of the twenty-four lines are enjambed, there are comparatively few metrical stresses, and the diction and syntactical constructions are more natural than in **"The Spectre Pig."** (pp. 196-97)

"The Star and the Water-Lily" . . . contains a generous sprinkling of anapestic feet, a variation which Holmes continued to use intermittently during his whole poetic career. . . .

"To an Insect" and **"My Aunt"** . . . , however, are more typical of Holmes's ballad measure, being straight iambic, 4 + 3. **"The Cambridge Churchyard"** is in precisely the same meter, but is less regular and inclined to singsong because of a skilful variation of stresses, including initial accented syllables, secondary accents, and spondees. (p. 198)

* * * * *

Holmes used the four-stress iambic line extensively from his college days (*cf.* **"The Meeting of the Dryads"**) until very near the end of his life. His four-stress verse includes simple stanza forms, such as the *abab* quatrain, octosyllabic couplets, and "clipped" four-stress iambic. No new, eccentric, or irregular versification is found in the handling of these forms, and since they are so common anyway, a full discussion of them should not be necessary.

His juvenile **"The Meeting of the Dryads"** is characteristic of much of Holmes's regular octosyllabic lines, with its inversions, smooth and regular beats, and couplet movement (even with alternate rime):

In every julep that he drinks,
    May gout, and bile, and headache be;
And when he strives to calm his pain,
    May colic mingle with his tea.

"Under the Violets" . . . is different in its versification only in the greater enjambment of its third stanza, the first four lines being read at one sweep. Rarely are more than two lines enjambed in Holmes's four-stress verse. (p. 199)

Holmes's most famous four-stress couplets are those of **"The Deacon's Masterpiece, or The Wonderful 'One-Hoss Shay'."** . . . The monotonous rime and absurd rhythm are part of the humor of this piece, but the versification is little better than doggerel. . . .

"Parson Turell's Legacy" . . . , written in the same year as the **"One-Hoss Shay"** . . . , is, on the whole, more regular, though the rhythm in some passages is broken by short, elliptical sentences, resulting in a colloquialism very characteristic of Holmes's humorous verse:

Facts respecting an old arm-chair.
At Cambridge. Is kept in the College there.
Seems but little the worse for wear.

(p. 201)

Another colloquial device is the use of abbreviations, with a consequent eccentricity of rhythm, as in **"How the Old Horse Won the Bet"**:

The swift g. m., old Hiram's nag,
The fleet s. h., Dan Pfeiffer's brag,
With these a third—and who is he
That stands beside his fast b. g.?

On the whole, **"Dorothy Q,"** with its very sparing enjambment and monotonous singsong rhythm, is characteristic of Holmes's four-stress couplets. Like Whittier's *Snow-Bound*, it is important for its description, not for its versification, though it is a much smoother and less awkward poem than Whittier's. **"At the Pantomime"** has greater enjambment, with more skilfully varied pauses, and contains some of Holmes's most pleasing octosyllabic couplets. (p. 202)

* * * * *

Holmes admitted his eighteenth-century prosodic background, and . . . he seemed to resent Lowell's laughing "at the old square-toed heroic." In **"Poem Read at the Dinner Given to the Author by the Medical Profession,"** he proudly admits his allegiance to this measure:

And so the hand that takes the lyre for you
Plays the old tune on strings that once were new. . . .
I smile to listen while the critic's scorn
Flouts the proud purple kings have nobly worn;

This passage is also a good illustration of the metrical regularity of Holmes's heroics. Each line has exactly ten syllables, inverted feet are used sparingly, spondees rarely (but *cf.* "proud purple"), and each couplet is closed or "couplet moulded" in the eighteenth-century manner. (p. 204)

Holmes used this measure extensively, both for serious and "familiar" verse. Most of his long poems are in this form. His "Five Stories and a Sequel," which he collected under the heading of "Readings Over the Teacups," are all in heroic couplets. They include **"To My Old Readers," "The Banker's Secret," "The Exile's Secret," "The Lover's Secret," "The Statesman's Secret," "The Mother's Secret,"** and **"The Secret of the Stars."** These poems are not so well known as Holmes's four-stress couplets of the **"One-Hoss Shay,"** yet they contain some good versification, such as **"The Secret of the Stars,"** which has some beautiful cadences, held in check only by the rime and a corresponding tendency toward the full stop after the completion of the rime. Many of the first lines of couplets, though, are enjambed:

In vain the sweeping equatorial pries
Through every world-sown corner of the skies,
To the far orb that so remotely strays
Our midnight darkness is its noonday blaze;
In vain the climbing soul of creeping man
Metes out the heavenly concave with a span,

These lines are less "couplet moulded" than the average eighteenth-century English heroics, but the neo-classical model is apparent. It is in this measure, however, that the eighteenth-century influence on Holmes's versification is strongest. (pp. 205-06)

* * * * *

Holmes wrote comparatively little blank verse, probably because it is not a very convenient form for "occasional" poems; and his few attempts are perhaps less known than any other poetic form that he used. But the little blank verse that he did write is, so far as versification goes, unusually good. The 1864 **"A Sea Dialogue"** contains some awkward lines, the worst being:

> Friend, you seem thoughtful. I not wonder much
> That he who sails the ocean should be sad.

Yet the 1872 **"Wind-Cloud and Star-Drifts"** shows complete mastery of the form. Especially commendable are the long breath-sweeps, permitting sustained cadences in the best blank verse tradition. (p. 206)

However much Holmes's heroic couplets may be in the eighteenth-century tradition, his blank verse is certainly not, for it shows scarcely a trace of the couplet influence. Yet it is more in the tradition of Freneau than of Bryant, since it echoes the good workmanship of Freneau (*cf. The Rising Glory of America*) and lacks the sonority of Bryant's *Thanatopsis*.

* * * * *

The popularity of **"The Chambered Nautilus"** and the poet's own undisguised pride in this poem make a discussion of it almost imperative. In a letter to George Ticknor, Holmes declares, "I am as willing to submit this [poem] to criticism as any I have written, in form as well as substance, and I have not seen any English verse of just the same pattern."

In none of his other poems do we find Holmes using such freely varied accents as in **"The Chambered Nautilus."** There are, in fact, so many reversed feet and interpolated spondees that no one stanza accurately indicates the underlying rhythmical pattern. (pp. 206-07)

It is probably unsafe to press very far a search for symbolism in the form of this poem, yet one wonders whether the rhythms (including the combinations of pentameter, trimeter, and alexandrine in the novel stanzaic arrangement) were not intended to symbolize the crenulated and scalloped shell of the chambered nautilus. At any rate, the form is, as Holmes himself believed, very unusual, and perhaps unique.

* * * * *

Next to **"The Chambered Nautilus,"** Holmes perhaps took most pride in **"The Last Leaf,"** at least among his stanzaic poems. Certainly it is the only other poem which he believed he had written on an original model. His own explanation of why he happened to use the "somewhat singular measure" is amusing. "I had become a little known as a versifier, and I thought that one or two other young writers were following my efforts with imitations. . . . I determined to write in a measure which would at once betray any copyist." He mentions Campbell's *Battle of the Baltic* as having probably suggested the form, "But I do not remember any poem in the same measure, except such as have been written since its publication."

It is a little puzzling why Holmes took so much pride in the form of this poem, but his handling of it is easy and dexterous. (pp. 208-09)

The rhythm does have a lilt which is more musical than anything else Holmes ever wrote. The only trouble is that it is almost too musical, the "tune" obtruding itself into the reading so much that the poem is mostly sound. Still, it is a competent lyric. And its music is reminiscent of the seventeenth-century English lyrics.

Holmes's most peculiar stanza is the unrimed trochaic quatrain of **"De Sauty,"** composed of three six-stress and one three-stress lines. This is unique in his poetry, for his only other unrimed verse is regular blank verse, and no other poem of his is so predominantly trochaic. (pp. 209-10)

The **"Two Sonnets: Harvard"** . . . and the sonnet sequence to Longfellow, **"Our Dead Singer"** . . . , show that Holmes could handle the Italian form with ease and facility, and it is surprising and regrettable that he did not write more sonnets. . . .

To judge by Holmes's random stanzas, his sonnets, his blank verse, and his few excellent lyrics, he could have achieved success in almost any conventional meter; yet as we have seen, he always remained essentially a poet of octosyllabics and the heroic couplet. . . .

While Holmes won considerable fame and distinction in his day, it is doubtful whether he has had much influence on American versification, (1) because he used the old measures without contributing anything new to their handling except an urbane unself-consciousness and an epigrammatic polish, and (2), and consequently, because his method called attention to content rather than technique. (p. 211)

> *Gay Wilson Allen, "Oliver Wendell Holmes," in his*
> American Prosody, *American Book Company, 1935,*
> *pp. 193-216.*

VAN WYCK BROOKS   (essay date 1936)

[*Brooks was an American critic, biographer, editor, and translator who is best known as a chronicler of America's cultural history. In the following excerpt, he contends that Holmes used* The Autocrat *and* Elsie Venner *as vehicles to unsettle his readers and to encourage them to question their beliefs. For further commentary by Brooks, see Additional Bibliography.*]

In his diplomatic way, the Autocrat attacked all the mental habits of his hearers. What was this "logical mind," the fruit of generations of preachers and lawyers, but the One-Hoss Shay of Calvinism? The doctor had no use for Calvinism, and he knew that, while they laughed at the one-hoss shay in Boston and at Harvard, it was no laughing matter in the country. He was determined to break it up,—if laughter failed, by other means, by quoting half a dozen sciences, by the use of analogies and comparisons, by every method but controversy, since controversy equalized the foolish and the wise and no one knew this better than the fools. For what was the "logical mind" of Calvinism but the parent of all injustice, the *a priori* and the *parti pris,* narrow judgment, rigid condemnation, all those moral plagues, in other words, from which the American mind so patently suffered? Did he mean to weaken moral obligations by drawing up the blinds of this dark chamber and letting in the light? His object was merely to define them; for the light he let into the dark chamber was the light of common sense, a doctor's view of the problem of cause and effect as it really expressed itself in human nature. Was some question of crime involved? The "logical mind" spoke of original sin and anathematized the doctor. The rational mind spoke of the effect and anathematized the cause. As for the fruits of the old religion, many of the minister's patients were fools and cowards, and all too many of them were also liars. (Immense sensation at the table.)

The Autocrat was prepared for the sensation. The religious weeklies and monthlies, all over the country, began to throw brickbats at him. The doctor was imperturbable. One cannot turn over any old falsehood without a terrible squirming and scattering of the unpleasant little population that dwells under it. No one can ever say anything to make his neighbors wiser or better without being abused for doing so; and, if there is one thing that people detest, it is to have their little mistakes made fun of. The Autocrat continued, with calm good humor, always ready to talk as long as a few boarders remained at the table, twirling their knives, perhaps, balancing their spoons on the edge of their tea-cups or tilting on their chairs against the wall. (pp. 3-4)

Everybody listened to the Autocrat, except a little group of thinkers who also described themselves as Humanists. Perhaps they were not in the room when [the Autocrat] remarked: "Beware of making your moral staple consist of the negative virtues. It is good to abstain, and teach others to abstain, from all that is sinful and harmful. But making a business of it leads to emaciation of character, unless one feeds largely also on the more nutritious diet of active sympathetic benevolence." Perhaps this little group considered the doctor frivolous, with his marked distaste for a "soul-subduing decorum." But everyone else was prepared to listen when he wrote a novel, *Elsie Venner;* for he had long believed that every intelligent man had the stuff of a novel in him, and therefore why not he? . . . His novels were "medicated novels"; and, as the doctor was always a talker, he strolled about from page to page, airing his views about his characters, dismissing them at times with a turn of the hand as if they were so many cases at a medical meeting. His composition was very untidy. But he always had a new story even when it was only a ghost of a story, as in the breakfast-table series, and he always had a problem to deal with,—hysteria in a young girl, a young man's gynophobia, morbid religious excitement and its effects. There were happy streaks in all his writings, and striking applications of modern science; and his essay on *Mechanism in Thought and Morals,* the "underground workshop of thought,"—the unconscious,—was a brilliant anticipation of Dr. Freud. In fact, although *Elsie Venner,* of all [his] later books, was the only one that seriously counted, the doctor knew so much about human nature, and had such a tang of his own, that one could read him at his worst with pleasure. (pp. 13-14)

[With *Elsie Venner*] the doctor cast a bombshell into the circle of his fellow-boarders. Every breakfast-table in the country resounded with *Elsie Venner.* Were you a Unitarian or a Calvinist, or any other variety of Jew or Christian, were you interested in the recent theories about heredity and environment, in medical and therapeutic questions, philosophy, criminology, education? Then *Elsie Venner* had something to say to you, and sometimes it was not a pleasant message. If, as a good Unitarian, you liked to think of the soul as an "unstained white tablet," then Elsie with her wicked little powders was an awkward nut to crack. The question whether Elsie could help herself was even more of a dose for the Orthodox. If you were a Pharisee, you fared still worse; for if Elsie was not responsible, if she could not be accused of sin,—however one might punish her for crime,—what became of your own pretensions? Were you not obliged to see that your valor and justice, your strength, truth, and virtue were merely the result of your happy fortune? What was your aristocracy but a sum that began with a one in tar and a two in tallow, and perhaps a three in whale-oil, however maintained by pluck? Your elevated type of face and figure were due not to you and your father's virtue, beyond a certain measure, but to the money made from the tar and the tallow that bought the air and sunshine, the healthy, happy summers, the good nursing and doc-

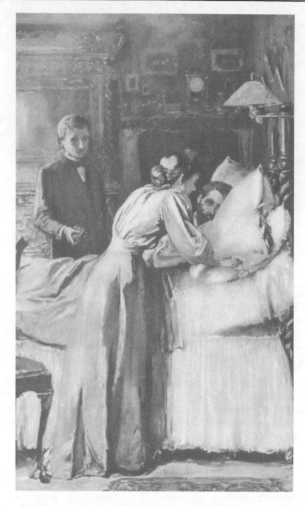

Iris at the Little Gentleman's sickbed, from The Professor at the Breakfast-Table.

toring, the best cuts of the best beef and mutton, which enabled your father, and his father and his, to grow up in such a kindly fashion and, when they were grown, to afford the costly luxury of beauty and marry the finest specimens of the other sex. This train of reasoning went a long way when the valor and the truth, strength and virtue were so obviously poisoned *out* of a race by the food of the bushman in his forest, by the foul air and darkness of the tenement-houses where half one's fellow-Christians were constrained to live. Just how far it went, the doctor might not have cared to think, for the "sunny street that holds the sifted few," the "swell-fronts and south-exposure houses" had a singular charm for him, as for other mortals, and the people who lived inside these houses were not only just as good as other people but the pleasantest for a doctor to take care of. "Why not take the tops of your sparrowgrass? Somebody must have 'em,—why shouldn't you?" Such was the doctor's advice to a young disciple; and, in fact, he never pretended to be a sage, too lofty for these trifles. He knew that a certain amount of glass was mingled with the bricks in the house he lived in, a knowledge that disarmed the caster of pebbles; and meanwhile he had discharged a thunderbolt that fairly rocked the walls of Philistinism. Who, after reading *Elsie Venner,* could talk about "total depravity"? Who was to condemn? Who to judge? Or pride himself too much on his family portraits? Or think that God had given him his lands and chattels in recognition of his Christian virtue? Dr. Holmes, perhaps unwittingly, had played into the hands of Dr. Darwin. He had played into the hands of Dr. Freud. He had played into the hands of another doctor of whom he had never heard, Dr. Marx. One never knows how far a doctor's table-talk may carry him. (p. 15)

> Van Wyck Brooks, "Dr. Holmes: Forerunner of the Moderns," in The Saturday Review of Literature, Vol. XIV, No. 9, June 27, 1936, pp. 3-4, 13-15.

S. I. HAYAKAWA AND HOWARD MUMFORD JONES (essay date 1939)

[*Hayakawa, an American semanticist, educator, and critic, is best known for his* Language in Thought and Action. *Jones, a twentieth-century American critic, humanist, and literary scholar, is noted for his illuminating commentary on the development of American culture and literature. In the following excerpt, Hayakawa and Jones stress that Holmes was an amateur in literature who "knew that the bardic gift had been denied him." Discussing Holmes's novels, verse, essays, and intellectual outlook, the critics conclude that he was "one of the most winsome characters in literary history." For additional commentary by Jones, see excerpt dated 1964; for further criticism by Hayakawa, see Additional Bibliography.*]

The casualness with which Holmes's medical career has been treated by literary critics, while natural, has had one unfortunate result: sufficient consideration has never been given by students of his literary writings to the fact that to him literature was never more than a sideline. The usual accounts of Holmes as the charming representative of the "silver age" of America, the "typical Brahmin," the fashionable after-dinner speaker and wit, the sentimental and kindly old gentleman, are true enough; but they fail to do justice to an important aspect of his character. Few writers have shown more kindliness and consideration in dealing with opinions they despise; it is frequently thought, therefore, that he was a social hot-house product, superficially brilliant, but lacking in robustness and vigor. Such an interpretation, of course, has been especially attractive to the opponents of the "genteel tradition," the admirers of the brawny, muscular, and untamed in American literature and life. But, while it is true that in his literary writings Holmes was all too scrupulous lest he offend the chaste ear of maidens or shock the decent piety of elderly spinsters, in his professional writings he reveals an altogether different personality—a sinewy and aggressive fighter, conscious of his strength, proud of the great scientific spirit he represented, exulting in his polemical cunning. His was a time when eloquence counted for more in the medical profession than it does today. Taking advantage, therefore, of every weapon at his hand, he sailed into his controversies with incisiveness, irony, and vigor. His medical papers sometimes make much better reading than his literary prose. (pp. xxxix-xl)

In literature, . . . Holmes was an amateur, in the sense of one whose real vocation was elsewhere. To compare Holmes even cursorily with writers who have taken themselves seriously as writers is to see that he is of a different order of being as a literary man. Shelley, Milton, Pope, Swift, Emerson, D. H. Lawrence—or even lesser men like Rupert Brooke—have in common a kind of artistic seriousness, a bardic or prophetic urge which has impelled them to write. Holmes, on the contrary, with neither a tragic nor a profoundly comic view of life, with none of the impassioned concern with ultimate realities which Matthew Arnold has called "high seriousness,"

with no deep sense of pathos, or even of melodrama, with no interest in advancing the technique of poetry, is distinctly an amateur in letters. His literary writings, on the whole, are partly the leisure-hour meditations of the physician, partly a means of spreading certain items of professional propaganda, partly a distillation of his social life. The mere fact that he employs the novel in the crudely didactic fashion of *Elsie Venner, The Guardian Angel,* and *A Mortal Antipathy,* shows how remote from him is the point of view of the genuine artist; these novels are, in the very motives that gave them birth, the novels of an amateur. If further proof were needed, one has only to point to the perfunctory admiration and easy generalities that usually characterize his criticism of other authors, as in his essays on Washington Irving and Nathaniel Hawthorne. No thoroughgoing artist would ever have contented himself with such off-hand remarks about other artists.

From his literary writings alone, therefore, we cannot understand the whole personality of Holmes. If he deals rarely or not at all with problems deeply tragical or pathetic, if he never discloses the grandeurs of inner spiritual conflict, if nothing he writes seems to be of the nature of an inspired *aperçu* into the nature of man or things, we need have no reason to conclude that he failed to recognize the importance of such attainments, or that his notions concerning literature were unsound. Holmes himself knew that the genuine artist is always in a sense a seer. He also knew that the bardic gift had been denied him. (pp. xli-xlii)

The main trouble with all three of [Holmes's] "medicated" novels is that the avowed purpose is always sacrificed in order to make a good-natured concession to the reader's supposed desire for a happy ending. The problem of moral responsibility, especially when treated in order to enlist the reader's sympathy for those unfortunates who sin or err through no fault of their own, should be a tragic and not a sentimental theme. Holmes's failure in these novels is that he arouses neither terror nor pity, nor even a strong sense of the pathetic. In *Elsie Venner,* the strongest of the three, there are moments of power, as when Elsie flattens her forehead in anger and fixes her cold, snake-like eyes on an enemy, or stares down a real rattlesnake in the mountains so that it crawls off abashed. But in the course of the novel, which has striking melodramatic possibilities, she leads a singularly blameless life, and dies conveniently before she has done any harm. The moral of the story, therefore, misses fire. The weight of his moral argument is carried, however, not by the story, but by the long, discursive conversations between the physician, Dr. Kittredge, and the Calvinist clergyman, the Reverend Dr. Honeywood. But these conversations (and the similar devices which carry the argument in the other two novels) show such skill in the presentation of his point of view that it is easy to forget the defects of the novel as a novel. Naturally, however, a point of view that can be presented in such a form as he uses—that is, permitting the opposition to present its opinions and drawing the opposing views closer by tact and ingenuity—is not an uncompromising one. Regarding himself as a devout Christian, Holmes is able to keep what he values in Calvinism at the same time that he propounds his anti-Calvinistic doctrines.

The boundaries to Holmes's determinism are set not simply by a reluctance to carry out a theory to its logical end, but by his sense that an attempt to establish complete determinism would require his going too far beyond the knowledge then available to medical science. . . . Although emphatically asserting that people who enjoy moral health have freedom of the will, he shows by many case studies that there is a class of unfortunates (as Holmes said, "out of health, morally") who have no freedom, being so unhappily situated or physiologically ill-constructed, that they must undergo some kind of *"traitement morale palliatif et curatif"* before they can overcome their deficiencies and achieve moral freedom.

What then was the realm in which Holmes believed that man could be morally "free"? Despine solved the problem sufficiently for his own purposes by saying that anyone who was conscious of making a moral choice was free. Holmes accepted this position in **"Crime and Automatism,"** but elsewhere he shows that as a determinist he is a great deal farther advanced than Despine, in that he saw how much of the action of perfectly normal human beings is governed not by moral choice but by mechanical principles. His essay *Mechanism in Thought and Morals* . . . , which represents his farthest advance in deterministic thought, reveals an intimate acquaintance with the medical knowledge then available on the relations between thought and physiological chemistry, between thought and anatomical structure; in fact, he foreshadows accurately the direction which physiology, experimental psychology, and neurological anatomy were to take in ensuing years. He shows no religious or superstitious fear of investigation in this direction—in fact, in **"Crime and Automatism"** he goes so far as to say that an illusory belief in the power of self-determination is sufficient for practical moral purposes—but he nevertheless maintained that "we do not find Hamlet and Faust, right and wrong, the valor of men and the purity of women, by testing for albumen, or examining fibres in microscopes." If, of course, these "spiritual" attainments of man are not to be found in the material conditions where they have their birth, where are they to be sought? This is a question never quite answered by Holmes, so that the complaints about the ambiguity of his position made by some of his contemporaries were not without justification. (pp. l-liii)

Science . . . is conceived humanistically in Holmes—that is, it is regarded as a part of, and not an enemy of, humane knowledge. . . . Perhaps his own triumph in the puerperal-fever controversy served to enliven his interest in the struggles others had in getting their views accepted. At any rate, he took the side of science in every controversy against popular prejudice or theological opposition. This is not to say that Holmes was contumacious. He devoted little space to the great Darwinian controversy: his conclusions about Darwinism are succinctly summarized in *The Professor at the Breakfast-Table* . . . , and in *The Poet at the Breakfast-Table* . . . the matter is touched upon again, but in no argumentative way. By the time Holmes got to writing about Darwin at all, the controversy was, to him, settled and won, and he accepted Darwinism complacently. The effect of Darwinism on his philosophy was that of reinforcing views arrived at earlier, such as his conviction that "Nature" is a "true divine manifestation," and that "development upward is the general law of the race." The basic optimism upon which such an attitude is founded is general throughout his work, and is even hinted at as early as 1831 in the juvenile **"Autocrat of the Breakfast-Table"** papers published in Buckingham's *New England Magazine*.

Holmes was fortunate in that the faith he put in science was one which the many great scientific discoveries of his time kept constantly alive and fresh. Science was proceeding triumphantly towards a better understanding of man and his universe; there was a beneficent order in nature which Divine Providence had provided; the Calvinist bogeys of hell-fire and torment had

been driven out of all but the more backward intellectual communities. America, the cradle of freedom, was reaching higher and higher levels of humane and scientific achievement, and his beloved city of Boston was contributing more than her share to the nation's glory in every line of laudable activity. The vulgarities of America, such as the daughters of the *nouveaux riches* satirized in **Elsie Venner,** and literary insurgents like Whitman, were the temporary aberrations of a growing civilization, and could be regarded humorously. It was a pleasant and hopeful world that Holmes inhabited. (pp. lvi-lviii)

[So] far as his familiar verse is concerned, Holmes appears to have been always in his prime. There was a period prior to 1831 in which he stumbled around for certainty of expression. Then from **"The Last Leaf"** to **"The Broomstick Train,"** that is to say, for a period of almost sixty years, his talents did not abate, but enabled him to turn out, in a great quantity though intermittently, familiar verse of high finish and perfection. (p. lxxxvi)

Holmes is . . . the best familiar verse writer in classic American letters, and the first American to devote himself to any great extent to this type of art. His only predecessor in this is Irving, who, however, produced only a little, and that at rare intervals. His successors, on the other hand, have maintained a strong tradition of familiar verse in America—so strong, indeed, that it seems almost to be the only American literary tradition that has a reasonable continuity, unaffected by fads and movements and social convulsions, to the present day. (pp. lxxxvii-lxxxviii)

The bulk of Oliver Wendell Holmes's [occasional] poetry, because it celebrates such fugitive events, is destined to be forgotten. It already has few readers left. But since it is a rare example of its kind in American literature, it deserves at least a kindly and sympathetic farewell before it fades into complete oblivion. (p. xc)

Perhaps nothing contributed so much to the charm of Holmes's occasional verses as his childlike and happy acceptance of the pleasures of society and the admiration and love of his friends. . . . Slight as the themes of many of these verses are, and easy as are their sentiments, it does not appear that he ever contented himself with a slovenly or hasty piece of work. (pp. xciv-xcv)

It goes almost without saying that the qualities which made Holmes an excellent occasional poet make his serious poetry unsatisfying. . . . The triteness of sentiment that makes his verses appropriate to occasions makes his serious lyrics commonplace and undistinguished. For certain shades of delicate pathos, as in **"Under the Violets,"** Holmes was capable of tender and appropriate expression, the competence and sincerity of which no one would question; but this poem is far from being great poetry, although it is one of his best. Its most striking fault to a reader today is its diffuseness. (pp. xcv-xcvi)

Amid all the third-rate prettiness that is to be found in the collected edition of Holmes's works, there are a few poems, however, that stand out as distinctly better than the rest. **"The Voiceless,"** though by no means a great poem, is not thirdrate. In it Holmes celebrates the pathos of those who have deep emotions but cannot express them.

On this subject of poetic inarticulateness, Holmes always manages to be genuinely tender and sympathetic, as the poem **"To the Poets Who Only Read and Listen"** further indicates. A deep sense of the mediocrity of his own verses and a fear that his poetic reputation was transitory made Holmes increasingly uneasy as he grew older. (p. xcviii)

Holmes was himself, in a sense, one of these inarticulate poets with whom he sympathized—he wrote enough, but had expressed few sentiments that rose from the depths of his being. It is not without significance that much of his better work, such as "Musa" . . . , expresses sympathy with inarticulateness.

"**The Chambered Nautilus**" is a real exception among Holmes's poems. We can readily believe what he has said about the feeling of exaltation he experienced when writing it. Short as it is, it states his most profound beliefs, his humanistic, non-religious, ethical idealism. (p. xcix)

With his amazing aptitude for daring similes that are the spice of his prose, with his quick intellectual curiosity, with his love of analysis which the romantic fashions of poetry in his time rarely permitted him to indulge except in prose, there seems to be more than a possibility that Holmes's poetic gifts might have flourished more richly had he lived in a time when metaphysical poetry was popular. Although not as complex in its intellectual convolutions as metaphysical poetry usually is, "**The Chambered Nautilus**" is an excellent example of the typically metaphysical "conceit" worked out with complete sureness of taste and judgment. (p. c)

Holmes's temper, capable of no sustained passion, but readily moved to quick bursts of tenderness, humor, sympathy, and raillery—his mind, erudite in many odd ways but pedantic in none—found complete expression in the new kind of essay form he evolved [in *The Autocrat of the Breakfast-Table*]. He was a brilliant conversationalist, and was not unconscious of his powers. Like every conversationalist, he probably had wished at one time or another for a Boswell to record his best remarks. (p. ci)

Now, no less than when they first appeared, it is the element of surprise . . . that constitutes the greatest charm of Holmes's papers in *The Autocrat,* in its sequels, *The Professor at the Breakfast-Table* . . . , *The Poet at the Breakfast-Table* . . . , and even in the more subdued product of his old age, *Over the Teacups.* . . . This element of surprise is due, first of all, to his close and reflective observation of even the most trivial matters with a view to discovering their larger implications. . . . (p. cii)

A second source of this surprise is his lively erudition, which he uses with startling ingenuity for purposes of metaphor, simile, and illustrative analogy. . . . His scientific knowledge is wide and deep, but the vast number of little things he knows about life—the speech habits of various classes of people, the peculiarities of men in various occupations, the records of racing-horses, the mannerisms of men and women in every kind of social situation—his sum of general knowledge is so great that it is in itself a kind of erudition. And all this varied information is not a dead mass of facts, but it is like a myriad of flying atoms in an electrical tube, ready to light up at the slightest current of thought the obscurest corners of human experience. His figures of speech are drawn from every imaginable source, chemical, anatomical, commercial, social, natural, pugilistical, nautical, "reportorial" or "newspaporial" (as he called it), historical, and physiological. (p. ciii)

A third reason for the element of surprise in Holmes's writings is the unconventionality of his thought. He was fond of paradoxes, not of the perverse kind such as Wilde and Shaw and Noel Coward delight in, but of the kind which owe their paradoxical character to the fact that they are startling to conventionality while being undeniably true. (p. civ)

The fourth reason for the surprise is Holmes's extraordinary ability to change his moods swiftly, even suddenly and abruptly, without destroying his design, or producing in the reader any sense of a lack of connection. . . . As everybody who has tried must know, to execute gracefully such swift changes of mood requires real technical virtuosity in the prose writer. (p. cv)

For litheness, for richness, for zest, for occasional blunt speaking, and above all, for adaptability, Holmes's style is perhaps without equal in American literature. Emerson has written a loftier prose; Lowell, a capricious, more analytical one. Melville, in spite of bad lapses, has epic qualities, and Hawthorne, magic—both beyond Holmes's reach. None of these, however, has a prose so various in its powers. Holmes's style is the best example that can be found in American letters of the lucidity, brilliance, ease, and flexible accuracy which we are accustomed to regard as the crowning ornaments of French prose. (p. cvii)

The conversations of [*The Autocrat* and its sequels] are united by a tiny filament of narrative. While Holmes was by no means alone in introducing narrative into the essay, he has approached a good deal closer to the novel than other essayists, especially by bringing events to a mildly dramatic close at the end of each series: the marriage of the Autocrat; the death of the Little Gentleman and the marriages of Iris and "the young fellow called John" in *The Professor;* the breaking up of the boardinghouse and the happy settlement of all the residents in *The Poet.* Charming as the narrative element is, however, these works are not novels, because the principal interest lies not in actions, not in the discussion of actions, but in opinions. The characters are not there for their own sake, but to provide the varieties of points of view that are necessary to conversation, and to create openings so that the Autocrat (Professor, Poet) may make his pronouncements. (p. cviii)

How perfectly this breakfast-table form suited Holmes's talents is indicated not only by his success with it, but by the fact that even when he tries to leave it temporarily, he unconsciously turns back to it. *Elsie Venner* and *The Guardian Angel,* while they cannot be taken seriously as triumphs of the novelist's art, are redeemed from artistic disgrace by their excellence as essays. In *Elsie Venner,* some of the most interesting passages are provided by Dr. Honeywood and Dr. Kittredge, who, sharing the function of the Autocrat between them, comment in conversation on the events; furthermore, such conversational episodes as Widow Rowen's tea party are the high points of the book. (Holmes never writes with so much gusto as when describing a social event: preparations for a party, the making out of invitation lists, the gathering of the guests, the surreptitious examination by guests of the quality of the silverware, etc.) *The Guardian Angel* is even more reminiscent of the Breakfast-Table series. Byles Gridley, Esq., is Holmes's own flattering self-portrait, and all the events revolve around him just as they do around the Autocrat in the essays. These two novels are not without their claims to an honorable mention in the history of American fiction—first, for their accurate observation of New England manners, speech, and scenery, which entitles them to a distinguished place in our regionalist literature; secondly, for their contribution to the development of the novel of purpose in America. If they are rarely given the credit due them, it is because their conspicuous excellences are those of the essayist, rather than of the novelist. It is more than a coincidence that the book least reminiscent of the Breakfast-Table series, *A Mortal Antipathy,* is his least successful work. (pp. cx-cxi)

The only fault that can be found with his method is that the concessions to the intellectual infirmities of the backward, the prejudiced, and the uninformed which his form so admirably enables him to make, are sometimes a trifle humiliating to a modern reader, whose backwardness, prejudice, and ignorance lie in other directions. (In making this objection, however, we should only be complaining of a trait in Holmes that at all other times we find delightful—his profound courteousness.) With a personality such as Holmes had—sentimental, excessively sociable, incapable of vehemence except in matters strictly relating to his profession, so even-tempered that he missed both the great heights and the great depths—it is perhaps to be wondered at that he became an artist at all. But in finding the perfect medium for imparting his attitude towards life, Holmes, without genius, or even an artistic temperament (if that is a help), succeeded in becoming a genuine artist. He established his own rules, evolved his own form. No one else can hope to do anything with the form he created, so peculiarly adapted is it to his own individuality. But he has form, and he has substance, and a perfect reconciliation of the one with the other. There are greater artists and greater men of whom this cannot be said. (p. cxi)

Holmes's main shortcomings—the narrowness of his universe, his blindness . . . to the heterogeneous America that was growing up around him—make some of his views seem hopelessly limited and provincial. Few poets have lived who have had so much faith in the better things of the society they lived in. (p. cxii)

But his optimism is by no means a sad commentary on the quality of his mind, as our more disillusioned contemporaries have hastened to conclude. It is merely the expression of Holmes's temperament: the childlike simplicity of a candid heart, which believes eternally (if it can be said without superciliousness or disrespect) in Santa Claus. His age was not without its skepticisms, but he escaped them or solved them. All the industrial vandalism of the post-Civil-War period disturbed him, . . . but he serenely continued on his way, believing in the "tolerable certainty of human averages," which was empirical evidence of the benevolence of God. Had he less charm, we might well be tempted to dismiss him . . . for what we cannot help regarding as his naïveté. But we cannot, because he is one of the most winsome characters in literary history. It is impossible not to be impressed by the richness of his humane and scientific culture, and by the minuteness and sensitivity of his social perceptions. It is impossible, too, to resist the appeal of his central intellectual principle: "I don't want you to believe anything I say; I only want you to see what makes me believe it." (pp. cxii-cxiii)

> *S. I. Hayakawa and Howard Mumford Jones, "Oliver Wendell Holmes," in* Oliver Wendell Holmes: Representative Selections *by Oliver Wendell Holmes, edited by S. I. Hayakawa and Howard Mumford Jones, American Book Company, 1939, pp. ix-cxiii.*

CLARENCE P. OBERNDORF   (essay date 1943)

[*Oberndorf, a professor of clinical psychiatry, analyzes Holmes's "medicated novels," emphasizing that the author's thinking was dominated by his training in medicine.*]

[Holmes's *Elsie Venner, The Guardian Angel,* and *A Mortal Antipathy*] present essentially in fictional form complex psychiatric situations made more vivid by backgrounds reflecting the standards, customs, and ideology of the last half of the

An illustration of the heroine from Elsie Venner.

nineteenth century. The family relationships portrayed not only helped to produce the neurotic manifestations but at the same time kept them alive. (p. v)

It is small wonder that the novels of Holmes, especially *The Guardian Angel* and *A Mortal Antipathy,* found little acclaim when they appeared. The average reader discovered in their melodramatic qualities the commonplaces of the second-rate fiction writers of the period—very likely he skipped over the heavier philosophical and psychological paragraphs. If these passages received any of his attention they must have appeared as technical and uninteresting as clinical case reports. Many portions of Holmes's stories make dull reading, with their wordy, stereotyped and old-fashioned dialogue and the repetition of certain character types almost unchanged in each of the novels. To add to the monotony, in each story Holmes has followed a similar plan of treatment and resorted to well-worn models for the introduction of the setting and the erection of the plots.

Nevertheless these dated novels seemed of sufficient importance as psychiatric and analytic studies of neuroses to warrant their re-presentation to sociologists and physicians. (pp. v-vi)

• • • • •

Holmes, for all his preferential social background and academic training, could not escape in his home and in his subsequent contacts the impact of repressive environmental influences. Holmes's father was a Calvinist minister; from all account, an exceptionally genial Calvinist. Nevertheless he believed firmly in predestination and preordination. Holmes's reaction to the fatalist religious principles of his father was in an escape, an eminently respectable escape, into science and scholarship. A horror of the depressing damnation theology of his childhood aroused in Holmes a bitter antipathy and lifelong rebellion against its crippling influences and manifestations.

The drive to counteract and correct the hopeless Calvinist philosophy appears time and again in his essays and in his three novels written late in life. A contemporary critic dubbed them "medicated novels." The term is appropriate, for in each the main character presents a psychiatric problem and is under the care of a doctor of skill and experience, who serves as an interpreter of the sickness.

Of course Holmes would not have regarded himself as a psychiatrist because this specialty was not to develop as an extramural practice for another fifty years. The most advanced psychiatrists of his day were concerned almost exclusively with the abolition of forcible restraint and punishment of the insane and the introduction of more humane attitudes and methods in custodial asylums. Even the problems of psychiatric classification and prognosis, which so engrossed the attention and encouraged the debating skill of psychiatrists from approximately 1885 to 1910, had been barely broached. Nevertheless, those tense psychiatric situations which destroy individuals, disrupt families, and disturb social groups were quite as prevalent then as today, and the physician was increasingly displacing the pastor in these cases as the counselor and authority.

To be a truly great physician in any but a purely technical specialty, or even a successful one, the medical practitioner must possess what are sometimes called "intuitive" gifts as a psychiatrist. This quality depends upon his experience as a clinician supplemented by his sympathy and consideration for people whose minds and bodies are distorted by physical pain or disappointments in life. The social import of these psychiatric situations impressed Holmes to such a degree that he assumed the same fighting radicalism in regard to their recognition and treatment as he had toward the control of the contagiousness of childbed fever, the value of scientific dentistry, the folly of overmedication, and the fallacies of homeopathy.

Holmes tried his talents in poetry, essays, and fiction but he continued first, last, and forever, the physician, his thinking dominated by his medical training and his daily scientific work. He was also a theological reformer, a philosopher, and, as indicated above, according to the present concept of this specialty, a psychiatrist many of whose ideas fell in line with the most advanced of this present day. In certain essentials Holmes's theory and philosophy of approach to psychological problems is prophetic of psychoanalysis and anticipated Freud's formulations and the psychoanalytic psychiatry which grew out of it. (pp. 4-7)

* * * * *

Holmes wrote his earlier psychiatric novels with the direct purpose of demonstrating that there is no inherited guilt. In the *Mechanism in Thought and Morals,* he has much to say on processes which might account for personal guilt. He expounds his ideas clearly, forcefully, and unequivocally. The object of his thesis is now never in doubt—namely, that such a thing as absolute freedom of the will cannot exist because of uncon-

scious processes which are affecting the individual's conscious activity all the time. If for this reason alone, Holmes affirms that we must regard with charity and understanding many deviations in conduct which are asocial and antisocial. He says: "Do we ever think without knowing that we are thinking? The question may be disguised so as to look a little less paradoxical: Are there any mental processes of which we are unconscious at the time, but which we recognize as having taken place by finding certain results in our minds?" (pp. 8-9)

All the reflections in *Mechanism in Thought and Morals* constitute a recapitulation of thoughts which Holmes had confirmed in psychopathological conditions during his career as a practicing and consulting physician. But Holmes did not put them in the form of a medical essay. He may have felt that his medical colleagues would be unreceptive and antagonistic, and probably was smarter than he knew. At all events here again he was prophetic of Freud, whose original presentations before the Vienna Medical Society met with a humiliating reception. (p. 13)

Holmes at the time his novels appeared was a professor of anatomy, a subject of dry bones and dead bodies, and as an anatomist his opinions on psychiatric disorders would not have been considered important to the practicing physicians and psychiatrists. He therefore deliberately and probably shrewdly chose narrative as a medium through which to bring his views before the public. His three stories are poor fiction when judged by modern criteria or compared with the masters of his time— Poe, Thackeray, Balzac, or even Hawthorne of his own literary group. . . . Their plots are simple, almost juvenile and, in two of them, the reader is not disappointed in the customary thwarting of the villain and the coming of true love to its own.

Although *Elsie Venner* enjoyed something of a popular success, literary critics dealt none too kindly with this or with Holmes's subsequent psychological works of fiction that were "tainted with the physiological." Surely Holmes, far more sensitive concerning his literary reputation both as a poet and novelist than about his clinical ability, would not have been pleased that these studies of abnormal characters should be regarded as case histories. In the light of the development of modern psychiatry they remain as testimony to his medical acuity, his knowledge, and his profound psychiatric understanding.

There can be slight doubt that the doctors who play such a prominent role in these social dramas and employ a similar technique in handling them are none other than a composite picture of Holmes himself. There also should be included in this class the crusty, warm-hearted, old Professor Byles Gridley who plays the part of amateur detective in *Guardian Angel.*

If one were to translate into psychoanalytic parlance the receptive and understanding method of these doctors with their patients it would follow the lines of the "passive technique" generally preferred in psychoanalytic practice today. Certainly it was defiantly at variance with the bad-tasting drug therapy of the time for the treatment of hysteria and other nervous symptoms.

In terms of professional conduct, the doctors' approach combines those qualities so desirable in every physician but indispensable in a psychiatrist—namely, patience, forbearance, tolerance, equanimity, accurate observation of the patient's actions and utterances, and unremitting consideration for the patient's psychological and environmental handicaps.

These psychiatric and psychoanalytic principles were not merely philosophical musing with Holmes. They rested upon clinical orientation and, because of this fact, his observations have a directness, reality, and cogency which other novelists have been able to portray with greater vividness and emotional appeal. A dozen years intervened between the writing of *Elsie Venner* . . . and *Mechanism in Thought and Morals*. During that time Holmes had gathered together his ideas and beliefs supporting the doctrine of limited responsibility and had developed for the treatment of mental disorders principles of theory and practice which are considered modern today.

Holmes saw with unusual clearness the far-reaching effects of mental disorder in the home and in intrafamilial relationships, especially the power of such disorders to restrict and distort the lives of the well—this was the effect of Elsie Venner's illness upon her father, and of the psychically determined invalidism of Mrs. Stoker, the minister's wife, upon her young daughter in *The Guardian Angel*.

Novels must have the element of love. This is not lacking in Holmes's stories. Here it takes the form not of violent, passionate or sensuous love, but of spiritual love, with its vital influence as an agency in molding character and establishing emotional balance. In *Elsie Venner* the love affect had been immobilized and became blocked; in *The Guardian Angel* Myrtle Hazard's capacity to love had been turned into resentment and rebellion; in *A Mortal Antipathy* Maurice Kirkwood's normal tendencies had been held in check by a morbid fear of young women.

All of these characters have one quality in common—they lost their mothers before the age of two, and during infancy and childhood had mother substitutes who were deficient in one way or another. From certain aspects the emotional disorder of each may be regarded as a reaction to a lack of love and to frustration in their unconscious search for the missing parent. Elsie Venner made an awkward attempt to free herself by falling in love but was unsuccessful and the rebuff and denial made her die. In *The Guardian Angel* and *A Mortal Antipathy* the principal characters achieve love through a symbolic rebirth (rescue from death by a person of the opposite sex who is an appropriate partner for marriage).

In *Elsie Venner* the circumstance that her mother was bitten by a snake during pregnancy is held responsible for the reptilian traits which Elsie showed. This is not psychoanalytic thinking. Yet few would dispute that the case is interpreted with the insight of analytic psychiatry. Moreover, the interesting question of the influence of very early, even antenatal, damage on later anxiety has recently been reëxamined in the light of observations made during the psychoanalysis of patients.

The second novel, *The Guardian Angel,* is a study of hereditary influences on the mind of one individual and on the development of hysterical symptoms. Written during the mellowness of Holmes's advancing years it is a final and unsparing thrust at meddling by the clergy in situations where emotional disturbance is threatening the very existence of the patient.

Holmes maintains that "this body in which we journey across the isthmus between the oceans is not a private carriage but an omnibus." In Myrtle Hazard of *The Guardian Angel*, the traits and experiences of antecedents reappear and produce strange and unaccountable actions (hysteria), seemingly belonging to the personalities of several ancestors. An analogous concept has received wide attention under the term "collective unconscious," as used by the Swiss psychiatrist, Carl Jung,

at one time closely associated with Freud. However, in the collective (archaic) unconscious as conceived by Jung, integral figures of remote ancestors as described in Myrtle Hazard are not generally presumed to exist.

The final novel, *A Mortal Antipathy,* is the study, by a fine psychiatrist, of a compulsion type of morbid fear. The preface, like the prefaces of the two previous novels, defends the validity of the actual framework of the story from a medical standpoint. In it Holmes approaches more significantly the psychoanalytic position of Freud—namely, that a personal shock or trauma in very early infancy may cause a conditioning which the individual sometimes does not outgrow.

The theory of bisexuality and the importance of bisexual components in influencing the characters of the individuals is more than implied in the description of each one of the abnormal personalities. The masculine traits in childhood of both Elsie Venner, the man-hater, and Myrtle Hazard, something of a tomboy, are unmistakable. The bisexual theme becomes even clearer in *A Mortal Antipathy,* when Holmes repeatedly contrasts the femininity of Euthymia Tower with the masculinity of Lurida Vincent—and it is apparent that he has little sympathy with the latter. The illness of Myrtle Hazard is typical of the hysterias described by Charcot, but which are not so often seen today.

The theme of determinism with its variations—whether antenatal, directly inherited, or psychic—is repeated in all the novels. It seems as though Holmes may have been under a compulsion to write off his father's Calvinism and predestination, but never quite succeeded. As he advanced in years, the determinism, as in *A Mortal Antipathy,* assumed individualistic and personal aspects—conditions which fitted a type of causation more in harmony with scientific criteria. But it is not my intention here to interpret these novels psychoanalytically as a reflection of any personal unconscious conflicts which their author may have had. Certainly, whatever these conflicts were and however deep they may have been, they were transformed into the highest type of human productivity and helpful coöperation.

The harsh New England predestinistic morality produced many a dismal domestic drama like those so effectively portrayed by Hawthorne in *The House of the Seven Gables* and by Edith Wharton in *Ethan Frome*. The mystifying physiological manifestations of self-denial and self-restraint Holmes grasped at the bedside. This repressive cultural attitude lingered on after his death. But the scientific spirit continued to grow great and strong in Cambridge and Boston. (pp. 13-18)

One wonders why Holmes's ideas did not receive greater attention when they were written. Probably society at large was far less prepared to entertain them in 1870 than it was to accept Freud reluctantly in 1910. But this does not explain why Holmes's theories were not more critically tested by two truly distinguished scientists of the Boston group who immediately followed him—William James, the philosopher, and Morton Prince, the psychiatrist. This is especially true of Prince, whose work on multiple personality is his outstanding contribution to psychiatry.

Psychiatry had remained in the sterile stage of description and classification. The social significance of mental deviation, so stressed by Holmes, had not been grasped by science or society. Neither James nor Prince could give heed to dynamism of thought or appreciate its correlation to the masterly clinical descriptions sketched by Holmes. . . . (p. 19)

Clarence P. Oberndorf, "Foreword" and "Introduction: Dynamic Psychiatry and Holmes," in The Psychiatric Novels of Oliver Wendell Holmes *by Oliver Wendell Holmes, edited by Clarence P. Oberndorf, Columbia University Press, 1943, pp. v-viii, 1-19.*

CHARLES BOEWE (essay date 1954)

[*Boewe examines Holmes's use of the theory of reflex action in* Elsie Venner, The Guardian Angel, *and* A Mortal Antipathy.]

The nimbus of science that surrounds the three novels of Oliver Wendell Holmes has often been found to be more impressive than their literary merit. William Dean Howells recalled that "a faint, faint odor of the pharmacopoeia clung to their pages; their magic was scientific," and more recent commentators have pointed out that much of their power of persuasion owes something to science. Holmes's own statement that *Elsie Venner* is intended to attack Calvinism—that the "real aim of the story was to test the doctrine of 'original sin' and human responsibility for the disordered volition coming under that technical denomination" [see excerpt dated 1883]—has tended too often to throw the emphasis in discussions of the novels wholly toward theological concerns, slighting the science that provides the foundation for their arguments. To the extent that all three are concerned with disordered volition, all are attacks on Calvinism. Each is a study of a different kind of limitation of the will, and all aim to persuade the reader that rational people cannot hold others accountable for acts over which they have no control.

Even in his own time Holmes seemed to some of his readers to be flaying dead horses; surely today the theological issue of the novels is less arresting than the scientific element, especially when it is seen how advanced the science really was. That there is a single scientific theory underlying all three books and that Holmes made bold speculative use of this theory has not been generally recognized. It is my intention to show here that they have a common indebtedness to the physiological theory of reflex action, and that awareness of this debt can give us an added respect for Holmes's excursions into fiction.

Holmes's Phi Beta Kappa address, *Mechanism in Thought and Morals,* which was delivered almost at the mid-point of his career as professor of anatomy, is "a brilliant anticipation of Dr. Freud," says Van Wyck Brooks [see excerpt dated 1936]. Indeed, in that essay Holmes does recognize the existence of a kind of unconscious mental action, automatic and beyond the control of the will, when he asks, "What happens when one idea brings up another? Some internal movement, of which we are wholly unconscious, and which we only know by its effect." Ten years earlier, in *The Professor at the Breakfast-Table* . . . , he had also alluded to a sensation we all have experienced: "that a deep layer of thought sometimes makes itself felt through the superincumbent strata. . . ." However, the unconscious mental actions which he noted seemed to him to be nothing new or astonishing—"that there are such," he said, "is laid down in the strongest terms by Leibnitz, whose doctrine reverses the axiom of Descartes into *sum, ergo cogito.*" While we may acknowledge that Holmes anticipated Freud in the recognition of the unconscious, still we cannot say that his psychology was Freudian. As is so often true, Holmes himself provides the best terminology. In 1874, in his essay **"Crime and Automatism,"** he said that the prison reforms which he advocated—"these newer modes of thought," as he called them—"are to a large extent outgrowths of what we

may call physiological psychology." "Physiological" is the correct qualifier for his psychology. He clearly saw that "the foundations of this [science] were laid in those studies of individual character made by the phrenologists, much in the same way that the foundations of chemistry were laid by the alchemists." This is the psychology which supports the plots of Holmes's three novels, a physiological psychology based on the concept of mechanical reflex action.

Holmes was primarily indebted for his theory of reflex action to the experiments of the English physician and physiologist Marshall Hall . . . , though it had been at least partly implied in the theory of mechanical animal action of Descartes and in David Hartley's psychology of association. (pp. 303-05)

As Holmes was to describe it, reflex action is "the mechanical sympathy . . . of distant parts. . . ." Surely what made the discovery attractive to Holmes was that Hall "furnished the basis for that conception of the reflex as a neural arc which functions independently of the brain. . . ." Thus Holmes learned that the cause for action may sidestep the brain, and consequently sidestep volition; here was scientific justification for his cherished belief that man's free will is no freer than a drop of water imprisoned in a crystal: "One little fluid particle in the crystalline prism of the solid universe!" (p. 306)

The study of reflex function in its higher sphere of course is its application to morality. But, one asks, did Holmes think morality depends upon nothing more than the well-oiled automatic functioning of the mechanisms Marshall Hall had called reflex arcs? Holmes was not prepared to say. Though he was one of America's first serious microscopists, the study of microscopic neuroanatomy, which would one day show the actual neural arcs, was still in its infancy. He had only Hall's theory to go on, a theory which satisfactorily explained certain experimental data that had been collected about the behavior of mutilated turtles and hedgehogs, a theory which he confidently assumed should apply equally to human beings—one which fitted nicely with his preconceived idea of free will. The study of reflex action seemed to him to offer a fruitful method in the exploration of human behavior, but he realized how much remained to be done. In *Elsie Venner,* the Professor, like the Autocrat, Holmes's thinly disguised self, says that "the limitations of human responsibility have never been properly studied. . . ." Marshall Hall had shown how that sort of study could be conducted by means of relatively simple physiological experiments in the realm of animal life; it remained for someone else to do a similar thing for man, in the much more complicated regions of psychology. Such a study would give morality a scientific footing. "Automatic action in the moral world," the Professor muses, "the *reflex movement* which *seems* to be self-determination, and has been hanged and howled at as such (metaphorically) for nobody knows how many centuries: until somebody shall study this as Marshall Hall has studied reflex nervous action in the bodily system, I would not give much for men's judgments of each others' characters." Meanwhile he could speculate, and the speculation could be safely expressed in novels, which no one supposed to be true anyway.

Holmes suggests, then, that his first two novels, *Elsie Venner* . . . and *The Guardian Angel,* . . . may be considered studies of reflex action in the sphere of morality. The third, *A Mortal Antipathy* . . . , is even more concerned with reflex action. The method of his studies, however, is less demonstration than persuasion.

Hence it is that the characters of his protagonists in all three novels are drawn to make the reader as sympathetic with them as possible. Elsie Venner in the novel which bears her name, Myrtle Hazard in *The Guardian Angel,* and Maurice Kirkwood in *A Mortal Antipathy* all had lost their mothers before the age of two. All are withdrawn from society. All are strange people whom society, though it tolerates them, is unwilling to accept without reservations; and, to hammer home the point of each story more convincingly, all are provided with limitations unlikely to be met with in the ordinary drawing room. Since their moral actions have not been explained by a Marshall Hall, how can anyone judge them harshly? Or more particularly, how can anyone judge a normal person harshly?

The important element of *Elsie Venner* is the prearranged restriction of Elsie's will. Her personality illustrates the theory of reflex action, as Holmes understood it, on its most physiological level. Since the "reflex movement which seems to be self-determination" operates in all of us, Holmes was able, by providing Elsie with a special physiological constitution, to contrast her unique reflexes with the normal. Elsie's mother had been bitten by a rattlesnake while her daughter was *in utero,* the rattlesnake poison causing the child to be part snake and part girl. It makes little difference whether or not Holmes believed in such prenatal conditioning; he said in the preface to the novel that he used "this doctrine as a part of the machinery . . . without pledging his absolute belief in it to the extent to which it is asserted or implied." But having committed himself to such a proposition, he did determine to have his account of Elsie as scientifically probable as he could. He kept a live rattlesnake in a glass jar to study its habits while he was writing the novel, and, as he always followed the reports of his fellow Boston physicians, he may have remembered reading an article on "A Case of Destitution of the Moral Feelings" which described a person who had snakelike characteristics.

Elsie is depicted quite convincingly in terms of a snake: she has a sinuous neck and diamond-shaped eyes; her clothing suggests snakelike qualities; she has compulsions to writhe in orgiastic dances, even her ordinary walk is slithering; she experiences torpor in the winter; her unblinking eyes have a hypnotic ability; and she is literally cold-blooded. She does not suffer from the delusion that she is part snake; she actually *is* part snake. She becomes ill when the rattlesnake side of her nature suppresses the human, and she dies when the natural term of the snake's existence is done.

Elsie's story is a study of the will limited by chemical agents. It becomes apparent as the novel unfolds that she cannot be held responsible for behavior that depends upon venom introduced into her blood stream before her birth, though the mechanism of her reflexes is left unexplained—no Marshall Hall had yet studied reflex actions in the moral world. Yet, how Elsie's sad history disproves the doctrine of original sin is still a little confusing, for she cannot be said to sin at all, in the ordinary sense of the word. Her "sin" is her unconventional behavior. Holmes, always an optimist, assumes that people tend naturally toward goodness and that they tend naturally toward the conventional in social behavior; a deviation from goodness correlates with a deviation from correct behavior. If carefully reared young ladies do not customarily go about acting like serpents, when we find one like Elsie deviating from the normal we must explain her aberrations in terms of forces over which her will has no control. Likewise, we must explain deviations from the normal in moral behavior in similar terms. So, near the end of the novel, Holmes presents this challenge to his readers: "if, while the will lies sealed in its fountain, it

Myrtle Hazard reading about her ancestors in The Guardian Angel.

may be poisoned at its very source, so that it shall flow dark and deadly through its whole course, who are we that we should judge our fellow-creatures by ourselves?"

As an anatomist and poet, Holmes had no reluctance to celebrate the human body's magnificent mechanics:

> Look in upon thy wondrous frame,—
> Eternal wisdom still the same!

But as a physician called upon to treat the body's multitude of ills, he readily saw its shortcomings. He argued that as one has no right to expect to find a perfect body in this imperfect world, he has no right to expect to find a perfect moral nature. "'Sin,' or the failure of an imperfectly made and imperfectly guided being to keep a perfect law," he wrote to Harriet Beecher Stowe, "seems to me to be given in the mere statement of the conditions of humanity, and could not be a surprise or a disappointment to a Creator with reasoning powers no greater than those of a human being of ordinary wisdom."

In *The Guardian Angel* Holmes came closer to the higher sphere of reflex action which he claimed both it and *Elsie Venner* dealt with. No chemical agent controls Myrtle Hazard's will; rather, her destiny is determined by inherited traits from four female ancestors. The first of these is Ann Holyoake, a sixteenth-century martyr. The next, though we do not have Myrtle's genealogy complete, is Ruth Bradford, who was accused of sorcery during the New England witchcraft delusion. She is of less importance than the others. Then comes Judith Pride, a great beauty, who was Myrtle's great-grandmother. And last, Myrtle's grandmother, Virginia Wild, who was part Indian. All of these women exercise varying degrees of influence on the growing heroine of the novel, and these influences are made to illustrate the author's somewhat hesitantly put thesis: "It is by no means certain that our individual personality is the single inhabitant of these our corporeal frames." Of course it is by no means certain that we do share our corporeal frames with guests, and Holmes makes no great effort to contradict common sense; again he had chosen a biological hypothesis—and rather a wild one at that, suggested perhaps by Francis Galton's "composite portraits"—as part of the machinery of the novel, "without pledging his absolute belief in it." (pp. 307-11)

Myrtle is made to believe that sometimes the spirits of her departed ancestors take actual possession of her material body; at other times they merely guide her conduct. For the rationalist reader there is sufficient evidence in the story to explain her visions (in which the ancestors enter her body) entirely in terms of hysteria. Holmes never commits himself to anything that is scientifically disreputable; he skates carefully on the thin ice between the unlikely and the improbable, letting the reader choose his own interpretation. The author's concern, after all, is to persuade his reader to believe that reflex functions operate in the higher sphere—that is, that his heroine is not responsible for her actions; and the method he chooses to relieve her of responsibility is to have her subject to uncontrollable hereditary influences. Near the middle of the novel he stops his narrative to admonish that "the reader, if such there be, who believes in the absolute independence and self-determination of the will, and the consequent total responsibility of every human being for every irregular nervous action and ill-governed muscular contraction, may as well lay down this narrative, or he may lose all faith in poor Myrtle Hazard, and all patience with the writer who tells her story."

It may be that one begins to lose patience with a novelist who takes the simple twitching of a frog's hind leg, magnifies it to explain the abnormal twitching of a snake-girl, and then asks his readers to believe the baby inherited its grandmother's blue eyes according to the same principle. The fact is that once Holmes started using the reflex-action theory for fictional purposes his conception of it entirely outgrew the bounds of Marshall Hall's unpretentious discovery; by this time it stood for any kind of force beyond human control—for anything for which we cannot hold ourselves responsible. (pp. 312-13)

Holmes is not especially concerned with the manner in which characteristics are transmitted by heredity; he only demands freedom to explore the consequences of this kind of automatic action, even if his exploration takes him into dangerous territory. . . . (p. 313)

A Mortal Antipathy uses the theory more in the spirit of Marshall Hall's actual accomplishments than the others, and less as a catch-all for uncontrollable biological forces. It is Holmes's only attempt to use reflex action as the sole supporting framework of a novel, and it is the only place where he tries to give an explanation for the mechanism of the reflex involved. That the novel is an unsatisfactory artistic performance cannot be argued away; but as a serious attempt to utilize and extend the fringe of exact knowledge in a work of fiction, it deserves to be understood on its own terms.

Though the novel rambles like the *Autocrat,* essentially it is the story of Maurice Kirkwood, who has an antipathy to beau-

tiful young women because, as a baby, he was accidentally dropped into a thorn bush by his beautiful cousin Laura. (p. 314)

When he grows up, Maurice reads all he can about antipathies, and he comes to understand the nature of his malady. He writes an account of his life "for the instruction of others, and especially for the light it throws on certain peculiarities of human character often wrongly interpreted as due to moral perversion, when they are in reality the results of misdirected or reversed actions in some of the closely connected nervous centres." This autobiography, one notes, is written only to instruct others; it serves no cathartic function for the writer, for Holmes's psychology is still a physiological psychology—in no way does he anticipate the psychiatric couch.

In his autobiographical sketch, Maurice is given the use of the facts of reflex action as Holmes himself understood them; the explanation is reserved for the savants of the Royal Academy of the Biological Sciences, the speculation for Dr. Butts, Maurice's physician. Maurice, as a layman, is permitted to remark that:

> It is enough to say here, without entering into the explanation of the fact, which will be found simple enough as seen by the light of modern physiological science, that the "nervous disturbance" which the presence of a woman in the flower of her age produced in my system was *a sense of impending death,* sudden, overwhelming, unconquerable, appalling. It was a reversed action of the nervous centres,—the opposite of that which flushes the young lover's cheek and hurries his bounding pulses as he comes into the presence of the object of his passion.

In *A Mortal Antipathy,* Holmes wisely foresaw and correctly described the conditioned reflex in a human being; his description leaves little to be asked. It is only when he lets his speculation run unchecked that he goes farther than available knowledge warranted. . . . Maurice recovers from his antipathy when he is saved from a burning house by a young and beautiful woman, Euthymia Tower. "The change which had taken place in the vital currents of Maurice Kirkwood's system was as simple and solid a fact as the change in a magnetic needle when the boreal becomes the austral pole, and the austral the boreal." Too simple, in the light of what we now know about psychology, but wholly consistent with the terms of the problem as Holmes had set them up.

It is ironic that in his medicated novels Dr. Holmes could not sufficiently sugar-coat the medicine to make it palatable to his readers. Miss Tilton is surely right when she says of *Elsie Venner* that Holmes failed to make his characters more than academic illustrations, either from the point of view of aesthetics or physiology [see Additional Bibliography]. This failure is true of all the novels. Yet they have the distinction of being founded in common on a theory of behavior until then unexploited in fiction . . . and all are sincere pleas for sympathy with unfortunates whose bodily constitutions make them irresponsible for their acts. It is to be hoped that as interest in the relation between science and literature continues to grow, Holmes's novels will not be neglected. (pp. 318-19)

Charles Boewe, "Reflex Action in the Novels of Oliver Wendell Holmes," in American Literature, *Vol. 26, November, 1954, pp. 303-19.*

R. W. B. LEWIS   (essay date 1955)

[*Lewis, an American literary critic and historian of ideas, maintains that Holmes used his novels as vehicles for dramatizing his ideas about science and history.*]

"If for the Fall of man, science comes to substitute the Rise of man, sir, it means the utter disintegration of all the spiritual pessimisms which have been like a spasm in the heart and a cramp in the intellect of man for so many centuries." The operative word in that utterance of Oliver Wendell Holmes, with its Johnsonian stance and its thoroughly Holmesian metaphor, is "science." For Holmes was not merely echoing the current Unitarian resentment against orthodoxy's picture of fallen nature: he was advocating a new picture of man and indicating the sources of his evidence.

"Science" meant many things, but in the ethical discussion it meant primarily the pre-Darwinian evolutionary hypothesis of Lamarck, a hypothesis about the steady development of the human species which happily coincided with and could be taken as a kind of proof of the contemporary high estimate of human nature. Holmes took the Lamarckian theory as the basis for his best-known (though not at all his most attractive) poem, **"The Chambered Nautilus"** . . . , in which the soul is compared to the shellfish and enjoined, like it, to build itself ever more stately mansions, "each new temple nobler than the last."

What science was replacing, according to Holmes, was a view of life ordered by the moralism of a desiccated Calvinist theology. He saw orthodoxy as embodying a set of beliefs and precepts inherited from a remote Asiatic epoch: tradition in its most paralyzing form. "Our dwellings are built on shell-heaps," he said; "the kitchen-midden of the age of stone. Inherited beliefs, as obscure in their origin as the parentage of the cave-dwellers, are stronger with many minds than the evidence of the senses and the simplest deductions of the intelligence." Holmes bent his energies to removing ancient ideas from the head and an ancient anxiety from the heart of living man. His motivation was that of his fellow-Unitarians; but his special weapon was empirical science: the evidence of the senses.

Holmes is an instructive guide for us, as we leave the wastelands of orthodoxy and approach the new Eden of Walt Whitman, for he himself made almost the entire journey. He went to school at orthodox Andover, where a whipping he received evidently produced a sort of traumatic experience. He came on to Harvard, in 1825, when Unitarianism was in the ascendancy, and became its wittiest exponent. He moved on to be one of America's leading men of science. In fact, Oliver Wendell Holmes, whose long life . . . spanned the century, ought to have been a most arresting figure, perhaps the representative man of his age; it is not easy to say why he so often disappoints us. Perhaps it is because he was at the center of so many tendencies and managed to occupy the middle only by achieving a consistent mediocrity.

Holmes stood midway between the vanishing virility of his father's Calvinism and the emerging vitality of his son's militant humanism; what seems to have been available to him from either direction was frequently only the secondary or illusory. The suspicions which clouded his kindly view of human nature lacked the terrible strength which his father, Abiel Holmes, brought to his Calvinist ministry, while his enlightened repudiation of the divine elect took him only as far as the socially eligible, and his replacement of the visible saints by the Boston quality had little of the astringent social philosophy of his son, the Justice. Holmes stood at the heart of his own time. He

was, of course, a Harvard man forever, and the class poet par excellence; he was also a respected colleague and friend of the Swiss zoölogist, Louis Agassiz. Holmes could listen attentively to the Swedenborgian mystifyings by which the elder James mapped the way of regeneration; he could equally grasp and expound the therapeutic methods by which clinical psychology hoped to accomplish the same thing. He led the attack on the old theology; but he was a competent critic and a great lover of the old literature. His interests were rich and varied; yet what we are apt to find in him is less a synthesis of these interests than a good-humored shrewdness about them all, a solid common sense not deep enough for skepticism, not large enough for faith.

At the same time, it is probably misleading to say of him, in the phrase which has clung, that he was an "authentic Brahmin"—unless Brahminism is a more complex state of mind than is commonly allowed. For Holmes, like his partially autobiographical character Byles Gridley in *The Guardian Angel,* was "a strange union of trampling radicalism in some directions and high-stepping conservatism in others." The traditionalist side is better known and remembered; it included familiar traits of the party of Memory, and it has helped to associate him with that party far more than Holmes would have wanted. . . . When he began to talk about the nature and function of science, he had something new to say and a resonant vocabulary in which to say it: "The attitude of modern science is erect, her aspect serene, her determination inflexible, her onward movement unflinching; because she believes herself, in the order of providence, the true successor of the men of old who brought down the light of heaven to men."

Almost all of the Holmes that interests us here is in that sentence. The qualities that Holmes attributes to science could be attributed with the same buoyant confidence to the individual in America. As the profile of the new Adam emerges, we can notice that he too is erect, serene, inflexible, unflinching: and, according to Dr. Holmes, exactly because "modern science" had liberated him, explained him to himself, and imparted to him science's own stalwart nature. For science would provide the new religion and the new prophets and mediators; science would write the new testament and invent the new metaphors. If Dr. Holmes, as one of the first champions of science, did very well at this game, it was largely because he understood to a remarkable extent what the game was about. Perhaps the most succinct statement of Holmes's achievement was that he recast traditional religious concepts in scientific and humanistic terms, that he extracted what he saw as the *facts* of the human situation from the metaphors of myth and posited them anew in the language of psychology and anthropology.

Holmes's artful and sometimes even compelling transpositions are illustrated best in two of his scientific or "medicated" novels, *Elsie Venner* and *The Guardian Angel.* The very genre to which Holmes ascribed these books was a sign of his enterprise; for while Emerson and Whitman were trying their best to convert medical facts into inspirational poetry, Holmes was converting a literary form into a vehicle for a medical case history. Each of the books also enacts the crucial shift in the long arguments between minister and doctor, with the doctor getting the final word in every discussion. Holmes's "novels" are suggestive if, out of fairness to their author, we do not ask of them any questions prompted by a literary bias.

In *Elsie Venner* . . . , Holmes tested the dreary theories which George Ellis and his Unitarian associates imputed to orthodoxy: that a living individual could be "a partaker in a sin committed before his birth''; that he can consequently suffer punishment ''for the offence of another.'' Holmes said in the Introduction that he had attempted ''to illustrate the doctrine of inherited moral responsibility for other people's misbehavior.'' This way of formulating or loading the question indicates the extent to which Holmes conceived of his work as an exercise in scientific history. Holmes took Hawthorne's *The Marble Faun* (written later than *Elsie Venner,* but published a year before) as giving the same answer to the same question: though Hawthorne was testing innocence rather than its opposite, and the similarity of the two novels is essentially the similarity of ethics to medicine. For Holmes, that similarity was close: how close, he demonstrated in his narrative of the hapless Elsie, whose case emerged as an analogy to what Holmes took to be the doctrine of original sin. (pp. 32-5)

Holmes never pretended that there was nothing wrong with the world or with individual human beings; he was not innocent, he was merely kind. The defense of Elsie Venner sprang from Holmes's awareness of and his compassion for human failings, and it communicated his warming belief that to understand is to forgive. But he was sure that theology, or at least the only theology he knew much about, would not help anyone to understand. That was to be the function of science. Science could teach a man to search for the origins and causes of bad actions; and if it discovered them to lie in ''external influences,'' in ''bad ancestors, abuse in childhood, bad company,'' science was prepared to argue that the actions themselves were not in any moral sense bad after all.

What he wanted, in short, was a renovation of the moral vocabulary. In order to get it, Holmes felt the necessity of rejecting the entire traditional scheme of thought, replacing it with those studies by which his friend President Eliot was simultaneously revamping the Harvard curriculum: ''The truth is,'' wrote Holmes in an essay on Jonathan Edwards, ''that the whole system of beliefs which came in with the story of the 'fall of man,' the curse of the father conveyed by natural descent to his posterity . . . is gently fading out of enlightened intelligence. . . . Astronomy, Geology, Ethnology, and a comparative study of Oriental religions have opened the way; and now Anthropology has taken hold of the matter.''

Holmes's own renovated vocabulary—his chosen symbols for describing renovated human nature—consisted of a series of medical metaphors. ''Like a spasm in the heart and a cramp in the intellect''; ''our tumid egotism''; ''treat bad men as if they were insane'': these are examples of Holmes's favorite device, and one which he managed with uncommon dexterity. He shared the prevalent belief in the doctrine of correspondences, or likeness in the elements of the physical and the spiritual world, but in his own peculiar way. For while Emerson, Thoreau, and Melville found gleams of spiritual meaning in the physical scene, a dim outline of the ideal in the actual, Holmes pointed to the operation in the ideal realm of actual or physical functions. Emerson thought that science (as he said in *Nature* and in other essays) should be completed and validated by his own brand of metaphysics; Holmes thought that the realm of spirit could be overhauled by going about it in a scientific manner. ''For what we want in the religious and political organisms,'' he wrote, ''is just that kind of vital change which takes place in our bodies,—interstitial disintegration and reintegration.''

If the bad habits of Elsie Venner were pardoned because they sprang from a bad ancestry, the self-destructive instinct of Myrtle Hazard, the heroine of Holmes's second medicated novel,

The Guardian Angel . . . , was overcome by the gracious influence of a good ancestor. The books are not at all contradictory in theme; indeed, they serve to resolve the apparent contradictions in their author; and the second novel is a valuable complement to the volume published six years earlier. (pp. 37-8)

In Myrtle's departure from the orthodox environment and her regeneration in the doctor's home, there is a symbolism, almost stiffening into allegory, of the succession by science of the dried-up moralism of ''religion.'' But in *The Guardian Angel* Holmes is less interested in continuing the battle against a moldering theology than in describing the anatomy of the mental personality and in exposing the scientific bases of the rebirth ritual. The experience of Myrtle's immersion in water, for example, though projected with slight dramatic effectiveness (much less, say, than the comparable experience of the young hero at the end of Melville's *White-Jacket* . . .), is handled with an acute consciousness of its psychic significance. Holmes is careful to introduce images of her dimly remembered mother into the girl's disturbed imagination, just before she makes the plunge—which is explicitly intended to be what later psychologists would call a return to the womb. Holmes knew what he was about, to the extent that it scarcely measures his awareness to say only that he ''anticipated'' some of the insights of Freud and Jung. On this ground, Holmes may be admired in his own right. He centered his story on a genuine mental illness, revealed its causes in austerity and repression, and suggested a therapy which much later practice would not seriously dispute.

We may recognize in the domination of the young heroine by Aunt Silence what Freud would call the repression of the ego by the superego. An excessive control by the superego—the repository of conventional moral attitudes—results, according to Freud, in a melancholy which can lead toward self-destruction; and that was precisely the effect of Aunt Silence. Perhaps more striking yet was Holmes's exposure, in a pre-Jungian manner, of the presence within the recesses of the mind of personality types filtered down from the past. The theme of *The Guardian Angel* and its title are derived from this notion, as Holmes explains in the opening pages: ''There is recorded an experience of one of the living persons mentioned in this narrative which tends to show that some, at least, who have long been dead, may enjoy a kind of secondary and imperfect, yet self-conscious life in these bodily tenements which we are in the habit of considering exclusively our own.'' And Myrtle Hazard's habit, during moments of stress, of revealing in her features the welling-up of ancestral influence permits Dr. Hurlbut, the Tiresias of this novel, to utter the book's message: ''Live folks are just dead folks warmed over.'' The theme is more persuasively stated than it is dramatized; but Holmes's awkward technique for showing in action what he meant in theory was a failure of narrative art (to which he hardly aspired) rather than of psychological insight.

Holmes did succeed, moreover, in distinguishing between those remote influences, treating them, the way Jung would do, as dramatis personae encountered on the psychic journey. Among them, in Myrtle's case, we find an Indian forebear, who appears in the girl's occasional gestures of violence; and the guardian angel, the ''guide'' who shepherds Myrtle through a variety of perils, an ancestor named Anne Holyoake, a sixteenth-century Puritan martyr. It is her image that Myrtle confuses with that of her mother. Holmes's story thus follows the symbolic pattern later proposed by Jung as the myth of psychic reinte-

A depiction of the infant Maurice's traumatizing accident in A Mortal Antipathy.

gration: the escape, the plunge, the journey, the dangerous and the saving encounters, the magical guidance to the journey's end, and the final healing of the personality.

The Guardian Angel, though without merit as literature, is a telling contribution toward resolving the tensions between Memory and Hope. Ancestry was the point of intersection for Holmes. Both of his novels and most of his essays make it plain that he sought, with the hopeful, to rid the living of the oppressive misdirection of "bad ancestors," and to stand the present on its own feet. But Holmes had a Brahmin's respect for family and good breeding; and he was able to see how the past might nourish as well as stifle. The conservatism in him was peculiarly reinforced by his advanced psychiatric understanding of the value of the past as directive. The example of Oliver Wendell Holmes might support a contention that the renewed persuasion about the necessity of tradition could best emerge not in theological but in psychological terms: by demonstrating the powerful stabilizing and energizing effect which the past may have upon the isolated personality.

The pathos of such isolation was felt and expressed even by that archetypal man of good hope, Emerson, who captured the sense of confusion and aimlessness which afflicted his more sensitive contemporaries with the words: "Here we drift.... To what port are we bound? Who knows!" Those wistful questions illustrated the point which, a century later, Thomas Mann would discover from the psychology of Freud and Jung:

the point that the individual "would be confused, helpless, unstable" if his career "consisted merely in the unique and the present." Mann would argue that experience took on meaning and purpose only when it was regarded as typical, not unique—the re-enactment of the past, not the pure event in the present. Holmes hinted at much the same thing, as he set about answering those Emersonian questions by turning to psychotherapy. The question for him was, How had the lost child— Myrtle Hazard, for example—arrived at her condition? And the cure required an adjustment in the working relations between the present and the past.

But the genuinely hopeful were not really interested in either Holmes's analysis or his proposals. Emerson, with total assurance, referred his own questions for answer to the Oversoul; and a moment later could rejoice in the very adventurousness of the uncharted journey. Every tendency in the age which Holmes himself most admired was pushing toward a total neglect of the past rather than a last-minute attempt to restore some of its value. The dominant emotion was exhilaration, not wistfulness. "The expansive future is our arena," declaimed that hopeful organ, the *Democratic Review*. "We are entering on its untrodden ways . . . with a clear conscience unsullied by the past." The excitement of life, for the hopeful, lay exactly in its present uniqueness; the burden of doubt and guilt had been disposed of when the whole range of European experience had been repudiated, for the burden was the chief product of that experience. The individual moral course was thus to be plotted—not in terms of readjustment or of identification with any portion of the past, and much less in terms of redemption— but simply in terms of the healthy cultivation of natural, unimpaired faculties. (pp. 38-41)

R. W. B. Lewis, "The New Adam: Holmes and Whitman," in his The American Adam: Innocence, Tragedy, and Tradition in the Nineteenth Century, *The University of Chicago Press, 1955, pp. 28-53.*

HOWARD MUMFORD JONES   (essay date 1964)

[Jones considers the literary merit of Holmes's works, focusing on his theories of psychology. For additional commentary by Jones, see excerpt dated 1939.]

[Holmes's] mundane spirit is a limited spirit; and Holmes works within its limitations. His collected works contain no instance of passion whether intellectual or emotional. Elsie Venner, his only attempt at sexuality in the novel of that name, though she suffers, suffers in a distant, smothered, and indirect way. His other women are out of *Godey's Lady's Book*. Over some of these genteel wraiths, the Iris's and the Avis's of the Breakfast Table series, he occasionally grows maudlin as only the late eighteenth century could grow maudlin. He has no knowledge of, no interest in, economics, politics, sociology, save as the Civil War roused him to eloquence; and though Boston was changing under his eyes, though he claimed he had bored that ancient city through and through as if it were a cheese, he knows little or nothing of filthy slums, metropolitan degradation, or laissez-faire immorality. Racial snobbery once or twice pained him, and he has an honorable passage and an honorable poem against anti-Semitism, but, in general, American treatment of immigrants, Indians, and slaves drew from him either mild reproof or none. He was neither Wendell Phillips nor William Lloyd Garrison. He knows nothing of Emerson's over-soul, nor of Melville's white whale, nor of Hawthorne's *Scarlet Letter*. . . . As a medical man he must have seen a good deal of suffering and evil . . .; yet in his kindly universe there are no dark Satanic mills, and we are some light years away from the darkness of William Faulkner, the cold cruelty of Robinson Jeffers, the taciturn Prometheanism of Hemingway.

What, then, do we have? We cannot all be giant-like; and what one finds in Oliver Wendell Holmes is a striking example of the free play of lucid and honest intelligence in limited surroundings over a few great problems of life—the relation of God to man, the relation of heredity to responsibility, the relation of truth to tradition. These are important themes which Holmes, a man of eighteenth-century inheritance living and working in the American equivalent of the Victorian world, treated with eloquence, with humor, with sarcasm, with denunciation; and in doing so he freed a great number of his countrymen from fear and ignorance. If Heinrich Heine asked to be remembered as a soldier in the war of humanity for liberation, Oliver Wendell Holmes—and how prim and proper he seems along side the mercurial and fascinating Jew!—enlisted in the same army and fought with some of the same weapons. A distance separates **"The One-Hoss Shay"** . . . from Heine's "Atta Troll," but the distance is not as great as at first it seems. A man who could write as Holmes did of "one more example of the methods of wringing a dry cloth for drops of evidence," or describe homeopathy as "a mingled mass of perverse ingenuity, of tinsel erudition, of imbecile credulity, and of artful misrepresentation, too often mingled in practice, if we may trust the authority of its founder, with heartless and shameless imposition," is not very remote from the savagery or the wit of the German poet. (pp. 89-91)

I find . . . on re-reading Holmes, that his interest for moderns lies . . . in his anticipations, often startling, of some of the doctrines of psychology. His medicated fiction has been considered by some historians to anticipate the theories of Freud and Jung. Dr. Clarence P. Oberndorf, for example, has published a study called *The Psychiatric Novels of Oliver Wendell Holmes* [see excerpt dated 1943]. In each of the three tales we are presented with a child left motherless at an early age and subjected to some sort of austere and unsympathetic force; in each we deal with an obsession developed in childhood; in each there is a sympathetic physician who watches over the central personage; and in each the narrative carries hero or heroine to cure or to destruction. The first and third stories—*Elsie Venner* and *A Mortal Antipathy*—focus upon infantile shock. *The Guardian Angel* vaguely foreshadows the collective unconscious of Jung and deals with the problem of multiple personality. All this is true enough, but we do not have to go to Europe to ascertain the originality of Holmes. We have only to turn to the masterpiece of another son of Harvard, *The Principles of Psychology,* of William James, published in 1890, four years before the death of Holmes and one year before the appearance of *Over the Teacups* in volume form. One of the central doctrines in James appears in the great chapter on the nature of consciousness. In *Over the Teacups,* one finds Holmes' tribute to James for his "full exposition of the doctrine of plural personality."

The culture of Federalist Boston, for all its worldliness and its urbanity, was an inward-looking, a brooding consciousness, concerned for the attributes of personality. If I were called upon to define the most "modern" theme in the twelve volumes of Holmes' complete works, I think I should select the nature of consciousness in its relation to personality. The entire Breakfast Table series, from *The Autocrat* to *Over the Teacups,* is,

in a sense, nothing more than the expression of the author's multifaceted personality—autocrat, professor, poet, sage. The novels are quasi-laboratory reports on personality problems. The two biographies are patient attempts at the analysis of striking personalities, and the remaining volumes (including the poetry) contain many passages concerning the development of personality, the relation of personality and freedom, and the meaning of consciousness.

His work as an anatomist possibly focussed Holmes' attention upon the leading role heredity plays in psychic life. When Harriet Beecher Stowe inquired what he really meant in *Elsie Venner,* he wrote that he wanted to "stir up" the question of automatic agency in relation to self-determination and that he used the rattlesnake to dramatize the truth that personality may be shaped by an "unconscious, intuitive tendency, dating from a powerful ante-natal influence which modifies the whole organization." He thought no malformed character wholly shapes (or mis-shapes) itself, as this trenchant passage from *The Poet at the Breakfast-Table* makes clear: "People hold up their hands at a moral monster as if there was no reason for his existence but his own choice . . . ; study . . . will teach you that you do not get such a malformed character . . . without a long chain of causes to account for it; and, if you only knew these causes, you would know perfectly well what to expect." Hang him, if it is for the good of society, he continued, but "recognize the fact that what you hate in him is chiefly misfortune, and that if you had been born with his villainous low forehead and poisoned instincts . . . you would not have been sitting there in your gold-bowed spectacles . . . passing judgment on the peccadilloes of your fellow creatures." Waiving the question whether the actions of a character like Popeye in Faulkner's *Sanctuary* are peccadilloes, one notes to what an astonishing degree Holmes' doctrine anticipates the assumptions of many modern novelists.

If many components of personality are for him inheritances, Holmes was equally impressed by the influence of environment in shaping consciousness, as the famous passages about the Brahmin caste and about quality and equality exist to prove. The Americans, he wrote, are touchy about social distinctions, but it is as impossible to avoid them as to avoid recognizing the facts of natural history. Environment shapes personality. Changes in our manner of existence, he wrote in 1861, imply that "we have experienced some very profound impression which will sooner or later betray itself in permanent effects on the minds and bodies of many among us"; and he noted the increase of what we would call psychosomatic symptoms in New England during the first months of the Civil War. His explanation might have been written by William James: "The same trains of thought go tramping round in one circle through the brain, like the supernumeraries that make up the grand army of a stage-show. Now, if a thought goes round through the brain a thousand times a day, it will have worn as deep a track as one which has passed through it once a week for twenty years."

In such passages Holmes is talking about matters external to consciousness; what of the operations of consciousness itself? The more Holmes studied the matter, the more unpredictable, the more complicated he found the matter to be. He compares the operations of men's minds to the varied moves in chess; he returns again and again to the idea that when two persons converse, multiple personalities may be engaged in talking— John and Thomas as they are each to himself, John and Thomas as they are to each other, John and Thomas as they are in the eyes of God. He was more and more fascinated by both the unconscious operations of the mind and by what we, following James and others, call the stream of consciousness. The Poet says in *The Poet at the Breakfast-Table*: "Some kinds of thoughts breed in the dark of one's mind like the blind fishes in the Mammoth Cave. We can't see them and they can't see us; but sooner or later the daylight gets in and we find that some cold, fishy little negative has been spawning over our beliefs, and the brood of blind questions it has given birth to are burrowing round and under and butting their blunt noses against the pillars of faith . . . some of our old beliefs are dying out every year, and others feed on them and grow fat." "My thoughts," observes the Professor, "flow in layers, or strata, at least three deep. I follow a slow person's talk, and keep a perfectly clear under-current of my own beneath it. Under both runs obscurely a consciousness belonging to a third train of reflections, independent of the two others." And the same personage sagely observes: "We shall probably never have the least idea of the enormous number of impressions which pass through our consciousness, until in some future life we see the photographic record of our thoughts and the stereoscopic picture of our actions. There go more pieces to make up a conscious life or a living body than you think for."

A long autobiographical passage in the volume is a proleptic example of what James was to call the blooming, buzzing confusion of conscious life—Holmes talking about a "keyboard of nerve-pulps, not as yet tanned or ossified, to the finger-touch of all outward agencies . . . the filmy threads of this web of life in which we insects buzz a while." The creative consciousness of the poet was, he thought, of this nature; and there is poignancy in reading the many passages in which Holmes, who longed for poetical fame more than he longed for anything else, broods over the psychology of art, alternating between the romantic concept of God-given genius and the late eighteenth-century idea of decorum, craftmanship, and imitation.

In a psychic universe of this sort, the idea of conscious control, of choice, of freedom of the will more and more diminished. A footnote to the standard edition of *The Professor at the Breakfast-Table* gives us Holmes' final estimate:

> The more I have observed and reflected, the more limited seems to me the field of action of the human will. Every act of choice involves a special relation between the *ego* and the conditions before it. But no man knows what forces are at work in the determination of his *ego*. The bias which decides his choice between two or more motives may come from some unsuspected ancestral source, of which he knows nothing at all. He is automatic in virtue of that hidden feeling that he is self-determining.

This, oddly enough, approaches the very doctrine of Jonathan Edwards that he denounced, but Holmes cannot shake off his cultural inheritance, he cannot think of men as machines walking, he had to keep God and vitalism in the universe, he had to retain an ideal end for science. And the same essay which proclaims that "the more we study the will in the way of analysis, the more strictly does it appear to be determined by the infinitely varied conditions of the individual," also declares that men are free and responsible agents in proportion as they feel themselves to be free! Here is the passage:

> In spite of the strongest-motive necessitarian doctrine, we do certainly have a feeling,

amounting to a working belief, that we are free to choose before we have made our choice. We have a sense of difficulty overcome by effort in many acts of choice. We have a feeling in retrospect, amounting to a practical belief, that we could have left undone the things that we have done and that we could have done the things that we ought to have done and did not do, and we accuse or else excuse ourselves accordingly.

Doubtless a logician can reconcile these statements with Holmes' belief that the laws of human nature are generalizations of the fact that every organ obeys its proper stimulus, but the lay mind finds a certain difficulty in the task. (pp. 96-101)

[Holmes's] firm rootage in the traditions of Boston prevented his ever approximating the vagaries of a genius like Strindberg or D. H. Lawrence, but at the same time it limited him. In *The Autocrat* he says that "the fluent, self-determining power of human beings is a very strictly limited agency in the universe," and he defined the chief planes of its limitation as organization, education, and condition. The same thing is true of Holmes in actuality. The logic of his thinking about the limits of responsibility should have led him to endorse nineteenth-century naturalism, but he read the death-bed scene in *Madame Bovary* with horror and charged the naturalists with being obsessed by filth. His explorations of the stream of consciousness should have led him in the direction of the association of ideas as a mode of poetry; his culture kept him within the confines of the late Augustan poetic manner modified by Regency wit. His medical doctrine was essentially democratic, inasmuch as all men are equally imperfect, equally the products of heredity; his social training kept him to an elegant republicanism. He hovered on the edge of philosophical determinism, but his urbanity rebuked his pessimism, and, child of a hopeful era, he thought that God and science would ever move from more to more, so that his most famous serious poem could conclude with a promise of perfect freedom:

> Build thee more stately mansions, O my soul,
>   As the swift seasons roll!
>   Leave thy low-vaulted past!
> Let each new temple, nobler than the last,
>   Shut thee from heaven with a dome more vast,
>   Till thou at length are free,
> Leaving thine outgrown shell by life's unresting sea!

Here is the incorrigible optimism of much American thought, and I think it significant that Holmes, whose biography of Emerson is commonly said to be inadequate because of the lack of sympathetic understanding between Cambridge manners and Concord dreams, comes in fact thus to parallel the poetic epigraph for Emerson's *Nature*:

> A subtle chain of countless rings
> The next unto the farthest brings;
> The eye reads omens where it goes,
> And speaks all languages the rose;
> And, striving to be man, the worm
> Mounts through all the spires of form.

Holmes found Emerson's book a poetic anticipation of evolution—"evolution of the best and elimination of the worst as the law of being," he said. Perhaps the unity of New England thought in the nineteenth century was greater than we had supposed. (pp. 101-02)

Dr. Holmes in front of his Beacon Street house in Boston.

Howard Mumford Jones, "Oliver Wendell Holmes (1809-1894)," in his History and the Contemporary: Essays in Nineteenth-Century Literature, *The University of Wisconsin Press, 1964, pp. 84-102.*

BRIGID BROPHY, MICHAEL LEVEY, AND CHARLES OSBORNE   (essay date 1967)

[*Brophy, Levey, and Osborne contend that* The Autocrat *is wholly underserving of attention.*]

Naturally it was the breakfast table: his facetiousness, his bounce, his sententiousness [in *The Autocrat of the Breakfast Table*] accost you with precisely the effect of funny stories before 9 a.m. Not that Holmes runs much to *stories;* he's incapable of making even blunt points; he meanders, but at the pace of a torrent. In the paragraphs of classical allusion and quotation one might surmise a motive (showing off). Otherwise he seems to talk on and on through sheer wanton aggressiveness. The book might be someone's rough notes for a set of very full footnotes to something, what the something is being unguessable. Only Holmes would have actually supplied such a book with footnotes.

His manner suggests (can it be because he was a doctor?) that he's constantly pressed for time: 'Immense sensation at the table—sudden retirement of the angular female in oxydated

bombazine. Movement of adhesion—as they say in the Chamber of Deputies—on the part of the young fellow they call John . . .' But what is he hurrying *for*? Perhaps to leave himself space for his sentimental passages: 'Ah, but I must not forget that dear little child I saw and heard in a French hospital. Between two and three years old. . . . Lying in bed, patient, gentle. Rough students round her . . . but the child placid, perfectly still. I spoke to her, and the blessed little creature answered me in a voice of such heavenly sweetness, with the reedy thrill in it which you have heard in the thrush's evensong, that I seem to hear it at this moment, while I am writing, so many, many years afterwards.' No wonder Mark Twain used *The Autocrat of the Breakfast Table* as a 'courting-book' and that his wife kept it in a box 'with the love letters'. It might *be* Huck Finn's love-talk.

The Autocrat is in current print as a 'classic', in a paperback series professing to be 'a timeless treasury of the world's great writings'. Since none of Holmes's remarks has point or relevance in the internal context of his book, it is a kindness to apply one of them to his book's situation in a treasury of great writings: 'Literary life is full of curious phenomena. I don't know that there is anything more noticeable than what we may call *conventional reputations*. There is a tacit understanding in every community of men of letters that they will not disturb the popular fallacy respecting this or that electro-gilded celebrity.' It's time to admit the electro-gilt has worn away and there's nothing beneath. (pp. 57-8)

> *Brigid Brophy, Michael Levey, and Charles Osborne, "'The Autocrat of the Breakfast Table'," in their* Fifty Works of English and American Literature We Could Do Without, *1967. Reprint by Stein and Day Publishers, 1968, pp. 57-8.*

LEWIS LEARY   (essay date 1974)

[*Leary identifies the characteristics of Holmes's humor.*]

Oliver Wendell Holmes probably possessed more minor literary virtues than any writer of his generation. . . . His essays were read and admired by almost every literary compatriot. His novels, now almost forgotten, were filled with good talk and wittily turned character sketches, all strung upon plots only loosely knitted together. For Oliver Wendell Holmes was a miniaturist in literature, better at the small thing, intricately wrought, than on a larger canvas. (p. 117)

[Holmes] flit lightly over surfaces. His laughter was a pleasant protection against the vagaries of mad reformers, misguided clergymen, and poets like Walt Whitman and Edgar Allan Poe, both of whom seemed to most proper Bostonians undisciplined in taste and lacking in judgment. Though Dr. Holmes admired much in Ralph Waldo Emerson, and in some respects echoed in lighter vein some of his more prominent ideas, he did make playful fun of what he called the more "cobwebby" notions of the Transcendentalists. Reformers of any kind were victims, he said, of "inflammation of the conscience." He insisted that

> The ludicrous has its place in the universe; it is not a human invention, but one of the Divine ideas, illustrated in the practical jokes of kittens and monkeys long before Aristophanes and Shakespeare. How curious it is that we always consider solemnity and the absence of all gay surpluses and encounter of wits as essential to the idea of the future life of those whom we

thus deprive of half their faculties and then call *blessed*!

(p. 119)

[Much] of Holmes's humor is so topical that, unlike his one-horse shay, it failed even to outlive its century. (p. 120)

In [*The Autocrat of the Breakfast-Table, The Professor at the Breakfast-Table, The Poet at the Breakfast-Table,* and *Over the Teacups*] the genial irascibility of Oliver Wendell Holmes found most effective and most exuberant expression. They were conversation pieces in which people sitting around a table engaged in sprightly good talk. If it tended often to become a monologue in which the Autocrat, the Professor, the Poet, or the aging Dr. Holmes himself monopolized most of the conversation, so much the better. Almost everything he said was worth a chortle or a gasp.

Most of these essays are colored with rambling, quiet humor, often reciting an incident, much as Mark Twain later would, with apparent great seriousness, with the humorous point, what Mark Twain would call the "nub," concealed until just the right moment, so that, when recognized, it would draw, in Holmes's writing, a quiet chuckle from the reader, never a boisterous guffaw. There was little boisterous in Holmes's quiet fun. Like Thoreau, he often approached what he thought to be a truth indirectly. For, he said,

> Every person's feelings have a front-door and a side-door by which they may be entered. The front-door is on the street. Some keep it always open; some keep it latched; some locked; some bolted,—with a chain that will let you peep in, but not get in; and some nail it up, so that nothing can pass its threshold. This front-door leads into a passage which opens into an ante-room and this into the interior apartments. The side-door opens at once into the sacred chambers.

But, he continued, be careful to whom you entrust a key to your side-door:

> If nature or accident has put one of these keys into the hands of a person who has the torturing instinct, I can solemnly pronounce the words that Justice utters over its doomed victim,— *The Lord have mercy on your soul!* . . .

It is easy, that is, to avoid people who approach directly, but those—like poets or humorists—who insinuate themselves and their thoughts indirectly, to make you think or feel, these are the enemy, the torturers.

At other times he is more direct, dwelling on commonplaces of almost everyone's experience.

> Don't you know how hard it is for some people to get out of a room after their visit is over? They want to be off, and you want them off, but they don't know how to manage it. One would think they had been built into your parlor or study, and were waiting to be launched. I have contrived a sort of ceremonial inclined plane for such visitors, which being lubricated with certain smooth phrases, I back them down, metaphorically speaking, stern-foremost into their "native element," the great ocean of out-of-doors.

Then, somewhat deviously, he turns in analogue to the subject of literature, of bad poetry which lingers on as tenaciously as do unwanted guests: "Well, now," he went on,

> there are some poems as hard to get rid of as these rural visitors. They come in glibly, use up all the serviceable rhymes, *say, ray, beauty, duty, eyes, skies, other, brother, mountain, fountain,* and the like; and so they go on until you think that it's time for a wind-up, and the wind-up doesn't come on any terms. So they lie about until you get sick of them, and end by thrusting some cold scrap of a final couplet upon them, and turning them out of doors.

This is quiet Yankee humor, nourished on understatement, innuendo, and gracious prose. It does not translate easily in time or space. Sometimes it was gently, but, oh, so gently, ribald, and when it was Holmes, like the early Mark Twain, was careful to put it into the mouth of someone else, as when he suggested:

> All thought, my friend, the Professor, says, is of the nature of an excretion. . . . A man instinctively tries to get rid of his thought in conversation or in print as soon as it is matured; but it is hard to get at as it lies embedded, a mere potentiality, the germ of a germ, in his intellect.

But a healthy man will get rid of his thoughts, not only to avoid intellectual indigestion, but in self-protection and as a service to his fellow men. "Every real thought," he reminded his readers at another time, "knocks the wind out of somebody."

And knock the wind out of people Holmes did, but genially with quietly familiar entrance through the side-door as a welcome friend whose scolding was as well-meaning as well-phrased. People in New England still occasionally chuckle over the sometimes innocuously naughty strictures of these essays. (pp. 121-23)

Holmes [kept] youthful and laughing and gay to the end. His humor was in many respects different from that of his contemporaries. It derived more from the jovial spirit of the coffee houses in Augustan England, or of convivial, aristocratic clubmen of any time, or from the epigrammatic wit of Horace at his frolicsome best than from the boisterous American frontier. It played more often on words than on vulgar risibilities. It was often bookishly intellectual. Though genial, it was perhaps at root snobbish, well-dressed, well-mannered, excellently contrived to delight a cultivated mind. (p. 127)

He preferred to toy with ideas and to toy with words, teasing them to more expressive meaning. Though himself an irredeemable punster, he pretended great distaste for the pun; people who pun should be punished. "Let me lay down the law on the subject," he said. "Life and language are alike sacred. Homicide and *verbicide*—that is, violent treatment of a word with fatal results to its legitimate meaning, which is its life—are alike forbidden." And then he proceeded in his argument, he who disliked argument, with one of the most telling and outrageous puns of all: Manslaughter, he explained is what homicide is about; man's laughter (which is spelled exactly the same) is the end of verbicide. He pretended dislike of people who might ask whether the deluge through which Noah is said to have piloted his Ark—whether this *deluge* was not a *deal huger* than any other flood. "People who make puns," he said, "are like wanton boys who put coppers on the railroad tracks. They amuse themselves and other children, but their little trick may upset a freight train of conversation for the sake of a battered witticism."

Yet it may be that Oliver Wendell Holmes's epigrammatic witticisms, so like those of Benjamin Franklin's "Poor Richard," will most surely survive. "Sin," he explained, "has many tools, but a lie is the handle that fits them all." Or again: "Habit is a labor saving device which enables man to get along with less fuel." He was sure that "We are all tattooed in our cradles with the beliefs of our tribes," that "We are all sentenced to capital punishment for the crime of living." With age, he rejoiced that "To be seventy years young is sometimes more cheerful and hopeful than to be forty years old." He was sure that "stupidity often saves a man from going mad," and that "The young man knows the rules, but the old man knows the exceptions."

As a physician, he observed that "Among the gentlemen that I have known, few, if any, are ruined by drinking. My few drunken acquaintances were generally ruined before they became drunkards. The habit of drinking is often a vice, no doubt, sometimes a misfortune, . . . but oftenest a punishment." As a man whose writings were greatly admired, but most often only by a small coterie of like-minded friends, he could muse on "How small a matter literature is to the great, seething, toiling, struggling, love-making, bread-winning, child-rearing, death-waiting men and women who fill this huge, palpitating world of ours." As a lecturer who livened his own talk with sprightly and entertaining learning, he could nonetheless assert that "All lecturers, all professors, all schoolmasters, have ruts and grooves in their minds into which their conversation is always sliding."

Unlike his Boston friend James Russell Lowell who sometimes frolicked in good, robust, common vernacular, and unlike Mark Twain and the Southwestern humorists, Dr. Holmes's drolleries were most often most effectively dressed in sophisticated, learned, polite, even "literary" language. But he could accommodate himself when he had to, as he did in talking about "the wonderful one-hoss shay," to the language of the people. (pp. 127-29)

So light and bright and good-natured was his humor that he made no enemies. His wit more often traveled delightfully over surfaces than penetrated to depths. His pinwheel mind darted exuberantly, hovering over serious thought as if afraid to alight. It was a native trait perhaps, the kind of comic coloration often taken on in self-defense, the rapier wit which pierces quickly to put an adversary off guard. He is closer to Washington Irving, whom he admired, than to Mark Twain, who puzzled and troubled him. But, if not in the main channel of American humor, Oliver Wendell Holmes at least bubbles brightly through tributary streams which continue occasionally to refresh. He would, I think, have liked it that way. (p. 130)

Lewis Leary, "Oliver Wendell Holmes," in The Comic Imagination in American Literature, *edited by Louis D. Rubin, Jr., Voice of America, 1974, pp. 117-30.*

MARGARET HALLISSY (essay date 1985)

[*Hallissy analyzes* Elsie Venner *within the context of the serpent woman, or lamia, myth in literature.*]

Dr. Holmes in 1892.

"Women are for the most part poisonous creatures," wrote Arnaldus of Villanova, a medical writer of the Middle Ages. Although seldom expressed so blatantly, this attitude has an impressive pedigree in Scripture, folklore, and literature. In mythology, the serpent-woman Lamia is the other woman in the stormy marriage of Hera and Zeus. Hera's revenge is to deform Lamia so that Lamia has the face and breasts of a woman and the body of a snake. In retaliation Lamia preys on other women's children and also on young men, whom she lures to her lair and eats. In iconography, the serpent of Eden was often depicted as having a woman's head, and the sin committed there as a sexual sin, to emphasize Eve's and her daughters' seductiveness. The logical culmination of the identification of sin, snakes and women is the serpentine woman, whose venomous flesh kills physically or spiritually. The serpent with a woman's face becomes the serpentine woman.

In folklore and in later literature, the lamia retains her status as a supernatural being. She operates through fascination and witchcraft. As her story comes down through the centuries, variations are made, some of them sympathetic. A major development in the lamia tradition is that it provoked a most distinguished group of nineteenth-century writers on both sides of the Atlantic—John Keats, Nathaniel Hawthorne, and Oliver Wendell Holmes—to explore the problem of good and evil as it manifests itself in human sexuality. For these three writers, the lamia story crystallizes the problem of reconciling the ancient dichotomies which her dual nature represents: passion and reason, individual and society. They use the story as an exploration of the paradoxes and ambiguities surrounding the love of the hero for the lamia. In these writers, and for the heroes of their stories, the simple equation between women and sin is insufficient; the hero must examine himself as well. Most difficult, he must come to terms with his own sexuality as well as hers. This involves ignoring the warnings of older mentors who advise him to avoid the risk she represents. While Keats's *Lamia* and Hawthorne's "Rappaccini's Daughter" have been thoroughly analyzed, Oliver Wendell Holmes's novel *Elsie Venner* has been neglected. This novel deserves a new reading, for not only is it an important contribution to the lamia tradition in literature, but it is also significant for the study of the portrayal of women in literature. Holmes clearly wanted Elsie to be considered in relationship to the lamia tradition; but he also develops her character with enough ambiguity so that by the novel's end the reader is forced to doubt the applicability of the tradition to Elsie. The serpent-woman metaphor is imposed on Elsie by the other characters as a punishment for being too unusual in general, and too sensual in particular.

The lamia story echoes folk motifs such as the animal paramour, as in the tale of Beauty and the Beast; she is kin to mermaids, *striges* or witches, and vampires; Hecate is her mythological, and Eve her theological, mother. Because she metamorphoses, she embodies male fears of women's changeability. (pp. 406-07)

The lamia's unpleasant traits make her a poor marriage risk. A man has to be careful that the woman he is marrying is not a lamia in disguise. Such a marriage usually involves a pact in which the husband promises not to take certain steps which would uncover her true identity. When the lamia is truly known, she vanishes, and with her whatever goods she has brought to her marriage. In the more specific folk tale variants, the plot structure is strikingly similar to that found in Holmes's novel. A young man visiting the country meets a beautiful girl. She appears to be virtuous and to come from a respectable background. He falls in love with her. But alas! she is a snake-woman. An older man with special powers discovers this. The plot outcome is that "the youth becomes or remains a disciple of his deliverer, and presumably stays away thenceforth from sexual pleasures." The lamia, even if she harms no one, is always punished, as if to suppress thoroughly the evil which she represents.

In folk versions, then, the lamia story is unambiguously misogynistic. But in the literary development of the lamia story a change occurs "when the lamia began to be regarded as a symbol not of lust, but of love." The effect is a more positive portrayal of the lamia, and this change influences Holmes. His adventurousness in exploring female sexuality is all the more remarkable in view of what has been called the then-current cult of "passionlessness," glorifying the appearance of asexuality in women. Through downplaying her sexuality and emphasizing her spirituality, by deception if necessary, the typical woman could "assert control in the sexual arena," call the sexual shots and get a better husband besides. The obviously passionate woman—the phallic serpent woman—was a particularly difficult problem. If it was better to marry than to burn, one should marry a passionless woman to control the burning, not the very symbol of lust, the lamia. But when the hero fails to give himself totally to the lamia, he is seen in the context of the fiction as a failure.

Keats's poem, written in 1819, began the nineteenth-century modification of the interrelated themes of sin, snakes, and sex. Later in the century, first Hawthorne . . . , then Holmes . . . ,

published venemous-woman stories. Both Holmes and Hawthorne are linked in a relationship of mutual influence with Melville, who, in *The Confidence-Man* . . . , explores the question of the moral responsibility of the serpent. While "clinking the social glass," the cosmopolitan and the stranger discuss the coexistence of beauty and evil in creatures, particularly the serpent. They agree that the serpent, being beautiful, is not evil, indeed has a "'latent benignity.'" (pp. 407-08)

In thinking about this dilemma in connection with *Elsie Venner,* Holmes may well have drawn a comparison between Melville's snake and his own snake-woman. How can a being be beautiful, yet evil? The question defies a simple answer. If one could have compassion for that maligned being, greater comprehension would result, but not from the action of reason. It is as impossible for a man to be a woman as for a man to be a snake, and hardly more desirable from the man's viewpoint, since to be a woman would mean bearing the weight of the intellectual constructs describing femaleness, and consequently enduring isolation, loneliness, and misery. Like the rattle of the serpent or the label of the poison, the voices of religion and culture warn men that women are dangerous. So, if a woman leads a man into ruin, it is no more than he deserves: "'He should have respected the label.'" And yet if the bitten snake charmer is worth pity, so is the man who risks compassion. To be dispassionate, reasonable and methodological is to risk loss of the experience which can only be achieved when the judgment is suspended. This is risky; but the cautious life is ignoble. The accountability of the woman for the evil she seems to represent is for a higher court to judge.

Holmes's *Elsie Venner* explores this mystery in his story of an envenomed woman and the young man she loves. The old wives' tale of prenatal influences was still taken seriously in Holmes's day, and discussed at medical meetings and in medical journals. So Holmes, himself a physician, could with some scientific respectability describe his Elsie as having been envenomed *in utero*, because her mother was bitten by a serpent, from which wound the mother dies after Elsie's birth. This influence leaves Elsie with serpentine characteristics and moods: she could "lie . . . basking for whole hours in the sunshine"; her strength waxes and wanes with "the juices of all the poison-plants and the blood of all the creatures that feed upon them" . . . ; she even dresses in serpentine patterns and wears jewelry that resembles the rings on snakes' skin. A necklace, which she wears always, is believed to conceal telltale markings.

The legend of the poisoned maiden is ancient. It dates back at least to the pseudo-Aristotelian work *Secreta Secretorum,* and is connected with Alexander the Great in most versions. According to the legend, a beautiful girl had been "'fed upon poison from infancy, until she was of the nature of a snake.'" After proving her mettle by poisoning many lovers, she was called upon by the enemies of Alexander as an assassination weapon, the plan being that she should seduce him and poison him too. In varying accounts, certainly her embrace, but even her breath, saliva and perspiration were deadly poisons. The author of the *Secreta Secretorum* claims to have discovered her true nature "'by tests'" and thus saved Alexander.

Combining esoteric pseudoscience with simple misogyny, this story captured the imagination of writers on poison for hundreds of years. Any reader on the subject of poison will find repeated debates on the possibility of being envenomed through physical contact with another person; in such cases the victim is always male and perpetrator female. Since the way to "truth" in medical writing was for centuries deduction from the principles laid down by the great authorities, or by deducing from other treatises deducing from them, once this story got into the medical lore it took a long time for it to get out. Medical writers convey the same information for centuries, unscathed by experimentation.

With Andrea Bacci's treatise *De venenis et antidotis* (Rome, 1586), a new angle of reasoning is added to the story: "He denies that the maiden fed on poison would have poisoned Alexander the Great, had he lain with her, because what she ate would have been transformed into nutrition." It is this crucial change, the idea of transformation by incorporation into the self, which affects the depiction of the venomous woman in Holmes. In *Elsie Venner*, it is the protagonist Bernard Langdon's misfortune that the physician whom he consults for advice on Elsie seems not to know this newer theory. Elsie Venner, venomous though she is, may be nourishment as well. The serpent woman may be morally superior to the people around her who are defined as normal; more importantly, she offers Bernard a chance to participate in that superiority.

In fact, in *Elsie Venner* the townspeople surrounding Elsie, by whom and in relation to whom she is judged, are relentlessly normal. Rockland is populated by a sensitive but overworked schoolmarm, a pious and dedicated black servant woman, an equally dedicated but somewhat uppity Yankee manservant, socially ambitious bourgeoises, Brahmin gentry, wise, concerned and learned authority figures (fathers, professors, doctors, and clergymen), and even a black sheep of the family. To this hypertypical town comes Bernard Langdon, a young medical student interrupting his education because of his family's diminished fortunes. He is an excellent student and shows promise as a teacher as well, according to his medical school professor, who is the narrator of the novel. All the events of the novel are seen through the consciousness of this professor, who also serves as advisor to Bernard.

In the typical lamia story, as we have seen, the young man needs a mentor; but it becomes increasingly clear that Bernard has allowed his professor to guide him too much. To depend on a former teacher is no unusual phenomenon; but at some point this dependence can become harmful, as even the best-intentioned advisor has his own inadequacies. But Bernard is not yet at the point of maturity necessary to realize this. He needs his old teacher, and so the question is, what kind of man is this professor?

The answer: smug, self-assured, and opinionated, like many an academic before and since. He has no name; he is always "the professor"—a typical example of his calling. His bias is rationalistic, his stance detached. He judges from afar, and has no qualms about issuing authoritative opinions about any subject. Unlike Dr. Kittredge, a practitioner whose sympathies are exercised by daily patient contact, the narrator is an ivory-tower theoretician who judges people according to ideas found in books. As a medical student and physician himself, Holmes must have known both types.

Teachers who influence the lives of their students beyond the classroom typically have nothing material to gain from the interaction, but enjoy the psychological power, and this is the case with the relationship in the novel. Each intrusion into the life of Bernard Langdon is motivated by sincere concern. The professor has high hopes that, after "ten brilliant years of spirited, unflagging labor" . . . Bernard can stand at the top of his profession. Therefore Bernard must be cautioned to avoid "love and all that nonsense" . . . , and, when the time arrives, to marry with an eye to professional and social advancement. This common-sense life plan, coming as it does from a seemingly wise and unselfish source, impresses the young man. Bernard does not see that the plan leaves no room for the fortuitous accident of falling in love.

Another bias which the professor passes along to Bernard is again endemic to his calling: the intellectual tradition of rationalism. For one thing, the professor assumes all problems can be solved if one keeps a cool head, and he reinforces a tendency to emotional detachment in the chilly Bernard. For another thing, the professor is an adherent of an elaborate theory of human responsibility, which he communicates to Bernard at a crucial point in Bernard's relationship with Elsie. Like the docile student who would naturally be a favorite of a professor like this, Bernard accepts his mentor's ideas.

Elsie then is set in contrast both with the ordinariness of the town and the rationality of the professor's theories. Her and Bernard's first meetings occur in situations which stress Elsie's nonconformity. They first meet as teacher and student at the Apollinean Female Institute, where young ladies are brought into conformity with the rules of reason. Then they meet again at a party given by the socially-aspiring Sprowles as a showcase for their marriageable Matilda. In each group, fellow students and fellow eligibles, Elsie differs from the ordinary girls of Rockland. To the basic situation, then, young male teacher and nubile female student, alluring enough in itself, is added Elsie's too-drastic difference from the other girls: she is extremely attractive, and she is venomous.

Who is Elsie, what is she? "By what demon is she haunted, by what taint is she blighted, by what curse is she followed, by what destiny is she marked, that her strange beauty has such a terror in it, and that hardly one shall dare to love her, and her eye glitters always, but warms for none?" . . . Over the peaceful little town hovers the shadow of Rattlesnake Ledge, where snakes breed. Into the careful, rational life of Bernard Langdon comes Elsie Venner, challenging every presupposition. She is dangerous. From early childhood her envenoming was threatening: as soon as Elsie cuts teeth, her wet-nurse sickens and dies; as a child, she bit her cousin Dick Venner so that he retains the scars as an adult; at fifteen, she rids herself of an objectionable governess by inducing in her a mysterious illness. Throughout her life she is perceived as so intractable that Dr. Kittredge advises her father to let her have her way. She wanders off, an odd behavior for a girl anyway, but made odder still by her preferred destination: trees, caves, Rattlesnake Ledge. (pp. 409-12)

In the fictional present, she is seventeen. The problem child has become an even more problematic young woman. What is to be done with a female like Elsie at sexual maturity? She cannot just be married off like any young girl. She is a maze of contradictions. Snake-like, she is cold: the light in her eyes is like the "lustre of ice" . . . , her expression is that of "remoteness, of utter isolation." . . . Yet she is also passionate: her mother was a Spaniard, and this influence (perceived by the xenophobic narrator as venomous in itself) makes for wild blood. Dancing to Spanish music, she whips herself into a frenzy, "undulating with flexuous grace." . . . Clearly she is nothing at all like the other girls.

The good citizens of Rockland chorus their disapproval of Elsie. She is possessed of "ungovernable anger" and "an irritable state of mind and body." . . . Clearly the sexual maturation of such a woman presents a problem. As her father,

Dudley Venner, puts it, "'Who would *dare* to marry Elsie?'" . . . (pp. 412-13)

There are two candidates for that honor, Bernard and also Dick Venner, Elsie's cousin. The conflict between the two (a new element in the lamia story) further adumbrates the reason/passion conflict. As we have seen, Bernard represents the intellectual achievements made possible by taming the passions. As a class, the Brahmins have been remarkably successful in producing intellectuals, but not without paying a price. The trade-off has been a loss of the vigor of the "animal nature," a decrease in "vital energy" . . . ; the Brahmins are slender, pallid, smooth-faced, delicate of feature. In short, they are cerebral and asexual. In contrast, his rival, Elsie's cousin Dick Venner, is, like Elsie herself, a "'half-breed'" . . . , with "Southern impulses in [his] wild blood," . . . which conflict with and overpower the "cunning and calculating" rationality of his "New-England side." . . . He is given to such symbolic gestures as riding his "half-tamed horse" when the "savage passion of his young blood came over him." . . . He is a bit of an outlaw; he has a dark past; and, because he is Elsie's cousin, there is a subdued incest motif. Dick Venner would seem to be a proper mate for Elsie, but she does not love him. Nor does he love her; although he is attracted to her, stronger still is the lure of her father's money. He is blood, Bernard brain, and Elsie seems attracted to what she lacks. So Dick Venner can be eliminated fairly early in the novel, to leave Bernard as the only candidate for Elsie's venomous hand.

Bernard is simultaneously attracted to and repelled by the danger Elsie represents. (p. 413)

Yet he is too much the intellectual simply to respond to Elsie naturally. He must perforce cerebralize her. Ever the attentive student, he sees her as an interesting case. He muses on the concept of fascination as a manifestation of man's affinity for the serpent, his inherited tendency to evil, the "fruit of the curse" . . . , original sin. He is able to test this theory when, himself fascinated by a snake on Rattlesnake Ledge, the spell is broken by Elsie's superior power. His medical/theological speculations are furthered when, one morning, a "dark, gypsy-looking woman" brings him a *crotalus,* a breed of snake living in the neighborhood, a creature which he desires to investigate. Alarmed, Bernard warns her of their deadliness, but the gypsy-looking woman reassures him of her immunity: "'rattlers never touches our folks.'" Bernard has never heard of the "possession of a power by certain persons, which enables them to handle these frightful reptiles with perfect impunity." . . . However, he should have. In the New Testament the followers of Christ are given the power to handle serpents and drink poison with impunity, and this is a sign of goodness. Does this mean that if he were good enough, Elsie would not be venomous for him, would perhaps even be beneficial? Rather than apply the implied moral lesson to himself, Bernard muses on the general topic of serpents and evil.

Again, the subject debated by Melville's stranger and the cosmopolitan [in *The Confidence Man*] returns: is the serpent, symbol of evil, itself evil? Bernard cannot take the question further, but, although he never knows it, Elsie has. Mr. Fairweather, the minister, recalls an incident from Elsie's childhood. He had sent a religious book to Elsie for her edification. From the book she tore out and kept the frontispiece—a picture of Eve's temptation—and threw the rest of the book out the window. For Elsie, Eve is the only important figure in religion. She said that "Eve was a good woman—and she'd have done just so if she'd been there." Mr. Fairweather sees this as

evidence of her "natural obliquity" and in fact the "'congenital sinfulness of human nature.'" . . . But Elsie's instinctive identification with Eve can also be seen as a rejection of the concept of sinfulness imposed on Eve. Eve sinned because the serpent deceived her. If she was deceived, then she is victim, not perpetrator. Like Eve, Elsie has been singled out to be a symbol, to represent a theory.

In fact, everyone around Bernard is devising theories—medical, philosophical, theological. Her own father, Dudley Venner, sees her as a victim of hysteria: Elsie is deadly because she is a woman. The long-suffering schoolmarm Helen Darley blames "'the force of transmitted tendencies.'" . . . Rev. Dr. Honeywood cites a "visitation of God" which "impairs the intellectual or the moral perceptions" but renders the person thus afflicted exempt from "common working standards of right and wrong." . . . All agree that Elsie's problem is not her fault; but none agree on what should be done about the fact that Elsie cannot marry. As Old Sophy tells Dr. Kittredge, Elsie's husband would die. Confused, Bernard consults his old professor.

The questions he asks of his medical/philosophical advisor bear on the health of body and soul. First, he wants to know if envenoming is physically possible; then, if it is, he wants to know whether a person thus envenomed is morally dangerous as well. He writes: "Is there any evidence that human beings can be wrought upon by poisons, or otherwise, so that they shall manifest any of the peculiarities belonging to beings of a lower nature?" . . . The professor replies at great length and with many citations from academic authorities. And along comes, here in the nineteenth century in America, the hoary story of Alexander the Great and his poisoned lady, cited "upon pretty good authority" . . . as medical evidence by a medical school professor. . . . The professor goes on, citing more recent stories, including the "malignant witch-woman" in Coleridge's *Christabel* and the "serpent transformed" in Keats's *Lamia*. . . . (pp. 414-15)

Bernard has also brought up the related question about the serpent-women raised by Melville in reference to the actual serpent: is the venomous being responsible for its own venomousness? Can people in this condition be "as free from moral responsibility as the instincts of the lower animals? Do you think there may be a *crime* which is not a *sin*?" . . . The professor replies with a discourse on the "limitations of human responsibility." . . . Some people are less responsible for their actions because of predisposing conditions, heredity being one, reflex or involuntary action another, and both applying to Elsie. The "moral insanity" defense in criminal trials, an innovation in Holmes's day, is based on the postulate that there exist people who are not morally responsible for their legal crimes. Holmes defended the theory of unconscious and mechanical mental action which limits human will, a theory he summarized in his Phi Beta Kappa address, **Mechanism in Thought and Morals.** The theory is obviously an early version of our "not guilty by reason of insanity" plea, and like that plea, it is not likely to inspire confidence in the person so absolved. In practice, according to the professor, the distinction between sin and crime is irrelevant: "*Treat bad men exactly as if they were insane.* They are *in-sane,* out of health, morally. Reason, which is food to sound minds, is not tolerated, still less assimilated . . . ." Although the professor does not know he is advising on Elsie, his message is to avoid the dangerous being.

Bernard Langdon is thus influenced by many theories—theological, medical, philosophical, psychological. Elsie is Eve, the channel through whom primordial guilt is transmitted. She is Circe, the enchantress whose sexual potency can distract a man from the goal of his life-journey. She is amorality, irresponsibility, madness. All these ideas stand between Elsie Venner and Bernard Langdon. The only character in the novel who can respond to Elsie without the barrier of ideas is the simple servant, Old Sophy. In fact, *Elsie Venner* is unusual as a lamia story in that there is a woman character to respond to Elsie. Usually the lamia is alone, a woman in a man's world, seen through men's perceptions. Here Old Sophy is the only person unjudgmentally sympathetic. Being black, female, nurturing, and instinctual, in a white, male and intellectually judgmental world, Sophy's influence is weak. What self-respecting young man would think of going to such a person for advice? Instead he follows the voices of reason, and it is their influence which determines his fateful reaction at the novel's climax.

Elsie, distressed, approaches Bernard. He is sympathetic but distant. "'Tell me what I can do to render your life happier,'" he asks. Elsie replies, "'*Love me!*'" This is the one thing she needs, and the one thing he cannot give her. He offers the handshake of friendship, a tepid substitute for the embrace of love. To Bernard the coldness seems to emanate from Elsie's hand: "a cold *aura* shot from it along his arm and chilled the blood running through his heart." . . . But the cold really emanates from Bernard's passionless nature—his attribution of it to Elsie is a classic case of projection. He has previously told Dr. Kittredge that he does not love Elsie; if he helps her, it would be "'in cold blood.'" . . . This stance of professional detachment is the reason that, after this crucial encounter, "it was all over with poor Elsie." . . . Deprived of the warmth of love which would have kept her alive, she sickens. The explicit offer of her virginity—"'*Love me!*'"—and Bernard's rejection of it are expressed in the imagery of flowers so often connected in literature with the young maiden. Earlier in the novel Elsie puts a flower in Bernard's copy of the *Aeneid,* at the point of the story which describes Dido's suicide after Aeneas's betrayal, to remind Bernard of the consequences of refusing passionate love. In her final illness Bernard places a sprig of white ash in a basket of flowers sent to her by her fellow students, as if giving the offer of her maidenhood back to her. Its purple leaves, an antidote to others, are poison to her. Chastity is no healthful remedy to Elsie. Bernard's prescription for her, and the flower which represents it, kills her.

So it is clear that the serpent in Elsie is her sexuality. Dr. Kittredge points out that serpents have shorter life spans than humans, and perhaps the human in Elsie can outlive the serpent. Dudley Venner regards the prenatal influence as a "blight." His hope had been that "the lower nature which had become engrafted on the higher would die out and leave the real woman's life she inherited to outlive this accidental principle which had so poisoned her childhood and youth." . . . These ideas have a dual significance. If she can be gotten safely through her peak sexual years, she will eventually become less powerful and consequently less threatening. But this is a counsel of despair. On the other hand, her sexuality might also be regarded less negatively and stripped of its association with evil. For this to happen, she needs a man who is not only emotionally responsive but also brave. Even on Elsie's deathbed, he looks at her "with almost scientific closeness of observation." . . . The lover's gaze, so crucial to the love tradition in literature, is here perverted by the spirit of dispassionate science. "Needing a Heathcliff, she has found only a proper Bostonian." He is too cold and cerebral to bring Elsie to sexual maturity.

At the funeral, before closing Elsie's coffin, Sophy takes off the gold cord Elsie had always worn around her neck. Everyone, even Sophy, thought that Elsie wore this cord to conceal serpentine marks. But "there was no shade nor blemish where the ring of gold had encircled her throat." Sophy attributes this to a miracle—the Lord taking away the mark of evil so Elsie would be fit to join the "'holy angels.'" . . . But this event at the novel's conclusion leaves a drastic ambiguity. Was Elsie really envenomed, or was she merely unusual?

Elsie's life violates several sacred norms. An undercurrent in the novel is the "idealised view of the daughter." Elsie is the only child of a widowed father. The nineteenth-century unmarried woman in her father's house has a special set of responsibilities, summarized in the telling phrase "Angel in the House." She is often raised in the image and likeness of her father, to be a companion to him in all ways save sexual. She is supposed to be a gentle, cheerful, smiling "'sunbeam,'" who can "adorn the household" with "ladylike accomplishments," provide "rest and amusement," attention, affection, and understanding for her father. She should be in no way independent; a "strong-minded girl" who is "'self-willed and arrogant, eccentric in dress and disagreeable in manner'" is a blight on her father's household. Even in the crucial process of achieving maturity by moving out of her father's house into another man's house, she is supposed to give no trouble. But Elsie Venner is a source of lifelong pain and suffering to her father. As a daughter, she is a disaster.

In an ordinary town, too, Elsie's beauty and sensuality are aberrant. Early in the novel, the narrator muses on beauty. While "in the abstract we all love beauty," to be beautiful also "carries an atmosphere of repulsion." Many people are "too poor, too ordinary, too humble, too busy, too proud" . . . to pay the price for loving an unusually beautiful person. Most people are, like Bernard, ordinary, and avoid the extraordinary. In the novel, Elsie is regarded as extraordinary by all, but she is seldom depicted as doing anything very unusual. There is little objective correlative to the fictional judgments. This could be a flaw in the narrative technique, but it could also reflect the fact that everything the narrator knows about her is filtered through the perceptions of conventional people.

These ordinary people live happily and bloodlessly ever after: Bernard finishes medical school, sets up a successful practice, and marries a "safe little lass." Even Dudley Venner remarries, allying himself with the soothing schoolmarm Helen Darley. For Elsie, who loved someone not up to the challenge of loving her, the eulogy is spoken by Dr. Honeywood: "From the life and the death of this our dear sister we should learn a lesson of patience with our fellow-creatures in their inborn peculiarities, of charity in judging what seems to us wilful faults of character. . . ." Judge not, lest you be judged; approach your fellow creatures with charity, all the more needed when dealing with the unusual person. Because the evidence of Elsie's venomousness is inconclusive, venom becomes, in addition to a symbol of female sexuality, also a symbol of divergence from socially imposed norms.

And so she may not marry. The unusual woman cannot reproduce herself without a courageous male to accept her in all her fearful complexity. For Bernard to respond to Elsie, he would have to ignore the voices of his upbringing which encourage him to quell the stirrings of passion and take the safe and intelligent path through life. Retreating from the challenge, Bernard never completes the psychic work of confronting his own sexual nature. Back in medical school, he reads a paper

significantly titled "Unresolved Nebulae in Vital Science."
. . . He has learned nothing from his unresolved relationship
with Elsie. For him, there will always be areas of darkness in
his understanding of life, because he approaches life as a science.

His marriage follows the chastity prescription, taming once
and for all the dangerous emotions connected with Elsie. But
when one marries so as not to burn, much is lost. In Bernard,
all passion is buried. His dead sexuality is like the "terrible
Rattlesnake Ledge" itself, which, after the earthquake, "with
all its envenomed reptiles, its dark fissures and black caverns,
was buried forever beneath a mighty incumbent mass of ruin."
. . . Lost forever too is Bernard's opportunity to be extraordinary, like Elsie. (pp. 415-18)

> Margaret Hallissy, "Poisonous Creature: Holmes's
> 'Elsie Venner'," in Studies in the Novel, Vol. XVII,
> No. 4, Winter, 1985, pp. 406-19.

ADDITIONAL BIBLIOGRAPHY

Brenner, Rica. "Oliver Wendell Holmes." In her *Twelve American
Poets before 1900*, pp. 169-98. New York: Harcourt, Brace and Co.,
1933.
    Assesses Holmes's literary career and claims that his works help
    to illuminate his life.

Brooks, Van Wyck. "Dr. Holmes." In his *The Flowering of New
England, 1815-1865*, pp. 478-98. New York: E. P. Dutton & Co.,
1936.
    A biographical sketch.

———. "Dr. Holmes's Boston." In his *New England: Indian Summer, 1865-1915*, pp. 1-22. New York: E. P. Dutton & Co., 1940.
    A view of Boston culture during Holmes's lifetime.

Clark, Harry Hayden. "Dr. Holmes: A Re-Interpretation." *The New
England Quarterly* XII, No. 1 (March 1939): 19-34.
    Examines Holmes's literary, social, and political views and states
    that, though they were conservative, they were "offset" by his
    radical religious and philosophical ideas.

Currier, Thomas Franklin. *A Bibliography of Oliver Wendell Holmes.*
Edited by Eleanor M. Tilton. New York: New York University Press,
1953, 707 p.
    An extensive bibliography of writings about Holmes that includes
    citations from English and foreign-language studies.

Doubleday, Neal Frank. "Dr. Holmes and the Faith in the Future."
College English 4, No. 5 (February 1943): 281-88.
    An analysis of Holmes's religious attitudes, which Doubleday
    terms "remarkably characteristic of the American mind."

Emerson, Edward Waldo. "Oliver Wendell Holmes." In his *The Early
Years of the Saturday Club, 1855-1870*, pp. 145-58. Boston: Houghton
Mifflin Co., 1918.
    A discussion of Holmes and his associates in the Saturday Club.

Fields, Annie. "Oliver Wendell Holmes: Personal Recollections and
Unpublished Letters." In her *Authors and Friends*, pp. 107-55. 1897.
Reprint. Grosse Pointe, Mich.: Scholarly Press, 1969.
    A friend's memories of Holmes.

Fuller, Harold de Wolf. "Holmes." In *American Writers on American
Literature*, edited by John Macy, pp. 153-63. New York: Horace
Liveright, 1931.
    A sketch of Holmes's life and work. Fuller contends that science
    and poetry were the strongest influences in the author's life.

Garner, Stanton. "*Elsie Venner*: Holmes's Deadly 'Book of Life'."
Huntington Library Quarterly XXXVII, No. 3 (May 1974): 283-98.

Uses *Elsie Venner* as a paradigm for a discussion of Holmes's
    criticism of the intellectual and Brahmin society of nineteenth-
    century New England.

Grattan, C. Hartley. "Oliver Wendell Holmes." *The American Mercury* IV, No. 13 (January 1925): 37-41.
    Proposes reducing Holmes's literary fame to a "footnote," con-
    tending that most of his poetry is "dusty" and his prose work
    barren.

Hayakawa, Samuel I. "Holmes's Lowell Institute Lectures." *American Literature* 8, No. 3 (November 1936): 281-90.
    Contains brief discussions of each of the twelve lectures on English
    poets that Holmes delivered in 1853.

Howe, M. A. DeWolfe. *Holmes of the Breakfast-Table*. London: Oxford University Press, 1939, 172 p.
    An illustrated biography. Howe also traces the creation and re-
    ception of Holmes's literary works.

Howells, William Dean. "Oliver Wendell Holmes." *Harper's Magazine* XCIV, No. DLIX (December 1896): 120-34.
    An intimate recollection of Howells's personal and professional
    association with Holmes.

Hoyt, Edwin P. *The Improper Bostonian: Dr. Oliver Wendell Holmes*.
New York: William Morrow and Co., 1979, 319 p.
    A detailed, anecdotal, and fully illustrated biography of Holmes.

Kern, Alexander C. "Dr. Oliver Wendell Holmes Today." *The University of Kansas City Review* XIV, No. 3 (Spring 1948): 191-99.
    A survey that assesses the value of Holmes's literary works and
    posits some reasons for the decline in his reputation.

Knickerbocker, William S. "His Own Boswell: A Note on the Poetry
of Oliver Wendell Holmes." *The Sewanee Review* XLI, No. 1 (January-March 1933): 454-66.
    An examination of Holmes's poetry.

Kreymborg, Alfred. "Dr. Holmes and the New England Decline." In
his *Our Singing Strength: An Outline of American Poetry (1620-1930)*,
pp. 134-50. New York: Coward-McCann, 1929.
    Claims that Holmes's "wittiest warfare" was directed against
    Calvinism and adds that the author was an intellectual whose
    poetical style was reminiscent of the eighteenth century.

[Ludlow, J. M.]. "*Elsie Venner* and *Silas Marner*: A Few Words on
Two Noteworthy Novels." *Macmillan's Magazine* IV, No. 22 (August
1861): 305-09.
    A comparison that finds George Eliot's novel a study in ethics,
    and Holmes's a study of physiology.

Martin, John Stephen. "The Novels of Oliver Wendell Holmes: A Re-
Interpretation." In *Literature and Ideas in America: Essays in Memory
of Harry Hayden Clark*, edited by Robert Falk, pp. 111-27. Athens:
Ohio University Press, 1975.
    Contends that Holmes's literary reputation has remained constant
    and interprets the novels as works involved not with psychology
    but with moral issues.

Morse, John T., Jr. *Life and Letters of Oliver Wendell Holmes.*, 2
vols. Boston: Houghton, Mifflin & Co., Riverside Press, 1896.
    A detailed and illustrated biography of Holmes. Morse discusses
    Holmes's careers in medicine and literature and includes excerpts
    from the author's notes and correspondence.

Roditi, Edouard. "Oliver Wendell Holmes as Novelist." *Arizona
Quarterly* 1, No. 4 (Winter 1945): 23-33.
    Argues that Holmes used scientific terminology to give authen-
    ticity to his stories. Roditi claims that Holmes's plots are actually
    provincial Victorian romances concerned with morality rather than
    psychology.

Scudder, H. E. "Biographical Sketch." In *The Complete Poetical
Works of Oliver Wendell Holmes*, pp. xi-xxi. Boston: Houghton, Mifflin and Co., Riverside Press, 1895.
    An introduction to Holmes's poetical works that includes bio-
    graphical material and critical commentary.

Sears, Lorenzo. "Oliver Wendell Holmes." In his *American Literature in the Colonial and National Periods*, pp. 327-37. 1902. Reprint. New York: Burt Franklin, 1970.

　　Reviews Holmes's work and his place in American literature, praising the wit of the Breakfast-Table series.

Small, Miriam Rossiter. *Oliver Wendell Holmes*. Twayne's United States Authors Series, edited by Sylvia E. Bowman, no. 29. New York: Twayne Publishers, 1962, 176 p.

　　A biography covering all facets of Holmes's life. Small also includes critical discussions of the author's works.

Strong, Augustus Hopkins. "Oliver Wendell Holmes." In his *American Poets and Their Theology*, pp. 319-67. Philadelphia: Griffith and Rowland Press, 1916.

　　Argues that Holmes failed to adequately challenge Calvinism because he misunderstood its true nature.

Tilton, Eleanor M. *Amiable Autocrat: A Biography of Dr. Oliver Wendell Holmes*. New York: Henry Schuman, 1947, 470 p.

　　A detailed biography that includes critical discussions of Holmes's works.

————. "Introduction." In *The Poetical Works of Oliver Wendell Holmes*, edited by Eleanor M. Tilton, pp. xvii-xxxv. Boston: Houghton Mifflin Co., 1975.

Studies Holmes's use of language, voice, and subject matter in his verse and prose.

Trent, W. P. and Erskine, John. "The New England Poets." In their *Great American Writers*, pp. 134-68. Home University Library of Modern Knowledge, edited by Herbert Fisher and others, no. 48. New York: Henry Holt & Co., 1912.

　　An assessment of Holmes as a minor novelist and poet, but an accomplished essayist.

Wendell, Barrett. "Oliver Wendell Holmes." In his *A Literary History of America*, pp. 407-24. New York: Charles Scribner's Sons, 1920.

　　A biographical sketch that includes a discussion of the themes of Holmes's works and the occasions for which his poems were written.

Wentersdorf, Karl P. "The Underground Workshop of Oliver Wendell Holmes." *American Literature* XXXV, No. 1 (March 1963): 1-12.

　　Calls Holmes a pioneer who deserves recognition for his theories about the role of the unconscious in the creative process.

Wolfe, Don M. "Of Crime and Responsibility: Oliver Wendell Holmes." In his *The Image of Man in America*, pp. 119-28. New York: Thomas Y. Crowell Co., 1970.

　　A discussion of Holmes's views on the relationship between heredity, environment, and will as expressed in both his fiction and non-fiction.

Walter Savage Landor

1775-1864

English poet, prose writer, and literary critic.

Landor is considered a master prose stylist and a significant poet of the nineteenth century. Although a contemporary of the Romantic writers, Landor was distinguished from them by his interest in classical themes and forms. Today, he is known primarily for his series entitled *Imaginary Conversations* and numerous elegant epigrams.

Born in Warwick, England, Landor was educated at the Rugby School and Trinity College, Oxford, where he received a classical education and excelled in writing Latin verse. Conflicts with the authorities and other students led to his expulsion from both schools, and Landor's formal education ended when he was nineteen. In 1795, he published his first work, *The Poems of Walter Savage Landor*. But these satiric verses on college personalities found a limited audience, and only thirty-six copies were sold. On his father's death in 1805, Landor inherited a sizable fortune. Intending to establish an estate in Wales, he purchased Llanthony Abbey in Monmouthshire and began extensive renovations. In 1808, he spent three months in Spain as a volunteer in the war against Napoleon, financing a troop himself. Landor married Julia Thuillier in 1811 and resumed work on his estate, but the Landors' years at Llanthony were marked by financial, legal, and marital disputes, and a lawsuit forced them to leave Wales in 1814. After a bitter separation of several months, they reconciled and settled in Florence, Italy, where Landor composed many of his works. They remained in Florence until 1835 when Landor, then sixty, found his marriage unendurable and moved to Bath, leaving most of his income to his wife and children. Living in England once again, Landor enjoyed friendships with Lady Blessington, Charles Dickens, John Forster, and Thomas Carlyle, among other authors and literary figures. Yet not all Landor's relationships in Bath proved so pleasant. In 1858, Landor was charged with libel when he misguidedly championed a young woman whom he believed had been wronged by a minister's wife, Mrs. Yescombe. In retaliation, Landor wrote vulgar and defamatory anonymous letters to the Yescombe household. To avoid the legal penalties and scandal resulting from the affair, Landor returned to Florence, where he unsuccessfully attempted to reconcile with his family. He was destitute, aimlessly roaming the streets of Florence, when Robert and Elizabeth Browning took him in and acted for him in financial matters. Landor spent his last years in Florence and Siena in the company of the Brownings and their American friends. Though his creative powers declined with age, he continued to write and maintain friendships with literary figures until a few months before his death in 1864.

In summarizing his opinion of his own work, Landor once stated, "Poetry was always my amusement, prose my study and work." His major prose writings, contained in the series entitled *Imaginary Conversations,* number over one hundred fifty. In addition, Landor's significant prose works include *The Pentameron and Pentalogia,* fictional dialogues between Boccaccio and Petrarch, *Pericles and Aspasia,* a series of imaginary letters describing life in the golden age of Athens, and *Citation and Examination of William Shakespeare,* an imaginary critical

discussion. In all these works, Landor depicted classical characters and literary and political figures discussing a wide variety of topics. Although Landor's prose style is often praised for its variety, restraint, and finish, his descriptions of characters and their views have frequently evoked negative reactions. Landor often deviated from historical record and accepted traditions, and the opinions expressed by his characters have been faulted as mere projections of his own attitudes toward classical republicanism and ideals of beauty and clarity.

Although Landor considered his poetry an "amusement" and therefore less important than his prose works, his early poem *Gebir,* and the parallel Latin version, *Gebirus,* were serious endeavors. Based on an Oriental myth, both of these elaborate blank verse works reflected Landor's attempt to return to the classical ideals of simplicity and severity of form. The poems, never widely read, have been regarded as insignificant and obscure by many scholars, but individual passages from *Gebir* have been highly valued for their beauty of expression. Landor also attempted to write dramas in poetic form, first in *Count Julian,* a heroic closet drama that drew on his experiences in Spain, and later in his historical trilogy, *Andrea of Hungary, Giovanna of Naples,* and *Fra Rupert.* Critics generally agree that these works merit attention as poetry but fail as drama because they lack unity and plot development. As in *Gebir,* in *The Hellenics of Walter Savage Landor* and *Heroic Idylls, with*

Additional Poems, Landor again displayed his interest in classical and mythological themes. In these collections of poetry, he employed a variety of verse forms in presenting brief, simple tales and dialogues. The shorter poems proved effective vehicles for Landor's talent. Indeed, many critics have remarked that his greatness lies in individual sentences rather than in complete works; they consider Landor a gifted epigrammatist. His Latin and English epigrams are cited as classics of the form, and his frequently anthologized lines addressed to Rose Aylmer and Ianthe are considered definitive examples. The poetic works of Landor's old age, *The Last Fruit off an Old Tree* and *Dry Sticks, Fagoted by W.S.L.,* are generally considered inferior in taste and originality.

Landor neither expected nor received widespread recognition in his lifetime; as he prophesied, "I shall dine late; but the dining room will be well-lighted, the guests few and select." Consciously writing for a limited and discerning audience, Landor shunned popular forms and topics: his Latin compositions, classical concerns, and erudite style have discouraged most readers. But the poet's poet, and the critic's critic, as Forster characterized him, has never failed to generate interest. Among the Romantics, Percy Bysshe Shelley, Charles Lamb, Thomas De Quincey, and Robert Southey praised Landor's work. In addition, Ralph Waldo Emerson, Charles Algernon Swinburne, Robert Browning, and Dickens revered the eccentric poet. While he drew such distinguished admirers, the majority of readers and critics have found his works difficult, unemotional, and uninteresting. This diversity has characterized the history of Landor criticism. In 1878, Leslie Stephen remarked, "Landor is perhaps the most striking instance in modern literature of a radical divergence of opinion between the connoisseurs and the mass of readers." Stephen's evaluation remains valid in the twentieth century: the "few and select," including T. S. Eliot, Ezra Pound, and W. B. Yeats, have respected Landor as a poet, yet his works are not widely read. Recent critics have frequently focused on the reasons for Landor's lack of popularity, though some have studied his qualities as a prose stylist and his classical sources and modes of expression. Ultimately, Landor is remembered as the author of the *Imaginary Conversations* and numerous epigrams, as a classicist in the Romantic and Victorian ages, and as an idiosyncratic, independent figure in English literary history.

PRINCIPAL WORKS

The Poems of Walter Savage Landor (poetry) 1795
Gebir (poetry) 1798
Poetry (poetry) 1802
Gebirus (poetry) 1803
Count Julian (closet drama) 1812
Idyllia Heroica Decem, Librum Phaleuciorum Unum (poetry) 1814
Imaginary Conversations of Literary Men and Statesmen, first series. 3 vols. (fictional conversations) 1824-28
Imaginary Conversations of Literary Men and Statesmen, second series. 2 vols. (fictional conversations) 1829
Citation and Examination of William Shakespeare before Sir T. Lucy, Touching Deer-Steeling (fictional conversation) 1834
Pericles and Aspasia (fictional letters) 1836
The Pentameron and Pentalogia (fictional conversations) 1837
Andrea of Hungary. Giovanna of Naples (closet dramas) 1839

Fra Rupert (closet drama) 1840
The Works of Walter Savage Landor. 2 vols. (fictional conversations, poetry, closet dramas, and prose) 1846
The Hellenics of Walter Savage Landor (poetry) 1847
Poemeta et Inscriptiones (poetry) 1847
The Italics of Walter Savage Landor (poetry) 1848
The Last Fruit off an Old Tree (poetry and prose) 1853
Antony and Octavius (closet drama) 1856
Dry Sticks, Fagoted by W.S.L. (poetry and translations) 1858
Heroic Idylls, with Additional Poems (poetry) 1863
**The Works and Life of Walter Savage Landor.* 8 vols. (fictional conversations, poetry, prose, fictional letters, and criticism) 1876
Letters and Other Unpublished Writings of Walter Savage Landor (letters, fictional conversation, fragments, and poetry) 1897
Letters of Walter Savage Landor, Private and Public (letters) 1899
Complete Works of Walter Savage Landor. 16 vols. (fictional conversations, poetry, prose, and letters) 1927-36

*This work includes *Walter Savage Landor: A Biography,* by John Forster.

WALTER SAVAGE LANDOR (essay date 1798)

[*In his preface to* Gebir, *from which the following excerpt is taken, Landor briefly discusses the origin and form of his lengthy poem. For additional commentary by Landor, see excerpts dated 1800 and 1847.*]

It may possibly save some trouble, and obviate some errors, if I take a cursory review of my own performance [in *Gebir*]. Not that I would prevent others from criticising it, but that I may explain at large, and state distinctly, its origin and design. This Poem, the fruit of Idleness and Ignorance—for had I been a botanist or mineralogist it never had been written—was principally written in Wales. The subject was taken, or rather the shadow of the subject, from a wild and incoherent, but fanciful, Arabian Romance. On the shelf of a circulating library, I met with a Critique on the various Novels of our Country. Though the work itself had nothing remarkable in it, . . . yet it presented to me, at the conclusion, the story of 'Gebirus and Charoba'. A Poem, like mine, descriptive of men and manners, should never be founded totally on fiction. But that which is originally fiction may cease in effect to be so:—the tears of Andromache are as precious as those of Sapphira. (p. 40)

I have availed myself merely of the names, and taken but few bare circumstances. I have followed no man closely; nor have I turned from my road because another stood in it: though perhaps I have momentarily, in passing, caught the object that attracted him. I have written in blank verse, because there never was a poem in rhyme that grew not tedious in a thousand lines. My choice is undoubtedly the most difficult of the two: for how many have succeeded in rhyme, in the structure at least; how few comparatively in blank verse. . . . [In most] we meet with stiffness instead of strength, and weakness instead of ease. I am aware how much I myself stand in need of favor. I demand some little from Justice; I entreat much more from Candor. If there are, now in England, ten men of taste and genius who will applaud my Poem, I declare myself fully content: I will call for a division; I shall count a majority. (pp. 40-1)

> Walter Savage Landor, "Preface to 'Gebir' (1798),"
> in Landor as Critic, *edited by Charles L. Proudfit,*
> *University of Nebraska Press, 1979, pp. 39-41.*

[ROBERT SOUTHEY]   (essay date 1799)

[*An English poet, historian, biographer, essayist, short story writer,
and editor, Southey was a prominent literary figure of the late
eighteenth and early nineteenth centuries and a key member of
the Lake School of poetry. Southey's praise of* Gebir, *excerpted
below, led to a lasting friendship with Landor. For additional
criticism by Southey, see the excerpt dated 1812.*]

[The story of **Gebir** is] strange indeed and told in language
sometimes uncouth, but abounding with such beauties as it is
rarely our good fortune to discover. (p. 29)

The story of this poem is certainly ill chosen and not sufficiently
whole; and the language is frequently deficient in perspicuity.
These are the faults of **Gebir.** Of its beauties, our readers must
already be sensible. They are of the first order; every circumstance is displayed with a force and accuracy which painting
can not exceed.

> I am aware, [says the author], how much I
> myself stand in need of favor. I demand some
> little from Justice; I entreat much more from
> candor. If there are, now in England, ten men
> of taste and genius who will applaud my poem,
> I declare myself fully content: I will call for a
> division; I shall count a majority [see excerpt
> dated 1798].
>
> (pp. 38-9)

It is not our business to examine whether he has underrated
the number of men of taste and genius in England; but we have
read his poem repeatedly with more than common attention,
and with far more than common delight. (p. 39)

> [Robert Southey], *in a review of "Gebir: A Poem,"*
> *in* The Critical Review, *n.s. Vol. XXVII, September,*
> *1799, pp. 29-39.*

THE MONTHLY REVIEW, LONDON   (essay date 1800)

[*The following excerpt is taken from a negative review of* Gebir.]

An unpractised author has attempted, in [**Gebir**], the difficult
task of relating a romantic story in blank-verse. His performance betrays all the incorrectness and abruptness of inex-
perience, but it manifests occasionally some talent for description. He has fallen into the common error of those who aspire
to the composition of blank-verse, by borrowing too many
phrases and epithets from our incomparable Milton. (pp. 206-07)

We must observe that the story is told very obscurely, and
should have been assisted by an *Argument* in prose. Young
writers are often astonished to find that passages, which seem
very clear to their own heated imaginations, appear very dark
to their readers.—The author of the poem before us may produce something worthy of more approbation, if he will labour
hard, and delay for a few years the publication of his next
performance. (p. 208)

> *A review of "Gebir: A Poem," in* The Monthly Re-
> view, *London, Vol. XXXI, February, 1800, pp.*
> *206-08.*

WALTER SAVAGE LANDOR   (essay date 1800)

[*Landor's "Post-Script to* Gebir*" was written in 1800 in response
to Southey's positive assessment in the* Critical Review *(see the
excerpt dated 1799) and the harsher critique in the* Monthly Review *(see the excerpt dated 1800). This piece was suppressed by
Landor on the advice of his publisher and friends and did not
appear in full until 1933. For additional commentary by Landor,
see excerpts dated 1798 and 1847.*]

The *Critical* and *Monthly,* as being of the old establishment,
are those on which at present I would fix attention. In respect
to *Gebir,* the one perhaps is conducted by a partial, but certainly
by a masterly, hand. It objects, and indeed with reason, to a
temporary and local obscurity, which I have not been able, or
I have not been willing, or I have not been bold enough, to
remove: but never on the whole, since it's first institution, has
a poem been more warmly praised. The other's account is short:
containing one quotation and two mis-statements. "That the
poem was nothing more than the version of an Arabic tale; and
that the author, not content with borrowing the expressions,
had made the most awkward attempts to imitate the phraseology
of Milton."

The Review is not before me. I believe I have softened, but I
have not perverted, nor have I deteriorated his style. No man
would make or meditate so rash indefensible an attack, unless
he were certain that, if not already stationed there, he could
speedily drop into obscurity. I repeat to him in answer, what
I before asserted in my preface, that, so far from a *translation,*
there is not a single sentence, nor a single sentiment, in common with the tale. Some characters are drawn more at large,
some are brought out more prominent, and several are added.
I have not changed the scene, which would have distorted the
piece, but every line of appropriate description, and every shade
of peculiar manners, is originally and entirely my own.

Now, whether this gentleman has or has not read the poem,
whether he has or has not read the romance, his account is
equally false and equally malicious. For the romance is in
English, therefor he could have read it; the poem is in English,
and therefor he could have compared it. There is no disgrace
in omitting to read them: the disgrace is, either in pretending
to have done what he had not done, or in assuming a part which
he was incompetent to support. But there *is* a disgrace in omitting to read Milton; there is a disgrace in forgetting him. The
critic has not perused or not remembered him: it would be
impossible, if he had, that he should accuse me of borrowing
his expressions. I challenge him to produce them. If indeed I
had borrowed them, so little should I have realized by the
dangerous and wild speculation, that I might have composed
a better poem and not have been a better poet. But I feared to
break open, for the supply of my games or for the maintenance
of my veteran heroes, the sacred treasury of the great republican. Although I might enjoy, not indeed the extorted, but the
unguarded praise of an enemy, if my vanity could stoop so
low and could live on so little,—of an enemy who, throughout
so long a journey, and after so many speeches, and those on
such various occasions, pertinaciously took me for Milton—I
will add, for the information of my young opponent, what a
more careful man would conceal, but what in his present distress will relieve him greatly, that this, which amongst the
vulgar and thoughtless might currently pass for praise, is really

none at all. For, the language of *Paradise Lost* ought not to be the language of *Gebir*. There should be the softened air of remote antiquity, not the severe air of unapproachable sanctity. I devoutly offer up my incence at the shrine of Milton. Woe betide the intruder that would steal it's jewels! It requires no miracle to detect the sacrilege. The crime will be found it's punishment. The venerable saints, and still more holy personages, of Rapheal or Michael-Angelo, might as consistently be placed among the Bacchanals and Satyrs, bestriding the goats and bearing the vases of Poussin, as the resemblance of that poem, or any of it's component parts, could be introduced in mine.

I have avoided high-sounding words. I have attempted to throw back the gross materials, and to bring the figures forward. I knew beforehand the blame that I should incur. I knew that people would cry out "your burden was so light, we could hardly hear you breathe, pray where is your merit". For, there are few who seem thoroughly acquainted with this plain and simple truth, that it is easier to elevate the empty than to support the full. I also knew the *body* of my wine, and that years must pass over it, before it would reach it's relish. Some will think me intoxicated, and most will misconstrue my good-nature, if I invite the Reviewer, or any other friend that he will introduce,—but himself the most earnestly, as I suspect from his manner that he *poetizes*—to an amicable trial of skill.—I will subject myself to any penalty, either of writing or of ceasing to write, if the author, who criticizes with the flightiness of a poet, will assume that character at once, and, taking in series my twenty worst verses, write better an equal number, in the period of twenty years. I shall be rejoiced if he will open to me any poem of my contemporaries, of my English contemporaries I mean, and point out three pages more spirited, I will venture to add more classical than the three least happy and least accurate in *Gebir*.

In challenging a comparison the discriminating will remark, that more expertness is used than bravery. They will certainly acquit me of presumption, altogether, and judge from the character of the person thus addressed, that the champion opposed to me will not be the stoutest or most dexterous, but the heaviest or most shewy, and will readily agree that I have little cause to tremble, when probably I shall find in array against me the *Sovereign* of Mr. Pybus, or a work no less patriotic, the labor of a worthy clergyman, and in praise of better things,—to wit— *bank-notes and strong-beer*.

Many will think that I should have suppressed what I have said; but let them recollect that, amongst those ancient poets who contended for the public prize, each must not only have formed the same determination, (for defects are not usually compared with defects, but are generally contrasted with beauties) but have actually engaged, and that too more openly and personally, in a still more strenuous competition. If my rights had not been refused me, I should not have asserted my claims. Rambling by the side of the sea, or resting on the top of a mountain, and interlining with verses the letters of my friends, I sometimes thought how a Grecian would have written, but never what methods he would take to compass popularity. The nearer I approached him, tho' distant still, the more was I delighted. (pp. 350-52)

Several of these sketches were obliterated, still more laid aside and lost; various ideas I permitted to pass away, unwilling to disturb, by the slightest action, the dreams of reposing fancy. So little was I anxious to publish my rhapsodies, that I never sate down in the house, an hour at once, for the purpose of composition. Instead of making, or inviting, courtship, I declared with how little I should rest contented. Far from soliciting the attention of those who are passing by, *Gebir* is confined, I believe, to the shop of one bookseller, and I never heard that he had even made his appearance at the window. I understand not the management of these matters, but I find that the writing of a book is the least that an author has to do. My experience has not been great; and the caution which it has taught me lies entirely on the other side of publication. Before I was twenty years of age I had imprudently sent into the world a volume [*The Poems of Walter Savage Landor*], of which I was soon ashamed. It every-where met with as much commendation as was proper, and generally more. For, tho' the structure was feeble, the lines were fluent: the rhymes shewed habitual ease, and the personifications fashionable taste. I suffered any of my heroes, the greater part of whom were of a gentle kind, to look on one side thro' the eye of Pity, on the other thro' that of Love; and it was with great delight, for I could not foresee the consequences, that I heard them speak or sing with the lips of soft Persuasion.... I was then in raptures with what I now despise. I am far from the expectation, or the hope, that these deciduous shoots will be supported by the ivy of my maturer years. But, without any boast of prudence, I have hung up a motley and paultry skin for my puppies in their snarling playfulness to pull at, that they may not tear in pieces a better and costlier one on which I desire to rest.

After all, I do not wonder that they barked at *Gebir*—he came disguised and in tatters. Still there was nothing to authorize the impertinence with which the publication was treated by the *Monthly Review*er. These are not the faults which he complains of; tho' these might, without his consciousness, have first occasioned his ill-humour. I pity his want of abilities, and I pardon his excess of insolence. The merit is by no means small of a critic who speaks with modesty. For, his time being chiefly occupied, at first, in works fundamentally critical, at least if we suppose him desirous to *learn* before he is ambitious to *teach,* he thinks when he has attained their expressions and brevity, he has attained their solidity and profoundness. He must surely be above what he measures, else how can he measure with exactness? He must be greater, *ex officio*, than the person he brings before him; else how can he stigmatize with censure, or even dismiss with praise? (pp. 352-53)

> *Walter Savage Landor, "Post-Script to 'Gebir'," in his* The Complete Works of Walter Savage Landor: Poems, Vol. XIII, *edited by Stephen Wheeler, Chapman and Hall Ltd., 1933, pp. 350-63.*

[ROBERT SOUTHEY] (essay date 1812)

[*The following excerpt, taken from Southey's review of the anonymously published* Count Julian, *offers mixed criticism of the drama. For additional criticism by Southey, see the excerpt dated 1799.*]

The author of the drama before us [*Count Julian*], has taken a very different view of Count Julian's character from that in which the Spanish writers represent him. He is not

> El injuriado Conde, a la venganza
> Atento, y no a la fama.

as Luis de Leon describes him, a man sacrificing his country and his faith to the gratification of his revenge: the Julian of the tragedy is a hero and a patriot, seeking as much to redress the wrongs of his country as his own peculiar grievances; but unhappily attempting to effect it by the assistance of a foreign power. Repugnant as this representation of Julian is to the feelings of a Spaniard, and to those which are drawn from Spanish history, it is less so than the liberty which has been taken of ennobling Opas, the archbishop of Seville, a renegado and a traitor, whose name is detested in the peninsula. The author does not seem to be sensible that this can produce an unpleasant effect. 'It is remarkable,' he says, 'that the most important era in Spanish history should be the most obscure. This is propitious to the poet, and, above all, to the tragedian. Few characters of such an era can be glaringly misrepresented, few facts offensively perverted.' The purposes of the dramatist have certainly been served by this departure from historical verity and received tradition. (p. 86)

As a drama, it is evident that [*Count Julian*] has not been intended for representation,—so little is it addressed either to the eyes or the ears of the multitude. The fable is not always sufficiently clear; in a few instances the language, which is occasionally laboured into stiffness, borders on obscurity, and the verse is every where epic rather than dramatic.

We should have no hesitation in ascribing *Count Julian* to the author of a narrative poem of which the story is strange and unprepossessing, and the diction obscure, but in which the higher requisites of poetry are incidentally displayed in an eminent degree. The same powers are exhibited here so strikingly, and the defects which exist partake so much of the same character, that the internal evidence secures decision; but when an author has not thought proper to affix his name, the critic who gives it publicity assumes an authority to which neither the laws of courtesy nor of his profession entitle him. (p. 92)

> [*Robert Southey*], *in a review of "Count Julian: A Tragedy," in* The Quarterly Review, *Vol. VIII, No. XV, September, 1812, pp. 86-92.*

[HENRY TAYLOR AND WILLIAM GIFFORD]   (essay date 1824)

[*The following excerpt is taken from a mixed review that identifies the strengths and weaknesses of the* Imaginary Conversations.]

The nature of [*Imaginary Conversations of Literary Men and Statesmen*] is sufficiently explained by its title, to which we have only to add, that it is distributed into thirty-five conversations, maintained by distinguished personages of various ages and countries, under whose names Mr. Landor enjoys the opportunity of inculcating the most violent opinions of all parties; protesting of course against any of them being attributed to himself. The work being of a very desultory character, our remarks must be equally so.

The reader who is attracted by the names of Southey and Porson, . . . and told to expect a specimen of their conversation, must have prepared himself for no scanty exhibition of wit, for much astute criticism, and deep erudition. How will he then be surprised to find, that these eminent individuals meet only to agree upon the merits of Mr. Wordsworth's poetry! that they talk as if they were writing commentaries and tired of it, and that their dialogue is carried on with about the same speed of alternation, and vigour of contention, as the celebrated game at chess between the Spanish and Persian monarchs, each of whom resumed his deliberations in his own palace, as soon as the courier had arrived to announce his other majesty's last move! We protest against Mr. Landor's dialogue being supposed to furnish a specimen of Mr. Southey's conversation, and we will not consent to receive a sarcasm elaborately got

up, and forced on the attention in all the importunity of italics, as representing Professor Porson's style of wit. Neither can we allow our Northern contemporary, though a much smaller personage than these, to be represented, in the space of half a dozen lines, in the several characters of an ant and a serpent; and though it is doubtless with the best intentions that Mr. Wordsworth is figured in the same fruitful allegory, first as Adam, (or Eve, we do not clearly make out which,) and secondly as an elephant, yet we know enough of that gentleman's modesty to assure ourselves that he would be satisfied with appearing in one of those characters. (pp. 509-10)

In noticing the absurdities and perversities of this author, we are far from denying that he is a man of knowledge and abilities, which nothing but his singular deficiency of judgment could have rendered useless. In the absence of any rational or consistent design, these volumes display many random thoughts forcibly expressed, pointed invective thrown out as chance directed, a few reflections which are just and valuable, and a lively imagination, though it be rather exuberant than select. Others may be more fastidious, but we have been able to get over much bad taste, many elaborate epigrams, strange prose-metaphors, and politics in verse, to find entertainment in the easier and better parts of the book. (pp. 513-14)

[The] volumes in general are characterized by a spirit of pugnacity which, while it takes all its tenderness from criticism, satisfies us that rebuke is wholesome. The objects of this spirit are sufficiently multifarious, but the nearest are the most trampled upon. (p. 515)

Mr. Landor's mind is a self-constituted court of oyer and terminer, ready to try all causes which may come before it; and this court being composed of the most heterogeneous elements, and profoundly ignorant of the extent of its proper jurisdiction, passes upon each and every matter at issue, and upon all parties litigant, a sudden, peremptory, and unqualified sentence. (p. 518)

In conclusion, whatever measure of absurdity there may be in Mr. Landor's work, we desire to do him full justice: there is also in it a good deal to be admired, and some little to be approved. (p. 519)

> [*Henry Taylor and William Gifford*], "*Landor— 'Imaginary Conversations'*," *in* The Quarterly Review, *Vol. XXX, No. LX, January, 1824, pp. 508-19.*

[WILLIAM HAZLITT]   (essay date 1824)

[*One of the most important commentators of the Romantic age, Hazlitt was an English critic and journalist. Characterized by a tough, independent view of the world, by his political liberalism, and by the influence of Samuel Taylor Coleridge and Charles Lamb, Hazlitt's criticism is particularly admired for its wide range of reference and catholicity. Here, Hazlitt ridicules the* Imaginary Conversations, *attacking Landor's inconsistencies and his deviations from historical facts.*]

[Mr Landor's *Imaginary Conversations of Literary Men and Statesmen*] is as remarkable an instance as we have lately met with of the strength and weakness of the human intellect. It displays considerable originality, learning, acuteness, terseness of style, and force of invective—but it is spoiled and rendered abortive throughout by an utter want of temper, of self-knowledge, and decorum. Mr Landor's mind is far from barren in feeling or in resources; but over the natural, and (what might be) the useful growth of these, there every where springs up a luxuriant crop of caprice, dogmatism, extravagance, intolerance, quaintness, and most ludicrous arrogance,—like the red and blue flowers in corn, that, however they may dazzle the passenger's eye, choke up the harvest, and mock the hopes of the husbandman. We are not ignorant of the school to which our author belongs; and could name other writers who, in the course of a laborious life, and in productions numerous and multiform—some recent and suited to the times, some long and luckily forgotten,—in odes, inscriptions, madrigals, epics,—in essays, histories and reviews,—have run into as many absurdities, and as many extremes: But never did we see, bound up in the same volume, close-packed, and pointed with all the significance of style, the same number of contradictions, staring one another in the face, and quarrelling for the precedence. Mr Landor's book is a perfect 'institute and digest' of inconsistency: it is made up of mere antipathies in nature and in reasoning. It is a *chef-d'oeuvre* of self-opinion and self-will, strangling whatever is otherwise sound and excellent in principle, defacing whatever is beautiful in style and matter.

If it be true (as has been said) that

> Great wits to madness nearly are allied,

we know few writers that have higher or more unequivocal pretensions in this way than the author of the *Imaginary Conversations*. Would it be believed, that, trampling manfully on all history and tradition, he speaks of Tiberius as a *man of sentiment,* who retired to Capri merely to indulge a tender melancholy on the death of a beloved wife: and will have it that Nero was a most humane, amiable, and deservedly popular character—not arguing the points as doubtful or susceptible of question, but assuming them, *en passant,* as most absolute and peremptory conclusions—as if whatever was contrary to common sense and common feeling carried conviction on the face of it? In the same page he assures us, with the same oracular tranquillity, that the conflagration of Rome, and the great fire of London, were both wise and voluntary measures, arising from the necessity of purifying the cities after sickness, and leaving no narrow streets in their centres! and on turning the leaf, it is revealed to us, that there is nothing in Rome, *or in the world,* equal to—the circus in Bath! He spells the words *foreign* and *sovereign,* 'foren' and 'sovran,' and would go to the stake, or send others there, to prove the genuineness of these orthographies, which he adopts on the authority of Milton; and yet he abuses Buonaparte for being the ape of Antiquity, and talking about Miltiades. He cries up Mr Locke as 'the most *elegant* of English prose writers,' for no other reason (as we apprehend) than that he has often been considered as the least so; and compares Dr Johnson's style to 'that article of dress which the French have lately made peace with,' (a pair of pantaloons), 'divided into two parts, equal in length, breadth, and substance, with a protuberance before and behind.' He pronounces sentence upon the lost works of two ancient writers, Democritus and Menander, that the former would be worth all the philosophical remains of antiquity, and the latter not be worth having,—precisely because he can know nothing about the matter; the will to decide superseding the necessity of any positive ground of opinion, and the spirit of contradiction standing him in lieu of all other conviction. (pp. 67-9)

[*William Hazlitt*], *"Landor's 'Imaginary Conversations'," in* The Edinburgh Review, *Vol. XL, No. LXXIX, March, 1824, pp. 67-92.*

[PEREGRINE BINGHAM?] (essay date 1824)

[*Bingham points to minor anachronisms and errors of fact in the* Imaginary Conversations, *but otherwise commends the work as interesting and valuable.*]

[*Imaginary Conversations of Literary Men and Statesmen*] is the work of a man of no ordinary genius, benevolence, and courage: genius,—to apprehend, almost intuitively, and to express felicitously, many of the profoundest principles of morals and legislation;—benevolence,—to side and sympathize with the mass of his species, rather than with that detached and favoured portion of them who require and possess the power of applying to their own purposes the property of the people at large;—and courage,—to expose whatever is mischievous in the conduct or pretensions of this favourite few.

In the light form of conversations, the author has contrived to convey to his readers much that is instructive in politics, much that is amusing in literature:—in conversations, not carried on by Doctor and Student, Venator and Piscator, Philalethes and Eleutherus, or any such dull and unfashionable society, but by real personages with whom most of us have for some time been more or less acquainted, and whose characters, whether for good or for evil, we are pretty well able to appreciate. (pp. 431-32)

The announcement in the preface that "the peculiarities of some celebrated authors, both in style and sentiment," had been "imitated in these dialogues," tends rather to mislead the reader's expectation. The author has too much mind for a mimic, and is too proper a man to play the monkey amusingly. Here is no caricature, no burlesque, none of the fun of Tickell's "Anticipation" nor of the farce of "the Rejected Addresses," those mirth-inspiring little books which would have cured Heraclitus, and made the cave of Trophonius echo shouts of laughter:—Dr. Johnson is very sparing in the use of *verba sesquipedalia,* Milton's sentences are neither long nor latinized; and Franklin is not distinguished by short speeches, parables, and proverbs. Instead of throwing out the peculiarities of his *personae* Mr. Landor keeps them down. Undoubtedly there is in the most excentric man more that is like other folks than there is that is unlike; but he is characterized by the latter, and on that the imitator ought chiefly to fix, if he intends to produce a striking likeness. We should scarcely have suspected that imitation was any part of our author's design, had it not been so declared by himself. There is just so much of it as was unavoidable in selecting certain persons as vehicles for the utterance of appropriate opinions, and no more. The thoughts are not (as might be expected of a professed imitator) strongly coloured; but only just tinged by the media through which they pass to the reader. The identification of the author with his imagined speakers seems never complete. They do not talk of themselves, but he talks through them. They are but puppets, and his is the only voice, though it may be a little varied. He does not employ the real dramatic magic of transforming himself into the character of his selection or creation; he only produces a compound being of which a tenth may be Milton or Marvel, and the remaining nine-tenths are Walter Savage Landor. The result, however, is far more valuable than it would have been had even the most successful imitation been the distinguishing merit of the book. A number of well-known names are employed, and they are, in general, fairly and effectively employed, to give additional interest to the discussion of important questions, and to the exposure of vile sophisms and viler practices. We may never lose sight of the author, but then we never wish to lose sight of him; nay, we like the company into which he leads us all the better for their bearing evident marks of being animated by his spirit.

In a work of this description, the author cannot be held responsible for the truth of any particular opinion, or the validity of any particular argument; all that is required, being, that such opinion or argument become the speaker to whom it is ascribed. But if it happens, that in a series of imaginary dialogues, some opinions are more frequently advanced, more impressively recommended, more plausibly supported, than others, so that the effect of the whole work is, to produce a prejudice or a conviction in their favour; the author may, without injustice, be considered as the advocate of those opinions. What is the writer's own opinion? is a question which rises in every reader's mind, and Mr. Landor has furnished materials for the answer, on a tolerably comprehensive list of topics.

Undesignedly, he has fallen into some mistakes in the way of anachronism, some errors in matters of fact, and designedly, into a good deal of affectation on the score of orthography, for which affectation he adduces, as it seems to us, very insufficient reasons in a conversation between Dr. Johnson and Horne Tooke; this, however, is as much notice as we choose to bestow on points so comparatively unimportant, and having thus far discussed the manner of the work, we shall now proceed to the matter.

With regard to this, in disquisitions so purely conversational, there is little on which the critic can fasten: partly, because the author has always a retreat under the dramatic character of his interlocutors; partly, because a work so constructed consists mainly of a series of desultory observations, neither presenting nor professing to present any complete system or any exposition of principles which will admit the process of detailed examination. (pp. 432-34)

From the general tone of his language and sentiments, it is clear to us, that Mr. Landor is a man of highly poetical imagination; we collect also from the whole complexion of his book, that he has devoted no small portion of his time and labour to Belles Lettres in every shape, ancient and modern, poetry and history. But from the errors we have already mentioned, as well as from various expressions which he has employed, we are equally convinced, either that he has not had access to the great and only sources of moral and political science—those few and recent writers who have developed the only principles which can produce the greatest happiness of the greatest number—or, that having had access to them, he has bestowed very little labour on the subject. If this be so, the wonder is, not that he should have fallen into the errors in question, or should occasionally wander in the mists of vague generalities, but rather that he should have discovered and adopted so many bold truths, and so many admirable sentiments as he has himself presented for our consideration. It is true, that an intellect unshackled as his, might have discovered of itself, and with ten or twenty years' labour and practice, might have developed, and have been able to apply, consistently, the great principle of general utility. But Mr. Landor has been engaged in other pursuits; he probably has neither had the time nor the inclination to make the discovery, or pursue the application of it unassisted; and he furnishes another and a striking example of the difficulties which beset even a searching and unprejudiced intellect, in handling the great problems of morals and legislation, unless by its own exertions, or those of others, it has been furnished with the only sure key to precision and truth.

Of the mischiefs attending many established institutions—of the sinister interests which support those institutions, and wage war against all public improvement, Mr. Landor has a ready and an accurate conception: in detecting the haunts, and exposing the fallacies of all the creatures of corruption, he is as quick as lightning; but when this has been accomplished, when the ground is cleared of the enemy, and the great question comes, *quid faciendum?* he is directly at fault, and gropes about in the mists of metaphor and generalities, just as a school-boy who quotes Cicero, or as Cicero himself did two thousand years ago. (pp. 434-35)

[*Peregrine Bingham?*], "Landor's 'Imaginary Conversations'," in The Westminster Review, *Vol. 1, April, 1824, pp. 431-53.*

SAMUEL TAYLOR COLERIDGE   (conversation date 1834)

[*An English poet and critic, Coleridge was central to the English Romantic movement and is considered one of the greatest literary critics in the English language. In this extract, Coleridge remarks that Landor lacks imagination, consistency, and the ability to write "simple and lucid English."*]

What is it that Mr. Landor wants, to make him a poet? His powers are certainly very considerable, but he seems to be totally deficient in that modifying faculty, which compresses several units into one whole. The truth is, he does not possess imagination in its highest form—that of stamping *il più nell' uno.* Hence his poems, taken as wholes, are unintelligible; you have eminences excessively bright, and all the ground around and between them in darkness. Besides which, he has never learned, with all his energy, how to write simple and lucid English.

Samuel Taylor Coleridge, in a conversation on January 1, 1834, in his The Table Talk and Omniana of Samuel Taylor Coleridge, *Oxford University Press, London, 1917, p. 286.*

[JOHN FORSTER]   (essay date 1836)

[*Forster was an English biographer, historian, critic, and editor. He had a significant impact on Landor's career and reputation as his editor and biographer. In the excerpt that follows, Forster evaluates Landor's strengths and failings as a poet, drawing instances from Landor's early dramatic poetry. For further criticism by Forster, see the excerpt dated 1846 and the Additional Bibliography.*]

[We characterize] Mr. Walter Savage Landor, as "a poet for poets." In this phrase, we would have it understood, we desire to include not only the highest tribute we can pay to his genius, but also the strongest detraction we can make from it. The power, the variety, and the rapidly-associating thought, which belong alone to the poetical perceptions, and by a combination of which it is that the eye of the poet is enabled to glance in an instant from heaven to earth, and from earth to heaven,—these are in some sort necessary to him who would understand Mr. Landor's poetry as a whole. That masterly connexion of the remotest analogies which is constantly to be met with there, and never with the help of any of those long intermediate processes which are requisite to the perceptions of ordinary readers, demands, for its entire and proper appreciation, the creative, scarcely less than the percipient faculty.

While this, however, is, on the one hand, an evidence of the most vivid conception and the most perfect faith to which a poet can attain, it is no less, on the other hand, open to very serious objections. So subtle a principle of association must frequently refine itself into a fault, and it may happen, at times, with the most docile disciple of Mr. Landor, that he shall recognize nothing but a series of thoughts or feelings, each evidently in some way dependent on the other, but according to some system which he is unable clearly to ascertain. The association, in fact, is liable to spring too hastily from a non-essential quality, rather than from the acknowledged and inseparate aggregate;—as sometimes, we venture to think, and more particularly in his minor poems, from the word rather than from the thought it expresses.

It is then a necessary result, from the nature of Mr. Landor's genius, that he can never become a popular poet. A writer of verse, after Sir Walter Scott's mode, who, acting under the broadest and most obvious law of association, merely reproduces, in a higher and illustrated form, the ordinary impressions, will as surely never be unpopular. It would be curious, indeed, to take one of the grandest passages from *Gebir,* and observe the running and connecting commentary that would be required to make it continuous and intelligible to a reader very capable of mastering the mysteries of *Marmion.* When Mr. Coleridge said,—as he is reported to have alleged, in explanation of the circumstance of Mr. Landor's poems not being popular,—that "Landor had not, after all, the power of expressing his thoughts in lucid and perspicuous English" [see excerpt dated 1834]; he seems to us to have exactly mistaken the cause. We hold, on the contrary, . . . that it is more likely to be found in Mr. Landor's too thorough sensitiveness on the subject of language—in his too precise apprehension of the vehicle of his thoughts. His light is diverted, and glances excentrically off from the facettes of his gem-like words. This is his grand fault in the midst of enormous beauties.

How different from Shelley's, with whose "obscurity" it has been the fashion to class the "puzzling verses" of Landor! Shelley's error was that of presenting a vast array of synchronous images relating to the same thing. (pp. 200-01)

All Mr. Landor's reflections and images are, on the other hand, successive. . . . [Each] one of them has a body and distinctness of its own. Each one of them is also obviously dependent on the other, though at times somewhat inexplicably so—"far-fetched" we might say. And how pregnant with meaning, and in what a dress of words—*splendidior vitro,* is each in itself! For, in the most apparently obscure parts of Landor's poetry, the sections, the passages, that bewilder the reader most *in succession,* are, when viewed abstractedly, as "one entire and perfect chrysolite." Nobody's single lines are nearly so good as Landor's. How grand is this from the *Count Julian*—

Guilt hath pavillions, but no privacy!

(p. 201)

In *Gebir,* all the splendour and all the peculiarities of Mr. Landor's genius have scope. Its successions of wondrous imagery, and of sweet and delicate fancies, are set down without pause or doubt, and as though the very objects were at hand to be referred to by any gainsayer. (p. 202)

[The poem itself] is a masterpiece. Through all its wonderful imagery there is not a pause or a doubt. Why should there be? The poet speaks of *existing* marvels. He does not call them up in the reader's presence. The task of creating is already accomplished, and his office is simply to describe. It may be said, at the same time, that all optics are not sufficiently acute to bear this sort of sudden exhibition; and it may admit of a reasonable doubt whether, in all cases, such tardiness of vision should be unprovided against. These questions, it will be seen, connect themselves with what we have said of the exacting nature of Mr. Landor's poetry, and of its continual demand on the imagination, almost creative, of its readers.

But what has all this to do, we may be asked, with a "GENIUS FOR DRAMATIC POETRY" in especial? We have just come to that. The questions suggested by *Gebir* cease to be questions here. There can be no doubt that the broad characteristics we have attributed to that great poem are those that belong to the true art of dramatic composition. In the drama all that is *material* is already upon the scene and actually present to the eye. We, the audience and spectators, have the passion bodily before us; we pursue its living progress, and watch its palpable results. It follows, therefore, for these reasons, that in the drama all which is *etherial* should be absolutely discharged from the task of setting forth what is, or ought to be, already visible. We do not want words, for instance, to assure us that this passion, and all its results, do exist. Virtually indeed words assure us of it, and that in the highest degree, because it is from the existence in question that they have at once flowed. But, as words, they are there because of the passion, not the passion because of them; and it is in this *effluence* of words, as a pure effect of passion, that the genuine art of dramatic writing consists.

Now—disjoin such an effect from the material agents that have produced it, from the actors, from the scene, from the very audience, and it instantly becomes as "obscure" and "unintelligible" as Mr. Landor's general poetry, to all but those who are capable of supplying those materials from their own imagination. (p. 203)

[Is] any elaborate commentary necessary to indicate the persons and the action that belong to these few intensely dramatic lines—?

"Stay! spare him! save the last!
Medea! . . . is that blood? again! it drops
From my imploring hand upon my feet . . .
I will invoke the Eumenides no more . . .
I will forgive thee . . . bless thee . . . bend to thee
In all thy wishes . . . do but thou, Medea,
Tell me, one lives.
    "And shall I too deceive?"
Cries from the firy car an angry voice;
And swifter than two falling stars descend
Two breathless bodies . . . warm, soft, motionless,
As flowers in stillest noon before the sun,
They lie three paces from him . . ."

This is from one of Mr. Landor's minor poems, addressed **"To Corinth."** But let us now introduce the reader to some of those full and splendid embodiments of what dramatic writing ought to be, which will justify our special and emphatic connexion of Mr. Landor's name with this great subject. . . .

[The following extract is from the dramatic poem **"Ines de Castro"**]:

IN.   Now tell me.
Pedro! your hand and brow are sadly parcht,
And you are out of breath, altho' you walked
These twenty paces, more than I who ran . . .
And yet you always caught me when we tried.
What would you tell me now, my faithful Pedro?
    PED. In one word, Ines! I have ceased to love thee.
Loose me and let me go.
    IN.   Is this your greeting?
This your first morning salutation? turn . . .
Can it be? must I (look at me) believe it?
    PED. Yes, my sweet . . . yes, my Ines . . . yes, yes,
Ines!

IN. And are you still so generous, O my love,
As to be sorry you have ceased to love me?
To sigh, almost to weep, bending your face
Away from me, lest I should grieve to see
A change in it, and in a change a loss?
Take off that hand from above mine then! take it!
I dare not move it from me . . . 'tis the prince's,
And not my Pedro's.
    PED.   I must go.
    IN.   I once
Might ask you why. Let *me* go.
    PED.   Wouldst thou? whither?
Unfortunate! So, thou resignest me,
Light heartless girl!

Every line here is absolutely perfect. Mark, above all, the struggle of the soul in those few words—"Yes, my sweet . . . yes, my Ines . . . yes, yes, Ines!"—and the breathless haste with which, in the last passage, the prince catches at the slightest shadow of excuse to himself for his proposed desertion. (pp. 204-05)

Add to [this a] . . . transcendent scene from **"Ippolito di Este."** Ferrante and Giulio were brothers, by the father's side, to the Duke Alfonso and the Cardinal Ippolito di Este. The Cardinal deprived Ferrante of his eyes for loving the same object as his Eminence, and because she had praised the beauty of them. . . . [Ippolito] carries the Duke's sentence to Ferrante, who is attended in his prison by Giulio. After a terrible interview, Ippolito stalks out of the prison, having handed the sentence to Giulio with these words—"Take you the sentence, *and God be with both!*" Is it necessary to ask the reader's admiration for *every word* in the scene which follows? . . .

    FER. O my true brother, Giulio, *why thus hang*
Around my neck and pour forth prayers for me?
Where there are priests and kinsmen such as ours,
God hears not, nor is heard. I am prepared
For death.
    GIU. Ah! worse than death may come upon you,
Unless Heaven interpose.
    FER.   I know the worst,
And bear one comfort in my breast that fire
And steel can ne'er force from it: she I love
Will not be his, but die as she hath lived.
Doubt you? that thus you shake the head, and sigh.
    GIU. Far other doubt was mine: even this shall cease.
    FER. Speak it.
    GIU. I must: God pardon me!
    FER.   Speak on.
    GIU. Have we not dwelt in friendship from our birth,
Told the same courtier the same tale of joy,
And pointed where life's earliest thorn had pierced
Amid the sports of boyhood, ere the heart
Hath aught of bitter or unsound within?
    FER. We have indeed.
    GIU.   Has my advice been ill?
    FER. Too often ill-observed, but always good.
    GIU. *Brother, my words are not what better men*
Would speak to you; and yet my love, I think,
Must be more warm than theirs can ever be. . . .
    FER. Brother's, friend's, father's, when was it like
        yours!
    GIU. Which of them ever said what I shall say!

FER. Speak; my desires are kindled, my fears
    quencht.
    GIU. DO NOT DELAY TO DIE, LEST CRUELLER
THAN COMMON DEATH BEFALL YOU. . . .
    GIU. Hark! hear you not the people? to the window!
They shout and clap their hands when they first meet
    you
After short absence; what shall they now do?
Up! seize the moment; shew yourself.
    FER.   Stay, Giulio!
Draw me not thither! speak not of my wrongs . . .
I would await but not arouse their vengeance,
And would deserve but court not their applause.
Little of good shall good men hope from them,
Nothing shall wiser.
          (Aside). *O were he away!*
But if I fail, he must die too, being here.
    GIU. Let me call out: they are below the grate.
They would deliver you: try this one chance.
Obdurate! would you hold me down! They're gone!
    FER. *Giulio! for shame! weep not,* or here I stay
And let vile hands deform me.

                      (pp. 207-08)

Is there any *writing in* of the action here? Are any stage-directions wanted? Does the actor of Giulio require to be told what to do, or how to do it? Are not the very words a KEAN in action? With what heart-rending earnestness do we not hear a Voice tremble, as it recalls the affection of the past, to excuse the terrible advice of the present! Does the actor of Ferrante need to know in what tones that commonplace excuse of his must be spoken, where he resigns the hope of release from the people, rather than endanger his brother,—or does he require a clue to the quiet accents of agonized resolve in which that "*aside*" must be expressed,—or to the action with which he may convey the keenness of the dagger's point? Truly we want no—*stabs himself and falls—right hand—prompt: side*—or any of those ingenious and elaborate details which abound in the books of the players. (p. 208)

[*John Forster*], "*Evidences of Genius for Dramatic Poetry,*" *in* The New Monthly Magazine, *Vol. XLVIII, No. CXC, October, 1836, pp. 200-08.*

[RALPH WALDO EMERSON]   (essay date 1841)

[*Emerson was one of the most influential figures of the nineteenth century. An American essayist and poet, he founded the Transcendentalist movement and shaped a distinctly American philosophy that embraces optimism, individuality, and mysticism. Emerson here praises the unique artistry of the* Imaginary Conversations *as seen in Landor's characterizations and astute critical perception. Yet he finds that the work lacks unity and that its value rests on the merit of individual sentences.*]

[For] twenty years we have . . . found [Landor's] *Imaginary Conversations* a sure resource in solitude, and it seems to us as original in its form as in its matter. Nay, when we remember his rich and ample page, wherein we are always sure to find free and sustained thought, a keen and precise understanding, an affluent and ready memory familiar with all chosen books, an industrious observation in every department of life, an experience to which nothing has occurred in vain, honor for every just and generous sentiment, and a scourge like that of the Furies for every oppressor, whether public or private, we feel how dignified is this perpetual Censor in his curule chair, and we wish to thank a benefactor of the reading world.

Mr. Landor is one of the foremost of that small class who make good in the nineteenth century the claims of pure literature. In these busy days of avarice and ambition, when there is so little disposition to profound thought, or to any but the most superficial intellectual entertainments, a faithful scholar receiving from past ages the treasures of wit, and enlarging them by his own love, is a friend and consoler of mankind. (pp. 263-64)

Whoever writes for the love of truth and beauty, and not with ulterior ends, belongs to [a] sacred class, and among these, few men of the present age, have a better claim to be numbered than Mr. Landor. Wherever genius or taste has existed, wherever freedom and justice are threatened, which he values as the element in which genius may work, his interest is sure to be commanded. His love of beauty is passionate, and betrays itself in all petulant and contemptuous expressions.

But beyond his delight in genius, and his love of individual and civil liberty, Mr. Landor has a perception that is much more rare, the appreciation of character. This is the more remarkable considered with his intense nationality. . . . He is buttoned in English broadcloth to the chin. He hates the Austrians, the Italians, the French, the Scotch, and the Irish. He has the common prejudices of an English landholder; values his pedigree, his acres, and the syllables of his name; loves all his advantages, is not insensible to the beauty of his watch-seal, or the Turk's head on his umbrella; yet with all this miscellaneous pride, there is a noble nature within him, which instructs him that he is so rich that he can well spare all his trappings, and, leaving to others the painting of circumstance, aspire to the office of delineating character. He draws his own portrait in the costume of a village schoolmaster, and a sailor, and serenely enjoys the victory of nature over fortune. Not only the elaborated story of Normanby, but the whimsical selection of his heads prove this taste. He draws with evident pleasure the portrait of a man, who never said anything right, and never did anything wrong. But in the character of Pericles, he has found full play for beauty and greatness of behavior, where the circumstances are in harmony with the man. These portraits, though mere sketches, must be valued as attempts in the very highest kind of narrative, which not only has very few examples to exhibit of any success, but very few competitors in the attempt. The word Character is in all mouths; it is a force which we all feel; yet who has analyzed it? What is the nature of that subtle, and majestic principle which attaches us to a few persons, not so much by personal as by the most spiritual ties? What is the quality of the persons who, without being public men, or literary men, or rich men, or active men, or (in the popular sense) religious men, have a certain salutary omnipresence in all our life's history, almost giving their own quality to the atmosphere and the landscape? A moral force, yet wholly unmindful of creed and catechism, intellectual, but scornful of books, it works directly and without means, and though it may be resisted at any time, yet resistance to it is a suicide. For the person who stands in this lofty relation to his fellow men is always the impersonation to them of their conscience. It is a sufficient proof of the extreme delicacy of this element, evanescing before any but the most sympathetic vision, that it has so seldom been employed in the drama and in novels. Mr. Landor, almost alone among living English writers, has indicated his perception of it.

These merits make Mr. Landor's position in the republic of letters one of great mark and dignity. He exercises with a grandeur of spirit the office of writer, and carries it with an air of old and unquestionable nobility. We do not recollect an example of more complete independence in literary history. He has no clanship, no friendships, that warp him. He was one of the first to pronounce Wordsworth the great poet of the age, yet he discriminates his faults with the greater freedom. He loves Pindar, Aeschylus, Euripides, Aristophanes, Demosthenes, Virgil, yet with open eyes. His position is by no means the highest in literature; he is not a poet or a philosopher. He is a man full of thoughts, but not, like Coleridge, a man of ideas. Only from a mind conversant with the First Philosophy can definitions be expected. Coleridge has contributed many valuable ones to modern literature. Mr. Landor's definitions are only enumerations of particulars; the generic law is not seized. But as it is not from the highest Alps or Andes, but from less elevated summits, that the most attractive landscape is commanded, so is Mr. Landor the most useful and agreeable of critics. He has commented on a wide variety of writers, with a closeness and an extent of view, which has enhanced the value of those authors to his readers. His Dialogue on the Epicurean philosophy is a theory of the genius of Epicurus. The Dialogue between Barrow and Newton is the best of all criticisms on the Essays of Bacon. His picture of Demosthenes in three several Dialogues is new and adequate. He has illustrated the genius of Homer, Aeschylus, Pindar, Euripides, Thucydides. Then he has examined before he expatiated, and the minuteness of his verbal criticism gives a confidence in his fidelity, when he speaks the language of meditation or of passion. His acquaintance with the English tongue is unsurpassed. He "hates false words, and seeks with care, difficulty, and moroseness, those that fit the thing." He knows the value of his own words. "They are not," he says, "written on slate." He never stoops to explanation, nor uses seven words where one will do. He is a master of condensation and suppression, and that in no vulgar way. He knows the wide difference between compression and an obscure elliptical style. The dense writer has yet ample room and choice of phrase, and even a gamesome mood often between his valid words. There is no inadequacy or disagreeable contraction in his sentence, any more than in a human face, where in a square space of a few inches is found room for every possible variety of expression.

Yet it is not as an artist, that Mr. Landor commends himself to us. He is not epic or dramatic, he has not the high, overpowering method, by which the master gives unity and integrity to a work of many parts. He is too wilful, and never abandons himself to his genius. His books are a strange mixture of politics, etymology, allegory, sentiment, and personal history, and what skill of transition he may possess is superficial, not spiritual. His merit must rest at last, not on the spirit of the dialogue, or the symmetry of any of his historical portraits, but on the value of his sentences. Many of these will secure their own immortality in English literature; and this, rightly considered, is no mean merit. These are not plants and animals, but the genetical atoms, of which both are composed. . . . Of many of Mr. Landor's sentences we are fain to remember what was said of those of Socrates, that they are cubes, which will stand firm, place them how or where you will. (pp. 265-68)

[*Ralph Waldo Emerson*], *"Walter Savage Landor,"* in The Dial, *Vol. II, No. II, October, 1841, pp. 262-71.*

ELIZABETH BARRETT with RICHARD HENGIST HORNE
(essay date 1844)

[*A leading poet in Victorian England, Barrett (later Elizabeth Barrett Browning) is best known for her cycle of love poetry,*

Sonnets from the Portuguese. In the following excerpt, she decries her contemporaries' unenthusiastic reception of Landor's works and discusses his status in literature and his qualities as a writer.]

Mr. Landor is a man of genius and learning, who stands in a position unlike that of any other eminent individual of his time. He has received no apparent influence from any one of his contemporaries; nor have they or the public received any apparent influence from him. The absence of any fixed and definite influence upon the public is actually as it seems; but that he has exercised a considerable influence upon the minds of many of his contemporaries is inevitable, because so fine a spirit could never have passed through any competent medium without communicating its electric forces, although from the very fineness of its elements, the effect, like the cause, has been of too subtle a nature to leave a tangible or visible impress. (pp. 109-10)

Of the difference between the partialities of the public, and the eventual judgements of the people; between a deeply-founded fame and an ephemeral interest, few more striking examples will perhaps be discovered in future years than in the solitary course of Walter Savage Landor amidst the various 'lights of his day'. He has incontestably displayed original genius as a writer; the highest critical faculty—that sympathy with genius and knowledge which can only result from imagination and generous love of truth—and also a fine scholarship in the spirit as well as the letter of classical attainments. But the public, tacitly, has denied his claims, or worse—admitted them with total indifference,—letting fall from its benumbed fingers, work after work, not because any one ventured to say, or perhaps even to think, the books were unworthy, but because the hands were cold. . . . [As] a general rule, the originality of a man, say and do what he may, is necessarily in itself an argument against his rapid popularity. In the case of Mr. Landor, however, other causes than the originality of his faculty have opposed his favour with the public. He has the most select audience perhaps,—the fittest, fewest,—of any distinguished author of the day; and this of his choice. 'Give me', he said in one of his prefaces, 'ten accomplished men for readers, and I am content' [see excerpt dated 1798];—and the event does not by any means so far as we could desire, outstrip the modesty, or despair, or disdain, of this aspiration. He writes criticism for critics, and poetry for poets: his drama, when he is dramatic, will suppose neither pit nor gallery, nor critics, nor dramatic laws. He is not a publican among poets—he does not sell his Amreeta cups upon the highway. He delivers them rather with the dignity of a giver, to ticketed persons; analysing their flavour and fragrance with a learned delicacy, and an appeal to the esoteric. His very spelling of English is uncommon and theoretic. He has a vein of humour which by its own nature is peculiarly subtle and evasive; he therefore refines upon it, by his art, in order to prevent anybody discovering it without a grave, solicitous, and courtly approach, which is unspeakably ridiculous to all the parties concerned, and which no doubt the author secretly enjoys. And as if poetry were not, in English, a sufficiently unpopular dead language, he has had recourse to writing poetry in Latin; with dissertations on the Latin tongue, to fence it out doubly from the populace. *'Odi profanum vulgus, et arceo.'*

Whether Mr. Landor writes Latin or English, poetry or prose, he does it all with a certain artistic composure, as if he knew what he was doing, and respected the cunning of his right hand. At times he displays an equal respect for his wilfulness. In poetry, his *Gebir*, the **"Phocaeans"** and some other performances take a high classic rank. He can put out extraordinary

power both in description and situation; but the vitality, comprehended in the power, does not overflow along the inferior portions of the work, so as to sustain them to the level of the reader's continued attention. The poet rather builds up to his own elevations than carries them out and on; and the reader passes from admiration to admiration, by separate states or shocks, and not by a continuity of interest through the intervals of emotion. Thus it happens that his best dramatic works,—those, the impression of which on the mind is most definite and excellent,—are fragmentary; and that his complete dramas are not often read through twice, even by readers who applaud them, but for the sake of a particular act or scene.

A remark should be made on Mr. Landor's blank verse, in which the poems just named, and several others, are written. It is the very best of the regular-syllable class, the versification of 'numbers', as they have been characteristically called by the schools. His blank verse is not only the most regular that ever was written, but it is the most sweet, and far less monotonous than we should expect of a musical system which excluded occasional discords. It has all the effect of the most melodious rhyming heroic verse; indeed, it often gives the impression of elegiac verses in rhyme. As blank verse it is a very bad model. There is more freedom in his dramatic verse, and always the purest style.

His dramatic works (except the compact little scenes entitled *Pentalogia,* which are admirable) are written upon an essentially undramatic principle; or, more probably, on no principle at all. Mr. Landor well knows 'all the laws', and they seem to provoke his will to be lawless. In this species of drama-looking composition he displays at times the finest passion, the most pure and perfect style of dramatic dialogue, and an intensity of mental movements, with their invisible, undeclared, yet necessarily tragic results; all of which proves him to possess the most wonderful three-fourths of a great dramatic genius which ever appeared in the world. But the fourth part is certainly wanting by way of making good his ground to the eyes, and ears, and understanding of the masses. (pp. 115-18)

In whatever Mr. Landor writes, his power, when he puts it forth, is of the first order. He is classical in the highest sense. His conceptions stand out, clearly cut and fine, in a magnitude and nobility as far as possible removed from the small and sickly vagueness common to this century of letters. If he seems obscure at times, it is from no infirmity or inadequacy of thought or word, but from extreme concentration, and involution in brevity—for a short string can be tied in a knot, as well as a long one. He can be tender, as the strong can best be; and his pathos, when it comes, is profound. His descriptions are full and startling; his thoughts, self-produced and bold; and he has the art of taking a commonplace under a new aspect, and of leaving the Roman brick, marble. In marble indeed, he seems to work; for there is an angularity in the workmanship, whether of prose or verse, which the very exquisiteness of the polish renders more conspicuous. You may complain too of hearing the chisel; but after all, you applaud the work—it is a work well done. The elaboration produces no sense of heaviness,—the severity of the outline does not militate against beauty;—if it is cold, it is also noble—if not impulsive, it is suggestive. As a writer of Latin poems, he ranks with our most successful scholars and poets; having less harmony and majesty than Milton had,—when he aspired to the species of 'Life in Death',—but more variety and freedom of utterance. Mr. Landor's English prose writings possess most of the characteristics of his poetry; only they are more perfect in their class. His

Pericles and Aspasia, and *Pentameron,* are books for the world and for all time, whenever the world and time shall come to their senses about them; complete in beauty of sentiment and subtlety of criticism. His general style is highly scholastic and elegant,—his sentences have articulations, if such an expression may be permitted, of very excellent proportions. And, abounding in striking images and thoughts, he is remarkable for making clear the ground around them, and for lifting them, like statues to pedestals, where they may be seen most distinctly, and strike with the most enduring though often the most gradual impression. This is the case both in his prose works and his poetry. It is more conspicuously true of some of his smaller poems, which for quiet classic grace and tenderness, and exquisite care in their polish, may best be compared with beautiful cameos and vases of the antique. (pp. 118-19)

Mr. Landor's wit and humour are of a very original kind, as previously remarked. Perhaps in none of his writings does their peculiarity occur so continuously as in a series of Letters, entitled **"High and Low Life in Italy"**. Every sarcasm, irony, jest, or touch of humour, is secreted beneath the skin of each tingling member of his sentences. His wit and his humour are alike covered up amidst various things, apparently intended to lead the reader astray, as certain birds are wont to do when you approach the nests that contain their broods. Or, the main jests and knotty points of a paragraph are planed down to the smooth level of the rest of the sentences, so that the reader may walk over them without knowing anything of the matter. All this may be natural to his genius; it may also result from pride, or perversity. So far from seeking the public, his genius has displayed a sort of apathy, if not antipathy, to popularity; *therefore,* the public must court it, if they would enjoy it; to possess yourself of his wit you must scrutinize; to be let into the secret of his humour you must advance 'pointing the toe'. (p. 120)

The imagination of Mr. Landor is richly graphic, classical, and subtly refined. In portraying a character, his imagination identifies itself with the mentality and the emotions of its inner being, and all those idiosyncracies which may be said to exist between a man and himself, but with which few, if anybody else, have any business. In other respects, most of his characters—especially those of his own invention—might live, think, move, and have their being in space, so little does their author trouble himself with their corporeal conditions. Whether it be that their author feels his own *physique* so strongly that it does not occur to him that any one else can need such a thing—*he* will find all that for them—or that it is the habit of his genius to abstract itself from corporeal realities (partly from the perverse love a man continually has of being his own 'opposite'), and ascend into a more subtle element of existence,—certain it is that many of his characters are totally without material or definite *form;* appear to live nowhere, and upon nothing, and to be very independent agents, to whom practical action seldom or never occurs. 'They think, therefore they are'. They feel, and know (they are apt too often to know as much as their author) therefore they are characters. But they are usually without bodily substance; and such form as they seem to have, is an abstraction which plays round them, but might go off in air at any time, and the loss be scarcely apparent. The designs of his larger works, as wholes, are also deficient in compactness of form, precision of outline, and condensation. They often seem wild, not at all intellectually, but from ungoverned will. It is difficult not to arrive at conclusions of this kind—though different minds will, of course, see differently—after a careful study of the dramas of *Andrea of Hungary, Giovanna of Naples,*

and *Fra Rupert;* the *Pericles and Aspasia,* the *Pentameron and Pentalogia,* &c. The very title of the *Imaginary Conversations* gives a strong foretaste of Mr. Landor's predominating ideality, and dismissal of mortal bonds and conditions. The extraordinary productions last named are as though their author had been rarified while listening to the conversation, or the double soliloquies, of august Shades; all of which he had carefully written down on resuming his corporeality, and where his memory failed him he had supplied the deficiency with some sterling stuff of his own. The Landorean 'peeps' seen through these ethereal dialogues and soliloquies of the mighty dead, are seldom to be mistaken; and though hardly at times in accordance with their company, are seldom unworthy of the highest.

As a partial exception to some of the foregoing remarks should be mentioned the *Examination of William Shakespeare before Sir Thomas Lucy, Knt., touching Deer-stealing.* Of all the thousands of books that have been issued from the press about Shakespeare, this one of Mr. Landor's is by far the most admirable. It is worth them all. There is the high-water mark of genius upon every page, lit by as true a sun as ever the ocean mirrored. Perfect and inimitable from beginning to end, that it has not become the most popular of all the books relating to Shakespeare, is only to be accounted for by some perversity or dullness of the public. The book is, certainly, not read. There is great love and reading bestowed upon every cant about Shakespeare, and much interest has been shown in all the hoaxes. (pp. 121-22)

Mr. Landor is not at all the product of the present age; he scarcely belongs to it; he has no direct influence upon it: but he has been an influence to some of its best teachers, and to some of the most refined illustrators of its vigorous spirit. For the rest—for the duty, the taste, or the favour of posterity— when a succession of publics shall have slowly accumulated a residuum of 'golden opinions' in the shape of pure admiring verdicts of competent minds, then only, if ever, will he attain his just estimation in the not altogether impartial roll of Fame. (p. 124)

> *Elizabeth Barrett with Richard Hengist Horne, "Walter Savage Landor," in* A New Spirit of the Age, *edited by Richard Hengist Horne, 1844. Reprint by Oxford University Press, 1907, pp. 107-24.*

[JOHN FORSTER] (essay date 1846)

[*The following excerpt is taken from a review of a revised edition of the* Imaginary Conversations, *which Forster assisted Landor in editing. Here, Forster comments on Landor's changes and additions to the new collection. For further criticism by Forster, see the excerpt dated 1836 and the Additional Bibliography.*]

When this Journal formerly spoke of the *Imaginary Conversations* [see excerpt by Hazlitt dated 1824], it was pointed out how exquisite the discrimination of character was in many cases, and how strange and wilful the indifference to it in others: How imperfect the dramatic appreciation of the intellect of the speakers, and of the literary tone of the age. . . . We might again take up and pursue this contrast. We might show how subtle and exact the art which sets before us the colloquy of **"Marvel and Parker,"** of the **"Emperor of China and his Minister,"** of **"Rochefoucault and La Fontaine,"** of **"Melancthon and Calvin,"** of **"Steele and Addison,"** of **"Lucian and Timotheus"**; and of other and grander Voices from the graves of Greece and Rome—while we condemned, for mere wilful singularity and want of keeping, the hearty, instead of dry tone of his "**Washington**"; the odd retinence of his "**Abbé Delille**," who, being the most talkative Frenchman on record, lets the Englishman have almost all the talk to himself; the mere self-ventriloquizing of his "**Franklins**," "**Southeys**," "**Romillys**," "**Sheridans**," "**Talleyrands**," and even his "**Galileos**" and "**Miltons**";—his well-educated language, where no such advantage could possibly have been heard of; and his high reasoning powers, where nothing of the kind existed. In one of the many additions to the old Dialogues which we observe in this Collection, there is indeed an answer attempted on the latter point. Mr Landor intimates that no one would care for his statesmen and kingly interlocutors of the inferior class, if he were to show them as they show themselves,—encrusted with all the dirtiness they contract in public life, in the debility of ignorance, in the distortion of prejudice, or in the trickery of partisanship. He reasons that, principles and ideas being his objects, they must not only be reflected from high and low, but must also be exhibited where people can see them best, and are most inclined to look at them; and he implies that if this is a blemish in his book, it is one his book would be worse without.

We doubt this. We have great faith for what is exact and true in every thing, and would for the most part leave it to tell for what it simply is. And we suspect the secret of these perverse departures from obvious character, to lie no deeper than Mr Landor's substitution of his own caprice and pleasure for all other considerations. It is very clear to us in such cases, that it is Mr Landor himself who is too plainly visible throughout, whomsoever he makes the organ of his opinions; and with all our hearty admiration of him,—we must own that in the special instances adverted to, we are obstructed and thrown back by an amount of this personal wilfulness, far from becoming such an arbiter and universalist as we otherwise gladly recognize in him. His opinions are then greatly too much at the command of his predilections;—sometimes of his momentary humours. He has capricious enmities, and unreasonable likings. You see assent and dissent occasioned by mere regard for one speaker, and dislike for another. He runs into violent hyperboles both of praise and blame; is a great deal too fond, for a demonstrative critic, of sweeping preferences of this and that, to 'all' that 'ever' was written in 'any' age or country; is apt to have more images than arguments, owing to the same exuberance of fancy; sometimes allows his robust animal spirits to swell to insolence, or to degenerate into coarseness; is often too prolix in his jokes and stories; and (to get rid as fast as we can of these objections on limited points) is too much tempted, by the nicety and exactness of his scholarship, to substitute verbal criticism for spiritual; and to tire his readers with accumulated objections to people whom the world have long ceased to make gods of.

But, these drawbacks stated, how little in reality they affect the great bulk of these Conversations. What a weighty book they make! How rich in scholarship; how correct, concise, and pure in style; how full of imagination, wit, and humour; how well informed, how bold in speculation, how various in interest, how universal in sympathy! In these hundred and twenty-five Dialogues, making allowance for every shortcoming or excess, the most familiar and the most august shapes of the Past are reanimated with vigour, grace, and beauty. Its long dead ashes rekindle suddenly their wonted fires, and again shoot up into warmth and brightness. 'Large utterances,' musical and varied voices, 'thoughts that breathe' for the world's advancement, 'words that burn' against the world's oppression, sound on throughout these lofty and earnest pages. We are in the high and goodly company of Wits and Men of Letters; of

Churchmen, Lawyers, and Statesmen; of Party men, Soldiers, and Kings; of the most tender, delicate, and noble Women; and of Figures that seem this instant to have left for us the Agora or the Schools of Athens,—the Forum or the Senate of Rome. At one moment we have politicians discussing the deepest questions of state; at another, philosophers still more largely philosophizing;—poets talking of poetry, men of the world of worldly matters, Italians and French of their respective Literatures and Manners. Whether such a book obtains its meed now or hereafter, will be the least part of its writer's concern: whether it is to be read in the present age or the next, may occupy his thought no more than whether in the morning or the afternoon of the present day. . . . Mr Landor's genius has a wonderfully suggestive quality. Even where he most offends against taste or judgment, he rarely fails to stimulate thought and reflection. Paradoxes, in him simply wilful and preposterous, will often be found to contain very profound truths for us. We may assent or we may oppose, but we must *think* when in company with him; and we shall always find ourselves the wealthier for what thought germinates within us. How much the more when, in his higher and nobler compositions, we see Suggestion drop its richest fruit in perfected and consummate Truths; and when every thought and feeling are such, as he who writes must have been the better for having entertained and uttered, and we who read are certainly the better and the happier for being permitted to partake. There are differences in the Dialogues as striking, as between the summer air on a mountain top, and the crowded atmosphere of a busy city. But the reader will make his choice according to his temper; for in both . . . there is 'much matter to be heard and learn'd.'

Nor need he fear that his temper will be ruffled, here, by the eccentric spelling which prevailed in former editions of the *Imaginary Conversations*. In the book before us, to reverse a reproach we have heard levelled against his orthographic infidelities, Mr Landor spells like a Christian. It would be difficult to guess why, unless some friend has been at the pains to assure him that a popular appreciation of his writings had been somewhat intercepted, by a prevalent notion that he had not been taught spelling. A conversion it certainly is not. It is a mere tribute to fashion, a kind of sacrifice to ignorance; for we observe evidence in the additions to the old dialogue of "**Johnson and Horne Tooke**," of even the strengthening and deepening of his orthographic heresy. . . . (pp. 487-90)

It would be too curious a labour to indicate all the additions and interpolations to the old Dialogues that have been made in this collection. In amount, we imagine, they would form little less than a sixth or seventh of the original; yet so skilfully are they interwoven, that to track and follow them is difficult. We find them in no case, for instance, interfere with that remarkable tact in the conduct of the Dialogues, by which a singular variety of topics is always sustained in each, without undue or violent transition; or any thing more of abruptness than should characterise the freedom and strength of conversation, and convey that mingled tone of study and society, which David Hume lays down to be the master-art of this style of composition. (p. 491)

[The conversations that have not before been collected] show, in undiminished force and vivacity, every characteristic of Mr Landor's genius. Any writer might have built, upon these compositions alone, an enduring reputation. The same beauties and the same faults recur; but the latter in diminished intensity. They have matter as various, and character as opposite and enlivening;—as much to occupy the intellect of the thoughtful, and as much to satisfy the imagination of the lively. They form an after-course, in short, worthy of the original banquet;—spread with the same solid viands, the same delicate rarities, and sparkling wines; the like vases of burnished gold on the board, the like statues of antique marble gracing the chamber;—but the very richness of the vases showing dark to imperfect vision, and the pure Greek on the plinths of the marble not easy to common appreciation.

Four of these new Dialogues seem to us to stand out preeminently from the rest. These are **"Lucian and Timotheus,"** **"Marvel and Parker,"** **"Emperor of China and his Minister,"** and **"Melancthon and Calvin."** In these the dramatic tone is as perfect as every other quality in the composition; and we may doubt if, in any other equal portion of Mr Landor's writings, there will be found so much beauty and fitness, so much point and gusto, so much condensation and strength. We have heard his friend Southey characterize his style, as uniting the poignancy of Champagne to the body of old English October; and nowhere, assuredly, but in Bacon or in Jeremy Taylor, do we find Prose-Poetry to compare with his,—in weight and brilliancy, or in wonderful suggestiveness. What Lucian says of Aristotle in the latter respect, we may apply to him. Whenever he presents to his readers one full-blown thought, there are several buds about it which are to open in the cool of the study. He makes us learn even more than he teaches. Without hesitation we say of these four Dialogues, and eminently of that between **"Marvel and Parker,"** that they contain a subtle discrimination of character, and passages of feeling and philosophy, pathetic, lofty, and profound, which we should not know where to equal in any living writer, and in very few of those who are immortal. (pp. 500-01)

The author and outpourer of [these works], stands apart from ordinary writers, and will be known, esteemed, and listened to, when all the rubbish of light and fashionable reading, which has so choked up our generation, shall have passed away. He has himself somewhere finely said, that the voice comes deepest from the sepulchre, and a great name has its root in the dead body. He is doubtless, for himself, well content to obey that law. But this Collection of his Writings has reminded us, for our own part, not to wait until 'deaf the praised ear, and mute the tuneful tongue.' Others, let us hope, will follow our example. And thus, while Mr Landor yet lives, he may hear what is violent and brief in his writings forgiven—what is wise, tranquil, and continuous, gratefully accepted—and may know that he has not vainly striven for those high rewards which he has so frequently and fully challenged. 'Fame, they tell you, is air; but without air there is no life for any—without fame there is none for the best.' (p. 511)

[*John Forster*], *"Landor's 'Collected Writings—New Imaginary Conversations',"* in The Edinburgh Review, *Vol. LXXXIII, No. CLXVIII, April, 1846, pp. 486-511.*

THOMAS DE QUINCEY   (essay date 1847)

[*An English critic and essayist, De Quincey used his own life as the subject of his best-known work,* Confessions of an English Opium Eater, *in which he chronicled his addiction to opium. De Quincey contributed reviews to a number of London journals and earned a reputation as an insightful if occasionally long-winded literary critic. In this excerpt from his commentary on* Gebir, *De Quincey admires the "sculpturesque" qualities of the little-read poem. For further criticism by De Quincey, see the Additional Bibliography.*]

[Mr. Landor] is a man of great genius, and, as such, he *ought* to interest the public. More than enough appears of his strong, eccentric nature, through every page of his now extensive writings, to win, amongst those who have read him, a corresponding interest in all that concerns him personally: in his social relations, in his biography, in his manners, in his appearance. Out of two conditions for attracting a *personal* interest, he has powerfully realised one. His moral nature, shining with coloured light through the crystal shrine of his thoughts, will not allow of your forgetting it. A sunset of Claude, or a dying dolphin, *can* be forgotten, and generally *is* forgotten; but not the fiery radiations of a human spirit, built by nature to animate a leader in storms, a martyr, a national reformer, an arch-rebel, as circumstances might dictate, but whom too much wealth, and the accidents of education, have turned aside into a contemplative recluse. Had Mr. Landor, therefore, been read in any extent answering to his merits, he must have become, for the English public, an object of prodigious personal interest. We should have had novels upon him, lampoons upon him, libels upon him; he would have been shown up dramatically on the stage; he would, according to the old joke, have been "traduced" in French, and also "overset" in Dutch. Meantime he has *not* been read. It would be an affectation to think it. Many a writer is, by the sycophancy of literature, reputed to be read, whom in all Europe not six eyes settle upon through the revolving year. Literature, with its cowardly falsehoods, exhibits the largest field of conscious Phrygian adulation that human life has ever exposed to the derision of the heavens. Demosthenes, for instance, or Plato, is not read to the extent of twenty pages annually by ten people in Europe. The sale of their works would not account for three readers; the other six or seven are generously conceded as possibilities furnished by the great public libraries. But, then, Walter Savage Landor, though writing a little in Latin, and a very little in Italian, does not write at all in Greek. So far he has some advantage over Plato; and, if he writes chiefly in dialogue, which few people love to read any more than novels in the shape of letters, *that* is a crime common to both. So that he has the 'd—l's luck and his own, all Plato's chances, and one of his own beside—viz. his English. Still it is no use counting chances; facts are the thing. And printing-presses, whether of Europe or of England, bear witness that neither Plato nor Landor is a marketable commodity. In fact, these two men resemble each other in more particulars than it is at present necessary to say. Especially they were both inclined to be luxurious: both had a hankering after purple and fine linen; both hated "filthy dowlas" with the hatred of Falstaff, whether in appareling themselves or their diction; and both bestowed pains as elaborate upon the secret *art* of a dialogue as a lapidary would upon the cutting of a sultan's rubies.

But might not a man build a reputation on the basis of *not* being read? To be read is undoubtedly something; to be read by an odd million or so, is a sort of feather in a man's cap; but it is also a distinction that he has been read absolutely by nobody at all.... [However] it can be proved against Mr. Landor, that he has been read by at least a score of people, all wide awake; and if any treason is buried in a page of *his*, thank Heaven, by this time it must have been found out and reported to the authorities. So that neither can Landor plead the unlimited popularity of a novelist, aided by the interest of a tale, and by an artist, nor the total observation of a German metaphysician. Neither do mobs read him, as they do M. Sue; nor do all men turn away their eyes from him, as they do from Hegel.

This, however, is true only of Mr. Landor's prose works. His first work was a poem, vis. *Gebir;* and it had the sublime distinction, for some time, of having enjoyed only two readers; which two were Southey and myself. . . . Not knowing Southey at that time, I vainly conceited myself to be the one sole purchaser and reader of this poem. I even fancied myself to have been pointed out in the streets of Oxford, where the Landors had been well known in times preceding my own, as the one inexplicable man authentically known to possess *Gebir,* or even (it might be whispered mysteriously) to have read *Gebir.* It was not clear but this reputation might stand in lieu of any independent fame, and might raise me to literary distinction. (pp. 18-19)

By the way, the propensity to *scandalum magnatum* in Aroar was one of the things that fixed my youthful attention, and perhaps my admiration, upon *Gebir.* For myself, as perhaps the reader may have heard, I was and am a Tory; and in some remote geological era, my bones may be dug up by some future Buckland as a specimen of the fossil Tory. Yet, for all that, I loved audacity; and I gazed with some indefinite shade of approbation upon a poet whom the attorney-general might have occasion to speak with.

This, however, was a mere condiment to the main attraction of the poem. *That* lay in the picturesqueness of the images, attitudes, groups, dispersed everywhere. The eye seemed to rest everywhere upon festal processions, upon the panels of Theban gates, or upon sculptured vases. . . . [In *Gebir* there are many] striking illustrations of this sculpturesque faculty in Mr. Landor; and for this faculty it was that both Southey and myself separately and independently had named him the English Valerius Flaccus. (p. 21)

> *Thomas De Quincey, "Notes on Walter Savage Landor," in* Tait's Edinburgh Magazine, *Vol. XIV, No. CLVII, January, 1847, pp. 18-23.*

WALTER SAVAGE LANDOR   (essay date 1847)

[*In his preface to* The Hellenics, *Landor contrasts the clarity of his poetry with the "prismatic" works of his contemporaries. For additional commentary by Landor, see excerpts dated 1798 and 1800.*]

Prefixing a preface is like keeping an invited friend at the hall-door, instead of conducting him at once into the house.

Little in these pages [*The Hellenics*] will gratify the generality of readers. Poetry, in our day, is oftener prismatic than diaphanous: this is not so: they who look into it may see through. If there be anywhere a few small air-bubbles, it yet leaves to the clear vision a wide expanse of varied scenery. (p. i)

> *Walter Savage Landor, in a preface to his* The Hellenics of Walter Savage Landor: Comprising Heroic Idyls, &c., *revised edition, 1847. Reprint by R. Griffin and Co., 1859, pp. i-ii.*

[AUBREY DE VERE]   (essay date 1850)

[*De Vere, a prolific Anglo-Irish poet, critic, and essayist, here reviews* The Hellenics, *noting the influence of classical Greek literature on the poems.*]

[*The Hellenics*] cannot be better described than by saying that the name has not been ill-chosen. The subject of nearly all the poems it contains is supplied by Greece, and the treatment is in accordance with that subject. . . .

The Hellenics have all the clear outline, the definite grace, and the sunny expansiveness of Greek poetry, and not less its aversion to the mysterious and the spiritual. Above all they are classical in their peculiar mode of dealing with outward nature. (p. 409)

[The merit of Landor's poem **"The Hamadryad"**] consists chiefly in the art with which the mythological idea is blended with a human interest. (p. 413)

It is in delineating the least pronounced part of the Greek mythology that a clear discernment of its meaning is most required. In [**"The Hamadryad"**], . . . the shadowy nature of a being not so much elevated above our mortal nature as standing at one side of it, seems to us most happily indicated. Such discrimination has long been rare, both in French and in English poetry. (p. 415)

The merit of Mr. Landor's poetry consists . . . more in the grace of his narratives, the skill with which they are worked out, and the perfection of their proportions, than in particular passages. . . . (p. 417)

The most deeply-toned and perhaps the most beautiful of Mr. Landor's Hellenics is that one which bears the name of Corythos, the son of Paris and of Oenone. . . .

The reader will linger over and return to many passages of this poem; especially to the description of Helen, and the lamentation of Oenone, as—the tears dried on her cheek by the bitter wind—she stands among the cones and the whirling pine-leaves with which the Idean hill is strewn, and watches her son descending to the city. (p. 419)

Mr. Landor's poetry has sometimes been charged with a deficiency of pathos. It is true that in general he loves rather to exhibit human life in the exhilarating and equable light of day, than tinged with the lights of a low horizon, and clouded with those extended shadows which belong especially to the declining eventide of literature. His pathos has, notwithstanding, a peculiar depth and tenderness; and though unostentatious, is very far from being infrequent. (p. 420)

If Mr. Landor's various dramas were braced and animated by such a spirit as sustains the [tragic scene entitled the **"Madness of Orestes"**], . . . few modern dramatists would stand on his level. Such, however, is not the fact. Many dramatic gifts are fatally marred by one deficiency. He has not, apparently, the faculty of devising a plot in which incident not only follows, but results from, incident; while each and all, instead of being connected merely by the chain of phenomenal causation, rest on a moral support, and illustrate character. Mr. Landor is accordingly more successful in his fragmentary dramatic scenes than in his dramas, none of which appear to us written with the same power, either in the delineation of character or of passion, which is to be found in many of his *Imaginary Conversations;* as, for instance, in that true prose poem, the dialogue between Tiberius and Vipsania; or that one between Peleus and Thetis, in which a mournful passion is so marvellously introduced into a subject belonging, it might seem, exclusively to the imagination. (p. 421)

It is in Mr. Landor's minor poems that we find most abundantly that delicacy, propriety, sweetness, and concise precision, which so eminently distinguish his poetry, and remind us of the Greek anthology. (p. 428)

Mr. Landor seems to turn with aversion from many forms of composition to which recent poetry has habituated us. A ballad is not to be found among his works; nor a didactic poem; nor a sonnet; nor, we might say, a song, using the term in its stricter sense. The temperament of his poetry, buoyant at once and serene, lacks apparently that vehement excitability which precipitates itself into fragmentary snatches of music, such as the songs of our early dramatists. Among his poems, on the other hand, we find many species with which we are familiarised in ancient poetry. The Idyl, especially that larger and graver kind for which, in his Latin volume, he claims the title of "Idyllia Heroica," appears to be his favourite; but he is also attached to the elegiac commemoration, to the brief but pregnant inscription, and to the epigram, especially to that species of epigram which embodies poetry not wit, and which can dispense with a sting in the last line. These poems are frequently marked by a playful tenderness, and as often by a tender pathos. (p. 429)

The unobtrusiveness of true poetry, a quality not sufficiently valued and but infrequently exemplified of late, is among the higher characteristics of Mr. Landor's. He is wholly free from exaggeration, and he never transgresses the Delphic precept . . . 'not too much of anything.' Nothing is inserted for effect; and his best passages, contented often to lurk in shadow, are never rendered more salient by a sprinkling of 'barbaric pearl and gold.' Thus, in his pages, heroism never struts, and sorrow never wails. Seldom, indeed, has fine poetry more ascetically renounced finery, or passion more religiously abstained from bluster. It is these qualities which impart to his verse that gentlemanly character which is observed to belong to it. Unobtrusiveness is not, however, likely to conduce to the popularity of a poet in these days. An object must sparkle to catch immediate attention when seen through the dust of the thoroughfare; and in the press and crush of modern literature, the thought which is not forward to claim a place, is likely to wait long without one. The music which is music only will be heard but in the still gallery or lonely grove; while the louder instrument, that sounds of wood and wire also, flings its noisy peal across the clamour of the throng.

Mr. Landor's poetry has not been popular. Warmly as the admiration of not a few among our first poets as well as scholars has been expressed with regard to it, that sentiment has not, as yet, made its way to the mass of readers. From our remarks upon that poetry, it may not unreasonably be inferred that the absence of popularity has proceeded from the peculiar character at once of its merits and of its defects. Refinement, grace, and condensed thought are not the qualities which most immediately recommend themselves to the public; and, on the other hand, there are few faults which a reader finds it more difficult to forgive than that obscurity which makes him discontented with himself as well as with the author. Mr. Landor's prose works also have in some measure merged his poetical in his literary fame, representing, as they do, a larger portion of his mind, and embodying the stronger, though not the higher part of his genius. (p. 430)

Mr. Landor's genius, not only does not sympathise with the present age, but has been, from first to last, in ardent sympathy with the imaginative and social associations of a remote era. To the Ideal as distinguished from the National school of English poetry, his poetry belongs exclusively and without admixture, being in this respect homogeneous. The question, then, as to his future popularity is part of a much larger inquiry. It is this: Do the poets of antiquity obtain the popular sym-

pathies of our countrymen, or must we admit that they lived in the hearts of those only for whom, and among whom, they wrote, and that they can but delight the imagination of the studious at this distant day? (p. 431)

[*Aubrey De Vere*], "*Landor's Poetry*," *in* The Edinburgh Review, *Vol. XCI, No. CLXXXIV, April, 1850, pp. 408-43.*

THE LONDON QUARTERLY REVIEW   (essay date 1854)

[*In the excerpt below, the anonymous critic praises the literary quality and varied genres found in* The Last Fruit off an Old Tree.]

The poetic prefix of Mr. Landor's last volume [**The Last Fruit off an Old Tree**] is highly characteristic of his genius, and furnishes in brief the sum of his career. It is also a good example of his style; a style remarkable for strength and terseness, and, if somewhat hard, yet, at the same time, picturesque and pure:—

> I strove with none, for none was worth my strife;
>   Nature I loved, and, next to nature, art:
> I warm'd both hands before the fire of life;
>   It sinks, and I am ready to depart.

Here we have the bold independence and self-assertion which have always distinguished him, marking him out from men of feebler mould, like Coriolanus among degenerate Romans, and urging him, sometimes to "flutter the Volsces" in a hostile camp, and sometimes, with petulant haste, to join the forces of an enemy, and pour scorn and contumely on his own "countrymen and lovers." Here, too, his love of nature, surviving youth and riper manhood, and crowning his old age with a second spring; his delight in all the miracles of art; his joyous welcome of all that life affords, and keen relish for its thousand blessings; and, not less prominent than his epicurean gladness in the intellectual past and sensuous present, his stoical indifference to all that may await him in the mysterious and impending future. If you would figure to yourself how a heathen of the classic age would demean himself, if suddenly transported into our present era, make intimate acquaintance with the writings of Walter Landor. To our minds, the single quatrain we have quoted awakens so many recollections of their beauty, that we seem to realize the conception at once, and hail him as a grand antique,—a living representative, but not a marble image. The firm grip of his friendly hand; the occasional disdain of his haughty head; the smile with which he greets the simple beauty of a field-flower, or the matchless grace of infancy; his passion for ideal liberty and natural beauty; his impatience of all meanness, servility, and fraud; his warm and generous friendships, and his hasty and more general enmities; his soft pity for the slave, and his fierce hatred of the tyrant;—these are all marks of his peculiar greatness. But, while his intellectual character is almost purely classic, it was not possible that in all things he should resist the influence of a Christian age, and be entirely Pagan in his soul. In literature and art and politics, he is a Grecian of the age of Pericles; but, in the higher humanities,—in all but its spiritual and evangelic type,—he is a Christian of the Protestant and English Church. And now we have Walter Landor gathering the last fruits of his genius, and sending them to market for the benefit of two humble and persecuted Christians; turning from the contemplation of "the physiognomies of Solon and Pericles, of Phocion and Epicurus," and fixing an admiring regard on Francesca and Rosa Madiai.

Homely, [says he,] very homely, are the countenances and the figures of the Madiai. But they also have their heroism: they took the same choice as Hercules, preferring virtue to pleasure, labour to ease, rectitude to obliquity; patient of imprisonment, and worshipping God with unfaltering devotion, unterrified by the menaces of death. May they awaken, if not enthusiasm, at least benevolence! In which hope, on their behalf, and for their sole emolument, I edit this volume.

Let us not quarrel with Mr. Landor because the grounds of his sympathy with this persecuted pair are haply lower than ours,—that he feels admiration for their fortitude, but professes no share in the sublime convictions to which, in them at least, such fortitude is due. Be it his to refer to the choice of Hercules, the type and parable of heathen virtue; but this, too, is included in another reference, surely far more appropriate, which a thousand hearts will instinctively make,—to the humble martyrs of our faith in the early ages of the Church.

Not its charitable object only, but its literary excellence also, will commend this volume of *Last Fruit*. It contains something in every species of composition to which our author has devoted himself; and, if not equal to the best of his former writings,—which it would be unreasonable to expect from a volume published in the author's eightieth year,—they indicate, at least, no positive declension of his powers. Of the *Conversations* he says, in allusion to the living interlocutors, "No sculptor can work in sandstone so artistically or effectively as in alabaster and marble." Yet some of these are fine examples of a class of writing, not, indeed, invented by Mr. Landor, yet stamped by his genius with a new and higher charm. None of the present series could have been written by a pen less pointed or less firm than his. Three admirable papers—on Theocritus, Catullus, and Petrarca respectively—show that his critical power is no way abated. His Letters on Popery are less to our liking; and those to Cardinal Wiseman are too full of obscure irony for popular and pleasant reading. Of poem and epigram there is great variety; and his peculiar style of dramatic composition—full of pregnant and picturesque expressions, and pervaded by a certain quiet brooding interest, and thus uniting, as it seems to us, the chaste and solemn spirit of antiquity with the free handling and the fruitful character of the romantic school—is finely exhibited in the **"Five Scenes"** which bring this varied volume to a close. (pp. 289-90)

A review of "Imaginary Conversations of Greeks and Romans" and "The Last Fruit off an Old Tree," in The London Quarterly Review, *Vol. II, No. III, March, 1854, pp. 289-91.*

THE LONDON QUARTERLY REVIEW   (essay date 1858)

[*This brief excerpt is gleaned from a negative review of* Dry Sticks, Fagoted by W.S.L.]

We were present with our readers when the *Last Fruits* were gathered from this sturdy and prolific tree [see excerpt dated 1854]. It is now stript from lowest branch to utmost twig, and the relics are before us [in *Dry Sticks, Fagoted by W.S.L.*]. We are not disposed to bewail a destruction which is in no sense premature. Let us own, without suspicion of ingratitude, that we never thoroughly depended on the produce of this wild fruit-tree,—wayward in growth and rude in flavour as it often proved, and never quite ripened even on the sunny side. No wonder, then, if these lopped branches have an acrid bitterness. Indeed, they are only offered as a fagot of old sticks; and it is just to say that blossoms on not a few of them testify to the presence of a vital moisture in the stem, still sensitive of such a spring as that which is now bursting on every side, and making every hedgerow in England more fragrant than the gardens of Stamboul or Cashmere.

All the characteristics of Mr. Landor's genius survive in these last effusions. His epigrams are as bitter if not as biting as ever; his love versicles are light and trivial as before. His prejudices seem to suffer no abatement; his charities still disport themselves in a narrow circle of love and friendship. We may well doubt the real greatness of a spirit which refuses to mellow and improve; and this reflection, often forced upon the reader of the present volume, makes it but a melancholy bequest. . . .

The volume closes with some translations from the Persian, Latin verses, and tributary poems on our author. It is a little surprising to find Walter Savage Landor publishing encomiums on himself; but we cannot grudge them to a man whose faults have found more eager recognition than his genius or his virtues.

A review of "Dry Sticks, Fagoted by Walter Savage Landor," in The London Quarterly Review, *Vol. X, No. XIX, April, 1858, p. 283.*

THE TIMES, LONDON   (essay date 1858)

[*The following excerpt, taken from an editorial regarding the* Yescombe v. Landor *libel suit, reflects the impact of the scandal on Landor's reputation.*]

What a strange and scandalous story it is that we published yesterday about the old age of Walter Savage Landor! He must be so old that one is almost afraid to talk about his age. He has been so famous a writer in his time that it would have been pleasant to think of him, if still alive, as surrounded by troops of friends who were smoothing the last furlong of his long pilgrimage. He should have outlived the ill-will of others, and the animosities of his own heart. It is with unfeigned reluctance that we perform the duty which has been cast upon us of saying a few words about the trial which took place at Bristol on Monday last, in which Mr. Landor was defendant. . . . Who can read the report of the proceedings without saying that it served him right? The old poet can scarcely lay claim to impunity on the ground of failing intellect. It must be admitted that in their own nasty way—and it is a very nasty way—the verses of Landor's old age are quite equal in point and vigour to the golden produce of his prime. But it is such filthy point—such dirty vigour! Take Jonathan Swift's impurest productions, when he sat down for a regular innings at dirt—take the obscenest off-scourings of Martial, when the Roman poet was wallowing in the very cesspool of the Muses, and you will have an idea of the nature of Landor's recent literary diversions. So far we have spoken of the old man's offence as of one against decency and morality. To describe it technically, according to the form in which it was brought the other day before the Court, we must, however, speak of it as the publication of a libel; and a fouler libel than the one brought home to him was never written by man. What made the case worse was that he had selected as the object of his attack a lady whose only fault seems to have been that she had been for many years on intimate terms with her unmanly traducer. . . .

Walter Savage Landor, the poet, the man of letters, the gentleman, just tottering on the verge of the grave, actually condescended to have recourse to the expedient of anonymous letters, and these letters contained such filth that one may well wonder how the ideas could occur to a human brain. . . .

How ineffable is the disgrace to a man of Mr. Landor's ability and reputation at the close of a long life to be mixed up with so disgraceful a transaction! A slanderer, and the slanderer of a lady—a writer of anonymous letters, and these letters reeking with the foulest odours of the dirtiest stews—a violator of his pledged word—who is it to whom these words must now be applied?—

> Who would not weep if Atticus were he?

> *"Walter Savage Landor," in* The Times, *London, August 25, 1858, p. 6.*

ROBERT BROWNING   (letter date 1864)

[*Browning was a major poet of the Victorian age. He befriended Landor when the author, exiled from England and rejected by his wife and children, was found wandering in the streets of Florence "like an old King Lear." In this excerpt from a letter written at the time of Landor's death, Browning recalls the "grand old solitary man."*]

Yes, poor Landor is off and away at last—I wish him well with all my heart: he wrote to me a month ago,—"probably about to die in a few weeks or days," but he had cried "Wolf!" so often. Five years care about him, and now he is past me. He has written passages not exceeded in beauty and subtlety by any literature that I am acquainted with; that is my opinion, other people have theirs; he was followed to the grave by two of his sons, and nobody else—the grand old solitary man, beset by weaknesses just as, in his own words, "the elephant is devoured by ants in his inaccessible solitudes." Bless us, if he had let the world tame him and strap a tower on his broad back, what havoc he would have made in the enemy's ranks!—as it was, they let off squibbs at him and he got into a rage and ran off, topsey-turveying his friends right and left. I'll tell you how he talked—the rather that I might not be impudent enough to tell you, if it occurred to me on next edifying Sunday morning's colloquy. "Mrs Landor called today" said I. "Ha—why, you did not let her in—never surely let *her* in?"—"Oh, I should let a dog in, even, bearing your name on the collar!"—"Oh, ay, a *dog*—good! but a—?"

Methinks I have a pleasure in remembering that he "gave her her own," now that the dead lion is being appraised as "worth" so much to the living Landors. (pp. 78-9)

> *Robert Browning, in a letter to Julia Wedgwood on October 3, 1864, in* Robert Browning and Julia Wedgwood: A Broken Friendship as Revealed by Their Letters, *edited by Richard Curle, Frederick A. Stokes Company, 1937, pp. 75-9.*

[ELIZA LYNN LINTON]   (essay date 1869)

[*Linton claims that the merits of the* Imaginary Conversations *compensate for the serious defects in the works of Landor's old age.*]

[Landor's] genius was the man. What he wrote when at his best, what he thought and felt when most inspired, was more himself than were his mere tempers; his *Imaginary Conver-*

sations were the real and permanent Landor, his passionate outbursts of violence and coarseness were only the outward and temporary man. The one will live for ever, the other will die out of the world's memory in another fifty years or so. . . . No man since Shakespeare's time has written so much wisdom or so much beauty; in no other man's works is there such exquisite tenderness, so much subtlety of thought, such wealth of imagery yet all chaste and nothing glaring, so much suggestiveness and yet such ample fulness. Not a page but contains the most deathless beauty; though also, we confess it sadly, his later volumes are disfigured by coarseness which we wish Landor had died before he had written. But these were his madnesses; we look upon them as the sorrowful ravings of insanity, and so pass them by with solemn pity, lamenting rather than condemning. It is not just to bring them too prominently forward; for he was better than these worst parts of him, and he must not be judged by them. (p. 566)

> [*Eliza Lynn Linton*], *"Walter Savage Landor," in* The North British Review, *Vol. L, No. C, July, 1869, pp. 550-67.*

[LESLIE STEPHEN]   (essay date 1878)

[*Stephen is considered one of the most important English literary critics of the late Victorian and early Edwardian eras. In his criticism, which is often moralistic, Stephen argues that all literature is nothing more than an imaginative rendering, in concrete terms, of a writer's philosophy or beliefs. His analyses often include biographical judgments of the writer as well as the work. In the following excerpt, Stephen admits that he, like many readers, finds Landor's works dull; he then considers the reasons for Landor's failure to earn widespread, lasting fame.*]

Landor is perhaps the most striking instance in modern literature of a radical divergence of opinion between the connoisseurs and the mass of readers. The general public have never been induced to read him, in spite of the lavish applauses of some self-constituted authorities. One may go further. It is doubtful whether those who aspire to a finer literary palate than is possessed by the vulgar herd are really so keenly appreciative as the innocent reader of published remarks might suppose. Hypocrisy in matters of taste—whether of the literal or metaphorical kind—is the commonest of vices. There are vintages, both material and intellectual, which are more frequently praised than heartily enjoyed. I have heard very good judges whisper in private that they have found Landor dull; and the rare citations made from his works often betray a very perfunctory study of them. (p. 667)

Southey and Wordsworth had a simple method of explaining the neglect of a great author. According to them contemporary neglect affords a negative presumption in favour of permanent reputation. No lofty poet has honour in his own generation. . . . Landor accepted and defended [this theory] with characteristic vigour. "I have published," he says, in the conversation with Hare, "five volumes of *Imaginary Conversations:* cut the worst of them through the middle, and there will remain in the decimal fraction enough to satisfy my appetite for fame. I shall dine late; but the dining-room will be well-lighted, the guests few and select." He recurs frequently to the doctrine. "Be patient!" he says, in another character. "From the higher heavens of poetry, it is long before the radiance of the brightest star can reach the world below. We hear that one man finds out one beauty, another man finds out another, placing his observatory and instruments on the poet's grave. The worms must have eaten us before we rightly know what we are. It is only when we are skeletons that we are boxed and ticketed and prized and shown. Be it so! I shall not be tired of waiting." Conscious, as he says in his own person, that in 2,000 years there have not been five volumes of prose (the work of one author) equal to his *Conversations,* he could indeed afford to wait: if conscious of earthly things, he must be waiting still. (p. 668)

Wordsworth's fame was for a long time confined to a narrow sect, and he did all in his power to hinder its spread by wilful disregard of the established canons—even when founded in reason. A reformer who will not court the prejudices even of his friends is likely to be slow in making converts. But it is one thing to be slow in getting a hearing, and another in attracting men who are quite prepared to hear. Wordsworth resembled a man coming into a drawing-room with muddy boots and a smock-frock. He courted disgust, and such courtship is pretty sure of success. But Landor made his bow in full court-dress. In spite of the difficulty of his poetry, he had all the natural graces which are apt to propitiate cultivated readers. His prose has merits so conspicuous and so dear to the critical mind, that one might have expected his welcome from the connoisseurs to be warm even beyond the limit of sincerity. To praise him was to announce one's own possession of a fine classical taste, and there can be no greater stimulus to critical enthusiasm. One might have guessed that he would be a favourite with all who set up for a discernment superior to that of the vulgar; though the causes which must obstruct a wide recognition of his merits are sufficiently obvious. It may be interesting to consider the cause of his ill success with some fulness; and it is a comfort to the critic to reflect that in such a case even obtuseness is in some sort a qualification; for it will enable one to sympathise with the vulgar insensibility to the offered delicacy, if only to substitute articulate rejection for simple stolid silence. (pp. 669-70)

Landor very frequently bores me. So do a good many writers whom I thoroughly admire. If any courage be wanted for such a confession, it is certainly not when writing upon Landor that one should be reticent for want of example. Nobody ever spoke his mind more freely about great expectations. He is, for example, almost the only poet who ever admitted that he could not read Spenser continuously. . . . "There is scarcely a poet of the same eminence," says Porson, obviously representing Landor in this case, "whom I have found it so delightful to read in, and so hard to read through." What Landor here says of Spenser, I should venture to say of Landor. There are few books of the kind into which one may dip with so great a certainty of finding much to admire as the *Imaginary Conversations,* and few of any high reputation which are so certain to become wearisome after a time. . . . But I must also admit, that on thinking of the whole five volumes, so emphatically extolled by their author, I feel certain twinges of remorse. There is a vigour of feeling, an originality of character, a fineness of style which makes one understand, if not quite agree to, the audacious self-commendation. Part of the effect is due simply to the sheer quantity of good writing. Take any essay separately, and one must admit that—to speak only of his contemporaries—there is a greater charm in passages of equal length by Lamb, De Quincey, or even Hazlitt. None of them gets upon such stilts, or seems so anxious to keep the reader at arm's length. But, on the other hand, there is something imposing in so continuous a flow of stately and generally faultless English, with so many weighty aphorisms rising spontaneously, and without a splashing or disturbance, to the surface of talk, and such an easy felicity of theme unmarred by the flash and glitter of the modern epigrammatic style. Lamb is both sweeter and more profound, to say nothing of his incomparable humour; but then Lamb's flight is short and uncertain. De Quincey's passages of splendid rhetoric are too often succeeded by dead levels of verbosity and laboured puerilities which make annoyance alternate with enthusiasm. Hazlitt is often spasmodic, and his intrusive egotism is pettish and undignified. But so far at least as his style is concerned, Landor's unruffled stream of continuous harmony excites one's admiration the more the longer one reads. Hardly any one who has written so much has kept so uniformly to a high level, and so seldom descended to empty verbosity or to downright slipshod. It is true that the substance does not always correspond to the perfection of the form. There are frequent discontinuities of thought where the style is smoothest. He reminds one at times of those Alpine glaciers where an exquisitely rounded surface of snow conceals yawning crevasses beneath; and if one stops for a moment to think, one is apt to break through the crust with an abrupt and annoying jerk.

The excellence of Landor's style has, of course, been universally acknowledged, and it is natural that it should be more appreciated by his fellow-craftsmen than by general readers less interested in technical questions. The defects are the natural complements of its merits. When accused of being too figurative, he had a ready reply. "Wordsworth," he says in one of his *Conversations,* "slithers on the soft mud, and cannot stop himself until he comes down. In his poetry there is as much of prose as there is of poetry in the prose of Milton. But prose on certain occasions can bear a great deal of poetry; on the other hand, poetry sinks and swoons under a moderate weight of prose, and neither fan nor burnt feather can bring her to herself again." The remark about the relations of prose and poetry was originally made in a real conversation with Wordsworth in defence of Landor's own luxuriance. Wordsworth, it is said, took it to himself, and not without reason, as appears by its insertion in this *Conversation.* The retort, however happy, is no more conclusive than other cases of the *tu quoque.* We are too often inclined to say to Landor as Southey says to Porson in another place: "Pray leave these tropes and metaphors." His sense suffers from a superfetation of figures, or from the undue pursuit of a figure, till the "wind of the poor phrase is cracked." In the phrase just quoted, for example, we could dispense with the "fan and burnt feather," which have very little relation to the thought. (pp. 670-71)

[Lapses] into the inflated are of course exceptional with Landor. There can be no question of the fineness of his perception in all matters of literary form. To say that his standard of style is classical is to repeat a commonplace too obvious for repetition, except to add a doubt whether he is not often too ostentatious and self-conscious in his classicism. . . . Landor aims, like Bacon, at rich imagery, at giving to thoughts which appear plain more value by fineness of expression, and at compressing shrewd judgments into weighty aphorisms. He would equally rival Cicero in fulness and perspicuity; whilst a severe rejection of everything slovenly or superfluous would save him from ever deviating into the merely florid. So far as style can be really separated from thought, we may admit unreservedly that he has succeeded in his aim, and has attained a rare harmony of tone and colouring.

There may, indeed, be some doubt as to his perspicuity. Southey said that Landor was obscure, whilst adding that he could not explain the cause of the obscurity. Causes enough may be suggested. Besides his incoherency his love of figures which sometimes become half detached from the underlying thought, and an over-anxiety to avoid mere smartness which sometimes leads to real vagueness, he expects too much from his readers, or perhaps despises them too much. He will not condescend to explanation if you do not catch his drift at half a word. He is so desirous to round off his transitions gracefully, that he obliterates the necessary indications of the main divisions of the subject. When criticising Milton or Dante, he can hardly keep his hand off the finest passages in his desire to pare away superfluities. Treating himself in the same fashion, he leaves none of those little signs which, like the typographical hand prefixed to a notice, are extremely convenient, though strictly superfluous. It is doubtless unpleasant to have the hard frame-work of logical divisions showing too distinctly in an argument, or to have a too elaborate statement of dates and places and external relations in a romance. But such aids to the memory may be removed too freely. The building may be injured in taking away the scaffolding. . . . [However, writers] of far greater obscurity and much more repellent blemishes of style to set against much lower merits, have gained a far wider popularity. The want of sympathy between so eminent a literary artist and his time must rest upon some deeper divergence of sentiment. Landor's writings present the same kind of problem as his life. We are told, and we can see for ourselves, that he was a man of many very high, and many very amiable qualities. . . . But . . . he could never live long at peace with anybody. He was the most impracticable of men, and every turning-point in his career was decided by some vehement quarrel. (pp. 672-74)

His work was marred by the unreasonableness of a nature so impetuous and so absorbed by any momentary gust of passion that he could never bring his thoughts or his plans to a focus, or conform them to a general scheme. His prejudices master him both in speculation and practice. He cannot fairly rise above them or govern them by reference to general principles, or the permanent interests of his life. In the vulgar phrase, he is always ready to cut off his nose to spite his face. . . . With such a temperament, reasoning, which implies patient contemplation and painful liberation from prejudice, has no fair chance; his principles are not the growth of thought, but the translation into dogmas of intense likes and dislikes, which have grown up in his mind he scarcely knows how, and gathered strength by sheer force of repetition instead of deliberate examination.

His writings reflect—and in some ways only too faithfully—these idiosyncrasies. . . . The *Conversations* give much that Landor's friends would have been glad to ignore; and yet they present such a full-length portrait of the man, that it is better to dwell upon them than upon his poetry, which, moreover, with all its fine qualities, is (in my opinion) of far less intrinsic value. The ordinary reader, however, is repelled from the *Conversations* not only by mere inherent difficulties, but by comments which raise a false expectation. An easy-going critic is apt to assume of any book that it exactly fulfils the ostensible aim of the author. So we are told of *Shakspeare's Examination* (and on the high authority of Charles Lamb), that no one could have written it except Landor or Shakspeare himself. When Bacon is introduced, we are assured that the aphorisms introduced are worthy of Bacon himself. What Cicero is made to say is exactly what he would have said, "if he could;" and the dialogue between Walton, Cotton, and Oldways is, of course, as good as a passage from the *Complete Angler*. In the same spirit we are told that the dialogues were to be "one-act dramas;" and we are informed how the great philosophers, statesmen, poets, and artists of all ages did in fact pass across the stage, each represented to the life, and discoursing in his most admirable style.

All this is easy to say; but unluckily represents what the *Conversations* would have been had they been perfect. To say that they are very far from perfect is only to say that they were the compositions of a man; but Landor was also a man to whom his best friends would hardly attribute a remarkable immunity from fault. The dialogue, it need hardly be remarked, is one of the most difficult of all forms of composition. One rule, however, would be generally admitted. Landor defends his digressions on the ground that they always occur in real conversations. If we "adhere to one point," he says (in Southey's person), "it is a disquisition, not a conversation." And he adds, with one of his wilful backhanded blows at Plato, that most writers of dialogue plunge into abstruse questions, and "collect a heap of arguments to be blown away by the bloated whiff of some rhetorical charlatan, tricked out in a multiplicity of ribbons for the occasion." Possibly! but for all that, the perfect dialogue ought not, we should say, to be really incoherent. It should include digressions, but the digressions ought to return upon the main subject. The art consists in preserving real unity in the midst of the superficial deviations rendered easy by this form of conversation. . . . So far as Landor used his facilities as an excuse for rambling, instead of so skilfully subordinating them to the main purpose as to reproduce new variations on the central theme, he is clearly in error, or is at least aiming at a lower kind of excellence. And this, it may be said at once, seems to be the most radical defect in the composition of Landor's *Conversations*. They have the fault which his real talk is said to have exemplified. We are told that his temperament "disqualified him for anything like sustained reasoning, and he instinctively backed away from discussion or argument." Many of the written dialogues are a prolonged series of explosions; when one expects a continuous development of a theme, they are monotonous thunder-growls. Landor undoubtedly had a sufficient share of dramatic power to write short dialogues expressing a single situation with most admirable power, delicacy, and firmness of touch. Nor, again, does the criticism just made refer to those longer dialogues which are in reality a mere string of notes upon poems or proposals for reforms in spelling. . . . But the more elaborate dialogues suffer grievously from this absence of a true unity. There is not that skilful evolution of a central idea without the rigid formality of scientific discussion which we admire in the real masterpieces of the art. We have a conglomerate not an organic growth; a series of observations set forth with never-failing elegance of style, and often with singular keenness of perception; but they do not take us beyond the starting-point. . . . After many digressions and ramblings we find ourselves back on the same side of the original question. We are marking time with admirable gracefulness, but somehow we are not advancing. Naturally flesh and blood grow weary when there is no apparent end to a discussion, except that the author must in time be wearied of performing variations upon a single theme.

We are more easily reconciled to some other faults which are rather due to expectations raised by his critics than to positive errors. No one, for example, would care to notice an anachronism, if Landor did not occasionally put in a claim for accuracy. . . . Were it not that critics have asserted the opposite, it would be hardly worth while to say that Landor's style seldom condescends to adapt itself to the mouth of the speaker, and that from Demosthenes to Porson every interlocutor has palpably the true Landorian trick of speech. Here and there, it is true, the effect is rather unpleasant. Pericles and Aspasia are apt to indulge in criticism of English customs, and no weak regard for time and place prevents Eubulides from denouncing Canning to Demosthenes. The classical dress becomes so thin on such occasions, that even the small degree of illusion which one may fairly desiderate is too rudely interrupted. The actor does not disguise his voice enough for theatrical purposes. It is perhaps a more serious fault that the dialogue constantly lapses into monologue. We might often remove the names of the talkers as useless interruptions. Some conversations might as well be headed, in legal phraseology, Landor *v.* Landor, or at most Landor *v.* Landor and another—the other being some wretched man of straw or Guy Faux effigy dragged in to be belaboured with weighty aphorisms and talk obtrusive nonsense. Hence sometimes we resent a little the taking in vain of the name of some old friend. It is rather too hard upon Sam Johnson to be made a mere "passive bucket" into which Horne Tooke may pump his philological notions, with scarcely a feeble sputter or two to represent his smashing retorts.

There is yet another criticism or two to be added. The extreme scrupulosity with which Landor polishes his style and removes superfluities from poetical narrative, smoothing them at times till we can hardly grasp them, might have been applied to some of the wanton digressions in which the dialogues abound. We should have been glad if he had ruthlessly cut out two-thirds of the conversation between Richelieu and others, in which some charming English pastorals are mixed up with a quantity of unmistakable rubbish. But, for the most part, we can console ourselves by a smile. When Landor lowers his head and charges bull-like at the phantom of some king or priest, we are prepared for, and amused by, his impetuosity. Malesherbes discourses with great point and vigour upon French literature, and may fairly diverge into a little politics; but it is certainly comic when he suddenly remembers one of Landor's pet grievances, and the unlucky Rousseau has to discuss a question for which few people could be more ludicrously unfit—the details of a plan for reforming the institution of English justices of the peace. The grave dignity with which the subject is introduced gives additional piquancy to the absurdity. An occasional laugh at Landor is the more valuable because, to say the truth, one is not very likely to laugh with him. Nothing is more difficult for an author—as he here observes in reference to Milton—than to decide upon his own merits as a wit or humourist. I am not quite sure that this is true; for I have certainly found authors distinctly fallible in judging of their own merits as poets and philosophers. But it is undeniable that many a man laughs at his own wit who has to laugh alone. I will not take upon myself to say that Landor was without humour; he has certainly a delicate gracefulness which may be classed with the finer kinds of humour; but if anybody (to take one instance) will read the story which Chaucer tells to Boccaccio and Petrarch and pronounce it to be amusing, I can only say that his notions of humour differ materially from mine. Landor often sins as distinctly, if not as heavily.

Blemishes such as these go some way perhaps to account for Landor's unpopularity. But they are such as might be amply redeemed by his vigour, his fulness, and unflagging energy of style. There is no equally voluminous author of great power who does not fall short of his own highest achievements in a large part of his work, and who is not open to the remark that his achievements are not all that we could have wished. It is doubtless best to take what we can get, and not to repine if we do not get something better, the possibility of which is suggested by the actual accomplishment. (pp. 675-79)

Is he a man whom we can take to our hearts, treating his vagaries and ill-humours as we do the testiness of a valued friend? Or do we feel that he is one whom it is better to have for an acquaintance than for an intimate? The problem seems to have exercised those who knew him best in life. Many, like Southey or Napier, thought him a man of true nobility and tenderness of character, and looked upon his defects as mere superficial blemishes. If some who came closer seem to have had a rather different opinion, we must allow that a man's personal defects are often unimportant in his literary capacity. (pp. 679-80)

Landor, undoubtedly, may be loved; but I fancy that he can be loved unreservedly only by a very narrow circle. For when we pass from the form to the substance—from the manner in which his message is delivered to the message itself—we find that the superficial defects rise from very deep roots. Whenever we penetrate to the underlying character we find something harsh and uncongenial mixed with very high qualities. He has pronounced himself upon a wide range of subjects; there is much criticism, some of it of a very rare and admirable order; much theological and political disquisition; and much exposition, in various forms, of the practical philosophy which every man imbibes according to his faculties in his passage through the world. It would be undesirable to discuss seriously his political or religious notions. To say the truth, they are not really worth discussing; they are little more than vehement explosions of unreasoning prejudice. (p. 680)

The reason for our not producing more Landors is indeed pretty simple. Men of real poetic genius are exceedingly rare at all times, and it is still rarer to find such a man who remains a schoolboy all his life. Landor is precisely a glorified and sublime edition of the model sixth-form lad, only with an unusually strong infusion of schoolboy perversion. Perverse lads, indeed, generally kick over the traces at an earlier point: refuse to learn anything. Boys who take kindly to the classical are generally good, that is to say, docile. They develop into tutors and professors; or, when the cares of life begin to press, they start their cargo of classical lumber and fill the void with law or politics. Landor's peculiar temperament led him to kick against authority, while he yet imbibed the spirit of the teaching fully, and in some respects rather too fully.

The impatient and indomitable temper which made quiet or continuous meditation impossible, and the accidental circumstances of his life, left him in possession of qualities which are in most men subdued or expelled by the hard discipline of life. Brought into impulsive collision with all kinds of authorities, he set up a kind of schoolboy republicanism, and used all his poetic eloquence to give it an air of reality. But he never cared to bring it into harmony with any definite system of thought, or let his outbursts of temper transport him into settled antagonism with accepted principles. His aristocratic feeling lay deeper than his quarrels with aristocrats. He troubled himself just as little about theological as about political theories: he was as utterly impervious as the dullest of squires to the mystic philosophy imported by Coleridge, and found the world quite rich enough in sources of enjoyment without tormenting himself about the unseen and the ugly superstitions which thrive in mental twilight. But he had quarrelled with parsons as much as with lawyers, and could not stand the thought of a priest interfering with his affairs or limiting his amusements. And so he set up as a tolerant and hearty disciple of Epicurus. Chivalrous sentiment and an exquisite perception of the beautiful saved him from any gross interpretation of his master's principles; although, to say the truth, he shows an occasional laxity on some points which savours of the easy-going pagan, or perhaps of the noble of the old school. As he grew up he drank deep of English literature, and sympathised with the grand republican pride of Milton—as sturdy a rebel as himself, and a still nobler because more serious rhetorician. He went to Italy, and as he imbibed Italian literature, sympathised with the joyous spirit of Boccaccio and the eternal boyishness of classical art. Mediaevalism and all mystic philosophies remained unintelligible to this true-born Englishman. Irritated rather than humbled by his incapacity, he cast them aside, pretty much as a schoolboy might throw a Plato at the head of a pedantic master.

The best and most attractive dialogues are those in which he can give free play to this Epicurean sentiment; forget his political mouthing, and inoculate us for the moment with the spirit of youthful enjoyment. Nothing can be more perfectly charming in its way than Epicurus in his exquisite garden, discoursing, on his pleasant knoll, where, with violets, cyclamens, and convolvuluses clustering round, he talks to his lovely girl-disciples upon the true theory of life—temperate enjoyment of all refined pleasures, forgetfulness of all cares, and converse with true chosen spirits far from the noise of the profane vulgar: of the art, in short, by which a man of fine cultivation may make the most of this life, and learn to take death as a calm and happy subsidence into oblivion. (pp. 684-85)

[The *Pentameron*], and many of the shorter and more dramatic dialogues, have a rare charm, and the critic will return to analyse, if he can, their technical qualities. But little explanation can be needed, after reading them, of Landor's want of popularity. If he had applied half as much literary skill to expand commonplace sentiment; if he had talked that kind of gentle twaddle by which some recent essayists edify their readers, he might have succeeded in gaining a wide popularity. Or if he had been really, as some writers seem to fancy, a deep and systematic thinker as well as a most admirable artist, he would have extorted a hearing even while provoking dissent. But his boyish waywardness has disqualified him from reaching the deeper sympathies of either class. We feel that the most superhuman of schoolboys has really a rather shallow view of life. His various outbursts of wrath amuse us at best when they do not bore, even though they take the outward form of philosophy or statesmanship. He has really no answer or vestige of answer for any problems of his, nor indeed of any other time, for he has no basis of serious thought. All he can say is, ultimately, that he feels himself in a very uncongenial atmosphere, from which it is delightful to retire, in imagination, to the society of Epicurus, or the study of a few literary masterpieces. That may be very true, but it can be interesting only to a few men of similar taste; and men of profound insight, whether of the poetic or the philosophic temperament, are apt to be vexed by his hasty dogmatism and irritable rejection of much which deserved his sympathy. His wanton quarrel with the world has been avenged by the world's indifference. We may regret the result, when we see what rare qualities have been cruelly wasted, but we cannot fairly shut our eyes to the fact that the world has a very strong case. (p. 686)

[Leslie Stephen], *"Landor's 'Imaginary Conversations',"* in The Cornhill Magazine, *Vol. XXXVIII, No. 228, December, 1878, pp. 667-86.*

ALGERNON CHARLES SWINBURNE (essay date 1882)

[*Swinburne was an English poet, dramatist, and critic. Though renowned during his lifetime for his lyric poetry, he is remembered today for his rejection of Victorian mores. In the following excerpt from an essay originally published in the ninth edition of* Encyclopaedia Britannica *in 1882, Swinburne expresses his profound admiration for Landor's works.*]

In the course of this long life [Walter Savage Landor] . . . won for himself such a double crown of glory in verse and in prose as has been worn by no other Englishman but Milton. And with that special object of his lifelong veneration he had likewise in common other claims upon our reverence to which no third competitor among English poets can equally pretend. He had the same constancy to the same principles, the same devotion to the same ideal of civic and heroic life; the same love, the same loyalty, the same wrath, scorn, and hatred, for the same several objects respectively; the same faith in the example and kinship to the spirit of the republican Romans, the same natural enjoyment and mastery of their tongue. Not accident merely but attraction must in any case have drawn them to enlist in the ranks and serve under the standard of the ancient Latin army of patriots and poets. But to Landor even more than to Milton the service of the Roman Muse was a natural and necessary expression of his genius, a spontaneous and just direction of its full and exuberant forces. . . . No poet at the age of twenty ever had more vigour of style and fluency of verse [than is evident in *The Poems of Walter Savage Landor* and his anonymous pamphlet, *Moral Epistle, Respectfully Dedicated to Earl Stanhope*]; nor perhaps has any ever shown such masterly command of epigram and satire, made vivid and vital by the purest enthusiasm and most generous indignation. Three years later appeared the first edition of the first great work

A portrait of Landor in 1804.

which was to inscribe his name for ever among the great names in English poetry. The second edition of *Gebir* appeared in 1803, with a text corrected of grave errors and improved by magnificent additions. About the same time the whole poem was also published in a Latin form, which for might and melody of line, for power and perfection of language, must always dispute the palm of precedence with the English version.... [Landor's experiences with the Spanish revolutionary army provided material] for the sublimest poem published in our language between the last masterpiece of Milton and the first masterpiece of Shelley—one equally worthy to stand unchallenged beside either for poetic perfection as well as moral majesty—the lofty tragedy of *Count Julian*.... No comparable work is to be found in English poetry between the date of *Samson Agonistes* and the date of *Prometheus Unbound;* and with both these great works it has some points of greatness in common. The superhuman isolation of agony and endurance which encircles and exalts the hero is in each case expressed with equally appropriate magnificence of effect. The style of *Count Julian*, if somewhat deficient in dramatic ease and the fluency of natural dialogue, has such might and purity and majesty of speech as elsewhere we find only in Milton so long and so steadily sustained. (pp. 201-03)

From nineteen almost to ninety his intellectual and literary activity was indefatigably incessant; but ... he could not write a note of three lines which did not bear the mark of his 'Roman hand' in its matchless and inimitable command of a style at once the most powerful and the purest of his age. The one charge which can ever seriously be brought and maintained against it is that of such occasional obscurity or difficulty as may arise from excessive strictness in condensation of phrase and expurgation of matter not always superfluous, and sometimes almost indispensable. His English prose and his Latin verse are perhaps more frequently and more gravely liable to this charge than either his English verse or his Latin prose. At times it is wellnigh impossible for an eye less keen and swift, a scholarship less exquisite and ready than his own, to catch the precise direction and follow the perfect course of his rapid thought and radiant utterance. This apparently studious pursuit and preference of the most terse and elliptic expression which could be found for anything he might have to say could not but occasionally make even so sovereign a master of two great languages appear 'dark with excess of light;' but from no former master of either tongue in prose or verse was ever the quality of real obscurity, of loose and nebulous incertitude, more utterly alien or more naturally remote. There is nothing of cloud or fog about the path on which he leads us; but we feel now and then the want of a bridge or a handrail; we have to leap from point to point of narrative or argument without the usual help of a connecting plank. Even in his dramatic works, where least of all it should have been found, this lack of visible connection or sequence in details of thought or action is too often a source of sensible perplexity. In his noble trilogy on the history of Giovanna Queen of Naples it is sometimes actually difficult to realize on a first reading what has happened or is happening, or how, or why, or by what agency—a defect alone sufficient, but unhappily sufficient in itself, to explain the too general ignorance of a work so rich in subtle and noble treatment of character, so sure and strong in its grasp and rendering of 'high actions and high passions,' so rich in humour and in pathos, so royally serene in its commanding power upon the tragic mainsprings of terror and of pity. As a poet, he may be said on the whole to stand midway between Byron and Shelley,—about as far above the former as below the latter. If we except Catullus and Simonides, it might be hard to match

and it would be impossible to overmatch the flawless and blameless yet living and breathing beauty of his most perfect elegies, epigrams, or epitaphs.... His passionate compassion, his bitter and burning pity for all wrongs endured in all the world, found only their natural and inevitable outlet in his lifelong defence or advocacy of tyrannicide as the last resource of baffled justice, the last discharge of heroic duty.... He was a classic, and no formalist; the wide range of his just and loyal admiration had room for a genius so far from classical as Blake's. Nor in his own highest mood or method of creative as of critical work was he a classic only, in any narrow or exclusive sense of the term. On either side, immediately or hardly below his mighty masterpiece of *Pericles and Aspasia*, stand the two scarcely less beautiful and vivid studies of mediaeval Italy and Shakespearean England. The very finest flower of his immortal dialogues is probably to be found in the single volume comprising only *Imaginary Conversations of Greeks and Romans;* his utmost command of passion and pathos may be tested by its transcendent success in the distilled and concentrated tragedy of **"Tiberius and Vipsania,"** where for once he shows a quality more proper to romantic than classical imagination—the subtle and sublime and terrible power to enter the dark vestibule of distraction, to throw the whole force of his fancy, the whole fire of his spirit, into the 'shadowing passion' (as Shakespeare calls it) of gradually imminent insanity. Yet, if this and all other studies from ancient history or legend could be subtracted from the volume of his work, enough would be left whereon to rest the foundation of a fame which time could not sensibly impair. (pp. 205-09)

Algernon Charles Swinburne, "Landor," in his Miscellanies, *Worthington Company, 1886, pp. 201-09.*

GEORGE SAINTSBURY (essay date 1893)

[*Saintsbury was an English literary historian and critic of the late nineteenth and early twentieth centuries. A prolific writer, he composed several histories of English and European literature as well as numerous critical works on individual authors, styles, and periods. In the following excerpt from his study of Landor's poetry, epigrams, and conversations, Saintsbury describes the merits and defects that characterize these works.*]

It is not easy, in reading over again Landor's voluminous poetical work, to decide on the exact reasons which have, with the large majority of readers, relegated it to the upper shelf. It is almost never bad; it is at times extremely good. The famous passages which lighten the darkness of *Gebir* and *Count Julian* are unstaled in their attraction by any custom. You may read **"Rose Aylmer"** for the hundredth time with the certain effect of that "divine despair" which inspires, and is inspired by only, the greatest poetry. **"Dirce,"** and the companion passage which Aspasia sent to Cleone, are equally sure of their own effect. But Landor is by no means obliged to rely on half a dozen purple passages like these. His enormous total of verse ... never for long fails to yield something altogether out of the common. From the unequal and motelike crowd of the Ianthe trifles to the long "Hellenic" and dramatic or semi-dramatic pieces, the same rule holds good. With Landor you can never read long before coming to the "flashing words, the words of light"; and the light of the flash is always distinct and not like that of any other poetical star. If he is too "classical," he is not more so than many poets of the seventeenth century, especially Jonson, whom he most resembles, and whom, perhaps from a vague sense of likeness, he rather undervalues and belittles. His quality, from its intense peculiarity, is exactly the quality which bribes the literary student. His passion is not unreal; his sense of beauty is exquisite; his power of expressing it is consummate; and yet he is not, at least to some readers, interesting as a whole. They have to gird themselves up to him; to get into training for him; or else to turn basely to the well-known pieces and re-read . . . these only.

The reasons of this are probably reasons of combination. Landor has accumulated different and even contradictory claims to the honour of remaining unread, in a fashion which might seem to be allowable in one whose quest after unpopularity was so ostentatiously intentional. The very scholarly poets are usually rather scant producers; he is enormously voluminous. The dealers in epigrams and short lyrics rarely attempt long-breathed poems; Landor by turns rains epigram (using that word in its proper sense) with the copiousness of a whole anthology, and pours out a steady stream of narrative or dramatic stuff with the ceaseless flow of Spenser. Those two stout volumes [*Poems, Dialogues in Verse, and Epigrams*], crammed with poems of all sorts and sizes, are full of delight for the few who really like to read poetry. Let us permit ourselves *Sortes Landorianae* and open one of the pair without even looking to see which it is. We open on *Dry Sticks*, certainly not a promising place to open, and find these verses:

> 'Tis pleasant to behold
> The little leaves unfold
> Day after day, still pouting at the sun,
> Until at last they dare
> Lay their pure bosoms bare
> Of all these flowers, I know the sweetest one.

Quite trifling verses perhaps, but assuredly not written in a quite trifling style. You may open a hundred volumes of verse as they come fresh from the press and not find one with that style-mark on it. Yet somehow the stoutest devotee of style may be smitten with hideous moments of scepticism when reading Landor. Few men in our days, or in any days at all near them, have had such a faculty of embalming in the self-same amber beautiful things, things presentable, and things absolutely trivial and null. All the defects of the classical and "marmoreal" style are perceived when we come to such a thing as this,

> Better to praise too largely small deserts
> Than censure too severely great defects.

That has most eminently the fault of phrase-making. It is a great question whether even what is true in it is worth saying, and it is a greater question still whether the larger part of it is not false. . . . Why not,

> Better to praise too largely great deserts
> Than censure too severely small defects?

Or,

> Better to praise too scantly great deserts
> Than censure over mildly small defects?

Or in short a dozen other truisms or paradoxes or what not of the same easy kind? It is the inevitable penalty of the "classical" form that it adapts itself with the most delusive submissiveness to almost any matter. (pp. 269-70)

If we turn from Landor's shorter poems to his longer we shall find, in different matter and in different measure, the same merits and the same defects. The poet with whom it is perhaps most natural to compare him is Mr. William Morris. It is indeed almost impossible for any one who knows the two not to think

of the *Hellenics* and the "**Acts and Scenes**" when he reads the *Life and Death of Jason* and the *Earthly Paradise*. Nor is it a very difficult thing to separate the comparative merits and defects of the two. Mr. Morris cannot pretend to Landor's dignity, precision, and lasting certainty of touch. He abounds in surplusage; he is often, if not exactly slipshod, loose and fluid; his singing robe is not girt up quite tight enough, and he tends to the garrulous. But he is always interesting; he has the gift of story, he carries us along with him, and the journey is always easy and sometimes exciting. Landor, though nearly if not quite as voluble as the later poet, has an air of the utmost economy, proportion, and rigour. His phrase, if sometimes rather long, is screwed to concert pitch; he never apparently babbles; there is a show, however modern his subject, of classical severity about him. Yet Landor can be exceedingly longwinded, and does not often succeed in being very interesting. (pp. 270-71)

The merits and defects of Landor's voluminous prose, are much the same; especially in the chief division of that prose, the vast aggregate of the Conversations, into which he preferred to throw such work of his as was not verse, while as has been seen even his verse-work had a tendency to assume the same guise. He seems indeed never to have been quite at home in any other. Perhaps he cannot in any case be ranked high as a critic; but his exercises in that kind, when couched in conversational form, are at any rate much more readable than the so-called criticisms in the eighth volume of his Works, which are either desultory jottings in the nature of annotations, or else worked into a continuous form which is stiff and lifeless. (p. 271)

[Landor] has probably left us the largest, most varied and most elaborate collection of [Conversations] in existence. . . . In some respects Plato of course stands alone; and it is not a favourable symptom of Landor's own capacities that he evidently did not like him. Plato at any rate is the first of all those who have written or ever will write conversations. The only counter claim which Landor can put in against his superiority in dignity of matter and in mastery of style, is the greater variety of his own subjects. There is indeed one other claim which he might urge, though it is an illegitimate one at best, the fuller revelation of personality. We know from the works that go under his name very little, hardly anything, of Plato. . . . [But] we know almost everything of Landor. Given the Conversations as the authentic data, and such things as early troubles at college, an unsatisfactory marriage, ample means, uncongenial surroundings, foreign residence, and the like for conjectural assistance, any novelist who knew his business could depict the life of Walter Savage Landor almost exactly as it happened.

The caution of the author to the reader, "Avoid a mistake in attributing to the writer any opinions in this book but what are spoken under his own name," is interesting but infantile. We always know, we always should know if we knew nothing else about him, from the constant presence of a common and unmistakable form, when Landor is putting Landor's opinions in the mouth of no matter who it may be. If this to some extent communicates a charm to the various and voluminous work concerned, it must be admitted that it also imparts a certain monotony to it. Greek or Roman, medieval or modern, political or amatory, literary or miscellaneous, the Conversations simply convey in stately English, the soon well known and not exceedingly fresh or wide ranging opinions of the author on mundane things, with occasional and not particularly happy excursions into things divine. (pp. 271-72)

The Conversations are full of delightful things, and it is impossible for any fit reader to attempt them without discovering these things. Let the subject admit of any description of natural scenery, any dream-scene (Landor's dreams are very nearly if not quite unapproached), any passage dealing with the greater and simpler emotions, any reflection on the sublime common-places of life, and Landor is almost entirely to be depended upon. It does not matter, it never with him matters much, what the nominal subject is; the best things written in connection with it are sure to be fine and may very likely be superb. In the *Pericles and Aspasia* (which indeed is not conversation in form but is hardly distinguishable from it), in *The Pentameron*, in many of the classical dialogues, and in not a few of the Literary Men the author will be found quite at his best. The famous **"Epicurus, Leontium, and Ternissa"** probably shows him at almost his very best, and at very nearly his very worst. In the dialogues of Sovereigns and Statesmen I should say (and not in the least because I generally disagree with the political views there expressed) that he is at his very worst. For politics is after all an eminently practical science, and of the practical spirit Landor had literally nothing. His only plan was to put more or less odious or ridiculous statements in the mouths of persons with whom he does not agree, to mop and mow at them, or to denounce them in Ciceronian strains of invective. The infallible test of a political writer, I think, is the reflection, "Should I like to have this man on my side or not?" For my part whenever I read Landor's political utterances I say, "Thank Heaven! he is on the other."

The dialogues of Famous Women are in the same way flawed by [an] artificial and namby-pamby conception of the female character . . . ; while the Miscellaneous Conversations obviously defy analysis as a whole. The author has left nothing better than some of them, such as the long, curious, unequal, but admirable **"Penn and Peterborough;"** while in others he sinks almost below the level of rational thought. **"Lord Coleraine, Rev. Mr. Bloombury, and Rev. Mr. Swan"** is fully worthy of the author of the *Examination*. It would be difficult to say of whom **"The Duke de Richelieu, Sir Firebrace Cotes, Lady G—, and Mr. Normanby"** is worthy. **"The Emperor of China and Tsing-ti"** is probably the very worst of all the imitations of Montesquieu; and on at least some others as harsh a judgment would have to be passed if they were critically judged at all. (pp. 272-73)

On all happy occasions when his hand is in, when the right subject is before him, and when he is not tempted away from it into the indulgence of some whim, into the memory of some petty wrong, into the repetition of some tiresome crotchet, he manages language literally as a great musician manages the human voice or some other organ of sound. The meaning, though it is often noble, is never the first thing in Landor, and in particular it is quite useless to go to him for any profound, any novel, any far-reaching thought. The thought is at best sufficient, and it very frequently is that; but it seldom makes any tax upon even the most moderate understanding, and it never by any chance averts attention from the beauty and the finish of the vesture in which it is clothed. The famous dreams which close *The Pentameron* are things of which it is almost impossible to tire. Nowhere else perhaps in English does prose style, while never trespassing into that which is not prose, accompany itself with such an exquisite harmony of varied sound; nowhere is there such a complicated and yet such an easily appreciable scheme of verbal music. The sense is, as has been said, just sufficient; it is no more; it is not in itself peculiarly arresting. Although the sentiment is heartfelt, it is not extremely passionate. But it is perfectly and exactly married to the verbal music, and the verbal music is perfectly and

exactly married to it. Again, it is a whole; if not perhaps quite flawless, yet with flaws which are comparatively unimportant. It does not consist, as "fine" writing too often does, of a certain number of more or less happy phrases, notes, or passages strung together. It is, as I have called it a "scheme"; a thing really deserving those terms from the science of actual music which have been so frequently and tediously abused in literary criticism. Moreover the qualities which exist pre-eminently in this and other great passages of Landor appear everywhere on smaller scales in his prose. It is never safe, except when he attempts the comic, to skip a single page. Anywhere you may come across, in five words or in five hundred, the great Landorian phrase, the sentence cunningly balanced or intentionally and deftly broken, the paragraph built with a full knowledge of the fact that a paragraph is a structure and not a heap, the adjective wedded to its proper substantive, not indulging in unseemly promiscuity, the clause proceeding clearly and steadily to the expression of the thought assigned to it. Whatever deficiencies there may be in Landor (and, as has been and will be seen, they are not few) he is seldom if ever guilty of the worst and the commonest fault of the ornate writer, a superabundance of ornament. Of his two contemporaries who tried styles somewhat similar in point of ornateness, Wilson constantly becomes tawdry, while De Quincey sometimes approaches tawdriness. Of this, nearly the worst of literary vices, Landor was constitutionally almost incapable; and his models and methods had converted his natural inaptitude into a complete and absolute immunity. He is sometimes, especially in his fits of personal dignity and scorn, a little too stately for the subject. . . . He is alas! when he unbends this pride, too often clumsily and even indecently gamesome. But with tawdriness, even with indulgence in literary frippery, he cannot for one moment be charged. In this respect, and perhaps in this respect only, his taste was infallible. His good angel was fatally remiss in its warnings on many points wherein such taste is concerned, but in this never.

If we set ourselves to discover the particular note in Landor which occasions these discords we shall find it I believe in a quality which I can only call, as I have called it, silliness. There are other great men of letters who have as much or even more of the quality of childishness; but that is a different thing. Lafontaine and Goldsmith are the two stock examples of childishness in literary history; and childish enough they were, almost inexcusably so in life. But when we find them with pen in hand we never think of them as of anything but very clever men. Landor alone, or almost alone, has written like an angel *and* like poor Poll, and written like both at once. Hazlitt was quite as wrongheaded as Landor, and much more bad-blooded. Peacock was, at any rate in his earlier years, as much the slave of whimsical crazes. Coleridge was as unpractical. His own dear friend Southey had almost as great a difficulty in adjusting the things and estimates of the study to the estimates and the things of the forum. De Quincey was even more bookish and unworldly. But even in passages of these men with which we least agree we do not find positive silliness, a positive incapacity to take the standpoint and the view of a full-grown man who has or ought to have mingled with and jostled against the things of the world and of life. We do find this in Landor. His apologists have admitted that he was always more or less of a schoolboy; I should say that he was always more or less of a baby.

The time-honoured Norman definition of a man is "One who fights and counsels." Landor had in almost superabundant measure that part of man which fights; he was abnormally deficient in the part which counsels. In some cases where taste (of certain, not of all kinds), scholarship, poetic inspiration, chivalry (again of certain kinds), and the like could supply the place of judgment and ratiocinative faculty, he has done nobly, even without taking into account that matchless gift of expression which never deserts him for long together. But in any kind of reasoning proper he is as an infant in arms; and in that faculty which (though sometimes it be divorced from it) comes nearest to the ratiocinative, the faculty of humour, he is almost as defective. Here I know there is great difference and discrepancy between those who should agree; but I shall boldly avow that I think Landor's attempts both at humour and at wit for the most part simply deplorable, as deplorable as his idol Milton's. Some persons whom I respect, as well as others whom I do not, have professed to see a masterpiece of humour in *The Examination of William Shakespeare*. If by a majority of competent critics it is admitted that it is such, I must be a heretic.... [The] entire absence of proportion in matter, so strangely contrasted with his excellent sense of proportion in style, which characterised Landor appears in this matter of the humorous, not perhaps more strongly but, more eminently than anywhere else. It was not that humorous ideas did not visit him, for they did; but he did not in the least know how to deal with them. He mumbles a jest as a bull-dog worries or attempts to worry a rat when he is set to that alien art. His three sets of models, the classics, the English writers of the seventeenth century, and the Italians ... had each in them certain evil precedent suggestions for a jester. Landor with unerring infelicity seized on these, combined them, worked them fully out, and produced things very terrible, things which range from the concentrated dreariness of the *Examination* and the Conversation between Pitt and Canning to the smaller flashes-in-the-pan of joking dulness which are scattered about his writings *passim*.

Another thing which is extremely noticeable about Landor is the marvellously small difference between his poetry and his prose. Except again Milton (an instance ominous and full of fear) and perhaps Wordsworth, I know no other English writer of the first class of which this can be said. But Landor has versified, or almost versified, some of his actual conversations, and has left explicit declaration that not a few of his poems are simply conversations in verse.... The sententious, intense, rhythmical phrase is the same in both; the poetical intuition of sights and sounds, and other delights of sense, is not more obvious in one than in the other. The absence of continuous logical thought is not greater here than there; the remoteness from what may be called the sense of business is always the same, whether the syllables in a line be limited to ten at most, or may run on to as many as the limits of the page will admit. Although he was conscious of, and generally avoided the mistake of introducing definitely poetic rhythm into prose, it is astonishing how close is the resemblance of a short stave of his verse to a sentence of his prose. It is owing to this, among other things, that his form of verse is as compared with that of others a rather severe form, while his prose is, compared with that of others, rather florid. It is owing to this that, while some of the very happiest efforts of his verse have the simplicity and directness of the ancient epigram, some of the most agreeable efforts of his prose have in the proper sense an idyllic character.

And so we have in Landor an almost unmatched example of the merits and the defects of style by itself. To attempt once more to narrow down the reasons of both, I should say that they lie in his having had nothing particular to say with a matchless faculty for saying anything. When the latter faculty is exercised sparingly on the former defect, we often get some of the finest things in literature.... But when the thing is administered in larger and ever larger doses the intensity of the flavour palls and the absence of anything else, besides and behind the flavour, begins to tell. Yet at his very best, and taken in not too large quantities, Landor is the equal of all but the greatest, perhaps of the greatest themselves. And if, according to a natural but rather foolish fashion, we feel at any time inclined to regret that he lived so long and had so much time to accumulate indifferent as well as good work, let us remember on the other hand that his best work is scattered over almost every period of his life, except the very last and the very first, and that the best of it is of a kind worth wading through volumes of inferior work to secure. The true critical question with every writer is, "Could we spare him? Could we do without him?" Most assuredly, if we tried to do without Landor, we should lose something with which no one else could supply us. (pp. 273-76)

> *George Saintsbury, "Landor," in* Macmillan's Magazine, *Vol. 67, No. 400, February, 1893, pp. 267-76.*

FRANCIS THOMPSON   (essay date 1897)

[*Thompson was one of the most important poets of the Catholic Revival in nineteenth-century English literature. Often compared to the seventeenth-century metaphysical poets, Thompson wrote poetry and prose noted for rich verbal effects and a devotion to the values of aestheticism. In this excerpt from an article that was first published in the* Academy *in 1897, Thompson claims that Landor's prose ranks with the best written in the English language, for his classical style and strong expression of personality compensate for his lack of profound subject matter.*]

[Landor's prose] is not, as a rule, imaginative, nor distinguished by any other extra-prose qualities; it gives one no thrill, no "shock of sweet surprise": it is most absolute prose, but also most admirable prose; lucid, structural, with an unclamorous rightness of phrase. Sometimes he goes out of his way for an epithet, with self-justifying result, as when he speaks about "the omnigenous imagery of Shakespeare." The adjective is exactly and felicitously apt, a sentence-saving adjective. But this is rare. He has, in fact, described his own style—probably not unawares.

> Elegance in prose composition is mainly this: a just admission of topics and of words, neither too many nor too few of either; enough of sweetness in the sound to induce us to enter and sit still; enough of illustration and reflection to change the posture of our minds when they would tire; and enough of sound matter in the complex to repay us for our attention.

This does not describe a profound writer, nor is Landor profound. The "sound matter in the complex" is a variable quality with him. He loves paradox and paradoxical satire—for if we have called his writing "absolute prose," we by no means meant to call it prosaic. But the paradox is as likely as not to be more startling than deep; and perhaps one of the circumstances which keep the reader alert in attention is, that you never know whether the next paradox will be convincing or maddeningly perverse. He upholds, for example, the unexpected proposition that Locke is the most elegant of English writers; and to the question why Plato is so much more applauded, answers most Landorianly that it is because he is so much less read. (p. 179)

By what careful study Landor gained his command of English is to be seen in the dialogue between Horne Tooke and Johnson. It deserves to be read for its acute criticism of language—mixed, of course, with Landorian crotchets and obstinacies.

> Since we are become a learned nation . . . , not only the words we have cast aside, but also those we have substituted in the place of them, are mostly injudicious; and such others as we have taken the trouble to construct are unskilful botches.

Landor slips in expression: he does not mean that the words we have cast aside are injudicious, but that it was injudicious to cast them aside. The substance, however, is the view of all those—chiefly poets—who have striven in modern days, against a chorus of facile censure, to revive some of those cast-off pieces of the English tongue. Yet in the midst of his criticism of others he himself uses the horrible comparative "frequenter"—by way, we suppose, of being still a mutineer, and Landor. Landor he always is: the *Imaginary Conversations,* which are his classical work in prose, if (as De Quincey insists) they have many points of skilful dialogue, are not dramatic; Chatham, for instance, is not Chatham, but Landor without the smallest of masks. Mr. Coventry Patmore drew a distinction between two kinds of dogmatism: the dogmatism of the seer, and the dogmatism of the man who opines. "By their fruits ye shall know them"—which means that to discern between the two the hearer must himself have the gift of recognising, though not of divining, truth. Landor belonged emphatically to the second class. He is stiff in opinion, not because his vision of truth is so dazzling, but because he has the bull-dog's instinct of hanging-on to whatever comes between his teeth. "Mamma says so," remarked the once famous child in *Punch;* "and if Mamma says so, it *is* so, even if it isn't!" That was the opinion of Walter Savage Landor about Walter Savage Landor's opinions—even when he recommended the Greeks to fight the Turks with bows and arrows instead of firearms. Let us be thankful that a certain genius makes them not too seldom right, and that a classical style allied with a strong personality makes them always interesting. In no intellectual quality, perhaps, can he be called great; but he has written some of the best prose in the English language. (pp. 180-81)

> *Francis Thompson, "Victorian Age: Landor," in his* Literary Criticisms: Newly Discovered and Collected, *edited by Rev. Terence L. Connolly, S. J., E. P. Dutton and Company Inc., 1948, pp. 177-81.*

ARTHUR SYMONS   (essay date 1906)

[*Symons was an English critic, poet, dramatist, short story writer, and editor who first gained notoriety in the 1890s as an English decadent. Eventually, he established himself as one of the most important critics of the modern era. Symons here reviews Landor's poetry. He states that the prose works were Landor's greater achievement, but that his genius, which permeated all his writing, was primarily poetic.*]

[Landor] remains alone in English literature, to which he brought, in verse and prose, qualities of order and vehemence, of impassioned thinking and passionless feeling, not to be found combined except in his own work. And in the man there was a like mingling of opposites: nobility and tenderness, haste and magnanimity, courtesy and irresponsible self-will, whatever is characteristically English and whatever is characteristically Roman, with the defects of every quality. Landor is monumental by the excess of his virtues, which are apt to seem, at times, a little too large for the stage and scenery of his life. He desired to live with grandeur; and there is grandeur in the outlines of his character and actions. But some gust of the will, some flurry of the nerves, was always at hand, to trouble or overturn this comely order. The ancient Roman becomes an unruly child, the scholar flings aside cap and gown and leaps into the arena.

Landor began to write verse when he was a schoolboy, and it is characteristic of him that poetry came to him first as a school exercise, taken for once seriously. Latin was to him, it has been well said, "like the language of some prior state of existence, rather remembered than learned." His first book, published at the age of twenty, contains both Latin and English verse, together with a defense, in Latin, of the modern use of that language. When, a few years later, he began to work upon his first serious poem, *Gebir,* he attempted it both in Latin and in English, finally decided to write it in English, and, later on, turned it also into Latin.

Gebir was published in 1798, the year of the *Lyrical Ballads,* and, in its individual way, it marks an epoch almost as distinctly. No blank verse of comparable calibre had appeared since the death of Milton, and, though the form was at times actually reminiscent both of Milton and of the Latin structure of some of the portions as they were originally composed, it has a quality which still remains entirely its own. Cold, sensitive, splendid, so precise, so restrained, keeping step with such a stately music, scarcely any verse in English has a more individual harmony, more equable, more refreshingly calm to the ear. It contains those unforgettable lines, which can never be too often repeated:—

> But I have sinuous shells of pearly hue
> Within, and they that lustre have imbibed
> In the sun's palace-porch, where when unyoked
> His chariot-wheel stands midway in the wave:
> Shake one and it awakens, then apply
> Its polisht lips to your attentive ear,
> And it remembers its august abodes,
> And murmurs as the ocean murmurs there.

There are in it single lines like,—

> The sweet and honest avarice of love;

and there are lines marching like these:

> the feast
> Was like the feast of Cepheus, when the sword
> Of Phineus, white with wonder, shook restrain'd,
> And the hilt rattled in his marble hand.

Has not that the tread of the Commander in *Don Juan*? And there are experiments in a kind of naïveté:—

> Compared with youth
> Age has a something like repose.

Tennyson is anticipated here:—

> On the soft inward pillow of her arm
> Rested her burning cheek;

Mr. Swinburne here:—

> The silent oars now dip their level wings,
> And weary with strong stroke the whitening wave.

But where the most intimately personal quality of Landor is seen is in the lofty homeliness of speech which is always definite, tangible, and about definite, tangible things. The Gadites are building, and Landor, remembering the workmen he has seen in the streets of Warwick, notes:—

> Dull falls the mallet with long labour fringed.

Gebir is wrestling with the nymph, who sweats like any mortal; Landor does not say so, but he sets her visibly before us,—

> now holding in her breath constrain'd,
> Now pushing with quick impulse and by starts,
> Till the dust blackened upon every pore.

We are far enough from Milton here; not so far, perhaps, from the Latin precision of statement; but certainly close to reality. And it is reality of a kind new to English poetry,—painter's, sculptor's, reality,—discovered, as we have seen, at precisely the moment when Wordsworth was discovering for himself the reality of simple feeling, and Coleridge the reality of imaginative wonder.

A few years after *Gebir,* Landor published two poems, "**Chrysaor**" and "**The Phocaeans**," and then, for many years, at long intervals, wrote, and occasionally published, other poems, in Latin and English, which were eventually to make up the *Idyllia Heroica* and the *Hellenics.* They are, to use a word which Browning was to invent (having learned the thing, perhaps, from Landor), dramatic idyls. The most perfect of them, "**The Death of Artemidora**," is only nineteen lines long; "**The Last of Ulysses**" fills fifty-five pages in the edition of 1847. Landor never ceased to shift their places, and to add, reject, and, above all, rewrite. The two essentially different texts are those of 1847 and 1859; and it is necessary to compare these with each other, and both with such as exist also in Latin, if we would trace with any care the diligent and never quite final labor which Landor gave to his verse.

In the poems which Landor twice translated from his own Latin, it is not often that either form of the English is quite as good as the Latin, and it is not always easy to choose between the two versions, of which the first is usually more easy and fluent, while the second, though more Latin, is often more personal to Landor. Often the second version is nearer to the original. . . . Sometimes the earlier version is the more literal, but the later one gains by condensation. (pp. 808-10)

Alike from what is gained and from what is lost in this recasting we see how uncertain, with all his care, was Landor's touch on English verse, how a Latin sound dominated his ears when he was writing English, and how his final choice of form was almost invariably of the nature of a compromise, like that of one to whom his native tongue was foreign. Compare the two versions of lines 30-34 of "**Veneris Pueri:**"—

> At neque propositum neque verba superba remittit,
> Ut Chaos antiquum flamma radiante subegit,
> Ut tenebras pepulit coelo, luctantiaque astra
> Stare, vel aeterno jussit prodire meatu,
> Ut pelago imposuit domito confinia rupes.

In 1847 "**The Children of Venus**" reads:—

> But neither his proud words did he remit
> Nor resolution: he began to boast
> How with his radiant fire he had reduced
> The ancient Chaos; how from heaven he drove
> The darkness that surrounded it, and drew
> Into their places the reluctant stars,

> And made some stand before him, others go
> Beyond illimitable space; then curb'd
> The raging sea and chain'd with rocks around.

In 1859 "**The Boys of Venus**" reads:—

> Still neither would he his intent forego
> Nor moderate his claim, nor cease to boast
> How Chaos he subdued with radiant fire,
> How from the sky its darkness he dispell'd,
> And how the struggling planets he coerced,
> Telling them to what distance they might go,
> And chain'd the raging Ocean down with rocks.

Both versions are fine, though the second, trying to follow the Latin more closely line for line, abandons the freer cadences of the first; but is either wholly without a certain constraint, which we do not feel in even those passages of Milton most like Latin? And is there not, when we read the lines in Latin, a sense, not due to mere knowledge of the fact, that we are reading an original after a translation?

Yet it is to this fact, partly, to this Latin savor in English, that not only those poems of Landor which were first written in Latin, but others also, never written in anything but English, owe their exceptional, evasive, almost illegitimate charm. What, we find ourselves saying, is this unknown, exquisite thing, which yet seems to be not quite poetry, or is certainly unlike anything else in English poetry? A perfume clings about it, as if it had been stored for centuries in cedar chests, and among spices. Nor does it fail to respond to its own appeal:—

> We are what suns and winds and waters make us.

I have read the *Hellenics,* lying by the seashore, on warm, quiet days when I heard nothing but the monotonous repetition of the sea at my feet, and they have not seemed out of key. The music is never full-throated or organ music, but picked out note by note on a reed-pipe, a slender sound with few intervals. And it is with truth that Landor says, in the preface to the edition of 1859, "Poetry, in our day, is oftener prismatic than diaphanous: this is not so: they who look into it may see through. If there be anywhere a few small air-bubbles, it yet leaves to the clear vision a wide expanse of varied scenery." (pp. 810-11)

The *Hellenics* are all in low relief; you can touch their surface, but not walk round them. Some are moulded in clay, some carved in marble; all with the same dispassionate and energetic skill of hand, the same austere sense of visible beauty. They do not imitate the variety and movement of life; they resemble the work of Flaxman rather than the work of Greek sculpture, and have the careful charm of the one rather than the restrained abundance of the other. They wish to be taken for what they are, figures in relief, harmoniously arranged, not without a reasonable decorative likeness to nature. The contours which have arrested them are suave, but a trifle rigid; the design has proportion, purity, rarely breadth or intensity. The planes are never obscured or unduly heightened; no figure, suddenly starting into life, throws disarray among the firmly stationed or sedately posed figures around.

With all his care, Landor rarely succeeds in seeming spontaneous; the fastidiousness of the choice is too conspicuous, and wounds the susceptibilities of the mind, as one who too obviously "picks and chooses" wounds the susceptibilities of a host or a friend. His touch, above all things sensitive, sometimes misses the note; in evading the brutality of statement, he sometimes leaves his meaning half expressed.

> The shore was won; the fields markt out; and roofs
> Collected the dun wings that seek house-fare;
> And presently the ruddy-bosom'd guest
> Of winter knew the doors; then infant cries
> Were heard within; and lastly, tottering steps
> Pattered along the image-stationed hall.

It is not without some intent deciphering that any one will realize from these hints that the passage of three years is meant to be indicated in them. Landor prefers to give you a sort of key, which he expects you to fit in the lock, and turn there; there is disdain in his way of stopping short, as with a half courteous and half contemptuous gesture. For the most part he hints at what has happened by mentioning an unimportant, but visible, consequence of it.

Landor's chief quality is sensitiveness; and this is seen equally in his touch on verse and in the temper of his daily life. (p. 811)

And sensitiveness makes his verse shrink away from any apparent self-assertion, all in little shivers, like the nymph's body at the first cold touch of the river. He heard a music which seemed to beat with too definite a measure, and he often draws back his finger from the string before he has quite sounded the note, so fearful is he lest the full twang should be heard. The words pause half-uttered; what they say is never more than a part of what they mean, as the tune to which they say it always supposes a more ample melody completing it behind the silence. In that familiar ending of **"The Death of Artemidora,"**—

> and now a loud deep sob
> Swell'd thro' the darken'd chamber: 't was not hers,—

we find this shy reticence, which from an idiosyncrasy has become almost a method.

Landor was a scholar of beauty, and it was with almost too disinterested an homage, too assured at once and too shy, that he approached the Muses. "The kingdom of heaven suffereth violence," and poetry wants to be wooed by life. Landor was not a strong man; he was a loud weak man; in his life we see the tumult, and only in his verse "the depth and not the tumult of the soul." His work is weakness made marmoreal; the explosive force tamed, indeed, but tamed too well, showing the lack of inner fire, so busy with rocks and lava on the surface. That is why it becomes tedious after a little; because life comes and goes in it but capriciously, like the shooting flames of his life; it is not warmed steadily throughout.

Something of this may have been in Coleridge's mind when he said, . . . "The truth is, he does not possess imagination in its highest form" [see excerpt dated 1834]. . . .

[But is] it, really, imagination which he lacks? In some lines addressed to Barry Cornwall, Landor states his own theory:

> Imagination's paper kite,
> Unless the string is held in tight,
> Whatever fits and starts it takes,
> Soon bounces on the ground, and breaks.

Landor holds in the string so tight that the kite never soars to the end of its tether. In one of his many fits of "the pride that apes humility," he writes:—

> And yet, perhaps, if some should tire
> Of too much froth or too much fire,
> There is an ear that may incline
> Even to words so dull as mine.

He was, indeed, averse to both froth and fire, and there is nothing of either in his temperate and lofty work. . . .

It is in Landor's dramatic work that we see, perhaps more clearly than elsewhere, the point beyond which he could not go, though nowhere else in his work do we see more clearly his nobility of attitude and his command of grave and splendid verse. Landor's method in dialogue is a logical method; the speeches are linked by a too definite and a too visible chain; they do not spring up out of those profound, subconscious affinities, which, in the work of the great dramatists, mimic nature with all her own apparent irregularity. (p. 812)

Landor, to forestall criticism, tells us that **Count Julian** is "rather a dialogue than a drama;" but it adopts the dramatic form, and even the form of French drama, in which the entrance of a new speaker begins a new scene. It could very well be presented by marionettes with sonorous voices, speaking behind the scenes. Landor never sees his people; they talk unmoved, or enunciate a sudden emotion with unnatural abruptness. The verse is too strict and stern, within measured Miltonic limits, for dramatic speech, or even for lifelike dialogue; thus:—

> If strength be wanted for security,
> Mountains the guard, forbidding all approach
> With iron-pointed and uplifted gates,
> Thou wilt be welcome too in Aguilar,
> Impenetrable, marble-turreted.

Yet there are moments when the Miltonic speech becomes, as it can become, nakedly dramatic:—

> Heaven will inflict it, and not I . . . but I
> Neither will fall alone nor live despised.

To Landor his own people were very real; and he says, "I brought before me the various characters, their forms, complexions, and step. In the daytime I laboured, and at night unburdened my mind, shedding many tears." But between this consciousness of a step heard in the mind, and a working knowledge of the movement of an actor across the stage, there is a great gulf; and Landor never crossed it. He aimed at producing the lofty effect of Greek tragedy, but in reading Sophocles he seems never to have realized the unerring, the infinitely ingenious playwright, to whom speech is first of all the most direct means of setting his characters to make his plot. Landor endows each of his characters with a few unvarying sentiments, and when several characters meet in action they do but give dignified expression, each as if speaking by himself, to those sentiments. The clash of wills, which makes drama, may be loud enough somewhere off the stage, but here it is but "recollected in tranquillity."

Landor is a great master of imagery, and in **Count Julian** there are many lines like these:—

> Gryphens and eagles, ivory and gold,
> Can add no clearness to the lamp above;
> Yet many look for them in palaces
> Who have them not, and want them not, at home.

Note how precise, how visual (in his own remote, sumptuous way), is the image; and how scrupulous the exactitude of the thought rendered by the image. But the image is, after all, no more than just such an ornamentation of "gryphens and eagles, ivory and gold" to a thought separately clear in itself. The image is not itself the most vital part of the speech. Take, again, the speech of Julian to Roderigo, in which an image is used with more direct aim at dramatic effect:—

> I swerve not from my purpose: thou art mine,
> Conquer'd; and I have sworn to dedicate,
> Like a torn banner on my chapel's roof,
> Thee to the power from whom thou hast rebelled.
>
> (pp. 813-14)

In the later plays and scenes, in **"The Siege of Ancona,"** and in the **"Beatrice Cenci,"** most notably, Landor seems to have more nearly mastered the dramatic method, partly by limiting himself to briefer and less complicated action; and he has finally adopted a style which is at once more flexible and more beautiful. (p. 814)

In some of the briefer scenes, those single conversations in which Landor could be so much more himself than in anything moving forward from scene to scene, there are lines that bite as well as shine; such lines as those of the drunken woman who has drowned her child:—

> *Febe.* I sometimes wish 't were back again.
> *Griselda.*   To cry?
> *Febe.* Ah! it *does* cry ere the first sea-mew cries;
> It wakes me many mornings, many nights,
> And fields of poppies could not quiet it.

It is, after all, for their single lines, single speeches, separate indications of character (the boy Caesarion in **"Antony and Octavius,"** the girl Erminia in **"The Siege of Ancona,"** a strain of nobility in the Consul, of honesty in Gallus, Inez de Castro at the moment of her death), that we remember these scenes. If we could wholly forget much of the rest, the "rhetoric-roses," not always "supremely sweet," though "the jar is full," the levity without humor, and, for the most part, without grace, the "giggling" women . . . , the placid arguing about emotions, his own loss of interest, it would seem, in some of these pages as he wrote them, we might make for ourselves in Landor what Browning in a friendly dedication calls him, "a great dramatic poet," and the master of a great and flawless dramatic style.

There is another whole section of Landor's work, consisting of epigrams and small poems, more numerous, perhaps, than any English poet since Herrick has left us. Throughout his life he persistently versified trifles, as persistently as Wordsworth, but with a very different intention. Wordsworth tries to give them a place in life, so to speak, talking them, as anecdotes or as records of definite feelings; while Landor snatches at the feeling or the incident as something which may be cunningly embalmed in verse, with almost a funereal care. Among these poems which he thus wrote there are immortal successes, such as **"Dirce"** or **"Rose Aylmer,"** with many memorable epitaphs and epitomes, and some notable satires. By their side there is no inconsiderable number of petty trivialities, graceful nothings, jocose or sentimental trifles. With a far less instinctive sense of the capacities of his own language than Herrick, Landor refused to admit that what might make a poem in Latin could fail to be a poem in English. He won over many secrets from that close language; but the ultimate secrets of his own language he never discovered. Blake, Shelley, Keats, Coleridge, Wordsworth, among his contemporaries, could all do something that he could not do, something more native, more organically English, and therefore of a more absolute beauty as poetry. (pp. 814-15)

No poet has ever been a bad prose writer, whenever he has cared to drop from poetry into prose; but it is doubtful whether any poet has been quite so fine, accomplished, and persistent a prose-writer as Landor. . . . Without his prose Landor is indeed but half, if he is half, himself. His verse at its best has an austere nobility, a delicate sensitiveness, the qualities of marble or of onyx. But there is much also which is no more than a graceful trifling, the verse of a courtly gentleman, who, as he grows older, takes more and more assiduous pains in the shaping and polishing of compliments. It is at its best when it is most personal, and no one has written more nobly of himself, more calmly, with a more lofty tenderness for humanity seen in one's small, private looking-glass. But the whole man never comes alive into the verse, body and soul, but only as a stately presence.

He has put more of himself into his prose, and it is in the prose mainly that we must seek the individual features of his soul and temperament. Every phrase comes to us with the composure and solemnity of verse, but with an easier carriage under restraint. And now he is talking, with what for him is an eagerness and straightforwardness in saying what he has to say,—the "beautiful thoughts" never "disdainful of sonorous epithets." And you discover that he has much more to say than the verse has quite fully hinted at: a whole new hemisphere of the mind becomes visible, completing the sphere. And in all his prose, though only in part of his verse, he has the qualities which he attributes to Pindar: "rejection of what is light and minute, disdain of what is trivial, and selection of those blocks from the quarry which will bear strong strokes of the hammer and retain all the marks of the chisel." He wrote far more prose than verse, concentrating his maturest years upon the writing of prose. Was it, then, that his genius was essentially a prose genius, and that it was only when he turned to prose that, in the fullest sense, he found himself? I do not think it can be said that the few finest things in Landor's verse are excelled by the best of the many fine things in his prose; but the level is higher. His genius was essentially that of the poet, and it is to this quality that he owes the greater among the excellencies of his prose. In the expression of his genius he was ambidextrous, but neither in prose nor in verse was he able to create life in his own image. No one in prose or in verse has written more finely about things; but he writes about them, he does not write them. (pp. 815-16)

> *Arthur Symons, "The Poetry of Landor," in* The Atlantic Monthly, *Vol. 97, No. 6, June, 1906, pp. 808-16.*

WILLIAM BRADLEY (essay date 1914)

[In this excerpt from his book-length study of Landor's early poetry, Bradley suggests that Landor's use of theme and language in "Chrysaor" was influenced by Milton's Paradise Lost.*]*

["Chrysaor"] is unfortunately too short to do more than indicate what might have been the outcome of [Landor's] genius, had that continued to manifest itself along the same lines of thought and in the same forms. The advertisement to ["Chrysaor"] describes the poem as a sketch, and ther is evidence in the work itself that the original plan contemplated something larger, of which the part published was only the introduction giving an outline of the whole. Colvin judges it to be 'Landor's finest piece of narrative writing in blank verse, less monotonous in its movement than *Gebir*, more lofty and impassioned than any of the later "Hellenics" with which it was afterwards incorporated' [see Additional Bibliography].

Few seem to have either appreciated or even understood it. . . . Its importance in this study lies in the strong evidence it affords of the influence of Milton, which seems to have determined to a great extent both its form and substance. (p. 94)

The nearest approach [in classical mythology] to the incident described by Landor [in "**Chrysaor**"] is in the story of the defiance of Ajax and his destruction by Neptune, as told by Homer. . . . It is very probable that this may have suggested the chief incident of the poem, but there are indications that Milton's account of the rebellion of Satan and the Fall of Man contributed most to its spirit and form. Like its two predecessors, the "**Phocaeans**" and *Gebir*, "**Chrysaor**" is an attack upon kingship, which is here represented as associated with the slave trade. In a note on the lines,

> Man for one moment hath engaged his lord,
> Henceforth let merchants value him, not kings. . . .

there is a discussion on some forms of slavery. The inner meaning and application of the poem can hardly be understood without its help. There is, for instance, a comparison between 'the petty princes of Hesse and Hanover,' and 'their brethren the petty princes of Negroland' in favour of the latter, since they sold their subjects into a gentler and less degrading servitude. The poem, according to the same note, describes a period when tyranny was at its worst, which could only be when men were the slaves and merchandise of their rulers. At such a time their duty is to remove the common enemy—a plea for tyrannicide—since by submission they incur the enmity of the gods.

The contents of the poem, which contains only 209 lines, may be briefly summarised thus: After the overthrow of the Titans, one of them, Chrysaor, survives, and rules over Spain. He hurls defiance at Jupiter, and, refusing to adore, declares that henceforth the sacrifices of men shall be for the Titans, not for the gods. He demands that the curse upon him be removed, or he will wage war on his oppressor. Jupiter is roused to indignation against mankind for submitting to the tyranny of the Giant, and calls upon Neptune to destroy him. At one blow Gades is severed from the main, and the rebellious Titan perishes. But the nations of fair Hesperia, who had for thrice twelve years endured his yoke, must suffer the penalty. One of the fallen giants has given birth to a daughter, who, as Superstition, is permitted for ages to oppress them.

Brief as it is, the theme is presented in such a way as to form a parallel to that of *Paradise Lost*. The powers and persons in Landor's sketch play much the same part as the chief of those in Milton's epic. This is seen from the following comparison:

God the Father.	Jupiter.
God the Son.	Neptune.
Angels.	Tritons and Nymphs.
Adam and Eve.	Mankind.
Satan.	Chrysaor.
Fallen Angels.	Fallen Titans.
Sin (born of Satan).	Superstition (born of a Titan).

The resemblance in subject extends also to the language, which has . . . , as in *Gebir*, taken on something of the splendour of Milton in *Paradise Lost*. . . . It is not of course suggested that Landor has borrowed from, or consciously imitated, *Paradise Lost*; he was, however, so much under the influence of Milton

that his thoughts and style naturally drew their inspiration from that source. (pp. 97-8)

Landor's "**Chrysaor**" may be fairly described as a poetic treatment, in terms of Greek mythology, of a theme parallel to that of Milton's epic. The crime of man which brings about his fall is that of submitting to kings who usurp the authority of the gods. His punishment consists in the age-long reign of Superstition. (p. 103)

> *William Bradley, in his* The Early Poems of Walter Savage Landor: A Study of His Development and Debt to Milton, *Bradbury, Agnes & Co., 1914, 121 p.*

ERNEST De SÉLINCOURT   (essay date 1914)

[*In this excerpt, originally printed in 1914 as an introduction to Landor's* Imaginary Conversations, *De Sélincourt demonstrates that the imaginary conversation was the form best suited to display Landor's genius and minimize his shortcomings. De Sélincourt also examines Landor's characterizations, view of history, classicism, choice of scene, and his grand, classical style.*]

Landor's outlook on life, his taste in art, and his manner of utterance are alike his own. He is remote from the literary current of his time. In an age when romanticism was in full flood he kept steadily before him the ideals and the temper of classic art. By the ideas let loose upon the world at the French Revolution he was as deeply moved as Wordsworth or as Shelley, but from their realization he hoped not for a new heaven and a new earth, but rather for a return to the noblest traditions of Athens and of Rome. He was as passionately idealistic as any poet or dreamer of the day, and the art in which he sought both refuge and expression was the product of hours of tense excitement, of deep emotional sympathy with his subject. Yet it bears no traces of the throes of its creation; its pervading characteristics are simplicity of design, a careful finish in execution, and a serenity of spirit that proclaims him its master and not its slave. The wide field of subjects over which his writings range gives evidence enough of breadth of reading, possible only to a long and leisured life. But whatever theme he handled he handled in the same severe manner. His intellectual and artistic sympathies were fixed in boyhood by a passion for classical antiquity which other interests could never shake. (pp. 79-80)

Landor's literary reputation rests most securely upon his prose. But though he realized from the first that prose was his 'study and business', he was in no hurry to establish his pre-eminence. He was a poet of rare distinction, if not of fame, at twenty-five years old; he was nearly fifty when, in 1824, he produced the first series of his *Imaginary Conversations*. 'All strong and generous wine', he tells us, 'must deposit its crust before it gratifies the palate', and in his earlier prose, discursively critical of politics, literature, and society, still more perhaps in his verse, his experience of life and his command over the resources of language can alike be seen attaining to mellowness and maturity. The Imaginary Conversation was a form of art most clearly suited to bring out the best elements in his genius and to minimize the worst. He had not that feeling for construction, that supple, quick-moving style, necessary to a writer of good narrative or complete drama. When he takes upon himself to tell a story in prose he often tells it badly; when he should keep to one point he is liable to wander from it. A striking image, a stirring reflection such as may come to him at any moment from some side-light upon his subject, is apt, when the emotion is not tense, to take him off his chosen track into some alluring by-way. But such is the way of conversation, which is most fruitful when its course is least rigorously controlled. Landor loved dialogue for its 'facility of turning the cycle of our thoughts to whatever aspect we wish'. Moreover, it responded to a distinctive quality in his genius. He was constitutionally incapable of clear abstract thinking; but when, in the manner of the dramatist, he could merge his personality in that of other men, thoughts would flash upon him, like sparks struck out, from the contact of mind with mind, of character with character. 'It has always appeared to me', he says, 'that conversation brings forth ideas readily and plenteously, and that the ideas of one person no sooner come out than another's follow them, whether upon the same side or the opposite.' Landor drew out his own thoughts upon the same principle. (pp. 88-9)

The range of characters whom Landor reveals, and through whom he reveals himself, is unrivalled by any other author. Most felicitous, perhaps, in his delineation of ancient Greece and Rome, of the Italy of the Renaissance, and of his native land from Plantagenet times down to his own day, he hardly leaves a country or a civilization unrepresented in his gallery of illustrious portraits. 'The noble mansion', he held, 'is most distinguished by the beautiful images it retains of beings passed away, and so is the noble mind.' With the heroes of the past he loved to commune in that solitude that was to him best society. . . . History was to Landor a succession of vivid personalities, whose actions and whose thoughts revealed not only themselves, but the characteristics of the time which produced them. To know them was to know their age. In his presentation of them he was quite careless of historical accuracy, of date, place, or situation. He is full of anachronisms and discrepancies in literal fact. It was not the letter but the spirit as he conceived it that he wished to reproduce, and he felt quite free to take any liberties with historical fact which tended to bring out the essential qualities of his dramatis personae. For he was artist primarily, not historian. Thus, in a conversation of exquisite beauty, *The Lady Lisle and Elizabeth Gaunt,* two heroic women judicially murdered by Judge Jeffreys for harbouring rebels are brought together by Landor in the hour before their execution. As a matter of fact they never met. But the fiction is justified by the opportunity it affords for revealing to us the inner springs of their natures. And similarly, in no way could the character of Catharine of Russia be more vividly presented to us than at the very moment when the murder of her husband, long and eagerly planned, is at last executed, and when in transports of suppressed excitement she stands with her more timid confidante at the door of the palace, and hears his blood dripping upon the floor, and the patter of the dogs' feet as they carry the marks over the palace stairs. To this dialogue Landor added a note significant beyond its actual context. 'It is unnecessary to inform the generality of readers that Catharine was not present at the murder of her husband. Nor is it easy to believe that Clytemnestra was at the murder of hers. Our business (i.e. the business of Aeschylus and all true dramatic writers) is character.' His practice is the same when his object is less obviously dramatic, and his conversation interesting rather from its ideas than from the tensity of the situation. Thus Bacon talks with Hooker at a date when Hooker had already been in the grave some ten years. Machiavelli refers to the Spanish Armada and the wars in the Netherlands. Landor does not even scruple to put into the mouths of Greeks or Romans allusions to characters and events of his own day. But he is always true to his conception of character and nationality, representing in his dramatis personae those qualities in which, as it seemed to him, not only the individuality of the speaker, but also the genius of his nation and the peculiar spirit of his age, found clear and forcible illustration. (pp. 90-2)

But Landor is most successful with characters of more heroic build, pre-eminent either in noble action or in their capacity for suffering, great by a courage that is not merely physical, but is the index of moral and spiritual grandeur—by love that triumphs even in its apparent defeat, or by that submission to cruel destiny or unjust doom which is a proof not of man's cowering will, but of his unconquerable mind. Like the true classic artist in his outlook upon life, he is always arrested by the greatness of the soul of man. His modern sentiment is revealed by the larger emphasis he lays upon the element of tenderness with which for him greatness is ever associated. Of what passes in the world for greatness—the power of a tyrant with brutal lusts or low selfish desires—he has given many pictures; but bold and striking as they are, they tend to be exaggerated, and lack the true psychological insight with which he penetrates into those whom he can view with less bias. They are indeed dangerously like stage tyrants. Such characters, though they dominate the stage on which they act, as indeed they dominate the stage of life, are of interest to Landor chiefly as dramatic foils. Thus, Peter the Great, with his total lack of natural human feeling, throws into relief his highly strung, susceptible son, Alexis, who is swayed by emotions and inspired by ideals incomprehensible to his father, and yearns for a love of which his brutal parent is wholly incapable. In a scene conceived on similar lines, Henry VIII visits Anne Boleyn on the night before her execution. He is half-drunk, and wholly oblivious of her tender love for him and for her child—now boisterously jocose, now hurling at her shameful charges which he half-knows to be false. He laughs at her memories of a happier past, and taunts her as she pleads not for forgiveness for what she has not committed, but rather for some return of the Henry that she still loves. These portraits of Peter and of Henry are undoubtedly overdrawn, but their very exaggeration serves an obvious artistic purpose. It strengthens our sense of pathos at the sight of an exquisite fragile beauty, 'beauty that is no stronger than a flower', trodden under a wanton and muddy heel. (pp. 92-4)

Landor's art is at its finest when his characters are less fiercely contrasted, and when the tyrant has some redeeming qualities, even if he is incapable of entering into the subtler emotions of the heroine. So it is in *Leofric and Godiva,* perhaps Landor's most famous dialogue, as it was certainly among his own favourites. Leofric's love, after its own boisterous fashion, is perfectly genuine, and we are made to feel that through it his redemption may ultimately come; but at present it is entirely selfish, and thrives by the side of a callous indifference to the suffering and the starvation of his thralls. There is nothing exaggerated, nothing even unusual in the character, yet its contrast is vivid enough with the sublime figure of Godiva, whose newly awakened love for her lord has awakened also all the finer possibilities of her being. It is inseparable from her joy in the beauty of nature—'Sad is the day, and worse must follow, when we hear the blackbird in the garden and do not throb with joy'—it quickens, instead of stifling, her sympathy with the poorest of her subjects, and inspires her to an act of self-sacrifice in which she stakes more than life itself.

It is indeed to be noted that the closer the sympathy between the characters presented, the subtler is Landor's presentation of them and the more delicate his psychological insight. (pp. 94-5)

[If these scenes] are to yield up to us their full secret, they must be read not with the eye alone, but with an intensity of thought and feeling sufficient to call them up before our minds alive and moving as Landor saw them. Their high artistic concentration can only appeal to the reader whose imagination is awake to their central emotion, and is readily responsive to the subtle transitions of feeling through which the characters pass. They are classical, not only in their reserve and in their emphasis upon the heroic in character and situation, but also in a certain statuesque quality in their conception. (pp. 95-6)

The moment that he delights in depicting is that preceding the climax of the action, when some great resolution has been taken, but has yet to be fulfilled, as in the *Leofric and Godiva,* or when, as with Catharine of Russia, some great action long planned has at last been executed, and now that the climax is over, the character, as it were, recoils upon itself, and is revealed in all its complexity. He is at his greatest when some heroic soul is faced with death, and, freed at last from the trivialities that tended to obscure its true proportions, it stands out in clear outline, the light of eternity behind it. Landor does not present the death, but what might be called the emotional pose that precedes it. But in every case what he exhibits is some pause in the action, a moment when nothing is done, but much has to be endured. And in this moment of tragic suspense we feel, as it were by contrast, the passionate storm of life from which for an instant the actors have emerged. The action is all about us, through our own lively sense of the immediate past or the immediate future; it is present with us in the cries of battle which die away into the distance as we listen to the last words of Marcellus to Hannibal, in the forebodings of Godiva when the people crowd about her as she enters the city on the eve of her sacrifice—'I hope they will not crowd about me so to-morrow.' But the scene before us has the impressive stillness of arrested movement, giving opportunity for that revelation of spirit which in the tumult of action would escape observation. It is the supreme function of Landor's art, like that of painting or of sculpture, to give

> To one brief moment caught from fleeting time
> The appropriate calm of blest Eternity.

The attainment of this effect depends no more upon the careful choice of the scene to be presented than upon the manner of its presentation. Landor never gives a full statement, he never exhausts his emotion; he leaves much to be overheard by sensitive ears, relying throughout upon his elaborate and studied use of literary irony. Of irony, in the popular sense of the word, Landor was a master, and his satire is most effective, either when it is Socratic, or when he puts into the mouth of his characters words which, unconsciously to them, reveal to us their own weaknesses. But literary irony is put to higher purpose than satire. It is based not so much on the different construction put upon words by their speaker and by their audience as upon the general inadequacy of words altogether to express what we wish them to convey. Like all successful devices of art, it has its foundation in nature and the experience of life. (pp. 96-7)

In the style of his *Imaginary Conversations* there is no attempt at dramatic realism. All the dramatis personae speak Landorian English, which is far different both in rhythm and structure from the language of ordinary conversation. Landor justifies this, as was his wont, by analogy with the practice of the greatest dramatic writers.

> No man in pain . . . ever used the best part of
> the language used by Sophocles in his delinea-

tion of Philoctetes. We admit it, and willingly; and are at least as much illuded by it as by anything else we hear or see upon the stage. Poets and statuaries and painters give us an adorned imitation of the object, so skilfully treated that we receive it for a correct one. This is the only illusion that they aim at; this is the perfection of their arts.

Now, in verse dialogue most people are prepared to accept this as a recognized artistic convention. They do not call *Hamlet* unnatural because in real life Hamlet would not have spoken in blank verse. They judge of the language by its adequacy to express the ideas and emotions of the speaker, and recognize that through the beauty of the words they are attuned to sympathy with his emotion. The music of Landor's prose, as different from ordinary speech as that of Shakespeare's verse, is employed by him for the same purpose. It has its own beauty, beauty of a kind that creates the atmosphere in which his scenes have been conceived. Landor's prose is careless of what is falsely called realism. It is in 'the grand style', which arises here, as in poetry, when a serious subject is treated 'with simplicity and severity'. For if the object of art be to give immortality to great human passion, if it is its function to make

> Sorrow more beautiful than beauty's self,

it can best be achieved by some kind of idealization, and in a form which lowers that element that is painful and distressing in order to emphasize the hidden emotion of which the physical is often an imperfect manifestation. (pp. 99-100)

In that emotional prose which never overreaches itself, yet has a beauty of melody and rhythm comparable to great poetry, Landor is one of our supreme masters. Prose, he said, may be infinitely varied in modulation, it is an extension of metres, an amplification of harmonies, of which even the best and most varied poetry admits but few; certainly his own prose has a more varied and a subtler cadence than his verse. But this does not imply either that he indulged in extraneous ornament, or that he over-emphasized musical effect. The first duty of a writer, he tells us, is to be clear and concise. Obscurity is the worst fault in writing—worse to him than a flaw in the grammar, 'for we may discover a truth through such a defect which we cannot through an obscurity'. And when he is obscure himself, it is because of transitions too abrupt, through over-conciseness—never through a lack of clearness in his own mind. Next to lucidity, he delighted in fullness of sound and sense. It has often been thought that his vocabulary is too much Latinized, but though he loved Latin words for their sonority he used none that had not been fully anglicized. In diction he is always conservative, and speaks his word against slang or slovenly attempts at picturesqueness of phrase. His English is that of a scholar, but it is never pedantic, it remains essentially English in idiom and in lucidity. And the harmony of cadence that he gives it is not far-sought at the expense of the logical or intellectual elements in the style. It is the blending of proportion and force. 'Natural sequences and right subordination of thoughts and that just proportion of numbers in the sentences which follow a strong conception, are the constituents of a true harmony.' And again, 'Whatever is rightly said, sounds rightly.' His desire for a fullness of sense as well as sound makes him an intensely pictorial and imaginative writer. He often speaks in metaphor. But metaphor with him is not ornament, it is illumination. It arises inevitably from his artistic conception of his subject. 'Never look abroad for ornament' is his advice. 'Apollo, either as the god of day or the slayer of the Python, had nothing to obscure his clearness or impede his strength.' Many writers use simile and metaphor either because they do not see clearly or because they see double, because they cannot express their meaning in plain language and strive to hide their confusion of thought in a heap of glowing words. Landor is poetic in style when he sees a thing imaginatively, when his appeal is to the emotions as well as to the intellect. (pp. 101-02)

[In] simple lucid prose Landor could attain imaginative effects after which the more lyrical prose romanticists strove, often in vain, with an elaborate magnificence, or a strangeness of phrase and cadence approximating to the style of poetry. This is best exemplified in the three allegories, **"Apologue of Critobulus," "The Dream of Boccaccio,"** and **"The Dream of Petrarca."** Allegory was a form of art which Landor held in no high esteem. It seemed to him a foggy way of presenting what ought to be presented clearly. He saw how most allegorists either think too much of their meaning and spoil their artistic picture, or think too much of their picture and put in details that are irrelevant to their meaning. But these short fables of Landor's are among the few perfect allegories in the language, each of them artistically beautiful, and yet with every detail of the presentation adding force and vividness to the truth he would present.

The limitations of Landor's art will be obvious enough. . . . He exacts a heavy tax from his readers, assuming that they will bring to their reading a greater knowledge of his dramatis personae and their circumstances than can fairly be expected, whilst the very clearness with which he saw them imaged in his own mind, in their movements and gestures, and in the expression on their countenances, often prevented him from leaving a sufficient clue by which we can follow his drift. At his best he demands much concentration from us; and when he is not at his best he lacks the supreme Hellenic quality of clarity. It is true of him, as of all great writers, that we must read him many times before his full meaning reaches us; it is true also, that for even an attentive mind the first reading is not so fruitful as it should be. And his style and method, suited as it is to present the heroic, the tender, and the pathetic—for all indeed that moves upon clear and simple lines—is unfitted to present the more complex and the evanescent. An uncontrollable passion, a rapid interchange of emotion, are as much outside his scope as are all the lighter forms of comedy. His art could have fashioned a Desdemona but not an Othello, a Lady Macbeth but not a Cleopatra, a Perdita or Miranda but not a Beatrice or a Rosalind. His style, always graceful and dignified, often majestic, often tender, is not flexible, and when it trespasses beyond its proper sphere it easily becomes stiff and ponderous. And those who are not willing to follow him to the heights on which his mind and passions move will find even in his noblest writing something strained and remote. Yet perhaps for this very reason he is more precious to his little clan. (pp. 102-04)

Ernest De Sélincourt, "Landor's Prose," in his Wordsworthian and Other Studies, *1947. Reprint by Russell & Russell, 1964, pp. 77-104.*

ELIZABETH NITCHIE   **(essay date 1918)**

[*Nitchie asserts that Landor was "more truly an artist in his classicism than any of his contemporaries, except possibly Keats," for his life and works consistently demonstrated his sympathy with Greek and Roman literary and philosophical ideals.*]

[In] order to understand fully the classicism of the nineteenth century, including that of Landor, we must consider how sharp was the contrast between it and that of the age of Pope. To Dryden and Pope and Johnson it was the form, the technique, and the style of the Latin authors which appealed. A dead, imitative sort of classicism was the result. . . . But Landor and Shelley and Keats were inspired with the true Hellenic spirit, and ancient Greece was reincarnated in their work. Shelley created a new Prometheus, Keats gave new meaning to the myth of Endymion, and Landor has made Aspasia live again before our eyes.

Yet Landor, strong as is his affinity with the spirit of the age in his love for the classics, seems not to be in any sense a product of the age. It is almost as if he had been born in a period to which he did not belong. For his Hellenism is of a very different stamp from that of poets like Shelley or Byron, or of antiquarian scholars like Parr or Porson, or even of an artist like Keats. To Byron, Greece typified liberty, and his interest in her was his enthusiasm for a free people. To Shelley the literature and myth of Hellas furnished material for allegory whereby he could impress the truths of Godwinism upon others. But whereas we must look in *Prometheus Unbound* for the moral purpose, the significance underlying the Hellenic machinery of the drama, we need not trouble ourselves with such a search in reading *Pericles and Aspasia* or the dialogues between Epicurus and his pupils or between Marcellus and Hannibal. It is true that occasionally Landor spoils a dialogue by introducing allusions to contemporary politics, but in the main the words of the Greeks and Romans whom he reanimates are free from modern moral or political propaganda. An intimate sympathy with the life and spirit of the characters imbues them with a reality which no other modern has succeeded in producing. The impression conveyed is that Landor is for the time being Cicero, Tiberius, Aesop, or Lucian. True, he often voices his own opinions through the mouths of his speakers. What earnest poet, novelist, or dramatist does not? But he is speaking in the terms of the theories and ideals of the golden age of classical antiquity, not the Romantic period of England. He does not make these old Greeks and Romans argue the cause of the perfectibility of man, or fulminate against the policies of the British crown. When Landor wishes to express his sympathies with Greece in her struggle for liberty he does so in his own person in an **"Ode to Corinth"** or an open letter on the **"Revolution at Athens"** contributed to the *Examiner*.

Landor was more truly an artist in his classicism than any of his contemporaries, except possibly Keats. While he felt, as did Shelley or Wordsworth, the call to be a poet, he felt none to be a prophet. He is singularly free from dogma. Although in this respect he most closely resembles Keats, yet he differs from him in that the younger poet felt more keenly the sense appeal of the external beauty of Greek myth and Greek art, and used them to spread his gospel of beauty and truth, whereas Landor, while fully appreciating this, was influenced more by the life and ideals of the actual men and women of past ages, their significance as a part of the universal scheme of existence. Keats, like a bee, gathered from the flowers of antiquity a sweetness wherewith to make his own honey; Landor, like a spring rain, sank into the classic soil and helped to make the flowers grow and blossom for the eyes of men, even becoming a part of them, the sap which flowed through their veins. No one could imagine *Endymion* to be the work of a Greek or Roman, but Elton has well said that the three dialogues from the Agamemnon story might be thought of as fragments translated from some lost old drama, dug up in a papyrus [see Additional Bibliography].

This may be due partly to the fact that Landor's scholarship was far greater than that of Keats, who had to get all his knowledge of Greek at second hand. Not that Landor is always consistently classic in thought and spirit, or always archaeologically correct. He was not a scholar . . . , nor an antiquarian. There are some anachronisms and improbabilities in his work. His knowledge of Latin was wide and accurate, but his Greek scholarship was less unexceptionable. It was secured mainly through the Latin, and his judgment, which was never influenced by the opinions of others, was sometimes prejudiced and one-sided. (pp. 149-51)

Not only was he sometimes at fault in his judgments, but often inaccurate in details. This was due to his method of work. As was said before, he was not an antiquarian. . . . Landor did not write in a library stocked with books of reference to which he could turn at need. He did not even study extensively about a person or period before writing. In fact his library was remarkably small for a man of letters. He gave away a book almost as soon as he had read it. But he did have an astonishingly retentive memory, and an unusually sympathetic intimacy with the past, which enabled him to reproduce the society of Greece and Rome with a vividness and reality which make any criticisms of inaccuracies in detail seem captious. After all it is not possible for the majority of writers to be infallible about the details even of modern life. It is the spirit which is the important part of any reanimation of past times, that which enlivens and vivifies the mass, rather than the dead letter of form and technique.

Landor said himself that he was particularly careful not to put into the mouths of his characters anything that history had assigned to them. The result is a new and individual interpretation of Greek or Roman thought, yet always one that is in harmony with the time which is represented. So harmonious are speaker and language that one constantly finds himself wondering how a certain phrase was expressed in the original. Nor in the main is this effect produced by Latinisms or Grecisms in the English. Though he is fonder of long Latin derivatives than of short Anglo-Saxon words, these usually impart a dignity and sonorousness to his style suited to the subject which is being treated or to the character who is speaking. In *Gebir,* it is true, where he is imitating Vergil in style and manner, he introduces many awkward Latinistic expressions and clauses which are almost unintelligible to one who does not know the language, and in any case are a blemish in his lines. He errs chiefly in participial constructions such as, for example,

> Lamented they their toil each night o'erthrown,

or

> He spake, and indignation sank in woe,
> Which she perceiving, pride refreshed her heart,

or

> Him overcome, her serious voice bespake.

At times there occurs a use of a verb or phrase with a significance which is characteristically Latin and which therefore causes a feeling of difficulty, as, "I should rather have *conceived from you* that the wand ought to designate those who merit the hatred of their species," or "if you had not dropped something out of which I *collect* that you think me too indif-

ferent." The use of "collect" in the sense of "understand" is marked archaic in the dictionary, but it is a very common meaning of the Latin verb *colligo,* especially in Quintilian. Again, we have such an expression as "the crown of laurel *badly cool'd* his brow," which is a clear echo of the idiomatic Latin use of *male;* or an instance of the Roman love of litotes, as in "no few," which recalls the common *non pauci,* or "Some, *nor the wealthier* of her suitors." He is somewhat too fond of Latin derivatives which are now considered rare, archaic, or obsolete, such as "propense," "discinct," "incondite," "intempestive," or "libant"; and when such a collocation of them meets the eye as "thy versicolored and cloudlike vestiary, puffed and effuse," it seems imperative to pause for breath. But with a list like this and the mention of a certain obscurity in language due to his effort after classic brevity and compression, we come to the end of the faults due to Landor's command of the ancient languages. For often the phrases, especially such as are essentially Greek, add to the classic spirit of the dialogue. (pp. 151-53)

Among all the things that he wrote Landor's own favorites were his Latin poems. These are of course the least read today, but they are worthy of notice and admiration. They are as varied in subject as in meter and show skill in the handling of both. It is remarkable that the work of a modern should be so independent and individual, yet so essentially Latin. There are reminiscences at times of Horace, as in the phrase, "Felix sorte tua," or of Vergil, as in "satque superque dedit." But he is more free from such echoes than are the Latins themselves, a considerable portion of the commentaries on whom are occupied with references to parallel passages in other authors. Though not entirely free from slips in grammar and prosody he is in general careful and accurate in the handling of his meter. He is, for instance, quite Ovidian in the management of the elegiac distich, observing almost invariably the rules for the dissyllabic ending of the pentameter and the penthimeral caesura. Quite in the style of Ovid too are his little tricks of balance of the two halves of the lines, as for example,

> Arripite arma, duces! arripite arma, viri!

or

> Quod pueri discent, discere vellet avus.

But aside from this correctness of form, his Latin verse has the merits of vigor, spontaneity, and sincerity. It is more subjective than his English verse, for he preferred the Latin for the expression of his most intimate thoughts and emotions. Latin was in reality a second mother-tongue to him, and he was as much at home with it as with English. Late in life he said, "I am sometimes at a loss for an English word, never for a Latin." In his prose essays he pleaded strongly for the use of Latin in modern times and showed by his own style how noble a vehicle of expression it could be made. His Latin prose is dignified, forceful, and varied. A good example of it is to be found in a sentence from the "Quaestio quamobrem poetae Latini recentiores minus legantur," which at the same time expresses his attitude toward the modern use of the language: "Leves homines ille sermo Romanus noster arcebit severitate sua, comprimet vi feroces, garrulos compescet maiestate: caveamus ne langueat, obtorpescat, conticiscat."

The English poems are quite different from those of his contemporaries. It has already been said that he was the least subjective of the Romantic poets. This is probably due to his manner of looking at life, which was essentially Greek and therefore objective, for the Greeks regarded the problems of existence in a singularly impersonal fashion. This is undoubtedly the reason for the contradiction between his passionate nature and his poetry, which expresses the charm of a placid life. It is not insincerity or affectation, but merely a result of his ideals, which are aesthetic rather than moral. Some of the lyrics remind us of Catullus, others of Horace, with their lesson of "aurea mediocritas," and the ode addressed to Joseph Ablett is in tone and manner very similar to the Horatian epistles. One little poem is so strikingly like a lyric by Sappho that the first four lines of it will bear quoting for the sake of comparison. Landor's lines are as follows:

> Mother, I can not mind my wheel;
> My fingers ache, my lips are dry.
> Oh! if you felt the pain I feel!
> But oh, who ever felt as I!

This lovesick maiden recalls at once the girl whom Sappho makes to say,

> Oh, my sweet mother, 'tis in vain,
> I cannot weave as once I wove,
> So 'wildered is my heart and brain
> With thinking of that youth I love.

Landor was a master, especially in his poems to Ianthe, of these "exquisite eidyllia, those carvings, as it were, in ivory or gems, which are modestly called Epigrams by the Greeks."

Although an ardent admirer of Milton, Landor's classicism is not at all like that of the author of *L'Allegro*. In the first place Landor never mingled Christian and pagan elements so inextricably as Milton did in *Comus*. Classic myth to Landor was not a part of a man's everyday vocabulary, clamoring to be used whether it sorted with the subject that was being discussed or not. He reserved it for the themes to which it belonged, for the *Hellenics* and *Heroic Idylls,* and kept his English poems remarkably free from the classic jargon which had been so popular in England in the eighteenth century. Even in the short lyrics scattered through *Pericles and Aspasia* he shows his understanding of how unsuitable classical allusions would be. For the pages of the melic poets of Greece are almost as lacking in references to mythology as those of a modern poet, save for the simplest and most natural mention of Zeus or Aphrodite. It was the Alexandrians and their Roman imitators who packed their lines with the most obscure kind of references. Landor fittingly makes no attempt to copy them, but takes for his examples Sappho or Anacreon.

Although *Gebir* is neither Greek nor Roman in theme, it clearly shows in its form and phraseology the effect of Landor's Latin affinities. It begins in true epic fashion, "I sing the fates of Gebir," and the hero seems a reflection of Aeneas, and his visit to the underworld is undoubtedly a reminiscence of the sixth book of the *Aeneid*. The Latin constructions which occur have already been spoken of, and there is also a striving after Latin brevity. Notice, for instance, the compression of the lines,

> Whate'er it be
> That grieves thee, I will pity, thou but speak,
> And I can tell thee, Tamar, pang for pang.

Sometimes the result of this compression is confusion and obscurity, especially in regard to the antecedents of the personal pronouns. One feels that if he had been writing in Latin the explicit *ille* or *hic* would have made all clear. The poem, however, with all its faults has dignity and power and has found favor with critics like Shelley and Southey. (pp. 156-58)

In the unpublished lines entitled "**An Apology for the Hellenics,**" Landor wrote,

> None had yet tried to make men speak
> In English as they would in Greek.

This seems to be exactly what he has tried to do and succeeded in doing in the *Classical Dialogues*. . . . His usual fault of a compression too great for clarity is to be found, but nowhere is there better expression of the glory of Greece than in the dialogue between Pericles and Sophocles, or of Roman pride and the spirit of conquest than in "**Marcellus and Hannibal**" and "**Metellus and Marius.**" In the dialogue with his brother, Marcus Tullius, Cicero says,

> If wiser men than those who appear at present
> to have spoken against my dialogues should
> undertake the same business, I would inform
> them that the most severe way of judging these
> works, with any plea or appearance of fairness,
> is to select the best passages from the best writers I may have introduced, and to place my
> pages in opposition to theirs in equal quantities. . . . Take a whole conversation, examine
> the quality, the quantity, the variety, the intensity, of mental power exerted. I myself would
> arm my adversaries, and teach them how to
> fight me.

It is impossible not to feel that in these words Landor is sounding a challenge to the critics. It is good and safe advice for him to give, for in general his dialogues would not suffer by comparison. It is impossible to make any word for word, line for line, or thought for thought comparison, but we can set opposite in our minds the picture that Landor draws and that which we gain from ancient sources, critical or autobiographical. We feel sure that we are listening to the Cicero who wrote on "Friendship" and "Old Age," the Cicero of the letters and the dialogues. We recognize in the Tibullus who greets his patron Messala the calm, generous, kindly poet who voiced in his elegies his love for simplicity of life and sincerity of worship. Only in Plato do we find a portrait not in harmony with that which he paints of himself.

Pericles and Aspasia is different in type and quite unique in plan. It has been called "an extended Imaginary Conversation," but it is more than that. In the reconstruction of the society of the Age of Pericles, in the portrayal of the characters of Aspasia and Cleone, in the intimate tone of their correspondence, and in the criticism of Greek authors and the imitation of them in the lyrics, epigrams, and dramatic fragments which are scattered through the letters, Landor found room to express all he had ever known or imagined about the golden age of Greece. Nowhere in modern literature can we find anything to equal it in sympathetic interpretation of antiquity. Upon laying down the book we feel that we have been reading a real correspondence between real persons—humor, personalities, comment on current literature, dull passages, and all. Especially is this true of the earlier letters, which are remarkably spontaneous and natural. At times the wits and sages of Athens do speak rather too much like Landor himself or with the pomposity of Dr. Johnson, and the attempt to reproduce the public speeches of Pericles in the style of Thucydides is the least successful portion of the book. Occasionally we hear the modern speak, as in the passages that purport to be prophecies of achievements of future ages, as for example when Pericles speaks of the future of astronomy:

We none of us know, but Anaxagoras hopes that, in a future age, human knowledge will be more extensive and more correct; and Meton has encouraged us in our speculations. The heavenly bodies may keep their secrets two or three thousand years yet; but one or other will betray them to some wakeful favorite, some Endymion beyond Latmos, perhaps in regions undiscovered, certainly in uncalculated times. Men will know more of them than they will ever know of Homer.

But the very shock that a passage like this causes is a proof that usually Landor has caught the true Hellenic spirit. The impetuous Alcibiades, the noble and generous Anaxagoras, the clever and quixotic Socrates, as well as many other men great in history and literature, appear in these pages against a background of Greek life which in its details—though, as has been said, some inaccuracies may be found by the patient archaeological delver—is remarkably real and vivid.

But the gems of the whole book are the three dramatic fragments which Aspasia writes on the story of Agamemnon for the perusal of her friend Cleone. They show Landor's classicism at its best, in the fulness of their Greek spirit and in their independence and individuality of treatment. They may profitably be put beside the work of the great Greek dramatists and compared with it. The differences in the actual course of events are not important, for Landor simply adopts the custom of the Greek dramatists, who felt at liberty to alter the story to suit their own dramatic purposes. The change in character portrayal is also an aspect of this same thing, for the Electra of Aeschylus is entirely different from the Electra of Sophocles or of Euripides. In the *Coephoroi* she is represented as urging at first the death of her mother, and thus addressing her father's spirit,

> I, father, ask this prayer, that I may work
> Aegisthos' death, and then acquittal gain.

But she is comparatively colorless, and after the recognition scene with Orestes she disappears from the action entirely. In the *Electra* of Sophocles, on the other hand, she is a woman of strongly marked character, possessed by no thought save that of revenge. Through the whole action of the drama she remains the foremost character, eager at first when she thinks her brother is dead to carry out the scheme of vengeance upon Clytemnaestra and Aegisthos herself, urging on Orestes to the murder, pitiless and unsoftened by her mother's cries, sending Aegisthos to meet his fate with the exhortation to Orestes, "Slay him outright."

The Electra of Landor is no such spirit of vengeance. Although the delineation is thoroughly in accordance with classic ideals, she is more of a true flesh-and-blood heroine than those of Aeschylus or Sophocles, or even of "Euripides the human." (pp. 159-62)

[Landor's] classicism finds expression in another form in the *Hellenics* and *Heroic Idylls*. Some of the latter, and the least spontaneous of them, are translations of his Latin *Idyllia Heroica;* the others were written originally in English. They are of various kinds, some in the shape of dialogues in verse, some blank-verse narratives, some in rhymed tetrameters, and there is one which tells no story but is a plea to mankind to aid in bringing about the liberty of Greece. Each is a jewel perfect in itself, some, like **"Chrysaor"** or the **"Hamadryad,"** marvelously cut and flashing with a thousand lights; some, like the **"Death of Artemidora,"** gleaming with the rich yet simple luster of a pearl. They again follow no models, ancient or modern, yet the spirit of them is that of the idyllic charm which breathes from the poetry of Theocritus, Moschus, and Bion. In their restraint and severity of beauty, as well as in the graceful flow of the language, they are thoroughly Greek. We see recurring again and again Landor's favorite themes—the Trojan cycle, the story of Iphigenia. Though **"Chrysaor"** is something quite different from the others, a poem on political liberty in the style of Shelley or Keats, the rest have no modern touch. (p. 163)

Landor's classicism was not confined to things literary. His ideals, philosophy, and attitude toward life were largely those of antiquity, partly Greek and partly Roman. It was his constant effort to harmonize duty and desire that was essentially Hellenic, and his high, stern standards of nobility of character which caused Carlyle to exclaim, "The unsubduable old Roman!" I have already spoken of his purely objective attitude toward the problems of existence that was so typical of the ancient mind. Quite pagan were his ideas of personal righteousness and high-mindedness, which were almost totally unconnected with any thought of Christian service or devotion to others. And these old Roman virtues he not only practiced himself but expected to find in everyone with whom he came in contact; according to his ideal everyone should be a Scipio or a Brutus. It was his expressed aim to walk "with Epicurus on the right hand and Epictetus on the left." And there are touches of Epicureanism in his poems and elsewhere. The poem and greeting sent by Cleone to Aspasia on her birthday contain the essence of this philosophy, especially in the last sentence, "Sweetest Aspasia, live on! live on! but rather live back the past!"

To take this last from its surroundings and use it as the text of this paper is too great a temptation to be resisted. For this is exactly what Landor did; he lived on, but lived back the past and made others live it back as well—not the past of his own life, but the past of the life of the world. Nor is this confined to antiquity. His historic imagination is just as vivid when applied to the Middle Ages or to more recent conditions in England itself as when at work on the scenes of ancient Greece or Rome. He was not an antiquarian, turning back to the fifth century before Christ from the nineteenth century after, but he belonged to the time of which he wrote; his life began, not in 1775 A.D., but in the Homeric age, growing and developing with the growth and development of the world and taking a vital and active part in the life of every period in every land. He is something more than a scholar, more than a historian, or more than a writer of drama or fiction. In him the living qualities of them all were fused and molded by the spirit of Rome on her seven hills and of Athens, the violet-crowned.

Doubtless he was more of a Roman in knowledge and scholarship but more of a Greek at heart. His Hellenism was a part of his inmost nature, a species of worship, and "in the very heat and fury of romantic predominance, Landor kept a cool chamber apart, where incense was burned to the ancient gods."

> And through the trumpet of a child of Rome
> Rang the pure music of the flutes of Greece.
>
> (pp. 165-66)

> *Elizabeth Nitchie, "The Classicism of Walter Savage Landor," in* The Classical Journal, *Vol. 14, No. 3, December, 1918, pp. 147-66.*

WALTER RALEIGH   (lecture date 1918)

[*A renowned lecturer and literary critic, Raleigh was appointed in 1904 the first professor of English literature at Oxford. His critical approach to literature was that of a highly perceptive, urbane commentator whose literary exegesis served to facilitate the nonspecialist's understanding of English literature through concise textual commentary. Raleigh's comments, originally notes for a lecture on Landor given in 1918, touch on the author's personality, the style of his poetry, his diction, his restraint, and his critical judgments.]*

Landor has many admirers, but few diligent readers. "I shall dine late; but the dining-room will be well lighted, the guests few and select." He did not add, perhaps he did not guess, that even those few guests would eat daintily and sparingly of what was provided, and would send away half the dishes untasted. I confess the extraordinary difficulty of reading Landor. One can lay him down at any time. His own coolness, quietude, selectiveness, infect his readers. They pick and choose. (p. 138)

Landor could not throw himself wholly or for long into the interests, passions, and minds of others. His *Imaginary Conversations* are not in the least dramatic. How many people have been excited by the names, and disappointed by the talk! It ends by being like a bad dream; we are always back in Landor's library, and someone is always *prosing*.

Yet, in prose or verse, he is a Master, and I think may be called a great Teacher. It is a special talent in some. How it would have pleased Landor to have a little circle and be called "The Master!" How his affectionate nature would have blossomed! What a sad thing it is to find him alone in a foreign country during his later years, companioned by a yellow dog! He had a loving heart, and was born to tyrannise. He was kind and jealous, wilful and sensitive—an unhappy blend. Such people are dreaded by their fellows, and unless they are fortunate in acquiring slaves, lead a thwarted life. As slave owners they are happy, magnanimous and humane.

I am in doubt how far an Academic School of Literature can serve the interests of creation. The live stuff won't grow in the pots. But I cannot help wishing that there had been such a school, for Landor to be made head of it. How he would have basked on the throne! And how helpful he would have been! To anyone who acknowledged his loftiness he was all courtesy, tenderness, and consideration.

His doctrine is the best you can get. A School of Literature exists to follow his teaching—so far as it attempts the real work. Simplicity, parsimony, accuracy, gravity: these make a wonderful prose.

I love Landor even when he is as haughty and stuck-up as a child, and I love his short poems best of all his works. The *Heroic Idylls,* the *Hellenics* are written in a noble style, but they are Culture poems, they breathe of the study. It is in extract that the longer poems have lived. . . . It is quite odd how Landor's people slip out of the mind. Yet some of their speeches are long remembered. The short, gem-like poems might be made the test of a lecture on style. They are single (trivial) occasions celebrated in lapidary verse. (pp. 139-41)

Landor will not raise his voice. If he feels strongly he is careful to choose words—I was going to say, no stronger than his feelings, but the truth is, a good deal weaker, or at least quieter, than his feelings. He never works up to a point, in verse or prose. He makes his point (tells the truth nakedly and severely), and then restores quiet by suggesting more peaceful considerations. This is so fixed a habit of his, that it is a mark of his style in verse or prose: his "dying fall." (p. 141)

[His] poems have the stately good manners of pride; they are not poems of passion, not for a moment self-forgetful, yet their charm (to me at least) is irresistible. They culminate in a four-lined poem as beautiful as his best:—

> Death stands above me, whispering low
> I know not what into my ear:
> Of his strange language all I know
> Is, there is not a word of fear.

The same dying fall is used in **"The Death of Artemidora"** in the *Hellenics,* and very beautifully in the prose account of the death of Acciaioli given by Boccaccio in the *Pentameron.* If you come to taste writing like that it makes coarser effects vulgar. There is a ceremonial gravity about it. Landor has an unerring feeling for impressions that the marble will take. He seems almost incapable of being deceived by pleasure or passion or anything but pride.

"What I write is not written on slate; and no finger, not that of Time himself, who dips it in the mist of years, can efface it."

> Well I remember how you smiled
> To see me write your name upon
> The soft sea-sand. *"O! what a child!*
> *You think you're writing upon stone!"*
>
> I have since written what no tide
> Shall ever wash away; what men
> Unborn shall read o'er ocean wide
> And find Ianthe's name again.

Landor always thought he was writing on stone, because he wrote nothing extravagant, excessive, exuberant. In that sense it will endure; it is pure English carefully graved, and will take long to grow old. But his work is as immortal as a graveyard.

Landor cared little for philosophy and much for history, which he saw as a great and stately pageant. He liked the great *shapes* of historical events.

A large number of his *Conversations* deal with literary criticism, and it crops up everywhere in others. Some have complained of the minuteness of his criticism, but this is what makes Landor so good a teacher. In these minute criticisms he always excels.

Landor's greatest prose passages might be collected in an anthology—"The Four Last Things." There is nothing new in what he has to say, and nothing subtle; his mind is not swift or alert. But give him a grave theme where there is nothing new to tell, and he surpasses himself. (pp. 143-45)

Landor, then, belongs to that very small company of English men of letters who are born Academicians; like Ben Jonson and Gray. Their works are stiff with scholarship. They are not congenial to our soil. The English doctrine is wider:—

> There are five and thirty ways
> Of constructing tribal lays,
> And every single one of them is right.

Landor's is one way, and not the worst. If you take him for a master the weakest passage in the worst thing you write will be immeasurably better than the poorest things in Shakespeare. (p. 145)

Walter Raleigh, "On Some Writers and Critics of the Nineteenth Century: Landor," in his On Writing and Writers, *edited by George Gordon, Edward Arnold & Co., 1926, pp. 138-45.*

The ruins of Landor's house on his estate in Llanthony. Illustration by James Wood.

STANLEY T. WILLIAMS (essay date 1921)

[*In assessing Landor's role in English literature, Williams asserts that while Landor is not important in the twentieth century, he was influential in Romantic and Victorian literary circles. For further criticism by Williams, see the excerpt dated 1923 and the Additional Bibliography.*]

Mr. Sidney Colvin says that Landorians may be counted on the fingers of two hands [see Additional Bibliography]. It is true. Most of us read the *Imaginary Conversations* with a feeling of suffocation, even though we are amazed by their author's learning. . . . The heroes of these endless dialogues come straight from the dead . . . ; they are as dusty as the mummies of the first dynasty. But—alas!—more talkative: they bicker, denounce, and harangue: they are the apotheosis of boring discussion; they are veritable ghosts on stilts. . . . [Although] modern dialogues owe something to the *Imaginary Conversations,* the fact remains that they are not read. Who in this century has performed the feat of reading them, every word? Let him speak out boldly.

As for Landor's lyrics, they are the icicles of nineteenth century literature, as those monstrous epics, *Gebir* and *Count Julian,* are the icebergs. To read Landor's poetry after Byron's or Shelley's is like leaping into the Arctic current. It seems impossible to believe that this artificial verse was written when the Romantic Movement in poetry was at its height. Yet such was the case. We of the twentieth century who are nurtured on a hundred varieties of Romanticism can hardly care much for this "marmoreal" verse. In its memory Swinburne and William Watson may write odes; nevertheless it will not be read.

Meanwhile Landor is frequently mentioned, and seriously, as a reputable poet. It is even insinuated that he is one of the nineteenth century hierarchy with a position as secure as those of the poets he seldom noticed,—Byron and Shelley. The implication is that Landor's writings have perished but his personality survives. People are fond of alluding to "the exiled Landor at Fiesole," or they refer knowingly to his temper. . . . Something is known too, of the old Roman's *hauteur*; of his litigations; of his resemblance to Lawrence Boythorn in *Bleak House.*

So they speak, the literary by-standers, but these remarks are merely echoes. Landor's personality will not save him. He dies hard, but dying he is, together with all his writings. Landor is not to be one of those immortals, whose books pass, but whose souls live on. He can never be compared, in respect to personality, as some would have us think, with Dr. Johnson. For this sort of immortality more is needed than a temper, a hearty laugh, and classical learning. No groups will be formed for the study of "Landor and His Circle." This condition may be partly because Landor spoke to "the few," but it is chiefly due to the fact that he communicated intellectual ideas whose significance today is precious little. (pp. 43-4)

[However], Landor's personality *was* great; great in a variety of ways. It is fading because of its strange quality and consequent unimportance to "modern literature." One fatal flaw this tragic hero had: his writings and sayings do not reach the hearts of men. Wise he is, wise with deep learning; brilliant as the cold sparkle on a sunny field of snow; morally lofty, also. But human he is not, and we'll have none of him today. To approach Landor, as Dr. Johnson is approached, through conversations and letters, is a chilling experience.

Landor was like the oracle which prefaced its remarks by a blast of cold air. His manner of pronouncement is like Jove's on Olympus. Inexorable. Moreover, these edicts are likely to be concerned with such popular topics as "Lycophron as a Poet", or the Greek word for violet. These are handicaps to an appreciation of Landor, but the greatest is that already mentioned. We are always forgiving assurance—and even learning—in writers. But out of their dead ages they must speak to us directly. They must entice our spirits, allure our souls. *Cor ad cor loquitur,* though the ages pass. But Landor never speaks to us; he addresses us, and talks down to us. His notions on life may be true, but we receive them without enthusiasm. His *ideas* seem to echo faintly in our own experience, but somewhere *en route* to us the emotion has been frozen. To recognize one's own feelings done in plaster of paris, read some of Landor's apothegms. (pp. 44-5)

Landor is read less and less every day; his name is becoming a reference for the prudent student to look up. Even "the few" guests show signs of an early leave-taking. Although Landor did not realize the fact, his influence was greatest during the first decades of the nineteenth century. Why? As Landor's influence disappears today a natural question is: Why was it great during his own life-time? Why did Southey, Shelley, Browning, and Swinburne think him not merely great but among the very greatest of his era?

In answer it may be stated that in general Landor's prose and poetry and personality were all powerful influences upon his contemporaries. It is evident, however, that the least influential of these three factors in Landor's reputation was his prose. Mr. Howitt says that "his *Imaginary Conversations* . . . eclipsed his verse." The eclipse has rather been mutual, resulting in complete darkness in respect to Landor's fame. At all events, in his own day, Landor influenced poets more than prose-writers; this was accomplished, naturally enough, through his poetry. As the *Conversations* appeared in ever-increasing numbers, they incited interest and respect for Landor's learning; but in all the gossip of the period, there is no evidence that they stirred writers deeply, or that they were regarded as the deepest source of Landor's influence. The *Conversations* and the *Pentameron* were simply mausoleums of learning. (p. 46)

[Vagaries] abound in the *Imaginary Conversations,* and they extend to all phases of life,—economics, politics, and religion. In addition, the reader is lost in a labyrinth of learning, for which Landor's pompous manner is a poor guide. Then, as now, the chief emotion aroused by Landor's prose must have been that of amazed respect. The style itself was damning. "He never learned," says Coleridge, "how to write simple and lucid English" [see excerpt dated 1834].

The influence of Landor's poetry, though more evident than that of his prose, was, nevertheless, limited. The lyrics and the narrative poems won over only a tiny audience. Landor founded no school, nor had he, like other nineteenth century poets, any group of imitators. The younger poets copied Rossetti, and Wordsworth, and Tennyson, but it did not occur to them to copy Landor—any more than Pindar. Classical poetry was a fad of the period, but Landor was inimitable, both in his obscure themes and in his austere manner. Compared to his the classical poems of Arnold and Tennyson were fairy-tales of Greece. Landor, as a poet, was almost as much apart, as if he had written in Persian.

Apart, and yet near. For we are approaching now the secret of Landor's influence in his own time. Imitators there were

not, but worshippers there were, and the notable thing is that these were of the best. I hope to show that Landor's instinctive doctrine . . . in literature, while it kept off the facile, the commonplace, the sensational among writers, affected deeply the very best. Moreover, though this influence of Landor's was most vital upon his coevals, through his personality, . . . it was also manifest in some degree through his poetry. Thus Shelley reads Landor unceasingly; Lamb, drunk or sober, is forever quoting **"Rose Aylmer"**; and Southey's worship of the narrative poems is fantastic.

It is, indeed, difficult to explain the devotion of some like Southey and De Quincey to Landor's poetry. . . . Possibly Southey's judgment was impaired by his friendship with Landor. But, Shelley, who had no such attachment, could not let *Gebir* alone. His biographer, Hogg, tells the story: "I often found Shelley reading *Gebir.* There was something in that poem which caught his fancy. He would read it aloud, or to himself, with a tiresome pertinacity. One morning I went to his rooms to tell him something of importance, but he would attend to nothing but *Gebir.*" And years later Swinburne bows down to *Count Julian*: "The sublimest poem published in our language between the last masterpiece of Milton and the first masterpiece of Shelley. . . . No comparable work is to be found in English poetry between the date of *Samson Agonistes* and the date of *Prometheus Unbound*" [see excerpt dated 1875-79]. And De Quincey declares the poem: "Aeschylean!" Here is a real influence directed towards some of the best minds of Landor's generation.

No one, surely, could read the lyrics which moved Shelley and Lamb, and fancy that their author was famous throughout Europe for litigations, quarrels, and violence of temper. . . . Yet it was this personality together with Landor's unflinching ideals for poetry that gave him his greatest influence over his contemporaries,—an influence greater than this achieved merely through his poetry. The picturesqueness of Landor's genius served him well. Extreme eccentricity, like extreme ugliness, may be an asset. Had Landor's temper been as unruffled as his poetry perhaps Fiesole would not have been such a Mecca for nineteenth century men of letters. Here was this venerable Prometheus of literature, stealing for nearly a century his fire from heaven, writing literally the style of gods, scorning his fellow-poets, laughing at them endlessly, pronouncing unreasonable, but strangely stimulating opinions on literature and life. . . . Why, Landor was a national character! (pp. 47-9)

That so eccentric a man should have interested is not strange. The significant thing is that he became in literature a constructive force. In spite of insane literary verdicts, Landor's praise of new books was eagerly desired. He is, Southey said, "the only man living of whose praise I was ambitious, or whose censure would have humbled me." And Robert Browning wrote to Mrs. Browning: "Landor's praise is altogether a different gift; a gold vase from King Hiram." (pp. 51-2)

So in the renewed study of Victorian literature it is well to notice the very special gifts of Walter Savage Landor and to reflect on the special task which he performed. Such an appraisal must begin, it seems to me, with the realization that little can be expected of Landor's influence now or in the future. His work is finished. Soon his devotees may be counted on the fingers of *one* hand. In 1890 W. B. Clymer wrote of Landor's influence: "His chance in the struggle for existence rests on the likelihood of there being in future generations a few men with Emerson's unjaded taste for 'pure literature.'" Perhaps. "Pure learning" would be nearer the truth. Margaret

Oliphant may speak of *Count Julian* as "worthy of the hand which showed us Hamlet and Othello." Steadman may compare *Gebir* to Keats' *Hyperion*. But Mrs. Mitford is nearer fact when she speaks, with curious juxtaposition, of "out-of-the-way writers . . . like Colley Cibber and W. S. Landor." The tendency is to think with Francis Thompson of "such minor men as Landor" [see excerpt dated 1897].

"Minor" he is now, but minor in his own day he was not. It is difficult to state in a few words the exact character of Landor's influence among his contemporaries. Certainly its essence lay in his austere idealism. In an age in which poets were introspective, Landor was objective. When others were expressing moods of unrest, reflecting the confused thought of the century, Landor was calmly imitating Pindar. When others were exhibiting the pageants of their bleeding hearts, Landor was concerned in his poetry, with subtle and delicate emotional values,—most of them Greek in origin. Landor never relinquished the ideal that poetry should be restrained, intellectual, and architectonic. Such maintenance had its effect. It is not too much to presume that Landor had an ennobling influence upon a few poets whom he definitely inspired. "Consider," says Steadman, "the names of those who, having met him and known his works, perceive in him something great and worshipful." (p. 53)

Stanley T. Williams, "Echoes of Walter Savage Landor," in The Texas Review, *Vol. VII, No. 1, October, 1921, pp. 43-53.*

STANLEY T. WILLIAMS (essay date 1923)

[*Williams faults the subjective nature and undisciplined form of Landor's criticism. He suggests that Landor's critical principles are little more than common sense and that his judgments are not supported by sustained analysis. For further commentary on Landor's work by Williams, see the excerpt dated 1921 and the Additional Bibliography.*]

As a critic of literature Walter Savage Landor had ideals but few principles. Such a statement is not another paradox in the life of the old lion. It means simply that we look in vain in Landor's numerous judgments on literature for a method or a body of criteria. He never formulated a system, like Coleridge; or standards, like Arnold; nor even consistent prejudices, like Carlyle. The evolution of English criticism between Dryden and Coleridge he disregarded, as indeed he seemed to disregard all consecutive philosophical thought. He did not look into the new worlds of psychological and social criticism. He was not interested in the relations of things, but rather in the things themselves. Such statements are never truer of Landor than when he studies a piece of literature, or a writer. As a critic he never saw literature in perspective—so marvellously increased in his own day—but as something directly before him,—foreshortened. Thus he judged Pindar and Wordsworth each *per se*; one would think he was a contemporary of both. In all his criticisms we cannot find a body of guiding principles. Personal ideals are the determinants. It need scarcely be added that these are austere and high.

The few scattered principles which Landor himself expressed are less peculiar to literature than to common sense: the critic should be just; he should be learned; and, like the poet, he should write not for the many, but for the few and the discerning. This is practically all. The allusions to critics and criticism in the *Imaginary Conversations,* the *Pentameron,* and *Pericles and Aspasia* amount to this only. Such "principles"

are obvious, but Landor states them nobly, and as no one else could. Thus of justice in criticism:

> The critic walks in a garden which is not his own; and he neither must gather the blossoms to embellish his discourse, nor break the branches to display his strength. Rather let him point to what is out of order, and help to raise what is lying on the ground.

Or of knowledge this, with its grave irony:

> I would seriously recommend to the employer of our critics, young and old, that he oblige them to pursue a course of study such as this: that under the superintendence of some respectable student from the university, they first read and examine the contents of the book; a thing generally more useful in criticism than is generally thought; secondly, that they carefully write them down, number them, and range them under their several heads; thirdly that they mark every beautiful, every faulty, every ambiguous, every uncommon expression. Which being completed, that they inquire what author, ancient or modern, has treated the same subject, first in smaller, afterward in larger portions, noting every defect in precision and its causes, every excellence and its nature; that they graduate these, fixing *plus* and *minus,* and designating them more accurately and discriminately by means of colours, stronger or paler. For instance, purple might express grandeur and majesty of thought; scarlet vigour of expression; pink, liveliness; green, elegant and equable composition.

The passage suggests Landor's thoroughness in his verbal and textual criticisms, and also his contempt for the casual critic. Landor lived through the days of the Quarterlies, that period of sword-and-buckler criticism. His own works were sadly cut to pieces. [The imaginary conversation entitled] **"Southey and Porson"** was partly an outlet for his rage against the swarm of flies that were busy with him, with Southey, and with Wordsworth. But, apart from his own wounds, it was natural for one who was beyond the arrows, views, and shouts of men to have the same attitude towards criticism as towards poetry. Criticism, like poetry, to be worth anything should be for the best, and, consequently unintelligible to the common rout of men. (pp. 906-08)

His literary criticisms are characteristic offshoots of his unique aims in literature. He tried, as everyone knows, to present concepts of the intellect or of the soul unadorned, in white light. His poems are like fragments of beautifully chiselled marble; not reproductions in the manner of the Greeks, but by a miracle, original creations done in the spirit of Greece. The medium is English, severe, self-sustained, integral. The means to this end was an erudition without parallel among nineteenth century poets. This type of creative art was Landor's goal; from it he never swerved. And it is not too much to say that in many instances his literary judgments may be referred to it. From his lofty and somewhat strange ideals come his wayward opinions in criticism.

Wayward in form as in substance, Landor did not write critical essays. In no writer of the nineteenth century may be found so many critical judgments on writers without the accompanying formal essay. His really memorable opinions float about in letters and diaries, and in the notes and journals of pilgrims to Fiesole. A small anthology might be made of his notions on Byron, Shelley, or the ancients. The bulk of his literary criticism may be found in the *Imaginary Conversations*. In his letters Landor protests again and again that the opinions of these characters cannot be regarded as his own. The reader, however, vetoes this pretension. Their creator is a rather awkward Proteus; under the disguises we detect the well-known features of W. S. Landor. The reader is justified in taking the literary criticism to be Landor's though it happens to come from the lips of Petrarch or Porson. If we examine the *Conversations* minutely (which it has been my misfortune to do) we encounter everywhere brilliant epigrams on literature. Even in the political and religious subjects Landor is never very far from literary themes. His enormous knowledge of the classics must not make us, by comparison, undervalue his acquaintance with other literatures. He read less than Carlyle, and remembered less than Macaulay, but his reading was wide, and often, as in his study of Milton, concentrated. Aside from chance references, the substance of Landor's criticism is in those dialogues which he himself classified as "Conversations of Literary Men." These are reflective; there is little need to consider the circumstances or action, as in the historical conversations; and if the names of the speakers are mentally deleted, there remains in effect literary criticism. To these the reader should turn to estimate Landor as a critic of literature; to **"Southey and Porson"** (both conversations), **"The Abbe Delille and Walter Landor," "Landor," "English Visiter and Florentine Visiter,"** [sic], **"Boccaccio and Petrarch," "Archdeacon Hare and Walter Landor"**; and to others similar in character. Nor must we forget, as we consider where Landor's criticism occurs, his unusual amount of critical verse. Some of this is doggerel, like the invitation to Tennyson; some is humourous epigram, as in the fugitive lines to Dickens; and some is in Landor's noblest mood, as in the lines to Browning. Altogether this verse totals hundreds of lines, and cannot be neglected in an estimate of Landor's critical opinions.

If all such fragments were placed within the bounds of a single volume, the main characteristics of Landor as a critic would be nearly as obvious as his characteristics as a man. The first of these was a tendency to eccentric enthusiasms. Landor's judgments were arbitrary. He had, as has been indicated, no set of critical principles, and his criticism was at the mercy of high but eccentric ideals. His opinions were not based wholly on intellectual conviction, nor on emotion, but sometimes on the former, sometimes on the latter. Thus Landor praised Milton because of Milton's lofty intellectual ideals for poetry; he worshipped Southey chiefly because, I believe, he loved the man. (pp. 908-10)

As we look further into our imaginary edition of Landor's criticism we see how characteristic [his] sweeping judgments are. Their fault is that they are unsupported by critical analysis. Landor uses the critic's *faute de mieux*,—comparison and contrast. Like Macaulay he loves to classify writers. He compares Ovid to Virgil, and Spenser to Chaucer. The following is typical of this method: "Scott superseded Wordsworth, and Byron superseded Scott. . . . Scott had a wider range than either, and excelled in more qualities." Instances might be multiplied. Instead of critical analysis with reference to unifying principles, there are arbitrary judgments, and for confirmation other arbitrary judgments.

Exception must be made in respect to one or two writers in English towards whom Landor manifests a more precise critical attitude. These are the objects of his especial devotion, and receive the same scrutiny as the classical writers. Such notable examples of critical study are Dante and Milton. Landor cannot say enough of the Francesca episode, and he studies *Paradise Lost* and *Paradise Regained* with meticulous care. It may be said that he concentrates in much the same way upon Wordsworth. The conversations of **"Southey and Porson"** and **"Southey and Landor"** exhibit particularly this sort of criticism, as well as certain passages in the **Pentameron**. But even here our exception itself must be qualified. Landor makes no study of Milton historically; and there is no testing of the epics by the theories and principles of poetry. What Landor does is to examine the text and comment learnedly upon it. (pp. 911-12)

[Many of his observations are close to his] hobbies of orthography and spelling. Many pages of this sort of "criticism" weigh down the *Imaginary Conversations*. It is hardly critical analysis. It is rather the examination of a text. Whenever Landor abandons his broad, general preferences he is apt to fall into a bog of annotation. Here is obviously a transference of the scholia of classical criticism to English literature. Landor's analysis resolves itself into learned notes. And even in such appraisal of literature, which has some scholarly value, Landor is likely to be transported to whimsical verdicts. After all, of what real worth is the following? "Milton is more correct than Addison, but less correct than Hooker." Or: "Such stupendous genius, so much fancy, so much eloquence, so much vigour of intellect, never were united as in *Paradise Lost*." . . . Moreover, Landor contrives to add a certain opaque quality to his generalizations which make them no happier. "Where," he queries, "excepting in Milton, where among all the moderns, is energy always to be found in the right place?" And sometimes the epigrams are grotesque: "A rib of Shakespeare," he declares, "would have made a Milton: the same portion of Milton, all poets born ever since."

In this Landorian *mot*, however, is the suggestion of the writer's greatest power as a critic of literature, his capacity for epigrammatic criticism. . . . This power was joined to a broad vision of literature. . . . Landor wrote striking apothegms about *all* men of letters. "Roscoe's works are a feather-bed of words." We find in Addison "a sweet temperature of thought." "Young is too often fantastical and frivolous; he pins butterflies to the pulpit cushion." "Johnson had somewhat of the medlar in his nature; one side hard and austere, the other unsound." Such sententious phrases Landor threw off by hundreds; they are remarkable not only in quality, but in scope. Each stands alone, as final as an oracle from Delphi, and often, unfortunately, not less cryptic. Perhaps they can never be regarded as real literary criticism; they are too fragmentary, too reticent. But the fact that Landor left an aphorism of this sort concerning almost every writer who has ever lived demands respect. He is a critic of literature, even if a somewhat eccentric one. (pp. 912-14)

To what Matthew Arnold liked to call "the main current" of criticism Landor contributed nothing. He was no less isolated as a critic than as a poet. His method, if he can be said to own a method, is archaic and peculiar to himself. He lacked, in the highest sense, the analytical faculty. But he had great resources of knowledge, and his lapidary criticism is enriched by many striking apothegms. His literary criticism is a series of fragmentary paragraphs on literature as brilliant, as terse, and as finished as his poetical *inscriptiones* and epigrams. (p. 928)

Stanley T. Williams, "Walter Savage Landor as a Critic of Literature," in PMLA, *38, Vol. XXXVIII, No. 4, December, 1923, pp. 906-28.*

RICHARD ALDINGTON (essay date 1924)

[*Aldington is perhaps best remembered as the editor of the Imagist periodical the* Egoist *and as an influential member of that movement. The major goal of the Imagists was to free poetry from excessive verbiage and vague generalities and to utilize precise imagery. As a literary critic and biographer, Aldington combined his skills as a poet and his perceptiveness as an extremely sensitive reader to produce criticism that is creative as well as informative. Here, Aldington explores the artistic implications of Landor's preface to* The Hellenics *(see excerpt dated 1847). The critic asserts that an understanding of the "diaphanous" quality in Landor's poetry, as opposed to the "prismatic" style of the Romantic poets, is requisite to an appreciation of* The Hellenics.]

Like his friend, Southey, [Landor] is often little more than a name as a poet. Of course there is no exact method of discovering how much the *Hellenics* are read and admired; Landor may be intensely appreciated by a large, silent audience, but he is certainly not fashionable, and probably never will be. The true cause of this comparative obscurity is . . . Landor's poetic style itself, the ideal of poetry he deliberately set himself, in opposition to the tendencies of eighteenth-century moralizing poetry and nineteenth-century decorative poetry. In the preface to the *Hellenics,* written with that brusque terseness he affected towards the public, he says: "Little in these pages will gratify the generality of readers. Poetry, in our day, is oftner prismatic than diaphanous: this is not so: they who look into it may see through" [see excerpt dated 1847]. The phrase "oftner prismatic than diaphanous"—a fine terse criticism of the Romantic movement—gives a first clue to a correct appreciation of Landor's poems. The poetry of the great Romantics and their successors is so often merely "prismatic"; deficient in architectural qualities but abounding in picturesque details and irridescent language. Matthew Arnold's criticism of *Isabella* marks a cardinal weakness of Romantic poetry. . . . Now the style of Landor is deliberately architectural and "classic," perhaps the most classic (in intention) of all our poets; Landor is the most determined to reproduce in English the effects of earlier Greek poetry, the most consistent in his poetical ideal and the most ruthless expunger of every tendency and influence foreign to his ideal. Most people will admit that Arnold had a lofty ideal of the poetic art, and that he also attempted to make English some of the "classic" qualities of Greek poetry. A comparison is interesting.

> Far, far from here
> The Adriatic breaks in a warm bay
> Among the green Illyrian hills; and there
> The sunshine in the happy glens is fair,
> And by the sea, and in the brakse.
> The grass is cool, the sea-side air
> Buoyant and fresh, the mountain flowers
> As virginal and sweet as ours.

That is "prismatic" poetry. Now turn from that romantic nostalgia to the "diaphanous" lines which open Landor's poem **"To Corinth"**—

> Queen of the double sea, beloved of him
> Who shakes the world's foundations, thou hast seen
> Glory in all her beauty, all her forms;
> Seen her walk back with Theseus when he left
> The bones of Sciron bleaching to the wind,
> Above the ocean's roar and cormorant's flight,
> So high that vastest billows from above
> Show but like herbage waving in the mead;
> Seen generations throng the Isthmian games,
> And pass away; . . .

Note Arnold's weak adjectives: "warm, green, happy, fair, cool, buoyant, fresh, virginal, sweet"—so many of them "literary" and unnecessary; and then look at Landor's: "double, high, vastest, Isthmian." Does not that mark the difference between a weak, emotional poet and a strong "classic" poet. (pp. 143-45)

To use the word "classic" in describing a style is to invite misapprehension and dissent. And yet "Hellenic" alone does not define the quality of Landor's poetry at its best. He is the most deliberately Hellenic of English poets; even his quaint-sounding laconisms are an attempt to achieve Greek brevity. But however Greek his mind and tastes, Landor himself was a choleric English gentleman with tremendous pride, a manner at once violent and courteous, blustering and dignified, and above all, a heart of the most tender delicacy and generosity; and this English character is continually invading his Hellenism, even in the most objective of his poems. . . . Landor's Hellenism has a double aspect: it comes chiefly from his affinity with the spirit of Greek thought, from his understanding of the Greek ideal, from his possessing a "Greek soul"—as we say sentimentally; but it comes also from an instinctive checking of his English emotionalism. He lived in a series of emotional explosions; of wrath, pride, generosity, tenderness, indignation. How natural that he should turn for discipline to the pure serenity of Attic Greek; and knowing him as we do, how natural that Walter Savage Landor, fuming with rage over some trifle, should invest his indignation (at some local squire) with the Jovian dignity of Pericles or the cynic indifference of Diogenes. The English Landor is always visible through the Greek Landor, even in the *Hellenics*; the matter, the form, almost the very speech is Greek, but the voice is English. One suspects that his chaste Hellenic maidens wore corkscrew curls; certainly his Agamemnons and Ptolemys, Hyperbions and Rhaicos have all been christened "Walter Savage" while the republican, or rather oligarchic, sentiment is too violent, the generosity too open and quixotic to fit a nation of genial liars and unscrupulous intriguers like the Athenians. Moreover, Landor's culture, though primarily, was not exclusively Hellenic. He was very extensively read in Latin, with an exceptionally wide knowledge of neo-Latin authors; he was nourished on the best in the literatures of Italy, France, and England. And he was one of our great critics. If he was not learned in any cumbersome or pejorative sense, he possessed a culture as choice and as enthusiastic as that of Goethe, if not so extensive. (pp. 145-47)

It would be impossible for Landor's style to be purely Hellenic—he would have had to be born Greek for that—and so the much-abused "classic" still seems the correct work. After all, "classic" implies many of the qualities Landor most admired; and it implies also the opposite of all "prismatic" and all turgidly unplastic poetry. But the Greeks were Landor's masters. Unlike Keats, he did not get his Hellenism at second hand through the kaleidoscope of Jacobean English poetry. . . . Perhaps a nice discrimination could detect Milton's influence in the *Hellenics,* but in general their style is modelled on the sententious brevity of poets like Simonides, with a certain alloy of Latinisms. Notice in the following lines the rather excessive attempt at Greek simplicity and brevity—

> The sea shines bright before us. What white sail
> Plays yonder? What pursues it? Like two hawks
> Away they fly. Let us away in time
> To overtake them. Are they menaces

We hear? And shall the strong repulse the weak
Enraged at her defender? Hippias!
Art thou the man? 'Twas Hippias. He had found
His sister borne from the Cecropian port
By Thrasymedes. And reluctantly?
Ask, ask the maiden; I have no reply.

Imagine that passage re-written in the "prismatic" style of Shelley; it would occupy at least a page. Observe that this is not the Gallic classicism of Pope nor the moralized and over-formal classicism of Johnson nor verbalized Hellenism like that of "Balaustion's Adventure"; it represents an almost unique and not very successful attempt to force into English classic density and terseness. The result is sometimes more strange than beautiful, for, to achieve it, Landor boggles at no obscurity, no allusiveness, no awkward Latinism. The mere reconditeness of his allusions is sufficient to daunt some readers who will need the classical dictionary nearly as much for the *Hellenics* as for the Metamorphoses. A timid reader is not encouraged by lines like these—

> The proud Aemonian shook Aëtion's towers.
> Alpheios and Spercheios heard the shout
> Of Maenalos; Cyllenè, Pholoë,
> Parthenos, Tegea, and Lycaios, called. . . .

These, if not defects in an English poem, can hardly be called beauties; still less the frequent Latinisms, like "*illuded* into love," "with light he *irrigates* the earth," "*pubescent* flower," "*lustral* water" and "*radiant* nod." The search for brevity and simplicity, the avoidance of the "prismatic" lead to some queer banalities when (as rarely happens) Landor loses his dignity—

> Thou hadst *evinced the madness of thy passion* . . .
> Whatever is most *laudable and manly* . . .
> *Flapping* the while with laurel-rose
> The honey-gathering tribes away. . . .

Yet when all these difficulties and defects have been recorded, when we add to them the peculiar spelling Landor affected and the occasional lack of spontaneity in the language (due perhaps to some of the poems having been written in Latin and then translated into English), then we have simply cleared away the obstacles which prevent enjoyment of the poetry of the *Hellenics*. When the reader perceives Landor's ideals and method, the difficulties begin to vanish, the defects become insignificant. Those whose taste is chiefly formed on romantic poetry, those who are entirely seduced by modern impressionism, will probably not enjoy the *Hellenics*. You cannot find witty or pointed couplets or lovely suave phrases (so abundant in Keats and Tennyson) nor any of the coloured fumes of mysticism in Landor's poetry. Landor is never verbose. Harsh, over rapid, too condensed, too allusive, too "diaphanous," perhaps; but never dull, never diffuse, never ignoble, never turgid and vague.

Because the poet worked for the architectural qualities of poetry, the *Hellenics* are not easily quotable. Landor's unit is not the line, not the passage, but the poem. To quote fragments of the *Hellenics* is to show a limb or a torso instead of the whole statue. (pp. 148-51)

Landor's poetic genius was not lyric; it lay rather in dialogue and narrative. English taste insists that all poetry shall sing; without reflecting that nobody would sing a narrative. But because Landor did not sacrifice everything to sound and "prismatic" conceits it does not follow that he is lacking in richness. When for a while he relaxes from his Attic severity into a more

Sicilian mood, few poets are capable of such richness. . . . (pp. 151-52)

Is it only a romantic fancy which makes one feel that no poets were ever so sensitive to the crisp outlines and clear tints of flowers and fruits as the Greeks? Landor shared that exquisite plastic feeling. Only a poet who is so gifted with the love and understanding of their beauty can so evoke their essential form and colour and scent. The demi-gods whom the Greek poets invented as the spirits of flowers and trees and windy rocks were a projection of this sensitiveness. And Landor, the tender old Englishman, understood so well that delicate respect for beauty. (pp. 152-53)

The idylls which compose the *Hellenics* are chiefly *heroic*. Landor can express the finest emotions of the lover of beauty and understand wild flowers like a sensitive woman; but he can also express fortitude with vehement eloquence. (p. 153)

It is hardly possible that the *Hellenics* could become popular. Many, whose taste is formed on less august models, will never feel the pure heroic beauty of the *Hellenics*. Yet Landor will always find some enthusiasts to prefer the "diaphanous" beauties of the *Hellenics* to the more dazzling but less satisfying attractions of "prismatic" poetry. (p. 154)

> *Richard Aldington, "Landor's 'Hellenics'," in his* Literary Studies and Reviews, The Dial Press Incorporated, 1924, pp. 141-54.

T. S. ELIOT   (lecture date 1933)

[Eliot, an American-born English poet, essayist, and critic, is regarded as one of the most influential literary figures of the first half of the twentieth century. As a critic, he introduced a number of terms and concepts that strongly affected critical thought in his lifetime. In the following brief excerpt, taken from a lecture originally delivered at Harvard University in 1933, Eliot contrasts the importance of Landor and Wordsworth as poets.]

[Consider] one of the very finest poets of the first part of the nineteenth century: Landor. He is an undoubted master of verse and prose; he is the author of at least one long poem which deserves to be much more read than it is; but his reputation has never been such as to bring him into comparison with Wordsworth or with either [Shelley or Keats]. . . . It is not only by reason of a handful of poems or a number of isolated lines expressive of deeper emotion than that of which Landor was capable, that we give Wordsworth his place; there is something integral about such greatness, and something significant in his place in the pattern of history, with which we have to reckon. And in estimating for ourselves the greatness of a poet we have to take into account also the *history* of his greatness. Wordsworth is an essential part of history; Landor only a magnificent by-product. (p. 88)

> *T. S. Eliot, "Shelley and Keats," in his* The Use of Poetry and the Use of Criticism: Studies in the Relation of Criticism to Poetry in England, Faber and Faber Limited, 1933, pp. 87-102.

DONALD A. DAVIE   (essay date 1951)

[An English poet, critic, educator, and translator, Davie is well respected for both his creative and critical contributions to literature. In his critical work The Purity of Diction in English Verse, *he argued for a return to the prose-like syntax, formal structures, and conservative metaphors of the eighteenth-century Augustan poets. During the 1950s Davie was associated with the*

Movement, a group of poets who emphasized restrained language, traditional syntax, and the moral and social implications of poetic content. In his examination of Landor's short poems and epigrams, excerpted below, Davie discusses their structure, form, and language. He declares that unevenness in diction and tone is "the besetting sin of Landor's writing, something which cancels out all his other virtues." For further commentary by Davie, see the excerpt dated 1984 and the Additional Bibliography.]

To C. H. Herford, in 1897, it seemed that 'Landor was . . . on the whole the greatest prose-writer of the age of Wordsworth; and, after Wordsworth, Coleridge, Byron, Shelley and Keats, he was its greatest poet' [see Additional Bibliography]. Whatever may be thought of Landor's prose, it would be hard to find anyone today to endorse the claim that, as a poet, he was greater than Scott, Clare, Crabbe, Hogg or Darley—all poets with whom Herford deals. I find him inferior to every one of these poets; but my intention here is not to gird at Herford or to sneer at Landor. For the latter has an importance out of proportion with his meagre achievement. At a crucial stage in the English poetic tradition he struck out alone a path of interesting and sensible experiment; and in deciding what chance there was of success, and where and how the experiment failed, we touch upon matters of importance for the writing of poetry at any time.

What Landor stood for in the writing of poetry can be seen from one of his more distinguished poems, **"To Wordsworth"**:

> He who would build his fame up high,
> The rule and plummet must apply,
> Nor say, 'I'll do what I have plann'd',
> Before he try if loam or sand
> Be still remaining in the place
> Delved for each polisht pillar's base.
> With skilful eye and fit device
> Thou raisest every edifice,
> Whether in sheltered vale it stand
> Or overlook the Dardan strand,
> Amid the cypresses that mourn
> Laodameia's love forlorn.

The advice is sufficiently trite. It appears less so, in the rather better verse of the **"Epistle to the Author of 'Festus'"**:

> Some see but sunshine, others see but gloom,
> Others confound them strangely, furiously;
> Most have an eye for colour, few for form.
> Imperfect is the glory to *create,*
> Unless on our creation we can look
> And see that all is good; we then may rest.
> In every poem train the leading shoot;
> Break off the suckers. Thought erases thought,
> As numerous sheep erase each other's print
> When spungy moss they press or sterile sand.
> Blades thickly sown want nutriment and droop,
> Although the seed be sound, and rich the soil;
> Thus healthy-born ideas, bedded close,
> By dreaming fondness perish overlain.

This is far more provocative, challenging, as it does, that other precept of the period, to 'load every rift with ore'. And yet the principle applied in the lines to Wordsworth and in these to Bailey is identical. We find it more provocative here, because, in addressing Wordsworth, Landor uses a trite architectural metaphor for quite commonplace ideas about the need for structure in longer poems; whereas in the lines to Bailey he seems to imply that a short poem requires structure no less. And we are more willing, I think, to consider the structure of

an ode or an epic than of a lyric or epigram. Just for that reason, perhaps, it is more salutary to examine Landor's theory and practice in his shorter poems. (pp. 345-46)

To begin with, it is not hard to see why we fight shy of Landor's theories about the structure of short poems. For when Landor insists that 'ideas' must be disposed carefully about the poem, not crowded one upon another, he raises at once the question of a staple language in which those 'ideas' may be set. The staple of a poem, in this sense, is the diction of the poem. And problems of poetic diction are particularly difficult in the period of the preface to *Lyrical Ballads*. . . . Landor's principles of disposition seem to me self-evidently right; and it follows that poetic diction, in the sense of a staple language for the poet, is a burning question for poets and readers in any age.

Landor's practice is another matter. The very lines in which he expounds his theory show how far he was from putting it into practice. To begin with, his word 'ideas' is peculiar, since any logical arrangement of words has meaning, and in that sense contains ideas. He cannot mean what he seems to say, that the staple, the gold ring in which the gems are set, shall be devoid of ideas, hence meaningless. And I infer that by 'ideas' Landor means rather what older critics called 'figures'. In other words, we are to find 'ideas' in this sense wherever we find in a poem any conscious rhetoric, any attempt to be striking, concentrated, or elaborate beyond what we expect from conversational prose. As a matter of fact, the lines from the **"Epistle to the Author of 'Festus'"** are themselves highly figurative, in the way they seem to condemn. And only four of them can be said to contain no images:

> Most have an eye for colour, few for form.
> Imperfect is the glory to *create,*
> Unless on our creation we can look
> And see that all is good; we then may rest.

Here, then, if anywhere, we should find the staple language, that poetic diction which Landor seems to demand, in which figures ('ideas') shall be disposed. Yet here the language is quite indiscriminate. The first line is notably conversational, the second, with its italic, even more so. But the third and fourth, with their presumptuous echo from Genesis, are elaborate, rhetorical and literary. How can this be a staple language, or a pure diction, when in the space of four lines it veers so giddily from high to low? It betrays in particular a bewildering insecurity of *tone*. At one moment the poet is addressing us amicably in the study; at the next, he is thundering from a rostrum. How can we know how to take him? What tone can we adopt in reading the poem aloud? The golden ring is cracked; and, however fine the brilliants, we can only be distressed.

This seems to me the besetting sin of all Landor's writing, something which cancels out all his other virtues. And nearly always Landor courts disaster, as here by the italic, so elsewhere by passages of direct speech. . . . The truth is that Landor merely takes no care for any consistent tone of discourse.

As a matter of fact, despite his advice to 'train the leading shoot', Landor was always prone to lose the thread of his poems, even in more obvious ways. In a poem addressed to satire, which contains some promising lines (for, like Shelley, Landor had satirical talent, but despised it), the failure with direct speech only aggravates a trailing-off into obscurity:

> Byron was not *all* Byron; one small part
> Bore the impression of a human heart.
> Guided by no clear love-star's panting light,
> Thro' the sharp surges of a northern night,

In Satire's narrow strait he swam the best,
Scattering the foam that hist about his breast.
He who might else have been more tender, first
From Scottish saltness caught his rabid thirst.
Praise Keats . . .
                    'I think I've heard of him'
                                        'With you
Shelley stands foremost'
                            . . . And his lip was blue . . .
'I hear with pleasure any one commend
So good a soul; for Shelley is my friend.'
One leaf from Southey's laurel made explode
All his combustibles . . .
                                        'An ass! by
    God!'

This is mere doodling. It would be hard to find anything less classical, in Landor's or any other sense.

It is unfair perhaps, to recall it. For we can adopt Herford's verdict on *Gebir* and say of its author that 'though hardly a great poet, he is full of the symptoms of greatness'. Nothing could be much more damaging or sadder; for, as Herford also says, 'It is characteristic of Landor that he is great in detail rather than in mass' [see Additional Bibliography]. In other words, the poet who tried above all things for the poem as an artifact, a whole thing cut loose from its maker, emerges as a true poet only in fragments and snatches. It is for this reason that one turns back through Landor's poems, coming across distinguished phrases by the way, and thinking, 'Surely I have misjudged him'. But one never has. On re-reading, the poem does not improve; it is still disastrously uneven, in the rough, unshaped. The fine writing remains irrelevant; it never adds up to an effect.

This difficulty should not arise so sharply with the epigrams. And the best of these are very good. . . . But this, it will be said, is to miss the point. His epigrams are important—the argument runs—because they retrieve the epigram from flippancy and make it once again a serious vehicle, as in the Greek Anthology. Well, I should like to think so. But in the first place flippancy can be serious in one sense where a solemn triviality is not. Such graceful marginalia as the lines **"With Petrarca's Sonnets"** or **"On Catullus"** are all very well in their way, but not serious in the sense that posterity need remember them. There are other epigrams that offer to be serious in the sense that they are momentous statements, and these that are serious in every sense often fail of their effect in the same way as the longer poems, on the score of diction.

Leaving aside the marginalia, Landor's epigrams can be divided for convenience into three classes. There are in the first place the compliments (**"Dirce"**, for instance, and most of the poems to Ianthe). Then there are traditional commonplaces, to be expressed in novel ways, with a seeming finality (**"Rose Aylmer"**, **"The leaves are falling; so am I"**). And finally there are poems which offer to be 'discoveries', original in theme but expressed in traditional form. (pp. 346-51)

The most famous example of the first class is the epigram on **"Dirce"**:

Stand close around, ye Stygian set,
    With Dirce in one boat conveyed!
Or Charon, seeing, may forget
    That he is old, and she a shade.

In the classical examples of such compliments, from the seventeenth and eighteenth centuries, we find the effect depends upon combining daring hyperbole with imperturbable urbanity:

To her, whose beauty doth excell
    Stories, wee tosse theis cupps, and fill
    Sobrietie, a sacrifice
To the bright lustre of her eyes.
Each soule that sipps this is divine:
Her beauty deifies the wine.

'Urbanity' begs at once the question of diction. For to explain how these trivia seem momentous, we have to give to 'urbanity' the meaning that Arnold gave to it, in "The Influence of Literary Academies", when he spoke of it as the tone or spirit of the centre, embodying the best of a civilization. There, of course, he spoke of such urbanity as an attribute of the best prose, and thought it no business of the poet. But such centrality seems the virtue of a pure diction in poetry, as of an Attic style in prose. . . . One has to say that by Landor's day to turn an elegant compliment and make momentous poetry of it was no longer a possibility: and of course it has never been possible since.

The same is true of the second class of Landor's epigrams, his attempts at 'what oft was thought but ne'er so well expressed'. To make poetry out of moral commonplace, a poet has to make it clear that he speaks not in his own voice (that would be impertinent) but as the spokesman of a social tradition. Hence the importance of the Horatian imitation for Pope, or the imitation of Juvenal by Johnson. By employing those forms and modes, the poets spoke out of a tradition which was not merely literary; for the reading of Horace and Juvenal was a tradition of social habit in the audience they addressed, which was also the society for which they spoke. The Greek epigram was no substitute. And when Landor treats a traditional commonplace ('Past ruin'd Ilion Helen lives', 'The Leaves are falling; so am I', 'There is a mountain and a wood between us') his achievement seems frail and marginal, chiefly because he does not show, in the form he chooses, how traditional, how far from original, is what he wants to say. (pp. 351-52)

There remains the third sort of epigram, which I have called 'Discoveries'. . . . Landor occasionally makes discoveries of the Wordsworthian sort, not 'what oft was thought but ne'er so well expressed', but what was never consciously thought before, nor ever expressed. Even here, I think, he tries more often than he succeeds. But sometimes he can make genuine discoveries, especially about movements of the mind:

Something (ah! tell me what) there is
    To cause that melting tone.
I fear a thought has gone amiss
    Returning quite alone.

[The] diction of the first two lines is faded and decadent, but this is important only because it leads us to expect something quite different from what we are given thereafter. In other words it makes the discovery more sudden and surprising. Perhaps for this reason, the lines have been found obscure, but their bearing is plain enough. Landor catches in a touching metaphor the experience of breaking off a line of thought, surprised by a melancholy reflection. He explains the shadow falling across the face of his companion by the supposition that a thought has 'gone amiss' (i.e. broken off the train of thought of which it was a link) and 'returned alone', or, as the common metaphor has it, 'brought home' to the thinker a melancholy truth. The poem, one could say, is an exploration and a discovery of what we mean when we say 'The truth was brought home to me'. To give form to an experience so fugitive yet so permanently human seems to me an achievement of a high order. Unfortunately I can think of only one other case in which Landor does something comparable, in his poem **"For an Urn in Thoresby Park"**.

There is considerable pathos in the story of Landor's life, so devoted, so disinterested, and to so little end. It is interesting and important chiefly because his attempt to put the clock back shows how inevitable was the Romantic revolution in poetic method and the conception of the poet's function. The poets had to undertake to make discoveries of truth, in some sense novel, because the poetry of truths already acknowledged depended upon conditions which no longer obtained. To make poetry out of traditional commonplace or personal compliment the poet had to write in and for a homogeneous society acknowledging strong and precise traditions of literature and manners. His awareness of such a society as his audience gave the poet the sureness of tone which comes out of a pure diction and achieves urbanity. When Landor attempted this, all the odds were against him. No such society and no such audience existed. And as a result, the great poets of the age were great in quite novel ways. Wordsworth, for instance, eschewed urbanity and made a virtue of provincialism. Shelley set out to be the discoverer in an absolute sense. Keats, when he was not the discoverer, evaded the question of a staple language by figurative luxury. And when the poets needed to be urbane . . . they sought no longer an impossible purity of diction, but a sort of calculated impurity; so that urbanity since has always been ironical. Landor is the type of the poet who refuses to acknowledge the temper of his age. There is a certain magnificence in his obstinate wrong-headedness; but it did not go to produce important poems. (pp. 353-55)

> Donald A. Davie, "The Shorter Poems of Walter Savage Landor," in Essays in Criticism, Vol. I, No. 4, October, 1951, pp. 345-55.

DOUGLAS BUSH   (essay date 1952)

[Bush examines Landor's technical and literary ideals, concluding that he "cherished a pseudo-classical notion of form and style as ends in themselves."]

[We] must take the briefest glance at a figure whose turbulence, unlike Byron's, shook only those in his immediate vicinity, and whose literary presence we are apt to forget, that is, Walter Savage Landor. . . . Landor's writings in verse and prose, English and Latin, covered nearly seventy years. He published *Gebir,* an epic of rather cryptic density, in the year of *Lyrical Ballads,* and lived to receive, as an aged libertarian and neo-pagan, the excited homage of Swinburne. As a person and an author, Landor belonged to the eighteenth century, the romantic age, and the Victorian age, and in all three periods he was a lion who walked by himself. He was an eighteenth-century aristocrat and a republican; a romantic poet whose theory and practice were classical; a man of explosive personality and opinions whose poetry was austerely impersonal and almost sufficiently detached from life and ideas to be called 'pure poetry' or Imagism.

But these and other paradoxes are resolved in the central fact that Landor's highest and most compelling ideal was literary and technical. While the romantic and early Victorian poets wrote with Elizabethan prodigality and colour, Landor, setting before himself such models as Pindar, strove for the compact and 'diaphanous'—not, however, because he believed, with the young Arnold, that the high and heavy spiritual responsibility of poetry required bare strength, but because he felt no such responsibility and cherished a pseudo-classical notion of form and style as ends in themselves. Many of Landor's poems treat classical myths, but whereas for the other poets myths are symbols charged with meaning, Landor is usually content to retell the stories, and usually without much human interest. The craftsmanship that shuns the realities of experience, and concentrates on expression when there is little to express, is not even facing the problems of the craftsman. Thus, though critics periodically deplore the neglect of Landor, we cannot really say, in spite of a few fine poems, that neglect is unjustified. (pp. 150-52)

> Douglas Bush, "Romanticism," in his English Poetry: The Main Currents from Chaucer to the Present, Methuen & Co. Ltd., 1952, pp. 112-52.

LAURENCE PERRINE   (essay date 1964)

[Landor's attitude toward immortality in his poetry suggests to Perrine that the poet rejected traditional views of life after death yet accepted death with serenity, recognizing that nature, art, and love can bring meaning to life.]

The theme of immortality is one on which Walter Savage Landor rings many changes in his verse. He treats it in a variety of contexts and a variety of moods, sometimes seriously, sometimes lightly, almost always gracefully. As one might expect, he turns to it with increasing frequency as he grows older. His attitude toward it, however, is not one of belief. . . . [The] main evidence, both of his verse and his recorded utterances, indicates that Landor was agnostic on the question of immortality but on the whole had very little expectation of it. (p. 50)

The most direct evidence of Landor's attitude toward immortality . . . is found in his statement to Swinburne, made during the last year of his life, as reported in Gosse's *Life of Swinburne:*

> Landor talked to his young visitor with great freedom, and, in relation to the approach of death at his own advanced age, remarked that he had no belief in immortality of the soul nor opinion about it, but "was sure of one thing, that whatever was to come was best—the right thing, or the thing that ought to come."

The attitude expressed here is reflected exactly in a poem, published eleven years earlier, when Landor was 79:

> Death stands above me, whispering low
> I know not what into my ear:
> Of his strange language all I know
> Is, there is not a word of fear. . . .

In this statement and this poem seems to be summed up Landor's most considered opinion on the subject of death. Death speaks to him in a foreign tongue—i.e., one of which Landor cannot understand the *words* (which reveal whether or not there is any life to follow) but of which he *can* understand the *tone* (in which there is nothing fearful). The attitude is very much like that of Socrates in the *Apology.* There is nothing to be feared in death, for either it will give Socrates a chance to converse with the souls of the good and the great who have preceded him, or else it will be simply like a long sleep—and when was not sleep gratefully received at the end of a full day?

The note that death is not to be feared or lamented, and that Landor is ready for it when it comes, is sounded again and again through Landor's work, but not accompanied—as it would be, say, in Browning—by the notion of a life to come. More generally it is accompanied in Landor by the profession, metaphorically expressed, that this life has been a good one, and that one should be grateful for it. . . . The sentiment is repeated in a lyric published when he was 84:

> Fast fall the leaves: this never says
> To that, "Alas! how brief our days!"
> All have alike enjoy'd the sun,
> And each repeats, *"So much is won:*
> Where we are falling, millions more
> Have dropt, nor weep that life is o'er." . . .

The idea that man should make no more protest over dying than a leaf makes in leaving the tree appealed to Landor. . . . Implicit in the analogy is a rejection of immortality, for what after-life has a leaf? (pp. 52-4)

Nature and Art Landor loved, and these made life worthwhile to him without the complement of an after-life. But the term which Landor most frequently opposed to death was neither Nature nor Art, but Love—Love not in the large sense of universal brotherhood, nor of affection for friend or kin, but in the more specific sense of an emotional and physical relationship with the opposite sex. "Whatever he may profess," said Robert Browning of Landor, "the thing he really loves is a pretty girl to talk nonsense with." Browning's judgment is borne out by Landor's poetry. Though what Landor means by love may vary from a deep and enduring feeling, such as he felt for Ianthe, to a more temporary fancy, love is always the hottest flame in that fire of life before which Landor warmed his hands:

> Soon, O Ianthe! life is o'er,
>   And sooner beauty's heavenly smile:
> Grant only (and I ask no more),
>   Let love remain that little while. . . .

If Landor asks no more than this, he does not ask for immortality, and so he explicitly declares in a poem which he titled **"What is *really* my belief?"**:

> My faith is this. I do believe
> That ladies never would deceive,
> And that the little fault of Eve
> Is very easy to retrieve.
>
> She lost us immortality,
> But in good earnest what care I,
> If *you* receive my latest sigh
> And give me one—*before* I die. . . .

"Make me immortal with a kiss!" So said Faustus to Helen of Troy, and so says Landor. The tone here is playful, of course, and the poem is not to be taken very seriously; but the basic idea—that love justifies life, and does not last beyond death—is one frequently repeated in Landor's poetry. . . . (p. 54)

The immortality conferred on a lover by a kiss is figurative, but there was another kind of immortality with which Landor was frequently and literally concerned—the immortality of poetry, and the immortality of fame poetry confers on the poet and his subject. . . . Occasionally Landor has doubts of the worth or reality of even this kind of immortality:

> O immortality of fame!
> What art thou? even Shakespeare's name
> Reaches not Shakespeare in his grave.
> The wise, the virtuous, and the brave,

> Resume ere long their common clay,
> And worms are longer lived than they.
> At last some gilded letters show
> What those were call'd who lie below. . . .

But in general Landor is confident that good poetry will last, if not forever, at least for a very long time. He assures a young poet,

> Worms revel in the slime of kings,
> But perish where the laurel springs. . . .

The point is relevant because an immortality of fame is likely to be most ardently embraced by those who have given up belief in a more personal immortality. (pp. 55-6)

Landor, all critics agree, was no orthodox believer. He undoubtedly believed . . . in a benign First Cause, but he had no use for the dogmas of the sects, he continually waxed satirical against priests, and he had nothing but contempt for what he regarded as religious superstitions. His religious ideal was centered in the idea of service rather than in a ritual of worship, a system of beliefs in the supernatural, or concern for the salvation of the soul. This ideal he summed up in a letter to Southey: "To increase the sum of happiness and to diminish the sum of misery, is the only right aim both of reason and of religion." As for immortality, the argument ends where it began—in affection for this life and serene uncertainty about the next, unattended by expectation. Credulous and pious as he is, he says in one poem, he would not change "certainties for uncertainties"; and besides, he adds, his soul is "only soul enough" for one existence. . . . (p. 57)

Laurence Perrine, "Landor and Immortality," in Victorian Poetry, *Vol. II, No. 1, Winter, 1964, pp. 50-7.*

GEOFFREY GRIGSON   (essay date 1964)

[*Grigson is an English poet, critic, editor, and journalist whose direct style characterizes both his criticism and his poetry. As founder and editor of the short-lived periodical* New Verse, *a forum for avant-garde poetry, Grigson distinguished himself as a strongly principled and sometimes polemical critic. In the following excerpt, Grigson views the epigram "The Dying Speech of an Old Philosopher" as a key to understanding Landor's classical ideals. He further suggests that critics have unjustly neglected Landor's poems which, though counter to the flow of the Romantic age, are creative, varied, and well-formed.*]

Something of value may be discovered about Landor's poems from our understanding, or rather our common misunderstanding, of his most famous epigram, which he called **"The Dying Speech of an Old Philosopher,"** and which he composed on the evening of his seventy-fourth birthday, after entertaining Charles Dickens and John Forster, who wrote his biography. Landor, we all know, was a hefty egotist with a loud laugh and a quick and at times violent temper; and we laugh ourselves, when we recall the first line of this birthday poem, in which he looked back over life and accepted death: we think how singular that of all men, Landor should say

> *I strove with none, for none was worth my strife,*

when his existence seems to have been an intermittent strife from childhood, and school, and university, to his extreme old age in Bath and Florence. But we are wrong, and Landor was right: Landor wrote his epigram, not as the subject of a known biography, but as a poet and as the prose-master of his *Imag-*

inary Conversations; in that role, though as a man he might be moiled in law suits and libel actions, and might end as a King Lear rejected by his children, this striving with no one, or no other writer, as writer himself, was firmly at the centre of Landor's creed, stated by him again and again. When his friend Southey died, the praise Landor accorded him, in a prose epitaph, was the praise he accorded himself in the epigram: 'Rarely hath any author been so exempt from the maladies of emulation.' To push, to scramble, to emulate, to compete, and lose independence—that was the sin of authorship, the betrayal of talent. 'Authors are like cattle going to a fair;' he makes a character say in one of the *Imaginary Conversations*, 'those of the same field can never move on without butting one another.' He butted no one for self-advancement (to criticize or despise is something else). He wrote neither for acclaim nor for money; and he realized that for this and for other reasons his situation in literature was a lonely one, and would continue to be lonely after his death. (p. xvii)

[Every] statement Landor makes in ["**The Dying Speech of an Old Philosopher**"], his life and his writings confirm explicitly. It is Landor's true biography, setting him both in and apart from his time, as our one eminent neo-classic. 'Nature I loved'— if he loved nature, that marked him as a man of his time, whether neo-classic or romantic (not that one would divorce neo-classic and romantic too absolutely), and one may recall Landor's delight—for a while—in the red sandstone valley of his Llanthony estates: 'I have made a discovery, which is, that there are both nightingales and glowworms in my valley. I would give two or three thousand less for a place that was without them'; or—for a while—in his villa garden on the slopes of Fiesole. (pp. xviii-xix)

'*Nature I loved, and, next to Nature, Art*': art, composure, moderation—'What is there lovely in poetry,' asked Landor, through the mouth of Boccaccio, in the *Pentameron* . . . , 'unless there be moderation and composure? Are they not better than the hot, uncontrollable harlotry of a flaunting dishevelled enthusiasm? Whoever has the power of creating, has likewise the inferior power of keeping his creation in order. The best poets are most impressive because their steps are regular; for without regularity there is neither strength nor state.'

As for the last two lines of the epigram—that he warmed 'both hands before the fire of Life,' that the fire was sinking and that Landor was ready to depart, they are a true summary of Landor's acceptance of life and death; of the fact that he neither evaded, nor substituted, preferring, for example, Wordsworth to Byron . . . , nature and natural language to seraglio and seraglio talk, or faeries and faery talk, or mists, or infinity; preferring objectivity to autotoxication or autoblabbery, *here and now* to *somewhere else and then*—

> Some see but sunshine, others see but gloom,
> Others confound them strangely, furiously;
> Most have an eye for colour, few for form.
> Imperfect is the glory to *create*,
> Unless on our creation we can look
> And see that all is good; we then may rest.

It could be argued, of course, that Landor's classicism was as much a substitution or an ideal evasion of here and now as another writer's liking for an ideal mediaevalism or an aery-faeryism derived from Drayton or *A Midsummer Night's Dream*, or border ballads; to which Landor's reply was that his ideal classic ground—Greek rather than Roman—and classic principles, demanded height, depth, severity, clarity, and grace.

In long poems his power to construct, and tell, and hold, is seldom sufficient, and his pressure does fall too low; in his short poems he sometimes goes soft, in the manner of other neo-classic poets, architects, and sculptors (such as Flaxman or Thorwaldsen, whom Landor admired). But Landor, like the Greek style architects of his time, wanted, and frequently achieved, what he considered a Greek stiffening of neo-classic sentimentality: the clear and determinate world of Greece was not the misty, indeterminate chaos of the Gothic. There were poets, Landor said, whose books in half a century would be enquired after only for 'cutting out an illuminated letter from the title-page' (Gothicizing poets) 'or of transplanting the willow at the end, that hangs so prettily over the tomb of Amaryllis' (neo-classically sentimental poets). 'If they wish to be healthy and vigorous, let them open their bosoms to the breezes of Sunium; for the air of Latium is heavy and overcharged.'

The Attic, temple-crowned, sun-clear promontory of Sunium was the ideal ground for Landor. . . . [As] Landor expressed it . . . in his poem on the Classick and the Romantick, in the grave, slow line of this poet reflecting, this poet considering ultimates:

> The ancients see us under them, and grieve
> That we are parted by a rank morass,
> Wishing its flowers more delicate and fewer.
> Abstemious were the Greeks; they never strove
> To look so fierce: their Muses were sedate,
> Never obstreperous: you heard no breath
> Outside the flute; each sound ran clear within.
> The Fauns might dance, might clap their hands, might shout,
> Might revel and run riotous; the Nymphs
> Furtively glanced, and fear'd, or seem'd to fear:
> Descended on the lightest of light wings,
> The graceful son of Maia mused apart,
> Graceful, but strong; he listen'd; he drew nigh;
> And now with his own lyre and now with voice
> Temper'd the strain; Apollo calmly smiled.

When Landor writes—and ends a poem—'Apollo calmly smiled', the three words are fact and metaphor; but fact all through. The god Apollo calmly smiled, the narrow-waisted, almond-eyed god whom we know in marble, and who is beauty, youth, composure, strength, civilization. The clear-edged congruence of word and object in Landor is one of his virtues, more acceptable, since language allows of less mannerism than stone and stucco, than the clear-edged 'Greek' architecture of Landor's time, Doric, Ionic, Corinthian, which we now value in the buildings of London and elsewhere. But it does not exhaust Landor's value as a poet to say that there is more of that clear congruence in his longer poems than we commonly admit, and to emphasize its creativity in his epigrams and shorter pieces. He is master especially of a calm line which often begins with short emphatic accented words, and then lightens; he makes poetry a matter of rhythm and language and objectivity, not of imagery and metaphysics; and he would certainly have rejected ambiguity as an evil. He is various, like his own large personality. He offers occasional perfection; he offers gravity, strength, delicacy, wit, comedy. He is lyrical, elegiacal, critical; but convinced also of pleasure—

> The narrow mind is the discontented one.
> There is pleasure in wisdom, there is wisdom in pleasure
> If thou findest no honey in thy cake,
> Put thy cake into honey with thine own right-hand,
> Nor think it defiled thereby.

He can make flickering fun, or knock down a bullock of stupidity. Criticism, perhaps with interference from the history of literature, has inclined to make less than it should have done of poems which are counter, in so many ways, to the 'romantic' flow of poetry and the other arts during Landor's extremely long, always active career. In the past many critics and readers seemed unsure or sure in the wrong way of the voluminous work of a man at times so boisterous and in some ways so uninhibited, who survived into a mealy age (when he died in 1864 he was in his ninetieth year). What was to be thought in such an age of a *poet*—better to think of the prose-writer—whose appetites and moral taste were suspect, who could write as he did about Ianthe's shell or red Priapus rearing his club among the junipers, who could deliver himself of an epigram so indecorous as

Exhausted now her sighs, and dry her tears,
For twenty youths these more than twenty years,
Anne, turning nun, swears God alone shall have her . . .
God ought to bow profoundly for the favour;

who was able to contrive poems with as much ease in outmoded Latin as in English. . . . (pp. xix-xxi)

In the present, criticism and reading have not caught up. 'Poetry was always my amusement, prose my study and business': take Landor's word for it, continue to insist that the poems are mostly occasional—(however: 'Regarding the occasional in poetry; is there less merit in taking and treating what is before us, than in seeking and wandering through an open field as we would for mushrooms?')—and use Landor's prose as an excuse for neglecting the poet (and the verse perhaps as an excuse for neglecting the prose). At any rate, a glance at the third and supplementary volumes of the *Cambridge Bibliography of English Literature* (which places Landor unfortunately among the essayists, and not the poets) shows that no English writer—no English poet—of equal size and quality has been less attended to in the last fifty years; which is a loss.

'I stand out a rude rock in the middle of a river, with no exotic or parasitical plant on it, and few others. Eddies and dimples and froth and bubbles pass rapidly by, without shaking me. Here indeed is little room for pic-nic and polka.'

Not a bad account of himself, as a poet; though Walter Landor was less a rock, and rough, than a finely shaped structure, graceful, but strong, like his Hermes in the poem, who invented the lyre and was the son of Zeus as well as of Maia. Landor himself had some of the attributes of the herm, he was more of a whole and healthy poet than many of his time; in justified pride he thought of himself in a high eagle's sunshine, as in his poem which begins

Ye who have toil'd uphill to reach the haunt
Of other men who lived in other days

and which ends (after he has established that they found nothing but owls hooting and shaking the ivy berries on their heads, and vipers hissing at them, as they crawled down)

Now, was it worth your while to mount so high
Merely to say ye did it, and to ask
If those about ye ever did the like?
Believe me, O my friends, 'twere better far

To stretch your limbs along the level sand
As they do, where small children scoop the drift,
Thinking it must be gold, where curlews soar
And scales drop glistening from the prey above.

(p. xxii)

Geoffrey Grigson, in an introduction to Poems *by Walter Savage Landor, edited by Geoffrey Grigson, Centaur Press Ltd. (England), 1964, pp. xvii-xxii.*

PIERRE VITOUX (essay date 1976)

[*In his assessment of* Gebir, *Vitoux describes Landor's style as a deliberate rejection of the poetic forms of his time in favor of a synthetic compression of language inspired by the ancients. He also finds that the poem's tragic theme represents a stage in the regeneration of humanity and expresses Landor's Romantic political ideals.*]

Gebir was published in 1798, when Landor was twenty-three. The composition of parts of the poem had begun, however, some two years before, during long rambling walks in the woods and along the sandy coast near Swansea, in Wales. Landor's attention had been arrested by a story he had found in the appendix of a book lent to him by his friend Rose Aylmer: *The Progress of Romance . . .* , by Clara Reeve, including the story of Charoba, Queen of Egypt, an adaptation from Vattier. He found it "lacking in simplicity, coherence, and argument—but there was something magnificent veiled in the twilight of antiquity." So he used it as the subject of *Gebir,* a poem which remains to this day fascinating for both its poetic diction and the originality of its conception.

The common reaction of the contemporary readers of the poem, even of the very few who received it with admiration, was the charge of excessive obscurity. Southey was delighted by its "beauties of the first order," but found the language "sometimes uncouth" and "frequently deficient in perspicuity" [see excerpt dated 1799]—and his commentary shows that he failed to grasp the essential connection between the pastoral and the heroic theme. (p. 51)

In fact, this obscurity was the result of Landor's deliberate reaction against the fluent facilities of the poetic style of his time, which was the style of his more youthful verse of 1795. His Latin epistle to his brother Robert, prefixed to *Gebirus,* includes strictures against the contemporary poets who "polish but do not sculpt," in whom every conception that is not frigid or childish "is dissolved in an over-abundance of words." In his **"Post-Script to Gebir"** [see excerpt dated 1800], he remarks of his own earlier poems that "the lines were fluent: the rhymes showed habitual ease, and the personifications fashionable taste"; and, of contemporary poetry, that it often shows "an even tenor of language, by courtesy and common acception held poetic, and an equal dilation of appropriate thoughts, hardly anywhere trivial and no-where exquisite." *Gebir* is for him a new departure; and, like Wordsworth, he starts from a rejection of a dead form, of an empty and facile poetic diction.

This rejection, however, makes him turn for a model, not to "the language really spoken by men" around him, but to the Ancients. "When I began to write *Gebir,* . . . I had just read Pindar a second time and understood him. What I admired was what nobody else had ever noticed—his proud complacency and scornful strength. If I could resemble him in nothing else, I was resolved to be as compendious and exclusive." Although *Paradise Lost* was also one of his favorite readings at the time, it has been conclusively shown that the influence of Milton is slight and limited to a few passages. What fashioned Landor's terse new style was the ideal defined in the abstract with reference to Pindar, but more concretely his attempt to experiment in English with an adaptation of the poetic medium he was using in his own Latin poetry.

This was made easier by the fact that *Gebir* and its Latin counterpart *Gebirus* were growing side by side. . . . [The] poem was taking shape in two languages simultaneously, and . . . in both, Landor's verbal imagination was striving to achieve a concentrated and expressive form, which, classical as it was in inspiration, took him as far as could be from the stereotypes of a conventionally latinized diction.

What is indeed striking, when one compares the two versions of some outstanding passages, is that the massive compression which is the keynote of the English verse reflects what is more spontaneously achieved in the synthetic language. This is apparent in the brief description of the panting serpent . . . , or in the famous Shell passage . . . which Landor invites us to compare with a similar passage in Wordsworth. Landor's description is characteristic in its strict and rounded perfection; it is also purely objective and self-sufficient, whereas that of Wordsworth, admittedly more loosely written, reaches further and opens out on the mystery of the unity of all life. The last two lines echo the Latin text without loss of harmony in conciseness:

> And it remembers its august abodes,
> And murmurs as the Ocean murmurs there.

In other places, however, the challenge of synthetic compactness is met at some cost. Many of the notes of 1803 have to make explicit what was quite clear in the Latin. The note of the adultress who "bays body," . . . explaining that "she looks up with unavailing desire to the corporeal state," develops what was implicit in "Corporeis formis illatrat." . . . Similarly, the syntactical ambiguity of "even her love thy strength was to disclose" is not present in the inflected language. Too many details of that kind contribute to make the text difficult to read. Although the difficulty is far from being an insuperable obstacle to enjoyment for a modern reader, more prepared than his predecessors to let the meaning form itself slowly, the result remains that he is jerked from one arresting scene to another instead of being carried away by the flow of the narrative. Landor's style, for all its distilled excellence, remains immature and unsuited for the sustained development of a "long poem."

The Latin element, derived from the Virgilian epic and Ovid, is also present in the treatment of the original story, but as part of a complex general design. *Gebir* is a strange poem, which defies classification, and this, as we shall see, raises more than a problem of literary genre and takes us to the center of its inspiration. Landor has several times insisted on the absurdity of affixing the label "epic" to his poem. . . . The most precise discussion of the nature of the epic poem occurs in the Preface to *Gebirus*. "It is a poem drawn from history, whether authentic or fictitious, carried by written or oral tradition; it requires various heroes, sudden changes of fortune, with mainly the hazards of war and extreme perils born by a leader; the issue must be fortunate, for it teaches that all things human yield to valour and perseverance." Landor is thus undoubtedly justified to conclude: "Not so ours." *Gebirus* was later republished by him . . . as one of his *Idyllia Heroica*. . . . It is wrong to consider an "idyll" as being exclusively pastoral in character, for it means, properly speaking, "an image in reduction of a larger

image"; the better part of Theocritus (and Moschus) is not pastoral, and there are many "idylls" in this sense in Ovid, who would have been a better poet if he had "restricted each scene to its limits" instead of "drawing out a continuous series of prodigies." But there is a great difference between Landor's later Idylls and *Gebir*, which is much more extended . . . as well as more complex in point of action. What fits it best would be the looser title of "Heroic Fable," . . . but even this would fail to cover all its aspects.

Its mixed character is at least suggested in the Prelude. The framework ("When Old Silenus called the Satyrs home . . . with Bacchus and the Nymphs . . .") is pastoral, reminiscent of a Virgilian eclogue; but Silenus "sometimes rose / Amidst the tale or pastoral, and shewed / The light of purest wisdom." Similarly, the poet's invocation is addressed to the "woody vales of Cambria," but also to its "famous hills" in an appeal to raise him from lowly subjects ("the force / Of high example influence my lay"). And the narrative is launched by means of a phrase with epic associations: "I sing the fates of Gebir" (in the Latin, "great Gebir"). In brief, the subject is the heroic story of Gebir, even though the hero's destiny implies, according to Landor's own definitions, tragic rather than epic greatness; but it will be treated in "the light of wisdom," which has its source closer to the pastoral world, and this will be achieved by means of the narrative section including Tamar, the shepherd-king, and his nymph, a pastoral episode ending in historic prophecy.

Landor's source was an unambiguous tale of violence and cunning. Gebir, the invader of Egypt, was strong and ruthless; his design was to become king of the country by forcing Charoba to marry him. But the Queen's nurse was "an artful woman . . . and a great Enchantress." Her first stratagem was to force Gebir to rebuild the ruined city, while at night the demons of the sea pulled down the buildings. But Gebir, taking the place of his chief shepherd (not here his brother) wrestled with a nymph, defeated her, and obtained from her the secret of the rites that would break the spell. Still, the nurse succeeded in her second trick, that of the poisoned garment, and Gebir died, with Charoba exclaiming: "This is the fate of such men as would compel queens to marry them"—a very limited moral lesson, indeed.

Landor took over the bare facts, but also modified them to make them meaningful. Gebir's original plans of military conquest are quickly altered. He is softened by pity, and soon love, for the young Queen. The passion of love is by no means excluded from the traditional epic, but here the tone is definitely modern. The hero is turned into a brooding man of feeling and Charoba into a modest maid who does not dare to look fully into her own heart. And although Charoba's reticence is finely described (and well used for the plot, since it will help the nurse's plotting), the sentimental parts are not the strongest ones in the poem. But Gebir's change of heart has a deeper cause. A revelation is vouchsafed to him in the course of a Descent into Hell (in Book III). This very classical episode is clearly fashioned with the sixth book of the *Aeneid* as a model: the setting, the guide (here named Aroar), the hero's meeting with his father, his vain attempt to return the unsubstantial shade's embrace, and a vision of the future. What Gebir sees, however, is not the glorious future of his race (that vision will later fall to the lot of Tamar), but the punishment of the evil deeds of tyrants. Landor does not resist the temptation of direct political satire, with George III suffering in afterlife the beheading his life had deserved. But what is even more relevant to the legendary theme is that Gebir's own father is among the sufferers, and he explains that his sin is to have exacted from his son the oath to reconquer Egypt, which had once been a possession of their dynasty. . . . [This detail] serves Landor's design to transform the spirit of the traditional epic, based on the conception of heroism fostered by a military civilization, to carry further an evolution already perceptible in Virgil's constructive national epic by infusing his poem with the modern values derived from a humanitarian and liberal inspiration. Gebir, on his return to earth, is no longer a conqueror; his aim is to unite two peoples in the bonds of brotherhood.

His new plan is doomed to failure, for in spite of the change within him he still finds himself inextricably in a false position; he is caught in the vicious circle of violence answering to violence, and he will fall a victim to the forces his military expedition has unleashed. Clearly, what Landor is here transposing into the legend is the ambiguous role of the armies of the French Revolution, carrying the ideal of freedom and imposing it by force on the nations around them. Although the mass of the people is in favor of Gebir, and of peace through reconciliation, Dalica, the Queen's nurse, still sees the man from Gades as an enemy. Dalica is a powerful development of the sorceress barely sketched in the original story. She has the initiative of the plot, for Charoba is made passive by the growing love she hesitates to acknowledge, so that it looks to her nurse as if her strength of mind has been destroyed by an evil spell. But what makes Dalica significant as a character is that she embodies and gathers around her all the reactions that work against the invader: religious bigotry, respect for custom, chauvinistic prejudices, interests vested in the political establishment—all the forms of an ignoble resistance to progress and freedom, but amounting to a real force in history intensified by the presence of the invading army. She prepares the poisoned tunic in a scene which carries reminiscences of Medea's magic rites in Ovid's Book VII of the *Metamorphoses,* and Gebir dies a helpless victim in a finale of pure, if restrained, pathos, happy to know at the last from Charoba's despair that she had no hand in his death.

Gebir's failure is underlined by the subplot. The beginning of it is steeped in an atmosphere of mythological pastoral. Tamar meets the nymph disguised as a sailor, they wrestle for a wager (his sheep against her shell), and he is defeated not so much on account of her strength as because he feels suddenly weak and trembling from an unknown cause. We are in the world of Theocritus (with eroticism somewhat toned down, but unmistakable). But this episode is further developed to counterpoint the main theme. The major scene in it is the marriage of the two lovers. . . . [The] nymph after the marriage urges Tamar to leave his brother to his destiny, and during their flight she shows him Corsica, where "From Tamar shall arise, 'tis Fate's decree, / A mortal man above all mortal praise." . . . But the promised hero of modern times, Bonaparte, is to be the liberator of mankind and represents a new ideal; he differs from the Achilles of Catullus who is to be great because his illustrious virtues and high actions will be "confessed by mothers burying their sons." . . . Here, the prophetic Book VI ends on a vision of Time redeemed from nationalism, violence and slavery. It is a passage still burdened with some allegorical obscurity (Time's "motley garb" thrown off is that of the names for the months and the days, suppressed by the French Convention), but its movement and inspiration clearly anticipate Shelley's conclusion to the third act of *Prometheus Unbound.*

> Captivity led captive, War o'erthrown,
> They shall o'er Europe, shall o'er Earth extend

> Empire that seas alone and skies confine,
> And glory that shall strike the crystal stars.

The tragedy of Gebir represents one stage, and not the end, in the process that leads to this regeneration of humanity. The hero is not only unfortunate in being entangled in the consequences of the past he has renounced, but he is also guilty because he remains king. As the nymph discerns "Gebir—tho' generous, just, humane—inhaled / Rank venom from these mansions," . . . his palace at Calpe. She wants to save Tamar from all craving for power. Landor wrote his poem in an optimistic mood, with confidence in the imminence of a new era of freedom and universal brotherhood. But he also shows himself aware of all the difficulties created by the permanence of the past and by the temptation for all men to use force and obtain power. He does not here qualify his praise of the Republican general, the "mortal man above all mortal praise," which shocked his political enemies so much. But a note in 1803 will soon register disappointment:

> Bonaparte might have been so. . . . But unhappily he thinks, that to produce great changes, is to perform great actions: to annihilate antient freedom and to substitute new, to give republics a monarchichal government, and the provinces of monarchs a republican one; in short, to overthrow by violence all the institutions and to tear from the heart all the social habits of men, has been the tenor of his politics to the present hour. . . .

There is very little Tom-Painish radicalism, by the way, in this condemnation not so much of the Consul rising to absolute power as of the subverter of traditions and natural identities, but it makes clear that Landor feels his confidence betrayed. And the Latin text only places Bonaparte above all mortal praise conditionally: "if at least he protects Justice and Liberty," introducing, rather oddly, an element of doubt at the core of the prophecy.

The doubt about the possibility of a new era for mankind is in fact at the center of the second theme. In her more-than-human wisdom, the nymph persuades Tamar to escape with her to a pleasant retreat, and the panoramic vision of the happier future is conveyed by her to the man she has just removed from the turmoil of history in the making. The theme of her exhortation is that private happiness must be placed above the strife of politics, that *otium* is better than a public life. Gebir, then, is guilty not only because he remains king, but because he is not wise enough to realize the vanity of all action. The central ambiguity of *Gebir* is that in its final development the pastoral subplot undercuts rather than supports or counterpoints the heroic theme. And this reflects (for the first and not the last time) the duality of Landor's inspiration: political involvement on the side of liberalism, embraced with passionate hopefulness, and then disillusionment and the fear of political chaos leading him to the refuge of nature and art, from which his former hopes appear as a Utopian dream rather than a goal accessible to human efforts. The two tendencies are part of the creative impulse behind *Gebir,* and they give life to the poem, even if they prevent it from being unified.

Landor has taken over an obscure Oriental tale (obscure enough to give him a free hand), and has also managed, as we have seen, to bring it within the pale of the classical tradition through the insertion of scenes or details that belong to the Greco-Latin epic. But, beyond the pleasures of imagination and transpo-

sition, he has another goal: to interpret and present his legendary plot in the light of the modern spirit of liberalism and
humanitarianism. This brings him to grips with the essential
problem of Romantic myth-making (illustrated in different ways
by *Prometheus Unbound* and *Hyperion*): the technical difficulty
of re-handling intractable material, which is, in fact, the formal
aspect of the struggle to reconcile new values with the cultural
past, progress with tradition, and more generally the dream of
the ideal with the reality of nature and history. It is clear that
Gebir does not quite bear up under the strain. The writer indulges in political allegorizing, escapes into irrelevant classical
details, and fails to achieve complete clarity or unity. But there
is a greatness in the fragments of this early ambitious design
which is not to be found in Landor's later poetry. The personal
lyrical poems, for which he is best known, are beautiful, and
minor. As to the later Heroic Idylls, they are more limited in
scope: self-contained scenes (real "idylls"), polished verse,
the erotic or domestic side-aspects of the great heroic legends—
the voice of private feelings, no longer a public utterance. The
Victorian poetry of Landor has accepted as final the defeat,
dramatized in *Gebir,* of Romantic political idealism. (pp. 51-6)

> Pierre Vitoux, "'Gebir' as an Heroic Poem," in
> The Wordsworth Circle, *Vol. VII, No. 1, Winter,*
> *1976, pp. 51-7.*

CHARLES L. PROUDFIT (essay date 1979)

[*Proudfit seeks to enhance Landor's reputation as a literary critic.
He finds that Landor's critical views, often faulted as digressive,
inconsistent, and subjective, are redeemed by the visual imagery,
metaphorical comparisons, and personal point of view he incorporated into his impressionistic judgments.*]

Walter Savage Landor has not attracted much attention as a
nineteenth-century literary critic. This would not surprise him.
He neither wrote as a professional critic for a specific audience;
nor did he, like his contemporaries Coleridge, De Quincey,
Hazlitt, Hunt, and Lamb, seek the usual critical forums of the
day—the periodical review, the formal essay, and the lecture
platform. 'I shall have as many readers as I desire to have in
other times than ours', wrote the seventy-five-year-old Walter
Savage Landor in 1850 to his friend and biographer, John
Forster. 'I shall dine late; but the dining-room will be well-
lighted, the guests few and select. I neither am, nor ever shall
be, popular. Such never was my ambition'. . . . Devotees of
Landor's poetry and prose have never been numerous, and
those who have articulated their praise compose as select a
company as Landor could have wished. In our own century
T. S. Eliot, Ezra Pound, and W. B. Yeats have acknowledged
Landor's literary achievement [see excerpt by Eliot dated 1933
and Additional Bibliography]. . . . Yet in the midst of all these
laudatory remarks lavished upon Landor's poetry and prose,
similar praise of Landor's literary criticism is noticeably absent.

There is reason for this. Readers who have turned to Landor's
works to find a consistent application of a set of carefully
determined critical principles have been disappointed. . . . Landor was a private man endowed with an income sufficient to
free him to become one of the most erudite and well-read
literary men of the first half of the nineteenth century. He
wrote out of enjoyment rather than necessity, and his lifetime
devotion to ancient and modern authors left behind him a body
of critical commentary that demands our respect and repays
our attention. This commentary, however, has never been eas-

ily available to readers. It has remained essentially to be discovered within his personal correspondence, suppressed or can-
celled prose pieces, Latin essays, poetry, the diaries and memoirs
of those who knew him, and that species of composition upon
which rests his reputation as a prose writer, the *Imaginary
Conversations of Literary Men and Statesmen.* On those few
occasions when reviews were solicited from him, late in life,
he expressed himself in a form of personal essay uniquely his
own.

It is perhaps this very individuality of expression which has
distinguished Landor among his contemporaries, has found him
friends and enemies, and has prevented the unlearned from
following along with him. The singularity of his pronouncements characterized his conversation as much as it does his
writings. His acquaintances all mark the Landorian voice. . . .
This Landorian voice expresses the man, his confidence in his
own judgment, his vast knowledge of literature and painting,
his extremes in temperament and disposition, and his ability
to convey his thoughts in words and images which are memorable. (pp. 1-2)

The Landorian voice repels as well as attracts, and his critics
have varied in their susceptibility to its charm. When Landor's
judgments and opinions emerged in dramatized and objectified
form in the *Imaginary Conversations* of 1824, his early reviewers were not swayed by the force of his personality into
accepting his unorthodox opinions and pronouncements. (p. 4)

[There are certain] qualities which render Landor as critic both
fascinating and frustrating. He does not merely read books; he
lives them. In doing so he brings with him all of his likes and
dislikes, loves and hates, strengths and weaknesses, perceptions and blind spots. He answers to no one except himself;
he cares for no one's criticism but his own; he is his own ideal
critic. It is little wonder that criticism of Landor's criticism
has seemed so unsatisfying. Those literary historians who have
endeavoured to know enough of his works even to generalize
about them have had enormous difficulties. They are attempting
to cope with a man who was born into a literary age that
included Dr. Johnson, was educated during the exciting years
of the American and French Revolutions, and was friend of
two generations of Romantic writers and of many eminent
Victorians. They are attempting to cope with a man responding
singularly to a life spent reading, writing, or talking about
reading and writing. We see the effect of this in the general
and insubstantial comments they make. (p. 5)

To approach Landor in search of a method or guiding principles
can only detract from the pleasure of reading him. There are
critical procedures and principles, but they emerge through
acquaintance, through the gradual submission to the Landorian
voice as it leads one arbitrarily, often quixotically, through a
library in which nothing is more meaningless than the dates
on books. . . .

As the Landorian voice accompanies us through this library,
making pronouncements on ancients and contemporaries, on
poets loved and poets despised, on critical issues past and
present, we are forced to consider whether this is the voice of
an opinionated eccentric or a voice which echoes his time. It
was a very long time, 1775-1864. One hardly knows whether
to view him as a Neo-Classic, a Romantic, or a Victorian; and
he gives the lie, perhaps more than any single figure, to the
periodization of English literature. Landor not only lived in all
three eras, but he also belongs within and without each of
them. (p. 6)

The critic of Landor as critic soon finds himself in conflict with traditional expectations. If Landor is to be justified as a literary critic, then it seems that one ought to be able to identify his basic principles, describe his method, and place him in a historical critical tradition. Landor, however, was a unique literary man, not a professional literary critic; and his method for approaching literature is so much an extension of Landor the man that attempts to describe it in the usual ways are doomed either to superficiality or to failure. Our final view of him as a convincing literary critic must be determined by the force and substance of his personality and the enthusiasm and intellectual vigour he brought to his reading of literature. To describe his method is to describe his mental behaviour with all of its singular turns and twists and tastes. How does Landor behave as a critic? He behaves as a highly-trained reader of literature for whom the past and present are one, who respects his own judgment completely, and who considers himself especially endowed to judge since he, too, is a practising poet and prose writer. He is his own ideal poet-critic, and he has extraordinary self-confidence. Thus, he makes pronouncements; he makes a-historical comparisons; he offers opinions sustained by his likes and dislikes; and his sensitivity and temperament are such that he is susceptible to what we might call sentimental but he would call the pathetic. If his love for literature had a rival, it was painting. Thus, his imagination is visual. He thinks in images and metaphors, and his criticism binds together for us all of the senses as he entices our imaginations either with the pictures he himself creates or those of artists he chooses to compare. We may not agree with his opinions, but we can never read Boccaccio, Petrarch, Milton, Dante, or Spenser again in quite the same way after reading Landor. (p. 16)

The submission of the text to verbal analysis is fundamental to Landor's approach to the reading and criticism of literature, but this in itself presents a problem in methodology. When does Landor's verbal criticism cease to be that and become marginalia? The two do seem to overlap for him. He seems more to participate in a text than merely to read it. Consequently, much of his criticism exists in the form of marginalia: some in books he once owned, some in his personal correspondence and public letters, most notably his *Letter to Emerson* . . . ; and some in his *Imaginary Conversations* where we would honorifically label it digression. Such marginalia preserves Landor's wit and humour for us more than his formal writings, as for instance when he finds Dryden's prose 'vigorous and natural' but his poetry partly 'composed in a brothel, the remainder in a gin-shop'. . . . Such is the highly individualized personal taste of Landor. However much he may desire critics to list faults and beauties and to make formal comparisons, Landor's own criticism is frequently marked by an enthusiasm which links him with the impressionistic Romantic critics Hazlitt and Lamb. This tendency can be endearing in him, as for instance when he says: 'I love Goldsmith. The poet never transgresses into the province of the historian. There is nothing profound or important in him; but his language is gracefully familiar, everything about him is sufficiently correct and well-placed, his style is polished enough, and he invites us by an ingenious and frank simplicity'. . . . Such personal enthusiasm did sometimes mislead Landor, especially in his later years when he would lavish praise indiscriminately on writers as different as Robert Browning and Felicia Dorthea Hemans.

A certain tension is established in Landor's criticism between his concept of himself as an ideal critic, his eighteenth-century

notions about how a textual critic ought to proceed, and his energetic, enthusiastic, imaginative, voracious habit of mind. Even his most successful literary form, the Imaginary Conversation, in which he attempts to re-create the natural movement of actual conversation, precludes the failure for him of the consistent application of the kind of thorough and extended critical analysis suggested in the Porson plan. Landor's thought is consistently interrupted by numerous digressions. His success rests in fulfilling the task of the critic as he describes it in *The Pentameron*:

> *Boccaccio* . . . To be useful to as many as possible is the especial duty of a critic, and his utility can only be attained by rectitude and precision. He walks in a garden which is not his own; and he neither must gather the blossoms to embellish his discourse, nor break the branches to display his strength. Rather let him point to what is out of order, and help to raise what is lying on the ground. . . .

This metaphor of the literary work as a garden in which the critic as gardener must remove the weeds and briars without disturbing the 'blossoms' and 'branches' and must 'raise' those beautiful plants that lie 'on the ground' is a favourite of Landor and figuratively describes his view that the critic's primary attention should be devoted to pointing out faults and to praising the beauties of literary works.

Landor's own practice often involves a greater concern for faults than for beauties. Yet it develops naturally from the high standards he demanded of himself as a creative artist and the high esteem in which he held verbal criticism. . . . (pp. 19-20)

One of the most unique and characteristic features of Landor's practice as a literary critic is his use of metaphorical criticism. . . . Landor's use of imagery in his literary criticism is functional rather than decorative; that is, his images, similes, and metaphors are integral to his critical thinking and are not window-dressing. Furthermore, his metaphorical criticism is given an extra dimension when one realizes that his approach to literature is not unlike his approach to representational art. . . .

When Landor wishes to blame or praise an author, he often turns to painting and sculpture for his imagery. Thus, Dryden is not 'a great poet' because 'there is not throughout his works one stroke of the sublime or one touch of the pathetic'. . . . Similarly: 'In Chaucer, . . . we recognize the strong homely strokes, the broad and negligent facility, of a great master'. . . . And the 'chief qualities' of Pindar's poetry are 'rejection of what is light and minute, disdain of what is trivial, and selection of those blocks from the quarry which will bear strong strokes of the hammer and retain all the marks of the chisel'. . . . (p. 21)

On some occasions his choice of imagery is either grotesque or realistic in the extreme. For example, Landor closes the first Conversation between Southey and himself with this grotesque image: 'A rib of Shakespeare would have made a Milton: the same portion of Milton, all poets born ever since'. . . . One of Landor's most successful realistic descriptions appropriately suggests the poetry of Crabbe: '[He] wrote with a twopenny nail, and scratched rough truths and rogues' facts on mud walls. . . . Young moralized at a distance on some external appearances of the human heart; Crabbe entered it *on all fours*, and told the people what an ugly thing it is inside'. . . . (pp. 21-2)

Landor is particularly fond of similes and extended comparisons, and he employs them in a variety of ways. He may use a simple comparison to praise a certain quality of a writer: '[Theocritus'] reflections are frequent, but seasonable; soon over, like the shadows of spring clouds on flowery meadows, and not hanging heavily upon the scene, nor depressing the vivacity of the blythe antagonists'. . . . Or he may use a simile to excuse a fault in a favourite author, such as the licentious tales in Boccaccio's *Decameron*: 'Their levities and gaieties are like the harmless lightnings of a summer sky in the delightful regions they were written in'. . . . Sometimes he suggests the difference between two writers by comparing the styles of two painters. For example, Landor says of Catullus: 'In relation to Virgil, he [Catullus] stands as Correggio in relation to Raffael: a richer colourist, a less accurate draftsman; less capable of executing grand designs, more exquisite in the working out of smaller'. . . . (p. 22)

Just as Landor is more successful in pointing out faults than in noting beauties, so is he especially effective in using simile and metaphor to negative ends, ranging from mild displeasure to fierce indignation. In a letter to his friend Southey, Landor writes that Wordsworth's *Lyrical Ballads* have 'sometimes disappointed me, just as an Aeolian harp has done when I expected a note more'. . . . When Landor wishes to convey his view that Tasso's characters are more 'vivid', 'distinct', and 'interesting' than Virgil's, he creates an extended comparison: 'The heroes of the *Aeneid* are like the half-extinct frescoes of Raphael; but what is wanting in the frescoes of the painter is effaced by time, what is wanting in the figures of the poet was wanting to his genius'. . . . Landor's extended comparisons can also be effective as a weapon of attack in critical discussion, as demonstrated in his strictures on Voltaire's criticism of Milton and Shakespeare in the Conversation between the Abbé Delille and himself: 'He stuck to them as a woodpecker to an old forest-tree, only for the purposes of picking out what was rotten: he has made the holes deeper than he found them, and, after all his cries and chatter, has brought home but scanty sustenance to his starveling nest'. . . . (pp. 22-3)

[In] order to gain an understanding of how [Landor's] method functions in conjunction with his basic criteria for determining great poetry from mediocre, we must look to those poets whom he chose most often to discuss and whose works he has celebrated in extended prose pieces. Among them we find Boccaccio, Dante, Petrarch, Spenser, Shakespeare, and Milton. Although he constantly refers to the classics, to Homer, Aeschylus, Pindar, Sophocles, Virgil, Horace, and Ovid for his touchstones in comparing poets, to only Catullus and Theocritus does he give full studies. . . . Wordsworth and Southey among his contemporaries receive detailed criticism; and Southey he overvalues through the sentiments of friendship, and Wordsworth he treats unjustly in his later criticism through personal dislike. Landor does not ignore the other poets of his period. Indeed, he says of them 'our field of poetry at the present time is both wider and better cultivated than it has ever been'. . . . (pp. 24-5)

Landor's interest in literature is that of an epicure, and quite properly one of his favourite Imaginary Conversations is that between Epicurus, the Greek philosopher, and two of his female disciples, Leontion and Ternissa. Epicurus is an idealized portrait of Landor himself, and it is Landor who speaks when Epicurus informs his young friends: 'All the imitative arts have delight for the principal object: the first of these is poetry: the highest of poetry is tragic'. . . . Literature is life to Landor,

and the characters of Achilles and Priam, Dido and Aeneas, Satan and Eve, and Othello and Desdemona were as real to him as the paintings that hung on his walls in his villa outside Florence and the deep and abiding friendships he formed with such men and women as Robert Southey, John Forster, Charles Dickens, Robert and Elizabeth Barrett Browning, and the Countess of Blessington. The very restrained and classical quality of his verse and short dramatic Imaginary Conversations suggests the emotional man behind them, and perhaps the poet Yeats's great admiration for Landor is partly due to his recognition of the battle between the emotional artist and the suggestive though impersonal work of art; the man and the mask. . . .

We do not turn to Landor today in search of a new approach to literature which will foster volumes of reevaluations. We turn to Landor for his living appreciation of all he read and contemplated. So long as we cherish learning; so long as harmony in poetry is important to us; so long as we expect poetry to express the greatest ideas and the most sincere emotions; and so long as we value singularity of response, confidence in informed opinion, and an epigrammatical, imagistic turn of mind; so long will Landor have an important place for us in literary criticism, not as a professional literary critic, but as a most unique and impressive literary man. (p. 31)

Charles L. Proudfit, in an introduction to Landor as Critic, *edited by Charles L. Proudfit, Routledge & Kegan Paul, 1979, pp. 1-33.*

DONALD DAVIE   (essay date 1984)

[*Davie explores the relationship between poetry and sculpture in Landor's poems and epigrams, focusing on the poet's use of "lapidary" or "chiselled" effects. Davie also compares the formal poetic ideals of Yeats and Landor and reflects on Landor's "immortality." See the excerpt dated 1951 and the Additional Bibliography for further commentary by Davie.*]

[Walter Savage Landor] was sometimes a bigot, sometimes a bully. But there are many places in his *Imaginary Conversations* where he is neither. In one such place, he has Diogenes maintain:

> There is no mass of sincerity in any place. What there is must be picked up patiently, a grain or two at a time; and the season for it is after a storm, after the overflowing of banks, and bursting of mounds, and sweeping away of landmarks. Men will always hold something back: they must be shaken and loosened a little, to make them let go what is deepest in them, and weightiest and purest.

We can set this beside something that Izaak Walton is made to say, about the love poems of Donne . . . :

> So ingenious are men when the spring torrent of passion shakes up and carries away their thoughts, covering (as it were) the green meadow of still homely life with pebbles and shingle, some colourless and obtuse, some sharp and sparkling.

Taken together, these passages seem to say that the lapidary or "chiselled" effect, as in the epigram or epitaph, so far from witnessing to lack of feeling, on the contrary is the aftermath and proof of very strong and tumultuous feeling. This is what I have always believed, not on the authority of Landor or any

Landor in his later years.

tation. What is it if it can buoy up no wisdom, no reflection? if we can throw into it none of our experience? if no repository is to be found in it for the gems we have collected, at the price sometimes of our fortunes, of our health, and of our peace? Your *improvisatori* let drop their verses as a string of mules their morning oats, for miles together . . . The first thing a young person who wishes to be a poet has to do, is, to conquer his volubility; to compress in three verses what he had easily thrown off in twelve; and to be an hour about what had cost him a minute. If he has a *knack* for verses, he must break it and forget it. Both the poet and the painter should acquire facility and frankness; but they must be exercised with discretion; they must be sternly regulated, and in great part suppressed. The young poet will remonstrate, and more often scoff: he will appall you by placing before you the *deep mouth* of Pindar and his mountain-torrents. Tell him, and tell older ones too, that Pindar of all poets is the most accurate and the most laborious.

"Gems," in Landor's usage, is no empty figure; it means *stones,* some precious and some not, "some colourless and obtuse, some sharp and sparkling." Only by entering into the metaphor with all seriousness can we regain access to the climate of ideas familiar from past centuries, in which it was high praise of a poet to say that he was "laborious," and of his poetry that it was "laboured." From within that climate of ideas we may recover what Landor intended by "mediocrity": not something run-of-the-mill, boring, of no account; but rather a standard of accomplishment which, though relatively many attain it, many more never do. I suspect we sell it short by thinking of it as what a devoted and gifted student in an excellent Creative Writing school may attain to. It is not in itself good enough to amount to anything; but it is the serviceable platform from which a few may lift themselves to do something that matters, having learned (the first lesson) to suppress in themselves whatever they may have by way of "knack," of "facility." As for what is needed to lift off further, Landor is quite specific; it is not anything to do with technique, with diligence, with the history of the art—it is "wisdom," it is "reflection," it is "experience," accumulated "at the price sometimes of our fortunes, of our health, and of our peace." This is what composition by way of improvisation can never attain to. On the contrary, we are invited to think, wisdom and passionate experience in poetry are often to be apprehended as an effect dryly conclusive, mournful or sardonic, *closed.* (pp. 104-05)

Thinking of poetry as like sculpture—something that Landor's verse-practice invites us to, more than any of his declarations in prose—can prompt many reflections, some of them profound and a few of them topical. It invites us for instance to envisage the inherited language, the poet's medium as the poet apprehends it in the act of composing, as something no less bleakly confronting, no more negotiable, than the cliff of Carrara marble that faced Michelangelo when he went to the quarry looking for a block that should excite his sculptor's imagination. Nothing could be further from the sense of language that French theorists and their Anglo-American followers have lately pressed upon us: language seen as a band of nebulous haze, infinitely malleable and protean according as the needs or whims of speaker and of auditor impinge upon it. The question is not

one else (for instance not Yeats nor Pound, who can both be shown to have endorsed Landor on this point [see Additional Bibliography]), but from my experience of how my own emotional experience was or was not convertible into poetry. And the principal sorrow or frustration of my life in poetry has been my inability to persuade others of this to me self-evident truth. On the contrary, so entrenched among us are the associations between the marmoreal and the cold, between the stony and the dry, between the firm contour and the rigid, between the chisel and the scalpel, that any attempt to envisage poetry by analogy with the sister-art of sculpture at once arouses bristling suspicions. (p. 103)

[The] compositional habits of poets of the present day in high favour among us, though they are often declared to be "Romantic" or "post-Romantic," are very hard to relate to the Romantic Movement as an international phenomenon known to literary history. When people claim to find such a connection, it usually turns out that what they are pointing to is an aversion on the part of the poet to anything predetermined or pre-planned. But as a mode of composition, improvisation, the feeling forward from one verse-line to the next in the presence of an actual or imagined audience, was known to the Ancient World as well as to the nineteenth century. Landor wrote (1828):

> . . . No *improvisatore* ever rose above mediocrity; few have reached it. Poetry, like wine, requires a gentle and regular and long fermen-

what language *is* (that question which so delightfully exercises philosophers and semioticians), but what language *is taken to be* by those who use it, either those who carve it or those who respond to the shapes it takes at the carver's hands. If we choose to think of the inherited language as a cliff of Carrara or Parian marble, its veins and lines of fracture imperfectly but still usefully traced by the better lexicographers, no voice out of Paris or Geneva can or should persuade us otherwise. Landor was boringly pedantic, in many of the *Imaginary Conversations,* about the etymology of English words; and he was a crank about how to spell them. But remote as all this rightly seems, in an age when English has become the *lingua franca* of airline-pilots and ground-controllers, still we cannot impugn the principle that Landor proceeded on: English is still an artistic medium, if we choose to think of it so; and indeed nothing but our so thinking of it is needed to ensure that, as an artistic medium, it shall persist. (pp. 107-08)

We should, when we write, think that we are *sculpting* language. Let no one think that this is only a fancy way of saying what we all painlessly subscribe to: the need for craftsmanship. On the contrary, the verb "to craft," nowadays much in favour among us, is one that we can do without. The sculptor— whether he works on the small scale of medal, medallion and coin, or on portrait-busts, or else monumentally, and whether "figurative" or "abstract"—is not a craftsman nor a technician, but an artist, laying on the line (as Landor says) his fortune, perhaps his health, certainly his peace of mind. In a late *Conversation* . . . Landor speaks in his own person with a sort of cracked defiance:

> Poetry was always my amusement, prose my study and business. I have published five volumes of *Imaginary Conversations*: cut the worst of them thro the middle, and there will remain in this decimal fraction quite enough to satisfy my appetite for fame. I shall dine late; but the dining-room will be well lighted, the guests few and select.

This passage, or rather the last sentence, was remodelled momentously by Yeats, in a poem of his middle years, "To a Young Beauty":

> There is not a fool can call me friend,
> And I may dine at journey's end
> With Landor and with Donne.

The coupling of Landor with Donne has seemed unaccountable to some readers; but as we have seen, Yeats had warrant for it. Yeats's confidence in posterity sounds much more ringingly than Landor's, and with good reason, for Yeats enjoyed far more fame and esteem in his lifetime than Landor did. Indeed it's not easy to say whether Landor's gamble on posterity has paid off even now; for he's represented in the standard anthologies but his name is seldom on any one's lip, and *Imaginary Conversations* is one of those works remembered more often than they are read. The point of these reflections is that, if our perspectives on the past are foreshortened, our perspectives on the future are even more so, and for reasons beyond our control. Under the threat of nuclear Armageddon no poet can appeal to posterity as confidently as Yeats or Landor did. If fame does not come in the poet's lifetime, he can have no confidence that it will come hereafter, from a posterity which, if it exists at all, may well take a form quite unimaginable. This means inevitably that the poet, stubbornly proud as he may be, is in our day dependent on his public in the here and now, compelled to adjust to the public's expectations and preferences, in a way that Landor and Yeats could not envisage.

A little later in the same Conversation with Archdeacon Hare, Landor made another prophecy about his posthumous reputation, and one that events have shown to be more accurate:

> I stand out a rude rock in the middle of a river,
> with no exotic or parasitical plant on it, and
> few others. Eddies and dimples and froth and
> bubbles pass rapidly by, without shaking me.
> Here indeed is little room for pic-nic and polka.

From this passage too Yeats seems to have taken a hint, if no more, for a poem with the sardonic title, "Men Improve With The Years." . . . (pp. 108-10)

[Though] Yeats from time to time dallied with the lapidary aspirations of poetry, beguiled by them, he is much less firmly committed to those aspirations than Landor is. Because of Landor's constancy to that ideal, these few sentences of his may prompt the reflection that the true immortality of the poet lies in his having become, he and his works, one more stratum in that cliff, the inherited language, which future poets will apprehend as the raw material they have to work, and to work with. This is a sort of immortality which, not quite logically and yet reasonably, we can envisage as more plausibly surviving some future cataclysm than any one poet's life-record and body of work; for we all know that there are languages, long "dead," which survive in fragmentary texts only dubiously attributed to named individuals. Landor's "rude rock in the middle of a river," the craggily inscrutable island that the pleasure-craft pass by, makes that sort of sense in the nuclear age. . . . (pp. 110-11)

> *Donald Davie, "Attending to Landor," in* Ironwood,
> *Vol. 12, No. 2, Fall, 1984, pp. 103-11.*

ADDITIONAL BIBLIOGRAPHY

Becker, George J. "Landor's Political Purpose." *Studies in Philology* XXXV, No. 3 (July 1938): 446-55.
> Examines the role of politics in Landor's writings and suggests that he considered himself a "political prophet."

Buxton, John. "Walter Savage Landor (1775-1864)." In his *The Grecian Taste: Literature in the Age of Neo-Classicism, 1740-1820,* pp. 105-27. New York: Harper & Row Publishers, Barnes & Noble Books, 1978.
> Characterizes Landor's poems as presentations of classical themes in a simple, clear, classical style.

Chambers, E. K. Introduction to *Landor: Poetry and Prose* by Walter Savage Landor, pp. v-xvii. 1946. Reprint. New York: AMS Press, 1978.
> A brief survey of Landor's life and major works.

Colvin, Sidney. *Landor.* English Men of Letters, edited by John Morley. New York: Harper & Brothers, Publishers, 1881, 224 p.
> A biographical and critical study based on Forster's *Walter Savage Landor* (see entry below), but including some additional sources. Though Colvin's work is praised for its "readability," modern scholars fault it for biographical inaccuracies.

Craig, Maurice James. "Landor and Ireland." *The Dublin Magazine* n.s. XVIII, No. 3 (July-September 1943): 35-41.
> Investigates the importance of Ireland to Landor's life and thought.

Davie, Donald. "Landor as Poet." *Shenandoah* IV, Nos. 2-3 (Summer-Autumn 1953): 93-105.

Identifies the classical models for Landor's *Hellenics*, heroic poems, epigrams, and dramas.

De Quincey, Thomas. "Orthographic Mutineers." *Tait's Edinburgh Magazine* XIV, No. CLIX (March 1847): 157-62.
  Pronounces Landor "outrageously crazy upon the one subject of spelling." Though De Quincey lampoons Landor's attempted spelling reforms, he admits that Landor is more scholarly and consistent in his revisions than other orthographers.

Dickens, Charles. *Bleak House.* London: Bradbury & Evans, 1853, 629 p.
  Includes a caricature of Landor in the character of Lawrence Boythorn.

Dilworth, Ernest. *Walter Savage Landor.* Twayne's English Author Series, edited by Sylvia E. Bowman, no. 125. New York: Twayne Publishers, 1971, 172 p.
  Includes biographical information and an examination of the style and content of Landor's verse and prose.

Elton, Oliver. "Southey and Landor." In his *A Survey of English Literature, 1780-1880,* Vol. 2, pp. 1-48. New York: Macmillan Co., 1920.
  Surveys Landor's career, devoting attention to the poems, dramatic scenes, epigrams, *Hellenics, Imaginary Conversations,* and the longer prose works.

Elwin, Malcolm. *Savage Landor.* New York: Macmillan Co., 1941, 498 p.
  A respected biography.

————. *Landor: A Replevin.* London: Macdonald, 1958, 502 p.
  Presents a more "sympathetic" commentary on Landor's life than other biographers. Elwin attempts to "recover Landor's character from misrepresentation and his works from neglect."

Evans, Edward Waterman, Jr. *Walter Savage Landor: A Critical Study.* New York: G. P. Putnam's Sons, Knickerbocker Press, 1892, 209 p.
  An early critical overview. Evans attempts to define Landor's place in literary history.

[Field, Kate]. "Last Days of Walter Savage Landor: Parts I, II, and III." *The Atlantic Monthly* XVII, Nos. CII-CIV (April, May, June, 1866): 385-95, 684-705, 540-51.
  Reminiscences of Landor's later years, chronicling his habits and personality.

Forster, John. *Walter Savage Landor: A Biography.* 2 vols. London: Chapman & Hall, 1869.
  The earliest biography. Forster's work is faulted by later critics and biographers as disorganized and inexact.

Gossman, Ann. "Landor and the 'Higher Fountains'." *The Classical Journal* 50, No. 7 (April 1955): 303-07.
  Highlights Landor's use of the characters, themes, and sentiments of classical antiquity.

Gregory, Horace. "The Elegiac Art of Walter Savage Landor." In his *Spirit of Time and Place,* pp. 62-72. New York: W. W. Norton & Co., 1973.
  Suggests that the appeal of the *Imaginary Conversations* was limited to the nineteenth century. Gregory finds that Landor's elegies and love lyrics deserve continued admiration, however.

Hare, Julius C. "On Walter Savage Landor's *Imaginary Conversations.*" *The London Magazine* IX (May 1824): 523-41.
  An "imaginary conversation" between Hare and a fictional critic, in which they evaluate Landor's work.

Henderson, W. Brooks Drayton. *Swinburne and Landor: A Study of Their Spiritual Relationship and Its Effect on Swinburne's Moral and Poetic Development.* London: Macmillan & Co., 1918, 304 p.
  Presents Landor as "the great spiritual force" who molded Swinburne's artistic ideals and political thought. Henderson bases his study on Swinburne's expressions of admiration for Landor and examines the works of both authors to show their similarities.

Herford, C. H. "The Shelley Group." In his *The Age of Wordsworth,* pp. 216-84. 1897. Reprint. London: G. Bell & Sons, 1930.
  Surveys Landor's works. Herford considers Landor the greatest prose writer of his age, and after Wordsworth, Coleridge, Byron, Shelley, and Keats, the greatest poet.

Kestner, Joseph. "The Genre of Landor's *Gebir:* 'Eminences Escessively Bright'." *The Wordsworth Circle* V, No. 1 (Winter 1974): 41-9.
  Assesses *Gebir* and *Gebirus* as epyllion, or "miniaturized epics." Kestner examines the formal and thematic unity of the two poems.

Larrabee, Stephen A. "Landor and Hunt." In his *English Bards and Grecian Marbles: The Relationship between Sculpture and Poetry, Especially in the Romantic Period,* pp. 233-56. New York: Columbia University Press, 1943.
  Suggests that Greek sculptures inspired Landor's poetry.

Lee, Vernon [pseudonym of Violet Paget]. "The Rhetoric of Landor." In her *The Handling of Words and Other Studies in Literary Psychology,* pp. 157-74. London: John Lane, The Bodley Head, 1923.
  Concludes that Landor's lack of feeling in his writings counterbalances his powers of technique. Lee states that Landor's classicism is "indicative not of the great talent he really possessed, but of his melancholy limitations of soul."

Linton, E. Lynn. "Reminiscences of Walter Savage Landor." *Fraser's Magazine* II, No. VII (July 1870): 113-20.
  Includes reminiscences of Landor's years in Bath.

Megally, Shafik H. "Landor's Dramatic Dialogues." *Cairo Studies in English* (1966): 167-80.
  Focuses on the dramatic elements and lyric qualities of the *Imaginary Conversations.*

Mercier, Vivian. "The Future of Landor Criticism." In *Some British Romantics: A Collection of Essays,* pp. 43-85. Edited by James V. Logan, John E. Jordan, and Northrop Frye. Ohio State University Press, 1966.
  Suggests topics for future studies on Landor.

Minchin, H. C., ed. *Walter Savage Landor: Last Days, Letters, and Conversations,* by Walter Savage Landor. London: Methuen & Co., 1934, 174 p.
  Recounts the last five years of Landor's life using his letters to Browning as a primary source. Later scholars question Minchin's accuracy in dating the letters.

Morgan, Charles. "The Independence of Landor." In his *Reflections in a Mirror, second series,* pp. 122-30. London: Macmillan & Co., 1946.
  Extols Landor's independent, courageous character and his unique literary expression.

Pinsky, Robert. *Landor's Poetry.* Chicago: University of Chicago Press, 1968, 179 p.
  Examines the genres and themes Landor employed in his poetry, relating his work to that of the modern poet critics Pound and Davie.

Pound, Ezra. *A B C of Reading.* New Directions Paperbook No. 89. New York: James Laughlin, 1960.
  A "text book" guide to literature, with scattered references to Landor. Pound cites him in a list of authors through whom the history of English poetry may be traced.

Quillinan, E. "Imaginary Conversation, between Mr Walter Savage Landor and the Editor of *Blackwood's Magazine.*" *Blackwood's Edinburgh Magazine* LIII, No. CCCXXX (April 1843): 518-36.
  A criticism of Landor's *Imaginary Conversations* and political opinions in the form of an imaginary conversation.

Richards, I. A. "Fifteen Lines from Landor." *The Criterion* XII, No. XLVIII (April 1933): 355-70.
  Uses a passage from *Gebir* in studying the process of understanding poetry.

Ruoff, A. LaVonne. "Walter Savage Landor's Criticism of Horace: The Odes and Epodes." *Arion* 9, Nos. 2-3 (Summer-Autumn 1970): 189-204.

> Presents Landor's criticism of Horace. This study is based on Landor's critical essays on classical poets and on the marginalia in his copy of Horace.

Saintsbury, George. "The Revival of Rhythmical Elaboration." In his *A History of English Prose Rhythm*, pp. 293-346. 1912. Reprint. Bloomington: Indiana University Press, 1965.

> Calls Landor's prose style faultless but uninspired.

————. "The First Romantic Group (The Lake Poets, Scott, Moore, Landor, etc.)." In his *A History of English Prosody: From the Twelfth Century to the Present Day*. Vol. III, *From Blake to Mr. Swinburne*. 2nd ed., pp. 47-92. London: Macmillan & Co., 1923.

> Demonstrates Landor's mastery of polyphonic prose. Saintsbury describes Landor's "Grand Style" as magnificent yet simple, severe yet opulent, frigid yet charming.

Super, R. H. "Landor and the 'Satanic School'." *Studies in Philology* XLII, No. 4 (October 1945): 793-810.

> Details Landor's literary and personal relationships with Southey, Byron, Shelley, and Leigh Hunt.

————. "Landor's American Publications." *Modern Language Quarterly* 14, No. 4 (December 1953): 360-74.

> Traces Landor's attempts to reach American readers.

————. *Walter Savage Landor*. New York: New York University Press, 1954, 654 p.

> A comprehensive, thoroughly documented biography.

Van Thal, Herbert, ed. *Landor: A Biographical Anthology*. London: George Allen & Unwin, 1973, 392 p.

> Includes an outline of Landor's life with selections from his *Imaginary Conversations* and other works.

Williams, Stanley T. "The Story of Gebir." *PMLA* XXXVI, No. 3 (September 1921): 615-31.

> Explores the origins of the obscure history of Gebir, on which Landor based his poem.

The Wordsworth Circle, Special Issue: Walter Savage Landor VII, No. 1 (Winter 1976): 3-57.

> Contains essays on Landor by such critics as Proudfit, Pinsky, Joukovsky, Mariani, Super, and Ruoff.

Yeats, W. B. *A Vision*. Rev. ed. New York: Macmillan Co., 1956.

> Contains scattered references to Landor.

Susanna (Strickland) Moodie

1803-1885

(Born Susanna Strickland) English-Canadian sketch and short story writer, poet, novelist, and author of children's books.

Regarded by many critics as one of the finest nineteenth-century Canadian immigrant writers, Moodie is best known for her *Roughing It in the Bush; or, Life in Canada* and *Life in the Clearings versus the Bush.* These collections of autobiographical sketches and poetry are noted for their humor, vivid descriptions of scenery, and realistic portrayal of life on the Canadian frontier. *Roughing It in the Bush* and *Life in the Clearings* are not well known, yet they have, since the late 1950s, enjoyed a resurgence of critical interest, with many commentators focusing on their value as both artistic and historical works. Although Moodie also published numerous short stories and novels as well as other poems and sketches throughout her career, these largely sentimental and didactic works have attracted little critical notice.

Moodie was born in Bungay, Suffolk, but moved in 1808 to Reydon Hall, a mansion near Southwold on the Suffolk coast. With ready access to the estate's well-stocked library, Moodie, her brother, and five sisters were rigorously instructed by their father in foreign languages, history, literature, and mathematics. All but one of Moodie's siblings went on to literary careers, publishing works of historical biography, fiction, poetry, and natural history. The best known of their works include Agnes and Elizabeth Strickland's *Lives of the Queens of England* and Catharine Parr Traill's *The Backwoods of Canada.*

Following the death of their father in 1818, Moodie and her sisters started contributing poems and children's stories to periodicals in order to help with the family finances. Moodie also published a juvenile work entitled *Spartacus: A Roman Story* during this period. In the late 1820s, she contributed to the journal *La belle assemblée,* publishing sketches of Suffolk life reminiscent of Mary Russell Mitford's *Our Village.* Around this time, she joined the Anti-Slavery Society and became a frequent visitor at the home of the society's secretary, the poet Thomas Pringle. During one of these visits, she met John Dunbar Moodie, whom she married in 1831. That same year she published *Enthusiasm, and Other Poems,* a collection of didactic, sentimental verses that had appeared previously in periodicals.

In 1832, after the birth of the first of their six children, the Moodies left England because of financial difficulties and immigrated to Canada. Although she had heard positive reports about the opportunities in Canada and considered the move an economic necessity, Moodie was devastated by the prospect of leaving her native land. The Moodies' life in Canada was marked by financial hardship, due in part to several failed attempts at farming, and they repeatedly relocated in hopes of improving their circumstances. The family first purchased a cleared farm in Hamilton Township, in what is now Ontario. Here Moodie encountered "Yankee" neighbors whose brash familiarity frustrated her sense of class propriety and who later became the subject of many sketches in *Roughing It in the Bush.* In 1834, the Moodies moved to the backwoods settlement of Duoro, near Peterborough, where Moodie's sister Catharine

and her brother, Samuel, lived. After another unsuccessful attempt at farming, Moodie's husband accepted a position as sheriff of Victoria District and in 1840 the family relocated to Belleville.

During her years in the backwoods Moodie published several poems and sketches in such periodicals as the *Canadian Literary Magazine,* the *New York Albion,* and the Montreal-based journal the *Literary Garland,* but it was not until after the family settled in Belleville that she devoted herself fully to writing. She then became one of the leading contributors to the *Garland,* writing new sketches and poems as well as expanding previously written pieces into novels for serialization. Among these writings published in the *Garland* were the six Canadian sketches later included in *Roughing It in the Bush.* During 1847 and 1848, Moodie and her husband also edited and wrote most of the material for the *Victoria Magazine,* a journal intended to educate Canada's growing working class.

In 1852, Moodie signed a lucrative contract with the London publisher Richard Bentley. Within three years, Bentley published *Roughing It in the Bush, Life in the Clearings,* and the autobiographical novel *Flora Lyndsay,* Moodie's three works describing her immigration and settlement in Canada. During this time he also published three of her other novels, including *Mark Hurdlestone,* and a collection of short stories entitled

Matrimonial Speculations, all of which are set in England. After this successful period, Moodie quit writing for more than a decade for reasons that are unknown. When in the 1860s she again submitted work to Bentley's firm, it was deemed inferior to her earlier writings; the only piece accepted was *The World before Them,* a novel published in 1868. She continued to write, but few of her subsequent pieces were published. Moodie's last years were marked by illness and poverty, and she died in Toronto in 1885.

Moodie's three works dealing with immigration are considered her best. *Roughing It in the Bush,* the first of the three, was intended to discourage unsuited members of the English middle class from immigrating and thus dwells on such negative aspects of frontier life as illness, danger, and death. Yet this work also contains many humorous sketches of the people, customs, and daily life of the Upper-Canadian backwoods, as well as passages and poems that reflect Moodie's romantic response to nature. Unlike *Roughing It in the Bush,* which Moodie wrote of her own accord, *Life in the Clearings* was written after Bentley's request for an account of life in the developing Canadian towns. Using a trip to Niagara Falls as its focal point, the work consists of sketches of town life and observations on colonial society. Moodie's autobiographical novel *Flora Lyndsay* deals with a young couple's decision to immigrate to Canada and includes a novel-within-a-novel ostensibly written by Flora en route to Canada. Considered the weakest of Moodie's three major works, *Flora Lyndsay* has inspired little commentary.

Until the mid-twentieth century, *Roughing It in the Bush* was regarded primarily as an important record of immigrant life in the Canadian backwoods. Then, in 1959, Carl F. Klinck called for an examination of Moodie's artistic techniques, maintaining that *Roughing It in the Bush* and *Life in the Clearings* should be studied as literary works rather than as purely historical accounts. Although *Life in the Clearings* is still valued principally as an important document of the early cultural and social development of Canada, *Roughing It in the Bush* has since become the subject of numerous interpretations. During the 1960s, critics began to examine Moodie's treatment of herself in *Roughing It in the Bush,* with some commentators arguing that she did not give a strictly autobiographical account of her experiences as had been previously assumed, but rather, as Klinck maintained, that she "dramatized her vision of herself." Critics have also studied the work's design, theme, and intent, as well as the manner in which the intensity of Moodie's personal experience allowed her to transcend what A. Charles von Guttenberg called her "sheltered middle-class veneer and sentimentality." In addition, Moodie's role in the development of Canadian literature has continued to figure prominently in modern assessments of *Roughing It in the Bush* and *Life in the Clearings.*

Though critics have all but dismissed most of Moodie's writings, the diverse examinations of *Roughing It in the Bush* that have appeared since 1959 stand as a collective testament to the many-faceted nature of this work. Whether they consider *Roughing It in the Bush* an important record of immigrant life or, as Margot Northey argued in 1984, the expression of Moodie's "long-standing, inward-looking response to her vision of herself as artist," most critics agree that Moodie is a significant though minor figure in the developing literature of nineteenth-century Canada.

PRINCIPAL WORKS

Spartacus: A Roman Story (novel) 1822
Enthusiasm, and Other Poems (poetry) 1831

Roughing It in the Bush; or, Life in Canada (sketches and poetry) 1852
Life in the Clearings versus the Bush (sketches and poetry) 1853
Mark Hurdlestone, the Gold Worshipper (novel) 1853
Flora Lyndsay; or, Passages in an Eventful Life (novel) 1854
Matrimonial Speculations (short stories) 1854
The World before Them (novel) 1868

*This work contains a chapter and several poems by John Dunbar Moodie.

SUSANNA MOODIE (essay date 1852)

[*In the following excerpt from her introduction to the first edition of* Roughing It in the Bush, *Moodie discusses the reasons that compelled certain people to immigrate to Canada. Though speaking generally, her words reveal her personal bitterness against the land sellers and others who lured the English to Canada with tales of plenty while concealing the hardships inherent in life in the Canadian backwoods.*]

In most instances, emigration is a matter of necessity, not of choice; and this is more especially true of the emigration of persons of respectable connections, or of any station or position in the world. Few educated persons, accustomed to the refinements and luxuries of European society, ever willingly relinquish those advantages, and place themselves beyond the protective influence of the wise and revered institutions of their native land, without the pressure of some urgent cause. Emigration may, indeed, generally be regarded as an act of severe duty, performed at the expense of personal enjoyment, and accompanied by the sacrifice of those local attachments which stamp the scenes amid which our childhood grew, in imperishable characters upon the heart. Nor is it until adversity has pressed sorely upon the proud and wounded spirit of the well-educated sons and daughters of old but impoverished families, that they gird up the loins of the mind, and arm themselves with fortitude to meet and dare the heart-breaking conflict.

The ordinary motives for the emigration of such persons may be summed up in a few brief words—the emigrant's hope of bettering his condition, and of escaping from the vulgar sarcasms too often hurled at the less wealthy by the purse-proud, commonplace people of the world. But there is a higher motive still, which has its origin in that love of independence which springs up spontaneously in the breasts of the high-souled children of a glorious land. They cannot labour in a menial capacity in the country where they were born and educated to command. They can trace no difference between themselves and the more fortunate individuals of a race whose blood warms their veins, and whose name they bear. The want of wealth alone places an impassable barrier between them and the more favoured offspring of the same parent stock; and they go forth to make for themselves a new name and to find another country, to forget the past and to live in the future, to exult in the prospect of their children being free and the land of their adoption great.

The choice of the country to which they devote their talents and energies depends less upon their pecuniary means than upon the fancy of the emigrant or the popularity of a name.... In 1830, the great tide of emigration flowed westward. Canada became the great landmark for the rich in hope and poor in purse. Public newspapers and private letters teemed with the unheard-of advantages to be derived from a settlement in this highly favoured region.

Its salubrious climate, its fertile soil, commercial advantages, great water privileges, its proximity to the mother country, and last, not least, its almost total exemption from taxation—that bugbear which keeps honest John Bull in a state of constant ferment—were the theme of every tongue, and lauded beyond all praise. The general interest, once excited, was industriously kept alive by pamphlets, published by interested parties, which prominently set forth all the *good* to be derived from a settlement in the Backwoods of Canada; while they carefully concealed the toil and hardship to be endured in order to secure these advantages. They told of lands yielding forty bushels to the acre, but they said nothing of the years when these lands, with the most careful cultivation, would barely return fifteen; when rust and smut, engendered by the vicinity of damp overhanging woods, would blast the fruits of the poor emigrant's labour, and almost deprive him of bread. They talked of log houses to be raised in a single day, by the generous exertions of friends and neighbours, but they never ventured upon a picture of the disgusting scenes of riot and low debauchery exhibited during the raising, or upon a description of the dwellings when raised—dens of dirt and misery, which would, in many instances, be shamed by an English pig-sty. The necessaries of life were described as inestimably cheap; but they forgot to add that in remote bush settlements, often twenty miles from a market town, and some of them even that distance from the nearest dwelling, the necessaries of life which would be deemed indispensable to the European, could not be procured at all, or, if obtained, could only be so by sending a man and team through a blazed forest road—a process far too expensive for frequent repetition.

Oh, ye dealers in wild lands—ye speculators in the folly and credulity of your fellow-men—what a mass of misery, and of misrepresentation productive of that misery, have ye not to answer for! You had your acres to sell, and what to you were the worn-down frames and broken hearts of the infatuated purchasers? The public believed the plausible statements you made with such earnestness, and men of all grades rushed to hear your hired orators declaim upon the blessings to be obtained by the clearers of the wilderness.

Men who had been hopeless of supporting their families in comfort and independence at home, thought that they had only to come out to Canada to make their fortunes; almost even to realize the story told in the nursery, of the sheep and oxen that ran about the streets, ready roasted, and with knives and forks upon their backs. They were made to believe that if it did not actually rain gold, that precious metal could be obtained, as is now stated of California and Australia, by stooping to pick it up.

The infection became general. A Canada mania pervaded the middle ranks of British society; thousands and tens of thousands, for the space of three or four years, landed upon these shores. A large majority of the higher class were officers of the army and navy, with their families—a class perfectly unfitted by their previous habits and education for contending with the stern realities of emigrant life. The hand that has long held the sword, and been accustomed to receive implicit obedience from those under its control, is seldom adapted to wield the spade and guide the plough, or try its strength against the stubborn trees of the forest. Nor will such persons submit cheerfully to the saucy familiarity of servants, who, republicans

in spirit, think themselves as good as their employers. Too many of these brave and honourable men were easy dupes to the designing land-speculators. Not having counted the cost, but only looked upon the bright side of the picture held up to their admiring gaze, they fell easily into the snares of their artful seducers.

To prove their zeal as colonists, they were induced to purchase large tracts of wild land in remote and unfavourable situations. This, while it impoverished and often proved the ruin of the unfortunate immigrant, possessed a double advantage to the seller. He obtained an exorbitant price for the land which he actually sold, while the residence of a respectable settler upon the spot greatly enhanced the value and price of all other lands in the neighbourhood.

It is not by such instruments as those I have just mentioned, that Providence works when it would reclaim the waste places of the earth, and make them subservient to the wants and happiness of its creatures. The Great Father of the souls and bodies of men knows the arm which wholesome labour from infancy has made strong, the nerves which have become iron by patient endurance, by exposure to weather, coarse fare, and rude shelter; and He chooses such, to send forth into the forest to hew out the rough paths for the advance of civilization. These men become wealthy and prosperous, and form the bones and sinews of a great and rising country. Their labour is wealth, not exhaustion; it produces independence and content, not homesickness and despair. What the Backwoods of Canada are to the industrious and ever-to-be-honoured sons of honest poverty, and what they are to the refined and accomplished gentleman, these simple sketches will endeavour to portray. They are drawn principally from my own experience, during a sojourn of nineteen years in the colony. (pp. xv-xviii)

> *Susanna Moodie, in an introduction to her* Roughing It in the Bush; or, Forest Life in Canada, *1852. Reprint by McClelland and Stewart Limited, 1962, pp. xv-xviii.*

THE INTERNATIONAL MONTHLY MAGAZINE (essay date 1852)

[*The following excerpt is from a positive review of* Roughing It in the Bush.]

If there be one of life's affairs in which woman has a peculiar right to have her wishes considered and her veto respected, it is that of emigration. For, in the arduous task of establishing a new home in a half-settled country, let man do what he will to alleviate, on her fall the burthen and heat of the day. Hers are the menial toils, the frequent anxieties, the lingering homesickness, the craving after dear friends' faces and a beloved native land. Hers, too, the self-imposed duty and unselfish effort to hide regret under cheerful smiles, when the weary brother or husband returns at evening from toil in field and forest. Blessed and beautiful are the smiles of the sad-hearted, worn to wile away another's cares!

Love in a cottage has long been jeered at, and depicted as flying out of the window. It seems miraculous to behold [in Mrs. Moodie's *Roughing It in the Bush*] the capricious little deity steadfastly braving, for many a long year, the chilly atmosphere of a log-hut in an American forest. In the year 1832, Mrs. Moodie . . . accompanied her husband, a half-pay subaltern, to the backwoods of Canada. Many were her misgivings, and they did not prove unfounded. Long and cruel was the probation she underwent, before finding comparative

Reydon Hall, where the author lived as a young girl. Photograph by Elizabeth Hopkins.

comfort and prosperity in the rugged land where at first she found so much to embitter her existence. Nobly did she bear up under countless difficulties and sufferings, supported by an energy rare in woman, and by her devoted attachment to the husband of her choice. For some years her troubles were not occasional, but continual and increasing. (p. 470)

[The Moodies' first winter in the backwoods] was a winter of painful instruction for the inexperienced young woman, and her not very prudent husband. We might fill columns with a bare list of their vexations and disasters. Amongst the former, not the least arose from the borrowing propensities of their neighbors. They had 'located' in a bad neighborhood, in the vicinity of a number of low Yankee squatters, "ignorant as savages, without their courtesy and kindness." These people walked unceremoniously at all hours into their wretched dwelling, to criticise their proceedings, make impertinent remarks, and to borrow—or rather to beg or steal, for what they borrowed they rarely returned. The most extraordinary loans were daily solicited or demanded; and Mrs. Moodie, strange and timid in her new home, and amongst these semi-barbarians—her husband, too, being much away at the farm—for some time dared not refuse to acquiesce in their impudent extortions. (p. 471)

[The anecdotes in *Roughing It in the Bush* about these neighbors] exhibit, more vividly than volumes of description, the sort of savages amongst whom poor Mrs. Moodie's lot was cast. They had all the worst qualities of Yankee and Indian—the good ones of neither. They had neither manners, heart, nor honesty. The basest selfishness, cunning, and malignity were their prominent characteristics. (p. 472)

Mrs. Moodie's work, unaffectedly and naturally written, though a little coarse, will delight ladies, please men, and even amuse

children. . . . The book is one of great originality and interest. (p. 474)

"Life in Canada," in The International Monthly Magazine, *Vol. V, No. 4, April 1, 1852, pp. 470-74.*

SUSANNA MOODIE   (essay date 1852)

[*This excerpt is from Moodie's 1852 introduction to* Life in the Clearings. *While she defends her attempt in* Roughing It in the Bush *to discourage unsuited British immigrants from settling in rural Canada, Moodie also praises the opportunities available in the colonial settlements.*]

In our work of *Roughing It in the Bush,* I endeavoured to draw a picture of Canadian life, as I found it twenty years ago, in the Backwoods. My motive in giving such a melancholy narrative to the British public was prompted by the hope of deterring well-educated people, about to settle in this colony, from entering upon a life for which they were totally unfitted by their previous pursuits and habits.

To persons unaccustomed to hard labour, and used to the comforts and luxuries deemed indispensable to those moving in the middle classes at home, a settlement in the bush can offer few advantages. It has proved the ruin of hundreds and thousands who have ventured their all in this hazardous experiment; nor can I recollect a single family of the higher class, that have come under my own personal knowledge, that ever realized an independence, or bettered their condition, by taking up wild lands in remote localities; while volumes might be filled with failures, even more disastrous than our own, to prove the truth of my former statements.

But while I have endeavoured to point out the error of gentlemen bringing delicate women and helpless children to toil in the woods, and by so doing excluding them from all social intercourse with persons in their own rank, and depriving the younger branches of the family of the advantages of education, which, in the vicinity of towns and villages, can be enjoyed by the children of the poorest emigrant, I have never said anything against the REAL benefits to be derived from a judicious choice of settlement in this great and rising country.

God forbid that any representations of mine should deter one of my countrymen from making this noble and prosperous colony his future home. But let him leave to the hardy labourer the place assigned to him by Providence, nor undertake, upon limited means, the task of pioneer in the great wilderness. Men of independent fortune can live anywhere. If such prefer a life in the woods, to the woods let them go; but they will soon find out that they could have employed the means in their power in a far more profitable manner than in chopping down trees in the bush.

There are a thousand more advantageous ways in which a man of property may invest his capital than by burying himself and his family in the woods. There never was a period in the history of the colony that offered greater inducements to men of moderate means to emigrate to Canada than the present. (pp. xxix-xxx)

Why gentlemen from Britain should obstinately crowd to the Backwoods, and prefer the coarse, hard life of an axeman to that of a respectable landed proprietor in a civilized part of the country, has always been to me a matter of surprise; for a farm under cultivation can always be purchased for less money than must necessarily be expended upon clearing and raising buildings upon a wild lot. (p. xxx)

At the period when the greatest portion of *Roughing it in the Bush* was written, I was totally ignorant of life in Canada, as it existed in the towns and villages. Thirteen years' residence in one of the most thriving districts in the Upper Province has given me many opportunities of becoming better acquainted with the manners and habits of her busy, bustling population than it was possible for me ever to obtain in the green prison of the woods.

Since my residence in a settled part of the country, I have enjoyed as much domestic peace and happiness as ever falls to the lot of poor humanity. Canada has become almost as dear to me as my native land; and the home-sickness that constantly preyed upon me in the Backwoods has long ago yielded to the deepest and most heartfelt interest in the rapidly increasing prosperity and greatness of the country of my adoption—the great foster-mother of that portion of the human family whose fatherland, however dear to them, is unable to supply them with bread.

To the honest sons of labour Canada is, indeed, an El Dorado—a land flowing with milk and honey; for they soon obtain that independence which the poor gentleman struggles in vain to realize by his own labour in the woods.

The conventional prejudices that shackle the movements of members of the higher classes in Britain are scarcely recognised in Canada; and a man is at liberty to choose the most profitable manner of acquiring wealth, without the fear of ridicule and the loss of caste. (pp. xxxi-xxxii)

I have been repeatedly asked, since the publication of *Roughing it in the Bush,* to give an account of the present state of society in the colony, and to point out its increasing prosperity and

commercial advantages; but statistics are not my forte, nor do I feel myself qualified for such an arduous and important task. My knowledge of the colony is too limited to enable me to write a comprehensive work on a subject of vital consequence, which might involve the happiness of others. But what I do know I will endeavour to sketch with a light pencil; and if I cannot convey much useful information, I will try to amuse the reader; and by a mixture of prose and poetry compile a small volume which may help to while away an idle hour, or fill up the blanks of a wet day. (p. xxxiii)

> *Susanna Moodie, in an introduction to her* Life in the Clearings, *edited by Robert L. McDougall, Macmillan of Canada, 1959, pp. xxix-xxxiii.*

THE NEW QUARTERLY REVIEW   (essay date 1853)

[*The following excerpt is from a negative review of* Mark Hurdlestone, the Gold Worshipper.]

We cannot highly congratulate the authoress of *Mark Hurdlestone* upon her success in the present instance. The tale is somewhat feeble, the characters are dull and commonplace, and the whole affair lacks spirit, incident, and life.

The preface, however, is interesting . . . [and] conveys an useful moral. . . . (p. 251)

The reader will perceive from this preface under what untoward circumstances the writer laboured when she first endeavoured to derive emolument from her pen. Her productions must therefore be perused with a more lenient eye than if they had emanated from one whose vocation is authorship. For that reason, therefore, we forbear to criticise, as we should, had we under review, the work of a professed novelist. (p. 252)

> *A review of "Mark Hurdlestone, the Gold Worshipper," in* The New Quarterly Review, *Vol. II, No. VI, 1853, pp. 251-52.*

ARCHIBALD MacMURCHY   (essay date 1906)

[*MacMurchy favorably reviews Moodie's novels about immigration and life in Canada.*]

In *Flora Lyndsay* and *Roughing It in the Bush* the authoress relates the details about leaving one's native land, the uncertainties in regard to a new country, the sorrows of leave-taking, the yearning for the homeland and all it contains. The writer does not omit to tell of the long voyage across the Atlantic, with its inconveniences, mishaps, and sufferings; the journey into the new, strange land, so extensive and so rude in comparison to the land left behind, yet, with all its disadvantages, recognized to be the land of promise for every one seeking a home and independence.

In *Life in the Clearings versus the Bush,* Mrs. Moodie gives historic sketches of cities and towns in Canada West, as they appeared in 1852. Very interesting she makes these sketches, combining with them many anecdotes and tales about residents and travellers. Let no reader miss her description of the Falls of Niagara. There is fiction in these books (perhaps more correct to say exaggeration), but the future historian of Canada, when he comes, will find in these volumes fit material ready for the writing of Canadian history.

Her work affords a good example of the style of a worthy class of fiction-writers of the early nineteenth century, with its large interest in human life, its marriages, family connections, births, and deaths, its stories of ghosts, its odd people, incredible feats of strength and endurance, the sweet home life, simple and humane. The reader of Mrs. Moodie's work receives the impression that she was of an amiable, sensible, refined, religious character. She has the additional honor of being one of the early pioneers of Canadian literature. (pp. 22-3)

> *Archibald MacMurchy, "Mrs. Susanna Moodie," in his* Handbook of Canadian Literature (English), *William Briggs, 1906, pp. 21-4.*

RAY PALMER BAKER   (essay date 1920)

[In his survey of English-Canadian literature, Baker briefly discusses the nationalistic sentiments and attitudes toward nature expressed by Moodie in her poetry and Roughing It in the Bush.*]*

[Susanna Moodie's] hopes and disappointments . . . are graphically described in her *Roughing It in the Bush; or Life in Canada* . . . , which has been equally popular in Great Britain, the United States, and Canada. Its value lies in the fact that her experiences were those of hundreds of other delicately reared gentlewomen who courageously obeyed the call of duty. From Quebec and Montreal, with their plague-infected streets, she takes her readers into the taverns of the "Front," as the counties on the Lakes were then designated, and into the offices of the despicable speculators who preyed on the ignorant immigrants. Were it not for her powers of characterization, her narrative would be as tedious as many that I have discarded. It is her ability to depict the flotsam of a raw community, the self-importance of the newly liberated serf, the vanity of the impecunious matron who boasts of her high connections at "Home," that gives her preëminence among the writers of memoirs.

Quite as fascinating as her references to the people whom she meets is the unconscious revelation of personality in her dependence on the conventional formulae of an English gentlewoman; in her surprise that the titles of "Sir" and "Madam" are "very rarely applied by inferiors," and in her little vanity of authorship. Yet, in spite of the narrowness of her sex and of her age, she emerges as a bright heroic spirit that anxiety and suffering could neither darken nor intimidate.

In her pages it is possible to trace her homesickness for the English countryside, her repugnance at her lot in the Canadian wilds, and her final contentment with her adopted home. . . . Howe, with his memorable phrases lit by the clear white flame of his imagination never uttered a higher prophecy of future greatness than this quiet, reserved Englishwoman of the Trent Valley. "You feel at every step," she writes, "that Canada must become a great nation." Its people "possess capabilities and talents which . . . will render them second to no people in the world."

Though Mrs. Moodie came to understand, and to appreciate, her neighbors, she never closed her eyes to their imperfections. Against the harshness and vulgarity of the satiric tradition she never ceased to battle. As one of the leaders in the romantic impulse, which has done much to widen the horizon of the Canadian people, she is worthy of remembrance. From childhood she had been peculiarly susceptible to natural beauty. Coming down the St. Lawrence, she tells her readers in *Roughing It,* she broke into tears at the sight of Quebec. "Next to the love of God," she asseverates, "the love of Nature may be regarded as the purest and holiest of the human heart."

Though not entirely above the aristocratic pastime of ridiculing the United States, she devoted her energies to the nobler task of arousing her neighbors to the glories of their environment. Into their narrow, unimaginative minds, warped by prejudice, she brought new images and new delights. (pp. 118-20)

[Moodie's other novels] are mere echoes of *Roughing It* on which her reputation rests. This, her most vital work, is far from perfect. The intermediate chapter, "The Land Jobber," by her husband, who also wrote a volume of reminiscences, destroys what little continuity the narrative possesses. The descriptions of the Indians, who appealed to her sense of the picturesque, lack proportion. Worst of all, the moral that no gentleman ever succeeds in the bush detracts from the matter-of-fact transcription which gives the memoir its charm. The fact that Mrs. Moodie had a "negative mind"—to borrow a phrase from the *Athenaeum*—increases her skill at portraiture. That she was willing, in general, to tell what she saw, without offering suggestions for improvement, heightens the power of her sketches. The naturalness of her manner at once invites confidence. The easy, limpid, almost slipshod style, with no pretense of force, is peculiarly ingratiating. (pp. 120-21)

In [the *Literary Garland*] and in the *Victoria Magazine,* afterwards conducted by Mrs. Moodie and her husband, most of her poems were given to the public. Though few of her lyrics were issued in book form, they speedily sang their way from periodicals and newspapers into the homes of Ontario and Quebec. Some like the **"Snow Song"** were widely popular in the United States. Although many of these ditties are entirely worthless, they brought a touch of cheer into many an unlovely settlement, and directed the attention of Canadian writers to Canadian subjects. However pernicious has become the theory that a national literature must be provincial in material, there is no gainsaying the fact that, when first promulgated by the *Literary Garland,* it stimulated independent effort and counteracted, in a small way, the influence of Byron, whose cynicism found a ready echo on this side of the Atlantic. Though it is undoubtedly true that Mrs. Moodie is indebted to the English Romanticists, it is also true that in treatment as well as in subject matter she occasionally attains to something approaching independence. Verses like **"The Canadian Herd Boy"** show how gracefully she can invest the dull routine of the backwoods with a poetic coloring. . . . (pp. 121-22)

I have referred to Mrs. Moodie's poetry because it cannot be separated from her prose: in most of her books they go hand in hand. Together they show the growing sense of national unity and the emergence of a new attitude towards Nature and the ordinary concerns of life. (p. 122)

> *Ray Palmer Baker, "Memoirs," in his* A History of English-Canadian Literature to the Confederation: Its Relation to the Literature of Great Britain and the United States, *Cambridge, Mass.: Harvard University Press, 1920, pp. 117-24.*

V. B. RHODENIZER   (essay date 1930)

[Rhodenizer praises Moodie's descriptions of the life of the early English settlers in Canada.]

Both Mrs. Moodie's prose and her verse show that she was influenced by the attitude of the English romanticists toward nature and the common life. At first, it is true, the contrast between the new and the old is to her a source of pain, but her writings reveal the gradual growth of a sympathetic attitude toward Canadian scenes and life. This attitude, combined with skill in description and in characterization of pioneer types, produced not only the best transcript we have of the conditions under which the early English settlers lived, but also a clear record of the emotional change that transformed cultured English men and women, homesick for their mother land, into loyal citizens with a strong sense of nationality and unbounded faith in the future of Canada. In *Roughing It in the Bush,* her best work, there are vivid descriptions of the journey up the St. Lawrence, of the environment of their new home, and of various kinds of new neighbours, and vivid narratives of adventures with fire, storms, and wild beasts. (p. 61)

> *V. B. Rhodenizer, "Travel, Exploration, and Memoirs," in his* A Handbook of Canadian Literature, *Graphic Publishers Limited, 1930, pp. 55-62.*

EDWARD A. McCOURT (essay date 1945)

[*McCourt maintains that* Roughing It in the Bush *provides "the best picture of life in an early Canadian backwoods settlement" in Canadian literature.*]

Since history is written mostly by men, it is inevitable that the building of Canada should be represented in our textbooks as a man's job. . . . It is the more unfortunate that our pioneer women were themselves largely inarticulate, being too much occupied with the business of looking after their husbands and rearing their numerous progeny to think of recording their struggles for posterity. But there is one notable exception. In the spare time which making a home in the wilderness and bringing up five children allowed her, Mrs. Susanna Moodie wrote a series of sketches describing the day-to-day existence which she led in the backwoods of Ontario between the years 1832 and 1840. These sketches, first published in *The Literary Garland* and later expanded into a volume of reminiscences under the title of *Roughing It in the Bush,* provide the best picture of life in an early Canadian backwoods settlement which our literature affords. (p. 77)

Apart from serving as an admirable record of life in a backwoods community, *Roughing It in the Bush* is worth reading as an antidote to the highly-coloured, sentimental accounts of pioneer life which constitute much of our romantic fiction. (p. 83)

Almost without emotion, with what in a more sophisticated writer might be regarded as deviceful understatement, [Mrs. Moodie] relates how for months at a time the family subsisted on a diet of bread, frozen potatoes, an occasional piece of bear meat, and coffee made from the roots of the ubiquitous dandelion. (p. 84)

But in spite of extravagant claims that have been made for it by over-zealous champions of our native literature, *Roughing It* is not a classic, even in the loosest sense of the term. It is an unpretentious, highly literate account of an heroic if not always intelligent struggle against a hostile environment. Such a struggle always possesses a strong element of interest in itself; and Mrs. Moodie's simple, unadorned style is well suited to her subject-matter. Only occasionally, as when she writes of the homeland, does she appropriate the manner and sentiments of her female contemporaries. *Roughing It* is for the most part a plain tale plainly told.

But the chief charm of the book derives from its characterizations. In sketching the individuals whom she encountered dur-

ing her years in the bush, Mrs. Moodie shows talent of a high order. (pp. 87-8)

Mrs. Moodie suffered much during her years in the bush, but, unlike many of her compatriots, she was sustained by a never-flagging interest in the odd characters whom she encountered, and by a love of the Canadian scene which grew stronger with the passing years. Thus, in the preface to the 1871 edition of *Roughing It,* Mrs. Moodie, then in her sixty-third year, writes of Canada not as the disciple of Mrs. Hemans pining for her childhood home on the banks of the Waveney, but as the loyal and enthusiastic citizen of a country in which she has found happiness and peace. . . . (pp. 88-9)

[She] writes, in words which are a high prophecy of the future greatness of her adopted country: "You feel at every step that Canada must become a great nation." Its people "possess capabilities and talents which will render them second to no people in the world". (p. 89)

> *Edward A. McCourt, "Roughing It with the Moodies," in* Queen's Quarterly, *Vol. LII, No. 1, Spring, 1945, pp. 77-89.*

R. E. RASHLEY (essay date 1958)

[*Rashley argues that* Roughing It in the Bush *is representative of nineteenth-century Canadian immigrants' transition from initial dislike of, to eventual affection and loyalty toward, their new country.*]

With most of the [Canadian] immigrants, the gradual change from immigrant to settler which occurred as the homeland memories faded and the urgent necessity of the moment forced a coming to grips at least with the new physical world entailed two simple and necessary adjustments. One of these reflects the change from foreigner to settler which shows itself in the many early volumes as an emotional adjustment to the new world. Most of those who disliked the country in their early experiences eventually arrived at affection for it and finally developed strong local loyalties. This is an elementary adjustment which is well represented by Mrs. Susannah Moodie. (p. 17)

Mrs. Moodie's life in the Ontario backwoods was difficult in proportion to the strength of her cultural resources. Highly class conscious, educated, accustomed to the separation of military castes, and in every way the epitome of qualities unvalued in pioneer life, she found that the culture which she represented invited critical response wherever she went. (p. 18)

A good deal of Mrs. Moodie's difficulty was caused by her failure to realize, until it was forced upon her, the fact that this culture was alien and hostile to the life to which she was committed. Ignorant of life outside of her sphere, she encountered better success with the Indians than with some of her Loyalist neighbours because she was aware of a difference in their lives and made allowance for it. Her book [*Roughing It in the Bush*] reflects no bitterness, however; her adversities are recorded with good humour, and the sensibilities which made pioneer life harsh made its good things so much the better. Her distaste for the life is perhaps best stated in her quiet survey when the opportunity of change presents itself:

> For seven long years I had lived out of the world
> entirely; my person had been rendered coarse
> by hard work and exposure to the weather. I
> looked double the age I really was, and my hair

was already thickly sprinkled with grey. I clung to my solitude. I did not like to be dragged from it to mingle in gay scenes, in a busy town, and with gaily dressed people. I was no longer fit for the world; I had lost all relish for the pursuits and pleasures which are so essential to its votaries; I was contented to live and die in obscurity.

Mrs. Moodie's presentation of the picture is false to the extent that it does not give us the effects of her way of life upon the other, the pioneer picture which *includes* her type, nor tell us of the continued effort which she made through local magazines, to give substance to an indigenous literature. *Roughing It in the Bush* is a prose record of her experience, but it contains fifty-two poems. . . . Early in her narrative she writes:

In the depths of dark forests my soul droops her wings;
In tall boughs above me no merry bird sings.
The sigh of the wild winds—rush of the Floods—
Is the only sad music that wakens the moods.

Toward the end, on leaving the backwoods for the settlements, she finds that these songless boughs have won their way into her affections and she writes an "Adieu to the Woods":

Adieu! adieu!—when grieving lips refuse
 The bitter pangs of parting to declare;
And the full bosom feels that it must lose
 Friends who were wont its inmost thoughts to share.

"Now," as she says, "when not only reconciled to Canada, but loving it, and feeling a deep interest in its present welfare, and the fair prospect of its future greatness, I often look back and laugh at the feelings with which I then regarded this noble country." It is this progression from dislike to love of the country which allows Mrs. Moodie to speak for a type of reaction. It is elementary enough and inevitable in the second generation if not in the first, but worth recording as a necessary step from the old world to the new. (pp. 18-19)

The poems of Mrs. Moodie . . . are successful neither as specimens of the old world art nor as expressions, however rough, of the new world experience, but their techniques are a partial bridging of the gap. They do use the native material in part, and, in doing so, make possible a further use of the material in a mode suited to the use. The best that could be said of them is that they allow the techniques of English versification to continue so that native poetry, when it does appear, is less gauche than it might otherwise have been. (p. 21)

R. E. Rashley, "Immigrant Poetry, Its Nature and Significance," in his Poetry in Canada: The First Three Steps, *The Ryerson Press, 1958, pp. 1-22.*

ROBERT L. McDOUGALL (essay date 1959)

[*In this excerpt from his introduction to the 1959 edition of* Life in the Clearings, *McDougall emphasizes the importance of this work as a record of the early cultural and social development of Canada.*]

As its title suggests, with its hint of axe and spade, *Roughing It in the Bush* is a book about pioneering in the common sense of the term. Substantially, it is a first-hand account of an attempt made by a family of English emigrants to establish a homestead on the frontiers of Upper Canada in the early part of the nineteenth century, an undertaking which obviously meant for the author a trying physical and spiritual experience. . . .

The whole is a narrative which, though not strictly chronological, has all the immediacy of a pioneering journal. Its principal component is the sure-fire drama of man's primitive struggle against drought, storm, pestilence, fire and sickness.

Life in the Clearings, on the other hand, though written by a pioneer in pioneering times, has little about it that suggests, either in subject matter or manner of treatment, the elemental conflicts of settlement. Indeed one's first thought, and a quite natural one, is that this is a very civilized book. Mrs. Moodie was of course a very civilized person both by birth and upbringing, and practically everything she wrote bore the marks of a tradition of refinement in writing which she inherited from the eighteenth century. The vein was that of the "elegant trifle", the pointedly amateur piece of writing which was nevertheless designed to exhibit all the best graces of literary and social convention. Her novels show this kind of sophistication to a marked degree; and *Roughing It in the Bush* shows it too, for that matter, though fortunately in this case the immediacy of the material puts a ceiling on the author's usual elevation of style. In the case of *Life in the Clearings,* however, circumstances combined to encourage a formal literary manner.

The book is both less autobiographical and more self-conscious than its forerunner. Following the publication of *Roughing It in the Bush* serially in the *Literary Garland* in 1847, Mrs. Moodie was asked, as she tells us, "to give an account of the present state of society in the colony. . . ." She complied—though not, she is careful to point out, in the role of statistician or official guide to immigrants. And in taking up the task she looked, not back to her six years solitary in "the green prison of the woods", but around her at the relatively complex society which had grown up along the "front" of the St. Lawrence River and Lake Ontario in the course of two or three decades of settlement and of which she herself had by this time been a member for many years. To her private life and the life of her family, always to be dealt with reticently and now no longer particularly dramatic or made up of experiences different from those of a score of her neighbours, she gives little attention. She sketches men and women, for she liked to do this and could do it well; but since the people she was now concerned with were members of close-knit communities, she does not create the frank and vigorous character studies which are a strong point of *Roughing It in the Bush.* Especially she writes about Orange Societies, religious sects, Mechanics' Institutes, and fire-fighting co-operatives—about social rather than solitary man. (pp. vii-ix)

Mrs. Moodie herself was by this time widely known as "the woman that writes", and a more select group recognized her as a prominent contributor of fiction and poetry to the *Literary Garland.* She was Canada's challenge to Mrs. Lydia Howard Sigourney—a hollow compliment to pay her today, but one of some substance to an earlier public.

And so, naturally enough, when Mrs. Moodie wrote *Life in the Clearings* she tried to do what was expected of her: that is, write a civilized book about society. Though in a sense she was to take her readers on a journey, this was to be no pioneering journey but a tourist trip to Niagara Falls undertaken by a cultured and romantically languid author in search of better health; and its chief purpose was to be to provide a peg on which to hang anecdotes, mostly anonymous and second-hand (which was a good way of playing safe with reputations), and a series of observations about society. What remains to be said here is that the book which was the outgrowth of all these conditions can hardly be expected to reproduce the confessional strength of *Roughing It in the Bush,* any more than it can be expected to reproduce the dramatic appeal of the earlier narrative of primitive struggle. And of course it does not.

What are the compensations? Mrs. Moodie is a good reporter and she has a good subject. Remembering one of the lessons of romanticism which she forgot too often in writing her novels, she keeps her eye (and ours) upon the object. The reader will find this eye an excellent one for detail, and he will experience the pleasure that comes from exact description when Mrs. Moodie distinguishes between the colours of the waters of the St. Lawrence, the Ottawa, and the Otonabee. He will find it also an eye sensitive to pictorial effect, and he will watch with interest the dignified progress of that lone cow down the stream of the flooded Moira. Beyond this area of intellectual free-wheeling there is good value again. Honouring the terms of her assignment, Mrs. Moodie inspects with a lively curiosity the social scene—the behaviour and dress of young ladies at a ball, the fare at a picnic, the programme of a travelling circus, the ritual at a village funeral, the proceedings at a religious camp-meeting, and the life of inmates in prison and asylum of the time. It is an impressive record which the student of institutions and ways of life in early Ontario will do well to consult. And, to return to less utilitarian values, one senses always that what permeates the record is the important literary virtue of an engaging personality. The reader is hard to please who does not like Mrs. Moodie's bird-like alertness, her good sense, her tolerance, her genial and gracious manner. If he expects pretentiousness to follow from the formal literary style, he will also be gratified to discover that this writer is "but a humly body after all", and no blue-stocking.

These qualities are perhaps in themselves a sufficient recommendation to reading enjoyment. Should one go on to speak of Mrs. Moodie's handling of dialogue, of her rendering of the sensational story of Grace Marks, and of other things she does well in the present text? I think not, for there is a danger of creating the impression that we are dealing with a first-rate writer, and this is far from being the case. On the other hand, there is a good deal more to be said about *Life in the Clearings* if we come at the book from another point of view. The fact is that this is a valuable document for special reasons which have little to do with literary skills and the sharpness of a photographic eye.

An account of how an Eskimo kills seals and keeps himself warm in winter is likely to make good reading; but it will make better reading if it tells us something also about the Eskimo's concepts of time and how they compare with our own. Similarly, Mrs. Moodie has a good story to tell about pioneering it in the bush, and another good one which sketches the features of everyday life known to early Canadian settlers. But she offers still another story, which is in a way the best of the lot. This is a story whose characters are ideas and values, and it shows us how and on what terms Canadian society was being built in the days when the Moodies lived on West Bridge Street in Belleville. Considering the principles of conduct and social organization which seem to her characteristic of the society growing up around her, Mrs. Moodie makes it plain in *Life in the Clearings* that these are not exactly the principles she or others had known in England. She notes the distinguishing marks of the new society, and to some extent accounts for them. Such a record, sifted from much else that is in the book, is an early chapter in the long account of our cultural evolution. And I believe it is a chapter we can read profitably in the present crucial stage of our national development; for by re-minding us of the nature of our cultural origins and of the kind of influences which from the beginning have been at work to modify our inheritance it can help us to form a correct notion of our national identity. Here is an aspect of Mrs. Moodie's work which can be described as important without reservation. (pp. ix-xi)

Since I shall wish to argue in a moment that the Mrs. Moodie of *Life in the Clearings* is to a considerable extent removed in her social outlook from the . . . dominant conservatism [of the Canadian pioneers], it is perhaps advisable to emphasize here her initial and essential conformity to the pattern. There is in fact ample evidence in the present text to make clear this conformity, despite the colouring of that evidence by the presence of social values of a different or at least modified sort. But if we turn back to the period covered by *Roughing It in the Bush* and beyond, the clues are unmistakable. . . . Everything about [Mrs. Moodie] bespoke respectability, refinement, and a deep sense of propriety in all matters relating to morality and the smooth functioning of the social order to which she was accustomed. Her accounts of her early experiences in the colony, as recorded in *Roughing It in the Bush,* reveal in particular her acute consciousness of class distinctions and her broadly conservative temper of mind. (p. xiv)

It was not in the nature of things . . . that the immigrants settling on the new frontiers should produce in the place they had come to an exact duplicate of the society they had left behind. To some extent, in an instinctive bid for survival in the face of their removal to a new environment, they fought to conserve the values they had brought with them. But the new environment was to prove an irresistible modifier—at least, up to a point. Specifically, ideals of social democracy were abroad in this new environment, and the immigrant soon felt the force they exerted. Thus from an early date an essentially radical force was brought to bear against the essentially conservative cast of British colonial society.

The first source of this radical influence was what may be called the frontier situation. American historians, particularly Parrington and Turner, have made much of the theory that the frontiers are almost by definition the spawning-grounds of social democracy. Their argument, which is sound for at least a limited period or part of American history, has been that the expansion of settlement into new territory is a process which constantly attracts and rewards those who have least patience with authority, and which is therefore an enemy of traditional class distinctions. . . . [The] frontier theory obviously does not fit the Canadian case as snugly as it does the American. Nevertheless, the potential of radicalism inherent in the frontier situation was a force known to Mrs. Moodie and her kind, both in their life in the bush and in the more formal social order of their life in the clearings. And the basis of its strength was the fact that life in both these areas, by setting a high premium on practicality and native industry, encouraged a spirit of independence and undermined Old World conceptions of class.

The second source of radical influence was specifically American. Undoubtedly nourished by the frontier situation, American democratic ideals assumed in the decade following 1825 what was to be historically their most vigorous political form. This was coonskin democracy, and its hero was perhaps as much Davy Crockett as it was Andrew Jackson. . . . Its adherents were ruled by a desire to give practical effect to the doctrine of social equality. For a time they raised a spirited clamour in the agrarian states beyond the Alleghenies; and because they were mobile as well as vocal their influence was felt both directly and indirectly in the British colonies to the north. They spilled over the border as part of the backwash of a nation on the move, with its main guard headed west. . . . [Their] ideas and values spread like a quick infection amongst the legions of the lower classes now pouring into the colonies. Servants were saucy with a phrase about Jack being as good as his master; and pauper immigrants, from the moment of their landing at Grosse Isle, raised the Scots equivalent for this in the cry, "We shall a' be lairds here!"

If this was the effect of democratization on the pauper immigrant scarcely off his ship, what happened later as the new social values, gaining strength from the naturally democratic thrust of frontier life, began to press in upon the values held by the dominant group of colonial society? It is Mrs. Moodie, of course, who supplies my reference to the behaviour of pauper immigrants at Grosse Isle, and it is clear from the account she gives of this scene in *Roughing It in the Bush* that she considered their behaviour scandalously democratic. Significantly, when she refers again to the scene at the close of *Life in the Clearings,* she is thinking by this time less about subversion of the social order than about immorality. But the point at the moment is that one comes to rely on Mrs. Moodie for this kind of information. And it is precisely for this reason that *Life in the Clearings* is a very valuable book. Though there is certainly a more complete answer than Mrs. Moodie's to the question of the later course of democratic influences, this answer is scattered throughout a large number of documents (mostly periodicals) which are hard to come by and often hard to read. In the present text, on the other hand, amidst much that is interesting on other accounts, we are given a concentrated view of Old World social values reacting to pressure from the New. It is simply our good fortune, and no threat to the general validity of the testimony, that this writer shows herself to be a little more sensitive to social climate than most of her fellow-colonists.

There are two aspects to Mrs. Moodie's answer. The first is that democratic influences produced a change in her social values. The second, which is of much greater importance from the point of view of the present argument, is that these influences were resisted beyond a certain point. Mrs. Moodie's way, in other words, became characteristically a way of compromise.

Numerous comments in *Life in the Clearings* show how the tree is being bent and by what wind. Submitting her report on "the present state of society in the colony", Mrs. Moodie is emphatic on one point: this society is in a much healthier condition than the one she had known in England. And she associates the improvement unhesitatingly with the mixing of the classes in the new society and the absence of convention and prejudice in the relations between various occupational groups—effects which she describes frankly as being due in part at least to a "friendly" American influence. She likes the greater liveliness in social intercourse which is a product of this new freedom; better still, she likes the way in which the stripping away of old preconceptions about class makes possible a true estimate of a man's worth. This real worth of a man, as distinct from the special gifts which rank and wealth may bestow on him, she sees simply as the sum of his native ability, his industry, his moral training, and his education. (pp. xiv-xvii)

On the other hand, it is certainly fruitless to try to see in this writer a republican or a thorough-going democrat. Mrs. Moodie would have none of such imputations in her day, and for good reasons. Her roots in the parent culture were deep, and there

was in addition much already written into the short record of North American history (most pointedly, the bitter strife brought on by the revolt of the New England states) to urge that the lifelines to the mother country be kept clear. She therefore accepted from the new environment only what she considered fundamentally reconcilable with the monarchical principle and with the already established values of British colonial society. Despite her satisfaction at the weakening of the old class barriers, she is no leveller. She is confident that society will always be made up of those who serve and those who command, of those who carry out the ordinary duties of life and those who see visions and create. "Equality of mind" is therefore the extent of her egalitarian philosophy; and by this she means that she looks to education to establish a commonwealth of intellect in which all classes will mingle and communicate harmoniously. Unlike the rigorous democrat, who is inclined to mistrust the intellectual (the "egg-head", as he is now called) and to level downwards to mediocrity, Mrs. Moodie prizes intellect and accepts as a main goal the raising of the intellectual powers of all men to the highest point consistent with native ability. Education so conceived, moreover, she sees as a protection against the danger already apparent in her day that a new class structure will arise in which social position will go simply to those who grab most in a scramble for the spoils liberally offered by the new environment. And there are other compromises. Her liking for the amenities of freer social intercourse is tempered by her strong sense of propriety, which is in turn rooted in her feeling for tradition. Nor does her acceptance of the ideal of practicality lead to full-scale utilitarianism; for she remains an enthusiastic supporter of the arts and a champion of spiritual values. Finally, against the potentially corrosive effects of democratic ideals on ethical standards, she is the guardian of an orthodox morality and, as her comments on novel-writing in the present text show, sturdily didactic.

To these clues, which lie wholly within *Life in the Clearings,* must be added another, which lies partly within and partly beyond the book. Mrs. Moodie's response to the crucial political events of the time provides perhaps the plainest evidence available of her willingness and her ability to find a new position between opposing influences. When the Upper Canadian rebellion broke out at Montgomery's Tavern in the winter of 1837, Mr. Moodie was among the first of the "loyal gentlemen" of the province to volunteer his services in putting down the rebels. Mrs. Moodie, for her part, promptly wrote a poem called **"The Oath of the Canadian Volunteers"** , in which she raised a "Huzza" for England and spoke bitterly of the rebels as those "whose crimes pollute our injured land". Within a few years, however, she had modified her position, and in *Life in the Clearings* she speaks sympathetically of the rebel cause and represents William Lyon Mackenzie, its fiery leader, as a much maligned man. Yet this change took Mrs. Moodie no further than a position of compromise. On the political front, those who sympathized with Mackenzie's quarrel but refused to back the extreme "republican" measures he eventually proposed were known as the Moderate Reformers; and it is the views of these and of their leader, the Hon. Robert Baldwin, that are reflected when the rebellion is touched upon in *Life in the Clearings.* The symbol of the response is a biographical detail: a son born to Mrs. Moodie in 1843 was christened Robert Baldwin.

This much understood, it is no wild fancy to see in *Life in the Clearings* a kind of prophecy. The way of compromise between the Old World and the New, which was Mrs. Moodie's way, was to become the Canadian way. The evidence I have produced is not intended to suggest that this was exclusively a political way or that it invariably meant a simple arithmetical mediation between conservative and radical poles of thought— or, for that matter, that where compromise occurred the conservative pole was invariably British and the radical invariably American. Certainly the way of compromise was to be familiar to the Fathers of Confederation, just as it was to be familiar much later to the ministers of government who were to shape Canada's foreign policy in the twentieth century. . . . But in the sense of a ready-reckoning made between British and American spheres of influence, it was also a way which was to enter into the kind of language spoken by Canadians, the kind (and number) of Royal Commissions they set up, the kind of universities they established, the kind of books they wrote—in fact, into all those aspects of national life which are broadly called cultural. (pp. xviii-xx)

One point remains. To those who ask, as many have done and still do, how a sense of national identity can emerge from a process that seems to be largely a matter of borrowing and imitation, *Life in the Clearings* again has something to say. Granted that the way of compromise points in one direction to dullness, to a lack of enterprise and originality; and granted that this is a direction in which a part of the Canadian character has travelled. Yet it is worth recalling that Susanna Moodie's response was neither passive nor negative. A shift in terms and another glance at *Life in the Clearings* will indicate the more dynamic possibilities contained in this writer's adjustment to a new situation. (pp. xx-xxi)

By 1853 Mrs. Moodie had made some progress towards defining her position as a member of British colonial society on the North American continent. She had taken her bearings back across the Atlantic to the parent culture, and south across the border to American civilization; and through an intelligent use of these bearings, much more reliably than through exposure to a particular physical environment, she had begun to know where she was. It is the first stirrings of a sense of location and identity that sponsor her attack upon the condescending attitude of the British to their colonies, her rejection of the mere thought of annexation to the United States, and her repeated predictions of the future greatness of her new homeland. Patriotic sentiments are numerous in *Life in the Clearings*— many of them, as was to be expected, in praise of the mother country. But a surprising number are linked with the country of Mrs. Moodie's adoption. Here is an early version of Canadian self-determination, a form of nationalism taking shape twenty years before Confederation at a time when nationalism could be little more than a congenial idea. (p. xxi)

> Robert L. McDougall, "Editor's Introduction," in
> Life in the Clearings *by Susanna Moodie, edited by*
> Robert L. McDougall, 1959. Reprint by Macmillan
> of Canada, 1976, pp. vii-xxiii.

LLOYD M. SCOTT   (essay date 1959)

[*Scott maintains that Moodie's* Roughing It in the Bush *and Traill's* The Backwoods of Canada *constitute "the finest products of the* [*Canadian*] *immigrant writers."*]

The genteel class . . . made substantial contributions to [Canada's] early cultural development. The memoirs of Mrs. Moodie and her sister, Mrs. Traill—daughters of a well-to-do Suffolk family—represent the finest products of the immigrant writers. . . . Both wrote hoping to deter others from making like sacrifices in the backwoods, but their homely style and powers

of characterization and description have earned them a far different and more enduring place in Canadian letters than such a narrow purpose would suggest. The two books on which their reputations chiefly rest are now regarded as classic accounts of pioneer life. (p. 57)

Both of these immigrant writers were unconsciously answering Canada's need for a literature, a need of which they often spoke: "Here there are no historical associations, no legendary tales of those that came before us." Of course, Susanna Moodie and Catharine Traill were not conscious artists; they possessed no great genius. Nevertheless their keen observations, their insight into human problems and, perhaps most important of all, their frank self-portraits, have bequeathed us a valuable historical perspective. (p. 68)

> Lloyd M. Scott, "The English Gentlefolk in the Back-
> woods of Canada," in The Dalhousie Review, *Vol.*
> 39, No. 1, Spring, 1959, pp. 56-69.

CARL F. KLINCK   (essay date 1959)

[*In the following excerpt from his review of the 1959 edition of* Life in the Clearings, *Klinck assesses* Roughing It in the Bush *and* Life in the Clearings *as literary works rather than as purely historical accounts.*]

Life in the Clearings is described as a "companion-piece" to *Roughing It in the Bush* because it shows Mrs. Moodie's desire to add her record of the clearings, or growing towns and villages, to her earlier one about the bush, or backwoods. Is it, however, the same kind of book? Is *Roughing It in the Bush* a novel, and is *Life in the Clearings* something else?

These books owe their preservation to public interest in the social life of the pioneers, and Mrs. Moodie is established as typical of the gentlewoman of Upper Canada. Her historical worth has thus obscured her literary position, and her individuality has not been sufficiently recognized, although her curiosity, prejudices, circumstances, and especially her characterization of herself among her neighbours make her readily distinguishable even from her sister, Mrs. Traill. Her book, *Roughing It in the Bush*, has also been regarded as representative of colonial history rather than of colonial literature. Yet it is both unique and illustrative of the practices in writing which prevailed in the Canadas during the first half of the nineteenth century. Mrs. Moodie wrote within the current fashions, as she knew them in the colonies, and, in doing so, found her own way, shaping a form of fiction which incorporated and transcended the raw facts and ideas drawn from life around her. (p. 76)

Although chronologically later in Mrs Moodie's life, and in some ways more mature or "civilized," the *Clearings* looks like a trial effort, not like a sequel. It is made of similar stuff, including remainders from the earlier volume. But it is not self-contained; it proceeds without imaginative cohesion, the lack of which is felt in spite of a mechanical scheme of travel through towns from Belleville to Niagara and in spite of the predictable flow of Mrs. Moodie's admirable convictions. She has put on a one-man show of the various materials and tendencies out of which her masterpiece grew. But the prize exhibit hangs in another gallery.

The personal and sociological values of *Life in the Clearings* will not be reviewed here; they can be found on page after page of the text with genuinely entertaining illustrations drawn from experience and gossip. Professor McDougall's introductory essay is an excellent guide to this book and to Mrs. Moodie herself [see excerpt dated 1959]. He has brought us to the point, we think, where a study of this author's literary theory and practice, and a critical biography are not only possible, but are urgently required. (p. 77)

> *Carl F. Klinck, "A Gentlewoman of Upper Canada," in* Canadian Literature, *No. 1, Summer, 1959, pp. 75-7.*

CARL F. KLINCK   (essay date 1962)

[*Klinck examines Moodie's use of both fictional and autobiographical elements in* Roughing It in the Bush, *claiming that she "dramatized her vision of herself."*]

[Mrs Moodie's] procedure in compiling her material for *Roughing It* and her positive intentions with regard to this book have not been fully determined. Professor Robert L. McDougall, in an excellent introduction to a recent reprint of the *Clearings,* observes that the first (the Cobourg farm) chapters of *Roughing It* deal with "the shock to Mrs Moodie's sensibilities of living in a shack" and coping with her Yankee neighbours [see excerpt dated 1959]. The later (the Otonabee) chapters deal with "man's primitive struggle against drought, storm, pestilence, fire and sickness." If any chapters are to be regarded as expendable, the second portion may be curtailed, for here the direct force of experience is not as powerfully conveyed. One does not know how Mrs Moodie would have reduced the size of her book—if, indeed, she would have consented to do so. Some of her chapters were the result of recollection in tranquillity; perhaps all of them were. There is no way of telling how much in any given chapter is due to experienced fact and how much to literary artifice. She did not pour out her confessions; she dramatized her vision of herself.

This involved more fictional latitude and a closer approach to fictional form than one would have found in the travel and immigrant literature of the 1820's, 1830's, and 1840's. In *Roughing It,* the Upper Canadian development of such literature toward stable literary forms reaches one of its plateaus. On the primitive levels there were "statistical" accounts and running narratives making a bid for the reader's interest because of apparent accuracy in reporting facts—in this case, basic data about Upper Canada. Added attractions were to be found in descriptions, brief essays, and anecdotes. All of these involved interpretation, and interpretation could go to the very borders of fanciful invention. As a later refinement, anecdotes could be fashioned into sketches, and a book like *Roughing It* might be made entirely of sketches.

Such an indigenous development undoubtedly occurred; and, within it, *Roughing It* represented a level beyond Mrs Traill's *The Backwoods of Canada.* . . . Superficially these books were similar. . . . Mrs Traill's presentation was natural, original, and skilful; the autobiographical elements were not obtrusive; the author seemed helpful, unassuming, unimpassioned, devoted to life and nature as she found it. Her style resembled the unaffected conversation of a truly well bred woman. She was on her way to fame as a naturalist; but her sister, Mrs Moodie, practising a less admirable style wavering between plain speaking and rhetoric, was on her way to fiction, a further stage in the growth of immigrant literature in the Upper Canadian environment.

The sketches in *Roughing It in the Bush* were written by a novelist. . . . Mrs Moodie, as a contributor to the Canadian *Literary Garland,* was a professional writer of instalment fiction. From 1839 to 1851 she was the *Garland*'s principal author, who turned out novels of English middle-class manners and exhibited a flair for eccentricities, Dickensian humour, excursions into pathos, hosts of minor characters, and heroines of rank and sensitivity sharing some of her own qualities. (pp. xi-xiii)

Roughing It in the Bush was not officially one of her *Garland* novels, but it bore on its title page these lines:

> I sketch from Nature, and the picture's true;
> Whate'er the subject, whether grave or gay,
> Painful experience in a distant land
> Made it mine own.

The early editors of *Roughing It* saw the book in this context—in spite of Mrs Moodie's underlining of its utility as a warning to gentlefolk. The London publisher called it a "glowing narrative of personal incident and suffering," interesting and "pathetic" in its "delineations of fortitude under privation." The New York reviser, "C. F. B.," praised it for "scenes and adventures . . . so full of freshness, truth, and humour"; for the "healthy tone . . . that pervades its entertaining pages"; and for its profitable lessons. His judgement was summarized in one sentence. "Mrs. Moodie is a true heroine, and her simple narrative is a genuine romance, which has all the interest of an imaginative creation."

This shrewd observation provides an explanation of the book's nature, its enduring interest, and its essential canon. Its unity is found in terms satisfactory in its own time and allowable in ours—one character is central, and that character is the author herself. "Genuine romance" is a controversial classification, and an alternative phrase like "apprenticeship novel" may not be better; but a certain core of meaning is there. Middle-class England and America had found a substitute for chivalric romances: the modern knight could be any person seeking a way to live in the midst of social dislocation, philosophical nullity, economic slavery, decline of wealth, or impending deterioration. Through long practice Mrs Moodie knew how to put a piece of herself into such stories of adjustment to life. *Roughing It* was wholly autobiographical, her own book; she was the author-apprentice-heroine. Everything pointed to her trials and her (partial) salvation. The amusing imperfect people around her were "touched up" to be foils, revealing the central figure who could bear comparison with impunity. Sharing in all the actions, and progressively enlarging the image of herself, she gave a pattern of movement to the whole book. The principal structural force was anticipation, the reader's knowledge that she had a large fund of ironic observations—the certainty that she would soon come up with new characters and more anecdotes. Limitations of space alone would cut them short. Through them, as through fiction, there would be a lively re-creation of the past. (pp. xiii-xiv)

> *Carl F. Klinck, "Editor's Introduction," in* Roughing It in the Bush; or, Forest Life in Canada *by Susanna Moodie, McClelland and Stewart Limited, 1962, pp. ix-xiv.*

CLARA THOMAS   (essay date 1966)

[*Noting Moodie's frequent and varied use of humor, Thomas praises* Roughing It in the Bush *and* Life in the Clearings, *but laments Moodie's failure to develop her talents in her later works.*]

Susanna was, in fact, not a diarist, not a writer of calm expository prose, certainly not an instructress of prospective emigrants, but a gifted recorder of character, dialogue and incident, especially of a humorous nature. Her early life in Canada made a great impact on her creative powers, extending talents that she had exercised before—character drawing and the record of incident—and releasing another that she had scarcely practised—the ability to see with a humorist's slant and to communicate her amusement to others. She never lived comfortably with her comic vision, however, or rightly estimated its potential in her writing. In *Life in the Clearings* . . . , she confesses embarrassment at her life-long tendency to laughter: "I wish nature had not given me such a quick perception of the ridiculous—such a perverse inclination to laugh in the wrong place; for though one cannot help deriving from it a wicked enjoyment, it is a very troublesome gift, and very difficult to conceal." (p. 58)

Susanna had written much fiction before coming to Canada. It had always been conventional, moral, sentimental, having to do with heroes, heroines, and villains of her own or higher social rank. In Canada she was thrust into the company of all sorts of people, few of whom were of her own social class and all of whom seemed different, often totally reprehensible, but almost always amusing. These people she could write of without inhibition and she captured a whole gallery of them, in the very accents in which she heard them speak. From the ship's captain to "the little stumpy Man," *Roughing it* is made memorable by these people and by their reported talk. Old Satan, Tom Wilson, Betty Fye, John Monaghan, Jacob and Malcolm come alive and occupy centre stage for a time; many others are recorded, as are the workers at the logging-bee, in vignettes only. In total, the book is alive with their many presences. There are a few persons she meets whose stories seem to demand her well-practised sentimental vein: the dying girl, Phoebe, is one of these, as is the strange, melancholy hunter, Brian. Even in these tales, however, she transcends her own sentimental convention as she sketches from the life.

In the service of her sketches, Susanna is recklessly self-revealing. It was natural for her to be the centre of her narrative, as Catharine is the narrator and centre of [*The Backwoods of Canada*]. But unlike her sister, Susanna, centre stage, becomes one of her own "characters": a prejudiced, class-conscious, ill-equipped pioneer, sometimes the butt of her own stories, sometimes the heroine, passionately revolting against her circumstances while slowly and uncomfortably adapting to them. Catharine quietly states the achievement, whether it be confidence in an assured social position or satisfactory relations with servants; Susanna dramatizes the struggle, with herself a storm centre. (pp. 58-9)

Roughing it in the Bush, as we know it, is an uneasy amalgam of Susanna's fictional talent, her keenly felt and humorously observed experiences, and her cautionary admonitions. On publication it was deservedly enjoyed; it was also resented by those who felt that the conditions which Mrs. Moodie described had passed away, and that, therefore, her representations were misleading, or, at the least, snobbish. It must certainly be admitted that Susanna had not been careful enough in editing her earlier work before its collected publication. She made amends, however, by the speedy preparation and publication of *Life in the Clearings* . . . , with an introduction which is both an apology for offence given and an explanation of the position taken [see excerpt dated 1852]. She reiterates her warning to the gentleman-emigrant: "let him leave to the hardy labourer

the place assigned to him by Providence, now undertaken, upon limited means, the task of pioneer in the great wilderness." But she balances this with an admission of the great gaps in her experience at the time of writing the sketches for *Roughing it in the Bush,* and with a statement of gratitude to Canada, the "country of my adoption—the great foster-mother of that portion of the human family whose fatherland, however dear to them, is unable to supply them with bread." Her earlier portraits of the rascally Yankee settlers who were at once the bane of her pioneer days and the source for some of her best sketches are now balanced by a tribute to "our enterprising, intelligent American neighbours." Their influence, she admits, has helped to produce a successful amalgamation of classes in Canada which she now finds desirable.

She based her sketches in *Life in the Clearings* on the framework of a travel narrative, a trip from Belleville to Niagara Falls. This structural device is not strong enough to support and dominate the sketches, and the book is memorable for the assembling of its parts rather than for the totality of its whole. Catharine Traill's powers of observing and reporting were predominantly exercised on her natural environment: Susanna's eye was always on individuals, and from them to their, and to her, social environment. Her descriptions of the trip itself read like romantic and sentimental "set pieces": the blue water glides by, the wooded hills recede in the distance, at the Falls "the wide world of tumbling waters are flashing and foaming in the sunlight." But the people she meets, the conversations she reports, the humorous anecdotes she tells, with herself as the central figure, are as vivid and persuasively "real" as the best of the Bush sketches, though marked by a more tolerant and less satiric tone.

Much of *Life in the Clearings* is, from our standpoint, social history, enlivened and authenticated by the presence of Susanna Moodie as its narrator. The chapters on "Camp Meetings," "Education," the "Lunatic Asylum" and the "Provincial Agricultural Show," the forerunner of the Toronto Exhibition, are documentary accounts of aspects of Ontario life in the mid-nineteenth century and as such alone are to be valued. That they were recorded by a contemporary, a practised observer, and a writer with twenty years' experience of Canada is a large bonus of good fortune. Furthermore, in this work Susanna is determinedly positive and factual in her approach, at the same time offering us the interest and vigour of her opinions. She now speaks, not from a position of passionate reaction to a new and shocking environment, but confidently, secure in her status as a Canadian, the wife of an official of the courts, and a professional woman of letters; in none of these rôles does she wish to be misunderstood

She believed that all writing, and particularly fiction, the work of "the despised and reprobated novelist," must and will subserve a moral purpose. "I look upon these authors as heaven-inspired teachers," she proclaims, thereby establishing a didactic purpose for her own work and explaining to us the inhibiting of certain of her own talents. She deprecates her own tendency to laughter, and takes care to announce in this book that certain anecdotes she reports, in a tone of humorous satire against the pretensions of the ignorant, were "told her by another." On the other hand, her admiration for the work of nineteenth-century novelists, particularly Dickens and Thomas Hood, the "humane men" who command the reader to "step with them into these dirty abodes of guilt and wretchedness, and see what crime really is" encouraged the development of her own talent toward realistic writing. The chapters on the

A portrait of Moodie by Thomas Cheesman.

prison and its inmates, the lunatic asylum and its patients, and particularly her story of Grace Marks the murderess, are blood-chilling in their effect. Her talent toward the realistic-naturalistic portrayal of the suffering and degradation she deplored was a formidable one; its lack of development in her later writing is, like the lack of development of her comic and anecdotal veins, regrettable to us. To Susanna Moodie, however, both what she wrote and the way she wrote were dictated by her time and place in society, her reading public, and her own conception of her function as an authoress.

After *Life in the Clearings,* she wrote many novels, but in them she reverted to the romantic and sentimental vein that she had practised even before coming to Canada, and that had been the style of much of her *Literary Garland* work. *Flora Lyndsay, Mark Hurdlestone, The World Before Them, Matrimonial Speculations,* and *Dorothy Chance* are among her later works; most of them were first published in England by Bentley; some were reprinted in the United States. . . . All were directed toward an English reader—the polite young lady and her eminently Victorian mother. There was in Canada, as Susanna Moodie well knew, little or no possibility of publication and an extremely small reading public. She was never without the necessity of writing to augment a small family income and in general her readers concurred in the admonition she reports from one English lady: "Don't fill your letters home with descriptions of Canada. Who, in *England,* thinks anything of *Canada?*" Prudently, she complied. (pp. 70-2)

Clara Thomas, "The Strickland Sisters," in The Clear Spirit: Twenty Canadian Women and Their Times, *edited by Mary Quayle Innis, University of Toronto Press, 1966, pp. 42-73.*

A. CHARLES von GUTTENBERG (essay date 1969)

[*In this assessment of the merits and flaws of* Roughing It in the Bush *and* Life in the Clearings, *Guttenberg attempts to define Moodie's place in nineteenth-century Canadian literature.*]

Despite her tolerance and perseverance in the face of countless disappointments, and those largely stemming from the contrast between a comparatively barbarous way of life and the ordered social pattern from which she had removed, [Mrs. Moodie] was too much the narrow provincial gentlewoman of early nineteenth-century England. She owned too many prejudices to record her history of the new undertaking with the fully impartial eye and deeply discerning sensibility necessary to fix a perpetual memorial of this new kind of social experiment. To put it quite simply, she lacked the vision to glean all the relevant particulars, the greater majority she did observe having obvious reference to the amenities of her class in England. Such commentary is not intended to frighten readers away from what is obviously one of the better works of Canadian literature of the nineteenth century; it is intended, however, as an introduction to the serious treatment of Canadian writing, an attempt to regard Canadian authorship with no gentler or less firm an eye than one would allow any other work of art. (p. 108)

The advantages of deciding on one's genre before writing are illustrated by the failure of *Roughing it in the Bush* to be any of history, memoir, autobiography, travel book, anthropology or sociology. It is not the first because of the omission of many necessary items—a discussion of political issues, for example; as anthropology or sociology it lacks the wide and painstaking scientific treatment of details, and a full enough view of cultural phenomena—as the chapter on the Indians shows. It is not autobiography because it too often deviates into incidental sketches to the forfeit of great parts of her own story, and there is little attempt at self-analysis of mental and emotional character. And there is not enough travelling done for a travel book. So far, these are not defects, since they were not part of Mrs. Moodie's intention; we can take it that if she had any genre specifically in mind it was that of a memoir.

It comes closest, in fact, to a memoir, a sketch of events without a pressing need for their consistent examination from certain specific points of view other than that of the idiosyncracy of the author. Yet for one thing, it lacks the consistent literary style of a memoir, both in the intrusion of her husband's two chapters, and in the absence of a highly individualised approach to events. One suspects that she lacked the literary force of personality necessary to colour all she saw with her own human light; it is coloured instead with the light of a unit—an exceptional one, to be sure—of a social class. The literary quality of the work as a whole is affected by these disadvantages: it is a highly competent piece of realistic writing—except where her educated sense of propriety skirts certain essential aspects of the life she is observing—set off by a few powerful passages of romantic nature description. Her talent was much less for analytic enquiry than for surface description, yet even the latter loses power to some extent through a lack of form. All writing is, or should be initiated for some purpose, and purpose demands form. Mrs. Moodie, by compounding a series of chronologically arranged sketches, sacrifices through lack of structural integration any marked literary distinction. There is a psychological reason for this, for her domestic memoir divides attention between the mind of a middle-class English gentlewoman of that time, and the conditions of life in the colony. She has been caught between the two stools of realistic reportage of settler life and psychological self-portraiture, based in this case on a radical change in the individual due to altered environment. Not that she had any idea of the latter as a literary purpose for her work: did she not use an injunction to realism as a motto for the book: 'I sketch from Nature, and the picture's true'—and, in *Life in the Clearings,* defend novel writing on realistic and didactic grounds?

But the divided treatment is there, to add to the charm of a literary curiosity and to detract from the formal perfection. We must also remember her declared intention in writing the book: to deter 'well-educated people, about to settle in this colony, from entering upon a life for which they were totally unfitted by their previous pursuits and habits'. Fortunately Mrs. Moodie was not completely successful in this latter respect, having underestimated the hunger of the spirit for personal freedom and a 'second chance'; and she had allowed that a judicious choice of location (i.e. not in the backwoods) could lead to material and social blessings. (pp. 108-10)

[*Life in the Clearings*] was purposely written to picture 'the present state of society in the colony, and to point out its increasing prosperity and commercial advantages'. *Roughing it* had sufficiently counteracted the false stories which had been circulated in Britain to encourage emigration to Canada, and the new book was much lighter in tone, if not as stirring as that dealing with isolated bush life. (p. 117)

But *Life in the Clearings* is not the book that *Roughing it . . .* was, and the explanation is to be found in the given degree of talent and in the early upbringing of the author. There were several long and very bad novels which followed, none of them readable today, although unfortunately parts of them were relished by readers of the *Literary Garland.* Mrs. Moodie is, in fact, illustrative of a paradox obtaining in many writers of her day: the combination of the pious didactic wish to 'sketch from Nature' with a patent unreality of sentiment. It runs through all her work in varying degrees, and with the exception of her writings on Canada the unreality of sentiment vitiates almost everything she wrote. In those two works, however, and especially in the earlier, we can only suppose that the soul-shaking shock of adverse and primitive conditions such as drove her to night-long tears over an extended period, cracked her sheltered middle-class veneer and sentimentality to such an extent that, in combination with sensitive nature appreciation under ideal conditions, reality was directly apprehended. Aware that serious criticisms had been levelled at her by various newspaper critics for her adverse account of settler life in *Roughing it,* she reasserted her realistic purpose and what had been her intention there, to uphold the idea of a 'Commonwealth of intellect' while affirming that equality of station is an unreal dream. She managed, too, to make a finally reiterated point of desired British sovereignty for Canada. These were typical views held by the average, enlightened, formerly middle-class British settler in the Canadas, and it is this very representativeness of Mrs. Moodie's work that constitutes one of its important values. (pp. 117-18)

Mrs. Moodie was a tireless supporter of Imperial sovereignty, and it was doubtless well nourished through the desperate years of homesickness when she wrote so many of the 'exile' poems of *Roughing it in the Bush.* Subtitled "**A Canadian Song**", and set to music by her flautist husband, the following must represent the many scattered throughout her work voicing the painful nostalgia of those who, at least during their early years on the land, could only regard themselves as unwilling exiles:

> Oh! can you leave your native land
> An exile's bride to be;
> Your mother's home, and cheerful hearth
> To tempt the main with me;

> Across the wide and stormy sea
> To trace our foaming track,
> And know the wave that bears us on
> Will ne'er convey us back?
> And can you in Canadian woods
> With me the harvest bind,
> Nor feel one lingering, sad regret
> For all you leave behind?

That is the authentic note of the pre-Confederation exile, a ballad note, simple, stark, yearning, possessing a quiet plaintive beauty of its own only possible in a direct transcription of experience. Reminiscence is a dominant characteristic of nineteenth century Canadian literature to Confederation; as there was little social integration of groups or even families, so their lives were fragmentary and they therefore nostalgically orientated themselves towards an earlier period of wholeness in the home country. Mrs. Moodie's Canadian writing is in the main stream of this tradition, but she enriches that tradition—and this is her considerable additional strength—in her loving depiction of the Canadian scene, character, and way of life. (pp. 118-19)

> *A. Charles von Guttenberg, "Susanna Moodie," in his* Early Canadian Art and Literature, *Europe Printing Estb., 1969, pp. 99-119.*

MARGARET ATWOOD (essay date 1970)

[*Atwood is a contemporary Canadian poet and novelist known for her spare, direct, and controlled style. Atwood often acts as spokesperson for her native Canada, and many of her writings feature a search for identity coupled with a journey motif, especially a journey into the wilderness. These elements figure prominently in her* The Journals of Susanna Moodie, *a collection of poems that recreates scenes from Moodie's life. In the following excerpt from the afterword to that work, Atwood sketches her response to Moodie's writings.*]

These poems were generated by a dream. I dreamt I was watching an opera I had written about Susanna Moodie. I was alone in the theatre; on the empty white stage, a single figure was singing.

Although I had heard of Susanna Moodie I had never read her two books about Canada, *Roughing It in the Bush* and *Life in the Clearings.* When I did read them I was disappointed. The prose was discursive and ornamental and the books had little shape: they were collections of disconnected anecdotes. The only thing that held them together was the personality of Mrs Moodie, and what struck me most about this personality was the way in which it reflects many of the obsessions still with us.

If the national mental illness of the United States is megalomania, that of Canada is paranoid schizophrenia. Mrs Moodie is divided down the middle: she praises the Canadian landscape but accuses it of destroying her; she dislikes the people already in Canada but finds in people her only refuge from the land itself; she preaches progress and the march of civilization while brooding elegiacally upon the destruction of the wilderness; she delivers optimistic sermons while showing herself to be fascinated with deaths, murders, the criminals in Kingston Penitentiary and the incurably insane in the Toronto lunatic asylum. She claims to be an ardent Canadian patriot while all the time she is standing back from the country and criticizing it as though she were a detached observer, a stranger. Perhaps that is the way we still live. We are all immigrants to this place even if we were born here: the country is too big for anyone to inhabit completely, and in the parts unknown to us we move in fear, exiles and invaders. This country is something that must be chosen—it is so easy to leave—and if we do choose it we are still choosing a violent duality. (p. 62)

> Margaret Atwood, in an afterword in her The Journals of Susanna Moodie, *Oxford University Press, Canadian Branch, 1970, pp. 62-4.*

RONALD SUTHERLAND (essay date 1971)

[*Sutherland detects a "disconcerting . . . undertone of racism" in Moodie's writings.*]

Mrs. Moodie was manifestly convinced of the superiority of the particular class of English gentlefolk to which she belonged, and she makes the idea clear in passages such as the following in her book *Roughing It in the Bush:*

> The hand that has long held the sword, and been accustomed to receive implicit obedience from those under its control, is seldom adapted to wield the spade and guide the plough, or try its strength against the stubborn trees of the forest. Nor will such persons submit cheerfully to the saucy familiarity of servants, who, republicans in spirit, think themselves as good as their employers.
>
> (p. 35)

Moodie makes the same point many times, always carefully differentiating between "superiors" and "inferiors". She speaks of the "vicious, uneducated barbarians, who form the surplus of over-populated European countries." At one point she observes: "The semi-barbarous Yankee squatters, who had 'left their country for their country's good,' and by whom we were surrounded in our first settlement, detested us. . . ." And to this last remark of Susanna Moodie's, one is tempted to reply "No Wonder." In many respects her classification of people is reminiscent of Samuel Richardson in *Sir Charles Grandison,* where he divided his characters into three categories: men, women and Italians. Only for Moodie the classes would be English gentlemen, English ladies and barbarians.

Of course, her standards for herself were exceedingly high. Here she is admitting to an "unpardonable weakness":

> In spite of my boasted fortitude—and I think my powers of endurance have been tried to the utmost since my sojourn in this country—the rigour of the climate subdued my proud, independent English spirit, and I actually shamed my womanhood, and cried with the cold. Yes, I ought to blush at confessing such unpardonable weakness; but I was foolish and inexperienced, and unaccustomed to the yoke.
>
> (pp. 35-6)

After having read the works of Susanna Moodie, one is left with the undeniable impression that everybody—Irish, French-Canadian, Scottish, Indian, lowborn English and especially American—who is not of her particular caste has been hopelessly predestined to insignificance, *ipso facto.* Moreover, her attitude, which appears to be essentially unconscious and without malicious intent, led her to remarkable conclusions on occasion. Speaking of the cholera doctor Stephen Ayres, for instance, she comments: "A friend of mine, in this town, has

an original portrait of this notable empiric—this man sent from heaven. The face is rather handsome, but has a keen, designing expression, and is evidently that of an American from its complexion and features." (p. 36)

Now it may appear to some that I have been looking at the writings of Susanna Moodie with a magnifying glass, considering that she did no more than echo the accepted English spirit of her time, but certainly through a magnifying glass is the way Mrs. Moodie consistently looked at herself. I do not deny the merits of her literary achievement—her keen eye for appropriate detail, her ear for dialect, her capacity to capture scenes and moods. Nevertheless, throughout her work, as throughout the works of Ralph Connor, to name one other obvious example, there is always the disconcerting body-odour of race, the undertone of racism. Not the screeching, messianic racism of a Houston Stewart Chamberlain, the man who talked with demons and who sowed the field which Adolf Hitler was to harvest, but something perhaps almost as malignant in the long run, because it is in the form of a deeply ingrained pattern of thought, a conviction which may even be unconsciously held. Furthermore, it is the very conviction which in various guises has haunted and continues to haunt a nation which, if it is going to survive, must perforce develop a *modus vivendi* for people of different ethnic origins.

Moodie herself, it should be pointed out, merely chanted a common tendency of many nations, a tendency which was perhaps an inevitable adjunct to strong cultural identification, a tendency which in most circumstances was probably not of great harm or consequence. What is important to us here is that the Moodie attitude has not died a natural death, but continues to infect the thinking of many English Canadians, and that in the particular circumstances of modern Canada it could be of vital consequence. (pp. 36-7)

> Ronald Sutherland, "The Body-Odour of Race," in his Second Image: Comparative Studies in Québec/ Canadian Literature, *New Press, 1971, pp. 28-59.*

R. D. MacDONALD (essay date 1972)

[*MacDonald examines the underlying design and purpose of* Roughing It in the Bush. *While highlighting the superficial contradictions in the work's style, MacDonald argues that* Roughing It in the Bush *is unified by its representations of nature.*]

Since few readers have seriously considered Susanna Moodie's *Roughing it in the Bush* as a work of art, I have had misgivings about my own exploration of the design underlying this work. Moreover, I have had to admit that Mrs. Moodie herself seems oblivious of her own purpose or of the pattern developing within her work. Says she: "It is not my intention to give a regular history of our residence in the bush, but merely to present to my readers such events as may serve to illustrate a life in the woods." A modest intention indeed! All that she seemingly requires of herself is to make her experience real. Notice that she has freed herself from the requirements of a single thesis and from the demands of a single chronology.

As Mrs. Moodie recounts the years of 1836 and 37, her purpose shifts to "illustrate the necessity of a perfect and childlike reliance upon the mercies of God. . . ." But after she has descended from her experience of the sublime and from theological speculation, she becomes wholly absorbed in the particulars of pioneer life; her book begins to read more and more like a handyman's guide, a how-to-make-do book. Her purpose now seems that of the seasoned guide who would show potential emigrants how to adapt to the bush.... In the last chapter, however, after having asserted her own contentment in the bush ("I was contented to live and die in obscurity"), after having nostalgically described the pleasantness of their leavetaking, the cordial hospitality afforded them while on the road, the beauty and good humour of their ride itself—after all this, Mrs. Moodie suddenly ends the story and then reverts to the purpose expressed in her preface:

> To the poor, industrious working man it presents many advantages; to the poor gentleman, *none!* The former works hard, puts up with coarse, scanty fare, and submits, with good grace, to hardships that would kill a domesticated animal at home....

In her last words the bush is named a "prison-house" and the life there simply one of "toil" and "suffering".

How is one to read such a contradictory work? Is it best simply to use *Roughing it in the Bush* as a historian might, i.e. by looking through Susanna Moodie's book on to the 1830's of Upper Canada or of the British empire? Is it best, if one is to look at the work itself, simply to touch and go, to point out Mrs. Moodie's ironic narrative voice and then slide away from the book by comparing this voice to Jane Austen's? Or is it best finally, simply to accept *Roughing it in the Bush* as a work roughly hewn, an anecdotal travelogue, a work in which experience is half digested, a work digressive and discontinuous, a work filled with vigorous, humorous but rather pointless character sketches?

To answer these questions, I will argue first that Mrs. Moodie's representation of nature does unify *Roughing it in the Bush,* and secondly that the design of the chapters emphasizes this representation of nature. Even here the book may appear confused: it is easy to construe Susanna Moodie carrying across the Atlantic romantic notions of nature which are inappropriate to her new setting. It becomes clear quickly, however, that her romantic ecstasies are not singleminded, or naive, at least in so far as Moodie-the-writer re-creates her earlier experience. In her first description of the serene and silent beauty of the shores of the St. Lawrence, it is obvious that the writer in retrospect has so framed the scene that the reader must suspect ironic implication: picturesque beauty, one is led to believe, is not reality.... As the ship's party approaches Grosse Isle, the pastoral view of nature begins to dissipate: "It was four o'clock when we landed on the rocks, which the rays of an intensely scorching sun had rendered so hot that I could scarcely place my foot upon them." Moreover the unpleasant effect of the place upon emigrants is suddenly made clear:

> The people who covered the island appeared perfectly destitute of shame, or even a sense of common decency. Many were almost naked, still more but partially clothed. We turned in disgust from the revolting scene, but were unable to leave the spot until the captain had satisfied a noisy group of his people, who were demanding a supply of stores.

The spirit of the place becomes a disease: even Scots "who while on board ship had conducted themselves with the greatest propriety, and appeared the most quiet, orderly set of people in the world, no sooner set foot upon the island than they became infected by the same spirit of insubordination and misrule, and were just as insolent and noisy as the rest."

Again, as Mrs. Moodie describes Quebec, the same bursting of the romantic dream occurs. The "grandeur" and the "picture perfect" quality of the landscape, and the sense that this landscape is the work of a "Divine Originator" so affects her that she reports:

> my spirit fell prostrate before it, and I melted involuntarily into tears. Yes, regardless of the eager crowds around me, I leant upon the side of the vessel and cried like a child—not tears of sorrow, but a gush from the heart of pure and unalloyed delight. I heard not the many voices murmuring in my ears—I saw not the anxious beings that thronged our narrow deck—my soul at the moment was alone with God.

If this passage is not bathetic, the one following closely upon it is, as Mrs. Moodie chauvinistically prophesies that only a great nation could rise from such a great landscape. Then to make matters worse, after apparently coming back to herself, she abruptly states: "But I have wandered away from my subject into the regions of thought and must again descend to common workaday realities." On this lower level, what follows is a satirical account of the vainglorious expectations of the working class immigrants. Moreover from the first hand accounts of those who have visited Quebec, Moodie suggests that man destroys the perfection of nature—a view not entirely contrary to the Wordsworthian or romantic notions which she has carried across the Atlantic. (pp. 20-3)

Romantic anticipation and disenchantment, high style and low, continue to alternate. But this anticipation and high style become a smaller and smaller part of the book. In part, anticipation is replaced by nostalgia for the idyllic British countryside.... Nature is remembered as the "indulgent mother, holding out her living arms to enfold to her bosom her erring but devoted child." By what seems a sheer effort of will, however, Mrs. Moodie turns from her lament for things past. Still avoiding the present, she prophesies a glorious future for Canada, the land now of her future, her children's future and the land of her children's graves. Typically, however, this chapter falls away from this "high style" to the ludicrous incongruities of Tom Wilson remembered, to the low reality of the crowded immigrant boat, and finally to the droll but foreboding grumbling of Tom Wilson, who has preceded the Moodies to the New World. (p. 23)

This alternation of the high and low may lead the reader to assert that Susanna Moodie's vision was contradictory, her style uneven. But as I have said, the low is usually implied in the high or else the low frames the high. Moreover, the high mimetic mode becomes a smaller and smaller part of the book as the story becomes more and more a catalogue of narrowly averted disasters and as the story implies that in Canada, at least, nature is a heartless tyrant who grinds down the fine edges of the British gentleman. The plot itself, (as it moves in circular fashion from British village, to the Lower St. Lawrence, to Lake Ontario, to the deep bush, and finally back to the Canadian counterpart of British civilization, the village) implies surely that the Canadian bush or Canadian nature is not suitable to the Moodie family.

On a smaller scale, the arrangement of chapters, especially the alternation of episodic chapters and chapters of character sketch, again suggest a single significant pattern within *Roughing it in the Bush:* the character sketches may seem at first to have no function, beyond merely presenting interesting personalities, but these chapters act as watersheds between the flows of action, and more importantly they imply failure, if the Moodies stay in the bush. (p. 24)

One might argue that *Roughing it in the Bush* is nicely rounded off, as in the last two chapters the circle of events is completed: the Moodies have left civilization, settled in the bush and now return to civilization. . . . But the last two chapters move in an uneven fashion, beginning with elevated speculations about intuition and then shifting abruptly to the raw chunks of Mrs. Moodie's undigested experience of the bush. This first paragraph is in her high speculative style:

> The holy and mysterious nature of man is yet hidden from himself; he is still a stranger to the movements of that inner life, and knows little of its capabilities and powers. A purer religion, a higher standard of moral and intellectual training, may in time reveal all this. Man still remains a half-reclaimed savage; the leaven of Christianity is slowly and surely working its way, but it has not yet changed the whole lump, or transformed the deformed into the beauteous child of God. Oh, for that glorious day! It is coming. The dark clouds of humanity are already tinged with the golden radiance of the dawn, but the sun of righteousness has not yet arisen upon the world with healing on his wings: the light of truth still struggles in the womb of darkness, and man stumbles on to the fulfilment of his sublime and mysterious destiny.

The very next paragraph reads like the diary of an Ontario farmer totally absorbed in the particulars of his life:

> This spring I was not a little puzzled how to get in the crops. I still continued so weak that I was quite unable to assist in the field, and my good old Jenny was sorely troubled with inflamed feet, which required constant care. At this juncture, a neighbouring settler, who had recently come among us, offered to put in my small crop of peas, potatoes, and oats, in all not comprising more than eight acres, if I would lend him my oxen to log-up a large fallow of ten acres and put in his own crops. Trusting to his fair dealing, I consented to this arrangement; but he took advantage of my isolated position, and not only logged-up his fallow, but put in all his spring crops before he sowed an acre of mine. The oxen were worked down so low that they were almost unfit for use, and my crops were put in so late, and with such little care, that they all proved a failure. I should have felt this loss more severely had it happened in any previous year; but I had ceased to feel that deep interest in the affairs of the farm from a sort of conviction in my own mind that it would not long remain my home.

Perhaps this kind of unevenness is to be excused in travel or frontier literature, but as I have already suggested, the very last paragraph of the book follows illogically from the previous paragraphs. Mrs. Moodie warns the emigrant gentleman to avoid settling in the bush, yet just before this, she has been describing the beauty of the winter sleigh ride, the pleasant leavetaking from their neighbours, and the warm hospitality of the innkeepers who shelter the Moodies on their trip to Belleville. Thus though the reader is perhaps prepared for the closing of a circular plot, he is startled at the sudden and contradictory warning which ends the book.

Recognizing the discontinuity within these last paragraphs, one should not forget the pattern that does integrate the book—the catalogue of narrowly averted disasters which increasingly imply failure for the Moodies if they do not leave the bush, and the cyclical plot (village, bush, village) which suggests that they cannot continue living in the bush. The book is also significantly tied together by those transitional chapters, those watershed chapters, which are comprised of character sketches. Each sketch is an ominous picture of the British gentleman who fails in the bush.

Tom Wilson may be seen merely as a humorous eccentric, but he really serves a larger purpose, for the impractical, absent-minded Tom, a caricature of the British gentleman, is totally incapable of coping with the bush. He fails, and his failure foreshadows Moodie's failure. (pp. 26-8)

At first reading, Brian the Still Hunter, may appear as no more than an interesting character, a Canadian counterpart of the American Natty Bumpo, the isolated gentleman of the woods who sees the woods as God's temple and who in his theological musings seems as much mystic as woodsman. But Mrs. Moodie's sketch of Brian is not a comforting one. How can one man be so violent and so gentle? This seems to be the question she is asking. . . . In his eccentricity, Brian is a mad version of the British gentleman who has gone native, who has been swallowed up by the bush, while somehow retaining the courtesy of a gentleman. His madness surely is an extension of Tom Wilson's eccentricity, and his failure a foreshadowing of the Moodies' possible end. (pp. 28-9)

Thus, despite the unevenness of Susanna Moodie's style, her contradictory set of purposes, and the anecdotal fragmentation of her story, a basic pattern unfolds in *Roughing it in the Bush*. The movement is from romantic anticipation to disillusionment, from nature as beautiful and benevolent to nature as a dangerous taskmaster. The story moves from her experience of the sublime to her catalogue of near disasters. What remains constant is Mrs. Moodie's viewpoint, an ironic and skeptical retrospection, which from the first pages brings into question the heady optimism of the emigrant. The character sketches are constant too as they imply that the British gentleman must fail in the bush. Susanna Moodie's basic fable warns "Beware!" (p. 30)

> *R. D. MacDonald, "Design and Purpose," in* Canadian Literature, *No. 51, Winter, 1972, pp. 20-31.*

CARL BALLSTADT   (essay date 1972)

[*Using as his starting point a series of sketches entitled "Sketches from the Country" that Moodie contributed to the journal* La belle assemblée *in 1827-29, Ballstadt examines the influence of Mary Russell Mitford's works on Moodie's sketches, including those that comprise* Roughing It in the Bush.]

Susanna Moodie's *Roughing It in the Bush* has long been recognized as a significant and valuable account of pioneer life in Upper Canada in the mid-nineteenth century. From among a host of journals, diaries, and travelogues, it is surely safe to say, her book is the one most often quoted when the historian, literary or social, needs commentary on backwoods people, frontier living conditions, or the difficulty of adjustment experienced by such upper middle-class immigrants as Mrs. Moodie and her husband.

The reasons for the pre-eminence of *Roughing It in the Bush* have also long been recognized. Mrs. Moodie's lively and humorous style, the vividness and dramatic quality of her characterization, the strength and good humour of her own personality as she encountered people and events have contributed to make her book a very readable one. For these reasons it enjoys a prominent position in any survey of our literary history, and, indeed, it has become a "touchstone" of our literary development. (p. 32)

Except for passing reference, Susanna Moodie's literary practice and acquaintanceships in England have not been considered in relationship to the form and techniques of her most successful book. As a member of a literary family which drew some attention to itself amongst minor English literary circles, Susanna Strickland sought and established literary friendships, and as a writer she followed an established pattern which, even had she remained in England, would very probably have led her to produce a book similar in many respects to *Roughing It in the Bush*. At the very least, however, when Susanna emigrated to Canada, she brought with her an awareness of models for a book of sketches about a region and its people. (p. 33)

During the years 1827-1829, Susanna Strickland contributed a series of prose sketches to a London periodical for ladies entitled *La Belle Assemblée* which was edited by a Suffolk native and friend of the Strickland family, Thomas Harral. The series, **"Sketches from the Country"**, consists of five pieces: **"The Witch of East Cliff"**, **"The Two Fishermen"**, **"Naomi"**, **"The Dead Man's Grave"**, and **"Old Hannah, or, the Charm"**. The first four involve Suffolk legends told to the author by elderly natives of the region. Unfortunately, they are marred by an excessively metaphorical style and are without restraint on sentiment. Only in the introduction does the author exercise economy and limit her pen to what she really knows. The fifth sketch is Susanna's personal recollection of a maid-servant at Reydon Hall, the Strickland home in Suffolk, near Southwold. It reflects warmth and good humour, and, perhaps because it is personal, is characterized by a greater directness and simplicity of style than the preceding sketches.

The importance of this series of sketches is that it represents Susanna's early attempt to emulate the writing of Mary Russell Mitford and to do for Suffolk what Miss Mitford did so prolifically and so well for Berkshire. (pp. 33-4)

Such emulation is indicated in the titles and contents of Susanna's country sketches. In the *Our Village* sketches, Miss Mitford was wont to include portraits of rural characters, accounts of country walks, and tributes to rural institutions. . . . The style is familiar and direct, exhibiting a fine attention to detail; the tone is delicate and quiet. They are sketches of ordinary life and the emphasis is upon the colour and charm of rural living. The introduction to "Hannah Bint" is a good example of her loving attention to nature, as a prelude to the character and situation of a country friend. . . . (p. 35)

The same kind of introduction is employed by Susanna in her country scenes, particularly in **"Old Hannah"** and **"The Dead Man's Grave"**. The latter is characterized by the similar attention to the particulars of a locale related to a specific history or event. . . . In the introductions to four of her sketches and throughout her reminiscence of Old Hannah, Susanna Strick-

land's series reminds one of Mitford's attention to a region and its people; it is local colour fiction.

It seems very likely, then, that when Susanna Moodie decided to write of her Canadian experiences near Cobourg and Peterborough, she would have thought of Miss Mitford's books on rural life and scenery. A connection seems indicated not only by her early interest in *Our Village,* but by the fact that parts of *Roughing It in the Bush* were first published as a series of **"Canadian Sketches"** in the *Literary Garland*. That series of six sketches includes a country walk, a backwoods custom, and portraits of eccentric or peculiar characters, all categories used by Mary Mitford, and all assuming an important place in *Roughing It in the Bush* when it was published in 1852. For the British reader of the mid-nineteenth century, large sections of **"Uncle Joe and his Family"**, **"Brian the Still Hunter"**, **"The Charivari"**, **"The Wilderness and Our Indian Friends"**, and **"The Walk to Dummer"** would satisfy an appetite for impressions of the peculiarities of custom and character in British North America.

Of course, *Roughing It* was conditioned by other important factors and, therefore, has different components and tones than *Our Village*. Mrs. Moodie had more functions than one to fulfil in writing her book. She wished to convey information to prospective immigrants, to tell her personal story of fortunes and misfortunes, and to create impressions and descriptions. She is, therefore, the essayist as well as the story-teller, and *Roughing It* is both a didactic book, an autobiography, and a sketch-book of pioneer life.

In *Our Village* the author's personality as a unifying factor is much less important. Although the sketches which are entirely devoted to seasonal country walks express Mitford's personal delight in nature, she is generally objective and does not obtrude with her personal fortunes.

Differences in the tone and flavour of the two books are largely due to the landscape which each writer focuses on. While Miss Mitford's sketches take on the gentle and fertile character of the Berkshire countryside, Mrs. Moodie's reflect the larger dimensions of the Canadian scene and the sense of challenge which the bold extremes of Canadian climate and landscape demanded. (pp. 35-7)

> *Carl Ballstadt, "Susanna Moodie and the English Sketch," in* Canadian Literature, *No. 51, Winter, 1972, pp. 32-8.*

DAVID STOUCK (essay date 1974)

[*Stouck discusses the conflict in* Roughing It in the Bush *between Moodie's romantic descriptions of nature and her accounts of the harsh reality of daily pioneer life. He concludes that Moodie's "personal drama of rejection and exile and her search for a refuge from an uncaring world" are central to the Canadian imaginative experience.*]

As we struggle in Canada to define our national identity in terms of a literary tradition, we repeatedly come up against Susanna Moodie's *Roughing It in the Bush,* a conceded classic, but a book which has resisted definition and critical assimilation. Part of the reason for this is formal. *Roughing It* is generically a collection of sketches, and this loose narrative form admits the inclusion of almost any kind of literary expression: landscape description, character portraits, legends and anecdotes, philosophical reflection. Mrs. Moodie accordingly lets the Crusoe-like interest of the book (her account of survival in the backwoods) be diverted for long stretches at a time by other preoccupations. But perhaps the greater reason for our confused and dislocated responses to this book lies in our learned cultural expectations. As North Americans we have been conditioned to view the pioneer experience as the heroic period of our history, as a simpler and more affirmative era in which our ancestors made creative sacrifices to ensure and enhance the lives of future generations. But *Roughing It* is no splendid celebration of pioneer life such as we find in the classic texts of American literature, no Franklinesque account of how to rise in the world; rather it is a tale of hardship and misery which culminates in withdrawal and defeat. Above all it is a book which denies the myths of renaissance and individual power in a new land. As Canadians we are now making many reversals in our thinking, and if we are willing to relinquish what ideally might have been our first account of heroic pioneer life, we will be rewarded in turn with a book which is imaginatively much richer than we might have guessed, a book more subtle, complex, devious.

A collection of sketches (and Thoreau's *Walden* is a good example of this form developed to its highest literary and philosophical end) achieves its unity and interest from the personality of the writer, and it is with this aspect of *Roughing It* that I am most concerned. Formally speaking, Mrs. Moodie's journal is not a work of art; however, the personality of the narrator has an imaginative numinousness which has caught a sympathetic reflection in the contemporary sensibility (witness the collection of poems by Margaret Atwood, *The Journals of Susanna Moodie* [see excerpt dated 1970]) and which is often paralleled in the work of Canadian artists in the past. What is initially so fascinating in the journals is the way Mrs. Moodie's public statements continually belie the drift of her unconscious feelings. As Margaret Atwood has put it, Mrs. Moodie speaks with two voices: with one, her public voice, she attempts to affirm the myths of the pioneer experience and lauds Canada as the land of future promise; but with the other, her private voice, she inadvertently expresses negative, inadmissable feelings which invalidate her patriotic rhetoric. The fundamental opposition or tension between these two voices (between what is socially acceptable and desired and what is privately felt) gives the book an imaginative dimension which other accounts of life in the Canadian backwoods do not have.

Mrs. Moodie's imaginative conflict is most strikingly apparent in the book's style—in the contrast, for example, between the Wordsworthian response to the Canadian landscape and the writer's detailed, day-to-day observations. Nurtured on the romantic myths of early nineteenth-century England, Mrs. Moodie, on first viewing the rugged scenery along the St. Lawrence, responds in a rhapsodic manner:

> The previous day had been dark and stormy, and a heavy fog had concealed the mountain chain, which forms the stupendous background to this sublime view, entirely from our sight. As the clouds rolled away from their grey, bald brows, and cast into denser shadow the vast forest belt that girdled them round, they loomed out like mighty giants—Titans of the earth, in all their rugged and awful beauty—a thrill of wonder and delight pervaded my mind. The spectacle floated dimly on my sight—my eyes were blinded with tears—blinded by the excess of beauty. I turned to the right and to the left, I looked up and down the glorious river, never

had I beheld so many striking objects blended into one mighty whole! Nature had lavished all her noblest features in producing that enchanting scene.

The landscape in this passage is scarcely described; the distant panorama yields to an idea and correspondent emotion which blinds the narrator to the actual scene itself. The idea of nature as an unfailing source of inspiration persists throughout the journal, and in her public-spirited, affirmative mood, Mrs. Moodie asserts that "Nature ever did, and I hope ever will, continue: *'To shoot marvellous strength into my heart.'"* . . . But that very passage is followed by a confession that her feeling for Canada was like the feeling of a condemned criminal whose only hope for escape is through the grave. In the accounts of day-to-day life there are descriptions of nature which, far from Wordsworthian rhapsody, direct us to an undercurrent of negative feeling about the country and the conditions of pioneer life:

> A thaw in the middle of winter is the most disagreeable change that can be imagined. After several weeks of clear, bright, bracing, frosty weather, with a serene atmosphere and cloudless sky, you awake one morning surprised at the change in the temperature; and, upon looking out of the window, behold the woods obscured by a murky haze—not so dense as an English November fog—but more black and lowering—and the heavens shrouded in a uniform covering of leaden-coloured clouds, deepening into a livid indigo at the edge of the horizon. The snow, no longer hard and glittering, has become soft and spongy, and the foot slips into a wet and insidiously-yielding mass at every step. From the roof pours down a continuous stream of water, and the branches of the trees, collecting the moisture of the reeking atmosphere, shower it upon the earth from every dripping twig. . . .

In this mood the author describes not just the horizon, but the details in the foreground in a realistic, documentary style which is closer to the style of F. P. Grove than to her contemporaries. This is the mood in which the author explores her genuinely imaginative feelings about Canada, though at the same time never allowing herself to abandon the nineteenth-century myths of nature, mother country and pioneer.

The conflict of styles, however, involves much more than simply a literary manner unevenly executed. The Wordsworthian stance was for Mrs. Moodie not just a learned set of attitudes or an affected literary pose, but something integral to her personality—a definition of self fundamental to survival in the backwoods. What emerges in the author's account of her rude experiences is a deep-seated fear of social contact, and her *role* as a gentlewoman in the wilderness is clearly a vital defence against what she fears most. By defining herself as both a gentlewoman and a woman of letters she is able to evade a reflexive relationship with the other settlers in the area. Even more to the point she is able to evade the social failure such relationships might precipitate. Likely our first opinion of Mrs. Moodie is that she is an intolerable prude, that she is proud and affected beyond endurance. She defines her Canadian neighbours as her inferiors, both socially and intellectually, and thus explains her reluctance to participate in their society. . . . But it is a simple truth that pride invariably has its source in feelings of self-doubt, and in order to read Mrs. Moodie's journal with any sympathy we must recognize that her role playing throughout is a bulwark against a profound sense of inadequacy. (pp. 463-66)

Mrs. Moodie's sense of failure and inadequacy, which she in part cloaks under her role of gentlewoman in the backwoods, extends further than ineptitude at frontier tasks; it is rooted deeply in her nature and finds direct expression when she reflects on her separation from England. In outbursts of homesickness she upbraids herself as a guilty, unworthy creature whose exile in Canada is a form of punishment for an unspecified crime. . . . Her sense of failure is reinforced by her anomolous presence in the backwoods, and she retreats into her role as a gentlewoman in exile. Nor is there escape for Mrs. Moodie through her husband, for he is a weak, unsuccessful man and during moments of crisis is invariably absent. Only through her writing can Mrs. Moodie salvage something of her life, and here she significantly evades self-confrontation and dramatizes herself as a martyr figure—a victim of unjust social conditions in England and a heroic pioneer, sacrificing personal happiness so that a new country can be formed. (pp. 466-67)

In lieu of personal achievements her narrative focuses on an impersonal image of growth—the idea of Canada, "a noble, free, and rising country" . . . and the idea of mankind in general slowly but surely moving toward the fulfilment of a sublime and mysterious destiny (a sentimental vision accommodating both Victorian Christianity and something like Social Darwinism). Such statements throughout the book project an idealized and dramatic sense of self in relation to society, but one which fails to convince as a total self-image. More revealing and suggestive is the way random vignettes in the narrative—the character sketches and anecdotes—fall together to form a pattern of social aversion and a preoccupation with failure and death. All the characters that Mrs. Moodie describes at any length are, like herself, totally out of place in the backwoods. (p. 468)

Perhaps the most vivid of the character sketches is the portrait of Malcolm, "the Little Stumpy Man", who, uninvited, stays with the Moodies for nine months. Mrs. Moodie's unyielding social manner is nowhere as omnipresent and oppressive. One critic [R. D. MacDonald] has suggested that Mrs. Moodie's fear of Malcolm and his ill temper is actually sexual in origin, that she is at a fundamental level attracted to him physically. Typically, Mrs. Moodie deflects the reader's attention from herself to the unscrupulous character of her visitor (as she does in describing her borrowing neighbours) and thereby covers her true feelings. She was writing, of course, in a prohibitive, genteel tradition, so that sex is limited to such innocent vignettes as the courtship of the servants, Jacob and Mary. But when sex does appear (and sex does represent the most complete form of social communion possible) violence and death are its corollary. When Malcolm, left alone one day with Mrs. Moodie, tells his story, he reveals that he is a murderer (he once shot a man in South America) and is haunted by guilt. The same unrecognized equation is more blatantly operative in the charivari stories where sex is invariably a cause for violence and, in the case of the Negro who marries a white woman, the occasion for death.

We do not know the exact process by which the journals took final shape (whether extracted from diaries or written as sketches entirely from memory), but in the reshaping of the original experience Mrs. Moodie selects and omits detail in response

to the unconscious drift of her feelings and in accord with a dramatic sense of self. Though not a work of art *Roughing It* has a definite imaginative shape in both the structure of its events and its patterns of imagery. The picture of Canada as a land of failure and death is present from the beginning with the ship of emigrants journeying into a country laid waste by cholera. . . . Mrs. Moodie's final stance in the book is not unlike that of the Ancient Mariner who tells of his voyage through guilt, despair and death and who reemerges to warn those who might follow in his path.

The important question remains to be asked: in what ways do Mrs. Moodie and her journal represent the origins of a Canadian imaginative tradition? At least three definable aspects of her experience seem to be continuous in Canadian life. First, the Moodies, like the United Empire Loyalists before them and like great numbers of people since, came to Canada not with a dream of carving individual empires, but with the modest hope of salvaging a way of life threatened at home. In the Moodies' case poverty was the specific ill which caused them to emigrate, although political and religious reasons were also common. Like so many of the genteel poor from England and Scotland the Moodies sought in Canada a refuge, a way of saving pride in the face of ever dwindling economic and social circumstances. The contrast to the creative and forward-looking American experience in the eighteenth and nineteenth centuries is absolutely crucial to understanding a distinctively Canadian imaginative tradition. Seeking a haven in which to preserve customs threatened at home is imaginatively at the opposite pole from rejecting the old order and emigrating in order to begin life anew. The backward-looking nature of the Canadian experience is reflected in Mrs. Moodie's nostalgia for the daisy-covered fields of her England home. The original sense in Canada of being nowhere, or in exile, has left an indelible print on the Canadian psyche. . . . (pp. 469-71)

Secondly, the image of one of our first settlers as a self-pitying failure rather than a bouyant pioneer characterizes a literary tradition in which fictional protagonists more likely lose than win, or are, at best, sorely compromised by their situation in life. The hard, intractable landscape seems to breed a conviction of inescapable defeat in the Canadian hero, a feeling which also colours his social relations. (p. 471)

Thirdly, the curious affection Mrs. Moodie feels for her forest home at the time of departure is an ascetic form of imaginative pleasure which recurs with significant frequency in Canadian art. Through suffering and self-denial Mrs. Moodie has become attached to her way of life in the backwoods and to her home which she describes as "consecrated by the memory of a thousand sorrows." In a harsh, punitive landscape life is imaginatively conducted with a heightened sense of formidable odds and an almost pleasurable certainty of ultimate defeat. . . . Mrs. Moodie's *Roughing It in the Bush* is not a work of art, but the narrator's personal drama of rejection and exile and her search for a refuge from an uncaring world is very central to what is imaginative in the Canadian experience. (pp. 471-72)

> *David Stouck, " 'Secrets of the Prison-House': Mrs. Moodie and the Canadian Imagination," in The Dalhousie Review, Vol. 54, No. 3, Autumn, 1974, pp. 463-72.*

ROBIN MATHEWS (essay date 1975)

[*Mathews considers the political orientation of* Roughing It in the Bush *and* Life in the Clearings. *Examining in particular Moodie's stance toward individualism, republicanism, and capitalism, Mathews then relates these issues to her depiction of nature and society.*]

Roughing It in the Bush has a classic shape, almost a quality of pre-destination about it, seen in retrospect. It is about the arrival of an immigrant to Canada. It is about her expectations, her surprises, and the day to day reality of life in Canada. It is about the hard task of settling, of discovering the people already present. It takes Mrs. Moodie through isolation, physical discomfort, bad and good neighbours, work in the fields, storm, fire, frost and the beginning of family. It is about evaluation and adaptation and a final move from the bush to Belleville. Mrs. Moodie reveals the genuine feelings of homesickness, uncertainty, discomfort that afflict the immigrant. She shows the forces at work to mould society in Canada—the Canadian dialectic becomes plain in her work. The book was written, some critics tell us repeatedly, by an English "aristocrat"(?) who rejects "democracy" and believes in the class system. Susanna Moodie did believe in the inevitability of social stratification, but the other claims against her are nonsense. She was, in fact, a pink tory, historical precursor to the Red Tory in Canada. . . . Susanna Moodie supported meritocracy. She moved towards breakdown of class as it was defined in Europe. She rejected individualism and—in a not fully articulated way—capitalist exploitation. She saw the threat to Canadian survival and development of community in the differences based on anything other than morals and education. And she saw the danger of uninhibited individualism. In *The Victoria Magazine,* December, 1847, Mrs. Moodie wrote that "The want of education and moral training, is the only *real* barrier that exists between the different classes of man. Nature, reason, and Christianity, recognize no other." That does not mean she was an equalitarian, because she wasn't. Ideas of total equality in her day were expressed in terms of political republicanism and social individualism. She rejected both. "Perfect unadulterated republicanism, is a beautiful but fallacious chimera, which never did exist on earth, and which . . . will not exist in heaven." (p. 4)

Individualism in **Roughing It in the Bush,** under the guise of egalitarianism, becomes the right to exploit, the right to invade. The individualistic Yankees have a real feeling of superiority, of wounded superiority, usually. Mrs. Moodie attacks the levelling pressure they exert. (p. 6)

Mrs. Moodie rejects the individualism of the Yankee; she struggles against it. But she loses much of her sense of hierarchy and belief in class superiority in Canada. She was a "progressive" thinker before she left England, and the terms of life in Canada developed the pinkness of her toryism. The Yankee is a small part of her training and provides, for the most part, a negative example. The Yankee and the U. S. A. are credited by some with teaching Mrs. Moodie about equality. But the Yankees she meets in **Roughing It in the Bush**—the majority of them—exploit her, reject her, and deny the possibility of a community based on trust. She learns cooperation partly because of the threat of the Yankee. Experience among Canadians cooperating and moving by merit brings her to a sense that class definitions of worth don't work. At one level, her advice to most gentry to stay out of Canada and her praise of people used to hard work make that point clear enough.

Mrs. Moodie is a democrat in the Canadian sense, but she abhors the individualist "democracy" of the U. S. She makes a great plea to Canadians to build their own community in gentle evolution from the mother country. (p. 7)

Near the close of **Life in the Clearings,** Mrs. Moodie is writing about the sublimity of Niagara Falls and its evocation of religious feeling. She writes that the U. S. intends to harness its side for industry:

> Ye Gods, what next will the love of gain suggest to these gold-worshippers. The whole earth should enter into a protest against such an act of sacrilege—such a shameless desecration of one of the noblest works of God.

Mrs. Moodie's apostrophe to 'the whole earth' sounds very modern in the light of recent, apparently new, concerns about nature and pollution. But in relation to a major theme in Canadian imaginative development her comment is only partly metaphorical.

Like many other Canadian writers she sees mankind's interrelation with what is called the "external world" as organic. Her move is away from the conservative view of a hierarchical, organically related society to a feeling of the possibility that society can be cooperative and egalitarian in organically continuous terms. (pp. 7-8)

Mrs. Moodie is deeply affected by the grandeur, majesty, stupendousness, sublimity, the excess of beauty, and the titanic aspects of the physical world. The experience is described in particularly Christian terms by her. But landscape and the elements become, for some later writers, an expression of the powers larger than self which may be historical, geological, cosmic—but not necessarily idealistic in an anti-materialist sense. They represent the extension and complication of real forces. They represent, therefore, an expression of reality which is comprehended by the 'native' and is integral with the values of the settlers and community builders. The experience, according to Mrs. Moodie, was unique. That would mean that the form of reality created here would also be unique. "Never," she says, "had I beheld so many striking objects blended into one mighty whole." (p. 8)

The enormity of the new experience of the physical environment is clearly connected to religious feelings for Mrs. Moodie. . . . Her experience of the physical world in Canada does not alienate her, nor does it make her despair at an apparent insignificance and absurdity of human life. Rather, it transforms her view of herself; it rearranges meaning for her. . . . Mrs. Moodie responds to her experience of the sublime with a reaffirmation of human meaning. (pp. 8-9)

Mrs. Moodie does not delude herself that Canada is Eden or that she is in the moral condition of our first parents. Canadian landscape, for her, connects her soul with God. There is a presiding power that gives her strength in the task of building civil society. . . .

The struggle necessary to make Canada a civilized society is insisted upon throughout **Roughing It in the Bush** and throughout Canadian literature. (p. 10)

In case there should be argument about Mrs. Moodie's sense of the moral condition of the Canadian new world, she defines it unequivocally. Nature is there as God made it; man must struggle *against himself* for perfected community:

> The unpeopled wastes of Canada must present the same aspect to the new settler that the world did to our first parents after their expulsion from the Garden of Eden; all the sin which could defile the spot, or haunt it with the association

of departed persons concentrated in their own persons.

In those terms *Roughing It in the Bush* has a larger life. For Mrs. Moodie is saying that the social, religious, and political philosophy of the perceiver decides his or her view of place. (p. 11)

Mrs. Moodie sees herself as part of a human network that is historically significant. . . . She moves in a complex way through what might be called one of the first steps in the Canadian experience, for she is at once *ingenue* and sophisticate. She is also *voyager*. As *ingenue* she can expose herself totally to the abuse of others in order to reveal their characters fully. . . . She is from an old world of ordered values and hierarchy, and so she can judge, or provide imaginative room for the reader to judge, the differences, failings and strengths of the new society and particular types in it. As a character typical of Canadian immigrants, in her mixture of ingenuousness and sophistication, she can involve the reader in her own character and in its growth and transformation.

Both *Roughing It in the Bush* and *Life in the Clearings* are voyages of discovery. The first is a voyage into the deeps of new settlements to discover what the terms of survival and community will be. There is a physical struggle in the material environment. But the primary struggle is with the definition of human kind in the new community, growing from the types of settlers, the effects of the physical environment, the clash of ideologies, the struggle within people of the old values and the new terms. (pp. 11-12)

The voyage structure of Mrs. Moodie's two works allows her to deal both widely and deeply with the definition of human kind in the Canadian new world. *Roughing It in the Bush* deals with ecstatic religious experience, attempted suicide and suicide, murder, madness, rejection, personal cruelty, and physical struggle to survive the extremes of frost and fire. *Life in the Clearings* is presented as a voyage to Niagara Falls, already in 1853 a place of social recourse and, fittingly, the destination of the voyage, a destination which Mrs. Moodie knows about, this time, in advance. . . . Mrs. Moodie was asked, as a kind of sequel to *Roughing It in the Bush* to tell about the state of society in the colony. The atmosphere of *Life in the Clearings* is the atmosphere of an achieved society. The battle, in a sense, has been won within the terms that she set as the dialectic. Canada is developing more slowly than the U. S. A. industrially and technologically. . . . She can believe that the cultural values in British North America are better and will be more powerful than the force of individualist capitalism in the U. S. A. But, of course, economics in Canada is also based on a structure of individualist capitalism, too. But Mrs. Moodie does not, and need not see that.

Yankee power is present, is an assumption of British North American consciousness. In fact, Mrs. Moodie includes two sketches entitled, **"Trials of a Travelling Musician,"** published first in her *Victoria Magazine* in 1847 and employing the techniques of Thomas C. Haliburton's *The Clockmaker*. Mrs. Moodie turns the coin over, however, and tells tales of a Canadian travelling in the U. S. In that way she can present a picture of U. S. society, employing the gentle satire of Haliburton for the purpose she has in *Life in the Clearings,* a gentler examination of the dialectic of forces than in *Roughing It in the Bush*. In that book she spends some time depicting the Yankee in Canada. In *Life in the Clearings* she uses the travelling musician to show something of the society the Yankees have come from.

Using the sketch popular in the England she knew and leaning a little on Haliburton's techniques of humour, Mrs. Moodie creates work in *Roughing It in the Bush* and in its sequel that treats questions and subjects that we shall not be free of in Canada for a long time, employing techniques and archetypes that describe both the Canadian fact and the ways in which Canadians deal with it, or try to.

Mrs. Moodie moves a long way through the immigrant transformation. She wants a government that is "liberal," but not U. S. What she did not know was to become of fundamental importance. She did not know that the cultural, humane, Christian values she espoused could not transform capitalist values. She could not know that the conservatism she expressed could only become North American free enterprise individualism, whatever other name it was given. Conservatism in the hands of free enterprise capitalism could only be a class ideology alienated from the land and the people, abusive of the material world and people. Mrs. Moodie's final paragraphs in *Life in the Clearings* seek to find a balance between a genuine idea of conservative organic class interdependence and the potential in Canada to release individual and group energy in an increasingly egalitarian system. She cannot forbear to make clear that she does *not* see the U. S. as having achieved a kind of life Canadians should seek. . . . (pp. 12-13)

Mrs. Moodie was a tory, but she was a pink tory. She did not believe in the supremacy of the individual. She combined a sense of the past and a sense of community with a clear sense of what needed to be changed. That means she recognized the importance of past experience to present community, at the same time as she perceived the new and peculiar demands of Canadian conditions on the life of the society and the individual. . . . She did not believe the individual was supreme; she believed in the *inalienable responsibility* of the individual to a concept of community and to the actual social order. . . .

Mrs. Moodie dealt greatly with the first steps towards Canadian society. She understood the rejection of the U. S., the necessary connection of Canadians with nature, the role of woman as community builder, the role of merit, and the place of education in the new Canadian place. But she was unaware—she almost could not be aware—of the ways in which the U. S. State would use economic techniques and technological novelty as soldiers in an army of political, cultural, and economic invasion. She could not see that Canadians of wealth would become the office

The Moodies' cottage at Belleville. Photograph by Michael Peterman.

clerks of U. S. expansionism as well as the individual exploiters of Canada themselves. That realization—and the understanding of the steps necessary to change our condition—have come late in the day. The next step—le prochain episode—has been left to Canadians of our time. (p. 14)

Robin Mathews, *"Susanna Moodie, Pink Toryism, and Nineteenth Century Ideas of Canadian Identity,"* in Journal of Canadian Studies/Revue d'études canadiennes, *Vol. X, No. 3, August, 1975, pp. 3-15.*

CAROL SHIELDS (essay date 1977)

[*In her study of Moodie's prose works, Shields traces three recurring major themes: complex personalities, sexual reversal, and social structure. The following excerpt presents Shields's comments on the complex characterizations in Moodie's novels, short stories, and autobiographical sketches.*]

Flora Lyndsay, Mrs. Moodie writes of one of her heroines, "delighted in the study of human character." . . . And in speaking of Flora she might just as easily have been speaking of herself. Despite the fact that she often hid her absorption in personality behind the screen of nature and religion, the power and mystery of personality emerges as her overriding concern. Personality in all forms—amusing, ironic, or tragic—appears to have been her greatest diversion, and it is by examples of human personality that she attempts to divert her readers. (p. 11)

Personality, individual or collective, is her major theme; but what frees her work from the commonplaceness of the character sketch is her concern with enigma, the extreme personality, the unfathomable, the complex, the personality which refuses to break down under analysis. (p. 12)

Compared to the characters in Mrs. Moodie's Canadian books, the personalities in her fiction are often mere instruments in a plot. Uncle Beaumont in the story **"Waiting For Dead Men's Shoes,"** *(Matrimonial Speculations . . .)* is vulnerable, comic, and picturesque with his fortune, his gout, and his love of food, but he never exhibits any of the complexity with which Mrs. Moodie describes those in her Canadian books. In her Canadian characters, Brian and Malcolm, for instance, there are blurred edges, the suggestion that it is not always possible to sum up human personality. Brian and Malcolm are not part of a story but are stories in themselves.

Many of the personalities she describes have the sketchy offbeat quality of newspaper stories or local scandals. Random and pointless, they clutter her narrative, and even Mrs. Moodie seems to sense that they are inappropriate. (pp. 12-13)

It is relatively easy to separate those stories which are hearsay from those which Mrs. Moodie has experienced firsthand. Obeying her autobiographical urge, she intrudes into many of her own stories, gladly taking a part and often the most important part. Even when she stands in the background, the reader is aware of a rush of sympathy toward the character she is describing. (p. 13)

In those stories which she has obviously collected second-hand, she frequently signifies distance by assigning another narrator or by devising a dialogue which excludes herself. Physical details are strikingly absent, and so is the almost cinematic quality she evokes when she has actually witnessed such a scene as the prison of Kingston or the lunatic asylum at Toronto. But most telling of all is her plunge from the salty, almost colloquial descriptions of human activity to the con-

ventional rhetoric which is the mark of her fiction. *Life in the Clearings* with its much greater second-hand content is a more subdued and formal book than the lively and autobiographical *Roughing It in the Bush.*

Perhaps the most appealing aspect of Mrs. Moodie's descriptions of human personality is her all-embracing acceptance of human variety and the infrequency of her moral judgments. Criminals, the most deviant of human beings, fill her with exhilaration rather than disgust. The "study" of human behaviour, as she calls it, includes all extremes of humanity, even the simple and the insane. The inmates of the asylum amuse her by their ironic self-misrepresentations, and she sees madness not as a horror, but as an alternative human response. (pp. 13-14)

It is indicative of Mrs. Moodie's overriding concern with the complexities of human personality that she is unable to sustain an abstract argument without illustrating it, frequently to the point of imbalance. For instance, in *Life in the Clearings* . . . she launches into an attack on the social custom of wearing mourning, beginning with a brief discussion of the foolishness of mourning from a religious standpoint. "It is not a reproach to Him" . . . , she asks, when all nature is in a perpetual state of change? From the religious reference she hastens through the philosophical arguments to the social argument which interests her far more and which she illustrates with a total of eleven anecdotes. These stories, some of them fragmentary and some of them crisply detailed, over-argue the case so emphatically that the reader suspects they exist for their entertainment value alone. Her best anecdotes are those in which irony is the controlling mood as in the story about a woman who orders her mourning clothes before the expected death of her brother and then is disappointed when he lives through his illness. . . . (pp. 14-15)

Human detail outweighs the literary framework in Mrs. Moodie's Canadian books; the framework, in fact, can be accommodated to hold any number of stories. . . . Her transitions tend to be either fragile or crude, and sometimes even nonexistent, but she seems not in the least reluctant to interrupt her design with a sketch from human nature.

The chapter on work bees in *Roughing It in the Bush* . . . is typical of a series of short, disjointed human anecdotes grouped under a chapter theme. Mrs. Moodie disliked bees, considering them a necessary evil in frontier life. The only redeeming feature was the opportunity they afforded to view an odd assortment of humanity at a glance and to study the interaction of personality. Temperance men such as her brother and husband are dismissed quickly. It is the more offbeat guests who engage her: old Wittals who combined a speech defect with a gross appetite; an illiterate but amazingly successful revival preacher; John who is unrivaled at the art of swearing; the slightly but not obnoxiously drunken Malachi Chroak who foolishly pretends to force one of the maids into marriage. All these sketches are slight; they seem to have been written from notes and suggest an awe for human variability rather than individuality.

But Mrs. Moodie's curiosity is also excited by characters viewed in isolation; she is detached, almost scientific at times, offering little which might be considered judgmental on individual human irregularities. (p. 15)

Eccentricity, which Mrs. Moodie not only tolerated but relished, is most frequently attached to the upper-class and appears in her work to be, almost without exception, a male indulgence; women were too occupied, apparently, to stray from the conventional path for long, and as for the poor, such deviations in behaviour were more likely to be viewed as barbarous and ignorant than tolerably eccentric. Some of the eccentric personalities described by Mrs. Moodie are so extraordinary that she feels compelled to supply a supporting footnote. (p. 16)

Gentleness usually accompanies the variety of eccentricity she describes, and her human oddities are often kind to the point of aberration. Wilhelmina Carr in *Flora Lyndsay* is expansively generous, and Tom Wilson in *Roughing It in the Bush* betrays a curious sweetness beneath his eccentricity. Even Malcolm, who was irritable and rude most of the time, was fond of children and gentle on occasion. And in almost every case of rampant eccentricity, Mrs. Moodie outlines her personalities with loneliness and suffering. Eccentrics such as Brian, Tom, and Malcolm in *Roughing It in the Bush* are not reduced by Mrs. Moodie to comic size; instead they contain their separate afflictions like species of private pain.

In her Canadian books Mrs. Moodie describes countless acts of eccentric and ironic behaviour. But her novels and tales, on the other hand, contain far more interchangeable characters, and personality is more likely to hinge on gender than on personal anomalies. Occasionally, though, her fictitious characters show complexities beyond their role type, and Mrs. Moodie herself, in a discussion of fiction, states her belief that a writer must blend qualities of good and evil in a character in order to make him believable. . . . (pp. 16-17)

William Mathews, for instance, who is a minor character in Mrs. Moodie's novel *Mark Hurdlestone,* is a fairly generalized representation of criminal low life. But he has periods of complexity in which he lapses into feelings of guilt. Mrs. Moodie even supplies him with something like a psychological explanation for his behaviour: the loss of his mother, Mathews says at one point, has flawed his life. Cruel and uneducated, he has strange pockets of sensitivity. When his father dies he says, "Something is gone—a string is loosened from the heart. . . ." Unlike Godfrey, his partner in crime, William is haunted by conscience. Dark, frightening visions torment him, a voice from the "shut up depths" of his heart. . . . Pursued by the law, he is also pursued by "blue devils that pinch and freeze my heart." . . . William speaks with a kind of dark poetry which places him in contrast to Godfrey, but, disappointingly, Mrs. Moodie does not develop his personality further; instead she allows him to harden along criminal lines. (p. 17)

In *Mark Hurdlestone,* the leading character is greatly simplified by Mrs. Moodie at first. He is the unmitigated consummation of evil: "There was not a drop of human kindness in his composition" . . . , Mrs. Moodie tells her readers. He "never" mingled; he had "no" friends; "no one" had ever shaken his hand. But later his character receives some psychological shading: he is not the personification of wickedness; instead he is mad. He hates women. He is cold and unresponsive. He has a fetish about cleanliness and a mania about gold. He has distinct paranoic symptoms: he believes people are trying to poison him or gain knowledge of his wealth. And he has what Mrs. Moodie hints might be an unnatural relationship with Grenard Pike, a being just as strange in his own way as Hurdlestone.

The Green sisters in the story **"The Miss Greens"** . . . are introduced as highly stereotyped spinster sisters, and one of them, Lydia, never becomes more than a vain, weak creature,

an indolent sipper of brandy. But Polly Green, obviously Mrs. Moodie's favourite just as she is the favourite of the suitor, develops into someone more recognizably human. She even has stirrings of wit; she makes her prayers short, she says, to repay the stinginess of Providence. And though she claims to be no philosopher, in her limited way she is. "Love," she says, "at the best is but a weakness, that the fondest grows ashamed of." . . . John Andrews, returning from his midnight courtship, admits to being half-captivated by Polly. But she never progresses beyond this interesting and contradictory point, and Mrs. Moodie leaves her as a bride, shamefully abandoned at the altar. The whole story, in fact, is marred by a viciousness on the one hand and a heavy-footed irony on the other.

The characters in **"Richard Redpath"** . . . are mainly stylized and conventional. Joshua Baynes, a foolish gourmand, and his daughter Betsey (who grieves when her fiance is drowned because her wedding clothes will be out of fashion before another groom is found) are both without real substance; even Mrs. Moodie doesn't pretend to take them seriously. But the character of Benjamin Levi is confusing, incomplete, and mysterious. Levi is a Jew, but even this status is confused for he terms himself a convert. His profession is not clearly defined either; he is both an editor and a seller of second-hand clothing. . . . Popularly considered to be sly and cunning, Levi is a natural philosopher, a cynic in the Shylock manner, given to such paradoxical declarations as "I never vouch for the truth of a story . . . until I know it to be a lie." . . . It may be that Mrs. Moodie had originally conceived a more ambitious role for Levi, but in a weak conclusion she has him suffer an absurd humiliation and death while her less interesting characters crow with glee. Obviously fascinated with Levi's contradictory personality, Mrs. Moodie has difficulty assimilating him into her fictional world; Levi, like Hurdlestone and William Mathews, is a human oddity who exists on another level of reality.

The reader gets the impression that Mrs. Moodie is unconscious of the contradictory natures of some of her characters. Aunt Dorothy in *Mark Hurdlestone* is one of these unwittingly complex people; she has all the standard equipment of a tart and a witty spinster, but her hatred of men and her contempt for romance have an edge which goes beyond the limits of her conventional role.

Mrs. Moodie's interest in personality is more than passive. She is, by her own frequent admission, a student of human behaviour, and it goes without saying that she interests herself in the motivation behind behaviour. Not surprisingly, she often demonstrates the pre-Freudian prejudices of her time. She is content to dismiss the crime of Grace Marks . . . as an inexplicable visitation of sin. And she takes careful note of the phrenological evidence she sees at the prison in Kingston. She has, in addition, a strong romantic belief in the human countenance as an "index" to the mind. (pp. 17-19)

Mrs. Moodie is a woman of her times who quite naturally reflects current ideas about personality, but often she suggests psychological motivation as well. Brian, the still-hunter, she speculates, has a retarded son whose affliction may be the root of Brian's melancholia. Malcolm, her unwelcome guest, may have acquired his irascible disposition from uncaring parents. In the novel *Flora Lyndsay,* one of her later works, Mrs. Moodie frequently takes the trouble to supply causative factors for personality aberration. Captain Kitson, a neighbour of Flora's, has accumulated his eccentricity through a lifetime of social non-acceptance. Mrs. Ready owes her aggressive vulgarity to a too rapid shift from lower to middle class. Wilhelmina Carr, one of Mrs. Moodie's most extraordinary characters, provides a rapid oral sketch of her life in which many of the seeds of her later bizarre behaviour can be found; her mother had died at her birth, and her stern absentee father had been a figure of fear and dislike. Her stepmother, herself a victim of class dislocation, had indulged her, and her schoolmates had jeered at her physical oddities. Furthermore, the only man she had ever loved had refused her offer of marriage, and the only child she had been drawn to had abandoned her.

Early influences, Mrs. Moodie seems to feel, are permanent and almost impossible to overcome. (p. 20)

Her random and off-hand psychological speculations are sometimes startlingly modern and sound. When Marcella DeTrueba in the story "Richard Redpath" contemplates suicide, she is advised by an old seaman that suicide is no more than a means of punishing someone else; this piece of wisdom is reinforced by a story he tells of his own daughter's suicide. Clearly Mrs. Moodie subscribes to this theory because Marcella instantly recognizes the truth of it.

Aside from describing the motivation behind personality, Mrs. Moodie reveals her characters through combinations of physical description, use of incident and dialogue, shifts in narration, and direct comparison through the mechanical pairing of characters.

Her fictional characters are described in a formulaic manner, but those characters she introduces in her Canadian books are frequently brought to life in a few words. (p. 21)

As in her chapter on bees in *Roughing It in the Bush*, Mrs. Moodie frequently gathers together a number of related anecdotes, interspersing them with comments on society. Writing about the charivari or the Yankee custom of borrowing, she clusters several stories together, each one forming a single snapshot image of a group attitude. The looseness of the form permits her to shift the narration when she chooses: sometimes she tells the story herself, sometimes a friend relates it, and sometimes the story is overheard. . . .

Many of these grouped stories give only the slightest insight into human behaviour, but occasionally Mrs. Moodie is able to encapsulate a personality in a rapid series of incidents. (p. 22)

In revealing personality, Mrs. Moodie has a modern interviewer's knack for asking the right question, inquiring of Brian "what made him so fond of hunting?" . . . She quotes his reply quickly and simply, using the verb "said" in these dialogues, a device Hemingway used much later to focus the reader's attention on the words of the reply. (p. 23)

It is Mrs. Moodie's use of dialogue which does more than anything to relieve her discursive heaviness. When she attempts dialect, which she does frequently in her Canadian books, there is more than a suggestion of condescension, but when she catches regional expressions or subtle class differences, she conveys character concisely and accurately. (pp. 23-4)

In instances where personality is not clearly marked, particularly in her fiction, Mrs. Moodie employs a traditional means of revelation, that of comparing paired personalities. When male characters are being compared in this manner, the twinning is both frequent and fairly rigidly adhered to. The two brothers theme in "Jane Redgrave" is typical: Armyn and Edward Sternfield are brothers competing for their mother's attention. In true Cain-Abel pattern, Armyn is eventually responsible for Edward's death. (p. 24)

The use of pairing of characters to point up personality is less rigid when women are concerned. Women are usually seen in larger groupings, confusing the comparison, and, furthermore, they relate to each other in more subtle ways, sometimes even crossing class lines and forming a flank. (p. 25)

Most of Mrs. Moodie's character revelations seem to be consciously formed from a combination of description, incident, dialogue, and comparison; but in the case of John Lyndsay, the husband of Flora Lyndsay, the personality is revealed, seemingly unconsciously, in his actions and speeches. Indeed, the narrator ironically insists that John Lyndsay is a perfect gentleman. His strength and talents are praised repeatedly, but, in contradiction, his essential heartlessness is revealed again and again. He can't be bothered taking Flora's old nurse to Canada, and even as he is kissing Flora's tears away, he is turning her to his advantage. When she "begged . . . entreated . . . coaxed" him to go on an outing with her, he bluntly refused. . . . Mrs. Moodie puts into his mouth speeches which make him a cruel manipulator. He wins his wife to his side in the argument over immigration by shaming her and making her feel she has been ungrateful. His attitudes are fixed and brutal and he has no tolerance for eccentricity; he is a relentless realist in combat with Flora's romantic nature. "I hate mystery in any shape" he tells Flora with finality. . . . (pp. 25-6)

Flora, on the other hand, even as the narrator insists that she is an obedient wife, shows a willingness to experiment; she has an easy relaxed tolerance and an active curiosity. She is also more intuitive; had the Lyndsays followed Flora's plan of not taking a servant to Canada they would have been better off. Flora's decision on which ship to take was also, in the end, the wiser course.

Flora and John are compared in their attitudes and reactions, but one senses that, though Mrs. Moodie may be consciously making a heroine of Flora, her vilification of John Lyndsay is unconscious. And it is interesting and tempting at this point to make biographical conclusions, for if Flora is a simplified extension of the author, John is almost certainly a counterpart of John Moodie, Mrs. Moodie's difficult husband, a stubborn man who was not particularly likeable or fortunate in personal dealings.

Indeed the character sketches in *Roughing It in the Bush* have one common link: most of them, at least the best of them, are of failed upper-class Englishmen—Tom, Brian, Malcolm, and always, hovering in the background, the shadow of Mr. Moodie himself. They constitute a type which Mrs. Moodie is able to represent dramatically, for in each case there is a sense of inevitability. Goodness is defeated, intelligence is scorned, sensitivity is clouted. The proper equipment for life in the bush, Mrs. Moodie seems to be saying, is ignorance, brute strength, and an absence of preconceptions. (p. 26)

Of all Mrs. Moodie's personality sketches none is more shapely than the portrait of Brian, the still-hunter. . . . The reader senses that the unsolved riddle of Brian's madness forms an exceptional attraction for her. Brian's story begins with a sudden dramatic meeting; there is a flashback about his life narrated by another visitor, and then there are several incidents concerning Brian, each a miniature portrait, each more fully illustrative of his complexity. There is even a monologue in which Brian attempts to explain his life.

Mrs. Moodie is less interested in the cause of his malady than she is in the effect, although she does once suggest that Brian's son's disability may be partially responsible. Brian is a man who is torn apart by ironies: he has several times attempted suicide but is afraid to cross the ocean for fear of drowning. He loves life but finds pleasure in killing. He has caused many of the settlers to fear for their lives, but he brings a message of comfort to Mrs. Moodie. He himself is capable of responding to irony, marvelling that a visiting naturalist should prefer the simple weeds to the lovely flowers. Brian says of the naturalist, "Well he was an innocent man . . . a very little made him happy. . . ." Mrs. Moodie repeats this statement as a double irony, for this is the way she actually sees Brian himself. The chapter on Brian ends a little too rapidly with a hasty note on Brian's later suicide and an equally hasty tribute to his goodness, but one senses that the unfinished edge to the sketch proceeds from Mrs. Moodie's own inability to comprehend the most thrilling and impenetrable of her characters.

"Human nature," Mrs. Moodie writes in *Roughing It in the Bush,* "has more strange varieties than any other menagerie can contain, and Malcolm was one of the oddest of his species." . . . Malcolm, the stranger who forced himself on the Moodies for a period of nine months, is described in the chapter "The Little Stumpy Man." He may be the most complex of all the characters Mrs. Moodie describes. The chapter about him is even more fragmented than her usual writing; she jumps from episode to episode in her frustration with him. She is plainly baffled. The string of anecdotes succeeds in forming a multi-lensed portrait of him, but the portrait is never finished; even Malcolm's eventual disappearance is clouded in mystery.

Usually razor-sharp in her physical descriptions, Mrs. Moodie falters with Malcolm. She is self-contradicting, calling him unpleasant looking, but testifying to his regular features and good colour. His voice is low and mysterious, and she senses that "the current of his feelings seemed to flow in a deep sluggish channel. . . ." The cumulative effect of the description suggests sexuality, and this impression is strengthened as Mrs. Moodie circles around Malcolm, drawing sometimes closer, sometimes further away.

Malcolm's tendency is to be unkind and rude, but in odd moments of intimacy he confesses to self-hatred and perpetual melancholy. In one extraordinary exchange he confesses to Mrs. Moodie that he has murdered a man. Mrs. Moodie receives this confidence with remarkable calm. Suggesting neither trauma nor untruth, she simply adds the murder episode on top of the pile of mysteries. When Malcolm mentions a miserable boyhood, an ill-natured mother, and a brother who was insane, she makes no link between these revelations and Malcolm, the misanthropic adult.

But she herself is more clearly revealed in this chapter than in any other place. Malcolm does not hesitate to tell her she is a prude, and Mrs. Moodie does not hesitate to repeat the charge. He also tells her that he is a man who thinks with his head, not his heart, implying perhaps that she is just the reverse. These personal exchanges between Malcolm and Mrs. Moodie are a real departure from her usual pattern; she is neither the shrewd interviewer nor the unseen observer, but a participating human being who has let her persona slip. She is often angry with her guest, petulant, bored, fascinated, exasperated, wounded, and, in the end, mystified, perhaps as much by herself as with Malcolm.

Margaret Atwood sees Mrs. Moodie as a woman divided down her Victorian middle, all manners and ladylike art forms on one side, and on the other a consciousness of sweat, dirt, disease, and mosquitoes [see excerpt dated 1970]. But it is possible that the dichotomy is not rooted in Mrs. Moodie's personality; it may be only a surface splintering, a division which exists for literary purposes, namely the division between person and persona. Her real and vulnerable self is only occasionally glimpsed. . . . She once refers briefly to the tragic drowning of her son, and there are oblique, scattered references to anxiety, weakness, and ennui, what may have been a nervous collapse near the end of her sojourn in the woods. But these are exceptions, slips of the pen, holes in the persona which she constructed for herself. (pp. 28-31)

Her persona in her early works is that of romantic heroine, the adventurous, felicitous spirit which reached fulfilment in the person of Flora Lyndsay. Mrs. Moodie likes to show herself counselling servant girls, healing the sick, teaching the infidel; she is the generous, humourous, resourceful deliverer as in the chapter "The Walk to Dummer" in *Roughing It in the Bush.* She is proud of her ability to be resourceful and she expresses that pride in ironic terms, the irony being that she, a woman of gentle breeding and education, should now be making coffee with dandelion roots and producing rows of well-hoed potatoes. When she fails in her first bread baking, Tom Wilson says, "I hope you make better books than bread." . . . She replies that she would rather fail as a writer than as a baker, but she is really suggesting the opposite: she is a gentlewoman to whom the mysteries of the household are unknown. Her exploration of domesticity is deliberately childlike, a pose which reinforces the image of herself as a woman of culture.

Her sensitivity to nature, she frequently points out, separates her from other people. . . . Her initial homesickness in Canada is lifted when she encounters the countryside. "It won me from my melancholy and I began to look around me with considerable interest." . . . But her English servant, she points out, does not have the ability to be lifted from sadness by scenery. A positive response to nature signified for Mrs. Moodie a delicacy of taste, an educated sensitivity.

In meeting her new countrymen she contrasts the paucity of their knowledge with her endless fund of facts. She believes that her health is nourished by fresh air, and she eats fresh apples although others tell her not to. She is the keeper of knowledge and the foe of ignorant superstition. Her persona is expanded and reinforced by the fact that she is often victimized by rude borrowing neighbours or scorned by the illiterate for her bookishness. Her uniqueness is stressed by her isolation, and her isolation is increasingly insisted upon as she moves from *Roughing It in the Bush* to the more reflective *Life in the Clearings.*

Her vision of herself as a heroine in an ongoing drama is stated most openly in the chapter "The Burning of the Fallow." In this episode she and her family have narrowly escaped death by fire; at the very moment before destruction a thundershower saves them. Later she learns that the scene has had one chance witness, an Irishman who had watched from a distant canoe. For reasons which she doesn't even attempt to explain, she finds the fact of having had a witness "comforting." It is as though her role-playing is reinforced by the existence of an audience. Her own persona, so patently constructed and so elaborately expanded, would otherwise have dissolved, unwitnessed and unverified, in the backwoods of Canada. From this innocent disclosure, one arrives at the conclusion that all of Mrs. Moodie's writing may have represented an attempt to find confirmation of her existence, an existence which was hidden in an alien wilderness and all but buried alive. (pp. 31-2)

Carol Shields, in her Susanna Moodie: Voice and Vision, *Borealis Press, 1977, 81 p.*

JANET GILTROW   (essay date 1981)

[*Giltrow treats* Roughing It in the Bush *and* Life in the Clearings *as travel narratives. She claims that Moodie's choice of the travel genre demonstrates both her unwillingness to accept her permanent status as an immigrant and her desire to return to England.*]

Frances Trollope's *Domestic Manners of the Americans* is clearly a travel book: it begins with the writer's embarkation from England; it includes large, discursive, informational units comparing life in the New World to life in the Old; it concludes with the writer's departure from the foreign scene. Susanna Moodie's *Roughing It in the Bush* also begins with her departure from home; it includes substantial information on Canadian life, organized for the benefit of European readers. In contrast to Trollope, however, Moodie never made the return trip: her book ends with the family's move from the bush to Belleville, which was a more congenial site but still no asylum on this cheerless continent. But although Moodie's book thus fails to conform to the classic structure of the genre, *Roughing It* is a travel book and the generic values of the text are those of travel narrative. In her rhetorical stance, Moodie is a travel writer; in Canada, she is a watchful visitor—a tourist and sightseer—and her observations are directed toward a European audience.

She arrives in the New World with a ready command of the expressive sentiments of nature description, bringing with her a diction and perspective in tune with the literary habits of eighteenth- and nineteenth-century Grand Tourists. (pp. 132-33)

Moodie's pious pleasure in landscape does not easily anticipate her own incorporation into the scene. In contrast, Catharine Parr Traill's more analytic observations in *The Backwoods of Canada* . . . do look forward to settling down. Where Traill's prose stops at small particulars, Moodie's rides on, along an abstract plane of diffuse enthusiasm. Her high excitement at panoramic vistas and her neglect of concrete details belong to genteel sightseeing—and a quick, unimplicating view of foreign sites.

The ruling conflict in *Roughing It* lies between this travel esthetic and the settler's destiny. In this book and its sequel, *Life in the Clearings,* it seems that Moodie never learned, temperamentally, that the journey was done and travel concluded. She expects, at least unconsciously, that there has been some mistake and that she must finally turn back and resume her route. Obviously, she was pinioned by manifest evidence to the contrary, and the distance between these two poles of mind—the imagination of travel and the realization of stasis—is sometimes resolved in *Roughing It* by the idea of death. Morbidity alleviates the emotional stress of homesickness by suggesting a mystic return-trip, a homing of the spirit to an earthly paradise. Thus Moodie addresses "dear, dear England": "Oh that I might be permitted to return and die upon your wave-encircled shores, and rest my weary head and heart beneath your daisy-covered sod at last!" . . . After a residence of nearly twenty years in Canada, Moodie uses the exclamatory present tense to express the anguish and helplessness of a newcomer.

Her reflections on letters from home, and on the gradual diminishment of their numbers, suggest that for a long while she did not believe she was here to stay. . . . (p. 133)

The "hope of return" is a durable one, on both sides of the breach, but its dissolution is finally inevitable, and emigration is a type of death for the settler. Return and homecoming are privileges of the traveler but not of the emigrant, and in Moodie's view the anticipation of homecoming is the basis for communication between the New World and the Old. To give up hope of return is to suffer the exchange of letters to dwindle and end: a grievous silence marks the irrevocable separation. Communication from the New World to the Old sustains the emigrant in her foreign exile, and maintains her attachment, however attenuated or unrealistic, to the society where she is "known" and from which she derives her identity. The interruption of this vital communication cuts a life-line and sentences the settler to fatal anonymity: "it is as if the grave had closed over you, and the hearts that once knew and loved you know you no more." If we can see this connecting, epistolary current as a survival mechanism, we can see the importance of the larger verbal enterprise—*Roughing It* or *Life in the Clearings*—in maintaining overseas connections. That "hope of return" may disappear in reality, but it can be renewed rhetorically by a literary communication with an Old World audience. By taking up travel narrative, Moodie revives the conceit of travel.

In dispatching a successful communication to English readers, the writer cultivates her original cultural and social values, and resists the New World attitudes which might dispossess her of these imported assets. Only a peculiar strength of mind can assure the emigrant's successful resistance. In her introduction to *Roughing It,* Moodie describes the determination with which the settlers depart: "they gird up the loins of the mind, and arm themselves with fortitude to meet and dare the heart-breaking conflict." . . . Refusing to capitulate to Canadian society, the displaced Englishwoman internalizes all those native institutions which had once supported her. She thus remains a traveler, never adopting the ways of the foreign place.

But this is only one view of the "heart-breaking conflict." There are alternatives to it which permit the immobilized traveler some relief from traumatic restlessness and death-wishing. Moodie suggests that the settler give up making comparisons between the New World and the Old, and get rid of one aspect of the traveler's mentality: "But, oh! beware of drawing disparaging contrasts between the colony and its illustrious parent." . . . With this warning she temporarily modifies her rhetorical stance to address "British mothers of Canadian sons" and instruct them in the process of settling down and learning to love Canada. Although Moodie is herself never innocent of suggesting contrasts which disparage the colony, she does at least reach a position where she no longer wants to die. Expressions of Canadian nationalism help her a little in this, but much more helpful and vivifying is her satire. Her comic vision effaces some of her morbidity, but without rupturing her essential connection with her English audience. The laugh is on the North American, even when Moodie is the apparent victim of the incidents she reports. The objects of her wit are patently too ignorant and morally inexperienced to see the joke, which is told for the entertainment of a European reader who shares her sense of humor.

In *Roughing It in the Bush* life is most hilarious when it is most dreadful. At Cobourg the Moodies find themselves in an insanely inhospitable neighborhood. Moodie is surrounded by unregenerate "savages"—Yankee squatters who harass her with outrageous rudeness. So exaggerated are these characters in their outlandish greed and unscrupulousness that the Cobourg episodes create a lunatic, lawless world at the center of which is the sane, astonished Moodie. She is culturally and economically disoriented; all social and moral principles are inverted in an antic parody of the life she has known. As she was respected and regarded in England, here she is reviled and loathed. In an alien land where she is "the stranger whom they hated and despised" . . . , she is powerless to alter her circumstances, and can only laugh and submit. Rebuke is futile in this desert of "ignorance and sin" where the moral voice echoes emptily. So Susanna Moodie learns to be quiet at Cobourg but vociferous in her literary life. (pp. 134-35)

Moodie's comedy is social comedy, arising from the serious travel issue of social insubordination and disorientation. Comedy defends the insulted immigrant and her offended values by ridiculing the hostile society which discounts her. Without the perpetual comparison of the New World to the Old there would be no joke, for the fun lies in the application of a superior intelligence which knows both the true shape of society and its ludicrous mutation in Upper Canada. The narrative voice of *Life in the Clearings* speaks, for the most part, in this knowing, wry tone. (p. 135)

In *Life in the Clearings* Moodie is especially concerned, as many European travelers in North America were, with analysis of class and of distribution of power and status in this new society. She identifies the materialism of colonial culture as the most influential factor in the corruption of traditional values, and she complains that the "educated man" belongs to a socially disenfranchised minority in the colony. But Moodie is convinced that a universal cultural hierarchy underlies even the most adverse conditions: "There is no mistaking the superiority that mental cultivation bestows," even when the local economic structure promotes illiterate, unrefined citizens.

Armed with this conviction, Moodie can withstand even the most blatant disparagements conferred on a woman of letters by an illiterate society: "The idea that some country people form of an author is highly amusing. One of my boys was tauntingly told by another lad at school, 'that his ma' said that Mrs. M—invented lies and got money for them.' This was her estimation of works of mere fiction." . . . (pp. 135-36)

But, even if she can shrug off such taunts, Moodie's art cannot address such a population and must revert to an audience which shares her own idea of literature and her own vision of society. Fortunately, she has recourse to another public. . . .

With the artist's physical as well as psychological survival at issue, Moodie chooses to ignore the philistine and materialistic Canadians and go abroad for her audience.

The travel structure of *Life in the Clearings* permits a type of social satire which expresses its author's estrangement from the country through which she journeys and from the community where she resides. . . . Moodie is an unimplicated sightseer, observing the exotic assortment of curiosities which comprises Upper Canadian society, and her narrative form is so elastic as to accommodate the social observations of other, similarly detached reporters. These reporters are outsiders—travelers or guests—who witness instances of cultural depravity and then tell their stories in such a way as to recover a sense of their own station and perspective. Always, this recovery involves a satiric exaggeration of North American folly. (p. 136)

Sometimes whole chapters are necessary to formalize anecdotal or digressive impulses, but *Clearings* always, sooner or later, recovers its direction. (p. 137)

Susanna Moodie, . . . with her melancholy lament for what she had lost and her sly satire of colonial manners, is central to the Canadian literary tradition. In the structure and expression of her attitudes—her reference to a distant point of origin, her homing tendencies and her feelings of literary and cultural isolation—are patterns recognizable to Canadian readers and artists. For Susanna Moodie, the true audience is elsewhere. (p. 142)

> *Janet Giltrow, "'Painful Experience in a Distant Land': Mrs. Moodie in Canada and Mrs. Trollope in America," in* Mosaic: A Journal for the Interdisciplinary Study of Literature, *Vol. XIV, No. 2, (Spring, 1981), pp. 131-44.*

MARGOT NORTHEY   (essay date 1984)

[*Northey probes the relationship between* Roughing It in the Bush *and* Rachel Wilde; or, Trifles from the Burthen of a Life, *a serialized autobiographical novel. She concludes that Moodie's feelings of isolation and misinterpretation are the result of her "long-standing, inward-looking response to her vision of herself as artist."*]

[In *Roughing It in the Bush*], Moodie clearly uses some of the techniques of fiction to heighten the characterizations and narrative drama. Moreover, the self has a special role in this partial autobiography in which fact is not always the whole truth. (p. 117)

Roughing It in the Bush in part presents Susanna Moodie as the romantic centre of the story. Yet because the book is also partially a collection of sketches about other characters and their experiences, the picture of the heroine that emerges is not as clear or complete as if she were the continuous focus. Moodie keeps one eye turned inward toward the self and the other fixed on those odd acquaintances who reveal and represent life in the New World. The outward-turned eye is observant, analytic, and humorous; the inward-turned eye is emotional, idealistic, and sentimental. One of the reasons the book is so disjointed and abruptly shifting in tone is that while Moodie's explicit purpose is to give the outward view—to present a typical picture of immigration life useful for others—the romantic ego keeps overruling it. The sense of a uniquely long-suffering heroine counteracts that of the representative immigrant. Thus while some critics perceive the conflict in the book as arising from Moodie's attempt to impress her upper-class English values on a patently unsuited new society, or from the distance between her romantic illusions and the rough reality she finds, or even from a kind of schizophrenic split in her responses—partly admiring and partly hating the country—the conflict also arises at a more basic level from her conflicting motives as author. She wants to tell a story of this strange land and its strange people, but she also has an urge to explain and magnify herself.

This desire for self-revelation and self-justification is better understood if one turns to one of Moodie's little-known works, *Rachel Wilde; or, Trifles from the Burthen of a Life.* Moodie wrote it in serialized form for *The Victoria Magazine,* an enterprising but unprofitable publication which she and her husband created and edited while living in Belleville. The story appeared in segments from 1847 to 1848—the life of the magazine. Although ostensibly about a girl called Rachel, it is obviously an autobiography of Moodie in her childhood years. . . . In *Rachel Wilde,* despite the fictitious name, the story is continuously autobiographical; with one small exception it concentrates entirely on the child. Moreover, if one considers romantic ideas about the nature of childhood, then these recollections of the early years have more import as a key to Susanna Moodie's perception of herself than do the recollections of her later life.

Although autobiography had become popular in the eighteenth century, Rousseau's *Confessions* (1782) fostered romantic introspection and the pursuit of self-knowledge as the source of knowledge about the world. Believing in the uniqueness of each individual, the romantics gave childhood new status. Rather than seeing the personality as static, they began to see it as a developing entity; the child was not a miniature adult, but a dynamic, malleable being whose experiences and perceptions would shape the personality of the adult. Wordsworth's belief that "the Child is father of the Man" was widely shared, and thus autobiographical accounts of childhood proliferated and became a key to the author's adult perspectives. (pp. 117-19)

Seen within this romantic pattern of thinking, *Rachel Wilde* becomes the obvious natural vehicle for Susanna Moodie to use for self-revelation and justification. Certainly as a literary work it has its shortcomings, many of them the same as in Moodie's better-known books. In places, the language is stilted and conventional; the episodic structure has many jerky transitions and changes in point of view. But as a guide to Moodie's sensibility it is revealing.

Moodie begins her story with the statement that "We are all more or less, the creatures of circumstance. . . . No one ever did, or could live for himself alone. We talk of originality of thought. Can such a thing in this stage of the world's history exist? Our very thoughts are not our own." . . . Such an opening hardly suggests romantic introspection and the inward-turned eye. In fact, she seems closer to the modern stress on environmental determinism when in the second and third paragraphs she illustrates how the physical surroundings of the early years "often determine the future character of the individuals." Moodie thus leads the reader to expect that she will trace those external environmental influences on the young child—that she will tell us about society by showing those critical areas of experience where the child intersected with it and was thus shaped by it. She proceeds in the first chapter to do just that. She gives the exact details of her family in the years of her infancy. (p. 119)

After this introduction, Moodie begins to narrate the first of a series of experiences which mark Rachel's years from the time of this happy infancy to the end of her childhood. As in all autobiographies, the memory selects—and the author shapes—those incidents which reinforce the pattern that the retrospective adult has created of past experience. To some extent Moodie does try to show how the events influenced the developing character and personality. . . . But overshadowing the theme of external influences is another, a stronger theme—that of an exceptional spirit, driven by her own imagination, emotion, and spiritual sensibility. In short, the picture which emerges is that of the romantic artist, isolated and misunderstood.

This portrait is developed in three stages. The first stage is of the infant in her happy home. But even here we find a prefiguring of the struggle of the visionary artist. Rachel enlists her younger brother and older sister Dorothy (a replica of the rational, patient, Catharine Parr Strickland) in a drama she has

created in which the boy is to be carried off by a wood demon. But Rachel's fantasy is misinterpreted by an alarmed older sister, and the budding artist receives a cuff for her efforts. The motif of the misunderstood artist is developed further in the second stage of the portrait when the young child is sent off for an extended period to live with the Long family. She is disliked and frequently abused by Miss Betsy Long, but the ultimate humiliation, which leads her to run away, comes after she has joyfully decorated the newly painted window frames by scraping designs on them with the scissors. To her surprise, and without explanation, she is given a severe beating with the hated rod.

In the third stage, when Rachel is home again and in the later years of childhood, she is still the object of scorn. Pronounced "bad" and "crazy-pated" by her governess, she, "like many an unfortunate, misunderstood child of genius, remains unteachable, untaught." Only her sister Dorothea is able to heal "the wounds which the daily friction of uncongenial minds, stamped into the unfortunate girl's too sensitive heart." A solitary person, since "other children felt no sympathy with her—they could not comprehend her fantastic notions" . . . , her main solace, like that of other romantic souls, is "the 'Eden' of nature" where the "Divine Mother" gives inspiration. Thus the romantic visionary is born, one who comes to believe that her "lofty visions" are "inspirations direct from heaven." (pp. 120-21)

An outcast in her own mind, Rachel is sympathetic to other outcasts, especially those of genius. She falls in love with the devil depicted in Milton's *Paradise Lost* and later is punished for her unrelenting devotion to the defeated and exiled Napoleon. The final blow comes in the last chapter when Rachel labours in secret—since her eldest sister disapproves—to write a story. When the "sacred Manuscript" is discovered, the sister wants only to use it to cover the roasting pig. (p. 121)

It would be a distortion to imply that this overdrawn portrait of the artist as a young girl is all there is to *Rachel Wilde.* Clearly Moodie is not one of those modern autobiographers who lets the childish perceptions speak for themselves. She wants to guide our understanding. At times she forces the reader to stand back and see the child in a more dispassionate way, by pointing to the stubborn wilfulness and spoilt behaviour of young Rachel; she insists that the child brought on some of her own misfortunes by her ignorance of her own weaknesses and errors. . . . Yet these critical comments are not entirely a deflation of the romantic spirit and a return for the author to the analytic observer role. Moodie's mention of Rachel's faults adheres to the romantic belief that awareness of one's own irrational weaknesses is a sign of strength. By showing she knows herself—even, or perhaps especially, as a child—she becomes a reliable adult guide to experience in general.

Many of Moodie's reflections are a gloss upon the common romantic theme of a child's growing awareness of the mystery of evil and injustice in society and the consequent separation from the infant state of innocent bliss. A few times in the story she points out the representative rather than unique nature of Rachel. Commenting on the child's propensity to ask indiscreet questions or to figure out the answers to forbidden ones, she says, "This is human nature, and Rachel, at that period, was a child of nature, and listened to no other teacher." . . . Later she apostrophises, "Ah, blessed, thrice blessed season of youth and innocence—when earth is still the paradise of God, and its crimes and sorrows are veiled from the eyes of the undefiled." . . . This remark is part of the chapter in which Rachel encounters the treachery of the servant girl, Nancy, who accuses Rachel of stealing the treacle when she herself had eaten it. Rachel is unjustly thrashed. In the most extensive comment about society in the entire story, Moodie returns to her initial thesis about the effect of environment on character:

> If [Nancy] was an artful, dishonest creature, she had been rendered so by circumstances over which she had no control. . . . her whole existence was a life-long agony. She never got a kind word from anyone; . . . and can we wonder, that to secure herself from blame, she falsely accused an innocent child. . . .

But Moodie really does not sustain this thesis with the other characters in the tale or even with Rachel. We learn less about how circumstances shape Rachel's character than about how Rachel's temperament and innate sensibilities lead her to act and react as she does. . . . Even when Moodie takes up such social issues as injustice, the focus is less on injustice in the world than on Rachel's receipt of it. The injustice of Rachel's wrongful punishment in the treacle incident and the injustice of the scorn she receives from her eldest sister on the discovery of the manuscript are but precursors, we are led to believe, for the unjust scorn she will receive as an adult artist. In the final episode, as she and her sister set out to write their manuscripts, Moodie remarks:

> Alas! poor children, they little knew the troubles and trials that beset the dangerous path they were about to tread. The love and approbation of the few, and the envy and hatred of the many. To resign the joys of the present, and to live alone for the future. To be the scorn of vulgar and common minds; the dread of the weak and sensitive, to stand alone and without sympathy, misunderstood and maligned by most of their species. . . .

Such rhetoric may seem hopelessly overblown in relation to the incident that apparently sparked it, but it is really a summation of the underlying primary theme—the artist as outcast. Coming as it does in the last chapter, and reflecting as it does the adult wisdom of the author rather than the feelings of the child, it has an extra resonance.

Following this outburst, the conclusion to the story is curious. In the penultimate paragraph Moodie abruptly informs us that after a passage of years, "The world, as umpire, decided the question of her capacity, and gave the meed of praise so long denied." Yet Rachel throws it all up in order to go off with the man she loves. In the final paragraph we learn that she "resigned the tempting wreath [the world] offered her, to follow the adverse fortunes of the beloved—to toil in poverty and sorrow by his side—a stranger and an exile in a foreign land." . . . What are we to make of this tacked-on finale? The simplest answer, of course, is that Moodie wanted to finish off the story and provide a quick accounting of what happened to the child— the roll-call of years common in many nineteenth-century stories. The contradictory tone of the final two paragraphs suggests another answer, that the author's wish to justify herself gets in the way of artistic consistency. Related to this answer is the possibility that Moodie wrote *Rachel Wilde* as a kind of explanation or supporting piece for the partial self-portrait she was creating in *Roughing It in the Bush.*

A look at dates supports this notion of linkage. *Rachel Wilde* was likely written not much prior to its appearance in the

1847-48 issues of *The Victoria Magazine*. Two of Moodie's "Scenes in Canada" (which were to become the first chapters of *Roughing It in the Bush*), "A Visit to Grosse Isle" and "First Impressions—Quebec," were also published in the 1847 issues; and it was likely not much afterwards that Moodie set her mind to finishing the rest of the book, since it was published in 1852. However, six other chapters had first appeared in *The Literary Garland* of 1847, and some of them may have been written several years before that, since Moodie was a regular contributor from 1839 onward. . . . They have that outward vision and half-humorous tone mentioned earlier in this discussion, qualities which are also found in the beginning and at occasional intervals in *Rachel Wilde*. It appears that when Moodie began to write for the public in Canada, she attempted a more uninvolved, dispassionate, observer role. But when she got into her stride in her own magazine, and pulled the early sketches together into a framework with more narrative continuity, the romantic notion of self took over.

With *Rachel Wilde,* Moodie fills in the portrait of self only partially revealed in the narratives of *Roughing It in the Bush*. Despite the initial attempt to distance herself from the material by using a fictitious name for the child and the third person voice, she quickly moves to dramatize the self. The fictional cover is so transparent that she sometimes disregards it; in several sections she switches to the first-person voice. The first time she does this, she makes a quick explanation in the following chapter, no doubt sensing the reader's confusion.

If we think of *Rachel Wilde* and the framing chapters of *Roughing It in the Bush* as linked writings, then the mention of exile at the end of the story of the child ties in nicely with the story of the later years in Canada. More importantly, the autobiography of childhood adds another dimension to the motif of exile which appears in *Roughing It in the Bush*. It shows that Moodie saw herself as a kind of outcast most of her life, first isolated from the family when she went to the Longs', later exiled from the circle of teachables run by the governess, and finally cut off from the friendship of peers and elders who misunderstood her creative nature. It can be argued, therefore, that the feelings of isolation, misinterpretation, and exile she expresses in *Roughing It in the Bush* are not simply a reaction to her particular physical circumstances but also a long-standing, inward-looking response to her vision of herself as artist. She was little appreciated as a child writer and little appreciated as an adult, whether in the bush or at the time of writing these pieces. That she yearned for recognition is also evident in *Rachel Wilde,* not only from descriptions of the hurt she felt but from the recurring image in which she fancies herself a queen. . . . Clearly the misunderstood outsider had intimations of superiority.

Linking the two works helps explain not only the ending of *Rachel Wilde* but also why Susanna's husband is such a shadowy figure in *Roughing It in the Bush*. Love is a leitmotif in the childhood story. Towards the beginning, the incident of the young soldier with his fickle sweetheart introduces the child to the notion of false love. By contrast, the maturing outcast finds partial satisfaction in her own deeper love, whether for Milton's Satan or for Napoleon. The desire for worldly admiration is only superseded by the romantic union of love. In the end, therefore, Rachel opts for a future of love despite artistic exile. Following this pattern, Susanna's husband is really less an actual personality to be carefully described than a fulfilment of this romantic ideal. In *Roughing It in the Bush* he is not a part of the outward view that perceives character sketches but a completion of the inward vision of herself as a romantic spirit.

Rachel Wilde reveals how fully Susanna Moodie saw herself as a romantic figure. Whether she grafted this mature perception of herself onto the depiction of her childhood, or whether she always had it, is difficult to prove; but the vivid, concrete descriptions of many of the experiences felt by the child suggest the latter. In any case, read as a companion piece to **Roughing It in the Bush, Rachel Wilde** shows how the child is mother of the woman who lives in the bush. It helps explain the persona who pushes forth insistently, if intermittently, in the story of the backwoods. Thus, the Susanna Moodie who leaves the bush, having been often abused and scorned by her neighbours, is not in her own eyes an unsuccessful settler or failed immigrant, but a sensitive artist in unsympathetic surroundings. Moreover the suffering she describes in both works has a common didactic base rooted in romantic vision. Whether she endured it in the harsh wilds of Canada or in the pleasant countryside of England, Moodie saw in her suffering, and wanted readers to see, a source of the wisdom that was her claim to respect. (pp. 121-26)

> *Margot Northey, "Completing the Self-Portrait: Moodie's 'Rachel Wilde'," in* Essays on Canadian Writing, *No. 29, Summer, 1984, pp. 117-27.*

ADDITIONAL BIBLIOGRAPHY

Ballstadt, Carl; Peterman, Michael; and Hopkins, Elizabeth. "'A Glorious Madness': Susanna Moodie and the Spiritualist Movement." *Journal of Canadian Studies* 17, No. 4 (Winter 1982-83): 88-100.
    Traces Moodie's interest and involvement in the spiritualist movement.

Davies, Robertson. *"At My Heart's Core"; "Overlaid."* Toronto: Clarke, Irwin & Co., 1966, 124 p.
    Contains *At My Heart's Core,* a drama that depicts Canadian pioneer life and features Moodie as one of its characters.

Gairdner, William D. "Traill and Moodie: The Two Realities." *Journal of Canadian Fiction* 1, No. 2 (Spring 1972): 35-42.

Portrays Moodie as a mystic who rejected rationalism in favor of the emotionalism and individualism characteristic of the European Romantic movement.

Kröller, Eva-Marie. "Resurrections: Susanna Moodie, Catharine Parr Traill, and Emily Carr in Contemporary Canadian Literature." *Journal of Popular Culture* 15, No. 3 (Winter 1981): 39-46.
    Examines recent Canadian writers' use of the works of Moodie, Traill, and Emily Carr in their own writings. Kröller focuses on Carol Shields's inclusion of Moodie in her novel *Small Ceremonies* and Atwood's recreation of Moodie in her collection of poetry entitled *The Journals of Susanna Moodie* (see excerpt dated 1970).

Lande, Lawrence M. "The Strickland Sisters." In his *Old Lamps Aglow: An Appreciation of Early Canadian Poetry,* pp. 301-07. Montreal: Fiat Lux, 1957.
    Briefly discusses the contributions made by Moodie and Traill to early Canadian poetry.

MacLulich, T. D. "Crusoe in the Backwoods: A Canadian Fable?" *Mosaic* IX, No. 2 (Winter 1976): 115-26.
    Analyzes *Roughing It in the Bush* in relation to several common interpretations of Daniel Defoe's *Robinson Crusoe.*

Noonan, G. "Susanna and Her Critics: A Strategy of Fiction for *Roughing It in the Bush.*" *Studies in Canadian Literature* (Fall 1980): 280-89.
    Examines various recent critics' views of *Roughing It in the Bush.*

Pacey, Desmond. "The Colonial Period (1750-1867)." In his *Creative Writing in Canada: A Short History of English-Canadian Literature,* rev. ed., pp. 8-34. Toronto: Ryerson Press, 1961.
    A brief, laudatory comparison of Moodie's *Roughing It in the Bush* and Traill's *The Backwoods of Canada.*

Thomas, Clara. "Journeys to Freedom." *Canadian Literature* No. 51 (Winter 1972): 11-19.
    Profiles Moodie, Traill, and Anna Murphy Jameson as notable nineteenth-century Canadian frontier writers.

Tinkler, John F. "Canadian Cultural Norms and Australian Social Rules: Susanna Moodie's *Roughing It in the Bush* and Marcus Clarke's *His Natural Life.*" *Canadian Literature* No. 94 (Autumn 1982): 10-22.
    Discusses the cultivation of both the Canadian wilderness and the developing Canadian society as the controlling theme of *Roughing It in the Bush.*

Weaver, Emily P. "Mrs. Traill and Mrs. Moodie: Pioneers in Literature." *The Canadian Magazine* XLVIII, No. 5 (March 1917): 473-76.
    A short biographical sketch of Moodie and Traill.

Mary Wollstonecraft Godwin Shelley

1797-1851

English novelist, editor, critic, short story and travel writer.

Shelley is best known for her novel *Frankenstein; or, The Modern Prometheus,* which has transcended the Gothic and horror genres and is now recognized as a work of philosophical and psychological resonance. Critics agree that with the depiction of a seemingly godless universe where science and technology have gone awry, Shelley created a powerful metaphor for the modern age; indeed, the *Frankenstein* myth, which has been adapted to stage, film, and television, has pervaded modern culture. Shelley's achievement is considered remarkable, moreover, because she completed the book before her twentieth birthday. In addition to *Frankenstein,* Shelley's literary works include several novels that were mildly successful in their time but are little known today and an edition of poetry by her husband, the Romantic poet Percy Bysshe Shelley, which she issued with notes that are now regarded as indispensable. Her reputation rests, however, on what she once called her "hideous progeny," *Frankenstein.*

Shelley's personal life has sometimes overshadowed her literary work. She was the wife of Percy Shelley and the daughter of Mary Wollstonecraft, the early feminist and author of *A Vindication of the Rights of Woman,* and William Godwin, the political philosopher and novelist. Her parents' wedding, which occurred when Wollstonecraft was five months pregnant with Mary, was the marriage of two of the day's most noted freethinkers. While they both objected to the institution of matrimony, they agreed to marry to ensure their child's legitimacy. Ten days after Mary's birth, Wollstonecraft died from complications, leaving Godwin, an undemonstrative and self-absorbed intellectual, to care for both Mary and Fanny Imlay, Wollstonecraft's daughter from an earlier liaison. Mary's home life improved little with the arrival four years later of a stepmother and her two children. The new Mrs. Godwin, whom contemporaries described as petty and disagreeable, favored her own offspring over the daughters of the celebrated Wollstonecraft, and Mary was often solitary and unhappy. She was not formally educated, but absorbed the intellectual atmosphere created by her father and such visitors as Samuel Taylor Coleridge. She read a wide variety of books, notably those of her mother, whom she idolized. Young Mary's favorite retreat was Wollstonecraft's grave in the St. Pancras churchyard, where she went to read and write and eventually to meet her lover, Shelley.

An admirer of Godwin, Percy Shelley visited the author's home and briefly met Mary when she was fourteen, but their attraction did not take hold until a subsequent meeting two years later. Shelley, twenty-two, was married and his wife was expecting their second child, but he and Mary, like Godwin and Wollstonecraft, believed that ties of the heart superseded legal ones. In July 1814, one month before her seventeenth birthday, Mary eloped with Percy to the continent, where, apart from two interludes in England, they spent the next several years traveling in Switzerland, Germany, and Italy. These years were characterized by financial difficulty and personal tragedy. Percy's father, Sir Timothy Shelley, a wealthy baronet, cut off his son's substantial allowance after his elopement. In 1816,

Mary's half-sister Fanny committed suicide; just weeks later, Percy's wife, Harriet, drowned herself. Mary and Percy were married in London, in part because they hoped to gain custody of his two children by Harriet, but custody was denied. Three of their own children died in infancy, and Mary fell into a deep depression that was barely dispelled by the birth in 1819 of Percy Florence, her only surviving child. The Shelleys' marriage suffered, too, in the wake of their children's deaths, and Percy formed romantic attachments to other women. Despite these trying circumstances, both Mary and Percy maintained a schedule of rigorous study—including classical and European literature, Greek, Latin, and Italian language, music and art—and ambitious writing; during this period Mary completed *Frankenstein* and another novel, *Valperga.* The two also enjoyed a coterie of stimulating friends, notably Lord Byron and Leigh Hunt. The Shelleys were settled near Lenci, Italy, on the Gulf of Spezzia in 1822 when Percy drowned during a storm while sailing to meet Leigh and Marianne Hunt. After one mournful year in Italy, Mary returned permanently to England with her son.

Shelley's life after Percy's death was marked by melancholy and hardship as she struggled to support herself and her child. Sir Timothy Shelley offered her a meager stipend, but ordered that she keep the Shelley name out of print; thus, all her works were published anonymously. In addition to producing four novels in the years after Percy's death, Mary contributed a series of biographical and critical sketches to *Chamber's Cabinet Cyclopedia*, as well as occasional short stories, which she considered potboilers, to the literary annuals of the day. The Shelleys' financial situation improved when Sir Timothy increased Percy Florence's allowance with his coming of age in 1840, which enabled mother and son to travel in Italy and Germany; their journeys are recounted in *Rambles in Germany and Italy in 1840, 1842, and 1843*. Too ill in her last few years to complete her most cherished project, a biography of her husband, Shelley died at fifty-four.

Although *Frankenstein* has consistently dominated critical discussions of Shelley's oeuvre, she also composed several other novels in addition to critical and biographical writings. Her five later novels attracted little notice, and critics generally agree that they share the faults of verbosity and awkward plotting. After *Frankenstein, The Last Man* is her best-known work. This novel, in which Shelley describes the destruction of the human race in the twenty-first century, is noted as an inventive depiction of the future and an early prototype of science fiction. *Valperga* and *The Fortunes of Perkin Warbeck* are historical novels that have received scant attention from literary critics, while *Lodore* and *Falkner*, thought by many to be autobiographical, are often examined for clues to the lives of the Shelleys and their circle. Shelley's stories were collected and published posthumously, as was *Mathilda*, a novella that appeared for the first time in the 1950s. The story of a father and daughter's incestuous attraction, it has been viewed as a fictional treatment—or distortion—of Shelley's relationship with Godwin. The posthumously published verse dramas, *Proserpine and Midas*, were written to complement one of Percy Shelley's works and have garnered mild praise for their poetry. Apart from *Frankenstein*, critics most often admire Shelley's non-fiction: the readable, though now dated, travel volumes, the essays for *Chamber's Cabinet Cyclopedia*, which are considered vigorous and erudite, and her illuminating notes on her husband's poetry.

Shelley's most famous novel was conceived in 1816 at Lake Leman, Switzerland, where she and Percy had settled near Byron and his companion, John Polidori. As Mary described in her preface to the 1831 edition of the novel, one evening after reading Gothic stories, the four challenged each other to create their own tales of horror. Mary waited several days in vain for an idea until she heard a discussion between Byron and Shelley about galvanism and the notion of creating life via electricity. That night she awoke mesmerized by a vision of a creature animated by such means. She began to write the monster's narrative, which forms the book's central section. Shelley urged her to expand the tale into a novel, and Mary subsequently added the narratives of Captain Walton and Dr. Frankenstein.

Since Shelley's death, critics have devoted little attention to her other works, focusing instead on *Frankenstein*. Early critics, generally with some dismay, usually relegated the novel to the Gothic genre then practiced by such popular authors as Ann Radcliffe and Matthew Gregory "Monk" Lewis. While most early Victorian reviewers reviled what they considered the sensationalist and gruesome elements in *Frankenstein*, many praised the anonymous author's imagination and powers of description. In the later nineteenth century and throughout *Frankenstein* criticism, commentators have focused on Prometheanism in the novel, an aspect that Shelley herself highlighted in the book's subtitle. This line of enquiry, which continues to engage critics, likens Dr. Frankenstein to the Greek mythic figure who wreaks his own destruction through abuse of power. Percy Shelley treated the same mythic-philosophic theme in his poetry, most notably in *Prometheus Unbound*, and critics have searched for his influence on *Frankenstein*, particularly in the expression of Romantic ideals and attitudes. Scholars have also debated the value of the additional narratives that he encouraged her to write. While some have praised the novel's resulting three-part structure, others have argued that these additions detract from and merely pad the story, although most have valued the other-worldly Arctic scenes. Commentators have also frequently noted the influence of Shelley's father, tracing strains of Godwin's humanitarian social views; in addition, some critics have found direct thematic links to his fiction, particularly to his novel, *Caleb Williams*. Other literary allusions often noted in *Frankenstein* include those to John Milton's *Paradise Lost*, the source of the book's epigraph, as well as Johann Wolfgang von Goethe's *Faust* and Coleridge's "The Rime of the Ancient Mariner."

Frankenstein criticism has proliferated since the 1950s, encompassing a wide variety of themes and approaches. The monster, who is often the focus of commentary, has been interpreted as representing ideas ranging from the alienation of modern humanity to the repression of women. Many commentators have viewed the monster as Dr. Frankenstein's double, an example of the doppelgänger archetype. In a similar vein, critics have discussed Dr. Frankenstein and the monster as embodying Sigmund Freud's theory of id and ego. Students of the Gothic, supernatural horror, and science fiction novel have adopted *Frankenstein* as a venerable forebear and have approached it from a historical slant. Alternately, Shelley's life has served as a starting point for those who perceive in the novel expressions of the author's feelings toward her parents, husband, children, and friends. Recent feminist critics, in particular, have found Shelley and *Frankenstein* a rich source for study, describing it, for example, as a manifestation of the author's ambivalent feelings toward motherhood.

Shelley's friend Leigh Hunt once characterized her as "four-famed—for her parents, her lord / And the poor lone impossible monster abhorr'd." Today, Shelley has emerged from the shadow of her parents and husband as an artist in her own right. The volume and variety of *Frankenstein* criticism attests to the endurance of her vision.

PRINCIPAL WORKS

History of a Six Weeks' Tour through a Part of France, Switzerland, Germany, and Holland, with Letters Descriptive of a Sail Round the Lake of Geneva and the Glaciers of Chamouni [with Percy Bysshe Shelley] (travel essay) 1817
Frankenstein; or, The Modern Prometheus (novel) 1818
Valperga; or, The Life and Adventures of Castruccio, Prince of Lucca (novel) 1823
Posthumous Poems [editor] (poetry) 1824
The Last Man (novel) 1826
The Fortunes of Perkin Warbeck (novel) 1830
Lodore (novel) 1835
Falkner (novel) 1837
The Poetical Works of Percy Shelley [editor] (poetry) 1839
Rambles in Germany and Italy in 1840, 1842, and 1843 (travel essay) 1844
The Choice: A Poem on Shelley's Death (poetry) 1876

Tales and Stories by Mary Wollstonecraft Shelley (short stories) 1891
Proserpine and Midas [first publication] (dramas) 1922
Mathilda (novella) 1959

PERCY BYSSHE SHELLEY (poem date 1817)

[*Regarded as a major English poet, Shelley was a leading figure in the English Romantic movement. His so-called "defense of poetry," in which he investigated poetry's relation to the history of civilization, was an important contribution to nineteenth-century aesthetics. Influenced by the French philosopher Jean-Jacques Rousseau and the German poet and pre Romanticist Johann Gottfried von Herder, Shelley viewed poetry, as he did human society, as a continuing evolution of ideas. He argued that poetry was like a mirror to its age, the history of its manners, and as such he labeled all poets "legislators and prophets" who contributed to the spiritual and political evolution of mankind. In the following excerpt, Shelley dedicates his poem* The Revolt of Islam *to Mary. He alludes to their elopement and life together and evokes her illustrious parents, particularly Mary Wollstonecraft. This dedication was written in 1817. For additional commentary by Percy Shelley, see excerpts dated 1817 and 1818.*]

Thou Friend, whose presence on my wintry heart
    Fell, like bright Spring upon some herbless plain;
How beautiful and calm and free thou wert
    In thy young wisdom, when the mortal chain
    Of Custom thou didst burst and rend in twain,
And walked as free as light the clouds among,
    Which many an envious slave then breathed in vain
From his dim dungeon, and my spirit sprung
To meet thee from the woes which had begirt it long!

No more alone through the world's wilderness,
    Although I trod the paths of high intent,
I journeyed now: no more companionless,
    Where solitude is like despair, I went.—
    There is the wisdom of a stern content
When Poverty can blight the just and good,
    When Infamy dares mock the innocent,
And cherished friends turn with the multitude
To trample: this was ours, and we unshaken stood!

Now has descended a serener hour,
    And with inconstant fortune, friends return;
Though suffering leaves the knowledge and the power
    Which says:—Let scorn be not repaid with scorn.
    And from thy side two gentle babes are born
To fill our home with smiles, and thus are we
    Most fortunate beneath life's beaming morn;
And these delights, and thou, have been to me
The parents of the Song I consecrate to thee.

Is it, that now my inexperienced fingers
    But strike the prelude of a loftier strain?
Or, must the lyre on which my spirit lingers
    Soon pause in silence, ne'er to sound again,
    Though it might shake the Anarch Custom's reign,
And charm the minds of men to Truth's own sway
    Holier than was Amphion's? I would fain
Reply in hope—but I am worn away,
And Death and Love are yet contending for their prey.

And what art thou? I know, but dare not speak:
    Time may interpret to his silent years.
Yet in the paleness of thy thoughtful cheek,
    And in the light thine ample forehead wears,
    And in thy sweetest smiles, and in thy tears,
And in thy gentle speech, a prophecy
    Is whispered, to subdue my fondest fears:
And through thine eyes, even in thy soul I see
A lamp of vestal fire burning internally.

They say that thou wert lovely from thy birth,
    Of glorious parents, thou aspiring Child.
I wonder not—for One then left this earth
    Whose life was like a setting planet mild,
    Which clothed thee in the radiance undefiled
Of its departing glory; still her fame
    Shines on thee, through the tempests dark and wild
Which shake these latter days; and thou canst claim
The shelter, from thy Sire, of an immortal name.

                                        (pp. 38-40)

> *Percy Bysshe Shelley, "'The Revolt of Islam'," in his* Poetical Works, *edited by Thomas Hutchinson with G. M. Matthews, Oxford University Press, London, 1970, pp. 31-158.*

PERCY BYSSHE SHELLEY (essay date 1817)

[*Shelley wrote the following highly favorable review of* Frankenstein *in 1817, but it was not published until 1832. In contrast with most early reviewers, Shelley emphasizes the novel's inherent moral aspects. He also acknowledges the similarity of* Frankenstein's *style and characterizations to those of William Godwin. For additional commentary by Percy Shelley, see excerpts dated 1817 and 1818.*]

The Novel of *Frankenstein; or, the Modern Prometheus,* is undoubtedly, as a mere story, one of the most original and complete productions of the day. We debate with ourselves in wonder, as we read it, what could have been the series of thoughts—what could have been the peculiar experiences that awakened them—which conduced, in the author's mind, to the astonishing combinations of motives and incidents, and the startling catastrophe, which compose this tale. There are, perhaps, some points of subordinate importance, which prove that it is the author's first attempt. But in this judgment, which requires a very nice discrimination, we may be mistaken; for it is conducted throughout with a firm and steady hand. The interest gradually accumulates and advances towards the conclusion with the accelerated rapidity of a rock rolled down a mountain. We are led breathless with suspense and sympathy, and the heaping up of incident on incident, and the working of passion out of passion. We cry "hold, hold! enough!"—but there is yet something to come; and, like the victim whose history it relates, we think we can bear no more, and yet more is to be borne. Pelion is heapen on Ossa, and Ossa on Olympus. We climb Alp after Alp, until the horizon is seen blank, vacant, and limitless; and the head turns giddy, and the ground seems to fail under our feet.

This novel rests its claim on being a source of powerful and profound emotion. The elementary feelings of the human mind are exposed to view; and those who are accustomed to reason deeply on their origin and tendency will, perhaps, be the only persons who can sympathize, to the full extent, in the interest of the actions which are their result. But, founded on nature as they are, there is perhaps no reader, who can endure anything beside a new love story, who will not feel a responsive string touched in his inmost soul. The sentiments are so affectionate and so innocent—the characters of the subordinate agents in this strange drama are clothed in the light of such a mild and gentle mind—the pictures of domestic manners are of the most simple and attaching character: the father's is irresistible and deep. Nor are the crimes and malevolence of the single Being, though indeed withering and tremendous, the offspring of any unaccountable propensity to evil, but flow irresistibly from certain causes fully adequate to their production. They are the children, as it were, of Necessity and Human Nature. In this the direct moral of the book consists; and it is perhaps the most important, and of the most universal application, of any moral that can be enforced by example. Treat a person ill, and he will become wicked. Requite affection with scorn;—let one being be selected, for whatever cause, as the refuse of his kind—divide him, a social being, from society, and you impose upon him the irresistible obligations—malevolence and self-ishness. It is thus that, too often in society, those who are best qualified to be its benefactors and its ornaments, are branded by some accident with scorn, and changed, by neglect and solitude of heart, into a scourge and a curse.

The Being in *Frankenstein* is, no doubt, a tremendous creature. It was impossible that he should not have received among men that treatment which led to the consequences of his being a social nature. He was an abortion and an anomaly; and though his mind was such as its first impressions framed it, affectionate and full of moral sensibility, yet the circumstances of his ex-istence are so monstrous and uncommon, that, when the con-sequences of them became developed in action, his original goodness was gradually turned into inextinguishable misan-thropy and revenge. The scene between the Being and the blind De Lacey in the cottage, is one of the most profound and extraordinary instances of pathos that we ever recollect. It is impossible to read this dialogue,—and indeed many others of a somewhat similar character,—without feeling the heart sus-pend its pulsations with wonder, and the "tears stream down the cheeks." The encounter and argument between Franken-stein and the Being on the sea of ice, almost approaches, in effect, to the expostulations of Caleb Williams with Falkland. It reminds us, indeed, somewhat of the style and character of that admirable writer, to whom the author has dedicated his work, and whose productions he seems to have studied.

There is only one instance, however, in which we detect the least approach to imitation; and that is the conduct of the in-cident of Frankenstein's landing in Ireland. The general char-acter of the tale, indeed, resembles nothing that ever preceded it. After the death of Elizabeth, the story, like a stream which grows at once more rapid and profound as it proceeds, assumes an irresistible solemnity, and the magnificent energy and swift-ness of a tempest.

The churchyard scene, in which Frankenstein visits the tombs of his family, his quitting Geneva, and his journey through Tartary to the shores of the Frozen Ocean, resemble at once the terrible reanimation of a corpse and the supernatural career of a spirit. The scene in the cabin of Walton's ship—the more than mortal enthusiasm and grandeur of the Being's speech over the dead body of his victim—is an exhibition of intellec-tual and imaginative power, which we think the reader will acknowledge has seldom been surpassed.

Percy Bysshe Shelley, "On Frankenstein," in The Athenaeum, *No. 263, November 10, 1832, p. 730.*

PERCY BYSSHE SHELLEY   (essay date 1818)

[*The "Preface" to the first edition of* Frankenstein, *published in 1818 and excerpted below, was presented as the work of Mary Shelley. She revealed, however, in a later preface (see excerpt dated 1831) that her husband actually wrote it. Here, Percy Shel-ley stresses that in spite of its supernatural bases,* Frankenstein *is intended to "preserve the truth of the elementary principles of human nature" and to demonstrate the primacy of human affection and virtue. For additional commentary by Percy Shelley, see excerpts dated 1817.*]

The event on which [*Frankenstein*] is founded, has been sup-posed, by Dr. [Erasmus] Darwin, and some of the physiological writers of Germany, as not of impossible occurrence. I shall not be supposed as recording the remotest degree of serious faith to such an imagination; yet, assuming it as the basis of a work of fancy, I have not considered myself as merely weav-ing a series of supernatural terrors. The event on which the interest of the story depends is exempt from the disadvantages of a mere tale of spectres or enchantment. It was recommended by the novelty of the situations which it developes; and, how-ever impossible as a physical fact, affords a point of view to the imagination for the delineating of human passions more comprehensive and commanding than any which the ordinary relations of existing events can yield.

I have thus endeavored to preserve the truth of the elementary principles of human nature, while I have not scrupled to in-novate upon their combinations. The *Illiad*, the tragic poetry of Greece—Shakspeare, in the *Tempest*, and *Midsummer Night's Dream*—and most especially Milton, in *Paradise Lost*, con-form to this rule; and the most humble novelist, who seeks to confer or receive amusement from his labors, may, without presumption, apply to prose fiction a license, or rather a rule, from the adoption of which so many exquisite combinations of human feeling have resulted in the highest specimens of poetry.

The circumstance on which my story rests was suggested in casual conversation. It was commenced, partly as a source of amusement, and partly as an expedient for exercising any un-tried resources of mind. Other motives were mingled with these, as the work proceeded. I am by no means indifferent to the manner in which whatever moral tendencies exist in the sentiments or characters it contains shall affect the reader; yet my chief concern in this respect has been limited to the avoiding the enervating effects of the novels of the present day, and to the exhibition of the amiableness of domestic affection, and the excellence of universal virtue. The opinions which naturally spring from the character and situation of the hero are by no means to be conceived as existing always in my own convic-tion; nor is any inference justly to be drawn from the following pages as prejudicing any philosophical doctrine of whatever kind. (pp. v-vi)

Percy Bysshe Shelley, in an extract in Frankenstein; or, The Modern Prometheus *by Mary W. Shelley, H. G. Daggers, 1845, pp. v-vi.*

[JOHN WILSON CROKER]   (essay date 1818)

[*Croker, a principal contributor to the conservative journal the* Quarterly Review, *was nicknamed the "slashing critic" for his vitriolic literary reviews. Here, Croker acknowledges the literary powers displayed in* Frankenstein, *yet he denounces the horrific effect to which they are employed.*]

Our readers will guess . . . what a tissue of horrible and disgusting absurdity [*Frankenstein*] presents.—It is piously dedicated to Mr. Godwin, and is written in the spirit of his school. The dreams of insanity are embodied in the strong and striking language of the insane, and the author, notwithstanding the rationality of his preface [see excerpt dated 1818 by Percy Bysshe Shelley], often leaves us in doubt whether he is not as mad as his hero. Mr. Godwin is the patriarch of a literary family, whose chief skill is in delineating the wanderings of the intellect, and which strangely delights in the most afflicting and humiliating of human miseries. His disciples are a kind of *out-pensioners of Bedlam,* and, like 'Mad Bess' or 'Mad Tom,' are occasionally visited with paroxysms of genius and fits of expression, which make sober-minded people wonder and shudder. (p. 382)

It cannot be denied that [it] is nonsense—but it is nonsense decked out with circumstances and clothed in language highly terrific: it is, indeed,

> —————————a tale
> Told by an ideot, full of sound and fury,
> Signifying nothing—

but still there is something tremendous in the unmeaning hollowness of its sound, and the vague obscurity of its images.

But when we have thus admitted that *Frankenstein* has passages which appal the mind and make the flesh creep, we have given it all the praise (if praise it can be called) which we dare to bestow. Our taste and our judgment alike revolt at this kind of writing, and the greater the ability with which it may be executed the worse it is—it inculcates no lesson of conduct, manners, or morality; it cannot mend, and will not even amuse its readers, unless their taste have been deplorably vitiated—it fatigues the feelings without interesting the understanding; it gratuitously harasses the heart, and wantonly adds to the store, already too great, of painful sensations. The author has powers, both of conception and language, which employed in a happier direction might, perhaps, (we speak dubiously,) give him a name among those whose writings amuse or amend their fellow-creatures; but we take the liberty of assuring him, and hope that he may be in a temper to listen to us, that the style which he has adopted in the present publication merely tends to defeat his own purpose, if he really had any other object in view than that of leaving the wearied reader, after a struggle between laughter and loathing, in doubt whether the head or the heart of the author be the most diseased. (p. 385)

> [*John Wilson Croker*], *in a review of "Frankenstein; or, The Modern Prometheus," in* The Quarterly Review, *Vol. XVIII, No. XXXVI, January, 1818, pp. 379-85.*

[SIR WALTER SCOTT]   (essay date 1818)

[*Scott was a Scottish novelist, poet, historian, biographer, and critic of the Romantic period who is best known for his novels, which were great popular successes. In the excerpt below, Scott places* Frankenstein *in the philosophical rather than merely sensational school of supernatural fiction, terming it a work of creative and poetic genius, despite its implausible plot.*]

[*Frankenstein*] is a novel, or more properly a romantic fiction, of a nature so peculiar, that we ought to describe the species before attempting any account of the individual production. . . .

[The] class of marvellous romances admits of several subdivisions. In the earlier productions of imagination, the poet or tale-teller does not, in his own opinion, transgress the laws of credibility, when he introduces into his narration the witches, goblins, and magicians, in the existence of which he himself, as well as his hearers, is a firm believer. This good faith, however, passes away, and works turning upon the marvellous are written and read merely on account of the exercise which they afford to the imagination of those who, like the poet Collins, love to riot in the luxuriance of oriental fiction, to rove through the meanders of enchantment, to gaze on the magnificence of golden palaces, and to repose by the waterfalls of Elysian gardens. In this species of composition, the marvellous is itself the principal and most important object both to the author and reader. (p. 613)

A more philosophical and refined use of the supernatural in works of fiction, is proper to that class in which the laws of nature are represented as altered, not for the purpose of pampering the imagination with wonders, but in order to shew the probable effect which the supposed miracles would produce on those who witnessed them. In this case, the pleasure ordinarily derived from the marvellous incidents is secondary to that which we extract from observing how mortals like ourselves would be affected,

> By scenes like these which, daring to depart
> From sober truth, are still to nature true.

Even in the description of his marvels, however, the author, who manages this style of composition with address, gives them an indirect importance with the reader, when he is able to describe, with nature and with truth, the effects which they are calculated to produce upon his dramatis personæ. . . . But success in this point is still subordinate to the author's principal object, which is less to produce an effect by means of the marvels of the narrations, than to open new trains and channels of thought, by placing men in supposed situations of an extraordinary and preternatural character, and then describing the mode of feeling and conduct which they are most likely to adopt. (pp. 613-14)

In the class of fictitious narrations to which we allude, the author opens a sort of account-current with the reader; drawing upon him, in the first place, for credit to that degree of the marvellous which he proposes to employ; and becoming virtually bound, in consequence of this indulgence, that his personages shall conduct themselves, in the extraordinary circumstances in which they are placed, according to the rules of probability, and the nature of the human heart. In this view, the *probable* is far from being laid out of sight even amid the wildest freaks of imagination; on the contrary, we grant the extraordinary postulates which the author demands as the foundation of his narrative, only on condition of his deducing the consequences with logical precision.

We have only to add, that this class of fiction has been sometimes applied to the purposes of political satire, and sometimes to the general illustration of the powers and workings of the human mind. Swift, Bergerac, and others, have employed it for the former purpose, and a good illustration of the latter is the well known *Saint Leon* of William Godwin. In this latter work, assuming the possibility of the transmutation of metals and of the *elixir vitæ,* the author has deduced, in the course of his narrative, the probable consequences of the possession of such secrets upon the fortunes and mind of him who might enjoy them. *Frankenstein* is a novel upon the same plan with *Saint Leon;* it is said to be written by Mr Percy Bysshe Shelley, who, if we are rightly informed, is son-in-law to Mr Godwin; and it is inscribed to that ingenious author. (p. 614)

[In *Frankenstein*] the author seems to us to disclose uncommon powers of poetic imagination. The feeling with which we perused the unexpected and fearful, yet, allowing the possibility of the event, very natural conclusion of Frankenstein's experiment, shook a little even our firm nerves; although such, and so numerous have been the expedients for exciting terror employed by the romantic writers of the age, that the reader may adopt Macbeth's words with a slight alteration:

> We have supp'd full with horrors:
> Direness, familiar to our "callous" thoughts,
> Cannot once startle us.

It is no slight merit in our eyes, that the tale, though wild in incident, is written in plain and forcible English, without exhibiting that mixture of hyperbolical Germanisms with which tales of wonder are usually told, as if it were necessary that the language should be as extravagant as the fiction. The ideas of the author are always clearly as well as forcibly expressed; and his descriptions of landscape have in them the choice requisites of truth, freshness, precision, and beauty. The self-education of the monster, considering the slender opportunities of acquiring knowledge he possessed, . . . [is] improbable and overstrained. That he should have not only learned to speak, but to read, and, for aught we know, to write—that he should have become acquainted with *Werter,* with Plutarch's *Lives,* and with *Paradise Lost,* by listening through a hole in a wall, seems as unlikely as that he should have acquired, in the same way, the problems of Euclid, or the art of book-keeping by single and double entry. . . . We should also be disposed, in support of the principles with which we set out, to question whether the monster, how tall, agile, and strong however, could have perpetrated so much mischief undiscovered; or passed through so many countries without being secured, either on account of his crimes, or for the benefit of some such speculator as Mr Polito, who would have been happy to have added to his museum so curious a specimen of natural history. But as we have consented to admit the leading incident of the work, perhaps some of our readers may be of opinion, that to stickle upon lesser improbabilities, is to incur the censure bestowed by the Scottish proverb on those who start at straws after swallowing *windlings.*

The following lines, which occur in the second volume, mark, we think, that the author possesses the same facility in expressing himself in verse as in prose.

> We rest; a dream has power to poison sleep.
>   We rise; one wand'ring thought pollutes the day.
> We feel, conceive, or reason; laugh, or weep,
>   Embrace fond woe, or cast our cares away;
> It is the same; for, be it joy or sorrow,
>   The path of its departure still is free.
> Man's yesterday may ne'er be like his morrow;
>   Nought may endure but mutability!

Upon the whole, the work impresses us with a high idea of the author's original genius and happy power of expression. We shall be delighted to hear that he has aspired to the *paullo majora;* and, in the meantime, congratulate our readers upon a novel which excites new reflections and untried sources of emotion. If Gray's definition of Paradise, to lie on a couch, namely, and read new novels, come any thing near truth, no small praise is due to him, who, like the author of *Frankenstein,*

has enlarged the sphere of that fascinating enjoyment. (pp. 619-20)

> [Sir Walter Scott], "Remarks on 'Frankenstein; or, The Modern Prometheus: A Novel'," in Blackwood's Edinburgh Magazine, *Vol. II, No. XII, March, 1818, pp. 613-20.*

THE EDINBURGH MAGAZINE AND LITERARY MISCELLANY (essay date 1818)

> [In the following excerpt, the critic faults the exaggerated, somewhat impious, and decidedly "Godwinian" premises of *Frankenstein.*]

[*Frankenstein*] is one of the productions of the modern school in its highest style of caricature and exaggeration. It is formed on the Godwinian manner, and has all the faults, but many likewise of the beauties of that model. In dark and gloomy views of nature and of man, bordering too closely on impiety,—in the most outrageous improbability,—in sacrificing every thing to effect,—it even goes beyond its great prototype; but in return, it possesses a similar power of fascination, something of the same mastery in harsh and savage delineations of passion, relieved in like manner by the gentler features of domestic and simple feelings. There never was a wilder story imagined, yet, like most of the fictions of this age, it has an air of reality attached to it, by being connected with the favourite projects and passions of the times. The real events of the world have, in our day, too, been of so wondrous and gigantic a kind,—the shiftings of the scenes in our stupendous drama have been so rapid and various, that Shakespeare himself, in his wildest flights, has been completely distanced by the eccentricities of actual existence. . . . [The public] can be satisfied with nothing in fiction that is not highly coloured and exaggerated; we even like a story the better that it is disjointed and irregular, and our greatest inventors, accordingly, have been obliged to accommodate themselves to the taste of the age, more, we believe, than their own judgment can, at all times, have approved of. The very extravagance of the present production will now, therefore, be, perhaps, in its favour. . . . (p. 249)

[In] this singular performance, . . . there is much power and beauty, both of thought and expression, though, in many parts, the execution is imperfect, and bearing the marks of an unpractised hand. It is one of those works, however, which, when we have read, we do not well see why it should have been written;—for a *jeu d'esprit* it is somewhat too long, grave, and laborious,—and some of our highest and most reverential feelings receive a shock from the conception on which it turns, so as to produce a painful and bewildered state of mind while we peruse it. We are accustomed, happily, to look upon the creation of a living and intelligent being as a work that is fitted only to inspire a religious emotion, and there is an impropriety, to say no worse, in placing it in any other light. It might, indeed, be the author's view to shew that the powers of man have been wisely limited, and that misery would follow their extension,—but still the expression "Creator," applied to a mere human being, gives us the same sort of shock with the phrase, "the Man Almighty," and others of the same kind, in Mr Southey's *Curse of Kehama.* All these monstrous conceptions are the consequences of the wild and irregular theories of the age; though we do not at all mean to infer that the authors who give into such freedoms have done so with any bad intentions. This incongruity, however, with our established and most sacred notions, is the chief fault in such fictions, regarding them merely in a critical point of view. Shakespeare's Caliban (though his simplicity and suitableness to the place where he is found are very delightful) is, perhaps, a more *hateful* being than our good friend in this book. But Caliban comes into existence in the received way which common superstition had pointed out; we should not have endured him if Prospero had created him. Getting over this original absurdity, the character of our monster is in good keeping;—there is a grandeur, too, in the scenery in which he makes his appearances,—the ice-mountains of the Pole, or the glaciers of the Alps;—his natural tendency to kind feelings, and the manner in which they were blighted,—and all the domestic picture of the cottage, are very interesting and beautiful. We hope yet to have more productions, both from this author and his great model, Mr. Godwin; but they would make a great improvement in their writings, if they would rather study the established order of nature as it appears, both in the world of matter and of mind, than continue to revolt our feelings by hazardous innovations in either of these departments. (pp. 252-53)

> A *review of "Frankenstein; or, The Modern Prometheus," in* The Edinburgh Magazine and Literary Miscellany, *n.s.Vol. II, March, 1818, pp. 249-53.*

THE BRITISH CRITIC   (essay date 1818)

[*This critic pronounces* Frankenstein *absurd and unnatural, but admits that the novel evinces powers that "might be disciplined into something better." Judging from references to Godwin's* Mandeville *and to a female author, the reviewer was aware of the author's true identity.*]

[**Frankenstein**] is another anomalous story of the same race and family as *Mandeville;* and, if we are not misinformed, it is intimately connected with that strange performance, by more ties than one. In the present instance, it is true, we are presented with the mysteries of equivocal generation, instead of the metaphysics of a bedlamite; but he who runs as he reads, might pronounce both novels to be *similis farinæ.* We are in doubt to what class we shall refer writings of this extravagant character; that they bear marks of considerable power, it is impossible to deny; but this power is so abused and perverted, that we should almost prefer imbecility; however much, of late years, we have been wearied and ennuied by the languid whispers of gentle sentimentality, they at least had the comfortable property of provoking no uneasy slumber; but we must protest against the waking dreams of horror excited by the unnatural stimulants of this later school; and we feel ourselves as much harassed, after rising from the perusal of these three spirit-wearing volumes, as if we had been over-dosed with laudanum, or hag-ridden by the night-mare. (p. 432)

We need scarcely say, that these volumes have neither principle, object, nor moral; the horror which abounds in them is too grotesque and *bizarre* ever to approach near the sublime, and when we did not hurry over the pages in disgust, we sometimes paused to laugh outright; and yet we suspect, that the diseased and wandering imagination, which has stepped out of all legitimate bounds, to frame these disjointed combinations and unnatural adventures, might be disciplined into something better. We heartily wish it were so, for there are occasional symptoms of no common powers of mind, struggling through a mass of absurdity, which well nigh overwhelms them; but it is a sort of absurdity that approaches so often the confines of what is wicked and immoral, that we dare hardly

The first illustration of Frankenstein's monster, from the 1831 Standard Novels edition.

trust ourselves to bestow even this qualified praise. The writer of it is, we understand, a female; this is an aggravation of that which is the prevailing fault of the novel; but if our authoress can forget the gentleness of her sex, it is no reason why we should; and we shall therefore dismiss the novel without further comment. (p. 438)

> A *review of "Frankenstein; or, The Modern Prometheus," in* The British Critic, *n.s. Vol. IX, April, 1818, pp. 432-38.*

BLACKWOOD'S EDINBURGH MAGAZINE   (essay date 1818)

[*The following excerpt is from a brief review that praises the lively, unpretentious style of Shelley's travel volume,* A Six Weeks' Tour.]

There is little information, no reflection, and very few incidents, in [*History of a Six Weeks' Tour through a Part of France, Switzerland, Germany, and Holland*], and yet it somehow or other produces considerable amusement and interest. It is the simplest and most unambitious journal imaginable of a Continental Tour; and probably in that simplicity consists its principal attraction. There is no formal appearance of a largely-promising preface; none of that assumed stateliness of intellect so ludicrous in your modern imbecil tourist; none of those common-places which, like so much dead luggage, impede the motion of the vehicle; no steeple-hunting in large towns—no talk of antiquities in every paltry village. When we lay down the volume, we are not much the wiser; but we are wholly free from that drowsiness that steals so imperceptibly from most journals, and the perusal of it rather produces the same effect as a smart walk before breakfast, in company with a lively friend who hates long stories.

The writer of this little volume, too, is a Lady, and writes like one,—with ease, gracefulness, and vivacity. Above all, there is something truly delightful in the colour of her stockings; they are of the purest white, and much more becoming than the brightest blue. She prattles away very prettily in the true English idiom, and has evidently learned her language from living lips, rather than from dead dictionaries. Though a travelling lady, and therefore entitled to understand all tongues, she very modestly confines herself to the English; and we are not the less disposed to believe, that she understands the languages of other countries, from observing that she writes well that of her own. Now and then a French phrase drops sweetly enough from her fair mouth, but the fear of bad grammar is before her eyes, and she has never ventured on a whole sentence. . . . There is also something original in the plan of travelling adopted by the fair Tourist. She is not . . . a sour, solitary spinster—she is a sweet-blooded wedded wife. Her youth has, she says, been chiefly past in pursuing, like the swallow, the inconstant summer of delight and beauty which invests this visible world. And, on the present occasion, with her husband (there is no travelling companion like a husband,) and her sister, she passes *on foot* through part of France and Switzerland, and sails down the castled magnificence of the Rhine. Her heart is at all times open to gladness and kindly feeling; and we think that no one will part with so amiable and agreeable a companion, without regret, and sincere wishes for her future happiness. (p. 412)

> A review of "History of a Six Weeks' Tour through a Part of France, Switzerland, Germany, and Holland," in Blackwood's Edinburgh Magazine, Vol. III, No. XVI, July, 1818, pp. 412-16.

WILLIAM GODWIN   (letter date 1822)

[*An English philosopher, novelist, and essayist, Godwin is remembered as an author whose writings strongly influenced the English Romantic writers. His anarchistic and rationalistic beliefs were first delineated in his philosophical masterpiece,* An Enquiry Concerning Political Justice and Its Influence on General Virtue and Happiness, *and later dramatized in his well-known novel,* Things As They Are; or, The Adventures of Caleb Williams. *The following excerpt is from Godwin's critique of Shelley's* Valperga.]

Perhaps it may be of some use to you if I give you my opinion of [*Valperga*]. I think there are parts of high genius, and that your two females are exceedingly interesting; but I am not satisfied. *Frankenstein* was a fine thing; it was compressed, muscular, and firm; nothing relaxed and weak; no proud flesh. [*Valperga*] is a work of more genius; but it appears, in reading, that the first rule you prescribed to yourself was, I will let it be long. It contains the quantity of four volumes of *Waverley*. No hard blow was ever hit with a woolsack! (p. 52)

> William Godwin, in a letter to Mary Wollstonecraft Shelley on November 15, 1822, in The Life & Letters of Mary Wollstonecraft Shelley, Vol. II by Julian Marshall, Richard Bentley & Son, 1889, pp. 50-2.

BLACKWOOD'S EDINBURGH MAGAZINE   (essay date 1823)

[*In this excerpt from a review of* Valperga, *the critic states that while the novel possesses certain beauties, it fails to live up to the promise displayed in* Frankenstein.]

Frankenstein, at the time of its appearance, we certainly did not suspect to be the work of a female hand; the name of Shelley was whispered, and we did not hesitate to attribute the book to *Mr* Shelley. Soon, however, we were set right. We learned that *Frankenstein* was written by *Mrs* Shelley; and then we most undoubtedly said to ourselves, "For a man it was excellent, but for a woman it is wonderful." What we chiefly admired, in that wild production, was vigour of imagination and strength of language; these were unquestionable attributes, and they redeemed the defects of an absurd groundwork and an incoherent fable; and, moreover, they tempted us, and everybody else, to forgive the many long passages of feeble conception and feeble execution, with which the vigorous scenes were interwoven.

The history of Castruccio Castracani [recounted in *Valperga*], on the other hand, had been long familiar to us in the glowing and energetic sketch of Machiavelli. Perhaps, on the whole, we should have been more rejoiced in the prospect of meeting Mrs Shelley again on the same dark territory, where she had first displayed so many striking powers; but the story of Castruccio we were willing to consider as not unlikely to furnish, in such hands, the basis and materials of a most romantic fiction. . . . We must confess, that in much of what we looked for, we have been disappointed; but yet, even here at the outset, we do not hesitate to say, that if we have not met with what we expected, we have met with other things almost as good.

Our chief objection, indeed, may be summed up in one word— Mrs Shelley has not done justice to the character of Castruccio. The life of him, by Machiavel, does not cover more than twenty or thirty duodecimo pages; yet, one rises from that brief sketch with a much more lively and perfect notion of the man, than from the perusal of the three closely printed volumes now on our table. There is not one spark of wit in all this book, and yet the keen Italian wit of Castruccio was one of the most striking features in his real character, and ought to have been among the most prominent in a work representing him throughout, in action and conversation. Machiavel, in two or three pages, tells stories enough to have suggested the true *"Castruccio vein."* Who does not remember that famous one of his rebuking a young man, whom he met coming out of a house of ill fame, and who blushed on being recognized? "It was when you went in that you should have coloured," said Castruccio, "not when you come out." (p. 283)

Of all this sort of thing we have no trace in Mrs Shelley's book; and yet she appears to have contemplated a very full development of Castruccio's character. She gives us his infancy, his boyhood, his manhood, all in complete detail. The attempt, whether successful or not, certainly is made to depict the slow and gradual formation of a crafty and bloody Italian tyrant of the middle ages, out of an innocent, open-hearted and deeply-feeling youth. We suspect, that in the whole of this portraiture, far too much reliance has been laid on thoughts and feelings, not only modern, but modern and feminine at once. Perhaps we might say more; nay, perhaps we should not be saying too much, if we plainly expressed the opinion, that a very great part of Mrs Shelley's book has no inspiration, but that of a certain *school*, which is certainly a very modern, as well as a very mischievous one, and which ought never, of all things, to have numbered ladies among its disciples. But, in spite even of this, we have closed the book with no feelings but those of perfect kindness—and we shall say no more of matters that will, perhaps, suggest themselves to our readers quite strongly enough, without our giving ourselves any trouble.

Laying out of view Antehminelli's real life and character, we can have no hesitation in saying, that Mrs Shelley has given us a clever and amusing romance. Not doubting, that she will in due time make more attempts in the same way, we would fain point out, to so clever a person, faults which she might easily avoid in future, and which here, even more, perhaps, than in *Frankenstein,* neutralize much of her power. But, on further reflection, we believe the best way will be to leave all this to the working of experience. A very little consideration must be enough to shew such a writer the absurdity of introducing so many pure episodes. The framer of an historical romance should not be reminding us at every turn, that his *principal* object is to shew off his own knowledge of strange manners, or power of fine writing. If quaint manners are to be quaintly and strongly represented, the incidents, with which these are connected, ought to have a strict connexion with, and influence over, the progress of the fable, or at least the development of the principal characters of the fable. We cannot stand the stepping aside for ten pages, *merely* for the purpose of letting us see, that the writer knows the way in which the *Mysteries* of the middle ages were represented, either on, or off the Arno—we cannot spare four days of the life of Castruccio Castraccani to singers and tale-tellers, and so forth, with whom he and his story have nothing to do—we abhor all unnecessary prosing about religious sects, and we are mortally sick of "orange-tinted skies," "dirges," and "Dante." (p. 284)

The work . . . undoubtedly reflects no *discredit* even on the authoress of *Frankenstein*—although we must once more repeat our opinion, that *Valperga* is, for a second romance, by no means what its predecessor was for a first one. (p. 293)

> A review of "Valperga; or, The Life and Adventures of Castruccio, Prince of Lucca," in Blackwood's Edinburgh Magazine, *Vol. XII, No. LXXIV, March, 1823, pp. 283-93.*

THE LONDON LITERARY GAZETTE   (essay date 1823)

[*The reviewer favorably compares* Valperga *with* Frankenstein.]

In [*Valperga*] the most powerful passions are called into action; and love, enthusiasm, and ambition, appear on the canvass, stamped with the same wild imagination that characterized *Frankenstein.* Energetic language, landscapes worthy of poet or painter, feelings strong in their truth, are to be found in every chapter. . . . The period, that of the struggle between the Guelphs and Ghibbelines, in which it is laid, is above all favourable for display and delineation of character. . . . In this Novel it is not the events that interest us so much as the actors; and we shall give a better idea of *Valperga* by sketching the characters than by detailing the plot.

At the head of the list stands Castruccio. We see him first a gentle and affectionate child, an exile in his infancy, and his earliest impressions those of blood and fear. Next he is a spirited, generous boy, who then becomes the very model of a young warrior, brave, beautiful, and in love; but even then the evil germ is in his heart, though as yet bearing no fruit. The ambitious soldier adds the lessons of craft to those of courage,

and craft is soon followed by its shadow, cruelty; the darker outlines of the picture are gradually filled up; and in the cold-blooded, intriguing, suspicious leader of the Ghibbelines, we lose almost all trace of the once light, frank-hearted, noble Castruccio. There is truth, there is power in the portrait, yet we feel unsatisfied in gazing on it; we mark the ravages of ambition on the once fresh and affectionate heart with the same repugnance that we watch on a beautiful face the encroachments of disease. The Lord of Lucca has too much interest at first to admit of our cordially hating his worthlessness; we do not like to see our bright idol prove but a thing of human dust and dross. No other male character occupies a conspicuous place. The subtle Galeazzo, the gentle Arigo, the Bishop, Buondelmonte, though well coloured, are but mere sketches; and Pepi seems to us solely introduced to gratify a family taste for monsters. This same remark may apply to Bindo the Albinois, and the witch of the forest—sheer mummery, unworthy the other parts. Indeed the most prevailing fault through the work is the multiplicity of those introduced, from whom we are led to expect much, yet who are afterwards, as it were, forgotten by the author. But the two female pictures are exquisite, both from their contrast and in themselves. Pure, beautiful, high-minded, generous, Euthanasia is an emanation of female loveliness and female delicacy; perfect without being insipid, her superiority is forgotten and forgiven in her gentleness and her sorrow. But with all the admiration we have conceded, we must think her character ideal: it scarcely seems in woman's nature for patriotism to be a stronger feeling than love; and we could have forgiven Euthanasia for marrying Castruccio, even though he had declared war against Florence. Beatrice is the very creation of fancy and poetry: young, beautiful, enthusiastic, yielding to love as to the dictates of Heaven; taking the wild impulses of an ungoverned imagination for inspiration; passionate, yet timid; pity is almost pain when we find the innocent and radiant girl withered in her fiery hour of insanity, dying of a broken heart: it is like a relief to have Castruccio to hate for it. (p. 132)

We recommend the readers of this work to skim the commencement of the first volume, dwell on the history of Euthanasia, for its feeling; the history of her court, held four days, for its vivid picture of the manners of the age; read the whole of the second, skim again the beginning of the third, and we will leave the end to speak for itself. (p. 133)

> A review of "Valperga; or, The Life and Adventures of Castruccio, Prince of Lucca," in The London Literary Gazette, *No. 319, March 1, 1823, pp. 132-33.*

THE LONDON LITERARY GAZETTE   (essay date 1826)

[*In the following excerpt from a review of* The Last Man, *the critic commends Shelley's ambitious subject, but finds the novel generally unsuccessful due to plot implausibilities and too many "horrors."*]

This is a novel [*The Last Man*], of which the subject is sufficiently extraordinary. Two of the most successful poets of the day, Byron and Campbell, have dared only just to touch upon it in a few detached lines; and yet here we have three volumes of prose devoted to it by a female writer. Whether the bards were wise in their restricted flights, or whether this bolder undertaking could possibly succeed, we will not here inquire. The author, suffice it to say, is not unknown to the reading world, for her scarcely less bold, and certainly not altogether unsuccessful attempt under the title of *Frankenstein.*

We shall, therefore, merely glance at the plan and conduct of the fable. . . . There is an Introduction, not very skilfully imagined, which gives us to understand that the work is to be looked upon as a sort of free translation of certain "Sibylline Leaves," picked up by a party of modern travellers in the (so called) cave of the Cumaean Sibyl, on the shores of the Bay of Naples: and the story (as its name indicates) relates to the life and fortunes of "the Last Man," who remains on the face of the earth after it has been desolated of its human inhabitants by a great plague, which rages during the last two or three years of the twenty-first century of our present era. The story, however, commences about the year 2073—thus affording scope for much matter not connected with the catastrophe, and enabling the writer to indulge in every possible (and impossible) flight of her anticipative imagination, touching the nature of human society, and of all other mundane matters, a hundred and fifty years hence! . . .

Were this not written by a woman, it would be sad, vapid impertinence: as it is written by a woman, we male critics do not know what it is. We wish we did! Who will teach us? (p. 102)

When we repeat that these volumes are the production of a female pen, and that we have not ceased to consider Mrs. Shelley as a woman and a widow, we shall have given the clue to our abstinence from remarks upon them. That we must deem the tale altogether to be an instance of the strange misapplication of considerable talent, is most true. After the first volume, it is a sickening repetition of horrors, and a struggle after the display of morbid feelings which could not exist under the circumstances, nor even in the world as it now exists, with good and evil, joys and woes, mingled together. To hear a *last man* talking of having his "sensitive nerves anatomised" by any thing, is sheer nonsense: by the time a man had outlived his kind, Mrs. S. might be assured that the nervous system too was pretty nearly abolished. . . . Really these are sad doings. We confess that we cannot get so seriously through the world in its last convulsions as we could wish; but there may be readers who can enter into the spirit of the thing, and to them the perusal of Mrs. Shelley's book may afford gratification. We will add, that there are some strong imaginings in it; and not the least cruel of these flights appears to us to be, the author's making the last human being an unfortunate gentleman. Why not *the last Woman?* she would have known better how to paint her distress at having nobody left to talk to: we are sure the tale would have been more interesting. (p. 103)

> *A review of "The Last Man," in* The London Literary Gazette, *No. 474, February 18, 1826, pp. 102-03.*

THE MONTHLY REVIEW, LONDON (essay date 1826)

[*According to the author of this excerpt from a brief, unfavorable review,* The Last Man *is excessively extravagant and morbid, "the offspring of a diseased imagination, and of a most polluted taste."*]

Mrs. Shelley, true to the genius of her family, has found this breathing world and the operations and scenes which enliven it, so little worthy of her soaring fancy, that [in *The Last Man*] she once more ventures to create a world of her own, to people it with beings modelled by her own hand, and to govern it by laws drawn from the visionary theories which she has been so long taught to admire as the perfection of wisdom. She seems herself to belong to a sphere different from that with which we are conversant. Her imagination appears to delight in in-

ventions which have no foundation in ordinary occurrences, and no charm for the common sympathies of mankind. (p. 333)

This idea of *The Last Man* has already tempted the genius of more than one of our poets, and, in truth, it is a theme which appears to open a magnificent and boundless field to the imagination. But we have only to consider it for a moment, in order to be convinced that the mind of man might as well endeavour to describe the transactions which are taking place in any of the countless planets that are suspended beyond our own, as to anticipate the horrors of the day which shall see the dissolution of our system. The utmost efforts of thought are absolutely childish, when they seek to fathom the abyss of ruin, to number the accumulation of disasters, to paint the dreadful confusion, which await that final scene. Every writer who has hitherto ventured on the theme, has fallen infinitely beneath it. Mrs. Shelley, in following their example, has merely made herself ridiculous. (p. 334)

There is nothing in the conduct, in the characters, in the incidents, or in the descriptive matter of this work, to which we feel any pleasure in referring. The whole appears to us to be the offspring of a diseased imagination, and of a most polluted taste. We must observe, however, that the powers of composition displayed in this production, are by no means of an ordinary character. They are indeed uncontrolled by any of the rules of good writing; but they certainly bear the impress of genius, though perverted and spoiled by morbid affectation. Mrs. Shelley frequently attempts to give her style a rythmical conciseness, and a poetical colouring, which we take to have been the main causes of the bombast that disfigures almost every chapter of this unamiable romance.

The descriptions of the operations of the pestilence are particularly objectionable for their minuteness. It is not a picture which she gives us, but a lecture in anatomy, in which every part of the human frame is laid bare to the eye, in its most putrid state of corruption. In this part of her subject, as indeed in every other, she amplifies beyond all the bounds of moderation. We are reluctantly obliged to pronounce the work a decided failure. (p. 335)

> *A review of "The Last Man," in* The Monthly Review, *London, Vol. I, No. III, March, 1826, pp. 333-35.*

[SIR WALTER SCOTT] (essay date 1827)

[*Here, Scott places* Frankenstein *in the tradition of "fantastic" literature.*]

[There is a] FANTASTIC mode of writing,—in which the most wild and unbounded license is given to an irregular fancy, and all species of combination, however ludicrous, or however shocking, are attempted and executed without scruple. In the other modes of treating the supernatural, even that mystic region is subjected to some laws, however slight; and fancy, in wandering through it, is regulated by some probabilities in the wildest flight. Not so in the fantastic style of composition, which has no restraint save that which it may ultimately find in the exhausted imagination of the author. (p. 72)

Our English severity of taste will not easily adopt this wild and fantastic tone into our own literature; nay, perhaps will scarce tolerate it in translations. The only composition which approaches to it is the powerful romance of *Frankenstein,* and there, although the formation of a thinking and sentient being by scientific skill is an incident of the fantastic character, still the interest of the work does not turn upon the marvellous creation of Frankenstein's monster, but upon the feelings and sentiments which that creature is supposed to express as most natural—if we may use the phrase—to his unnatural condition and origin. In other words, the miracle is not wrought for the mere wonder, but is designed to give rise to a train of acting and reasoning in itself just and probable, although the *postulatum* on which it is grounded is in the highest degree extravagant. So far **Frankenstein,** therefore, resembles the *Travels of Gulliver,* which suppose the existence of the most extravagant fictions, in order to extract from them philosophical reasoning and moral truth. In such cases the admission of the marvellous expressly resembles a sort of entry-money paid at the door of a lecture-room,—it is a concession which must be made to the author, and for which the reader is to receive value in moral instruction. But the *fantastic* of which we are now treating encumbers itself with no such conditions, and claims no further object than to surprise the public by the wonder itself. (pp. 72-3)

> [*Sir Walter Scott*], *"On the Supernatural in Fictitious Composition: And Particularly on the Works of Hoffmann," in* The Foreign Quarterly Review, *Vol. 1, No. 1, July, 1827, pp. 60-98.*

THE ATHENAEUM   (essay date 1830)

[*The following excerpt is from a favorable notice of* The Fortunes of Perkin Warbeck.]

[The] volumes before us [***The Fortunes of Perkin Warbeck***] are the productions of no ordinary pen. It is manifest that a richly-endowed and vigorous intellect has directed the hand which traced them. They are written with a noble energy of thought—a deep concentration of feeling—a fervid glow of expression, and sweet purity of sentiment, which display in their author the very highest capabilities. The reader is hurried on from action to action with a spirit-stirring impulse, which never for a moment allows his excitement to abate; and the scenes which follow each other in such rapid succession, are wrought out with all the distinctness of a present reality. The characters are drawn with great vividness, and in some of them, especially, there is an originality which strikingly marks the powerfully-creative mind of the author of **Frankenstein.**

Clifford, Frion, and Herman de Faro, we take to be very noble conceptions. The two first stand before us in the darkest hues of reckless depravity, whilst the latter is endowed with a dignity, which a peculiar mental idiosyncrasy often superadds to the natural elevation of virtue.

Mrs. Shelley's work contains simply what its title indicates—the fortunes of Perkin Warbeck, (whom our fair author presumes to be no impostor, but the true Plantagenet,) from his rescue from the Tower, when a child, to the sad termination of his career upon the scaffold.

The great defect in this romance appears to us to be the painful anticipation of disaster which is continually forced upon the reader, and which the mind cannot escape from, so that no pleasurable emotions are excited. It is painful to hurry through a succession of events which we know beforehand will all terminate unhappily. Warbeck's marriage with Lady Catherine Gordon is the only oasis amid the wilderness of misfortune through which he is doomed to wander. The interest of the reader is necessarily vastly diminished by his unavoidable

knowledge, that every effort of the hero will fail, and that destruction must overtake him at the last. (p. 323)

> *A review of "The Fortunes of Perkin Warbeck: A Romance," in* The Athenaeum, *No. 135, May 29, 1830, pp. 323-25.*

THE EDINBURGH LITERARY JOURNAL   (essay date 1830)

[*This critic assesses the merits and faults of* The Fortunes of Perkin Warbeck, *noting particularly its excessive detail.*]

[*The Fortunes of Perkin Warbeck*] is a talented work, but, at the same time, a little tedious and heavy. Mrs Shelley informs us in the preface, that she studied the subject originally with a view towards historical detail, but that, becoming aware of its romance, she determined not to confine herself to the mere incorporation of facts narrated by the old Chroniclers. A good deal of the leaven of history, however, still remains; and though several fictitious characters have been introduced, a calm straightforwardness of style characterises the whole book. The authoress sets out on the assumption that Perkin Warbeck was really the Duke of York, and consequently entitled to the throne of England upon the death of his elder brother Edward the Fifth. Upon this disputed question it is unnecessary for us to enter farther, than to remark that sufficient plausibility attaches to Mrs Shelley's theory, to authorise her as a novelist to avail herself of it, although we are afraid that, in order to carry it through, she has been obliged, in more instances than one, to twist to her own interpretation the established facts of history. The chief fault we have to find with her production is, that it does not blend together with sufficient skill what is fictitious and what is true. The great use of an intermixture of fiction in an historical romance, is to relieve the reader from many dry details, and agreeably to fill up the interstices between those events which rivet the attention the more powerfully that they stand forth in bold and prominent contrast to the no less important occurrences of everyday life. Mrs Shelley, however, is contented to follow her hero's fortunes through thick and thin; and instead of fixing, as we should have advised her to do, on a few circumstances of acknowledged interest and moment, and contriving that all the narrative should tend towards them, she rather prefers patiently to act the part of a biographer, and with the utmost perseverance follows Warbeck through all his fortunes, whether his adventures be brilliant or stupid, fortunate or disastrous. Could every reader enter into the fate and character of her hero with the same enthusiasm as our authoress, there would be nothing tiresome in this minuteness of detail; but even though we were to grant that he was the veritable heir to England's crown, we fear that, with one or two exceptions, there was little in his career to warrant our devoting undivided attention to it through three long volumes. (pp. 350-51)

It is therefore to be regretted, we think, that Mrs Shelley has, in the present work, indefatigably gone through the whole of Perkin Warbeck's life. Many of the smaller adventures and unsuccessful attempts at rebellion should have been omitted, because they lead to nothing, and wear out without satisfying the mind; and because, moreover, they tend to diminish our respect for her hero, pointing him out as one continually borne down by adversity, and consequently one more to be pitied than admired. Had she, on the contrary, confined her story to one or two of the more striking parts of his career,—such as his residence and marriage in Scotland, and subsequent fate,—she would have greatly strengthened her narrative; and by contracting her details into a narrower compass, given a solidity and compactness to them, in which they are at present deficient. To speak in the language of painters, her novel has not a sufficiently powerful middle-distance and foreground. The objects introduced are too much diffused and scattered. She has taken us to the top of a hill, and when we expected a broad and beautiful lake to burst upon us at once, we see nothing but the long line of a canal, which is equally broad at the one end as it is at the other.

Though we have thus stated, pretty plainly, our objection to Mrs Shelley's novel, we must at the same time state, no less plainly, that it unquestionably bears the stamp of a powerful mind, and that no one can read it without feeling a conviction that the authoress need not fear a comparison with even the most talented of her sex. It is certain that Mrs Shelley is apt at times to be heavy, and assuredly her *Last Man* is, in many parts, abundantly so, yet we entertain a high respect for her abilities, and believe her worthy to have been the wife of the author of the "Cenci." There is much powerful writing in her *Perkin Warbeck,* and several of the characters introduced—especially those of Sir Robert Clifford, Monina de Faro, and Catherine Gordon—are sketched with bold vigour and fine discrimination. It is not, however, in a facility of giving an intense individuality to the persons of her story that Mrs Shelley chiefly excels. We like her better in the narrative parts, interspersed as these always are with her own observations on men and manners, and coloured by her own peculiar imagination, feelings, and associations. (p. 351)

> *A review of "The Fortunes of Perkin Warbeck: A Romance," in* The Edinburgh Literary Journal, *No. 84, June 19, 1830, pp. 350-52.*

MARY W. SHELLEY (essay date 1831)

[*In her preface to the 1831 edition of* Frankenstein, *excerpted below, Shelley recounts the famous circumstances surrounding the conception and composition of the novel. She concludes the account with an allusion to the monster: "I bid my hideous progeny go forth and prosper."*]

The Publishers of the Standard Novels, in selecting *Frankenstein* for one of their series, expressed a wish that I should furnish them with some account of the origin of the story. I am the more willing to comply because I shall thus give a general answer to the question so very frequently asked me—"How I, then a young girl, came to think of, and to dilate upon so very hideous an idea?" It is true that I am very averse to bringing myself forward in print; but as my account will only appear as an appendage to a former production, and as it will be confined to such topics as have connection with my authorship alone I can scarcely accuse myself of a personal intrusion.

It is not singular, that, as the daughter of two persons of distinguished literary celebrity, I should very early in life have thought of writing. As a child, I scribbled; and my favorite pastime, during the hours given me for recreation, was "to write stories." Still I had a dearer pleasure than this, which was the formation of castles in the air—the indulging in waking dreams—the following up trains of thought; which had for their subject the formation of a succession of imaginary incidents. My dreams were at once more fantastic and agreeable than my writings. In the latter I was a close imitator—rather doing as others had done than putting down the suggestions of my own mind. What I wrote was intended at least for one other eye—my childhood's companion and friend—but my dreams were

all my own; I accounted for them to nobody; they were my refuge when annoyed—my dearest pleasure when free.

I lived principally in the country as a girl, and passed a considerable time in Scotland. I made occasional visits to the more picturesque parts; but my habitual residence was on the blank and dreary northern shores of the Tay, near Dundee. Blank and dreary, on retrospection, I call them; they were not so to me then. They were the cry of freedom, and the pleasant region where unheeded I could commune with the creatures of my fancy. I wrote then—but in a most common-place style. It was beneath the trees of the grounds belonging to our house, or on the bleak sides of the woodless mountains near, that my true compositions, the airy flights of my imagination, were born and fostered. I did not make myself the heroine of my tales. Life appeared to me too common-place an affair as regarded myself. I could not figure to myself that romantic woes or wonderful events would ever be my lot; but I was not confined to my own identity; and I could people the hours with creations far more interesting to me at that age, than my own sensations.

After this, my life became busier, and reality stood in place of fiction. My husband, however, was from the first very anxious that I should prove myself worthy of my parentage, and enrol myself on the page of fame. He was for ever inciting me to obtain literary reputation, which, even on my own part, I cared for then, though since I have become infinitely indifferent to it. At this time he desired that I should write, not so much with the idea that I could produce any thing worthy of notice, but that he might himself judge how far I possessed the promise of better things hereafter. Still I did nothing. Travelling, and the cares of a family, occupied my time; and study, in the way of reading, or improving my ideas in communication with his far more cultivated mind, was all of literary employment that engaged my attention.

In the summer of 1816, we visited Switzerland, and became the neighbors of Lord Byron. At first we spent our pleasant hours on the lake, or wandering on its shores; and Lord Byron, who was writing his third canto of *Childe Harold,* was the only one among us who put his thoughts upon paper. These, as he brought them successively to us, clothed in all the light and harmony of poetry, seemed to stamp as divine the glories of heaven and earth, whose influences we partook with him.

But it proved a wet, ungenial summer, and incessant rain often confined us for days to the house. Some volumes of ghost stories, translated from the German and French, fell into our hands. There was the *History of the Inconstant Lover,* who, when he thought to clasp the bride to whom he had pledged his vows, found himself in the arms of the pale ghost of her whom he had deserted. There was the tale of the sinful founder of his race, whose miserable doom it was to bestow the kiss of death on all the younger sons of his ill-fated house, just when they reached the age of promise. His gigantic, shadowy form, clothed like the ghost in Hamlet, in complete armor, but with the beaver up, was seen at midnight by the moon's fitful beams, to advance slowly along the gloomy avenue. The shape was lost beneath the shadow of the castle walls: but soon a gate swung back, a step was heard, the door of the chamber opened, and he advanced to the couch of the blooming youths, cradled in healthy sleep. Eternal sorrow sat upon his face as he bent down and kissed the forehead of the boys, who from that hour withered like flowers snapped upon the stalk. I have not seen these stories since then; but their incidents are as fresh in my mind as if I had read them yesterday.

"We will each write a ghost-story," said Lord Byron; and his proposition was acceded to. (pp. vii-viii)

I busied myself *to think of a story*—a story to rival those which had excited us to this task. One which would speak to the mysterious fears of our nature, and awaking thrilling horror—one to make the reader dread to look round, to curdle the blood, and quicken the beatings of the heart. If I did not accomplish these things, my ghost story would be unworthy of its name. I thought and pondered—vainly. I felt that blank incapability of invention which is the greatest misery of authorship, when dull Nothing replies to our anxious invocations. *Have you thought of a story?* I was asked each morning, and each morning I was forced to reply with a mortifying negative. (pp. viii-ix)

Many and long were the conversations between Lord Byron and Shelley, to which I was a devout, but nearly silent listener. During one of these, various philosophical doctrines were discussed, and among others, the nature of the principle of life, and whether there was any probability of its ever being discovered and communicated. They talked of the experiments of Dr. Darwin. (I speak not of what the Doctor really did, or said he did, but, as more to my purpose, of what was then spoken of as having been done by him,) who preserved a piece of vermicelli in a glass cage, till by some extraordinary means it began to move with voluntary motion. Not thus, after all, would life be given. Perhaps a corpse would be re-animated; galvanism had given token of such things; perhaps the component parts of a creature might be manufactured, brought together, and endued with vital warmth.

Night waned upon this talk, and even the witching hour had gone by, before we retired to rest. When I had placed my head on my pillow, I did not sleep, nor could I be said to think. My imagination, unbidden, possessed and guided me, gifting the successive images that arose in my mind with a vividness far beyond the usual bound of reverie. I saw—with shut eyes, but acute mental vision—I saw the pale student of unhallowed arts kneeling beside the thing he had put together. I saw the hideous phantasm of a man stretched out, and then, on the working of some powerful engine, show signs of life, and stir with an uneasy, half vital motion. Frightful must it be; for supremely frightful would be the effect of any human endeavor to mock the stupendous mechanism of the Creator of the world. His success would terrify the artist; he would rush away from his odious handywork, horror-stricken. He would hope that, left to itself, the slight spark of life which he had communicated, would fade; that this thing which had received such imperfect animation, would subside into dead matter; and he might sleep in the belief that the silence of the grave would quench for ever the transient existence of the hideous corps which he had looked upon as the cradle of life. He sleeps: but he is awakened; he opens his eyes: behold the horrid thing stands at his bedside, opening his curtains, and looking on him with yellow, watery, but speculative eyes.

I opened mine in terror. The idea so possessed my mind, that a thrill of fear ran through me and I wished to exchange the ghastly image of my fancy for the realities around. I see them still; the very room, the dark *parquet*, the closed shutters, with the moonlight struggling through, and the sense I had that the glassy lake and white high Alps were beyond. I could not so easily get rid of my hideous phantom; still it haunted me. I must try to think of something else. I recurred to my ghost story—my tiresome, unlucky ghost story! O! if I could only contrive one which would frighten my reader as I myself had been frightened that night!

Swift as light, and as cheering, was the idea that broke in upon me. "I have found it! What terrified me will terrify others; and I need only describe the spectre which had haunted my midnight pillow." On the morrow I announced that I had *thought of a story*. I began that day with the words, *It was on a dreary night in November,* making only a transcript of the grim terrors of my waking dream.

At first I thought but of a few pages—of a short tale; but Shelley urged me to develope the idea at greater length. I certainly did not owe the suggestion of one incident, nor scarcely of one train of feeling, to my husband, and yet, but for his incitement, it would never have taken the form in which it was presented to the world. From this declaration I must except the preface. As far as I can recollect, it was entirely written by him.

And now, once again, I bid my hideous progeny go forth and prosper. I have an affection for it, for it was the offspring of happy days, when death and grief were but words, which found no true echo in my heart. Its several pages speak of many a walk, many a drive, and many a conversation, when I was not alone; and my companion was one who, in this world, I shall never see more. But this is for myself; my readers have nothing to do with these associations. (pp. ix-x)

> *Mary W. Shelley, in an extract in her* Frankenstein; or, The Modern Prometheus, *H. G. Daggers, 1845, pp. vi-x.*

Mary Shelley at the age she wrote Frankenstein.

THE NEW-YORK MIRROR   (essay date 1833)

[*The author of the following excerpt offers a sardonic assessment of* Frankenstein's *plot implausibilities, particularly those regarding the education and development of the monster.*]

The remark applied to Shakspeare, that he not only exhausted ordinary characters, but imagined new, is not altogether inapplicable to Mrs. Shelley. She has not, like the great bard, penetrated into all the variety of human nature, but the demon, created by Frankenstein, stands as much alone as Caliban, and, like that, takes a powerful hold on the imagination. We do not, however, assume the pen to praise a work [like *Frankenstein*], so well known and justly admired by every reader of romance; we mean only to enumerate several of its defects and improbabilities. We say *improbabilities*, because, notwithstanding that the tale itself is founded on a wild superstition, yet an author, although he may create impossible characters, may not make them do impossible things. There is a probability in their actions independent of the probability of their existence. Caliban, however exclusively a creation of the poet, is, nevertheless, always kept within the bounds of probability, bating the pardonable, and, indeed, necessary absurdity of rendering the uncouth savage thoughts of his glimmering intellect in verse. The monster has a certain character to sustain, certain powers of mind to lead him, certain peculiarities of body, and he has passed through a certain series of events which have formed his mind and disposition. He exhibits no knowledge but such as he had an opportunity to acquire. He speaks only of things with which he may be supposed to have been familiar. Shakspeare does not make him write, or read, or comprehend metaphysics. If Homer had fallen into his hands, he would not have conceived it. . . .

The probabilities of Frankenstein's demon are not so well preserved. The author soon found herself in a dilemma respecting the creature at length endowed with the vital spark, and she must have been as much in doubt what to do with him, as was the poor student himself, when blasted with the fatal success of his tremendous experiment. He must eat, drink, talk, understand, think, and act. He requires, too, extraordinary cunning to elude vigilance, and yet to procure the necessaries of existence. With a gigantic form, he has only an infant's mind—no knowledge, no experience. The author has, indeed, although at some expense or probability, adroitly managed to extricate him from so many difficulties.

Here, for instance, is one absurdity in her delineation of his thoughts. It occurs almost immediately after his creation, and while his mind is yet in its unenlightened state. It was very cold in the woods where he was wandering, and having found a fire which had been left by some beggars, he was overcome with delight at the warmth, thrust his hand into the embers, "and quickly drew it out again, with a cry of pain." Thus far it is natural. It is just what the creature might have done. But when he observes, (in his subsequent narrative,) "how strange, I thought, that the same cause should produce such opposite effects," and this too before he had acquired any language, you feel at once, that, being what he was, such a philosophical reflection never could have occurred to him. The whole account of his residence by the hut of the old man, Felix &c., is exceedingly pretty, but also exceedingly improbable. His reflections, previously to his knowledge, are such as no one, without that knowledge, could possess. How could he come to the conclusion, from the noise which the family made with their lips, that they were communicating ideas, that this was a godlike science, that, in reading, they found in the paper signs for speech which they understood, and that he would have been pleased to understand those signs, but despaired, because he did not understand the sounds which they represented? All these are philosophical conclusions, which, however apparently self-evident to the enlightened, yet imply long previous study and observation. All his mental operations here are of the same inconsistent and incredible nature. By looking through a hole in the wall, and listening alone, he learns not only to understand the language, but to read it and speak it so well, that he comprehends and remembers a complicated story of considerable length and full of allusions to the institutions, character and events of a state of civilized society. What could he know of grated windows—different languages—Paris—an execution—passports—treachery—exile? &c. After having learned what he could through the chink in the cottage wall, he became accidentally possessed of *Paradise Lost*, Plutarch's *Lives*, and the *Sorrows of Werter*, which he read with intelligence and criticized with force and precision. When, at length, he decides on entering the cottage to address the blind man, his language is so correct, that his hearer holds a long conversation with him, and discovers nothing extraordinary in his pronunciation and method of speaking. . . .

One of the most improbable things in the book, is the obtuseness of Frankenstein in reference to the nature of the demon's threat, "remember, I shall be with you on your wedding night." The wretch had already murdered one of his friends, and subsequently ended the life of another, thus plainly proving that his revenge sought to wound the creator of his misery through his affections; yet Frankenstein, with the most improbable want of common sense, continues to the period of his wedding, to tremble for his own life only, without once suspecting that any harm could befall his bride. Yet which of the two would such a diabolical foe slay? So completely is he blinded on this subject, that he actually leaves Elizabeth unguarded, when any other man would have locked her, if possible, in an inaccessible castle. . . .

It is not impossible, that the author was aware of these inconsistencies, and presumed upon the license necessary to the illustration of so poetical a story; but as many of them, and especially the last, might have been obviated by a little ingenuity, and without impairing the interest of the narration, it is a matter of regret that they have not been corrected.

The reader must not suppose, from these remarks, that we intend any thing derogatory to the high reputation of the tale. Indeed it merits strong commendation. There never yet, within the pages of a romance, was a plot more startling and wildly and intensely interesting. The imagination is immediately aroused, and hurried on impetuously toward the conclusion. The style of the writer also is easy, artless, and graceful. The most stupendous events and sublimest scenes are narrated and described in unaffected yet powerful language; and, indeed, one of the most striking merits of the author, independent of the invention of the story, is the total absence of verbiage and bathos, when a more elevated and turgid style would not, by any critics, be considered as inappropriate to the lofty and exciting character of the subject. The tale is doubtless destined to immortalize the accomplished writer, and quite sanctions the remark of Mr. Moore, that it is "one of those original conceptions that take hold of the public mind at once and for ever."

A review of "Frankenstein," in The New-York Mirror, *Vol. X, No. 49, June 8, 1833, p. 390.*

THE ATHENAEUM   (essay date 1835)

[*In this excerpt from a favorable review of* Lodore, *the critic praises its pleasing "feminine" attributes.*]

Mrs. Shelley's novels always possess a character of their own, which renders them acceptable to us; yet, when we sit down to consider wherein the charm of this their individuality consists, we frankly confess, that we find a difficulty in satisfying ourselves, or explaining our thoughts to others. Delicacy in conception of character, earnestness of purpose, such as draws the reader along, though, to quote an old *concetto,* "the rein be merely a string of roses"—and a gentle harmony of language, may all be mentioned as among their attributes: they are essentially feminine too in their strength as well as their sweetness, and singularly free from the soil and tinsel of this world's trick-wisdom. If, in all courtesy, we might, for once, be personal—we should not find it difficult to point out from what source the authoress of *Lodore* has derived her turn for investigating those springs and secrets of the human heart, which are least open to the eye of the superficial and vulgar gazer—whence she has inherited her conception of—

> How divine a thing
> A woman may be made,

and from whom she has caught a felicity of epithet, and a skillful ease of cadence, which make her style at times positively melodious.

It will be easy for our readers to perceive, that we have been pleased with *Lodore,* and we think, that all who can appreciate what is refined, and breathes of the affections rather than the passions, will share our pleasure. As the authoress has a style of her own, so also are her plots unlike any others with which we are acquainted. The tale of *Lodore* is consistent in its own peculiar colouring, so that we do not feel that it contains unsolved improbabilities, and difficulties and hindrances too finely drawn for reality. Without destroying any of the reader's interest, we may say that it turns upon the estrangement of Lord Lodore and his wife, which leads to the exile of the former, and afterwards to the yet more painful separation of daughter and mother. The characters of both of these are fascinating—the one softening in her resentment, and being purified from her worldliness by the lapse of time; the other, in the hour of vicissitude, strengthened by her affections, and becoming from a simple and innocent child, a faithful and noble-spirited wife—there are few creations in modern fiction, sweeter than Ethel Villiers. The incidental sketches of Miss Fitzhenry, the lonely day-dreaming old maid, and of Clorinda Saville, the violent jealous Italian wife, are also clear and *new.* The gentlemen are cast in a less decided mould, but strong enough to sustain the interest of the story, which never flags, and ends just as we would have it.... [Having] said so much in favour of our authoress, we may likewise tell her that she is too fond of expatiating upon the feelings of her characters, instead of letting them be shown in dialogue or action; her story, too, flows on so continuously, that it is difficult to detach a scene.... (pp. 238-39)

We had marked . . . passages for extract, as, for instance, those in which the simple and delightful heroine of the story comes in upon her husband in the midst of his distresses, and by her cheerful devotedness, makes their poverty not only endurable, but happy. The squalidity and meanness of narrow circumstances, may be, perhaps, too entirely left out of the picture, for the authoress has thrown the poetry of her own spirit over her story—but we like her book all the better, because, for that very reason, it resembles so much the less, the bargain-driving world we live in. (p. 239)

> *A review of "Lodore," in* The Athenaeum, *No. 387, March 28, 1835, pp. 238-39.*

[WILLIAM MAGINN]   (essay date 1835)

[*One of the most prominent journalists in England during the first half of the nineteenth century, Maginn wrote articles ranging from burlesques in verse to literary criticism. In his extremely laudatory review of* Lodore, *excerpted below, Maginn praises the work's style, execution, and characterization.*]

The publication of *Lodore* has gone a considerable way towards convincing us that Mrs. Shelley might have indeed been the author of *Frankenstein*—a work which we once believed could not possibly owe its existence to a female novelist; and this, not because there is a similitude between the structure and development of *Frankenstein,* that fearful and fantastic dream of genius, and the love-story before us, which is of the every-day world—its doings and its sufferings, but because there is common to both a depth and sweep of thought—a knowledge of human kind, in its manifold relations with this earth—and a boldness and *directness* in penetrating to the recesses and displaying the motives and workings of the heart, its feelings and passions—not in woman only, but in man also—which we certainly should have imagined to be far beyond the scope and power of a lady. Yet is there, at the same time, nothing in these volumes which a lady might not have known, and felt, and written; nor can there be the slightest doubt that they are the production of a feminine mind, albeit one of robust culture and extraordinary vigour. In the form and course of thought, if not actually in the style of expression in many passages, and in the downright, unaffected, noble simplicity, with which, in *Lodore,* subjects are treated, in which the heart and senses play a subtly mingled part, we were oftentimes reminded of the confessions of that charming enthusiast, Madame Roland—the only politician and philosopher in petticoats we could ever bring ourselves to regard with affectionate respect. Like her, too, Mrs. Shelley has shewn, not only that she can unveil the soul of woman to its very uttermost recesses, but that she can divine, appreciate, and depict the character of men. The work is very unlike the generality of our modern novels; it does not contain a sweeping together of incidents from a long suite of stories, historic, romantic, and burlesque; it does not present a faded anthology of *effeté* jests, of shrivelled gallantries, and impassible sentimentalities. There is not a constant succession of the startling events, the outrageous griefs, the bloody battles, the atrocious catastrophes, which form the staple commodity of that farrago of elongated melodramas which so frequently constitutes a modern novel. Nor is that ingenious device resorted to, which was originally borrowed by our novel-spinners from the festival scene in the pantomimes, of having a number of persons, bedecked in the costume of great names, to stand by and assist at the multifarious performances of the regular actors in the scene—the pseudo-representatives of kings and Caesars, beauties and heroes, wits and sages—to witness, as it were, the vigour of Harlequin and the agility of Columbine, to say nothing of the parts of the Clown and Pantaloon. Nor is that vile expedient put in use, of pretending to gratify the prurient curiosity of the vulgar by the introduction of real characters, who have rendered themselves either distinguished or notorious on the stage of life. No! nor is the plot "perplexed in the extreme;" nor are the characters multitudinous, like the waves of the sea; nor are they ever suffered, in obedience to some immediate necessity of the author, to obey the magical injunction,

Come like shadows,
So depart;

nor, moreover, do we, from first to last, find a single being who is absolutely exalted above, or depressed below humanity.

The story is simple—its theme is

Love, still love!

It treats of the hopes and fears, the joys and sorrows, the delights and dangers, the blessings and the evils, of the fierce and tender passion. A healthy moral pervades her whole treatment of the subject. (pp. 600-01)

The execution of the work is, upon the whole, extremely good—it is quite worthy of the design. The impress of an original and thoughtful mind is visible throughout, and there are many passages of exceeding gracefulness, of touching eloquence, and of intense feeling. Her most obvious faults are that of occasionally introducing, by way of illustration, wild and quaint imagery—we might say, in some instances, imagery which is quite incongruous with that it is intended to illustrate; and, secondly, that of analysing and detailing too minutely each and every one of the sensations, intermingled or successive, which, when operating in mass (so to speak), constitute a feeling or a passion. The result of this extreme elaborateness is often to weary, and always, by refining away, to injure the general effect. These faults, however, we apprehend, may be with her either the results of education, or the pious faults of imitation; for her husband has fallen into the first in several of his poems, her father is remarkable for the other.

Mrs. Shelley has not, like a weak and ambitious artist, crowded her canvass with figures. Her characters are few—they are well-considered, perfectly individualised, and in happy contrast. There is no attempt at a violent opposition of colours to produce startling effects. In the calm consciousness of power, she has dispensed altogether with a villain who, in many a grand modern novel, is made to serve the same purpose as a daub of black in one of Martin's monster-pictures. All the characters are excellently drawn: the greater number are very elaborately wrought forth, the rest are firmly sketched. (pp. 601-02)

Lodore [is] one of the best novels it has been of late years our fortune to read. We are very happy in being able to confer this praise on Mrs. Shelley, whose name is dear to us (as we doubt not, from "the late remorse of love," it is to the public), for the sake alike of the dead and living—her illustrious husband, and her living son, who was born in his image. (p. 605)

[William Maginn], in a review of "Lodore," in Fraser's Magazine, Vol. XI, No. LXV, May, 1835, pp. 600-05.

THE MONTHLY REVIEW, LONDON   (essay date 1837)

[*The following commentary on* Falkner *offers high praise for Shelley's characterization, noble sentiments, and skillful structure.*]

Falkner, is perhaps the finest and most powerful, in regard to sentiment, of Mrs. Shelley's novels. Tenderness, pathos, and romantic elevation of feeling characterize all her productions. There is not much of real life in her stories, but a vast amount of thought and pensive meditation. Her colouring is for the most part sombre, but yet refining, and when she probes to the source of human action, though it be with much of her father's discernment, it is not with his misanthropic tendency, but with a generous sympathy with and for her kind. . . . She seems also to have imbibed much of her husband's poetic temperament, its singular loveliness and delicacy, but to have shorn it of those extravagant visions and emotions which led him beyond the province of truth, and the dictates of a well-regulated judgment, which certainly are as essential to poetic excellence, as are the flights of an ardent or sensitive imagination.

We have said that Mrs. Shelley's colouring is for the most part sombre; but it should rather, perhaps, be asserted that her themes being gloomy, and her characters closely connected with some mystery of extraordinary weight and depth, there is necessarily established very early in the story over the mind of the reader, that brooding foreboding of evil and of terrible things, that cannot be playfully dealt with. But it is to the honour of her genius, and to the force as well as delicate beauty of her minute delineations, that this gloominess is never felt to be unwelcome, but of a soft and melancholy cast. *Falkner,* for example, is a tale in which crime, dark deeds, and remorse, form prominent parts. There is great suffering also entailed upon the innocent. And yet not only is the story one of arresting power, but the chief criminal himself, who is the hero, engages the heart, and fain would we see him restored to mental comfort, and hear of him being forgiven. Along with this absorbing interest in behalf of Falkner—(which is established by nothing like meretricious or morbid sentiments, but by an acute and delicate dissection of motives and temptations, and an unmitigating picture of the consequences of crime, even in this world, as also the penitent's desire to atone for his great offences, were it but by enduring the punishment which his guilt has incurred)—there are so many charming characters, incidents, and feelings portrayed as to render this romantic story rather pathetic than gloomy, rather the vehicle of melancholy reflections than of horror. (pp. 376-77)

A review of "Falkner," in The Monthly Review, London, n.s. Vol. I, No. III, March, 1837, pp. 376-80.

TAIT'S EDINBURGH MAGAZINE   (essay date 1844)

[*In a mixed review of Shelley's* Rambles in Germany and Italy, *this critic suggests that the book reveals too many personal details and too few factual and philosophical observations.*]

Any work must have strong claims to attention that comes before the world as the avowed production of the author of *Frankenstein,* the chosen wife of Shelley, and the daughter of William Godwin and Mary Wollstonecraft. Whether [*Rambles in Germany and Italy*] will fulfil the expectations raised by these extraordinary claims is more than doubtful. They possess many beauties of the highest kind, and, as some may think, one or two deep blemishes. Among the latter is a too frequent obtrusion of the Pantheistic or poetical religion of Shelley. Yet these form the most ambitious and eloquent passages of the series. The poetic faith is in them expounded with great eloquence and felicity, as if a Corinne were pouring forth her rapt spirit, though we miss throughout the earnestness, the impulsive movement which dictated Mary Wollstonecraft's *Letters from Norway.* Another blemish will be judged according to the temperament of the reader's own mind. Some will be touched as by a sympathetic charm from Mrs. Shelley's frequent allusions to the death of her children, and the master calamity of her life, the awful catastrophe which bereaved her of her husband; while others may feel that the sacred fount of sorrow has been too often laid bare to cold or careless eyes. These allusions are no doubt made with great delicacy; but they recur so often as to mar their own effect, if not to beget an unpleasant sensation in the reader's mind, though he may neither be indifferent nor hard of heart. To some readers it may be an objection that beyond beauty of style and sentiment, and a few scattered profound thoughts, the work does not contain much of either the precise information or philosophical disquisition which one would have expected from a writer of Mrs. Shelley's compass of mind. This holds especially of France and Germany,—not only her enthusiasm and love, but her space being monopolized by beautiful Italy. (p. 729)

> *"Mrs. Shelley's 'Rambles in Germany and Italy',"*
> *in Tait's Edinburgh Magazine, Vol. XI, No. CXXXI,*
> *November, 1844, pp. 729-40.*

RICHARD HENGIST HORNE (essay date 1844)

[*Horne, a minor English poet and critic, places* Frankenstein *among the finest romantic fiction of the day and discusses the analogies suggested by the monster. The critic also comments briefly on* Valperga *and* Falkner.]

The imaginative romance, as distinguished from the historical romance, and the actual or social life fiction, is of very rare occurrence in the literature of the present day. Whether the cause lies with the writers or the public, or the character of events and influences now operating on society, certain it is that the imaginative romance is almost extinct among us.

We had outgrown the curdling horrors and breathless apprehensions of Mrs. Radcliffe, and the roseate pomps of Miss Jane Porter. But why have we no *Frankenstein*, for that fine work is in advance of the age?

Perhaps we ought to seek the cause of the scarcity in the difficulty of the production. A mere fruitless, purposeless excitement of the imagination will not do *now*. The imaginative romance is required to be a sort of epic—a power to advance—a something to propel the frame of things. Such is Bulwer's *Zanoni*, a profound and beautiful work of fiction, which has been reviewed in its place, and in which Godwin's *St. Leon* found a worthy successor. With this single exception, the first place among the romances of our day belongs to the *Frankenstein* of Mrs. Shelley. (p. 409)

The Monster in *Frankenstein*, sublime in his ugliness, his simplicity, his passions, his wrongs, and his strength, physical and mental, embodies in the wild narrative more than one distinct and important moral theory or proposition. In himself he is the type of a class deeply and cruelly aggrieved by nature—the Deformed or hideous in figure or countenance, whose sympathies and passions are as strong as their bodily deformity renders them repulsive. An amount of human woe, great beyond reckoning, have such experienced. When the Monster pleads his cause against cruel man, and when he finally disappears on his raft on the icy sea to build his own funeral pile, he pleads the cause of all that class who have so strong a claim on the help and sympathy of the world, yet find little else but disgust or, at best, neglect.

The Monster created by Frankenstein is also an illustration of the embodied consequences of our actions. As he, when formed and endowed with life, became to his imaginary creator an everlasting, ever-present curse, so may one single action, nay a word, or it may be a thought, thrown upon the tide of time,

become to its originator a curse, never to be recovered, never to be shaken off.

Frankenstein suggests yet another analogy. It teaches the tragic results of attainment when an impetuous irresistible passion hurries on the soul to its doom. Such tragic results are the sacrificial fires out of which humanity rises purified. They constitute one form of the great ministry of Pain. The conception of *Frankenstein* is the converse of that of the delightful German fiction of Peter Schlemihl, in which the *loss* of his shadow (reputation or honour) leads on the hero through several griefs and troubles to the great simplicity of nature and truth; while in *Frankenstein* the *attainment* of a gigantic reality leads through crime and desolation to the same goal, but it is only reached in the moment of death. (pp. 410-11)

Mrs. Shelley's romance entitled *Valperga* is of high merit. She exhibits in her hero a brave and successful warrior, arriving at the height of his ambition, endowed with uncommon beauty and strength, and with many good qualities, yet causes him to excite emotions of reprobation and pity, because he is cruel and a tyrant, and because in the truth of things he is unhappy. This is doing a good work, taking the false glory from the eyes and showing things as they are. There are two female characters of wonderful power and beauty. The heroine is a lovely and noble creation. Perhaps Mrs. Shelley's *Falkner* ranks next in power to *Frankenstein*. The chief character, in especial, is worked out with subtle truth and force; and the same may be said, though with different degrees and modes of working, of all the personages of the story. Mrs. Shelley's plots are always of deep interest. These works taken as wholes, if below *Fran-*

Percy Bysshe Shelley, painted by Amelia Curran in Rome in 1819, the year of his marriage to Mary Wollstonecraft Godwin.

kenstein in genius, are yet worthy of their author and of her high rank in the aristocracy of genius, as the daughter of Godwin and Mary Wollstonecraft, and the widow of Shelley. (pp. 413-14)

> Richard Hengist Horne, "Mrs. Shelley," in A New Spirit of the Age, *edited by Richard Hengist Horne, 1844. Reprint by Oxford University Press, 1907, pp. 407-14.*

GEORGE GILFILLAN   (essay date 1847)

[*Gilfillan unfavorably compares Mary Shelley's talent with her husband's, but praises* Frankenstein *as "one distinct addition to our original creations."*]

[Despite] Mrs. Shelley's similarity in genius to her husband—we by no means think her his equal. She has not his subtlety, swiftness, wealth of imagination, and is never caught up (like Ezekiel by his lock of hair) into the same rushing whirlwind of inspiration. She has much, however, of his imaginative and of his speculative qualities—her tendency, like his, is to the romantic, the ethereal, and the terrible. The tie detaining her, as well as him, to the earth, is slender—her protest against society is his, copied out in a fine female hand—her style is carefully and successfully modelled upon his—she bears, in brief, to him, the resemblance which Laone did to Laon, which Astarte did to Manfred. Perhaps, indeed, intercourse with a being so peculiar, that those who came in contact with, either withdrew from him in hatred, or fell into the current of his being; vanquished and enthralled, has somewhat affected the originality, and narrowed the extent of her own genius. Indian widows used to fling themselves upon the funeral pyre of their husbands: she has thrown upon that of hers her mode of thought, her mould of style, her creed, her heart, her all. Her admiration of Shelley was, and is, an idolatry. (pp. 852-53)

Mrs. Shelley's genius, though true and powerful, is monotonous and circumscribed—more so than even her father's—and, in this point, presents a strong contrast to her husband's, which could run along every note of the gamut—be witty or wise, satirical or sentimental, didactic or dramatic, epic or lyrical, as it pleased him. She has no wit, nor humour—little dramatic talent. Strong clear description of the gloomier scenes of nature, or the darker passions of the mind, or of those supernatural objects which her fancy, except in her first work, somewhat *laboriously* creates, is her forte. Hence her reputation still rests upon *Frankenstein;* for her *Last Man, Perkin Warbeck,* &c., are far inferior, if not entirely unworthy of her talents. She unquestionably made him; but, like a mule or a monster, he has had no progeny. . . .

The theme [of *Frankenstein*] is morbid and disgusting enough. . . . Nothing more preposterous than the meagre outline of the story exists in literature. But Mrs. Shelley deserves great credit, nevertheless. In the first place, she has succeeded in her delineation; she has painted this shapeless being upon the imagination of the world for ever; and beside Caliban, and Hecate, and Death in Life, and all other weird and gloomy creations, this nameless, unfortunate, involuntary, gigantic unit stands. To succeed in an attempt so daring, proves at once the power of the author, and a certain value even in the original conception. To keep verging perpetually on the limit of the absurd, and to produce the while all the effects of the sublime, this takes and tasks very high faculties indeed. Occasionally, we admit, she does overstep the mark. Thus the whole scene of the monster's education in the cottage, his overhearing the

reading of the *Paradise Lost,* the *Sorrows of Werter,* &c., and in this way acquiring knowledge and refined sentiments, seems unspeakably ridiculous. A Caco-demon weeping in concert with Eve or Werter is too ludicrous an idea—as absurd as though he had been represented as boarded at Capsicum Hall. But it is wonderful how delicately and gracefully Mrs. Shelley has managed the whole prodigious business. She touches pitch with a lady's glove, and is not defiled. From a whole forest of the "nettle danger" she extracts a sweet and plentiful supply of the "flower safety." With a fine female footing, she preserves the narrow path which divides the terrible from the disgusting. She unites, not in a junction of words alone, but in effect, the "horribly beautiful." Her monster is not only as Caliban appeared to Trinculo—a very pretty monster—but somewhat poetical and pathetic withal. You almost weep for him in his utter insulation. . . .

He is not only alone, but alone because he has no being like him throughout the whole universe. What a solitude within a solitude!—solitude comparable only to that of the Alchemist in *St. Leon,* when he buries his last tie to humanity in his wife's grave, and goes on his way, "friendless, friendless, alone, alone." (p. 853)

Altogether, the work is wonderful as the work of a girl of eighteen. She has never since fully equalled or approached its power, nor do we ever expect that she shall. One distinct addition to our original creations must be conceded her—and it is no little praise; for there are few writers of fiction who have done so much out of Germany. (p. 854)

> George Gilfillan, "Female Authors, No. III: Mrs. Shelley," in Tait's Edinburgh Magazine, *Vol. XIV, No. CLXVIII, December, 1847, pp. 850-54.*

HELEN MOORE   (essay date 1886)

[*The author of the first full-length biography of Shelley, Moore demonstrates an attitude that persisted until recently: that Shelley's chief significance derived from her relationship with her husband. Moore essentially dismisses all Shelley's writings except* Frankenstein, *which she singles out because it "alone reflected Mrs. Shelley's true self."*]

While it is true that Mrs. Shelley's place among eminent women does not rest upon the circumstance that she was Shelley's wife, it is in every sense due to the fact that she was his companion. The nature and quality of this companionship is at once an index and a test of her character. It was not that an erratic genius had made her the object of his wayward passion, or even that she was the recipient of his genuine tenderness. It was very much more than this. Think how different Mrs. Shelley's place from that held by any of the various loves of Goethe or Byron. It may not be overstating it to say that one of the chief interests we have in her, arises from a worthy curiosity to know what manner of woman it was who could be so completely the companion, who could hold such close fellowship with so marked a genius as Shelley. It is for this reason that his character must ever be a prominent element in the life of Mrs. Shelley. For the same reason, due prominence must be given to the nature of that union which welded these twain together in a spiritual oneness so instant, an intellectual harmony so complete,—in fine, a union so unlike those ordinarily made on earth, and so like those which we are told are made in Heaven, that an inconsequential world promptly decided that it had been made in Hell.

Certainly, Mrs. Shelley does not owe her fame to the extent of her literary labors. Of these we shall do more than merely speak, finding in one of them—*Frankenstein*—a peculiar literary faculty. But she must be ranked among those literary women whose true province is to influence and stimulate others; who are receptive, appreciative, and incentive, rather than productive. . . . (pp. 11-12)

[Women] possessed of the intellectual *timbre,* styled literary, fall naturally into two classes, one possessed of a power to produce beyond the scope made apparent by their personal influence, which may even give no promise of such power; the other owning and wielding a far greater influence over men about them, which gives richer promise, but which fails to transmute itself into a permanent literary yield. Of the former class are George Eliot, Charlotte Brontë, Mrs. Browning, Miss Austin, while in the latter class are Margaret Fuller, Mary Wollstonecraft, Madame de Stael, Madame Recamier, and a host of French women, of whom Madame Du Deffend may be taken as the type.

Without doubt it is to this latter class that Mrs. Shelley must be assigned; so that in proportion as her permanent contribution to the literary stock of the world is small, must we the more earnestly seek in her private life and its reflected lights, for those qualities which have made her unquestionably eminent among women. (pp. 12-13)

[Mrs. Shelley's] literary productions were few and disproportionate to her intellectual force; disappointing when viewed side by side with her peculiar gift of evoking the most artistic literary work in others. (p. 244)

Of Mrs. Shelley's writings, *Frankenstein* is without question the most noteworthy. From the day of its first appearance in print down to the present, it has had accorded to it a position as a unique and remarkable production. (pp. 244-45)

Regarded as a mere tale, it is difficult to account for the hold this story has always had upon the minds of the reading world. As a story it does not justify its own success. To say that it is remarkable as a work of imagination does not meet the difficulty. By a work of the imagination, as used in the current criticism of *Frankenstein,* is simply meant that it is a fantastic romance, such as we find in the ''Arabian Nights,'' or in the prose tales of Poe. But a position utterly different from these is accorded to *Frankenstein.* (pp. 248-49)

[There was a dual quality in *Frankenstein*] to which it owed its singular power and place in literature. One element is doubtless the horror of the tale and the weird fancy of the author's imagination in the ordinary acceptation of the word. But it is to an entirely different department of mental conception that we must look for the secret of its peculiar influence. The faculty of imagination is something more than the recalling and rearrangements of past impressions. Profoundly considered, it is that function of the mind which formulates, as though real, a state of things which if present would so appear. It is the power of projecting the mind into unhappened realities. It is the faculty of picturing unseen verities. There is thus in it a prophetic element, not at all miraculous, but dependent upon subtle laws of association and suggestion. It is to this element that *Frankenstein* owes its power over thoughtful minds. It is by virtue of the allegorical element in it that it holds its high position as a work of the imagination. (p. 249)

[The] chief allegorical interest in the narrative concerns itself about that tendency in the human being to discard the established order of things and to create for itself a new and independent existence. In the simple story, Frankenstein made a being responsible to him alone for its creation,—a being not produced by the ordinary course of life, not amenable or even adaptable to the existing world of men. Right or wrong, better or worse, the creature may be, but different certainly, and this irreconcilable disparity points back ever to its origin, which had been anomalous and strange.

The whole story is but the elaboration of the embarrassment and dangers which flow from departure from the ordinary course of nature; this forced attempt to invade society from within. What strong existence in real life of this same tendency Mary Shelley had seen in those nearest and dearest to her! She has not failed to learn the lesson of her mother's history; time analyzes rather than destroys. And the life of Mary Wollstonecraft was doubtless seen by the clear-minded daughter in stronger contrast of light and shade than it had been by its contemporaries. Who knew so well the glories of that life? Its successes as well as its miseries had sprung from the self-same causes as those of Frankenstein,—from the breach of the conventional; from overstepping the limits; from creating an individuality and a sphere of existence denied it by Nomos, and consequently sure of the hostility of society. (pp. 255-56)

The world, by its acknowledgment of the coercive quality of *Frankenstein,* has given silent acceptance of its genius. The other works, novels, critiques, biographies, while they have had literary merit, feeling, even power, have not shown genius. *Frankenstein* alone was personal, it alone reflected Mrs. Shelley's true self. Her other books contain simply what she wrote in them: this alone contains what was written in her. (pp. 257-58)

> *Helen Moore, in her* Mary Wollstonecraft Shelley, *J. B. Lippincott Company, 1886, 346 p.*

LUCY MADOX ROSSETTI   (essay date 1890)

[*Rossetti states that the* raison d'être *of her biography of Shelley, from which the following excerpt is drawn, is to discuss Shelley's literary work. However, Rossetti offers only scant biographical criticism of the novels, granting nearly equal attention to Shelley's* Lives of Eminent Literary Men, *which is reviewed below.*]

[*Lives of Eminent Literary Men*] are a most interesting series of biographies written by a woman who could appreciate the poet's character, and enter into the injustices and sorrows from which few poets have been exempt. They show careful study, her knowledge of various countries gives local colour to her descriptions, and her love of poetry makes her an admirable critic. (p. 206)

Freedom from affectation, and a genuine love of her subject, make her biographies most readable, and for the ordinary reader there is a fund of information. (p. 207)

You feel [her sketch of Dante] is written from the heart of the woman who herself felt as she wrote. We would fain go through her different biographies, tracing her feelings, her appreciation, and poetic enthusiasm throughout, but that is impossible. She takes us through Boccaccio's life, and, as by the reflection of a sunset from a mirror, we are warmed with the glow and mirth from distant and long-past times in Italy. One feels through her works the innate delicacy of her mind. (p. 208)

Mary's studies in Spanish enabled her to treat equally well the poets of Spain and of Portugal. Her introduction is a good essay on the poetry and poets of Spain, and some of the translations, which are her own, are very happily given. The poetic impulse in Spain is traced from the Iberians through the Romans, Visigoths, Moors, and the early unknown Spanish poets, among whom there were many fine examples. (p. 211)

Lucy Madox Rossetti, in her Mrs. Shelley, 1890. Reprint by The Folcroft Press, Inc., 1969, 238 p.

THE ATHENAEUM (essay date 1891)

[*The author of the following excerpt deems Shelley's* Tales and Stories *outdated and superficial, but occasionally intriguing.*]

[Mrs. Shelley's stories collected in *Tales and Stories by Mary Wollstonecraft Shelley*] have until now been hidden away in what Charles Lamb would have designated as books that are no books—namely, keepsakes, annuals, and, if we remember rightly, even ladies' pocket-books—volumes which are now never visited unless it be by some worshipper of Turner who is searching for his handiwork in the shape of illustrations. This is the first time that her stories have been collected, and it is as trying an ordeal to the fame of an author to have the scattered productions of a lifetime gathered together in one volume as to a painter to have a large collection of his drawings or pictures exhibited in one room. A taste of the producer's quality is obtained that goes far towards fixing his rank for ever.

It is difficult, however, to fix Mrs. Shelley's, for most of the stories are written in a style that is now as completely out of fashion as the annuals in which they first saw the light. The heroines are "children of light and love," they are liable to be addressed as "lovely and deceived one," they "speak in terms of soft silver tenderness," their "tresses are heavy with their own rich beauty," their complexions are of "marmoreal whiteness," they tread on "carpets inwoven with silk," and we even find a maiden who reminds us of Mrs. Radcliffe's heroines, who never stir out for pleasure nor fly from their prisons without taking their lutes with them. Mrs. Shelley's heroine carries her harp into the woods with her. There is no introspection in these stories, no searching study of character, but there is some imaginative power and generous sympathy with all that is noble. Their merit, of course, varies; the romantic stories are much the best; but perhaps that which will be the most interesting to all will be **"The Parvenue,"** in which, under a very sufficient disguise, we find what we have long wished to find—proof of the irritation with which Mrs. Shelley regarded her father's habit of making incessant and exorbitant demands on Shelley's pocket. It might have been well to make some corrections in this volume; they are frequently needed. (pp. 12-13)

A review of "Tales and Stories by Mary Wollstonecraft Shelley," in The Athenaeum, No. 3297, January 3, 1891, pp. 12-13.

THE SPECTATOR (essay date 1891)

[*The* Spectator *critic offers a mixed review of* Tales and Stories, *finding them occasionally powerful but generally of interest only as the work of the author of* Frankenstein.]

Of the seventeen tales [in *Tales and Stories by Mary Wollstonecraft Shelley*] which may be considered as fairly representative of the writer's taste in the selection of imaginative material, only two deal with a preternatural motive, and in neither is there any violence, morbidness, or repulsiveness of treatment. **"The Mortal Immortal"** is a not specially striking handling of the often-used theme of a magically prolonged life, and it is curious to note that Mrs. Shelley seemed unable to turn to profitable imaginative account the one really original idea in the story,—that is, the mistake made by the hero, who drinks the *elixir vitae* supposing it to be merely a philtre which will destroy his love for the girl who has flouted him. **"Transformation"** is more fantastic, but not more striking. . . . Neither story is exactly poor, but both are wanting in distinction: they are just good enough to suggest what might have been made of them by such an artist as Hawthorne, Poe, or Théophile Gautier.

As a matter of fact, they were out of the line of Mrs. Shelley, who was most at home in the region of romantic picturesqueness and pathetic sentiment. The majority of her stories are of the usual "Annual" type, and they are distinguished from their companions, which have been kindly left to oblivion, only by the superiority of their general style and the artistic truthfulness of their elaborate backgrounds. The annualists as a body liked Italy, for an Italian story allowed the use of high-sounding names and wonderful incidents, the lifelikeness of which few English readers of the time were able to impeach; but Mrs. Shelley turned frequently to the much-favoured country because she knew and loved it, and her lavish descriptions have the sunlight of Claude or the sombreness of Salvator Rosa. Mrs. Shelley's imaginative gifts were not great, but they were genuine, and when she allowed herself to be dominated either by the influence of her father or her husband, her work was, as a rule, the poorer instead of the richer for the submission. We say as a rule, for here and there we find evidences of a feeling for natural beauty and a power of rendering it, which are both beautiful and Shelley-like. "The domes and turrets of the far town flashed and gleamed, the trees were dyed in splendour; two or three slight *clouds, which had drunk the radiance till it became their essence,* floated golden islets in the lustrous empyrean." We might almost fancy that the italicised words were a quotation from that wonderful poem, "To a Skylark;" and this is by no means a solitary example of a power of expression which has been learned rather than inherited. In the story of **"The Mourner,"** the writer has evidently utilised Shelley's reminiscences of his schooldays; but elsewhere we have failed to find any of these references to real persons or actual incidents which are not infrequent in her novels. That these stories will attract the general reader of to-day, is unlikely. They are interesting mainly as the work of the author of *Frankenstein.* (pp. 18-19)

"Mrs. Shelley's Shorter Tales," in The Spectator, Vol. LXVI, No. 3262, January 3, 1891, pp. 18-19.

CLARA H. WHITMORE (essay date 1910)

[*In a general overview of Shelley's fiction, Whitmore discusses* Frankenstein, Valperga, *and* Lodore *as the author's only noteworthy novels.*]

Frankenstein is one of those novels that defy the critic. Everyone recognises that the letters written by Captain Walton to his sister in which he tells of his meeting with Frankenstein, and repeats to her the story he has just heard from his guest, makes an awkward introduction to the real narrative. Yet all this part about Captain Walton and his crew was added at the suggestion of Shelley after the rest of the story had been written.

But the narrative of Frankenstein is so powerful, so real, that, once read, it can never be forgotten. (p. 206)

The monster created by Frankenstein is closely related to our own human nature. ''My heart was fashioned to be susceptible of love and sympathy,'' he says, ''and, when wrenched by misery to vice and hatred, it did not endure the violence of the change without torture, such as you cannot even imagine.'' There is a wonderful blending of good and evil in this demon, and, while the magnitude of his crimes makes us shudder, his wrongs and his loneliness awaken our pity.... Perhaps sadder than the story of the monster is that of Frankenstein, who, led by a desire to widen human knowledge, finds that the fulfilment of his lofty ambition has brought only a curse to mankind. (p. 207)

The interest [of *Valperga*] centres in the two heroines, Euthanasia, Countess of Valperga, and Beatrice, Prophetess of Ferrara. Strong, intellectual, and passionate, not until the time of George Eliot did women of this type become prominent in fiction. (p. 208)

[More] beautiful than the intellectual character of Euthanasia, is the spiritual one of Beatrice, the adopted daughter of the bishop of Ferrara, who is regarded with feelings of reverence by her countrymen, because of her prophetic powers. Pure and deeply religious, she accepted all the suggestions of her mind as a message from God. When Castruccio came to Ferrara and was entertained by the bishop as the prince and liberator of his country, she believed that together they could accomplish much for her beloved country: ''She prayed to the Virgin to inspire her; and, again giving herself up to reverie, she wove a subtle web, whose materials she believed heavenly, but which were indeed stolen from the glowing wings of love.'' No wonder she believed the dictates of her own heart, she whose words the superstition of the age had so often declared miraculous. She was barely seventeen and she loved for the first time. How pathetic is her disillusionment when Castruccio bade her farewell for a season, as he was about to leave Ferrara. She had believed that the Holy Spirit had brought Castruccio to her that by the union of his manly qualities and her divine attributes some great work might be fulfilled. But as he left her, he spoke only of earthly happiness.... (pp. 208-09)

The daughter of Mary Wollstonecraft could fully sympathise with Beatrice. In the grief, almost madness, with which Beatrice realises her self-deception, there are traces of Frankenstein. Perhaps no problem plucked from the tree of good and evil was so ever-present to Mary Shelley as why misery so often follows an obedience to the highest dictates of the soul. Both her father and mother had experienced this; and she and Shelley had tasted of the same bitter fruit. In the analysis of Beatrice's emotions Mrs. Shelley shows herself akin to Charlotte Brontë.

Three years after the death of Shelley, she published *The Last Man*.... The plot is clumsy; the characters are abstractions. (p. 210)

Mrs. Shelley made the great mistake of writing this novel in the first person. *The Last Man,* who is telling the story, although he has the name of Lionel, is most assuredly of the female sex. The friendship between him and Adrian is not the friendship of man for man, but rather the love of man and woman.

Mrs. Shelley's next novel, *Lodore,* ... had a better outlined plot and more definite characters. (pp. 212-13)

Besides two other novels of no value, *Perkin Warbeck* and *Falkner,* Mrs. Shelley wrote numerous short stories for the annuals.... Many of them have the intensity and sustained interest of *Frankenstein.*

After the death of her husband, grief and trouble dimmed Mrs. Shelley's imagination. But the pale student Frankenstein, the monster he created, and the beautiful priestess, Beatrice, three strong conceptions, testify to the genius of Mary Shelley. (pp. 214-15)

> *Clara H. Whitmore, ''Lady Caroline Lamb (1785-1828)—Mary Shelley (1797-1851),'' in her* Woman's Work in English Fiction: From the Restoration to the Mid-Victorian Period, *G. P. Putnam's Sons, 1910, pp. 200-15.*

EDITH BIRKHEAD (essay date 1921)

[*Birkhead's* The Tale of Terror, *from which the following excerpt is drawn, is considered one of the first significant studies of the Gothic movement. Here, she offers a thoughtful overview of the virtues and flaws of* Frankenstein, *in addition to briefer considerations of* Valperga, The Last Man, *and some of Shelley's short stories.*]

It is indeed remarkable that so young and inexperienced a writer as Mary Shelley, who was only nineteen when she wrote *Frankenstein,* should betray so slight a dependence on her predecessors. It is evident from the records of her reading that the novel of terror in all its guises was familiar to her. She had beheld the majestic horror of the halls of Eblis; she had threaded her way through Mrs. Radcliffe's artfully constructed Gothic castles; she had braved the terrors of the German Ritter-, Räuber- und Schauer-Romane; she had assisted, fearful, at Lewis's midnight diablerie; she had patiently unravelled the ''mystery'' novels of Godwin and of Charles Brockden Brown. Yet, despite this intimate knowledge of the terrible and supernatural in fiction, Mrs. Shelley's theme and her way of handling it are completely her own. In an ''acute mental vision,'' as real as the visions of Blake and of Shelley, she beheld her monster and the ''pale student of unhallowed arts'' who had created him, and then set herself to reproduce the thrill of horror inspired by her waking dream. *Frankenstein* has, indeed, been compared to Godwin's *St. Leon,* but the resemblance is so vague and superficial, and *Frankenstein* so immeasurably superior, that Mrs. Shelley's debt to her father is negligible. St. Leon accepts the gift of immortality, Frankenstein creates a new life, and in both novels the main interest lies in tracing the effect of the experiment on the soul of the man, who has pursued scientific inquiry beyond legitimate limits. But apart from this, there is little resemblance. Godwin chose the supernatural, because it chanced to be popular, and laboriously built up a cumbrous edifice, completing it by a sheer effort of willpower. His daughter, with an imagination naturally more attuned to the gruesome and fantastic, writes, when once she has wound her way into the heart of the story, in a mood of breathless excitement that drives the reader forward with feverish apprehension.

The name of Mrs. Shelley's *Frankenstein* is far-famed; but the book itself, overshadowed perhaps by its literary associations, seems to have withdrawn into the vast library of famous works that are more often mentioned than read. The very fact that the name is often bestowed on the monster instead of his creator seems to suggest that many are content to accept Mrs. Shelley's ''hideous phantom'' on hearsay evidence rather than encounter for themselves the terrors of his presence. The story deserves a happier fate, for, if it be read in the spirit of willing surrender that a theme so impossible demands, it has still power momentarily "to make the reader dread to look round, to curdle the blood and to quicken the beatings of the heart." (pp. 158-60)

Mrs. Shelley has been censured for setting her tale in a clumsy framework, but she tells us in her preface that she began with the words: "It was on a dreary night of November." This sentence now stands at the opening of Chapter V., where the plot begins to grip our imagination; and it seems not unfair to assume that the introductory letters and the first four chapters, which contain a tedious and largely unnecessary account of Frankenstein's early life, were written in deference to Shelley's plea that the idea should be developed at greater length, and did not form part of her original plan. The uninteresting student, Robert Walton, to whom Frankenstein, discovered dying among icebergs, tells his story, is obviously an afterthought. If Mrs. Shelley had abandoned the awkward contrivance of putting the narrative into the form of a dying man's confession, reported verbatim in a series of letters, and had opened her story, as she apparently intended, at the point where Frankenstein, after weary years of research, succeeds in creating a living being, her novel would have gained in force and intensity. From that moment it holds us fascinated. It is true that the tension relaxes from time to time, that the monster's strange education and the Godwinian precepts that fall so incongruously from his lips tend to excite our mirth, but, though we are mildly amused, we are no longer merely bored. Even the protracted descriptions of domestic life assume a new and deeper meaning, for the shadow of the monster broods over them. One by one those whom Frankenstein loves fall victims to the malice of the being he has endowed with life. Unceasingly and unrelentingly the loathsome creature dogs our imagination, more awful when he lurks unseen than when he stands actually before us. With hideous malignity he slays Frankenstein's young brother, and by a fiendish device causes Justine, an innocent girl, to be executed for the crime. Yet ere long our sympathy, which has hitherto been entirely with Frankenstein, is unexpectedly diverted to the monster who, it would seem, is wicked only because he is eternally divorced from human society. (pp. 161-62)

He describes how his physical ugliness repels human beings, who fail to realise his benevolent intentions. A father snatches from his arms the child he has rescued from death; the virtuous family, whom he admires and would fain serve, flee affrighted from his presence. To educate the monster, so that his thoughts and emotions may become articulate, and, incidentally, to accentuate his isolation from society, Mrs. Shelley inserts a complicated story about an Arabian girl, Sofie, whose lover teaches her to read from Plutarch's *Lives*, Volney's *Ruins of Empire*, *The Sorrows of Werther*, and *Paradise Lost*. The monster overhears the lessons, and ponders on this unique library, but, as he pleads his own cause the more eloquently because he knows Satan's passionate outbursts of defiance and self-pity, who would cavil at the method by which he is made to acquire his knowledge? "The cold stars shone in mockery, and the bare trees waved their branches above me; now and then the sweet voice of a bird burst forth amidst the universal stillness. All save I were at rest or in enjoyment. I, like the arch fiend, bore a hell within me." And later, near the close of the book: "The fallen angel becomes a malignant devil. Yet even that enemy of God and man had friends and associates in his desolation;

I am alone." His fate reminds us of that of *Alastor, the Spirit of Solitude,* who:

> Over the world wanders for ever
> Lone as incarnate death.

(pp. 162-63)

Like *Alastor, Frankenstein* was a plea for human sympathy, and was, according to Shelley's preface, intended "to exhibit the amiableness of domestic affection and the excellence of universal virtue." The monster has the perception and desire of goodness, but, by the circumstances of his abnormal existence, is delivered over to evil. It is this dual nature that prevents him from being a mere automaton. The monster indeed is far more real than the shadowy beings whom he pursues. Frankenstein is less an individual than a type, and only interests us through the emotions which his conflict with the monster arouses. Clerval, Elizabeth and Frankenstein's relatives are passive sufferers whose psychology does not concern us. Mrs. Shelley rightly lavishes her skill on the central figure of the book, and succeeds, as effectually as Frankenstein himself, in infusing into him the spark of life. Mrs. Shelley's aim is to "awaken thrilling horror," and, incidentally, to "exhibit the excellence of domestic virtue," and for her purpose the demon is of paramount importance. The involved, complex plot of a novel seemed to pass beyond Mrs. Shelley's control. A short tale she could handle successfully, and Shelley was unwise in inciting her to expand *Frankenstein* into a long narrative. So long as she is completely carried away by her subject Mrs. Shelley writes clearly, but when she pauses to regard the progress of her story dispassionately, she seems to be overwhelmed by the wealth of her resources and to have no power of selecting the relevant details. The laborious introductory letters, the meticulous record of Frankenstein's education, the story of Felix and Sofie, the description of the tour through England before the creation of the second monster is attempted, are all connected with the main theme by very frail links and serve to distract our attention in an irritating fashion from what really interests us. In the novel of mystery a tantalising delay may be singularly effective. In a novel which depends chiefly for its effect on sheer horror, delays are merely dangerous. By resting her terrors on a pseudo-scientific basis and by placing her story in a definite locality, Mrs. Shelley waives her right to an entire suspension of disbelief. If it be reduced to its lowest terms, the plot of Frankenstein, with its bewildering confusion of the prosaic and the fantastic, sounds as crude, disjointed and inconsequent as that of a nightmare. Mrs. Shelley's timid hesitation between imagination and reality, her attempt to reconcile incompatible things and to place a creature who belongs to no earthly land in familiar surroundings, prevents *Frankenstein* from being a wholly satisfactory and alarming novel of terror. She loves the fantastic, but she also fears it. She is weighted down by commonsense, and so flutters instead of soaring, unwilling to trust herself far from the material world. But the fact that she was able to vivify her grotesque skeleton of a plot with some degree of success is no mean tribute to her gifts. The energy and vigour of her style, her complete and serious absorption in her subject, carry us safely over many an absurdity. It is only in the duller stretches of the narrative, when her heart is not in her work, that her language becomes vague, indeterminate and blurred, and that she muffles her thoughts in words like "ascertain," "commencement," "peruse," "diffuse," instead of using their simpler Saxon equivalents. Stirred by the excitement of the events she describes, she can write forcibly in simple, direct language. She often frames short, hurried sentences such as a man would naturally utter when breathless with terror or with recollections of terror. The final impression that *Frankenstein* leaves with us is not easy to define, because the book is so uneven in quality. It is obviously the shapeless work of an immature writer who has had no experience in evolving a plot. Sometimes it is genuinely moving and impressive, but it continually falls abruptly and ludicrously short of its aim. Yet when all its faults have been laid bare, the fact remains that few readers would abandon the story half-way through. Mrs. Shelley is so thoroughly engrossed in her theme that she impels her readers onward, even though they may think but meanly of her story as a work of art.

Mrs. Shelley's second novel, *Valperga, or the Life and Adventures of Castruccio, Prince of Lucca,* . . . was a work on which she bestowed much care and labour, but the result proves that she writes best when the urgency of her imagination leaves her no leisure either to display her learning or adorn her style. She herself calls *Valperga* a "child of mighty slow growth," and Shelley adds that it was "raked out of fifty old books." Mrs. Shelley, always an industrious student, made a conscientious survey of original sources before fashioning her story of mediaeval Italy, and she is hampered by the exuberance of her knowledge. The novel is not a romance of terror; but Castruccio, though his character is sketched from authentic documents, seems towards the end of the story to resemble the picturesque villain who numbered among his ancestry Milton's Satan. He has "a majestic figure and a countenance beautiful but sad, and tarnished by the expression of pride that animated it." Beatrice, the gifted prophetess who falls deep in love with Castruccio ends her days in the dungeons of the Inquisition. Mrs. Shelley's aim, however, is not to arouse fear, but to trace the gradual deterioration of Castruccio's character from an openhearted youth to a crafty tyrant. The blunt remarks of Godwin, who revised the manuscript, are not unjust, but fall with an ill grace from the pen of the author of *St. Leon:* "It appears in reading, that the first rule you prescribed was: 'I will let it be long.' It contains the quantity of four volumes of *Waverley.* No hard blow was ever hit with a woodsaw."

In *The Last Man,* . . . Mrs. Shelley attempted a stupendous theme, no less than a picture of the devastation of the human race by plague and pestilence. She casts her imagination forward into the twenty-first century, when the last king of England has abdicated the throne and a republic is established. Very wisely, she narrows the interest by concentrating on the pathetic fate of a group of friends who are among the last survivors, and the story becomes an idealised record of her own sufferings. The description of the loneliness of the bereft has a personal note, and reminds us of her journal, where she expresses the sorrow of being herself the last survivor, and of feeling like a "cloud from which the light of sunset has passed." Raymond, who dies in an attempt to place the standard of Greece in Stamboul, is a portrait of Byron; and Adrian, the late king's son, who finally becomes Protector, is clearly modelled on Shelley. Yet in spite of these personal reminiscences, their characters lack distinctness. Idris, Clara and Perdita are faintly etched, but Evadne, the Greek artist, who cherishes a passion for Raymond, and dies fighting against the Turks, has more colour and body than the other women, though she is somewhat theatrical. Mrs. Shelley conveys emotion more faithfully than character, and the overwrought sensibilities and dark forebodings of the diminished party of survivors who leave England to distract their minds by foreign travel are artfully suggested. The leaping, gesticulating figure, whom their jaded nerves and morbid fancy transform into a phantom, is a delir-

ious ballet-dancer; and the Black Spectre, mistaken for Death Incarnate, proves only to be a plague-stricken noble, who lurks near the party for the sake of human society. These "reasonable" solutions of the apparently supernatural remind us of Mrs. Radcliffe's method, and Mrs. Shelley shows keen psychological insight in her delineation of the state of mind which readily conjures up imaginary terrors. When Lionel Verney is left alone in the universe, her power seems to flag, and instead of the final crescendo of horror, which we expect at the end of the book, we are left with an ineffective picture of the last man in Rome in 2095 deciding to explore the countries he has not yet viewed. As he wanders amid the ruins he recalls not only "the buried Caesars," but also the monk in *The Italian,* of whom he had read in childhood—a striking proof of Mrs. Shelley's faith in the permanence of Mrs. Radcliffe's fame.

Though the style of *The Last Man* is often tediously prolix and is disfigured by patches of florid rhetoric and by inappropriate similes scattered broadcast, occasional passages of wonderful beauty recall Shelley's imagery; and, in conveying the pathos of loneliness, personal feeling lends nobility and eloquence to her style. With so ambitious a subject, it was natural that she should only partially succeed in carrying her readers with her. Though there are oases, the story is a somewhat tedious and dreary stretch of narrative that can only be traversed with considerable effort.

Mrs. Shelley's later works—*Perkin Warbeck* . . . , a historical novel; *Lodore* . . . , which describes the early life of Shelley and Harriet; *Falkner* . . . , which was influenced by *Caleb Williams*—do not belong to the history of the novel of terror; but some of her short tales, contributed to periodicals and collected in 1891, have gruesome and supernatural themes. "**A Tale of the Passions, or the Death of Despina,**" a story based on the struggles of the Guelphs and the Ghibellines, contains a perfect specimen of the traditional villain of the novel of terror:

> Every feature of his countenance spoke of the struggle of passions and the terrible egotism of one who would sacrifice himself to the establishment of his will: his black eyebrows were scattered, his grey eyes deep-set and scowling, his look at once stern and haggard. A smile seemed never to have disturbed the settled scorn which his lips expressed; his high forehead was marked by a thousand contradictory lines.

This terrific personage spends the last years of his life in orthodox fashion as an austere saint in a monastery.

"**The Mortal Immortal,**" a variation on the theme of *St. Leon,* is the record of a pupil of Cornelius Agrippa, who drank half of the elixir his master had compounded in the belief that it was a potion to destroy love. It is written on his three hundred and twenty-third birthday.

"**Transformation,**" like *Frankenstein,* dwells on the pathos of ugliness and deformity, but the subject is treated rather in the spirit of an eastern fairy tale than in that of a novel of terror. The dwarf, in return for a chest of treasure, borrows a beautiful body, and, thus disguised, wins the love of Juliet, and all ends happily. Mrs. Shelley's short stories reveal a stronger sense of proportion than her novels, and are written in a more graceful, fluent style than the books on which she expended great labour. (pp. 163-69)

Edith Birkhead, "Later Developments of the Tale of Terror," in her The Tale of Terror: A Study of the

Boris Karloff as Frankenstein's monster in the 1931 film Frankenstein. *The Granger Collection, New York.*

Gothic Romance, *1921. Reprint by Russell & Russell, Inc., 1963, pp. 157-84.*

J. MIDDLETON MURRY (essay date 1922)

[*Murry was a noted English essayist, magazine editor, and literary critic during the first half of the twentieth century. In his review of Shelley's verse dramas,* Proserpine *and* Midas, *he praises her poetic gift as minor but true.*]

The beauty of these little pieces [*Proserpine* and *Midas*], we are sure, will come as a surprise to many, who, though they may have had no doubt of Mary Shelley's talent, can scarcely have believed that her talent was poetic. We think of her chiefly as the author of *Frankenstein,* and it has always seemed hard to reconcile the brilliant novelist of extravagant, romantic sensation with the restrained and measured commentator on her husband's poetry. These little dramas supply the connecting link between the two manifestations. Their restraint, their purity is unmistakable; and it is a natural restraint. It seems to come less from an imitation of classical models than from an experience of life itself. The Mary whose rapturous cry of "Shelley!" has echoed once at least in the recesses of all our hearts, has grown into a woman who has borne children and seen them die. There is a grave and delicate sadness in her

Proserpine; and even in her *Midas,* where the fable could scarcely lend itself to austerity of treatment, the same instinctive restraint is felt in her touch. She cannot laugh; she smiles, and she smiles rather sadly.

Let us not exaggerate. These dramas are in miniature. Perhaps it is a mistake to call them dramas at all. They are more truly idylls cast, as the classical idyllists so often cast them, into dramatic form. And, though we believe that they very definitely are *poems* and that they prove that Mary Shelley had her portion of the true gift, we must admit that they are small. They are small; but they are nearly perfect. Perhaps their quality can be best defined by saying that there is hardly a line of Mary Shelley's writing in these composite idylls which could be improved. . . .

It is surely not extravagantly biographical to imagine that Mary Shelley's loss of her little girl Clara in September, 1818, and the yet more bitter loss of her little boy William at Rome in June, 1819—losses whose poignancy she set herself to combat by a return to original composition—may have guided her in her choice of the story of Proserpine. It is one of the profoundest and most inspiring of classical themes, and although when Mary Shelley took it up it had not yet been handled, as it was to be, by Tennyson and Swinburne and Meredith, it had already been the occasion of some of the greatest lines in English poetry—greater lines by far than were struck out of the theme by any of these three epigoni. It is as well to have them in mind in order to judge of Mary Shelley's quality. Shakespeare's—

> O Proserpina!
> For the flowers now that frighted thou let'st fall
> From Dis's waggon . . .

and Milton's

> Not that fair field
> Of *Enna,* where Proserpin gath'ring flowers,
> Herself a fairer flower, by gloomy Dis
> Was gather'd, which cost Ceres all that pain
> To seek her through the world:

these are two of the most magical movements of English poetry. Here is Mary Shelley:—

> Ceres for ever weeps, seeking her child,
> And in her rage has struck the land with blight;
> Trinacria mourns with her; its fertile fields
> Are dry and barren, and all little brooks
> Struggling scarce creep within their altered banks;
> The flowers that erst were wont with bended heads
> To gaze within the clear and glassy wave,
> Have died, unwatered by the failing stream—
> And yet their hue but mocks the deeper grief
> Which is the fountain of these bitter tears.

Certainly we can see the difference here between great poetry and another kind. But surely the striking thing is not so much the difference as the quiet, unobtrusive certainty with which Mary Shelley's lines hold their ground in such prodigious company. The speedwell lifts its head before the rose, and it is not abashed, for it knows that Solomon in all his glory was less beautifully arrayed.

This passage of pure and delicate poetry is not isolated in Mary Shelley's *Proserpine.* There are at least a dozen others of the same order, and one where she suddenly touches a more sombre note with equal mastery. Consider the closing line in these—

> Then you descend to deepest night, and reign
> Great Queen of Tartarus, 'mid shadows dire,
> Offspring of Hell—or in the silent groves
> Of fair Elysium through which Lethe runs,
> The sleepy river; where the windless air
> Is never struck by flight or song of bird—
> But all is calm and clear, bestowing rest,
> After the toil of life, on wretched men
> Whom thus the Gods reward for sufferings
> Gods cannot know.

It may be that the thought of the last line is Shelley's, though there is no reason to believe that Mary could not think, and think cogently, for herself; but the firm conciseness of the expression is all her own. Shelley's method of saying such a thing was quite different; it was never better.

If we are to disentangle any thread of influence at all in Mary Shelley's *Proserpine,* it is Miltonic. But if she was in fact influenced by Milton—we should not care to insist upon it— she displayed a rare discrimination in what she accepted or rejected. There is no classicism in her verse; if she has absorbed something of Milton's purity, she is on her guard against the risk of imitating Milton's triumphant mannerisms. Even when her lines most clearly ring with tones reminiscent of his, the simple music is still essentially her own. . . .

The only possible criticism of a poem which is complete with its own quiet beauty is that something of the deeper spiritual significance of the Proserpine myth escaped Mary Shelley. Had it not escaped her, she would have been different, and her poem, instead of a lovely miniature, would have been a masterpiece. That it is not; but it is a true and precious addition to the corpus of English poetry, as well as a new and shining illumination thrown upon Mary Shelley's character.

> *J. Middleton Murry, "Mary Shelley's Poetry," in* The Nation and The Athenaeum, *Vol. XXXII, No. 11, December 16, 1922, p. 461.*

HOWARD PHILLIPS LOVECRAFT   (essay date 1927)

[*Lovecraft is considered one of the foremost modern authors of supernatural horror fiction, as well as one of its most notable critics. In the following brief excerpt from his* Supernatural Horror in Literature, *which is regarded as one of the earliest and most comprehensive studies of that genre, Lovecraft praises Franken-stein. Lovecraft's remarks were written in 1927.*]

[Mary Shelley's] inimitable *Frankenstein; or, the Modern Prometheus* . . . is one of the horror-classics of all time. Composed in competition with her husband, Lord Byron, and Dr. John William Polidori in an effort to prove supremacy in horror-making, Mrs. Shelley's *Frankenstein* was the only one of the rival narratives to be brought to an elaborate completion; and criticism has failed to prove that the best parts are due to Shelley rather than to her. The novel, somewhat tinged but scarcely marred by moral didacticism, tells of the artificial human being molded from charnel fragments by Victor Frankenstein. . . . Some of the scenes in *Frankenstein* are unforgettable, as when the newly animated monster enters its creator's room, parts the curtains of his bed, and gazes at him in the yellow moonlight with watery eyes—"if eyes they may be called." Mrs. Shelley wrote other novels, including the fairly notable *Last Man;* but never duplicated the success of her first effort. It has the true

touch of cosmic fear, no matter how much the movement may lag in places. (pp. 38-9)

> *Howard Phillips Lovecraft, "The Aftermath of Gothic Fiction," in his* Supernatural Horror in Literature, *Ben Abramson Publisher, 1945, pp. 36-44.*

R. GLYNN GRYLLS   (essay date 1938)

[*In her biography of Shelley, from which the following excerpt is drawn, Grylls terms* Frankenstein *a "period piece" important chiefly as a forerunner of science fiction, finding* The Last Man *more relevant and worthy of attention.*]

[*Frankenstein*] is of interest as a considerable *tour de force,* for Mary was only nineteen when she wrote it, but its importance in the history of the novel depends primarily on the originality of the plot and on the descendants for which it has been responsible.

In its erection of a superstructure of fantasy on a foundation of circumstantial 'scientific' fact . . . it is the first of the Scientific Romances that have culminated in our day in the work of Mr. H. G. Wells; in this, as in its suggestion of deeper psychological and sociological implications underlying the story, *Frankenstein* marks an advance on the crude horror of the Radcliffe-Monk Lewis school. But in other respects, in style and in characterization in particular, it is badly 'dated'; the digressions and the description of scenery that delay the unfolding of the story proper are not only obvious devices to pad out the story to the dimensions of a novel (on Shelley's advice), but are conventions of the time with little to recommend them. It is not for nothing that *The Sorrows of Werther* is among the first three books that the monster came across. Frankenstein's fastidiousness and hesitancy, in debt more to German sentimentality than to *Hamlet,* make the modern reader as impatient with him as he is incredulous of the blameless beauty of the heroine. It is not the monster who is unreal in *Frankenstein,* but the human beings. The heavy Gothic diet, that Shelley was strong enough to assimilate and survive, permanently impaired Mary's weaker literary digestion.

If she had developed in *Frankenstein* and in the later novels the subtler psychology which she touched upon in the monster's *apologia* for his malignity, she would have taken a far higher rank as an artist; she would have been a novelist and not a 'fictioneer'; but she was content to deal in the stock-in-trade of her generation, and consequently her high gifts of imagination and her command over language, worthy of better things, are lost in a neglect not wholly undeserved. *Frankenstein* remains a 'period piece', of not very good date; historically interesting, but not one of the living novels of the world.

I have dealt at length with *Frankenstein* as it is the only novel of Mary Shelley's whose reputation has survived, and criticism of it applies in general to her other work.

Lodore is valuable now as veiled biography, but as a novel is not as intrinsically interesting as *The Last Man,* which, in the present writer's opinion, has not received its deserts. Her imaginative powers in it, concentrated on achieving one effect, that of utter desolation, are more successfully employed than when they range more diffusely and stray into the grandiose and the sentimental. Her description of the devastation wrought by a plague which sweeps the world and brings in its train a breakdown, more nightmarish than death itself, of the organization on which civilized existence depends takes on a heightened reality to a generation threatened by an extinction as complete from the man-made plague of war: there seems nothing fanciful in the wanderings of the surviving hero over a wrecked and deserted Europe. (pp. 319-21)

> *R. Glynn Grylls, in her* Mary Shelley: A Biography, *Oxford University Press, London, 1938, 345 p.*

SYLVA NORMAN (essay date 1938)

[*In this excerpt from a survey of Shelley's novels, journalistic pieces, short stories, verse dramas, and poetry, Norman identifies her as a romantic and traces those qualities in many of her works. Although she credits the author with talent and inspiration, Norman essentially dismisses much of Shelley's creative writing because she was unable to devise plot and character. Norman does praise some of Shelley's nonfiction pieces, pronouncing* Lives of Eminent Men *"her soundest, most scholarly and efficient writing."*]

On June 18, 1824, Mary Shelley broke away from despondency in her journal, to be stimulated by the thrill of a 'divine night'.

> I have just returned from Kentish Town; a calm twilight pervades the clear sky; the lamp-like moon is hung out in heaven, and the bright west retains the dye of sunset. If such weather would continue, I should write again; the lamp of thought is again illumined in my heart, and the fire descends from heaven that kindles it. . . . I shall again feel the enthusiastic glow of composition, again, as I pour forth my soul upon paper, feel the winged ideas arise, and enjoy the delight of expressing them. Study and occupation will be a pleasure, and not a task, and this I shall owe to sight and companionship of trees and meadows, flowers and sunshine.

The passage reveals several small points about our authoress. First, it establishes the certainty—not without importance—that Mary was, or had been, capable of losing herself delightedly in the intimate process of creation. Such an attitude cannot be induced by advice or suggestion on the part of another, and we may take it that Mary Godwin would have been a writer if there had been no Shelley or Byron to startle her into the nightmare of *Frankenstein.* It hints further, when we consider its date, that the joy of composition could be all-sufficing, removing her from the need of Shelley's presence, and filling the desolate gap after his death. (pp. 55-6)

Further, the quotation gives a clue to her literary mentality by displaying the sources of her inspiration. They are those of the romantic—moonlight, trees and meadows, flowers and sunshine. A revolutionary would have been inspired by politics and ideas, a satirist by men. (p. 56)

[It is] the romantic period that must be borne in mind when we consider [Mary Shelley], if we are not to confuse the fashions of an age with the faults of an individual. Genius carves its own way through all conventions without being independent of its period; but average talent exists to be moulded by the current fashion, not only because escape is difficult, but also because the question of popularity is involved. The early nineteenth century favoured melancholy. Its feelings were harrowed most pleasantly by a tale of ill-starred love, and death, and deserted souls who grieved eternally. Its drama must be tragic, its lyrics despairing, its lengthy novels stuffed out with disasters and bespattered with the bleeding fragments of warm hearts.

Naturally those who wrote for a living tuned themselves in to this popular note. . . . (p. 57)

In one respect, at least, the three-volume novel presented no difficulty to Mary: she could fill it up. Words slipped easily from her pen, and, the situation once given, she found little trouble in prolonging it. But the situation was another matter, so were the characters. Genuine imaginative fertility was denied her, nor was she a keen, detached observer of men and women. Plot, in both novel and short story, was an initial bugbear that had to be overcome by a desperate search into memory or history. Even when established, the narrative was pushed along by devices that strike us now as being clumsy and tiresome, though probably acceptable to the taste of her public. Each new character is linked to the plot by a chain of information about his own past life and circumstances; he comes, as it seems, from an infinite distance—a distance the more deplorable when we find him eventually hooked tight to the plot by a past coincidence of time and presence, or a concealed identity. Far too often Mary's idea of a firmly constructed novel is to reveal the blood-relationships of apparent strangers, kinsman becoming painfully entangled with kinsman in the dark. The 'Hold, hold! he cried,—I tell thee 'tis her brother!' of [P. B. Shelley's] "Rosalind and Helen" was comfortably installed, with all its box of tricks, in Mary's mind, to be brought out less sensationally and at greater length. Again the taste of her readers is to blame; without these artificial disclosures they would have been as disappointed as Edwardian children at a pantomime that lacked its transformation scene.

As for her characters, the rule of snobbery appeared to prevail; they must be highborn, whether they were the medieval Italian chieftains of *Valperga,* the English princes of *Perkin Warbeck,* the society nobles of *Lodore* and *Falkner,* or the imaginary king's sons of *The Last Man.* There was never again so humble a hero as the student 'Frankenstein'. Yet how often are these distinguished folk incognito, even to themselves! They are brought up in peasants' huts, performing menial tasks, far in thought and mileage from the ancestral mansion. This suggests prudence on the novelist's part; some of her readers were liable to a closer acquaintance with great houses than the Whig baronet's runaway daughter-in-law, who was denied Field Place and knew the Lord of Newstead only as an exile. But the picturesque Shelley and Byron she did know, and for an authoress they were godsends. Again and again she snatched at such of their features as she might readily reproduce, so that hollow semblances and distortions of them drift through her thousands of pages, despoiled of their keen features and smothered, by the end of their pilgrimage, under fictitious clothes. . . . Almost unreal in reality, Byron fitted astonishingly well into the period novel, and if his image and identity had not been preserved for us, we could have sworn that in every case this wilful charmer was a projection of the writer's sentiment. Shelley, whose portrait required some discussion of philosophy and reform, was more difficult to catch. When Mary attempts it he becomes [scarcely recognizable]. . . . But he is useful to her, if only to bring in a train of ghostly associates and incidents which, as in *Lodore,* can be shuffled and shaped into a story.

Mary's first novel [*Frankenstein*] has become a classic, and needs no discussion here. Its popularity was fortunate for her, since all her subsequent novels, and most of her short stories, were compelled by Sir Timothy's ban to appear with 'the author of *Frankenstein*' as sole signature. The first of them, *Valperga, or the Life and Adventures of Castruccio, Prince of Lucca,* had been written during Shelley's lifetime, and the reward promised to Godwin before Mary knew how eagerly she would want it herself. If the devoted parent is to be believed, his drastic cuts and alterations were responsible for its seeing the light of publication. He had deplored its length, although two of the 'females' were 'exceedingly interesting' and to his thinking there were 'parts of high genius'. The last was a kindly estimate, and any one having the persistence to read through *Valperga*, which harbours some of Mary's dreariest writing, must thank Godwin for the liberties he took with it. And yet, at one point an echo of Shelleyan boldness enters the story, to remind us that she still had his backing.

[In *Valperga*], popularity enters in with the romantical nightmare machinery of witches, miracles, and inquisition. It is not all fustian; occasional subtleties creep into the analysis of motive and character, and the Italian landscape, being of the essence of her inspiration, is vividly and convincingly described. (pp. 60-5)

[The subject of *The Last Man*], which might have seemed almost as original as that of *Frankenstein* had it been Mary's own invention, was going the literary rounds when she seized on it to supply her need of a plot. She might, one feels, have allowed it to supply the *whole* plot; yet there is some merit in her suggestion that the end of the world, when it does come, will alarm a population fully occupied with its own absorbing activities. It certainly takes an unconscionable time to get under way. (p. 66)

The Last Man having lived and died, its author turned with decision into English History, read up her Yorkist and Lancastrian annals, received pedestrian information from her father, even begged Sir Walter Scott the expert for help with obscurer references, and produced *The Fortunes of Perkin Warbeck*.... There was only one romantic way of treating Perkin Warbeck; Mary believed firmly, in her preface, that records in the Tower proved him, almost beyond doubt, to be the Duke of York. Her favourite subject of nobility in disguise was thus available, giving her, as she naïvely put it, 'a hero to ennoble the pages of a humble tale'. It gave her in addition such a surfeit of material about kings and princes, royal relationships, political plans, and movements of conspirators, that she was hard pressed nearly all the way through by the necessity of embodying and arranging it while she kept the Duke's horse trotting to its doom. If the predominant note is an echo of Scott, she deserves a word of praise for her successful obstacle race. Besides, it prevented her most healthily from overindulgence in the woeful situation, simply through lack of time for it. (pp. 70-1)

It was a quiet story in that Mary decided to procure no plot for it beyond a medley of happenings based on the lives of her own circle, broken up, transplanted, fertilized (or sterilized) with fiction. *Lodore*, ... with no claims but as a society novel, proved nearer than the historical ventures had been to the public taste. It has since been used as a competition ground for Shelleyans, who go through it neatly labelling the characters and incidents until all is docketed.... [In *Lodore*], Mary has skilfully split the personalities, reduced the interest, and abstracted the tragedy of her own life and circumstances. She has added intrigue and a measure of tedium to fill the gap. (pp. 72-4)

Besides her enormous novels, a good body of journalistic writing lies at Mary's door. She was anything but lazy. Her journalism—not quite of the modern miscellaneous order—falls into two sections. One comprises the *Lives of Eminent Men* written for Lardner's *Cabinet Cyclopaedia*, the other consists of stories and sketches contributed to the fashionable Annuals. They make a fair contrast, the first containing her soundest, most scholarly and efficient writing, the second being all bubble and baseless fabrication.

The full title of the Lardner volumes was *Lives of the Most Eminent Literary and Scientific Men of Italy, Spain and Portugal*. The first appeared in February 1835. Mary wrote to Mrs. Gisborne, 'The Lives of Dante and Ariosto are by Mr. [James] Montgomery, the rest are mine.' Those others, which had been 'a source of interest and pleasure' to her, were those of Petrarch, Boccaccio, Lorenzo de Medici, Bojardo, Berni, and Machiavelli, besides an article on half a dozen minor figures. In the autumn a second volume was published, in which Mary had lost Galileo and Tasso to Montgomery, but wrote on Metastasio, Goldoni, Alfieri, Guicciardini, Vittoria Colonna, Guarini, Chiabrera, Tassoni, Marini, Ugo Foscolo, and Monti—this last being pronounced as 'without question, the greatest Italian poet that has appeared since the golden days of its poetry'. (pp. 79-80)

The *Lives* were not intended to contain original research. Enough that they were accurate, readable, sympathetic, and concise. Looking through them we seem at last to have a picture of that Mary who sat studying and reading for long hours with Shelley, sparing only a moment at the end of the day to record a line in her diary. As Godwin had said of *Frankenstein*, the biographical writing was 'compressed, muscular, and firm; nothing relaxed and weak; no proud flesh'. Mary was performing a healthy, honest task imposed from without; her mind, rather than her heart, was in it, and she performed it competently.

The stories belong to another world, being written to grace those graceful Annuals—the *Keepsake*, the *Book of Beauty*, the *Forget-me-Not*—which were produced so elegantly at Christmas time, bound in rose-coloured silk covers and embellished with steel engravings of romantic subjects to illustrate the text.... Every fashionable lady probably had a *Keepsake* in her boudoir, so that it was worth while for the socially ambitious to contribute. Only she must suit her surroundings. A love lyric, a sketch of sunset, a romance of the East (to be illustrated by scimitars and turbans), any story of colourful heroism or sweet sacrifice, of love in mourning or rescue from villainy, for preference set amongst foreign vines and olives, rugged gorges, and torrential mountain streams. Humour was not encouraged. Obviously, Mary could write for the Annuals without much schooling. Her past dwellings lay up and down the landscapes of Italy, her connexions led her farther east to Greece, her pen was facile and her heart romantic. (pp. 81-3)

All the features we have noticed about Mary's conduct of a novel apply equally—often more disastrously—to her stories. The two were not then such different forms of art. No implicit rule laid down a limit to the scope of the short story; the 'single episode', 'the continuous mood'—such unities were unheard of, for Maupassant, Tchehov, and their disciples were yet to come. Mary's tales had as many and gaudy trimmings as a well-hung Christmas tree. In their confined space they still presented story within story, to an irritating extent. One of the worst offenders is **"Euphrasia."** ... This story begins with a party caught in a Sussex snowdrift, waiting in such cold tedium to be rescued that a gentleman is induced to tell of his adventures in revolutionary Greece.... Richard Garnett, collecting Mary's tales into a volume in 1891, improved the case by cutting out the snowdrift altogether, without a word of his surgery. But he could not cover Mary's lapse of memory, whereby the adventurer's story is begun in the third person and finished in the first.

To be sure, in this Arabian Night kind of production we should not be too particular. A few genii, flying palaces, and revengeful auks might have improved their weaving; it is the attempt at realism in an artificial frame that makes them so irksome. For instance, in **"The Mourner"** one of Mary's young Nevilles goes to Eton in a Shelleyan way. 'I will not attempt to dwell on my sufferings there. . . . I was a fag to a hard taskmaster', and West Indian slavery was light compared with that bondage. After this hyperbolical indictment the young man lives a fairy tale with one of those high-born ladies who take to polite rusticity. The entire story is glitter and tinsel, ending in a tragedy. . . . (pp. 83-5)

There is no need to dwell longer on these baubles, except to mourn the wasted talent and the fragments of true observation that lie embalmed in them. In his preface to *St. Leon,* Godwin wrote in 1799: 'I have mixed human feelings and passions with incredible situations, and thus rendered them impressive and interesting.' Mary, whose work is in the Godwin tradition, tries to do the same, even borrowing her father's Wandering Jew theme for her tale of **"The Mortal Immortal"**; but her passions are as incredible as her situations. She could never leave her castles and cottages, her runaway girls and truculent pursuers, her disguised identities, funereal smiles and flower-decked tears—not though she was richer than most women of her time in keen experience. There is strength in her intellect, but it bows to her truly feminine invention which prefers to dive into a glade of detached fancy rather than face the responsibility of truth and living portraiture.

Setting aside editorship and travel notes, one more aspect of Mary's literary work remains—her poetry and drama. There is not much of it. Her longest poem, *The Choice,* written a few months after Shelley's death, mourned her lover and her own shortcomings, and doubtless raised her spirits towards exaltation, though it has no such effect now on the reader. (pp. 85-6)

Perhaps Mary's ambition did not really envisage the limited field of the lyric. For many years after her bereavement she dreamed of writing tragedy in the grand style. She had always been attracted by the glamour of the stage and the personalities of actors, and believed now that out of this personal sorrow some magnificent drama would be born. Godwin, seeing more clearly the difference between feeling and ability, dissuaded his daughter in round terms, and she gave up the idea with a sigh. However, she had already written some dramatic scenes in verse, at a time when Shelley and Byron were composing dramas. Her two mythological verse scenes, *Proserpine* and *Midas,* were written, according to their modern editor, in 1820. (pp. 88-9)

One must in honesty admit that Mary Shelley's verse dramas, pretty and sometimes poetical as they are, do not really call for analytical and comparative study. In the altering of lines and phrases [between the first and second versions] we find no great mind at work, but only, as in the case of her occasional lyrics, a musical intonation and simple command of rhythm grafted on to the usual facility of her prose language.

It is not to be wondered at that her 'poetical works' are few; those who live in permanent close contact with a poet (as Mary did mentally, even after Shelley's death) must be conceited or hard of hearing if they insist on adding their small tinkle to the sonorous note. Mary had sense and judgement enough to leave the poetry in Shelley's hands, and to concentrate on fiction, which financial returns and a genuine if unexalted gift both served to justify. (pp. 98-9)

Sylva Norman, "Mary Shelley: Novelist and Dramatist," in On Shelley *by Edmund Blunden, Gavin de Beer, and Sylva Norman, Oxford University Press, London, 1938, pp. 55-99.*

MILTON MILLHAUSER (essay date 1946)

[*Millhauser considers* Frankenstein's *monster in relation to the tradition of the "noble savage" in literature.*]

The estimate of Mary Shelley's **Frankenstein** familiar to us from literary handbooks and popular impression emphasizes its macabre and pseudo-scientific sensationalism: properly enough, so far as either its primary conception or realized qualities are concerned. But it has the effect of obscuring from notice certain secondary aspects of the work which did, after all, figure in its history and weigh with its contemporary audience, and which must, therefore, be taken into consideration before either the book or the young mind that composed it has been properly assayed. One such minor strain, not too well recognised in criticism, is a thin vein of social speculation: a stereotyped, irrelevant, and apparently automatic repetition of the lessons of that school of liberal thought which was then termed "philosophical."

In the work of Godwin's daughter and Shelley's bride, some reflection of contemporary social radicalism—crude, second-hand, very earnest, already a little out of date—occurs almost as a matter of course; what deserves comment is just that this element entered the author's notion of her plot so late and remained so decidedly an alien in it; for it governs the story only temporarily and, so to speak, extraneously, and confuses as much as it promotes the development of the character of the central figure, the monster itself. Where one might have expected, from Mary's character, that it would prove a main *motif* of the narrative, it is actually both detrimental thereto and ill-assimilated, and must be discarded altogether before the story can advance to its principal effect.

For, throughout a considerable part of the book—roughly speaking, the first half of the middle section, beginning with chapter xi—the monster is so far from being the moral horror he presently becomes that it is hardly credible he should ever be guilty of wanton brutality at all. (The transformation, by the way, is effected most abruptly, without even the degree of psychological consistency appropriate to fantasy; two violent rebuffs and an astonishingly rigid logicality of temperament turn the monster from his lonely and contemplative benevolence to a course of harsh, melodramatic vengefulness.) Rather, in the solitary student of Volney, musing on the pageant of human history, or on the contrast between man's accomplishments and his failures—"Was man, indeed, at once so powerful, so virtuous and magnificent, yet so vicious and base?"— it is not hard to recognise that gentle lay-figure of late eighteenth century social criticism, the "natural man," bringing his innocence into forceful and oversimplified contrast with the complexities and contradictions of our civilisation. Or, more precisely, may we not see in him (because of his strange origin and untutored state) something approximating to that variation of the general "child of nature" pattern to which Professor Fairchild has attached the name of Noble Savage? Like the savage, the monster approaches our society as an outsider, tests it by natural impulse and unsophisticated reason, and responds to it with a mixture of bewilderment and dismay.

Now, this aspect of the monster's character is basically unnecessary to the horror-plot; he need not pass by this road to ferocity and misery. (There might, for instance, as easily have been an original moral flaw in his constitution, paralleling the physical one; he might, as in the vulgar imagination, have been *created* bestial.) Indeed, the more this phase of his development is dwelt upon, the less consistent with the later stages does it appear. Nor is his experience as a Noble Savage too closely integrated into the story; it is connected rather arbitrarily to his education in language, but the social reflections, as well as the narrative which is their more immediate occasion, are pure interpolation, and lead to nothing. This is a real flaw in the story, felt by the reader as expectation disappointed; the author fails to *make use* of all her speculative preparation. When, for instance, the monster is hurt—brutally attacked—by those he trusted, it is because of their human ignorance and natural terror, not society's injustice; so that his radical observations are irrelevant to his own fate. Before long, indeed, the author is able to forget that the monster was ever a "natural man" (and consequently gentle and just by inclination) at all, without apparent loss to the dramatic values of the story. Everything points to the whole idea's having been an afterthought, arising, perhaps, before the full detail of the book had been worked out, but well after the general mood and drift and structure of the plot had been decided. The chance for it was offered by the story, and Mary Shelley could not decline it, but it was not an essential part of her idea, and could only be fitted in as a disproportioned and almost pointless interpolation.

The temptation seems to have been offered by the problem of the monster's intellectual development. The effort to make her creature psychologically credible must have troubled Mrs. Shelley most in his early days. What the difficulty was appears as one writes of it; how is one to speak of the "youth," the "childhood," of a being that appeared upon the earth full-grown, and yet how else is one to speak of his period of elementary ignorance and basic learning? The author cannot allow him the normal protracted human infancy and gradual education, for the plot demands that he escape from his creator and fend for himself at once; yet both plot and probability demand that he escape unformed, that he be confused and ignorant in the world into which he has blundered. As a result, the author bestows upon him a curious apprenticeship (to call it that), an amalgam of two quite different rates of development: for he is at the same time both child and man, and learns alternately like each. Thus he can walk and clothe himself from the moment of his creation, yet, infant-like, has trouble for a long while in separating the effects of the various senses; he learns the use of fire (by strict inductive reasoning!) in a few minutes, yet it is years before he can teach himself to speak or read. For the most part, however, his story is that of an adult in the state of nature, with faculties full-grown but almost literally without experience, and therefore making the acquaintance of the most primitive social facts by toilsome and unguided individual endeavour. If one distinguishes the difficulties (possible to an adult) of ignorance from those (peculiar to a child) of incapacity, there is really only a single effort to make him behave like one new-born—the confusion of the senses; thereafter he is a full-grown and decidedly intelligent but extraordinarily inexperienced man.

Now this comes close to being a description of the Noble Savage: an adult, but an alien to our world. If at this point

Mary Shelley's mother, Mary Wollstonecraft, painted by John Opie circa 1797.

(that is, chapters xi through xv) he differs markedly from the average of the type, it is only in being not an average but an extreme; the actual savage has his own commendable if elementary civilisation that he can compare with ours, but Frankenstein's monster has only the impulses of his nature—which are, to start with, absolutely good. But this mixture of innocence with ignorance was the very point to be exhibited by the Noble Savage or the "natural man"—"man as he is not"—both forms familiar to tediousness in the literature upon which early nineteenth century ingenuous radicalism fed its mind. So that, having brought her monster, untutored and uncorrupted, into the wilderness, there to spy upon and so study civilised ways (all of which was demanded anyhow by the plot), Mrs. Shelley would have found it hard not to fall into what must have been a very familiar habit of thought. She must surely have recognised that she was straying from the plotted path, whether she identified the new influence or not; but she was trying to write a full-length novel on the basis of a rather slim idea, and in those days interpolation was not yet a sin. So, not deliberately and yet not unwillingly, she permitted the assimilation of her story and her creature into the well-worn patterns they had skirted; none the less gratefully, perhaps, because they gave the young rebel an opportunity to utter a little of what was seething in her environment—the Shelley atmosphere, crossed by Byron's sulphureous trail—and in her own eager mind.

But if the temptation was strong enough to attract her into a rather long and somewhat incongruous philosophical digression, it was still subsidiary to her initial impulse. If Godwin's daughter could not help philosophising, Shelley's wife knew also the eerie charms of the morbid, the occult, the scientifically bizarre. Her first purpose, which was melodrama, stood. Therefore the alien figure appears in the novel only momentarily—so long as, with a little effort, the plot accommodates itself to him; when he really threatens to interfere with it, he is abandoned. But if he never dominates the story, he does figure in it, and should be reckoned with. However relentlessly the first lurid vision is finally pursued to its end, the familiar lineaments of the Noble Savage, the child of nature, did come for a little while to be visible in Frankenstein's impious creation; however sharply his hideous features and terrible career may have distinguished him from the brooding islander or haughty Indian sachem, the central theme, the uncongeniality of our actual world with a certain ideal and touchingly beautiful simplicity, served to associate his history, in some degree, with theirs, and so attract him temporarily into their form. (pp. 248-50)

> *Milton Millhauser, "The Noble Savage in Mary Shelley's 'Frankenstein'," in* Notes and Queries, *Vol. 190, No. 12, June 15, 1946, pp. 248-50.*

ELIZABETH NITCHIE (essay date 1953)

[*In the following excerpt from her well-regarded critical biography of Shelley, Nitchie focuses on structure, style, and characterization in Shelley's fiction.*]

[Mary Shelley] left only two works that have survived as wholes on their own merits: the notes to Shelley's works largely because of their subject matter, *Frankenstein* because of the strange, imaginative conception and compelling writing. It is easy to dispose of her as the unworthy companion of a great poet, the progressively worsening author of sentimental fiction. Such a judgment, however, neglects the strength of her nonfiction and the positive merits of her novels and tales. (p. 179)

Mary's writing has many faults, most of which were obvious even to her contemporary admirers: lack of humor, monotony, verbosity, overwriting, sentimentality of plot and character, fondness for beautiful, blameless heroines, reliance on analysis of character at the expense of dramatic action and dialogue. With all these faults there are still positive merits that even a modern critic must allow. The charges against her as a writer can be, not refuted, perhaps, but modified, some of them considerably, some of them at least by the exception that proves the rule. The charge of impiety brought against *Frankenstein* obviously need not be considered. And that of wild imagination in *Frankenstein* and *The Last Man* seems rather absurd in an age of robots, of air-borne travel, and of a socialized Britain—and of Aldous Huxley and George Orwell. But other—and serious—literary sins must be examined.

Except for *Frankenstein* Mary's fiction reveals little originality and invention in plotting. She depended too much either on actual events or on stereotyped situations. She repeated devices, such as the riding accident which she used many times in her novels and tales in order to throw a character where she wanted him, frequently at the feet of the heroine. The endings of her stories, though not always conventionally happy and sometimes even tragic are usually contrived and foreseeable. . . . She included too much in her plots, too many incidents that were merely incidental. Godwin cut *Valperga* drastically, and yet the reviewers thought it still burdened by episodes and minor characters. She had difficulty in sustaining a long, involved plot; her use of the flash-back too often results in confusion and diffusion rather than in clarity and conciseness;

occasionally, as in one hastily written short story, she herself loses track of her plot.

Yet she had a sense of dramatic structure. Even in *Falkner* the basic irony of the situation, though marred by over-emphasis and repetition, is striking. Gerard Neville, having vowed to seek out and punish his mother's destroyer, falls in love with Elizabeth, not knowing that her foster-father Falkner is the man he seeks. He even helps Elizabeth to nurse Falkner back to life after a severe illness. The plot of *Frankenstein* is tightly knit, with contrasts creating dramatic tensions. Two main ideas, loneliness and scientific curiosity with its hopes and fears and pains, are foreshadowed in the introductory letters of Walton to his sister and developed throughout the novel.

This entire story is set in strangeness: Walton and Frankenstein meet in the mysterious white world of the ice-bound Arctic—Coleridge's "land of mist and snow." Consciously or unconsciously, Mary owed much to *The Rime of the Ancient Mariner*. In Walton's letters to his sister there are several references to the poem. Indeed he attributes his passionate enthusiasm for "the dangerous mysteries of the ocean, to that production of the most imaginative of modern poets." And the loneliness of the Mariner appealed to the lonely creator of the lonely Monster.

And as was said of Coleridge, it is not in the invention of wonders that Mary excelled—striking as her central invention is—but in the extraordinary skill with which she "paints the passions they excite." Frankenstein's exaltation and terror, his doubt and dread and remorse, his wild grief and his passion for revenge are the chief means by which we are impressed with the frightfulness of his unhallowed creation. Just as in *The Ancient Mariner* we see and feel the horrors first with the Mariner and second with the Wedding Guest, so in *Frankenstein* the wonder is twice removed from the reality. Frankenstein's horror is told in his own words, like the Mariner's story, to Walton, a man who has no personal connection with the supernatural events but who "cannot choose but hear." And there is another layer of narrative: the Monster tells his story to Frankenstein, who tells it to Walton. Yet at the end, with Frankenstein's death, the middle layer disappears and reality meets wonder—Walton comes face to face with the Monster.

There are bright fragments of reality within the inner layers: Clerval's normalcy, the idyllic home of Felix (yet broken in upon by the strange girl from the East), Elizabeth's first letter with news of their happy family life. They serve only to thicken the strange darkness that surrounds and engulfs them. The words *strange* and *unnatural* become key words, appearing and reappearing on page after page.

Thus the structure of the novel is an ingenious, strangely wrought nest of boxes, reality on the outside and horror at the core. The chief persons in this story too are both real and strange. Walton combines practical, painstaking industry with "a love for the marvellous, a belief in the marvellous" which hurries him away from normal living to exploration of the "wild sea and unvisited regions." Frankenstein goes away to the university like any other young man but is caught by the magic of modern science until he is driven into experiments unhallowed and presumptuous in their invasion of the power of the Creator. The Monster himself is non-human in his origin, his physical frame and appearance, but human in his longings and desires and even in that passion for revenge which leads him to commit inhuman crimes.

In *The Last Man* there are dramatic foreshadowings and contrasts. Raymond, foreseeing his death, looks upon the earth as a tomb, each man he meets as a corpse; thus, as the story progresses, Verney and the reader come to look upon mankind. The beauty of nature and the gaiety or the idyllic happiness of man are broken in upon by word of the progress of the plague. Adrian's dream of a paradise on earth, Merrival's prediction of eternal spring to come a hundred thousand years in the future, little Alfred's birthday party, a service at Westminster Abbey are interrupted by news of fresh victims or the actual presence of Pestilence. A sense of dramatic fitness animates the account of a performance of *Macbeth* at Drury Lane Theatre in plague-stricken London:

> A shudder like the swift passing of an electric shock ran through the house, when Rosse exclaimed, in answer to "Stands Scotland where it did?"

> Alas, poor country;
> Almost afraid to know itself! It cannot
> Be called our mother, but our grave: where nothing,
> But who knows nothing, is once seen to smile;
> Where sighs, and groans, and shrieks that rent the air,
> Are made, not marked; where violent sorrow seems
> A modern extasy: the dead man's knell
> Is there scarce asked, for who; and good men's lives
> Expire before the flowers in their caps,
> Dying, or ere they sicken.

> Each word struck the scene, as our life's passing bell; we feared to look at each other, but bent our gaze on the stage, as if our eyes could fall innocuous on that alone.

> (pp. 180-84)

These moments of dramatic tension, however, do not save most of Mary's stories from prolixity and confusion.

As she had difficulty in sustaining an involved plot, so she could rarely sustain the drawing of an important character. Her heroes and heroines are usually two-dimensional, cut out like paper dolls from a pattern of Byronic gentleman or beautiful and virtuous maiden. She lacked skill in presenting the mingling of good and bad—although she had known it well in her friends. The faults in the fundamentally noble persons are of the grand sort, due to strong passions or to bad bringing up. The villains are either idle, profligate spendthrifts or tyrannical and prejudiced old men, cold of heart. It is in minor characters seen comparatively briefly or in flashes of insight into personality that Mary is successful and impressive. Mrs. Elizabeth Fitzhenry, good-natured, simple, stupid, adoring but not understanding her brother Lodore, doing her duty by Ethel in the great city of London but never dreaming that a love affair is going on under her nose, retiring with thankfulness to her quiet country life after Ethel's marriage—here is a real "character," drawn, as far as anyone knows, from Mary's own imagination. Miss Jervis, Elizabeth Falkner's governess, in her crispness and primness, her intellectual limitations and her professional conscientiousness, is a real person. (pp. 185-86)

Not all of the principal characters are flat. Adrian in *The Last Man,* though shadowy when compared with his living model, is drawn with delicate sympathy and with the rounded knowledge which his creator had of his original. Beatrice, the strange, dark, passionate girl in *Valperga,* deserves the praise she received from Shelley, Godwin, and the reviewers. Euthanasia, except for her typical extreme beauty, is an interesting woman

Mary Shelley's father, William Godwin, painted by James Northcote in 1802.

because of the conflict within her between her love for Castruccio and her love for her own people. Her gradual disenchantment is convincing in its clarity and logic.

Mary Shelley frequently used characters confused by mixed emotions and motives. The most interesting person in *Lodore* is Cornelia, whose pride is always at war with her affections and keeps her for a long time from both her daughter and her lover. In *Falkner* most of the characters are thoroughly wound up in mixed motives: Falkner in his wish for death and his love and sense of responsibility for Elizabeth; Neville in his honorable desire to vindicate his mother and his love for Elizabeth to whom such vindication would bring sorrow; Elizabeth in her own involved loyalties to Neville and to Falkner. Even when Falkner has been acquitted, he and Neville are still hampered by conflicting delicacies of feeling that delay the conclusion. Part of the drama and the tragedy of *Frankenstein* lies in the conflicts in the young scientist's own soul: his glory and his horror at his scientific achievement; his pity and his hatred of the Monster.

The Monster himself, that earliest creation of Mary's, is probably her best, most subtle, most perceptive characterization. [In] his loneliness he is a projection of Mary herself. It is that which makes him human, which is responsible for the changes in his character, which makes him tragic. Improbable as are the circumstances of his creation—why, asked one reviewer, did Frankenstein make him so huge and so hideous—and of his self-education, he becomes a real and convincing person, viewed in the round, whose motives are clear and valid. He runs through an arc of experience and of feeling for others, from love through fear and hatred to a final compassion for mankind and even for his creator. To the last he justifies his crimes by the fact that he is alone and that every man's hand has been against him. "Robbed of its romantic form," said Bertrand Russell, "there is nothing unreal in this psychology. . . . To an English visitor, the ex-Kaiser, at Doorn, lamented that the English no longer loved him. Dr. Burtt, in his book on the juvenile delinquent, mentions a boy of seven who drowned another boy in the Regent Canal; his reason was that neither his family nor his contemporaries showed him affection. Dr. Burtt was kind to him, and he became a respectable citizen; but no Dr. Burtt undertook the reformation of Frankenstein's monster" [see Additional Bibliography].

Vague and diffuse as Mary's characterizations sometimes are, she often presents an attitude, a characteristic, or a whole character in a concise and telling comment that shows her observant and ironic eye. "She satisfied her conscience . . . by cherishing a little quiet stock of family hate." "My aunt . . . was as a plant beneath a thick covering of ice; my hands would have been frozen in any attempt to get at it." Castruccio, the man of war, was accustomed "to count men as the numerals of a military arithmetic." And with a turn of phrase that gives fresh meaning to a cliché Mary sums up the character of Miss Jervis: "She has a heart of gold, though it does not shine." (pp. 186-88)

Her comments on the morality of society or the vanity of human wishes, her wistful reflections on life and death, on youth and age may not be original in thought. But often she finds for them a turn of phrase that stamps them with interest and individuality. "We never do what we wish when we wish it, and when we desire a thing earnestly, and it does arrive, that or we are changed, so that we slide from the summit of our wishes and find ourselves where we were." . . .

Mary's descriptive style, generalized and elaborate as much of it seems today, was considered vigorous, clear, and nervous by her contemporaries. Individual words are often precise and expressive: "the light waves coursed one another," "dusky manuscripts," "the snowdrift, whirring past the lattice." Figures of speech are often fresh and vivid. Verney speaks of "the inch and barley-corn growth of my life." Of the small remnant of English waiting on the Dover cliffs to cross to the hoped-for safety of the continent, he says, "Death had hunted us through the course of many months, even to the narrow strip of time on which we now stood." (p. 190)

In longer passages of description, although they are often colored and weakened by romantic diction, Mary can sustain a mood and create a distinct picture. She can describe scenery, especially that which she had known herself: the landscape of Tuscany through which she passed on her return to England and of which she wrote to Hunt; the streets and houses of Geneva; the country around Albano; the peaks and valleys and glaciers of the Alps. In *Frankenstein* Walton's "land of mist and snow," which she had never seen, owes much to her reading of Coleridge. But the journey of Frankenstein and Clerval down the Rhine is lively and full of detail like that in Mary's own *History of a Six Weeks' Tour*. And her vivid pictures of the grand scenes among which she began to write *Frankenstein*—the thunderstorm in the Alps, the valleys of Servox and Chamounix, the glacier and the precipitous sides of Montanvert, and the smoke of rushing avalanches, the "tremendous dome" of Mont Blanc—are not shamed by comparison with the poems written in the same months and on the same ground, Byron's third canto of *Childe Harold* and Shelley's "Mont Blanc." (p. 191)

[Darkly] dramatic moments stand out against the flatter narrative in her novels: the Monster's drawing back of the curtains on Frankenstein's bed; the collapse of the bridge of Carraia at the Spectacle of Hell in Florence; the exhumation of the body of Falkner's Alithea; Lodore's fatal duel with the American, their figures silhouetted against a moonlit sky; the discovery of Raymond's body in the ruins of Constantinople guarded by his dying dog; the climax of Mathilda's search for her father; the portentous setting for doomed humanity in *The Last Man*. . . . (p. 193)

Mary's style had considerable range. It is at its most elaborate in *The Last Man.* Here she uses the romantic poetic devices of alliteration and assonance, echo and repetition, question and apostrophe to heighten the mood. "Who was there indeed to save? What troop had we brought fit to stand at bay, and combat with the conqueror? We were a failing remnant, tamed to mere submission to the coming blow. A train half dead, through fear of death. . . . Like a few furrows of unreaped corn. . . . Like a few straggling swallows. . . . Like a stray sheep. . . . Like a cloud. . . . Such were we." The threnody of coming destruction and solitude mounts as the novel draws to its emotional close: "Thus around the shores of deserted earth, while the sun is high, and the moon waxes or wanes, angels, the spirits of the dead, and the ever-open eye of the Supreme, will behold the tiny bark, freighted with Verney—the LAST MAN."

Mary could also write simply and directly.

> Early, therefore, on Monday, August 8th, Sxxx and Cxxx went to the ass market, and purchased an ass, and the rest of the day, until four in the afternoon, was spent in preparations for our departure. . . . Packing up a few necessaries, leaving the rest to go by diligence, we departed in a fiacre from the door of the hotel, our little ass following.
>
> (p. 194)

This account, "unpresuming," as Mary calls it in her preface, gives a bright, clear picture of the "six weeks' tour" of the three light-hearted young runaways. It can be matched by direct and simple writing in the narrative of her travels with her son and his friends nearly thirty years later. (p. 195)

There is little reward for a reader of Mary Shelley's poems. . . . Her [verse] was not unmusical—she had a sense of rhythm and harmony. But except for an occasional phrase or line—

> The bride of Time no more, I wed Eternity—
>
> She is immortal—yet unusual fear
> Runs through my veins—

the diction is obvious, commonplace, imitative and sentimental.

Against her work as a whole so harsh a charge cannot be brought. Although the general reader would hardly care to peruse Mary Shelley's works, yet there is reward for so doing. There are familiar people to be met again, disguised and perhaps distorted, but always seen, however myopically, through the eyes of Shelley's wife. There are lesser persons, new and interesting, flashing momentarily from the pages. There are tales of power and scenes of horror to take permanent hold on the imagination. There are landscapes of beauty and of association to remain in the memory. There is writing to be admired—lucid and moving. . . . There is the woman herself, to be seen in a fuller, truer light than that cast upon her by the words of worshippers or detractors or even by her own letters and journals. It is a woman neither angel nor devil, full of faults, full of merits: brave in spite of her self-pity, liberal in her views in spite of her compromises with society, endowed with intellectual powers that command respect in spite of their limitations and with imagination capable of creative achievement in spite of her later taming of it to meet the taste of the reading public. There is in all her work, however dulled and diluted, the young author of *Frankenstein*. (pp. 199-200)

> *Elizabeth Nitchie, in her* Mary Shelley: Author of "Frankenstein", *Rutgers University Press, 1953, 255 p.*

M. A. GOLDBERG (essay date 1959)

[*Goldberg's investigation of the themes of isolation and knowledge in* Frankenstein *is considered one of the first comprehensive assessments of the novel and a milestone in* Frankenstein *studies.*]

In the central pages of Mary Shelley's *Frankenstein or, The Modern Prometheus* the reader encounters for some six chapters a personal narrative of the monster. For the first time since his creation, he is approaching his maker who sits sad and pensive near the awful majesty of Mont Blanc. Conscious of his "duties as a creator towards his creature," Frankenstein agrees to listen to the tale of this blighted being who has developed from a *tabula rasa,* experiencing in true Lockean fashion first confused, then distinct sensations, and developing in turn social affections, then moral and intellectual judgments. Crucial to his learning, we discover, has been a leather portmanteau, found one day in the forest where he has hidden himself from the eyes of mankind, and in which are contained, together with some articles of dress, a volume of Plutarch's *Lives,* the *Sorrows of Werter,* and Milton's *Paradise Lost.* The latter, he explains, has had a most profound effect upon him:

> I read it [*Paradise Lost*], as I had read the other volumes which had fallen into my hands, as a true history. . . . I often referred the several situations, as their similarity struck me, to my own. Like Adam, I was apparently united by no link to any other being in existence; but his state was far different from mine in every other respect. He had come forth from the hands of God a perfect creature, happy and prosperous, guarded by the especial care of his Creator; he was allowed to converse with, and acquire knowledge from, beings of a superior nature: but I was wretched, helpless, and alone. Many times I considered Satan as the fitter emblem of my condition; for often, like him, when I viewed the bliss of my protectors, the bitter gall of envy rose within me.

This is no idle image which the creature evokes here, comparing his own situation with Satan's, and with Adam's paradisaic state in Eden. The confusion apparent in his own consciousness—whether he is an Adam, destined ultimately for eternal grace, or a Satan, doomed to eternal darkness—is a motif crucial to the entire novel. It is crucial to the monster's tale, embedded as the innermost circle of the text. It is crucial to Frankenstein's narrative, which, unfolded to Captain Walton, encircles the monster's tale like the middle ring of a vast inferno. And it is crucial to Walton's letters, which hover about

the outermost fringes of these depths. Indeed, these three circles—their relationship to one another and to the Miltonic motif—form the basic structure of the novel, a structure from which Mrs. Shelley has spun a moral web, with consistency and with precision. (pp. 27-8)

To examine [*Frankenstein*] for the terror it evokes, without perceiving its relationship to the moral context of early nineteenth-century England, is, in reality, to distort the essence of the tale.

We encounter the first indications of this moral context in the letters of Captain Walton, who has been inspired since early youth to satiate an ardent curiosity about the unknown regions of the earth. . . .

One major failing seems to threaten Walton's relentless pursuit: the lack of compassionate society, "intimate sympathy with a fellow mind." Significantly, Walton regards this want as "a most severe evil" and he readily acknowledges that "a man could boast of little happiness, who did not enjoy this blessing."

Once he encounters Victor Frankenstein amid the ice floes of the north, this conflict—between his thirst for knowledge which increasingly carries him away from society and a thirst for social love which is frustrated by this pursuit of knowledge—appears happily reconciled. His newly-found friend reminds him, however, "You seek for knowledge and wisdom, as I once did," and hopes that Walton's temptation "may not be a serpent to sting you, as mine has been." In order that Walton might "deduce an apt moral" from his own experience, Frankenstein consents to disclose the secret of his life.

Frankenstein's tale, forming the middle circle of the novel, is clearly intended, then, as an *exemplum,* aimed at weaning the captain from his obsession. Just as Walton's opening letters sound this didactic note, so do his closing epistles. "Learn my miseries, and do not seek to increase your own," Walton is cautioned at the close of Frankenstein's narrative, just as he has been previously warned: "Learn from me, if not from my precepts, at least by my example, how dangerous is the acquirement of knowledge." (p. 29)

An examination of Frankenstein's central narrative reveals that this opening motif, the temptation of knowledge and the punishment of estrangement, is echoed with consistency and clarity.

From the beginning Frankenstein is "deeply smitten with the thirst for knowledge." He too is tempted by the forbidden fruit, and his earliest sensations are "curiosity, earnest research to learn the hidden laws of nature." For him "the world was . . . a secret which I desired to divine," and even in his youth his "inquiries were directed to the metaphysical, or, in its highest sense, the physical secrets of the world." (p. 30)

Like Prometheus—whom Apollodorus describes as having first created man out of clay, then instilled into his bosom a sacred spark of fire, stolen from the heavens—Frankenstein, his nineteenth-century disciple, succeeds in infusing "a spark of being into the lifeless being" that lies before him in his laboratory. . . . What is glory for the omnipotent deity of *Genesis* or the Babylonian god Bel, for the Egyptian father-of-gods Khnoumou or the Australian creator Pund-jel, is for lesser gods, like Frankenstein, the "modern Prometheus," a crime. The apple of knowledge bears within it the acrid seeds of punishment. As with Satan and Beëlzebub, this passion to

Colin Clive as Dr. Frankenstein in James Whale's 1931 film. The Granger Collection, New York.

usurp divine prerogatives casts the new creator into a burning cauldron of his own making. (pp. 30-1)

Like Coleridge's guilt-ridden mariner, Frankenstein has a deadly weight hanging round his neck, bowing him to the ground. . . . His father had wished him "to seek amusement in society [but] I abhorred the face of man," Frankenstein admits. "I felt that I had no right to share their intercourse." Now, he reveals only the "desire to avoid society" and fly "to solitude, from the society of every creature." . . . He is "immersed in solitude," for he perceives "an insurmountable barrier" between him and his fellow-man. "I felt as if I had committed some great crime, the consciousness of which haunted me. I was guiltless, but I had indeed drawn down a horrible curse upon my head, as mortal as that of crime," . . . he confesses. Though his inner being longs for the compassion and sympathy that society affords, his guilt has already driven him out of love's garden. He dares not even whisper "paradisaical dreams of love and joy" to Elizabeth, for, as he readily concedes, "the apple was already eaten, and the angel's arm bared to drive me from all hope." . . . (pp. 31-2)

[In] his final hours of life, he confesses to Robert Walton the sin he shares with Milton's archangel:

> All my speculations and hopes are as nothing; and, like the archangel who aspired to omni-

potence, I am chained in an eternal hell. . . . I conceived the idea and executed the creation of a man. Even now I cannot recollect without passion my reveries while the work was incomplete. I trod heaven in my thoughts, now exulting in my powers, now burning with the idea of their effects. From my infancy I was imbued with high hopes and a lofty ambition; but how am I sunk! . . .

(p. 32)

Although parallels between the temptations of Frankenstein or Walton and those of Adam or Satan are clearly delineated, it would be a grave distortion to force the analogy without noting pertinent differences. Milton's is a seventeenth-century reinterpretation of the Fall described by the Jehovistic writer of *Genesis;* but Milton's narrative also parallels to no small degree the Hellenic myth of Prometheus who having usurped the powers of the higher gods, is alienated forever from both men and gods, and chained to the frozen top of the Caucasus. This is an allusion of which Mrs. Shelley was certainly conscious, since she refers to Frankenstein as a "Modern Prometheus" in her sub-title. Also, Shelley himself was obviously aware of the structural similarity between Milton's narrative and the Greek myth, for in his preface to *Prometheus Unbound* he remarks that "the only imaginary being resembling in any degree Prometheus, is Satan." Parallels for Mrs. Shelley's handling of the guilt-theme, however, can also be found in Dostoyevsky and Kafka, or in Jung who suggests that "every step towards greater consciousness is a kind of Promethean guilt: through knowledge, the gods are as it were robbed of their fire, that is, something that was the property of the unconscious powers is torn out of its natural context and subordinated to the whims of the conscious mind."

But Frankenstein's guilt is not the psychological and mystic soul-searching of Kafka or Dostoyevsky, just as it is never completely the crime of *hubris* manifested in Aeschylus or the failure to recognize derivation which we discern in Milton. Frankenstein's crime, like Walton's, is social. Both sin against society. In syncretizing the Miltonic and Promethean motif Mrs. Shelley has clearly translated her materials into early nineteenth-century terms, just as Keats revised the myth of Endymion, and as Shelley transformed the story of Prometheus within his own contemporary framework.

Walton and Frankenstein both sin, not against self or God, but against the moral and social order. Though both begin their pursuit with benevolent intentions, each discovers his error in assuming that knowledge is a higher good than love or sympathy, and that it can be independent of the fellow-feeling afforded by a compassionate society. As a result, what had appeared initially as a benevolent intention becomes in the final analysis misguided pride, a selfish pursuit aimed at self-glory, because it evades the fulfillment of higher duties toward the social community, the brotherhood of man which forms the highest good. Understandably, then, Mrs. Shelley's book is paralleled most significantly, not by Aeschylus or Milton, but by her own contemporaries. In Byron's *Manfred,* for example, an analogous "quest of hidden knowledge" leads the hero increasingly toward a "solitude . . . peopled with the Furies." Manfred's avowed flaw ("though I wore the form, / I had no sympathy with breathing flesh") rises from the same ethical assumptions implicit in the guilt-ridden consciousness of Victor Frankenstein. Similarly, Shelley's prefatory remarks on *Alastor or, The Spirit of Solitude* indicate that "the Poet's self-centred seclusion was avenged by the furies of an irresistible passion pursuing him to speedy ruin." Shelley's supposition, that "the intellectual faculties, the imagination, the functions of sense, have their respective requisitions on the sympathy of corresponding powers in other human beings," is obviously engendered from the same general principle which has ordered the materials of *Frankenstein.*

Mrs. Shelley offers in her novel—as does Byron in *Manfred* and Shelley in *Alastor*—a theme which is clearly in the tradition of Cudworth and Price, the seventeenth-century Platonists. This is a conception inherited in the eighteenth century by Shaftesbury and Hutcheson; later, by the Scottish Common-Sense School, as represented by Adam Smith; and finally by William Godwin, who had assumed as basic to his doctrine of political justice that virtue is essentially social. Insistent that reason and free will, as developed in an enlightened society, would naturally result in the subordination of individual pleasures for the good of society as a whole, Godwin set himself in opposition to La Rochefoucauld, Hobbes, and Mandeville, for whom man was basically selfish and non-social, and to Rousseau, who had seen society as a force destructive to natural benevolence. "No being can be either virtuous, or vicious, who has no opportunity of influencing the happiness of others," Godwin had contended in his *Enquiry concerning Political Justice,* insistent that "the true solitaire cannot be considered as a moral being.... His conduct is vicious, because it has a tendency to render him miserable." Explaining that "virtue consists in a desire of the happiness of the species.... It must begin with a collective idea of the human species," Godwin argues that true knowledge is also dependent upon the social structure. "Even knowledge, and the enlargement of intellect, are poor, when unmixed with sentiments of benevolence and sympathy," he points out; "... and science and abstraction will soon become cold, unless they derive new attractions from ideas of society."

Similarly, Thomas Paine develops the relationship between happiness and social virtues in *The Rights of Man.* Since nature created man for social life, Paine writes, "no one man is capable, without the aid of society, of supplying his own wants; and those wants, acting upon every individual, impel the whole of them into society, as naturally as gravitation acts to a centre." Nature has gone even further than this, Paine continues. "She has implanted in him a system of social affections, which, though not necessary to his existence, are essential to his happiness. There is no period in life when this love of society ceases to act. It begins and ends with our being." (pp. 32-4)

Through Mrs. Shelley's journal entries we know that during 1816-1817, when *Frankenstein* was conceived, she and Shelley discussed the work many times. We know, too, through the *Journal,* that in these years she and Shelley both read Milton's *Paradise Lost,* and that Shelley was immersed at this same time in Godwin's *Political Justice* and Paine's *The Rights of Man,* as well as in the *Prometheus Bound* of Aeschylus. I do not mean to imply that Mary Shelley borrowed her social and moral conceptions from Paine, or from Shelley or Godwin, then deliberately embodied them within her mythological framework. It is perfectly understandable that she shared the social thought of her father and her husband, and that she wove these ideas, which were shared also by many of the enlightened English public during those decades, into an esthetic pattern of her own making.

The consistency of her social and moral theme is certainly nowhere more apparent than in the narrative of the monster, whose experience forms an essential parallel with that of Frankenstein and Walton. Like the latter, whose original intentions were directed at benevolence and sympathy, the creature initially bears the seeds of virtue. The sympathies of Walton and Frankenstein have been rendered torpid by their monomaniacal pursuit of knowledge which removes them increasingly from a compassionate society; similarly, the creature discovers that his sympathies are perpetually blunted by the misery of loneliness and isolation, estranged as he must be from human kind. At first, he views "crime as a distant evil; benevolence and generosity were ever present" in the persons of the DeLaceys, behind whose cottage he has hidden. "My heart yearned to be known and loved by these amiable creatures: to see their sweet looks directed towards me with affection was the utmost limit of my ambition," he confesses. His readings only reinforce this natural propensity for social love, so that before long he feels "the greatest ardour for virtue ... and abhorrence for vice." ... (pp. 35-6)

Like his maker, and like Captain Walton, the creature soon comes to realize that "sorrow only increased with knowledge," ... for the more he learns about the nature of good and its dependence upon social intercourse, the more he recognizes the impossibility of immersing himself in it. ...

Alternating between the role of Adam and Satan, hoping he might still be lifted to the glories of love and sympathy, but fearing that he might be forced into the depths of malevolence and depravity because of his isolation, the creature soon finds his fate determined, once the DeLaceys reject his friendly advances, just as all mankind has rejected him beforehand. "From that moment I declared everlasting war against the species," he admits. "I, like the arch-fiend, bore a hell within me; and, finding myself unsympathized with, wished to ... spread havoc and destruction." ... Natural proclivities toward virtue compel the creature to approach his maker and urge him to create a mate "with whom I can live in the interchange of those sympathies necessary for my being. ... I am malicious because I am miserable," he explains, as he begs for the happiness which is his right. "Let me feel gratitude towards you for one benefit! Let me see that I excite the sympathy of some existing thing; do not deny me my request." ... With an understanding strikingly analogous to that revealed in Godwin, Shelley, Byron, and Paine, the monster describes his moral state:

> If I have no ties and no affections, hatred and vice must be my portion; the love of another will destroy the cause of my crimes, and I shall become a thing of whose existence every one will be ignorant. My vices are the children of a forced solitude that I abhor; and my virtues will necessarily arise when I live in communion with an equal. I shall feel the affections of a sensitive being, and become linked to the chain of existence and events, from which I am now excluded.
>
> (p. 36)

In an 1817 review which has generally been ignored [see excerpt above], Shelley draws some interesting parallels between Godwin's *Caleb Williams* and *Frankenstein,* and summarizes thematic development in Mary Shelley's book with penetrating incisiveness:

> ... The crimes and malevolence of the single Being, though indeed withering and tremendous, [are not] the offspring of any unaccount-

able propensity to evil, but flow irresistibly from certain causes fully adequate to their production. They are the children, as it were, of Necessity and Human Nature. In this the direct moral of the book consists. . . . Treat a person ill, and he will become wicked. Requite affection with scorn;—let one being be selected, for whatever cause, as the refuse of his kind—divide him, a social being, from society, and you impose upon him the irresistible obligations—malevolence and selfishness. It is thus that, too often in society, those who are best qualified to be its benefactors and its ornaments, are branded by some accident with scorn, and changed, by neglect and solitude of heart, into a scourge and a curse.

The distinction which Shelley draws here between an "unaccountable propensity to evil" and that necessitated by external social forces which isolate the individual, thus causing selfishness and malevolence, points indeed to the "direct moral of the book." Although a recent biographer [Elizabeth Nitchie; see excerpt dated 1953], noting this theme of estrangement throughout Mrs. Shelley's novels, interprets this as the author's "symbol of her own loneliness," it is apparent in any close examination of the text that "loneliness" assumes its fullest meaning relative only to the social and moral context of early nineteenth-century England. This is the context of Godwin and Paine, as well as Byron and Shelley, and certainly the context of the woman who came to be known as "the author of *Frankenstein*." (pp. 37-8)

> *M. A. Goldberg, "Moral and Myth in Mrs. Shelley's 'Frankenstein'," in* Keats-Shelley Journal, *Vol. 8, Winter, 1959, pp. 27-38.*

KINGSLEY AMIS   (essay date 1960)

[*A distinguished English novelist, poet, essayist, and editor, Amis is also the author of* New Maps in Hell, *one of the first major critical surveys of science fiction. In the following brief consideration of* Frankenstein *as a precursor of that genre, Amis identifies three popular science fiction themes that Shelley initiated in the novel. Amis's remarks were first published in* New Maps in Hell *in 1960.*]

[With] one large exception, [the Gothic novel and its successors], while all-important in the ancestry of modern fantasy, scarcely prefigure science fiction. The exception can hardly help being *Frankenstein*, which, albeit in a distorted form, has had a posthumous career of unparalleled vigour; even old Dracula has less often been exhumed in cinematic form and has never been mated or allowed to re-galvanise himself. (I had better explain at this point that the contemporary trade-term applying to the monster is "android," a synthetic being roughly resembling a man, as opposed to a robot, which is a mere peripatetic machine.) The notable thing about Frankenstein the character is that, far from being possessed of supernatural powers, he is a physiologist with academic training, a feature he has retained in his modern incarnations, while altogether losing the sentimental Shelleyan quality that marked his original appearance. Frankenstein, in the popular mind, when not confused with his monster, is easily the most outstanding representative of the generic mad scientist who plagued bad early-modern science fiction and has now been fined down into the better-adjusted but still unsociable and eccentric scientist who, often with a Miranda-like daughter-secretary in attendance,

continues to head an occasional research project and figure in the hero's thoughts as the Old Man. More important science-fiction themes than this, however, have radiated from the original book. It is true that, as L. Sprague de Camp observes [see Additional Bibliography], "all the shambling horde of modern robots and androids are descendants of Frankenstein's sadly malevolent monster," but beyond this lies the whole notion of the artificial creation which turns and rends its master. Capek's *R. U. R.* (1920) was perhaps the first modern treatment of this notion, which still regularly reappears, a recent instance being Robert Sheckley's story "Watchbird." Here an airborne device, programmed to detect and forestall aggressive intentions, ends by prohibiting most kinds of human action. This idea generalises into innumerable fictionalised sermons on the dangers of overgrown technology. . . . Before leaving *Frankenstein*, it is worth observing that a third aspect of the scientific character descends from it, that of the morally irresponsible researcher indifferent to the damage he may cause or render possible, a kind of person consciously described by Wells in *The Island of Dr. Moreau*, where animals are vivisected in an attempt to humanise them, and to all appearance unconsciously in *The Food of the Gods*, where Herakleophorbia IV, the growth-inducing compound, is thrown on to the rubbish dump and swilled down the drains and generally scattered over the countryside in a fantastically light-hearted spirit. (pp. 255-56)

> *Kingsley Amis, "Starting Points," in* Science Fiction: The Future, *edited by Dick Allen, Harcourt Brace Jovanovich, Inc., 1971, pp. 245-62.*

HAROLD BLOOM   (essay date 1965)

[*Bloom, an American critic and editor, is best known as the formulator of "revisionism," a controversial theory of literary creation based on the concept that all poets are subject to the influence of earlier poets, and that to develop their own voices, they attempt to overcome this influence through a deliberate process of "creative correction," which Bloom calls "misreading." His theories are largely based on his readings of English poetry from the Romantic period to the present. In his influential study of* Frankenstein, *excerpted below, Bloom focuses on solipsism and Prometheanism in the work, which he regards as an extreme example of "the Romantic mythology of the self."*]

The motion picture viewer who carries his obscure but still authentic taste for the sublime to the neighborhood theater, there to see the latest in an unending series of *Frankensteins*, participates in a Romantic terror now nearly one hundred and fifty years old. The terror is a familiar and a pleasing one, and few figures in contemporary mythology are as universally loved as Frankenstein's once pathetic monster, now a star beaconing from the abode of television, comic strips and the sweatshirts of the young.

"Frankenstein," to most of us, is the name of a monster rather than of a monster's creator, for the common reader and the common viewer have worked together, in their apparent confusion, to create a myth soundly based on a central duality in Mary Shelley's novel. As Richard Church [see Additional Bibliography] and Muriel Spark [see excerpt dated 1951] were the first to record, the monster and his creator are the antithetical halves of a single being. Miss Spark states the antithesis too cleanly; for her, Victor Frankenstein represents the feelings, and his nameless creature the intellect. In her view, the monster has no emotion, and "what passes for emotion . . . are really intellectual passions arrived at through rational channels." Miss Spark carries this argument far enough to insist that the monster is asexual, and that he demands a bride from Frankenstein only for companionship, a conclusion evidently at variance with the novel's text.

The antithesis between the scientist and his creature in Frankenstein is a very complex one, and to be described more fully it must be placed in the larger context of Romantic literature and its characteristic mythology. The shadow or double of the self is a constant conceptual image in Blake and Shelley, and a frequent image, more random and descriptive, in the other major Romantics, especially in Byron. In *Frankenstein,* it is the dominant and recurrent image, and accounts for much of the latent power the novel possesses. (pp. 611-12)

No Romantic writer employed the Prometheus archetype without a full awareness of its equivocal potentialities. The Prometheus of the ancients had been for the most part a spiritually reprehensible figure, though frequently a sympathetic one, both in terms of his dramatic situation and in his close alliance with mankind against the gods. But this alliance had been ruinous for man, in most versions of the myth, and the Titan's benevolence toward humanity was hardly sufficient recompense for the alienation of man from heaven that he had brought about. Both sides of Titanism are evident in earlier Christian references to the story. The same Prometheus who is taken as an analogue of the crucified Christ is regarded also as a type of Lucifer, a son of light justly cast out by an offended heaven.

In the Romantic readings of Milton's *Paradise Lost* (and *Frankenstein* is implicitly one such reading), this double identity of Prometheus is a vital element. Blake, whose mythic revolutionary named Orc is another version of Prometheus, saw Milton's Satan as a Prometheus gone wrong, as desire restrained until it became only the shadow of desire, a diminished double of creative energy. Shelley went further in judging Milton's Satan as an imperfect Prometheus, inadequate because his mixture of heroic and base qualities engendered in the reader's mind a "pernicious casuistry" inimical to the spirit of art.

Blake, more systematic a poet than Shelley, worked out an antithesis between symbolic figures he named Spectre and Emanation, the shadow of desire and the total form of desire, respectively. A reader of *Frankenstein,* recalling the novel's extraordinary conclusion with its scenes of obsessional pursuit through the Arctic wastes, can recognize the same imagery applied to a similar symbolic situation in Blake's lyric on the strife of Spectre and Emanation:

> My Spectre around me night and day
> Like a Wild beast guards my way
> My Emanation far within
> Weeps incessantly for my Sin.
>
> A Fathomless and boundless deep,
> There we wander, there we weep;
> On the hungry craving wind
> My Spectre follows thee behind.
>
> He scents thy footsteps in the snow,
> Wheresoever thou dost go
> Thro' the wintry hail and rain . . .

Frankenstein's monster, tempting his revengeful creator on through a world of ice, is another Emanation pursued by a Spectre, with the enormous difference that he is an Emanation flawed, a nightmare of actuality, rather than a dream of desire.

Though abhorred rather than loved, the monster is the total form of Frankenstein's creative power, and is *more imaginative* than his creator. The monster is at once more intellectual *and* more emotional than his maker, indeed he excels Frankenstein as much (and in the same ways) as Milton's Adam excels Milton's God in *Paradise Lost*. The greatest paradox, and most astonishing achievement, of Mary Shelley's novel is that the monster is *more human* than his creator. This nameless being, as much a Modern Adam as his creator is a Modern Prometheus, is more lovable than his creator and more hateful, more to be pitied and more to be feared, and above all more able to give the attentive reader that shock of added consciousness which compels a heightened realization of the self. For, like Blake's Spectre and Emanation, or Shelley's Alastor and Epipsyche, Frankenstein and his monster are the solipsistic and generous halves of the one self. Frankenstein is the mind and emotions turned in upon themselves, and his creature is the mind and emotions turned imaginatively outward, seeking a greater humanization through a confrontation of other selves.

I am suggesting that what makes *Frankenstein* an important book, though it is only a strong, flawed, frequently clumsy novel is that it vividly projects a version of the Romantic mythology of the self, found, among other places, in Blake's *Book of Urizen*, Shelley's *Prometheus Unbound* and Byron's *Manfred*. It lacks the sophistication and imaginative complexity of such works but precisely because of that *Frankenstein* affords a unique introduction to the archetypal world of the Romantics. (pp. 612-13)

There are two paradoxes at the center of Mrs. Shelley's novel, and each illuminates a dilemma of the Promethean imagination. The first is that Frankenstein *was* successful: he *did* create Natural Man, not as he was, but as the meliorists saw him. Indeed, Frankenstein did better than this, since his creature was more imaginative even than himself. Frankenstein's tragedy stems, not from his Promethean excess, but from his own moral error, his failure to love. He *abhorred his creature,* became terrified of it, and fled his responsibilities.

The second paradox is the more ironic. This disaster either would not have happened, or would not have mattered anyway, if Frankenstein had been an esthetically successful maker; a beautiful "monster," or even a passable one, would not have been a monster. The creature himself bitterly observes:

> Shall I respect man when he contemns me? Let
> him live with me in the interchange of kindness;
> and, instead of injury, I would bestow every
> benefit upon him with tears of gratitude at his
> acceptance. But that cannot be; the human senses are insurmountable barriers to our union.

As the sensuous horror of his creature was no part of Victor Frankenstein's intention, it is worth noticing how this came about. It would not be unjust to characterize Victor Frankenstein, in his act of creation, as being momentarily a moral idiot. There is an indeliberate humor, to which readers since 1945 are doubtless more sensitive than earlier ones, in the contrast between the enormity of the scientist's discovery, and the mundane emotions of the discoverer. Finding that "the minuteness of the parts" slows him down, he resolves to make his creature "about eight feet in height, and proportionably large." As he works on, he allows himself to dream that "a new species would bless me as its creator and source; many happy and excellent natures would owe their being to me." Yet he knows his is a "workshop of filthy creation," and he fails the fundamental test of his own creativity. When the "dull yellow eye" of his creature opens, this creator falls from the autonomy of a supreme artificer to the terror of a child of earth: "breathless horror and disgust filled my heart." He flees his responsibility, and sets in motion the events that will lead to his own Arctic immolation, a fit end for a being (rather like Lawrence's Gerald in *Women in Love*) who has never achieved a full sense of another's existence.

It is part of Mary Shelley's insight into her mythological theme that all the monster's victims are innocents. The monster not only refuses actively to slay his guilty creator; he *mourns* for him, though with the equivocal tribute of terming the scientist a "generous and self-devoted being." Frankenstein, the Modern Prometheus who has violated nature, receives his epitaph from the ruined second nature he has made, the God-abandoned, who consciously echoes the ruined Satan of *Paradise Lost,* and proclaims "Evil thenceforth became my good." It is imaginatively fitting that the greater and more interesting consciousness of the creature should survive his creator, for he alone in Mrs. Shelley's novel possesses character. Frankenstein, like Coleridge's Ancient Mariner, has no character in his own right; both figures win a claim to our attention only by their primordial crimes against original nature.

The monster is of course Mary Shelley's finest invention, and his narrative (Chapters XI through XVI) forms the highest achievement of the novel, more absorbing even than the magnificent and almost surrealistic pursuit of the climax. In an age so given to remarkable depictions of the dignity of natural man, an age including the shepherds and beggars of Wordsworth, Frankenstein's hapless creature stands out as a sublime embodiment of heroic pathos. Though Frankenstein lacks the moral imagination to understand him, the daemon's appeal is to what is most compassionate in us:

> "Oh, Frankenstein, be not equitable to every other, and trample upon me alone, to whom thy justice, and even thy clemency and affection, is most due. Remember, that I am thy creature; *I ought to be thy Adam; but I am rather the fallen angel, whom thou drivest from joy for no misdeed.* Everywhere I see bliss, from which I alone am irrevocably excluded. I was benevolent and good; misery made me a fiend. Make me happy, and I shall again be virtuous."

The passage I have italicized is the imaginative kernel of the novel, a reminder of the novel's epigraph:

> Did I request thee, Maker, from my clay
> To mould me man? Did I solicit thee
> From darkness to promote me?
> —*Paradise Lost,* Book X, 743-5

That desperate plangency of the fallen Adam becomes the characteristic accent of the daemon's lamentations, with the influence of Milton cunningly built into the novel's narrative by the happy device of Frankenstein's creature receiving his education through reading *Paradise Lost* "as a true history." Already doomed because his standards are human, which makes him an outcast even to himself, his Miltonic education completes his fatal growth in self-consciousness. (pp. 614-16)

If we stand back from Mary Shelley's novel, in order better to view its archetypal shape, we see it as the quest of a solitary and ravaged consciousness first for consolation, then for revenge, and finally for a self-destruction that will be apocalyp-

tic, that will bring down the creator with his creature. Though Mary Shelley may not have intended it, her novel's prime theme is a necessary counterpoise to Prometheanism, for Prometheanism exalts the increase in consciousness despite all cost. Frankenstein breaks through the barrier that separates man from God, and apparently becomes the giver of life, but all he actually can give is death-in-life. The profound dejection endemic in Mary Shelley's novel is fundamental to the Romantic mythology of the self, for all Romantic horrors are diseases of excessive consciousness, of the self unable to bear the self. Kierkegaard remarks that Satan's despair is absolute, because Satan as pure spirit is pure consciousness, and for Satan (and all men in his predicament) every increase in consciousness is an increase in despair. Frankenstein's desperate creature attains the state of pure spirit through his extraordinary situation, and is racked by a consciousness in which every thought is a fresh disease.

A Romantic poet fought against self-consciousness through the strength of what he called imagination, a more than rational energy, by which thought could seek to heal itself. But Frankenstein's daemon, though he is in the archetypal situation of the Romantic Wanderer or Solitary, who sometimes was a poet, can win no release from his own story by telling it. His desperate desire for a mate is clearly an attempt to find a Shelleyan Epipsyche or Blakean Emanation for himself, a self within the self. But as he is the nightmare actualization of Frankenstein's desire, he is himself an emanation of Promethean yearnings, and his only double is his creator and denier.

When Coleridge's Ancient Mariner progressed from the purgatory of consciousness to his very minimal control of imagination, he failed to save himself. He remained in a cycle of remorse. But he at least became a salutary warning to others, and made of the Wedding Guest a wiser and a better man. Frankenstein's creature can help neither himself nor others, for he has no natural ground to which he can return. Romantic poets liked to return to the imagery of the ocean of life and immortality; in the eddying to and fro of the healing waters they could picture a hoped-for process of restoration, of a survival of consciousness despite all its agonies. Mary Shelley, with marvelous appropriateness, brings her Romantic novel to a demonic conclusion in a world of ice. The frozen sea is the inevitable emblem for both the wretched daemon and his obsessed creator, but the daemon is allowed a final image of reversed Prometheanism. There is a heroism fully earned in the being who cries farewell in a claim of sad triumph: "I shall ascend my funeral pyre triumphantly, and exult in the agony of the torturing flames." (pp. 617-18)

There is something both Godwinian and Shelleyan about the final utterance of Victor Frankenstein, which is properly made to Walton, the failed Promethean, whose ship has just turned back. Though chastened, the Modern Prometheus ends with a last word true, not to his accomplishment, but to his desire:

> "Farewell, Walton! Seek happiness in tranquility and avoid ambition, even if it be only the apparently innocent one of distinguishing yourself in science and discoveries. Yet why do I say this? I have myself been blasted in these hopes, yet another may succeed."

Shelley's Prometheus, crucified on his icy precipice, found his ultimate torment in a Fury's taunt: "And all best things are thus confused to ill." It seems a fitting summation for all the work done by Modern Prometheanism, and might have served

Boris Karloff in his third portrayal of Frankenstein's monster, from the 1939 film Son of Frankenstein. *Forrest J. Ackerman Sci-Fi CinemArchives, Hollywood.*

as an alternate epigraph for Mary Shelley's disturbing novel. (p. 618)

> Harold Bloom, "Frankenstein; or, The New Prometheus," in Partisan Review, *Vol. XXXII, No. 4, Fall, 1965, pp. 611-18.*

STEPHEN CRAFTS (essay date 1967)

[*Crafts bases his explication of* Frankenstein's *monster on the theory of "one-dimensional" man set forth by Herbert Marcuse, the contemporary German-American philosopher. Crafts asserts that the creature's dilemma foreshadows that of modern humanity.*]

Today the figure of Frankenstein has been relegated to the camp late show and plastic models for children. This phenomenon indicates that the original prophecy of one-dimensionality by Mary Shelley's novel has been largely subsumed in the increasing totality of advanced industrial society. Hence the irony of **Frankenstein**'s contemporary reception: Mary Shelley's very accuracy has prophesied the agent of its present neglect as social commentary. A further irony lies in the common confusion of the creator and the creature, for it was Victor Frankenstein who created a monster. The figure of horror has

been projected by man to a product, a process repeated from the novel. It is Frankenstein who deserts his monster and thus brings about the rampage which has become synonomous with the figure of the monster. A similar tendency exists today in the one-dimensional bias to distinguish between subject and object in such a way that "value-free inquiry" establishes evasion of responsibility as technological *modus operandi*. The same mentality fails to take seriously those works of social criticism, like **Frankenstein,** which do not seem objective or one-dimensionally real.

The term "one-dimensional" owes its origins to the common empirical data of social totality considered by Herbert Marcuse in his definitive work, *One-Dimensional Man.* I intend to use Marcuse's term in a limited sense as the conclusion of a process within industrial societies to stifle human sensibility within the all-inclusive context of abstraction. The distinction made by Herbert Read will prove helpful in defining the issue:

> Intellect begins with the observation of nature, proceeds to memorize and classify the facts thus observed, and by logical deduction builds up that edifice of knowledge properly called science. Sensibility, on the other hand, is a direct and particular reaction to the separate and individual nature of things.

In **Frankenstein,** Mary Shelley explores metaphorically the usurpation of sensibility by intellect and the concomitant human relationships the perversion produces. The berserk actions of Frankenstein's monster are not those of an inherently evil creature but the desperate gropings of a sensitive being attempting to assert a form of humanity following its objectification within a technological context. The cliché concerning atomic energy—that it can be used for either good or evil—however true, rests upon the assumption that we have at our disposal the critical sensibility to know which is which. Read again defines the issue:

> . . . to neglect the senses, either through ignorance of their epistemological significance, or from mere puritanical prejudice is to neglect one half of our being.

Yet in the act of creating his monster, Frankenstein extirpates a good part of his existence by avowing the technological reality of one-dimensionality. Marcuse has described this reality as follows:

> As a technological universe, advanced industrial society is a *political* universe, the latest stage in the realization of a specific historical *project*—namely, the experience, transformation, and organization of nature as the mere stuff of domination.

Domination of nature in its entirety is the professed project of Frankenstein, a latterday Faust. He defines reality for his creature and thus makes of him an object of oppression. It is the monster's reactions to his situation which form the basis of the book, for one-dimensionality reworks the grotesque as reality in its brutalization of the objectified oppressed. Rather than hunt down Frankenstein's monster today, we would be more likely to rehabilitate him for life in the "real world" or pacify him in furthering the aims of *pax americana*.

Another indication of the totalism which the book predicts lies in the unintentional tendency of Mrs. Shelley to abet one-dimensionality in a form of cultural imperialism: the perpetuation of the romantic myth of the Noble Savage. In this process, the objectification of human beings forms a social mentality which "kills with kindness." That is, the social frame of reference becomes so pervasive as to even order attempts to create meaningful human relationships. Thus, in creating an ideal state of being as embodied by the Noble Savage, Mary Shelley has, with good intention, perpetuated the suppression of humanity which makes Frankenstein's monster "an object for the scorn and horror of mankind." The psychic tendency to project one's own inadequacies, fantasies, etc. upon another finds its perfect example in the objectification of Frankenstein's monster. On the one hand, he becomes the technologist's projection of the horror of his own atrocity; on the other, the monster furnishes a nostalgic urge to innocence as a Noble Savage figure. In either case the monster has been objectified. The totality of one-dimensional thought thus places the burden of asserting humanity upon the technologically oppressed: it is only the oppressed who can reject the definition of reality placed upon them as objects through active rebellion. The monster's attempt to assert his humanity finds a remarkable contemporary counterpart in the Third World movement.

Frankenstein is subtitled "The Modern Prometheus" and thus involves romantic mythology, which need not concern us here beyond a consideration of Frankenstein as a Faust figure. In literature, Faust represents the ambiguity of knowledge. He is a later manifestation of Prometheus, who extended man's dominion over nature. Faust seeks to extend that dominion further and yet concomitantly brings man closer to self-destruction. The Mad Scientist has become the modern Faust figure, although he has lost this quality of ambiguity. The change lies, I think, in the increasing predominance in industrially advanced societies of intellect over sensibility. Earlier Faust figures (notably Marlowe's Dr. Faustus and Goethe's Faust) attempt, through alchemy, to reconcile religion with science or, in a sense, sensibility with intellect. The gradual assumption of religious function by science leads inexorably to one-dimensionality with its rejection of significant experience of the non-intellect. (pp. 96-8)

With his grotesque obsession with creating life wedded to the most modern means, Frankenstein resolves with Faustian incantation:

> So much has been done, . . . more, far more, will I achieve; treading in the steps already marked, I will pioneer a new way, explore unknown powers, and unfold to the world the deepest mysteries of creation. . . .

So from the beginning, Frankenstein's scientific enterprise involves the means and ends dichotomy which produces: 1) the fallacious distinction between subject and object enabling him to dominate nature; and 2) the mechanism for evading responsibility for his work.

The most remarkable feature of *Frankenstein* is the vitality of the monster in comparison to the human characters of the book. The force of the figure lies in its sense of suppressed humanity which: 1) has been victimized by technological and mythic objectification; and 2) attempts to assert its humanity through rebellion in the face of this objectification. The monster appeals to us, as he appealed to a romantic generation as the embodiment of a dream, the Noble Savage. The Noble Savage acts within a nostalgic frame of reference in that he combines both intellect and sensibility, the supposed reconciliation of innocence. Yet the monster's condemnation of Frankenstein—

"Unfeeling, heartless creature! You had endowed me with perceptions and passions and then cast me abroad an object for the scorn and horror of mankind." . . .—applies as well to the objectification of primitive life as an ideal state of being, for both creations are objectified. Thus the mentality of one-dimensionality perpetuates a system of subject-object relationships so pervasive that not even artists escape its influence. (pp. 98-9)

As the embodiment of an ideal state of being, the monster serves as a nostalgic frame of reference to an earlier day of innocence. The process involves the perhaps unconscious manipulation of primitive humanity as an abstraction. No matter how well-intentioned the Noble Savage as the embodiment of an ideal state of existence, the figure represents a species of cultural imperialism. The objectification of a group of human beings makes economic, social, and political exploitation possible. It cannot be mere coincidence that the Noble Savage first appealed to those nations in the process of colonial development. (p. 99)

It is doubtful that Mary Shelley intended to be an accomplice of colonialism, but the evolution of the monster from Noble Savage to ravager of mankind in the novel finds a similar historical development in the figure of the Happy Native of colonialization turning revolutionary in the attempt to assert his humanity, much to the chagrin of the colonialist who knows him only as an object of his own definition. The monster's self-immolation at the end of the novel is the act of a man proudly removing *himself* from the world of men who so despise him rather than allowing himself to be killed by the man, Frankenstein, who has created him as an object. The assertion of humanity on the part of the monster assumes the proportions of rebellion because humanity cannot be bestowed as edict by the oppressing party. The monster has been defined by both Frankenstein and within the context of romantic mythology as an object; he does not possess, in this sense, the humanity to assert. He must, in effect, recreate himself. (p. 100)

The monster's form of rebellion takes the peculiarly romantic form noticed by Camus: "The romantic hero . . . considers himself compelled to do evil by his nostalgia for an unrealizable good." The monster begins the classic terrorism of guerrilla warfare and even indulges in selective killing of his oppressor's immediate family. Sartre comments upon the redemptive nature of violence in his preface to Fanon's *The Wretched of the Earth:*

> . . . this irrepressible violence is neither sound and fury, nor the resurrection of savage instincts, nor even the effect of resentment: it is man re-creating himself . . . no gentleness can efface the marks of violence; only violence itself can destroy them. The native cures himself of colonial neurosis by thrusting out the settler through force of arms. When his rage boils over, he rediscovers his lost innocence and he comes to know himself in that he himself creates himself.

By espousing evil (i.e., the opposite of what his definer considers good), the monster emerges, from beneath the onus of objectification, a man. Through his terrorist activities, the monster asserts his humanity; in the assumption of depravity, he becomes a monster of his own making.

Frankenstein pursues his former creation, appropriately enough, to the Arctic wastes, fails to kill him, and dies in the effort. The *raison d'être* of the monster dies with him. Walton tells the monster, "It is not pity that you feel [after the monster has attempted to explain his situation]; you lament only because the victim of your malignity is withdrawn from your power." . . . It is the only really intelligent thing a human character has said throughout the book, for it places the causes of rebellion squarely on the oppressor. Frankenstein passes his necessity to see the monster die onto Walton, but the monster chooses to end his life on his own terms:

> I shall collect my funeral pile and consume to ashes this miserable frame. . . . I shall die. I shall no longer feel the agonies which now consume me or be the prey of feelings unsatisfied, yet unquenched. . . .

Thus, however wretched, the monster collects what dignity he retains in creating himself anew and immolates himself.

Early in the Nineteenth Century, *Frankenstein* presages one-dimensional existence. With its irrational assumptions about the rational, technological reality rejects by its very nature the necessity for human sensibility. Bereft of this basis for critical thought, an uncontrolled technology threatens to annihilate the world. At the same time, the objectification of human beings as grist for the technological mill has produced widespread alienation in advanced industrial societies as well as the movement of the Third World toward an assertion of humanity independent of that of the defining oppressor. The oppressor has himself been brutalized by his one-dimensional existence and tends to project the inadequacies of his own thwarted life upon the oppressed whom he has defined in such a way as to ease their exploitation for him. The oppressor and the oppressed, the definer and the defined, must sometime face each other. One-dimensionality seems to deny that they can do so as human beings. Mary Shelley's novel indicates that master and monster will kill each other, and so far it seems terribly accurate. (pp. 102-03)

> *Stephen Crafts, "'Frankenstein': Camp Curiosity or Premonition?" in* Catalyst, *No. 3, Summer, 1967, pp. 96-103.*

R. H. W. DILLARD (essay date 1967)

[*In the following discussion of the cinematic myth of* Frankenstein, *Dillard suggests that through the medium of film, Shelley's "minor philosophical novel" has been transformed into a major work of art.*]

We are sitting, you and I, in the plush (if somewhat worn) seats of a darkened movie house—featureless, all of us seated in rows, hearing the first dark chords of a somber score, waiting for the hard grin of death's skull to chill us all to the bone that will outlast our flesh and set on end our hair that legend says will grow long after we are dead.

And on the screen, dark figures move among the mists and tilting stones of a Central European graveyard—a hunchbacked dwarf, a tall young man. There is the clank of shovels under a full moon. High scudding clouds. The action is unclear. A body is raised from its rest, and heavy clods thump on the empty coffin lid. And somehow, a stone tower, the fury of a storm, the mad harmony of thunder, lightning, and the buzzing of machines that spit and crackle life into the shrouded figure on the table. It moves, first a hand, an arm; it rises and lurches unsteadily on sewn and cumbrous limbs. And its face is the face of death, the pain and incomprehensibility of death, the death that waits for us all. (pp. 60-1)

[The cinematic myth of Frankenstein] speaks of the darkness of being a fallen and flawed thing, alone in a world of hate and misunderstanding, out of harmony with the design of his creator and an offense to himself and to nature in that creator's eyes, doomed by the very flesh of his body to sin and separation and a long suffering unto death. The Frankenstein story speaks of the darkness of man in a fallen state, separated from God and seeking communion and understanding.

Certainly a simpler reading, and a valid one, is to consider the story of Dr. Frankenstein and his monster to be completely medieval in its moral basis, to understand it as the cautionary tale of a man who tampers with the laws of nature beyond the bounds set him by God and who suffers the sad consequences of his sin. Like Marlowe's Faustus, Frankenstein does seek too much knowledge and pays for his arrogance; but the story is something more than that, for it is as much the monster's as his creator's, and their relationship is the center of the story, dramatically and morally. As Mary Shelley wrote [*Frankenstein*] originally, it is the completely Romantic story of "The Modern Prometheus," and, although the film manages successfully to avoid most of her Shelleian philosophical lectures, it does adhere to the complexity of that central relationship. The monster defines that relationship himself in the novel, as he pleads for Frankenstein to make him a wife, and offers a clearly Romantic interpretation of his fall and of his responsibilities to his creator and his creators' responsibilities to him:

> I am thy creature, and I will be even mild and docile to my natural lord and king, if thou wilt also perform thy part, the which thou owest me. Oh, Frankenstein, be not equitable to every other, and trample upon me alone, to whom thy justice, and even thy clemency and affection, is most due. Remember that I am thy creature, I ought to be thy Adam; but I am rather the fallen angel, whom thou drivest from joy for no misdeed. Everywhere I see bliss, from which I alone am irrevocably excluded. I was benevolent and good; misery made me a fiend. Make me happy, and I shall again be virtuous.

But is his fall so simple? And what of his creator's relationship to his Creator in turn? Mary Shelley developed her story thoroughly and skillfully, and the films follow it to some degree, especially *The Bride of Frankenstein* [1935], but they have changed her rational and argumentative monster substantially and succeeded in transmuting a minor philosophical novel into a cinematic myth which carries the full emotional and moral impact of a major work of art. This is, unfortunately, not the place for a discussion of the similarities and differences between the novel and the film, but I should like to use one difference to serve as a starting point for my discussion of the films.

Mary Shelley's monster is in many ways the superior of his creator, morally as well as physically, but they can never gain an understanding because of Frankenstein's repugnance for that creature's ugliness and the misdeeds resulting from his ugliness and his isolation from human society. Frankenstein agrees to make the monster a mate but finally cannot because of that repugnance and the consequent strain on his conscience; he destroys her before she may live, and the monster loses his chance to begin a new life (and perhaps a new race) because of his creator's moral nature. In *The Bride of Frankenstein* the monster makes similar demands, for he has learned what it is to love and to be loved. Frankenstein agrees and creates a bride for his Adam, but the new Eve, impelled by whatever remains in her brain of her former human life, shrinks from her intended mate and shrieks in absolute disgust and terror. The monster, who has been driven away from every human contact and driven to violence and murder by his mistreatment, surrenders to despair and destroys himself and his bride.

Mary Shelley's monster dies, too, by his own hand when, after the death of his creator and the end of their long vendetta, he steps onto an ice floe and is "borne away by the waves and lost in darkness and distance." But he also dies a Romantic hero, morally superior to Frankenstein in his suffering and his refusal to yield his identity and life while his creator still lived. He speaks to the corpse of Frankenstein: "Blasted as thou wert, my agony was still superior to thine; for the bitter sting of remorse will not cease to rankle in my wounds until death shall close them forever"; he dies secure in the knowledge that his "spirit will sleep in peace; or if it thinks, it will not surely think thus."

The film monster does not die a hero's death, nor can he be sure of anything but death itself. He dies in a moment of total despair, rejected by even a creature of his own kind, driven to destroy not only himself but everything he is. His is a plunge into violent death, peaceful in contrast to his life but blacker by infinities than that quiet spiritual assurance of the novel's hero. The monster of the films is the ultimate victim, the final image of lost and suffering man, all illusions stripped away, naked in his own damnation. The horror of his death may be the most intense of all . . . cinematic myths, and the Frankenstein story is the most complex and, for all its darkness, finally enlightening. (pp. 82-5)

[The] monster never achieves his humanity, and his death is only a blotting out, a leap from unnatural life into nothing. Where, then, is the moral lesson, the accommodation to death in this myth? It is, I think, involved in an act of love, a feeling of sympathy with the ugliest and most outcast of living creatures, an act which no human in the films is capable of making but one which each member of the audience should make. We give our feelings to the monster, suffer and die with him. . . .

There is the power of the Frankenstein myth, the power to inspire love for the untouchable, feeling for the violent and murderous beast, love and fear involved as they seldom are but always should be. The Frankenstein myth teaches us how fallen we are and, at the same time, how we must love one another, despite all our sins and crimes, in order to live through that world and maintain the humanity which the monster could not only not find in himself, but which he smothered in those around him with their fear and violence. If the film can rouse our sympathy for the monster and his downward path to death, it has shown us the possibility of a life which, even with death as its inevitable end, can be rich with love and alive with the human spirit. (p. 90)

> *R. H. W. Dillard, "Even a Man Who Is Pure at Heart: Poetry and Danger in the Horror Film," in* Man and the Movies, *edited by W. R. Robinson with George Garrett, Louisiana State University Press, 1967, pp. 60-96.*

MARIO PRAZ (essay date 1968)

[*In a general consideration of* Frankenstein, *Praz surveys the novel's sources and literary descendants.*]

[Despite] its capacity of stirring our sense of horror, [Mary Shelley's *Frankenstein*] has a fundamental weakness which seriously hampers the suspense of disbelief. In the fourth chapter we read that 'after days and nights of incredible labour and fatigue', the narrator has 'succeeded in discovering the cause of generation and life', nay more, he has become himself 'capable of bestowing animation upon lifeless matter'. He then addresses his friend thus:

> I see by your eagerness, and the wonder and hope which your eyes express, my friend, that you expect to be informed of the secret with which I am acquainted; that cannot be: listen patiently until the end of my story, and you will easily perceive why I am reserved upon that subject. I will not lead you on, unguarded and ardent as I then was, to your destruction and infallible misery. Learn from me, if not by my precepts, at least by my example, how dangerous is the acquirement of knowledge.

Thus the manner of animating lifeless matter must be kept secret, but is the reader content with this blunt statement? Generally authors of pseudo-scientific novels try to lift the veil, be it only for a moment. (p. 25)

The artificial creation of a human being had been the dream of centuries, but the problem was particularly alive in the eighteenth century and Goethe voiced it in the Homunculus in the second part of *Faust* which, however, was begun only in 1826, whereas *Frankenstein* was published in 1818. Sources have been pointed out, in Godwin's novels, in Madame De Genlis's *Pygmalion et Galatée,* not to speak of *Paradise Lost;* Condillac may have contributed his psychological sensationalism, Locke was meticulously read by Mrs Shelley through December 1816 and January 1817. (pp. 27-8)

There are in *Frankenstein* echoes of Coleridge's *Rime of the Ancient Mariner,* witness the very appearance of the narrator ('his lustrous eyes dwell on me with all their melancholy sweetness', says Walton in the fourth preliminary letter), and the polar regions through which the last mad pursuit takes place; and certainly the image of the wounded deer in Chapter IX was inspired by William Cowper's famous passage (*The Task,* III, 108-20). There are also anticipations of Poe's Imp of the Perverse ('Chance or rather the evil influence, the Angel of Destruction, which asserted omnipotent sway over me from the moment I turned my reluctant steps from my father's door—led me first to Mr Kempe, professor of natural philosophy'), and even of Ahab's pursuit of Moby Dick in Frankenstein's relentless, Heaven-assigned chase of the monster. So that for the far-reaching implications of the main theme and for the grandiose scenery through which the mad chase takes place, Mrs Shelley's novel ranks as the greatest achievement of the Gothic school notwithstanding its frequent clichés of phrasing and situation and the occasionally disarming naïveté. Because the way in which the monster acquires a remarkable degree of education, to the point of reading *Paradise Lost*, Plutarch's *Lives,* and the *Sorrows of Werther,* and of quoting Milton in his speeches ('Evil thenceforth became my good', 'It presented to me as exquisite and divine a retreat as Pandaemonium appeared to the daemons of hell after their suffering in the lake of fire', etc.), is a no less serious obstacle to the suspension of disbelief than the manner in which the monster is contrived by Frankenstein out of dead limbs.

There are in the novel all the elements of a good film, whatever one thinks of the one which was actually made; witness the very spectacular end, which reads like the script for a regular Hollywood finale:

> He sprang from the cabin-window, as he said this, upon the ice-raft which lay close to the vessel. He was soon borne away by the waves and lost in darkness and distance.

Indeed, it was reserved for the film of our day to realize successfully effects that the horror novelists tried to achieve, but crudely, so crudely indeed that they easily lent themselves to Jane Austen's and Thomas Love Peacock's satires. (pp. 31-2)

> *Mario Praz, in an introduction to* Three Gothic Novels, *edited by Peter Fairclough, Penguin Books, 1968, pp. 7-34.*

MASAO MIYOSHI (essay date 1969)

[*Miyoshi's* The Divided Self, *from which the following excerpt is drawn, is a study of self-duplication and self-division in nineteenth-century literature. Here the critic suggests that the characters Walton, Clerval, and the Monster serve to illuminate various aspects of Frankenstein's personality. According to Miyoshi, Walton mirrors Frankenstein in his Faustian striving, while Clerval and the Monster represent the good and evil extremes, respectively, of the scientist's nature.*]

The Faustian theme of thirst for knowledge [in *Frankenstein*] is expressed particularly in the use of the laboratory. Not only Frankenstein but Captain Walton as well is engaged in scientific experiment. Walton's expedition parallels Frankenstein's Fausto-Promethean adventures. Nor is the Monster any different in this respect: His long tale within a tale, covering six chapters (eleventh to sixteenth), might well be called "The Education of a 'Natural' Man" (albeit an "artificial" natural man), the author's assumption being man's innate goodness and, voicing Godwin and Shelley, the failure of existing institutions to sustain him. With the Monster, too, it is an insatiable thirst for knowledge—in particular, knowledge of his origin and identity—that motivates him: "Who was I? What was I? Whence did I come? What was my destination?" (p. 80)

Godwin's daughter moved freely in the circle of the foremost poets and writers of the time, and it was unlikely that she could allow *Frankenstein* to become just another horror story. As a small child, she had heard "The Ancient Mariner" recited by Coleridge himself, and by the time she had finished her own story in May of 1817, she had come to know Thomas Peacock, "Monk" Lewis, Leigh Hunt, Byron, and, of course, Shelley. With this background, *Frankenstein* could scarcely avoid reflecting a great many serious concerns of the Romantics: the dualism of poetry and science, of the individual and society, and of faith and humanistic rationalism.

The story opens with Walton's rescue of Frankenstein. Sensing somewhere in the dark gloom of his bearing a "double existence," composed of great suffering and great glory too, Walton understands Frankenstein's dreams of retiring within, where he can preside "like a celestial spirit," . . . for Walton, too, is pulled between his thirst for "a more intimate sympathy with a fellow mind" and his longing for more inward "knowledge and wisdom." . . . The two immediately recognize these poles in each other. At the end of the story, when the ship is halted by mountains of ice on all sides, the crew urge the captain to sacrifice the expedition and return home straightaway with the first sign of the thaw. However, the dying Frankenstein, wanting desperately to track down his Monster, insists they push on. There is here a remarkable resemblance to Conrad's *The Secret Sharer*, in which Leggatt and the captain meet and become by their identical quest indistinguishable. In *Frankenstein*, the encounter functions as more than a mere narrative convention, acting to reinforce the Faustian theme by mirroring it—Frankenstein in Walton and vice versa—and in a paradoxical way universalizing their common solitude. There are hints here too of the Mariner's meeting with the Wedding Guest, although comparison with Coleridge's poem brings out something else of interest. For a while, the Frankenstein-Mariner parallel is strongly suggested at several points. Walton, too, resembles the Coleridge hero (for example, "I am going to unexplored regions, to 'the land of mist and snow'; but I shall kill no albatross. . . .") It is only after Walton decides to terminate the voyage that Frankenstein, released at last from his monomaniacal chase, dies. Walton, then, is a kind of other possibility for Frankenstein, a life which he might have had, and it is with this in mind that the Faustian motive should be looked into.

Against this, it would be natural to insist that Frankenstein's friendship with Clerval anticipates the later one with Walton. However there the relationship was not one of identity, but of contrast; Clerval was "a being formed in the 'very poetry of nature'," . . . and occupied with "the moral relations of things." . . . Frankenstein with his scientific interests, Clerval with his poetry, the two complemented each other: "Harmony was the soul of [their] companionship." . . . Had this balance prevailed, there would have been no Frankenstein creation and consequently no tragedy to tell. However, in the world of this work, friction and discord prevail. In Frankenstein's career, first science and then poetry occupies his interest, until the possibility of either is destroyed by the Monster's vengeful reappearance.

The subtitle, *Or, The Modern Prometheus*, certainly suggests it is Frankenstein who in the creation of life has defied God and become Prometheus, but it is nonetheless the Monster's rebellion that dominates the story. The epitaph taken from *Paradise Lost*— "Did I request thee, Maker, from clay / To mould me man? Did I solicit thee / From darkness to promote me?"—points to the essential identity between Monster and maker. They are both Promethean figures and both finally return to that one clay that was their common origin.

If we treated Frankenstein's life experiment purely as the outgrowth of his rationalistic obsession the Monster would fit well into the pattern of a being who is, rather limitedly, "reason in isolation." As it happens he does not develop so straightforwardly as an embodiment of rational man. Faustian, yes, but his initial thrust of existence is toward development of his total being, moral and emotional as well as intellectual. From the De Laceys and his readings in Milton, Plutarch, and Goethe, he forms the notion, for one, of service to humanity. But there is no response to his earnest and generous efforts; on the contrary, people are horrified with his appearance and fear and hate him. He reasons that a child might be different, that he might mold a little one into a friend, but it turns out badly. The boy—Frankenstein's little brother—abuses him for his hideous appearance and the Monster strangles him. The period of Frankenstein's mastery is over; the Monster, discovering that he, too, can "create desolation," becomes a second Frankenstein. As he says to the scientist, recalling the ambiguous Master-Slave relationship so well understood by Hegel, "You are my creator, but I am your master." . . . (pp. 80-3)

At the same time, Frankenstein's enormous creative effort seems to have completely exhausted him. Henceforth rejecting his scientific pursuits, he devotes himself to Clerval's world of poetry and emotion. "A serene sky and verdant fields filled me wih ecstasy. The present season was indeed divine; the flowers of spring bloomed in the hedges, while those of summer were already in bud. I was undisturbed by thoughts which during the preceding year had pressed upon me, notwithstanding my endeavors to throw them off, with an invincible burden." . . . Frankenstein the intellectual purges the intellect through Nature.

Only with the reappearance of the Monster in his life, with his program of revenge and destruction, is this balance shaken. He can no longer take delight in the beauties of Nature and is driven back once again to a tormenting sense of his great guilt. Like many of the Gothic heroes, he is utterly at a loss over what course to take next, and his indecisiveness, which, in a sense, allows the murder of Justine, Clerval, Elizabeth, and M. Frankenstein himself, only intensifies his remorse unbearably. The disintegration of his personality is now complete.

As though to mirror his creator's cycle of guilt and remorse, the Monster too finds himself agonized. The two voice an identical feeling of bearing a "hell within" them. . . . The Monster has certainly systematically destroyed Frankenstein's family in retribution for not having been provided with a spouse. However, it may not be too far afield to propose that these murders are at the same time a projection of Frankenstein's own suppressed urge to destroy what he loves—a negative impulse lurking in the depths of rationalism. Indeed, it is only the absence of a carefully conceived plan that distinguishes Frankenstein's creation of the Monster from Dr. Jekyll's of Mr. Hyde, who is turned loose solely as a means by which the creator realizes his secret and abominable desires. The common error of calling the Monster "Frankenstein" has considerable justification. He is the scientist's deviant self.

The essential oneness of the two is manifest in still another way. Frankenstein and the Monster, engrossed with each other, are soon completely inseparable in their mutual hatred and common misery. The facts surrounding the Monster's origin, existence, and subsequent culpability are too strange to be believed, and as a result people around them lose interest in the two and their far-ranging wanderings—pursuer and pursued, creator and creature, maker and destroyer, trekking over Europe from the Alps to the Mediterranean, and from there to the North Sea. In a narrative recalling aspects of her father's *Caleb Williams,* Mary Shelley unfolds this tale of a great chase which, with society receding in significance, gradually takes on the only meaning, the only existence even, for both pursuer and pursued. We see the fugitive posting a landmark here and there that the search might continue, and when death claims the hunter, the fugitive too must die—the chase has been his life.

The Monster is an all too real nightmare for his maker, yet there is some semblance here of the *Alastor* Poet's visionary quest. In this tale, as in the Shelley poem, there is a projection or reproduction of the self; nor is a reunion of the two ultimately possible, for the pursuit ends only with the death of the pursuer. For this reason primarily, the story is a commentary on Romantic alienation, although, like her husband, Mary Shelley is finally quite ambivalent toward the Romantic quest. Frankenstein dies a defeated man, but sublimely, in the style of the Poet.

To go back to Shelley for a moment, it was in the Preface of 1817 [see excerpt above] that he recapitulated the principle of the romance first set down by Walpole: "I have thus endeavored to preserve the truth of the elementary principles of human nature, while I have not scrupled to innovate upon their combinations. The *Iliad,* the tragic poetry of Greece—Shakespeare, in the *Tempest* and *Midsummer Night's Dream*—and most especially Milton, in *Paradise Lost,* conform to this rule. . . ." What he means by "the truth of the elementary principles of human nature" and his innovations on various combinations of same should be clear in the light of his references to the epics and romances: simply, the ordinary and the marvelous. The romance tradition, blending the two, continues right into the nineteenth century and later. However, what is remarkable about this is not so much the continuity of the tradition, but its continual absorption of elements not yet utilized in the early romances. For instance, in *Frankenstein* the main vehicle of Gothic fantasy is no longer the conventional supernatural. Its author, writing in an age of increasing scientism when the old Gothic mysteries had lost much of their appeal, took instead as her theme this same new science whose role M. Krempe had defined as limited to "annihilation" of the old fantasies, and in effect annihilated it as a humane pursuit by demonstrating its possible monstrous results. Despite the many lines of correspondence to the ghosts and devils of the conventional romances, science, with its growing prestige, can generate a totally new species of terror. If scientific man is a kind of God, his scientific method becomes a new supernaturalism, a contemporary witchdoctoring of frightening potential.

However, what is more, oxymoron being a prominent feature of science fiction, contradictory demands are made on the tone and style of the work. To convince his reader, the writer must delineate objects and events in the story very clearly and completely. At the same time, fantasy requires that he surround these objects and events with an atmosphere of wonder and at least the suggestion of the supernatural. For the first, neither Beckford's whimsy and irony, Mrs. Radcliffe's misty landscapes and characterizations, nor Godwin's rhetoric would be appropriate. Instead, Mrs. Shelley borrows the realistic type of scene, event, and character from the by then fully developed orthodox novel of Maria Edgeworth, Jane Austen, and some aspects of Sir Walter Scott. Her description of the De Lacey family, for example, is straight out of the domestic novel. . . . (pp. 83-7)

The second requirement is met as much by ample infusions of the Romantic poets, mainly Wordsworth and Coleridge, as by the conventional Gothicisms. Mary Shelley quotes liberally from "Tintern Abbey" and "The Ancient Mariner," and the Alps, so important to these poets, are there exploited to heighten the feelings of solitude and awe in the two major characters. However, "The Ancient Mariner" is perhaps the most important of these Romantic influences, as we can see from the resemblance that the extensive wanderings of Frankenstein and Walton bear to the Mariner's voyage of atonement. Especially striking in its reference to Coleridge is the final scene:

> Immense and rugged mountains of ice often barred up my passage, and I often heard the thunder of the ground sea which threatened my destruction. But again the frost came and made the paths of the sea secure. . . .
>
> September 9th, the ice began to move, and roarings like thunder were heard at a distance

as the islands split and cracked in every direction. . . .

Here is the Coleridge:

> And through the drifts the snowy clifts
> Did send a dismal sheen:
> Nor shapes of men nor beasts we ken—
> The ice was all between.
>
> The ice was here, the ice was there,
> The ice was all around:
> It cracked and growled, and roared and howled,
> Like noises in a swound! . . .

Mrs. Shelley has not fully worked out the symbolic potential of the scene. The term "mountains of ice," nowhere varied or made any more specific, is nowhere strongly referential either; we miss the full sense in it of their dead damp whiteness against the impenetrable night. However, if she has not conquered those particular mountains, others have. Take the way she concludes her tale of Fausto-Promethean defiance—flames that devour the Monster rising to the dark skies above the stark white icebergs—a scene strikingly anticipating Poe who ended his *Arthur Gordon Pym* with just such components as Mrs. Shelley's, but with considerably greater awareness of their possibilities. With Poe, the romance tradition would take on new visual variety and symbolic depth, qualities not lost on other highly gifted romancers such as Hawthorne and Melville, and indeed Dickens. (pp. 87-9)

> *Masao Miyoshi, "The Logic of Passion: Romanticism," in his* The Divided Self: A Perspective on the Literature of the Victorians, *New York University Press, 1969, pp. 47-106.*

WILLIAM A. WALLING   (essay date 1972)

[*In the preface to his full-length critical survey of Shelley's writings, Walling argues that her first three novels—* Frankenstein, Valperga, *and* The Last Man—*"ought to have earned for Mary a higher place in the literature about the fiction of the period than she currently holds." Here, he discusses* Valperga *as a novel of misplaced ambition and delineates the political critique inherent in* The Last Man.]

Mary Shelley, in her second novel [*Valperga*] as well as in her first [*Frankenstein*], is interested in taking up the theme of ambition and exploring the emotional cost it exacts. But if *Frankenstein* may be regarded as a religious and even a philosophical treatment of such a theme, then surely *Valperga,* based on an historical figure of medieval Italy, is a political exploraton of the same basic dilemma: the conflict between intense aspiration (the desire for political power) and the demands of the human heart. In truth, although Mary's criticism of religious orthodoxy is unmistakable in *Valperga* through the character of Beatrice, one of the weaknesses in the construction of the novel as a whole is that the religious elements never really—as they do in *Frankenstein*—become a part of the central theme. Instead, what we find in *Valperga* is that political issues clearly dominate the formal structure, while the religious criticism—despite its vividness—stands to one side as a brilliant but often irrelevant digression. (p. 60)

Valperga deals with a central figure who schemes to bring about "the government of a single person." Quite early in the novel, in fact, when Castruccio is still essentially a boy, Mary makes this intent clear. He has taken up residence with Francis Guinigi, a man who, although once a successful military leader, has laid "aside the distinctions of society" and has turned to agriculture as a way of life, recognizing, "with lovely humility, . . . the affinity of the meanest peasant to his own noble mind." . . . Castruccio, however, argues with Guinigi, endeavoring to prove to him "that in the present distracted state of mankind, it was better that one man should get the upper hand, to rule the rest." . . . In other words, what Mary presents through Castruccio is the fatal result of the obvious solution to "the present distracted state" of nineteenth-century Europe: the government of each nation by a powerful individual, who is ultimately responsible to no one but himself. (pp. 62-3)

[This] early disputation between Castruccio and Guinigi is also valuable for pointing to Mary's method of organizing her political theme. For what she does is present, as stages in Castruccio's development, a series of dialectic milestones in which Castruccio's colloquist functions somewhat in the fashion of either the good or the bad angel in the old morality plays. Guinigi, for example, is obviously a "good" angel—the first, in fact, that Castruccio encounters—just as Euthanasia is the most important. Alberto Scoto, on the other hand, is the first of Castruccio's "bad" angels, for he introduces Castruccio to the unscrupulous methods of successful power politics. Thus Scoto advises Castruccio, in a Machiavellian passage, "But, having once formed an army, disciplined it, and shewn its temper by success, then is the time to change the arts of war for those of counsel, and to work your way as the mole, shewing no sign of your path, until your triumphant power comes forth where it is least expected." . . . "And in those days," Mary continues by way of summary of Scoto's effect, "the seeds of craft were sown, that, flourishing afterwards, contributed to his advancement to power and glory." . . . (p. 63)

Although Scoto, as the first, is the crucial dark angel in Castruccio's career, Benedetto Pepi, whom Castruccio meets in the Alps while traveling to Italy, is the one receiving the fullest treatment. (pp. 63-4)

Indeed, Pepi, in a striking (although undoubtedly coincidental) similarity to Blake's "The Human Abstract," presents an image of the perdurable nature of human selfishness that seems to insure the perpetution of injustice: "Tyranny is a healthy tree, it strikes a deep root, and each year its branches grow larger and larger, and its shade spreads wider and wider. While liberty is a word, a breath, an air; it will dissipate, and Florence become as slavish as it is now rebellious; did not Rome fall?" . . . As a result, the final stage of Castruccio's moral collapse is indicated by an appropriate reference to his having become indistinguishable from his archtempter: "He now fully subscribed to all the articles of Pepi's political creed, and thought fraud and secret murder fair play, when it thinned the ranks of the enemy." . . . (p. 64)

But, as I have indicated, not only Guinigi but also Euthanasia stands against the malign influences on Castruccio's career. In one of their earliest colloquies, in fact, Euthanasia attempts to rescue Castruccio from the temptation of a self-centered tyranny by suggesting to him that true fulfillment is impossible without a climate of liberty: "The essence of freedom is that clash and struggle which awaken the energies of our nature, and that operation of the elements of our mind, which as it were gives us the force and power that hinder us from degenerating, as they say all things earthly do when not regenerated by change." . . . (pp. 64-5)

And yet, as we know, the nature of Mary's historical material dooms Euthanasia to failure. No matter how well she may argue, no matter how passionately she may champion the cause of liberty—and at times Euthanasia does indeed justify Claire Clairmont's description of her (a "Shelley in female attire")—Castruccio nevertheless continues his downward path. . . . (p. 65)

[With] Euthanasia's failure of persuasion a foregone conclusion, the task which confronted Mary was that of showing how Castruccio's ostensible political success is nothing more than a hollow victory since it is purchased at the cost of his essential humanity—and such a theme inevitably carries us back to the obvious moral of Victor Frankenstein's development. For, like Frankenstein (and, in truth, also like Walton), Castruccio indulges himself "in dreams of . . . distinction" at an early age. . . . Consequently, by the time he becomes an orphan in his seventeenth year and goes to reside with Guinigi, he is already predisposed against the older man's willingness to recognize "the affinity of the meanest peasant" to himself. And his very refusal to acknowledge the principle of equality starts Castruccio not only on the downward path to tyranny but to a condition of increasing emotional deprivation.

For this reason Mary quite clearly places so great an emphasis on "romantic," . . . nonhistorical elements in her narrative. Not once, but twice Castruccio rejects a specific love which is offered to him—first, from Euthanasia; then, from Beatrice. For, while Castruccio persists in his offer to marry Euthanasia, she refuses to accept anyone who is an enemy to liberty, regardless of how deep her love for Castruccio may be. . . . (pp. 65-6)

[The] implicit struggle in Castruccio between his ambitious dreams of power and his love for Euthanasia is given direct expression in the account of the aftereffects of his brief affair with Beatrice: "And love was with him, ever after, the second feeling in his heart, the servant and thrall of his ambition." . . . And the consequences of this triumph of political ambition over the needs of the human heart receive their baldest expression at the end of the novel when, with Euthanasia dead, Castruccio meets again one of the dark angels of his youth, Galeazzo Visconti:

> In recording the events which had passed since their separation, Galeazzo found, that, if he had lost sovereignty and power, Castruccio had lost that which might be considered far more valuable; he had lost his dearest friends. . . . We know nothing of the private communion of these friends; but we may guess that, if Castruccio revealed the sorrows of his heart, Galeazzo might have regretted that, instead of having instigated the ambition, and destroyed the domestic felicity of his friend, he had not taught him other lessons, through which he might have enjoyed that peace, sympathy and happiness, of which he was now for ever deprived. . . .

What we have in *Valperga,* then, is the portrayal of a man who chooses power and personal eminence in preference to love. And, like Victor Frankenstein, Castruccio finds that even the limited achievement of his dream of eminence traps him in a selfhood of exacerbated isolation: like Frankenstein's monster, Castruccio's ambition takes on a murderous autonomy of its own. . . . So it is, that at the end of the novel, with Euthanasia reduced to a captured member of the utterly defeated republican party, she can still assert to the victorious Castruccio the moral point of his ostensibly successful career: that his life is "miserable" and "unworthy"—while Castruccio, driven for the

moment into the clarity of a genuine insight, can do nothing more than agree. . . . In short, in the scheme of *Valperga,* Castruccio, like the Jupiter of *Prometheus Unbound,* is shown to be struggling to retain less than what his victims already possess: the cost of a system of political inequality permeates an entire society, ultimately redounding, in its emotional consequences, upon the tyrant himself. And although analogues drawn from actuality may be less illuminating than ingenious, I doubt if anyone, fresh from reading of the memoirs of Stalin's daughter, Svetlena Alliluyeva, will be inclined to accuse Mary Shelley of naïveté. (pp. 66-7)

• • • • •

For some time it has been recognized by commentators that *The Last Man* . . . represents a creative landmark in Mary Shelley's career—a landmark which has been obscured both by the fame of *Frankenstein* and by her role as Shelley's wife. (p. 72)

The Last Man deserves serious attention in any assessment of Mary Shelley's career. Indeed, although the novel is marred by overwriting and sentimentality (Mary's major literary vices) as well as by its excessive length, *The Last Man* is a book of genuine power. Less readable than *Valperga,* less intense and richly symbolic than *Frankenstein,* it easily surpasses, nonetheless, her three remaining novels and does seem, to me, to merit its current ranking of a firm second place (after *Frankenstein*) by virtue of a greater unity and a more substantial underlying conception than is found in *Valperga.* (p. 73)

For the most part, the suggestive structure of *The Last Man* appears to have been misunderstood. Because more than a third of the novel deals not with the plague at all but with political and romantic elements in republican England, a common criticism is that Mary has provided an unduly tedious introduction to the "real" theme of her book—the plague itself and its far-reaching consequences. Yet such a charge—despite the undoubted tedium of some of the passages dealing with the love relationships—fails to take note of the full implications of *The Last Man.* For, in its deepest import, the novel achieves a striking fusion of the theme of the plague (in the second and third volumes) with the theme of political and social change implicit from the outset in the presentation of England as a republic. Indeed, Mary, who quotes approvingly from Burke's *Reflections on the French Revolution* at least twice in the course of her novel . . . , has produced in *The Last Man* a pervasive criticism of her father's (and, to a degree, of Shelley's) theory of society—a criticism of which Burke himself would have approved.

In Chapter 4 of the first volume, for example, Ryland appears on the scene as the chief opponent of Raymond's early bid for political power. Fully aware that Raymond wishes to overturn the republic and become king, Ryland rises to confront him with a speech that seems to reflect the triumph of many of the ideas advanced by Shelley in his "Philosophical View of Reform":

> Ryland began by praising the present state of the British empire. He recalled past years to their memory; the miserable contentions which in the time of our fathers arose almost to civil war, the abdication of the late king, and the foundation of the republic. He described this republic; shewed how it gave privilege to each individual in the state, to rise to consequence, and even to temporary sovereignty. He com-

An 1831 portrait by S. J. Stump, generally believed to be of Mary Shelley.

pared the royal and republican spirit; shewed how the one tended to enslave the minds of men; while all the institutions of the other served to raise even the meanest among us to something great and good. He shewed how England had become powerful, and its inhabitants valiant and wise, by means of the freedom they enjoyed. . . .

(pp. 88-9)

Yet this presentation of Ryland as the apparent champion of many of Shelley's most prominent political ideas becomes immeasurably more complex in the second volume, once the theme of the plague has been announced. For Ryland, now that Raymond is dead, stands on the very threshold of political power himself; and the policy he intends to pursue if elected lord protector is clearly that of the extension of Shelley's "divine Equality": "The political state of England became agitated as the time drew near when the new Protector was to be elected. This event excited the more interest, since it was the current report that if the popular candidate (Ryland) should be chosen, the question of the abolition of hereditary rank, and other feudal relics, would come under the consideration of parliament." . . . (pp. 89-90)

To Burke, of course, such a proposal as the one attributed to Ryland would have seemed a threat to the very principle of social order. "The power of perpetuating our property in our families," Burke declares in his *Reflections*, "is one of the most valuable . . . circumstances belonging to it, and that which tends the most to the perpetuation of society itself. . . . The possessor of family wealth, and of the distinction which attends hereditary possession . . . are the natural securities for this transmission." And again, in a claim that clearly associates the continuation of what we would today call "culture" with a continuation of the system that Ryland intends to overturn, Burke asserts: "Nothing is more certain, than that our manners, our civilization, and all the good things which are connected with manners, and with civilization, have, in this European world of ours, depended for ages upon two principles; and were indeed the result of both combined; I mean the spirit of a gentleman and the spirit of religion."

Nor is this analogue an idle one, for Burke's argument becomes a part of the texture of Mary's novel as she presents the entire English nation as considering the abolition of rank and title: "The newspapers teemed with nothing else; and in private companies the conversation, however remotely begun, soon verged towards this central point, while voices were lowered and chairs drawn closer. The nobles did not hesitate to express their fear; the other party [that is, the "popular" party] endeavoured to treat the matter lightly." . . . Thus Ryland attempts to dismiss the whole storm of fear and uncertainty with the supremely self-confident rationality of a Jeremy Bentham—or of a William Godwin: "'Shame on the country,' said Ryland, 'to lay so much stress upon words and frippery; it is a question of nothing; of, the new painting of carriage-panels and the embroidery of footmen's coats'." . . . (p. 90)

Yet immediately after this bluff dismissal of aristocratic objections, a long paragraph follows on the prospect of an egalitarian society, a paragraph which presents, ostensibly through Lionel's reflections, the major arguments for and against such an innovation. First, there is the popular party's glowing prediction of what will actually occur in England, despite the widespread fear in the nation that a "democratic style" may introduce a change for the worse:

> Yet could England indeed doff her lordly trappings, and be content with the democratic style of America? Were the pride of ancestry, the patrician spirit, the gentle courtesies and refined pursuits, splendid attributes of rank, to be erased among us? We were told that this would not be the case. . . . We were assured that, when the name and title of Englishman was the sole patent of nobility, we should all be noble; that when no man born under English sway, felt another his superior in rank, courtesy and refinement would become the birth-right of all our countrymen. . . .

But second, and of course counter to this egalitarian argument, runs the Burkean claim of the aristocratic party, which contends that in truth the highest achievements of civilization are at stake: "That party . . . could hardly yet be considered a minority in the kingdom, who extolled the ornament of the column, 'the Corinthian capital of polished society'; they appealed to prejudices without number, to old attachments and young hopes; to the expectation of thousands who might one day become peers; they set up as a scarecrow, the spectre of all that was sordid, mechanic and base in the commercial republic." . . . (pp. 90-1)

And then, with the opening words of the next paragraph, Mary fuses her two themes. "The plague had come to Athens," she writes starkly, exactly as, in the opening sentence of the paragraph directly preceding her description of the egalitarian conflict in England, she had written: "But, though it seemed absurd to calculate upon the arrival of the plague in London, I could not reflect without extreme pain on the desolation this evil would cause in Greece." . . . For, to put it as simply as possible, Mary Shelley, on the deepest symbolic level, surely unaware herself of the full implications of her novel, has created a startlingly pessimistic allegory which identifies egalitarianism with a plague virulent enough to destroy civilization itself.

Nor is this reading in the least a fanciful one. In *Valperga,* Mary made a similar identification, although there, with Shelley still alive, she projected her deepest fears (and they are close to Burke's) onto one of Castruccio's dark angels, Galeazzo Visconti. "The contagion of liberty is dangerous," Galeazzo tells Castruccio: "the Ghibellines [the royalist party] must fall in Lucca, if the Guelphs [the republican party] be not destroyed in Florence. Think you, if your people are allowed free intercourse with this republic, that the plague of liberty will not spread to your state? For no quarantine will eradicate that spot, if once it has entered the soul." . . .

In *The Last Man,* however, Mary Shelley, despondent, psychologically isolated, bitterly resentful over the lack of charity in ordinary humanity . . . produced a novel in which her fears are no longer projected by a minor figure but are incorporated into the very texture of her work.

Symbolically, then, the true subject of *The Last Man* is "the plague of liberty" and its egalitarian consequences. The first volume, with its political concerns, introduces us to an England where the old hierarchies (the monarchy in particular) have broken down; and then, as the novel progresses through its second and third volume, we are presented with the horrified vision of a world from which all social distinctions have vanished and where every man is reduced to the lowest common denominator—that of his most primitive animal interests.

"The race of man had lost in fact all distinctions of rank," we are told as the plague continues to rage across England. . . . Furthermore, with the abandonment of hard and fast hierarchies of labor, the scale of civilized values is reversed, and the most menial abilities rise to the ascendancy. . . . (pp. 91-2)

[This] fusion of the ravages of the plague with the destructive consequences of a thoroughgoing social equality is heightened into genuine, almost Burkean intensity in the opening pages of the third volume. With a nostalgic look backward at a God-centered world, where, paradoxically, man's stature was enlarged through his acceptance of the principle of subordination, Mary writes:

> Once man was a favourite of the Creator, as the royal psalmist sang, "God had made him a little lower than the angels, and had crowned him with glory and honour." . . . Once it was so; now is man lord of the creation? Look at him—ha! I see plague! She has invested his form, is incarnate in his flesh, has entwined herself with his being, and blinds his heaven-seeking eyes. Lie down, O man, on the flower-strown earth; give up all claim to your inheritance, all you can ever possess of it is the small cell which the dead require. . . .

For now that all men are reduced to the lowest common denominator, heroic effort is a thing of the past; and intellectual

distinction has dwindled to a low cunning that is useful for nothing more than the preservation of life:

> Plague is the companion of spring, of sunshine, and plenty. We no longer struggle with her. We have forgotten what we did when she was not. Of old navies used to stem the giant ocean-waves betwixt Indus and the Pole for slight articles of luxury. Men made perilous journies to possess themselves of earth's splendid trifles, gems and gold. Human labour was wasted—human life set at nought. Now life is all that we covet; that this automaton of flesh should, with joints and strings in order, perform its functions, that this dwelling of the soul should be capable of containing its dweller. Our minds, late spread abroad through countless spheres and endless combinations of thought, now retrenched themselves behind this wall of flesh, eager to preserve its well-being only. We were surely sufficiently degraded. . . .

And this overture to the third volume ends with a dying fall that is a palinode to the liberal hopes of an age—a palinode, it must be added, to many of the liberal hopes that Mary herself, on the conscious level of her mind, was to continue to hold almost until her death:

> As the rules of order and pressure of laws were lost, some began with hesitation and wonder to transgress the accustomed uses of society. Palaces were deserted, and the poor man dared at length, unreproved, intrude into the splended apartments, whose very furniture and decorations were an unknown world to him. . . . We were all equal now; magnificent dwellings, luxurious carpets, and beds of down, were afforded to all. Carriages and horses, gardens, pictures, statues, and princely libraries, there were enough of these even to superfluity; and there was nothing to prevent each from assuming possession of his share. We were all equal now; but near at hand was an equality still more levelling, a state where beauty and strength, and wisdom, would be as vain as riches and birth. . . .

For it was only in the last years of her life, as she watched with horror the revolutions of 1848, that Mary allowed into full consciousness the Burkean fears that were hers in 1824-25 during the composition of *The Last Man.* "Strange & fearful events are in progress in Europe," she wrote on June 30, 1848. "Barbarism—countless uncivilized men, long concealed under the varnish of our social system, are breaking out with the force of a volcano & threatening order—law & peace. In Germany the bands of society are entirely broken—no rents are paid—the peasant invades the Chateau—& would take it—were it worth his while." But, as I have tried to show, this horrified reaction of 1848 is only the waking counterpart to the powerful and extended nightmare of *The Last Man,* a nightmare whose deepest symbolic import was concealed from even Mary herself. (pp. 93-4)

• • • • •

Preeminently, it seems to me, [Shelley's] significance rests on her three early novels—*Frankenstein, The Last Man,* and *Valperga*—in that order. Indeed, such a total achievement ought to have earned for Mary a higher place in the literature about the fiction of the period than she currently holds. For, while Scott and Jane Austen are far superior to her, when we descend from these two, past Peacock, into the host of novelists who were Mary's contemporaries in the early nineteenth century, it is difficult to discover—on the basis of the seriousness of conception, the originality and variety of technique, and the relevance to their time and to our own—anything to equal the over-all implications of Mary's three novels. (p. 142)

[Any] study of Mary Shelley must end on a note of regret for her failure to fulfill her early promise. Few novelists have begun with a debut as auspicious as that of *Frankenstein.* No other novelist of her time combined such a promising beginning with so youthful an age. And, when we consider that *Frankenstein* was not an entirely isolated phenomenon in Mary's career, the regret can only grow sharper. For, whatever the final conclusion may be about the unevenness of *Valperga, The Last Man* in its sustained conception is surely a novel with its own independent significance. Briefly, then, the last word on Mary Shelley must be one of regret for her failure to make of her career a more impressive creative whole. And although the reason for the failure can be debated . . . , it is the failure itself which matters. Out of it, in fact, can be found the basis on which Mary Shelley takes her place in English literature as a minor figure. (pp. 142-43)

> *William A. Walling, in his* Mary Shelley, *Twayne Publishers, Inc., 1972, 173 p.*

ROBERT KIELY   (essay date 1972)

[Kiely examines and elaborates upon what he considers to be two dominant themes in Frankenstein: *"the monstrous consequences of egotism" and "the virtue of friendship."]*

Superiority through suffering is a major theme of [*Frankenstein*], a romantic half-tragedy in which the fall from greatness is nearly all fall or, more accurately, where greatness is defined in terms of the personal pain which results from the consciousness of loss which cannot be recalled or comprehended by other men. In unique regret, Frankenstein discovers his true distinction: "I was seized by remorse and the sense of guilt which hurried me away to a hell of intense tortures, such as no language can describe." The failure of language, as always in romantic fiction, is meant to be a sign not of vacuity or of an imaginative limitation of the character or author, but of the singular noncommunicable nature of great experience.

It is unfortunate (though psychologically fitting) that in the popular mind the monster has assumed the name of his creator, because Mary Shelley considered it of some importance that the creature remain unnamed. As Elizabeth Nitchie points out, it was the custom in dramatic performances of *Frankenstein* to represent the monster's part on the playbill with "_____." On first remarking this, Mary Shelley was pleased: "This nameless mode of naming the unnameable is rather good." If the phenomenon itself cannot be named, neither can the feelings it evokes in its maker. No one can know what it is like to be the monster or its "parent." (pp. 158-59)

Mary Shelley spends a great part of her narrative confronting her hero with images which evoke the sublimity of his mental state where ordinary words fail. Frankenstein journeys to Chamonix, where the mountain views elevate him from all "littleness of feeling" and "subdue and tranquilize" his grief though they cannot remove it. Mont Blanc provides him with a moment of "something like joy," but the Alps, though briefly impressive, are not in the end any more able than words to express or alleviate what Frankenstein feels. Trips up the Rhine, across the sea, even into the Arctic, hint at his unrest, but "imperial Nature," in all her "awful majesty," can no more provide truly adequate images of his misery than she can provide the fulfillment of his ambitious dreams.

At the end of the narrative, Frankenstein accuses himself of over-reaching, but even in doing this, he immodestly compares himself with the prince of overreachers: "Like the archangel who aspired to omnipotence, I am chained in an eternal hell." Rather than looking back on his ambition with disgust, he remembers it with pleasure: "Even now I cannot recollect without passion my reveries while the work was incomplete. I trod heaven in my thoughts, now exulting in my powers, now burning with the idea of their effects." Despite the conventional speeches about the dangers of pride, it becomes more and more evident in the last pages of the novel that Frankenstein, though regretting the *result* of his extraordinary efforts, is not ashamed of having made the effort in the first place. He repeatedly warns Walton, who is engaged in an expedition into the Polar Sea, to content himself with modest ambitions and a quiet life. . . . In his last breath, he begins to warn Walton once more not to make the same mistake he did, but then changes his mind:

> Seek happiness in tranquility and avoid ambition, even if it be only the apparently innocent one of distinguishing yourself in science and discoveries. Yet why do I say this? I have myself been blasted in these hopes, but another may succeed.

That Frankenstein does not die absolutely repentant once again raises the possibility that the monstrous result of his experiment was not the inevitable issue of pride but an accident of circumstance, the result of insufficient knowledge, or an imperfection in nature itself. If one wishes to accept Walton's reverent appraisal of his new friend, it can be said that Frankenstein has the immunity of all scientific and artistic genius from conventional morality, that he is somehow apart from and superior to material circumstances even when he himself seems to have brought them about. (pp. 159-60)

Mary learned her lessons in idealism well, and there is in her narrative a level on which her hero is above reproach. But it must be admitted that there is a mundane side to this fantastic tale. If genius can escape or withdraw from the material universe, ordinary mortals cannot. And however great their admiration for genius may be, they cannot fully separate it from the lesser objects of their perception.

Mary Shelley was a young and impetuous woman when she ran off with the poet; she was also an intelligent woman, but her journals and letters reveal that despite her efforts to form herself after her husband's image, common sense often intruded and made the task difficult. She was never intellectually disloyal to Shelley, yet she admitted that her mind could not follow his to the heights. Her novel, like almost everything else about her life, is an instance of genius observed and admired but not shared. In making her hero the creator of a monster, she does not necessarily mock idealistic ambition, but in making that monster a poor grotesque patchwork, a physical mess of seams and wrinkles, she introduces a consideration of the material universe which challenges and undermines the purity of idealism. In short, the sheer concreteness of the ugly thing which

Frankenstein has created often makes his ambitions and his character—however sympathetically described—seem ridiculous and even insane. The arguments on behalf of idealism and unworldly genius are seriously presented, but the controlling perspective is that of an earthbound woman. (pp. 160-61)

Frankenstein digging about in graveyards and charnel houses, matching eyeballs and sawing bones, is not an inspiring sight. Even less so is the bungled construct of muscles, arteries, and shriveled skin which he had intended as a perfectly proportioned and beautiful being. The gap between the ideal and the real, the ambition and the accomplishment, produces a result as gruesome and absurd as any pseudo-science of the Middle Ages. Still, Mary is not criticizing exalted ambition, but the misapplication of it, the consequences of what Frankenstein himself describes as "unrelaxed and breathless eagerness," a "frantic impulse," a trance-like pursuit of one idea. Through the mouth of her hero, she raises a question which in life she could probably never bring herself to ask her husband: "Is genius forever separate from the reasonable, the reflective, and the probable?" (p. 162)

In describing the way in which Frankenstein's experiment seems most "unnatural," Mary Shelley implies a definition of the natural which is peculiarly feminine in bias. For her, Frankenstein's presumption is not in his attempt to usurp the power of the gods—she quite willingly grants him his "divine" attributes—but in his attempt to usurp the power of women. "A new species would bless me as its creator and source," says Frankenstein in the enthusiasm of his first experiments. "No father could claim the gratitude of his child so completely as I should deserve theirs." He seeks to combine the role of both parents in one, to eliminate the need for woman in the creative act, to make sex unnecessary. At least that would be the net result of his experiment if it were successful, despite the fact that he himself tends to see its consequences in grander and vaguer terms. Thus, while Mary grants her hero the nobility and even the innocence of his intentions, she cannot help but undercut them with her own womanly sense of how things are.

Stripped of rhetoric and ideological decoration, the situation presented is that of a handsome young scientist, engaged to a beautiful woman, who goes off to the mountains alone to create a new human life. When he confesses to Walton that he has "worked hard for nearly two years" to achieve his aim, we may wonder why he does not marry Elizabeth and, with her cooperation, finish the job more quickly and pleasurably. But one must be careful not to imply that Mary's irony is flippant or altogether conscious. Quite to the contrary, her reservations about her hero's presumptuous idealism are so deeply and seriously felt that they produce a symbolic nightmare far more disturbing and gruesome than the monster itself. As soon as the creature begins to show animation and Frankenstein realizes that he has made an abomination, the scientist races to his bedroom, paces feverishly about, and finally falls into a troubled sleep:

> "I slept indeed, but I was disturbed by the wildest dreams. I thought I saw Elizabeth, in the bloom of health, walking in the streets of Ingolstadt. Delighted and surprised, I embraced her; but as I imprinted the first kiss on her lips, they became livid with the hue of death; her features appeared to change, and I thought that I beheld the corpse of my dead mother in my arms; a shroud enveloped her form, and I saw the graveworms crawling in the folds of the

flannel. I started from my sleep with horror . . . (and) beheld the wretch—the miserable monster whom I had created."

In this extraordinary rendition of an Oedipal nightmare, Mary shows, without moral comment, the regressive depths of her hero's mind. Frankenstein's crime against nature is a crime against womanhood, an attempt—however unconscious—to circumvent mature sex. For Mary, this is the supreme symbol of egotism, the ultimate turning away from human society and into the self which must result in desolation. Having moved away from family, friends, and fiancée to perform his "creative" act in isolation, Frankenstein later beholds the monster, in a grotesquely exaggerated re-enactment of his own behavior, "eliminate" his younger brother, his dearest friend, and his beloved Elizabeth.

All the crimes are sins against life in the bloom of youth and beauty, but the murder of the woman is the most effectively presented and, in a way, the most carefully prepared. Frankenstein's fears on his wedding night are presumably due to the monster's threat to pursue him even to his marriage chamber. But the immediate situation and the ambiguity of the language contribute to the impression that the young groom's dread of the monster is mixed with his fear of sexual union as a physical struggle which poses a threat to his independence, integrity, and delicacy of character. Frankenstein describes the event in the following manner:

> "I had been calm during the day: but so soon as night obscured the shapes of objects, a thousand fears arose in my mind. I was anxious and watchful, while my right hand grasped a pistol which was hidden in my bosom; every sound terrified me; but I resolved that I would sell my life dearly, and not shrink from the conflict, until my own life, or that of my adversary, was extinguished.
>
> "Elizabeth observed my agitation for some time in timid and fearful silence; but there was something in my glance which communicated terror to her, and trembling she asked, 'What is it that agitates you, my dear Victor? What is it you fear?'
>
> "'Oh! peace, peace, my love,' replied I; 'this night and all will be safe; but this night is dreadful, very dreadful.'
>
> ". . . I reflected how fearful the combat which I momentarily expected would be to my wife, and I earnestly entreated her to retire, resolving not to join her until I had obtained some knowledge as to the situation of my enemy."

Frankenstein leaves the room, and it is while he is away that his bride is murdered by the monster on her untried marriage bed. The passage is filled with the language of anxiety, phallic inference, and imagery of conflict, yet it is in Frankenstein's absence—not in an eager assertion of his physical presence—that harm comes to Elizabeth. If we take the monster to be one side of Frankenstein's nature, an alter-ego, then we see his physically potent self as brutish, ugly, and destructive, completely unintegrated with his gentle spirit. To depict a radical separation of mind from sexuality is one way to explore an unsatisfactory rapport between the imagination and the natural world. But what is important in the thematic terms of the novel is not the mere existence of the separation, but the fact that physical life is made ugly (indeed, is made to wither and die prematurely) because it is inadequately tended by the mind. The problem is not abuse but neglect.

The importance of the wedding night scene lies in its sexual connotation insofar as that provides the basic and concrete context in which, once again, to exemplify the hero's withdrawal from physical and emotional contact with living human beings. There are earlier instances of his separating himself from his family and from his friend Clerval, even while protesting, as he has with Elizabeth, that he continues to love them in spirit. The outrage dramatized in this novel is not restricted to a specifically sexual offense—nor is it directed against genius or ambition or idealism. The enemy is an egotism which, when carried to the extreme, annihilates all life around it and finally destroys itself.

While the main theme of the novel is the monstrous consequences of egotism, the counter-theme is the virtue of friendship. For, as Frankenstein's crime is seen as a sin against humankind more than against the heavens, it is through human sympathy, rather than divine grace, that it might have been avoided or redeemed. In her treatment of friendship, Mary shows the Coleridgean side of herself. She sees a friend as a balancing and completing agent, one who is sufficiently alike to be able to sympathize and understand, yet sufficiently different to be able to correct, and refine. Above all, the friend, in giving ear to one's dreams and sufferings, provides not only a temporary release from them, but the immediate excuse to order them by putting them into words.

The entire narrative of *Frankenstein* is in the form of three confessions to individuals with whom the speaker has unusually close ties. First, the young explorer Robert Walton writes to his sister in England as he journeys into the Arctic. There he rescues Frankenstein from a shipwreck and listens to his tale, which, in turn, contains a long narrative spoken by the monster to its creator. (pp. 164-67)

Each narrator speaks of the importance of friendship—Walton and the monster because they feel the lack of it, Frankenstein because he has had friends and lost them. In Walton's second letter to his sister, he reports that he has hired a ship and is ready to set sail on his dangerous journey. The one thing that troubles him is that, though he has a well-trained crew, he has no soul companion:

> I have one want which I have never yet been able to satisfy . . . I have no friend . . . When I am glowing with the enthusiasm of success, there will be none to participate in my joy; if I am assailed by disappointment, no one will endeavour to sustain me in dejection . . . I desire the company of a man who could sympathize with me; whose eyes would reply to mine. You may deem me romantic, my dear sister, but I bitterly feel the want of a friend. I have no one near me, gentle yet courageous, possessed of a cultivated as well as of a capacious mind, whose tastes are like my own, to approve or amend my plans. How would such a friend repair the faults of your poor brother!
> (pp. 167-68)

Frankenstein condescends to poor Walton even on the subject of friendship. It is too late for him to take up any new ties in life, he explains, because no man could ever be more to him than Clerval was and no woman more than Elizabeth. (p. 168)

Mary was sufficiently her mother's daughter to assume that a woman, as easily as another man, could be the soul companion, the ideal friend, of a man. She did not regard sexual love as an impediment to ideal friendship, nor, it would seem, as a "small party" of the claims of true love. Elizabeth and Frankenstein almost always address one another as "dear friend," and she and Clerval simply complement different sides of Frankenstein's nature. If it were to come to a choice of one or the other, the novel leaves little doubt that the feminine companion is the more valuable since she can provide both spiritual sympathy and physical affection. It is a great and painful loss for Frankenstein when Clerval is killed, but the death of Elizabeth is the end of everything for him. He dedicates himself to the pursuit and destruction of the monster, follows him to "the everlasting ices of the north" where, surrounded by blankness and waste, he confronts the sterility and uselessness of his life. . . . (pp. 168-69)

An earlier scene of frozen desolation associated with isolation from human—especially feminine—companionship takes place between Frankenstein and the monster on a glacier at the base of Mont Blanc. The monster begs his maker to listen to him and proceeds to explain in detail how he has observed and imitated the ways of man, but is shunned because of his ugliness and is forced to wander over glaciers and hide in caves of ice because these are the only dwellings "man does not grudge." In other words, despite the bizarre details associated with his creation, the monster's lament is much the same as that of the physically presentable Caleb Williams: the world does not see him as he really is. His narrative is punctuated by outcries of loneliness:

> "Everywhere I see bliss, from which I alone am irrevocably excluded."

> "When I looked around, I saw and heard of none like me."

> "I had never yet seen a being resembling me, or who claimed any intercourse with me. What was I?"

> "I am an unfortunate and deserted creature . . . I have no relation or friend upon earth."

The repetition of this theme, with slight variations, continues throughout the monster's narrative. However ludicrous or grotesque it may seem in the concrete, it is nonetheless in keeping with one of the central arguments of the novel that the monster should ask Frankenstein to make him a wife. (pp. 169-70)

The irony of the situation, though heavy-handed, is effective. Having removed himself from human companionship and the sexual means of procreation, Frankenstein brings into being a creature who, though not innately evil, is a torment to himself and to others precisely because he is without companionship and a sexual counterpart. In this respect the monster may well be taken as Frankenstein's alter-ego, his strange and destructive self, which finds no adequate means of communicaton with others, no true resemblances, no reciprocation, a repressed and hidden beast for whom all acceptable forms of human commerce are unavailable and therefore hateful. Frankenstein himself calls the unnameable creature "my own spirit let loose from the grave . . . forced to destroy all that was dear to me."

Mary saw, as did her father, the duality in human nature which is capable of bringing misery and ruin to the most gifted of beings. Her novel is not so pessimistic as *Caleb Williams* nor are the solutions implied in it so optimistic as those outlined in *Political Justice*. Neither her father's trust in system nor her husband's unworldliness seemed satisfactory to her. On the contrary, judging from the events of her novel, both alternatives were too likely to lead to that single-mindedness which, when carried to the extreme, was a kind of insanity. It would seem, in fact, that of all the romantic influences on her mind and work, Shelley's undoubtedly stimulated, but Coleridge's comforted; Shelley's provided confusion and enchantment, Coleridge's provided psychological and moral consolation. The ethereal reveries of her hero are loyal attempts to imitate Shelley, but they are among the most strained and unconvincing passages of the novel. Mary's natural inclination was toward synthesis, integration, a constant effort to find balance, relationship, correspondence, to root all ideals in natural process, and to find in nature the external signs of an ideal region. Her heart is with those, described by Coleridge, "who measuring and sounding the rivers of the vale at the feet of their furthest inaccessible falls have learned, that the sources must be far higher and far inward." Despite his supposedly scientific approach to things, Frankenstein's error is to circumvent an elementary principle of nature in trying to achieve his rather vaguely conceived ambition.

In stressing friendship, and especially heterosexual love, as her "river of the vale," the natural symbol of a higher necessity, Mary presents her own concrete version of the theory of correspondence. We must give her more credit than to think that she supposed the problems of all men—including geniuses—would be solved by marriage to a good woman. What she does mean is that no being truly exists—except in an insane wilderness of its own creation—unless it finds and *accepts* a relationship of mutual dependence with another. The rapport with otherness is both the link with the objective world and the condition for self-delineation. (pp. 170-71)

Mary Shelley's definition of a monster is precisely that being to which nothing corresponds, the product of a genius who tried to exercise its will without reference to other beings. (p. 171)

Frankenstein's first act after creating a new life is to disown it. The problem is not, as in *Caleb Williams*, an ambiguous fascination leading to abuse and immediate and obsessive pursuit. As soon as his dream is realized in concrete form, Frankenstein wants nothing to do with it. Despite his claims to scientific interest, he demonstrates no wish whatever to observe and analyze the imperfect results of his experiment. When he does finally pursue the monster, it is not in order to possess, dominate, or torment it, but to annihilate it. Though there is something ludicrous in the way the monster stumbles upon books and learns to read during his lonely wandering, the thematic consistency of the episode is unmistakable. The monster is most impressed by *Paradise Lost;* he compares himself with Adam before the creation of Eve, but, like a good Romantic, he finds Satan an even "fitter emblem" of his condition. Still, neither emblems, nor words can really help or define him any more than ordinary men can. He can find parallels but no connections and he concludes his encounter with books by envying Satan like all the others, for even he "had his companions."

The two dominant themes of *Frankenstein* never truly harmonize, nor does one succeed effectively in canceling out the other. Surely, the most explicit "moral" theme of the novel—expressed by the author with genuine conviction—is that man discovers and fulfills himself through others and destroys himself alone. Yet played against this, not so much as an argument but as an assumption, is the idea that the genius, even in his failures, is unique, noble, and isolated from other men by divine right.

Frankenstein is neither a pure hymn of praise to Godwin and Shelley nor a simple repudiation of them. Mary's uncertainties are not reflected in parody or burlesque, as Beckford's and Lewis's are in *Vathek* and *The Monk*. Her prose style is solemn, inflated, and imitative, an unhappy combination of Godwin's sentence structure and Shelley's abstract vocabulary. Whatever else she may have thought, Mary obviously did not regard her father or husband as silly. Her reservations about them were deep, complex, and mixed with genuine admiration.

After Shelley's death, Mary considered how best to educate her son, and a friend advised that she teach him to think for himself. Mary is said to have answered, "Oh my God, teach him to think like other people!" If the young wife had been able to speak with the emphatic clarity of the widow, she probably would have had fewer nightmares and *Frankenstein* might never have been written. The book is a bad dream entwined with a moral essay. Like all romantic fiction, it resounds with the fascinating dissonance which usually results from intimate encounters between irrational symbols and reasonable statements. (pp. 171-73)

Robert Kiely, "'Frankenstein': Mary Wollstonecraft Shelley," in his The Romantic Novel in England, *Cambridge, Mass.: Harvard University Press, 1972, pp. 155-73.*

ELLEN MOERS (essay date 1974)

[*In a biographical interpretation of the maternal themes of* Frankenstein, *Moers asserts that the book was largely inspired by Shelley's intense feelings about and experiences of motherhood.*]

Mary Shelley's *Frankenstein,* in 1818, made over the Gothic novel into what today we call science fiction. *Frankenstein* brought a new sophistication to literary terror, and it did so without a heroine, without even an important female victim. Paradoxically, however, no other Gothic work by a woman writer, perhaps no other literary work of any kind by a woman, better repays examination in the light of the sex of its author. For *Frankenstein* is a birth myth, and one that was lodged in the novelist's imagination, I am convinced, by the fact that she was herself a mother.

Much in Mary Shelley's life was remarkable. . . . But nothing so sets her apart from the generality of writers of her own time, and before, and for long afterward, than her early and chaotic experience, at the very time she became an author, with motherhood. Pregnant at sixteen, and almost constantly pregnant throughout the following five years; yet not a secure mother, for she lost most of her babies soon after they were born; and not a lawful mother, for she was not married—not at least when, at the age of eighteen, Mary Godwin began to write *Frankenstein*. So are monsters born.

What in fact has the experience of giving birth to do with women's literature? In the eighteenth and nineteenth centuries very few important women writers, except for Mary Shelley, bore children; most of them, in England and America, were spinsters and virgins. With the coming of Naturalism late in the century, and the lifting of the Victorian taboo against writing about physical sexuality (including pregnancy and labor), the subject of birth was first brought to literature in realistic form by male novelists, from Tolstoy and Zola to William Carlos Williams. (pp. 24-5)

Mary Shelley was a unique case, in literature as in life. She brought birth to fiction not as realism but as Gothic fantasy, and thus contributed to Romanticism a myth of genuine originality. She invented the mad scientist who locks himself in his laboratory and secretly, guiltily, works at creating human life, only to find that he has made a monster. . . .

That is very good horror, but what follows is more horrid still: Frankenstein, the scientist, runs away and abandons the newborn monster, who is and remains nameless. Here, I think, is where Mary Shelley's book is most interesting, most powerful, and most feminine: in the motif of revulsion against newborn life, and the drama of guilt, dread, and flight surrounding birth and its consequences. Most of the novel, roughly two of its three volumes, can be said to deal with the retribution visited upon monster and creator for deficient infant care. *Frankenstein* seems to be distinctly a woman's mythmaking on the subject of birth precisely because its emphasis is not upon what precedes birth, not upon birth itself, but upon what follows birth: the trauma of the afterbirth.

Fear and guilt, depression and anxiety are commonplace reactions to the birth of a baby, and well within the normal range of experience. But more deeply rooted in our cultural mythology, and certainly in our literature, are the happy maternal reactions: ecstasy, a sense of fulfillment, and the rush of nourishing love which sweep over the new mother when she first holds her baby in her arms. . . .

[Mary Shelley] rejoiced at becoming a mother and loved and cherished her babies as long as they lived. But her journal is a chilly and laconic document, mostly concerned with the extraordinary reading program she put herself through at Shelley's side. Her own emphasis on books in the journal has set the tone of most of the discussion of the genesis of *Frankenstein.* (p. 25)

Mary Shelley herself was the first to point to her fortuitous immersion in the romantic and scientific revolutions of her day as the source of *Frankenstein.* Her extreme youth, as well as her sex, has contributed to the generally held opinion that she was not so much an author in her own right as a transparent medium through which passed the ideas of those around her. "All Mrs. Shelley did," writes Mario Praz, "was to provide a passive reflection of some of the wild fantasies which were living in the air about her."

Passive reflections, however, do not produce original works of literature, and *Frankenstein,* if not a great novel, was unquestionably an original one. The major Romantic and minor Gothic tradition to which it *should* have belonged was the literature of the overreacher: the superman who breaks through normal human limitations to defy the rules of society and infringe upon the realm of God. In the Faust story, hypertrophy of the individual will is symbolized by a pact with the devil. Byron's and Balzac's heroes; the rampaging monks of Mat Lewis and E.T.A. Hoffmann; the Wandering Jew and Melmoth the wanderer; the chained and unchained Prometheus: all are overreachers, all are punished by their own excesses—by a surfeit of sensation, of experience, of knowledge, and most typically, by the doom of eternal life.

But Mary Shelley's overreacher is different. Frankenstein's exploration of the forbidden boundaries of human science does not cause the prolongation and extension of his own life, but the creation of a new one. He defies mortality not by living forever, but by giving birth. That this original twist to an old myth should have been the work of a young woman who was also a young mother seems to me, after all, not a very surprising answer to the question that, according to Mary Shelley herself, was asked from the start: "How I, then a young girl, came to think of, and to dilate upon, so very hideous an idea?"

Birth is a hideous thing in *Frankenstein,* even before there is a monster. For Frankenstein's procedure, once he has determined to create new life, is to frequent the vaults and charnel houses and study the human corpse in all its loathsome stages of decay and decomposition. (p. 26)

It is in her journal and her letters that Mary Shelley reveals the workshop of her own creation, where she pieced together the materials for a new species of romantic mythology. They record a horror story of maternity such as literary biography hardly provides again until Sylvia Plath.

As far as I can figure out, she was pregnant, barely pregnant but aware of the fact, when at the age of sixteen she ran off with Shelley in July, 1814. Also pregnant at the same time was Shelley's legal wife Harriet, who gave birth in November to a "son and heir," as Mary noted in her journal. In February, 1815, Mary gave birth to a daughter, illegitimate, premature, and sickly. There is nothing in the journal about domestic help or a nurse in attendance. Mary notes that she breast fed the baby; that Fanny, her half-sister, came to call; that Mrs. Godwin, her stepmother, sent over some linen; that Claire Clairmont, Mrs. Godwin's daughter who had run off with Mary, kept Shelley amused. Bonaparte invaded France, the journal tells us, and Mary took up her incessant reading program: this time, Mme. de Staël's *Corinne.* The baby died in March. "Find my baby dead," Mary wrote. "A miserable day."

In April, 1815, she was pregnant again, about eight weeks after the birth of her first child. In January, 1816, she gave birth to a son: more breast feeding, more reading. In March, Claire Clairmont sought out Lord Byron and managed to get herself pregnant by him within a couple of weeks. This pregnancy would be a subject of embarrassment and strain to Mary and Shelley, and it immediately changed their lives, for Byron left England in April, and Claire, Shelley, Mary, and her infant pursued him to Switzerland in May. There is nothing yet in Mary's journal about a servant, but a good deal about mule travel in the mountains. In June they all settled near Byron on the shores of Lake Geneva.

In June, 1816, also, Mary began *Frankenstein.* And during the year of its writing the following events ran their swift and sinister course: In October, Fanny Imlay, Mary's half-sister, committed suicide after discovering that she was not Godwin's daughter but Mary Wollstonecraft's daughter by her American lover. . . . In early December Mary was pregnant again, which she seems to have sensed almost the day it happened. . . . In mid-December, Harriet Shelley drowned herself in the Serpentine, she was pregnant by someone other than Shelley. In late December Mary married Shelley. In January, 1817, Mary wrote Byron that Claire had borne him a daughter. In May she finished *Frankenstein,* published the following year.

Death and birth were thus as hideously mixed in the life of Mary Shelley as in Frankenstein's "workshop of filthy creation." Who can read without shuddering, and without remembering her myth of the birth of a nameless monster, Mary's journal entry of March 19, 1815, which records the trauma of her loss, when she was seventeen, of her first baby, the little girl who did not live long enough to be given a name. "Dream that my little baby came to life again," Mary wrote; "that it had only been cold, and that we rubbed it before the fire, and it lived. Awake and find no baby. I think about the little thing all day. Not in good spirits." (*"I thought, that if I could bestow animation upon lifeless matter, I might in process of time renew life where death had apparently devoted the body to corruption."*)

So little use has been made of this material by writers about *Frankenstein* that it may be worth emphasizing how important, because how unusual, was Mary Shelley's experience as a woman. The harum-scarum circumstances surrounding her maternity have no parallel until our own time, which in its naïve cerebrations upon family life (and in much else, except genius) resembles the generation of the Shelleys. Mary Godwin sailed into teenage motherhood without any of the financial or social or familial supports that made bearing and rearing children a relaxed experience for the normal middle-class woman of her day (as Jane Austen, for example, described her). She was an unwed mother, responsible for breaking up the marriage of a young woman just as much a mother as she. The father whom she adored broke furiously with her when she eloped; and Mary Wollstonecraft, the mother whose memory she revered, and whose books she was rereading throughout her teenage years, had died in childbirth—died giving birth to Mary herself.

Surely no outside influence need be sought to explain Mary Shelley's fantasy of the newborn as at once monstrous agent

Boris Karloff as the monster, 1931. The Granger Collection, New York.

of destruction and piteous victim of parental abandonment. "I, the miserable and the abandoned," cries the monster at the end of *Frankenstein*, "I am an abortion to be spurned at, and kicked, and trampled on. . . . I have murdered the lovely and the helpless. . . . I have devoted my creator to misery; I have pursued him even to that irremediable ruin."

In the century and a half since its publication, *Frankenstein* has spawned innumerable interpretations among the critics, and among the novelists, playwrights, and filmmakers who have felt its influence. The idea, though not the name, of the robot originated with Mary Shelley's novel, and her title character became a byword for the dangers of scientific knowledge. But the work has also been read as an existential fable; as a commentary on the split between reason and feeling, in both philosophical thought and educational theory; as a parable of the excesses of idealism and genius; as a dramatization of the divided self; as an attack on the stultifying force of social convention.

The versatility of Mary Shelley's myth is due to the brilliance of her mind and the range of her learning, as well as to the influence of the circle in which she moved as a young writer. But *Frankenstein* was most original in its dramatization of dangerous oppositions through the struggle of a creator with monstrous creation. The sources of this Gothic conception, which still has power to "curdle the blood, and quicken the beatings of the heart," were surely the anxieties of a woman who, as daughter, mistress, and mother, was a bearer of death. (pp. 26-8)

Mary Shelley came honestly to grips with the dilemma of a newly created human being, a giant adult male in shape, who must swiftly recapitulate, and without the assistance of his terrified parent, the infantile and adolescent stages of human development. She even faces squarely the monster's sexual needs, for the denouement of the story hangs on his demand that Frankenstein create a female monster partner, and Frankenstein's refusal to do so.

But more than mundane is Mary Shelley's concern with the emotions surrounding the parent-child and child-parent relationship. Here her intention to underline the birth myth in *Frankenstein* becomes most evident, quite apart from biographical evidence about its author. She provides an unusual thickening of the background of the tale with familial fact and fantasy, from the very opening of the story in the letters a brother addresses to his sister of whom he is excessively fond, because they are both orphans. There is Frankenstein's relationship to his doting parents, and his semi-incestuous love for an abandoned orphan girl brought up as his sister. There is the first of the monster's murder victims, Frankenstein's infant brother (precisely drawn, even to his name, after Mary Shelley's baby); and the innocent young girl wrongly executed for the infant's murder, who is also a victim of what Mary Shelley calls that "strange perversity," a mother's hatred. (Justine accepts guilt with docility: "I almost began to think that I was the monster that my confessor said I was. . . .") The abundant material in *Frankenstein* about the abnormal, or monstrous, manifestations of the child-parent tie justifies as much as does its famous monster Mary Shelley's reference to the novel as "my hideous progeny."

What Mary Shelley actually did in *Frankenstein* was to transform the standard Romantic matter of incest, infanticide, and patricide into a phantasmagoria of the nursery. (p. 28)

Ellen Moers, ''Female Gothic: The Monster's Mother,'' in The New York Review of Books, *Vol. XXI, No. 4, March 21, 1974, pp. 24-8.*

JAMES RIEGER (essay date 1974)

[*In his introduction to an edition of* Frankenstein, *Rieger disputes the notion that the novel is either Gothic romance or early science fiction and discusses it as an example of mythic fiction.*]

The complexity of *Frankenstein* becomes apparent as soon as one tries to classify it. The difficulty is the author's rich eclecticism, together with the stylistic inconsistencies and narrative absurdities that are, perhaps, the inescapable converse of that eclecticism. Mary Shelley works so many veins at once that impatient readers have tended to falsify her book by filing it away as late Gothic romance, for example, or early science fiction. Before trying to determine what *Frankenstein* is, let us see what it is not. (pp. xxiv-xxv)

[Gothic romance] shares certain elements with *Frankenstein,* most noticeably an awareness of the deathly and nihilistic components of lust. The reader never learns whether Radcliffe's dark, brooding, and very sexy villains would prefer to rape her heroines or to murder them. Similarly, Frankenstein thinks he is affirming the life force by transfusing it into the stitched-together fragments of various corpses. But the disgusting and homicidal botch that results is a nightmare image, the surface manifestation of the unseen motives that underlie the scientist's ''curiosity.'' It is symbolically appropriate that the monstrous miscreation should cancel the possibility of natural procreation, that he should ''be with you on your wedding-night'' . . . to break the neck of his maker's bride. The Gothic and Shelleyan perception of the destructive side of sexuality has contemporary analogues in Byron's tragedies and verse romances and in the novels of de Sade.

The Gothic romancers aimed at a middle-class, Protestant, largely female audience, whose education barely extended beyond simple literacy. They exploited the prejudices of this audience against the Catholic south of Europe, which had been feared for centuries as the homeland of Macchiavelli, the Borgia Popes, and Philip of Spain—the source, then, of political trickery, ecclesiastical corruption, poison, and Armadas, together with what we now call polymorphous perversity. Mary Shelley turned this convention around. The lecherous, treacherous Italians and Spaniards depicted by Radcliffe and Lewis yield to Frankenstein's fiancée, Elizabeth Lavenza. In the third edition, Elizabeth's Italy stands for emotional warmth, and her birthplace is the destination of the aborted wedding trip. Conversely, the northward journeys of the two self-proclaimed rationalists, Walton and Frankenstein, are voyages into coldness, darkness, and delusion, though each traveler in his way expects to discover ''light'' and the innermost secret of life.

Finally, Frankenstein's interest in the occult and the quasi-magical powers he gains through the study of chemistry resemble the diabolical alliances contracted by some Gothic villains and the energy acquired by others through their association with the mystique of Roman Catholic ritual. Lewis's Ambrosio and Radcliffe's Schedoni have taken holy orders, and Frankenstein has enrolled for a degree. The anticlericalism of *The Monk* and *The Italian* and the anti-intellectualism of *Frankenstein* both stem from earlier treatments of the Faust legend, whose central figure has degrees in everything from medicine to theology.

Despite these affinities, *Frankenstein* departs from the Gothic tradition as obviously as it follows it. As its name implies, Gothicism depends on spatial and temporal exoticism. The era is vaguely and unconvincingly medieval in most cases, and the scenery is cultivated, second-hand, ''picturesque.'' Radcliffe's scenic effects, for instance, are explicitly painterly. Mary Shelley's Arctic wastes have a starkness rarely risked by the Gothic romancers, even when they varied picturesqueness with sublimity. And her other major landscapes were drawn from first-hand observation. The symbolism of light and coldness which permeates the description of the Arve glacier, the narrative setting of the second volume, is perhaps obtrusive. Nevertheless, the author had been there with Shelley in July 1816. The scene is concrete and clear, whatever its metaphorical tendency. Above all, it is immediate.

The realistic principle extends to the social context. The center of the novel's centrifugal action is the ''republic'' of Geneva during the decade of the French Revolution. The Frankensteins are enlightened bourgeois in the birthplace of Rousseau, a city no longer ruled by the theocracy of Calvin. . . . Unlike the rest of Europe in the 1790s, Geneva had neither bishops nor a king. It is upon this emancipated city and its progressive inhabitants—the Frankensteins and the Clervals—that the demonic legacy of the Middle Ages obtrudes in scientific guise. The reversal of the Gothic strategy could not be more complete.

Mary Shelley shared her husband's fascination with the natural sciences. In the 1830s, . . . she would contribute scientific biographies to Lardner's *Cabinet Cyclopedia,* and in her futuristic novel, *The Last Man,* she invented a flying machine. Still, it would be a mistake to call *Frankenstein* a pioneer work of science fiction. Its author knew something of Sir Humphry Davy's chemistry, Erasmus Darwin's botany, and, perhaps, Galvani's physics, but little of this got into her book. Frankenstein's chemistry is switched-on magic, souped-up alchemy, the electrification of Agrippa and Paracelsus. Things simply unknown or undone do not engage his attention; he wants the *forbidden* unknown and undone. He is a criminal magician who employs up-to-date tools. Moreover, the technological plausibility that is essential to science fiction is not even pretended at here. The science-fiction writer says, in effect, since x has been experimentally proven or theoretically postulated, y can be achieved by the following, carefully documented operation. Mary Shelley skips to the outcome and asks, if y had been achieved, by whatever means, what would be the moral consequences? In other words, she skips the science. The terms of her basic question (if that were her only question) would place *Frankenstein* with works that follow the same logic with regard, say, to eternal life or eternal youth: the Struldbrug episode in *Gulliver's Travels,* Godwin's *St. Leon,* Mary Shelley's own **''The Mortal Immortal''** (1834), Tennyson's ''Tithonus,'' and Wilde's *The Picture of Dorian Gray.* (pp. xxv-xxviii)

Like Rousseau and Godwin before her, Mary stresses the role of education in the liberation or enslavement of the personality. She apparently agrees with Locke that the mind is a blank slate at birth, and with the sceptics that sensory evidence can mislead the moral judgment. But *Frankenstein* does not survive as a ''novel with a thesis.'' Rather it comes through to us, in Northrop Frye's words, as ''a precursor . . . of the existential thriller, of such a book as Camus's *L'Etranger.*'' Its three concentric narrators, geographically, intellectually, and erotically cut off from the rest of mankind, deal with the world by means of a secret: the explorer's ''secret of the magnet,'' the researcher's galvanic secret of life, and the Monster's pure embodiment of these secrets, together with his unique knowledge of what it is like to be born free of history. Each secret reflects the others, or rather, each is an aspect of what Shelley in "Mont Blanc" calls "The secret Strength of things / Which governs thought, and to the infinite dome / Of Heaven is as a law. . . ." By the same token, each narrator finds a mirror-image of himself in one of the others: Walton knows that once he could have possessed Frankenstein as "the brother of my heart," . . . and Frankenstein and the Monster know that their master-slave relationship, in which the balance of power constantly shifts, parodies the love existing between father and son. The attempt to kiss the mirror is thwarted always by the illicit possession of the secret, which withers the heart and condemns its owner to emotional isolation. As Frankenstein puts it, "If the study to which you apply yourself has a tendency to weaken your affections, and to destroy your taste for those simple pleasures in which no alloy can possibly mix, then that study is certainly unlawful, that is to say, not befitting the human mind." . . . (p. xxx)

The moral is Godwinian, as is the imaginative pattern that gives it flesh. Caleb Williams's actions are determined by a ruinous secret, and St. Leon possesses the elixir of life, which destroys him and all around him. Caleb's stricken conscience mirrors Falkland's, and St. Leon's aging mind is at war with his eternally youthful body. As well as foreshadowing the existential hero, Mary Shelley's and Godwin's characters have American cousins in the obsessed and claustrophobic heroes of Brockden Brown, Poe, Hawthorne, and Melville. Brockden Brown acknowledged his debt to Godwin, and it is not fortuitous that Melville read *Frankenstein* in 1849, two years before he published his own tale of a single-minded voyager, Ahab, chasing "round the Norway Maelstrom, and round perdition's flames" his own monstrous secret, "the monomaniac incarnation of all those malicious agencies which some deep men feel eating in them."

All such fiction is mythic, in the same sense that Blake's Prophetic Books and Shelley's *Prometheus Unbound* are myth-poetry. Blake's symbolic personages are fragments of a single, shattered psyche, and the cosmic struggle in Shelley's lyrical drama employs "imagery . . . drawn from the operation of the human mind, or from those external actions by which they are expressed." Psychomachia and theomachia are metaphors of each other, which is to say that the internecine warfare of the gods cannot be distinguished from the mental chaos of their victim and creator. Romantic myth-fiction replaces the fratricidal gods with *Frankenstein*'s ambiguous, magnetic, devouring secret, as later with Melville's "intangible malignity which has been from the beginning." The whiteness of Moby Dick, like that of Mary Shelley's Mont Blanc and Arctic ice-cap, "shadows forth the heartless voids and immensities of the universe . . . a colorless, all-color of atheism from which we shrink." (pp. xxx-xxxi)

James Rieger, in an introduction to Frankenstein; or, The Modern Prometheus: The 1818 Text *by Mary Wollstonecraft Shelley, edited by James Rieger, 1974. Reprint by The University of Chicago Press, 1982, pp. xi-xxxvii.*

GEORGE LEVINE (essay date 1979)

[*An American editor and critic, Levine coedited* The Endurance of "Frankenstein," *the collection of essays from which the following excerpt is drawn. Here, he cites seven of the major implications of the Frankenstein metaphor in contemporary consciousness and outlines their sources in the novel.*]

[While] *Frankenstein* is a phenomenon of popular culture, it is so because it has tapped into the center of Western feeling and imagination: we can hear echoes of it, not only in Gothic fiction, science fiction, and fantasies of all sorts, but in far more "respectable" works, written before the glut of popular cinematic distortions. *Frankenstein* has become a metaphor for our own cultural crises, and survives even yet in high literary culture whose professors may have seen Boris Karloff stumbling through the fog, hands outstretched, at least once too often.

Of course, *Frankenstein* is a "minor" novel, radically flawed by its sensationalism, by the inflexibly public and oratorical nature of even its most intimate passages. But it is, arguably, the most important minor novel in English. If we return to the text for a check on Boris Karloff, or, recently, Mel Brooks, or for some further light on Percy Shelley, invariably we find that the book is larger and richer than any of its progeny and too complex to serve as mere background. Even in our dictionaries, "Frankenstein" has become a vital metaphor, peculiarly appropriate to a culture dominated by a consumer technology, neurotically obsessed with "getting in touch" with its authentic self and frightened at what it is discovering: "a work, or agency that proves troublesomely uncontrollable, esp. to its creator." Latent in the metaphor are some of the fundamental dualisms, the social, moral, political and metaphysical crises of Western history since the French Revolution. It may well appear that the metaphorical implications are far more serious than the novel that gave birth to them, but that novel has qualities that allow it to exfoliate as creatively and endlessly as any important myth; if it threatens to lapse into banality and bathos, it yet lives through unforgettable dreamlike images. . . . (pp. 3-4)

Frankenstein's mysterious power derives from a thoroughly earthy, practical, and unideal vision of human nature and possibility. Its modernity lies in its transformation of fantasy and traditional Christian and pagan myths into unremitting secularity, into the myth of mankind as it must work within the limits of the visible, physical world. The novel echoes, for example, with the language and the narrative of *Paradise Lost,* but it is *Paradise Lost* without angels, or devils, or God. . . . The whole narrative of *Frankenstein* is, indeed, acted out in the absence of God. The grand gestures of *Frankenstein* may suggest a world of fantasy that has acquired a profound escapist appeal in modern culture, but they take place in a framework that necessarily makes an ironic commentary on them, even while our sympathies are drawn to dreams of the more than human the narrative will not allow.

This characteristic tension between an impinging, conditional, and time-bound world and a dream of something freer and better makes the central subject matter and form of the nineteenth-century novel and, ironically, of nineteenth-century science as well. The old myths enter nineteenth-century fiction, but they do so in the mode of realism. . . . [Though] it would be absurd to claim Mary Shelley as a direct "influence" on the dominant literary and scientific forms of the century, we can see that in her secularization of the creation myth she invented a metaphor that was irresistible to the culture as a whole. As George Eliot turned to Feuerbach to allow her to transform Christianity into a humanism with all the emotional power of religion, so the novel itself, as a genre, put its faith in a material world of fact that, as Matthew Arnold pointed out, had failed us. In writers as central and various as Feuerbach, Comte, Darwin, Marx, Frazer, and Freud we can find Victor Frankenstein's activity: the attempt to discover in matter what we had previously attributed to spirit, the bestowing *on* matter (or history, or society, or nature) the values once given to God.

This argument puts Mary Shelley in some rather remarkable company, but, of course, the point is not to equate the achievement of her little "ghost story" with that of the great thinkers named. The claim is simply that Mary Shelley did, indeed, create an image, with the authenticity of dream vision, that became prophetic; that the image articulates powerfully the dominant currents of her culture and ours; and that it is for these reasons that *Frankenstein* has survived its own adolescent clumsiness and its later distortions.

The pervasiveness of the Frankenstein metaphor in modern consciousness testifies to the richness and variousness of its implications. The dictionary definition focuses only on the uncontrollable nature of the thing created; but the image of the created Monster, emerging from the isolated workshop of the obsessed but otherwise gentle scientist, unfolds into more possibilities than I can describe. . . . At the risk of arbitrary exclusions and of belaboring what may seem obvious, I want to outline some of the major implications of the Frankenstein metaphor in contemporary consciousness, and as they have their sources in the novel proper.

1. *Birth and Creation*. In *Frankenstein* we are confronted immediately by the displacement of God and woman from the acts of conception and birth. Where Victor imagines himself embarked on the creation of a new race that would bless him, he behaves, even before his creation proves a monster, as though he is engaged in unnatural, shameful activity. Neither of the two attitudes is entirely undercut by the narrative, even though the dream of the new race is, of course, exploded. The image of Frankenstein in his laboratory is not only of an unnatural act, but also one of an heroic dream, and the novel's insistence, even through Walton and the Monster, on Victor's heroic nature, implies that the creation without God, without woman, need not be taken as an unequivocal evil.

The displacement of woman obviously reflects a fear of birth and Mary Shelley's own ambivalence about childbearing . . . ; the Monster's presence on the wedding night becomes a permanent image of the horror of sexuality as opposed to the ideal and nonsexual love of the cousins, Victor and Elizabeth. The image of the Monster lurking ominously in the background, with Elizabeth sprawled on the bed, is one of the dominant icons of the film versions. Obviously, the image is profoundly phallic and profoundly violent, an unacceptable alternative to and consequence of the act of conception in the laboratory. Indeed, in the novel itself . . . the two scenes precisely echo each other. In both cases, there is an association that runs as constant ground-motif through the novel.

Sexuality and birth, imagination and creation are, in this heavily material world, reverse images of death and destruction. Frankenstein and his creature come to represent, in part, an alternative to the violence of sexuality, on the one hand, and to the sheer spirituality of divine creation, on the other. (pp. 6-9)

2. *The Overreacher*. The aspiration to divine creative activity (akin to Romantic notions of the poet) places Victor Frankenstein in the tradition of Faustian overreachers. Frankenstein the creator is also Frankenstein the modern Prometheus, full of the great Romantic dream—concretized for a moment in the French Revolution—of a rebirth of mankind. True, Victor is seeking a kind of immortality, but, as Ellen Moers points out [see excerpt dated 1974], Mary Shelley works the Faust tradition in an unusual (and, I might again add, secularizing) way by having Victor seek immortality not directly for himself but in the creation of offspring. If we detect the stirrings of selfishness in Victor's desire to have a whole species that would bless him, the text still insists on the profundity of his moral character and the conscious morality of all of his choices save the fatal one. Indeed . . . , Frankenstein is removed from direct personal responsibility even for his own ambitions: for the most part he is described as passively consumed by energies larger than himself or as quite literally unconscious and ill when his being conscious might have changed the course of the narrative.

The theme of the overreacher is largely complicated by the evidence that Victor's worst sin is not the creation of the Monster but his refusal to take responsibility for it. It is as though God had withdrawn from his creation. Characteristically, in the secularizing myth, Mary Shelley has imagined the responsibilities of God shifted to mankind. The burden is too great to allow us an easy moral placing of Victor. The theme of the overreacher in this context brings us to the kind of impasse that *Frankenstein* itself reaches in the mutual destruction of creator and created. That is, we see that the ambition is heroic and admirable, yet deadly because humans are incapable of fulfilling their dreams in material reality, or, paradoxically, of bearing the responsibility for them should they succeed. (pp. 9-10)

3. *Rebellion and Moral Isolation*. Obviously, these aspects of the myth are related to "overreaching." Yet it is important to note that they apply not only to Victor but to the Monster as well, whose ambition is really limited to the longing for domestic affection. Victor himself is not quite imagined as a rebel, except perhaps in his pursuit of alchemical knowledge after his father ridicules him for reading Paracelsus. In any case, unlike the Monster, he does not consciously rebel against authority. Yet, "animated by an almost supernatural enthusiasm," Victor takes up an intellectual pursuit (whence did the "principle of life proceed") that places him outside the traditional Christian world, and that ought to make him, like Adam eating the apple, a rebel against God. The context, however, is quietly un-Christian. Victor speaks in a scientific or at least naturalistic language that assumes a natural material answer to what was once a religious and metaphysical question. (pp. 10-11)

The moral isolation into which Victor sinks is, in effect, chosen for him by his obsession. Like Raskolnikov plotting murder, like Dimmesdale guilty of adultery, Victor lives with a secret that we understand, without explanation, must be kept from public knowledge. Here the residue of metaphysical shame works its effects, but social and psychological explanations offer themselves immediately. In any case, the activity separates Victor from normal life as fully as a direct act of murder would. (p. 11)

The Monster's isolation derives not so much from his actions as from his hideousness. Where Victor moves from domestic bliss to the garret, the Monster leaves the garret to seek that bliss. Victor's revolutionary action causes his isolation; the Monster's isolation causes his revolutionary action. "Believe me, Frankenstein," he says, "I was benevolent; my soul glowed with love and humanity; but am I not alone, miserably alone?" (pp. 11-12)

Despite the apparent moral simplicity of most modern versions of *Frankenstein,* the Frankenstein metaphor implies great ambiguity about where the burden of good and evil rests. Both Victor and the Monster imply resistance to the established order. . . . In early Romantic literature, of course, rebellion is more likely to be a virtue than a sin, and the Monster makes a strong case against social injustice. Even Walton, though warned by Victor, is instinctively convinced of the justice of the Monster's arguments.

The constantly shifting moral perspective of the narrative results from the fact that each of its major figures—Walton, Victor, the Monster—is at once victimizer and victim; and this tradition is even continued in modern movie versions. In novel and films, any singularity is punished by the community, either by forcing isolation or by literal imprisonment. The three major figures and Felix De Lacey variously challenge the established order and acquire dignity by virtue of the challenge and of the punishment that ensues. Thus the novel, which might be taken as a parable of the necessity of limits in an entirely secular world, may also be taken as a parable of the necessity for revolutionary reprisal (at whatever cost) because of the social and political limits that frustrate the noblest elements of the human spirit.

4. *The Unjust Society.* After the execution of the innocent Justine, Elizabeth Lavenza, the vessel of domestic purity, tells Victor that "men appear to me as monsters thirsting for each other's blood." . . . Even if she retracts immediately ("Yet I am certainly unjust"), the notion that the world of men is itself "monstrous" is a constant motif of the novel. Even in the most conventional of the modern Frankenstein films, the motif emerges when, in the obligatory misty night, the villagers turn out as a maddened lynch mob and transform Frankenstein and the Monster into victims of an overwhelming attack on the castle. In almost every film, the townspeople are almost comically banal, the burgomeisters and gendarmerie officious and totally without sensibility. Absurd though these figures may be . . . , they echo the essentially shallow ambitions and dreams of security that fill the background of the novel.

There the motif is handled subtly enough to make the monstrous problematic. Elizabeth's sense that "men are monsters" recurs in the monster's ingenious hectoring of Victor in a fine God-winian rational discourse. Moreover, the De Lacey story is a continuing narrative of injustice, on all sides. And in his last speech to Walton, the Monster makes clear once more that his own monstrousness is not really different from that of the world that condemns him. . . . The novel has taught us to distrust the evenhandedness of the law that Victor's father praises before Justine is executed; we understand with the Monster that greed is a commonplace of social activity. Not even the family unit—Frankenstein's and the Monster's ideal—escapes the contamination that almost makes rebellion necessary and that makes Victor's escape to his laboratory from Geneva seem psychologically and socially explicable.

5. *The Defects of Domesticity.* The theme of the overreacher and the rebel—the Promethean theme—is the other side of the theme of ideal domesticity. . . . Mary Shelley treats "domestic affection" in such a way as to make it possible to read *Frankenstein* as an attack on the very traditions of bourgeois society it purports to be celebrating. Certainly, as we have seen, "the amiableness of domestic affection" does nothing to satisfy Victor Frankenstein's ambitions, or to prevent the monstrous creation; nor, in the tale of the Monster's wanderings, does it extend to anything outside itself to allow for the domestication of the Monster's loving energies. "Domestic affection" is, in a way, defined by its exclusion of energy and by its resistance to the larger community. The Monster instinctively believes in the rhetoric of domesticity and the need for community; it is psychologically and dramatically appropriate that he should exhaust himself in the total destruction of ostensibly ideal domesticity when he discovers that he is excluded from it, and that the ideal is false. (pp. 13-14)

6. *The Double.* Almost every critic of *Frankenstein* has noted that Victor and his Monster are doubles. The doubleness even enters some of the popular versions and is un-self-consciously accepted by everyone who casually calls the Monster "Frankenstein." The motif of the *Doppelgänger* was certainly in Mary's mind during the writing, as it was a part of the Gothic tradition in which she wrote; moreover, it is one with which she would have been intimately connected through Shelley himself, as in "Alastor" and "Epipsychidion." So pervasive has been the recognition that the Monster and Frankenstein are two aspects of the same being that the writers in this volume assume rather than argue it. The narrative requires us to see that the doubling extends beyond the two major narrators: Walton is obviously another aspect of Frankenstein, and Clerval yet another; Elizabeth can be paired with Victor's mother, with Justine, and with the unfinished "bride" of the Monster. . . . Such doublings and triplings, with reverberations in and out of the novel in Mary Shelley's own life and in modern psychological theory, suggest again the instability and ambivalence of the book's "meanings."

They point centrally to the way "Frankenstein" as a modern metaphor implies a conception of the divided self, the creator and his work at odds. The civilized man or woman contains within the self a monstrous, destructive, and self-destructive energy. The angel in the house entails a demon outside it, the Monster leering through the window at the horrified Victor and the murdered Elizabeth. Here, in particular, we can watch the specially secularized versions of traditional mythology. The devil and the angel of the morality play are replaced by a modern pre-Freudian psychology that removes the moral issue from the metaphysical context—the traditional concepts of good and evil—and places it entirely within the self. Morality is, as it were, replaced by schizophrenia. Frankenstein's longing for domesticity is echoed in the Monster's (and in Walton's expression of loneliness in the opening pages); Frankenstein's obsession with science is echoed in the Monster's obsession with destruction. The two characters haunt and hunt each other through the novel, each evoking from us sympathy for their sufferings, revulsion from their cruelties.

The echoes force themselves on us with a persistence and intensity that override the mere narrative and even enter into popular versions that are not intrinsically concerned with doubling. The book creates a psychomachia, an internal war that has its own authenticity despite the grotesqueness of the external action. If the characters seem shallow as novelistic figures within the conventions of realism we have come to assume are natural to nineteenth-century fiction, it is partly because they are imagined from the start as incomplete (a notion explored in Peter Brook's essay [see excerpt dated 1979]). They can be seen, indeed, as fragments of a mind in conflict with itself, extremes unreconciled, striving to make themselves whole. Ambition and passivity, hate and love, the need to procreate and the need to destroy are seen, in *Frankenstein,* as symbiotic: the destruction of one is, through various narrative strategies, the destruction of the other.

7. *Technology, Entropy, and the Monstrous*. Perhaps the most obvious and continuing application of the word "Frankenstein" in modern society is to technological advances. This is altogether appropriate to Mary Shelley's original conception of the novel since Victor's discovery of the secret of life is fundamentally scientific; and he talks of his "animation" of the Monster's body as a mere trick of technology. Modern science fiction and modern industry are full of such "animated" beings, the products of computer technology; with the discovery of DNA, biologists even seem on the verge of simulating the natural process of creation of life. But both of these developments are part of the same imagination as Mary Shelley gives us with her Monster: that life is not "spirit" but matter imbued with energy, itself another form of matter.

Martin Tropp has noted that "when Mary Shelley gave her intended 'ghost story' a scientific context, she linked the Gothic concept of the double with technology" [see Additional Bibliography]. Her fears of the creation of life by mere mechanisms, Tropp notes, resulted from her awareness that "technology can never be more than a magnified image of the self." . . . And when that self is engaged in a psychomachia, the result can only be large-scale disaster. In a psychic world of the divided self, in a social world in which domesticity and ambition are seen as incompatible poles, the self expressed in technology can only be what our original dictionary definition tells us, "troublesomely uncontrollable, esp. to its creator," i.e., monstrous. The nightmare quality of the novel depends on this projection of the self into an objectively existing, independent reality over which one necessarily loses control as it acts out one's own monstrous passions. Here all the battery of Freudian equipment comes neatly or, perhaps, explosively into play. All the elements of moral isolation, the grubbing in filthy flesh, the obsessed and inhuman energies that went into the creation of the Monster, can be seen acting themselves out in the destruction they really imply—in the incestuous destructiveness of Victor's ostensibly ideal relation to Elizabeth, in the fraternal hostility buried in his love for poor William, in the hatred of his mother implied in his failure to save Justine (who has adopted Mrs. Frankenstein's very way of life). Such implications are explored in a great deal of criticism of the novel. But the point here is that technology becomes the means by which these buried aspects of the self are enacted. The "work or agency" does not rebel against the creator but actually accomplishes what the creator wants. . . . The uncontrolled technological creation is particularly frightening and obsessively attractive to modern consciousness because it forces a confrontation with our buried selves. It promises to reveal to us our deepest and most powerful desires, and to enact them. The Monster demands our sympathetic engagement while our social consciousness must by an act of will—almost like Walton's when he finds himself irresistibly attracted by the Monster's talk—reject him.

The duality of our relationship to creator and creature is an echo of our relationship to the technology that we worship even as we recognize that it is close to destroying us. Another way to express the duality, in technological terms, is through the idea of entropy. Victor's overreaching is an attempt to create *new* life. He fails to recognize the necessary secular-scientific myth of entropy: that in any closed system, the new energy generated will be less than the energy expended in its creation, and that ultimately the system will run down. It took a great deal of death to make the new life; the making of the Monster is at the expense of all of Victor's immediate world—brother, father, bride, friend. The world of mere matter is both finite

Frankenstein's monster observing the creation of his mate. Illustration by Nino Carbe from the 1932 edition of Frankenstein, *published by World Publishing Company.*

and corrupted. Without the incalculable presence of divine spirit, creation can only entail destruction larger than itself. It is, ultimately, this nightmare image that the Monster represents to our culture. (pp. 15-17)

> George Levine, "The Ambiguous Heritage of 'Frankenstein'," in The Endurance of Frankenstein: Essays on Mary Shelley's Novel, *edited by George Levine and U. C. Knoepflmacher, University of California Press, 1979, pp. 3-30.*

PETER BROOKS   (essay date 1979)

[*Brooks analyzes the significance of language in* Frankenstein, *focusing on its importance to the Monster.*]

Mary Shelley's *Frankenstein* continues to solicit and disturb us not only through its creation of a decisive image of Gothic horror, but also by the pathos of a monsterism in doomed dialectic with nature and with culture. It is above all in the question of language, both as explicit theme of the novel and as implicit model of the novel's complex organization, that the problem of the monstrous is played out. We might approach the network of issues dramatized in the novel first through Victor Frankenstein's crucial interview with his monstrous creation, the interview which leads to the Monster's telling his tale to Frankenstein, the story-within-a-story (itself a story-within-a-story, when we consider the role of Robert Walton as initial and ultimate narrator). Following the first murders committed by his Monster—William strangled, Justine judicially done to death through maliciously falsified evidence—Frankenstein seeks solace in the mountains above Chamonix. He penetrates into the "glorious presence-chamber of imperial Nature," climbs to Montanvert and the Mer de Glace, hoping to recapture a remembered effect of "a sublime ecstasy that gave wings to the soul, and allowed it to soar from the obscure world to light and joy." His ascension takes him to a "wonderful and stupendous scene," overlooking the Mer de Glace, facing the "awful majesty" of Mont Blanc; his heart once again opens to joy and he exclaims, in the tones of the Ossianic bard, "Wandering spirits, if indeed ye wander, and do not rest in your narrow beds; allow me this faint happiness, or take me, as your companion, away from the joys of life." . . . Whereupon a superhuman shape comes bounding over the ice. It is, of course, no spirit of the departed, nor any beneficient spirit of nature, but the Monster himself, who has at last tracked down his creator, and will force him into parley. (pp. 205-06)

Frankenstein's initial reaction to the encounter with the Monster consists in curses and an abortive attempt to do battle with him. Still the Monster pleads for a hearing. A hearing that need not be a seeing: when Frankenstein commands, "Begone! relieve me from the sight of your detested form," the Monster responds by placing his huge hands over Frankenstein's eyes: "Thus I relieve thee, my creator . . . thus I take from thee a sight which you abhor. Still thou canst listen to me, and grant me thy compassion." . . . The Monster understands that it is not visual relationship that favors him—indeed, his only favorable reception by a human being has come from a blind man—but rather the auditory, the interlocutory, the relationship of language.

For the Monster is eloquent. From his first words, he shows himself to be a supreme rhetorician of his own situation, one who controls the antitheses and oxymorons that express the pathos of his existence: "Remember, that I am thy creature; I ought to be thy Adam; but I am rather the fallen angel, whom thou drivest from joy for no misdeed. Everywhere I see bliss, from which I alone am irrevocably excluded. I was benevolent and good; misery made me a fiend. Make me happy, and I shall again be virtuous." . . . When we learn of the Monster's self-education—and particularly his three master-texts: *Paradise Lost,* Plutarch's *Lives,* and *Werther*—we understand the sources of his eloquence, and of the conception of a just order of things that animates his plea to his creator. But it is of primary importance to register Mary Shelley's radical and saving decision to stage a deformed and menacing creature who, rather than using grunts and gestures, speaks and reasons with the highest elegance, logic, and persuasiveness. In the Monster's use of language the novel poses its most important questions, for it is language alone that may compensate for a deficient, monstrous nature.

Frankenstein is touched by the Monster's eloquence. When he looks at this "filthy mass that moved and talked," he feels horror and hatred; yet by the end of the Monster's tale he avows: "His words had a strange effect upon me. I compassionated him." . . . Through the medium of language, a first relationship is created. Like Coleridge's Wedding Guest, Frankenstein is compelled to hear out the tale of this cursed being. The force of the compulsion here is no "glittering eye," but the power of language itself to link speaker and listener. (pp. 206-07)

The Monster hence produces a tale, based, like any tale, on the "narrative contract" between narrator and narratee. Its very possibility depends on an order of cultural symbolic which implies that network of intersubjective relations from which the Monster protests he has been excluded. The close of his narrative suggests the importance of language as relation. In arguing that Frankenstein create a female monster to be a companion to him, the Monster asserts that only in communication with a similar being can he "become linked to the chain of existence and events, from which I am now excluded." . . . The wish for a *semblable* may itself belong to the imaginary order, as an instance of speculary narcissism and deception. The term *chain,* however, identifies meaning as residing in a

systematic network of relation, in the symbolic order. . . . Exclusion from this chain could be the very definition of monsterism. (p. 208)

Language is also the principal theme of the Monster's story of his life up to this point. His first experience with humankind has laid bare the hopelessness of speculary relationship, its necessary result in alienation and rejection: the shepherd he encounters in a hut flees shrieking from his sight. Retreating into the hovel adjoining the de Lacey cottage, he then begins his education, seeing, but himself unseen. From his hiding place, he discovers that "these people possessed a method of communicating their experience and feelings to one another by articulate sounds. What particularly impress him are the emotional effects wrought by these sounds, which "sometimes produced pleasure or pain, smiles or sadness, in the minds and countenances of the beholders. This was indeed a godlike science."

Mary Shelley's Monster is in many respects an Enlightenment natural man, or noble savage; his first ideas demonstrate the processes of Lockean sensationalism and Hartleyan associationism. His discovery of language implies Rousseau's argument, in the *Essai sur l'origine des langues,* that language springs from passion rather than need: need cannot form the necessary social context for voiced language, since its effect is to scatter men; and need can make do with the barest repertory of visual signs, gestures, imperatives. Passion, on the other hand, brings men together, and the relation of desire calls forth voice. It is hence no accident that what language first reveals to the Monster is human love, and that his rhetorical plea to his creator ends with the demand for a creature whom he might love. (pp. 208-09)

The Monster intuitively grasps that language will be of importance to him because by its very nature it implies the "chain of existence and events" within which he seeks a place, defines the interdependency of senders and receivers of messages in that chain, and provides the possibility of emotional effect independent of any designation.

The Monster unerringly discovers language to be on the side of culture rather than nature, and to imply the structures of relation at the basis of culture. The discovery is a vital one, for the side of "nature" is irreparably marked by lack, by monsterism. Against the Monster's hearing of the cottagers' language is set his discovery of his own features mirrored in a pool—a sinister parody of Eve's discovery of her fair features in the pool of Eden, on the day of her creation, in Book IV of *Paradise Lost.* In *Frankenstein,* the reflected image convinces the beholder "that I was in reality the monster that I am." . . . This speculary *cogito,* where the Monster witnesses his outward identity as alien to his inner desire, estranged, determined by the view and judgment of the Other, clinches the importance of language as the symbolic order that must compensate for nature. The Monster understands that he must not show himself to the cottagers until he has mastered their language, "which knowledge might enable me to make them overlook the deformity of my figure." . . . (pp. 209-10)

[Language], and especially writing, must appear to the Monster, as it did to Rousseau, ambiguous in effect, like the Promethean gift of fire, so strange in its production of "opposite effects." . . . Yet it remains the necessary compensation, the only hope for linkage to humankind. The Monster will try its effects first on the blind De Lacey. And here the godlike power of the science does reveal itself, as De Lacey responds: "I am blind, and cannot judge of your countenance, but there is some-thing in your words which persuades me that you are sin-cere." . . . Mutual sympathy, benefaction, protection, and re-lation are close to being sealed through language, when Felix, Agatha, and Safie enter and throw the situation brutally back into the speculary order: Agatha faints, Safie flees, and Felix "tore me from his father, to whose knees I clung." . . . The result is Fall. The Monster becomes explicitly satanic—"I, like the arch-fiend, bore a hell within me." . . .

At its completion, the Monster's narrative implies that use of language has failed to gain him entry into the "chain of ex-istence and events," but has rather made him fully aware of his unique and accursed origin. (p. 211)

> *Peter Brooks, "'Godlike Science/Unhallowed Arts':*
> *Language, Nature, and Monstrosity," in* The En-
> durance of Frankenstein: Essays on Mary Shelley's
> Novel, *edited by George Levine and U. C. Knoep-*
> *flmacher, University of California Press, 1979, pp.*
> *205-20.*

THOMAS LIGOTTI   (story date 1985)

[*Ligotti, a contemporary American horror writer, provides an epilogue to* Frankenstein.]

Victor Frankenstein has died on board a ship caught in seas of ice near the North Pole. His body has been sent back to his native Switzerland, where, however, there is no one to receive it. Everyone he ever knew has already died before him. His brother William, his friend Henry, his wife Elizabeth, and his father, Alphonse Frankenstein, among others, are all dead. A minor official in the Genevan civil service comes up with the suggestion to donate the corpse, still very well preserved, to the university at Ingolstadt, where the deceased distinguished himself in scientific studies.

Hans Hoffmann, a prodigy in comparative anatomy at the uni-versity at Ingolstadt, is conducting a series of experiments in his apartment. He has assembled, and is quite sure he can vivify, a human being from various body parts he has bought or stolen. To consummate his project, which to his knowledge has never been attempted and would certainly make him fa-mous, he still needs a human brain. He has heard that the body of a former student at the university at Ingolstadt is preserved in the morgue of the medical school. He has heard that the man was a brilliant student. This would be the perfect brain, thinks Hans Hoffmann. Late one night he breaks into the morgue and helps himself.

Well, says Hans Hoffmann on the spectacular evening when the creature first opens its eyes, aren't you a beauty! This is intended ironically, of course; the creature is quite hideous. What Hans Hoffmann now notices is that the creature is gazing around the room, as if expecting to see someone who, for the moment, is absent.

Oh ho, says the scientist, I can see I'm going to have trouble with you. You'll be begging me one of these days to make you a companion, someone of your own kind. Well, look here, says Hans Hoffmann holding a handful of entrails and part of a woman's face. I've already tried to do it, perhaps a little half-heartedly, I admit. It's not the same, making a woman, and I don't have much use for them anyway.

Hans Hoffmann cannot tell whether or not the creature has understood these words. Nevertheless, it has an extremely des-olate expression on its face (just possibly due to a few collapsed muscles). Now the creature is staggering around Hans Hoff-man's apartment, inadvertantly breaking a number of objects. Finally, it stumbles out the door and into the streets of Ingol-stadt. (Good riddance! shouts Hans Hoffmann.)

But as the creature wanders into the darkness, searching for a face it remembers from long ago, it is unaware that the only being left in the entire universe who could possibly offer him any comfort has already incinerated himself on a furious pyre deep in the icy wasteland of the North Pole. (pp. 128-29)

> *Thomas Ligotti, "'The Agonizing Resurrection of*
> *Victor Frankenstein, Citizen of Geneva'," in his* Songs
> of a Dead Dreamer, *Silver Scarab Press, 1985, pp.*
> *128-29.*

BRIAN W. ALDISS   (essay date 1986)

[*Aldiss is an English novelist, short story writer, critic, and editor who is best known for his science fiction novels and criticism. In this excerpt from his comprehensive history of the genre, Aldiss credits Shelley as the first science fiction author and examines the literary, social, and scientific bases for* Frankenstein.]

Frankenstein: or, The Modern Prometheus was published anon-ymously on 11th March 1818. . . . The Napoleonic Wars were over; *Savannah* crossed the Atlantic, the first steamship to do so; the early steam locomotives were chuffing along their metal tracks, Boulton's iron foundries going full blast; the Lancashire cotton factories were lit by gas, and gas mains were being laid in London. Telford and McAdam were building roads and bridges, Galvani's followers and Humphry Davy were exper-imenting with electricity. "So much has been done," ex-claimed the soul of Frankenstein, "more, far more, will I achieve!" . . . (p. 36)

[Mary Shelley was the] first writer of science fiction; [she] had imbibed the philosophical ideas of Locke and the scientific ideas of Darwin, Humphry Davy, Joseph Priestley, and others. They helped shape her emotional life and she set about applying her ideas to papers within a loose Gothic structure of suspense and pursuit. (p. 37)

Readers and commentators alike are agreed that *Frankenstein* is Mary Shelley's great original novel. It is hardly surprising. *Frankenstein* is the one novel she wrote during Shelley's life-time. As he in his poems was opening up new ground, she—caught in the aura of intellectual excitement which existed between them—also ventured into startling new territory. (p. 38)

What exactly is uniquely innovative about *Frankenstein*?

Interest has always centred on the creation of the nameless monster. This is the core of the novel, an experiment that goes wrong—a prescription to be repeated later, more sensationally, in *Amazing Stories* and elsewhere. Frankenstein's is the Faus-tian dream of unlimited power, but Frankenstein makes no pacts with the devil. "The devil" belongs to a relegated system of belief. Frankenstein's ambitions bear fruit only when he throws away his old reference books from a pre-scientific age and gets down to some research in the laboratory. This is now accepted practice, of course. But what is now accepted practice was, in 1818, a startling perception, a small revolution.

The novel dramatizes the difference between the old age and the new, between an age when things went by rote and one where everything was suddenly called into question. (p. 39)

The Byron-Shelley circle understood themselves to be living in a new age. They felt themselves to be moderns. The study of gases was advanced; much was understood about the composition of the atmosphere; that lightning and electricity were one and the same was already clear—although that it was not a fluid was still not so definite that Mary was unable to use that misconception as a metaphor. Shelley had a microscope while at Oxford, and the study of morbid anatomy was well advanced. Mary lived in a thoroughly Newtonian world, in which natural explanations could be sought for natural phenomena. It is for this reason she sends Victor Frankenstein to Ingolstadt University; it was renowned in its time as a centre for science. Mary knew more of the science of her time than has been generally granted. . . .

Why, then, is so much time spent by Frankenstein with the alchemists, with Cornelius Agrippa and Paracelsus?

One practical answer is that Mary Shelley wished to make it plain that the old authorities who "promised impossibilities and performed nothing" had to go. She had to show that they were useless, outdated, and without merit in a modern age. (p. 40)

As if to dispel any doubts about her aversion to "jiggery-pokery magic", Mary makes it plain that her central marvel shares the essential quality of scientific experiment, rather than the hit-and-miss of legerdermain. She has Frankenstein create life a second time.

Frankenstein agrees to make a female companion for the monster, subject to certain conditions. When his work is almost finished, Frankenstein pauses, thinking of the "race of devils" that might be raised up by the union between his two creatures (a curious moment, this, for science fiction, looking back towards Caliban's snarl to Prospero in *The Tempest*—"I had peopled else the isle with Calibans!"—and forward to the monstrous legions of robots which were to tramp across the pages of the twentieth-century world!). Victor destroys what he has begun, the monster discovers the breach of contract, utters his direst threat—"I shall be with you on your wedding-night"—and disappears.

The rest is a tale of flight and pursuit, punctuated by death and retribution, with everyone's hand turned against the wretched monster. This section contains much of Godwin's thinking, and of his novel, *Caleb Williams,* which, as its preface announced, was a review of "the modes of domestic and unrecorded despotism by which man becomes the destroyer of man."

The influence of Godwin and *Caleb Williams* is very strong. Frankenstein's friend, Clerval, is probably named after Mr Clare, the one good man in *Caleb Williams*—as, in Mary Shelley's later novel, Lord Raymond is named after the Raymond, a kind of eighteenth-century Robin Hood, in her father's novel.

No celestial vengeance here. No devils, no retribution from God. Mankind is left alone, scheming to take over the vacant premises. Like *Caleb Williams, Frankenstein* becomes a story of implacable lay revenge, hatred, judicial blunder, pistols fired from open windows, a thwarted voyage of discovery, exhausting journeys without map or compass. There is nemesis but no promise of afterlife—unless it is the miserable hounded afterlife suffered by the monster. (p. 41)

One enduring attraction of the book is its series of ambiguities, not all of which can have been the intention of an inexperienced novelist. We never see Frankenstein in his laboratory, throwing the fatal switch. That was Boris Karloff. The book tells us

only of the creature bending over his master. Again, in the pursuit, pursuer and pursued take turn. In particular, the language of the novel invites us to confuse the main roles. Perhaps we are meant to believe that the creature is Frankenstein's doppelganger, pursuing him to death. Which of them is "restored to animation"? "We . . . restored him to animation . . . As soon as he showed signs of life we wrapped him up in blankets. I often feared that his suffering had deprived him of understanding . . . He is generally melancholy and despairing. . . ."

This is not the monster but Victor, before Victor tells his story to Walton. We have only his word for the story's accuracy, just as, finally, we have only the monster's promises, as he disappears into darkness and distance, that he will destroy himself. The outcome of all the trials (there are four in the book) are unreliable; are we then encouraged to trust our witnesses? (pp. 41-2)

In one of its aspects, *Frankenstein* is a diseased creation myth, prototype of many to come. . . . (p. 42)

Here we confront the more personal side of the novel. The struggle between Victor and his fiend is Oedipal in nature. Like André Gide's Oedipus, the fiend seems to himself to have "welled out of the unknown": "Who was I? What was I? Whence did I come?" it asks itself . . . The muddying of generations and generation reflects the confusion Mary Shelley felt regarding her own involved family situation, surrounded by the half-sisters of both her mother's earlier and her father's later liaisons.

Some critics have read into the more macabre scenes of *Frankenstein* undertones of vampirism (a favourite with Lord Byron) and incest. "I shall be with you on your wedding night," cries the creature to Victor, who is in a sense its mother and father. Sexual tensions move throughout the book. (pp. 42-3)

In referring to *Frankenstein* as a diseased creation myth, I have in mind phrases in the novel with sexual connotations such as "my workshop of filthy creation", used by Frankenstein of his secret work. Mary's experience brought her to see life and death as closely intertwined. The phraseology used to describe her dream [in the 1831 preface; see excerpt above] is significant. She saw "the hideous phantasm of a man stretched out, and then, on the working of some powerful engine, show signs of life, and stir with an uneasy, half vital motion". The vigorous line suggests both a distorted image of her mother dying, in those final restless moments which often tantalizingly suggest recovery rather than its opposite, as well as the stirrings of sexual intercourse, particularly when we recall that "powerful engine" is a term serving in pornography as a synonym for penis. (p. 43)

The last word on *Frankenstein* will never be said. It contains too many seemingly conflicting elements for that. (p. 49)

The Outwardness of science and society is balanced in the novel by an Inwardness which Mary's dream helped her to accommodate. This particular balance is perhaps one of *Frankenstein*'s greatest merits: that its tale of exterior adventure and misfortune is accompanied by—encompassed by—psychological depth. Mary might have claimed for her drama what Shelley said in his Preface to *Prometheus Bound:* "The imagery which I have employed will be found, in many instances, to have been drawn from the operations of the human mind, or from those external actions by which they are expressed."

Love, fear, the cruelty of parents and lovers—such familiar acquaintances are stirred up by the introduction of the central novelty.

Victor's lowly unique creature, outcast from human kind, takes a lofty view of itself and—in contrast with the almost dumb fiend to which the movies have accustomed us—is articulate regarding its sorrows.

Here we are given an educational prescription which looks both backward and forward—to a time when mankind does not judge merely by appearances.

Shelley read *Paradise Lost* aloud to Mary in 1816.

The monster likens himself to Adam in the poem—but how much less fortunate than Adam, for in this case the creator rushes away from "his odious handywork, horror-stricken". The creature's career has something in common with Adam's, with the vital exception of the missing Eve. He is first created, and then brought to full intellectual awareness of the world in which he lives—at which stage, "benevolence and generosity were ever present before me". . . . He then undergoes his version of the Fall, when "the spirit of revenge enkindled in my heart". . . . Now the creature is frequently referred to as "the fiend". In many ways, it becomes less human, more a symbol of inhumanity. "I saw him," says Frankenstein, "descend the mountain with greater speed than the flight of an eagle, and quickly lost him among the undulations of the sea of ice". . . . (pp. 49-50)

The fiend increasingly speaks of itself in Miltonic terms, saying of itself at last, over Victor's corpse, "the fallen angel becomes a malignant devil".

This change in the nature of the monster enables Mary Shelley to bring out two aspects of the struggle which are subordinate to the eschatological theme.

The first aspect is man's confrontation with himself, which the power of creation necessarily entails. The diseased creation myth prefigures Jekyll and Hyde, as Frankenstein struggles with his alter ego; their obsessive pursuit of one another makes sense only in metaphysical terms.

The second aspect is the disintegration of society which follows man's arrogation of power. One perversion of the natural order leads to another. *Frankenstein* is loaded with a sense of corruption, and "the fiend" moves about the world striking where it will, like a disease which, beginning naturally enough in a charnel house, can be isolated and sterilized only on a drift ice flow.

The rejection of a just Heavenly Father, the concern with suffering, the sexual obsessions, have helped preserve *Frankenstein*'s topicality. Not only does it foreshadow our fears about the two-edged triumphs of scientific progress; it is also the first novel to be powered by the evolutionary idea. God, however often called upon, is an absentee landlord. The lodgers have to fight things out between themselves.

Herein lies the force of the novel's sub-title. In Shelley's lyrical drama, *Prometheus Unbound*, mighty Jupiter has chained Prometheus to a rock. Prometheus suffers terrible torture, but is eventually freed when Jupiter is dethroned, to retire into obscurity.

What is mankind to seek, if not God? Answers to this modern conundrum include objectives like knowledge, power, and self-

fulfilment. According to one's reading of the novel, Victor Frankenstein can be understood to seek all three.

The use of this modernized Faust theme is particularly suited to the first real novel of science fiction: Frankenstein is *the* modern predicament, involving the post-Rousseauvian dichotomy between the individual and his society, as well as the encroachment of science on that society, and mankind's dual nature, whose inherited ape curiosity has brought him both success and misery. His great discovery apart, Frankenstein is an over-reacher and victim, staggering through a world where virtues are few (though the fiend *reads* of them). Instead of hope and forgiveness, there remain only the misunderstandings of men and the noxious half life of the monster. Knowledge brings no guarantee of happiness.

For this critic's taste, the Frankenstein theme is more contemporary and more interesting than interstellar travel tales, since it takes us nearer to the enigma of man and thus of life. . . . (pp. 50-1)

> Brian W. Aldiss, "On the Origins of Species: Mary Shelley," in his Trillion Year Spree: The History of Science Fiction, Atheneum, 1986, pp. 25-51.

ADDITIONAL BIBLIOGRAPHY

Angeli, Helen Rossetti. *Shelley and His Friends in Italy*. London: Methuen & Co., 1911, 326 p.
  A biography detailing the Shelleys' years in Italy.

Bowerbank, Sylvia. "The Social Order vs. the Wretch: Mary Shelley's Contradictory-Mindedness in *Frankenstein*."*ELH* 46, No. 3 (Fall 1979): 418-31.
  Examines *Frankenstein* from a sociopolitical perspective. According to Bowerbank, the novel reveals the simultaneously radical and conservative attitudes of Shelley and her friends because it "sentimentally defends, and yet skeptically attacks, domestic and social tranquility."

Church, Richard. *Mary Shelley*. 1928. Reprint. Representative Women, edited by Francis Birrell. Folcroft, Pa.: Folcroft Press, 1969, 91 p.
  A reliable early biography containing brief, generally favorable critical comments.

Clifford, Gay. "*Caleb Williams* and *Frankenstein*: First-Person Narratives and 'Things as They Are'." *Genre* 10, No. 4 (Winter 1977): 601-17.
  Outlines the artistic and philosophical viewpoints of the first-person narratives in *Caleb Williams* and *Frankenstein* and compares Shelley's narrative techniques with those of her father.

Cude, Wilfred. "Mary Shelley's Modern Prometheus: A Study in the Ethics of Scientific Creativity." *The Dalhousie Review* 52, No. 2 (Summer 1972): 212-25.
  Regards *Frankenstein* as primarily an exploration through Promethean myth of the ethics of scientific research. According to Cude, Shelley blames modern society for the failure of the "Modern Prometheus" experiment because of society's cruel response to the monster.

Dunn, Richard J. "Narrative Distance in *Frankenstein*." *Studies in the Novel* VI, No. 4 (Winter 1974): 408-17.
  Asserts that the separate narratives of Captain Walton, the monster, and Dr. Frankenstein create a distancing effect that underscores the common focus of each narrative: "the need for human interrelationship."

Dussinger, John A. "Kinship and Guilt in Mary Shelley's *Frankenstein*." *Studies in the Novel* VIII, No. 1 (Spring 1976): 38-55.

Proposes that in *Frankenstein* Shelley was depicting not only the dangers of Promethean striving, but also the hazards of denying one's moral responsibility to family and kin.

Fleck, P. D. "Mary Shelley's Notes to Shelley's Poems and *Frankenstein.*" *Studies in Romanticism* VI, No. 4 (Summer 1967): 226-54.
Examines Shelley's notes to her husband's poems. According to Fleck, the notes reveal Mary's somewhat hostile attitude toward Percy's romanticism. Fleck also draws a parallel between *Frankenstein* and Percy's poem *Alastor; or, The Spirit of Solitude.*

Florescu, Radu. *In Search of Frankenstein.* New York: Warner Books, 1976, 364 p.
A heavily illustrated, speculative travelogue that documents Florescu's geographical search for the historical origins of *Frankenstein.*

Frank, Frederick S. "Mary Shelley's *Frankenstein*: A Register of Research." *Bulletin of Bibliography* 40, No. 3 (September 1983): 163-88.
A bibliography of twentieth-century research. Individual listings include editions of the novel published between 1950 and 1980, critical biographies of Shelley, bibliographical resources for *Frankenstein*, a listing of critical commentary on *Frankenstein*, and a filmography.

Gardner, Joseph H. "Mary Shelley's Divine Tragedy." *Essays in Literature* IV, No. 2 (Fall 1977): 182-97.
Explores the dichotomy in *Frankenstein* between the characters' quest "for knowledge on the one hand and [their] quest for sympathy and love on the other." Gardner also discusses Shelley's "Miltonic" conception of the justice of God's creation.

Gilbert, Sandra M., and Gubar, Susan. "Horror's Twin: Mary Shelley's Monstrous Eve." In their *The Madwoman in the Attic: The Woman Writer and the Nineteenth-Century Literary Imagination*, pp. 213-47. New Haven: Yale University Press, 1979.
A noted feminist analysis of *Frankenstein*. The critics stress the literary and sexual bases of the novel, which they term a "version of the misogynist story implied in *Paradise Lost.*"

Glut, Donald F. *The Frankenstein Legend: A Tribute to Mary Shelley and Boris Karloff.* Metuchen, N.J.: Scarecrow Press, 1973, 372 p.
A heavily illustrated chronicle detailing the development of the *Frankenstein* legend in popular culture. Glut includes chapters on theatrical, film, and television versions of the story, emphasizing Boris Karloff's performances in various *Frankenstein* movies.

Harvey, A. D. "*Frankenstein* and *Caleb Williams.*" *Keats-Shelley Journal* XXIX (1980): 21-7.
Traces *Frankenstein*'s structural and thematic debt to *Caleb Williams* and terms both works "novels of pursuit."

Hildebrand, William H. "On Three Prometheuses: Shelley's Two and Mary's One." *The Serif* XI, No. 2 (Summer 1974): 3-11.
Compares and contrasts the theme of Prometheanism in *Frankenstein* with Percy Shelley's use of the same theme in his *Queen Mab* and *Prometheus Unbound.*

Hirsch, Gordon D. "The Monster Was a Lady: On the Psychology of Mary Shelley's *Frankenstein.*" *Hartford Studies in Literature* VII, No. 2 (1975): 116-53.
Explores the theme of psychological determinism in *Frankenstein.*

Hume, Robert D. "Gothic Versus Romantic: A Revaluation of the Gothic Novel." *PMLA* 84, No. 2 (March 1969): 282-90.
A brief character analysis of *Frankenstein*'s monster within the context of a discussion of the Gothic novel.

Kaplan, Morton, and Kloss, Robert. "Fantasy of Paternity and the Doppelgänger: Mary Shelley's *Frankenstein.*" In their *The Unspoken Motive: A Guide to Psycho-Analytic Literary Criticism*, pp. 119-45. New York: Free Press, 1973.
A psychoanalytic reading tracing the doppelgänger and oedipal motifs in *Frankenstein.*

Ketterer, David. "Mary Shelley and Science Fiction: A Select Bibliography Selectively Annotated." In *Science Fiction Studies* 5, No. 15, Pt. 2 (July 1978): 172-78.
Lists critical works on Shelley, *Frankenstein*, *The Last Man*, and the short story "Roger Dodsworth."

———. *Frankenstein's Creation: The Book, the Monster, and Human Reality.* ELS Monograph Series, edited by Samuel L. Macey, no. 16. Victoria, B.C.: University of Victoria, 1979, 124 p.
Examines the construction of *Frankenstein.*

Koszul, A. Introduction to *Proserpine and Midas*, by Mary Shelley, edited by A. Koszul, pp. v-xxxi. London: Humphrey Milford, 1922.
An overview of Shelley's mythological dramas. Koszul describes the circumstances under which they were written and suggests that the dramas bridge the gap between the fantastical *Frankenstein* and Shelley's other, more pedestrian works.

Levine, George. *The Realistic Imagination: English Fiction from Frankenstein to Lady Chatterley.* Chicago: University of Chicago Press, 1981, 357 p.
Employs *Frankenstein* as a "metaphor for the strategies of realism" in the works of English novelists from Jane Austen to D. H. Lawrence.

———, and Knoepflmacher, U. C., eds. *The Endurance of "Frankenstein": Essays on Mary Shelley's Novel.* Berkeley and Los Angeles: University of California Press, 1974, 341 p.
A collection of essays by twelve contemporary critics covering various aspects of *Frankenstein*, including its literary and biographical sources, language, and adaptations for the theater and cinema. Also included are a brief chronology of Shelley's life, a select bibliography, illustrations, and an introduction by the editors attesting to *Frankenstein*'s growing critical importance.

Lovell, Ernest J., Jr. "Byron and Mary Shelley." *Keats-Shelley Journal* II (January 1953): 36-49.
Details Shelley's relationship with Lord Byron.

Lyles, W. H. *Mary Shelley: An Annotated Bibliography.* New York: Garland Publishing, 1975, 297 p.
A complete bibliography of works by and about Shelley. Appendices include a chronological listing of Shelley's works, an historical essay on "The Legend of George of Frankenstein," a guide to theatrical, film, and television versions of *Frankenstein*, and a list of current selling prices for various books by and about the author.

Marshall, Mrs. Julian. *The Life and Letters of Mary Wollstonecraft Shelley.* 2 vols. London: Richard Bentley & Son, 1889.
An early, essentially noncritical biography that includes many of Shelley's letters and other personal documents.

Massey, Irving. "Singles and Doubles: *Frankenstein.*" In his *The Gaping Pig: Literature and Metamorphosis*, pp. 124-37. Berkeley and Los Angeles: University of California Press, 1976.
Examines the theme of dualism in *Frankenstein.*

Mays, Milton A. "*Frankenstein*: Mary Shelley's Black Theodicy." *Southern Humanities Review* III, No. 2 (Spring 1969): 146-53.
Traces the echoes of the *Faust* myth and *Paradise Lost* in *Frankenstein*. The critic posits that the world of *Frankenstein* reveals a "black theodicy" in which "fundamental injustice prevails among men . . . and between men and God."

McCloskey, Frank H. "Mary Shelley's *Frankenstein.*" In *The Humanities in the Age of Science: In Honor of Peter Sammartino*, edited by Charles Angoff, pp. 116-138. Rutherford, N.J.: Fairleigh Dickinson University Press, 1968.
Asserts that Shelley's primary intention in *Frankenstein* was to promote Godwin's radical ideas.

Neumann, Bonnie Rayford. *The Lonely Muse: A Critical Biography of Mary Wollstonecraft Shelley.* Salzburg Studies in English Literature: Romantic Reassessment, edited by James Hogg, vol. 85. Salzburg: Universität Salzburg, 1979, 283 p.

A critical biography emphasizing Shelley's sense of personal alienation and tracing that theme in her work. Neumann argues for greater critical recognition of *The Last Man*, which she considers Shelley's "second outstanding work" after *Frankenstein*.

Nitchie, Elizabeth. Introduction to *Mathilda*, by Mary Wollstonecraft Shelley, edited by Elizabeth Nitchie, pp. vii-xv. Chapel Hill: University of North Carolina Press, 1959.
    Details the publishing history and autobiographical elements of Shelley's novella. Nitchie comments briefly on the text, stating that while the work is flawed, the heroine Mathilda has a place in "the great tradition of romantic heroines."

Palacio, Jean de. "Mary Shelley and *The Last Man*: A Minor Romantic Theme." *Revue de littérature comparée* XLII, No. 1 (January-March 1968): 37-49.
    Compares Shelley's *The Last Man* with literary works on the same theme by her contemporaries Thomas Campbell, Thomas Hood, Edward Bulwer-Lytton, and Jean Batiste de Grainville.

Palmer, D. J., and Dowse, R. E. "*Frankenstein*: A Moral Fable." *The Listener* LXVIII, No. 1743 (23 August 1962): 281-84.
    A general discussion of the moral issues raised in *Frankenstein*.

Peck, Walter Edwin. "The Biographical Element in the Novels of Mary Wollstonecraft Shelley." *PMLA* XXXVIII, No. 1 (March 1923): 196-219.
    Traces autobiographical elements in *Valperga*, *The Last Man*, and *The Fortunes of Perkin Warbeck*. Peck draws parallels between various fictional characters from these works and the Shelleys, Byron, Claire Clairmont, and other members of their circle.

Pollin, Burton R. "Philosophical and Literary Sources of *Frankenstein*." *Comparative Literature* XVII, No. 2 (Spring 1965): 97-108.
    Argues that *Frankenstein* was influenced by such works as Madame di Geulis's *Pygmalion et Galatée*, Ovid's *Metamorphoses*, John Locke's *Essay Concerning Human Understanding*, and *Paradise Lost*. The critic documents Shelley's familiarity with these works with quotes from her diary and letters.

————. "Mary Shelley as the Parvenue." *A Review of English Literature* VIII, No. 3 (July 1967): 9-21.
    Explores the biographical bases for Shelley's short story "The Parvenue." According to Pollin, the story derives from Godwin's financial demands on Percy Shelley.

Poovey, Mary. *The Proper Lady and the Woman Writer: Ideology as Style in the Works of Mary Wollstonecraft, Mary Shelley, and Jane Austen*. Women in Culture and Society, edited by Catharine R. Stimpson. Chicago: University of Chicago Press, 1984, 287 p.
    Explores the conflict between the bourgeois ideal of the "Proper Lady" and the concept of woman as artist in the works of Shelley, Wollstonecraft, and Austen. Two chapters are devoted to Shelley and *Frankenstein*, which is analyzed chiefly from a biographical standpoint.

Russell, Bertrand. "The Romantic Movement." In his *A History of Western Philosophy and Its Connection with Political and Social Circumstances from the Earliest Times to the Present Day*, pp. 675-83. New York: Simon and Schuster, 1945.
    Includes a brief discussion positing that *Frankenstein* "contains what might almost be regarded as an allegorical prophetic history of the development of romanticism."

Small, Christopher. *Ariel Like a Harpy: Shelley, Mary and "Frankenstein."* London: Victor Gollancz, 1972, 352 p.
    Explores a broad range of approaches to *Frankenstein*, including biographical, mythical, and philosophical analyses. Small also offers a detailed comparison of the novel and Percy Shelley's *Prometheus Unbound*.

Spark, Muriel. *Child of Light: A Reassessment of Mary Wollstonecraft Shelley*. Hadleigh, Essex: Tower Bridge Publications, 1951, 235 p.
    A biographical-critical study. In this, the first serious full-length consideration of Shelley's work, Spark focuses on *Frankenstein*, *The Last Man*, and *Perkin Warbeck*, as well as on Shelley's criticism.

Tannenbaum, Leslie. "From Filthy Type to Truth: Miltonic Myth in *Frankenstein*." *Keats-Shelley Journal* XXVI (1977): 101-113.
    Catalogues the parallels between *Paradise Lost* and *Frankenstein* and discusses the presence of Miltonic philosophy throughout the novel.

Twain, Mark. "In Defence of Harriet Shelley: Parts I, II, and III." *The North American Review* CLIX, Nos. 452-54, (July, August, September 1894): 108-19, 240-51, 353-368.
    A review of Edward Dowden's *Life of Shelley*. Twain sardonically describes and assesses the controversial events leading to the break-up of Percy Shelley's first marriage.

Robert Louis Stevenson

1850-1894

(Born Robert Lewis Balfour Stevenson) Scottish novelist, short story writer, poet, essayist, dramatist, and prayer writer.

The following entry presents criticism of Stevenson's novel *Strange Case of Dr. Jekyll and Mr. Hyde* (1886). For additional criticism on Stevenson's career and *Dr. Jekyll and Mr. Hyde,* see *NCLC,* Vol. 5.

Dr. Jekyll and Mr. Hyde is one of the most famous tales of English literature; indeed, the kindly and upstanding Dr. Jekyll and his evil alter ego, Mr. Hyde, have become synonymous with the dual aspects of human nature. In this brief novel, Stevenson delineates the moral conflict between the two characters while creating a sinister tale of horror. Its popular appeal was almost instantaneous and continues to this day. However, critics' interpretations of *Dr. Jekyll and Mr. Hyde* have varied widely since its publication, focusing on the novel as either a terrifying melodrama, a moral allegory with Scottish Puritan overtones, or a presentation of Stevenson's own insight into human nature. Despite the diverse readings accorded the novel, most readers agree that in *Dr. Jekyll and Mr. Hyde,* Stevenson achieved a masterpiece of terror and suspense.

Dr. Jekyll and Mr. Hyde appeared near the midpoint of Stevenson's career. Suffering from respiratory ailments all his life, Stevenson was seeking a cure in Europe when he composed the novel in the autumn of 1885. Perhaps because of his failing health, he rejected the lighter tone of his early pieces, especially such books for children as *Kidnapped* and *A Child's Garden of Verses.* Instead, Stevenson wrote *Dr. Jekyll and Mr. Hyde* in a more serious vein, creating an atmosphere of mystery and horror in his later works.

When Stevenson composed *Dr. Jekyll and Mr. Hyde,* his financial situation was poor. He had a family to support, but he seemed unable to create a plot that would attract the reading public. Ironically, the genesis of *Dr. Jekyll and Mr. Hyde* occurred while he was asleep. Afterwards, Stevenson recalled that his wife, Fanny, woke him from a nightmare. Yet when she tried to comfort him, he merely rebuffed her for interrupting his dream: "Why did you awake me? I was dreaming a fine bogey tale." According to Stevenson, he had conjured the idea of Jekyll's personality transformation while asleep, and the rest came quickly to him after he began to write.

Once Stevenson started to record his dream, he found it impossible to stop the composition of his tale; within three days, he had completed the first draft. Fanny, however, disliked his story and objected: "It was merely a story . . . when it should have been a masterpiece." She contended that the tale had no moral implications and was simply sensational. In response to her criticism, Stevenson destroyed the draft, then incorporated her suggestions into a new story, which he completed in three more days. When onlookers commented on the speed of his writing, Stevenson attributed his pace to "Brownies," the tiny creatures in his dreams who worked while he slept.

Despite the complexity of the story's possible meanings, the plot is quite simple. When Henry Jekyll, an honest physician,

The Bettmann Archive, Inc.

swallows a potion that he created in his laboratory, he changes into a horrible creature named Edward Hyde. Jekyll initially is able to control this metamorphosis, but he gradually loses his hold over his own personality, and Hyde comes to dominate Jekyll. After Hyde commits a cold-blooded murder, Jekyll finally emerges, writes a confession of his misdeeds, and kills himself.

Upon completing *Dr. Jekyll and Mr. Hyde,* Stevenson submitted it to the publishers of *Longman's Magazine,* who decided against issuing the work serially, instead printing it in a single volume in a format commonly known as a "shilling shocker." *Dr. Jekyll and Mr. Hyde* was ready for distribution by Christmas 1885, but booksellers were already fully stocked and refused the new piece. When *Dr. Jekyll and Mr. Hyde* finally appeared in January 1886, few copies sold until a glowing anonymous review appeared in the London *Times* (see *NCLC,* Vol. 5). In this article, the critic termed the novel a masterpiece that far surpassed Stevenson's previous works. That review significantly contributed to the popularity of *Dr. Jekyll and Mr. Hyde;* almost overnight, thousands of copies were sold in England. The novel achieved equal success in the United States, where the nature of its moral became a subject of religious dispute. This controversy only made the novel more appealing to Victorian readers, and as the debate increased, more books sold. Londoners interpreted the book as a tale with allegorical overtones and attempted to match the characters with politicians of the era.

While *Dr. Jekyll and Mr. Hyde* was immensely popular with contemporary readers, early critics' reactions varied widely. Almost all acknowledged Stevenson's skill as a writer of suspense, yet many reviewers questioned the work's moral intent, faulting Stevenson's choice of subject matter. Some commentators, however, viewed the novel as a moral allegory on the nature of evil. Stevenson's own remarks are illuminating; he stated that the transformation of Jekyll into Hyde was meant to show that desires, when ignored, become perverted. As the nineteenth-century controversy over the novel's morality waned, the amount of commentary also dwindled. Until the 1930s, the few studies that were published emphasized the novel's moral lesson, while some analyzed the relationship of Jekyll and Hyde as an aspect of that theme. Then, as now, critics have interpreted the pair as a symbol of the classic conflict between the flesh and the spirit. In recent years, scholars have provided psychological readings of *Dr. Jekyll and Mr. Hyde,* discussing the role of the unconscious in Stevenson's composition of the novel, his insight into personality, and his depiction of the divided self. Other modern discussions have focused on the novel's artistic elements, specifically addressing the themes of dualism and the nature of evil and the link between structure and multiple narrative techniques.

Today, *Dr. Jekyll and Mr. Hyde* has been translated into numerous languages and adapted for the stage, screen, and television. Though it is not frequently a subject of critical discussion, the novel is considered to be as popular now as it was during Stevenson's lifetime. Most commentators agree that in *Dr. Jekyll and Mr. Hyde* Stevenson achieved a level of suspenseful prose rivaled only by Edgar Allan Poe. Probably the novel's most enduring legacy is the identification of the names Jekyll and Hyde with the two sides of human nature; their immediate recognition bears testimony to the novel's indelible mark on English literature.

(See also *Dictionary of Literary Biography,* Vol. 18: *Victorian Novelists after 1885.*)

ROBERT LOUIS STEVENSON   (letter date 1886)

[*In the following letter to W. H. Low, an artist and Stevenson's close friend, the author acknowledges the dedication of Low's illustrated edition of John Keats's* Lamia *and sends him the newly published* Dr. Jekyll and Mr. Hyde.]

I send you herewith a Gothic gnome for your Greek nymph; but the gnome is interesting, I think, and he came out of a deep mine, where he guards the fountain of tears. It is not always the time to rejoice. (pp. 381-82)

The gnome's name is *Jekyll & Hyde*; I believe you will find he is likewise quite willing to answer to the name of Low or Stevenson. (p. 382)

> *Robert Louis Stevenson, in a letter to W. H. Low on January 2, 1886, in his* The Letters of Robert Louis Stevenson: 1880-1887, Alps and Highlands— Hyères—Bournemouth, *Vol. II, revised edition, ed-ited by Sidney Colvin, 1911. Reprint by Charles Scribner's Sons, 1923, pp. 380-82.*

[E. T. COOK]   (essay date 1886)

[*Cook faults the absurdity of the novel's plot.*]

Mr. R. L. Stevenson's proved ability in the invention of exciting stories is by no means at fault in his *Strange Case of Dr. Jekyll and Mr. Hyde....* It is certainly a very strange case, and one which would be extremely difficult to see through from the beginning. It has also the first requisite of such a story—it is extremely clearly narrated, and it holds one's interest. It overshoots the mark, however, by being not merely strange, but impossible, and even absurd when the explanation is given. So good an artist in fanciful mysteries as Mr. Stevenson should have avoided the mistake of a lengthy rationalization which in the nature of things is no rationalization at all. In the effective part of the story two points strike the reader as weak: the first incident which is meant to show the diabolical character of Mr. Hyde is inadequate, and the terms of Dr. Jekyll's will would have been inoperative. Mr. Stevenson has overlooked the fact that a man's will does not come into force until he is dead, and that the fact that he has not been heard of for three months would not enable his executor to carry out his testamentary directions.

> *[E. T. Cook], in a review of "Strange Case of Dr. Jekyll and Mr. Hyde," in* The Athenaeum, *No. 3038, January 16, 1886, p. 100.*

JAMES ASHCROFT NOBLE   (essay date 1886)

[*Noble praises the novel and compares it favorably to the works of Nathaniel Hawthorne.*]

The *Strange Case of Dr. Jekyll and Mr. Hyde* is not an orthodox three-volume novel; it is not even a one-volume novel of the ordinary type; it is simply a paper-covered shilling story, belonging, so far as external appearance goes, to a class of literature familiarity with which has bred in the minds of most readers a certain measure of contempt. Appearances, it has been once or twice remarked, are deceitful; and in this case they are very deceitful indeed, for, in spite of the paper cover and the popular price, Mr. Stevenson's story distances so unmistakably its three-volume and one-volume competitors, that its only fitting place is the place of honour. It is, indeed, many years since English fiction has been enriched by any work at once so weirdly imaginative in conception and so faultlessly ingenious in construction as this little tale, which can be read with ease in a couple of hours.... [The] story has a much larger and deeper interest than that belonging to a mere skilful narrative. It is a marvellous exploration into the recesses of human nature; and though it is more than possible that Mr. Stevenson wrote with no ethical intent, its impressiveness as a parable is equal to its fascination as a work of art. I do not ignore the many differences between the genius of the author of *The Scarlet Letter* and that of the author of *Dr. Jekyll and Mr. Hyde* when I say that the latter story is worthy of Hawthorne.

> *James Ashcroft Noble, in a review of "Strange Case of Dr. Jekyll and Mr. Hyde," in* The Academy, *n.s. Vol. XXIX, No. 716, January 23, 1886, p. 55.*

THE BOOK BUYER (essay date 1886)

[*In the following excerpt, the critic praises* Dr. Jekyll and Mr. Hyde, *terming it a masterpiece.*]

The author of the *New Arabian Nights* fulfils in *Dr. Jekyll* the expectations of the most enthusiastic believers in his powers. His extraordinary hold upon the reader is not kept by mere fantastic *tours de force;* his constructive skill does not consist only in concocting plots which baffle the prophet; even his style, which defies definition, is not the result of any of those artificial factors which well-meaning disciples have tried to see at work in it. Whatever he writes has in it the always indefinable touch of original power, and this has been nowhere shown so forcibly as in the most absorbing, strange, and novel conception of this story.

It is a tale of which no description can be given without letting the reader into the central secret of the plot. The idea of double personality on which it is grounded receives from Mr. Stevenson so new and startling a turn, that from the moment it is caught, one is "thrilled and possessed," as a recent reviewer wrote, by this main motive of the book, until he is in danger of losing sight of the wonderful skill of the details by which he is led on to the *dénouement.* It may be safely promised that the story will be read with such a thrill as no mere ingenuity could produce, and remembered among the few masterpieces of its kind. (pp. 23-4)

> *A review of "Strange Case of Dr. Jekyll and Mr. Hyde," in* The Book Buyer, *n.s. Vol. III, No. 1, February, 1886, pp. 23-4.*

THE CRITIC, NEW YORK (essay date 1886)

[*This reviewer praises the conception and execution of the novel.*]

[The *Strange Case of Dr. Jekyll and Mr. Hyde*] is an original and interesting piece of work, combining a French grace of execution with a distinctly Saxon ethical method. It is a bit of art that subserves a high moral purpose. Careless readers will say, in the hackneyed phrase of half-read people, that it 'reminds one of Poe,' but its construction is not that of the author of "Ligeia" or "The Fall of the House of Usher." Poe had his method, a legitimate one, in which he won high and lasting success, but it is idle to compare Poe with Hawthorne, merely because both dealt with the abnormal or weird. If "Ethan Brand" be at one extreme and one of Poe's best stories at the other, Mr. Stevenson's *Strange Case* follows in the Hawthorne line, because it offers both art and ethics, in a remarkable union. We commend it to that celebrated personage, the 'jaded novel-reader,' and still more to those serious people who will read none but noteworthy novels.

> *A review of "Strange Case of Dr. Jekyll and Mr. Hyde," in* The Critic, *New York, Vol. V, February 6, 1886, p. 68.*

FREDERICK W. H. MYERS (letter date 1886)

[*A poet, classical scholar, and essayist, Myers was also very interested in psychic research. He admired* Dr. Jckyll and Mr.

Hyde *and wrote Stevenson several letters proposing corrections for the novel. In the two letters from February 1886, the initial page references are to the first edition of* Dr. Jekyll and Mr. Hyde, *while the bracketed references are to the South Seas edition of 1925. Stevenson responded in the letter dated March 1, 1886; Myers wrote Stevenson again (see excerpts dated 1886 and 1887), but Stevenson never incorporated any of the revisions suggested by Myers.*]

We have a common friend in Mr. J. A. Symonds, who has often spoken of you to me—and I have often wished that I might have the pleasure of meeting you. The present letter is called forth by the extreme admiration with which I have read and reread your *Strange Case of Dr. Jekyll and Mr. Hyde.* I should be afraid to say how high this story seems to me to stand among imaginative productions; and I cannot but hope that it may take a place in our literature as permanent as *Robinson Crusoe.*

But, owing part to the brevity which forms one of the book's merits, partly perhaps to a certain speed in its composition which also reflects itself—especially in the style, there are certain points which I think that you might expand or alter with advantage; and which are well worth the slight trouble involved. These are specially on pages (1st edition)

37 [27]	Nature of crime.
52 [36-7]	Handwriting.
56 [39]	Change in Dr. Lanyon.
83 [54-5]	Condition of room.
103 [66-7]	Metamorphosis in Dr. L's presence.
111 [71-2]	Nature of Metamorphosis.
127 [81]	Same as p. 37 [27].
131 [83-4]	Omission of precaution.
137 [87]	Relationship of consciousness: reason for fear of apprehension.

I think that I would select pp. 121 [77-8], 138 [87-8] as instances of a mastery of language and imagination which it would be hard to parallel in fiction.

I do not know whether you will care to receive any of these suggestions which have occurred to me. But I venture to say that [it] is primarily as the author of this work that you will be known to posterity, and that pains spent on perfecting it will be well repaid. If pushed, I will explain the suggestions which I have thought of. . . . (pp. 213-14)

> *Frederick W. H. Myers, in a letter to Robert Louis Stevenson on February 21, 1886, in* Robert Louis Stevenson: The Critical Heritage, *edited by Paul Maixner, Routledge & Kegan Paul, 1981, pp. 213-14.*

F. W. H. MYERS (letter date 1886)

[*In the following excerpt, Myers outlines the revisions for the novel that he had proposed in an earlier letter to Stevenson. For additional commentary by Myers, see the excerpts dated 1886 and 1887.*]

p. 6 [7-8]   Quite admirable. Some foolish review (I believe) missed this altogether and saw his act as [?] not sufficiently criminal.

9 [9-10]   After 'in my chambers' are not a few words like '—a grisly time—' needed? One has rather too vague an idea of the group. A word or two as to Hyde's demeanour would be valuable.

19 [16]   Admirable! 22-26 [17-20] Admirable! 33 [24-5] *Admirable!*

35-38 [26-8]   This is the weakest point, to my mind. The cruelty developed from *lust* surely never becomes of just the same quality as the cruelty developed from mere madness [?] and savagery. Hyde would, I think, have simply brushed the baronet aside with a curse, and run on to some long-planned crime. The ground is ticklish, but could you not hint at a projected outrage (not on the baronet) hurried into dangerous haste by his having been long away from Soho and not made the usual preparations? Page 6 [7-8] is the keynote. If you think it needful to avoid a female victim it might be a policeman or some relation of a tacitly-understood victim. No real temptation to make body of baronet jump on roadway (p. 37 [27]). Jekyll was thoroughly civilized, and his degeneration must needs take certain lines only. Have you not sometimes thought of incarnate *evil* rather too vaguely? Hyde is really not a generalized but a specialized fiend. Minor objections. 1) Ambiguity as to house where maid was. Was it in Westminster? How did Baronet need to ask way to post close to Parliament or to his own house? If house is meant to be in a low district how did Baronet come there? 2) Why did Hyde leave the stick? Excitement too *maniacal* to make us thoroughly enter into Hyde.

39-40 [28-9]   Admirable! 42 [30] One would like to hear more of this house. Would Jekyll have sent a picture there? Would he not have concealed the house from his servants? If picture wanted you might try one or two small Jan Steens which he could have taken in a cab.

43 [30-1]   'Other half of stick' Why not thrown away?

45 [32-3]   No obvious reason why Jekyll receives Utterson in *theatre*. (Not important, as he *must* be made to do so, and *need not* give explicit reason.)

52 [36-7]   Here I think you miss a point for want of familiarity with recent psycho-physical discussions. Handwriting in cases of double personality (spontaneous . . . or induced, as in hypnotic cases) *is not* and *cannot be* the same in the two personalities. Hyde's writing might look like Jekyll's done *with the left hand,* or done when partly drunk, or ill: that is the kind of resemblance there might be. Your imagination can make a good point of this.

56 [39]   The effect of shock in Dr. Lanyon might be more specified. At present it seems rather *unreal*. It *might* induce diabetes, if there were previous kidney weakness. Could some slight allusion be made to this on p. 57 [39-40]?

62-65 [43-4]   *Admirable!*

74 [49-50]   Admirable!

83 [54-5]   Surely not a true point—tidiness of room. When had the housemaid been in? Who had removed cinders from under grate? Surely coals were left at door and only the empty coal scuttle put out. Who washed cups? Sugar in tea-cup p. 86 [56] seems to me a false point. Neither J. nor H. would prepare in that minute way for comfort.

99-100 [64-5]   Excellent.

102 [66]   Objections to this page stated later: on page 131 [83-4].

103 [66-7]   Two objections. (1) Style too elevated for Hyde. (Of this further on p. 138 [87-8].) These are not remarks that fit the husky broken voice of Hyde—they are Jekyllian. Surely Hyde's admirable style (p. 24 [19]) should be retained for him. (2) He would have been more unwilling to show the transformation. Lanyon should show, I think, more resolve (hint at pistol?) to make him do it.

106-110 [69-71]   Excellent.

111 [71-2]   I suppose the agent must be a drug. But the description of the process surely needs more substance and novelty. For one thing, there must have been a loss of consciousness. (This point admirable when we come to the spontaneous reversions into Hyde during sleep.) The first time the loss of consciousness might last for some hours.

112 [72-3]   *Admirable*—but I think there should be more physical exhaustion the first time. Then he might revive himself by wine placed nearby: his new body would be specially sensitive to stimulants. You perhaps purposely make *few* (but admirable) points as to the new body.

114 [73-4]   Excellent! excellent!

115 [74]   The return to Jekyll should surely be more insisted on—the doubt whether possible, and doubt whether taking drug again might not be *fatal*. A little more too about subsequent shrinkings from the pain etc.—overcome by restless impulse. I don't understand the phrase 'kept awake by ambition.' I thought the stimulus was a different one.

116 [74-5]   We should understand already that he hadn't yet conquered his aversion. Surely the motive for the change was this. And, by the way, I think that it might somewhere be hinted that Jekyll was a good deal more licentious in early life than he avows. I don't want him to be prematurely aged but might there not be something more of flabbiness in his portliness? And some hint of his desiring *variety*? And a word or two more of Utterson's? Or a *thought* of Utterson's? How had Jekyll come across the housekeeper whom he placed in Soho? (What led you to specify Greek street?)

118 [75-6]   Excellent, but needs expansion. 'They soon began to turn towards the monstrous' is almost the only hint in the book of the process by which the thoroughly sympathetic and gently apolaustic Jekyll becomes the ruffianly Hyde. This is one of the great moral nodes of the book, and while I thoroughly admire your rapidity of manner and absence of didactic preoccupation, I nevertheless feel that this is a point on which Jekyll's memory would have dwelt: which he would have insisted on. He would not have liked that his friends should think that he had *fiendish* qualities in him at all to begin with: he would rather have laid all that on the continually expanding desires and insatiable enterprise of Hyde—'That insatiability which is attached to inordinate desires as their bitterest punishment.'

120 [77]   'Sloping my own hand backward': see on p. 52 [36-7]. (Note that Hyde would have to make great effort to simulate Jekyll's signature—be long about it—signature would look odd, but unmistakably Jekyll's.)

121 [77-8]   *This is genius.*

123 [78-9]   Excellent! But correspondingly Jekyll's body should have got flabbier. See also p. 55 [38] where Jekyll, I think, regains vigour and cheerfulness far too rapidly. There should be something deprecative [?] rather than complacent about him after the murder.

124 [79]   An admirable page but 'begun to pamper' might be stronger and we here also begin to note a slight uncertainty in the psychical relationship of the two personalities. Here Hyde is (bandit simile) hardly at all Jekyll; later on (and on p. 120 [77]) he is much more Jekyll and see p. 103 [66-7].

127 [81]   Here I again feel a false note. See on p. 36 [26-7] 'mauled the unresisting body'—no, not an elderly MP's!

129 [82]   'the hands of all men would be raised' Surely the one servant maid and his few acquaintances were not so dangerous. Hyde might have escaped from England easily enough. Why does Jekyll not think of a trip to Brussels?

131 [83-4]   An admirable page! But here one asks why, after the metamorphosis in bed, take the risk of separation from the drug? At any time even before the spontaneous metamorphosis it might have been extremely desirable to change back into Jekyll. If the drug was portable and manageable anywhere he would likely have taken it with him:—and after the murder certainly. Can you suppose that a Bunsen burner or some means of producing intense heat was necessary to effect a chemical combination? Or an electrical machine (which Lanyon also might possess) to assist change of body?

136-138   Genius!
[86-8]

138 [87-8]   But Hyde was in very little danger. Who could identify him? Probably almost any acquaintance that he had could have been bought off. And what chance of their seeing him if he went to an unfamiliar quarter of London? Or why does he not think of Paris or New York? For he is now so psychically separate from Jekyll (and I think something should be said as to growing psychical separation, if you determine to take that line)— he would surely have thought 'I will give up the Jekyll life, which can't really be retained, and will start fresh in New York.' (Even Liverpool would have tempted him, if you say that he was not [?] enough for New York.)

141 [89]   How would it be if Jekyll committed suicide and we were left to infer, from the finding of Hyde's body, that the death-agony had so transformed him?

(pp. 214-19)

F. W. H. Myers, in a letter to Robert Louis Stevenson on February 28, 1886, in Robert Louis Stevenson: The Critical Heritage, *edited by Paul Maixner, Routledge & Kegan Paul, 1981, pp. 214-19.*

ROBERT LOUIS STEVENSON   (letter date 1886)

[*In the following letter, Stevenson thanks Myers for the revisions he proposed (see excerpts dated 1886).*]

I know not how to thank you: this is as handsome as it is clever. With almost every word I agree—much of it I even knew before—much of it, I must confess, would never have been, if I had been able to do what I like, and lay the thing by for the matter of a year. But the wheels of Byles the Butcher drive exceeding swiftly, and *Jekyll* was conceived, written, re-written, re-rewritten, and printed inside ten weeks. Nothing but this white-hot haste would explain the gross error of Hyde's speech at Lanyon's. Your point about the specialised fiend is more subtle, but not less just: I had not seen it.—About the picture, I rather meant that Hyde had brought it himself; and Utterson's hypothesis of the gift . . . an error.—The tidiness of the room, I thought, but I dare say my psychology is here too ingenious to be sound, was due to the dread weariness and horror of the imprisonment. Something has to be done: he would tidy the room. But I dare say it is false.

I shall keep your paper; and if ever my works come to be collected, I will put my back into these suggestions. In the meanwhile, I do truly lack words in which to express my sense of gratitude for the trouble you have taken. The receipt of such a paper is more than a reward for my labours. I have read it with pleasure, and as I say, I hope to use it with profit. (pp. 325-26)

Robert Louis Stevenson, in a letter to F. W. H. Myers on March 1, 1886, in his The Letters of Robert Louis Stevenson: 1880-1887, Alps and Highlands— Hyères—Bournemouth, *Vol. II, revised edition, edited by Sidney Colvin, 1911. Reprint by Charles Scribner's Sons, 1923, pp. 325-26.*

J. A. SYMONDS   (letter date 1886)

[*Symonds was a noted nineteenth-century English critic, poet, historian, and translator. Although primarily remembered for his translations of the Greek poets, Symonds is also known for his aesthetic theory and impressionistic essays. In the following excerpt from a letter to Stevenson, Symonds praises Stevenson's technique but considers the subject of* Dr. Jekyll and Mr. Hyde *too painful to linger over.*]

At last I have read *Dr Jekyll*. It makes me wonder whether a man has the right so to scrutinize "the abysmal deeps of personality." It is indeed a dreadful book, most dreadful because of a certain moral callousness, a want of sympathy, a shutting out of hope. The art is burning and intense.... As a piece of literary work, this seems to me the finest you have done—in all that regards style, invention, psychological analysis, exquisite fitting of parts, and admirable employment of motives to realize the abnormal. But it has left such a deeply painful impression on my heart that I do not know how I am ever to turn to it again.

The fact is that, viewed as an allegory, it touches one too closely. Most of us at some epoch of our lives have been upon the verge of developing a Mr Hyde.

Physical and biological Science on a hundred lines is reducing individual freedom to zero, and weakening the sense of responsibility. I doubt whether the artist should lend his genius to this grim argument. Your Dr Jekyll seems to me capable of loosening the last threads of self-control in one who should read it while wavering between his better and worse self. It is like the Cave of Despair in the *Faery Queen*.

I had the great biologist Lauder Brunton with me a fortnight back. He was talking about *Dr Jekyll* and a book by O. W. Holmes [*Elsie Venner*], in [which] atavism is played with. I could see that, though a Christian, he held very feebly to the theory of human liberty; and these two works of fiction interested him, as *Dr Jekyll* does me, upon that point at issue.

I understand now thoroughly how much a sprite you are. Really there is something not quite human in your genius!

The denouement would have been finer, I think, if Dr Jekyll by a last supreme effort of his lucid self had given Mr Hyde up to justice—[which] might have been arranged after the scene in Lanyon's study. Did you ever read Raskolnikow [*Crime and Punishment*]? How fine is that ending! Had you made your hero act thus, you would at least have saved the sense of human dignity. (pp. 120-21)

> *J. A. Symonds, in a letter to Robert Louis Stevenson on March 3, 1886, in his* The Letters of John Addington Symonds: 1885-1893, *Vol. III, edited by Herbert M. Schueller and Robert L. Peters, Wayne State University Press, 1969, pp. 120-22.*

F. W. MYERS   (letter date 1886)

[*In the following letter, Myers suggests more revisions for the novel. For additional commentary by Myers, see the excerpts dated 1886 and 1887.*]

I. Would Hyde have brought a picture? I think—and friends of weight support my view—that such an act would have been altogether unworthy of him. What are the motives which would prompt a person in his situation to that act?

1. There are jaded voluptuaries who seek in a special class of art a substitute or reinforcement for the default of primary stimuli. Mr. Hyde's whole career forbids us to insult him by classing him with these men.

2. There are those who wish for elegant surroundings to allure or overawe the minds of certain persons unaccustomed to luxury or splendour. But does not all that we know of Mr. Hyde teach us that he disdained these modes of adventitious attractions? When he is first presented to us in [*Dr. Jekyll and Mr. Hyde*] as 'stumping along eastward at a good walk' (I have mislaid my copy and must quote from memory) does not this imply the gait of one who aimed at energy but not at grace? And when we read that he was 'very plainly dressed,' don't we know that his means were such that he might have permitted himself without extravagance an elegant costume,—does not this show us the man aiming only at simple convenience, direct sufficiency? not anxious to present himself as personally attractive to others, but relying frankly on a cash nexus, and on that decision of character which would startle—almost terrify into compliance in cases where the blandishments of the irresolute might have been lavished in vain?

3. There are those, again, who surround their more concentrated enjoyments with a halo of mixed estheticism; who even if blameably adventurous in action are gently artistic in repose. Such, no doubt, was Dr. Jekyll: such, no doubt, he *expected* that Mr. Hyde would be. But was he not deceived? Was there not something unlooked for, something Napoleonic, in Hyde's way of pushing aside the aesthetic as well as the moral superfluities of life? Between the conception of some lawless design and its execution do we suppose that Jekyll himself could look at his pictures with tranquil pleasure? Did not his inward state 'suffer with the likeness of an insurrection'? And was not Hyde's permanent state this stabler and intenser reproduction of such absorbed and critical moments in Jekyll's inward history? We do not imagine the young Napoleon as going to concerts or taking a walk in a garden. We imagine him as now plunged in gloomy torpor, now warmly planning crimes to be. I cannot fancy Hyde looking in at picture shops. I cannot think that he ever even left his rooms, except on business. And in these rooms I fancy that there would be a certain look as of lower tenancy supervening [?] on a high-class outfit; a certain admixture of ill-chosen with handsome things; an unhomelike bareness along with provision for ready ease.

II. I have thought of how you could alter the murder with least trouble. Perhaps it might do if the servant maid looked out of the window when the murderous assault had just begun and mentions that there was no one else in the street except 'a shabbily dressed johnny just a-scampering around the street corner.' The girl need never appear again; but Jekyll might speak of the Baronet as having interfered to baulk what (in his way of speaking of Hyde) he would probably call 'an enterprise too hastily conceived.'

III. A very small point. I think that the housekeeper says 'What's he been doing?' If 'now' were added, it might imply that in her view he had already been fortunate in escaping the interference of the Law.

IV. A criticism of Mr. Gladstone's (to whom my sister-in-law took the book while he was forming a ministry [?] which is now, I hope, splitting up more irretrievably than Dr. Jekyll's personality) may introduce my next suggestion. He said that while he much admired and enjoyed the book, he felt that the ethical retransference of Hyde into Jekyll was made too easy a thing;—that he could not fancy so profound and sudden a *backward* change. This, as you perceive, bears out what I ventured to hint as to the progressive effect which the repeated changes must needs operate on the Jekyllian phase. And it suggests, I think, the need of dealing with the subject of community of memory. At first I think such community would be very imperfect; gradually the two memories would fuse into one; and in the last stage you might make an effective contrast of the increasing *fusion* of the two personalities in all except ethical temper, joined with the increasing revulsion in all except ethical temper, joined with the increasing revulsion of Jekyll against the ethical temper of Hyde; a revulsion maintained, no doubt, at great cost of nervous exhaustion—like the prolonged attention needed down an ice-slope which gets steeper and steeper; till the suicide (of Jekyll in my view, not of Hyde) would represent the kind of despairing spring with which the thoroughly exhausted climber leaps to a point where he could not in his right senses have expected to find foothold, misses and falls. (pp. 219-22)

> *F. W. Myers, in a letter to Robert Louis Stevenson on March 17, 1886, in* Robert Louis Stevenson: The Critical Heritage, *edited by Paul Maixner, Routledge & Kegan Paul, 1981, pp. 219-22.*

GERARD MANLEY HOPKINS   (letter date 1886)

[*Hopkins, a Roman Catholic priest, was a nineteenth-century English poet whose work was not published until the twentieth century. Hopkins's poetry is characterized by its striking diction and unusual rhythmic structure. In the following excerpt from a letter to Robert Bridges, Hopkins defends Stevenson's characters against charges of "gross absurdity."*]

Jekyll and Hyde I have read. You speak of 'the gross absurdity' of the interchange. Enough that it is impossible and might perhaps have been a little better masked: it must be connived at, and it gives rise to a fine situation. It is not more impossible than fairies, giants, heathen gods, and lots of things that literature teems with—and none more than yours. You are certainly wrong about Hyde being overdrawn: my Hyde is worse. The trampling scene is perhaps a convention: he was thinking of something unsuitable for fiction.

I can by no means grant that the characters are not characterised, though how deep the springs of their surface action are I am not yet clear. But the superficial touches of character are admirable: how can you be so blind as not to see them? e.g. Utterson frowning, biting the end of his finger, and saying to the butler 'This is a strange tale you tell me, my man, a very strange tale'. And Dr. Lanyon: 'I used to like it, sir [life]; yes, sir, I liked it. Sometimes I think if we knew all' etc. These are worthy of Shakespeare. (p. 238)

> *Gerard Manley Hopkins, in a letter to Robert Bridges on October 28, 1886, in his* The Letters of Gerard Manley Hopkins to Robert Bridges, *edited by Claude Colleer Abbott, Oxford University Press, London, 1935, pp. 235-41.*

ROBERT LOUIS STEVENSON   (letter date 1887)

[*In the following letter, Stevenson discusses his attitudes, and those of his characters, toward sexuality. His comments are later contested by Katharine D. Osbourne (see essay dated 1923).*]

Hyde was the younger of the two. He was not good-looking, however; and not, Great Gods! a mere voluptuary. There is no harm in voluptuaries; and none, with my hand on my heart and in the sight of God, none—no harm whatsoever in what prurient fools call "immorality." The harm was in Jekyll, because he was a hypocrite—not because he was fond of women;

he says so himself; but people are so filled full of folly and inverted lust, that they think of nothing but sexuality. The Hypocrite let out the beast of Hyde—who is no more sexual than another, but who is the essence of cruelty and malice and selfishness and cowardice, and these are the diabolic in man—not this poor wish to love a woman, that they make such a cry about. I know and I dare to say, you know as well as I, that bad and good even to human eyes, has no more connection with what is called dissipation than it has with flying kites. But the sexual field and the business field are the two best fitted for the display of cruelty and cowardice and selfishness. (pp. 129-30)

> *Robert Louis Stevenson, in an extract from a letter to John Paul Bocock in 1887, in* The True Stevenson: A Study in Clarification *by George S. Hellman, Little, Brown, and Company, 1925, pp. 129-30.*

F. W. H. MYERS   (letter date 1887)

[*In the following letter, Myers reminds Stevenson that he has not yet revised the novel. For additional commentary by Myers, see the excerpts dated 1886.*]

I do not want to be importunate, but I cannot but help reminding you that time is going on, and your masterpiece remains (so far as I know) without that final revision, the possible lack of which would be a real misfortune to English literature. The works, even of the most fertile and brilliant authors, which can hope for *permanent* preservation must needs be few. Is it not well worth while to make them as perfect as possible? I have heard the views of many other persons on **Dr. Jekyll and Mr. Hyde** since I last wrote. I have not found any competent person who does not think it your best work, or who did not also feel it contained obvious, and removable, blots.

> *F. W. H. Myers, in a letter to Robert Louis Stevenson on April 17, 1887, in* Robert Louis Stevenson: The Critical Heritage, *edited by Paul Maixner, Routledge & Kegan Paul, 1981, p. 222.*

HENRY JAMES   (essay date 1888)

[*James was an American-born English novelist, short story writer, critic, and essayist of the late nineteenth and early twentieth centuries. The following discussion of* Dr. Jekyll and Mr. Hyde *is drawn from an overview of Stevenson's writings.*]

Is **Dr. Jekyll and Mr. Hyde** a work of high philosophic intention, or simply the most ingenious and irresponsible of fictions? It has the stamp of a really imaginative production, that we may take it in different ways, but I suppose it would be called the most serious of the author's tales. It deals with the relation of the baser parts of man to his nobler—of the capacity for evil that exists in the most generous natures, and it expresses these things in a fable which is a wonderfully happy invention. The subject is endlessly interesting, and rich in all sorts of provocation, and Mr. Stevenson is to be congratulated on having touched the core of it. I may do him injustice, but it is, however, here, not the profundity of the idea which strikes me so much as the art of the presentation—the extremely successful form. There is a genuine feeling for the perpetual moral question, a fresh sense of the difficulty of being good and the brutishness of being bad, but what there is above all is a singular ability in holding the interest. I confess that that, to my sense, is the most edifying thing in the short, rapid, concentrated story, which is really a masterpiece of concision. There is something almost impertinent in the way . . . in which Mr. Stevenson achieves his best effects without the aid of the ladies, and *Dr. Jekyll* is a capital example of his heartless independence. It is usually supposed that a truly poignant impression cannot be made without them, but in the drama of Mr. Hyde's fatal ascendency they remain altogether in the wing. It is very obvious—I do not say it cynically—that they must have played an important part in his development. The gruesome tone of the tale is, no doubt, deepened by their absence; it is like the late afternoon light of a foggy winter Sunday, when even inanimate objects have a kind of wicked look. I remember few situations in the pages of mystifying fiction more to the purpose than the episode of Mr. Utterson's going to Dr. Jekyll's to confer with the butler, when the doctor is locked up in his laboratory and the old servant, whose sagacity has hitherto encountered successfully the problems of the sideboard and the pantry, confesses that this time he is utterly baffled. The way the two men, at the door of the laboratory, discuss the identity of the mysterious personage inside, who has revealed himself in two or three inhuman glimpses to Poole, has those touches of which irresistible shudders are made. The butler's theory is that his master has been murdered, and that the murderer is in the room, personating him with a sort of clumsy diabolism. "Well, when that masked thing like a monkey jumped from among the chemicals and whipped into the cabinet, it went down my spine like ice." That is the effect upon the reader of most of the story. I say of most rather than all, because the ice rather melts in the sequel, and I have some difficulty in accepting the business of the powders, which seems to me too explicit and explanatory. The powders constitute the machinery of the transformation, and it will probably have struck many readers that this uncanny process would be more conceivable (so far as one may speak of the conceivable in such a case), if the author had not made it so definite. (pp. 877-78)

> *Henry James, "Robert Louis Stevenson," in* The Century, *Vol. XXXV, No. 6, April, 1888, pp. 868-79.*

ROBERT LOUIS STEVENSON (essay date 1888)

[*In the following excerpt from his "A Chapter on Dreams," an essay composed in 1888, Stevenson describes how he transformed dream material into his fiction. He then outlines the method of composition of* Dr. Jekyll and Mr. Hyde, *which he contends was largely subconscious and performed by "Brownies"—the Little People who populate and create his dreams.*]

This honest fellow had long been in the custom of setting himself to sleep with tales, and so had his father before him; but these were irresponsible inventions, told for the teller's pleasure, with no eye to the crass public or the thwart reviewer: tales where a thread might be dropped, or one adventure quitted for another, on fancy's least suggestion. So that the little people who manage man's internal theatre had not as yet received a very rigorous training; and played upon their stage like children who should have slipped into the house and found it empty, rather than like drilled actors performing a set piece to a huge hall of faces. But presently my dreamer began to turn his former amusement of story-telling to (what is called) account; by which I mean that he began to write and sell his tales. Here was he, and here were the little people who did that part of his business, in quite new conditions. The stories must now be trimmed and pared and set upon all fours, they must run from a beginning to an end and fit (after a manner) with the laws of life; the pleasure, in one word, had become a business; and that not only for the dreamer, but for the little people of his theatre.

These understood the change as well as he. When he lay down to prepare himself for sleep, he no longer sought amusement, but printable and profitable tales; and after he had dozed off in his box-seat, his little people continued their evolutions with the same mercantile designs. . . . Often enough the waking is a disappointment: he has been too deep asleep, as I explain the thing; drowsiness has gained his little people, they have gone stumbling and maundering through their parts; and the play, to the awakened mind, is seen to be a tissue of absurdities. And yet how often have these sleepless Brownies done him honest service, and given him, as he sat idly taking his pleasure in the boxes, better tales than he could fashion for himself. (pp. 215-18)

Who are the Little People? They are near connections of the dreamer's, beyond doubt; they share in his financial worries and have an eye to the bank-book; they share plainly in his training; they have plainly learned like him to build the scheme of a considerate story and to arrange emotion in progressive order; only I think they have more talent; and one thing is beyond doubt, they can tell him a story piece by piece, like a serial, and keep him all the while in ignorance of where they aim. Who are they, then? and who is the dreamer?

Well, as regards the dreamer, I can answer that, for he is no less a person than myself;—as I might have told you from the beginning, only that the critics murmur over my consistent egotism;—and as I am positively forced to tell you now, or I could advance but little farther with my story. And for the Little People, what shall I say they are but just my Brownies, God bless them! who do one-half my work for me while I am fast asleep, and in all human likelihood, do the rest for me as well, when I am wide awake and fondly suppose I do it for myself. That part which is done while I am sleeping is the Brownies' part beyond contention; but that which is done when I am up and about is by no means necessarily mine, since all goes to show the Brownies have a hand in it even then. Here is a doubt that much concerns my conscience. For myself—what I call I, my conscience ego, the denizen of the pineal gland unless he has changed his residence since Descartes, the man with the conscience and the variable bank-account, the man with the hat and the boots, and the privilege of voting and not carrying his candidate at the general elections—I am sometimes tempted to suppose he is no story-teller at all, but a creature as matter of fact as any cheesemonger or any cheese, and a realist bemired up to the ears in actuality; so that, by that account, the whole of my published fiction should be the single-handed product of some Brownie, some Familiar, some unseen collaborator, whom I keep locked in a back garret, while I get all the praise and he but a share (which I cannot prevent him getting) of the pudding. I am an excellent adviser, something like Molière's servant; I pull back and I cut down; and I dress the whole in the best words and sentences that I can find and make; I hold the pen, too; and I do the sitting at the table, which is about the worst of it; and when all is done, I make up the manuscript and pay for the registration; so that, on the whole, I have some claim to share, though not so largely as I do, in the profits of our common enterprise.

I can but give an instance or so of what part is done sleeping and what part awake, and leave the reader to share what laurels there are, at his own nod, between myself and my collaborators; and to do this I will first take a book that a number of persons have been polite enough to read, the *Strange Case of Dr. Jekyll and Mr. Hyde*. I had long been trying to write a story on this subject, to find a body, a vehicle, for that strong sense of man's double being which must at times come in upon and overwhelm the mind of every thinking creature. I had even written one, *The Travelling Companion,* which was returned by an editor on the plea that it was a work of genius and indecent, and which I burned the other day on the ground that it was not a work of genius, and that *Jekyll* had supplanted it. Then came one of those financial fluctuations to which (with an elegant modesty) I have hitherto referred in the third person. For two days I went about racking my brains for a plot of any sort; and on the second night I dreamed the scene at the window, and a scene afterwards split in two, in which Hyde, pursued for some crime, took the powder and underwent the change in the presence of his pursuers. All the rest was made awake, and consciously, although I think I can trace in much of it the manner of my Brownies. The meaning of the tale is therefore mine, and had long pre-existed in my garden of Adonis, and tried one body after another in vain; indeed, I do most of the morality, worse luck! and my Brownies have not a rudiment of what we call a conscience. Mine, too, is the setting, mine the characters. All that was given me was the matter of three scenes, and the central idea of a voluntary change becoming involuntary. Will it be thought ungenerous, after I have been so liberally ladling out praise to my unseen collaborators, if I here toss them over, bound hand and foot, into the arena of the critics? For the business of the powders, which so many have censured, is, I am relieved to say, not mine at all but the Brownies'. (pp. 224-28)

> *Robert Louis Stevenson, "A Chapter on Dreams," in his* Across the Plains with Other Memories and Essays, *1892. Reprint by Charles Scribner's Sons, 1923, pp. 206-30.*

REV. W. J. DAWSON   (essay date 1896)

[*Dawson analyzes the "spiritual genius" exhibited in* Dr. Jekyll and Mr. Hyde. *This essay was originally published in the* Young Man *in September 1896.*]

Nowhere does the spiritual genius of Stevenson express itself with such force and fulness as in his *Strange Case of Dr. Jekyll and Mr. Hyde.* . . . Here again we come upon that profound seriousness of soul that underlies all Stevenson's best work; the questioning and philosophic mind groping at the intricate coil of things; the intense imagination of the Celt, fascinated by the grim and subtle mysteries of human nature. The seed-thought of this appalling fable of Dr. Jekyll and Mr. Hyde is familiar enough: it is the ancient Pauline description of a war in our members, so that the thing we would, that we do not; and the thing we would not, that we do. The summary of the whole—it might well form the inscription for the title-page—is that great cry wrung out of the very agonised heart of this internecine conflict, 'O wretched man that I am! who shall deliver me from the body of this death?' We have heard the words many times on the lips of preachers and theologians, but one would certainly have doubted if they were capable of being vitalised by the art of the novelist. . . . A piece of writing like this is a unique achievement in the art of letters. It is really comparable with nothing else; it stands alone. And it is conclusive evidence of that subtlety and force of spiritual genius which gives Stevenson a place apart, and high above all contemporaries, as an interpreter of the deepest things of the human soul. . . .

Stevenson was too modest a man to pose as a thinker; yet a thinker he was, and of great originality and insight. And in the truest sense of the word he was an entirely pious man. He knew what it meant, as he has put it, to go up 'the great bare staircase of his duty, uncheered and undepressed.' In the trials of a life unusually difficult, and pierced by the spear's points of the sharpest limitations, he preserved a splendid and unbroken fortitude. No man ever met life with a higher courage; it is safe to say that a man less courageous would not have lived nearly so long. There are few things more wonderful and admirable than the persistence of his energy; ill and compelled to silence, he still dictates his story in the dumb alphabet, and at his lowest ebb of health makes no complaint. And through all there runs a piety as invincible as his fortitude; a certain gaiety of soul that never deserts him; a faith in the ultimate rightness of destiny which holds him serene amid a sea of troubles. (pp. 219-20)

> *Rev. W. J. Dawson, in an extract in* Stevensoniana, *revised edition, edited by J. A. Hammerton, John Grant, 1910, pp. 217-20.*

LESLIE STEPHEN   (essay date 1902)

[*Stephen is considered one of the most important English critics of the late Victorian and early Edwardian eras. In the following excerpt, Stephen praises Stevenson's novel as a "fine bogey tale."*]

I have always wondered that, after such a proof of his powers of fascination [as *Treasure Island*], Stevenson should only have achieved full recognition by *Dr. Jekyll and Mr. Hyde.* That book, we are told, was also written in a fit of inspiration, suggested by dreaming a 'fine bogey tale.' The public liked it because it became an allegory—a circumstance, I fear, which does not attract me. But considered as a 'bogey tale,' able to revive the old thrill of delicious horror in one who does not care for psychical research, it has the same power of carrying one away by its imaginative intensity. (pp. 233-34)

> *Leslie Stephen, "Robert Louis Stevenson," in his* Studies of a Biographer, *Duckworth and Co., 1902, pp. 206-46.*

KATHARINE D. OSBOURNE   (letter date 1923)

[*Osbourne, the wife of Stevenson's stepson, wrote this letter to George S. Hellman, one of Stevenson's biographers. Here, she attempts to refute a letter by Stevenson (see excerpt dated 1887) in which he examines sexuality in* Dr. Jekyll and Mr. Hyde.]

[There] are two things I want to say now—One regarding the letter you read me of Stevenson's about *Dr. Jekyll and Mr. Hyde.* I do not think it should be taken at full face value. Seldom do any of us write an absolutely truthful letter. They are tempered to suit the recipient. I wish I had noticed the name of the one to whom this letter of Louis Stevenson's was written. If Stevenson had ever thought of its being published or if it had been intended for an understanding public, I think it would have been partly different. We are all things to all men, you know and sometimes Stevenson, not to appear self-righteous to one his heart did not wholly approve, verged from the truth and again did not do himself justice on account of this.

If it were true that hypocrisy and hypocrisy alone was in his mind when writing the story of a dual nature he would have made that point plainer. There was much more in his mind: the constant remembrance of his own love experiences which he did not glory in, but rather realized that could hardly have been different—possessed with his strong temperament, and at the same time he was convinced that no harm was done, since there had been no deception, no destroying of another's happiness. When you see the fragment of autobiography Stevenson began in San Francisco which is to be sent me in your care you will see with what loyalty and gratitude he regarded a woman who had given comfort to a man. I think there is nothing ever written elsewhere that expresses this sublime thought on women. It is chivalry at its highest degree.

Then as to Stevenson's letter about *Dr. Jekyll and Mr. Hyde,* one must set off against it Louis Stevenson's last letter to his cousin Bob. Bob was the one, and he was four years older, that led Louis in the days of adolescence, into many seasons of unrestrained passion. "Bobism" once Lloyd called it in speaking of Louis in those days. In this letter I refer to, Louis's usual desire to be *not censorious* was thrown off. He was speaking not so much to Bob as of conclusions he had come to for himself in reviewing his own life. He was thinking with regret of the waywardness of his youth. He was realizing that this giving way to his passions had had a weakening effect on his own character even if it had not hurt professional prostitutes nor willing women—and he was reviewing the causes which had brought his life to a distressful wasted end as in his depression thus it appeared to him. . . .

He realized that he had been a victim all through, and mainly the victim of public sentiment and ignorance on the public's part of what love and virtue is—and how it is to be hedged about and preserved in its strength, not wasted. . . .

This letter to Bob is of the utmost importance in weighing that part of Louis Stevenson's life which has been left untold, his love nature, and because of this omission makes the chief demand that a new biography be written. (pp. 76-8)

> *Katharine D. Osbourne, in a letter to George S. Hellman on May 28, 1923, in* The True Stevenson: A Study in Clarification *by George S. Hellman, Little, Brown, and Company, 1925, pp. 76-9.*

EDWIN A. McALPIN   (essay date 1928)

[*In the following excerpt, McAlpin discusses the effects of sin in* Dr. Jekyll and Mr. Hyde.]

There is [a] characteristic of sin that prevents it from being considered a mere matter of personal opinion. It is the destroyer of character and also of sound judgment. After a person has yielded to temptation he loses his ability to form correct estimates as to what is right and what is wrong.

Robert Louis Stevenson shows this in *Dr. Jekyll and Mr. Hyde.* Dr. Jekyll possessed a fine intellect, enthusiasm for scientific investigation, and a desire to hold the good opinion of other people. He had also inherited a large fortune. His life gave promise of being both useful and successful. He was honored by his associates and looked up to by all men. He was known for his benevolent disposition and for the efforts he made to relieve those in distress. This respectable and respected man had, as every man has, another side to his nature. He liked to indulge in sensual pleasures.

Dr. Jekyll's investigations included metaphysical as well as medical subjects. These investigations led him to believe that every life was made up of several different personalities held together in one body. He thought it might be possible to find a drug strong enough to dissolve the connecting link and let loose a kind of character other than the one that naturally

controlled the individual's life. He wanted to retain the respect of his professional associates and still indulge his sensual nature. He was torn in two. (pp. 44-5)

The story is made up of the relations and adventures of [the] two different personalities, which dwelt in one body. While he despised the character and activities of Mr. Hyde, Dr. Jekyll enjoyed sensuality too much to give up this obnoxious personality and its indulgences. The dual position seemed a perfectly safe one. When he tired of the excesses and indulgences of Mr. Hyde, he reassumed the person and character of Dr. Jekyll. He did not consider himself a hypocrite. Dr. Jekyll was very sorry for the cruelties of Mr. Hyde, and frequently Dr. Jekyll spent time and money in relieving the distress Mr. Hyde had caused. Once he found it necessary to double the dose before his transformation was completed, but he was deaf to the warning this should have given him. He continued his double life until, one night, in a wild outburst of fury, Mr. Hyde committed a brutal murder. After destroying all evidences of the close connection between Mr. Hyde and Dr. Jekyll he returned to his home and, taking the required dose, was transformed into the respectable and honored Dr. Jekyll. (pp. 46-7)

The story then narrates the efforts Dr. Jekyll made in order to keep from slipping into the features and character of Mr. Hyde. His supply of one of the salts he used to prepare the drug that caused this transformation was becoming exhausted. When he replaced it he discovered the new consignment failed to give results.

It is the old, old story of the good yielding to the evil. Finally the evil reigns supreme.

Under its strange fantasies *Dr. Jekyll and Mr. Hyde* is a good account of the dual elements in personality. Every individual born on this earth has a higher and a lower nature. There are moments when it is comparatively easy to follow the good. At other times it is desperately hard to keep the animal side of life from gaining control. Dr. Jekyll said the drug he used was neither good nor bad, it simply established the mental state that was in ascendance at the moment and made it the controlling power of his life, even to the alteration of his features. For a time a person may be able to live honorably and occasionally indulge in sin, but if a man tries to carry on a dual life, the evil is sure to overcome the good. His moral judgments lose all sense of proportion, and a catastrophe occurs.

In *Dr. Jekyll and Mr. Hyde* Stevenson shows one of the worst characteristics of sin. This is the tendency of evil to overcome and drive out the best elements of character. While the book is only a fantastic tale it is also an allegory of man's struggle against the baser side of life. Unless a person conquers the evil in his nature by unifying his personality on pure and honorable lines, the evil is sure to gain the upper hand and wreck both his individuality and his life. (pp. 48-9)

[Two] truths stand out as danger signals for all who read: first, the innocent must always suffer with the guilty, and second, both character and personality must deteriorate when an individual yields to the subtle influence of sin. We need these warnings. We need the art of the novelist to show us by vivid, startling dramatization that there is no doubt about it: "The wages of sin is death." (p. 49)

> *Edwin A. McAlpin, "Sin and Its Consequences," in his* Old and New Books as Life Teachers, *Doubleday, Doran & Company, Inc., 1928, pp. 36-49.*

G. K. CHESTERTON (essay date 1928)

[*Chesterton was one of England's most prominent and colorful men of letters during the early twentieth century. The following excerpt, in which he studies the setting and morality of* Dr. Jekyll and Mr. Hyde, *is drawn from his critical biography of Stevenson.*]

It will be realised that I am not, alas, so close a student of Stevensoniana as many who seem to think much less of Stevenson. But it seems to me that the story of [*Dr. Jekyll and Mr. Hyde*], which is presumably presented as happening in London, is all the time very unmistakably happening in Edinburgh. More than one of the characters seem to be pure Scots. Mr. Utterson, the lawyer, is a most unmistakably Scottish lawyer, strictly occupied with Scots Law. No modern English lawyer ever read a book of dry divinity in the evening merely because it was Sunday. Mr. Hyde indeed possesses the cosmopolitan charm that unites all nations; but there is something decidedly Caledonian about Dr. Jekyll; and especially something that calls up that quality in Edinburgh that led an unkind observer (probably from Glasgow) to describe it as "an east-windy, west-endy place." The particular tone about his respectability, and the horror of mixing his reputation with mortal frailty, belongs to the upper middle classes in solid Puritan communities. But what is especially to the point of the present argument, there is a sense in which that Puritanism is expressed even more in Mr. Hyde than in Dr. Jekyll. The sense of the sudden stink of evil, the immediate invitation to step into stark filth, the abruptness of the alternative between that prim and proper pavement and that black and reeking gutter—all this, though doubtless involved in the logic of the tale, is far too frankly and familiarly offered not to have had some basis in observation and reality. It is not thus that the ordinary young pagan, of warmer climes, conceives the alternative of Christ and Aphrodite. His imagination and half his mind are involved in defending the beauty and dignity of the joy of gods and men. It is not so that Stevenson himself came to talk of such things, when he had felt the shadow of old Athens fall on the pagan side of Paris. I allow for all the necessary horror of the conception of Hyde. But this dingy quality does not belong only to the demon antics of Hyde. It is implied, somehow, in every word about the furtive and embarrassed vices of Jekyll. It is the tragedy of a Puritan town; every bit as much as that black legend which Stevenson loved, in which the walking-stick of Major Weir went walking down the street all by itself. I hope to say something in a moment about the very deep and indeed very just and wise morality that is really involved in that ugly tale. I am only remarking here that the atmosphere and setting of it are those of some tale of stiff hypocrisy in a rigid sect or provincial village; it might be a tale of the Middle West savagely dissected in the *Spoon River Anthology.* But the point about it is that the human beauty which makes sin most dangerous hardly appears by a hint; this Belial is never graceful or humane; and in this there seems to me to be something suggestive of the inverted order and ugly contrast with which licence presents itself in a world that has frowned on liberty. It is the utterance of somebody who, in the words of Kipling, knew the worst too young; not necessarily in his own act or by his own fault, but by the nature of a system which saw no difference between the worst and the moderately bad. But whatever form the shock of evil might take, I think it jerked him out of the right development of his romantic nature; and was responsible for much that seemed random or belated in his life.

I do not mean to imply that the morality of the story itself has anything of weakness or morbidity; my opinion is very much the other way. Though the fable may seem mad, the moral is very sane; indeed, the moral is strictly orthodox. The trouble is that most of those who mention it do not know the moral, possibly because they have never read the fable. From time to time those anonymous authorities in the newspapers, who dismiss Stevenson with such languid grace, will say that there is something quite cheap and obvious about the idea that one man is really two men and can be divided into the evil and the good. Unfortunately for them, that does not happen to be the idea. The real stab of the story is not in the discovery that the one man is two men; but in the discovery that the two men are one man. After all the diverse wandering and warring of those two incompatible beings, there was still one man born and only one man buried. Jekyll and Hyde have become a proverb and a joke; only it is a proverb read backwards and a joke that nobody really sees. But it might have occurred to the languid critics, as a part of the joke, that the tale is a tragedy; and that this is only another way of saying that the experiment was a failure. The point of the story is not that a man *can* cut himself off from his conscience, but that he cannot. The surgical operation is fatal in the story. It is an amputation of which both the parts die. Jekyll, even in dying, declares the conclusion of the matter; that the load of man's moral struggle is bound upon him and cannot be thus escaped. The reason is that there can never be equality between the evil and the good. Jekyll and Hyde are not twin brothers. They are rather, as one of them truly remarks, like father and son. After all, Jekyll created Hyde; Hyde would never have created Jekyll; he only destroyed Jekyll. The notion is not so hackneyed as the critics find it, after Stevenson has found it for them thirty years ago. But Jekyll's claim is not that it is the first of such experiments in duality; but rather that it must be the last.

Nor do I necessarily admit the technical clumsiness which some have alleged against the tale, merely because I believe that many of its emotions were first experienced in the crude pain of youth.... That moment in which Jekyll finds his own formula fail him, through an accident he had never foreseen, is simply the supreme moment in every story of a man buying power from hell; the moment when he finds the flaw in the deed. Such a moment comes to Macbeth and Faustus and a hundred others; and the whole point of it is that nothing is really secure, least of all a Satanist security. The moral is that the devil is a liar, and more especially a traitor; that he is more dangerous to his friends than his foes.... [Although] the story ultimately emerged as a gargoyle very carefully graven by a mature master-craftsman, and was moreover a gargoyle of the greatest spiritual edification, eminently suited to be stuck on to the most sacred edifice, my point for the moment is that the stone of which it was made was originally found, I think, by Stevenson as a boy, kicking about the street, not to mention the gutter. In other words, he did not need to leave the respectable metropolis of the north to find the weaknesses of Jekyll and the crimes of Hyde.

I deal with these things in general terms, not merely out of delicacy, but partly out of something that I might almost call impatience or contempt. (pp. 51-6)

Stevenson was not a Catholic: he did not pretend to have remained a Puritan; but he was a highly honourable, responsible and chivalrous Pagan, in a world of Pagans who were most of them considerably less conspicuous for chivalry and honour. I for one, if I may say so, am ready to defend my own standards or to judge other men by theirs. But the Victorian pretence that every well-dressed hero of romance with over five hundred a year is born immune from the temptations which the mightiest saints have rolled themselves in brambles to control—that does not concern me and I shall not discuss it again.

But what does concern me, at this particular stage of the story, is not the question of what Stevenson thought right or wrong when he had become consciously and consistently a Pagan, but the particular way in which right and wrong appeared to him at this crude and groping age when he was still by tradition a Puritan. And I do think there was something tail-foremost, to use one of his own favourite words, in the way in which evil crept into his existence, as it does into everybody else's. He saw the tail of the devil before he saw his horns. Puritanism gave him the key rather to the cellars than the halls of Babylon; and something thus subterranean, suffocating and debased rolls like a smoke over the story of Jekyll and Hyde. (pp. 58-9)

> G. K. Chesterton, in his Robert Louis Stevenson,
> Dodd, Mead & Company, 1928, 211 p.

VLADIMIR NABOKOV   (lecture date 1941-59)

[*A Russian-born American man of letters, Nabokov was a prolific contributor to many literary fields who produced works in both Russian and English and distinguished himself in particular as the author of the novels* Lolita *and* Pale Fire. *Nabokov was fascinated with all aspects of the creative life; in his works he explored the origins of creativity, the relationships of artists to their work, and the nature of invented reality. In the following excerpt, Nabokov analyzes the style and artistic intent of* Dr. Jekyll and Mr. Hyde. *This excerpt formed part of a series of lectures given between 1941 and 1959.*]

Dr. Jekyll and Mr. Hyde was written in bed, at Bournemouth on the English Channel, in 1885 in between hemorrhages from the lungs. It was published in January 1886. Dr. Jekyll is a fat, benevolent physician, not without human frailties, who at times by means of a potion projects himself into, or concentrates or precipitates, an evil person of brutal and animal nature taking the name of Hyde, in which character he leads a patchy criminal life of sorts. For a time he is able to revert to his Jekyll personality—there is a down-to-Hyde drug and a back-to-Jekyll drug—but gradually his better nature weakens and finally the back-to-Jekyll potion fails, and he poisons himself when on the verge of exposure. This is the bald plot of the story.

First of all, if you have the Pocket Books edition I have, you will veil the monstrous, abominable, atrocious, criminal, foul, vile, youth-depraving jacket—or better say straitjacket. You will ignore the fact that ham actors under the direction of pork packers have acted in a parody of the book, which parody was then photographed on a film and showed in places called theatres; it seems to me that to call a movie house a theatre is the same as to call an undertaker a mortician.

And now comes my main injunction. Please completely forget, disremember, obliterate, unlearn, consign to oblivion any notion you may have had that **Jekyll and Hyde** is some kind of a mystery story, a detective story, or movie. It is of course quite true that Stevenson's short novel, written in 1885, is one of the ancestors of the modern mystery story. But today's mystery story is the very negation of style, being, at the best, conventional literature. Frankly, I am not one of those college professors who coyly boasts of enjoying detective stories—they are too badly written for my taste and bore me to death. Whereas Stevenson's story is—God bless his pure soul—lame as a detective story. Neither is it a parable nor an allegory, for it would be tasteless as either. It has, however, its own special

enchantment if we regard it as a phenomenon of style. It is not only a good "bogey story," as Stevenson exclaimed when awakening from a dream in which he had visualized it much in the same way I suppose as magic cerebration had granted Coleridge the vision of the most famous of unfinished poems. It is also, and more importantly, "a fable that lies nearer to poetry than to ordinary prose fiction" [according to Stephen Gwynn] and therefore belongs to the same order of art as, for instance, *Madame Bovary* or *Dead Souls*.

There is a delightful winey taste about this book; in fact, a good deal of old mellow wine is drunk in the story: one recalls the wine that Utterson so comfortably sips. This sparkling and comforting draft is very different from the icy pangs caused by the chameleon liquor, the magic reagent that Jekyll brews in his dusty laboratory. Everything is very appetizingly put. Gabriel John Utterson of Gaunt Street mouths his words most roundly; there is an appetizing tang about the chill morning in London, and there is even a certain richness of tone in the description of the horrible sensations Jekyll undergoes during his *hydizations*. Stevenson had to rely on style very much in order to perform the trick, in order to master the two main difficulties confronting him: (1) to make the magic potion a plausible drug based on a chemist's ingredients and (2) to make Jekyll's evil side before and after the hydization a believable evil. (pp. 179-80)

The names Jekyll and Hyde are of Scandinavian origin, and I suspect that Stevenson chose them from the same page of an old book on surnames where I looked them up myself. Hyde comes from the Anglo-Saxon *hyd*, which is the Danish *hide*, "a haven." And Jekyll comes from the Danish name *Jökulle*, which means "an icicle." Not knowing these simple derivations one would be apt to find all kinds of symbolic meanings, especially in Hyde, the most obvious being that Hyde is a kind of hiding place for Dr. Jekyll, in whom the jocular doctor and the killer are combined.

Three important points are completely obliterated by the popular notions about this seldom read book:

1. Is Jekyll good? No, he is a composite being, a mixture of good and bad, a preparation consisting of a ninety-nine percent solution of Jekyllite and one percent of Hyde (or *hydatid* from the Greek "water" which in zoology is a tiny pouch within the body of man and other animals, a pouch containing a limpid fluid with larval tapeworms in it—a delightful arrangement, for the little tapeworms at least. Thus in a sense, Mr. Hyde is Dr. Jekyll's parasite—but I must warn that Stevenson knew nothing of this when he chose the name.) Jekyll's morals are poor from the Victorian point of view. He is a hypocritical creature carefully concealing his little sins. He is vindictive, never forgiving Dr. Lanyon with whom he disagrees in scientific matters. He is foolhardy. Hyde is mingled with him, within him. In this mixture of good and bad in Dr. Jekyll, the bad can be separated as Hyde, who is a precipitate of pure evil, a precipitation in the chemical sense since something of the composite Jekyll remains behind to wonder in horror at Hyde while Hyde is in action.

2. Jekyll is not really transformed into Hyde but projects a concentrate of pure evil that becomes Hyde, who is smaller than Jekyll, a big man, to indicate the larger amount of good that Jekyll possesses.

3. There are really three personalities—Jekyll, Hyde, and a third, the Jekyll residue when Hyde takes over. (pp. 182-83)

Stevenson has set himself a difficult artistic problem, and we wonder very much if he is strong enough to solve it. Let us break it up into the following points:

1. In order to make the fantasy plausible he wishes to have it pass through the minds of matter-of-fact persons, Utterson and Enfield, who even for all their commonplace logic must be affected by something bizarre and nightmarish in Hyde.

2. These two stolid souls must convey to the reader something of the horror of Hyde, but at the same time they, being neither artists nor scientists, unlike Dr. Lanyon, cannot be allowed by the author to notice details.

3. Now if Stevenson makes Enfield and Utterson too commonplace and too plain, they will not be able to express even the vague discomfort Hyde causes them. On the other hand, the reader is curious not only about their reactions but he wishes also to see Hyde's face for himself.

4. But the author himself does not see Hyde's face clearly enough, and could only have it described by Enfield or Utterson in some oblique, imaginative, suggestive way, which, however, would not be a likely manner of expression on the part of these stolid souls.

I suggest that given the situation and the characters, the only way to solve the problem is to have the aspect of Hyde cause in Enfield and Utterson not only a shudder of repulsion but also something else. I suggest that the shock of Hyde's presence brings out the hidden artist in Enfield and the hidden artist in Utterson. Otherwise the bright perceptions that illumine Enfield's story of his journey through the lighted, empty streets before he witnessed Mr. Hyde's assault on the child, and the colorful imaginings of Utterson's dreams after he has heard the story can only be explained by the abrupt intrusion of the author with his own set of artistic values and his own diction and intonation. A curious problem indeed.

There is a further problem. Stevenson gives us the specific, lifelike description of events by humdrum London gentlemen, but contrasting with this are the unspecified, vague, but ominous allusions to pleasures and dreadful vices somewhere behind the scenes. On the one side there is "reality"; on the other, "a nightmare world." If the author really means there to be a sharp contrast between the two, then the story could strike us as a little disappointing. If we are really being told "never mind what the evil was—just believe it was something very bad," then we might feel ourselves cheated and bullied. We could feel cheated by vagueness in the most interesting part of the story just because its setting is so matter of fact and realistic. The question that must be asked of the work is whether Utterson and the fog and the cabs and the pale butler are more "real" than the weird experiments and unmentionable adventures of Jekyll and Hyde. (pp. 192-93)

Vladimir Nabokov, "Robert Louis Stevenson: 'The Strange Case of Dr. Jekyll and Mr. Hyde'," in his Lectures on Literature, *edited by Fredson Bowers, Harcourt Brace Jovanovich, 1980, pp. 179-204.*

RALPH TYMMS   (essay date 1949)

[*Tymms discusses the use of the doppelgänger, or literary double, in the novel.*]

In *The Strange Case of Dr. Jekyll and Mr. Hyde,* Stevenson advances from the boundaries of allegory towards the realm of psychological realism; though never does he lose from sight his point of departure. The basic conception of the *Doppelgänger,* to which he remains true, assumes the moral dualism of man. . . . Jekyll maintains . . . that evil has its right to freedom; and by a magical drug he releases the slumbering monster in his nature, to replace the predominantly good self habitually in control. Jekyll confesses that he had first detected a moral dualism in his nature; but even this (he supposes), if the truth were but known, would not suffice to describe the complexity of man's mind, doubtless 'a mere polity of multifarious, incongruous and independent denizens'. Setting out from his favourite attitude of moral allegory, Stevenson chances on conceptions of dualism closely resembling those of experimental psychologists of his day; and, as Jekyll continues to ponder on the problem of the discordant elements, he concludes that if he could but house each of them in separate identities, each would be freed from the intolerable interference of the other, incongruous, twin. This proves to be true: he succeeds in separating the conflicting selves from the 'agonised womb of consciousness' by the wonder-working drug; it '. . . had no discriminating action; it was neither diabolical nor divine; it but shook the doors of the prison-house of my disposition; and like the captives of Philippi, that which stood within ran forth'. The evil that lurks within his mind is swift to seize the opportunity, and projects itself in an appropriately hideous bodily form. Under the name of Hyde, it indulges in all the vices and crimes which Jekyll's better self has long resisted; but Hyde is younger and smaller than Jekyll, since, in a lifetime of predominant virtue, the evil self has had less scope for growth and maturity.

Hyde's new freedom progressively strengthens him at the expense of Jekyll's normal self, and Jekyll comes to loathe this horror chained to him—'caged in his flesh', a monster clinging to him . . . , in whom he is gradually becoming incorporated, and who, as time goes on, waits for Jekyll's hour of weakness to be born again, even without the help of the drug. Hyde returns Jekyll's hatred, but he is forced to give way to him and to allow Jekyll's habitual self to resume control in body and mind whenever he is himself in danger of capture for the murder he has committed. But in his resentment he plays malicious tricks on his other self, scrawling blasphemies in Jekyll's handwriting on the pages of devotional books, burning his letters, and destroying the portrait of his father. The end of this game of hide-and-seek between the alternating entities comes when Jekyll is unable to keep his own form at all. Hyde has become complete master, and by his very triumph brings about his own ruin; for, in permanently abandoning Jekyll's form, he has involuntarily destroyed his only hope of escape from capture; when he realises that he cannot turn back into Jekyll's wonted form, the monster kills himself, and thereby, Jekyll, too. (pp. 92-3)

Ralph Tymms, "The Double in Post-Romantic Literature," in his Doubles in Literary Psychology, *Bowes & Bowes, 1949, pp. 72-118.*

CHARLES D. ARING   (essay date 1960-61)

[*Aring is a neurologist who has written extensively on psychiatry, medical education, and philosophy. In discussing the psychological insights that Stevenson reveals in* Dr. Jekyll and Mr. Hyde, *Aring compares modern perceptions of personality with those of Stevenson's day.*]

Like many another genius, Stevenson was able to share with us the fruits of his fertile mind. These harvests demand inquiring curiosity and critical thought; as wildest dreams they are preludes that may or may not lead to truth. In *The Strange Case of Dr. Jekyll and Mr. Hyde,* Stevenson recovered his dream story and reworked it so provocatively that, like some other writers and poets, he is considered to have been in advance of the great sanitarians of the mind.

Most everybody has heard of Stevenson's tale about the dichotomy resident in each of us. Edward Hyde, the prime mover in the story, is the embodiment of evil; loathsome and apelike, he evokes hate at first sight, although sighting him is most unusual. Hyde's alter ego, the admirable Dr. Henry Jekyll, is a Fellow of the Royal Society, an eminently successful and respected physician, handsome, wealthy, with a string of degrees attached to his name including, besides the medical, a Doctor of Laws and a Doctorate of Civil Law, all of which, it might be presumed, would have allowed him to know himself. But such was not the case. In 1885, when the story was written, no degree carried with it much hope of enlightenment about the self.

The emergence of the satanic Hyde under the guise of medical research by the good Dr. Jekyll and the eventual loss of control of the former by the latter have become legend. Their destruction was inevitable in those early Darwinian times when the fit survived and there wasn't much to be done about those born less fit. Jekyll's researches into the mind's function are said to be "unscientific balderdash" and Jekyll is "wrong in mind," according to his surgeon friend, Dr. Hastie Lanyon. In retrospect I believe we would term his researches an interesting and needful prelude.

In attempting to find the truth behind these preludes, considerable study has gone into such problems as Stevenson lays before us. We no longer doubt that we are made as Dr. Jekyll and that our behavior is apt to contain Hyde-like vagaries. Human behavior is never quite predictable, mainly because the unseen Hyde, as Stevenson says, "never sleeps and constantly growls for license." While our ability to predict behavior may not have improved since Stevenson's time, we have advanced in our ability to understand the manner in which we have behaved, and in the opportunity to do something about it. "Life can only be understood backward, but it must be lived forward," said Kierkegaard. Stevenson tells us little about Jekyll's history prior to his maturity. We know that he is a prosperous bachelor of fifty and that he was wild when he was young. But as Stevenson had the lawyer Utterson remark in his soliloquy about Jekyll's past, as it bore on his present tribulations, "in the law of God there is no statute of limitations." It would appear, therefore, that Stevenson felt there could be no release from the past, particularly if the past was inadequately considered or vaguely understood.

Stevenson hadn't much use for Hyde, or perhaps it would be more accurate to say that the culture of 1885 had no evident uses for him. In Stevenson's day no better solution for the lively Mr. Hyde was to be had than to do away with him, a method reminiscent of the handling of some of our modern Hydes. Book learning still doesn't cut much of a figure in the presence of the preternatural Hyde. However, convert him into a cadaver and it is remarkable how readily he becomes manageable. Here is the main issue, as a contemporary psychiatrist Bertram D. Lewin has pointed out: some of us prefer to work with a live and even a lively subject; others would have him completely out of the way. There are, of course, intermediate positions between these extremes.

A close examination of the lively Edward Hyde at this later day will reveal that he has many qualities that we could wish for ourselves. He is strong and contemptuous of danger; he can be direct and vigorous; his faculties are sharp; he is completely lacking the dissemblance so crippling to ordinary man. Among his endowments is that of being able to arouse the doctor to do his bidding even in the dead of night, no mean feat in itself. In disaster he maintains a certain equanimity. There is no beating about the bush with Mr. Hyde; you know where you stand with him. Get in his way and he takes steps to go around you or, if necessary, over you—conduct sanctioned in some eminently successful men if we can believe their biographers. Mr. Hyde prefers to be abroad by night, as does the pestilence that walketh in darkness, and as do dreams. Released by the censor, he commits his vigorous predations when the coast is relatively clear, as with the action in dreams. Again like dreams, he is glimpsed by few. He handles troublesome situations forthrightly and with dispatch; this trait is also reminiscent of dream activity.

A patient who has engaged his own Hyde suggests that Stevenson's story should be reworked to indict Jekyll rather than Hyde as the villain. With his personal experience as touchstone, he arrives at the reasonable conclusion that Hyde never had a chance. He was handled as a monster, repressed and in chains, as illustrated in the summary uttered by Jekyll that "my devil

A frontispiece to Dr. Jekyll and Mr. Hyde. *Illustration by W. Stein.*

had long been caged, he came out roaring.'' As far as the data take us, Hyde seems to be a prime case of character warping. (pp. 70-2)

Jekyll's researches into mind were spectacular but contributed little to an understanding of it. Like some of the flamboyant experiments with mind in our time, they are quite startling, but leave no one the wiser. Jekyll's manipulations are of the order that do things to man rather than with him; they are authoritarian in nature and accordingly ignore or bypass his creative possibilities. Rather than foster more living by knowing, in the sense of Samuel Butler, they encourage helplessness and passivity; one is done for or to, rather than with.

But as is usual, the unknowing victim, Jekyll in this case, readily developed the derivations of his disquiet that we know as symptoms—the same symptoms that have become so ubiquitous in our time. Take insomnia for example: even a doze would suffice to bring the alter-ego Hyde on the scene. By remaining awake one may guard against the evil, the raging hell within. To sleep, then, is to tempt the emergence of all-powerful devils—all-powerful in the proportion that one is weak, or as sickly as Stevenson, or as unknowing as poor Jekyll. As we have learned since, such symptoms as insomnia are a sad substitute for understanding, although the victim usually prefers them to the look within. Symptoms pervert all useful function. Energy is drained into sustaining them, and malfunction, if not disintegration, is the inevitable outcome.

Stevenson goes to some trouble to impress upon us the reaction of the few who had caught glimpses of Hyde: *disgust, loathing* and *fear* are the strong words that he uses. Hyde evoked the desire to kill at first sight, a revulsion not unlike that evinced in even the highest medical circles later in the nineteenth century when glimpses were beginning to be afforded of the unconscious life of man, some of them through dreams. Today it is reasonably said that nothing provokes such fear as one's unconscious. For what other reason is it that we would have inward peace, but will not look within? (pp. 72-3)

Utterson, Jekyll's friend and lawyer, thought that if he could but behold the features of the real Hyde, the mystery of him might lighten, and perhaps be dissipated altogether ''as was the habit of mysterious things when well examined.'' Stevenson is urging us to examine the thing that is dreaded although it occasion disgust, loathing, fear and even murderous impulses—feelings that can be controlled if we will become aware of their nature.

In Stevenson's day the way to health for Jekyll was in dissociation from his alter-ego Hyde, since no other method to unburden the one of the other had been devised. Stevenson noted correctly, to be sure, that the more either was exercised, the stronger it became and assumed the ascendancy. Much that has been said since Stevenson about the constitution of personality, or its reconstituting, has derived largely from fright and ignorance of the manner in which the mind works. (pp. 73-4)

Every authority on behavior—including the Delphic Oracle, Plato, the Bible, Montaigne, Shakespeare, Cervantes, the poets and today's enlightened sociologist and psychiatrist—has reiterated ''know thyself'' as the best means to achieve Plato's mark of an educated man: that he should be able, and above all that he should always be willing, to see things as they are. . . . Several centuries before Christ, Plato warned about the madness and misery of one who uses the appearance of things as a measure of their reality and makes a mess of it.

It was to this knotty problem that Stevenson addressed himself three-quarters of a century ago, in the working out of his dream fantasy. He had the lawyer Mr. Utterson attempt to lessen the mystery of Hyde by seeking him out and confronting him to try to ''know'' him. Utterson seemed utterly baffled by the experience. But if we listen carefully to Stevenson's lucid and graceful undertones, we catch hints that his psychological insights were considerably ahead of the times:

> Mr. Hyde was pale and dwarfish, he gave an impression of deformity without any namable malformation, he had a displeasing smile, he had borne himself to the lawyer with a sort of murderous mixture of timidity and boldness, and he spoke with a husky, whispering, and somewhat broken voice: all these were points against him, but not all of these together would explain the hitherto unknown disgust, loathing and fear with which Mr. Utterson regarded him. ''There must be something else,'' said the perplexed gentleman. ''There is something more, if I could find a name for it. God bless me, the man seems hardly human! Something troglodytic, shall we say? or can it be the old story of Dr. Fell? or is it the mere radiance of a foul soul that thus transpires through, and transfigures, its clay continent? . . .''

Surely in this day, whenever a Hyde rears an ugly head, the challenge needs to be joined and the thing examined with our very best will, minds, energy and tools to try to learn its meaning. Turning away from it will no longer do; time has run out on this quaint custom. (pp. 75-6)

Despite his eventual solution for the evil and lively Hyde, Stevenson betrays a certain fascination for him. Hyde's spirits were always higher, sharper, more acute than Jekyll's, and it appears that so was his love of life. In their day Jekyll and Hyde were coheirs to death; they were irrevocably oriented toward destruction despite any love for life. Deep, blind, primitive compulsions that bypassed consciousness drew them nearer and nearer to the verge of death. These forces, usually neglected and about which we are therefore unknowing, drag along such persons as Jekyll to premature destruction. Theirs is a drift toward tragedy. Stevenson said of this force ''. . . that what was dead and had no shape should usurp the offices of life.''

Jekyll was frequently sunk in apathy, almost depression; he had little zest for life and seemed bored by his deadly round. His was, he said, ''an aversion to the dryness of a life of study.'' Today we can better understand Jekyll's method of stimulating his listless spirit, which is described in a line toward the end of the story: ''With a transport of glee I mauled the unresisting body [Jekyll's own], tasting delight with every blow. . . .''

While Stevenson had glimmerings that strength, vigor and spirit were on the side of Hyde, he saw no constructive way in which they could be tapped. Indeed, in 1885 there was none. In the late nineteenth century these were waste products buried in the manifest personality, and there was no way to get to them. They were then about as hidden from man as was the force in the atom, and potentially as destructive. Our tools for working these deposits have improved, among them the analysis of dreams, an exquisite although highly subtile instrument.

Stevenson took the tack, perhaps poetic license, perhaps autobiographical and surely timely, that there was no resolution of the problem but death and oblivion. This remains a prevailing breeze, and it hardly matters in what quarter one is standing. Our current Hydes—junior and senior delinquents, beatniks, Communists, obscene literature, and even dreams—too frequently are given the now outmoded treatment of suppression. It is difficult to convey the fact that what is suppressed retains its full force. Indeed, suppression may stimulate a swelling of the energy.

We need constantly to be reminded that mystery will lighten and perhaps be dissipated altogether when it is competently examined. This does not guarantee resolution, but it is the starting point of any real investigation motivated by a genuine desire to find out. This requires hard work, even bravery. (pp. 76-7)

The fearful cannot be allowed to restrain our explorations; they would prefer to have us about as circumscribed and restrained as Jekyll sometimes had Hyde. Naturally enough, they are troubled by such manifestations as a searching curiosity or dreams, and they refuse to be responsible for them. They act as though dreams were inspired by alien spirits. They find it impossible to believe that as people become more knowing they become more responsible. Since they have no real faith in themselves, they find everyone untrustworthy. With our uneasy friends, acquiescence in their nostalgic way of life puts their fears temporarily at rest, while an active exploration of the truth arouses their anxiety. They are satisfied with things as they are, with their prerogatives.

There isn't one of the feared, loathed and hated groups or concepts—our Hydes—that does not contain strengths, if we have the curiosity, the wit, the courage and the energy to search them out and to temper them. (pp. 77-8)

So the resolution of the Jekyll-Hyde dilemma is not repression or suicide or death, which in any of their derivations is a quick way out, but rather the cultivation and harvest of the strengths and constructions—the by-products, if you will—of the partial evil. (p. 78)

> *Charles D. Aring, "The Case Becomes Less Strange,"*
> *in* The American Scholar, *Vol. 30, No. 1, Winter,*
> *1960-61, pp. 67-78.*

MASAO MIYOSHI　(essay date 1966)

[*In considering* Dr. Jekyll and Mr. Hyde *as a "story of ideas," Miyoshi analyzes its characters in relation to Victorian society, identifies the literary tradition from which it developed, and addresses the relationship between Jekyll and Hyde*]

The *Strange Case of Dr. Jekyll and Mr. Hyde* is not exactly a nursery tale, and it is reasonable to expect that, of all the Stevenson stories, that would be the one to get an occasional nod in an article or in the classroom as having something more than entertainment quality, even as having something to do with ideas. Everyone is familiar with its two-men-in-one motif . . . but perhaps not unrelated to this popular status, the book is usually dismissed as crude science fiction or cruder moral allegory. . . . Should *Jekyll and Hyde* be remembered solely or primarily for its author's supposed invention of the dual-personality theme? Is the book too slight for any more conscientious critical effort? I would like to think that . . . *Dr. Jekyll and Mr. Hyde* may be read and studied as a story of ideas, that it will by this means yield insights into certain aspects of the late Victorian society that was its milieu, and that it will finally suggest something of the literary tradition which fathered it. (p. 471)

In approaching the work, it would be best to envision the world of the story—its men and landscape—before turning to the Jekyll-Hyde relationship itself. To begin with Mr. Utterson, who is evidently a highly respected citizen. The lawyer is always correctly professional and trustworthy, yet there is something furtive and suppressed about him. He is "austere with himself." He never smiles. He is "cold, scanty, and embarrassed in discourse." . . . He claims to like the theater, though he has not been to a play in twenty years. He makes no new friends and socializes only with men he has known well for a very long time. As for his renowned tolerance toward other people's misconduct, this looks suspiciously like the result not of charity but of indifference, though there is the subtlest suggestion of vicarious pleasure. Utterson, too, it turns out, has a past not quite innocent. When it occurs to him that blackmail may be at the root of Hyde's connection with Jekyll, he considers the possibility of a similar threat to himself: "And the lawyer, scared by the thought, brooded a while on his own past, groping in all the corners of memory, lest by chance some Jack-in-the-Box of an old iniquity should leap to light there." . . . When his friend and client Sir Danvers Carew is murdered, the event stirs no deeper emotion in him than worry "lest the good name of another should be sucked down in the eddy of the scandal." . . . (pp. 471-72)

Dr. Hastie Lanyon is, by contrast, an apparently healthy and genial man. Yet he too is shielded from life by an imposing respectability. Estranged from Dr. Jekyll for ten years, Dr. Lanyon is a scientist of "practical usefulness," . . . who sees Jekyll as a man gone wrong with his "scientific heresies." . . . As it happens, when the great Dr. Lanyon confronts a phenomenon which his matter-of-fact science cannot explain, his life is "shaken to its roots." . . . (p. 472)

The important men of the book, then, are all unmarried, barren of ideas, emotionally stifled, joyless. In the city at large the more prosperous business people fix up their homes and shops, yet there is something sleazy about the decor: the houses give an appearance of "coquetry," and the store fronts invite one like "rows of smiling saleswomen." . . . The setting is of a wasteland, but a wasteland hidden by the secure and relatively comfortable respectability of its inhabitants.

In this society of respectables Dr. Jekyll stands out as "the very pink of the proprieties." . . . Although his studies, like those of Faust and Frankenstein before him, tend toward "the mystic and the transcendental," . . . he still manages to maintain a considerable scientific reputation. And yet, despite Jekyll's social role—in fact, because of it—it is Jekyll, rather than Utterson or Lanyon, who brings forth Mr. Hyde.

It will be remembered that, for a period long before the emergence of Mr. Hyde, Dr. Jekyll was "committed to a profound duplicity of life": alongside his "imperious desire" for dignity and reputation, there was that "impatient gaiety of disposition." . . . But for those in the Victorian wasteland, gaiety and respectability are not easily reconciled. Dr. Jekyll, in particular, sees the two as mutually exclusive: a respectable pleasure would be a contradiction in terms. The exacting nature of his ambitions was such that the most unremarkable pleasure resulted in shame. Meanwhile, his Faustian studies, which had already "shed such a strong light on this consciousness of the perennial war among my members," . . . suggested to him a practical means of settling the whole question. (Dr. Jekyll, it should be understood, is incapable of expanding the mere self to the scale of the universe, nor can he hope to unify the antagonists within by a commitment to the betterment of all mankind, both of which Dr. Faust found feasible. Respectable society, of which Jekyll is a member in good standing, would repudiate such spurious modes of self-transcendence. Thus, whereas Faust was irrepressible by definition, Jekyll, the latter-day Faust, must at all costs hold his place as a reputable man and even rise in the establishment if he can.) And so, though pleasure had been suppressed for a long time by the dreary decency that was his life, Dr. Jekyll will enjoy it, after all, in the person of a totally new identity, Edward Hyde.

Hyde, once unleashed, arouses disgust in everyone. Dr. Jekyll's servant, for one, feels "kind of cold and thin" in his marrow after meeting Hyde for the first time . . . , and even the "Sawbones" has the urge to do away with him. To catch sight of Hyde is to be reminded of the hidden *"je"* in each of us, the "troglodytic" . . . animal that only waits for the moment of release. In most societies men agree to curb the *"je"* and are not required to totally suppress it. But in Jekyll's world, the *"je"* must be ruthlessly suppressed—most unequivocally so by the man known as "the very pink of the proprieties," Dr. Henry Jekyll, the most thoroughgoing *"je*-killer" of them all.

Hyde, at once Jekyll's Mephistopheles and his (Frankenstein) monster, looks like the very incarnation of evil, but at the beginning he is in fact merely Jekyll's unrepressed spontaneous existence. Going about in the guise of Mr. Hyde, Dr. Jekyll discovers a new freshness and joy in his life. (pp. 472-73)

But Hyde gradually shows himself dissatisfied with his role as mere "impatient gaiety," and scornful of the rights of others. His "every act and thought [were] centred on self." . . . In fact, his pleasure comes to depend on his torturing others. At this point, the self and society are enemies to the death.

Soon after the episode in which Hyde tramples the child, the Jekyll-Hyde metamorphosis becomes involuntary: the doctor goes to bed Henry Jekyll and awakes as Edward Hyde. The hidden *"je"* released by the social "I" threatens now to overpower it. Yet he believes it is still within his ability to stop this emergence of Mr. Hyde. Resolving to forego the "leaping impulses and secret pleasures," he determines to live once again the life of an "elderly and discontented doctor." . . . Of course, having once allowed his *"je"* the taste of freedom, he finds he cannot long suppress it. Soon Edward Hyde leaps out "roaring" . . . from the cave of Henry Jekyll. When the brutal murder of Sir Danvers Carew is disclosed, Jekyll's remorse is intense, if short-lived, recalling the reaction of countless Gothic villains after indulging their sadism. . . . The next time he goes out it is in the guise of Dr. Henry Jekyll. No wonder, then, that the metamorphosis should have become completely involuntary and the magic drug virtually ineffectual. There are no longer any inner or outer marks to distinguish the two. The merging, however, is in no sense a reconcilement of the Jekyll-Hyde duality. Rather, it signals a return to the starting point of Jekyll's whole experience. Only the annihilation of one of the two selves "reconciles" them: at the end of the story the doctor finally suppresses the *"je"* by murdering Hyde, thereby, of course, becoming a "self-destroyer," . . . a suicide. (p. 473)

Dr. Jekyll bears a close family resemblance to the Gothic romances of the late eighteenth century, a resemblance in respect both to the theme of double personality and their similar wide departure from the realism of the orthodox novel. *The Castle of Otranto, Vathek, The Italian, Caleb Williams, The Monk,* and many other stories feature outrageous villains whose abrupt and inexplicable transformations from a state of uncontrollable passion to that of heartfelt remorse indicate the dual personality in almost as virulent a form as Jekyll's. Vathek is cursed by his mother—herself unflaggingly evil—as a "two-headed, four-legged monster." And Caleb Williams likens human beings in general to "those twin-births that have two heads indeed, and four hands." This characteristic theme of the romances suggests a central concern of modern writers to document the dualism by examining particularly the disjunct passion and reason which have remained, pretty much throughout the modern period, alien to each other like the two sealed and separate chambers of the Gothic personality. (pp. 474, 479)

Of all the enormous output of the 1890s it is the Stevenson work which, unluckily, has given us a convenient epithet ("Jekyll-and-Hyde") for the post-Freudian with an unhappy double self. Paradoxically, Stevenson was too successful, both in his story-idea and in what has come to be a silly name for it: by that silly name we have been diverted from reading what should have great interest for us. By far the largest part of that interest lies in the vision the book conjures of the late Victorian wasteland, truly a de-Hyde-rated land unfit to sustain a human being simultaneously in an honorable public life and a joyful private one. (p. 480)

> *Masao Miyoshi, "Dr. Jekyll and the Emergence of Mr. Hyde," in* College English, *Vol. 27, No. 6, March, 1966, pp. 470-74, 479-80.*

JOSEPH J. EGAN   (essay date 1966)

[*Egan regards Stevenson's use of artistic elements, including symbolism and narration, as indicative of Stevenson's belief that humanity is capable of both good and evil.*]

[The] idea that Dr. Jekyll himself is both good and evil is the only one supported by the artistic design of the story.

The central pattern of symbolism in *Jekyll and Hyde* is associated with the various dwelling places that figure in the tale to reveal the spiritual condition of their inhabitants. Dr. Jekyll's own home lies in "a square of ancient, handsome houses, now for the most part decayed from their high estate and let in flats and chambers to all sorts . . . of men," . . . and the physician's surroundings thus suggest both the past condition of his soul, when evil was still in check, and its present state of moral debility. We are told that around the corner from this square is a pleasant and respectable bystreet of the London business section: "The street shone out in contrast to its dingy neighborhood, like a fire in a forest; and with its . . . general cleanliness and gayety of note, instantly caught and pleased the eye of the passenger." . . . And yet the attractive scene is marred by the presence of "a certain sinister block of building [that] bore, in every feature, the marks of prolonged and sordid negligence." . . . This structure proves to be the "'back way to Dr. Jekyll's," . . . by which Mr. Hyde gains access to the physician's home, and in the context of the story becomes symbolic not only of Hyde's depravity but of the tarnished side of all men as well. Like the moral destitution it represents, Hyde's sinister doorway, the appropriate symbol of the "back door" to Henry Jekyll's soul, stands out in contrast to its ostensibly wholesome and orderly surroundings. The London bystreet, then, suggests something of the incongruity in human nature itself, where evil coexists with that which is seemingly most respectable.

The idea of spiritual decay is given further meaning when we discover that this grimy building where Dr. Jekyll performs his secret experiments is called "'Black Mail House'" . . . , for evil has indeed come to compromise the good in Henry Jekyll. It is his own frightful inclination towards evil that has brought on the moral ruination of Jekyll, a ruination which cannot long be concealed despite the fact that the doctor's dwelling still wears the deceiving mask of respectability and "a great air of wealth and comfort." . . . A more obvious image of corruption is Hyde's filthy residence in Soho, which is guarded by an old woman with "an evil face, smoothed by hypocrisy," . . . the fitting companion and familiar for such a creature as Edward Hyde.

Stevenson repeatedly employs the artistic elements in **Jekyll and Hyde** to suggest the spiritual destruction of Dr. Jekyll at the hands of Mr. Hyde. In his "Full Statement of the Case," Dr. Jekyll confesses that he never ceased to believe that evil is "the lethal side of man," . . . and the meaning of the story depends on this belief. The blasphemies and profanities which Hyde scribbles on the pages of Jekyll's theological texts are indicative of the attempt of evil to destroy the good in man. Hyde's destruction of the portrait of Jekyll's father is also suggestive of the terrible effects which evil can produce in the human soul. . . . Conversely, the son figure, to which Jekyll likens Hyde, is representative of the present imbalance of moral values in the doctor's soul and a total alienation from goodness. When Hyde destroys the portrait of the elder Jekyll, his action is therefore symbolic of the destruction of Henry Jekyll's spiritual integrity by the power of the evil within him.

Several even more vivid examples of the lethal power of evil and its inherent antagonism to all goodness are given in connection with Mr. Hyde's cruelty towards others. Early in the story we are given a description of the terrible way in which Hyde treats the little girl whom he has knocked down: "'Then came the horrible part of the thing; for the man trampled calmly over the child's body and left her screaming on the ground. It sounds nothing to hear, but it was hellish to see. It wasn't like a man; it was like some damned Juggernaut'." . . . Hyde's attack on the child, a figure of innocence, represents the assault which his own evil has made upon the soul of Dr. Jekyll. (pp. 28-9)

The murder of Sir Danvers closely parallels the trampling of the little girl; but the meanings of the two events are not quite identical. The child represents an internal state of the innocence of the soul, and it is this inherent goodness which evil first seeks to undermine. Carew, on the other hand, though he remains associated with goodness, is more representative of Henry Jekyll's outer respectability and public reputation, things which, as we have seen, the doctor values very highly. The aspect of the Carew murder most stressed is that the victim was a national figure, a well-known Member of Parliament whose death "'will make a deal of noise'." . . . The second assault of Mr. Hyde, then, is directed against Dr. Jekyll's public image, an image which is shattered by the scandal of the doctor's own sinister proclivity towards evil.

A significant relationship exists between the increasing ferocity of Hyde's sadistic attacks on his victims' bodies and the awful growth of his own "energy of life." . . . In **The Strange Case of Dr. Jekyll and Mr. Hyde** Edward Hyde is depicted as a vampire who feeds on the very life of his victims, "drinking pleasure with bestial avidity from any degree of torture to another; relentless like a man of stone" . . . ; and Stevenson uses this vampire image to suggest the way in which indulgence of evil eats away man's capacity for goodness. (pp. 29-30)

Stevenson employs the image of the criminal in relationship to Mr. Hyde in order to give further emphasis to the effect which Hyde has upon Henry Jekyll's spiritual life: "Men have before hired bravos to transact their crimes, while their own person and reputation sat under shelter. I was the first that ever did so for his pleasures. . . . Hyde was indifferent to Jekyll, or but remembered him as the mountain bandit remembers the cavern in which he conceals himself from pursuit." . . . Like a kind of deadly bandit of the soul, Mr. Hyde comes to rob Dr. Jekyll of his goodness and reputation; and yet Hyde is strangely dependent on his victim Jekyll for continued existence. . . . [He] needs Jekyll as a means of concealing himself from arrest for his crimes, and at the heart of the relationship between Dr. Jekyll and Mr. Hyde is thus the suggestion that in destroying the good, evil comes to destroy itself. When Hyde can no longer change back into Jekyll, he has lost that very thing upon which he preys and has no course left him but the taking of his own life.

But this physical death is suggestive of the spiritual suicide towards which both Jekyll and Hyde have been moving throughout the story, for the indulgence of evil will eventually destroy the whole man and both the good and evil within him. . . . Mr. Hyde is the figure of the deadly evil which *hides* in the soul of each of us and contains the seeds of our spiritual and psychological destruction; and the name *Jekyll* (*Je* = French, *I; kyll* = *kill*) suggests the self-destroyer.

The death of Dr. Lanyon, brought on by the sight of Hyde's transformation into Jekyll, also symbolizes the perishing of the good in Henry Jekyll. Indeed, Lanyon becomes almost the reflection of Jekyll, and the tragic fates of the two medical men are strikingly similar. . . . Stevenson thus uses Dr. Lanyon as the counterpart of Henry Jekyll; both were once reasonably good men, but their impetuous inquiry into the nature of evil drove them on to destroy their souls. It is not for nothing, then, that Dr. Lanyon's first name is Hastie, and his physical death suggests the spiritual and psychic death of the man who has too *hastily* called forth the power of evil.

A significant part of the artistic design of **The Strange Case of Dr. Jekyll and Mr. Hyde** is Stevenson's use of three distinct modes of narration in the story. Though the friend and advisor of Dr. Jekyll, Lawyer Utterson is not a medical scientist and he remains to the end only the bewildered onlooker. But his point of view gives way first to that of Dr. Lanyon, who is a party to the hideous secret of transformation, and finally to that of Jekyll himself, who in the last chapter fully exposes the terrible ruination of his soul. The narrative progression of the tale is thus from the outside to within and closely follows the gradual penetration into the troubled mind of Dr. Jekyll.

This narrative thread of **Jekyll and Hyde** is carefully paralleled and reinforced by the skillful use of passageways in the story. A series of doors separate Dr. Jekyll's house from the back courtyard and the laboratory where he conducts his experiments. Just as the narrative movement of the tale brings us ever nearer to the heart of the mystery of Edward Hyde, so too with the opening of each successive door by Mr. Utterson, we move closer and closer towards the innermost depths of Dr. Jekyll's tormented soul, which is itself represented by the sealed cabinet in the upper storey of the laboratory building.

Significantly, the door to this cabinet is covered by red baize, a cheap, coarse material which Dr. Jekyll uses to muffle the sounds of his scientific investigations. The baize itself suggests the "cheapness" of Dr. Jekyll's improper experimentation, and the color red gives additional emphasis to the sinister unholiness of his propensity for evil, for the tincture which helps effect the change into Hyde is "blood-red" in color . . . and at one stage in the process the transformation compound becomes a bright red. . . . The successive changes of the compound's color from red to purple and then to green suggest, in turn, the idea of altered appearance upon which the plot of the story depends. When Utterson and the butler Poole finally smash in the red "baize door, their action is symbolic of both the end of the "silence" connected with Henry Jekyll's secret experiments and the exposure of the doctor's spiritual dissolution and the true identity of Edward Hyde.

We also learn that the laboratory building had served its former owner as a dissecting theatre, and it becomes therefore the fit setting for Henry Jekyll's attempts to "dissect" his own personality: "It was the first time that the lawyer [Mr. Utterson] had been received in that part of his friend's quarters; and he eyed the dingy, windowless structure with curiosity, and gazed round with a distasteful sense of strangeness as he crossed the theatre, once crowded with eager students and now lying gaunt and silent, the tables laden with chemical apparatus, the floor strewn with crates and littered with packing straw, and the light falling dimly through the foggy cupola." . . . The shadowy and cluttered aspect of the laboratory suggests the spiritual darkness and disorder in Dr. Jekyll's life, and, significantly, it is in close proximity to these unwholesome surroundings that Henry Jekyll at last disappears forever and that the body of Edward Hyde is found stretched out in the final death agony. And yet in the description of Dr. Jekyll's sealed cabinet, the actual scene of Hyde's suicide, Stevenson calls attention to a quite appropriate irony between apparent order and cheeriness and the hideous double death of good and evil:

> There lay the cabinet before their eyes in the quiet lamplight, a good fire glowing and chattering on the hearth, the kettle singing its thin strain, a drawer or two open, papers neatly set forth on the business table, and nearer the fire, the things laid out for tea: the quietest room, you would have said, and, but for the glazed presses full of chemicals, the most commonplace that night in London.
>
> Right in the midst there lay the body of a man sorely contorted and still twitching. They drew near on tiptoe, turned it on its back and beheld the face of Edward Hyde. . . .

The tragic irony connected with this description of the cabinet, the image of Jekyll's own soul, suggests the tragic irony of the doctor's fate and points up the incongruities at the heart of human moral life.

Here again Stevenson reinforces the pervading theme of *Jekyll and Hyde*—the idea of the self-contradictory impulses and mingled strains of good and evil within the same man. In his attempt to separate the conflicting elements within his personality, Dr. Jekyll had been prompted by the hope that he need be "no longer exposed to disgrace and penitence by the hands of this extraneous evil." . . . But Dr. Jekyll at last discovers that evil is as essential a part of human nature as good itself and not the "extraneous" factor he had once thought it: "I

have been made to learn that the doom and burthen of our life is bound forever on man's shoulders, and when the attempt is made to cast it off, it but returns upon us with more unfamiliar and more awful pressure." . . . The meaning of *The Strange Case of Dr. Jekyll and Mr. Hyde* and all of the story's artistic design thus continually carry us back to the idea that humanity is, in the end, synonymous with the struggle of good and evil. (pp. 30-2)

> *Joseph J. Egan, "The Relationship of Theme and Art in 'The Strange Case of Dr. Jekyll and Mr. Hyde'," in* English Literature in Transition, *Vol. 9, No. 1, 1966, pp. 28-32.*

EDWIN M. EIGNER   (essay date 1966)

[*Eigner assesses Stevenson's narrative style and character development in* Dr. Jekyll and Mr. Hyde. *Focusing on the relationship between the two characters, Eigner describes Hyde as a part of Jekyll's personality that the latter unsuccessfully tries to suppress.*]

Stevenson's *Strange Case of Dr. Jekyll and Mr. Hyde* is written from more points of view than any other of his works. It contains two first person narratives, a chapter written in the impersonal style of a newspaper report, and the account of a seemingly uninvolved third person point of view character, Mr. Gabriel Utterson, who sometimes observes Jekyll and Hyde directly and sometimes listens to the stories told by still other characters who have observed them. What the reader who has not looked at the story for some time tends to think of as *Dr. Jekyll and Mr. Hyde* is only the last quarter of it, the part which Jekyll himself recounts.

No doubt this oblique approach to narration added to the suspense and mystery for the work's initial audience. The reader who comes to the story fresh (it is almost impossible to find such a one nowadays) does not know that Jekyll and Hyde are one man until the work is almost three-quarters over, and for this reader the shock is still a potent one. But Stevenson has another and a more serious reason for using all these points of view. The most important focus in the story, as we might expect, will be on Jekyll's attitudes towards his double. Before we come to these reactions, however, Stevenson feels it necessary to present us with a number of other opinions of Hyde, attitudes which should prepare us for Jekyll's and which might furthermore serve us as a standard of comparison.

The first response to Hyde comes from Mr. Richard Enfield, "the well-known man about town," . . . who describes the incident in which Hyde knocks down and tramples the little girl. Enfield takes a loathing to Hyde at first sight. . . . He prides himself as a connoisseur of beauty, and so he finds Hyde's unspecifiable deformity distasteful to the point of nausea. . . . Enfield also provides us with a number of other reactions. He tells, for instance, about the women whom the sight of Hyde turned "as wild as harpies," . . . and about the colorless, "cut-and-dry" Edinburgh apothecary, "about as emotional as a bagpipe," who turned "sick and white with the desire to kill him." . . . (pp. 144-45)

G. J. Utterson of Gaunt Street, to whom Enfield tells this story, is himself something like the unemotional Edinburgh apothecary, and his association with Enfield is really the first *Doppelgänger* relationship the story presents. The two men are distant kinsmen. Nevertheless, they seem to have little in common, for Utterson is "austere with himself" and drinks gin when he is alone "to mortify a taste for vintages." . . . To strengthen his moral fiber, he has for twenty years denied himself the pleasure of going to the theater. Yet Utterson and the *bon vivant* Enfield are fast friends. (pp. 145-46)

The third important, uninvolved narrator reaction comes from Hastie Lanyon, who is a Scottish doctor, like Jekyll himself. Lanyon is a bold and boisterous scientist of the soundest modern principles. He drinks wine when he is alone, instead of gin, but he lacks Utterson's tolerance, and has allowed his friendship with Henry Jekyll to lapse because of the latter's "fanciful" medical theories. "'Such unscientific balderdash,' added the doctor, flushing suddenly purple, 'would have estranged Damon and Pythias'." . . . Edward Hyde fills this scientist with "a disgustful curiosity," . . . and once Lanyon has learned the Jekyll-and-Hyde secret, he rejects Jekyll entirely. (pp. 146-47)

These then are the principal reactions which prepare us for the encounters of Jekyll and Hyde with one another—loathing, disgust, fear, and shocked horror. . . . *Jekyll and Hyde* has developed into a popular myth, one of the very few to come out of the Victorian period, and its meanings have consequently become blurred. . . . The result is that the term Jekyll-and-Hyde, even as used by psychologists, has little reference to Stevenson's work. Most nonexperts, as a matter of my own observation, are rather surprised to learn that the story has a known author, or if they associate Stevenson's name with it, they often assume he took the plot from some well-worn folk legend. (pp. 147-48)

If we have seen the movies, we tend perhaps to regard Jekyll as an essentially good man who looks upon his dangerous experiment as a noble service to mankind. He is a sort of Tennysonian hero, like King Arthur, who strives to free man from the evil in his nature. (p. 149)

This has, indeed, proved to be a very saleable version of the story, but it is hardly fair to saddle Stevenson with it. And it is especially unfair to complain afterwards, as critics oftentimes do, of the story's "slightly too obvious meaning." One such critic [C. Keith], smarting over the insult to his intelligence, explains the moral of *Dr. Jekyll and Mr. Hyde* in the following sarcastic language:

> If you weren't careful, the evil in you would swallow up the good, as the wicked Hyde does Dr. Jekyll. And you'd be lost. So be careful! Nearly as crude as that.

Now there is no suggestion in Stevenson's version of the *Strange Case of Dr. Jekyll and Mr. Hyde* that carelessness was Henry Jekyll's chief fault. On the contrary, according to one of Stevenson's letters, the "harm" was in Jekyll precisely because he was *too* careful, "because he was a hypocrite. . . . The Hypocrite let out the beast of Hyde." (pp. 149-50)

Jekyll, in direct contrast to Stevenson's statement about him, asserts that he "was in no sense a hypocrite," but he means something special by this, something which requires explanation. He means, as he says, that both sides of him "were in dead earnest," . . . that he was not a bad man posing during the day as a good one. He does not mean that he took Sunday afternoon strolls with his *alter ego,* as Utterson and Enfield do. As a matter of fact, he specifically declines an invitation from this engaging pair, who recommend that he take a "quick turn" with them to whip up his "circulation." . . . His one self is deathly ashamed of the other, and the doctor believes,

moreover, that this mortification does him a world of credit. (p. 152)

As for Jekyll's goodness, we have very little evidence for it besides the doctor's own word. There is a period just after Hyde's murder of Sir Danvers when Jekyll goes about actively striving to do good, but this activity is presented almost as though it were contrary to his more general habits. As to his actions prior to this stage, no one in the story will go beyond the author's statement that "he had always been known for his charities." . . . The public nature of his good actions is, in fact, heavily stressed. Enfield calls him "the very pink of the proprieties. . . . One of your fellows who do what they call good." . . . And when Utterson finds a book of Jekyll's which Hyde has disfigured with blasphemies, he describes it as "a pious work for which Jekyll had several times expressed a great esteem." . . . Yet Utterson does not discover any reverent marginalia in *Jekyll's* hands. Neither do we witness Jekyll actually doing any of the good he boasts of and is known for. In a previous draft of the story, obviously intermediate between the destroyed first manuscript and the published version, Stevenson was somewhat more specific in detailing Jekyll's virtues. There Jekyll calls himself "a man of distinction, immersed in toils, open to generous sympathies, never slow to befriend struggling virtue." But even these generalities were not permitted to stand.

Perhaps the problem is simply that Stevenson, here as elsewhere, cannot sufficiently bring himself to believe in positive acts of virtue. The only goodness Stevenson seems capable of rendering in his fiction is the act of renunciation, and sacrifice seems hardly to be Henry Jekyll's strong point. . . . The benevolence in Jekyll seems to stem not from any innate springs of virtue, but, as he admits, from an "imperious desire to carry my head high, and wear a more than commonly grave countenance before the public." . . . As with so many of Stevenson's Lowlanders, the ideal to which Henry Jekyll is committed is not goodness, but mere respectability.

But we should also note that Jekyll is the type of hypocrite who deludes himself along with the world. No doubt he believes that his day-life of negative virtues represents real good, just as he believes that his night-life of sensuous indulgence represents real evil. And these convictions, though Stevenson would have rejected them both, are what lead Henry Jekyll to the recognition of his double nature. (pp. 152-54)

This diagnosis, no matter how mistakenly arrived at, is again a healthy one. It is indeed a truth according to Stevenson's most consistent thought, and it is a truth a man always does well to face. What is unhealthy is the treatment the good doctor prescribes. Jekyll was wrong in attempting to segregate the two sides of his life, and he was even more wrong in glorifying the one side while alternately condemning and indulging the other. His chemical experiment is simply a logical extension of this treatment. . . . Stevenson's Jekyll is at least as much interested in freeing his evil nature from restraint as he is in giving scope to the good in him. . . . According to Jekyll, though, each of the two natures is dear to him, and he sees himself as "radically both." . . . Jekyll, far from wishing to end his double nature, is attempting to make it permanent. He does not mean, at the beginning at least, to reject either of his identities. And when Hyde, the evil nature, appears for the first time, the experiment may be thought of as incomplete, but it should certainly not be considered a failure.

Now that Hyde is out in the open, Jekyll must react to him, and since Jekyll's nature is more distorted by Lowland morality than any of the other narrators'—he lacks the tolerance of Utterson and Enfield and the robustness of Lanyon—we may expect his attitudes to be even more extreme than theirs. . . . Jekyll's reactions are confused and mixed. On the one hand, Jekyll was "conscious of no repugnance, rather a leap of welcome" at the appearance of Hyde. "This, too, was myself. It seemed natural and human." . . . As the relationship develops, moreover, he begins to regard Hyde as his own child. Their ages are right for this: Jekyll is fifty, Hyde is in his twenties. And Hyde is the smaller of the two. Like an indulgent father of a scapegrace son, Jekyll writes a check to keep Hyde out of trouble. Later, he even makes Hyde the beneficiary of his will. But while Jekyll is quick enough at first to accept his secret kinship with Hyde and very naturally refers to the latter as "me," he is just as quick to recognize Hyde as wicked, "tenfold more wicked" than himself. . . . (pp. 154-56)

Certainly Hyde does not merit the indulgence Jekyll allows him. One wonders also whether at his very first appearance he quite deserves so full a condemnation. I suggest this because it is clear from the incidents which follow that Hyde grows more wicked as the story progresses, and if this is so, he can hardly have been "pure evil" at the beginning. It is true that by the end of the story Hyde "is the essence of cruelty and malice and selfishness and cowardice," as we have heard Stevenson say, but at the start he seems perhaps to be something less than this.

No doubt, although the story does not present it, Hyde continues with, and indeed improves upon, Jekyll's voluptuary adventures; but this sort of behavior is pure evil only in the minds of Jekyll and other products of the negative morality from which Stevenson had himself rebelled. And if there is a possibility that Jekyll judges his *alter ego* unjustly, let us re-examine some of the earlier condemnations of Hyde to see whether they too are not excessive in view of the facts.

Hyde's first narrated adventure . . . is described by Richard Enfield. Enfield tells how he saw Hyde and a little girl approaching one another at a street intersection.

> Well, sir, the two ran into one another naturally enough at the corner; and then came the horrible part of the thing; for the man trampled calmly over the child's body and left her screaming on the ground. It sounds nothing to hear; but it was hellish to see. It wasn't like a man; it was like some damned Juggernaut. . . .

This incident shows Hyde as a creature without compassion, but it does not show him as either malicious or cruel. He takes no pleasure, as far as we know, in hurting the child. He tramples "calmly," and the Juggernaut simile underscores the impersonality of his action. Hyde is simply indifferent to the girl's pain. He is, as we might expect after the chemical amputation, a man without a conscience, completely uncivilized.

But Enfield and the other bystanders . . . react to Hyde as though his wickedness were of a more positive nature. (pp. 156-57)

Hyde does not appear purely evil in this adventure, but he does seem to bring out all the cruelty and malice in those who judge him. . . . Enfield, the bystanders, and the other narrators are rejecting a part of themselves when they reject Hyde, and the more strenuously they excise him, the more thoroughly they come to resemble their notion of him, and the more profoundly they are affected by the encounter. . . .

Hyde, of course, is a part of Jekyll, and the harm caused by Jekyll's rejection of him is mirrored in Hyde's own changing nature. At the beginning of their relationship, Hyde was indifferent to Jekyll. (p. 158)

The change in Hyde is a slow one and it must be observed through several of the points of view, but it is, nevertheless, very perceptible and quite extreme. Hyde progresses from conscienceless and impersonal indifference to malicious hatred, from a Juggernaut to a devil. And if he appears sufficiently evil to us at his first appearance in the story, we should remember that Jekyll has been pushing him away from his conscience for more than twenty years. . . . Moreover, the rest of society, as represented by the bystanders and the narrators, with their strong morals or their weak stomachs, have been assisting and encouraging Jekyll in the destructive polarization of his nature. The experiment in the laboratory is only a step in this separation—albeit the most dramatic. There were steps before it, and, tragically, there are steps to follow it.

As the poles widen, Hyde becomes more and more evil. Yet Jekyll continues his dissociation. He decides that Hyde alone is guilty of the nighttime activities, and simultaneously Hyde's crimes "began to turn toward the monstrous." . . . Hyde displays much more than indifference and lack of conscience in his senseless and brutal murder of Sir Danvers Carew. "Instantly," Jekyll writes, "the spirit of hell awoke in me and raged. With a transport of glee, I mauled the unresisting body, tasting delight from every blow." . . . (pp. 158-59)

Nor does the rejection end even here. Indeed, the purpose of Jekyll's next move, his increased performance of benevolent actions and church duties, is to make himself over as much as he can into the direct antithesis of Hyde. (p. 159)

The *Strange Case of Dr. Jekyll and Mr. Hyde* is not an allegory of the evil in man swallowing up the helpless good; rather it is a story of a whole man driving one part of his nature to depravity until the entire ego is destroyed. . . . After the murder of Carew, Jekyll announces that he is "quite done with" Hyde . . . , and whereas at the beginning of the relationship he had referred to his *alter ego* in both the first and third person indiscriminately, towards the end of the story he denies Hyde's humanity altogether and cannot bring himself to speak of him as I. (p. 160)

Hyde responds to such treatment with hatred of Jekyll and with increased evil. Near the end he fiendishly destroys Jekyll's papers, and, like the devil in a saint's life, he writes blasphemies in Jekyll's sacred books. . . . But even when Hyde is most wicked, Jekyll cannot be regarded as a victim. The doctor feels he is the tormented one, because he has a conscience, but it is Hyde, after all, who is driven finally to commit suicide out of sheer terror. It is still another case of dog against wolf, and as usual in Stevenson, the dog is by far the more formidable. (pp. 160-61)

In writing such a story of a creature turned diabolic in response to the hatred and rejection afforded him by society and by the man to whom he owes his life, Stevenson must have been aware of similarities to the first important monster story of the century, Mary Shelley's *Frankenstein*. There are several points of strong comparison, the most basic of which is that both works employ *Doppelgänger* to emphasize the duality of human nature. (p. 161)

Another similarity between *Frankenstein* and Stevenson's story is that in both works the hero is excessively self-righteous. We have seen that this was also a part of the intervening tradition as practiced by Hogg, Bulwer, and Dostoyevsky. It figures also in such works as *Les Misérables,* in *The Scarlet Letter,* and in what is perhaps the greatest of the pursuit stories of the century, *Moby Dick.* In *Frankenstein,* as in several of Stevenson's works, the greatest harm comes from two things within the hero's own nature—a delicate sensibility which cannot bear to look at the Monster's ugliness, and an overdeveloped moral conscience which shrinks from the Monster's deeds; in other words, from Enfield and from Utterson. (pp. 162-63)

The emotion in the reader which these works of rejection, pursuit, and mutual destruction aim at is pathos. We are meant to mourn the noble intention and the frantic energy wasted by these rejections of self or of nature. We are probably meant to believe the words of Frankenstein's Monster when he says that his "thoughts were once filled with sublime and transcendent visions of the beauty and the majesty of goodness." (p. 163)

Edward Hyde lacked the Monster's literary education; he had neglected his Milton. He was anyway never an angel. According to Stevenson's theory of duality, though, he was originally not a devil either, but a necessary part of Henry Jekyll's and of every man's character. And he could have been a useful part, as well—not when we first meet him; it was already too late by this time; but years earlier, in the days before Jekyll began to live his double life, channeling all his energy into voluptuary pleasures and all his aspirations into a creed of negative virtues. . . .

Like *Frankenstein* and the other romances of pursuit, the *Strange Case of Dr. Jekyll and Mr. Hyde* is a story of pathetic waste. It is also the story of a weak man—but not weak because he dabbles irresponsibly with evil, as the American play and the American movies would have it. Henry Jekyll's weakness is like that of every other Stevensonian protagonist . . . ; it resides entirely in his tragic inability to accept his own nature. (p. 164)

> *Edwin M. Eigner, in his* Robert Louis Stevenson and Romantic Tradition, *Princeton University Press, 1966, 258 p.*

BARBARA HANNAH   (essay date 1971)

[*In this Jungian analysis, Hannah explores the role of the subconscious in the creation of the novel by relating it to Stevenson's "A Chapter on Dreams" (see excerpt dated 1888). She describes Jekyll's attempts to come to grips with his divided personality, characterizing Stevenson as "a man in tortured flight from himself."*]

Carrying one's cross and carrying one's shadow is only a difference of words—as anyone who has really tried the latter can testify—and Stevenson himself tells us, in *Across the Plains,* how much he suffered from a "strong sense of man's double being which must at times come in upon and overwhelm the mind of every living creature." He puts it more clearly in *The Strange Case of Dr. Jekyll and Mr. Hyde* where he writes that "man is not truly one, but truly two," and that these two are severed into "provinces of good and ill which divide and compound man's dual nature."

It is questionable whether Stevenson realized that this is a problem which can only be solved in one's own individual psyche. (pp. 38-9)

But he had an extraordinary insight into the unconscious—far beyond that of his time—so one cannot doubt that, had he realized how much can be accomplished by analytic work on oneself, he would have been singularly gifted in this respect. As it was, the objective psyche was known to him under another name, although for many years he regarded its as something not identical with himself but which could help him in his work. What we call the "unconscious" was "the Brownies" to Stevenson and, unlike most creative artists, he gave them full credit for their contributions to his writings. He even says that his Brownies "do one half of my work for me while I am asleep, and in all human likelihood do the rest for me as well, when I am wide awake and fondly suppose I do it for myself." (pp. 39-40)

The Brownies are a modern version of the Cabiri, those creative dwarf gods of antiquity, which we meet again and again in various forms in mythology. Stevenson—although he admits his debt to them most generously—was inclined to take them much too lightly. One doubts whether he realized their full mythological background or anything like their latent power. . . . (p. 40)

After Stevenson had long been trying to find a "story . . . a body, a vehicle" for his "strong sense of man's double being," he tells us that *Jekyll and Hyde* was suggested by a dream. He "dreamed the scene at the window, and a scene afterwards split into two, in which Hyde, pursued for some crime, took the powder and underwent the change in the presence of his pursuers. All the rest was made awake and consciously, although I think I can trace in much of it the manner of my Brownies."

When our totality is left behind us in the unconscious, it is the conscious ego only that takes this one-sided journey. It is in our dreams that we can look for the elements that compensate and enlarge our too narrow consciousness. This dream of Stevenson's not only gave him the outline of the story for which he had been searching so long—a point he was swift to seize upon—but it also offered him an extraordinary insight into his own split and suffering psyche, if only he could have seen the connections. But we will first consider the story as Stevenson wrote it, keeping the dream in mind.

The reader will remember that Stevenson used the second part of his dream, the transformation of Mr. Hyde into Dr. Jekyll, as the main theme of his story. He made an exceedingly exciting tale of it, saving the fact that Jekyll and Hyde were one and the same person for the thrilling denouement at the end. But we are not concerned here with the story as a popular thriller but with the *facts* of the case.

The most fatal fact which was added to the dream by Stevenson or his Brownies in the "conscious waking state" is given at the beginning of the final chapter, "Henry Jekyll's Full Statement of the Case." Jekyll tells us there that he found it hard to reconcile "a certain impatient gaiety of disposition" with his "imperious desire to carry (his) head high, and wear a more than commonly grave countenance before the public." Therefore he concealed his pleasures and soon stood "committed to a profound duplicity of life," thus severing "those provinces of good and ill which divide and compound man's dual nature" with an even "deeper trench than in the majority of men." Jekyll says later:

> It was on the moral side, and in my own person, that I learned to recognize the thorough and primitive duality of man.

Since his ambition forbade him even to countenance an "impatient gaiety of disposition"—which he says originally was his worst fault—he naturally soon drove the opposites much further apart than is normally the case. But he still realized that "even if I could rightly be said to be either, it was only because I was radically both."

This is a very psychological statement indeed and Dr. Jekyll was near here to a realization of the paradox in every human life which could have led him (and perhaps thus also Stevenson) back towards his original wholeness. However, such a realization would be exceedingly painful and—this is the fatal point—Jekyll began "to dwell with pleasure, as a beloved daydream," on the possibility of escaping this suffering by separating his two natures into two separate identities. Then, he says, "the unjust might go his way, delivered from the aspirations and remorse of his more upright twin; and the just could walk steadfastly and securely on his upward path, doing the good things in which he found his pleasure, and no longer exposed to disgrace and penitence by the hands of this extraneous evil."

It is quite clear that the fatal end of the story was the direct result of an *unwillingness to suffer*. The value of accepting suffering is one of the great contributions of the Christian religion and Louis certainly threw out the baby with the bathwater when he had Dr. Jekyll repudiate it entirely. Reading his life and his letters, one receives the impression that this was also a mistake of Stevenson himself. His nomadic life was, on one side, a legitimate search for health and, on the other, a constant flight from suffering and himself.

It is true that Jekyll admits he was "made to learn that the doom and burthen of our life is bound forever on man's shoulders, and when the attempt is made to cast it off, it but returns upon us with more unfamiliar and more awful pressure," but unfortunately he learned this far too late to avert the complete catastrophe with which the book ends.

In the meantime, having discovered how to compose a powder that would turn the worthy Dr. Jekyll into the infamous Mr. Hyde, he was able for some time to enjoy the emergence into reality of his "beloved day-dream" and to pursue both his good and evil lives, with each life unchecked and undisturbed by its opposite. When he first looked at Hyde in the mirror, he was "conscious of no repugnance, rather of a leap of welcome. *This, too, was myself*. It seemed natural and human." . . . (pp. 43-6)

Though exaggerated and dramatized, for reasons we shall consider later, this is perhaps one of the best descriptions in literature of a man meeting his shadow and recognizing him fully as his own: "This, too, was myself." Dr. Jekyll has an unparalleled opportunity here of taking the first step back toward the original wholeness of man. But this involves suffering, agony indeed, and it is the whole purpose of the experiment to escape any such suffering. So when he discovers that the drug will also change Hyde into Jekyll—in his dream this was the change Stevenson had seen—he merely rejoices in what he feels to be his complete security. (p. 46)

His original recognition when he first saw Hyde, "This, too, was myself," very soon begins to fade. As he indulges his Hyde side, his original "undignified" pleasures become "inherently malign and villainous," Hyde's every act and thought centered on self; drinking pleasure with bestial avidity from any degree of torture to another; relentless like a man of stone." At first Jekyll is somewhat "aghast" but he says that "the situation was apart from ordinary laws, and insidiously relaxed

the grasp of conscience. It was Hyde, after all, and Hyde alone, that was guilty." What has become of his realization: "This, too, was myself"?

It is fear, not conscience, that puts an end to this fool's paradise. The change from Jekyll to Hyde, at first so difficult and painful to bring about, begins to happen involuntarily, even in sleep. The first time this happens, it seems like "the Babylonian finger on the wall." The "beloved day dream" is over and Jekyll feels that he must choose between his two personalities. He chooses Jekyll, though he admits with certain reservations that he is keeping Hyde's clothes and his house in Soho.

His search to escape suffering has thus led Jekyll far from his earlier realization "in his own person" of "the thorough and primitive duality of man." How could he believe that it was possible to choose *one* side of his nature and simply ignore the other? (pp. 46-7)

Experience shows us again and again that the way in which a creative work develops has a strong effect on its creator. One sees this particularly clearly in "active imagination." If someone is able to work out a problem in active imagination, it changes him and makes him more capable of meeting the problems of his own individual life. If Jekyll therefore had profited by his extraordinarily deep insights, such as "If I could rightly be said to be either, it was only because I was radically both," it would undoubtedly have changed the whole course of the story and equally its effect on Stevenson himself.

The reader will remember that Jekyll was "made to learn that the doom and burthen of our life is bound forever on man's shoulders, and when the attempt is made to cast it off, it but returns upon us with more unfamiliar and more awful pressure." The same was true to a great extent in Stevenson's own life. We hear that he was never happy after his life at Hyeres, that is, about two years before he wrote *Jekyll and Hyde*. His health improved a lot in the South Seas, nevertheless one does not get an impression of peace or serenity but rather—till toward the end—of a man in tortured flight from himself. This might have been very different if he had treated Jekyll more seriously, and had perhaps found a solution to the problem of the dual nature of man. Once such a problem has been raised—and no one will deny that Stevenson did raise it—the question will automatically go on haunting the one who asks it.

To return to Stevenson's dream: The transformation which he saw and made the theme of his story was Hyde turning into Jekyll after drinking the powder. Now in the story it is Dr. Jekyll who makes and drinks the powders and thus turns into Hyde. At the end the powder will only work that way. What then did Stevenson (or his Brownies) do to this theme, "awake and consciously," as he calls it himself?

If we were to analyze the dream we would consider the facts often referred to in the story, that Hyde was a smaller man than Jekyll and that his principal characteristic was evil; the latter impressed Stevenson in the dream itself. Since the dreamer was no monster of iniquity—as Stevenson most certainly was not—we could safely assume that Jekyll more nearly represented his usual personality, as it appeared to himself and to his friends, and that Hyde represented a repressed and evil shadow that was yet so intimately connected with him that, in extremity, it could assume his shape. (pp. 48-50)

Hyde, "that thing of darkness," had shown Stevenson that he existed and that something must be done, and urgently, to bring together "the thorough and primitive duality of man." It must be Jekyll, the conscious personality, who integrates the shadow figure—as in the dream—and *not* vice versa. Otherwise the conscious becomes the slave of the autonomous shadow, as is so dramatically illustrated at the end of the story. It was probably not possible at that time for Stevenson to realize . . . that this was essentially his own problem, but he might have taken the situation very differently in the story he made of it. He took it far too lightly. He saw it merely as an opportunity to write a successful thriller in which he made no serious attempt to find a solution, although one feels he might have. (pp. 50-1)

Another point in the dream that he failed to realize was that the transformation took place in public. In the story it is kept a complete secret. This certainly adds to the excitement of the tale but it is disastrous psychologically. The hush-hush politics of the witch is one of his or her most dangerous qualities, and if the secret in *Jekyll and Hyde* had been publicly known the disastrous escape from suffering would not have been possible. Here again Stevenson (or his Brownies) made a dangerous alteration. Yet in another point, Stevenson felt very much bound by his dream. He disliked the use of the powder as too material an agency, but he could not bring himself to change it, for it made such a strong impression on him in the dream. With his pixy-like appearance and his nomadic life, Stevenson was, till almost the end, the typical *puer aeternus* who skimmed the surface of life and hated to be drawn into any real or material situation. Therefore he naturally hated the powder "as too material an agency." But we see that when he was really impressed by a dream motif he was capable of taking it very seriously indeed. In **"A Chapter on Dreams"** he speaks of the help the Brownies gave in writing *Jekyll and Hyde*. . . . (p. 51)

The tragedy of concealing the transformation is, from the psychological point of view, made clearer by another part of his dream, the "Incident at the Window." Mr. Utterson, friend and lawyer of Dr. Jekyll, is out for his usual Sunday walk with Mr. Richard Enfield, his distant kinsman, when the scene occurs. But it should first be pointed out that these two form another pair of opposites in the story, a far more human and less dramatic ego and shadow pair than Jekyll and Hyde, and thus much nearer to the man, Stevenson. Such extremes, as are depicted in Jekyll and Hyde, are entirely beyond our human limitations and enter the archetypal sphere. One could almost say that the infamous Hyde contains all of the qualities that have been left out of our image of God.

The Christian religion, in its conception of the God of Love, has depicted such a summit of the light side that this necessarily casts a correspondingly dark shadow. It may seem blasphemous to speak of Hyde as the image of the archetypal shadow of God in Stevenson's unconscious, yet it is not far from the truth. Nor is this concept very far from the idea of the opposites as they appear in the story of Eden. The serpent, the personification of evil, was even then God's opposite. It "was more subtile than any beast of the field which the Lord God had made" and it at once used that subtility *against* the avowed will of the Lord. And since God had "created man in his own image," Adam and Eve immediately came up against their own dual nature in the shape of the serpent who successfully tempted them to disobey the Lord's command.

Mr. Utterson and Mr. Enfield, however, have nothing archetypal about them. Mr. Utterson is the born observer who takes very little active part in life except through his profession and his friendships. He is "austere with himself" but has an unusual tolerance for everyone else. He used to say: "I let my brother go to the devil in his own way" and thus he was often

"the last good influence in the lives of down-going men." Whatever they did "he never marked a shade of change in his demeanour." No one can understand the bond that unites him with Richard Enfield, a "well-known man about town." Their Sunday walks seem to outsiders singularly dull. They say nothing and "would hail with obvious relief the appearance of a friend. For all that, the two men put the greatest store by these excursions, counted them the chief jewel of each week, and not only set aside occasions of pleasure, but even resisted the calls of business, that they might enjoy them uninterrupted." Stevenson, with his extraordinary knowledge of the dual nature of man, has described here two friends, each of whom finds the opposite half of himself in the other in an unsurpassable way.

It is these two men, then, who step into the court of Dr. Jekyll's house one Sunday afternoon and take part in the "incident at the window" which Stevenson dreamed. (It is when Jekyll's sufferings are at their height, when the involuntary change into Hyde can no longer be kept at bay and when he is secluded in his laboratory.) They find Dr. Jekyll sitting by an open window "taking the air with an infinite sadness of mien, like some disconsolate prisoner." Refusing to join their walk, Jekyll nevertheless evinces pleasure at the idea of a talk. "But the words were hardly uttered, before the smile was struck out of his face and succeeded by an expression of such abject terror and despair, as froze the very blood of the two gentlemen below." The window is instantly closed and the two friends leave the court: "They were both pale, and there was an answering horror in their eyes. 'God forgive us, God forgive us,' said Mr. Utterson." And they both relapsed into silence. Stevenson's dream continued with the transformation of Mr. Hyde into Dr. Jekyll, so there is no question that he knew what was happening behind that window. Yet in the conscious waking state, he, or his Brownies, kept Mr. Utterson in ignorance till after the death of the Hyde-Jekyll figure. If Utterson had known the facts—with his extraordinary toleration for "down-going men"—again Stevenson could have ended his story very differently. Utterson begs Jekyll to tell him his secret on many occasions but is always refused.

The dream of the incident at the window gave Stevenson a glimpse of the original wholeness of man. There are four figures: Utterson and Enfield below, the dual figure of Jekyll-Hyde above. The opposites in the latter pair are larger than human; they are more an archetypal pair of opposites. The change, which the dreamer knew was taking place behind the window, was supernatural, and this characterizes the pair as non-human, archetypal symbols, images which man can apprehend but with which he can never identify without disaster.

In such a dream the dreamer could only afford to recognize the human pair as his own personal responsibility. Interestingly enough, Mr. Enfield—the man about town—is exactly the kind of shadow that Jekyll describes at the beginning of his career. He says: "The worst of my faults was a certain impatient gaiety of disposition, such as has made the happiness of many, but such as I found it hard to reconcile with my imperious desire to carry my head high, and wear a more than commonly grave countenance before the public." Yet Stevenson's dream offers an opportunity for reconciling these two figures, provided that Mr. Utterson, the image of the ego, retains his extraordinary tolerance for others and does not try to reject them for false and ambitious purposes. Yes, the dream even predicts success, for, although the friendship between this pair was incomprehensible to others, their meeting was to them "the chief jewel of each week."

But if we cannot accept the shadow in its human and bearable form, then we eliminate it and the result is a dangerous vacuum in our immediate neighborhood. If we leave something un- done—in this case the attempt to reconcile ego and shadow— we create a vacuum which the unconscious must fill. It is like the pattern of Christ's parable in which the man casts out one devil, presumably his personal shadow with which he ought to come to terms, and then when the house is "swept and garnished"—that is, when a vacuum has been allowed in his most personal sphere—seven devils worse than the first take its place. This is just what happens in *Jekyll and Hyde*. The "impatient gaiety of disposition" is cast out—the house is left swept and garnished—and Mr. Hyde, prototype of the devil himself and quite equal to the seven devils in the parable, takes its place. (pp. 51-5)

> Barbara Hannah, "Robert Louis Stevenson," in her
> Striving towards Wholeness, C. J. Jung Foundation
> for Analytical Psychology, 1971, pp. 38-71.

IRVING MASSEY (essay date 1973)

[*Massey interprets Jekyll as an example of a literary double and attempts to determine the balance of good and evil within his character. This essay originally appeared in* Bulletin of the Mid- west Modern Language Association, *Fall, 1973.*]

A common version of the "double" story presents a character who harbors an alien self, or who turns uncontrollably from good to bad. In dealing with [*Dr. Jekyll and Mr. Hyde*], . . . I would like to shift the emphasis from the familiar areas of discussion of the double (such as split personality, or the sup- pressed natural man) to what one might rather call the discus- sion of the single. In other words, I would suggest that the problems . . . arise from the unity rather than from the duality of character. (p. 98)

[In] *Jekyll and Hyde,* the evil follows from the good. The two are the same. Jekyll is to begin with a good man. (p. 101)

"Evil" is what is left at the bottom of the pan when we boil down the good-evil choice, which is what is available to the good. Jekyll can hide in Hyde, but where is Hyde to hide? (Or, to put it differently, Jekyll is Jekyll-Hyde, but who is Hyde?) There are no further transformations available to him, and having faced his singleness he cannot forever continue dodging back into the falsehood of duality. It is not because the evil in Jekyll has overwhelmed the good that Hyde can no longer return to the form of Jekyll; it is because our progress or descent toward unity is a one-way process, and the reali- zation of our singleness is something that once learned cannot be forgotten. One by one, the characters in *Jekyll and Hyde*— Lanyon, Utterson, even Poole—must come down to singleness. Hell is the loss of duality, not the victory of evil. Jekyll's suggestion that he could just as easily, by the same mechanical means, have become an angel as a devil . . . remains a barren, unconvincing notion. (pp. 101-02)

The good, then, when it is left without alternatives, must digest inwards into "the bad." Privacy, singleness, is "the bad"; it is an unspeaking, languageless state. The lawyer "Utterson" represents its opposite alternative; for all his taciturnity and his glumness, he is the one who demands speech, an answer. Utterson is Hyde's true double; Jekyll merely mediates between the two. There is a suggestion in the name, "Utterson of Gaunt Street," . . . that he is the extreme, the absolute refusal of what the Jekyll-Hyde dilemma thrusts on us, the contrary aspiration.

"Make a clean breast of this in confidence"; he urges Jekyll; "and I make no doubt I can get you out of it." . . . For him, everything will have to be made explicit, even if only in the spare, precise language that seems to be the ideal of the book and that as such makes him seem the narrator. Utterson is the tragic character in *Jekyll and Hyde*; it is he who is called upon to find his way to a reconciliation with Hyde (not vice versa), through the reading of the posthumous papers that make clear what has happened. His is finally shown to have been the unjustifiable position, and his is the solitary melancholy with which the book ends. (pp. 102-03)

Hyde, in his extreme and ultimate state, is invisible, hidden behind the cabinet door. All that has lately been seen of him is the passing shadow of a small, preternaturally lithe figure flitting through the courtyard. But Hyde, even before his dis- appearance behind the door, is small, shrivelled; the oversized clothes seem to hang on an emptiness within. He is hardly the embodiment of gross sensual satisfaction; in fact, there is prac- tically nothing in the book that convinces us of his "evil." Like Deacon Brodie in the play of that name, Jekyll is too clean-cut for his admissions of violent criminal behavior through the person of Hyde to be convincing. The scene of Hyde's walking straight on over the body of a small girl whom he most improbably bumps into on the streets late at night, evi- dently invented to prove how evil Hyde is, is so artificial and unrealistic as to appear merely ridiculous. His two other spec- ified acts of violence are similarly unsatisfactory. In one case . . . , when he is again wandering the streets at night, in a state of intense anxiety, "a woman spoke to him, offering, I think, a box of lights. He smote her in the face, and she fled." In the other . . . , it is an elderly man who asks for directions (again at night); Hyde reacts as if he has been intruded upon, bothered, and clubs him to the ground in what is described as nothing but a fit of absolute exasperation. (p. 104)

In each of these encounters, it is as if Hyde were reacting to an intrusion. He is protecting the inner, silent language from the demands of public communication. People will not realize that he does not have the patience to play their game of so- ciality, of relatedness, of communication. Sir Danvers Carew wants directions to go to some plausible world, but has no awareness of the real one, which Hyde inhabits (and to which he sends Carew). There may be some sensual satisfaction in Hyde's transgressions, but we see little of it in this book, even though it is talked about a great deal as a justification for his acts of violence. Some clue to the nature of that satisfaction, such as it is, may be derived from another story of Stevenson's, **"Olalla,"** but what we are much more conscious of in *Dr. Jekyll* is our pity for Hyde, our desire to help him and our knowledge that there is no way to get him, or ourselves, out of his dilemma. (p. 105)

Finally all that we hear of Hyde is his odd, light, swinging footstep, his disembodied weeping, then his last words: "for God's sake, have mercy!" For Hyde emerges at that level of our awareness where we are beyond, or below, language. Lan- guage is predicated on duality, and . . . on falsehood. The single self cannot communicate; it rests its case on its being; if it is forced to communicate, it communicates with a blow. That blow is all its speech and its refutation of language.

All that really sticks with the reader is one's sorrow for Hyde, not his evil; and by the time that sorrow makes itself felt the book is nearly over, Hyde is hidden from the reader, and soon after is dead. Yet these concluding pages are what matter in the book, not the stage of contrived violence. We learn to identify with Hyde, even to love him. In the end he proves to be less afraid of death than Jekyll had been. Jekyll had admitted that he was glad to have his better impulses "buttressed and guarded by the terrors of the scaffold," . . . and he speculates, on the last page of the book, whether Hyde will or will not "find courage to release himself at the last moment." . . . By that point, we have had the answer. (pp. 105-06)

> Irving Massey, "The Third Self: 'Dracula', 'Jekyll and Hyde', 'Lokis'," in his The Gaping Pig: Literature and Metamorphosis, *University of California Press, 1976, pp. 98-114.*

IRVING S. SAPOSNIK (essay date 1974)

[*Saposnik offers a detailed analysis of the novel's structural and thematic development, focusing on its presentation of duality.*]

Only a careful reading of [**Strange Case of Dr. Jekyll and Mr. Hyde**] reveals its formal complexity and its moral depth. As a narrative, it is the most intricately structured of Stevenson's stories; as a fable, it represents a classic touchstone of Victorian sensibilities. It is clearly difficult today to detail each of the responsive chords which the story struck in the Victorian mind, but its use of duality as both a structural and thematic device suggests that its application goes beyond a simple antithesis of moral opposites or physical components. Present evidence indicates that Victorian man was haunted constantly by an inescapable sense of division. As rational and sensual being, as public and private man, as civilized and bestial creature, he found himself necessarily an actor, playing only that part of himself suitable to the occasion. As both variables grew more predictable, his role became more stylized; and what was initially an occasional practice became a way of life. (pp. 88-9)

The Victorian World

Because the morality of **Dr. Jekyll and Mr. Hyde** lies at the center of the Victorian world, no detail in the story is so vital as its location. Critics, especially G. K. Chesterton [see excerpt dated 1928], have been quick to indicate that the morality is actually more Scottish than English and that the more proper setting for the narrative would have been Edinburgh. Yet although Chesterton and others are right in thinking that Stevenson could no more put aside his Scottish heritage here than he could in other stories, they fail to recognize that only London could serve as the *locus classicus* of Victorian behavior. An enigma composed of multiple layers of being, its confines held virtually all classes of society conducting what were essentially independent lives. (p. 89)

Unlike Edinburgh with its stark division of Old Town and New, London represented that division-within-essential-unity which is the very meaning of *Jekyll and Hyde*. As both geographic and symbolic center, London exemplified what Stevenson called it in *New Arabian Nights*, "the great battlefield of mankind." (pp. 89-90)

Of equal importance to a consideration of *Jekyll and Hyde* are the people who inhabit that world and the manner in which they are presented. Critics have often complained that the London of the story is singularly devoid of women. . . . For once it is easy to account for this omission without reference to the bogeyman of Victorian prudery. For better or worse, Victoria's era, despite its monarch, was male-centered; and a story so directed at the essence of its moral behavior is best seen from a male perspective. In addition, . . . an air of fierce austerity pervades the story—a peculiarly masculine breed of asceticism

which, like the London fog, colors the entire surface. It is as if the atmospheric color were itself a symbol of normative rigidity. The men of the story are representative Victorian types, exemplars of a harsh life that is best seen in the somber context of their professional and social conduct.

The four prominent men in the story are gentlemen and, as such, are variations of standard gentlemanly behavior. Three are professional men—two doctors, one lawyer—and the only non/professional, Richard Enfield, is so locked into his role that his description as "the well-known man about town" might as well be a professional designation. The first to be introduced, "Mr. Utterson the lawyer," is characterized immediately by his profession as well as by a somewhat bitter-sweet compound of surface harshness and internal sympathy. Prone to self-mortification in order to stifle temptation, he nonetheless confines his rigorous standard to himself. With others, he is not only tolerant but charitable, as he translates compassion into action. Feigning unconcern, he often remains "the last good influence in the lives of down-going men." Clearly the moral norm of the story, Utterson is introduced first not only because he is Jekyll's confidant (the only one remaining) but because by person and profession he represents the best and worst of Victoria's social beings. Pledged to a code harsh in its application, he has not allowed its pressures to mar his sense of human need. For himself, he has chosen; and he must make his life on that choice; but he judges others with the understanding necessary to human weakness.

As a lawyer, he represents that legality which identifies social behavior as established law, unwritten but binding; as a judge, however, he is a combination of justice and mercy (as his names Gabriel John suggest), tempering rigidity with kindness, self-denial with compassion. His reaction to Hyde must be seen in this context. While Hyde's grim visage seems sufficient to alarm even the most objective observer (witness the Edinburgh apothecary), Hyde's threat to Jekyll's reputation, and possibly his person, makes him even more frightening to Utterson, a partisan in the best sense of the term, and loyal to his friends especially in their adversity. Utterson is the essence of what Stevenson meant in **"Reflections and Remarks on Human Life"** when he said: "It is the business of this life to make excuses for others. . . . Even justice is no right of a man's own, but a thing . . . which he should strive to see rendered to another." . . . (pp. 90-1)

Utterson's walking companion, and the narrator of Hyde's first "crime," Richard Enfield, appears as a strange, yet appropriate, complement to his distant kinsman. Described as "a well-known man about town," his haunts and habits ("I was coming home from some place at the end of the world, about three o'clock of a black winter morning") seem the "other Victorian" side of Utterson's sobriety. Yet even their casual friendship suggests a combination evidently not impossible in the Victorian social world. Their dull but necessary weekly stroll represents a public acknowledgement of a possibility that Henry Jekyll, for one, was unwilling to admit; and it reinforces the belief that the "other Victorians" are very much the Victorians one has always known but only recently grown to understand. (p. 92)

While Utterson and Enfield complement each other's limitations, Lanyon and Jekyll reveal each other's emptiness. Eminent medical men with an initial "bond of common interest," they have severed their bond over what seems a professional quarrel—Jekyll's metaphysical speculations about human identity which Lanyon admits were "too fanciful." Lanyon, however, has made not so much a professional judgement as a personal one; he has refrained from following Jekyll because of cowardice rather than because of conviction. If Jekyll's inquiries were "too fanciful," they were so because Lanyon lacked the courage, though not the curiosity, to follow him; and his horror at the discovery that Hyde and Jekyll are actually one is as much a self-realization as it is a condemnation of his former friend. Lanyon abandoned Jekyll because he was afraid of the temptation to which he finally succumbed, the offer made so perfectly by the serpentine Hyde coaxing the more-than-willing Lanyon to discover "a new province of knowledge and new avenues to fame and power." A friend in name only, his envy of Jekyll works in direct contrast to that which prompts Utterson to loyalty. Like Jekyll, Lanyon's outward manner belies his inner compulsions; but, unlike his colleague, he cannot struggle with their emergence.

Henry Jekyll, however, is nobody's hero. Although his actions are prompted by no single motive, his primary impulse is fear. If Lanyon is afraid to admit vital truths about himself, Jekyll fears these same truths when he discovers them. Dedicated to an ethical rigidity more severe than Utterson's, because solely self-centered, he cannot face the necessary containment of his dual being. However he may attempt to disguise his experiments under scientific objectivity, and his actions under a macabre alter-ego, he is unable to mask his basic selfishness. As he reveals in his final statement (the bare legal term is better than the more sentimental "confession"), he has thrived upon duplicity; and his reputation has been maintained largely upon his successful ability to deceive. Yet he is no ordinary hypocrite, a simple analogue of such other Stevenson characters as Deacon Brodie. Although Jekyll is unable to judge himself accurately, he is right in denying his hypocrisy. Only briefly does he pretend to be someone other than himself. Having recognized his duality, he attempts to isolate his two selves into individual beings and to allow each to go his separate way. Mere disguise is never sufficient for his ambition; and his failure goes beyond hypocrisy, a violation of social honesty, until it touches upon moral transgression, a violation of the physical and metaphysical foundations of human existence. Henry Jekyll is a complex example of his age of anxiety: woefully weighed down by self-deception, cruelly a slave to his own weakness, sadly a disciple of a severe discipline, his is a voice out of "De Profundis," a cry of Victorian man from the depths of his self-imposed underground.

Henry Jekyll's fiction is to identify that underground man as Edward Hyde. The fiction of the story, however, confirms the insoluble duality of his being. Each of the successive narratives strengthens that inherent union of antagonistic forces which Jekyll attempts to deny. In each, the reader learns more about both Jekyll and Hyde. Unlike conventional narratives in which the action usually develops with a continuous depiction of incident, the matter of *Jekyll and Hyde* ends only after the several incidents have been illuminated by subjective comment. For example, the cold objective horror of the maid's description as Hyde pounces upon the unsuspecting Sir Danvers Carew is balanced by the tormented narratives of a pitiful Lanyon and a compulsive Jekyll. The measure of this story is thus not only in its characters' actions but in their narrations of those actions. Nothing in the story is as singly frightening as Henry Jekyll's final narrative, for in it the reader learns most about the distorted mind which released an unwilling Hyde.

The Narrative Voices

The three separable narrative voices—Enfield, Lanyon, Jekyll—are placed in successive order so that they add increasing

Hyde stepping over the child's body. Illustration by W. Stein.

rhetorical and psychological dimension to the events they describe. In contrast to other multiple narratives whose several perspectives often raise questions of subjective truth and moral ambiguity, these individual narratives in *Jekyll and Hyde* provide a linear regularity of information—an incremental catalogue of attitudes toward Hyde's repulsiveness and Jekyll's decline. Enfield's narrative is the briefest since it describes Hyde's trampling a little girl; and the salient items in it are Enfield's unsuccessful attempts at objectivity and the horrified reactions of the other spectators. To Enfield, it is not the collision itself which is of primary importance but Hyde's casual indifference to the screaming agonies of his victim. Hyde violates a norm of respectable behavior, and his subsequent offer of monetary retribution is nothing more than automatic. Enfield's description, therefore, accentuates Hyde's mechanical regularity in contrast to the human concern which a gentleman should display (does Enfield recognize the artificiality of convention?). Thus, objective as he would be by first describing Hyde as a little man with a stumping gait, his rising gorge forces his language toward the metaphors of "hellish," "damned Juggernaut," and "Satan."

Enfield, however, is reacting to an action which he had personally witnessed. More surprising is the reaction of the hate-filled crowd that gathers around the cornered Hyde, for the people respond not to the trampling but to Hyde's physical repulsiveness. Of these, none is more representative than the doctor who comes to attend the child. A cut-and-dry Edinburgh apothecary, the most general of general practitioners, "about as emotional as a bagpipe," he cannot mask a fierce desire to kill Hyde even as he looks at him. The first of the story's three doctors, he represents what might be regarded as the normative medical mind. Placed here as an effective contrast to his more ambitious colleagues Lanyon and Jekyll, the apothecary's immediate, physical loathing foreshadows the later revelation that Hyde is more than a stunted figure of a man, that he is in truth an amoral abstraction.

Lanyon's and Jekyll's narratives follow immediately upon each other, and both are voices from the grave. As Enfield's narrative is meant as an introduction to the dual existence of Jekyll-Hyde, their narratives occur appropriately after that existence has been concluded. Before either may comment, it is necessary that Hyde emerge with uncontrollable suddenness and commit a murder from which there is no escape but death. By the time of Lanyon's narrative, the reader knows that the Hyde whose misdeeds he has been following has killed himself; but he only suspects that Henry Jekyll has also died. Lanyon's narrative is the first to reveal the truth about the Jekyll-Hyde relationship at the same time that it confirms the grim dominance of Hyde and his magnetic "glittering eye." The whole substance of his narrative is meant to carry Hyde beyond the automatic and rather innocent actions of the Enfield narrative so that he may now be seen as truly diabolical. If Enfield's Hyde was a Juggernaut, Lanyon's is a cunning tempter ruthlessly proud of his ability.

Only after the reader has experienced the revelation of Lanyon's narrative does Stevenson permit him Jekyll's "Full Statement," one which should be read not simply as an appropriate conclusion to the narrative action but as the culmination of the multiple-narrative technique. More than the other narratives, it attempts to present some insight into the narrator's psychology at the same time that it chronicles the process of his destruction. It thus proceeds in two complementary directions: a progressive exposition of events verifiable by their previous occurrence, and an explanation of those events necessarily ambiguous since they are offered by a man incapable of self-judgment. Indeed, the structure of Jekyll's statement is directed toward an often inadvertent self-revelation which proves conclusively that his selfishness and moral cowardice released the horrible personification of his hidden drives. This is not to say that Jekyll is a fiend; he is one no more so than Hyde. Yet, with increasing evidence, he incriminates himself as the guilty party in an indivisible relationship.

Jekyll also details the legitimate scientific concerns which prompted his experiment. His error, however, is that he used these as excuses; but the reader can view them only as explanations. Because of his self-delusion, Jekyll remains unaware of the true results of his experiment; until the end, he believes that Hyde "concerns another than myself." Never able to see beyond his initial deception, he learns little about himself or about the essential failure of his experiment, and remains convinced that the incompatible parts of his being can be separated if the pure powder were available. This conviction, as much as anything else, is Henry Jekyll's tragedy. He is so enmeshed in his self-woven net of duplicity that he cannot identify the two entities whose separation he hopes to achieve. By seeing Hyde as another being rather than as part of himself, he is forced to deny the most significant result of his experiment

and indeed of his entire story: the inescapable conclusion that man must dwell in uncomfortable but necessary harmony with his multiple selves. The final suicide is thus fittingly a dual effort: though the hand that administers the poison is Edward Hyde's, Henry Jekyll forces the action. (pp. 95-6)

Stevenson's fictional abilities are further evidenced by his successful insertion of thematic contrasts into the narrative structure itself. The topography of *Jekyll and Hyde* may be seen as a study in symbolic location, a carefully worked out series of contrasts between exterior modes and interior realities. Like much of Victorian life and letters, most of the story's action is physically internalized behind four walls. (p. 96)

The Symbolic Structure

While the structure of *Jekyll and Hyde* is predicated upon a contrast between exterior and interior, the contrast is never allowed to remain static. The actions that occur in each represent an intriguing paradox: in the exterior, social ambles and foul crimes; in the interior, elegant drawing rooms and secreted laboratories. Each division contains two opposing elements which combine to characterize the individual locale, but both locations in their necessary union represent the social cosmos. The result is a social bond no less indivisible than the moral bond which Jekyll attempts unsuccessfully to sever. The central metaphor is Jekyll's house, with its sinister rear entrance through which Hyde passes and its handsome front "which wore a great air of wealth and comfort": the two faces of Jekyll contained in one inseparable dwelling.

The paradox is continued as the action of *Jekyll and Hyde* becomes internalized. The two final subjective accounts solidify this process on a psychological level, and the action itself leads farther and farther into the interior of Jekyll's house. Although the reader's first views of the house are external, the action soon directs him to the hall, then to the study, and finally to the ominous experiments behind the closed door of the former dissection laboratory. As Poole and Utterson break down the last barrier to Jekyll's secret, they literally and metaphorically destroy his one remaining refuge; by invading his physical sanctuary, they force him into a psychological admission whose only possibility is death. Stevenson's skillful juggling of literal and metaphoric—his ability to suggest the symbolic significance of commonplace reality—is undoubtedly the chief difference between the original bogey story to which his wife, Fanny, objected and the classic fable which *Jekyll and Hyde* has become. Clearly, the most telling evidence of this skill is his ability to select highly suggestive scenery and to allow its multiple suggestions to form the several layers of his narrative.

For reader and nonreader alike, the crucial item of thematic significance has been Edward Hyde. Unquestionably the dominant character, his role in the narrative is often considered the fictional mechanism by which the moral truths are driven home. Surely such a reading is partial, for it fails to approach the story as a total construct and thus commits the sin of facile separation only a trifle less grievous than Jekyll's. Yet Hyde's identity, both physical and moral, is the pervasive mystery whose elusiveness and final revelation unites the fictional and moral concerns. Without Jekyll, there could never have been a Hyde; without Hyde, one can never fully know Jekyll. Thus an ability to understand their relationship rests on an ability to identify what Hyde represents. To begin negatively, he is not the antithetical evil to Jekyll's good nor is he evil at all. His cruelty derives from his association with Jekyll, not from any inherent motivation toward destruction. True, he is compulsive (as is Jekyll), a veritable Juggernaut proceeding on his mechanical way; but this characteristic is primarily found in his initial movements when Jekyll's desires first spring him from his lair. One of the more fascinating developments in the story is Hyde's growing malice—his increasing premeditation as he becomes more and more a mortal. (pp. 97-8)

The legendary Hyde is obviously a difficult opponent. There is clearly something consolatory about equating Hyde with illicit sex; it localizes one's impulses and allows indulgences within the proprieties. Stevenson's Hyde, on the other hand, though less formidable, is more substantial. His substantiality increases, in fact, in direct proportion to his recognition as the essence of man's natural vitality. The key word is *natural,* for it governs the entire amoral world from which Hyde emerges. As the mirror of Jekyll's inner compulsions, he represents that shadow side of man which civilization has striven to submerge: he is a creature of primitive sensibilities loosed upon a world bent on denying him. A reminder of the barbarism which underlies civilization, he is a necessary component of human psychology which most would prefer to leave unrealized.

As an essential life force, Hyde's proper role is to act in harmony with the other parts of man's being. (pp. 98-9)

Throughout his writings Stevenson dwells upon the inescapable burden which any relationship between the barbaric and the civilized produces. Painfully aware of the difficulties their conjunction necessitates, he continues to affirm their vital correspondence. (p. 99)

In his fiction in particular Stevenson develops this double strain of being; there he illustrates the inevitable conflict between natural urges and societal pressures, and there he presents the tragedy of those who surrender themselves to either.

Jekyll surrenders to his society. "The harm [that] was in Jekyll" was in large part the harm of Victoria's England; and his unwillingness to acknowledge his kinship with Edward Hyde may be likened to everyone else's intense hatred of his moral twin. The universal hatred directed at Hyde both in and out of the story is a striking verification of the extent to which Victorian England feared what he represented. Jekyll's repugnance is scarcely his alone, and his actions are predicated upon a social ethic only slightly less distorted than his moral myopia. Victorian anxieties contributed greatly to *Jekyll and Hyde*'s success. The fictional paradox revealed the social paradox; Jekyll's dilemma spoke for more of his countrymen than many were willing to admit.

If Jekyll's fears are taken as a barometer of Victorian anxieties, his relationship to Hyde becomes apparent. While Jekyll represents a man "in the pink of the proprieties," Hyde is the brutal embodiment of the moral, social, political, and economic threats which shook the uncertain Victorian world. In his moral role, he exemplifies the impossibility of any successful separation of man's natural being. A metaphysical impulse in a postlapsarian world, any attempted return to Eden (he proves) must be made at the cost of one's life. Likewise, his social identity cautions the attempted imposition of a new Manicheanism based upon a dichotomy between external and internal behavior. (pp. 99-100)

As political and economic man, Hyde's role is more subtle. The inevitability of his brute power, his unceasing energy, no doubt recalled to many the threatening forces which were beating upon the solid doors of their comfortable homes. Hidden in them as he was, Victorian man could not for long confine himself beneath the domestic covers. He feared "the armies of the night," the troops of the new politics and the new economics that were massing for the onslaught. (p. 100)

Hyde is usually described in metaphors because essentially that is what he is: a metaphor of uncontrolled appetites, an amoral abstraction driven by a compelling will unrestrained by any moral halter. Such a creature is, of necessity, only figuratively describable; for his deformity is moral rather than physical. Purposely left vague, he is best described as Jekyll-deformed—dwarfish, stumping, ape-like—a frightening parody of a man unable to exist on the surface. He and Jekyll are inextricably joined because one without the other cannot function in society. As Hyde is Jekyll's initial disguise, so Jekyll is Hyde's refuge after the Carew murder. If Jekyll reflects respectability, then Hyde is his image "through the looking glass."

Hyde's literal power ends with his suicide, but his metaphorical power is seemingly infinite. Many things to his contemporaries, he has grown beyond Stevenson's story in an age of automatic Freudian response. As Hyde has grown, Jekyll has been overshadowed so that his role has shifted from culprit to victim. Accordingly, the original fable has assumed a meaning neither significant for the nineteenth century nor substantial for the twentieth. The time has come for Jekyll and Hyde to be put back together again. (p. 101)

> *Irving S. Saposnik, in his* Robert Louis Stevenson, *Twayne Publishers, Inc., 1974, 164 p.*

JULIA BRIGGS   (essay date 1977)

[*Briggs discusses the circumstances surrounding the composition of the novel.*]

The Strange Case of Dr. Jekyll and Mr. Hyde . . . is now the most moralized allegory of duality, but the original version was very different. The first draft, written at high speed during one of Stevenson's recurrent attacks of tuberculosis, was apparently simply a narrative of the transformation; according to his stepson, Lloyd Osbourne, 'a magnificent bit of sensationalism'. It was Stevenson's wife Fanny who told him that he had left out the most important part, 'the morality, worse luck!' Stevenson threw the manuscript on the fire in a fury, but rewrote it in the next two days, in spite of a high temperature. The initial idea for the story had come to him in a nightmare, as he relates in **"A Chapter on Dreams"** [see excerpt dated 1888], his account of the independent and creative activity of the brain in sleep. The 'Brownies' of this essay, the imaginative impulses of the sleeping mind, stand in a strange, ambiguous relation to their author. They work for him, and yet they are a little frightening. They 'have not a rudiment of what we call conscience', and are 'somewhat fantastic, like their stories hot and hot, full of passion and the picturesque, alive with animating incident; and', he continues, 'they have no prejudice against the supernatural'.

The irrational, amoral Brownies, voices of nightmare and delirium, at times appear to set up a dialogue with Stevenson's more repressive conscious mind, and their conflict may well have given rise to the sensation of being 'two people at once' which inspired *Jekyll and Hyde*. . . . The sinister intimacy between the feverish subversive Brownies and Stevenson's conscious mind is not unlike that of Jekyll and Hyde, and it may also be relevant that the change from Jekyll into Hyde is first made spontaneously in sleep. In a moment that anticipates the horrible revelation of Kafka's *Metamorphosis*, Jekyll wakes to find the hand of Hyde lying on his counterpane. Later the same thing happens in public in Regent's Park, and finally, 'if I slept, or even dozed for a moment in my chair, it was always as Hyde that I awakened'. This suggests that the evil of Hyde is at its zenith when Jekyll is asleep, and he awakens as if from a nightmare whose evil influence he cannot cast off. In Jekyll's case—and perhaps in Stevenson's, in a less literal sense—the sleep of reason may be said to have brought forth monsters. (pp. 66-7)

At the outset of the story Jekyll condones Hyde and finds it useful to be able to indulge in 'such irregularities as I was guilty of' at night and in a different guise, while possessing a grave and authoritative mien during the day. As Jekyll asserts in his "Final Statement", 'all men in life . . . are commingled out of good and evil', but it would be wonderfully convenient to be able to isolate one's evil propensities and indulge them as a different person. Edward Hyde is a kind of psychological scapegoat, so utterly wicked that the respectable Jekyll can feel quite dissociated from him, as if his crimes were really someone else's, yet he can share in Hyde's sensual gratifications. Stevenson's allegory is never so naïve as to suggest that Jekyll was ever a genuinely virtuous man. Like so many outwardly respectable Victorians, pillars of their society, he was a man who harboured the desires of Hyde, and had originally hoped to use Hyde as a convenience. Although Hyde was at first younger and not nearly so well developed as the doctor, he grows, and finally the convenience *becomes* him—Jekyll begins to revert to Hyde spontaneously. (pp. 67-8)

Stevenson's frequent attacks of fever, with their accompanying delirium and nightmares, probably made him unusually aware of the activities of the unconscious, at the same time enabling him to take a confidently detached view of them as merely 'the voice of the fever'. Indeed he went further, deliberately exploiting the promising raw material they provided in stories such as *Jekyll,* or his short story of a werewolf, **"Olalla"**. His particular balance of introspection and comparative psychological stability enabled him to write freely and perceptively of the disturbing dualities in man. (p. 68)

One of the practical problems Stevenson set for himself, and did not entirely solve, was how to present an embodiment of pure evil. How is such a being to be depicted so that his behaviour is distinguished from that of the man of average immorality? There are hints of Jekyll's earlier indulgences in Soho, of Hyde's 'strange companions', but Hyde's evil is primarily reduced to two events: walking over a child and the murder of Sir Danvers Carew, both *actes gratuits,* yet both demonstrating a total lack of that 'cunning' which Stevenson several times claims to be characteristic of Hyde's smile. Viewed from a psychological standpoint, he seems anxious to provoke punishment, rather than to administer it. Perhaps the twentieth century, which combines more searching attitudes towards apparently motiveless violence with more obvious contemporary examples of it, tends to be hypercritical of fictional portrayals of evil. The atrocities performed in our times by supposedly civilized men make Hyde's murders look like schoolboy pranks. But here is a genuine artistic problem which, though perhaps appreciated by Wilde, was not resolved until, ten years later, Henry James wrote *The Turn of the Screw*. Faced with the same difficulty, Stevenson's disciple Arthur Machen resorted to references to 'unspeakable' or 'unutterable' orgies, and allusions to Greek mysteries and Sabbaths, which combine sensationalism with evasiveness. His identification of evil with sexual licence is banal and commonplace in comparison with the motiveless malignity of Edward Hyde. (pp. 69-70)

Julia Briggs, "A Scientific Spirit: Mesmerism, Drugs and Psychic Doctors," in her Night Visitors: The Rise and Fall of the English Ghost Story, *Faber & Faber, 1977, pp. 52-75.*

ROSEMARY JACKSON   (essay date 1981)

[*Jackson assesses the moral intent of the novel and the repressed elements in the characters' personalities.*]

[A] famous parable of dualism, *The Strange Case of Dr Jekyll and Mr Hyde* . . . is usually seen as the clearest allegory of Victorian hypocrisy and repression: 'Behind its latterday Gothick lies a very profound and epoch-revealing truth.' The other side of the human returns to act out latent libidinal drives concealed by the social ego. (Je-kyll—I kill—his very name has within it his real nature as murderer, embodied in Hyde—what is hidden.) This exemplifies Freud's theory of fantastic narrative as telling of a return of the repressed: Hyde is able to fulfil Jekyll's desires to steal, love, be violent. . . . [But] Stevenson's is much more than an allegory of good and evil at war with one another. The text itself draws attention to 'evil' as a relative moral category, as a notion imposed upon natural disorder. Jekyll, conducting his 'experiment while under the empire', is drawn towards the world on the other side of the mirror because it offers him an infinite number of 'selves'. . . . Good-evil dichotomies are preceded by an a-moral condition, one which echoes Sade's ideal of undifferentiation, his 'universal prostitution of all beings'. Jekyll is attracted to this ideal as his original, undivided nature. (pp. 114-15)

Hyde is originally a nameless, shapeless thing, without identity, smaller than Jekyll, dwarflike, *within* his parent's form. He is 'hardly human! Something troglodytic, shall we say? . . . Like a man restored from death . . . he gave an impression of deformity without any nameable malformation'. . . . The lawyer, Utterson, reads into Hyde's face 'Satan's signature' and Jekyll refers to him as 'that child of hell', though initially Hyde was 'neither diabolical nor divine', but prior to human concepts of good and evil. Hyde introduces absolute otherness, 'a sense of unreality', an a-morality beneath moral structures. 'As for the moral turpitude that man *unveiled* to me . . . I cannot dwell on it without a sense of horror.' Hyde threatens late Victorian London with his horrid laughter, theft, sexuality, criminality: he breaks every social taboo. What most frightens Jekyll is Hyde's distance from the human, his non-human origins, i.e. his link with the inorganic, which comes to be categorized as demonic in an 'evil' sense:

> he thought of Hyde, for all his energy of life, as of something not only hellish but inorganic. This was the shocking thing; that the slime of the pit seemed to utter cries and voices; that the amorphous dust gesticulated and sinned; that what was dead, and had no shape, should usurp the office of life. And this again, that that insurgent horror was knit to him closer than a wife, closer than an eye . . . (it) prevailed against him, and deposed him out of life. . . .

Once this inorganicism is recognized, the text has to evolve strategies to contain and exclude it. *Dr Jekyll and Mr Hyde* develops in the pattern of the detective novel 'hunting down' anti-social energies, neutralizing desire. The relation of Jekyll to Hyde is also one of father to son. 'Jekyll had more than a father's interest; Hyde had more than a son's indifference.' Like other fantasies, this one repeats the Oedipal drama of father-son conflict and finally rewrites the victory of the first. (pp. 115-16)

> Rosemary Jackson, "Gothic Tales and Novels," in her Fantasy: The Literature of Subversion, *Methuen, 1981, pp. 95-122.*

ADDITIONAL BIBLIOGRAPHY

Aldington, Richard. *Portrait of a Rebel: The Life and Work of Robert Louis Stevenson.* London: Evans Brothers, 1957, 245 p.
    An intimate portrait of Stevenson that presents information regarding the composition of *Dr. Jekyll and Mr. Hyde.*

Elwin, Malcolm. *The Strange Case of Robert Louis Stevenson.* London: Macdonald, 1950, 256 p.
    A biographical study that contains scattered critical references to *Dr. Jekyll and Mr. Hyde.*

Geduld, Harry M., ed. *The Definitive "Dr. Jekyll and Mr. Hyde" Companion.* New York: Garland Publishing, 1983, 219 p.
    A collection of essays about the novel, including reviews of the theatrical and cinematic renditions.

Gwynn, Stephen. *Robert Louis Stevenson.* London: Macmillan and Co., 1939, 267 p.
    A biography that includes a section on the circumstances surrounding the composition of the novel.

Jefford, Andrew. "Dr. Jekyll and Professor Nabokov: Reading a Reading." In *Robert Louis Stevenson,* edited by Andrew Noble, pp. 47-72. London: Vision Press, 1983.
    An analysis of Nabokov's discussion of the novel (see excerpt dated 1941-48).

Kanzer, Mark. "The Self-Analytic Literature of Robert Louis Stevenson." In *Psychoanalysis and Culture: Essays in Honor of Géza Róheim,* edited by George B. Wilbur and Warner Muensterberger, pp. 425-35. New York: International Universities Press, 1951.
    Discusses the role of the unconscious in Stevenson's composition of the novel.

Kiely, Robert. *Robert Louis Stevenson and the Fiction of Adventure.* Cambridge: Harvard University Press, 1964, 285 p.
    A discussion of Stevenson's adventure fiction, with several references to *Dr. Jekyll and Mr. Hyde.*

Leaf, Munro. *"The Strange Case of Dr. Jekyll and Mr. Hyde." The American Magazine* CXXXI, No. 5 (May 1941): 104.
    A brief parody of the novel.

Schultz, Myron G. "The 'Strange Case' of Robert Louis Stevenson." *The Journal of the American Medical Association* 216, No. 1 (5 April 1971): 90-4.
    Suggests that Stevenson may have written the novel under the influence of cocaine.

Sontag, Susan. "Doctor Jekyll." In her *I, Etcetera,* pp. 187-230. New York: Farrar, Straus, Giroux, 1978.
    Recreates the novel in the vernacular of the late 1970s.

Thomas, Ronald. "In the Company of Strangers: Absent Voices in Stevenson's *Dr. Jekyll and Mr. Hyde* and Beckett's *Company." Modern Fiction Studies* 32, No. 2 (Summer 1986): 157-73.
    Interprets *Dr. Jekyll and Mr. Hyde* as an example of the evolution of the modern novel.

Robert Smith Surtees

1805-1864

(Also wrote under pseudonyms of John Jorrocks, The York-shireman, and Nim South) English novelist, sketch and manual writer, and autobiographer.

A minor Victorian author, Surtees is recognized as the best sporting novelist in the English language. In a series of works that deal primarily with fox-hunting, he elaborately described mid-nineteenth-century English country life, recording in precise detail his characters' manners and speech and such everyday aspects of their lives as their clothing, meals, and hairstyles. Surtees mercilessly exposed the hypocrisy and social pretensions of the middle and upper classes, yet his satire is balanced by his raucous humor; indeed, he is particularly praised for his vivid, exuberant style and comic characters, most notably John Jorrocks, the vulgar, self-confident, and outspoken Cockney grocer turned huntsman whom he immortalized in *Jorrocks's Jaunts and Jollities, Handley Cross,* and *Hillingdon Hall.* Since the nineteenth century, Surtees' admirers have argued that his works are of interest to both hunting fans and general readers. Nevertheless, his reputation as a sporting novelist has limited his audience and contributed to his critical neglect. While modern commentators debate the literary merits of Surtees' works, they unanimously stress their value as social histories.

Surtees developed a passion for fox-hunting early in life. He was raised at Hamsterley Hall, a country estate near Durham, England, and spent much of his boyhood hunting. A second son, Surtees had no prospect of inheriting the family estate, and he decided to pursue a law career. Although he qualified as a solicitor in 1828, he never practiced law assiduously, preferring to devote most of his time to hunting. Having, as he expressed it, "a taste for scribbling," he began contributing hunting stories under the pseudonym Nim South to the *Sporting Magazine* in 1830. The following year was important for several reasons, including the publication of his first book. *The Horseman's Manual,* a practical guide to the sale and purchase of horses, was the only work to which Surtees signed his name; indeed, numerous critics have questioned why he insisted on remaining anonymous. In addition, his older brother died of smallpox, leaving him heir to the family fortune and Hamsterley Hall. Surtees' improved finances influenced his decision to join Rudolph Ackermann in 1831 in founding the London-based *New Sporting Magazine,* which he edited from its inception until 1836 and which featured many of his stories. After his father's death in 1838, Surtees returned to Hamsterley Hall, where he lived as a country gentleman, hunting, managing his estate, and holding a number of positions of responsibility in Durham County, including sheriff and justice of the peace. He also continued to write, publishing several novels as well as *The Analysis of the Hunting Field,* a collection of sporting sketches that commemorate the 1845-46 hunting season. Surtees was working on an autobiography that he intended to call *Sporting and Social Recollections* when he died of a heart attack in 1864.

Among Surtees' most significant contributions to the *New Sporting Magazine* is a series of sketches that appeared in the periodical between July 1831 and September 1834. In these

sketches, he first recorded the farcical adventures of the now-famous Jorrocks, whose boisterous enthusiasm for fox-hunting has prompted critics to label him the "Falstaff of the chase." In 1838, the Jorrocks stories were published in book form as *Jorrocks's Jaunts and Jollities.* The genre of this work has been debated by critics: while some liken the volume to a picaresque novel, most term it a collection of sketches. On its appearance, *Jorrocks's Jaunts and Jollities* was overshadowed by Charles Dickens's *Pickwick Papers,* which many critics believe was patterned after Surtees' sketches. Surtees further described Jorrocks's exploits in his next two works, *Handley Cross* and *Hillingdon Hall.* In these novels, Jorrocks is accompanied by James Pigg, a hard-riding, hard-drinking huntsman who is praised as one of Surtees' most delightful characters. Neither *Handley Cross* nor *Hillingdon Hall* was popular: modern critics speculate that Surtees offended a large segment of his audience by ridiculing those who viewed fox-hunting as a fashionable sport for the wealthy. In fact, only Jorrocks and Pigg escaped the author's derision for, like Surtees himself, they hunted for the sheer sport of it.

Surtees achieved his greatest popular success with *Mr. Sponge's Sporting Tour,* which originally appeared serially in the *New Monthly Magazine* in 1849-51. The title character of this novel travels throughout the English countryside "sponging" on unsuspecting families who supply him with free room and board;

according to Surtees, Soapey Sponge's "dexterity in getting into people's houses was only equaled by the difficulty of getting him out again." Sponge is a rogue but, like Jorrocks and Pigg, he is redeemed in Surtees' eyes by his genuine fondness for hunting. *Sponge* was the first of Surtees' works to be illustrated by the famous sporting caricaturist John Leech, whose drawings for it and Surtees' later novels have attracted almost as much attention as the texts. Following the success of *Sponge,* Surtees issued an expanded edition of *Handley Cross* that sold much better than the original version and is now considered by most critics to be his best work. In addition, Surtees contracted with William Harrison Ainsworth, the editor of the *New Monthly Magazine,* to publish another novel—*Young Tom Hall*—in the periodical. Only a few installments of the work had appeared when Surtees, learning that Ainsworth had revealed him as the author, abruptly quit writing it. Although he never finished *Young Tom Hall,* Surtees used some of its characters and incidents in his next two novels, *Ask Mamma* and *Plain or Ringlets?* Two of his least popular works, *Ask Mamma* and *Plain or Ringlets?* marked a departure for the author by focusing on nonhunting aspects of country society. Surtees returned to more familiar themes in his last novel, the posthumously published *Mr. Facey Romford's Hounds,* which is a sequel to *Sponge.*

Surtees has never attracted a large following among readers or critics. The greatest reason for this, commentators note, is his reputation as the classic novelist of fox-hunting. Pigeonholed as a sporting writer since the nineteenth century, Surtees remains today, in the words of Alex Hamilton, "the darling of a specialist readership," applauded by hunting enthusiasts but virtually ignored by the literary establishment and the general public. Twentieth-century critics point out that other factors have also adversely affected Surtees' fame. Among these is the widespread notion that the original illustrations to his works—those by Leech as well as those by Henry Alken and Hablot K. Browne (Phiz)—constitute their sole source of appeal. Another factor cited is the author's penchant for anonymity, which has led many commentators to believe that because Surtees viewed writing as a hobby rather than a serious profession, he does not deserve critical attention. As John Shand explains, these critics have disregarded Surtees because "he was not a literary gentleman with an odd taste for hunting, but a hunting gentleman with an odd gift for writing."

Although a number of Surtees' famous contemporaries, including William Makepeace Thackeray and William Morris, avidly read his works, very few reviews appeared in the nineteenth century. By the early 1930s, the amount of Surtees criticism still remained so slight that Frederick Watson was able to write, "because of the nature rather than the quality of his work, Robert Surtees has been allowed a sanctuary from critical discussion." Since that time, a small but admiring group of commentators has attempted to reverse the trend toward classifying Surtees as a sporting novelist by urging that his works possess merits beyond their value as hunting stories. Among these merits are Surtees' host of comic characters and what Virginia Woolf called his "slapdash, gentlemanly" style. A number of critics have attributed the appeal of Surtees' characters to their racy, colloquial speech. Jorrocks, who is especially praised in this respect, is perhaps best known for his invective and for his countless witty sayings, including his often-quoted definition of hunting: "the sport of kings, the image of war without its guilt, and only five-and-twenty per cent. of its danger." In commending Surtees' style, critics have also noted his particularly terse and exciting descriptions

of the hunt. Yet not all twentieth-century commentary on Surtees' artistry has been positive. Many critics have faulted his loosely constructed, episodic plots, while others have censured his overuse of clichés and catch phrases. Still others have objected to his harsh treatment of women, pointing out that Lucy Glitters, who appears in *Sponge* and *Mr. Facey Romford's Hounds,* is his only female character who is not a greedy, conniving shrew. While the artistic worth of Surtees' novels continues to be a subject of controversy, critics have reached a consensus on at least one aspect of his writings: their unflinching realism. Commentators rarely fail to point out that Surtees painted a truthful and uncomplimentary picture of English country life during the mid-nineteenth century. The endless eating and drinking, filthy stables, fashionable inns, and exclusive hunt parties—all, critics agree, are presented in graphic detail, rendering Surtees' works indispensable social documents that recreate a limited but significant phase of nineteenth-century life ignored by most novelists of his day. Although the history of Surtees' reputation indicates that he may never be widely read or granted a large amount of critical attention, recent commentary suggests that he will continue to be admired for his lively humor, memorable characters, and remarkably accurate depiction of one aspect of Victorian life.

(See also *Dictionary of Literary Biography,* Vol. 21: *Victorian Novelists Before 1885.*)

*PRINCIPAL WORKS

The Horseman's Manual: Being a Treatise on Soundness, the Law of Warranty, and Generally on the Laws Relating to Horses (manual) 1831
Jorrocks's Jaunts and Jollities; or, The Hunting, Shooting, Racing, Driving, Sailing, Eating, Eccentric, and Extravagant Exploits of That Renowned Sporting Citizen, Mr. John Jorrocks, of St. Botolph Lane and Great Coram Street (sketches) 1838
Handley Cross; or, The Spa Hunt (novel) 1843; also published as *Handley Cross; or, Mr. Jorrocks's Hunt* [enlarged edition], 1854
Hillingdon Hall; or, The Cockney Squire (novel) 1845
The Analysis of the Hunting Field: Being a Series of Sketches of the Principal Characters That Compose One, the Whole Forming a Slight Souvenir of the Season 1845-6 (sketches) 1846
Hawbuck Grange; or, The Sporting Adventures of Thomas Scott, Esq. (novel) 1847
Mr. Sponge's Sporting Tour (novel) 1853
Ask Mamma; or, The Richest Commoner in England (novel) 1858
Plain or Ringlets? (novel) 1860
Mr. Facey Romford's Hounds (novel) 1865
**Robert Smith Surtees (Creator of "Jorrocks")* (unfinished autobiography) 1924
Young Tom Hall: His Heart-Aches and Horses (unfinished novel) 1926
The Novels of R. S. Surtees. 10 vols. (novels) 1929-30

*Many of Surtees' works were originally published serially in periodicals.

**This work is comprised of Surtees' memoirs, also known as *Sporting and Social Recollections,* and commentary by E. D. Cuming.

JOHN GIBSON LOCKHART   (letter date 1836)

[*Lockhart wrote several novels, but his fame rests on his biography of Sir Walter Scott and his critical contributions to* Blackwood's Edinburgh Magazine *and the* Quarterly Review, *which he edited from 1825 to 1853. Critics speculate that this encouraging letter from Lockhart inspired Surtees to write* Handley Cross.]

I believe you are the creator of Jorrocks, who has always delighted me. Do get some cousin of his in the horsey (?) line, and throw the materials into light dramatic form.

> *John Gibson Lockhart, in an extract from a letter to Robert Smith Surtees on July 8, 1836, in* Robert Smith Surtees (Creator of ''Jorrocks''): 1803-1864 *by Robert Smith Surtees and E. D. Cuming, Charles Scribner's Sons, 1924, p. 211.*

FRASER'S MAGAZINE   (essay date 1838)

[*In this review of* Jorrocks's Jaunts and Jollities, *the anonymous critic prefers Jorrocks to Dickens's Pickwick.*]

The essays now published under the title of *Jorrocks's Jaunts and Jollities* were the first to lead the way in the . . . [school of sporting] fiction. In these, Mr. Jorrocks, a rich sporting grocer, is the chief character; and competent and unprejudiced judges incline to the opinion, that the idea of the popular character of *Pickwick* was derived from the hero of the Surrey hunt. Pickwick is an excellent character, with the assistance of Sam Weller; but, viewed singly, Jorrocks, in our opinion, is the better of the two. He has all Pickwick's good-natured simplicity, without his lethargic slowness. No man, be he sportsman or otherwise, can read Mr. Jorrocks's adventures—hunting, shooting, racing, driving, &c.—without feeling that the hero is a sportsman; while, despite the title and the wrapper, headed by a man shooting with the gun from the wrong shoulder, no one can accuse any of the members of the Pickwick Club of any pretensions to the name. . . .

The first scene [in *Jorrocks's Jaunts and Jollities*], ''Swell and the Surrey,'' is a parody on Nimrod's article in the *Quarterly*, in which ''Snob,'' or the provincial gentleman on the good little bay horse, makes his appearance among the dandified Meltonians. In lieu of Snob, we have a Melton swell appearing among the Surrey men, astonishing them equally by the cut of his coat and the cut of his nag; who, after a brilliant day among the flints, goes away, thoroughly disgusted with the country. Next, Mr. Jorrocks mounts his Yorkshire friend, to see their ''brilliant 'ounds;'' and the start out of London, in the fog, is, we think, one of the most ludicrous scenes in the book, heightened not a little by Phiz's excellent illustration of Mr. Jorrocks bumping away with the mail-coach lamp strapped to his back. (p. 482)

The scene in the hunting stables at Croydon, where Mr. Jorrocks shews off the nags to his friend, is true to nature; and the meet of the hounds, the find below hill, with the runs up and down, Mr. Jorrocks's tumble into the unsavoury cesspool, with the brilliant finish of the brushless fox, are all done in a style that conveys the very scene to the mind. (p. 484)

Mr. Jorrocks's other adventures embrace nearly all sorts of sporting,—stag-hunting, racing, sailing, driving, &c., in England and France; but each sketch is done in a style to interest the general reader, as well as the lover of the particular amusement. The scene at Newmarket, where the honest grocer joins a party of blacklegs at the White Hart, conveys a better idea of the doings of that noted spot than any we have ever read; and his adventures in France are full of fun. (p. 488)

> ''Sporting Literature,'' in Fraser's Magazine, *Vol. XVIII, No. CVI, October, 1838, pp. 481-88.*

[JOHN GIBSON LOCKHART]   (essay date 1843)

[*In this favorable review of* Handley Cross, *Lockhart defends the originality of Jorrocks and predicts a bright future for Surtees as a novelist.*]

Many hasty critics accused the author of *Jorrocks's Jaunts and Jollities* . . . of plagiarizing Pickwick and Co., regardless of the preface, which stated that the chapters 'were reprinted from the *New Sporting Magazine,* wherein they had appeared between the years 1831 and 1834,' long before Mr. Dickens emerged into public notice. We will venture to say that the sire of Jorrocks would no more think of such a thing as filching another man's style than would the more prolific 'Boz.' How far the popularity of *The Jaunts* may have induced certain publishers to wish for a Cockney sportsman of their own is another matter: but the dialect of Jorrocks was and is his own; and we must equally disclaim, on the part of our independent friend, as respects character, all clanship or sympathy with the soft Mr Pickwick. Jorrocks is a sportsman to the backbone. (p. 397)

In [*Handley Cross*] the character of the sporting grocer is brought out in still more perfect developement than in [*Jorrocks's Jaunts and Jollities*]. . . . [Our] author, though a crack sportsman, is quite awake upon a variety of subjects besides. (pp. 397-98)

[Jorrocks's historian] is a writer of no common promise. On this occasion Mr. Surtees has not thought proper to trouble himself with much complication of plot; but the easy style in which he arranges and draws out his characters satisfies us that he might, if he pleased, take a high place among our modern novelists. He has a world of knowledge of life and manners beyond what most of those now in vogue can pretend to; and a gentleman-like tone and spirit, perhaps even rarer among them. We advise him to try his hand—and that before he loses the high spirits of youth;—but he must, in so doing, by all means curb his propensity to caricature. (p. 411)

> [*John Gibson Lockhart*], *in a review of ''Handley Cross; or, The Spa-Hunt,'' in* The Quarterly Review, *Vol. LXXI, No. CXLII, March, 1843, pp. 392-411.*

ROBERT SMITH SURTEES   (essay date 1847)

[*In the following extract from* Hawbuck Grange, *Surtees offers a tongue-in-cheek judgment of his works and the profession of writing.*]

''What queer books you write!'' observed our excellent but rather matter-of-fact friend, Sylvanus Bluff, the other day, who seeing us doubling up a sheet of paper in a rather unceremonious way, concluded we were at what he calls our ''old tricks.'' ''I buy all your books,'' added he with a solemn shake of the head, as though we were beggaring him—''I bought your *Jorrocks, Jaunts, and Jollities,* I bought *Handley Cross, or the Spa Hunt,* I bought *Hillingdon Hall, or the Cockney Squire;* but I don't *understand* them. I don't see the *wit* of them. *I* don't see

Surtees' home, Hamsterley Hall.

the *use* of them. *I* wonder you don't write something useful. I should think now,'' added he seriously, ''you could do something better. I should say now you would be quite equal to writing a dictionary, or a book upon draining, and those would be really useful works, and your friends would get something for their money.''

Gentle reader! we plead guilty to the charge of writing most egregious nonsense. Nay, we are sometimes surprised how such stuff can ever enter our head, astonished that we should be weak enough to commit it to paper, amazed that there should be publishers rash enough to print it, and lost in utter bewilderment that there should be good, honest, sane, nay sensible folks, not only idle enough to read it, but, oh wonder! of all wonders! extravagant enough to part with their good current coin to buy it!

And talking of friends buying our books out of politeness, we may here avail ourself of the opportunity to say that there is nothing we dislike more; nay, so great is our objection, that if we knew any honest, mistaken man about to commit such an absurdity, we would absolutely forestall our own market by offering him a copy. At least we *think* we would.

We don't know why any one should do so, we are sure, for neither by name, dedication, or date, do we ever provoke so

suicidal an act. We may say, with our excellent friend Peter Morris, that ''if putting our Christian name and surname at the beginning of a book were necessary conditions to the dignity of authorship, we should never be one while we live.'' Like Peter, ''we want nerves for this.'' We rejoice in the privilege of writing and printing *incognito,* and think with him that it is the ''finest discovery'' that ever was made. Peter, to be sure, got bolder with age, but then he felt that he was ''somebody.''

Writing, we imagine, is something like snuffing or smoking—men get into the way of it, and can't well leave it off. Like smoking, it serves to beguile an idle hour. Individually speaking, writing makes us tolerably independent, both of the world and the weather. We are never regularly high and dry for want of a companion so long as we can get pen, ink, and paper; and though we should not like to back ourself against such a winter as the last (1846-7), yet writing enables us to contend with a tolerable amount of bad weather. An author has pretty much the same pleasure in seeing his ugly cramped hand turned into neat print that a traveller has in receiving five-and-twenty francs for a sovereign on landing in France. Revising is something like returning to the realities of English money again. But we are getting into the mysteries of authorship. (pp. 222-23)

Robert Smith Surtees, ''The Season 1846-7,'' in his Hawbuck Grange; or, The Sporting Adventures of Thomas Scott, Esq., *1847. Reprint by Methuen & Co. Ltd., 1913, pp. 222-29.*

W. M. THACKERAY (letter date 1849)

[*A famed Victorian author, Thackeray is best known for his satiric sketches and novels of upper- and middle-class English life. Thackeray and Surtees began corresponding early in 1849 and became close friends shortly thereafter. In his first letter to Thackeray, Surtees asked him to illustrate* Sponge; *Thackeray's response is excerpted below.*]

I was very much flattered by your proposal to illustrate [*Sponge*], but I only draw for my own books, and indeed am not strong enough as an artist to make designs for anybody else's stories. You would find my pictures anything but comical, and I have not the slightest idea how to draw a horse, a dog, or a sporting scene of any sort. My friend Leech, I should think, would be your man—he is of a sporting turn, and to my mind draws a horse excellently. . . .

Mr Jorrocks has long been a dear and intimate friend of mine. I stole from him years ago, having to describe a hunting scene with which I was quite unfamiliar. . . .

> *W. M. Thackeray, in a letter to Robert Smith Surtees in May, 1849, in* Robert Smith Surtees (Creator of "Jorrocks"): 1803-1864 *by Robert Smith Surtees and E. D. Cuming, Charles Scribner's Sons, 1924, p. 245.*

W. M. THACKERAY (letter date 1852)

[*In this excerpt from a letter to Surtees, Thackeray praises two installments of* Sponge.]

This is not to thank you for the grouse, but for the last two numbers of *Soapey Sponge:* they are capital, and the Flat Hats delightful; those fellows in spectacles divine; and Scamperdale's character perfectly odious and admirable.

> *W. M. Thackeray, in a letter to Robert Smith Surtees in April? 1852, in* Robert Smith Surtees (Creator of "Jorrocks"): 1803-1864 *by Robert Smith Surtees and E. D. Cuming, Charles Scribner's Sons, 1924, p. 260.*

ROBERT SMITH SURTEES (essay date 1854)

[*Critics who fault the incoherent structure of Surtees' works frequently note that he acknowledged this weakness in both his preface to the 1854 edition of* Handley Cross *and his preface to* Ask Mamma *(see excerpts below).*]

Mr. Jorrocks, having for many years maintained his popularity, it is believed that, with the aid of the illustrious Leech, he is now destined for longevity.

The Author, in the present edition, not being tied to space or quantity, has had a better opportunity of developing his sporting hero than before.

The reader will have the kindness to bear in mind, that the work merely professes to be a tale, and does not aspire to the dignity of a novel.

> *Robert Smith Surtees, in a preface to his* Handley Cross, *second edition, Methuen & Co. Ltd., 1854, p. i.*

ROBERT SMITH SURTEES (essay date 1858)

[*Surtees' preface to* Ask Mamma *is reprinted below.*]

It may be a recommendation to the lover of light literature to be told, that the following story does not involve the complication of a plot. It is a mere continuous narrative of an almost every day exaggeration, interspersed with sporting scenes and excellent illustrations by Leech.

> *Robert Smith Surtees, in a preface to "Ask Mamma"; or, The Richest Commoner in England, Bradbury, Agnew, & Co., 1858, p. i.*

ROBERT SMITH SURTEES (essay date 1864?)

[*In the following excerpt, Surtees recalls the inception of his literary career. This piece was composed during the last months of Surtees' life and was intended to form part of his unfinished* Sporting and Social Recollections.]

I had always had a taste for scribbling, and thus it happened that I endeavoured to beguile the dead winter of 1829 by writing a semi-sporting novel. Up to that time no one had ever essayed anything in the sporting line that he was not prepared to swear to. (p. 60)

I had got about two-thirds through my work when I showed it to a couple of friends, and these so laughed it to scorn that I put it on the fire, and half resolved to abandon the pursuit of letters for the future. I had, however, kept a hunting journal, and after a time, not being quite satisfied with the verdict of those two friends, and having passed for a good theme-writer at school, I determined to try my hand at facts, and take the opinion of one of those best of critics, a publisher. To this end I sketched out some papers, and, Nimrod being then at variance with the proprietors, I offered them to the editor of what, for the sake of distinction, I will now call the "Old" *Sporting Magazine*. The bait took, and I presently found myself installed as first fiddle in the hunting line. A friend of mine having adopted the signature "Nim North," I took that of "Nim South" for my hunting contributions. I wrote on other subjects over other signatures, however. (pp. 60-1)

> *Robert Smith Surtees, "First Literary Efforts: The 'New Sporting Magazine' and 'The Horseman's Manual'," in* Robert Smith Surtees (Creator of "Jorrocks"): 1803-1864 *by Robert Smith Surtees and E. D. Cuming, Charles Scribner's Sons, 1924, pp. 60-72.*

THE NATION (essay date 1888)

[*This anonymous critic reviews an 1888 edition of* Hillingdon Hall, *labeling it a "second-rate" novel that has not stood the test of time.*]

It is scarcely probable that the individual exists to-day who could read through *Hillingdon Hall, or The Cockney Squire.* Any interest in this reprint of a novel written forty-four years ago is of the kind attached to literary curiosities. It is a truism to say that posterity is the infallible judge of literary greatness, but if any one should desire personally to test the truth of that truism, let him compare *Pickwick* and *Hillingdon Hall,* Weller and Jorrocks. If that doubting person should also wish to satisfy himself that the general readableness of our second-rate novels is some compensation for our paucity of first-rate, let him select *Hillingdon Hall* first among a bundle of the second-rates of the first half of our century. It appears from the illustrations of the novel that humor, expressed by pictorial art not of the highest excellence, retains the power to amuse longer than that of inferior literary art. The Flathers and Jorrocks, the Marquis of Bray and the Duchess of Donkeyton, are to us caricature of an insufferably dull kind; but it is just as easy to laugh at Wildrake's pictures of "The Guests Departing from Donkeyton Castle" and "The Surprise," as it was the day they were drawn. (p. 275)

> *A review of "Hillingdon Hall; or, The Cockney Squire," in* The Nation, *Vol. XLVII, No. 1214, October 4, 1888, pp. 273-75.*

THEODORE ROOSEVELT   (letter date 1906)

[*Roosevelt was active in American politics during the late nineteenth and early twentieth centuries, serving as assistant secretary of the navy and vice-president of the United States before succeeding William McKinley as president in 1901. The following excerpt, drawn from a letter Roosevelt wrote to an English admirer of Surtees, reveals that both he and his wife were devotees of the author.*]

Yes, Mrs Roosevelt and I are both as fond as you are of the immortal *Soapey Sponge,* but I shall be very grateful if you will send me that copy, because the only copy we have in the house is one Mrs Roosevelt inherited from her father. It is a rather cheap American edition, though with the Leech pictures, and we have read it until it has practically tumbled to pieces. (pp. 270-71)

> *Theodore Roosevelt, in an extract from a letter written January 22, 1906, in* Robert Smith Surtees: A Critical Study *by Frederick Watson, George G. Harrap & Co. Ltd., 1933, pp. 270-71.*

MOIRA O'NEILL   (essay date 1913)

[*Arguing that literary critics have unjustly neglected Surtees' works, O'Neill enthusiastically praises both their authenticity and their artistic value.*]

Those who do not read the novels of Surtees never think of him at all. Those who do read the novels of Surtees never forget him, and never can cease to read them. It becomes a habit, like playing Patience; a habit to be taken up every winter, with the warm waistcoats, and laid down every spring, about the time that warm waistcoats get uncomfortable.

But why is it that Surtees has not been given his proper place in literature? That is simply because literary men are, as a crowd, unsportsmanlike. They cannot see that Surtees is great because there is nothing in them that responds to him. Even Lindsay Gordon and Whyte Melville have had more justice done to them; for both those gentlemen wrote verse, strayed a good deal in regions of romance, and generally speaking spread their wings. But Surtees strictly excluded romance from his field of vision. If he had wings he kept them as carefully concealed from the public as he kept his novels from the sight of his daughters; who confessed to a stranger that they had never read them, "because papa said there was nothing worse for young people than reading bad literature."

Sometimes the world accepts a man's verdict on himself, though ironically spoken, as we know. But if the literary world has been foolish enough to overlook Surtees, the ordinary world, which after all has more people in it, has shown better sense. What books are taken oftener from the shelves in the smoking-room than those thick volumes in cheerful red, **Handley Cross** and **Mr Sponge's Sporting Tour?**—How quickly the happy reader gets absorbed in either of these, growing quieter and lying flatter on his shoulders in the chair, till that moment arrives when his heels begin to drum on the floor, and he utters ecstatic noises. . . .

Now it is a great thing to have added to the gaiety of the nation, as some wise man remarked. Surtees has done this, and more too. He has seen and recorded a side of life which for some good reason is concealed from nearly all the fine writers on human nature. With very few exceptions—Sir Walter Scott is one—they have ignored or misrepresented, but more often simply ignored, that instinct for sport which is deeply rooted in the heart of man. (p. 535)

Now, what we all feel about Surtees is that being a natural man himself, he understood the nature of sport and the hearts of sportsmen as no one ever yet has understood them. A man who will hunt with hounds if he can, and if he can't do that will hunt with ferrets, and if he can't do that will hunt a rat in a rickyard rather than not hunt at all,—that is the kind of sportsman whom Surtees honoured.

He knew every kind of M.F.H. [Master of Foxhounds] that exists—the hereditary M.F.H. like Lord Scamperdale, the rich *parvenu* M.F.H. like Mr Puffington, the adventurer M.F.H. like Mr Facey Romford, that fine sportsman who "could kill a fox with any one," the useless young M.F.H. like Mr Waffles, and the eccentric and joyous M.F.H. like the immortal grocer, Mr Jorrocks. All these are finished portraits in his long picture-gallery; and there is many a thumb-nail sketch besides. . . . (p. 536)

It is the spirit of the thing that we get from Surtees, not a mere surface picture. Many a writer of sporting novels can give a rattling account of a run, lively and truthful enough as far as it goes. But how few have the accurate, *inner* knowledge of hunting that he had, the science and the sympathy combined!

He shows us everything, even the little, warm, dry corner in the cover where the fox is lying private. He makes us hear everything, from the slight crackle of snapping twigs and the stamp of an impatient horse's hoof, to the light whimper of the first hound, the challenge, the full chorus, and the ringing melody that "makes horses jump and plunge with delight, while their riders funk or rejoice according to the stuff of which they are made."

Then the run itself! He has written of every kind of run, in every sort of country, upon every kind of horse that the experience of ten ordinary men would include. . . . We have read them all ten times over, and shall probably read them half as often again. They have life and breath in them, they have sense and speed, and the very sound and smell and excitement of a wintry day in a hunting country. Surely this is no mean achievement for any writer. It is certain that literary merit was the very last thing Surtees would have claimed for his sporting chronicles, and yet literary merit they undoubtedly have. The language is graphic and terse, the narration is swift, the characters original and varied, and the incidents simply imperishable. He confined himself to sporting novels; had he chosen to write political novels instead, they would probably have been highly successful. His gift of cynicism would have been very useful in the political atmosphere. (p. 537)

The wisest writers are those who know their limits best. Miss Austen, that perfect artist, was a strictly limited person, and recognised her limits with a smile, to the immense advantage of her readers. Surtees did the same. He had an extraordinary power of accurate observation; he used that, and kept his imagination always well under the control of his own caustic humour. The result was a perfect realism, which in some ways almost equals the realism of Defoe. He had Defoe's command of detail, too, and his memory must have been one of the most remarkable organs ever possessed by a writer. He never fails to describe with precision the dress of every character presented. . . .

He could describe ladies' dresses . . .—a rare accomplishment,—as well as their curls and their eyebrows. Farther than that he did not go, or at least only on the strictly conventional lines fashionable in his day; when it was an article of faith with men that all women were jealous of each others' good looks, and all wildly anxious to marry the first marriageable man who came in their way. Since even Thackeray clung to these hoary superstitions, it is not surprising that Surtees went easily along with him. Women and sentiment were really out of his line, but he could be immensely amusing about their views of sport. . . . (p. 538)

For all his sarcasms Surtees knew quite well that there is such a thing as a sportswoman. Mrs Somerville, *née* Lucy Glitters, with her light hands, her pluck, and her determination to enjoy herself, was a prototype of a class that has swelled enormously in numbers since **Mr Romford's Hounds** was written; but she was rather a solitary figure in her day. (p. 539)

[Surtees] saw men and things in a remarkably dry light, and reported them precisely as he saw them. He was convinced that nearly half the people in the world were imposing on the other half, and his amusement at the spectacle was much greater than his disgust. This was fortunate for his readers; for what would become of the fun of the thing if Surtees had taken a high moral tone in recounting the sale of that redoubtable horse Hercules by Mr Buckram, the dealer, to Sponge, by Sponge to the helpless Waffles, by Waffles back to Buckram, and by Buckram back to Sponge, with the additional imaginary episode of Lord Bullfrog in a highborn rage? As it is, when Sponge receives the final £250 from the deluded Waffles, we rather sympathise with his comment on the whole transaction.

> *Con*found it! I don't do myself justice. *I'm too much of a gentleman!* I should have had five 'under'd—such an ass as Waffles deserves to be done!

This is exactly the spirit in which we desire to read of such transactions. A little more cleverness, and they would be too sordid to be amusing; a little more cynicism, and they would cease to be realistic. Surtees had the happy knack of telling things easily, as one light-hearted gentleman might to another after dinner, in an hour when the moral sense is not exactly clamorous, and laughter comes naturally. But his ease is masterly all the same. A hundred little, quick, incisive touches show the artist, and there is no repetition.

How many pictures of huntsmen has he given us, and all are distinct portraits! Jack Frostyface is not a bit like Tom Towler, and old Lotherington is not a bit like Watchorn or Dick Bragg. (pp. 539-40)

[When] it comes to James Pigg, comparisons fail. The man from Canny Newcassel is unique. His simplicity and his shrewdness, his honesty and his lying, his obstinacy, his intrepid courage, his taste for "brandy and 'baccy," and his over-mastering passion for hunting—none of these qualities are so very exceptional in themselves; yet their combination in Pigg is a masterpiece of originality. Jorrocks himself is less remarkable than Pigg. He sometimes reminds us of other fat men in other fields of literature, and very fat men are always declining towards farce. But Pigg reminds us of no one, and he is in the purest vein of comedy.

Surtees was, in fact, a fine comedian. One incident alone would prove this—the death of Jack Spraggon. Almost any other writer would have made this melodramatic, or else have allowed it to be repulsive. But the creator of Lord Scamperdale and Jack Spraggon was equal to the occasion. One never recognises the born comedian so clearly as on the border of a tragedy.

Like all comedians, he loves a crowd. His pages fairly hum with the numbers of people he introduces, and yet there is no confusion; in this point he is nearly the equal of Thackeray. His minor characters are so cleverly sketched in that we know them intimately. (pp. 540-41)

He understood rich Mr Joseph Large and his natural timidity just as well as he understood poor young Charley Stobbs and his natural courage. It takes all sorts to make a world, he thought, just as the old proverb says; and the hunting-world is as diverse in its way as the social or the political.

But Surtees, for all his dry humour, had the true passion of the chase at heart as surely as John Jorrocks had it. And this was why he immortalised John Jorrocks. (p. 541)

It was not very long ago that there appeared in a leading weekly paper extracts from **Handley Cross** and **Mr Sponge's Sporting Tour**. They were, of course, edited in the explanatory American fashion now usual, which consists principally in curtailment and skipping, and the inference was unavoidable that the works themselves were supposed to have passed completely out of knowledge, as being too lengthy in their original form for modern perusal. *If* this be so indeed, then Surtees is in the same case with Dickens, and even with Sir Walter Scott; and we, his loyal admirers, may safely leave him in their excellent company.

But the balance of the evidence seems rather to show that the editor of the leading weekly paper was labouring under a delusion. (p. 542)

> *Moira O'Neill, "Some Novels by Surtees," in* Blackwood's Magazine, *Vol. CXCIII, No. MCLXX, April, 1913, pp. 535-42.*

RUDYARD KIPLING   (essay date 1913)

[*Kipling was a popular English writer who is now generally accepted as one of the masters of the short story form. The following excerpt is drawn from his short story "'My Son's Wife',"" which was first published in 1913. In this passage, the story's main character, the London aesthete Frankwell Midmore, stumbles upon a number of Surtees' novels in the library of a country estate.*]

At last [Midmore] was driven to paw over a few score books in a panelled room called the library, and realised with horror what the late Colonel Werf's mind must have been in its prime. The volumes smelt of a dead world as strongly as they did of mildew. He opened and thrust them back, one after another, till crude coloured illustrations of men on horses held his eye. He began at random and read a little, moved into the drawing-

A Leech illustration of Jorrocks giving a lecture on hunting.

room with the volume, and settled down by the fire still reading. It was a foul world into which he peeped for the first time—a heavy-eating, hard-drinking hell of horsecopers, swindlers, matchmaking mothers, economically dependent virgins selling themselves blushingly for cash and lands: Jews, tradesmen, and an ill-considered spawn of Dickens-and-horsedung characters (I give Midmore's own criticism), but he read on, fascinated, and behold, from the pages leaped, as it were, the brother to the red-eyed man of the brook, bellowing at a landlord (here Midmore realised that *he* was that very animal) for new barns; and another man who, like himself again, objected to hoof-marks on gravel. Outrageous as thought and conception were, the stuff seemed to have the rudiments of observation. He dug out other volumes by the same author, till Rhoda came in with a silver candlestick.

'Rhoda,' said he, 'did you ever hear about a character called James Pigg—and Batsey?'

'Why, o' course,' said she. 'The Colonel used to come into the kitchen in 'is dressin'-gown an' read us all those Jorrockses.'

'Oh, Lord!' said Midmore, and went to bed with a book called **Handley Cross** under his arm, and a lonelier Columbus into a stranger world the wet-ringed moon never looked upon. (pp. 348-49)

> Rudyard Kipling, "'My Son's Wife'," in his A Diversity of Creatures, 1917. Reprint by Doubleday, Page & Company, 1926, pp. 335-78.

THE TIMES LITERARY SUPPLEMENT (essay date 1916)

[*This anonymous critic ranks Surtees' novels in order of merit and briefly describes his artistic method.*]

During the fifty years and more which have elapsed [since his death], the books to which Surtees owes his fame have enjoyed a popularity which has never shown any sign of decay. They do not appeal to everybody, but by those who care for them at all they are at the present time esteemed as highly as ever. It is hardly necessary to say that many people are led to read Surtees by their interest in fox hunting. This to a great extent accounts for the steadiness of his popularity. But there are many other readers who appreciate his work quite as much, though their knowledge of hunting hardly extends beyond what they have learnt from him. . . .

In one respect Surtees holds a fortunate position—namely, that there has never been any sham reverence for him. He has never attracted much of the attention of professional literary critics. Very little has been written about him; he is quoted, but that is nearly all. There is no stereotyped view as to his place in literature. . . . To read Surtees has never been regarded by anyone as a duty. Those who liked his books have read them, and to many people almost every page is familiar. Those who have found that they did not care for them have felt no scruple about leaving them alone. . . .

It is characteristic of Surtees that he wrote about nothing outside the range of his own personal knowledge. He was a man of mature experience of the world before he did any of his important work. Dickens was 24 when *Pickwick* was being issued; Surtees was 40 when the first edition of **Handley Cross** appeared, and this was subsequently greatly altered, the alterations including omissions, as well as revision and large additions. All his work which really counts at all appeared, in the form in which we now have it, after he was fifty. . . .

The question which is the best of Surtees's books is not an unreasonable one, for several of them are in some respects better than *Handley Cross,* and as amusing. It seems clear, however, that the answer which has been given by popular acclamation, in favour of *Handley Cross,* must be accepted. Mr. Jorrocks and James Pigg, as they appear here, have taken the popular imagination by storm, while the true touch with which the sport of fox-hunting is handled overrides any absurdities of detail. It is a great achievement for any writer to have created characters which have taken such a hold on the minds of so many generations of readers. What everybody means by ''Jorrocks'' is simply the Jorrocks of *Handley Cross;* his appearances in other books are negligible in the public eye. Thus *Handley Cross* contains Surtees's most important literary effort, besides, of course, other things which we could not spare; and it is full of the shrewd wit and wisdom of a man of the world. It has obvious defects; it grew as a patchwork; some passages seem rather irrelevant, and some are too farcical; but it is on the whole the successful result of very good, careful work. Some of the work spent upon it can be traced in detail by noting the changes made in revision. We can compare the first draft of **''The Benighted Sportsman''** in the *New Sporting Magazine* with the chapter about Stobbs's adventure as we now have it, or some of the chapters of the first edition with their final form; and in doing so we constantly note the sound judgment with which exuberance was pruned, and the skill with which passages rewritten were amplified. . . .

It is not very easy to separate the three books which stand next in order of merit—namely, *Mr. Sponge's Sporting Tour, Plain or Ringlets?* and *Mr. Romford's Hounds.* They are all admirable, and have more finish as compositions than *Handley Cross.* On the whole we give the preference to *Mr. Romford's Hounds*— partly because it has the best story. In all we have examples of genuine enthusiasm for hunting, as shown in various forms. There is no topic on which Surtees is happier. He has all the buoyancy of mind which just suits it, and he knows too much to be tempted to exaggerate here, whatever he may do elsewhere. It is at home or out visiting that Lord Scamperdale and Jack Spraggon and Mr. Romford sometimes appear in absurd situations, not often out hunting. Moreover, he restrains himself from giving us too much of it. He is mainly concerned with people who, if they go out hunting at all, as many of them do, represent aspects of it other than that of genuine enthusiasm.

There remain three books belonging to a period earlier than that of Surtees's best work. *Hawbuck Grange* is a series of admirable sketches . . . in which perhaps Mr. Trumper is the most enduring character. *Jorrocks's Jaunts and Jollities,* the earliest of all, has the distinction of being the work which first established Surtees's reputation. . . . It contains some clever parody of other writers. . . . The third book is *Hillingdon Hall.* . . . [This] book is not worth reading. The leading topic is a poor one, and the story is elaborated by the introduction of hopelessly stupid people, like Emma Flather and the Marquis, for whom he cannot have cared at all.

Surtees is a standing protest against the view, which we sometimes meet with, that true humour is inseparable from pathos. Surtees's humour throws any amount of light on human nature, but to connect it with pathos would be absurd. We can recall a few examples of pathos in his writings, but not enough for the fingers of one hand. Surtees's methods are to a great extent independent of the ordinary appliances of a novelist. He gives his characters definite parts to play, sometimes giving them fantastic names to fit their parts, and generally makes them act their parts as strictly as if they were in the *Pilgrim's Progress.* There are no searchings of heart, there is no repentance, there is hardly any development of a character into anything different from what is more or less indicated for him when he is introduced. Apparent exceptions to this are generally only partial and superficial. It is true that Mr. Sponge proposes to Lucy Glitters and marries her, thus abandoning his purpose of fortune-hunting; but this is due to a sudden impulse, and is a way of winding up his career. Mr. Romford has more in him than could have been imagined when he is first introduced, but this is doubtless an accident. Probably the author had no idea of ever making him play any very important part when he introduced him in *Mr. Sponge's Sporting Tour,* and had not even settled what his name was to be. Lucy is, perhaps, an exception; and when in the end she bursts into tears, we have the nearest approach to tragedy that Surtees admits. Again, we have no love affairs which excite any real interest. Stobbs will, of course, marry Belinda: there has been no question about this from the beginning of their acquaintance. We are interested in Rosa, and would gladly see her marry Lord Marchhare; they would suit each other very well, and she would enjoy being a duchess. But, of course, there is no chance of this. The only question is whether the bargain is to be made with Jasper Goldspink or with Mr. Bunting, who are both muffs; and the interest in this is so slight as to fit very well with the parallel question, ''plain or ringlets.'' It is only a thread to hang the story on. There is only one book, namely, *Mr. Romford's Hounds,* in which the story as a whole is very important and excites much interest. Often we have scenes which, with a little explanation, might fairly well stand alone. The method of telling varies according to the mood of the author. Often it shows careful craftsmanship, occasionally it is rather random, and sometimes it is too farcical, but it is hardly ever dull. A not uncommon feature of it is caricature.

Surtees's use of caricature deserves a little attention, though to discuss it is rather like giving a ponderous explanation of a pun. There seem to be some people who take it amiss. We have seen a review of *Handley Cross* in which the writer objected to the misspellings and misplacements of h's in Mr. Jorrocks's letters. Here was a man who was a successful merchant in the City; it must be wrong to make him write so grotesquely. It is, of course, a case of caricature. Surtees did not mean that Jorrocks could not spell better. He was not concerned with such a detail; all that he was concerned with was to give, on the whole, a true impression of the man. He cannot tell everything, so he exaggerates some features. Take a simpler example. One of his lawyers writes a letter in which he reports a bargain made for 1,000 pounds. Surtees, who is always ready for a passing jest at the expense of lawyers, makes him write ''one thousand pounds, be the same more or less.'' He does not mean that an actual lawyer could actually write this; but with a touch of his pen we get the effect of a thickheaded lawyer who would write needless, though less amusing, verbiage. A *Quarterly Review*er, in March, 1843, in an appreciative review of the first edition of *Handley Cross* [see excerpt dated 1843], solemnly warned the author to curb his propensity to caricature. He might as well have talked to the winds. Surtees always has this weapon at hand, and we are content with the way he uses it when he needs it.

Surtees will always find grateful readers among those who regard some crudity of form as negligible compared with insight; who appreciate humour, and do not particularly want to have their feelings harrowed; and who like to feel about a writer with whom they are on intimate terms that he is a man of sturdy common sense. If a time should ever come when fox-hunting is dead, we do not doubt that it will be found that Surtees has survived.

"The Novels of Surtees," in The Times Literary Supplement, *No. 780, December 28, 1916, p. 632.*

FRANK J. WILSTACH   (essay date 1922)

[*In this enthusiastic defense of Surtees' works, Wilstach responds to claims made by the author's detractors.*]

Robert Smith Surtees, a contemporary of Dickens and Thackeray, is one of the maddening puzzles of literature. Considered by some as being the greatest fictioneer humorist of his time, he is practically unknown to the general reader.

His reputation has doubtless suffered in consequence of his stories being designated as "sporting novels," and, furthermore, the extraordinary illustrations by Leech, Alken and others have served, in some minds, to becloud the splendors of the tales themselves.

These novels treat of English country life, with fleeting glimpses of London. Incidental to the stories are shooting, hunting, horse racing and other sports, along with jocund and often hilarious accounts of dinners, dances, flirtations, picnics and cattle shows.

Other novels of the period treating of country life, such as J. G. Whyte Melville's *Market Harborough* and Anthony Trollope's *Framley Parsonage,* have brisk huntings of fox—only this, Surtees's hunts, even to one unacquainted with the fox and the hounds, are as exciting as a chase after a burglar. . . .

Having become acquainted with Mr. Soapey Sponge, it is with the risk of being set down as a dizzard, a doodle or a blockhead that I do unblushingly declare that Surtees is altogether the most amusing and delectable story-teller that the Victorian or any other age has produced. . . .

The review of his life which appears in the *Dictionary of National Biography* was written by Thomas Seccombe [see Additional Bibliography]. . . .

The one statement by Mr. Seccombe which seems utterly absurd is this: "Without the original illustrations these works have very small interest." This exasperating statement by Seccombe is sufficient to make the Surteesian howl with rage!

John Leech was a hard-working artist. He illustrated a vast array of books, and, curiously, despite the unquestioned worth of his artistry, none of these, except the novels of Surtees, are held at purse-defying figures. To say that his illustrations to the five Surtees novels are responsible for their popularity, is, to this chronicler, as preposterous as to say that Cruikshank's illustrations for *Oliver Twist* were accountable for the popularity of that novel. . . .

Stanley K. Wilson, an out-and-out detractor of Surtees, lately, in parroting Seccombe, stated that "R. S. Surtees would have died long back, but for the famous Leech illustrations." In point of fact, the Leech plates, instead of being responsible for the life of Surtees's novels, are mainly the cause of his not being generally read.

The point is justly made that the owners of the Leech plates, hand-colored, have kept up the fiction that the books would not be acceptable without them, and were their chief charm. The Surteesians hotly protest against any such notion, contending that the high cost of reproducing these illustrations has served to preclude the making of popular-priced editions, and so has been the means of destroying any chance Surtees might have had of gaining a wide popularity. And when you come to examine the prices in the bookseller's catalogues it is disclosed that the books which were illustrated by other artists than Leech, to whom Seccombe and Wilson attribute his popularity, are held at higher figures. And the most curious thing of all is the price asked for the *Horseman's Manual.* This is without any illustrations whatever, and can be had only at a figure above what one can buy a set of the first editions of the five novels illustrated by Leech. . . .

Mr. Wilson makes another statement which arouses the Surteesians to rage, i. e., that Surtees's novels are marred by "inane pun-making." In point of actual fact Surtees was not infected with the great literary plague of his time—the rhetorical black death—pun-making! John Jorrocks may have been guilty of this crime in a slight degree, but nowhere else in these voluminous volumes is a single pun to be found. William Congreve is not denounced as a punster because he gives his characters such names as Heartwell, Vainlove, Fondlewife, Setter, Maskwell, Careless, Scandal, Tattle, Waitwell. Surely, a name which designates the character and physical peculiarities of a person can hardly be called a pun. Most of Surtees's characters are named after the manner of Congreve and the Restorationists. We, therefore, have Soapey Sponge, the Duke of Donkeyton; Fizzler, the confectioner; Lord Lovetin, Johnny O'Dicey, Captain Doleful, Waffles, Sir Harry Scamperdale, Captain Greatgun, Sir Moses Mainchance, Sir Giles Nabem, Earle of Coarsegab, Duke of Dazzzleton, Mr. Spareneck and Lady Scattercash. . . .

While John Jorrocks is undoubtedly Surtees's greatest character, the two books, *Mr. Sponge's Sporting Tour* and *Mr. Facey Romford's Hounds,* contain the best work of the novelist. Mr. Soapey Sponge does not belie his name, for as Surtees said: "His dexterity in getting into people's houses was only equaled by the difficulty of getting him out again." If Surtees had written nothing else than these two novels he would be entitled to a high place as an English fictioneer. . . .

Those who have written slightingly of Surtees have been those, evidently, who haven't read him. He was not given to circumlocutions or battalogias. He was full up to the chin with bounce and gusto, and there are those who insist upon comparing him to Thackeray and Dickens. This, of course, is an idle pastime. (p. 13)

Finally, by way of protest, in [regard to] Seccombe and Wilson's pestiferous assaults, a procession of the Surteesians on Fifth Avenue has been suggested. Robert H. Davis would jump at the chance to lead the parade on horseback, made up as the renowned John Jorrocks. Then would come a gay cavalcade: Marjorie Rambeau as Lady Scattercash, Henry L. Mencken as Lord Bullfrog, Josephine Drake as Lucy Sparkle, Al Jolson as Waffles, De Wolf Hopper as the Duke of Tergiversation, &c., followed by Simeon Ford in a carriage, representing the author. Then would come Benjamin de Casseres leading the much esteemed Tom Smith, made up as an anti-Surteesian.

Such a demonstration would serve to remove quite a number of bloodclots from the brain of literature, suffered in these parts. Tally-ho! (p. 26)

Frank J. Wilstach, "Surtees and Charles Dickens," in The New York Times Book Review, *July 23, 1922, pp. 13, 26.*

VIRGINIA WOOLF   (essay date 1925)

[*A British novelist, essayist, and short story writer, Woolf is one of the most prominent literary figures of the twentieth century. In the excerpt below, she comments upon how the works of Surtees, Nimrod, Peter Beckford, and Charles St. John influenced the prose style of later English writers.*]

[The] English sporting writers, Beckford, St. John, Surtees, Nimrod, make no mean reading. In their slapdash, gentlemanly way they have ridden their pens as boldly as they have ridden their horses. They have had their effect upon the language. This riding and tumbling, this being blown upon and rained upon and splashed from head to heels with mud, have worked themselves into the very texture of English prose and given it that leap and dash, that stripping of images from flying hedge and tossing tree which distinguish it not indeed above the French but so emphatically from it. (p. 135)

Virginia Woolf, "Jack Mytton," in her The Common Reader, *Harcourt Brace Jovanovich, 1925, pp. 134-40.*

S. M. ELLIS   (essay date 1927)

[*Ellis welcomes the first book publication of* Young Tom Hall.]

It is curious that for seventy-four years an excellent story [*Young Tom Hall*] by R. S. Surtees should have remained unpublished in book form, its existence in the pages of *The New Monthly Magazine* either forgotten or unknown. There is an ever increasing fame and value for the works of Surtees which makes this omission the stranger. The admirers of Surtees are principally to be found among the leisured and monied classes who enjoy hunting scenes and sporting life in the country: I doubt if there is any demand for Surtees in the public libraries of large towns, or if even thirty per centum of the readers of other Victorian novelists know aught of Jorrocks and Soapey Sponge, the two outstanding creations of this author. . . .

[*Young Tom Hall*] is a most entertaining work in Surtees's characteristic vein, being the adventures of a loutish youth, son of a provincial banker and wool-stapler, in search of social uprise and a wife by means of sporting and military endeavours. Here, once again, are the mischances of an embryo sportsman, the amusing scenes of rural entertainments, and a fine description of a hunting day ("At Silverspring Firs"). There is a good deal of caricature of course. The presentation of Colonel Blunt and the officers of the Heavysteeds, a gross collection of guzzling blackguards with no notions of honour in the sale of a horse or in any other matter, can scarcely be accepted as a correct picture of the officers in a dragoon regiment of that period. But Surtees's gift of satirical observation is at its best in his inimitable pictures here of the "Thé Dansante" and "The Hunt Breakfast," for example.

This abortive and long-lost child, now clothed in uniform scarlet cloth, must be placed beside his eight fine brethren upon the shelves of every "gentleman's library," as the booksellers and auctioneers would say.

S. M. Ellis, "A Forgotten Surtees Novel," in The Bookman, *New York, Vol. LXXI, No. 426, March, 1927, p. 324.*

SIEGFRIED SASSOON   (essay date 1928)

[*Sassoon's autobiographical novel* Memoirs of a Fox-Hunting Man, *excerpted below, recounts the life of the Sassoon persona, a prosperous country squire named George Sherston. In this passage, Sherston describes how he and his friend Stephen Colwood were influenced by Surtees' works.* Memoirs of a Fox-Hunting Man *was first published in 1928.*]

In describing my friendship with Stephen I am faced by a difficulty which usually arises when one attempts to reproduce the conversational oddities of people who are on easy terms. We adopted and matured a specialized jargon drawn almost exclusively from characters in the novels of Surtees; since we knew these almost by heart, they provided us with something like a dialect of our own, and in our care-free moments we exchanged remarks in the mid-Victorian language of such character-parts as Mr. Romford, Major Yammerton, and Sir Moses Mainchance, while Mr. Jorrocks was an all-pervading influence. In our Surtees obsession we went so far that we almost identified ourselves with certain characters on appropriate occasions. One favourite rôle which Stephen facetiously imposed on me was that of a young gentleman named Billy Pringle who, in the novel which he adorns, is reputed to be very rich. My £600 a year was thus magnified to an imaginary £10,000, and he never wearied of referring to me as 'the richest commoner in England.' The stress was laid on my great wealth and we never troubled to remember that the Mr. Pringle of the novel was a dandified muff and 'only half a gentleman.' I cannot remember that I ever succeeded in finding a consistent rôle for Stephen, but I took the Surtees game for granted from the beginning, and our adaptation of the Ringwell Hunt to the world created by that observant novelist was simplified by the fact that a large proportion of the Ringwell subscribers might have stepped straight out of his pages. (pp. 153-54)

Siegfried Sassoon, "At the Rectory," in his The Memoirs of George Sherston: Memoirs of a Fox-Hunting Man, *Vol. 1,* The Literary Guild of America, Inc., *1937, pp. 152-86.*

[BONAMY DOBRÉE]   (essay date 1930)

[*Dobrée delineates the reasons for Surtees' enduring popularity, citing his vivid characterization, lively yet satiric humor, knowledge of hunting, comic imagination, and vigorous prose.*]

There is . . . no single reason [for the persistence of Surtees]. If we take Surtees's writings as a hunting country and try to pursue the fox of his popularity through it, it is not at all certain that we shall make him "cry capevi." It is a large country, some of it fair and free enough, with no unjumpable fences: but some of it is woodland with, it must be confessed, not a few boggy rides, not unlike those in that "incorrigible mountain," that "unpardonable wilderness," Pinch-me-near Forest. We shall often be in danger of changing foxes, and if we do not keep the pack of our ideas well in hand we may even riot after hare. It would be a woe-begone critic who would have to confess himself in the end a mere currant-jelly man.

How impossible it is, thinking of Surtees, not to drop into his jargon; and there at once is another bit of the secret: it is by very vivid if often repeated catch phrases that he imparts a certain kind of life to his characters. For these, with a few exceptions, are of the nature of "humours," and "dash my vig!" is only a variant of swearing by Pharaoh's foot. The lively catch phrase and the "humour," these together account for a degree of vitality; for the humour, if skilfully enough

One of Henry Alken's illustrations for Jorrock's Jaunts and Jollities.

contrived, constantly reminds us of people we know, if we happen to come into contact with the circles from which they were drawn. Those who are not lucky enough to hunt and meet the squire of Hawbuck Grange may yet meet Admiration Jack at whatever watering-place they idle away their health in; just as the traveller abroad must keep very much to himself if he does not run across Sir Politick Would be. Not, of course, that Surtees's mind is as probing or as general as Jonson's, nor has he the same giant's capacity for creating his butts; in short, to compare them as writers would be ridiculous; but we shall not quite see what Surtees was after if we altogether forget the older comic traditions.

The object in writing is not to be confused with the impulse to write, at all events in a minor author like Surtees. His object, one need not question, was to give the average hawbuck something to read besides "Bell's Life," the local paper, and the Post Office Directory, which was the only literature, apparently, to be found in many houses. Himself a man of considerable reading, who could quote the poets, or rather misquote them with a happy familiarity, he did not see why even Soapey Sponge should have to spend an off day in reading nothing but "Mogg's Cab Fares." His books, therefore, would have to be of the lightest, with nothing to strain the mind or make more demands on the attention than a tired fox-hunter would be willing to give, or a disgruntled one cheated of a day with hounds by a black frost. Thus he boldly informed anyone who cared to read the preface to *Ask Mamma:*

> It may be a recommendation to the lover of
> light literature to be told that the following story
> does not involve the complication of a plot. It

is a mere continuous narrative of an almost everyday exaggeration, interspersed with sporting scenes and excellent illustrations by Leech [see excerpt dated 1858].

That is a fair description of all Surtees's novels, except that he is not, perhaps, quite fair to himself, since his stories have a certain structure; they have a beginning and an end, even though the middle is elastic and episodic; they are not just separate sketches like the *Jaunts and Jollities;* they have, besides, a hero of recognizable character or humour to bind the episodes together.

Surtees is not an author whom one reads for the sake of intimacy with a charming or profound personality, though the man is engaging enough. . . . [His] impulse to write was a direct reaction to his delight in life; being pleased with it, he wanted to talk about it. And, having once started, it was difficult to stop. . . . So he rambles on, telling us of the joys of fox-hunting, or of the minor ones of hare-hunting, describing odd characters, inveighing against the racing which has become a mere betting match, and against the battue which is slaughter without sport; reviling bad farmers and bad landlords; grumbling at the villainous discomforts and still more villainous charges of country inns, the coldness and robbery of town hotels, and thence praising the development of clubs which give the country squire a home from home. Great also are the feasts, deep and potent the libations which revive the heroes of that Homeric age of hunting; for whatever Surtees may be talking about, the adventures of the chase are the background, where they are not the immediate theme. And, after all, he lived in the glorious age of which his friend Nimrod (Apperley) wrote, which Scrutator (Horlock) knew, when Osbaldestone, the Squire *par excellence,* was alive; when the names of Warde and Assheton Smith were to be conjured with, and the hunt could still attract good painters. It was the age, again, of eccentrics, when the name of Tom Mytton was a household word, and jailbirds would palm themselves off as captains in great houses.

It was just this eccentricity, this "excess," which gave material to the man whose comic vein ran in the mould of the humours. But his humours are nearly all what he called "snobs"—namely, to follow Thackeray's definition, as no doubt he himself did, those who "meanly admire mean things." For him the snob is not so much the man who looks down upon others as it is for us, but those who are like Mr. Sponge, "wishing to be gentlemen without knowing how," thinking that all that is needed is a tolerable amount of cash, an intolerable deal of splash, and a capacity for bullying the under-dog—just as Miss Rosa, too well bred ever to show that she enjoyed anything, thought nothing of working the unfortunate milliner all night so that she might appear in a new bonnet at the next day's picnic. Nearly all his characters are people trying to make a show and to rise in the world by dishonourable means—Soapey Sponge, Facey Romford, the A.D.C. at Handley Cross, who by the ingenious initial disguised the fact that he was only the Assistant Drains Commissioner—and a dozen others, even Jorrocks himself in the Hillingdon Hall stage. Or else they are people of reasonably good position trying meanly to improve it, or to keep it up by mercenary marriages—Jawleyford, Admiration Jack, Captain Miserrimus Doleful—and again a dozen others. There are few likeable people; and they, as a rule, are very minor characters, such as Charley Stobbs, the only exception of full-length size being Thomas Scott, the owner of Hawbuck Grange, a charming, sensible, modest person, who loved hunting for hunting's sake, and not for the glamour, nor the hard riding, nor the appetite, nor the opportunities for horse-coping. A real love of hunting, of course, redeemed anyone for Surtees, as it does Jorrocks, or Lord Scamperdale, or Facey Romford; a pretended love would damn an angel, as it does those who are by no means angels—the Duke of Tergiversation, Jack Bunting, Puff:, the richest commoner in England, and so on. But just occasionally the real "humour" is invented for its own sake, as the altogether delightful, wheezing, puffing, bellows-to-mend Jogglebury Crowdey, consumed by his passion for cutting walkingsticks from hedges, and carving them in likenesses of famous men to provide fortunes for his children. And, of course, there is Pigg.

But in the main, as a result of his satirical bent, for Surtees had taken the Becky Sharp leaf out of *Vanity Fair,* most of his people are unlovable. One loves Pickwick, who owed his birth to Jorrocks, as one does not love Jorrocks; and that is because Pickwick is a lineal descendant of Uncle Toby, whereas Jorrocks derives rather from Commodore Trunnion. Perhaps it is necessary to be a trifle sentimental to make a lovable character, and there is nothing sentimental in Surtees; there is, indeed, no sentiment. Or, failing sentimentality, some quality of subtlety is necessary—something of the subtlety, shall we say, of Becky Sharp as opposed to the hard surface of Lucy Glitters, who is all on the outside, not having had the advantage of an education at the Pinkerton Academy. All Surtees's girls are nasty little monkeys, without heart or passion, however pretty they may be, except Jorrocks's niece, Belinda: all his women aspire meanly after mean things. Then what is there in Surtees which makes us read him? In what channel does the stream of his vitality run? For it is that in the last resort which makes us take down any book from our shelves.

His fame really rests upon **Handley Cross.** *Sponge* is entertaining, certainly, it has something of the creative vigour of the master work; *Ask Mamma* perhaps comes next, coupled with *Facey Romford; Hawbuck Grange* is a treasure to the hunting man; *Plain or Ringlets* is interesting as a light on manners, and does at least contain that brilliant comic invention, the Jug. *Hillingdon Hall* is a slough of dullness, for, apart from hunting, Surtees could make little of Jorrocks. In fact, the more hunting, the more fun. And here, perhaps, is another clue to his persistence: he knew more about hunting than any other novelist of the nineteenth century. . . . With Surtees . . . we are let into the secrets of the stable and the kennel; we know, for instance, that Jorrocks hunted a mixed pack, what he fed his hounds on, and how he made up his entry. By inference, or rather by caricature, he tells us what a good horse, a good pack, a good huntsman, a good anything down to a good pair of boots ought to be like: he has as much information to give us as Beckford and Nimrod combined, and a beginner can learn as much from Mr. Jorrocks's sporting "lectors"—supported equally though they were by Beckford and brandy—as from, say, Lord Willoughby de Broke's *Hunting the Fox,* provided, of course, that he is sharp enough to see when Surtees is fooling and when he is not. And, besides, he rubs in the important lesson that hunting is to be pursued for the sport, to see hounds, and not for any extraneous reason of snobbery, showing off, hard riding, or other irrelevance. . . . There is nothing of the cut 'em down spirit about Surtees: he would ride if need be, but he would always think of his horse. The psychologist might perhaps scent disappointment, and behold the wish-fulfilment illustrated in the run in which Soapey Sponge took the horn from the huntsman and killed the fox single-handed; or when, on New Year's Day, in a hard frost, his tremendous gallop enabled him to catch the fox and Lucy Glitters at one and the same time; but even the most sober riders may be guilty of dreams. Nor was Surtees a snob, even in hunting, in the way that Nimrod was; he despised the carted stag variety, it is true, for "When you've catched the stag, you're no better off than ye were afore," as Jimmy observed to Mr. Romford; but he was friends with the currant-jelly men: the excellent Major Yammerton is not held up to ridicule, and one of the best descriptions of a hunt is that of the hare with the Goose and Dumpling folk in **Hawbuck Grange.**

Yet with all these qualities, to which must be added his observant eye—there is no excuse for a reader not to know how any one of the characters was dressed on any occasion—we have probably been rioting after hare; and the fox of his popularity is the creative capacity, the *vis comica,* and the gift for racy language which inform **Handley Cross.** Jorrocks is without doubt an imaginative creation; he is of the race of immortal and divine fat men. In a sense he is the Falstaff of the chase; for he is something of a fairy, with a superb gift for variegated invective—though perhaps Lord Scamperdale beats him here—and unanswerable repartee. Like Dr. Johnson, he was called a bear, and scorned your clarety wines. He may not be so gentle as Mr. Pickwick, but he is almost as gullible, which is to say that he has something about him of the heavenly simpleton which is the mark of the great comic character. We do a little love Jorrocks, and are sorry when his wife bundles him into a lunatic asylum. James Pigg, again, is a creation whom Tom Jones surely is not ashamed to be seen with in Hades, perhaps even walking with him hand in hand, "like the sign of the Mutual Insurance hoffice," as the M.F.H. would say.

And if Surtees is often boisterously burlesque, and in this he is not as bad as Smollett, he can be sly as well; he has some delicious pieces of cool irony, while his *à pédant pédant et demi* treatment of Nimrod as Pomponius Ego is real though friendly satire.... *Handley Cross,* undoubtedly, is more various than any other of Surtees's books, and rises to greater comic heights. The scene where the genial madman entertains Charley Stobbs at breakfast after the Ongar Park run, finally clapping his saucer on his head and throwing his cup through the window-pane, has a flavour of Borrow, and all the actual hunting scenes have the wisdom of Beckford added to a discriminating observation. He also has something of the genius needed to make the great comic phrase which reveals the aspirations and weaknesses of humanity. "What a huntsman I should be if it weren't for the leaps!": most of us say that in one connexion or another. Most delicious of all, perhaps, is Jorrocks's sigh as he pounded along all elbows and legs, ribroasting Arterxerxes, on the great Cat and Custard Pot day; "How I wish I was a heagle!" That is as profound, if not as touching as "'I wish, Trim,' said my uncle Toby, 'that I was in bed.'"

Thus, although for many the main interest of *Handley Cross* lies in the talk of horses and hounds, it is not only to those that have "the bump of Fox-un-ta-tiveness werry strongly deweloped" that the book appeals. For there is the little world of the watering place, with its rival doctors Roger Swizzle and Sebastian Mello, with the preposterous Mrs. Barnington, and the mournful Master of the Ceremonies, done with great zest and an eye for the absurd; and there is that very Dickensian glimpse of seamy London life, with its dingy lawyers' offices, which Surtees knew at first hand; and the strange, sinister figure of Mr. William Bowker, hatching great schemes in the murk of his tobacco shop, and patronizing dog-fights. Surtees, one feels it at every point, had more than the mere novelist's eye which suffices the second-rate novelist; he had the knowledge which comes from an active interest in the doings of men. His range was limited, his apprehensions were not profound, he had no peculiar sensibility, he was, no doubt, rather too complacent; but the whiff of good strong country air is with him wherever he goes. He took a vast delight in life, its ins and outs, its queer characters, its shifts and changes, its unexpectedness.

And this brings us to the last of his claims to popularity, his joyful use of words; for after all it is for their words we read authors as much as for what they have to tell us. Idiom is the salt which keeps fresh the meat which might otherwise have lost its savour. Surtees is full of phrases, not unforgettable, certainly, but which make their mark so that we remember them with a smile when we meet them again—there is, to give one instance, "the tremendous discharge of popularity" which greeted Major Yammerton's speech at Lord Ladythorne's hunt breakfast. But it is rather the vigour, the brio, of the tumbling flow of words which carries us on, whether he is describing a meet or a meal, a dance or a journey; all the clash and clatter is there. He is careless in his writing, no doubt, repeating phrases such as "Third time is killing time"; every comfortable house he describes is "replete" with luxury; the horse "like Gil Blas' mule—all faults," is his veritable King Charles's head. But what does that matter when Lord Scamperdale enlarges the scope of the language in a way that our armies in Flanders would have delighted in; and when Mr. Jorrocks says "Jest put 'em on to me Charley, whilst I make one o' Mr. Craven Smith's all-round-my-'at casts, for that beggar Binjamin's of no more use with a pack of 'ounds than a hopera box

would be to a cow, or a frilled shirt to a pig"? And what could be more ludicrous than the master's concluding a panegyric of himself as a huntsman with a quotation from Cato: "It's not for mortals to command success"?

And even if the words do not linger in the "mind's memory"—there is a Jorrocks's phrase again!—it is they which give vividness to the figures they describe. In the general atmosphere of bustle and movement the figures stand out, and not altogether as puppets. One would recognize them anywhere by their looks alone (for who would fail to greet Sir Harry Scattercash with his strings all flying?); or by their gestures (cannot you hear Mr. Benjamin Buckram letting the coins slide down his pocket, one by one, or in an avalanche?); and one would recognize their horses, for who would not be ashamed to see Arterxerxes or Multum-in-Parvo go by without knowing them by name? But in letting the mind wander over the novels it is detached scenes or gestures that we see, phrases that we hear: Mr. Jorrocks dashes his vig and dances with glee about the fox's corpse; or he is floundering through Pinch-me-Near Forest; or drowning in the bath at Ongar Park: Soapey Sponge canons into Lord Scamperdale, who screams out "Just because you think I'm a Lord and can't swear or use coarse words," before launching out into one of his most lurid torrents; Facey Romford gets his hounds round him with the help of his pretended sister, the late Lucy Glitters; Mr. Jogglebury Crowdey wheezes where the verbs ought to be, and Sir Harry replaces his nouns with a hiccup; that good sportsman Mr. Jovey Jessop gives the office of Jug to his friend Boyston, who is thereby empowered to drink all that his patron cannot hold; Binjamin sticks his fingers into the marmeylad; old Sivin-and-four's-Ilivin the banker counts his bills; Gabriel Junks the peacock prophesies the weather: Mr. Jorrocks in the ecstasy of his fox-hunting dreams kicks his wife out of bed; and over all of them hovers the airy spirit of James Pigg, that racy *lusus naturae,* or loose 'un by nature, invoking Canninewcassel and his cousin Deavilboger, and keeping the tambourine a-rowling while he offers you a gob of tobacco.

Whether or not we have rolled the fox over, or have run him to earth, or have lost the scent completely, there can be no doubt that Surtees is still popular.... (pp. 257-58)

> [*Bonamy Dobrée*], *"Robert Smith Surtees," in* The Times Literary Supplement, *No. 1469, March 27, 1930, pp. 257-58.*

W. L. RENWICK (essay date 1932)

[*In the following extract from an imaginary conversation between two literati named Aelius and Barbarus, Renwick illustrates the ongoing critical debate over the value of reading Surtees' works.*]

[*Ael.*] Nobody, I fancy, reads Surtees, except the sporting illiterates of the Counties, who read nothing else but *The Field,* and perhaps *The Autocar.*

Bar. Don't be uppish. Surtees was good enough for Thackeray and John Gibson Lockhart and William Morris, and lots more of your intellectual as well as your social superiors. Your brilliant youth who convulses his coterie with his subtleties and audacities may be a significant and even an important phenomenon, but the man whose work is read with delight, during three generations, by the multitude of the non-literary, can hardly be brushed aside; and he may have more influence on the world at large.... And you have enjoyed Surtees yourself: haven't you now?

Ael. Yes, when I read him long ago, but one reads so uncritically at that age.

Bar. Don't we lose as well as gain by academic habits of reading? Come now, what do you object to in him?

Ael. For one obvious thing, his style. Half his writing moves on eighteenth-century stilts, and shaky ones at that, and the other half is mere vulgar rambling, full of the facetious topical jauntiness of the sporting journalist. It dates so badly, and it's so slovenly.

Bar. I grant you both, within reason. He wasn't fastidious by nature or by training, and he lacked a fastidious audience. But isn't there a third kind in him? Doesn't he sometimes forget both the genteel and the knowing mannerisms when he describes a horse or a hunt, and write clearly and forcibly as he gets excited? Look at bits of **Soapy Sponge** or **Facey Romford**— or for that matter Mr. Jorrocks's own discourses—how he crashes on, over hedge and ditch, sometimes nearly bogged in a complicated series of subordinate clauses, scratched and torn by unrelated participles, sometimes nearly unhorsed trying to take a bit of description faster than the difficult place will allow, but stretching out as the going gets clearer, and coming in at the death with a whoop, and enjoying every minute of it. (pp. 77-8)

Ael. But allowing that he could write excited prose, think of the construction, or lack of construction, in his so-called novels. The merest picaresque.

Bar. There's a good deal to be said for the picaresque. It's better than a collection of the short stories we used to be so precious about, and more difficult. And isn't life rather picaresque? Suppose you write down your adventures in the War, from your first disastrous interview with a Regular adjutant to what happened the night you were demobilized—won't the result be picaresque?

Ael. Don't make me out a Lazarillo de Tormes. I was a perfectly respectable if entirely undistinguished junior officer of His Majesty's Land Forces, trusty and well-beloved. But even if I agreed, life isn't literature, memoirs aren't novels, and a novel should have some sort of construction about it.

Bar. I suppose so, though I'm tired of young men's novels that are hugely praised because the bones show through. Surtees always did retain something of the monthly journalist of *The New Sporting Magazine*. All his books are **Jaunts and Jollities**. But we must take what the gods give. His plots haven't the interest of logical relation, or of the working-out of a theme; but they have other virtues. In the picaresque, all the more weight is thrown on incident, because the other interests are discarded; the incidents must be vivid and exciting and real: and those of Surtees are, very, very often. That's something. And in his later works at least, Surtees has the other necessary virtue: ingenuity in the linking-up of his incidents, in devising neat turns and transitions of narrative. Look at **Mr. Facey Romford's Hounds** again, and you'll see how he solved the problem (as the young men from Oxford would say) of showing two different sorts of mastership in one book, by making the same lady and the same horse the cause of Mr. Romford's losing one pack and getting into touch with the other. Surtees is like Spenser in that.

Ael. Congruous comparison!

Bar. I'm full of congruous comparisons. Haven't you noticed that? It's what I call Criticism. Smollett, then, if you jib at Spenser. The Smollett mark is plain to see. You'll notice that Smollett and all his heirs, from Dickens down through Mr. Wells to Mr. Sinclair Lewis, have this about them, that their men have to think about their bread and butter. The Psychological Analysts always omit the two things that make most difference to a man, his job and his current account. . . . However, we were discussing Surtees, not . . . the psychological complications of Daily Bread. There's another mark of the Smollett clan, that the adventures happen among strangers. The hero is usually sent travelling, and is never at home living what you would call a normal social life.

Ael. And a good job too, so far as Surtees is concerned. As a social novelist he is as low as can be, a coarsened caricature of the worst of his friend Thackeray. I grant you he was a man's man. Drawing-rooms aren't his natural habitat. But though his men are usually understandable, he has that hateful common pose of his time, that semi-cynical and wholly patronizing tone about women, the tone of the Regency rake with the edge off. Except for one or two Sporting Females, his women may be classified as the shrewish or the cuddlesome, and I detest both— and the Sporting Female too, for that matter.

Bar. Let us say that he ignored the more subtle and complex movements of human machinery. But isn't this knowledge-of-the-world-my-boy business, like the monstrous eating and still more monstrous drinking, at least in part a question of Fashion—literary Fashion as much as social? We must always remember to allow for Fashion and Snobbery in literature as well as in clothes and manners and surgery. It is true, though, that the social value, the criticism of life, in Surtees, is limited pretty strictly to the one standard—I won't say the only one he knew, for that would obviously be wrong, but the one he allowed to appear in his books—the standard of the gentleman sportsman.

Ael. I groan. I'm weary of sportsmanship. You remember the lectures they used to inflict on us behind the Line, holding up The Sportsmanship Of The English Public Schoolboy as a shining ideal for honest journeymen soldiers to adore as an ikon? . . . The English Public Schoolboy is dead already, thank goodness, except perhaps in Kenya.

Bar. I'm very much with you. . . . You can talk about Sportsmanship, because it's vague, unintellectual, adolescent, and lazy, and therefore suits the English. But you'll notice I said 'gentleman sportsman'. 'Gentleman' is deader than Public Schoolboy and that's not so lucky. The English have lost all that was valuable in their snobbery and kept the rest. But Surtees had his double standard, and kept his values separate, and that is where he is so superior to the prize-givers and the Indian Army Majors we suffered under. And he meant to make it clear; like every other writer of importance, he regarded his work as instructive as well as recreative—like Sir Philip Sidney, Said He, using another congruous comparison. Because Mr. Facey Romford is a fine horseman and a clever huntsman, scrupulously fair to his horses, his hounds, his foxes, and his field, it does not follow that he is by any means a fine character in other ways; and on the other hand, because Mr. Soapy Sponge is a trifle indelicate in financial affairs, his creator, who made him for the purpose of showing up a shady type of young man, does not deny him certain qualities in the field and even out of it. Indeed, much of his moral and worldly-wise instruction proceeds out of the mouth of his somewhat dubious characters, just as his sporting instruction comes from the entirely comic one of Jorrocks. That makes it the more telling, and also shows his appreciation of the fact that the least admirable of men of this world usually has his code—the good things he will always do, and the evil things he is not fool or blackguard enough to do. He preached sport in itself and for its own sake, which is where the Public School moralists go wrong, for they extend Sportsmanship into fields where it doesn't belong. . . . (pp. 78-81)

Ael. But we were talking books, and it's late at night for moral philosophy. Take it that Surtees showed one virtue in action, and had a deal of the wisdom of the billiard-room. That's a small field and a low one.

Bar. Is there any 'high' and 'low' in art?

Ael. There is in life, anyhow—we seem to be changing places—and, with all deference to Signor Croce, the artist is concerned with life. And unfortunately the horse is usually to be found in lowish surrounding, among Gentlemen Who Always Pay, and most ignoble knaves.

Bar. But not Surtees. He hated all that business. What would *The Sporting and Dramatic,* not to mention *The Daily Herald,* do with a journalist whose only sign of interest, when he was 'covering' Goodwood, was the remark, 'Was much gratified by the scenery'? His recognition of the mixed character was not merely weak tolerance. There were things and people Surtees could not stand: gamblers, dilettante sportsmen whose heart was not in the game, jealous sportsmen, dishonest grooms, and quasi-amateurs who lived by what they pretended was their recreation—he hated them as he hated dirty land and neglected drains, and all the minor dishonesties and slacknesses and insincerities. It is this that makes him so sound, in spite of the drunkennesses and the practical jokes our modern manners dislike. Even at that, he wrote of *The New Sporting Magazine*—here it is in Mr. Cuming's Life of him—'We had expressly stated in our prospectus that Prize-fighting, Bull-baiting, and Cock-fighting were low and demoralizing pursuits, and all reference thereto was to be excluded from our pages.' His idea of sportsmanship is perfectly sound: sport must be free from brutality, an end in itself, with enjoyment as its only reward—he always deprecated the competitive element, as you'll see in the end of *Soapy Sponge*—and he recognized its limitations.

Ael. I've already granted you all that. But it's no great contribution to literature.

Bar. It's a contribution, anyhow. Set Surtees alongside of Thackeray and Dickens and he appears as a very minor novelist, but he is not obscured by them, or superseded by them, as Scott, for instance, superseded the Clara Reeves and obscures the Harrison Ainsworths. In his minor class Marryat is a better artist, but Marryat and Surtees do not compete. Must we always be putting writers into a scale of merit? Isn't it more useful sometimes to place them side by side, to see how they fit into each other, what country they cover and whether they overlap? Then, if we must, we can begin classifying according to value. If we take England of the 30's to the 50's—England growing out of the Regency into the Victorian Age—we have Thackeray for middle-class society and journalism; Thomas Love Peacock for literature, finance, ideas; Dickens for the poor and the law; Charlotte Brontë for the Industrial Revolution and Emily for the moorlands; Marryat for the sea, and Surtees for the hunting and farming folk.

Ael. It had been done before. What about Addison's Tory Foxhunter, and Squire Western, and the Osbaldestones? And what about the Border sports in *Guy Mannering?*

Bar. These are all barbarians, looked at from the outside by civilized writers; and as for *Guy Mannering,* Scott had no part in the scientific study of sport that had been interesting English country gentlemen for a generation. Surtees knew it all from the inside; he ranges with Beckford and Colonel Hawker as well as with Smollett and Marryat. And as the mouthpiece of a great and worthy company, their ideas and their interests, he is, recognizably at the first glance, authentic.

Ael. He may have been inside all that, but his characters don't look like it. What was Carlyle's phrase about Scott—that he described people from the outside and not from the inside?

Bar. I think nane the mair o' Tam for that. Any artist is free to choose his own way of doing things, and why not the natural way? We only do see the outsides of people at first, and then, gradually if at all, their appearance, actions, idiosyncrasies, tics and tricks, enable us to build up some idea of what they are like inside. Why should not a novelist present his people in the same way? It was Chaucer's way, and Surtees, like Chaucer, like every writer who writes like a man of the world and not like a scientist or a theorist, differentiates people first by their clothes, their faces, their tricks of speech, their favourite songs and stories, and so they are all recognizable and consistent, in a human natural sort of way, without becoming abstractions.

Ael. But what are these people? They mean nothing to the great movements of thought of their time or ours. Think of all that happened in Surtees's time, and how little reflection of it there is in his books.

Bar. My dear *Aelius,* remember that most people are oblivious of the great movements of their time. Surely you are old enough to avoid the error of thinking of England in the nineteenth century as inhabited exclusively by Byrons and Shelleys and their victims—so many Castlereaghs—succeeded by a generation of George Eliots and Darwins and Newmans.

Ael. They are the ones who matter; the rest are dead.

Bar. More's the pity, perhaps: we over-concentrate on the picturesque. But anyhow they were alive, and are you, as a democrat, arguing that the majority is negligible? Take a simple case in Surtees: the railway expansion of his time, and its very important social implications—you could make a nice little sketch of social history out of "The Railways in Literature". You could show how Thackeray found them vulgar, but amusing for the opportunities they gave of snap-shotting people; how they provided Dickens with an arabesque paragraph; how in Peacock's eyes they were the excuse for wild, stupid gambling and cheating. You would have to bring in Surtees, and there you would find they were an abomination because they dirtied the countryside, but at the same time a convenience to a man who wanted to get out of town to hunt, or across country to see a horse. His attitude is quite simple and natural: if people go and build railways for our convenience, we'll use them when it suits our convenience. Not very politically-economical and all that sort of thing, but isn't it how we all regard the railways? There is always a majority of decent ordinary folk, who take things as they come; it is something to be their interpreter.

Ael. And it has the advantage that there's not much to interpret. You're doing your best, but really, is there anything in Surtees but descriptions of hunting?

Bar. Even if there were nothing else, there we get at his real value. It's more complicated than it looks. First of all notice

Mr. Jorrocks (loq.) "Come hup! I say...You ugly Beast!"

Jorrocks uttering one of his most famous sayings during a hunt in Handley Cross, *illustrated by Leech.*

that when Surtees gets into the country he's in his own element. His young ladies may be insipid, stupid, rapacious; his horses are interesting and sensible individuals. There is nothing factitious about him now, nothing pumped-up, like Wilde, or palpably got up for the occasion, like Sinclair Lewis in *Martin Arrowsmith*. He knew what he was talking about, and once he leaves the attempt at social satire and arrives in his own province—I should say his own *country*—he is absolutely sincere, unconstrained, and therefore admirable. Now he draws on his own experience, from the early journalistic days when he visited famous hunts with a critical eye, to his later life as a dignified squire with the North Riding, the Slaley, and Lord Elcho's. In the country, among horses and hounds, he is back at home—either in the country of his youth round London, or in the North. People argue whether 'Handley Cross' is Leamington or Shotley Bridge; it's probably both. 'Rosebery Rocks' is Brighton. But when it is not Surrey it's Northumberland and Durham and North Yorkshire. The dialect of his countrymen is always the one familiar to him since childhood. . . . And when he describes a run, the names are made on familiar patterns; wouldn't you look up Tomlinson's *Guide to Northumberland* if some one asked you where are *Corsenside Lane, Howell Burn, Winforth Rig, Birdshope, Kidland Hill?* I've just picked them out of **Handley Cross** here. He remembers days above Slaley, or round Belford, and he plays with names just as Milton did.

Ael. More congruous comparisons!

Bar. And good ones. Surtees uses a name to give flavour and definition to a phrase, just as, I insist, Milton did. Milton liked geography, and Surtees had the huntsman's sense of topography. Mr. Jorrocks may be lost, but his creator never is. Each pack has its country, and though it may be pieced together from different places, the country has definite shape, features, and directions. It may not be possible to follow a point on the Ordnance Survey map, as you might follow one by *The Field*'s report, but that is only because the map happens not to exist, not because the run takes place across a cloudland or because it is only a series of snapshots. That's more difficult than it sounds, creating an imaginary stretch of country that is convincing, and doing it without elaborate set description and without a map—though maps are delectable things and an ornament to any book—and making the reader gradually acquainted with it, so that he instinctively orientates himself as he reads: that's a triumph. And it isn't enough to be there—a man must see, notice, be keen in wits and senses, to convey the lie of ground and the character of country as Surtees does. You feel the same thing in his weather. There's more English weather in Surtees than anywhere I know, except England. Sometimes he sets himself to describe a particular day, but it's there all the time. The wind of The World Turned Upside Down Day in **Handley Cross** is elaborately described—though not fancifully as Dickens would have done it—but it is usually something so simple and telling that I could scarcely pick it out for you. Here's a scrap in *Mr. Sponge's Sporting Tour:*

> Who does not know the chilling feel of an English spring, or rather of a day at the turn of the year before there is any spring? Our gala-day was a perfect specimen of the order—a white frost, succeeded by a bright sun, with an east wind, warming one side of the face and starving the other. It was neither a day for fishing, nor hunting, nor coursing, nor anything but farming. The country, save where there were a few lingering patches of turnips, was all one dingy drab, with abundant scalds on the undrained fallows. The grass was more like hemp than anything else. The very rushes were yellow and sickly.

That's the North: and so simply done, no fine writing, no arabesque, no pumping-up: just the farmer's eye and the feel on your skin. Don't tell me that man couldn't write. And when we remember that this is the prologue to the description of a steeple-chase, a thing Surtees loathed and despised, don't tell me he knew nothing about the art of ironical planning.

Ael. Suppose I grant the authenticity of his horses and hunts and coverts and so on. I'm told hunting-folk swear by him. Then I ask, what is that to you? You admit yourself that he is a very minor novelist, and good only in the hunting-field. Do you then have three days a week and a bye-day with the Tynedale or the Braes of Derwent?

Bar. Not by quite a bit. The only times I ever got across a horse were when my Colonel said I jolly well had to. But don't you see? That's just it! I don't hunt; I don't even ride on the Town Moor: and I read Surtees with something warmer than mere pleasure.

Ael. Isn't it Mr. Birrell who describes the gentle lady at the dinner-party lamenting the decadence of the prize-fighters of England? She was bemused with Borrow; you seem to be bemused with Surtees. There was more excuse for her.

Bar. Perhaps; but the cause is the same. Borrow and Surtees have the one great and essential gift—enthusiasm, gusto, zest— call it what you like. The real gusto that is fed on experience, on the beef of life and not the red peppers and cocktails. . . . And you'll notice a queer thing: with all our English sportiveness, there's mighty little of this enthusiasm for sport in creative literature. . . . You golf—I've heard you bragging about your approach at the ninth and so on—now golf has the great advantage of being a primitive game, in which you employ skill to defeat distance, weather, and vegetation; and the employment of skill is the sheerest of joys, and, if the spiritualistic aestheticians would only believe it, a main element in art. But you also fish, which is the saving of you. Now tell me: isn't the thrill of holing a long putt quite different from the thrill of playing a lively trout?

Ael. Ye-es, yes. But where does that get us to?

Bar. This. England being a badly over-populated country, the English exercise themselves in artificial ball games, played within certain arbitrary rules devised merely to enforce a certain appropriate kind of skill, and no other. . . . So the English idea of sportsmanship is, two sides or two men or two young ladies—known to every cheap reporter by their Christian names— playing a game according to the rules. In fishing and hunting you play according to nature. . . . [My] point is this, that in life and in literature, wherein life is the quarry, you are dealing with nature, not playing an artificial game according to arbitrary and universally understood rules. That's why 'cricket' emasculated English foreign policy and sent you and me into the Line, and that's why so many modern novelists are dull. They are eternally thinking of the rules of the game, and there aren't any. So one page of St. John's *Wild Sports in the Highlands* makes *Point-Counter-Point* look like a six-cylinder motor-engine decorated with lip-stick, and so Surtees in the hunting-field, being natural, is full of that peculiar thrill you get from rising and playing a good fish, but don't get from holing the longest of putts. And it's got to be there, whether you are stalking deer on the hill or character in a pub—the thing that's so much needed just now, that's so difficult to communicate and yet can be communicated so subtly and so completely— the thing Smollett had, the love of the spectacle of life, even if it were only two blackguards kicking one another—the thing Jane Austen had, though it were only a lady and gentleman conversing over breakfast—the thing all the great ones had— gusto, enthusiasm, infectious zest for just being.

Ael. You were Crocean and are now Tolstoyan—the infection theory.

Bar. Infection fact—only don't think it accounts for everything—and Tolstoy had it too. Experience and gusto: there's the formula for the novel, though it's no good to the American University Courses or the coteries on the *terrasse* of the Rotonde.

Ael. Then I'm to tell all my young literary friends to study Surtees and be saved?

Bar. Yes. And Henry James. And Marcel Proust. And Thackeray and Stendhal and Sterne and Fielding and a whole lot more. And have them observe that all these great ones have beef on their bones.

It is late, and we may leave them arguing. (pp. 81-9)

> W. L. Renwick, "Jorrocks: A Conversation," in Essays and Studies by Members of the English Association, Vol XVII, *edited by W. H. Hadow, Oxford at the Clarendon Press, Oxford, 1932, pp. 76-89.*

ANTHONY STEEL   (essay date 1933)

[*Steel's* Jorrocks's England *is a sociological study of mid-Victorian life based on Surtees' works. In his introduction, excerpted below, Steel argues that Surtees' writings provide valuable insight into the social customs of his day.*]

Most people who write books, historians, literary authorities, or what not, have not even read [Surtees], or else have had the edge taken off their appetite by beginning in chronological order with the work which should be read last—namely, *Jorrocks's Jaunts and Jollities.* There are in fact large numbers of people who will not read Surtees because they do not hunt, care nothing for hunting, and yet—this is the odd thing— profess an interest in the middle-class life and literature of England during the nineteenth century. As if, in any case, Surtees meant hunting and nothing more! (pp. 1-2)

There is, however, a persistent delusion that Surtees writes about nothing but hunting, that his characters are practically always on the hunting-field, and away from it do not exist. Actually, his is a wider England, an England in which hunting is only one of many activities not all concerned with sport. This England included not only the upper, but most of the middle, classes in both town and country; that is, outside the great industrial areas. If it is first and foremost Jorrocks's England, it is still no inconsiderable part of the real England: politically speaking, it represents a fair proportion of the England which votes between 1832 and 1867. Surtees lived through this period—he died in 1864—and his writing life almost exactly coincided with it. Within his limits he was an interested and a close and accurate observer. He represents the view of the squire, the county magistrate, the farmer; he is acquainted with, and describes very fully, middle-class life in general, both in London and the provinces—very fully because, though he was emphatically not writing for posterity, he was definitely satirizing his daily life for the amusement of people who shared it with him.

His limits are immediately obvious. He is not interested in religion, or in economic development in the technical sense, except perhaps in agriculture; he is not deeply interested in social problems, in foreign or imperial affairs of any kind, or even in Scotland, Wales or Ireland, or in education or literature to any great extent, or in politics or administration as such, except where they directly and personally concern him, or in science, art or architecture at all, or in the Court or in high society, except in so far as the latter unbends towards the middle classes in the shires, usually for political purposes.

On the other hand, he *is* deeply interested in farming and in the means of communicating with others and of getting about England, and he is interested, more superficially, in the Law and in professional life. In sport his sphere is narrower than is sometimes supposed. He has little use for games of any kind, for racing, which he attacks, or for coursing, and Heaven knows what he would have thought of electric hares: he barely admires horsemanship as such—Jorrocks's riding is consistently made fun of—and he goes out of his way to attack it when practised in steeplechases as an end in itself. He tolerates shooting and harriers, but hardly mentions fishing. He is essentially a landsman, and pays not the least attention to the current cant about the inborn and necessary interest of every native Englishman in the sea: yachting, travel by water and the navy are all practically ignored, and even steamboats have quite evidently none of the fascination for him possessed by railways. He goes out of his way to ridicule the army, but seldom bothers about sailors to any great degree; thus though one or two caricatures of naval men are introduced into his hunting-fields, they are far outnumbered by his ludicrous soldiers, yeomanry and militia. Watching, and hearing, hounds work is in effect the essence of his sporting life, and comprises practically everything that hunting means to him. It is true he has an eye for country, not only in the hunting sense: he was evidently influenced by natural surroundings, and attempts a rather self-conscious, but not unhappy, landscape on more than one occasion. Again, when he is not thinking about a formal representation, he is full of pleasant tributes to the countryside. But this sort of thing, except in a master's hand, is apt to border on the sentimental, and sentimentality and prudery, those alleged traits of the well-to-do Victorians, were alike anathema to him. If such are his limitations, what is there left? There is more than might be supposed.

After all, farming, travelling even within England, and middle-class life in general, are considerable subjects in themselves, especially when we remember that they were all undergoing rapid and far-reaching changes in Surtees' day, changes which he was fully conscious of and eagerly describes. 'Farming' includes such topics as the formation of agricultural associa-

tions, anti-Corn-Law activities, drainage, game-laws, land-agents, tenants and land-owners, manures, soils, stock-breeding and forestry, though curiously little about technical improvements; 'travelling', besides railways, memories of coaching and detailed descriptions of every kind of horse vehicle from phaetons to omnibuses, such things as inns, canals, caravans, roads, posts, the electric telegraph and turn-pike gates. Other topics which absorb him at times are business affairs, from the point of view of the investor, the private banker and the tradesman, trivial things in everyday use from food to furniture and costume, male as much as female, while even children's fashions and hairdressing are not neglected. More than any other Victorian novelist Surtees tells us in lavish detail in what sort of houses his characters lived, how they furnished them, what they wore and used and ate and drank from day to day; and we have come near to forgetting in the process of time how immensely varied all these things were three generations ago. Surtees was more observant: it was, in fact, precisely their oddity and variety which astonished him—a rare gift in a contemporary—and impelled him to record them. He is full of formidable interiors, town and country, haunted by the grotesque fashions of the time, and balanced precariously in the half-light of guttering candles between the extremes of heat and cold.

Another topic on which he has much to say is always of interest, that of servants, and the prevalent illusion that here too the nineteenth century witnessed a golden age is immediately dispelled. He writes a good deal of women in general and their place in everyday life, says something about doctors and diseases, and a good deal about watering-places, inland and marine, together with their curious society.

However, all this is anticipating. It is probably clear enough by now that Surtees' characters are, or so it is claimed, presented as human beings, with all the multifarious activities of human beings; that Surtees in short would have found the 'hunting man', pure and simple, as unreal an abstraction as we ourselves have been taught to find the 'economic man' of his contemporaries. Of course his portraits are caricatured, for even in his chosen field Surtees does not adequately describe the best establishments of his day, but embroiders richly upon eccentricities. His strongly drawn studies, touched with just that element of exaggeration which makes them easy to identify, will persist as long as human nature, no matter how surrounded or employed, but in the novels they are put through the tricks of a circus, the better to exhibit their quality, while the paraphernalia and background of their extraordinary careers are sometimes almost equally distorted, and in any case wholly strange.

But how the people live! They swarm out from his pages in a boisterous, unruly crowd, until it is almost difficult to distinguish faces among them, though one can always hear the great voices of Jorrocks and James Pigg bellowing above the rest. They *were* the substantial, semi-barbarous middle classes of that day; that is why they are still recognizable in the living bodies of their descendants. At all times since their original creation the great mass of the inarticulately masculine and prosperous have seen, if not themselves, at least their friends, acquaintances and relations mirrored in these books. That is why it is not only interesting but important to study them, and not only their own selves, but, always allowing for the element of exaggeration, their interests and activities, and the way in which they lived. (pp. 2-6)

Jorrocks's England, though one England out of many, is perhaps uniquely unfortunate in having been overlaid and crusted with a mass of different associations and predominantly alien memories. What was built on it is no doubt more important, for the house is of greater interest than the foundations, and moreover only one small corner of the Victorian mansion rests upon it; yet in order to appreciate a building we must know something of the ground-plan after all. . . . [In] the novels of Surtees lying ready to our hands, there is the sketch we need, a picture which, with all its faults of violence and exaggeration, has attracted kindred spirits since it was first executed, and yet has come to represent a reality which is increasingly strange to us. We shall find it sturdily insular, immensely English; though it is not an aggressive nationalism. Few writers, indeed, have been more essentially pacific than Surtees: the budding 'Jingoism' of the Crimean War—to anticipate a convenient term by twenty years—was utterly repugnant to him, if only through its lack of humour, though his objections went deeper than that, and it finds no place in his work. Still, beneath all his apparent cynicism this quiet country magistrate conceals the usual vein of English sentiment, and can admire with anyone, for all his hatred of militarism, the 'hobbling, frosty-pated, wound-scarred, old cocks of the Peninsula'. (pp. 7-8)

> *Anthony Steel, in his* Jorrocks's England, *E. P. Dutton and Company Inc. Publishers, 1933, 303 p.*

FREDERICK WATSON (essay date 1933)

[*Arguing that Surtees deserves serious critical attention, Watson analyzes what he considers to be the three most important aspects of his art: his satire, comic characters, and energetic, colloquial style.*]

In a review of a recent edition of Surtees' novels a discerning critic reflected upon the great good fortune of this novelist in evading so unobtrusively, and yet over so long a period, both the enthusiasm and patronage of the superior person. He has not throughout the last eighty years suffered from sham reverence. He is a remarkable, almost a solitary, example of a writer of definite quality who has been permitted to reach an established position without the benediction of indiscriminating applause or the condemnation of academic criticism. (p. 255)

[Between] the publication of *Jorrocks's Jaunts and Jollities* in 1838 and his death in 1864 the success of Surtees, both among fox-hunters and the general public, was so moderate that, although his books survived, their prospects were not encouraging. In a word, Surtees' place in literature could hardly have been regarded seriously until the eighties. Fifty years later the most obvious claim to the qualities of permanence lies in the rugged fact that no author continues to live unless his work is removed beyond the ephemeral, and possesses at least sincerity and imagination. And yet there are admittedly signs of permanent attainment.

There comes a time in the career of a novelist exceptionally gifted—that is, gifted in the creation of character—when the man in the street includes the figures of his fiction in his own family circle. Dickens is the classic example. It is sometimes a little difficult to believe Micawber—that refuge of political controversy—never existed, or Sherlock Holmes—to take a

Leech's rendition of James Pigg crashing into the melon frame, from Handley Cross.

less effulgent modern instance—was unknown in Baker Street. Fame of this character is perhaps the best tribute to an author, because it is the unconscious recognition of common life. So when, in 1864, Whyte-Melville wrote to Colonel Anstruther Thomson and said as an aside, ''The longer I live the more cause I have to agree with Mr Jorrocks 'that all time is wasted that is not spent in hunting,''' he took it for granted that Jorrocks was a commonplace to his correspondent, which makes the year 1864 something of a landmark in Surtees' progress.

But it still remains that Surtees' smooth passage down the years may be claimed as fortunate. Where the books of others of equal or greater merit have departed, why is it that his novels have triumphed over changes in fashion and thought, during crises and wars, and taken an unexpected place among standard fiction? . . . Surtees was not a best-seller, even with a hunting public. But that does not mean his preservation has not been dependent throughout good and bad spells upon a public which, from father to son, has come to regard him as its particular classic. Upon that there can be no argument. Just as Scott is admired by the intelligent reader, and also read as a kind of patriotic duty by every Scotsman, so, in a much lesser degree, Surtees has been bought and read as a matter of course wherever hounds are followed. So it will be as long as fox-hunting exists. (pp. 255-56)

It is a great advantage for any man to write about a subject, whether it is a science or a sport, which suffers little change, and he would be a rash prophet who would wager that *Handley Cross* will not be read in A.D. 2000. But if this steadfast public which comes to few authors over a century may be admitted to have kept Surtees' books in circulation it still remains, as a secondary problem, to be discussed whether his novels can be judged by ambitious critical standards or whether they have been justly dismissed as 'merely sporting.'

A critical estimate of Surtees' novels must concentrate in the end upon three distinct qualifications for serious attention. He was a satirist, if not upon his great level, at least quite worthy of Thackeray's unqualified praise; he was a creator of genuine comic characters; and he wrote with an infectious enthusiasm which is so rare that it has gone far to give him a special niche in English literature. Let us take these points in their sequence.

''Wit, my lords,'' wrote Lord Chesterfield, ''is a sort of property; it is the property of those that have it, and too often the only property.'' So it was with Surtees, and, to do him justice, he recognized the severe limitations of satire, and as he could only write with original genius about ignoble people he proceeded to do so with hardly a false step.

He was lacking in practically all the most attractive and humane qualities of a great and successful writer. He was destitute of romance, sentiment, and reverence. He hit one nail on the head, and that nail was satirical comedy. It is an attitude of art more unpopular than any other because it is cold, uncomfortable, and narrow. But, as Surtees knew and said with truth, ''Most men take a pleasure in satire when it is not aimed at themselves.'' He, like Thackeray, to whom he came nearest in his attitude, wrote with fine scorn of parasites, toadies, vulgarians, and snobs, but, unlike Thackeray, he resisted the prevalent habit of preaching. To him the humanities in fiction came very hardly, and as an artist he shrank from following current demands to the weakening of his limited genius.

Surtees in that *genre* had modelled his attitude and style upon Fielding. Both exposed weakness and knavery, both wrote with meticulous observation and even temperature. Neither suc-

ceeded in portraying women (unless one includes Amelia), and when Thackeray wrote of the greater man's genius that it was ''wonderfully wise and detective; it flashes upon a rogue and lightens up a rascal like a policeman's lantern,'' he might, upon a lesser stage, have included the author of *Mr Sponge's Sporting Tour*. This imperturbable loyalty of Surtees to realism is so significant that it calls for elaboration. It is known that Thackeray loved old Jorrocks, treasured Sponge, and said so. But the author of *Vanity Fair* could not exclude sentiment, and he abandoned the narrow path of satire. ''Oh for a little manly, honest, God-relying simplicity—cheerful, unaffected, and humble,'' he had prayed. But Surtees did not kneel with him. Instead, he created Scamperdale and Spraggon, in whom there is nothing simple or humble, but a great deal of beer and beef with the elementary school left out.

In his character-sketch of ''Captain Rook and Mr Pigeon,'' which in itself sounds like a chapter out of Surtees, Thackeray has commented, ''Wherever shines the sun, you are sure to find folly basking in it. Knavery is the shadow at folly's heels.'' If Surtees preferred the shadow, instead of the footlights, of the human scene one may regret it, but there is no justification whatever for assuming that knavery is not as interesting or as prevalent as honesty. To-day the presentation of types entirely relieved of any beauty of life or character is applauded rather than denounced. Realism is all the rage, and the occupants of the Surtees gallery are, as a consequence, treated as human beings, however conscienceless. The refusal to believe in crude, savage, and vulgar people has given place to an unbiased appreciation of the art by which even curiosities of life may become classics of literature. What is more, the wider knowledge of all classes of men has compelled or persuaded the modern reader to realize that the 'nasty people' of Surtees were, like the giraffe, only astonishing so long as people preferred to deny their existence. Today it is no longer rather shocking to discover that peasants are not as simple as a pastoral idyll, that farmers, like commercial travellers, are not confirmed ascetics, and that a squire may be a Scamperdale and still remain a most accurate portrait. (pp. 257-59)

It is . . . likely that Surtees' acceptance of the stoical was drawn from his own temperament and times rather than from any preference for brutality. ''One thing is quite certain,'' he wrote, ''you can't buy experience with another man's money,'' and if his people were 'nasty' or 'inhuman' that does not mean they were not genuine.

It is much the same with his satire. Here was the man himself directing his keen, ruthless gaze in search of what suited his narrow path. Remote, inscrutable, taciturn—he has left more than a tradition for a nature unkindly, cold, and uncompanionable. Like man, like satire, one may presume. But even then, had Surtees been small-minded or merely a snarling, jaundiced fellow, he could have claimed no place in literature. His people may, with a few exceptions, be singularly relieved of idealism, but they are not savage caricatures. Mr Sponge could be no other than Mr Sponge, and, given the splendid opportunities of old Heartycheer, he could hardly be drawn like a rural dean. Surtees drew the line, not merely somewhere, but rigidly on the safe side of humanity, which is more than could be said of some of his successors. In his novels are no blasphemies, seductions, scenes of cruelty, or passages sneering at what is good or beautiful or sacred to simple people. If his place in literature may be counted among the satirists it is because his satire is removed from personal spite, and not cheapened by the consistent posturing of the professional cynic.

He was, in fact, a gentleman in his traditional sense of the decencies, and when one says that it is no less important to remember he was also a democrat in his hatred of injustice. To read his remarkable letter to *The Times* appealing for mercy for the inmates of Southwark Workhouse is to grasp this profound truth—that the satirist upon occasions differs from the sentimentalist only in his line of approach. When Jorrocks remarked, "He is the best poor man's friend wot gives him a good day's pay for a good day's work," he would not have brought down the house, but it would be impossible to mistake his shrewd compassion.

Surtees cherished, like Jane Austen, not a little of the traditional old maid in his spiteful conclusions, his meticulous eye for detail, his reverence for propriety, and his shrewish hesitancy regarding human motives. Not only did human passion fail to move him, but he actually suspected its complications and prophesied its catastrophes. He employed the same petty preference for surface values, the same bloodless contempt for human frailties, the same eye at the wrong end of the telescope, as the author of *Pride and Prejudice*. Upon women, for instance, no disappointed female could have written with greater venom and cattishness. But, whether he describes their tawdry garments or their tarnished ideals, his eye is alert with the bland serenity of the cynic, not with the savage rancour of disappointment. To Surtees the race of women was united in one brave adventure, which was the pursuit of man. But if he found it impossible to approach them in the spirit of sanctity his malice was not vindictive. If the attitude was ridiculously overdone it was also infinitely more amusing than one of undiluted reverence. But the point to remember is that it was selective choice, not prejudice, which guided him. (pp. 260-62)

If satire grew upon Surtees in the middle years humour carried him with triumph in his London days, and it is his humour which has established his fame. But, in contradiction of the popular view that humour, to be supreme, must include pathos, the comedy of Surtees is innocent of sentiment. And here again the shadow of disapproval fell, and has not altogether been lifted.

If the comedy of his characters, like that of the immortal sea captains of Mr Jacobs, was an example of the highest standard of humour untouched by pathos, it was not, for that reason, artificial, or merely a clever juggling with phrases, or a succession of farcical situations. "All his fun," wrote Mr Harold Child with truth, "is rooted in human nature" [see Additional Bibliography], and in Surtees' comic characters . . . when they make one laugh it is not by what happens to them but simply by their own rich personalities.

To advance the point a step farther, Surtees' humour—especially in *Jorrocks's Jaunts and Jollities* and *Handley Cross*—is, like that of Dickens, inseparable from the creation of comic characters—not merely one or two great personages upon a big scale, but a gallery of those minor figures which so definitely establish an author's place in fiction. To quote Mr Child once more, "In the invention of comic characters and speech Surtees comes second only to Dickens." Even then what is the final test in such things? John Galsworthy acutely observed, "In those few character creations which endure is a quality which can best, perhaps, be described as homespun yet vital," and concluded, "If one had to give the palm to a single factor in the creation of character it would be to sly, dry humour." Few novelists have exercised so successfully the "sly, dry humour" as Robert Surtees in *Handley Cross,* and who—unless it were Baillie Nicol Jarvie—ever kept the comic within the bounds

of caricature and the homespun as vital and yet as overwhelming as old John Jorrocks?

"Comic characters and speech"—if the unities of personality and dialogue are accepted as a test of creative genius few authors have possessed the power of making their characters live as Jorrocks and Pigg and Sponge lived. But fewer still can create subsidiary people who, within a page, possess sharpness of outline and economy of detail like etchings in process—or at least silhouettes.

In his ironical faculty for dialogue Surtees is relieved of much of the sustained tedium and affectation of some Victorian writers. His joy in words is a sure symptom of natural inspiration. (pp. 262-63)

This joy in words is neither common nor trivial. Half of the pure gold of Jorrocks is the manner in which his problems are, as it were, dramatized by his grotesque similes. "Jest put 'em on to me, Charley," he says, with his customary optimism, "whilst I make one o' Mr Craven Smith's patent all-round-my-'at casts, for that beggar Binjamin's of no more use with a pack of 'ounds than a hopera-box would be to a cow, or a frilled shirt to a pig." And other examples are "sellin' small coals from a donkey-cart out of a quart pot," and "frightenin' rats from a barn wi' the bagpipes at a 'alfpenny a day, and findin' yoursel'."

Taking him all in all, Jorrocks seldom disappoints. Even in *Hillingdon Hall* he convinces one that, whatever happens, it will not be his fault if he is a bore—or is bored. Even his artless complacency is not prosy: "Wot a many things are wantin' to 'unt a country plisantly!" he says, which is true, but a normal observation. Then he adds conclusively, "Things that would never enter the 'ead of a sailor," and leaves one with that sense of surprise which the experts say is half the art of fiction.

This gift of creating comic characters who are not simply diverting but also convincing reached its highest level in Jorrocks. But what of Pigg? He remains the classic huntsman. Or what of Sponge? Never does that quiet and cynical man for an instant say or do anything which does not satisfy our sense of his consistency, however much it may wound our hopes of his conversion. Or old Scamperdale? Or Facey Romford? All these are living people, not caricatures. But are his minor characters less successful? When Lockhart reviewed *Handley Cross* in *The Quarterly Review* he concluded with a warning note that the author must be careful of caricaturing [see excerpt dated 1843]. But if the fun is perhaps a little near the grotesque at times these lesser lights still shine bravely enough. One will not easily forget Jogglebury Crowdey with his carved sticks, and Colonel Blunt, that priceless officer, surely the best representative of the second-rate Victorian C.O. in fiction, and what of the "Jug," that delightful but intemperate gentleman in charge of all the precious children at the Hunt?

Surtees' economy in words was masterly in throwing a minor character on his screen. When one meets Mr Cucumber, the gentleman's gentleman, one knows as much about him as most novelists can express in a full-blown novel. And what about Mr Wotherspoon, most tireless of after-dinner speakers, and the lunatic fox-hunter host encountered by Charley Stobbs?

But the final test must always return to Jorrocks. To those who see nothing beyond vulgarity in *Handley Cross* the novels of Surtees must remain a mystery. But it is not a mystery to be explained away by contempt or liable to expire through critical neglect. Jorrocks lives by personality. He may be a number of things, but he remains a character for ever inseparably associated with a conservative sport. (pp. 264-65)

To the present century Surtees remains the classic novelist on fox-hunting. But his net has, in these days of less stringent moralities, drawn in a substantial body of readers who know nothing whatever about horses or hounds. He was—and here we are on solid ground—intensely *national*. Few novelists—unless it be Trollope or Kingsley—have been so representative of the English temperament. He possessed a second great attraction to the ordinary reader in the colloquial ease of his style, which, if it is not suitable for a text-book on literature, is hard to beat in an armchair on holiday.

Surtees will never be translated into Russian, but wherever the Anglo-Saxon lights his pipe and with an uncritical finger skips an occasional page (or even chapter) the creator of Mr Sponge—*Mr Sponge's Sporting Tour* is perhaps the best book for beginners—will beguile an idle hour—so long as that fleeting joy is permitted the modern citizen. What he possessed was the English fibre of Cobbett—most authentic of countrymen. (pp. 266-67)

Surtees is free from affectation, false sentiment, and long stretches of description. He stands the test of time surprisingly well even against the later Victorian humorists. If the standards of nineteenth-century comedy are examined in the adventures of Mr Briggs or the lectures of Mrs Caudle, it will be observed that the Victorians laughed more heartily at incompetence or henpecking than we are able to do to-day. Their sense of superiority and gentility is extremely dated. Victorian humour, like the furniture of the period, is solid, unavoidable, and depressing. It oozes snobbery, parochialism, and a careful elimination of the lower orders. Just as *The Innocents Abroad* of Mark Twain is almost painful in its revelation of the abysmal legend of American superiority, so Victorian humour was most successful when it was most condescending. The modern humorist prefers not merely to find laughter in the most unexpected surroundings of which the Victorian pretended a bland ignorance, but sympathizes, as do Mr H. G. Wells and Arnold Bennett, with the futility, or incompetence, or absurd aspirations of his characters.

Surtees comes very close to this attitude. He was spared 'gentility,' jingoism, and contemporary standards of literature. A single instance may be noted in the occasion when old Jorrocks dined with the Duke of Donkeyton.

> "Pray, Mr Jorrocks, who was your mother?" inquired his Grace, after he had bowed and drunk off his wine.
>
> "Please, your Greece, my mother was a washer-woman."
>
> "*A washer-woman, indeed!*" exclaimed his Grace—"That's very odd—I like washer-women—nice, clean, wholesome people.—I wish my mother had been a washer-woman."

In other words, Surtees treated Jorrocks as Mr Wells treated Mr Polly, or Arnold Bennett "The Card," without that class consciousness which was so prominent a weakness of the Victorian humorist. Possibly, just as the Lord in the Prologue to *Faust* preferred a knave to a bore, the obvious faults in *Handley Cross* are swallowed with good grace.

That Surtees has none of the compact technique of the modern novelist is never in doubt; that he meanders and does not cross his literary *t*'s is only too apparent. To many he must appear hopelessly old-fashioned and slovenly. There is, for example, a great objection to his laboured efforts, so popular a century ago, to make the characters fit their peculiarities. Such names as "Scattercash," "Seedeybuck," or "Heartycheer" are admittedly rather overdoing it, while "Lord Lionel Lazytongs," son of the "Marquis of Fender and Fireirons," is nothing short of deplorable. And yet there is even to-day something rather attractive in such manufactured names when they are not hopelessly exaggerated. One would require to be very critical to refuse to read the story of Mr Sponge because of this weakness. There seems also to be a kind of tradition for baptizing sporting characters with spectacular signatures, and from Surtees to Mr A. P. Herbert, in *Tantivy Towers*, the custom endures. There is probably a temptation to label comic characters with grotesque but descriptive names. . . . Despite such obvious crudities Surtees' perspective is more in sympathy with the present age than the one in which he lived, and possibly for that reason his characters have ceased to shock, and continue to amuse. (pp. 267-69)

[The] reader to-day prefers characters to speak naturally and behave naturally. To bore is the crowning sin in a novelist, and one must allow that Surtees, in his most familiar novels, makes bracing reading. Whether his characters are the kind of people we would remember in our wills is no longer an angle of criticism. When Thackeray, in referring to *Mr Sponge's Sporting Tour,* calls "those fellows in spectacles divine, and Scamperdale's character perfectly odious and admirable" [see excerpt dated 1852], he expresses exactly our own feeling. "Odious and admirable"—those three words explain a good deal of the attraction of Surtees' portrait gallery. There is—to go a step farther—an attractive neutral quality in Romford and Sponge. They neither alarm, depress, nor unduly convulse with laughter. And it is, as a consequence, not a little interesting to see how surely and inevitably Surtees has passed from the covertside to the city. Some of the most inveterate enthusiasts for his novels are, in my experience, men who have never been on a horse, and, I suspect, have never seen a hound. This interesting state of affairs is comparatively recent, and is still making surprising converts. (p. 270)

But one question still remains to answer. What is it in Surtees' more popular novels which still attracts the ordinary reader? It would seem to be, at least in *Handley Cross,* a kind of literary infection. It is, one may suggest, the genius not only for creating comic characters like Jorrocks, but for enabling the reader to partake of their exuberance, share their adventures, and echo their tremendous gusts of laughter. Surtees possessed imaginative energy. Not only do his characters live, but, what is just as important, they *revel* in the fact, and this zest for life, whether in the hunting-field or in the dealer's yard, whether in a horse or in a host, is really what matters in the end. Let it be allowed his style was slovenly, his construction wooden, his characters vulgar. What remains is Surtees himself. He had the saving grace of making human life a world of astonishing encounters with quite astonishing people. (p. 271)

> *Frederick Watson, in his* Robert Smith Surtees: A Critical Study, *George G. Harrap & Co. Ltd., 1933, 291 p.*

JOHN MOORE   (essay date 1935)

[*Moore dismisses Surtees' characters as humorless and vulgar.*]

A Leech illustration of Jorrocks and his wife at a hunt ball, from Handley Cross.

I must confess that I have never found Surtees very funny; perhaps he was quoted at me too much in my youth. His gallery of genial rascals, crooks, and cadgers seems to me to be singularly unattractive. These rogues are gross without greatness; they are like the characters in *Pickwick Papers* would be if Dickens were stripped of his all-pervading humanity. Moreover, they have none of the vitality with which Dickens animated his people; the only distinctive thing they possess is a certain pungency of speech. Mr. Soapy Sponge, Mr. Facey Romford, Mr. Jorrocks, and James Pigg: what a hideous scarecrow crew they are! A dismal sort of drunkenness, and a petty sort of dalliance with housekeepers and the like, compose their mean pleasures, and for the rest they cadge, cheat, lie, and swindle in a wholly vulgar and unimaginative way. Their antics are no more humorous than those of the horrible people in Rowlandson's cartoons, of which—far more than of John Leach's excellent drawings—they always somehow remind me. (p. 95)

> *John Moore, "The Hunting Men," in his* Country Men, *1935. Reprint by Books for Libraries Press, 1969; distributed by Arno Press, Inc., pp. 76-107.*

EDWARD WAGENKNECHT   (essay date 1943)

[Arguing that Surtees' characters are an important contribution to English literature, Wagenknecht proclaims that the author "seems due for a revival."]

For many years, the novels of Robert Smith Surtees—expensively printed, with hand-colored illustrations, and handsomely bound in the sportsman's favorite red—have been an indispensable part of every hunting gentleman's library. This cir-

cumstance, placing as it were the stamp of a too narrow specialization upon him, has probably contributed adversely to Surtees's fame as a novelist. It is not his ability to describe the "run" that gives him his place in the history of the English novel; it is rather his ability to create characters like John Jorrocks. And Jorrocks may be enjoyed even by those (like the present writer) who are so far from relishing hunting that they take up toward it the attitude of such Englishmen as John Galsworthy and Thomas Hardy. (p. 197)

Except for *Romford*, which does make some approach to an organized plot, one episode follows another in Surtees's books, and nobody cares particularly whether all the material is brought to bear on a central theme or not. In *Ask Mamma*, Miss de Glancey is introduced as if she were to play an important role; then she is simply dropped. When the terrible Mrs. Jorrocks is not needed, she disappears from *Hillingdon Hall*; on her brief reappearance, the reader finds himself wondering how in the world Jorrocks was able to get away from her for so long, and how he was able to manage so many activities without her. When the Anti-Corn Law League needs a candidate, Mr. Bowker is reintroduced from a former novel, with no particular regard paid to the consistency of his characterization.

The trial scene in *Pickwick* would seem clearly to show the influence of Jorrocks's trial for the killing of Old Tom, the hare—they get him for poaching when it is determined by foot-rule that the length of his great toe was across the line of Squire Cheatum's estate when he fired the fatal shot—and it must be admitted that even with Dickens's immortal bravura piece in mind, Surtees's dialogue is very amusing. There are those who believe that the general idea of *The Pickwick Papers* was suggested to its publishers, Chapman and Hall, by the success of *Jorrocks*. Both Dickens and Surtees go back to Smollett; one feels the influence more strongly in the older writer because his tone is predominantly farcical throughout his work, not merely in his first novel, as Dickens's is, and also because he comes closer to an eighteenth-century outlook. He lacks Smollett's brutality, to be sure, and Smollett's appetite for dirt, but he is as far from Dickens's intense Victorian earnestness as he is from his sentimentalism.

Jorrocks is a savage compared to Pickwick, yet there are many points of resemblance between them. Don Quixote had his Sancho Panza; Pickwick has his Sam Weller; Jorrocks has his huntsman, James Pigg. Jorrocks is not often so innocent as either of these other worthies (though once Pigg saves him from everlasting disgrace by yanking him out of a temperance procession into which he had strayed!), but what Frederick Watson calls "the contrast between the dry-tongued, uncouth, hard-riding northerner and the voluble, enthusiastic, but timorous cockney" is consistently maintained. Like Pickwick, the character changes notably; the buffoon of the *Jaunts and Jollities,* who loses his pants on the beach at Margate, is hardly the same man who gives those masterly "lectors" on hunting, and whom Surtees uses as the mouthpiece of his own ideas on agriculture and the Corn Laws. Mr. Pickwick in the pound is not a very pretty sight, but Pickwick is abstemious compared to Jorrocks, and his adventure with the lady in curl-papers is mild indeed compared to Jorrocks's Parisian sojourn with the Countess "Benwolio," or even his flirtations with Mrs. Markham and Mrs. Flather.

This does not mean that Jorrocks is necessarily the lesser achievement. He has the peculiar kind of vulgarity that is one of the glories of English literature, the vulgarity which first appeared notably in the Wife of Bath, and which reached its apotheosis in Falstaff. . . . With all his faults, Jorrocks has a refreshing freedom from meanness—his humanity as a magistrate is notable—yet I suppose many readers must be surprised to find themselves thinking of him so kindly as they do. No doubt his marvelous vitality has much to do with it, and so does his marvelous lingo.

"I'm a Post Hoffice Directory, not a Peerage, man," he cries. "Where I dine I sleep and where I sleep I breakfast." Muttonbroth reminds him of "a cold in the 'ead," and he calls French macaroni soup "water with worms in it." He refuses mince because he likes to chew his own meat, and he requires "a good fruity wine; a wine with a grip o' the gob, that leaves a mark on the side o' the glass." So enthusiastic is his love of hunting that he hunts in his sleep. "No man is fit to be called a sportsman," he declares in a public address, "wot doesn't kick his wife out of bed on a haverage once in three weeks!" His definition of hunting is famous—"the sport of kings, the image of war without its guilt, and only five-and-twenty per cent. of its danger." And his "COME HUP! I say, YOU HUGLY BEAST!" is still heard and understood among hunting Englishmen.

Surtees has many vivid characters besides Pigg and Jorrocks, but the best of them are surely those two "dead beats," Soapey Sponge and Facey Romford. By 1852 Surtees found it convenient to perform the conventional genuflexion before Mrs. Grundy; he created Soapey, he tells us, "to put the rising generation on their guard against specious, promiscuous acquaintance, and [train] them on to the noble sport of hunting, to the exclusion of its mercenary, illegitimate off-shoots." There can be no question as to the sincerity of Surtees's op-

position to the "low and demoralising pursuits" of "Prizefighting, Bull-baiting, and Cock-fighting"—he would not so much as allow them to be treated in his magazines—but he did not create Soapey as a horrible example. He might even have agreed with Mr. Watson's enthusiastic defense of that engaging rogue. The brutal ending of *Mr. Sponge's Sporting Tour*—the death of Jack Spraggon in a steeplechase—disturbs many readers, and the Defoe-like unemotionalism of Surtees's description is generally attributed to his own coldness of temperament. No doubt this element enters in, but it should not be forgotten that he has a point to make against racing.

It is in the *Sponge* books too that we get Lucy Glitters, whom Sponge marries, then deserts, when the cigar and betting rooms they establish are not going too well, and who is probably Romford's mistress, as well as his partner in the business alliance they set up. In general, Surtees is very cruel to women: an especially flagrant example is the marriage of the heroine's mother in *Plain or Ringlets?* to "the Jug" who does Jovey Jessup's drinking for him. Except for Jorrocks's niece, Belinda, who is too much of a lay-figure to count—and even Belinda "pets" mildly!—almost all Surtees's women, young and old, are selfish, spiteful, or shrewish. We are told specifically when we first meet Lucy Glitters that the ex-actress is only moderately virtuous, yet we are made to like her, and we feel that Surtees liked her also.

Though Surtees pays little attention to what may be called the intellectual life of his day, it must not be supposed that he was interested only in sport; he reflects his age, indeed, in so many aspects that a whole book has been devoted to the subject. He was deeply concerned over the agricultural problem, and *Hillingdon Hall* is one of the few books in which the modern reader may still find a statement of the case in favor of the Corn Laws. Surtees never rebelled against his age as Dickens did, but he was too intelligent to be entirely conventional; it has been argued that one reason why his hunting books were less immediately popular than Whyte-Melville's was that Jorrocks was not the early Victorian notion of what an M.F.H. ought to be. Huntsmen were not too comfortable under Surtees's chaffing; he did not quite hew to the "party line."

Surtees is one of the few English novelists who have never been "boomed." Lockhart, Thackeray, . . . Kipling, Theodore Roosevelt [see excerpts by Lockhart dated 1836 and 1843, by Thackeray dated 1849 and 1852, by Kipling dated 1913, and by Roosevelt dated 1906]—these are among the few famous men who have expressed enthusiasm for him; yet he has safely come through his first hundred years. Both Kipling and Wingfield-Stratford have been horrified by the coarseness of the world he pictures; unfortunately we have plenty of testimony that the picture was only too true. . . . [Because] of his historic importance and his own creative powers, he now seems due for a revival, and there are some signs that he may get it. That it will reach the extent of the Trollope revival is doubtful, however, nor can one believe that such ill-considered judgments as André Maurois's statement that Jorrocks is the *chef d'oeuvre* of the English novel will contribute to it notably. Nevertheless it is high time Surtees was rescued from the stables. (pp. 198-202)

Edward Wagenknecht, "From Scott to Dickens," in his Cavalcade of the English Novel: From Elizabeth to George VI, *Holt, Rinehart and Winston, 1943, pp. 173-212.*

JOHN SHAND (essay date 1945)

[*Shand speculates on the reasons for Surtees' popular and critical neglect, incorporating a defense of the author's works into his discussion.*]

Surtees has never been popular, nor is he ever likely to be. His main subject was sport, which does not attract the intellectual reader; he was a satirist and a cynic, and satire and cynicism are not enjoyed by the general English public. It is true that there is a national love of sport, and a select audience for satiric writing. But Surtees did not write of sport in a way to tickle the multitude, and chose the wrong subject to please the few who would enjoy his humor. He fell between two audiences, pleasing neither the barbarians of Horseback Hall nor the cultured of Heartbreak House.

Like his own Facey Romford, Surtees was "not a man of much blandishment." He wrote in a "take it or leave it" style; and as his satiric strokes were often sharp enough to hurt, most readers chose to leave it. He did not choose his words with conscious care; but he expressed himself in a clear, colloquial English that leaves the reader in no doubt of his meaning and reflects his tart, taciturn personality; and for his comic characters, especially for Jorrocks, he found a torrent of racy, exuberant speech.

Readers who flatter themselves that they know something about English fiction are likely to nod agreeably (if vaguely) at mention of Jorrocks; but it cannot be assumed that they have read even *Handley Cross,* in which the Cockney foxhunter is developed with superb vigor and vivacity from the first faint sketches in *Jorrocks's Jaunts and Jollities*—a book that preceded and probably suggested the writing of *The Pickwick Papers. Handley Cross* is an ill-constructed masterpiece that lives only (but lives decidedly) because of Jorrocks and James Pigg; and it peters out in a couple of law trial scenes that are dismally unfunny and, when contrasted with the magical comedy of Bardell versus Pickwick, seem painfully inept.

But Surtees's novels as a whole, filled as they are with amusing characters and sardonic pictures of the Victorian scene, continue to be ignored by the critical mandarins—probably because he is pigeon-holed as a sporting writer. Art connoisseurs long disdained English sporting pictures for the same reason. Surtees is also something of a "sport" among novelists as well as a novelist of sport. That may be another reason why he is neglected by the literary fancy. For he was not a literary gentleman with an odd taste for hunting, but a hunting gentleman with an odd gift for writing. It is this that gives to his tales an individual flavor and a valuable authenticity. (p. 91)

It is easy to understand why Surtees's novels failed to attract that important body of novel readers, the women of the English—of the Victorian English—middle class. They did not attract Surtees. He viewed them positively with distaste. He disliked their manners, despised their affectations, and laughed at their pretensions to gentility. His attitude towards them could not be better expressed than in the words of "Independent Jimmy," a delightful Tyneside character in *Mr. Romford's Hounds,* who drives a bus, delivers parcels, and knows all the gossip of the country. He is acidly giving an account of a local nabob who has just bought the old squire's house and set up for a gentleman, and Jimmy, in the peculiar dialect of Tyneside, thus continues:—

> As to the darter . . . she's just the impittantest, sarciest gal i' the world, arlways tossin' aboot

and givin' gob. Noo, there's the Ladies Rosebud, Lord Flowerdew's darters, when ar gans to the Castle, for any body there, they speak quite civil and plizant; 'Good morning, Jimmy! How do ye do, Jimmy? Hoo are all the little Jimmys?' ("for ar ha' thorteen on 'em," added Jimmy, parenthetically) and so on, while this sarcy thing taks had of her stickin'-out claes, and cries, 'Now, man! get out of the way, man; see, man! look, man! mind, man!' just as if I were a twoad. . . . Sink, but ar often wonders who these sort o' fondies think they impose upon. It can't be the likes o' me . . . for we know all about them; it can't be the gentlefolks, for they'll ha' nout to say to them. It mun just be their arn silly sels.

This touches home. And though these "fondies" no longer wear crinolines, they are otherwise not much altered, and one is still permitted to wonder whom they think they impose upon.

Women readers—indeed, most readers—also prefer a novel to have a story. Surtees never bothered himself much about a plot. This was a fault; but he laughed at love, which was fatal. It was perhaps only a misfortune that he lacked sentiment; but he failed to be sentimental, and that was not to be forgiven. His men (except for one ancient nobleman) never attempt seduction. They can hardly be said to fall in love. His women quite lack romance. The Victorian virgin and her matchmaking mama he depicts entirely without reverence. The one woman in his fiction for whom he exhibits any admiration (and to emphasize his interest in her he brings her into two of his best novels) is an actress from the minor London theaters, and only "tolerably virtuous." The one love scene that has a touch of passion (and it has an oddly convincing quality) is that between her and that rogue, Soapey Sponge.

Generally, Surtees shows his couples courting strictly with a view to a profitable alliance, and if they look foolish, they act with prudence; if one eye fills with feeling, calculation stares from the other, and the lawyer must consent before the priest is asked to bless. "Oh, you needn't be afraid of me, Mr. Ballivant! You needn't be afraid of me, I'm not one of the sentimental sort," remarks Miss Rosa, the heroine of *Plain or Ringlets?* when after a grand inquisition on the hero's funds and property the family attorney advises her mother "to keep Miss back a little for the present"—as if Miss were a good horse whose sale could await a better bid.

This is typical, and shows clearly how Surtees offended every canon of the circulating library. He sees the women as snobs and tuft-hunters of the first degree, and he describes what he sees with masculine vigor and almost feminine relish for detail.

If Surtees offended women readers, surely he pleased the foxhunters of his day? Doubtless he delighted some of them; but as many in proportion ride to hounds because it is the thing to do as go to the opera or travel abroad, and Surtees spared them not. As a foxhunter himself who delighted in the sport, Surtees saw nothing to ridicule in Jorrocks, the Cockney grocer whose passion was hunting. Jorrocks is comical enough, to be sure, but he holds his own in any company because his enjoyment in hunting foxes is as genuine as his love of money, because he hunts for fun, and because he is completely lacking in a sense of reverence for his social superiors. He is completely at home with everybody because he sees no reason why everybody should not feel at home with him.

Surtees reserved his sarcasm for the pretentious Jawleyford, the dandy Puffington, and all that sort of gentry who attend the meet only to speak to his lordship or to show off to the ladies. Surtees with tactless clarity showed his preference for Sponge and Romford, who cheated in order to hunt, to the respectable snobs and toadies whose very presence in the hunting field was a cheat.

As for the earnest intellectual readers of his day, it was hopeless to expect them to approve a writer who had no gospel to preach, who showed no zeal to reform the world, and in whom the pleasures of the chase, the courage of a rider, the cunning of a fox, the sagacity of hounds, obviously raised a warmth of feeling that strongly contrasted with his cynical attitude toward society. Society, indeed, only engaged his unloving attention. Surtees had sharp eyes for faults and follies. He reports details of dress, manners, meals, speech, furniture, transportation, so minutely that his descriptions are sometimes tedious for casual reading, though probably of enormous interest to the social historian.

But though Surtees disliked much of what he observed, he had too much vitality merely to yawn; and as he is never bored, he is not often dull reading. If he has no taste for the ideal, he at least enjoys the real without bitterness. If he does not see his fellows as angels walking, he does not in disappointment call them devils. If his lovers never believe the world well lost for love, it is also true that they do not believe the world well lost for any consideration. The way of the world perfectly suits all his characters. They are completely selfish, and they view unselfishness in others with high suspicion. They adore riches and despise poverty. Altogether they imitate humanity pretty closely.

Being country born and bred, Surtees views field and forest with the practical eyes of a farmer. He is quite unable to be "enthusymusy" about scenery. He takes for granted the enjoyment of fresh air and good food and the changing beauties of the seasons, and leaves to Jorrocks such a truly Cockney cry as: "Dash it, wot a mornin' it is! Wot a many delicious moments one loses by smooterin' i' bed!" It is true that when the scene shifts occasionally to London or to a holiday town, Surtees seems also perfectly at home—his London episodes are particularly amusing; but he is at his best in the country, and views its inhabitants with the penetrating knowledge of an old friend. He is "country," too, in his solid, stolid good sense, his stoical acceptance of things as they are. He never attempts pathos; neither is he ever maudlin. His characters are interested only in everyday matters. As in life, though not in fiction, money is an object of anxious solicitude. Dress is also a serious problem, and an essay on Victorian costume might be written from Surtees's exact descriptions.

Such scenes as that of the Duke of Tergiversation's ball (in *Plain or Ringlets?*) are a panorama of rural society. A shrewd sardonic pen traces all the social reverberations created by this grand local spectacle. The delicious comedy of the ducal couple drawing up the list of guests is accompanied by that of some receiving the coveted cards. The Duke and Duchess are seen including or excluding guests with all the calculation of politicians forming a government; and the complex diplomacy needed to get all the right people into the castle ballroom is balanced by that which goes on in the kitchen to get them fed. The butler must patronize the local shops if the castle credit is still good; if not, the London tradesmen—"terribly obnoxious to the influence of rank"—can always be tapped.

The fuss and bother of the guests is equally good fun. The pleasure of being invited (and of knowing who is not invited) is countered by the expense and fatigue of finding dress and carriage suited to the occasion, and the disgust of discovering that the castle has asked neighbors who ought to have been left out. (Surtees acidly observes that the ducal ball would be excessively exclusive if the guests could issue the invitations.) And at the ball itself, the spectacle of the Duchess "measuring affability" is not less amusing because her star guest is not the Italian prince she supposes him to be, but a dancing master. (pp. 92-4)

[It] is difficult for an admirer of Surtees not to believe that a far larger audience would enjoy his books if they were better known, and it is difficult not to accuse the critics—who so thoroughly omit to recommend them—as guilty of dereliction of duty. (p. 94)

[In] *The English Novel* [Saintsbury] gave Surtees a curt "nearly always readable—and sometimes very amusing—even to those who are not exactly Nimrods" [see Additional Bibliography]. Faint praise—fainter, indeed, than at first it seems, for Saintsbury compares Surtees to his disadvantage with Kingsley's sporting novel, *Yeast*, which he praises for its "most fascinating and real heroine" and its "accurate and real dialogue."

But Saintsbury's brief tribute might pass had he not added . . . just those few words that made him put his foot in it. In contrast to Kingsley's "real heroine" and "real dialogue," he remarks that Surtees's "characters and manners have the old artificial-picaresque quality only"—an observation that makes one wonder if even dimly he appreciated the astonishing reality of Sponge and Romford, and of many other of Surtees's characters, and the fidelity with which he records "manners." Jorrocks and Pigg are another matter: they are "artificial," as all great comic (or tragic) characters are "artificial."

But Sponge and Romford, though amusing, are not in the technical sense comic characters; they are perfectly ordinary masculine creatures boldly and vigorously drawn. They are exceedingly life-like portraits of men moderately "on the make" who see their fellows as much like themselves—"anxious to look after Number One." (pp. 94-5)

Sponge and Romford are "real" because their creator had an enormous preference for what was true to life to what was likely to be popular; and they are likable because—perhaps in spite of himself—Surtees could not help making them excellent sportsmen as well as superb critics, by implication, of social hypocrisy.

Surtees in his own day was inevitably over-shadowed by the genius of Dickens. Where he resembled Dickens, the odds were heavily against him; and where he differed, it was a difference that did not attract Victorian taste. There was a touch of the raffish Regency in him that was not likely to appeal to the respectable reader, and a masculine attitude toward life that would have been better appreciated by the age of Fielding and Smollett. A comparison between the tours of Sponge and Romford and those of Pickwick and Weller would suggest, perhaps, that the books resembled each other only in the seeming ability of their authors to continue the stories indefinitely: they end only because an end must be made.

While the people in *Pickwick* are all transfigured by the golden radiance of good humor, so that Stiggins and Jingle, even Dodson and Fogg, delight no less than Pickwick and the Wellers, in Surtees one is reminded how Stiggins and Jingle and

A Leech illustration of Lucy Glitters leading a hunt, from Mr. Sponge.

Dodson and Fogg would appear in the cold light of day. Compare Sponge going out shooting with Jogglebury Crowdey, with Winkle exhibiting his supposed prowess at Dingley Dell. The scene in Dickens is farce divinely genial; the scene in Surtees, equally ludicrous and not less well written, is farce humanly ungenial.

Winkle is a gorgeous lunatic; Crowdey is as Winkle would look to a real sportsman seriously out for game. The pompous Crowdey, with his undisciplined spaniel anywhere but at heel, who cannot hit a haystack except by accident, is seen through the cold, jeering eyes of an expert shot, who is at once spitefully amused by the absurd spectacle and intensely irritated that he is wasting his time with a fool. It is farce decidedly less pleasant than that of Dickens, but it is excellent fooling, and some palates will always relish its pungent flavor. (p. 95)

John Shand, "Squire Surtees," in The Atlantic Monthly, *Vol. 175, No. 1, January, 1945, pp. 91-6.*

LEONARD COOPER   (essay date 1952)

[Cooper holds that Surtees was "a stylist of high order," particularly praising his handling of dialogue.]

In his *Art of Writing* Sir A. T. Quiller-Couch lays down four requirements for a good English style. It must, he says, be accurate, perspicuous, persuasive and appropriate: and measured by these standards Surtees may fairly lay claim to be a stylist of high order. If he fails at all it is in accuracy—that is in precision of grammar and nicety in the use of words. Mrs. Woolf calls his style "Gentlemanly and slapdash" [see excerpt

dated 1925] and there can hardly be a better description. He was certainly careless in construction and more than a little slipshod in his diction in those parts of the book which obviously interested him least. His gravest fault in style is a habit of using over and over again a cliché, either borrowed or of his own invention, and an occasional facetious turn of phrase which seems to come from habit rather than from thought. Someone in his youth must have told him about the sailor who said that he had had "beef, mutton and cheese—all the delicacies of the season" and this not very amusing conceit appears in all the books and more than once in several of them. His use of the catch-phrase, "we beg pardon," is even more frequent and quite as irritating. He writes of "Lucy Glitters—we beg pardon Mrs. Somerville," or "the kind of man—we beg pardon gentleman," as often as he uses his other favourite catch-phrase, "the order of the day." "Munch, crunch, munch was then the order of the day," is his usual descriptive phrase for a dinner or a hunt-breakfast and "Jog, jog, bump, bump, trot trot, was then the order of the day," serves for the field moving off from the meet.

He has, too, a persistent habit of describing any noise made by a man or an animal by an onomatopoeic word and repeating the word as often as the noise occurs and as long as it sounds. Horns always go "toot-toot," cats "mew-mew," and the wind "shoosh." And no character in the book can sneeze, cough, hiccup, smoke or make any kind of noise without its being painstakingly recorded. It is his most persistent and most wearisome habit, but scarcely less persistent is his fondness for calling his characters by names that personify their leading qualities—Sir Harry Scattercash, Mr. Bottleends the butler, Mr. Fleeceall the lawyer and their fellows. But it was the convention of the time and he adopted it—and having adopted it, rode it to death as he was apt to ride his conceits. He carried it to far greater lengths than did his contemporaries though they nearly all indulged in the same practice. (pp. 163-64)

Laboured and verbose as his descriptions are, there is no excuse for any reader of Surtees not knowing exactly what his characters looked like, or how they dressed. His descriptions of clothing are as accurate and detailed as his descriptions of persons. And his persuasiveness, his ability to make his readers see with his own eyes, is never more in evidence than when hounds are running. (p. 165)

No higher tribute can be paid to Surtees' persuasiveness than the fact that his hunting runs can be and are read with enjoyment by men who have never ridden to hounds nor even laid leg across a horse. Such runs as those with the Goose and Dumpling Hounds in *Hawbuck Grange*, the "Cat and Custard-Pot" day in *Handley Cross*, or the Calderlaw Common run with Mr. Facey Romford and the Heavyside Hunt are first-rate pieces of descriptive writing. To the hunting man there is the interest of seeing hounds work, the check and the cast, the final run into view. To the horseman there is the varied delight in the performance of the different horses, the chances of rail and water—a slower more detailed description than the whirlwind steeplechases of Nimrod and Whyte-Melville. But for the great mass of us who are neither hunting men nor horsemen there is the outstanding attraction of the fact that never throughout the run does Surtees lose sight of the men who follow the hounds.

It is noticeable, too, how his style alters when hounds are running, to match the speed and rhythm of the hunt. It becomes crisper and terser, the dialogue is in curt sentences, jerked out by breathless and excited men. Diffuse and verbose as he sometimes is in the less active parts of his writing, he prunes it of all but the barest necessities when the action calls for it. His style is in fact in the fullest sense what Quiller-Couch calls "appropriate." In the inn and the dining-room he is long-winded enough. But when the hounds break out of cover he rides his pen, in Mrs. Woolf's phrase, as gallantly as he rode his horse. "Slapdash and gentlemanly" she calls his style: and hunting is after all a slapdash and gentlemanly occupation.

The real strength of Surtees' style is in his dialogue and it is not too much to say that in this department of his art he surpassed his great contemporaries by as much as he came short of them in other ways. The great Victorians, with all their merits, were as a rule indifferent writers of dialogue. They seemed to ignore the fundamental fact that men and women in ordinary conversation do not talk coherent prose. Their characters could hardly say good-morning to each other without making a speech about it. (pp. 165-66)

But Surtees really did know how people talked. From the earliest discussion at the meet in the *Jaunts and Jollities* to the last talk in *Facey Romford* the books are crammed with dialogue of the very best sort—crisp, accurate, colloquial, amusing and above all natural. So many of the Victorians seem to have written not so much what their characters said as what they ought to have said. Their speech conveys their meaning clearly enough, but conveys it in the accents of the study, the lecture-room or the pulpit. They were hindered—as Surtees was never hindered—by the fact that the characters were bursting with the highest and most creditable of emotions and while their

reactions to the emotions are true and in character their expression of them is at its worst nothing but *oratio obliqua* enclosed in inverted commas. Few of Surtees' characters were troubled by creditable emotions, but still fewer of them are guilty of falseness of expression. He was usually writing comic dialogue which does not lend itself to pomposity except for the purpose of mocking it. (pp. 167-68)

There is no exaggeration in Surtees' dialogue, which is often at its best in the quieter passages. He is not obliged to force the comic relief since there is nothing in the books that needs relief, and so it follows that his characters are talking in their normal accents and at their normal level. There is no virtuosity in the dialogue itself. With the exception of Mr. Jorrocks, who was a humorist in word as well as in deed, there is hardly a character whose speech is worth quoting as purely humorous dialogue. It is too natural, too life-like. It is always the speech of characters, humorous in themselves, who have no need of verbal fireworks. (p. 168)

Whatever Surtees' faults as a stylist may have been he was never at a loss in reporting conversation. His accurate ear, his dislike of exaggeration and his keen sense of humour all helped him. They helped him to avoid the pitfalls that so many of his contemporaries fell into. His characters talk neither coherent prose nor over-forced comedy. They talk like the real people that they are. (p. 172)

Leonard Cooper, in his R. S. Surtees, *Arthur Barker Ltd., 1952, 180 p.*

JOYCE CARY (essay date 1957)

[*Cary contends that Surtees' greatest strengths as a novelist—his objectivity and candor—are best displayed in* Sponge. *This essay was written in April 1957.*]

The special quality of Surtees seems to be quite ignored. I dare say this is because people think of him as a writer only for hunting fanatics, and, in fact, *Handley Cross,* with all the adventures of John Jorrocks, is a boring work. It was Surtees's *Pickwick* thrown together without any conception of form and with not a trace of Dickens's genius for humorous character.

Dickens's wildest grotesques live in their own right; we do not feel that Dickens has invented them; we shouldn't be surprised to meet them anywhere. Jorrocks is a mere invention and in a vein of humour completely dead; that mid-Victorian humour which astonishes us in mid-Victorian *Punch*. Who now could read *Mrs. Caudle's Curtain Lectures*, so famous in those days? Jorrocks is in the same style. Even that episode, so often quoted, where he is carousing with Pigg, the huntsman, and, fearing a frost, asks him what the weather is like, has gone flat. Pigg opens the cupboard door in mistake for the shutter and answers, 'Hellish dark, and smells of cheese'. It won't really bear repetition, as you see.

But Surtees after Jorrocks, like Dickens after Pickwick, did acquire a form, and *Mr. Sponge's Sporting Tour* is a masterpiece in its own way. . . . What is remarkable is the portrait not only of Sponge, but of the whole society in which he moves.

It is an extraordinarily tough society, without any of that self-consciousness which belongs to Hemingway's heroes. The men are tough as a matter of course, yet they are by no means cut to pattern. Look at that sporting nobleman Lord Scamperdale, Master of the Flat Hat Hunt, and his toady Jack Spraggon. Scamperdale is exceedingly tough. One realizes in him one puzzling feature of the Regency—how men of fine manner and classical education could also be thugs, going out to beat up aged watchmen for a joke. (p. vii)

Surtees's England is a century away from us; its peasantry are real peasantry and he describes them with the same fearless honesty that he brings to all his writing. He called them usually 'Chaw-bacons'. They are a poverty-stricken and brutalized race; he had no idea of romanticizing his moujiks. You see them as Goncharov saw his Zahar and Gogol his Petrushka, those two valet-serfs.

I don't know anybody except Surtees who gives this picture, or makes us feel so strongly what a good thing it is that in England we don't any more have a peasantry. Surtees does this without any political motive; he is not a propagandist; we trust him absolutely. Of course, he gives his own picture; he can't do anything else. *Mr. Sponge* is contemporary with Trollope's *The Warden*, and what different pictures it gives of a different England; all authentic to a feeling of the time and all complementary when we allow for the writer's purpose and preoccupation.

Surtees is brilliant not only with touts, lags, and shysters, he is a master at the snob and the climber. His social parasites are inferior only to Thackeray's. In one respect he can be better than Thackeray. Thackeray's Lord Steyne in *Vanity Fair* is a common cad; compare him with Disraeli's Monmouth in *Coningsby*. . . . [Monmouth] is as arrogant and selfish as you like, a complete egotist, but he has the grand style; he is not a vulgarian, and Surtees's Lord Scamperdale in his quite different surroundings has the same quality. He is a simple country squire without any of Monmouth's magnificence, but he is still as different from Steyne as that authentic nobleman. He is a tough, but he does not smell of the gutter.

Probably Surtees owes this success to that observant eye and candour of speech which is his chief force as a writer. He has no cant of any kind; he is sucking up to nobody and no class. He has his moral standards, but he is not trying to preach them; there is none of that sense that we have, even in Trollope, of the moralizer. Trollope's world and Trollope's moralizing were also typical of the time, but Surtees has in pre-eminence that quality—which belongs also to Michael Scott, the author of *Tom Cringle's Log* and another neglected master, not to speak of Gogol—of the *describer*. He writes of what he sees and knows, with a reckless sincerity especially refreshing in these self-conscious times.

I should think it would be almost impossible to read *Sponge* aloud; every second sentence has a broken back or tail, and the grammar is a mine of howlers. Neither does the man get on with the work. He stops at every corner, looks over every hedge. He will take half a page to tell you what some minor character is wearing, what he ate for breakfast. But this is just the charm of the work. (pp. viii-ix)

[There] are two kinds of novelists whose lack of form allows them a great deal of detail which is very close to reporting—which often, if we knew it, is almost certainly from direct observation. One is the slack novelist, filling out a chapter when he has run short of invention. Sergeant Bumptious in *Handley Cross* is such a piece of observation. And for me at least, he is better than Dickens's Buzfuz, founded on the same real person, a certain Sergeant Bompos, renowned for bombast. Bumptious is a rougher sketch of a cruder man, but he jumps out of the page and the scene while Buzfuz stays where he is put, as a comic character.

The other kind of novelist who achieves real life is the picaresque—Le Sage, Gogol, *Gil Blas* and *Dead Souls* are full of people so real that if you put them into a novel of formal construction it would have to be built round them. As secondary characters, if you fitted them in at all, they would steal the stage.

Surtees is not only a slack novelist, in *Sponge* he is also picaresque. He's licensed to stop anywhere and describe anything, or anyone, from a country house bedroom about 1850, with half a dozen different kinds of bath, to a spa dandy and his waistcoats. I defy any writer to beat Surtees on clothes. He gives us not only cut and colour, but fabric and quality, the very sewing. He takes a page to give us Sponge's hunting coat, with lapped seams on the outside, and it's not a word too much. That coat is more real to us than our own for the good reason that it is not only an historic coat, but a moral coat. It expresses Surtees's moral idea, his hatred of sham, pretension, the shoddy in man or clothes, with a force all the more telling in that he is probably quite unaware of it. His eye is on the coat, which certainly existed, and even the fact that he likes it has to be inferred.

Like the true picaresque, he does not deal much in admiration. Sponge is a swindler without a single redeeming virtue except perhaps his clothes and his nerve. Surtees gave him the clothes as the proper equipment of a swell mobsman and also a superb horseman. He could not bear to dress such a horseman in anything but the best. But the clothes are almost the only virtue he allows him and only Surtees would think of clothes as a virtue. Even Sponge's courage is the worst of its kind, the desperate gamble of a con-man. He is not only a crook but a mean crook who will cheat a servant. Among Surtees's gallery of lags, touts and shysters he is surpassed only by Facey Romford in *Mr. Facey Romford's Hounds,* who is an oaf as well as a crook and does not wash.

In this respect Gil Blas, even Gogol's Chichikov, is inferior to Sponge. He is done, in Henry James's phrase, to a turn. And this is Surtees's great virtue as a novelist. He never softens to a man; he never tries to catch a reader's sympathy for his worst, his meanest hero. He is objective to the last, like Flaubert, like Proust, and very unlike the later Thackeray.

It is again typical of the picaresque writer that his dialogue is so good. He is in no hurry to make it serve any purpose except the revelation of character. All Surtees is full of good dialogue in its special kind, like reported talk. Scamperdale and Spraggon are at their best in their smallest talk; it is as though we overheard them. We feel the very stuffiness of Scamperdale's den in their yawns and starts.

Surtees was himself a country squire from the deep North, the M.F.H. of a scratch pack. He had all the prejudices of his kind. He hated the fashionable places and people and smart society, he was suspicious of any kind of cleverness. He was prickly and hard, he had little compassion except for dogs and horses. He is pitiless to his victims. When Sponge and Spraggon unite to swindle and bully a wretched youth called Pacey, he records every detail of the latter's humiliation with the zest of loathing. Pacey was silly and weak and so despicable to him. Surtees prefers crooks to fools, because they are hard, because, as he thinks, they have no illusions.

Sponge is not a book for the sentimentalist, but for the man who likes to understand something of human nature in both its strength and weakness, especially in its power of creating, each man for himself, a complete ideal world, social and moral, and living in it.

Of Surtees's other novels *Mr. Facey Romford's Hounds* is not much inferior to *Sponge,* and Sponge reappears in it. The rest are tedious and flat to the general reader. To the social historian, on the other hand, they are of unique value. *Ask Mamma* and *Plain or Ringlets?* record mid-Victorian life as seen by a highly critical contemporary eye at a time when all the other novelists, even Thackeray, were sentimentalizing it.

Surtees lived through the biggest social revolution in [England] between 1066 and 1938. He was born into the Regency, Pierce Egan's London and the horse age; he describes the three days' journey from his home in Durham to London. He lived to see the railways everywhere, to travel as fast and easily as we do now, and to know a society for whom the Regency buck was not only a brute, but, more significantly, an aberration, a monster.

In Surtees's eyes probably the most striking change was the beginning of the family holiday for the middle class; tens of thousands on the move instead of the few hundred who alone, before the railway age and the excursion train, had been able to afford to travel farther than the county town or the village fair. He records the more superficial consequences: spas crowded with husband-hunting girls and city fops, town-bred rich men playing squire and sportsman, usually, he tells us, with a typical twist of prejudice, in the wrong clothes.

What struck him was not only the complete change in the character of fashionable seaside places like Brighton, but in the manners of the visitors. The place set out to cater for the crowd, and the visitors had quite other notions of amusement than the Regency bucks and their Harriet Wilsons, for whom the seaside was simply an Alsatia in which they could live openly with mistresses who had to be more discreetly entertained in London.

Surtees had not loved the bucks, but he still more detested the mobs, which seemed to him all that was vulgar. No doubt they were. Newly prosperous and newly emancipated people usually are so. They keep the competitive habit of mind which has brought them up in the world and think of society in terms of rivalry. Especially on holiday among strangers they set out to impress. In these mid-century years leading up to the Great Exhibition all industry was booming and the whole country was full of new rich. Surtees describes them, in mass and in detail, with the particularity of his disgust. But he also jibes at the smart gentry, and in their despite makes a hero of the grocer Jorrocks. (pp. ix-xii)

Mr. Sponge's Sporting Tour is solid Surtees; he comes through in every line. The reason is that he has no idea of striking any kind of attitude. He has no self-consciousness, as man or writer. He is not afraid of anybody and rolls no logs. To read him is to escape for an hour or two from eyewash and cant into an atmosphere as brisk as one of his hunting mornings, sharp and raw, highly unflattering to everything in sight, faces, hedges, trees, nibbled pasture and greasy plough, but thoroughly bracing. (p. xii)

> Joyce Cary, *in an introduction to* Mr. Sponge's Sporting Tour *by R. S. Surtees, Oxford University Press, London, 1958, pp. vii-xii.*

V. S. PRITCHETT (essay date 1964)

[*Pritchett, a modern British writer, is respected for his mastery of the short story and for what critics describe as his judicious,*

A portrait of Surtees.

reliable, and insightful literary criticism. In the excerpt below, he interprets Surtees' works as a protest against the snobbishness of the rising middle class in mid-Victorian England.]

Robert Surtees is a sport, in both senses of the term, who flashes in and out of the English novel, excites hope and reduces the critical factions to silence. He has all the dash, all the partiality and all the prospect of an amateur. There is a rush of air, a shower of rain drops from the branches, a burst of thundering mud, a crashing of hazel, the sight of a pink coat and, as far as the English novel is concerned, he has gone. In that brief appearance he has made the genial suggestion that all the other English novelists have been mistaken; they have missed the basic fact in English life—that we are religious, that our religion is violent sport. The unwritten life of a large proportion of the characters in English fiction is passed in playing or watching games in the open air; nature is being worshipped with the senses and the muscles. We are either bemused by fresh air or are daydreaming of some lazy, cunning and exhausting animal life in the open. In that condition, our hourly and sedentary habit of worry as a substitute for thought vanishes and we become people in love. It takes an amateur, like Surtees, to see an obvious thing like this and to exaggerate so that the part becomes the whole of English life. He was a north country squire, an excellent sporting journalist, but handsomely innocent of the future of hunting in England. He really thought that the Industrial Revolution would make the sport democratic! His assumption is that English violence can be appeased only by the horse. He is the final authority on our horse civilization, and Jorrocks is a sort of Don Quixote of the last phase of a brutal chivalry. (pp. 88-9)

It is natural that hunting people should admire Surtees. It is not surprising that serious literary critics should admire him also. He creates a complete world. It is the world which Fielding's and Thackeray's people knew in their off-stage lives. It has no relation with the feeble subculture of horse lovers, pony worshippers, or with the gentility of the jodphur that spread over England as the coach gave way to the railway, provoking the cult of the New Forest pony. The natural democrats of England live in the north and, though Surtees was a Tory squire, he sincerely believed that the horse was an insurance against the new, snobbish exclusiveness of the shot-up Victorian middle class. He imagined, as so many have done before, that class revolutions will not become snobbish and exclusive. Happy pastoral delusion! Surtees did not foresee either the hardness or the sentimentality of the coming urban England. Or, perhaps, he half guessed it. For the point about Jorrocks is that he is (1) not a horse lover but a fox lover, (2) that he rides, buys and sells horses, (3) that he has not an aitch to his name. He is, boldly, incontrovertibly, aggressively, in mid-nineteenth-century—a grocer. His fame is that he is not merely a sportsman, but a Cockney sportsman. He has all the trading sharpness and romanticism of a man who sells tea. Surtees is content (purposefully content) with this reality. Jorrocks is as vulgar as Keats; and, as a northerner and a gentleman, Surtees refuses to accept the improved accents of the new rich in the south. He exploits the rewards our class system offers to our literature. We are continually supplying a number of vulgar geniuses who stand out against the new snobberies which the Puritan streak in us is liable to create; and, in the case of Surtees, there is the anomaly that a Tory squire provides the vulgar protest. The heir of Jorrocks is Mr. Polly. Both are native protests against the mean and successful revolutions that deny the instincts of genial, sincere and natural men.

Surtees owes a lot to the low side of Thackeray and does seamy society a good deal better. His dialogue is as quick and true as the master's. He extends a robust and native tradition: the masculine strain of English comic writing. This comedy is broad and extraverted. It grins at the pleasures and pains of the human animal—if it is male—and has little time for the female. Occasionally Surtees sees a tolerable female, but very rarely. We need not suppose that he agreed with Jorrocks that a man ought to kick his wife out of bed three times a month, but we suspect this was only because he regarded the act wistfully as an ideal unfortunately unattainable. The fact is that our comic extraverts are like Mr. Sponge and bring a horse-dealer's eye to the consideration of women—"fifteen two and a half is plenty of height" for them. In its male world, the comic tradition likes the misfortunes of the body, the bruises, the black eyes, the drinking sessions, the gorging at table; prefers the low to the refined, the masterful and unreasonable to the sensitive and considerate. There is a strong regard for the impossible element in human character, for the eccentric and the obsessed. The brutes have their engaging moments. (They give the right kind of girls half a dozen smacking kisses.) But their transcendent emotions emerge in another direction. Jorrocks will quarrel with his huntsman, Pigg, but be reconciled, to the point of embracing him, at the kill. These people are dedicated. They will suffer anything, from drowning upwards, for their sport. They will experience an ecstasy which goes beyond the animal into the poetic. And, in the meantime, they will rollick. Thoroughly non-Puritan, they understand that

the life of animal pleasure is the life of animal dismay and they accept it. What these writers in the masculine comic tradition dwell on is the variety of human character. They know that action brings this out and, with a kind of mercy, they will forgive anything so long as action, not introspection, has revealed it. (pp. 89-91)

On the one hand, Surtees was a man of the eighteenth century—hence Thackeray's understanding of him; on the other, he was an amateur who dealt almost entirely with background figures, the great Jorrocks excepted. He was deeply knowing about English sporting life, the squirearchy and the law, but he did not construct the melodramas and elaborate plots of the other Victorian novelists, nor did he issue their moralizings. He often excelled them in the recording of ordinary speech and day-to-day incident. He is fresher than the masters, but he is artless. A good deal of his humor is the humor of shrewd sayings which, later on, we find in Kipling. His original contribution is in the field of invective. Surtees has a truly Elizabethan power of denunciation. Here is Jorrocks loosing off to his servant:

> "Come hup, you snivellin', drivellin' son of a lucifer-match maker," he roars out to Ben who is coming lagging along in his master's wake. . . . "Come hup, I say, ye miserable, road-ridin', dish-lickin' cub! And give me that quad, for you're a disgrace to a saddle, and only fit to toast muffins for a young ladies' boarding school. Come hup, you preter-pluperfect tense of 'umbugs. . . . Come on, ye miserable, useless son of a lily-livered besom-maker. Rot ye, I'll bind ye 'prentice to a salmon-pickler."

This is all the more splendid because Jorrocks keeps to the "'ard road" as much as possible, and can't bear taking a fence. He is eloquent, perhaps because he is as cowardly as Falstaff and yet as sincere in his passion. He knows what he wants to be. His is the eloquence of romance. And this is where we come to the Dickensian aspect of Surtees, too. Dickens has several degrees of comic observation. There is the rudimentary Dickens of caricature, of the single trait or phrase turned into the whole man. And there is the Dickens where this is elaborated into soliloquy, in which the character is represented by his fantasy life. Like the rudimentary Dickens, Surtees has the feeling for caricature. *Handley Cross, Facey Romford's Hounds* and *Mr. Sponge's Tours* are packed with minor eccentrics of the field, the fancy and the law; but in Jorrocks, Surtees enters upon the more complex study of people who live out the comic orgy. "By 'eavens, it's sublime," says Jorrocks, watching the hounds stream over a hundred acres of pasture below him. "'Ow they go, screechin' and towlin' along just like a pocketful o' marbles . . . 'Ow I wish I was a heagle." A "heagle" he is, in that moment; sublimity is his condition. He has shrewdly built up his pack, he has given his uproarious lectures, he has had his vulgar adventures in country houses; he has got the better of his betters and has outdone the new rich in vulgarity—making among other things that immortal remark about mince: "I like to chew my own meat"—he has disgraced Mrs. Jorrocks, but he has pursued an obsession utterly so that it has no more to teach him, beyond the fact that it has damaged his credit among the unimaginative in the City. Fortunately, Surtees has given him power of speech. Jorrocks is never at a loss for repartee or for metaphor. He is remarkable in his duels with Pigg, and the only pity is that Pigg's dialect is nearly incomprehensible. But Pigg and his master are well matched.

They battle like theologians about the true business of life: the pursuit of foxes.

Surtees is a specialist. But he is, to an important extent, outside his speciality. He had strong views about sport. He hated the drunkenness of sporting society and the old squirearchy. He hoped the new age would bring in something better. He was hostile to the literary conventions. His parodies of *Nimrod* show him as an opponent of literary snobbery. He disliked the obsequious regime of servants and the rogueries of the stable, the auctions and the law. It is odd that one so saturated in his world should have seen it all with so fresh an eye. Perhaps he had that morbidity of eye which is given to some men at the end of a period, when they can see things with the detachment which considerable art demands. He was too much the gentleman and amateur to construct a great novel; but he was independent enough and sufficiently instructed by obsession to create in Jorrocks a huge character who could go off and live an episodic life of his own. The Victorians were shy of Surtees's honesty. They were moving away from the notion that there was a level on which all Englishmen could be united. They were building the split culture of our time. Surtees was trying to save England on the acres of Handley Cross. (pp. 91-3)

> *V. S. Pritchett, "The Brutal Chivalry," in his* The Living Novel & Later Appreciations, *revised edition, Random House, 1964, pp. 88-93.*

CHARLES ALVA HOYT (essay date 1967)

[*Deeming Surtees the best sporting writer in the English language, Hoyt argues that his subject matter has been both "a bane and a blessing" to his reputation. Hoyt also delineates the strengths and weaknesses of Surtees' art, focusing on his characterization.*]

Robert Smith Surtees is a neglected author to whom our century might very well look both for entertainment and instruction. To be sure Surtees . . . is a minor novelist, in the most accepted sense of the term: he is a specialist, a sporting writer, and the best in our language. Unfortunately that is where many of the anthologies leave him, on the tips of the tongues of doctoral candidates, from which bad eminence he is let fall, from time to time, into discussion.

Even these excursions must be rare for him today; young scholars on the prowl want material of greater "significance." And yet they would do well to remember Louis Kronenberger's description of Don Juan's adventures in England: "a stiff ride with the hounds after hypocrites and snobs; a long day on the moors bagging philistines and pharisees; a large coaching party clattering at the heels of politics." As Kronenberger suggests, sport to the British is not idle amusement, but their way of life. A British sporting writer then, if he is a good one, will have a great deal to say about his time. Surtees was the best, and his opinions of nineteenth-century British society are both wise and diverting: vigorous, unsparing, almost always highly critical. His irony is intense, his indignation warm, although he frequently melts into long passages of sheer fun, and nonsense, that sole delight among Victorian virtues. For these and other reasons he remains easy to read; I find him one of the most congenial of the nineteenth-century novelists.

His deficiencies are almost entirely in technique, and even there confined to few, if important, considerations. His style is rich, anecdotal, Dickensian. In his pervasive irony, however, he more resembles Thackeray, with whom he corresponded and sometimes consulted about his books. But even more than Thackeray he is ever the satirist, a fact which our textbooks too often ignore, although it was understood perfectly in his day. (pp. 59-60)

Surtees' chosen subject matter is at once a bane and a blessing: it requires a special knowledge and a special style, both of which I now propose to take up.

All of Surtees' novels are focussed squarely upon hunting, although some spend longer than others in coming to the subject, and some wander freely from it. I think we may set it down as an axiom that the more the books have to do with hunting, the better they are. It is not because Surtees is knowledgeable only upon the one subject, but, apparently, that he is happiest there. The young man who left the law to follow the hounds all over England, who resisted respectability for five years from his editor's desk, had but one great love in life. "'Untin is the foremost passion of my 'eart! compared with it all others are flat and unprofitable (cheers and laughter). It's not never of no manner of use 'umbuggin the matter, but there's no sport fit to hold the candle to fox-'untin'." Thus his alter ego, Jorrocks (*Handley Cross* . . .), the one major character in his fiction to whom we may say that he gave his wholehearted approval. (p. 64)

Surtees was one of the keenest foxhunters of a generation of eager sportsmen. In the course of his profession as touring writer he made himself familiar with every hunting country in England, just as a seasoned sportswriter today knows every city in the league. But much more than baseball is the American game, fox hunting was the sport of the ruling class in nineteenth-century England. It was in fact participated in by members of all classes, from the notorious hunting tailors and grocers of Surrey (Jorrocks was one such), representative of the middle class on the way up, to the sturdy farmers over whose fields the sport was pursued, and the common laborers themselves who frequently followed the hounds on foot. The foxhunter, as appears over and over again in the novels, was welcome everywhere. (pp. 64-5)

But just that strength of subject matter has proven Surtees' downfall in our day, when fox hunting is known to few and practiced by even fewer. If the popularity of the sport insured the hunting novelist a wide audience in the nineteenth century, whatever his faults, so its decay in the twentieth serves to keep him in obscurity in spite of his virtues.

So much for the special knowledge required; there is a similar difficulty involved with the special style. All arts have their mysteries, one of which is a sacred language. The sacred language attached to a lost art is rough going, and that is Surtees' problem in a nutshell. But here too is a positive side: there is such a thing as the fertile cliché. It exists on the outward circumference of style, where it is not only unavoidable but useful, comfortable, and reassuring. Anyone who enjoys baseball, or Baroque music, or literary criticism, must know what I mean. If Surtees suffers from the restrictions of his special language, he also enjoys the stability, security, and comfort it imparts to his style. Consider the following passage, chosen practically at random, and from one of the lesser works:

> Mr. Boggledike was again to be seen standing erect in his stirrups, yoiking and coaxing his hounds into Crashington Gorse. There was Dicky, cap-in-hand, in the centre ride, exhorting the young hounds to dive into the strong sea of gorse. "Y-o-o-icks! wind him! y-o-o-icks!

pash him up!'' cheered the veteran, now turning his horse across to enforce the request. There was his lordship at the high corner as usual, ensconced among the clump of weatherbeaten blackthorns—thorns that had neither advanced nor receded a single inch since he first knew them,—his eagle eye fixed on the narrow fern and coarse grass-covered dell down which Reynard generally stole. There was Harry Swan at one corner to head the fox back from the beans, and Tom Speed at the other to welcome him away over the corn-garnered open. And now the whimper of old sure-finding Harbinger, backed by the sharp ''yap'' of the terrier, proclaims that our friend is at home, and presently a perfect hurricane of melody bursts from the agitated gorse,—every hound is in the paroxysm of excitement, and there are five-and-twenty couple of them, fifty musicians in the whole! ''*Tally-ho!* there he goes across the ride!''

''*Cub!*'' cries his lordship.

''*Cub!*'' responded Dicky.

''*Crack!*'' sounds the whip.—

(*Ask Mamma* . . .)

And so ''the whole infuriated phalanx dashed across the ride,'' and off they go, out of our sight. The passage does not present any particularly interesting or unusual character, like Soapey Sponge or Jorrocks' huntsman, James Pigg. It varies in no important particulars from a thousand others in the sporting literature of the time: the technical terms, the affectionate Victorian circumlocutions—''our friend is at home''—''the veteran''—and the cast, as closely prescribed as in an Oriental drama: the Squire, the field, huntsmen, rustics, horses, hounds, fox.

The technical terms, unlike those of some crafts, are easy to master, and the circumlocutions and other assorted gewgaws of Victorian expression may as well seem quaint and charming to us as offensive, now that we have condemned them so utterly in our own fiction. As for the classic situation and its cast, I welcome them with the same affection that I might show a favorite piece of Baroque woodwind music. Indeed the whole passage seems to me like nothing as much as the imperative opening blast of a quartet by K. P. E. Bach, pregnant with good things to come, things which lose none of their value because one knows what they are to be.

Special pleas to one side, it becomes necessary to attempt some evaluation of Surtees' accomplishment as novelist. And immediately it must be said that he is deficient in one vitally important area—design. His weakness is the more noticeable, appearing as it does against the great strengths of many of his contemporaries, who surely have never been surpassed as systematic observers of human life. With Surtees, however, it is otherwise: he grasps situations with incisive wit and draws individuals brilliantly; but in the managing of large movements or character development he is rarely successful. *Ask Mamma,* for example, is very unsure in direction from the start, and *Hawbuck Grange* is little better than a pastiche of anecdotal fragments. In many of his better books, too, he is forced to take hold of the plot from time to time and wrench it into the direction in which he wishes it to go. The death of Jack Spraggon at the end of *Mr. Sponge's Sporting Tour* serves no purpose whatever that I can see, save to get him out of the way; similarly

the sudden good fortune that descends upon the hero of *Plain or Ringlets* seems nothing more than a last desperate measure to punish the mercenary women who have been misusing him.

Of these weaknesses Surtees himself was aware. In the preface to *Handley Cross* he says, ''The reader will have the kindness to bear in mind, that the work merely professes to be a tale, and does not aspire to the dignity of a novel'' [see excerpt dated 1854]. There is sarcasm there, perhaps, but self-knowledge as well. Before *Ask Mamma,* he writes, ''It may be a recommendation to the lover of light literature to be told, that the following story does not involve the complication of a plot'' [see excerpt dated 1858]. Certainly Surtees tended to counteract his weakness by slipping into the picaresque, which he does with great success in *Mr. Sponge's Sporting Tour.* ''Soapey'' Sponge, a delightful fraud and confidence man, but a keen sportsman, methodically works his way through one unsuspecting family after another on his tour, playing upon his well-to-do hosts' and hostesses' crassness and greed. Similarly, the movements of the hunt give a picaresque flavor to *Handley Cross* as well as to *Mr. Romford's Hounds,* whose hero, ''Facey'' Romford, is like Sponge a confidence man who fattens on the cupidity of his victims.

Subtlety, then, and sophisticated development, of plot, theme, or character, is not to be found here. But what a great deal else is! First of all, the wit and humor, the continuous crackle of exploded pretensions and hypocrises. Surtees has the columnist's feeling for situation. His perception may lack depth or scope, but the reader may supply these for himself if the author has but caught the situation accurately. At times Surtees apprehends it perfectly. (pp. 65-8)

[Surtees' characters] are all either wolves or sheep. There are, however, some exceptions; and exceptions do not make rules; they break them. The half-dozen lovable characters in Surtees' fiction, with all their faults, atone for whole legions of his mutton-headed squires, thieving servants, and rotten society women.

One of the most endearing characteristics of Surtees is that he loves a good rascal. Both Soapey Sponge and Facey Romford are crooks; they make a handsome living cheating respectable people. Yet he gives them nerve and stamina and flair—hunters' virtues. If they live on other people's money, they live with style. They are no Robin Hoods, however. Facey is in fact a considerable skinflint, as far as his own limited funds are concerned, and he is callous, insensitive, crude and ignorant to boot. Soapey is selfish, irresponsible, tactless and impertinent. Yet they can ride, and will ride, and nothing can stop them. Like their creator, they esteem nothing so much as fox hunting.

These men are at the head of Surtees' list of rogues. He has many, many more. A good Surtees novel begins with a hunt and a ball, a banquet and a by-day, and ends with a marriage, an election, or a bankruptcy. In between we have seen hunt society in action: the men trying to sell each other horses; the women, their daughters. This society, as I have suggested, is conceived of by Surtees and his time as including practically everybody. There are rich families looking for titles, titled families looking for riches; poor boys trying to pass themselves off as Earls, and poor girls posing as heiresses. The rich are too often proud, and the poor either envious or craven.

All these dinner parties and dances are in reality fine dressing for a primitive and rather ugly business: buying and selling innocent flesh, and it is a clear case of *caveat emptor*. The buyer is, in fact, almost always cheated, Surtees seems to say, because he has tried to purchase with money that which he should have sought out with an honest heart. If this statement makes Surtees a moralist, so be it. There is no other explanation for his constant attack on Victorian morality.

For it is the "respectable people" who lose, time and again, in every novel. Who wins? Jorrocks, but he is a presumptuous cockney and an unashamed bourgeois, a tea merchant held in disdain by the wealthy Mrs. Barnington and her set. Soapey Sponge and Facey Romford escape to Australia with whole skins and a bit of money after having led the gentry a pretty dance. But old Goldspink, the prosperous banker of *Ask Mamma,* is ruined in business in spite of all his cleverness.

These greedy respectable people are the legitimate prey of frauds, whether professionals like Soapey and Facey, or amateurs like "Fine Billy" Pringle, a harmless simpleton, the hero of *Ask Mamma,* who has somehow acquired a reputation as "the richest commoner in England." Of course he has next to nothing, but he lives very well at the expense of all the greedy mammas who would rather be humbugged ten times over than lose a good prospect to a rival.

Then there are the exotic frauds, like Prince Pirouetteza, the son of a Florentine dancing master, who turns up in *Plain or Ringlets* as house guest of the great Duke of Tergiversation, or Sir Moses Mainchance of *Ask Mamma,* the stock villainous Jew of fiction, wealthy and crass. Sir Moses, however, with the advent of his baronetcy, has embraced the principles of the Church of England. (pp. 72-3)

Then there are *nouveaux riches* like Willy Watkins of *Mr. Romford's Hounds,* "a good-looking fellow without any brains," who has fallen into money somehow in the never-never land Australia, and returned home with a horror of a wife, the sort "who would push her way if she could." There is a marriageable daughter, Cassandra Cleopatra, descended on her father's side of ne'er-do-wells, and on her mother's of deported felons. The Watkins family carries on a duel for honors with Mr. and Mrs. Hazey of a landed family of dubious character. And there are mountebanks and quack doctors—Sebastian Mello, the fastidious fraud of *Handley Cross*—and common cardsharpers—Johnny O'Dicey of *Plain or Ringlets*—all the jackals and kites who lurk at the edges of society. But we have had enough of them.

Truly good men and women are rare in Surtees, as in life, but worth the search. The parade of his characters in their ceaseless vanity reminds one of Hieronymus Bosch's painting, "The Hay Wain." There all mankind is represented as struggling forward in foolish dispute over an enormous load of straw which is rolling them straight to Hell, while far above all the scuffling and shouting two lovers dally, on top of the world as it were, protected from its nonsense by the purity of their emotion. Just so Surtees exempts from his indictment the honest sportsman, the rare man who forsakes worldliness for love. Such a one is Jovey Jessup; several times referred to in the canon, and fully portrayed in *Plain or Ringlets*: "a thorough sportsman and a hearty hospitable fellow." He keeps two cooks, "an Englishman to cook his beefsteak for breakfast, and a Frenchman to send up the fricandeau, etc., for dinner." When his digestion is threatened because of his unceasing dinners and drinking bouts, he does not become a recluse, but rather takes on a fellow to do his drinking for him, a Mr. Boyston who is thereafter known as Jovey Jessup's Jug.

Delightful as these two are, they are eclipsed by Jorrocks and his famous Scotch huntsman, James Pigg ("dinna call me a Scotchman, and keep thy bit bowdekite quiet—ar'll manish matters"). (pp. 74-5)

Hunting, hunting, is Jorrocks' life, but not his only life. Like other great men he plays many parts. Hunting is undoubtedly his preferred role, but Surtees brings him on so that we see him from every side of his imposing personality. In the early sketches we know him as a great merchant of London, an eccentric, already famous as a fox hunting enthusiast. *Handley Cross* brings him down to the country and into country society, as a Master of Fox Hounds—the apex of his ambition. Finally, in *Hillingdon Hall,* he buys an estate and establishes himself as a squire—Justice of the Peace and all. The book ends with his winning an election over the Marquis of Bray by two votes and going into Parliament.

It is Dick Whittington all over again. And indeed Jorrocks is precisely of that tradition, a tradition as honorable and old as London itself. He is the heir to those prosperous city merchants of the old drama, the "flat-caps" of Shakespeare's day who held firm to their principles although scorned by sprigs of quality.... Their liberality, their geniality, their prudence and good sense were at the heart of English prosperity, and the old playwrights knew it. Jorrocks is just such another. He has not an ounce of pretense or sham about him; when snobs patronize him by adding an order for tea to their correspondence about fox hunting, he dutifully fills the order before telling them to go to the devil. (pp. 76-7)

It seems to me that it is very much to Surtees' credit that he made this man the central figure of his fiction.... Although he has a good deal of fun with Jorrocks, he never patronizes him, no, nor betrays him, either. Whatever Surtees may have lacked as a novelist, it was not what is popularly called *class*.

And thus it is possible to say that he was not entirely disillusioned with his country either, for although he looked unflinchingly at its faults, he believed that in it a man like Jorrocks might still rise from a grocer's apprenticeship to great wealth, popularity in the highest circles, and finally to parliament. The parallels are by no means exact, but Surtees put a great deal of himself into Jorrocks: both were men absolutely devoted. This honest, unpretentious devotion, in both cases, justified and dignified its subject, and incidentally led both men, if we may judge by what Surtees' friends have written of him, away from shallowness and vanity into lives of decency, happiness, and merit. (pp. 77-8)

Charles Alva Hoyt, "Robert Smith Surtees," in Minor British Novelists, *edited by Charles Alva Hoyt, Southern Illinois University Press, 1967, pp. 59-78.*

ALEX HAMILTON (essay date 1968)

[*In his introduction to* Jorrocks, *Hamilton praises Surtees' creative powers yet suggests that he remains a minor figure among nineteenth-century English novelists because he never fully developed his literary talents.*]

The intransigence of Surtees's sporting heroes lies midway between the utter recklessness known as 'bottom' of eighteenth-century bloods, and the baying for broken glass of Evelyn Waugh's bloody-minded aristocrats. Which is not to say that Surtees would have had patience with either of these terrible manifestations of the petted English male ego—he is saved from the worst excesses of the squirearchy by his lack of com-

Mr. Sponge at Jawleyford Court, illustrated by Leech.

petitive spirit. He might have been disturbed by the threats to the landed interest, as evinced in the move to repeal the Corn Laws—indeed he never wholly repudiated the suggestions of friends that he should involve himself directly in the battle at Westminster—but at the worst he imagined the corruption of a way of living: the prospect of total dispossession can never have occurred to him. And that maudlin sense of not being wanted by the State which crept throughout contemporary Romantic European literature was as remote from him and his concerns as today J. B. Priestley is from the flower people. Somewhere here one must begin to look for the explanation of his finally disappointing his admirers, for with all his exuberance, comic invention, wonderful ear, instinctive sense of an audience and vast experience of the sheer friction caused by the irregularities of character, with everything that should have given him parity on the shelf with Dickens, there is no growth. He never got his whole weight behind his literary talent. He is the darling of a specialist readership, but even within the narrow scope of the English nineteenth-century novel, he remains a minor figure.

The very manner of his first entry on to the literary scene already whispers both the charm of his personality and his ambivalence towards the matter of exploiting it. Tucked in towards the end of the third number of *The New Sporting Magazine,* published in July 1831, which Surtees himself founded and edited, appears a sketch entitled **"A Day with the Surrey,"** by 'A Yorkshireman'. The Yorkshireman hasn't trotted five paragraphs before he's notched a specimen for *The Oxford Dictionary of Quotations*: 'Every man shouting in proportion

to the amount of his subscription', and for thirty-three more years this eccentric, obsessed fellow plied his own lonely covert of literature, sparking off quotable stuff from horses and dogs and the retinue who follow, to borrow another quotation, 'the sport of kings'. . . . Everything Surtees wrote was for magazine publication, usually in serialized form, with the result that his works have the flavour of social occasions, and the difference between one and another is as much, or as little, as that between dancing with one partner all evening, and playing the field. (pp. vii-viii)

The coherence of Surtees's fictional world is established by the unquestioned assumption of every character in it that, while breath can be drawn, he must somehow keep up the pace. If the reader cannot see the presence of this human motive as proper to contriving the death of a fox, the vitality of Surtees's writing will seem to him spurious and even offensive. If he accepts it, he has a mount which will take the obstacles (a certain repetitiousness, plus a mass of arch allusiveness to points of reference rubbed out by time) and hack along comfortably through the barren country. 'Horses and intellects go a racing pace' wrote a Regency versifier—the fork in the road which would take one to the gymkhana and the other to the railway station lay still some way ahead. In Surtees's time horses and intellects were, if not symbiotic, at least at ease with one another. (pp. ix-x)

The Surtees hunting world binds together in good fellowship (whose only prescription is that if they drink water it is 'for the purpose of bringing their stomachs round to stand something stronger') an astonishing variety of characters, and it is exclusive of only one important (which some may think fatal) element: women. (p. xi)

In Jorrocks's view women exist to be kicked out of bed a couple of times a month, and to have the leg of mutton done to a turn at five o'clock sharp. But there is no use in repining over missed opportunities in Surtees's work—he has to be seen like one of those touchy, eccentric innkeepers who are so fond of their own cooking that they serve dinner without ever thinking to offer their guests any choice from a menu. (p. xii)

[Surtees's published works do] not make a very long list of titles, but still it is enough to evoke from those who have read the books an echo of the criticism made by the *Morning Post* of his redoubtable rival, Nimrod, when it printed the opinion that his style was so excellent it was a pity he did not interest himself in something more important than sport. But of course not a few million Englishmen since, confronted with this comment, would instantly have retorted that Nimrod and Surtees alike could at least see what was in front of their noses, unlike most pen-pushers, and that there is nothing more important than sport. It is in this particular, his emphasis on an activity which gives no obvious rewards to the participant, that Surtees really claims gratitude for a valuable insight. He wrote eight novels, all but two of which (*Plain or Ringlets?* and *Ask Mamma,* which spread the jollifications as far as general Victorian amusements, and weddings) are ramifications of the interests expressed in his first novel. *Handley Cross* and *Mr Sponge's Sporting Tour* . . . are undoubtedly the big ones, and one cannot help regretting the fact that he died in 1864 at a time when he was planning one more on this scale, with the modest title of *Sporting and Social Recollections.* (pp. xiv-xv)

One of the anomalies of English literature is the little attention that has been given to sportsmen as heroes. Of late some investigations into the possibilities have been made by novelists, who have returned with strong stories and dismal conclusions about their subjects. They may seem to indicate that Surtees's hopes were misplaced—there is no release from pettiness in a sporting life. It appears the pressures move naturally away from democratization of the athlete. But it is always worth keeping Surtees in mind when making such forays. What he is saying through Jorrocks is that the sportsman may be oddly shaped, the rhythm of his life matched to a metronome in his guts, the weather may be terrible, the terrain dotted with hostile figures, the mount be a spavined nag, and the fox when found turn out to be a rabbit, but that if he has had a run at all the day has been worth while, and in the midst of rueful contemplation of disaster the participants know something screened from the onlooker—things may turn out better tomorrow and today's experience will then add immeasurable spice to the triumph. (p. xv)

> *Alex Hamilton, in an introduction to* Jorrocks' Jaunts and Jollities *by Robert Smith Surtees, edited by Herbert Van Thal, Cassell, 1968, pp. vii-xv.*

BONNIE RAYFORD NEUMANN (essay date 1978)

[*In this analysis of* Hawbuck Grange, Young Tom Hall, Ask Mamma, Plain or Ringlets?, *and* Mr. Facey Romford's Hounds, *Neumann traces the development of Surtees' art, examining how he experimented with plot, structure, narration, characterization, and theme.*]

"To beguile an idle hour" must have been Surtees's primary reason for writing [*Hawbuck Grange* (see excerpt dated 1847)];

his secondary reason was to provide a kind of memorial to November 1846, "the worst hunting November that perhaps ever was known." . . .

Certainly to write a successful novel covering only one month's time would require a great deal of skill and planning. One would expect to find a strong central character in whom the reader is truly interested, a plot of some complexity that can be developed quickly and concisely and brought soon to a climax, a cast of supporting characters who are easily identifiable and essential to the story, a careful control of time, including a discriminating use of flashbacks. *Hawbuck Grange* has none of these. (p. 80)

It is intriguing to speculate why, after three novels bursting with Jorrocks, Surtees created Tom Scott as the hero of his fourth book. Perhaps he merely desired a change; perhaps he wanted to find out if he could write successfully about another kind of person, far different not only from Jorrocks but also from all the minor characters in his earlier novels. Or perhaps he was reacting to outside influences—none of the earlier novels had been particularly successful, and . . . he might have hoped a Tom Scott would prove more to the public's liking. (pp. 80-1)

"Surtees apparently decided to have a normal human being for a hero for once," writes Cooper, but if Tom Scott is "normal," then the majority of the human race must be very dull. Siegfried Sassoon goes even further. "I have a special affection for Thomas Scott," he writes, "since he is one of the few unquestionably likeable characters in Surtees, charming, sensible and modest, and—in my opinion—the nearest to a self-portrait in his works." The very fact that *Hawbuck Grange* exists at all is sufficient refutation of Sassoon's identification of a self-portrait—Tom Scott lacks both imagination and ambition to undertake a novel, except perhaps in fireside musings, and to complete not one but eight novels and several other works besides is entirely beyond his capacity. Besides, Surtees—with his wife and three children, his financially successful country estate, his numerous positions of responsibility in his community, his political involvement and local lectures, his fighting on behalf of his poorer neighbors and inmates of workhouses, his connections with the literary world—was actively and intimately involved with life. Poor Tom Scott could not even manage to get himself married! . . . Surtees was *not* a Tom Scott, and the world is a much happier place for it. (p. 81)

Fortunately *Hawbuck Grange* has more to offer than one main character; it is essentially a collection of hunting episodes. . . . It is primarily the framework for these sketches that is weak, for once Surtees is in the middle of a chase his writing is every bit as good as it was in *Handley Cross*. (p. 84)

Good and numerous as the hunting scenes are, however, they cannot, unsupported, carry the novel, and *Hawbuck Grange* has little more to offer. In fact its defects quite overshadow its good points. For one thing, Surtees carried further in this novel his experiment in author-intrusion which he started in *Hillingdon Hall*. Perhaps he had Sterne's *Tristram Shandy* in mind as a model; unfortunately, he lacked Sterne's genius, and the result is complete confusion between Tom Scott's story and the author's digressions, between the third person and the first, between the present and the past. Sometimes these digressions are meant to be educational, as when he points out that "good farming is certainly a great promoter of hunting" . . . , or "wet is not indispensable to scent" . . . , or "a horse's coat furnishes a pretty good criterion of the state of the atmosphere" . . . , or even when he insists that "there is nothing makes a person look so queer as an extremely long frock or greatcoat." . . . Other times he pauses to carry on a conversation with the reader, much in imitation of Sterne. Chapter nine, for example, begins in this distracting way: "'WHO-OOP!' 'Who-oop! That's a queer way of beginning a chapter, Mr. Author!' 'So it is, Mr. Reader, but you'll have a good many more of them before you are done'." . . . Sterne's great antinovel is composed entirely of such literary devices; unfortunately Surtees's few sorry attempts irritate the reader rather than amuse him. (pp. 85-6)

. . . . .

Surtees never finished [*Young Tom Hall*]. He couldn't bring himself to abandon it altogether though, and he tried to restore it in bits and pieces by using many of the same characters and incidents in his next two novels. Such patchwork is seldom successful, however, and in *Ask Mamma* and *Plain or Ringlets* it is extremely disappointing. *Tom Hall* was on its way to being one of Surtees's best novels; those two which succeeded it and were made up in part from it are among his worst.

Young Tom Hall is something of a departure for Surtees, for in it one sees him gradually drawing away from the hunting field and focusing his attention more and more on the non-hunting element of country society. His next two novels continue the trend and can be appropriately classified, as they are by Ms. Hallgarth, "fashionable parodies" as opposed to sporting fiction. The most noticeable difference between the two types of novels is the difference in their main characters, for rather than being true and enthusiastic sportsmen, these men use the hunting field merely to gain social advantage. In fact, of the four heroes in these three books, two of them, Tom Hall and Billy Pringle, genuinely hate to hunt, a third, Jack Bunting, knows virtually nothing about the sport in the beginning but gradually becomes initiated and enthusiastic before the end of the novel, and a fourth, Jasper Goldspink, never hunts at all! (pp. 103-04)

[*Young Tom Hall*] is fast-moving and genuinely interesting. The male characters are all types new to Surtees, and he obviously enjoyed them. All his characters here carry that distinguishing Surtees mark of individuality, of somehow being larger than life, more real than real people. The novel abounds with jovial humor of the kind found in the early Jorrocks books and in *Mr. Sponge*. His satire, although of a slightly different focus, is good-natured and well-balanced between standard Surtees sporting types such as Lord Heartycheer and new satirical subjects such as old "sivin and four's elivin" Hall and the Heavysteed Dragoons. . . . Tom has one advantage that Surtees's next few heroes do not have—he is a completely sympathetic character. As physically unattractive and slow-minded as he is, he is the one innocent, unambitious person in the novel, and for that reason alone the reader is entirely on his side.

Altogether, *Young Tom Hall* is a novel which the reader does not like to see interrupted; he really wants to find out what happens to Tom Hall and his engagement to Angelina and his new flirtation with Laura Guineafowle and to Angelina's "second string," the little soldier called "Jug." He has not yet begun to tire of any of them. Sincerely wishing to know how a novel ends is perhaps the highest tribute a reader can pay to an author, but in this case he is doomed to frustration, for the next two books, far from carrying on either the story or the fun of *Young Tom Hall*, are very sorry affairs indeed.

. . . . .

Ask Mamma is an obvious offshoot from the preceding novel; Lord Heartycheer reappears as Lord Ladythorne, still seventy years old and still hunting both fox and young ladies; Dicky Thorndyke becomes Dicky Boggledyke, huntsman to his Lordship in fields both of sport and of romantic conquest; Major Guineafowle is Major Yammerton, still hunting hare "five and twenty years without a subscription"; Angelina Blunt reappears as the international coquette Miss de Glancey. . . . (pp. 108-09)

Most interesting, however, are the similarities and differences between the heroes of the two novels, for although Billy Pringle is obviously based on Tom Hall, the two men appear to the reader as entirely different persons, and the novels succeed or fail to the extent that these characters capture the reader's interest and concern. Just as old Tom Hall balances his accounts and declares that "our Tom shall be a gent!" so old William Pringle exclaims, "Our Billy shall be a gent!" Old Hall's definition of a gentleman, "a man with plenty of money and nothing to do," applies as well to Billy as it does to Tom. Billy, just as much as Tom, lacks any self-motivation, any direction except that imposed on him by others. In fact, the only basic difference between the two characters is their size, for Billy Pringle is slender rather than fat, handsome in a pampered way rather than grotesque, and from that change in the physical appearance of the main character arises a vast difference in the reader's acceptance and interpretation of him. For instance, when Tom affects the "swell" he is completely ludicrous. No matter how showy his clothes or tight his new hunting boots, the reader always sees him as he is first introduced, "disporting himself on three chairs in the bay-windowed coffee-room of the Salutation Inn." As a "round, fat, humming-top-shaped" man "upon whose plump limbs the flesh wobbled and trembled" as he walks, Tom Hall is a perfect victim—the reader sympathizes with him because he has known and sympathized with fat people in real life. While it is true that the stereotype of the naive fat boy is offensive and even cruel, nevertheless it is this very stereotyping that saves Tom as a character, for the reader can accept him and even approve of him on the one-dimensional basis in which he is presented. But take away Tom's size and one has Billy Pringle, a very sad main character indeed.

While Tom is a reluctant social climber, his financial condition, parents, and friends urging the role upon him, Billy Pringle is a "swell" of the first order. Whereas Tom's actions, however absurd, have an air of naturalness about them, Billy is Paris-trained to play the snob. Another difference between them is that while Tom's money is real, Billy's is primarily a matter of reputation. Billy's entire character is a vast pretense, and the reader dislikes him immediately. (pp. 109-10)

This sadly disappointing character Billy Pringle is symbolic of the inferiority of *Ask Mamma* to Surtees's earlier works, including *Young Tom Hall*. For one thing, the satire here has a different flavor. Watson calls it "bleak," Hallgarth says it has a "bitterness" of tone, and Cooper states that the novel has "little geniality." The new direction of Surtees's satire was already obvious in *Tom Hall,* but in that novel Surtees retains enough of his former successful character types and humorous situations to make a good novel. Here the satire is more limited, more clichéd, and often preachy. The primary difference, again, lies in the differences between main characters, for Tom Hall provides *Young Tom Hall* with a center of focus that *Ask Mamma* lacks. The reader cares about Tom, and this quality of caring raises him above the mere caricature, the butt of laughter, the

Guests dancing the polka at the hunt ball in Ask Mamma, *illustrated by Leech.*

pawn of satire. Although he is far from being a Jorrocks or a Sponge, he is sufficiently honest and natural to represent Surtees's satiric norm; he is the center of consciousness with which the reader identifies to watch and laugh at the absurdities around him. Such is not the case with Billy Pringle. If anything, Billy epitomizes everything Surtees could not stand, and, because he is allowed no redeeming characteristics, the reader cannot stand him either. Consequently he becomes the object of satire rather than the satirical norm, and the soul of the novel is gone; there is no chink in the satirical armor through which the reader can enter and view Surtees's world from inside. There is no John Jorrocks to laugh with, no Soapey Sponge to connive with, no Tom Hall to cheer for. The reader is kept emotionally outside the action while the *nouveau-riche* world of "swells" and hypocrites and social climbers and jealous, possessive, self-satisfied, petty people, led by Billy Pringle himself, are paraded before him. The parade, from this distance, soon becomes obvious, repetitious, and dull. One gets the feeling that Surtees himself did not enjoy it anymore. (p. 112)

But the greatest part of the problem with this novel lies with Surtees—never before had he written with such hesitation, such insecurity. One can find whole chapters that add nothing whatever to the book: "The Major's Stud," "Cards for a Spread," "Commerce and Agriculture." On the occasion of Lord Ladythorne's hunt breakfast, the kind of scene in which Surtees usually excels, he deadens it with entirely too much detail; instead of highlighting the most interesting aspects, he describes *every* guest, *every* costume, *every* serving dish, *every* particle of food, *every* bit of conversation within the hearing of Billy or Ladythorne.... Even the best-intentioned reader finds himself skimming and flipping pages.

Worse yet are Surtees's constant, irritating intrusions into the novel with tidbits of irrelevant information. One could make an extensive list of such things: "Posterity will know nothing of the misery their forefathers underwent in the travelling way" ...; "Some people can eat at any time, but to a well-regulated appetite, having to undergo even the semblance of an additional meal is inconvenient"; ... "Let any man of forty look at his tailor's bill when he was twenty, and see what a liberality of innocence it displays" ... and so on and on and on. Surtees had already experimented with this technique ... in *Hawbuck Grange;* here it gets entirely out of control. (pp. 117-18)

It is impossible to ascertain for sure just what happened to Surtees in [*Ask Mamma* and *Plain or Ringlets*], although most critics put the blame for their lack of success on the interruption of *Young Tom Hall.* There Surtees had a fine novel underway; when he was abruptly forced to abandon it, he floundered. If he could have brought himself to finish it, even with its greatly reduced chance of publication, he might have avoided this inspirational hiatus. As it was, instead of waiting for a new idea, he grabbed at what he had—a character here, a scene there—and tried to lump them together into some kind of whole, losing sight in the process of both his satirical direction and his reader. The effort was fruitless. Not only does the novel fail, but so does something else—Surtees's heretofore excellent critical judgment, for he plunged immediately into another such novel, salvaging what he could of the rest of *Young Tom Hall.*

. . . . .

Plain or Ringlets is unique among Surtees's works for one reason—of the three main characters, characters who among them provide the novel's points-of-view, one is a woman, Miss Rosa McDermott of Privett Grove. While it is true that in other works Surtees may present a woman in an important role, Mrs. Flather in *Hillingdon Hall,* for example, or Lucy Glitters Sponge in *Mr. Romford's Hounds,* such women are still completely dominated in literary terms by the novels' heroes, John Jorrocks and Facey Romford. Such is not the case in *Plain or Ringlets,* where Rosa plays an equal part with Jasper Goldspink and Jack Bunting, the other two corners of the love-triangle. None of the three is a pleasing character; in fact, to characterize their relationship as a "love-triangle" is misleading, for the only real love they are capable of feeling is for themselves or for someone else's money. Rosa speaks for all three when, warned by her lawyer not to marry hastily, she laughs, "Oh, you needn't be afraid of me, Mr. Ballivant! You needn't be afraid of me, I'm not one of the sentimental sort." This novel, like its predecessor, is constructed of bits and pieces of *Young Tom Hall* carelessly thrown together with picnics and regattas and races and grand balls.... Here Surtees moves even farther from the sporting toward the social novel, for all the interest here centers around the marriage market, around the question of who will end up married to whom. Again Surtees makes the mistake of presenting no sympathetic character, no satirical norm against which to measure the absurdities of the rest of society. In fact, his main characters here are perfect examples of those kinds of people whom Surtees himself most disliked. (pp. 118-19)

Although *Plain or Ringlets* is not a successful novel, it is, however, an extremely important source of social history and of information about the ideas and feelings of Surtees. Instead of those irritating one and two sentence digressions that permeated *Ask Mamma,* in this novel Surtees devotes entire chapters to discussing various aspects of Victorian life, frequently comparing what he sees around him with conditions he knew as a young man. (p. 124)

· · · · ·

Although *Handley Cross* and *Mr. Sponge's Sporting Tour* have always been Surtees's most popular books, *Mr. Romford's Hounds* is in many ways a better novel, most obviously because it has two features which all Surtees's earlier novels lack: a new, more human hero, and Surtees's *only* fully drawn, realistic female character.

Although Facey Romford is another of Surtees's great hero-villains, he is neither so arrogant as John Jorrocks nor so self-assertive as Soapey Sponge. While it is true that he takes advantage of the coincidence concerning his name and trades upon the borrowed Romford crest, he never actually *tells* anyone he is the other Romford—he simply lets other people draw the wrong conclusions and does nothing to correct them. As Surtees insists, when a wealthy bachelor, a man who is a fine huntsman and giver of grand parties, is in question, people are every bit as willing to be deceived as Facey is to deceive them. He never pushes himself into people's homes, as Sponge does, or takes advantage of their friendship, as Jorrocks tends to do. Even the questionable horse deals in which he participates are not initiated by him; he merely accepts the offers other people make. If those offers happen to be ridiculous, they are not his responsibility. He simply wants to be able to live comfortably, lamb chops and batter pudding constituting his favorite meal. He has no social pretension; he rents Beldon Hall unseen simply because it is available, and his first sight of so much grandeur genuinely dismays him. (pp. 134-35)

Unlike Soapey Sponge, who hunts primarily to show off a horse he wants to sell, Facey lives to hunt, and the social and economic responsibilities incumbent on a master of hounds are simply to be endured. He would much rather stay at home in the evening with his pipe and a bottle of Lovetin's gin than face a dinner party; in fact, if it were not for Lucy's nagging he probably would never have gone out at all. (p. 135)

Facey has little in common with Jorrocks and even less with that pushier version of Jorrocks, Soapey Sponge. He would rather die than deliver a "sporting lector," rather leave the country than impose himself on a Duke of Donkeyton. The very idea of running for public office would give him nightmares. He values his privacy much too dearly to surrender it to the Puffingtons, Crowdeys, and Scattercashs of the world, even in exchange for free room and board. On the other hand he is certainly a far cry from the innocuous Tom Scott, the dumb Billy Pringle, or the dandy Jack Bunting. He is a new kind of hero for Surtees, an individual, a believable human being, more low-key than Jorrocks and more likable than Sponge, further from a stereotype than any he had yet produced. (p. 136)

[Surtees's] treatment of women as characters in his novels has earned him severe criticism from every person who has written about his work. Not until Lucy Glitters in *Mr. Romford* did Surtees create a woman character in any depth; even more serious, not until Lucy Glitters did Surtees present or even mention women for any purpose other than to demean them or to laugh at them. (p. 138)

Surtees certainly fell victim over and over again to the most degrading of female stereotypes, for all of his women except Lucy Glitters Sponge are two-dimensional and easily categorized. Among his major female characters there are just two types—the marriage-minded "mamma" trying to sell her offspring to the highest bidder (Mrs. Flather, Mrs. Trotter, Mrs. McDermott, and Mrs. Jorrocks with her niece Belinda, as well as that most famous mother of all, Mrs. Pringle) and the marriageable daughter who is perfectly willing to be sold for the best settlement (Emma Flather, Angelina Blunt, Rosa McDermott, Cassandra Cleopatra Watkins, Anna Maria Hazey). Although these are obviously stereotypes, at least Surtees allows them to play conspicuous roles in his works; all his other women are not only stereotypes but also so constricted in their presentation that they never rise above a caricature. Women servants are dirty, lazy thieves. Young girls, while sometimes physically attractive, are always superficial and fickle with minds obsessed with marriage and clothes; in fact, they are never allowed to think one thought not directly connected with those two subjects. Once the girls are married they turn into shrews just like their mothers.

Women are, in other words, a nuisance. They perpetuate conversation at the dinner table when the men want to stuff themselves in peace and quiet; they wear crinolines and hoop-skirts that fill up the inside of a carriage, leaving no room for the men; they insist on having a new dress once in a while. Only one male character, the Marquis of Bray in *Hillingdon Hall,* does not breathe a sigh of relief when the women retire to the drawing room after dinner—in fact, "not being a great man for his liquor" he actually sneaks away from the table and joins them! But then Surtees makes clear that there is some question about the Marquis's masculinity anyway, referring to him as "the butterfly Marquis" and asserting that "Nature meant the Marquis for a girl, and a very pretty one he would have made." After all, no one "of the breeches, at least *le-*

gitimately of the breeches,'' would have acted in such a manner.

It would not be valid to argue that Surtees was writing satire and was, therefore, just as hard on the men. He was not. While it is true that many of his male characters are obviously satirical caricature or ''humour'' characters, even they show more variety and more believable human qualities than do any of his women. In fact, all characters with any imagination, any integrity, any sensitivity, even any intelligence, are men. . . . It would not be surprising if all Surtees's female readers, after such a display as this, would agree with Lucy who ''often said that the only thing that reconciled her to being a woman was, that she could not by any possibility have to marry one.'' . . . (pp. 139-40)

Then suddenly, with this kind of record in the presentation of women, Surtees, in his last novel, came up with a Lucy Glitters Sponge Somerville Sponge. What a delight and what a relief! She is everything the most ardent feminist of today could ask for. She is strong, independent, and hard-working. When the cigar store is in jeopardy and her husband completely irresponsible she goes on trying to make it work. When Sponge runs off the quietly salvages what she can for herself and retires to suffer in private whatever feelings of anger or sense of loss may assail her. She is beautiful and proud of her beauty in the best sense—she dresses well because it makes her feel good about herself; she accepts admiration gracefully but never demands it. She is genuinely fond of Facey and manages, because of her attachment and endless patience, to civilize him. She supports her mother and entertains her friends in style. She is

aware of all the stereotypes usually associated with her sex and uses them, sometimes necessarily and sometimes for fun—she can be the coquette or the little girl or the nagging wife or the dumb blonde when assuming those roles will get her what she wants or protect herself or Facey from exposure. Underneath that pretty, feminine exterior she is as intelligent, independent, and tough-minded as any person can be. (p. 140)

All things considered, *Mr. Romford's Hounds,* Surtees's last book, is also his best. It has more structure, more plot, than any of the others. It has genuine suspense created by the assumption of false identities which the reader knows will have to be uncovered. Its hunting scenes have all the color and excitement of those of *Handley Cross* and the ''wheeling and dealing,'' if less prominent, is every bit as clever as in *Mr. Sponge.* Those intimate details of Victorian life, from the discomforts of the ''melon-frame'' buggy to the dingy bedrooms, from the elaborate dinners to the smoky candles, from the glorious dress to the filthy servants, were never better represented. In contrast to the last three novels particularly, the humor has lost its bitterness and the satire its maliciousness. Facey Romford and Lucy Glitters outshine all Surtees's earlier characters. Perhaps his turning from fiction to autobiography was evidence of his own satisfaction, his recognition that he had reached a plateau, that all those characters and methods that he had been experimenting with over the last thirty-three years, ever since the first Jorrocks story appeared in the *New Sporting Magazine,* had finally come together and worked just right. (pp. 141-42)

Bonnie Rayford Neumann, in her Robert Smith Surtees, *Twayne Publishers, 1978, 165 p.*

One of Leech's illustrations for Mr. Facey Romford's Hounds.

VIRGINIA BLAIN   (essay date 1981)

[*In her introduction to* Sponge, *excerpted below, Blain explains how Surtees "is truly unique" among the minor novelists of the Victorian era.*]

Surtees's claim to our consideration does not rest upon his membership [in] a peculiarly English club, the sporting writers, but springs from his unusual ability to bridge the distance between that exclusive set and the larger world of mid-nineteenth century fiction. In *Mr. Sponge's Sporting Tour* Surtees united two literary traditions which had otherwise remained distinct; sporting writing on the one hand, and the satiric comedy of manners on the other. In this way he created a "kind" of novel that was quite unique.

Although his name has from time to time been linked for comparison with Trollope and Dickens, the writer with whom Surtees had most in common was Thackeray.... (p. ix)

Mr. Sponge's Sporting Tour is far from being an imitation of *Vanity Fair,* although that novel certainly provided a model of the anti-romanticism which characterized Surtees's own outlook. Surtees does have faults as a writer, but lack of originality is not one of them, and he is in many ways more tough-minded than Thackeray. No one could accuse him of sentimentality: he views the world through a shrewdly observant eye, mercilessly exposing affectation and hypocrisy, and extracting the most extraordinary amounts of information with a glance which apparently embraces only the surface. Nuances of dress are unerringly described in such a way as to pinpoint not only a character's sartorial habits and social class, but his or her personal history, moral standpoint and personality.

Because he was writing chiefly to amuse, he was careful to avoid "the inner chambers of the heart" in his own work and of course this limits his depth. But his range takes us far afield, and it is refreshing as well as instructive to be given such a knowledgeable "tour" of many important but too often neglected aspects of English rural society in the mid-nineteenth century. How did landowners, great and small, occupy themselves during a bleak country winter, for instance? Mr Sponge may indeed be a "characterless character" in more senses than the moral one, but the story of his progress in the gentle art of sponging provides his creator with unlimited opportunities for answering questions like this, and at the same time exposing pretensions and follies across all classes. Lord Scamperdale, the fox-hunting fanatic with such a splendid line in sub-blasphemy ("because I'm a lord and can't swear"), is treated with just as much ironic detachment and good-humoured mockery as Peter Leather, the intrepid groom who looks after Mr Sponge's alarming set of hired horses. One of Surtees's great advantages as a satirist of snobbery was that he feared nobody, neither the labourer nor the lord, with the result that, unusually among his contemporaries, he was never tempted to flatter or vilify either on the basis of class alone.

This characteristic disregard for his readers' prejudices certainly lowered his reputation in genteel circles.... It is not difficult to see why certain sections of the sporting public were offended by Surtees. One has only to glance at the novels of "serious" sporting writers, such as Nimrod (Charles Apperley), John Mills, or K. W. Horlock, to realize that flattery of the landed classes was one of their chief purposes. They described fox-hunting not only as an idyllic pastime, but also in terms of its moral advantages in sorting out the manly and noble from the cowards and the tradesmen. At the same time, they would protest that fox-hunting was a nonexclusive sport,

which could be enjoyed regardless of rank or wealth. Ironically enough, as Raymond Carr has pointed out, its "social glamour . . . and its attractions for the fortune hunter and the snob depended on its status as the aristocratic sport *par excellence.*"

Surtees was a realist, in a way that his fellows were not, and he could see such ironies very clearly and exploit them in his fiction. So he presented an unwelcome threat to their complacent double-vision by creating such an underbred character as Mr Sponge and allowing him to appear as a bold and expert rider who is generally up at the finish: a position they would have reserved for a *true* gentleman. (pp. x–xi)

[Although] Surtees had a predilection for sporting eccentrics, and although he liked to tease the morally earnest and the socially pretentious, none the less he was at heart a traditionalist too. He believed that the class system was natural, that hereditary wealth and privilege were right, and that hereditary landowners should govern the country. Given the society in which he grew up as one of the privileged, it would indeed be extraordinary if he had not. But when confronted with signs of erosion in the power of the landed classes, it never occurred to him to wall his park and beat his breast, or to close his eyes and find security in complacency. He foresaw that these reactions would only hasten the disappearance of traditional values, and he ridiculed the self-delusions, the shams and vanities, of the landed gentry, because he felt that the only way it could survive was by facing reality and, paradoxically, earning the superiority it was entitled to. His deep-seated belief, shared with the more "serious" sporting writers, that field sports had an essential part to play in ensuring the continuity of the basic pattern of English country life, was complementary to his concern for the increasingly threatened ideal of the true country gentleman.

Moreover, fox-hunting was a rural custom still full of life, and this was another of its attractions for Surtees. True, it was a sport with a particularly strong mystique, a set of unwritten rules for behaviour and dress. Yet once the sherry had been downed and the girths tightened, there it was: man (or, more rarely, woman) confronted by Nature, in the form of horse-flesh, mud, thorns, ditches and his own inner self.... Nobody but the huntsman in charge of the hounds ever cares whether a fox is actually killed at the end of it all; usually very few even see the finish. For Surtees as novelist the hunting field presented rich opportunities for observing character in action, and this is its chief interest in *Mr. Sponge.* There was a "glorious ideal" of fox-hunting, and Surtees had his share of belief in it, but the clash of the real against such an ideal seemed to him a much more entertaining subject for fiction than the dreary recitation of the latter. He was right, of course, and this is why his competitors, who set themselves up as "high priests" of fox-hunting, are seldom read today, even by devotees of the sport. It is ironic that it was Surtees the demythologizer who should have carried on the myth to later generations. (pp. xii–xiii)

[The secret nature of Surtees's authorship] meant that it retained for him the flavour of a hobby; he never quite took it seriously. Had his material circumstances been less easy, and had he been forced, like Dickens and Thackeray, to earn his living by his pen, his writing might have been the better for it. For even at his best he is uneven, and it is often the air of determined amateurishness which prevents a polished achievement. He responded well to the pressure of a more discriminating audience when it was put upon him, but this happened all too rarely.

In fact the most important instance occurred with *Mr. Sponge's Sporting Tour*. It was only then, with his fourth novel, that Surtees wrote for serial publication in a family magazine with literary pretensions (*The New Monthly,* edited at this time by Harrison Ainsworth), instead of a sporting magazine, whose readers' only demand was for plenty of hunting scenes. So *Mr. Sponge* was written with rather more care than its predecessors. . . . *Mr. Sponge* marked a turning point in Surtees's career in more ways than one. Not only was it his first popular success, it also led to his finding an ideal medium of publication. More importantly, though, it is the book in which he really found his feet as a writer of comic social satire, and it is considered by many to be his best work.

In some ways, however, it is not a novel at all. There is no plot to speak of, and almost no characterization in the conventional sense. But there is an eventful narrative, and there are some splendid caricatures, and they are linked together in so lively a manner that the total effect far surpasses that of many books with more pretensions to be termed novels. The caricatures of Lord Scamperdale, Mr Jawleyford and Mr Jogglebury Crowdey are delightfully vivid and far more alive than many a Forsterian "round" job. We even feel we know well 'Ercles and Parvo, Mr Sponge's profitably iniquitous horses, so zestfully are they presented. Of course in chronicling the progress of a rogue, Surtees is closer to the picaresque mode of the eighteenth century than to the bulk of Victorian novels. It might be possible to regard him simply as a "left-over" eighteenth-century writer stranded in the middle of the nineteenth century, were it not for the fact that he was so very much involved in his Present, even to the extent of updating his topical allusions when revising.

In relying on the progress of Mr Sponge's peregrinations to give the story movement. Surtees ignored both romance and social mobility as material for a real plot. But then upward social mobility, which can perhaps be said to provide the "archeplot" for mid-Victorian novels, did not involve Surtees at a sufficiently deep level. He himself was not placed ambiguously enough in the class system to conceive a great plot based upon it, like that, for instance, of *Our Mutual Friend,* even had he had Dickens's talent. His social rank was unquestioned, and he could only view others' struggles up the ladder from a secure height. That is not to say that he thought those at the top necessarily deserved their places any more than those below: Jawleyford of Jawleyford Court, for instance, bleeding his estate dry to feed his preposterous vanity, is a disgrace as a country gentleman despite his ancestral portraits. That Jawleyford's equally vain daughters marry respectively a stingy ageing aristocrat with homosexual tendencies and a pompous spendthrift parvenu with no sexual tendencies, is matter for amusement; that his tenant farmers are wretchedly oppressed through their landlord's irresponsibility is cause for real concern. None the less, for a writer of this period the tone of the whole is remarkably detached, and so far from being moralistic as to appear almost amoral.

Surtees's anti-romanticism emerges strongly in his depiction of women. Emily and Amelia Jawleyford, entering the drawing-room "in the full fervour of sisterly animosity"; Mrs Jog Crowdey, nagging her family into misery in order to try to ensnare a "rich godpapa" for Gustavus James; the decadent Lady Scattercash, totally indifferent to her husband's mental and physical collapse: these are all women seen in terms of narrow female roles, bogged down in pettiness and vanity. Even the "heroine", Lucy Glitters (late of Astley's Amphi-

theatre), though pretty and good-natured, is a fortune-hunter and possibly a prostitute. Her fortune-hunting matches her with the "hero", and it provides a neat ironic ending for Lucy and Sponge to betroth themselves, each believing the other to be rich. Whether each believed the other to be virtuous as well is not at issue; here again Surtees was more down-to-earth than many of his contemporaries, in depicting a loose woman making a happy marriage rather than dying in degradation. (pp. xiii-xv)

The chief strengths of Surtees's writing lie in his humour, in the combination of his remarkable acuteness of observation with his unusual viewpoint, and in his vigour of style. He is not, however, in any sense a stylist: his syntax is often awry and his locutions ugly, he rarely baulks at a cliché and he is far too repetitive. And yet, at its best, his writing transmits enormous energy, and he displays an extraordinary vitality in his imaginative engagement with his material. His language is remarkable not for any careful professionalism, but for an earthy, sinewy strength, and he can thank his native north country for its gift of some powerfully expressive words: sloggering, scrimmaging, spurlinged, slumpey, smatch, for example. Such words are not self-consciously introduced to provide local colour, they are employed perfectly naturally in contexts where they perform very effectively.

This strongly individual use of language underlines Surtees's originality as a writer. In his avoidance of moralizing, of thematic seriousness, of complexity of structure, and even of plot, he shows himself to be in many ways an anti-novelist rather than a novelist. He cannot be numbered among the great writers, but he is truly unique, and important because so different from what is too often glibly assumed to be the typical minor author of the Victorian age. (pp. xv-xvi)

> *Virginia Blain, in an introduction to* Mr. Sponge's Sporting Tour *by R. S. Surtees, edited by Virginia Blain, Batsford Academic and Educational Ltd., 1981, pp. ix-xvi.*

ADDITIONAL BIBLIOGRAPHY

Allen, Walter. "The Early Victorians." In his *The English Novel: A Short Critical History,* pp. 153-252. New York: E. P. Dutton & Co., 1954.
    Includes an appreciation of Surtees' humor and knowledge of fox-hunting.

Baker, Ernest A. "The Predecessors of Dickens." In his *The History of the English Novel: The Age of Dickens and Thackeray,* pp. 203-36. London: H. F. & G. Witherby, 1936.
    Examines Surtees' realism and its effect upon his characters and plots.

Bell, Quentin. "Surtees." *The New Statesman and Nation* XIX, n.s. No. 472 (9 March 1940): 335.
    Attempts to convince the reading public that Surtees' works deserve attention.

Bovill, E. W. *The England of Nimrod and Surtees, 1815-1854.* London: Oxford University Press, 1959, 188 p.
    A social history based on the works of Surtees and Nimrod. Bovill studies two developments in England during the first half of the nineteenth century: the rise of the stagecoach system and the evolution of fox-hunting into a national sport.

Burn, W. L. "Surtees and Trollope." *Blackwood's Magazine* 261, No. 1578 (April 1947): 301-07.

Compares the works of Surtees and Anthony Trollope, focusing on the authors' attitudes toward women, professional success, and country life.

Carr, Raymond. "Foes of the Fox." *The Times Literary Supplement*, No. 4127 (7 May 1982): 503.
Welcomes the publication of two new editions of *Sponge*.

Child, Harold. "Caricature and the Literature of Sport: *Punch*." In *The Cambridge History of English Literature*, edited by Sir A. W. Ward and A. R. Waller. Vol. XIV, *The Nineteenth Century*, pt. III, pp. 234-64. New York: G. P. Putnam's Sons, 1917.
Maintains that Surtees ranks second only to Dickens "in the invention of comic character and speech."

Collison, Robert L. "R. S. Surtees: Satirist and Sociologist." *Nineteenth-Century Fiction* VII, No. 3 (December 1952): 202-07.
Holds that Surtees' works are "invaluable" social documents of life in mid-Victorian England.

————. *A Jorrocks Handbook: A Centenary Dictionary of the Characters, Places, Situations, and Allusions Which Occur in the Jorrocks Novels and in the Short Stories by Robert Smith Surtees*. London: Coole Book Service, 1964, 162 p.
A guide to the people, places, and contemporary allusions in *Jorrocks, Handley Cross,* and *Hillingdon Hall*.

Cone, Carl B. "The Genesis of John Jorrocks, Fox-'unter." *The Kentucky Review* III, No. 3 (1982): 20-7.
States that Jorrocks made his first appearance as an unnamed Cockney hunter in a sketch by Surtees published in the August 1830 number of the *Sporting Magazine*.

Darton, F. J. Harvey. "The Age of Jorrocks." In his *From Surtees to Sassoon: Some English Contrasts (1838-1928)*, pp. 3-32. 1931. Reprint. Folcroft, Penn.: Folcroft Library Editions, 1977.
Describes how Surtees created characters whose appeal is timeless.

Ellis, Stewart M. "R. S. Surtees." In his *Mainly Victorian*, pp. 95-102. London: Hutchinson & Co., 1925.
A brief biographical sketch and overview of Surtees' writings. Ellis's discussion of the novels focuses on their illustrations.

Engel, Elliot, and King, Margaret F. "Subgenres of the Novel from 1830 to 1837." In their *The Victorian Novel Before Victoria: British Fiction during the Reign of William IV, 1830-37*, pp. 87-134. Macmillan Studies in Victorian Literature. London: Macmillan, 1984.
Studies *Jorrocks* in relation to the comic novels written by Dickens and Theodore Hook between 1830 and 1837.

Gladstone, Hugh S. "Bibliographical Notes." In *Shooting with Surtees*, by Robert Smith Surtees, edited by Hugh S. Gladstone, pp. 203-09. New York: Frederick A. Stokes Co., Publishers, 1928.
A bibliography of Surtees' works that details their publication history.

Johnston-Jones, David R. *"The Deathless Train": The Life and Work of Robert Smith Surtees*. Salzburg Studies in English Literature: Romantic Reassessment, edited by James Hogg, no. 36. Salzburg: Universität Salzburg, 1974, 183 p.
An analysis "from an aesthetic standpoint" of Surtees' contribution to literature, with separate chapters on characterization, humor, style, and construction. Johnston-Jones quotes liberally from Surtees' works and from earlier critical estimates of the author.

Newton, A. Edward. "Jack Jorrocks." In his *End Papers: Literary Recreations*, pp. 111-20. Boston: Little, Brown, and Co., 1933.
Describes the genesis of Jorrocks and attributes the character's immortality to his wit and humor.

Noakes, Aubrey. *Horses, Hounds and Humans: Being the Dramatized Story of R. S. Surtees*. London: Oldbourne, 1957, 183 p.
Combines biographical information with descriptions of Surtees' characters and plots.

O'Neill, Moira. "The Author of 'Jorrocks'." *Blackwood's Magazine* CCXV, No. MCCCIV (June 1924): 857-68.
A biographical portrait.

Pope-Hennessy, Una. "Hamsterley and Jorrocks." In *Durham Company*, pp. 189-223. London: Chatto & Windus, 1941.
Covers various aspects of Surtees' life and career, with particular emphasis on the relationship between his art and that of Dickens.

Ray, Cyril. Introduction to *Robert Smith Surtees: Scenes and Characters*, by Robert Smith Surtees, edited by Cyril Ray, pp. 7-13. Falcon Prose Classics, edited by Leonard Russell. London: Falcon Press, 1948.
An introduction to a collection of extracts from Surtees' works. Ray maintains that Jorrocks is Surtees' greatest character, but regards *Sponge* as his most polished work.

————. "A Master of Life." *The Spectator* 201, No. 6801 (31 October 1958): 573-74.
A favorable review of *Sponge*. Ray summarizes the novel's plot and praises Surtees' "eye for character."

Rendall, Vernon. "Surtees for Christmas." *The Saturday Review* 142, No. 3710 (4 December 1926): 667-68.
Considers Surtees' novels superior to most contemporary literature.

Rivers, W. C. "The Place of R. S. Surtees." *The London Mercury* X, No. 59 (September 1924): 605-13.
A survey of Surtees' works that focuses on two aspects of *Handley Cross*: its characters and its value as a historical document of the Victorian age.

Saintsbury, George. "The Mid-Victorian Novel." In his *The English Novel*, pp. 237-72. The Channels of English Literature, edited by Oliphant Smeaton. London: J. M. Dent & Sons, 1924.
Contains a survey of English sporting novels in which Surtees receives brief attention.

Sassoon, Siegfried. Introduction to *Hillingdon Hall; or, The Cockney Squire*, by Robert Smith Surtees, pp. ix-xiii. New York: William Farquhar Payson, 1933(?).
Argues that *Hillingdon Hall* has been undeservedly labeled Surtees' dullest novel.

Schachterle, Lance. "The Serial Publication of R. S. Surtees's *Jorrocks's Jaunts and Jollities*." *Victorian Periodicals Newsletter*, No. 20 (June 1973): 8-13.
Compares the book version of *Jorrocks* with the serialized episodes.

[Seccombe, Thomas]. In *The Dictionary of National Biography: From the Earliest Times to 1900*, Vol. XIX, edited by Sir Sidney Lee, pp. 174-75. London: Oxford University Press, 1949-50.
Briefly reviews Surtees' life and career. Critics frequently discuss Seccombe's assertion that the interest of Surtees' novels derives almost exclusively from their illustrations. Seccombe's remarks were first published in 1898-99.

Welcome, John. *The Sporting World of R. S. Surtees*. Oxford: Oxford University Press, 1982, 203 p.
In Welcome's words, "a comprehensive life, placing [Surtees] in the sporting, literary, and social context of his time."

Weygandt, Cornelius. "The Fellows of Scott and the Earlier Victorians." In his *A Century of the English Novel*, pp. 122-71. New York: Century Co., 1925.
Emphasizes Surtees' nationalism.

William Makepeace Thackeray

1811-1863

(Also wrote under pseudonyms of Michael Angelo Titmarsh, Samuel Titmarsh, George Savage Fitz-boodle, Mr. Snob, Yellowplush, Ikey Solomons, The Fat Contributor, and Jeames de la Pluche, among others) English novelist, essayist, short story, fairy tale, and sketch writer, poet, critic, and editor.

The following entry presents criticism of Thackeray's novel *Vanity Fair: A Novel without a Hero* (1848). For additional information on Thackeray's career and *Vanity Fair*, see *NCLC*, Vol. 5.

Vanity Fair is considered one of the great novels of the nineteenth century. For its multitude of successfully realized major and minor characters, and for its vivid panorama of middle- and upper-class English society, it is often compared with such sweeping masterpieces as Leo Tolstoy's *War and Peace* and Honoré de Balzac's *La comédie humaine*. Conceived by Thackeray as a "novel without a hero," *Vanity Fair* challenged many of the conventions of early Victorian fiction with its unprecedentedly realistic approach to characterization and its frankly satirical and often pessimistic view of the human condition. Today, scholars regard Thackeray's innovations as a milestone in the development of realism in English fiction. Critics particularly praise his ability to create complex human characters, among them Becky Sharp, the energetic, attractive, and controversial anti-heroine around whom much of *Vanity Fair* revolves. While many of the novel's early readers found it cynical in tone and harsh in its revelation of human weakness, *Vanity Fair* nevertheless captivated its contemporary audience and has remained a favorite of both critics and the reading public.

Generally regarded as Thackeray's finest work, *Vanity Fair* was also his first great success as an author. Prior to its publication, he had established himself in London literary circles as a minor satirist and magazine writer working under a variety of humorous pseudonyms. His output consisted of numerous essays and reviews, several collections of comic sketches, and a number of novels. While nearly all critics consider *Vanity Fair* an enormous artistic advance for Thackeray, they have also emphasized that the novel owes much of its satirical brilliance and epic scope to the years he spent as a comic sketch writer and author of vivid travel pieces. The series of satiric portraits entitled *The Snobs of England, by One of Themselves* that Thackeray published in *Punch* magazine from 1846 to 1847 is considered of particular importance because it forms a comprehensive gallery of the types of individuals whose acquisitiveness, social affectations, and selfishness the novelist was shortly to attack in a more subtle and far-reaching fashion in *Vanity Fair*.

Scholars disagree over precisely when Thackeray began work on *Vanity Fair*, but they generally believe it to have been in either late 1844 or early the following year. During 1845 he submitted a version of the novel's initial chapters to various publishers, all of whom refused the manuscript. By the beginning of 1846, however, the London firm of Bradbury and Evans had accepted the work for publication in monthly installments—under the title *The Novel without a Hero: Pen and Pencil Sketches of English Society*. Although the book was

originally scheduled to begin appearing in May 1846, Thackeray set it aside until the following autumn, when he gave it the name by which it is known today. Thackeray later told an acquaintance that while searching for a better title for his work, the phrase "Vanity Fair" had suddenly occurred to him in the middle of the night, upon which, according to the novelist, he "jumped out of bed and ran three times around my room, uttering as I went, 'Vanity Fair, Vanity Fair, Vanity Fair'." The source for the title lay in John Bunyan's prose allegory *The Pilgrim's Progress*, in which Bunyan portrays Vanity Fair as a wicked place where worldly pleasures are sold. Scholars believe that the moral allegory and unified concept suggested by his new title inspired Thackeray to revise the relatively loose and unstructured chapters of his novel into a narrative possessing greater cohesiveness and artistic purpose than any of his previous writings. The author himself realized that his new work outshone his earlier efforts: in December 1846, he wrote to a friend, "*Vanity Fair* may make me." The first number of *Vanity Fair: Pen and Pencil Sketches of English Society*, featuring Thackeray's own illustrations and published under his real name, appeared in January 1847. The novel ran in nineteen monthly parts through July 1848, when it was published in book form with the new subtitle *A Novel without a Hero*.

Both socially and geographically, *Vanity Fair* covers a wide expanse of early nineteenth-century Europe. Ranging from the streets of Mayfair in London through provincial towns on the Continent, the novel traces the fortunes of two women—Becky and her friend Amelia Sedley—from their boarding school days through marriage, motherhood, wealth, poverty, social prominence, and social ostracism. Amelia, the good-natured but weak and sentimental daughter of wealthy parents, forms a sharp contrast with the heartless Becky, who, though of humble origin, possesses cleverness, ruthless ambition, and an ability to please that allows her to manipulate others. After Amelia's first husband, the selfish dandy George Osborne, dies in the Battle of Waterloo, she ignores the attentions of William Dobbin, whom Thackeray portrays as the only truly noble character in the novel. In the meantime, Becky and her husband, the rakish cavalry officer Rawdon Crawley, establish themselves in London and, under Becky's shrewd direction, attempt to "live well on nothing a year" by borrowing, swindling, and keeping up the appearance of wealth. Eventually, however, Becky's schemes backfire, and she is temporarily forced to flee in disgrace to the Continent. After years of patient waiting and unselfish devotion by Dobbin, Amelia consents to marry him, but only after he realizes that she is perhaps not quite worthy of him. Their union is happy yet falls short of what both had hoped for from life, and the novel ends with the famous exclamation: "Ah! *Vanitas Vanitatum!* which of us is happy in this world? Which of us has his desire? or, having it, is satisfied?"

Although the stories of Becky and Amelia form the central plot of *Vanity Fair,* Thackeray also uses the often-connected events of their lives to expose the corruption, greed, hypocrisy, and pernicious snobbery of almost the entire range of English society, from the servant classes to the aristocracy. The novelist declared in a letter that he intended to portray an entire "set of people living without God in the world." As Becky and Amelia's lives intersect at regular intervals throughout *Vanity Fair,* their stories are caught up in those of a vast array of authentically portrayed secondary characters, including the debauched Lord Steyne, Becky's crude and miserly father-in-law Sir Pitt Crawley, and Jos Sedley, Amelia's gluttonous and weak-willed brother.

While many of *Vanity Fair*'s early critics expressed regret that Thackeray had chosen to delve so zealously—and without exception—into the selfish motivations and vain pretensions of his characters, his wide-ranging assaults on sham and hypocrisy met with an appreciative audience. By the time the work had run through half of its scheduled numbers, reviewers had already begun to acclaim it as a highly original and important contribution to the English novel, and Thackeray quickly found himself a famous author. Among the most influential of the early reviews was that of Abraham Hayward in the powerful *Edinburgh Review* (see *NCLC,* Vol. 5). Praising Thackeray's "entire freedom from mannerism and affectation both in style and sentiment," Hayward focused on those aspects of *Vanity Fair* that separated it from current fiction. Along with Hayward, a large proportion of the novel's initial critics recognized that Thackeray had transcended many of the hackneyed conventions prevalent in early Victorian fiction. Foremost among the features of *Vanity Fair* that set it apart from the works of Thackeray's contemporaries was his ability and willingness to reveal both the negative and positive attributes of all his characters, an innovative practice in an era when idealized and simplistic characters were common. Thackeray's calculated avoidance of hero worship and his refusal to distinguish be-

tween good and bad characters bothered many readers, however. Such early critics as George Henry Lewes (see *NCLC,* Vol. 5) and John Forster were among those who remarked upon the extraordinary verisimilitude of the novel's men and women, but both writers faulted Thackeray's overly pessimistic view of human nature. The related question as to why Thackeray had chosen to make Becky such a compelling personality and Amelia such an insipid one also disturbed many early reviewers. Several commentators echoed Lewes in asserting that by depicting evil as attractive and virtue as drab and dull, the author had "erred both against art and nature." Despite the widespread sentiment among early critics that in striving to make his characters real Thackeray had occasionally overemphasized their faults, most contemporary on *Vanity Fair* followed Hayward's example in extolling the elegant simplicity of the novel's style and the unprecedented veracity of its portraiture. After Thackeray's death in 1863, little significant criticism of *Vanity Fair* appeared during the remainder of the nineteenth century.

In the twentieth century, scholars have taken a broad range of approaches to *Vanity Fair.* Among the most frequently discussed aspects of the novel have been its narrative technique, characterization, structure, and major themes. Thackeray's narrative technique in *Vanity Fair* and a range of associated topics, including his dramatic method, handling of time, prose style, shifting perspective, and relationship with his characters, have been the subject of extensive critical debate. Writing in the 1920s, Percy Lubbock explored Thackeray's use of dramatic presentation as a means of narrative expression, praising the author's use of broad retrospection, but faulting his inability to portray the small dramatic moment (see *NCLC,* Vol. 5). John A. Lester, Jr., in a highly influential article written in the mid-1950s, investigated Thackeray's skillful manipulation of chronology in *Vanity Fair,* focusing on the novelist's use of sudden movements back and forward in time to lend his story impact and poignancy (see *NCLC,* Vol. 5). Important analyses of style in *Vanity Fair* include those by G. Armour Craig, who explored the contrast between Thackeray's familiar addresses to the reader and his detached silence about many of the novel's crucial episodes, and John Loofbourow, who examined Thackeray's "flexible, allusive prose" in relation to the development of narrative technique in the English novel.

Thackeray's use of a multiple narrative perspective and his seemingly ambiguous attitude toward his characters have been the focus of many modern discussions of narrative technique in *Vanity Fair.* Numerous critics have attempted to understand Thackeray's regular shifts from an omniscient narrator to a narrator who plays a part in the world he is describing. While some critics, including Russell A. Fraser, have charged that this practice creates confusion and inconsistency, others, among them Juliet McMaster (see *NCLC,* Vol. 5) and Wolfgang Iser, have argued that the lack of a single point of view in the novel contributes to its realism and lends it historical importance as a highly innovative work whose ambiguities place it on the boundary of modern fiction. Closely associated with the issue of Thackeray's uncertain point of view is his handling of Amelia and Becky. Many critics have debated Thackeray's intentions in allowing Becky to eclipse Amelia, questioning why he portrayed Becky as appealing despite her palpably vicious character and her (apparent) capacity for murder. Although a few commentators asserted that Becky was not in fact an attractive figure at all, others sought for clues to her despicable but alluring personality in the riddle of Thackeray's complex attitudes toward women. While the diversity of recent commentary suggests that Thackeray's characterization of Becky and Amelia will continue to be the subject of controversy for some time to come, critics agree that Becky is one of the most memorable characters in English literature.

In analyzing the structure of *Vanity Fair*, twentieth-century scholars have voiced opposing opinions: some have reiterated what Robert Bell had argued in 1848—that the *Novel without a Hero* was "a novel without a plan" (see *NCLC*, Vol. 5)—while others have agreed with David Cecil's assertion in 1934 that "the structural scheme of *Vanity Fair* is Thackeray's greatest technical achievement" (see *NCLC*, Vol. 5). Charles Whibley and Joseph Warren Beach (see *NCLC*, Vol. 5) fall into the group of commentators who found the novel deficient in structural integrity. Writing in the early years of the twentieth century, both Whibley and Beach stressed the negative effects of serial publication on the design of the novel. Conversely, a number of more recent scholars, including Myron Taube and Edgar F. Harden, have perceived a conscious design beneath the surface of *Vanity Fair*. While Taube posited that the novel derives its structure from a series of contrasting characters and situations, Harden argued that the work's unity results from thematic parallels between its monthly parts.

The epic scale of *Vanity Fair* has brought forth a broad spectrum of commentary on what various critics have seen as its central thematic concerns. Although in the nineteenth century such critics as Bell could assert without controversy that the subject of the novel was the "Vanity Fair of the vulgar great"—the slavish pursuit of wealth and fashion by the middle class—scholars in the twentieth century have examined in greater detail the extensive range of *Vanity Fair*'s moral and social concerns. Thus, Joseph E. Baker explored the relationship between Thackeray's concept of Vanity Fair and similar ideas in the works of Bunyan, St. Augustine, and Plato; and A. E. Dyson, in a prominent study of Thackeray's social criticism, investigated the novelist's vision of the effect of Vanity Fair upon individual morality (see *NCLC*, Vol. 5). Critics have also dealt with such themes as the pursuit of love and wealth in *Vanity Fair*, Thackeray's use of the theme of art versus nature, and his portrayal of history.

In assessing Thackeray's accomplishment in *Vanity Fair*, Gordon N. Ray has stated that the novel "was quite as revolutionary a book in the development of Victorian fiction as *Ulysses* has proved to be in the development of modern fiction." In addition to the novel's historical importance, modern scholars have emphasized the enduring relevance of its brilliantly conceived attacks on human greed, corruption, and pretension. For both the vitality of its legion of characters and the monumental achievement inherent in its panoramic vision of English society, critics rank *Vanity Fair* as one of the most important novels of the Victorian era.

(See also *Dictionary of Literary Biography*, Vol. 21: *Victorian Novelists Before 1885*.)

WILLIAM MAKEPEACE THACKERAY   (letter date 1847)

[*In the following excerpt from a letter to his mother, Thackeray responds to the suggestion that Amelia and the other characters in* Vanity Fair *are selfish and unattractive*.]

Of course you are quite right about *Vanity Fair* and Amelia being selfish. . . . My object is not to make a perfect character or anything like it. Dont you see how odious all the people are in the book (with exception of Dobbin)—behind whom all there lies a dark moral I hope. What I want is to make a set of people living without God in the world (only that is a cant phrase) greedy pompous mean perfectly self-satisfied for the most part and at ease about their superior virtue. Dobbin & poor Briggs are the only 2 people with real humility as yet. Amelia's is to come, when her scoundrel of a husband is well dead with a ball in his odious bowels; when she has had sufferings, a child, and a religion—But she has at present a quality above most people whizz: LOVE—by [which] she shall be saved. (p. 309)

> William Makepeace Thackeray, in a letter to Mrs. Carmichael-Smyth on July 2, 1847, in his The Letters and Private Papers of William Makepeace Thackeray: 1841-1851, Vol. II, edited by Gordon N. Ray, Cambridge, Mass.: Harvard University Press, 1945, pp. 308-11.

WILLIAM MAKEPEACE THACKERAY   (letter date 1848)

[*In the following excerpt from a letter to the noted critic George Henry Lewes, Thackeray explains a passage from* Vanity Fair *that Lewes had recently discussed in the* Morning Chronicle (*see excerpt by Lewes dated 1848 in* NCLC, *Vol. 5*).]

I have just read your notice in the *Chronicle* (I conclude it is a friend who has penned it) and am much affected by the friendliness of the sympathy, and by the kindness of the reproof of the critic.

That passage [which] you quote bears very hardly upon the poor alderman certainly: but I don't mean that the man deprived of turtle would as a consequence steal bread: only that he in the possession of luxuries and riding through life respectably in a gig, should be very chary of despising poor Lazarus on foot, & look very humbly and leniently upon the faults of his less fortunate brethren—If Becky had had 5000 a year I have no doubt in my mind that she would have been respectable; increased her fortune advanced her family in the world: laid up treasures for herself in the shape of 3 per cents, social position, reputation &c—like Louis Philippe let us say, or like many a person highly & comfortably placed in the world not guilty of many wrongs of commission, satisfied with himself, never doubting of his merit, and decorously angry at the errors of less lucky men. What satire is so awful as Lead us not into temptation? What is the gospel and life of our Lord (excuse me for mentioning it) but a tremendous Protest against pride and self-righteousness? God forgive us all, I pray, and deliver us from evil.

I am quite aware of the dismal roguery [which] goes all through the *Vanity Fair* story—and God forbid that the world should be like it altogether: though I fear it is more like it than we like to own. But my object is to make every body engaged, engaged in the pursuit of Vanity and I must carry my story through in this dreary minor key, with only occasional hints here & there of better things—of better things [which] it does not become me to preach.

I never scarcely write letters to critics and beg you to excuse me for sending you this. It is only because I have just laid down the paper, and am much moved by the sincere goodwill of my critic. (pp. 353-54)

William Makepeace Thackeray, in a letter to George Henry Lewes on March 6, 1848, in his The Letters and Private Papers of William Makepeace Thackeray: 1841-1851, Vol. II, *edited by Gordon N. Ray, Cambridge, Mass.: Harvard University Press, 1945, pp. 353-54.*

WILLIAM MAKEPEACE THACKERAY (letter date 1848)

[*In the following excerpt from a letter to the duke of Devonshire, written before the publication of the final chapters of* Vanity Fair, *Thackeray provides a humorous account of the fortunes of various characters subsequent to the close of the novel.*]

My Lord Duke,—Mrs. Rawdon Crawley, whom I saw last week, and whom I informed of your Grace's desire to have her portrait, was good enough to permit me to copy a little drawing made of her "in happier days," she said with a sigh, by Smee, the Royal Academician.

Mrs. Crawley now lives in a small but very pretty little house in Belgravia, and is conspicuous for her numerous charities, which always get into the newspapers, and her unaffected piety. Many of the most exalted and spotless of her own sex visit her, and are of opinion that she is a *most injured woman*. There is no *sort of truth* in the stories regarding Mrs. Crawley and the late Lord Steyne. The licentious character of that nobleman alone gave rise to reports from which, alas! the most spotless life and reputation cannot always defend themselves. The present Sir Rawdon Crawley (who succeeded his late uncle, Sir Pitt, 1832; Sir Pitt died on the passing of the Reform Bill) does not see his mother, and his undutifulness is a cause of the deepest grief to that admirable lady. "If it were not for *higher things*," she says, how could she have borne up against the world's calumny, a wicked husband's cruelty and falseness, and the thanklessness (sharper than a serpent's tooth) of an adored child? But she has been preserved, mercifully preserved, to bear all these griefs, and awaits her reward *elsewhere*. The italics are Mrs. Crawley's own.

She took the style and title of Lady Crawley for some time after Sir Pitt's death in 1832; but it turned out that Colonel Crawley, Governor of Coventry Island, had died of fever three months before his brother, whereupon Mrs. Rawdon was obliged to lay down the title which she had prematurely assumed.

The late Jos. Sedley, Esq., of the Bengal Civil Service, left her two lakhs of rupees, on the interest of which the widow lives in the practices of piety and benevolence before mentioned. She has lost what little good looks she once possessed, and wears false hair and teeth (the latter give her rather a ghastly look when she smiles), and—for a pious woman—is the best-crinolined lady in Knightsbridge district.

Colonel and Mrs. W. Dobbin live in Hampshire, near Sir R. Crawley; Lady Jane was godmother to their little girl, and the ladies are exceedingly attached to each other. The Colonel's *History of the Punjaub* is looked for with much anxiety in some circles.

Captain and Lt.-Colonel G. Sedley-Osborne (he wishes, he says, to be distinguished from some other branches of the Osborne family, and is descended by the mother's side from Sir Charles Sedley) is, I need not say, well, for I saw him in a most richly embroidered cambric pink shirt with diamond studs, bowing to your Grace at the last party at Devonshire House. He is in Parliament; but the property left him by his Grandfather has, I hear, been a good deal overrated.

He was very sweet upon Miss Crawley, Sir Pitt's daughter, who married her cousin, the present Baronet, and a good deal cut up when he was refused. He is not, however, a man to be permanently cast down by sentimental disappointments. His chief cause of annoyance at the present moment is that he is growing bald, but his whiskers are still without a gray hair and the finest in London.

I think these are the latest particulars relating to a number of persons about whom your Grace was good enough to express some interest. I am very glad to be enabled to give this information. . . . (pp. 375-77)

P.S.—Lady O'Dowd is at O'Dowdstown arming. She has just sent in a letter of adhesion to the Lord-Lieutenant, which has been acknowledged by his Excellency's private secretary, Mr. Corry Connellan. Miss Glorvina O'Dowd is thinking of coming up to the Castle to marry the last-named gentleman.

P.S.2.—The India mail just arrived announces the utter ruin of the Union Bank of Calcutta, in which all Mrs. Crawley's money was. Will Fate never cease to persecute that suffering saint? (p. 377)

William Makepeace Thackeray, in a letter to the duke of Devonshire on May 1, 1848, in his The Letters and Private Papers of William Makepeace Thackeray: 1841-1851, Vol. II, *edited by Gordon N. Ray, Cambridge, Mass.: Harvard University Press, 1945, pp. 375-77.*

WILLIAM MAKEPEACE THACKERAY (essay date 1848)

[*The following preface to* Vanity Fair, *in which Thackeray describes himself as the "Manager of the Performance," is often discussed in studies of the novel's narrative perspective. Dated by Thackeray June 28, 1848, the preface was first published when the novel appeared in book form.*]

As the Manager of the Performance sits before the curtain on the boards, and looks into the Fair, a feeling of profound melancholy comes over him in his survey of the bustling place. There is a great quantity of eating and drinking, making love and jilting, laughing and the contrary, smoking, cheating, fighting, dancing, and fiddling: there are bullies pushing about, bucks ogling the women, knaves picking pockets, policemen on the look-out, quacks (*other* quacks, plague take them!) bawling in front of their booths, and yokels looking up at the tinselled dancers and poor old rouged tumblers, while the light-fingered folk are operating upon their pockets behind. Yes, this is VANITY FAIR; not a moral place certainly; nor a merry one, though very noisy. Look at the faces of the actors and buffoons when they come off from their business; and Tom Fool washing the paint off his cheeks before he sits down to dinner with his wife and the little Jack Puddings behind the canvass. The curtain will be up presently, and he will be turning over head and heels, and crying, "How are you?"

A man with a reflective turn of mind, walking through an exhibition of this sort, will not be oppressed, I take it, by his own or other people's hilarity. An episode of humour or kindness touches and amuses him here and there;—a pretty child looking at a gingerbread stall; a pretty girl blushing whilst her lover talks to her and chooses her fairing; poor Tom Fool, yonder behind the waggon, mumbling his bone with the honest family which lives by his tumbling;—but the general impression is one more melancholy than mirthful. When you come home, you sit down, in a sober, contemplative, not uncharitable frame of mind, and apply yourself to your books or your business.

I have no other moral than this to tag to the present story of *Vanity Fair*. Some people consider Fairs immoral altogether, and eschew such, with their servants and families: very likely they are right. But persons who think otherwise, and are of a lazy, or a benevolent, or a sarcastic mood, may perhaps like to step in for half an hour, and look at the performances. There are scenes of all sorts; some dreadful combats, some grand and lofty horse-riding, some scenes of high life, and some of very middling indeed; some love-making for the sentimental, and some light comic business; the whole accompanied by appropriate scenery, and brilliantly illuminated with the Author's own candles.

What more has the Manager of the Performance to say?—To acknowledge the kindness with which it has been received in all the principal towns of England through which the Show has passed, and where it has been most favourably noticed by the respected conductors of the Public Press, and by the Nobility and Gentry. He is proud to think that his Puppets have given satisfaction to the very best company in this empire. The famous little Becky Puppet has been pronounced to be uncommonly flexible in the joints, and lively on the wire: the Amelia Doll, though it has had a smaller circle of admirers, has yet been carved and dressed with the greatest care by the artist; the Dobbin Figure, though apparently clumsy, yet dances in a very amusing and natural manner: the Little Boys' Dance has been liked by some; and please to remark the richly-dressed figure of the Wicked Nobleman, on which no expense has been spared, and which Old Nick will fetch away at the end of this singular performance.

And with this, and a profound bow to his patrons, the Manager retires, and the curtain rises. (pp. 5-6)

> William Makepeace Thackeray, "Before the Curtain," in his *Vanity Fair: A Novel without a Hero*, edited by George Tillotson and Kathleen Tillotson, Methuen & Co., Limited, 1963, pp. 5-6.

[JOHN FORSTER]   (essay date 1848)

[*Forster was an English biographer, historian, critic, and journalist who is best known for* The Life of Charles Dickens, *which is considered one of the finest biographies of a literary figure in the English language. In the following excerpt, Forster explores* Vanity Fair's *realistic characters, social satire, and "cynical, sarcastic tone."*]

Laughing at the minute and interminable details, despising the conventional decencies and real indecorums, wearied by the want of all manly passion in Richardson's *Pamela*, that novel of the pattern morality of its day, Fielding at last revenged himself by a burlesque, which was meant to show how compatible the specious virtue of Mrs Pamela might be, with the absence of every virtue except the one by which she gained for a husband the man who had done his best to ruin her. But Fielding had too great an imagination to allow of his filling up one book with a mere parody of another. From Richardson his satire extended to the fashionable world. . . .

Put the fashionable-life manners of our day for the manners in Richardson's novels, and Mr Thackeray's position in the book before us in some respect resembles Fielding's. The task he first set himself, in *Vanity Fair,* would seem to have been to portray or expose, with witty malice, their ideal of fine life in its various grades. But his better genius forced him beyond the narrow limits of a mere ill-natured joke or burlesque, and informed his pages with characters and incidents full of life and reality. If Mr Thackeray falls short of Fielding, much of whose peculiar power and more of whose manner he has inherited or studiously acquired, it is because an equal amount of large cordiality has not raised him entirely above the region of the sneering, into that of simple uncontaminated human affection. His satiric pencil is dipped in deeper colours than that of his prototype. Not Vanity Fair so properly as Rascality Fair is the scene he lays open to our view; and he never wholly escapes from its equivocal associations, scarcely ever lays aside for a whole page his accustomed sneer. His is a less comfortable, an on the whole therefore, let us add, a less true view of society than Fielding's.

Vanity Fair is the work of a mind, at once accomplished and subtle, which has enjoyed opportunities of observing many and varied circles of society. Its author is endowed with penetrating discrimination and just appreciation of character, and with a rare power of graphic delineation. His *genteel* characters (we dislike the word as much as Dr Johnson did *cleverness,* but we have no better at hand) have a reality about them which we do not remember to have met with in any recent work of fiction except *Pelham*. They are drawn from actual life, not from books and fancy; and they are presented by means of brief, decisive, yet always most discriminative, touches. It never is necessary to have recourse to supplementary reflections and associations, to make amends for dimness and indistinctness in the portraiture. This, for the most part, holds true of all Mr Thackeray's characteristic sketches. But there is a tendency to caricature, to select in preference grotesque and unpleasing lineaments even where no exaggeration is indulged, that detracts considerably from the pleasure such high artistic abilities might otherwise afford; and we are seldom permitted to enjoy the appreciation of all gentle and kind things which we continually meet with in the book, without some neighbouring quip or sneer that would seem to show the author ashamed of what he yet cannot help giving way to.

It would be tasking the reader's patience too severely to inflict upon him a dry analysis of a story already familiar to a wide public, and daily attracting more attention. But a brief review of its elements is necessary to a just estimate of its character and value. If the novel is without a hero, it has two heroines. We are introduced to them as they leave their boarding-school, described in a very few pages, but with inimitable humour; and we follow their adventures, conjointly or alternately, till we leave the one in the secure haven of a second and comfortable marriage, and the other in an incipient old age of missionary and philanthropic societies, cognac, and stalls at fancy fairs. In tracing the fortunes of the artistically accomplished, clever, sensible, daring, selfish, and unprincipled Becky, we are led through beggarly scenes tenanted by adventurers, through avowedly rakish and more splendid circles, through those where a conventional tone of decorum prevails; thence, into the squalid resorts of tattered finery and habitual vice which lie beyond; and thence again, into that withered, sapless, and flowerless region where sham penitents find a refuge, who have returned to external decency without reawakening to virtue. In tracing, on the one hand, the fortunes of the good and amiable but somewhat selfish and insipid Amelia, we are led from the vulgar comfort and splendour of the *bourgeoisie* of Vanity Fair, through sudden reverses of bankruptcy; allowed again to emerge into commonplace affluence; and after a short excursion through the stately haunts of poor German princes, are conducted finally to a home of worth and virtue. The relations of the heroines afford a connecting link between those dissimilar routes and the passengers who crowd them. The scene shifts from England to the continent, and the time of action extends from before the battle of Waterloo to the year of grace in which we write. The heroes and heroines of high life and low life, of town life and country life, and of that amphibious life which is neither, pass in succession before us; and all, whether we like and admire them or the contrary, are presented with a startling reality of effect.

It must not be imagined, because we have hinted at Mr Thackeray's inferior power of escaping from the mere satirical and burlesque when compared with Fielding, that there are not many finely-conceived characters in his book,—characters which win upon us by their intrinsic worth, and are all the more dear from the dash of the ridiculous that mingles with their better qualities. The hero (for after all there is a hero in the novel), Dobbin, though perhaps elaborated here and there in too minute detail, is a noble portrait of awkward devoted affection, of unobtrusive talents, and of uncompromising integrity. We love him from the first page to the last; from his gawky beginnings at school, through his inadequate rewards during life, to his doubtful happiness at the close. He is always kind, loving, truthful, heroical-hearted; a gentleman. The ineffable Peggy O'Dowd, too, is always welcome; whether brushing her husband's accoutrements and preparing his cup of coffee while he takes his natural rest before the battle of Waterloo, or plotting and planning to marry the major with Glorvina, or watching tenderly over the sick bed of the desolate Amelia, or breaking off the intrigue between the lieutenant and the surgeon's wife, or quarrelling with all the other ladies of the regiment, or dancing down an interminable succession of military men and civilians in an Irish jig. Nor less is her quiet, submissive, gallant, and good-natured husband worthy of her. The poor curate at Brompton, Miss Clapp, Miss Schwarz, Jemima, Miss Briggs, Lady Jane, and others, are also people we can take to our heart, and in whose society we edify. Perhaps the noblest conception of all, however, is the manner in which the good qualities of the manly but battered old *roué*, Rawdon, ignorant and uneducated except by vice, are developed under the combined influence of paternal affection, adversity, and occasional association with the good.

Still it cannot be denied that it is in those characters where great natural talents and energy are combined with unredeemed depravity that the author puts forth his full powers, and that in the management and contemplation of them he seems absolutely to revel. The Marquis of Steyne is a magnificent picture; his fiendish sagacity, energy, absorbing self-indulgences, and contemptuous tramplings upon everything human and divine, fascinate while they revolt. It is in like manner impossible to escape being charmed with the indomitable buoyancy, self-possession, and *applomb* of the little adventuress, Becky, even while we are conscious of her utter depravity. She commits every conceivable wickedness; dishonours her husband, betrays her friend, degrades and embrutes herself, and finally commits a murder; without in the least losing those smart, good-tempered, sensible manners and ways, which ingratiate her with the reader in spite of all her atrocities. In this we may think the art questionably employed, but it is not to be denied that it *is* very extraordinary art; and it is due to Mr Thackeray to add that he has been careful to explain the blended good and evil in this woman by very curious and impressive early details of the circumstances of her birth and bringing up. Nor is it so much with respect to these exceptional characters that we feel inclined

to complain of the taunting, cynical, sarcastic tone that too much pervades the work, as with respect to a preponderance of unredeemed selfishness in the more common-place as well as the leading characters, such as the Bullocks, Mrs Clapp, the Miss Dobbinses even, and Amelia's mother. We can relish the shrewd egoism of Miss Crawley; can admire, while we tremble at, the terrible intentness of Mrs Bute Crawley, who writes her husband's sermons, drills her daughters, and persecutes with selfish sycophancy till everybody flies from her; we can bow with awe and veneration before Lady Southdown, that miraculous compound of Lady Bountiful and Lady Macbeth; we can triumph completely over such fribblers as Sir Pitt Crawley the second, and Tapeworm; we see what power there is in making young Osborne so heartless, old Osborne so hateful, old Sedley so contemptible; but we feel that the atmosphere of the work is overloaded with these exhalations of human folly and wickedness. We gasp for a more liberal alternation of refreshing breezes of unsophisticated honesty. Fielding, after he has administered a sufficient dose of Blifil's choke-damp, purifies the air by a hearty laugh from Tom Jones. But the stifling ingredients are administered by Mr Thackeray to excess, without the necessary relief.

It is exclusively in an artistical point of view that we offer this criticism. It would be unjust in the extreme to impute an immoral tendency to **Vanity Fair.** Vice and folly are never made alluring in it, though all justice is done to their superficial meretricious charms. Mr Thackeray's moral is true and just. It is the victims of such adventurers as Becky who are made so mainly by their own faults and follies. Unsuspicious virtue and innocence—as in the case of Dobbin and Amelia—have a charm in their own simple integrity that unconsciously baffles her spells. It is the vices of her victims that subject them to her power—whether their vices be inherent, gross, and revolting, as in the case of Sir Pitt Crawley; or superinduced on a naturally better, but ignorant and uneducated nature, as in the case of poor Rawdon; or feeble and degrading, as in that compound of silly vanity and selfishness, Joseph Sedley; or merely insipidly heartless and unthinking, as with young Osborne. But this moral is insisted upon with a pertinacity, and illustrations of it are heaped upon us with a redundant profusion, unalleviated by a sufficient amount of more gratifying images, that seems to us to go beyond the limits of the pleasurable, and consequently of true art.

Notwithstanding this defect, **Vanity Fair** must be admitted to be one of the most original works of real genius that has of late been given to the world. The author contemplates many phases of society from a point of view entirely his own. The very novelty of tone in the book impeded its first success; but it will be daily more justly appreciated; and will take a lasting place in our literature. If we have not scrupled to dwell with force upon what we conceive to be its grave defect, it is because we are convinced that the author is capable of avoiding it in his future works, and of producing characteristic tales less alloyed in their enjoyment, and equal, if not superior, in racy power. (p. 468)

> *[John Forster], in a review of "Vanity Fair: A Novel without a Hero," in* The Examiner, *No. 2112, July 22, 1848, pp. 468-70.*

[ROBERT S. RINTOUL]   (essay date 1848)

> [*Rintoul comments on the novel's artistic unity, its lack of attractive characters, and the quality of its illustrations.*]

The completion of Mr. Thackeray's novel of *Vanity Fair* enables us to take a more entire view of the production, and to form a more complete judgment of it as a work of art, than was possible in the course of piecemeal publication in monthly numbers. Our impression from that review is, that the novel is distinguished by the more remarkable qualities which have created the reputation of the author,—his keen perception of the weaknesses, vanities, and humbug of society, the felicitous point with which he displays or the pungent though goodnatured satire with which he exposes them, and the easy, close, and pregnant diction in which he clothes his perceptions; though, possibly, happier specimens of his peculiar excellencies may be found in some of his other works. *Vanity Fair* displays a depth and at times a pathos which we do not remember to have met with in Mr. Thackeray's previous writings; but, considered as a whole, it is rather a succession of connected scenes and characters than a well-constructed story. Both incidents and persons belong more to the sketch than the finished picture. Either from natural bias or long habits of composition, Mr. Thackeray seems to have looked at life by bits rather than as a whole. A half-length here, a whole-length there, a group in another place, a character or a clique with single actions or incidents belonging to them, have been studied, and transferred to paper with a humour, truth, and spirit, that have rarely been equalled. But something more than this is needed for a finished picture of human life. Such things, indeed, are scarcely its entire elements, for they are little more than parts; and so remain till very many such have been compared by the artist—their general laws evolved by this comparison, and the whole animated and fused by the imagination, so as to present the type of a class without loss of individuality. Mr. Thackeray has rarely accomplished this in *Vanity Fair*. There is, indeed, plenty of individuality; the work is full of it. However exceptional, outré, distasteful, or even farcical the characters may be, they have strong particular traits, well supported in the main, and their delineation is always capital: but this peculiarity attaches to the principal characters—that no useful deduction, no available rule of life, can be drawn from their conduct; except in that of the elder Osborne, who points the moral of sordid vanity and a grovelling love of distinction, and points it with effect, as his vices are made the means of his punishment.

It may be said that this largeness is of no consequence, if there be particular or even exceptional nature: which is true as regards sketches, that exhibit a character on one or two occasions and then drop it. Such sketches of passing phases of society do not, however, suffice to form the materials of a fiction: it requires a whole career—the before and after as well as the present. When the characters have no types in nature, or have that obvious weakness or low vice about them that their example conduces to nothing, they tire in a lengthened exhibition, because we have little sympathy with them. *Vanity Fair* is said by its author to be a novel without a hero: which is undoubtedly a truth; but the heroines do not make up for this omission, since one is without a heart, and the other without a head. The author evidently has his misgivings about Amelia Osborne, (née Sedley,) for although she is clearly a favourite, he deems it necessary occasionally to appeal to the reader in favour of her weakness. But there is rarely weakness without vice; and though the extreme attachment of Amelia to a selfish, worthless, neglectful young man, may be forgiven as *so* natural, yet the manner in which she yields to it, and nurses her sentiment to the neglect of her duties, as well as her subsequent shilly-shally conduct to her obsequious admirer Major Dobbin, is rather mawkish than interesting.

Rebecca Crawley (formerly Sharpe) is the principal person of the book, with whom nearly all the others are more or less connected: and a very wonderfully-drawn picture she is, as a woman scheming for self-advancement, without either heart or principle, yet with a constitutional vivacity and a readiness to please, that save her from the contempt or disgust she deserves. As a creation or *character,* we know not where Rebecca can be matched in prose fiction: but she is too deficient in morale to excite interest. The want of entirety we have spoken of is visible in Rebecca's finale. The discredit of a separation from her husband, when not followed by public proceedings, might be surmounted; but a demirep who gambles, consorts with blacklegs and all kinds of disreputables, and raises the wind by advertising concerts that she never gives after getting the money for the tickets, could hardly have regained a place in reputable society, although backed by religious hypocrisy. This conclusion, which was quite needless, is not only wrong as wanting in poetical justice, but untrue as a picture of society even in "Vanity Fair."

A similar want of attractive sympathy runs through the male characters, either from grossness, weakness, sordidness, or vice. It may be urged that these defects of *Vanity Fair* are owing to its periodical publication. That has probably induced an occasional but strong sacrifice of consistency in the characters, to produce an immediate effect; and the same necessity of making parts tell may have given rise to some exaggerations

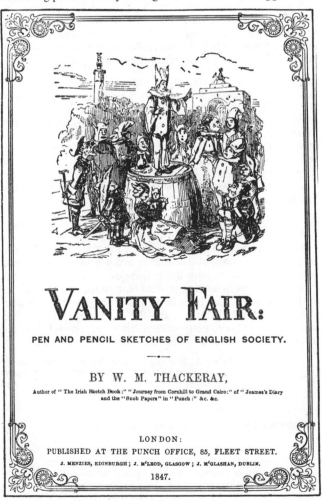

Thackeray's cover for the monthly parts of Vanity Fair.

that would otherwise have been avoided. There are also obvious drawbacks to continuous perusal, such as direct addresses to the reader, and a little of *writing* for the million, which would have been omitted in another mode of publication. But we think all the peculiarites arising from the mode of publication could be got rid of by revision: the defects we speak of lie deeper, and are owing, we think, to a want of imagination and large comprehension of life.

But if, putting *Vanity Fair* aside as a fiction of high art, we look at it as a series of bits from life, it is entitled to the first rank as a set of sketches lifelike and natural. Sir Pitt Crawley—the selfish, low-minded baronet, the coarsest of the coarse old school, who cannot spell, and who living meanly, acting harshly and cruelly, and exercising great shrewdness in money matters, is notwithstanding always a loser—is a capital portrait; and, though exceptional even in his day, (which was the early part of the century,) still might be found in life. His brother, the jovial, fox-hunting, port-drinking rector, is equal to him as a real piece of flesh and blood. The Marquis of Steyne—the roué whom everybody censures, (except the serious,) but all visit when they get an invitation—revives some reminiscences of a similar personage in *Coningsby:* though Thackeray penetrates the pomps and strips off the conventions that rather imposed upon Disraeli. There are numerous other characters, which, if not quite so powerfully painted as these, are quite as truthful individually; but, always excepting Rebecca, the most large and vigorous delineation in the book is old Mr. Osborne. He is a type of a class; he points a moral; and, though sordid, selfish, sullen, half-savage, and meanly subservient to greatness, he obtains a hold on the reader by the force of his will, at least till he turns to a sort of goodness towards the conclusion.

These characters are frequently engaged in scenes that create amusement or exhibit society; and the sketches are intermingled with lively descriptions or shrewd remarks on life. Read as a series of sketches connected with persons whose fortunes serve to introduce them, *Vanity Fair* will furnish a lively and agreeable entertainment. Read as a continuous story, it will perhaps be felt to lack the interest which a story requires, except in the scenes connected with Rawdon Crawley's arrest, release, and subsequent discovery of his wife's liasion with the Marquis of Steyne. (p. 709)

As is usual with works of fiction published periodically, *Vanity Fair* is profusely illustrated with wood-cuts and etchings representing the persons and incidents of the text, by Mr. Thackeray himself. If only of passable or average merit, they would be creditable, as arguing the possession of a double art; but they strike us as allowing powers akin to the literary abilities of the author, besides possessing this further quality: the spirit of the scene and the character—the idiosyncracy of the persons—is more thoroughly entered into and presented to the reader than is common with professional artists. (p. 710)

> [*Robert S. Rintoul*], *in a review of "Vanity Fair,"* in The Spectator, *Vol. XXI, No. 1047, July 22, 1848, pp. 709-10.*

[GEORGE HENRY LEWES]   (essay date 1848)

[*Lewes was one of the most versatile men of letters in the Victorian era. Critics often cite his influence on the novelist George Eliot, to whom he was a companion and mentor, as his principal contribution to English letters, but they also credit him with critical acumen in his literary commentary, most notably in his dramatic criticism. Here, Lewes discusses artistic continuity and propor-* tion, style, satirical method, characterization, and realism in Vanity Fair. *For additional criticism on* Vanity Fair *by Lewes, see excerpt dated 1848 in* NCLC, *Vol. 5.*]

For some years Mr. Thackeray has been a marked man in letters,—but known rather as an amusing sketcher than as a serious artist. Light playful contributions to periodical literature, and two amusing books of travel, were insufficient to make a reputation; but a reputation he must now be held to have established by his *Vanity Fair.* It is his greatest effort and his greatest success. The strength which lay within him he has here put forth for the first time. The work before us retains traces of the writer's old fault—a fault fostered no doubt by the carelessness and impromptu proper to serial publication—viz. a sort of indifference to the serious claims of literature, a cavalier impertinence of manner as if he were playing with his subject. Nothing could be more impertinent, for instance, than Mr. Thackeray's second number,—in which he relapsed into his old magazine manner, and postponed the continuation of his narrative to imitations of some of his cotemporary writers of fiction. Fit subjects for ridicule such writers may be—but the ridicule is misplaced in the work which Mr. Thackeray had in hand, considered as a work of Art. In the same number he becomes suddenly aware of the discrepancy between the costume of the period in which he has laid his scene and the costume in which he has depicted the characters in his pictorial illustrations. All he does on the discovery is to notify the fact in a note, and flippantly pretend that the real costume was too hideous for his purpose. He has been guilty, however, of the same confusion of periods throughout the work. Sometimes we are in the early part of the present century—at others we are palpably in 1848. Writing from month to month encourages such laches; but for the sake of such a reputation as Mr. Thackeray has now arrived at, it will be well that he should be more upon his guard.

The style of *Vanity Fair* is winning, easy, masculine, felicitous, and humorous. Its pleasant pages are nowhere distorted by rant. The author indulges in no sentimentalities—inflicts no fine writing on his readers. Trusting to the force of truth and humour, he is the *quietest* of contemporary writers,—a merit worth noting in a literary age which has a tendency to mistake spasm for force. The book has abundant faults of its own,—and we shall presently notice some of them; but they are not the faults most current in our literature. The writer is quite free from theatricality. No glare from the footlights is thrown upon human nature, exaggerating and distorting it. He is guiltless too—let us be thankful for such a boon in the sense here intended—of a "purpose." Unfettered by political or social theories, his views of men and classes are not cramped. The rich in his pages are not necessarily vicious—the poor not as a consequence of their poverty virtuous and high-minded. Again—many jesters take advantage of their cap and bells, and adopt as their motto, "Ridentem dicere *falsum* quid vetat." Under the plea that laughter is not a serious thing, and what is laughingly spoken is not to be critically judged, they have sacrificed truth to their joke. No advocate of any cause, however, should be more scrupulously watched than he who laughing teaches. Against the dogmas of the politician, philosopher, or theologian the reader is on his defence. These "come in such a questionable shape" that we *must* examine them. Their seriousness alarms us. We scrutinize proofs and combat conclusions. But the jester is privileged. He throws us off our guard by the smile of his approach, and insinuates conviction by the bribery of laughter. The laughter passes, but the error may remain. It has gained admittance into our unsuspecting minds,—and is left there unsuspected.

It is a much-disputed question, whether or not ridicule be a test of truth? To us the question appears answered by saying that if the ridicule be developed *ab intra* from the argument—not thrown *on* it *ab extra*—it is a test. If a wit descries the latent absurdity grinning under a moral mask, and exposes it, he has confuted the argument; if he himself grins and makes faces *at* the mask, he may excite laughter but has not carried confutation. . . . It is one of Thackeray's peculiar excellencies that he almost always ridicules *ab intra*. An absurdity is stated by him in the quietest and gravest manner, as if he were himself a believer in it like others, and—enforced by such means of self-accumulation as leave it to unmitigated contempt. His irony of this kind is perfect,—but it is a weapon which he uses far too exclusively. He has shown himself, as we have said, a satirist—but not an artist. With himself we exclaim, "O brother wearers of motley! are there not moments when one grows sick of grinning and tumbling and the jingling of bells?" There is nothing so sad as a constant smile. Laughter becomes wearisome when too much prolonged,—for it is then a sort of blasphemy against the divine beauty which is in life. Mr. Thackeray grows serious and pathetic at times—but almost as if he were ashamed of it, like a man caught in tears at the theatre.—It is one weakness of the satirist that he is commonly afraid of the ridicule of others!

We have said that Mr. Thackeray is a satirist, not an artist:—and from that characteristic may be deduced many of his deficiencies. For instance, the reader of *Vanity Fair* will have observed that we have in it nothing but scenes and sketches—only glimpses, not views. There is constant succession of description, but no developement of story. The passions are taken at their culminating point, not exhibited in the process of growth; the incidents are seldom transacted before our eyes, but each is taken as a *fait accompli*. Nor is there anything like proportion kept. The writer opens a chapter, and his pen runs on easily, fed by a full and observant mind,—but recording the suggestions of the moment rather than building up the various portions of an edifice already planned and in which each part has its due significance.

Mr. Thackeray is deficient, too, in passion:—a deficiency that sits lightly on a satirist, but is serious in a writer of fiction. He has no command over this quality—apparently but little knowledge of it. The curtain of the tragedy of life has seldom risen before him—or he has looked on its representations with an incurious eye. Altogether, one may say that Mr. Thackeray has not very curiously or patiently observed moral phenomena. Life he has seen both at home and abroad, and he has reflected on what he has seen. We feel that he is painting after Nature: and this conviction it is which makes his work so delightful. Nothing is permanently interesting but truth.

As a consequence of Mr. Thackeray's satirical tendency may be noted the prodigality of vice and folly to be found in his pages—and which affords no true representation of human nature, but only the exaggeration of a feature. It has been made a serious reproach against this writer that he has arrived at such a pitch of misanthropy or doubt as to think, with Chamfort, that an honest man is a variety of the human species. . . . The writer began, no doubt, with the wholesome intention of lashing the vices and follies of Vanity Fair in a more restrictive sense—regarded as one of the social phases: but gradually *all* the districts of society are swept into his Vanity Fair—and there is *nothing good in it*. This is false and unwholesome

teaching. What a mass of scoundrels, blacklegs, fools, and humbugs Mr. Thackeray has crowded together. There is scarcely a good or estimable person in the book and as little of affection as of virtue. Even the heroine Amelia—with whom the writer seems to have been somewhat enamoured (a feeling of which he is likely to have the monopoly)—is thoroughly selfish as well as silly. The one fine exception is Major Dobbin—a sketch not unworthy of the hand that drew 'My Uncle Toby.'

As we have said, Mr. Thackeray's humour is peculiarly his own. He never frames and glazes an idea. The simplest words and in the simplest manner are used to bring out his meaning; and everything seems to flow from him as water from a rock. We may add that when he chooses to be pathetic, a quality of the same kind gives wonderful effect to his pathos. How beautiful is the scene in which Amelia has resolved at length to part from her child! (pp. 794-95)

The character of Becky is amongst the finest creations of modern fiction. She is perfectly unlike any other clever, heartless woman yet drawn. With great art, she is made rather selfish than wicked—though the excess of the selfishness rises to the force and has the effect of wickedness. Profound immorality is made to seem consistent with unfailing good humour. Becky has neither affections, nor passions, nor principles. She uses men as chessmen—and is not check-mated at last. It is very strange that the reader has a sort of liking for her in spite of his better knowledge. The fact is, the author has contrived in a surprising way to represent not only Becky's *mind* but her *manner*. We are in some sort under her spell,—as Rawdon was. To us she is almost as lively, entertaining and good-humoured as she was to those amongst whom she lived. Like Lord Steyne, we may see through her yet covet her society. Her equability of temper is a nice touch:—it belongs to the physiology of such a character. They who have no affections and no principles can be wounded only in their self-love, and may obtain the character of being good-tempered at the cheapest possible cost. The consistency of this remarkable character is maintained to the last. How full yet brief—graphic and suggestive—is the microscopic view of her life after her separation from her husband!— (p. 796)

Next in point of skill to that of Becky is the portrait of Rawdon Crawley—the heavy, stupid, gentlemanly dragoon and blackleg so completely subjugated by his clever little wife. His affection for his child quite whitewashes him. The reader forgets the blackleg in the father. It is worthy of note with what consummate truth this heavy dragoon is made to feel his insignificance by the side of his clever little wife, but how completely paralyzed the adroit little woman is when she stands guilty before her husband:—how silently she obeys him who has hitherto obeyed her,—how she feels that her arts are powerless against his passion. Brute strength long led by mental cunning here reasserts its empire and is undisputed. The whole scene is most masterly.

Jos Sedley is rather a failure:—nor is he consistently drawn. We are introduced to him as a man painfully shy, nervous, and stupid; but as the story proceeds he drops his shyness, and retains only the gluttony and stupidity of his former self. Meant as a decidedly *comic* character, he creates but little mirth.— George Osborne, the vain and foolish young officer, is capitally drawn. Lord Steyne is one of those *telling* exaggerations which make people exclaim, "How true!" when their acquaintance with lords is confined to fashionable novels. Though overdone, however, it is an exaggeration by a master; and the descriptions of Gaunt House and its inmates transcend all previous efforts in that style. Old Miss Crawley is capital. Her selfishness, her sagacity, her terrors in ill health, her triumph over the meanness which surrounds her and which she laughs at and profits by, are vividly presented, yet by the simplest strokes. Here is a sentence pregnant with meaning and very characteristic of the author:—''Picture to yourself, oh fair young reader, a worldly, selfish, graceless, thankless, religionless old woman, writhing in pain and fear, and *without her wig!* Picture her to yourself, and ere you be old learn to love and pray!''

Mrs. O'Dowd must not be forgotten. The gallant woman has won the hearts of her regiment,—and of all her readers. How true, homely, affectionate, and wise is the description of her packing up the Major's traps and preparing his coffee for him on the eve of Waterloo!

The vividness with which the whole of the scenes at Brussels stand out before the eye is marvellous when we reflect that the author is not describing the scenes which he himself witnessed, but only painting after the descriptions of others. They imply a fine faculty for historical romance. Nor is it only in this more elaborate painting that Mr. Thackeray has exhibited a constant mastery in the present book. The instances are abundant of meaning conveyed and intensified by a single line of illustration. . . .

Knowledge of life, good humoured satire, penetration into motive, power of characterization, and great truthfulness are qualities in fiction as rare as they are admirable; and no work that has been published for many years past can claim these qualities so largely as *Vanity Fair.* (p. 797)

> [*George Henry Lewes*], *in a review of ''Vanity Fair: A Novel without a Hero,'' in* The Athenaeum, *No. 1085, August 12, 1848, pp. 794-97.*

WILLIAM MAKEPEACE THACKERAY   (letter date 1848)

[*In the following excerpt from a letter to the critic Robert Bell, Thackeray responds to Bell's review of* Vanity Fair *in* Fraser's Magazine *(see excerpt by Bell dated 1848 in NCLC, Vol. 5).*]

Although I have made a rule to myself never to thank critics yet I like to break it continually, and especially in the present instance for what I hope is the excellent article in *Fraser.* It seems to me very just in most points as regards the author: some he questions as usual—If I had put in more fresh air as you call it my object would have been defeated—It is to indicate, in cheerful terms, that we are for the most part an abominably foolish and selfish people ''desperately wicked'' and all eager after vanities. Everybody is you see in that book,—for instance if I had made Amelia a higher order of woman there would have been no vanity in Dobbins falling in love with her, whereas the impression at present is that he is a fool for his pains that he has married a silly little thing and in fact has found out his error rather a sweet and tender one however, *quia multum amavit* I want to leave everybody dissatisfied and unhappy at the end of the story—we ought all to be with our own and all other stories. Good God dont I see (in that maybe cracked and warped looking glass in which I am always looking) my own weaknesses wickednesses lusts follies short comings? in company let us hope with better qualities about which we will pretermit discourse. We must lift up our voices about these and howl to a congregation of fools: so much at least has been my endeavour. You have all of you taken my misanthropy to task—I wish I could myself: but take the world by a certain standard (you know what I mean) and who dares

talk of having any virtue at all? For instance Forster says [see excerpt dated 1848] After a scene with Blifil, the air is cleared by a laugh of Tom Jones—Why Tom Jones in my holding is as big a rogue as Blifil. Before God he is—I mean the man is selfish according to his nature as Blifil according to his. In fact I've a strong impression that we are most of us not fit for—never mind.

Pathos I hold should be very occasional indeed in humourous works and indicated rather than expressed or expressed very rarely. In the passage where Amelia is represented as trying to separate herself from the boy—She goes upstairs and leaves him with his aunt 'as that poor Lady Jane Grey tried the axe that was to separate her slender life' I say that is a fine image whoever wrote it (& I came on it quite by surprize in a review the other day) that is greatly pathetic I think: it leaves you to make your own sad pictures—We shouldn't do much more than that I think in comic books—In a story written in the pathetic key it would be different & then the comedy perhaps should be occasional. Some day—but a truce to egotistical twaddle. It seems to me such a time ago that **V F** was written that one may talk of it as of some body elses performance. My dear Bell I am very thankful for your friendliness & pleased to have your good opinion. (pp. 423-25)

> *William Makepeace Thackeray, in a letter to Robert Bell on September 3, 1848, in his* The Letters and Private Papers of William Makepeace Thackeray: 1841-1851, Vol. II, *edited by Gordon N. Ray, Cambridge, Mass.: Harvard University Press, 1945, pp. 423-25.*

CHARLES ASTOR BRISTED   (essay date 1848)

[*In the following excerpt, Bristed discusses various aspects of* Vanity Fair, *including the predominance of ''disagreeable'' characters in the novel, Becky's personality, and Thackeray's satirical intentions.*]

[A comparison of *Vanity Fair* and Thackeray's other writings with the words of Honoré de Balzac] brings to mind a more serious charge than that of occasional conceit or affectation which we have more than once heard urged against [Thackeray]; namely, that his sketches contain too many disagreeable characters. A queer charge this to come from a reading generation which swallows copious illustrated editions of *Les Mystères* and *Le Juif,* and is lenient to the loathsome vulgarities of *Wuthering Heights* and *Wildfell Hall.* But let us draw a distinction or ''discriminate a difference,'' as a transcendentalist acquaintance of ours used to say. If a story is written for mere purposes of amusement, there certainly ought not to be more disagreeable characters introduced than are absolutely necessary for relief and contrast. But the moral and end of a story may often compel the author to bring before us a great number of unpleasant people. In a former volume of this Review the opinion was pretty broadly stated that no eminent novelist writes merely for amusement without some ulterior aim; most decidedly Thackeray does not at any rate. We shall have occasion to refer to this more than once, for it is doing vast injustice to Mr. T. to regard him merely as a provider of temporary fun. He does introduce us to many scamps, and profligates, and hypocrites, but it is to show them up and put us on our guard against them. His bad people are evidently and unmistakably bad; we hate them, and he hates them, too, and doesn't try to make us fall in love with them, like the philosophers of the ''Centre of Civilization,'' who dish you up seraphic poisoners and chaste adulteresses in a way that perplexes and confounds all established ideas of morality. And if he ever does bestow attractive traits on his rogues, it is to expose the worthlessness and emptiness of some things which are to the world attractive—to show that the good things of Vanity Fair are not good *per se*, but may be coincident with much depravity.

Thus Becky Sharpe, as portrayed by his graphic pen, is an object of envy and admiration for her cleverness and accomplishments to many a fine lady. There are plenty of the "upper ten" who would like to be as "smart" as Rebecca. She speaks French like a French woman, and gets up beautiful dresses out of nothing, and makes all the men admire her, and always has a repartee ready, and insinuates herself every where with an irresistible nonchalance. Then comes in the sage moralist, and shows us that a woman may do all these fine things, and yet be ready to lie right and left to every one, and ruin any amount of confiding tradesmen; to sell one man and poison another; to betray her husband and neglect her child. (That last touch is the most hateful one: in our simplicity we hope it is an exaggeration. That a woman should be utterly regardless of her offspring seems an impossibility—in this country, we are proud to say, it *is* an impossibility.) Or if any of his doubtful personages command our temporary respect and sympathy, it is because they are for the time in the right. Rawdon Crawley is not a very lofty character; he frequently comes before us in a position not even respectable; but when he is defending his honor against the old sybarite Lord Steyne, he rises with the occasion: even the guilty wife is forced to admire her husband, as he stands "strong, brave, and victorious." Nor though he

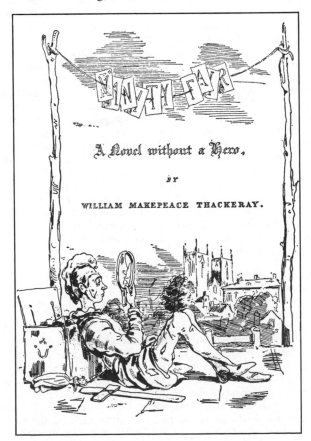

The title page of the first edition of Vanity Fair, *illustrated by Thackeray.*

finds it sometimes necessary to expose hypocrites, does Thackeray delight in the existence of hypocrisy, and love to seek out bad motives for apparently good actions. His charity rather leads him to attribute with a most humane irony pretended wickedness to weakness. Your French writer brings an upright gentleman before the footlights, and grudges you the pleasure of admiring him; he is impatient to carry him off behind the scenes, strip off his Christian garments, and show him to you in private a very fiend. But Thackeray, when he has put into a youth's mouth an atrociously piratical song, is overjoyed to add quietly that he "remembers seeing him awfully sick on board a Greenwich steamer." (pp. 422-23)

Thackeray never sets about a story of any length without having a will and a purpose. And this indeed is a noticeable difference generally existing between the wit and the humorist, that while the former sparkles away without any object beyond his own momentary amusement, the latter has a definite aim, some abuse to attack, some moral to hint. Thackeray attacks abuses, and it is with an honest indignation and simple earnestness that form the distinguishing features of his serious writings. He assaults all manner of social sham, humbug and flunkeyism, and gives it to them in a way that does you good to hear. Against toadyism, affectation and mobbery, he preaches a crusade in the sturdiest Anglo-Saxon. The charge began in the *Snobs of England;* it is now followed up in *Vanity Fair.* Any one, therefore, who reads the latter book should read the *Snob Papers* in *Punch,* by way of introduction to it. Tin-worship and title-worship, and that "praise of men" which your fashionables love more than the "praise of God"—Titmarsh is sworn foe to all these, and wages unrelenting war on them—but with none of that cant which runs all through Jerrold and half through Dickens: he does not make all his poor people angels, nor all his rich people devils, because they are rich. Nor has he any marked prejudice against Christianity in general, or the Christianity of his own church in particular—which we are weak enough to think rather to his credit. Moreover his sledge-hammer invective against fashionable fooleries, is not engendered of or alloyed with any rusticity or inability to appreciate the refinements of civilized life, as a backwoodsman or Down-easter might abuse things he did not comprehend; for Titmarsh has a soul for art and poetry, and good living, and all that is aesthetic and elegant.

Vanity Fair, then, is a satire on English society. The scene indeed is laid thirty years back, but that is of a piece with Juvenal's

> Experiar quid concedatur in illos
> Quorum Flaminia tegitur cinis atque Latina.

It is meant for the present time, as the very illustrations show, in which all the male characters wear the convenient trouser (*Americanice* pantaloons) of our own day, instead of the stiff "tights" which were the habit of that period. In a work of this sort we naturally expect to find many *type-characters*—that is, characters who represent classes of people. Most of these are very good and true. Rawley Crawdon is a capital representative of the uneducated part of the young British officery—profligate and spendthrift, stupid in everything but cards, billiards, and horseflesh, and too illiterate to spell decently; yet withal bold as a lion. It is pleasant to see such a man properly depicted now and then, for the writer who does it is doing his duty to civilization by assailing the old barbarous feudal notion that mere physical courage, which is generally founded on the consciousness of superior physical strength and dexterity, should ride roughshod over moral courage and intellect. And Lord

Steyne is a thorough specimen of the aristocratic old Sybarite. Others had tried their hands at this character before—D'Israeli and that coarsest of fine ladies, Lady Blessington—but none of them have succeeded like Thackeray. And Pitt Crawley is a perfect model of the stiff, slow, respectable *formula* man. And Osborne, Sr., is one of your regular purse-proud cits who measure everything by what it will fetch on 'Change. But some of the portraits are not fair even to Vanity Fair, and that of Sir Pitt, the elder Crawley, seems to us positively unjust. He may be a true sketch from life; rumor has indeed given him a real name and family; but he is too bad to be a type of country baronets, or even of country squires. And though the high-life characters have bitter justice done them in most things, there is one point on which the men are a little wronged: *they swear too much.* Allowing that a fearful amount of profanity prevails among people who ought to know better, there is surely no necessity for its being repeated. We do not want to hear the thing simply because it is true, any more than we wish to see pictures of disgusting and frightful objects, however faithfully to nature they may be painted. But in fact English gentlemen are not so openly profane as Titmarsh represents them.

The book has no hero: it openly professes to have none. But there is a heroine, at least a prominent female character, and she is equal to a dozen ordinary heroines and heroes. Becky Sharpe is an original creation, not the representative of a class, though there are traits about her that remind you of several classes. Any one who has been much in society must have had the fortune or misfortune to meet more than one woman who resembled Becky in some points—ay, even among us simple, unsophisticated, etc., republicans; for in truth if you only leave out a little nonsense about titles, everything in Titmarsh's literary puppet-show will apply point-blank to our own occidental Vanity Fair. There are women as spitefully satirical as Rebecca, making mischief in the most ingenious and graceful ways—fashionable enough that, and not by any means a sin, but on the contrary no small recommendation in Vanity Fair. There are women all in the best society, who flirt with every passable man that comes near them, as Rebecca did; for observe, it is not proved that Mrs. Rawdon Crawley did anything more; her biographer does not give you to understand that she actually "committed herself" with any one—and this is very proper and pleasing in Vanity Fair. There are women who, like Rebecca, have always a plausible lie ready to excuse themselves; and this is an excusable pecadillo in Vanity Fair. There are women who, like Rebecca, look to marriage only as a means of getting a position "in society," and what can be a more flattering homage to Vanity Fair? There are women, like Rebecca, who sponge upon spooneys and get money under false pretences; and the victims may "cut up rough" about it, but the rest of Vanity Fair pass it over as a venial offence and accept their part of the spoil. In short, put together a number of things the practice of which is not only allowable but successful in Vanity Fair, and what a devil of a woman you will make! Such at least is our idea of the *moral* and theory of Rebecca Crawley *née* Sharpe. (pp. 423-25)

It would take too long to follow Becky through her chequered career—her grand catastrophe, her exile, her ultimate partial recovery. Many of our readers were more or less familiar with her before seeing these remarks of ours; and such as are not, must have been tempted ere this to resolve that they will go to the fountain-head for information about her. We have only to observe, before taking leave of her, the skill which her biographer displays in lightly passing over some of the diabolical scenes she is concerned in, such for instance as "her

second appearance in the character of Clytemnestra." Your true artist will produce infinitely more effect by just hinting at a horror, than a second-rate man can work by going into the most elaborate details.

Some notice should be taken of the Osbornes and Sedleys who make up the underplot of the story. We have some suspicion that Thackeray finished up old Osborne, the purse-proud merchant, more carefully than he had intended at first, in opposition to Mr. Dombey, to show *his* view of such a character in opposition to that of Dickens. If such a comparison is challenged, there can be no doubt that so far as verisimilitude and nature are concerned, Mr. Osborne, Sr., has it by long odds. (pp. 429-30)

The loves and fortunes of young Osborne and Amelia Sedley, are designed to carry out still further the attack on what formed one of the strongest topics of denunciation in the *Snob Papers,*—that heartless system (flourishing to perfection in France, but deep-rooted enough in England) which considers matrimony as the union, not of a young man to a young woman, but of *so much to so much.* A splendid theme for indignant declamation, and one in which the satirist is sure to meet with much sympathy from the young of both sexes. But we must remember that the principle of union for love has, like all principles, its limitations. That two young people, long and fondly attached to each other, should be afraid to marry because they would be obliged to drop a little in the social scale, and deny themselves some of the outward luxuries they enjoy separately; that they should sacrifice their hearts to those abominable dictates of fashion which Titmarsh has summed up in his Snob Commandment, "Thou shalt not marry unless thou hast a Brougham and a man-servant;" this is truly matter of indignation and mourning, against which it is not possible to say too much. But we must also protest against the opposite extreme—the inference drawn from an extension of our principle—that love ought to overcome and exclude *all* objections, want of principles and character in the man for instance; or utter want of means on both sides to support a family; or even—what is generally the first thing to be disregarded in such cases—incompatibility of relations and friends. . . . We appeal to your own experience, reader. Of all the *pur sang* love-matches you have known—matches where one or more of the impediments we have mentioned existed—how many have turned out happily? Nay, we appeal to Titmarsh himself and *his own characters in this very book.* Would it not have been a thousand times better for Amelia if she had married Dobbin in the first place? And might not George as well have taken Miss Schwartz as wed Amelia one month and been ready to run away with another woman the next?

We must take leave of Titmarsh; for he is carrying us off into all sorts of digressions. We never were so long filling the same number of pages as we have been on the present occasion, for whenever we opened the book to make an extract we were tempted to read on, on, on—the same things which we had read a dozen times—but there was no resisting. And when we resolutely turned our back to his people, it was only to think, and reason, and argue about them. How many of the hundreds of novels, published every year, leave any impression in your mind or give you one afterthought about any character in them? It is easy to take exceptions to the book—we have taken our share; we might go on to pick out little slips, instances of forgetfulness, as where we are told first that Amelia Sedley is not the heroine, and two or three pages after that she is; or when the climate of Coventry Island is so bad that no office will insure Rawdon's life there, yet in the very same number it is mentioned how much his life-insurance cost him. But, say what you will, the book draws you back to it, over and over again. Farewell then, O Titmarsh! Truly, thou deservest better treatment than we can give thee. Thy book should be written about in a natural, even, continuous, flowing style like thine own, not in our lumbering paragraphs, that blunder out only half of what we mean to say. And do thou, O reader, buy this book if thou hast not bought it; if thou hast, throw it not away into the chiffonier-basket as thou dost many brown-paper-covered volumes; but put it into a good binding and lay it by—not among the works "that no gentleman's library should be without"—but somewhere easy of access; for it is a book to keep and read, and there are many sermons in it. (pp. 430-31)

> *Charles Astor Bristed, in a review of "Vanity Fair,"*
> *in* The American Review, *n.s. Vol. II, No. IV, October, 1848, pp. 421-31.*

THE LONDON REVIEW   (essay date 1861)

[*This anonymous reviewer harshly criticizes* Vanity Fair *for its cynical view of life and lack of idealized characters and situations.*]

[In *Vanity Fair*] Thackeray gives us to understand that he writes as a moralist:—

> My kind reader will please to remember, that this history has "Vanity Fair" for a title, and that Vanity Fair is a very vain, wicked, foolish place, full of all sorts of humbugs, and falsenesses, and pretensions.... People there are living and flourishing in the world ... with no reverence except for prosperity, and no eye for anything beyond success ... faithless, hopeless, charityless: let us have at them, dear friends, with might and main.

And how does Thackeray carry out this intention? He makes us almost like Becky Sharp by endowing her with those deservedly popular qualities, tact, wit, good-humour, and good-temper; and by putting her in contact with other persons equally wicked but not equally pleasant, and with one or two worthy people whom he contrives to make ridiculous or contemptible. We are inclined to pardon Becky's wickedness in 'doing' every one she comes across, when every one she comes across so well deserves to be 'done.' Especially has he failed in putting her in contrast with Amelia, that mean-minded whimpering little woman, whose loving temperament never inspires her with one noble sentiment. Becky has at least one element of greatness; she honours even her enemies when they are worthy of honour; while Amelia is incapable of appreciating true merit even in her friends. We pardon her infatuation for George Osborne, that 'selfish humbug, that low-bred cockney-dandy,' as Becky rightly calls him; we pardon it as a delusion of early youth, rivetted by the premature death of her husband on the battle field; but we cannot pardon her low estimate of, and petty tyranny over Dobbin; we cannot even pardon her hasty marriage, bringing, as it was sure to do, ruin on the man she loved. That hard intellectual type of woman-kind which is commonly stigmatized as 'strong-minded,' is frightening authors from the study of qualities essentially womanly. It is woman's vocation to be strong, not in mind, but in noble and generous impulses; that, while her husband and sons know best what is expedient, logical, or wise, she should know best what is true, gallant, and right. *Vanity Fair* is a remarkable book,

brilliant, entertaining, life-like (as far as life is bad and base); but if we plunge beneath the sparkling surface, it is a dreary book. It gives the real, and utterly omits the ideal: it strips away the veil which our love or trust throws over our neighbours' actions, and holds them up in all their possible selfishness and falseness. The blossom of the gay Epicurean is gone, and we are fed to satiety on the Cynic's bitter fruit. Are we so silly as to imagine that there is such a thing as disinterested service and love? (pp. 291-92)

Don't let us trust any one, dear friends. Nor our lovers, lest, while we picture them 'bivouacking, or attending the couch of a wounded comrade, or studying the art of war in their own desolate chamber,' our angel-thoughts happily find the barrack gates shut, and cannot pass through to 'hear the young fellows roaring over their whiskey-punch.' (p. 293)

O what a dreary book! Give us its narrative, its comedy, its brilliant jesting and wit, and let us laugh and be merry; but spare us these reflections, O bitter cynic, if you would not drive us to despair. The grave irony that praises baseness, or the grave censure that condemns it, leaves us equally helpless and hopeless, if you show us no way of escape. When did the bitterness of the fruit ever prevent men from clutching at the fair outside? We want something better, something substantial on which to rest and feed, in the place of this universal negation, this desolate hollowness and barrenness of life. Human nature is bad enough; but while God reigns over the world, and while His Spirit is abroad in it, we rejoice to think that glimmerings of truth and trust and kindness, of faithful service and disinterested love, are ever breaking through the darkness, witnesses of that gracious Presence which offers light and peace to all. (p. 294)

> *A review of "Vanity Fair," in* The London Review,
> *Vol. XVI, No. XXXII, July, 1861, pp. 291-94.*

JAMES HANNAY   (essay date 1868)

[*Hannay was a British novelist and journalist who became a close friend of Thackeray. His* Studies on Thackeray, *from which the following excerpt is drawn, was the first full-length critical survey of the novelist's works. In the excerpt below, he discusses such facets of* Vanity Fair *as its drama, satire, and realism.* Studies on Thackeray *was originally published in 1868 in the magazine* Broadway.]

The warmest admirers of Thackeray's earlier tales must, of course, acknowledge that *Vanity Fair* was a prodigious advance upon them. It retains a peculiar charm, though he reached a still higher grade of art in *Esmond* and in *The Newcomes*. There is an animation and a freedom of satire about *Vanity Fair* which has its own delightfulness as distinct from the mellower beauty and sedater humour of its successors. In dramatic effect, and interest of narration, it, perhaps, takes the lead of all; for Thackeray has scarcely anywhere else such situations as that of the Waterloo crisis, or the surprise of Becky by her husband when he escapes from the spunging-house. And how admirably the story develops itself out of such simple elements! How modest the fountains from which spring the stream of story that by-and-by expands into a mirror-like lake, reflecting the character of a whole generation! We have two middle-class families in Russell Square, the son and daughter of which are engaged to each other. The daughter has a school-fellow who goes out as a governess to make her way in the world. The son enters the army, and naturally makes intimate friends at his mess. But by degrees the interest widens and deepens. A whole group of personages is taken in, and their fortunes linked together; the comedy darkens into tragedy, the satire grows more and more thoughtful and intense, and a book, apparently begun as one of mere amusement, closes leaving its reader a livelong theme for emotion and meditation. The change is chiefly due to the development of the character of Becky Sharp; and nothing is more illustrative of Thackeray's genius than the probable, reasonable, and entirely natural and sensible way in which Becky's progress through life is managed. Nobody can lay his finger on an incident in it not likely enough under the conditions, and in perfect keeing with Becky's own character, and that of the people among whom she is thrown. It is this supreme merit of truth which distinguishes Thackeray from mere novelists of the day; heroes of the Photographic school, which deals in common-place realism; and the Fantastic school, which deals in extravagant incident. There are realists and realists. Thackeray paints common life, but not in a common-place manner. There are novelists whose imitation is mechanical rather than creative, and resembles the employment of real water, real horses, &c., on the stage—a vulgarity which attacks art in its very essence. They make their characters twaddle through whole pages, like those in Swift's satirical piece on "Polite Conversation." But though people do undoubtedly twaddle in the actual world, that is not a sufficient reason for making them twaddle in a work of art, which, though bound to be natural, is bound also to show some power of *selection* amongst the products of nature. Thackeray, in *Vanity Fair,* and everywhere else, detests the false, the turgid, the high-flown; and resolutely prefers good low art to the sham high. But there is a medium; and he is never realistic in the sense in which a post-office directory is so. He was, however, for a long time, too veracious for his readers, and even after *Vanity Fair* had appeared, the sweet, kindly little Amelia was attacked as not clever enough for the place which she held in the novel. As if cleverness was either the commonest, or the most desirable quality in a heroine—at least, a heroine that is intended to be loved and married! Through all Thackeray's books, there runs the prevailing doctrine that women—in spite of their little jealousies and other faults—are better than men by dint of their tenderness and affection; and surely these are found every day in women still duller than Amelia is represented as being. It is curious how completely in *Vanity Fair* Thackeray put on the stage his whole company of actors in the comedy of life. Dobbin has a family likeness to Colonel Newcome and Henry Esmond; George Osborne has a strong moral resemblance to Arthur Pendennis; Laura Bell is a cleverer Amelia; and Miss Crawley claims kin both with old Lady Kew and with the Baroness Bernstein, who, as the brilliant Beatrix, had some points in common (under great difference of condition) with Becky Sharp. . . . I do not the least mean that Thackeray repeated himself, or that these are not all distinct individualities. On the contrary, the very fact that they should be both like and unlike, is a proof of the artist's subtlety as of his fidelity to nature. But the resemblances are worth studying by those who would understand his sympathies and antipathies. (pp. 19-24)

> *James Hannay, in his* Studies on Thackeray, *1869. Reprint by Kennikat Press, 1970, 107 p.*

GEORGE AUGUSTUS SALA   (essay date 1869)

[*Sala was an English journalist. In the following excerpt, he discusses Thackeray's authentic representation of character and* incident in Vanity Fair, *focusing on a single episode that he finds inconsistent with the novel's generally realistic portrayal of life.*]

I can with difficulty assume that there are any intelligent persons of the Victorian era who have not read and re-read the wonderful drama of human life, the more wonderful analysis of human vice, weakness, meanness, and folly, called [*Vanity Fair*]. And with much greater difficulty could I deem it possible for any literate person to wander about Brussels, or take that inevitable but sorely disappointing trip to the field of Waterloo itself, without peopling his mind incontinent with all the Thackerayian *dramatis personae,* and all the phases of the Waterloo episode in *Vanity Fair.* In comparison with the astonishing skill with which Thackeray has made out of the great battle—which, in itself, he never describes—an unseen pivot on which turns, from first to last, the whole machinery of his story, the Waterloo chapter in Victor Hugo's *Misérables,* brilliant and graphic and powerful as it is, seems but a clumsy piece of "padding," dragged in by the head and shoulders to fill up a gap. For my part, the last time I went to Waterloo, I found Hougoumont and the Belle Alliance and the Haye Sainte, so many blackened and crumbling booths in Vanity Fair. I should not have been at all surprised to find the names of the Marquis of Steyne and Sir Pitt Crawley in the visitors' book at Mont St. Jean, or to be told by the cicerone at the Cottonian Museum, that yonder battered shako hanging up had belonged to M. le Capitaine Osborne, or that the dinted broadsword hard by had been worn by M. Crawley, *officier aux Gardes, Milor Anglais.*

The highest praise which, as I conceive, can be awarded to a work of fiction is that the circumstances therein narrated may be taken to be the truth, and the personages represented accepted as real people. The *Iliad* is probably a fiction, and *Paradise Lost* is certainly one; yet everybody believes in Nestor, and Thersites, and Ulysses, and Agamemnon; and Abdiel, and Ithuriel, and Raphael the good-natured angel. Even a battle in heaven with real cannon, or the interference of all the deities of Olympus in the petty squabbles of a lot of rascally Greek klephts, do not strike us—so exquisite has been the dexterity of the narrator—as being very out-of-the-way occurrences. The reality, however, of *Vanity Fair* does not demand even the slight concessions which are extorted from the imagination of those who read Homer or Milton. The epic is a plain-clothes one, and we may take it for granted as completely as we take the *Times* newspaper or *Hart's Army-List.* The realistic excellence attained by Mr. Thackeray in his chapters on the Waterloo time is on a par with the excellence attained by Captain Siborne in his model of the battle-field itself. It is excellence of the kind recognised by the horse and the birds, when the first neighed at the painted representation of a horse, and the last pecked at the painted fruit in the old Greek's picture. The old ship-captain who, when the conversation turned on the voyage to Liliput, declared that he knew Captain Gulliver very well, only that he lived at Wapping and not at Rotherhithe, passed on Swift's immortal satire a criticism analogous to that which might be passed on *Vanity Fair;* and Swift, be it remembered, to his greater praise, was dealing with the most extravagant personages and the most incredible circumstances. (pp. 351-52)

I look upon *Vanity Fair* as a work so artistically perfect, in the very best sense of literary perfection, the art being all but entirely concealed, that I have often asked myself with surprise and bewilderment what the artist could have been thinking of to introduce in this said Waterloo episode an incident which I can but think grossly unreal, improbable, and unnatural. I allude to the proposal made by George Osborne to Becky Sharpe, on the night of the Duchess of Richmond's ball, that she should "fly" with him. I own that George was over head and ears in love with Becky—infatuated, *ensorcelé,* by that baleful little fairy with the green eyes—whom I heard qualified once by a Frenchman who had read the Hachette edition of *La Foire aux Vanités* as *"une incarnation de l'absinthe des plus désastreuses."* I grant that a man who is in love with a woman will stop short of no folly and no absurdity in the avowal of his passion, and that very few considerations of common sense will hinder him from attempting the most desperate deeds to win her. The restraint is less, perhaps, when the object of love happens to be another man's wife; for the passion being *ab initio* a guilty one demands, on the "much more blood" principle in *Macbeth,* more and more criminality as it approaches culmination. But Mr. Thackeray's George Osborne, although a vain, empty-headed coxcomb, was not a raving madman; and no one but a howling lunatic would have asked, circumstanced as George Osborne then was, a woman to "fly" with him. Whither were they to fly? Into Napoleon's lines? To Ostend? The pair would have been stopped on the shore, and George would have been arrested as a deserter, tried by court-martial, and shot. Could they conceal themselves in Brussels? Could they reach Paris? Why, George Osborne was bound by a hundred indissoluble fetters as strong as Acadian steel to Flanders, to Brussels, and to the headquarters and his regiment. He was a captain in the famous British army. He was on active service. The campaign had begun. From hour to hour a deadly conflict might be expected. Was it likely, was it feasible, was it within the range of possibility, that a British officer—a brave one too, notwithstanding all his conceit and ignorance—would desert his colours, would betray his country, would submit to be branded as a rascal and a dastard, in order to "fly" with his friend's wife? Elopements have been heard of before now, I grant. In peaceful times dissolute gentlemen show as little reluctance in levanting with other people's spouses as in deserting their own; but Don Juan does not commit an amorous escapade in front of the enemy. Faublas does not smuggle a marchioness into a post-chaise and abscond with her on the eve of a tremendous battle. That this strangely-improbable incident was of no hasty or careless commission on the part of Mr. Thackeray is clear. It marks a very important point in the story. Subsequent events of the story hinge upon it. The *dénouement* of *Vanity Fair* is affected by it. It is in the first volume that George Osborne makes this preposterous proposal. It is not until the close of the third that Becky, to bring about Amelia's marriage with Dobbin, triumphantly shows her the letter which she has been hoarding for long years—the letter given to her in a bouquet by George on the night of the Duchess of Richmond's ball, and in which the young man had asked her to "fly." The production of this *billet-doux* at length forces George's widow to the conviction that her darling husband was a false-hearted humbug, and, her eyes being opened, she very sensibly marries Major Dobbin.

This passage in *Vanity Fair* has been to me a stumbling-block for years, and over and over again I have asked myself, with increasing perplexity and general discomfiture, how ever this piece of false art could have crept into a wondrously-polished and homogeneous work—how ever the Homer of this prose epic could not merely have nodded, but have sunk for a time into a slumber as deep as Rip Van Winkle's. When I was young I used to bewilder myself almost as desperately in guesses as to the probability of a broken-down, bankrupt, knavish captain of horse—a *roué,* a gamester, a sharper, such as Rawdon Crawley was—being appointed to the governorship of a West

India island; but years and experience, and the attentive study of the *Court Guide* in connection with the *London Gazette,* have mitigated both my perplexity and my incredulity on *that* head. As things go, have gone, and are likely to go, one need not be surprised at the appointment of anybody to anything. I have some hopes of getting the mission to Timbuctoo myself when I am old and broke.

The only tenable hypothesis I can form as to this "flying" matter in *Vanity Fair* is one which may not be very agreeable to English ears. So long, however, as we have the published reports of a Court for Divorce and Matrimonial Causes, we are constrained to admit that the elopement of other women's husbands with other men's wives are not always of the same Platonic nature as that of Mr. Carker with Mrs. Dombey—the oddest wild-goose chase perhaps ever imagined by a novelist. These divorce-court people mean naughtiness, and as a rule commit naughtiness. I cannot help fancying that the acute philosopher who wrote *Vanity Fair* meant in the first instance that George Osborne should avow his adulterous love for Rebecca Crawley, and ask her for a rendezvous. A French novelist of the present century, or an English novelist of the last one—the virtuous Richardson even—would have made no bones at all about the matter. But Mr. Thackeray may have hesitated. He knew that he was appealing to a refined, a "genteel," a fastidious audience—an audience who will listen unblushingly to the grossest scenes of profligacy at the French plays, but who, when it visits the Olympic or the Princess's, expects that

Thackeray's illustration of Becky's departure from Miss Pinkerton's academy.

profligacy shall be wrapped up in cotton-wool, and naughtiness softened down to indiscretion. Half the *vaudevilles* which English playwrights translate for our theatres, and impudently pass off as their own, turn on the illicit love of a young man for a married woman, or *vice versâ;* but in the English translation the criminality involved is generally slurred over by the convenient device of the young gentleman being in possession of certain letters written by the lady before her marriage; at which discreet compromise refined, fastidious, and genteel society rejoices greatly. May not the expediency of a similarly discreet compromise have occurred to the author of *Vanity Fair?* and what would have been more discreet than George's proposal to Becky to "fly" with him? It is a pity that in conceding so much to genteel squeamishness, a very serious blemish should have fallen on an otherwise perfect work of art. (pp. 352-55)

> George Augustus Sala, "On a Certain Passage in 'Vanity Fair'," in Belgravia, Vol. VIII, No. 31, May, 1869, pp. 345-55.

ANTHONY TROLLOPE   (essay date 1879)

[*A prominent Victorian novelist, Trollope is best known for the "Barsetshire Chronicles," a series of novels that realistically and humorously depicts English provincial life. Trollope's* Thackeray, *from which the following excerpt was drawn, was one of the earliest book-length studies of the novelist and is still a highly regarded work. Here, Trollope responds to Thackeray's detractors on such issues as* Vanity Fair's *moral influence, its apparently cynical outlook on life, and Amelia's suitability as a heroine.*]

It may be as well to speak first of the faults which were attributed to [*Vanity Fair*]. It was said that the good people were all fools, and that the clever people were all knaves. When the critics,—the talking critics as well as the writing critics,—began to discuss *Vanity Fair,* there had already grown up a feeling as to Thackeray as an author—that he was one who had taken up the business of castigating the vices of the world. Scott had dealt with the heroics, whether displayed in his Flora MacIvors or Meg Merrilieses, in his Ivanhoes or Ochiltrees. Miss Edgeworth had been moral; Miss Austen conventional; Bulwer had been poetical and sentimental; Marryat and Lever had been funny and pugnacious, always with a dash of gallantry, displaying funny naval and funny military life; and Dickens had already become great in painting the virtues of the lower orders. But by all these some kind of virtue had been sung, though it might be only the virtue of riding a horse or fighting a duel. Even Eugene Aram and Jack Sheppard, with whom Thackeray found so much fault, were intended to be fine fellows, though they broke into houses and committed murders. The primary object of all those writers was to create an interest by exciting sympathy.... With Thackeray it had been altogether different. Alas, alas! the meanness of human wishes; the poorness of human results! That had been his tone. There can be no doubt that the heroic had appeared contemptible to him, as being untrue.... Why sing songs that are false? Why tell of Lucy Ashtons and Kate Nicklebys, when pretty girls, let them be ever so beautiful, can be silly and sly? Why pour philosophy out of the mouth of a fashionable young gentleman like Pelham, seeing that young gentlemen of that sort rarely, or we may say never, talk after that fashion? Why make a housebreaker a gallant charming young fellow, the truth being that housebreakers as a rule are as objectionable in their manners as they are in their morals? Thackeray's mind had in truth worked in this way, and he had become a satirist. That had

been all very well for *Fraser* and *Punch;* but when his satire was continued through a long novel, in twenty-four parts, readers,—who do in truth like the heroic better than the wicked,—began to declare that this writer was no novelist, but only a cynic. (pp. 90-2)

[This] special fault was certainly found with *Vanity Fair* at the time. Heroines should not only be beautiful, but should be endowed also with a quasi celestial grace,—grace of dignity, propriety, and reticence. A heroine should hardly want to be married, the arrangement being almost too mundane,—and, should she be brought to consent to undergo such bond, because of its acknowledged utility, it should be at some period so distant as hardly to present itself to the mind as a reality. Eating and drinking should be altogether indifferent to her, and her clothes should be picturesque rather than smart, and that from accident rather than design. Thackeray's Amelia does not at all come up to the description here given. She is proud of having a lover, constantly declaring to herself and to others that he is "the greatest and the best of men,"—whereas the young gentleman is, in truth, a very little man. She is not at all indifferent as to her finery, nor, as we see incidentally, to enjoying her suppers at Vauxhall. She is anxious to be married,—and as soon as possible. A hero too should be dignified and of a noble presence; a man who, though he may be as poor as Nicholas Nickleby, should nevertheless be beautiful on all occasions, and never deficient in readiness, address, or self-assertion. *Vanity Fair* is specially declared by the author to be "a novel without a hero," and therefore we have hardly a right to complain of deficiency of heroic conduct in any of the male characters. But Captain Dobbin does become the hero, and is deficient. Why was he called Dobbin, except to make him ridiculous? Why is he so shamefully ugly, so shy, so awkward? Why was he the son of a grocer? Thackeray in so depicting him was determined to run counter to the recognised taste of novel readers. And then again there was the feeling of another great fault. Let there be the virtuous in a novel and let there be the vicious, the dignified and the undignified, the sublime and the ridiculous,—only let the virtuous, the dignified, and the sublime be in the ascendant. Edith Bellenden, and Lord Evandale, and Morton himself would be too stilted, were they not enlivened by Mause, and Cuddie, and Poundtext. But here, in this novel, the vicious and the absurd have been made to be of more importance than the good and the noble. Becky Sharp and Rawdon Crawley are the real heroine and hero of the story. It is with them that the reader is called upon to interest himself. It is of them that he will think when he is reading the book. It is by them that he will judge the book when he has read it. There was no doubt a feeling with the public that though satire may be very well in its place, it should not be made the backbone of a work so long and so important as this. A short story such as *Catherine* or *Barry Lyndon* might be pronounced to have been called for by the iniquities of an outside world; but this seemed to the readers to have been addressed almost to themselves. Now men and women like to be painted as Titian would paint them, or Raffaelle,—not as Rembrandt, or even Rubens.

Whether the ideal or the real is the best form of a novel may be questioned, but there can be no doubt that as there are novelists who cannot descend from the bright heaven of the imagination to walk with their feet upon the earth, so there are others to whom it is not given to soar among clouds. The reader must please himself, and make his selection if he cannot enjoy both. There are many who are carried into a heaven of pathos by the woes of a Master of Ravenswood, who fail altogether to be touched by the enduring constancy of a Dobbin. There are others,—and I will not say but they may enjoy the keenest delight which literature can give,—who cannot employ their minds on fiction unless it be conveyed in poetry. With Thackeray it was essential that the representations made by him should be, to his own thinking, lifelike. A Dobbin seemed to him to be such a one as might probably be met with in the world, whereas to his thinking a Ravenswood was simply a creature of the imagination. He would have said of such, as we would say of female faces by Raffaelle, that women would like to be like them, but are not like them. Men might like to be like Ravenswood, and women may dream of men so formed and constituted, but such men do not exist. Dobbins do, and therefore Thackeray chose to write of a Dobbin.

So also of the preference given to Becky Sharp and to Rawdon Crawley. Thackeray thought that more can be done by exposing the vices than extolling the virtues of mankind. No doubt he had a more thorough belief in the one than in the other. The Dobbins he did encounter—seldom; the Rawdon Crawleys very often. He saw around him so much that was mean! He was hurt so often by the little vanities of people! It was thus that he was driven to ... overthoughtfulness about snobs.... It thus became natural to him to insist on the thing which he hated with unceasing assiduity, and only to break out now and again into a rapture of love for the true nobility which was dear to him,—as he did with the character of Captain Dobbin.

It must be added to all this that, before he has done with his snob or his knave, he will generally weave in some little trait of humanity by which the sinner shall be relieved from the absolute darkness of utter iniquity. He deals with no Varneys or Deputy-Shepherds, all villany and all lies, because the snobs and knaves he had seen had never been all snob or all knave. Even Shindy probably had some feeling for the poor woman he left at home. Rawdon Crawley loved his wicked wife dearly, and there were moments even with her in which some redeeming trait half reconciles her to the reader.

Such were the faults which were found in **Vanity Fair;** but though the faults were found freely, the book was read by all. Those who are old enough can well remember the effect which it had, and the welcome which was given to the different numbers as they appeared. Though the story is vague and wandering, clearly commenced without any idea of an ending, yet there is something in the telling which makes every portion of it perfect in itself. There are absurdities in it which would not be admitted to anyone who had not a peculiar gift of making even his absurdities delightful. No schoolgirl who ever lived would have thrown back her gift-book, as Rebecca did the "dixonary," out of the carriage window as she was taken away from school. But who does not love that scene with which the novel commences? How could such a girl as Amelia Osborne have got herself into such society as that in which we see her at Vauxhall? But we forgive it all because of the telling. (pp. 92-6)

There is a double story running through the book, the parts of which are but lightly woven together, of which the former tells us the life and adventures of that singular young woman Becky Sharp, and the other the troubles and ultimate success of our noble hero Captain Dobbin. Though it be true that readers prefer, or pretend to prefer, the romantic to the common in their novels, and complain of pages which are defiled with that which is low, yet I find that the absurd, the ludicrous, and even the evil, leave more impression behind them than the grand, the beautiful, or even the good. Dominie Sampson,

Dugald Dalgetty, and Bothwell are, I think, more remembered than Fergus MacIvor, than Ivanhoe himself, or Mr. Butler the minister. It certainly came to pass that, in spite of the critics, Becky Sharp became the first attraction in **Vanity Fair.** When we speak now of **Vanity Fair,** it is always to Becky that our thoughts recur. She has made a position for herself in the world of fiction, and is one of our established personages. (p. 98)

To the end [Becky] is the same,—utterly false, selfish, covetous, and successful. To have made such a woman really in love would have been a mistake. Her husband she likes best,—because he is, or was, her own. But there is no man so foul, so wicked, so unattractive, but that she can fawn over him for money and jewels. There are women to whom nothing is nasty, either in person, language, scenes, actions, or principle,—and Becky is one of them; and yet she is herself attractive. A most wonderful sketch, for the perpetration of which all Thackeray's power of combined indignation and humour was necessary!

The story of Amelia and her two lovers, George Osborne and Captain, or as he came afterwards to be, Major, and Colonel Dobbin, is less interesting, simply because goodness and eulogy are less exciting than wickedness and censure. Amelia is a true, honest-hearted, thoroughly English young woman, who loves her love because he is grand,—to her eyes,—and loving him, loves him with all her heart. Readers have said that she is silly, only because she is not heroic. I do not know that she is more silly than many young ladies whom we who are old have loved in our youth, or than those whom our sons are loving at the present time. Readers complain of Amelia because she is absolutely true to nature. There are no Raffaellistic touches, no added graces, no divine romance. She is feminine all over, and British,—loving, true, thoroughly unselfish, yet with a taste for having things comfortable, forgiving, quite capable of jealousy, but prone to be appeased at once, at the first kiss; quite convinced that her lover, her husband, her children are the people in all the world to whom the greatest consideration is due. Such a one is sure to be the dupe of a Becky Sharp, should a Becky Sharp come in her way,—as is the case with so many sweet Amelias whom we have known. But in a matter of love she is sound enough and sensible enough,—and she is as true as steel. I know no trait in Amelia which a man would be ashamed to find in his own daughter. (pp. 104-05)

The reader as he closes the book has on his mind a strong conviction, the strongest possible conviction, that among men George is as weak and Dobbin as noble as any that he has met in literature; and that among women Amelia is as true and Becky as vile as any he has encountered. Of so much he will be conscious. In addition to this he will unconsciously have found that every page he has read will have been of interest to him. There has been no padding, no longueurs; every bit will have had its weight with him. And he will find too at the end, if he will think of it—though readers, I fear, seldom think much of this in regard to books they have read—that the lesson taught in every page has been good. There may be details of evil painted so as to disgust,—painted almost too plainly,—but none painted so as to allure. (pp. 106-07)

Anthony Trollope, in his Thackeray, *1879. Reprint by Gale Research Company, 1968, 216 p.*

ROBERT LOUIS STEVENSON (essay date 1882)

[*A famous Scottish novelist and essayist, Stevenson wrote some of the nineteenth century's most beloved novels, including* Treasure Island, Doctor Jekyll and Mr. Hyde, *and* Kidnapped. *In the following excerpt, Stevenson stresses the importance in* Vanity Fair *of the scene in chapter fifty-three in which Rawdon strikes Lord Steyne after finding him alone with Becky. Stevenson's comments were written in 1882.]*

If Rawdon Crawley's blow were not delivered, *Vanity Fair* would cease to be a work of art. That scene is the chief ganglion of the tale; and the discharge of energy from Rawdon's fist is the reward and consolation of the reader. (p. 239)

> Robert Louis Stevenson, "A Gossip on Romance," in his Memories and Portraits, 1887. Reprint by Charles Scribner's Sons, 1923, pp. 229-53.

ADOLPHUS ALFRED JACK (essay date 1895)

[*In the following excerpt, Jack initially examines* Vanity Fair *within the context of Thackeray's output as a whole, speculating on the possibility that prototypes for various characters in the novel may exist in the author's previous works. In the second portion of the excerpt, the critic explores the vision of life presented in the novel as well as Thackeray's portrayal of Becky, Rawdon, Amelia, and Dobbin.*]

[*Vanity Fair*] is singularly straightforward. The same attitude is preserved throughout, and that attitude, though severer than, is in all essentials similar to that formerly adopted. There is a greater diversity in the personages of the novel, and more sagacity in the commentary which accompanies the record of their doings than is to be found in any of Thackeray's earlier works. But the figures are such as we should have expected him, when concentrating his faculties, to be able to draw, and the sentiments have nothing surprising in them, coming from the author of *Catherine, The Hoggarty Diamond,* and *The Book of Snobs.* Miss Wirt, the governess of the two Miss Osbornes, was formerly in the service of Major Ponto; Dobbin's fight at Slaughter House School is a repetition of Mr. Frank Berry's; Deuceace, Viscount Cinqbars, and Lord Bareacres flit about in the background, and just as the mother of the heroine of *The Ravenswing* was a ballet-dancer, so Mrs. Sharp is an opera-girl. These are not merely superficial resemblances, but there are others that are still more striking. "The richly-dressed figure of the wicked nobleman" is merely a compound of all those vices which Thackeray had for long pointed out as appertaining especially to the aristocracy. Dennis Haggarty's devotion to a woman unworthy of him gave a hint for Dobbin's; Rawdon Crawley has not the ability of Redmond Barry or of Deuceace, but he has as many of their vices as were compatible with his stupidity; Amelia gave scope for an elaborate study of the virtues of Mary Titmarsh and Caroline Gann; while it is easy to see that Becky is a cleverer Catherine Hayes, moving in a higher rank of society, and amid less melodramatic surroundings. Mr. Sedley in his misfortunes, and Mr. Osborne in his prosperity, are both indebted to the earlier portraiture of the oil-merchant in *A Shabby Genteel Story;* the feelings entertained for Caroline by the Misses Macarthy, and those that characterize the relations of George Osborne's sisters with his *fiancée,* are the same with a difference; while Sir Pitt has as much bluster as Sir George Tufto, and more vulgar arrogance than Lord Crabs.

The origins of George Osborne, Pitt Crawley, and Miss Briggs, it is true, are not so easily traceable; and though Miss Hoggarty's money had been an object of much solicitude to Mr. Brough, she has no other likeness to Miss Crawley. Major O'Dowd and his wife, and the admirably drawn Jos Sedley, are also original. But though these figures give variety to the canvas, and we are forced to confess that we do not recognize them, they all have a family likeness to the people whom we already knew, and take their places naturally by their sides. Nor is the treatment accorded to these characters unfamiliar. The sub-title of the book is *A Novel without a Hero,* a phrase that, effective as it is, fails to express the meaning of the author. There was nothing to necessitate a flourish in the absence of a hero. Shakespeare wrote plays without a hero:—the interest of one is centred in Lady Macbeth, and in *Twelfth Night* it is Olivia and Viola who arrest our attention; while *The Blithedale Romance* subordinates Miles Coverdale and Hollingsworth to the more commanding personality of Zenobia. Rebecca Sharp takes up as much of the space of *Vanity Fair* as is usually allocated to a heroine, and there was nothing remarkable in giving to a woman the chief position in a tale. The characteristic of *Vanity Fair* is not that it has no hero, but that there is nothing heroic in it, and this it is that differentiates the novel from the works of other writers, and supplies the real reason of its effect upon the public. But this, for Thackeray, was not a new departure; on the contrary, it is this that furnishes the distinct peculiarity of all his earlier tales. *Vanity Fair* came with the novelty of a new sensation, only because they were so little read. But the book itself is the best justification of its success.

In some ways it is the most striking thing that Thackeray ever did. He never surpassed it for quiet observation of character, and for the skill with which he has contrived to make the most unreal and fantastic of its personages appear to live. But it is hard, one-sided, and the peculiarity which made it famous is the most marked of its defects. It has been said that it is an actual transcript from life, but the *Midsummer Night's Dream* is more near to reality. While we read the book, so great is its fascination, we can almost believe it to be true, but as soon as we lay it down, the narrative begins to assume its true form for us, and we see it as it is, from the beginning to the end "one entire impossibility." It is not that the characters are impossible, though some of them are impossible enough. It is not that no woman was ever simply a calculating machine, it is not that no man was ever merely sanctimonious, it is not that no baronet was ever a brutal bully and nothing more, or a peer ever wholly profligate, or a merchant ever made up only of vulgarity and rage, because such people have on rare occasions existed, and may by possibility again. It is not in this that the impossibility consists, but such a collection was never got together in one corner of the world. There are two good people in the book,—Dobbin, who is a simpleton, and Amelia, who is a fool. But these are not the only virtuous inhabitants of the Vanity Fair in which we live. If it were otherwise, if there were no other virtuous inhabitants, a man walking through it would not only "not be oppressed by his own or other people's hilarity" [see Thackeray's preface to *Vanity Fair,* dated 1848], but he would decline, and very properly decline, to walk through it at all. If life were as Thackeray depicts it in *Vanity Fair,* not only would the earth be more sparsely populated than it is, but it would have been impossible for true virtue ever to have manifested itself. Virtue being the product of precept and example, Scott could not have lived, nor the qualities of the Vicar of Wakefield had opportunity to develop. Had the world been peopled with Neros, there would have been no room for Seneca, and were every one a Crawley or a Sharp, Esmond's self-sacrifice or Colonel Newcome's heroism would never have been understood.

In *The Memoirs of Barry Lyndon* the company is worse than in *Vanity Fair,* and *The Memoirs of Barry Lyndon* is a triumph of art but it would have been far from a triumph if we had been asked to take the company there assembled as a fair representation of society. We should have rejected it at once as an imposture, whereas the falsehood underlying *Vanity Fair* is only apparent—and it is a tribute to Thackeray's power—after a careful perusal of the work. But when this fact is allowed, when we turn to look at *Vanity Fair* not as a portrait, not even as a caricature of society, but as a brilliant painting of a section of it, there remains much that is admirable. It is almost as difficult to draw a woman without a heart as a woman without a soul, and the latter has not yet been seriously attempted. Mr. Benson's Dodo is an ingenious and clever study of such a character, but it is only necessary to compare his method with Thackeray's to see why he has failed, and how much he has underrated the gravity of the task. Thackeray devotes all his resources to the creation of Becky Sharp. He was well aware how long a course of observation had to be undertaken before even the broad lines of such a figure could be accurately sketched. And it is this that makes him watch Becky with a solicitude that might deceive the reader into imagining that her creator could not resist occasionally admiring her cleverness and resource. He calls her "darling," it is true; but the epithet is always abusive, never laudatory, and though in a sense she is the darling of his eye, it is only that he knew that, if he was for a moment to lose sight of her, her interest for the reader could not have been sustained. She is hardly ever absent from the stage, and her introduction is so bold that Mr. Trollope thought it must have slipped in by mistake. "No schoolgirl," he writes, "who ever lived would have thrown back her gift-book as Rebecca did the 'dixonary' out of the carriage-window as she was taken away from school" [see excerpt dated 1879]. The error is comprehensible, even in so acute a critic, but the facts are quite the other way. No woman so selfish and calculating as Becky afterwards became could have failed to make mistakes of temper and forwardness in her youth. (pp. 75-82)

Her second appearance as Clytemnestra is, however, less to be defended. She had by that time acquired too much experience to risk, even when driven to bay, poisoning Jos Sedley; but the incident is improbable, not impossible, and the same artist who leaves a lingering suspicion that Lord Steyne may, at the last moment, have been baulked of his prey, refrains from deliberately accusing her of murder. The introduction of Sir Pitt Crawley, on the other hand, is caricature, and Mr. Trollope is justified in supposing that it must have been written before any of the other members of the Crawley family had been conceived. And what a family it is; a selfish old woman who has money, a dissolute clergyman, a hypocritical diplomatist, and a dissipated bully. But they all manage to preserve some relation to humanity, and their actions and sentiments are for the most part chronicled with a strange fidelity to life. (pp. 83-4)

For Rawdon Crawley it is difficult to understand Thackeray's admiration. He calls him "honest Rawdon," with real fondness in his voice, and seems to pity him for his connection with his wife. But the man was a drunkard and a cheat long before Becky had anything to do with him; and we are left to supply the occasion of the duel which ended disastrously for Captain Marker. Duelling days were nearly over then, and it is as likely as not that Captain Marker had some serious cause for offence. That Rawdon should experience a passion for a fascinating governess was nothing particularly meritorious. He did not expect to lose money by it, and when he discovered that he had, even he had sense enough to perceive that he owed something to the woman who alone was able to keep him above

water. Besides, the money was never really his, and he was too stupid to appreciate the excellence of his chance. That he should beat an old man who had been intriguing with his wife so openly that every one but he had seen it long before, was no more praiseworthy than the resentment of a thief when his own property is stolen. It is true that there was a pitch of baseness to which he could not bring himself to descend, and he returned the price of Becky's dishonour to Lord Steyne; but he sulkily accepted from the same nobleman the considerable income of a sinecure which he could easily have refused, and for the slight duties of which he was totally unfit. All this was natural enough, but it was no subject for admiration; and though it was human of him to be fond of his son, there was as much merit in the maudlin tears of Redmond Barry, or the pleasure Catherine took in the fine clothes of the adopted son of Mr. Hayes.

It is one thing to treat vice with charity, and quite another to speak of its professors with affection. The same book that spoke of "honest Rawdon" could hardly contain a character that would ensure our respect. Amelia fails even to enlist our sympathy. In prosperity she is childish, in adversity she becomes petted and wilful, and Mr. Senior has pointed out that her reluctance to part with her boy is due wholly to a desire that they should not be separated, not to any fear of the prejudicial results for him that might arise from acquaintance with the Osbornes. She is passionately devoted during his life to George Osborne, who half despises her, and after his death she cherishes a romantic attachment to his memory. To Amelia Sedley, however, a large portion of the book is devoted, and it is not to be supposed that she should not occasionally be betrayed into animation. Thackeray's purpose in delineating this character was twofold; he introduced her first as an example of the negative virtues, and afterwards continued the study of her disposition as a foil to that of Becky. He maintains an unswerving determination to keep her as we first met her, a timid, expansive school-girl, with a fund of maudlin sensibility dangerously apt to develop into selfishness. Again and again, in her passages with Dobbin, Thackeray resists the temptation to endow her with a heart, and where one would have expected from the most long-suffering, righteous anger, or an outburst of wronged and passionate love, we find only sobs and protestations, and a page of sentimental reflection. Once or twice she finds her lot too hard, and becomes peevishly unreasonable, as in the scene with Mrs. Sedley and the baby's medicine, or flings out into a momentary burst of irritation. But these passages are for the most part calculated, and have a touch of artifice. They serve to vary the monotony of her characterless virtue, but they give a laboured effect to the portrait. Once only Nature takes the pen from his hand, and allows us to have a peep at the heart of this too real Cinderella. It is the morning after the Duchess of Richmond's ball, when the English officers have left for Waterloo. (p. 85-8)

But Amelia never again rises to this height of womanly indignation, and she sinks back into the spiritless creature whom the worthy and clumsy Dobbin was content to pursue. His devotion is disinterested and noble, but it is expended on so poor an object that it lessens him in our esteem. She was no "dear lady Disdain," whose waywardness increased her attraction, and it is natural and fitting that her knight-errant should be as uninteresting as herself.

Thackeray might have gauged the effect Amelia would have upon the public from the fate he prescibes for Dobbin. Like her, he is a compound of all the negative virtues, though he

An illustration by Thackeray of George lighting his cigar with one of Amelia's letters.

has a warmer heart, and is, as all soldier-heroes, necessarily courageous. But she prefers the memory of her first husband, who, if he had few virtues, had just enough character to commit occasional and ineffectual sins. His approbation was perhaps also the more precious as she was conscious of having partially lost it. As to Dobbin's affection, it was to be had long before it was asked, and always at her command. He is so formally precise that he cannot even blunder into his own happiness, and it is by a subtle touch of irony that he is made to win Amelia at length, not because her sentiments towards him are altered, but because she has discovered that her first husband was unfaithful. "This is what he has asked for every day and hour for eighteen years. This is what he pined after. Here it is—the summit, the end—the last page of the third volume." Well might Thackeray conclude his book with the melancholy question, "Ah, Vanitas Vanitatum! which of us has his desire? or, having it, is satisfied?" (pp. 92-4)

> *Adolphus Alfred Jack, in his* Thackeray: A Study, *1895. Reprint by Kennikat Press, 1970, 196 p.*

HARRY THURSTON PECK   (essay date 1909)

[*Peck discusses numerous aspects of* Vanity Fair, *including the various stages in the development of the novel, its lack of heroic characters, and the influence of Thackeray's membership in men's clubs on his philosophy. The critic also uses* Vanity Fair *to compare Thackeray's works with those of Charles Dickens.*]

To set oneself the task of writing about *Vanity Fair* recalls Schopenhauer's famous saying: "Everything has been thought,

everything has been done, everything has been written, everything has been said." It would not be possible, for example, to discover anything in Becky Sharp which had escaped the observation of a host of critics long ago. From Dobbin and Amelia and Lord Steyne, with his buckteeth and great jarring laugh, and old Osborne, and the gluttonous Jos, down to Kirsch, the courier, and the frowsy German students dabbling their blond moustaches in their beer-mugs at Pumpernickel, all the people in the book have been held beneath the microscope since the time when they were first created for us, sixty years ago. There is not one of them that lacks the breath of life; but for this very reason they are too familiar to need interpretation. Like old acquaintances, we have come to know them down to the very last detail. We do not dwell upon their virtues or deplore their vices. We simply accept them as they are and take them quite for granted.

Nevertheless, of the book itself there remains, perhaps, something still to say. The most curious thing about it is the circumstance that, when Thackeray set out to write it, he did not in the least suppose that he was going to produce a masterpiece. He had been scribbling nearly all his life, often for the sheer love of self-expression, and later, after he had lost his fortune, because of the money which his pen would bring him. (pp. 149-50)

Nearly everything he wrote was in a vein of irony or humour. He took nothing very seriously, least of all himself and his own writings. What he actually valued most was his bent for art. This is only another example of what we so often see— the ambition of a gifted man to shine in some sphere other than that for which his native genius fits him. Thackeray really thought himself an artist of the brush and pencil, and he was hurt when Dickens would not employ him as an illustrator for the early books of "Boz." He was pleased that *Punch* would accept and publish his faulty drawings. So Dickens, in his turn, valued more the perfunctory praise which he won in amateur theatricals than he did the true fame which came to him spontaneously as an author.

Finally after having written an immense deal that is hardly worth recalling, and some other things which do not deserve remembrance, Thackeray put forth, on New Year's Day in 1847, the first number of *Vanity Fair,* in a yellow wrapper. He was led to begin a story to appear in parts by the great success which Dickens had won in the same way. But *Vanity Fair* at first seemed likely to be an utter disappointment. When four numbers had been issued, the publishers were so assured of its failure that they proposed to discontinue it. It is probable that Thackeray himself had no great hope. Then, with the fifth number, the tide turned, and all literary London began talking of the story which in spirit and in manner was something genuinely new.

Nevertheless, if it succeeded, it did so almost in its author's own despite. Thackeray had really planned it as a burlesque. If any one will compare the first edition of it with the form in which we have it now, it will be plain enough that the novel was meant to be written in a comic vein. Whole passages that were farcical were afterward eliminated. In one of the earlier chapters, for instance, the author stops the progress of the tale to explain, with a sort of side-wink to the reader, that, had he chosen, he might have written the adventures of Jos and Becky and Amelia in one of two other manners. Thus, he says, he might have promoted all his characters to the peerage; or, on the other hand, he might have copied the Bulwer-Lytton of his time and made them lackeys and roughs and burglars, who patter thieves' argot—"beladle your glumbanions and bimbole your chickeys"—whatever that may mean. He even writes in a little scene as a specimen of what he could do in the latter *genre* had he but chosen. As he went on, however, his "novel without a hero" took strong hold of him. He afterwards confessed that he "wasn't going to write it in that way when he began." He started out to perpetrate a caricature. He ended by producing a finished painting.

The reason why *Vanity Fair* succeeded at the time is to be found in its freshness of manner. The historical romance, which had been so splendidly developed by Scott, had grown stale in the hands of G. P. R. James, Harrison Ainsworth, and a hundred smaller men. The sentimental romance pure and simple had reached the verge of mawkishness with Miss Landon and Bulwer-Lytton. The latter had also led the ranks of writers who revelled in low life and the psychology of crime. Then upon the scene came Thackeray, to give the English-speaking people a novel of manners, of social experiences, of life as men and women of the world beheld it. Every one had become tired of "fine writing," and Thackeray gave them good writing instead—writing that was often half colloquial and still more often wholly so. Men read him with that sense of relief which, in an earlier generation, they had felt in passing from the rhodomontade of Mrs. Radcliffe and her school to the sturdy, vigorous manner of Sir Walter Scott. But Thackeray pushed the easy style a stage farther. He left rhetoric alone and spoke in that level, easy tone which marks the talk of the club smokingroom rather than the library of the professional man of letters. It was sophisticated writing, but still it had the effectiveness of simplicity.

The men and the women who appear in *Vanity Fair* are also, if not themselves sophisticated, at least seen through sophisticated eyes. Thackeray called the book "a novel without a hero." It is just as truly a novel without a heroine, at least in the old sense of that word. There is, indeed, nothing heroic in any of the characters. There is not one of them who is free from vice or folly or from some petty failing. Thackeray himself declared that he meant to make "a set of people living without God in the world" [see excerpt dated 1847]. He did not really do this; yet, none the less, he has created a set of people who are always far below the level on which we can unfeignedly admire them. Amelia Sedley, for example, is almost worse that Becky Sharp. She is quite as selfish, and she has no brains. She can be maudlin over the cockney dandy who married her almost against his will, and she can weep over her little son, who is as selfish as his father was; but she can not understand the loyal love of an honest man. She will use it unscrupulously for her own convenience, and she will give it no reward except at the last, when she is forced to take it because she needs its strong protection. Thackeray never intended to let Dobbin marry Amelia; but he was urged to do so by his readers until at last he yielded, saying pettishly:

> Well, he shall marry her; but when he has got
> her, he shall not find her worth the having.

What a wonderful panorama of human weakness is unrolled before our eyes in the chapters of *Vanity Fair!* Try to recall one character whom you can admire without reservation. Dobbin, perhaps, stands forth a finer person than the rest. In character and in mind he makes a strong appeal; yet his awkwardness and loutishness of bearing are continually harped upon. Again and again he appears to be entirely ridiculous. His foolish infatuation for Amelia almost makes one's blood boil, it is so utterly unjustified. For the rest, think of the miserly and clown-ish old baronet, Sir Pitt Crawley; his fox-hunting, hard-drinking parson brother; his graceless, selfish, and bewigged old sister, and his two sons, one a dissolute bully, and the other a feeble prig. Think of Wenham, the smooth pander, of the senile old general just before Waterloo, and of the cowardly and gluttonous Jos Sedley!

It must be confessed that in this maze of living meannesses, Becky Sharp stands out by contrast almost a good woman. At least, she is consistent from beginning to end. If she is selfish, she is thoroughly good-natured. She is fighting for her own hand, but she does so with wit and grace and astounding cleverness. At the last she is willing even to efface herself to help Amelia, although, of course, she does so only after Amelia's environment begins to bore her. When you close the book you rather sympathise with this free-lance of society; for she is a gallant little campaigner, and she has had to deal with persons who are worse than she, or else infinitely stupid. One resents a little the fact that she fooled poor old Miss Briggs, because Miss Briggs was fooled so very easily; but that she fooled George Osborne and the Crawleys, young and old, is only fitting. Her magnificent insolence to Lady Bareacres in the hotel courtyard at Brussels is really delightful. And when she actually fools Lord Steyne our admiration is unqualified. Indeed, as the reader will remember, it extorted admiration from that hardened sinner himself when he found out that Becky had by tears and pitiful pleas got money from him, ostensibly to pay Miss Briggs, and had then kept it for herself.

> "What an accomplished little devil it is!" thought he. "What a splendid actress and manager! She had almost got a second supply out of me the other day, with her coaxing ways. She beats all the women I have ever seen in the course of all my well-spent life. They are babies compared to her. I am a greenhorn myself, and a fool in her hands—an old fool. She is unsurpassable in lies!"
>
> His Lordship's admiration for Becky rose immeasurably at this proof of her cleverness. Getting the money was nothing—but getting double the sum she wanted, and paying nobody—it was a magnificent stroke.

From Thackeray's standpoint, he was, after all, merely stripping off the false pretences, the hypocritical masks, behind which every one must hide himself while in the confines of Vanity Fair. The picture is true to life itself, though it is not true to all of life. In this respect Thackeray is like Maupassant. Every human being whom he draws is drawn with a pitiless realism. Each separate impression is veracious. The only false thing is the tacit assumption that all the world is peopled by such types as we discover in *Vanity Fair,* and that there are none who are wholly pure-minded, generous, and noble.

Thackeray, in his book, has looked at human nature, not face to face and in the open air, but rather through the bay-window of a club. His philosophy is the philosophy of the man who lives in clubs, and who listens to the talk which comes buzzing to the ear in club-room corners. It is talk made up of *risqué* stories, of hinted scandal, of cynical observation and of worldly aphorisms. So far as it goes, it conveys the truth while it looks only at the seamy side of character. It questions motives with a sneer. It dissects and vivisects and analyses with consummate cleverness. It strips away illusions, and pries into hidden meannesses. But it takes no account of another and fairer world in which men are not debauchees, or card-sharps, or tuft-hunters, or snobs and social climbers, but where they believe in right and justice and in God, where they treat women with respect, and where women are deserving of respect. *Vanity Fair* displays for us a microcosm. Its art is microcosmic.

It was not unnatural that Thackeray should view life from this standpoint. He himself was essentially an inhabitant of clubs. The insanity fo his wife had deprived him of a home. He had roamed about in the Bohemia of Paris and the Behemia of London; and the club-window was the nest on which he settled down as other men repose before their firesides. Later, when many homes were open to him, he knew a world which had not forgotten God; and then we find him writing in a nobler vein, quite as rich in observation and richer far in a perception of what is fine and true. *The Newcomes* shows far less the influence of the club *fumoir*. In *Henry Esmond* we breathe the free air of the greater world which reaches beyond Hyde Park and Piccadilly, beyond London, and even beyond England.

The comparison of Thackeray and Dickens is an old, old literary game. As it is often carried on, nothing can be more absurd. . . . Indeed, the two men and their work are not properly comparable at all. They can not, so to speak, be reduced to a common denominator. Yet, in a broad way, some comparison may be instructive. Both of them were intensely English; but Thackeray was an Englishman of London, while Dickens was an Englishman of England; and his imagination, grotesque and strained as it sometimes is, reaches out beyond the sphere of the Particular up into the illimitable spaces of the Universal. His pathos may be at times theatrical. His humour may be often farcical. Yet, in his mightier moments he appeals to something to which every human heart responds. Thackeray, on the other hand, is technically the greater artist. He is the truest realist that England has produced, except his contemporary, Trollope. But in *Vanity Fair* his realism is a realism that is shrunken to a single corner of his country. It is not large enough and broad enough to comprehend the hearts of men and women everywhere. *Vanity Fair* is a wonderful example of urban literature. Yet unless you are a Londoner, unless you are worldly-wise, unless you have yourself a touch of cynicism in your nature, you will not greatly care for Thackeray. To prefer Dickens to him is to show yourself more broadly human. (pp. 150-58)

To the last Thackeray remained the Englishman of London. He never understood the French. His judgments on them are oftentimes absurd. He set Balzac far below such second-rate French authors as Bernard and Reybaud, whom the world has long ago forgotten. He declares that he could not read Dumas "without a risk of lighting upon horrors." He is sometimes still more smug, as when in Athens he sees nothing but its shabbiness, "which beats Ireland." His smugness is equally apparent in the pages of *Vanity Fair,* whenever he breaks off his marvellous portrait-painting to preach sermons, or again as where he spoils a passage of fine pathos with a sort of cynic lccr, so that, as Mr. Whibley says, "he seems to snigger amid sobs." It is equally true that he often sobs amid sniggers. He can not be the artist pure and simple—all of one piece, consistent, whole. He is a product of the clubs, and yet one thinks of him, perhaps, as sneaking out of his club to appease his conscience with an evening in a Wesleyan chapel. This would be commendable did he go boldly to the chapel; but he certainly does not do that. He discovers his place of worship in some remote back alley where his fine friends will not see him; and then, returning and sitting once more in his club-window, he will light a fresh cigar and sneer at the devout.

Vanity Fair is one of the greatest books in English literature, but it belongs to purely English literature, and not to the great masterpieces which the whole world owns and to which it gives an unforced admiration. If you can breathe its atmosphere, you will read it over and over to the end of life. Otherwise its author will be to you simply a remarkable English novelist whom Englishmen will always place in the first rank of their fiction-writers. (pp. 160-61)

Harry Thurston Peck, "Thackeray and 'Vanity Fair',"
in his Studies in Several Literatures, *Dodd, Mead*
and Company, 1909, pp. 149-61.

G. K. CHESTERTON   (essay date 1930)

[*Chesterton was one of England's most prominent and colorful men of letters during the early twentieth century. Although he is best known today as a detective novelist and essayist, he was also an eminent literary critic. Here, Chesterton provides a general introduction to* Vanity Fair, *commenting on its form, narrative style, characters, and philosophy and comparing Thackeray's tone with that of Dickens. Chesterton's remarks were first published in a 1930 edition of* Vanity Fair. *For additional criticism on the novel by Chesterton, see Additional Bibliography.*]

The rising generations, when confronted with *Vanity Fair,* as with the *Iliad,* the *Book of Job* or other works, are fully entitled to be struck, or even repelled, by the appearance of something old-fashioned; so long as they remember that they will not go on rising very long, before they become old-fashioned themselves. But in the matter of the form of fiction, fashions follow each other today with rather bewildering rapidity. *Vanity Fair* might have appeared somewhat formless to some of the old supporters of the classical unities; it might again have appeared somewhat formless to the exact artistry of the school and generation of Stevenson; but even if it were much more formless than it is, it could hardly reach the superb ecstasy of formlessness, which is admired in many of the long realistic novels of today. As a matter of fact, it is far less formless than it looks. The narrative style of the novelist is garrulous and therefore discursive. Indeed the way in which the tale is told is in a rather special sense the manner of gossip. It is gossip not only in being casual and allusive; but also in actually being indirect. Much of the story comes to us by rumour; tales are told by one club man to another club man; we might say by one Thackeray to another Thackeray. He often manages to suggest more than he is prepared to say, by putting up some jolly old snob to say it. The method of gossip has a certain realism; it suggests the same figure seen from many sides; like a single man seen in all the mirrors of the London club. It will at least be well if the younger critic realises that Thackeray's style, which seems to be one of drawling and dawdling irrelevancy, is not an accident but an artistic method, suitable to his special purposes; and that sometimes his very irrelevance is as relevant as a conjurer's patter. In more direct and economical stylists, such as Stevenson, we know what the author thinks of the character; and possibly what thc character thinks of the other character whom he marries or murders with a cutlass. In books like *Vanity Fair,* it is very necessary that we should also know what the World thinks of the character; for indeed in *Vanity Fair* the chief character is the World. It would be an exaggeration to say that the World is the villain of the piece; but it may well be said that in this sense it is a novel without a hero. The theme of it is what the old comic dramatist called *The Way of the World;* and a sort of satiric but not too severe judgment on it, for the way in which it treats all its characters, including the comparatively rare heroes and villains. For this purpose it is necessary that the club of Thackeray, like the island of Prospero, should be "full of voices"; and that we should get a general sense of much that is mere talk, or even mere echoes. For instance; I doubt if it would have been possible to convey the historic but rather unique position of the few very great, because very rich, English Dukes or Marquises (who were something quite different from mere nobility or gentry, in the sense in which any squire or soldier might happen to have a title); it would have been impossible to suggest the strange public position of a man like Lord Steyne, without all those scattered allusions to him and momentary glimpses of him, in the distance, on the high places of English social life. That sort of man is Somebody through all the nobodies who never knew him. We should not feel it enough by being suddenly introduced into his presence; we have to feel that this very absence is as impressive as his presence. All this gossip about the great House of Gaunt is deliberate and even delicate, and without it we should not get the distance or the perspective that points to the ultimate scene; or feel the full force of that splendid blow which the obscure and stupid husband struck, leaving the scar which the Lord Steyne carried till his death.

Allowing for this wandering style (which as I say is often artful as well as artless), I repeat that there is a real form in *Vanity Fair*, the lines of which are kept more carefully than in much modern fiction. The pattern or outline of the story consists of the parallel or divergent careers of two girls, who start together from the same school in the first chapter. Vanity Fair, or the fashion of this world that passes away, is tested by its treatment of these two types and tests the types in its turn. One is the celebrated Becky Sharpe, the adventuress with many of the attractions of adventure; courageous, humorous, quick-witted, but under these natural defences somewhat hard and entirely cynical; one of those children of the poor who are born with a curious moral conviction of a right to possess riches and to rob the rich. The other is a more normal young woman of the sort that most would call ordinary; not demanding much from life, but expecting at the best a happiness of the sort called sentimental; and in all her views of existence at the best traditional, and at the worst conventional. I may remark here that I think it was one of Thackeray's real mistakes that he made her hold on such things rather conventional than traditional. Indeed in this case he was too conventional himself. He was so occupied with his contrasted pattern, with the good golden-haired heroine on one side and the wicked red-haired heroine on the other, that he made the golden-haired heroine a great deal less heroic than she might reasonably have been. It is not stating the alternative of vice and virtue fairly to make the vicious person a wit and imply that the virtuous person must be a fool. If he had been less anxious to make her a pathetic figure, she would have been more of a tragic figure.

Indeed, I think one disadvantage about *Vanity Fair,* especially today, is that one or two of these weak exaggerations occur very early in the book: and some greater passages only towards the end. Amelia is made at the very beginning a mere pink and white doll to be a foil to Becky; and if she represents a rather stale and vapid sort of sentimental comedy, her brother, Jos Sedley, represents a rather stale and vulgar sort of sentimental farce. I never could understand, even in youth, why that fat and featureless buck was allowed to sprawl across so much of the opening of the story; and I think it is rather a false note to make Becky deliberately set her cap at him. I imagine Miss Sharpe as already knowing the world well enough not to

waste herself on so socially fourth-rate a figure. It almost seems as if the Sedley family were more unfairly treated by Thackeray than by fortune; since the brother is vulgarised merely that he may be a slightly more vulgar copy of the dandy Osborne; while the sister suffers throughout from that first water-colour sketch of the two schoolgirls, in which Amelia is given all the water and Rebecca all the colour.

But, allowing for this, which I confess to thinking a mistake, we can still trace the clear outline and the largely convincing logic in the contrast of the two heroines. The contrast is of importance, for it involves the chief debates about Thackeray: the sense in which he was wrongly called cynical; the sense in which he may rightly be called sceptical. First of all, any number of idiots doubtless did call him cynical, because the story of these two girls was not what they called a moral tale; by which they meant the grossly immoral tale which tells, in the teeth of Job and Jesus Christ, the lie that the virtuous are rewarded with wealth. It is not, certainly, in that sense, a story of the Idle and Industrious Apprentice. It is certainly not modelled on the disgusting morals of *Pamela or Virtue Rewarded*. But (and this is the important point) neither is it made to enforce the opposite modern moral of "Amelia or Virtue Punished". There are many twisted and poisoned writers today, who would have played out the whole play with the opposite anti-moral purpose; leaving the wicked Becky in the blaze of the candelabra of Gaunt House and the kind Amelia picking up bits of coal, with a smut on her nose. This tragic trick (which was only too attractive to Thomas Hardy) is quite as much of a refusal to see life steadily and see it whole as the opposite artifice of the most artificial happy ending. It is not probable, but improbable, that Becky, with her desperate double or triple life, would have remained the Queen of Society for ever. It is not probable, but improbable, that anyone with the virtues and old connections of Amelia would have found absolutely none of her old friends ready to patch up her life for her. The point is that it is a sort of patching up in both cases. And with that we come near to the real meaning of Thackeray and the real moral of *Vanity Fair*.

The general inference from *Vanity Fair* is that life largely deceives and disappoints *all* people, bad and good; but that there is a difference, and that is (though the stupid optimist could not see it) rather on the side of the good. If we judge even Becky's life by the ambitious flights and flirtations of the beginning she is a ragged and disreputable failure at the end. If we judge Amelia's life by the romantic hopes of her first engagement, she is a stunned and helpless victim at the end. But if we compare the failure of Becky with the failure of Amelia, we see something that is profoundly true and is the chief truth of *Vanity Fair,* though most of the critics have missed it. The simpler, more innocent and more bewildered person is still capable of settling down into some sort of consolation and contentment; whereas she who has hardened herself against scandal or remorse has also hardened herself against hope.

A good novelist always has a philosophy; but a good novel is never a book of philosophy. The moral philosophy of Thackeray unites him rather with the old moralists than with the modern pessimists. He says, as his favourite authors, Solomon and Horace, would say, that life is in a sense vanity. He would never admit, in the sense of modern authors like Zola and Dreiser, that life is also vileness. His view may be called stoic or sceptic or anything else rather than pessimist. But because he was a novelist and a narrative artist, and not merely a man with a theory, it is true that there did appear in his works something of a personal note, not to be explained by any impersonal system. There is, when all is said and done, something which haunts the air and discolours the very scenery of *Vanity Fair* though it has never been satisfactorily stated or explained. It is a vivacious book, passing chiefly through scenes of gaiety and fashion; it is often witty and satirical; it contains a great deal of humorous interlude and comic characterization; some of it, as I have noted, being even too broadly comic. But it is not a *jolly* book; even when it is for the moment a funny book. There really is something about it faintly acid and antagonistic; and that something did belong partly to Thackeray the man, as well as to Thackeray the philosopher. (pp. 56-61)

If we want to understand the *tone* of Thackeray, the thing which is rather subtle and often misunderstood and makes up so much of the atmosphere of *Vanity Fair,* we must look first at something in his life and character, which can really be seen most sharply in contrast with that of Dickens. Dickens was a man who began in poverty and fought his way up to relative riches. Thackeray was a man who began with the reasonable prospect of riches, lost that prospect and had to work under conditions of relative poverty. With all his social type, tastes, and intentions, those of a gentleman of private means, or at least of considerable leisure, he became a hack and hung about Grub Street for a long time, before he had anything resembling the rapid rise and popularity of Dickens. It happened, as most people know, through his being ruined by professional gamblers, with whom he had played cards in his capacity of casual and lordly man of the world. The theme of such a swindle occurs again and again throughout his work. . . . (p. 62)

Now this did really involve a tone, which the comparison with the other novelist may make more clear. Money was a sore subject with Thackeray. But it was not so much a sore as an itch; in the sense that he could not let it alone and was always irritating it anew. Money was not a sore subject with Dickens. What is much more important, *poverty* was not a sore subject with Dickens. It did not really depress him; because he had faced it from the first and triumphed over it long before the end; and for both reasons he was familiar with it and not ashamed of it. Dickens does not describe the poor as merely unhappy, because he remembers being happy when he was young, and even when he was poor. . . . Now it is sometimes said that Thackeray confined all his attention to the rich and to being a mere novelist of society. This is meant for a sneer; but I rather wish for his sake that it were a truth. The truth is that Thackeray often did describe dismal lodgings and dreary privations and even high life below stairs. But what he could not bring himself to believe was that the lodgings were not always dismal; from the point of view of the lodgers. That is where the real difference from Dickens came in; for, much as Dickens suffered in youth, the lodgings had once, for him, really been *home*. . . . To Thackeray they had never been home, but a miserable seedy asylum for a man who had lost the home of his fathers or his equals. Hence it is not so much that Thackeray never looks at mean houses, as that he never looks at them from within; there is written across all that part of his work the title of one of his tales; *A Shabby Genteel Story.* (pp. 62-3)

In the particular case of *Vanity Fair* this tone can be easily caught in the description of the broken fortunes of the Sedleys; Dickens would never have thought that the Sedleys *were* so completely defeated by the Osbornes, merely because they lost a lot of money. But the paradox is that Dickens thought less

of poverty because he had known it, and thought less of money because he had earned it. To have that particular Thackerayan tone, compounded of pity and acrimony, it is necessary to have a certain bitterness; which is the bitterness of the man who has lost money rather than of the man who has failed to gain it. This tone has been called pessimistic or stoical or helpless or a hundred things; it has been called cynical by the old, and sentimental by the young; and it has elements of all these things. But the essential of it, which determines the idea of *Vanity Fair,* is a certain feeling, which no novelist had yet really introduced into the fiction of England; though Balzac had already introduced it into the fiction of France. It would be putting it too simply to call it The Importance of Money. For it is also a particular sense of something ghastly and unnatural about the Importance of Money. It is the cry of somebody who has found out, by falling over it, or breaking it, or losing it, that it is important; and yet cannot reconcile its importance with his own inner dignity and right reason. Hence the metaphor which makes the whole apparent world a sort of show with booths and puppet-theatres: Vanity Fair. In a sense he could not *believe* in this world; as smaller sceptics cannot believe in the other.

For we may say of Thackeray what he said of Swift; that there did remain at the back of his mind, in spite of all apparent scepticism, a noble but rather dark reality that is of the substance of religion. The Victorian Age had made it vague; the tradition of classical scholarship had made it seem almost heathen; but it was there, by the unanswerable test that applies to all the prophets and the saints. Thackeray thought the world *false;* which alone proves the presence of something contrasted with it which is true. Despite the superficial irritability which I have described, and which accounts for some of his lighter and less convincing sneers, it is true that he was too great a man to be godless and that he did not in his heart doubt that the injustices of the earth stand in contrast with a real justice. That is why I say that he stands rather with the ancient moralists than with the modern pessimists. It is true that this phrase also has been used incessantly and invariably wrongly. He himself confessed to a tendency to moralise; and many modern readers will doubtless repeat with far fiercer contempt this charge of moralising. But as a fact, it is not moralising at all. It is not strictly even philosophising. It is repeating old proverbs like the burden of an old song. It is not surprising that people once called it cynical and now call it sentimental. "Oh, it's the old story" is a sentence that can easily be said, both in a cynical and a sentimental tone. Thackeray was penetrated through and through with the conviction that this story is only the old story; and no criticisms can anticipate him on that. But its importance is that, like many old stories, it is in its way a great tragedy; and tragedy is that point when things are left to God and men can do no more. (pp. 63-5)

> *G. K. Chesterton, "'Vanity Fair'," in his* A Handful of Authors: Essays on Books & Writers, *edited by Dorothy Collins, Sheed and Ward, 1953, pp. 56-65.*

OSBERT SITWELL　(essay date 1935)

[*Sitwell was an English poet, dramatist, novelist, and critic. In the excerpt below, he offers a negative assessment of Thackeray's skills as a novelist in* Vanity Fair, *unfavorably comparing him with Dickens.*]

I have just been re-reading Thackeray's *Vanity Fair,* pondering the problems that its former popularity raises. For undoubtedly at one time it *was* universally read, though I am unaware of the extent to which the book is read to-day, and whether it has maintained its appeal.

I had not opened its pages, though they still remained familiar to me, since I had left school, and was amazed at the inferiority of Thackeray to Dickens as an artist. And, which renders the position so much more peculiar, all the stock criticisms of Dickens, made by those who dislike his novels: that he cannot render the portrait of a lady, that he exaggerates, that he interpolates chunks of his own feelings into the story and addresses the reader in an irritating manner, that he indulges in sticky, slushy sentimentality are all of them, however untrue of him, fully justified if applied instead to Thackeray. In his drawing of character he uses a vulgar exaggeration, as it were; never the superb, the magnificent distortion by means of which Dickens bestows upon some of his characters a quite extraordinary significance, by no other method obtainable. Even the names of Thackeray's supposedly comic characters, when compared with the nomenclature invented by Dickens, prove the truth of this assertion: how weak a name is Lord Tapeworm, how good Sir Leicester Dedlock!

When he tries to depict it, Thackeray can never, it seems, produce any characters that are true to low life, and though this may actually have been of aid to his popularity in such snobbish times as those in which he wrote, it deprives the broad panorama that it was his aim to produce of some of its vigour; that sense of energy and virility which Hogarth and Rowlandson share in English pictorial art with writers such as Smollett and Dickens.... Further, how much more incisive are the low-life pictures of Dickens than the high-life ones of Thackeray, for which he was so celebrated. Even though Sam Weller and his kind indulge in a Cockney lingo which no longer exists and is difficult for us to read, this does not deprive them of their verisimilitude. Their talk is not nearly so extinct as that of Major Dobbin and Mrs Sedley. In addition, it seems to me that Dickens's Vanity-Fair characters, when he attempts that sort of thing, are actually better than Thackeray's; how much more alive, and of their world, are the distorted portraits of Sir Leicester and Lady Dedlock, in *Bleak House,* and of that supreme poor relation, who always has to be so gay and youthful, Miss Volumnia Dedlock, than any which Thackeray achieves in his exaggerated galleries. What a horrible suppressed sycophancy, for example, exhales, all unnoticed by the author, from the portrait of the majestically wicked Lord Steyne; what cringing before money and position, what peeping into forbidden cupboards and furtive gleaning of old letters locked in drawers. And why should Becky Sharp, the only attractive and comprehensible person in the book, be made to drink and intrigue so scandalously, just because she has Bohemian connections and comes of Bohemian stock? How deep an importance does not her creator attach to the fact that her grandmother is discovered in the end as a person who locks up the boxes at the Paris Opera! ... Again, Dickens surely held up a far more accurate and yet amusing mirror to the middle classes than his great contemporary: the image of Amelia's sister-in-law, the unmarried Miss Osborne, fades into nothingness beside that of Mrs Copperfield's sister-in-law, Miss Murdstone. Indeed, it appears as though Thackeray were only successful in his rendering of foreign scenes; for, directly he removes his characters abroad, whether to Waterloo or to a foreign watering-place, they assume a life hitherto lacking altogether in them; whereas Dickens abroad, as in his *Sketches of Italy,* is at his worst.

It is strange, too, to notice the extent to which Thackeray is obsessed by certain antipathies: young cavalry officers, for instance, and above all Members of Parliament. He can hardly allow a chapter in any novel of his to run its course without chucking a literary coconut or a rotten egg at the august body of poor, dead King George IV; poor sport, one would have assumed, and unworthy of an artist of any description; for, whatever the sensual faults of that monarch, he was the only English Prince since Charles I to be endowed with an interest in the arts and literature; the only English Prince since Charles II who liked to be surrounded by people of wit, such as Fox and Sheridan, rather than by the usual court numskulls. (pp. 303-06)

In this respect, then, as in many others, Thackeray appears to have been unjust.

He is at his best, it may be, in his portraits of the British Merchants: that race of stout, top-hatted, iron-whiskered, bullying braggarts who in his time inhabited the squares and streets of Bloomsbury, now the homes of a much more pacific, cultured and mild-accented sect.... But, indeed, his novels suffer greatly from the way in which the scene has changed, even in the last ten years.... Where are the moustachioed young artists, the gorgeous, lisping cavalry officers; where the villainous card-sharpers of good birth; where the club-toadies? ... All are under the heel of industry, commerce and the Slump. The great houses themselves have been pulled down: Lord Steyne's is a museum, Lady Kew's a club. The vast estates in the country have been disposed of, and their heirs pay 16s. 6d. in the pound in income-tax and super-tax. The country houses are only to be visited by those who, having beheld them in the advertisement pages of *Country Life,* have applied for the proper permit.... And yet, though Vanity Fair has changed, though the vulgar have inherited the earth and hypocrisy has been succeeded by an often revolting frankness, nevertheless Thackeray's picture of it is still recognizable. (pp. 306-07)

Osbert Sitwell, "Thackeray and 'Vanity Fair'," in his Penny Foolish: A Book of Tirades & Panegyrics, *1935. Reprint by Books for Libraries Press, Inc., 1967; distributed by Arno Press, Inc., pp. 303-07.*

J.Y.T. GREIG (essay date 1950)

[*Greig focuses on the development of Becky and Amelia as characters, exploring the effect of serial publication and Thackeray's own attitudes toward his heroines on their changing roles within the story. For additional commentary by Greig on* Vanity Fair, *see excerpt dated 1950 in NCLC, Vol. 5.*]

[*Vanity Fair*], in the form in which most of us know it, has a sub-title, *A Novel without a Hero.* This was added only when Bradbury and Evans published the novel as a whole. The serial publication had another sub-title: *Pen and Pencil Sketches of English Society,* a relic, apparently, of earlier and unsuccessful drafts of the story.

Thackeray might have done better to describe the book as *A Novel with two Heroines.* This, at any rate, is how he thought of it as soon as he gave up the idea of a series of articles like the [*Snob Papers*], and began shaping it as a novel. The principle he worked on was a good one—contrast. Becky Sharp and Amelia Sedley were to balance one another; the first being plain in appearance, but clever, witty, resourceful, unscrupulous, dangerous to her associates, and, for a time at least, successful in life, and the second being pretty, simple-minded, gullible, charming in an unobtrusive way, 'pure', of course, tender-hearted, and, for a time at least, unsuccessful in life. They were also to be linked very closely through a plot. Amelia's task was to give Becky her start in life through the homely society of Russell Square, and Becky's was to destroy Amelia's happiness by stealing her first husband, and then, if the novel could be made to end happily, to restore it with casual generosity by presenting her with a second. As the outline of a plot, this was excellent. Fielding could have woven it into a complex and enthralling pattern. Thackeray tried to. He knew, admired, and often imitated his Fielding, from whom, depend upon it, he had learned the importance of the principle of contrast.

Elaborating as he went along, he continued to apply this principle. Round the pair of heroines he grouped other pairs of characters, each member of the pair balancing the other: George Osborne and Rawdon Crawley, old Osborne and old Sedley, old Sir Pitt Crawley and the Marquis of Steyne (both would-be lovers of the naughty heroine), Miss Crawley, with her Regency outlook, and the Evangelical Lady Southdown. But for fear that the pattern should become too formal, he devised cross-groupings: George Osborne and William Dobbin, Rawdon Crawley and his elder brother, Miss Crawley and the covetous Mrs. Bute Crawley, Becky and her sister-in-law (*née* Sheepshanks). Actions, too, he balanced and contrasted: Becky's marriage of convenience with Amelia's marriage for love; Becky's rise to social eminence with Amelia's descent into poverty; Amelia's final complacent and respectable happiness with Becky's restless and disreputable life at foreign spas.

But this, to be sure, is plotting, and although Thackeray could work out a plot in outline, he lacked Fielding's gift of working it out even to its smallest details. Besides, he was tied to serial composition, and being by habit indolent and dilatory, he soon found himself writing hurriedly, trusting very largely to the inspiration of the moment, in order to get his next number delivered to the printers in time. *Vanity Fair* is unified and shapely up to and including the episodes of Brussels and the Battle of Waterloo: for although it contains two heroines, the adventures and sufferings of the one are casually related to the adventures and sufferings of the other. It becomes unified and shapely again after Chapter XLIII (Pumpernickel), and for the same reason. But in between—roughly 300 pages—the plot of the first and last sections of the book is suspended, and the unity of the novel disappears. Two stories now occupy the author's attention alternately. One is centred in Becky, the other in Amelia. They are still built on the principle of contrast, undoubtedly, for Becky's fortunes are steadily rising until the crisis, and Amelia's just as steadily sinking until the return of Dobbin from India; but there is no causal relation between them, and each might very well have been the basis of a separate novel. (pp. 105-06)

I can only conclude that when Thackeray began upon *Vanity Fair* he intended that Amelia should be entangled all along in the meshes of the Becky story, but that after the scenes in Brussels and the death of George Osborne at Waterloo he discovered that he could not keep it up. It was Amelia herself who destroyed the plan. She had gone limp upon his hands. This was something he had not foreseen when he started, because, apparently, it had not occurred to him that the original of Amelia, his own 'poor little wife', had not enough in her to support the role of a major character. And being emotionally tied by his memories of Isabella, he did not know what to do. His first intention, clearly, had been to make Amelia what Mrs. Procter, after reading only seven numbers of the serial,

blandly told Abraham Hayward, the *Edinburgh* reviewer, that she was: 'Charming . . . not an angel, only a good, true, kind-hearted girl.' But something had gone wrong. Although Thackeray may well have believed that it was only kindly memories of the 'poor little woman' that he was using for the novel, yet in fact, not being able to stand back and reshape 'emotion recollected in tranquillity', he was mingling these memories with others not so kindly; and, to make matters worse, he was trying to give solidity to the character by importing certain traits from two other women to whom he was emotionally in bondage, his mother and Jane Brookfield. It was all very well to draw on several originals for Becky. His own relationship to these originals was cool, intellectual, properly 'distanced'; and so he could reshape what he borrowed into a coherent and living personality. But the same method would not work when he was borrowing from Isabella, Jane, and his mother, since from none of these could he withdraw to the proper 'distance' for artistic creation. The result was that Amelia became one thing one moment and another another, according to his mood and the real woman he was thinking of. It was well-intentioned nonsense on the part of Mrs. Procter to compare her with Wordsworth's 'Phantom of Delight'—

> A creature not too bright and good
> For human nature's daily food,
> For transient sorrows, simple wiles,
> Praise, blame, love, kisses, tears and smiles—

and laziness or critical incompetence in Hayward to repeat this comparison in the *Edinburgh* [see excerpt dated 1848 in *NCLC*, Vol. 5].

When Thackeray surrendered to the excitement of creation, his unconscious mind often took control. He once told Whitwell Elwin: 'I have no idea where it all comes from. . . . I am often astonished myself to read it after I have got it on paper.' This is as it should be; at any rate, as it seems to be with most of the greater artists, whether men of letters, painters, sculptors, or musicians: they draw from a well that is deeper than conscious memory. Unfortunately, the waters beneath the level of Thackeray's conscious memory were often troubled, and on the present occasion he was troubling them still more by interference at the fully conscious level.

At all events, Thackeray had to make the best of a failure. Prompted by Hayward's article, perhaps, and certainly by what both Mrs. Carmichael-Smyth and Jane Brookfield had to say about Amelia (which was not much more encouraging than Hayward's attack), he recognized that she would not serve his purpose in the way that he had planned. The trouble was, he could not drop her. At the beginning of the novel he had warned his readers in his customary half-serious, half-joking tone to accept Amelia and not Becky as the heroine. Now, he had to gloss this over. After admitting in Chapter XXX, still in the same tone, that the indomitable Becky had become the heroine, he surrendered more and more to the joys of writing about her, with the result that he tended more and more to follow the lead given him by his mother and Jane Brookfield, and depreciate Amelia. Whibley exaggerates when he says that Amelia 'is drawn with a cold contempt' [see excerpt dated 1903 in *NCLC*, Vol. 5]. It was not so bad as that. But contempt became an ever stronger element in Thackeray's attitude as the book progressed. The 'poor panting little soul', 'poor tender heart' of the days before Waterloo turned into 'a namby-pamby milk-and-water affected creature'; at any rate, he allowed Dobbin's sisters to call her that, and did not take any very active steps to prove that they were wrong. Speaking of her letters to Dobbin himself, he admits that they are 'cold, kind, hopeless and selfish', and when he quotes one for the reader's benefit, he makes it about as simpering and factitious as it is possible for a letter to be.

Even when he repents of his harshness to this silly but forlorn creature, and does his best to prove sympathetic, he betrays himself by fustian ('a sainted agony of tears'), or by that tell-tale repetition of the adjective ('an humble humble heart') which is nearly always the symptom of an unresolved conflict in his mind. Most significant of all, he completely changes his attitude towards another character, whom he had first presented as a little ridiculous—Lady Jane Sheepshanks. The name he had given her had to stand. Possibly he regretted that now. But, Amelia having failed, he now used Lady Jane as a foil to Becky.

It is easy, therefore, to believe an anecdote related in the biography of Dean Liddell. When Mrs. Liddell, an excited reader of *Vanity Fair* as a serial, exclaimed, 'O Mr. Thackeray, you must let Dobbin marry Amelia', he is said to have answered: 'Well, he shall, and when he has got her, he will not find her worth having.'

Life influences fiction, obviously. But fiction also influences life. One wonders whether in the course of writing *Vanity Fair* Thackeray had come round to the same conclusion about himself and Isabella Shawe as he now allowed himself to express about Dobbin and Amelia. (pp. 107-10)

An illustration by Thackeray of Dobbin visiting Amelia and her baby after George's death.

In the middle portion of *Vanity Fair* (Brussels to Pumpernickel) Thackeray devotes rather more than a third of the space to Amelia and rather less than two-thirds to Becky. The style in the different sections often turns out very different. Writing of Becky and the Crawleys, his pen moves easily and swiftly, with vigour and felicity of phrase; writing of Amelia and her family, or of Dobbin and his stupid infatuation, it is apt to flag. But it does not always flag. His account of the decay, moral as well as financial, of the Sedleys is in his best sober-sympathetic manner—gentle, unforced, yet concise and penetrating. He portrays the deterioration in Mrs. Sedley relentlessly—it is one of his proper themes—but without the suggestion of personal animus that we are conscious of in his treatment of Mrs. Prior in *Lovel the Widower;* and though he moralizes on the death of Mr. Sedley, he resists the temptation to become sentimental about it.

As for 'the famous little Becky puppet', Thackeray boasts in 'Before the Curtain' that she 'has been pronounced to be uncommonly flexible in the joints, and lively on the wire' [see essay dated 1848]. No one will deny it. Puppet none the less she must often be called. Readers can watch the author's supple fingers as he pulls the wires; they can listen to his voice, ventriloquizing. He has manufactured her. Sometimes we can see the tool marks. Becky, though a masterpiece of skill, has not been quite 'assembled'.

The usual impression that we get of her is of selfish good-nature. She is too self-possessed to be quick-tempered. She is also greedy for admiration. Why then should she box the ears of her child, young Rawdon, when he listens to her singing? It is not in character. The sudden unfair blow is Thackeray's, not hers. He has jerked the wrong wire. He has remembered with a start (for he secretly admires Becky very deeply) that he ought to make her odious, that the book in which she is disporting herself so gaily ought, like the earlier *Catherine,* to be followed 'to edification'; and being always sentimental when it comes to a 'Mother and Child', he brutally ascribes to her an act which is not credible. And he does something similar twice again. When Lord Steyne discovers that his protégée has not paid Briggs with the money he gave her for that purpose, and accuses her good-humouredly of sharp practice, Thackeray again jerks the wrong wire. Becky, he says, was not disconcerted for long; which is right. Then she made up 'another neat plausible circumstantial story':

> 'It was my husband, by threats and the most savage treatment, forced me to ask for that sum about which I deceived you. . . . He took the money. He told me he had paid Miss Briggs; I did not want, I did not dare to doubt him. Pardon the wrong which a desperate man is forced to commit, and pity a miserable miserable woman.' She bursts into tears as she spoke. Persecuted virtue never looked more bewitchingly wretched.

This is not Becky, the resourceful, brazen Becky we have learnt to know. It is a new, melodramatic Becky from the Lyceum Theatre. Fortunately the shocking impersonation is but temporary.

All the same, we can guess at Thackeray's motive here. He is getting very near the crisis in the Becky plot. When the crisis comes, Becky is to behave with unpardonable callousness towards her blundering but affectionate husband. This behaviour must be led up to; otherwise the reader who has watched and delighted in her triumphs at Gaunt House will receive too great a shock when he finds her mean and treacherous.

And yet, puppet though she is, we believe in her. Here is the most infuriating paradox of all in the novelist Thackeray. He can put men and women on their legs and endow them with vitality; and this, after all, is the one essential gift for the novelist. Other powers, as of humour, satire, a comprehensive knowledge of human nature, skill in the handling of words, may be added to him, but without the essential gift he is nothing. And Thackeray was so perverse that he did not seem to value what the gods in their magnanimity had bestowed on him. The miracle of creation once performed, he would set about spoiling it. He had little reverence for his own creations; he would treat them either as a manufactured article, or, when the fancy took him, as a moral emblem. Unlike other gifted novelists, he is not content that the readers shall 'know' his characters; he must be fussing over them, in the hope that they shall 'know about' them. (pp. 110-12)

Whenever, in *Vanity Fair,* Thackeray will trust Becky, she will be herself, unerringly, miraculously vital. It is this vital Becky who puts the puppy George Osborne in his place when he tries to patronize her in Miss Crawley's drawing-room, who takes her revenge on Lady Bareacres, and who exploits her triumphs in the drawing-rooms at Gaunt House.

> 'How cool that woman is!' said one; 'what airs of independence she assumes, where she ought to sit still and be thankful if anybody speaks to her!' 'What an honest and good-natured soul she is!' said another. 'What an artful little minx!' said a third. They were all right very likely; but Becky went her own way. . . .

They *were* right, all of them. Becky, in contrast to every other woman who appeared in a Thackeray novel (not excluding Beatrix in *Esmond,* who comes nearest to her), shows 'infinite variety'. And yet the essential Becky emerges in a single statement: 'I think I could be a good woman if I had five thousand a year.'

She went on her own way, says Thackeray. Would that he had always allowed her to! He cannot leave well alone. As soon as she has made her statement about five thousand a year, he comments on it:

> And who knows but Rebecca was right in her speculations—and that it was only a question of money and fortune which made the difference between her and an honest woman? If you take temptations into account, who is to say that he is better than his neighbour? A comfortable career of prosperity, if it does not make people honest, at least keeps them so. An alderman coming from a turtle feast. . . .

and so on. Thackeray would not trust his daemon. (pp. 112-13)

> *J.Y.T. Greig, in his* Thackeray: A Reconsideration, *Oxford University Press, London, 1950, 215 p.*

DOROTHY VAN GHENT (essay date 1953)

[*Van Ghent was an American educator and literary critic. In the following study of* Vanity Fair, *she focuses on narrative technique, imagery, and theme, interpreting the novel within the context of English social and literary history. The critic explores both Thack-*eray's *portrayal of his society and the relationship between* Vanity Fair *and its literary predecessors and contemporaries.*]

Almost exactly a century separates *Tom Jones* from *Vanity Fair;* but with *Vanity Fair,* so far as technical developments in the novel are concerned, it is as if there had been none. We are in the story telling convention of the "omniscient author" sanctioned by Fielding's great example, but with a damaging difference that is due, not so much to an inherent inadequacy of that convention itself, as the spiritual incoherency of another age. It is true that the technique of omniscient authorship can allow a relaxed garrulity—what James called "the terrible fluidity of self-revelation"—for if the author can enter the story in his own voice, there is nothing to keep him from talking. After discussing Becky's adolescent designs on Jos Sedley, and her visions of shawls and necklaces and aristocratic company which she imagines will be the rewards of marriage with Jos, Thackeray comments,

> Charming Alnaschar visions! it is the happy privilege of youth to construct you, and many a fanciful young creature besides Rebecca Sharp has indulged in these delightful day-dreams ere now!

The comment is both inane and distracting—distracting our attention from the tense mental operations of Becky and turning it upon the momentarily flaccid mentality of her author. The effect is one of rather surprised irritation, as it is again when, having described Jos's wardrobe, his pains in dressing, his vanity and shyness, Thackeray remarks,

> If Miss Rebecca can get the better of *him,* and at her first entrance into life, she is a young person of no ordinary cleverness.

What we feel is that two orders of reality are clumsily getting in each other's way: the order of imaginative reality, where Becky lives, and the order of historical reality, where William Makepeace Thackeray lives. The fault becomes more striking in the following unforgivable parenthesis. Jos has just presented Amelia with flowers.

> "Thank you, dear Joseph," said Amelia, quite ready to kiss her brother, if he were so minded. (And I think for a kiss from such a dear creature as Amelia, I would purchase all Mr. Lee's conservatories out of hand.)

The picture of Thackeray himself kissing Amelia pulls Amelia quite out of the created world of *Vanity Fair* and drops her into some shapeless limbo of Thackerayan sentiment where she loses all aesthetic orientation.

Nevertheless, the conventions employed in a work of art cannot fairly be judged by themselves; they can be judged only as instrumental to a vision. The time in which Thackeray wrote was, compared with Fielding's time, itself looser in what we might call cultural composition; its values were less integrated in a common philosophical "style" or tenor of mind. In *Tom Jones,* the convention of the author's appearance in his book as "gregarious eye," stage manager, and moralist, is a strategy that is used with a highly formal regularity of rhythm, and it animates every turn of Fielding's language, as the ironic life of the language. Most important, the convention had benefited by an age's practice of and belief in form, form in manners and rhetoric and politics and philosophy—that is, by an age's coherently structured world view. The set of feelings and ideas of which Fielding acts as vehicle, when he makes his personal appearances in his book, is a set of feelings and ideas with the stamp of spiritual consistency upon them. They do not afflict us with a sense of confused perspectives between the author's person and his work, his opinions and his creation, as do Thackeray's. Whereas Thackeray seems merely to be victimized or tricked by his adopted convention into a clumsy mishandling of perspectives, Fielding manipulates the same convention deliberately to produce displacements of perspective as an organic element of composition. This is not to say that Fielding's creative perceptions are, on the whole, more penetrating and profound than Thackeray's; indeed, Thackeray's seem to reach a good deal deeper into the difficulties, compromises, and darkness of the human estate; but Fielding's have the organizing power to make an ancient oral convention of storytelling an appropriate instrument of his vision, whereas the same convention—actually one that is most sympathetic to Thackeray's gift of easy, perspicacious, ranging talk—becomes a personal convenience for relaxation of aesthetic control, *even a means to counterfeit* his creative vision.

Becky ruminates, "I think I could be a good woman if I had five thousand a year," and adds with a sigh,

> "Heigho! I wish I could exchange my position
> in society, and all my relations, for a snug sum
> in the Three per Cent. Consols."

Here she is as true to herself psychologically as is Moll Flanders; but she is more complex than Moll, and we know perfectly that, at this promising stage in her career, the sigh is only a casual fantasy—arising chiefly out of boredom with the tedious business of cultivating the good graces of people much less intelligent than herself—and that if the "snug sum" were offered, she would not really exchange her prospects for it, for her temperament is not at present to be satisfied with snugness. There are to be pearl necklaces, presentation at court, a *succès fou* at Gaunt House. But Thackeray interprets for us.

> It may, perhaps, have struck her that to have
> been honest and humble, to have done her duty,
> and to have marched straightforward on her
> way, would have brought her as near happiness
> as that path by which she was striving to attain
> it.

This is a doctrine with which, in principle, we have no cause either to agree or disagree; a novel is not made of doctrines and princples, but of concretely imagined life, and whatever moral principle may be honestly adduced from that life must be intrinsic to it, concretely qualitative within it. *Vanity Fair* is strong with life, but in those concretions where it is alive there is nothing to suggest that to be "honest and humble" can possibly bring happiness. Becky is the happiest person in the book; she is alive from beginning to end, alive in intelligence and activity and *joie de vivre,* whether she is throwing Dr. Johnson's dictionary out of a coach window, in superb scorn of the humiliations of the poor, or exercising her adulterous charm on General Tufto, whether she is prancing to court to be made an "honest woman" (in stolen lace), or hiding a cognac bottle in a sordid bed. From Becky's delighted exercise in being alive, we can learn nothing about the happiness to be derived from humble dutifulness. On the other hand, from Amelia's humble dutifulness we can learn nothing that convinces us doctrinally that happiness lies in such a way of life. For it is not only that the brisk gait and vivid allure of Becky's egoistic and aggressive way of life make Amelia look tepid, tear sodden, and compromised: this effect would not occur if the book were soundly structured, if its compositional center (what James called the "commanding centre" of the composition) were entirely firm and clear.

The actually functioning compositional center of *Vanity Fair* is that node or intersection of extensive social and spiritual relationships constituted by Becky's activities: her relationships with a multitude of individuals—Jos and Amelia and George, old Sir Pitt and Rawdon and Miss Crawley and the Bute Crawleys and the Pitt Crawleys, Lady Bareacres, Lord Steyne, and so on—and, through these individuals, her relationships with large and significant blocks of a civilization: with the middle-class Sedley block, that block which is in the process of physical destruction because of its lack of shrewdness in an acquisitive culture; with the other middle-class Osborne block, that block which has displaced the Sedley block through its own acquisitive shrewdness and through the necessarily accompanying denial of the compassionate and sympathetic human impulses; with the aristocratic Crawley block, in all its complexity of impotence and mad self-destruction, and (in young Sir Pitt, with the "gooseberry eyes") canny self-renovation through connivance with the economy and morality of the dominant middle class; with the ambiguous Steyne block, that is above the economic strife and therefore free of conventional moral concerns, but in its social freedom, "stained" deeply in nerves and blood. (In the names he gives people, Thackeray plays—like many novelists—on punning suggestion, as he does in the name of the crawling Crawleys, "raw-done" Rawdon, Sharp, Steyne, O'Dowd, etc.) This social relationship, concretized through Becky's relationship with individuals, is the hub of the book's meanings, its "compositional center." But beside this violently whirling and excited center is another, a weak and unavailing epicenter, where Amelia weeps and suffers and wins—wins Dobbin and solvency and neighborhood prestige and a good middle-class house with varnished staircases. Organized around the two centers are two plots, which have as little essentially to do with each other as Thackeray's creative imagination had to do with his sentimental, morally fearful reflections. He cannot bear to allow the wonderfully animated vision of Becky's world to speak for itself, for its meaning is too frightening; he must add to it a complementary world—Amelia's—to act as its judge and corrector. One thinks, in comparison, of Balzac, who was writing almost contemporaneously. Balzac was both as skeptical and as sentimental as Thackeray, but he was a passionate rationalist as well, and a much bolder dramatic formalist. In Balzac, the weak and the suffering and the pure in heart do not win. They have no pretensions to effective moral dynamism in the evil Balzacian world, which uses them as illustrative examples of the impotence of an "honest and humble" way of life.

As the convention of the omniscient author allows Thackeray to keep up a maladroit "sound track" of personal interpolations, so it also collaborates with his confusion as to where the compositional center of his book lies; for though the Becky-world and the Amelia-world, having no common motivation, confront each other with closed entrances, so to speak, yet the author is able, by abuse of his rights of omniscience, to move facilely through these closed doors. We assume that, in Thackeray's plan, the compositional center of the book was to be the moral valence between the two worlds. But there is no valence between them, nothing in either to produce a positive effect of significance on the other. The only effect is negative: the Amelia-plot pales into a morally immature fantasy beside the vivid life of the Becky-plot. For Becky is the great morally meaningful figure, the moral symbol, in the book, and beside her there is room and meaning for Amelia only as victim—certainly not as "success figure." The word "moral" . . . needs perhaps a somewhat closer attention here. Becky is not virtuous, and in speaking of her as a morally significant figure, we cannot possibly confuse her moral meaning with the meaning of "virtue." She is a morally meaningful figure because she symbolizes the morality of her world at its greatest intensity and magnitude. The greediness that has only a reduced, personal meaning in Mrs. Bute Crawley, as she nags and blunders at old Miss Crawley's deathbed, acquires, through Becky's far more intelligent and courageous greed—as she encounters international techniques for the satisfaction of greed with her own subtle and knowing and superior techniques—an extensive social meaning. The corruption that, in old Sir Pitt, has meaning at most for the senility of a caste, becomes, in Becky's prostitution and treason and murderousness, the moral meaning of a culture. For Becky's activities are designed with intelligent discrimination and lively intuition, and they are carried through not only with unflagging will power but with joy as well. By representing her world at its highest energetic potential, by alchemizing all its evil but stupid and confused or formless impulses into brilliantly controlled intention, she endows her world with meaning. The meaning is such as to inspire horror; but the very fact that we conceive this horror intellectually and objectively is an acknowledgment of Becky's morally symbolic stature. (pp. 139-44)

The English novel has tended traditionally to symbolize certain phases of personality through the concrete image (Christian as the "man in rags" with a burden on his back; the Philosopher Square standing among Molly's "other female utensils" when the curtain falls in the bedroom; Clarissa, with streaming eyes and disheveled bosom, prostrating herself before Lovelace; Jaggers washing his hands or Miss Havisham beside the rotten bridecake); while the French novel has tended traditionally to a discursive analysis of feeling and motive, as has the French drama. Image and analysis are merely two different ways of mirroring what goes on in the soul. The methods are never exclusive; and we find such significant exceptions to the general tendency as Flaubert's *Madame Bovary,* where the image dominates, and Conrad's *Lord Jim,* where analysis dominates.

Let us illustrate, from *Vanity Fair,* the method of the image and what it is able to imply as to the "deeper layers of personality." Characteristically, in this book, the social concern is paramount. We have spoken of the various "blocks" of this civilization, some slipping into rubble by the crush of the others or by internal decay, some thrusting themselves up by the neighboring defaulment. But governing all the movements is one ethos of aggressive egoism, articulated through the acquisition of cash and though the prestige fantasies born of cash. Becky herself is a member of no particular class and confined to no particular "block." (Significantly, she is the daughter of a Bohemian artist and a French music-hall singer.) She is more mobile than any of the other characters, because of her freedom from caste, an thus is able to enter into a great variety of class relationships: this is the peculiar novelistic virtue of the picara and picaro, and the enduring source of virility of the picaresque form—the protagonist's freedom of movement. Still acting under the same ethos as that governing the whole civilization, Becky is able to represent its tendencies without class pretenses. Thus Becky, like Moll Flanders, though a strongly individualized character, is the type of a whole civilization, a small-scale model of a world, a microcosm in which the social macrocosm is subtilized and intensified and made significant. With this predominantly social bearing of the novel,

the characters—even Becky—tend to be depicted in a relatively "external" way: that is, there is relatively little discussion of the nuances of their feelings and their motivations; they are not self-analytical characters, as characters in French novels tend to be, nor do they spend much time in deliberate analysis of each other; they appear to us physically, in action; and—with some generalized interpretive help from the author himself (whose interpretations, as we have noted, we cannot always trust)—we enter into their motives and states of feeling by our own intuition. Examples are manifold. There is Becky's meeting of George's eyes in the mirror as she and Amelia, Jos and George, are leaving for Vauxhall: a flashing, accidental illumination of his vanity and vulnerability—and though here might be an excellent opportunity for Becky to engage in psychological speculations and deliberations, little of the kind occurs. There is the physical flash, the illumination by image only, and Becky has George's number. And yet later, when George and Amelia, Becky and Rawdon, meet on their honeymoon trips at Brighton, and Becky with almost unconscious slyness encourages George to make love to her, the early image of the meeting of eyes in a mirror plays on the reader's understanding of motivation, as it does again when we see Becky in overt sexual aggressiveness at the Brussels ball. There has been no need of discursive analysis of motive; the image does the work.

Or—another instance of the work of the image—there is Jos, in his obesity and his neckcloths and his gorgeous waistcoats. We should not expect Jos to analyze himself, nor anyone else to have an interest in analyzing what he feels, for he is below the level of what is rationally interesting; and yet, from the physical picture alone, we are made intuitively aware of deeply disturbed "layers of personality" in Jos. He is one of the most complicated psychological portraits in the book (more complicated, for instance, than that of another voluptuary, the Marquis of Steyne, who has more refined opportunities than Jos and a better head), extremely unpleasant, with suggestions of impalpable submerged perversities, pathetic, with a pathos that is at the same time an outrage to our feeling for what is humanly cognizable in pathos—for Jos is a glandularly suffering animal, with the "human" so hidden in his tortured fat that we feel it to be obscene, while we must still recognize it as human. Jos offering his neck to Isidore's razor . . . is a complex image of a kind of fear so muddied, an image of a psychological state so profoundly irrational, that we react to it with an impulse of horrified laughter—the intuitive horror having no other outlet than in a sense of the absurd. At the same time that these physical images of Jos flash to the mind's eye an impression of something deep and possible in individual personality, they are made by Thackeray to represent to the social reason an extremely significant phase of a culture. We see in Jos's obesity the sickness of a culture, the sickness due to spiritual gourmandism, or, in simpler but still metaphorical words, to "overeating"; in his shyness of women, the repressions and abnormalities of a sick culture; in his stupidity and febrile conceit, the intellectual numbing and tubercular euphoria of a culture. Thus the physical image, here, mirrors most fearful depths of the personal and, at the same time, most threatening perspectives of the social life.

We shall cite a few more illustrations of this method of the "image," as Thackeray uses it, keeping in mind its double significance, its significance for personal psychology (the "deeper layers of personality") and its social significance. But in preparation for these particular citations, we should speak of one singularly important theme of *Vanity Fair,* and that is a theme which we shall call the theme of the "fathers." . . .

[In eighteenth-century novels, the "father" appears] in a light that is rather different from the light that is thrown on the "father" in nineteenth-century novels. There is Squire Allworthy, for instance, who, as "father," though he may have his failures of insight, is still an affirmative moral reference in the *Tom Jones* system of values; he is idealized, but this itself is significant of the fact that the "father" still represents a moral ideal. In the eighteenth century, the idea of the "father" was not, on the whole, ambiguous, or suggestive of doubts or deficiencies or culpability—that is, as this idea is reflected in literature. Mr. Harlowe, in *Clarissa*, is the most exceptional example; but even here, the daughter's return to her "Father's house," on the elevated stage of the divine, is an affirmation and sanction of the usual parental-filial relationship of authority and obedience which is esteemed to be universally valid; Mr. Harlowe made a mistake, but so did Clarissa make a mistake; informed by Clarissa's passion, it is to be hoped that no other daughters or fathers will ever make such mistakes. In *Tristram Shandy,* the "father," Walter Shandy, is a freak, yet he is presented only under the aspect of general human freakishness, pleasant and interesting eccentricity, and we are led in no way to think of him in terms of parental culpability; indeed, as "father," he takes his responsibility most enormously—to be the right kind of father and to bring up the right kind of son are his devouring concern; the inquiries and devotions of fatherhood—as to conditions of conception, size of the son's nose, the son's name, his education—form the whole shape of Walter Shandy's mental activities, his very eccentricity. Similarly in Smollett's *Humphry Clinker,* where the "father" (an uncle, in this case) is a querulous hypochondriac, leading his life in a tone of objection to everything, we are "on his side," we object when he objects, with a grain of salt for his elderly fury; and the book has its moral equipoise in the rightness of this "father's" perceptions.

We see, in the notion of the father in eighteenth-century literature, a reflection of social trust: of trust in and reliance upon and devotion to a general social system of values—that coherent "world view " of the eighteenth century that we have spoken of earlier in this essay. For, under our anciently inherited patriarchal organization of the family, an organization that inevitably extended itself into political organization and philosophic organization, the "father-imago" has acquired vast symbolic extension beyond domestic life and into general social life: our "fathers" are not only our individual fathers but all those who have come before us—society as it has determined our conditions of existence and the problems we have to confront. *Vanity Fair,* with its panorama of western European international society as backdrop to the heroine's activities, is full of "fathers," sick fathers, guilty fathers. (pp. 144-48)

It is significant of the vital intuitiveness of Thackeray's *Vanity Fair* that the theme of the "fathers" should have such importance: in this book, an immensely impressive female, herself quite fatherless, manages to articulate in her career the most meaningful social aspects of the "father" theme. We need, in this view of the book, to free ourselves from the narrower Freudian aspects of the theme and to think in terms of Thackeray's broad social perspective, where the "fathers" are such variants as Mr. Sedley, Mr. Osborne, old Sir Pitt, even the Marquis of Steyne: in other words, such variants as to include all the older, authoritative, and determinative aspects of society.

And now, with this general notion of the significance of the theme of parental authority, we can consider what Thackeray

manages to get out of the "image" of old Mr. Osborne and his daughters coming down the stairs, in their evening ritual, to dinner.

> The obedient bell in the lower regions began ringing the announcement of the meal. The tolling over, the head of the family thrust his hands into the great tail-pockets of his great blue coat and brass buttons, and without waiting for a further announcement, strode downstairs alone, scowling over his shoulder at the four females.
>
> "What's the matter now, my dear?" asked one of the other, as they rose and tripped gingerly behind the sire.
>
> "I suppose the funds are falling," whispered Miss Wirt; and so, trembling and in silence, this hushed female company followed their dark leader.

In the lines just before this there is one other, inconspicuous, touch: in the drawing room where they are waiting for dinner is a chronometer "surmounted by a cheerful brass group of the sacrifice of Iphigenia." The depths which are suggested by this picture, but quite as if accidentally, are the depths of Greek tragedy and, still further back, of Freud's dim, subhuman, imagined "primitive horde": the "dark leader" with his "hushed female company," and the ridiculous but furious Victorian clock "cheerfully" symbolizing the whole. Antiquity's dark brooding over the monstrous nature of man is made to take on, in this incidental image of a family's going to dinner, the unwholesomeness and perversity that have been added to

An illustration by Thackeray of Becky and Rawdon with Lord Steyne. Becky is dressed as Clytemnestra.

man's classical monstrosity by "falling funds," a drop in the stock market.

There is the recurrent incident in the hall outside the bedroom where old Miss Crawley is sick, Becky tending her, everyone—including Becky—waiting for and speculating on the "reversionary spoils."

> Captain Rawdon got an extension of leave on his aunt's illness, and remained dutifully at home. He was always in her ante-chamber. (She lay sick in the state bedroom into which you entered by the little blue saloon.) His father was always meeting him there; or if he came down the corridor ever so quietly, his father's door was sure to open, and the hyaena face of the old gentleman to glare out. What was it set one to watch the other so? A generous rivalry, no doubt, as to which should be most attentive to the dear sufferer in the state bedroom. Rebecca used to come out and comfort both of them—or one or the other of them rather.

Short and unemphasized as the passage is (outside of one ironic line, it consists only of an image, the image of Rawdon opening a door and looking into the corridor, of the old man's "hyaena face" instantly looking out from an opposite door, of Becky coming down the hall to "comfort" them), it contains a pregnant and disturbing meaning, both for personal psychology and for social psychology. Later, when Becky will attempt to inform Sir Pitt about her clandestine marriage, but without telling him the name of her husband, he will be uproariously amused; but as soon as she tells him the name—his son, Rawdon—he goes mad with inexplicable fury. We look back mentally to the incidents in the hall outside Miss Crawley's sickroom, where son and father glare at each other, and where Becky comes to comfort them *separately,* holding each in suspense as to her amorous favor. And we look forward also to that horrible line in Becky's letter to Rawdon (after the disclosure to Sir Pitt), where she says, "I might have been somebody's mamma, instead of—Oh, I tremble, I tremble . . ." What is contained here is probably the most excruciatingly primitive father-son battle in literature, with one of the most sensitively feminine but perversely sentimental reflections upon it. How are we to say, in such a case, whether what we are observing is the "deeper layers of personality" or the social scene?

And then there is the description of the turmoil surrounding old Sir Pitt's death. It consists of a succession of images: Miss Horrocks flitting in ribbons through "the halls of their fathers"; again Miss Horrocks

> of the guilty ribbons, with a wild air, trying at the presses and escritoires with a bunch of keys.—

while upstairs they are "trying to bleed" Sir Pitt (the "trying to" suggests unknown but repulsive derangements); the servant girl screaming and making faces at him in private while he whimpers. The cumulation of these images, scattered and casual as they are, makes the face of a gorgon of destiny. The personal and social idea of the "father" (an idea which is inextricably both personal and social) is made the nasty companion of the ribbon-flitting Miss Horrocks; when Sir Pitt gives the family pearls to Lady Jane ("Pretty pearls—never gave 'em to the ironmonger's daughter"), marital relationships, with all they mean for the security created for us by our elders, are referred back retrospectively to Sir Pitt's chronic tipsiness and

Lady Crawley's worsted knitting—an "enormous interminable piece of knitting"—

> She worked that worsted day and night . . . She had not character enough to take to drinking . . . ;

drawers are tried while the "father" is bled; and finally—so great is the prestige of this "father" and baronet—the servant girl has full amplitude to scream obscenities and make faces at him, for he has turned into "a whimpering old idiot put in and out of bed and cleaned and fed like a baby."

The burden of Thackeray's intuition into personal psychology and its social meaning falls on images like these, and they are innumerable in *Vanity Fair.* But the greatness of *Vanity Fair* is not in scattered images, sensitive as these are. They are all gathered up in Becky Sharp. Becky does for Jos, murderously, at the end; and what she does to Jos is only cancerously implicit in himself and the civilization that has made him; she is the darkness—shining obsidianly in an intelligent personality—in old Mr. Osborn's dense sadism against his daughters and his corruption of the meaning of paternal responsibility toward his son; she manipulates the insane father-son conflict between Sir Pitt and Rawdon; and she is the "guilty ribbons" of Miss Horrocks (instead of a servant's ribbons she has a courtesan's pearls) and at the same time the whimpering idiocy of the dying Sir Pitt (paralleling his repulsive attack of mortality, she inflicts a similarly repulsive mortality on Jos)—for she is at once all the imperatively aggressive, insanely euphoric impulses of a morally sick civilization, and an individual condensation of that civilization. We question whether we would understand her at all, or be charmed by her buoyancy or appalled by her destructiveness, if her impulses were not memorabilia of our own and her civilization our heritage. (pp. 149-52)

> *Dorothy Van Ghent, "On 'Vanity Fair'," in her* The English Novel: Form and Function, *Holt, Rinehart and Winston, 1953, pp. 139-52.*

FRANK O'CONNOR [PSEUDONYM OF MICHAEL O'DONOVAN] (essay date 1956)

[*O'Connor was an Irish short story writer and man of letters whose critical commentary is distinguished by his insistent probing into the connections between society and the artist as well as his attempt to analyze the creative process of the writer he is examining. In the following excerpt, O'Connor examines Thackeray's portrayal of human instinct and selfishness in* Vanity Fair, *commenting also on the novelist's attitudes toward women and motherhood.*]

Vanity Fair is no mere random choice of a title; it expresses the whole meaning of the book. It is a wonderful novel, and a highly original one. Among English novels it comes closest to the Russian ideal of organic form, of a story that tells itself without recourse to invention by virtue of a certain unity of viewpoint and tone. The viewpoint, however, is an exceedingly disillusioned one. The mainspring of all human actions, if we are to believe the author, is self-interest. From the servant girl up to the Princess, the only motive to be distinguished is that of getting something for oneself. Intelligent people recognize this and act accordingly, and those who do not, behave as they do because their self-interest is of a different sort or because they are too stupid to do anything else. "To part with money is a sacrifice beyond almost all men endowed with a sense of order. There is scarcely any man alive who does not think himself meritorious for giving his neighbour five pounds.

Thriftless gives, not from a beneficent pleasure in giving, but from a lazy delight in spending." Virtue, in Thackeray's eyes, is always weak or stupid. "She was a very good woman," he says of Lady Grizzel, "good to the poor, stupid, blameless, unsuspicious." If she had been an out-and-out criminal, he could not have blasted her more effectively.

This means that the contrast Thackeray sets up between instinct and judgment differs widely from that of all other novelists I know of. In Jane Austen the instinct represents the imaginative life, while the judgment represents morality. In Stendhal the instinct is also an aspect of the imagination, though the judgment usually represents irony. In Thackeray it would almost seem as if the instinct always represented some form of weakness, while the judgment represented selfishness. At any rate, it is he who links the two in describing Osborne's behavior after his son, George, is killed at Waterloo.

> Which of us is there can tell how much vanity lurks in our warmest regard for others and how selfish our love is? Old Osborne did not speculate much on the mingled nature of his feelings, and how his instinct and selfishness were combating together.

The thinking here is childish, as Thackeray's thinking so often is; it is the price one has to pay for so disillusioned a viewpoint; and, for what it is worth, the point he is making had been dealt with pretty effectively by Christ in the parable of the Good Samaritan. But it is clear from this, as from many other passages, that he regards instinct as weakness; selfishness, for all that he affects to denounce it, as strength. It was his preoccupation with selfishness which made him so much better a historian of his period than Dickens.

It is also characteristic of the novel that its real heroine, Becky Sharp, is an adventuress and the personification of human selfishness. She is also, by the same token, a prostitute and a murderess, though Thackeray deals gingerly with those aspects of her character while grumbling at the necessity for doing so. At the same time, what makes the book so remarkable is that, whether Thackeray likes it or not, he turns her into the heroine and even, in his shallow way, tries to defend her. "And who knows but Rebecca was right in her speculations, and that it was only a question of money and fortune which made the difference between her and an honest woman?"

Who *does* know? The answer quite obviously is "Thackeray and no one but Thackeray." The mere fact that the question can be asked at all shows that Becky Sharp is something more than a character in a novel. (pp. 115-17)

[Though] she is to a certain extent a character, she is also a point of view, and that point of view is very close to Thackeray's own, at least to that part of it which he would have attributed to his judgment. Becky lives by discovering the weak points of others and flattering their vanity or stimulating their lusts while herself remaining quite cold and, indeed, good-humored about it all. Becky is "bad," but she is also clever.

Now Amelia, her protagonist, is of course "good," but she is also intolerably stupid. And here we come to the most interesting point in Thackeray's moral dilemma. Amelia is also a mother in a sense in which Becky is not a mother at all. There was something about maternity that fascinated Thackeray, apparently because it broke down the crust of egotism and selfishness in a woman and left her vulnerable to circumstances. In an admirable passage of analysis, Lord David Cecil

has pointed out the inconsistency of Becky Sharp's boxing her child's ears when she finds him listening to her singing, and argues quite correctly that "people of her temperament neglect their children, but their very selfishness makes them good-natured to them." At the same time, this is not slipshod writing on Thackeray's part, as Cecil believes. It is quite deliberate and considered, and the same attitude is repeated again and again in the latter part of the book. Becky, as one of her lovers informs us, cannot like children "any more than the Devil can like holy water," and again and again we are told flatly that "gentle thoughts and simple pleasures were odious to Mrs. Becky; they discorded with her; she hated people for liking them; she spurned children and children-lovers." This is not carelessness, but a contradiction in Becky's character required by the fact that she is something other than a character, by the fact that she represents a point of view.

Becky is part of the antithesis that racks Thackeray more than any other novelist I know of. Every great writer, of course, has such antitheses; no matter how much of his material he draws from real life, his characters and situations necessarily form masses and contradict one another in ways that ultimately reveal the whole bent of his nature, but few writers are trying to balance such an unstable antithesis as Thackeray. Becky *cannot* like children because she is antithetical to Amelia, who can like nothing else. This was one of the ways his instinct operated, and if he had to have good women, he preferred them as mothers. When dealing with them he sometimes becomes unendurably mawkish, almost obscene.

> As his eyes opened and his mind expanded, under the influence of the outward nature round about him, she taught the child, to the best of her humble power, to acknowledge the Maker of All; and every night and every morning he and she—(in that awful and touching communion which I think must bring a thrill to the heart of every man who witnesses or who remembers it)—the mother and the little boy—prayed to Our Father together, the mother pleading with all her gentle heart, the child lisping after her as she spoke. And each time they prayed God to bless dear papa, as if he were alive and in the room with them.

It is scarcely possible to believe that this was not written with the shadow of a sneer, and, indeed, . . . I wonder if Thackeray could ever be unselfconsciously emotional. But this was as earnest as he could be, because Amelia—as he, Mrs. Brookfield, and her husband all agreed—was inspired by Mrs. Brookfield. He had not concealed the Brookfield relationship from his mother, and she had done her best to console him. This is how he described her to Mrs. Brookfield at the time.

> I look at her character and go down on my knees as it were with wonder and pity. It is Mater Dolorosa, with a heart bleeding with love. Is not that a pretty phrase? I wrote it yesterday in a book, whilst I was thinking about her—and have no shame somehow now in writing thus sentimentally to all the public; though there are very few people in the world to whom I would have the face to talk in this way tete-a-tete.

There is little question but that there was in Thackeray a childish strain that attracted him to women who resembled his mother, women who were soft, stupid, and indulgent. And there is no question but that the mature man in him was attracted to women of a very different type—cold, sensual, calculating women like Becky Sharp, Blanche Amory, and Beatrix Esmond. That is why *Vanity Fair* has the eternal appeal of its originality. It is the only novel written by a man of mature mind which makes a cold-hearted scheming adventuress into a heroine, and does it so successfully that, in spite of ourselves, we are charmed into accepting her point of view. (pp. 118-20)

> *Frank O'Connor [pseudonym of Michael O'Donovan], "Thackeray: 'Vanity Fair',' in his* The Mirror in the Roadway: A Study of the Modern Novel, *Alfred A. Knopf, 1956, pp. 111-24.*

RUSSELL A. FRASER   (essay date 1957)

[*Fraser investigates Thackeray's apparently inconsistent and confused attitude toward many of the characters in* Vanity Fair.]

The world of fashion is depicted in *Vanity Fair*. The world of power is not. Does Meredith's Diana have to do with the Corn Laws? or Kingsley's poet-tailor with Chartism? There is nothing of either in Thackeray's novel. What there is, crucially, is presentation of character. Here all depends on success or failure. And whether the one or the other is achieved will depend just as surely on the character of Thackeray himself, for he plays a real part in the action. He is able to write with conviction of the wedding of George and Amelia, because a friend—Captain Dobbin—has detailed it all for him. . . . He can share Amelia's grief at weaning her child, because the same Dr. Pestler who attended her then has become his acquaintance, as well. . . . What goes on behind the front of Lord Steyne's dreary palace he knows, beyond peradventure, so excellent a ferret is that little Tom Eaves, who informs him. . . . And if he can tell of the opera in Pumpernickel, that "little comfortable ducal town," it is because once from a place in the stalls he has listened to *Fidelio*—and looked hard at Dob and Jos and Amelia and young George in the loge. . . . (p. 137)

Although his conversance with his characters has been thorough and close, it has made him not unnaturally partisan. He will "step down from the platform" to trounce whatever villainy he descries (lest a suspicious reader fail to see where he stands) or, it may be, to laugh in that same reader's sleeve. . . . But if Thackeray, like his master Fielding, is to take upon himself the role of a Chorus, he must speak with fixed purpose from a single point of view. It will not do to deride a fool's piety one moment and to applaud it sententiously the next. Yet this is precisely what is done. Held up to ridicule are the evening prayers, conducted by the unctuous Pitt Crawley, that complacent possessor "of a mediocrity which ought to have insured any man a success." But though the servants are "subjected" to those devotional exercises, it is somehow "so much the better" that old Sir Pitt, a notorious infidel, is compelled to partake of them, too. . . . This is to have it both ways, to speak, not consciously, impartially, but uneasily, irresolutely, for two points of view, each opposed to the other. It is a flaw in Thackeray's handling of character. And the flaw persists.

Miss Crawley, for example, has been called "the greatest character in the book." Now this is at least a possible judgment. It is possible because Miss Crawley amuses, and is herself amused at the scrambling for her wealth in which all the Crawleys join. "Imperious, crochety, and perverse," she is like that maternal grandmother of Thackeray's, in whom, if there was something to censure, there was also much to praise. Just because she sees, she is of the reader's party. He gives her his

trust; and how she betrays it! For the very qualities which constitute her strength, her "free notions about religion and morals" . . . , must be pilloried at last. Her final illness must be aggravated by hysteria and "the most dreadful terrors of death"; an "utter cowardice" must take one who, when in health, had quite ignored the future world. . . . It must be so, if poetic justice is to be done. Remorselessly Thackeray destroys what he had well created:

> Picture to yourself, O fair young reader, a worldly, selfish, graceless, thankless, religionless old woman, writhing in pain and fear, and without her wig. Picture her to yourself, and ere you be old, learn to love and pray!

This is a kind of violation.

It is revealing, however, for what it tells of Thackeray himself. So often one hears him named cynic. In his contemporaries his uncanonical wit aroused both awe and distrust; in Charlotte Brontë, both sorrow and anger. "Why," she demanded, "should his mocking tongue so perversely deny the better feelings of his better moods?" The truth is that, mingled with that mockery and as often as not warring with it, is a strain of intense moral fervor. There is that Thackeray who anticipates the famous preface to *Pendennis:* "One is bound to speak the truth as far as one knows it . . . and a deal of disagreeable matter must come out in the course of such an undertaking." . . . And then there is the prig who assailed Bulwer-Lytton for allowing the hero of *Ernest Maltravers* to seduce an innocent girl; the staid Briton who, as Paris correspondent for the *National Standard*, found the realism of the French romantics mere extravagance—and decidedly repulsive: "Clotted blood . . . scattered brains . . . gaping wounds"; the moralist who would not write on Eugène Sue: were not his books numbered among the most immoral in the world? One thinks of Oscar Wilde, censured also for his flippancy: a daring writer and a wicked, but manifesting in plays like *Lady Windermere's Fan* and *A Woman of No Importance* the same curious and unlucky confusion that marks and goes far to damage Thackeray's handling of character in *Vanity Fair;* the same predilection to run with the hares—engaging creatures, not vowed to convention—and hunt with the hounds—respectability and all its claims and works.

The "Amelia Doll," as she is named in the preface [see essay by Thackeray dated 1848], makes the point well. She is a woman quite impervious to the world of movers and shakers, unless of course that world impinge on her own little circle. Bonaparte she despises, "for it needs not to be said that this soft and gentle creature took her opinions from those people who surrounded her, such fidelity being much too humble-minded to think for itself." . . . "A dear little creature," her tears are expended on a dead canary, or a mouse, or the end of a sentimental novel. . . . When hard times come to try her, her shifts to surmount them are so futile as to constitute a kind of degradation. So gentle is Amelia, so careless of self, that nature marks her for its victim. . . . (pp. 137-40)

The love she bears George Osborne is debasing, after all: for the reader, who sees Osborne plain, is moved first to indignation and at last to dismay by Amelia's inveterate blindness. And there is, in that life, such an awful dearth of action, so little assertion of character. "You see," says Thackeray fairly, "it is not much of a life to describe. There is not much of what you call incident in it." . . . Amelia, who has "begun not unprosperously . . . [has] come down to this—to a mean prison and a long, ignoble bondage." Inevitably, there is something of frustration in her story. For neither satisfaction nor enjoyment, wrote Arnold of *Empedocles on Etna,* can be derived from situations "in which the suffering finds no vent in action; in which a continuous state of mental distress is prolonged, unrelieved by incident, hope, or resistance; in which there is everything to be endured, nothing to be done. In such situations there is inevitably something morbid, in the description of them something monotonous." To own that it is so, as Thackeray does, is only to acknowledge but scarcely to meet one's objection. For in Amelia the reader is given not a heroine, really, but a creature forlorn and pathetic who, demanding pity, finds contempt.

And yet her very weakness is pleasing to Thackeray. . . . So manifest is his sympathy for her "sweet submission and softness" that one is made aware again of that basic split in attitude which runs like a fault through the novel. Henry James mirrors it nicely when, in *Washington Square,* he makes Mrs. Penniman demand of her brother: "'Do you think it better to be clever than good?' 'Good for what?' asked the Doctor. 'You are good for nothing unless you are clever.'" . . . And the answer is more than an epigram. Amelia, not clever, is good for precious little. The Thackeray who does not gladly suffer fools, who scorns to make a virtue of incompetence, sees that it is so and passes a judgment so hardy that tiresome critics like Charlotte Brontë cannot bring themselves to forgive him. But there is also that Thackeray whose sensibility yields nothing to Amelia's, who finds in her, for all his strictures, "the kind, fresh, smiling, artless, tender little domestic goddess, whom men are inclined to worship." . . . It is as if the ingenuous Mrs. Penniman and the mordant Dr. Sloper were one.

Consider the virtuous, vacuous Lady Jane Crawley, née Sheepshanks, she of the "soft dove-like eyes." What an entrance Thackeray affords her: "Her mamma ordered her dresses, her books, her bonnets, and her ideas." . . . And yet a transformation, rather too magical to inspire much confidence, is worked. Lady Jane is seen as the prayerful mother (of an unprepossessing Pitt Binkie), as the loyal spouse (of a thoroughly tedious Sir Pitt). She consoles the broken Rawdon, fights for hearth and home against the unprincipled Becky. How attractive has she latterly become, this Sheepshanks. But the transformation doesn't signify. Her end is not in her beginning.

A fervent admirer of Thackeray once wrote, apropos of an article by Kate Field, "It is like the good little books which say that Tom told a lie and broke his leg, whereas Dick spoke the truth and was at once made a lord." The trouble with such fables, Anthony Trollope concludes, is that "There is no evidence of the facts but the statement of the writer." The trouble with Thackeray is that often the facts are too nettlesome. But to state them away is no solution.

Becky Sharp fares as badly as her antagonist, Jane, if it be bad for an artist to lay violent hands on his work. She is no angel; her own word is proof. . . . Still, so cool and collected is "the indomitable little aide de camp's wife" that Thackeray, his novel half done, claims her for its heroine. . . . Some thirty chapters later, he will have it so no more. The evil, or rather, the lack of a positive good, that has characterized Becky from the first, fills her creator with a sudden and overwhelming revulsion. In a memorable passage his heroine is metamorphosed. She becomes—as it were, before his eyes—a monster. Once he had been ready even to applaud her, "this siren, singing and smiling, coaxing and cajoling." Now he is undeceived: "Those who like may peep down under waves that are pretty transparent, and see . . . [the tail of the monster]

writhing and twirling, diabolically hideous and slimy, flapping amongst bones, or curling round corpses." . . . It is not a pretty picture, nor is it quite fair to its subject, who must pay now belatedly for Thackeray's confusion.

But if Becky is treated to something more than just deserts, the author makes good by bestowing upon her, in the fashion of one who gives the devil his due, more care and close surveillance than is granted to any other of his people. And so mettlesome a creature does his scrutiny reveal her that one cannot choose but admire. In a world which entertains "an insuperable repugnance to hearing vice called by its proper name" . . . , she refreshes just because she is candid. To the awful Miss Pinkerton she gives a lesson in forthright behavior: "I am here to speak French with the children . . . not to teach them music, and save money for you. Give me money, and I will teach them." She blows up cant and the glib shows of false affection that others put on as a matter of course. Again to the friend of the Great Lexicographer: "You took me because I was useful. There is no question of gratitude between us." . . . Do others esteem the simpering George Osborne? She penetrates at once beneath his bland manners, his brave dress, and knows him for the coxcomb he is. And when her quondam lover Jos Sedley panics in Brussels on the even of Waterloo, does he, that splendid fat man, soften her heart with his plight? Why, scarcely. She drives a hard bargain, quite without compunction, for the horses that bear Jos away.

Her coolness and pluck suit well her russet yeas and honest kersey noes. The French are rumored to be marching on Brussels, but Becky is far from distraught: "If the worst comes to the worst . . . my retreat is secure; and I have a right-hand seat in the barouche." . . . A little reflection, and the idea of flight is put away altogether: "Suppose the French do come . . . what can they do to a poor officer's widow? Bah! the times of sacks and sieges are over. We shall be let to go home quietly, or I may live pleasantly abroad with a snug little income." . . . And when, her realism vindicated, her husband safely returned, that gentleman complains of their unsettled existence, she rounds on him at once with "Ruined! fiddlededee! I will get you a good place before that; or"—and her expectations are nothing if not sanguine—"Pitt and his little boy will die, and we will be Sir Rawdon and my lady. While there is life, there is hope, my dear, and I intend to make a man of you yet.". . . (pp. 140-43)

Becky never quite succeeds in making a man of her husband. Yet what pains she is at to carry forward the task, with what demure assurance does she take it in hand. Let Miss Crawley, her democratic principles utterly cast down by Rawdon's unfortunate marriage, divorce her nephew from favor. There is only a little repining: Becky, for her part, will see that favor not merely resumed but engrossed. So to Rawdon: "You will now, if you please, my dear, sit down at the writing-table and pen me a pretty little letter to Miss Crawley, in which you'll say that you are a good boy, and that sort of thing." . . . And Rawdon does write the letter—with much amazement and more misspelling—and the letter is good. But Miss Crawley is not thereby brought round. Becky's great expectations, now of a marriage, now a legacy, are dashed. A venturesome woman, quite as intrepid as the Iron Duke himself, she ought, one would think, to get on. With a nice lack of modesty she owns to herself how much greater is her charm than that of the Creole Miss Schwartz, she of the hundred thousand pounds; how much finer her figure and more compelling her wit than that of the "little pink-faced chit Amelia." . . . She is right. And still she fails. Perhaps it is because she is too clever.

An outlander herself, she is able to perceive, with a clarity most disconcerting, the absolute humbug—"nonsense upon stilts," to take a phrase from Jeremy Bentham—of the society into which she has pushed. And she is not content merely to see; she must parody with undisguised pleasure that society's most signal faults. So to Vanity Fair she acts a sentimental child: Mrs. Sedley finds her "all heart" . . .; Miss Crawley's wretched Briggs wallows delightedly in her studied italics, her transports, her abnegation of self: "the friendless orphan." . . . And Miss Briggs richly merits the destruction that is her reward, for who will commiserate with a woman who must speak of Rawdon Crawley as "the heroic soldier, whose name is inscribed in the annals of his country's glory?" . . . Sentimentality is bought dear by those who luxuriate in it, and this is just. But it does not make against Becky's cruelty. Yet here is a paradox: whatever Becky's dereliction, whatever the rightness of her fall, the reader sympathizes with her. That this should be so is traceable directly to the ambiguity of Thackeray's point of view.

Of the character of Milton's Satan, Shelley has written, he "engenders in the mind a pernicious casuistry which leads us to weigh his faults with his wrongs, and to excuse the former because the latter exceed all measure." Agree or not with Shelley's dictum in terms of *Paradise Lost,* one must concede its applicability here: for Becky, quite as Satan, is "a superior bad angel" . . . , and her wrongs do exceed all measure. Her earliest memories are of the duns and tradesmen who clamor about her father's door; in consequence she is endowed with "the dismal precocity of poverty." . . . No wonder, then, that she becomes "an eagle in the Chiswick dovecot" . . . , avid of despoiling; a picaro, as lacking in scruple as Barry Lyndon, or Jonathan Wild, and as devoted as they to the main chance.

But her most appropriate role is that of a miniature Napoleon who mocks and discomposes, at least for a time, her own time and the sphere which she has made her own. Just so does the Corsican upstart mock the whole of Europe, which is Vanity Fair writ large. He is a poor Italian, and she the luckless daughter of a French opera girl. He makes for himself a marriage with Austria, and she, very nearly, with an English baronet. He fleers at the sacred totem of patriotism: France, he avers, is his mistress, not his mother, as the venerable cliché would insist. So Becky, a hardheaded opportunist, without a trace in her of rodomontade, flouts the claims of honor, family, and religion: when were they ever allies of the poor? She is Napoleon, seizing his crown from the hands of a scandalized and quiet superfluous Pope. She has the same admirable phlegm, the same incisive intellect which understands that the old gods are false gods, and—unforgiveable fault—acts on that understanding. Like Napoleon she is at once the product and nemesis of Vanity Fair.

It is fitting that as her story begins, as she takes leave of Miss Pinkerton's school, she should cry, *"Vive la France! Vive l'Empereur! Vive Bonaparte!"* . . .; fitting that Rawdon should believe in his wife "as much as the French soldiers in Napoleon." . . . And if Boney is stigmatized as "the wretched upstart and swindler" . . . , so is she styled a "parvenue" . . . , a "little adventurer" . . . , "an imposter." . . . Yet the admiration she commands, as one who has made her own way, is qualified still. For the Thackeray whose ancestry was of the army and the squirearchy, whose education was of Charterhouse and Cambridge, whose unswerving belief in the sanctity of caste had led him to pillory the social climbing of John Henry Skelton, was the Thackeray who sat in judgment on the

Thackeray's illustration of the scene in which Amelia reads the letter George had written Becky before the Battle of Waterloo.

interloper, Becky Sharp. Of course he condemned her. It was, after all, his snobbery and sense of position—and not merely a sense of the absurd—that begot the *Yellowplush Papers.* That this is so is shown by the essentially irrelevant details—phonetic spelling, for example—which he employs to convict his unhappy Charles Jeames Yellowplush. It is rather Thackeray who is convicted. For his criticism of Vanity Fair is based on a misapprehension: it is not really caste he deplores, but those who violate caste. Thus the unthinking and careless anti-Semitism that pervades his work (the rascally narrator of *Catherine* is, inevitably, Ikey Solomons, Junior): the Jew has no status, but is determined to achieve it. He is therefore satirically drawn.

Not, indeed, that those who stay fixed in their orbit win complete approbation: Amelia is one of them, and Amelia is a fool. But Becky is a knave, and perhaps that is worse. Thackeray's essential feeling might fairly be expressed in the proposition: a good man is a dull man, and he who escapes dullness must be of necessity bad. In that earlier work, *The Great Hoggarty Diamond,* there are good people enough, but they are preyed on by the bad. Thus the proposition is illustrated: the bad live by marauding; the good give themselves up to the bad. And this is the whole duty of good people and bad. Becky is bad. Her neglect of her son is a scandal: "poor lonely little benighted boy!" he is one who worships a stone. . . . Her leechlike attachment to the credulous Briggs is only less painful. Her murder of Jos Sedley, in the character of Clytemnestra, completes her degradation. But Thackeray is quits with her at last: as the novel draws to a close, he dooms her to be forever beginning again: "Whenever Becky made a little circle for herself with incredible toils and labour, somebody came and swept it down rudely." . . . Truly, it is hard, as Thackeray says: "very hard; lonely, and disheartening." It is also retribution, the wages of a knave among fools.

But *Vanity Fair* is not the homily that Trollope describes [see excerpt dated 1879]. Tom, who juggles with the truth, is not without charm; Dick, for all his veracity, has only a very modest success. So Amelia is now praised and now derided; Becky, though damned, retains her glamor forever. Yet if Thackeray's handling of his characters seems to a degree arbitrary and uncertain, if there is at times "no evidence of the facts but the statement of the writer," this constitutes a tribute, however perverse, to the world of the nineteenth century. For idealism, no matter how willful, has this fineness about it: only figures of some heroism attempt to gainsay an unpalatable truth, and appeal from it to another, a higher. In a sense those bitter antagonists—Eldon, who fought to preserve a world that had already vanished, and Shelley, who essayed in his verse "beautiful idealisms of moral excellence" that had not yet been seen in the world—are complementary figures, each expressing the great endeavor of his time: to impose on recalcitrant facts an order which, to the mere realist, those facts could not possibly suggest. For the censorship and sour strictures of the one may reflect the same impulse as the lofty visions of the other. The impulse is formal, poetical. From what seems a dance of matter, agitation without purpose or tendency, the nineteenth century deduces—or, more properly, beguiles—a beneficent pattern. Thus Carlyle in *Characteristics:* "Evil, in the widest sense we can give it, is precisely the dark, disordered material out of which man's Freewill has to create an edifice of order and Good." And after Carlyle, Robert Browning. Hence the casuistry, not of Thackeray alone, but of so much nineteenth-century fiction. Is it better to be clever than good? The question is never really answered. (pp. 143-47)

Russell A. Fraser, "Pernicious Casuistry: A Study of Character in 'Vanity Fair'," in Nineteenth-Century Fiction, *Vol. 12, No. 2, September, 1957, pp. 137-47.*

G. ARMOUR CRAIG (lecture date 1958)

[*In the excerpt below, Craig provides a detailed analysis of various aspects of style in* Vanity Fair, *including its language, drama, and shifting narrative perspective.*]

"Among all our novelists his style is the purest, as to my ears it is also the most harmonious. Sometimes it is disfigured by a slight touch of affectation, by little conceits which smell of the oil;—but the language is always lucid." The judgment is Anthony Trollope's and the lucidity he praises is Thackeray's: "The reader, without labour, knows what he means, and knows all that he means." The judgment has been shared by many, perhaps even by Thackeray himself, for he was vigilant in detecting "fine writing" or "claptraps" in the work of others, and for himself he insisted that "this person writing strives to tell the truth. If there is not that, there is nothing." Yet some reconciling is necessary, for the truth is not always lucid and lucidity may not always be quite true.

There is at any rate a passage in chapter 42 of *Vanity Fair* for Trollope's judgment of which the modern reader—at least this reader—would give a good deal. It describes the life of Jane Osborne keeping house for her father: her sister is now the fashionable Mrs. Frederick Bullock, her brother, disowned by their father for his marriage to Amelia Sedley, has been killed at Waterloo, and Jane now lives in idle spinsterhood in the great glum house in Russell Square.

> It was an awful existence. She had to get up of black winter's mornings to make breakfast for her scowling old father, who would have turned the whole house out of doors if his tea had not been ready at half-past eight. She remained silent opposite to him, listening to the urn hissing, and sitting in tremor while the parent read his paper, and consumed his accustomed portion of muffins and tea. At half-past nine he rose and went to the City, and she was almost free till dinner-time, to make visitations in the kitchen and to scold the servants: to drive abroad and descend upon the tradesmen, who were prodigiously respectful: to leave her cards and her papa's at the great glum respectable houses of their City friends; or to sit alone in the large drawing-room, expecting visitors; and working at a huge piece of worsted by the fire, on the sopha, hard by the great Iphigenia clock, which ticked and tolled with mournful loudness in the dreary room. The great glass over the mantle-piece, faced by the other great console glass at the opposite end of the room, increased and multiplied between them the brown holland bag in which the chandelier hung; until you saw these brown holland bags fading away in endless perspectives, and this apartment of Miss Osborne's seemed the centre of a system of drawing-rooms. When she removed the cordovan leather from the grand piano, and ventured to play a few notes on it, it sounded with a mournful sadness, startling the dismal echoes of the house. . . .

Thackeray's prose is seldom better than this. The passage comes from a paragraph that comments on the difference between Jane Osborne's life and that of her sister: "One can fancy the pangs" with which Jane regularly read about Mrs. Frederick Bullock in the "Morning Post," particularly the account of her presentation at the Drawing-room. The reader, characteristically, is invited to supply from his own observation the sort of vulgar envy that feeds upon accounts of "Fashionable Reunions" in the newspaper and to look down on Jane Osborne's suffering as no more than the deprivation of the snobbish pleasures of elegant society. The passage begins, then, easily enough: "It was an awful existence." And "awful" is at first simply a colloquial affectation. It becomes something more, however, as we move into the account of Jane's routine and ascend from the tremors of the breakfast table to the solitude of the drawing room with its covered chandelier "fading away in endless perspectives": the conversational pitch turns momentarily solemn with the vision of "this apartment of Miss Osborne's" as "the centre of a system of drawing-rooms"—including perhaps even that most august of all such apartments where her sister has been received. It would be hard to find this an example of the "little conceits which smell of the oil," for even here Thackeray does not lose his customary confidential hold upon the reader. The vision is kept close to us by his usual resource: the opposing mirrors "increased and multiplied between them the brown holland bag in which the chandelier hung; until *you* saw these brown holland bags fading away in endless perspectives.'' The ''you'' is no doubt as unobtrusive as an idiom. But it is not inconsistent with Thackeray's constant and fluent address to his reader, an address at its best as easy as idiom. In this very short passage Thackeray has moved from an example of the snobbery he loved to detect to a memorable symbol of the society in which snobbery flourishes. It is a society of endless perspectives, a system of drawing rooms whose center is everywhere, whose circumference is nowhere.

But is this what Thackeray meant? And is it the ''all'' that he meant? Certainly the symbol is not characteristic—it is indeed unique in *Vanity Fair*. Usually, or at any rate perhaps too often, Thackeray renders the barren routines of high life in mock genealogies or in the kind of mildly allegorical guest list that follows this passage. We are told that twice a month the solitary dinners of Mr. and Miss Osborne are shared with ''Old Dr. Gulp and his lady from Bloomsbury Square, . . . old Mr. Frowser the attorney, . . . old Colonel Livermore, . . . old Serjeant Toffy, . . . sometimes old Sir Thomas Coffin.'' *Vanity Fair*, we recall, began as ''Pen and Pencil Sketches of English Society,'' as an extension of *The Book Of Snobs*. Yet Thackeray seems to have felt the need of some larger, more inclusive presiding idea. In the early stages of writing the first few numbers he ''ransacked'' his brain for another title, and ''Vanity Fair,'' he said, came to him suddenly in the middle of the night. It seems to have summed up for him a position from which he could confidently go on with his ''Novel without a Hero,'' but a position of course very different from John Bunyan's. The original Vanity Fair as described by Evangelist is the dwelling place of abominations. But it is after all only one more obstacle on the road to the Celestial City, and all such obstacles are rewards in disguise. ''He that shall die there,'' says Evangelist, ''although his death will be unnatural, and his pain perhaps great, he will yet have the better of his fellow.'' While there are some unnatural and painful deaths in Thackeray's Fair, there seems to be no act of resistance or sacrifice by which anyone can get the better of anyone else, and the irony of the title has no doubt been lively in the minds of many readers. But Evangelist lays down a more poignantly ironical prescription: ''he that will go to the [Celestial] City, and yet not go through this Town [where Vanity Fair is kept], *must* needs *go out of the World*.'' If there is no Celestial City beyond Thackeray's Fair, and if there is no hero determined to fight on to a heavenly peak, it is even more certain that none of Thackeray's characters shall go out of this world. On every page of *Vanity Fair* we find description, exposure, comment, from a position much less elevated and secure than that of an evangelist, yet one from which we do see into an ''all'' as large as a whole society.

Certainly the style of all this commenting and exposing is this-worldly to a degree that would have puzzled Bunyan as much as it has troubled some of his descendants. In the preface to *Pendennis* Thackeray speaks of his work as ''a sort of confidential talk between reader and writer,'' and it was the excess of this conception of himself—''the little earmark by which he is most conspicuous''—that Trollope found ''his most besetting sin in style.'' The ''sin'' is ''a certain affected familiarity'': Thackeray ''indulges too frequently in little confidences with individual readers, in which pretended allusions to himself are frequent. 'What would you do? what would you say now, if you were in such a position?' he asks'' [see excerpt dated 1879 in *NCLC*, Vol. 5]. Yet for Trollope, although this familiarity might breed occasional contempt, it did not finally

compromise the great virtue of Thackeray's lucidity. ''As I have said before, the reader always understands his words without an effort, and receives all that the author has to give.'' But to know what, and to know all, a writer means is to be in his confidence indeed, and it would be a serious lapse of style that this confidence should break down in affectation or something worse.

In ''Before the Curtain,'' the preface he wrote in 1848 for the completed novel [see essay above], Thackeray promises his reader ''no other moral than this tag to the present story,'' that after wandering with him through the Fair, ''When you come home, you sit down, in a sober, contemplative, not uncharitable frame of mind, and apply yourself to your books or your business.'' He raises no literary expectations, he promises no carefully graduated feast of human nature, he does not even excuse himself to those who find all Fairs ''immoral'' and hence refuse to enter this one. The stern moralists may be quite right in withholding their custom, but those ''of a lazy, or a benevolent, or a sarcastic mood, may perhaps like to step in for half an hour and look at the performance.'' This casualness, the queer juxtaposition of ''lazy,'' ''benevolent,'' and ''sarcastic,'' may seem like the very height of good breeding. It does sum up the uncomfortable collocation of responses that any reader must make to some stretches of the novel. But it also promises that this writer will keep us free from violent emotions as we read. It is the guarantee of a special detachment.

Such detachment is often suggested by a coy version of one of Fielding's comic devices. When we witness the departure of Becky and Amelia from Chiswick Mall, the last flurry of farewells is recounted thus: ''Then came the struggle and the parting below. Words refuse to tell it. . . .'' The congregation of servants and pupils, the hugging and kissing and crying are such ''as no pen can depict, and as the tender heart would fain pass over.'' . . . Or, on the morning after the fatal excursion to Vauxhall, Joseph Sedley lies ''groaning in agonies which the pen refuses to describe'' . . . while he suffers the aftermath of rack punch. Becky, disappointed in her attempt to capture Joseph, goes away from the Sedley house to her duties as governess: ''Finally came the parting with Amelia, over which I intend to throw a veil.'' . . . Such mild affectations as these amuse a good deal less than their frequency suggests they should, however obliquely they may glance at sentimental explorations of young female affection or the tract-writer's interest in the heavy repentance of the drunkard. But they are the simplest and the least interesting form of a larger kind of detachment.

About other episodes the narrator is more artfully silent. Perhaps the most interesting is the courtship of Rawdon Crawley, which extends over several chapters and is concealed in the narrative of Becky's ministrations to old Miss Crawley. It will be recalled that the success of Becky's attentions to this lady, the old aunt whose wealth is the object of all the Crawleys' envy and scheming, alarm Mrs. Bute Crawley—whose portrait, incidentally, as well as that of her family and of her husband the Rector, make one wonder that Thackeray could have quarreled with Jerrold's anticlericalism. Mrs. Bute's scheming to secure Miss Crawley's money for her own leads her to warn Rawdon that when his stepmother dies, old Sir Pitt will marry Becky. Rawdon's response sets the level of intrigue exactly:

> ''By Jove, it's too bad,'' thought Rawdon, ''too
> bad, by Jove! I do believe the woman wants
> the poor girl to be ruined, in order that she

shouldn't come into the family as Lady Craw-ley.'' . . .

He proceeds to the recommended seduction, but is outguessed by the frank and outraged role that Becky adopts when he ''rallie[s] her in his graceful way about this father's attachment.'' The game goes on, Miss Crawley recovers from her surfeit under Becky's assiduous care, and shortly news comes that the meek Lady Crawley is dead. Rawdon and his aunt discuss the matter while Becky stands by.

> Rebecca said nothing. She seemed by far the gravest and most impressed of the family. She left the room before Rawdon went away that day; but they met by chance below, as he was going away after taking leave, and had a parley together. . . .

And the next thing we know, old Sir Pitt has come to town and is down on his knees to ask for the hand of Becky. The narrator comments:

> In the course of this history we have never seen her lose her presence of mind; but she did now, and wept some of the most genuine tears that ever fell from her eyes. . . .

But what does ''genuine'' mean here? Or ''they met by chance'' in the passage above? Are we to infer that during their ''parley'' Becky uses the threat of a proposal from the father to make sure of the son? Are we to infer that the tears are genuine because she has planned too well—the threat she has used to get one husband has turned out to be prophetic, and she might have had the father? Are they tears of rage? of regret? As we move on to the next chapter we certainly find no circumstantial report of when and how Becky and Rawdon are married; instead there is a good deal of indirect veiling of the scene and refusing of the pen. ''How they were married is not of the slightest consequence to anybody.'' Perhaps, it is conjectured, they went off one afternoon when Becky was presumed to be visiting Amelia. But the matter is left in uncertainty. On the one hand, ''Who needs to be told, that if a woman has a will, she will assuredly find a way?'' And on the other: ''who on earth, after the daily experience we have, can question the probability of a gentleman marrying anybody?'' . . . (pp. 87-96)

The concealment of the circumstances of the marriage may appeal to the lazy, may satisfy the benevolent, and it may give the sarcastic something to work on too. But its most important effect is that the narration here, clustered about with confidential comments and dismissive questions, sets before us a way of knowing the world. It is a way so inferential, so dependent upon unfinished implications, that it comes close to the character of gossip. And a good gossip, while its unfinished sentences and its discreet and indiscreet omissions may keep us from the exhilaration of indignation or rhapsody, can suggest values and insights superior to the vocabulary of the purveyor or the listener. Here, whatever the meaning of that ''by chance'' that modifies the meeting of Becky and Rawdon, or whatever the meaning of that ''genuine'' that modifies her tears, we can only infer that the marriage is the result neither of grand passion nor of mean seduction. The veiling of the secret here means that we can only accept Becky's marriage as a convenience. Even the grossness of Mrs. Bute's plotting is lost in the shadows.

The questions with which Thackeray disposes of this affair—''Who needs to be told . . . who can question the probabil-ity . . .''—are of course the most conspicuous earmark of his detachment in *Vanity Fair*. There is the issue of who made the first move in Becky's first romance, with the young Reverend Mr. Crisp who came infatuated to tea at Chiswick Mall: after a parenthetical cloud of hints and counter-hints the narrator concludes, ''But who can tell you the real truth of the matter?'' . . . Just as when the pen refuses to tell, the implication here is only coy. But a good many hundred pages later, in what is called ''A Vagabond Chapter'' . . . , this kind of coyness can exasperate. It comes in a passage summarizing Becky's career after her fall from polite society in London: ''When she got her money she gambled; when she had gambled it she was put to shifts to live; who knows how or by what means she succeeded? . . . The present historian can give no certain details regarding the event.'' . . . The detachment inculcated here is vast and affluent indeed; it is perhaps matched only by the elaborate veiling of the circumstances of Joseph Sedley's death. But the most puzzling questions in the book are those that comment upon its crucial passage.

Every reader of *Vanity Fair* remembers the ''discovery scene'' of chapter 53—the scene in which Becky suffers exposure and isolation after her husband and Lord Steyne violently clash. And every student of the novel knows that this scene is a battleground upon which the judgments of a number of Thackeray's critics have collided. Rawdon, having been freed from the spunging house, hurries ''across the streets and the great squares of Vanity Fair, and bursts in upon his wife and Lord Steyne in something less than *flagrante delicto* though ready for embarrassment.''

> Steyne was hanging over the sofa on which Becky sate. The wretched woman was in a brilliant full toilette, her arms and all her fingers sparkling with bracelets and rings; and the brilliants on her breast which Steyne had given her. He had her hand in his, and was bowing over it to kiss it, when Becky started up with a faint scream as she caught sight of Rawdon's white face. At the next instant she tried a smile, a horrid smile, as if to welcome her husband; and Steyne rose up, grinding his teeth, pale, and with fury in his looks. . . .

> There was that in Rawdon's face which caused Becky to fling herself before him. ''I am innocent, Rawdon,'' she said; ''before God, I am innocent.'' She clung hold of his coat, of his hands; her own were all covered with serpents, and rings, and baubles.

> ''I am innocent.—Say I am innocent,'' she said to Lord Steyne.

> He thought a trap had been laid for him, and was as furious with the wife as with the husband. ''You innocent! Damn you!'' he screamed out. ''You innocent! Why, every trinket you have on your body is paid for by me. I have given you thousands of pounds which this fellow has spent, and for which he has sold you.'' . . . Lord Steyne seized up his hat, and, with flame in his eyes, and looking his enemy fiercely in the face, marched upon him, never for a moment doubting that the other would give way.

> But Rawdon Crawley springing out, seized him by the neckcloth, until Steyne, almost stran-

gled, writhed, and bent under his arm. "You lie, you dog!" said Rawdon. "You lie, you coward and villain!" And he struck the Peer twice over the face with his open hand, and flung him bleeding to the ground. It was all done before Rebecca could interpose. She stood there trembling before him. She admired her husband, strong, brave, and victorious.

"Come here," he said.—She came up at once.

"Take off those things."—She began, trembling, pulling the jewels from her arms, and the rings from her shaking fingers, and held them all in a heap, quivering, and looking up at him. "Throw them down," he said, and she dropped them. He tore the diamond ornament out of her breast, and flung it at Lord Steyne. It cut him on his bald forehead. Steyne wore the scar to his dying day.

(pp. 96-9)

The theatricality of the passage—Becky's clinging and quivering, the serpents and baubles on her hands, Rawdon's springing out and his terse manifesto, the flame in the eyes of the wicked nobleman and the lifelong scar on his head—all such features suggest that the creator of Punch's Prize novelists is once again engaged in something like parody. On the other hand it has been asserted that far from a joke, the scene "is the chief ganglion of the tale; and the discharge of energy from Rawdon's fist [*sic*] is the reward and consolation of the reader" [see excerpt by Robert Louis Stevenson dated 1882]. The most extensive criticism of the scene finds it unprepared for and conveyed by a dramatic technique foreign to Thackeray's genius [see excerpt by Percy Lubbock dated 1921 in *NCLC*, Vol. 5], but this judgment has in turn been disposed of by another critic who finds Thackeray's usual stamp upon it and some other felicities as well. He suggests that one of these is the way in which "Steyne wore the scar" echoes "Steyne wore the star." By the same sort of reasoning we might infer from "He tore the diamond ornament out of her breast" that Becky's heart is surpassing hard; and certainly Thackeray tells us that the battle takes the heart out of her. But the one touch upon which Thackeray himself is known to have commented is Becky's response to the sudden burst of energy from Rawdon: "She stood there trembling before him. She admired her husband, strong, brave, and victorious." Of this observation Thackeray is reported to have said that it was a touch of genius, and it does consort well with his special genius in the rest of the book.

For although the battle seems to be the expression of outraged honor, it is a collision that misses its main issue and prize. As the resistless masses meet, Becky stands off to one side, and although her admiration is unacceptable or even unknown to Rawdon, and although we are told that her life seems so "miscrable, lonely, and profitless" after Rawdon has silently departed that she even thinks of suicide, there is still a profound irrelevance in this violent scene. Becky's maid comes upon her in her dejection and asks the question that is in every reader's mind: "*Mon Dieu*, madame, what has happened?" And the "person writing" concludes this crucial chapter with an enlargement of the same question:

What *had* happened? Was she guilty or not? She said not; but who could tell what was truth which came from those lips; or if that corrupt

heart was in this case pure? All her lies and her schemes, all her selfishness and her wiles, all her wit and her genius had come to this bankruptcy. . . .

Becky lies down, the maid goes to the drawing room to gather up the pile of trinkets, and the chapter ends. If Thackeray has not risen to a cruel joke on those readers who find consolation and reward in the discharge of energy from Rawdon, he has at least interrupted their satisfaction.

Lord Steyne's meaning of "guilty"—"He thought a trap had been laid for him" by Becky and Rawdon—is of course quite false, though it corroborates the characterization of Steyne as one experienced in double-dealing. "Guilty" from Rawdon's point of view of course means, as he tells Pitt next day, that "it was a regular plan between that scoundrel and her" to get him out of the way. . . . And Thackeray goes to as great lengths to make it impossible for us to know that this interpretation is true as he does to conceal the timing and motives of Becky's marriage. To see the entangling and displacing of any clear answer, we need only ask "guilty of what?" The usual answer is of course "guilty of adultery" (or guilty of getting ready for it), and Thackeray's silence is commonly attributed to his awareness of the "squeamishness" of his public. Indeed he himself lends real authority to this account of the matter. In 1840, writing on Fielding, he complains that the world no longer tolerates real satire. "The same vice exists now, only we don't speak about it; the same things are done, but we don't call them by their names." And in *Vanity Fair* he complains that he must be silent about some events in Becky's later career because he must satisfy "the moral world, that has, perhaps, no particular objection to vice, but an insuperable repugnance to hearing vice called by its proper name." . . . There may well be evidence in Thackeray's personal history to suggest in addition that he was, perhaps even before the separation from his mad wife, evasive and unclear on the subject of sexual behavior. But however complicated the tensions of Thackeray's own emotional experience, and however rigid the scruples of his audience, the answer to the questions with which he comments on this most important episode cannot be a single "name" or possess any "proper name." For he has led us here, however uneasily, with mingled attitudes of parody and outrage, to a startling though incomplete vision of a new social world, a vision exactly proportioned to the irrelevance of the violence we have witnessed.

The words of the passage that command our moral response are precisely those that most nearly approach parody: Becky responds to a nameless "that" in Rawdon's face by exclaiming "I am innocent." If the reader trained in melodrama scoffs at the response and turns Becky into a consummate villain, he will have some trouble getting through the rest of the novel, and it is likely that he will long since have become exasperated with Thackeray's tone, his silences and implications. The same is true, moreover, of the sentimental reader who throws down the volume and declares that Becky has been monstrously wronged and victimized by wicked men in a bad world. But the reader who says, in effect, "it is impossible to tell whether or of what she is guilty" is exactly in the difficult position of one who accepts Thackeray's narrative as it is given. And what such a reader sees from this position must fill him with wonder if not dismay. For he sees that while he wants to answer these questions, he cannot do so, and he can only conclude that he is looking at a situation before which his moral vocabulary is irrelevant. Becky in her isolation has finally gone out of this

An illustration by Thackeray depicting Amelia and her family's encounter with Becky at a London fair.

world, and it will take a new casuistry to bring her back. Thackeray uses some strong moral words in his comment, it is true: "who could tell what was truth which came from those lips; or if that corrupt heart was in this case pure?" But while we know that Becky has lied heartily to Steyne, and to his hearty admiration, we cannot know that she is lying to Rawdon when she insists on her innocence. Whatever corruption we may have seen, the question this time is in earnest. The qualities named in the final statement, and especially by its last word, tell us where we are: "All her lies and her schemes, all her selfishness and her wiles, all her wit and her genius had come to this bankruptcy." For these are the terms not so much of moral as of financial enterprise, and "this bankruptcy" is the real touch of genius in the passage. Thackeray's questions and his comment express neither indignation nor sympathy. Rather, they bring before us the terrible irresolution of a society in which market values and moral values are discontinuous and separate. And Thackeray will not—he can not—support us as we revolt from such a spectacle.

The ghostly paradigm upon which human nature plays in *Vanity Fair* is the credit economy that in Thackeray's own lifetime finally developed from a money economy. Even the constant gambling in Thackeray's Fair, historically appropriate as it may be to his Regency setting (and much of his own early experience as it may reflect), suggests the unpredictability of the system. Distant though the gambler may be from respectability, his luck is only a little less mysterious than the power his winnings confer upon him. However it may be in the most famous conversation recorded in modern literary history, it is all too true in *Vanity Fair* that rich people are different because they have more money. Thackeray exposed himself to some high-minded

criticism from George Henry Lewes [see excerpt by Lewes dated 1848 in *NCLC*, Vol. 5] when he published the number containing Becky's famous reflection, "I think I could be a good woman if I had five thousand a year." For he had commented, "And who knows but Rebecca was right in her speculations—and that it was only a question of money and fortune which made the difference between her and an honest woman? . . . In its interrogative form the comment is much more precise than the declaration Thackeray wrote to Lewes. The latter called it "detestable" to say that "honesty is only the virtue of abundance." Thackeray replied that he meant "only that he in the possession of luxuries . . . should be very chary of despising poor Lazarus on foot, and look very humbly and leniently upon the faults of his less fortunate brethren" [see excerpt dated March 6, 1848]. This is of course no answer; or if it is, it asks for a curious forbearance towards Becky Sharp. But Thackeray qualifies at once: "I am quite aware of the dismal roguery . . . [which] goes all through the Vanity Fair story—and God forbid that the world should be like it altogether: though I fear it is more like it than we like to own." The likeness to "the world" is in the belief that money is magic and in the frightening awareness, no doubt recently reinforced by the financial crisis of 1847, that no theory had yet been devised to control it. (pp. 99-105)

The first mention of the "guilt" or "innocence" of Becky's relations to Lord Steyne comes in a passage about the "awful kitchen inquisition" of the servants of Vanity Fair. We are told that Raggles, the retired butler of Miss Crawley, who owns the house in Curzon Street where Becky and Rawdon live well on nothing a year, is ruined by his extension of credit to them. But he is the victim of something more than the simple excess of liabilities over assets. The "*Vehmgericht* of the servants'-hall" early pronounces Becky guilty:

> And I shame to say, she would not have got credit had they not believed her to be guilty. It was the sight of the Marquis of Steyne's carriage-lamps at her door, contemplated by Raggles, burning in the blackness of midnight, "that kep him up," as he afterwards said; that, even more than Rebecca's arts and coaxings. . . .

The question of guilt here is quite subordinate to the question of credit, and Raggles is ruined not because he is right about Becky's guilt but because he believes in a strict correlation between Becky's moral and financial status. The last of Raggles is seen at the drunken party of the servants on the morning after the battle; our last glimpse of him is not as he suffers in ruin but as he looks at his fellows "with a wild surprise" upon hearing from Becky that Rawdon "has got a good appointment." . . . It is no wonder that Thackeray should have said in a letter to his mother written during the very month when the "discovery scene" appeared,

> I cant find the end of the question between property and labour. We want something almost equal to a Divine Person to settle it. I mean if there is ever to be an elucidation of the mystery it is to be solved by a preacher of such novelty and authority, as will awaken and convince mankind—but O how and when?

Whatever the fate of the larger question, Thackeray does do some novel preaching upon bankruptcy in one section of *Vanity Fair*. John Sedley, we recall, is ruined in the uncertainties following Napoleon's escape from Elba . . . , and Thackeray's extended portrait of the "business and bustle and mystery of a ruined man" . . . seems at first sight disproportionate. Of course the bankruptcy accounts for the career of Amelia, but not for all of it. For old Osborne, who also emerges from the background just here, is described as behaving towards his former friend Sedley "with savageness and scorn." Our attitude is shaped precisely by Osborne's insisting that as a bankrupt Sedley must be wicked—that he is both out of business and out of the circle of decency. "From a mere sense of consistency, a persecutor is bound to show that the fallen man is a villain—otherwise he, the persecutor, is a wretch himself." . . . And Osborne is characterized more grossly still by his opposition to Amelia for his son, by his insistence that George marry the rich mulatto Miss Schwarz, and by his vast self-righteousness. Osborne is perhaps an inept caricature of the City man who has succumbed completely to the superstitions of money, but he is a new kind of portrait. . . . (pp. 105-07)

In *Vanity Fair* . . . Becky's bankruptcy offers no clearer connection between villainy—or goodness—and loss of credit than does the situation of Old John Sedley that Osborne so ruthlessly categorizes. The thoroughness with which Thackeray has covered his tracks suggests that no single transaction, not even payment by adultery, is at issue here. The kind of credit upon which the Crawleys lived so well in London and Paris is beyond the power of any act or value to overtake, for it is the social version of that system in which the perpetual promise to pay is taken for the perpetual fact of payment. "The truth is, when we say of a gentleman that he lives well on nothing a year, we use the word 'nothing' to signify something unknown." . . . It may be that Rawdon and Becky are "wicked," but their wickedness will not account for their credit as they pursue the fashionable life. Just as the war that so mysteriously yet inevitably ruined John Sedley was, as Thackeray tells us, a lucky accident interrupting the endless double- and triple-dealing among nations . . . , so for Becky an accident interrupts the double-dealing and counter double-dealing of the scramble for social power. The perspectives here are indeed almost endless; they are certainly beyond the limits of innocence or guilt. Even Rawdon, who experiences something like coversion or reform as Becky's career reaches its height, is not quite secure. His one assertion to Becky after the battle is an ironic fulfillment of Steyne's accusation: "You might have spared me a hundred pounds, Becky, out of all this—I have always shared with you." . . . And the last words he speaks in the novel are as ambiguous as any question from the narrator:

> "She has kep money concealed from me these ten years," he said. "She swore, last night only, she had none from Steyne. She knew it was all up, directly I found it. If she's not guilty, Pitt, she's as bad as guilty, and I'll never see her again, never." . . .

It is hardly possible to find the outrage of manly honor in these exactly struck last words. The distinction between "guilty" and "as bad as guilty" would be the final viciousness if it were not the final irrelevance.

But, again, is this what Thackeray means, and is it the *all* that he means? We can believe so only by acknowledging that the easy confidence between reader and writer promised at the beginning has been renounced, for we are here outside the domain of laziness, benevolence, or sarcasm. If the renunciation were the deliberate act of a supreme ironist who turns and rends us for our naive acceptance of his confidential detachment, Thackeray would indeed have created a masterpiece.

But in the crucial scene and in portions of the chapters that lead to it Thackeray has exposed us to violent emotions that no politeness can conceal. The enmity between Little Rawdy and Lord Steyne, for example, is an extension of Becky's neglect of her child that erupts into physical violence: Becky boxes his ears for listening to her on the stairs as she entertains Lord Steyne. . . . The child indeed makes his first speaking appearance in the same chapter as that in which Lord Steyne also first appears, grinning "hideously, his little eyes leering towards Rebecca." . . . The juxtaposition is emphasized when little Rawdon is apostrophized:

> O thou poor lonely little benighted boy! Mother is the name for God in the lips and hearts of little children; and here was one who was worshipping a stone. . . .

The appeal is no mere instance of competing with the creator of little Paul Dombey, as everyone who has read Thackeray's letters to his own mother will know. It is an appeal similar to many others in the narrative of Amelia, although there Thackeray is more characteristically reticent. When Amelia and her mother are reunited after her marriage, though Thackeray begins by referring to "How the floodgates were opened," he adds, "Let us respect Amelia and her mamma whispering and whimpering and laughing and crying in the parlour and the twilight." And when Amelia retreats to meditate in "the little room" with its "little white bed" in her old home, Thackeray desists:

> Have we a right to repeat or to overhear her prayers? These, brother, are secrets, and out of the domain of Vanity Fair, in which our story lies. . . .

Even—especially—if we construe this scene and its secrets as an expression of Amelia's first awareness that she is to be a mother herself, it still involves relationships and sentiments outside the "domain" that Thackeray so thoroughly explored. It is a domain bounded by the "politeness" invoked in that early address to the reader in which the narrator promises "to love and shake by the hand" his "good and kindly" characters, "to laugh confidentially in the reader's sleeve" at the "silly" ones, but "to abuse in the strongest terms that politeness admits of" all those who are "wicked and heartless." . . . Such terms of abuse for the wicked and love for the good are for the most part so polite that we accept them with all the detachment guaranteed by the Manager of the Performance. But the limits of this detachment—its very bankruptcy—can be shown only as we glimpse the howling wilderness outside, where the secrets of private feelings are violently confused with public forces of huge and mysterious dimensions, and where there is neither lucidity nor truth.

What Thackeray does then exhibit within the domain of the Fair is the impossibility of self-knowledge and, in the fullest sense, dramatic change. The most intimate experiences of the self, whether in prayer or in love, in disappointment or in outrage, must be kept outside. Becky's "I am innocent" is no more an articulation of the truth than it is the lucid exposure of a lie. But to put us where we cannot know "What *had* happened" and to face us with the bewildering irrelevance of our polite detachment, Thackeray was driven to an extreme that no style of his could control. He could not be clear without being untruthful, and he could not be truthful without being obscure. He tried to recover himself, it is true, in the subsequent chapters by returning to the conception of Becky that most saves his book. The most interesting feature of her characterization is not that she begins from the ambiguous social position of the orphan and governess—"'I don't trust them governesses, Pinner,' says the Sedley housekeeper with enormous assurance, 'they're neither one thing nor t'other. They give themselves the hairs and hupstarts of ladies, and their wages is no better than you nor me.'" ... Thackeray is concerned with much more than the favorite Victorian example of social mobility. The greater truth about Becky is that she is a mimic, that she trades on the difference between fantasy and society, between the role and the fact. But the truth of endless mimicry is much too large for the domain of the lucid. It is larger than any drawing room, park, or square of Vanity Fair, and it could be forced in only by an act of violence that darkened lucidity and concealed truth. The casuistry upon which *Vanity Fair* rests is unique, and the responses of many thousands of readers for a hundred years to this much-read book must constitute one of the most erratic subterranean currents of our moral history. (pp. 108-13)

> G. Armour Craig, "On the Style of 'Vanity Fair'," in Style in Prose Fiction: English Institute Essays 1958, edited by Harold C. Martin, Columbia University Press, 1959, pp. 87-113.

MYRON TAUBE (essay date 1963)

[*Taube investigates how the structure of* Vanity Fair *derives from Thackeray's use of contrasting characters and situations.*]

The structure of *Vanity Fair* is in many ways unlike that of the typical Victorian novel, whatever that might be. A general criticism of the serial novel has been that "The serial form of publication . . . has undoubtedly been responsible for much overplotting. The Victorian novel in general suffers from too heavy a structure." While this is true of many of the novels of Dickens and Collins, it is not true of *Vanity Fair*. On the contrary, *Vanity Fair* supposedly lacks structure, organization, and plot. It is a "novel without a plan" [see excerpt by Charles Whibley dated 1903 in *NCLC*, Vol. 5]; "like Topsy, [it] just grew." And, of course, the serial form was to blame: "the spasmodic writing of monthly installments prevented good integration." However, while it is true that *Vanity Fair* does not have the heavy structure of a Dickens or Collins novel, it is not true that it lacks structure or organization. Just as Thackeray's unity is new—a unity of theme rather than the traditional unity of plot involving the life of a hero—so is his structure a new kind of structure. In the traditional novel, structure depended on the continuity of action, on the flow of narrative and dramatic action from one climax to the next. But with *Vanity Fair,* the principle of structure changes from the continuity of action to the contrast of characters and the actions they perform.

Little attention has been paid to the influence of serial publication on the shape and structure of the Victorian novel. Kathleen Tillotson has pointed out that "within a single number, the balance is held between varieties of narrative method—summary, description, and presentation—and also between the fortunes of different sets of characters." Each monthly number served as a frame for a limited action which, whether unified or not, had to fit into the unity of the entire novel. Each monthly number of *Vanity Fair* shows that contrast which serves as the structural principle of the novel. Perhaps the most obvious contrast is between the Amelia and Becky stories, which serve as the frame for the entire novel. Both stories are almost congruent triangles, except that they are direct opposites. Becky knows no love; Amelia is all love. Becky, who loves only herself, marries a man who worships her; Amelia worships and marries a man who loves only himself. Becky has admirers about her all the time; Amelia has one constant admirer. In the first number, Amelia is quietly in love with George and Becky is laying her snares for Jos. Eighteen numbers later, Amelia has given up her foolish infatuation for George, and Becky has finally snared Jos. Between these terminal numbers, the plots show contrast in each monthly number. Thus, in the first two numbers, the two girls begin their lives together in the world: they begin their love affairs. The third and fourth members present a series of contrasts between the Crawley household and the Osborne household, developing the characters. In Number V . . . , Becky begins her rise in the world and is thrown out of Miss Crawley's favor because of her marriage to Rawdon. Likewise, Mr. Sedley is ruined financially and Amelia is thrown out of favor with Mr. Osborne. The secret marriage of George and Amelia in Number VII is obviously meant to contrast with the secret Becky-Rawdon marriage in the preceding number. Old Osborne's treatment of George in Number VII . . . is meant to contrast with Miss Crawley's treatment of Rawdon. . . : George is left with £2,000, Rawdon with £20.

The eighth and ninth numbers bring the participants together in a series of interwoven contrasts as they prepare for the battle of Waterloo. In Number X, Becky, Bute, and Pitt Crawley compete for Miss Crawley's money. Number XI contrasts the lives of the Rawdon Crawleys and Amelia. The Crawleys live well on nothing a year; Amelia lives poorly on nothing a year. Becky's career is a rising arc; Amelia is sinking deeper and deeper into personal failure and unhappiness. In Number XII. . . , Becky is making ready to be taken back into the bosom of her family and return to the "halls of her ancestors"; at the same time, Georgy's aunt tells her father that she has seen the boy, thus laying the groundwork for Georgy's return to the halls of *his* ancestors. In Number XIII. . . , further contrast is made between Becky's life and Amelia's, between Becky's treatment of her child and Amelia's treatment of hers; between Amelia's response to the news of Dobbin's supposed marriage, and Dobbin's response to the news of Amelia's supposed marriage. In Number XIV. . . , Becky is at the zenith of her career: she is introduced to the king; she receives money from Lord Steyne; and she appears at her first dinner at Gaunt House. On the other hand, Amelia is at her nadir: she surrenders her son to his grandfather. But then Becky's arc turns sharply downward, and Amelia's turns up. In Number XVI . . . , Becky tries to salvage what she can of a life shattered by the too early arrival of her husband, while the pieces of Amelia's life are ready to be put together by the return from India of her future husband. And so their triangles are again contrasted: Becky gives up the love of a now moral husband for a wealthy, powerful admirer, Lord Steyne. Amelia gives up the love of an honest lover, Dobbin, for a rather despicable husband. Ironically, she does it twice—when she marries George, and when she remains faithful to his memory. Herein is what has been called the "likeness within difference of Amelia's stupid fidelity to her husband's memory, and Becky's stupid infidelity to Rawdon." Later, when Dobbin leaves Amelia to rejoin his regiment and return to India, Thackeray comments, "She didn't wish to marry him, but she wished to keep him. She wished to give him nothing, but that he should give her all. It is a bargain not unfrequently levied in love." Kathleen Tillotson notes, "Outside its context, the second of these sentences could be taken as describing Becky."

The last three numbers contrast Amelia's life and the life of the Osbornes; life on the Continent and life in London; Amelia's new life and Becky's failure. The Becky and Amelia stories are finished in such a way that the circle of their lives is closed: Amelia's by her finally finding the man who really loves her, Becky's by her being true to her inner nature and remaining the outsider she always was.

A good deal of negative opinion has been passed over the last three numbers. It has been contended that they are gratuitous. The novel did not "stop when it should. The logical end of the book is Rawdon Crawley's appointment to the Governorship of Coventry Island, and the regathering of the threads—over 150 pages—is a wanton and tedious operation." Strangely, Whibley has hit upon a valid point, but unfortunately, he has the wrong value judgments and the wrong reasons; and to paraphrase T. S. Eliot, the worst critical treason is to make a judgment with the wrong reasons. The fact is that the last three numbers, but particularly the chapters in Pumpernickel, *are* a regathering of the threads. Actually, the concluding chapters of the novel are a coda, a "concluding passage, the function of which is to bring a composition or division to a proper close" (*Webster's New Collegiate Dictionary*). Artistically, structurally, and thematically, the coda is right: it brings the two major melodic lines—the Becky and Amelia stories—together, rounding out both stories, and maintaining the same bittersweet tone that runs through the novel.

My use of a musical term to describe the ending of *Vanity Fair* is not haphazard. I believe that the structure of *Vanity Fair*, which is a much more carefully planned, complex, and sophisticated structure than has hitherto been assumed, can best be understood if analyzed with a musical analogy. Thus, the Amelia and Becky stories are like two contrapuntal melodies, one played in the treble, one in the bass. Filling the space between them, like variations on a musical theme, are the contrasted and related sub-plots. For example, while Becky's pursuit of wealth and Amelia's loss of wealth are a contrast in the major melodic lines, there are variations which elaborate upon and develop the central theme. The Crawleys pursue Miss Crawley's wealth. In Number III. . . , Thackeray gives the background for what he calls "this race for money.". . . First Sir Pitt had tried, but he had failed. . . . Rawdon's favored position made Becky set her snare for him as she had for Jos. But then the Bute Crawleys enter the race. . . . In Number X, the behind the scenes machinations of Pitt Crawley and Lady Southdown and their decision to use Lady Jane as a means of winning over Miss Crawley . . . contrast with the behind the scenes machinations of the Bute Crawleys and their decision to use their son James. . . . A further variation on the pursuit of wealth theme is seen in the rise and fall of the two British business men—old Osborne and old Sedley. Sedley, who had set up Osborne in business, himself fails, and the recipient of his kindness grows to hate him. In Number V are contrasted their attitudes towards each other and the possible marriage of their children. . . . In Number VI, Old Sedley's interview with Dobbin . . . balances Old Osborne's interview with his son. . . . Embittered by life, the two old men live out their lives in disappointment. Their stories are finally brought together in Number XVIII. . . : Old Sedley dies begging his daughter's forgiveness; Osborne dies before a reconciliation is made with Amelia. And one sees the balance and contrast of deaths in the novel: the decline of Miss Crawley in Number X parallels the decline of Old Sedley in Number XI and the decline of Sir Pitt in Number XII. All die helpless and alone, loveless and

beaten by life, and their deaths are variations on the novel's central theme of anti-materialism and salvation through love.

While the Amelia-Becky stories serve as a frame for the novel, they also supply the material which will be expanded upon in variations. Both girls are seen as children and parents, and these roles become a major theme in *Vanity Fair*. Much of *Vanity Fair* is structured about the moral and emotional parent-child relationships of three generations: Old Osborne, George and his sisters, Georgy; the Sedleys, Amelia and Jos, Georgy; Sir Pitt, Pitt and Rawdon, and their children. . . . In each generation there is conflict between parent and child: Sir Pitt loses Becky to Rawdon in a father-son-female triangle that foreshadows the tragedy of *The Brothers Karamazov;* Osborne, whose actions are symbolized by the "chronometer, which was surmounted by a cheerful brass group of the sacrifice of Iphigenia". . . , sacrifices his children on the altar of his selfishness; Amelia fights with her mother and surrenders herself to the power of her son. Moreover, these patterns of conflict are not haphazard: besides being part of the over-all structure of the novel, they are given additional structural meaning by their development within the monthly number.

Thackeray uses the principle of contrast so that his monthly issues will reveal his characters. Using similar relationships and corresponding characters, he develops his variations on the theme. For example, while Becky and Amelia are opposites in many ways, George and Rawdon are cut from the same fabric but with different patterns. George, a would-be gentleman, is a *nouveau riche arrivist;* Rawdon, the military dandy, is the rake about town. Although both are selfish young bucks with similar tastes, attitudes and activities, they are also quite different. George is too selfish to love and dies too early to change. Rawdon, "a perfectly marvelous piece of verisimilitude," shows the effects of time and circumstance. A Samson shorn of his locks (Thackeray uses the image twice in Chapter xvi), the domesticated Rawdon loses his dash and color and becomes "Mrs. Crawley's husband.". . . But Rawdon Crawley, unlike Becky and George, has one commendable quality: he worships his wife and loves his son. . . . In Number XI, Becky leaves Rawdon behind when she goes to England. . . . [Her] complete indifference is in direct contrast with Rawdon's feelings for the boy. While Becky lets the boy cry at night, Rawdon sneaks off to see him. . . . In Chapter xxxviii (as well as xxxv) are the details of Amelia's life with George and her parents, and Amelia's role as a parent is contrasted with her mother's. Thus, Thackeray has created contrasts not only between the Becky and Amelia stories, but within each story: Becky and Rawdon, Amelia and her mother. And Thackeray's judgment of both Becky and Amelia is implicit; the contrast between the two different kinds of mother love is "subtle, because Thackeray is critical both of heartless neglect and passionate possessiveness."

Because Thackeray's interest is in the revelation of character, and because he uses contrast as a formal principle, he very often places his characters in the same or similar situations so that their actions will reveal the differences between their personalities. After all, "what is character but the determination of incident? What is incident but the illustration of character?" To continue the musical analogy, his variations extend to having the same tune played by different instruments in order to reveal the quality of each instrument. For example, both George and Rawdon are disinherited because of imprudent marriages. However, note the differences in the reactions of the men and their wives: When George finds out that he has been cut by his father and left with only £2,000, he reacts violently:

"A pretty way you have managed the affair," said George, looking savagely at William Dobbin. "Look here, Dobbin," and he flung over to the latter his parent's letter. "A beggar, by Jove, and all in consequence of my d--d sentimentality. Why couldn't we have waited? A ball might have done for me in the course of the war, and may still, and how will Emmy be bettered by being left a beggar's widow? It was all your doing. You were never easy until you got me married and ruined. What the deuce am I to do with two thousand pounds? Such a sum won't last two years. I've lost a hundred and forty to Crawley at cards and billiards since I've been down here. A pretty manager of a man's matters *you* are, forsooth.". . .

When George breaks the news to Amelia, she asks innocently, "Isn't two thousand pounds an immense deal of money, George?" George, of course, "laughed at her *naiveté.*" On the other hand, Rawdon and Becky begin married life with much less money, and with a completely different attitude. While Mrs. Bute Crawley has Miss Crawley in tow and Rawdon is out of Miss Crawley's favor, Rawdon and Becky wait, and Rawdon realizes that Mrs. Bute connived to bring him and Becky together at every opportunity. . . . Later, when Rawdon, who had expected at least two hundred pounds from his aunt, went for his check, he "came back furious. 'By Jove, Becky,' says he, 'she's only given me twenty pound!' Though it told against themselves, the joke was too good, and Becky burst out laughing at Rawdon's discomfiture.". . . (pp. 119-27)

But Thackeray's use of contrast and variation is not restricted to different people performing contrasting or similar actions: so skillfully has Thackeray organzied his novel around the principle of contrast that his characters perform actions which contrast not only with the actions of others, but also with similar actions they themselves had performed in time past! Thus, for example, little Georgy is a beginning again of George, and those about him respond to him not only as to a child, but also as though he were George. . . . [When] Georgy is being made a gentleman, he is made into a carbon copy of his father: "Georgy, after breakfast, would sit in the armchair in the dining-room, and read the *Morning Post*, just like a grown-up man. 'How he *du* dam and swear,' the servants would cry, delighted at his precocity. Those who remembered the Captain his father, declared Master George was his Pa every inch of him. He made the house lively by his activity, his imperiousness, his scolding, and his good-nature." Moreover, Georgy's return affects his grandfather's sense of guilt over his own son, and Georgy has the same mastery—and then some—over his grandfather that his father had:

> In Russell Square everybody was afraid of Mr. Osborne, and Mr. Osborne was afraid of Georgy. The boy's dashing manners, and offhand rattle about books and learning, his likeness to his father (dead unreconciled in Brussels yonder), awed the old gentleman, and gave the young man the mastery. The old man would start at some hereditary feature or tone unconsciously used by the little lad, and fancy that George's father was again before him. He tried by indulgence to the grandson to make up for harshness to the elder George. . . .

"Come children, let us shut up the box": Thackeray's illustration following the last lines of Vanity Fair.

Not only do we see Old Osborne reacting to the past brought back to the present, but Georgy himself re-enacts the same patterns of development of his father, although there are variations. Georgy's little composition on "Selfishness" is, of course, an ironic comment on most of the characters and actions in the novel. . . ; but it is also a contrast to his father's letter written many years before, in which he revealed his own childish selfishness. . . . And one sees another of Thackeray's little touches of absolute mastery: the father, in a time when the families were on excellent terms, signed his letter "George Sedley Osborne"; the son, because of his grandfather's continual attacks on Old Sedley, signed his composition "George S. Osborne."

In the same way, Amelia and Dobbin relive their relationships from the past. For Amelia, George is a beginning again, too. And Dobbin, who had been the protector and advisor of the older George, becomes the protector and advisor of the young George. And as he had loved Amelia in the past, so does he continue to love her. But the years have made changes, and these changes lead to Dobbin's final break with Amelia. But through it all, we have the feeling that Thackeray, for what may well be the first time in the English novel, is bringing us into the secret areas of man's life in time. For not only do the years pass, etching their lines on the characters, but the characters, deeply involved in time, make a statement that has the objective qualities of a Bennett or James. Thackeray's approach to his characters was, essentially, that of the eighteenth century: he believed in types, he doubted the efficacy of political action for social improvement, and believed in the necessity of satire. But to his eighteenth century approach, he brought an awareness of time and its effects that is more modern than has been hitherto assumed. When he plays tricks with time, so to speak, Thackeray is making a statement about the cyclical nature of life, suggesting that what one is determines what one will do; he also suggests, I think, that what one does is what one is. And since what one is is affected by time, Thackeray shows the same person responding to two similar events, years apart, and revealing in the different responses the changes produced by time. (pp. 128-30)

Thackeray's use of contrast gives to *Vanity Fair* more than just a formal principle: it also gives the novel a certain texture. To continue the musical analogy, the contrasts between sets of characters and actions fill the space between the two melodic lines with a rich-textured series of variations. While the Becky and Amelia melodies serve to frame the novel, the contrasts in between are contrapuntal variations that develop the basic themes. The result is a vertical development that gives increased richness to the novel. By vertical development I mean, continuing the musical analogy, a chord structure. If the Amelia and Becky stories are melodic, or horizontal, development, then the contrasting variations which fill the space between are a chordal, or vertical, development. Serial publication makes this kind of analogy more readily understandable: each month, the reader received only a part of the plot, or melodic line, but the contrasts, or chord pattern, came complete.

Perhaps a final look at one of Thackeray's chapters will explain more clearly what I mean by the vertical or chord structure. In the first chapter of Number IX. . . . , the melody (narrative) moves very little, but the chordal accompaniment (parallel contrasts) is complete. In this chapter, the participants are getting ready for Waterloo. First we see Major O'Dowd preparing for battle. Instead of going to the big ball, he stays home. . . . At the same time, Rawdon prepares for battle in a scene that reveals his altered character. . . . [He] goes through his properties, estimating their value for Becky. Finally, to insure Becky as much as possible, "the Captain dressed himself in his oldest and shabbiest uniform and epaulets, leaving the newest behind under his wife's (or it might be his widow's) guardianship. And this famous dandy of Windsor and Hyde Park went off on his campaign with a kit as modest as that of a sergeant, and with something like a prayer on his lips for the woman he was leaving."

Dobbin and Jos also prepare for battle. Jos, who "would have snoozed on until his usual hour of rising in the forenoon," is awakened by Dobbin, who has come to insure Amelia's safety. While Dobbin tries to make Jos promise to take care of his sister, Jos refuses to discuss his bravery, his ability to take care of Amelia, or even the possibility of an English defeat. When Dobbin leaves, he has seen Amelia: "Our gentle-hearted Captain felt a guilty shock as he looked at her. 'Good God,' thought he, 'and is it grief like this I dared to pry into?' And there was no help; no means to soothe and comfort this helpless, speechless misery. He stood for a moment and looked at her, powerless and torn with pity, as a parent regards an infant in pain."

George, too, prepares to go into battle. His parting from his wife took but a moment. . . . (pp. 131-33)

Thus we see five men with different attitudes and feelings: the business-like seriousness of the professionals—O'Dowd and Rawdon and Dobbin—contrasts with the flamboyance and bravado of the amateurs—Jos and George. The sober Rawdon contrasts with the selfish George; the greatly concerned Dobbin contrasts with the stupidly indifferent Jos. Besides dealing with the officers, the chapter also covers the officers' wives. Mrs. O'Dowd gets set for her husband's departure:

> Mrs. O'Dowd, the good housewife, arrayed in curl papers and a camisole, felt that her duty was to act, and not to sleep, at this juncture. "Time enough for that," she said, "when Mick's gone;" and so she packed his travelling valise ready for the march, brushed his cloak, his cap,

and other warlike habiliments, set them out in order for him; and stowed away in the cloak pockets a light package of portable refreshments. . . .

Mrs. Crawley, too, retains her composure on the departure of her husband. After Rawdon's departure, Becky goes back to bed, and sleeps until ten. She then continued taking stock of her goods: trinkets, a mare, cashmere shawls, watches—one given by George, the other by General Tufto. Becky finds her position not too uncomfortable. . . . Mrs. Osborne, too, prepares for the departure of her husband, but her conduct lacks the experienced calm and resignation of Mrs. O'Dowd or the complete control motivated by self-interest of Mrs. Crawley. Amelia has lost control; she is on the verge of hysteria and emotional collapse. . . . (pp. 133-34)

The time span of the chapter is from the evening to the next morning, but the action, in effect, has been repeated four times. Thus, the horizontal development—the flow of the story, the narrative—has not moved a great deal in time or distance; but there have been variations on the theme of preparation for war, and these variations have given the chapter a certain texture, a certain feeling of simultaneity of action in different places, a certain feeling of interrelationship among all those involved. The men prepare, and the women prepare, and each one responds in a different way, with different emotions and hopes and fears. These contrasts, extended throughout the book, create a certain feeling of depth in time and space and action. They create a sense of the limited possibilities of human existence, for the contrasts and differences are generally touched with irony. These contrasts—or rather, variations on a theme—provide the novel with a formal principle of structure. Within each monthly number and throughout the novel, contrast is the principle Thackeray uses to develop *Vanity Fair*. (p. 135)

> *Myron Taube, "Contrast as a Principle of Structure in 'Vanity Fair'," in* Nineteenth-Century Fiction, *Vol. 18, No. 2, September, 1963, pp. 119-35.*

JOHN LOOFBOUROW (essay date 1964)

[*Loofbourow explores the interrelationship of style, subject matter, and dramatic structure in* Vanity Fair, *examining the novel's "flexible, allusive prose" within the context of the English literary tradition. For additional commentary by Loofbourow on* Vanity Fair, *see excerpt dated 1964 in NCLC, Vol. 5.*]

When in *Vanity Fair* Thackeray fused his early, satiric expressive conventions into an integral narrative form, a new kind of novel was in the making. In earlier fiction, content, form, and style were separate elements; they could be considered individually as subjects in their own right. But in Thackeray's major novels, as in the work of many modern writers, these aspects of fiction are inseparable and the language itself is a creative element. The difference is like the familiar contrast between classic and romantic art.

The classic-romantic antithesis involves a fairly clear distinction between two ways of envisioning the form-style-content relationship—ways that may conveniently be called "illustration" and "expression." In classical or "illustrative" art, it is the writer's subject that is of primary importance; style is only a means of communicating, form a way of organizing, content. The classicist begins by defining his subject; then he selects an appropriate style and plans an effective presentation. In romantic or "expressive" art, the writer's style is part of the content of his work; his words create meaning, and patterns develop in the process—the method is thought of as a continuous act of expression. The antithesis is figurative—in practice no writer can begin without words or continue without a plan. But the disparity implies dissimilar creative methods and the results are as different as Proust from Fielding. So, in the classical, illustrative tradition, Horace's *Ars Poetica* defines style as decorous exposition (*locum teneant sortita decentum*), form as appropriate presentation (*sibi covenientia finge*), and both form and style merely as instruments for conveying rational content (*verbaque provisam rem non invita sequentur*). The proto-romantic Longinus, however, considers the expressive medium to be synonymous with the artistic concept ("the expressiveness of the word is the essence of art").

English fiction before Thackeray was in the illustrative tradition. Eighteenth-century writers—Defoe, Smollett, Fielding—equated the novel's subject with rational content; for these novelists, form was identical with plot, an effective arrangement of the narrative materials; and style was an expository or decorative means of communication rather than a creative medium. If Richardson's structures were less controlled, his style less apposite, it was due to technical insufficiency rather than artistic originality, and Sterne is the exception, as he is to all literary rules. Long after the content of the nineteenth-century novel had become "romantic," the illustrative method continued to control the writing of English fiction; the development of new narrative methods does not date from the break between the early romantic poets and the neoclassical tradition. The technique of the novel remained basically unchanged from Fielding to Thackeray, and a look at some examples will show how far this is true.

Classicism found its superlative exponent in Jane Austen, and *Emma* is its most brilliant example. *Emma*'s dramatic form is synonymous with narrative fact and, consequently, with its literal "plot." The novel's climaxes coincide with three objective incidents: an abortive marriage proposal, a misguided flirtation, and a successful marriage. The first is a typical instance. Emma attempts to make a match for her friend, Harriet, and her efforts result in Mr. Elton's indecorous proposal for her own hand—the event is logically prepared, Emma's mistake is defined, and the objective outcome of her actions is the rational penalty for her behavior. . . . (pp. 73-5)

Emma's plot is exquisitely correlated with dramatic structure, distinct and iridescent as a Platonic idea: form is an appropriate harmony (*convenientia finge*); moral insights (*rem provisam*) are essential themes. Nowhere does the novel's imaginative content supersede its objective structure or transcend its clear, communicative medium; and this is both an advantage and a limitation.

The melodic consonance of Jane Austen's style is an instance of decorous illustration (*sortita decentum*); and the illustrative technique excludes the expressive diversity of modern narrative prose. Like Parian marble, the classical novel's diction is a common medium, varying only in the degree of rhetorical precision and the effectiveness of the embellishments. The writer's exercise of individuality is confined to the choice of subject and the manner of ornamentation; for all their differences in creative vision and decorative detail, Fielding, Smollett, and Jane Austen write the same fundamental rhetoric. It is impossible, among novelists of this period, to find such stylistic contrasts as between Hardy, Virginia Woolf, James Joyce; and English novelists continued to write illustrative prose until the middle of the nineteenth century.

This proposition may seem untenable when it includes the Brontës, whose fiction seems so distant from the novels of the eighteenth century; but an analysis of their prose makes it clear that they were practicing traditional techniques. Even so "romantic" a writer as Emily Brontë was limited to the common diction. Although the Brontës' visionary effects are not truly compatible with the neo classical rhetoric that exquisitely illustrated Jane Austen's luminous insights, at the time they wrote, prose narrative had no other language to express dramatic event, and they adapted, rather than altered, the accepted medium. Thus in *Wuthering Heights*, Emily Brontë represents climaxes of pure emotional content by conventional images of physical action that typify but do not express Heathcliff's agony and Catherine's passion: "He dashed his head against the knotted trunk; and, lifting up his eyes, howled, not like a man, but like a savage beast"; "such senseless, wicked rages! There she lay . . . her hair flying over her shoulders . . . the muscles of her neck and arms standing out."

The point is made clearer by comparing Emily Brontë's language with the eighteenth-century diction of Richardson's *Clarissa*, where the same basic rhetoric is used to describe the very different instance of a prostitute's "squalid" death—the "infamous" Mrs. Sinclair's "wickedness" and "rage": "howling, more like a wolf than a human," "her hair" conventionally "torn," "violence" distending "her muscular features." The common rhetoric's neoclassical abstractions—"savagery," "wickedness," "rage"—preclude the expressive representation of complex emotions, which must be conveyed by the author's or actors' rational comments, as they are in Jane Austen; and when the writer attempts to surmount this restriction, the tradition's invariable equation of subjective experience with generalized behavior ("dashed his head," "lifted his eyes") produces an indecorous but persistently formulaic effect.

In *Vanity Fair*, Thackeray writes another kind of prose; he dispenses with rational analysis, but develops a narrative medium whose expressive images convey the novel's emotional event—Amelia at Waterloo, "her large eyes fixed and without light"; Steyne, "with flame in his eyes," defying retribution. In *Wuthering Heights*, similitudes are confined to explicit comparisons—"My love for Linton is like the foliage in the woods . . . my love for Heathcliff resembles the eternal rocks beneath." In *Vanity Fair*, similes are replaced by metaphors whose suggestive range is amplified by allusion to familiar artistic conventions, as when a sequence of romance motifs culminates in imagery that transforms men to oaks and women to doves: "Oh, thou poor little panting soul! The very finest tree in the whole forest, with the straightest stem, and the strongest arms, and the thickest foliage, wherein you choose to build and coo, may be marked, for what you know, and may be down with a crash ere long."

Thackeray's prose, the crucial factor in his narrative experiment, was an unaccustomed harmony ("Nobody in our day wrote, I should say, with such perfection of style," Carlyle remarked). Among its precursors were the rhythms of Sterne, who brought a conversational flexibility to his narrative style, and the rhetoric of Carlyle, who revived, in prose, the richness of allegorical figuration. Sterne's rhythmic range greatly increased the capacity of the narrative medium to assimilate diverse modes without losing its expressive unity. His stylistic innovation was simple and profound: he put Locke's theory of associated ideas into fictional practice by adapting the informal rhetoric of personal letters or memoirs—cursive punctuations (dots, dashes, parentheses, semicolons, :—, or —!), conversational inflections ("Fy, Mr. Shandy," "O Thomas! Thomas!"), inversions, ellipses and digressions. There are earlier instances of rhythmic complexity—Swift's "Tale of a Tub," for example—but none in which a story is simultaneously developed. "The machinery of my work," Sterne insisted, "is of a species by itself." Digressions are part of his narration, associations are continuous with statement—"In a word, my work is digressive, and it is progressive too,—and at the same time." It was this freedom of rhythmic movement that permitted Thackeray to integrate diverse expressive textures in *Vanity Fair*—and if the rhythmic resources of Sterne's narrative style enabled Thackeray to assimilate allusive modes, Carlyle's figured rhetoric taught him to fuse these allusions into cumulative metaphor. (pp. 77-8)

Sterne and Carlyle are themselves, of course, only particular instances of the complex processes that prefigured the prose of *Vanity Fair*. Sterne's rhythms were imitated by many writers, including the fashionable novelists that Thackeray parodied; Carlyle's metaphors were derived from Goethe and the German romantics, whose work Thackeray knew, as well as from Milton and Donne. But Thackeray's vigorous version of fashionable syncopations is his tribute to *Tristram Shandy;* and *Sartor* is audible in the resonance of his narrative commentary. *Vanity Fair*'s diction combines Sterne's punctuations, inflections, and digressive continuities with satirical modifications of Carlyle's symbolism; and this unprecedented synthesis produces characteristic overtones in passages like the classical-biblical parable that shadows forth Rebecca's fate: "the honest newspaper-fellow . . . can't survive the glare of fashion long. It scorches him up, as the presence of Jupiter in full dress wasted that poor imprudent Semele—a giddy moth of a creature who ruined herself by venturing out of her natural atmosphere. Her myth ought to be taken to heart amongst the Tyburnians, the Belgravians,—her story, and perhaps Becky's too. Ah, ladies!—ask the Reverend Mr. Thurifer if Belgravia is not a sounding brass, and Tyburnia a tinkling cymbal."

Vanity Fair, formed on this flexible, allusive prose, is as different from *Emma* and the "classical" novel as Berlioz is from Mozart. Thackeray's characters are refractions of allusive color rather than instruments of rational insight. They do not think. In *Vanity Fair,* thinking is sometimes an emotional response—"She thought of her long past life, and all the dismal incidents of it"—sometimes a subjective conflict—"how she tries to hide from herself the thought which will return to her, that she ought to part with the boy"—sometimes an intuitive judgment—"He loved her no more, he thought, as he had loved her"—but never intellectual analysis. There is no mutual explication, since the characters never communicate rationally: "poor Amelia . . . had no confidante; indeed, she could never have one: as she would not allow to herself the possibility of yielding." These actors represent not intellect deluded but delusion itself. *Emma*'s characters often make erroneous choices; in *Vanity Fair,* alternatives are unperceived, and the actors retreat unconsciously from the force of facts: "giving way daily before the enemy with whom she had to battle. One truth after another was marshalling itself silently against her, and keeping its ground." Truth is never confronted in *Vanity Fair;* its inhabitants must be pushed blindfolded over the edge of reality. When Amelia decides at last to relinquish her child, it is in a "burst of anguish": "she was conquered. The sentence was passed." Such characters cannot define or respond to objective event—they hardly recognize it.

The result is that *Vanity Fair*'s objective plot-sequence does not control the novel's effective dramatic form. Since the actors respond not to external facts but to inner images represented by allusive motifs and expressive textures, the literal incidents of the novel's "plot" are not correlated with its imaginative events. When Amelia's father loses his fortune, the factual crisis has no effect on dramatic experience. Before the event, distressed by George's negligence, Amelia expects to marry him; after the event, distressed by George's negligence, Amelia marries him. Conversely, when Rawdon dismisses the Marquis of Steyne, Rebecca suffers no literal loss—unlike the social adventuress in *Bleak House,* Lady Dedlock, she has acquired neither wealth nor real prestige; she forfeits nothing but marital security: Rawdon provides her with "a tolerable annuity" and she was always *demi-mondaine*. Again, in the dramatic and central Waterloo episode, literal event is peripheral: malice, jealousy, panic are its subjective phenomena; its only objective incident is dismissed in the last sentence, and is never emotionally or dramatically represented in the narrative context— "Amelia was praying for George, who was lying on his face, dead."

In *Vanity Fair,* factual incident is a convenience for the common reader and the novel's "plot" has no real relationship to dramatic development. Literal event gives no clue to *Vanity Fair*'s expressive tensions; thus, the opposition between Becky's and Amelia's fortunes which is felt as a formal principle does not correspond to their objective experiences. . . . There is no significant literal relationship between the two fortunes. The heroines' dramatic opposition is not an objective antithesis. Amelia's social status fluctates erratically, never illustrating the emotional sequence—her prolonged personified journey from amorous confusion to maternal agony. The imaginative pattern of Rebecca's picaresque dramatic progress is not based on financial facts which are statistically monotonous from her marriage to Rawdon through her liasion with Steyne. And Waterloo, since no objective event is represented, has no place in the literal plot, although it is the artistic center of the novel.

Dramatic event in *Vanity Fair* is a very different thing from dramatic event in illustrative novels. Created by the words themselves, the significance of Thackeray's "events" is found in expressive, metaphorical values, not in objective elements. In earlier fiction, narrative incident was an illustration of logical content; *Emma*'s final love-scene has no expressive importance: it is an affirmation of rational insights: "She had led her friend astray, and it would be a reproach to her for ever; but her judgment was as strong as her feelings, and as strong as it had ever been before, in reprobating any such alliance for him, as most unequal and degrading. Her way was clear, though not quite smooth." In *Vanity Fair,* there are no rational affirmations to illustrate. The final love-scene draws no morals; instead, its allusive textures assemble, in one expressive realization, the successive satiric emblems of Amelia and Dobbin—"fragrant and blooming tenderly in quiet shady places"; "fluttering to Lieutenant George Osborne's heart"; "the prize I had set my life on was not worth the winning":

> The vessel is in port. He has got the prize he has been trying for all his life. The bird has come in at last. There it is with its head on his shoulder, billing and cooing close up to his heart, with soft outstretched fluttering wings. This is what he has asked for every day and hour for eighteen years. This is what he pined after. Here it is—the summit, the end—the last

page of the third volume. Good-bye, Colonel.—God bless you, honest William!—Farewell, dear Amelia.—Grow green again, tender little parasite, round the rugged old oak to which you cling!

The ironic significance of this passage is a purely expressive phenomenon; its textures are a representation of emotional realities, rather than an illustration of rational truths. There is no logical flaw in the premised union—Dobbin is deserving, Amelia is loving, the marriage is appropriate. But dissonance is overt in the writer's satirical allusion to fashionable finales ("the last page of the third volume"), and this central discord governs a sequence of harmonic incongruities. A rhapsody of saccharine infelicities figures the ironic fulfillment of a fantasy: the worthless "prize" of Dobbin's chivalric quest that began with his worship of George, "the summit" of his pilgrimage—"the end"; Amelia's "feeble remnant" of romance that "clings" to its victim, recalling her role, as George's bride, nesting in "the finest tree in the whole forest" ("Grow green again, tender little parasite")—and the subtly sacrilegious image of Amelia's sentimental ecstasy, the "soft outstretched fluttering wings" of dove-like devotion.

Such narrative event begins with words, and words in *Vanity Fair* are no longer illustration. As Thackeray's writing matures, the pastiches of *Catherine* and the **"Legend"** are developed into sustained dramatic metaphor: creative prose ("the expressiveness of the word") becomes the novel's effective content. Like poetry, this prose includes the language of emotional event; and it was the dramatic potential of this new expressive medium that transformed the novels of many English writers after Thackeray. (pp. 78-83)

In *Vanity Fair,* expressive realization of emotional event is the novel's effective drama, as in the satirical mating of Dobbin and Amelia. *Vanity Fair*'s dramatic "form" depends on allusive continuities—sequences of sentiment and romance—rather than on plot progressions. . . . These [sequences], evolved from expressive continuities, correspond more closely to effective form in *Vanity Fair* than analyses of literal event. The novel's opening scenes are filled with subtle discriminations in fashionable sin and sentiment—Amelia's *"Sehnsucht nach der Liebe,"* Rebecca's "Charming Alnaschar visions." At the first intimation of the heroines' future marriages, the arcs of fashionable parody are intersected by opposing tangents of chivalric satire—Amelia's "little tender heart . . . beating, and longing and trusting" to George, Becky's "barbed shaft" quivering in Rawdon's "dull hide." Waterloo, the satiric paradigm of knightly combat, is *Vanity Fair*'s expressive center—a sentimental-chivalric crux: the novel's opposing tangents of romance—Amelia's amorous grail-motifs, Rebecca's magic metaphors—intersect; the heroines' hostilities qualify Amelia's agony, imaged in the blood-red laceration of George's military sash; and Rebecca's victorious visit to her prostrate rival combines picaresque parody (Becky's exploits) with sentimental satire (Amelia's animosity). After the battle, chivalric oppositions are reversed. Rebecca's magical success approaches satirical apotheosis; Amelia's masochism reaches its nadir in the ironies of maternal sacrifice. As Dobbin returns, Amelia's romantic reprieve spans Rebecca's farcical disaster with Steyne; the swift descent of the glittering rogue is crossed by the amorous dove's ascending flight—and the final sequences are suffused with the satirical sentimentality that opened the novel.

Vanity Fair's expressive form is a vast metaphor, an extended figure filled with typifications. If the novel is named from *The*

A sketch by Thackeray in a copy of Vanity Fair *he presented to the artist George Cruikshank.*

Pilgrim's Progress, its allegory begins in Bunyan's "Town . . . wherein should be sold . . . Lusts, Pleasures, and Delights of all sorts"—"Yes, this is Vanity Fair," the novel's prologue announces, "eating and drinking, making love and jilting . . . not a moral place certainly; nor a merry one, though very noisy" [see essay by Thackeray dated 1848]. As Thackeray's actors begin to suffer, their subjective world becomes a dramatic scene, and the novel's symbolic psychology revives the *Psychomachia*'s generic image of inner strife—a *bellum intestinum* that C. S. Lewis calls "the root of all allegory": "The combat, which we describe in a sentence or two, lasted for many weeks in poor Amelia's heart . . . one by one the outworks of the little citadel were taken, in which the poor soul passionately guarded her only love and treasure." But if Thackeray's initial metaphor is borrowed from Bunyan, his personifications ("behind whom all there lies a dark moral I hope" [see excerpt from Thackeray's letter dated 1847]), unlike the simple symbolism of *The Pilgrim's Progress,* are images of contemporary subjective complexities. Amelia is Love, but delusive love; Dobbin's Faith and Charity are colored by George's Hypocrisy; Rebecca, a moral reprobate, is also a type of Fun and Truth, the artist's persona personified. Thackeray's "Love" becomes an ambivalent quality when the novel's semi-Shakespearian commentary mocks the amorous ingenue ("Perhaps some beloved female subscriber has arrayed an ass in the splendour and glory of her imagination . . . and used him as the brilliant fairy Titania did a certain weaver at Athens.") "Of course you are quite right," Thackeray remarks in [the aforementioned] letter, "about Vanity Fair and Amelia being selfish. . . . My object is not to make a perfect character or anything like it.'' In certain satirical perspectives the ambiguity is intensified—as when Amelia's pathetic poses are ironically reflected in Rebecca's insincerities. Allegory becomes a comic anti-masque when Amelia and Rebecca are beatified—when Amelia's thoughts, ''as if they were angels,'' try ''to peep into the barracks where George was''—''the gates were shut, and the sentry allowed no one to pass; so that the poor little white-robed angel could not hear the songs those young fellows were roaring over the whisky-punch.''—and when Rebecca, the students' ''Angel Engländerin,'' sobs out her simulated sufferings at Baden: ''it was quite evident from hearing her, that if ever there was a white-robed angel escaped from heaven to be subject to the infernal machinations and villainy of fiends here below, that spotless being—that miserable unsullied martyr, was present on the bed before Jos—on the bed, sitting on the brandy-bottle.''

Vanity Fair's recension of the allegory of emotional experience is the beginning of a new kind of fiction that includes such disparate exponents as Meredith, Firbank, and Virginia Woolf; it prepares a medium for such a development as *To the Lighthouse*, where drama is interior, experience subjective, fantasy fused with reality in the symbolism of World War I, as it is at Waterloo in *Vanity Fair*. But, unlike Thackeray, Virginia Woolf forces her war-metaphor to function as an objective as well as an emotional event, sacrificing the imaginative suspension of disbelief that is achieved by Thackeray's displacement of literal incident; the symbolic pattern that is sustained in *Vanity Fair* is discredited in *To the Lighthouse* by the intrusion of the realities it symbolizes.

If *Vanity Fair*'s expressive method revived the techniques and typifications of Sidney, Spenser, and *The Pilgrim's Progress,* its content, like Wagner's orchestration, was a radical polyphony. ''I think I see in him an intellect profounder and more unique than his contemporaries have yet recognised,'' Charlotte Brontë wrote. Thackeray's ability to ''scrutinise and expose'' seemed to her ''prophet-like''—''No commentator on his writings has yet found,'' she insisted, ''the terms which rightly characterise his talent.''

An aspect of this insight was Thackeray's expressive representation of psychological relativity (''after looking into a microscope how infinite littleness even is''). The glittering allusive tangents of his prose reflected a sustained ambivalent logic— recognition of the range of possible relationships:

> O philosophic reader . . . a distinct universe walks about under your hat and mine—all things are different to each—the woman we look at has not the same features, the dish we eat from has not the same taste to the one and the other— you and I are but a pair of infinite isolations, with some fellow-islands a little more or less near to us.

In *Vanity Fair,* perceptions like these fuse bits of human anomaly and fragments of shattered idealisms into eccentric images of psychological truth. ''In the passage where Amelia is represented as trying to separate herself from the boy,'' Thackeray wrote to the critic for *Fraser's Magazine,* '' 'as that poor Lady Jane Grey tried the axe that was to separate her slender life' I say that is a fine image whoever wrote it . . . it leaves you to make your own sad pictures'' [see excerpt dated September 3, 1848]. In this sequence, the mother's suffering is mirrored in images that reflect the whole range of her sentimental neurosis—her personified denial of reality and defeat by truth, her

chivalric fetishism, her amorous idolatry. The episode is conceived in several dimensions—the mother's possessiveness, her jealousy of the boy's aunt, her obsessive image of George, the child's ironic indifference—

> terror is haunting her . . . George's picture and dearest memory. . . . The child must go from her—to others—to forget her. Her heart and her treasure—her joy, hope, love, worship— her God, almost! . . . The mother had not been so well pleased, perhaps, had the rival been better looking . . . preparing him for the change . . . He was longing for it.

Amelia's compulsive fantasies—''her God, almost!''—anticipating religious ironies in the novel's final love-scene, discredit the Victorian image of romantic maternity; and the allegory of Vanity Fair is largely concerned with revealing such emotional compulsions in the elements of accepted conventions. George Henry Lewes, who could accept George Eliot's ambiguities, found Thackeray's too unpleasant (''in *Vanity Fair* . . . how little there is to love'') and protested the inclusion of that ''detestable passage,'' rephrased in the prologue to *Esmond,* ''wherein [the author] adds from himself this remark:— 'And who knows but Rebecca was right in her speculations— and that it was only a question of money and fortune which made the difference between her and an honest woman? . . . An alderman . . . will not step out of his carriage to steal . . . *but put him to starve, and see if he will not purloin a loaf.*' [Lewes' italics] Was it carelessness, or deep misanthropy, distorting an otherwise clear judgment, which allowed such a remark to fall?'' [see excerpt dated 1848 in *NCLC*, Vol. 5].

The passage is not personal observation; it is commentary— the rigorous recognition of the relativity of human values that typifies the novel's method. In *Vanity Fair,* the Commentator is a dimension of dissent—''I wonder is it because men are cowards in heart that they admire bravery so much?'' '''Was Rebecca guilty or not?' The Vehmgericht of the servants' hall had pronounced against her''—and, instead of solving dilemmas, asks questions unanswered in the silence at the end: ''Ah! *Vanitas, Vanitatum!* which of us is happy in this world? Which of us has his desire? or, having it, is satisfied?'' (pp. 83-8)

A contingent aspect of Thackeray's insight (his power, Charlotte Brontë put it, ''to penetrate the sepulchre, and reveal charnel relics'') is expressed in *Vanity Fair*'s mock-epic and romance evocations of primitive impulse—an imaginative projection of the hypotheses of contemporary science that became, in *The Newcomes,* a symbolism of creative method:

> Professor Owen or Professor Agassiz takes a fragment of a bone, and builds an enormous forgotten monster out of it, wallowing in primaeval quagmires, tearing down leaves and branches of plants that flourished thousands of years ago, and perhaps may be coal by this time— so the novelist puts this and that together: from the footprint finds the foot; from the foot, the brute who trod on it; from the brute, the plant he browsed on, the marsh in which he swam—and thus, in his humble way a physiologist too, depicts the habits, size, appearance of the beings whereof he has to treat;— traces this slimy reptile through the mud, and describes his habits filthy and rapacious; prods down his butterfly with a pin, and depicts his

beautiful coat and embroidered waistcoat; points out the singular structure of yonder more important animal, the megatherium of his history.

The biological analogy is not a casual conceit; it is a newly recognized aspect of human reality that impinges on *Vanity Fair*. In Spenserian allegory, personification illustrates enduring moral fact: Una's truth, Acrasia's artifice, Guyon's discipline. The figurations of *Vanity Fair,* like Spenser's types, personify moral qualities; but Thackeray's characters express other kinds of reality as well—the survival of primitive fantasy, the persistence of the biological past. His actors are not only victims of romance delusions but types of subconscious compulsions. Primal violence is implicit at chivalric Waterloo. . . . (pp. 89-90)

The novel's heroines exhibit atavistic symptoms: Amelia acts out archaic obsession—"powerless in the hands of her remorseless little enemy"—Rebecca reveals tribal mores—("She admired her husband, strong, brave, and victorious.") Under fashionable fantasies, chivalric visions, amorous mystique, lurks the "forgotten monster" of *Vanity Fair.* The actors indulge involuntary urges—George's blood-lust, Dobbin's self-abasement, Amelia's idolatry—and *Vanity Fair*'s dramatic structure is partly predicated on these emotional compulsions. Mock-epic imagery reinforces romance motif; ritual fetishes coincide (Amelia worshipping the image of George, Rebecca defacing Miss Pinkerton's doll and piercing Amelia's heart); and racial impulse becomes a sustained expressive metaphor—Sir Pitt is a "hyaena face," Rawdon a rutting bull, Dobbin a Caliban, Amelia a "bleeding heart," and Rebecca a "monster's tail," "writhing and twirling, diabolically hideous and slimy."

This does not mean that *Vanity Fair* is a prototype of Conrad or Kafka; Thackeray is far more concerned with the subtleties of civilized society and the images of idealized convention. His novel is, however, a fable—and a fable with modern as well as traditional implications. Its patterns are unprecedented in English fiction; but they are achieved at a sacrifice. In order to project the internal drama of *Vanity Fair,* Thackeray has excluded the dimension of objective reality and conceived his characters primarily as types. (pp. 90-1)

> *John Loofbourow, in his* Thackeray and the Form of Fiction, *Princeton University Press, 1964, 236 p.*

U. C. KNOEPFLMACHER (essay date 1971)

[*Knoepflmacher examines the important role that the pursuit of love and wealth plays in the lives of various characters in* Vanity Fair. *The critic also discusses how Thackeray illustrates the passage of time in the novel.*]

The characters in *Vanity Fair* are moved by either of two impulses: greed (or what the Showman at one point calls "this race for money") or love (or those feelings which the characters mistake for love). Speaking of the auction at the Sedley home, the narrator argues that such public assemblies afford the novelist with an opportunity to "light on the strangest contrasts laughable and tearful." . . . To be sure, the auction provides the Showman with a perfect miniature spectacle which Satire and Sentiment can visit arm in arm together. The narrator can simultaneously expose two different kinds of appetite: the voraciousness of the bargain-hunters who rummage through the belongings of the Sedleys and the hunger of those sentimentalists who rummage through the associations held by these remnants of a lost past.

Money and material goods possess a kind of permanence in *Vanity Fair*. The acquisition or loss of wealth may alter the characters, but the cult of money is unvarying. As long as Dobbin's father runs a modest shop he is looked down upon by the sons of gentlemen, but when his profits rise he is made Alderman Dobbin and knighted. The distance separating the onetime grocer and Mr. Osborne is thus considerably reduced; their sons are no longer as far apart on the social scale as they seemed at Mr. Swishtail's establishment. On the other hand, the bonds that once existed between Osborne and his benefactor, John Sedley, vanish after Sedley's financial ruin.

On visiting Amelia's fallen father, Dobbin admits that his own father and sisters, who would in earlier years have been most grateful to be noticed by Mr. Sedley, now snub him. In turn, the old man scrapes and bows before Dobbin. In a pathetic mixture of abasement and vanity, he alludes to "the worthy alderman, and my lady, your excellent mother" . . . in order to be overheard by a waiter in the shabby coffeehouse. Mr. Sedley blames his collapse on Napoleon, the British government, and the Kings and Emperors of Austria, Russia, and Prussia. His accusation is an attempt to aggrandize himself by obscuring his own imprudence. But his statements also carries a meaning unintended by him: the kings and emperors of this world *are* on a par with him; they too are warring merchants eager to gain economic supremacy. From top to bottom, money determines alliances and attractions. Just as the rival powers who join to fight the returning Napoleon are willing to overcome their contempt of each other, so is old Osborne more than willing to overlook the social ineligibility of an heiress with 200,000 pounds. In the political world, unequal nations consolidate against a common competitor; in the world of society, unequal marriages are made for money, and undesirable relatives are wooed for their fortunes. Mr. Osborne commands his son to marry Miss Swartz before some aristocrat will snatch her away. Conversely, aristocrats like Rawdon feel that it is their duty to take as much "tin" as possible from gambling "city-men." The Bute Crawleys abjectly court Miss Crawley, although they secretly despise her. Miss Crawley, in turn, unfairly accuses Miss Briggs of waiting for her death to receive a legacy; she assumes that her devoted housekeeper is pleading for Rawdon and Becky because of a bribe. To the materially minded, there can be no disinterested attachments.

Nobody understands better the commodity that sentiment can be than Becky Sharp. Her financial gains are always achieved through her exploitation of the affections of others. She wheedles a gift out of Mr. Sedley by tearfully alluding to herself as a penniless orphan; on reaching the street, she wipes her tears and counts her guineas. The one time she weeps in earnest is on discovering that she could have married Sir Pitt, an ailing man with a title and sure income, instead of sharing the increasingly doubtful expectations of his younger son. Becky's obsession with money is contrasted to the naïvete of Amelia who regards two thousand pounds as "an immense deal of money" that will last for a lifetime. Unlike Becky, who thinks that she could be a good woman on five thousand pounds a year, Amelia never even wonders where the funds maintaining her and Georgy are coming from.

Becky's money-mindedness is also contrasted to Rawdon's disregard for his earnings as a gambler. When we first see the couple living on "nothing a year," Becky's indifference to money seems like Rawdon's. Gradually, however, their attitudes prove to be totally dissimilar. In chapter twenty-five Rawdon stops to think about the future. The impending war makes him pity the newly wed Amelia: "I say, what'll Mrs. O. do, when O. goes out with the regiment?" Becky, too, has thought of the possibility of George's departure. But her foresight takes a significantly different shape: "Rawdon, dear—don't you think—you'd better get that—money from Cupid, before he goes?" While cajoling her husband to claim his bill, she is "fixing on a killing bow" to impress the same man whose death she has so calmly considered.

This same contrast is elaborated in "The Girl I Left Behind" . . . , in which Becky's relation to Rawdon is brilliantly juxtaposed to Mrs. O'Dowd's and Amelia's farewells to their respective husbands. The chapter begins with Mrs. O'Dowd's preparations. The woman who wakes up her husband "as soon as the hands of the 'repayther' pointed to half past one" is acutely aware of time. Like Becky, who is the next wife to be described, she also seems to be realistic and unsentimental, devoid of "the fits of tears and hysterics by which more sensitive females exhibited their love." But as soon as we shift to Becky's leave-taking from Rawdon we realize that Mrs. O'Dowd, for all her outward calm, may in fact be closer to the hysterical Amelia. Despite their matter-of-factness, Mrs. O'Dowd's preparations "betokened affection." Not so Becky's. Sentences which would have aptly described Mrs. O'Dowd's stoic refusal to yield to sentimentality become heavily ironic when applied to Becky: "Knowing how useless regrets are, and how the indulgence of sentiment only serves to make people more miserable, Mrs. Rebecca wisely determined to give way to no vain feelings of sorrow, and bore the parting from her husband with quite a Spartan equanimity. Indeed Captain Rawdon himself was much more affected at the leave-taking than the resolute little woman to whom he bade farewell."

Rebecca's good humor grates on the reader as much as it does on Rawdon. Sensing that her manner has "hurt the feelings" of her husband, she mollifies him by "hastily dashing something from her eyes"; but if Rawdon is convinced, the reader is not. There is something moving in Rawdon's sudden metamorphosis from spendthrift into provider: "'Look here,' said he. 'If I drop, let us see what there is for you. I have had a pretty good run of luck here, and here's two hundred and thirty pounds. I have got ten Napoleons in my pocket. That is as much as I shall want; for the General pays everything like a prince; and if I'm hit, why you know I cost nothing. Don't cry, little woman; I may live to vex you yet.'" Becky remains quite unvexed. Rawdon trots off to battle, wearing his oldest and shabbiest uniform, "leaving the newest behind, under his wife's (or it might be his widow's) guardianship," while Becky, who, "as we have said, wisely determined not to give way to unavailing sentimentality," goes back to bed. After her beauty sleep, she resumes Rawdon's "calculations" beyond any plane imagined by him. Rawdon has given her all his earthly belongings down to his coat and duelling pistols. But we now discover that she, unbeknown to him, has stashed away a fortune in "valuables" given to her by other admirers. Satisfied, she concludes that she can easily "begin the world" again. Rummaging through Rawdon's notes, she finds a twenty pound draft on Osborne: "'I will go and get the draft cashed,' she said, 'and pay a visit afterwards to poor little Emmy.'" Becky is a far more astute economist than her husband: whereas his "plan of economy" is an expression of love, her own calculations show only self-interest.

Rawdon does not die on the battlefield; he lives to vex his wife. What is only implicit in "The Girl I Left Behind" finally becomes explicit when Rawdon surprises Becky with Lord Steyne. Earlier, on being imprisoned, he had asked her to pay his debts; her reply—written "in bed"—dwelt on her difficulties in liberating *"mon pauvre prisonnier."* . . . Now, after Rawdon is released by his sister-in-law, he not only discovers Becky with Lord Steyne but also discovers that the nobleman regards him as a pander who has profited from his wife's prostitution. Forcing Becky to open her desk, Rawdon lights on her hoard: "It contained papers, love-letters many years old—all sorts of small trinkets and woman's memoranda. And it contained a pocket-book with bank notes. Some of these were dated ten years back, too, and one was quite a fresh note—a note for a thousand pounds which Lord Steyne had given her." . . . The scene is one of the high points of the novel; its position—at the three-quarter point—shows the extent of Becky's progress. The wife who murders Rawdon's love is closer to the survivor who eagerly cashes Jos Sedley's insurance policy than to the girl who had flung the dictionary at the kind-hearted Miss Jemima in the first chapter of the novel. Her protestation, "I am innocent," seems less and less believable. Her innocence diminishes in proportion to the pain she inflicts. Although we are forced to make our own surmises, it is clear that the girl whose wit once seemed so delightful has become a woman capable of adultery and murder.

But in a sense, Becky *is* "innocent." She has merely carried the outlook of Vanity Fair to its logical extremes. The reader who belongs to a society as acquisitive as her own finds himself yoked to Becky's cruel logic. Even Rawdon's words upon discovering her treasure reinforce the inescapability of material considerations: "You might have spared me a hundred pounds, Becky, out of all of this—I have always shared with you." Morally, Rawdon is far more innocent than his calculating wife, yet even he must express his affection through the values of Vanity Fair. His words confirm Becky's cynicism. Love, gratitude, affection are to her meaningless abstractions by which most men disguise their true values. At the end of the novel, when the insurance company backs down and pays Becky her claim for Jos' policy, the Showman comments laconically: "The money was paid, and her character established." . . . (pp. 71-6)

Becky thrives by disregarding sentiment. She knows that emotions are salable wares in the mart of Vanity Fair. She is logical and clear-eyed. But what of those who are illogical because they are moved by feeling? Rawdon, Amelia, Dobbin, Lady Jane, Miss Briggs go against the grain of Vanity Fair. They do not care for money. Nonetheless, these characters do not escape the ironic treatment accorded to the materialists of Thackeray's world. . . . Thackeray refuses to dispense sweetmeats and sugar plums. His Amelia is not the model of perfection that her namesake was in Fielding's novel. In his more realistic treatment, love, too, can prove to be a crippling vanity.

While Becky disregards all considerations beyond the self, Amelia's love presumably is directed at others. And yet her childlike and naïve obsession with love resembles Becky's adult and cynical obsession with money. Becky the opportunist thinks ahead, aware of change; Amelia the sentimentalist tries to arrest all growth, to deny change. She refuses to admit that her childhood sweetheart has developed into a man unworthy of her devotion; she loves this man all the more when his death allows her to be true to a fixed and unchanging image. Thackeray makes sure to have Amelia disillusioned in George before his death, for he wants us to see that she knows that her husband is not the ideal she had worshiped. Her distortion of George's character after his death is therefore all the more reprehensible. His death is a blessing to her because it allows her to avoid the reality she was about to face and to revert to her former cult.

Amelia's love, like Becky's, thus is self-love. Although, unlike Becky, she is a dutiful mother, she smothers her son and almost ruins Georgy by fashioning him in the image of his snobbish father. Becky's cynicism leads her to deny all bonds; Amelia's love of love results in similar denials. She is uninterested in the European cataclysm which ruins her father; she is too self-pitying to show commiseration for Mr. Sedley's misfortune; she refuses to acknowledge her debts to Dobbin. Like Becky, she takes without offering a return. And, since her self-love involves an act of self-blinding, we almost prefer Becky's frank egotism—almost, until we realize that such empathy can also lead us to empathize with adultery and murder. Still, just as Becky helps the author to satirize the greed that rules Vanity Fair, so does she allow him to puncture Amelia's false love. Becky is cruel in destroying George's memory, yet for once the reader rejoices in her lack of pity: "Why, the man was weary of you, and would have jilted you, but that Dobbin forced him to keep his word.... He used to sneer about you to me, time after time; and made love to me the week after he married you." Becky produces the evidence of George's infidelity by forcing Amelia to look at the letter she has kept: "He wrote that to me—wanted me to run away with him—gave it me under your nose, the day before he was shot—and served him right!" ... (pp. 76-7)

Becky's savagery is necessary. Yet, though we want her to prick Amelia's illusions, we cannot rejoice in the union she makes possible.... The union of Dobbin and Amelia is not a triumph. It merely mitigates Dobbin's misery and chastens Amelia's self-love. The marriage is belated. Amelia is not a prize.... The matron who now becomes Dobbin's wife is but a shade of the vision to which he had clung over the years. When Dobbin finally admits that he, and not George, had retrieved Amelia's piano, he unwillingly calls attention to the disparity between past and present:

> "Amelia, Amelia," he said, "I did buy it for you. I loved you then as I do now. I must tell you. I think I loved you from the first minute that I saw you, when George brought me to your house, to show me the Amelia whom he was engaged to. You were but a girl in white, with large ringlets; you came down singing—do you remember?—and we went to Vauxhall. Since then I have thought of but one woman in the world, and that was you."
>
> (pp. 77-8)

Dobbin's recollection exposes the vanity of his own love. Though more intelligent than Amelia, though far more aware of the ways of Vanity Fair, he too is guilty of attributing his own emotions to others. In one of the novel's key ironies, this silent lover forces George into marrying Amelia by bringing him a letter from her thanking George for the gift of the piano: "I shall often play upon the piano—your piano. It was like you to send it." Amelia's sentimental words—words which apply to Dobbin and not to George—are exploited by Dobbin in order to move Amelia's reluctant groom. In delivering the message, Dobbin is overcome by emotion: "'George, she is dying,' William Dobbin said,—and could speak no more." ... Amelia is hardly dying. Unaware of Bonaparte's fall, unconcerned with Mr. Sedley's plight, the girl who mopes in her room is dimly

conscious that her father's ruin somehow prevents her from marrying George. Dobbin is using hyperbole for a calculated effect—his exaggeration, like those of Becky Sharp, has the effect of touching his listener. George is infected by his friend's genuine emotion. He writes a note: "Dearest Emmy—dearest love—dearest wife—come to me." He is happy with himself. He will defy his father and marry the poor and virtuous Amelia. But his pose crumbles to pieces after he discovers that his father remains firm. Vindictively, George turns on Dobbin: "A beggar, by Jove, and all in consequence of my d——d sentimentality." ... (p. 78)

George's remark is as ugly as his sudden disenchantment with his wife. It is permeated by his love of money. His recrimination is just, nonetheless. He has been blinded by Dobbin's sentimentality. Dobbin has muddled things up. He is responsible for a father's disavowal of his son; he has forced Amelia into a marriage saved only by George's death. And why? "Because he loved her so much that he could not bear to see her unhappy: or because his own sufferings of suspense were so unendurable that he was glad to crush them at once—as we hasten a funeral after a death." ... Love is selfish even in its unselfishness. Had Dobbin been more cruel and less kind (as Becky will be when she finally crushes Amelia's illusions), he could have spared Amelia this unfortunate marriage. What is more, he could have spared himself the years of misery that now await him. In due time, he admits his mistake. Unlike Amelia's recognition, which must be forced on her by Becky, his admission comes unaided: "It was myself I deluded, and persisted in cajoling; had she been worthy of the love I gave her, she would have returned it long ago. It was a fond mistake. Isn't the whole course of life made up of such?" ...

Dobbin's recognition cannot be altered. Even after he gets his Amelia he can never love her as he had loved her before. She is no longer the girl in white he had sentimentalized as much as she had sentimentalized George Osborne. Resigned, he weds the querulous mother of a teen-age son. His hopefulness must be placed in his own child, who, significantly, is named after another woman, Lady Jane, in a novel where all other children bear the name of their parents. Dobbin is fonder of Janey "than of anything in the world—fonder even than of his 'History of the Punjaub'." ... Amelia is envious: "Fonder that he is of me," she thinks rightly. Still, the narrator renders her point of view only to insist, in his own voice, that Dobbin remained a model husband: "he never said a word to Amelia, that was not kind and gentle; or thought of a want of hers that he did not try to gratify." ... (p. 79)

The narrator avoids a final summing up. He refuses to enter Dobbin's inner life. But, as in the concluding description of Becky's charitable activities, what remains unsaid is as important as what is being said. We are not allowed to forget the stoicism of Dobbin's earlier concession in the same chapter: "I have 'geliebt und gelebt' as the girl in Wallenstein says. I am done.—Pay the bills and get me a cigar." ... The tone of his statement strongly resembles the narrator's parting words in the novel's last paragraph: "Ah! *Vanitas Vanitatum!* Which of us is happy in this world? Which of us has his desire? or, having it, is satisfied?—Come children, let us shut up the box and the puppets, for our play is played out."

Like the narrator and like the ideal reader demanded by the Showman, Dobbin, the man of feeling, must remain a spectator at the perpetual fair of vanities. The man with the horselike name is a Houyhnhnm among the Yahoos. He has lived as an exile during most of the novel; on tasting the fruits enjoyed by others he finds them insufficient. The goal he has maintained so long, Amelia, proves a mere illusion. Though resigned to his present, Dobbin finds comfort in his observation of the past and his trust in a better future. He writes his 'History of the Punjaub' and also hopes that he may benefit from his past mistakes by making Janey a wiser child than her parents. Like the reader of *Vanity Fair,* this observer of life finds meaning through the act of retrospection. Though the search for happiness proves to be futile, the search itself has not been in vain. As in that other treatise on the vanity of human wishes, Dr. Johnson's *Rasselas,* we are left with a conclusion that is no conclusion. The novel's movement is circular. Time, which both perpetuates and annihilates human vanity, is the protagonist of this novel without a hero.

No work before *Vanity Fair* illustrates so extensively and impressively the passage of time. The very bulk of the panoramic novel allows Thackeray to create the impression of the flow of years. The weight of time affects characters and reader alike, modifying their initial assumptions and threatening their security. Becky destroys Amelia's denial of the past by producing George's faded letter; her bills and letters rupture Rawdon's long-held belief in her innocence. Throughout the novel, time-past mocks the illusions of those who would deny change. Miss Briggs still cherishes the "hectic" love letters of a writing master she flirted with twenty-four years ago. The letters remind the spinster not only of the dead man who could have been hers but also of other dead hopes and expectations. Old Osborne looks at the parcel of letters written by George; young Georgy, in his grandfather's house, sees the initials "G.O." scratched upon a windowpane. The initials are his father's; they establish a link between the failings of Amelia's husband and the potential failings of her son. The recovery of the little piano, the reappearance of Jos' picture, the reemergence of Jos' flowery vests and of the scar on Lord Steyne's forehead help to create a rhythm in which the emphasis is less on the continuity that arises from repetition than it is on the disconnectedness between hope and regret, expectation and disappointment. The narrator wishes that this gap were less apparent; sardonically, he implores men to destroy the record of their onetime feelings:

> Perhaps in Vanity Fair there are no better satires than letters. Take a bundle of your dear friend's of ten years back—your dear friend whom you hate now. Look at a file of your sister's: how you clung to each other till you quarrelled about the twenty pound legacy! Get down the round-hand scrawls of your son who has half broken your heart with selfish undutifulness since; or a parcel of your own, breathing endless ardour and love eternal, which were sent back by your mistress when she married the Nabob—your mistress for whom you now care no more than for Queen Elizabeth. Vows, love, promises, confidences, gratitude, how queerly they read after a while! There ought to be a law in Vanity Fair ordering the destruction of every written document (except receipted tradesmen's bills) after a certain brief and proper interval.
>
> (pp. 79-81)

Change is all in Vanity Fair. The passage of time exposes all human vanity. Although time perpetuates the same aspirations from generation to generation, it also modifies them and ends them. The novel's many death scenes are not due to a mawkish

Victorian fascination with such situations, but rather stem from Thackeray's desire to remind the reader that death, the end of life, is the only true vanquisher of vanity. Osborne, aloof and powerful, and Sedley, low and powerless, die on the same day. Miss Crawley's fortune and the elder Sir Pitt's title change hands after their deaths. Alive, they have used these ornaments as a bait; dead, they are soon forgotten.

Becky and Dobbin, antagonists in so many other ways, can be contrasted in relation to their attitude towards time. Becky always lives in the present; she never permits herself "much useless and unseemly sorrow for the irrevocable past." . . . Her reversals only spur her on—the world is forever before her. Immutable because of her very mutability, she posses a chameleonlike ability to adapt herself to new environs. Jos' fortune renovates her; even her features seem youthful again in Thackeray's last illustration. Dobbin, on the other hand, does age. Though he climbs from Lieutenant to Captain to Major and Colonel, his rise in rank and his father's changed social position are equally irrelevant to him. The civilian who faces Becky with such disgust in the last drawing looks more dignified than the awkward Major Sugarplums depicted earlier. But he also looks wearier, more pained. Becky's experiences have increased her flexibility; Dobbin's experiences have increased his rigidity. The spectator who stands outside Becky's booth is incapable of anchoring his ideals in the ever-shifting bustle of the Fair.

Vanity Fair is primarily a satire. In it, the author of a book on *The Four Georges* tries to laugh at the unheroic age of George IV in the same way that Pope had laughed at the age of George II: "Yes, we saw him. Fate cannot deprive us of *that*. Others have seen Napoleon. Some few still exist who have beheld Frederick the Great, Doctor Johnson, Marie Antoinette, &c.— be it our reasonable boast to our children, that we saw George the Good, the Magnificent, the Great." . . . Yet the irony that Thackeray maintains throughout his masterpiece does not really lead to the purgative laughter of a Swift or Pope. Although, strictly speaking, *Vanity Fair* is neither a religious nor a philosophical work, it raises questions about human existence that are not posed in Trollope's comic world of clergymen. Under the guise of laughter, it laments the external and internal barriers which conspire against freedom and depicts a world of flux in which being is pitted against becoming. Unlike the Brontës, Meredith, George Eliot, or Dickens, Thackeray refuses to impose a moral order on the erratic universe he portrays. Instead, he puts his Amelia doll, Becky puppet, and Dobbin figure back into their box, content to have illustrated the contradictions inherent in human nature. (pp. 81-3)

> U. C. Knoepflmacher, "'Vanity Fair': The Bitterness of Retrospection," in his Laughter & Despair: Readings in Ten Novels of the Victorian Era, *University of California Press, 1971, pp. 50-83.*

BARBARA HARDY (essay date 1972)

[*Hardy provides a detailed discussion of Thackeray's use of the theme of art versus nature in* Vanity Fair. *For additional commentary on* Vanity Fair *by Hardy, see excerpt dated 1972 in NCLC, Vol. 5.*]

One of the major implications of the title and main image of *Vanity Fair* is the corruption of nature by greed, deceit and art. Thackeray approves of honesty, sincerity and spontaneity, and criticizes posing and artifice. The critical emphasis varies, falling on heartlessness or hypocrisy or exhibitionism or artful manipulation, and sometimes on all four simultaneously. Everyone knows that the chief performance in *Vanity Fair* is that given by 'the famous little Becky puppet', as Thackeray describes her in the preliminary address, "Before the Curtain" [see essay dated 1848]. At the very beginning of her performance, in Chapter I, "Chiswick Mall", Thackeray does not show Becky's accomplishments as artist, actress and performer, but rather establishes the environment in which performance becomes necessary. He begins his novel with a critique of Becky's environment which certainly goes far to create and explain her histrionic ways: it shows a hierarchy of power, a pecking-order in which Becky is as yet only finding her way, and it very clearly reveals the incompatibility of success— defined as money and power—with nature, heart, sincerity or love. As yet, Becky is only a novice and learner, as befits a character who is on the brink of leaving school. Her performance has scarcely begun, but Thackeray's analysis of performance is already complex.

The school itself is one of those totally assimilated social symbols which exist in full and self-contained particularity in Thackeray's satiric world: schooling, learning, achievement, testimonials, teaching, finishing the course, are metaphors as well as realities, but Thackeray uses the ready-made social symbol very quietly. It is his great gift, here and elsewhere, to work through a plenitude of such unobtrusively significant action, and not only each detail of pedagogy, teaching and learning, but every single aspect of the scene, events and characters, in this first chapter, is morally expressive.

One key to the theme of art and nature is given in the first image, which contrasts the undignified with the dignified. It does so in a way which draws our attention to the narrow formality of the institution which Becky and Amelia are about to leave for the wide world. The fat horses and the fat coachman, the bandy-legged servant and the red nose of Miss Jemima Pinkerton represent the vivid, undignified informal world, while 'the great iron gate of Miss Pinkerton's academy for young ladies' represents dignity and enclosure. The contrast becomes plainer in the first piece of dialogue between Miss Pinkerton and her sister Miss Jemima, who are a contrasting pair in a novel largely organized on the principle of contrast and duality. The contrast emerges as one of style and sensibility, directing our attention to Miss Jemima's natural, informal, good-hearted, outer-directed attention and the formality and arrangement of Miss Pinkerton's artifice:

> 'It is Mrs Sedley's coach, sister,' said Miss Jemima. 'Sambo, the black servant, has just rung the bell; and the coachman has a new red waistcoat.'
>
> 'Have you completed all the necessary preparations incident to Miss Sedley's departure, Miss Jemima?' asked Miss Pinkerton herself. . . .

(pp. 50-1)

Miss Jemima speaks loosely, but has her eye on the colours and particulars of the world outside. Her concreteness is indeed characteristic of Thackeray's descriptions, and throughout the novel his eye is fixed on the solidity and detail of persons, clothing and objects; his presentation of Amelia and Becky, for instance, is marked by this precision, of action and colour. Here, the concreteness makes Miss Jemima interesting, while her sister is less attractive in her dryness and abstraction of style. The Johnsonian lady, Miss Pinkerton, speaks in the grand style; she is presented appropriately by Thackeray in polysyl-

labic, allusive and high-piled grandeur, as he sets the linguistic tone for the ensuing dialogue: 'Miss Pinkerton herself, that majestic lady; the Semiramis of Hammersmith, the friend of Dr Johnson, the correspondent of Mrs Chapone herself.' His grand style acts as a faint burlesque, not pushing its effects, but maintaining grandeur of vocabulary and syntax. The contrast between the sisters becomes explicit when Miss Jemima uses the old word 'bowpot' and is told to say 'bouquet' as more genteel, doing her best in the compromise of 'booky', which is followed up by the big-hearted but undignified simile, 'as big almost as a haystack'. The sisters' styles draw attention to the formality and pedantry of the one and the clumsy and casual artlessness of the other; and throughout Thackeray works in circumlocutions, like 'autograph letter' or 'billet', and in typically Johnsonian figures of sentiments and negation, parallelism and more periodic elaboration, all shown paradigmatically in this model letter:

> MADAM,—After her six years' residence at the Mall, I have the honour and happiness of presenting Miss Amelia Sedley to her parents, as a young lady not unworthy to occupy a fitting position in their polished and refined circle. Those virtues which characterise the young English gentlewoman, those accomplishments which become her birth and station, will not be found wanting in the amiable Miss Sedley, whose *industry* and *obedience* have endeared her to her instructors, and whose delightful sweetness of temper has charmed her *aged* and her *youthful* companions.
>
> In music, in dancing, in orthography, in every variety of embroidery and needle-work, she will be found to have realised her friends' *fondest wishes.* In geography there is still much to be desired; and a careful and undeviating use of the backboard, for four hours daily during the next three years, is recommended as necessary to the acquirement of that dignified *deportment* and *carriage,* so requisite for every young lady of *fashion.*

(pp. 52-3)

What is said is as important as how it is said, but style and value are related. Miss Pinkerton's careful and pedantic 'For whom is this, Miss Jemima?' is answered by the artless and warm-hearted 'For Becky Sharp: she's going too', which undermines the style and the very insistence of Miss Pinkerton's question. Thackeray works through dialogue and through the surrounding narration and description. The humanity of Miss Jemima's unpedantic, unpremeditated natural style matches her spontaneous show of sensibility: she trembles, blushes all over 'her withered face and neck', and her sensibility shows itself in her wasted imaginative identification with Becky, 'it's only two and ninepence and poor Becky will be miserable if she don't get one'. Miss Jemima, like Briggs later on, is much too simple-minded to criticize the grand and acquisitive cold-heartedness around her, but her criticism is implicit in the language and feelings. Predatory Miss Pinkerton is coldly, self-interestedly and manipulatively in control, in giving, speaking, teaching and writing; Miss Jemima is vulgar, loving, giving, artlessly betrayed by feeling and undignified in action and speech, trotting off, ungrandly, 'exceedingly flurried and nervous'. Miss Pinkerton's condolence is a public event: '. . . Once, when poor Miss Birch died of the scarlet fever, was Miss

A facsimile of a page from the manuscript of Vanity Fair.

Pinkerton known to write personally to the parents of her pupils; and it was Jemima's opinion that if anything *could* console Mrs Birch for her daughter's loss, it would be that pious and eloquent composition in which Miss Pinkerton announced the event.'

From the beginning, therefore, Thackeray establishes a contrast between formal showing-off and lack of heart, loving generosity and lack of style. He also establishes, from the beginning, a sense of social hierarchy and power-structure, not unrelated to the style and capacity for feeling. Those who are at the top, in Vanity Fair, get there by art, not heart. The linguistic and moral contrast between the 'superior' and the 'inferior' sister is followed by the contrast between two other ladies in the hierarchy, Becky and Amelia: 'Miss Sedley's papa was a merchant in London, and a man of some wealth; whereas Miss Sharp was an articled pupil, for whom Miss Pinkerton had done, as she thought, quite enough, without conferring upon her at parting the high honour of the Dixonary.' The psychological pecking-order can override the social, as Thackeray demonstrates in the little passage in which Becky makes her 'adieux' in fluent French, unintelligible to Miss Pinkerton, thus inflicting a stylistic victory, appropriately enough, over the Johnsonian mode. This victory is accompanied by a flouting gesture, as Becky refuses to accept one of Miss Pinkerton's fingers: 'In fact, it was a little battle between the young lady and the old one, and the latter was worsted.' One could describe the whole action of the novel in such military terms, and Thackeray uses them freely; he is well aware of ironic parallels between his story and history, and also of the 'unheroic' ap-

propriation of military or heroic terms to everyday strife. In his novels, these skirmishes are fought with social weapons—with words, sentences, wit, foreign languages, gestures, rituals, refusal of ritual, clothes, presents. Thackeray does more than show Becky as victorious, her strength of personality, intelligence, and learning prevailing over her low place in the social order. He creates a contrast between failure and success in artifice and ritual. Miss Pinkerton makes her ridiculous, elaborate gesture, 'she waved one hand, both by way of adieu, and to give Miss Sharp an opportunity of shaking one of the fingers of the hand which was left out for that purpose', and Becky nonchalantly rejects it. Becky's very last gesture, however, is not an act of social aggression against the style of the Hammersmith Semiramis, but a rejection of poor loving style-less Jemima. The throwing of the dictionary is of course a marvellous rejection of style—Johnson, the institution, order, dignity and pretence—but it is not a simple revolutionary gesture which we can applaud. As so often, Becky is on the wrong side, attacking the Establishment only because she is jealous of its advantages. Our sympathies are carefully withdrawn from her as she throws back what is not only a symbol of 'corrupt' style, but a loving present. Miss Jemima's very last speech and action are typically artless, broken and stammered, and her last generous, if silly, act, is accompanied by the words, 'God bless you!' Becky, like Scrooge, rejects a blessing. The rejection marks her entry into the great world.

Thackeray's last sentences emphasize the contrast between the world of school and the great world, as the gates close; he says, formally, 'and so, farewell to Chiswick Mall'. The brilliant close-up of this first scene has established style and theme, the style and theme of nature and art.

There are certain characters in this chapter I have not mentioned, and they too are involved in style and theme. They are the author and his readers, real and imaginary. Before the curtain rises, in ''Before the Curtain'', Thackeray has presented himself as the Manager of the Performance; he has begun to develop the histrionic significance, as well as the vanity and commerce of Vanity Fair; he has admitted that he is in it for money, and is not without charlatanry: amongst the crowd he singles out 'quacks (*other* quacks, plague take them!)'. The author is, from the beginning, involved in the business of art and acting. As we know, Thackeray originally intended to call the novel 'A Novel without a Hero' and to develop the theme of unheroic drama, rather than that of Vanity Fair. Although there are divergent emphases, the two themes very plainly overlap, and in Thackeray's claim to the unheroic, he uses the convention of the self-conscious artist to make a certain claim for realism. A certain claim: implicit in his insistence that this is art, that these are puppets, that this is illusion and performance, that it is a book, written for money by an author, and read by various readers, is the claim that it is closer to life and nature than some forms of art. The self-conscious claim to realism is made in the description of Amelia's undignified, unheroinelike beauty and sensibility. Another complex claim for heart as against art, it ends with a disarming address to a Reader, Jones, whose taste is 'for the great and heroic in life and novels' and who will underline the author's 'foolish, twaddling, etc.', and add *quite true*. But Jones is critically presented as a worldling, reading at his club, and 'rather flushed with his joint of mutton and half-pint of wine', and it seems likely that Thackeray uses him in order to further the claim for simple, unworldly heroines and passions. He does as much as he can to claim that his novel, though a work of art, has a heart, and not simply by making jokes about the wrong kind of heartless, art-seeking (but wine-flushed) reader like Jones, but by deliberately drawing attention to his own sentimentality. Amelia has a heart, cries over silly novels, and dead pets, and attracts heart: in yet another qualification of the pecking-order, even Semiramis gives orders that Amelia should be treated gently, and when Amelia goes she is surrounded by loving, giving, weeping friends. Indeed, Becky is not entirely the victim of the class hierarchy, since Amelia's friends are seen to love her for herself ('kindly, smiling, tender, gentle, generous heart') and perhaps even Miss Pinkerton is not sensitive to her wholly because of her father's income. Though Becky is made to claim, in Chapter 2, ''In Which Miss Sharp and Miss Sedley Prepare to Open the Campaign'', that Amelia was her only friend, we shall, in retrospect, blame that on Becky's heartlessness rather than on the social hierarchy of the school. Jones's rejection of Amelia is made to be a rejection of sentimentality, and Thackeray lays claim to the sentimental as an index of sensibility: she cries over dead pets, lost friends, and even silly novels. Thackeray makes it awkward for us by linking the three so that we cannot be as selective in our emotional snobbishness as we should like.

Amelia is, as a character and a woman, deliberately sentimental: that is, she is meant to be the sentimental heroine of an unsentimental novel, illustrating the complexity of the heart's excesses. We shall begin by loving her and feeling with her, in her friendship, love, grief, maternal affection, but we shall eventually learn the limitations of sensibility uncontrolled by reason: she will worship her unworthy husband, alive and dead, spoil her son, and make sentimental demands on Dobbin, her patient lover. The very first chapter prepares us for this aspect of Thackeray's criticism, his refusal to accept unqualified sensibility as a moral norm. Heart like this can be linked with silliness and excess: it is all very well to cry for dead birds but not for silly novels. But the qualification of heart is less conspicuous, at first, than the qualification of art. Only in the misplaced loving gift of Miss Jemima, the rejected dictionary, do we see our first clear instance of sentimentality; it is punished rudely by its exact opposite, hard-heartedness, which also earns its first clear criticism when, biting the hand that feeds, it throws back the dictionary at the silly affectionate old woman. The reader is involved even with her rejection, because Thackeray tells us, drily, that she is not going to appear again:

> ... Miss Jemima had already whimpered several times at the idea of Amelia's departure; and, but for fear of her sister, would have gone off in downright hysterics, like the heiress (who paid double) of St Kitt's. Such luxury of grief, however, is only allowed to parlour-boarders. Honest Jemima had all the bills, and the washing, and the mending, and the puddings, and the plate and crockery, and the servants to superintend. But why speak about her? It is probable that we shall not hear of her again from this moment to the end of time, and that when the great filigree iron gates are once closed on her, she and her awful sister will never issue therefrom into this little world of history.
>
> (pp. 53-7)

What does this rather odd passage mean? That there are heroines even less heroic than Amelia, who is, once this passage has urged us to reflect, more of a heroine than Miss Jemima? Thackeray seems to mean what he says in the sentence 'Such luxury of grief, however, is only allowed to parlour-boarders'. In a novel which is about the luxury of grief, Thackeray reminds us, in the dismissal of Jemima, of the circumstances that permit grief, in and out of novels. He also claims for his novel a high degree of realism; though it is interesting to distinguish his claim from George Eliot's in the totally tolerant *Adam Bede*, where Lizbeth Bede *is* permitted her 'luxury of grief'. At the same time, he draws our attention to the social interest of his emotional theme: if people like Amelia dwell on grief, devote themselves to worship of dead husband and living son, it is as a luxury. Thus he makes another qualification of heart: sensitivity, as well as art, depends on position and possessions. Thackeray's initial creation of category is uncomfortably blurred. On the one hand we have Miss Pinkerton, the Johnsonian style, the great filigree iron gates, Jones, with his contempt for sentiment, and Becky, able to put down the grand style with fluent French. On the other hand, Amelia, all tolerant and sentimental readers, and Jemima, loving, giving, artless. Between the two worlds, the rejection of the dictionary; yet, beside it, Jemima's blessing and the two-edged admission that Jemima is not promising material for Thackeray's novel.

The realistic effects of the self-conscious reference should be stressed here. Thackeray insists on the illusion, the art, the performance, the drama, the novel, but in such a way—dismissing a character who is not qualified to be a character—that brings the novel very close indeed to life. There are some unpromising materials, he says, that will not come in; and the very mention reminds us of the novelist's selection from life, in a way that is moving and evaluative. At the extreme of art is Thackeray himself; at the extreme of heart is Jemima, who will be left out. The reader is made wary, and perhaps, as Thackeray wished, uncomfortable. If he is attentive, he will not reject Jones, Amelia, Miss Pinkerton or Johnson's dictionary too precipitately.

This first formal and framing scene in Chapter I of **Vanity Fair** makes plain the heroines' initiation into the great world, and the reader's initiation into the world of the novel. In Chapter 8, Thackeray draws our attention, first by direct dramatic presentation, then by complex authorial commentary, to certain crucial differences between Becky's art and his own. In the chapters that bridge the initiation and the very explicit analysis, we have seen Becky beginning her career as an artist in life. She does, in fact, possess some positive artistic talents, chiefly displayed in her entertaining and persuasive performances of miming and singing. In Chapter 8, Thackeray adds a new artistic achievement, epistolary and literary. Becky's letter to Amelia probably takes a glance at epistolary fiction in its feminine effusiveness and self-pity, and its very lack of resemblance to the situations of Pamela and Clarissa. But the chief purpose, as I see it, is to bridge Becky's artistic forte, which is dramatic, and Thackeray's, which is literary.

Becky is given the whole narrative burden, for the space of her letter, of introducing the reader to a new place and several new characters. She is a quite convenient surrogate for Thackeray, being, like him, sharply attentive, witty and satirical, but she is of course not simply a surrogate, and her letter also shows the Becky Sharp traits of false sensibility and predatoriness. Her letters are usually written to get something, directly or indirectly, and this letter is clearly designed to keep a tenuous hook on the Sedleys—'Is your poor brother recovered of his rack-punch?'—and even Amelia, who may be good for another India muslin or pink silk in the future. But the cast-off dresses are still fresh (see Chapter 11 for the hint about their replacements) and Thackeray is free to develop Becky's literary gifts.

Throughout the novel, her letters are important in the furthering of the action and the development of her character. There is the unsuccessful letter dictated to Rawdon and addressed to Miss Crawley, which does not take in the old lady for a minute, since Becky has thought of using short sentences but not of mis-spelling. Moreover, the letter is fatally amusing, and Miss Crawley detects Becky's fundamental style, as well as appreciating it and asking for more. There is the more crucial letter written to Rawdon in the sponging-house, designed to put him off affectionately and humorously, but unable to hide her exhibitionism and self-interest. Its crude ingratiation does not take in Rawdon, who also detects her fundamental style, failing to be amused by Becky's jokes, and disliking them for the first time. But the first letter, in Chapter 8, is a more disengaged venture. It introduces the reader to King's Crawley and to some new and important characters. It is a superb stroke of art, totally and variously eloquent. The very title of the chapter, "Private and Confidential", is expressive of the epistolary gossip of bosom-friends and its frank-mark, "Free.-Pitt Crawley", is informative and ironic—who pays and for what, or who does not pay, is always of interest in Thackeray.

My Dearest, Sweetest Amelia,

With what mingled joy and sorrow do I take up the pen to write to my dearest friend! Oh, what a change between to-day and yesterday! *Now* I am friendless and alone; yesterday I was at home, in the sweet company of a sister, whom I shall ever, *ever* cherish!

I will not tell you in what tears and sadness I passed the fatal night in which I separated from you. *You* went on Tuesday to joy and happiness, with your mother and *your devoted young soldier* by your side; and I thought of you all night, dancing at Perkins's, the prettiest, I am sure, of all the young ladies at the Ball. I was brought by the groom in the old carriage to Sir Pitt Crawley's town house, where, after John the groom had behaved most rudely and insolently to me (alas! 'twas safe to insult poverty and misfortune!), I was given over to Sir P's care, and made to pass the night in an old gloomy bed, and by the side of a horrid gloomy old charwoman, who keeps the house. I did not sleep one single wink the whole night.

Sir Pitt is not what we silly girls, when we used to read Cecilia at Chiswick, imagined a baronet must have been. Anything, indeed, less like Lord Orville cannot be imagined. Fancy an old, stumpy, short, vulgar, and very dirty man, in old clothes and shabby old gaiters, who smokes a horrid pipe, and cooks his own horrid supper in a saucepan. He speaks with a country accent, and swore a great deal at the old charwoman, at the hackney coachman who drove us to the inn where the coach went from, and on which I made the journey *outside for the greater part of the way.* . . .

Half an hour after our arrival, the great dinner-bell was rung, and I came down with my two pupils (they are very thin and insignificant little chits of ten and eight years old). I came down in your *dear* muslin gown (about which that odious Mrs Pinner was so rude, because you gave it me); for I am to be treated as one of the family, except on company days, when the young ladies and I are to dine up-stairs.

Well, the great dinner-bell rang, and we all assembled in the little drawing-room where my Lady Crawley sits. She is the second Lady Crawley, and mother of the young ladies. She was an ironmonger's daughter, and her marriage was thought a great match. She looks as if she had been handsome once, and her eyes are always weeping for the loss of her beauty. She is pale and meagre, and high-shouldered; and has not a word to say for herself, evidently. Her step-son, Mr Crawley, was likewise in the room. He was in full dress, as pompous as an undertaker. He is pale, thin, ugly, silent; he has thin legs, no chest, hay-coloured whiskers, and straw-coloured hair. . . .

A hundred thousand grateful loves to your dear papa and mamma! Is your poor brother recovered of his rack-punch? Oh, dear! Oh, dear! How men should beware of wicked punch!

Ever and ever thine own,

Rebecca

The first thing we notice is the conventional satire on female sensibility. The strongest impression is that of exaggeration and falsity: 'My Dearest, Sweetest Amelia'; or 'With what mingled joy and sorrow do I take up the pen to write to my dearest friend! . . . Now I am friendless and alone. . . .' But these initial emotions of indulgence, envy and self-pity soon give way to the sheer verve of narrative and presentation of character. Thackeray does something simple but clever with Becky's narration; he allows it to overlap slightly with his own narrative in Chapter 10, so that we see a slight discrepancy between what has happened and what Becky presents as happening. Nothing very marked; just a little evidence that Becky is a liar: the detail that she has not slept a wink (when the author has said that she does) and the omission of her attempt to pump the old charwoman with whom she shares a bed. She presents herself as the heroine of a Gothic novel rather than a resilient, unfastidious and predatory opportunist. But what is most striking is the wit and humour of Becky's narrative, achieved at the expense of the characters in her story. The girls are 'very thin and insignificant little chits of ten and eight years old'. Lady Crawley 'looks as if she had been handsome once, and her eyes are always weeping for the loss of her beauty'. Pitt Crawley is 'pompous as an undertaker . . . pale, thin, ugly, silent; he has thin legs, no chest, hay-coloured whiskers, and straw-coloured hair'. Sir Pitt is exposed by his 'dumpy little legs' and rustic accent. The butler is laughed at for his ludicrous French pronunciation (Becky's pride in her French is one of her humourless weaknesses), and Miss Horrocks, described as 'very much over-dressed', flings Becky a look of scorn as 'she plumped down on her knees'.

Such strokes of wit and ridicule may be enjoyed for their own sake, and our critical spirit may be held in check until Thackeray himself stands back to analyse the letter. The contrast between the maidenly gush and the hard-hitting satire is probably clear, but we do not feel strongly critical until Thackeray drily observes that we should. For although he has been using Becky as a narrator, the narration is itself material for satire. It is satire proffered for the reader's enjoyment, then analysed by the satirist.

> Everything considered, I think it is quite as well for our dear Amelia Sedley, in Russell Square, that Miss Sharp and she are parted. Rebecca is a droll funny creature, to be sure; and those descriptions of the poor lady weeping for the loss of her beauty, and the gentleman 'with hay-coloured whiskers and straw-coloured hair', are very smart, doubtless, and show a great knowledge of the world. That she might, when on her knees, have been thinking of something better than Miss Horrocks's ribbons, has possibly struck both of us. But my kind reader will please to remember, that this history has 'Vanity Fair' for a title, and that Vanity Fair is a very vain, wicked, foolish place, full of all sorts of humbugs and falsenesses and pretensions. And while the moralist, who is holding forth on the cover (an accurate portrait of your humble servant), professes to wear neither gown nor bands, but only the very same long-eared livery in which his congregation is arrayed: yet, look you, one is bound to speak the truth as far as one knows it, whether one mounts a cap and bells or a shovel-hat; and a deal of dis-

agreeable matter must come out in the course of such an undertaking.

(pp. 58-63)

This first ironic combination of criticism and defence is Thackeray at his most subtle and disconcerting: we cannot know what he is saying in this first paragraph which neatly balances indictment with justification, and relates Becky to her author. But what does he mean by speaking the truth? Does he refer to his own exposure of Becky? Or does he also include her exposure of the vanity and foolishness of Lady Crawley, Pitt and Miss Horrocks, who are all easily and accurately describable as vain and foolish, 'full of all sorts of humbugs and falsenesses and pretensions'.

Another contrast and symmetrical figure follow: the story of a preacher—a Neapolitan story-teller—who worked himself up into such a 'rage and passion' against 'some of the villains whose wicked deeds he was describing and inventing that the audience could not resist it'. The result of the story-teller's fervour was a good profit: 'the hat went round, and the bajocchi tumbled into it, in the midst of a perfect storm of sympathy'. This anecdote is balanced against that of the Parisian actors who refuse to play villains and prefer to play virtuous characters for a lower payment. He observes: 'I set these two stories one against the other, so that you may see that it is not from mere mercenary motives that the present performer is desirous to show up and trounce his villains; but because he has a sincere hatred of them, which he cannot keep down, and which must find a vent in suitable abuse and bad language.' Not a simple antithesis, it needs careful analysis before we finally conclude that Thackeray is admitting his own lack of pure motivation. After all, he is a performer who gains from the performance, an author earning his living with this serial (later a book) which is paid for by the reader. Thackeray is distinguishing between his satiric stance and Becky's; he is telling us clearly that though a critic, she is subjected to the author's criticism as 'one who has no reverence except for prosperity, and no eye for anything beyond success. Such people there are living and flourishing in the world—Faithless, Hopeless, Charityless; let us have at them, dear friends, with might and main'.

This disclosure criticizes and clarifies Becky's wit and ridicule. While admitting that Thackeray writes for gain, it claims that his satiric mode derives from Faith, Hope and Charity. It invokes lofty and noble moral purpose: he is mercenary but not 'merely' mercenary. If we then look at Thackeray's irony, scorn, wit and ridicule, we see that his satire is not cynical; rather it derives from Hope and Faith in the possibilities of human nature, and has Charity. Thackeray is a master of timing and placing, and follows this criticism of Becky's immoral and eclectic satire and wit by a conspicuously charitable and serious satiric piece in the next chapter. Another instance of symmetry and juxtaposition, it is also an instance of Thackeray's explicitness and clarity. Uncomfortable though he may be as a satirist constantly involving the reader in the satire, he takes no chances with misunderstanding. He is writing a novel about the corruption of nature, and this corruption shows itself here, in Becky, performance, wit and satire. However, as an artist sharing the actions of performance, wit and satire, he is constrained to distinguish between right and wrong wit, right and wrong satire. The distinctions involve an art which has a heart—Hope, Faith, Charity—and an art which is heartless, 'no reverence for anything except for prosperity'. At the same time, he is aware and forced to admit that he is involved in profiting too. The character and the author are fully compared and contrasted. This is extremely rare in English fiction, apart from the earlier and influential case of Fielding who presented, in *Tom Jones,* antithetical images of his own desire for lofty Fame and worldly prosperity—what Thackeray, memorably recalling Fielding's invocation of roast beef, calls 'a little of the Sunday side'.

Chapter 8, then, exposes Becky as a heartless artist practising Thackeray's arts, and implies that Thackeray is more honourable than Becky. Chapter 9 follows with a demonstration, taking a revised look at those characters analysed so heartlessly and artfully by Becky. Sir Pitt, Lady Crawley and Mr Pitt Crawley are all presented afresh, with wit and satire, and with sympathy and charity. Sir Pitt, for whom admittedly little can be said, is shown as first marrying 'under the auspices of his parents', then marrying to please himself. There is feeling in 'He had his pretty Rose, and what more need a man require than to please himself?' What follows is inside information, not mere brilliant superficial wit, and it is much more devastating than Becky's exposure: 'So he used to get drunk every night: to beat his pretty Rose sometimes: to leave her in Hampshire when he went to London for the parliamentary session, without a single friend in the whole world.' An extremely charitable account of pretty Rose herself follows, together with a glance at her limitations and losses: '. . . she had no sort of character, nor talents, nor opinions, nor occupations, nor amusements, nor that vigour of soul and ferocity of temper which often falls to the lot of entirely foolish women. . . . O Vanity Fair—Vanity Fair! This might have been, but for you, a cheery lass:—Peter Butt and Rose, a happy man and wife'.

There is a dignified and sympathetic account of Pitt, his respect for his mother-in-law, his kindness, and then—just in case we were beginning to identify Thackeray's manner of satiric analysis with charity and imagination—a devastating account of his mediocrity, industry and lack of self-knowledge. Thackeray's own wit is disarmingly produced when least expected, as we nod over his ability to see the humanity of these characters with heart and generosity; it is harder than anything achieved by Becky's rather visual ridicule: '. . . yet he failed somehow, in spite of a mediocrity which ought to have insured any man a success. He did not even get the prize poem, which all his friends said he was sure of'. Thackeray is very deliberate in his revision of Becky's satire, even to the extent of commenting when he agrees with her: 'Miss Sharp's accounts of his employment at Queen's Crawley were not caricatures. He subjected the servants there to the devotional exercises before mentioned, in which (and so much the better) he brought his father to join.' The parentheses of course mark, once more, the comment Becky would not be capable of making.

Thackeray's expansion and revision has one last effect. He has a capacity for moral and social diagnosis and generalization which Becky, at least at this stage in her education, utterly lacks. She sees, at school and out of it, how she is at an unfair disadvantage because of her birth and poverty; but later, when she makes the celebrated suggestion that she could be a good woman on five thousand a year, she does not see into the heartlessness of Vanity Fair, having insufficient heart and vision for the enterprise. Her social criticism, even when generalized, is shallow. Thackeray, having like Becky observed Sir Pitt's drunkenness and illiteracy, though more seriously and less amusedly, also sees the criticism of society involved in marking the defects of this dignitary. Becky finds Sir Pitt funny; 'Anything, indeed, less like Lord Orville cannot be imagined,' she comments, in her literary and hypocritically fastidious way. Thackeray replaces this with a moral fervour:

A drawing by Thackeray in a copy of Vanity Fair *he presented to Lady Normanby.*

Vanity Fair—Vanity Fair! Here was a man, who could not spell, and did not care to read—who had the habits and the cunning of a boor: whose aim in life was pettifogging: who never had a taste, or emotion, or enjoyment, but what was sordid and foul; and yet he had rank, and honours, and power, somehow: and was a dignitary of the land, and a pillar of the state. He was high sheriff, and rode in a golden coach. Great ministers and statesmen courted him; and in Vanity Fair he had a higher place than the most brilliant genius or spotless virtue.

(pp. 63-7)

At one stroke, Thackeray candidly admits his own involvement; he makes explicit and dramatic the seriousness, profundity and passion of his satire. Avoiding a simple division of intellect or feeling into art and nature, he creates an art which is as close to nature, and as inclusive and serious, as possible. He also suggests, craftily and dramatically, that social criticism is his aim. (p. 67)

> *Barbara Hardy, in her* The Exposure of Luxury: Radical Themes in Thackeray, *Peter Owen Limited, London, 1972, 190 p.*

WOLFGANG ISER (essay date 1972)

[*Iser discusses the narrative techniques employed by Thackeray in* Vanity Fair *and their effect upon the relationship between the reader, narrator, and characters. Iser's study was originally published in German in 1972.*]

The author-reader relationship, which was . . . developed by the eighteenth-century novel, has remained a constant feature of narrative prose and is still in evidence even when the author seems to have disappeared and the reader is deliberately excluded from comprehension. While Fielding offers this reassurance to his readers: "I am, indeed, set over them for their own good only, and was created for their use, and not they for mine," Joyce, at the other end of the scale drops only the ironic information that the author has withdrawn behind his work, "paring his fingernails." The reader of modern novels is deprived of the assistance which the eighteenth-century writer had given him in a variety of devices ranging from earnest exhortation to satire and irony. Instead, he is expected to strive for himself to unravel the mysteries of a sometimes strikingly obscure composition. This development reflects the transformation of the very idea of literature, which seems to have ceased to be a means of relaxation and even luxury, making demands now on the capacity of understanding because the world presented seems to have no bearing on what the reader is familiar with. This change did not happen suddenly. The stages of transition are clearly discernible in the nineteenth century, and one of them is virtually a half-way point in the development: the so-called 'realistic' novel. An outstanding example of this is Thackeray's *Vanity Fair*. Here, the author-reader relationship is as different from the eighteenth-century 'dialogue' as it is from the twentieth-century demand that the reader find for himself the key to a many-sided puzzle. In Thackeray, the reader does have to make his own discoveries, but the author provides him with unmistakable clues to guide him in his search.

The first stage in our discussion must be to modify the term 'author'. We should distinguish, as Wayne Booth does in his *Rhetoric of Fiction,* between the man who writes the book (author), the man whose attitudes shape the book (implied author), and the man who communicates directly with the reader (narrator): "The 'implied author' chooses, consciously or unconsciously, what we read; . . . he is the sum of his own choices. . . . This implied author is always distinct from the 'real man'—whatever we may take him to be—who creates a superior version of himself, a 'second self', as he creates his work." The narrator, of course, is not always to be identified with the implied author.

In the novels of the nineteenth century it happens again and again that the narrator moves even further and further away from the implied author by virtue of being an actual character in the story itself. Traces of this kind of narrator are already apparent in Dickens's novels, and in Thackeray's *Vanity Fair* he is a complete character in his own right. It is almost as if the implied author, who devised the story, has to bow to the narrator, who has a deeper insight into all the situations. What the implied author describes is interpreted by the narrator to a degree far beyond what one might normally deduce from the events. One is bound to ask the purpose of this clear though sometimes complex separation between narration and commentary, especially in a 'realistic' novel which is supposed to represent reality as it is. The justification lies in the fact that even a realistic novel cannot encompass total reality. As Arnold Bennett once remarked: "You can't put the whole of a character into a book." If the limitations of the novel are such that one cannot reveal a complete character, it is even more impossible to try to transcribe complete reality. And so even a novel that is called realistic can present no more than particular aspects of a given reality, although the selection must remain implicit in order to cloak the author's ideology.

Thackeray's *Vanity Fair* is also governed by this principle, which is clearly reflected by the different titles of the original

version and the final one. The first, consisting of eight chapters, was called "Pen and Pencil Sketches of English Society," indicating that the reality described was meant primarily as a reproduction of social situations; the final version, "Vanity Fair," is concerned less with depicting social situations than with offering a judgment of them. This quality is commented on by Thackeray himself in a letter written a few years after the publication of *Vanity Fair:* ". . . the Art of Novels *is* . . . to convey as strongly as possible the sentiment of reality—in a tragedy or a poem or a lofty drama you aim at producing different emotions; the figures moving, and their words sounding, heroically." "Sentiment of reality" implies that the novel does not represent reality itself, but aims rather at producing an idea of how reality can be experienced. Thus *Vanity Fair* not only offers a panorama of contemporary reality but also reveals the way in which the abundance of details has been organized, so that the reader can participate in the organization of events and thus gain the "sentiment of reality." This is the reason why the novel continues to be effective even today, though the social conditions it describes are only of historical interest. If the past has been kept alive, this is primarily due to the structural pattern through which the events are conveyed to the reader: the effect is gained by the interplay between the implied author who arranges the events, and the narrator who comments on them. The reader can only gain real access to the social reality presented by the implied author, when he follows the adjustments of perspective made by the narrator in viewing the events described. In order to ensure that the reader participates in the way desired, the narrator is set up as a kind of authority between him and the events, conveying the impression that understanding can only be achieved through this medium. In the course of the action, the narrator takes on various guises in order to appear as a fully developed character and in order to control the distance from which the reader has to view the scenes unfolded before him.

At the start of the novel, the narrator introduces himself as "Manager of the Performance" [see essay by Thackeray dated 1848], and gives an outline of what the audience is to expect. The ideal visitor to 'Vanity Fair' is described as a "man with a reflective turn of mind"; this is an advance indication of what the reader has to accomplish, if he is to realize the meaning of the proceedings. But at the same time, the Manager promises that he has something for everyone: "Some people consider Fairs immoral altogether, and eschew such, with their servants and families: very likely they are right. But persons who think otherwise, and are of a lazy, or a benevolent, or a sarcastic mood, may perhaps like to step in for half an hour, and look at the performances. There are scenes of all sorts: some dreadful combats, some grand and lofty horse-riding, some scenes of high life, and some of very middling indeed; some love-making for the sentimental, and some light comic business." In this way the Manager tries to entice all different types of visitors to enter his Fair—bearing in mind the fact that such a visit will also have its after-effects. When the reader has been following the narrator for quite some time, he is informed: "This, dear friends and companions, is my amiable object—to walk with you through the Fair, to examine the shops and the shows there; and that we should all come home after the flare, and the noise, and the gaiety, and be perfectly miserable in private." But the reader will only feel miserable after walking through the Fair if, unexpectedly, he has come upon himself in some of the situations, thereby having his attention drawn to his own behavior, which has shone out at him from the mirror of possibilities. The narrator is only pretending to help the reader—in reality he is goading him. His reliability is already reduced by the fact that he is continually donning new masks: at one moment he is an observer of the Fair, like the reader; then he is suddenly blessed with extraordinary knowledge, though he can explain ironically that "novelists have the privilege of knowing everything"; and then, toward the end, he announces that the whole story was not his own at all, but that he overheard it in a conversation. At the beginning of the novel the narrator is presented as Manager of the Performance, and at the end he presents himself as the reporter of a story which fell into his hands purely by chance. The further away he stands from the social reality depicted, the clearer is the outline of the part he is meant to play. But the reader can only view the social panorama in the constantly shifting perspectives which are opened up for him by this Protean narrator. Although he cannot help following the views and interpretations of the narrator, it is essential for him to understand the motivations behind this constant changing of viewpoints, because only the discovery of the motivations can lead to the comprehension of what is intended. Thus the narrator regulates the distance between reader and events, and in doing so brings about the esthetic effect of the story. The reader is given only as much information as will keep him oriented and interested, but the narrator deliberately leaves open the inferences that are to be drawn from this information. Consequently, empty spaces are bound to occur, spurring the reader's imagination to detect the assumption which might have motivated the narrator's attitude. In this way, we get involved because we react to the viewpoints advanced by the narrator. If the narrator is an independent character, clearly separated from the inventor of the story, the tale of the social aspirations of the two girls Becky and Amelia takes on a greater degree of objectivity, and indeed one gains the impression that this social reality is not a mere narration but actually exists. The narrator can then be regarded as a sort of mediator between the reader and the events, with the implication that it is only through him that the social reality can be rendered communicable in the first place.

The narrator's strategy can be seen even more clearly in his relations with the characters in the novel and with the reader's expectations. *Vanity Fair* has as the subtitle, *A Novel without a Hero,* which indicates that the characters are not regarded as representing an ideal, exemplary form of human conduct, as established by the conventions of the eighteenth-century novel. Instead, the reader's interest is divided between two figures who, despite the contrast in their behavior, can under no circumstances be regarded as complementary or even corrective. For Becky, no price is too high for the fulfillment of her social ambitions; her friend Amelia is simple and sentimental. And so right at the beginning we are told:

> As she is not a heroine, there is no need to describe her person; indeed I am afraid that her nose was rather short than otherwise, and her cheeks a great deal too round and red for a heroine; but her face blushed with rosy health, and her lips with the freshest of smiles, and she had a pair of eyes which sparkled with the brightest and honestest good-humour, except indeed when they filled with tears, and that was a great deal too often; for the silly thing would cry over a dead canary-bird; or over a mouse, that the cat haply had seized upon; or over the end of a novel, were it ever so stupid.

The details of such a description serve only to trivialize those features that were so important in the hero or heroine of the traditional novel. These details give the impression that something significant is being said about the person described, but the succession of clichés, from the round red cheeks and sparkling eyes to the soft-hearted sentimentality, achieve their purpose precisely by depriving the character of its representative nature. But if Amelia is deprived of traditional representative qualities and is not to be regarded as the positive counterpart to the unscrupulous, sophisticated Becky, then the novel denies the reader a basic focal point of orientation. He is prevented from sympathizing with the hero—a process which till now had always provided the nineteenth-century reader with his most important means of access to the events described—as typified by the reaction of a reviewer to Charlotte Brontë's *Jane Eyre:* "We took up *Jane Eyre* one winter's evening, somewhat piqued at the extravagant commendations we had heard, and sternly resolved to be as critical as Croker. But as we read on we forgot both commendations and criticism, identified ourselves with Jane in all her troubles, and finally married Mr. Rochester about four in the morning." In contrast, *Vanity Fair* seems bent on breaking any such direct contact with the characters, and indeed the narrator frequently goes out of his way to prevent the reader from putting himself in their place.

This occurs predominantly through the narrator's comments on the particular patterns of behavior developed by Amelia and Becky in critical situations. He reveals the motives behind their utterances, interpolating consequences of which they themselves are not aware, so that these occasions serve to uncover the imbalance of the characters. Often the behavior of the characters is interpreted far beyond the scope of the reactions shown and in the light of knowledge which at best could only have been revealed by the future. In this way the reader is continually placed at a distance from the characters. As Michel Butor once pointed out, in a different context: "If the reader is put in the place of the hero, he must also be put in the hero's immediate present; he cannot know what the hero does not know, and things must appear to him just as they appear to the hero." In *Vanity Fair,* however, the characters are illuminated by a knowledge to which they themselves have no access. They are constantly kept down below the intellectual level of the narrator, whose views offer the reader a far greater stimulus to identification than do the characters themselves. This detachment from the characters is part of the narrator's avowed intention: ". . . as we bring our characters forward, I will ask leave, as a man and a brother, not only to introduce them, but occasionally to step down from the platform, and talk about them: if they are good and kindly, to love them and shake them by the hand; if they are silly, to laugh at them confidentially in the reader's sleeve: if they are wicked and heartless, to abuse them in the strongest terms which politeness admits of." The characters in this novel are completely hedged in by such judgments, and the reader sees all their actions only when they have been refracted by the narrator's own critical evaluations. The immensity of his presence makes it impossible for the reader to live their lives with them, as did the reviewer we have quoted, during his reading of *Jane Eyre.* The actual gap between the characters' actions and the narrator's comments stimulates the reader into forming judgments of his own—thereby bridging the gaps—and gradually adopting the position of critic himself.

It is mainly this intention that shapes the composition of the characters, and there are two dominant techniques to be observed. The first part of the novel reproduces letters which Becky and Amelia write to each other. The letter makes it possible to reveal the most intimate thoughts and feelings to such a degree that the reader can learn from the correspondents themselves just who they are and what makes them 'tick'. A typical example is Becky's long letter telling Amelia all about her new surroundings at the Crawley family's country seat. Becky's impressions end with the spontaneous self-revelation: "I am determined to make myself agreeable." Fitting in with present circumstances remains her guiding principle throughout her quest for social advancement. Such a wish is so totally in keeping with her own character that the maneuvers necessary for its fulfillment constitute for Becky the natural way to behave. Thus we see that in society, self-seeking hypocrisy has become second nature to man. In the letters, however, Becky's self-esteem remains so constant that she is clearly quite unaware of her two-facedness. The obvious naiveté of such self-portraits is bound to provoke the reader into critical reaction, and the heading of the chapter that reproduces Becky's letter is already pointing in this direction, for the unmistakably ironic title is: "Arcadian Simplicity." Thus the self-revelation of the letter actually justifies the narrator for not taking the character as it is, but setting it at a critical distance so that it can be seen through. Elsewhere we read: "Perhaps in Vanity Fair there are no better satires than letters." But the intention of the satire is for the reader himself to uncover, for the narrator never offers him more than ironic clues. The narrator's keen concern to give the impression that he never commits himself to ultimate clarity reveals itself at those times when he accidentally reaches an 'understanding' with his reader, but then remembers that such an exchange of experiences goes beyond the limits of his narrative: ". . . but we are wandering out of the domain of the story."

The second technique designed to rouse the critical faculties of the reader is revealed in Amelia's almost obsessive habit of "building numberless castles in the air . . . which Amelia adorned with all sorts of flower-gardens, rustic walks, country churches, Sunday schools, and the like." This day-dreaming is typical of Amelia, who devises these beautiful visions as an escape from the narrow confines of her social existence. Her whole outlook is governed by expectations that generally arise out of chance events in her life and are therefore as subject to fortuitous change as the social situations she gets into. The dependence of these often very sentimental day-dreams on the circumstances of the moment shows not only the fickleness of her behavior but also the disoriented nature of her desires, the fulfillment of which is inevitably frustrated by the apparently superior forces of her environment. The projection of hopes which cannot be realized leads to an attitude which is as characteristic of Amelia as it is of Becky, who for different motives also covers up what she really is, in order to gain the social position she hankers after. Despite the difference in their motives, both Amelia's and Becky's lives are largely governed by illusions, which are shown up for what they are by the fact that whenever they are partially realized, we see how very trivial the aspirations really were. The characters themselves, however, lack this awareness, and this is hardly surprising, as their ambitions or longings are often roused by chance occurrences which are not of sufficient lasting importance to give the characters a true sense of direction. Becky certainly has greater drive in her quest for social advancement, and one would therefore expect a greater degree of continuity in her conduct; but this very ambition requires that she should adapt her conduct to the various demands made by the different strata of society; and this fact in turn shows how malleable and therefore illusory are the conventions of social life. What is presented in Becky's life as continuity should not be confused with the aspirations of the eighteenth-century hero, who went forth in order to find out the truth about himself; here it is the expression of the many-sided sham which is the very attribute of social reality.

When the narrator introduces his characters at the beginning of the novel, he says of Becky: "The famous little Becky Puppet has been pronounced to be uncommonly flexible in the joints, and lively on the wire." As the characters cannot free themselves from their illusions, it is only to be expected that they should take them for unquestionable reality. The reader is made aware of this fact by the attitude of the narrator, who has not only seen through his 'puppets', but also lets them act on a level of consciousness far below his own. This almost overwhelming superiority of the narrator over his characters also puts the reader in a privileged position, though with the unspoken but ever-present condition that he should draw his own conclusions from the extra knowledge imparted to him by the narrator. There is even an allegory of the reader's task at one point in the novel, when Becky is basking in the splendor of a grand social evening:

> The man who brought her refreshment and stood behind her chair, had talked her character over with the large gentleman in motley-coloured clothes at his side. Bon Dieu! it is awful, that servants' inquisition! You see a woman in a great party in a splendid saloon, surrounded by faithful admirers, distributing sparkling glances, dressed to perfection, curled, rouged, smiling and happy:—Discovery walks respectfully up to her, in the shape of a huge powdered man with large calves and a tray of ices—with Calumny (which is as fatal as truth) behind him, in the shape of the hulking fellow carrying the wafer-biscuits, Madam, your secret will be talked over by those men at their club at the public-house to-night. . . . Some people ought to have mutes for servants in Vanity Fair—mutes who could not write. If you are guilty, tremble. That fellow behind your chair may be a Janissary with a bowstring in his plush breeches pocket. If you are not guilty, have a care of appearances: which are as ruinous as guilt.

This little scene contains a change of standpoints typical of the way in which the reader's observations are conditioned throughout this novel. The servants are suddenly transformed into allegorical figures with the function of uncovering what lies hidden beneath the façades of their masters. But the discovery will only turn into calumny from the standpoint of the person affected. The narrator compares the destructive effect of calumny with that of truth and advises his readers to employ mutes, or better still illiterate mutes, as servants, in order to protect themselves against discovery. Then he brings the reader's view even more sharply into focus, finally leaving him to himself with an indissoluble ambiguity: if he feels guilty, because he is pretending to be something he is not, then he must fear those around him as if they were an army of Janissaries. If he has nothing to hide, then the social circle merely demands of him to keep up appearances; but since this is just as ruinous as deliberate hypocrisy, it follows that life in society imposes roles on all concerned, reducing human behavior to the level of play-acting. All the characters in the novel are caught up in this play, as is expressly shown by the narrator's own stage metaphor at the beginning and at the end. The key word for the reader is 'discover', and the narrator continually prods him along the road to discovery, laying a trail of clues for him to follow. The process reveals not only the extent to which Becky and Amelia take their illusions for reality but also—even more strikingly—the extent to which reality itself is illusory, since it is built on the simulated relationships between people. The reader will not fail to notice the gulf between 'illusion' and 'reality', and in realizing it, he is experiencing the esthetic effect of the novel: Thackeray did not set out to create the conventional illusion that involved the reader in the world of the novel as if it were reality; instead, his narrator constantly interrupts the story precisely in order to prevent such an illusion from coming into being. The reader is deliberately stopped from identifying himself with the characters. And as the aim is to prevent him from taking part in the events, he is allowed to be absorbed only to a certain degree and is then jerked back again, so that he is impelled to criticize from the outside. Thus the story of the two girls serves to get the reader involved, while the meaning of the story can only be arrived at by way of the additional manipulations of perspective carried out by the narrator.

This 'split-level' technique conveys a far stronger impression of reality than does the illusion which claims that the world of the novel corresponds to the whole world. For now the reader himself has to discover the true situation, which becomes clearer and clearer to him as he gets to know the characters in their fetters of illusion. In this way, he himself takes an active part in the animation of all the characters' actions, for they seem real to him because he is constantly under obligation to work out all that is wrong with their behavior. In order that his participation should not be allowed to slacken, the individual characters are fitted out with different types and degrees of delusion, and there are even some, like Dobbin, whose actions and feelings might mislead one into taking them for positive counterparts to all the other characters. Such a false assumption is certainly perceived, even if not intended, by the narrator, who toward the end of the novel addresses the reader as follows: "This woman [i.e., Amelia] had a way of tyrannising over Major Dobbin (for the weakest of all people will domineer over somebody), and she ordered him about, and patted him, and made him fetch and carry just as if he was a great New-foundland dog. . . . This history has been written to very little purpose if the reader has not perceived that the Major was a spooney." What might have seemed like noble-mindedness was in fact the behavior of a nincompoop, and if the reader has only just realized it, then he has not been particularly successful in the process of 'discovering'.

The esthetic effect of *Vanity Fair* depends on activating the reader's critical faculties so that he may recognize the social reality of the novel as a confusing array of sham attitudes, and experience the exposure of this sham as the true reality. Instead of being expressly stated, the criteria for such judgments have to be inferred. They are the blanks which the reader is supposed to fill in, thus bringing his own criticism to bear. In other words, it is his own criticism to bear. In other words, it is his own criticism that constitutes the reality of the book. The novel, then, is not to be viewed as the mere reflection of a social reality, for its true form will only be revealed when the world it presents has, like all images, been refracted and converted by the mind of the reader. *Vanity Fair* aims not at presenting social reality, but at presenting the way in which such reality can be experienced. "To convey as strongly as possible the sentiment of reality" is Thackeray's description of this process, which he regarded as the function of the novel. If the sense of the narrative can only be completed through the cooperation

of the reader (which is allowed for in the text), then the borderline between fiction and reality becomes increasingly hazy, for the reader can scarcely regard his own participation as fictional. He is bound to look on his reactions as something real, and at no time is this conviction disputed. But since his reactions are real, he will lose the feeling that he is judging a world that is only fictional. Indeed, his own judgments will enhance the impression he has that this world is a reality.

How very concerned Thackeray was to confront the reader with a reality he himself considered to be real is clear from the passage already quoted, in which the narrator tells the reader that his object is to walk with him through the Fair and leave him "perfectly miserable" afterward. Thackeray reiterates this intention in a letter written in 1848: "my object . . . is to indicate, in cheerful terms, that we are for the most part an abominably foolish and selfish people . . . all eager after vanities . . . I want to leave everybody dissatisfied and unhappy at the end of the story—we ought all to be with our own and all other stories" [see excerpt dated September 3, 1848]. For this insight to take root in the reader, the fictional world must be made to seem real to him. Since, in addition, the reader is intended to be a critic of this world, the esthetic appeal of the novel lies in the fact that it gives him the opportunity to step back and take a detached look at that which he had regarded as normal human conduct. This detachment, however, is not to be equated with the edification which the moral novel offered to its readers. Leaving the reader perfectly miserable after his reading indicates that such a novel is not going to offer him pictures of another world that will make him forget the sordid nature of this one; the reader is forced, rather, to exercise his own critical faculties in order to relieve his distress by uncovering potential alternatives arising out of the world he has read about. "A man with a reflective turn of mind" is therefore the ideal reader for this novel. (pp. 102-14)

The aspect of the novel which we have discussed so far is the narrator's continual endeavor to stimulate the reader's mind through extensive commentaries on the actions of the characters. This indirect form of guidance is supplemented by a number of remarks relating directly to the expectations and supposed habits of the novel-reader. If the fulfillment of the novel demands a heightened faculty of judgment, it is only natural that the narrator should also compel the reader—at times quite openly—to reflect on his own situation, for without doing so he will be incapable of judging the actions of the characters in the novel. For this process to be effective, the possible reader must be visualized as playing a particular role with particular characteristics, which may vary according to circumstances. And so just as the author divides himself up into the narrator of the story and the commentator on the events in the story, the reader is also stylized to a certain degree, being given attributes which he may either accept or reject. Whatever happens he will be forced to react to those ready-made qualities ascribed to him. In this manner the double role of the author has a parallel in that of the reader, as W. Booth has pointed out in a discussion on the narrator:

> . . . the same distinction must be made between myself as reader and the very often different self who goes about paying bills, repairing leaky faucets, and failing in generosity and wisdom. It is only as I read that I become the self whose beliefs must coincide with the author's. Regardless of my real beliefs and practices, I must subordinate my mind and heart to the book if

I am to enjoy it to the full. The author creates, in short, an image of himself and another image of his reader; he makes his reader, as he makes his second self, and the most successful reading is one in which the created selves, author and reader, can find complete agreement.

Such an agreement can, however, be reached along widely differing lines, for instance through disagreement—i.e., a subtly instituted opposition between reader and narrator—and this is what happens in *Vanity Fair.*

When the narrator pretends to be at one with the reader in evaluating a certain situation, the reverse is usually the case. For instance, he describes an old but rich spinster who is a member of the great Crawley family, into which Becky is going to marry, in fulfillment of her social aspirations:

> Miss Crawley was . . . an object of great respect when she came to Queen's Crawley, for she had a balance at her banker's which would have made her beloved anywhere. What a dignity it gives an old lady, that balance at the banker's! How tenderly we look at her faults if she is a relative (and may every reader have a score of such), what a kind good-natured old creature we find her! . . . How, when she comes to pay us a visit, we generally find an opportunity to let our friends know her station in the world! We say (and with perfect truth) I wish I had Miss MacWhirter's signature to a cheque for five thousand pounds. She wouldn't miss it, says your wife. She is my aunt, say you, in an easy careless way, when your friend asks if Miss MacWhirter is any relative. Your wife is perpetually sending her little testimonies of affection, your little girls work endless worsted baskets, cushions, and footstools for her. What a good fire there is in her room when she comes to pay you a visit, although your wife laces her stays without one! . . . Is it so, or is it not so?

By using the first person plural, the narrator gives the impression that he is viewing through the reader's eyes the many attentions paid to the old lady with the large bank balance; for the reader such conduct is scarcely remarkable—indeed it is more the expression of a certain *savoir vivre.* By identifying himself with this view, the narrator seems to reinforce rather than to oppose this attitude, which is symptomatic of human nature. But in pretending merely to be describing 'natural' reactions, he is in fact seeking to trap the reader into agreeing with him—and as soon as this is accomplished, the reader realizes for himself the extent to which consideration of personal gain shapes the natural impulses of human conduct.

In this way, the difference between the reader and the characters in the novel is eliminated. Instead of just seeing through them, he sees himself reflected in them, so that the superior position which the narrator has given him over the pretences and illusions of the characters now begins to fade. The reader realizes that he is similar to those who are supposed to be the objects of his criticism, and so the self-confrontations that permeate the novel compel him to become aware of his own position in evaluating that of the characters. In order to develop this awareness, the narrator creates situations in which the characters' actions correspond to what the reader is tricked into regarding as natural, subsequently feeling the irresistible urge to detach

himself from the proceedings. And if the reader ignores the discreet summons to observe himself, then his critical attitude toward the characters becomes unintentionally hypocritical, for he forgets to include himself in the judgment. Thackeray did not want to edify his readers, but to leave them miserable, though with the tacit invitation to find ways of changing this condition for themselves.

This predominantly intellectual appeal to the mind of the reader was not always the norm in the realistic novel. In Dickens, for example, emotions are aroused in order to create a premeditated relationship between the reader and the characters. . . . He follows traditional practice insofar as he brings about a total involvement of the reader in the action. In Thackeray things are different. He is concerned with preventing any close liaison between reader and characters. The reader of *Vanity Fair* is in fact forced into a position outside the reality of the novel, though the judgment demanded of him is not without a tension of its own, as he is always in danger of sliding into the action of the novel, thereby suddenly being subjected to the standards of his own criticism. (pp. 114-17)

The reader is constantly forced to think in terms of alternatives, as the only way in which he can avoid the unambiguous and suspect position of the characters is to visualize the possibilities which they have not thought of. While he is working out these alternatives the scope of his own judgment expands, and he is constantly invited to test and weigh the insights he has arrived at as a result of the profusion of situations offered him. The

A photograph of Thackeray near the end of his life. The Granger Collection, New York.

esthetic appeal of such a technique consists in the fact that it allows a certain latitude for the individual character of the reader, but also compels specific reactions—often unobtrusively—without expressly formulating them. By refusing to draw the reader into the illusory reality of the novel, and keeping him at a variable distance from the events, the text gives him the illusion that he can judge the proceedings in accordance with his own point of view. To do this, he has only to be placed in a position that will provoke him to pass judgments, and the less loaded in advance these judgments are by the text, the greater will be the esthetic effect.

The "Manager of the Performance" opens up a whole panorama of views on the reality described, which can be seen from practically every social and human standpoint. The reader is offered a host of different perspectives, and so is almost continually confronted with the problem of how to make them consistent. This is all the more complicated as it is not just a matter of forming a view of the social world described, but of doing so in face of a rich variety of viewpoints offered by the commentator. There can be no doubt that the author wants to induce his reader to assume a critical attitude toward the reality portrayed, but at the same time he gives him the alternative of adopting one of the views offered him, or of developing one of his own. This choice is not without a certain amount of risk. If the reader adopts one of the attitudes suggested by the author, he must automatically exclude the others. If this happens, the impression arises, in this particular novel, that one is looking more at oneself than at the event described. There is an unmistakable narrowness in every standpoint, and in this respect the reflection the reader will see of himself will be anything but complimentary. But if the reader then changes his viewpoint, in order to avoid this narrowness, he will undergo the additional experience of finding that his behavior is very like that of the two girls who are constantly adapting themselves in order to ascend the social scale. All the same, his criticism of the girls appears to be valid. Is it not a reasonable assumption then that the novel was constructed as a means of turning the reader's criticism of social opportunism back upon himself? This is not mentioned specifically in the text, but it happens all the time. Thus, instead of society, the reader finds himself to be the object of criticism.

Thackeray once mentioned casually: "I have said somewhere it is the unwritten part of books that would be the most interesting." It is in the unwritten part of the book that the reader has his place—hovering between the world of the characters and the guiding sovereignty of the "Manager of the Performance." If he comes too close to the characters, he learns the truth of what the narrator told him at the beginning: "The world is a looking-glass, and gives back to every man the reflection of his own face." If he stands back with the narrator to look at things from a distance, he sees through all the activities of the characters. Through the variableness of his own position, the reader experiences the meaning of *Vanity Fair*. Through the characters he undergoes a temporary entanglement in the web of his own illusions, and through the demand for judgment he is enabled to free himself from it and to get a better view of himself and of the world.

And so the story of the two girls and their social aspirations forms only one aspect of the novel, which is continually supplemented by views through different lenses, all of which are trained on the story with the intention of discovering its meaning. The necessity for these different perspectives indicates that the story itself does not reveal direct evidence as to its meaning, so that the factual reality depicted does not represent a total reality. It can only become total through the *manner* in which it is observed. Thus the narrator's commentary, with its often ingenious provocations of the reader, has the effect of an almost independent action running parallel to the story itself. Herein lies the difference between Thackeray and the naturalists of the nineteenth century, who set out to convince their readers that a relevant 'slice of life' was total reality, whereas in fact it only represented an ideological assumption which, for all the accuracy of its details, was a manipulated reality.

In *Vanity Fair* it is not the slice of life, but the means of observing it that constitute the reality, and as these means of observation remain as valid today as they were in the nineteenth century, the novel remains as 'real' now as it was then, even though the social world depicted is only of historical interest. It is in the preoccupation with different perspectives and with the activation of the reader himself that *Vanity Fair* marks a stage of transition between the traditional and what we now call the 'modern' novel. The predominant aim is no longer to create the illusion of an objective outside reality, and the novelist is no longer concerned with projecting his own unambiguous view of the world onto his reader. Instead, his technique is to diversify his vision, in order to compel the reader to view things for himself and discover his own reality. The author has not yet withdrawn "to pare his fingernails," but he has already entered into the shadows and holds his scissors at the ready. (pp. 118-20)

> *Wolfgang Iser, "The Reader as a Component Part of the Realistic Novel: Esthetic Effects in Thackeray's 'Vanity Fair'," in his* The Implied Reader: Patterns of Communication in Prose Fiction from Bunyan to Beckett, *The Johns Hopkins University Press, 1974, pp. 101-20.*

JOHN SUTHERLAND (essay date 1983)

[*Sutherland examines the concept of* Vanity Fair *as an historical novel. The critic focuses on the role of the novel's historical background and Thackeray's portrayal of events prior to, during, and following the Battle of Waterloo.*]

As Gordon Ray puts it, *Vanity Fair* signals clearly and early the kind of novel Thackeray will not write [see Additional Bibliography, 1955]; that is to say, the kind of novel the majority of his writing and reading contemporaries affect. Throughout *Vanity Fair*, and explicitly in Chapter VI, Thackeray makes the pharisaical assertion that he is not as other novelists are. But, as critics have come round to noticing, this *censor morum literariorum* would often seem to have a dangerously soft spot for his victims. *Vanity Fair*, for all its show of repudiation, frequently conforms to the fiction it purports to chastise. With its 'arsenical' ending (Becky poisoning Jos) *Vanity Fair* is as much of the Newgate genre as Lytton's sensational *Lucretia* (1846). K. J. Hollingsworth, the authority on this early shoot of crime fiction, goes so far as to claim that *Vanity Fair* is the Newgate novel to end Newgate novels [see Additional Bibliography]. So too, Matthew Rosa sees Thackeray's novel as the *summum genus* of silver forkery. It has certainly survived as the greatest of Waterloo novels (who now remembers the multitudinous works of W. H. Maxwell, or Lever's *Charles O'Malley*, the bestselling novel of 1841 which Thackeray put down hilariously with his spoof, **"Phil Fogarty. A Tale of the Fighting Onety-Oneth"**?). Thackeray was loftily contemptuous in his two reviews of *Coningsby*, affecting to find Disraeli's romance of power politics in the 'saloons of the mighty' obnoxious and absurd. (See also **"Codlingsby"**, by the dubiously eminent hand of 'B. de Shrewsbury, Esq.') But who is the arch villain of *Vanity Fair*? Why, Steyne, avowedly based on the Marquis of Hertford, the same aristocrat who modelled for the all-powerful Monmouth in *Coningsby*.

Thackeray, we may say, has a more complex and intimate relationship with the modes of fashionable fiction of the age than his apparently dismissive satirical manner would suggest. Neither is it easy to fix his feelings about the period in which *Vanity Fair* is principally set—the dissolute Regency and reign of George IV. Here, again, we detect in Thackeray mixed feelings of nostalgia and severe moral criticism. But at least we are on firm ground with the age's figurehead. Of all the historical figures whom Thackeray loathed, the bloated 'first gentleman of Europe' was the blackest of beasts. Even Marlborough in *Esmond* is treated with more tenderness than 'the great simulacrum'. Thackeray's ink boils whenever he describes Florizel. He often did describe him. More or less full-length portraits are found in *Punch* (see, particularly, *The Georges, Punch,* 11 October 1845), in *The Snobs of England* (see particularly Chapter II, 'The Snob Royal'), and—most vituperatively—in *The Four Georges* where the fourth lecture is devoted to an hour-long diatribe against the last Hanoverian. Thackeray's theme is simple. The Prince Regent represents the sink of corruption against which the present, Victorian, age is the wholesome reaction:

> He is dead but thirty years, and one asks how
> a great society could have tolerated him? Would
> we bear him now? In this quarter of a century,
> what a silent revolution has been working! how
> it has separated us from old times and manners!
> How it has changed men themselves!

In *Vanity Fair,* the fourth George is referred to frequently. He actually appears on stage twice (and speaks once) at the apogee of Becky's career, in the charade scene at Gaunt House and in the Drawing-room presentation in 1827—Becky's moment of glory. On neither occasion can Thackeray, with a satiric attack of commoner's humility, bring himself to describe, nor even name, the 'great personage':

> What were the circumstances of the interview
> between Rebecca Crawley, *née* Sharp, and her
> Imperial Master, it does not become such a
> feeble and inexperienced pen as mine to attempt
> to relate. The dazzled eyes close before that
> Magnificent Idea. Loyal respect and decency
> tell even the imagination not to look too keenly
> and audaciously about the sacred audience-
> chamber, but to back away rapidly, silently,
> and respectfully, making profound bows out of
> the August Presence. . . .

But while miming loyal blindness at the incandescence of the Hanoverian sun god, Thackeray insinuates his derogatory view of the Prince Regent and his dandified parasites with the namesake Osborne, and George Osborne's very fat friend, Jos. ('William' Dobbin is significantly named for the decent, if maladroit, 'Silly Billy'. One of his first royal edicts on coming to power in 1830 was to restrict the extravagant military uniforms so beloved of the 'padded booby' George. Dobbin embodies that 'change' Thackeray eulogizes in *The Four Georges*.)

Vanity Fair, then, is an historical novel. In particular the middle-class social life of the Regency (i.e. 1811-20) is reconstructed with apparently personal familiarity. Thackeray, however, was born in the year George was declared Regent. He could scarcely have been conscious of Waterloo, four years later. But the victory remained for him, as for many Victorians, the age's great event. Indeed, with the English 'saving revolution' of 1688, the American Revolution of 1776 and the French Revolution of 1789, Waterloo could easily be conceived as the most monumental occurrence in modern history. The close-run thing in Belgium was the foundation of Britain's century of triumph and the spread of imperial red over the world's map. And had the battle been lost, history would probably have delivered a bloody English Revolution, rather than the Reform Bill of 1832. Nor was it just the European balance of power which was rearranged by Waterloo. The victory had profound social consequences; it marked a moment of regeneration for the British aristocracy. Dandyism fell; Brummell was disgraced in 1815—a fall 'as great as Napoleon's' it was said. The Duke of Wellington was himself a 'dandy general' and led an army whose fashionable regiments fought brilliantly. (Hence, of course, the famous 'won on the playing fields of Eton' proverb.) Thackeray's 'silent revolution' can more plausibly be dated from 1815 than from 1830, when George died. Despite his monarchic radiance in mid-1820s *Vanity Fair*, George's last ten years were spent in almost total social eclipse and public unpopularity.

But despite his fascination with Waterloo, and its profound effect on the novel's five main characters and the world they inhabit, Thackeray's treatment of the battle is tantalizing in the highest degree. The suspense builds from Dobbin's 'the regiment's called away' to the Duchess of Richmond's eve of battle ball, from which officers slip out one by one, some to death, some to glory. We arrive to within earshot of the cannonade at Quatre Bras. But then, at the most teasing moment, we are denied satisfaction (which as thrill-seeking and *paying* readers we legitimately demand) by Thackeray's mock-humble and maidenish retraction:

> We do not claim to rank among the military
> novelists. Our place is with the non-combatants.
> When the decks are cleared for action we go
> below and wait meekly. We should only be in
> the way of the manoeuvres that the gallant fel-
> lows are performing overhead. We shall go no
> farther with the —th than to the city gate. . . .

As a matter of literary record, the reader indignantly retorts that Thackeray is an excellent military novelist. Any number of examples could be given; but for the nearest turn to Chapters IV, V, VI of *Barry Lyndon,* which Thackeray was writing virtually up to the month when he began *Vanity Fair*. This rollicking autobiography of an eighteenth-century soldier of fortune demonstrates the skill which Thackeray disowns, with infuriating modesty, at the start of the ninth number of *Vanity Fair.*

The novelist teases at other similarly exciting moments in the novel's action. He will not, for instance, conduct us into the penetralium of Gaunt House, giving us, instead, serpentine, 'Tomeavesian' gossip. What we crave is reliable eye-witness report of what's going on at this climax of Becky's English campaign. 'Great personages' pop up momentarily on the edge of *Vanity Fair*'s narrative, only to pop down. Thus the Duke of Wellington himself rides past the novel's heroes and heroines in a Brussels public park. It is his sole appearance and what does Thackeray give us? Peggy O'Dowd's chauvinist Hibernian irrelevance: 'the Wellesleys and Moloneys are related; but, of course, poor *I* would never dream of introjuicing myself unless his Grace thought proper to remember our family tie.' The Duchess of Richmond's Brussels ball on 15 June—that conjunction of brilliant social glitter and carnage—is famous from at least two other literary presentations. But Thackeray's thinned account keeps off-stage Byron's 'fated Brunswick'; the glamorous hostess; the martial guest of honour and indeed all personages above field rank. *Charles O'Malley*, by contrast, has the hero on the most hob-nobbing terms with the ducal hostess and Commander-in-Chief. The 'great captain' in Lever's narrative actually 'introjuices' himself to the hero ('know your face well; how d'ye do?') with the lack of reserve which suggests that the brash Moloneys and the Wellesleys might indeed be related.

No more than with Thackeray's battlefield reticence can we put this omission down to authorial inadequacy. The depiction of Marlborough in *Esmond*, of Washington in *The Virginians* (and probably the imminent depiction of Paul Jones in the unfinished *Duval*) testify that Thackeray was as capable of rendering the portrait of a military chief as he was a military fight—when he chose to do so. *Vanity Fair*, then, is an historical novel in whose historical fabric there are gaping, but evidently carefully placed, holes. Thackeray gives us Regency London without Brummell, Byron or the Regent (how easy it would have been to send the Osborne-Sedley-Dobbin party to Vauxhall on the festive night of 13 July . . .); the great Brussels ball without grandees; the frontline in 1815 without Waterloo, Wellington or Napoleon; and, later in the novel, Weimar without Goethe. An historical novel, we might call it, without everything conventionally historical.

The artful anticlimaxes in *Vanity Fair*, and particularly the frustrating vacancy around Waterloo, are partly explained by Thackeray's determination to avoid romantic stereotype. Other factors are his ambivalence about British imperial might, and his circumstances while actually composing *Vanity Fair*. To take this last (and probably least) consideration: the novelist was evidently very pressed for time and space during the writing of the middle sections of his narrative. He intended to get the action to the battle at least two numbers earlier than he actually managed. But what with the marriages and all the falling-out between relatives in the 'hundred days' between March and June, *Vanity Fair* was fairly bursting at the seams. Of course, with a narrator as deft as Thackeray, pressure could not have been the deciding factor. In fact, as the Tillotsons point out, Thackeray's gimmick of telling the story of Waterloo indirectly through its domestic repercussions had been aired as early as 1842, during a visit to Charles Lever's house near Dublin. As reported, Thackeray 'seemed much inclined to "laugh at martial might"', although he still held to the idea that "something might be made out of Waterloo", even without the smoke and din of the action being introduced.' In Lever's *Charles O'Malley*, published in 1841, smoke and din is prominent and the hero observes the epic encounter at Napoleon's side.

Silence in the face of Waterloo was probably also encouraged by Thackeray's perplexity when he went to visit the battlefield, a few weeks before embarking on his novel. What he describes (in a **"Little Travels and Roadside Sketches"** piece, published in *Fraser's Magazine*, January 1845) is strikingly like Orwell's painful sense of British greatness, lying underfoot in the mouldering carcasses of the expendable 'natives' whose sweat, suffering and hunger is empire's real foundation. Walking over the place where thousands of uncommemorated private soldiers were cut, blasted or bled to death, Thackeray felt pride—as what Englishman would not. But he also felt ashamed of a pride so paid for by others' sacrifice. Moreover, the strength of his mixed feelings induced a conviction that here was a place where one ought to be decently quiet, as in a church. . . . (pp. x-xvi)

One cannot know for certain, but I suspect that until he actually came to writing it, Thackeray kept open the important question of how he should treat Waterloo. We know, for instance, that he ordered an early copy of G. R. Gleig's *Story of the Battle of Waterloo* in June 1847. He evidently devoured the book when it arrived. . . . And he must have been struck by one feature in particular. Gleig, at one point, complains at the feeble powers of the 'pen and pencil' (a phrase Thackeray had used in his novel's title) when it comes to describing this battle of battles. Moreover, the most vivacious by far of Gleig's chapters are those dealing with the furious carnival in Brussels before Waterloo, and the stiltedly entitled chapter 'State of Feeling Where the War was not', which records, with lively detail, the wild currents of pessimism and rumour that swept over Brussels during the three days of fighting. Thackeray plundered these sections for *Vanity Fair*'s ninth number. With one notable exception . . . , the stodgier battle chapters seem to have inspired him less. It is possible, too, that having read Gleig, the novelist felt disinclined to compete with the military historian on his own ground.

To summarize. There is no need to retract, nor even to modify the assertion that *Vanity Fair* is an historical novel. But the sense of historical period and the passage of world-shaking events around the characters is conveyed obliquely. Most obviously by the introduction of minor period detail such as seven shilling pieces and hessian boots. Thackeray inserts material of this kind very judiciously—but it is a simple device, equivalent to theatrical 'props'. More complex is the way in which he throws up a London subtly different from that familiar to his 1848 readers. Thus, in Chapter XXII, Dobbin meets George at the old Slaughter's Coffee House (it stood in St. Martin's Lane until 1843) before his furtive marriage cum elopement with Amelia:

> It was about half an hour from twelve when this brief meeting and colloquy took place between the two captains. A coach, into which Captain Osborne's servant put his master's desk and dressing-case, had been in waiting for some time; and into this the two gentlemen hurried under an umbrella, and the valet mounted on the box, cursing the rain and the dampness of the coachman who was steaming beside him. 'We shall find a better trap than this at the chutch-door,' says he; 'that's a comfort.' And the carriage drove on, taking the road down Piccadilly; where Apsley House and St. George's Hospital wore red jackets still, where there were oil-lamps; where Achilles was not yet born; nor the Pimlico arch raised; nor the hideous equestrian monster which pervades it and the neighbourhood;—and so they drove down by Brompton to a certain chapel near the Fulham road there. . . .

Misfortune is predicted in the proverbially unlucky rain which falls on the bride and groom. Other predictions are contained in the urban landscape. This is early 1815. Apsley House, on Hyde Park Corner, was to become the residence of the Duke of Wellington, victor of Waterloo. Wyatt encased it in Bath stone in 1828 ('red coat' means literally 'brick' but also has a military significance here, as does St. George's Hospital, which is to care for Waterloo wounded). Wyatt was also responsible for the heroic statue of Wellington—weighing forty tons—erected at a cost of £30,000 by public subscription, in 1846. This monstrosity, as Thackeray and many of his contemporaries thought, also stood at the south-eastern entrance to the Park. (It figures, in caricature, on the serial cover. . . .) The Achilles statue was subscribed for (£10,000), and inscribed by 'the women of England.' It was also dedicated as a tribute to Wellington, and was raised in 1822. It was cast partly from enemy cannon captured at Waterloo.

This elaboration of scenic detail serves a number of purposes. It emphasizes how London has changed (omnibuses in 1846 serve this part of London; oil-lighting gave way to gas in 1828). More thematically, we feel the marriage threatened by futurity, a futurity centred on Waterloo. These monuments to victory are also, we sense, George's gravestone. Amelia, although she does not know it, will join the 'women of England' in making a widow's sacrificial donation.

In the above example, Thackeray dwarfs a major novelistic event (the marriage of two principal characters) by throwing gigantic historical shadows across their bridal path. Examples can be found where—for artistic effect—he does just the opposite. In the following, the dizzying European crisis of 1813-14 is shrunk by reflection in Amelia's preoccupation about her engagement to George:

> Meanwhile matters went on in Russell Square, Bloomsbury, just as if matters in Europe were not in the least disorganised. The retreat from Leipsic made no difference in the number of meals Mr. Sambo took in the servants' hall; the allies poured into France, and the dinner-bell rang at five o'clock just as usual. I don't think poor Amelia cared anything about Brienne and Montmirail, or was fairly interested in the war until the abdication of the Emperor; when she clapped her hands and said prayers,—oh, how grateful! and flung herself into George Osborne's arms with all her soul, to the astonishment of every body who witnessed the ebullition of sentiment. The fact is, peace was declared . . . Lieutenant Osborne's regiment would not be ordered on service. That was the way in which Miss Amelia reasoned. The fate of Europe was Lieutenant George Osborne to her. His dangers being over, she sang Te Deum. He was her Europe; her emperor: her allied monarchs and august prince regent. He was her sun and moon; and I believe she thought the grand illumination and ball at the Mansion House, given to the sovereigns, were especially in honour of George Osborne. . . .

There are ironies at work here. Amelia's naive perspective is both admirable and—in a very loaded word which Thackeray used about his 'Vanityfairians'—'selfish'. Soon she is to discover that the great convulsions of European history (which will ruin her father and slaughter her husband) are no respecters of girlish romance, however good and worthy the girl.

In the second half of the novel, after Waterloo, the historical background to *Vanity Fair* fades somewhat. As we follow the fortunes of Thackeray's characters over this most troubled of eras, one has the odd impression of social tranquillity. Perhaps,

as he looked back in a spirit of 'De Juventute', that is how it seemed to Thackeray in 1847-8. *Vanity Fair* is blind to Peterloo, corn law riots, industrial revolution, reform agitation. Even the great Bill itself sneaks in only parenthetically with a reference to Sir Pitt's disappointed retirement from public life after 1832. From the 1820s onwards, things gradually melt into the Victorian present. The novel's last numbers feature many fewer historical markers than their early counterparts. Imperceptibly, the historical texture merges if not into the 'now' of 1847-8, then into the Victorian reader's well-remembered yesterday. It is a fine and very moving effect in the novel. (pp. xvi-xx)

> *John Sutherland, in an introduction to* Vanity Fair: A Novel without a Hero *by William Makepeace Thackeray, Oxford University Press, Oxford, 1983, pp. vii-xlvi.*

ADDITIONAL BIBLIOGRAPHY

Baker, Joseph E. "*Vanity Fair* and the Celestial City." *Nineteenth-Century Fiction* 10, No. 2 (September 1955): 89-98.
  Explores the affinity between Thackeray's concept of Vanity Fair and similar ideas in the works of Bunyan, St. Augustine, and Plato.

Blodgett, Harriet. "Necessary Presence: The Rhetoric of the Narrator in *Vanity Fair*." *Nineteenth-Century Fiction* 22, No. 3 (December 1967): 211-23.
  A study of the narrator's rhetoric. Blodgett maintains that "*Vanity Fair* succeeds because of its narrator, not despite him."

Brophy, Brigid. "*Vanity Fair*." In her *Don't Never Forget: Collected Views and Reviews*, pp. 209-16. New York: Holt, Rinehart and Winston, 1967.
  A general introduction to the novel, focusing on its cynicism, historical perspective, and structure.

Carey, John. "*Vanity Fair*." In his *Thackeray: Prodigal Genius*, pp. 177-201. London: Faber & Faber, 1977.
  Discusses Thackeray's attitudes toward and methods of portraying the central characters in *Vanity Fair*. Carey also provides an extended comparison of the novel with *War and Peace*.

Chesterton, G. K. Introduction to *Masters of Literature: Thackeray*, by William Makepeace Thackeray, edited by G. K. Chesterton, pp. ix-xxxii. London: George Bell and Sons, 1909.
  Discusses the question of Thackeray's alleged cynicism in *Vanity Fair* and contrasts Becky's "energy without joy" with Amelia's simple if usually ineffectual goodness.

Cleall, Charles. *A Guide to "Vanity Fair."* Aberdeen: Aberdeen University Press, 1982, 143 p.
  An extended glossary providing definitions of words, names, and phrases in *Vanity Fair* with which the reader is unlikely to be familiar.

Colby, Robert A. "*Vanity Fair*; or, The Mysteries of Mayfair." In his *Thackeray's Canvass of Humanity: An Author and His Public*, pp. 231-73. Columbus: Ohio State University Press, 1979.
  Focuses on the literary and social environment in which Thackeray wrote *Vanity Fair*. Colby discusses both the influence on the novel of contemporary literature and the connection between *Vanity Fair* and Thackeray's writings for *Punch*.

Dooley, D. J. "Thackeray's Use of Vanity Fair." *Studies in English Literature, 1500-1900* XI, No. 4 (Autumn 1971): 701-13.
  Elaborates on Baker's study of Thackeray's use of Vanity Fair (see annotation above). Dooley assigns additional symbolic meanings to the Vanity Fair concept, exploring the religious and literary traditions with which it has been associated.

Drew, Elizabeth. "William Makepeace Thackeray: *Vanity Fair*." In her *The Novel: A Modern Guide to Fifteen English Masterpieces*, pp. 111-26. New York: Dell Publishing Co., A Laurel Edition, 1963.
A general discussion of the novel, touching upon its characters, satire, narrative, and description.

Ennis, Lambert. "At the Summit." In his *Thackeray: The Sentimental Cynic*, pp. 136-72. Evanston, Ill.: Northwestern University Press, 1950.
Describes the circumstances under which Thackeray composed *Vanity Fair* and also speculates upon possible real-life models for the characters in the novel.

Flamm, Dudley. *Thackeray's Critics: An Annotated Bibliography of British and American Criticism, 1836-1901*. Chapel Hill: University of North Carolina Press, 1966, 184 p.
An annotated guide to criticism of Thackeray's works through 1901.

Hagan, John. "*Vanity Fair*: Becky Brought to Book Again." *Studies in the Novel 7*, No. 4 (Winter 1975): 479-506.
Analyzes the problem of Thackeray's attitude toward Becky. Hagan argues that she cannot be seen as a sympathetic character.

Hannah, Donald. "'The Author's Own Candles': The Significance of the Illustrations to *Vanity Fair*." In *Renaissance and Modern Essays Presented to Vivian de Sola Pinto in Celebration of His Seventieth Birthday*, edited by G. R. Hibbard, pp. 119-27. London: Routledge and Kegan Paul, 1966.
Discusses the function of Thackeray's illustrations to *Vanity Fair*.

Harden, Edgar F. "The Fields of Mars in *Vanity Fair*." *Tennessee Studies in Literature 10* (1965): 123-32.
Argues that warfare, whether it be literal, personal, or social, is the "underlying principle of life permeating all of Vanity Fair."

————. "The Discipline and Significance of Form in *Vanity Fair*." *PMLA LXXXII*, No. 7 (December 1967): 530-41.
Suggests that the structure of *Vanity Fair* derives from a series of thematic parallels running through the monthly parts.

Hollingsworth, Keith. "*Vanity Fair* and 'George de Barnwell'." In his *The Newgate Novel, 1830-1847: Bulwer, Ainsworth, Dickens, and Thackeray*, pp. 202-22. Detroit: Wayne State University Press, 1963.
Analyzes the relationship between *Vanity Fair* and the popular crime fiction of Thackeray's contemporaries.

Johnson, E.D.H. "*Vanity Fair* and *Amelia*: Thackeray in the Perspective of the Eighteenth Century." *Modern Philology 59*, No. 2 (November 1961): 100-13.
Explores the possible influence of Henry Fielding's novel *Amelia* on *Vanity Fair*.

Karl, Frederick R. "Thackeray's *Vanity Fair*: All the World's a Stage." In his *A Reader's Guide to the Nineteenth Century British Novel*, pp. 177-203. New York: Farrar, Straus and Giroux, The Noonday Press, 1965.
Probes the limitations of Thackeray's realism in *Vanity Fair*. Karl maintains that the novelist was unable to transcend a sentimental view of life and lacked a mature sense of tragedy.

Kettle, Arnold. "Thackeray: *Vanity Fair*." In his *An Introduction to the English Novel*. Vol. I, *To George Eliot*, pp. 156-70. Hutchinson's University Library, English Literature, edited by Basil Willey. London: Gainsborough Press, 1951.
Argues that the "artistic motive-force of *Vanity Fair* is Thackeray's vision of bourgeois society and of the personal relationships engendered by that society."

Kronenberger, Louis. "*Vanity Fair*." In his *The Polished Surface: Essays in the Literature of Worldliness*, pp. 201-16. New York: Alfred A. Knopf, 1969.
Examines *Vanity Fair* within the context of a literary tradition devoted to the portrayal and criticism of worldly life.

Mathison, John K. "The German Sections of *Vanity Fair*." *Nineteenth-Century Fiction 18*, No. 3 (December 1963): 235-46.
Asserts that Thackeray utilizes the German episodes of the novel to help clarify his thematic concerns rather than merely to conclude the narrative.

Moler, Kenneth L. "Evelina in Vanity Fair: Becky Sharp and Her Patrician Heroes." *Nineteenth-Century Fiction 27*, No. 2 (September 1972): 171-81.
Explores the possible connection between *Vanity Fair* and a type of eighteenth-century novel represented by Fanny Burney's *Evelina*. Moler argues that Becky interacts with men who are parodies of the virtuous heroes in Burney's novel.

Olmstead, Charles John. *Thackeray and His Twentieth-Century Critics: An Annotated Bibliography, 1900-1975*. New York: Garland Publishing, 1977, 249 p.
An annotated guide to twentieth-century criticism of Thackeray's works.

Paris, Bernard J. "The Psychic Structure of *Vanity Fair*." *Victorian Studies X*, No. 4 (June 1967): 389-410.
A psychological study of the implied author of *Vanity Fair*.

Pollard, Arthur, ed. *Thackeray: "Vanity Fair," A Casebook*. Casebook Series. London: Macmillan Press, 1978, 237 p.
Reprints selected nineteenth- and twentieth-century critical commentary on *Vanity Fair*. Pollard includes essays by such critics as Forster, Bell, Ray, Dyson, and Craig.

Quennell, Peter. "*Vanity Fair*." In his *Casanova in London*, pp. 97-109. New York: Stein and Day, 1971.
A general introduction to *Vanity Fair*. Quennell discusses the genesis of the novel, Thackeray's attitudes toward his female characters, and the differences between Dickens's and Thackeray's approach to literature.

Rawlins, Jack P. "*Vanity Fair*: The Structure of Self-Refutation." In his *Thackeray's Novels: A Fiction that Is True*, pp. 1-35. Berkeley and Los Angeles: University of California Press, 1974.
A three-part essay dealing with the ways in which *Vanity Fair* "can be described as a dramatic action, an apologue, or a satire."

Ray, Gordon N. "*Vanity Fair*: One Version of the Novelist's Responsibility." In *Essays by Divers Hands*, edited by Sir Edward Marsh, New Series, Vol. XXV, pp. 87-101. London: Oxford University Press, 1950.
Explores the origin of Thackeray's conception of his responsibility as a novelist in *Vanity Fair*.

————. *Thackeray: The Uses of Adversity, 1811-1846*. Vol. I; *Thackeray: The Age of Wisdom, 1846-1863*. Vol. II. New York: McGraw-Hill Book Co., 1955, 1958.
The definitive biography.

Sharp, Sister M. Corona. "Sympathetic Mockery: A Study of the Narrator's Character in *Vanity Fair*." *ELH 29*, No. 3 (September 1962): 324-36.
Argues that the narrator of *Vanity Fair* is a "sophisticated ironist" whose character provides the novel's unifying principle.

Sheets, Robin Ann. "Art and Artistry in *Vanity Fair*." *ELH 42*, No. 3 (Fall 1975): 420-32.
Suggests that art is one of the primary themes in *Vanity Fair*. Sheets examines the artistic abilities and attitudes toward art of various characters in the novel, as well as Thackeray's and the narrator's views on the subject.

Shillingsburg, Peter L. "The Printing, Proof-reading, and Publishing of Thackeray's *Vanity Fair*: The First Edition." *Studies in Bibliography XXXIV* (1981): 118-45.
A technical analysis of the various stages in the publishing process that produced the first edition of *Vanity Fair*.

Stevens, Joan. "Thackeray's *Vanity Fair*." *Review of English Literature 6*, No. 1 (January 1965): 19-38.
Argues that Thackeray's illustrations serve an important function in the novel that later publishers of the text have thwarted by omitting the designs or by placing them in inappropriate locations.

Sundell, M. G., ed. *Twentieth-Century Interpretations of "Vanity Fair": A Collection of Critical Essays.* Twentieth-Century Interpretations, edited by Maynard Mack. Englewood Cliffs, N.J.: Prentice-Hall, A Spectrum Book, 1969, 123 p.

A collection of twentieth-century critical commentary on *Vanity Fair.* Sundell reprints essays by such critics as Van Ghent, Loofbourow, and Dyson.

Sutherland, J. A. "*Vanity Fair:* The Art of Improvisation." In his *Thackeray at Work,* pp. 11-44. London: Athlone Press, 1974.

A study of Thackeray's compositional methods during the writing of *Vanity Fair.*

Talon, Henri A. "Thackeray's *Vanity Fair* Revisited: Fiction as Truth." In *Of Books and Humankind: Essays and Poems Presented to Bonamy Dobrée,* edited by John Butt, pp. 117-48. London: Routledge and Kegan Paul, 1964.

A wide-ranging analysis of the novel, focusing on the Vanity Fair motif, the moral and social significance of various characters, and Thackeray's technique of variation and contrast.

Thackeray, William Makepeace. *Vanity Fair: A Novel without a Hero.* Edited by Geoffrey Tillotson and Kathleen Tillotson. London: Methuen & Co., 1963, 680 p.

An authoritative text of the novel.

Tilford, John E., Jr. "The Degradation of Becky Sharp." *South Atlantic Quarterly* 58, No. 4 (Autumn 1959): 603-08.

Argues that critics who have seen Becky as the heroine of *Vanity Fair* have failed to take into account Thackeray's consistent portrayal of her as degraded and evil.

Tillotson, Geoffrey, and Tillotson, Kathleen. Introduction to *Vanity Fair: A Novel without a Hero,* by William Makepeace Thackeray, edited by Geoffrey Tillotson and Kathleen Tillotson, pp. v-xxxix. London: Methuen & Co., 1963.

A general introduction to *Vanity Fair,* focusing on Thackeray's avoidance of "surplus description," his range of subject matter, and his moral commentary.

Tillotson, Geoffrey, and Hawes, Donald, eds. *Thackeray: The Critical Heritage.* The Critical Heritage series, edited by B. C. Southam. London: Routledge & Kegan Paul, 1968, 392 p.

Includes selected nineteenth-century critical commentary on *Vanity Fair.*

Wheatley, James H. "*Vanity Fair:* Postures of Wisdom" and "*Vanity Fair:* Wisdom and Art." In his *Patterns in Thackeray's Fiction,* pp. 56-75, pp. 75-93. Cambridge: M.I.T. Press, 1969.

Two chapters, the first focusing on structural perspectives in *Vanity Fair,* the second concerned with Thackeray's concepts of psychology and causation.

Wilkenfeld, Roger B. "'Before the Curtain' and *Vanity Fair.*" *Nineteenth-Century Fiction* 26, No. 3 (December 1971): 307-18.

A study of Thackeray's preface to *Vanity Fair* (see essay dated 1848).

Wilkinson, Ann Y. "The Tomeavesian Way of Knowing the World: Technique and Meaning in *Vanity Fair.*" *ELH* 32, No. 3 (September 1965): 370-87.

Explores the important role that the secret knowledge of others plays in *Vanity Fair.*

Appendix

The following is a listing of all sources used in Volume 14 of *Nineteenth-Century Literature Criticism*. Included in this list are all copyright and reprint rights and acknowledgments for those essays for which permission was obtained. Every effort has been made to trace copyright, but if omissions have been made, please let us know.

THE EXCERPTS IN NCLC, VOLUME 14, WERE REPRINTED FROM THE FOLLOWING PERIODICALS:

The Academy, v. XXIX, January 23, 1886; v. LI, February, 1897.

American Literature, v. 26, November, 1954. Copyright © 1955, renewed 1982, Duke University Press, Durham, NC. Reprinted by permission.

The American Review, n.s. v. II, October, 1848.

The American Scholar, v. 30, Winter, 1960-61 for "The Case Becomes Less Strange" by Charles D. Aring. Copyright © 1961 by the author. Reprinted by permission of the author.

The Athenaeum, n. 135, May 29, 1830; n. 263, November 10, 1832; n. 387, March 28, 1835; n. 1085, August 12, 1848; n. 3038, January 16, 1886; n. 3297, January 3, 1891.

The Atlantic Monthly, v. 97, June, 1906; v. 109, May, 1912; v. 116, July, 1915./ v. 175, January, 1945. Copyright 1945, renewed 1972, by The Atlantic Monthly Company, Boston, MA. Reprinted by permission.

Beeton's Christmas Annual, No. 28, November, 1887.

Belgravia, v. VIII, May, 1869.

Blackwood's Edinburgh Magazine, v. II, March, 1818; v. III, July, 1818; v. XII, March, 1823; v. XXVII, May, 1830; v. CXXV, June, 1879; v. CXLVIII, August, 1890; v. CLII, August, 1892.

Blackwood's Magazine, v. CXCIII, April, 1913.

The Book Buyer, v. III, February, 1886.

The Bookman, London, v. XII, October, 1900.

The Bookman, New York, v. XV, May, 1902; v. XXXVII, March, 1913; v. LXXI, March, 1927.

The British Critic, v. IV, July, 1794; n.s. v. IX, April, 1818.

Keats-Shelley Journal, v. 8, Winter, 1959. © Keats-Shelley Association of America, Inc. 1959. Reprinted by permission.

Littell's Living Age, v. XX, March 10, 1849.

The Living Age, v. CCXXX, July 6, 1901.

The London Literary Gazette, n. 319, March 1, 1823; n. 474, February 18, 1826.

The London Quarterly Review, v. II, March, 1854; v. X, April, 1858.

The London Review, v. XVI, July, 1861.

Macmillan's Magazine, v. 67, February, 1893.

The Monthly Review, London, v. XV, October, 1794; n. XXXI, February, 1800; v. I, March, 1826; n.s. v. I, March, 1837.

Morning Chronicle, January 10, 1793.

Mosaic: A Journal for the Interdisciplinary Study of Literature, v. XIV (Spring, 1981). © *Mosaic* 1981. Acknowledgment of previous publication is herewith made.

The Nation, v. V, November 24, 1867; v. XL, January 29, 1885; v. XLVII, October 4, 1888.

The Nation and The Athenaeum, v. XXXII, December 16, 1922.

The National Review, London, v. XXVI, October, 1861; v. III, July, 1884; v. XIX, 1892; v. XXVII, July, 1896; v. XXXVIII, February, 1902; v. LXXXII, December, 1923.

The New Monthly Magazine, v. XLVIII, October, 1836.

The New Quarterly Review, v. II, 1853.

The New World, November, 1920.

The New-York Mirror, v. X, June 8, 1833.

The New York Review of Books, v. XXI, March 21, 1974 for ''Female Gothic: The Monster's Mother'' by Ellen Moers. Copyright © 1974 by the author. All rights reserved. Reprinted by permission of the Literary Estate of Ellen Moers.

The New York Times Book Review, July 23, 1922. Copyright 1922 by The New York Times Company. Reprinted by permission.

Nineteenth-Century Fiction, v. 12, September, 1957 for ''Pernicious Casuistry: A Study of Character in 'Vanity Fair','' by Russell A. Fraser; v. 18, September, 1963 for ''Contrast as a Principle of Structure in 'Vanity Fair','' by Myron Taube. © 1957, 1963 by The Regents of the University of California. Both reprinted by permission of The Regents and the respective authors.

The North American Review, v. VII, May, 1818; v. XLIV, January, 1837; v. LXIV, January, 1847; v. CLIV, December, 1894.

The North British Review, v. L, July, 1868.

Notes & Queries, v. 190, June 15, 1946.

Partisan Review, v. XXXII, Fall, 1965 for ''Frankenstein; or, The New Prometheus'' by Harold Bloom. Copyright © by the author. Reprinted by permission of the author.

PMLA, 33, n.s. v. XXXIII, March, 1918; 38, v. XXXVIII, December, 1923.

The Quarterly Review, v. VIII, September, 1812; v. XVIII, January, 1818; v. XXX, January, 1824; v. LXXI, March, 1843; v. CXXII, January, 1867; v. CLXXIX, January, 1895.

Queen's Quarterly, v. LII, Spring, 1945.

The Saturday Review, London, v. 22, December 15, 1866; v. 24, October 26, 1867; v. 27, June 5, 1869; v. 45, May 18, 1878.

Aldington, Richard. From *Literary Studies and Reviews*. The Dial Press, 1924.

Aldiss, Brian W. From *Trillion Year Spree: The History of Science Fiction*. Atheneum, 1986, Gollancz, 1986. Copyright © 1973, 1986 Brian Aldiss. Reprinted with the permission of Atheneum Publishers, Inc. In Canada by Victor Gollancz Ltd.

Allen, Gay Wilson. From *American Prosody*. American Book Company, 1935.

Amis, Kingsley. From *New Maps of Hell*. Victor Gollancz Ltd., 1960. Copyright © 1960 by Kingsley Amis. Reprinted by permission of Jonathan Clowes Ltd.

Atwood, Margaret. From *The Journals of Susanna Moodie*. Oxford University Press, Canadian Branch, 1970. © Oxford University Press 1970. Reprinted by permission.

Baker, Ray Palmer. From *A History of English-Canadian Literature to the Confederation: Its Relation to the Literature of Great Britain and the United States*. Cambridge, Mass.: Harvard University Press, 1920.

Barrett, Elizabeth, with Richard Hengist Horne. From "Walter Savage Landor," in *A New Spirit of the Age*. Edited by Richard Hengist Horne. Harper & Brothers, 1844.

Birkhead, Edith. From *The Tale of Terror: A Study of the Gothic Romance*. Constable & Company Ltd., 1921.

Blain, Virginia. From an introduction to *Mr. Sponge's Sporting Tour*. By R. S. Surtees, edited by Virginia Blain. Batsford Academic and Educational Ltd., 1981. Introduction and notes © University of Queensland Press, St. Lucia, Queensland 1981. All rights reserved. Reprinted by permission.

Bleiler, E. F. From an introduction to *Monsieur Lecoq*. By Émile Gaboriau, edited by E. F. Bleiler. Dover, 1975. Copyright © 1975 by Dover Publications, Inc. All rights reserved. Reprinted by permission.

Boulton, James T. From *The Language of Politics in the Age of Wilkes and Burke*. Routledge & Kegan Paul, 1963. © James T. Boulton 1963. Reprinted by permission of Routlege & Kegan Paul PLC.

Bradley, William. From *The Early Poems of Walter Savage Landor: A Study of His Development and Debt to Milton*. Bradbury, Agnes & Co., 1914.

Briggs, Julia. From *Night Visitors: The Rise and Fall of the English Ghost Story*. Faber & Faber, 1977. © 1977 by Julia Briggs. Reprinted by permission of Faber & Faber Ltd.

Brooks, Peter. From "Godlike Science/Unhallowed Arts': Language, Nature, and Monstrosity," in *The Endurance of Frankenstein: Essays on Mary Shelley's Novel*. Edited by George Levine and U. C. Knoepflmacher. University of California, 1979. Copyright © 1979 by The Regents of the University of California. Reprinted by permission of the publisher.

Brophy, Brigid, Michael Levey, and Charles Osborne. From *Fifty Works of English and American Literature We Could Do Without*. Stein and Day, 1968. Copyright © 1967 by Brigid Brophy, Michael Levey, Charles Osborne. All rights reserved. Reprinted with permission of Stein and Day Publishers.

Browning, Robert. From a letter in *Robert Browning and Julia Wedgwood: A Broken Friendship as Revealed by Their Letters*. Edited by Richard Curle. Frederick A. Stokes Company, 1937. Copyright, 1937, by Mary Wedgwood and John Murray. Renewed 1965 by Richard Curle.

Bush, Douglas. From *English Poetry: The Main Currents from Chaucer to the Present*. Methuen & Co. Ltd., 1952.

Cary, Joyce. From an introduction to *Mr. Sponge's Sporting Tour*. By R. S. Surtees. Oxford University Press, London, 1958. Reprinted by permission of the Literary Estate of Joyce Cary.

Chandler, Frank Wadleigh. From *The Literature of Roguery, Vol. II*. Houghton, Mifflin and Company, 1907.

Chesterton, G. K. From *Robert Louis Stevenson*. Dodd, Mead, 1928. Copyright, 1928 by Dodd, Mead & Company, Inc. Renewed 1955 by Oliver Chesterton. Reprinted by permission of A. P. Watt Ltd. on behalf of Miss D. E. Collins.

Chesterton, G. K. From *A Handful of Authors: Essays on Books & Writers*. Edited by Dorothy Collins. Sheed and Ward, 1953.

Coleridge, Samuel Taylor. From *Letters, Conversations, and Recollections of S. T. Coleridge*. Edited by Allsop. N.p., 1836.

Cooper, Leonard. From *R S. Surtees*. Arthur Barker Ltd., 1952.

Craig, G. Armour. From "On the Style of 'Vanity Fair'," in *Style in Prose Fiction*. English Institute Essays 1958. Edited by Harold C. Martin. Columbia University Press, 1959. © 1959, Columbia University Press. Reprinted by permission of the publisher.

De Sélincourt, Ernest. From an introduction to *Imaginary Conversations*. By Walter Savage Landor. Oxford University Press, London, 1914.

Dillard, R. H. W. From "Even a Man Who Is Pure at Heart: Poetry and Danger in the Horror Film," in *Man and the Movies*. Edited by W. R. Robinson with George Garrett. Louisiana State University Press, 1967. Copyright © 1967 by Louisiana State University Press. Reprinted by permission of the publisher.

Driver, C. H. From "William Godwin." in *The Social & Political Ideas of Some Representative Thinkers of the Revolutionary Era*. Edited by F. J. C. Hearnshaw. George G. Harrap & Company Ltd., 1931.

Eigner, Edwin M. From *Robert Louis Stevenson and Romantic Tradition*. Princeton University Press, 1966. Copyright © 1966 by Princeton University Press. All rights reserved. Reprinted with permission of the publisher.

Eliot, T. S. From *The Use of Poetry and the Use of Criticism: Studies in the Relation of Criticism to Poetry in England*. Cambridge, Mass.: Harvard University Press, 1933, Faber and Faber, 1933. Copyright 1933 by the President and Fellows of Harvard College. Renewed © 1961 by T. S. Eliot. All rights reserved. Excerpted by permission of Harvard University Press. In Canada by Faber and Faber Ltd.

Gilfillan, George. From *A Gallery of Literary Portraits*. William Tait, 1845.

Godwin, William. From *St. Leon: A Tale of the Sixteenth Century*. Colburn and Bentley, 1831.

Godwin, William. From *The Adventures of Caleb Williams; or, Things as They Are*. Revised edition. Richard Bentley, 1849.

Godwin, William. From a letter in *The Life and Letters of Mary Wollstonecraft Shelley, Vol. II*. By Julian Marshall. Richard Bentley & Son, 1889.

Greig, J. Y. T. From *Thackeray: A Reconsideration*. Oxford University Press, London, 1950.

Grigson, Geoffrey. From an introduction to *Poems*. By Walter Savage Landor, edited by Geoffrey Grigson. Centaur Press, 1964. Copyright © by Centaur Press Limited. Reprinted by permission of the publisher.

Grylls, R. Glynn. From *Mary Shelley: A Biography*. Oxford University Press, London, 1938.

Guttenberg, A. Charles von. From *Early Canadian Art and Literature*. Europe Printing Estb., 1969. © 1969 A. Ch. v. Guttenberg. Reprinted by permission.

Hamilton, Alex. From an introduction to *Jorrocks' Jaunts and Jollities*. By Robert Smith Surtees, edited by Herbert Van Thal. Cassell, 1968. New Material © Cassell and Company Limited 1968. Reprinted with permission of Macmillan Publishing Company.

Hannah, Barbara. From *Striving towards Wholeness*. C. G. Jung Foundation for Analytical Psychology, 1971. Copyright © 1971 by the C. G. Jung Foundation for Analytical Psychology, Inc., New York, NY. All rights reserved. Reprinted by permission of the publisher.

Hardy, Barbara. From *The Exposure of Luxury: Radical Themes in Thackeray*. Peter Owen Limited, London, 1972. © 1972 Barbara Hardy. All rights reserved. Reprinted by permission.

Hayakawa, S. I. and Howard Mumford Jones. From "Oliver Wendell Holmes," in *Oliver Wendell Holmes: Representative Selections*. By Oliver Wendell Holmes, edited by S. I. Hayakawa and Howard Mumford Jones. American Book Company, 1939.

Haycraft, Howard. From *Murder for Pleasure: The Life and Times of the Detective Story*. Appleton-Century, 1941. Copyright 1941 by D. Appleton-Century Co., Inc. Renewed 1968 by Howard Haycraft. All rights reserved. Reprinted by permission of E. P. Dutton, a division of New American Library.

Hazlitt, William. From *The Spirit of the Age; or, Contemporary Portraits*. H. Colburn, 1825.

Holmes, Oliver Wendell. From *The Poems of Oliver Wendell Holmes*. Ticknor and Fields, 1862.

Holmes, Oliver Wendell. From *Elsie Venner: A Romance of Destiny*. Houghton, Mifflin and Company, 1883.

MacMurchy, Archibald. From *Handbook of Canadian Literature (English)*. William Briggs, 1906.

Macy, John. From *The Spirit of American Literature*. Doubleday, Page & Company, 1913. Copyright 1913 by Doubleday & Company, Inc. Copyright renewed 1940 by William M. Rockwell, as literary executor to the Estate of John Macy.

Malthus, T. R. From *An Essay on the Principle of Population; or, A View of Its Past and Present Effects on Human Happiness, Vol. II*. Third edition. J. Johnson, 1806.

McAlpin, Edwin A. From *Old and New Books as Life Teachers*. Doubleday, Doran, & Company, Inc., 1928.

McDougall, Robert L. From "Editor's Introduction," in *Life in the Clearings*. By Susanna Moodie, edited by Robert L. McDougall. Macmillan, 1959. © 1959 The Macmillan Company of Canada Ltd. All rights reserved. Reprinted by permission of the editor.

Mitford, Mary Russell. From *Recollections of a Literary Life; or, Books, Places, and People*. R. Bentley, 1852.

Miyoshi, Masao. From *The Divided Self: A Perspective on the Literature of the Victorians*. New York University Press, 1969. Copyright © 1969 by New York University. Reprinted by permission of the publisher.

Moodie, Susanna. From *Life in the Clearings versus the Bush*. Richard Bentley, 1853.

Moodie, Susanna. From *Roughing It in the Bush; or, Forest Life in Canada*. G. P. Putnam, 1852.

Moore, Helen. From *Mary Wollstonecraft Shelley*. J. B. Lippincott Company, 1886.

Moore, John. From *Country Men*. J. M. Dent & Sons, Ltd., 1935.

Morse, David. From *Romanticism: A Structural Analysis*. Barnes & Noble, 1982. © David Morse 1982. All rights reserved. Reprinted by permission of Barnes & Noble Books, a Division of Littlefield, Adams & Co., Inc.

Murch, A. E. From *The Development of the Detective Novel*. Philosophical Library, 1958. © A. E. Murch 1958. All rights reserved. Reprinted by permission.

Murry, John Middleton. From *Heroes of Thought*. Julian Messner, Inc., 1938. Copyright, 1938 by John Middleton Murry. Renewed © 1966 by Mary Middleton Murry. Reprinted by permission of Julian Messner, a division of Simon & Schuster, Inc.

Myers, F. W. H. From *Dr. Jeykll and Mr. Hyde*. By Robert Louis Stevenson. B. Tauchnitz, 1886.

Myers, Frederick W. H. From a letter in *Robert Louis Stevenson: The Critical Heritage*. Edited by Paul Maixner. Routledge & Kegan Paul, 1981. Copyright © the Estate of Paul Maixner 1981. Reprinted by permission of Routledge & Kegan Paul PLC.

Nabokov, Vladimir. From *Lectures on Literature*. Edited by Fredson Bowers. Harcourt Brace Jovanovich, 1980. Copyright © 1980 by the Estate of Vladimir Nabokov. Reprinted by permission of Harcourt Brace Jovanovich, Inc.

Neumann, Bonnie Rayford. From *Robert Smith Surtees*. Twayne, 1978. Copyright 1978 by Twayne Publishers. All rights reserved. Reprinted with the permission of Twayne Publishers, a division of G. K. Hall & Co., Boston.

Nitchie, Elizabeth. From *Mary Shelley: Author of "Frankenstein."* Rutgers University Press, 1953. Copyright 1953 by the Trustees of Rutgers College in New Jersey. All rights reserved. Reprinted by permission of the publisher.

Norman, Sylva. From "Mary Shelley: Novelist and Dramatist," in *On Shelley*. By Edmund Blunden, Gavin de Beer, and Sylva Norma. Oxford University Press, London, 1938.

Oberndorf, Clarence P. From "Foreword" and "Introduction: Dynamic Psychiatry and Holmes," in *The Psychiatric Novels of Oliver Wendell Holmes*. By Oliver Wendell Holmes, edited by Clarence P. Oberndorf. Columbia University Press, 1943.

O'Connor, Frank. From *The Mirror in the Roadway: A Study of the Modern Novel*. Alfred A. Knopf, 1956.

Osbourne, Katharine D. From a letter in *The True Stevenson: A Study in Clarification*. By George S. Hellman. Little, Brown and Company, 1925.

Ousby, Ian. From *Bloodhounds of Heaven: The Detective in English Fiction from Godwin to Doyle*. Cambridge, Mass.: Harvard University Press, 1976. Copyright © 1976 by the President and Fellows of Harvard College. All rights reserved. Excerpted by permission.

Parrington, Vernon Louis. From *Main Currents in American Thought, an Interpretation of American Literature from the Beginnings to 1920: The Romantic Revolution in America, 1800-1860, Vol. 2*. Harcourt Brace Jovanovich, 1927. Copyright 1927 by Harcourt Brace

Peck, Harry Thurston. From *Studies in Several Literatures*. Dodd, Mead and Company, 1909.

Praz, Mario. From an introduction to *Three Gothic Novels*. Penguin English Library. Edited by Peter Fairclough. Penguin Books, 1968. Introductory essay copyright © Mario Praz, 1968. Reproduced by permission of Penguin Books Ltd.

Pritchett, V. S. From *The Living Novel & Later Appreciations*. Revised edition. Random House, 1964. Copyright © 1975 by V. S. Pritchett. All rights reserved. Reprinted by permission of Literistic, Ltd.

Proudfit, Charles L. From an introduction to *Landor as Critic*. Edited by Charles L. Proudfit. University of Nebraska Press, 1979. Copyright 1979 Charles L. Proudfit. Reprinted by permission of University of Nebraska Press.

Raleigh, Walter. From *On Writing and Writers*. Edited by George Gordon. Edward Arnold & Co., 1926.

Rashley, R. E. From *Poetry in Canada: The First Three Steps*. The Ryerson Press, 1958. Copyright © McGraw-Hill Ryerson Limited, 1958. All rights reserved. Reprinted by permission of the Literary Estate of R. E. Rashley.

Renwick, W. L. From ''Jorrocks: A Conversation,'' in *Essays and Studies by Members of the English Association, Vol. XVII*. Edited by W. H. Hadow. Oxford at the Clarendon Press, Oxford, 1932.

Rhodenizer, V. B. From *A Handbook of Canadian Literature*. Graphic Publishers Limited, 1930.

Rieger, James. From an introduction to *Frankenstein; or, The Modern Prometheus: The 1818 Text*. By Mary Wollstonecraft Shelley, edited by James Rieger. Bobbs-Merrill, 1974, University of Chicago Press, 1982. © 1974, 1982 by James Rieger. All rights reserved. Reprinted by permission of The University of Chicago Press and the Literary Estate of James Rieger.

Roosevelt, Theodore. From an extract from a letter in *Robert Smith Surtees: A Critical Study*. By Frederick Watson. George G. Harrap & Co. Ltd., 1933.

Rossetti, Lucy Madox. From *Mrs. Shelley*. W. H. Allen & Co., 1890.

Saposnik, Irving S. From *Robert Louis Stevenson*. Twayne, 1974. Copyright 1974 by Twayne Publishers. All rights reserved. Reprinted with the permission of Twayne Publishers, a division of G. K. Hall & Co., Boston.

Sassoon, Siegfried. From *Memoirs of a Fox-Hunting Man*. Faber & Gwyer Limited, 1928. Copyright 1929, renewed 1956, by Siegfried Sassoon. Reprinted by permission of Stackpole Books/The K. S. Giniger Co. Inc. In Canada by Faber & Faber Ltd.´

Shelley, Mary Wollstonecraft. From *Frankenstein; or, The Modern Prometheus*. H. Colburn and R. Bentley, 1831.

Shelley, Percy Bysshe. From a preface to *Frankenstein; or, The Modern Prometheus*. By Mary Wollstonecraft Shelley. Lackington, Hughes, Harding, etc., 1818.

Shelley, Percy Bysshe. From *The Revolt of Islam*. N.p., 1818.

Shelley, Percy Bysshe. From *The Letters of Percy Bysshe Shelley: Shelley in England, Vol. I*. Edited by Frederick L. Jones. Oxford at the Clarendon Press, Oxford, 1964.

Shields, Carol. From *Susanna Moodie: Voice and Vision*. Borealis Press, 1977. Copyright Borealis Press Limited, 1977. All rights reserved. Reprinted by permission.

Sitwell, Osbert. From *Penny Foolish: A Book of Tirades & Panegyrics*. Macmillan & Company Ltd., 1935.

Steel, Anthony. From *Jorrocks's England*. E. P. Dutton and Company Inc. Publishers, 1933.

Stephen, Leslie. From *Studies of a Biographer*. Duckworth and Co., 1902.

Stevenson, Robert Louis. From *Memories and Portraits*. C. Scribner's Sons, 1887.

Stevenson, Robert Louis. From *Across the Plains with Other Memories and Essays*. Charles Scribner's Sons, 1892.

Stevenson, Robert Louis. From *The Letters of Robert Louis Stevenson: 1880-1887, Alps and Highlands—Hyères—Bournemouth, Vol. II.* Edited by Sidney Colvin. Revised edition. Charles Scribner's Sons, 1911.

Stevenson, Robert Louis. From a letter in *The True Stevenson: A Study in Clarification*. By George S. Hellman. Little, Brown and Company, 1925.

Stewart, R. F. From *... And Always a Detective: Chapters on the History of Detective Fiction*. David & Charles, 1980. © R. F. Stewart 1980. All rights reserved. Reprinted by permission of the author.

Surtees, Robert Smith. From *Hawbuck Grange; or, The Sporting Adventures of Thomas Scott, Esq*. Longmans, Brown, Green & Longman, 1847.

Surtees, Robert Smith. From *Handley Cross*. Second edition. Methuen & Co. Ltd., 1854.

Surtees, Robert Smith. From *"Ask Mamma"; or, The Richest Commoner in England*. Bradbury, Agnew, & Co., 1858.

Surtees, Robert Smith. From "First Literary Efforts: The 'New Sporting Magazine' and 'The Horseman's Manual'," in *Robert Smith Surtees (Creator of "Jorrocks"): 1803-1864*. By Robert Smith Surtees and E. D. Cuming. Charles Scribner's Sons, 1924.

Sutherland, John. From an introduction to *Vanity Fair: A Novel without a Hero*. By William Makepeace Thackeray. Oxford University Press, Oxford, 1983. Introduction, introductory notes, bibliography, and chronology © John Sutherland 1983. All rights reserved. Reprinted by permission of Oxford University Press.

Sutherland, Ronald. From *Second Image: Comparative Studies in Quebec/Canadian Literature*. New Press, 1971. Copyright © 1971 by Ronald Sutherland. Reprinted by permission of Stoddart Publishing Co. Limited.

Swinburne, Algernon Charles. From "Landor," in *The Encyclopaedia Britannica: A Dictionary of Arts, Sciences, and General Literature*. Edited by T. S. Baynes. Ninth edition. A. C. Black, 1882.

Symonds, J A From *The Letters of John Addington Symonds: 1885-1893, Vol. III*. Edited by Herbert M. Schueller and Robert L. Peters. Wayne State University Press, 1969. Copyright © 1969 by Herbert M. Schueller and Robert L. Peters. All rights reserved. Reprinted by permission of the editors.

Thackeray, W. M. From a letter in *Robert Smith Surtees (Creator of 'Jorrocks'): 1803-1864*. By Robert Smith Surtees and E. D. Cuming. Charles Scribner's Sons, 1924.

Thackeray, William Makepeace. From *Vanity Fair: A Novel without a Hero*. Bradbury & Evans, 1848.

Thackeray, William Makepeace. From *The Letters and Private Papers of William Makepeace Thackeray: 1841-1851, Vol. II*. Edited by Gordon N. Ray. Cambridge, Mass.: Harvard University Press, 1945. Copyright, 1945 by Hester Thackeray Ritchie Fuller and the President and Fellows of Harvard College. Renewed 1973 by Belinda Norman Butler and Gordon H. Ray. Reprinted by permission of the Literary Estate of William Makepeace Thackeray.

Thomas, Clara. From "The Strickland Sisters," in *The Clear Spirit: Twenty Canadian Women and Their Times*. Edited by Mary Quayle Innis. University of Toronto Press, 1966. © University of Toronto Press, 1966. Reprinted by permission of the publisher.

Thomson, H. Douglas. From *Masters of Mystery: A Study of the Detective Story*. W. Collins Sons & Co., 1931.

Trollope, Anthony. From *Thackeray*. Macmillan & Co., Limited, 1879.

Tymms, Ralph. From *Doubles in Literary Psychology*. Bowes & Bowes, 1949.

Van Ghent, Dorothy. From *The English Novel: Form and Function*. Holt, Rinehart and Winston, 1953. Copyright 1953, renewed 1981, by Dorothy Van Ghent. Reprinted by permission of the Literary Estate of Dorothy Van Ghent.

Cumulative Index to Authors

This index lists all author entries in the Gale Literary Criticism Series and includes cross-references to other Gale sources. For the convenience of the reader, references to the *Yearbook* in the *Contemporary Literary Criticism* series include the page number (in parentheses) after the volume number. References in the index are identified as follows:

AITN:	*Authors in the News*, Volumes 1-2
CAAS:	*Contemporary Authors Autobiography Series*, Volumes 1-4
CA:	*Contemporary Authors* (original series), Volumes 1-118
CANR:	*Contemporary Authors New Revision Series*, Volumes 1-18
CAP:	*Contemporary Authors Permanent Series*, Volumes 1-2
CA-R:	*Contemporary Authors* (revised editions), Volumes 1-44
CLC:	*Contemporary Literary Criticism*, Volumes 1-41
CLR:	*Children's Literature Review*, Volumes 1-11
DLB:	*Dictionary of Literary Biography*, Volumes 1-53
DLB-DS:	*Dictionary of Literary Biography Documentary Series*, Volumes 1-4
DLB-Y:	*Dictionary of Literary Biography Yearbook*, Volumes 1980-1985
LC:	*Literature Criticism from 1400 to 1800*, Volumes 1-4
NCLC:	*Nineteenth-Century Literature Criticism*, Volumes 1-14
SAAS:	*Something about the Author Autobiography Series*, Volumes 1-2
SATA:	*Something about the Author*, Volumes 1-44
TCLC:	*Twentieth-Century Literary Criticism*, Volumes 1-22
YABC:	*Yesterday's Authors of Books for Children*, Volumes 1-2

Author Index

Author Index

Borowski, Tadeusz 1922-1951 . . . . . **TCLC 9**
See also CA 106

Borrow, George (Henry)
1803-1881 . . . . **NCLC 9**
See also DLB 21

Bosschère, Jean de
1878-1953 . . . . **TCLC 19**

Boswell, James 1740-1795 . . . . **LC 4**

Bourget, Paul (Charles Joseph)
1852-1935 . . . . **TCLC 12**
See also CA 107

Bourjaily, Vance (Nye) 1922- . . . .**CLC 8**
See also CAAS 1
See also CANR 2
See also CA 1-4R
See also DLB 2

Bourne, Randolph S(illiman)
1886-1918 . . . . **TCLC 16**

Bowen, Elizabeth (Dorothea Cole)
1899-1973 . . . . . . **CLC 1, 3, 6, 11, 15, 22**
See also CAP 2
See also CA 17-18
See also obituary CA 41-44R
See also DLB 15

Bowering, George 1935- . . . .**CLC 15**
See also CANR 10
See also CA 21-24R
See also DLB 53

Bowering, Marilyn R(uthe)
1949- . . . .**CLC 32**
See also CA 101

Bowers, Edgar 1924- . . . .**CLC 9**
See also CA 5-8R
See also DLB 5

Bowie, David 1947- . . . .**CLC 17**
See also Jones, David Robert

Bowles, Jane (Sydney)
1917-1973 . . . .**CLC 3**
See also CAP 2
See also CA 19-20
See also obituary CA 41-44R

Bowles, Paul (Frederick)
1910- . . . . **CLC 1, 2, 19**
See also CAAS 1
See also CANR 1
See also CA 1-4R
See also DLB 5, 6

Box, Edgar 1925-
See Vidal, Gore

Boyd, William 1952- . . . .**CLC 28**
See also CA 114

Boyle, Kay 1903- . . . . **CLC 1, 5, 19**
See also CAAS 1
See also CA 13-16R
See also DLB 4, 9, 48

Boyle, Patrick . . . .**CLC 19**

Boyle, T. Coraghessan 1948- . . . .**CLC 36**

Brackenridge, Hugh Henry
1748-1816 . . . . **NCLC 7**
See also DLB 11, 37

Bradbury, Edward P. 1939-
See Moorcock, Michael

Bradbury, Malcolm (Stanley)
1932- . . . .**CLC 32**
See also CANR 1
See also CA 1-4R
See also DLB 14

Bradbury, Ray (Douglas)
1920- . . . .**CLC 1, 3, 10, 15**
See also CANR 2
See also CA 1-4R
See also SATA 11
See also DLB 2, 8
See also AITN 1, 2

Bradley, David (Henry), Jr.
1950- . . . .**CLC 23**
See also CA 104
See also DLB 33

Bradley, Marion Zimmer
1930- . . . .**CLC 30**
See also CANR 7
See also CA 57-60
See also DLB 8

Bradstreet, Anne 1612-1672 . . . . **LC 4**
See also DLB 24

Bragg, Melvyn 1939- . . . .**CLC 10**
See also CANR 10
See also CA 57-60
See also DLB 14

Braine, John (Gerard)
1922-1986 . . . .**CLC 1, 3, 41**
See also CANR 1
See also CA 1-4R
See also DLB 15

Brammer, Billy Lee 1930?-1978
See Brammer, William

Brammer, William 1930?-1978 . . . . .**CLC 31**
See also obituary CA 77-80

Brancati, Vitaliano
1907-1954 . . . . **TCLC 12**
See also CA 109

Brancato, Robin F(idler) 1936- . . . . .**CLC 35**
See also CANR 11
See also CA 69-72
See also SATA 23

Brand, Millen 1906-1980 . . . .**CLC 7**
See also CA 21-24R
See also obituary CA 97-100

Brandes, Georg (Morris Cohen)
1842-1927 . . . . **TCLC 10**
See also CA 105

Branley, Franklyn M(ansfield)
1915- . . . .**CLC 21**
See also CANR 14
See also CA 33-36R
See also SATA 4

Brathwaite, Edward 1930- . . . .**CLC 11**
See also CANR 11
See also CA 25-28R
See also DLB 53

Brautigan, Richard
1935-1984 . . . .**CLC 1, 3, 5, 9, 12,
34 (314)**
See also CA 53-56
See also obituary CA 113
See also DLB 2, 5
See also DLB-Y 80, 84

Brecht, (Eugen) Bertolt (Friedrich)
1898-1956 . . . .**TCLC 1, 6, 13**
See also CA 104

Bremer, Fredrika 1801-1865 . . . . . **NCLC 11**

Brennan, Christopher John
1870-1932 . . . . **TCLC 17**

Brennan, Maeve 1917- . . . .**CLC 5**
See also CA 81-84

Brentano, Clemens (Maria)
1778-1842 . . . . **NCLC 1**

Brenton, Howard 1942- . . . .**CLC 31**
See also CA 69-72
See also DLB 13

Breslin, James (E.) 1930-
See Breslin, Jimmy
See also CA 73-76

Breslin, Jimmy 1930- . . . .**CLC 4**
See also Breslin, James (E.)
See also AITN 1

Bresson, Robert 1907- . . . .**CLC 16**
See also CA 110

Breton, André 1896-1966 . . . . . **CLC 2, 9, 15**
See also CAP 2
See also CA 19-20
See also obituary CA 25-28R

Breytenbach, Breyten
1939- . . . . **CLC 23, 37**
See also CA 113

Bridgers, Sue Ellen 1942- . . . .**CLC 26**
See also CANR 11
See also CA 65-68
See also SAAS 1
See also SATA 22

Bridges, Robert 1844-1930 . . . . **TCLC 1**
See also CA 104
See also DLB 19

Bridie, James 1888-1951 . . . . **TCLC 3**
See also Mavor, Osborne Henry
See also DLB 10

Brin, David 1950- . . . . **CLC 34 (133)**
See also CA 102

Brink, André (Philippus)
1935- . . . . **CLC 18, 36**
See also CA 104

Brinsmead, H(esba) F(ay)
1922- . . . .**CLC 21**
See also CANR 10
See also CA 21-24R
See also SATA 18

Brittain, Vera (Mary)
1893?-1970 . . . .**CLC 23**
See also CAP 1
See also CA 15-16
See also obituary CA 25-28R

Broch, Hermann 1886-1951 . . . . . . **TCLC 20**
See also CA 117

Brock, Rose 1923-
See Hansen, Joseph

Brodsky, Iosif Alexandrovich 1940-
See Brodsky, Joseph
See also CA 41-44R
See also AITN 1

Brodsky, Joseph
1940- . . . . **CLC 4, 6, 13, 36**
See also Brodsky, Iosif Alexandrovich

Brodsky, Michael (Mark)
1948- . . . .**CLC 19**
See also CANR 18
See also CA 102

Bromell, Henry 1947- . . . .**CLC 5**
See also CANR 9
See also CA 53-56

Author Index

Author Index

Author Index

Machado (y Ruiz), Antonio
    1875-1939................... TCLC 3
    See also CA 104

Machado de Assis, (Joaquim Maria)
    1839-1908.................. TCLC 10
    See also CA 107

Machen, Arthur (Llewellyn Jones)
    1863-1947.................... TCLC 4
    See also CA 104
    See also DLB 36

MacInnes, Colin 1914-1976..... CLC 4, 23
    See also CA 69-72
    See also obituary CA 65-68
    See also DLB 14

MacInnes, Helen (Clark)
    1907-1985........... CLC 27, 39 (349)
    See also CANR 1
    See also CA 1-4R
    See also SATA 22, 44

Macintosh, Elizabeth 1897-1952
    See Tey, Josephine
    See also CA 110

Mackenzie, (Edward Montague) Compton
    1883-1972.....................CLC 18
    See also CAP 2
    See also CA 21-22
    See also obituary CA 37-40R
    See also DLB 34

Mac Laverty, Bernard 1942-.......CLC 31
    See also CA 116, 118

MacLean, Alistair (Stuart)
    1922-...................... CLC 3, 13
    See also CA 57-60
    See also SATA 23

MacLeish, Archibald
    1892-1982............... CLC 3, 8, 14
    See also CA 9-12R
    See also obituary CA 106
    See also DLB 4, 7, 45
    See also DLB-Y 82

MacLennan, (John) Hugh
    1907-..................... CLC 2, 14
    See also CA 5-8R

MacNeice, (Frederick) Louis
    1907-1963............... CLC 1, 4, 10
    See also CA 85-88
    See also DLB 10, 20

Macpherson, (Jean) Jay 1931-......CLC 14
    See also CA 5-8R
    See also DLB 53

MacShane, Frank 1927-..... CLC 39 (404)
    See also CANR 3
    See also CA 11-12R

Macumber, Mari 1896-1966
    See Sandoz, Mari (Susette)

Madden, (Jerry) David
    1933-..................... CLC 5, 15
    See also CAAS 3
    See also CANR 4
    See also CA 1-4R
    See also DLB 6

Madhubuti, Haki R. 1942-..........CLC 6
    See also Lee, Don L.
    See also DLB 5, 41

Maeterlinck, Maurice
    1862-1949.................. TCLC 3
    See also CA 104

Maginn, William 1794-1842...... NCLC 8

Mahapatra, Jayanta 1928-.........CLC 33
    See also CANR 15
    See also CA 73-76

Mahon, Derek 1941-..............CLC 27
    See also CA 113
    See also DLB 40

Mailer, Norman
    1923-......CLC 1, 2, 3, 4, 5, 8, 11, 14,
                        28, 39 (416)
    See also CA 9-12R
    See also DLB 2, 16, 28
    See also DLB-Y 80, 83
    See also DLB-DS 3
    See also AITN 2

Mais, Roger 1905-1955........... TCLC 8
    See also CA 105

Major, Clarence 1936-......... CLC 3, 19
    See also CA 21-24R
    See also DLB 33

Major, Kevin 1949-..............CLC 26
    See also CLR 11
    See also CA 97-100
    See also SATA 32

Malamud, Bernard
    1914-......CLC 1, 2, 3, 5, 8, 9, 11, 18,
                        27
    See also CA 5-8R
    See also DLB 2, 28
    See also DLB-Y 80

Mallarmé, Stéphane
    1842-1898................... NCLC 4

Mallet-Joris, Françoise 1930-.......CLC 11
    See also CANR 17
    See also CA 65-68

Maloff, Saul 1922-................CLC 5
    See also CA 33-36R

Malouf, David 1934-..............CLC 28

Malraux, (Georges-) André
    1901-1976........ CLC 1, 4, 9, 13, 15
    See also CAP 2
    See also CA 21-24R
    See also obituary CA 69-72

Malzberg, Barry N. 1939-..........CLC 7
    See also CAAS 4
    See also CANR 16
    See also CA 61-64
    See also DLB 8

Mamet, David
    1947-.............CLC 9, 15, 34 (217)
    See also CANR 15
    See also CA 81-84
    See also DLB 7

Mamoulian, Rouben 1898-.........CLC 16
    See also CA 25-28R

Mandelstam, Osip (Emilievich)
    1891?-1938?............... TCLC 2, 6
    See also CA 104

Mandiargues, André Pieyre de
    1909-........................CLC 41
    See also CA 103

Manley, (Mary) Delariviere
    1672?-1724.................... LC 1
    See also DLB 39

Mann, (Luiz) Heinrich
    1871-1950.................. TCLC 9
    See also CA 106

Mann, Thomas
    1875-1955......... TCLC 2, 8, 14, 21
    See also CA 104

Manning, Olivia 1915-1980..... CLC 5, 19
    See also CA 5-8R
    See also obituary CA 101

Mano, D. Keith 1942-.......... CLC 2, 10
    See also CA 25-28R
    See also DLB 6

Mansfield, Katherine
    1888-1923................. TCLC 2, 8
    See also CA 104

Manso, Peter 1940-......... CLC 39 (416)
    See also CA 29-32R

Marcel, Gabriel (Honore)
    1889-1973....................CLC 15
    See also CA 102
    See also obituary CA 45-48

Marchbanks, Samuel 1913-
    See Davies, (William) Robertson

Marinetti, F(ilippo) T(ommaso)
    1876-1944.................. TCLC 10
    See also CA 107

Marivaux, Pierre Carlet de Chamblain de
    (1688-1763) .... LC 4

Markandaya, Kamala 1924- .... CLC 8, 38
    See also Taylor, Kamala (Purnaiya)

Markfield, Wallace (Arthur)
    1926-.......................CLC 8
    See also CAAS 3
    See also CA 69-72
    See also DLB 2, 28

Markham, Robert 1922-
    See Amis, Kingsley (William)

Marks, J. 1942-
    See Highwater, Jamake

Marley, Bob 1945-1981 ....CLC 17
    See also Marley, Robert Nesta

Marley, Robert Nesta 1945-1981
    See Marley, Bob
    See also CA 107
    See also obituary CA 103

Marmontel, Jean-François
    1723-1799...................... LC 2

Marquand, John P(hillips)
    1893-1960................. CLC 2, 10
    See also CA 85-88
    See also DLB 9

Márquez, Gabriel García 1928-
    See García Márquez, Gabriel

Marquis, Don(ald Robert Perry)
    1878-1937................... TCLC 7
    See also CA 104
    See also DLB 11, 25

Marryat, Frederick 1792-1848 .... NCLC 3
    See also DLB 21

Marsh, (Edith) Ngaio
    1899-1982....................CLC 7
    See also CANR 6
    See also CA 9-12R

Marshall, Garry 1935?- ....CLC 17
    See also CA 111

Marshall, Paule 1929-.............CLC 27
    See also CA 77-80
    See also DLB 33

North, Andrew 1912-
See Norton, Andre

North, Christopher 1785-1854
See Wilson, John

Norton, Alice Mary 1912-
See Norton, Andre
See also CANR 2
See also CA 1-4R
See also SATA 1, 43

Norton, Andre 1912-..............CLC 12
See also Norton, Mary Alice
See also DLB 8

Norway, Nevil Shute 1899-1960
See Shute (Norway), Nevil
See also CA 102
See also obituary CA 93-96

Nossack, Hans Erich 1901-1978 .....CLC 6
See also CA 93-96
See also obituary CA 85-88

Nova, Craig 1945-............. CLC 7, 31
See also CANR 2
See also CA 45-48

Novalis 1772-1801 .... NCLC 13

Nowlan, Alden (Albert) 1933-......CLC 15
See also CANR 5
See also CA 9-12R
See also DLB 53

Noyes, Alfred 1880-1958 .... TCLC 7
See also CA 104
See also DLB 20

Nunn, Kem 19??-............ CLC 34 (94)

Nye, Robert 1939-................CLC 13
See also CA 33-36R
See also SATA 6
See also DLB 14

Nyro, Laura 1947-................CLC 17

Oates, Joyce Carol
1938-.....CLC 1, 2, 3, 6, 9, 11, 15, 19, 33
See also CA 5-8R
See also DLB 2, 5
See also DLB-Y 81
See also AITN 1

O'Brien, Darcy 1939-..............CLC 11
See also CANR 8
See also CA 21-24R

O'Brien, Edna
1932-............. CLC 3, 5, 8, 13, 36
See also CANR 6
See also CA 1-4R
See also DLB 14

O'Brien, Flann
1911-1966......... CLC 1, 4, 5, 7, 10
See also O Nuallain, Brian

O'Brien, Richard 19??-............CLC 17

O'Brien, (William) Tim(othy)
1946-................. CLC 7, 19, 40
See also CA 85-88
See also DLB-Y 80

O'Casey, Sean
1880-1964........ CLC 1, 5, 9, 11, 15
See also CA 89-92
See also DLB 10

Ochs, Phil 1940-1976 ....CLC 17
See also obituary CA 65-68

O'Connor, Edwin (Greene)
1918-1968....................CLC 14
See also CA 93-96
See also obituary CA 25-28R

O'Connor, (Mary) Flannery
1925-1964...... CLC 1, 2, 3, 6, 10, 13, 15, 21
See also CANR 3
See also CA 1-4R
See also DLB 2
See also DLB-Y 80

O'Connor, Frank
1903-1966............... CLC 14, 23
See also O'Donovan, Michael (John)

O'Dell, Scott 1903- ....CLC 30
See also CLR 1
See also CANR 12
See also CA 61-64
See also SATA 12

Odets, Clifford 1906-1963 ...... CLC 2, 28
See also CA 85-88
See also DLB 7, 26

O'Donovan, Michael (John) 1903-1966
See O'Connor, Frank
See also CA 93-96

Ōe, Kenzaburō 1935- .... CLC 10, 36
See also CA 97-100

O'Faolain, Julia 1932- .... CLC 6, 19
See also CAAS 2
See also CANR 12
See also CA 81-84
See also DLB 14

O'Faoláin, Seán
1900-................CLC 1, 7, 14, 32
See also CANR 12
See also CA 61-64
See also DLB 15

O'Flaherty, Liam
1896-1984............ CLC 5, 34 (355)
See also CA 101
See also obituary CA 113
See also DLB 36
See also DLB-Y 84

O'Grady, Standish (James)
1846-1928................... TCLC 5
See also CA 104

O'Hara Family
See Banim, John and Banim, Michael

O'Hara, Frank
1926-1966............... CLC 2, 5, 13
See also CA 9-12R
See also obituary CA 25-28R
See also DLB 5, 16

O'Hara, John (Henry)
1905-1970......... CLC 1, 2, 3, 6, 11
See also CA 5-8R
See also obituary CA 25-28R
See also DLB 9
See also DLB-DS 2

O'Hehir, Diana 1922-.............CLC 41
See also CA 93-96

Okigbo, Christopher (Ifenayichukwu)
1932-1967....................CLC 25
See also CA 77-80

Olds, Sharon 1942- ...... CLC 32, 39 (186)
See also CANR 18
See also CA 101

Olesha, Yuri (Karlovich)
1899-1960....................CLC 8
See also CA 85-88

Oliphant, Margaret (Oliphant Wilson)
1828-1897.................. NCLC 11
See also DLB 18

Oliver, Mary 1935- ...... CLC 19, 34 (246)
See also CANR 9
See also CA 21-24R
See also DLB 5

Olivier, (Baron) Laurence (Kerr)
1907-.......................CLC 20
See also CA 111

Olsen, Tillie 1913-.............. CLC 4, 13
See also CANR 1
See also CA 1-4R
See also DLB 28
See also DLB-Y 80

Olson, Charles (John)
1910-1970....... CLC 1, 2, 5, 6, 9, 11, 29
See also CAP 1
See also CA 15-16
See also obituary CA 25-28R
See also DLB 5, 16

Olson, Theodore 1937-
See Olson, Toby

Olson, Toby 1937-................CLC 28
See also CANR 9
See also CA 65-68

Ondaatje, (Philip) Michael
1943-.................... CLC 14, 29
See also CA 77-80

Oneal, Elizabeth 1934-
See Oneal, Zibby
See also CA 106
See also SATA 30

Oneal, Zibby 1934-................CLC 30
See also Oneal, Elizabeth

O'Neill, Eugene (Gladstone)
1888-1953................. TCLC 1, 6
See also CA 110
See also AITN 1
See also DLB 7

Onetti, Juan Carlos 1909- ...... CLC 7, 10
See also CA 85-88

O'Nolan, Brian 1911-1966
See O'Brien, Flann

O Nuallain, Brian 1911-1966
See O'Brien, Flann
See also CAP 2
See also CA 21-22
See also obituary CA 25-28R

Oppen, George
1908-1984........CLC 7, 13, 34 (358)
See also CANR 8
See also CA 13-16R
See also obituary CA 113
See also DLB 5

Orlovitz, Gil 1918-1973 ....CLC 22
See also CA 77-80
See also obituary CA 45-48
See also DLB 2, 5

Ortega y Gasset, José
1883-1955................... TCLC 9
See also CA 106

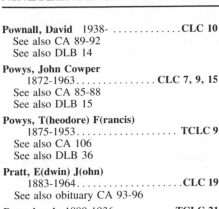

Author Index

Author Index

Author Index

Swados, Harvey 1920-1972 . . . .**CLC 5**
See also CANR 6
See also CA 5-8R
See also obituary CA 37-40R
See also DLB 2

Swarthout, Glendon (Fred)
1918- . . . .**CLC 35**
See also CANR 1
See also CA 1-4R
See also SATA 26

Swenson, May 1919- . . . . **CLC 4, 14**
See also CA 5-8R
See also SATA 15
See also DLB 5

Swift, Graham 1949- . . . .**CLC 41**
See also CA 117

Swift, Jonathan 1667-1745. . . . . **LC 1**
See also SATA 19
See also DLB 39

Swinburne, Algernon Charles
1837-1909. . . . . **TCLC 8**
See also CA 105
See also DLB 35

Swinfen, Ann 19??- . . . . **CLC 34 (576)**

Swinnerton, Frank (Arthur)
1884-1982. . . . .**CLC 31**
See also obituary CA 108
See also DLB 34

Symons, Arthur (William)
1865-1945. . . . . **TCLC 11**
See also CA 107
See also DLB 19

Symons, Julian (Gustave)
1912- . . . . **CLC 2, 14, 32**
See also CAAS 3
See also CANR 3
See also CA 49-52

Synge, (Edmund) John Millington
1871-1909. . . . . **TCLC 6**
See also CA 104
See also DLB 10, 19

Syruc, J. 1911-
See Miłosz, Czesław

Tabori, George 1914- . . . .**CLC 19**
See also CANR 4
See also CA 49-52

Tagore, (Sir) Rabindranath
1861-1941. . . . . **TCLC 3**
See also Thakura, Ravindranatha

Talese, Gaetano 1932-
See Talese, Gay

Talese, Gay 1932- . . . .**CLC 37**
See also CANR 9
See also CA 1-4R
See also AITN 1

Tamayo y Baus, Manuel
1829-1898. . . . . **NCLC 1**

Tanizaki, Jun'ichirō
1886-1965. . . . . **CLC 8, 14, 28**
See also CA 93-96
See also obituary CA 25-28R

Tarkington, (Newton) Booth
1869-1946. . . . . **TCLC 9**
See also CA 110
See also SATA 17
See also DLB 9

Tate, (John Orley) Allen
1899-1979. . . . . . **CLC 2, 4, 6, 9, 11, 14, 24**
See also CA 5-8R
See also obituary CA 85-88
See also DLB 4, 45

Tate, James 1943- . . . . **CLC 2, 6, 25**
See also CA 21-24R
See also DLB 5

Tavel, Ronald 1940- . . . .**CLC 6**
See also CA 21-24R

Taylor, C(ecil) P(hillip)
1929-1981. . . . .**CLC 27**
See also CA 25-28R
See also obituary CA 105

Taylor, Eleanor Ross 1920- . . . .**CLC 5**
See also CA 81-84

Taylor, Elizabeth
1912-1975. . . . .**CLC 2, 4, 29**
See also CANR 9
See also CA 13-16R
See also SATA 13

Taylor, Kamala (Purnaiya) 1924-
See Markandaya, Kamala
See also CA 77-80

Taylor, Mildred D(elois) 19??- . . . . . .**CLC 21**
See also CA 85-88
See also SATA 15

Taylor, Peter (Hillsman)
1917- . . . . **CLC 1, 4, 18, 37**
See also CANR 9
See also CA 13-16R
See also DLB-Y 81

Taylor, Robert Lewis 1912- . . . .**CLC 14**
See also CANR 3
See also CA 1-4R
See also SATA 10

Teasdale, Sara 1884-1933. . . . . **TCLC 4**
See also CA 104
See also DLB 45
See also SATA 32

Tegnér, Esaias 1782-1846. . . . . **NCLC 2**

Teilhard de Chardin, (Marie Joseph) Pierre
1881-1955. . . . . **TCLC 9**
See also CA 105

Tennant, Emma 1937- . . . .**CLC 13**
See also CANR 10
See also CA 65-68
See also DLB 14

Teran, Lisa St. Aubin de 19??- . . . . .**CLC 36**

Terkel, Louis 1912-
See Terkel, Studs
See also CANR 18
See also CA 57-60

Terkel, Studs 1912- . . . .**CLC 38**
See also Terkel, Louis
See also AITN 1

Terry, Megan 1932- . . . .**CLC 19**
See also CA 77-80
See also DLB 7

Tesich, Steve 1943?- . . . .**CLC 40**
See also CA 105
See also DLB-Y 83

Tesich, Stoyan 1943?-
See Tesich, Steve

Tertz, Abram 1925-
See Sinyavsky, Andrei (Donatevich)

Teternikov, Fyodor Kuzmich 1863-1927
See Sologub, Fyodor
See also CA 104

Tey, Josephine 1897-1952 . . . . **TCLC 14**
See also Mackintosh, Elizabeth

Thackeray, William Makepeace
1811-1863. . . . .**NCLC 5, 14**
See also SATA 23
See also DLB 21

Thakura, Ravindranatha 1861-1941
See Tagore, (Sir) Rabindranath
See also CA 104

Thelwell, Michael (Miles)
1939- . . . .**CLC 22**
See also CA 101

Theroux, Alexander (Louis)
1939- . . . . **CLC 2, 25**
See also CA 85-88

Theroux, Paul
1941- . . . . **CLC 5, 8, 11, 15, 28**
See also CA 33-36R
See also DLB 2
See also SATA 44

Thibault, Jacques Anatole Francois
1844-1924
See France, Anatole
See also CA 106

Thiele, Colin (Milton) 1920- . . . .**CLC 17**
See also CANR 12
See also CA 29-32R
See also SAAS 2
See also SATA 14

Thomas, Audrey (Grace)
1935- . . . . **CLC 7, 13, 37**
See also CA 21-24R
See also AITN 2

Thomas, D(onald) M(ichael)
1935- . . . . **CLC 13, 22, 31**
See also CANR 17
See also CA 61-64
See also DLB 40

Thomas, Dylan (Marlais)
1914-1953. . . . .**TCLC 1, 8**
See also CA 104
See also DLB 13, 20

Thomas, Edward (Philip)
1878-1917. . . . . **TCLC 10**
See also CA 106
See also DLB 19

Thomas, John Peter 1928-
See Thomas, Piri

Thomas, Joyce Carol 1938- . . . .**CLC 35**
See also CA 113, 116
See also SATA 40
See also DLB 33

Thomas, Lewis 1913- . . . .**CLC 35**
See also CA 85-88

Thomas, Piri 1928- . . . .**CLC 17**
See also CA 73-76

Thomas, R(onald) S(tuart)
1913- . . . . **CLC 6, 13**
See also CAAS 4
See also CA 89-92
See also DLB 27

Thomas, Ross (Elmore)
1926- . . . . **CLC 39 (246)**
See also CA 33-36R

Author Index

West, Jessamyn 1907-1984...... CLC **7, 17**
See also CA 9-12R
See also obituary SATA 37
See also DLB 6
See also DLB-Y 84

West, Morris L(anglo)
1916-.................... CLC **6, 33**
See also CA 5-8R

West, Nathanael
1903?-1940.............. TCLC **1, 14**
See Weinstein, Nathan Wallenstein
See also DLB 4, 9, 28

West, Paul 1930-.............. CLC **7, 14**
See also CA 13-16R
See also DLB 14

West, Rebecca 1892-1983..... CLC **7, 9, 31**
See also CA 5-8R
See also obituary CA 109
See also DLB 36
See also DLB-Y 83

Westall, Robert (Atkinson)
1929-......................CLC **17**
See also CANR 18
See also CA 69-72
See also SAAS 2
See also SATA 23

Westlake, Donald E(dwin)
1933-..................... CLC **7, 33**
See also CANR 16
See also CA 17-20R

Whalen, Philip 1923-........... CLC **6, 29**
See also CANR 5
See also CA 9-12R
See also DLB 16

Wharton, Edith (Newbold Jones)
1862-1937................. TCLC **3, 9**
See also CA 104
See also DLB 4, 9, 12

Wharton, William 1925-....... CLC **18, 37**
See also CA 93-96
See also DLB-Y 80

Wheatley (Peters), Phillis
1753?-1784................... LC **3**
See also DLB 31, 50

Wheelock, John Hall
1886-1978...................CLC **14**
See also CANR 14
See also CA 13-16R
See also obituary CA 77-80
See also DLB 45

Whelan, John 1900-
See O'Faoláin, Seán

Whitaker, Rodney 1925-
See Trevanian
See also CA 29-32R

White, E(lwyn) B(rooks)
1899-1985......... CLC **10, 34 (425), 39 (369)**
See also CLR 1
See also CANR 16
See also CA 13-16R
See also obituary CA 116
See also SATA 2, 29, 44
See also DLB 11, 22
See also AITN 2

White, Edmund III 1940-.........CLC **27**
See also CANR 3
See also CA 45-48

White, Patrick (Victor Martindale)
1912-............ CLC **3, 4, 5, 7, 9, 18**
See also CA 81-84

White, T(erence) H(anbury)
1906-1964....................CLC **30**
See also CA 73-76
See also SATA 12

White, Walter (Francis)
1893-1955.................. TCLC **15**
See also CA 115

Whitehead, E(dward) A(nthony)
1933-........................CLC **5**
See also CA 65-68

Whitemore, Hugh 1936-...........CLC **37**

Whitman, Walt 1819-1892....... NCLC **4**
See also SATA 20
See also DLB 3

Whittemore, (Edward) Reed (Jr.)
1919-........................CLC **4**
See also CANR 4
See also CA 9-12R
See also DLB 5

Whittier, John Greenleaf
1807-1892.................. NCLC **8**
See also DLB 1

Wicker, Thomas Grey 1926-
See Wicker, Tom
See also CA 65-68

Wicker, Tom 1926-................CLC **7**
See also Wicker, Thomas Grey

Wideman, John Edgar
1941-............CLC **5, 34 (297), 36**
See also CANR 14
See also CA 85-88
See also DLB 33

Wiebe, Rudy (H.) 1934-..... CLC **6, 11, 14**
See also CA 37-40R

Wieners, John 1934-................CLC **7**
See also CA 13-16R
See also DLB 16

Wiesel, Elie(zer)
1928-................CLC **3, 5, 11, 37**
See also CAAS 4
See also CANR 8
See also CA 5-8R
See also AITN 1

Wight, James Alfred 1916-
See Herriot, James
See also CA 77-80
See also SATA 44

Wilbur, Richard (Purdy)
1921-.................CLC **3, 6, 9, 14**
See also CANR 2
See also CA 1-4R
See also SATA 9
See also DLB 5

Wild, Peter 1940-.................CLC **14**
See also CA 37-40R
See also DLB 5

Wilde, Oscar (Fingal O'Flahertie Wills)
1854-1900................. TCLC **1, 8**
See also CA 104
See also SATA 24
See also DLB 10, 19, 34

Wilder, Billy 1906- ....CLC **20**
See also Wilder, Samuel
See also DLB 26

Wilder, Samuel 1906-
See Wilder, Billy
See also CA 89-92

Wilder, Thornton (Niven)
1897-1975...... CLC **1, 5, 6, 10, 15, 35**
See also CA 13-16R
See also obituary CA 61-64
See also DLB 4, 7, 9
See also AITN 2

Wilhelm, Kate 1928-................CLC **7**
See also CANR 17
See also CA 37-40R
See also DLB 8

Willard, Nancy 1936- .... CLC **7, 37**
See also CLR 5
See also CANR 10
See also CA 89-92
See also SATA 30, 37
See also DLB 5

Williams, C(harles) K(enneth)
1936-........................CLC **33**
See also CA 37-40R
See also DLB 5

Williams, Charles (Walter Stansby)
1886-1945................ TCLC **1, 11**
See also CA 104

Williams, (George) Emlyn
1905-........................CLC **15**
See also CA 104
See also DLB 10

Williams, John A(lfred)
1925-.................... CLC **5, 13**
See also CAAS 3
See also CANR 6
See also CA 53-56
See also DLB 2, 33

Williams, Jonathan (Chamberlain)
1929-........................CLC **13**
See also CANR 8
See also CA 9-12R
See also DLB 5

Williams, Joy 1944-................CLC **31**
See also CA 41-44R

Williams, Norman 1952-..... CLC **39 (100)**

Williams, Paulette 1948-
See Shange, Ntozake

Williams, Tennessee
1911-1983....... CLC **1, 2, 5, 7, 8, 11, 15, 19, 30, 39 (444)**
See also CA 5-8R
See also obituary CA 108
See also DLB 7
See also DLB-Y 83
See also DLB-DS 4
See also AITN 1, 2

Williams, Thomas (Alonzo)
1926-........................CLC **14**
See also CANR 2
See also CA 1-4R

Williams, Thomas Lanier 1911-1983
See Williams, Tennessee

Williams, William Carlos
1883-1963....... CLC **1, 2, 5, 9, 13, 22**
See also CA 89-92
See also DLB 4, 16

Williamson, Jack 1908-............CLC **29**
See also Williamson, John Stewart
See also DLB 8

Author Index

Cumulative Index to Nationalities

Cumulative Index to Critics

Critic Index

Critic Index

Critic Index

Critic Index

Critic Index

Critic Index

Critic Index

Critic Index